NATIONAL ACCOUNTS STATISTICS: MAIN AGGREGATES AND DETAILED TABLES, 1987

PART II

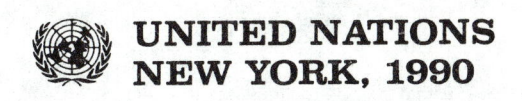

UNITED NATIONS
NEW YORK, 1990

NOTE

Symbols of United Nations documents are composed of capital letters combined with figures. Mention of such a symbol indicates a reference to a United Nations document.

The first 14 editions of the *Yearbook* were issued without series symbols.

ST/ESA/STAT/SER.X/13

UNITED NATIONS PUBLICATION

Sales No. E.90.XVII.2, Part II

10000
(not to be sold separately)
ISBN 92-1-161312-4

Inquiries should be directed to:

PUBLISHING DIVISION
UNITED NATIONS
NEW YORK, N.Y. 10017

Copyright © United Nations, 1990
All rights reserved
Manufactured in the United States of America

CONTENTS

	Page
Introduction	v
I. System of National Accounts (SNA)	ix
II. System of Material Product Balances (MPS)	xxi
III. Country tables	863

Country	Page	Country	Page
Lebanon	865	Rwanda	1273
Lesotho	867	Saint Kitts and Nevis	1284
Liberia	872	Saint Lucia	1287
Libyan Arab Jamahiriya	876	Saint Vincent and the Grenadines	1289
Luxembourg	890	Samoa	1291
Madagascar	902	Saudi Arabia	1292
Malawi	906	Senegal	1296
Malaysia	911	Seychelles	1299
Maldives	918	Sierra Leone	1307
Mali	921	Singapore	1317
Malta	924	Solomon Islands	1321
Martinique	942	Somalia	1326
Mauritania	944	South Africa	1330
Mauritius	947	Spain	1341
Mexico	960	Sri Lanka	1368
Mongolia	970	Sudan	1385
Montserrat	971	Suriname	1399
Morocco	975	Swaziland	1402
Mozambique	979	Sweden	1414
Myanmar	980	Switzerland	1465
Nepal	985	Syrian Arab Rep.	1470
Netherlands	988	Thailand	1476
Netherlands Antilles	1027	Togo	1494
New Caledonia	1033	Tonga	1499
New Zealand	1037	Trinidad and Tobago	1505
Nicaragua	1053	Tunisia	1515
Niger	1057	Turkey	1521
Nigeria	1062	Uganda	1527
Norway	1068	Ukrainian SSR	1530
Oman	1115	United Arab Emirates	1531
Pakistan	1120	United Kingdom	1535
Panama	1128	United Rep. of Tanzania	1580
Papua New Guinea	1141	United States	1586
Paraguay	1151	Uruguay	1639
Peru	1159	USSR	1644
Philippines	1192	Venezuela	1646
Poland	1205	Viet Nam	1660
Portugal	1217	Yemen	1661
Puerto Rico	1261	Yugoslavia	1668
Qatar	1267	Zaire	1670
Reunion	1268	Zambia	1673
Romania	1270	Zimbabwe	1683

INTRODUCTION

This is the thirty-first issue of *National Accounts Statistics: Main Aggregates and Detailed Tables*, [1/] showing detailed national accounts estimates for 168 countries and areas. Like the first 30 issues, it has been prepared by the Statistical Office of the Department of International Economic and Social Affairs of the United Nations Secretariat with the generous co-operation of national statistical services. It is issued in accordance with the request of the Statistical Commission, [2/] that the most recent available data on national accounts for as many countries and areas as possible be published regularly.

The present publication (Parts I and II) forms part of a *National Accounts Statistics* series. Another publication in the same series, issued separately is *National Accounts Statistics: Analysis of Main Aggregates*, [3/] presenting in the form of analytical tables a summary of main national accounts aggregates extracted from this publication and supplemented by estimates made by the Statistical Office where official data are not available.

SCOPE OF PUBLICATION

National accounts estimates for countries or areas with market economies are shown, where available, for each of the subjects below. Estimates for the matrix tables are shown for some or all of the years 1980 through 1987. For other tables, estimates are shown for some or all of the years 1970, 1975, 1978 through 1987.

Part 1. Summary information

1.1 Expenditures on the gross domestic product (current prices)

1.2 Expenditures on the gross domestic product (constant prices)

1.3 Cost components of the gross domestic product

1.4 General government current receipts and expenditures, summary

1.5 Current income and outlay of corporate and quasi-corporate enterprises, summary

1.6 Current income and outlay of households and non-profit institutions, summary

1.7 External transactions on current account, summary

1.8 Capital transactions of the nation, summary

1.9 Gross domestic product by institutional sector of origin

1.10 Gross domestic product by kind of activity (current prices)

1.11 Gross domestic product by kind of activity (constant prices)

1.12 Relations among national accounting aggregates

Part 2. Final expenditures on gross domestic product: detailed breakdowns and supporting tables

2.1 General government final consumption expenditure by function (current prices)

2.2 General government final consumption expenditure by function (constant prices)

2.3 Total government outlays by function and type (current prices)

2.4 Composition of general government social security benefits and social assistance grants to households

2.5 Private final consumption expenditure by type (current prices)

2.6 Private final consumption expenditure by type (constant prices)

2.7 Gross capital formation by type of good and owner (current prices)

2.8 Gross capital formation by type of good and owner (constant prices)

2.9 Gross capital formation by kind of activity of owner, ISIC major divisions (current prices)

2.10 Gross capital formation by kind of activity of owner, ISIC major divisions (constant prices)

2.11 Gross fixed capital formation by kind of activity of owner, ISIC divisions (current prices)

2.12 Gross fixed capital formation by kind of activity of owner, ISIC divisions (constant prices)

2.13 Stocks of reproducible fixed assets, by type of good and owner (current prices)

2.14 Stocks of reproducible fixed assets, by type of good and owner (constant prices)

2.15 Stocks of reproducible fixed assets by kind of activity (current prices)

2.16 Stocks of reproducible fixed assets by kind of activity (constant prices)

2.17 Exports and imports of goods and services, detail

Part 3. Institutional sector accounts: detailed flow accounts [4/]

1. General government

3.11 Production account

3.12 Income and outlay account

3.13 Capital accumulation account

3.14 Capital finance account

2. Corporate and quasi-corporate enterprises

    3.21 Production account: total and subsectors

    3.22 Income and outlay account: total and subsectors

    3.23 Capital accumulation account: total and subsectors

    3.24 Capital finance account: total and subsectors

3. Households and private unincorporated enterprises

    3.31 Production account: total and subsectors

    3.32 Income and outlay account: total and subsectors

    3.33 Capital accumulation account: total and subsectors

    3.34 Capital finance account: total and subsectors

4. *Private non-profit institutions serving households*

    3.41 Production account

    3.42 Income and outlay account

    3.43 Capital accumulation account

    3.44 Capital finance account

5. *External transactions*

    3.51 Current account, detail

    3.52 Capital accumulation account

    3.53 Capital finance account

Part 4. Production by kind of activity: detailed breakdowns and supporting tables

   4.1 Derivation of value added by kind of activity (current prices)

   4.2 Derivation of value added by kind of activity (constant prices)

   4.3 Cost components of value added

For the countries with centrally planned economies, estimates are shown, where available, in terms of the System of Material Product Balances (MPS), for each of the following subjects, as a rule, for some or all of the years 1970, 1975, 1978 through 1987.

1. Net material product by use

2. Net material product by kind of activity of the material sphere

3. Primary incomes by kinds of activity of the material sphere

4. Primary incomes from net material product

5. Supply and disposition of goods and material services

6. Capital formation by kind of activity of the material and non-material spheres

7. Final consumption

8. Personal consumption according to source of supply of goods and material services

9. Total consumption of the population by object, commodity and service, and mode of acquisition.

CONCEPTUAL REFERENCES

The form and concepts of the statistical tables in the present publication generally conform, for the countries or areas with market economies, to the recommendations in *in A System of National Accounts*, Studies in Methods, Series F, No. 2, Rev. 3. For the countries with centrally planned economies, the form and concepts generally conform to the recommendations in *Basic Principles of the System of Balances of the National Economy Studies in Methods, Series F, No.17. A summary of the conceptual framework of both systems, their classifications and definitions of transactions items, is provided in chapters I and II of the present publication.*

COMPILATION OF DATA

To compile the large volume of national accounts data, the Statistical Office each year sends to countries or areas with market economies a national accounts questionnaire; those with centrally planned economies receive a material balances questionnaire. The recipients of the questionnaires are also requested to indicate where the scope and coverage of the country estimates differ for conceptual or statistical reasons from the definitions and classifications recommended in the System of National Accounts (SNA) or in MPS. Data obtained from these replies are supplemented by information gathered from correspondence with the national statistical services and from national and international source publications.

In the present publication, the data for each country or area are presented in separate chapters, as far as possible, under uniform table headings and classifications of SNA or the material balances questionnaire, as the case may be. Each country chapter contains a brief introductory text (source and general note). The general note describes the extent to which the estimates conform conceptually to the recommendations of SNA or the material balances questionnaire. Important deviations from the two systems, where known, are described in the general note, while differences in definition and coverage of specific items are indicated in footnotes to the relevant tables.

Country data in chapter III are presented in alphabetical order. Unless otherwise stated, the data in the country tables relate to the calendar year against which they are shown.

COMPARABILITY OF THE NATIONAL ESTIMATES

Every effort has been made to present the estimates of the various countries or areas in a form designed to facilitate international comparability. To this end, important differences in concept, scope, coverage and classification have been described in the notes which precede and accompany the country tables. Such differences should be taken into account if misleading comparisons among countries or areas are to be avoided.

REVISIONS

The figures shown are the most recent estimates and revisions available at the time of compilation. In general, figures for the most recent year are to be regarded as provisional. For more up to date information, reference is made to the December issue of the *United Nations Monthly Bulletin of Statistics*.

EXPLANATION OF SYMBOLS

The following symbols have been employed:

Data not available . . . .

Category not applicable . . . .

Magnitude nil or less than
half of the unit employed . . . . . . -

Decimal figures are always
preceded by a point . . . . (.)

When a series is not homogeneous, this is indicated by presenting the figures in separate rows.

Details and percentages in tables do not necessarily add to totals shown because of rounding.

GENERAL DISCLAIMER

The designations employed and the presentation of material in this publication do not imply the expression of any opinion whatsoever on the part of the Secretariat of the United Nations concerning the legal status of any country, territory, city or area or of its authorities, or concerning the delimitation of its frontiers or boundaries.

Where the designation "country or area" appears in the headings of tables, it covers countries, territories, cities or areas. In prior issues of this publication, where the designation "country" appears in the headings of tables, it covers countries, territories, cities or areas.

In some tables, the designations "developed" and "developing" economies are intended for statistical convenience and do not, necessarily, express a judgement about the stage reached by a particular country or area in the development process.

---

[1] United Nations publication. The first 25 editions of this publication were issued under the title *Yearbook of National Accounts Statistics* under the following sales number: 1957, 58.XVII.3; 1958, 59.XVII.3; 1959, 60.XVII.3; 1960, 61.XVII.4; 1961, 62.XVII.2; 1962, 63.XVII.2;. 1963, 64.XVII.4; 1964, 65.XVII.2; 1965, 66.XVII.2; 1966, 67.XVII.14; 1967, 69.XVII.6; 1968, vol. I, 70.XVII.2, vol. II. 70.XVII.3; 1969, vol. I, 71.XVII.2, vol. II. 71.XVII.3; 1970 ,72.XVII.3, vol. I, 72.XVII.3, vol. II; 1971, (3 volumes), E.73.XVII.3; 1972, (3 volumes), E.74.XVII.3; 1973, (3 volumes), E.75.XVII.2; 1974, (3 volumes), E.75.XVII.5; 1975, (3 volumes), E.76.XVII.2; 1976 (2 volumes) E.77.XVII.2; 1977, (2 volumes), E.78.XVII.2; 1978, (2 volumes) E.79.XVII.8; 1979, (2 volumes), E.80.XVII.11; l980, (2 volumes) E.82.XVII.6; 1981, (2 volumes), E.83.XVII.3. Beginning with the twenty-sixth edition, this publication replaced Volume I, Individual country data, of the Yearbook and it was issued under the following sales number: 1982, E.85.XVII.4; 1983, E.86.XVII.3; 1984, E.86.XVII.26; 1985,E.87.XVII.10; 1986, E.89.XVII.7(Part I and Part II).
[2] See Official Records of the Economic and Social Council, First Year, Second Session, (E/39), annex III, chap. IV.
[3] United Nations publication. Sales No. E.87.XVII.11.
[4] Institutional sector accounts are shown only for those countries which have tables for all the institutional sectors.
[5] United Nations publication, Sales No. E.69.XVII.3. The first addition of the report, published in 1953, was prepared by an expert committee appointed by the Secretary-General of the United Nations.
[6] United Nations publication, Sales. No. E.71.XVII.10.
[7] United Nations publication, ST/ESA/STAT/SER.Q.

I. SYSTEM OF NATIONAL ACCOUNTS (SNA)

The revised System of National Accounts (SNA) was adopted by the Statistical Commission at its fifteenth session [1] for the use of national statistical authorities and in the international reporting of comparable national accounting data. The present System [2] is a revision and extension of the former SNA which was first formulated in 1952.

A. STRUCTURE OF SNA

SNA provides a comprehensive and detailed framework for the systematic and integrated recording of transaction flows in an economy. It brings together into an articulated and coherent system data ranging in degree of aggregation from consolidated accounts of the nation to detailed input-output and flow-of-funds tables. It includes production and goods and services and outlay and capital finance accounts for institutional sectors and subsectors.

The country tables are divided into four parts. These are listed in the above introduction. Part 1 contains summary but comprehensive information, at current and, where appropriate, constant prices. This part includes not only the basic gross domestic product (final expenditures and cost composition) but also summary information on government receipts and disbursements, enterprise and household income and outlay, and external transactions, a summary capital transactions account, information on gross product by institutional sector of origin and kind of activity and, finally, a table showing the relations among the aggregate concepts used in the revised SNA and also commonly in national statistical systems. Tables 1.1, 1.3, 1.4, 1.5, 1.6, 1.7 and 1.8 form a simple, closed and balancing set of flow accounts, drawn from the much more complex and elaborate standard accounts of SNA; these tables can therefore be used not only to provide an overview of the operation of the economic system but also as a guide to the more detailed data that follow and as a framework to enforce conceptual and statistical consistency.

Part 2 shows detailed breakdowns of the final expenditure components on gross domestic product (consumption, capital formation, imports and exports), in current and constant prices, together with supporting tables giving additional information on government outlays and capital stock. This part also shows tables relating to stocks of reproducible tangible assets at current and constant prices.

Part 3 shows detailed institutional sector accounts. For each sector and subsector, five accounts are given: a production account, an income and outlay account, a capital formation account, a capital finance account, and a balance sheet. The latter four are standard SNA accounts, as shown in annex 8.3 to *A System of National Accounts* [2] and in annex 8.2 to *Provisional Guidelines on National and Sector Balance Sheets and Reconciliation Accounts of the System of National Accounts.* [4]

The SNA standard accounts do not include institutional sector production accounts, but provision is made for this information in the supporting tables.

The sectors and subsectors distinguished in part 3 are: general government (central, state or provincial, local, social security funds), corporate and quasi-corporate enterprises (non-financial, financial), households and private unincorporated enterprises (farm entrepreneurial, other farm, non-farm entrepreneurial, non-farm wage earner, other) and non-profit institutions serving households.

Part 4 contains kind-of-activity breakdowns. Two levels of detail are employed. All of the information is asked for at the major division (1-digit) level of the *International Standard Industrial Classification of All Economic Activities* [5] (ISIC). In some cases, data are also asked for at the ISIC division (2-digit) level, with a very small amount of further breakdown to the 3-digit level. Where appropriate, both current and constant prices are specified. The tables show the derivation of value added (gross output less intermediate consumption), the cost components of value added, and employment.

B. STANDARD CLASSIFICATIONS OF THE SNA

Detailed discussions of definitions and classifications are to be found in *A System of National Accounts*, [2] and in the other publications on SNA cited above. SNA distinguishes between transactor and transaction classifications. Below is a short summary of the main characteristics of each of the classifications used by the system.

I. *Classifications of transactors*

1. *Kind of activity*

The kind-of-activity classification employed is the major division (1-digit) level or, in some tables the division (2-digit) level of ISIC.

In SNA, this classification is intended to be applied to establishment-type units, defined as the smallest units for which separate production accounts can be compiled. SNA also employs a much broader kind of activity classification which divides producers into "industries" and three categories of "other producers". Industries are, broadly, establishments whose activities are intended to be self-sustaining, whether through production for the market or for own use, and it is to this category that the ISIC breakdown is generally applied.

All establishments falling into ISIC major divisions 1-8 should be classed as industries. Producers of government services, private non-profit services to households, and domestic services are classed as "other producers"; all of these should fall into ISIC category 9 "Community, social and personal services". ISIC category 9 also may, of course, include some establishments classed as industries. Where countries consider, however, that some establishments classed as other producers should appear in ISIC categories other than 9, the nature of the exceptions would be specified in footnotes to tables 1.10 and 1.11.

2. *Institutional sectors*

The basic SNA institutional sectoring is given in *A System of National Accounts,* [3/] table 5.1.

Institutional sectoring, in SNA, is intended to be applied to enterprise-type units, that is, units for which complete accounts can be compiled, as opposed to the establishment-type units employed in the kind-of-activity classification. This distinction is applicable mainly to the corporate and quasi-corporate enterprise sector.

The sectoring and subsectoring employed in the institutional sector accounts in part 3 is as follows:

General government

    Central
    State or provincial
    Local
    Social security funds

Corporate and quasi-corporate enterprises

    Non-financial
    Financial

Households and private unincorporated enterprises

    Farm entrepreneurial
    Other farm
    Non-farm entrepreneurial
    Non-farm wage earner
    Other

Non-profit institutions serving households

Rest of the world

(a) *General government.* This sector includes (1) *producers of government services,* all bodies, departments and establishments of any level of government that engage in administration, defence, regulation of the public order and health, cultural, recreational and other social services and social security arrangements that are furnished but not normally sold to the public; and (2) *industries of government,* ancillary departments and establishments mainly engaged in supplying goods and services to other units of government, such as printing plants, central transport pools and arsenals, and agencies mainly selling goods and services to the public but operating on a small scale and financially integrated with general government, such as government restaurant facilities in public buildings.

Non-profit institutions which, while not an official part of any organ of government, are wholly or mainly financed and controlled by it should be included in producers of government services. Ancillary agencies may occur in any kind of activity. Producers of government services normally occur only in major division 9 (which of course may also include ancillary agencies). .

Provision is made for four subsectors of general government, all of which may include the two components noted above. However, it is not intended that artificial distinctions should be introduced where they do not exist in the institutions of a particular country. It will, for instance, usually be desirable to separate state or provincial government from local government only in countries in which state or provincial governments exercise a considerable degree of autonomy. Similarly, social security funds should in general be distinguished separately only where they are organized separately from the other activities of general government and exercise substantial autonomy in their operations.

(b) *Corporate and quasi-corporate enterprises.* SNA defines this sector to include enterprises which meet any one of the following criteria: (1) they are incorporated; (2) they are owned by a non-resident; (3) they are relatively large partnerships or proprietorships with complete income statements and balance sheets; (4) they are non-profit institutions mainly serving business and financed and controlled by business; or (5) they are engaged in financial activities. Because of the difficulty that may be encountered in compiling separate production account data for incorporated and unincorporated units, a combined production account for these two sectors has also been provided for.

(c) *Households and private unincorporated enterprises.* This sector includes all private unincorporated enterprises not classed as quasi-corporations. SNA also includes in this sector private non-profit institutions serving households that employ less than the equivalent of two full-time persons.

The criterion for classifying the subsectors of the household sector in these tables differs slightly from that tentatively proposed in SNA. There, the subsectoring is based on the occupational status of the person designated "head of household". Here, the classification is based on the most important source of household income, taking all household members into account. It is considered that this criterion more accurately reflects both changing social views and changing labour force participation practices; it also responds to recent directives relating to the elimination of sex-based stereotypes.

(d) *Private non-profit institutions serving households.* This sector includes institutions, not mainly financed and controlled by general governments and employing the equivalent of two or more persons, that furnish educational, health, cultural, recreational and other social and community services to households free of charge or at prices that do not fully cover their costs of production.

As in the case of general government, SNA includes two components in this sector: (1) *producers of private non-profit services to households,* which engage in the activities enumerated above, and (2) *commercial activities* of these institutions, such as owning and letting dwellings, operating eating and lodging facilities, and publishing and selling books, for which it is possible to compile separate production accounts but not complete separate financial accounts. (Where separate financial accounts can be compiled, such activities would be classed as ordinary quasi-corporations.) In SNA, these commercial activities are considered to be "industries" and should be classed in the appropriate ISIC categories, whereas the non-profit services proper will all fall into ISIC category 9.

II. Classifications of transactions

1. Classification of the functions of government

Table 5.3 of *A System of National Accounts* [3/] contains a classification of the purposes of government, the 1-digit level of which was used in previous publications for classifying general government outlays. This classification has now been superseded by the *Classification of the Functions of Government.* [6/]

2. Household consumption expenditure

Table 6.1 of SNA provides a classification of household goods and services. The classification used in the present publication is a slightly condensed version of the second level of this classification, in which some second-level categories have been combined.

3. Purposes of private non-profit bodies serving households

This classification appears in table 5.4 of SNA. It is used for classifying the final consumption expenditures of private non-profit institutions serving households.

4. Gross capital formation

Table 6.2 of SNA classifies stocks according to type, and table 6.3 classifies gross fixed capital formation according to type. These classifications are used in the present publication in slightly modified form, calling for less detail in some areas and slightly more detail in others (specifically, transport equipment).

5. Exports and imports of goods and services

This classification is given in table 6.4 of SNA.

6. Transfers

Table 7.1 of SNA contains a classification of unrequired current transfers, including direct taxes. This classification is not employed directly in the present publication but it is the source of the definitions of a number of flows, and will be referred to in that connection.

7. Financial assets and liabilities

Table 7.2 of SNA gives a classification of items appearing in the capital finance account.

8. Balance sheet categories

Classifications of the various types of assets not included in the previous classification are given in tables 5.1 and 5.2 of *Provisional Guidelines on National and Sector Balance Sheets and Reconciliation Accounts of the System of National Accounts,* [4/], which deal respectively, with stocks and fixed assets, and non-reproducible tangible assets. These classifications are used in the capital stock tables in part 2 and the balance sheet tables in part 3 of the present publication.

C. DEFINITIONS OF FLOWS

The following section briefly defines the content of the flows appearing in the SNA tables of chapter III of the present publication.

I. Total supply of goods and services

1. Gross output of goods and services

Gross output of goods and services covers both the value of goods and services produced for sale and the value of goods and services produced for own use. It includes (a) the domestic production of goods and services which are either for sale or for transfer to others, (b) net additions to work in progress valued at cost and to stocks of finished goods valued in producers' prices; (c) products made on own account for government or private consumption or for gross fixed capital formation; and (d) rents received on structures, machinery and equipment (but not on land) and imputed rent for owner-occupied dwellings.

Production for own consumption of households includes all own-account production of primary products (agricultural, fishing, forestry, mining and quarrying), own-account production of such items as butter, flour, wine, cloth or furniture made from primary products, and other goods and services that are also commonly sold. Gross output of the distributive trades is defined as the difference between sales and purchase values of goods sold. Gross output of banks and similar financial institutions is defined as the sum of actual service charges and imputed service charges; the latter is equal to the excess of property income received over interest paid out on deposits. For casualty insurance companies, gross output is defined as the excess of premiums received over claims paid, and for life insurance schemes it is the excess of premiums received over the sum of claims paid and net additions to actuarial reserves, excluding the accrued interest of the policy-holders in these reserves. Gross output of general government includes the market value of sales and goods and services produced for own use. The latter should be valued at cost, that is, the sum of net purchases of goods and services for intermediate consumption (at purchasers' prices), consumption of fixed capital, compensation of employees and any indirect taxes paid.

The concept of gross output appears in the tables in both part 3 and part 4. In part 3, each sector production account aggregates to its gross output. In part 4, gross output of various kind-of-activity sectors appears in tables 4.1 - 4.2 and 4.5 - 4.10. In the sector production accounts (tables 3.11, 3.21, 3.31 and 3.41) and the supply tables (4.5, 4.6, 4.9 and 4.10), gross output is divided into marketed and non-marketed components. The marketed component includes all output offered for sale (whether or not a buyer is actually found) or valued on the basis of a market transaction, even if it reaches the ultimate recipient through a transfer.

2. *Imports of goods and services*

Imports of goods and services include broadly the equivalent of general imports of merchandise as defined in external trade statistics, plus imports of services and direct purchases abroad made by resident households and by the government on current account. Transfer of migrants' household and personal effects and gifts between households are also included. The following additions and deductions are required, however, to move from the general trade concept to the national accounting concept. Additions required include (1) the value of purchases of bankers, stores and ballast for ships, aircraft, etc., (2) fish and salvage purchased from foreign vessels, and (3) purchases from abroad of gold ore and gold for industrial uses Deductions required include (4) goods imported solely for improvement or repair and subsequently re-exported; and (5) leased or rented machinery, equipment and other goods; the value of the repairs or leasing and rental services is included, however. The valuation of imports is c.i.f. In principle, transactions should be recorded at the moment the transfer of ownership takes place and not when goods physically enter the domestic territory, but in practice the time of recording used in the national accounts usually must follow that used in the external trade statistics.

Total imports of goods and services appear in tables 1.1, 1.2, 1.7 and 3.51. A detailed breakdown is given in table 2.17.

II. *Disposition of total supply: intermediate and final uses*

1. *Intermediate consumption*

Intermediate consumption covers non-durable goods and services used up in production, including repair and maintenance, research and development and exploration costs. It also includes indirect outlays on financing capital formation, such as flotation costs for loans and transfer costs involved in the purchase and sale of intangible assets and financial claims. Intermediate consumption is, as far as possible, valued in purchasers' prices at the moment of use.

For producers of government services and private non-profit services to households, intermediate consumption includes (1) purchases of goods and services on current account *less* sales of similar second-hand goods and scraps and wastes, (2) value of goods in kind received as transfers or gifts from foreign governments, except those received for distribution to households without renovation or alteration, (3) durable goods acquired primarily for military purposes, and (4) goods and services paid for by government but furnished by private suppliers to individuals (e.g., medical services), provided that the individuals have no choice of supplier. However, intermediate consumption of these producers does not include (1) goods and services acquired for use in constructing capital assets, such as roads or buildings, (2) goods and services paid for by government but furnished by private suppliers to individuals, when the individuals can choose the supplier and (3) purchases of strategic materials for government stockpiles.

Intermediate consumption appears in each institutional sector production account in part 3, and in tables 4.1-4.2 by kind of activity. In addition to the flow numbers assigned in SNA, flow numbers have been introduced for two categories of intermediate consumption not separately numbered in *A System of National Accounts*. [3] The first is imputed bank service charges. The imputed bank service charge is defined as the excess of property income accruing to banks and similar financial institutions from the investment of deposits over the interest accruing to their depositors. This imputation is made because of the view that banks perform services for depositors for which no explicit payment is made, in return for the use of the deposits as earning assets. It is not possible to allocate the imputation to specific recipients of the services, however, so that it cannot be included, as would be desirable, as part of the intermediate consumption of each reception. It is therefore deducted as a lump-sum adjustment. The adjustment appears in the tables showing kind-of-activity breakdowns of value added or intermediate consumption, including tables 1.10, 1.11 and 4.1-4.2. The second addition is intermediate consumption of industries of government, required for constructing a production account for general government (table 3.11).

2. *Government final consumption expenditure*

Government final consumption expenditure is equal to the service produced by general government for its own use. Since these services are not sold, they are valued in the gross domestic product at their cost to the government. This cost is defined as the sum of (1) intermediate consumption, (2) compensation of employees, (3) consumption of fixed capital and (4) payments of indirect taxes, *less* (5) the value of own-account production of fixed assets, and *less* (6) sales of goods and services.

The latter item, government sales, includes all payments made by individuals for services received (whether nominal or full cost) and it also includes the provision of second-hand goods from government stores as transfers in kind to foreign governments. Sales of such items as timber from forest preserves, seeds from agricultural experiment stations and government publications would also appear here. Compensation of employees, consumption of fixed capital and indirect taxes paid (if any) should preferably relate to all general government activity, with intra-governmental purchases and sales of goods and services eliminated in order to avoid double counting. With this treatment, there will be no operating surplus for any general government unit. Where countries consider that ancillary agencies and/or unincorporated government enterprises selling to the general public are operated on commercial principles and that the prices charged reflect market values, treatment of these entities on a net basis is an acceptable alternative. In this treatment, their sales to other government agencies will appear as intermediate consumption of the latter, and their operating surplus will appear as an item of general government income. This treatment has a number of disadvantages: the boundary between ancillary agencies and other government agencies is very difficult to specify precisely, and variations in treatment are likely to lead to incomparability among countries. Also, the net treatment makes it impossible to obtain figures for such flows as total compensation of general government employees. Finally, the level of gross domestic product will vary when the government's internal transfer prices are altered, a result that is somewhat incongruous.

Total government consumption expenditures appear in tables 1.1, 1.2, 4.7 and 4.8. A breakdown by government subsectors appears in table 3.12. Tables 2.1-2.2 show detailed breakdowns by function.

3. *Private final consumption expenditure*

Private consumption expenditure measures the final consumption expenditure of all resident non-governmental units. Thus, it is the sum of final consumption expenditure of households and that of private non-profit institutions serving households.

(a) *Private non-profit institutions serving households*. Final consumption expenditure of these units, as in the case of government, is equal to services they produce for their own use and is valued at cost. Cost includes purchases and the value (in purchasers' prices) of transfers of goods and services received in kind, compensation of employees, consumption of fixed capital, and indirect taxes paid by these institutions, *less* their sales of goods and services. The definitions of purchases and sales on current account are much the same as those for general government. Private non-profit institutions serving households are defined to include units employing the equivalent of two or more full-time persons and providing educational, health, cultural, recreational, and other social and community services to households free of charge or at prices that are not intended to cover the full costs of their production. Units mainly financed and controlled by general government, however, are included in general government rather than here. Units primarily serving business, such as trade associations, are included with corporate and quasi-corporate enterprises. In applying these definitions, some judgement is required, and it will often be necessary to examine intent, as well as outcome. A normally profit-making unit that sustains a loss does not thereby become a non-profit institution.

Final expenditures of private non-profit institutions serving households appear in tables 1.1, 1.2 and 3.42, and a breakdown by purpose appears in tables 2.5 and 2.6. Definitions of the purpose categories are given in SNA classification 5.4

(b) *Resident households*. What is wanted as a component of the final uses of gross domestic product is the final consumption expenditure of resident households. What is most commonly available in the statistics, however, is not expenditure of resident units but expenditure in the domestic market. To adjust expenditure in the domestic market to expenditure of resident units, purchases abroad and net gifts in kind received from abroad have been added, and subtracted are purchases in the domestic market of non-resident units. Corresponding adjustments are made to exports (to ensure that they include purchases of non-residents in the domestic market) and to imports (to ensure that they include purchases of residents abroad). These adjustments include expenditures by tourists, ships' crews, border and seasonal workers and diplomatic and military personnel on goods and services, including local transportation, but they exclude expenditures reimbursible as travel expenses (which are counted as intermediate consumption). These adjustments are shown in tables 2.5 and 2.6.

Household final consumption expenditure includes outlays on non-durable and durable goods and services, *less* sales of second-hand goods and of scraps and wastes. In addition to market purchases, household final consumption expenditure includes the imputed gross rent of owner-occupied dwellings, food and other items produced on own account and consumed, and items provided as wages and salaries in kind by an employer, such as food, shelter or clothing, and other fringe benefits included in compensation of employees, except those considered to add to household saving. The imputed gross rent of owner-occupied dwellings should, in principle, be valued at the rent of similar facilities on the market but has been approximated by costs, including operating maintenance and repair charges, depreciation, mortgage interest, and interest on the owner's equity. Other non-marketed output included in final consumption is valued at producers' prices.

Total resident final consumption expenditure appears in tables 1.1, 1.2, 1.6 and 1.12. It is broken down by institutional subsectors in tables 3.32, and in tables 4.7 and 4.8 it is broken down by industrial origin. A detailed breakdown by type of good is shown in tables 2.5 and 2.6. The type-of-good categories are defined in SNA classification 6.1.

4. *Gross capital formation*

Gross capital formation is the sum of the increase in stocks and gross fixed capital formation, defined below. It appears in tables 1.1, 1.2 and 1.8. Breakdowns of gross capital formation appear in tables 2.7-2.12, 4.7 and 4.8. Gross capital formation of individual institutional sectors appears in tables 3.13, 3.23, 3.33. and 3.43.

(a) *Increase in stocks*. This flow includes the value of the physical change in (a) stocks of raw materials, work in progress and finished goods held by private producers, and (b) stocks of strategic materials held by the government. Work put in place on buildings and other structures, roads and other construction projects is treated as gross fixed capital formation rather than increase in stocks but is distinguished separately there to facilitate analysis. Increases in livestock raised for slaughter should be included in the increase in stocks, but breeding and draft animals, dairy cattle, and animals raised for wool clips are treated as fixed capital. The physical change in stocks during a period of account should be valued at average purchasers' prices during the period. In some cases, the available data relate to the change in the value of stocks held rather than the value of the physical change.

A classification of the increase in stocks by type is given in tables 2.7 and 2.8, and defined in SNA classification 6.2. The increase in stocks by kind of activity of owner is shown in tables 2.9 and 2.10.

(b) *Gross capital formation*. This flow is defined to include purchases and own-account production of new producers' durable goods, reduced by net sales to the rest of the world of similar second-hand or scrapped goods. Outlays of producers of government services for military purposes (except on land and certain civilian-type items, such as schools, hospitals, family-type housing and, in some cases, roads when for civilian use) are, however, considered to be current expenditures. "Military purposes" are here construed in terms of final expenditures: they include the military airport, but not the bulldozer used in constructing the airport. Gross fixed capital formation includes outlays on reclamation and improvement of land and development and extension of timber tracts, mines, plantations, orchards, vineyards etc., and on breeding and dairy cattle, draft animals, and animals raised for wool. Outlays on alteration or extension of fixed assets, which significantly extend their life or increase their productivity, are included, but outlays on repair and maintenance to keep fixed assets in good working order are not. All costs are included that are directly connected with the acquisition and installation of the fixed assets, such as customs duties and other indirect taxes, transport, delivery and installation charges, site clearing, planning and designing costs, legal fees and other transfer costs with respect to transactions in land, mineral deposits, timber tracts etc. However, the costs of financing, such as flotation costs, underwriters' commissions and the cost of advertising bond issues, are excluded; these items are included in intermediate consumption. The acquisition of fixed assets is to be recorded at the moment that the ownership of the goods passes to the buyer. In the case of construction projects, this is taken to be the time that the work is put in place but, as noted above, uncompleted construction projects are shown separately from completed ones.

A classification of fixed assets by type is given in tables 2.7 and 2.8, and the categories are defined in SNA classification 6.3. A classification by kind of activity of purchaser is given in tables 2.9, 2.10, 2.11 and 2.12, and a classification by producing industry is given in tables 4.7 and 4.8. Breakdowns by institutional sector are given in tables 3.13, 3.23, 3.33 and 3.43.

5. *Exports of goods and services*

Exports of goods and services are defined to be parallel to the definition of imports given above, and they are shown in the same tables and classifications. Exports are, however, valued f.o.b., whereas imports are valued c.i.f.

III. *Cost components and income shares*

1. *Value added and gross domestic product*

The value added of industries at producers' prices is equal to the gross output of the industries at producers' prices *less* the value of their intermediate consumption at purchasers' prices. Value added for the total of all domestic producers (*plus* import duties and value added tax which are not included in the value added of any domestic producer, and *less* imputed bank service charges which are deducted in a single line) is equal to the gross domestic product is shown in tables 1.9-1.11, and 4.1 - 4.2. Gross domestic product may be defined alternatively as the sum of final expenditures in the domestic economy (tables 1.1 and 1.2) or as the sum of incomes received in the domestic economy (tables 1.3, 1.9 and 4.3). In principle, all three methods should yield the same result but in statistical practice there are likely to be small discrepancies. Such statistical discrepancies are shown where they exist.

2. Compensation of employees

Compensation of employees appears in SNA as a domestic concept and as a national concept. Table 1.3 employs the domestic concept, that is, compensation of employees paid by resident producers. This includes payments to non-resident employees working in the country but excludes payments to resident employees temporarily working abroad. In order to show the relation of this concept to compensation received by resident households (shown in tables 1.6 and 3.32) and compensation paid to the rest of the world (shown in tables 1.7 and 3.51), the two components are shown separately in table 1.3. Each component includes (a) wages and salaries, (b) employers' contributions to social security schemes and (c) employers' contributions to private pension, insurance and similar schemes. The national concept of compensation of employees is shown in the household sector income and outlay account (tables 1.6 and 3.31), where compensation received by resident households from domestic producers and that received from the rest of the world are gathered together. The portion paid by resident producers appears in table 1.3; that paid by the rest of the world appears in table 1.7.

Wages and salaries include all payments to employees for their labour, whether in cash or in kind, before deduction of employee contributions to social security schemes, withholding taxes and the like. They include commissions, bonuses and tips, and cost of living, vacation and sick leave allowances paid directly by the employers to the employee but exclude reimbursement for travel and other expenses incurred by employees for business purposes, which is included in intermediate consumption. The pay and allowances of members of the armed forces, the fees, salaries and bonuses of members of boards of directors, managing directors, executives and other employees of incorporated enterprises and the fees of ministers of religion are included. Wages and salaries in kind are valued at their cost to the employer, and include goods and services furnished to employees free of charge or at markedly reduced cost that are clearly and primarily of benefit to the employees as consumers.

Employers' contributions to social security schemes include all social security contributions that employers make on behalf of their employees, but not the employees' own share of such contributions. Social security contributions may be broader than payments to social security funds, since not all social security arrangements are funded.

Employers' contributions to pension, insurance and similar schemes include paid and imputed contributions by employers on behalf of their employees to private funds, reserves or other schemes for providing pensions, family allowances, lay-off and severance pay, maternity leave, workmen's compensation, health and other casualty insurance life insurance and the like. Where employers make payments to employees for such benefits without the establishment a formal fund for this purpose, the contributions that would be required to support such a fund are imputed both here and subsequently as an imputed transfer from households to their employers, since of course the employees do not control the use of the fund.

3. Operating surplus

Operating surplus is the balancing item in the SNA production account. For an individual establishment, it is defined as the excess of value added over the sum of compensation of employees, consumption of fixed capital, and net indirect taxes. The operating surplus of all types of establishments -- corporate, quasi-corporate, and unincorporated, public and private -- is included in the figure shown in table 1.3. Operating surplus for each of the institutional sectors individually is shown in tables 3.11, 3.21 and 3.31; its breakdown by kind of activity is shown in table 4.3 . It is also included in the totals for property and entrepreneurial income shown in tables 1.4, 1.5 and 1.6.

4. Consumption of fixed capital

Consumption of fixed capital includes allowances for normal wear and tear, foreseen obsolescence and probable (normally expected) accidental damage to fixed capital not made good by repair, all valued at current replacement cost. Unforeseen obsolescence, damages due to calamities, and depletion of natural resources are not included, since these are capital losses and should appear as changes in the balance sheet. Also not included is the revaluation of past allowances for consumption of fixed capital due to changes in the current replacement cost of fixed assets; this also will appear as part of the change in accumulated allowances shown in the balance sheet. Total consumption of fixed capital appears in tables 1.3, 1.8 and 1.12, consumption of fixed capital of individual institutional sectors in tables 3.11, 3.21, 3.31 and 3.41, and consumption of fixed capital by kind of activity in table 4.3. The accumulated consumption of fixed capital for specific types of assets and kind-of-activity sectors appears as the difference between the gross and net capital stock in tables 2.13-2.16, and for individual institutional sectors it appears in tables 3.15, 3.25, 3.35 and 3.45.

5. Indirect taxes

Indirect taxes are defined as taxes chargeable to the cost of production or sale of goods and services. They include (a) import and export duties, (b) excise, sales, entertainment and turnover taxes, (c) real estate and land taxes, unless they are merely an administrative device for collecting income tax, (d) levies on value added and the employment of labour (but not social security contributions), (e) motor-vehicle, driving-test, licence, airport and passport fees, when paid by producers, and (f) the operating surplus of government fiscal monopolies on such items as alcoholic beverages and tobacco (in principle reduced by the normal profit margin of similar business units). In the present publication, indirect taxes paid and subsidies received from supranational organizations (e.g., the European Economic Community) are shown separately. Also, the net treatment of value added taxes recommended by the European Economic Community has been employed.

Unlike all other indirect taxes, SNA does not allocate import duties among producers in tables by kind of activity. Indirect taxes are only allocated to a particular kind of activity where they are levied directly on the output of that activity (e.g., excise duties) or on the process of producing that output (e.g., employment taxes). Import duties, however, are levied on the output of foreign rather than domestic producers, and are therefore shown separately in tables by kind of activity, including tables 1.10, 1.11, 4.1, 4.2, 4.3, 4.5 and 4.6.

Total indirect taxes appear in table 1.3. Indirect taxes paid by individual institutional sectors appear in tables 3.11, 3.21, 3.31, and 3.41. Indirect taxes paid to supranational organizations appear in tables 1.7 and 1.12. Indirect taxes retained by government are shown in table 3.12.

6. *Subsidies*

Subsidies are grants on current account by the government to (a) private enterprises and public corporations, or (b) unincorporated public enterprises when clearly intended to compensate for losses resulting from the price policies of government. Total subsidies, including those paid by supranational organizations, as well as by government, appear in table 1.3; subsidies paid by supranational organizations in tables 1.7 and 1.12; and those paid by government in tables 1.4 and 3.12. Subsidies received by individual institutional sectors appear in tables 3.21, 3.31 and 3.41.

7. *Withdrawals from quasi-corporations*

Withdrawals from the entrepreneurial income of quasi-corporations consist of the actual payments made to the proprietors of quasi-corporations from the entrepreneurial income of these units. Entrepreneurial income of quasi-corporations is equal to their income from production (net operating surplus) *plus* their net income (receipts *less* payments) from property. In some cases, the whole of the entrepreneurial income will be treated as if paid out to the proprietors; in other cases, some of it is retained as net saving within the quasi-corporation. Withdrawals from quasi-corporations also include withdrawals from foreign branches of domestic companies or from domestic branches of foreign companies, since both of these categories are treated as quasi-corporations. The withdrawals may be negative, since proprietors may provide funds to the enterprises to compensate for losses.

SNA assigns separate flow numbers to withdrawals as they appear in the paying sectors (flow 4.4) and in the receiving sectors (flow 4.5). As disbursements, they appear in table 3.22 and as part of a larger total in table 1.5. As receipts, they appear in tables 3.12, 3.22, 3.32 and 3.42, and as parts of the larger total in tables 1.4, 1.5 and 1.6

8. *Property income*

Property income consists of payments of interest, dividends and land rents and royalties, all of which are assigned separate SNA flow numbers, both as payments and as receipts. Interest is defined as income payable and receivable on financial claims, such as bank and other deposits, bills and bonds, including public debt, and the equity of households in life insurance actuarial reserves and pension funds. Dividends consist of income payable and receivable on corporate equity securities and other forms of participation in the equity of private incorporated enterprises, public corporations and co-operatives. Rent payments include, in addition to net land rent, royalty payments for concessions to exploit mineral deposits or for the use of patents, copyrights, trademarks and the like. They exclude rent payments on machinery and equipment or buildings, which are treated as the purchase of a service rather than property income and appear in gross output of the seller and intermediate consumption of the purchaser. Payments of land rent are always treated as a domestic flow since the foreign owners are, for national accounting purposes, dealt with as residents of the country in which the land is located. When it is not possible to separate rent of buildings and rent of the land on which the buildings stand, the whole flow is attributed to the buildings, that is, excluded from property income and included in intermediate consumption.

Property income paid and received by individual institutional sectors is shown in tables 3.12, 3.22, 3.32 and 3.42. As part of a larger total it appears in the summary tables 1.4, 1.5 and 1.6.

IV. *Taxes and unrequited transfers*

The categories of taxes and unrequited transfers are classified and defined in SNA classification 7.1. SNA does not provide the full articulation of the to-whom from-whom relationships of these flows, but assigns flow numbers to the various combinations of them used in specific standard tables and accounts. In order to define less ambiguously the flows used in the present publication, a somewhat fuller listing of individual flow components is used.

1. *Casualty insurance transactions*

Casualty insurance transactions refer to health, accident fire, theft, unemployment and similar insurance schemes. The total of net premiums for the economy as a whole is equal to the total premiums payable *less* an imputed service charge which in turn is defined to be equal to the difference between premiums and claims. As a consequence, for the economy as a whole, net premiums and claims are equal. However, the total service charge is distributed to sectors of receipt and disbursement in proportion to the total (not net) premiums paid, so that net premiums and claims are not necessarily equal for each sector. In the former SNA, these insurance transactions were considered to be in part capital items, and this practice continues in the accounts of a number of countries. In the revised SNA, however, all casualty insurance transactions, including compensation for capital losses, are considered to be current flows. They are shown in detail in tables 3.12, 3.22, 3.32 and 3.42.

2. *Taxes and other government receipts*

Taxes and other government receipts include direct taxes, compulsory fees, fines and penalties, social security contributions, and other current transfers received by general government.

Direct taxes include two components. Direct taxes on income cover levies by public authorities at regular intervals (except social security contributions) on income from employment, property, capital gains or any other source. Real estate and land taxes are included only if they are merely administrative procedures for the assessment and collection of income tax. Other direct taxes cover levies by public authorities at regular intervals on the financial assets and the net of total worth of enterprises, private non-profit institutions and households, and on the possession or use of goods by households. Direct taxes received are shown in tables 1.4 and 3.2; payments of other sectors are shown in tables 3.22, 3.32 and 3.42.

Compulsory fees are payments to public authorities by households for services that are obligatory and unavoidable in the only circumstances in which they are useful. Examples of such fees are payments by households for driving tests and licenses, airport and court fees and the like. Similar payments by business units are treated as indirect taxes. Fines and penalties, however, include not only those paid by households but also those paid by corporate and quasi-corporate enterprises and private non-profit institutions serving households. They appear in the same tables as direct taxes.

Social security contributions consist of contributions for the account of employees, whether made by employees or by employers on their behalf, to the social security arrangements that are imposed, controlled or financed by the government for the purpose of providing social security benefits for the community or large sections of the community. They appear as receipts in tables 1.4 and 3.12, and as payments in tables 1.6 and 3.32.

Current transfers n.e.c. received by general government consist primarily of transfers received from the rest of the world and imputed employee welfare contributions. Transfers from the rest of the world include grants between governments to finance military outlays, outlays for health and educational purposes, and similar transfers in kind of military equipment, food, clothing etc. Payments and assessments and other periodic contributions to international organizations are also included. In addition to actual transfers, this item also includes imputed transfers arising from the obligation of the government as an employer to pay directly to its employees pensions, family allowances, severance and lay-off pay and other welfare benefits when there is no special fund, reserve or insurance for these purposes. In these circumstances, SNA provides for the establishment of an imputed fund to which imputed contributions are made, of a magnitude sufficient to support the unfunded benefit payments. The imputed contributions are included in compensation of employees, as an addition to actual payments, and are then shown as an imputed payment by the employees back to the government as an employer. These transfers appear in table 1.4 as an aggregate, and in table 3.12 in more detail.

3. *Household transfer receipts*

Household transfer receipts include social security benefits, social assistance grants, and unfunded employee welfare benefits. These flows, in varying detail, are shown in tables 1.6, 2.4 and 3.32.

Social security benefits are payments to individuals under the social security arrangements described above. The payments are often made out of a special fund and may be related to the income of individuals from employment or to contributions to social security arrangements made on their behalf. Examples are unemployment insurance benefits, old-age, disability and survivors' pensions, family allowances and reimbursements for medical and hospital expenses. It may be difficult to distinguish social security benefits from social assistance grants, on the one hand, and insurance benefits, on the other. The main criterion is method of finance; the actual content will vary from country to country. Medical services, for instance, may be supplied as social assistance, as a part of social security, as a casualty insurance benefit, or as a free government service.

Social assistance grants are cash grants to individuals and households, except social security benefits and unfunded employee welfare benefits. They may be made by public authorities, private non-profit institutions, or corporate and quasi-corporate enterprises. Examples are relief payments;

widows', guardians' and family allowances and payments of medical and dental expenses which are not part of social insurance schemes; war bonuses, pensions and service grants; and scholarships, fellowships and maintenance allowances for educational, training and similar purposes. They include payments made by public authorities for services provided by business enterprises and private non-profit institutions directly and individually to persons, whether these payments are made to the individuals or directly to the providers of the services that the persons are considered to have purchased. They exclude, however, transfers to persons or households as indemnities for property losses during floods, wars and similar calamities; these are considered to be capital items.

Unfunded employee welfare benefits are pensions, family allowances, severance and lay-off pay, maternity leave pay, workmen's and disability compensation and reimbursements for medical expenses and other casualties which employers pay directly to their former or present employees when there is no special fund, reserve or insurance for these purposes.

4. *Transfers received by private non-profit institutions*

Transfers received by private non-profit institutions serving households include grants and gifts, in cash and in kind, to non-profit institutions serving households which are intended to cover partially the cost of the provision of services by these institutions. They also include membership dues paid to political organizations, fraternal bodies and the like. They appear as a receipt in table 3.42, and as payments sometimes as part of a larger total, in tables 3.12, 3.22 and 3.32.

5. *Other current transfers n.e.c.*

Other current transfers n.e.c. include transfers to and from resident sectors that are not specifically included in any other flows. They may include migrants' remittances, transfers of immigrants' personal and household goods, and transfers between resident and non-resident households, in cash and in kind. They include allowances for bad debts.

V. *Finance of gross accumulation*

1. *Net saving*

Net saving is the balancing item in the SNA income and outlay account. It is defined as the difference between current receipts and current disbursements. Net saving for the nation as a whole appears in tables 1.8 and 1.12. Net saving for individual institutional sectors appears in tables 3.12, 3.13, 3.22, 3.23, 3.32, 3.33, 3.42 and 3.43.

2. *Surplus of the nation on current transactions*

The surplus of the nation on current transactions is the balancing item in the external transactions current accounts (tables 1.7 and 3.51). It also appears in table 1.8, the capital transactions account, in table 1.12, the table showing relationships among the national accounting aggregates, and table 3.52, the external transactions capital accumulation account.

3. *Purchases of land, net*

Purchases of land, net, include purchases *less* sales of land, subsoil deposits, forests and inland waters, including any improvements that are an integral part of these assets except buildings and other structures. The purchases and sales are valued at the transaction (sales) price of the land, forests etc., not including the transfer costs involved; such transfer costs are included in gross capital formation. Purchases and sales are assumed to take place when the legal title to the land is passed. They are considered to take place between resident institutions only. Where the land is purchased by a non-resident, a nominal resident institution is considered to be the owner of the land. The foreign owner is assigned equity in the resident institution equivalent to the purchase price of the land. The value recorded in the flow is the same for both the buyer and the seller. For the country as a whole, therefore, purchases and sales will cancel out. If the sales value of the structures situated on the land cannot be separated from the sales value of the land itself, the entire transaction should be recorded as a purchase and sale of structures (i.e., of second-hand assets), unless the structures are intended for immediate demolition. Purchases of land appear in the capital accumulation accounts of the individual institutional sectors, (tables 3.13, 3.23, 3.33 and 3.43).

4. *Purchases of intangible assets, net*

Purchases of intangible assets, net, are defined as purchases, *less* sales, of exclusive rights to mineral, fishing and other concessions and of patents, copyrights etc. These transactions involve the once-and-for-all relinquishment and acquisition of the exclusive rights, although they may be paid for over a period of years; they do not include concessions, leases, licences to use patents and permission to publish copyrighted materials which involve the periodic payment of royalties or rents, with eventual reversion of the rights to the seller. The purchases and sales are valued at the transaction (sales) value of the mineral concession, lease, patent, etc., not including any transfer costs involved. (The transfer costs are included in gross capital formation.) Purchases of intangible assets appear in the individual institutional sector capital accumulation accounts (tables 3.13, 3.23, 3.33, and 3.43) as a part of gross accumulation. Purchases from the rest of the world appear in table 3.52.

5. *Capital transfers*

Capital transfers are defined as unrequited transfers, in cash or in kind, which are used for purposes of capital formation or other forms of capital accumulation, are made out of wealth, or are non-recurrent. Examples of capital transfers are grants from one government to another to finance deficits in external trade, investment grants, unilateral transfers of capital goods, legacies, death duties and inheritance taxes, migrants' transfers of financial assets and indemnities in respect of calamities. Mixed transfers, considered by one party to the transaction as capital and the other as current, are treated as capital. Capital transfers appear in tables 3.13, 3.23, 3.33, 3.43 and 3.52.

6. *Net lending*

Net lending is defined as the excess of the sources of finance of accumulation (i.e., net saving, consumption of fixed capital and capital transfers received) over the uses of these funds for gross capital formation, net purchases of land and intangibles, and capital transfers paid. It appears in the capital accumulation accounts of the individual institutional sectors (tables 3.13, 3.23, 3.33 and 3.43), and in the external transactions capital accumulation account (table 3.52). Net lending is also equal to the difference between a sector's net acquisition of financial assets and its net incurrence of financial liabilities. It thus also appears in the institutional sector capital finance accounts (tables 3.14, 3.24, 3.34, 3.44 and 3.53). Although not for all countries, net lending derived in these two different ways are statistically identical.

VI. *Financial assets and liabilities*

Net acquisition of financial assets is defined as the difference between, on the one hand, acquisitions or purchases and, on the other, relinquishment or sales by given transactors of financial claims on second parties. Net incurrence of liabilities is equal to the issue or sale *less* redemption or payment of financial claims of second parties. A classification and definitions of financial assets and liabilities is given in SNA classification 7.2. Changes in financial assets and liabilities for individual institutional sectors appear in the capital finance accounts (tables 3.14, 3.24, 3.34, 3.44 and 3.53). Their total amount is shown in the sector balance sheets (tables 3.15, 3.25, 3.35 and 3.45).

VII. *Other assets*

1. *Reproducible tangible assets*

Reproducible tangible assets are classified and defined in table 5.1 of the *Provisional Guidelines on National and Sector Balance Sheets and Reconciliation Accounts of the System of National Accounts.* [4] They appear, classified by type of asset and broad sector, in tables 2.13 and 2.14, by kind of activity in tables 2.15 and 2.16 and for individual institutional sectors, in the sector balance sheets in tables 3.15, 3.25, 3.35 and 3.45

2. *Non-reproducible tangible assets*

Non-reproducible tangible assets are classified and defined in table 5.2 of the *Provisional Guidelines* (see above). Only the total appears in the tables, in the sector balance sheets (tables 3.15, 3.25, and 3.45).

3. *Non-financial intangible assets*

Non-financial intangible assets include the mineral, fishing and other concessions, leases, patents, copyrights etc., the purchase and sale of which is recorded in the capital accumulation account. These intangible assets are created at the time of the purchase or sale, that is, when a once-and-for-all lump-sum payment has been made for the lease, concession, patent or copyright. They appear in the sector balance sheets (tables 3.15, 3.25, 3.35 and 3.45).

---

[1] *Official records of the Economic and Social Council, Forty-fourth Session, Supplement No. 10, (E/4471),* paras. 8-24.

[2] The present system is published in *A System of National Accounts,* Studies in Methods, Series F, No. 2, Rev. 3 (United Nations publication, Sales No. E.69.XVII.3).

[3] *Ibid*

[4] Statistical Papers, Series M, No. 60 United Nations publication, Sales No. 77.XVII.10.

[5] Statistical Papers, Series M, No. 4, Rev. 2, Add. 1 (United Nations publication, Sales No. E.71.XVII.8).

[6] Statistical Papers, Series M, No. 70 (United Nations publication, Sales No. 80.XVII.17).

II. SYSTEM OF MATERIAL PRODUCT BALANCES (MPS)

The System of Material Product Balances (MPS) furnishes the means for standardizing the national accounting data which the Statistical Office of the the Department of International Economic and Social Affairs of the United Nations Secretariat receives from countries with centrally planned economies. Data collection follows the principles found in the *Basic Methodological Rules for the Compilation of the Statistical Balance of the National Economy.* [1] This system is also described in the *Basic Principles of the System of Balances of the National Economy.* [2]

A. STRUCTURE OF MPS

MPS is based on a system of balances. It includes material and financial balances, the balance of manpower resources and the balance of fixed capital and indicators of national wealth. The material balance is a presentation of the volume of the supply of goods and material services originating in domestically produced global product and imports and their disposition to consumption, capital formation and exports, classified by different production activity categories. The financial balance is a presentation of income flows generated in production in the material sphere, their redistribution through transactions in the non-material sphere and through other transfers flows and, finally, their disbursement to consumption and capital formation. The income flows of the financial balance are classified by institutional (social) sectors. The presentation is therefore comparable to that of production, income and outlay and capital finance accounts by institutional sectors in the System of National Accounts (SNA). The third type of balance, that is, the manpower balance, presents the allocation of available manpower to production activities and institutional or social sectors. This balance is expressed in the number of persons employed. The last balance is the one of national wealth and capital assets. It is a presentation of the volume of the stocks of tangible fixed and other assets available at the beginning and the end of the year and the increase that has taken place during the year. The tangible assets are classified by type of asset and by form of ownership and production activities of the national economy.

The MPS tables that are presented in chapter III and are listed in the introduction provide further detail on the material balances. Table 1 on net material product by use is similar to the SNA table on gross domestic product by kind of economic activity. Data regarding the production and goods and services transactions are included in tables 2, 3, 4 and 5 which present, respectively, activity breakdowns of net material product and of primary incomes, of the population and of enterprises, a breakdown by socio-economic sectors of these two types of primary incomes, and a breakdown of supply and disposition of goods and material services by kind of activity of the producers. Tables 6, 7, 8 and 9 present further details on the expenditure categories, such as a breakdown of fixed capital formation by kind of economic activity and by socio-economic sector and of increases in material circulating assets and of stocks by kind of activity, and a classification of final consumption, personal consumption and of total consumption of the population by type of expenditure.

B. DIFFERENCES BETWEEN MPS AND SNA

Apart from the differences in structure of the two systems, there are considerable differences between the coverage of the concepts used in MPS and in SNA. Since these differences limit the use of MPS and SNA data in cross-country types of analyses, a summary of those that are relevant to the MPS data published in chapter III of the present publication is reproduced below. [3]

1. *The treatment of material and non-material services*

In MPS there is a distinction different to that made in SNA, between the production of material and non-material services. Only the production of material services, together with that of goods, is covered by the gross output (global product) concept of MPS. The production of non-material services is excluded. Material goods and services used as input in the production of non-material services are considered to be a part of final consumption expenditure, while income flows resulting from this type of production are treated as income transfers. The material services are those that are directly linked to the production of goods and cover the services related to the repair, transportation and distribution of goods. All other services are treated as non-material services. This important difference between MPS and the present SNA results in the following concrete differences between the two systems:

(a) Expenditures by enterprises on cultural, sports and similar facilities for their employees are excluded in MPS from intermediate consumption. Instead, a transfer between enterprises and households is included, while the material goods and services involved in the above expenditures are allocated to final consumption of the population. SNA treats these expenditures as intermediate consumption;

(b) Depreciation of dwellings and other material goods and services involved in the provision of housing are allocated in MPS to final consumption expenditure. Since these are non-material services, no value-added contribution is included in net material product. In SNA, this contribution is included in gross domestic product;

(c) Travel expenses in connection with business are not included in intermediate consumption in MPS as they are in the present SNA. Instead, they are treated as a part of compensation of employees and the material goods and services involved are allocated to private final consumption expenditure;

(d) In SNA and MPS a different distinction is drawn between uniforms to be treated as intermediate consumption and those to be included in compensation of employees and final consumption expenditure of households. In SNA, the distinction is drawn between civilian (intermediate consumption) and military uniforms and in MPS, between dress and working uniforms;

(e) Tips are treated in SNA as a part of compensation of employees, while in MPS they are treated as income transfers, when they exceed the normal service charge.

2. *Capital formation*

The MPS and SNA guidelines differ, on the one hand, with regard to the treatment of capital gains and losses and the coverage of depreciation and, on the other, in the coverage of fixed capital formation and increases in stocks. The main differences are the following:

(a) In MPS, depreciation, as well as the replacement for losses due to certain foreseeable and non-forseeable damages to fixed assets and stocks, including those caused by accidents and calamities, are deducted in order to arrive at net fixed capital formation. In SNA, generally uses the concept of gross fixed capital formation only is generally used. However, if net capital formation were to be estimated, only depreciation on fixed assets would have to be deducted in that system. Losses in stocks or fixed assets would never be considered for deduction. Losses on fixed assets would be treated as capital losses and dealt with outside the national accounts flows, while losses in stocks would be treated as a part of intermediate consumption or as capital losses, depending on whether they are due to normal events in production or to calamities. The dividing line between losses and depreciation of fixed assets also differs in the two systems. In SNA, depreciation is assumed to cover, among other things, the average amount of accidental damage to fixed assets that is not made good by repair or replacement of parts--for example, damage arising from fire and accidents. In MPS, such damages are not reflected in depreciation but covered under losses;

(b) Depreciation in MPS is based on the original cost of the assets. However, every eight to ten years, adjustments to replacement cost are made to this asset value and these adjustments are also reflected in a corrected value of depreciation. Furthermore, differences that arise between the actual value and the written-off book value at the moment the assets are scrapped or sold are included in the value of depreciation for the year in which the sale or scrapping occurs. In SNA, instead, the replacement value of the assets is used as a basis for depreciation. Any change in this value, whether it happens at the moment the asset is sold or during the time it is used, is considered to be a capital gain or loss and is not accounted for in the national accounting flows;

(c) In addition, in MPS, depreciation includes capital consumption allowances with respect to afforestation, land improvements, roads, bridges and similar structures. In SNA, no imputations for depreciation of this type of asset are included;

(d) Expenditures on fixed assets for military purposes are treated in MPS as a part of net fixed capital formation. In SNA, these outlays are allocated to government final consumption expenditure, except for outlays by government on the construction and alteration of family dwellings for personnel of the armed forces, which are included in gross fixed capital formation;

(e) Transfer cost with regard to purchases and sales of existing fixed assets are treated in MPS as transfers since these are non-material services. In SNA, these costs are included in gross fixed capital formation;

(f) Work put in place on structures, roads, dams, ports and other forms of construction is allocated in MPS to increases in material circulating assets and stocks. Only when the construction is finished is its total value transferrred to net fixed capital formation. In SNA, these outlays are immediately allocated to gross fixed capital formation.

3. *External transactions*

The third area in which MPS and SNA differ is in the coverage of exports and imports of goods and services, in the distinction between residents and non-residents and in the treatment of monetary, as opposed to non-monetary gold. The differences are the following:

(a) In MPS, embassies, consulates and international bodies are treated as residents of the country in which they are located, while in SNA they are treated as residents of the country they represent. This difference in the residence concept has consequences for the allocation between countries of capital formation and government final consumption expenditure and also for the allocation of the income flows. Wages and salaries paid to local employees of these extraterritorial bodies are not included in SNA concept of gross domestic product. They are dealt with, however, as factor income from abroad and therefore accounted for in the national income concept in SNA. In MPS, such wages and salaries, if earned in the sphere of material production, are included in primary incomes of the population, as well as in net material product;

(b) In MPS, the territorial concept of final consumption expenditure, which includes purchases by non-residents in the domestic market and excludes purchases abroad by residents, is used. As a result, such flows are not accounted for in exports or imports. On the other hand, it does include, in exports and imports, transactions that, though they take place in the domestic market, are conducted in foreign currency. These transactions are treated as if they were transactions with non-residents. In SNA, the national concept of final consumption expenditure is used; taken into account in exports and imports, respectively, are the direct purchases in the domestic market by non-residents and the direct purchases abroad by non-residents. Furthermore, no distinction is made in SNA between transactions that are conducted in local or in foreign currency;

(c) Purchases and sales by external trade organizations of goods that do not cross the border of the country in question and also imported goods that are re-exported without being processed are treated in MPS as part of respectively, imports and exports. In SNA, they are not accounted for in the export and import flows, except for the margins received by resident units as payments for services rendered;

(d) Gifts in kind by households to and from abroad are included in exports and imports in SNA. In MPS, they are excluded from these flows;

(e) Transactions in intangible assets (patents, copyrights, trade-marks, exclusive rights to exploit mineral deposits etc.) with the rest of the world are included in MPS in exports and imports. In SNA, they are treated as property income or as sales or purchases of intangible assets to or from abroad, depending on whether the payment is for the use of the rights or for the outright transfer of those rights;

(f) Transactions with the rest of the world in monetary and non-monetary gold are included in MPS in exports and imports. In SNA, included in exports and imports are actual transactions in non-monetary gold only. Exports in addition include newly mined gold (whether actually exported or not) in order to transform gold as a commodity into a financial asset.

C. STANDARD CLASSIFICATIONS OF MPS

Two classifications are used in the MPS standard tables presented, that is, the kind-of-activity classification and the classification by socio-economic group. Contrary to SNA usage with respect to the activity and institutional classifications for different groups of transactions, the two MPS classifications are parallel ones that are applied to the same transaction categories: net material product and its component primary incomes and capital formation. Each of these classifications is described briefly below.

1. *Kind of activity*

All forms of activity in production are classified according to groups or branches, depending on the nature and results of the application of labour. The two major categories constitute branches of the material sphere and branches of the non-material sphere. The first category covers the production of goods, and services that are related to the production of goods, such as repair services, transportation services and goods distribution services. The second category includes the remaining services-producing activities. Each of the two categories is further broken down by branches which are similar in character to the ISIC categories used in SNA. The unit of classification is not the organizational unit (i.e., enterprise) but a smaller unit that performs one type of activity (i.e., establishment). If an enterprise or institution or other organizational unit carries on more than one type of economic activity, it is considered to consist of two or more establishments that perform different activities.

For the subclassification of net material product by kind of activity, only the activity breakdown of the material sphere is used since net material product originates in this sphere only. For capital formation, however, the activity categories of the non-material sphere are also used, since capital formation relates not only to the material sphere but also to non-material branches.

A rough correspondence based on the names of the activity categories can be established between the activity categories presented in SNA and in the MPS branches. The user should be aware, however, of the limitations that such a linkage may entail, as indicated in the following points:

(a) Mining and quarrying, manufacturing, and electricity, gas and water are shown as three separate categories in the SNA presentation and as one category (industrial production), in the MPS presentation;

(b) Hunting and the collection of forestry products is treated as a part of agriculture in the SNA presentation and as a part of forestry and logging in MPS;

(c) The distribution of gas, electricity and water to households is treated in MPS as a non-material service (including in housing). This activity is therefore not reflected in net material product, while its capital formation is dealt with as capital formation of the non-material sphere. In SNA, these distribution activities are an integral part of the activity category for electricity, gas and water;

(d) Printing and publishing, which is treated as a material activity in MPS, is allocated to the MPS category known as "other activities of the material sphere". In SNA, this activity is included with manufacturing;

(e) Cleaning, dyeing and repair services are included with industrial activity (manufacturing) in the MPS presentation and with community, social and personal services in SNA;

(f) In comparing the activity breakdown of net material product and gross domestic product, the user should be aware that the coverage of the MPS category known as "other activities of the material sphere" falls far short of the combined coverage of the two SNA categories for finance, insurance, real estate and business services and for community, social and personal services. The SNA categories include all non-material activities that are excluded from the MPS coverage of net material product. In addition, the shifts between activity categories that were outlined in the previous points affect this group. Other activities in the presentation of net material product include telegraph, news-gathering and editorial agencies, industrial services other than architectural design services, printing and publishing services, the production of motion pictures, phonograph records and prerecorded tapes, data-processing and tabulating services, waterway-maintenance services and the operation of flood-control systems, and services related to the conservation of natural resources and the protection of the environment.

2. Socio-economic sectors

The rates of development of the national economy and the basic features of production that support this development are largely determined by the social structure of the community. In order to study the process, the various activities involved in the production of material goods and services are classified in MPS by socio-economic sector. This classification is based on the form of ownership of the fixed and circulating capital. The form of ownership of the means of production determines the forms of ownership of the product and of the incomes generated by its disposal.

The basic socio-economic sectors are the socialist sector and the private sector.

The socialist sector embraces the enterprises and institutions in public, socialist ownership. The fixed and circulating assets of these enterprises are public property. The socialist sector also includes the personal plots of employees and members of co-operatives.

Within the socialist sector, the following socio-economic subsectors are distinguished: the state subsector; the co-operative subsector, which includes agricultural producers' co-operatives; associations; personal plots of employees; personal plots of members of co-operatives.

The state subsector includes the enterprises and institutions in state ownership. The State furnishes them with the fixed and circulating assets required for their operation. These economic units are administratively subordinated to central or local organs of state authority. The production of the state subsector and the income generated in it belong to the people as a country.

The co-operative subsector embraces the enterprises and institutions in collective or group onwership. The fixed and circulating assets of these economic bodies are originally built up from the entrance fees (initiation fees) of their members and the proceeds of sales of shares to them; and are later supplemented from part of their operating surplus. The output and income of the enterprises and institutions of the co-operative subsector are the property of their members.

The association subsector includes the enterprises and institutions owned by voluntary or semi-voluntary associations. The fixed and circulating assets of the economic bodies of this subsector are built up from the voluntary contributions of their members and from part of the operating surplus of such bodies. The output and income of this subsector belong to the associations.

The personal plots of employees and members of co-operatives embrace agricultural output, construction and other forms of activity (gathering of wild fruits and berries, scrap collection etc.).

The private sector includes the enterprises and institutions, the fixed and circulating assets of which are privately owned. The classification of enterprises and institutions of the private sector is based on the specific economic conditions in the country concerned. Within this sector, the subsector of craftsmen, artisans and peasants who are not members of co-operatives may be distinguished.

Peasants, craftsmen and artisans who do not belong to co-operatives operate small private ventures in which the productive process is carried out by their owners in person, as a rule without recourse to hired labour. This group also includes the subsidiary activities of the population occupied in the private sector of the national economy.

D. DEFINITIONS OF FLOWS

Given below are the definitions of the flows that appear in the MPS standard tables of chapter III. To make possible a comparison between SNA and MPS data, a description of the differences between the MPS and the SNA coverage is added to each of the sections. The items needed in order to convert the MPS coverage into a coverage that conforms to the SNA definition are only summarily indicated. For more information on these items, the user is therefore referred to the description of the differences between the two systems in section B above. The items described below have been grouped together into categories similar to those used for the SNA flows (see chap. I above, sect. C).

I. Total supply and disposition of goods and material services

1. Gross output

Global product covers the value of goods and material services produced. Deliveries of goods and material services within the same enterprise are generally excluded. Included are, among other things, the value of own-account constructed capital goods and capital repairs to fixed assets, the value of work-in-progress and the value of finished goods added to stocks. Covered is, furthermore, the value of goods and material services provided free to employees (the material services are valued at the material cost involved). Included in the contribution to global product by agriculture are seeds and feed produced and consumed at the same farm and agricultural and other goods produced on personal plots for own consumption or for sale, including the cost of their processing. This concept of gross output appears in MPS table 5.

To derive gross output in producers' prices as defined in SNA, global product as described above needs to be increased by:

plus: the gross output value of non-material services (including those of government), including the transfer cost on purchases and sales of existing second-hand fixed assets and land.

2. *Trade margins and transport charges*

The gross output of material goods and services is valued at both producers' and purchasers' values. The difference between the two sets of values gives the distributive trade margins (including restaurants, cafés and other catering) and the transportation margins. The gross output of the distributive-trade units is equal to the value of their gross margins on internal and external trade.

The gross margins on external trade are equivalent to the sum in domestic currency of (a) the value of imports of goods and material services in the domestic market *less* the actual value at which these imports are purchased from abroad and (b) the actual value at which exports of goods and material services are sold to abroad *less* the value of these exports in the domestic market. Trade margins and transport charges appear in MPS table 5.

3. *Intermediate material consumption, including depreciation*

Intermediate material consumption consists of the value of the goods and material services used up in the process of production during a period of account by units of the material sphere, including the consumption of fixed assets during the period. Consistent with the scope of the gross output of goods and material services included in intermediate consumption are certain items, for example, seeds and animal feed, which are produced and used by the same unit. The intermediate output of raw materials etc., is valued net of the value of scraps and wastes originating in the process of production. Purchased items are valued at purchasers' values; items produced on own account are valued at cost in the case of state and co-operative enterprises and at average purchasers' prices in the case of personal plots of households. This concept of intermediate material consumption appears in MPS table 5.

Depreciation or consumption of fixed assets includes an allowance for normal wear and tear and foreseen obsolescence of fixed assets based on standard rates of depreciation and, furthermore, the difference between the book value of scrapped fixed assets and their scrap value. The allowances for depreciation are often based on the original cost of the assets which may be periodically adjusted to replacement cost.

To arrive from intermediate material consumption, including depreciation as defined above, at the SNA concept of intermediate consumption, the MPS coverage needs to be increased and decreased by the following items:

plus: (i) material cost of non-material services;

plus: (ii) material expenditures by enterprises on cultural, sports and similar facilities for their employees;

plus: (iii) reimbursable expenditures for material goods and services purchased during business trips;

minus: (iv) consumption of fixed capital in the material sphere.

4. *Personal consumption*

This consists of all consumer goods, irrespective of durability, and material services (repair, transport, communication and similar services) which are purchased by households, received in kind as payment for work in state and collective enterprises and in private plots, or produced on own account on personal plots. Excluded is the purchase by households of dwellings (which is dealt with as capital formation) but included is the maintenance and depreciation of dwellings. Also included are reimbursable expenditures for material goods and services purchased during business trips. This concept of personal consumption appears in MPS tables 1 and 7. It appears according to source of supply of goods and material services in MPS table 8. In MPS, the domestic concept of consumption is used, so that direct purchases by foreign tourists, diplomatic personnel and other non-residents in the domestic market are included, while similar purchases abroad by residents are excluded.

5. *Material consumption in the units of the non-material sphere serving individuals*

This flow covers expenditures on non-durable goods and material services by units of the non-material sphere serving individuals, reduced by the increases in their stocks of goods. Also included is consumption of fixed assets used by these units. It appears in MPS tables 1 and 7.

6. *Material consumption in the units of the non-material sphere serving the community as a whole*

This flow consists of non-durable goods and material services purchased during a period of account by units of the non-material sphere serving the community as a whole, reduced by the increases in their stocks of goods during the period of account. Also included is consumption of fixed assets of these units. It appears in MPS tables 1 and 7.

To arrive from this concept at government final consumption expenditure as defined in SNA, the following additions to and subtraction from the MPS concept have to be made:

plus: (i) the difference between the value of non-material services produced by government and their material cost and depreciation

plus: (ii) government expenditures on fixed assets that have military uses;

plus: (iii) the difference between consumption expenditures (i.e., material and non-material cost, depreciation and compensation of employees) of extraterritorial bodies that represent the country abroad *minus* consumption expenditures incurred by extraterritorial bodies of other countries and international organizations located in the country in question;

plus: (iv) material expenditures by government (units in the non-material sphere serving individuals) on education, health, culture and other services provided free to individuals.

7. *Final consumption*

This flow is equal to the sum of personal consumption and material consumption in the units of the non-material sphere serving individuals and of those serving the community as a whole. Each of these concepts has been defined above. They appear in MPS tables 5 and 7.

8. *Consumption of the population*

Consumption of the population is the sum of personal consumption and material consumption in the units of the non-material sphere serving individuals. This concept is comparable to private final consumption expenditure in SNA, which can be derived from this MPS concept by adding and subtracting the following items:

plus: (i) the difference between the value of non-material services purchased by households, including housing services and the material cost and depreciation included in the value of these services;

minus: (ii) material expenditures by government (units in the non-material sphere serving individuals) on education, health, culture and other services provided free to individuals;

plus: (iii) the difference between direct purchases abroad by resident households and direct purchases in the domestic market by non-resident households as well as the difference between gifts sent abroad by household *minus* gifts received from abroad;

minus: (iv) reimbursable expenditures for material goods and services purchased during business trips;

minus: (v) material expenditures by enterprises on cultural sports and similar facilities for their employees.

9. *Total consumption of the population*

Total consumption of the population covers the consumption by the population of goods and material services and of non-material services, whether purchased by households or furnished free of charge. It therefore exceeds the consumption of the population (i.e., the sume of personal consumption and material consumption in the units of the non-material sphere serving individuals) by the value of the services of the units of the non-material sphere serving individuals, reduced by the consumption of goods and material services by these units. The value of the services of the units is equivalent to their costs of production, including operating surplus in some instances. In the case of dwellings provided by these units, their depreciation is not included when evaluating costs of production, since charges in respect of depreciation of these dwellings are included in personal consumption. Total consumption of the population appears classified by object in MPS table 9.

10. *Net fixed capital formation*

Net fixed capital formation consists of the value of new fixed assets purchased or constructed on own account and of completed capital repairs to these assets reduced by consumption of fixed assets for renewal of assets and capital repairs, and capital losses due to fire, floods and other calamities and furthermore reduced by the remaining value of scrapped fixed assets. Thus, it measures the net increase in the value of fixed assets during a period of account. This flow appears in MPS tables 5 and 6.

Fixed assets include completed dwellings, buildings and other structures; machinery, equipment and other durable goods acquired by units of the material and non-material sphere; cattle, excluding young cattle and cattle raised for meat; perennial plants; and expenditures on the improvement of land, forests and other natural resources. New fixed assets put into use are generally valued inclusive of acquisition and installation cost.

Capital repairs cover outlays on repairs that make up at least in part for the physical depreciation of the fixed assets and/or significantly raise the capacity and productivity of the fixed assets.

In order to convert the MPS concept of net fixed capital formation into gross fixed capital formation as defined in SNA, the following additions to and substractions from the MPS concept have to be made:

plus: (i) consumption of fixed capital in the material and non-material sphere, including that on afforestation, roads, bridges and similar structures;

plus: (ii) losses due to foreseeable as well as non-foreseeable damages to fixed assets;

plus: (iii) transfer cost with regard to purchases and sales of existing second-hand fixed assets, including land;

plus: (iv) work in progress on the construction of structures, roads, dams and ports on other forms of construction;

plus: (v) the difference between outlays on fixed capital formation by extraterritorial bodies representing the country in question abroad, *less* similar outlays by extraterritorial bodies of other countries and international organizations located in the country in question;

minus: (vi) government expenditures on fixed assets that have military uses.

11. *Gross fixed capital formation*

Gross fixed capital formation is equal to net fixed capital formation as defined above *plus* depreciation. Depreciation is defined in section 3 above, together with intermediate material consumption. Gross fixed capital formation classified by kind of activity appears in MPS table 6.

12. *Increases in material circulating assets and stocks*

This item consists of increases during the period of account in the stocks of enterprises in the material sphere, including wholesale and retail trade units, reduced by losses. Also covered are increases in government stockpiles, including stocks of defense items and state reserves of precious metals and precious stones. The stocks in the material sphere consist of raw materials, fuels, supplies and other non-durable goods; young cattle and cattle raised for meat; work in progress, including uncompleted construction projects; and finished goods not yet sold. Increases in material circulating assets and stocks appear in MPS tables 1 and 6.

In order to convert the MPS concept of increases in material circulating assets and stocks into increases in stocks as defined in SNA, the following addition to and subtractions from the MPS concept are needed:

plus: (i) losses due to foreseeable and non-foreseeable damages to stocks;

minus: (ii) work in progress on the construction of structures, roads, dams and ports and on other forms of construction;

minus: (iii) net increases in the holdings of gold ingots and other monetary gold.

13. *Losses*

This item is the sum of the value of the losses in fixed assets and losses in material circulating assets and stocks. Included are losses (a) due to fires, floods and other calamities, (b) in adult productive and working cattle, (c) due to abandoned or interrupted construction works and (d) in agricultural products in storage at state and co-operative agricultural enterprises and at farms. This flow appears in MPS tables 1 and 5.

In SNA, this final demand category is not identified separately from gross capital formation.

14. *Exports and imports of goods and material services*

Exports are defined to include: (a) outward-bound goods thast cross the border of the country, including imported goods which are exported without being processed; (b) goods which are purchased outside the country by an external trade organization of the country in question and shipped directly to a third country; (c) outward-bound monetary and non-monetary gold and other precious metals; (d) unilateral transfers of goods by the government and public organizations of the country (uncompensated foreign aid); (e) material services, such as transport, forwarding and communication services, rental, including rental payments for time-charter of ships and other transport equipment and, furthermore, export contract services rendered to other countries. The imports cover the same categories of goods and material services which are inward bound. Exports are valued f.o.b. while imports are valued c.i.f. They appear in MPS tables 1 and 5.

To arrive at the SNA coverage of exports of goods and services, the following additions to and subtractions from the MPS concept are needed:

plus: (i) the difference between the export value of non-material services and the material cost and depreciation included in these services;

plus: (ii) consumption expenditure (material and non-material cost, depreciation and compensation of employees) and outlays on fixed capital formation by extraterritorial bodies of foreign governments and international organizations located in the country in question;

plus: (iii) direct purchases in the domestic market by non-resident households and gifts sent abroad by households;

minus: (iv) sales abroad by an external trade organization of the country of goods that have not crossed the border of the country in question; as well as of goods that have crossed the border but that are re-exported without being processed;

minus: (v) the difference between exported monetary gold and the value of sales of newly produced gold ingots and bars.

MPS imports have to be adjusted in a similar manner. To be added are the import value of non-material services *minus* material cost and depreciation, consumption expenditure and fixed capital formation of extraterritorial bodies that represent the country abroad and direct purchases abroad by residents. To be deducted are re-exports and purchases abroad by external trade organizations of goods that do not cross the border of the country, and also the value of imported monetary gold and gifts received households from abroad.

III. Cost components and income shares

1. *Net material product*

Net material product is defined in MPS and is used in countries with centrally planned economies. It can be estimated from the production income and expenditure side in the same manner, as is indicated in chapter I above, section C.III, in which the SNA coverage of gross domestic product is described. Following the production approach, net material product is the difference between global product (i.e., gross output) of goods and material services and intermediate material consumption, including consumption of fixed assets. Net material product defined from the income side is the sum of primary incomes of the population (comparable to compensation of employees in SNA) and primary incomes of enterprises (comparable to operating surplus in SNA). The expenditure approach finally defines net material product as the sum of the final uses of goods and material services, that is, personal consumption, and material consumption of units in the non-material sphere serving individuals and that of similar units serving the community as a whole, net capital formation (i.e., net of depreciation), replacement for losses and the balance between exports and imports of goods and material services. These three different methods for deriving net material product are shown in MPS tables 1, 2 and 4.

To arrive at the SNA concept of gross domestic product, net material product needs to be increased and reduced as follows:

plus: (i) the excess value of non-material services (i.e., the gross output value *minus* material cost and depreciation) consumed by households and by government *plus* the difference between these excess values of exported and imported non-material services;

minus: (ii) material expenditures by enterprises on cultural, sports and similar facilities for their employees;

minus: (iii) reimbursable expenditures for material goods and services purchased during business trips;

plus: (iv) consumption of fixed capital in the material and non-material sphere, including that on afforestation, roads, bridges and similar structures;

plus: (v) losses of fixed assets and stocks due to accidental damage, such as fire, accidents etc.;

plus: (vi) transfer cost with regard to purchases and sales of existing second-hand fixed assets, including land.

2. *Primary income of the population*

The primary income of the population consists of (a) wages and salaries, including receipts in kind, and related income, such as bonuses and reimbursements of expenses on business trips received from state, co-operative and private units of the material sphere; (b) the net material product (net value added) originating from the personal plots of households; and (c) the net material product of self-employed craftsmen, artisans and peasants. This flow appears in MPS tables 3 and 4.

Primary income of the population is roughly comparable to the SNA concept of compensation of employees. However, several differences remain and in order to arrive from the MPS concept at compensation of employees as defined in SNA, the following additions and subtractions are needed:

plus: (i) compensation of employees, including employers' contributions to social security funds, paid out in connection with non-material activities, inclusive of those that are paid out in connection with the provision of cultural, sports and similar facilities by industries in the material sphere;

plus: (ii) employers' contributions to social security funds paid out in connection with material activities;

minus: (iii) income from private enterprises;

minus: (iv) reimbursable expenditures for material goods and services purchased during business trips.

3. *Primary income of enterprises*

Primary income of enterprises consists of the sum of the net material product of the units of the material sphere which have employees *less* the wages and salaries and related incomes which they pay out. The primary incomes of these units are the source of such items as their net income, turnover taxes, contributions to social insurance, payments of taxes, fines and other compulsory items, finance of purchases of non-material services, insurance premiums, interest on bank loans and other business costs. This flow appears in MPS tables 3 and 4.

Although the coverage of primary income of enterprises is similar to that of operating surplus in SNA, the following additions to and subtractions from the MPS concept are needed in order to arrive at operating surplus as defined in SNA:

plus: (i) the remaining value of non-material services (i.e., the gross output value *minus* material cost, depreciation and compensation of employees) consumed by households and government, *plus* the difference between the remaining values of exported and imported non-material services;

minus: (ii) material expenditures by enterprises on cultural, sports and similar facilities for their employees;

plus: (iii) consumption of fixed capital in the material and non-material sphere, including that on afforestation, roads, bridges and similar structures;

plus: (iv) losses of fixed assets and stocks due to accidental damage, such as fire, accidents etc.;

plus: (v) transfer cost with regard to purchases and sales of existing fixed assets, including land;

minus: (vi) employers' contributions to social security funds, paid out in connection with material activities;

plus: (vii) income from private plots and private enterprises.

1/ Standing Statistical Commission, Council of Mutual Economic Assistance (Moscow, 1969).

2/ Studies in Methods, Series F, No. 17 (United Nations publication, Sales No. E.71.XVII.10).

3/ For a more exhaustive list of differences between MPS and SNA, the user should refer to *Comparisons of the System of National Accounts and the System of Balances of the National Economy*, part One, *Conceptual Relationships* (United Nations publication, Sales No. 77.XVII.6).

III. COUNTRY TABLES

Lebanon

Source. Reply to the United Nations National Accounts Questionnaire from the Direction Centrale de la Statistique, Ministere du plan, Beyrouth. The official estimates are published annually by the Direction Centrale de la Statistique in 'Les Comptes Economiques'.

General note. The official estimates of Lebanon have been adjusted by the Direction Centrale de la Statistique to conform to the United Nations System of National Accounts so far as the existing data would permit.

1.1 Expenditure on the Gross Domestic Product, in Current Prices

Million Lebanese pounds

	1970	1975	1978	1979	1980	1981	1982	1983	1984	1985	1986	1987
1 Government final consumption expenditure	512	...	2012	2559	3515	4219	4850	...	...	...	...	...
2 Private final consumption expenditure	4197	...	7627	9661	12905	15488	15840	...	...	...	...	...
3 Gross capital formation	905	...	1640	2010	2196	3459	1179	...	...	...	...	...
A Increase in stocks	-33	...	...	...	...	...	...	...	...	...	...	...
B Gross fixed capital formation	938	...	...	...	...	...	...	...	...	...	...	...
4 Exports of goods and services	1149	...	2120	4168	5460	5724	5255	...	...	...	...	...
5 Less: Imports of goods and services	1897	...	4600	7248	10076	12090	14525	...	...	...	...	...
Equals: Gross Domestic Product	4866	...	8799	11150	14000	16800	12599	...	...	...	...	...

1.3 Cost Components of the Gross Domestic Product

Million Lebanese pounds

	1970	1975	1978	1979	1980	1981	1982	1983	1984	1985	1986	1987
1 Indirect taxes, net	344	...	509	682	683	436	306	...	...	...	...	...
A Indirect taxes	464	...	...	...	...	...	...	...	...	...	...	...
B Less: Subsidies	120	...	...	...	...	...	...	...	...	...	...	...
2 Consumption of fixed capital	275	...	...	...	...	...	...	...	...	...	...	...
3 Compensation of employees paid by resident producers to:	4247	...	...	...	...	...	...	...	...	...	...	...
4 Operating surplus		...	...	...	...	...	...	...	...	...	...	...
Equals: Gross Domestic Product	4866	...	8799	11150	14000	16800	12599	...	...	...	...	...

1.7 External Transactions on Current Account, Summary

Million Lebanese pounds

	1970	1975	1978	1979	1980	1981	1982	1983	1984	1985	1986	1987
Payments to the Rest of the World												
1 Imports of goods and services	1897	...	...	...	...	...	...	...	...	...	...	...
2 Factor income to the rest of the world	299	...	...	...	...	...	...	...	...	...	...	...
3 Current transfers to the rest of the world	...	...	...	...	...	...	...	...	...	...	...	...
4 Surplus of the nation on current transactions	-38	...	...	...	...	...	...	...	...	...	...	...
Payments to the Rest of the World and Surplus of the Nation on Current Transactions	2158	...	...	...	...	...	...	...	...	...	...	...
Receipts From The Rest of the World												
1 Exports of goods and services	1149	...	...	...	...	...	...	...	...	...	...	...
2 Factor income from rest of the world	1009	...	...	...	...	...	...	...	...	...	...	...
3 Current transfers from rest of the world	...	...	...	...	...	...	...	...	...	...	...	...
Receipts from the Rest of the World on Current Transactions	2158	...	...	...	...	...	...	...	...	...	...	...

1.10 Gross Domestic Product by Kind of Activity, in Current Prices

Million Lebanese pounds

	1970	1975	1978	1979	1980	1981	1982	1983	1984	1985	1986	1987
1 Agriculture, hunting, forestry and fishing	445	...	751	952	1288	1435	1076	...	...	...	...	...
2 Mining and quarrying	661	...	...	...	...	...	...	...	...	...	...	...
3 Manufacturing		...	1148	1455	1702	2192	1644	...	...	...	...	...
4 Electricity, gas and water	113	...	478	605	708	911	683	...	...	...	...	...
5 Construction	219	...	300	381	447	575	431	...	...	...	...	...
6 Wholesale and retail trade, restaurants and hotels	1527	...	2490	3155	4008	4753	3565	...	...	...	...	...
7 Transport, storage and communication	401	...	676	857	530	628	471	...	...	...	...	...
8 Finance, insurance, real estate and business services	595	...	1112	1408	2349	2785	2089	...	...	...	...	...
9 Community, social and personal services	482	...	948	1201	1526	1809	1357	...	...	...	...	...

Lebanon

1.10 Gross Domestic Product by Kind of Activity, in Current Prices
(Continued)

Million Lebanese pounds

	1970	1975	1978	1979	1980	1981	1982	1983	1984	1985	1986	1987
Total, Industries	4442	...	7903	10014	12557	15087	11316	...	...	...	...	...
Producers of Government Services	424	...	897	1136	1443	1712	1284	...	...	...	...	...
Other Producers	...	...	...	...	...	...	...	...	...	...	...	...
Subtotal	4866	...	8799	11150	14000	16800	12600	...	...	...	...	...
Less: Imputed bank service charge	...	...	...	...	...	...	...	...	...	...	...	...
Plus: Import duties	...	...	...	...	...	...	...	...	...	...	...	...
Plus: Value added tax	...	...	...	...	...	...	...	...	...	...	...	...
Equals: Gross Domestic Product	4866	...	8799	11150	14000	16800	12600	...	...	...	...	...

1.12 Relations Among National Accounting Aggregates

Million Lebanese pounds

	1970	1975	1978	1979	1980	1981	1982	1983	1984	1985	1986	1987
Gross Domestic Product	4866	...	...	...	...	...	...	...	...	...	...	...
Plus: Net factor income from the rest of the world	165	...	...	...	...	...	...	...	...	...	...	...
Equals: Gross National Product	5031	...	...	...	...	...	...	...	...	...	...	...
Less: Consumption of fixed capital	275	...	...	...	...	...	...	...	...	...	...	...
Equals: National Income	4756	...	...	...	...	...	...	...	...	...	...	...
Plus: Net current transfers from the rest of the world	...	...	...	...	...	...	...	...	...	...	...	...
Equals: National Disposable Income	...	...	...	...	...	...	...	...	...	...	...	...
Less: Final consumption	4709	...	...	...	...	...	...	...	...	...	...	...
Equals: Net Saving	...	...	...	...	...	...	...	...	...	...	...	...
Less: Surplus of the nation on current transactions	...	...	...	...	...	...	...	...	...	...	...	...
Equals: Net Capital Formation	630	...	...	...	...	...	...	...	...	...	...	...

Lesotho

General note. The preparation of national accounts statistics in Lesotho is undertaken by the Bureau of Statistics, Maseru. The official estimates together with methodological notes on sources and methods are published in a series of reports entitled 'National Accounts'. The estimates are generally in accordance with the classifications and definitions recommended in the United Nations System of National Accounts (SNA). The following tables have been prepared from successive replies to the United Nations national accounts questionnaire. When the scope and coverage of the estimates differ for conceptual or statistical reasons from the definitions and classifications recommended in SNA, a footnote is indicated to the relevant tables.

Sources and methods:

(a) Gross domestic product. Gross domestic product if estimated mainly through the production approach.

(b) Expenditure on the gross domestic product. All items of GDP by expenditure type are estimated through the expenditure approach. Government final consumption expenditure, consisting of wages and salaries and purchases of goods and services, is obtained from government accounts. The government expenditure is classified by the type of service provided by the central authorities. The estimates of private final consumption expenditure are based on the rural household survey undertaken in 1967-1969 and on the urban household survey carried out in six district towns from May 1972 to May 1973. Recently, this item has been estimated as a residual. Increase in stocks is estimated mainly from questionnaires and surveys carried out for the agricultural sector. Gross fixed capital formation consists of the value of purchases and own-account construction of fixed assets by government, private and public enterprises, individuals and non-profit institutions. Various sources such as questionnaires are used to collect the information. For the agricultural sector only, increase in stocks is included in this item. Estimates of exports and imports of merchandise are obtained from foreign trade statistics with adjustments made for differences in coverage and valuation. Exports are recorded f.o.b. at the border of Lesotho and imports are also recorded f.o.b. at the point of dispatch. Gross domestic product by expenditure type is not estimated at constant prices.

(c) Cost-structure of the gross domestic product. Wages and salaries are derived from the government accounts and other returns. Estimates of operating surplus are derived as residuals from the production accounts of all sectors. Depreciation is obtained from returned questionnaires and no estimate is available for the government or subsistence sectors. Indirect taxes consist mainly of revenue received by Lesotho as a member of the customs agreement with Botswana, South Africa and Swaziland. Subsidy figures consist of government contributions to defray part of the operating expenses of government and other enterprises.

(d) Gross domestic product by kind of economic activity. The table of GDP by kind of economic activity is prepared in factor values. The production approach is used to estimate the value added of the different industries except for producers of government services in which case the income approach is used. The Agricultural Division of the Bureau of Statistics carries out regular annual surveys. The 1970 census of agriculture and the 1973 agricultural survey are used to derive estimates of cereal production, assuming a wastage of 6 per cent during the various stages of harvest. The 1967-69 rural household survey is used for fruit and vegetable production estimates. For livestock, balance sheets prepared by the Agricultural Division of the Bureau of Statistics provide changes in stock estimates, to which the average values for different types of livestock are applied. For meat production, average carcass weights are applied to the numbers of livestock slaughtered which are obtained from the Ministry of Health and annual production surveys. The value of diamonds sold to licenced dealers by diggers is regarded as the value of diamonds exported from Lesotho. The receipts from diamonds are regarded as a contribution by the mining sector to GDP. Data on quantities and values of diamonds are obtained monthly from the Department of Mines and Geology. For manufacturing, data are derived from questionnaires prepared specially for manufacturing enterprises while data for handicrafts are based on the 1967-1969 rural household consumption and expenditure survey. Data for electricity and water are obtained from the balance sheets of the electricity corporation and accounts of the concerned ministry. Special questionnaires filled in by building contractors are used for the construction sector. Estimates of own-account contribution are included. For the trade sector, questionnaires are used for large enterprises while the results of a survey conducted in 1970-1971 are used for small enterprises. Estimates of the public transport and communication sector are based on government accounts supplemented by inquiries while estimates of private transport are obtained from the concerned enterprises. For the financial sector, special inquiries directed at the banks and the headquarters of insurance companies are used. For ownership of dwellings, government accounts provide information for the public sector while questionnaires returned by businesses and institutions are used for the private sector. The 1972-73 urban household survey is used to estimate imputed rent. Information relating to general government services is obtained from the government accounts. Data on other services are obtained through questionnaires and special inquiries. GDP by kind of economic activity is not estimated at constant prices.

1.1 Expenditure on the Gross Domestic Product, in Current Prices

Million Lesotho maloti

		1970	1975	1978	1979	1980	1981	1982	1983	1984	1985	1986	1987
1	Government final consumption expenditure	6.2	23.1 / 21.3	40.9	52.4	98.9	108.6	99.0	111.2	124.9	168.3	194.6	...
2	Private final consumption expenditure	63.2	183.9 / 167.2	300.7	353.7	395.3	473.7	593.4	707.9	804.4	879.1	1002.3	...
3	Gross capital formation	6.0	27.3 / 20.7	60.1	84.6	100.7	116.3	140.5	100.5	160.7	183.0	215.1	...
A	Increase in stocks	0.8	3.8 / -	9.1	10.9	7.2	8.9	-2.5	0.3	10.1	-2.3	2.0	...
B	Gross fixed capital formation	5.1	23.5 / 20.7	51.0	73.7	93.5	107.4	143.0	100.2	150.6	185.3	213.1	...
	Residential buildings	...	3.2 / 11.2[a]										...
	Non-residential buildings	...	5.8 / ...	30.3	40.3	52.3	55.2	83.2	59.7	72.5	84.0	96.0	...
	Other construction and land improvement etc.	...	3.2 / ...										...
	Other	2.7	11.4 / 9.5	20.7	33.4	41.2	52.2	59.8	40.5	78.1	101.3	117.1	...
4	Exports of goods and services	5.7	16.2 / 14.6	36.4	50.0	61.9	63.4	63.9	59.8	69.7	83.3	95.4	...
5	Less: Imports of goods and services	28.6	139.5 / 113.2	206.3	296.4	359.5	433.6	527.6	584.3	689.0	743.2	860.2	...
	Equals: Gross Domestic Product [b]	52.5	111.0 / 110.6	231.8	244.3	297.3	328.4	369.2	395.1	470.7	570.5	647.2	...

a) Including item 'Residential buildings' through 'Other construction and land improvement etc.'.
b) First series, estimates refer to year beginning 1 April.

Lesotho

1.3 Cost Components of the Gross Domestic Product

Million Lesotho maloti

	1970	1975	1978	1979	1980	1981	1982	1983	1984	1985	1986	1987
1 Indirect taxes, net	4.7	12.9 / 13.2	46.3	28.8	32.9	41.8	69.5	86.7	95.5	113.8	130.5	...
2 Consumption of fixed capital	...	3.0	...	...	...	...	...	...	...	...	...	...
3 Compensation of employees paid by resident producers to:	...	30.3 / 97.4[a]										...
A Resident households	...	30.3 / ...	185.5	215.5	264.4	286.6	299.7	308.4	375.2	456.7	516.7	
B Rest of the world	...	- / ...										...
4 Operating surplus	42.5	64.8 / ...										
Equals: Gross Domestic Product [b]	52.5	111.0 / 110.6	231.9	244.3	297.3	328.4	369.2	395.1	470.7	570.5	647.2	...

a) Including item 'Compensation of employees paid by resident producers to:' through 'Operating surplus'.
b) First series, estimates refer to year beginning 1 April.

1.7 External Transactions on Current Account, Summary

Million Lesotho maloti

	1970	1975	1978	1979	1980	1981	1982	1983	1984	1985	1986	1987
Payments to the Rest of the World												
1 Imports of goods and services	...	139.5 / 113.2	206.3	296.4	359.5	433.6	527.6	584.3	689.0	743.2	860.2	...
A Imports of merchandise c.i.f.	...	137.8 / 106.7	195.9	275.2	331.5	405.5	497.7	539.4	629.1	654.9	744.3	...
B Other	...	1.7 / 6.5	10.4	21.2	28.8	28.1	29.9	44.9	59.9	88.3	115.9	...
2 Factor income to the rest of the world	...	3.2 / 4.8	4.4	5.0	5.7	7.7	16.4	13.9	16.3	20.0	23.7	...
A Compensation of employees	...	...	...	...	...	...	...	...	...	...	...	...
B Property and entrepreneurial income	...	... / 4.8	4.4	5.0	5.7	7.7	16.4	13.9	16.3	20.0	23.7	...
3 Current transfers to the rest of the world [a]	...	0.3	...	...	...	...	...	...	...	...	...	...
4 Surplus of the nation on current transactions	...	-11.5 / 1.5	12.2	1.4	-8.7	-42.9	-41.6	-11.5	7.7	23.4	-30.9	...
Payments to the Rest of the World and Surplus of the Nation on Current Transactions [b]	...	131.6 / 119.5	222.9	302.8	356.5	398.4	502.4	586.7	713.0	786.6	853.0	...
Receipts From The Rest of the World												
1 Exports of goods and services	...	16.2 / 14.6	36.4	50.0	61.9	63.4	63.9	59.8	69.7	83.3	95.4	...
A Exports of merchandise f.o.b.	...	10.6 / 9.2	28.7	38.9	46.6	44.6	40.6	34.6	41.8	51.8	59.9	...
B Other	...	5.7 / 5.4	7.7	11.1	15.3	18.8	23.3	25.2	27.9	31.5	35.5	...
2 Factor income from rest of the world	...	104.2 / 93.9	157.7	183.2	210.7	262.5	389.3	437.0	503.5	534.3	607.1	...
A Compensation of employees	...	100.4 / 90.4	154.3	178.9	205.0	255.0	378.0	421.0	475.9	499.0	583.6	...
B Property and entrepreneurial income	...	3.8 / 3.5	3.4	4.3	5.7	7.5	11.3	16.0	27.6	35.3	23.5	...
3 Current transfers from rest of the world [a]	...	11.1 / 11.0	28.8	69.6	83.9	72.5	49.2	89.9	139.8	169.0	150.5	...
Receipts from the Rest of the World on Current Transactions [b]	...	131.6 / 119.5	222.9	302.8	356.5	398.4	502.4	586.7	713.0	786.6	853.0	...

a) Current transfers from the rest of the world is net of current transfers to the rest of the world.
b) First series, estimates refer to year beginning 1 April.

Lesotho

1.8 Capital Transactions of The Nation, Summary

Million Lesotho maloti

	1970	1975	1978	1979	1980	1981	1982	1983	1984	1985	1986	1987
Finance of Gross Capital Formation												
Gross saving	...	15.8 / 22.2	72.3	86.0	92.0	73.4	98.9	89.0	168.4	206.4	184.2	...
1 Consumption of fixed capital	...	3.0 / ...	...	...	...	...	...	...	...	...	...	...
2 Net saving	...	12.8 / ...	...	...	...	...	...	...	...	...	...	...
Less: Surplus of the nation on current transactions	...	-11.5 / 1.5	12.2	1.4	-8.7	-42.9	-41.6	-11.5	7.7	23.4	-30.9	...
Finance of Gross Capital Formation [a]	...	27.3 / 20.7	60.1	84.6	100.7	116.3	140.5	100.5	160.7	183.0	215.1	...
Gross Capital Formation												
Increase in stocks	...	3.8 / -	9.1	10.9	7.2	8.9	-2.5	0.3	10.1	-2.3	2.0	...
Gross fixed capital formation	...	23.5 / 20.7	51.0	73.7	93.5	107.4	143.0	100.2	150.6	185.3	213.1	...
1 General government	...	12.6 / 10.8	40.6	44.4	44.4	61.0	64.3	59.2	69.0	73.7	84.8	...
2 Corporate and quasi-corporate enterprises	...	10.9 / 9.9	10.4	29.3	49.1	46.4	78.7	41.0	81.6	111.6	128.3	...
A Public	...	... / ...	...	...	...	...	...	...	...	...	...	...
B Private	...	10.9 / 9.9	10.4	29.3	49.1	46.4	78.7	41.0	81.6	111.6	128.3	...
3 Other	...	... / ...	...	...	...	...	...	...	...	...	...	...
Gross Capital Formation [a]	...	27.3 / 20.7	60.1	84.6	100.7	116.3	140.5	100.5	160.7	183.0	215.1	...

a) First series, estimates refer to year beginning 1 April.

1.10 Gross Domestic Product by Kind of Activity, in Current Prices

Million Lesotho maloti

	1970	1975	1978	1979	1980	1981	1982	1983	1984	1985	1986	1987
1 Agriculture, hunting, forestry and fishing	16.7	31.1 / 31.7	55.2	65.7	70.0	74.1	63.9	75.3	98.0	111.0	108.6	121.3
2 Mining and quarrying	0.7	0.5 / 0.5	15.4	18.6	20.7	16.0	13.5	0.8	0.6	1.6	1.9	1.9
3 Manufacturing [a]	2.1	5.6 / 5.6	10.1	11.9	13.9	16.8	22.2	29.1	40.5	45.7	59.2	76.3
4 Electricity, gas and water	0.2	0.8 / 0.8	1.8	2.0	2.2	2.0	2.5	2.1	3.4	4.7	5.0	7.8
5 Construction	1.4	6.0 / 6.0	16.2	21.5	28.0	29.5	44.5	31.9	38.8	50.0	57.5	73.3
6 Wholesale and retail trade, restaurants and hotels	11.2	21.5 / 21.6	27.8	28.7	33.2	36.8	44.7	52.6	63.7	77.7	92.5	110.3
7 Transport, storage and communication	0.6	2.6 / 2.6	4.9	3.6	3.7	4.3	4.7	6.8	9.3	11.4	13.5	15.3
8 Finance, insurance, real estate and business services	7.4	13.5 / 13.5	23.2	23.5	26.4	34.8	42.9	50.6	60.5	65.2	74.6	73.3
9 Community, social and personal services	0.5	0.8 / 6.9	11.5	16.7	27.2	31.0	28.2	29.6	31.6	41.0	47.4	50.1
Total, Industries	40.7	82.4 / 89.2	166.1	192.2	225.3	245.3	267.1	278.8	346.4	408.3	460.2	529.6
Producers of Government Services	4.3	7.8 / 7.2	17.2	22.2	38.7	47.3	44.5	45.9	49.3	67.0	78.6	76.1
Other Producers	2.8	7.9 / 1.0	2.2	3.2	3.2	3.6	4.1	3.4	3.9	4.7	5.4	6.4
Subtotal [b]	47.8	98.1 / 97.4	185.5	217.6	267.2	296.2	315.7	328.1	399.6	480.0	544.2	612.1
Less: Imputed bank service charge	...	... / ...	...	2.1	2.8	9.6	16.0	19.7	24.4	23.3	27.5	18.4
Plus: Import duties	...	... / ...	...	...	...	...	...	...	...	...	...	...
Plus: Value added tax	...	... / ...	...	...	...	...	...	...	...	...	...	...
Plus: Other adjustments [c]	4.7	12.9 / 13.2	46.3	28.8	32.9	41.8	69.5	86.7	95.5	113.8	130.5	156.1
Equals: Gross Domestic Product [d]	52.5	111.0 / 110.6	231.8	244.3	297.3	328.4	369.2	395.1	470.7	570.5	647.2	749.8

a) Item 'Manufacturing' includes handicrafts.
b) Gross domestic product in factor values.
c) Item 'Other adjustments' refers to indirect taxes net of subsidies.
d) First series, estimates refer to year beginning 1 April.

Lesotho

1.11 Gross Domestic Product by Kind of Activity, in Constant Prices

Million Lesotho maloti

	1970	1975	1978	1979	1980	1981	1982	1983	1984	1985	1986	1987
					At constant prices of: 1980							
1 Agriculture, hunting, forestry and fishing	...	...	...	...	70.0	68.3	59.7	66.5	71.6	74.4	65.1	70.8
2 Mining and quarrying	...	...	...	...	20.7	11.6	15.7	1.4	1.4	2.6	2.1	2.2
3 Manufacturing a	...	...	...	...	13.9	15.0	17.3	19.8	24.5	24.2	27.7	32.0
4 Electricity, gas and water	...	...	...	...	2.2	2.5	2.7	2.6	2.7	2.9	3.1	3.5
5 Construction	...	...	...	...	28.0	25.7	32.5	19.8	21.4	24.4	33.2	28.6
6 Wholesale and retail trade, restaurants and hotels	...	...	...	...	33.2	32.9	35.0	37.1	41.5	43.1	46.6	46.8
7 Transport, storage and communication	...	...	...	...	3.7	3.8	4.0	5.2	5.8	6.3	6.9	7.2
8 Finance, insurance, real estate and business services	...	...	...	...	26.4	30.5	33.7	36.7	39.9	37.8	39.1	42.2
9 Community, social and personal services	...	...	...	...	27.2	28.8	26.3	27.6	29.5	28.2	32.7	34.4
Total, Industries	...	...	...	...	225.3	219.1	226.9	216.7	238.3	243.9	256.5	267.7
Producers of Government Services	...	...	...	...	38.7	44.0	41.5	42.8	45.9	44.7	52.4	50.7
Other Producers	...	...	...	...	3.2	3.2	3.2	2.4	2.5	2.6	2.8	2.9
Subtotal b	...	...	...	...	267.2	266.3	271.6	261.9	286.7	291.2	311.7	321.3
Less: Imputed bank service charge	...	...	...	...	2.8	8.4	12.4	14.0	15.9	13.0	14.0	15.5
Plus: Import duties	...	...	...	...	...	...	...	...	...	...	...	...
Plus: Value added tax	...	...	...	...	...	...	...	...	...	...	...	...
Plus: Other adjustments c	...	...	...	...	32.9	35.2	36.7	35.1	35.4	33.0	31.7	35.7
Equals: Gross Domestic Product d	...	...	...	...	297.3	293.1	295.9	283.0	306.2	311.2	329.4	341.5

a) Item 'Manufacturing' includes handicrafts.
b) Gross domestic product in factor values.
c) Item 'Other adjustments' refers to indirect taxes net of subsidies.
d) First series, estimates refer to year beginning 1 April.

1.12 Relations Among National Accounting Aggregates

Million Lesotho maloti

	1970	1975	1978	1979	1980	1981	1982	1983	1984	1985	1986	1987
Gross Domestic Product a	52.5	111.0 / 110.6	231.8	244.3	297.3	328.4	369.2	395.1	470.7	570.5	647.2	...
Plus: Net factor income from the rest of the world	22.3	101.0 / 89.1	153.3	178.2	205.0	254.8	372.9	423.1	487.2	514.3	583.4	...
Factor income from the rest of the world	...	104.2 / 93.9	157.7	183.2	210.7	262.5	389.3	437.0	503.5	534.3	607.1	...
Less: Factor income to the rest of the world	...	3.2 / 4.8	4.4	5.0	5.7	7.7	16.4	13.9	16.3	20.0	23.7	...
Equals: Gross National Product	74.8	212.0 / 199.7	385.1	422.5	502.3	583.2	742.1	818.2	957.9	1084.8	1230.6	...
Less: Consumption of fixed capital	...	3.0	...	...	...	...	...	...	...	...	...	...
Equals: National Income ba	...	209.0 / 199.7	385.1	422.5	502.3	583.2	742.1	818.2	957.9	1084.8	1230.6	...
Plus: Net current transfers from the rest of the world	...	10.8 / 11.0	28.8	69.6	83.9	72.5	49.2	89.9	139.8	169.0	150.5	...
Current transfers from the rest of the world	...	11.1	...	...	...	...	...	...	...	...	...	...
Less: Current transfers to the rest of the world	...	0.3	...	...	...	...	...	...	...	...	...	...
Equals: National Disposable Income ca	...	219.8 / 210.7	413.9	492.1	586.2	655.7	791.3	908.1	1097.7	1253.8	1381.1	...
Less: Final consumption	...	207.0 / 188.5	341.6	406.1	494.2	582.3	692.4	819.1	929.3	1047.4	1196.9	...
Equals: Net Saving da	...	12.8 / 22.2	72.3	86.0	92.0	73.4	98.9	89.0	168.4	206.4	184.2	...
Less: Surplus of the nation on current transactions	...	-11.5 / 1.5	12.2	1.4	-8.7	-42.9	-41.6	-11.5	7.7	23.4	-30.9	...
Equals: Net Capital Formation ea	...	24.3 / 20.7	60.1	84.6	100.7	116.3	140.5	100.5	160.7	183.0	215.1	...

a) First series, estimates refer to year beginning 1 April.
b) Item 'National income' includes consumption of fixed capital.
c) Item 'National disposable income' includes consumption of fixed capital.
d) Item 'Net saving' includes consumption of fixed capital.
e) Item 'Net capital formation' includes consumption of fixed capital.

Lesotho

2.1 Government Final Consumption Expenditure by Function, in Current Prices

Million Lesotho maloti

	1970	1975	1978	1979	1980	1981	1982	1983	1984	1985	1986	1987
1 General public services	...	5.7 / 5.3	10.1	13.8	26.4	35.4	21.2	28.1	33.6	47.7	59.4	56.6
2 Defence	...	...	...	...	...	...	...	...	...	...	...	...
3 Public order and safety	...	3.8 / 3.5	7.7	9.6	20.4	20.7	24.8	24.5	28.0	41.0	46.0	50.0
4 Education	...	6.4 / 5.8	10.1	12.8	25.6	24.8	24.3	27.1	29.9	36.5	42.4	46.1
5 Health	...	1.6 / 1.5[a]	2.9	4.2	7.3	7.1	8.3	10.5	10.8	14.0	15.9	18.1
6 Social security and welfare	...	...										
7 Housing and community amenities	...	...										
8 Recreational, cultural and religious affairs	...	...	...	...	...	...	...	...	...	...	...	...
9 Economic services	...	5.6 / 5.2	10.1	12.0	19.3	20.5	20.3	21.0	22.5	29.0	30.9	36.5
A Fuel and energy	...	...	...	...	...	...	...	...	...	...	...	...
B Agriculture, forestry, fishing and hunting	...	2.0 / 2.0	4.8	5.8	10.4	9.6	9.0	9.4	10.5	13.0	14.1	16.1
C Mining, manufacturing and construction, except fuel and energy	...	... / 0.3	1.1	0.6	1.0	1.4	0.9	0.8	1.2	1.6	1.8	2.2
D Transportation and communication	...											
E Other economic affairs	...	3.5 / 2.9	4.2	5.6	7.8	9.6	10.3	10.7	10.8	14.4	15.0	18.2
10 Other functions	...	...	...	...	...	...	...	...	...	...	...	...
Total Government Final Consumption Expenditure [b]	6.2	23.1 / 21.3	40.9	52.5	99.0	108.6	99.0	111.2	124.8	168.3	194.6	207.3

a) Including item 'Social security and welfare'.
b) First series, estimates refer to year beginning 1 April.

Liberia

General note. The preparation of national accounts statistics in Liberia is undertaken by the Ministry of Planning and Economic Affairs, Monrovia. The official estimates are published annually in 'Economic Survey of Liberia'. A description of the sources and methods used for the national accounts estimation is found in 'Sources and Methods of Estimation of National Product, 1970-1973' and 'The New Series and Methodology for Estimating Gross Domestic Product, 1973' published in 1975 and 1978 respectively. The estimates are generally in accordance with the classifications and definitions recommended in the United Nations System of National Accounts (SNA). The following tables have been prepared from successive replies to the United Nations national accounts questionnaire. When the scope and coverage of the estimates differ for conceptual or statistical reasons from the definitions and classifications recommended in SNA, a footnote is indicated to the relevant tables.

Sources and methods:

(a) Gross domestic product. Gross domestic product is estimated mainly through the income approach.

(b) Expenditure on the gross domestic product. The expenditure approach is used to estimate government final consumption expenditure, increase in stocks and exports and imports of goods and services. The commodity-flow approach is used to estimate private final consumption expenditure and gross fixed capital formation. The main sources used for estimating government final consumption expenditure are the monthly revenue and expenditure reports contained in 'Government Accounts of Liberia'. For private expenditure on imported goods, the c.i.f. value and import duties are obtained directly from the import statistics of consumer goods while the trade and transport margin is put at 35 per cent of the c.i.f. value. For local production, estimates are obtained from the production statistics of goods and services. Changes in stocks are estimated for iron-ore only. The sources used are the annual reports of the iron-ore companies and an analysis based on the difference between production and exports. The estimate is obtained by finding the difference between the quantities produced and the quantities exported and applying the average export prices. Gross fixed capital formation is estimated as value of local production plus imports minus exports plus transport costs, trade mark-ups, duties paid, etc. For machinery and equipment, the estimates are based on foreign trade statistics. For construction, the estimates are prepared by analysing import and local production of construction materials, the data of which are obtained from import statistics and the survey of establishments. The estimates of imports and exports of goods and services are based on the foreign trade statistics. Figures on exports and imports are supplemented by estimates for non-factor services. Constant price series of government expenditure is estimated by using employment data to extrapolate the base-year figures. The base-year value for stocks of iron-ore is extrapolated by using a volume indicator. For the remaining components of GDP by expenditure type, the current values are deflated by price indexes.

(c) Cost-structure of the gross domestic product. The estimates of compensation of employees, operating surplus and consumption of fixed capital are obtained from income tax files, replies to the national accounts questionnaires and from annual reports and financial accounts. The estimates of indirect taxes and subsidies are based on income tax returns for the main activities.

(d) Gross domestic product by kind of economic activity. The table of GDP by kind of economic activity is prepared in factor values. The income approach is used to estimate the value added of most industries. When data are available, the production and expenditure approaches are also used. For the agricultural sector, value added of rubber production is estimated from the financial accounts of the rubber concessions, the income tax statements of all rubber companies, and from information obtained from local rubber farmers. For other agricultural crops and fishing, value added is obtained from the income tax files. The value added of forestry is arrived at from an input-output study of the industry, based on the national accounts surveys. For the mining of iron-ore, value added is obtained directly from the financial accounts of the companies. Information of production components of manufacturing is obtained from income tax files, semi-annual questionnaires and other supplementary series. An extrapolation is made for non-reporting establishments. The value added of electricity, gas and water is obtained directly from the annual reports and accounts of concerned enterprises and their replies to the national accounts questionnaires. Estimates of the construction sector are derived mainly by using the commodity-flow approach. Domestic production of commodities used in construction is estimated and adjusted for exports, imports and changes in stocks and supplementary data on transport costs, dealers' margins, etc. is added. The value of imported construction materials and production statistics of locally produced construction are obtained. Information on substantial development of land undertaken is supplied by the companies. A combination of the production approach and the income approach is used for the trade sector. The output is equal to the gross margin. The income tax data and the technique of extrapolation are used to arrive at value added. The extrapolation process involves separating the large establishments from the others, extrapolating the value added by the change registered by comparable establishments and finally indentifying new establishments and treating them as an additional contributor to value added. The estimates of the transport sector are derived from various sources such as national accounts questionnaire, income tax files and reports of the Motor Vehicle Division. The gross output of the financial sector is equal to the sum of actual service charges and imputed service charges. The data required for the value added are obtained through a questionnaire. The estimates of real estate and ownership of dwellings are obtained by extrapolating the 1967 estimate by means of the population growth rate and the rent component of the consumer price index. For producers of government services, the main source is the detailed analysis of the government accounts. The value added of other private services are extrapolated by the change in compensation of employees, interest, depreciation and operating surplus obtained from the income tax files. For the constant price estimates, price deflation is used for manufacturing, construction and trade sectors. For the remaining sectors, value added is extrapolated by using volume indexes.

1.1 Expenditure on the Gross Domestic Product, in Current Prices

Million Liberian dollars

	1970	1975	1978	1979	1980	1981	1982	1983	1984	1985	1986	1987
1 Government final consumption expenditure	45.1	73.2	139.0	156.6	182.0	200.1	222.4	169.1	160.2	137.3	135.8	...
2 Private final consumption expenditure	206.4	257.6	402.0	436.2	430.0	647.2	650.4	723.0	710.2	706.8	662.6	...
3 Gross capital formation	88.4	216.7	218.6	280.0	245.2	198.1	236.0	190.8	194.6	134.3	122.8	...
A Increase in stocks [a]	8.4	55.5	-41.5	-17.6	49.1	18.5	42.9	7.7	25.7	7.8	7.8	...
B Gross fixed capital formation	80.0	161.2	260.1	297.6	196.1	179.6	193.1	183.1	168.9	126.5	115.0	...
4 Exports of goods and services	240.1	403.7	500.0	553.6	613.5	540.7	510.6	463.5	489.0	470.2	459.4	...
5 Less: Imports of goods and services	172.2	371.9	548.6	587.4	614.0	560.9	478.5	479.2	411.5	322.8	370.2	...
Statistical discrepancy	...	30.3	62.7	52.3	59.9	29.1	-47.6	18.4	-69.6	-69.0	24.4	...
Equals: Gross Domestic Product	407.8	609.6	773.7	891.3	916.6	1054.3	1093.3	1085.6	1072.9	1056.8	1034.8	...

a) Item 'Increase in stocks' includes only increase in iron ore stocks. Beginning 1981, it includes increase in iron ore and rubber stocks.

Liberia

1.2 Expenditure on the Gross Domestic Product, in Constant Prices

Million Liberian dollars

	1970	1975	1978	1979	1980	1981	1982	1983	1984	1985	1986	1987
					At constant prices of:							
				1971					1981			
1 Government final consumption expenditure	49.6	48.8	60.2	64.0	61.0	58.5 / 200.1	218.9	169.0	156.8	136.9	134.3	...
2 Private final consumption expenditure	209.5	161.5	217.0	202.0	171.0	163.5 / 647.2	620.9	650.0	621.1	625.0	593.4	...
3 Gross capital formation	76.4	116.6	97.1	122.0	116.9	87.1 / 198.1	234.3	193.4	173.3	120.2	104.4	...
A Increase in stocks	-4.3[a]	26.6[a]	-28.2[a]	-11.3[a]	21.7[a]	-4.5[a] / 18.5	40.5	5.4	20.6	6.5	6.5	...
B Gross fixed capital formation	80.7	90.0	125.3	133.3	95.2	91.6 / 179.6	193.8	188.0	152.7	113.7	97.9	...
4 Exports of goods and services	261.0	211.7	239.1	236.0	237.0	217.4 / 540.7	471.0	460.1	489.5	473.0	449.0	...
5 Less: Imports of goods and services	187.2	187.5	223.6	267.0	187.0	169.0 / 560.9	454.0	473.1	375.1	317.4	314.6	...
Statistical discrepancy	...	23.4	29.2	82.0	12.5	17.9 / 29.1	-18.3	36.5	-35.8	-28.7	25.8	...
Equals: Gross Domestic Product	409.3	374.5	419.0	439.0	411.4	395.4 / 1054.3	1072.8	1035.9	1029.8	1009.0	992.3	...

a) Item 'Increase in stocks' includes only increase in iron ore stocks. Beginning 1981, it includes increase in iron ore and rubber stocks.

1.3 Cost Components of the Gross Domestic Product

Million Liberian dollars

	1970	1975	1978	1979	1980	1981	1982	1983	1984	1985	1986	1987
1 Indirect taxes, net	28.5	50.5	103.7	114.2	115.8	116.5	118.2	106.8	103.0	96.0	86.6	...
2 Consumption of fixed capital	54.8	...	...	...	...	...	...	...	...	...	...	...
3 Compensation of employees paid by resident producers to:	324.5	...	...	...	...	...	...	...	...	...	...	...
4 Operating surplus		...	...	...	...	...	...	...	...	...	...	...
Equals: Gross Domestic Product	407.8	609.6	773.7	891.3	916.6	1054.3	1093.3	1085.6	1072.9	1056.8	1034.8	...

1.10 Gross Domestic Product by Kind of Activity, in Current Prices

Million Liberian dollars

	1970	1975	1978	1979	1980	1981	1982	1983	1984	1985	1986	1987
1 Agriculture, hunting, forestry and fishing	94.4	62.6	118.3	139.7	159.0	297.0	284.8	334.5	358.7	352.8	335.1	...
2 Mining and quarrying	115.6	231.8	130.2	134.8	153.0	127.4	150.3	123.2	107.4	128.2	129.6	...
3 Manufacturing	15.2	36.3	53.7	82.0	77.0	62.9	65.2	59.6	68.5	64.8	64.7	...
4 Electricity, gas and water	5.6	8.5	13.2	17.2	19.1	22.7	25.0	28.9	22.5	16.6	18.3	...
5 Construction	18.4	28.8	50.1	63.0	32.5	37.0	39.7	39.8	34.6	32.2	29.0	...
6 Wholesale and retail trade, restaurants and hotels	42.6	49.2	85.0	93.0	79.0	59.1	74.9	70.4	62.5	60.2	56.7	...
7 Transport, storage and communication	31.8	40.7	59.2	66.0	61.0	76.2	77.0	80.4	80.7	71.4	75.3	...
8 Finance, insurance, real estate and business services	23.7	40.2	55.6	68.2	76.6	85.8	90.2	100.9	110.3	109.0	115.2	...
9 Community, social and personal services	9.0	21.4	...	...	31.5	28.6	29.6	31.7	27.7	31.4	31.0	...
Total, Industries	356.3	520.5	...	...	688.7	796.7	836.7	869.4	872.9	866.7	854.9	...
Producers of Government Services	23.0	43.8	...	...	123.6	154.4	154.9	127.1	121.7	114.4	113.0	...

Liberia

1.10 Gross Domestic Product by Kind of Activity, in Current Prices
(Continued)

Million Liberian dollars

	1970	1975	1978	1979	1980	1981	1982	1983	1984	1985	1986	1987
Other Producers	3.4	...	...	...	...	...	...	...	...	...	...	...
Subtotal a	382.7	564.3	675.0	791.4	812.3	951.1	991.6	996.5	994.6	981.1	967.9	...
Less: Imputed bank service charge	3.4	4.7	5.0	14.1	11.5	13.3	16.5	17.7	24.7	20.3	19.7	...
Plus: Import duties	18.1	33.2	72.1	77.4	67.6	80.3	67.3	60.3	57.0	57.5	...	...
Plus: Value added tax	...	...	...	...	...	...	...	...	...	...	...	...
Plus: Other adjustments b	10.4	16.8	31.6	36.8	48.2	36.2	50.9	46.5	46.0	37.8	...	...
Equals: Gross Domestic Product	407.8	609.6	773.7	891.3	916.6	1054.3	1093.3	1085.6	1072.9	1056.8	1034.8	...

a) Gross domestic product in factor values.
b) Item 'Other adjustments' refers to net indirect taxes other than import duties.

1.11 Gross Domestic Product by Kind of Activity, in Constant Prices

Million Liberian dollars

	1970	1975	1978	1979	1980	1981	1982	1983	1984	1985	1986	1987
		\multicolumn{5}{c}{At constant prices of: 1971}	\multicolumn{6}{c}{1981}	
1 Agriculture, hunting, forestry and fishing	89.3	50.1	59.9	62.8	63.0	49.4 / 297.0	297.9	305.0	323.2	339.2	342.3	...
2 Mining and quarrying	121.2	116.2	93.3	99.1	111.0	100.8 / 127.4	120.9	96.0	99.4	92.0	94.3	...
3 Manufacturing	15.7	23.1	30.7	33.0	26.0	23.6 / 62.9	66.0	65.4	68.3	67.2	65.1	...
4 Electricity, gas and water	4.9	6.6	7.9	8.0	7.8	7.9 / 22.7	26.9	23.4	23.6	24.0	24.0	...
5 Construction	17.4	14.1	22.0	25.0	15.0	18.0 / 37.0	33.3	38.2	29.8	30.5	26.7	...
6 Wholesale and retail trade, restaurants and hotels	40.4	27.6	30.2	31.0	25.0	23.0 / 59.1	68.9	67.1	56.9	57.4	52.4	...
7 Transport, storage and communication	32.7	35.5	43.0	44.0	35.0	33.4 / 76.2	88.8	86.4	84.7	72.7	71.1	...
8 Finance, insurance, real estate and business services	24.1	26.7	28.0	30.0	30.0	31.1 / 85.8	83.6	88.7	86.3	86.5	87.3	...
9 Community, social and personal services	9.1	18.7	...	...	17.0	16.0 / 28.6	30.5	31.4	27.1	30.0	28.0	...
Total, Industries	354.8	318.6	...	...	330.3	303.2 / 796.7	816.8	801.6	799.3	799.5	791.2	...
Producers of Government Services	25.2	29.2	...	...	39.6	50.4 / 154.4	154.9	152.5	146.0	137.3	135.6	...
Other Producers	3.4	...	...	...	...	...	...	...	...	...	...	...
Subtotal	383.4 a	347.8 a	372.2 a	393.5 a	369.9 a	353.6 a / 951.1	971.7	954.1	945.3	936.8	926.8	...
Less: Imputed bank service charge	3.3	4.3	4.0	4.5	3.7	4.3 / 13.3	12.4	14.7	11.1	13.0	13.7	...
Plus: Import duties	...	...	...	...	...	...	...	...	...	...	...	...
Plus: Value added tax	...	...	...	...	...	...	...	...	...	...	...	...
Plus: Other adjustments	29.2 b	31.0 b	50.8 b	50.0 b	45.2 b	45.8 b / 116.5	113.5	96.5	95.6	85.2	79.2	...
Equals: Gross Domestic Product	409.3	374.5	419.0	439.0	411.4	395.4 / 1054.3	1072.8	1035.9	1029.8	1009.0	992.3	...

a) Gross domestic product in factor values.
b) Item 'Other adjustments' refers to net indirect taxes other than import duties.

Liberia

1.12 Relations Among National Accounting Aggregates

Million Liberian dollars

	1970	1975	1978	1979	1980	1981	1982	1983	1984	1985	1986	1987
Gross Domestic Product	...	...	...	...	...	1054.3	1093.3	1085.6	1072.9	1056.8	1034.8	...
Plus: Net factor income from the rest of the world	...	...	...	...	...	-125.2	-175.5	-141.9	-170.1	-70.6	-110.9	...
Equals: Gross National Product	...	...	...	...	...	929.1	917.8	943.7	902.8	986.2	923.9	...
Less: Consumption of fixed capital	...	...	...	...	...	118.3	115.8	115.8	98.6	85.2	90.8	...
Equals: National Income	...	...	...	...	...	810.8	802.0	827.9	804.2	901.0	833.1	...
Plus: Net current transfers from the rest of the world	...	...	...	...	...	...	...	...	...	...	...	...
Equals: National Disposable Income	...	...	...	...	...	...	...	...	...	...	...	...
Less: Final consumption	...	...	...	...	...	...	...	...	...	...	...	...
Equals: Net Saving	...	...	...	...	...	...	...	...	...	...	...	...
Less: Surplus of the nation on current transactions	...	...	...	...	...	...	...	...	...	...	...	...
Equals: Net Capital Formation	...	...	...	...	...	...	...	...	...	...	...	...

Libyan Arab Jamahiriya

General note. The preparation of national accounts statisticis in Libyan Arab Jamahiriya is undertaken by the Ministry of Planning, Tripoli. The official estimates are published in a series of publications entitled 'National Accounts of Libya'. A detailed description of the sources and methods used for the national accounts estimation is contained in a publication entitled 'National Accounts Statistics of the Libyan Arab Republic - Sources and Methods' published in 1972. The estimates are generally in accordance with the classifications and definitions recommended in the United Nations System of National Accounts (SNA). The following tables have been prepared from successive replies to the United Nations national accounts questionnaire. When the scope and coverage of the estimates differ for conceptual or statistical reasons from the definitions and classifications recommended in SNA, a footnote is indicated to the relevant tables.

Sources and methods:

(a) Gross domestic product. Gross domestic product is estimated mainly through the production approach.

(b) Expenditure on the gross domestic product. The expenditure approach is used to estimate government final consumption expenditure and imports and exports of goods and services. This approach is also used for gross fixed capital formation, although supported by the commodity-flow method for machinery and equipment. The commodity-flow method is used for the estimation of private expenditure on goods while other approaches are used for the estimation of expenditure on services. For government final consumption expenditure, the estimates are obtained from actual revenue and expenditure data supplied by the Ministry of Finance, by municipalities and by the National Social Insurance Institutions. The estimates are classified both by purpose and by kind of expenditure. The estimates of private expenditures on goods are obtained from the external trade statistics by commodity and from data on locally produced goods, import duties, trade margins and average retail prices. The estimates of capital formation for the petroleum sector are obtained from Annual Survey of Petroleum Mining Industry and for the general government, the most important source is the data on actual expenditure in the central government development budgets. For machinery and equipment, external trade data are used, adding duties paid and other costs and deducting value of re-export from c.i.f. value of imports. Exports and imports of goods and services are estimated from data supplied by the Bank of Libya. For the constant price estimates, price deflation is used for most of the expenditure items, the current values being deflated by various price indexes such as nation-wide cost of living index, price index of imported consumer goods and appropriate unit value indexes for different capital goods. Personal expenditures on items such as food and transport equipment are extrapolated by quantity indicators.

(c) Cost-structure of the gross domestic product. In estimating the cost-structure components of GDP, depreciation of the petroleum sector is obtained from the Annual Survey of Petroleum Mining Industry. For other sectors, depreciation is estimated as a certain percentage of gross domestic product according to international experience and judgement about the prevailing situation in the Libyan economy. Indirect taxes are estimated from the central government and local authorities' annual accounts, while subsidies are estimated on the basis on the ordinary and the development budgets. No information for compensation of employees and operating surplus is available about the methods of estimation.

(d) Gross domestic product by kind of economic activity. The table of gross domestic product by kind of economic activity is prepared at market prices, i.e. producers' values. The production approach is used to estimate value added of the majority of industries. The income approach is used for transport, storage and communication, public administration and defence and other services. The expenditure approach is used for the construction sector, whereas value added of the trade sectors is based upon the use of the commodity-flow method. All data required for the estimation of the agriculture sector are supplied by the Ministry of Agriculture. The agricultural statistics are based on reports made by the local authorities of the Ministry of Agriculture and data derived from the reporting system are verified by the agricultural census held in 1974. Petroleum mining, which accounts for more than two-thirds of GDP, is carried out by petroleum mining concession holding units and by non-concession holding units which are engaged in prospecting and drilling activities on a contract basis. Gross output of the concession holding units is made up of value of exports, value of domestic sales, value of changes in stocks, cost of surveys and exploration, value of work done for others and miscellaneous sources of income. The value of exports based on f.o.b. values, is reported by crude petroleum exporting companies, while the value of the other output is contained in the Annual Survey of Petroleum Mining Industry. The total value of inputs consists of the cost of materials consumed and the value of services purchased. For the activities of the non-concession holding units, a survey is undertaken on an annual basis since 1970. The basic source of information for manufacturing is the annual survey conducted since 1965 and published in 'Report of the Annual Survey of Large Manufacturing Establishments'. The data derived from the surveys are adjusted to exclude trade activity. Estimates for gross output and value added are then worked out for all establishments, including those engaging less than 20 persons which are not covered by the annual surveys. The main sources of information for the construction sector are the government budgets, statements by the municipalities and the annual surveys of the petroleum mining industry and of the large manufacturing establishments. The value added of construction is estimated as a percentage of the total expenditure on construction made by all sectors of the economy. There are no comprehensive statistics which could be used for a direct compilation of value added originating in trade. The estimation is instead based on an indirect method, according to which the income accruing to the trade sector is estimated as a percentage of the value of goods transacted during the year. The value added of road transport is based on the number of vehicles in operation and the estimated value added per vehicle. Transport data are supplied by Ministry of Communication Road Department and Libyan Arab Airline. Data for banking and insurance are supplied by Bank of Libya. The income accrued from ownership of dwellings is based on the estimation of the number of dwelling units existing each year and on the application of an average annual rent per unit. Estimates for the producers of government services are based on actual revenue and expenditure of the government sectors. Other services estimates are derived by applying an average gross income per person to the number of persons engaged in the different activities. For the constant price estimates, double deflation is used for the agricultural sector with the quantity of output and input valued at average 1963-1965 prices. Value added of crude oil production, electricity, gas and water, construction and transport is extrapolated by quantity indexes of output. For other activities in the petroleum sector, the current value is deflated by a price index roughly reflecting changes in the cost of its main goods and services. For manufacturing, trade, financial sector and other services, different kinds of price indexes are used, such as cost of living index and price index of domestic manufacturing goods.

1.1 Expenditure on the Gross Domestic Product, in Current Prices

Million Libyan dinars

	1970	1975	1978	1979	1980	1981	1982	1983	1984	1985	1986	1987
1 Government final consumption expenditure	220.7	1044.3	1691.8	2006.6	2350.5	2720.5	2965.5	...	...	...	...	...
2 Private final consumption expenditure	395.5	1193.5	1665.2	1894.7	2327.5	3127.3	3383.8	...	...	...	...	...
3 Gross capital formation	246.3	1154.7	1552.0	1965.3	2518.8	2930.9	2311.8	...	...	...	...	...
A Increase in stocks	3.6	100.0	20.0	110.0	95.0	120.0	-50.0	...	...	...	...	...
B Gross fixed capital formation	242.7	1054.7	1532.0	1855.3	2423.8	2810.9	2361.8	...	...	...	...	...
Residential buildings	...	235.5	256.5	214.8	250.6	325.2	...	...	...	...	...	...
Non-residential buildings	...	166.5	255.6	356.9	419.9	540.5	...	...	...	...	...	...
Other construction and land improvement etc.	...	285.7	535.6	659.7	914.2	999.3	...	...	...	...	...	...
Other	...	367.0	484.3	623.9	839.1	945.9	...	...	...	...	...	...
4 Exports of goods and services	870.0	2053.2	2978.1	4801.4	6737.0	4868.4	4104.5	...	...	...	...	...
5 Less: Imports of goods and services	403.2	1665.7	2199.5	2821.7	3398.7	4306.2	3920.0	...	...	...	...	...
Equals: Gross Domestic Product	1329.3	3780.0	5687.6	7846.4	10535.1	9340.9	8845.6	8531.0	7574.0	7203.0	6473.0	...

Libyan Arab Jamahiriya

1.2 Expenditure on the Gross Domestic Product, in Constant Prices

Million Libyan dinars

	1970	1975	1978	1979	1980	1981	1982	1983	1984	1985	1986	1987
		At constant prices of:										
		1975						1980				
1 Government final consumption expenditure	...	1044.3	1619.0	1884.1	2141.0 / 2350.5	2566.5	2696.0	...	...	...	...	...
2 Private final consumption expenditure	...	1193.5	1518.6	1679.9	1995.3 / 2327.5	3053.9	3026.3	...	...	...	...	...
3 Gross capital formation	...	1154.7	1307.1	1538.2	1781.5 / 2518.8	2746.2	2095.2	...	...	...	...	...
A Increase in stocks	...	100.0	15.0	100.0	90.0 / 95.0	112.0	-45.5	...	...	...	...	...
B Gross fixed capital formation	...	1054.7	1292.1	1438.2	1691.5 / 2423.8	2634.2	2140.7	...	...	...	...	...
Residential buildings	...	235.5	243.2	265.6	180.1 / ...	...	...	...	...	...	...	...
Non-residential buildings	...	166.5	225.9	246.5	332.8 / ...	...	...	...	...	...	...	...
Other construction and land improvement etc.	...	285.7	437.3	475.9	635.4 / ...	...	...	...	...	...	...	...
Other	...	367.0	385.7	450.2	543.2 / ...	...	...	...	...	...	...	...
4 Exports of goods and services	...	2053.2	2728.3	2958.1	2443.1 / 6737.0	4314.2	4549.1	...	...	...	...	...
5 Less: Imports of goods and services	...	1665.7	1949.8	2369.2	2630.8 / 3398.7	4102.5	3685.0	...	...	...	...	...
Equals: Gross Domestic Product	...	3780.0	5223.2	5691.1	5730.1 / 10535.1	8578.3	8681.6	...	...	...	...	...

1.3 Cost Components of the Gross Domestic Product

Million Libyan dinars

	1970	1975	1978	1979	1980	1981	1982	1983	1984	1985	1986	1987
1 Indirect taxes, net	41.0	105.7	191.5	243.4	297.9	385.9	315.6	...	...	...	...	...
A Indirect taxes	50.5	219.9	307.3	393.3	509.4	575.8	528.0	...	...	...	...	...
B Less: Subsidies	9.5	114.2	115.8	149.9	211.5	189.9	212.4	...	...	...	...	...
2 Consumption of fixed capital	109.0	166.1	237.4	263.2	338.3	392.4	475.9	...	...	...	...	...
3 Compensation of employees paid by resident producers to:	268.8	1048.2	1635.4	1848.9	2162.7	2546.7	2635.2	...	...	...	...	...
A Resident households	217.5	976.5	...	...	...	...	...	...	...	...	...	...
B Rest of the world	51.3	71.7	...	...	...	...	...	...	...	...	...	...
4 Operating surplus	910.5	2460.0	3623.3	5490.9	7736.2	6015.9	5418.9	...	...	...	...	...
A Corporate and quasi-corporate enterprises	...	...	...	...	...	...	...	...	...	...	...	...
B Private unincorporated enterprises	...	...	...	...	...	...	...	...	...	...	...	...
C General government	...	3.3	...	...	...	...	...	...	...	...	...	...
Equals: Gross Domestic Product	1329.3	3780.0	5687.6	7846.3	10535.1	9340.9	8845.6	...	...	...	...	...

1.4 General Government Current Receipts and Disbursements

Million Libyan dinars

	1970	1975	1978	1979	1980	1981	1982	1983	1984	1985	1986	1987
				Receipts								
1 Operating surplus	...	3.3	3.1	10.9	15.9	...	...	...	...	...	...	...
2 Property and entrepreneurial income	490.1	1408.4	2405.0	3950.5	6497.9	...	...	...	...	...	...	...
3 Taxes, fees and contributions	80.5	363.4	595.4	740.3	919.8	...	...	...	...	...	...	...
A Indirect taxes	50.5	219.9	307.3	393.3	509.4	...	...	...	...	...	...	...

Libyan Arab Jamahiriya

1.4 General Government Current Receipts and Disbursements
(Continued)

Million Libyan dinars

	1970	1975	1978	1979	1980	1981	1982	1983	1984	1985	1986	1987
B Direct taxes	16.2	83.4	195.9	225.5	283.9	...	...	...	...	...	...	...
C Social security contributions	8.9	48.8	75.4	76.9	86.0	...	...	...	...	...	...	...
D Compulsory fees, fines and penalties	4.9	11.3	16.8	44.6	40.5	...	...	...	...	...	...	...
4 Other current transfers	7.2	9.5	3.7	2.5	1.7	...	...	...	...	...	...	...
Total Current Receipts of General Government	577.8	1784.7	3007.2	4704.2	7435.4	...	...	...	...	...	...	...

Disbursements

	1970	1975	1978	1979	1980	1981	1982	1983	1984	1985	1986	1987
1 Government final consumption expenditure	220.7	1044.3	1691.8	2006.6	2350.5	...	...	...	...	...	...	...
A Compensation of employees	...	413.9	...	...	...	...	...	...	...	...	...	...
B Consumption of fixed capital	...	20.5	...	...	...	...	...	...	...	...	...	...
C Purchases of goods and services, net	...	...	...	...	...	...	...	...	...	...	...	...
D Less: Own account fixed capital formation	...	...	...	...	...	...	...	...	...	...	...	...
E Indirect taxes paid, net	...	...	...	...	...	...	...	...	...	...	...	...
2 Property income	...	...	...	...	...	...	...	...	...	...	...	...
3 Subsidies	9.5	114.2	115.8	149.9	211.5	...	...	...	...	...	...	...
4 Other current transfers	68.4	90.3	160.7	216.4	337.6	...	...	...	...	...	...	...
A Social security benefits	...	30.6	43.9	52.3	49.9	...	...	...	...	...	...	...
B Social assistance grants	6.5	9.0	34.2	49.3	81.3	...	...	...	...	...	...	...
C Other	68.4	50.7	82.7	114.9	206.4	...	...	...	...	...	...	...
5 Net saving	279.2	536.0	1038.9	2331.0	4535.7	...	...	...	...	...	...	...
Total Current Disbursements and Net Saving of General Government	577.8	1784.7	3007.2	4704.2	7435.4	...	...	...	...	...	...	...

1.7 External Transactions on Current Account, Summary

Million Libyan dinars

	1970	1975	1978	1979	1980	1981	1982	1983	1984	1985	1986	1987

Payments to the Rest of the World

	1970	1975	1978	1979	1980	1981	1982	1983	1984	1985	1986	1987
1 Imports of goods and services	403.2	1665.7	2199.5	2821.7	3398.7	4306.2	3920.0	...	...	...	...	...
A Imports of merchandise c.i.f.	372.2	1454.8	1957.6	2469.0	3057.8	...	...	...	...	...	...	...
B Other	31.0	210.9	241.9	352.7	340.9	...	...	...	...	...	...	...
2 Factor income to the rest of the world	252.6	495.3	535.8	678.9	668.2	860.1	836.4	...	...	...	...	...
A Compensation of employees	51.3	71.7	161.5	301.9	311.5	453.2	466.2	...	...	...	...	...
B Property and entrepreneurial income	201.3	423.6	374.3	377.0	356.7	406.9	370.2	...	...	...	...	...
3 Current transfers to the rest of the world	43.4	50.1	37.7	70.1	30.1	41.7	39.1	...	...	...	...	...
4 Surplus of the nation on current transactions	208.1	-93.6	304.1	1362.0	3025.3	149.6	-424.6	...	...	...	...	...
Payments to the Rest of the World and Surplus of the Nation on Current Transactions	907.3	2117.5	3077.1	4932.7	7122.3	5357.6	4370.9	...	...	...	...	...

Libyan Arab Jamahiriya

1.7 External Transactions on Current Account, Summary
(Continued)

Million Libyan dinars

	1970	1975	1978	1979	1980	1981	1982	1983	1984	1985	1986	1987
Receipts From The Rest of the World												
1 Exports of goods and services	870.0	2053.2	2978.1	4801.4	6737.0	4868.4	4104.5	...	...	...	...	...
A Exports of merchandise f.o.b.	857.6	2011.8	2941.0	4766.4	6697.4	...	...	...	...	...	...	...
B Other	12.4	41.4	37.1	35.0	39.6	...	...	...	...	...	...	...
2 Factor income from rest of the world	36.6	63.5	93.9	125.8	379.5	481.6	256.9	...	...	...	...	...
A Compensation of employees	-	-	-	-	...	...	...	...	...	...	...	...
B Property and entrepreneurial income	36.6	63.5	93.9	125.8	...	...	...	...	...	...	...	...
3 Current transfers from rest of the world	0.7	0.8	5.1	5.8	5.8	7.6	9.5	...	...	...	...	...
Receipts from the Rest of the World on Current Transactions	907.3	2117.5	3077.1	4932.7	7122.3	5357.6	4370.9	...	...	...	...	...

1.8 Capital Transactions of The Nation, Summary

Million Libyan dinars

	1970	1975	1978	1979	1980	1981	1982	1983	1984	1985	1986	1987
Finance of Gross Capital Formation												
Gross saving	454.3	1061.1	1856.1	3327.3	5544.1	3080.5	1887.2	...	...	...	...	...
1 Consumption of fixed capital	109.0	166.1	237.4	263.2	338.3	392.4	475.9	...	...	...	...	...
A General government	...	18.4	37.6	50.3	63.7	...	...	...	...	...	...	...
B Corporate and quasi-corporate enterprises	...	...	...	...	...	...	...	...	...	...	...	...
C Other	...	...	...	...	...	...	...	...	...	...	...	...
2 Net saving	345.3	895.0	1618.7	3064.1	5205.8	2688.1	1411.3	...	...	...	...	...
A General government	279.2	536.0	1038.9	2331.0	4535.7	...	...	...	...	...	...	...
B Corporate and quasi-corporate enterprises	...	...	...	...	...	...	...	...	...	...	...	...
C Other	...	...	...	...	...	...	...	...	...	...	...	...
Less: Surplus of the nation on current transactions	208.1	-93.6	304.1	1362.0	3025.3	149.6	-424.6	...	...	...	...	...
Finance of Gross Capital Formation	246.3	1154.7	1552.0	1965.3	2518.8	2930.6	2311.8	...	...	...	...	...
Gross Capital Formation												
Increase in stocks	3.6	100.0	20.0	110.0	95.0	120.0	-50.0	...	...	...	...	...
Gross fixed capital formation	242.7	1054.7	1532.0	1855.3	2423.8	2810.9	2361.8	...	...	...	...	...
1 General government	3.3	834.1	1284.4	1672.6	2223.3	...	...	...	...	...	...	...
2 Corporate and quasi-corporate enterprises	...	...	...	...	...	...	...	...	...	...	...	...
3 Other	...	...	...	...	...	...	...	...	...	...	...	...
Gross Capital Formation	246.3	1154.7	1552.0	1965.3	2518.8	2930.9	2311.8	...	...	...	...	...

Libyan Arab Jamahiriya

1.10 Gross Domestic Product by Kind of Activity, in Current Prices

Million Libyan dinars

	1970	1975	1978	1979	1980	1981	1982	1983	1984	1985	1986	1987
1 Agriculture, hunting, forestry and fishing	33.1	82.9	122.1	140.4	164.9	204.3	217.2	...	...	...	...	...
2 Mining and quarrying [a]	814.3	1981.8	2842.0	4586.8	6620.7	4709.4	4265.2	...	...	...	...	...
3 Manufacturing	22.5	65.5	148.7	185.8	213.9	240.8	304.9	...	...	...	...	...
4 Electricity, gas and water	6.2	17.6	31.0	40.0	49.7	55.7	69.2	...	...	...	...	...
5 Construction	87.8	434.7	682.8	726.7	935.7	1202.5	1053.9	...	...	...	...	...
6 Wholesale and retail trade, restaurants and hotels	47.0	224.6	338.9	383.2	481.7	556.5	522.7	...	...	...	...	...
7 Transport, storage and communication	43.2	175.8	250.9	291.2	335.3	385.5	387.3	...	...	...	...	...
8 Finance, insurance, real estate and business services	67.9	229.9	348.2	383.4	441.3	495.4	467.6	...	...	...	...	...
9 Community, social and personal services	68.2	201.9	318.8	351.0	381.0	421.1	469.9	...	...	...	...	...
Total, Industries	1190.2	3414.7	5083.4	7088.5	9624.2	8271.2	7757.9	...	...	...	...	...
Producers of Government Services	98.1	258.3	410.8	512.5	611.1	683.8	772.1	...	...	...	...	...
Other Producers	...	1.3	1.9	2.0	2.0	-	-	...	...	...	...	...
Subtotal [b]	1288.3	3674.3	5496.1	7603.0	10237.3	8955.0	8530.0	...	...	...	...	...
Less: Imputed bank service charge	...	...	...	...	...	...	...	...	...	...	...	...
Plus: Import duties	...	...	...	...	...	...	...	...	...	...	...	...
Plus: Value added tax	...	...	...	...	...	...	...	...	...	...	...	...
Plus: Other adjustments [c]	41.0	105.7	191.5	243.4	297.9	385.9	315.6	...	...	...	...	...
Equals: Gross Domestic Product	1329.3	3780.0	5687.6	7846.4	10535.1	9340.9	8845.6	...	...	...	...	...

a) Item 'Mining and quarrying' includes oil and gas production.
b) Gross domestic product in factor values.
c) Item 'Other adjustments' refers to indirect taxes net of subsidies.

1.11 Gross Domestic Product by Kind of Activity, in Constant Prices

Million Libyan dinars

	1970	1975	1978	1979	1980	1981	1982	1983	1984	1985	1986	1987
		1964		1975	At constant prices of:		1980					
1 Agriculture, hunting, forestry and fishing	17.2	82.9	85.9	91.2	104.9 / 164.9	177.9	185.9	...	...	...	...	...
2 Mining and quarrying	660.4	1981.8[a]	2647.6[a]	2853.1[a]	2478.0[a] / 6620.7[a]	4200.3[a]	4414.8[a]	...	...	...	...	...
3 Manufacturing	20.5	65.5	141.0	136.0	157.0 / 213.9	220.8	280.5	...	...	...	...	...
4 Electricity, gas and water	4.7	17.6	31.0	40.0	49.7 / 49.7	54.1	64.2	...	...	...	...	...
5 Construction	41.8	434.7	559.7	567.7	660.9 / 935.7	1085.5	942.8	...	...	...	...	...
6 Wholesale and retail trade, restaurants and hotels	37.5	224.6	294.7	314.1	349.1 / 481.7	515.3	493.1	...	...	...	...	...
7 Transport, storage and communication	36.5	175.8	223.6	246.2	274.1 / 335.3	376.0	373.4	...	...	...	...	...
8 Finance, insurance, real estate and business services	50.3	229.9	320.0	339.6	376.8 / 441.3	476.2	452.4	...	...	...	...	...
9 Community, social and personal services	51.0	203.2	318.2	348.3	376.6 / 382.9	411.1	440.3	...	...	...	...	...

Libyan Arab Jamahiriya

1.11 Gross Domestic Product by Kind of Activity, in Constant Prices
(Continued)

Million Libyan dinars

	1970	1975	1978	1979	1980	1981	1982	1983	1984	1985	1986	1987
		1964		1975	At constant prices of:			1980				
Total, Industries	919.9	3416.0	4621.7	4936.2	4827.1 / 9626.1	7517.2	7647.4	...	...	...	...	...
Producers of Government Services	73.4	258.3	410.0	511.5	605.1 / 611.1	670.2	718.6	...	...	...	...	...
Other Producers	...	...	...	...	...	...	...	...	...	...	...	...
Subtotal	993.3	3674.3	5031.7	5447.7	5432.2 / 10237.2	8187.4	8366.0	...	...	...	...	...
Less: Imputed bank service charge	...	...	...	...	...	...	...	...	...	...	...	...
Plus: Import duties	...	...	...	...	...	...	...	...	...	...	...	...
Plus: Value added tax	...	...	...	...	...	...	...	...	...	...	...	...
Equals: Gross Domestic Product	993.3	3674.3[b]	5031.7[b]	5447.7[b]	5432.2[b] / 10237.2[b]	8187.4[b]	8366.0[b]	...	...	...	...	...

a) Item 'Mining and quarrying' includes oil and gas production.
b) Gross domestic product in factor values.

1.12 Relations Among National Accounting Aggregates

Million Libyan dinars

	1970	1975	1978	1979	1980	1981	1982	1983	1984	1985	1986	1987
Gross Domestic Product	1329.3	3780.0	5687.6	7846.3	10535.1	9340.9	8845.6	...	...	...	...	...
Plus: Net factor income from the rest of the world	-216.0	-431.8	-441.9	-553.1	-288.7	-378.5	-579.5	...	...	...	...	...
Factor income from the rest of the world	36.6	63.5	93.9	125.8	379.5	481.6	256.9	...	...	...	...	...
Less: Factor income to the rest of the world	252.6	495.3	535.8	678.9	668.2	860.1	836.4	...	...	...	...	...
Equals: Gross National Product	1113.3	3348.2	5245.7	7293.2	10246.4	8962.4	8266.1	...	...	...	...	...
Less: Consumption of fixed capital	109.0	166.1	237.4	263.2	338.3	392.4	475.9	...	...	...	...	...
Equals: National Income	1004.3	3182.1	5008.3	7030.0	9908.1	8570.0	7790.2	...	...	...	...	...
Plus: Net current transfers from the rest of the world	-42.7	-49.3	-32.6	-64.3	-24.3	-34.1	-29.6	...	...	...	...	...
Current transfers from the rest of the world	0.7	0.8	5.1	5.8	5.8	7.6	9.5	...	...	...	...	...
Less: Current transfers to the rest of the world	43.4	50.1	37.7	70.1	30.1	41.7	39.1	...	...	...	...	...
Equals: National Disposable Income	961.6	3132.8	4975.7	6965.7	9883.8	8535.9	7760.6	...	...	...	...	...
Less: Final consumption	616.2	2237.8	3357.0	3901.3	4678.0	5847.8	6349.3	...	...	...	...	...
Equals: Net Saving	345.3	895.0	1618.7	3064.1	5205.8	2688.1	1411.3	...	...	...	...	...
Less: Surplus of the nation on current transactions	208.1	-93.6	304.1	1362.0	3025.3	149.6	-424.6	...	...	...	...	...
Equals: Net Capital Formation	137.3	988.6	1314.6	1702.1	2180.5	2538.5	1835.9	...	...	...	...	...

Libyan Arab Jamahiriya

2.1 Government Final Consumption Expenditure by Function, in Current Prices

Million Libyan dinars

	1970	1975	1978	1979	1980	1981	1982	1983	1984	1985	1986	1987
1 General public services	47.7					...	...	...	...	...	...	...
2 Defence	91.2	763.9	1201.6	1381.2	1617.7	...	...	...	...	...	...	...
3 Public order and safety						...	...	...	...	...	...	...
4 Education	33.0	132.0	210.5	237.8	271.2	...	...	...	...	...	...	...
5 Health	16.2	65.1	121.8	144.5	174.4	...	...	...	...	...	...	...
6 Social security and welfare	1.4	17.7	34.9	55.0	54.4	...	...	...	...	...	...	...
7 Housing and community amenities	7.0	18.1	32.0	34.7	29.3	...	...	...	...	...	...	...
8 Recreational, cultural and religious affairs	6.0	12.2	24.3	20.4	21.3	...	...	...	...	...	...	...
9 Economic services	18.2	35.0	66.7	133.0	182.1	...	...	...	...	...	...	...
10 Other functions	...	...	...	...	...	...	...	...	...	...	...	...
Total Government Final Consumption Expenditure	220.7	1044.3	1691.8	2006.6	2350.5	...	...	...	...	...	...	...

2.2 Government Final Consumption Expenditure by Function, in Constant Prices

Million Libyan dinars

	1970	1975	1978	1979	1980	1981	1982	1983	1984	1985	1986	1987
				At constant prices of:1975								
1 General public services	...					...	...	...	...	...	...	...
2 Defence	...	763.9	1142.3	1282.8	1454.1	...	...	...	...	...	...	...
3 Public order and safety	...					...	...	...	...	...	...	...
4 Education	...	132.4	206.4	231.4	258.4	...	...	...	...	...	...	...
5 Health	...	65.1	117.1	136.2	159.3	...	...	...	...	...	...	...
6 Social security and welfare	...	17.7	34.1	53.9	53.1	...	...	...	...	...	...	...
7 Housing and community amenities	...	18.1	30.5	32.8	27.3	...	...	...	...	...	...	...
8 Recreational, cultural and religious affairs	...	12.2	23.7	19.7	20.2	...	...	...	...	...	...	...
9 Economic services	...	34.9	64.9	127.3	168.6	...	...	...	...	...	...	...
10 Other functions	...	...	...	...	...	...	...	...	...	...	...	...
Total Government Final Consumption Expenditure	...	1044.3	1619.0	1884.1	2141.0	...	...	...	...	...	...	...

2.5 Private Final Consumption Expenditure by Type and Purpose, in Current Prices

Million Libyan dinars

	1970	1975	1978	1979	1980	1981	1982	1983	1984	1985	1986	1987
				Final Consumption Expenditure of Resident Households								
1 Food, beverages and tobacco	152.0	...	...	...	...	...	...	...	...	...	...	...
A Food	136.5	...	...	...	...	...	...	...	...	...	...	...
B Non-alcoholic beverages	3.2	...	...	...	...	...	...	...	...	...	...	...
C Alcoholic beverages	1.1	...	...	...	...	...	...	...	...	...	...	...
D Tobacco	11.2	...	...	...	...	...	...	...	...	...	...	...
2 Clothing and footwear	39.6	...	...	...	...	...	...	...	...	...	...	...
3 Gross rent, fuel and power	71.6	...	...	...	...	...	...	...	...	...	...	...
4 Furniture, furnishings and household equipment and operation	17.6	...	...	...	...	...	...	...	...	...	...	...
A Household operation	5.3	...	...	...	...	...	...	...	...	...	...	...
B Other	12.3	...	...	...	...	...	...	...	...	...	...	...
5 Medical care and health expenses	11.8	...	...	...	...	...	...	...	...	...	...	...
6 Transport and communication	51.0	...	...	...	...	...	...	...	...	...	...	...
A Personal transport equipment	7.4	...	...	...	...	...	...	...	...	...	...	...
B Other	43.6	...	...	...	...	...	...	...	...	...	...	...
7 Recreational, entertainment, education and cultural services	14.6	...	...	...	...	...	...	...	...	...	...	...
8 Miscellaneous goods and services	24.5	...	...	...	...	...	...	...	...	...	...	...

Libyan Arab Jamahiriya

2.5 Private Final Consumption Expenditure by Type and Purpose, in Current Prices
(Continued)

Million Libyan dinars

	1970	1975	1978	1979	1980	1981	1982	1983	1984	1985	1986	1987
A Personal care	18.4	...	...	...	...	...	...	...	...	...	...	...
B Expenditures in restaurants, cafes and hotels	5.2	...	...	...	...	...	...	...	...	...	...	...
C Other	0.9	...	...	...	...	...	...	...	...	...	...	...
Total Final Consumption Expenditure in the Domestic Market by Households, of which	382.7	...	...	...	...	...	...	...	...	...	...	...
A Durable goods	38.0	...	...	...	...	...	...	...	...	...	...	...
B Semi-durable goods	54.9	...	...	...	...	...	...	...	...	...	...	...
C Non-durable goods	187.0	...	...	...	...	...	...	...	...	...	...	...
D Services	102.8	...	...	...	...	...	...	...	...	...	...	...
Plus: Direct purchases abroad by resident households	19.5	...	...	...	...	...	...	...	...	...	...	...
Less: Direct purchases in the domestic market by non-resident households	10.1	...	...	...	...	...	...	...	...	...	...	...
Equals: Final Consumption Expenditure of Resident Households	392.1	...	...	...	...	...	...	...	...	...	...	...

Final Consumption Expenditure of Private Non-profit Institutions Serving Households

	1970	1975	1978	1979	1980	1981	1982	1983	1984	1985	1986	1987
Equals: Final Consumption Expenditure of Private Non-profit Organisations Serving Households	...	...	...	...	...	...	...	...	...	...	...	...
Statistical discrepancy	3.4	...	...	...	...	...	...	...	...	...	...	...
Private Final Consumption Expenditure	395.5	...	...	...	...	...	...	...	...	...	...	...

2.6 Private Final Consumption Expenditure by Type and Purpose, in Constant Prices

Million Libyan dinars

	1970	1975	1978	1979	1980	1981	1982	1983	1984	1985	1986	1987

At constant prices of: 1964

Final Consumption Expenditure of Resident Households

	1970	1975	1978	1979	1980	1981	1982	1983	1984	1985	1986	1987
1 Food, beverages and tobacco	118.6	...	...	...	...	...	...	...	...	...	...	...
A Food	107.1	...	...	...	...	...	...	...	...	...	...	...
B Non-alcoholic beverages	3.0	...	...	...	...	...	...	...	...	...	...	...
C Alcoholic beverages	0.7	...	...	...	...	...	...	...	...	...	...	...
D Tobacco	7.8	...	...	...	...	...	...	...	...	...	...	...
2 Clothing and footwear	36.9	...	...	...	...	...	...	...	...	...	...	...
3 Gross rent, fuel and power	56.0	...	...	...	...	...	...	...	...	...	...	...
4 Furniture, furnishings and household equipment and operation	16.9	...	...	...	...	...	...	...	...	...	...	...
A Household operation	4.2	...	...	...	...	...	...	...	...	...	...	...
B Other	12.7	...	...	...	...	...	...	...	...	...	...	...
5 Medical care and health expenses	7.9	...	...	...	...	...	...	...	...	...	...	...
6 Transport and communication	36.9	...	...	...	...	...	...	...	...	...	...	...
A Personal transport equipment	6.5	...	...	...	...	...	...	...	...	...	...	...
B Other	30.4	...	...	...	...	...	...	...	...	...	...	...
7 Recreational, entertainment, education and cultural services	14.1	...	...	...	...	...	...	...	...	...	...	...
8 Miscellaneous goods and services	16.2	...	...	...	...	...	...	...	...	...	...	...
A Personal care	11.9	...	...	...	...	...	...	...	...	...	...	...
B Expenditures in restaurants, cafes and hotels	3.6	...	...	...	...	...	...	...	...	...	...	...

Libyan Arab Jamahiriya

2.6 Private Final Consumption Expenditure by Type and Purpose, in Constant Prices
(Continued)

Million Libyan dinars

	1970	1975	1978	1979	1980	1981	1982	1983	1984	1985	1986	1987
					At constant prices of: 1964							
C Other	0.7	...	...	...	...	...	...	...	...	...	...	...
Total Final Consumption Expenditure in the Domestic Market by Households, of which	303.5	...	...	...	...	...	...	...	...	...	...	...
Plus: Direct purchases abroad by resident households	15.5	...	...	...	...	...	...	...	...	...	...	...
Less: Direct purchases in the domestic market by non-resident households	7.6	...	...	...	...	...	...	...	...	...	...	...
Equals: Final Consumption Expenditure of Resident Households	311.4	...	...	...	...	...	...	...	...	...	...	...

Final Consumption Expenditure of Private Non-profit Institutions Serving Households

Equals: Final Consumption Expenditure of Private Non-profit Organisations Serving Households	...	...	...	...	...	...	...	...	...	...	...	...
Statistical discrepancy	4.5	...	...	...	...	...	...	...	...	...	...	...
Private Final Consumption Expenditure	315.9	...	...	...	...	...	...	...	...	...	...	...

2.7 Gross Capital Formation by Type of Good and Owner, in Current Prices

Million Libyan dinars

	1980			
	TOTAL	Total Private	Public Enterprises	General Government
Increase in stocks, total	95.0	...	...	...
Gross Fixed Capital Formation, Total	2423.8	200.5	...	2223.3
1 Residential buildings	250.6	53.3	...	197.4
2 Non-residential buildings	419.9	5.0	...	414.9
3 Other construction	726.0	40.2	...	685.8
4 Land improvement and plantation and orchard development	188.2	0.6	...	187.6
5 Producers' durable goods	653.3	77.1	...	576.1
A Transport equipment	81.2	38.6	...	42.6
B Machinery and equipment	572.1	38.5	...	533.5
6 Breeding stock, dairy cattle, etc.	9.4	3.9	...	5.5
Statistical discrepancy [a]	176.4	20.4	...	156.0
Total Gross Capital Formation	2518.8	...	...	...

a) Item 'Statistical discrepancy' refers to furnishing and supplies and other assets.

2.8 Gross Capital Formation by Type of Good and Owner, in Constant Prices

Million Libyan dinars

	1980				1981			
	TOTAL	Total Private	Public Enterprises	General Government	TOTAL	Total Private	Public Enterprises	General Government
	At constant prices of: 1975							
Increase in stocks, total	90.0	...	...	...	...	...	...	...
Gross Fixed Capital Formation, Total	1691.5	...	...	...	1853.5	...	...	...
1 Residential buildings	180.1	...	...	...	342.0	...	...	...
2 Non-residential buildings	332.8	...	...	...	317.0	...	...	...
3 Other construction	499.1	...	...	...	461.0	...	...	...
4 Land improvement and plantation and orchard development	136.3	...	...	...	152.0	...	...	...
5 Producers' durable goods	421.8	...	...	...	444.5	...	...	...
A Transport equipment	54.8	...	...	...	46.5	...	...	...
B Machinery and equipment	367.0	...	...	...	398.0	...	...	...
6 Breeding stock, dairy cattle, etc.	7.6	...	...	...	5.0	...	...	...
Statistical discrepancy [a]	113.8	...	...	...	132.0	...	...	...
Total Gross Capital Formation	1781.5	...	...	...	...	...	...	...

a) Item 'Statistical discrepancy' refers to furnishing and supplies and other assets.

Libyan Arab Jamahiriya

2.11 Gross Fixed Capital Formation by Kind of Activity of Owner, ISIC Divisions, in Current Prices

Million Libyan dinars

	1970	1975	1978	1979	1980	1981	1982	1983	1984	1985	1986	1987
					All Producers							
1 Agriculture, hunting, forestry and fishing	...	149.9	217.5	234.2	334.2	375.9	247.7	...	...	...	...	...
2 Mining and quarrying	...	28.4	102.0	89.8	102.3	70.0	55.0	...	...	...	...	...
3 Manufacturing	...	121.5	163.2	269.8	431.8	442.9	342.7	...	...	...	...	...
4 Electricity, gas and water	...	135.1	205.5	284.3	370.8	261.3	252.0	...	...	...	...	...
5 Construction	...	28.4	16.2	20.0	22.8	25.0	30.0	...	...	...	...	...
6 Wholesale and retail trade, restaurants and hotels	...	5.9	23.4	59.9	83.2	107.0	90.0	...	...	...	...	...
7 Transport, storage and communication	...	157.7	268.1	320.8	439.4	703.8	690.4	...	...	...	...	...
8 Finance, insurance, real estate and business services	...	235.7	257.4	215.9	251.7	324.0	234.7	...	...	...	...	...
9 Community, social and personal services	...	100.7	125.9	177.2	197.5	305.3	265.1	...	...	...	...	...
Total Industries	...	963.3	1379.2	1671.9	2233.7	2615.2	2207.6	...	...	...	...	...
Producers of Government Services	...	91.4	152.6	183.6	190.1	195.7	154.2	...	...	...	...	...
Private Non-Profit Institutions Serving Households	...	...	...	...	...	...	...	...	...	...	...	...
Total	...	1054.7	1532.0	1855.3	2423.8	2810.9	2361.8	...	...	...	...	...

2.12 Gross Fixed Capital Formation by Kind of Activity of Owner, ISIC Divisions, in Constant Prices

Million Libyan dinars

	1970	1975	1978	1979	1980	1981	1982	1983	1984	1985	1986	1987
				At constant prices of:1975								
				All Producers								
1 Agriculture, hunting, forestry and fishing	...	149.9	185.5	185.4	244.4	...	...	...	...	...	...	...
2 Mining and quarrying	...	28.4	83.0	68.0	70.0	...	...	...	...	...	...	...
3 Manufacturing	...	121.5	134.3	200.9	277.5	...	...	...	...	...	...	...
4 Electricity, gas and water	...	135.1	168.7	213.0	255.4	...	...	...	...	...	...	...
5 Construction	...	28.4	13.7	15.5	16.4	...	...	...	...	...	...	...
6 Wholesale and retail trade, restaurants and hotels	...	5.9	19.8	47.7	59.9	...	...	...	...	...	...	...
7 Transport, storage and communication	...	157.7	227.2	252.0	311.8	...	...	...	...	...	...	...
8 Finance, insurance, real estate and business services	...	235.7	222.9	171.8	182.4	...	...	...	...	...	...	...
9 Community, social and personal services	...	100.7	107.8	139.7	139.3	...	...	...	...	...	...	...
A Sanitary and similar services	...	...	...	...	...	...	...	...	...	...	...	...
B Social and related community services	...	...	...	...	...	...	...	...	...	...	...	...
Educational services	...	73.1	63.7	77.9	83.5	...	...	...	...	...	...	...
Medical, dental, other health and veterinary services	...	26.2	43.2	60.7	47.7	...	...	...	...	...	...	...
C Recreational and cultural services	...	...	...	...	...	...	...	...	...	...	...	...
D Personal and household services	...	1.4	0.9	1.1	0.7	...	...	...	...	...	...	...
Total Industries	...	963.3	1162.9	1294.0	1557.1	...	...	...	...	...	...	...
Producers of Government Services	...	91.4	129.2	144.2	134.4	...	...	...	...	...	...	...
Private Non-Profit Institutions Serving Households	...	...	...	...	...	...	...	...	...	...	...	...
Total	...	1054.7	1292.1	1438.2	1691.5	...	...	...	...	...	...	...

Libyan Arab Jamahiriya

2.17 Exports and Imports of Goods and Services, Detail

Million Libyan dinars

	1970	1975	1978	1979	1980	1981	1982	1983	1984	1985	1986	1987
Exports of Goods and Services												
1 Exports of merchandise, f.o.b.	857.6	2011.8	2941.0	4766.4	6697.4	...	...	...	...	...	...	...
2 Transport and communication												
3 Insurance service charges						...	...	...	...	...	...	...
4 Other commodities	12.4	41.4	37.1	35.0	39.6	...	...	...	...	...	...	...
5 Adjustments of merchandise exports to change-of-ownership basis												
6 Direct purchases in the domestic market by non-residential households						...	...	...	...	...	...	...
7 Direct purchases in the domestic market by extraterritorial bodies												...
Total Exports of Goods and Services	870.0	2053.2	2978.1	4801.4	6737.0	...	...	...	...	...	...	...
Imports of Goods and Services												
1 Imports of merchandise, c.i.f.	372.2	1454.8	1957.6	2469.0	3057.8	...	...	...	...	...	...	...
2 Adjustments of merchandise imports to change-of-ownership basis	...	...										
3 Other transport and communication					340.9	...						
4 Other insurance service charges							...					...
5 Other commodities	31.0	210.9	241.9	352.7		...						...
6 Direct purchases abroad by government						...	...	...	...	...	...	...
7 Direct purchases abroad by resident households						...						...
Total Imports of Goods and Services	403.2	1665.7	2199.5	2821.7	3398.7	...	...	...	...	...	...	...
Balance of Goods and Services	466.8	387.5	778.6	1979.7	3338.3	...	...	...	...	...	...	...
Total Imports and Balance of Goods and Services	870.0	2053.2	2978.1	4801.4	6737.0	...	...	...	...	...	...	...

4.1 Derivation of Value Added by Kind of Activity, in Current Prices

Million Libyan dinars

	1980 Gross Output	Intermediate Consumption	Value Added
All Producers			
1 Agriculture, hunting, forestry and fishing	233.7	68.8	164.9
A Agriculture and hunting	227.7	67.2	160.5
B Forestry and logging	1.1	0.2	0.9
C Fishing	4.9	1.4	3.5
2 Mining and quarrying [a]	6862.2	241.5	6620.7
A Coal mining	-	-	-
B Crude petroleum and natural gas production	6801.2	229.3	6571.9
C Metal ore mining	-	-	-
D Other mining	61.0	12.2	48.8

Libyan Arab Jamahiriya

4.1 Derivation of Value Added by Kind of Activity, in Current Prices
(Continued)

Million Libyan dinars

		1980	
	Gross Output	Intermediate Consumption	Value Added
3 Manufacturing	623.0	409.1	213.9
A Manufacture of food, beverages and tobacco	110.7	74.5	36.2
B Textile, wearing apparel and leather industries	26.9	17.7	9.2
C Manufacture of wood and wood products, including furniture	21.3	14.4	6.9
D Manufacture of paper and paper products, printing and publishing	12.5	4.9	7.6
E Manufacture of chemicals and chemical petroleum, coal, rubber and plastic products [b]	363.8	252.1	111.7
F Manufacture of non-metallic mineral products, except products of petroleum and coal [b]	41.6	21.2	20.4
G Basic metal industries	34.3	17.5	16.8
H Manufacture of fabricated metal products, machinery and equipment			
I Other manufacturing industries	11.9	6.8	5.1
4 Electricity, gas and water	107.4	57.7	49.7
A Electricity, gas and steam	106.0	57.3	48.7
B Water works and supply	1.4	0.4	1.0
5 Construction	1701.5	765.8	935.7
6 Wholesale and retail trade, restaurants and hotels	598.6	116.9	481.7
A Wholesale and retail trade	558.3	102.7	455.6
B Restaurants and hotels	40.3	14.2	26.1
7 Transport, storage and communication	455.5	120.2	335.3
A Transport and storage	454.3	119.9	334.4
B Communication	1.2	0.3	0.9
8 Finance, insurance, real estate and business services	457.5	16.2	441.3
A Financial institutions	204.4	10.5	193.9
B Insurance	19.4	1.8	17.6
C Real estate and business services	233.7	3.9	229.8
Real estate, except dwellings	21.0	1.6	19.4
Dwellings	212.7	2.3	210.4
9 Community, social and personal services	496.7	115.8	380.9
A Sanitary and similar services	-	-	-
B Social and related community services	445.6	110.1	335.5
Educational services	271.2	50.4	220.8
Medical, dental, other health and veterinary services	174.4	59.7	114.7
C Recreational and cultural services	5.3	1.1	4.2
D Personal and household services	45.8	4.6	41.2
Total, Industries	11536.1	1912.0	9624.2
Producers of Government Services	1934.7	1323.6	611.1
Other Producers	2.8	0.8	2.0
Total [c]	13473.6	3236.4	10237.3
Less: Imputed bank service charge	...	...	...
Import duties	...	...	...
Value added tax	...	...	...
Total	...	...	...

a) Item 'Mining and quarrying' includes oil and gas production.
b) Petroleum products and liquified gas industries are included in item 'Manufacture of non-metallic mineral products'.
c) Gross domestic product in factor values.

Libyan Arab Jamahiriya

4.3 Cost Components of Value Added

Million Libyan dinars

	Compensation of Employees	Capital Consumption	Net Operating Surplus	Indirect Taxes	Less: Subsidies Received	Value Added
			1980			
			All Producers			
1 Agriculture, hunting, forestry and fishing	46.3	24.5	94.1	...	...	164.9
A Agriculture and hunting	44.0	23.9	92.6	...	...	160.5
B Forestry and logging	0.7	0.1	0.1	...	...	0.9
C Fishing	1.6	0.5	1.4	...	...	3.5
2 Mining and quarrying [a]	128.5	73.3	6418.9	...	...	6620.7
A Coal mining	...	...	...	...	...	...
B Crude petroleum and natural gas production	108.8	63.5	6399.6	...	...	6571.9
C Metal ore mining	...	...	...	...	...	...
D Other mining	19.7	9.8	19.3	...	...	48.8
3 Manufacturing	71.6	24.8	117.5	...	...	213.9
A Manufacture of food, beverages and tobacco	18.8	10.1	7.3	...	...	36.2
B Textile, wearing apparel and leather industries	8.5	1.2	-0.5	...	...	9.2
C Manufacture of wood and wood products, including furniture	6.5	1.4	-1.0	...	...	6.9
D Manufacture of paper and paper products, printing and publishing	4.9	0.8	1.9	...	...	7.6
E Manufacture of chemicals and chemical petroleum, coal, rubber and plastic products [b]	12.2	6.7	92.8	...	...	111.7
F Manufacture of non-metallic mineral products, except products of petroleum and coal [b]	10.9	3.0	6.5	...	...	20.4
G Basic metal industries	7.7	1.3	7.8	...	...	16.8
H Manufacture of fabricated metal products, machinery and equipment	...	...	...	...	...	...
I Other manufacturing industries	2.1	0.3	2.7	...	...	5.1
4 Electricity, gas and water	30.5	19.2	-	...	...	49.7
A Electricity, gas and steam	29.7	19.0	-	...	...	48.7
B Water works and supply	0.8	0.2	-	...	...	1.0
5 Construction	692.1	53.9	189.7	...	...	935.7
6 Wholesale and retail trade, restaurants and hotels	80.6	10.4	390.7	...	...	481.7
A Wholesale and retail trade	69.5	7.0	379.1	...	...	455.6
B Restaurants and hotels	11.1	3.4	11.6	...	...	26.1
7 Transport, storage and communication	152.2	53.8	129.3	...	...	335.3
A Transport and storage	152.0	53.7	128.7	...	...	334.4
B Communication	0.2	0.1	0.6	...	...	0.9
8 Finance, insurance, real estate and business services	22.7	36.4	382.2	...	...	441.3
A Financial institutions	15.6	1.7	176.6	...	...	193.9
B Insurance	2.5	0.4	14.7	...	...	17.6
C Real estate and business services	4.6	34.3	190.9	...	...	229.8
Real estate, except dwellings	3.5	1.9	14.0	...	...	19.4
Dwellings	1.1	32.4	176.9	...	...	210.4
9 Community, social and personal services	339.6	27.9	13.5	...	...	381.0
A Sanitary and similar services	-	-	-	...	...	-
B Social and related community services	308.7	26.8	-	...	...	335.5
Educational services	206.3	14.5	-	...	...	220.8
Medical, dental, other health and veterinary services	102.4	12.3	-	...	...	114.7
C Recreational and cultural services	1.1	0.5	2.6	...	...	4.2
D Personal and household services	29.8	0.5	10.9	...	...	41.2

Libyan Arab Jamahiriya

4.3 Cost Components of Value Added
(Continued)

Million Libyan dinars

	\multicolumn{6}{c}{1980}
	Compensation of Employees	Capital Consumption	Net Operating Surplus	Indirect Taxes	Less: Subsidies Received	Value Added
Total, Industries c	1564.1	324.2	7735.9	...	...	9624.2
Producers of Government Services	...	...	...	...	...	...
Other Producers	...	...	...	...	...	...
Total	...	...	...	...	...	...
Less: Imputed bank service charge	...	...	...	...	...	...
Import duties	...	...	...	...	...	...
Value added tax	...	...	...	...	...	...
Total	...	...	...	...	...	...

a) Item 'Mining and quarrying' includes oil and gas production.
b) Petroleum products and liquified gas industries are included in item 'Manufacture of non-metallic mineral products'.
c) Gross domestic product in factor values.

Luxembourg

Source. Reply to the United Nations National Accounts Questionnaire from the Service Central de la Statistique et des Etudes Economiques, Ministere de L'Economie Nationale, Luxembourg. The official estimates and descriptions are published by the Service in 'Cahiers Economiques, Serie B, Comptes Nationaux'.
General note. The official estimates have been adjusted by the Service to conform to the United Nations System of National Accounts so far as the existing data would permit. It should be noted that in the National Accounts published by the Service Central de la Statistique et des Etudes Economiques of Luxembourg, imputed bank services provided to non-residents are not deducted in calculating GDP. For this reason estimates of GDP published by the Luxembourg authorities are somewhat higher than those shown here, particularly for the recent years.

1.1 Expenditure on the Gross Domestic Product, in Current Prices

Million Luxembourg francs

	1970	1975	1978	1979	1980	1981	1982	1983	1984	1985	1986	1987
1 Government final consumption expenditure	5781	12951	17553	19517	22182	24668	26097	27556	29756	32306	35521	37297
2 Private final consumption expenditure [a]	27802	50117	65023	70649	78085	86252	95756	104180	112602	120524	126631	132149
3 Gross capital formation	14392	20118	28380	27234	34204	35228	39900	42960	48248	44373	48402	52642
A Increase in stocks	1691	-3941	1392	-2542	-1830	-791	334	5814	9619	6180	2301	2185
B Gross fixed capital formation	12701	24059	26988	29776	36034	36019	39566	37146	38629	38193	46101	50457
Residential buildings	2448	6962	5903	6659	7278	7325	6800	5970	6200	6500	7200	...
Non-residential buildings	5087	10307	11078	12873	15490	16547	18192	16821	16579	18199	20106	...
Other construction and land improvement etc.												...
Other	5166	6790	10007	10244	13266	12147	14574	14355	15850	13494	18804	...
4 Exports of goods and services	48893	80245	93998	111058	117308	122498	141101	157403	195709	222292	224305	225183
5 Less: Imports of goods and services	41826	76689	92739	106313	118850	126955	144068	157416	192649	212029	214320	223746
Equals: Gross Domestic Product	55042	86742	112215	122145	132929	141691	158786	174683	193666	207466	220539	223525

a) Item 'Private consumption expenditure' refers to expenditure in the domestic market only.

1.2 Expenditure on the Gross Domestic Product, in Constant Prices

Million Luxembourg francs

	1970	1975	1978	1979	1980	1981	1982	1983	1984	1985	1986	1987
At constant prices of: 1980												
1 Government final consumption expenditure	16436	19544	21048	21518	22182	22493	22825	22661	23061	23872	24837	25720
2 Private final consumption expenditure [a]	52851	67955	73522	75971	78085	79359	79509	79404	81322	82725	86230	87416
3 Gross capital formation	32818	30149	32628	30473	34204	33243	33986	34392	37788	36751	36503	38075
A Increase in stocks	5168	-1971	1657	-1771	-1830	-365	501	4780	8281	8216	3450	3277
B Gross fixed capital formation	27650	32120	30971	32244	36034	33608	33485	29612	29507	28535	33053	34798
Residential buildings	6101	9608	6886	7305	7278	6783	5807	4803	4713	4761	5081	...
Non-residential buildings	11828	13779	12862	14043	15490	15382	15821	14089	13317	14119	14946	...
Other construction and land improvement etc.												...
Other	9721	8733	11223	10896	13266	11443	11857	10720	11477	9655	13026	...
4 Exports of goods and services	84263	99569	108364	118685	117308	113122	113965	119856	140883	153498	160410	173238
5 Less: Imports of goods and services	84663	99077	107555	115245	118850	115558	115581	117703	135905	144225	148246	160800
Equals: Gross Domestic Product	101705	118140	128007	131402	132929	132659	134704	138610	147149	152621	159734	163649

a) Item 'Private consumption expenditure' refers to expenditure in the domestic market only.

1.3 Cost Components of the Gross Domestic Product

Million Luxembourg francs

	1970	1975	1978	1979	1980	1981	1982	1983	1984	1985	1986	1987
1 Indirect taxes, net	4716	8897	11259	11572	14029	13862	16526	20465	23623	25888	27985	30067
A Indirect taxes	5412	11367	15688	16347	19024	20542	24118	30132	32638	35139	37677	40094
B Less: Subsidies	696	2470	4429	4775	4995	6680	7592	9667	9015	9251	9692	10027
2 Consumption of fixed capital	7863	12365	12808	14602	15921	16961	18144	20180	22610	23980	25100	26400
3 Compensation of employees paid by resident producers to:	25594	54890	71274	77057	85181	93545	100045	106740	115253	121490	131856	141416
A Resident households	23817	49589	64207	69504	76699	84289	89931	95497	102879	107614	115394	122441
B Rest of the world	1777	5301	7067	7553	8482	9256	10114	11243	12374	13876	16462	18975
4 Operating surplus	16869	10590	16874	18914	17798	17323	24071	27298	32180	36108	35598	25642
A Corporate and quasi-corporate enterprises	...	...	...	...	...	...	...	...	...	...	...	...
B Private unincorporated enterprises	...	...	...	...	...	...	...	...	...	...	...	...
C General government	769	1433	2249	2226	2679	2729	3009	3139	3257	3342	3816	...
Equals: Gross Domestic Product	55042	86742	112215	122145	132929	141691	158786	174683	193666	207466	220539	223525

Luxembourg

1.4 General Government Current Receipts and Disbursements

Million Luxembourg francs

	1970	1975	1978	1979	1980	1981	1982	1983	1984	1985	1986	1987
Receipts												
1 Operating surplus	769	1433	2249	2226	2679	2729	3009	3139	3257	3342	3816	...
2 Property and entrepreneurial income	1249	2492	3251	4098	5331	5923	6376	6228	6192	7227	6269	...
3 Taxes, fees and contributions	16881	36759	54395	54924	60120	64408	72550	85322	91539	99864	103496	...
A Indirect taxes	5341	11086	15394	16041	18094	19233	22552	27921	30045	32797	34346	...
B Direct taxes	6674	14709	23779	22775	24015	25699	28844	35060	36953	41485	41812	...
C Social security contributions	4866	10964	15222	16108	18011	19476	21154	22341	24541	25582	27338	...
D Compulsory fees, fines and penalties	...	...	...	...	...	...	...	...	...	...	...	...
4 Other current transfers	589	1436	2089	2369	2712	3226	3423	3515	3946	4390	4554	
Total Current Receipts of General Government	19488	42120	61984	63617	70842	76286	85358	98204	104934	114823	118135	...
Disbursements												
1 Government final consumption expenditure	5781	12951	17553	19517	22182	24668	26097	27556	29756	32306	35521	...
2 Property income	622	738	1062	1006	1127	1281	1650	1844	2099	2305	2363	...
A Interest	622	738	1062	1006	1127	1281	1650	1844	2099	2305	2363	...
B Net land rent and royalties	-	-	-	-	-	-	-	-	-	-	-	...
3 Subsidies	696	2189	3424	4191	4484	6460	7370	9376	8766	8956	9495	...
4 Other current transfers	8671	19580	28029	30326	33449	37562	40796	43282	46862	49580	53192	...
A Social security benefits	7504	16850	24586	26881	30245	33855	37028	39606	42840	45127	48768	...
B Social assistance grants	...	...	...	...	...	...	...	...	...	...	...	...
C Other	1167	2730	3443	3445	3204	3707	3768	3676	4022	4453	4424	...
5 Net saving	3718	6662	11916	8577	9600	6315	9445	16146	17451	21676	17564	...
Total Current Disbursements and Net Saving of General Government	19488	42120	61984	63617	70842	76286	85358	98204	104934	114823	118135	...

1.7 External Transactions on Current Account, Summary

Million Luxembourg francs

	1970	1975	1978	1979	1980	1981	1982	1983	1984	1985	1986	1987
Payments to the Rest of the World												
1 Imports of goods and services	41826	76689	92739	106313	118850	126955	144068	157416	192649	212029	214320	...
A Imports of merchandise c.i.f.	38213	69234	83351	95088	105622	111326	124638	136168	168990	186696	188110	...
B Other	3613	7455	9388	11225	13228	15629	19430	21248	23659	25333	26210	...
2 Factor income to the rest of the world	11548	73426	115807	194573	326329	538580	565862	464767	532139	528547	486813	...
A Compensation of employees	1777	5301	7067	7553	8482	9256	10114	11243	12374	13876	16462	...
B Property and entrepreneurial income	9771	68125	108740	187020	317847	529324	555748	453524	519765	514671	470351	...
3 Current transfers to the rest of the world	1235	3043	4589	5163	5704	6396	7411	8347	9455	10067	11548	...
A Indirect taxes to supranational organizations	71	281	294	306	930	1309	1566	2211	2593	2342	3331	...
B Other current transfers	1164	2762	4295	4857	4774	5087	5845	6136	6862	7725	8217	...
4 Surplus of the nation on current transactions	7708	10237	14639	20676	18216	17729	23641	28190	34677	46050	43256	...
Payments to the Rest of the World and Surplus of the Nation on Current Transactions	62317	163395	227774	326725	469099	689660	740982	658720	768920	796693	755937	...
Receipts From The Rest of the World												
1 Exports of goods and services	48893	80245	93998	111058	117308	122498	141101	157403	195709	222292	224305	...
A Exports of merchandise f.o.b.	42517	65309	72328	85817	87907	88587	101924	111503	145598	168071	166227	...

Luxembourg

1.7 External Transactions on Current Account, Summary
(Continued)

Million Luxembourg francs

	1970	1975	1978	1979	1980	1981	1982	1983	1984	1985	1986	1987
B Other	6376	14936	21670	25241	29401	33911	39177	45900	50111	54221	58078	...
2 Factor income from rest of the world	12844	81018	130048	212203	348095	563264	595529	496774	568190	568655	525078	...
A Compensation of employees	1412	4179	6489	7384	8030	9250	10754	11544	12743	13378	14908	...
B Property and entrepreneurial income	11432	76839	123559	204819	340065	554014	584775	485230	555447	555277	510170	...
3 Current transfers from rest of the world	580	2132	3728	3464	3696	3898	4352	4543	5021	5746	6554	...
A Subsidies from supranational organisations	-	281	1005	584	511	220	222	291	249	295	197	...
B Other current transfers	580	1851	2723	2880	3185	3678	4130	4252	4772	5451	6357	...
Receipts from the Rest of the World on Current Transactions	62317	163395	227774	326725	469099	689660	740982	658720	768920	796693	755937	...

1.8 Capital Transactions of The Nation, Summary

Million Luxembourg francs

	1970	1975	1978	1979	1980	1981	1982	1983	1984	1985	1986	1987
Finance of Gross Capital Formation												
Gross saving	22722	34631	50074	53468	59295	65599	94921	112138	124184	135234	135279	126394
1 Consumption of fixed capital	7863	12365	12808	14602	15921	16961	18144	20180	22610	23980	25100	26400
A General government	505	880	1253	1351	1499	1722	1654	1557	1838	2080	2712	...
B Corporate and quasi-corporate enterprises	...	...	...	...	...	...	...	...	...	...	...	...
C Other	...	...	...	...	...	...	...	...	...	...	...	...
2 Net saving	14859	22266	37266	38866	43374	48638	76777	91958	101574	111254	110179	99994
A General government	3718	6662	11916	8577	9600	6315	9445	16146	17451	21676	17564	...
B Corporate and quasi-corporate enterprises	...	...	...	...	...	...	...	...	...	...	...	...
C Other	...	...	...	...	...	...	...	...	...	...	...	...
Less: Surplus of the nation on current transactions	8330	14513	21694	26234	25091	30371	55021	69178	75936	90861	86877	73752
Finance of Gross Capital Formation	14392	20118	28380	27234	34204	35228	39900	42960	48248	44373	48402	52642
Gross Capital Formation												
Increase in stocks	1691	-3941	1392	-2542	-1830	-791	334	5814	9619	6180	2301	2185
Gross fixed capital formation	12701	24059	26988	29776	36034	36019	39566	37146	38629	38193	46101	50457
1 General government	1788	5223	5931	6950	8398	8909	9358	9097	8848	10071	11260	...
2 Corporate and quasi-corporate enterprises	...	...	...	...	...	...	...	...	...	...	...	...
3 Other	...	...	...	...	...	...	...	...	...	...	...	...
Gross Capital Formation	14392	20118	28380	27234	34204	35228	39900	42960	48248	44373	48402	52642

1.10 Gross Domestic Product by Kind of Activity, in Current Prices

Million Luxembourg francs

	1970	1975	1978	1979	1980	1981	1982	1983	1984	1985	1986	1987
1 Agriculture, hunting, forestry and fishing	2119	2947	3481	3619	3460	3900	5413	4963	5290	5632	5922	...
2 Mining and quarrying	675	720	446	467	501	468	177	192	180	166	157	...
3 Manufacturing	23789	25363	33536	36849	37807	39331	46768	49825	57392	63803	62877	...
4 Electricity, gas and water	1520	2429	2907	3086	3088	3638	4129	4183	4479	4801	4787	...
5 Construction	3452	7488	7926	8368	10026	10100	10107	10784	10882	11138	12884	...
6 Wholesale and retail trade, restaurants and hotels	6922	13861	17861	20135	22150	24218	27321	29550	31725	33804	35361	...
7 Transport, storage and communication	2708	4230	5997	6798	7054	7405	7485	8952	10577	10825	12529	...
8 Finance, insurance, real estate and business services [a]	1867	9235	14928	16398	17113	19911	22483	24012	26528	31262	35314	...
9 Community, social and personal services [a]	6811	12483	17223	18592	20483	22226	24347	26864	29007	30203	31687	...

Luxembourg

1.10 Gross Domestic Product by Kind of Activity, in Current Prices
(Continued)

Million Luxembourg francs	1970	1975	1978	1979	1980	1981	1982	1983	1984	1985	1986	1987
Total, Industries	49863	78756	104305	114312	121682	131197	148230	159325	176060	191634	201518	...
Producers of Government Services	4464	9918	13700	15139	17121	19104	20100	21707	23517	25167	27805	...
Other Producers	156	344	506	545	600	687	746	824	893	989	1063	...
Subtotal	54483	89018	118511	129996	139403	150988	169076	181856	200470	217790	230386	...
Less: Imputed bank service charge	1536	8814	14459	16337	17325	20814	23506	24056	26147	30733	31640	...
Plus: Import duties	929	2089	2460	2600	4279	3811	4142	6375	6853	7179	7491	...
Plus: Value added tax	1166	4449	5703	5886	6572	7706	9074	10508	12490	13230	14302	...
Equals: Gross Domestic Product [b]	55042	86742	112215	122145	132929	141691	158786	174683	193666	207466	220539	...

a) Business services are included in item 'Community, social and personal services'.
b) The branch breakdown used in this table (GDP by kind of activity) is according to the classification NACE/CLIO.

1.11 Gross Domestic Product by Kind of Activity, in Constant Prices

Million Luxembourg francs	1970	1975	1978	1979	1980	1981	1982	1983	1984	1985	1986	1987
					At constant prices of:1980							
1 Agriculture, hunting, forestry and fishing	3802	3645	3771	3710	3460	3645	4332	3806	4076	4018	4124	...
2 Mining and quarrying	1234	844	493	493	501	427	162	165	145	133	130	...
3 Manufacturing	33041	33709	36787	38205	37807	35892	37121	38814	43255	46299	46918	...
4 Electricity, gas and water	2385	3202	3280	3228	3088	3089	2919	2713	2677	2774	2841	...
5 Construction	7626	9806	9149	9257	10026	9999	9440	9521	9328	9245	10286	...
6 Wholesale and retail trade, restaurants and hotels	12795	18575	20332	21728	22150	22414	23360	23458	23797	24376	25295	...
7 Transport, storage and communication	4335	5556	6490	7060	7054	7137	7210	7393	8391	8654	9209	...
8 Finance, insurance, real estate and business services [a]	3328	9974	12895	14656	17113	17790	17709	18221	18448	19662	22523	...
9 Community, social and personal services [a]	14455	16781	19108	19643	20483	20763	21043	21714	22522	22880	23750	...
Total, Industries	83001	102092	112305	117980	121682	121156	123296	125805	132639	138041	145076	...
Producers of Government Services	13701	15134	16384	16617	17121	17383	17828	18166	18561	18926	19508	...
Other Producers	422	505	560	580	600	622	645	667	688	710	733	...
Subtotal	97124	117731	129249	135177	139403	139161	141769	144638	151888	157677	165317	...
Less: Imputed bank service charge	2602	9152	12451	14709	17325	18277	18481	18098	17967	18819	20016	...
Plus: Import duties	2929	3503	4691	4559	4279	4677	4498	4618	4902	5263	5297	...
Plus: Value added tax	4254	6058	6518	6375	6572	7098	6918	7452	8326	8500	9136	...
Equals: Gross Domestic Product [b]	101705	118140	128007	131402	132929	132659	134704	138610	147149	152621	159734	...

a) Business services are included in item 'Community, social and personal services'.
b) The branch breakdown used in this table (GDP by kind of activity) is according to the classification NACE/CLIO.

1.12 Relations Among National Accounting Aggregates

Million Luxembourg francs	1970	1975	1978	1979	1980	1981	1982	1983	1984	1985	1986	1987
Gross Domestic Product	55042	86742	112215	122145	132929	141691	158786	174683	193666	207466	220539	223525
Plus: Net factor income from the rest of the world	1918	11868	21296	23188	28641	37326	61047	72995	77310	84919	81886	78406
Factor income from the rest of the world	12844	80965	128948	210543	346129	560261	593837	495986	566280	568058	515626	522749
Less: Factor income to the rest of the world	10926	69097	107652	187355	317488	522935	532790	422991	488970	483139	433740	444343
Equals: Gross National Product	56960	98610	133511	145333	161570	179017	219833	247678	270976	292385	302425	301931
Less: Consumption of fixed capital	7863	12365	12808	14602	15921	16961	18144	20180	22610	23980	25100	26400
Equals: National Income	49097	86245	120703	130731	145649	162056	201689	227498	248366	268405	277325	275531
Plus: Net current transfers from the rest of the world	-655	-911	-861	-1699	-2008	-2498	-3059	-3804	-4434	-4321	-4994	-6091
Current transfers from the rest of the world	580	2132	3728	3464	3696	3898	4352	4543	5021	5746	6554	...
Less: Current transfers to the rest of the world	1235	3043	4589	5163	5704	6396	7411	8347	9455	10067	11548	...
Equals: National Disposable Income	48442	85334	119842	129032	143641	159558	198630	223694	243932	264084	272331	269440
Less: Final consumption	33583	63068	82576	90166	100267	110920	121853	131736	142358	152830	162152	169446
Equals: Net Saving	14859	22266	37266	38866	43374	48638	76777	91958	101574	111254	110179	99994
Less: Surplus of the nation on current transactions	8330	14513	21694	26234	25091	30371	55021	69178	75936	90861	86877	73752
Equals: Net Capital Formation	6529	7753	15572	12632	18283	18267	21756	22780	25638	20393	23302	26242

Luxembourg

2.5 Private Final Consumption Expenditure by Type and Purpose, in Current Prices

Million Luxembourg francs

	1970	1975	1978	1979	1980	1981	1982	1983	1984	1985	1986	1987
Final Consumption Expenditure of Resident Households												
1 Food, beverages and tobacco	7902	12911	16446	17378	18480	20440	24159	26872	27782	29295	29612	...
A Food	6598	10054	12250	12592	13103	14202	15681	16832	18014	18697	19121	...
B Non-alcoholic beverages	176	230	281	332	355	426	511	560	567	685	771	...
C Alcoholic beverages	528	906	1075	1232	1423	1620	1750	1784	1787	1885	1963	...
D Tobacco	600	1721	2840	3222	3599	4192	6217	7696	7414	8028	7757	...
2 Clothing and footwear	2623	4429	5268	5572	5875	6400	6745	7373	7460	8270	8846	...
3 Gross rent, fuel and power	4865	9069	12537	13829	15200	17262	19406	22068	24364	26403	26340	...
A Fuel and power	1486	2600	3927	4798	5610	6538	7792	9108	9979	10803	9771	...
B Other	3379	6469	8610	9031	9590	10724	11614	12960	14385	15600	16569	...
4 Furniture, furnishings and household equipment and operation	2624	5356	6312	6620	7498	8191	8741	9412	10581	11565	12203	...
5 Medical care and health expenses	1490	3220	4883	5243	5863	6362	7043	7287	7941	8390	9070	...
6 Transport and communication	3029	6534	9800	11272	13359	15454	17818	18976	20028	21282	22065	...
7 Recreational, entertainment, education and cultural services	1109	2010	2530	2530	2707	2930	3457	3833	4193	4336	4729	...
8 Miscellaneous goods and services	4186	7290	8837	10099	11310	11740	12563	13793	15226	16293	18483	...
Total Final Consumption Expenditure in the Domestic Market by Households, of which	27828	50819	66613	72543	80292	88779	99932	109614	117575	125834	131348	...
Plus: Direct purchases abroad by resident households	1356	2442	3195	3435	3770	4324	5033	5540	5980	6458	6797	...
Less: Direct purchases in the domestic market by non-resident households	1382	3144	4785	5329	5977	6851	9209	10974	10953	11768	11514	...
Equals: Final Consumption Expenditure of Resident Households [a]	27802	50117	65023	70649	78085	86252	95756	104180	112602	120524	126631	...
Final Consumption Expenditure of Private Non-profit Institutions Serving Households												
Equals: Final Consumption Expenditure of Private Non-profit Organisations Serving Households	...	...	...	...	...	...	...	...	...	...	...	...
Private Final Consumption Expenditure	27802	50117	65023	70649	78085	86252	95756	104180	112602	120524	126631	...

a) Item 'Final consumption expenditure of resident households' includes consumption expenditure of private non-profit institutions serving households.

2.6 Private Final Consumption Expenditure by Type and Purpose, in Constant Prices

Million Luxembourg francs

	1970	1975	1978	1979	1980	1981	1982	1983	1984	1985	1986	1987
At constant prices of:1980												
Final Consumption Expenditure of Resident Households												
1 Food, beverages and tobacco	14228	16729	17406	17915	18480	18742	19803	20346	19648	19892	19471	...
A Food	12059	12946	13009	13066	13103	13138	13145	13125	13134	13179	13203	...
B Non-alcoholic beverages	283	325	318	356	355	386	448	458	449	526	561	...
C Alcoholic beverages	841	1115	1128	1259	1423	1460	1435	1353	1298	1328	1317	...
D Tobacco	1045	2343	2951	3234	3599	3758	4775	5410	4767	4859	4390	...
2 Clothing and footwear	5064	6252	6086	6036	5875	5960	5938	6073	5846	6181	6264	...
3 Gross rent, fuel and power	10067	12836	14857	15194	15200	15634	15712	16211	17472	17371	17857	...
A Fuel and power	3585	4153	5315	5600	5610	5724	5900	6328	6481	6726	6928	...

Luxembourg

2.6 Private Final Consumption Expenditure by Type and Purpose, in Constant Prices
(Continued)

Million Luxembourg francs

	1970	1975	1978	1979	1980	1981	1982	1983	1984	1985	1986	1987
					At constant prices of:1980							
B Other	6482	8683	9542	9594	9590	9910	9812	9883	10991	10645	10929	...
4 Furniture, furnishings and household equipment and operation	4267	6601	6967	7077	7498	7700	7474	6907	7329	7795	7919	...
5 Medical care and health expenses	2996	4178	5414	5538	5863	5932	6181	6021	6268	6207	6350	...
6 Transport and communication	5939	9535	11979	12818	13359	14037	14020	14005	13955	14349	15990	...
7 Recreational, entertainment, education and cultural services	1927	2482	2733	2664	2707	2805	3065	3097	3110	3107	3313	...
8 Miscellaneous goods and services	8412	10294	9877	10765	11310	10874	10784	10886	11285	11467	12279	...
Total Final Consumption Expenditure in the Domestic Market by Households, of which	52900	68907	75319	78007	80292	81684	82977	83546	84913	86369	89443	...
Plus: Direct purchases abroad by resident households	2578	3311	3613	3694	3770	3978	4179	4222	4319	4433	4628	...
Less: Direct purchases in the domestic market by non-resident households	2627	4263	5410	5730	5977	6303	7647	8364	7910	8077	7841	...
Equals: Final Consumption Expenditure of Resident Households a	52851	67955	73522	75971	78085	79359	79509	79404	81322	82725	86230	...
			Final Consumption Expenditure of Private Non-profit Institutions Serving Households									
Equals: Final Consumption Expenditure of Private Non-profit Organisations Serving Households	...	...	...	...	...	...	...	...	...	...	...	...
Private Final Consumption Expenditure	52851	67955	73522	75971	78085	79359	79509	79404	81322	82725	86230	...

a) Item 'Final consumption expenditure of resident households' includes consumption expenditure of private non-profit institutions serving households.

2.11 Gross Fixed Capital Formation by Kind of Activity of Owner, ISIC Divisions, in Current Prices

Million Luxembourg francs

	1970	1975	1978	1979	1980	1981	1982	1983	1984	1985	1986	1987
					All Producers							
1 Agriculture, hunting, forestry and fishing	664	1149	1046	1122	1166	1310	1693	1987	1620	1359	1153	...
2 Mining and quarrying	152	47	21	59	55	4	12	15	4	10	10	...
A Coal mining	-	-	-	-	-	-	-	-	-	-	-	...
B Crude petroleum and natural gas production	-	-	-	-	-	-	-	-	-	-	-	...
C Metal ore mining	126	34	2	-	1	-	-	-	-	-	-	...
D Other mining	26	13	19	59	54	4	12	15	4	10	10	...
3 Manufacturing	4549	5275	6167	7145	7834	8737	7601	7855	7668	9181	9951	...
A Manufacturing of food, beverages and tobacco	411	638	389	462	514	699	540	602	626	866	938	...
B Textile, wearing apparel and leather industries	13	408	66	48	54	43	86	35	19	180	196	...
C Manufacture of wood, and wood products, including furniture a	...	...	...	...	...	...	...	...	...	...	...	...
D Manufacture of paper and paper products, printing and publishing	35	99	323	199	157	157	179	182	241	160	173	...
E Manufacture of chemicals and chemical petroleum, coal, rubber and plastic products	902	601	403	438	988	814	1525	1686	1890	2347	2554	...
F Manufacture of non-metalic mineral products except products of petroleum and coal	146	536	298	390	814	2229	591	838	448	674	730	...
G Basic metal industries	2526	2701	4365	5115	4498	3416	3414	3718	3165	3444	3725	...
H Manufacture of fabricated metal products, machinery and equipment	493	262	289	444	726	1330	1227	731	1195	1459	1580	...
I Other manufacturing industries a	23	30	34	49	83	49	39	63	84	51	55	...
4 Electricity, gas and water	553	1016	891	872	1011	1115	1074	1225	1091	1231	1350	...
5 Construction	315	348	550	581	884	686	774	783	782	624	669	...
6 Wholesale and retail trade, restaurants and hotels	889	1256	1841	2085	2530	2748	3261	3663	5196	4944	5275	...
A Wholesale and retail trade	641	924	1561	1725	1962	2033	2232	2452	3183	3427	3650	...
B Restaurants and hotels	248	332	280	360	568	715	1029	1211	2013	1517	1625	...
7 Transport, storage and communication	667	1421	2656	2232	4090	2038	2795	2203	1754	-1913	2621	...

Luxembourg

2.11 Gross Fixed Capital Formation by Kind of Activity of Owner, ISIC Divisions, in Current Prices
(Continued)

Million Luxembourg francs

	1970	1975	1978	1979	1980	1981	1982	1983	1984	1985	1986	1987
A Transport and storage	476	974	1727	1495	3288	1280	1821	1750	1319	-2695	1779	...
B Communication	191	447	929	737	802	758	974	453	435	782	842	...
8 Finance, insurance, real estate and business services [b]	243	851	639	1070	1587	1936	2947	2615	3197	3716	3972	...
A Financial institutions	215	834	621	969	1289	1546	2735	2463	...	...	...	...
B Insurance	28	17	18	101	226	206	165	105	...	...	...	...
C Real estate and business services	...	...	...	...	...	...	...	...	...	...	...	...
9 Community, social and personal services [b]	2876	7465	7224	7651	8469	8522	10018	7656	8390	8931	9798	...
Total Industries	10908	18828	21035	22817	27626	27096	30175	28002	29702	28083	34799	...
Producers of Government Services	1788	5223	5931	6950	8398	8909	9358	9097	8848	10071	11260	...
Private Non-Profit Institutions Serving Households	5	8	22	9	10	14	33	47	79	39	42	...
Total	12701	24059	26988	29776	36034	36019	39566	37146	38629	38193	46101	...

a) Item 'Manufacture of wood and wood products, including furniture' is included in item 'Other manufacturing industries'.
b) Business services are included in item 'Community, social and personal services'.

2.12 Gross Fixed Capital Formation by Kind of Activity of Owner, ISIC Divisions, in Constant Prices

Million Luxembourg francs

	1970	1975	1978	1979	1980	1981	1982	1983	1984	1985	1986	1987
					At constant prices of: 1980							
					All Producers							
1 Agriculture, hunting, forestry and fishing	1645	1641	1201	1218	1166	1243	1481	1666	1254	1002	811	...
2 Mining and quarrying	286	61	24	64	55	4	10	12	3	7	7	...
A Coal mining	-	-	-	-	-	-	-	-	-	-	-	...
B Crude petroleum and natural gas production	-	-	-	-	-	-	-	-	-	-	-	...
C Metal ore mining	236	44	2	-	1	-	-	-	-	-	-	...
D Other mining	50	17	22	64	54	4	10	12	3	7	7	...
3 Manufacturing	9191	6869	6947	7637	7834	8168	6198	5886	5557	6493	6825	...
A Manufacturing of food, beverages and tobacco	823	846	439	495	514	654	442	456	455	613	646	...
B Textile, wearing apparel and leather industries	24	524	75	51	54	40	70	27	14	135	142	...
C Manufacture of wood, and wood products, including furniture [a]	...	...	...	...	...	...	...	...	...	...	...	...
D Manufacture of paper and paper products, printing and publishing	70	127	366	215	157	147	145	139	175	112	118	...
E Manufacture of chemicals and chemical petroleum, coal, rubber and plastic products	1870	773	454	469	988	761	1244	1274	1371	1716	1802	...
F Manufacture of non-metalic mineral products except products of petroleum and coal	281	718	339	419	814	2083	488	633	328	469	493	...
G Basic metal industries	5050	3500	4906	5462	4498	3193	2767	2757	2280	2379	2498	...
H Manufacture of fabricated metal products, machinery and equipment	1026	342	329	473	726	1244	1010	553	871	1033	1087	...
I Other manufacturing industries [a]	47	39	39	53	83	46	32	47	63	36	39	...
4 Electricity, gas and water	1232	1319	1026	943	1011	1037	933	1027	893	977	1026	...
5 Construction	626	451	630	625	884	640	631	590	560	430	452	...
6 Wholesale and retail trade, restaurants and hotels	1658	1610	2083	2241	2530	2584	2725	2865	3917	3628	3806	...
A Wholesale and retail trade	1144	1187	1769	1855	1962	1911	1857	1897	2386	2495	2620	...
B Restaurants and hotels	514	423	314	386	568	673	868	968	1531	1133	1186	...
7 Transport, storage and communication	1415	1843	3056	2416	4090	1904	2374	1776	1451	-1076	1922	...
A Transport and storage	995	1279	2006	1622	3288	1194	1545	1405	1107	-1669	1297	...

Luxembourg

2.12 Gross Fixed Capital Formation by Kind of Activity of Owner, ISIC Divisions, in Constant Prices
(Continued)

Million Luxembourg francs

	1970	1975	1978	1979	1980	1981	1982	1983	1984	1985	1986	1987
					At constant prices of:1980							
B Communication	420	564	1050	794	802	710	829	371	344	593	625	...
8 Finance, insurance, real estate and business services b	529	1128	725	1154	1587	1816	2474	2038	2372	2683	2820	
Real estate except dwellings	...	...	...	...	...	...	...	...	...	...	...	
Dwellings	6101	9608	6886	7305	7270	6854	6020	6060	...	...	...	
9 Community, social and personal services b	6887	10261	8390	8374	8469	7912	8496	6134	6375	6557	6979	...
Total Industries	23469	25183	24082	24672	27626	25308	25322	21994	22382	20701	24648	
Producers of Government Services	4173	6927	6864	7562	8398	8287	8135	7580	7065	7805	8375	
Private Non-Profit Institutions Serving Households	8	10	25	10	10	13	28	38	60	29	30	
Total	27650	32120	30971	32244	36034	33608	33485	29612	29507	28535	33053	

a) Item 'Manufacture of wood and wood products, including furniture' is included in item 'Other manufacturing industries'.
b) Business services are included in item 'Community, social and personal services'.

2.17 Exports and Imports of Goods and Services, Detail

Million Luxembourg francs

	1970	1975	1978	1979	1980	1981	1982	1983	1984	1985	1986	1987
					Exports of Goods and Services							
1 Exports of merchandise, f.o.b.	42517	65309	72328	85817	87907	88587	101924	111503	145598	168071	166227	...
2 Transport and communication												...
3 Insurance service charges	4994	11792	16885	19912	23424	27060	29968	34926	39158	42453	46564	...
4 Other commodities												...
5 Adjustments of merchandise exports to change-of-ownership basis												...
6 Direct purchases in the domestic market by non-residential households	1382	3144	4785	5329	5977	6851	9209	10974	10953	11768	11514	
7 Direct purchases in the domestic market by extraterritorial bodies	...	...	...	...	...	...	...	...	...	...	...	
Total Exports of Goods and Services	48893	80245	93998	111058	117308	122498	141101	157403	195709	222292	224305	...
					Imports of Goods and Services							
1 Imports of merchandise, c.i.f.	38213	69234	83351	95088	105622	111326	124638	136168	168990	186696	188110	
2 Adjustments of merchandise imports to change-of-ownership basis												...
3 Other transport and communication												...
4 Other insurance service charges	2257	5013	6193	7790	9458	11305	14397	15708	17679	18875	19413	
5 Other commodities												...
6 Direct purchases abroad by government												
7 Direct purchases abroad by resident households	1356	2442	3195	3435	3770	4324	5033	5540	5980	6458	6797	
Total Imports of Goods and Services	41826	76689	92739	106313	118850	126955	144068	157416	192649	212029	214320	...
Balance of Goods and Services	7067	3556	1259	4745	-1542	-4457	-2967	-13	3060	10263	9985	...
Total Imports and Balance of Goods and Services	48893	80245	93998	111058	117308	122498	141101	157403	195709	222292	224305	...

4.3 Cost Components of Value Added

Million Luxembourg francs

	1980						1981					
	Compensation of Employees	Capital Consumption	Net Operating Surplus	Indirect Taxes	Less: Subsidies Received	Value Added	Compensation of Employees	Capital Consumption	Net Operating Surplus	Indirect Taxes	Less: Subsidies Received	Value Added
					All Producers							
1 Agriculture, hunting, forestry and fishing	212	...	3494	...	...	3460	219	...	3866	...	...	3900
A Agriculture and hunting	...	...	...	...	...	3053	...	...	...	...	...	3481
B Forestry and logging	...	...	...	...	...	407	...	...	...	...	...	413
C Fishing	...	...	...	...	...	...	...	...	...	...	...	...
2 Mining and quarrying	428	...	70	...	...	501	418	...	106	...	...	468
A Coal mining	...	...	...	...	...	-	...	...	...	...	...	-
B Crude petroleum and natural gas production	...	...	...	...	...	-	...	...	...	...	...	-
C Metal ore mining	301	...	22	...	...	323	292	...	42	...	...	273

Luxembourg

4.3 Cost Components of Value Added
(Continued)

Million Luxembourg francs

	1980						1981					
	Compensation of Employees	Capital Consumption	Net Operating Surplus	Indirect Taxes	Less: Subsidies Received	Value Added	Compensation of Employees	Capital Consumption	Net Operating Surplus	Indirect Taxes	Less: Subsidies Received	Value Added
D Other mining	127	...	48	...	...	178	126	...	64	...	...	195
3 Manufacturing	26995	...	9518	...	...	37807	28169	...	9929	...	...	39331
A Manufacture of food, beverages and tobacco	1555	...	1250	...	...	3517	1720	...	1281	...	...	3858
B Textile, wearing apparel and leather industries	402	...	559	...	...	976	446	...	547	...	...	1037
C Manufacture of wood and wood products, including furniture	...	...	...	...	...	...	...	...	...	...	...	...
D Manufacture of paper and paper products, printing and publishing	853	...	341	...	...	1210	922	...	442	...	...	1388
E Manufacture of chemicals and chemical petroleum, coal, rubber and plastic products	3423	...	1859	...	...	5438	3674	...	2276	...	...	6193
F Manufacture of non-metallic mineral products, except products of petroleum and coal	1319	...	917	...	...	2300	1477	...	835	...	...	2388
G Basic metal industries	14930	...	2895	...	...	18048	15079	...	2679	...	...	17610
H Manufacture of fabricated metal products, machinery and equipment	4273	...	1551	...	...	5923	4606	...	1735	...	...	6469
I Other manufacturing industries	240	...	146	...	...	395	245	...	134	...	...	388
4 Electricity, gas and water	1149	...	1807	...	...	3088	1224	...	2269	...	...	3638
5 Construction	7287	...	2565	...	...	10026	7463	...	2462	...	...	10100
6 Wholesale and retail trade, restaurants and hotels	11269	...	10200	...	...	22150	12305	...	11210	...	...	24218
A Wholesale and retail trade	9913	...	8528	...	...	19038	10829	...	9366	...	...	20806
B Restaurants and hotels	1356	...	1672	...	...	3112	1476	...	1844	...	...	3412
7 Transport, storage and communication	7717	...	2501	...	...	7054	8441	...	2686	...	...	7405
A Transport and storage	6110	...	1742	...	...	4681	6666	...	1787	...	...	4722
B Communication	1607	...	759	...	...	2373	1775	...	899	...	...	2683
8 Finance, insurance, real estate and business services [a]	7756	...	6894	...	...	17113	9113	...	7897	...	...	19911
9 Community, social and personal services [a]	6210	...	12496	...	...	20483	8196	...	12951	...	...	22226
Total, Industries [b]	69023	...	49545	...	...	121682	75548	...	53376	...	...	131197
Producers of Government Services	15558	...	1499	...	...	17121	17310	...	1722	...	...	19104
Other Producers	600	...	-	...	...	600	687	...	-	...	...	687
Total [b]	85181	...	51044	...	...	139403	93545	...	55098	...	...	150988
Less: Imputed bank service charge	...	...	17325	...	...	17325	...	...	20814	...	...	20814
Import duties	...	...	...	...	...	4279	...	...	...	...	...	3811
Value added tax	...	...	...	...	...	6572	...	...	...	...	...	7706
Total [cb]	85181	...	33719	...	...	132929	93545	...	34284	...	...	141691

	1982						1983					
	Compensation of Employees	Capital Consumption	Net Operating Surplus	Indirect Taxes	Less: Subsidies Received	Value Added	Compensation of Employees	Capital Consumption	Net Operating Surplus	Indirect Taxes	Less: Subsidies Received	Value Added
				All Producers									
1 Agriculture, hunting, forestry and fishing	234	...	5366	...	...	5413	235	...	5004	...	...	4963
A Agriculture and hunting	...	...	...	...	...	4967	...	...	...	...	...	4511
B Forestry and logging	...	...	...	...	...	446	...	...	...	...	...	473
C Fishing	...	...	...	...	...	...	...	...	...	...	...	...
2 Mining and quarrying	132	...	42	...	...	177	135	...	53	...	...	192
A Coal mining	...	...	...	...	...	-	...	...	...	...	...	-
B Crude petroleum and natural gas production	...	...	...	...	...	...	...	...	...	...	...	...
C Metal ore mining	-	...	-	...	...	-	-	...	-	...	...	-
D Other mining	132	...	42	...	...	177	135	...	53	...	...	192

Luxembourg

4.3 Cost Components of Value Added
(Continued)

Million Luxembourg francs

	1982						1983					
	Compensation of Employees	Capital Consumption	Net Operating Surplus	Indirect Taxes	Less: Subsidies Received	Value Added	Compensation of Employees	Capital Consumption	Net Operating Surplus	Indirect Taxes	Less: Subsidies Received	Value Added
3 Manufacturing	29925	...	15401	...	...	46768	29874	...	19770	...	...	49825
A Manufacture of food, beverages and tobacco	1820	...	1625	...	...	4570	1951	...	1893	...	...	5183
B Textile, wearing apparel and leather industries	459	...	487	...	...	1001	492	...	538	...	...	1071
C Manufacture of wood and wood products, including furniture	...	...	...	...	...	...	...	...	...	...	...	...
D Manufacture of paper and paper products, printing and publishing	985	...	466	...	...	1475	1113	...	503	...	...	1641
E Manufacture of chemicals and chemical petroleum, coal, rubber and plastic products	3916	...	3505	...	...	7711	4327	...	4198	...	...	8900
F Manufacture of non-metallic mineral products, except products of petroleum and coal	1684	...	1389	...	...	3174	1863	...	1553	...	...	3535
G Basic metal industries	15774	...	6045	...	...	21511	14632	...	9021	...	...	21803
H Manufacture of fabricated metal products, machinery and equipment	5044	...	1714	...	...	6906	5245	...	1890	...	...	7258
I Other manufacturing industries	243	...	170	...	...	420	251	...	174	...	...	434
4 Electricity, gas and water	1318	...	2646	...	...	4129	1418	...	2561	...	...	4183
5 Construction	7636	...	2295	...	...	10107	7769	...	2750	...	...	10784
6 Wholesale and retail trade, restaurants and hotels	13330	...	13252	...	...	27321	14292	...	14468	...	...	29550
A Wholesale and retail trade	11744	...	11089	...	...	23471	12589	...	12144	...	...	25413
B Restaurants and hotels	1586	...	2163	...	...	3850	1703	...	2324	...	...	4137
7 Transport, storage and communication	8731	...	2897	...	...	7485	9269	...	4327	...	...	8952
A Transport and storage	6831	...	2015	...	...	4694	7211	...	3088	...	...	5646
B Communication	1900	...	882	...	...	2791	2058	...	1239	...	...	3306
8 Finance, insurance, real estate and business services [a]	10632	...	8435	...	...	22483	12384	...	8201	...	...	24012
9 Community, social and personal services [a]	8978	...	13733	...	...	24347	10466	...	12843	...	...	26864
Total, Industries [b]	80916	...	64067	...	...	148230	85842	...	69977	...	...	159325
Producers of Government Services	18383	...	1654	...	...	20100	20074	...	1557	...	...	21707
Other Producers	746	...	-	...	...	746	824	...	-	...	...	824
Total [b]	100045	...	65721	...	...	169076	106740	...	71534	...	...	181856
Less: Imputed bank service charge	...	...	23506	...	...	23506	...	...	24056	...	...	24056
Import duties	...	...	...	...	...	4142	...	...	...	...	...	6375
Value added tax	...	...	...	...	...	9074	...	...	...	...	...	10508
Total [cb]	100045	...	42215	...	...	158786	106740	...	47478	...	...	174683

	1984						1985					
	Compensation of Employees	Capital Consumption	Net Operating Surplus	Indirect Taxes	Less: Subsidies Received	Value Added	Compensation of Employees	Capital Consumption	Net Operating Surplus	Indirect Taxes	Less: Subsidies Received	Value Added

All Producers

1 Agriculture, hunting, forestry and fishing	266	...	5285	...	...	5290	275	...	5513	...	...	5632
A Agriculture and hunting	...	...	...	...	...	4823	...	...	...	...	...	...
B Forestry and logging	...	...	...	...	...	470	...	...	...	...	...	...
C Fishing	...	...	...	...	...	...	...	...	...	...	...	...
2 Mining and quarrying	131	...	45	...	...	180	121	...	41	...	...	166
A Coal mining	...	...	...	...	...	-	...	...	...	...	...	-
B Crude petroleum and natural gas production	...	...	...	...	...	...	...	...	...	...	...	-
C Metal ore mining	-	...	-	...	...	...	-	...	...	...	...	-
D Other mining	131	...	45	...	...	180	121	...	41	...	...	166

899

Luxembourg

4.3 Cost Components of Value Added
(Continued)

Million Luxembourg francs

	1984						1985					
	Compensation of Employees	Capital Consumption	Net Operating Surplus	Indirect Taxes	Less: Subsidies Received	Value Added	Compensation of Employees	Capital Consumption	Net Operating Surplus	Indirect Taxes	Less: Subsidies Received	Value Added
3 Manufacturing	32416	...	22693	...	...	57392	32767	...	28499	...	...	63803
A Manufacture of food, beverages and tobacco	2067	...	1790	...	...	5344	2137	...	2037	...	...	5806
B Textile, wearing apparel and leather industries	526	...	484	...	...	1047	481	...	698	...	...	1224
C Manufacture of wood and wood products, including furniture	...	...	...	...	...	...	...	...	...	...	...	...
D Manufacture of paper and paper products, printing and publishing	1385	...	373	...	...	1790	1492	...	428	...	...	1955
E Manufacture of chemicals and chemical petroleum, coal, rubber and plastic products	5112	...	4134	...	...	9718	5377	...	4566	...	...	10479
F Manufacture of non-metallic mineral products, except products of petroleum and coal	2060	...	1841	...	...	4021	2187	...	1773	...	...	4086
G Basic metal industries	15060	...	11221	...	...	26235	14364	...	15088	...	...	29410
H Manufacture of fabricated metal products, machinery and equipment	5924	...	2716	...	...	8812	6462	...	3730	...	...	10387
I Other manufacturing industries	282	...	134	...	...	425	267	...	179	...	...	456
4 Electricity, gas and water	1517	...	2722	...	...	4479	1608	...	2938	...	...	4801
5 Construction	8074	...	2602	...	...	10882	8135	...	2794	...	...	11138
6 Wholesale and retail trade, restaurants and hotels	15511	...	15352	...	...	31725	16608	...	16267	...	...	33804
A Wholesale and retail trade	13461	...	13009	...	...	27215	14254	...	13818	...	...	28873
B Restaurants and hotels	2050	...	2343	...	...	4510	2354	...	2449	...	...	4931
7 Transport, storage and communication	10024	...	5188	...	...	10577	10376	...	5221	...	...	10825
A Transport and storage	7823	...	3661	...	...	6840	8118	...	3627	...	...	6964
B Communication	2201	...	1527	...	...	3737	2258	...	1594	...	...	3861
8 Finance, insurance, real estate and business services [a]	13450	...	9277	...	...	26528	15085	...	11521	...	...	31262
9 Community, social and personal services [a]	11375	...	15935	...	...	29007	12523	...	15947	...	...	30203
Total, Industries [b]	92764	...	79099	...	...	176060	97498	...	88741	...	...	191634
Producers of Government Services	21596	...	1838	...	...	23517	23003	...	2080	...	...	25167
Other Producers	893	...	-	...	...	893	989	...	-	...	...	989
Total [b]	115253	...	80937	...	...	200470	121490	...	90821	...	...	217790
Less: Imputed bank service charge	...	...	26147	...	...	26147	...	...	30733	...	...	30733
Import duties	...	...	...	...	...	6853	...	...	...	...	...	7179
Value added tax	...	...	...	...	...	12490	...	...	...	...	...	13230
Total [cb]	115253	...	54790	...	...	193666	121490	...	60088	...	...	207466

	1986					
	Compensation of Employees	Capital Consumption	Net Operating Surplus	Indirect Taxes	Less: Subsidies Received	Value Added

All Producers

1 Agriculture, hunting, forestry and fishing	286	...	5741	...	...	5922
A Agriculture and hunting	...	...	...	...	...	...
B Forestry and logging	...	...	...	...	...	...
C Fishing	...	...	...	...	...	...
2 Mining and quarrying	133	...	19	...	...	157
A Coal mining	...	...	...	...	...	-
B Crude petroleum and natural gas production	...	...	...	...	...	...
C Metal ore mining	-	...	-	...	...	-
D Other mining	133	...	19	...	...	157

Luxembourg

4.3 Cost Components of Value Added
(Continued)

Million Luxembourg francs

	Compensation of Employees	Capital Consumption	Net Operating Surplus	Indirect Taxes	Less: Subsidies Received	Value Added
	\multicolumn{6}{c	}{1986}
3 Manufacturing	34633	...	25477	...	...	62877
A Manufacture of food, beverages and tobacco	2226	...	2196	...	...	6173
B Textile, wearing apparel and leather industries	478	...	575	...	...	1092
C Manufacture of wood and wood products, including furniture	...	...	...	...	...	...
D Manufacture of paper and paper products, printing and publishing	1587	...	482	...	...	2106
E Manufacture of chemicals and chemical petroleum, coal, rubber and plastic products	5763	...	4183	...	...	10521
F Manufacture of non-metallic mineral products, except products of petroleum and coal	2330	...	2149	...	...	4620
G Basic metal industries	14960	...	12088	...	...	27041
H Manufacture of fabricated metal products, machinery and equipment	7023	...	3569	...	...	10812
I Other manufacturing industries	266	...	235	...	...	512
4 Electricity, gas and water	1656	...	2873	...	...	4787
5 Construction	8756	...	3886	...	...	12884
6 Wholesale and retail trade, restaurants and hotels	17553	...	16840	...	...	35361
A Wholesale and retail trade	15060	...	14246	...	...	30141
B Restaurants and hotels	2493	...	2594	...	...	5220
7 Transport, storage and communication	11131	...	6585	...	...	12529
A Transport and storage	8643	...	4536	...	...	7992
B Communication	2488	...	2049	...	...	4537
8 Finance, insurance, real estate and business services [a]	17328	...	13198	...	...	35314
9 Community, social and personal services [a]	14319	...	15007	...	...	31687
Total, Industries [b]	105795	...	89626	...	...	201518
Producers of Government Services	24998	...	2712	...	...	27805
Other Producers	1063	...	-	...	...	1063
Total [b]	131856	...	92338	...	...	230386
Less: Imputed bank service charge	...	...	31640	...	...	31640
Import duties	...	...	...	...	...	7491
Value added tax	...	...	...	...	...	14302
Total [cb]	131856	...	60698	...	...	220539

a) Business services are included in item 'Community, social and personal services'.
b) Column 'Consumption of fixed capital' is included in column 'Net operating surplus'.
c) The branch breakdown used in this table (GDP by kind of activity) is according to the classification NACE/CLIO.

Madagascar

Source. Reply to the United Nations National Accounts Questionnaire from the Institut National de la Statistique et de la Recherche Economique, Ministere des Finances et du Commerce, Tananarive.

General note. The official estimates of Madagascar have been adjusted by the Institut National de la Statistique et de la Recherche Economique to conform to the United Nations System of National Accounts so far as the existing data would permit.

1.1 Expenditure on the Gross Domestic Product, in Current Prices

Million Malagasy francs

	1970	1975	1978	1979	1980	1981	1982	1983	1984	1985	1986	1987
1 Government final consumption expenditure	46100	60400	81600	103000	117800	129100	149500	165300	185000	209700	...	...
2 Private final consumption expenditure [a]	167200	301100	360600	444300	526100	604600	799000	973400	1058100	1208600	...	...
3 Gross capital formation	38900	50600	70400	150800	162400	142500	133000	160700	185700	217700		
A Increase in stocks	...	...	...	...	4800	-5800	3600	...	...	...		
B Gross fixed capital formation	...	...	...	...	157600	148300	129400	...	...	...		
4 Exports of goods and services	56800	74500	96100	95300	96800	96400	125700	139700	214200	225000		
5 Less: Imports of goods and services	59600	91400	122100	198300	213300	183600	211100	218000	273900	307600		
Equals: Gross Domestic Product	249400	395200	486600	595100	689800	789000	996100	1221100	1369100	1553400	1806900	

a) Item 'Private final consumption expenditure' has been obtained as a residual.

1.2 Expenditure on the Gross Domestic Product, in Constant Prices

Million Malagasy francs

	1970	1975	1978	1979	1980	1981	1982	1983	1984	1985	1986	1987
	At constant prices of: 1970								1984			
1 Government final consumption expenditure	46100	44600	49800	57100	59600	59500	57700	57900	185000	189600	...	...
2 Private final consumption expenditure [a]	167200	167200	163600	175100	175800	157400	161700	162700	1058100	1070500	...	...
3 Gross capital formation	38900	37600	28700	51900	49200	34300	28000	27800	185700	189300	...	...
A Increase in stocks	2500	...	...	...	...	...	...	...	...	...		
B Gross fixed capital formation	36400	...	...	...	...	...	...	...	...	...		
4 Exports of goods and services	56800	58400	50700	51400	48700	37300	38100	33400	214200	223300		
5 Less: Imports of goods and services	59600	50400	44100	62400	58000	37000	38600	32900	273900	272500		
Equals: Gross Domestic Product	249400	257400	248700	273100	275300	251500	246900	248900	1369100	1400200	...	...

a) Item 'Private final consumption expenditure' has been obtained as a residual.

1.3 Cost Components of the Gross Domestic Product

Million Malagasy francs

	1970	1975	1978	1979	1980	1981	1982	1983	1984	1985	1986	1987
1 Indirect taxes, net	29700	33600	56400	67400	...	...	...	...	...	...	...	...
A Indirect taxes	32400	36400	...	...								
B Less: Subsidies	2700	2800	...	...								
2 Consumption of fixed capital	...	...	6200	7000								
3 Compensation of employees paid by resident producers to:	...	...	414200	507500								
4 Operating surplus	...	...										
Equals: Gross Domestic Product	249400	395200	486600	595100	...	...	...	...	...	...	...	...

1.7 External Transactions on Current Account, Summary

Million Malagasy francs

	1970	1975	1978	1979	1980	1981	1982	1983	1984	1985	1986	1987
	Payments to the Rest of the World											
1 Imports of goods and services	51599	103744	...	...	...	...	...	...	...	...	...	...
A Imports of merchandise c.i.f.	39534	88862	...	...	...	...	...	...	...	...	...	...
B Other	12065	14882	...	...	...	...	...	...	...	...	...	...
2 Factor income to the rest of the world	11002	8473	...	...	...	...	...	...	...	...	...	...

Madagascar

1.7 External Transactions on Current Account, Summary
(Continued)

Million Malagasy francs

	1970	1975	1978	1979	1980	1981	1982	1983	1984	1985	1986	1987
A Compensation of employees	6904	6291	...	...	...	...	...	...	...	...	...	...
B Property and entrepreneurial income	4098	2182	...	...	...	...	...	...	...	...	...	...
By general government	353	701	...	...	...	...	...	...	...	...	...	...
By corporate and quasi-corporate enterprises	3745	1481	...	...	...	...	...	...	...	...	...	...
By other	...	...	...	...	...	...	...	...	...	...	...	...
3 Current transfers to the rest of the world	1267	2202	...	...	...	...	...	...	...	...	...	...
4 Surplus of the nation on current transactions	-1007	-22677	...	...	...	...	...	...	...	...	...	...
Payments to the Rest of the World and Surplus of the Nation on Current Transactions	62861	91742	...	...	...	...	...	...	...	...	...	...

Receipts From The Rest of the World

	1970	1975	1978	1979	1980	1981	1982	1983	1984	1985	1986	1987
1 Exports of goods and services	45671	76124	...	...	...	...	...	...	...	...	...	...
A Exports of merchandise f.o.b.	40222	68506	...	...	...	...	...	...	...	...	...	...
B Other	5449	7618	...	...	...	...	...	...	...	...	...	...
2 Factor income from rest of the world	...	8684	...	...	...	...	...	...	...	...	...	...
A Compensation of employees	...	7619	...	...	...	...	...	...	...	...	...	...
B Property and entrepreneurial income	516	1065	...	...	...	...	...	...	...	...	...	...
By general government	20	...	...	...	...	...	...	...	...	...	...	...
By corporate and quasi-corporate enterprises	-	...	...	...	...	...	...	...	...	...	...	...
By other	496	1065	...	...	...	...	...	...	...	...	...	...
3 Current transfers from rest of the world	18688	6934	...	...	...	...	...	...	...	...	...	...
Receipts from the Rest of the World on Current Transactions	62861	91742	...	...	...	...	...	...	...	...	...	...

1.10 Gross Domestic Product by Kind of Activity, in Current Prices

Million Malagasy francs

	1970	1975	1978	1979	1980	1981	1982	1983	1984	1985	1986	1987
1 Agriculture, hunting, forestry and fishing	73800	162400	187600	212500	249100	313600	409700	525300	580600	653200	...	...
2 Mining and quarrying											...	...
3 Manufacturing	46000	70600	93600	114500	124300	125300	149900	185400	213900	254100		
4 Electricity, gas and water												
5 Construction											...	...
6 Wholesale and retail trade, restaurants and hotels											...	...
7 Transport, storage and communication	82700	104900	122100	163500	197700	230100	298700	361500	400600	451300		
8 Finance, insurance, real estate and business services											...	...
9 Community, social and personal services												
Total, Industries	202500	337900	403300	490500	571100	669000	858300	1072200	1195100	1358600	...	...
Producers of Government Services	33700	42400	59600	72600	83600	90400	107600	115200	128000	142000		
Other Producers a	...	...	...	...	...	...	...	...	...	...		
Subtotal	236200	380300	462900	563100	654700	759400	965900	1187400	1323100	1500600		
Less: Imputed bank service charge	...	...	...	...	...	...	...	...	...	...		
Plus: Import duties	13200	14900	23700	32000	35100	29600	30200	33700	46000	52800	...	...
Plus: Value added tax												
Equals: Gross Domestic Product	249400	395200	486600	595100	689800	789000	996100	1221100	1369100	1553400	...	...

a) Item 'Other producers' is included in item 'Community, social and personal services'.

Madagascar

1.11 Gross Domestic Product by Kind of Activity, in Constant Prices

Million Malagasy francs

	1970	1975	1978	1979	1980	1981	1982	1983	1984	1985	1986	1987
					At constant prices of: 1970					1984		
1 Agriculture, hunting, forestry and fishing	73800	80900	71300	76400	78300	74800	77800	79700	... 580600	591700	...	...
2 Mining and quarrying											...	...
3 Manufacturing	46000	51400	50100	56500	55000	42400	36400	36900	... 213900	223500	...	...
4 Electricity, gas and water											...	...
5 Construction											...	...
6 Wholesale and retail trade, restaurants and hotels											...	...
7 Transport, storage and communication	82600	83900	80700	90100	90700	84500	83600	82900	... 400600	409200	...	...
8 Finance, insurance, real estate and business services											...	...
9 Community, social and personal services											...	...
Total, Industries	202400	216200	202100	223000	224000	201700	197800	199500	... 1195100	1224400	...	...
Producers of Government Services	33700	32200	37300	40000	41700	43800	44200	44700	... 128000	129200	...	...
Other Producers a	...	...	...	...	...	...	...	...	...	...	...	...
Subtotal	236100	248400	239400	263000	265700	245500	242000	244200	... 1323100	1353600	...	...
Less: Imputed bank service charge	...	...	...	...	...	...	...	...	...	...	...	...
Plus: Import duties	13200	9000	9300	10100	9600	6000	4900	4700	... 46000	46600	...	...
Plus: Value added tax	...	...	...	...	...	...	...	...	...	...	...	...
Equals: Gross Domestic Product	249400	257400	248700	273100	275300	251500	246900	248900	... 1369100	1400200	...	...

a) Item 'Other producers' is included in item 'Community, social and personal services'.

1.12 Relations Among National Accounting Aggregates

Million Malagasy francs

	1970	1975	1978	1979	1980	1981	1982	1983	1984	1985	1986	1987
Gross Domestic Product	249400	395200	486600	595100	689800	...	...	...	...	...	...	...
Plus: Net factor income from the rest of the world	-6300	211	-600	-900	-1000	...	...	...	...	...	...	...
Factor income from the rest of the world	...	8684	...	...	...	...	...	...	...	...	...	...
Less: Factor income to the rest of the world	...	8973	...	...	...	...	...	...	...	...	...	...
Equals: Gross National Product	243100	395411	486000	594200	688800	...	...	...	...	...	...	...
Less: Consumption of fixed capital	...	...	6200	7000	...	...	...	...	...	...	...	...
Equals: National Income	...	...	479800	587200	...	...	...	...	...	...	...	...
Plus: Net current transfers from the rest of the world	17421	4732	...	...	...	...	...	...	...	...	...	...
Current transfers from the rest of the world	18688	6934	...	...	...	...	...	...	...	...	...	...
Less: Current transfers to the rest of the world	1267	2202	...	...	...	...	...	...	...	...	...	...
Equals: National Disposable Income	...	...	...	...	...	...	...	...	...	...	...	...
Less: Final consumption	...	...	...	...	...	...	...	...	...	...	...	...
Equals: Net Saving	...	...	...	...	...	...	...	...	...	...	...	...
Less: Surplus of the nation on current transactions	...	...	...	...	...	...	...	...	...	...	...	...
Equals: Net Capital Formation	...	...	...	...	...	...	...	...	...	...	...	...

Madagascar

2.17 Exports and Imports of Goods and Services, Detail

Million Malagasy francs

	1970	1975	1978	1979	1980	1981	1982	1983	1984	1985	1986	1987
Exports of Goods and Services												
1 Exports of merchandise, f.o.b.	40268	68480	...	...	...	...	...	...	...	...	...	...
2 Transport and communication	...	3020	...	...	...	...	...	...	...	...	...	...
3 Insurance service charges	...	...	...	...	...	...	...	...	...	...	...	...
4 Other commodities	...	...	...	...	...	...	...	...	...	...	...	...
5 Adjustments of merchandise exports to change-of-ownership basis	...	...	...	...	...	...	...	...	...	...	...	...
6 Direct purchases in the domestic market by non-residential households	...	...	...	...	...	...	...	...	...	...	...	...
7 Direct purchases in the domestic market by extraterritorial bodies	...	...	...	...	...	...	...	...	...	...	...	...
Total Exports of Goods and Services	45669	80600	...	...	...	...	...	...	...	...	...	...
Imports of Goods and Services												
1 Imports of merchandise, c.i.f.	...	84730	...	...	...	...	...	...	...	...	...	...
A Imports of merchandise, f.o.b.	39434	71040	...	...	...	...	...	...	...	...	...	...
B Transport of services on merchandise imports	...	12190	...	...	...	...	...	...	...	...	...	...
C Insurance service charges on merchandise imports	...	1500	...	...	...	...	...	...	...	...	...	...
By residents	...	...	...	...	...	...	...	...	...	...	...	...
By non-residents	...	1500	...	...	...	...	...	...	...	...	...	...
2 Adjustments of merchandise imports to change-of-ownership basis	...	...	...	...	...	...	...	...	...	...	...	...
3 Other transport and communication	...	...	...	...	...	...	...	...	...	...	...	...
4 Other insurance service charges	...	...	...	...	...	...	...	...	...	...	...	...
5 Other commodities	...	...	...	...	...	...	...	...	...	...	...	...
6 Direct purchases abroad by government	...	...	...	...	...	...	...	...	...	...	...	...
7 Direct purchases abroad by resident households	...	...	...	...	...	...	...	...	...	...	...	...
Total Imports of Goods and Services	51599	91400	...	...	...	...	...	...	...	...	...	...
Balance of Goods and Services	-5930	-10800	...	...	...	...	...	...	...	...	...	...
Total Imports and Balance of Goods and Services	45669	80600	...	...	...	...	...	...	...	...	...	...

Malawi

General note. The preparation of national accounts statistics in Malawi is undertaken by the National Statistical Office, Zomba. The official estimates are published in a series of reports entitled 'National Accounts Report'. A detailed description of the sources and methods used for national accounts estimates is found in 'National Accounts Handbook, Sources and Methods' published in 1985. The estimates are generally in accordance with the classifications and definitions recommended in the United Nations System of National Accounts (SNA). The following tables have been prepared from successive replies to the United Nations national accounts questionnaire. When the scope and coverage of the estimates differ for conceptual or statistical reasons from the definitions and classifications recommended in SNA, a footnote is indicated to the relevant tables.

Sources and methods:

(a) Gross domestic product. Gross domestic product is estimated mainly through the production approach.

(b) Expenditure on the gross domestic product. The expenditure approach is used to estimate government final consumption expenditure, increase in stocks, investment in building and construction and exports and imports of goods and services. The commodity-flow approach is used to estimate the gross capital formation of transport equipment, plant and machinery whereas private final consumption expenditure is estimated as a residual. Government expenditure is estimated by netting out rent from the total of Malawi Government Revenue Expenditure on Revenue and Development Account Expenditure and final consumption as shown in 'Public Sector Financial Statistics'. Changes in recorded stocks of the monetary sector are obtained from the annual economic surveys and annual reports of the Agricultural Development and Marketing Corporation. Unrecorded stocks, i.e., imported goods, are estimated on the basis of information received from businessmen and the Ministry of Trade and Industry. Estimates of non-monetary stocks are estimated from annual economic surveys, reports of the Veterinary Department and from the Agricultural Development and Marketing Corporation. Estimates of investments in building and construction are obtained directly from large enterprises and government. For fixed operating and auxiliary equipment, installation costs are estimated at 25 per cent of the price of deliveries. Other equipment is valued at estimated delivered prices. 15 per cent of the private cars and bicycles are assumed to be imported by government and private industry and are treated as capital formation. Export and imports of goods and services are based on the balance of payments report. For the constant price estimates, price deflation is used to estimate all items of GDP by expenditure type.

(c) Cost-structure of the gross domestic product. Estimates of compensation of employees, operating surplus and consumption of fixed capital are based on data obtained from the annual survey of ecomomic activities. Data on indirect taxes and subsidies are taken from the financial statistics of the public sector.

(d) Gross domestic product by kind of economic activity. The table of GDP by kind of economic activity is prepared in factor values. The production approach is used to estimate the value added of most industries. The value added of large and medium-scale establishments, was generally taken from the Annual Economic Survey 1973-1979 and from the Medium Business Annual Review. Estimates of agricultural output are based mainly on the annual reports of the Agricultural Development and Marketing Corporation and on agricultural surveys undertaken by the National Statistical Office. Net income of farmers from sales of crops to the corporation is derived by deducting from total farm receipts the expenditure on cotton spraying and 50 per cent of the expenditure on fertilizers, seeds and tools. Income from sales of crops to other dealers is calculated as 50 per cent of the free-on-rail export value of the crops, whereas income from sales in local village and urban markets is calculated from estimates of the annual consumption of main food crops by the African population. For livestock production, estimates are based on live-weight purchases by butchers and the Cold Storage Commission which are published in the annual reports of the Veterinary Department. Increase in herds is estimated from the annual livestock censuses and the national sample survey of agriculture. For forestry, the National Statistical Office makes estimates of the retail value of firewood sales less the cost of axes and hatchets. An assumption on the quantities of firewood consumed per household is made for nonmarketed firewood. The Fisheries Department provides estimates for the fishing sector. Own-consumption of fish is estimated as 10 per cent of the landed value of the total fish catch. The estimates of large mining entreprises are based on the annual economic survey. For large manufacturing enterprises employing 20 persons or more, the annual economic survey is used to estimate gross output and intermediate consumption. The estimates of enterprises such as grain-milling, tailoring, fish-curing, handicrafts, etc. are based on agricultural sample surveys, information from the Ministry of Trade and Industry, data supplied by the Buildings Department, etc. The sources for the estimates of electricity, gas and water are the annual ecomomic surveys and the public sector financial statistics. For government construction, the annual reports of the Ministry of Works and Supplies and the estimates prepared by the National Statisticial Office are used as sources. For private construction, the quarterly building inquiries and the annual economic surveys are used for the larger enterprises while data from agricultural surveys are used for other construction including own-account construction. It is assumed that the ratio of value added to total receipts for the large construction enterprises also applies to small operators. The annual economic survey is the source used to estimate activity of larger trade enterprises while the annual reviews of small businesses are used for other enterprises. The wage component of gross output is derived from data on average employment per store and minimum wage rates. For the transport sector, the annual economic survey is also used for the larger enterprises while the annual reports of the Road Traffic Commissioner are used for the small transport operators. It is assumed that average value added per vehicle for the larger operators applies equally to the small enterprises. Value added of the financial institutions is estimated on the basis of the quarterly employment inquiries, documents of banks, information from the Ministry of Finance and the Accountant-General's annual reports. Rental value are obtained from various sources such as the public sector financial statistics, the Accountant-General's annual reports and reports of the Commissioner for Taxes.ng income survey, respectively. Value added of public administration and defence is obtained from the detailed analysis of government accounts. For private services, estimates are based on quarterly employment and earnings inquiries, agricultural surveys, annual inquiries of domestic servants, annual economic surveys and information supplied by the Ministry of Trade and Industry. GDP by kind of economic activity is not estimated at constant prices.

1.1 Expenditure on the Gross Domestic Product, in Current Prices

Million Malawi kwacha

	1970	1975	1978	1979	1980	1981	1982	1983	1984	1985	1986	1987
1 Government final consumption expenditure	41.0	74.7	134.2	164.2	193.9	198.0	218.3	235.9	268.0	344.0	433.8	488.6
2 Private final consumption expenditure a	192.3	365.2	502.2	577.0	728.6	806.5	923.1	1111.6	1183.0	1432.8	1601.2	1965.2
3 Gross capital formation	69.6	178.6	307.8	261.4	...	...	...	...	...	...	...	...
A Increase in stocks a	8.5	46.8	60.7	29.5	...	...	...	...	...	...	...	...
B Gross fixed capital formation	61.1	131.8	247.1	231.9	223.1	167.8	181.7	197.3	185.7	264.4	242.9	332.9
Residential buildings	26.0	...	...	...	...	...	...	...	...	...	...	...
Non-residential buildings	...	...	...	...	...	...	...	...	...	...	...	...
Other construction and land improvement etc.	...	...	...	...	...	...	...	...	...	...	...	...
Other	35.1	...	...	...	...	...	...	...	...	...	...	...
4 Exports of goods and services	58.7	-88.8	-143.5	-170.7	249.7	284.4	280.2	298.2	484.4	475.0	504.7	658.2
5 Less: Imports of goods and services	94.5				390.1	348.6	359.3	407.1	451.2	568.2	551.8	724.9
Equals: Gross Domestic Product	267.1	529.7	800.7	831.9	1005.2	1108.1	1244.0	1435.9	1706.9	1943.1	2230.7	2720.1

a) Beginning 1980, item 'Increase in stocks' is included in item 'Private final consumption expenditure'.

Malawi

1.2 Expenditure on the Gross Domestic Product, in Constant Prices

Million Malawi kwacha

	1970	1975	1978	1979	1980	1981	1982	1983	1984	1985	1986	1987
			1964		At constant prices of:				1978			
1 Government final consumption expenditure	38.6	...	...	...	157.2	150.6	153.9	153.5	165.9	183.6	203.3	201.3
2 Private final consumption expenditure	167.2	...	...	...	543.1[a]	541.3[a]	571.6[a]	603.0[a]	555.9[a]	600.6[a]	580.2[a]	565.2[a]
3 Gross capital formation	52.3	...	...	...	...	...	...	...	...	...	...	...
A Increase in stocks	7.1	...	...	...	...	...	...	...	...	...	...	...
B Gross fixed capital formation	45.2	...	...	...	174.0	118.0	114.8	111.9	108.5	108.0	74.4	83.2
4 Exports of goods and services	-32.1	...	...	...	273.6	224.7	202.3	209.0	277.4	295.2	281.1	282.3
5 Less: Imports of goods and services		...	...	...	308.8	239.7	228.7	232.8	217.5	259.0	195.2	189.5
Equals: Gross Domestic Product	226.0	...	...	...	839.1	794.9	813.9	844.6	890.2	930.3	943.3	942.4

a) Beginning 1980, item 'Increase in stocks' is included in item 'Private final consumption expenditure'.

1.3 Cost Components of the Gross Domestic Product

Million Malawi kwacha

	1970	1975	1978	1979	1980	1981	1982	1983	1984	1985	1986	1987
1 Indirect taxes, net	17.8	35.0	58.2	74.1	103.5	107.8	116.1	139.6	178.1	216.0	216.4	268.3
A Indirect taxes	18.2	...	...	...	...	...	...	...	...	...	...	...
B Less: Subsidies	0.4	...	...	...	...	...	...	...	...	...	...	...
2 Consumption of fixed capital [a]	...	29.8	56.7	56.5	...	...	...	...	...	...	...	...
3 Compensation of employees paid by resident producers to:	69.4	130.3	207.2	223.1	...	...	...	...	...	...	...	...
A Resident households	64.6	...	...	...	...	...	...	...	...	...	...	...
B Rest of the world	4.9	...	...	...	...	...	...	...	...	...	...	...
4 Operating surplus [a]	179.8	334.6	478.6	478.2	...	...	...	...	...	...	...	...
Equals: Gross Domestic Product	267.1	529.7	800.7	831.9	1005.2	1108.1	1244.0	1435.9	1706.9	1943.1	2230.7	2720.1

a) Item 'Operating surplus' includes consumption of fixed capital.

1.4 General Government Current Receipts and Disbursements

Million Malawi kwacha

	1970	1975	1978	1979	1980	1981	1982	1983	1984	1985	1986	1987
					Receipts							
1 Operating surplus	...	...	...	...	...	...	...	...	...	...	...	...
2 Property and entrepreneurial income	...	...	...	...	...	...	...	...	...	...	...	...
3 Taxes, fees and contributions	...	75.0	123.1	140.7	175.1	184.4	208.8	...	...	...	...	...
A Indirect taxes	...	35.0	58.2	74.1	98.4	113.2	122.4	...	...	...	...	...
B Direct taxes	...	30.5	57.2	59.4	64.9	61.9	79.9	...	...	...	...	...
C Social security contributions	...	...	...	...	...	...	...	...	...	...	...	...
D Compulsory fees, fines and penalties	...	9.5	7.7	7.2	11.8	9.3	6.5	...	...	...	...	...
4 Other current transfers	...	7.3	32.8	38.1	40.6	41.4	34.5	...	...	...	...	...
Total Current Receipts of General Government	...	82.3	155.9	178.8	215.7	225.8	243.3	...	...	...	...	...
					Disbursements							
1 Government final consumption expenditure	...	74.7	134.2	164.2	193.9	198.0	218.3	235.9	268.0	344.0	412.8	...

Malawi

1.4 General Government Current Receipts and Disbursements
(Continued)

Million Malawi kwacha

	1970	1975	1978	1979	1980	1981	1982	1983	1984	1985	1986	1987
A Compensation of employees	...	39.8	61.3	68.3	74.1	84.4	99.0	111.7	127.3	149.5	172.4	...
B Consumption of fixed capital	...	3.7	5.9	5.7	...	...	...	...	...	...	...	...
C Purchases of goods and services, net	...	31.2	67.0	90.2	119.8	113.6	119.3	124.2	140.7	194.5	240.4	...
D Less: Own account fixed capital formation	...	...	...	...	...	...	...	...	...	...	...	...
E Indirect taxes paid, net	...	...	...	...	...	...	...	...	...	...	...	...
2 Property income	...	...	...	...	...	...	...	...	...	...	...	...
3 Subsidies	...	...	...	...	...	...	...	...	...	...	...	...
4 Other current transfers	...	...	...	...	...	...	...	...	...	...	...	...
5 Net saving	...	7.6	21.7	14.6	17.6	4.1	14.5	...	...	...	...	...
Total Current Disbursements and Net Saving of General Government	...	82.3	155.9	178.8	215.7	225.8	243.3	...	...	...	...	...

1.7 External Transactions on Current Account, Summary

Million Malawi kwacha

	1970	1975	1978	1979	1980	1981	1982	1983	1984	1985	1986	1987
Payments to the Rest of the World												
1 Imports of goods and services	94.5	...	...	...	...	...	...	...	...	...	...	...
A Imports of merchandise c.i.f.	77.3	...	...	...	...	...	...	...	...	...	...	...
B Other	17.2	...	...	...	...	...	...	...	...	...	...	...
2 Factor income to the rest of the world	16.1	...	...	...	...	...	...	...	...	...	...	...
A Compensation of employees	4.9	...	...	...	...	...	...	...	...	...	...	...
B Property and entrepreneurial income	11.2	...	...	...	...	...	...	...	...	...	...	...
3 Current transfers to the rest of the world	0.3	...	...	...	...	...	...	...	...	...	...	...
4 Surplus of the nation on current transactions	-34.7	...	...	...	...	...	...	...	...	...	...	...
Payments to the Rest of the World and Surplus of the Nation on Current Transactions	76.2	...	...	...	...	...	...	...	...	...	...	...
Receipts From The Rest of the World												
1 Exports of goods and services	58.7	...	...	...	...	...	...	...	...	...	...	...
A Exports of merchandise f.o.b.	47.9	...	...	...	...	...	...	...	...	...	...	...
B Other	10.8	...	...	...	...	...	...	...	...	...	...	...
2 Factor income from rest of the world	10.0	...	...	...	...	...	...	...	...	...	...	...
A Compensation of employees	8.2	...	...	...	...	...	...	...	...	...	...	...
B Property and entrepreneurial income	1.9	...	...	...	...	...	...	...	...	...	...	...
3 Current transfers from rest of the world	7.5	...	...	...	...	...	...	...	...	...	...	...
Receipts from the Rest of the World on Current Transactions	76.2	...	...	...	...	...	...	...	...	...	...	...

1.10 Gross Domestic Product by Kind of Activity, in Current Prices

Million Malawi kwacha

	1970	1975	1978	1979	1980	1981	1982	1983	1984	1985	1986	1987
1 Agriculture, hunting, forestry and fishing [a]	139.8	194.9	296.5	319.7	...	...	...	...	...	...	...	...
2 Mining and quarrying	0.4	...	...	...	...	...	...	...	...	...	...	...
3 Manufacturing	24.8	69.1	99.1	110.1	...	...	...	...	...	...	...	...
4 Electricity, gas and water	2.9	7.9	12.5	15.7	...	...	...	...	...	...	...	...
5 Construction	8.5	23.8	46.3	29.9	...	...	...	...	...	...	...	...

Malawi

1.10 Gross Domestic Product by Kind of Activity, in Current Prices
(Continued)

Million Malawi kwacha

	1970	1975	1978	1979	1980	1981	1982	1983	1984	1985	1986	1987
6 Wholesale and retail trade, restaurants and hotels	24.6	74.6	104.9	97.7	...	...	...	...	...	...	...	...
7 Transport, storage and communication	9.5	35.9	45.0	40.4	...	...	...	...	...	...	...	...
8 Finance, insurance, real estate and business services	6.6	24.6	43.4	51.1	...	...	...	...	...	...	...	...
9 Community, social and personal services	14.5	20.8	26.9	30.8	...	...	...	...	...	...	...	...
Total, Industries	231.6	451.6	674.6	695.4	...	...	...	...	...	...	...	...
Producers of Government Services	17.9	43.5	67.2	74.0	...	...	...	...	...	...	...	...
Other Producers	2.5	19.6	29.3	33.7	...	...	...	...	...	...	...	...
Subtotal	252.0	514.7	771.1	803.1	...	...	...	...	...	...	...	...
Less: Imputed bank service charge	2.7	9.0	12.1	23.8	...	...	...	...	...	...	...	...
Plus: Import duties	...	22.0	38.1	49.0	...	...	...	...	...	...	...	...
Plus: Value added tax	...	2.9	3.6	3.6	...	...	...	...	...	...	...	...
Plus: Other adjustments	17.8	...	...	...	...	...	...	...	...	...	...	...
Equals: Gross Domestic Product	267.1	529.7	800.7	831.9	...	...	...	...	...	...	...	...

a) Item 'Agriculture, hunting, forestry and fishing' includes all non-monetary output.

1.11 Gross Domestic Product by Kind of Activity, in Constant Prices

Million Malawi kwacha

	1970	1975	1978	1979	1980	1981	1982	1983	1984	1985	1986	1987
			At constant prices of:1978									
1 Agriculture, hunting, forestry and fishing	...	230.3	294.9	304.1	284.1	260.7	278.7	290.6	309.8	308.0	310.0	320.2
2 Mining and quarrying	...	...	...	...	...	...	...	...	...	...	...	...
3 Manufacturing	...	81.1	84.8	88.5	89.0	92.0	91.8	98.3	100.8	101.1	101.0	100.5
4 Electricity, gas and water	...	10.8	12.5	13.2	14.1	14.3	14.6	15.8	16.3	16.4	17.3	18.7
5 Construction	...	33.9	46.2	42.7	43.4	35.8	36.0	33.0	33.8	39.3	49.5	32.5
6 Wholesale and retail trade, restaurants and hotels	...	91.9	104.8	105.1	108.5	96.1	93.8	97.7	101.8	113.9	108.8	104.9
7 Transport, storage and communication	...	43.9	44.7	51.5	51.8	48.2	46.8	47.3	46.7	49.5	52.3	48.8
8 Finance, insurance, real estate and business services	...	31.0	43.3	50.6	51.4	47.4	47.0	50.3	51.3	54.9	55.9	52.5
9 Community, social and personal services	...	26.1	26.9	28.1	29.1	30.5	31.0	33.2	34.3	35.2	37.7	37.4
Total, Industries	...	549.0	658.1	683.8	671.4	624.9	639.7	666.2	694.8	718.3	732.5	715.5
Producers of Government Services	...	58.2	67.2	72.3	79.0	85.1	89.8	93.9	96.1	108.2	118.0	134.5
Other Producers	...	22.6	29.3	31.5	32.3	31.7	32.6	33.9	35.2	36.2	37.2	36.9
Subtotal	...	629.8	754.6	787.6	782.7	741.7	762.1	794.0	826.1	862.7	887.7	886.9
Less: Imputed bank service charge	...	11.3	12.1	20.4	20.7	19.0	19.0	20.3	20.7	22.1	22.5	21.1
Plus: Import duties	...	...	...	...	...	...	...	...	...	...	...	...
Plus: Value added tax	...	...	...	...	...	...	...	...	...	...	...	...
Equals: Gross Domestic Product [a]	...	618.5	742.5	767.2	762.0	722.7	743.1	773.7	805.4	840.6	865.2	865.8

a) Gross domestic product in factor values.

1.12 Relations Among National Accounting Aggregates

Million Malawi kwacha

	1970	1975	1978	1979	1980	1981	1982	1983	1984	1985	1986	1987
Gross Domestic Product	267.1	529.7	800.7	831.9	1005.2	1108.1	1244.0	1435.9	1706.9	1943.1	2230.7	2720.1
Plus: Net factor income from the rest of the world	-6.1	10.7	-4.0	-34.8	-81.1	-74.3	-74.0	-75.4	-78.8	-90.9	-112.9	-125.7
Factor income from the rest of the world	10.0	...	...	...	...	...	...	...	...	...	...	...
Less: Factor income to the rest of the world	16.1	...	...	...	...	...	...	...	...	...	...	...
Equals: Gross National Product	261.0	540.4	796.7	797.1	924.1	1033.8	1170.0	1360.5	1628.1	1852.2	2117.8	2594.4

Malawi

1.12 Relations Among National Accounting Aggregates
(Continued)

Million Malawi kwacha

	1970	1975	1978	1979	1980	1981	1982	1983	1984	1985	1986	1987
Less: Consumption of fixed capital	...	29.8	56.7	56.5	...	...	...	...	...	...	...	...
Equals: National Income	...	510.6	740.0	740.6	...	...	...	...	...	...	...	...
Plus: Net current transfers from the rest of the world	7.3	12.2	37.8	37.8	40.6	41.4	38.3	34.7	34.5	42.1	51.0	...
Equals: National Disposable Income	...	522.8	777.8	778.4	...	...	...	...	...	...	...	...
Less: Final consumption	233.3	439.9	636.4	741.2	...	...	...	...	...	...	...	...
Equals: Net Saving	...	82.9	141.4	37.2	...	...	...	...	...	...	...	...
Less: Surplus of the nation on current transactions	-34.7	...	...	...	...	...	...	...	...	...	...	...
Equals: Net Capital Formation	...	...	...	...	...	...	...	...	...	...	...	...

2.17 Exports and Imports of Goods and Services, Detail

Million Malawi kwacha

		1970	1975	1978	1979	1980	1981	1982	1983	1984	1985	1986	1987
	Exports of Goods and Services												
1	Exports of merchandise, f.o.b.	47.9	...	...	...	...	...	...	...	...	...	...	...
2	Transport and communication	3.7	...	...	...	...	...	...	...	...	...	...	...
A	In respect of merchandise imports	0.8	...	...	...	...	...	...	...	...	...	...	...
B	Other	2.9	...	...	...	...	...	...	...	...	...	...	...
3	Insurance service charges	1.1	...	...	...	...	...	...	...	...	...	...	...
4	Other commodities	2.2	...	...	...	...	...	...	...	...	...	...	...
5	Adjustments of merchandise exports to change-of-ownership basis	...	...	...	...	...	...	...	...	...	...	...	...
6	Direct purchases in the domestic market by non-residential households	3.8	...	...	...	...	...	...	...	...	...	...	...
7	Direct purchases in the domestic market by extraterritorial bodies	...	...	...	...	...	...	...	...	...	...	...	...
	Total Exports of Goods and Services	58.7	...	...	...	...	...	...	...	...	...	...	...
	Imports of Goods and Services												
1	Imports of merchandise, c.i.f.	77.3	...	...	...	...	...	...	...	...	...	...	...
A	Imports of merchandise, f.o.b.	68.4	...	...	...	...	...	...	...	...	...	...	...
B	Transport of services on merchandise imports	9.0	...	...	...	...	...	...	...	...	...	...	...
	By residents	...	...	...	...	...	...	...	...	...	...	...	...
	By non-residents	9.0	...	...	...	...	...	...	...	...	...	...	...
C	Insurance service charges on merchandise imports	...	...	...	...	...	...	...	...	...	...	...	...
2	Adjustments of merchandise imports to change-of-ownership basis	...	...	...	...	...	...	...	...	...	...	...	...
3	Other transport and communication	4.9	...	...	...	...	...	...	...	...	...	...	...
4	Other insurance service charges	2.8	...	...	...	...	...	...	...	...	...	...	...
5	Other commodities	3.0	...	...	...	...	...	...	...	...	...	...	...
6	Direct purchases abroad by government	6.5	...	...	...	...	...	...	...	...	...	...	...
7	Direct purchases abroad by resident households	...	...	...	...	...	...	...	...	...	...	...	...
	Total Imports of Goods and Services	94.5	...	...	...	...	...	...	...	...	...	...	...
	Balance of Goods and Services	-35.9	...	...	...	...	...	...	...	...	...	...	...
	Total Imports and Balance of Goods and Services	58.7	...	...	...	...	...	...	...	...	...	...	...

Malaysia

General note. The preparation of national accounts statistics in Malaysia is undertaken by the Department of Statistics, Kuala Lumpur. The official estimates are published in a series of reports entitled 'Malaysia National Accounts Statistics'. The estimates are generally in accordance with the classifications and definitions recommended in the United Nations System of National Accounts (SNA, 1968). Since 1970, the publication of estimates of National Accounts have been on a Malaysia basis. The following tables have been prepared from successive replies to the United Nations National Accounts Questionnaire. When the scope and coverage of the estimates differ for conceptual or statistical reasons from the definitions and classifications recommended in SNA, a footnote is indicated to the relevant tables.

Sources and methods:

(a) Gross domestic product. Gross domestic product is estimated mainly through the production approach

(b) Expenditure on the gross domestic product. All components of GDP by expenditure type are estimated through the expenditure approach (by 'commodity flow'). Data on government final consumption expenditure are obtained from the annual accounts of the various levels of government. Estimates of private consumption expenditure have been made by allocating the available supply of consumer goods and services from import and local production to consumption accounts for the various component items. Estimates of changes in stocks are derived from annual censuses and government accounts. Gross fixed capital formation includes not only building, construction, machinery and equipment but also investment in plantation and small-holders' perennial crops. For building and construction, information is obtained from the annual surveys of construction industries for the private enterprises, institutions and households and from annual financial reports and analysis of accounts of the general government and public corporations. For machinery and equipment, mark-ups derived from the 1967 census of distributive trades, transport charges, indirect taxes etc. are added to the c.i.f. values to obtain the final value of capital formation. Data on domestic production are provided by the annual surveys of manufacturing industries. Information for the estimation of investment in perennial crops is derived from the annual censuses of the various crops. Export and import data are recorded at the time of crossing the customs boundaries. GDP by expenditure type is not estimated at constant prices.

(c) Cost-structure of the gross domestic product. Estimates for compensation of employees are derived from statistics covering output, input and government accounts for all sectors except for the agricultural sector which is obtained from the census of population and the labour force survey. Indirect taxes are obtained from government accounts. The allocation according to industries and households are based on information from the production statistics, tax regulations and assumed relationships to known items. Operating surplus including depreciation is obtained as a residual.

(d) Gross domestic product by kind of economic activity. The table of GDP by kind of economic activity is prepared at market prices, i.e., producers' values. The production approach is used to estimate the value added of all industries except government services and part of the private services which are estimated through the income approach. Information on the production volume of the various agricultural crops, except paddy, is based on the 1973 household budget survey and updated with acreage, yield and price data. Input are obtained from the relevant agricultural economic bulletins. For paddy, data on production from the Ministry of Agriculture are used while the prices are derived from the National Padi Board's approved buying prices, rice mills' purchase prices and retail prices prior to 1972. Since 1972, the Department compiles a producer price index for all goods. Information on intermediate consumption is based on input coefficients extracted from reports of the economic survey of paddy production in 1967/68. Data on the production of palmoil, coconut, copra and tea, are obtained from monthly and annual reports submitted by the estates. Statistics on livestock, forestry and fishing are obtained from the Veterinary Services, the Department of Forestry and the Department of Fishery, respectively. Salting, drying and other forms of fish preservation are treated as manufacturing and therefore are not included in the value of fishing. For the mining sector the value of production, inputs and other related information are obtained from the oil companies for crude oil, from annual censuses for mining and from an annual survey for stone-quarrying. The annual surveys of manufacturing industries are used for estimating the gross value of production and intermediate consumption of manufacturing. For industries not covered, censuses of manufacturing industries in 1968 and 1973 have been used as bench-marks. Data relating to electricity and water are obtained from the detailed accounts of the producers. For construction, the information is obtained from the annual survey of construction industries supplemented by the analysis of government accounts and public corporations. The value of services rendered by the trade sector is calculated as the gross mark-up. Mark-ups are added to the producers' values of commodities, the total of which is treated as deliveries from the 'distributive trades' industry to other industries. Mark-ups and intermediate consumption are calculated from sources such as the census of distributive trades, import prices, ex-factory prices and retail prices. For restaurants and hotels, estimates are based on the 1971 census of selected service trades in the urban areas. The estimates of the value of production for road transport are made on the basis of the number of vehicle registered and the 1971 census of selected industries. For the financial sector, information is obtained from concerned institutions. The household expenditure survey in 1973 is used as the basis for the calculation of rent paid on dwellings and imputed rent of owner-occupied dwellings. Business services rendered by professionals in the private sector are valued by means of data collected from the annual census of professions and institutions. Information on producers of government services is derived from the analysis of government financial statements. For private services, estimates are obtained from a variety of sources such as the census of professions and institutions, the 1971 census of selected industries and employment data. For the constant price estimates, value added of agriculture, mining and quarrying, manufacturing, electricity and water transport sectors is extrapolated by a quantity index for output. For education and health, trends in the number of persons engaged are used. For the remaining industries, construction, trade, ownership of dwellings and public services, estimates of current prices are retained.

1.1 Expenditure on the Gross Domestic Product, in Current Prices

Million Malaysian ringgit

		1970	1975	1978	1979	1980	1981	1982	1983	1984	1985	1986	1987
1	Government final consumption expenditure	1742	3924	6090	6475	8811	10425	11469	11015	11741	11844	12127	12239
2	Private final consumption expenditure	6349	13086	19584	22406	26946	30594	33226	36458	39594	40360	36574	37964
3	Gross capital formation	2016	5221	10104	13423	16217	20157	23338	26466	26697	21367	17977	19386
	A Increase in stocks	315	-381	723	1173	-380	-602	593	1253	1306	-1757	-888	1106
	B Gross fixed capital formation	1701	5602	9381	12250	16597	20759	22745	25213	25391	23124	18865	18280
	Residential buildings	250	...	1058	...	...	...	...	2702	...	...	...	...
	Non-residential buildings	288	...	2270	...	...	...	...	3067	...	...	...	...
	Other construction and land improvement etc.	378	...	1682	...	...	...	...	7064	...	...	...	...
	Other	785	...	4371	...	...	...	...	12380	...	...	...	...
4	Exports of goods and services	4332	10172	18585	26004	30676	30154	31846	35795	43171	42537	40707	50714
5	Less: Imports of goods and services	3851	10071	16477	21884	29342	33717	37300	39793	41653	38561	36241	39694
	Equals: Gross Domestic Product	10588	22332	37886	46424	53308	57613	62579	69941	79550	77547	71144	80609

Malaysia

1.2 Expenditure on the Gross Domestic Product, in Constant Prices

Million Malaysian ringgit

	1970	1975	1978	1979	1980	1981	1982	1983	1984	1985	1986	1987
			At constant prices of:									
		1970						1978				
1 Government final consumption expenditure	1742	3117	3931 / 6090	6195	7750	8784	9552	9989	9500	9417	9536	9676
2 Private final consumption expenditure	6349	9631	12398 / 19584	21698	24445	25686	26531	27376	29142	29299	26369	27055
3 Gross capital formation	2016	3670	5418 / 10104	11455	13612	15952	18245	19638	20713	16626	13816	14788
A Increase in stocks	315	-266	299 / 723	285	-319	-498	478	445	952	-1262	-785	834
B Gross fixed capital formation	1701	3936	5119 / 9381	11170	13931	16450	17767	19193	19761	17888	14601	13954
4 Exports of goods and services	4332	7179	9410 / 18585	21924	22619	22431	24826	27889	31733	31875	37541	41312
5 Less: Imports of goods and services	3851	6232	8893 / 16477	19844	23914	25251	28724	31310	33347	30067	29403	31985
Equals: Gross Domestic Product	10588	17365	22264 / 37886	41428	44512	47602	50430	53582	57741	57150	57859	60846

1.3 Cost Components of the Gross Domestic Product

Million Malaysian ringgit

	1970	1975	1978	1979	1980	1981	1982	1983	1984	1985	1986	1987
1 Indirect taxes, net	1549	3366	6099	7671	9066	8836	8758	10882	12066	11650	9943	9972
A Indirect taxes	1551	...	6099	...	...	...	...	...	...	...	...	...
B Less: Subsidies	2	...	-	...	...	...	...	...	...	...	...	...
2 Consumption of fixed capital [a]	...	...	...	...	...	...	...	...	...	...	...	...
3 Compensation of employees paid by resident producers to:	3726	...	11966	...	...	...	...	23579	...	...	...	...
4 Operating surplus [a]	5313	...	19821	...	...	...	...	35480	...	...	...	...
Equals: Gross Domestic Product	10588	22332	37886	46424	53308	57613	62579	69941	79550	77547	71144	80609

a) Item 'Operating surplus' includes consumption of fixed capital.

1.7 External Transactions on Current Account, Summary

Million Malaysian ringgit

	1970	1975	1978	1979	1980	1981	1982	1983	1984	1985	1986	1987
Payments to the Rest of the World												
1 Imports of goods and services	3851	...	16477	...	...	...	...	39793	...	...	...	...
A Imports of merchandise c.i.f.	3401	...	14690	...	...	...	...	33466	...	...	...	...
B Other	450	...	1787	...	...	...	...	6327	...	...	...	...
2 Factor income to the rest of the world	536	...	2581	...	...	...	...	5815	...	...	...	...
3 Current transfers to the rest of the world	470	...	280	...	...	...	...	186	...	...	...	...
4 Surplus of the nation on current transactions	-30	...	304	...	...	...	...	-8416	...	...	...	...
Payments to the Rest of the World and Surplus of the Nation on Current Transactions	4827	...	19642	...	...	...	...	37378	...	...	...	...
Receipts From The Rest of the World												
1 Exports of goods and services	4332	...	18585	...	...	...	...	35795	...	...	...	...
A Exports of merchandise f.o.b.	4105	...	17067	...	...	...	...	31432	...	...	...	...
B Other	227	...	1518	...	...	...	...	4363	...	...	...	...
2 Factor income from rest of the world	219	...	881	...	...	...	...	1404	...	...	...	...
3 Current transfers from rest of the world	276	...	176	...	...	...	...	179	...	...	...	...
Receipts from the Rest of the World on Current Transactions	4827	...	19642	...	...	...	...	37378	...	...	...	...

1.10 Gross Domestic Product by Kind of Activity, in Current Prices

Million Malaysian ringgit

	1970	1975	1978	1979	1980	1981	1982	1983	1984	1985	1986	1987
1 Agriculture, hunting, forestry and fishing	3051	...	9513	...	...	...	...	13100	...	...	...	...
2 Mining and quarrying	735	...	3912	...	...	...	...	9756	...	...	...	...
3 Manufacturing	1554	...	7189	...	...	...	...	13376	...	...	...	...
4 Electricity, gas and water	203	...	531	...	...	...	...	1024	...	...	...	...
5 Construction	395	...	1571	...	...	...	...	3846	...	...	...	...

Malaysia

1.10 Gross Domestic Product by Kind of Activity, in Current Prices
(Continued)

Million Malaysian ringgit

	1970	1975	1978	1979	1980	1981	1982	1983	1984	1985	1986	1987
6 Wholesale and retail trade, restaurants and hotels	1269	...	4156	...	...	...	...	8084	...	...	...	...
7 Transport, storage and communication	549	...	1867	...	...	...	...	3656	...	...	...	...
8 Finance, insurance, real estate and business services	912	...	3177	...	...	...	...	6587	...	...	...	...
9 Community, social and personal services	221	...	798	...	...	...	...	1905	...	...	...	...
Total, Industries	8889	...	32714	...	...	...	...	61334	...	...	...	...
Producers of Government Services	1268	...	4105	...	...	...	...	7171	...	...	...	...
Other Producers	67	...	102	...	...	...	...	185	...	...	...	...
Subtotal	10224	...	36921	...	...	...	...	68690	...	...	...	...
Less: Imputed bank service charge	106	...	585	...	...	...	...	1895	...	...	...	...
Plus: Import duties	470	...	1550	...	...	...	...	3146	...	...	...	...
Plus: Value added tax	...	...	...	...	...	...	...	...	...	...	...	...
Equals: Gross Domestic Product	10588	22332	37886	...	...	...	...	69941	...	...	...	...

1.11 Gross Domestic Product by Kind of Activity, in Constant Prices

Million Malaysian ringgit

	1970	1975	1978	1979	1980	1981	1982	1983	1984	1985	1986	1987
		At constant prices of 1970			At constant prices of 1978							
1 Agriculture, hunting, forestry and fishing	3051	4804	5610 / 9513	10060	10189	10684	11375	11302	11623	11914	12389	13311
2 Mining and quarrying	735	792	1054 / 3912	4586	4487	4289	4617	5342	6073	5985	6433	6442
3 Manufacturing	1554	2850	4081 / 7189	8004	8742	9155	9668	10429	11711	11263	12111	13663
4 Electricity, gas and water	203	365	499 / 530	584	640	689	721	798	890	948	1027	1109
5 Construction	395	654	919 / 1572	1761	2066	2367	2598	2867	2988	2738	2355	2077
6 Wholesale and retail trade, restaurants and hotels	1269	2219	2824 / 4156	4669	5383	5694	6104	6583	7107	6911	6147	6423
7 Transport, storage and communication	549	1071	1415 / 1867	2107	2542	2847	2984	3138	3464	3630	3851	4055
8 Finance, insurance, real estate and business services	912	1468	1823 / 3177	3434	3687	3953	4231	4570	4892	5093	5073	5355
9 Community, social and personal services	221	388	498 / 798	841	912	950	1024	1076	1130	1181	1231	1271
Total, Industries	8889	14611	18723 / 32714	36046	38648	40628	43322	46105	49878	49663	50617	53706
Producers of Government Services	1268	2210	2831 / 4106	4375	4563	5649	6027	6328	6817	6957	7253	7543
Other Producers	67	90	97 / 101	107	109	115	117	117	119	119	121	122
Subtotal	10224	16911	21651 / 36921	40528	43320	46392	49466	52550	56814	56739	57991	61371
Less: Imputed bank service charge	106	211	302 / 585	733	854	877	1152	1397	1595	1834	1891	2175
Plus: Import duties	470	665	915 / 1550	1633	2046	2087	2116	2429	2522	2245	1759	1650
Plus: Value added tax	...	...	...	...	...	...	...	...	...	...	...	...
Equals: Gross Domestic Product	10588	17365	22264 / 37886	41428	44512	47602	50430	53582	57741	57150	57859	60846

1.12 Relations Among National Accounting Aggregates

Million Malaysian ringgit

	1970	1975	1978	1979	1980	1981	1982	1983	1984	1985	1986	1987
Gross Domestic Product	10588	22332	37886	46424	53308	57613	62579	69941	79550	77547	71144	80609
Plus: Net factor income from the rest of the world	-317	-726	-1700	-2070	-1918	-2011	-2889	-4411	-5368	-5508	-4780	-5270
Factor income from the rest of the world	219	...	881	...	...	...	...	1404	...	...	...	...
Less: Factor income to the rest of the world	536	...	2581	...	...	...	...	5815	...	...	...	...
Equals: Gross National Product	10271	21606	36186	44354	51390	55602	59690	65530	74182	72039	66364	75339
Less: Consumption of fixed capital	...	...	...	...	...	...	...	...	...	...	...	...

Malaysia

1.12 Relations Among National Accounting Aggregates
(Continued)

Million Malaysian ringgit

	1970	1975	1978	1979	1980	1981	1982	1983	1984	1985	1986	1987
Equals: National Income a	10271	...	36186	...	...	...	...	65530	...	...	...	...
Plus: Net current transfers from the rest of the world	-194	...	-104	...	...	...	...	-7	...	...	...	...
Current transfers from the rest of the world	276	...	176	...	...	...	...	179	...	...	...	...
Less: Current transfers to the rest of the world	470	...	280	...	...	...	...	186	...	...	...	...
Equals: National Disposable Income b	10077	...	36082	...	...	...	...	65523	...	...	...	...
Less: Final consumption	8091	17010	25674	...	...	...	...	47473	...	...	...	...
Equals: Net Saving c	1986	...	10408	...	...	...	...	18050	...	...	...	...
Less: Surplus of the nation on current transactions	-30	...	304	...	...	...	...	-8416	...	...	...	...
Equals: Net Capital Formation d	2016	...	10104	...	...	...	...	26466	...	...	...	...

a) Item 'National income' includes consumption of fixed capital.
b) Item 'National disposable income' includes consumption of fixed capital.
c) Item 'Net saving' includes consumption of fixed capital.
d) Item 'Net capital formation' includes consumption of fixed capital.

2.1 Government Final Consumption Expenditure by Function, in Current Prices

Million Malaysian ringgit

		1970	1975	1978	1979	1980	1981	1982	1983	1984	1985	1986	1987
1	General public services	444	...	1261	...	...	...	...	2346	...	...	...	...
2	Defence	442	...	1645	...	...	...	...	3371	...	...	...	...
3	Public order and safety		...		...	...	...	...		...	...	...	...
4	Education	434	...	1636	...	...	...	...	2649	...	...	...	...
5	Health	150	...	601	...	...	...	...	961	...	...	...	...
6	Social security and welfare		...		...	...	...	...		...	...	...	...
7	Housing and community amenities	272	...	933	...	...	...	...	1688	...	...	...	...
8	Recreational, cultural and religious affairs		...		...	...	...	...		...	...	...	...
9	Economic services		...		...	...	...	...		...	...	...	...
10	Other functions	...	...	14	...	...	...	...	...	...	...	...	...
	Total Government Final Consumption Expenditure	1742	3924	6090	6475	8811	10425	11469	11015	11741	11844	12127	12239

2.5 Private Final Consumption Expenditure by Type and Purpose, in Current Prices

Million Malaysian ringgit

		1970	1975	1978	1979	1980	1981	1982	1983	1984	1985	1986	1987

Final Consumption Expenditure of Resident Households

		1970	1975	1978	1979	1980	1981	1982	1983	1984	1985	1986	1987
1	Food, beverages and tobacco	2875	...	7908	...	...	...	...	11546	...	...	...	...
	A Food	2392	...	6623	...	...	...	...	9113	...	...	...	...
	B Non-alcoholic beverages	37	...	163	...	...	...	...	309	...	...	...	...
	C Alcoholic beverages	129	...	382	...	...	...	...	752	...	...	...	...
	D Tobacco	317	...	740	...	...	...	...	1372	...	...	...	...
2	Clothing and footwear	348	...	1109	...	...	...	...	1540	...	...	...	...
3	Gross rent, fuel and power	862	...	2051	...	...	...	...	3628	...	...	...	...
4	Furniture, furnishings and household equipment and operation	392	...	1479	...	...	...	...	2742	...	...	...	...
	A Household operation	162	...	421	...	...	...	...	670	...	...	...	...
	B Other	230	...	1058	...	...	...	...	2072	...	...	...	...
5	Medical care and health expenses	133	...	420	...	...	...	...	902	...	...	...	...
6	Transport and communication	856	...	3481	...	...	...	...	7410	...	...	...	...
	A Personal transport equipment	180	...	1221	...	...	...	...	2967	...	...	...	...
	B Other	676	...	2260	...	...	...	...	4443	...	...	...	...
7	Recreational, entertainment, education and cultural services	347	...	1252	...	...	...	...	4123	...	...	...	...
	A Education	50	...	101	...	...	...	...	219	...	...	...	...
	B Other	297	...	1151	...	...	...	...	3904	...	...	...	...
8	Miscellaneous goods and services	519	...	1623	...	...	...	...	3512	...	...	...	...
	A Personal care	217	...	622	...	...	...	...	1062	...	...	...	...
	B Expenditures in restaurants, cafes and hotels	248	...	798	...	...	...	...	1904	...	...	...	...
	C Other	54	...	203	...	...	...	...	546	...	...	...	...
	Total Final Consumption Expenditure in the Domestic Market by Households, of which	6332	...	19323	...	...	...	...	35403	...	...	...	...
	A Durable goods	356	...	2391	...	...	...	...	5787	...	...	...	...

Malaysia

2.5 Private Final Consumption Expenditure by Type and Purpose, in Current Prices
(Continued)

Million Malaysian ringgit

	1970	1975	1978	1979	1980	1981	1982	1983	1984	1985	1986	1987
B Semi-durable goods	831	...	2527	...	...	...	...	4505	...	...	...	...
C Non-durable goods	3501	...	9883	...	...	...	...	16534	...	...	...	...
D Services	1644	...	4522	...	...	...	...	8577	...	...	...	...
Plus: Direct purchases abroad by resident households	184	...	883	...	...	...	...	2630	...	...	...	...
Less: Direct purchases in the domestic market by non-resident households	167	...	622	...	...	...	...	1575	...	...	...	...
Equals: Final Consumption Expenditure of Resident Households [a]	6349	...	19584	...	...	...	...	36458	...	...	...	...

Final Consumption Expenditure of Private Non-profit Institutions Serving Households

	1970	1975	1978	1979	1980	1981	1982	1983	1984	1985	1986	1987
Equals: Final Consumption Expenditure of Private Non-profit Organisations Serving Households	...	...	...	...	...	...	...	...	...	...	...	...
Private Final Consumption Expenditure	6349	...	19584	...	...	...	...	36458	...	...	...	...

a) Item 'Final consumption expenditure of resident households' includes consumption expenditure of private non-profit institutions serving households.

2.11 Gross Fixed Capital Formation by Kind of Activity of Owner, ISIC Divisions, in Current Prices

Million Malaysian ringgit

	1970	1975	1978	1979	1980	1981	1982	1983	1984	1985	1986	1987

All Producers

	1970	1975	1978	1979	1980	1981	1982	1983	1984	1985	1986	1987
1 Agriculture, hunting, forestry and fishing	294	...	990	...	...	...	...	2194	...	...	...	...
2 Mining and quarrying	101	...	585	...	...	...	...	2761	...	...	...	...
3 Manufacturing	321	...	1639	...	...	...	...	2605	...	...	...	...
4 Electricity, gas and water	85	...	537	...	...	...	...	1989	...	...	...	...
5 Construction	87	...	769	...	...	...	...	1790	...	...	...	...
6 Wholesale and retail trade, restaurants and hotels	67	...	337	...	...	...	...	1019	...	...	...	...
7 Transport, storage and communication	112	...	1236	...	...	...	...	3037	...	...	...	...
8 Finance, insurance, real estate and business services	254	...	2294	...	...	...	...	5257	...	...	...	...
9 Community, social and personal services	9	...	103	...	...	...	...	233	...	...	...	...
Total Industries	1330	...	8490	...	...	...	...	20885	...	...	...	...
Producers of Government Services	371	...	891	...	...	...	...	4328	...	...	...	...
Private Non-Profit Institutions Serving Households	...	...	...	...	...	...	...	...	...	...	...	...
Total	1701	...	9381	...	...	...	...	25213	...	...	...	...

2.17 Exports and Imports of Goods and Services, Detail

Million Malaysian ringgit

	1970	1975	1978	1979	1980	1981	1982	1983	1984	1985	1986	1987

Exports of Goods and Services

	1970	1975	1978	1979	1980	1981	1982	1983	1984	1985	1986	1987
1 Exports of merchandise, f.o.b.	4105	...	17067	...	...	...	...	31432	...	...	...	...
2 Transport and communication	5	...	696	...	...	...	...	1097	...	...	...	...
3 Insurance service charges	...	...	16	...	...	...	...	2	...	...	...	...
4 Other commodities	5	...	184	...	...	...	...	1688	...	...	...	...
5 Adjustments of merchandise exports to change-of-ownership basis	50	...	...	...	...	...	...	...	...	...	...	...
6 Direct purchases in the domestic market by non-residential households	167	...	622	...	...	...	...	1576	...	...	...	...
7 Direct purchases in the domestic market by extraterritorial bodies	...	...	...	...	...	...	...	...	...	...	...	...
Total Exports of Goods and Services	4332	10172	18585	...	...	...	...	35795	...	...	...	...

Imports of Goods and Services

	1970	1975	1978	1979	1980	1981	1982	1983	1984	1985	1986	1987
1 Imports of merchandise, c.i.f.	3401	...	14690	...	...	...	...	33466	...	...	...	...

Malaysia

2.17 Exports and Imports of Goods and Services, Detail
(Continued)

Million Malaysian ringgit

	1970	1975	1978	1979	1980	1981	1982	1983	1984	1985	1986	1987
2 Adjustments of merchandise imports to change-of-ownership basis	...	...	...	...	...	...	...	...	...	...	...	...
3 Other transport and communication	85	...	381	...	...	...	...	1044	...	...	...	...
4 Other insurance service charges	11	...	39	...	...	...	...	142	...	...	...	...
5 Other commodities	170	...	484	...	...	...	...	2511	...	...	...	...
6 Direct purchases abroad by government	...	...	[883]	...	...	...	...	[2630]	...	...	...	...
7 Direct purchases abroad by resident households	184	...		...	...	...	...		...	...	...	...
Total Imports of Goods and Services	3851	10071	16477	...	...	...	...	39793	...	...	...	...
Balance of Goods and Services	481	101	2108	...	...	...	...	-3998	...	...	...	...
Total Imports and Balance of Goods and Services	4332	10172	18585	...	...	...	...	35795	...	...	...	...

4.3 Cost Components of Value Added

Million Malaysian ringgit

1983

	Compensation of Employees	Capital Consumption	Net Operating Surplus	Indirect Taxes	Less: Subsidies Received	Value Added
All Producers						
1 Agriculture, hunting, forestry and fishing	2721	...	8931	...	...	13100
A Agriculture and hunting	1896	...	5962	...	...	8155
B Forestry and logging	568	...	1569	...	...	3271
C Fishing	257	...	1400	...	...	1674
2 Mining and quarrying	742	...	6432	...	...	9756
3 Manufacturing	3877	...	6503	...	...	13376
A Manufacture of food, beverages and tobacco	535	...	1503	...	...	2686
B Textile, wearing apparel and leather industries	341	...	210	...	...	620
C Manufacture of wood and wood products, including furniture	522	...	323	...	...	1079
D Manufacture of paper and paper products, printing and publishing	286	...	278	...	...	612
E Manufacture of chemicals and chemical petroleum, coal, rubber and plastic products	555	...	1566	...	...	3067
F Manufacture of non-metallic mineral products, except products of petroleum and coal	232	...	418	...	...	676
G Basic metal industries	344	...	471	...	...	940
H Manufacture of fabricated metal products, machinery and equipment	[1062]	...	[1734]	...	...	[3696]
I Other manufacturing industries		...		...	...	
4 Electricity, gas and water	241	...	773	...	...	1024
5 Construction	2544	...	1264	...	...	3846
6 Wholesale and retail trade, restaurants and hotels	2606	...	5289	...	...	8084
A Wholesale and retail trade	...	...	...	...	...	6930
B Restaurants and hotels	...	...	...	...	...	1154
7 Transport, storage and communication	1446	...	2174	...	...	3656
8 Finance, insurance, real estate and business services	1438	...	5083	...	...	6587
9 Community, social and personal services	610	...	926	...	...	1905

Malaysia

4.3 Cost Components of Value Added
(Continued)

Million Malaysian ringgit

	1983					
	Compensation of Employees	Capital Consumption	Net Operating Surplus	Indirect Taxes	Less: Subsidies Received	Value Added
Total, Industries	16225	...	37375	...	...	61334
Producers of Government Services	6988	183	...	...	...	7171
Other Producers	185	...	...	...	...	185
Total	23398	183	37375	...	...	68690
Less: Imputed bank service charge	...	...	1895	...	...	1895
Import duties	...	...	...	...	...	3146
Value added tax	...	...	...	...	...	...
Total	23396	183	35480	10882	...	69941

Maldives

Source. Reply to the United Nations National Accounts Questionnaire from the Department of information and broadcasting, Male. Official estimates are published by the ministry of planning and development in the Statistical Yearbook.

General note. The estimates shown in the following tables have been prepared in accordance with the United Nations System of National Accounts so far as the existing data would permit.

1.1 Expenditure on the Gross Domestic Product, in Current Prices

Million Maldivian Rufiyaa

	1970	1975	1978	1979	1980	1981	1982	1983	1984	1985	1986	1987
1 Government final consumption expenditure	...	...	...	...	56.8	49.0	65.0	76.0	94.8	...	...	...
2 Private final consumption expenditure	...	...	...	...	270.3	344.0	367.0	385.0	416.0	...	...	...
3 Gross capital formation	...	...	...	...	117.4	99.0	105.0	178.0	220.0	...	...	...
A Increase in stocks	...	...	...	...	...	...	1.6	12.0	8.0	...	...	...
B Gross fixed capital formation	...	...	...	...	...	...	103.0	166.0	212.0	...	...	...
4 Exports of goods and services	...	...	...	...	142.4	196.0	240.0	288.0	300.0	...	...	...
5 Less: Imports of goods and services	...	...	...	...	231.3	313.0	345.0	464.0	495.0	...	...	...
Equals: Gross Domestic Product [a]	...	...	...	...	355.6	376.0	432.0	466.0	537.0	596.0	...	...

a) Data for this table have not been revised, therefore, data for some years are not comparable with those of other tables.

1.2 Expenditure on the Gross Domestic Product, in Constant Prices

Million Maldivian Rufiyaa

	1970	1975	1978	1979	1980	1981	1982	1983	1984	1985	1986	1987
				At constant prices of:								
			1980				1982			1984			
1 Government final consumption expenditure	...	...	37.1	42.6	56.8 / 45.0	46.0	60.0	70.0 / 83.6	94.8	...	...	...
2 Private final consumption expenditure	...	...	182.4	237.7	270.3 / 321.0	354.0	363.0	374.0 / 380.8	416.0	...	...	...
3 Gross capital formation	...	...	41.6	48.6	117.4 / 87.0	105.0	105.0	109.0 / 178.0	220.0	...	...	...
A Increase in stocks	...	...	...	...	...	...	...	12.0	8.0	...	...	...
B Gross fixed capital formation	...	...	...	...	...	...	...	166.0	212.0	...	...	...
4 Exports of goods and services	...	...	108.7	133.1	142.4 / 175.0	225.0	239.0	261.0 / 288.0	300.0	...	...	...
5 Less: Imports of goods and services	...	...	98.8	162.1	231.3 / 254.0	312.0	322.0	352.0 / 464.0	495.0	...	...	...
Equals: Gross Domestic Product	...	...	271.0	299.9	355.6 / 374.0	418.0	445.0	462.0 / 475.4	537.0	...	...	...

1.10 Gross Domestic Product by Kind of Activity, in Current Prices

Million Maldivian Rufiyaa

	1970	1975	1978	1979	1980	1981	1982	1983	1984	1985	1986	1987
1 Agriculture, hunting, forestry and fishing	...	...	...	...	111.5	130.5	130.3	149.3	167.5	176.3	212.7	...
2 Mining and quarrying	...	...	...	...	5.8	10.3	10.7	11.1	11.4	11.7	12.0	...
3 Manufacturing	...	...	...	...	14.3	16.8	21.4	27.2	30.4	33.5	38.1	...
4 Electricity, gas and water	...	...	...	...								...
5 Construction	...	...	...	...	30.2	27.7	32.8	34.2	40.7	48.9	52.9	...
6 Wholesale and retail trade, restaurants and hotels	...	...	...	...	40.0	36.6	49.5	69.4	87.7	97.2	103.5	...
7 Transport, storage and communication	...	...	...	...	17.2	84.2	41.6	58.7	101.3	135.7	159.3	...
8 Finance, insurance, real estate and business services	...	...	...	...	8.2	11.7	13.4	15.4	19.6	26.0	29.3	...
9 Community, social and personal services	...	...	...	...	54.5	7.7	9.6	16.5	41.5	38.0	34.1	...

Maldives

1.10 Gross Domestic Product by Kind of Activity, in Current Prices
(Continued)

Million Maldivian Rufiyaa

	1970	1975	1978	1979	1980	1981	1982	1983	1984	1985	1986	1987
Total, Industries	...	...	...	...	281.1	325.6	309.3	381.8	500.1	567.3	641.9	...
Producers of Government Services	...	...	...	...	39.5	18.5	22.2	37.6	42.7	45.8	55.5	...
Other Producers	...	...	...	...	...	...	...	...	...	...	...	...
Subtotal	...	...	...	...	320.6	344.1	331.5	381.8	542.8	613.1	697.4	...
Less: Imputed bank service charge	...	...	...	...	...	...	...	...	...	...	...	...
Plus: Import duties	...	...	...	...	...	...	...	...	...	...	...	...
Plus: Value added tax	...	...	...	...	...	...	...	...	...	...	...	...
Equals: Gross Domestic Product	...	...	...	...	320.6	344.1	331.5	381.8	542.8	613.1	697.4	...

1.11 Gross Domestic Product by Kind of Activity, in Constant Prices

Million Maldivian Rufiyaa

	1970	1975	1978	1979	1980	1981	1982	1983	1984	1985	1986	1987
			At constant prices of:									
			1980		1982				1985			
1 Agriculture, hunting, forestry and fishing	...	...	98.1	96.9	114.9 / 128.7	138.9 / 150.2	140.7	145.6	157.3	176.3	174.3	194.4
2 Mining and quarrying	...	...	3.2	4.8	5.6 / 5.6	5.4 / 9.0	9.6	10.4	11.0	11.7	12.4	13.2
3 Manufacturing	...	...	10.0	12.5	14.9 / 12.7 [a]	16.0 / 19.3	25.9	29.8	32.1	33.5	36.0	39.6
4 Electricity, gas and water	...	...	1.7	0.7	0.9 / ...							
5 Construction	...	...	25.6	35.4	42.0 / 39.6	28.6 / 28.5	33.4	34.4	40.8	48.9	52.8	58.1
6 Wholesale and retail trade, restaurants and hotels	...	...	...	...	... / 44.0	44.3 / 36.6	49.5	69.4	87.7	97.2	103.5	...
7 Transport, storage and communication	...	...	15.5	18.4	21.8 / 19.4	21.0 / 82.8	39.7	53.6	92.5	122.7	145.6	37.1
8 Finance, insurance, real estate and business services	...	...	62.5	74.4	88.2 / 12.5	14.7 / 15.3	16.2	17.5	20.9	26.0	28.3	...
9 Community, social and personal services	...	...	8.0	9.6	11.4 / 58.4	72.1 / 8.2	10.0	17.1	42.2	38.0	33.4	...
Total, Industries	...	...	224.4	252.7	299.6 / 320.9	340.9 / 349.9	325.0	377.8	484.5	554.3	586.3	...
Producers of Government Services	...	...	46.6	47.2	56.0 / 44.9	54.9 / 18.5	22.2	37.6	42.7	45.8	55.5	...
Other Producers	...	...	...	...	... / ...	... / ...	...	...	...	...	...	...
Subtotal	...	...	271.0	299.9	355.6 / 365.8	395.8 / 368.4	347.2	415.4	527.2	600.1	641.8	709.7
Less: Imputed bank service charge	...	...	...	...	... / ...	... / ...	...	...	...	...	...	...
Plus: Import duties	...	...	...	...	... / ...	... / ...	...	...	...	...	...	...
Plus: Value added tax	...	...	...	...	... / ...	... / ...	...	...	...	...	...	...
Equals: Gross Domestic Product	...	...	271.0	299.9	355.6 / 365.8	395.8 / 368.4	347.2	415.4	527.2	600.1	641.8	709.7

a) Including item 'Electricity, gas and water'.

2.1 Government Final Consumption Expenditure by Function, in Current Prices

Million Maldivian Rufiyaa

	1970	1975	1978	1979	1980	1981	1982	1983	1984	1985	1986	1987
1 General public services	...	...	...	...	...	...	19.6	27.5	31.3	36.2	44.9	...
2 Defence	...	...	...	...	...	...	11.4	14.1	16.1	18.1	22.6	...
3 Public order and safety	...	...	...	...	...	...						...
4 Education	...	...	...	...	...	...	9.7	13.1	15.0	17.5	22.5	...
5 Health	...	...	...	...	...	...	7.4	7.1	8.1	9.5	11.5	...

Maldives

2.1 Government Final Consumption Expenditure by Function, in Current Prices
(Continued)

Million Maldivian Rufiyaa

	1970	1975	1978	1979	1980	1981	1982	1983	1984	1985	1986	1987
6 Social security and welfare	...	...	...	...	...	...	27.1	13.7	7.0	6.8	7.4	...
7 Housing and community amenities	...	...	...	...	...	...	4.4	5.2	6.0	9.7	10.8	...
8 Recreational, cultural and religious affairs	...	...	...	...	...	...						...
9 Economic services	...	...	...	...	...	...	9.0	10.1	14.3	14.3	7.8	...
A Fuel and energy	...	...	...	...	...	...	...	...	...	...	...	...
B Agriculture, forestry, fishing and hunting	...	...	...	...	...	...	1.2	1.5	1.8	1.7	2.6	...
C Mining, manufacturing and construction, except fuel and energy	...	...	...	...	...	...	...	...	...	...	...	...
D Transportation and communication	...	...	...	...	...	...	6.8	6.9	10.2	10.4	2.3	...
E Other economic affairs	...	...	...	...	...	...	1.0	1.7	2.3	2.2	2.9	...
10 Other functions	...	...	...	...	...	...	4.2	4.4	5.1	8.8	11.3	...
Total Government Final Consumption Expenditure	...	...	...	...	...	...	92.8	95.2	102.9	120.9	138.8	...

Mali

Source. Reply to the United Nations National Accounts Questionnaire from the Direction Nationale de la Statistique et de l'informatique, Ministere du Plan, Bamako, Mali. Official estimates are published by the same office annually in 'Comptes Economiques du Mali'. On 1 June 1984, Mali joined the French Community in Africa of which the legal tender is CFA francs. Two Mali francs is equivalent to one CFA franc.

General note. The estimates shown in the following tables have been prepared in accordance with the United Nations System of National Accounts so far as the existing data would permit.

1.1 Expenditure on the Gross Domestic Product, in Current Prices

Thousand Million CFA francs

	1970	1975	1978	1979	1980	1981	1982	1983	1984	1985	1986	1987
1 Government final consumption expenditure	...	...	9.4	11.3	12.6	36.6	39.6	44.9	50.1	56.2	58.1	...
2 Private final consumption expenditure	...	...	172.8	213.6	246.5	315.6	360.4	386.5	423.8	445.3	444.0	...
3 Gross capital formation	...	...	46.1	47.5	50.6	93.0	71.0	59.9	70.5	92.9	149.2	...
A Increase in stocks	...	...	4.0	3.8	3.0	...	-0.4	-15.1	-14.1	-11.5	14.2	...
B Gross fixed capital formation	...	...	42.1	43.8	47.6	...	71.4	75.0	84.6	104.4	135.0	146.4
4 Exports of goods and services	...	...	30.0	37.2	53.3	55.6	62.6	78.6	107.2	99.4	86.3	96.8
5 Less: Imports of goods and services	...	...	65.4	76.9	90.0	120.6	130.0	158.6	188.1	218.8	194.7	171.6
Equals: Gross Domestic Product	76.3	129.5	217.8	259.6	300.6	380.2	403.6	411.3	463.5	475.0	542.9	569.2

1.2 Expenditure on the Gross Domestic Product, in Constant Prices

Thousand Million CFA francs

	1970	1975	1978	1979	1980	1981	1982	1983	1984	1985	1986	1987
					At constant prices of:1982							
1 Government final consumption expenditure	...	...	...	...	...	...	...	...	...	...	...	...
2 Private final consumption expenditure	...	...	...	...	...	...	...	...	...	...	...	...
3 Gross capital formation	...	...	...	...	...	...	...	...	...	...	...	...
4 Exports of goods and services	...	...	...	...	...	...	...	...	...	...	...	...
5 Less: Imports of goods and services	...	...	...	...	...	...	...	...	...	...	...	...
Equals: Gross Domestic Product	...	...	...	...	...	...	403.6	383.2	385.7	382.3	453.6	...

1.3 Cost Components of the Gross Domestic Product

Thousand Million CFA francs

	1970	1975	1978	1979	1980	1981	1982	1983	1984	1985	1986	1987
1 Indirect taxes, net	...	...	13.6	16.9	14.5	28.9	30.6	...	...	...	...	...
A Indirect taxes	...	...	17.6	17.7	17.3	30.9	33.0	...	...	...	...	...
B Less: Subsidies	...	...	4.0	0.8	2.8	2.0	2.5	...	...	...	...	...
2 Consumption of fixed capital	...	...	...	...	...	22.6	24.3	...	...	...	...	...
3 Compensation of employees paid by resident producers to:	...	...	49.5	59.2	68.5	81.0	90.7	...	...	...	...	...
4 Operating surplus [a]	...	...	154.0	180.2	208.6	197.6	221.0	...	...	...	...	...
Equals: Gross Domestic Product [b]	...	...	217.8	259.6	300.6	330.0	366.5	...	...	...	...	...

a) Item 'Operating surplus' includes consumption of fixed capital.
b) Data for this table have not been revised, therefore, data for some years are not comparable with those of other tables.

1.4 General Government Current Receipts and Disbursements

Thousand Million CFA francs

	1970	1975	1978	1979	1980	1981	1982	1983	1984	1985	1986	1987
					Receipts							
1 Operating surplus	...	...	...	...	...	-	-	...	...	...	...	...
2 Property and entrepreneurial income	...	...	...	...	...	-	0.3	...	...	...	...	...
3 Taxes, fees and contributions	...	...	...	...	...	45.8	48.5	...	...	...	...	...
A Indirect taxes	...	...	...	...	...	30.9	33.0	...	...	...	...	...

Mali

1.4 General Government Current Receipts and Disbursements
(Continued)

Thousand Million CFA francs

	1970	1975	1978	1979	1980	1981	1982	1983	1984	1985	1986	1987
B Direct taxes	...	...	...	...	...	10.0	10.8	...	...	...	...	...
C Social security contributions	...	...	...	...	...	4.4	4.1	...	...	...	...	...
D Compulsory fees, fines and penalties	...	...	...	...	...	0.6	0.7	...	...	...	...	...
4 Other current transfers	...	...	...	...	...	30.8	31.8	...	...	...	...	...
Total Current Receipts of General Government [a]	...	...	...	...	...	76.7	80.7	...	...	...	...	...

Disbursements

	1970	1975	1978	1979	1980	1981	1982	1983	1984	1985	1986	1987
1 Government final consumption expenditure	...	...	...	...	...	35.0	38.1	...	...	...	...	...
2 Property income	...	...	...	...	...	3.9	7.0	...	...	...	...	...
3 Subsidies	...	...	...	...	...	2.0	2.5	...	...	...	...	...
4 Other current transfers	...	...	...	...	...	12.8	11.2	...	...	...	...	...
A Social security benefits	...	...	...	...	...	1.7	1.9	...	...	...	...	...
B Social assistance grants	...	...	...	...	...	...	...	...	...	...	...	...
C Other	...	...	...	...	...	11.2	9.3	...	...	...	...	...
5 Net saving	...	...	...	...	...	22.9	21.9	...	...	...	...	...
Total Current Disbursements and Net Saving of General Government [a]	...	...	...	...	...	76.7	80.7	...	...	...	...	...

a) Data for this table have not been revised, therefore, data for some years are not comparable with those of other tables.

1.7 External Transactions on Current Account, Summary

Thousand Million CFA francs

	1970	1975	1978	1979	1980	1981	1982	1983	1984	1985	1986	1987

Payments to the Rest of the World

	1970	1975	1978	1979	1980	1981	1982	1983	1984	1985	1986	1987
1 Imports of goods and services	...	...	...	...	...	120.6	130.0	158.6	188.1	218.8	194.7	...
A Imports of merchandise c.i.f.	...	...	...	...	...	104.6	109.2	134.6	160.9	187.7	159.6	...
B Other	...	...	...	...	...	16.0	20.8	24.0	27.2	31.1	35.1	...
2 Factor income to the rest of the world	...	...	...	...	...	8.0	12.6	13.7	17.2	15.5	16.2	...
A Compensation of employees	...	...	...	...	...	4.1	4.7	5.0	5.1	6.2	7.7	...
B Property and entrepreneurial income	...	...	...	...	...	3.9	7.9	8.7	12.1	9.3	8.5	...
3 Current transfers to the rest of the world	...	...	...	...	...	1.3	1.7	2.0	1.8	2.0	2.0	...
4 Surplus of the nation on current transactions	...	...	...	...	...	-31.0	-44.3	-49.7	-39.2	-63.5	-75.3	...
Payments to the Rest of the World and Surplus of the Nation on Current Transactions	...	...	...	...	...	98.9	100.0	124.6	167.9	172.8	137.6	...

Receipts From The Rest of the World

	1970	1975	1978	1979	1980	1981	1982	1983	1984	1985	1986	1987
1 Exports of goods and services	...	...	...	...	...	55.6	62.6	78.6	107.2	99.4	86.3	...
A Exports of merchandise f.o.b.	...	...	...	...	...	42.0	47.9	63.0	89.4	81.1	68.6	...
B Other	...	...	...	...	...	13.6	14.7	15.6	17.8	18.3	17.7	...
2 Factor income from rest of the world	...	...	...	...	...	12.5	12.9	13.9	14.2	15.8	14.0	...
A Compensation of employees	...	...	...	...	...	12.5	12.9	13.9	14.2	15.8	14.0	...
B Property and entrepreneurial income	...	...	...	...	...	...	...	...	...	...	...	...
3 Current transfers from rest of the world	...	...	...	...	...	30.8	24.5	32.1	46.5	57.6	37.3	...
Receipts from the Rest of the World on Current Transactions	...	...	...	...	...	98.9	100.0	124.6	167.9	172.8	137.6	...

1.10 Gross Domestic Product by Kind of Activity, in Current Prices

Thousand Million CFA francs

	1970	1975	1978	1979	1980	1981	1982	1983	1984	1985	1986	1987
1 Agriculture, hunting, forestry and fishing	...	...	...	...	...	224.5	232.0	219.9	233.4	225.1	285.8	...
2 Mining and quarrying	...	...	...	...	...	...	5.7	7.4	7.2	7.3	7.1	...
3 Manufacturing [a]	...	...	...	...	...	15.9	19.1	22.0	33.9	40.3	34.8	...
4 Electricity, gas and water	...	...	...	...	...	20.8	14.2	16.2	18.7	22.5	25.6	...
5 Construction	...	...	...	...	...							...

Mali

1.10 Gross Domestic Product by Kind of Activity, in Current Prices
(Continued)

Thousand Million CFA francs

	1970	1975	1978	1979	1980	1981	1982	1983	1984	1985	1986	1987
6 Wholesale and retail trade, restaurants and hotels	...	...	...	...	...	53.6	61.3	65.8	75.8	74.4	75.5	...
7 Transport, storage and communication	...	...	...	...	...	13.0	12.9	15.0	21.0	24.3	25.4	...
8 Finance, insurance, real estate and business services	...	...	...	...	...	16.4	16.5	18.0	19.8	24.3	28.8	...
9 Community, social and personal services	...	...	...	...	...							...
Statistical discrepancy	...	...	...	...	...	-4.3	-3.8	-4.0	-4.4	-5.7	-7.3	...
Total, Industries	...	...	...	...	...	339.8	357.9	360.3	405.4	412.5	475.7	...
Producers of Government Services	...	...	...	...	...	26.6	29.3	33.6	37.9	41.7	44.0	...
Other Producers	...	...	...	...	...	...	...	...	...	...	...	...
Subtotal	...	...	...	...	...	366.4	387.2	393.9	443.3	454.2	519.7	...
Less: Imputed bank service charge	...	...	...	...	...	...	...	...	...	...	...	...
Plus: Import duties	...	...	...	...	...	13.8	16.3	17.5	20.0	20.8	23.2	...
Plus: Value added tax	...	...	...	...	...	...	...	...	...	...	...	...
Equals: Gross Domestic Product	...	...	...	...	...	380.2	403.6	411.3	463.5	475.0	542.9	...

a) Item 'Manufacturing' includes handicrafts.

1.12 Relations Among National Accounting Aggregates

Thousand Million CFA francs

	1970	1975	1978	1979	1980	1981	1982	1983	1984	1985	1986	1987
Gross Domestic Product	76.3	129.5	217.8	259.6	300.6	380.2	403.6	411.3	463.5	475.0	542.9	...
Plus: Net factor income from the rest of the world	0.9	4.2	-8.9	-7.4	-7.4	4.5	0.3	0.2	-3.0	0.3	-2.2	...
Factor income from the rest of the world	...	...	...	...	...	12.5	12.9	13.9	14.2	15.8	14.0	...
Less: Factor income to the rest of the world	...	...	...	...	...	8.0	12.6	13.7	17.2	15.5	16.2	...
Equals: Gross National Product	77.2	183.7	208.9	252.4	293.2	384.7	403.9	411.5	460.5	475.3	540.7	...
Less: Consumption of fixed capital	3.0	...	...	...	...	...	...	...	...	...	...	...
Equals: National Income a	74.2	...	...	...	...	384.7	403.9	411.5	460.5	475.3	540.7	...
Plus: Net current transfers from the rest of the world	...	...	...	...	...	29.5	22.8	30.1	44.7	55.6	35.3	...
Current transfers from the rest of the world	...	...	...	...	...	30.8	24.5	32.1	46.5	57.6	37.3	...
Less: Current transfers to the rest of the world	...	...	...	...	...	1.3	1.7	2.0	1.8	2.0	2.0	...
Equals: National Disposable Income b	...	...	...	...	...	414.2	426.7	441.6	505.2	530.9	576.0	...
Less: Final consumption	...	...	...	...	...	352.2	400.0	431.4	473.9	501.5	502.1	...
Equals: Net Saving c	...	...	...	...	...	62.0	26.7	10.2	31.3	29.4	73.9	...
Less: Surplus of the nation on current transactions	...	...	...	...	...	-31.0	-44.3	-49.7	-39.2	-63.5	-75.3	...
Equals: Net Capital Formation d	...	...	...	...	...	93.0	71.0	59.9	70.5	92.9	149.2	...

a) Item 'National income' includes consumption of fixed capital.
b) Item 'National disposable income' includes consumption of fixed capital.
c) Item 'Net saving' includes consumption of fixed capital.
d) Item 'Net capital formation' includes consumption of fixed capital.

Malta

General note. The preparation of national accounts statistics in Malta is undertaken by the Central Office of Statistics, Valetta. The offical estimates and methodological notes are published annually in 'National Accounts of the Maltese Islands'. The estimates are generally in accordance with the definitions and classifications recommended in the United Nations System of National Accounts (SNA). Input-output tables are published in the above-mentioned publication. The following tables have been prepared from successive replies to the United Nations national accounts questionaire. When the scope and coverage of the estimates differ for conceptual or statistical reasons from the definitions and classification recommended in SNA, a footnote is indicated to the relevant tables.

Sources and methods:

(a) Gross domestic product. Gross domestic product is estimated mainly through the income approach.

(b) Expenditure on the gross domestic product. The expenditure approach is used to estimate government final consumption expenditure and exports and imports of goods and services. This approach, in combination with the commodity-flow approach is used for gross fixed capital formation and private final consumption expenditure. Increase in stocks is obtained as a residual. The estimates of government consumption expenditure is based on returns from all government departments. Excluded are current expenditure on national insurance benefits, subsidies and grants to persons and expenditure on fixed capital assets and on addition to stocks. Private consumption expenditure represents expenditure on consumer goods and services by persons and non-profit making bodies at market prices. Gross fixed capital formation constitutes expenditure on fixed assets for the replacement of and addition to existing assets. The estimates are based on an analysis of government expenditure, import data and censuses of production. The estimates of exports and imports of goods and services are based on data available from trade returns, banking statistics and estimates of expenditure on services, supplemented by ad hoc inquiries. For the constant price estimates, government final consumption expenditure, gross fixed capital formation and exports and imports of goods and services are deflated by appropriate indexes. For private consumption expenditure, extensive use is made of the various subindexes that make up the retail price index.

(c) Cost-structure of the gross domestic product. Compensation of employees includes employers' contributions to national insurance. For the private sector, employees' incomes are taken from annual reports of labours inspectors except in the manufacturing, quarrying and construction sectors, for which data are taken from the censuses of production. Government wages and salaries are estimated on the basis of department returns, while the services submit actual figures of their wage and salary bill. Profits are estimated from income tax data for professionals, annual censuses of production for manufacturing and ad hoc inquiries for other activities. For trade, gross profits are arrived at by assessing wholesale and retail profits on the basis of calculated turnovers. Income from property is estimated on the basis of actual rents received by the government plus rents earned by the private sector which is based on data obtained in the census of population, housing and employment in 1967 and interest earned from local sources. Indirect taxes cover items such as customs and excise duties, business licenses, stamp duties, motor vehicle licenses, etc. While subsidies include grants to farmers, price-stabilization payment, loss incurred on water and milk supplies, etc.

(d) Gross domestic product by kind of economic activity. The table of GDP by kind of economic activity is prepared in factor values. The income approach is used to estimate the value added of most industries except agriculture and fishing, for which the production approach is used. For most sectors of GDP by economic activity, separate estimates are available for wages and salaries, income from self-employment and other trading income. The contribution of each industry also includes provision for depreciation. The sources of these estimates are described in the cost-structure of GDP above. GDP by kind of economic activity is not estimated at constant prices.

1.1 Expenditure on the Gross Domestic Product, in Current Prices

Thousand Maltese pounds

	1970	1975	1978	1979	1980	1981	1982	1983	1984	1985	1986	1987
1 Government final consumption expenditure	18350	30523	46091	53678	63364	75407	85216	82257	80321	84309	89508	98249
2 Private final consumption expenditure	73855	118660	186371	206006	253485	279434	305724	306705	317475	333239	347895	358284
3 Gross capital formation	31034	38957	65104	82992	96457	118154	145625	137090	133233	133754	130506	151076
A Increase in stocks [a]	3221	1475	4789	4795	9383	12557	25504	5460	6780	7883	8179	-2377
B Gross fixed capital formation	27813	37482	60315	78197	87074	105597	120121	131630	126453	125871	122327	153453
Residential buildings	4946	5509	17629	21065	20875	30155	38634					
Non-residential buildings	4750	2497						50960	48661	41197	44779	49103
Other construction and land improvement etc.	2960	6397	10896	9867	10658	11215	11317					
Other	15157	23079	31790	47265	55541	64227	70170	80670	77792	84674	77548	104350
4 Exports of goods and services	47098	137327	229569	290769	356647	355918	319799	307647	323539	345155	365702	422496
5 Less: Imports of goods and services	75516	159710	249518	307666	377989	392462	394578	376143	393516	420475	421742	480934
Equals: Gross Domestic Product	94821	165757	277617	325779	391964	436451	461786	457556	461052	475982	511869	549171

a) Item 'Increase in stocks' includes a statistical discrepancy.

1.2 Expenditure on the Gross Domestic Product, in Constant Prices

Thousand Maltese pounds

	1970	1975	1978	1979	1980	1981	1982	1983	1984	1985	1986	1987
	1954	At constant prices of: 1973										
1 Government final consumption expenditure	11300	26700	34600	38200	38900	41800	44300	43800	42700	45100	47100	51400
2 Private final consumption expenditure	60300	101900	136300	140400	149100	154000	158500	160700	167100	175400	180300	182500
3 Gross capital formation	20200	28900	40000	44000	48900	58900	78500	67000	64000	62800	58300	63100
A Increase in stocks [a]	3200	1500	4800	4800	9400	12600	25400	5500	6800	7900	8200	-2400
B Gross fixed capital formation	17000	27400	35200	39200	39500	46300	53100	61500	57200	54900	50100	65500
4 Exports of goods and services	32200	105600	146800	171500	192000	170100	146600	143900	149700	160800	169900	190500
5 Less: Imports of goods and services	58800	110900	135600	148700	166200	153400	150400	139500	145000	158400	158500	178000
Equals: Gross Domestic Product	65200	152200	222100	245400	262700	271400	277600	275900	278500	285700	297100	309500

a) Item 'Increase in stocks' includes a statistical discrepancy.

Malta

1.3 Cost Components of the Gross Domestic Product
Thousand Maltese pounds

	1970	1975	1978	1979	1980	1981	1982	1983	1984	1985	1986	1987
1 Indirect taxes, net	12620	12813	26357	32128	43352	45917	44041	40426	39675	45432	50103	53721
A Indirect taxes	14828	20002	30116	36159	45744	47897	46852	43794	43706	49452	54885	58595
B Less: Subsidies	2208	7189	3759	4031	2392	1980	2811	3368	4031	4020	4782	4874
2 Consumption of fixed capital	2927	5432	10040	11085	12896	14363	15738	19753	20990	21423	23200	25977
3 Compensation of employees paid by resident producers to:	47147	82975	131460	152669	180553	203805	228625	223584	217928	222942	231617	254706
4 Operating surplus	32127	64537	109760	129897	155163	172366	173382	173793	182459	186185	206949	214767
A Corporate and quasi-corporate enterprises	...	...	50454	65646	77597	73736	74167	69052	69425	73345	76513	79604
B Private unincorporated enterprises	...	...	55983	59894	71287	83587	88491	92466	97810	101151	108507	109863
C General government a	...	...	3323	4357	6279	15043	10724	12275	15224	11689	21929	25300
Equals: Gross Domestic Product	94821	165757	277617	325779	391964	436451	461786	457556	461052	475982	511869	549171

a) Public enterprises is included in general government.

1.4 General Government Current Receipts and Disbursements
Thousand Maltese pounds

	1970	1975	1978	1979	1980	1981	1982	1983	1984	1985	1986	1987
Receipts												
1 Operating surplus	...	...	151	590	2295	7581	3566	2997	6250	2752	14290	18645
2 Property and entrepreneurial income	...	...	26979	35223	50911	56584	59969	46139	52434	48276	39825	33075
3 Taxes, fees and contributions	...	...	66022	87987	108634	121039	127618	123744	118437	126801	131338	130681
A Indirect taxes a	...	...	30116	36159	45744	47897	46852	43794	43706	49452	54885	58595
B Direct taxes	...	...	21865	32902	36521	40908	45994	44974	41310	42666	41570	36425
C Social security contributions	...	...	14041	18926	26369	32234	34772	34976	33421	34683	34883	35661
D Compulsory fees, fines and penalties a	...	...	...	...	...	...	...	...	...	...	...	...
4 Other current transfers	...	...	3596	3897	4001	4558	4603	5081	5697	5792	5695	5683
Total Current Receipts of General Government b	...	...	96748	127697	165841	189762	195756	177961	182818	183621	191148	188084
Disbursements												
1 Government final consumption expenditure	...	...	46091	53678	63364	75407	85216	82257	80321	84309	89508	98249
A Compensation of employees	...	...	33348	38756	44444	51513	58152	57348	56090	58534	62317	68862
B Consumption of fixed capital	...	...	...	...	...	...	...	...	...	...	...	...
C Purchases of goods and services, net	...	...	12743	14922	18920	23894	27064	24909	24231	25775	27191	29387
D Less: Own account fixed capital formation	...	...	...	...	...	...	...	...	...	...	...	...
E Indirect taxes paid, net	...	...	...	...	...	...	...	...	...	...	...	...
2 Property income	...	...	1672	1667	1666	1641	1630	1611	1700	1705	1716	1717
A Interest	...	...	1672	1667	1666	1641	1630	1611	1700	1705	1716	1717
B Net land rent and royalties	...	...	...	...	...	...	...	...	...	...	...	...
3 Subsidies	...	...	3759	4031	2392	1980	2811	3368	4031	4020	4782	4874
4 Other current transfers	...	...	28704	31695	40312	51410	59402	61484	65351	65021	66668	68392
A Social security benefits	...	...	28468	31408	40035	51125	59130	61211	65100	64726	66412	68075
B Social assistance grants	...	...										
C Other	...	...	236	287	277	285	272	273	251	295	256	317
5 Net saving	...	...	16522	36626	58107	59324	46697	29241	31415	28566	28474	14852
Total Current Disbursements and Net Saving of General Government b	...	...	96748	127697	165841	189762	195756	177961	182818	183621	191148	188084

a) Item 'Fees, fines and penalties' is included in item 'Indirect taxes'.
b) Public enterprises is included in general government.

Malta

1.5 Current Income and Outlay of Corporate and Quasi-Corporate Enterprises, Summary

Thousand Maltese pounds

	1970	1975	1978	1979	1980	1981	1982	1983	1984	1985	1986	1987
Receipts												
1 Operating surplus	9493	26770	43838	46404	52235	59863	68790	69703	72729	76329	74824	82851
2 Property and entrepreneurial income received	576	945	1395	3107	4618	5474	5412	3826	3876	4209	4387	5719
3 Current transfers	...	...	...	...	...	...	...	...	...	...	...	...
Total Current Receipts [a]	10069	27715	45233	49511	56853	65337	74202	73529	76605	80538	79211	88570
Disbursements												
1 Property and entrepreneurial income	4015	10307	18606	27908	29296	31397	33484	32107	35279	38009	35066	32556
2 Direct taxes and other current payments to general government	1934	3064	7142	10705	10260	11376	17065	16032	14728	15194	15354	16612
3 Other current transfers	...	...	...	...	...	...	...	...	...	...	...	...
4 Net saving	4120	14344	19485	10898	17297	22564	23653	25390	26598	27335	28791	39402
Total Current Disbursements and Net Saving [a]	10069	27715	45233	49511	56853	65337	74202	73529	76605	80538	79211	88570

a) Public enterprises is included in general government.

1.6 Current Income and Outlay of Households and Non-Profit Institutions

Thousand Maltese pounds

	1970	1975	1978	1979	1980	1981	1982	1983	1984	1985	1986	1987
Receipts												
1 Compensation of employees	47147	82975	131460	152669	180553	203805	228625	223584	217928	222942	231617	254706
2 Operating surplus of private unincorporated enterprises	19668	28968	45572	47574	57940	66268	72020	73370	75774	79082	84042	83352
3 Property and entrepreneurial income	11706	23472	29036	39538	48676	50878	50767	49599	53845	54036	54419	56059
4 Current transfers	13591	27549	43177	45457	53668	64994	74126	77252	81334	79638	80236	83476
A Social security benefits	4000	15759	28468	31408	40035	51125	59130	61211	65100	64726	66412	68075
B Social assistance grants												
C Other	9591	11790	14709	14049	13633	13869	14996	16041	16234	14912	13824	15401
Total Current Receipts	92112	162964	249245	285238	340837	385945	425538	423805	428881	435698	450314	477593
Disbursements												
1 Private final consumption expenditure	73855	118660	186371	206006	253485	279434	305724	306705	317475	333239	347895	358284
2 Property income	...	...	...	...	...	...	...	...	...	...	...	...
3 Direct taxes and other current transfers n.e.c. to general government	2359	17058	29022	41435	52968	62042	64060	64347	60471	62603	61483	55762
A Social security contributions	795	5981	12390	16758	23464	28450	30482	31304	29492	30766	31466	32396
B Direct taxes	1476	10824	16374	24365	29166	33316	33219	32614	30511	31389	29633	23078
C Fees, fines and penalties	88	253	258	312	338	276	359	429	468	448	384	288
4 Other current transfers	2047	3222	4850	5432	6095	7053	6308	6499	8095	7420	7530	8114
5 Net saving	13851	24024	29002	32365	28289	37416	49446	46254	42840	32436	33406	55433
Total Current Disbursements and Net Saving	92112	162964	249245	285238	340837	385945	425538	423805	428881	435698	450314	477593

1.7 External Transactions on Current Account, Summary

Thousand Maltese pounds

	1970	1975	1978	1979	1980	1981	1982	1983	1984	1985	1986	1987
Payments to the Rest of the World												
1 Imports of goods and services	75516	159710	249518	307666	377989	392462	394578	376143	393516	420475	421742	480934
2 Factor income to the rest of the world	3503	5623	12233	22019	19929	19679	11801	9874	9199	10758	17195	8850
A Compensation of employees	...	...	...	...	...	...	...	...	...	...	...	...
B Property and entrepreneurial income	3503	5623	12233	22019	19929	19679	11801	9874	9199	10758	17195	8850
3 Current transfers to the rest of the world	1309	1730	2445	2654	2915	3156	2383	2173	3185	2465	2560	3108
4 Surplus of the nation on current transactions	-11694	6795	9945	7982	20132	15513	-10091	-16452	-11390	-23994	-16635	-15412
Payments to the Rest of the World and Surplus of the Nation on Current Transactions	68634	173858	274141	340321	420965	430810	398671	371738	394510	409704	424862	477480

Malta

1.7 External Transactions on Current Account, Summary
(Continued)

Thousand Maltese pounds

	1970	1975	1978	1979	1980	1981	1982	1983	1984	1985	1986	1987
				Receipts From The Rest of the World								
1 Exports of goods and services	47098	137327	229569	290769	356647	355918	319799	307647	323539	345155	365702	422496
2 Factor income from rest of the world	10781	23880	29166	34983	50479	60923	63829	47997	54669	49543	45251	39511
A Compensation of employees	...	...	...	...	...	...	...	...	...	...	...	...
B Property and entrepreneurial income	10781	23880	29166	34983	50479	60923	63829	47997	54669	49543	45251	39511
3 Current transfers from rest of the world	10755	12651	15406	14569	13839	13969	15043	16094	16302	15006	13909	15473
Receipts from the Rest of the World on Current Transactions	68634	173858	274141	340321	420965	430810	398671	371738	394510	409704	424862	477480

1.8 Capital Transactions of The Nation, Summary

Thousand Maltese pounds

	1970	1975	1978	1979	1980	1981	1982	1983	1984	1985	1986	1987
				Finance of Gross Capital Formation								
Gross saving	19340	45752	75049	90974	116589	133667	135534	120638	121843	109760	113871	135664
1 Consumption of fixed capital	2927	5432	10040	11085	12896	14363	15738	19753	20990	21423	23200	25977
A General government [a]	654	1808	2899	2731	3127	3746	4996	5624	5972	5917	6778	7569
B Corporate and quasi-corporate enterprises	715	1820	4627	5501	6718	7087	7285	10097	11594	12269	12946	15077
Public	...	...	...	...	...	...	...	...	...	...	...	...
Private	715	1820	4627	5501	6718	7087	7285	10097	11594	12269	12946	15077
C Other	1558	1804	2514	2853	3051	3530	3457	4032	3424	3237	3476	3331
2 Net saving	16413	40320	65009	79889	103693	119304	119796	100885	100853	88337	90671	109687
A General government	-1558	1952	16522	36626	58107	59324	46697	29241	31415	28566	28474	14852
B Corporate and quasi-corporate enterprises	4120	14344	19485	10898	17297	22564	23653	25390	26598	27335	28791	39402
Public	...	...	...	...	...	...	...	...	...	...	...	...
Private	4120	14344	19485	10898	17297	22564	23653	25390	26598	27335	28791	39402
C Other	13851	24024	29002	32365	28289	37416	49446	46254	42840	32436	33406	55433
Less: Surplus of the nation on current transactions	-11694	6795	9945	7982	20132	15513	-10091	-16452	-11390	-23994	-16635	-15412
Finance of Gross Capital Formation	31034	38957	65104	82992	96457	118154	145629	137090	133233	133754	130506	151076
				Gross Capital Formation								
Increase in stocks [b]	3221	1475	4789	4795	9383	12557	25504	5460	6780	7883	8179	-2377
Gross fixed capital formation	27813	37482	60315	78197	87074	105597	120121	131630	126453	125871	122327	153453
1 General government [a]	10074	17982	21868	21885	25543	30609	33375	23747	25124	25330	25795	33093
2 Corporate and quasi-corporate enterprises	3470	7551	17129	32186	38903	44043	43354	72964	60601	57982	53344	91864
A Public	...	...	...	...	...	...	...	...	...	...	...	...
B Private	3470	7551	17129	32186	38903	44043	43354	72964	60601	57982	53344	91864
3 Other	14269	11949	21318	24126	22628	30945	43392	34919	40728	42559	43188	28496
Gross Capital Formation	31034	38957	65104	82992	96457	118154	145625	137090	133233	133754	130506	151076

a) Public enterprises is included in general government.
b) Item 'Increase in stocks' includes a statistical discrepancy.

1.10 Gross Domestic Product by Kind of Activity, in Current Prices

Thousand Maltese pounds

	1970	1975	1978	1979	1980	1981	1982	1983	1984	1985	1986	1987
1 Agriculture, hunting, forestry and fishing	5813	9210	11357	11529	13289	15038	16767	18731	19346	19375	20419	21429
2 Mining and quarrying [a]	6206	9209	11662	13533	15655	17073	23546	23511	19660	20758	18869	21051
3 Manufacturing	17865	46684	84445	99976	115358	121384	125024	120036	124706	126929	134676	136427
4 Electricity, gas and water [b]	4289	5859	10340	11661	15635	23586	21958	21119	24985	22278	34704	42119
5 Construction [a]	...	...	...	...	...	...	...	...	...	...	...	...
6 Wholesale and retail trade, restaurants and hotels [c]	13597	21732	39139	45766	51001	57421	63184	64010	66077	66696	67647	70847
7 Transport, storage and communication	2845	6686	11863	14679	22230	22596	20396	24050	23391	23955	26240	30204
8 Finance, insurance, real estate and business services [d]	7287	14511	22934	29252	37269	45519	50303	51475	53517	57131	61255	62782
9 Community, social and personal services [cd]	4268	9253	21082	28129	33731	36404	38415	36850	33605	34894	35639	41729
Total, Industries	62170	123144	212822	254525	304168	339021	359593	359782	365287	372016	399449	426588
Producers of Government Services	19221	28728	37291	39126	44444	51513	58152	57348	56090	58534	62317	68862

Malta

1.10 Gross Domestic Product by Kind of Activity, in Current Prices
(Continued)

Thousand Maltese pounds

	1970	1975	1978	1979	1980	1981	1982	1983	1984	1985	1986	1987
Other Producers	810	1072	1147	...	...	...	...	...	...	...	...	...
Subtotal e	82201	152944	251260	293651	348612	390534	417745	417130	421377	430550	461766	495450
Less: Imputed bank service charge	...	...	...	...	...	...	...	...	...	...	...	...
Plus: Import duties	...	...	...	...	...	...	...	...	...	...	...	...
Plus: Value added tax	...	...	...	...	...	...	...	...	...	...	...	...
Plus: Other adjustments f	12620	12813	26357	32128	43352	45917	44041	40426	39675	45432	50103	53721
Equals: Gross Domestic Product	94821	165757	277617	325779	391964	436451	461786	457556	461052	475982	511869	549171

a) Item 'Construction' is included in item 'Mining and quarrying'.
b) Item 'Electricity, gas and water' refers to all government enterprises.
c) Restaurants and hotels are included in item 'Community, social and personal services'.
d) Business services are included in item 'Community, social and personal services'.
e) Gross domestic product in factor values.
f) Item 'Other adjustments' refers to indirect taxes net of subsidies.

1.12 Relations Among National Accounting Aggregates

Thousand Maltese pounds

	1970	1975	1978	1979	1980	1981	1982	1983	1984	1985	1986	1987
Gross Domestic Product	94821	165757	277617	325779	391964	436451	461786	457556	461052	475982	511869	549171
Plus: Net factor income from the rest of the world	7278	18257	16933	12964	30550	41244	52028	38123	45470	38785	28056	30661
Factor income from the rest of the world	...	...	29166	34983	50479	60923	63829	47997	54669	49543	45251	39511
Less: Factor income to the rest of the world	...	...	12233	22019	19929	19679	11801	9874	9199	10758	17195	8850
Equals: Gross National Product	102099	184014	294550	338743	422514	477695	513814	495679	506522	514767	539925	579832
Less: Consumption of fixed capital	2927	5432	10040	11085	12896	14363	15738	19753	20990	21423	23200	25977
Equals: National Income	99172	178582	284510	327658	409618	463332	498076	475926	485532	493344	516725	553855
Plus: Net current transfers from the rest of the world	9446	10921	12961	11915	10924	10813	12660	13921	13117	12541	11349	12365
Current transfers from the rest of the world	10755	12651	15406	14569	13839	13969	15043	16094	16302	15006	13909	15473
Less: Current transfers to the rest of the world	1309	1730	2445	2654	2915	3156	2383	2173	3185	2465	2560	3108
Equals: National Disposable Income	108618	189503	297471	339573	420542	474145	510736	489847	498649	505885	528074	566220
Less: Final consumption	92205	149183	232462	259684	316849	354841	390940	388962	397796	417548	437403	456533
Equals: Net Saving	16413	40320	65009	79889	103693	119304	119796	100885	100853	88337	90671	109687
Less: Surplus of the nation on current transactions	-11694	6795	9945	7982	20132	15513	-10091	-16452	-11390	-23994	-16635	-15412
Equals: Net Capital Formation	28107	33525	55064	71907	83561	103791	129887	117337	112243	112331	107306	125099

2.1 Government Final Consumption Expenditure by Function, in Current Prices

Thousand Maltese pounds

	1970	1975	1978	1979	1980	1981	1982	1983	1984	1985	1986	1987
1 General public services	2968	7360	7921	9284	9583	9819	10887	10718	9575	10804	11478	12844
2 Defence	2743	4170	6674	8150	9264	11419	14339	14169	13826	14636	15265	17366
3 Public order and safety												
4 Education	5594	6842	10930	13397	15500	18252	20266	19666	18528	19484	20197	22885
5 Health	4135	6222	10902	11923	15133	17587	20731	20723	20680	21108	22980	25565
6 Social security and welfare	423	658	1014	1344	1449	1950	1792	1704	2160	2146	2385	2009
7 Housing and community amenities	1750	4514	7453	8292	10711	14265	14428	12606	12768	13314	14041	14014
8 Recreational, cultural and religious affairs	...	...	...	...	...	...	...	...	...	...	...	...
9 Economic services	499	757	1197	1288	1724	2115	2773	2671	2784	2817	3162	3566
10 Other functions	238	-	-	-	-	-	-	-	-	-	-	-
Total Government Final Consumption Expenditure	18350	30523	46091	53678	63364	75407	85216	82257	80321	84309	89508	98249

2.5 Private Final Consumption Expenditure by Type and Purpose, in Current Prices

Thousand Maltese pounds

	1970	1975	1978	1979	1980	1981	1982	1983	1984	1985	1986	1987
Final Consumption Expenditure of Resident Households												
1 Food, beverages and tobacco	32801	53120	81798	93447	114993	127180	133047	131847	131301	141513	140887	150799
A Food	23445	37618	56270	60828	74501	83668	92140	93762	92954	101225	98285	107015
B Non-alcoholic beverages	2626	3222	3415	3938	5248	6932	9938	9907	10811	12920	13599	15066
C Alcoholic beverages	3638	5462	13426	18391[a]	21626	22559	17354	15545	14810	14840	16224	15458
D Tobacco	3092	6818	8687	10290	13618	14021	13615	12633	12726	12528	12779	13260
2 Clothing and footwear	9333	13877	19140	23914	29375	29725	25951	25184	27014	33039	36247	37000
3 Gross rent, fuel and power	5845	9953	14385	19655	25042	26296	21867	22225	22423	22828	24102	25560
A Fuel and power	...	...	5100	5813	8232	8827	6730	7196	8102	8032	8525	8676

Malta

2.5 Private Final Consumption Expenditure by Type and Purpose, in Current Prices
(Continued)

Thousand Maltese pounds

	1970	1975	1978	1979	1980	1981	1982	1983	1984	1985	1986	1987
B Other	...	...	9285	13842	16810	17469	15137	15029	14321	14796	15577	16884
4 Furniture, furnishings and household equipment and operation	8696	16377	25318	30804	37639	35917	35771	35141	35517	33534	35252	37754
A Household operation	1359	4469	6981	7854	8966	9037	10310	9766	10925	10888	9544	10129
B Other	7337	11908	18337	22950	28673	26880	25461	25375	24592	22646	25708	27625
5 Medical care and health expenses	2210	6820	10498	10625	10675	10404	12198	12593	13404	12524	14620	15268
6 Transport and communication	5988	18647	30884	38198	50689	50870	51151	50726	51042	57969	60127	66126
A Personal transport equipment	4499	12705	20700	24579	32420	31796	32819	31425	33893	37189	38974	43249
B Other	1489	5942	10184	13619	18269	19074	18332	19301	17149	20780	21153	22877
7 Recreational, entertainment, education and cultural services	5179	9667	15187	16749	21953	23169	23114	21009	22527	21490	24949	26392
A Education	...	...	987	1096	1731	1342	1470	1406	1547	1547	1677	1721
B Other	...	...	14200	15653	20222	21827	21644	19603	20930	19943	23272	24671
8 Miscellaneous goods and services	7637	13690	28663	37004	56717	61696	55498	52976	54457	56749	63976	77075
A Personal care	3208	4266	8278	11641	11421	12020	13109	10645	11048	10777	10903	11790
B Expenditures in restaurants, cafes and hotels	...	7177	18006	22154	41083	46490	37455	38181	39240	41531	48744	60681
C Other	...	2247	2379	3209	4213	3186	4934	4150	4169	4441	4329	4604
Total Final Consumption Expenditure in the Domestic Market by Households, of which	77689	142151	225873	270396	347083	365257	358597	351701	357685	379646	400160	435974
Plus: Direct purchases abroad by resident households	2051	4596	10250	11837	18336	19591	23707	22804	22890	23443	27085	35310
Less: Direct purchases in the domestic market by non-resident households	5885	28087	49752	76227	111934	105414	76580	67800	63100	69850	79350	113000
Equals: Final Consumption Expenditure of Resident Households [a]	73855	118660	186371	206006	253485	279434	305724	306705	317475	333239	347895	358284

Final Consumption Expenditure of Private Non-profit Institutions Serving Households

Equals: Final Consumption Expenditure of Private Non-profit Organisations Serving Households	...	...	...	...	...	...	...	...	...	...	...	...
Private Final Consumption Expenditure	73855	118660	186371	206006	253485	279434	305724	306705	317475	333239	347895	358284

a) Item 'Final consumption expenditure of resident households' includes consumption expenditure of private non-profit institutions serving households.

2.6 Private Final Consumption Expenditure by Type and Purpose, in Constant Prices

Thousand Maltese pounds

	1970	1975	1978	1979	1980	1981	1982	1983	1984	1985	1986	1987
	1954				**At constant prices of:**		**1973**					

Final Consumption Expenditure of Resident Households

	1970	1975	1978	1979	1980	1981	1982	1983	1984	1985	1986	1987
1 Food, beverages and tobacco	25362	48951	65159	70787	71139	69605	67851	68081	68583	74885	72805	77093
A Food	18075	36212	45832	47718	49096	48375	48370	50067	50433	56105	53027	56836
B Non-alcoholic beverages	2951	1591	1712	1974	2581	2507	3490	3482	3799	4541	4779	5295
C Alcoholic beverages	2777	4819	10287	12938	10585	9954	7578	6816	6468	6481	7086	6751
D Tobacco	1559	6329	7328	8157	8877	8769	8413	7716	7883	7758	7913	8211
2 Clothing and footwear	9156	12675	17198	20691	24392	24026	19323	18730	20156	24540	25590	25910
3 Gross rent, fuel and power	5517	8776	11526	15568	18526	19043	16102	16329	16120	16501	17434	18632
A Fuel and power	...	...	3088	3098	3418	3515	2689	3013	3457	3426	3661	3710
B Other	...	...	8438	12470	15108	15528	13413	13316	12663	13075	13773	14922
4 Furniture, furnishings and household equipment and operation	7046	14125	19122	21115	24330	21869	20766	20976	20963	19723	20943	22371
A Household operation	1070	3613	5023	4634	4577	4366	4838	4752	5321	5303	4560	4849

Malta

2.6 Private Final Consumption Expenditure by Type and Purpose, in Constant Prices
(Continued)

Thousand Maltese pounds

	1970	1975	1978	1979	1980	1981	1982	1983	1984	1985	1986	1987
		1954			At constant prices of:			1973				
B Other	5976	10512	14099	16481	19753	17503	15928	16224	15642	14420	16383	17522
5 Medical care and health expenses	1991	6014	8426	8335	8036	8376	7488	7421	7904	7415	8577	8705
6 Transport and communication	4386	12308	16453	17552	18854	16823	15292	15326	15437	17698	18549	21147
A Personal transport equipment	3121	6662	10475	10330	11163	9692	9369	8786	9166	10603	11132	12834
B Other	1265	5646	5978	7222	7691	7131	5923	6540	6271	7095	7417	8313
7 Recreational, entertainment, education and cultural services	4406	8399	12518	13438	15012	14089	13874	12538	13482	12854	14489	15217
A Education	...	...	721	801	1265	981	1075	1028	1131	1131	1226	1258
B Other	...	...	11797	12639	13747	13108	12799	11510	12351	11723	13263	13959
8 Miscellaneous goods and services	5714	11711	21060	25297	34978	32701	31538	31159	32016	33367	37615	45317
Total Final Consumption Expenditure in the Domestic Market by Households, of which	63578	122959	171462	192783	215267	207252	192234	190559	194661	206983	216002	234392
Plus: Direct purchases abroad by resident households	1298	3304	4999	5091	6739	6660	7141	6602	6489	6182	6725	8382
Less: Direct purchases in the domestic market by non-resident households	4580	24377	40197	57504	72940	59956	40862	36422	34027	37761	42401	60228
Equals: Final Consumption Expenditure of Resident Households [a]	60296	101886	136264	140370	149066	153956	158513	160739	167123	175404	180326	182546

Final Consumption Expenditure of Private Non-profit Institutions Serving Households

Equals: Final Consumption Expenditure of Private Non-profit Organisations Serving Households	...	...	...	...	...	...	...	...	...	...	...	...
Private Final Consumption Expenditure	60296	101886	136264	140370	149066	153956	158513	160739	167123	175404	180326	182546

a) Item 'Final consumption expenditure of resident households' includes consumption expenditure of private non-profit institutions serving households.

2.7 Gross Capital Formation by Type of Good and Owner, in Current Prices

Thousand Maltese pounds

	1980				1981				1982			
	TOTAL	Total Private	Public Enterprises	General Government	TOTAL	Total Private	Public Enterprises	General Government	TOTAL	Total Private	Public Enterprises	General Government
Increase in stocks, total	9383	2036	6971	376	12557	7160	5856	-459	25504	19229	3096	3179
Gross Fixed Capital Formation, Total	87074	61531	5070	20473	105597	74988	13466	17143	120121	86746	19214	14161
1 Residential buildings	20875	...	...	...	30155	25760	...	4395				
2 Non-residential buildings		...	...	...		...	...		50020	33366	5635	11019
3 Other construction	10658	...	...	...	11215	...	...	...				
4 Land improvement and plantation and orchard development		...	...	...		...	...	...				
5 Producers' durable goods	55541	44782	3115	7644	64227	49228	10004	4995	70101	53380	13579	3142
A Transport equipment	13153	13040	...	...	13828	13595	...	...	14508	14273	...	...
B Machinery and equipment	42388	31742	...	...	50399	35633	...	...	55593	39107	...	...
6 Breeding stock, dairy cattle, etc.	...	...	...	...	...	...	...	...	...	...	...	...
Total Gross Capital Formation	96457	63567	12041	20849	118154	82148	19322	16684	145625	105975	22310	17340

Malta

2.7 Gross Capital Formation by Type of Good and Owner, in Current Prices
Thousand Maltese pounds

	1983 TOTAL	1983 Total Private	1983 Public Enterprises	1983 General Government	1984 TOTAL	1984 Total Private	1984 Public Enterprises	1984 General Government	1985 TOTAL	1985 Total Private	1985 Public Enterprises	1985 General Government
Increase in stocks, total	5460	9479	-7588	3569	6780	-1372	5197	2955	7883	9446	-5000	3437
Gross Fixed Capital Formation, Total	131630	107883	11371	12376	126453	101329	14199	10925	125871	100541	16453	8877
1 Residential buildings												
2 Non-residential buildings	50960	37400	4035	9527	48661	37076	2964	8621	41197	30806	3382	7009
3 Other construction												
4 Land improvement and plantation and orchard development												
5 Producers' durable goods	80670	70483	7338	2849	77792	64253	11235	2304	84674	69735	13071	1868
A Transport equipment	33135	32972	...	...	14559	14449	...	...	15939	15755	...	...
B Machinery and equipment	47535	37511	...	...	63233	49804	...	...	68735	53980	...	...
6 Breeding stock, dairy cattle, etc.	...	...	...	...	...	...	...	...	...	...	...	...
Total Gross Capital Formation	137090	117362	3783	15945	133233	99957	19396	13880	133754	109987	11453	12314

	1986 TOTAL	1986 Total Private	1986 Public Enterprises	1986 General Government	1987 TOTAL	1987 Total Private	1987 Public Enterprises	1987 General Government
Increase in stocks, total	8179	3500	324	4355	-2377	-1783	-214	-380
Gross Fixed Capital Formation, Total	122327	96532	16210	9585	153453	120360	14652	18441
1 Residential buildings					49103	25608	6645	16850
2 Non-residential buildings	44779	32925	3607	8247	...	...	...	...
3 Other construction					...	...	...	...
4 Land improvement and plantation and orchard development					...	...	...	...
5 Producers' durable goods	77548	63607	12603	1338	104350	94752	8007	1591
A Transport equipment	16676	16491	...	...	41515	41382	...	...
B Machinery and equipment	60872	47116	...	...	62835	53370	...	...
6 Breeding stock, dairy cattle, etc.	...	...	...	...	...	...	...	...
Total Gross Capital Formation	130506	100032	16534	13940	151076	118577	14438	18061

2.11 Gross Fixed Capital Formation by Kind of Activity of Owner, ISIC Divisions, in Current Prices
Thousand Maltese pounds

	1970	1975	1978	1979	1980	1981	1982	1983	1984	1985	1986	1987
					All Producers							
1 Agriculture, hunting, forestry and fishing	292	468	1000	1010	1180	1270	1447	1363	1603	1355	1697	1404
2 Mining and quarrying [a]	1182	1472	2222	3725	1432	2692	4976	4761	6340	5743	5598	6116
3 Manufacturing	4918	7670	10951	18936	22693	28095	24882	23301	26298	30578	23620	28836
4 Electricity, gas and water	4153	617	1611	...	...	...	...	...	...	...	...	...
5 Construction [a]	...	...	...	...	...	...	...	...	...	...	...	...
6 Wholesale and retail trade, restaurants and hotels	2053	1770	3470	8230	12085	7912	6721	4143	4606	4829	10000	16591
7 Transport, storage and communication	3617	5004	9255	9416	11184	14415	15582	37345	31486	32016	27326	44185
8 Finance, insurance, real estate and business services [b]	4578	3305	10421	11928	9792	18179	29274	32985	26898	22821	24195	19377
9 Community, social and personal services [b]	1099	1276	3578	3067	2165	2425	3864	3985	4098	3199	4096	3851
Total Industries	21892	21582	42508	56312	61531	74988	86746	107883	101329	100541	96532	120360
Producers of Government Services	5921	15900	17807	21885	25543	30609	33375	23747	25124	25330	25795	33093
Private Non-Profit Institutions Serving Households	...	...	...	...	...	...	...	...	...	...	...	...
Total	27813	37482	60315	78197	87074	105597	120121	131630	126453	125871	122327	153453

a) Item 'Construction' is included in item 'Mining and quarrying'.
b) Finance, insurance and business services are included in item 'Community, social and personal services'.

Malta

3.13 General Government Capital Accumulation Account: Total and Subsectors

Thousand Maltese pounds

	1980					1981				
	Total General Government	Central Government	State or Provincial Government	Local Government	Social Security Funds	Total General Government	Central Government	State or Provincial Government	Local Government	Social Security Funds

Finance of Gross Accumulation

1 Gross saving	61234	...	...	...	...	63070	...	...	...	...
A Consumption of fixed capital	3127	...	...	...	...	3746	...	...	...	...
B Net saving	58107	...	...	...	...	59324	...	...	...	...
2 Capital transfers	6351	...	...	...	...	19995	...	...	...	...
A From other government subsectors	...	...	...	...	...	...	...	...	...	...
B From other resident sectors	1753	...	...	...	...	1955	...	...	...	...
C From rest of the world	4598	...	...	...	...	18040	...	...	...	...
Finance of Gross Accumulation [a]	67585	...	...	...	...	83065	...	...	...	...

Gross Accumulation

1 Gross capital formation	32890	...	...	...	...	36006	...	...	...	...
A Increase in stocks	7347	...	...	...	...	5397	...	...	...	...
B Gross fixed capital formation	25543	...	...	...	...	30609	...	...	...	...
2 Purchases of land, net	-	...	...	...	...	-	...	...	...	...
3 Purchases of intangible assets, net	-	...	...	...	...	-	...	...	...	...
4 Capital transfers	759	...	...	...	...	1086	...	...	...	...
A To other government subsectors	...	...	...	...	...	1	...	...	...	...
B To other resident sectors	759	...	...	...	...	1085	...	...	...	...
C To rest of the world	...	...	...	...	...	...	...	...	...	...
Net lending	33936	...	...	...	...	45973	...	...	...	...
Gross Accumulation [a]	67585	...	...	...	...	83065	...	...	...	...

	1982					1983				
	Total General Government	Central Government	State or Provincial Government	Local Government	Social Security Funds	Total General Government	Central Government	State or Provincial Government	Local Government	Social Security Funds

Finance of Gross Accumulation

1 Gross saving	51693	...	...	...	...	34865	...	...	...	...
A Consumption of fixed capital	4996	...	...	...	...	5624	...	...	...	...
B Net saving	46697	...	...	...	...	29241	...	...	...	...
2 Capital transfers	10776	...	...	...	...	9393	...	...	...	...
A From other government subsectors	...	...	...	...	...	...	...	...	...	...
B From other resident sectors	1721	...	...	...	...	1824	...	...	...	...
C From rest of the world	9055	...	...	...	...	7569	...	...	...	...
Finance of Gross Accumulation [a]	62469	...	...	...	...	44258	...	...	...	...

Gross Accumulation

1 Gross capital formation	39650	...	...	...	...	19728	...	...	...	...
A Increase in stocks	6275	...	...	...	...	-4019	...	...	...	...
B Gross fixed capital formation	33375	...	...	...	...	23747	...	...	...	...
2 Purchases of land, net	-	...	...	...	...	-	...	...	...	...
3 Purchases of intangible assets, net	-	...	...	...	...	-	...	...	...	...
4 Capital transfers	591	...	...	...	...	435	...	...	...	...
A To other government subsectors	...	...	...	...	...	...	...	...	...	...
B To other resident sectors	591	...	...	...	...	435	...	...	...	...
C To rest of the world	...	...	...	...	...	...	...	...	...	...
Net lending	22228	...	...	...	...	24095	...	...	...	...
Gross Accumulation [a]	62469	...	...	...	...	44258	...	...	...	...

	1984					1985				
	Total General Government	Central Government	State or Provincial Government	Local Government	Social Security Funds	Total General Government	Central Government	State or Provincial Government	Local Government	Social Security Funds

Finance of Gross Accumulation

1 Gross saving	37387	...	...	...	...	34483	...	...	...	...
A Consumption of fixed capital	5972	...	...	...	...	5917	...	...	...	...
B Net saving	31415	...	...	...	...	28566	...	...	...	...
2 Capital transfers	9298	...	...	...	...	2040	...	...	...	...

Malta

3.13 General Government Capital Accumulation Account: Total and Subsectors
(Continued)

Thousand Maltese pounds

	1984					1985				
	Total General Government	Central Government	State or Provincial Government	Local Government	Social Security Funds	Total General Government	Central Government	State or Provincial Government	Local Government	Social Security Funds
A From other government subsectors	...	...	...	...	...	...	...	...	...	...
B From other resident sectors	2116	...	...	...	...	1596	...	...	...	...
C From rest of the world	7182	...	...	...	...	444	...	...	...	...
Finance of Gross Accumulation [a]	46685	...	...	...	...	36523	...	...	...	...
Gross Accumulation										
1 Gross capital formation	33276	...	...	...	...	23767	...	...	...	...
A Increase in stocks	8152	...	...	...	...	-1563	...	...	...	...
B Gross fixed capital formation	25124	...	...	...	...	25330	...	...	...	...
2 Purchases of land, net	-	...	...	...	...	-	...	...	...	...
3 Purchases of intangible assets, net	-	...	...	...	...	-	...	...	...	...
4 Capital transfers	543	...	...	...	...	246	...	...	...	...
A To other government subsectors	...	...	...	...	...	...	...	...	...	...
B To other resident sectors	543	...	...	...	...	246	...	...	...	...
C To rest of the world	...	...	...	...	...	...	...	...	...	...
Net lending	12866	...	...	...	...	12510	...	...	...	...
Gross Accumulation [a]	46685	...	...	...	...	36523	...	...	...	...

	1986					1987				
	Total General Government	Central Government	State or Provincial Government	Local Government	Social Security Funds	Total General Government	Central Government	State or Provincial Government	Local Government	Social Security Funds
Finance of Gross Accumulation										
1 Gross saving	35252	...	...	...	...	22421	...	...	...	...
A Consumption of fixed capital	6778	...	...	...	...	7569	...	...	...	...
B Net saving	28474	...	...	...	...	14852	...	...	...	...
2 Capital transfers	2923	...	...	...	...	2033	...	...	...	...
A From other government subsectors	...	...	...	...	...	...	...	...	...	...
B From other resident sectors	1584	...	...	...	...	1972	...	...	...	...
C From rest of the world	1339	...	...	...	...	61	...	...	...	...
Finance of Gross Accumulation [a]	38175	...	...	...	...	24454	...	...	...	...
Gross Accumulation										
1 Gross capital formation	30474	...	...	...	...	32499	...	...	...	...
A Increase in stocks	4679	...	...	...	...	-594	...	...	...	...
B Gross fixed capital formation	25795	...	...	...	...	33093	...	...	...	...
2 Purchases of land, net	-	...	...	...	...	-	...	...	...	...
3 Purchases of intangible assets, net	-	...	...	...	...	-	...	...	...	...
4 Capital transfers	206	...	...	...	...	2648	...	...	...	...
A To other government subsectors	...	...	...	...	...	...	...	...	...	...
B To other resident sectors	691	...	...	...	...	2648	...	...	...	...
C To rest of the world	...	...	...	...	...	...	...	...	...	...
Net lending	7010	...	...	...	...	-10693	...	...	...	...
Gross Accumulation [a]	38175	...	...	...	...	24454	...	...	...	...

a) Public enterprises is included in general government.

3.22 Corporate and Quasi-Corporate Enterprise Income and Outlay Account: Total and Sectors

Thousand Maltese pounds

	1980			1981			1982			1983		
	TOTAL	Non-Financial	Financial	TOTAL	Non-Financial	Financial	TOTAL	Non-Financial	Financial	TOTAL	Non-Financial	Financial
Receipts												
1 Operating surplus	52235	43201	9034	59863	53807	6056	68790	59316	9474	69703	62505	7198
2 Property and entrepreneurial income	4618	4618	-	5474	5474	-	5412	5412	-	3826	3826	-
A Withdrawals from quasi-corporate enterprises	4618	4618	-	5474	5474	-	5412	5412	-	3826	3826	-
B Interest	...	...	...	...	...	...	...	...	...	...	...	...
C Dividends	...	...	...	...	...	...	...	...	...	...	...	...
D Net land rent and royalties	...	...	...	...	...	...	...	...	...	...	...	...

Malta

3.22 Corporate and Quasi-Corporate Enterprise Income and Outlay Account: Total and Sectors
(Continued)

Thousand Maltese pounds

	1980			1981			1982			1983		
	TOTAL	Non-Financial	Financial	TOTAL	Non-Financial	Financial	TOTAL	Non-Financial	Financial	TOTAL	Non-Financial	Financial
3 Current transfers	...	...	...	...	...	...	...	...	...	...	...	...
Total Current Receipts	56853	47819	9034	65337	59281	6056	74202	64728	9474	73529	66331	7198
Disbursements												
1 Property and entrepreneurial income	29296	26315	2981	31397	28852	2545	33484	29460	4024	32107	28497	3610
A Withdrawals from quasi-corporations	9970	9970	-	6129	6129	-	6268	6268	-	3547	3547	-
B Interest	19326	16345	2981	25268	22723	2545	27216	23192	4024	28560	24950	3610
C Dividends	...	...	...	...	...	...	...	...	...	...	...	...
D Net land rent and royalties	...	...	...	...	...	...	...	...	...	...	...	...
2 Direct taxes and other current transfers n.e.c. to general government	10260	7324	2936	11376	9408	1968	17065	13986	3079	16032	13693	2339
A Direct taxes	10260	7324	2936	11376	9408	1968	17065	13986	3079	16032	13693	2339
On income	10260	7324	2936	11376	9408	1968	17065	13986	3079	16032	13693	2339
Other	...	...	...	...	...	...	...	...	...	...	...	...
B Fines, fees, penalties and other current transfers n.e.c.	...	...	...	...	...	...	...	...	...	...	...	...
3 Other current transfers	...	...	...	...	...	...	...	...	...	...	...	...
Net saving	17297	14180	3117	22564	21021	1543	23653	21282	2371	25390	24141	1249
Total Current Disbursements and Net Saving	56853	47819	9034	65337	59281	6056	74202	64728	9474	73529	66331	7198

	1984			1985			1986			1987		
	TOTAL	Non-Financial	Financial	TOTAL	Non-Financial	Financial	TOTAL	Non-Financial	Financial	TOTAL	Non-Financial	Financial
Receipts												
1 Operating surplus	72729	65309	7420	76329	67289	9040	74824	65722	9102	82851	76726	6125
2 Property and entrepreneurial income	3876	3876	-	4209	4209	-	4387	4387	-	5719	5719	-
A Withdrawals from quasi-corporate enterprises	3876	3876	-	4209	4209	-	4387	4387	-	5719	5719	-
B Interest	...	...	...	...	...	...	...	...	...	...	...	...
C Dividends	...	...	...	...	...	...	...	...	...	...	...	...
D Net land rent and royalties	...	...	...	...	...	...	...	...	...	...	...	...
3 Current transfers	...	...	...	...	...	...	...	...	...	...	...	...
Total Current Receipts	76605	69185	7420	80538	71498	9040	79211	70109	9102	88570	82445	6125
Disbursements												
1 Property and entrepreneurial income	35279	30774	4505	38009	35239	2770	35066	32480	2586	32556	31003	1553
A Withdrawals from quasi-corporations	4820	4820	-	6842	6842	-	4743	4743	-	5207	5207	-
B Interest	30459	25954	4505	31167	28397	2770	30323	27737	2586	27349	25796	1553
C Dividends	...	...	...									
D Net land rent and royalties	...	...	...	...	...	...	...	...	...	...	...	...
2 Direct taxes and other current transfers n.e.c. to general government	14728	12317	2411	15194	12256	2938	15354	12396	2958	16612	14621	1991
A Direct taxes	14728	12317	2411	15194	12256	2938	15354	12396	2958	16612	14621	1991
On income	14728	12317	2411	15194	12256	2938	15354	12396	2958	16612	14621	1991
Other	...	...	...	...	...	...	...	...	...	...	...	...
B Fines, fees, penalties and other current transfers n.e.c.	...	...	...	...	...	...	...	...	...	...	...	...
3 Other current transfers	...	...	...	...	...	...	...	...	...	...	...	...
Net saving	26598	26094	504	27335	24003	3332	28791	25233	3558	39402	36821	2581
Total Current Disbursements and Net Saving	76605	69185	7420	80538	71498	9040	79211	70109	9102	88570	82445	6125

Malta

3.23 Corporate and Quasi-Corporate Enterprise Capital Accumulation Account: Total and Sectors

Thousand Maltese pounds

	1980 TOTAL	1980 Non-Financial	1980 Financial	1981 TOTAL	1981 Non-Financial	1981 Financial	1982 TOTAL	1982 Non-Financial	1982 Financial	1983 TOTAL	1983 Non-Financial	1983 Financial
Finance of Gross Accumulation												
1 Gross saving	24015	20415	3600	29651	27899	1752	30938	28325	2613	35487	33983	1504
A Consumption of fixed capital	6718	6575	143	7087	6878	209	7285	7043	242	10097	9842	255
B Net saving	17297	13840	3457	22564	21021	1543	23653	21282	2371	25390	24141	1249
2 Capital transfers	...	...	...	...	...	...	...	...	...	...	...	...
Finance of Gross Accumulation	24015	20415	3600	29651	27899	1752	30938	28325	2613	35487	33983	1504
Gross Accumulation												
1 Gross capital formation	40914	40914	-	50782	50782	-	62394	62394	-	82193	82193	-
A Increase in stocks	2011	2011	-	6739	6739	-	19040	19040	-	9229	9229	-
B Gross fixed capital formation	38903	38903	-	44043	44043	-	43354	43354	-	72964	72964	-
2 Purchases of land, net	...	...	...	...	...	...	...	...	...	...	...	...
3 Purchases of intangible assets, net	...	...	...	...	...	...	...	...	...	...	...	...
4 Capital transfers	...	...	...	...	...	...	...	...	...	...	...	...
Net lending	-16899	-20499	3600	-21131	-22883	1752	-31456	-34069	2613	-46706	-48210	1504
Gross Accumulation	24015	20415	3600	29651	27899	1752	30938	28325	2613	35487	33983	1504

	1984 TOTAL	1984 Non-Financial	1984 Financial	1985 TOTAL	1985 Non-Financial	1985 Financial	1986 TOTAL	1986 Non-Financial	1986 Financial
Finance of Gross Accumulation									
1 Gross saving	38192	37397	795	39604	35961	3643	41737	37836	3901
A Consumption of fixed capital	11594	11303	291	12269	11958	311	12946	12603	343
B Net saving	26598	26094	504	27335	24003	3332	28791	25233	3558
2 Capital transfers	...	...	...	...	...	...	...	...	...
Finance of Gross Accumulation	38192	37397	795	39604	35961	3643	41737	37836	3901
Gross Accumulation									
1 Gross capital formation	59271	59271	-	67028	67028	-	56344	56344	-
A Increase in stocks	-1330	-1330	-	9046	9046	-	3000	3000	-
B Gross fixed capital formation	60601	60601	-	57982	57982	-	53344	53344	-
2 Purchases of land, net	...	...	...	...	...	...	...	...	...
3 Purchases of intangible assets, net	...	...	...	...	...	...	...	...	...
4 Capital transfers	...	...	...	...	...	...	...	...	...
Net lending	-21079	-21874	795	-27424	-31067	3643	-14607	-18508	3901
Gross Accumulation	38192	37397	795	39604	35961	3643	41737	37836	3901

3.32 Household and Private Unincorporated Enterprise Income and Outlay Account

Thousand Maltese pounds

	1970	1975	1978	1979	1980	1981	1982	1983	1984	1985	1986	1987
Receipts												
1 Compensation of employees	47147	82975	131460	152669	180553	203805	228625	223584	217928	222942	231617	254706
A Wages and salaries	46259	79323	125265	144290	168821	189580	213384	207932	203182	207559	215884	238508
B Employers' contributions for social security	888	3652	6195	8379	11732	14225	15241	15652	14746	15383	15733	16198
C Employers' contributions for private pension & welfare plans	...	...	...	...	...	...	...	...	...	...	...	...
2 Operating surplus of private unincorporated enterprises	19668	28968	45572	47574	57940	66268	72020	73370	75774	79082	84042	83352
3 Property and entrepreneurial income	11706	23472	29036	39538	48676	50878	50767	49599	53845	54036	54419	56059
A Withdrawals from private quasi-corporations	...	...	...	...	...	...	...	...	...	...	...	...
B Interest												
C Dividends	11706	23472	29036	39538	48676	50878	50767	49599	53845	54036	54419	56059
D Net land rent and royalties												

Malta

3.32 Household and Private Unincorporated Enterprise Income and Outlay Account
(Continued)

Thousand Maltese pounds

	1970	1975	1978	1979	1980	1981	1982	1983	1984	1985	1986	1987
3 Current transfers	13591	27549	43177	45457	53668	64994	74126	77252	81334	79638	80236	83476
A Casualty insurance claims	...	...	...	...	...	...	...	...	...	...	...	...
B Social security benefits	4000	15759	28468	31408	40035	51125	59130	61211	65100	64726	66412	68075
C Social assistance grants												
D Unfunded employee pension and welfare benefits	-	-	-	-	-	-	-	-	-	-	-	...
E Transfers from general government	...	...	...	...	...	...	...	...	...	...	...	...
F Transfers from the rest of the world	9591	11790	14709	14049	13633	13869	14996	16041	16234	14912	13824	15401
G Other transfers n.e.c.	...	...	...	...	...	...	...	...	...	...	...	...
Total Current Receipts	92112	162964	249245	285238	340837	385945	425538	423805	428881	435698	450314	477593

Disbursements

	1970	1975	1978	1979	1980	1981	1982	1983	1984	1985	1986	1987
1 Final consumption expenditures	73855	118660	186371	206006	253485	279434	305724	306705	317475	333239	347895	358284
A Market purchases	...	...	...	...	...	...	...	...	...	...	...	...
B Gross rents of owner-occupied housing	1251	2135	2657	2778	2965	3586	3758	3884	3932	4184	4307	4455
C Consumption from own-account production	...	...	...	...	...	...	...	...	...	...	...	...
2 Property income	...	...	...	...	...	...	...	...	...	...	...	...
3 Direct taxes and other current transfers n.e.c. to government	2359	17058	29022	41435	52968	62042	64060	64347	60471	62603	61483	55762
A Social security contributions	795	5981	12390	16758	23464	28450	30482	31304	29492	30766	31466	32396
B Direct taxes	1476	10824	16374	24365	29166	33316	33219	32614	30511	31389	29633	23078
Income taxes	1476	10824	16374	24365	29166	33316	33219	32614	30511	31389	26216	19812
Other	...	...	...	...	...	...	...	...	...	...	3417	3266
C Fees, fines and penalties	88	253	258	312	338	276	359	429	468	448	384	288
4 Other current transfers	2047	3222	4850	5432	6095	7053	6308	6499	8095	7420	7530	8114
A Net casualty insurance premiums	...	...	...	...	...	...	...	...	...	...	...	...
B Transfers to private non-profit institutions serving households	...	...	...	...	...	...	...	...	...	...	...	...
C Transfers to the rest of the world	959	1476	2209	2367	2638	2871	2111	1900	5161	5250	5226	5323
D Other current transfers, except imputed	1088	1746	2641	3065	3457	4182	4197	4599	2934	2170	2304	2791
E Imputed employee pension and welfare contributions	-	-	-	-	-	-	-	-	-	-	-	...
Net saving	13851	24024	29002	32365	28289	37416	49446	46254	42840	32436	33406	55433
Total Current Disbursements and Net Saving	92112	162964	249245	285238	340837	385945	425538	423805	428881	435698	450314	477593

3.33 Household and Private Unincorporated Enterprise Capital Accumulation Account

Thousand Maltese pounds

	1970	1975	1978	1979	1980	1981	1982	1983	1984	1985	1986	1987

Finance of Gross Accumulation

	1970	1975	1978	1979	1980	1981	1982	1983	1984	1985	1986	1987
1 Gross saving	15409	25828	31516	35218	31340	40946	52903	50286	46264	35673	36882	58764
A Consumption of fixed capital	1558	1804	2514	2853	3051	3530	3457	4032	3424	3237	3476	3331
B Net saving	13851	24024	29002	32365	28289	37416	49446	46254	42840	32436	33406	55433
2 Capital transfers [a]	-862	615	2689	4806	3389	5228	7960	5829	7802	11376	...	18065
Total Finance of Gross Accumulation	14547	26443	34205	40024	34729	46174	60863	56115	54066	47049	...	76829

Gross Accumulation

	1970	1975	1978	1979	1980	1981	1982	1983	1984	1985	1986	1987
1 Gross Capital Formation	15804	10295	21597	24406	22653	31366	43581	35169	40686	42959	43688	27783
A Increase in stocks	1535	-1654	279	280	25	421	189	250	-42	400	500	-713
B Gross fixed capital formation	14269	11949	21318	24126	22628	30945	43392	34919	40728	42559	43188	28496
2 Purchases of land, net	...	...	...	...	...	...	...	...	...	...	...	...
3 Purchases of intangibles, net	...	...	...	...	...	...	...	...	...	...	...	...
4 Capital transfers	...	...	...	...	...	...	...	...	...	...	...	...
Net lending	-1257	16148	12608	15618	12076	14808	17282	20946	13380	4090	7713	49046
Total Gross Accumulation	14547	26443	34205	40024	34729	46174	60863	56115	54066	47049	51401	76829

a) Capital transfers received are recorded net of capital transfers paid.

Malta

3.51 External Transactions: Current Account: Detail

Thousand Maltese pounds

	1970	1975	1978	1979	1980	1981	1982	1983	1984	1985	1986	1987
	\multicolumn{12}{c}{Payments to the Rest of the World}
1 Imports of goods and services	75516	159710	249518	307666	377989	392462	394578	376143	393516	420475	421742	480934
2 Factor income to the rest of the world	3503	5623	12233	22019	19929	19679	11801	9874	9199	10758	17195	8850
A Compensation of employees	...	...	...	...	...	...	...	...	...	...	...	...
B Property and entrepreneurial income	3503	5623	12233	22019	19929	19679	11801	9874	9199	10758	17195	8850
3 Current transfers to the rest of the world	1309	1730	2445	2654	2915	3156	2383	2173	3185	2465	2560	3108
A Indirect taxes by general government to supranational organizations	...	...	...	...	...	...	...	...	...	...	...	...
B Other current transfers	1309	1730	2445	2654	2915	3156	2383	2173	3185	2465	2560	3108
By general government	350	254	236	287	277	285	272	273	251	295	256	317
By other resident sectors	959	1476	2209	2367	2638	2871	2111	1900	2934	2170	2304	2791
4 Surplus of the nation on current transactions	-11694	6795	9945	7982	20132	15513	-10091	-16452	-11390	-23994	-16635	-15412
Payments to the Rest of the World, and Surplus of the Nation on Current Transfers	68634	173858	274141	340321	420965	430810	398671	371738	394510	409704	424862	477480
	\multicolumn{12}{c}{Receipts From The Rest of the World}
1 Exports of goods and services	47098	137327	229569	290769	356647	355918	319799	307647	323539	345155	365702	422496
2 Factor income from the rest of the world	10781	23880	29166	34983	50479	60923	63829	47997	54669	49543	45251	39511
A Compensation of employees	...	...	...	...	...	...	...	...	...	...	...	...
B Property and entrepreneurial income	10781	23880	29166	34983	50479	60923	63829	47997	54669	49543	45251	39511
3 Current transfers from the rest of the world	10755	12651	15406	14569	13839	13969	15043	16094	16302	15006	13909	15473
A Subsidies to general government from supranational organizations	...	...	...	...	...	...	...	...	...	...	...	...
B Other current transfers	10755	12651	15406	14569	13839	13969	15043	16094	16302	15006	13909	15473
To general government	1164	861	697	520	206	100	47	53	68	94	85	72
To other resident sectors	9591	11790	14709	14049	13633	13869	14996	16041	16234	14912	13824	15401
Receipts from the Rest of the World on Current Transfers	68634	173858	274141	340321	420965	430810	398671	371738	394510	409704	424862	477480

3.52 External Transactions: Capital Accumulation Account

Thousand Maltese pounds

	1970	1975	1978	1979	1980	1981	1982	1983	1984	1985	1986	1987
	\multicolumn{12}{c}{Finance of Gross Accumulation}
1 Surplus of the nation on current transactions	-11694	6795	9945	7982	20132	15513	-10091	-16452	-11390	-23994	-16635	-15412
2 Capital transfers from the rest of the world	9394	18257	20669	10764	8981	24138	18145	14787	16557	13170	16751	17450
A By general government	6500	17037	16474	5042	4598	18040	9055	7569	7182	444	1339	61
B By other resident sectors	2894	1220	4195	5722	4383	6098	9090	7218	9375	12726	15412	17389
Total Finance of Gross Accumulation	-2300	25052	30614	18746	29113	39651	8054	-1664	5167	-10824	116	2038
	\multicolumn{12}{c}{Gross Accumulation}
1 Capital transfers to the rest of the world	...	...	...	...	...	...	...	...	...	...	...	...
2 Purchases of intangible assets, n.e.c., net, from the rest of the world	-	-	-	-	-	-	-	-	-	-	-	...
Net lending to the rest of the world	-2300	25052	30614	18746	29113	39651	8054	-1665	5167	-10824	116	2038
Total Gross Accumulation	-2300	25052	30614	18746	29113	39651	8054	-1665	5167	-10824	116	2038

4.1 Derivation of Value Added by Kind of Activity, in Current Prices

Thousand Maltese pounds

	\multicolumn{3}{c}{1980}	\multicolumn{3}{c}{1981}	\multicolumn{3}{c}{1982}	\multicolumn{3}{c}{1983}
	Gross Output	Intermediate Consumption	Value Added	Gross Output	Intermediate Consumption	Value Added	Gross Output	Intermediate Consumption	Value Added	Gross Output	Intermediate Consumption	Value Added
	\multicolumn{12}{c}{All Producers}
1 Agriculture, hunting, forestry and fishing	...	...	13289	...	...	15038	...	...	16767	...	...	18731
2 Mining and quarrying [a]	...	...	15655	...	...	17073	...	...	23546	...	...	23511
3 Manufacturing	...	...	115358	...	...	121384	...	...	125024	...	...	120036
A Manufacture of food, beverages and tobacco	...	...	15543	...	...	18413	...	...	20814	...	...	19903

937

Malta

4.1 Derivation of Value Added by Kind of Activity, in Current Prices
(Continued)

Thousand Maltese pounds

	1980 Gross Output	1980 Intermediate Consumption	1980 Value Added	1981 Gross Output	1981 Intermediate Consumption	1981 Value Added	1982 Gross Output	1982 Intermediate Consumption	1982 Value Added	1983 Gross Output	1983 Intermediate Consumption	1983 Value Added
B Textile, wearing apparel and leather industries	...	...	36559	...	...	36531	...	...	36189	...	...	33665
C Manufacture of wood and wood products, including furniture	...	...	5306	...	...	5622	...	...	6223	...	...	5466
D Manufacture of paper and paper products, printing and publishing	...	...	8266	...	...	7790	...	...	6829	...	...	6979
E Manufacture of chemicals and chemical petroleum, coal, rubber and plastic products	...	...	7423	...	...	6879	...	...	6325	...	...	7005
F Manufacture of non-metallic mineral products, except products of petroleum and coal	...	...	2786	...	...	2957	...	...	3448	...	...	3965
G Basic metal industries	...	...	4319	...	...	-	...	...	-	...	...	-
H Manufacture of fabricated metal products, machinery and equipment	...	...	25558	...	...	34823	...	...	35710	...	...	32537
I Other manufacturing industries	...	...	9598	...	...	8369	...	...	9486	...	...	10516
4 Electricity, gas and water [b]	...	...	15635	...	...	23586	...	...	21958	...	...	21119
5 Construction [a]	...	...	...	...	...	...	...	...	...	...	...	...
6 Wholesale and retail trade, restaurants and hotels [c]	...	...	51001	...	...	57421	...	...	63184	...	...	64010
7 Transport, storage and communication	...	...	22230	...	...	22596	...	...	20396	...	...	24050
8 Finance, insurance, real estate and business services [d]	...	...	37269	...	...	45519	...	...	50303	...	...	51475
9 Community, social and personal services [cd]	...	...	33731	...	...	36404	...	...	38415	...	...	36850
Total, Industries	...	...	304168	...	...	339021	...	...	359593	...	...	359782
Producers of Government Services	...	...	44444	...	...	51513	...	...	58152	...	...	57348
Other Producers												
Total [e]	...	...	348612	...	...	390534	...	...	417745	...	...	417130
Less: Imputed bank service charge	...	...	...	...	...	...	...	...	...	...	...	...
Import duties	...	...	...	...	...	...	...	...	...	...	...	...
Value added tax	...	...	...	...	...	...	...	...	...	...	...	...
Other adjustments [f]	...	...	43352	...	...	45917	...	...	44041	...	...	40426
Total	...	...	391964	...	...	436451	...	...	461786	...	...	457556

	1984 Gross Output	1984 Intermediate Consumption	1984 Value Added	1985 Gross Output	1985 Intermediate Consumption	1985 Value Added	1986 Gross Output	1986 Intermediate Consumption	1986 Value Added	1987 Gross Output	1987 Intermediate Consumption	1987 Value Added
						All Producers						
1 Agriculture, hunting, forestry and fishing	...	...	19346	...	...	19375	...	...	20419	...	...	21429
2 Mining and quarrying [a]	...	...	19660	...	...	20758	...	...	18869	...	...	21051
3 Manufacturing	...	...	124706	...	...	126929	...	...	134676	...	...	136427
A Manufacture of food, beverages and tobacco	...	...	20431	...	...	22813	...	...	25390	...	...	...
B Textile, wearing apparel and leather industries	...	...	35052	...	...	35091	...	...	35809	...	...	...
C Manufacture of wood and wood products, including furniture	...	...	5065	...	...	4220	...	...	4994	...	...	...
D Manufacture of paper and paper products, printing and publishing	...	...	8661	...	...	8383	...	...	7818	...	...	...
E Manufacture of chemicals and chemical petroleum, coal, rubber and plastic products	...	...	7962	...	...	8352	...	...	8314	...	...	...
F Manufacture of non-metallic mineral products, except products of petroleum and coal	...	...	4891	...	...	3626	...	...	2887	...	...	...
G Basic metal industries	...	...	-	...	...	-	...	...	-	...	...	...
H Manufacture of fabricated metal products, machinery and equipment	...	...	31607	...	...	33431	...	...	35653	...	...	...
I Other manufacturing industries	...	...	11037	...	...	11013	...	...	13811	...	...	...
4 Electricity, gas and water [b]	...	...	24985	...	...	22278	...	...	34704	...	...	42119

Malta

4.1 Derivation of Value Added by Kind of Activity, in Current Prices
(Continued)

Thousand Maltese pounds

	1984 Gross Output	1984 Intermediate Consumption	1984 Value Added	1985 Gross Output	1985 Intermediate Consumption	1985 Value Added	1986 Gross Output	1986 Intermediate Consumption	1986 Value Added	1987 Gross Output	1987 Intermediate Consumption	1987 Value Added
5 Construction [a]	...	...	...	...	...	...	...	...	...	...	...	...
6 Wholesale and retail trade, restaurants and hotels [c]	...	...	66077	...	...	66696	...	...	67647	...	...	70847
7 Transport, storage and communication	...	...	23391	...	...	23955	...	...	26240	...	...	30204
8 Finance, insurance, real estate and business services [d]	...	...	53517	...	...	57131	...	...	61255	...	...	62782
9 Community, social and personal services [cd]	...	...	33605	...	...	34894	...	...	35639	...	...	41729
Total, Industries	...	...	365287	...	...	372016	...	...	399449	...	...	426588
Producers of Government Services	...	...	56090	...	...	58534	...	...	62317	...	...	68862
Other Producers	...	...		...	...		...	...		...	...	
Total [e]	...	...	421377	...	...	430550	...	...	461766	...	...	495450
Less: Imputed bank service charge	...	...	...	...	...	...	...	...	...	...	...	...
Import duties	...	...	...	...	...	...	...	...	...	...	...	...
Value added tax	...	...	...	...	...	...	...	...	...	...	...	...
Other adjustments [f]	...	...	39675	...	...	45432	...	...	50103	...	...	53721
Total	...	...	461052	...	...	475982	...	...	511869	...	...	549171

a) Item 'Construction' is included in item 'Mining and quarrying'.
b) Item 'Electricity, gas and water' refers to all government enterprises.
c) Restaurants and hotels are included in item 'Community, social and personal services'.
d) Business services are included in item 'Community, social and personal services'.
e) Gross domestic product in factor values.
f) Item 'Other adjustments' refers to indirect taxes net of subsidies.

4.3 Cost Components of Value Added

Thousand Maltese pounds

	1980 Compensation of Employees	1980 Capital Consumption	1980 Net Operating Surplus	1980 Indirect Taxes	1980 Less: Subsidies Received	1980 Value Added	1981 Compensation of Employees	1981 Capital Consumption	1981 Net Operating Surplus	1981 Indirect Taxes	1981 Less: Subsidies Received	1981 Value Added
					All Producers							
1 Agriculture, hunting, forestry and fishing	1366	...	11923	...	...	13289	1699	...	13339	...	...	15038
2 Mining and quarrying [a]	12337	...	3318	...	...	15655	12936	...	4137	...	...	17073
3 Manufacturing	67560	...	47798	...	...	115358	73420	...	47964	...	...	121384
4 Electricity, gas and water [b]	10213	...	5422	...	...	15635	12259	...	11327	...	...	23586
5 Construction [a]	...	...	...	...	...	...	...	...	...	...	...	...
6 Wholesale and retail trade, restaurants and hotels [c]	8253	...	42748	...	...	51001	10282	...	47139	...	...	57421
7 Transport, storage and communication	9757	...	12473	...	...	22230	11215	...	11381	...	...	22596
8 Finance, insurance, real estate and business services [d]	5137	...	32132	...	...	37269	5839	...	39680	...	...	45519
9 Community, social and personal services [cd]	21486	...	12245	...	...	33731	24642	...	11762	...	...	36404
Total, Industries	136109	...	168059	...	...	304168	152292	...	186729	...	...	339021
Producers of Government Services	44444	...	...	...	...	44444	51513	...	...	...	...	51513
Other Producers		...	...	...	...			...	...	...	...	
Total [ef]	180553	...	168059	...	...	348612	203805	...	186729	...	...	390534
Less: Imputed bank service charge	...	...	...	...	...	...	...	...	...	...	...	...
Import duties	...	...	...	...	...	...	...	...	...	...	...	...
Value added tax	...	...	...	...	...	...	...	...	...	...	...	...
Other adjustments [g]	...	...	...	45744	2392	43352	...	...	...	47897	1980	45917
Total	180553	...	168059	45744	2392	391964	203805	...	186729	47897	1980	436451

	1982 Compensation of Employees	1982 Capital Consumption	1982 Net Operating Surplus	1982 Indirect Taxes	1982 Less: Subsidies Received	1982 Value Added	1983 Compensation of Employees	1983 Capital Consumption	1983 Net Operating Surplus	1983 Indirect Taxes	1983 Less: Subsidies Received	1983 Value Added
					All Producers							
1 Agriculture, hunting, forestry and fishing	2072	...	14695	...	...	16767	1975	...	16756	...	...	18731
2 Mining and quarrying [a]	16804	...	6742	...	...	23546	16923	...	6588	...	...	23511
3 Manufacturing	78328	...	46696	...	...	125024	75103	...	44933	...	...	120036
4 Electricity, gas and water [b]	13396	...	8562	...	...	21958	12498	...	8621	...	...	21119

Malta

4.3 Cost Components of Value Added
(Continued)

Thousand Maltese pounds

	1982						1983					
	Compensation of Employees	Capital Consumption	Net Operating Surplus	Indirect Taxes	Less: Subsidies Received	Value Added	Compensation of Employees	Capital Consumption	Net Operating Surplus	Indirect Taxes	Less: Subsidies Received	Value Added
5 Construction a	...	...	...	...	...	...	...	...	...	...	...	...
6 Wholesale and retail trade, restaurants and hotels c	11668	...	51516	...	...	63184	11931	...	52079	...	...	64010
7 Transport, storage and communication	11674	...	8722	...	...	20396	11945	...	12105	...	...	24050
8 Finance, insurance, real estate and business services d	7942	...	42361	...	...	50303	7933	...	43542	...	...	51475
9 Community, social and personal services cd	28589	...	9826	...	...	38415	27928	...	8922	...	...	36850
Total, Industries	170473	...	189120	...	...	359593	166236	...	193546	...	...	359782
Producers of Government Services	58152					58152	57348					57348
Other Producers												
Total ef	228625	...	189120	...	...	417745	223584	...	193546	...	...	417130
Less: Imputed bank service charge	...	...	...	...	...	...	...	...	...	...	...	...
Import duties	...	...	...	...	...	...	...	...	...	...	...	...
Value added tax	...	...	...	...	...	...	...	...	...	...	...	...
Other adjustments g	...	...	...	46852	2811	44041	...	...	...	43794	3368	40426
Total	228625	...	189120	46852	2811	461786	223584	...	193546	43794	3368	457556

	1984						1985					
	Compensation of Employees	Capital Consumption	Net Operating Surplus	Indirect Taxes	Less: Subsidies Received	Value Added	Compensation of Employees	Capital Consumption	Net Operating Surplus	Indirect Taxes	Less: Subsidies Received	Value Added
				All Producers								
1 Agriculture, hunting, forestry and fishing	1830	...	17516	...	...	19346	1783	...	17592	...	...	19375
2 Mining and quarrying a	14224	...	5436	...	...	19660	14495	...	6263	...	...	20758
3 Manufacturing	75470	...	49236	...	...	124706	76029	...	50900	...	...	126929
4 Electricity, gas and water b	12763	...	12222	...	...	24985	13609	...	8669	...	...	22278
5 Construction a	...	...	...	...	...	...	...	...	...	...	...	...
6 Wholesale and retail trade, restaurants and hotels c	12294	...	53783	...	...	66077	12452	...	54244	...	...	66696
7 Transport, storage and communication	12491	...	10900	...	...	23391	12901	...	11054	...	...	23955
8 Finance, insurance, real estate and business services d	7988	...	45529	...	...	53517	8254	...	48877	...	...	57131
9 Community, social and personal services cd	24778	...	8827	...	...	33605	24885	...	10009	...	...	34894
Total, Industries	161838	...	203449	...	...	365287	164408	...	207608	...	...	372016
Producers of Government Services	56090					56090	58534					58534
Other Producers												
Total ef	217928	...	203449	...	...	421377	222942	...	207608	...	...	430550
Less: Imputed bank service charge	...	...	...	...	...	...	...	...	...	...	...	...
Import duties	...	...	...	...	...	...	...	...	...	...	...	...
Value added tax	...	...	...	...	...	...	...	...	...	...	...	...
Other adjustments g	...	...	...	43706	4031	39675	...	...	...	49452	4020	45432
Total	217928	...	203449	43706	4031	461052	222942	...	207608	49452	4020	475982

	1986						1987					
	Compensation of Employees	Capital Consumption	Net Operating Surplus	Indirect Taxes	Less: Subsidies Received	Value Added	Compensation of Employees	Capital Consumption	Net Operating Surplus	Indirect Taxes	Less: Subsidies Received	Value Added
				All Producers								
1 Agriculture, hunting, forestry and fishing	1774	...	18645	...	...	20419	2054	...	19375	...	...	21429
2 Mining and quarrying a	13676	...	5193	...	...	18869	15518	...	5533	...	...	21051
3 Manufacturing	80856	...	53820	...	...	134676	85879	...	50548	...	...	136427
4 Electricity, gas and water b	13636	...	21068	...	...	34704	15905	...	26214	...	...	42119
5 Construction a	...	...	...	...	...	...	...	...	...	...	...	...
6 Wholesale and retail trade, restaurants and hotels c	12834	...	54813	...	...	67647	13005	...	57842	...	...	70847
7 Transport, storage and communication	12569	...	13671	...	...	26240	14441	...	15763	...	...	30204
8 Finance, insurance, real estate and business services d	8983	...	52272	...	...	61255	10660	...	52122	...	...	62782
9 Community, social and personal services cd	24972	...	10667	...	...	35639	28382	...	13347	...	...	41729

Malta

4.3 Cost Components of Value Added
(Continued)

Thousand Maltese pounds

	1986						1987					
	Compensation of Employees	Capital Consumption	Net Operating Surplus	Indirect Taxes	Less: Subsidies Received	Value Added	Compensation of Employees	Capital Consumption	Net Operating Surplus	Indirect Taxes	Less: Subsidies Received	Value Added
Total, Industries	169300	...	230149	...	...	399449	185844	...	240744	...	...	426588
Producers of Government Services	62317	...	...	...	...	62317	68862	...	...	...	...	68862
Other Producers		...	...	...	...			...	...	...	...	
Total e)	231617	...	230149	...	...	461766	254706	...	240744	...	...	495450
Less: Imputed bank service charge	...	...	...	...	...	...	...	...	...	...	...	...
Import duties	...	...	...	...	...	...	...	...	...	...	...	...
Value added tax	...	...	...	...	...	...	...	...	...	...	...	...
Other adjustments g)	...	...	...	54885	4782	50103	...	...	...	...	...	53721
Total	231617	...	230149	54885	4782	511869	254706	...	240744	58595	4874	549171

a) Item 'Construction' is included in item 'Mining and quarrying'.
b) Item 'Electricity, gas and water' refers to all government enterprises.
c) Restaurants and hotels are included in item 'Community, social and personal services'.
d) Business services are included in item 'Community, social and personal services'.
e) Gross domestic product in factor values.
f) Column 'Consumption of fixed capital' is included in column 'Net operating surplus'.
g) Item 'Other adjustments' refers to indirect taxes net of subsidies.

Martinique

Source. Reply to the United Nations National Accounts Questionnaire from the Institute national de la statistique et des studes economiques (INSEE), Paris.
General note. The estimates shown in the following tables have been adjusted by the INSEE to conform to the United Nations System of National Accounts so far as the existing data would permit.

1.1 Expenditure on the Gross Domestic Product, in Current Prices

Million French francs

	1970	1975	1978	1979	1980	1981	1982	1983	1984	1985	1986	1987
1 Government final consumption expenditure	489.6	1140.5	1668.9	1919.6	2236.5	2567.9	3065.8	3534.9	3896.1	4212.8	...	...
2 Private final consumption expenditure	1395.3	2714.5	4211.1	4892.0	5499.4	6549.5	8013.4	9038.9	9840.7	10948.8	...	...
3 Gross capital formation	366.5	567.7	795.3	1027.6	1461.5	1460.3	1698.6	2001.6	1978.1	2085.1	...	...
A Increase in stocks	-10.2	-44.4	38.5	15.8	187.4	92.3	13.6	-28.3	-61.6	-52.7	...	...
B Gross fixed capital formation	376.7	612.1	756.8	1011.8	1274.1	1368.0	1685.0	2029.9	2039.7	2137.8	...	...
4 Exports of goods and services	166.8	407.7	564.1	567.4	528.6	894.6	992.8	1261.8	1355.7	1458.9	...	...
5 Less: Imports of goods and services	817.7	1472.9	2268.9	2868.6	3624.4	4227.3	4896.4	5722.9	6050.9	6128.7	...	...
Equals: Gross Domestic Product	1600.5	3357.5	4970.7	5538.0	6101.6	7245.0	8874.2	10114.3	11019.7	12576.9	...	...

1.3 Cost Components of the Gross Domestic Product

Million French francs

	1970	1975	1978	1979	1980	1981	1982	1983	1984	1985	1986	1987
1 Indirect taxes, net	186.9	339.1	499.5	555.3	687.7	790.5	958.6	...	...	...	...	...
A Indirect taxes	208.4	372.7	565.9	631.8	775.3	939.2	1123.4	...	...	...	...	...
B Less: Subsidies	21.5	33.6	66.4	76.5	87.6	148.7	164.8	...	...	...	...	...
2 Consumption of fixed capital [a]	...	...	...	...	...	...	...	...	...	...	...	...
3 Compensation of employees paid by resident producers to:	1037.4	2194.1	3334.7	3809.8	4432.1	5092.0	6159.5	...	...	...	...	...
4 Operating surplus [a]	376.2	824.3	1136.5	1172.9	981.8	1362.5	1756.1	...	...	...	...	...
Equals: Gross Domestic Product	1600.5	3357.5	4970.7	5538.0	6101.6	7245.0	8874.2	10114.3	11019.7	12576.9	...	...

a) Item 'Operating surplus' includes consumption of fixed capital.

1.7 External Transactions on Current Account, Summary

Million French francs

	1970	1975	1978	1979	1980	1981	1982	1983	1984	1985	1986	1987
Payments to the Rest of the World												
1 Imports of goods and services	817.7	1472.9	2268.8	2868.6	3624.4	4227.3	4896.4	...	...	...	...	...
2 Factor income to the rest of the world	31.2	88.8	158.4	182.9	213.4	275.3	322.3	...	...	...	...	...
A Compensation of employees	-	-	-	-	-	-	-	...	...	...	...	...
B Property and entrepreneurial income	31.2	88.8	158.4	182.9	213.4	275.3	322.3	...	...	...	...	...
3 Current transfers to the rest of the world	16.1	17.9	49.2	58.2	80.9	104.8	117.9	...	...	...	...	...
4 Surplus of the nation on current transactions	-123.8	70.8	-54.3	-336.1	-639.3	-513.2	-590.6	...	...	...	...	...
Payments to the Rest of the World and Surplus of the Nation on Current Transactions	741.2	1650.4	2422.1	2773.6	3279.4	4094.2	4746.0	...	...	...	...	...
Receipts From The Rest of the World												
1 Exports of goods and services	166.8	407.7	564.1	567.3	528.6	894.6	992.8	...	...	...	...	...
2 Factor income from rest of the world	8.9	18.4	60.0	74.9	114.2	174.7	201.0	...	...	...	...	...
A Compensation of employees	-	-	-	-	-	-	-	...	...	...	...	...
B Property and entrepreneurial income	8.9	18.4	60.0	74.9	114.2	174.7	201.0	...	...	...	...	...
3 Current transfers from rest of the world	565.5	1224.3	1798.0	2131.4	2636.6	3024.9	3552.2	...	...	...	...	...
Receipts from the Rest of the World on Current Transactions	741.2	1650.4	2422.1	2773.6	3279.4	4094.2	4746.0	...	...	...	...	...

1.10 Gross Domestic Product by Kind of Activity, in Current Prices

Million French francs

	1970	1975	1978	1979	1980	1981	1982	1983	1984	1985	1986	1987
1 Agriculture, hunting, forestry and fishing	...	344.1	506.7	424.5	372.9	531.2	691.1	...	...	...	...	...
2 Mining and quarrying	...	207.1	267.1	306.1	303.5	419.7	527.9	...	...	...	...	...
3 Manufacturing	...							...	...	...	...	...
4 Electricity, gas and water	...	80.9	83.5	106.9	97.9	87.8	89.6	...	...	...	...	...
5 Construction	...	170.6	170.1	167.5	225.8	258.5	310.4	...	...	...	...	...

Martinique

1.10 Gross Domestic Product by Kind of Activity, in Current Prices
(Continued)

Million French francs

	1970	1975	1978	1979	1980	1981	1982	1983	1984	1985	1986	1987
6 Wholesale and retail trade, restaurants and hotels	...	599.3	841.2	990.8	1037.3	1196.3	1478.2	...	...	...	...	...
7 Transport, storage and communication	...	105.0	147.7	199.6	220.3	269.2	372.5	...	...	...	...	...
8 Finance, insurance, real estate and business services	...	282.1	491.5	556.0	427.8	627.6	762.6	...	...	...	...	...
9 Community, social and personal services	...	398.0	703.1	812.6	1118.4	1288.9	1512.9	...	...	...	...	...
Total, Industries	...	2187.1	3210.9	3564.0	3803.9	4679.2	5745.2	...	...	...	...	...
Producers of Government Services	...	991.5	1500.0	1682.7	1985.6	2254.4	2712.8	...	...	...	...	...
Other Producers	...	51.4	95.3	104.6	115.4	137.4	162.0	...	...	...	...	...
Subtotal	1505.2	3230.0	4806.2	5351.3	5904.9	7071.0	8620.0	...	...	...	...	...
Less: Imputed bank service charge	45.0	116.0	196.4	231.7	308.6	418.0	479.8	...	...	...	...	...
Plus: Import duties	77.0	113.3	174.3	205.6	247.5	284.2	344.5	...	...	...	...	...
Plus: Value added tax	63.3	130.2	186.6	212.9	257.8	307.8	389.5	...	...	...	...	...
Equals: Gross Domestic Product	1600.5	3357.5	4970.7	5538.1	6101.6	7245.0	8874.2	10114.3	11019.7	12576.9	...	...

1.12 Relations Among National Accounting Aggregates

Million French francs

	1970	1975	1978	1979	1980	1981	1982	1983	1984	1985	1986	1987
Gross Domestic Product	1600.5	3357.5	4970.7	5538.0	6101.6	7245.0	8874.2	10114.3	11019.7	12576.9	...	...
Plus: Net factor income from the rest of the world	-22.3	-70.4	-98.4	-108.0	-99.2	-100.6	-121.3	...	...	...	...	...
Factor income from the rest of the world	8.9	18.4	60.0	74.9	114.2	174.7	201.0	...	...	...	...	...
Less: Factor income to the rest of the world	31.2	88.8	158.4	182.9	213.4	275.3	322.3	...	...	...	...	...
Equals: Gross National Product	1578.2	3287.1	4872.3	5430.0	6002.4	7144.4	8752.9	...	...	...	...	...
Less: Consumption of fixed capital	...	...	...	...	...	...	...	...	...	...	...	...
Equals: National Income	...	...	...	...	...	...	...	...	...	...	...	...
Plus: Net current transfers from the rest of the world	549.4	1206.4	1748.8	2073.2	2555.7	2920.1	3434.4	...	...	...	...	...
Current transfers from the rest of the world	565.5	1224.3	1798.0	2131.4	2636.6	3024.9	3552.3	...	...	...	...	...
Less: Current transfers to the rest of the world	16.1	17.9	49.2	58.2	80.9	104.8	117.9	...	...	...	...	...
Equals: National Disposable Income	...	...	...	...	...	...	...	...	...	...	...	...
Less: Final consumption	1884.9	3855.0	5880.1	6811.7	7773.6	9117.4	11079.2	...	...	...	...	...
Equals: Net Saving	...	...	...	...	...	...	...	...	...	...	...	...
Less: Surplus of the nation on current transactions	-123.8	70.8	-54.3	-336.1	-639.3	-513.3	-590.5	...	...	...	...	...
Equals: Net Capital Formation	...	...	...	...	...	...	...	...	...	...	...	...

Mauritania

Source. Reply to the United Nations National Accounts Questionnaire from the Direction de la Statistique et des Etudes Economiques, Ministere de la Planification et du Developpement Industriel, Nouakchott. The official estimates are published annually in 'Comptes Economiques'.

General note. The estimates shown in the following tables have been prepared in accordance with the United Nations System of National Accounts so far as the existing data would permit.

1.1 Expenditure on the Gross Domestic Product, in Current Prices

Million Mauritanian ouguiyas

		1970	1975	1978	1979	1980	1981	1982	1983	1984	1985	1986	1987
1	Government final consumption expenditure	1853	5060	9370	9523	9183	9224	9885	10127	10189	...	...	...
2	Private final consumption expenditure	5998	11652	17407	22126	28504	32381	30733	32214	33180	...	...	...
3	Gross capital formation	2559	9144	6713	8078	10200	15925	18708	19682	16280	...	...	...
	A Increase in stocks	220	2128	2673	2172	2400	6353	8108	8317	1580	...	...	...
	B Gross fixed capital formation	2339	7016	4040	5906	7800	9572	10600	11365	14700	...	...	...
4	Exports of goods and services	4760	7986	7421	8821	11566	12128	15434	18820	18821	...	...	...
5	Less: Imports of goods and services	3840	13247	16003	17648	21383	26419	32091	34922	33970	...	...	...
	Equals: Gross Domestic Product [a]	11330	20595	24908	30853	38070	43239	42669	45921	44500	...	...	...

a) Data in this table have been revised, therefore they are not strictly comparable with the unrevised data in the other tables.

1.7 External Transactions on Current Account, Summary

Million Mauritanian ouguiyas

		1970	1975	1978	1979	1980	1981	1982	1983	1984	1985	1986	1987
	Payments to the Rest of the World												
1	Imports of goods and services	...	13247	16003	17648	21383	26419	32091	32549	32644	...	...	...
	A Imports of merchandise c.i.f.	...	8987	12048	13117	14751	18653	22083	20732	19276	...	...	...
	B Other	...	4260	3955	4531	6632	7766	10008	11817	13368	...	...	...
2	Factor income to the rest of the world	...	262	922	1049	1023	2076	1874	2373	1325	...	...	...
	A Compensation of employees	...	7	12	15	18	16	15	17	10	...	...	...
	B Property and entrepreneurial income	...	255	910	1034	1005	2060	1859	2356	1315	...	...	...
3	Current transfers to the rest of the world	...	1344	1523	1987	2202	1509	2155	1938	1904	...	...	...
4	Surplus of the nation on current transactions	...	-2781	-3295	-4485	-6171	-10747	-14348	-11690	-7534	...	...	...
	Payments to the Rest of the World and Surplus of the Nation on Current Transactions	...	12072	15153	16199	18437	19257	21772	25170	28339	...	...	...
	Receipts From The Rest of the World												
1	Exports of goods and services	...	7986	7421	8821	11566	12128	15434	20241	20567	...	...	...
	A Exports of merchandise f.o.b.	...	7212	5474	6754	9013	9411	12426	17286	18745	...	...	...
	B Other	...	774	1947	2067	2553	2717	3008	2955	1822	...	...	...
2	Factor income from rest of the world	...	232	180	558	815	1018	1008	550	595	...	...	...
	A Compensation of employees	...	17	35	40	46	46	50	50	55	...	...	...
	B Property and entrepreneurial income	...	215	145	518	769	972	958	500	540	...	...	...
3	Current transfers from rest of the world	...	3854	7552	6820	6056	6111	5330	4929	7177	...	...	...
	Receipts from the Rest of the World on Current Transactions	...	12072	15153	16199	18437	19257	21772	25170	28339	...	...	...

1.10 Gross Domestic Product by Kind of Activity, in Current Prices

Million Mauritanian ouguiyas

		1970	1975	1978	1979	1980	1981	1982	1983	1984	1985	1986	1987
1	Agriculture, hunting, forestry and fishing	3114	5137	6131	8769	12262	15223	13028	11982	8564	...	...	...
2	Mining and quarrying	2810	4028	2476	3079	4505	4831	5342	4369	4426	...	...	...
3	Manufacturing	525	918	1444	1615	1997	2337	2408	3685	3808	...	...	...
4	Electricity, gas and water										...	...	...
5	Construction	700	1114	1179	1929	2314	2726	2888	3175	3505	...	...	...
6	Wholesale and retail trade, restaurants and hotels	660	2239	2533	2968	3424	3100	3834	4708	5688	...	...	...
7	Transport, storage and communication	605	966	1940	2371	2584	2710	3007	3179	3188	...	...	...
8	Finance, insurance, real estate and business services	927	1416	2078	2350	2632	2500	2500	2585	2685	...	...	...
9	Community, social and personal services										...	...	...

Mauritania

1.10 Gross Domestic Product by Kind of Activity, in Current Prices
(Continued)

Million Mauritanian ouguiyas

	1970	1975	1978	1979	1980	1981	1982	1983	1984	1985	1986	1987
Total, Industries	9341	15818	17781	23081	29718	33427	33007	33683	31864	...	...	...
Producers of Government Services	1297	3059	5165	5616	5943	6938	6166	7720	7800	...	...	...
Other Producers	...	...	...	...	...	...	...	...	...	...	...	...
Subtotal [a]	10638	18877	22946	28697	35661	40365	39173	41403	39664	...	...	...
Less: Imputed bank service charge	...	...	...	...	...	...	...	...	...	...	...	...
Plus: Import duties	...	...	...	...	...	...	...	...	...	...	...	...
Plus: Value added tax	...	...	...	...	...	...	...	...	...	...	...	...
Plus: Other adjustments [b]	692	1718	1962	2156	2409	2874	3496	4518	4836	...	...	...
Equals: Gross Domestic Product [c]	11330	20595	24908	30853	38070	43239	42669	45921	44500	...	...	...

a) Gross domestic product in factor values.
b) Item 'Other adjustments' refers to indirect taxes net of subsidies.
c) Data in this table have been revised, therefore they are not strictly comparable with the unrevised data in the other tables.

1.11 Gross Domestic Product by Kind of Activity, in Constant Prices

Million Mauritanian ouguiyas

	1970	1975	1978	1979	1980	1981	1982	1983	1984	1985	1986	1987
					At constant prices of:1973							
1 Agriculture, hunting, forestry and fishing	4653	3743	3287	3528	3317	4464	3884	3398	2743	...	...	...
2 Mining and quarrying	2930	2471	1548	1866	2189	2336	2115	2127	2129	...	...	...
3 Manufacturing	720	712	902	1011	997	1297	1216	1412	1403	...	...	...
4 Electricity, gas and water										...	...	...
5 Construction	917	779	674	1037	1157	1250	1162	1280	1300	...	...	...
6 Wholesale and retail trade, restaurants and hotels	824	1722	1490	1604	1712	1670	1706	1803	1812	...	...	...
7 Transport, storage and communication	755	732	965	1270	1119	1320	1310	1325	1358	...	...	...
8 Finance, insurance, real estate and business services	1157	1089	1222	1270	1316	...	...	...	...	...	...	...
9 Community, social and personal services												
Total, Industries	11956	11248	10088	10715	11807							
Producers of Government Services	961	2683	3689	3694	3552	3304	2680	3027	3037	...	...	...
Other Producers	...	...	...	...	...	...	...	...	...	...	...	...
Subtotal [a]	12917	13931	13777	15280	15359	15641	14070	14372	13782	...	...	...
Less: Imputed bank service charge	...	...	...	...	...	...	...	...	...	...	...	...
Plus: Import duties	...	...	...	...	...	...	...	...	...	...	...	...
Plus: Value added tax	...	...	...	...	...	...	...	...	...	...	...	...
Plus: Other adjustments [b]	...	1507	1401	1418	1456	1844	2076	2179	2110	...	...	...
Equals: Gross Domestic Product [c]	12917	15438	15178	16698	16815	17485	16149	16551	15892	...	...	...

a) Gross domestic product in factor values.
b) Item 'Other adjustments' refers to indirect taxes net of subsidies.
c) Data in this table have been revised, therefore they are not strictly comparable with the unrevised data in the other tables.

1.12 Relations Among National Accounting Aggregates

Million Mauritanian ouguiyas

	1970	1975	1978	1979	1980	1981	1982	1983	1984	1985	1986	1987
Gross Domestic Product	11330	20595	24908	30853	38070	43239	42669	45921	44500	...	...	...
Plus: Net factor income from the rest of the world	...	-30	-742	-491	-208	-1058	-866	-1823	-730	...	...	...
Factor income from the rest of the world	...	232	180	25	815	1018	1008	550	595	...	...	...
Less: Factor income to the rest of the world	...	262	922	541	1023	2076	1874	2373	1325	...	...	...
Equals: Gross National Product	...	20565	24166	30362	37862	42181	41803	44098	43770	...	...	...
Less: Consumption of fixed capital	...	...	...	...	...	...	...	...	...	...	...	...
Equals: National Income [a]	...	20565	24166	30362	37862	42181	41803	44098	43770	...	...	...
Plus: Net current transfers from the rest of the world	...	2510	6029	4833	3854	4602	3175	2991	5273	...	...	...
Current transfers from the rest of the world					6056	6111	5330	4929	7177	...	...	...
Less: Current transfers to the rest of the world	...	...	...	...	2202	1509	2155	1938	1904	...	...	...
Equals: National Disposable Income [b]	...	23075	30195	35195	41716	46783	44978	47089	49043	...	...	...
Less: Final consumption	...	...	...	...	...	...	...	...	...	...	...	...
Equals: Net Saving	...	...	...	...	...	...	...	...	...	...	...	...
Less: Surplus of the nation on current transactions	...	...	...	...	...	...	...	...	...	...	...	...
Equals: Net Capital Formation	...	...	...	...	...	...	...	...	...	...	...	...

a) Item 'National income' includes consumption of fixed capital.
b) Item 'National disposable income' includes consumption of fixed capital.

Mauritania

2.1 Government Final Consumption Expenditure by Function, in Current Prices

Million Mauritanian ouguiyas

	1970	1975	1978	1979	1980	1981	1982	1983	1984	1985	1986	1987
1 General public services	...	1285.7	...	...	...	...	...	...	...	...	...	...
2 Defence	...	439.9	...	...	...	...	...	...	...	...	...	...
3 Public order and safety	...		...	...	...	...	...	...	...	...	...	...
4 Education	...	598.0	...	...	...	...	...	...	...	...	...	...
5 Health	...	191.7	...	...	...	...	...	...	...	...	...	...
6 Social security and welfare	...	29.1	...	...	...	...	...	...	...	...	...	...
7 Housing and community amenities	...	-	...	...	...	...	...	...	...	...	...	...
8 Recreational, cultural and religious affairs	...	145.5	...	...	...	...	...	...	...	...	...	...
9 Economic services	...	320.7	...	...	...	...	...	...	...	...	...	...
10 Other functions	...	2187.4	...	...	...	...	...	...	...	...	...	...
Total Government Final Consumption Expenditure	...	5198.0	...	...	...	...	...	...	...	...	...	...

2.17 Exports and Imports of Goods and Services, Detail

Million Mauritanian ouguiyas

	1970	1975	1978	1979	1980	1981	1982	1983	1984	1985	1986	1987
Exports of Goods and Services												
1 Exports of merchandise, f.o.b.	...	7212	5474	6754	9013	9411	12426	17286	18745	...	...	...
2 Transport and communication	...	207	578	736	725	1001	1046	566	559	...	...	...
A In respect of merchandise imports	...	66	2	6	1	-	-	-	-	...	...	...
B Other	...	141	576	730	724	1001	1046	566	559	...	...	...
3 Insurance service charges	...	...	...	...	...	...	...	...	...	...	...	...
4 Other commodities	...	136	247	48	99	435	693	922	593	...	...	...
5 Adjustments of merchandise exports to change-of-ownership basis	...	-	-	-	...	...	...	...	...	...	...	...
6 Direct purchases in the domestic market by non-residential households	...	207	845	1039	1420	960	840	519	670	...	...	...
7 Direct purchases in the domestic market by extraterritorial bodies	...	244	277	244	309	321	429	382	439	...	...	...
Total Exports of Goods and Services	4760	7986	7421	8821	11566	12128	15434	20241	20567	...	...	...
Imports of Goods and Services												
1 Imports of merchandise, c.i.f.	...	8987	12048	13117	14751	18653	22083	20732	19276	...	...	...
A Imports of merchandise, f.o.b.	...	8987	12048	13117	14751	18653	22083	20732	19276	...	...	...
B Transport of services on merchandise imports	...	...	...	...	...	...	...	...	...	...	...	...
C Insurance service charges on merchandise imports	...	...	...	...	...	...	...	...	...	...	...	...
2 Adjustments of merchandise imports to change-of-ownership basis	...	...	...	...	...	...	...	...	...	...	...	...
3 Other transport and communication	...	1861	1728	2184	3862	4693	4937	6137	6421	...	...	...
4 Other insurance service charges	...				...					...	...	...
5 Other commodities	...	1827	1247	1395	1584	2145	3617	4366	5194	...	...	...
6 Direct purchases abroad by government	...	185	504	445	587	245	497	354	791	...	...	...
7 Direct purchases abroad by resident households	...	396	476	507	599	683	957	960	962	...	...	...
Total Imports of Goods and Services	3840	13247	16003	17648	21383	26419	32091	32549	32644	...	...	...
Balance of Goods and Services	920	-5261	-8582	-8827	...	...	...	...	...	...	...	...
Total Imports and Balance of Goods and Services	4760	7986	7421	8821	...	...	...	...	...	...	...	...

Mauritius

General note. The preparation of national accounts statistics in Mauritius is undertaken by the Central statistical Office, Rose Hill. The official estimates are published periodically in 'National Accounts of Mauritius'. The following presentation on sources and methods is mainly based on information received from the central Statistical Office. The estimates are generally in accordance with the Clasifications and definitions recommended in the United Nations System of National Accounts (SNA). The following tables have been prepared from successive replies to the United Nations national accounts questionnaire. When the scope and coverage of the estimates differ for conceptual or statistical reasons from the definitions and classifications recommended in SNA, a footnote is indicated to the relevant tables.

Sources and methods:

(a) Gross domestic product. Gross domestic product is estimated mainly through the production approach.

(b) Expenditure on the gross domestic product. The expenditure approach is used to estimate government final consumption expenditure and exports and imports of goods and services. This approach, in combination with the commodity-flow approach is used to estimate gross fixed capital formation. The commodity-flow approach is used for private final consumption expenditure supplemented by the expenditure approach for expenditure on services. Government consumption expenditure is estimated on the basis of the annual financial reports of the government and the municipal and town councils. The sources of data for private expenditure on goods include the 1972 census of population, the annual trade reports of the Customs Department, the annual financial reports of the government and special surveys of wholesale and retail margins, costs and profits. Figures of imported goods are extracted and reclassified from the foreign trade statistics and added to the figures for local production, both valued at market prices. Expenditure on services and private expenditure abroad are estimated on the basis of data from financial reports of the government, the censuses, records of income Tax Office and annual reports of the Ministry of Education. Information of investment on new buildings is obtained from records of building permits issued, records of the municipal and town councils and from returns of industrial and building companies. Investment on plantations is estimated from the returns of agricultural concerns and reports of the Chamber of Agriculture and the Tobacco Board. For machinery and equipment, figures on imports are derived from the annual trade reports and returns from industrial firms. Charges for transport, trade margins and installation costs are added to the c.i.f. values. Domestic production figures are obtained from the annual returns of manufacturing firms. Estimates of exports and imports of goods and services are based on sources such as the annual trade reports of the Customs Department, monthly returns from banks, records of Post Office and balance-of-payments. GDP by expenditure type at constant prices has not been estimated since 1966.

(c) Cost-structure of the gross domestic product. Information on compensation of employees for large establishments of all sectors, except the sugar industry is available from questionnaires sent out in connexion with the census of production and income tax returns. For the sugar sector, detailed figures of payments in cash and in kind are supplied by all sugar estates with factories while figures from employment records, statutory wage rates and the quantity of canes produced are used for the remaining sugar industry. Wages and salaries for the public sector are obtained from a bi-annual survey of all government departments and ministries. Operating surplus is estimated through the use of questionnaires and income-tax statistics for the private sector and production accounts for the government sector. For consumption of fixed capital, all sugar estates with factories provide data on a replacement cost basis while for other capital goods, the estimates are based on expected lifetime. Data on indirect taxes and subsidies are obtained from government and municipal council records.

(d) Gross domestic product by kind of economic activity. The table of GDP by kind of economic activity is prepared in factor values. The production approach is used to estimate value added of most industries. The income approach is used for some private services and for public administration and defence. For the agricultural sector, estimates are made on an item-by-item basis using annual statistical returns, annual surveys and reports supplemented by direct inquiries among producers and distributors. Sources used for sugar production are reports of the Chamber of Agriculture and financial statements of the Mauritius Sugar Syndicate. The estimates for mining and quarrying refer only to salt production and sand quarries and are provided directly by the concerned enterprises. The estimates for manufacturing are obtained through similar methods as those used for the agricultural sector. For sugar and related products, data are obtained from returns furnished by the factories and distilleries, reports and statistics of the Chamber of Agriculture and financial statements of the Mauritius Sugar Syndicate. The estimates of electricity and water are based on information provided by the concerned enterprises and the financial reports of the government. Information on private construction is obtained from records of building permits issued and from the municipal and town councils. Information furnished by the building contractors and financial reports of the government are used for public construction. For trade, information is obtained from the Income Tax Office and from imports and local production statistics. Special questionnaires on receipts and expenditure are sent to large hotel and restaurant enterprises as well as to large transport enterprises. Informatiom on public transport is available from the Accountant-General's records. For the financial sector, the most important sources are the Central Bank, income-tax returns of commercial banks and annual reports of the Registrar of insurance Companies. Special questionnaires are also sent to insurance companies. The estimates for ownership of dwellings are based on the 1972 census of population and records of building permits issued. For public administration and defence, detailed information is available from treasury records. For the private services, information is obtained from the population census and special questionnaires sent to large enterprises. For the constant price estimates, current values are generally deflated by appropriate price indexes. In cases where production is homogeneous, e.g. Sugar production value added is extrapolated by volume indexes.

1.1 Expenditure on the Gross Domestic Product, in Current Prices

Million Mauritius rupees	1970	1975	1978	1979	1980	1981	1982	1983	1984	1985	1986	1987
1 Government final consumption expenditure	166	443	933	1009	1224	1422	1624	1706	1835	1915	2068	2480
2 Private final consumption expenditure	734	1878	4174	5144	6562	7269	8301	8874	9841	11118	12000	13930
3 Gross capital formation	145	1138	1923	2385	1803	2578	2130	2229	3165	3900	4320	5970
A Increase in stocks	...	...	153	420	-225	338	30	-71	570	800	430	880
B Gross fixed capital formation	145	1138	1770	1965	2028	2240	2100	2300	2595	3100	3890	5090
Residential buildings	33	264	588	718	685	730	735	700	740	730	775	850
Non-residential buildings	23	201	264	235	223	248	245	277	350	635	660	800
Other construction and land improvement etc.	40	180	319	345	327	402	480	527	495	425	635	715
Other	49	493	599	667	793	860	640	796	1010	1310	1820	2725
4 Exports of goods and services	22	2184	2705	3260	4450	4566	5529	5953	6989	8895	11919	15745
5 Less: Imports of goods and services		2227	3477	4158	5342	5626	5859	5999	7470	9210	10607	15140
Equals: Gross Domestic Product [a]	1067	3416	6258	7640	8697	10209	11725	12763	14360	16618	19700	22985

a) Data in this table have been revised, therefore they are not strictly comparable with the unrevised data in the other tables.

Mauritius

1.2 Expenditure on the Gross Domestic Product, in Constant Prices

Million Mauritius rupees

	1970	1975	1978	1979	1980	1981	1982	1983	1984	1985	1986	1987
			\multicolumn{5}{c}{At constant prices of: 1976}	\multicolumn{6}{c}{1982}					
1 Government final consumption expenditure	...	...	695	682	688	713	727 / 1624	1665	1727	1727	1755	1880
2 Private final consumption expenditure	...	...	3210	3240	3059	2965	3071 / 8301	8463	8844	9295	9835	11310
3 Gross capital formation	...	...	1608	1685	988	1213	908 / 2130	2097	2520	2690	3565	5466
A Increase in stocks	...	...	138	308	-132	173	14 / 30	-70	220	160	530	1681
B Gross fixed capital formation	...	...	1470	1377	1120	1040	894 / 2100	2167	2300	2530	3035	3785
Residential buildings	...	...	500	517	418	382	348 / 735	667	662	631	650	685
Non-residential buildings	...	...	220	165	130	120	107 / 245	263	311	540	545	630
Other construction and land improvement etc.	...	...	265	238	185	189	204 / 480	502	445	364	520	560
Other	...	...	485	457	387	349	235 / 640	735	882	995	1320	1910
4 Exports of goods and services	...	...	2701	2790	2843	2701	2971 / 5529	5580	5810	6554	8736	10826
5 Less: Imports of goods and services	...	...	3010	3010	2733	2462	2265 / 5859	6035	6578	7081	9381	13392
Equals: Gross Domestic Product	...	...	5204	5387	4845	5130	5412 / 11725a	11770a	12323a	13185a	14510a	16090a

a) Data in this table have been revised, therefore they are not strictly comparable with the unrevised data in the other tables.

1.3 Cost Components of the Gross Domestic Product

Million Mauritius rupees

	1970	1975	1978	1979	1980	1981	1982	1983	1984	1985	1986	1987
1 Indirect taxes, net	155	326	... / 764	1100	1308	1444	1705	2150	2310	2738	3250	3900
A Indirect taxes	155	359	... / 825	1136	1326	1455	1717	2180	2355	2784	3348	4054
B Less: Subsidies	-	33	... / 61	36	18	11	12	30	45	46	98	154
2 Consumption of fixed capital a	...	...	...	...	...	...	...	...	...	...	...	...
3 Compensation of employees paid by resident producers to:	516	1568	... / 3046	3470	3953	4482	4972	5400	5915	6570	7365	8675
4 Operating surplus a	396	1522	... / 2448	3070	3436	4283	5048	5213	6135	7310	9085	10410
Equals: Gross Domestic Product b	1067	3416	... / 6258	7640	8697	10209	11725	12763	14360	16618	19700	22985

a) Item 'Operating surplus' includes consumption of fixed capital.
b) Data in this table have been revised, therefore they are not strictly comparable with the unrevised data in the other tables.

1.4 General Government Current Receipts and Disbursements

Million Mauritius rupees

	1970	1975	1978	1979	1980	1981	1982	1983	1984	1985	1986	1987
			\multicolumn{10}{c}{Receipts}									
1 Operating surplus	...	...	...	...	...	23	43	62	67	92	98	115
2 Property and entrepreneurial income	13	46	80	106	125	129	176	180	135	303	328	404
3 Taxes, fees and contributions	205	957	1205	1615	1845	2193	2492	3042	3263	3754	4474	5516
A Indirect taxes	155	359	826	1136	1326	1455	1717	2180	2355	2784	3347	4054
B Direct taxes	50	598	354	367	379	464	457	509	529	545	650	918
C Social security contributions	...	...	9	90	115	248	287	322	344	387	423	478
D Compulsory fees, fines and penalties	...	...	16	22	25	26	31	31	35	38	54	66
4 Other current transfers	8	62	...	1	3	14	72	29	51	30	30	30
Total Current Receipts of General Government	226	1065	1285	1722	1973	2359	2783	3313	3516	4179	4930	6065

Mauritius

1.4 General Government Current Receipts and Disbursements
(Continued)

Million Mauritius rupees

	1970	1975	1978	1979	1980	1981	1982	1983	1984	1985	1986	1987
Disbursements												
1 Government final consumption expenditure	166	443	933	1009	1224	1422	1624	1706	1835	1915	2068	2480
A Compensation of employees	...	...	774	872	1043	1242	1421	1471	1522	1598	1718	2037
B Consumption of fixed capital	...	...	...	...	...	...	...	...	...	...	...	...
C Purchases of goods and services, net	...	...	159	137	180	180	203	235	313	317	350	443
D Less: Own account fixed capital formation	...	...	...	...	...	...	...	...	...	...	...	...
E Indirect taxes paid, net	...	...	...	...	...	...	...	...	...	...	...	...
2 Property income	...	...	133	253	332	410	866	759	848	929	965	913
3 Subsidies	1	33	61	36	18	11	12	30	45	46	98	154
4 Other current transfers	37	345	388	481	478	659	825	860	774	880	880	995
A Social security benefits [a]	...	...	...	...	...	...	328	389	449	503	563	630	705
B Social assistance grants	...	...	...	...	...	...						
C Other	...	...	...	...	...	...	331	436	411	271	317	250	290
Statistical discrepancy	...	75	...	...	...	...	...	...	...	...	...	...
5 Net saving	22	169	-230	-57	-79	-143	-544	-42	14	409	919	1523
Total Current Disbursements and Net Saving of General Government	226	1065	1285	1722	1973	2359	2783	3313	3516	4179	4930	6065

a) Item 'Social security benefits' includes unfounded employee welfare benefits.

1.5 Current Income and Outlay of Corporate and Quasi-Corporate Enterprises, Summary

Million Mauritius rupees

	1970	1975	1978	1979	1980	1981	1982	1983	1984	1985	1986	1987
Receipts												
1 Operating surplus	...	...	...	...	...	...	2067	1925	2522	3125	4442	...
2 Property and entrepreneurial income received	...	...	...	...	...	...	666	699	740	1156	1313	...
3 Current transfers	...	...	...	...	...	...	346	396	472	436	441	...
Total Current Receipts	...	...	...	...	...	...	3079	3020	3734	4717	6196	...
Disbursements												
1 Property and entrepreneurial income	...	...	...	...	...	...	777	923	1049	1604	1923	...
2 Direct taxes and other current payments to general government	...	...	...	...	...	...	181	204	188	233	327	...
3 Other current transfers	...	...	...	...	...	...	302	363	462	371	339	...
4 Net saving	...	...	...	...	...	...	1819	1530	2035	2509	3607	...
Total Current Disbursements and Net Saving	...	...	...	...	...	...	3079	3020	3734	4717	6196	...

1.6 Current Income and Outlay of Households and Non-Profit Institutions

Million Mauritius rupees

	1970	1975	1978	1979	1980	1981	1982	1983	1984	1985	1986	1987
Receipts												
1 Compensation of employees	516	1568	...	...	...	...	4972	5400	5915	6570	7365	...
2 Operating surplus of private unincorporated enterprises	...	...	...	...	...	...	2939	3227	3546	4093	4545	...
3 Property and entrepreneurial income	256	832	...	...	...	...	419	473	576	629	778	...
4 Current transfers	46	271	...	...	...	...	1052	1156	1162	1333	1384	...
A Social security benefits [a]	...	...	...	...	...	...	389	449	503	563	630	...
B Social assistance grants	...	...	...	...	...	...						...
C Other	...	...	...	...	...	...	663	707	659	770	754	...
Statistical discrepancy	...	-9	...	...	...	...	...	...	...	...	...	...
Total Current Receipts	818	2662	...	...	...	...	9382	10256	11199	12625	14072	...

Mauritius

1.6 Current Income and Outlay of Households and Non-Profit Institutions
(Continued)

Million Mauritius rupees

		1970	1975	1978	1979	1980	1981	1982	1983	1984	1985	1986	1987
					Disbursements								
1	Private final consumption expenditure	734	1832	...	...	...	...	8301	8874	9891	11118	12000	...
2	Property income	...	...	...	...	...	...	110	161	180	255	260	...
3	Direct taxes and other current transfers n.e.c. to general government	30	135	...	...	...	...	595	658	720	737	799	...
	A Social security contributions	...	...	...	...	...	...	287	322	344	387	422	...
	B Direct taxes	...	...	...	...	...	...	283	311	348	320	334	...
	C Fees, fines and penalties	...	...	...	...	...	...	25	25	28	30	43	...
4	Other current transfers	6	8	...	...	...	...	122	147	146	194	217	...
5	Net saving	48	687	...	...	...	...	254	416	262	321	796	...
	Total Current Disbursements and Net Saving	818	2662	...	...	...	...	9382	10256	11199	12625	14072	...

a) Item 'Social security benefits' includes unfounded employee welfare benefits.

1.7 External Transactions on Current Account, Summary

Million Mauritius rupees

		1970	1975	1978	1979	1980	1981	1982	1983	1984	1985	1986	1987
				Payments to the Rest of the World									
1	Imports of goods and services	515	2227	3477	4158	5342	5626	5859	5999	7470	9210	10608	15141
	A Imports of merchandise c.i.f.	414	1965	3051	3602	4661	4922	5008	5164	6528	8083	9292	13113
	B Other	101	262	426	556	681	704	851	835	942	1127	1315	2028
2	Factor income to the rest of the world	12	45	83	130	216	470	541	514	666	730	805	713
	A Compensation of employees	-	-	-	-	-	-	-	-	-	-	-	-
	B Property and entrepreneurial income	12	45	83	130	216	470	541	514	666	730	805	713
3	Current transfers to the rest of the world	10	23	30	47	60	64	53	80	75	76	85	118
4	Surplus of the nation on current transactions	42	127	-735	-927	-911	-1321	-457	-237	-716	-459	1253	914
	Payments to the Rest of the World and Surplus of the Nation on Current Transactions	579	2422	2855	3408	4707	4839	5996	6356	7495	9557	12750	16886
				Receipts From The Rest of the World									
1	Exports of goods and services	531	2268	2705	3259	4450	4566	5529	5953	6989	8895	11919	15745
	A Exports of merchandise f.o.b.	388	1848	1969	2427	3332	2999	3985	4346	5201	6639	9056	11599
	B Other	143	420	736	832	1118	1567	1544	1607	1788	2256	2863	4146
2	Factor income from rest of the world	17	61	35	24	38	62	43	29	40	30	76	180
	A Compensation of employees	-	1	-	-	-	-	-	-	-	-	-	-
	B Property and entrepreneurial income	17	60	35	24	38	62	43	29	40	30	76	180
3	Current transfers from rest of the world	31	93	115	125	219	211	424	374	466	632	755	961
	Receipts from the Rest of the World on Current Transactions [a]	579	2422	2855	3408	4707	4839	5996	6356	7495	9557	12750	16886

a) Data in this table have been revised, therefore they are not strictly comparable with the unrevised data in the other tables.

1.10 Gross Domestic Product by Kind of Activity, in Current Prices

Million Mauritius rupees

		1970	1975	1978	1979	1980	1981	1982	1983	1984	1985	1986	1987
1	Agriculture, hunting, forestry and fishing	222	1034	977	1224	914	1257	1530	1465	1736	2123	2510	2830
2	Mining and quarrying	1	4	11	12	15	16	17	18	19	20	22	25
3	Manufacturing	146	564	801	972	1127	1377	1560	1678	2183	2864	3830	4605
4	Electricity, gas and water	29	69	118	161	209	188	260	245	296	397	462	490
5	Construction	48	217	506	552	561	588	625	655	690	775	880	1000

Mauritius

1.10 Gross Domestic Product by Kind of Activity, in Current Prices
(Continued)

Million Mauritius rupees

	1970	1975	1978	1979	1980	1981	1982	1983	1984	1985	1986	1987
6 Wholesale and retail trade, restaurants and hotels	91	279	630	779	1050	1219	1290	1455	1640	1834	2300	2930
7 Transport, storage and communication	108	281	563	653	837	997	1112	1230	1372	1510	1775	2035
8 Finance, insurance, real estate and business services	90	160	981	1139	1416	1635	1883	2044	2232	2446	2641	2815
9 Community, social and personal services	126	342	251	303	361	442	525	569	593	624	646	722
Total, Industries	861	2950	4838	5795	6490	7719	8802	9359	10761	12593	15066	17452
Producers of Government Services	51	140	705	793	952	1104	1275	1327	1379	1447	1560	1840
Other Producers	...	...	39	46	54	60	71	81	92	96	130	133
Subtotal [a]	912	3090	5582	6634	7496	8883	10148	10767	12232	14136	16756	19425
Less: Imputed bank service charge	...	...	88	94	107	118	128	154	182	256	306	340
Plus: Import duties	...	...	...	...	...	...	...	...	...	...	...	...
Plus: Value added tax	...	...	...	...	...	...	...	...	...	...	...	...
Plus: Other adjustments [b]	155	326	764	1100	1308	1444	1705	2150	2310	2738	3250	3900
Equals: Gross Domestic Product [c]	1067	3416	6258	7640	8697	10209	11725	12763	14360	16618	19700	22985

a) Gross domestic product in factor values.
b) Item 'Other adjustments' refers to indirect taxes net of subsidies.
c) Data in this table have been revised, therefore they are not strictly comparable with the unrevised data in the other tables.

1.11 Gross Domestic Product by Kind of Activity, in Constant Prices

Million Mauritius rupees

	1970	1975	1978	1979	1980	1981	1982	1983	1984	1985	1986	1987
			At constant prices of: 1976					1982				
1 Agriculture, hunting, forestry and fishing	...	...	939	977	643	784	936 / 1530	1331	1341	1492	1652	1614
2 Mining and quarrying	...	...	7	7	7	7	7 / 17	17	17	17	18	19
3 Manufacturing	...	...	717	754	701	762	802 / 1560	1576	1768	2038	2450	2795
4 Electricity, gas and water	...	...	89	97	97	97	117 / 250	243	267	315	343	360
5 Construction	...	...	400	370	307	292	280 / 625	633	646	698	768	834
6 Wholesale and retail trade, restaurants and hotels	...	...	538	582	558	568	542 / 1290	1373	1455	1527	1677	2010
7 Transport, storage and communication	...	...	431	437	423	434	454 / 1112	1151	1209	1260	1345	1465
8 Finance, insurance, real estate and business services	...	...	734	763	761	794	831 / 1765	1812	1872	1935	1993	2070
9 Community, social and personal services	...	...	231	252	252	265	286 / 596	627	646	652	675	710
Total, Industries	...	...	4086	4239	3749	4003	4255 / 8745	8763	9221	9934	10921	11877
Producers of Government Services	...	...	547	563	569	591	604 / 1275	1300	1320	1330	1343	1383
Other Producers	...	...	...	...	...	...	...	...	...	...	...	...
Subtotal [a]	...	...	4633	4802	4318	4594	4859 / 10020	10063	10541	11264	12264	13260
Less: Imputed bank service charge	...	...	...	...	...	...	...	...	...	...	...	...
Plus: Import duties	...	...	...	...	...	...	...	...	...	...	...	...
Plus: Value added tax	...	...	...	...	...	...	...	...	...	...	...	...
Plus: Other adjustments [b]	...	...	571	585	527	536	553 / 1705	1707	1782	1921	2246	2830
Equals: Gross Domestic Product	...	...	5204	5387	4845	5130	5412 / 11725[c]	11770[c]	12323[c]	13185[c]	14510[c]	16090[c]

a) Gross domestic product in factor values.
b) Item 'Other adjustments' refers to indirect taxes net of subsidies.
c) Data in this table have been revised, therefore they are not strictly comparable with the unrevised data in the other tables.

Mauritius

1.12 Relations Among National Accounting Aggregates

Million Mauritius rupees

	1970	1975	1978	1979	1980	1981	1982	1983	1984	1985	1986	1987
Gross Domestic Product	1067	3416	6258	7640	8697	10209	11725	12763	14360	16618	19700	22985
Plus: Net factor income from the rest of the world	7	17	-48	-106	-178	-408	-498	-485	-626	-700	-729	-533
Factor income from the rest of the world	...	...	35	24	38	62	43	29	40	30	76	180
Less: Factor income to the rest of the world	...	...	83	130	216	470	541	514	666	730	805	713
Equals: Gross National Product	1074	3433	6210	7534	8519	9801	11227	12278	13734	15918	18971	22452
Less: Consumption of fixed capital	...	...	...	...	...	...	...	...	...	...	...	...
Equals: National Income [a][b]	1074	3433	6210	7534	8519	9801	11227	12278	13734	15918	18971	22452
Plus: Net current transfers from the rest of the world	11	35	85	78	159	147	371	294	391	556	670	843
Current transfers from the rest of the world	...	...	115	125	219	211	424	374	466	632	755	961
Less: Current transfers to the rest of the world	...	...	30	47	60	64	53	80	75	76	85	118
Equals: National Disposable Income [c][b]	1085	3467	6295	7612	8678	9948	11598	12572	14125	16474	19641	23295
Less: Final consumption	900	2321	5107	6153	7786	8691	9925	10580	11676	13033	14068	16410
Equals: Net Saving [d]	185	1146	1188	1459	892	1257	1673	1992	2449	3441	5573	6885
Less: Surplus of the nation on current transactions	...	...	...	...	...	...	...	...	...	...	...	...
Equals: Net Capital Formation [b]	...	...	...	...	...	...	...	...	...	...	...	...

a) Item 'National income' includes consumption of fixed capital.
b) Data in this table have been revised, therefore they are not strictly comparable with the unrevised data in the other tables.
c) Item 'National disposable income' includes consumption of fixed capital.
d) Item 'Net saving' includes consumption of fixed capital.

2.1 Government Final Consumption Expenditure by Function, in Current Prices

Million Mauritius rupees

	1970	1975	1978	1979	1980	1981	1982	1983	1984	1985	1986	1987
1 General public services	...	...	152	142	147	173	208	215	254	298	329	...
2 Defence	...	...	-	-	22	27	34	34	42	38	42	...
3 Public order and safety	...	...	112	154	157	171	193	208	221	247	269	...
4 Education	...	...	211	232	299	349	384	435	419	440	480	...
5 Health	...	...	170	184	228	256	283	296	328	336	364	...
6 Social security and welfare	...	...	22	22	27	29	30	37	48	56	63	...
7 Housing and community amenities	...	...	77	80	84	90	105	116	105	72	81	...
8 Recreational, cultural and religious affairs	...	...	19	19	23	26	36	32	34	35	39	...
9 Economic services	...	...	170	176	237	301	351	333	384	393	408	...
A Fuel and energy	...	...	4	1	1	1	1	1	1	1	1	...
B Agriculture, forestry, fishing and hunting	...	...	52	53	82	88	135	123	145	169	180	...
C Mining, manufacturing and construction, except fuel and energy	...	...	75	85	108	160	172	167	172	164	172	...
D Transportation and communication	...	...	3	4	3	4	5	7	8	8	9	...
E Other economic affairs	...	...	36	33	43	48	38	35	58	51	46	...
10 Other functions	...	...	-	-	-	-	-	-	-	-	-	...
Total Government Final Consumption Expenditure	...	...	933	1009	1224	1422	1624	1706	1835	1915	2075	...

Mauritius

2.3 Total Government Outlays by Function and Type

Million Mauritius rupees

		Final Consumption Expenditures Total	Compensation of Employees	Other	Subsidies	Other Current Transfers & Property Income	Total Current Disbursements	Gross Capital Formation	Other Capital Outlays	Total Outlays
					1982					
1	General public services	208	141	67	4	9	221	...	...	...
2	Defence	34	28	6	-	-	34	...	...	...
3	Public order and safety	193	181	12	-	-	193	...	...	...
4	Education	384	368	16	-	130	514	...	...	...
5	Health	283	231	52	-	2	285	...	...	...
6	Social security and welfare	30	32	-2	-	392	422	...	...	...
7	Housing and community amenities	105	93	13	-	2	107	...	...	...
8	Recreation, culture and religion	36	30	6	3	5	44	...	...	...
9	Economic services	351	318	33	5	285	641	...	...	...
	A Fuel and energy	1	1	-	-	-	1	...	...	...
	B Agriculture, forestry, fishing and hunting	135	132	3	-	2	137	...	...	...
	C Mining (except fuels), manufacturing and construction	172	149	23	5	-	177	...	...	...
	D Transportation and communication	5	5	-	-	-	5	...	...	...
	E Other economic affairs	38	31	7	-	283	321	...	...	...
10	Other functions	-	-	-	-	866	866	...	...	...
	Total	1624	1421	203	12	1691	3327	...	...	...
					1983					
1	General public services	215	148	67	-	9	224	...	...	...
2	Defence	34	30	4	-	-	34	...	...	...
3	Public order and safety	208	187	21	-	-	208	...	...	...
4	Education	435	387	48	-	125	560	...	...	...
5	Health	296	238	58	-	1	297	...	...	...
6	Social security and welfare	37	37	-	-	452	489	...	...	...
7	Housing and community amenities	116	106	10	-	1	117	...	...	...
8	Recreation, culture and religion	32	25	7	3	6	41	...	...	...
9	Economic services	333	313	20	27	266	627	...	...	...
	A Fuel and energy	1	1	-	-	1	2	...	...	...
	B Agriculture, forestry, fishing and hunting	123	128	-5	15	7	146	...	...	...
	C Mining (except fuels), manufacturing and construction	167	145	22	8	-	175	...	...	...
	D Transportation and communication	7	7	-	4	-	11	...	...	...
	E Other economic affairs	35	32	3	-	258	293	...	...	...
10	Other functions	-	-	-	-	759	759	...	...	...
	Total	1706	1471	235	30	1619	3355	...	...	...
					1984					
1	General public services	254	162	92	-	18	272	...	...	...
2	Defence	42	31	11	-	-	42	...	...	...
3	Public order and safety	221	196	25	-	-	221	...	...	...
4	Education	419	393	26	-	144	563	...	...	...
5	Health	328	242	86	-	2	330	...	...	...
6	Social security and welfare	48	40	8	-	507	555	...	...	...
7	Housing and community amenities	105	96	9	-	9	114	...	...	...
8	Recreation, culture and religion	34	27	7	3	7	44	...	...	...
9	Economic services	384	335	49	42	87	513	...	...	...
	A Fuel and energy	1	1	-	-	1	2	...	...	...
	B Agriculture, forestry, fishing and hunting	145	148	-3	26	8	179	...	...	...
	C Mining (except fuels), manufacturing and construction	172	146	26	11	-	183	...	...	...
	D Transportation and communication	8	7	1	5	1	14	...	...	...
	E Other economic affairs	58	33	25	-	77	135	...	...	...
10	Other functions	-	-	-	-	848	848	...	...	...
	Total	1835	1522	313	45	1622	3502	...	...	...

Mauritius

2.3 Total Government Outlays by Function and Type
(Continued)

Million Mauritius rupees

	Final Consumption Expenditures Total	Compensation of Employees	Other	Subsidies	Other Current Transfers & Property Income	Total Current Disbursements	Gross Capital Formation	Other Capital Outlays	Total Outlays
1985									
1 General public services	298	195	103	-	10	308	...	...	...
2 Defence	38	31	7	-	-	38	...	...	...
3 Public order and safety	247	214	33	-	-	247	...	...	...
4 Education	440	414	26	-	147	587	...	...	...
5 Health	336	248	88	-	4	340	...	...	...
6 Social security and welfare	56	48	8	-	563	619	...	...	...
7 Housing and community amenities	72	70	2	9	1	82	...	...	...
8 Recreation, culture and religion	35	26	9	2	7	44	...	...	...
9 Economic services	393	352	41	35	148	576	...	...	...
A Fuel and energy	1	1	-	-	1	2	...	...	...
B Agriculture, forestry, fishing and hunting	169	161	8	24	4	197	...	...	...
C Mining (except fuels), manufacturing and construction	164	149	15	5	-	169	...	...	...
D Transportation and communication	8	7	1	6	5	19	...	...	...
E Other economic affairs	51	34	17	-	138	189	...	...	...
10 Other functions	-	-	-	-	929	929	...	...	...
Total	1915	1598	317	46	1809	3770	...	...	...
1986									
1 General public services	329	207	122	-	17	346	...	...	...
2 Defence	42	32	10	-	-	42	...	...	...
3 Public order and safety	269	233	36	-	-	269	...	...	...
4 Education	480	449	31	-	149	629	...	...	...
5 Health	364	272	92	-	3	367	...	...	...
6 Social security and welfare	63	51	12	-	603	666	...	...	...
7 Housing and community amenities	81	77	4	10	-	91	...	...	...
8 Recreation, culture and religion	39	27	12	2	7	48	...	...	...
9 Economic services	408	377	31	87	75	570	...	...	...
A Fuel and energy	1	1	-	-	2	3	...	...	...
B Agriculture, forestry, fishing and hunting	180	176	4	77	1	257	...	...	...
C Mining (except fuels), manufacturing and construction	172	159	13	5	-	177	...	...	...
D Transportation and communication	9	8	1	6	1	16	...	...	...
E Other economic affairs	46	33	13	-	71	117	...	...	...
10 Other functions	-	-	-	-	963	963	...	...	...
Total	2075	1725	350	100	1817	3992	...	...	...

2.7 Gross Capital Formation by Type of Good and Owner, in Current Prices

Million Mauritius rupees

	1980 TOTAL	Total Private	Public Enterprises	General Government	1981 TOTAL	Total Private	Public Enterprises	General Government	1982 TOTAL	Total Private	Public Enterprises	General Government
Increase in stocks, total	-225	...	...	...	338	...	...	...	30	...	...	...
Gross Fixed Capital Formation, Total	2028	1298	...	730	2240	1375	...	865	2100	1345	...	755
1 Residential buildings	685	573	...	112	730	637	...	93	735	655	...	80
2 Non-residential buildings	223	120	...	103	248	143	...	105	245	164	...	81
3 Other construction	327	27	...	300	402	31	...	371	480	46	...	434

Mauritius

2.7 Gross Capital Formation by Type of Good and Owner, in Current Prices
(Continued)

Million Mauritius rupees

	1980 TOTAL	1980 Total Private	1980 Public Enterprises	1980 General Government	1981 TOTAL	1981 Total Private	1981 Public Enterprises	1981 General Government	1982 TOTAL	1982 Total Private	1982 Public Enterprises	1982 General Government
4 Land improvement and plantation and orchard development	...	...	...	...	...	...	...	...	...	...	...	...
5 Producers' durable goods	793	578	...	215	860	564	...	296	640	480	...	160
A Transport equipment	246	208	...	38	242	136	...	106	120	86	...	34
Passenger cars	46	43	...	3	52	37	...	15	45	41	...	4
Other	200	165	...	35	190	99	...	91	75	45	...	30
B Machinery and equipment	547	370	...	177	618	428	...	190	520	394	...	126
6 Breeding stock, dairy cattle, etc.	...	...	...	...	...	...	...	...	...	...	...	...
Total Gross Capital Formation	1803	...	...	...	2578	...	...	...	2130	...	...	...

	1983 TOTAL	1983 Total Private	1983 Public Enterprises	1983 General Government	1984 TOTAL	1984 Total Private	1984 Public Enterprises	1984 General Government	1985 TOTAL	1985 Total Private	1985 Public Enterprises	1985 General Government
Increase in stocks, total	-73	...	...	...	570	...	...	...	800	...	...	...
Gross Fixed Capital Formation, Total	2300	1485	...	815	2595	1770	...	825	3100	2100	...	1000
1 Residential buildings	700	634	...	66	740	685	...	55	730	678	...	52
2 Non-residential buildings	277	207	...	70	350	260	...	90	635	375	...	260
3 Other construction	527	50	...	477	495	74	...	421	425	60	...	365
4 Land improvement and plantation and orchard development	...	...	...	...	...	...	...	...	...	...	...	...
5 Producers' durable goods	796	594	...	202	1010	751	...	259	1310	987	...	323
A Transport equipment	151	89	...	62	201	159	...	42	270	197	...	73
Passenger cars	40	35	...	5	56	47	...	9	85	75	...	10
Other	111	54	...	57	145	112	...	33	185	122	...	63
B Machinery and equipment	645	505	...	140	809	592	...	217	1040	790	...	250
6 Breeding stock, dairy cattle, etc.	...	...	...	...	...	...	...	...	...	...	...	...
Total Gross Capital Formation	2229	...	...	...	3165	...	...	...	3900	...	...	...

	1986 TOTAL	1986 Total Private	1986 Public Enterprises	1986 General Government
Increase in stocks, total	...	...	...	...
Gross Fixed Capital Formation, Total	3915	...	...	...
1 Residential buildings	775	...	...	...
2 Non-residential buildings	660	...	...	...
3 Other construction	645	...	...	...
4 Land improvement and plantation and orchard development	...	...	...	...
5 Producers' durable goods	1835	...	...	...
A Transport equipment	485	...	...	...
Passenger cars	155	...	...	...
Other	330	...	...	...
B Machinery and equipment	1350	...	...	...
6 Breeding stock, dairy cattle, etc.	...	...	...	...
Total Gross Capital Formation	3915	...	...	...

2.11 Gross Fixed Capital Formation by Kind of Activity of Owner, ISIC Divisions, in Current Prices

Million Mauritius rupees

	1970	1975	1978	1979	1980	1981	1982	1983	1984	1985	1986	1987
					All Producers							
1 Agriculture, hunting, forestry and fishing	23	120	... 119	135	102	127	135	102	123	130	130	...
2 Mining and quarrying	-	-	... -	-	-	-	-	-	-	-	-	...
3 Manufacturing	16	292	... 268	296	279	302	315	337	503	740	1070	...
4 Electricity, gas and water	12	71	... 144	100	170	243	350	467	316	285	230	...

Mauritius

2.11 Gross Fixed Capital Formation by Kind of Activity of Owner, ISIC Divisions, in Current Prices
(Continued)

Million Mauritius rupees

	1970	1975	1978	1979	1980	1981	1982	1983	1984	1985	1986	1987
5 Construction	5	22	45	48	62	74	45	36	29	80	135	...
6 Wholesale and retail trade, restaurants and hotels	5	37	80	85	101	111	90	131	184	330	300	...
7 Transport, storage and communication	32	184	308	405	380	374	235	330	453	435	955	...
8 Finance, insurance, real estate and business services	36	265	611	748	760	773	780	744	788	815	875	...
9 Community, social and personal services	16	103	28	33	40	50	70	63	95	135	75	...
Total Industries	145	1094	1603	1850	1894	2054	2020	2210	2491	2950	3770	...
Producers of Government Services	-	44	167	115	134	186	80	90	104	150	145	...
Private Non-Profit Institutions Serving Households	...	...	...	...	...	...	...	...	...	...	...	...
Total	145	1138	1770	1965	2028	2240	2100	2300	2595	3100	3915	...

2.12 Gross Fixed Capital Formation by Kind of Activity of Owner, ISIC Divisions, in Constant Prices

Million Mauritius rupees

	1970	1975	1978	1979	1980	1981	1982	1983	1984	1985	1986	1987
		1970	At constant prices of: 1976					1982				
			All Producers									
1 Agriculture, hunting, forestry and fishing	23	56	100	95	58	60	53 / 135	107	122	120	115	...
2 Mining and quarrying	-	-	-	-	-	-	-	-	-	-	-	...
3 Manufacturing	16	119	220	205	141	127	117 / 315	314	442	580	805	...
4 Electricity, gas and water	12	29	116	68	88	104	136 / 350	438	280	231	180	...
5 Construction	5	10	36	33	30	30	18 / 45	33	25	60	97	...
6 Wholesale and retail trade, restaurants and hotels	5	14	66	59	56	50	40 / 90	123	162	269	236	...
7 Transport, storage and communication	32	72	248	274	192	158	92 / 235	300	388	341	721	...
8 Finance, insurance, real estate and business services	36	87	519	538	458	401	367 / 780	708	704	697	725	...
9 Community, social and personal services	...	...	24	24	22	26	34 / 70	60	86	110	59	...
Total Industries	129	387	1329	1296	1045	956	857 / 2020	2083	2209	2408	2938	...
Producers of Government Services	16	...	141	81	75	84	37 / 80	84	91	122	113	...
Private Non-Profit Institutions Serving Households	...	58	...	...	...	...	...	...	...	...	...	...
Total	145	445	1470	1377	1120	1040	894 / 2100	2167	2300	2530	3051	...

Mauritius

2.17 Exports and Imports of Goods and Services, Detail

Million Mauritius rupees

	1970	1975	1978	1979	1980	1981	1982	1983	1984	1985	1986	1987
					Exports of Goods and Services							
1 Exports of merchandise, f.o.b.	388	1848	1969	2427	3332	2999	3985	4346	5201	6639	9045	...
2 Transport and communication	68	168	291	333	449	507	669	712	777	985	1143	...
A In respect of merchandise imports	14	14	5	...	20	35	33	34	26	30	38	...
B Other	54	154	286	333	429	472	636	678	751	955	1105	...
3 Insurance service charges	2	5	11	11	17	214	11	12	14	10	13	...
A In respect of merchandise imports	-	-	-	-	-	-	-	-	-	-	-	...
B Other	2	5	11	11	17	214	11	12	14	10	13	...
4 Other commodities	29	77	149	186	267	344	334	327	302	342	466	...
5 Adjustments of merchandise exports to change-of-ownership basis	-	-	-	-	-	-	-	-	-	-	-	...
6 Direct purchases in the domestic market by non-residential households	27	135	230	260	325	433	450	503	631	845	1190	...
7 Direct purchases in the domestic market by extraterritorial bodies	17	35	55	42	60	69	80	53	64	74	50	...
Total Exports of Goods and Services	531	2268	2705	3259	4450	4566	5529	5953	6989	8895	11907	...
					Imports of Goods and Services							
1 Imports of merchandise, c.i.f.	414	1965	3051	3602	4661	4922	5008	5164	6528	8083	9183	...
A Imports of merchandise, f.o.b.	360	1679	2580	3055	3965	4260	4313	4516	5727	7056	8197	...
B Transport of services on merchandise imports	54	286	471	547	696	662	695	648	801	1027	986	...
C Insurance service charges on merchandise imports	...	...	...	...	...	...	...	...	...	...	...	...
2 Adjustments of merchandise imports to change-of-ownership basis	...	...	...	...	...	...	...	...	...	...	...	...
3 Other transport and communication	59	85	161	216	296	305	342	302	349	468	460	...
4 Other insurance service charges	4	38	43	53	68	57	98	83	95	128	129	...
5 Other commodities	11	36	87	92	95	119	143	173	183	198	306	...
6 Direct purchases abroad by government	27	103	135	195	222	223	268	277	315	333	420	...
7 Direct purchases abroad by resident households												...
Total Imports of Goods and Services	515	2227	3477	4158	5342	5626	5859	5999	7470	9210	10498	...
Balance of Goods and Services	16	41	-772	-899	-892	-1060	-330	-46	-481	-315	1409	...
Total Imports and Balance of Goods and Services	531	2268	2705	3259	4450	4566	5529	5953	6989	8895	11907	...

4.1 Derivation of Value Added by Kind of Activity, in Current Prices

Million Mauritius rupees

	1980			1981			1982			1983		
	Gross Output	Intermediate Consumption	Value Added	Gross Output	Intermediate Consumption	Value Added	Gross Output	Intermediate Consumption	Value Added	Gross Output	Intermediate Consumption	Value Added
					All Producers							
1 Agriculture, hunting, forestry and fishing	1523	609	914	1984	727	1257	2345	815	1530	2316	861	1455
2 Mining and quarrying	34	19	15	35	19	16	38	21	17	40	22	18
3 Manufacturing	5008	3397	1611	6198	4210	1988	7038	4789	2249	7498	5104	2394
4 Electricity, gas and water	381	172	209	456	268	188	502	242	260	558	313	245
5 Construction	1558	997	561	1653	1065	588	1700	1075	625	1780	1124	656
6 Wholesale and retail trade, restaurants and hotels	1839	737	1102	2076	802	1274	2254	902	1352	2431	928	1503
7 Transport, storage and communication	1514	666	848	1760	748	1012	1962	839	1123	2201	960	1241
8 Finance, insurance, real estate and business services	1734	299	1436	1982	325	1657	2296	383	1913	2470	397	2073
9 Community, social and personal services	633	222	411	729	229	500	829	229	600	892	231	661

Mauritius

4.1 Derivation of Value Added by Kind of Activity, in Current Prices
(Continued)

Million Mauritius rupees

	1980			1981			1982			1983		
	Gross Output	Intermediate Consumption	Value Added	Gross Output	Intermediate Consumption	Value Added	Gross Output	Intermediate Consumption	Value Added	Gross Output	Intermediate Consumption	Value Added
Total, Industries	14225	7118	7107	16873	8393	8480	18964	9295	9669	20186	9940	10246
Producers of Government Services	1170	218	952	1328	224	1104	1520	245	1275	1608	281	1327
Other Producers	58	5	54	66	7	60	76	5	71	86	5	81
Total	15454	7341	8113	18267	8624	9644	20560	9545	11015	21880	10226	11654
Less: Imputed bank service charge	...	-107	107	...	-118	118	...	-128	128	...	-154	154
Import duties	691	...	691	684	...	684	839	...	839	1262	...	1262
Value added tax	...	...	...	...	...	...	...	...	...	...	...	...
Total	16145	7448	8697	18951	8742	10210	21399	9673	11726	23142	10380	12762

	1984			1985		
	Gross Output	Intermediate Consumption	Value Added	Gross Output	Intermediate Consumption	Value Added
	All Producers					
1 Agriculture, hunting, forestry and fishing	2607	886	1721	3098	990	2108
2 Mining and quarrying	42	23	19	44	24	20
3 Manufacturing	9160	6323	2837	11610	7999	3611
4 Electricity, gas and water	648	351	297	797	400	397
5 Construction	1910	1226	684	2148	1380	768
6 Wholesale and retail trade, restaurants and hotels	2537	842	1695	2849	941	1908
7 Transport, storage and communication	2512	1129	1383	2891	1372	1519
8 Finance, insurance, real estate and business services	2799	532	2267	3056	573	2483
9 Community, social and personal services	964	275	689	1036	310	726
Total, Industries	23179	11587	11592	27529	13989	13540
Producers of Government Services	1717	338	1379	1785	338	1447
Other Producers	97	5	92	100	4	96
Total	24993	11930	13063	29414	14331	15083
Less: Imputed bank service charge	...	-181	181	...	-256	256
Import duties	1478	...	1478	1791	...	1791
Value added tax	...	...	...	...	...	...
Total	26471	12111	14360	31205	14587	16618

4.3 Cost Components of Value Added

Million Mauritius rupees

	1980					1981				
	Compensation of Employees	Capital Consumption	Net Operating Surplus	Indirect Taxes	Less: Subsidies Received	Value Added	Compensation of Employees	Capital Consumption	Net Operating Surplus	Indirect Taxes	Less: Subsidies Received	Value Added

	All Producers										
1 Agriculture, hunting, forestry and fishing	737	...	177	-	...	914	840	...	417	-	...	1257
2 Mining and quarrying	8	...	7	-	...	15	8	...	8	-	...	16
3 Manufacturing	589	...	538	484	...	1611	684	...	694	610	...	1988
4 Electricity, gas and water	114	...	95	-	...	209	121	...	67	-	...	188
5 Construction	376	...	185	-	...	561	380	...	208	-	...	588
6 Wholesale and retail trade, restaurants and hotels	333	...	717	52	...	1102	377	...	842	55	...	1274
7 Transport, storage and communication	485	...	352	11	...	848	556	...	441	15	...	1012
8 Finance, insurance, real estate and business services	152	...	1264	20	...	1436	177	...	1458	22	...	1657
9 Community, social and personal services	153	...	208	50	...	411	175	...	267	58	...	500
Total, Industries ab	2947	...	3543	617	...	7107	3318	...	4402	760	...	8480
Producers of Government Services	952	...	...	...	...	952	1104	...	...	...	...	1104
Other Producers	54	...	...	...	...	54	60	...	...	...	...	60
Total ab	3953	...	3543	617	...	8113	4482	...	4402	760	...	9644
Less: Imputed bank service charge	...	...	107	...	...	107	...	...	118	...	...	118
Import duties	...	...	...	691	...	691	...	...	...	684	...	684
Value added tax	...	...	...	...	...	...	...	...	...	...	...	...
Total ab	3953	...	3436	1308	...	8697	4482	...	4284	1444	...	10210

Mauritius

4.3 Cost Components of Value Added

Million Mauritius rupees

1982 / 1983

	Compensation of Employees	Capital Consumption	Net Operating Surplus	Indirect Taxes	Less: Subsidies Received	Value Added	Compensation of Employees	Capital Consumption	Net Operating Surplus	Indirect Taxes	Less: Subsidies Received	Value Added
					All Producers							
1 Agriculture, hunting, forestry and fishing	900	...	630	-	...	1530	974	...	491	-10	...	1455
2 Mining and quarrying	9	...	8	-	...	17	9	...	9	-	...	18
3 Manufacturing	754	...	806	689	...	2249	841	...	836	717	...	2394
4 Electricity, gas and water	140	...	120	-	...	260	150	...	95	-	...	245
5 Construction	400	...	225	-	...	625	420	...	235	1	...	656
6 Wholesale and retail trade, restaurants and hotels	420	...	870	61	...	1351	469	...	986	234	...	1698
7 Transport, storage and communication	596	...	515	12	...	1123	660	...	570	11	...	1241
8 Finance, insurance, real estate and business services	205	...	1678	30	...	1913	248	...	1796	29	...	2073
9 Community, social and personal services	202	...	324	74	...	600	221	...	348	92	...	661
Total, Industries [ab]	3626	...	5176	866	...	9668	3992	...	5366	1074	...	10432
Producers of Government Services	1275	...	...	...	...	1275	1327	...	...	...	...	1327
Other Producers	71	...	...	...	...	71	81	...	...	...	...	81
Total [ab]	4972	...	5176	866	...	11014	5400	...	5366	1074	...	11840
Less: Imputed bank service charge	...	...	128	...	...	128	...	...	154	...	...	154
Import duties	...	...	...	839	...	839	...	...	...	1076	...	1076
Value added tax	...	...	...	...	...	...	...	...	...	...	...	...
Total [ab]	4972	...	5048	1705	...	11725	5400	...	5212	2150	...	12762

1984 / 1985

	Compensation of Employees	Capital Consumption	Net Operating Surplus	Indirect Taxes	Less: Subsidies Received	Value Added	Compensation of Employees	Capital Consumption	Net Operating Surplus	Indirect Taxes	Less: Subsidies Received	Value Added
					All Producers							
1 Agriculture, hunting, forestry and fishing	994	...	742	-15	...	1721	1043	...	1080	-15	...	2108
2 Mining and quarrying	10	...	9	-	...	19	10	...	10	-	...	20
3 Manufacturing	1043	...	1139	655	...	2837	1320	...	1543	748	...	3611
4 Electricity, gas and water	156	...	141	-	...	297	155	...	242	-	...	397
5 Construction	450	...	240	-6	...	684	480	...	295	-7	...	768
6 Wholesale and retail trade, restaurants and hotels	523	...	1116	273	...	1912	650	...	1184	74	...	1908
7 Transport, storage and communication	753	...	619	11	...	1383	791	...	719	9	...	1519
8 Finance, insurance, real estate and business services	284	...	1947	36	...	2267	329	...	2117	37	...	2483
9 Community, social and personal services	231	...	363	95	...	689	249	...	376	101	...	726
Total, Industries [ab]	4444	...	6316	1049	...	11809	5027	...	7566	947	...	13540
Producers of Government Services	1379	...	...	...	...	1379	1447	...	...	...	...	1447
Other Producers	92	...	...	...	...	92	96	...	...	...	...	96
Total [ab]	5915	...	6316	1049	...	13280	6570	...	7566	947	...	15083
Less: Imputed bank service charge	...	...	181	...	...	181	...	...	256	...	...	256
Import duties	...	...	...	1261	...	1261	...	...	...	1791	...	1791
Value added tax	...	...	...	...	...	...	...	...	...	...	...	...
Total [ab]	5915	...	6135	2310	...	14360	6570	...	7310	2738	...	16618

a) Column 4 refers to indirect taxes less subsidies received.
b) Column 'Consumption of fixed capital' is included in column 'Net operating surplus'.

Mexico

General note. The preparation of national accounts statistics in Mexico is undertaken by the Direccion General de Estadistica of the Instituto Nacional de Estadistica, Geografia e Informatica (Ministry of Programming and the Budget). The official estimates are published annually in 'Sistema de Cuentas Naconales de Mexico'. The estimates are generally in accordance with the classifications and definitions recommended in the United Nations System of National Accounts (SNA). Input-output tables for 1950, 1960, 1970 and 1975 have been published. The following tables have been prepared from successive replies to the United Nations national accounts questionnaire. A revision of the national accounts estimates is presently undertaken by the Direccion General de Estadistica. The new series will be published in the 1981 edition of this publication. When the scope and coverage of the estimates differ for conceptual or statistical reasons from the definitions and classifications recommended in SNA, a footnote is indicated to the relevant tables.

Sources and methods:

(a) Gross domestic product. The main approach used to estimate GDP is the production approach.

(b) Expenditure on the gross domestic product. The expenditure approach is used to estimate government final consumption expenditure, increase in stocks, and exports and imports of goods and services. The estimates of gross fixed capital formation is largely based on the commodity-flow approach, whereas private final consumption expenditure is calculated as a residual. The estimates of government consumption expenditure are based on government accounts. For gross fixed capital formation the values from the input-output table of 1960 are extrapolated by value indexes for each of the principal components. The indexes are constructed by using special quantity and price indexes. Exports and imports of goods are estimated from the table of external transactions, which is based on the balance of payments. For the calculation of constant prices, general government expenditure is deflated by a specially constructed price index covering wages and salaries as well as prices of goods and services. As in the case of current prices, private consumption expenditure in constant prices is calculated as a residual. Gross domestic investment is first estimated in constant prices and later converted into current prices. Exports and imports of goods and services are deflated by specially constructed price indexes.

(c) Cost-structure of the gross domestic product. The estimates of compensation of employees for general government, petroleum and electricity production, financial institutions and partly for the transport sector, are based on direct current information on wages, salaries, etc. In the case of manufacturing, mining and private services the estimates are based on ratios of wages and salaries to gross output taken from sample surveys. For construction, trade and agriculture, employment indexes are constructed on the basis of data on occupation from the population censuses of 1960 and 1970, projected by production indexes and indexes of average wages. The estimates of consumption of fixed capital, are based on an approximation to the perpetual inventory method. Each year depreciation of the capital stock, valued at replacement cost, is estimated, based on assumptions regarding the economic life of the fixed assets. The price indexes required are derived implicitly from the estimation of gross fixed capital at 1960 prices. Government accounts are used in the estimation of indirect taxes and subsidies. Operating surplus is estimated as a residual.

(d) Gross domestic product by kind of economic activity. The table of GDP by kind of economic activity is prepared at market prices, i.e. producers' values. The production approach is used to estimate value added of all industries with direct relation to the input-output table of 1960. The income approach or the expenditure approach are used for some sectors. The estimation of gross output, intermediate consumption and value added is based on the 1960 input-output table, from which extrapolations are made by means of value indexes. These value indexes are, in general, the products of price indexes and volume indexes. The volume index for agricultural production is based on statistics of gross output of more than 60 commodities. The index for livestock production is based on statistics of animals slaughtered for domestic consumption and export, live animals exported and inventory changes. The intermediate consumption of crop and livestock production in 1960 is extrapolated by value indexes for the principal components and commodities used. For petroleum and other mining, the volume indexes are based on data from the concerned authorities. The intermediate consumption of 1960 is extrapolated by value indexes for the principal components and commodities used, based on various surveys. The volume index for manufacturing, which covers 200 products, is based on data from several authorities and through direct inquiries to industry associations and manufacturers. Input is extrapolated by value indicators. The index for construction is compiled on the basis of the apparent consumption of a few construction materials. Fixed input-output coefficients of 1960 are used. The volume index for trade is based on estimates of trade margins on locally produced and imported goods. Gross margins are based on data from the commercial censuses and special surveys. Input is extrapolated by a weighed value index. The volume index for transport and communications is based on data from the concerned authorities and companies. Input is extrapolated by quantity indexes. Value added of financial institutions and insurance is estimated through the income approach. For real estate output is extrapolated by value index for housing construction and industrial rents. Fixed input-output coefficients are used at constant prices. Current prices are obtained through the use of a specially constructed price index of principal commodities. The population censuses and household budget surveys are used to impute the rents of owner-occupied dwellings. The volume index for public administration and defense is obtained by compiling an index of wages, salaries and other compensation paid to the government employees. For the computation of constant prices, double deflation is used for all sectors, except the community, social and personal services sector. Output is extrapolated by means of output or volume indexes in all sectors in which double deflation is used. The input of the base-year is extrapolated by quantity indexes in all sectors except for the electricity, construction, restaurants and hotels, financing and services sectors, in which cases either deflation by price indexes is done or constant input-output coefficients are assumed. In the community, social and personal services sector, various approaches are used to estimate output in constant prices, such as double deflation, extrapolation of value added and deflation by price indexes.

1.1 Expenditure on the Gross Domestic Product, in Current Prices

Thousand Million Mexican pesos

	1970	1975	1978	1979	1980	1981	1982	1983	1984	1985	1986	1987
1 Government final consumption expenditure	32	113	255	334	463 / 449	660	1026	1574	2722	4374	7235	16741
2 Private final consumption expenditure	320	756	1544	1976	2651 / 2909	3945	6036	10882	18590	30575	54185	126486
3 Gross capital formation	101	261	552	796	1203 / 1214	1678	2244	3710	5853	10035	14394	35858
A Increase in stocks	12	25	59	78	170 / 107	61	-4	573	566	987	-1021	-627
B Gross fixed capital formation	89	236	492	718	1033 / 1107	1617	2249	3137	5287	9048	15415	36485
Residential buildings	21	61	109	151	206 / 199	276	431	744	1231	2079	3638	8883
Non-residential buildings	12	25	47	66	96 / 144	209	322	397	713	1080	1514	3897
Other construction and land improvement etc.	18	50	133	188	286 / 278	422	600	737	1146	1887	3164	6663
Other	38	100	204	314	445 / 486	710	896	1259	2197	4003	7098	17041
4 Exports of goods and services	34	76	245	343	537 / 479	638	1502	3397	5122	7305	13655	38076
5 Less: Imports of goods and services	43	106	258	382	578 / 580	793	1011	1684	2815	4897	10025	24226
Equals: Gross Domestic Product	444	1100	2337	3068	4276 / 4470	6128	9798	17879	29472	47392	79443	192935

Mexico

1.2 Expenditure on the Gross Domestic Product, in Constant Prices

Thousand Million Mexican pesos

	1970	1975	1978	1979	1980	1981	1982	1983	1984	1985	1986	1987
			At constant prices of:									
			1970					1980				
1 Government final consumption expenditure	32	54	62	68	75 / 449	495	505	519	553	558	570	565
2 Private final consumption expenditure	320	425	491	534	575 / 2909	3123	3046	2883	2977	3083	3016	3014
3 Gross capital formation	101	151	164	193	236 / 1214	1393	1055	770	817	901	698	714
A Increase in stocks	12	19	22	22	39 / 107	107	-16	2	-	20	-79	-59
B Gross fixed capital formation	89	132	143	172	197 / 1107	1286	1070	768	817	881	777	772
Residential buildings	21	32	32	35	36 / 199	214	218	205	215	232	229	239
Non-residential buildings	12	13	13	15	17 / 144	164	159	103	116	115	88	97
Other construction and land improvement etc.	18	27	37	44	52 / 278	329	285	204	201	204	181	168
Other	38	61	61	79	93 / 486	580	409	255	284	329	280	268
4 Exports of goods and services	34	43	64	72	77 / 479	534	650	739	781	746	770	845
5 Less: Imports of goods and services	43	64	70	91	120 / 580	683	424	281	331	367	322	336
Equals: Gross Domestic Product	444	610	712	777	842 / 4470	4862	4832	4629	4796	4920	4732	4802

1.3 Cost Components of the Gross Domestic Product

Thousand Million Mexican pesos

	1970	1975	1978	1979	1980	1981	1982	1983	1984	1985	1986	1987
1 Indirect taxes, net	22	63	138	207	355 / 343	458	858	1326	2375	4435	6631	19240
A Indirect taxes	25	79	175	260	434 / 432	579	1135	1924	3164	5688	8537	23523
B Less: Subsidies	3	16	37	53	80 / 89	122	277	598	789	1254	1907	4283
2 Consumption of fixed capital	24	60	136	178	237 / 384	527	956	2176	3359	5331	10875	26474
3 Compensation of employees paid by resident producers to:	158	419	886	1157	1542 / 1611	2295	3450	5248	8445	13590	22517	51008
4 Operating surplus	240	559	1177	1525	2143 / 2133	2847	4533	9129	15293	24036	39420	96212
Equals: Gross Domestic Product	444	1100	2337	3068	4276 / 4470	6128	9798	17879	29472	47392	79443	192935

1.7 External Transactions on Current Account, Summary

Thousand Million Mexican pesos

	1970	1975	1978	1979	1980	1981	1982	1983	1984	1985	1986	1987
					Payments to the Rest of the World							
1 Imports of goods and services	43	106	258	382	578 / 580	793	1011	1684	2815	4897	10025	24226
A Imports of merchandise c.i.f.	31	82	190	287	449 / 456	615	722	1141	2000	3535	7187	17861
B Other	12	24	68	95	129 / 124	178	288	544	815	1362	2838	6365
2 Factor income to the rest of the world	8	22	68	96	143 / 157	257	640	1269	2042	2753	5374	12007
A Compensation of employees	-	-	-	-	- / ...	...	...	...	...	...	...	...
B Property and entrepreneurial income	8	22	68	96	143 / 157	257	640	1269	2042	2753	5374	12007
3 Current transfers to the rest of the world	-	-	1	1	1 / 1	1	1	5	4	8	8	26
4 Surplus of the nation on current transactions	-13	-46	-61	-111	-152 / -224	-365	-50	704	765	615	-331	5964
Payments to the Rest of the World and Surplus of the Nation on Current Transactions	38	81	265	368	570 / 514	686	1602	3661	5627	8273	15077	42223

Mexico

1.7 External Transactions on Current Account, Summary
(Continued)

Thousand Million Mexican pesos

	1970	1975	1978	1979	1980	1981	1982	1983	1984	1985	1986	1987
Receipts From The Rest of the World												
1 Exports of goods and services	34	76	245	343	537 / 479	638	1502	3397	5122	7305	13655	38076
A Exports of merchandise f.o.b.	34	76	245	343	537 / 347	476	1211	2655	3994	5523	9762	27940
B Other	-	-	-	-	- / 131	162	292	743	1128	1783	3892	10136
2 Factor income from rest of the world	2	4	15	19	26 / 29	40	82	214	424	632	1119	3214
A Compensation of employees	2	2	6	5	4 / 4	5	10	23	44	89	205	506
B Property and entrepreneurial income	1	1	9	13	22 / 24	35	72	191	380	542	914	2708
3 Current transfers from rest of the world	1	2	5	6	7 / 7	8	18	50	80	336	303	934
Receipts from the Rest of the World on Current Transactions	38	81	265	368	570 / 514	686	1602	3661	5627	8273	15077	42223

1.10 Gross Domestic Product by Kind of Activity, in Current Prices

Thousand Million Mexican pesos

	1970	1975	1978	1979	1980	1981	1982	1983	1984	1985	1986	1987
1 Agriculture, hunting, forestry and fishing	54	123	240	281	357 / 368	503	720	1392	2533	4307	7466	16825
2 Mining and quarrying [a]	11	31	77	129	288 / 141	144	298	1264	1647	2190	2868	9742
3 Manufacturing [a]	105	258	553	717	988 / 991	1329	2037	3780	6633	11096	19589	49759
4 Electricity, gas and water	5	10	24	31	42 / 44	56	88	167	282	449	994	2016
5 Construction	24	66	139	194	276 / 287	427	635	804	1298	2070	3383	7721
6 Wholesale and retail trade, restaurants and hotels	115	277	560	743	1000 / 1250	1695	2903	5073	8362	13306	21128	52524
7 Transport, storage and communication	21	63	150	200	279 / 286	395	606	1172	2004	3165	5708	13824
8 Finance, insurance, real estate and business services	51	107	215	269	349 / 396	554	843	1440	2310	3659	6501	14128
9 Community, social and personal services	38	90	204	273	377 / 401	569	926	1700	2693	4410	7599	17117
Total, Industries	425	1024	2164	2838	3956 / 4165	5673	9055	16793	27762	44652	75237	183657
Producers of Government Services	25	88	199	263	368 / 353	521	830	1232	2065	3293	5232	11979
Other Producers	...	...	...	...	...	...	...	...	...	...	...	...
Subtotal	450	1112	2363	3101	4324 / 4518	6194	9884	18025	29827	47945	80469	195637
Less: Imputed bank service charge	5	12	26	33	48 / 48	66	86	146	355	554	1026	2702
Plus: Import duties	...	...	...	...	...	...	...	...	...	...	...	...
Plus: Value added tax	...	...	...	...	...	...	...	...	...	...	...	...
Equals: Gross Domestic Product	444	1100	2337	3068	4276 / 4470	6128	9798	17879	29472	47392	79443	192935

a) Basic petroleum manufacturing is included in item 'Mining and quarrying'.

Mexico

1.11 Gross Domestic Product by Kind of Activity, in Constant Prices

Thousand Million Mexican pesos

	1970	1975	1978	1979	1980	1981	1982	1983	1984	1985	1986	1987
			At constant prices of:									
			1970					1980				
1 Agriculture, hunting, forestry and fishing	54	63	72	71	76 / 368	391	383	391	401	416	405	410
2 Mining and quarrying [a]	11	15	19	22	27 / 141	162	177	175	179	179	172	181
3 Manufacturing [a]	105	148	177	196	210 / 991	1055	1026	946	993	1054	994	1019
4 Electricity, gas and water	5	8	11	12	13 / 44	49	54	55	58	62	65	66
5 Construction	24	33	37	41	46 / 287	329	305	247	260	267	240	243
6 Wholesale and retail trade, restaurants and hotels	115	158	179	200	216 / 1250	1382	1370	1267	1298	1312	1227	1233
7 Transport, storage and communication	21	38	48	55	63 / 286	314	291	283	298	306	296	304
8 Finance, insurance, real estate and business services	51	68	77	81	82 / 396	421	440	456	481	499	518	530
9 Community, social and personal services	38	48	57	61	66 / 401	428	433	435	431	430	411	411
Total, Industries	425	578	676	738	800 / 4165	4532	4480	4254	4400	4525	4326	4397
Producers of Government Services	25	39	44	49	53 / 353	385	409	434	459	458	470	471
Other Producers	...	...	...	...	... / ...	...	...	...	...	...	...	...
Subtotal	450	617	721	787	853 / 4518	4916	4889	4688	4858	4983	4797	4868
Less: Imputed bank service charge	5	7	9	10	11 / 48	54	57	59	62	63	64	66
Plus: Import duties	...	...	...	...	... / ...	...	...	...	...	...	...	...
Plus: Value added tax	...	...	...	...	... / ...	...	...	...	...	...	...	...
Equals: Gross Domestic Product	444	610	712	777	842 / 4470	4862	4832	4629	4796	4920	4732	4802

a) Basic petroleum manufacturing is included in item 'Mining and quarrying'.

1.12 Relations Among National Accounting Aggregates

Thousand Million Mexican pesos

	1970	1975	1978	1979	1980	1981	1982	1983	1984	1985	1986	1987
Gross Domestic Product	444	1100	2337	3068	4276 / 4470	6128	9798	17879	29472	47392	79443	192935
Plus: Net factor income from the rest of the world	-6	-18	-53	-77	-117 / -129	-217	-558	-1055	-1618	-2122	-4255	-8793
Factor income from the rest of the world	2	4	15	19	26 / 29	40	82	214	424	632	1119	3214
Less: Factor income to the rest of the world	8	22	68	96	143 / 157	257	640	1269	2042	2753	5374	12007
Equals: Gross National Product	439	1082	2285	2990	4159 / 4341	5911	9240	16824	27854	45270	75188	184142
Less: Consumption of fixed capital	24	60	136	178	237 / 384	527	956	2176	3359	5331	10875	26474

Mexico

1,12 Relations Among National Accounting Aggregates
(Continued)

Thousand Million Mexican pesos

	1970	1975	1978	1979	1980	1981	1982	1983	1984	1985	1986	1987
Equals: National Income	415	1022	2149	2812	3923 3958	5383	8283	14648	24495	39939	64313	157668
Plus: Net current transfers from the rest of the world	1	2	4	5	6 6	7	17	45	76	329	295	907
Current transfers from the rest of the world	1	2	5	6	7 7	8	18	50	80	336	303	934
Less: Current transfers to the rest of the world	-	-	1	1	1 1	1	1	5	4	8	8	26
Equals: National Disposable Income	416	1024	2153	2817	3929 3964	5390	8300	14693	24571	40268	64608	158575
Less: Final consumption	352	869	1799	2310	3114 3358	4605	7062	12455	21312	34949	61420	143227
Equals: Net Saving	64	155	354	507	815 607	785	1238	2238	3260	5319	3188	15349
Less: Surplus of the nation on current transactions	-13	-46	-61	-111	-152 -224	-365	-50	704	765	615	-331	5964
Equals: Net Capital Formation	77	201	415	618	966 830	1150	1288	1534	2494	4704	3519	9384

2.5 Private Final Consumption Expenditure by Type and Purpose, in Current Prices

Thousand Million Mexican pesos

	1970	1975	1978	1979	1980	1981	1982	1983	1984	1985	1986	1987
Final Consumption Expenditure of Resident Households												
1 Food, beverages and tobacco	129	319	626	760	989	1304	2042	3742	6404	...	...	...
2 Clothing and footwear	37	82	169	223	304	402	654	1179	1843	...	...	...
3 Gross rent, fuel and power	40	78	148	182	236	314	502	869	1467	...	...	...
4 Furniture, furnishings and household equipment and operation	40	90	195	263	355	462	764	1338	2141	...	...	...
5 Medical care and health expenses	9	25	57	75	107	155	274	530	899	...	...	...
6 Transport and communication	25	66	148	197	273	375	642	1264	2227	...	...	...
7 Recreational, entertainment, education and cultural services	15	37	80	110	149	203	327	528	873	...	...	...
8 Miscellaneous goods and services	29	75	158	210	285	400	687	1223	2059	...	...	...
Total Final Consumption Expenditure in the Domestic Market by Households, of which	325	772	1581	2021	2698	3616	5891	10672	17912	...	...	...
A Durable goods	29	68	153	212	290	383	602	897	1455	...	...	...
B Semi-durable goods	194	467	924	1158	1531	2017	3260	6017	10221	...	...	...
C Non-durable goods										...	...	...
D Services	102	237	503	651	877	1216	2030	3758	6237	...	...	...
Plus: Direct purchases abroad by resident households	9	17	49	68	94	153	231	288	408	...	...	...
Less: Direct purchases in the domestic market by non-resident households	15	33	86	112	140	184	346	604	852	...	...	...
Equals: Final Consumption Expenditure of Resident Households [a]	320	756	1544	1976	2651	3584	5776	10356	17469	...	...	...
Final Consumption Expenditure of Private Non-profit Institutions Serving Households												
Equals: Final Consumption Expenditure of Private Non-profit Organisations Serving Households	...	...	...	...	...	...	...	...	...	...	...	...
Private Final Consumption Expenditure	320	756	1544	1976	2651	3584	5776	10356	17469	...	...	...

a) Item 'Final consumption expenditure of resident households' includes consumption expenditure of private non-profit institutions serving households.

Mexico

2.6 Private Final Consumption Expenditure by Type and Purpose, in Constant Prices

Thousand Million Mexican pesos

	1970	1975	1978	1979	1980	1981	1982	1983	1984	1985	1986	1987
	\multicolumn{12}{c}{At constant prices of:1970}
	\multicolumn{12}{c}{Final Consumption Expenditure of Resident Households}
1 Food, beverages and tobacco	129	169	190	201	215	226	234	232	...	...	...	...
2 Clothing and footwear	37	49	57	63	65	69	71	65	...	...	...	...
3 Gross rent, fuel and power	40	49	55	58	60	63	67	68	...	...	...	...
4 Furniture, furnishings and household equipment and operation	40	52	63	71	75	78	82	71	...	...	...	...
5 Medical care and health expenses	9	17	21	24	26	28	30	30	...	...	...	...
6 Transport and communication	25	38	47	53	59	65	64	56	...	...	...	...
7 Recreational, entertainment, education and cultural services	15	21	27	30	32	34	35	30	...	...	...	...
8 Miscellaneous goods and services	29	39	44	49	52	55	59	54	...	...	...	...
Total Final Consumption Expenditure in the Domestic Market by Households, of which	325	434	504	547	583	619	641	605	621	...	...	...
A Durable goods	29	43	53	61	67	72	69	50	51	...	...	...
B Semi-durable goods	194	257	293	317	337	358	376	358	369	...	...	...
C Non-durable goods										...	...	...
D Services	102	134	157	169	179	189	197	197	202	...	...	...
Plus: Direct purchases abroad by resident households	9	12	16	19	23	32	20	11	15	...	...	...
Less: Direct purchases in the domestic market by non-resident households	15	20	29	33	32	34	38	40	45	...	...	...
Equals: Final Consumption Expenditure of Resident Households [a]	320	425	491	534	575	617	623	577	591	...	...	...
	\multicolumn{12}{c}{Final Consumption Expenditure of Private Non-profit Institutions Serving Households}
Equals: Final Consumption Expenditure of Private Non-profit Organisations Serving Households	...	...	...	...	...	...	...	...	...	...	...	...
Private Final Consumption Expenditure	320	425	491	534	575	617	623	577	591	...	...	...

a) Item 'Final consumption expenditure of resident households' includes consumption expenditure of private non-profit institutions serving households.

4.1 Derivation of Value Added by Kind of Activity, in Current Prices

Thousand Million Mexican pesos

	\multicolumn{3}{c	}{1980}	\multicolumn{3}{c	}{1981}	\multicolumn{3}{c	}{1982}	\multicolumn{3}{c}{1983}
	Gross Output	Intermediate Consumption	Value Added	Gross Output	Intermediate Consumption	Value Added	Gross Output	Intermediate Consumption	Value Added	Gross Output	Intermediate Consumption	Value Added
	\multicolumn{12}{c}{All Producers}
1 Agriculture, hunting, forestry and fishing	...	...	368	...	...	503	...	...	720	...	...	1392
2 Mining and quarrying [a]	...	...	141	...	...	144	...	...	298	...	...	1264
A Coal mining	...	...	2	...	...	3	...	...	4	...	...	12
B Crude petroleum and natural gas production	...	...	82	...	...	83	...	...	196	...	...	1039
C Metal ore mining	...	...	34	...	...	26	...	...	48	...	...	126
D Other mining	...	...	23	...	...	31	...	...	49	...	...	87

Mexico

4.1 Derivation of Value Added by Kind of Activity, in Current Prices
(Continued)

Thousand Million Mexican pesos

	1980 Gross Output	1980 Intermediate Consumption	1980 Value Added	1981 Gross Output	1981 Intermediate Consumption	1981 Value Added	1982 Gross Output	1982 Intermediate Consumption	1982 Value Added	1983 Gross Output	1983 Intermediate Consumption	1983 Value Added
3 Manufacturing [a]	...	...	991	...	...	1329	...	...	2037	...	...	3780
A Manufacture of food, beverages and tobacco	...	...	243	...	...	322	...	...	522	...	...	979
B Textile, wearing apparel and leather industries	...	...	136	...	...	175	...	...	257	...	...	491
C Manufacture of wood and wood products, including furniture	...	...	42	...	...	54	...	...	80	...	...	141
D Manufacture of paper and paper products, printing and publishing	...	...	54	...	...	74	...	...	113	...	...	214
E Manufacture of chemicals and chemical petroleum, coal, rubber and plastic products	...	...	153	...	...	206	...	...	339	...	...	716
F Manufacture of non-metallic mineral products, except products of petroleum and coal	...	...	69	...	...	95	...	...	146	...	...	269
G Basic metal industries	...	...	61	...	...	80	...	...	113	...	...	214
H Manufacture of fabricated metal products, machinery and equipment	...	...	216	...	...	298	...	...	428	...	...	696
I Other manufacturing industries	...	...	17	...	...	25	...	...	38	...	...	59
4 Electricity, gas and water	...	...	44	...	...	56	...	...	88	...	...	167
5 Construction	...	...	287	...	...	427	...	...	635	...	...	804
6 Wholesale and retail trade, restaurants and hotels	...	...	1250	...	...	1695	...	...	2903	...	...	5073
7 Transport, storage and communication	...	...	286	...	...	395	...	...	606	...	...	1172
8 Finance, insurance, real estate and business services	...	...	396	...	...	554	...	...	843	...	...	1440
9 Community, social and personal services	...	...	401	...	...	569	...	...	926	...	...	1700
Total, Industries	...	...	4165	...	...	5673	...	...	9055	...	...	16793
Producers of Government Services	...	...	353	...	...	521	...	...	830	...	...	1232
Other Producers	...	...	...	...	...	...	...	...	...	...	...	...
Total	...	...	4518	...	...	6194	...	...	9884	...	...	18025
Less: Imputed bank service charge	...	...	48	...	...	66	...	...	86	...	...	146
Import duties	...	...	...	...	...	...	...	...	...	...	...	...
Value added tax	...	...	...	...	...	...	...	...	...	...	...	...
Total [b]	...	...	4470	...	...	6128	...	...	9798	...	...	17879

	1984 Gross Output	1984 Intermediate Consumption	1984 Value Added	1985 Gross Output	1985 Intermediate Consumption	1985 Value Added	1986 Gross Output	1986 Intermediate Consumption	1986 Value Added
All Producers									
1 Agriculture, hunting, forestry and fishing	...	...	2533	...	...	4307	...	...	7466
2 Mining and quarrying [a]	...	...	1647	...	...	2196	...	...	2871
A Coal mining	...	...	26	...	...	45	...	...	57
B Crude petroleum and natural gas production	...	...	1312	...	...	1672	...	...	1814
C Metal ore mining	...	...	147	...	...	175	...	...	405
D Other mining	...	...	163	...	...	305	...	...	595

Mexico

4.1 Derivation of Value Added by Kind of Activity, in Current Prices
(Continued)

Thousand Million Mexican pesos

	1984 Gross Output	1984 Intermediate Consumption	1984 Value Added	1985 Gross Output	1985 Intermediate Consumption	1985 Value Added	1986 Gross Output	1986 Intermediate Consumption	1986 Value Added
3 Manufacturing [a]	...	...	6633	...	...	11093	...	...	19589
A Manufacture of food, beverages and tobacco	...	...	1719	...	...	2884	...	...	5573
B Textile, wearing apparel and leather industries	...	...	770	...	...	1237	...	...	2087
C Manufacture of wood and wood products, including furniture	...	...	245	...	...	429	...	...	724
D Manufacture of paper and paper products, printing and publishing	...	...	379	...	...	639	...	...	1153
E Manufacture of chemicals and chemical petroleum, coal, rubber and plastic products	...	...	1208	...	...	1991	...	...	3566
F Manufacture of non-metallic mineral products, except products of petroleum and coal	...	...	461	...	...	801	...	...	1406
G Basic metal industries	...	...	443	...	...	638	...	...	1085
H Manufacture of fabricated metal products, machinery and equipment	...	...	1295	...	...	2278	...	...	3676
I Other manufacturing industries	...	...	112	...	...	196	...	...	318
4 Electricity, gas and water	...	...	282	...	...	449	...	...	987
5 Construction	...	...	1298	...	...	2065	...	...	3373
6 Wholesale and retail trade, restaurants and hotels	...	...	8362	...	...	13332	...	...	21149
7 Transport, storage and communication	...	...	2004	...	...	3152	...	...	5636
8 Finance, insurance, real estate and business services	...	...	2310	...	...	3659	...	...	6477
9 Community, social and personal services	...	...	2693	...	...	4410	...	...	7599
Total, Industries	...	...	27762	...	...	44663	...	...	75147
Producers of Government Services	...	...	2065	...	...	3293	...	...	5232
Other Producers	...	...	...	...	...	...	...	...	...
Total	...	...	29827	...	...	47956	...	...	80380
Less: Imputed bank service charge	...	...	355	...	...	554	...	...	1026
Import duties	...	...	...	...	...	...	...	...	...
Value added tax	...	...	...	...	...	...	...	...	...
Total [b]	...	...	29472	...	...	47403	...	...	79353

a) Basic petroleum manufacturing is included in item 'Mining and quarrying'.
b) Data for this table have not been revised, therefore, data for some years are not comparable with those of other tables.

4.2 Derivation of Value Added by Kind of Activity, in Constant Prices

Thousand Million Mexican pesos

	1980 Gross Output	1980 Intermediate Consumption	1980 Value Added	1981 Gross Output	1981 Intermediate Consumption	1981 Value Added	1982 Gross Output	1982 Intermediate Consumption	1982 Value Added	1983 Gross Output	1983 Intermediate Consumption	1983 Value Added
At constant prices of:1980 — All Producers												
1 Agriculture, hunting, forestry and fishing	...	...	368	...	...	391	...	...	383	...	...	391
2 Mining and quarrying [a]	...	...	141	...	...	162	...	...	177	...	...	175
A Coal mining	...	...	2	...	...	3	...	...	3	...	...	3
B Crude petroleum and natural gas production	...	...	82	...	...	96	...	...	111	...	...	108
C Metal ore mining	...	...	34	...	...	39	...	...	39	...	...	43
D Other mining	...	...	23	...	...	25	...	...	24	...	...	22

Mexico

4.2 Derivation of Value Added by Kind of Activity, in Constant Prices
(Continued)

Thousand Million Mexican pesos

	1980 Gross Output	1980 Intermediate Consumption	1980 Value Added	1981 Gross Output	1981 Intermediate Consumption	1981 Value Added	1982 Gross Output	1982 Intermediate Consumption	1982 Value Added	1983 Gross Output	1983 Intermediate Consumption	1983 Value Added
						At constant prices of:1980						
3 Manufacturing [a]	...	...	991	...	...	1055	...	...	1026	...	...	946
A Manufacture of food, beverages and tobacco	...	...	243	...	...	254	...	...	265	...	...	262
B Textile, wearing apparel and leather industries	...	...	136	...	...	144	...	...	137	...	...	130
C Manufacture of wood and wood products, including furniture	...	...	42	...	...	42	...	...	41	...	...	38
D Manufacture of paper and paper products, printing and publishing	...	...	54	...	...	57	...	...	57	...	...	53
E Manufacture of chemicals and chemical petroleum, coal, rubber and plastic products	...	...	153	...	...	167	...	...	171	...	...	168
F Manufacture of non-metallic mineral products, except products of petroleum and coal	...	...	69	...	...	71	...	...	69	...	...	64
G Basic metal industries	...	...	61	...	...	64	...	...	58	...	...	54
H Manufacture of fabricated metal products, machinery and equipment	...	...	216	...	...	237	...	...	208	...	...	163
I Other manufacturing industries	...	...	17	...	...	20	...	...	19	...	...	15
4 Electricity, gas and water	...	...	44	...	...	49	...	...	54	...	...	55
5 Construction	...	...	287	...	...	329	...	...	305	...	...	247
6 Wholesale and retail trade, restaurants and hotels	...	...	1250	...	...	1382	...	...	1370	...	...	1267
7 Transport, storage and communication	...	...	286	...	...	314	...	...	291	...	...	283
8 Finance, insurance, real estate and business services	...	...	396	...	...	421	...	...	440	...	...	456
9 Community, social and personal services	...	...	401	...	...	428	...	...	433	...	...	435
Total, industries	...	...	4165	...	...	4532	...	...	4480	...	...	4254
Producers of Government Services	...	...	353	...	...	385	...	...	409	...	...	434
Other Producers	...	...	...	...	...	...	...	...	...	...	...	...
Total	...	...	4518	...	...	4916	...	...	4889	...	...	4688
Less: Imputed bank service charge	...	...	48	...	...	54	...	...	57	...	...	59
Import duties	...	...	...	...	...	...	...	...	...	...	...	...
Value added tax	...	...	...	...	...	...	...	...	...	...	...	...
Total [b]	...	...	4470	...	...	4862	...	...	4832	...	...	4629

	1984 Gross Output	1984 Intermediate Consumption	1984 Value Added	1985 Gross Output	1985 Intermediate Consumption	1985 Value Added	1986 Gross Output	1986 Intermediate Consumption	1986 Value Added
			At constant prices of:1980						
			All Producers						
1 Agriculture, hunting, forestry and fishing	...	...	401	...	...	416	...	...	405
2 Mining and quarrying [a]	...	...	179	...	...	179	...	...	172
A Coal mining	...	...	3	...	...	3	...	...	3
B Crude petroleum and natural gas production	...	...	109	...	...	107	...	...	99
C Metal ore mining	...	...	43	...	...	45	...	...	45
D Other mining	...	...	23	...	...	25	...	...	24

Mexico

4.2 Derivation of Value Added by Kind of Activity, in Constant Prices
(Continued)

Thousand Million Mexican pesos

At constant prices of: 1980

	1984 Gross Output	1984 Intermediate Consumption	1984 Value Added	1985 Gross Output	1985 Intermediate Consumption	1985 Value Added	1986 Gross Output	1986 Intermediate Consumption	1986 Value Added
3 Manufacturing [a]	...	...	993	...	...	1053	...	...	993
A Manufacture of food, beverages and tobacco	...	...	265	...	...	275	...	...	274
B Textile, wearing apparel and leather industries	...	...	131	...	...	134	...	...	127
C Manufacture of wood and wood products, including furniture	...	...	40	...	...	40	...	...	39
D Manufacture of paper and paper products, printing and publishing	...	...	56	...	...	61	...	...	59
E Manufacture of chemicals and chemical petroleum, coal, rubber and plastic products	...	...	179	...	...	189	...	...	182
F Manufacture of non-metallic mineral products, except products of petroleum and coal	...	...	68	...	...	73	...	...	68
G Basic metal industries	...	...	61	...	...	61	...	...	57
H Manufacture of fabricated metal products, machinery and equipment	...	...	177	...	...	200	...	...	170
I Other manufacturing industries	...	...	17	...	...	19	...	...	17
4 Electricity, gas and water	...	...	58	...	...	62	...	...	64
5 Construction	...	...	260	...	...	266	...	...	239
6 Wholesale and retail trade, restaurants and hotels	...	...	1298	...	...	1313	...	...	1223
7 Transport, storage and communication	...	...	298	...	...	306	...	...	296
8 Finance, insurance, real estate and business services	...	...	481	...	...	499	...	...	515
9 Community, social and personal services	...	...	431	...	...	430	...	...	411
Total, Industries	...	...	4400	...	...	4525	...	...	4318
Producers of Government Services	...	...	459	...	...	458	...	...	470
Other Producers	...	...	...	...	...	...	...	...	...
Total	...	...	4858	...	...	4983	...	...	4789
Less: Imputed bank service charge	...	...	62	...	...	63	...	...	63
Import duties	...	...	...	...	...	...	...	...	...
Value added tax	...	...	...	...	...	...	...	...	...
Total [b]	...	...	4796	...	...	4920	...	...	4725

a) Basic petroleum manufacturing is included in item 'Mining and quarrying'.
b) Data for this table have not been revised, therefore, data for some years are not comparable with those of other tables.

Mongolia

Source. The official data are published annually in 'National Economy of the Mongolian People's Republic'.

General note. The estimates shown in the following tables have been prepared in accordance with the System of Material Product Balances. Therefore, these estimates are not comparable in concept and coverage with those conforming to the United Nations System of National Accounts.

2a Net Material Product by Kind of Activity of the Material Sphere in Current Market Prices

Percentages

	1970	1975	1978	1979	1980	1981	1982	1983	1984	1985	1986	1987
1 Agriculture and forestry	25.3	22.4	19.5	18.0	15.0	16.4	17.9	18.0	17.0	16.2	21.0	18.8
2 Industrial activity	22.6	24.7	27.3	27.8	29.3	29.4	30.9	32.2	32.3	32.6	33.7	33.7
3 Construction	5.8	5.4	5.4	5.7	6.1	5.6	5.1	4.8	5.0	5.0	5.8	6.7
4 Wholesale and retail trade and restaurants and other eating and drinking places	36.5	36.2	35.4	35.9	36.3	35.9	33.8	32.8	33.0	33.0	25.7	27.2
5 Transport and communication	7.5	9.1	10.2	10.5	11.2	10.9	10.5	10.5	11.0	11.5	11.7	11.5
A Transport	6.9	8.2	9.3	9.5	10.1	9.7	9.3	9.2	9.6	10.1	10.2	10.0
B Communication	0.6	0.9	0.9	1.0	1.1	1.2	1.2	1.3	1.4	1.4	1.5	1.5
6 Other activities of the material sphere	2.3	2.2	2.2	2.1	2.0	1.8	1.8	1.7	1.7	1.7	2.1	2.1
Net material product	100.0	100.0	100.0	100.0	100.0	100.0	100.0	100.0	100.0	100.0	100.0	100.0

2b Net Material Product by Kind of Activity of the Material Sphere in Constant Market Prices

Index numbers 1970=100

	1970	1975	1978	1979	1980	1981	1982	1983	1984	1985	1986	1987
					At constant prices of:1970							
1 Agriculture and forestry	100	111	98	97	81	95	109	109	99	109	115	108
2 Industrial activity	100	181	240	273	295	321	355	390	424	447	457	470
3 Construction	100	135	152	172	188	188	190	193	202	210	232	276
4 Wholesale and retail trade and restaurants and other eating and drinking places [a]	100	122	142	153	160	171	179	187	194	200	211	230
5 Transport and communication	100	175	226	246	266	285	306	327	347	376	422	430
A Transport	100	172	225	243	262	277	295	312	330	359	404	409
B Communication	100	200	246	286	313	379	426	493	532	559	621	657
6 Other activities of the material sphere	100	139	153	155	157	157	171	176	175	175	198	200
Net material product	100	138	161	175	181	196	213	226	236	249	262	272

a) Item 'Other activities of the material sphere' is included in item 'Wholesale and retail trade and restaurants and other eating and drinking places'.

6b Capital Formation by Kind of Activity of the Material and Non-Material Spheres in Constant Market Prices

Million Mongolian tugriks

	1970	1975	1978	1979	1980	1981	1982	1983	1984	1985	1986	1987
					At constant prices of:1960							
					Gross Fixed Capital Formation							
1 Agriculture and forestry	293	...	...	...	...	...	...	...	...	...	...	...
2 Industrial activity	327	...	...	...	...	...	...	...	...	...	...	...
3 Construction	52	...	...	...	...	...	...	...	...	...	...	...
4 Wholesale and retail trade and restaurants and other eating and drinking places	28	...	...	...	...	...	...	...	...	...	...	...
5 Transport and communication	95	...	...	...	...	...	...	...	...	...	...	...
6 Other activities of the material sphere	...	...	...	...	...	...	...	...	...	...	...	...
Total Material Sphere	794	...	...	...	...	...	...	...	...	...	...	...
7 Housing except owner-occupied, communal and miscellaneous personal services	109	...	...	...	...	...	...	...	...	...	...	...
8 Education, culture and art	96	...	...	...	...	...	...	...	...	...	...	...
9 Health and social welfare services and sports	42	...	...	...	...	...	...	...	...	...	...	...
Total Non-Material Sphere Serving Individuals	247	...	...	...	...	...	...	...	...	...	...	...
10 Government	...	...	...	...	...	...	...	...	...	...	...	...
11 Finance, credit and insurance	...	...	...	...	...	...	...	...	...	...	...	...
12 Research, scientific and technological institutes	...	...	...	...	...	...	...	...	...	...	...	...
13 Other activities of the non-material sphere	...	...	...	...	...	...	...	...	...	...	...	...
Total Non-Material Sphere Serving the Community as a Whole	21	...	...	...	...	...	...	...	...	...	...	...
14 Owner-occupied dwellings	...	...	...	...	...	...	...	...	...	...	...	...
Total Gross Fixed Capital Formation	1062	...	...	...	...	...	...	...	...	...	...	...

Montserrat

Source. Government of Montserrat, Statistics Office, 'National Accounts Statistics 1975-82'.
General note. The estimates shown in the following tables have been prepared in accordance with the United Nations System of National Accounts so far as the existing data would permit.

1.1 Expenditure on the Gross Domestic Product, in Current Prices

Million East Caribbean dollars

	1970	1975	1978	1979	1980	1981	1982	1983	1984	1985	1986	1987
1 Government final consumption expenditure	...	6.3	7.8	9.9	12.2	14.1	16.9	17.9	19.3	20.3	21.3	...
2 Private final consumption expenditure	...	27.1	37.2	47.4	71.2	76.5	81.9	83.7	90.2	96.4	102.1	...
3 Gross capital formation	...	8.7	14.2	19.6	26.8	33.7	32.1	25.6	24.7	26.2	40.8	...
A Increase in stocks	...	0.3	2.3	1.4	5.2	4.3	1.5	2.0	2.5	1.5	3.2	...
B Gross fixed capital formation	...	8.4	11.9	18.2	21.6	29.4	30.6	23.6	22.2	24.7	37.6	...
Residential buildings	...											...
Non-residential buildings	...	6.2	6.6	11.0	11.4	14.4	18.6	12.9	13.9	16.0	19.1	...
Other construction and land improvement etc.	...											...
Other	...	2.2	5.3	7.2	10.2	15.0	12.0	10.7	8.3	8.7	18.5	...
4 Exports of goods and services	...	1.5	5.6	3.1	4.8	8.9	10.5	18.5	12.7	11.7	11.5	...
5 Less: Imports of goods and services	...	18.2	29.6	37.7	49.7	59.9	60.4	59.2	53.3	54.5	61.5	...
Equals: Gross Domestic Product	...	25.4	35.2	43.2	65.4	73.3	81.0	86.5	93.6	100.1	114.1	...

1.2 Expenditure on the Gross Domestic Product, in Constant Prices

Million East Caribbean dollars

	1970	1975	1978	1979	1980	1981	1982	1983	1984	1985	1986	1987
					At constant prices of:1977							
1 Government final consumption expenditure	...	6.9	7.0	7.0	7.5	8.3	9.1	9.4	9.4	10.1	9.8	...
2 Private final consumption expenditure	...	32.9	31.0	37.4	40.4	38.8	40.0	38.2	38.9	42.4	41.4	...
3 Gross capital formation	...	12.4	12.6	15.0	18.0	20.6	18.6	13.2	12.3	13.5	20.2	...
A Increase in stocks	...	0.5	2.1	1.0	3.0	2.3	0.8	1.1	0.7	0.8	1.6	...
B Gross fixed capital formation	...	11.9	10.5	14.0	15.0	18.3	17.6	12.1	11.6	12.7	18.6	...
Residential buildings	...											...
Non-residential buildings	...	8.5	5.9	8.7	8.2	8.9	10.6	6.9	7.4	8.5	10.2	...
Other construction and land improvement etc.	...											...
Other	...	3.4	4.6	5.3	6.8	9.4	7.0	5.2	4.1	4.2	8.4	...
4 Exports of goods and services	...	2.0	5.6	2.5	3.3	5.8	6.0	9.2	6.3	5.8	5.6	...
5 Less: Imports of goods and services	...	22.7	23.8	25.7	29.3	32.4	30.7	28.4	24.6	27.5	30.4	...
Equals: Gross Domestic Product	...	31.3	32.4	36.2	39.9	41.1	42.8	41.6	42.3	44.3	46.6	...

1.4 General Government Current Receipts and Disbursements

Thousand East Caribbean dollars

	1970	1975	1978	1979	1980	1981	1982	1983	1984	1985	1986	1987
					Receipts							
1 Operating surplus	...	...	...	...	...	...	...	...	...	...	...	...
2 Property and entrepreneurial income	...	529	653	1073	1090	1994	...	...	...	...	...	...
3 Taxes, fees and contributions	...	4471	6198	9021	12840	15453	...	...	...	...	...	...
A Indirect taxes	...	2551	3438	5305	7948	9807	10020	9980	10554	11890	...	...
B Direct taxes	...	1000	1705	2358	2853	3299	4040	5210	5686	5100	...	...
C Social security contributions	...	-	-	-	-	-	-	...	...	...	...	...
D Compulsory fees, fines and penalties	...	920	1055	1358	2039	2347	...	...	...	...	...	...
4 Other current transfers	...	66	706	432	763	570	785	865	1099	349	...	...
Total Current Receipts of General Government	...	5066	7557	10526	14693	18017	19776	20920	21559	22119	...	...
					Disbursements							
1 Government final consumption expenditure	...	6280	7786	9906	12242	14119	16877	17929	19279	20279	...	...

Montserrat

1.4 General Government Current Receipts and Disbursements
(Continued)

Thousand East Caribbean dollars

	1970	1975	1978	1979	1980	1981	1982	1983	1984	1985	1986	1987
A Compensation of employees	...	4709	5439	7281	8700	8828	10792	12109	13400	14068	...	...
B Consumption of fixed capital	...	...	...	...	...	...	...	...	...	...	...	...
C Purchases of goods and services, net	...	1571	2347	2625	3542	5291	6085	5820	5879	6211	...	...
D Less: Own account fixed capital formation	...	...	...	...	...	...	...	...	...	...	...	...
E Indirect taxes paid, net	...	...	...	...	...	...	...	...	...	...	...	...
2 Property income	...	80	54	45	57	303	370	326	268	257	...	...
A Interest	...	80	54	45	57	303	370	326	268	257	...	...
B Net land rent and royalties	...	-	-	-	-	-	-	-	-	-	...	...
3 Subsidies	...	116	93	80	120	135	-	130	139	155	...	...
4 Other current transfers	...	674	789	873	1096	1175	1378	1593	1668	1105	...	...
5 Net saving	...	-2084	-1165	-378	1178	2285	1151	942	205	323	...	...
Total Current Disbursements and Net Saving of General Government	...	5066	7557	10526	14693	18017	19776	20920	21559	22119	...	...

1.10 Gross Domestic Product by Kind of Activity, in Current Prices

Million East Caribbean dollars

	1970	1975	1978	1979	1980	1981	1982	1983	1984	1985	1986	1987
1 Agriculture, hunting, forestry and fishing	...	1.2	1.5	2.0	2.4	3.0	3.3	3.3	3.9	4.1	4.8	...
2 Mining and quarrying	...	0.2	0.4	0.4	0.4	0.5	1.1	0.7	1.1	1.2	1.3	...
3 Manufacturing	...	1.4	2.3	3.0	3.4	4.1	4.0	5.3	5.6	5.1	6.5	...
4 Electricity, gas and water	...	0.7	1.1	1.0	1.9	2.0	2.1	3.0	3.3	3.3	3.7	...
5 Construction	...	2.8	3.0	4.9	5.3	6.4	8.3	5.7	6.2	7.1	8.5	...
6 Wholesale and retail trade, restaurants and hotels	...	4.2	6.8	6.6	10.6	15.0	16.1	16.1	16.0	17.0	20.5	...
7 Transport, storage and communication	...	1.5	3.1	3.6	4.3	5.2	6.5	8.5	9.7	11.0	12.2	...
8 Finance, insurance, real estate and business services	...	6.7	7.9	8.9	17.7	15.7	16.7	19.8	20.7	21.5	24.2	...
9 Community, social and personal services	...	2.8	4.1	5.0	8.6	10.0	16.6	11.4	13.1	14.1	13.9	...
Total, Industries	...	21.5	30.2	35.4	54.6	61.9	68.9	73.8	79.6	84.4	95.6	...
Producers of Government Services	...	0.8	3.0	4.0	4.9	4.9	5.8	6.6	7.7	8.3	10.4	...
Other Producers	...	...	...	...	...	...	...	...	...	...	...	...
Subtotal [a]	...	22.3	33.2	39.4	59.5	66.8	74.7	80.4	87.3	92.7	106.0	...
Less: Imputed bank service charge	...	-0.8	1.2	1.3	1.9	2.8	3.7	3.6	4.0	4.1	4.8	...
Plus: Import duties	...	...	...	...	...	...	...	...	...	...	...	...
Plus: Value added tax	...	...	...	...	...	...	...	...	...	...	...	...
Plus: Other adjustments [b]	...	2.3	3.3	5.2	7.8	9.3	10.0	9.7	10.3	11.5	12.9	...
Equals: Gross Domestic Product	...	25.4	35.2	43.2	65.4	73.3	81.0	86.5	93.6	100.1	114.1	...

a) Gross domestic product in factor values.
b) Item 'Other adjustments' refers to indirect taxes net of subsidies.

1.11 Gross Domestic Product by Kind of Activity, in Constant Prices

Million East Caribbean dollars

	1970	1975	1978	1979	1980	1981	1982	1983	1984	1985	1986	1987
					At constant prices of:1977							
1 Agriculture, hunting, forestry and fishing	...	1.6	1.3	1.6	1.5	1.7	1.6	1.4	1.7	1.8	1.9	...
2 Mining and quarrying	...	0.3	0.3	0.3	0.3	0.3	0.7	0.3	0.5	0.5	0.5	...
3 Manufacturing	...	1.7	2.4	2.8	3.1	3.5	3.4	3.6	3.5	3.5	3.8	...
4 Electricity, gas and water	...	0.8	1.0	1.0	1.1	1.1	1.1	1.2	1.3	1.3	1.4	...
5 Construction	...	3.8	2.6	3.8	3.6	4.0	4.7	3.1	3.3	3.8	4.5	...
6 Wholesale and retail trade, restaurants and hotels	...	6.3	6.5	6.8	7.7	8.1	8.2	8.0	7.6	8.0	8.2	...
7 Transport, storage and communication	...	1.9	2.5	2.6	2.8	2.9	3.1	3.2	3.2	3.5	3.5	...
8 Finance, insurance, real estate and business services	...	7.5	7.8	8.2	8.5	8.7	8.8	8.9	9.2	9.4	9.8	...
9 Community, social and personal services	...	3.3	3.5	3.6	5.0	4.9	4.7	4.5	4.6	4.7	4.2	...
Total, Industries	...	27.2	28.0	30.8	33.7	35.2	36.3	34.2	34.9	36.5	37.8	...
Producers of Government Services	...	2.6	2.8	2.9	3.2	3.1	3.3	3.6	3.9	4.1	4.8	...

Montserrat

1.11 Gross Domestic Product by Kind of Activity, in Constant Prices
(Continued)

Million East Caribbean dollars

	1970	1975	1978	1979	1980	1981	1982	1983	1984	1985	1986	1987
				At constant prices of:1977								
Other Producers	...	...	...	...	...	...	...	...	...	...	...	...
Subtotal a	...	29.8	30.8	33.7	36.9	38.3	39.6	37.8	38.8	40.6	42.6	...
Less: Imputed bank service charge	...	1.4	1.1	1.3	1.6	1.6	1.6	1.6	1.7	1.7	1.8	...
Plus: Import duties	...	...	...	...	...	...	...	...	...	...	...	...
Plus: Value added tax	...	...	...	...	...	...	...	...	...	...	...	...
Plus: Other adjustments b	...	3.0	2.9	3.8	4.6	4.4	4.8	5.4	5.2	5.3	5.8	...
Equals: Gross Domestic Product	...	31.3	32.4	36.2	39.9	41.1	42.8	41.6	42.3	44.2	46.6	...

a) Gross domestic product in factor values.
b) Item 'Other adjustments' refers to indirect taxes net of subsidies.

2.1 Government Final Consumption Expenditure by Function, in Current Prices

Thousand East Caribbean dollars

		1970	1975	1978	1979	1980	1981	1982	1983	1984	1985	1986	1987
1	General public services	...	1066	1254	2066	2281	2378	3109	2715	3786	3802	...	...
2	Defence	...	20	24	34	71	43	56	63	59	59	...	...
3	Public order and safety	...	847	889	1205	1373	1486	1752	1961	2031	2301	...	...
4	Education	...	1371	1427	1987	2222	2513	2772	3170	3727	4533	...	...
5	Health	...	1239	1456	1853	2298	2502	2822	3121	3063	3093	...	...
6	Social security and welfare	...	552	856	711	1225	1174	1522	1652	1275	982	...	...
7	Housing and community amenities	...	54	53	89	75	148	141	135	-45	188	...	...
8	Recreational, cultural and religious affairs	...	29	40	55	64	75	175	249	120	341	...	...
9	Economic services	...	1114	1703	1876	2500	3793	4475	4832	5250	4963	...	...
	A Fuel and energy	...	-8	35	43	54	63	69	191	-	-	...	...
	B Agriculture, forestry, fishing and hunting	...	285	349	454	732	661	732	914	1380	1569	...	...
	C Mining, manufacturing and construction, except fuel and energy	...	224	351	341	457	956	1416	2436	3391	2433	...	...
	D Transportation and communication	...	577	716	912	1173	1641	1959	868	420	927	...	...
	E Other economic affairs	...	36	252	126	84	472	299	423	59	34	...	...
10	Other functions	...	-12	84	30	133	7	38	-	13	17	...	...
	Total Government Final Consumption Expenditure	...	6280	7786	9906	12242	14119	16862	17929	19279	20279	...	...

4.1 Derivation of Value Added by Kind of Activity, in Current Prices

Million East Caribbean dollars

		1980			1981		
		Gross Output	Intermediate Consumption	Value Added	Gross Output	Intermediate Consumption	Value Added
				All Producers			
1	Agriculture, hunting, forestry and fishing	...	...	2.4	...	...	3.0
	A Agriculture and hunting	...	...	1.7	...	...	2.3
	B Forestry and logging	...	...	0.4	...	...	0.4
	C Fishing	...	...	0.3	...	...	0.3
2	Mining and quarrying	...	...	0.4	...	...	0.5
3	Manufacturing	...	...	3.5	...	...	4.1
4	Electricity, gas and water	...	...	1.9	...	...	2.0
5	Construction	...	...	5.3	...	...	6.4
6	Wholesale and retail trade, restaurants and hotels	...	...	10.7	...	...	15.0
	A Wholesale and retail trade	...	...	8.9	...	...	12.6
	B Restaurants and hotels	...	...	1.7	...	...	2.4
	Restaurants	...	...	0.1	...	...	0.2
	Hotels and other lodging places	...	...	1.6	...	...	2.2
7	Transport, storage and communication	...	...	4.3	...	...	5.2
	A Transport and storage	...	...	3.5	...	...	4.3
	B Communication	...	...	0.8	...	...	0.9
8	Finance, insurance, real estate and business services	...	...	17.7	...	...	15.7
	A Financial institutions	...	...	2.3	...	...	2.7

Montserrat

4.1 Derivation of Value Added by Kind of Activity, in Current Prices
(Continued)

Million East Caribbean dollars

	1980 Gross Output	1980 Intermediate Consumption	1980 Value Added	1981 Gross Output	1981 Intermediate Consumption	1981 Value Added
B Insurance	...	...	0.4	...	...	0.8
C Real estate and business services	...	...	15.0	...	...	12.2
Real estate, except dwellings	...	...	1.2	...	...	1.5
Dwellings	...	...	13.8	...	...	10.7
9 Community, social and personal services	...	...	8.6	...	...	10.0
A Sanitary and similar services	...	...	-	...	...	-
B Social and related community services	...	...	5.8	...	...	7.2
C Recreational and cultural services	...	...	2.0	...	...	1.9
D Personal and household services	...	...	0.8	...	...	0.9
Total, Industries	...	...	54.6	...	...	61.9
Producers of Government Services	...	...	4.9	...	...	4.9
Other Producers	...	...	...	...	...	...
Total [a]	...	...	59.5	...	...	66.8
Less: Imputed bank service charge	...	...	1.9	...	...	2.8
Import duties	...	...	...	...	...	...
Value added tax	...	...	...	...	...	...
Other adjustments [b]	...	...	7.8	...	...	9.3
Total	...	...	65.4	...	...	73.3
Memorandum Item: Mineral fuels and power	...	...	1.4	...	...	...

a) Gross domestic product in factor values.
b) Item 'Other adjustments' refers to indirect taxes net of subsidies.

Morocco

Source. Reply to the United Nations National Accounts Questionnaire from the Division du Plan et des Etudes Economiques, Rabat. Official estimates are published by the Division in 'Comptes de la Nation'.

General note. The estimates have been adjusted by the Division du Plan et des Etudes Economiques to conform to the United Nations System of National Accounts so far as the existing data would permit. It should be noted that the domestic territory is defined to include all de facto residents, such as foreign diplomats and troops.

1.1 Expenditure on the Gross Domestic Product, in Current Prices

Thousand Million Moroccan Dirhams

	1970	1975	1978	1979	1980	1981	1982	1983	1984	1985	1986	1987
1 Government final consumption expenditure	2.40	5.86	11.47	13.23	13.59	15.08	17.00	16.63	17.48	20.52	23.59	23.37
2 Private final consumption expenditure	14.53	24.80	36.44	40.81	49.50	53.70	61.49	66.55	77.42	84.48	95.38	100.93
3 Gross capital formation	3.70	9.25	14.03	15.19	17.93	20.64	26.22	23.78	28.40	35.13	44.59	40.76
A Increase in stocks	0.71	0.21	0.30	0.32	1.45	0.13	0.84	-0.45	2.45	5.20	11.50	8.78
B Gross fixed capital formation	2.99	9.04	13.73	14.87	16.48	20.51	25.38	24.23	25.95	29.93	33.09	31.98
4 Exports of goods and services	3.54	8.43	9.35	10.83	13.04	16.22	18.14	21.10	26.95	32.20	33.02	35.52
5 Less: Imports of goods and services	4.15	11.93	16.14	18.02	19.97	26.60	29.94	28.92	37.91	42.81	41.94	41.58
Equals: Gross Domestic Product	20.02	36.41	55.15	62.04	74.09	79.03	92.90	99.14	112.34	129.51	154.62	159.00

1.2 Expenditure on the Gross Domestic Product, in Constant Prices

Thousand Million Moroccan Dirhams

	1970	1975	1978	1979	1980	1981	1982	1983	1984	1985	1986	1987
	\multicolumn{12}{c}{At constant prices of:1960}											
1 Government final consumption expenditure	2.36	4.17	...	...	...	...	...	...	...	...	...	...
2 Private final consumption expenditure	14.34	17.21	...	...	...	...	...	...	...	...	...	...
3 Gross capital formation	2.81	5.61	...	...	...	...	...	...	...	...	...	...
A Increase in stocks	0.07	0.13	...	...	...	...	...	...	...	...	...	...
B Gross fixed capital formation	2.74	5.48	...	...	...	...	...	...	...	...	...	...
4 Exports of goods and services	3.54	3.96	...	...	...	...	...	...	...	...	...	...
5 Less: Imports of goods and services	4.15	6.47	...	...	...	...	...	...	...	...	...	...
Equals: Gross Domestic Product	18.89	24.49	...	...	...	...	...	...	...	...	...	...

1.3 Cost Components of the Gross Domestic Product

Thousand Million Moroccan Dirhams

	1970	1975	1978	1979	1980	1981	1982	1983	1984	1985	1986	1987
1 Indirect taxes, net	2.55	3.20	6.37	7.50	9.70	...	...	...	...	...	...	...
2 Consumption of fixed capital	...	...	...	...	...	...	...	...	...	...	...	...
3 Compensation of employees paid by resident producers to:	6.47	11.69	17.54	20.55	23.22	...	...	...	...	...	...	...
4 Operating surplus [a]	11.00	21.53	31.24	34.00	41.17	...	...	...	...	...	...	...
Equals: Gross Domestic Product	20.02	36.41	55.15	62.04	74.09	...	...	...	...	...	...	...

a) Item 'Operating surplus' includes consumption of fixed capital.

1.7 External Transactions on Current Account, Summary

Thousand Million Moroccan Dirhams

	1970	1975	1978	1979	1980	1981	1982	1983	1984	1985	1986	1987
	\multicolumn{12}{c}{Payments to the Rest of the World}											
1 Imports of goods and services	4.15	11.93	16.14	18.02	19.97	26.60	29.94	28.92	37.91	42.81	41.94	41.58
A Imports of merchandise c.i.f.	...	...	...	...	18.39	24.54	27.48	26.38	35.13	39.57	37.19	37.87
B Other	...	...	...	...	1.58	2.06	2.46	2.54	2.78	3.24	4.75	3.71
2 Factor income to the rest of the world	0.45	0.66	1.74	2.22	2.79	4.32	5.00	5.09	5.46	8.17	6.81	6.89
A Compensation of employees	0.03	0.03	0.04	0.04	0.01	0.01	0.01	0.01	0.02	0.02	0.03	0.03
B Property and entrepreneurial income	0.42	0.63	1.70	2.18	2.78	4.31	4.99	5.08	5.44	8.15	6.78	6.86
3 Current transfers to the rest of the world	0.25	0.38	0.49	0.55	0.64	0.68	0.71	0.80	0.85	0.69	0.46	0.54
4 Surplus of the nation on current transactions	-0.57	-2.05	-5.40	-5.77	-5.30	-9.15	-10.92	-6.11	-8.32	-8.05	-1.50	1.80
Payments to the Rest of the World and Surplus of the Nation on Current Transactions	4.28	10.91	12.96	15.01	18.10	22.45	24.73	28.70	35.90	43.62	47.70	50.81
	\multicolumn{12}{c}{Receipts From The Rest of the World}											
1 Exports of goods and services	3.54	8.43	9.35	10.83	13.04	16.22	18.14	21.10	26.95	32.20	33.02	35.52

Morocco

1.7 External Transactions on Current Account, Summary
(Continued)

Thousand Million Moroccan Dirhams

	1970	1975	1978	1979	1980	1981	1982	1983	1984	1985	1986	1987
A Exports of merchandise f.o.b.	...	...	...	...	9.65	12.00	12.47	14.76	19.12	21.75	22.11	23.39
B Other	...	...	...	...	3.39	4.22	5.67	6.34	7.83	10.45	10.91	12.13
2 Factor income from rest of the world	0.13	0.45	0.62	0.76	0.25	0.31	0.33	0.23	0.37	0.52	0.49	0.44
A Compensation of employees	0.04	0.23	0.35	0.42	0.03	0.04	0.05	0.05	0.07	0.08	0.10	0.10
B Property and entrepreneurial income	0.09	0.22	0.27	0.34	0.22	0.27	0.28	0.18	0.30	0.44	0.39	0.34
3 Current transfers from rest of the world	0.61	2.02	2.98	3.43	4.79	5.96	6.25	7.37	8.55	10.88	14.19	14.85
Receipts from the Rest of the World on Current Transactions	4.28	10.91	12.96	15.01	18.10	22.45	24.73	28.70	35.90	43.62	47.70	50.81

1.10 Gross Domestic Product by Kind of Activity, in Current Prices

Thousand Million Moroccan Dirhams

	1970	1975	1978	1979	1980	1981	1982	1983	1984	1985	1986	1987
1 Agriculture, hunting, forestry and fishing	3.99	6.52	10.44	11.12	13.65	10.21	14.22	15.03	16.85	21.50	29.80	23.99
2 Mining and quarrying	0.66	3.30	2.08	2.75	3.41	4.41	3.95	4.11	5.31	5.63	4.45	4.44
3 Manufacturing	3.25	6.23	9.37	10.44	12.47	14.30	16.09	18.22	20.74	24.03	25.99	28.63
4 Electricity, gas and water	0.64	0.90	1.34	2.14	2.40	2.36	3.01	4.05	4.96	6.19	11.24	11.68
5 Construction	0.85	2.38	4.51	4.94	4.65	5.85	6.58	6.57	6.38	7.39	7.67	7.37
6 Wholesale and retail trade, restaurants and hotels	3.92	6.25	8.57	9.16	10.61	11.38	13.46	13.33	15.57	18.25	22.60	24.45
7 Transport, storage and communication	0.84	1.55	2.47	2.64	3.38	4.46	5.14	5.98	7.20	8.32	9.13	10.35
8 Finance, insurance, real estate and business services	0.30	0.71	1.20	1.33	1.88	2.02	2.11	2.41	3.25	3.86	4.45	4.81
9 Community, social and personal services [a]	4.71	8.05	12.72	14.80	8.14	8.93	10.11	11.06	12.58	14.13	15.81	16.66
Total, Industries	...	...	...	...	61.09	63.92	74.67	80.76	92.84	109.30	131.14	132.38
Producers of Government Services	...	...	...	...	8.79	10.43	11.77	13.18	14.01	14.84	16.67	17.71
Other Producers [a]	...	...	...	...	...	...	...	...	...	...	...	...
Subtotal	19.16	35.89	52.69	59.30	69.88	74.35	86.44	93.94	106.85	124.14	147.81	150.09
Less: Imputed bank service charge	0.28	0.69	1.11	1.20	1.57	1.80	1.78	2.39	2.97	3.67	4.20	4.53
Plus: Import duties	1.14	1.21	3.57	3.94	5.79	6.48	8.24	7.59	8.48	9.05	11.02	13.45
Plus: Value added tax	...	...	...	...	...	...	...	...	...	...	...	...
Equals: Gross Domestic Product	20.02	36.41	55.15	62.04	74.09	79.03	92.90	99.14	112.34	129.51	154.62	159.00

a) Item 'Other producers' is included in item 'Community, social and personal services'.

1.11 Gross Domestic Product by Kind of Activity, in Constant Prices

Thousand Million Moroccan Dirhams

	1970	1975	1978	1979	1980	1981	1982	1983	1984	1985	1986	1987
	At constant prices of: 1969				1980							
1 Agriculture, hunting, forestry and fishing	3.72	3.47	4.14	4.07	4.32 / 13.65	9.75	13.15	11.79	12.23	14.48	20.01	15.22
2 Mining and quarrying	0.65	0.72	0.92	0.98	0.93 / 3.41	3.47	3.29	3.42	3.64	3.62	3.44	3.37
3 Manufacturing	3.21	4.33	5.19	5.27	5.52 / 12.47	12.65	13.32	13.88	14.48	15.50	15.64	16.22
4 Electricity, gas and water	0.64	0.89	1.02	1.62	1.33 / 2.40	2.36	2.44	2.56	2.62	2.75	2.91	3.12
5 Construction	0.78	1.60	1.67	1.62	1.47 / 4.65	5.03	5.12	4.64	4.10	4.40	4.40	4.19
6 Wholesale and retail trade, restaurants and hotels	3.61	4.81	5.55	5.66	6.41 / 10.61	10.32	11.27	11.05	11.57	12.23	12.89	12.96
7 Transport, storage and communication	0.84	1.09	1.49	1.53	1.56 / 3.88	4.04	4.25	4.54	4.67	4.86	4.93	5.14
8 Finance, insurance, real estate and business services	0.30	0.50	0.63	0.63	0.67 / 1.88	1.80	1.69	1.82	2.19	2.41	2.56	2.68
9 Community, social and personal services [a]	4.91	6.06	7.93	8.53	9.23 / 8.14	8.12	8.40	8.67	8.85	9.22	9.53	9.75

Morocco

1.11 Gross Domestic Product by Kind of Activity, in Constant Prices
(Continued)

Thousand Million Moroccan Dirhams

	1970	1975	1978	1979	1980	1981	1982	1983	1984	1985	1986	1987
			At constant prices of:									
			1969						1980			
Total, Industries	...	...	...	...	61.09	57.54	62.93	62.37	64.35	69.47	76.31	72.65
Producers of Government Services	...	...	...	...	8.79	9.87	10.74	12.02	12.78	13.30	14.62	15.26
Other Producers	...	...	...	...	...	...	...	...	...	...	...	...
Subtotal	18.64	23.47	28.53	29.92	31.25 / 69.88	67.41	73.67	74.39	77.13	82.77	90.93	87.91
Less: Imputed bank service charge	0.28	0.48	0.57	0.58	0.61 / 1.57	1.60	1.44	1.81	2.01	2.30	2.41	2.53
Plus: Import duties	0.99	1.63	1.62	1.66	1.76 / 5.79	6.24	6.73	5.94	6.82	6.63	6.39	6.79
Plus: Value added tax	...	...	...	...	...	...	...	...	...	...	...	...
Equals: Gross Domestic Product	19.35	24.62	29.58	31.00	32.13 / 74.09	72.04	78.97	78.53	81.93	87.11	94.90	92.17

a) Item 'Other producers' is included in item 'Community, social and personal services'.
b) Items 'Other producers' and 'Producers of government services' are included in item 'Community, social and personal services'.

1.12 Relations Among National Accounting Aggregates

Thousand Million Moroccan Dirhams

	1970	1975	1978	1979	1980	1981	1982	1983	1984	1985	1986	1987
Gross Domestic Product	20.02	36.41	55.15	62.04	74.09	79.03	92.90	99.14	112.34	129.51	154.62	159.00
Plus: Net factor income from the rest of the world	-0.32	-0.19	-1.11	-1.46	-2.54	-4.01	-4.67	-4.86	-5.09	-7.65	-6.32	-6.45
Factor income from the rest of the world	0.13	0.45	0.62	0.76	0.25	0.31	0.33	0.23	0.37	0.52	0.49	0.44
Less: Factor income to the rest of the world	0.45	0.66	1.74	2.22	2.79	4.32	5.00	5.09	5.46	8.17	6.81	6.89
Equals: Gross National Product	19.70	36.22	54.04	60.58	71.55	75.02	88.23	94.28	107.25	121.86	148.30	152.55
Less: Consumption of fixed capital	...	...	...	...	...	...	...	...	...	...	...	...
Equals: National Income [a]	19.70	36.22	54.04	60.58	71.55	75.02	88.23	94.28	107.25	121.86	148.30	152.55
Plus: Net current transfers from the rest of the world	0.36	1.64	2.50	2.89	4.15	5.28	5.54	6.57	7.70	10.19	13.73	14.31
Current transfers from the rest of the world	0.61	2.02	2.98	3.43	4.79	5.96	6.25	7.37	8.55	10.88	14.19	14.85
Less: Current transfers to the rest of the world	0.25	0.38	0.48	0.54	0.64	0.68	0.71	0.80	0.85	0.69	0.46	0.54
Equals: National Disposable Income [b]	20.06	37.86	56.54	63.47	75.72	80.26	93.76	100.85	114.99	132.06	162.04	166.86
Less: Final consumption	16.93	30.66	47.91	54.04	63.09	68.77	78.49	83.18	94.90	104.99	118.96	124.30
Equals: Net Saving [c]	3.13	7.20	8.63	9.43	12.63	11.49	15.30	17.67	20.09	27.07	43.08	42.56
Less: Surplus of the nation on current transactions	-0.57	-2.05	-5.40	-5.77	-5.30	-9.15	-10.92	-6.11	-8.32	-8.05	-1.50	1.80
Equals: Net Capital Formation [d]	3.70	9.25	14.03	15.19	17.93	20.64	26.22	23.78	28.40	35.13	44.59	40.76

a) Item 'National income' includes consumption of fixed capital.
b) Item 'National disposable income' includes consumption of fixed capital.
c) Item 'Net saving' includes consumption of fixed capital.
d) Item 'Net capital formation' includes consumption of fixed capital.

2.17 Exports and Imports of Goods and Services, Detail

Thousand Million Moroccan Dirhams

		1970	1975	1978	1979	1980	1981	1982	1983	1984	1985	1986	1987
						Exports of Goods and Services							
1	Exports of merchandise, f.o.b.					9.65	12.00	12.47	14.76	19.12	21.75	22.11	23.39
2	Transport and communication	2.46	6.94	6.26	7.62	1.16	1.37	1.86	1.65	1.88	2.21	2.40	2.45
3	Insurance service charges					0.03	0.04	0.06	0.06	0.05	0.07	0.07	0.07
4	Other commodities	0.41	0.31	1.44	1.54	0.20	0.50	0.90	1.01	1.21	1.55	1.13	1.22
5	Adjustments of merchandise exports to change-of-ownership basis	...	...	...	...	...	...	...	...	...	...	...	...
6	Direct purchases in the domestic market by non-residential households [a]	0.67	1.18	1.65	1.67	1.91	2.20	2.70	3.46	4.49	6.39	6.99	8.06
7	Direct purchases in the domestic market by extraterritorial bodies	...	...	...	...	0.09	0.12	0.16	0.17	0.20	0.24	0.33	0.33
	Total Exports of Goods and Services	3.54	8.43	9.35	10.83	13.04	16.22	18.14	21.10	26.95	32.20	33.02	35.52

Morocco

2.17 Exports and Imports of Goods and Services, Detail
(Continued)

Thousand Million Moroccan Dirhams

	1970	1975	1978	1979	1980	1981	1982	1983	1984	1985	1986	1987
Imports of Goods and Services												
1 Imports of merchandise, c.i.f.					18.39	24.54	27.48	26.38	35.13	39.57	37.19	37.87
A Imports of merchandise, f.o.b.	3.47	11.05	15.10	16.96	...	...	...	...	...	...	...	...
B Transport of services on merchandise imports					...	...	...	...	...	...	...	...
C Insurance service charges on merchandise imports					...	...	...	...	...	...	...	...
2 Adjustments of merchandise imports to change-of-ownership basis	...	...	...	...	...	...	...	...	...	...	...	...
3 Other transport and communication	...	...	...	...	0.27	0.29	0.36	0.25	0.25	0.34	0.33	0.36
4 Other insurance service charges	...	...	...	...	0.01	0.02	0.02	0.01	0.02	0.03	0.03	0.03
5 Other commodities	0.68	0.88	1.04	1.05	0.74	1.08	1.36	1.46	1.64	1.72	3.14	1.83
6 Direct purchases abroad by government	...	...	...	...	0.08	0.09	0.11	0.11	0.11	0.12	0.16	0.18
7 Direct purchases abroad by resident households	...	...	...	...	0.48	0.58	0.62	0.71	0.76	1.03	1.10	1.31
Total Imports of Goods and Services	4.15	11.93	16.14	18.02	19.97	26.60	29.94	28.92	37.91	42.81	41.94	41.58
Balance of Goods and Services	-0.61	-3.50	-6.79	-7.19	-6.93	-10.38	-11.80	-7.82	-10.96	-10.61	-8.92	-6.06
Total Imports and Balance of Goods and Services	3.54	8.43	9.35	10.83	13.04	16.22	18.14	21.10	26.95	32.20	33.02	35.52

a) Item 'Direct purchases in the domestic market by non-resident households' refers to foreign tourists and agencies.

Mozambique

Source. The estimates are published by the Direccao Nacional de Estatistica in 'Infermacao Estadistica'.

General note. The estimates shown in the following tables have been prepared in accordance with the United Nations System of National Accounts so far as the existing data would permit.

1.1 Expenditure on the Gross Domestic Product, in Current Prices

Thousand Million Mozambique Meticais

	1970	1975	1978	1979	1980	1981	1982	1983	1984	1985	1986	1987
1 Government final consumption expenditure	...	...	...	...	14	17	19	21	22	24	...	...
2 Private final consumption expenditure	...	...	...	...	64	65	77	80	93	127	...	...
3 Gross capital formation	...	...	...	...	15	16	18	9	11	10	...	...
4 Exports of goods and services	...	...	...	...	-14	-16	-21	-19	-18	-15	...	...
5 Less: Imports of goods and services	...	...	...	...							...	...
Equals: Gross Domestic Product	...	...	...	...	78	82	92	91	109	147	...	...

1.3 Cost Components of the Gross Domestic Product

Thousand Million Mozambique Meticais

	1970	1975	1978	1979	1980	1981	1982	1983	1984	1985	1986	1987
1 Indirect taxes, net	...	...	...	...	8	8	8	8	9	6	...	...
A Indirect taxes	...	...	...	...	8	9	9	9	10	7	...	...
B Less: Subsidies	...	...	...	...	-	1	1	1	1	1	...	...
2 Consumption of fixed capital	...	...	...	...	5	5	5	4	4	4	...	...
3 Compensation of employees paid by resident producers to:	...	...	...	...	65	69	79	79	96	137	...	...
4 Operating surplus	...	...	...	...							...	...
Equals: Gross Domestic Product	...	...	...	...	78	82	92	91	109	147	...	...

1.12 Relations Among National Accounting Aggregates

Thousand Million Mozambique Meticais

	1970	1975	1978	1979	1980	1981	1982	1983	1984	1985	1986	1987
Gross Domestic Product	...	...	...	...	78	82	92	91	109	147	...	...
Plus: Net factor income from the rest of the world	...	...	...	...	1	-	-1	1	-	-	...	...
Equals: Gross National Product	...	...	...	...	79	81	91	92	109	147	...	...
Less: Consumption of fixed capital	...	...	...	...	5	5	5	4	4	4	...	...
Equals: National Income	...	...	...	...	74	76	86	88	105	143	...	...
Plus: Net current transfers from the rest of the world	...	...	...	...	...	...	...	...	...	...	...	...
Equals: National Disposable Income	...	...	...	...	...	...	...	...	...	...	...	...
Less: Final consumption	...	...	...	...	...	...	...	...	...	...	...	...
Equals: Net Saving	...	...	...	...	...	...	...	...	...	...	...	...
Less: Surplus of the nation on current transactions	...	...	...	...	...	...	...	...	...	...	...	...
Equals: Net Capital Formation	...	...	...	...	...	...	...	...	...	...	...	...

Myanmar

Source. Reply to the United Nations National Accounts Questionnaire from the Planning Department, Ministry of Planning and Finance, Rangoon. The official estimates and descriptions are published annually in the 'National Income of Burma', by the same Department.

General note. The estimates shown in the following tables have been prepared in accordance with the United Nations System of National Accounts so far as the existing data would permit.

1.1 Expenditure on the Gross Domestic Product, in Current Prices

Million Myanmarese kyats

	1970	1975	1978	1979	1980	1981	1982	1983	1984	1985	1986	1987
1 Government final consumption expenditure	9168	21389	27404	29088	31775	35217	39747	42685	47395	49532	52802	53859
2 Private final consumption expenditure												
3 Gross capital formation	1453	2339	5778	7876	8293	9841	10375	8962	8110	8693	7460	8802
A Increase in stocks	293	659	414	487	1065	1206	331	-95	-367	44	-1157	-1620
B Gross fixed capital formation	1160	1680	5364	7389	7228	8635	10044	9057	8477	8649	8617	10422
4 Exports of goods and services	535	1192	1842	2679	3176	3432	3003	3373	3133	2566	2433	2099
5 Less: Imports of goods and services	896	1443	3224	4310	4635	5611	6314	5197	5041	4802	3936	4100
Equals: Gross Domestic Product ab	10260	23477	31800	35333	38609	42879	46811	49823	53597	55989	58759	60660

a) For 1970-1974, all estimates refer to year ending 30 September.
b) Constant price data are valued at 1969-1970 average market prices, thus, data for current and constant prices do not agree in the base year.

1.2 Expenditure on the Gross Domestic Product, in Constant Prices

Million Myanmarese kyats

At constant prices of: 1970

	1970	1975	1978	1979	1980	1981	1982	1983	1984	1985	1986	1987
1 Government final consumption expenditure	9026	10410	12038	12464	13461	14276	15321	16147	17469	17908	18095	18468
2 Private final consumption expenditure												
3 Gross capital formation	1311	1158	2033	2372	2517	2872	2888	2477	2244	2386	2094	2273
A Increase in stocks	158	350	181	166	359	418	101	-26	-96	17	-263	-437
B Gross fixed capital formation	1153	808	1852	2206	2158	2454	2787	2503	2340	2369	2357	2710
4 Exports of goods and services	535	448	555	747	811	810	815	919	822	807	916	839
5 Less: Imports of goods and services	896	454	783	1021	1071	1241	1370	1114	1080	1024	835	864
Equals: Gross Domestic Product ab	9976	11562	13843	14562	15718	16717	17654	18429	19455	20077	20270	20716

a) For 1970-1974, all estimates refer to year ending 30 September.
b) Constant price data are valued at 1969-1970 average market prices, thus, data for current and constant prices do not agree in the base year.

1.3 Cost Components of the Gross Domestic Product

Million Myanmarese kyats

	1970	1975	1978	1979	1980	1981	1982	1983	1984	1985	1986	1987
1 Indirect taxes, net	974	2270	3119	3417	3709	4063	4363	4336	4288	4725	4830	4883
A Indirect taxes	974	2270	3119	3417	3709	4063	4363	4336	4288	4725	4830	4883
B Less: Subsidies	...	...	...	...	...	...	...	...	...	...	...	...
2 Consumption of fixed capital	711	1903	2724	3152	3415	3784	4166	4484	4871	5056	5294	5526
3 Compensation of employees paid by resident producers to:	4202	9494	12045	13462	14596	16190	17812	18998	20637	21478	22380	23275
4 Operating surplus	4373	9810	13912	15302	16889	18842	20470	22005	23801	24730	26255	26976
Equals: Gross Domestic Product a	10260	23477	31800	35333	38609	42879	46811	49823	53597	55989	58759	60660

a) For 1970-1974, all estimates refer to year ending 30 September.

Myanmar

1.10 Gross Domestic Product by Kind of Activity, in Current Prices

Million Myanmarese kyats — Fiscal year beginning 1 April

	1970	1975	1978	1979	1980	1981	1982	1983	1984	1985	1986	1987
1 Agriculture, hunting, forestry and fishing	3899	11051	14058	16203	17970	20330	22319	23711	25795	26983	29535	30668
2 Mining and quarrying	111	136	316	410	427	430	501	504	545	533	499	533
3 Manufacturing	1072	2106	3172	3363	3683	4009	4350	4775	5280	5561	5427	5597
4 Electricity, gas and water [a]	61	66	98	126	135	167	210	227	263	278	279	282
5 Construction	212	221	419	503	647	692	833	872	946	945	961	977
6 Wholesale and retail trade, restaurants and hotels [b]	2611	6846	9283	9669	10121	10714	11512	12273	12886	13389	13348	13469
7 Transport, storage and communication	618	740	960	1215	1357	1612	1834	1985	2106	2218	2320	2439
8 Finance, insurance, real estate and business services [c]	112	123	564	648	829	1039	1096	1172	1254	1332	1421	1499
9 Community, social and personal services [bca]	749	864	1243	1430	1603	1854	1941	2038	2125	2182	2257	2327
Total, Industries	9445	22153	30113	33567	36772	40847	44596	47557	51200	53421	56047	57791
Producers of Government Services	815	1324	1687	1766	1837	2032	2215	2266	2397	2568	2712	2869
Other Producers	...	...	...	...	...	...	...	...	...	...	...	...
Subtotal [de]	10260	23477	31800	35333	38609	42879	46811	49823	53597	55989	58759	60660
Less: Imputed bank service charge	...	...	...	...	...	...	...	...	...	...	...	...
Plus: Import duties	...	...	...	...	...	...	...	...	...	...	...	...
Plus: Value added tax	...	...	...	...	...	...	...	...	...	...	...	...
Equals: Gross Domestic Product [de]	10260	23477	31800	35333	38609	42879	46811	49823	53597	55989	58759	60660
Memorandum Item: Mineral fuels and power	...	...	...	...	4269	4909	5242	...	...	...	...	...

a) Item 'Electricity, gas and water' refers to electricity only. Gas and water are included in item 'Community, social and personal services'.
b) Restaurants and hotels are included in item 'Community, social and personal services'.
c) Insurance, real estate and business services are included in item 'Community, social and personal services'.
d) For 1970-1974, all estimates refer to year ending 30 September.
e) Constant price data are valued at 1969-1970 average market prices, thus, data for current and constant prices do not agree in the base year.

1.11 Gross Domestic Product by Kind of Activity, in Constant Prices

Million Myanmarese kyats — Fiscal year beginning 1 April

At constant prices of: 1970

	1970	1975	1978	1979	1980	1981	1982	1983	1984	1985	1986	1987
1 Agriculture, hunting, forestry and fishing	3707	4219	5033	5299	5846	6297	6674	7001	7310	7482	7563	7665
2 Mining and quarrying	111	120	169	196	190	197	214	221	253	263	262	260
3 Manufacturing	1071	1200	1419	1475	1585	1705	1795	1854	2007	2050	1997	2043
4 Electricity, gas and water [a]	61	97	136	150	171	207	243	262	302	319	331	366
5 Construction	212	200	313	368	444	455	483	507	549	548	553	562
6 Wholesale and retail trade, restaurants and hotels [b]	2519	2863	3250	3336	3483	3568	3694	3844	4032	4170	4103	4118
7 Transport, storage and communication	619	625	719	780	835	937	1041	1110	1175	1221	1263	1315
8 Finance, insurance, real estate and business services [c]	112	146	436	496	621	679	702	739	789	837	875	916
9 Community, social and personal services [bca]	749	859	914	943	971	1000	1022	1072	1117	1142	1175	1207

Myanmar

1.11 Gross Domestic Product by Kind of Activity, in Constant Prices
(Continued)

Million Myanmarese kyats — Fiscal year beginning 1 April

	1970	1975	1978	1979	1980	1981	1982	1983	1984	1985	1986	1987
				At constant prices of:1970								
Total, Industries	9161	10329	12389	13043	14146	15045	15868	16610	17534	18032	18122	18452
Producers of Government Services	815	1233	1454	1519	1572	1672	1786	1819	1921	2045	2148	2264
Other Producers	...	...	...	...	...	...	...	...	...	...	...	...
Subtotal [de]	9976	11562	13843	14562	15718	16717	17654	18429	19455	20077	20270	20716
Less: Imputed bank service charge	...	...	...	...	...	...	...	...	...	...	...	...
Plus: Import duties	...	...	...	...	...	...	...	...	...	...	...	...
Plus: Value added tax	...	...	...	...	...	...	...	...	...	...	...	...
Equals: Gross Domestic Product [de]	9976	11562	13843	14562	15718	16717	17654	18429	19455	20077	20270	20716

a) Item 'Electricity, gas and water' refers to electricity only. Gas and water are included in item 'Community, social and personal services'.
b) Restaurants and hotels are included in item 'Community, social and personal services'.
c) Insurance, real estate and business services are included in item 'Community, social and personal services'.
d) For 1970-1974, all estimates refer to year ending 30 September.
e) Constant price data are valued at 1969-1970 average market prices, thus, data for current and constant prices do not agree in the base year.

1.12 Relations Among National Accounting Aggregates

Million Myanmarese kyats — Fiscal year beginning 1 April

	1970	1975	1978	1979	1980	1981	1982	1983	1984	1985	1986	1987
Gross Domestic Product [a]	10260	23477	31800	35333	38609	42879	46811	49823	53597	55989	58759	60660
Plus: Net factor income from the rest of the world	2	-77	-93	-145	-160	-168	-347	-510	-517	-581	-658	-672
Equals: Gross National Product [a]	10262	23400	31707	35188	38449	42711	46464	49313	53080	55408	58101	59988
Less: Consumption of fixed capital	711	1903	2724	3152	3415	3784	4166	4484	4871	5056	5294	5526
Equals: National Income [a]	9551	21497	28983	32036	35034	38927	42298	44829	48209	50352	52807	54462
Plus: Net current transfers from the rest of the world	...	...	...	...	...	...	...	...	...	...	...	...
Equals: National Disposable Income	...	...	...	...	...	...	...	...	...	...	...	...
Less: Final consumption	...	...	...	...	...	...	...	...	...	...	...	...
Equals: Net Saving	...	...	...	...	...	...	...	...	...	...	...	...
Less: Surplus of the nation on current transactions	...	...	...	...	...	...	...	...	...	...	...	...
Equals: Net Capital Formation	...	...	...	...	...	...	...	...	...	...	...	...

a) For 1970-1974, all estimates refer to year ending 30 September.

4.1 Derivation of Value Added by Kind of Activity, in Current Prices

Million Myanmarese kyats — Fiscal year beginning 1 April

	1980 Gross Output	1980 Intermediate Consumption	1980 Value Added	1981 Gross Output	1981 Intermediate Consumption	1981 Value Added	1982 Gross Output	1982 Intermediate Consumption	1982 Value Added	1983 Gross Output	1983 Intermediate Consumption	1983 Value Added
						All Producers						
1 Agriculture, hunting, forestry and fishing	21847	3877	17970	24769	4439	20330	26898	4579	22319	28648	4937	23711
2 Mining and quarrying	790	363	427	803	373	430	846	345	501	850	346	504
3 Manufacturing	20534	16851	3683	22275	18266	4009	24061	19711	4350	26438	21663	4775
4 Electricity, gas and water [a]	214	79	135	264	97	167	313	103	210	338	111	227
5 Construction	2099	1452	647	2248	1556	692	2729	1896	833	2859	1987	872
6 Wholesale and retail trade, restaurants and hotels [b]	13066	2945	10121	14159	3445	10714	15259	3747	11512	16244	3971	12273
7 Transport, storage and communication	2358	1001	1357	2775	1163	1612	3178	1344	1834	3344	1359	1985
8 Finance, insurance, real estate and business services [c]	1230	401	829	1551	512	1039	1804	708	1096	1919	747	1172
9 Community, social and personal services [abc]	1874	271	1603	2177	323	1854	2278	337	1941	2388	350	2038

Myanmar

4.1 Derivation of Value Added by Kind of Activity, in Current Prices
(Continued)

Million Myanmarese kyats — Fiscal year beginning 1 April

	1980 Gross Output	1980 Intermediate Consumption	1980 Value Added	1981 Gross Output	1981 Intermediate Consumption	1981 Value Added	1982 Gross Output	1982 Intermediate Consumption	1982 Value Added	1983 Gross Output	1983 Intermediate Consumption	1983 Value Added
Total, Industries [d]	64012	27240	36772	71021	30174	40847	77366	32770	44596	83028	35471	47557
Producers of Government Services	3491	1654	1837	3970	1938	2032	4211	1996	2215	4298	2032	2266
Other Producers	...	...	...	...	...	...	...	...	...	...	...	...
Total [d]	67503	28894	38609	74991	32112	42879	81577	34766	46811	87326	37503	49823
Less: Imputed bank service charge	...	...	...	...	...	...	...	...	...	...	...	...
Import duties	...	...	...	...	...	...	...	...	...	...	...	...
Value added tax	...	...	...	...	...	...	...	...	...	...	...	...
Total [d]	67503	28894	38609	74991	32112	42879	81577	34766	46811	87326	37503	49823

	1984 Gross Output	1984 Intermediate Consumption	1984 Value Added	1985 Gross Output	1985 Intermediate Consumption	1985 Value Added	1986 Gross Output	1986 Intermediate Consumption	1986 Value Added	1987 Gross Output	1987 Intermediate Consumption	1987 Value Added
All Producers												
1 Agriculture, hunting, forestry and fishing	31566	5771	25795	33242	6259	26983	35819	6284	29535	37176	6508	30668
2 Mining and quarrying	959	414	545	904	371	533	832	333	499	888	355	533
3 Manufacturing	29254	23974	5280	31191	25630	5561	30583	25156	5427	31524	25927	5597
4 Electricity, gas and water [a]	379	116	263	398	120	278	424	145	279	460	178	282
5 Construction	3096	2150	946	3078	2133	945	3109	2148	961	3124	2147	977
6 Wholesale and retail trade, restaurants and hotels [b]	17227	4341	12886	18112	4723	13389	18075	4727	13348	18249	4780	13469
7 Transport, storage and communication	3536	1430	2106	3694	1476	2218	3829	1509	2320	4002	1563	2439
8 Finance, insurance, real estate and business services [c]	2051	797	1254	2147	815	1332	2328	907	1421	2439	940	1499
9 Community, social and personal services [abc]	2498	373	2125	2571	389	2182	2671	414	2257	2764	437	2327
Total, Industries [d]	90566	39366	51200	95337	41916	53421	97670	41623	56047	100626	42835	57791
Producers of Government Services	4547	2150	2397	4886	2318	2568	5140	2428	2712	5418	2549	2869
Other Producers	...	...	...	...	...	...	...	...	...	...	...	...
Total [d]	95113	41516	53597	100223	44234	55989	102810	44051	58759	106044	45384	60660
Less: Imputed bank service charge	...	...	...	...	...	...	...	...	...	...	...	...
Import duties	...	...	...	...	...	...	...	...	...	...	...	...
Value added tax	...	...	...	...	...	...	...	...	...	...	...	...
Total [d]	95113	41516	53597	100223	44234	55989	102810	44051	58759	106044	45384	60660

a) Item 'Electricity, gas and water' refers to electricity only. Gas and water are included in item 'Community, social and personal services'.
b) Restaurants and hotels are included in item 'Community, social and personal services'.
c) Insurance, real estate and business services are included in item 'Community, social and personal services'.
d) Constant price data are valued at 1969-1970 average market prices, thus, data for current and constant prices do not agree in the base year.

4.2 Derivation of Value Added by Kind of Activity, in Constant Prices

Million Myanmarese kyats — Fiscal year beginning 1 April

	1980 Gross Output	1980 Intermediate Consumption	1980 Value Added	1981 Gross Output	1981 Intermediate Consumption	1981 Value Added	1982 Gross Output	1982 Intermediate Consumption	1982 Value Added	1983 Gross Output	1983 Intermediate Consumption	1983 Value Added
At constant prices of:1970												
All Producers												
1 Agriculture, hunting, forestry and fishing	7005	1159	5846	7567	1270	6297	7939	1265	6674	8321	1320	7001
2 Mining and quarrying	322	132	190	342	145	197	350	136	214	363	142	221
3 Manufacturing	7331	5746	1585	7871	6166	1705	8221	6426	1795	8531	6677	1854
4 Electricity, gas and water [a]	215	44	171	264	57	207	313	70	243	338	76	262
5 Construction	1283	839	444	1303	848	455	1466	983	483	1532	1025	507
6 Wholesale and retail trade, restaurants and hotels [b]	4363	880	3483	4657	1089	3568	4775	1081	3694	4942	1098	3844
7 Transport, storage and communication	1417	582	835	1570	633	937	1761	720	1041	1840	730	1110
8 Finance, insurance, real estate and business services [c]	871	250	621	999	320	679	1116	414	702	1185	446	739
9 Community, social and personal services [abc]	1171	200	971	1209	209	1000	1233	211	1022	1293	221	1072

Myanmar

4.2 Derivation of Value Added by Kind of Activity, in Constant Prices
(Continued)

Million Myanmarese kyats — Fiscal year beginning 1 April

	1980 Gross Output	1980 Intermediate Consumption	1980 Value Added	1981 Gross Output	1981 Intermediate Consumption	1981 Value Added	1982 Gross Output	1982 Intermediate Consumption	1982 Value Added	1983 Gross Output	1983 Intermediate Consumption	1983 Value Added
					At constant prices of:1970							
Total, Industries [d]	23978	9832	14146	25782	10737	15045	27174	11306	15868	28345	11735	16610
Producers of Government Services	2744	1172	1572	2978	1306	1672	3153	1367	1786	3214	1395	1819
Other Producers	...	...	...	...	...	...	...	...	...	...	...	...
Total [d]	26722	11004	15718	28760	12043	16717	30327	12673	17654	31559	13130	18429
Less: Imputed bank service charge	...	...	...	...	...	...	...	...	...	...	...	...
Import duties	...	...	...	...	...	...	...	...	...	...	...	...
Value added tax	...	...	...	...	...	...	...	...	...	...	...	...
Total [d]	26722	11004	15718	28760	12043	16717	30327	12673	17654	31559	13130	18429

	1984 Gross Output	1984 Intermediate Consumption	1984 Value Added	1985 Gross Output	1985 Intermediate Consumption	1985 Value Added	1986 Gross Output	1986 Intermediate Consumption	1986 Value Added	1987 Gross Output	1987 Intermediate Consumption	1987 Value Added
					At constant prices of:1970 — All Producers							
1 Agriculture, hunting, forestry and fishing	8734	1424	7310	8939	1457	7482	9020	1457	7563	9121	1456	7665
2 Mining and quarrying	430	177	253	449	186	263	439	177	262	434	174	260
3 Manufacturing	9077	7070	2007	9243	7193	2050	8914	6917	1997	9032	6989	2043
4 Electricity, gas and water [a]	380	78	302	398	79	319	424	93	331	460	94	366
5 Construction	1650	1101	549	1640	1092	548	1655	1102	553	1665	1103	562
6 Wholesale and retail trade, restaurants and hotels [b]	5200	1168	4032	5375	1205	4170	5321	1218	4103	5346	1228	4118
7 Transport, storage and communication	1939	764	1175	2003	782	1221	2060	797	1263	2128	813	1315
8 Finance, insurance, real estate and business services [c]	1264	475	789	1322	485	837	1420	545	875	1489	573	916
9 Community, social and personal services [abc]	1350	233	1117	1386	244	1142	1433	258	1175	1464	257	1207
Total, Industries [d]	30024	12490	17534	30755	12723	18032	30686	12564	18122	31139	12687	18452
Producers of Government Services	3398	1477	1921	3635	1590	2045	3803	1655	2148	4003	1739	2264
Other Producers	...	...	...	...	...	...	...	...	...	...	...	...
Total [d]	33422	13967	19455	34390	14313	20077	34489	14219	20270	35142	14426	20716
Less: Imputed bank service charge	...	...	...	...	...	...	...	...	...	...	...	...
Import duties	...	...	...	...	...	...	...	...	...	...	...	...
Value added tax	...	...	...	...	...	...	...	...	...	...	...	...
Total [d]	33422	13967	19455	34390	14313	20077	34489	14219	20270	35142	14426	20716

a) Item 'Electricity, gas and water' refers to electricity only. Gas and water are included in item 'Community, social and personal services'.
b) Restaurants and hotels are included in item 'Community, social and personal services'.
c) Insurance, real estate and business services are included in item 'Community, social and personal services'.
d) Constant price data are valued at 1969-1970 average market prices, thus, data for current and constant prices do not agree in the base year.

Nepal

Source. Reply to the United Nations National Accounts Questionnaire from the National Income Division, Central Bureau of Statistics, Kathmandu.

General note. The official estimates of Nepal have been prepared in accordance with the United Nations System of National Accounts so far as the existing data would permit.

1.1 Expenditure on the Gross Domestic Product, in Current Prices

Million Nepalese rupees — Fiscal year ending 15 July

	1970	1975	1978	1979	1980	1981	1982	1983	1984	1985	1986	1987
1 Government final consumption expenditure	...	1257	1471	1889	1565	1922	2638	3416	3644	4371	5197	6225
2 Private final consumption expenditure	...	13652	15721	17741	19195	22411	25488	27287	31809	34778	40415	45600
A Households	...	13494	15567	17557	19040	22190	25333	27014	31491	34430	40011	45144
B Private non-profit institutions serving households	...	158	154	184	155	221	155	273	318	348	404	456
3 Gross capital formation	...	2402	3507	3514	4270	4808	5098	6799	7402	9055	10859	12264
A Increase in stocks	...	179	213	251	589	509	-151	52	444	798	1168	1073
B Gross fixed capital formation	...	2223	3294	3263	3681	4299	5249	6747	6958	8257	9691	11191
Residential buildings	...	...	803	875	1021	1203	...	...	...	...	...	...
Non-residential buildings	...	...	1626	1713	1765	2140	...	...	...	...	...	...
Other construction and land improvement etc.	...	...					...	...	...	...	...	...
Other	...	...	865	675	895	956	...	...	...	...	...	...
4 Exports of goods and services	...	1475	2086	2618	2695	3523	3592	3455	4196	5372	6506	7563
5 Less: Imports of goods and services	...	2215	3053	3547	4374	5357	5828	7196	7661	9317	11218	13148
Equals: Gross Domestic Product	...	16571	19732	22215	23351	27307	30988	33761	39390	44259	51759	58504

1.3 Cost Components of the Gross Domestic Product

Million Nepalese rupees — Fiscal year ending 15 July

	1970	1975	1978	1979	1980	1981	1982	1983	1984	1985	1986	1987
1 Indirect taxes, net	...	635	1306	1436	1465	1841	1951	2117	2386	2861	3300	3510
2 Consumption of fixed capital	...	698	959	1088	1091	1283	1427	1583	1748	2055	2387	2627
3 Compensation of employees paid by resident producers to:	...	9944	11433	12069	13251	16328	16665	18603	...	...	...	...
4 Operating surplus	...	5294	6034	7622	7544	7855	10945	11458	...	...	...	...
Equals: Gross Domestic Product	...	16571	19732	22215	23351	27307	30988	33761	39390	44259	51759	58504

1.4 General Government Current Receipts and Disbursements

Million Nepalese rupees — Fiscal year ending 15 July

	1970	1975	1978	1979	1980	1981	1982	1983	1984	1985	1986	1987
Receipts												
1 Operating surplus	...	...	...	...	...	...	...	...	...	...	...	...
2 Property and entrepreneurial income	...	...	...	...	93	...	...	...	...	...	...	...
3 Taxes, fees and contributions	...	...	...	...	2216	...	...	...	...	...	...	...
A Indirect taxes	...	...	...	...	1465	...	...	...	...	...	...	...
B Direct taxes	...	...	...	...	115	...	...	...	...	...	...	...
C Social security contributions	...	...	...	...	413	...	...	...	...	...	...	...
D Compulsory fees, fines and penalties	...	...	...	...	223	...	...	...	...	...	...	...
4 Other current transfers	...	...	...	...	319	...	...	...	...	...	...	...
Total Current Receipts of General Government	...	...	...	...	2628	...	...	...	...	...	...	...
Disbursements												
1 Government final consumption expenditure	...	...	...	...	1565	...	...	...	...	...	...	...
A Compensation of employees	...	...	...	...	867	...	...	...	...	...	...	...
B Consumption of fixed capital	...	...	...	...	...	...	...	...	...	...	...	...
C Purchases of goods and services, net	...	...	...	...	699	...	...	...	...	...	...	...
D Less: Own account fixed capital formation	...	...	...	...	...	...	...	...	...	...	...	...
E Indirect taxes paid, net	...	...	...	...	...	...	...	...	...	...	...	...
2 Property income	...	...	...	...	...	...	...	...	...	...	...	...
3 Subsidies	...	...	...	...	5	...	...	...	...	...	...	...
4 Other current transfers	...	...	...	...	67	...	...	...	...	...	...	...
5 Net saving	...	...	...	...	991	...	...	...	...	...	...	...
Total Current Disbursements and Net Saving of General Government	...	...	...	...	2628	...	...	...	...	...	...	...

Nepal

1.7 External Transactions on Current Account, Summary

Million Nepalese rupees — Fiscal year ending 15 July

	1970	1975	1978	1979	1980	1981	1982	1983	1984	1985	1986	1987
Payments to the Rest of the World												
1 Imports of goods and services	...	2215	3053	3547	4374	5357	5828	7196	7661	9317	11218	13148
A Imports of merchandise c.i.f.	...	1815	2516	2912	3569	4443	4948	6333	6534	7767	9373	10905
B Other	...	400	537	635	805	914	880	863	1127	1550	1845	2243
2 Factor income to the rest of the world	...	46	29	38	53	57	59	56	84	124	164	190
3 Current transfers to the rest of the world	...	-	-	-	-	-	-	-	-	-	...	...
4 Surplus of the nation on current transactions	...	-119	-291	40	-341	-296	-393	-1671	-1342	-1848	-2471	-2916
Payments to the Rest of the World and Surplus of the Nation on Current Transactions	...	2142	2791	3625	4086	5118	5494	5581	6403	7593	8911	10422
Receipts From The Rest of the World												
1 Exports of goods and services	...	1475	2086	2618	2695	3523	3592	3455	4196	5372	6506	7563
A Exports of merchandise f.o.b.	...	890	1065	1304	1166	1613	1496	1136	1710	2746	3086	2991
B Other	...	585	1021	1314	1529	1910	2096	2319	2486	2626	3420	4572
2 Factor income from rest of the world	...	313	320	428	547	644	674	753	709	785	873	1359
3 Current transfers from rest of the world	...	354	385	579	844	951	1228	1373	1498	1436	1532	1500
Receipts from the Rest of the World on Current Transactions	...	2142	2791	3625	4086	5118	5494	5581	6403	7593	8911	10422

1.10 Gross Domestic Product by Kind of Activity, in Current Prices

Million Nepalese rupees — Fiscal year ending 15 July

	1970	1975	1978	1979	1980	1981	1982	1983	1984	1985	1986	1987
1 Agriculture, hunting, forestry and fishing	5922	9949 / 11435	11616	13365	13520	15510	17715	19082	22570	23927	27713	...
2 Mining and quarrying	4	3 / 22	25	34	42	58	66	85	111	140	166	...
3 Manufacturing [a]	787	1458 / 664	794	848	936	1049	1243	1460	1816	1840	2185	...
4 Electricity, gas and water	18	34 / 34	42	48	60	67	82	127	158	196	233	...
5 Construction	192	172 / 583	1338	1559	1570	1974	2342	2377	2576	3583	4255	...
6 Wholesale and retail trade, restaurants and hotels	363	738 / 540	707	724	889	953	1068	1199	1520	1837	2181	...
7 Transport, storage and communication	192	453 / 690	1093	1248	1541	1889	1992	2129	2468	2764	3282	...
8 Finance, insurance, real estate and business services	857	1119 / 1095	1534	1613	1833	2077	2366	2594	2937	3420	4061	...
9 Community, social and personal services [b]	256	544 / 873	1277	1340	1495	1889	2163	2591	2848	3691	4383	...
Total, Industries	8591	14470 / 15936	18426	20779	21886	25466	29037	31644	37004	41398	48459	...
Producers of Government Services [b]	177	332	...	...	...	...	...	...	...	...	...	...
Other Producers [b]	...	...	...	...	...	...	...	...	...	...	...	...
Subtotal [c]	8768	14802 / 15936	18426	20779	21886	25466	29037	31644	37004	41398	48459	...
Less: Imputed bank service charge	...	...	...	...	...	...	...	...	...	...	...	...
Plus: Import duties	...	...	...	...	...	...	...	...	...	...	...	...
Plus: Value added tax	...	...	...	...	...	...	...	...	...	...	...	...
Plus: Other adjustments [d]	...	635	1306	1436	1465	1841	1951	2117	2386	2861	3300	...
Equals: Gross Domestic Product	8768	14802 / 16571	19732	22215	23351	27307	30988	33761	39390	44259	51759	...

a) Item 'Manufacturing' includes cottage industries.
b) Items 'Other producers' and 'Producers of government services' are included in item 'Community, social and personal services'.
c) Gross domestic product in factor values.
d) Item 'Other adjustments' refers to indirect taxes net of subsidies.

Nepal

1.11 Gross Domestic Product by Kind of Activity, in Constant Prices

Million Nepalese rupees — Fiscal year ending 15 July

	1970	1975	1978	1979	1980	1981	1982	1983	1984	1985	1986	1987
		1965			At constant prices of:			1975				
1 Agriculture, hunting, forestry and fishing	5922	4530 11550	11141	11480	10933	12066	12616	12478	13668	13990	14589	14735
2 Mining and quarrying	...	... ...	...	...	...	...	...	...	...	...	...	...
3 Manufacturing	...	... ...	...	...	...	...	...	...	...	...	...	...
4 Electricity, gas and water	...	... ...	...	...	...	...	...	...	...	...	...	...
5 Construction	...	... ...	...	...	...	...	...	...	...	...	...	...
6 Wholesale and retail trade, restaurants and hotels	...	... ...	...	...	...	...	...	...	...	...	...	...
7 Transport, storage and communication	...	... ...	...	...	...	...	...	...	...	...	...	...
8 Finance, insurance, real estate and business services	...	... ...	...	...	...	...	...	...	...	...	...	...
9 Community, social and personal services	...	... ...	...	...	...	...	...	...	...	...	...	...
Total, Industries	...	... ...	...	...	...	...	...	...	...	...	...	...
Producers of Government Services	...	... ...	...	...	...	...	...	...	...	...	...	...
Other Producers	...	... ...	...	...	...	...	...	...	...	...	...	...
Subtotal	...	... ...	...	...	...	...	...	...	...	...	...	...
Less: Imputed bank service charge	...	... ...	...	...	...	...	...	...	...	...	...	...
Plus: Import duties	...	... ...	...	...	...	...	...	...	...	...	...	...
Plus: Value added tax	...	... ...	...	...	...	...	...	...	...	...	...	...
Equals: Gross Domestic Product	6367	6965 16571	18607	19048	18606	20158	20920	20297	22262	24012	24959	25561

1.12 Relations Among National Accounting Aggregates

Million Nepalese rupees — Fiscal year ending 15 July

	1970	1975	1978	1979	1980	1981	1982	1983	1984	1985	1986	1987
Gross Domestic Product	...	16571	19732	22215	23351	27307	30988	33761	39390	44259	51759	58504
Plus: Net factor income from the rest of the world	...	267	291	390	494	587	615	697	625	661	709	1169
Factor income from the rest of the world	...	313	320	428	547	644	674	753	709	785	873	1359
Less: Factor income to the rest of the world	...	46	29	38	53	57	59	56	84	124	164	190
Equals: Gross National Product	...	16838	20023	22605	23845	27894	31603	34458	40015	44920	52468	59673
Less: Consumption of fixed capital	...	698	959	1088	1091	1283	1427	1583	1748	2055	2387	2627
Equals: National Income	...	16140	19064	21517	22754	26611	30176	32875	38267	42865	50081	57046
Plus: Net current transfers from the rest of the world	...	354	385	579	844	951	1228	1373	1498	1436	1532	1500
Current transfers from the rest of the world	...	354	385	579	844	951	1228	1373	1498	1436	1532	1500
Less: Current transfers to the rest of the world	...	-	-	-	-	-	-	-	-	-	-	-
Equals: National Disposable Income	...	16494	19449	22096	23598	27562	31404	34248	39765	44301	51613	58546
Less: Final consumption	...	14909	17192	19630	20760	24333	28126	30703	35453	39149	45612	51825
Equals: Net Saving	...	1585	2257	2466	2838	3229	3278	3545	4312	5152	6001	6721
Less: Surplus of the nation on current transactions	...	-119	-291	40	-341	-296	-393	-1671	-1342	-1848	-2471	-2916
Equals: Net Capital Formation	...	1704	2548	2426	3179	3525	3671	5216	5654	7000	8472	9637

Netherlands

General note. The preparation of national accounts statistics in the Netherlands is undertaken by the Central Bureau of Statistics, Voorburg. The official estimates together with methodological notes are published annually in 'Nationale Rekeningen' (National Accounts). The estimates are generally in accordance with the classifications and definitions recommended in the United Nations System of National Accounts (SNA). The first annual publication on input-output tables, covering the years 1948-1957, was issued in 1960. The following tables have been prepared from successive replies to the United Nations national accounts questionnaire. When the scope and coverage of the estimates differ for conceptual or statistical reasons from the definitions and classifications recommended in SNA, a footnote is indicated to the relevant tables.

Sources and methods:

(a) Gross domestic product. The main approach used to estimate GDP is the production approach.

(b) Expenditure on the gross domestic product. The expenditure approach is used to estimate government final consumption expenditure, gross fixed capital formation and exports and imports of goods and services. A combination of the commodity-flow approach and the expenditure approach is used for the estimation of private final consumption expenditure, private gross fixed capital formation and increase in stocks. The main sources for estimating general government consumption expenditure are the final accounts of the various agencies. The data sources for exports and imports of goods and services are foreign trade statistics for merchandise and balance of payments data and survey data for services. Constant prices are obtained through deflation with price indexes for all expenditure components, except government consumption expenditure referring to wages and salaries, which is extrapolated by employment data.

(c) Cost-structure of the gross domestic product. The main source for the compilation of compensation of employees is data from the social security institutions in the case of employees in enterprises and accounts data in the case of general government employees. Operating surplus is obtained as a residual within the framework of the annual input-output tables. Estimates of the consumption of fixed capital are made by the Central Bureau of Statistics, based on the perpetual inventory method. Information on indirect taxes and subsidies is provided by government agencies.

(d) Gross domestic product by kind of economic activity. The table on GDP by kind of economic activity is prepared at market prices net of value added tax for which breakdown by kind of economic activity is not available. The production approach is used to estimate value added of most industries. This is done within the framework of detailed input-output tables using the commodity-flow approach. The income approach is used to estimate value added of producers of government services, business services and most community, social and personal services. For the agricultural sector, the main sources of information are the annual surveys of crop production and unpublished reports of statutory trade offices. Data on the structure of production costs are provided by annual farm management surveys. Statistics on sales of horticulture produce in special markets are also available. Net increase of livestock is evaluated on the basis of frequent samples, and on average annual prices per category. Regarding crude petroleum and natural gas production the information base consists of data supplied by all individual enterprises. The information base for manufacturing consists mainly of an annual survey of all enterprises with more than 10 employees. Recent bench-mark information is given by a census of establishments conducted for 1978. The census covers all establishments and collects information on kind of economic activity and employment. For the private construction sector, annual production surveys are available. For general government, data are available on the capital expenditure. The production of buildings is covered by quarterly progress reports from the municipalities. The production value is estimated on the basis of the production of work completed. Bench-mark data for wholesale and retail trade are available for certain years. For some parts of the trade sector annual production surveys are available. Surveys are planned to be held for other parts. Annual surveys are carried out for the transport sector. Information on railways and communications is derived directly from the few existing enterprises. Inter-urban public transportation by bus is covered by statements by government agencies. For the estimation of value added of credit institutions, the required data are collected on the basis of an annual survey. Data of insurance companies are obtained both from an annual survey and from the companies' accounts. The value of dwellings corresponds to total rents, including the imputed rents of owner-occupied houses. Cost accounts for houses are published by housing corporations. For producers of government services the main sources are the accounts of the agencies. Considerable gaps exist regarding some sub-sectors of private services. In these cases date are collected from various sources such as income tax data and social security information. For the constant price estimates, double deflation is used for agriculture and fishing. Current output quantities are valued at base-year prices where quantities are available, otherwise deflated by representative price indexes. Some input categories are valued at base year prices while others are deflated by price index. Value added of mining and quarrying, manufacturing, electricity, gas, water, transport and communication is calculated by double deflation. For trade, output at constant prices is extrapolated by quantity indicators for output, input categories are deflated by price indexes. Value added at constant prices of financing, insurance and business services is generally extrapolated by means of volume indexes of material output and factor input. For producers of government services, net value added at constant prices is extrapolated by means of a value added index based on quantity data of factor services. For private services value added is extrapolated by indexes of employment.

1.1 Expenditure on the Gross Domestic Product, in Current Prices

Million Netherlands guilders

		1970	1975	1978	1979	1980	1981	1982	1983	1984	1985	1986	1987
1	Government final consumption expenditure	18660	38250	52610	57170	60260	62750	65120	66580	66390	67670	68540	69700
2	Private final consumption expenditure	70820	128950	179170	192430	205780	213230	221830	229860	236750	247720	256260	262960
3	Gross capital formation	33810	45380	65120	67990	72510	64490	66140	70020	76300	82750	87080	87130
	A Increase in stocks	2450	-940	1820	1500	1720	-3090	-1020	560	1990	2500	700	-390
	B Gross fixed capital formation	31360	46320	63300	66490	70790	67580	67160	69460	74310	80250	86380	87520
	Residential buildings	7240	11690	17730	18280	20840	20130	19540	19470	20400	20380	21450	22510
	Non-residential buildings	6520	8700	12460	13740	15120	13710	12900	11960	12310	12480	13610	14710
	Other construction and land improvement etc.	4380	6470	7240	7240	8030	8010	7630	7360	7960	8030	7720	7280
	Other	13220	19460	25870	27230	26800	25730	27090	30670	33640	39360	43600	43020
4	Exports of goods and services	54300	109720	133340	155060	176810	204620	212600	219770	248560	265540	232650	226610
5	Less: Imports of goods and services	56410	102340	133230	156690	178620	192240	196830	205210	227750	245500	214650	214580
	Equals: Gross Domestic Product	121180	219960	297010	315960	336740	352850	368860	381020	400250	418180	429880	431820

1.2 Expenditure on the Gross Domestic Product, in Constant Prices

Million Netherlands guilders

		1970	1975	1978	1979	1980	1981	1982	1983	1984	1985	1986	1987
		\multicolumn{12}{c}{At constant prices of:1980}
1	Government final consumption expenditure	46180	52100	58260	59920	60260	61460	61860	62630	62260	63090	64330	64920
2	Private final consumption expenditure	145980	173880	199810	205760	205780	200610	198260	199990	201990	206930	212880	219080
3	Gross capital formation	72960	65030	75100	73410	72510	60920	60000	62430	66420	71150	75870	76470
	A Increase in stocks	3340	-1030	2390	1950	1720	-2500	-840	330	970	1260	240	-380
	B Gross fixed capital formation	69620	66060	72710	71460	70790	63420	60840	62100	65450	69890	75630	76850
	Residential buildings	18890	17900	20950	19910	20840	18840	17790	17720	18510	18430	19370	19970
	Non-residential buildings	16260	13370	14750	14990	15120	12920	11910	11070	11340	11600	12620	13490
	Other construction and land improvement etc.	11220	9960	8590	7910	8030	7540	6990	6670	7040	6940	6740	6350
	Other	23250	24830	28420	28650	26800	24120	24150	26640	28560	32920	36900	37040
4	Exports of goods and services	107320	145450	162170	174180	176810	179540	179510	185820	199560	210310	213600	222600
5	Less: Imports of goods and services	119670	140510	169210	179410	178620	168160	169970	176580	185380	197540	205290	216810
	Equals: Gross Domestic Product	252770	295950	326130	333860	336740	334370	329660	334290	344850	353940	361390	366260

Netherlands

1.3 Cost Components of the Gross Domestic Product

Million Netherlands guilders

	1970	1975	1978	1979	1980	1981	1982	1983	1984	1985	1986	1987
1 Indirect taxes, net	11550	20210	29300	29800	32020	32900	32700	33920	35380	37190	39800	40780
A Indirect taxes	13600	24140	37000	38580	41120	41720	42760	45140	47990	50700	53710	57420
B Less: Subsidies	2050	3930	7700	8780	9100	8820	10060	11220	12610	13510	13910	16640
2 Consumption of fixed capital	10260	20010	26670	29290	32490	35620	37860	39190	41190	42870	43450	44770
3 Compensation of employees paid by resident producers to:	67170	131170	172770	185920	197840	201530	207480	209640	210000	216770	225710	231480
A Resident households	66780	130510	172020	185120	196930	200520	206340	208520	208880	215550	224500	230410
B Rest of the world	390	660	750	800	910	1010	1140	1120	1120	1220	1210	1070
4 Operating surplus	32200	48570	68270	70950	74390	82800	90820	98270	113680	121350	120920	114790
A Corporate and quasi-corporate enterprises	32200	48570	68270	70950	74390	82800	90820	98270	113680	121350	120920	114790
B Private unincorporated enterprises												
C General government	...	...	...	...	...	...	...	...	...	...	...	...
Equals: Gross Domestic Product	121180	219960	297010	315960	336740	352850	368860	381020	400250	418180	429880	431820

1.4 General Government Current Receipts and Disbursements

Million Netherlands guilders

	1970	1975	1978	1979	1980	1981	1982	1983	1984	1985	1986	1987
						Receipts						
1 Operating surplus	...	...	...	...	...	...	...	...	...	...	...	...
2 Property and entrepreneurial income	2960	8690	14230	16710	20000	25290	26950	28170	32530	35790	29430	21100
3 Taxes, fees and contributions	46580	96520	132680	141130	153570	159040	167330	178160	179390	186870	193160	204310
A Indirect taxes	13590	22550	34570	35040	37450	37990	38710	41000	43400	45690	48070	51470
B Direct taxes	15810	34530	45500	48500	53500	53280	54290	51890	51030	52870	57620	60800
C Social security contributions	16760	38530	51420	56310	61220	66140	72490	83300	82860	85990	85000	89130
D Compulsory fees, fines and penalties	420	910	1190	1280	1400	1630	1840	1970	2100	2320	2470	2910
4 Other current transfers	1360	3100	4210	4660	4270	4300	4320	4220	4440	4530	4610	4730
Total Current Receipts of General Government	50900	108310	151120	162500	177840	188630	198600	210550	216360	227190	227200	230140
						Disbursements						
1 Government final consumption expenditure	18660	38250	52610	57170	60260	62750	65120	66580	66390	67670	68540	69700
A Compensation of employees	13510	28880	39140	41980	44080	45020	46720	46950	46410	46910	47500	48140
B Consumption of fixed capital	800	1600	2080	2150	2400	2560	2420	2300	2620	2750	2800	2950
C Purchases of goods and services, net	4520	8080	11640	13300	14000	15390	16170	17490	17580	18170	18300	18610
D Less: Own account fixed capital formation	210	460	550	560	580	580	570	560	640	590	520	480
E Indirect taxes paid, net	40	150	300	300	360	360	380	400	420	430	460	480
2 Property income	4160	8250	11850	13260	15660	19340	23180	26500	29860	32170	32630	31120
A Interest	4160	8250	11850	13260	15660	19340	23180	26500	29860	32170	32630	31120
B Net land rent and royalties	...	...	...	...	...	...	...	...	...	...	...	...
3 Subsidies	1570	2140	4070	4240	4980	5520	6220	6710	7410	7860	8130	9880
4 Other current transfers	21930	55580	80680	87300	94260	102730	112860	118420	119370	121360	123740	126310
A Social security benefits	16760	39960	58730	64720	70920	75690	80610	81400	81570	82960	84610	86960
B Social assistance grants	2410	7770	10660	11590	12700	15600	20490	24730	24870	22510	22690	22880
C Other	2760	7850	11290	10990	10640	11440	11760	12290	12930	15890	16440	16470
5 Net saving	4580	4090	1910	530	2680	-1710	-8780	-7660	-6670	-1870	-5840	-6870
Total Current Disbursements and Net Saving of General Government	50900	108310	151120	162500	177840	188630	198600	210550	216360	227190	227200	230140

Netherlands

1.5 Current Income and Outlay of Corporate and Quasi-Corporate Enterprises, Summary

Million Netherlands guilders

	1970	1975	1978	1979	1980	1981	1982	1983	1984	1985	1986	1987
Receipts												
1 Operating surplus	32200	48570	68270	70950	74390	82800	90820	98270	113680	121350	120920	114790
2 Property and entrepreneurial income received [a]	11210	32540	46530	58440	73520	89240	93600	91000	97200	102070	99580	102180
3 Current transfers	3590	6810	10290	11020	11540	12840	12710	13210	13600	14210	15300	16830
Total Current Receipts	47000	87920	125090	140410	159450	184880	197130	202480	224480	237630	235800	233800
Disbursements												
1 Property and entrepreneurial income [a]	34270	69300	98510	113120	132540	154080	165560	165370	179920	189810	187060	183780
2 Direct taxes and other current payments to general government	3050	7410	8300	8260	10170	11100	11340	10850	10300	13060	14370	16030
3 Other current transfers	3590	6810	10290	11020	11540	12840	12710	13210	13600	14210	15300	16830
4 Net saving	6090	4400	7990	8010	5200	6860	7520	13050	20660	20550	19070	17160
Total Current Disbursements and Net Saving	47000	87920	125090	140410	159450	184880	197130	202480	224480	237630	235800	233800

a) For the period 1970-1976, property and entrepreneurial income paid by non-financial corporate and quasi-corporate enterprises is net of property income received.

1.6 Current Income and Outlay of Households and Non-Profit Institutions

Million Netherlands guilders

	1970	1975	1978	1979	1980	1981	1982	1983	1984	1985	1986	1987
Receipts												
1 Compensation of employees	67200	131260	172850	186020	197960	201640	207690	209810	210150	216850	225690	231600
A From resident producers	66780	130510	172020	185120	196930	200520	206340	208520	208880	215550	224500	230410
B From rest of the world	420	750	830	900	1030	1120	1350	1290	1270	1300	1190	1190
2 Operating surplus of private unincorporated enterprises	...	...	...	...	...	...	...	...	...	...	...	...
3 Property and entrepreneurial income [a]	24790	36210	50160	52070	55850	59890	69490	74830	81100	86380	91650	93160
4 Current transfers	23400	57780	83670	91890	98960	107570	117480	123270	123920	126190	128950	132610
A Social security benefits	16660	39750	58310	64230	70370	75100	79900	80730	80870	82230	83810	86170
B Social assistance grants	2450	7870	10770	11700	12820	15710	20600	24840	25010	22640	22820	23020
C Other	4290	10160	14590	15960	15770	16760	16980	17700	18040	21320	22320	23420
Total Current Receipts	115390	225250	306680	329980	352770	369100	394660	407910	415170	429420	446290	457370
Disbursements												
1 Private final consumption expenditure	70820	128950	179170	192430	205780	213230	221830	229860	236750	247720	256260	262960
2 Property income [a]	...	...	1320	1670	1910	2070	1890	1740	1700	1660	1680	1670
3 Direct taxes and other current transfers n.e.c. to general government	29940	66560	89810	97830	105950	109950	117280	126310	125690	128120	130720	136810
A Social security contributions	16760	38530	51420	56310	61220	66140	72490	83300	82860	85990	85000	89130
B Direct taxes	12760	27120	37200	40240	43330	42180	42950	41040	40730	39810	43250	44770
C Fees, fines and penalties	420	910	1190	1280	1400	1630	1840	1970	2100	2320	2470	2910
4 Other current transfers	3450	7370	10530	11760	11890	12370	12480	12700	13280	13930	14700	16690
5 Net saving	11180	22370	25850	26290	27240	31480	41180	37300	37750	37990	42930	39240
Total Current Disbursements and Net Saving	115390	225250	306680	329980	352770	369100	394660	407910	415170	429420	446290	457370

a) For 1970-1976, property income received is net of property income paid.

1.7 External Transactions on Current Account, Summary

Million Netherlands guilders

	1970	1975	1978	1979	1980	1981	1982	1983	1984	1985	1986	1987
Payments to the Rest of the World												
1 Imports of goods and services	56410	102340	133230	156690	178620	192240	196830	205210	227750	245500	214650	214580
A Imports of merchandise c.i.f.	49140	90890	115680	137550	156120	168420	171710	179580	200240	216610	185260	184900
B Other	7270	11450	17550	19140	22500	23820	25120	25630	27510	28890	29390	29680
2 Factor income to the rest of the world	4180	8990	11610	15730	22710	31090	32400	27810	31370	32200	28840	29880
A Compensation of employees	390	660	750	800	910	1010	1140	1120	1120	1220	1210	1070
B Property and entrepreneurial income	3790	8330	10860	14930	21800	30080	31260	26690	30250	30980	27630	28810
By general government	...	...	...	...	...	...	...	...	...	...	...	...
By corporate and quasi-corporate enterprises	3790	8330	10860	14930	21800	30080	31260	26690	30250	30980	27630	28810

Netherlands

1.7 External Transactions on Current Account, Summary
(Continued)

Million Netherlands guilders

	1970	1975	1978	1979	1980	1981	1982	1983	1984	1985	1986	1987
By other	...	...	...	...	...	...	...	...	...	...	...	...
3 Current transfers to the rest of the world	1120	4690	7400	7820	8400	9160	9600	9830	10860	11790	12700	14010
A Indirect taxes to supranational organizations	10	1590	2430	3540	3670	3730	4050	4140	4590	5010	5640	5950
B Other current transfers	1110	3100	4970	4280	4730	5430	5550	5690	6270	6780	7060	8060
4 Surplus of the nation on current transactions	-1700	5490	-2700	-3870	-4900	7760	11640	11860	16630	17310	11890	6910
Payments to the Rest of the World and Surplus of the Nation on Current Transactions	60010	121510	149540	176370	204830	240250	250470	254710	286610	306800	268080	265380

Receipts From The Rest of the World

	1970	1975	1978	1979	1980	1981	1982	1983	1984	1985	1986	1987
1 Exports of goods and services	54300	109720	133340	155060	176810	204620	212600	219770	248560	265540	232650	226610
A Exports of merchandise f.o.b.	43010	88960	107460	128460	147080	171330	177620	185010	210630	225950	195830	188250
B Other	11290	20760	25880	26600	29730	33290	34980	34760	37930	39590	36820	38360
2 Factor income from rest of the world	4740	8970	10930	15000	22090	30130	32020	28370	30870	32880	28110	29870
A Compensation of employees	420	750	830	900	1030	1120	1350	1290	1270	1300	1190	1190
B Property and entrepreneurial income	4320	8220	10100	14100	21060	29010	30670	27080	29600	31580	26920	28680
By general government	...	50	60	40	40	110	100	80	70	130	70	70
By corporate and quasi-corporate enterprises	...	7710	9310	13240	20100	27830	29140	25470	27940	29520	25040	26760
By other	...	460	730	820	920	1070	1430	1530	1590	1930	1810	1850
3 Current transfers from rest of the world	970	2820	5270	6310	5930	5500	5850	6570	7180	7860	7960	9160
A Subsidies from supranational organisations	480	1790	3630	4540	4120	3300	3840	4510	5200	5650	5780	6760
B Other current transfers	490	1030	1640	1770	1810	2200	2010	2060	1980	2210	2180	2400
Statistical discrepancy [a]	...	...	...	...	...	...	...	...	...	520	-640	-260
Receipts from the Rest of the World on Current Transactions	60010	121510	149540	176370	204830	240250	250470	254710	286610	306800	268080	265380

a) The surplus of the nation on current transactions corresponds to gross national saving less gross capital formation, plus from 1985 onwards a statistical discrepancy. This discrepancy is a consequence of the difference between on the one hand the surplus of the nation on current transactions (estimated by the Dutch Central Bank in cooperation with the Central Bureau of Statistics) and on the other hand the sum of the balance of exports and imports and the net current distributive transactions with the rest of the world. For the years 1983 and 84 there were also statistical discrepancies. However, these have been eliminated by altering the imports with destination increase in stocks.

1.8 Capital Transactions of The Nation, Summary

Million Netherlands guilders

	1970	1975	1978	1979	1980	1981	1982	1983	1984	1985	1986	1987

Finance of Gross Capital Formation

	1970	1975	1978	1979	1980	1981	1982	1983	1984	1985	1986	1987
Gross saving	32110	50870	62420	64120	67610	72250	77780	81880	92930	99540	99610	94300
1 Consumption of fixed capital	10260	20010	26670	29290	32490	35620	37860	39190	41190	42870	43450	44770
A General government	800	1600	2080	2150	2400	2560	2420	2300	2620	2750	2800	2950
B Corporate and quasi-corporate enterprises [a]	9460	18410	24590	27140	30090	33060	35440	36890	38570	40120	40650	41820
C Other [a]	...	...	...	...	...	...	...	...	...	...	...	...
2 Net saving	21850	30860	35750	34830	35120	36630	39920	42690	51740	56670	56160	49530
A General government	4580	4090	1910	530	2680	-1710	-8780	-7660	-6670	-1870	-5840	-6870
B Corporate and quasi-corporate enterprises	6090	4400	7990	8010	5200	6860	7520	13050	20660	20550	19070	17160
C Other	11180	22370	25850	26290	27240	31480	41180	37300	37750	37990	42930	39240
Less: Surplus of the nation on current transactions	-1700	5490	-2700	-3870	-4900	7760	11640	11860	16630	17310	11890	6910
Statistical discrepancy	...	...	...	...	...	...	...	...	...	520	-640	-260
Finance of Gross Capital Formation	33810	45380	65120	67990	72510	64490	66140	70020	76300	82750	87080	87130

Gross Capital Formation

	1970	1975	1978	1979	1980	1981	1982	1983	1984	1985	1986	1987
Increase in stocks	2450	-940	1820	1500	1720	-3090	-1020	560	1990	2500	700	-390
Gross fixed capital formation	31360	46320	63300	66490	70790	67580	67160	69460	74310	80250	86380	87520
1 General government	5670	8640	9640	9800	10970	11100	10620	10190	11190	10940	10180	9960
2 Corporate and quasi-corporate enterprises [a]	25690	37680	53660	56690	59820	56480	56540	59270	63120	69310	76200	77560
3 Other [a]	...	...	...	...	...	...	...	...	...	...	...	...
Gross Capital Formation	33810	45380	65120	67990	72510	64490	66140	70020	76300	82750	87080	87130

a) Item 'Other' is included in item 'Corporate and quasi-corporate enterprises'.

Netherlands

1.9 Gross Domestic Product by Institutional Sectors of Origin

Million Netherlands guilders

	1970	1975	1978	1979	1980	1981	1982	1983	1984	1985	1986	1987
	\multicolumn{12}{c}{Domestic Factor Incomes Originating}											
1 General government	13510	28880	39140	41980	44080	45020	46720	46950	46410	46910	47500	48140
2 Corporate and quasi-corporate enterprises [a]	85860	150860	201900	214890	228150	239310	251580	260960	277270	291210	299130	298130
A Non-financial	84770	149260	198910	211610	224630	236070	248570	257900	273950	287750	295440	293970
B Financial	1090	1600	2990	3280	3520	3240	3010	3060	3320	3460	3690	4160
3 Households and private unincorporated enterprises [a]	...	...	...	...	...	...	...	...	...	...	...	...
4 Non-profit institutions serving households [a]	...	...	...	...	...	...	...	...	...	...	...	...
Subtotal: Domestic Factor Incomes	99370	179740	241040	256870	272230	284330	298300	307910	323680	338120	346630	346270
Indirect taxes, net	11550	20210	29300	29800	32020	32900	32700	33920	35380	37190	39800	40780
A Indirect taxes	13600	24140	37000	38580	41120	41720	42760	45140	47990	50700	53710	57420
B Less: Subsidies	2050	3930	7700	8780	9100	8820	10060	11220	12610	13510	13910	16640
Consumption of fixed capital	10260	20010	26670	29290	32490	35620	37860	39190	41190	42870	43450	44770
Gross Domestic Product	121180	219960	297010	315960	336740	352850	368860	381020	400250	418180	429880	431820

a) The estimates of Households and private unincorporated enterprises and Non-profit institutions serving households are included in item 'Corporate and quasi-corporate enterprises'.

1.10 Gross Domestic Product by Kind of Activity, in Current Prices

Million Netherlands guilders

	1970	1975	1978	1979	1980	1981	1982	1983	1984	1985	1986	1987
1 Agriculture, hunting, forestry and fishing	6696	9752	11772	11330	11676	14557	15932	16124	17259	17141	18250	17130
2 Mining and quarrying	1897	8883	12555	14545	19151	25563	25972	27328	31091	35372	23710	15440
3 Manufacturing	31320	48234	57952	60084	60365	59780	64670	67463	72569	75231	81450	80540
4 Electricity, gas and water	2608	4908	6509	6639	7172	7606	8159	8412	8367	8551	8840	8700
5 Construction	9380	14936	20690	21508	23760	23056	22444	21413	21357	21264	23150	24310
6 Wholesale and retail trade, restaurants and hotels [a]	17238	29617	39614	42106	43437	44575	47051	48461	51175	53743	56480	59320
7 Transport, storage and communication	8768	14186	18740	20271	21298	22265	22395	23152	24590	26083	27880	28200
8 Finance, insurance, real estate and business services	11593	24881	38962	43251	46893	50314	54273	60108	63012	65836	69440	71970
9 Community, social and personal services [b,a]	10247	22839	31976	34656	37528	39452	41626	42776	43278	44390	47140	48920
Statistical discrepancy	13	-6	-10	...	...	12	8	13	12	9	...	...
Total, Industries	99760	178230	238760	254390	271280	287180	302530	315250	332710	347620	356340	354530
Producers of Government Services	14350	30630	41520	44430	46840	47940	49520	49650	49450	50090	50760	51570
Other Producers	500	750	990	1020	1050	1060	1090	1070	1090	1140	1170	1190
Subtotal	114610	209610	281270	299840	319170	336180	353140	365970	383250	398850	408270	407290
Less: Imputed bank service charge	2340	6360	9310	10590	11460	12660	14080	16150	16420	16730	16760	16550
Plus: Import duties	1820	2920	3800	4300	4440	4220	4580	4770	5130	5650	6100	6880
Plus: Value added tax [c]	7090	13790	21250	22410	24590	25110	25220	26430	28290	30410	32270	34200
Equals: Gross Domestic Product	121180	219960	297010	315960	336740	352850	368860	381020	400250	418180	429880	431820

a) Repair services are included in item 'Community, social and personal services'.
b) Item 'Manufacturing' includes manufacture of medical, surgical and dental equipment.
c) Item 'Value added tax' includes selective investment levy.

1.11 Gross Domestic Product by Kind of Activity, in Constant Prices

Million Netherlands guilders

	1970	1975	1978	1979	1980	1981	1982	1983	1984	1985	1986	1987
	\multicolumn{12}{c}{At constant prices of: 1980}											
1 Agriculture, hunting, forestry and fishing	7930	9670	10910	11370	11680	13290	14270	14740	15650	15220	16640	15510
2 Mining and quarrying												
3 Manufacturing	62980	79900	85410	87750	86680	85070	80980	83980	87140	90480	90440	90060
4 Electricity, gas and water												
5 Construction	26560	25460	24860	23460	23760	21860	20730	20110	20730	20890	21780	22250
6 Wholesale and retail trade, restaurants and hotels [a]												
7 Transport, storage and communication	103320	123080	140630	146470	149160	149610	150090	151720	157430	162160	166760	170830
8 Finance, insurance, real estate and business services												
9 Community, social and personal services [b,a]												

Netherlands

1.11 Gross Domestic Product by Kind of Activity, in Constant Prices
(Continued)

Million Netherlands guilders

	1970	1975	1978	1979	1980	1981	1982	1983	1984	1985	1986	1987
					At constant prices of:1980							
Total, Industries	200790	238110	261810	269050	271280	269830	266070	270550	280950	288750	295620	298650
Producers of Government Services	36500	41480	45280	46050	46840	47680	47820	47690	47760	48230	47780	48950
Other Producers	1230	1040	1070	1060	1050	1030	1000	980	990	1020	1020	1020
Subtotal	238520	280630	308160	316160	319170	318540	314890	319220	329700	338000	344420	348620
Less: Imputed bank service charge	5960	9200	10460	11250	11460	11910	12380	12360	12330	12450	12850	13060
Plus: Import duties	3360	3690	4270	4490	4440	4250	4400	4550	4380	4770	5200	5400
Plus: Value added tax [c]	16850	20830	24160	24460	24590	23490	22750	22880	23100	23620	24620	25300
Equals: Gross Domestic Product	252770	295950	326130	333860	336740	334370	329660	334290	344850	353940	361390	366260

a) Repair services are included in item 'Community, social and personal services'.
b) Item 'Manufacturing' includes manufacture of medical, surgical and dental equipment.
c) Item 'Value added tax' includes selective investment levy.

1.12 Relations Among National Accounting Aggregates

Million Netherlands guilders

	1970	1975	1978	1979	1980	1981	1982	1983	1984	1985	1986	1987
Gross Domestic Product	121180	219960	297010	315960	336740	352850	368860	381020	400250	418180	429880	431820
Plus: Net factor income from the rest of the world	560	-20	-680	-730	-620	-960	-380	560	-500	680	-730	-10
Factor income from the rest of the world	4740	8970	10930	15000	22090	30130	32020	28370	30870	32880	28110	29870
Less: Factor income to the rest of the world	4180	8990	11610	15730	22710	31090	32400	27810	31370	32200	28840	29880
Equals: Gross National Product	121740	219940	296330	315230	336120	351890	368480	381580	399750	418860	429150	431810
Less: Consumption of fixed capital	10260	20010	26670	29290	32490	35620	37860	39190	41190	42870	43450	44770
Equals: National Income	111480	199930	269660	285940	303630	316270	330620	342390	358560	375990	385700	387040
Plus: Net current transfers from the rest of the world	-150	-1870	-2130	-1510	-2470	-3660	-3750	-3260	-3680	-3930	-4740	-4850
Current transfers from the rest of the world	970	2820	5270	6310	5930	5500	5850	6570	7180	7860	7960	9160
Less: Current transfers to the rest of the world	1120	4690	7400	7820	8400	9160	9600	9830	10860	11790	12700	14010
Equals: National Disposable Income	111330	198060	267530	284430	301160	312610	326870	339130	354880	372060	380960	382190
Less: Final consumption	89480	167200	231780	249600	266040	275980	286950	296440	303140	315390	324800	332660
Equals: Net Saving	21850	30860	35750	34830	35120	36630	39920	42690	51740	56670	56160	49530
Less: Surplus of the nation on current transactions	-1700	5490	-2700	-3870	-4900	7760	11640	11860	16630	17310	11890	6910
Statistical discrepancy [a]	...	...	...	...	...	...	...	...	...	520	-640	-260
Equals: Net Capital Formation	23550	25370	38450	38700	40020	28870	28280	30830	35110	39880	43630	42360

a) The surplus of the nation on current transactions corresponds to gross national saving less gross capital formation, plus from 1985 onwards a statistical discrepancy. This discrepancy is a consequence of the difference between on the one hand the surplus of the nation on current transactions (estimated by the Dutch Central Bank in cooperation with the Central Bureau of Statistics) and on the other hand the sum of the balance of exports and imports and the net current distributive transactions with the rest of the world. For the years 1983 and 84 there were also statistical discrepancies. However, these have been eliminated by altering the imports with destination increase in stocks.

2.1 Government Final Consumption Expenditure by Function, in Current Prices

Million Netherlands guilders

	1970	1975	1978	1979	1980	1981	1982	1983	1984	1985	1986	1987
1 General public services [a]	...	...	...	...	...	...	...	...	...	...	...	...
2 Defence	3880	6460	8770	9720	10170	10790	11430	12360	12230	11930	12100	...
3 Public order and safety	...	...	...	...	...	...	...	...	...	...	...	...
4 Education [b]	6410	14010	18770	20140	21130	21650	21970	21480	21200	21570	21880	...
5 Health [a]	...	...	...	...	...	...	...	...	...	...	...	...
6 Social security and welfare [c]	630	1330	1910	2140	2400	2650	2890	2990	3070	3140	3160	...
7 Housing and community amenities [a]												...
8 Recreational, cultural and religious affairs	7740	16450	23160	25170	26560	27660	28830	29750	29890	30910	31100	...
9 Economic services												...
10 Other functions [a]												...
Total Government Final Consumption Expenditure [d]	18660	38250	52610	57170	60260	62750	65120	66580	66390	67550	68240	...

a) Items 'General public service' and 'Health' are included in items 'Housing and community amenities' through 'Other functions'.
b) Item 'Education' refers to school only.
c) Item 'Social security and welfare' refers to social security only.
d) Data for this table have not been revised, therefore, data for some years are not comparable with those of other tables.

Netherlands

2.3 Total Government Outlays by Function and Type

Million Netherlands guilders

	Final Consumption Expenditures Total	Compensation of Employees	Other	Subsidies	Other Current Transfers & Property Income	Total Current Disbursements	Gross Capital Formation	Other Capital Outlays	Total Outlays
1980									
1 General public services [a]	...	...	...	...	...	...	...	...	...
2 Defence	10170	6460	3710	-	500	10670	-	10	10680
3 Public order and safety	...	...	...	...	...	...	...	...	...
4 Education [b]	21130	17160	3970	-	1400	22530	1630	10	24170
5 Health [a]	...	...	...	...	...	...	...	...	...
6 Social security and welfare [c]	2400	1510	890	-	70940	73340	-	90	73430
7 Housing and community amenities [a]									
8 Recreation, culture and religion	26560	18950	7610	4980	33860	65400	9340	8750	83490
9 Economic services									
10 Other functions [a]									
Total [d]	60260	44080	16180	4980	106700	171940	10970	8860	191770
1981									
1 General public services [a]	...	...	...	...	...	...	...	...	...
2 Defence	10790	6640	4150	-	520	11310	-	200	11510
3 Public order and safety	...	...	...	...	...	...	...	...	...
4 Education [b]	21650	17470	4180	-	1450	23100	1510	-	24610
5 Health [a]	...	...	...	...	...	...	...	...	...
6 Social security and welfare [c]	2650	1640	1010	-	75790	78440	-	80	78520
7 Housing and community amenities [a]									
8 Recreation, culture and religion	27660	19270	8390	5520	40630	73810	9590	10150	93550
9 Economic services									
10 Other functions [a]									
Total [d]	62750	45020	17730	5520	118390	186660	11100	10430	208190
1982									
1 General public services [a]	...	...	...	...	...	...	...	...	...
2 Defence	11430	6840	4590	-	540	11970	-	110	12080
3 Public order and safety	...	...	...	...	...	...	...	...	...
4 Education [b]	21970	17890	4080	-	1420	23390	1460	10	24860
5 Health [a]	...	...	...	...	...	...	...	...	...
6 Social security and welfare [c]	2890	1840	1050	-	80720	83610	-	70	83680
7 Housing and community amenities [a]									
8 Recreation, culture and religion	28830	20150	8680	6220	49220	84270	9160	10450	103880
9 Economic services									
10 Other functions [a]									
Total [d]	65120	46720	18400	6220	131900	203240	10620	10640	224500
1983									
1 General public services [a]	...	...	...	...	...	...	...	...	...
2 Defence	12360	6840	5520	-	510	12870	-	10	12880
3 Public order and safety	...	...	...	...	...	...	...	...	...
4 Education [b]	21480	17600	3880	-	1440	22920	1210	-	24130
5 Health [a]	...	...	...	...	...	...	...	...	...
6 Social security and welfare [c]	2990	1900	1090	-	81500	84490	-	70	84560
7 Housing and community amenities [a]									
8 Recreation, culture and religion	29750	20610	9140	6710	56630	93090	8980	10290	112360
9 Economic services									
10 Other functions [a]									
Total [d]	66580	46950	19630	6710	140080	213370	10190	10370	233930

Netherlands

2.3 Total Government Outlays by Function and Type
(Continued)

Million Netherlands guilders

	Final Consumption Expenditures Total	Compensation of Employees	Other	Subsidies	Other Current Transfers & Property Income	Total Current Disbursements	Gross Capital Formation	Other Capital Outlays	Total Outlays
1984									
1 General public services [a]	...	...	...	...	...	...	...	...	...
2 Defence	12230	6930	5300	-	570	12800	-	10	12810
3 Public order and safety	...	...	...	...	...	...	...	...	...
4 Education [b]	21200	17170	4030	-	1480	22680	1300	-	23980
5 Health [a]	...	...	...	...	...	...	...	...	...
6 Social security and welfare [c]	3070	1930	1140	-	81690	84760	-	80	84840
7 Housing and community amenities [a]									
8 Recreation, culture and religion	29890	20380	9510	7410	59490	96790	9890	11780	118460
9 Economic services									
10 Other functions [a]									
Total [d]	66390	46410	19980	7410	143230	217030	11190	11870	240090
1985									
1 General public services [a]	...	...	...	...	...	...	...	...	...
2 Defence	11930	6800	5130	-	580	12510	-	20	12530
3 Public order and safety	...	...	...	...	...	...	...	...	...
4 Education [b]	21570	17340	4230	-	1590	23160	1250	-	24410
5 Health [a]	...	...	...	...	...	...	...	...	...
6 Social security and welfare [c]	3140	1990	1150	-	83380	86520	-	90	86610
7 Housing and community amenities [a]									
8 Recreation, culture and religion	30910	20680	10230	8110	62160	101180	9270	11750	122200
9 Economic services									
10 Other functions [a]									
Total [d]	67550	46810	20740	8110	147710	223370	10520	11860	245750
1986									
1 General public services [a]	...	...	...	...	...	...	...	...	...
2 Defence	12100	6860	5240	-	630	12730	-	20	12750
3 Public order and safety	...	...	...	...	...	...	...	...	...
4 Education [b]	21880	17710	4170	-	1770	23650	1130	-	24780
5 Health [a]	...	...	...	...	...	...	...	...	...
6 Social security and welfare [c]	3160	2000	1160	-	84700	87860	-	100	87960
7 Housing and community amenities [a]									
8 Recreation, culture and religion	31100	20530	10570	7710	62230	101040	8420	14270	123730
9 Economic services									
10 Other functions [a]									
Total [d]	68240	47100	21140	7710	149330	225280	9550	14390	249220

a) Items 'General public service' and 'Health' are included in items 'Housing and community amenities' through 'Other functions'.
b) Item 'Education' refers to school only.
c) Item 'Social security and welfare' refers to social security only.
d) Data for this table have not been revised, therefore, data for some years are not comparable with those of other tables.

2.5 Private Final Consumption Expenditure by Type and Purpose, in Current Prices

Million Netherlands guilders

	1970	1975	1978	1979	1980	1981	1982	1983	1984	1985	1986	1987
Final Consumption Expenditure of Resident Households												
1 Food, beverages and tobacco	18250	28350	35990	37620	39610	41840	43860	44750	46510	47200	47670	47940
A Food	14430	21860	27790	28780	30630	32390	33910	34520	36020	36700	37040	37360
B Non-alcoholic beverages	...	...	940	1050	1090	1140	1310	1360	1300	1330	1340	1310
C Alcoholic beverages	...	...	3730	4120	4060	4340	4620	4690	4790	4740	4860	4750
D Tobacco	1830	2760	3530	3670	3830	3970	4020	4180	4400	4430	4430	4520
2 Clothing and footwear	7490	11770	14480	15340	16170	15770	15690	15690	15770	17010	18460	19160
3 Gross rent, fuel and power [a]	8810	17960	25520	29170	32640	36410	39670	42540	44820	48000	48680	47460
A Fuel and power	2550	5190	7440	9200	10530	12150	12770	13200	14000	15870	14630	11620
B Other	6260	12770	18080	19970	22110	24260	26900	29340	30820	32130	34050	35840
4 Furniture, furnishings and household equipment and operation	8160	12810	17650	17720	18590	17590	17190	17400	17260	17920	19070	20290
A Household operation	1770	2750	3530	3690	3940	4070	4300	4310	4460	4630	4830	4980

Netherlands

2.5 Private Final Consumption Expenditure by Type and Purpose, in Current Prices
(Continued)

Million Netherlands guilders

	1970	1975	1978	1979	1980	1981	1982	1983	1984	1985	1986	1987
B Other	6390	10060	14120	14030	14650	13520	12890	13090	12800	13290	14240	15310
5 Medical care and health expenses	5950	14480	20890	22750	24830	26560	28410	29220	29750	30640	31570	32370
6 Transport and communication	6600	13790	19740	21620	21810	22500	23070	24330	24710	26580	27730	29440
A Personal transport equipment	2380	4940	8110	8420	6760	6630	6950	7990	7960	8950	10520	11170
B Other	4220	8850	11630	13200	15050	15870	16120	16340	16750	17630	17210	18270
7 Recreational, entertainment, education and cultural services	5930	12470	17890	18700	20050	20300	20380	21250	21960	22590	23680	24550
A Education	...	...	550	600	660	700	710	730	740	760	810	860
B Other	...	...	17340	18100	19390	19600	19670	20520	21220	21830	22870	23690
8 Miscellaneous goods and services	9030	16370	23130	25220	27310	28180	29150	30050	31820	32970	34180	35760
A Personal care	1970	3120	4420	4740	5100	5190	5150	5390	5650	5830	6170	6400
B Expenditures in restaurants, cafes and hotels	3720	5900	8170	8860	9660	10050	10560	10880	11770	12020	12270	12600
C Other	3340	7350	10540	11620	12550	12940	13440	13780	14400	15120	15740	16760
Total Final Consumption Expenditure in the Domestic Market by Households, of which	70220	128000	175290	188140	201010	209150	217420	225230	232600	242910	251040	256970
A Durable goods	...	...	24830	24670	23270	21830	21550	22740	22250	23600	26270	28040
B Semi-durable goods	...	...	28940	30890	33120	32850	32410	32870	33570	35790	38460	40470
C Non-durable goods	...	...	55020	59740	64790	69560	72670	74210	77550	80540	79210	77100
D Services	...	...	66500	72840	79830	84910	90790	95410	99230	102980	107100	111360
Plus: Direct purchases abroad by resident households	2470	4470	7670	8180	9450	9410	9630	9870	10200	10940	11320	12090
Less: Direct purchases in the domestic market by non-resident households	1870	3520	3790	3890	4680	5330	5220	5240	6050	6130	6100	6100
Equals: Final Consumption Expenditure of Resident Households [b]	70820	128950	179170	192430	205780	213230	221830	229860	236750	247720	256260	262960

Final Consumption Expenditure of Private Non-profit Institutions Serving Households

	1970	1975	1978	1979	1980	1981	1982	1983	1984	1985	1986	1987
Equals: Final Consumption Expenditure of Private Non-profit Organisations Serving Households	...	...	...	...	...	...	...	...	...	...	...	...
Private Final Consumption Expenditure	70820	128950	179170	192430	205780	213230	221830	229860	236750	247720	256260	262960

a) Item 'Gross rent, fuel and power' includes maintenance expenditure.
b) Item 'Final consumption expenditure of resident households' includes consumption expenditure of private non-profit institutions serving households.

2.6 Private Final Consumption Expenditure by Type and Purpose, in Constant Prices

Million Netherlands guilders

	1970	1975	1978	1979	1980	1981	1982	1983	1984	1985	1986	1987

At constant prices of:1980

Final Consumption Expenditure of Resident Households

	1970	1975	1978	1979	1980	1981	1982	1983	1984	1985	1986	1987
1 Food, beverages and tobacco	30830	35430	38520	39700	39610	39770	39620	40040	40100	40320	40990	41860
A Food	24810	27140	29310	29900	30630	30790	30720	31080	31510	31920	32530	33550
B Non-alcoholic beverages	...	...	1000	1120	1090	1140	1180	1260	1170	1140	1200	1190
C Alcoholic beverages	...	...	4160	4540	4060	4160	4120	4170	4140	4040	4080	3960
D Tobacco	3170	4000	4050	4140	3830	3680	3600	3530	3280	3220	3180	3160
2 Clothing and footwear	16010	15750	16180	16420	16170	15180	14500	14320	14180	14780	15550	16250
3 Gross rent, fuel and power [a]	20400	26880	30410	32300	32640	32610	32730	33330	34170	35630	36340	37060
A Fuel and power	7670	9020	9970	11140	10530	9880	9240	9230	9410	10210	10160	10180
B Other	12730	17860	20440	21160	22110	22730	23490	24100	24760	25420	26180	26880
4 Furniture, furnishings and household equipment and operation	15080	16050	19230	18760	18590	16720	15750	15740	15490	15760	16440	17300
A Household operation	3610	3600	3920	3950	3940	3930	3970	3940	4010	4090	4150	4240
B Other	11470	12450	15310	14810	14650	12790	11780	11800	11480	11670	12290	13060
5 Medical care and health expenses	17730	21190	23400	24000	24830	25120	25490	25760	26360	26910	27130	27840
6 Transport and communication	13620	18250	22690	23710	21810	21000	20710	21060	20960	21930	23280	23880
A Personal transport equipment	4490	6450	8770	8950	6760	6380	6250	6830	6680	7250	8130	8200
B Other	9130	11800	13920	14760	15050	14620	14460	14230	14280	14680	15150	15680
7 Recreational, entertainment, education and cultural services	10910	15130	19000	19450	20050	19510	18860	19080	19440	19550	20170	20760
A Education	...	...	620	640	660	650	610	590	570	570	590	620

Netherlands

2.6 Private Final Consumption Expenditure by Type and Purpose, in Constant Prices
(Continued)

Million Netherlands guilders

	1970	1975	1978	1979	1980	1981	1982	1983	1984	1985	1986	1987
					At constant prices of:1980							
B Other	...	...	18380	18810	19390	18860	18250	18490	18870	18980	19580	20140
8 Miscellaneous goods and services	19260	22900	25210	26450	27310	27060	26900	26890	27810	28350	28970	29550
A Personal care	4110	4220	4840	5040	5100	5060	4920	5070	5290	5370	5650	5810
B Expenditures in restaurants, cafes and hotels	7490	8470	8930	9290	9660	9450	9440	9350	9740	9760	9730	9770
C Other	7660	10210	11440	12120	12550	12550	12540	12470	12780	13220	13590	13970
Total Final Consumption Expenditure in the Domestic Market by Households, of which	143840	171580	194640	200790	201010	196970	194560	196220	198510	203230	208870	214500
A Durable goods	...	...	26440	25840	23270	21040	19990	20640	20120	20850	22730	23670
B Semi-durable goods	...	...	31810	32870	33120	31570	30130	30010	30260	31330	32780	34490
C Non-durable goods	...	...	62110	65150	64790	63880	63020	63220	63720	64750	65730	66760
D Services	...	...	74280	76930	79830	80480	81420	82350	84410	86300	87630	89580
Plus: Direct purchases abroad by resident households	5790	7060	9330	9080	9450	8630	8320	8290	8370	8550	8830	9340
Less: Direct purchases in the domestic market by non-resident households	3650	4760	4160	4110	4680	4990	4620	4520	4890	4850	4820	4760
Equals: Final Consumption Expenditure of Resident Households b	145980	173880	199810	205760	205780	200610	198260	199990	201990	206930	212880	219080

Final Consumption Expenditure of Private Non-profit Institutions Serving Households

Equals: Final Consumption Expenditure of Private Non-profit Organisations Serving Households	...	...	...	...	...	...	...	...	...	...	...	...
Private Final Consumption Expenditure	145980	173880	199810	205760	205780	200610	198260	199990	201990	206930	212880	219080

a) Item 'Gross rent, fuel and power' includes maintenance expenditure.
b) Item 'Final consumption expenditure of resident households' includes consumption expenditure of private non-profit institutions serving households.

2.7 Gross Capital Formation by Type of Good and Owner, in Current Prices

Million Netherlands guilders

	1980				1981				1982			
	TOTAL	Total Private	Public Enterprises	General Government	TOTAL	Total Private	Public Enterprises	General Government	TOTAL	Total Private	Public Enterprises	General Government
Increase in stocks, total a	1720	1720	...	...	-3090	-3090	...	...	-1020	-1020	...	...
Gross Fixed Capital Formation, Total ba	70790	59820	...	10970	67580	56480	...	11100	67160	56540	...	10620
1 Residential buildings	20840	20840	...	...	20130	20130	...	...	19540	19540	...	...
2 Non-residential buildings	15120	11960	...	3160	13710	10600	...	3110	12900	9820	...	3080
3 Other construction	8030	1700	...	6330	8010	1570	...	6440	7630	1480	...	6150
4 Land improvement and plantation and orchard development			...				...				...	
5 Producers' durable goods	24740	23260	...	1480	23900	22350	...	1550	25320	23930	...	1390
A Transport equipment	7080	6760	...	320	6160	5820	...	340	7310	6990	...	320
Passenger cars	2640	...	...	...	2520	...	...	...	2760	...	...	...
Other	4440	...	...	...	3640	...	...	...	4550	...	...	...
B Machinery and equipment	17660	16500	...	1160	17740	16530	...	1210	18010	16940	...	1070
6 Breeding stock, dairy cattle, etc.	60	60	...	...	150	150	...	...	140	140	...	...
Statistical discrepancy c	2000	2000	...	...	1680	1680	...	...	1630	1630	...	...
Total Gross Capital Formation ba	72510	61540	...	10970	64490	53390	...	11100	66140	55520	...	10620

	1983				1984				1985			
	TOTAL	Total Private	Public Enterprises	General Government	TOTAL	Total Private	Public Enterprises	General Government	TOTAL	Total Private	Public Enterprises	General Government
Increase in stocks, total a	560	560	...	...	1990	1990	...	...	2500	2500	...	...
Gross Fixed Capital Formation, Total ba	69460	59270	...	10190	74310	63120	...	11190	80250	69310	...	10940
1 Residential buildings	19470	19470	...	...	20400	20400	...	...	20380	20380	...	...
2 Non-residential buildings	11960	9080	...	2880	12310	9420	...	2890	12480	9840	...	2640
3 Other construction	7360	1320	...	6040	7960	1220	...	6740	8030	1400	...	6630
4 Land improvement and plantation and orchard development			...				...				...	

Netherlands

2.7 Gross Capital Formation by Type of Good and Owner, in Current Prices
(Continued)

Million Netherlands guilders

	1983 TOTAL	1983 Total Private	1983 Public Enterprises	1983 General Government	1984 TOTAL	1984 Total Private	1984 Public Enterprises	1984 General Government	1985 TOTAL	1985 Total Private	1985 Public Enterprises	1985 General Government
5 Producers' durable goods	28590	27320	...	1270	31960	30400	...	1560	37650	35980	...	1670
A Transport equipment	9410	9120	...	290	9100	8770	...	330	10360	10040	...	320
Passenger cars	3330	...	...	...	3600	...	...	...	4280	...	...	...
Other	6080	...	...	...	5500	...	...	...	6080	...	...	...
B Machinery and equipment	19180	18200	...	980	22860	21630	...	1230	27290	25940	...	1350
6 Breeding stock, dairy cattle, etc.	190	190	...	...	-150	-150	...	...	-270	-270	...	...
Statistical discrepancy [c]	1890	1890	...	...	1830	1830	...	...	1980	1980	...	...
Total Gross Capital Formation [ba]	70020	59830	...	10190	76300	65110	...	11190	82750	71810	...	10940

	1986 TOTAL	1986 Total Private	1986 Public Enterprises	1986 General Government	1987 TOTAL	1987 Total Private	1987 Public Enterprises	1987 General Government
Increase in stocks, total [a]	700	700	...	...	-390	-390	...	...
Gross Fixed Capital Formation, Total [ba]	86380	76200	...	10180	87520	77560	...	9960
1 Residential buildings	21450	21450	...	...	22510	22510	...	...
2 Non-residential buildings	13610	11230	...	2380	14710	12220	...	2490
3 Other construction	7720	1620	...	6100	7280	1630	...	5650
4 Land improvement and plantation and orchard development			...				...	
5 Producers' durable goods	41340	39640	...	1700	40990	39170	...	1820
A Transport equipment	11690	11400	...	290	11210	10910	...	300
Passenger cars	5170	...	...	...	5470	...	...	...
Other	6520	...	...	...	5740	...	...	...
B Machinery and equipment	29650	28240	...	1410	29780	28260	...	1520
6 Breeding stock, dairy cattle, etc.	-170	-170	...	...	-550	-550	...	...
Statistical discrepancy [c]	2430	2430	...	...	2580	2580	...	...
Total Gross Capital Formation [ba]	87080	76900	...	10180	87130	77170	...	9960

a) Column 'Public enterprises' is included in column 'Total private'.
b) Gross capital formation are estimated by user rather than by owner base.
c) Item 'Statistical discrepancy' refers to transfers costs on existing fixed capital goods.

2.8 Gross Capital Formation by Type of Good and Owner, in Constant Prices

Million Netherlands guilders

	1980 TOTAL	1980 Total Private	1980 Public Enterprises	1980 General Government	1981 TOTAL	1981 Total Private	1981 Public Enterprises	1981 General Government	1982 TOTAL	1982 Total Private	1982 Public Enterprises	1982 General Government
	At constant prices of: 1980											
Increase in stocks, total [a]	1720	1720	...	...	-2500	-2500	...	...	-840	-840	...	...
Gross Fixed Capital Formation, Total [ba]	70790	59820	...	10970	63420	52960	...	10460	60840	51120	...	9720
1 Residential buildings	20840	20840	...	...	18840	18840	...	...	17790	17790	...	...
2 Non-residential buildings	15120	11960	...	3160	12920	10000	...	2920	11910	9070	...	2840
3 Other construction	8030	1700	...	6330	7540	1470	...	6070	6990	1360	...	5630
4 Land improvement and plantation and orchard development			...				...				...	
5 Producers' durable goods	24740	23260	...	1480	22160	20690	...	1470	22150	20900	...	1250
A Transport equipment	7080	6760	...	320	5890	5560	...	330	6560	6270	...	290
Passenger cars	2640	...	...	...	2470	...	...	...	2540	...	...	...
Other	4440	...	...	...	3420	...	...	...	4020	...	...	...
B Machinery and equipment	17660	16500	...	1160	16270	15130	...	1140	15590	14630	...	960
6 Breeding stock, dairy cattle, etc.	60	60	...	...	130	130	...	...	100	100	...	...
Statistical discrepancy [c]	2000	2000	...	...	1830	1830	...	...	1900	1900	...	...
Total Gross Capital Formation [ba]	72510	61540	...	10970	60920	50460	...	10460	60000	50280	...	9720

Netherlands

2.8 Gross Capital Formation by Type of Good and Owner, in Constant Prices

Million Netherlands guilders

	1983 TOTAL	1983 Total Private	1983 Public Enterprises	1983 General Government	1984 TOTAL	1984 Total Private	1984 Public Enterprises	1984 General Government	1985 TOTAL	1985 Total Private	1985 Public Enterprises	1985 General Government
				At constant prices of:1980								
Increase in stocks, total a	330	330	...	...	970	970	...	...	1260	1260	...	...
Gross Fixed Capital Formation, Total ba	62100	52830	...	9270	65450	55480	...	9970	69890	60300	...	9590
1 Residential buildings	17720	17720	...	...	18510	18510	...	...	18430	18430	...	...
2 Non-residential buildings	11070	8400	...	2670	11340	8660	...	2680	11600	9130	...	2470
3 Other construction	6670	1190	...	5480	7040	1070	...	5970	6940	1230	...	5710
4 Land improvement and plantation and orchard development			...				...				...	
5 Producers' durable goods	24370	23250	...	1120	26680	25360	...	1320	30980	29570	...	1410
A Transport equipment	8050	7800	...	250	7550	7290	...	260	8390	8130	...	260
Passenger cars	2930	...	...	...	3000	...	...	...	3480	...	...	...
Other	5120	...	...	...	4550	...	...	...	4910	...	...	...
B Machinery and equipment	16320	15450	...	870	19130	18070	...	1060	22590	21440	...	1150
6 Breeding stock, dairy cattle, etc.	140	140	...	...	-140	-140	...	...	-230	-230	...	...
Statistical discrepancy c	2130	2130	...	...	2020	2020	...	...	2170	2170	...	...
Total Gross Capital Formation ba	62430	53160	...	9270	66420	56450	...	9970	71150	61560	...	9590

	1986 TOTAL	1986 Total Private	1986 Public Enterprises	1986 General Government	1987 TOTAL	1987 Total Private	1987 Public Enterprises	1987 General Government
				At constant prices of:1980				
Increase in stocks, total a	240	240	...	...	-380	-380	...	...
Gross Fixed Capital Formation, Total ba	75630	66660	...	8970	76850	68130	...	8720
1 Residential buildings	19370	19370	...	...	19970	19970	...	...
2 Non-residential buildings	12620	10390	...	2230	13490	11190	...	2300
3 Other construction	6740	1430	...	5310	6350	1440	...	4910
4 Land improvement and plantation and orchard development			...				...	
5 Producers' durable goods	34480	33050	...	1430	34870	33360	...	1510
A Transport equipment	9320	9090	...	230	8720	8500	...	220
Passenger cars	4040	...	...	...	4080	...	...	...
Other	5280	...	...	...	4640	...	...	...
B Machinery and equipment	25160	23960	...	1200	26150	24860	...	1290
6 Breeding stock, dairy cattle, etc.	-170	-170	...	...	-530	-530	...	...
Statistical discrepancy c	2590	2590	...	...	2700	2700	...	...
Total Gross Capital Formation ba	75870	66900	...	8970	76470	67750	...	8720

a) Column 'Public enterprises' is included in column 'Total private'.
b) Gross capital formation are estimated by user rather than by owner base.
c) Item 'Statistical discrepancy' refers to transfers costs on existing fixed capital goods.

2.11 Gross Fixed Capital Formation by Kind of Activity of Owner, ISIC Divisions, in Current Prices

Million Netherlands guilders

	1970	1975	1978	1979	1980	1981	1982	1983	1984	1985	1986	1987
					All Producers							
1 Agriculture, hunting, forestry and fishing	1150	1870	3880	4510	3870	3120	3390	3820	3760	4170	4850	4110
A Agriculture and hunting	...	...	3880	4490	3810	2970	3160	3470	...	...	...	...
B Forestry and logging	...	...	...	...	...	...	...	...	...	...	...	...
C Fishing	...	...	-	20	60	150	120	150	...	...	...	...
2 Mining and quarrying	400	1430	1200	1070	1060	1370	1690	1470	1530	2230	1790	...
A Coal mining	...	...	-	-	-	-	-	-	...	...	...	...
B Crude petroleum and natural gas production	...	...	1200	1070	1060	1370	1700	...	...	...	...	...
C Metal ore mining	...	...	...	...	...	...	...	...	...	...	...	...
D Other mining	...	...	...	...	...	...	...	...	...	...	...	...

Netherlands

2.11 Gross Fixed Capital Formation by Kind of Activity of Owner, ISIC Divisions, in Current Prices
(Continued)

Million Netherlands guilders

	1970	1975	1978	1979	1980	1981	1982	1983	1984	1985	1986	1987
3 Manufacturing [a]	6970	7450	10310	11330	11970	11230	11260	11730	13980	16350	19230	26130
A Manufacturing of food, beverages and tobacco	...	...	2330	2820	3050	2660	2590	...	...	...	...	...
B Textile, wearing apparel and leather industries	...	...	290	330	310	240	310	...	...	...	...	...
C Manufacture of wood, and wood products, including furniture	...	...	290	300	280	200	200	...	...	...	...	...
D Manufacture of paper and paper products, printing and publishing	...	...	900	1280	1120	1190	1140	...	...	...	...	...
E Manufacture of chemicals and chemical petroleum, coal, rubber and plastic products	...	...	2910	2710	2750	2900	3140	...	...	...	...	...
F Manufacture of non-metalic mineral products except products of petroleum and coal	...	...	720	660	830	640	450	...	...	...	...	...
G Basic metal industries	...	...	280	370	430	490	420	...	...	...	...	...
H Manufacture of fabricated metal products, machinery and equipment	...	...	2450	2670	3050	2740	2930	...	...	...	...	...
I Other manufacturing industries	...	...	140	190	150	170	160	...	...	...	...	...
4 Electricity, gas and water	1860	2950	2710	2770	3070	3080	2540	2280	2440	2530	3670	...
5 Construction	620	700	1360	1200	1150	1040	890	1120	1250	1600	1230	...
6 Wholesale and retail trade, restaurants and hotels [ba]	2100	2710	3840	4160	4240	3700	3600	3630	4120	4800	5700	6060
7 Transport, storage and communication	2510	4750	6020	6190	6020	5540	6530	8110	7590	8380	9040	8450
A Transport and storage	...	...	4650	4840	4560	4150	5130	6340	...	...	...	...
B Communication	...	...	1370	1350	1460	1390	1380	1450	...	...	...	...
8 Finance, insurance, real estate and business services [c]	7760	12750	19750	20170	22470	21520	20890	21070	21990	22080	23540	24740
A Financial institutions	170	170	200	200	210	230	250	270	300	320	360	390
B Insurance	80	80	90	90	100	110	120	130	140	150	160	170
C Real estate and business services [c]	7510	12500	19460	19880	22160	21180	20520	20670	21550	21610	23020	24180
Real estate except dwellings	...	...	...	...	...	...	...	...	...	...	...	...
Dwellings	7510	12500	19460	19880	22160	21180	20520	20670	21550	21610	23020	24180
9 Community, social and personal services [bc]	2320	3070	4590	5290	5970	5880	5750	6040	6460	7170	7150	8070
Total Industries [d]	25690	37680	53660	56690	59820	56480	56540	59270	63120	69310	76200	77560
Producers of Government Services	5670	8640	9640	9800	10970	11100	10620	10190	11190	10940	10180	9960
Private Non-Profit Institutions Serving Households [d]	...	...	...	...	...	...	...	...	...	...	...	...
Total [e]	31360	46320	63300	66490	70790	67580	67160	69460	74310	80250	86380	87520

a) Repair services are included in item 'Manufacturing'.
b) Restaurants and hotels are included in item 'Community, social and personal services'.
c) Business services are included in item 'Community, social and personal services'.
d) Item 'Private non-profit institutions serving households' is included with various industries above.
e) Gross capital formation are estimated by user rather than by owner base.

2.12 Gross Fixed Capital Formation by Kind of Activity of Owner, ISIC Divisions, in Constant Prices

Million Netherlands guilders

	1970	1975	1978	1979	1980	1981	1982	1983	1984	1985	1986	1987
	At constant prices of: 1980											
	All Producers											
1 Agriculture, hunting, forestry and fishing	2520	2640	4440	4860	3870	2930	3060	3390	3240	3560	4140	3520
2 Mining and quarrying												
3 Manufacturing [a]	18090	16130	17400	17430	17250	15510	14430	14350	16330	19070	22160	22890
4 Electricity, gas and water												

Netherlands

2.12 Gross Fixed Capital Formation by Kind of Activity of Owner, ISIC Divisions, in Constant Prices
(Continued)

Million Netherlands guilders

	1970	1975	1978	1979	1980	1981	1982	1983	1984	1985	1986	1987
At constant prices of: 1980												
5 Construction	...	...	...	...	...	...	...	...	...	...	...	...
6 Wholesale and retail trade, restaurants and hotels [b,a]	4140	3800	4350	4480	4240	3510	3260	3210	3580	4110	4840	5100
7 Transport, storage and communication	4560	6080	6650	6550	6020	5150	5770	6920	6410	6960	7640	7210
8 Finance, insurance, real estate and business services [b,c]	25880	24350	28550	27500	28440	25860	24600	24960	25920	26600	27880	29410
9 Community, social and personal services [c]	...	...	...	...	...	...	...	...	...	...	...	...
Total Industries [d]	55190	53000	61390	60820	59820	52960	51120	52830	55480	60300	66660	68130
Producers of Government Services	14430	13060	11320	10640	10970	10460	9720	9270	9970	9590	8970	8720
Private Non-Profit Institutions Serving Households [d]	...	...	...	...	...	...	...	...	...	...	...	...
Total [e]	69620	66060	72710	71460	70790	63420	60840	62100	65450	69890	75630	76850

a) Repair services are included in item 'Manufacturing'.
b) Restaurants and hotels are included in item 'Finance, insurance, real estate and business services'.
c) Item 'Community, social and personal services' is included in item 'Finance, insurance, real estate and business services'.
d) Item 'Private non-profit institutions serving households' is included with various industries above.
e) Gross capital formation are estimated by user rather than by owner base.

2.17 Exports and Imports of Goods and Services, Detail

Million Netherlands guilders

	1970	1975	1978	1979	1980	1981	1982	1983	1984	1985	1986	1987
Exports of Goods and Services												
1 Exports of merchandise, f.o.b.	43010	88960	107460	128460	147080	171330	177620	185010	210630	225950	195830	188250
2 Transport and communication	6360	8930	10680	11950	13760	15350	15180	15560	16930	17890	16600	16480
A In respect of merchandise imports	370	360	280	340	380	430	430	400	500	550	430	420
B Other	5990	8570	10400	11610	13380	14920	14750	15160	16430	17340	16170	16060
3 Insurance service charges	270	450	850	800	830	1100	920	1030	860	910	950	1090
4 Other commodities	2790	7860	10560	9960	10460	11510	13660	12930	14090	14660	13170	14690
5 Adjustments of merchandise exports to change-of-ownership basis	...	...	...	...	...	...	...	...	...	...	...	...
6 Direct purchases in the domestic market by non-residential households	1870	3520	3790	3890	4680	5330	5220	5240	6050	6130	6100	6100
7 Direct purchases in the domestic market by extraterritorial bodies												
Total Exports of Goods and Services	54300	109720	133340	155060	176810	204620	212600	219770	248560	265540	232650	226610
Imports of Goods and Services												
1 Imports of merchandise, c.i.f.	49140	90890	115680	137550	156120	168420	171710	179580	200240	216610	185260	184900
A Imports of merchandise, f.o.b.	45920	85540	109080	129610	147200	158330	161810	170390	188700	203770	175220	175210
B Transport of services on merchandise imports	3080	5080	6240	7530	8480	9620	9460	8770	11030	12320	9620	9280
By residents	370	360	280	340	380	430	430	400	500	550	430	420
By non-residents	2710	4720	5960	7190	8100	9190	9030	8370	10530	11770	9190	8860
C Insurance service charges on merchandise imports	140	270	360	410	440	470	440	420	510	520	420	410
By residents	...	...	...	...	...	...	...	...	...	...	...	...
By non-residents	140	270	360	410	440	470	440	420	510	520	420	410
2 Adjustments of merchandise imports to change-of-ownership basis	...	...	...	...	...	...	...	...	...	...	...	...
3 Other transport and communication	240	480	670	750	960	1040	1140	1120	1200	1260	1060	1070
4 Other insurance service charges	330	590	700	820	930	1000	1040	1050	1090	1160	1240	1280
5 Other commodities	4230	5910	8510	9390	11160	12370	13310	13590	15020	15530	15770	15240
6 Direct purchases abroad by government												
7 Direct purchases abroad by resident households	2470	4470	7670	8180	9450	9410	9630	9870	10200	10940	11320	12090
Total Imports of Goods and Services	56410	102340	133230	156690	178620	192240	196830	205210	227750	245500	214650	214580
Balance of Goods and Services	-2110	7380	110	-1630	-1810	12380	15770	14560	20810	20040	18000	12030
Total Imports and Balance of Goods and Services	54300	109720	133340	155060	176810	204620	212600	219770	248560	265540	232650	226610

Netherlands

3.11 General Government Production Account: Total and Subsectors

Million Netherlands guilders

	1980					1981				
	Total General Government	Central Government	State or Provincial Government	Local Government	Social Security Funds	Total General Government	Central Government	State or Provincial Government	Local Government	Social Security Funds
Gross Output											
1 Sales	3200	1750	...	1450	-	3290	1730	...	1560	-
2 Services produced for own use	60260	27010	...	30850	2400	62750	28200	...	31900	2650
3 Own account fixed capital formation	580	-	...	580	-	580	-	...	580	-
Gross Output a	64040	28760	...	32880	2400	66620	29930	...	34040	2650
Gross Input											
Intermediate Consumption	17200	9970	...	6340	890	18680	10780	...	6890	1010
Subtotal: Value Added	46840	18790	...	26540	1510	47940	19150	...	27150	1640
1 Indirect taxes, net	360	130	-	230	-	360	120	-	240	-
A Indirect taxes	360	130	...	230	-	360	120	...	240	-
B Less: Subsidies	-	-	...	-	-	-	-	...	-	-
2 Consumption of fixed capital	2400	660	...	1740	-	2560	710	...	1850	-
3 Compensation of employees	44080	18000	...	24570	1510	45020	18320	...	25060	1640
A To residents	44080	18000	...	24570	1510	45020	18320	...	25060	1640
B To the rest of the world	-	-	...	-	-	-	-	...	-	-
4 Net Operating surplus	-	-	...	-	-	-	-	...	-	-
Gross Input a	64040	28760	...	32880	2400	66620	29930	...	34040	2650

	1982					1983				
	Total General Government	Central Government	State or Provincial Government	Local Government	Social Security Funds	Total General Government	Central Government	State or Provincial Government	Local Government	Social Security Funds
Gross Output											
1 Sales	3700	1900	...	1800	-	4040	2110	...	1930	-
2 Services produced for own use	65120	29310	...	32920	2890	66580	30660	...	32930	2990
3 Own account fixed capital formation	570	-	...	570	-	560	-	...	560	-
Gross Output a	69390	31210	...	35290	2890	71180	32770	...	35420	2990
Gross Input											
Intermediate Consumption	19870	11520	...	7300	1050	21530	12920	...	7520	1090
Subtotal: Value Added	49520	19690	...	27990	1840	49650	19850	...	27900	1900
1 Indirect taxes, net	380	140	-	240	-	400	130	-	270	-
A Indirect taxes	380	140	...	240	-	400	130	...	270	-
B Less: Subsidies	-	-	...	-	-	-	-	...	-	-
2 Consumption of fixed capital	2420	630	...	1790	-	2300	670	...	1630	-
3 Compensation of employees	46720	18920	...	25960	1840	46950	19050	...	26000	1900
A To residents	46720	18920	...	25960	1840	46950	19050	...	26000	1900
B To the rest of the world	-	-	...	-	-	-	-	...	-	-
4 Net Operating surplus	-	-	...	-	-	-	-	...	-	-
Gross Input a	69390	31210	...	35290	2890	71180	32770	...	35420	2990

	1984					1985				
	Total General Government	Central Government	State or Provincial Government	Local Government	Social Security Funds	Total General Government	Central Government	State or Provincial Government	Local Government	Social Security Funds
Gross Output											
1 Sales	4360	2310	...	2050	-	4580	2380	...	2200	-
2 Services produced for own use	66390	30720	...	32600	3070	67670	31260	...	33290	3120
3 Own account fixed capital formation	640	-	...	640	-	590	-	...	590	-
Gross Output a	71390	33030	...	35290	3070	72840	33640	...	36080	3120
Gross Input											
Intermediate Consumption	21940	13040	...	7760	1140	22750	13440	...	8180	1130
Subtotal: Value Added	49450	19990	...	27530	1930	50090	20200	...	27900	1990
1 Indirect taxes, net	420	150	-	270	-	430	160	-	270	-
A Indirect taxes	420	150	...	270	-	430	160	...	270	-
B Less: Subsidies	-	-	...	-	-	-	-	...	-	-
2 Consumption of fixed capital	2620	800	...	1820	-	2750	860	...	1890	-
3 Compensation of employees	46410	19040	...	25440	1930	46910	19180	...	25740	1990
A To residents	46410	19040	...	25440	1930	46910	19180	...	25740	1990
B To the rest of the world	-	-	...	-	-	-	-	...	-	-
4 Net Operating surplus	-	-	...	-	-	-	-	...	-	-
Gross Input a	71390	33030	...	35290	3070	72840	33640	...	36080	3120

Netherlands

3.11 General Government Production Account: Total and Subsectors

Million Netherlands guilders

	1986 Total General Government	1986 Central Government	1986 State or Provincial Government	1986 Local Government	1986 Social Security Funds	1987 Total General Government	1987 Central Government	1987 State or Provincial Government	1987 Local Government	1987 Social Security Funds
				Gross Output						
1 Sales	5100	2810	...	2290	-	5100	2620	...	2480	-
2 Services produced for own use	68540	31890	...	33430	3220	69700	32640	...	33720	3340
3 Own account fixed capital formation	520	-	...	520	-	480	-	...	480	-
Gross Output a	74160	34700	...	36240	3220	75280	35260	...	36680	3340
				Gross Input						
Intermediate Consumption	23400	14250	...	8020	1130	23710	14380	...	8140	1190
Subtotal: Value Added	50760	20450	...	28220	2090	51570	20880	...	28540	2150
1 Indirect taxes, net	460	180	-	280	-	480	190	...	290	-
A Indirect taxes	460	180	...	280	-	480	190	...	290	-
B Less: Subsidies	-	-	...	-	-	-	-	...	-	-
2 Consumption of fixed capital	2800	930	...	1870	-	2950	1020	...	1930	-
3 Compensation of employees	47500	19340	...	26070	2090	48140	19670	...	26320	2150
A To residents	47500	19340	...	26070	2090	48140	19670	...	26320	2150
B To the rest of the world	-	-	...	-	-	-	-	...	-	-
4 Net Operating surplus	-	-	...	-	-	-	-	...	-	-
Gross Input a	74160	34700	...	36240	3220	75280	35260	...	36680	3340

a) Local Government includes provincial government and other regional government entities.

3.12 General Government Income and Outlay Account: Total and Subsectors

Million Netherlands guilders

	1980 Total General Government	1980 Central Government	1980 State or Provincial Government	1980 Local Government	1980 Social Security Funds	1981 Total General Government	1981 Central Government	1981 State or Provincial Government	1981 Local Government	1981 Social Security Funds
				Receipts						
1 Operating surplus	...	...	...	...	...	...	...	...	...	...
2 Property and entrepreneurial income	20000	14120	...	4890	990	25290	18830	...	5440	1020
A Withdrawals from public quasi-corporations	2600	550	...	2050	-	2900	630	...	2270	-
B Interest	6690	3170	...	2530	990	7560	3720	...	2820	1020
C Dividends	10710	10400	...	310	-	14830	14480	...	350	-
D Net land rent and royalties			...					...		
3 Taxes, fees and contributions	153570	88730	...	3620	61220	159040	88660	...	4240	66140
A Indirect taxes	37450	35250	...	2200	-	37990	35480	...	2510	-
B Direct taxes	53500	52760	...	740	-	53280	52350	...	930	-
Income	50680	50680	...	-	-	50410	50410	...	-	-
Other	2820	2080	...	740	-	2870	1940	...	930	-
C Social security contributions	61220	-	...	-	61220	66140	-	...	-	66140
D Fees, fines and penalties	1400	720	...	680	-	1630	830	...	800	-
4 Other current transfers	4270	1990	...	46050	11500	4300	1950	...	49830	9880
A Casualty insurance claims	80	20	...	60	-	100	-	...	100	-
B Transfers from other government subsectors	...	-	...	43790	11480	...	-	...	47510	9850
C Transfers from the rest of the world	140	140	...	-	-	140	140	...	-	-
D Other transfers, except imputed	330	90	...	240	-	340	90	...	250	-
E Imputed unfunded employee pension and welfare contributions	3720	1740	...	1960	20	3720	1720	...	1970	30
Total Current Receipts a	177840	104840	...	54560	73710	188630	109440	...	59510	77040
				Disbursements						
1 Government final consumption expenditure	60260	27010	...	30850	2400	62750	28200	...	31900	2650
2 Property income b	15660	7090	...	8560	10	19340	9420	...	9840	80
A Interest	15660	7090	...	8560	10	19340	9420	...	9840	80
B Net land rent and royalties	...	...	...	...	...	...	...	...	...	...
3 Subsidies	4980	2940	...	2040	...	5520	3380	...	2140	...

Netherlands

3.12 General Government Income and Outlay Account: Total and Subsectors
(Continued)

Million Netherlands guilders

	1980					1981				
	Total General Government	Central Government	State or Provincial Government	Local Government	Social Security Funds	Total General Government	Central Government	State or Provincial Government	Local Government	Social Security Funds
4 Other current transfers	94260	65130	...	13460	70940	102730	68230	...	16140	75720
A Casualty insurance premiums, net	80	20	...	60	-	100	-	...	100	-
B Transfers to other government subsectors	...	55270	...	-	-	...	57360	...	-	-
C Social security benefits	70920	-	...	-	70920	75690	-	...	-	75690
D Social assistance grants	12700	2980	...	9720	-	15600	3380	...	12220	-
E Unfunded employee pension and welfare benefits	3720	1740	...	1960	20	3720	1720	...	1970	30
F Transfers to private non-profit institutions serving households	5140	3450	...	1690	-	5700	3900	...	1800	-
G Other transfers n.e.c.	220	190	...	30	-	260	210	...	50	-
H Transfers to the rest of the world	1480	1480	...	-	-	1660	1660	...	-	-
Net saving	2680	2670	...	-350	360	-1710	210	...	-510	-1410
Total Current Disbursements and Net Saving a	177840	104840	...	54560	73710	188630	109440	...	59510	77040

	1982					1983				
	Total General Government	Central Government	State or Provincial Government	Local Government	Social Security Funds	Total General Government	Central Government	State or Provincial Government	Local Government	Social Security Funds

Receipts

1 Operating surplus	...	...	...	...	...	...	...	...	...	...
2 Property and entrepreneurial income	26950	20330	...	5840	780	28170	21060	...	6430	680
A Withdrawals from public quasi-corporations	3300	850	...	2450	-	3400	700	...	2700	-
B Interest	7890	4250	...	2860	780	8810	4910	...	3220	680
C Dividends	15760	15230	...	530	-	15960	15450	...	510	-
D Net land rent and royalties			...					...		
3 Taxes, fees and contributions	167330	90080	...	4760	72490	178160	90000	...	4860	83300
A Indirect taxes	38710	35890	...	2820	-	41000	38230	...	2770	-
B Direct taxes	54290	53210	...	1080	-	51890	50760	...	1130	-
Income	51300	51300	...	-	-	48850	48850	...	-	-
Other	2990	1910	...	1080	-	3040	1910	...	1130	-
C Social security contributions	72490	-	...	-	72490	83300	-	...	-	83300
D Fees, fines and penalties	1840	980	...	860	-	1970	1010	...	960	-
4 Other current transfers	4320	2040	...	58170	7840	4220	1990	...	61680	3600
A Casualty insurance claims	80	-	...	80	-	70	-	...	70	-
B Transfers from other government subsectors	...	-	...	55920	7810	...	-	...	59480	3570
C Transfers from the rest of the world	190	190	...	-	-	160	160	...	-	-
D Other transfers, except imputed	320	100	...	220	-	320	100	...	220	-
E Imputed unfunded employee pension and welfare contributions	3730	1750	...	1950	30	3670	1730	...	1910	30
Total Current Receipts a	198600	112450	...	68770	81110	210550	113050	...	72970	87580

Disbursements

1 Government final consumption expenditure	65120	29310	...	32920	2890	66580	30660	...	32930	2990
2 Property income b	23180	12450	...	10620	110	26500	15230	...	11170	100
A Interest	23180	12450	...	10620	110	26500	15230	...	11170	100
B Net land rent and royalties	...	...	...	...	...	...	...	...	...	...
3 Subsidies	6220	3480	...	2740	...	6710	3800	...	2910	...

Netherlands

3.12 General Government Income and Outlay Account: Total and Subsectors
(Continued)

Million Netherlands guilders

	1982					1983				
	Total General Government	Central Government	State or Provincial Government	Local Government	Social Security Funds	Total General Government	Central Government	State or Provincial Government	Local Government	Social Security Funds
4 Other current transfers	112860	75670	...	20280	80640	118420	76120	...	23920	81430
A Casualty insurance premiums, net	80	-	...	80	-	70	-	...	70	-
B Transfers to other government subsectors	...	63730	...	-	-	...	63050	...	-	-
C Social security benefits	80610	-	...	-	80610	81400	-	...	-	81400
D Social assistance grants	20490	4200	...	16290	-	24730	4860	...	19870	-
E Unfunded employee pension and welfare benefits	3730	1750	...	1950	30	3670	1730	...	1910	30
F Transfers to private non-profit institutions serving households	5870	3950	...	1920	-	6460	4460	...	2000	-
G Other transfers n.e.c.	250	210	...	40	-	270	200	...	70	-
H Transfers to the rest of the world	1830	1830	...	-	-	1820	1820	...	-	-
Net saving	-8780	-8460	...	2210	-2530	-7660	-12760	...	2040	3060
Total Current Disbursements and Net Saving [a]	198600	112450	...	68770	81110	210550	113050	...	72970	87580

	1984					1985				
	Total General Government	Central Government	State or Provincial Government	Local Government	Social Security Funds	Total General Government	Central Government	State or Provincial Government	Local Government	Social Security Funds

Receipts

1 Operating surplus	...	...	...	...	...	...	...	...	...	...
2 Property and entrepreneurial income	32530	24750	...	6960	820	35790	27500	...	7440	850
A Withdrawals from public quasi-corporations	3400	610	...	2790	-	3900	980	...	2920	-
B Interest	10500	6050	...	3630	820	10780	6170	...	3760	850
C Dividends	18630	18090	...	540	-	21110	20350	...	760	-
D Net land rent and royalties			...					...		
3 Taxes, fees and contributions	179390	91510	...	5020	82860	186870	95340	...	5540	85990
A Indirect taxes	43400	40540	...	2860	-	45690	42500	...	3190	-
B Direct taxes	51030	49860	...	1170	-	52870	51620	...	1250	-
Income	47790	47790	...	-	-	49480	49480	...	-	-
Other	3240	2070	...	1170	-	3390	2140	...	1250	-
C Social security contributions	82860	-	...	-	82860	85990	-	...	-	85990
D Fees, fines and penalties	2100	1110	...	990	-	2320	1220	...	1100	-
4 Other current transfers	4440	2200	...	60790	2940	4530	2250	...	62470	2750
A Casualty insurance claims	80	-	...	80	-	90	-	...	90	-
B Transfers from other government subsectors	...	-	...	58580	2910	...	-	...	60220	2720
C Transfers from the rest of the world	270	270	...	-	-	360	360	...	-	-
D Other transfers, except imputed	400	180	...	220	-	290	70	...	220	-
E Imputed unfunded employee pension and welfare contributions	3690	1750	...	1910	30	3790	1820	...	1940	30
Total Current Receipts [a]	216360	118460	...	72770	86620	227190	125090	...	75450	89590

Disbursements

1 Government final consumption expenditure	66390	30720	...	32600	3070	67670	31260	...	33290	3120
2 Property income [b]	29860	17920	...	11830	110	32170	20020	...	12050	100
A Interest	29860	17920	...	11830	110	32170	20020	...	12050	100
B Net land rent and royalties	...	...	...	...	...	...	...	...	...	...
3 Subsidies	7410	3920	...	3490	...	7860	3600	...	4260	...

Netherlands

3.12 General Government Income and Outlay Account: Total and Subsectors
(Continued)

Million Netherlands guilders

		1984				1985				
		Total General Government	Central Government	State or Provincial Government	Local Government	Social Security Funds	Total General Government	Central Government	State or Provincial Government	Local Government	Social Security Funds
4	Other current transfers	119370	74800	...	24460	81600	121360	76690	...	24620	82990
	A Casualty insurance premiums, net	80	-	...	80	-	90	-	...	90	-
	B Transfers to other government subsectors	...	61490	...	-	-	...	62940	...	-	-
	C Social security benefits	81570	-	...	-	81570	82960	-	...	-	82960
	D Social assistance grants	24870	4450	...	20420	-	22510	4550	...	17960	-
	E Unfunded employee pension and welfare benefits	3690	1750	...	1910	30	3790	1820	...	1940	30
	F Transfers to private non-profit institutions serving households	6510	4510	...	2000	-	9060	4480	...	4580	-
	G Other transfers n.e.c.	250	200	...	50	-	240	190	...	50	-
	H Transfers to the rest of the world	2400	2400	...	-	-	2710	2710	...	-	-
Net saving		-6670	-8900	...	390	1840	-1870	-6480	...	1230	3380
Total Current Disbursements and Net Saving [a]		216360	118460	...	72770	86620	227190	125090	...	75450	89590

		1986					1987				
		Total General Government	Central Government	State or Provincial Government	Local Government	Social Security Funds	Total General Government	Central Government	State or Provincial Government	Local Government	Social Security Funds

Receipts

1	Operating surplus	...	...	...	...	...	...	...	...	...	...
2	Property and entrepreneurial income	29430	21400	...	7280	750	21100	13950	...	6340	810
	A Withdrawals from public quasi-corporations	3800	970	...	2830	-	2900	410	...	2490	-
	B Interest	10610	6170	...	3690	750	8720	4850	...	3060	810
	C Dividends	15020	14260	...	760	-	9480	8690	...	790	-
	D Net land rent and royalties								...		
3	Taxes, fees and contributions	193160	102580	...	5580	85000	204310	108900	...	6280	89130
	A Indirect taxes	48070	44990	...	3080	-	51470	48200	...	3270	-
	B Direct taxes	57620	56360	...	1260	-	60800	59470	...	1330	-
	Income	54130	54130	...	-	-	57110	57110	...	-	-
	Other	3490	2230	...	1260	-	3690	2360	...	1330	-
	C Social security contributions	85000	-	...	-	85000	89130	-	...	-	89130
	D Fees, fines and penalties	2470	1230	...	1240	-	2910	1230	...	1680	-
4	Other current transfers	4610	2210	...	62790	2160	4730	2210	...	59900	1970
	A Casualty insurance claims	100	-	...	100	-	110	-	...	110	-
	B Transfers from other government subsectors	...	-	...	60420	2130	...	-	...	57410	1940
	C Transfers from the rest of the world	340	340	...	-	-	310	310	...	-	-
	D Other transfers, except imputed	280	60	...	220	-	290	60	...	230	-
	E Imputed unfunded employee pension and welfare contributions	3890	1810	...	2050	30	4020	1840	...	2150	30
Total Current Receipts [a]		227200	126190	...	75650	87910	230140	125060	...	72520	91910

Disbursements

1	Government final consumption expenditure	68540	31890	...	33430	3220	69700	32640	...	33720	3340
2	Property income [b]	32630	20750	...	11790	90	31120	20870	...	10160	90
	A Interest	32630	20750	...	11790	90	31120	20870	...	10160	90
	B Net land rent and royalties	...	...	...	...	...	...	...	...	...	...
3	Subsidies	8130	3940	...	4190	...	9880	5350	...	4530	...

Netherlands

3.12 General Government Income and Outlay Account: Total and Subsectors
(Continued)

Million Netherlands guilders

	1986 Total General Government	1986 Central Government	1986 State or Provincial Government	1986 Local Government	1986 Social Security Funds	1987 Total General Government	1987 Central Government	1987 State or Provincial Government	1987 Local Government	1987 Social Security Funds
4 Other current transfers	123740	77380	...	24270	84640	126310	76690	...	21980	86990
A Casualty insurance premiums, net	100	-	...	100	-	110	-	...	110	-
B Transfers to other government subsectors	...	62550	...	-	-	...	59350	...	-	-
C Social security benefits	84610	-	...	-	84610	86960	-	...	-	86960
D Social assistance grants	22690	5310	...	17380	-	22880	7670	...	15210	-
E Unfunded employee pension and welfare benefits	3890	1810	...	2050	30	4020	1840	...	2150	30
F Transfers to private non-profit institutions serving households	9300	4590	...	4710	-	9350	4870	...	4480	-
G Other transfers n.e.c.	230	200	...	30	-	240	210	...	30	-
H Transfers to the rest of the world	2920	2920	...	-	-	2750	2750	...	-	-
Net saving	-5840	-7770	...	1970	-40	-6870	-10490	...	2130	1490
Total Current Disbursements and Net Saving [a]	227200	126190	...	75650	87910	230140	125060	...	72520	91910

a) Local Government includes provincial government and other regional government entities.
b) Item 'Property income' includes payments and receipts of property income from other subsectors of general government.

3.13 General Government Capital Accumulation Account: Total and Subsectors

Million Netherlands guilders

	1980 Total General Government	1980 Central Government	1980 State or Provincial Government	1980 Local Government	1980 Social Security Funds	1981 Total General Government	1981 Central Government	1981 State or Provincial Government	1981 Local Government	1981 Social Security Funds
			Finance of Gross Accumulation							
1 Gross saving	5080	3330	...	1390	360	850	920	...	1340	-1410
A Consumption of fixed capital	2400	660	...	1740	-	2560	710	...	1850	-
B Net saving	2680	2670	...	-350	360	-1710	210	...	-510	-1410
2 Capital transfers	1200	1070	...	2160	200	1360	1350	...	2750	200
A From other government subsectors	...	30	...	2000	200	...	150	...	2590	200
B From other resident sectors	1100	940	...	160	-	1260	1100	...	160	-
C From rest of the world	100	100	...	-	-	100	100	...	-	-
Finance of Gross Accumulation [a]	6280	4400	...	3550	560	2210	2270	...	4090	-1210
			Gross Accumulation							
1 Gross capital formation	10970	3160	...	7810	-	11100	3300	...	7800	-
A Increase in stocks	-	-	...	-	-	-	-	...	-	-
B Gross fixed capital formation	10970	3160	...	7810	-	11100	3300	...	7800	-
Own account	580	-	...	580	-	580	-	...	580	-
Other	10390	3160	...	7230	-	10520	3300	...	7220	-
2 Purchases of land, net	...	...	...	...	...	...	...	...	...	...
3 Purchases of intangible assets, net	...	...	...	...	...	...	...	...	...	...
4 Capital transfers	8860	10190	...	810	90	10430	12120	...	1170	80
A To other government subsectors	...	2200	...	30	-	...	2790	...	150	-
B To other resident sectors	8250	7380	...	780	90	9670	8570	...	1020	80
C To rest of the world	610	610	...	-	-	760	760	...	-	-
Net lending [b]	-13550	-8950	...	-5070	470	-19320	-13150	...	-4880	-1290
Gross Accumulation [a]	6280	4400	...	3550	560	2210	2270	...	4090	-1210

	1982 Total General Government	1982 Central Government	1982 State or Provincial Government	1982 Local Government	1982 Social Security Funds	1983 Total General Government	1983 Central Government	1983 State or Provincial Government	1983 Local Government	1983 Social Security Funds
			Finance of Gross Accumulation							
1 Gross saving	-6360	-7830	...	4000	-2530	-5360	-12090	...	3670	3060
A Consumption of fixed capital	2420	630	...	1790	-	2300	670	...	1630	-
B Net saving	-8780	-8460	...	2210	-2530	-7660	-12760	...	2040	3060
2 Capital transfers	1510	1320	...	3170	200	1690	1510	...	3400	200

Netherlands

3.13 General Government Capital Accumulation Account: Total and Subsectors
(Continued)

Million Netherlands guilders

	1982					1983				
	Total General Government	Central Government	State or Provincial Government	Local Government	Social Security Funds	Total General Government	Central Government	State or Provincial Government	Local Government	Social Security Funds
A From other government subsectors	...	90	...	2890	200	...	90	...	3130	200
B From other resident sectors	1430	1150	...	280	-	1550	1280	...	270	-
C From rest of the world	80	80	...	-	-	140	140	...	-	-
Finance of Gross Accumulation a	-4850	-6510	...	7170	-2330	-3670	-10580	...	7070	3260
Gross Accumulation									
1 Gross capital formation	10620	2870	...	7750	-	10190	2880	...	7310	-
A Increase in stocks	-	-	...	-	-	-	-	...	-	-
B Gross fixed capital formation	10620	2870	...	7750	-	10190	2880	...	7310	-
Own account	570	-	...	570	-	560	-	...	560	-
Other	10050	2870	...	7180	-	9630	2880	...	6750	-
2 Purchases of land, net	...	...	...	...	...	...	...	...	...	...
3 Purchases of intangible assets, net	...	...	...	...	...	...	...	...	...	...
4 Capital transfers	10640	12630	...	1120	70	10370	12310	...	1410	70
A To other government subsectors	...	3090	...	90	-	...	3330	...	90	-
B To other resident sectors	9830	8730	...	1030	70	9750	8360	...	1320	70
C To rest of the world	810	810	...	-	-	620	620	...	-	-
Net lending b	-26110	-22010	...	-1700	-2400	-24230	-25770	...	-1650	3190
Gross Accumulation a	-4850	-6510	...	7170	-2330	-3670	-10580	...	7070	3260

	1984					1985				
	Total General Government	Central Government	State or Provincial Government	Local Government	Social Security Funds	Total General Government	Central Government	State or Provincial Government	Local Government	Social Security Funds
Finance of Gross Accumulation									
1 Gross saving	-4050	-8100	...	2210	1840	880	-5620	...	3120	3380
A Consumption of fixed capital	2620	800	...	1820	-	2750	860	...	1890	-
B Net saving	-6670	-8900	...	390	1840	-1870	-6480	...	1230	3380
2 Capital transfers	2080	1610	...	3910	200	2060	1790	...	4090	180
A From other government subsectors	...	10	...	3430	200	...	20	...	3800	180
B From other resident sectors	1960	1480	...	480	-	1910	1620	...	290	-
C From rest of the world	120	120	...	-	-	150	150	...	-	-
Finance of Gross Accumulation a	-1970	-6490	...	6120	2040	2940	-3830	...	7210	3560
Gross Accumulation									
1 Gross capital formation	11190	3190	...	8000	-	10940	3150	...	7790	-
A Increase in stocks	-	-	...	-	-	-	-	...	-	-
B Gross fixed capital formation	11190	3190	...	8000	-	10940	3150	...	7790	-
Own account	640	-	...	640	-	590	-	...	590	-
Other	10550	3190	...	7360	-	10350	3150	...	7200	-
2 Purchases of land, net	...	...	...	...	...	...	...	...	...	...
3 Purchases of intangible assets, net	...	...	...	...	...	...	...	...	...	...
4 Capital transfers	11870	13790	...	1640	80	11880	14040	...	1750	90
A To other government subsectors	...	3630	...	10	-	...	3980	...	20	-
B To other resident sectors	11380	9670	...	1630	80	11370	9550	...	1730	90
C To rest of the world	490	490	...	-	-	510	510	...	-	-
Net lending b	-25030	-23470	...	-3520	1960	-19880	-21020	...	-2330	3470
Gross Accumulation a	-1970	-6490	...	6120	2040	2940	-3830	...	7210	3560

	1986					1987				
	Total General Government	Central Government	State or Provincial Government	Local Government	Social Security Funds	Total General Government	Central Government	State or Provincial Government	Local Government	Social Security Funds
Finance of Gross Accumulation									
1 Gross saving	-3040	-6840	...	3840	-40	-3920	-9470	...	4060	1490
A Consumption of fixed capital	2800	930	...	1870	-	2950	1020	...	1930	-
B Net saving	-5840	-7770	...	1970	-40	-6870	-10490	...	2130	1490
2 Capital transfers	2250	2000	...	3590	180	2860	2560	...	3620	170

1008

Netherlands

3.13 General Government Capital Accumulation Account: Total and Subsectors
(Continued)

Million Netherlands guilders

	1986 Total General Government	1986 Central Government	1986 State or Provincial Government	1986 Local Government	1986 Social Security Funds	1987 Total General Government	1987 Central Government	1987 State or Provincial Government	1987 Local Government	1987 Social Security Funds
A From other government subsectors	...	10	...	3330	180	...	10	...	3310	170
B From other resident sectors	2150	1890	...	260	-	2720	2410	...	310	-
C From rest of the world	100	100	...	-	-	140	140	...	-	-
Finance of Gross Accumulation [a]	-790	-4840	...	7430	140	-1060	-6910	...	7680	1660

Gross Accumulation

1 Gross capital formation	10180	3130	...	7050	-	9960	3120	...	6840	-
A Increase in stocks	-	-	...	-	-	-	-	...	-	-
B Gross fixed capital formation	10180	3130	...	7050	-	9960	3120	...	6840	-
Own account	520	-	...	520	-	480	-	...	480	-
Other	9660	3130	...	6530	-	9480	3120	...	6360	-
2 Purchases of land, net	...	...	...	...	...	...	...	...	...	...
3 Purchases of intangible assets, net	...	...	...	...	...	...	...	...	...	...
4 Capital transfers	14210	16070	...	1570	90	15610	17540	...	1460	100
A To other government subsectors	...	3510	...	10	-	...	3480	...	10	-
B To other resident sectors	13570	11920	...	1560	90	14980	13430	...	1450	100
C To rest of the world	640	640	...	-	-	630	630	...	-	-
Net lending [b]	-25180	-24040	...	-1190	50	-26630	-27570	...	-620	1560
Gross Accumulation [a]	-790	-4840	...	7430	140	-1060	-6910	...	7680	1660

a) Local Government includes provincial government and other regional government entities.
b) Net lending of the capital accumulation account and the capital finance account have not been reconciled and are different due to different statistical sources.

3.14 General Government Capital Finance Account, Total and Subsectors

Million Netherlands guilders

	1980 Total General Government	1980 Central Government	1980 State or Provincial Government	1980 Local Government	1980 Social Security Funds	1981 Total General Government	1981 Central Government	1981 State or Provincial Government	1981 Local Government	1981 Social Security Funds

Acquisition of Financial Assets

1 Gold and SDRs	...	...	...	...	...	...	...	...	...	...
2 Currency and transferable deposits	1624	1581	...	39	4	-650	-548	...	-130	28
3 Other deposits	-1116	-	...	-909	-207	-974	-	...	329	-1303
4 Bills and bonds, short term [a]	26	-	...	4	22	18	-	...	-4	22
5 Bonds, long term	-56	-	...	-	-56	-73	-	...	-	-73
6 Corporate equity securities	-	-	...	-	-	-	-	...	-	-
7 Short-term loans, n.e.c. [a]	-270	-368	...	-65	163	-179	-	...	-39	-140
8 Long-term loans, n.e.c.	11834	5637	...	6010	187	13920	7420	...	6470	30
9 Other receivables	...	...	...	...	...	...	...	...	...	...
10 Other assets	...	...	...	...	...	...	...	...	...	...
Total Acquisition of Financial Assets [b]	12042	6850	...	5079	113	12062	6872	...	6626	-1436

Incurrence of Liabilities

1 Currency and transferable deposits	207	207	...	-	-	146	146	...	-	-
2 Other deposits	-89	-89	...	-	-	-1073	-1073	...	-	-
3 Bills and bonds, short term [a]	3319	3319	...	-	-	2215	2215	...	-	-
4 Bonds, long term	5355	5976	...	-621	-	8790	9381	...	-591	-
5 Short-term loans, n.e.c. [a]	3190	53	...	3021	222	-223	-100	...	-710	587
6 Long-term loans, n.e.c.	14851	7450	...	7221	180	22039	9718	...	12225	96
7 Other payables	...	...	...	...	...	...	...	...	...	...
8 Other liabilities	...	...	...	...	...	...	...	...	...	...
Total Incurrence of Liabilities	26833	16810	...	9621	402	31894	20287	...	10924	683
Statistical discrepancy	-1241	-1010	...	528	-759	-512	-265	...	582	-829
Net Lending [c]	-13550	-8950	...	-5070	470	-19320	-13150	...	-4880	-1290
Incurrence of Liabilities and Net Worth [b]	12042	6850	...	5079	113	12062	6872	...	6626	-1436

Netherlands

3.14 General Government Capital Finance Account, Total and Subsectors

Million Netherlands guilders

	1982					1983				
	Total General Government	Central Government	State or Provincial Government	Local Government	Social Security Funds	Total General Government	Central Government	State or Provincial Government	Local Government	Social Security Funds
Acquisition of Financial Assets										
1 Gold and SDRs	...	...	...	...	...	...	...	...	...	...
2 Currency and transferable deposits	378	320	...	64	-6	-1	-190	...	159	30
3 Other deposits	-402	-	...	-72	-330	1509	-	...	566	943
4 Bills and bonds, short term a	-142	-	...	3	-145	-44	-	...	6	-50
5 Bonds, long term	-8	-	...	-	-8	-	-	...	-	-
6 Corporate equity securities	-	...	...	...	...	...	...	...	...	...
7 Short-term loans, n.e.c. a	251	-	...	306	-55	-400	-	...	338	-738
8 Long-term loans, n.e.c.	11490	6200	...	5550	-260	10172	5247	...	4990	-65
9 Other receivables	...	...	...	...	...	...	...	...	...	...
10 Other assets	...	...	...	...	...	...	...	...	...	...
Total Acquisition of Financial Assets b	11567	6520	...	5851	-804	11236	5057	...	6059	120
Incurrence of Liabilities										
1 Currency and transferable deposits	53	53	...	-	-	45	45	...	-	-
2 Other deposits	-9	-9	...	-	-	-379	-379	...	-	-
3 Bills and bonds, short term a	1239	1239	...	-	-	-255	-255	...	-	-
4 Bonds, long term	16177	16645	...	-468	-	20604	21264	...	-660	-
5 Short-term loans, n.e.c. a	-2506	310	...	-3375	559	-1932	-123	...	-401	-1408
6 Long-term loans, n.e.c.	19912	9436	...	10858	-382	17686	9672	...	7901	113
7 Other payables	...	...	...	...	...	...	...	...	...	...
8 Other liabilities	...	...	...	...	...	...	...	...	...	...
Total Incurrence of Liabilities	34866	27674	...	7015	177	35769	30224	...	6840	-1295
Statistical discrepancy	2811	856	...	536	1419	107	833	...	959	-1685
Net Lending c	-26110	-22010	...	-1700	-2400	-24640	-26000	...	-1740	3100
Incurrence of Liabilities and Net Worth b	11567	6520	...	5851	-804	11236	5057	...	6059	120

a) Bills are included in item 'Short-term loans, n.e.c.'.
b) Local Government includes provincial government and other regional government entities.
c) Net lending of the capital accumulation account and the capital finance account have not been reconciled and are different due to different statistical sources.

3.21 Corporate and Quasi-Corporate Enterprise Production Account: Total and Sectors

Million Netherlands guilders

	1980				1981				1982			
	Corporate and Quasi-Corporate Enterprises			ADDENDUM: Total, including Unincorporated	Corporate and Quasi-Corporate Enterprises			ADDENDUM: Total, including Unincorporated	Corporate and Quasi-Corporate Enterprises			ADDENDUM: Total, including Unincorporated
	TOTAL	Non-Financial	Financial		TOTAL	Non-Financial	Financial		TOTAL	Non-Financial	Financial	
Gross Output												
1 Output for sale	573070	561520	11550	573070	610000	598300	11700	610000	629030	617200	11830	629030
2 Imputed bank service charge	11460	...	11460	11460	12660	...	12660	12660	14080	...	14080	14080
3 Own-account fixed capital formation	1720	1720	...	1720	1970	1970	...	1970	2020	2020	...	2020
Gross Output a	586250	563240	23010	586250	624630	600270	24360	624630	645130	619220	25910	645130
Gross Input												
Intermediate consumption	296350	277760	18590	296350	319720	299570	20150	319720	325790	303870	21920	325790
1 Imputed banking service charge	11460	...	11460	11460	12660	...	12660	12660	14080	...	14080	14080
2 Other intermediate consumption	284890	277760	7130	284890	307060	299570	7490	307060	311710	303870	7840	311710
Subtotal: Value Added	289900	285480	4420	289900	304910	300700	4210	304910	319340	315350	3990	319340
1 Indirect taxes, net	31660	31020	640	31660	32540	31860	680	32540	32320	31650	670	32320
A Indirect taxes	40760	40110	650	40760	41360	40680	680	41360	42380	41700	680	42380
B Less: Subsidies	9100	9090	10	9100	8820	8820	-	8820	10060	10050	10	10060
2 Consumption of fixed capital	30090	29830	260	30090	33060	32770	290	33060	35440	35130	310	35440
3 Compensation of employees	153760	145030	8730	153760	156510	147230	9280	156510	160760	150870	9890	160760
A To residents	152850	144120	8730	152850	155500	146220	9280	155500	159620	149730	9890	159620
B To the rest of the world	910	910	...	910	1010	1010	...	1010	1140	1140	...	1140
4 Net operating surplus	74390	79600	-5210	74390	82800	88840	-6040	82800	90820	97700	-6880	90820
Gross Input a	586250	563240	23010	586250	624630	600270	24360	624630	645130	619220	25910	645130

Netherlands

3.21 Corporate and Quasi-Corporate Enterprise Production Account: Total and Sectors

Million Netherlands guilders

	1983				1984				1985			
	\multicolumn{3}{c}{Corporate and Quasi-Corporate Enterprises}	ADDENDUM: Total, including Unincorporated	\multicolumn{3}{c}{Corporate and Quasi-Corporate Enterprises}	ADDENDUM: Total, including Unincorporated	\multicolumn{3}{c}{Corporate and Quasi-Corporate Enterprises}	ADDENDUM: Total, including Unincorporated
	TOTAL	Non-Financial	Financial		TOTAL	Non-Financial	Financial		TOTAL	Non-Financial	Financial	

Gross Output

1 Output for sale	649480	637190	12290	649480	700680	687660	13020	700680	731510	717600	13910	731510
2 Imputed bank service charge	16150	...	16150	16150	16420	...	16420	16420	16730	...	16730	16730
3 Own-account fixed capital formation	2070	2070	...	2070	2370	2370	...	2370	2300	2300	...	2300
Gross Output a	667700	639260	28440	667700	719470	690030	29440	719470	750540	719900	30640	750540

Gross Input

Intermediate consumption	336330	312030	24300	336330	368670	343720	24950	368670	382450	356500	25950	382450
1 Imputed banking service charge	16150	...	16150	16150	16420	...	16420	16420	16730	...	16730	16730
2 Other intermediate consumption	320180	312030	8150	320180	352250	343720	8530	352250	365720	356500	9220	365720
Subtotal: Value Added	331370	327230	4140	331370	350800	346310	4490	350800	368090	363400	4690	368090
1 Indirect taxes, net	33520	32770	750	33520	34960	34140	820	34960	36760	35890	870	36760
A Indirect taxes	44740	43980	760	44740	47570	46740	830	47570	50270	49390	880	50270
B Less: Subsidies	11220	11210	10	11220	12610	12600	10	12610	13510	13500	10	13510
2 Consumption of fixed capital	36890	36560	330	36890	38570	38220	350	38570	40120	39760	360	40120
3 Compensation of employees	162690	152510	10180	162690	163590	153280	10310	163590	169860	159130	10730	169860
A To residents	161570	151390	10180	161570	162470	152160	10310	162470	168640	157910	10730	168640
B To the rest of the world	1120	1120	...	1120	1120	1120	...	1120	1220	1220	...	1220
4 Net operating surplus	98270	105390	-7120	98270	113680	120670	-6990	113680	121350	128620	-7270	121350
Gross Input a	667700	639260	28440	667700	719470	690030	29440	719470	750540	719900	30640	750540

	1986				1987			
	\multicolumn{3}{c}{Corporate and Quasi-Corporate Enterprises}	ADDENDUM: Total, including Unincorporated	\multicolumn{3}{c}{Corporate and Quasi-Corporate Enterprises}	ADDENDUM: Total, including Unincorporated
	TOTAL	Non-Financial	Financial		TOTAL	Non-Financial	Financial	

Gross Output

1 Output for sale	705710	690750	14960	705710	700620	684550	16070	700620
2 Imputed bank service charge	16760	...	16760	16760	16550	...	16550	16550
3 Own-account fixed capital formation	2360	2360	...	2360	2400	2400	...	2400
Gross Output a	724830	693110	31720	724830	719570	686950	32620	719570

Gross Input

Intermediate consumption	345710	319020	26690	345710	339320	312250	27070	339320
1 Imputed banking service charge	16760	...	16760	16760	16550	...	16550	16550
2 Other intermediate consumption	328950	319020	9930	328950	322770	312250	10520	322770
Subtotal: Value Added	379120	374090	5030	379120	380250	374700	5550	380250
1 Indirect taxes, net	39340	38380	960	39340	40300	39310	990	40300
A Indirect taxes	53250	52280	970	53250	56940	55940	1000	56940
B Less: Subsidies	13910	13900	10	13910	16640	16630	10	16640
2 Consumption of fixed capital	40650	40270	380	40650	41820	41420	400	41820
3 Compensation of employees	178210	166980	11230	178210	183340	171730	11610	183340
A To residents	177000	165770	11230	177000	182270	170660	11610	182270
B To the rest of the world	1210	1210	...	1210	1070	1070	...	1070
4 Net operating surplus	120920	128460	-7540	120920	114790	122240	-7450	114790
Gross Input a	724830	693110	31720	724830	719570	686950	32620	719570

a) Corporate and quasi-corporate enterprise include unincorporated enterprise and private non-profit institutions serving households.

3.22 Corporate and Quasi-Corporate Enterprise Income and Outlay Account: Total and Sectors

Million Netherlands guilders

	1980			1981			1982			1983		
	TOTAL	Non-Financial	Financial	TOTAL	Non-Financial	Financial	TOTAL	Non-Financial	Financial	TOTAL	Non-Financial	Financial

Receipts

1 Operating surplus	74390	79600	-5210	82800	88840	-6040	90820	97700	-6880	98270	105390	-7120
2 Property and entrepreneurial income a	73520	10370	63140	89240	11620	77620	93600	10860	82740	91000	10100	80900
A Withdrawals from quasi-corporate enterprises	1080	...	1080	1140	...	1140	1200	...	1200	1370	...	1370
B Interest	66530	5700	60830	81310	6200	75110	85260	5500	79760	81860	4600	77260
C Dividends	5910	4670	1230	6790	5420	1370	7140	5360	1780	7770	5500	2270
D Net land rent and royalties												

1011

Netherlands

3.22 Corporate and Quasi-Corporate Enterprise Income and Outlay Account: Total and Sectors
(Continued)

Million Netherlands guilders

	1980 TOTAL	1980 Non-Financial	1980 Financial	1981 TOTAL	1981 Non-Financial	1981 Financial	1982 TOTAL	1982 Non-Financial	1982 Financial	1983 TOTAL	1983 Non-Financial	1983 Financial
3 Current transfers	11540	3250	8290	12840	3560	9280	12710	3480	9230	13210	3570	9640
A Casualty insurance claims	2550	2330	220	3150	2680	470	2910	2640	270	3110	2750	360
B Casualty insurance premiums, net, due to be received by insurance companies	7830	-	7830	8570	-	8570	8720	-	8720	9040	-	9040
C Current transfers from the rest of the world	-	-	-	-	-	-	-	-	-	-	-	-
D Other transfers except imputed	150	-	150	150	-	150	150	-	150	150	-	150
E Imputed unfunded employee pension and welfare contributions	1010	920	90	970	880	90	930	840	90	910	820	90
Total Current Receipts [b]	159450	93220	66220	184880	104020	80860	197130	112040	85090	202480	119060	83420

Disbursements

	1980 TOTAL	1980 Non-Financial	1980 Financial	1981 TOTAL	1981 Non-Financial	1981 Financial	1982 TOTAL	1982 Non-Financial	1982 Financial	1983 TOTAL	1983 Non-Financial	1983 Financial
1 Property and entrepreneurial income [a]	132540	80180	52360	154080	88520	65560	165560	96170	69390	165370	99570	65800
A Withdrawals from quasi-corporations	3680	3610	70	4040	4030	10	4500	4490	10	4770	4770	-
B Interest	67880	34500	33380	82380	38700	43680	83690	39600	44090	75690	38500	37190
C Dividends	60980	42070	18910	67660	45790	21870	77370	52080	25290	84910	56300	28610
D Net land rent and royalties												
2 Direct taxes and other current transfers n.e.c. to general government	10170	8760	1410	11100	9680	1420	11340	10100	1240	10850	9730	1120
A Direct taxes	10170	8760	1410	11100	9680	1420	11340	10100	1240	10850	9730	1120
On income	10170	8760	1410	11100	9680	1420	11340	10100	1240	10850	9730	1120
Other	-	-	-	-	-	-	-	-	-	-	-	-
B Fines, fees, penalties and other current transfers n.e.c.	-	-	-	-	-	-	-	-	-	-	-	-
3 Other current transfers	11540	3250	8290	12840	3560	9280	12710	3480	9230	13210	3570	9640
A Casualty insurance premiums, net	2550	2330	220	3150	2680	470	2910	2640	270	3110	2750	360
B Casualty insurance claims liability of insurance companies	7830	-	7830	8570	-	8570	8720	-	8720	9040	-	9040
C Transfers to private non-profit institutions	-	-	-	-	-	-	-	-	-	-	-	-
D Unfunded employee pension and welfare benefits	1010	920	90	970	880	90	930	840	90	910	820	90
E Social assistance grants	150	-	150	150	-	150	150	-	150	150	-	150
F Other transfers n.e.c.	...	...	...	...	...	...	...	...	...	...	...	...
G Transfers to the rest of the world	-	-	-	-	-	-	-	-	-	-	-	-
Net saving	5200	1030	4160	6860	2260	4600	7520	2290	5230	13050	6190	6860
Total Current Disbursements and Net Saving [b]	159450	93220	66220	184880	104020	80860	197130	112040	85090	202480	119060	83420

	1984 TOTAL	1984 Non-Financial	1984 Financial	1985 TOTAL	1985 Non-Financial	1985 Financial	1986 TOTAL	1986 Non-Financial	1986 Financial	1987 TOTAL	1987 Non-Financial	1987 Financial

Receipts

	1984 TOTAL	1984 Non-Financial	1984 Financial	1985 TOTAL	1985 Non-Financial	1985 Financial	1986 TOTAL	1986 Non-Financial	1986 Financial	1987 TOTAL	1987 Non-Financial	1987 Financial
1 Operating surplus	113680	120670	-6990	121350	128620	-7270	120920	128460	-7540	114790	122240	-7450
2 Property and entrepreneurial income [a]	97200	10370	86830	102070	12950	89120	99580	11190	88390	102180	11580	90600
A Withdrawals from quasi-corporate enterprises	1470	...	1470	1570	...	1570	1710	...	1710	1840	...	1840
B Interest	87910	5300	82610	90430	6100	84330	89220	6300	82920	91320	6700	84620
C Dividends	7820	5070	2750	10070	6850	3220	8650	4890	3760	9020	4880	4140
D Net land rent and royalties												

Netherlands

3.22 Corporate and Quasi-Corporate Enterprise Income and Outlay Account: Total and Sectors
(Continued)

Million Netherlands guilders

		1984 TOTAL	1984 Non-Financial	1984 Financial	1985 TOTAL	1985 Non-Financial	1985 Financial	1986 TOTAL	1986 Non-Financial	1986 Financial	1987 TOTAL	1987 Non-Financial	1987 Financial
3	Current transfers	13600	3700	9900	14210	3700	10510	15300	3790	11510	16830	4000	12830
	A Casualty insurance claims	3060	2880	180	3090	2890	200	3260	3040	220	3650	3300	350
	B Casualty insurance premiums, net, due to be received by insurance companies	9480	-	9480	10070	-	10070	11090	-	11090	12250	-	12250
	C Current transfers from the rest of the world	-	-	-	-	-	-	-	-	-	-	-	-
	D Other transfers except imputed	140	-	140	130	-	130	130	-	130	140	-	140
	E Imputed unfunded employee pension and welfare contributions	920	820	100	920	810	110	820	750	70	790	700	90
Total Current Receipts [b]		224480	134740	89740	237630	145270	92360	235800	143440	92360	233800	137820	95980

Disbursements

		TOTAL	Non-Financial	Financial	TOTAL	Non-Financial	Financial	TOTAL	Non-Financial	Financial	TOTAL	Non-Financial	Financial
1	Property and entrepreneurial income [a]	179920	108040	71880	189810	115260	74550	187060	113330	73730	183780	107980	75800
	A Withdrawals from quasi-corporations	4870	4700	170	5470	4920	550	5510	5040	470	4740	4730	10
	B Interest	79960	39700	40260	80210	40500	39710	77620	40400	37220	78100	39800	38300
	C Dividends	95090	63640	31450	104130	69840	34290	103930	67890	36040	100940	63450	37490
	D Net land rent and royalties												
2	Direct taxes and other current transfers n.e.c. to general government	10300	8900	1400	13060	11910	1150	14370	13120	1250	16030	14740	1290
	A Direct taxes	10300	8900	1400	13060	11910	1150	14370	13120	1250	16030	14740	1290
	On income	10300	8900	1400	13060	11910	1150	14370	13120	1250	16030	14740	1290
	Other	-	-	-	-	-	-	-	-	-	-	-	-
	B Fines, fees, penalties and other current transfers n.e.c.												
3	Other current transfers	13600	3700	9900	14210	3700	10510	15300	3790	11510	16830	4000	12830
	A Casualty insurance premiums, net	3060	2880	180	3090	2890	200	3260	3040	220	3650	3300	350
	B Casualty insurance claims liability of insurance companies	9480	-	9480	10070	-	10070	11090	-	11090	12250	-	12250
	C Transfers to private non-profit institutions												
	D Unfunded employee pension and welfare benefits	920	820	100	920	810	110	820	750	70	790	700	90
	E Social assistance grants	140	-	140	130	-	130	130	-	130	140	-	140
	F Other transfers n.e.c.	...	...	...	...	...	...	...	...	...	...	...	...
	G Transfers to the rest of the world	-	-	-	-	-	-	-	-	-	-	-	-
Net saving		20660	14100	6560	20550	14400	6150	19070	13200	5870	17160	11100	6060
Total Current Disbursements and Net Saving [b]		224480	134740	89740	237630	145270	92360	235800	143440	92360	233800	137820	95980

a) For the period 1970-1976, property and entrepreneurial income paid by non-financial corporate and quasi-corporate enterprises is net of property income received.
b) Private unincorporated enterprises are included in non-financial corporate and quasi-corporate enterprises. Private non-profit institutions serving households are included partly in households, partly in private unincorporated enterprises.

3.23 Corporate and Quasi-Corporate Enterprise Capital Accumulation Account: Total and Sectors

Million Netherlands guilders

		1980 TOTAL	1980 Non-Financial	1980 Financial	1981 TOTAL	1981 Non-Financial	1981 Financial	1982 TOTAL	1982 Non-Financial	1982 Financial	1983 TOTAL	1983 Non-Financial	1983 Financial

Finance of Gross Accumulation

1	Gross saving	35290	30860	4430	39920	35030	4890	42960	37420	5540	49940	42750	7190
	A Consumption of fixed capital	30090	29830	260	33060	32770	290	35440	35130	310	36890	36560	330
	B Net saving	5200	1030	4170	6860	2260	4600	7520	2290	5230	13050	6190	6860
2	Capital transfers	7690	7300	390	9090	8710	380	9220	8710	510	9110	8570	540
	A From resident sectors	7690	7300	390	9090	8710	380	9220	8710	510	9110	8570	540
	B From the rest of the world	-	-	-	-	-	-	-	-	-	-	-	-
Finance of Gross Accumulation [a]		42980	38160	4820	49010	43740	5270	52180	46130	6050	59050	51320	7730

Gross Accumulation

1	Gross capital formation	61540	61230	310	53390	53050	340	55520	55150	370	59830	59430	400
	A Increase in stocks	1720	1720	-	-3090	-3090	-	-1020	-1020	-	560	560	-
	B Gross fixed capital formation	59820	59510	310	56480	56140	340	56540	56170	370	59270	58870	400

1013

Netherlands

3.23 Corporate and Quasi-Corporate Enterprise Capital Accumulation Account: Total and Sectors
(Continued)

Million Netherlands guilders

	1980 TOTAL	1980 Non-Financial	1980 Financial	1981 TOTAL	1981 Non-Financial	1981 Financial	1982 TOTAL	1982 Non-Financial	1982 Financial	1983 TOTAL	1983 Non-Financial	1983 Financial
Own account	1720	1720	-	1970	1970	-	2020	2020	-	2070	2070	-
Other	58100	57790	310	54510	54170	340	54520	54150	370	57200	56800	400
2 Purchases of land, net	...	...	...	...	...	...	...	...	...	...	...	...
3 Purchases of intangible assets, net	...	...	...	...	...	...	...	...	...	...	...	...
4 Capital transfers [b]	640	360	280	740	480	260	1110	720	390	1290	870	420
A To resident sectors	640	360	280	740	480	260	1110	720	390	1290	870	420
B To the rest of the world	-	-	-	-	-	-	-	-	-	-	-	-
Net lending [c]	-19200	-23430	4230	-5120	-9790	4670	-4450	-9740	5290	-2070	-8980	6910
Gross Accumulation [a]	42980	38160	4820	49010	43740	5270	52180	46130	6050	59050	51320	7730

	1984 TOTAL	1984 Non-Financial	1984 Financial	1985 TOTAL	1985 Non-Financial	1985 Financial	1986 TOTAL	1986 Non-Financial	1986 Financial	1987 TOTAL	1987 Non-Financial	1987 Financial
Finance of Gross Accumulation
1 Gross saving	59230	52320	6910	60670	54160	6510	59720	53470	6250	58980	52520	6460
A Consumption of fixed capital	38570	38220	350	40120	39760	360	40650	40270	380	41820	41420	400
B Net saving	20660	14100	6560	20550	14400	6150	19070	13200	5870	17160	11100	6060
2 Capital transfers	10690	9820	870	10650	9890	760	12860	12240	620	14260	13640	620
A From resident sectors	10690	9820	870	10650	9890	760	12860	12240	620	14260	13640	620
B From the rest of the world	-	-	-	-	-	-	-	-	-	-	-	-
Finance of Gross Accumulation [a]	69920	62140	7780	71320	64050	7270	72580	65710	6870	73240	66160	7080
Gross Accumulation
1 Gross capital formation	65110	64670	440	71810	71340	470	76900	76380	520	77170	76610	560
A Increase in stocks	1990	1990	-	2500	2500	-	700	700	-	-390	-390	-
B Gross fixed capital formation	63120	62680	440	69310	68840	470	76200	75680	520	77560	77000	560
Own account	2370	2370	-	2300	2300	-	2360	2360	-	2400	2400	-
Other	60750	60310	440	67010	66540	470	73840	73320	520	75160	74600	560
2 Purchases of land, net	...	...	...	...	...	...	...	...	...	...	...	...
3 Purchases of intangible assets, net	...	...	...	...	...	...	...	...	...	...	...	...
4 Capital transfers [b]	1890	1150	740	1710	1090	620	1620	1170	450	2020	1580	440
A To resident sectors	1890	1150	740	1710	1090	620	1620	1170	450	2020	1580	440
B To the rest of the world	-	-	-	-	-	-	-	-	-	-	-	-
Net lending [c]	2920	-3680	6600	-2200	-8380	6180	-5940	-11840	5900	-5950	-12030	6080
Gross Accumulation [a]	69920	62140	7780	71320	64050	7270	72580	65710	6870	73240	66160	7080

a) Private unincorporated enterprises are included in non-financial corporate and quasi-corporate enterprises. Private non-profit institutions serving households are included partly in households, partly in private unincorporated enterprises.
b) Capital transfers from financial enterprises to resident sectors on imputed transaction that is equal to the capital transfer received by pension funds from general government in order to supplement the net equity of households in life insurance and pension funds.
c) Net lending of the capital accumulation account and the capital finance account have not been reconciled and are different due to different statistical sources.

3.24 Corporate and Quasi-Corporate Enterprise Capital Finance Account: Total and Sectors
Million Netherlands guilders

	1980 TOTAL	1980 Non-Financial	1980 Financial	1981 TOTAL	1981 Non-Financial	1981 Financial	1982 TOTAL	1982 Non-Financial	1982 Financial	1983 TOTAL	1983 Non-Financial	1983 Financial
Acquisition of Financial Assets
1 Gold and SDRs	96	-	96	422	-	422	532	-	532	-732	-	-732
2 Currency and transferable deposits	6329	3250	3079	-2293	-1236	-1057	11212	6974	4238	7875	7039	836
3 Other deposits	27387	10468	16919	37911	19466	18445	6458	11116	-4658	3456	2770	686
4 Bills and bonds, short term	3293	-166	3459	2197	-98	2295	1381	86	1295	-211	126	-337
5 Bonds, long term	6262	3540	2722	9408	3967	5441	17274	6530	10744	23181	8448	14733
6 Corporate equity securities	479	1073	-594	2407	2407	...	1200	-262	1462	2609	-494	3103
7 Short term loans, n.e.c.	14749	1529	13220	15356	5467	9889	1269	907	362	8905	1764	7141
8 Long term loans, n.e.c.	47479	4782	42697	43792	5897	37895	38953	3303	35650	37787	3965	33822
9 Trade credits and advances	...	...	...	...	...	...	...	...	...	...	...	...
10 Other receivables	...	...	...	...	...	...	...	...	...	...	...	...
11 Other assets	26396	26396	...	26718	26718	...	30042	30042	...	32670	32670	...
Total Acquisition of Financial Assets [a]	132470	50872	81598	135918	62588	73330	108321	58696	49625	115540	56288	59252
Incurrence of Liabilities
1 Currency and transferable deposits	5240	-	5240	539	-	539	9153	-	9153	7606	-	7606

Netherlands

3.24 Corporate and Quasi-Corporate Enterprise Capital Finance Account: Total and Sectors
(Continued)

Million Netherlands guilders

	1980 TOTAL	1980 Non-Financial	1980 Financial	1981 TOTAL	1981 Non-Financial	1981 Financial	1982 TOTAL	1982 Non-Financial	1982 Financial	1983 TOTAL	1983 Non-Financial	1983 Financial
2 Other deposits	37736	14	37722	41485	-160	41645	8118	25	8093	10970	157	10813
3 Bills and bonds, short term [b]	...	...	...	...	...	...	...	...	...	...	...	...
4 Bonds, long term	4398	910	3488	1485	182	1303	490	-173	663	932	-394	1326
5 Corporate equity securities	953	1799	-846	901	1165	-264	2913	2695	218	2115	1248	867
6 Short-term loans, n.e.c. [b]	7476	4739	2737	6917	4424	2493	-2004	-2320	316	3879	818	3061
7 Long-term loans, n.e.c.	38761	34238	4523	28254	29920	-1666	23959	25815	-1856	25367	23392	1975
8 Net equity of households in life insurance and pension fund reserves [c]	26206	-	26206	26398	-	26398	29752	-	29752	32430	-	32430
9 Proprietors' net additions to the accumulation of quasi-corporations	...	...	...	...	...	...	...	...	...	...	...	...
10 Trade credit and advances	...	...	...	...	...	...	...	...	...	...	...	...
11 Other accounts payable	...	...	...	...	...	...	...	...	...	...	...	...
12 Other liabilities	249	-	249	276	-	276	-	-	-	-	-	-
Total Incurrence of Liabilities [a]	121019	41700	79319	106255	35531	70724	72381	26042	46339	83299	25221	58078
Statistical discrepancy	3901	5842	-1941	3723	5787	-2064	330	2334	-2004	-2869	3047	-5916
Net Lending [d]	7550	3330	4220	25940	21270	4670	35610	30320	5290	35110	28020	7090
Incurrence of Liabilities and Net Lending [a]	132470	50872	81598	135918	62588	73330	108321	58696	49625	115540	56288	59252

a) Private unincorporated enterprises are included in non-financial corporate and quasi-corporate enterprises. Private non-profit institutions serving households are included partly in households, partly in private unincorporated enterprises.
b) Bills are included in item 'Short-term loans, n.e.c.'.
c) Item 'Net equity of households in life insurance and pension fund reserves' includes technical reserves of casualty insurance.
d) Net lending of the capital accumulation account and the capital finance account have not been reconciled and are different due to different statistical sources.

3.32 Household and Private Unincorporated Enterprise Income and Outlay Account

Million Netherlands guilders

	1970	1975	1978	1979	1980	1981	1982	1983	1984	1985	1986	1987
Receipts												
1 Compensation of employees	67200	131260	172850	186020	197960	201640	207690	209810	210150	216850	225690	231600
A Wages and salaries	53940	101360	133850	143360	152080	155080	160320	159850	160550	166100	173160	178870
B Employers' contributions for social security	8870	20090	26500	29270	31350	32300	33250	35360	35410	37040	38750	39240
C Employers' contributions for private pension & welfare plans	4390	9810	12500	13390	14530	14260	14120	14600	14190	13710	13780	13490
2 Operating surplus of private unincorporated enterprises	...	...	...	...	...	...	...	...	...	...	...	...
3 Property and entrepreneurial income [a]	24790	36210	50160	52070	55850	59890	69490	74830	81100	86380	91650	93160
A Withdrawals from private quasi-corporations	...	...	-	-	-	-	-	-	-	-	-	-
B Interest	...	...	8600	9890	12530	14220	15910	14460	14610	15930	14600	14650
C Dividends	...	...	41560	42180	43320	45670	53580	60370	66490	70450	77050	78510
D Net land rent and royalties	...	...	-	-	-	-	-	-	-	-	-	-
3 Current transfers	23400	57780	83670	91890	98960	107570	117480	123270	123920	126190	128950	132610
A Casualty insurance claims	1350	2760	4130	4550	4870	5190	5360	5570	5860	6400	7220	8080
B Social security benefits	16660	39750	58310	64230	70370	75100	79900	80730	80870	82230	83810	86170
C Social assistance grants	2450	7870	10770	11700	12820	15710	20600	24840	25010	22640	22820	23020
D Unfunded employee pension and welfare benefits	1450	3400	4710	5270	4730	4690	4660	4580	4610	4710	4710	4810
E Transfers from general government	1260	3490	5030	5210	5210	5810	5970	6580	6620	9170	9400	9450
F Transfers from the rest of the world	230	510	720	930	960	1070	990	970	950	1040	990	1080
G Other transfers n.e.c.	-	-	-	-	-	-	-	-	-	-	-	-
Total Current Receipts [b]	115390	225250	306680	329980	352770	369100	394660	407910	415170	429420	446290	457370
Disbursements												
1 Final consumption expenditures	70820	128950	179170	192430	205780	213230	221830	229860	236750	247720	256260	262960
2 Property income [a]	...	...	1320	1670	1910	2070	1890	1740	1700	1660	1680	1670
A Interest	...	...	1320	1670	1910	2070	1890	1740	1700	1660	1680	1670
B Net land rent and royalties	...	...	...	...	...	...	...	...	...	...	...	...
3 Direct taxes and other current transfers n.e.c. to government	29940	66560	89810	97830	105950	109950	117280	126310	125690	128120	130720	136810
A Social security contributions	16760	38530	51420	56310	61220	66140	72490	83300	82860	85990	85000	89130
B Direct taxes	12760	27120	37200	40240	43330	42180	42950	41040	40730	39810	43250	44770

Netherlands

3.32 Household and Private Unincorporated Enterprise Income and Outlay Account
(Continued)

Million Netherlands guilders

	1970	1975	1978	1979	1980	1981	1982	1983	1984	1985	1986	1987
Income taxes	12050	25790	34970	37710	40510	39310	39960	38000	37490	36420	39760	41080
Other	710	1330	2230	2530	2820	2870	2990	3040	3240	3390	3490	3690
C Fees, fines and penalties	420	910	1190	1280	1400	1630	1840	1970	2100	2320	2470	2910
4 Other current transfers	3450	7370	10530	11760	11890	12370	12480	12700	13280	13930	14700	16690
A Net casualty insurance premiums	1350	2760	4130	4550	4870	5190	5360	5570	5860	6400	7220	8080
B Transfers to private non-profit institutions serving households	...	...	...	...	...	...	...	...	...	...	...	...
C Transfers to the rest of the world	470	990	1400	1650	1960	2150	2140	2230	2410	2530	2490	3510
D Other current transfers, except imputed	180	220	290	290	330	340	320	320	400	290	280	290
E Imputed employee pension and welfare contributions	1450	3400	4710	5270	4730	4690	4660	4580	4610	4710	4710	4810
Net saving	11180	22370	25850	26290	27240	31480	41180	37300	37750	37990	42930	39240
Total Current Disbursements and Net Saving [b]	115390	225250	306680	329980	352770	369100	394660	407910	415170	429420	446290	457370

a) For 1970-1976, property income received is net of property income paid.
b) Private unincorporated enterprises are included in non-financial corporate and quasi-corporate enterprises. Private non-profit institutions serving households are included partly in households, partly in private unincorporated enterprises.

3.33 Household and Private Unincorporated Enterprise Capital Accumulation Account

Million Netherlands guilders

	1970	1975	1978	1979	1980	1981	1982	1983	1984	1985	1986	1987
Finance of Gross Accumulation												
1 Gross saving	11180	22370	25850	26290	27240	31480	41180	37300	37750	37990	42930	39240
A Consumption of fixed capital	-	-	-	-	-	-	-	-	-	-	-	-
B Net saving	11180	22370	25850	26290	27240	31480	41180	37300	37750	37990	42930	39240
2 Capital transfers	780	1580	1360	1440	1150	1230	1540	1600	1930	2010	1840	1950
A From resident sectors [a]	640	1360	1100	1110	840	840	1000	1060	1430	1340	1160	1160
B From the rest of the world	140	220	260	330	310	390	540	540	500	670	680	790
Total Finance of Gross Accumulation [b]	11960	23950	27210	27730	28390	32710	42720	38900	39680	40000	44770	41190
Gross Accumulation												
1 Gross Capital Formation	...	...	...	...	...	...	...	...	...	...	...	...
2 Purchases of land, net	...	...	...	...	...	...	...	...	...	...	...	...
3 Purchases of intangibles, net	...	...	...	...	...	...	...	...	...	...	...	...
4 Capital transfers	430	600	1020	1190	1330	1410	1470	1290	1430	1480	2030	2450
A To resident sectors	270	360	590	710	740	780	710	680	810	820	980	1140
B To the rest of the world	160	240	430	480	590	630	760	610	620	660	1050	1310
Net lending	11530	23350	26190	26540	27060	31300	41250	37610	38250	38520	42740	38740
Total Gross Accumulation [b]	11960	23950	27210	27730	28390	32710	42720	38900	39680	40000	44770	41190

a) Capital transfers from financial enterprises to resident sectors on imputed transaction that is equal to the capital transfer received by pension funds from general government in order to supplement the net equity of households in life insurance and pension funds.
b) Private unincorporated enterprises are included in non-financial corporate and quasi-corporate enterprises. Private non-profit institutions serving households are included partly in households, partly in private unincorporated enterprises.

3.51 External Transactions: Current Account: Detail

Million Netherlands guilders

	1970	1975	1978	1979	1980	1981	1982	1983	1984	1985	1986	1987
Payments to the Rest of the World												
1 Imports of goods and services	56410	102340	133230	156690	178620	192240	196830	205210	227750	245500	214650	214580
A Imports of merchandise c.i.f.	49140	90890	115680	137550	156120	168420	171710	179580	200240	216610	185260	184900
B Other	7270	11450	17550	19140	22500	23820	25120	25630	27510	28890	29390	29680
2 Factor income to the rest of the world	4180	8990	11610	15730	22710	31090	32400	27810	31370	32200	28840	29880
A Compensation of employees	390	660	750	800	910	1010	1140	1120	1120	1220	1210	1070
B Property and entrepreneurial income	3790	8330	10860	14930	21800	30080	31260	26690	30250	30980	27630	28810
By general government	...	...	...	...	...	...	...	...	...	...	...	...
By corporate and quasi-corporate enterprises	3790	8330	10860	14930	21800	30080	31260	26690	30250	30980	27630	28810

Netherlands

3.51 External Transactions: Current Account: Detail
(Continued)

Million Netherlands guilders

	1970	1975	1978	1979	1980	1981	1982	1983	1984	1985	1986	1987
By other	...	...	...	...	...	...	...	...	...	...	...	...
3 Current transfers to the rest of the world	1120	4690	7400	7820	8400	9160	9600	9830	10860	11790	12700	14010
A Indirect taxes by general government to supranational organizations	10	1590	2430	3540	3670	3730	4050	4140	4590	5010	5640	5950
B Other current transfers	1110	3100	4970	4280	4730	5430	5550	5690	6270	6780	7060	8060
By general government	410	1740	2810	1930	2060	2290	2580	2530	3100	3440	3720	3540
By other resident sectors	700	1360	2160	2350	2670	3140	2970	3160	3170	3340	3340	4520
4 Surplus of the nation on current transactions	-1700	5490	-2700	-3870	-4900	7760	11640	11860	16630	17310	11890	6910
Payments to the Rest of the World, and Surplus of the Nation on Current Transfers	60010	121510	149540	176370	204830	240250	250470	254710	286610	306800	268080	265380

Receipts From The Rest of the World

	1970	1975	1978	1979	1980	1981	1982	1983	1984	1985	1986	1987
1 Exports of goods and services	54300	109720	133340	155060	176810	204620	212600	219770	248560	265540	232650	226610
A Exports of merchandise f.o.b.	43010	88960	107460	128460	147080	171330	177620	185010	210630	225950	195830	188250
B Other	11290	20760	25880	26600	29730	33290	34980	34760	37930	39590	36820	38360
2 Factor income from the rest of the world	4740	8970	10930	15000	22090	30130	32020	28370	30870	32880	28110	29870
A Compensation of employees	420	750	830	900	1030	1120	1350	1290	1270	1300	1190	1190
B Property and entrepreneurial income	4320	8220	10100	14100	21060	29010	30670	27080	29600	31580	26920	28680
By general government	...	50	60	40	40	110	100	80	70	130	70	70
By corporate and quasi-corporate enterprises	...	7710	9310	13240	20100	27830	29140	25470	27940	29520	25040	26760
By other	...	460	730	820	920	1070	1430	1530	1590	1930	1810	1850
3 Current transfers from the rest of the world	970	2820	5270	6310	5930	5500	5850	6570	7180	7860	7960	9160
A Subsidies to general government from supranational organizations	480	1790	3630	4540	4120	3300	3840	4510	5200	5650	5780	6760
B Other current transfers	490	1030	1640	1770	1810	2200	2010	2060	1980	2210	2180	2400
To general government	30	150	160	140	140	140	190	160	270	360	340	310
To other resident sectors	460	880	1480	1630	1670	2060	1820	1900	1710	1850	1840	2090
Statistical discrepancy [a]	...	...	...	...	...	...	...	...	...	520	-640	-260
Receipts from the Rest of the World on Current Transfers	60010	121510	149540	176370	204830	240250	250470	254710	286610	306800	268080	265380

a) The surplus of the nation on current transactions corresponds to gross national saving less gross capital formation, plus from 1985 onwards a statistical discrepancy. This discrepancy is a consequence of the difference between on the one hand the surplus of the nation on current transactions (estimated by the Dutch Central Bank in cooperation with the Central Bureau of Statistics) and on the other hand the sum of the balance of exports and imports and the net current distributive transactions with the rest of the world. For the years 1983 and 84 there were also statistical discrepancies. However, these have been eliminated by altering the imports with destination increase in stocks.

3.52 External Transactions: Capital Accumulation Account

Million Netherlands guilders

	1970	1975	1978	1979	1980	1981	1982	1983	1984	1985	1986	1987

Finance of Gross Accumulation

	1970	1975	1978	1979	1980	1981	1982	1983	1984	1985	1986	1987
1 Surplus of the nation on current transactions	-1700	5490	-2700	-3870	-4900	7760	11640	11860	16630	17310	11890	6910
2 Capital transfers from the rest of the world	260	310	390	450	410	490	620	680	620	820	780	930
A By general government	120	90	130	120	100	100	80	140	120	150	100	140
B By other resident sectors	140	220	260	330	310	390	540	540	500	670	680	790
Total Finance of Gross Accumulation	-1440	5800	-2310	-3420	-4490	8250	12260	12540	17250	18130	12670	7840

Gross Accumulation

	1970	1975	1978	1979	1980	1981	1982	1983	1984	1985	1986	1987
1 Capital transfers to the rest of the world	500	530	800	1030	1200	1390	1570	1230	1110	1170	1690	1940
A By general government	340	290	370	550	610	760	810	620	490	510	640	630
B By other resident sectors	160	240	430	480	590	630	760	610	620	660	1050	1310
2 Purchases of intangible assets, n.e.c., net, from the rest of the world	...	...	...	...	...	...	...	...	...	...	...	...
Net lending to the rest of the world [a]	-1940	5270	-3110	-4450	-5690	6860	10690	11310	16140	16960	10980	5900
Total Gross Accumulation	-1440	5800	-2310	-3420	-4490	8250	12260	12540	17250	18130	12670	7840

a) Net lending of the capital accumulation account and the capital finance account have not been reconciled and are different due to different statistical sources.

Netherlands

3.53 External Transactions: Capital Finance Account

Million Netherlands guilders

	1970	1975	1978	1979	1980	1981	1982	1983	1984	1985	1986	1987
Acquisitions of Foreign Financial Assets											
1 Gold and SDR's	316	-	-	255	249	276	-	-	...	...	...	...
2 Currency and transferable deposits	534	320	592	-296	226	2803	1578	628	...	...	...	...
3 Other deposits	5181	10657	16705	18689	28782	21702	-811	5373	...	...	...	...
4 Bills and bonds, short term	...	...	...	...	...	...	...	...	...	...	...	...
5 Bonds, long term	2105	1044	2409	2386	4240	1826	2119	1352	...	...	...	...
6 Corporate equity securities	913	936	1206	1931	2496	1617	3769	1670	...	...	...	...
7 Short-term loans, n.e.c.	2464	-641	-124	1383	178	1325	-1032	-2310	...	...	...	...
8 Long-term loans	2428	2275	2142	4022	3466	5022	2355	6834	...	...	...	...
9 Prporietors' net additions to accumulation of quasi-corporate, non-resident enterprises	...	...	...	...	...	...	...	...	...	...	...	...
10 Trade credit and advances	...	...	...	...	...	...	...	...	...	...	...	...
11 Other [a]	6	10	-80	-80	-190	-320	-290	-240	...	...	...	...
Total Acquisitions of Foreign Financial Assets	13947	14601	22850	28290	39447	34251	7688	13307	...	...	...	...
Incurrence of Foreign Liabilities											
1 Currency and transferable deposits [b]	3948	3785	109	1706	2732	-825	3962	851	...	...	...	...
2 Other deposits	2467	10120	9525	10350	17406	18227	-2864	-253	...	...	...	...
3 Bills and bonds, short term	...	...	...	...	...	...	...	...	...	...	...	...
4 Bonds, long term	-12	219	804	45	693	886	2718	2997	...	...	...	...
5 Corporate equity securities	2110	3499	2641	997	2022	3123	2056	2164	...	...	...	...
6 Short-term loans, n.e.c.	901	-110	1520	4228	3991	9808	4998	4248	...	...	...	...
7 Long-term loans	1527	3660	6787	10297	9167	12441	8927	11740	...	...	...	...
8 Non-resident proprietors' net additions to accumulation of resident quasi-corporate enterprises	...	...	...	...	...	...	...	...	...	...	...	...
9 Trade credit and advances	...	...	...	...	...	...	...	...	...	...	...	...
10 Other [c]	762	102	-838	-2127	96	422	532	-732	...	...	...	...
Total Incurrence of Liabilities	11703	21275	20548	25496	36107	44082	20329	21015	...	...	...	...
Statistical discrepancy	304	-1724	-478	-1286	-2660	-3211	-3141	2762	...	...	...	...
Net Lending [d]	1940	-4950	2780	4080	6000	-6620	-9500	-10470	...	...	...	...
Total Incurrence of Liabilities and Net Lending	13947	14601	22850	28290	39447	34251	7688	13307	...	...	...	...

a) Item 'Other' of 'Acquisitions of foreign financial assets' refers to insurance technical reserves.
b) For 1979, item 'Currency and transferable deposits' includes 3979 million guilders in European Currency Units.
c) Item 'Other' of 'Incurrence of liabilities' refers to SDRs and financial gold.
d) Net lending of the capital accumulation account and the capital finance account have not been reconciled and are different due to different statistical sources.

4.1 Derivation of Value Added by Kind of Activity, in Current Prices

Million Netherlands guilders

	1980			1981			1982			1983		
	Gross Output	Intermediate Consumption	Value Added	Gross Output	Intermediate Consumption	Value Added	Gross Output	Intermediate Consumption	Value Added	Gross Output	Intermediate Consumption	Value Added
All Producers											
1 Agriculture, hunting, forestry and fishing	27370	15694	11676	31442	16885	14557	33493	17561	15932	34724	18600	16124
A Agriculture and hunting	26746	15399	11347	30701	16528	14173	32690	17143	15547	33830	18149	15681
B Forestry and logging												
C Fishing	624	295	329	741	357	384	803	418	385	894	451	443
2 Mining and quarrying	21893	2742	19151	28764	3201	25563	30049	4077	25972	31501	4173	27328
A Coal mining	...	...	...	...	...	...	...	...	...	...	...	...
B Crude petroleum and natural gas production	20868	2217	18651	27760	2729	25031	28947	3530	25417	30229	3495	26734
C Metal ore mining	...	...	...	...	...	...	...	...	...	...	...	...
D Other mining	1025	525	500	1004	472	532	1102	547	555	1272	678	594

Netherlands

4.1 Derivation of Value Added by Kind of Activity, in Current Prices
(Continued)

Million Netherlands guilders

	1980 Gross Output	1980 Intermediate Consumption	1980 Value Added	1981 Gross Output	1981 Intermediate Consumption	1981 Value Added	1982 Gross Output	1982 Intermediate Consumption	1982 Value Added	1983 Gross Output	1983 Intermediate Consumption	1983 Value Added
3 Manufacturing	220709	160344	60365	235777	175997	59780	242374	177704	64670	251817	184354	67463
A Manufacture of food, beverages and tobacco	56578	45812	10766	63168	51873	11295	66969	54518	12451	69467	56917	12550
B Textile, wearing apparel and leather industries	8609	6060	2549	8158	5742	2416	8351	5825	2526	8286	5843	2443
C Manufacture of wood and wood products, including furniture	5157	3145	2012	4917	3090	1827	4695	2971	1724	4747	3075	1672
D Manufacture of paper and paper products, printing and publishing	16822	10267	6555	17357	10712	6645	17719	10749	6970	17942	10746	7196
E Manufacture of chemicals and chemical petroleum, coal, rubber and plastic products	63586	51823	11763	70240	59456	10784	70388	58146	12242	76839	62363	14476
F Manufacture of non-metallic mineral products, except products of petroleum and coal	5822	3282	2540	5665	3364	2301	5520	3323	2197	5488	3260	2228
G Basic metal industries	8755	6246	2509	9182	6817	2365	9282	6359	2923	9509	6667	2842
H Manufacture of fabricated metal products, machinery and equipment	52325	31830	20495	53950	33092	20858	56224	33930	22294	56069	33443	22626
I Other manufacturing industries	3055	1879	1176	3140	1851	1289	3226	1883	1343	3470	2040	1430
4 Electricity, gas and water	18511	11339	7172	22219	14613	7606	23145	14986	8159	23759	15347	8412
A Electricity, gas and steam	17112	11068	6044	20781	14332	6449	21583	14695	6888	22078	15051	7027
B Water works and supply	1399	271	1128	1438	281	1157	1562	291	1271	1681	296	1385
5 Construction	55239	31479	23760	52469	29413	23056	50324	27880	22444	48847	27434	21413
6 Wholesale and retail trade, restaurants and hotels	68101	24664	43437	69541	24966	44575	72704	25653	47051	74281	25820	48461
A Wholesale and retail trade	58292	20596	37696	59328	20721	38607	61954	21162	40792	63238	21276	41962
B Restaurants and hotels	9809	4068	5741	10213	4245	5968	10750	4491	6259	11043	4544	6499
7 Transport, storage and communication	34215	12917	21298	36791	14526	22265	37103	14708	22395	37651	14499	23152
A Transport and storage	26745	11858	14887	28885	13378	15507	28671	13501	15170	28811	13289	15522
B Communication	7470	1059	6411	7906	1148	6758	8432	1207	7225	8840	1210	7630
8 Finance, insurance, real estate and business services	59336	12443	46893	63406	13092	50314	68016	13743	54273	74128	14020	60108
A Financial institutions	13815	2863	10952	15141	3064	12077	16805	3288	13517	19300	3513	15787
B Insurance	9188	4266	4922	9221	4436	4785	9106	4547	4559	9140	4649	4491
C Real estate and business services	36333	5314	31019	39044	5592	33452	42105	5908	36197	45688	5858	39830
Real estate, except dwellings	...	...	...	...	...	...	...	...	...	...	...	...
Dwellings	19153	2797	16356	21276	2888	18388	23765	3006	20759	26142	2934	23208
9 Community, social and personal services [a]	49181	11653	37528	51997	12545	39452	54915	13289	41626	56488	13712	42776
A Sanitary and similar services	...	...	...	...	...	...	...	...	...	...	...	...
B Social and related community services	23778	4910	18868	25432	5459	19973	27215	5960	21255	28068	6180	21888
Educational services	...	...	...	...	...	...	...	...	...	...	...	...
Medical, dental, other health and veterinary services	23778	4910	18868	25432	5459	19973	27215	5960	21255	28068	6180	21888
C Recreational and cultural services	5647	2059	3588	5924	2113	3811	6300	2176	4124	6773	2320	4453
D Personal and household services [a]	19756	4684	15072	20641	4973	15668	21400	5153	16247	21647	5212	16435
Statistical discrepancy	1615	1615	...	1834	1822	12	2117	2109	8	2234	2221	13
Total, Industries	556170	284890	271280	594240	307060	287180	614240	311710	302530	635430	320180	315250
Producers of Government Services	64040	17200	46840	66620	18680	47940	69390	19870	49520	71180	21530	49650
Other Producers	1050	...	1050	1060	...	1060	1090	...	1090	1070	...	1070
Total	621260	302090	319170	661920	325740	336180	684720	331580	353140	707680	341710	365970
Less: Imputed bank service charge	...	-11460	11460	...	-12660	12660	...	-14080	14080	...	-16150	16150
Import duties	4440	...	4440	4220	...	4220	4580	...	4580	4770	...	4770
Value added tax [b]	24590	...	24590	25110	...	25110	25220	...	25220	26430	...	26430
Total	650290	313550	336740	691250	338400	352850	714520	345660	368860	738880	357860	381020

Netherlands

4.1 Derivation of Value Added by Kind of Activity, in Current Prices

Million Netherlands guilders

		1984			1985	
	Gross Output	Intermediate Consumption	Value Added	Gross Output	Intermediate Consumption	Value Added

All Producers

1	Agriculture, hunting, forestry and fishing	36630	19371	17259	36676	19535	17141
	A Agriculture and hunting	35661	18876	16785	35569	19013	16556
	B Forestry and logging						
	C Fishing	969	495	474	1107	522	585
2	Mining and quarrying	35291	4200	31091	39533	4161	35372
	A Coal mining	...	...	...	...	...	...
	B Crude petroleum and natural gas production	33933	3526	30407	37971	3376	34595
	C Metal ore mining	...	...	...	...	...	...
	D Other mining	1358	674	684	1562	785	777
3	Manufacturing	279477	206908	72569	286122	210891	75231
	A Manufacture of food, beverages and tobacco	76054	62934	13120	76766	63805	12961
	B Textile, wearing apparel and leather industries	8864	6365	2499	9468	6880	2588
	C Manufacture of wood and wood products, including furniture	4743	3095	1648	4893	3152	1741
	D Manufacture of paper and paper products, printing and publishing	19592	12148	7444	21018	12945	8073
	E Manufacture of chemicals and chemical petroleum, coal, rubber and plastic products	86640	70029	16611	85503	68689	16814
	F Manufacture of non-metallic mineral products, except products of petroleum and coal	5876	3468	2408	6204	3641	2563
	G Basic metal industries	11764	8256	3508	11884	8174	3710
	H Manufacture of fabricated metal products, machinery and equipment	62139	38366	23773	66404	41267	25137
	I Other manufacturing industries	3805	2247	1558	3982	2338	1644
4	Electricity, gas and water	25200	16833	8367	27410	18859	8551
	A Electricity, gas and steam	23483	16523	6960	25673	18533	7140
	B Water works and supply	1717	310	1407	1737	326	1411
5	Construction	51008	29651	21357	52523	31259	21264
6	Wholesale and retail trade, restaurants and hotels	79350	28175	51175	84239	30496	53743
	A Wholesale and retail trade	67428	23200	44228	72085	25477	46608
	B Restaurants and hotels	11922	4975	6947	12154	5019	7135
7	Transport, storage and communication	40110	15520	24590	42798	16715	26083
	A Transport and storage	30966	14238	16728	33068	15240	17828
	B Communication	9144	1282	7862	9730	1475	8255
8	Finance, insurance, real estate and business services	77803	14791	63012	81786	15950	65836
	A Financial institutions	19776	3689	16087	20458	4002	16456
	B Insurance	9663	4849	4814	10180	5219	4961
	C Real estate and business services	48364	6253	42111	51148	6729	44419
	Real estate, except dwellings	...	...	...	...	...	...
	Dwellings	27574	3063	24511	28834	3251	25583
9	Community, social and personal services [a]	57513	14235	43278	59497	15107	44390
	A Sanitary and similar services	...	...	...	...	...	...
	B Social and related community services	28467	6361	22106	29133	6760	22373
	Educational services	...	...	...	...	...	...
	Medical, dental, other health and veterinary services	28467	6361	22106	29133	6760	22373
	C Recreational and cultural services	6959	2434	4525	7184	2531	4653
	D Personal and household services [a]	22087	5440	16647	23180	5816	17364
	Statistical discrepancy	2578	2566	12	2756	2747	9

Netherlands

4.1 Derivation of Value Added by Kind of Activity, in Current Prices
(Continued)

Million Netherlands guilders

	1984			1985		
	Gross Output	Intermediate Consumption	Value Added	Gross Output	Intermediate Consumption	Value Added
Total, Industries	684960	352250	332710	713340	365720	347620
Producers of Government Services	71390	21940	49450	72840	22750	50090
Other Producers	1090	...	1090	1140	...	1140
Total	757440	374190	383250	787320	388470	398850
Less: Imputed bank service charge	...	-16420	16420	...	-16730	16730
Import duties	5130	...	5130	5650	...	5650
Value added tax b	28290	...	28290	30410	...	30410
Total	790860	390610	400250	823380	405200	418180

a) Repair services are included in item 'Community, social and personal services'.
b) Item 'Value added tax' includes selective investment levy.

4.3 Cost Components of Value Added

Million Netherlands guilders

	1980						1981					
	Compensation of Employees	Capital Consumption	Net Operating Surplus	Indirect Taxes	Less: Subsidies Received	Value Added	Compensation of Employees	Capital Consumption	Net Operating Surplus	Indirect Taxes	Less: Subsidies Received	Value Added
						All Producers						
1 Agriculture, hunting, forestry and fishing	2492	1800	7127	435	178	11676	2577	1970	9583	500	73	14557
A Agriculture and hunting	2342	1730	7005	431	161	11347	2400	1890	9437	495	49	14173
B Forestry and logging												
C Fishing	150	70	122	4	17	329	177	80	146	5	24	384
2 Mining and quarrying	528	780	17803	40	-	19151	576	930	24014	43	-	25563
A Coal mining	...	...	...	...	-	...	...	...	...	...	-	...
B Crude petroleum and natural gas production	357	690	17584	20	...	18651	405	820	23784	22	...	25031
C Metal ore mining	...	...	...	...	...	...	...	...	...	...	...	...
D Other mining	171	90	219	20	...	500	171	110	230	21	...	532
3 Manufacturing	43678	8340	5971	5847	3471	60365	44482	9220	3340	6014	3276	59780
A Manufacture of food, beverages and tobacco	6913	1670	2338	2886	3041	10766	7197	1870	1818	2990	2580	11295
B Textile, wearing apparel and leather industries	2280	400	-115	24	40	2549	2066	420	-57	25	38	2416
C Manufacture of wood and wood products, including furniture	1627	200	186	7	8	2012	1549	210	67	7	6	1827
D Manufacture of paper and paper products, printing and publishing	4832	650	1040	37	4	6555	4918	710	985	38	6	6645
E Manufacture of chemicals and chemical petroleum, coal, rubber and plastic products	6589	2540	-89	2743	20	11763	6876	2850	-1743	2824	23	10784
F Manufacture of non-metallic mineral products, except products of petroleum and coal	1808	430	289	14	1	2540	1764	480	43	15	1	2301
G Basic metal industries	1836	590	59	24	-	2509	1883	650	-184	16	-	2365
H Manufacture of fabricated metal products, machinery and equipment	17005	1780	1954	110	354	20495	17431	1940	2000	96	609	20858
I Other manufacturing industries	788	80	309	2	3	1176	798	90	411	3	13	1289
4 Electricity, gas and water	2557	2410	2158	47	-	7172	2612	2720	2223	51	-	7606
A Electricity, gas and steam	2141	2050	1806	47	-	6044	2190	2320	1888	51	-	6449
B Water works and supply	416	360	352	-	-	1128	422	400	335	-	-	1157
5 Construction	17704	1090	4910	120	64	23760	16300	1190	5487	130	51	23056
6 Wholesale and retail trade, restaurants and hotels	26012	3280	13974	598	427	43437	26473	3470	14270	656	294	44575
A Wholesale and retail trade	23836	2940	10827	505	412	37696	24222	3110	11007	550	282	38607
B Restaurants and hotels	2176	340	3147	93	15	5741	2251	360	3263	106	12	5968
7 Transport, storage and communication	15418	4690	3221	320	2351	21298	15792	5090	3655	349	2621	22265
A Transport and storage	11308	3590	2033	307	2351	14887	11629	3900	2270	329	2621	15507
B Communication	4110	1100	1188	13	-	6411	4163	1190	1385	20	-	6758
8 Finance, insurance, real estate and business services	17784	5770	21750	3330	1741	46893	18899	6350	23458	3299	1692	50314
A Financial institutions	5486	130	5204	138	6	10952	5873	150	5897	161	4	12077

Netherlands

4.3 Cost Components of Value Added
(Continued)

Million Netherlands guilders

	1980						1981					
	Compensation of Employees	Capital Consumption	Net Operating Surplus	Indirect Taxes	Less: Subsidies Received	Value Added	Compensation of Employees	Capital Consumption	Net Operating Surplus	Indirect Taxes	Less: Subsidies Received	Value Added
B Insurance	3241	130	1042	510	1	4922	3407	140	719	520	1	4785
C Real estate and business services	9057	5510	15504	2682	1734	31019	9619	6060	16842	2618	1687	33452
Real estate, except dwellings	...	...	...	...	...	...	...	...	...	...	...	...
Dwellings	581	5100	11055	1343	1723	16356	620	5600	12285	1561	1678	18388
9 Community, social and personal services [a]	26536	1930	8936	196	70	37528	27734	2120	9432	214	48	39452
A Sanitary and similar services	...	...	...	...	...	...	...	...	...	...	...	...
B Social and related community services	11770	1450	5538	111	1	18868	12356	1600	5905	115	3	19973
Educational services	...	...	...	...	...	...	...	...	...	...	...	...
Medical, dental, other health and veterinary services	11770	1450	5538	111	1	18868	12356	1600	5905	115	3	19973
C Recreational and cultural services	2625	120	831	23	11	3588	2764	130	894	26	3	3811
D Personal and household services [a]	12141	360	2567	62	58	15072	12614	390	2633	73	42	15668
Statistical discrepancy	1	...	...	-3	-2	...	5	...	-2	14	5	12
Total, Industries	152710	30090	85850	10930	8300	271280	155450	33060	95460	11270	8060	287180
Producers of Government Services	44080	2400	-	360	-	46840	45020	2560	-	360	-	47940
Other Producers	1050	...	-	-	-	1050	1060	...	-	-	-	1060
Total	197840	32490	85850	11290	8300	319170	201530	35620	95460	11630	8060	336180
Less: Imputed bank service charge	...	...	11460	...	...	11460	...	...	12660	...	...	12660
Import duties	...	...	...	4440	...	4440	...	...	...	4220	...	4220
Value added tax [b]	...	...	...	24590	...	24590	...	...	...	25110	...	25110
Other adjustments	...	...	...	800	800	...	...	...	...	760	760	...
Total	197840	32490	74390	41120	9100	336740	201530	35620	82800	41720	8820	352850

	1982						1983					
	Compensation of Employees	Capital Consumption	Net Operating Surplus	Indirect Taxes	Less: Subsidies Received	Value Added	Compensation of Employees	Capital Consumption	Net Operating Surplus	Indirect Taxes	Less: Subsidies Received	Value Added
					All Producers							
1 Agriculture, hunting, forestry and fishing	2727	2100	10683	556	134	15932	2926	2200	10656	565	223	16124
A Agriculture and hunting	2543	2000	10568	549	113	15547	2736	2090	10505	557	207	15681
B Forestry and logging												
C Fishing	184	100	115	7	21	385	190	110	151	8	16	443
2 Mining and quarrying	645	1070	24215	42	-	25972	691	1150	25442	45	-	27328
A Coal mining	...	...	...	...	-	...	...	...	...	...	-	...
B Crude petroleum and natural gas production	465	940	23990	22	...	25417	512	1010	25187	25	...	26734
C Metal ore mining	...	...	...	...	...	...	...	...	...	...	...	...
D Other mining	180	130	225	20	...	555	179	140	255	20	...	594

Netherlands

4.3 Cost Components of Value Added
(Continued)

Million Netherlands guilders

	1982						1983					
	Compensation of Employees	Capital Consumption	Net Operating Surplus	Indirect Taxes	Less: Subsidies Received	Value Added	Compensation of Employees	Capital Consumption	Net Operating Surplus	Indirect Taxes	Less: Subsidies Received	Value Added
3 Manufacturing	45658	9900	6528	6214	3630	64670	45626	10240	8779	6833	4015	67463
A Manufacture of food, beverages and tobacco	7515	2020	2652	3257	2993	12451	7652	2100	2553	3576	3331	12550
B Textile, wearing apparel and leather industries	1974	430	161	27	66	2526	1895	440	164	29	85	2443
C Manufacture of wood and wood products, including furniture	1478	220	30	7	11	1724	1403	220	54	9	14	1672
D Manufacture of paper and paper products, printing and publishing	5075	760	1100	40	5	6970	5122	800	1238	42	6	7196
E Manufacture of chemicals and chemical petroleum, coal, rubber and plastic products	7229	3070	-771	2736	22	12242	7544	3190	774	2993	25	14476
F Manufacture of non-metallic mineral products, except products of petroleum and coal	1746	510	-72	15	2	2197	1684	520	11	16	3	2228
G Basic metal industries	1941	700	267	15	-	2923	2000	720	106	16	-	2842
H Manufacture of fabricated metal products, machinery and equipment	17869	2090	2747	114	526	22294	17492	2150	3381	147	544	22626
I Other manufacturing industries	831	100	414	3	5	1343	834	100	498	5	7	1430
4 Electricity, gas and water	2664	2940	2504	51	-	8159	2695	3020	2642	55	-	8412
A Electricity, gas and steam	2268	2500	2069	51	-	6888	2308	2570	2095	54	-	7027
B Water works and supply	396	440	435	-	-	1271	387	450	547	1	-	1385
5 Construction	15591	1270	5539	132	88	22444	14830	1330	5234	131	112	21413
6 Wholesale and retail trade, restaurants and hotels	26769	3680	16196	724	318	47051	27464	3820	16792	839	454	48461
A Wholesale and retail trade	24424	3300	12757	608	297	40792	25030	3430	13210	719	427	41962
B Restaurants and hotels	2345	380	3439	116	21	6259	2434	390	3582	120	27	6499
7 Transport, storage and communication	16323	5480	3444	378	3230	22395	16700	5770	3605	393	3316	23152
A Transport and storage	12002	4160	1876	362	3230	15170	12299	4390	1772	377	3316	15522
B Communication	4321	1320	1568	16	-	7225	4401	1380	1833	16	-	7630
8 Finance, insurance, real estate and business services	20028	6710	25920	3393	1778	54273	20708	6950	31042	3637	2229	60108
A Financial institutions	6329	160	6859	176	7	13517	6558	170	8854	214	9	15787
B Insurance	3563	150	341	507	2	4559	3619	160	170	545	3	4491
C Real estate and business services	10136	6400	18720	2710	1769	36197	10531	6620	22018	2878	2217	39830
Real estate, except dwellings	...	...	...	...	...	...	...	...	...	...	...	...
Dwellings	669	5910	14225	1708	1753	20759	715	6110	16867	1712	2196	23208
9 Community, social and personal services [a]	29257	2290	9880	280	81	41626	29981	2410	10223	266	104	42776
A Sanitary and similar services	...	...	...	...	...	...	...	...	...	...	...	...
B Social and related community services	13177	1730	6174	179	5	21255	13573	1810	6367	144	6	21888
Educational services	...	...	...	...	...	...	...	...	...	...	...	...
Medical, dental, other health and veterinary services	13177	1730	6174	179	5	21255	13573	1810	6367	144	6	21888
C Recreational and cultural services	2927	140	1034	28	5	4124	2989	150	1291	30	7	4453
D Personal and household services [a]	13153	420	2672	73	71	16247	13419	450	2565	92	91	16435
Statistical discrepancy	8	...	-9	10	1	8	-1	...	5	6	-3	13
Total, Industries	159670	35440	104900	11780	9260	302530	161620	36890	114420	12770	10450	315250
Producers of Government Services	46720	2420	-	380	-	49520	46950	2300	-	400	-	49650
Other Producers	1090	-	-	-	-	1090	1070	-	-	-	-	1070
Total	207480	37860	104900	12160	9260	353140	209640	39190	114420	13170	10450	365970
Less: Imputed bank service charge	...	...	14080	...	...	14080	...	...	16150	...	...	16150
Import duties	...	...	...	4580	...	4580	...	...	...	4770	...	4770
Value added tax [b]	...	...	...	25220	...	25220	...	...	...	26430	...	26430
Other adjustments	...	...	...	800	800	...	...	...	...	770	770	...
Total	207480	37860	90820	42760	10060	368860	209640	39190	98270	45140	11220	381020

Netherlands

4.3 Cost Components of Value Added

Million Netherlands guilders

	1984 Compensation of Employees	1984 Capital Consumption	1984 Net Operating Surplus	1984 Indirect Taxes	1984 Less: Subsidies Received	1984 Value Added	1985 Compensation of Employees	1985 Capital Consumption	1985 Net Operating Surplus	1985 Indirect Taxes	1985 Less: Subsidies Received	1985 Value Added
All Producers												
1 Agriculture, hunting, forestry and fishing	2957	2340	11488	575	101	17259	3081	2470	10911	622	-57	17141
A Agriculture and hunting	2755	2210	11348	567	95	16785	2855	2340	10689	612	-60	16556
B Forestry and logging	...	...	...	...	...	...	...	...	...	...	...	...
C Fishing	202	130	140	8	6	474	226	130	222	10	3	585
2 Mining and quarrying	736	1250	29062	43	-	31091	814	1350	33157	51	-	35372
A Coal mining	...	...	...	...	-	...	...	...	...	...	-	...
B Crude petroleum and natural gas production	562	1100	28723	22	...	30407	633	1190	32745	27	...	34595
C Metal ore mining	...	...	...	...	...	...	...	...	...	...	...	...
D Other mining	174	150	339	21	...	684	181	160	412	24	...	777
3 Manufacturing	45666	10630	13638	7407	4772	72569	47650	11040	14464	6937	4860	75231
A Manufacture of food, beverages and tobacco	7704	2180	3644	3681	4089	13120	7935	2250	3383	3644	4251	12961
B Textile, wearing apparel and leather industries	1841	430	282	28	82	2499	1881	420	323	30	66	2588
C Manufacture of wood and wood products, including furniture	1353	220	81	9	15	1648	1358	220	166	9	12	1741
D Manufacture of paper and paper products, printing and publishing	5235	850	1323	43	7	7444	5490	890	1656	43	6	8073
E Manufacture of chemicals and chemical petroleum, coal, rubber and plastic products	7570	3320	2294	3449	22	16611	8060	3460	2333	2989	28	16814
F Manufacture of non-metallic mineral products, except products of petroleum and coal	1680	530	185	16	3	2408	1730	550	269	17	3	2563
G Basic metal industries	2025	740	726	17	-	3508	2133	760	803	14	...	3710
H Manufacture of fabricated metal products, machinery and equipment	17413	2250	4498	159	547	23773	18166	2380	4894	186	489	25137
I Other manufacturing industries	845	110	605	5	7	1558	897	110	637	5	5	1644
4 Electricity, gas and water	2640	3090	2579	58	-	8367	2662	3140	2687	62	-	8551
A Electricity, gas and steam	2255	2620	2028	57	-	6960	2270	2660	2149	61	-	7140
B Water works and supply	385	470	551	1	-	1407	392	480	538	1	-	1411
5 Construction	14828	1380	5129	135	115	21357	14808	1410	4997	136	87	21264
6 Wholesale and retail trade, restaurants and hotels	27726	3960	19219	783	513	51175	28912	4080	20218	792	259	53743
A Wholesale and retail trade	25190	3550	15309	661	482	44228	26313	3660	16201	668	234	46608
B Restaurants and hotels	2536	410	3910	122	31	6947	2599	420	4017	124	25	7135
7 Transport, storage and communication	16810	6160	4665	412	3457	24590	17526	6490	5184	346	3463	26083
A Transport and storage	12417	4710	2670	388	3457	16728	13061	4920	2985	325	3463	17828
B Communication	4393	1450	1995	24	-	7862	4465	1570	2199	21	...	8255
8 Finance, insurance, real estate and business services	21263	7220	33599	3717	2787	63012	22350	7490	35822	4089	3915	65836
A Financial institutions	6651	180	9039	227	10	16087	6928	180	9089	267	8	16456
B Insurance	3661	170	393	593	3	4814	3798	180	372	614	3	4961
C Real estate and business services	10951	6870	24167	2897	2774	42111	11624	7130	26361	3208	3904	44419
Real estate, except dwellings	...	...	...	...	...	...	...	...	...	...	...	...
Dwellings	758	6330	18401	1772	2750	24511	761	6560	20128	2018	3884	25583
9 Community, social and personal services [a]	29864	2540	10720	265	111	43278	30912	2650	10642	280	94	44390
A Sanitary and similar services	...	...	...	...	...	...	...	...	...	...	...	...
B Social and related community services	13354	1910	6704	144	6	22106	13664	2010	6556	148	5	22373
Educational services	...	...	...	...	...	...	...	...	...	...	...	...
Medical, dental, other health and veterinary services	13354	1910	6704	144	6	22106	13664	2010	6556	148	5	22373
C Recreational and cultural services	2965	160	1376	31	7	4525	3025	160	1441	34	7	4653
D Personal and household services [a]	13545	470	2640	90	98	16647	14223	480	2645	98	82	17364
Statistical discrepancy	10	...	1	5	4	12	5	...	-2	5	-1	9

Netherlands

4.3 Cost Components of Value Added
(Continued)

Million Netherlands guilders

	1984						1985					
	Compensation of Employees	Capital Consumption	Net Operating Surplus	Indirect Taxes	Less: Subsidies Received	Value Added	Compensation of Employees	Capital Consumption	Net Operating Surplus	Indirect Taxes	Less: Subsidies Received	Value Added
Total, Industries	162500	38570	130100	13400	11860	332710	168720	40120	138080	13320	12620	347620
Producers of Government Services	46410	2620	-	420	-	49450	46910	2750	-	430	-	50090
Other Producers	1090	...	-	-	-	1090	1140	...	-	-	-	1140
Total	210000	41190	130100	13820	11860	383250	216770	42870	138080	13750	12620	398850
Less: Imputed bank service charge	...	...	16420	...	...	16420	...	...	16730	...	...	16730
Import duties	...	...	...	5130	...	5130	...	...	...	5650	...	5650
Value added tax [b]	...	...	...	28290	...	28290	...	...	...	30410	...	30410
Other adjustments	...	...	...	750	750	...	...	...	...	890	890	...
Total	210000	41190	113680	47990	12610	400250	216770	42870	121350	50700	13510	418180

	1986						1987					
	Compensation of Employees	Capital Consumption	Net Operating Surplus	Indirect Taxes	Less: Subsidies Received	Value Added	Compensation of Employees	Capital Consumption	Net Operating Surplus	Indirect Taxes	Less: Subsidies Received	Value Added

All Producers

1 Agriculture, hunting, forestry and fishing	3200	2580	11760	670	-40	18250	3240	2670	10550	700	30	17130
A Agriculture and hunting	...	...	...	...	...	...	...	...	...	...	...	...
B Forestry and logging	...	...	...	...	...	...	...	...	...	...	...	...
C Fishing	...	...	...	...	...	...	...	...	...	...	...	...
2 Mining and quarrying	880	1410	21370	50	...	23710	880	1420	13080	60	...	15440
A Coal mining	...	...	...	...	...	...	...	...	...	...	...	...
B Crude petroleum and natural gas production	...	...	...	...	...	...	...	...	...	...	...	...
C Metal ore mining	...	...	...	...	...	...	...	...	...	...	...	...
D Other mining	...	...	...	...	...	...	...	...	...	...	...	...
3 Manufacturing	49920	11160	18680	7060	5370	81450	51270	11310	17750	7380	7170	80540
A Manufacture of food, beverages and tobacco	...	...	...	...	...	...	...	...	...	...	...	...
B Textile, wearing apparel and leather industries	...	...	...	...	...	...	...	...	...	...	...	...
C Manufacture of wood and wood products, including furniture	...	...	...	...	...	...	...	...	...	...	...	...
D Manufacture of paper and paper products, printing and publishing	...	...	...	...	...	...	...	...	...	...	...	...
E Manufacture of chemicals and chemical petroleum, coal, rubber and plastic products	...	...	...	...	...	...	...	...	...	...	...	...
F Manufacture of non-metallic mineral products, except products of petroleum and coal	...	...	...	...	...	...	...	...	...	...	...	...
G Basic metal industries	...	...	...	...	...	...	...	...	...	...	...	...
H Manufacture of fabricated metal products, machinery and equipment	...	...	...	...	...	...	...	...	...	...	...	...
I Other manufacturing industries	...	...	...	...	...	...	...	...	...	...	...	...
4 Electricity, gas and water	2710	3110	2950	70	...	8840	2770	3100	2760	70	...	8700
A Electricity, gas and steam	...	...	...	...	...	...	...	...	...	...	...	...
B Water works and supply	...	...	...	...	...	...	...	...	...	...	...	...
5 Construction	15910	1400	5760	140	60	23150	16350	1390	6480	150	60	24310
6 Wholesale and retail trade, restaurants and hotels	30270	4170	21540	930	430	56480	31520	4380	23020	1140	740	59320
A Wholesale and retail trade	...	...	...	...	...	...	...	...	...	...	...	...
B Restaurants and hotels	...	...	...	...	...	...	...	...	...	...	...	...
7 Transport, storage and communication	18410	6460	6050	360	3400	27880	18940	6700	5600	390	3430	28200
A Transport and storage	...	...	...	...	...	...	...	...	...	...	...	...
B Communication	...	...	...	...	...	...	...	...	...	...	...	...
8 Finance, insurance, real estate and business services	23430	7610	37740	4460	3800	69440	24270	7980	39230	4730	4240	71970
A Financial institutions	...	...	...	...	...	...	...	...	...	...	...	...
B Insurance	...	...	...	...	...	...	...	...	...	...	...	...
C Real estate and business services	...	...	...	...	...	...	...	...	...	...	...	...
Real estate, except dwellings	...	...	...	...	...	...	...	...	...	...	...	...

Netherlands

4.3 Cost Components of Value Added
(Continued)

Million Netherlands guilders

	1986						1987					
	Compensation of Employees	Capital Consumption	Net Operating Surplus	Indirect Taxes	Less: Subsidies Received	Value Added	Compensation of Employees	Capital Consumption	Net Operating Surplus	Indirect Taxes	Less: Subsidies Received	Value Added
Dwellings	...	...	...	...	...	...	...	...	...	...	...	...
9 Community, social and personal services [a]	32310	2750	11830	320	70	47140	32910	2870	12870	340	70	48920
A Sanitary and similar services	...	...	...	...	...	...	...	...	...	...	...	...
B Social and related community services	...	...	...	...	...	...	...	...	...	...	...	...
Educational services	...	...	...	...	...	...	...	...	...	...	...	...
Medical, dental, other health and veterinary services	...	...	...	...	...	...	...	...	...	...	...	...
C Recreational and cultural services	...	...	...	...	...	...	...	...	...	...	...	...
D Personal and household services [a]	...	...	...	...	...	...	...	...	...	...	...	...
Statistical discrepancy	...	...	...	...	...	...	...	...	...	...	...	...
Total, Industries	177040	40650	137680	14060	13090	356340	182150	41820	131340	14960	15740	354530
Producers of Government Services	47500	2800	-	460	-	50760	48140	2950	...	480	...	51570
Other Producers	1170	...	-	-	-	1170	1190	...	...	...	...	1190
Total	225710	43450	137680	14520	13090	408270	231480	44770	131340	15440	15740	407290
Less: Imputed bank service charge	...	...	16760	...	...	16760	...	...	16550	...	...	16550
Import duties	...	...	...	6100	...	6100	...	...	...	6880	...	6880
Value added tax [b]	...	...	...	32270	...	32270	...	...	...	34200	...	34200
Other adjustments	...	...	...	820	820	...	...	...	...	900	900	...
Total	225710	43450	120920	53710	13910	429880	231480	44770	114790	57420	16640	431820

a) Repair services are included in item 'Community, social and personal services'.
b) Item 'Value added tax' includes selective investment levy.

Netherlands Antilles

Source. Reply to the United Nations National Accounts Questionnaire from the Bureau Voor de Statistiek, Curacao. Official estimates together with detailed information on concepts, definitions, sources and methods of estimation utilized are published in 'Nationale Rekeningen, 1975'.

General note. The official estimates have been adjusted by the Bureau to conform to the United Nations System of National Accounts so far as the existing data would permit. It should be noted that estimates for Windward Islands are not included.

1.1 Expenditure on the Gross Domestic Product, in Current Prices

Million Netherlands Antillian guilders

	1970	1975	1978	1979	1980	1981	1982	1983	1984	1985	1986	1987
1 Government final consumption expenditure	...	...	...	469.1	568.3	649.1	726.7	...	...	...	...	...
2 Private final consumption expenditure	...	...	...	1305.1	1467.8	1702.9	1891.3	...	...	...	...	...
3 Gross capital formation	...	...	...	351.0	433.3	479.5	463.4	...	...	...	...	...
A Increase in stocks	...	...	...	88.7	49.3	64.9	35.3	...	...	...	...	...
B Gross fixed capital formation	...	...	...	262.3	384.0	414.6	428.1	...	...	...	...	...
4 Exports of goods and services [a]	...	...	...	1478.8	1791.2	1886.5	1787.6	...	...	...	...	...
5 Less: Imports of goods and services [a]	...	...	...	1730.4	2186.6	2313.9	2311.1	...	...	...	...	...
Equals: Gross Domestic Product	...	...	...	1873.6	2074.0	2404.1	2557.9	...	...	...	...	...

a) Exports and imports of merchandise are recorded on the basis of the crossing of frontiers. No data are available on the basis of changes in the ownership of the goods. Imports and exports are recorded on a cash basis and the imports and exports of oil refineries are not included in the estimates.

1.3 Cost Components of the Gross Domestic Product

Million Netherlands Antillian guilders

	1970	1975	1978	1979	1980	1981	1982	1983	1984	1985	1986	1987
1 Indirect taxes, net	...	...	...	120.3	137.5	131.8	123.3	...	...	...	...	...
A Indirect taxes	...	...	...	168.3	188.2	183.2	200.7	...	...	...	...	...
B Less: Subsidies	...	...	...	48.0	50.7	51.4	77.4	...	...	...	...	...
2 Consumption of fixed capital	...	...	...	140.0	158.1	187.4	206.1	...	...	...	...	...
3 Compensation of employees paid by resident producers to: [a]	...	...	...	1223.0	1442.1	1681.5	1865.8	...	...	...	...	...
A Resident households	...	...	...	1209.4	1403.3	1645.0	1823.6	...	...	...	...	...
B Rest of the world	...	...	...	13.6	38.8	36.5	42.2	...	...	...	...	...
4 Operating surplus	...	...	...	390.3	336.3	403.4	362.7	...	...	...	...	...
Equals: Gross Domestic Product [a]	...	...	...	1873.6	2074.0	2404.1	2557.9	...	...	...	...	...

a) The oil refineries in the Netherlands Antilles are now considered non-resident producers. Consequently, their compensation of employees to resident households is treated as wages and salaries paid by the rest of the world. Other cost components of these oil refineries are not included in GDP.

1.4 General Government Current Receipts and Disbursements

Million Netherlands Antillian guilders

	1970	1975	1978	1979	1980	1981	1982	1983	1984	1985	1986	1987
Receipts												
1 Operating surplus	...	...	...	-	-	-	-	...	...	...	...	...
2 Property and entrepreneurial income	...	...	...	20.4	8.2	28.5	12.7	...	...	...	...	...
3 Taxes, fees and contributions	...	...	...	511.9	608.5	707.6	741.1	...	...	...	...	...
A Indirect taxes	...	...	...	168.3	188.2	183.2	200.7	...	...	...	...	...
B Direct taxes [a]	...	...	...	264.8	328.7	409.7	410.7	...	...	...	...	...
C Social security contributions	...	...	...	73.3	86.1	107.5	124.4	...	...	...	...	...
D Compulsory fees, fines and penalties	...	...	...	5.5	5.5	7.2	5.3	...	...	...	...	...
4 Other current transfers [a]	...	...	...	148.1	215.3	289.1	434.5	...	...	...	...	...
Total Current Receipts of General Government	...	...	...	680.4	832.0	1025.2	1188.3	...	...	...	...	...
Disbursements												
1 Government final consumption expenditure	...	...	...	469.1	568.3	649.1	726.7	...	...	...	...	...
A Compensation of employees	...	...	...	342.2	395.5	469.1	536.4	...	...	...	...	...
B Consumption of fixed capital	...	...	...	7.2	8.1	9.9	11.1	...	...	...	...	...
C Purchases of goods and services, net	...	...	...	127.6	173.3	179.9	191.0	...	...	...	...	...
D Less: Own account fixed capital formation	...	...	...	8.4	9.1	10.4	12.4	...	...	...	...	...
E Indirect taxes paid, net	...	...	...	0.5	0.5	0.6	0.6	...	...	...	...	...
2 Property income	...	...	...	31.0	31.0	33.4	39.4	...	...	...	...	...
A Interest	...	...	...	31.0	31.0	33.4	39.4	...	...	...	...	...
B Net land rent and royalties	...	...	...	-	-	-	-	...	...	...	...	...

Netherlands Antilles

1.4 General Government Current Receipts and Disbursements
(Continued)

Million Netherlands Antillian guilders

	1970	1975	1978	1979	1980	1981	1982	1983	1984	1985	1986	1987
3 Subsidies	...	...	...	48.0	50.7	51.4	77.4	...	...	...	...	...
4 Other current transfers	...	...	...	147.5	172.3	206.0	236.1	...	...	...	...	...
A Social security benefits	...	...	...	71.3	80.4	102.2	116.3	...	...	...	...	...
B Social assistance grants	...	...	...	22.0	25.2	30.2	35.6	...	...	...	...	...
C Other	...	...	...	54.2	66.7	73.6	84.2	...	...	...	...	...
5 Net saving	...	...	...	-15.2	9.7	85.3	108.7	...	...	...	...	...
Total Current Disbursements and Net Saving of General Government	...	...	...	680.4	832.0	1025.2	1188.3	...	...	...	...	...

a) The profit taxes paid by the petroleum refineries and the off-shore companies are now considered as current transfers from the rest of the world.

1.7 External Transactions on Current Account, Summary

Million Netherlands Antillian guilders

	1970	1975	1978	1979	1980	1981	1982	1983	1984	1985	1986	1987
Payments to the Rest of the World												
1 Imports of goods and services [a]	...	...	...	1730.4	2186.6	2313.9	2311.1	...	...	...	...	...
A Imports of merchandise c.i.f.	...	...	...	1318.6	1610.0	1531.2	1636.4	...	...	...	...	...
B Other	...	...	...	411.8	576.6	782.7	674.7	...	...	...	...	...
2 Factor income to the rest of the world	...	...	...	101.6	141.0	110.8	111.8	...	...	...	...	...
A Compensation of employees	...	...	...	13.6	38.8	36.5	42.2	...	...	...	...	...
B Property and entrepreneurial income	...	...	...	88.0	102.2	74.3	69.6	...	...	...	...	...
By general government	...	...	...	21.5	21.8	17.9	17.2	...	...	...	...	...
By corporate and quasi-corporate enterprises	...	...	...	66.5	80.4	56.4	52.4	...	...	...	...	...
By other	...	...	...	-	-	-	-	...	...	...	...	...
3 Current transfers to the rest of the world	...	...	...	51.8	57.4	69.4	90.9	...	...	...	...	...
A Indirect taxes to supranational organizations	...	...	...	-	-	-	-	...	...	...	...	...
B Other current transfers	...	...	...	51.8	57.4	69.4	90.9	...	...	...	...	...
4 Surplus of the nation on current transactions	...	...	...	0.3	-89.0	44.0	109.2	...	...	...	...	...
Payments to the Rest of the World and Surplus of the Nation on Current Transactions	...	...	...	1884.1	2296.0	2538.1	2623.0	...	...	...	...	...
Receipts From The Rest of the World												
1 Exports of goods and services [a]	...	...	...	1478.8	1791.2	1886.5	1787.6	...	...	...	...	...
A Exports of merchandise f.o.b.	...	...	...	204.7	243.8	191.7	179.0	...	...	...	...	...
B Other	...	...	...	1274.1	1547.4	1694.8	1608.6	...	...	...	...	...
2 Factor income from rest of the world	...	...	...	254.6	288.6	360.1	416.6	...	...	...	...	...
A Compensation of employees [b]	...	...	...	202.0	231.6	255.4	287.5	...	...	...	...	...
B Property and entrepreneurial income	...	...	...	52.6	57.0	104.7	129.1	...	...	...	...	...
By general government	...	...	...	-	-	-	-	...	...	...	...	...
By corporate and quasi-corporate enterprises	...	...	...	39.9	39.2	33.5	41.9	...	...	...	...	...
By other	...	...	...	12.7	17.8	71.2	87.2	...	...	...	...	...
3 Current transfers from rest of the world	...	...	...	150.7	216.2	291.5	418.8	...	...	...	...	...
A Subsidies from supranational organisations	...	...	...	-	-	-	-	...	...	...	...	...
B Other current transfers	...	...	...	150.7	216.2	291.5	418.8	...	...	...	...	...
Receipts from the Rest of the World on Current Transactions	...	...	...	1884.1	2296.0	2538.1	2623.0	...	...	...	...	...

a) Exports and imports of merchandise are recorded on the basis of the crossing of frontiers. No data are available on the basis of changes in the ownership of the goods. Imports and exports are recorded on a cash basis and the imports and exports of oil refineries are not included in the estimates.

b) The oil refineries in the Netherlands Antilles are now considered non-resident producers. Consequently, their compensation of employees to resident households is treated as wages and salaries paid by the rest of the world. Other cost components of these oil refineries are not included in GDP.

Netherlands Antilles

1.8 Capital Transactions of The Nation, Summary

Million Netherlands Antillian guilders	1970	1975	1978	1979	1980	1981	1982	1983	1984	1985	1986	1987
Finance of Gross Capital Formation											
Gross saving	...	...	...	351.3	344.3	523.5	572.6	...	...	...	...	...
1 Consumption of fixed capital	...	...	...	140.0	158.1	187.4	206.1	...	...	...	...	...
A General government	...	...	...	7.2	8.1	9.9	11.1	...	...	...	...	...
B Corporate and quasi-corporate enterprises	...	...	...	132.8	150.0	177.5	195.0	...	...	...	...	...
C Other	...	...	...	...	...	...	...	...	...	...	...	...
2 Net saving	...	...	...	211.3	186.2	336.1	366.5	...	...	...	...	...
A General government	...	...	...	-15.2	9.7	85.3	108.8	...	...	...	...	...
B Corporate and quasi-corporate enterprises	...	...	...	89.5	176.5	250.8	257.7	...	...	...	...	...
C Other	...	...	...	137.0	...	...	...	...	...	...	...	...
Less: Surplus of the nation on current transactions	...	...	...	0.3	-89.0	44.0	109.2	...	...	...	...	...
Finance of Gross Capital Formation	...	...	...	351.0	433.3	479.5	463.4	...	...	...	...	...
Gross Capital Formation											
Increase in stocks	...	...	...	88.7	49.3	64.9	35.3	...	...	...	...	...
Gross fixed capital formation	...	...	...	262.3	384.0	414.6	428.1	...	...	...	...	...
1 General government	...	...	...	57.4	44.9	39.4	51.0	...	...	...	...	...
2 Corporate and quasi-corporate enterprises	...	...	...	204.9	339.1	375.2	377.1	...	...	...	...	...
3 Other	...	...	...	...	...	...	...	...	...	...	...	...
Gross Capital Formation	...	...	...	351.0	433.3	479.5	463.4	...	...	...	...	...

1.9 Gross Domestic Product by Institutional Sectors of Origin

Million Netherlands Antillian guilders	1970	1975	1978	1979	1980	1981	1982	1983	1984	1985	1986	1987
Domestic Factor Incomes Originating											
1 General government	...	...	...	342.2	395.5	469.1	536.4	...	...	...	...	...
2 Corporate and quasi-corporate enterprises	...	...	...					...	...	...	...	...
3 Households and private unincorporated enterprises	...	...	...	1271.1	1382.9	1615.8	1692.1	...	...	...	...	...
4 Non-profit institutions serving households	...	...	...					...	...	...	...	...
Subtotal: Domestic Factor Incomes	...	...	...	1613.3	1778.4	2084.9	2228.5	...	...	...	...	...
Indirect taxes, net	...	...	...	120.3	137.5	131.8	123.3	...	...	...	...	...
A Indirect taxes	...	...	...	168.3	188.2	183.2	200.7	...	...	...	...	...
B Less: Subsidies	...	...	...	48.0	50.7	51.4	77.4	...	...	...	...	...
Consumption of fixed capital	...	...	...	140.0	158.1	187.4	206.1	...	...	...	...	...
Gross Domestic Product	...	...	...	1873.6	2074.0	2404.1	2557.9	...	...	...	...	...

1.10 Gross Domestic Product by Kind of Activity, in Current Prices

Million Netherlands Antillian guilders	1970	1975	1978	1979	1980	1981	1982	1983	1984	1985	1986	1987
1 Agriculture, hunting, forestry and fishing	...	...	...	9.1	11.5	10.3	10.8	...	...	...	...	...
2 Mining and quarrying	...	...	...					...	...	...	...	...
3 Manufacturing	...	...	...	133.5	159.8	172.9	185.6	...	...	...	...	...
4 Electricity, gas and water	...	...	...	38.6	40.3	57.3	54.9	...	...	...	...	...
5 Construction	...	...	...	155.6	186.8	190.1	198.3	...	...	...	...	...
6 Wholesale and retail trade, restaurants and hotels	...	...	...	489.5	531.8	636.0	668.7	...	...	...	...	...
7 Transport, storage and communication	...	...	...	337.0	353.8	379.0	336.0	...	...	...	...	...
8 Finance, insurance, real estate and business services	...	...	...	274.4	293.4	351.2	387.3	...	...	...	...	...
9 Community, social and personal services	...	...	...	146.2	161.7	205.0	250.4	...	...	...	...	...

Netherlands Antilles

1.10 Gross Domestic Product by Kind of Activity, in Current Prices
(Continued)

Million Netherlands Antillian guilders

	1970	1975	1978	1979	1980	1981	1982	1983	1984	1985	1986	1987
Total, Industries	...	...	...	1583.9	1739.1	2001.8	2092.0	...	...	...	...	...
Producers of Government Services	...	...	...	349.9	404.1	479.6	548.1	...	...	...	...	...
Other Producers	...	...	...	...	...	...	...	...	...	...	...	...
Subtotal	...	...	...	1933.8	2143.2	2481.4	2640.1	...	...	...	...	...
Less: Imputed bank service charge	...	...	...	60.2	69.2	77.3	82.2	...	...	...	...	...
Plus: Import duties	...	...	...	...	...	...	...	...	...	...	...	...
Plus: Value added tax	...	...	...	...	...	...	...	...	...	...	...	...
Equals: Gross Domestic Product	...	...	...	1873.6	2074.0	2404.1	2557.9	...	...	...	...	...

1.12 Relations Among National Accounting Aggregates

Million Netherlands Antillian guilders

	1970	1975	1978	1979	1980	1981	1982	1983	1984	1985	1986	1987
Gross Domestic Product	...	...	...	1873.6	2074.0	2404.1	2557.9	...	...	...	...	...
Plus: Net factor income from the rest of the world	...	...	...	153.0	147.6	249.3	304.8	...	...	...	...	...
Factor income from the rest of the world	...	...	...	254.6	288.6	360.1	416.6	...	...	...	...	...
Less: Factor income to the rest of the world	...	...	...	101.6	141.0	110.8	111.8	...	...	...	...	...
Equals: Gross National Product	...	...	...	2026.6	2221.6	2653.4	2862.7	...	...	...	...	...
Less: Consumption of fixed capital	...	...	...	140.0	158.1	187.4	206.1	...	...	...	...	...
Equals: National Income	...	...	...	1886.6	2063.5	2466.0	2656.6	...	...	...	...	...
Plus: Net current transfers from the rest of the world	...	...	...	98.9	158.8	222.1	327.9	...	...	...	...	...
Current transfers from the rest of the world	...	...	...	150.7	216.2	291.5	418.8	...	...	...	...	...
Less: Current transfers to the rest of the world	...	...	...	51.8	57.4	69.4	90.9	...	...	...	...	...
Equals: National Disposable Income	...	...	...	1985.5	2222.3	2688.1	2984.5	...	...	...	...	...
Less: Final consumption	...	...	...	1774.2	2036.1	2352.0	2618.0	...	...	...	...	...
Equals: Net Saving	...	...	...	211.3	186.2	336.1	366.5	...	...	...	...	...
Less: Surplus of the nation on current transactions	...	...	...	0.3	-89.0	44.0	109.2	...	...	...	...	...
Equals: Net Capital Formation	...	...	...	211.0	275.2	292.1	257.3	...	...	...	...	...

2.1 Government Final Consumption Expenditure by Function, in Current Prices

Million Netherlands Antillian guilders

	1970	1975	1978	1979	1980	1981	1982	1983	1984	1985	1986	1987
1 General public services	...	...	...	72.7	82.1	106.6	130.3	...	...	...	...	...
2 Defence	...	...	...	-	20.5	10.9	1.7	...	...	...	...	...
3 Public order and safety	...	...	...	47.0	49.7	69.1	81.6	...	...	...	...	...
4 Education	...	...	...	120.3	150.9	179.7	198.4	...	...	...	...	...
5 Health [a]	...	...	...	36.6	42.0	48.2	51.6	...	...	...	...	...
6 Social security and welfare	...	...	...	82.7	101.2	114.7	130.1	...	...	...	...	...
7 Housing and community amenities [a]	...	...	...	...	...	...	...	...	...	...	...	...
8 Recreational, cultural and religious affairs	...	...	...	11.5	12.3	14.8	16.6	...	...	...	...	...
9 Economic services	...	...	...	60.4	66.0	66.2	69.5	...	...	...	...	...
A Fuel and energy	...	...	...					...	...	...	...	...
B Agriculture, forestry, fishing and hunting	...	...	...	31.0	37.5	45.2	44.2	...	...	...	...	...
C Mining, manufacturing and construction, except fuel and energy	...	...	...					...	...	...	...	...
D Transportation and communication	...	...	...	29.4	28.5	21.0	25.3	...	...	...	...	...
E Other economic affairs	...	...	...	-	-	-	-	...	...	...	...	...
10 Other functions	...	...	...	37.9	43.6	38.9	46.9	...	...	...	...	...
Total Government Final Consumption Expenditure [b]	...	...	...	469.1	568.3	649.1	726.7	...	...	...	...	...

a) Housing and community amenities are included in health.
b) The estimates of government final consumption expenditure include estimates of non-commodity sales and commodities produced for which there is no available breakdown.

Netherlands Antilles

2.3 Total Government Outlays by Function and Type

Million Netherlands Antillian guilders

		Final Consumption Expenditures			Other Current	Total Current	Gross Capital	Other Capital	Total
		Total	Compensation of Employees	Other	Subsidies	Transfers & Property Income	Disbursements	Formation	Outlays	Outlays

1980

1	General public services [a]	82.1	67.3	14.8	-	38.1	120.2	9.4	...	...
2	Defence	20.5	-	20.5	-	-	20.5	-	...	...
3	Public order and safety	49.7	43.4	6.3	-	-	49.7	5.2	...	...
4	Education	150.9	131.6	19.3	-	14.8	165.7	10.5	...	...
5	Health [b]	42.0	28.4	13.6	1.4	-	43.4	3.1	...	...
6	Social security and welfare	101.2	43.0	58.2	-	108.7	209.9	0.3	...	...
7	Housing and community amenities [b]	...	...	...	...	...	...	...	...	...
8	Recreation, culture and religion	12.3	6.9	5.4	-	2.1	14.4	2.0	...	...
9	Economic services	66.0	32.5	33.5	49.2	-	115.2	13.1	...	...
	A Fuel and energy								...	...
	B Agriculture, forestry, fishing and hunting	37.5	24.4	13.1	48.5	-	86.0	6.0		
	C Mining (except fuels), manufacturing and construction								...	...
	D Transportation and communication	28.5	8.1	20.4	0.7	-	29.2	7.1	...	...
	E Other economic affairs	-	-	-	-	-	-	-	...	...
10	Other functions	43.6	35.7	7.9	0.1	39.6	83.3	1.3	...	...
	Total [c]	568.3	388.8	179.5	50.7	203.3	822.3	44.9	64.9	932.1

1981

1	General public services [a]	106.6	84.7	21.9	-	41.6	148.2	8.5	...	...
2	Defence	10.9	0.1	10.8	-	-	10.9	-	...	...
3	Public order and safety	69.1	60.0	9.1	-	-	69.1	2.0	...	...
4	Education	179.7	157.3	22.4	-	16.8	196.5	6.8	...	...
5	Health [b]	48.2	33.4	14.8	-	-	48.2	4.8	...	...
6	Social security and welfare	114.7	45.0	69.7	0.4	136.7	251.8	1.2	...	...
7	Housing and community amenities [b]	...	...	...	...	...	...	...	...	...
8	Recreation, culture and religion	14.8	8.0	6.8	0.2	2.0	17.0	3.6	...	...
9	Economic services	66.2	38.6	27.6	50.5	-	116.7	9.7	...	...
	A Fuel and energy								...	...
	B Agriculture, forestry, fishing and hunting	45.2	28.3	16.9	45.3	-	90.5	6.6		
	C Mining (except fuels), manufacturing and construction								...	...
	D Transportation and communication	21.0	10.3	10.7	5.2	-	26.2	3.1	...	...
	E Other economic affairs	-	-	-	-	-	-	-	...	...
10	Other functions	38.9	34.1	4.8	0.3	42.3	81.5	2.8	...	...
	Total [c]	649.1	461.2	187.9	51.4	239.4	939.9	39.4	63.3	1042.6

1982

1	General public services [a]	130.2	103.1	27.1	-	50.2	180.4	7.3	...	...
2	Defence	1.7	0.1	1.6	-	-	1.7	-	...	...
3	Public order and safety	81.6	69.4	12.2	-	-	81.6	2.5	...	...
4	Education	198.4	172.9	25.5	-	15.8	214.2	6.0	...	...
5	Health [b]	51.7	38.5	13.2	5.5	-	57.2	10.2	...	...
6	Social security and welfare	130.1	52.1	78.0	-	156.8	286.9	0.4	...	...
7	Housing and community amenities [b]	...	...	...	...	...	...	...	...	...
8	Recreation, culture and religion	16.6	9.6	7.0	0.3	2.4	19.3	8.4	...	...
9	Economic services	69.5	43.7	25.8	70.7	-	140.2	13.3	...	...

Netherlands Antilles

2.3 Total Government Outlays by Function and Type
(Continued)

Million Netherlands Antillian guilders

	Final Consumption Expenditures Total	Compensation of Employees	Other	Subsidies	Other Current Transfers & Property Income	Total Current Disbursements	Gross Capital Formation	Other Capital Outlays	Total Outlays
A Fuel and energy								...	...
B Agriculture, forestry, fishing and hunting	44.2	31.0	13.2	63.9	-	108.1	9.6	...	...
C Mining (except fuels), manufacturing and construction								...	...
D Transportation and communication	25.3	12.7	12.6	6.8	-	32.1	3.7	...	...
E Other economic affairs	-	-	-	-	-			...	...
10 Other functions	46.9	38.5	8.4	0.9	50.3	98.1	2.9	...	...
Total c	726.7	527.9	198.8	77.4	275.5	1079.6	51.0	72.4	1203.0

a) General public services of column 5 includes the total amount of unfunded employee pension and welfare benefits for which there is no available breakdown.
b) Housing and community amenities are included in health.
c) The estimates of government final consumption expenditure include estimates of non-commodity sales and commodities produced for which there is no available breakdown.

2.17 Exports and Imports of Goods and Services, Detail

Million Netherlands Antillian guilders

	1970	1975	1978	1979	1980	1981	1982	1983	1984	1985	1986	1987
Exports of Goods and Services												
1 Exports of merchandise, f.o.b.	...	...	...	204.7	243.8	191.7	179.0	...	...	...	...	...
2 Transport and communication	...	...	...	439.3	493.2	474.2	377.3	...	...	...	...	...
3 Insurance service charges	...	...	...					...	...	...	...	...
4 Other commodities	...	...	...	135.1	188.8	239.9	247.4	...	...	...	...	...
5 Adjustments of merchandise exports to change-of-ownership basis	...	...	...	...	...	...	...	...	...	...	...	...
6 Direct purchases in the domestic market by non-residential households	...	...	...	569.7	714.7	785.7	759.4	...	...	...	...	...
7 Direct purchases in the domestic market by extraterritorial bodies	...	...	...	130.0	150.7	195.0	224.5	...	...	...	...	...
Total Exports of Goods and Services a	...	...	...	1478.8	1791.2	1886.5	1787.6	...	...	...	...	...
Imports of Goods and Services												
1 Imports of merchandise, c.i.f.	...	...	...	1318.6	1610.0	1531.2	1636.4	...	...	...	...	...
2 Adjustments of merchandise imports to change-of-ownership basis	...	...	...	...	...	...	...	...	...	...	...	...
3 Other transport and communication	...	...	...	98.7	113.3	165.6	153.9	...	...	...	...	...
4 Other insurance service charges	...	...	...	...	...	...	...	...	...	...	...	...
5 Other commodities	...	...	...	211.5	346.6	485.7	366.4	...	...	...	...	...
6 Direct purchases abroad by government	...	...	...	8.6	12.7	13.4	12.9	...	...	...	...	...
7 Direct purchases abroad by resident households	...	...	...	93.0	104.0	118.0	141.5	...	...	...	...	...
Total Imports of Goods and Services a	...	...	...	1730.4	2186.6	2313.9	2311.1	...	...	...	...	...
Balance of Goods and Services	...	...	...	-251.6	-395.4	-427.4	-523.5	...	...	...	...	...
Total Imports and Balance of Goods and Services	...	...	...	1478.8	1791.2	1886.5	1787.6	...	...	...	...	...

a) Exports and imports of merchandise are recorded on the basis of the crossing of frontiers. No data are available on the basis of changes in the ownership of the goods.

New Caledonia

Source. Reply to the United Nations National Accounts Questionnaire from the Institute national de la statistique et des etudes economiques (INSEE), Paris.

General note. The estimates shown in the following tables have been adjusted by the INSEE to conform to the United Nations System of National Accounts so far as the existing data would permit.

1.1 Expenditure on the Gross Domestic Product, in Current Prices

Million CFP francs

	1970	1975	1978	1979	1980	1981	1982	1983	1984	1985	1986	1987
1 Government final consumption expenditure [a,b]	2852	12514	19313	21851	25334	29473	35631	39773	46037	52831	...	...
2 Private final consumption expenditure [a]	19686	33256	39483	44240	49575	57147	65935	68606	72488	76497	...	...
3 Gross capital formation	18641	18553	15245	13285	19772	16362	19637	19145	18405	19579	...	...
A Increase in stocks	450	...	-1442	-5900	-619	-904	-1247	-817	-2933	-1963	...	...
B Gross fixed capital formation	18191	...	16687	19185	20391	17266	20884	19962	21338	21542	...	...
Residential buildings	...	3084	...	...	...	...	...	...	...	...	...	...
Non-residential buildings	...	...	...	...	...	...	...	...	...	...	...	...
Other construction and land improvement etc.	...	...	...	...	...	...	...	...	...	...	...	...
Other	...	...	...	...	...	...	...	...	...	...	...	...
4 Exports of goods and services	19647	26650	20051	30184	31908	33794	30295	30964	42951	46680	...	...
5 Less: Imports of goods and services	24437	27966	25759	29643	37050	40631	43719	44763	53211	55484	...	...
Statistical discrepancy [b,c]	1815	636	1087	1089	1308	159	314	436	-181	-453	...	...
Equals: Gross Domestic Product	38204	63643	69420	81006	90847	96304	108093	114161	126489	139650	...	...

a) Beginning 1972, education and health are included in item 'Government final consumption expenditure' rather than in item 'Private final consumption expenditure'.
b) Government final consumption expenditure estimates are under-estimated since the system of national accounts used treats the government sector separately. Therefore this under estimation is rectified as a statistical discrepancy.
c) The accounting reconciliation is done at the level of the gross domestic production instead of gross domestic product. Therefore the statistical discrepancy reflects mainly the domestic salaries not accounted for elsewhere.

1.3 Cost Components of the Gross Domestic Product

Million CFP francs

	1970	1975	1978	1979	1980	1981	1982	1983	1984	1985	1986	1987
1 Indirect taxes, net	4152	3266	3142	4540	3159	3708	3611	3543	4400	2837	...	...
A Indirect taxes	4742	4712	...	...	...	7312	8036	8372	9617	8567	...	...
B Less: Subsidies	590	1446	...	...	...	3604	4425	4829	5217	5730	...	...
2 Consumption of fixed capital	16699	11911	9979	12161	13694	9881	11594	10083	11482	11887	...	...
3 Compensation of employees paid by resident producers to:	15984	32833	41956	46563	55190	51492	61318	66930	73810	82201	...	...
4 Operating surplus	1369	15633	14343	17742	18804	31223	31570	33605	36797	42725	...	...
Equals: Gross Domestic Product	38204	63643	69420	81006	90847	96304	108093	114161	126489	139650	...	...

1.4 General Government Current Receipts and Disbursements

Million CFP francs

	1970	1975	1978	1979	1980	1981	1982	1983	1984	1985	1986	1987
Receipts												
1 Operating surplus	...	...	...	...	...	...	...	...	...	...	...	...
2 Property and entrepreneurial income	...	...	...	...	...	...	...	...	...	...	...	...
3 Taxes, fees and contributions	...	...	...	...	...	19268	21359	24217	28279	...	...	...
A Indirect taxes	...	...	...	...	...	7312	8036	8372	9617	...	...	...
B Direct taxes	...	...	...	...	...	4983	5082	6490	7417	...	...	...
C Social security contributions	...	...	...	...	...	6973	8241	9355	11245	...	...	...
D Compulsory fees, fines and penalties	...	...	...	...	...	...	...	...	...	...	...	...
4 Other current transfers	...	...	...	...	...	30013	35952	40370	42875	...	...	...
Total Current Receipts of General Government	...	...	...	...	...	49281	57311	64587	71154	...	...	...
Disbursements												
1 Government final consumption expenditure	...	...	...	...	...	29473	35631	39773	46037	...	...	...
A Compensation of employees	...	...	...	...	...	21703	26084	29337	33679	...	...	...
B Consumption of fixed capital	...	...	...	...	...	...	...	...	...	...	...	...
C Purchases of goods and services, net	...	...	...	...	...	6339	7840	8236	9185	...	...	...
D Less: Own account fixed capital formation	...	...	...	...	...	...	...	...	...	...	...	...
E Indirect taxes paid, net	...	...	...	...	...	1431	1707	2200	3173	...	...	...
2 Property income	...	...	...	...	...	...	...	...	...	...	...	...

New Caledonia

1.4 General Government Current Receipts and Disbursements
(Continued)

Million CFP francs

	1970	1975	1978	1979	1980	1981	1982	1983	1984	1985	1986	1987
3 Subsidies	...	...	...	...	...	3604	4425	4829	5217	...	...	...
4 Other current transfers	...	...	...	...	...	11663	14307	16938	18403	...	...	...
A Social security benefits	...	...	...	...	...	3921	4713	5936	7021	...	...	...
B Social assistance grants	...	...	...	...	...	5107	6116	6698	7588	...	...	...
C Other	...	...	...	...	...	2635	3478	4304	3794	...	...	...
5 Net saving	...	...	...	...	...	4541	2948	3047	1497	...	...	...
Total Current Disbursements and Net Saving of General Government	...	...	...	...	...	49281	57311	64587	71154	...	...	...

1.5 Current Income and Outlay of Corporate and Quasi-Corporate Enterprises, Summary

Million CFP francs

	1970	1975	1978	1979	1980	1981	1982	1983	1984	1985	1986	1987
					Receipts							
1 Operating surplus	...	...	...	...	...	41104	43164	43688	48279	...	...	...
2 Property and entrepreneurial income received	...	...	...	...	...	717	784	1675	2193	...	...	...
3 Current transfers	...	...	...	...	...	...	...	...	...	...	...	...
Total Current Receipts	...	...	...	...	...	41821	43948	45363	50472	...	...	...
					Disbursements							
1 Property and entrepreneurial income	...	...	...	...	...	18383	20995	22286	22616	...	...	...
2 Direct taxes and other current payments to general government	...	...	...	...	...	3979	3253	3746	3670	...	...	...
3 Other current transfers	...	...	...	...	...	3034	3903	3888	4231	...	...	...
4 Net saving	...	...	...	...	...	16425	15797	15443	19955	...	...	...
Total Current Disbursements and Net Saving	...	...	...	...	...	41821	43948	45363	50472	...	...	...

1.6 Current Income and Outlay of Households and Non-Profit Institutions

Million CFP francs

	1970	1975	1978	1979	1980	1981	1982	1983	1984	1985	1986	1987
					Receipts							
1 Compensation of employees	...	...	...	...	...	43801	52226	56677	61563	...	...	...
2 Operating surplus of private unincorporated enterprises	...	...	...	...	...	18383	20995	22286	22616	...	...	...
3 Property and entrepreneurial income	...	...	...	...	...	...	...	...	...	...	...	...
4 Current transfers	...	...	...	...	...	13070	16281	19082	20948	...	...	...
A Social security benefits	...	...	...	...	...	3921	4713	5936	7021	...	...	...
B Social assistance grants	...	...	...	...	...	5107	6116	6698	7588	...	...	...
C Other	...	...	...	...	...	4042	5452	6448	6339	...	...	...
Total Current Receipts	...	...	...	...	...	75254	89502	98045	105127	...	...	...
					Disbursements							
1 Private final consumption expenditure	...	...	...	...	...	57147	65935	68606	72488	...	...	...
2 Property income	...	...	...	...	...	...	...	...	...	...	...	...
3 Direct taxes and other current transfers n.e.c. to general government	...	...	...	...	...	1208	2070	3010	4074	...	...	...
A Social security contributions	...	...	...	...	...	204	241	266	327	...	...	...
B Direct taxes	...	...	...	...	...	1004	1829	2744	3747	...	...	...
C Fees, fines and penalties	...	...	...	...	...	...	...	...	...	...	...	...
4 Other current transfers	...	...	...	...	...	2193	2955	3932	4240	...	...	...
5 Net saving	...	...	...	...	...	14706	18542	22497	24325	...	...	...
Total Current Disbursements and Net Saving	...	...	...	...	...	75254	89502	98045	105127	...	...	...

1.7 External Transactions on Current Account, Summary

Million CFP francs

	1970	1975	1978	1979	1980	1981	1982	1983	1984	1985	1986	1987
				Payments to the Rest of the World								
1 Imports of goods and services	24437	27966	25759	29643	37050	40631	43719	44763	53211	55484	...	...
A Imports of merchandise c.i.f.	23069	27049	...	...	...	...	...	...	...	...	...	...
B Other	1368	917	...	...	...	...	...	...	...	...	...	...
2 Factor income to the rest of the world	...	...	...	...	...	...	...	...	...	...	...	...

New Caledonia

1.7 External Transactions on Current Account, Summary
(Continued)

Million CFP francs

	1970	1975	1978	1979	1980	1981	1982	1983	1984	1985	1986	1987
3 Current transfers to the rest of the world	59	109	312	375	470	...	...	...	...	...	...	...
4 Surplus of the nation on current transactions	-1256	7857	11159	20847	18952	20238	18612	21842	27372	34152	...	...
Payments to the Rest of the World and Surplus of the Nation on Current Transactions	23240	35932	37230	50865	56472	60869	62331	66605	80583	89636	...	...
Receipts From The Rest of the World												
1 Exports of goods and services	19647	26650	20051	30184	31908	33794	30295	30964	42951	46680	...	...
A Exports of merchandise f.o.b.	19277	25809	...	...	...	...	...	...	...	...	...	...
B Other	370	841	...	...	...	...	...	...	...	...	...	...
2 Factor income from rest of the world	...	...	...	...	...	...	...	...	...	...	...	...
3 Current transfers from rest of the world	3593	9282	17179	20681	24565	27075	32036	35641	37632	42956	...	...
Receipts from the Rest of the World on Current Transactions	23240	35932	37230	50865	56472	60869	62331	66605	80583	89636	...	...

1.10 Gross Domestic Product by Kind of Activity, in Current Prices

Million CFP francs

	1970	1975	1978	1979	1980	1981	1982	1983	1984	1985	1986	1987
1 Agriculture, hunting, forestry and fishing	1643	1901	2196	2340	2719	1429	1820	2155	2252	2581	...	...
2 Mining and quarrying	10981	16368	7106	12902	14472	15901	13476	10591	16379	21739	...	...
3 Manufacturing	1373	4003	4289	4872	5231	4030	4985	5892	6215	6497	...	...
4 Electricity, gas and water	594	1658	1588	1810	2319	2332	2091	2318	2491	3239	...	...
5 Construction	1488	8588	7760	8240	8279	5432	6782	5290	5301	4749	...	...
6 Wholesale and retail trade, restaurants and hotels [a]	13158	12889	15339	16952	19351	24287	28395	30483	31274	33277	...	...
7 Transport, storage and communication	1178	2611	2408	2769	3395	4288	4761	4917	4227	4741	...	...
8 Finance, insurance, real estate and business services	3605	4192	11972	12226	13377	14549	16900	19814	20169	20153	...	...
9 Community, social and personal services [a]		629									...	...
Total, Industries	34020	52839	52658	62111	69142	72248	79210	81460	88308	96976	...	...
Producers of Government Services	3847	10068	15775	17806	20447	23134	27791	31537	36852	41407	...	...
Other Producers	337	736	987	1089	1258	922	1092	1164	1329	1267	...	...
Subtotal	38204	63643	69420	81006	90847	96304	108093	114161	126489	139650	...	...
Less: Imputed bank service charge	...	...	...	...	...	...	...	...	...	...	...	...
Plus: Import duties	...	...	...	...	...	...	...	...	...	...	...	...
Plus: Value added tax	...	...	...	...	...	...	...	...	...	...	...	...
Equals: Gross Domestic Product	38204	63643	69420	81006	90847	96304	108093	114161	126489	139650	...	...

a) Restaurants and hotels are included in item 'Community, social and personal services'.

2.17 Exports and Imports of Goods and Services, Detail

Million CFP francs

	1970	1975	1978	1979	1980	1981	1982	1983	1984	1985	1986	1987
Exports of Goods and Services												
1 Exports of merchandise, f.o.b.	19277	25809	...	...	...	...	...	...	...	...	...	...
2 Transport and communication	...	...	...	...	...	...	...	...	...	...	...	...
3 Insurance service charges	...	...	...	...	...	...	...	...	...	...	...	...
4 Other commodities	...	...	...	...	...	...	...	...	...	...	...	...
5 Adjustments of merchandise exports to change-of-ownership basis	...	...	...	...	...	...	...	...	...	...	...	...
6 Direct purchases in the domestic market by non-residential households	370	841	...	...	...	...	...	...	...	...	...	...
7 Direct purchases in the domestic market by extraterritorial bodies	...	...	...	...	...	...	...	...	...	...	...	...
Total Exports of Goods and Services	19647	26650	...	...	...	...	...	...	...	...	...	...
Imports of Goods and Services												
1 Imports of merchandise, c.i.f.	23069	27049	...	...	...	...	...	...	...	...	...	...

New Caledonia

2.17 Exports and Imports of Goods and Services, Detail
(Continued)

Million CFP francs

	1970	1975	1978	1979	1980	1981	1982	1983	1984	1985	1986	1987
2 Adjustments of merchandise imports to change-of-ownership basis	...	...	...	...	...	...	...	...	...	...	...	...
3 Other transport and communication	...	...	...	...	...	...	...	...	...	...	...	...
4 Other insurance service charges	...	...	...	...	...	...	...	...	...	...	...	...
5 Other commodities	...	...	...	...	...	...	...	...	...	...	...	...
6 Direct purchases abroad by government	1368	917	...	...	...	...	...	...	...	...	...	...
7 Direct purchases abroad by resident households			...	...	...	...	...	...	...	...	...	...
Total Imports of Goods and Services	24437	27966	...	...	...	...	...	...	...	...	...	...
Balance of Goods and Services	-4790	-1316	...	...	...	...	...	...	...	...	...	...
Total Imports and Balance of Goods and Services	19647	26650	...	...	...	...	...	...	...	...	...	...

New Zealand

Source. Reply to the United Nations National Accounts Questionnaire from the Department of Statistics, Wellington. The official estimates and descriptions are published by the Department in the 'Annual Series National Income and Expenditure' and as appendices to the 'Monthly Abstract of Statistics'.

General note. The official estimates of New Zealand have been adjusted by the Department of Statistics to conform to the United Nations System of National Accounts so far as the existing data would permit.

1.1 Expenditure on the Gross Domestic Product, in Current Prices

Million New Zealand dollars — Fiscal year beginning 1 April

	1970	1975	1978	1979	1980	1981	1982	1983	1984	1985	1986	1987
1 Government final consumption expenditure	770	1732	2882	3314	4134	4988	5554	5839	6208	7321	8815	10424
2 Private final consumption expenditure	3742	7098	10353	12105	14244	16626	18640	20134	22777	26861	31290	35621
A Households	...	7010	10197	11921	14023	16348	18347	19846	22459	26488	30828	35082
B Private non-profit institutions serving households	...	88	156	184	221	278	293	288	318	373	462	539
3 Gross capital formation	1418	3705	3634	4537	4797	6887	8145	8997	11087	12076	13040	12723
A Increase in stocks a	204	459	-246	470	43	290	318	542	1482	632	1197	-368
B Gross fixed capital formation	1214	3246	3880	4067	4754	6597	7827	8455	9605	11444	11843	13091
Residential buildings	...	769	716	731	881	1180	1333	1556	1785	2081	2416	2695
Non-residential buildings	...	612	762	747	821	1034	1182	1243	1471	2001	2421	3067
Other construction and land improvement etc.	...	512	657	679	808	1136	1327	1372	1365	1480	1504	1194
Other	...	1352	1744	1909	2244	3247	3985	4285	4984	5881	5502	6135
4 Exports of goods and services	1296	2666	4687	5996	7003	8249	9116	10699	13317	14037	15052	16468
5 Less: Imports of goods and services	1456	3430	4647	6256	7272	9168	10318	11090	14859	15093	15048	16072
Statistical discrepancy	62	-102	-52	-9	41	163	-41	-272	307	-342	-69	94
Equals: Gross Domestic Product	5832	11668	16856	19688	22947	27745	31097	34307	38838	44861	53079	59257

a) From 1977 onward, stock valuation adjustment is made for the estimates of value of physical increase in stocks.

1.2 Expenditure on the Gross Domestic Product, in Constant Prices

Million New Zealand dollars — Fiscal year beginning 1 April

	1970	1975	1978	1979	1980	1981	1982	1983	1984	1985	1986	1987
				At constant prices of:1982								
1 Government final consumption expenditure	...	...	...	...	...	...	5554	5701	5722	5867	5957	6104
2 Private final consumption expenditure	...	...	...	...	...	...	18640	19089	19756	19852	20449	20811
A Households	...	...	...	...	...	...	18347	18795	19450	19526	20095	20455
B Private non-profit institutions serving households	...	...	...	...	...	...	293	294	306	326	354	356
3 Gross capital formation	...	...	...	...	...	...	8145	8555	9670	9057	8920	8571
A Increase in stocks a	...	...	...	...	...	...	318	283	1105	123	649	-238
B Gross fixed capital formation	...	...	...	...	...	...	7827	8272	8565	8934	8271	8809
Residential buildings	...	...	...	...	...	...	1333	1473	1558	1593	1487	1503
Non-residential buildings	...	...	...	...	...	...	1182	1201	1341	1632	1749	2077
Other construction and land improvement etc.	...	...	...	...	...	...	1327	1330	1235	1194	1077	809
Other	...	...	...	...	...	...	3985	4265	4430	4514	3958	4420
4 Exports of goods and services	...	...	...	...	...	...	9116	9756	10516	10811	11163	11695
5 Less: Imports of goods and services	...	...	...	...	...	...	10317	10283	11588	11185	11429	12766
Statistical discrepancy	...	...	...	...	...	...	-41	-875	-352	-131	-325	226
Equals: Gross Domestic Product	...	...	...	...	...	...	31097	31943	33724	34271	34735	34641

a) From 1977 onward, stock valuation adjustment is made for the estimates of value of physical increase in stocks.

New Zealand

1.3 Cost Components of the Gross Domestic Product

Million New Zealand dollars

Fiscal year beginning 1 April

	1970	1975	1978	1979	1980	1981	1982	1983	1984	1985	1986	1987
1 Indirect taxes, net	518	712	1297	1646	1996	2336	2685	3192	3944	4476	6320	8442
A Indirect taxes	577	1103	1725	1998	2344	2914	3440	3847	4545	4848	6610	8711
B Less: Subsidies	59	391	428	352	348	578	755	655	601	372	290	269
2 Consumption of fixed capital	523	940	1297	1465	1679	1925	2222	2623	3133	3636	4096	4562
3 Compensation of employees paid by resident producers to:	2945	6269	9399	10961	13026	15689	17195	17496	19028	22093	25830	28815
A Resident households	2945	6269	9399	10961	13026	15689	17195	17496	19028	22093	25830	28815
B Rest of the world	-	-	...	-	-	-	-	-	-	-	-	-
4 Operating surplus	1846	3747	4862	5615	6246	7797	8996	10997	12733	14656	16833	17437
Equals: Gross Domestic Product a	5832	11668	16856	19688	22947	27746	31097	34307	38838	44861	53079	59257

a) From 1977 onward, stock valuation adjustment is made for the estimates of value of physical increase in stocks.

1.7 External Transactions on Current Account, Summary

Million New Zealand dollars

Fiscal year beginning 1 April

	1970	1975	1978	1979	1980	1981	1982	1983	1984	1985	1986	1987
Payments to the Rest of the World												
1 Imports of goods and services	...	3430	4647	6256	7272	9168	10318	11090	14859	15093	15048	16072
A Imports of merchandise c.i.f.	...	...	3540	4906	5576	7086	7888	8589	11697	11945	11396	12054
B Other	...	...	1107	1350	1696	2082	2430	2501	3162	3148	3652	4018
2 Factor income to the rest of the world	...	240	492	539	604	803	1068	1530	2179	2365	2663	3268
A Compensation of employees	...	-	-	-	-	-	-	-	-	-	-	-
B Property and entrepreneurial income	...	240	492	539	604	803	1068	1530	2179	2365	2663	3268
3 Current transfers to the rest of the world a	...	119	199	212	262	311	295	370	442	525	607	560
A Indirect taxes to supranational organizations	...	...	...	...	...	...	...	...	...	...	...	...
B Other current transfers	...	119	199	212	262	311	295	370	442	525	607	560
4 Surplus of the nation on current transactions	...	-905	-402	-709	-740	-1502	-1944	-1605	-3236	-2916	-1973	-2052
Payments to the Rest of the World and Surplus of the Nation on Current Transactions	...	2884	4936	6298	7398	8780	9737	11385	14244	15067	16346	17847
Receipts From The Rest of the World												
1 Exports of goods and services	...	2666	4687	5996	7003	8249	9116	10699	13317	14037	15051	16467
A Exports of merchandise f.o.b.	...	...	3820	4919	5715	6624	7230	8381	10423	10805	11527	12730
B Other	...	...	867	1077	1288	1625	1886	2318	2894	3232	3524	3737
2 Factor income from rest of the world	...	75	83	79	93	188	208	232	275	321	448	517
A Compensation of employees	...	-	-	-	-	-	-	-	-	-	-	-
B Property and entrepreneurial income	...	75	83	79	93	188	208	232	275	321	448	517
3 Current transfers from rest of the world a	...	143	166	223	302	343	413	454	652	709	846	862
A Subsidies from supranational organisations	...	...	...	...	...	...	...	...	...	...	...	...
B Other current transfers	...	143	166	223	302	343	413	454	652	709	846	862
Receipts from the Rest of the World on Current Transactions	...	2884	4936	6298	7398	8780	9737	11385	14244	15067	16346	17847

a) Item 'Current transfers to/from the rest of the world' includes also capital transfers.

New Zealand

1.10 Gross Domestic Product by Kind of Activity, in Current Prices

Million New Zealand dollars — Fiscal year beginning 1 April

	1970	1975	1978	1979	1980	1981	1982	1983	1984	1985	1986	1987
1 Agriculture, hunting, forestry and fishing	...	1163	1607	2395	2517	2661	2561	2941	3690	4035	4328	4676
2 Mining and quarrying	...	45	165	153	188	227	367	280	414	520	527	476
3 Manufacturing	...	2597	3771	4442	5082	6517	7236	7852	9169	10059	11192	11748
4 Electricity, gas and water	...	201	439	654	715	828	962	1066	1101	1440	1882	1010
5 Construction	...	868	933	969	1115	1461	1620	1764	1987	2342	2682	3155
6 Wholesale and retail trade, restaurants and hotels	...	2522	3246	3465	4400	5334	6205	7084	7558	8640	9437	8703
7 Transport, storage and communication	...	840	1429	1635	1861	2172	2527	2943	3218	3500	4122	4461
8 Finance, insurance, real estate and business services	...	1669	2499	2773	3185	3958	4630	5268	6134	8049	10127	13351
9 Community, social and personal services	...	453	649	742	863	1026	1173	1257	1467	1692	1936	2158
Total, Industries	...	10359	14740	17229	19925	24184	27280	30455	34739	40276	46232	49736
Producers of Government Services	...	1302	2137	2481	3106	3715	4088	4202	4389	5136	6276	7449
Other Producers	...	104	178	211	251	289	293	277	302	342	408	473
Subtotal	...	11765	17055	19921	23282	28188	31661	34934	39430	45754	52915	57658
Less: Imputed bank service charge	...	241	389	473	603	834	977	1121	1277	1531	2079	2557
Plus: Import duties	...	124	166	212	231	337	362	432	604	535	668	847
Plus: Value added tax	...	...	...	...	...	...	...	...	...	...	1407	3099
Plus: Other adjustments [a]	...	19	24	28	37	55	51	62	81	103	168	210
Equals: Gross Domestic Product [b]	...	11668	16856	19688	22947	27746	31097	34307	38838	44861	53080	59257

a) Item 'Other adjustments' relates to other indirect taxes and import duties not allocated to industries.
b) From 1977 onward, stock valuation adjustment is made for the estimates of value of physical increase in stocks.

1.11 Gross Domestic Product by Kind of Activity, in Constant Prices

Million New Zealand dollars — Fiscal year beginning 1 April

At constant prices of: 1982

	1970	1975	1978	1979	1980	1981	1982	1983	1984	1985	1986	1987
1 Agriculture, hunting, forestry and fishing	...	...	1938	2195	2467	2457	2561	2447	2445	2926	2959	...
2 Mining and quarrying	...	...	349	253	228	250	367	288	385	554	578	...
3 Manufacturing	...	...	6413	6713	6612	7183	7235	7435	8223	7864	8042	...
4 Electricity, gas and water	...	...	830	908	933	956	962	1062	1071	1107	1124	...
5 Construction	...	...	1636	1501	1484	1601	1620	1758	1830	1929	1921	...
6 Wholesale and retail trade, restaurants and hotels	...	...	6200	6132	6038	6359	6205	6399	6628	6520	6437	...
7 Transport, storage and communication	...	...	2364	2425	2421	2487	2527	2716	3006	3043	3151	...
8 Finance, insurance, real estate and business services	...	...	4269	4371	4488	4618	4630	4926	5192	5449	5805	...
9 Community, social and personal services	...	...	1389	1403	1420	1478	1466	1531	1601	1676	1691	...
Total, Industries	...	...	25388	25901	26091	27389	27573	28562	30381	31068	31708	...
Producers of Government Services	...	...	3931	3957	3977	4053	4088	4135	4133	4108	4130	...
Other Producers	...	...	...	...	...	...	...	...	...	...	...	...
Subtotal	...	...	29319	29858	30068	31442	31661	32697	34514	35176	35838	...
Less: Imputed bank service charge	...	...	919	941	931	954	977	1135	1261	1399	1603	...
Plus: Import duties	...	...	...	...	...	...	...	...	...	...	...	...
Plus: Value added tax	...	...	...	...	...	...	...	...	...	...	...	...
Plus: Other adjustments [a]	...	...	297	362	346	449	413	382	474	493	499	...
Equals: Gross Domestic Product [b]	...	...	28697	29277	29482	30940	31097	31943	33724	34271	34735	...

a) Item 'Other adjustments' relates to other indirect taxes and import duties not allocated to industries.
b) From 1977 onward, stock valuation adjustment is made for the estimates of value of physical increase in stocks.

New Zealand

1.12 Relations Among National Accounting Aggregates

Million New Zealand dollars — Fiscal year beginning 1 April

	1970	1975	1978	1979	1980	1981	1982	1983	1984	1985	1986	1987
Gross Domestic Product	5832	11668	16856	19688	22947	27746	31097	34307	38838	44861	53079	59257
Plus: Net factor income from the rest of the world	-41	-165	-409	-460	-511	-615	-860	-1298	-1904	-2044	-2215	-2751
Factor income from the rest of the world	...	75	83	79	93	188	208	232	275	321	448	517
Less: Factor income to the rest of the world	...	240	492	539	604	803	1068	1530	2179	2365	2663	3268
Equals: Gross National Product	5791	11503	16447	19228	22436	27131	30237	33009	36934	42817	50864	56506
Less: Consumption of fixed capital	523	940	1297	1465	1679	1925	2222	2623	3133	3636	4096	4562
Equals: National Income	5268	10563	15150	17763	20757	25206	28015	30386	33800	39180	46768	51944
Plus: Net current transfers from the rest of the world [a]	-9	24	-33	11	40	32	118	84	210	184	239	303
Current transfers from the rest of the world	...	143	166	223	302	343	413	454	652	709	846	862
Less: Current transfers to the rest of the world	...	119	199	212	262	311	295	370	442	525	607	560
Equals: National Disposable Income	5259	10587	15117	17774	20797	25238	28133	30470	34010	39364	47007	52247
Less: Final consumption	4512	8830	13235	15419	18378	21615	24194	25974	28985	34182	40105	46045
Equals: Net Saving	747	1757	1882	2354	2419	3624	3939	4497	5025	5182	6903	6202
Less: Surplus of the nation on current transactions	-209	-905	-402	-709	-740	-1502	-1944	-1605	-3236	-2916	-1973	-2052
Statistical discrepancy	-62	102	52	9	-41	-163	41	272	-307	342	69	-94
Equals: Net Capital Formation [b]	895	2764	2336	3072	3118	4963	5924	6374	7954	8440	8945	8160

a) Item 'Current transfers to/from the rest of the world' includes also capital transfers.
b) From 1977 onward, stock valuation adjustment is made for the estimates of value of physical increase in stocks.

2.5 Private Final Consumption Expenditure by Type and Purpose, in Current Prices

Million New Zealand dollars — Fiscal year beginning 1 April

Final Consumption Expenditure of Resident Households

	1970	1975	1978	1979	1980	1981	1982	1983	1984	1985	1986	1987
1 Food, beverages and tobacco	...	...	...	...	...	...	3563	3824	4195	4732	5549	6296
A Food	...	...	...	...	...	...	2525	2684	2939	3321	3818	4432
B Non-alcoholic beverages	...	...	...	...	...	...	632	676	744	848	1044	995
C Alcoholic beverages	...	...	...	...	...	...	...	...	...	...	...	...
D Tobacco	...	...	...	...	...	...	406	464	512	563	687	869
2 Clothing and footwear	...	...	...	...	...	...	1363	1418	1583	1787	2143	2282
3 Gross rent, fuel and power	...	...	...	...	...	...	2945	3212	3652	4830	5704	6631
A Fuel and power	...	...	...	...	...	...	440	463	483	575	724	846
B Other	...	...	...	...	...	...	2505	2749	3169	4255	4980	5785
4 Furniture, furnishings and household equipment and operation	...	...	...	...	...	...	1703	1811	2033	2267	2704	2884
5 Medical care and health expenses	...	...	...	...	...	...	857	919	1024	1259	1592	1943
6 Transport and communication	...	...	...	...	...	...	3434	3724	4332	5112	5380	6066
A Personal transport equipment	...	...	...	...	...	...	1154	1200	1471	1587	1696	1843
B Other [a]	...	...	...	...	...	...	2280	2524	2861	3525	3684	4223
7 Recreational, entertainment, education and cultural services	...	...	...	...	...	...	1679	1836	2041	2311	2773	3130
8 Miscellaneous goods and services	...	...	...	...	...	...	2936	3243	3716	4436	5247	6052
A Personal care	...	...	...	...	...	...	603	651	727	862	1027	1174
B Expenditures in restaurants, cafes and hotels [b]	...	...	...	...	...	...	1526	1694	1940	2308	2668	3022
C Other [a]	...	...	...	...	...	...	807	898	1049	1266	1552	1856
Total Final Consumption Expenditure in the Domestic Market by Households, of which	...	...	...	...	...	...	18480	19988	22575	26734	31091	35284

New Zealand

2.5 Private Final Consumption Expenditure by Type and Purpose, in Current Prices
(Continued)

Million New Zealand dollars — Fiscal year beginning 1 April

	1970	1975	1978	1979	1980	1981	1982	1983	1984	1985	1986	1987
A Durable goods	...	...	...	...	...	...	5695	6063	6961	7799	9026	9725
B Semi-durable goods	...	...	...	...	...	...	...	...	...	...	...	...
C Non-durable goods	...	...	...	...	...	...	5600	5994	6595	7601	8727	9928
D Services [a]	...	...	...	...	...	...	7185	7931	9019	11334	13338	15631
Plus: Direct purchases abroad by resident households	...	...	...	...	...	...	326	358	471	529	738	1016
Less: Direct purchases in the domestic market by non-resident households	...	...	...	...	...	...	459	500	587	774	1002	1219
Equals: Final Consumption Expenditure of Resident Households	...	...	...	...	...	...	18347	19846	22459	26488	30828	35082

Final Consumption Expenditure of Private Non-profit Institutions Serving Households

	1970	1975	1978	1979	1980	1981	1982	1983	1984	1985	1986	1987
Equals: Final Consumption Expenditure of Private Non-profit Organisations Serving Households	...	...	...	...	...	...	293	288	318	373	462	539
Private Final Consumption Expenditure	...	...	...	...	...	...	18640	20134	22777	26861	31290	35621

a) Item 'Other' includes fringe benefits received by households.
b) Item 'Expenditures in restaurants, cafes and hotels' includes expenditure on alcohol consumed in chartered clubs, taverns and hotels and restaurants.

2.6 Private Final Consumption Expenditure by Type and Purpose, in Constant Prices

Million New Zealand dollars — Fiscal year beginning 1 April

At constant prices of: 1982

Final Consumption Expenditure of Resident Households

	1970	1975	1978	1979	1980	1981	1982	1983	1984	1985	1986	1987
1 Food, beverages and tobacco	...	...	...	...	...	...	3563	3644	3709	3652	3756	...
A Food	...	...	...	...	...	...	2525	2578	2627	2610	2671	...
B Non-alcoholic beverages	...	...	...	...	...	...	...	...	...	...	...	...
C Alcoholic beverages	...	...	...	...	...	...	632	652	671	662	744	...
D Tobacco	...	...	...	...	...	...	406	414	411	380	341	...
2 Clothing and footwear	...	...	...	...	...	...	1363	1326	1405	1405	1471	...
3 Gross rent, fuel and power	...	...	...	...	...	...	2945	3007	3054	3087	3162	...
A Fuel and power	...	...	...	...	...	...	440	465	470	456	487	...
B Other	...	...	...	...	...	...	2505	2542	2584	2631	2675	...
4 Furniture, furnishings and household equipment and operation	...	...	...	...	...	...	1703	1757	1866	1840	1906	...
5 Medical care and health expenses	...	...	...	...	...	...	857	892	938	979	1046	...
6 Transport and communication	...	...	...	...	...	...	3434	3489	3591	3580	3526	...
A Personal transport equipment	...	...	...	...	...	...	1154	1106	1145	1053	973	...
B Other	...	...	...	...	...	...	2280	2383	2446	2527	2553	...
7 Recreational, entertainment, education and cultural services	...	...	...	...	...	...	1679	1738	1799	1863	2015	...
8 Miscellaneous goods and services	...	...	...	...	...	...	2936	3132	3262	3356	3429	...
A Personal care	...	...	...	...	...	...	603	636	674	700	748	...
B Expenditures in restaurants, cafes and hotels	...	...	...	...	...	...	1526	1640	1690	1739	1733	...
C Other	...	...	...	...	...	...	807	856	898	917	948	...
Total Final Consumption Expenditure in the Domestic Market by Households, of which	...	...	...	...	...	...	18480	18985	19624	19762	20311	...
Plus: Direct purchases abroad by resident households	...	...	...	...	...	...	...	...	...	...	...	...
Less: Direct purchases in the domestic market by non-resident households	...	...	...	...	...	...	133	187	175	234	216	...
Equals: Final Consumption Expenditure of Resident Households	...	...	...	...	...	...	18347	18798	19449	19528	20095	20455

Final Consumption Expenditure of Private Non-profit Institutions Serving Households

	1970	1975	1978	1979	1980	1981	1982	1983	1984	1985	1986	1987
Equals: Final Consumption Expenditure of Private Non-profit Organisations Serving Households	...	...	...	...	...	...	293	294	306	326	354	356
Private Final Consumption Expenditure	...	...	...	...	...	...	18640	19092	19755	19854	20449	20811

New Zealand

2.7 Gross Capital Formation by Type of Good and Owner, in Current Prices

Million New Zealand dollars — Fiscal year beginning 1 April

	1980 TOTAL	1980 Total Private	1980 Public Enterprises	1980 General Government	1981 TOTAL	1981 Total Private	1981 Public Enterprises	1981 General Government	1982 TOTAL	1982 Total Private	1982 Public Enterprises	1982 General Government
Increase in stocks, total [a]	43	...	...	...	290	...	...	...	318	...	...	...
Gross Fixed Capital Formation, Total	4754	3289	...	1466	6597	4617	...	1980	7827	5313	...	2514
1 Residential buildings	881	828	...	53	1180	1142	...	38	1333	1268	...	65
2 Non-residential buildings	821	460	...	361	1034	634	...	400	1182	736	...	446
3 Other construction	592	115	...	476	862	258	...	604	1056	233	...	822
4 Land improvement and plantation and orchard development	216	166	...	51	274	211	...	63	271	196	...	75
5 Producers' durable goods	2244	1720	...	525	3247	2373	...	874	3985	2882	...	1104
A Transport equipment	812	674	...	139	1217	883	...	334	1246	994	...	252
B Machinery and equipment	1432	1046	...	386	2030	1490	...	540	2739	1888	...	852
6 Breeding stock, dairy cattle, etc.	...	...	...	...	...	...	...	...	...	...	...	...
Total Gross Capital Formation	4797	...	...	...	6887	...	...	...	8145	...	...	...

	1983 TOTAL	1983 Total Private	1983 Public Enterprises	1983 General Government	1984 TOTAL	1984 Total Private	1984 Public Enterprises	1984 General Government	1985 TOTAL	1985 Total Private	1985 Public Enterprises	1985 General Government
Increase in stocks, total [a]	542	...	...	...	1482	...	...	...	632	...	...	...
Gross Fixed Capital Formation, Total	8455	5776	...	2680	9605	7152	...	2453	11444	8211	...	3233
1 Residential buildings	1556	1485	...	71	1785	1714	...	71	2081	1950	...	131
2 Non-residential buildings	1243	794	...	449	1471	992	...	478	2001	1393	...	608
3 Other construction	1122	258	...	864	1109	294	...	815	1280	295	...	986
4 Land improvement and plantation and orchard development	250	180	...	70	256	179	...	77	200	135	...	65
5 Producers' durable goods	4285	3058	...	1227	4984	3973	...	1011	5881	4439	...	1442
A Transport equipment	1192	999	...	193	1694	1556	...	138	2077	1536	...	541
B Machinery and equipment	3093	2059	...	1035	3290	2417	...	873	3804	2903	...	901
6 Breeding stock, dairy cattle, etc.	...	...	...	...	...	...	...	...	...	...	...	...
Total Gross Capital Formation	8997	...	...	...	11087	...	...	...	12076	...	...	...

	1986 TOTAL	1986 Total Private	1986 Public Enterprises	1986 General Government
Increase in stocks, total [a]	1197	...	...	...
Gross Fixed Capital Formation, Total	11843	8586	...	3257
1 Residential buildings	2416	2291	...	125
2 Non-residential buildings	2421	1716	...	705
3 Other construction	1343	218	...	1125
4 Land improvement and plantation and orchard development	161	91	...	70
5 Producers' durable goods	5502	4271	...	1231
A Transport equipment	1857	1652	...	205
B Machinery and equipment	3645	2619	...	1026
6 Breeding stock, dairy cattle, etc.	...	...	...	...
Total Gross Capital Formation	13040	...	...	...

a) From 1977 onward, stock valuation adjustment is made for the estimates of value of physical increase in stocks.

2.9 Gross Capital Formation by Kind of Activity of Owner, ISIC Major Divisions, in Current Prices

Million New Zealand dollars — Fiscal year beginning 1 April

	1980 Total Gross Capital Formation	1980 Increase in Stocks	1980 Gross Fixed Capital Formation	1981 Total Gross Capital Formation	1981 Increase in Stocks	1981 Gross Fixed Capital Formation	1982 Total Gross Capital Formation	1982 Increase in Stocks	1982 Gross Fixed Capital Formation	1983 Total Gross Capital Formation	1983 Increase in Stocks	1983 Gross Fixed Capital Formation
All Producers												
1 Agriculture, hunting, fishing and forestry	967	329	638	1165	345	820	1033	223	810	1454	609	845
2 Mining and quarrying	65	-5	70	65	14	51	62	-4	66	122	7	115
3 Manufacturing	550	-183	733	1264	-41	1305	2170	-53	2223	2001	-199	2200
4 Electricity, gas and water	379	-27	406	493	-17	510	598	6	592	656	42	614

New Zealand

2.9 Gross Capital Formation by Kind of Activity of Owner, ISIC Major Divisions, in Current Prices
(Continued)

Million New Zealand dollars — Fiscal year beginning 1 April

	1980 TGCF	1980 IS	1980 GFCF	1981 TGCF	1981 IS	1981 GFCF	1982 TGCF	1982 IS	1982 GFCF	1983 TGCF	1983 IS	1983 GFCF
5 Construction	154	4	150	215	2	213	185	21	164	174	16	158
6 Wholesale and retail trade, restaurants and hotels	368	-96	464	621	-6	627	755	90	665	831	7	824
7 Transport, storage and communication	424	-1	425	721	-3	724	785	35	750	767	45	722
8 Finance, insurance, real estate and business services	1149	-	1149	1545	-	1545	1708	-	1708	2046	-	2046
9 Community, social and personal services	70	-2	72	83	-6	89	83	-3	86	118	10	108
Total Industries	4128	20	4108	6172	288	5884	7379	314	7065	8171	539	7632
Producers of Government Services	602	23	579	635	2	633	693	4	689	737	3	734
Private Non-Profit Institutions Serving Households	67	-	67	81	-	81	74	-	74	90	-	90
Total [a]	4797	43	4754	6887	290	6597	8145	318	7827	8997	542	8455

	1984 TGCF	1984 IS	1984 GFCF	1985 TGCF	1985 IS	1985 GFCF	1986 TGCF	1986 IS	1986 GFCF
	All Producers									
1 Agriculture, hunting, fishing and forestry	1707	764	943	1868	1221	647	1464	905	559
2 Mining and quarrying	137	2	135	196	6	190	316	1	315
3 Manufacturing	2473	306	2167	2387	-5	2392	1577	-218	1795
4 Electricity, gas and water	567	5	562	519	-29	548	706	117	589
5 Construction	218	24	194	251	-5	256	246	-15	261
6 Wholesale and retail trade, restaurants and hotels	1372	279	1093	549	-678	1227	1838	527	1311
7 Transport, storage and communication	986	90	896	1681	145	1536	1311	-115	1426
8 Finance, insurance, real estate and business services	2563	-	2563	3366	-	3366	4113	-	4113
9 Community, social and personal services	170	10	160	170	-24	194	223	3	220
Total Industries	10190	1478	8712	10987	631	10356	11795	1205	10590
Producers of Government Services	803	5	798	986	1	985	1126	-7	1133
Private Non-Profit Institutions Serving Households	96	-	96	103	-	103	119	-	119
Total [a]	11087	1482	9605	12076	632	11444	13040	1197	11843

a) From 1977 onward, stock valuation adjustment is made for the estimates of value of physical increase in stocks.

2.11 Gross Fixed Capital Formation by Kind of Activity of Owner, ISIC Divisions, in Current Prices

Million New Zealand dollars — Fiscal year beginning 1 April

	1970	1975	1978	1979	1980	1981	1982	1983	1984	1985	1986	1987
	All Producers											
1 Agriculture, hunting, forestry and fishing	...	246	406	530	638	820	810	845	943	647	559	...
A Agriculture and hunting	...	225	371	483	593	770	760	791	880	575	479	...
B Forestry and logging	...	22	25	26	36	43	27	31	35	32	36	...
C Fishing	...	...	10	21	9	7	23	23	28	40	44	...
2 Mining and quarrying	...	142	120	81	70	51	66	115	135	190	315	...

New Zealand

2.11 Gross Fixed Capital Formation by Kind of Activity of Owner, ISIC Divisions, in Current Prices
(Continued)

Million New Zealand dollars — Fiscal year beginning 1 April

	1970	1975	1978	1979	1980	1981	1982	1983	1984	1985	1986	1987
3 Manufacturing	...	361	460	547	733	1305	2223	2200	2167	2392	1795	...
A Manufacturing of food, beverages and tobacco	...	124	165	222	348	393	394	393	440	429	378	...
B Textile, wearing apparel and leather industries	...	27	40	39	31	35	68	65	86	102	103	...
C Manufacture of wood, and wood products, including furniture	...	32	22	27	32	27	42	41	111	151	133	...
D Manufacture of paper and paper products, printing and publishing	...	50	70	71	86	115	137	141	213	211	271	...
E Manufacture of chemicals and chemical petroleum, coal, rubber and plastic products	...	39	62	62	98	382	1067	1009	779	634	306	...
F Manufacture of non-metalic mineral products except products of petroleum and coal	...	20	16	17	20	53	63	39	42	41	24	...
G Basic metal industries	...	9	21	20	29	172	301	343	284	560	324	...
H Manufacture of fabricated metal products, machinery and equipment	...	59	61	86	86	125	148	160	202	252	245	...
I Other manufacturing industries	...	1	3	3	3	3	3	8	10	12	11	...
4 Electricity, gas and water	...	305	411	377	406	510	592	614	562	548	589	...
5 Construction	...	77	74	115	150	213	164	158	194	256	261	...
6 Wholesale and retail trade, restaurants and hotels	...	224	300	454	464	627	665	824	1093	1227	1311	...
7 Transport, storage and communication	...	417	539	321	425	724	750	722	896	1536	1426	...
A Transport and storage	...	339	455	258	327	605	555	445	598	1092	802	...
B Communication	...	78	84	63	98	119	195	277	298	444	624	...
8 Finance, insurance, real estate and business services	...	1024	976	1011	1149	1545	1708	2046	2563	3366	4113	...
9 Community, social and personal services	...	...	51	63	72	89	86	108	160	194	220	...
Total Industries	...	2797	3339	3500	4108	5884	7065	7632	8712	10356	10590	...
Producers of Government Services	...	408	492	513	579	633	689	734	798	985	1133	...
Private Non-Profit Institutions Serving Households	...	40	49	54	67	81	74	90	96	103	119	...
Total	...	3246	3880	4067	4754	6598	7828	8456	9606	11444	11842	...

4.1 Derivation of Value Added by Kind of Activity, in Current Prices

Million New Zealand dollars — Fiscal year beginning 1 April

	1980 Gross Output	1980 Intermediate Consumption	1980 Value Added	1981 Gross Output	1981 Intermediate Consumption	1981 Value Added	1982 Gross Output	1982 Intermediate Consumption	1982 Value Added	1983 Gross Output	1983 Intermediate Consumption	1983 Value Added
All Producers											
1 Agriculture, hunting, forestry and fishing	5231	2714	2517	5808	3147	2661	6061	3500	2561	7028	4088	2941
A Agriculture and hunting [a]	4549	2388	2161	4992	2749	2243	5092	2975	2117	5891	3486	2405
B Forestry and logging	502	206	296	593	252	341	699	343	356	787	357	431
C Fishing [a]	180	120	61	223	146	78	270	182	90	350	245	105
2 Mining and quarrying	431	243	188	540	313	227	758	392	367	868	589	280

New Zealand

4.1 Derivation of Value Added by Kind of Activity, in Current Prices
(Continued)

Million New Zealand dollars — Fiscal year beginning 1 April

	1980 Gross Output	1980 Intermediate Consumption	1980 Value Added	1981 Gross Output	1981 Intermediate Consumption	1981 Value Added	1982 Gross Output	1982 Intermediate Consumption	1982 Value Added	1983 Gross Output	1983 Intermediate Consumption	1983 Value Added
3 Manufacturing	15732	10652	5082	19932	13414	6517	22007	14771	7236	23472	15620	7852
A Manufacture of food, beverages and tobacco	4701	3307	1394	5767	4119	1647	6656	4670	1986	7200	4842	2358
B Textile, wearing apparel and leather industries	1605	1046	560	1931	1216	716	2132	1376	756	2140	1432	708
C Manufacture of wood and wood products, including furniture	1043	676	367	1377	905	472	1374	932	442	1452	936	516
D Manufacture of paper and paper products, printing and publishing	1710	1104	606	2049	1325	724	2175	1372	803	2380	1535	844
E Manufacture of chemicals and chemical petroleum, coal, rubber and plastic products	1748	1278	470	2168	1573	595	2320	1651	668	2537	1860	677
F Manufacture of non-metallic mineral products, except products of petroleum and coal	539	312	227	764	427	337	872	499	373	904	506	399
G Basic metal industries	606	433	173	773	556	217	873	575	298	998	664	335
H Manufacture of fabricated metal products, machinery and equipment	3645	2416	1229	4913	3186	1726	5404	3565	1839	5642	3707	1934
I Other manufacturing industries	135	80	56	190	107	83	201	131	71	219	138	81
4 Electricity, gas and water	1468	753	715	1710	882	828	2084	1123	962	2237	1171	1066
5 Construction	3853	2738	1115	4911	3451	1461	5691	4071	1620	6227	4463	1764
6 Wholesale and retail trade, restaurants and hotels	9973	5573	4400	11972	6638	5334	13654	7449	6205	14858	7773	7084
7 Transport, storage and communication	3490	1630	1861	4108	1936	2172	4767	2239	2527	5191	2248	2943
A Transport and storage	2749	1517	1232	3253	1811	1442	3703	2086	1616	4016	2101	1915
B Communication	741	113	629	855	125	730	1064	153	911	1175	147	1028
8 Finance, insurance, real estate and business services	4852	1667	3185	6009	2051	3958	7177	2548	4630	8061	2793	5268
9 Community, social and personal services	1750	887	863	2154	1128	1026	2485	1313	1173	2745	1488	1257
Total, Industries	46783	26857	19925	57144	32960	24184	64685	37405	27280	70687	40232	30455
Producers of Government Services	4482	1376	3106	5398	1682	3715	6026	1938	4088	6353	2152	4202
Other Producers	439	188	251	507	218	289	539	246	293	531	254	277
Total	51704	28422	23282	63049	34861	28188	71249	39588	31661	77572	42637	34934
Less: Imputed bank service charge	...	-603	603	...	-834	834	...	-977	977	...	-1121	1121
Import duties	231	...	231	337	...	337	362	...	362	432	...	432
Value added tax	...	...	...	...	...	...	...	...	...	...	...	...
Other adjustments [b]	37	...	37	55	...	55	51	...	51	62	...	62
Total [c]	51972	29025	22947	63441	35695	27746	71662	40565	31097	78066	43758	34307

	1984 Gross Output	1984 Intermediate Consumption	1984 Value Added	1985 Gross Output	1985 Intermediate Consumption	1985 Value Added	1986 Gross Output	1986 Intermediate Consumption	1986 Value Added	1987 Gross Output	1987 Intermediate Consumption	1987 Value Added
						All Producers						
1 Agriculture, hunting, forestry and fishing	8635	4944	3690	8671	4636	4035	8995	4667	4328	...	...	4676
A Agriculture and hunting [a]	7224	4269	2954	6878	3889	2989	6945	3821	3124	...	...	3427
B Forestry and logging	1024	413	612	1349	474	875	1497	485	1012	...	...	1091
C Fishing [a]	387	262	124	444	273	171	553	361	192	...	...	158
2 Mining and quarrying	1042	628	414	1307	788	520	1258	731	527	...	...	476

New Zealand

4.1 Derivation of Value Added by Kind of Activity, in Current Prices
(Continued)

Million New Zealand dollars — Fiscal year beginning 1 April

		1984			1985			1986			1987	
		Gross Output	Intermediate Consumption	Value Added	Gross Output	Intermediate Consumption	Value Added	Gross Output	Intermediate Consumption	Value Added	Gross Output	Intermediate Consumption	Value Added
3	Manufacturing	28119	18952	9169	30817	20758	10059	33779	22589	11192	...	...	11748
	A Manufacture of food, beverages and tobacco	7903	5403	2499	8574	5992	2582	9704	6502	3202	...	...	3646
	B Textile, wearing apparel and leather industries	2633	1800	834	2894	1934	960	3300	2290	1010	...	...	829
	C Manufacture of wood and wood products, including furniture	1767	1153	614	2037	1334	703	2133	1424	710	...	...	686
	D Manufacture of paper and paper products, printing and publishing	2985	1851	1135	3321	2138	1183	3859	2560	1299	...	...	1544
	E Manufacture of chemicals and chemical petroleum, coal, rubber and plastic products	3136	2309	827	3536	2504	1032	3972	2677	1295	...	...	1339
	F Manufacture of non-metallic mineral products, except products of petroleum and coal	1040	604	436	1221	719	501	1346	764	582	...	...	568
	G Basic metal industries	1245	803	442	1154	703	451	1134	713	421	...	...	406
	H Manufacture of fabricated metal products, machinery and equipment	7102	4834	2269	7729	5229	2501	8003	5440	2563	...	...	2640
	I Other manufacturing industries	308	195	113	351	205	146	328	219	110	...	...	90
4	Electricity, gas and water	2497	1395	1101	3140	1700	1440	3675	1794	1882	...	...	1010
5	Construction	6997	5009	1987	8730	6389	2342	9298	6615	2682	...	...	3155
6	Wholesale and retail trade, restaurants and hotels	16352	8793	7558	18508	9868	8640	19868	10431	9437	...	...	8703
7	Transport, storage and communication	6001	2782	3218	7036	3537	3500	7971	3849	4122	...	...	4461
	A Transport and storage	4693	2570	2123	5518	3201	2318	5978	3421	2557	...	...	2499
	B Communication	1308	212	1095	1518	336	1182	1993	428	1565	...	...	1962
8	Finance, insurance, real estate and business services	9400	3266	6134	11750	3701	8049	14803	4677	10127	...	...	13351
9	Community, social and personal services	3216	1749	1467	3846	2154	1692	4463	2527	1936	...	...	2158
	Total, Industries	82257	47518	34739	93806	53530	40276	104111	57879	46232	...	...	49736
	Producers of Government Services	6790	2401	4389	8052	2916	5136	9775	3499	6276	...	...	7449
	Other Producers	575	273	302	673	331	342	809	401	408	...	...	473
	Total	89622	50192	39430	102532	56778	45754	114695	61780	52915	...	...	57658
	Less: Imputed bank service charge	...	-1277	1277	...	-1531	1531	...	-2079	2079	...	...	2557
	Import duties	604	...	604	535	...	535	668	...	668	...	...	847
	Value added tax	...	...	...	...	...	...	1407	...	1407	...	...	3099
	Other adjustments b	81	...	81	103	...	103	168	...	168	...	...	210
	Total c	90307	51469	38838	103170	58309	44861	116939	63859	53080	...	...	59257

a) Hunting is included in item 'Fishing'.
b) Item 'Other adjustments' relates to other indirect taxes and import duties not allocated to industries.
c) From 1977 onward, stock valuation adjustment is made for the estimates of value of physical increase in stocks.

4.2 Derivation of Value Added by Kind of Activity, in Constant Prices

Million New Zealand dollars — Fiscal year beginning 1 April

		1980			1981			1982			1983		
		Gross Output	Intermediate Consumption	Value Added	Gross Output	Intermediate Consumption	Value Added	Gross Output	Intermediate Consumption	Value Added	Gross Output	Intermediate Consumption	Value Added

At constant prices of: 1982

All Producers

1	Agriculture, hunting, forestry and fishing	...	...	2467	...	...	2457	...	...	2561	...	...	2447
	A Agriculture and hunting a	...	...	2038	...	...	2015	...	...	2117	...	...	2000
	B Forestry and logging	...	...	349	...	...	358	...	...	356	...	...	365
	C Fishing a	...	...	81	...	...	86	...	...	90	...	...	97
2	Mining and quarrying	...	...	228	...	...	250	...	...	367	...	...	288

New Zealand

4.2 Derivation of Value Added by Kind of Activity, in Constant Prices
(Continued)

Million New Zealand dollars — Fiscal year beginning 1 April

	1980 Gross Output	1980 Intermediate Consumption	1980 Value Added	1981 Gross Output	1981 Intermediate Consumption	1981 Value Added	1982 Gross Output	1982 Intermediate Consumption	1982 Value Added	1983 Gross Output	1983 Intermediate Consumption	1983 Value Added
						At constant prices of:1982						
3 Manufacturing	...	...	6612	...	...	7183	...	...	7235	...	...	7435
A Manufacture of food, beverages and tobacco	...	...	1824	...	...	1872	...	...	1986	...	...	1998
B Textile, wearing apparel and leather industries	...	...	701	...	...	745	...	...	756	...	...	736
C Manufacture of wood and wood products, including furniture	...	...	436	...	...	489	...	...	442	...	...	468
D Manufacture of paper and paper products, printing and publishing	...	...	815	...	...	832	...	...	803	...	...	871
E Manufacture of chemicals and chemical petroleum, coal, rubber and plastic products	...	...	642	...	...	689	...	...	668	...	...	716
F Manufacture of non-metallic mineral products, except products of petroleum and coal	...	...	298	...	...	360	...	...	373	...	...	377
G Basic metal industries	...	...	258	...	...	285	...	...	298	...	...	334
H Manufacture of fabricated metal products, machinery and equipment	...	...	1639	...	...	1911	...	...	1909	...	...	1935
I Other manufacturing industries	...	...	...	...	...	...	...	...	...	...	...	...
4 Electricity, gas and water	...	...	933	...	...	956	...	...	962	...	...	1062
5 Construction	...	...	1484	...	...	1601	...	...	1620	...	...	1758
6 Wholesale and retail trade, restaurants and hotels	...	...	6038	...	...	6359	...	...	6205	...	...	6399
7 Transport, storage and communication	...	...	2421	...	...	2487	...	...	2527	...	...	2716
A Transport and storage	...	...	1623	...	...	1641	...	...	1623	...	...	1811
B Communication	...	...	827	...	...	874	...	...	909	...	...	963
8 Finance, insurance, real estate and business services	...	...	4488	...	...	4618	...	...	4630	...	...	4926
9 Community, social and personal services	...	...	1420	...	...	1478	...	...	1466	...	...	1531
Total, Industries	...	...	26091	...	...	27389	...	...	27573	...	...	28562
Producers of Government Services	...	...	3977	...	...	4053	...	...	4088	...	...	4135
Other Producers	...	...	...	...	...	...	...	...	...	...	...	...
Total	...	...	30068	...	...	31442	...	...	31661	...	...	32697
Less: Imputed bank service charge	...	...	931	...	...	954	...	...	977	...	...	1135
Import duties	...	...	...	...	...	...	...	...	...	...	...	...
Value added tax	...	...	...	...	...	...	...	...	...	...	...	...
Other adjustments [b]	...	...	346	...	...	449	...	...	413	...	...	382
Total [c]	...	...	29483	...	...	30937	...	...	31097	...	...	31944

	1984 Gross Output	1984 Intermediate Consumption	1984 Value Added	1985 Gross Output	1985 Intermediate Consumption	1985 Value Added	1986 Gross Output	1986 Intermediate Consumption	1986 Value Added
			At constant prices of:1982						
			All Producers						
1 Agriculture, hunting, forestry and fishing	...	...	2445	...	...	2926	...	...	2959
A Agriculture and hunting [a]	...	...	1975	...	...	2512	...	...	...
B Forestry and logging	...	...	378	...	...	406	...	...	...
C Fishing [a]	...	...	95	...	...	95	...	...	...
2 Mining and quarrying	...	...	385	...	...	554	...	...	578

New Zealand

4.2 Derivation of Value Added by Kind of Activity, in Constant Prices
(Continued)

Million New Zealand dollars — Fiscal year beginning 1 April

	1984 Gross Output	1984 Intermediate Consumption	1984 Value Added	1985 Gross Output	1985 Intermediate Consumption	1985 Value Added	1986 Gross Output	1986 Intermediate Consumption	1986 Value Added
			At constant prices of:1982						
3 Manufacturing	...	...	8223	...	...	7864	...	...	8042
A Manufacture of food, beverages and tobacco	...	...	2085	...	...	1926	...	...	...
B Textile, wearing apparel and leather industries	...	...	819	...	...	797	...	...	...
C Manufacture of wood and wood products, including furniture	...	...	521	...	...	505	...	...	...
D Manufacture of paper and paper products, printing and publishing	...	...	986	...	...	990	...	...	...
E Manufacture of chemicals and chemical petroleum, coal, rubber and plastic products	...	...	818	...	...	791	...	...	...
F Manufacture of non-metallic mineral products, except products of petroleum and coal	...	...	412	...	...	427	...	...	...
G Basic metal industries	...	...	371	...	...	315	...	...	...
H Manufacture of fabricated metal products, machinery and equipment	...	...	2212	...	...	2115	...	...	...
I Other manufacturing industries	...	...	...	...	...	...	...	...	...
4 Electricity, gas and water	...	...	1071	...	...	1107	...	...	1124
5 Construction	...	...	1830	...	...	1929	...	...	1921
6 Wholesale and retail trade, restaurants and hotels	...	...	6628	...	...	6520	...	...	6437
7 Transport, storage and communication	...	...	3006	...	...	3043	...	...	3151
A Transport and storage	...	...	1948	...	...	1893	...	...	...
B Communication	...	...	1046	...	...	1134	...	...	...
8 Finance, insurance, real estate and business services	...	...	5192	...	...	5449	...	...	5805
9 Community, social and personal services	...	...	1601	...	...	1676	...	...	1691
Total, Industries	...	...	30381	...	...	31068	...	...	31708
Producers of Government Services	...	...	4133	...	...	4108	...	...	4130
Other Producers	...	...	...	...	...	...	...	...	...
Total	...	...	34514	...	...	35176	...	...	35838
Less: Imputed bank service charge	...	...	1261	...	...	1399	...	...	1603
Import duties	...	...	...	...	...	...	...	...	...
Value added tax	...	...	...	...	...	...	...	...	...
Other adjustments [b]	...	...	474	...	...	493	...	...	499
Total [c]	...	...	33727	...	...	34270	...	...	34734

a) Hunting is included in item 'Fishing'.
b) Item 'Other adjustments' relates to other indirect taxes and import duties not allocated to industries.
c) From 1977 onward, stock valuation adjustment is made for the estimates of value of physical increase in stocks.

4.3 Cost Components of Value Added

Million New Zealand dollars — Fiscal year beginning 1 April

	1980 Compensation of Employees	1980 Capital Consumption	1980 Net Operating Surplus	1980 Indirect Taxes	1980 Less: Subsidies Received	1980 Value Added	1981 Compensation of Employees	1981 Capital Consumption	1981 Net Operating Surplus	1981 Indirect Taxes	1981 Less: Subsidies Received	1981 Value Added
					All Producers							
1 Agriculture, hunting, forestry and fishing	509	312	1650	86	40	2517	610	345	1875	104	274	2661
A Agriculture and hunting [a]	373	290	1450	81	33	2161	446	322	1639	98	262	2243
B Forestry and logging	110	11	177	4	6	296	135	13	198	4	10	341
C Fishing [a]	26	11	23	1	1	61	29	10	38	2	2	78
2 Mining and quarrying	55	33	80	22	1	188	66	30	105	27	-	227

New Zealand

4.3 Cost Components of Value Added
(Continued)

Million New Zealand dollars — Fiscal year beginning 1 April

	1980						1981					
	Compensation of Employees	Capital Consumption	Net Operating Surplus	Indirect Taxes	Less: Subsidies Received	Value Added	Compensation of Employees	Capital Consumption	Net Operating Surplus	Indirect Taxes	Less: Subsidies Received	Value Added
3 Manufacturing	3422	393	948	416	101	5082	4184	446	1486	512	107	6517
A Manufacture of food, beverages and tobacco	916	119	145	256	42	1394	1091	140	156	301	40	1647
B Textile, wearing apparel and leather industries	407	30	123	6	7	560	494	32	194	7	11	716
C Manufacture of wood and wood products, including furniture	246	24	95	3	2	367	314	26	131	3	2	472
D Manufacture of paper and paper products, printing and publishing	387	63	140	19	4	606	470	72	162	23	3	724
E Manufacture of chemicals and chemical petroleum, coal, rubber and plastic products	326	52	97	36	40	470	385	54	153	44	41	595
F Manufacture of non-metallic mineral products, except products of petroleum and coal	121	18	85	3	1	227	151	21	163	4	2	337
G Basic metal industries	104	15	53	1	-	173	129	16	72	2	1	217
H Manufacture of fabricated metal products, machinery and equipment	880	69	198	87	5	1229	1105	81	427	121	7	1726
I Other manufacturing industries	35	3	12	5	-	56	45	4	28	7	-	83
4 Electricity, gas and water	213	85	419	4	6	715	263	97	469	5	6	828
5 Construction	752	56	306	14	13	1115	896	66	489	18	9	1461
6 Wholesale and retail trade, restaurants and hotels	2041	227	1192	983	44	4400	2435	269	1486	1173	28	5334
7 Transport, storage and communication	1345	211	357	83	135	1861	1584	247	383	101	143	2172
A Transport and storage	910	162	215	78	133	1232	1061	194	232	94	140	1442
B Communication	435	49	142	5	2	629	523	53	151	7	3	730
8 Finance, insurance, real estate and business services	931	293	1577	386	2	3185	1158	346	1969	488	3	3958
9 Community, social and personal services	445	42	318	64	8	863	541	52	370	73	9	1026
Total, Industries	9712	1655	6849	2057	348	19925	11735	1898	8631	2498	578	24184
Producers of Government Services	3094	-	-	12	-	3106	3700	-	-	15	-	3715
Other Producers	220	25	-	7	-	251	254	27	-	8	-	289
Total	13026	1678	6849	2075	348	23282	15689	1925	8631	2521	578	28188
Less: Imputed bank service charge	...	...	603	...	...	603	...	...	834	...	...	834
Import duties	...	...	...	231	...	231	...	...	...	337	...	337
Value added tax	...	...	...	...	...	...	...	...	...	...	...	...
Other adjustments [b]	...	...	...	37	...	37	...	...	...	55	...	55
Total [cd]	13026	1678	6246	2343	348	22947	15689	1925	7797	2913	578	27746

	1982						1983					
	Compensation of Employees	Capital Consumption	Net Operating Surplus	Indirect Taxes	Less: Subsidies Received	Value Added	Compensation of Employees	Capital Consumption	Net Operating Surplus	Indirect Taxes	Less: Subsidies Received	Value Added

All Producers

1 Agriculture, hunting, forestry and fishing	636	380	1872	121	447	2561	658	417	2103	128	365	2941
A Agriculture and hunting [a]	478	351	1611	114	437	2117	485	386	1761	120	347	2405
B Forestry and logging	124	16	220	5	9	356	129	14	299	5	17	431
C Fishing [a]	34	13	41	2	1	90	44	17	43	3	1	105
2 Mining and quarrying	78	39	206	43	-	367	87	59	87	47	-	280

New Zealand

4.3 Cost Components of Value Added
(Continued)

Million New Zealand dollars — Fiscal year beginning 1 April

1982 | 1983

	Compensation of Employees	Capital Consumption	Net Operating Surplus	Indirect Taxes	Less: Subsidies Received	Value Added	Compensation of Employees	Capital Consumption	Net Operating Surplus	Indirect Taxes	Less: Subsidies Received	Value Added
3 Manufacturing	4561	519	1684	571	99	7236	4482	617	2196	635	76	7852
A Manufacture of food, beverages and tobacco	1225	160	294	343	37	1986	1192	186	606	397	23	2358
B Textile, wearing apparel and leather industries	514	38	207	8	11	756	494	47	168	8	8	708
C Manufacture of wood and wood products, including furniture	325	29	86	4	2	442	316	36	162	5	2	516
D Manufacture of paper and paper products, printing and publishing	509	86	186	25	3	803	540	98	180	29	3	844
E Manufacture of chemicals and chemical petroleum, coal, rubber and plastic products	405	60	194	47	37	668	404	80	192	34	32	677
F Manufacture of non-metallic mineral products, except products of petroleum and coal	173	26	172	4	2	373	159	31	204	7	2	399
G Basic metal industries	146	25	126	2	1	298	150	32	151	2	1	335
H Manufacture of fabricated metal products, machinery and equipment	1220	91	403	131	6	1839	1183	102	510	144	5	1934
I Other manufacturing industries	44	4	16	7	-	71	44	5	23	9	...	81
4 Electricity, gas and water	278	109	575	5	5	962	294	137	635	5	5	1066
5 Construction	1009	84	513	21	7	1620	1050	102	595	22	6	1764
6 Wholesale and retail trade, restaurants and hotels	2682	322	1785	1445	28	6205	2733	394	2381	1606	30	7084
7 Transport, storage and communication	1701	290	576	121	159	2527	1741	354	882	128	162	2943
A Transport and storage	1148	226	286	113	156	1616	1193	267	494	120	159	1915
B Communication	553	64	290	8	3	911	548	87	388	8	3	1028
8 Finance, insurance, real estate and business services	1327	388	2327	590	2	4630	1409	446	2755	661	2	5268
9 Community, social and personal services	600	64	436	82	9	1173	621	71	485	90	10	1257
Total, Industries	12870	2193	9973	2999	755	27280	13074	2595	12118	3324	655	30455
Producers of Government Services	4069	-	-	18	-	4088	4182	-	-	20	-	4202
Other Producers	256	28	-	9	-	293	239	28	-	10	-	277
Total	17195	2222	9973	3027	755	31661	17496	2623	12118	3353	655	34934
Less: Imputed bank service charge	...	...	977	...	...	977	...	...	1121	...	...	1121
Import duties	...	...	...	362	...	362	...	...	...	432	...	432
Value added tax	...	...	...	...	...	...	...	...	...	...	...	...
Other adjustments [b]	...	...	...	51	...	51	...	...	...	62	...	62
Total [c,d]	17195	2222	8996	3440	755	31097	17496	2623	10997	3847	655	34307

1984 | 1985

	Compensation of Employees	Capital Consumption	Net Operating Surplus	Indirect Taxes	Less: Subsidies Received	Value Added	Compensation of Employees	Capital Consumption	Net Operating Surplus	Indirect Taxes	Less: Subsidies Received	Value Added
					All Producers							
1 Agriculture, hunting, forestry and fishing	740	499	2631	142	323	3690	805	505	2660	162	96	4035
A Agriculture and hunting [a]	554	464	2045	130	240	2954	602	455	1875	145	88	2989
B Forestry and logging	138	14	536	6	82	612	145	20	710	7	7	875
C Fishing [a]	48	21	50	6	1	124	58	30	75	10	1	171
2 Mining and quarrying	95	81	181	57	-	414	103	113	226	78	-	520

New Zealand

4.3 Cost Components of Value Added
(Continued)

Million New Zealand dollars — Fiscal year beginning 1 April

	1984 Compensation of Employees	Capital Consumption	Net Operating Surplus	Indirect Taxes	Less: Subsidies Received	Value Added	1985 Compensation of Employees	Capital Consumption	Net Operating Surplus	Indirect Taxes	Less: Subsidies Received	Value Added
3 Manufacturing	4939	736	2826	746	79	9169	5551	877	2870	810	49	10059
A Manufacture of food, beverages and tobacco	1296	230	555	448	29	2499	1305	248	576	467	14	2582
B Textile, wearing apparel and leather industries	544	54	230	10	5	834	620	61	270	14	4	960
C Manufacture of wood and wood products, including furniture	349	39	222	6	2	614	406	48	242	8	1	703
D Manufacture of paper and paper products, printing and publishing	596	116	390	36	4	1135	723	129	291	44	4	1183
E Manufacture of chemicals and chemical petroleum, coal, rubber and plastic products	444	104	268	41	31	827	527	158	323	42	18	1032
F Manufacture of non-metallic mineral products, except products of petroleum and coal	170	31	228	9	2	436	200	38	253	11	1	501
G Basic metal industries	168	34	239	2	1	442	191	35	223	3	2	451
H Manufacture of fabricated metal products, machinery and equipment	1321	122	650	181	5	2269	1517	152	631	206	5	2501
I Other manufacturing industries	51	6	43	13	-	113	62	8	61	15	-	146
4 Electricity, gas and water	305	163	630	7	3	1101	390	181	860	13	4	1440
5 Construction	1144	121	701	26	4	1987	1326	129	859	32	4	2342
6 Wholesale and retail trade, restaurants and hotels	3056	462	2196	1875	31	7558	3642	551	2547	1922	21	8640
7 Transport, storage and communication	1849	404	929	183	148	3218	2099	478	877	228	182	3500
A Transport and storage	1267	303	523	175	146	2123	1458	343	483	215	181	2318
B Communication	582	101	406	8	2	1095	641	135	394	13	1	1182
8 Finance, insurance, real estate and business services	1590	553	3303	689	2	6134	2009	674	4553	815	2	8049
9 Community, social and personal services	684	84	612	98	11	1467	775	96	734	100	12	1692
Total, Industries	14404	3102	14010	3823	601	34739	16699	3602	16187	4160	372	40276
Producers of Government Services	4364	-	-	26	-	4389	5097	-	-	39	-	5136
Other Producers	260	32	-	10	-	302	296	34	-	12	-	342
Total	19028	3133	14010	3860	601	39430	22093	3636	16187	4210	372	45754
Less: Imputed bank service charge	...	...	1277	...	...	1277	...	...	1531	...	...	1531
Import duties	...	...	...	604	...	604	...	...	...	535	...	535
Value added tax	...	...	...	...	...	...	...	...	...	...	...	...
Other adjustments [b]	...	...	...	81	...	81	...	...	...	103	...	103
Total [cd]	19028	3133	12733	4545	601	38838	22093	3636	14656	4848	372	44861

	1986 Compensation of Employees	Capital Consumption	Net Operating Surplus	Indirect Taxes	Less: Subsidies Received	Value Added
All Producers						
1 Agriculture, hunting, forestry and fishing	881	486	2800	207	45	4328
A Agriculture and hunting [a]	651	436	1907	164	34	3124
B Forestry and logging	155	21	839	8	10	1012
C Fishing [a]	75	29	54	35	1	192
2 Mining and quarrying	119	117	204	89	3	527

New Zealand

4.3 Cost Components of Value Added
(Continued)

Million New Zealand dollars — Fiscal year beginning 1 April

	Compensation of Employees	Capital Consumption	Net Operating Surplus	Indirect Taxes	Less: Subsidies Received	Value Added
3 Manufacturing	6265	1007	3197	751	24	11192
A Manufacture of food, beverages and tobacco	1577	266	858	507	6	3202
B Textile, wearing apparel and leather industries	649	69	282	14	3	1010
C Manufacture of wood and wood products, including furniture	433	61	208	9	1	710
D Manufacture of paper and paper products, printing and publishing	863	142	265	32	2	1299
E Manufacture of chemicals and chemical petroleum, coal, rubber and plastic products	578	221	470	34	8	1295
F Manufacture of non-metallic mineral products, except products of petroleum and coal	225	38	311	9	-	582
G Basic metal industries	202	34	182	4	-	421
H Manufacture of fabricated metal products, machinery and equipment	1670	167	597	133	4	2563
I Other manufacturing industries	68	9	24	9	-	110
4 Electricity, gas and water	480	199	1187	18	2	1882
5 Construction	1426	138	1087	35	3	2682
6 Wholesale and retail trade, restaurants and hotels	4249	656	2619	1923	10	9437
7 Transport, storage and communication	2355	561	1165	229	188	4122
A Transport and storage	1614	377	545	208	188	2557
B Communication	741	184	620	21	-	1565
8 Finance, insurance, real estate and business services	2593	794	5795	946	2	10127
9 Community, social and personal services	889	100	857	102	13	1936
Total, Industries	19257	4056	18912	4297	290	46232
Producers of Government Services	6219	-	-	57	-	6276
Other Producers	355	40	-	13	-	408
Total	25830	4096	18912	4366	290	52915
Less: Imputed bank service charge	...	...	2079	...	...	2079
Import duties	...	...	...	668	...	668
Value added tax	...	...	...	1407	...	1407
Other adjustments [b]	...	...	...	168	...	168
Total [c,d]	25830	4096	16833	6609	290	53080

a) Hunting is included in item 'Fishing'.
b) Item 'Other adjustments' relates to other indirect taxes and import duties not allocated to industries.
c) From 1977 onward, stock valuation adjustment is made for the estimates of value of physical increase in stocks.
d) For year 1986, fringe benefits and fringe benefits tax are not included.

Nicaragua

Source. Reply to the United Nations National Accounts Questionnaire from the Departamento de Estudios Economicos, Banco Central de Nicaragua, Managua. The official estimates are published by the Banco Central in the 'Informe Anual'.

General note. The estimates shown in the following tables have been prepared in accordance with the United Nations System of National Accounts so far as the existing data would permit.

1.1 Expenditure on the Gross Domestic Product, in Current Prices

Million Nicaraguan cordobas

		1970	1975	1978	1979	1980	1981	1982	1983	1984	1985	1986	1987
1	Government final consumption expenditure	521	1007	1762	2591	4107	5371	6646	10351	15913	41235	154039	589130
2	Private final consumption expenditure	4038	8732	10901	10739	18381	18094	19237	18655	24965	55616	243194	1387850
3	Gross capital formation	1011	2385	1850	-833	3364	5777	5323	7401	10010	26702	73609	259270
	A Increase in stocks	120	-126	-282	-1800	482	539	624	1011	1273	2782	13293	71420
	B Gross fixed capital formation	891	2510	2132	967	2882	5238	4699	6390	8737	23920	60316	187850
	Residential buildings	89	417	221	...	...	...	...	...	...	...	...	...
	Non-residential buildings	125	555	445	...	...	...	...	...	...	...	...	...
	Other construction and land improvement etc.	140	165	143	...	...	...	...	...	...	...	...	...
	Other	537	1373	1324	...	...	...	...	...	...	...	...	...
4	Exports of goods and services	1453	3122	5160	6100	5039	5470	4530	6387	7404	17041	55672	527910
5	Less: Imports of goods and services	1587	4113	4686	4083	8999	10229	7386	9874	13262	25188	90770	374650
	Equals: Gross Domestic Product	5436	11133	14988	14514	21892	24483	28350	32920	45030	115404	435742	2389500

1.2 Expenditure on the Gross Domestic Product, in Constant Prices

Million Nicaraguan cordobas

		1970	1975	1978	1979	1980	1981	1982	1983	1984	1985	1986	1987
					At constant prices of:1958								
1	Government final consumption expenditure	293.9	407.6	625.6	...	...	...	...	...	...	...	...	...
2	Private final consumption expenditure	3365.7	4329.0	4475.1	...	...	...	...	...	...	...	...	...
3	Gross capital formation	928.1	1049.7	772.5	...	...	...	...	...	...	...	...	...
	A Increase in stocks	102.6	-101.3	-95.9	...	...	...	...	...	...	...	...	...
	B Gross fixed capital formation	825.5	1151.0	868.4	...	...	...	...	...	...	...	...	...
	Residential buildings	80.8	207.5	119.9	...	...	...	...	...	...	...	...	...
	Non-residential buildings	113.0	282.1	224.3	...	...	...	...	...	...	...	...	...
	Other construction and land improvement etc.	126.9	83.3	59.7	...	...	...	...	...	...	...	...	...
	Other	504.8	578.1	464.5	...	...	...	...	...	...	...	...	...
4	Exports of goods and services	1403.2	2058.0	2205.0	...	...	...	...	...	...	...	...	...
5	Less: Imports of goods and services	1326.6	1731.6	1741.9	...	...	...	...	...	...	...	...	...
	Equals: Gross Domestic Product	4664.3	6112.7	6336.3	...	...	...	...	...	...	...	...	...

1.3 Cost Components of the Gross Domestic Product

Million Nicaraguan cordobas

		1970	1975	1978	1979	1980	1981	1982	1983	1984	1985	1986	1987
1	Indirect taxes, net	459.2	1032.8	1329.8	...	...	...	...	...	...	...	...	...
2	Consumption of fixed capital	217.4	445.3	599.5	...	...	...	...	...	...	...	...	...
3	Compensation of employees paid by resident producers to:	2906.1	6044.3	8366.9	...	...	...	...	...	...	...	...	...
4	Operating surplus	1853.4	3610.6	4691.8	...	...	...	...	...	...	...	...	...
	A Corporate and quasi-corporate enterprises	1861.2	3624.1	4745.6									
	B Private unincorporated enterprises				...	...	...	...	...	...	...	...	...
	C General government	-7.8	-13.5	-53.8	...	...	...	...	...	...	...	...	...
	Equals: Gross Domestic Product	5436.1	11133.0	14988.0	...	...	...	...	...	...	...	...	...

1.4 General Government Current Receipts and Disbursements

Million Nicaraguan cordobas

		1970	1975	1978	1979	1980	1981	1982	1983	1984	1985	1986	1987
					Receipts								
1	Operating surplus	-7.8	-13.5	-53.8	...	...	...	...	...	...	...	...	...
2	Property and entrepreneurial income	...	...	...	...	...	...	...	...	...	...	...	...
3	Taxes, fees and contributions	637.6	1483.5	1894.1	...	...	...	...	...	...	...	...	...
	A Indirect taxes [a]	459.2	1032.8	1329.8	...	...	...	...	...	...	...	...	...

Nicaragua

1.4 General Government Current Receipts and Disbursements
(Continued)

Million Nicaraguan cordobas

	1970	1975	1978	1979	1980	1981	1982	1983	1984	1985	1986	1987
B Direct taxes	178.4	450.7	564.3	...	...	...	...	...	...	...	...	...
C Social security contributions	...	...	...	...	...	...	...	...	...	...	...	...
D Compulsory fees, fines and penalties	...	...	...	...	...	...	...	...	...	...	...	...
4 Other current transfers	30.8	87.4	68.8	...	...	...	...	...	...	...	...	...
Total Current Receipts of General Government	660.6	1557.4	1909.1	...	...	...	...	...	...	...	...	...

Disbursements

	1970	1975	1978	1979	1980	1981	1982	1983	1984	1985	1986	1987
1 Government final consumption expenditure	521.4	1007.3	1762.4	...	...	...	...	...	...	...	...	...
2 Property income	...	...	...	...	...	...	...	...	...	...	...	...
3 Subsidies [a]	...	...	...	...	...	...	...	...	...	...	...	...
4 Other current transfers	60.8	114.9	176.2	...	...	...	...	...	...	...	...	...
A Social security benefits	...	...	...	...	...	...	...	...	...	...	...	...
B Social assistance grants	...	...	...	...	...	...	...	...	...	...	...	...
C Other	60.8	114.9	176.2	...	...	...	...	...	...	...	...	...
5 Net saving	78.4	435.2	-29.5	...	...	...	...	...	...	...	...	...
Total Current Disbursements and Net Saving of General Government	660.6	1557.4	1909.1	...	...	...	...	...	...	...	...	...

a) Item 'Subsidies' is netted out of item 'Indirect taxes'.

1.7 External Transactions on Current Account, Summary

Million Nicaraguan cordobas

	1970	1975	1978	1979	1980	1981	1982	1983	1984	1985	1986	1987

Payments to the Rest of the World

	1970	1975	1978	1979	1980	1981	1982	1983	1984	1985	1986	1987
1 Imports of goods and services	1586.9	4112.5	4685.8	...	...	...	...	...	...	...	...	...
A Imports of merchandise c.i.f.	1250.4	2626.2	4521.8	...	...	...	...	...	...	...	...	...
B Other	336.5	1486.3	164.0	...	...	...	...	...	...	...	...	...
2 Factor income to the rest of the world	255.5	543.2	627.9	...	...	...	...	...	...	...	...	...
3 Current transfers to the rest of the world	11.0	5.6	3.8	...	...	...	...	...	...	...	...	...
4 Surplus of the nation on current transactions	-266.4	-1282.3	72.9	...	...	...	...	...	...	...	...	...
Payments to the Rest of the World and Surplus of the Nation on Current Transactions	1587.0	3379.0	5390.4	...	...	...	...	...	...	...	...	...

Receipts From The Rest of the World

	1970	1975	1978	1979	1980	1981	1982	1983	1984	1985	1986	1987
1 Exports of goods and services	1453.2	3122.0	5159.7	...	...	...	...	...	...	...	...	...
A Exports of merchandise f.o.b.	1250.4	2626.2	4521.8	...	...	...	...	...	...	...	...	...
B Other	202.8	495.8	637.9	...	...	...	...	...	...	...	...	...
2 Factor income from rest of the world	79.1	127.4	153.3	...	...	...	...	...	...	...	...	...
3 Current transfers from rest of the world	54.7	129.6	77.4	...	...	...	...	...	...	...	...	...
Receipts from the Rest of the World on Current Transactions	1587.0	3379.0	5390.4	...	...	...	...	...	...	...	...	...

1.8 Capital Transactions of The Nation, Summary

Million Nicaraguan cordobas

	1970	1975	1978	1979	1980	1981	1982	1983	1984	1985	1986	1987

Finance of Gross Capital Formation

	1970	1975	1978	1979	1980	1981	1982	1983	1984	1985	1986	1987
Gross saving	743.9	1095.3	1917.7	...	...	...	...	...	...	...	...	...
1 Consumption of fixed capital	217.4	445.3	599.5	...	...	...	...	...	...	...	...	...
A General government	...	...	...	...	...	...	...	...	...	...	...	...
B Corporate and quasi-corporate enterprises	217.4	445.3	599.5	...	...	...	...	...	...	...	...	...
C Other	...	...	...	...	...	...	...	...	...	...	...	...
2 Net saving	526.5	650.0	1318.2	...	...	...	...	...	...	...	...	...
A General government	78.4	435.2	-29.5	...	...	...	...	...	...	...	...	...
B Corporate and quasi-corporate enterprises	342.7	695.1	940.2	...	...	...	...	...	...	...	...	...

Nicaragua

1.8 Capital Transactions of The Nation, Summary
(Continued)

Million Nicaraguan cordobas	1970	1975	1978	1979	1980	1981	1982	1983	1984	1985	1986	1987
C Other	105.4	-480.3	407.5	...	...	...	...	...	...	...	...	...
Less: Surplus of the nation on current transactions	-266.4	-1282.3	72.9	...	...	...	...	...	...	...	...	...
Finance of Gross Capital Formation	1010.8	2384.6	1850.3	...	...	...	...	...	...	...	...	...
Gross Capital Formation												
Increase in stocks	119.6	-125.7	-281.6	...	...	...	...	...	...	...	...	...
Gross fixed capital formation	891.2	2510.3	2131.9	...	...	...	...	...	...	...	...	...
Gross Capital Formation	1010.8	2384.6	1850.3	...	...	...	...	...	...	...	...	...

1.10 Gross Domestic Product by Kind of Activity, in Current Prices

Million Nicaraguan cordobas	1970	1975	1978	1979	1980	1981	1982	1983	1984	1985	1986	1987
1 Agriculture, hunting, forestry and fishing	1353.2	2490.6	3701.2	...	...	...	...	...	...	...	...	...
2 Mining and quarrying [a]	33.5	39.1	45.5	...	...	...	...	...	...	...	...	...
3 Manufacturing [b]	1110.8	2459.9	3149.0	...	...	...	...	...	...	...	...	...
4 Electricity, gas and water	84.1	174.8	302.5	...	...	...	...	...	...	...	...	...
5 Construction	173.3	603.9	429.2	...	...	...	...	...	...	...	...	...
6 Wholesale and retail trade, restaurants and hotels [c]	1153.3	2397.2	3540.3	...	...	...	...	...	...	...	...	...
7 Transport, storage and communication	293.1	606.0	795.8	...	...	...	...	...	...	...	...	...
8 Finance, insurance, real estate and business services [d]	494.8	923.2	1176.5	...	...	...	...	...	...	...	...	...
9 Community, social and personal services [cde]	365.2	728.8	766.1	...	...	...	...	...	...	...	...	...
Total, Industries	5061.3	10423.5	13906.1	...	...	...	...	...	...	...	...	...
Producers of Government Services	374.8	709.5	1081.9	...	...	...	...	...	...	...	...	...
Other Producers [e]	...	...	...	...	...	...	...	...	...	...	...	...
Subtotal	5436.1	11133.0	14988.0	...	...	...	...	...	...	...	...	...
Less: Imputed bank service charge	...	...	...	...	...	...	...	...	...	...	...	...
Plus: Import duties	...	...	...	...	...	...	...	...	...	...	...	...
Plus: Value added tax	...	...	...	...	...	...	...	...	...	...	...	...
Equals: Gross Domestic Product	5436.1	11133.0	14988.0	...	...	...	...	...	...	...	...	...

a) Item 'Mining and quarrying' refers to metal ore mining only.
b) For 1972, item 'Manufacturing' excludes damages by earthquake amounting to 21.7 million cordobas at current prices, and 17.9 million cordobas at constant prices.
c) Restaurants and hotels are included in item 'Community, social and personal services'.
d) Business services are included in item 'Community, social and personal services'.
e) Domestic service of households is included in item 'Community, social and personal services'.

1.11 Gross Domestic Product by Kind of Activity, in Constant Prices

Million Nicaraguan cordobas	1970	1975	1978	1979	1980	1981	1982	1983	1984	1985	1986	1987
				At constant prices of:1958								
1 Agriculture, hunting, forestry and fishing	1073.1	1427.9	1594.0	...	...	...	...	...	...	...	...	...
2 Mining and quarrying [a]	32.3	25.8	13.4	...	...	...	...	...	...	...	...	...
3 Manufacturing [b]	1071.0	1426.6	1598.0	...	...	...	...	...	...	...	...	...
4 Electricity, gas and water	125.5	175.3	210.7	...	...	...	...	...	...	...	...	...
5 Construction	158.3	304.2	199.9	...	...	...	...	...	...	...	...	...
6 Wholesale and retail trade, restaurants and hotels [c]	1008.1	1316.4	1260.8	...	...	...	...	...	...	...	...	...
7 Transport, storage and communication	256.2	334.6	301.4	...	...	...	...	...	...	...	...	...
8 Finance, insurance, real estate and business services [d]	443.0	472.0	507.2	...	...	...	...	...	...	...	...	...
9 Community, social and personal services [cde]	319.2	397.4	302.2	...	...	...	...	...	...	...	...	...
Total, Industries	4486.7	5880.2	5987.6	...	...	...	...	...	...	...	...	...
Producers of Government Services	211.3	287.1	384.1	...	...	...	...	...	...	...	...	...
Other Producers [e]	...	...	...	...	...	...	...	...	...	...	...	...
Subtotal	4698.0	6167.3	6371.7	...	...	...	...	...	...	...	...	...
Less: Imputed bank service charge	33.7	54.6	35.4	...	...	...	...	...	...	...	...	...
Plus: Import duties	...	...	...	...	...	...	...	...	...	...	...	...
Plus: Value added tax	...	...	...	...	...	...	...	...	...	...	...	...
Equals: Gross Domestic Product	4664.3	6112.7	6336.3	...	...	...	...	...	...	...	...	...

a) Item 'Mining and quarrying' refers to metal ore mining only.
b) For 1972, item 'Manufacturing' excludes damages by earthquake amounting to 21.7 million cordobas at current prices, and 17.9 million cordobas at constant prices.
c) Restaurants and hotels are included in item 'Community, social and personal services'.
d) Business services are included in item 'Community, social and personal services'.
e) Domestic service of households is included in item 'Community, social and personal services'.

Nicaragua

1.12 Relations Among National Accounting Aggregates

Million Nicaraguan cordobas

	1970	1975	1978	1979	1980	1981	1982	1983	1984	1985	1986	1987
Gross Domestic Product	5436.1	11133.0	14988.0	14514.0	21892.0	24483.0	28350.0	32920.0	...	...	...	...
Plus: Net factor income from the rest of the world	-176.4	-415.8	-474.6	-801.0	-922.0	-1016.0	-1380.0	-671.0	...	...	...	...
Equals: Gross National Product	5259.7	10717.2	14513.4	13713.0	20970.0	23467.0	26970.0	32249.0	...	...	...	...
Less: Consumption of fixed capital	217.4	445.3	599.5	1204.0	876.0	1038.0	1182.0	1473.0	...	...	...	...
Equals: National Income	5042.3	10271.9	13913.9	12509.0	20094.0	22429.0	25788.0	30776.0	...	...	...	...
Plus: Net current transfers from the rest of the world	43.7	124.0	73.6	...	...	...	...	...	...	...	...	...
Current transfers from the rest of the world	54.7	129.6	77.4	...	...	...	...	...	...	...	...	...
Less: Current transfers to the rest of the world	11.0	5.6	3.8	...	...	...	...	...	...	...	...	...
Equals: National Disposable Income	5086.0	10395.9	13987.5	...	...	...	...	...	...	...	...	...
Less: Final consumption	4559.0	9738.9	12663.8	...	...	...	...	...	...	...	...	...
Statistical discrepancy	-0.5	-7.0	-5.5	...	...	...	...	...	...	...	...	...
Equals: Net Saving	526.5	650.0	1318.2	...	...	...	...	...	...	...	...	...
Less: Surplus of the nation on current transactions	-266.4	-1282.3	72.9	...	...	...	...	...	...	...	...	...
Statistical discrepancy	0.5	7.0	5.5	...	...	...	...	...	...	...	...	...
Equals: Net Capital Formation	793.4	1939.3	1250.8	...	...	...	...	...	...	...	...	...

2.17 Exports and Imports of Goods and Services, Detail

Million Nicaraguan cordobas

		1970	1975	1978	1979	1980	1981	1982	1983	1984	1985	1986	1987
	Exports of Goods and Services												
1	Exports of merchandise, f.o.b.	1250.4	2626.2	4521.8	...	...	...	...	...	...	...	...	...
2	Transport and communication	202.8	495.8	637.9	...	...	...	...	...	...	...	...	...
3	Insurance service charges				...	...	...	...	...	...	...	...	...
4	Other commodities	...	...	...	...	...	...	...	...	...	...	...	...
5	Adjustments of merchandise exports to change-of-ownership basis				...	...	...	...	...	...	...	...	...
6	Direct purchases in the domestic market by non-residential households				...	...	...	...	...	...	...	...	...
7	Direct purchases in the domestic market by extraterritorial bodies	...	...	...	...	...	...	...	...	...	...	...	...
	Total Exports of Goods and Services	1453.2	3122.0	5159.7	...	...	...	...	...	...	...	...	...
	Imports of Goods and Services												
1	Imports of merchandise, c.i.f.	1250.4	2626.2	4521.8	...	...	...	...	...	...	...	...	...
2	Adjustments of merchandise imports to change-of-ownership basis	...	...	...	...	...	...	...	...	...	...	...	...
3	Other transport and communication				...	...	...	...	...	...	...	...	...
4	Other insurance service charges	336.5	1486.3	164.0	...	...	...	...	...	...	...	...	...
5	Other commodities				...	...	...	...	...	...	...	...	...
6	Direct purchases abroad by government	...	...	...	...	...	...	...	...	...	...	...	...
7	Direct purchases abroad by resident households	...	...	...	...	...	...	...	...	...	...	...	...
	Total Imports of Goods and Services	1586.9	4112.5	4685.8	...	...	...	...	...	...	...	...	...
	Balance of Goods and Services	-133.7	-990.5	473.9	...	...	...	...	...	...	...	...	...
	Total Imports and Balance of Goods and Services	1453.2	3122.0	5159.7	...	...	...	...	...	...	...	...	...

Niger

Source. Reply to the United Nations National Accounts Questionnaire from the Service de la Statistique et de la Mecanographie, Niamey.
General note. The estimates shown in the following tables have been adjusted by the Service to conform to the United Nations System of National Accounts so far as the existing data would permit.

1.1 Expenditure on the Gross Domestic Product, in Current Prices
Million CFA francs

	1970	1975	1978	1979	1980	1981	1982	1983	1984	1985	1986	1987
1 Government final consumption expenditure	13500	23600	34019	40958	53958	70230	81031	87512	89706	97200	102700	107200
2 Private final consumption expenditure	94900	138600	264602	311108	381735	410608	483160	522824	473300	488141	...	...
3 Gross capital formation	10500	43000	113536	141008	169104	168355	181191	106994	94600	111400	...	...
A Increase in stocks	3000	6300	22888	28247	32389	4501	25975	-12370	-21500	6600	...	...
B Gross fixed capital formation	7500	36700	90648	112761	136715	163854	155216	119364	116100	104800	...	...
4 Exports of goods and services	16700	34600	71173	109740	128824	141805	139817	143729	143300	128400	...	...
5 Less: Imports of goods and services	24700	59500	124172	159575	197413	189539	222177	173917	162500	178000	...	...
Equals: Gross Domestic Product [a]	111000	180300	359158	443239	536208	601459	663022	687142	638406	647141	643362	649846

a) Data in this table have been revised, therefore they are not strictly comparable with the unrevised data in the other tables.

1.3 Cost Components of the Gross Domestic Product
Million CFA francs

	1970	1975	1978	1979	1980	1981	1982	1983	1984	1985	1986	1987
1 Indirect taxes, net	...	11834	26749	35130	50725	51708	50566	49063	...	...	...	...
A Indirect taxes	...	12071	27102	35802	51079	54977	57105	52730	...	...	...	...
B Less: Subsidies	...	237	353	672	354	3269	6539	3667	...	...	...	...
2 Consumption of fixed capital	...	10107	21981	31282	40951	48224	57583	64175	...	...	...	...
3 Compensation of employees paid by resident producers to:	...	37827	55459	69051	86552	106882	119171	121084	...	...	...	...
4 Operating surplus	...	120532	254969	307776	357980	394645	435702	452820	...	...	...	...
A Corporate and quasi-corporate enterprises	...	...	...	...	...	...	...	...	...	...	...	...
B Private unincorporated enterprises	...	...	...	...	...	...	...	...	...	...	...	...
C General government	...	-27	43	-4	-2	...	...	...	...	...	...	...
Equals: Gross Domestic Product [a]	...	180300	359158	443239	536208	601459	663022	687142	638406	647141	643362	649846

a) Data in this table have been revised, therefore they are not strictly comparable with the unrevised data in the other tables.

1.4 General Government Current Receipts and Disbursements
Million CFA francs

	1970	1975	1978	1979	1980	1981	1982	1983	1984	1985	1986	1987
Receipts												
1 Operating surplus	...	...	...	...	...	...	...	...	...	...	...	...
2 Property and entrepreneurial income	...	1505	...	...	...	...	...	...	...	...	...	...
3 Taxes, fees and contributions	...	20265	...	...	...	...	...	...	...	...	...	...
A Indirect taxes	...	12071	...	...	...	...	...	...	...	...	...	...
B Direct taxes	...	6580	...	...	...	...	...	...	...	...	...	...
C Social security contributions	...	1301	...	...	...	...	...	...	...	...	...	...
D Compulsory fees, fines and penalties	...	313	...	...	...	...	...	...	...	...	...	...
4 Other current transfers	...	20312	...	...	...	...	...	...	...	...	...	...
Statistical discrepancy	...	-27	...	...	...	...	...	...	...	...	...	...
Total Current Receipts of General Government	...	42055	...	...	...	...	...	...	...	...	...	...
Disbursements												
1 Government final consumption expenditure	...	23634	...	...	...	...	...	...	...	...	...	...
A Compensation of employees	...	14384	...	...	...	...	...	...	...	...	...	...
B Consumption of fixed capital	...	1664	...	...	...	...	...	...	...	...	...	...
C Purchases of goods and services, net	...	7610	...	...	...	...	...	...	...	...	...	...
D Less: Own account fixed capital formation	...	...	...	...	...	...	...	...	...	...	...	...
E Indirect taxes paid, net	...	-24	...	...	...	...	...	...	...	...	...	...
2 Property income	...	684	...	...	...	...	...	...	...	...	...	...

Niger

1.4 General Government Current Receipts and Disbursements
(Continued)

Million CFA francs

	1970	1975	1978	1979	1980	1981	1982	1983	1984	1985	1986	1987
3 Subsidies	...	237	...	...	...	...	...	...	...	...	...	...
4 Other current transfers	...	11717	...	...	...	...	...	...	...	...	...	...
A Social security benefits	...	3130	...	...	...	...	...	...	...	...	...	...
B Social assistance grants	...	[ ]	...	...	...	...	...	...	...	...	...	...
C Other	...	8587	...	...	...	...	...	...	...	...	...	...
5 Net saving	...	5783	...	...	...	...	...	...	...	...	...	...
Total Current Disbursements and Net Saving of General Government	...	42055	...	...	...	...	...	...	...	...	...	...

1.7 External Transactions on Current Account, Summary

Million CFA francs

	1970	1975	1978	1979	1980	1981	1982	1983	1984	1985	1986	1987
Payments to the Rest of the World												
1 Imports of goods and services	...	59501	124172	159575	197413	189539	222177	173917	162500	...	...	...
2 Factor income to the rest of the world	...	3314	14394	17436	18133	23057	26512	25713	30729	...	...	...
A Compensation of employees	...	...	158	198	231	256	193	283	...	...	...	...
B Property and entrepreneurial income	...	3314	14236	17238	17902	22801	26319	25430	...	...	...	...
3 Current transfers to the rest of the world	...	6990	10561	13350	14725	17038	20367	21206	21626	...	...	...
4 Surplus of the nation on current transactions	...	-12777	-55343	-65355	-76740	-60222	-92752	-43916	-33249	...	...	...
Payments to the Rest of the World and Surplus of the Nation on Current Transactions [a]	...	57028	93784	125006	153531	169412	176304	176920	181606	...	...	...
Receipts From The Rest of the World												
1 Exports of goods and services	...	34603	71173	109740	128824	141805	139817	143729	143300	...	...	...
2 Factor income from rest of the world	...	2814	2856	3500	6653	4792	6102	4417	6162	...	...	...
A Compensation of employees	...	1759	1624	1689	2043	1097	1561	1336	...	...	...	...
B Property and entrepreneurial income	...	1055	1232	1811	4610	3695	4541	3081	...	...	...	...
3 Current transfers from rest of the world	...	19611	19755	11766	18054	22815	30385	28774	32144	...	...	...
Receipts from the Rest of the World on Current Transactions [a]	...	57028	93784	125006	153531	169412	176304	176920	181606	...	...	...

a) Data in this table have been revised, therefore they are not strictly comparable with the unrevised data in the other tables.

1.8 Capital Transactions of The Nation, Summary

Million CFA francs

	1970	1975	1978	1979	1980	1981	1982	1983	1984	1985	1986	1987
Finance of Gross Capital Formation												
Gross saving	...	30248	...	...	...	...	...	...	...	...	...	...
1 Consumption of fixed capital	...	10107	...	...	...	...	...	...	...	...	...	...
A General government	...	1664	...	...	...	...	...	...	...	...	...	...
B Corporate and quasi-corporate enterprises	...	...	...	...	...	...	...	...	...	...	...	...
C Other	...	...	...	...	...	...	...	...	...	...	...	...
2 Net saving	...	20141	...	...	...	...	...	...	...	...	...	...
A General government	...	5783	...	...	...	...	...	...	...	...	...	...
B Corporate and quasi-corporate enterprises	...	...	...	...	...	...	...	...	...	...	...	...
C Other	...	...	...	...	...	...	...	...	...	...	...	...
Less: Surplus of the nation on current transactions	...	-12777	...	...	...	...	...	...	...	...	...	...
Finance of Gross Capital Formation	...	43025	...	...	...	...	...	...	...	...	...	...

Niger

1.8 Capital Transactions of The Nation, Summary
(Continued)

Million CFA francs

	1970	1975	1978	1979	1980	1981	1982	1983	1984	1985	1986	1987
Gross Capital Formation												
Increase in stocks	...	6280	...	...	...	...	...	...	...	...	...	...
Gross fixed capital formation	...	36745	...	...	...	...	...	...	...	...	...	...
1 General government	...	15770	...	...	...	...	...	...	...	...	...	...
2 Corporate and quasi-corporate enterprises	...	20967	...	...	...	...	...	...	...	...	...	...
3 Other	...	8	...	...	...	...	...	...	...	...	...	...
Gross Capital Formation	...	43025	...	...	...	...	...	...	...	...	...	...

1.9 Gross Domestic Product by Institutional Sectors of Origin

Million CFA francs

	1970	1975	1978	1979	1980	1981	1982	1983	1984	1985	1986	1987
Domestic Factor Incomes Originating												
1 General government	...	14357	...	...	...	...	...	...	...	...	...	...
2 Corporate and quasi-corporate enterprises	...	...	...	...	...	...	...	...	...	...	...	...
3 Households and private unincorporated enterprises	...	123551	...	...	...	...	...	...	...	...	...	...
4 Non-profit institutions serving households	...	121	...	...	...	...	...	...	...	...	...	...
Subtotal: Domestic Factor Incomes	...	158412	...	...	...	...	...	...	...	...	...	...
Indirect taxes, net	...	11834	...	...	...	...	...	...	...	...	...	...
A Indirect taxes	...	12071	...	...	...	...	...	...	...	...	...	...
B Less: Subsidies	...	237	...	...	...	...	...	...	...	...	...	...
Consumption of fixed capital	...	10107	...	...	...	...	...	...	...	...	...	...
Gross Domestic Product	...	180353	...	...	...	...	...	...	...	...	...	...

1.10 Gross Domestic Product by Kind of Activity, in Current Prices

Million CFA francs

	1970	1975	1978	1979	1980	1981	1982	1983	1984	1985	1986	1987
1 Agriculture, hunting, forestry and fishing	...	88585	166059	188746	228097	246815	279121	285712	228312	237777	231901	219070
2 Mining and quarrying	...	10643	36956	63074	67397	50633	50724	56818	52693	52242	47454	49386
3 Manufacturing	...	13844	15174	18228	19819	36007	40585	42840	44819	46250	49320	56642
4 Electricity, gas and water	...	872	1240	1153	2361	4626	6906	9941	11048	14151	16130	17900
5 Construction	...	5055	17086	24638	32120	36075	35667	29377	29309	22693	28893	33375
6 Wholesale and retail trade, restaurants and hotels	...	17594	40279	51059	62101	92773	99093	104996	109732	101971	90661	88859
7 Transport, storage and communication	...	7485	14587	18031	22632	20843	24780	26471	25432	27328	26428	26942
8 Finance, insurance, real estate and business services	...	13168	22585	27193	33565	39963	42393	42729	41331	43431	45973	48426
9 Community, social and personal services	...	1644	8236	9490	10985	5624	6242	6582	7000	8104	7882	8353
Total, Industries	...	158890	322202	401612	479077	533359	585510	605466	549676	553947	544642	548953
Producers of Government Services	...	16024	22836	25137	33809	47749	54243	62734	66139	69895	74290	79294
Other Producers	...	865	1501	2153	2536	2100	2211	2328	3002	3185	3494	4001
Subtotal	...	175779	346539	428902	515422	583208	641964	670528	618817	627027	622426	632248
Less: Imputed bank service charge	...	2336	3004	4757	6302	8828	9576	8673	6654	5530	3771	3436
Plus: Import duties	...	6910	15623	19094	27088	27079	30633	25287	26243	25644	24707	21034
Plus: Value added tax	...	...	...	...	...	...	...	...	...	...	...	...
Equals: Gross Domestic Product [a]	...	180353	359158	443239	536208	601459	663022	687142	638406	647141	643362	649846

a) Data in this table have been revised, therefore they are not strictly comparable with the unrevised data in the other tables.

1.12 Relations Among National Accounting Aggregates

Million CFA francs

	1970	1975	1978	1979	1980	1981	1982	1983	1984	1985	1986	1987
Gross Domestic Product	...	180300	359158	443239	536208	601459	663022	687142	638406	...	...	...
Plus: Net factor income from the rest of the world	...	-500	-11538	-13936	-11480	-18265	-20410	-21296	-24567	...	...	...
Factor income from the rest of the world	...	2814	2856	3500	6653	4792	6102	4417	6162	...	...	...
Less: Factor income to the rest of the world	...	3314	14394	17436	18133	23057	26512	25713	30729	...	...	...
Equals: Gross National Product	...	179800	347620	429303	524728	583194	642612	665846	613839	...	...	...
Less: Consumption of fixed capital	...	10107	21981	31282	40951	48224	57583	64175	66604	...	...	...

Niger

1.12 Relations Among National Accounting Aggregates
(Continued)

Million CFA francs

	1970	1975	1978	1979	1980	1981	1982	1983	1984	1985	1986	1987
Equals: National Income [a]	...	169693	325639	398021	483777	534970	585029	601671	547235	...	...	...
Plus: Net current transfers from the rest of the world	...	12621	9194	-1584	3329	5777	10018	7568	10518	...	...	...
Current transfers from the rest of the world	...	19611	19755	11766	18054	22815	30385	28774	32144	...	...	...
Less: Current transfers to the rest of the world	...	6990	10561	13350	14725	17038	20367	21206	21626	...	...	...
Equals: National Disposable Income [a]	...	182314	334833	396437	487106	540747	595047	609239	557753	...	...	...
Less: Final consumption	...	162200	298621	352066	435693	480838	564191	610336	563006	...	...	...
Equals: Net Saving [a]	...	20114	36212	44371	51413	59909	30856	-1097	-5253	...	...	...
Less: Surplus of the nation on current transactions	...	-12777	-55343	-65355	-76740	-60222	-92752	-43916	-33249	...	...	...
Equals: Net Capital Formation [a]	...	32891	91555	109726	128153	120131	123608	42819	27996	...	...	...

a) Data in this table have been revised, therefore they are not strictly comparable with the unrevised data in the other tables.

2.11 Gross Fixed Capital Formation by Kind of Activity of Owner, ISIC Divisions, in Current Prices

Million CFA francs

	1970	1975	1978	1979	1980	1981	1982	1983	1984	1985	1986	1987
					All Producers							
1 Agriculture, hunting, forestry and fishing	...	10601	...	...	...	...	...	...	...	...	...	...
A Agriculture and hunting	...	6002	...	...	...	...	...	...	...	...	...	...
B Forestry and logging	...	4599	...	...	...	...	...	...	...	...	...	...
C Fishing	...	...	...	...	...	...	...	...	...	...	...	...
2 Mining and quarrying	...	3182	...	...	...	...	...	...	...	...	...	...
3 Manufacturing	...	1580	...	...	...	...	...	...	...	...	...	...
A Manufacturing of food, beverages and tobacco	...	483	...	...	...	...	...	...	...	...	...	...
B Textile, wearing apparel and leather industries	...	422	...	...	...	...	...	...	...	...	...	...
C Manufacture of wood, and wood products, including furniture	...	4	...	...	...	...	...	...	...	...	...	...
D Manufacture of paper and paper products, printing and publishing	...	49	...	...	...	...	...	...	...	...	...	...
E Manufacture of chemicals and chemical petroleum, coal, rubber and plastic products	...	72	...	...	...	...	...	...	...	...	...	...
F Manufacture of non-metalic mineral products except products of petroleum and coal	...	391	...	...	...	...	...	...	...	...	...	...
G Basic metal industries	...	...	...	...	...	...	...	...	...	...	...	...
H Manufacture of fabricated metal products, machinery and equipment	...	159	...	...	...	...	...	...	...	...	...	...
I Other manufacturing industries	...	...	...	...	...	...	...	...	...	...	...	...
4 Electricity, gas and water	...	542	...	...	...	...	...	...	...	...	...	...
5 Construction	...	681	...	...	...	...	...	...	...	...	...	...
6 Wholesale and retail trade, restaurants and hotels	...	1896	...	...	...	...	...	...	...	...	...	...
A Wholesale and retail trade	...	1870	...	...	...	...	...	...	...	...	...	...
B Restaurants and hotels	...	26	...	...	...	...	...	...	...	...	...	...
7 Transport, storage and communication	...	1932	...	...	...	...	...	...	...	...	...	...
A Transport and storage	...	1185	...	...	...	...	...	...	...	...	...	...
B Communication	...	747	...	...	...	...	...	...	...	...	...	...
8 Finance, insurance, real estate and business services	...	481	...	...	...	...	...	...	...	...	...	...
A Financial institutions	...	316	...	...	...	...	...	...	...	...	...	...
B Insurance	...	...	...	...	...	...	...	...	...	...	...	...
C Real estate and business services	...	165	...	...	...	...	...	...	...	...	...	...
9 Community, social and personal services	...	72	...	...	...	...	...	...	...	...	...	...
A Sanitary and similar services	...	...	...	...	...	...	...	...	...	...	...	...
B Social and related community services	...	39	...	...	...	...	...	...	...	...	...	...

Niger

2.11 Gross Fixed Capital Formation by Kind of Activity of Owner, ISIC Divisions, in Current Prices
(Continued)

Million CFA francs

	1970	1975	1978	1979	1980	1981	1982	1983	1984	1985	1986	1987
Educational services	...	39	...	...	...	...	...	...	...	...	...	...
Medical, dental, other health and veterinary services	...	-	...	...	...	...	...	...	...	...	...	...
C Recreational and cultural services	...	10	...	...	...	...	...	...	...	...	...	...
D Personal and household services	...	23	...	...	...	...	...	...	...	...	...	...
Total Industries	...	20967	...	...	...	...	...	...	...	...	...	...
Producers of Government Services	...	15770	...	...	...	...	...	...	...	...	...	...
Private Non-Profit Institutions Serving Households	...	8	...	...	...	...	...	...	...	...	...	...
Total	...	36745	...	...	...	...	...	...	...	...	...	...

Nigeria

General note. The preparation of national accounts statistics in Nigeria is undertaken by the Federal Office of Statistics, Lagos. The official estimates together with methodological notes on sources and methods are published in 'Gross Domestic Product of Nigeria'. Another publication 'National Accounts of Nigeria' with estimates dating back to 1958/59, was published in 1978. The estimates are generally in accordance with the definitions and classifications recommended in the United Nations System of National Accounts (SNA). Input-output tables have been published for the year 1959/60 in 'An Input-Output Analysis of the Nigerian Economy'. The following tables have been prepared from successive replies to the United Nations national accounts questionnaire. Estimates relate to fiscal year beginning 1 April. When the scope and coverage of the estimates differ for conceptual or statistical reasons from the definitions and classifications recommended in SNA, a footnote is indicated to the relevant tables.

Sources and methods:

(a) Gross domestic product. Gross domestic product is estimated mainly through the production approach.

(b) Expenditure on the gross domestic product. The expenditure approach is used to estimate government final consumption expenditure, exports and imports of goods and services and buildings and other construction of gross fixed capital formation. This approach, in combination with the commodity-flow approach is used to estimate investment in machinery and equipment. Private final consumption expenditure, which includes increase in stocks, is estimated as a residual. Government consumption expenditure is estimated from the annual economic analysis of the accounts of the public authorities. Useful information on private consumption expenditure will become available when the urban consumer survey and the rural consumption inquiry for 1974/75 are completed. The estimates of gross fixed capital formation for machinery, transport and other equipment are based on foreign trade statistics supplemented by information on import duties. A mark-up for trade, transport and installation charges of 33.3 per cent and 10 per cent is added to the import values of machinery and transport equipment respectively. The values of small concrete buildings are based on the value of cement used and of mud-walled houses on the estimated population in need of such houses. For the oil sector, the estimates of gross capital formation are compiled from the returns obtained from the oil companies. Sources for other sectors include the accounts of the Nigerian Coal Corp., the reports of the Nigerian Steel Development Authority, the Nigerian Railway Corp.and the Nigerian Shipping Line Ltd., and the accounts of the government. The main sources of information for exports and imports of goods and services are the balance-of-payments accounts.

(c) Cost-structure of the gross domestic product. Compensation of employees, operating surplus, and consumption of fixed capital are obtained as a residual by deducting net indirect taxes from the GDP. For indirect taxes and subsidies, the annual government accounts are used.

(d) Gross domestic product by kind of economic activity. The table of GDP by kind of economic activity is prepared in factor values. The production approach is used to estimate the value added of most industries. The income approach is used for producers of government services. Production estimates for 13 harvested agricultural crops are obtained from the national agriculture sample census in 1974/75 and the annual rural economic surveys. Estimates of output for green vegetables, tomatoes, oranges, bananas, sugar cane, coconut, pawpaw and pineapple are based on the average expenditure per household contained in the reports on inquiries into the income and expenditure patterns of lower and middle income households supplemented by export data. The values are reduced by 50 per cent for trade and transport charges. Foreign trade statistics provide the information for all other crops, except cocoa and tobacco which is estimated from information supplied by the Nigerian Produce Marketing CO., and from manufacturing companies. For livestock and its products, estimates are based on such data as foreign trade statistics, number of animals slaughtered, number of cattle that are milked, Lagos retail prices, etc. Non-monetary activities are covered in the estimates. The output of timber is estimated from the data on logs exported or used locally. Data on the production of fish are obtained from the Federal Fisheries Department. The annual reports of the Petroleum Division in the Federal Ministry of Mines and Power furnish information on production and f.o.b. values of crude oil and the quantity of gas sold. The same Ministry also furnishes data on production of metalliferious ores. This output is valued at f.o.b. prices. Information on the values of manufacturing output and intermediate consumption are obtained from the annual surveys of large establishments. Adjustment is made of value added by 20 per cent to cover small establishments. The estimates of electricity are based on annual reports of the concerned companies The sources of information on water supply are the actual expenditure of the Government bodies and annual accounts of water boards of corporations. Data for estimating value added in construction are obtained from accounts of public authorities and corporations government enterprises and the survey of large establishments engaged in mining, manufacturing and distributive activities. For smaller construction activities, sources such as the value of cement used,questionnaire and actual of approved expenditure of public authorities are used. Trade is assumed to be 12.5 per cent of GDP in the base year 1958/59. For other years, value added is extrapolated by indexes. The bench-mark value added of road transport is based on the number of commercial vehicles. Other years' estimates are made by projecting the 1958/59 figure by the estimated number of tractors and commercial vehicles and using the CPI of transport services for five urban centres. The value added of railways, harbours, water and air transports are estimated from annual reports of concerned enterprises. The sources of information for estimating the value added of government services are the Accountant-General's reports and budget of the public authorities. For education, estimates are based on information obtained from the Federal Ministry of Education and the National Universities Commission for private institutions and on the number of teachers and an assumed average salary per teacher for other institutions. For private health institutions, the expenditure on personal emoluments is regarded as value added and assumed to grow at the same rate as for government institutions. The value added of other services, which includes the financial sector, is assumed to grow at an average annual rate of 13.8 per cent. For the constant price estimates, price deflation is used for the manufacturing, construction, part of transport and services sectors. For agriculture, the production of corps is either revalued at 1962/63 prices or deflated by retail prices. Value added of mining, electricity, trade and transport relating to passenger-miles and ton-miles is extrapolated by appropriate indicators.

1.1 Expenditure on the Gross Domestic Product, in Current Prices

Million Nigerian naira — Fiscal year beginning 1 April

	1970	1975	1978	1979	1980	1981	1982	1983	1984	1985	1986	1987
1 Government final consumption expenditure	577.6	2236.9	4999.3	4881.7	5051.4	5503.5	5504.0	5560.7	...	...	...	...
2 Private final consumption expenditure	4143.4	13688.5	23271.9	23847.0	28436.6	33853.3	36834.8	33843.0	...	...	...	...
3 Gross capital formation	882.7	5514.1	9886.3	9580.2	11565.8	13991.7	11320.4	9316.6	...	...	...	...
A Increase in stocks	...	494.3	500.0	500.0	589.9	673.5	450.0	391.5	...	...	...	...
B Gross fixed capital formation	882.7	5019.8	9386.3	9080.2	10976.0	13318.2	10870.4	8925.1	...	...	...	...
Residential buildings	...	552.3							...	...	...	...
Non-residential buildings	...	1469.2	6191.7	6383.7	7342.3	8003.2	7206.3	6536.6	...	...	...	...
Other construction and land improvement etc.	...	1311.3							...	...	...	...
Other	...	1687.0	3194.6	2696.5	3633.7	5315.0	3664.1	2388.5	...	...	...	...
4 Exports of goods and services	953.8	5317.7	6881.6	11016.9	14908.8	11375.8	9650.2	7806.7	...	...	...	...
5 Less: Imports of goods and services	937.0	4978.4	10024.2	8243.1	11705.4	16081.9	12119.3	7875.3	...	...	...	...
Equals: Gross Domestic Product	5620.5	21778.7	35014.9	41082.7	48257.2	48642.5	51190.1	48651.7	...	...	...	...

Nigeria

1.2 Expenditure on the Gross Domestic Product, in Constant Prices

Million Nigerian naira — Fiscal year beginning 1 April

	1970	1975	1978	1979	1980	1981	1982	1983	1984	1985	1986	1987
					At constant prices of:1977							
1 Government final consumption expenditure	...	2667.8	4125.1	3149.5	2591.6	2930.4	2826.3	2848.8	...	...	...	...
2 Private final consumption expenditure	...	16374.0	19206.9	15387.7	14594.2	18031.0	18914.0	17340.9	...	...	...	...
3 Gross capital formation	...	6628.2	9336.1	8012.3	9218.2	10511.4	7990.0	6368.5	...	...	...	...
A Increase in stocks	...	642.8	498.2	468.5	562.1	625.3	416.9	365.8	...	...	...	...
B Gross fixed capital formation	...	5985.4	8837.9	7543.8	8656.1	9885.2	7573.1	6002.7	...	...	...	...
Residential buildings	...	799.9	...	...	...	...	...	...	...	...	...	...
Non-residential buildings	...	2127.8	5786.6	5556.8	6112.0	6408.2	5349.1	4624.4	...	...	...	...
Other construction and land improvement etc.	...	1311.3							...	...	...	...
Other	...	1746.4	3051.3	1987.0	2544.1	3477.0	2224.0	1378.3	...	...	...	...
4 Exports of goods and services	...	6809.7	6844.6	10206.5	13294.8	9605.5	7426.7	5662.4	...	...	...	...
5 Less: Imports of goods and services	...	5131.9	9002.4	6718.6	8613.3	10711.3	7296.8	4319.3	...	...	...	...
Equals: Gross Domestic Product	...	27347.8	30510.3	30037.3	31085.5	30366.2	29860.1	27861.3	...	...	...	...

1.3 Cost Components of the Gross Domestic Product

Million Nigerian naira — Fiscal year beginning 1 April

	1970	1975	1978	1979	1980	1981	1982	1983	1984	1985	1986	1987
1 Indirect taxes, net	415.4	821.1	1543.5	1176.2	1216.4	1597.1	1819.7	1879.0	...	...	...	...
A Indirect taxes	423.5	833.5	1611.2	1233.8	1423.8	1887.5	2048.3	2136.2	...	...	...	...
B Less: Subsidies	8.1	12.4	67.7	57.6	207.4	290.4	228.6	257.2	...	...	...	...
2 Consumption of fixed capital	5205.1	759.8	1032.5	998.8	1207.4	1465.0	1195.7	981.8	...	...	...	...
3 Compensation of employees paid by resident producers to:		5726.1	10058.9	10221.7	11915.0	14003.2	15064.2	14019.8	...	...	...	...
A Resident households	...	5673.6	9727.7	9932.7	11480.8	13486.8	14508.7	13659.4	...	...	...	...
B Rest of the world	...	52.5	331.2	289.0	434.2	516.4	555.6	360.4	...	...	...	...
4 Operating surplus	...	14471.0	22380.0	28686.1	33918.5	31577.2	33110.5	31771.0	...	...	...	...
Equals: Gross Domestic Product	5620.5	21778.7	35014.9	41082.7	48257.2	48642.5	51190.1	48651.7	...	...	...	...

1.7 External Transactions on Current Account, Summary

Million Nigerian naira — Fiscal year beginning 1 April

	1970	1975	1978	1979	1980	1981	1982	1983	1984	1985	1986	1987
				Payments to the Rest of the World								
1 Imports of goods and services	937.0	4978.4	10024.2	8243.1	11705.4	16081.9	12119.3	7875.3	...	...	...	...
2 Factor income to the rest of the world	118.8	534.5	660.1	781.2	1468.6	1348.8	1317.4	1040.1	...	...	...	...
A Compensation of employees	...	52.5	331.2	289.0	434.2	516.4	555.6	360.4	...	...	...	...
B Property and entrepreneurial income	...	482.0	328.9	492.2	1034.4	832.4	761.8	679.7	...	...	...	...
3 Current transfers to the rest of the world	31.8	92.8	178.0	247.6	332.6	366.7	308.5	198.4	...	...	...	...
4 Surplus of the nation on current transactions	-50.0	42.6	-3787.2	1924.1	1798.0	-5962.5	-3920.8	-1242.3	...	...	...	...
Payments to the Rest of the World and Surplus of the Nation on Current Transactions	1037.6	5648.3	7075.1	11196.0	15304.6	11834.9	9824.4	7871.5	...	...	...	...

Nigeria

1.7 External Transactions on Current Account, Summary
(Continued)

Million Nigerian naira — Fiscal year beginning 1 April

Receipts From The Rest of the World

	1970	1975	1978	1979	1980	1981	1982	1983	1984	1985	1986	1987
1 Exports of goods and services	953.8	5317.7	6881.6	11016.9	14908.8	11375.8	9650.2	7806.7	...	...	...	...
2 Factor income from rest of the world	7.0	314.6	186.1	165.0	378.4	438.9	155.1	54.5	...	...	...	...
A Compensation of employees	...	5.0	2.2	5.6	6.9	7.7	6.7	5.0	...	...	...	...
B Property and entrepreneurial income	...	309.6	183.9	159.4	371.5	431.2	148.4	49.5	...	...	...	...
3 Current transfers from rest of the world	76.8	16.0	7.4	14.1	17.4	20.2	19.1	10.3	...	...	...	...
Receipts from the Rest of the World on Current Transactions	1037.6	5648.3	7075.1	11196.0	15304.6	11834.9	9824.4	7871.5	...	...	...	...

1.10 Gross Domestic Product by Kind of Activity, in Current Prices

Million Nigerian naira — Fiscal year beginning 1 April

	1970	1975	1978	1979	1980	1981	1982	1983	1984	1985	1986	1987
1 Agriculture, hunting, forestry and fishing	2495.2	5354.7	8053.9	9101.4	10079.3	9863.1	12410.3	12165.7	...	...	...	...
2 Mining and quarrying	540.7	4668.4	8415.5	11339.5	15066.5	12400.1	11555.4	9923.0	...	...	...	...
3 Manufacturing	378.4	1170.4	1785.0	2037.1	2354.4	2647.5	2726.3	2372.5	...	...	...	...
4 Electricity, gas and water	38.0	63.4	127.9	199.7	244.6	309.7	386.0	460.3	...	...	...	...
5 Construction	304.5	1814.6	3077.2	3192.3	3671.2	4001.6	3603.0	3268.3	...	...	...	...
6 Wholesale and retail trade, restaurants and hotels	673.5	4378.6	7104.1	8821.4	9722.9	10564.8	10593.8	10490.3	...	...	...	...
7 Transport, storage and communication	146.9	673.6	1211.1	1447.0	1762.6	2129.0	2396.5	2187.7	...	...	...	...
8 Finance, insurance, real estate and business services	220.8	609.9	796.0	806.1	815.0	1161.7	1398.1	1494.3	...	...	...	...
9 Community, social and personal services	...	871.3	1135.5	1216.5	1309.6	1398.1	1492.0	1499.0	...	...	...	...
Total, Industries	4798.0	19604.7	31706.2	38161.0	45026.0	44475.6	46561.3	43861.1	...	...	...	...
Producers of Government Services	407.1	1352.9	1765.2	1745.6	2014.9	2570.0	2809.1	2911.5	...	...	...	...
Other Producers	...	...	...	...	...	...	...	...	...	...	...	...
Subtotal a	5205.1	20957.6	33471.4	39906.6	47040.9	47045.4	49370.4	46772.6	...	...	...	...
Less: Imputed bank service charge	...	...	...	...	...	...	...	...	...	...	...	...
Plus: Import duties	...	...	...	...	...	...	...	...	...	...	...	...
Plus: Value added tax	...	...	...	...	...	...	...	...	...	...	...	...
Plus: Other adjustments b	415.4	821.1	1543.5	1176.1	1216.3	1597.1	1819.7	1879.1	...	...	...	...
Equals: Gross Domestic Product	5620.5	21778.7	35014.9	41082.7	48257.2	48642.5	51190.1	48651.7	...	...	...	...
Memorandum Item: Mineral fuels and power	...	-47.7	-391.9	-283.4	...	...	...	...	...	...	...	...

a) Gross domestic product in factor values.
b) Item 'Other adjustments' refers to indirect taxes net of subsidies.

Nigeria

1.11 Gross Domestic Product by Kind of Activity, in Constant Prices

Fiscal year beginning 1 April
Million Nigerian naira

	1970	1975	1978	1979	1980	1981	1982	1983	1984	1985	1986	1987
		1962			At constant prices of:			1977				
1 Agriculture, hunting, forestry and fishing	1835.8	6947.2	6673.7	5785.8	6071.0	5720.7	6495.6	6155.0	...	...	...	...
2 Mining and quarrying	508.9	6276.5	7073.7	8240.1	7406.7	5302.1	4645.3	4461.5	...	...	...	...
3 Manufacturing	317.6	1186.5	1778.4	1908.6	2244.8	2458.3	2526.5	2216.7	...	...	...	...
4 Electricity, gas and water	24.5	86.0	110.3	136.8	143.3	169.5	189.4	199.4	...	...	...	...
5 Construction	266.2	1932.5	2875.9	2778.8	3056.0	3204.1	2674.5	2312.2	...	...	...	...
6 Wholesale and retail trade, restaurants and hotels	515.3	5457.1	6112.9	5744.8	6533.2	6941.3	6359.2	6092.7	...	...	...	...
7 Transport, storage and communication	138.2	964.2	1083.7	1162.3	1311.4	1458.0	1523.8	1299.6	...	...	...	...
8 Finance, insurance, real estate and business services	192.7	679.2	746.0	713.8	689.7	932.6	1066.4	1089.8	...	...	...	...
9 Community, social and personal services	...	1047.5	1074.4	1077.2	1091.5	1105.9	1120.8	1070.8	...	...	...	...
Total, Industries	3799.2	24576.8	27528.9	27548.3	28547.5	27292.3	26601.5	24897.7	...	...	...	...
Producers of Government Services	387.4	1581.0	1650.9	1584.3	1687.5	2150.8	2280.4	2143.0	...	...	...	...
Other Producers	...	...	...	...	...	...	...	...	...	...	...	...
Subtotal [a]	4186.6	26157.8	29179.7	29132.6	30235.0	29443.1	28881.8	27040.7	...	...	...	...
Less: Imputed bank service charge	...	...	...	...	...	...	...	...	...	...	...	...
Plus: Import duties	...	...	...	...	...	...	...	...	...	...	...	...
Plus: Value added tax	...	...	...	...	...	...	...	...	...	...	...	...
Plus: Other adjustments	...	1190.0[b]	1330.6[b]	904.7[b]	850.5[b]	923.1[b]	978.3[b]	820.6[b]	...	...	...	...
Equals: Gross Domestic Product	4186.6[a]	27347.8	30510.3	30037.3	31085.5	30366.2	29860.1	27861.3	...	...	...	...

a) Gross domestic product in factor values.
b) Item 'Other adjustments' refers to indirect taxes net of subsidies.

1.12 Relations Among National Accounting Aggregates

Fiscal year beginning 1 April
Million Nigerian naira

	1970	1975	1978	1979	1980	1981	1982	1983	1984	1985	1986	1987
Gross Domestic Product	...	21778.7	35014.9	41082.7	48257.2	48642.5	51190.1	48651.7	...	...	...	...
Plus: Net factor income from the rest of the world	...	-219.9	-474.0	-616.2	-1090.2	-909.9	-1162.3	-985.6	...	...	...	...
Factor income from the rest of the world	...	314.6	186.1	165.0	378.4	438.9	155.1	54.5	...	...	...	...
Less: Factor income to the rest of the world	...	534.5	660.1	781.2	1468.6	1348.8	1317.4	1040.1	...	...	...	...
Equals: Gross National Product	...	21558.8	34540.9	40466.5	47167.0	47732.6	50027.8	47666.1	...	...	...	...
Less: Consumption of fixed capital	...	759.8	1032.5	998.8	1207.4	1465.0	1195.7	981.8	...	...	...	...
Equals: National Income	...	20799.0	33508.4	39467.7	45959.6	46267.6	48832.1	46684.3	...	...	...	...
Plus: Net current transfers from the rest of the world	...	-76.8	-170.6	-233.5	-315.2	-346.5	-289.4	-188.1	...	...	...	...
Current transfers from the rest of the world	...	16.0	7.4	14.1	17.4	20.2	19.1	10.3	...	...	...	...
Less: Current transfers to the rest of the world	...	92.8	178.0	247.6	332.6	366.7	308.5	198.4	...	...	...	...
Equals: National Disposable Income	...	20722.2	33337.8	39234.2	45644.4	45921.1	48542.7	46496.2	...	...	...	...
Less: Final consumption	...	15925.4	28271.2	28728.7	33488.0	39356.8	42338.8	39403.7	...	...	...	...
Equals: Net Saving	...	4796.9	5065.6	10505.5	12156.4	6564.3	6203.9	7092.5	...	...	...	...
Less: Surplus of the nation on current transactions	...	42.6	-3787.2	1924.1	1798.0	-5962.5	-3920.8	-1242.3	...	...	...	...
Equals: Net Capital Formation	...	4754.3	8853.8	8581.4	10358.4	12526.8	10124.7	8334.8	...	...	...	...

Nigeria

4.1 Derivation of Value Added by Kind of Activity, in Current Prices

Million Nigerian naira

Fiscal year beginning 1 April

	1980 Gross Output	1980 Intermediate Consumption	1980 Value Added	1981 Gross Output	1981 Intermediate Consumption	1981 Value Added	1982 Gross Output	1982 Intermediate Consumption	1982 Value Added	1983 Gross Output	1983 Intermediate Consumption	1983 Value Added
						All Producers						
1 Agriculture, hunting, forestry and fishing	...	...	10079.3	...	...	9863.1	...	...	12410.3	...	...	12165.7
A Agriculture and hunting	...	...	8545.7	...	...	7952.4	...	...	10092.8	...	...	9369.5
B Forestry and logging	...	...	315.0	...	...	321.7	...	...	329.7	...	...	337.7
C Fishing	...	...	1218.6	...	...	1589.0	...	...	1987.8	...	...	2458.5
2 Mining and quarrying	...	...	15066.5	...	...	12400.1	...	...	11555.4	...	...	9923.0
A Coal mining	...	...	0.1	...	...	0.1	...	...	-	...	...	-
B Crude petroleum and natural gas production	...	...	14192.7	...	...	11512.7	...	...	10758.6	...	...	9201.4
C Metal ore mining	...	...	16.8	...	...	16.6	...	...	12.7	...	...	10.4
D Other mining	...	...	856.8	...	...	870.8	...	...	784.1	...	...	711.3
3 Manufacturing	...	...	2354.4	...	...	2647.5	...	...	2726.3	...	...	2372.5
4 Electricity, gas and water	...	...	244.6	...	...	309.7	...	...	386.0	...	...	460.8
A Electricity, gas and steam	...	...	227.3	...	...	285.7	...	...	352.2	...	...	417.3
B Water works and supply	...	...	17.3	...	...	24.0	...	...	33.8	...	...	43.5
5 Construction	...	...	3671.2	...	...	4001.6	...	...	3603.0	...	...	3268.3
6 Wholesale and retail trade, restaurants and hotels	...	...	9722.9	...	...	10564.8	...	...	10593.8	...	...	10489.9
A Wholesale and retail trade	...	...	9617.2	...	...	10449.7	...	...	10463.6	...	...	10344.6
B Restaurants and hotels	...	...	105.7	...	...	115.1	...	...	130.1	...	...	145.3
7 Transport, storage and communication	...	...	1762.6	...	...	2128.9	...	...	2396.6	...	...	2187.7
A Transport and storage	...	...	1692.6	...	...	2055.0	...	...	2321.9	...	...	2109.6
B Communication	...	...	70.0	...	...	73.9	...	...	74.7	...	...	78.1
8 Finance, insurance, real estate and business services	...	...	815.0	...	...	1161.7	...	...	1398.1	...	...	1494.3
A Financial institutions	...	...	558.7	...	...	869.7	...	...	1069.0	...	...	1117.5
B Insurance	...	...	141.2	...	...	172.4	...	...	205.0	...	...	248.1
C Real estate and business services	...	...	115.1	...	...	119.6	...	...	124.1	...	...	128.7
9 Community, social and personal services	...	...	1309.6	...	...	1398.1	...	...	1492.0	...	...	1498.9
Total, Industries	...	...	45026.0	...	...	44475.6	...	...	46561.3	...	...	43861.1
Producers of Government Services	...	...	2014.9	...	...	2569.9	...	...	2809.1	...	...	2911.5
Other Producers	...	...	...	...	...	...	...	...	...	...	...	...
Total [a]	...	...	47040.9	...	...	47045.4	...	...	49370.4	...	...	46772.6
Less: Imputed bank service charge	...	...	...	...	...	...	...	...	...	...	...	...
Import duties	...	...	...	...	...	...	...	...	...	...	...	...
Value added tax	...	...	...	...	...	...	...	...	...	...	...	...
Total	...	...	...	...	...	...	...	...	...	...	...	...

a) Gross domestic product in factor values.

4.2 Derivation of Value Added by Kind of Activity, in Constant Prices

Million Nigerian naira

Fiscal year beginning 1 April

	1980 Gross Output	1980 Intermediate Consumption	1980 Value Added	1981 Gross Output	1981 Intermediate Consumption	1981 Value Added	1982 Gross Output	1982 Intermediate Consumption	1982 Value Added	1983 Gross Output	1983 Intermediate Consumption	1983 Value Added
					At constant prices of: 1977							
						All Producers						
1 Agriculture, hunting, forestry and fishing	...	...	6071.0	...	...	5720.7	...	...	6495.6	...	...	6155.0
A Agriculture and hunting	...	...	5069.2	...	...	4699.8	...	...	5449.9	...	...	4976.8
B Forestry and logging	...	...	270.6	...	...	264.5	...	...	259.4	...	...	255.4
C Fishing	...	...	731.1	...	...	756.5	...	...	786.3	...	...	922.8
2 Mining and quarrying	...	...	7406.7	...	...	5302.1	...	...	4645.3	...	...	4461.5
A Coal mining	...	...	0.1	...	...	0.1	...	...	-	...	...	-
B Crude petroleum and natural gas production	...	...	6748.2	...	...	4613.1	...	...	4071.7	...	...	3966.2
C Metal ore mining	...	...	16.6	...	...	16.1	...	...	11.9	...	...	9.7
D Other mining	...	...	641.8	...	...	672.9	...	...	561.6	...	...	485.6
3 Manufacturing	...	...	2244.8	...	...	2458.3	...	...	2526.5	...	...	2216.7
4 Electricity, gas and water	...	...	143.3	...	...	169.5	...	...	189.4	...	...	199.4
A Electricity, gas and steam	...	...	129.3	...	...	151.4	...	...	165.0	...	...	169.8
B Water works and supply	...	...	13.9	...	...	18.2	...	...	24.3	...	...	29.6

Nigeria

4.2 Derivation of Value Added by Kind of Activity, in Constant Prices
(Continued)

Million Nigerian naira — Fiscal year beginning 1 April

At constant prices of: 1977

	1980 Gross Output	1980 Intermediate Consumption	1980 Value Added	1981 Gross Output	1981 Intermediate Consumption	1981 Value Added	1982 Gross Output	1982 Intermediate Consumption	1982 Value Added	1983 Gross Output	1983 Intermediate Consumption	1983 Value Added
5 Construction	...	...	3056.0	...	...	3204.1	...	...	2674.5	...	...	2312.2
6 Wholesale and retail trade, restaurants and hotels	...	...	6533.2	...	...	6941.3	...	...	6359.2	...	...	6092.7
A Wholesale and retail trade	...	...	6432.1	...	...	6831.6	...	...	6236.5	...	...	5956.8
B Restaurants and hotels	...	...	101.1	...	...	109.7	...	...	122.7	...	...	135.9
7 Transport, storage and communication	...	...	1311.4	...	...	1458.0	...	...	1523.8	...	...	1299.6
A Transport and storage	...	...	1247.0	...	...	1390.9	...	...	1457.2	...	...	1230.9
B Communication	...	...	64.4	...	...	67.1	...	...	66.6	...	...	68.7
8 Finance, insurance, real estate and business services	...	...	689.7	...	...	932.6	...	...	1066.4	...	...	1089.8
A Financial institutions	...	...	462.6	...	...	682.3	...	...	769.0	...	...	792.7
B Insurance	...	...	161.6	...	...	136.0	...	...	153.4	...	...	176.8
C Real estate and business services	...	...	65.5	...	...	114.2	...	...	144.0	...	...	120.2
Real estate, except dwellings	...	...	6.0	...	...	5.8	...	...	5.0	...	...	4.7
Dwellings	...	...	...	...	...	...	...	...	...	...	...	...
9 Community, social and personal services	...	...	1091.5	...	...	1105.9	...	...	1120.8	...	...	1070.8
Total, Industries	...	...	28547.5	...	...	27292.3	...	...	26601.5	...	...	24897.7
Producers of Government Services	...	...	1687.5	...	...	2150.8	...	...	2280.4	...	...	2143.0
Other Producers	...	...	...	...	...	...	...	...	...	...	...	...
Total [a]	...	...	30235.0	...	...	29443.1	...	...	28881.8	...	...	27040.7
Less: Imputed bank service charge	...	...	...	...	...	...	...	...	...	...	...	...
Import duties	...	...	...	...	...	...	...	...	...	...	...	...
Value added tax	...	...	...	...	...	...	...	...	...	...	...	...
Total	...	...	...	...	...	...	...	...	...	...	...	...

a) Gross domestic product in factor values.

Norway

General note. The preparation of national accounts statistics in Norway is undertaken by the Central Bureau of Statistics, Oslo. The official estimates are published annually in 'Nasjonalregnskap (National Accounts)'. A detailed description of the sources and methods is found in 'National Accounts of Norway - System and Methods of Estimation', No. 45 in the series Samfunnsokononieske Studier (Norwegian text) and No. 81/1 in the series RAPPORTER (English text), published in 1981. The estimates are generally in accordance with the classifications and definitions recommended in the United Nations system of National Accounts (SNA). Estimates conforming to the present SNA were published for the first time in 'Okonomisk Utsyn (Economic Survey) 1972'. The corresponding changes of concepts and classifications were published in 'Revidert Nasjonalregnskap (Revised National Accounts)' in 1975. Input-output tables were published in 1968 in 'Input-output data 1954, 1959 and 1964'. The following tables have been prepared from successive replies to the United Nations national accounts questionnaire. When the scope and coverage of the estimates differ for conceptual or statistical reasons from the definitions and classifications recommended in SNA, a footnote is indicated to the relevant tables.

Sources and methods:

(a) Gross domestic product. The main approach used to estimate GDP is the production approach.

(b) Expenditure on the gross domestic product. The expenditure approach is used to estimate all components of GDP by expenditure type, within the framework of detailed input-output tables using the commodity-flow method. Change in stocks, however, is primarily calculated as the difference between supply and other uses for each commodity. Government final consumption expenditure is mainly based on government accounts. Estimates of private consumption expenditure relating to consumer goods are based on turnover statistics and extrapolated by value indexes. Gross fixed capital formation is recorded at purchasers' prices which includes investment levies, but excludes value added tax. Exports and imports of goods and services are mainly based on foreign exchange statistics from the Bank of Norway and external trade statistics of the Central Bureau of Statistics. For the constant price estimates, double deflation and the commodity-flow approach are used within the framework of detailed annual input-output tables for all expenditure components. Current values are deflated by appropriate price indexes.

(c) Cost-structure of the gross domestic product. The value of compensation of employees is obtained through adding up wages and salaries by branch of activity. Censuses provide bench-mark data, while data from government accounts, quarterly earnings statistics and annual industrial statistics are used as extrapolators for the inter-censal years. Operating surplus is arrived at as a residual. Consumption of fixed capital is estimated by using the perpetual inventory method. Time series of gross investment at constant prices provide the basis for calculating consumption of fixed capital. Commodity taxes and subsidies are calculated on accrual basis through the commodity-flow method.

(d) Gross domestic product by kind of economic activity. The table of GDP by kind of economic activity is prepared at market prices, i.e. producers' values. The production approach is used to estimate value added of almost all industries. This is done within the framework of detailed input-output tables using the commodity-flow method. The income approach is used for producers of government services and part of other private services. The expenditure approach is used in the case of the trade sector. Agricultural production is estimated from data prepared by the Agricultural Budgeting Board. Information on prices is obtained from the Agricultural Price Reporting Office and from the marketing cooperatives. For mining and quarrying estimates are extracted from the annual industrial statistics, which include crude oil and natural gas production in the North Sea. For manufacturing use is made of the annual industrial statistics which supply detailed information on gross output and intermediate consumption by industrial activity and by commodity for all establishments employing five or more persons. The annual statistics of building and construction work give information on the number of establishments, persons engaged, value of production, cost of materials and gross fixed capital formation. Gross output of the trade sector is measured as the total of trade and transport margins plus some minor items. The margins are estimated as the aggregate difference between purchasers' values and producers' values, except for bench-mark years when mark-ups are estimated from information from government agencies, business organizations, surveys of consumer expenditure or from price data. The estimation of intermediate consumption is to a large extent based on ratios from bench-mark years. The estimates for railway, tramway, subway and suburban railway transport as well as air transport are based on detailed accounting data. For other land transport the statistical sources are the annual scheduled road transport statistics, data from censuses of establishments, etc. Summary accounts for financial institutions exist in the annual credit market statistics. For insurance the annual insurance statistics and extracts of accounts are used. Operating surplus of dwellings in the bench-mark year has been fixed as a certain percentage of reduced replacement cost of the dwelling stock in the base-year. For subsequent years gross output is extrapolated by using information on investments, repairs and clearing of old dwellings. Bench-mark estimates for business services are made from the censuses of establishments held every ten years and extrapolated by value indices based on annual statistics on services. For government services data are obtained from the municipal accounts and central government accounts including social insurance administration. For private services bench-mark estimates are to a large extent based on the censuses of establishments, and extrapolated by use of employment estimates and components of consumer price index. For the estimation of constant prices, double deflation and the commodity-flow approach are used within the framework of detailed annual input-output tables. In most sectors output is deflated by appropriate price indexes. However, output of crop and livestock products is valued at base-year prices, and extrapolation by quantity indicators is undertaken for restaurants and hotels, transport of goods and financial institutions.

1.1 Expenditure on the Gross Domestic Product, in Current Prices

Million Norwegian kroner

	1970	1975	1978	1979	1980	1981	1982	1983	1984	1985	1986	1987
1 Government final consumption expenditure	13533	28702	43543	46585	53478	62616	70408	78214	84099	92653	102005	116325
2 Private final consumption expenditure	43047	77615	110670	120104	135242	155205	175310	192979	210921	245439	278764	294796
3 Gross capital formation	24326	52335	60765	65727	78902	84032	96071	99116	116267	121145	151648	157866
A Increase in stocks	3131	1544	-6941	-459	8104	-7761	3809	-4332	-1300	11103	5515	1654
B Gross fixed capital formation	21195	50791	67706	66186	70798	91793	92262	103448	117567	110042	146133	156212
Residential buildings [a]	3984	8138	11765	12552	13535	15055	17465	18526	19171	20523	25566	...
Non-residential buildings	4102	8982	12798	12910	14482	16138	16289	17047	17918	21326	27805	...
Other construction and land improvement etc. [b]	3842	13734	19681	17116	17682	29112	24379	36175	46106	33527	52271	...
Other	9268	19937	23461	23607	25098	31488	34130	31702	34372	34666	40491	...
4 Exports of goods and services	33403	62189	87221	105407	134795	156288	165023	183921	214077	235564	194629	199731
5 Less: Imports of goods and services	34431	72139	89119	99154	117371	130467	144543	152031	172852	194602	212469	211794
Equals: Gross Domestic Product	79878	148702	213080	238669	285046	327674	362269	402199	452512	500199	514577	556924

a) Item 'Residential buildings' includes also summer cottages, temporary dwellings, logging camps, fishermens' quarters etc.. b) The estimates of 'Other construction' include oil drilling rigs, oil production platforms etc., pipelines for gas, oil and gas exploration and drilling.

Norway

1.2 Expenditure on the Gross Domestic Product, in Constant Prices

Million Norwegian kroner

	1970	1975	1978	1979	1980	1981	1982	1983	1984	1985	1986	1987
		\[1970\]	\[1975\]			At constant prices of: \[1980\]				\[1984\]		\[1986\]
1 Government final consumption expenditure	13533	17510 / 28702	34068	35277	37191 / 53478	56763	58985	61727	63238 / 84099	86842	90712 / 102005	105813
2 Private final consumption expenditure	43047	52069 / 77615	86606	89389	91488 / 135242	136784	139199	141303	145139 / 210921	231825	244994 / 278764	272597
3 Gross capital formation	24326	33813 / 52335	46053	48263	52525 / 78902	76461	77337	75509	87173 / 116267	112004	129818 / 151648	143591
A Increase in stocks	3131	1548 / 1544	-5418	-649	4344 / 8104	-7024	3041	-3109	-51 / -1300	10834	4495 / 5515	914
B Gross fixed capital formation	21195	32265 / 50791	51471	48912	48181 / 70798	83485	74296	78618	87224 / 117567	101170	125323 / 146133	142677
Residential buildings a	3984	5311 / 8138	9361	9594	9376 / 13535	13695	14533	14420	14255 / 19171	19696	22484 / 25566	...
Non-residential buildings	4102	5914 / 8982	10212	10053	10345 / 14482	14975	14016	13897	14068 / 17918	20135	24391 / 27805	...
Other construction and land improvement etc. b	3842	8885 / 13734	15621	12828	11952 / 17682	25289	17861	26366	31619 / 46106	31298	46298 / 52271	...
Other	9268	12156 / 19937	16277	16438	16508 / 25098	29526	27887	23935	27282 / 34372	30041	32151 / 40491	...
4 Exports of goods and services	33403	43319 / 62189	77718	79723	81393 / 134795	136651	136451	146786	158841 / 214077	228754	233006 / 194629	195302
5 Less: Imports of goods and services	34431	46487 / 72139	72459	71954	74298 / 117371	119113	123467	123449	135177 / 172852	183044	202044 / 212469	198149
Equals: Gross Domestic Product	79878	100224 / 148702	171986	180698	188299 / 285046	287546	288505	301876	319214 / 452512	476381	496486 / 514577	519153

a) Item 'Residential buildings' includes also summer cottages, temporary dwellings, logging camps, fishermens' quarters etc.. b) The estimates of 'Other construction' include oil drilling rigs, oil production platforms etc., pipelines for gas, oil and gas exploration and drilling.

1.3 Cost Components of the Gross Domestic Product

Million Norwegian kroner

	1970	1975	1978	1979	1980	1981	1982	1983	1984	1985	1986	1987
1 Indirect taxes, net	10450	17197	21500	24363	29064	33901	38085	45294	52491	64101	70225	73933
A Indirect taxes	14568	26455	37946	41106	49025	55695	61747	69733	78200	91037	99794	104710
B Less: Subsidies	4118	9258	16446	16743	19961	21794	23662	24439	25709	26936	29569	30777
2 Consumption of fixed capital	11026	21089	34598	36878	41358	48053	55007	59614	62513	66512	72708	81434
3 Compensation of employees paid by resident producers to:	41879	86186	123964	129392	145421	164165	183355	198235	216350	239667	271632	304323
A Resident households	41801	86120	123900	129308	145331	163917	183086	197974	216070	239347	271312	304003
B Rest of the world	77	66	64	84	90	248	270	261	280	320	320	320
4 Operating surplus	16522	24229	33017	48035	69201	81554	85823	99055	121159	129920	100012	97236
A Corporate and quasi-corporate enterprises	...	8830	8450	24653	42423	50576	51361	62069	80354	88229	54392	46668
B Private unincorporated enterprises	...	15399	24567	23381	26780	30977	34462	36985	40805	41691	45620	50567
C General government	...	-	-	-	-	-	-	-	-	-	-	-
Equals: Gross Domestic Product	79877	148701	213079	238668	285044	327673	362270	402198	452513	500200	514577	556926

Norway

1.4 General Government Current Receipts and Disbursements

Million Norwegian kroner

	1970	1975	1978	1979	1980	1981	1982	1983	1984	1985	1986	1987
Receipts												
1 Operating surplus	-	-	-	-	-	-	-	-	-	-	-	
2 Property and entrepreneurial income	1846	2288	4611	5940	7049	9639	11507	14089	19928	23054	30855	33239
3 Taxes, fees and contributions	32909	70152	103669	115319	144657	160250	176332	194120	216898	249303	247000	268308
A Indirect taxes	14568	26455	37946	41106	49024	55696	61747	69733	78200	91037	99795	104710
B Direct taxes	10591	23790	37900	44201	61260	65657	70604	76722	87637	100599	79290	84167
C Social security contributions	7730	19863	27757	29914	34224	38699	43494	47149	50511	57304	67442	78084
D Compulsory fees, fines and penalties	20	44	66	98	149	198	487	516	550	363	473	1347
4 Other current transfers	...	...	...	...	...	...	...	...	3000	3078	3078	578
Total Current Receipts of General Government	34755	72440	108280	121259	151706	169889	187839	208209	239826	275435	280933	302125
Disbursements												
1 Government final consumption expenditure	13533	28701	43543	46585	53478	62616	70408	78213	84099	92654	102005	116325
A Compensation of employees	8833	19550	30145	32087	36574	42504	48526	53655	58470	64173	71054	80471
B Consumption of fixed capital	578	1154	1868	2026	2327	2658	2980	3186	3339	3742	4236	4806
C Purchases of goods and services, net	4122	7997	11530	12472	14577	17454	18902	21372	22291	24739	26718	31050
D Less: Own account fixed capital formation	...	...	...	...	...	...	...	...	...	...	...	...
E Indirect taxes paid, net	...	...	...	...	...	...	...	...	...	...	...	...
2 Property income	1430	2557	5873	7628	9664	10721	11529	13414	15018	17393	22324	24073
A Interest	1430	2557	5873	7628	9664	10721	11529	13414	15018	17393	22324	24073
B Net land rent and royalties	...	...	...	...	...	...	...	...	...	...	...	...
3 Subsidies	4118	9258	16446	16743	19960	21795	23662	24439	25708	26936	29569	30777
4 Other current transfers	10084	21036	33674	38961	43172	50255	57789	66076	71787	78029	86472	96725
A Social security benefits	9785	20154	31916	37023	40975	47636	54516	62212	67917	73820	81525	91503
B Social assistance grants	...	...	...	...	...	...	...	...	...	...	...	...
C Other [a]	299	882	1758	1938	2197	2619	3273	3864	3870	4209	4947	5222
5 Net saving	5590	10888	8744	11342	25432	24502	24451	26067	43212	60422	40561	34224
Total Current Disbursements and Net Saving of General Government	34755	72440	108280	121259	151706	169889	187839	208209	239824	275434	280931	302124

a) Item 'Other' of Other current transfers refers to transfers to the rest of the world.

1.5 Current Income and Outlay of Corporate and Quasi-Corporate Enterprises, Summary

Million Norwegian kroner

	1970	1975	1978	1979	1980	1981	1982	1983	1984	1985	1986	1987
Receipts												
1 Operating surplus	...	8830	8450	24653	42423	50576	51361	62069	80354	88229	54392	46668
2 Property and entrepreneurial income received	...	15331	27764	32559	41855	53244	65299	74114	84083	104138	141342	167345
3 Current transfers	...	5278	9789	10568	11484	14408	16823	18968	20360	20381	19489	19449
Total Current Receipts	...	29439	46003	67780	95762	118228	133483	155151	184797	212748	215223	233462
Disbursements												
1 Property and entrepreneurial income	...	16111	31806	38513	47237	60442	73947	83196	98276	113342	146191	169659
2 Direct taxes and other current payments to general government	...	3400	7494	11577	23531	26004	27965	32642	39025	47862	20290	17920
3 Other current transfers	...	5646	10388	11194	12227	15150	17711	19944	24650	24429	24274	23076
4 Net saving	...	4282	-3685	6496	12767	16632	13860	19369	22847	27115	24468	22807
Total Current Disbursements and Net Saving	...	29439	46003	67780	95762	118228	133483	155151	184798	212748	215223	233462

1.6 Current Income and Outlay of Households and Non-Profit Institutions

Million Norwegian kroner

	1970	1975	1978	1979	1980	1981	1982	1983	1984	1985	1986	1987
Receipts												
1 Compensation of employees	...	86161	123960	129376	145397	164002	183182	198070	216178	239467	271438	304135
A From resident producers	...	86120	123900	129310	145330	163919	183085	197974	216070	239347	271312	304003
B From rest of the world	...	42	60	66	66	84	96	96	108	120	126	132
2 Operating surplus of private unincorporated enterprises	...	15399	24567	23381	26779	30977	34462	36985	40805	41691	45620	50567

Norway

1.6 Current Income and Outlay of Households and Non-Profit Institutions
(Continued)

Million Norwegian kroner

		1970	1975	1978	1979	1980	1981	1982	1983	1984	1985	1986	1987
3	Property and entrepreneurial income	...	3493	6180	7739	9612	11793	13711	16885	20392	23076	28630	36526
4	Current transfers	...	21518	33979	39230	43575	50675	58014	65938	72096	77993	86718	97591
	A Social security benefits	...	20154	31916	37023	40975	47636	54516	62212	67916	73820	81525	91503
	B Social assistance grants	...	...	...	...	...	...	...	...	...	...	...	...
	C Other	...	1364	2063	2207	2600	3039	3498	3726	4180	4173	5193	6088
	Total Current Receipts	...	126571	188686	199726	225363	257447	289369	317878	349471	382227	432406	488819

Disbursements

		1970	1975	1978	1979	1980	1981	1982	1983	1984	1985	1986	1987
1	Private final consumption expenditure	...	77615	110670	120104	135241	155205	175310	192980	210921	245439	278764	294796
2	Property income	...	4343	8199	9525	11231	14024	17572	21316	24080	28838	41289	52150
3	Direct taxes and other current transfers n.e.c. to general government	...	40245	58017	62419	71833	78255	86160	91280	99199	110104	126559	144372
	A Social security contributions	...	19863	27757	29914	34224	38699	43495	47151	50512	57305	67442	78084
	B Direct taxes	...	20382	30260	32505	37609	39556	42665	44129	48687	52799	59117	66287
	C Fees, fines and penalties	...	-	-	-	-	-	-	-	-	-	-	-
4	Other current transfers	...	985	1698	1946	2265	2656	3427	3594	3649	4067	4794	5679
5	Net saving	...	3384	10102	5732	4793	7307	6899	8709	11623	-6222	-19001	-8178
	Total Current Disbursements and Net Saving	...	126572	188686	199726	225363	257447	289368	317879	349472	382226	432405	488819

1.7 External Transactions on Current Account, Summary

Million Norwegian kroner

Payments to the Rest of the World

		1970	1975	1978	1979	1980	1981	1982	1983	1984	1985	1986	1987
1	Imports of goods and services	34431	72139	89119	99154	117371	130469	144543	152031	172852	194602	212469	211795
	A Imports of merchandise c.i.f.	26651	54366	61979	70433	84543	90516	100458	102520	116541	133927	153072	151581
	B Other	7780	17773	27140	28721	32828	39953	44085	49510	56311	60675	59397	60214
2	Factor income to the rest of the world	1676	3706	9635	12663	14841	19319	23431	23394	26651	27733	29438	29967
	A Compensation of employees	77	66	64	84	90	248	270	261	280	320	320	320
	B Property and entrepreneurial income	1599	3640	9571	12579	14751	19071	23161	23133	26371	27413	29118	29647
3	Current transfers to the rest of the world	487	1356	2478	2799	3212	3796	4791	5522	5506	6189	7208	8039
	A Indirect taxes to supranational organizations	-	-	-	-	-	-	-	-	-	-	-	-
	B Other current transfers	487	1356	2478	2799	3212	3796	4791	5522	5506	6189	7208	8039
4	Surplus of the nation on current transactions	-1728	-12692	-11005	-5278	5448	12460	4146	14645	23929	26682	-32913	-27579
	Payments to the Rest of the World and Surplus of the Nation on Current Transactions	34866	64509	90227	109338	140872	166044	176911	195592	228938	255206	216202	222222

Receipts From The Rest of the World

		1970	1975	1978	1979	1980	1981	1982	1983	1984	1985	1986	1987
1	Exports of goods and services	33403	62189	87221	105407	134795	156288	165022	183921	214078	235563	194630	199732
	A Exports of merchandise f.o.b.	17715	38140	57863	70007	92863	106899	114798	133249	156822	173254	136003	144945
	B Other	15688	24049	29358	35400	41932	49390	50224	50672	57256	62309	58627	54787
2	Factor income from rest of the world	1056	1791	2453	3337	5321	8740	10727	10392	13509	18227	20266	21007
	A Compensation of employees	24	42	60	66	66	84	96	96	108	120	126	132
	B Property and entrepreneurial income	1031	1749	2393	3271	5255	8656	10631	10296	13401	18107	20140	20875
3	Current transfers from rest of the world	408	529	553	594	756	1016	1161	1278	1350	1415	1307	1483
	A Subsidies from supranational organisations	-	-	-	-	-	-	-	-	-	-	-	-
	B Other current transfers	408	529	553	594	756	1016	1161	1278	1350	1415	1307	1483
	Receipts from the Rest of the World on Current Transactions	34867	64509	90227	109338	140872	166044	176910	195591	228937	255205	216203	222222

Norway

1.8 Capital Transactions of The Nation, Summary

Million Norwegian kroner

	1970	1975	1978	1979	1980	1981	1982	1983	1984	1985	1986	1987
Finance of Gross Capital Formation												
Gross saving	22597	39643	49759	60448	84350	96492	100218	113760	140197	147827	118735	130284
1 Consumption of fixed capital	11024	21089	34598	36878	41358	48053	55007	59614	62513	66512	72707	81434
A General government	578	1155	1868	2026	2327	2658	2979	3187	3339	3742	4234	4805
B Corporate and quasi-corporate enterprises	10446	14415	23842	25363	28552	32808	38099	41467	43903	46209	50328	56343
Public	1476	3268	5234	5774	6806	7955	9052	10493	11096	13993	16210	18643
Private	8970	11147	18608	19589	21746	24853	29047	30974	32807	32216	34118	37700
C Other [a]	...	5520	8888	9489	10479	12587	13928	14961	15271	16561	18146	20287
2 Net saving	11573	18554	15161	23570	42992	48439	45211	54146	77684	81315	46028	48850
A General government	5590	10888	8744	11342	25432	24502	24451	26067	43212	60422	40561	34224
B Corporate and quasi-corporate enterprises	5983	4282	-3685	6496	12767	16632	13860	19369	22847	27116	24468	22808
Public	...	675	1669	421	6420	7989	12085	13118	13181	7020	15411	25280
Private	...	3607	-5354	6075	6347	8643	1775	6251	9666	20096	9057	-2472
C Other [a]	...	3384	10102	5732	4793	7307	6899	8709	11623	-6222	-19000	-8178
Less: Surplus of the nation on current transactions	-1728	-12692	-11005	-5278	5448	12460	4146	14644	23929	26682	-32913	-27579
Finance of Gross Capital Formation	24325	52335	60764	65726	78902	84032	96072	99116	116268	121145	151648	157863
Gross Capital Formation												
Increase in stocks	3131	1544	-6941	-460	8104	-7761	3809	-4332	-1300	11103	5515	1654
Gross fixed capital formation	21194	50791	67705	66186	70798	91793	92262	103448	117567	110042	146133	156212
1 General government	3578	7121	10737	10343	11454	11602	11525	12411	12857	13288	16458	19699
2 Corporate and quasi-corporate enterprises	17617	31356	37620	37679	39221	60596	56988	67353	78853	64934	91293	95336
A Public	3166	8120	12557	12628	14811	19762	17885	26649	23751	27856	36798	36555
B Private	14451	23236	25063	25051	24410	40834	39103	40704	55102	37078	54495	58781
3 Other [a]	...	12314	19348	18164	20123	19595	23747	23684	25856	31819	38382	41177
Gross Capital Formation	24325	52335	60764	65726	78902	84032	96071	99116	116267	121145	151648	157866

a) Beginning 1972, item 'Other' includes households and private unincorporated enterprises and non-profit institutions serving households.

1.9 Gross Domestic Product by Institutional Sectors of Origin

Million Norwegian kroner

	1970	1975	1978	1979	1980	1981	1982	1983	1984	1985	1986	1987
Domestic Factor Incomes Originating												
1 General government	8833	19550	30145	32087	36574	42504	48526	53654	58470	64173	71054	80471
2 Corporate and quasi-corporate enterprises [a]	49568	90864	126836	145340	178049	203216	220652	243635	279039	305414	300590	321091
3 Households and private unincorporated enterprises	...	...	...	...	...	...	...	...	...	...	...	...
4 Non-profit institutions serving households	...	...	...	...	...	...	...	...	...	...	...	...
Subtotal: Domestic Factor Incomes	58401	110415	156981	177427	214622	245719	269178	297290	337509	369587	371644	401559
Indirect taxes, net	10450	17197	21500	24363	29064	33901	38085	45294	52491	64101	70225	73933
A Indirect taxes	14568	26455	37946	41106	49025	55695	61747	69733	78200	91037	99794	104710
B Less: Subsidies	4118	9258	16446	16743	19961	21794	23662	24439	25709	26936	29569	30777
Consumption of fixed capital	11026	21089	34598	36878	41358	48053	55007	59614	62513	66512	72708	81434
Gross Domestic Product	79877	148701	213079	238668	285044	327673	362270	402198	452513	500200	514577	556926

a) The estimates of Households and private unincorporated enterprises and Non-profit institutions serving households are included in item 'Corporate and quasi-corporate enterprises'.

1.10 Gross Domestic Product by Kind of Activity, in Current Prices

Million Norwegian kroner

	1970	1975	1978	1979	1980	1981	1982	1983	1984	1985	1986	1987
1 Agriculture, hunting, forestry and fishing	4460	7115	9815	10137	10969	12957	13437	13135	15042	15150	16714	19348
2 Mining and quarrying	591	4493	13756	21788	42078	51185	56514	68231	84778	91009	51431	51712
3 Manufacturing	17259	32270	37528	43820	45635	48575	51383	56724	64524	70127	75074	82994
4 Electricity, gas and water	2165	4303	6491	7486	8237	10158	11981	14312	16571	18278	19660	22715
5 Construction	5593	10320	15289	15254	16952	19673	22711	23848	24353	27070	30888	36000

Norway

1.10 Gross Domestic Product by Kind of Activity, in Current Prices
(Continued)

Million Norwegian kroner

	1970	1975	1978	1979	1980	1981	1982	1983	1984	1985	1986	1987
6 Wholesale and retail trade, restaurants and hotels	9943	17816	26501	27685	33264	38475	42765	45475	49445	53897	62166	68396
7 Transport, storage and communication	11780	16458	20929	23116	26890	30755	31289	33852	37077	37976	44970	45664
8 Finance, insurance, real estate and business services	7286	14369	21310	24730	28244	34155	40859	45633	49318	56383	68582	75195
9 Community, social and personal services	3780	7239	10637	11339	12478	14009	15722	17701	18750	21408	24523	27681
Total, Industries	62856	114383	162257	185354	224747	259941	286660	318912	359858	391297	394008	429705
Producers of Government Services	9412	20705	32013	34114	38901	45162	51505	56841	61808	67965	75346	85337
Other Producers	...	...	...	...	...	...	...	...	...	...	...	...
Subtotal	72268	135087	194270	219468	263648	305103	338165	375753	421667	459261	469354	515042
Less: Imputed bank service charge	1709	4061	6158	7278	8724	11349	14318	15960	15443	15431	20630	21434
Plus: Import duties [a]	1328	2380	2974	3253	3692	4248	5203	5764	6006	9320	11758	9716
Plus: Value added tax [b]	7734	14312	20143	21612	24703	28024	31536	34623	37794	44150	50527	53219
Plus: Other adjustments [c]	256	983	1851	1613	1726	1649	1683	2017	2489	2900	3569	383
Equals: Gross Domestic Product	79877	148702	213080	238668	285045	327675	362269	402197	452512	500201	514578	556926
Memorandum Item: Mineral fuels and power	2387	8182	19726	30873	49587	59777	67331	80842	99676	107846	69373	...

a) Item 'Import duties' includes collection of customs duties, value added tax on imports and special excises or taxes on imports.
b) Item 'Value added tax' excludes value added tax on imports which is included in item 'Import duties'.
c) Item 'Other adjustments' refers to collection of investment levy on fixed capital formation and subsidies on residential and social buildings and a statistical discrepancy.

1.11 Gross Domestic Product by Kind of Activity, in Constant Prices

Million Norwegian kroner

	1970	1975	1978	1979	1980	1981	1982	1983	1984	1985	1986	1987
	\multicolumn{12}{c}{At constant prices of:}											
	1970		1975		1980				1984		1986	
1 Agriculture, hunting, forestry and fishing	4460	4943 / 7115	7155	7368	7515 / 10969	11959	12446	12319	13356 / 15042	13682	13264 / 16714	17990
2 Mining and quarrying	591	2964 / 4493	11722	14083	17360 / 42078	40498	40719	47866	55141 / 84778	87815	91850 / 51431	57917
3 Manufacturing	17259	20328 / 32270	30891	31883	31535 / 45635	45191	44887	44555	47113 / 64524	66893	67126 / 75074	76029
4 Electricity, gas and water	2165	2831 / 4303	4590	5022	4791 / 8237	8954	9094	10287	10614 / 16571	16109	15727 / 19660	21064
5 Construction	5593	6922 / 10320	12543	12354	12487 / 16952	16735	17031	17563	17768 / 24353	25319	26481 / 30888	31130
6 Wholesale and retail trade, restaurants and hotels	9943	12803 / 17816	19858	20560	20757 / 33264	32521	31907	31823	33351 / 49445	53663	58669 / 62166	59985
7 Transport, storage and communication	11780	14038 / 16458	19615	20263	21037 / 26890	27545	26530	27149	28501 / 37077	38374	42808 / 44970	43694
8 Finance, insurance, real estate and business services	7286	8493 / 14369	16515	17399	18141 / 28244	29310	30209	30274	31494 / 49318	53417	56833 / 68582	72398
9 Community, social and personal services	3780	4525 / 7239	8207	8551	8524 / 12478	12542	12699	13031	12965 / 18750	20093	21160 / 24523	25344

Norway

1.11 Gross Domestic Product by Kind of Activity, in Constant Prices
(Continued)

Million Norwegian kroner

	1970	1975	1978	1979	1980	1981	1982	1983	1984	1985	1986	1987
					At constant prices of:							
		1970		1975			1980			1984		1986
Total, Industries	62856	77845 114383	131095	137482	142147 224747	225254	225521	234866	250302 359858	375366	393916 394008	405549
Producers of Government Services	9412	12403 20705	25120	26209	27686 38901	41141	43393	44993	46248 61808	63768	65071 75346	77046
Other Producers	...	...	...	...	...	...	...	...	...	...	...	...
Subtotal	72268	90248 135087	156215	163691	169833 263648	266396	268914	279858	296550 421667	439135	458987 469354	482595
Less: Imputed bank service charge	1709	1947 4061	4480	4610	4797 8724	8985	9205	9543	10157 15443	16393	17829 20630	23023
Plus: Import duties a	1328	1907 2380	1917	2218	2475 3692	3869	4253	4092	4189 6006	9141	9762 11758	9045
Plus: Value added tax b	7734	9712 14312	16046	16659	16942 24703	25000	25399	25951	27309 37794	41820	45238 50527	49368
Plus: Other adjustments c	256	304 983	2289	2741	3846 1726	1267	-855	1518	1324 2489	2680	328 3569	1173
Equals: Gross Domestic Product	79877	100224 148702	171987	180699	188299 285045	287546	288506	301877	319215 452512	476382	496486 514578	519153
Memorandum Item: Mineral fuels and power	2387	5159 8182	15694	18418	21355 49587	48837	49455	57607	65289 99676	102457	106017 69373	...

a) Item 'Import duties' includes collection of customs duties, value added tax on imports and special excises or taxes on imports.
b) Item 'Value added tax' excludes value added tax on imports which is included in item 'Import duties'.
c) Item 'Other adjustments' refers to collection of investment levy on fixed capital formation and subsidies on residential and social buildings and a statistical discrepancy.

1.12 Relations Among National Accounting Aggregates

Million Norwegian kroner

	1970	1975	1978	1979	1980	1981	1982	1983	1984	1985	1986	1987
Gross Domestic Product	79877	148701	213079	238668	285045	327674	362270	402198	452512	500200	514578	556925
Plus: Net factor income from the rest of the world	-621	-1915	-7182	-9326	-9520	-10579	-12704	-13002	-13142	-9506	-9172	-8960
Factor income from the rest of the world	1056	1791	2453	3337	5321	8740	10727	10392	13509	18227	20266	21007
Less: Factor income to the rest of the world	1677	3706	9635	12663	14841	19319	23431	23394	26651	27733	29438	29967
Equals: Gross National Product	79255	146786	205897	229342	275525	317095	349565	389195	439370	490694	505405	547962
Less: Consumption of fixed capital	11024	21089	34598	36878	41358	48053	55007	59614	62512	66512	72707	81434
Equals: National Income	68232	125697	171299	192464	234167	269042	294559	329581	376858	424182	432698	466528
Plus: Net current transfers from the rest of the world	-79	-827	-1925	-2205	-2456	-2780	-3630	-4244	-4156	-4774	-5901	-6556
Current transfers from the rest of the world	408	529	553	594	756	1016	1161	1278	1350	1415	1307	1483
Less: Current transfers to the rest of the world	487	1356	2478	2799	3212	3796	4791	5522	5506	6189	7208	8039
Equals: National Disposable Income	68153	124870	169374	190259	231711	266262	290929	325337	372702	419408	426797	459972
Less: Final consumption	56579	106316	154213	166689	188719	217821	245718	271192	295018	338093	380769	411122
Equals: Net Saving	11573	18554	15161	23570	42992	48441	45211	54146	77684	81315	46028	48850
Less: Surplus of the nation on current transactions	-1728	-12692	-11005	-5278	5448	12460	4146	14645	23929	26682	-32913	-27579
Equals: Net Capital Formation	13301	31246	26166	28848	37544	35981	41064	39501	53755	54633	78940	76431

Norway

2.1 Government Final Consumption Expenditure by Function, in Current Prices

Million Norwegian kroner

		1970	1975	1978	1979	1980	1981	1982	1983	1984	1985	1986	1987
1	General public services	1156	2436	3627	3684	4001	4564	5088	5735	6270	6993	7676	8929
2	Defence	2821	4750	6360	6789	8033	10243	11160	12569	13011	14441	15338	18204
3	Public order and safety	541	1220	1864	1971	2207	2598	2910	3169	3422	3736	4172	4957
4	Education	3881	7959	12073	12884	14419	16347	18578	20263	21790	24067	26100	28461
5	Health	1927	5331	8953	9734	11547	13471	15396	17699	19464	21507	24095	28284
6	Social security and welfare	690	2118	3541	3912	4642	5524	6312	6745	7191	8167	9291	11429
7	Housing and community amenities	135	106	-10	-14	235	99	35	-1	-141	-185	-178	-580
8	Recreational, cultural and religious affairs	367	827	1361	1469	1641	1933	2241	2512	2732	3005	3280	3688
9	Economic services	1944	3884	5681	5882	6562	7495	8424	9340	10047	10641	11539	12348
	A Fuel and energy	15	61	132	163	99	120	159	138	9	-42	98	224
	B Agriculture, forestry, fishing and hunting	240	465	623	668	725	870	965	1063	1195	1257	1383	1464
	C Mining, manufacturing and construction, except fuel and energy	18	42	38	22	46	64	91	99	69	73	83	96
	D Transportation and communication	1342	2435	3570	3649	4854	5468	6079	6637	7118	7551	8232	8715
	E Other economic affairs	330	881	1319	1379	838	974	1131	1403	1657	1802	1744	1849
10	Other functions	73	71	92	274	190	342	265	182	313	282	691	606
	Total Government Final Consumption Expenditure	13533	28702	43543	46585	53478	62616	70408	78214	84099	92653	102005	116326

2.2 Government Final Consumption Expenditure by Function, in Constant Prices

Million Norwegian kroner

At constant prices of:

		1970	1975	1978	1979	1980	1981	1982	1983	1984	1985	1986	1987
		1970	**1975**			**1980**				**1984**			
1	General public services	1156	1474 / 2436	2838	2800	2923 / 4001	4130	4259	4544	4710 / 6270	6605	6928	...
2	Defence	2821	2952 / 4750	4959	5137	5456 / 8033	9250	9304	9913	10026 / 13011	13561	14086	...
3	Public order and safety	541	738 / 1220	1458	1499	1551 / 2207	2353	2438	2511	2569 / 3422	3517	3775	...
4	Education	3881	4812 / 7959	9451	9800	10045 / 14419	14939	15737	16100	16473 / 21790	22626	23091	...
5	Health	1927	3216 / 5331	6965	7305	8069 / 11547	12136	12822	13811	14296 / 19464	20010	20930	...
6	Social security and welfare	690	1273 / 2118	2770	2971	3264 / 4642	4967	5240	5266	5300 / 7191	7674	8186	...
7	Housing and community amenities	135	63 / 106	-8	-10	-11 / 235	89	43	33	-35 / -141	-192	-136	...
8	Recreational, cultural and religious affairs	367	510 / 827	1074	1114	1197 / 1641	1754	1865	1928	1994 / 2732	2811	2885	...
9	Economic services	1944	2430 / 3884	4490	4453	4540 / 6562	6835	7057	7476	7669 / 10047	9965	10341	...

Norway

2.2 Government Final Consumption Expenditure by Function, in Constant Prices
(Continued)

Million Norwegian kroner

	1970	1975	1978	1979	1980	1981	1982	1983	1984	1985	1986	1987
					At constant prices of:							
	1970		1975				1980			1984		
A Fuel and energy	15	37	103	124	62	109	133	110	7	-39	89	...
		61			99				9			
B Agriculture, forestry, fishing and hunting	240	281	487	505	501	791	812	846	902	1180	1244	...
		465			725				1195			
C Mining, manufacturing and construction, except fuel and energy	18	25	30	17	47	57	75	78	50	68	73	...
		42			46				69			
D Transportation and communication	1342	1557	2840	2765	2827	4996	5091	5335	5477	7067	7398	...
		2435			4854				7118			
E Other economic affairs	330	530	1030	1043	1103	882	946	1108	1232	1689	1538	...
		881			838				1657			
10 Other functions	73	43	72	208	159	309	222	145	235	265	625	...
		71			190				313			
Total Government Final Consumption Expenditure	13533	17510	34068	35277	37191	56763	58985	61727	63238	86842	90712	...
		28702			53478				84099			

2.5 Private Final Consumption Expenditure by Type and Purpose, in Current Prices

Million Norwegian kroner

	1970	1975	1978	1979	1980	1981	1982	1983	1984	1985	1986	1987
				Final Consumption Expenditure of Resident Households								
1 Food, beverages and tobacco	13883	23175	30478	32464	36201	41360	46420	50743	54932	61601	68642	72623
A Food	10504	17304	23115	24280	27285	31381	35744	38758	41858	46707	51694	53391
B Non-alcoholic beverages	467	808	1158	1246	1327	1377	1726	1824	2008	2309	2841	...
C Alcoholic beverages	1650	3146	3782	4368	4826	5412	5393	6144	6629	7521	8199	...
D Tobacco	1261	1917	2423	2570	2764	3190	3557	4017	4436	5064	5908	...
2 Clothing and footwear	4535	6940	9751	10501	11934	12975	13950	14352	15802	19076	21521	20871
3 Gross rent, fuel and power	6084	10844	16544	18493	21271	24881	28769	32708	36611	40858	45011	50145
A Fuel and power	1736	3022	5165	6173	7406	8846	10285	11570	13114	14848	16102	17730
B Other	4348	7823	11379	12320	13864	16036	18484	21138	23497	26009	28910	32415
4 Furniture, furnishings and household equipment and operation	3606	7155	10069	10721	11878	13215	14099	15102	16507	19060	21735	23133
A Household operation [a]	837	1840	2633	2717	3069	3418	3672	4055	4398	4884	5536	...
B Other	2769	5315	7437	8004	8810	9798	10428	11047	12110	14177	16199	...
5 Medical care and health expenses	1729	3504	4906	5249	5676	6387	7407	8180	8586	9298	10095	11073
6 Transport and communication	5036	10056	15090	17353	20220	23086	26502	29188	31811	41337	47194	45837
A Personal transport equipment	1715	3674	5113	6419	7406	8089	9694	10393	11363	18296	21841	17198
B Other	3321	6382	9977	10934	12814	14997	16808	18795	20448	23041	25353	28639
7 Recreational, entertainment, education and cultural services	3313	6575	9612	10361	11626	13403	14488	15979	17572	20196	23658	24811
A Education	233	415	528	557	647	618	695	775	850	980	1126	...
B Other	3080	6160	9084	9803	10979	12785	13794	15204	16722	19215	22531	...
8 Miscellaneous goods and services	4257	7628	10668	11478	12968	15174	17139	19511	21742	25078	29575	33681
A Personal care	738	1422	1939	2003	2335	2710	3112	3546	3987	4602	5441	...
B Expenditures in restaurants, cafes and hotels	1564	2992	4240	4560	5150	6042	6960	8066	9147	10488	11734	...
C Other	1955	3214	4489	4915	5483	6421	7068	7899	8609	9988	12400	...
Total Final Consumption Expenditure in the Domestic Market by Households, of which	42442	75876	107120	116620	131773	150481	168774	185762	203563	236503	267431	282175
A Durable goods	4526	9444	13422	15270	16932	18851	20809	22127	24495	33817	39938	...
B Semi-durable goods	6973	11795	16670	18061	20766	23235	25163	26282	28800	34599	39423	...
C Non-durable goods	18537	31935	44184	47917	54529	62683	70534	77533	84513	94732	104835	...

Norway

2.5 Private Final Consumption Expenditure by Type and Purpose, in Current Prices
(Continued)

Million Norwegian kroner

	1970	1975	1978	1979	1980	1981	1982	1983	1984	1985	1986	1987
D Services	12406	22701	32844	35373	39545	45713	52269	59820	65755	73356	83235	...
Plus: Direct purchases abroad by resident households	1849	3864	6761	6986	7414	9411	11592	12535	13197	15918	19706	21620
Less: Direct purchases in the domestic market by non-resident households	1245	2125	3211	3501	3945	4687	5056	5319	5839	6982	8373	8998
Equals: Final Consumption Expenditure of Resident Households [b]	43047	77615	110670	120104	135242	155205	175310	192979	210921	245439	278764	294796

Final Consumption Expenditure of Private Non-profit Institutions Serving Households

Equals: Final Consumption Expenditure of Private Non-profit Organisations Serving Households	...	...	...	...	...	...	...	...	...	...	...	...
Private Final Consumption Expenditure	43047	77615	110670	120104	135242	155205	175310	192979	210921	245439	278764	294796

a) Item 'Household operations' also includes repair of furniture and household goods.
b) Item 'Final consumption expenditure of resident households' includes consumption expenditure of private non-profit institutions serving households.

2.6 Private Final Consumption Expenditure by Type and Purpose, in Constant Prices

Million Norwegian kroner

	1970	1975	1978	1979	1980	1981	1982	1983	1984	1985	1986	1987
	At constant prices of:											
	1970	1975			1980				1984		1986	

Final Consumption Expenditure of Resident Households

	1970	1975	1978	1979	1980	1981	1982	1983	1984	1985	1986	1987
1 Food, beverages and tobacco	13883	15426 / 23175	24030	24811	25746 / 36201	34998	34498	34741	35261 / 54932	58117	59430 / 68642	67663
A Food	10504	11528 / 17304	18441	18669	19291 / 27285	27057	27203	27313	27566 / 41858	43821	44513 / 51694	50247
B Non-alcoholic beverages	467	530 / 808	938	993	987 / 1327	1195	1313	1320	1371 / 2008	2177	2468 / 2841	...
C Alcoholic beverages	1650	2105 / 3146	2823	3219	3453 / 4826	4275	3752	3845	3961 / 6629	7285	7343 / 8199	...
D Tobacco	1261	1263 / 1917	1829	1931	2016 / 2764	2472	2230	2263	2363 / 4436	4834	5106 / 5908	...
2 Clothing and footwear	4535	4713 / 6940	7528	7688	7968 / 11934	11627	11585	11308	11776 / 15802	17785	18427 / 21521	19120
3 Gross rent, fuel and power	6084	7375 / 10844	12778	13353	13709 / 21271	21817	22420	23068	23855 / 36611	38632	40628 / 45011	46709
A Fuel and power	1736	1894 / 3022	3520	3761	3706 / 7406	7380	7354	7232	7434 / 13114	13993	14814 / 16102	16560
B Other	4348	5482 / 7823	9259	9593	10003 / 13864	14437	15066	15836	16422 / 23497	24639	25814 / 28910	30148
4 Furniture, furnishings and household equipment and operation	3606	4615 / 7155	8148	8242	8192 / 11878	11623	11246	11174	11649 / 16507	18218	19405 / 21735	21324
A Household operation [a]	837	1020 / 1840	2096	2036	2073 / 3069	3079	2972	3052	3122 / 4398	4621	4930 / 5536	...

Norway

2.6 Private Final Consumption Expenditure by Type and Purpose, in Constant Prices
(Continued)

Million Norwegian kroner

	1970	1975	1978	1979	1980	1981	1982	1983	1984	1985	1986	1987
					At constant prices of:							
		1970			1975					1984		
B Other	2769	3595	6053	6206	6120						1986	
		5315			8810	8544	8274	8122	8527	13597	14475	
									12110		16199	...
5 Medical care and health expenses	1729	2204	3851	3983	3705							
		3504			5676	5771	6126	6345	6271	8672	8724	
									8586		10095	10522
6 Transport and communication	5036	6813	11533	12485	12997							
		10056			20220	20662	21663	21857	22514	39575	42292	
									31811		47194	41496
A Personal transport equipment	1715	2547	3845	4324	4765							
		3674			7406	7708	8568	8290	8273	17050	17779	
									11363		21841	14961
B Other	3321	4266	7688	8162	8232							
		6382			12814	12955	13095	13567	14241	22525	24513	
									20448		25353	26535
7 Recreational, entertainment, education and cultural services	3313	4716	7954	8343	8705							
		6575			11626	12428	12128	12505	13162	19205	21266	
									17572		23658	23045
A Education	233	257	404	414	458							
		415			647	563	564	586	604	916	967	
									850		1126	...
B Other	3080	4459	7550	7929	8247							
		6160			10979	11865	11564	11919	12558	18289	20299	
									16722		22531	...
8 Miscellaneous goods and services	4257	4892	8123	8357	8505							
		7628			12968	13154	13191	13568	14393	23494	24919	
									21742		29575	30751
A Personal care	738	940	1569	1584	1675							
		1422			2335	2372	2389	2468	2619	4314	4734	
									3987		5441	...
B Expenditures in restaurants, cafes and hotels	1564	1952	3021	3155	3331							
		2992			5150	5005	4812	4979	5319	9927	10219	
									9147		11734	12563
C Other	1955	2000	3533	3618	3498							
		3214			5483	5777	5989	6121	6455	9253	9966	
									8609		12400	...
Total Final Consumption Expenditure in the Domestic Market by Households, of which	42442	50754	83946	87262	89527							
		75876			131773	132081	132856	134566	138881	223697	235091	
									203563		267431	260628
A Durable goods	4526	6772	10897	11547	11756							
		9444			16932	17462	18019	17662	18438	31949	34018	
									24495		39938	...
B Semi-durable goods	6973	7936	13112	13452	14065							
		11795			20766	20840	20813	20596	21499	32614	34620	
									28800		39423	...
C Non-durable goods	18537	21065	34261	35514	36500							
		31935			54529	53342	52988	53402	54372	89701	93296	
									84513		104835	...

Norway

2.6 Private Final Consumption Expenditure by Type and Purpose, in Constant Prices
(Continued)

Million Norwegian kroner

	1970	1975	1978	1979	1980	1981	1982	1983	1984	1985	1986	1987
					At constant prices of:							
	1970	**1975**			**1980**				**1984**		**1986**	
D Services	12406	14982 22701	25676	26748	27206 39545	40437	41036	42906	44572 65755	69433	73156 83235	...
Plus: Direct purchases abroad by resident households	1849	2736 3864	5155	4723	4596 7414	8829	10159	10385	10036 13197	14753	17209 19706	20232
Less: Direct purchases in the domestic market by non-resident households	1245	1421 2125	2495	2595	2635 3945	4126	3816	3648	3778 5839	6625	7306 8373	8263
Equals: Final Consumption Expenditure of Resident Households [b]	43047	52069 77615	86606	89389	91488 135242	136784	139199	141303	145139 210921	231825	244994 278764	272597

Final Consumption Expenditure of Private Non-profit Institutions Serving Households

Equals: Final Consumption Expenditure of Private Non-profit Organisations Serving Households	...	...	...	...	...	...	...	...	...	...	...	...
Private Final Consumption Expenditure	43047	52069 77615	86606	89389	91488 135242	136784	139199	141303	145139 210921	231825	244994 278764	272597

a) Item 'Household operations' also includes repair of furniture and household goods.
b) Item 'Final consumption expenditure of resident households' includes consumption expenditure of private non-profit institutions serving households.

2.7 Gross Capital Formation by Type of Good and Owner, in Current Prices

Million Norwegian kroner

	1980				1981				1982			
	TOTAL	Total Private	Public Enterprises	General Government	TOTAL	Total Private	Public Enterprises	General Government	TOTAL	Total Private	Public Enterprises	General Government
Increase in stocks, total	8104	8104	...	...	-7761	-7761	...	...	3809	3809	...	...
1 Goods producing industries	6369	6369	...	...	-4282	-4282	...	...	4231	4231	...	...
A Materials and supplies	...	...	...	...	...	...	...	...	...	...	...	...
B Work in progress [a]	6284	6284	...	...	-4191	-4191	...	...	4278	4278	...	...
C Livestock, except breeding stocks, dairy cattle, etc. [b]	85	85	...	...	-91	-91	...	...	-47	-47	...	...
D Finished goods	...	...	...	...	...	...	...	...	...	...	...	...
2 Wholesale and retail trade	...	...	...	...	...	...	...	...	...	...	...	...
3 Other, except government stocks	1735	1735	...	...	-3479	-3479	...	...	-422	-422	...	...
4 Government stocks	...	...	...	...	...	...	...	...	...	...	...	...
Gross Fixed Capital Formation, Total	70798	59344	...	11454	91793	80190	...	11602	92262	80737	...	11525
1 Residential buildings [c]	13535	13489	...	46	15055	14986	...	69	17465	17693	...	-228
2 Non-residential buildings	14482	9405	...	5078	16138	10985	...	5153	16289	10949	...	5340
3 Other construction [d]	17146	12482	...	4665	28536	23968	...	4568	23775	19308	...	4467
4 Land improvement and plantation and orchard development	536	536	...	...	576	576	...	...	605	605	...	...
5 Producers' durable goods	24978	23312	...	1666	31412	29600	...	1812	34176	32230	...	1946
A Transport equipment	7359	7179	...	179	12341	11876	...	465	15043	14838	...	205
Passenger cars [e]	1585	1547	...	38	2305	1987	...	318	2369	2325	...	44
Other	5774	5633	...	142	10036	9890	...	147	12673	12513	...	161
B Machinery and equipment	17620	16133	...	1487	19071	17724	...	1347	19133	17392	...	1741
6 Breeding stock, dairy cattle, etc.	120	120	...	...	76	76	...	...	-46	-46	...	...
Total Gross Capital Formation	78902	67448	...	11454	84032	72429	...	11602	96071	84546	...	11525

Norway

2.7 Gross Capital Formation by Type of Good and Owner, in Current Prices

Million Norwegian kroner

	1983 TOTAL	1983 Total Private	1983 Public Enterprises	1983 General Government	1984 TOTAL	1984 Total Private	1984 Public Enterprises	1984 General Government	1985 TOTAL	1985 Total Private	1985 Public Enterprises	1985 General Government
Increase in stocks, total	-4332	-4332	...	...	-1300	-1300	...	...	11103	11103	...	...
1 Goods producing industries	2116	2116	...	...	-2613	-2613	...	...	10960	10960	...	...
A Materials and supplies	...	...	...	...	...	...	...	...	...	...	...	...
B Work in progress [a]	2112	2112	...	...	-2649	-2649	...	...	10987	10987	...	...
C Livestock, except breeding stocks, dairy cattle, etc. [b]	4	4	...	...	36	36	...	...	-27	-27	...	...
D Finished goods	...	...	...	...	...	...	...	...	...	...	...	...
2 Wholesale and retail trade												
3 Other, except government stocks	-6448	-6448	...	...	1313	1313	...	...	143	143	...	...
4 Government stocks												
Gross Fixed Capital Formation, Total	103448	91037	...	12410	117567	104709	...	12858	110042	96754	...	13288
1 Residential buildings [c]	18526	19035	...	-509	19171	19636	...	-465	20523	21304	...	-781
2 Non-residential buildings	17047	11158	...	5889	17918	12098	...	5820	21326	15595	...	5732
3 Other construction [d]	35608	30689	...	4919	45579	40410	...	5169	33072	27571	...	5501
4 Land improvement and plantation and orchard development	567	567	...	...	527	527	...	...	455	455	...	...
5 Producers' durable goods	31700	29589	...	2111	34406	32071	...	2335	34750	31913	...	2836
A Transport equipment	13150	12932	...	219	11725	11484	...	241	7740	7482	...	258
Passenger cars [e]	2535	2483	...	52	2521	2467	...	54	3632	3563	...	69
Other	10615	10449	...	166	9204	9017	...	187	4108	3918	...	190
B Machinery and equipment	18550	16657	...	1893	22681	20587	...	2094	27010	24432	...	2578
6 Breeding stock, dairy cattle, etc.	...	...	...	...	-34	-34	...	...	-84	-84	...	...
Total Gross Capital Formation	99116	86705	...	12410	116267	103409	...	12858	121145	107857	...	13288

	1986 TOTAL	1986 Total Private	1986 Public Enterprises	1986 General Government	1987 TOTAL	1987 Total Private	1987 Public Enterprises	1987 General Government
Increase in stocks, total	5515	5515	...	...	1654	1654	...	...
1 Goods producing industries	-2375	-2375	...	...	...	...	...	...
A Materials and supplies	...	...	...	...	...	...	...	...
B Work in progress [a]	-2426	-2426	...	...	...	...	...	...
C Livestock, except breeding stocks, dairy cattle, etc. [b]	51	51	...	...	...	...	...	...
D Finished goods	...	...	...	...	...	...	...	...
2 Wholesale and retail trade	...	...	...	...	...	...	...	...
3 Other, except government stocks	7891	7891	...	...	...	...	...	...
4 Government stocks								
Gross Fixed Capital Formation, Total	146133	129675	...	16458	156212	136513	...	19699
1 Residential buildings [c]	25566	25914	...	-348	...	...	...	...
2 Non-residential buildings	27805	20677	...	7128	...	...	...	...
3 Other construction [d]	51829	45449	...	6380	...	...	...	...
4 Land improvement and plantation and orchard development	442	442	...	...	...	...	...	...
5 Producers' durable goods	40653	37355	...	3298	44253	40750	...	3503
A Transport equipment	9351	9039	...	312	...	...	...	...
Passenger cars [e]	5391	5303	...	88	...	...	...	...
Other	3960	3736	...	224	...	...	...	...
B Machinery and equipment	31302	28316	...	2986	...	...	...	...
6 Breeding stock, dairy cattle, etc.	-161	-161	...	...	...	...	...	...
Total Gross Capital Formation	151648	135190	...	16458	157866	138167	...	19699

a) Item 'Work in progress' includes work in progress in mining and manufacturing, ships, oil drilling and oil production platforms.
b) Item 'Livestock except breeding stocks, dairy cattles etc.' includes increase in stocks of fodder, timber and firewood.
c) Item 'Residential buildings' includes also summer cottages, temporary dwellings, logging camps, fishermens' quarters etc..
d) The estimates of 'Other construction' include oil drilling rigs, oil production platforms etc., pipelines for gas, oil and gas exploration and drilling.
e) Item 'Passenger cars' includes station wagons.

Norway

2.8 Gross Capital Formation by Type of Good and Owner, in Constant Prices
Million Norwegian kroner

	1984 TOTAL	1984 Total Private	1984 Public Enterprises	1984 General Government	1985 TOTAL	1985 Total Private	1985 Public Enterprises	1985 General Government	1986 TOTAL	1986 Total Private	1986 Public Enterprises	1986 General Government
				At constant prices of:1984								
Increase in stocks, total	-1300	-1300	...	...	10834	10834	...	...	4495	4495	...	...
1 Goods producing industries	-2613	-2613	...	...	10263	10263	...	...	-1926	-1926	...	...
A Materials and supplies	...	...	...	...	...	...	...	...	...	...	...	...
B Work in progress a	-2649	-2649	...	...	10288	10288	...	...	-1969	-1969	...	...
C Livestock, except breeding stocks, dairy cattle, etc. b	36	36	...	...	-25	-25	...	...	43	43	...	...
D Finished goods	...	...	...	...	...	...	...	...	...	...	...	...
2 Wholesale and retail trade	...	...	...	...	...	...	...	...	...	...	...	...
3 Other, except government stocks	1313	1313	...	...	571	571	...	...	6421	6421	...	...
4 Government stocks	...	...	...	...	...	...	...	...	...	...	...	...
Gross Fixed Capital Formation, Total	117567	104709	...	12858	101170	88778	...	12392	125323	110826	...	14498
1 Residential buildings c	19171	19636	...	-465	19696	20449	...	-754	22484	22796	...	-312
2 Non-residential buildings	17918	12098	...	5820	20135	14724	...	5412	24391	18078	...	6313
3 Other construction d	45579	40410	...	5169	30877	25807	...	5070	45913	40279	...	5634
4 Land improvement and plantation and orchard development	527	527	...	...	421	421	...	...	385	385	...	...
5 Producers' durable goods	34406	32071	...	2335	30112	27448	...	2664	32287	29425	...	2863
A Transport equipment	11725	11484	...	241	4455	4220	...	235	4749	4494	...	255
Passenger cars e	2521	2467	...	54	3208	3148	...	60	4104	4037	...	67
Other	9204	9017	...	187	1247	1072	...	174	645	457	...	188
B Machinery and equipment	22681	20587	...	2094	25657	23228	...	2429	27539	24931	...	2608
6 Breeding stock, dairy cattle, etc.	-34	-34	...	...	-71	-71	...	...	-136	-136	...	...
Total Gross Capital Formation	116267	103409	...	12858	112004	99612	...	12392	129818	115321	...	14498

a) Item 'Work in progress' includes work in progress in mining and manufacturing, ships, oil drilling and oil production platforms.
b) Item 'Livestock except breeding stocks, dairy cattles etc.' includes increase in stocks of fodder, timber and firewood.
c) Item 'Residential buildings' includes also summer cottages, temporary dwellings, logging camps, fishermens' quarters etc..
d) The estimates of 'Other construction' include oil drilling rigs, oil production platforms etc., pipelines for gas, oil and gas exploration and drilling.
e) Item 'Passenger cars' includes station wagons.

2.11 Gross Fixed Capital Formation by Kind of Activity of Owner, ISIC Divisions, in Current Prices
Million Norwegian kroner

	1970	1975	1978	1979	1980	1981	1982	1983	1984	1985	1986	1987
					All Producers							
1 Agriculture, hunting, forestry and fishing	1398	2943	5216	4882	5795	6258	5897	5186	5359	6135	7246	6809
A Agriculture and hunting	973	2121	3689	3717	4812	5156	4776	3955	3867	4390	4480	4148
B Forestry and logging	131	231	310	317	326	369	361	386	415	442	469	596
C Fishing	294	591	1218	848	657	733	760	845	1077	1303	2297	2065
2 Mining and quarrying	518	4381	8531	6964	6833	18343	11578	15401	28388	20111	36521	32183
A Coal mining	7	30	56	29	41	111	19	22	34	44	55	...
B Crude petroleum and natural gas production	313	4069	8184	6594	6360	17696	11145	15042	28039	19705	36018	31848
C Metal ore mining	72	161	94	128	205	300	200	136	119	109	243	...
D Other mining	126	121	196	213	226	237	215	201	195	253	204	...

Norway

2.11 Gross Fixed Capital Formation by Kind of Activity of Owner, ISIC Divisions, in Current Prices
(Continued)

Million Norwegian kroner

	1970	1975	1978	1979	1980	1981	1982	1983	1984	1985	1986	1987
3 Manufacturing	3234	6650	8343	7331	9031	10855	9105	8258	9311	11975	16828	20510
A Manufacturing of food, beverages and tobacco	613	879	1451	1580	1593	1946	1897	1880	1970	2054	2377	2997
B Textile, wearing apparel and leather industries	99	110	239	237	282	222	217	126	142	189	272	220
C Manufacture of wood, and wood products, including furniture	246	465	590	594	584	782	676	724	761	710	840	1081
D Manufacture of paper and paper products, printing and publishing	383	886	1276	1270	2155	2039	970	980	1304	1550	2310	3540
E Manufacture of chemicals and chemical petroleum, coal, rubber and plastic products	414	1591	1688	745	962	1177	1235	1150	1208	1835	3697	...
F Manufacture of non-metalic mineral products except products of petroleum and coal	141	235	452	335	350	492	517	288	401	606	792	...
G Basic metal industries	594	824	773	768	1181	1939	1511	967	1287	2108	2981	1542
H Manufacture of fabricated metal products, machinery and equipment	730	1636	1820	1758	1870	2189	2056	2103	2207	2863	3473	...
I Other manufacturing industries	15	25	54	43	55	68	24	40	32	60	86	...
4 Electricity, gas and water	1726	3267	6013	6321	7000	7721	7960	8073	8266	8079	8203	8626
A Electricity, gas and steam	1567	2877	5392	5694	6380	7130	7353	7469	7665	7541	7516	7806
B Water works and supply	159	390	622	627	620	591	608	604	601	538	687	820
5 Construction [a]	431	1789	2405	1628	1588	1549	3165	3312	2382	3545	4868	3770
6 Wholesale and retail trade, restaurants and hotels [b]	967	1976	3056	3090	3285	3770	4141	4467	4464	5791	7321	7495
A Wholesale and retail trade	922	1895	2938	2966	3152	3618	3972	4286	4283	5565	7072	7237
B Restaurants and hotels	44	82	119	125	133	152	169	181	181	227	249	258
7 Transport, storage and communication [c]	4351	11954	8065	9043	7696	11595	15090	20250	18191	8054	7058	9606
A Transport and storage	3912	10531	5630	6382	4910	8720	11841	16709	14413	3918	2883	...
B Communication	439	1423	2436	2661	2785	2875	3249	3541	3778	4136	4176	...
8 Finance, insurance, real estate and business services [d]	4619	10029	14341	15540	16952	18732	22293	24437	26611	30516	38830	44365
A Financial institutions	250	490	760	1061	1299	1926	1341	2359	2840	3562	3724	4440
B Insurance	...	...	...	...	...	...	...	...	...	...	...	...
C Real estate and business services	4369	9538	13582	14479	15653	16806	20952	22077	23770	26955	35106	...
Real estate except dwellings	430	1418	1847	1973	2169	1825	3264	3047	4139	5655	9196	...
Dwellings	3939	8120	11735	12506	13484	14981	17688	19030	19631	21300	25910	29088
9 Community, social and personal services [e]	374	682	998	1043	1166	1369	1509	1654	1737	2547	2801	3150
Total Industries	17617	43670	56969	55843	59344	80190	80737	91037	104709	96754	129675	136514
Producers of Government Services	3578	7121	10737	10343	11454	11602	11525	12410	12858	13288	16458	19699
Private Non-Profit Institutions Serving Households	...	...	...	...	...	...	...	...	...	...	...	...
Total	21195	50791	67706	66186	70798	91792	92262	103447	117567	110042	146133	156213

a) Item 'Construction' also includes oil and natural gas exploration and drilling.
b) Item 'Wholesale and retail trade, restaurants and hotels' includes producers' durable goods, otherwise included in real estate.
c) Item 'Transport, storage and communication' includes pipeline transport for crude oil and natural gas.
d) Business services are included in item 'Community, social and personal services'.
e) Item 'Community, social and personal services' includes other private and business services but excludes commercial buildings.

Norway

2.12 Gross Fixed Capital Formation by Kind of Activity of Owner, ISIC Divisions, in Constant Prices

Million Norwegian kroner

	1970	1975	1978	1979	1980	1981	1982	1983	1984	1985	1986	1987
At constant prices of:	1970	1975			1980				1984		1986	

All Producers

	1970	1975	1978	1979	1980	1981	1982	1983	1984	1985	1986	1987
1 Agriculture, hunting, forestry and fishing	1398	1953 / 2943	4080	3562	3791 / 5795	5781	5042	4176	4181 / 5359	5730	6315 / 7246	6224
A Agriculture and hunting	973	1377 / 2121	2736	2688	3133 / 4812	4774	4126	3183	2991 / 3867	4111	3919 / 4480	3788
B Forestry and logging	131	154 / 231	239	236	222 / 326	340	309	312	320 / 415	412	410 / 469	541
C Fishing	294	423 / 591	1104	638	437 / 657	667	608	681	869 / 1077	1208	1987 / 2297	1895
2 Mining and quarrying	518	2881 / 4381	6659	5113	4275 / 6833	15334	7334	10522	19408 / 28388	18906	32397 / 36521	29877
A Coal mining	7	21 / 30	47	24	33 / 41	103	16	18	28 / 34	41	48 / 55	...
B Crude petroleum and natural gas production	313	2668 / 4069	6383	4822	3935 / 6360	14719	6954	10217	19082 / 28039	18525	31957 / 36018	29572
C Metal ore mining	72	109 / 161	77	102	146 / 205	286	175	115	114 / 119	103	213 / 243	...
D Other mining	126	84 / 121	152	164	161 / 226	227	189	172	184 / 195	238	179 / 204	...

1083

Norway

2.12 Gross Fixed Capital Formation by Kind of Activity of Owner, ISIC Divisions, in Constant Prices
(Continued)

Million Norwegian kroner

	1970	1975	1978	1979	1980	1981	1982	1983	1984	1985	1986	1987
					At constant prices of:							
		1970		1975			1980			1984		1986
3 Manufacturing	3234	4603 / 6650	6635	5858	6573 / 9031	10330	7997	7087	8718 / 9311	11360	14825 / 16828	18662
A Manufacturing of food, beverages and tobacco	613	607 / 879	1159	1267	1169 / 1593	1843	1659	1598	1801 / 1970	1945	2082 / 2377	2733
B Textile, wearing apparel and leather industries	99	77 / 110	189	189	206 / 282	212	191	109	134 / 142	178	237 / 272	201
C Manufacture of wood, and wood products, including furniture	246	320 / 465	475	474	430 / 584	743	592	624	700 / 761	673	739 / 840	986
D Manufacture of paper and paper products, printing and publishing	383	621 / 886	1000	1011	1538 / 2155	1950	856	848	1254 / 1304	1476	2037 / 2310	3255
E Manufacture of chemicals and chemical petroleum, coal, rubber and plastic products	414	1092 / 1591	1353	593	691 / 962	1124	1086	996	1132 / 1208	1739	3271 / 3697	...
F Manufacture of non-metalic mineral products except products of petroleum and coal	141	162 / 235	359	265	256 / 350	469	453	249	371 / 401	572	695 / 792	...
G Basic metal industries	594	573 / 824	606	607	868 / 1181	1842	1334	831	1202 / 1287	1992	2625 / 2981	1413
H Manufacture of fabricated metal products, machinery and equipment	730	1134 / 1636	1452	1418	1372 / 1870	2082	1806	1799	2092 / 2207	2728	3066 / 3473	...
I Other manufacturing industries	15	17 / 25	44	35	42 / 55	64	21	34	32 / 32	56	75 / 86	...
4 Electricity, gas and water	1726	2111 / 3267	4846	4816	4909 / 7000	7264	6917	6724	6581 / 8266	7696	7284 / 8203	7789
A Electricity, gas and steam	1567	1861 / 2877	4337	4327	4466 / 6380	6718	6406	6231	6118 / 7665	7193	6687 / 7516	7054
B Water works and supply	159	250 / 390	509	489	443 / 620	547	511	493	463 / 601	503	597 / 687	735

Norway

2.12 Gross Fixed Capital Formation by Kind of Activity of Owner, ISIC Divisions, in Constant Prices
(Continued)

Million Norwegian kroner

	1970	1975	1978	1979	1980	1981	1982	1983	1984	1985	1986	1987
					At constant prices of:							
	1970	**1975**			**1980**				**1984**		**1986**	
5 Construction a	431	1167 1789	1714	1042	1024 1588	1460	2453	2179	1756 2382	3317	4278 4868	3631
6 Wholesale and retail trade, restaurants and hotels b	967	1503 1976	2238	2188	2323 3285	3612	3604	3836	4022 4464	5296	6078 7321	6939
A Wholesale and retail trade	922	1439 1895	2152	2100	2225 3152	3467	3464	3684	3853 4283	5087	5873 7072	6699
B Restaurants and hotels	44	65 82	87	88	98 133	145	140	152	169 181	209	205 249	240
7 Transport, storage and communication c	4351	5942 11954	4625	5772	4630 7696	10460	10894	12575	9410 18191	4965	3302 7058	9166
A Transport and storage	3912	4866 10531	2649	3662	2589 4910	7701	7931	9258	5733 14413	1083	-350 2883	...
B Communication	439	1076 1423	1976	2109	2040 2785	2760	2963	3317	3676 3778	3883	3652 4176	...
8 Finance, insurance, real estate and business services d	4619	6580 10029	11447	11932	11833 16952	17152	18755	19459	20580 26611	29124	33921 38830	39758
A Financial institutions	250	362 490	611	831	941 1299	1805	1179	2068	2610 2840	3355	3258 3724	4059

Norway

2.12 Gross Fixed Capital Formation by Kind of Activity of Owner, ISIC Divisions, in Constant Prices
(Continued)

Million Norwegian kroner

	1970	1975	1978	1979	1980	1981	1982	1983	1984	1985	1986	1987
					At constant prices of:							
	1970		1975		1980				1984		1986	
B Insurance	...	...	...	...	...	...	...	...	...	...	...	...
		...			...				...		...	
C Real estate and business services	4369	6219	10836	11101	10893	15347	17576	17391	17971	25769	30662	...
		9538			15653				23770		35106	
Real estate except dwellings	430	920	1500	1544	1553	1721	2863	2566	3354	5324	7870	...
		1418			2169				4139		9196	
Dwellings	3939	5299	9336	9557	9340	13626	14713	14825	14617	20445	22792	26001
		8120			13484				19631		25910	
9 Community, social and personal services [e]	374	581	785	813	873	1324	1388	1635	1898	2384	2426	2917
		682			1166				1737		2801	
Total Industries	17617	27321	43029	41096	40231	72717	64384	68194	76553	88778	110826	124963
		43670			59344				104709		129675	
Producers of Government Services	3578	4944	8443	7817	7950	10769	9913	10425	10671	12392	14498	17712
		7121			11454				12858		16458	
Private Non-Profit Institutions Serving Households	...	...	...	...	...	...	...	...	...	...	...	...
		...			...				...		...	
Total	21195	32265	51472	48913	48181	83486	74297	78619	87224	101170	125324	142676
		50791			70798				117567		146133	

a) Item 'Construction' also includes oil and natural gas exploration and drilling.
b) Item 'Wholesale and retail trade, restaurants and hotels' includes producers' durable goods, otherwise included in real estate.
c) Item 'Transport, storage and communication' includes pipeline transport for crude oil and natural gas.
d) Business services are included in item 'Community, social and personal services'.
e) Item 'Community, social and personal services' includes other private and business services but excludes commercial buildings.

2.13 Stocks of Reproducible Fixed Assets, by Type of Good and Owner, in Current Prices

Million Norwegian kroner

	TOTAL Gross	TOTAL Net	Total Private Gross	Total Private Net	Public Enterprises Gross	Public Enterprises Net	General Government Gross	General Government Net
				1980				
1 Residential buildings [a]	...	238433	...	238433	...	...	...	...
2 Non-residential buildings	...	223155	...	142440	...	...	...	80715
3 Other construction [b]	...	282185	...	173976	...	...	...	108210
4 Land improvement and plantation and orchard development	...	42776	...	42776	...	...	...	...
5 Producers' durable goods	...	220515	...	210060	...	...	...	10455
A Transport equipment	...	91841	...	91169	...	...	...	672
Passenger cars [c]	...	5450	...	5346	...	...	...	103
Other	...	86391	...	85822	...	...	...	569
B Machinery and equipment	...	128674	...	118891	...	...	...	9783
6 Breeding stock, dairy cattle, etc.	...	3933	...	3933	...	...	...	...
Total	...	1011000	...	811618	...	...	...	199380

Norway

2.13 Stocks of Reproducible Fixed Assets, by Type of Good and Owner, in Current Prices
(Continued)

Million Norwegian kroner

	TOTAL Gross	TOTAL Net	Total Private Gross	Total Private Net	Public Enterprises Gross	Public Enterprises Net	General Government Gross	General Government Net
1981								
1 Residential buildings [a]	...	269938	...	269938	...	...	...	...
2 Non-residential buildings	...	251193	...	159925	...	...	...	91269
3 Other construction [b]	...	329514	...	207611	...	...	...	121903
4 Land improvement and plantation and orchard development	...	53235	...	53235	...	...	...	...
5 Producers' durable goods	...	240516	...	228994	...	...	...	11523
A Transport equipment	...	99868	...	98936	...	...	...	933
Passenger cars [c]	...	5872	...	5536	...	...	...	336
Other	...	93996	...	93399	...	...	...	597
B Machinery and equipment	...	140648	...	130058	...	...	...	10590
6 Breeding stock, dairy cattle, etc.	...	4435	...	4435	...	...	...	...
Total	...	1148830	...	924138	...	...	...	224695
1982								
1 Residential buildings [a]	...	314114	...	314114	...	...	...	...
2 Non-residential buildings	...	281116	...	179022	...	...	...	102094
3 Other construction [b]	...	379268	...	240741	...	...	...	138527
4 Land improvement and plantation and orchard development	...	56426	...	56426	...	...	...	...
5 Producers' durable goods	...	263458	...	250716	...	...	...	12742
A Transport equipment	...	108076	...	107110	...	...	...	966
Passenger cars [c]	...	7129	...	6771	...	...	...	358
Other	...	100947	...	100339	...	...	...	608
B Machinery and equipment	...	155382	...	143606	...	...	...	11776
6 Breeding stock, dairy cattle, etc.	...	4432	...	4432	...	...	...	...
Total	...	1298810	...	1045450	...	...	...	253363
1983								
1 Residential buildings [a]	...	346259	...	346259	...	...	...	...
2 Non-residential buildings	...	306603	...	194132	...	...	...	112471
3 Other construction [b]	...	407193	...	260251	...	...	...	146942
4 Land improvement and plantation and orchard development	...	53205	...	53205	...	...	...	...
5 Producers' durable goods	...	274326	...	261640	...	...	...	12686
A Transport equipment	...	114360	...	113398	...	...	...	962
Passenger cars [c]	...	7582	...	7244	...	...	...	339
Other	...	106778	...	106154	...	...	...	624
B Machinery and equipment	...	159966	...	148242	...	...	...	11723
6 Breeding stock, dairy cattle, etc.	...	4315	...	4315	...	...	...	...
Total	...	1391900	...	1119800	...	...	...	272099
1984								
1 Residential buildings [a]	...	376232	...	376232	...	...	...	...
2 Non-residential buildings	...	329161	...	208831	...	...	...	120330
3 Other construction [b]	...	461360	...	301499	...	...	...	159862
4 Land improvement and plantation and orchard development	...	62894	...	62894	...	...	...	...
5 Producers' durable goods	...	257396	...	244773	...	...	...	12623
A Transport equipment	...	101243	...	100322	...	...	...	921
Passenger cars [c]	...	7315	...	7039	...	...	...	275
Other	...	93928	...	93283	...	...	...	645
B Machinery and equipment	...	156153	...	144452	...	...	...	11701
6 Breeding stock, dairy cattle, etc.	...	4663	...	4663	...	...	...	...
Total	...	1491705	...	1198890	...	...	...	292814

Norway

2.13 Stocks of Reproducible Fixed Assets, by Type of Good and Owner, in Current Prices
(Continued)

Million Norwegian kroner

	TOTAL Gross	TOTAL Net	Total Private Gross	Total Private Net	Public Enterprises Gross	Public Enterprises Net	General Government Gross	General Government Net
1985								
1 Residential buildings a	...	407077	...	407077	...	...	...	...
2 Non-residential buildings	...	362952	...	232374	...	...	...	130578
3 Other construction b	...	506135	...	327034	...	...	...	179101
4 Land improvement and plantation and orchard development	...	66826	...	66826	...	...	...	...
5 Producers' durable goods	...	263265	...	248465	...	...	...	14801
A Transport equipment	...	87646	...	86734	...	...	...	913
Passenger cars c	...	8609	...	8372	...	...	...	237
Other	...	79038	...	78362	...	...	...	676
B Machinery and equipment	...	175619	...	161731	...	...	...	13888
6 Breeding stock, dairy cattle, etc.	...	5195	...	5195	...	...	...	...
Total	...	1611450	...	1286970	...	...	...	324480
1986								
1 Residential buildings a	...	463080	...	463080	...	...	...	...
2 Non-residential buildings	...	406844	...	263759	...	...	...	143085
3 Other construction b	...	557707	...	364497	...	...	...	193210
4 Land improvement and plantation and orchard development	...	68353	...	68353	...	...	...	...
5 Producers' durable goods	...	285510	...	267964	...	...	...	17545
A Transport equipment	...	82119	...	81204	...	...	...	915
Passenger cars c	...	11255	...	11058	...	...	...	197
Other	...	70864	...	70146	...	...	...	718
B Machinery and equipment	...	203391	...	186761	...	...	...	16630
6 Breeding stock, dairy cattle, etc.	...	5366	...	5366	...	...	...	...
Total	...	1786860	...	1433020	...	...	...	353841

a) Item 'Residential buildings' includes also summer cottages, temporary dwellings, logging camps, fishermens' quarters etc..
b) The estimates of 'Other construction' include oil drilling rigs, oil production platforms etc., pipelines for gas, oil and gas exploration and drilling.
c) Item 'Passenger cars' includes station wagons.

2.14 Stocks of Reproducible Fixed Assets, by Type of Good and Owner, in Constant Prices

Million Norwegian kroner

	TOTAL Gross	TOTAL Net	Total Private Gross	Total Private Net	Public Enterprises Gross	Public Enterprises Net	General Government Gross	General Government Net
At constant prices of: 1984								
1984								
1 Residential buildings a	...	376232	...	376232	...	...	...	...
2 Non-residential buildings	...	329161	...	208831	...	...	...	120331
3 Other construction b	...	461360	...	301499	...	...	...	159861
4 Land improvement and plantation and orchard development	...	62894	...	62894	...	...	...	...
5 Producers' durable goods	...	257396	...	244773	...	...	...	12623
A Transport equipment	...	101243	...	100322	...	...	...	921
Passenger cars c	...	7315	...	7039	...	...	...	276
Other	...	93928	...	93283	...	...	...	645
B Machinery and equipment	...	156153	...	144452	...	...	...	11701
6 Breeding stock, dairy cattle, etc.	...	4663	...	4663	...	...	...	...
Total d	...	1491710	...	1198890	...	...	...	292815

Norway

2.14 Stocks of Reproducible Fixed Assets, by Type of Good and Owner, in Constant Prices
(Continued)

Million Norwegian kroner

		TOTAL Gross	TOTAL Net	Total Private Gross	Total Private Net	Public Enterprises Gross	Public Enterprises Net	General Government Gross	General Government Net
				At constant prices of:1984					
				1985					
1	Residential buildings a	...	390761	...	390761	...	...	...	...
2	Non-residential buildings	...	342094	...	219236	...	...	...	122858
3	Other construction b	...	471823	...	306892	...	...	...	164931
4	Land improvement and plantation and orchard development	...	63331	...	63331	...	...	...	...
5	Producers' durable goods	...	248506	...	234597	...	...	...	13908
	A Transport equipment	...	81572	...	80742	...	...	...	830
	Passenger cars c	...	7645	...	7435	...	...	...	210
	Other	...	73927	...	73307	...	...	...	620
	B Machinery and equipment	...	166934	...	153856	...	...	...	13079
6	Breeding stock, dairy cattle, etc.	...	4611	...	4611	...	...	...	...
	Total d	...	1521130	...	1219430	...	...	...	301697
				1986					
1	Residential buildings a	...	407398	...	407398	...	...	...	...
2	Non-residential buildings	...	358174	...	231524	...	...	...	126650
3	Other construction b	...	495982	...	325417	...	...	...	170565
4	Land improvement and plantation and orchard development	...	63730	...	63730	...	...	...	...
5	Producers' durable goods	...	249229	...	233949	...	...	...	15280
	A Transport equipment	...	70242	...	69487	...	...	...	755
	Passenger cars c	...	8620	...	8471	...	...	...	149
	Other	...	61622	...	61016	...	...	...	606
	B Machinery and equipment	...	178986	...	164462	...	...	...	14525
6	Breeding stock, dairy cattle, etc.	...	4476	...	4476	...	...	...	...
	Total d	...	1578990	...	1266490	...	...	...	312495

a) Item 'Residential buildings' includes also summer cottages, temporary dwellings, logging camps, fishermens' quarters etc..
b) The estimates of 'Other construction' include oil drilling rigs, oil production platforms etc., pipelines for gas, oil and gas exploration and drilling.
c) Item 'Passenger cars' includes station wagons.
d) Column 8 (General government, net) refers to stocks of reproducible fixed assets outside general government.

2.15 Stocks of Reproducible Fixed Assets by Kind of Activity, in Current Prices

Million Norwegian kroner

		1980 Gross	1980 Net	1981 Gross	1981 Net	1982 Gross	1982 Net	1983 Gross	1983 Net	1984 Gross	1984 Net	1985 Gross	1985 Net
1	Residential buildings a	...	238433	...	269938	...	314114	...	346259	...	376232	...	407077
2	Non-residential buildings	...	223155	...	251193	...	281116	...	306603	...	329161	...	362952
	A Industries	...	142440	...	159925	...	179022	...	194132	...	208831	...	232374
	1 Agriculture	...	35945	...	40362	...	44333	...	47237	...	49932	...	53539
	2 Mining and quarrying	...	1224	...	1425	...	1549	...	1650	...	1722	...	4284
	3 Manufacturing	...	44272	...	49831	...	55411	...	59460	...	63044	...	68071
	4 Electricity, gas and water	...	15427	...	17222	...	19379	...	21248	...	22499	...	24242
	5 Construction	...	2132	...	2513	...	3063	...	3659	...	4078	...	4734
	6 Wholesale and retail trade	...	...	...	...	...	...	...	...	...	...	...	...
	7 Transport and communication	...	2078	...	2355	...	2670	...	2910	...	3175	...	3527
	8 Finance, etc.	...	41362	...	46217	...	52617	...	57968	...	64381	...	73978
	9 Community, social and personal services	...	...	...	...	...	...	...	...	...	...	...	...
	B Producers of government services	...	80715	...	91269	...	102094	...	112471	...	120331	...	130578
	C Other producers	...	...	...	...	...	...	...	...	...	...	...	...
3	Other construction b	...	282185	...	329514	...	379268	...	407193	...	461360	...	506135
	A Industries	...	173976	...	207611	...	240741	...	260251	...	301499	...	327034
	1 Agriculture c	...	2414	...	2745	...	3150	...	3429	...	3804	...	4411
	2 Mining and quarrying d	...	44908	...	66040	...	81808	...	84607	...	103329	...	112787
	3 Manufacturing	...	6179	...	6737	...	7442	...	8035	...	8469	...	10070
	4 Electricity, gas and water	...	67330	...	75290	...	84526	...	89967	...	98339	...	105848

Norway

2.15 Stocks of Reproducible Fixed Assets by Kind of Activity, in Current Prices
(Continued)

Million Norwegian kroner

	1980 Gross	1980 Net	1981 Gross	1981 Net	1982 Gross	1982 Net	1983 Gross	1983 Net	1984 Gross	1984 Net	1985 Gross	1985 Net
5 Construction e	...	6728	...	6925	...	8670	...	8515	...	11023	...	11037
6 Wholesale and retail trade	...	...	...	...	...	...	...	...	...	...	...	...
7 Transport and communication f	...	46416	...	49874	...	55145	...	65698	...	76535	...	82882
8 Finance, etc.	...	...	...	...	...	...	...	...	...	...	...	...
9 Community, social and personal services	...	...	...	...	...	...	...	...	...	...	...	...
B Producers of government services	...	108210	...	121903	...	138527	...	146942	...	159861	...	179101
C Other producers	...	...	...	...	...	...	...	...	...	...	...	...
4 Land improvement and development and plantation and orchard development	...	42776	...	53235	...	56426	...	53205	...	62894	...	66826
5 Producers' durable goods	...	220515	...	240516	...	263458	...	274326	...	257396	...	263265
A Industries	...	210060	...	228994	...	250716	...	261640	...	244773	...	248465
1 Agriculture c	...	21832	...	23984	...	25869	...	27193	...	27839	...	29957
2 Mining and quarrying d	...	3062	...	3516	...	3787	...	3750	...	5131	...	5886
3 Manufacturing	...	55564	...	60289	...	66346	...	66870	...	59868	...	65282
4 Electricity, gas and water	...	14664	...	16196	...	18673	...	20718	...	22411	...	24519
5 Construction e	...	6979	...	7118	...	7373	...	7318	...	6247	...	6975
6 Wholesale and retail trade	...	14827	...	15526	...	16940	...	17364	...	17348	...	20162
7 Transport and communication	...	85280	...	93560	...	101647	...	107887	...	94746	...	81141
8 Finance, etc. g	...	1535	...	1870	...	2380	...	2788	...	3422	...	4944
9 Community, social and personal services g	...	6318	...	6938	...	7701	...	7753	...	7760	...	9598
B Producers of government services	...	10455	...	11523	...	12742	...	12686	...	12623	...	14801
C Other producers	...	...	...	...	...	...	...	...	...	...	...	...
6 Breeding stock, dairy cattle, etc.	...	3933	...	4435	...	4432	...	4315	...	4663	...	5195
Total	...	1011000	...	1148830	...	1298810	...	1391900	...	1491710	...	1611450
Memorandum Item: Mineral Fuels and Power	...	133292	...	164919	...	193130	...	204709	...	235265	...	258257

	1986 Gross	1986 Net
1 Residential buildings a	...	463080
2 Non-residential buildings	...	406844
A Industries	...	263759
1 Agriculture	...	57759
2 Mining and quarrying	...	5542
3 Manufacturing	...	75421
4 Electricity, gas and water	...	26188
5 Construction	...	5581
6 Wholesale and retail trade	...	...
7 Transport and communication	...	3939
8 Finance, etc.	...	89328
9 Community, social and personal services	...	...
B Producers of government services	...	143085
C Other producers	...	...
3 Other construction b	...	557707
A Industries	...	364497
1 Agriculture c	...	5540
2 Mining and quarrying d	...	135921
3 Manufacturing	...	11285
4 Electricity, gas and water	...	114375
5 Construction e	...	11612
6 Wholesale and retail trade	...	...
7 Transport and communication f	...	85765

Norway

2.15 Stocks of Reproducible Fixed Assets by Kind of Activity, in Current Prices
(Continued)

Million Norwegian kroner

		1986 Gross	1986 Net
	8 Finance, etc.	...	...
	9 Community, social and personal services	...	...
	B Producers of government services	...	193210
	C Other producers	...	...
4	Land improvement and development and plantation and orchard development	...	68353
5	Producers' durable goods	...	285510
	A Industries	...	267964
	1 Agriculture c	...	32691
	2 Mining and quarrying d	...	6781
	3 Manufacturing	...	75723
	4 Electricity, gas and water	...	27677
	5 Construction e	...	8022
	6 Wholesale and retail trade	...	24185
	7 Transport and communication	...	74294
	8 Finance, etc. g	...	6888
	9 Community, social and personal services g	...	11704
	B Producers of government services	...	17545
	C Other producers	...	...
6	Breeding stock, dairy cattle, etc.	...	5366
Total		...	1786860
Memorandum Item: Mineral Fuels and Power		...	296782

a) Item 'Residential buildings' includes also summer cottages, temporary dwellings, logging camps, fishermens' quarters etc..
b) The estimates of 'Other construction' include oil drilling rigs, oil production platforms etc., pipelines for gas, oil and gas exploration and drilling.
c) Item 'Agriculture' refers to agriculture, forestry and fishing.
d) Item 'Mining and quarrying' also includes crude petroleum and natural gas production.
e) Item 'Construction' also includes oil and natural gas exploration and drilling.
f) Item 'Transport, storage and communication' includes pipeline transport for crude oil and natural gas.
g) Business services are included in item 'Community, social and personal services'.

2.16 Stocks of Reproducible Fixed Assets by Kind of Activity, in Constant Prices

Million Norwegian kroner

		1984 Gross	1984 Net	1985 Gross	1985 Net	1986 Gross	1986 Net
				At constant prices of:1984			
1	Residential buildings a	...	376232	...	390761	...	407398
2	Non-residential buildings	...	329161	...	342094	...	358174
	A Industries	...	208831	...	219236	...	231524
	1 Agriculture	...	49932	...	50248	...	50400
	2 Mining and quarrying	...	1722	...	4055	...	4936
	3 Manufacturing	...	63044	...	64427	...	67229
	4 Electricity, gas and water	...	22499	...	22957	...	23353
	5 Construction	...	4078	...	4485	...	4978
	6 Wholesale and retail trade	...	...	...	...	...	...
	7 Transport and communication	...	3175	...	3317	...	3468
	8 Finance, etc.	...	64381	...	69748	...	77160
	9 Community, social and personal services	...	...	...	...	...	...
	B Producers of government services	...	120331	...	122858	...	126650
	C Other producers	...	...	...	...	...	...
3	Other construction b	...	461360	...	471823	...	495982
	A Industries	...	301499	...	306892	...	325417
	1 Agriculture c	...	3804	...	4124	...	4816
	2 Mining and quarrying d	...	103329	...	105674	...	121240
	3 Manufacturing	...	8469	...	9048	...	9691
	4 Electricity, gas and water	...	98339	...	100531	...	102576

Norway

2.16 Stocks of Reproducible Fixed Assets by Kind of Activity, in Constant Prices
(Continued)

Million Norwegian kroner

	1984 Gross	1984 Net	1985 Gross	1985 Net	1986 Gross	1986 Net
	\multicolumn{6}{c}{At constant prices of:1984}					
5 Construction e	...	11023	...	10475	...	10518
6 Wholesale and retail trade	...	...	...	...	...	...
7 Transport and communication f	...	76535	...	77040	...	76576
8 Finance, etc.	...	...	...	...	...	...
9 Community, social and personal services	...	...	...	...	...	...
B Producers of government services	...	159861	...	164931	...	170565
C Other producers	...	...	...	...	...	...
4 Land improvement and development and plantation and orchard development	...	62894	...	63331	...	63730
5 Producers' durable goods	...	257396	...	248506	...	249229
A Industries	...	244773	...	234597	...	233949
1 Agriculture c	...	27839	...	28125	...	28748
2 Mining and quarrying d	...	5131	...	5643	...	6024
3 Manufacturing	...	59868	...	62482	...	66757
4 Electricity, gas and water	...	22411	...	23519	...	24308
5 Construction e	...	6247	...	6610	...	7016
6 Wholesale and retail trade	...	17348	...	18614	...	20402
7 Transport and communication	...	94746	...	75969	...	64561
8 Finance, etc. g	...	3422	...	4639	...	5972
9 Community, social and personal services g	...	7760	...	8997	...	10162
B Producers of government services	...	12623	...	13908	...	15280
C Other producers	...	...	...	...	...	...
6 Breeding stock, dairy cattle, etc.	...	4663	...	4611	...	4476
Total	...	1491710	...	1521130	...	1578990
Memorandum Item: Mineral Fuels and Power	...	235265	...	244321	...	265318

a) Item 'Residential buildings' includes also summer cottages, temporary dwellings, logging camps, fishermens' quarters etc..
b) The estimates of 'Other construction' include oil drilling rigs, oil production platforms etc., pipelines for gas, oil and gas exploration and drilling.
c) Item 'Agriculture' refers to agriculture, forestry and fishing.
d) Item 'Mining and quarrying' also includes crude petroleum and natural gas production.
e) Item 'Construction' also includes oil and natural gas exploration and drilling.
f) Item 'Transport, storage and communication' includes pipeline transport for crude oil and natural gas.
g) Business services are included in item 'Community, social and personal services'.

2.17 Exports and Imports of Goods and Services, Detail

Million Norwegian kroner

	1970	1975	1978	1979	1980	1981	1982	1983	1984	1985	1986	1987
\multicolumn{13}{c}{Exports of Goods and Services}												
1 Exports of merchandise, f.o.b.	17715	38140	57863	70007	92863	106899	114798	133249	156822	173254	136003	144945
2 Transport and communication	13164	18054	19808	26276	31500	36506	35246	34921	40191	43342	38820	34270
A In respect of merchandise imports	241	470	464	498	505	516	517	551	580	610	546	503
B Other	12923	17584	19344	25778	30995	35990	34729	34370	39611	42732	38275	33767
3 Insurance service charges	47	88	120	139	168	186	206	204	234	282	305	311
A In respect of merchandise imports	47	88	120	139	168	179	200	197	226	265	300	300
B Other	-	-	-	-	-	7	6	7	7	17	5	11
4 Other commodities	1206	3711	6205	5461	6287	8022	9729	10240	11004	11703	11129	11208
5 Adjustments of merchandise exports to change-of-ownership basis	...	...	...	...	...	...	...	...	...	...	...	...
6 Direct purchases in the domestic market by non-residential households	1271	2196	3225	3524	3977	4430	4727	4910	5388	6590	7949	8485
7 Direct purchases in the domestic market by extraterritorial bodies						245	317	397	440	392	424	514
Total Exports of Goods and Services	33403	62189	87221	105407	134795	156288	165022	183921	214078	235563	194630	199732
\multicolumn{13}{c}{Imports of Goods and Services}												
1 Imports of merchandise, c.i.f.	26651	54366	61979	70433	84543	90516	100458	102520	116541	133927	153072	151581

Norway

2.17 Exports and Imports of Goods and Services, Detail
(Continued)

Million Norwegian kroner

	1970	1975	1978	1979	1980	1981	1982	1983	1984	1985	1986	1987
A Imports of merchandise, f.o.b.	25956	52861	60484	68805	82787	88586	98462	99945	113707	130617	149663	148024
B Transport of services on merchandise imports	554	1197	1154	1212	1255	1392	1397	1985	2155	2515	2509	2658
By residents	241	470	464	498	505	516	517	551	580	610	546	503
By non-residents	313	727	690	714	750	876	880	1434	1574	1905	1964	2155
C Insurance service charges on merchandise imports	141	308	341	416	501	538	598	590	679	795	900	899
By residents	-	-	-	-	-	-	-	-	-	-	-	-
By non-residents	141	308	341	416	501	538	598	590	679	795	900	899
2 Adjustments of merchandise imports to change-of-ownership basis	...	...	...	...	...	...	...	...	...	...	...	...
3 Other transport and communication	5355	9275	11704	15246	17936	21056	22038	24360	28281	29047	25410	23907
4 Other insurance service charges	43	503	253	306	663	405	356	579	903	924	18	93
5 Other commodities	527	4012	8264	6067	6709	9105	10122	12061	13954	14785	14263	14594
6 Direct purchases abroad by government	1855	3983	6919	7102	7520	109	125	126	139	158	170	181
7 Direct purchases abroad by resident households						9279	11443	12385	13034	15761	19536	21439
Total Imports of Goods and Services	34431	72139	89119	99154	117371	130469	144543	152031	172852	194602	212469	211795
Balance of Goods and Services	-1028	-9950	-1898	6253	17424	25819	20479	31890	41226	40961	-17839	-12063
Total Imports and Balance of Goods and Services	33403	62189	87221	105407	134795	156288	165022	183921	214078	235563	194630	199732

3.12 General Government Income and Outlay Account: Total and Subsectors

Million Norwegian kroner

	1980					1981				
	Total General Government	Central Government	State or Provincial Government	Local Government	Social Security Funds	Total General Government	Central Government	State or Provincial Government	Local Government	Social Security Funds

Receipts

1 Operating surplus	-	...	...	-	...	-	...	...	-	...
2 Property and entrepreneurial income [a]	7049	5935	...	-336	1450	9639	8321	...	-334	1652
A Withdrawals from public quasi-corporations [a]	-2216	-1214	...	-1002	...	-1894	-845	...	-1049	...
B Interest	9132	7016	...	666	1450	11415	9048	...	715	1652
C Dividends	133	133	...	...	...	118	118	...	...	...
D Net land rent and royalties	...	...	...	...	...	...	...	...	...	...
3 Taxes, fees and contributions	144657	88665	...	25217	30775	160250	94388	...	29409	36453
A Indirect taxes	49024	48399	...	487	138	55696	54940	...	609	147
B Direct taxes	61260	36530	...	24730	...	65657	36857	...	28800	...
Income [b]	38379	14299	...	24080	...	40599	12484	...	28115	...
Other	22881	22231	...	650	...	25058	24373	...	685	...
C Social security contributions	34224	3587	...	...	30637	38699	2393	...	...	36306
D Fees, fines and penalties	149	149	...	...	...	198	198	...	...	...
4 Other current transfers	...	3847	...	17762	10922	...	4450	...	20623	12944
A Casualty insurance claims	...	-	...	...	...	...	-	...	...	...
B Transfers from other government subsectors	...	3847	...	17762	10922	...	4450	...	20623	12944
C Transfers from the rest of the world	...	-	...	...	...	...	-	...	...	...
D Other transfers, except imputed	...	...	...	...	...	...	...	...	...	...
E Imputed unfunded employee pension and welfare contributions	...	...	...	...	...	...	...	...	...	...
Total Current Receipts [c]	151706	98447	...	42643	43147	169889	107159	...	49698	51049

Disbursements

1 Government final consumption expenditure	53478	20417	...	32225	836	62616	24929	...	36737	950
2 Property income	9664	7813	...	1851	...	10721	8435	...	2286	...
A Interest	9664	7813	...	1851	...	10721	8435	...	2286	...
B Net land rent and royalties	...	...	...	...	...	...	...	...	...	...
3 Subsidies	19960	18845	...	866	249	21795	19656	...	1831	308

Norway

3.12 General Government Income and Outlay Account: Total and Subsectors
(Continued)

Million Norwegian kroner

	1980					1981				
	Total General Government	Central Government	State or Provincial Government	Local Government	Social Security Funds	Total General Government	Central Government	State or Provincial Government	Local Government	Social Security Funds
4 Other current transfers	43172	30146	...	5239	40317	50255	35710	...	5734	46828
A Casualty insurance premiums, net	-	-	...	...	...	-	-	...	...	...
B Transfers to other government subsectors	...	24595	...	998	6937	...	29387	...	1186	7444
C Social security benefits	40975	3354	...	4241	33380	47636	3704	...	4548	39384
D Social assistance grants	...	...	...	...	...	...	...	...	...	...
E Unfunded employee pension and welfare benefits	...	...	...	...	...	...	...	...	...	...
F Transfers to private non-profit institutions serving households	...	...	...	...	...	...	...	...	...	...
G Other transfers n.e.c.	11	11	...	...	...	2	2	...	...	...
H Transfers to the rest of the world	2186	2186	...	...	...	2617	2617	...	...	...
Net saving	25432	21226	...	2462	1745	24502	18429	...	3110	2963
Total Current Disbursements and Net Saving [c]	151706	98447	...	42643	43147	169889	107159	...	49698	51049

	1982					1983				
	Total General Government	Central Government	State or Provincial Government	Local Government	Social Security Funds	Total General Government	Central Government	State or Provincial Government	Local Government	Social Security Funds

Receipts

1 Operating surplus	-	...	...	...	...	-	...	...	-	...
2 Property and entrepreneurial income [a]	11507	9757	...	-152	1903	14089	11816	...	37	2236
A Withdrawals from public quasi-corporations [a]	-2208	-1167	...	-1041	...	-1510	-589	...	-921	...
B Interest	13218	10426	...	889	1903	15085	11891	...	957	2236
C Dividends	497	497	...	...	...	514	514	...	...	...
D Net land rent and royalties	...	...	...	...	...	...	...	...	...	...
3 Taxes, fees and contributions	176332	102995	...	32690	40647	194120	115060	...	34872	44188
A Indirect taxes	61747	60794	...	771	182	69733	68600	...	931	202
B Direct taxes	70604	38685	...	31919	...	76722	42781	...	33941	...
Income [b]	42892	11751	...	31141	...	44674	11593	...	33081	...
Other	27712	26934	...	778	...	32048	31188	...	860	...
C Social security contributions	43494	3029	...	...	40465	47149	3163	...	...	43986
D Fees, fines and penalties	487	487	...	...	...	516	516	...	...	...
4 Other current transfers	...	5477	...	24204	14995	...	5472	...	26445	18026
A Casualty insurance claims	...	-	...	...	...	...	-	...	...	...
B Transfers from other government subsectors	...	5477	...	24204	14995	...	5472	...	26445	18026
C Transfers from the rest of the world	...	-	...	...	...	...	-	...	...	...
D Other transfers, except imputed	...	...	...	...	...	...	...	...	...	...
E Imputed unfunded employee pension and welfare contributions	...	...	...	...	...	...	...	...	...	...
Total Current Receipts [c]	187839	118229	...	56742	57545	208209	132348	...	61354	64450

Disbursements

1 Government final consumption expenditure	70408	27472	...	41940	997	78213	30456	...	46635	1122
2 Property income	11529	8767	...	2762	...	13414	10237	...	3177	...
A Interest	11529	8767	...	2762	...	13414	10237	...	3177	...
B Net land rent and royalties	...	...	...	...	...	...	...	...	...	...
3 Subsidies	23662	21326	...	2021	315	24439	22225	...	2209	6

Norway

3.12 General Government Income and Outlay Account: Total and Subsectors
(Continued)

Million Norwegian kroner

1982 / 1983

	Total General Government	Central Government	State or Provincial Government	Local Government	Social Security Funds	Total General Government	Central Government	State or Provincial Government	Local Government	Social Security Funds
4 Other current transfers	57789	41949	...	6596	53921	66076	47402	...	7474	61144
A Casualty insurance premiums, net	-	...	...	...	...	-	...	...	...	...
B Transfers to other government subsectors	...	34547	...	1376	8753	...	38844	...	1529	9570
C Social security benefits	54516	4129	...	5219	45168	62212	4694	...	5945	51573
D Social assistance grants	...	...	...	...	...	...	...	...	...	...
E Unfunded employee pension and welfare benefits	...	...	...	...	...	...	...	...	...	...
F Transfers to private non-profit institutions serving households	...	...	...	...	...	...	...	...	...	...
G Other transfers n.e.c.	2	2	...	...	...	14	14	...	...	...
H Transfers to the rest of the world	3271	3271	...	...	...	3850	3850	...	...	...
Net saving	24451	18715	...	3423	2312	26067	22029	...	1859	2179
Total Current Disbursements and Net Saving [c]	187839	118229	...	56742	57545	208209	132349	...	61354	64451

1984 / 1985

	Total General Government	Central Government	State or Provincial Government	Local Government	Social Security Funds	Total General Government	Central Government	State or Provincial Government	Local Government	Social Security Funds
Receipts										
1 Operating surplus	-	...	...	-	...	-	...	...	...	...
2 Property and entrepreneurial income [a]	19928	16934	...	418	2576	23054	19468	...	746	2841
A Withdrawals from public quasi-corporations [a]	-1595	-833	...	-762	...	-2776	-2081	...	-695	...
B Interest	20552	16796	...	1180	2576	24780	20498	...	1441	2841
C Dividends	971	971	...	...	...	1050	1050	...	...	...
D Net land rent and royalties	...	...	...	...	...	...	...	...	...	...
3 Taxes, fees and contributions	216898	131825	...	37436	47637	249303	153018	...	42807	53478
A Indirect taxes	78200	76936	...	1062	202	91037	89545	...	1283	209
B Direct taxes	87637	51263	...	36374	...	100599	59075	...	41524	...
Income [b]	49647	14308	...	35339	...	55554	15267	...	40287	...
Other	37989	36954	...	1035	...	45045	43808	...	1237	...
C Social security contributions	50511	3076	...	...	47435	57304	4035	...	...	53269
D Fees, fines and penalties	550	550	...	...	...	363	363	...	...	...
4 Other current transfers	3000	8486	...	31050	21584	3078	10321	...	34492	21497
A Casualty insurance claims	...	-	...	...	...	...	-	...	...	...
B Transfers from other government subsectors	...	5486	...	31050	21584	...	7243	...	34492	21497
C Transfers from the rest of the world	...	...	...	...	...	...	-	...	...	...
D Other transfers, except imputed	3000	3000	...	...	...	3078	3078	...	...	...
E Imputed unfunded employee pension and welfare contributions	...	...	...	...	...	...	...	...	...	...
Total Current Receipts [c]	239826	157245	...	68904	71797	275435	182807	...	78045	77816
Disbursements										
1 Government final consumption expenditure	84099	31999	...	50958	1142	92654	34525	...	56819	1310
2 Property income	15018	11219	...	3799	...	17393	13300	...	4093	...
A Interest	15018	11219	...	3799	...	17393	13300	...	4093	...
B Net land rent and royalties	...	...	...	...	...	...	...	...	...	...
3 Subsidies	25708	23340	...	2363	6	26936	24355	...	2574	7

Norway

3.12 General Government Income and Outlay Account: Total and Subsectors
(Continued)

Million Norwegian kroner

	1984 Total General Government	1984 Central Government	1984 State or Provincial Government	1984 Local Government	1984 Social Security Funds	1985 Total General Government	1985 Central Government	1985 State or Provincial Government	1985 Local Government	1985 Social Security Funds
4 Other current transfers	71787	53445	...	8447	68015	78029	58272	...	9471	73518
A Casualty insurance premiums, net	-	-	...	...	...	-	-	...	...	...
B Transfers to other government subsectors	...	44664	...	1559	11897	...	48806	...	1531	12895
C Social security benefits	67917	4911	...	6888	56118	73820	5257	...	7940	60623
D Social assistance grants	...	...	...	...	...	...	...	...	...	...
E Unfunded employee pension and welfare benefits	...	...	...	...	...	...	...	...	...	...
F Transfers to private non-profit institutions serving households	...	...	...	...	...	...	...	...	...	...
G Other transfers n.e.c.	...	...	...	...	...	...	...	...	...	...
H Transfers to the rest of the world	3870	3870	...	...	...	4209	4209	...	...	...
Net saving	43212	37241	...	3337	2633	60422	52355	...	5088	2981
Total Current Disbursements and Net Saving [c]	239824	157244	...	68904	71796	275434	182807	...	78045	77816

	1986 Total General Government	1986 Central Government	1986 State or Provincial Government	1986 Local Government	1986 Social Security Funds	1987 Total General Government	1987 Central Government	1987 State or Provincial Government	1987 Local Government	1987 Social Security Funds
Receipts										
1 Operating surplus	-	...	...	-	...	-	...	...	-	...
2 Property and entrepreneurial income [a]	30855	26228	...	1227	3400	33239	27442	...	1538	4259
A Withdrawals from public quasi-corporations [a]	-4046	-3076	...	-970	...	-7878	-6878	...	-1000	...
B Interest	33289	27692	...	2197	3400	39959	33162	...	2538	4259
C Dividends	1612	1612	...	...	...	1158	1158	...	...	...
D Net land rent and royalties	...	...	...	...	...	...	...	...	...	...
3 Taxes, fees and contributions	247000	136727	...	48218	62058	268308	142643	...	53187	72478
A Indirect taxes	99795	98051	...	1575	169	104710	102723	...	1802	185
B Direct taxes	79290	32647	...	46643	...	84167	32782	...	51385	...
Income [b]	63118	17709	...	45409	...	71014	20987	...	50027	...
Other	16172	14938	...	1234	...	13153	11795	...	1358	...
C Social security contributions	67442	5553	...	...	61889	78084	5791	...	...	72293
D Fees, fines and penalties	473	476	...	...	...	1347	1347	...	...	...
4 Other current transfers	3078	10150	...	37062	18714	578	7990	...	40502	18659
A Casualty insurance claims	...	-	...	...	...	...	-	...	...	...
B Transfers from other government subsectors	...	7072	...	37062	18714	...	7412	...	40502	18659
C Transfers from the rest of the world	...	...	...	...	...	...	...	...	...	...
D Other transfers, except imputed	3078	3078	...	...	...	578	578	...	...	...
E Imputed unfunded employee pension and welfare contributions	...	...	...	...	...	...	...	...	...	...
Total Current Receipts [c]	280933	173105	...	86507	84172	302125	178075	...	95227	95396
Disbursements										
1 Government final consumption expenditure	102005	37842	...	62782	1382	116325	43363	...	71520	1443
2 Property income	22324	17811	...	4513	...	24073	18923	...	5150	...
A Interest	22324	17811	...	4513	...	24073	18923	...	5150	...
B Net land rent and royalties	...	...	...	...	...	...	...	...	...	...
3 Subsidies	29569	26211	...	3350	8	30777	27174	...	3594	9

Norway

3.12 General Government Income and Outlay Account: Total and Subsectors
(Continued)

Million Norwegian kroner

	1986 Total General Government	1986 Central Government	1986 State or Provincial Government	1986 Local Government	1986 Social Security Funds	1987 Total General Government	1987 Central Government	1987 State or Provincial Government	1987 Local Government	1987 Social Security Funds
4 Other current transfers	86472	60170	...	9774	79376	96725	61914	...	11557	89827
A Casualty insurance premiums, net	-	-	...	...	...	-	-	...	...	...
B Transfers to other government subsectors	...	49466	...	899	12483	...	50120	...	1620	14833
C Social security benefits	81525	5757	...	8875	66893	91503	6572	...	9937	74994
D Social assistance grants	...	...	...	...	...	...	...	...	...	...
E Unfunded employee pension and welfare benefits	...	...	...	...	...	...	...	...	...	...
F Transfers to private non-profit institutions serving households	...	...	...	...	...	...	...	...	...	...
G Other transfers n.e.c.	-	-	...	...	...	-	-	...	...	...
H Transfers to the rest of the world	4947	4947	...	...	...	5222	5222	...	...	...
Net saving	40561	31068	...	6088	3406	34224	26701	...	3406	4117
Total Current Disbursements and Net Saving c	280931	173102	...	86507	84172	302124	178075	...	95227	95396

a) Beginning 1975, loss on capital investments are deducted from item 'Withdrawals from public quasi-corporations.
b) Beginning 1975, income includes ordinary taxes on income and property.
c) Central government includes also sector for tax collection, i.e. values shown on accrued basis.

3.13 General Government Capital Accumulation Account: Total and Subsectors

Million Norwegian kroner

	1980 Total General Government	1980 Central Government	1980 State or Provincial Government	1980 Local Government	1980 Social Security Funds	1981 Total General Government	1981 Central Government	1981 State or Provincial Government	1981 Local Government	1981 Social Security Funds
Finance of Gross Accumulation										
1 Gross saving	27759	21835	...	4180	1745	27160	19115	...	5082	2963
A Consumption of fixed capital	2327	610	...	1717	...	2658	686	...	1972	...
B Net saving	25432	21225	...	2463	1745	24502	18429	...	3110	2963
2 Capital transfers	...	...	...	...	...	...	...	...	...	...
Finance of Gross Accumulation a	27759	21835	...	4180	1745	27160	19115	...	5082	2963
Gross Accumulation										
1 Gross capital formation	11454	3627	...	7786	41	11602	3780	...	7787	36
A Increase in stocks	...	...	...	...	...	...	...	...	...	...
B Gross fixed capital formation	11454	3627	...	7786	41	11602	3780	...	7787	36
2 Purchases of land, net	...	...	...	...	...	...	...	...	...	...
3 Purchases of intangible assets, net	...	...	...	...	...	...	...	...	...	...
4 Capital transfers	...	...	...	...	...	...	...	...	...	...
Net lending	16305	18208	...	-3606	1705	15558	15335	...	-2705	2927
Gross Accumulation a	27759	21835	...	4180	1746	27160	19115	...	5082	2963

	1982 Total General Government	1982 Central Government	1982 State or Provincial Government	1982 Local Government	1982 Social Security Funds	1983 Total General Government	1983 Central Government	1983 State or Provincial Government	1983 Local Government	1983 Social Security Funds
Finance of Gross Accumulation										
1 Gross saving	27430	19465	...	5653	2312	29254	22812	...	4262	2179
A Consumption of fixed capital	2979	750	...	2229	...	3187	783	...	2404	...
B Net saving	24451	18715	...	3424	2312	26067	22029	...	1858	2179
2 Capital transfers	...	...	...	...	...	...	...	...	...	...
Finance of Gross Accumulation a	27430	19465	...	5653	2312	29254	22812	...	4262	2179
Gross Accumulation										
1 Gross capital formation	11525	3811	...	7694	20	12410	4254	...	8130	26
A Increase in stocks	...	...	...	...	...	...	...	...	...	...
B Gross fixed capital formation	11525	3811	...	7694	20	12410	4254	...	8130	26
2 Purchases of land, net	...	...	...	...	...	...	...	...	...	...
3 Purchases of intangible assets, net	...	...	...	...	...	...	...	...	...	...
4 Capital transfers	...	...	...	...	...	...	...	...	...	...
Net lending	15905	15654	...	-2041	2292	16844	18558	...	-3868	2153
Gross Accumulation a	27430	19465	...	5653	2312	29254	22812	...	4262	2179

Norway

3.13 General Government Capital Accumulation Account: Total and Subsectors
Million Norwegian kroner

	\multicolumn{5}{c	}{1984}	\multicolumn{5}{c	}{1985}
	Total General Government	Central Government	State or Provincial Government	Local Government	Social Security Funds	Total General Government	Central Government	State or Provincial Government	Local Government	Social Security Funds

Finance of Gross Accumulation

1 Gross saving	46551	38054	...	5863	2633	64164	53275	...	7909	2981
A Consumption of fixed capital	3339	813	...	2526	...	3742	921	...	2821	...
B Net saving	43212	37241	...	3337	2633	60422	52354	...	5088	2981
2 Capital transfers	...	...	...	...	...	...	...	...	...	...
Finance of Gross Accumulation [a]	46551	38054	...	5863	2633	64164	53275	...	7909	2981

Gross Accumulation

1 Gross capital formation	12858	4691	...	8094	73	13288	5044	...	8105	139
A Increase in stocks	...	...	...	...	...	...	...	...	...	...
B Gross fixed capital formation	12858	4691	...	8094	73	13288	5044	...	8105	139
2 Purchases of land, net	...	...	...	...	...	...	...	...	...	...
3 Purchases of intangible assets, net	...	...	...	...	...	...	...	...	...	...
4 Capital transfers	...	...	...	...	...	...	...	...	...	...
Net lending	33693	33363	...	-2231	2560	50876	48231	...	-196	2842
Gross Accumulation [a]	46551	38054	...	5863	2633	64164	53275	...	7909	2981

	\multicolumn{5}{c	}{1986}	\multicolumn{5}{c	}{1987}
	Total General Government	Central Government	State or Provincial Government	Local Government	Social Security Funds	Total General Government	Central Government	State or Provincial Government	Local Government	Social Security Funds

Finance of Gross Accumulation

1 Gross saving	44795	32111	...	9279	3406	39029	27887	...	7025	4117
A Consumption of fixed capital	4234	1043	...	3191	...	4805	1186	...	3619	...
B Net saving	40561	31068	...	6088	3406	34224	26701	...	3406	4117
2 Capital transfers	...	...	...	...	...	...	...	...	...	...
Finance of Gross Accumulation [a]	44795	32111	...	9279	3406	39029	27887	...	7025	4117

Gross Accumulation

1 Gross capital formation	16458	5627	...	10754	77	19699	6688	...	12988	23
A Increase in stocks	...	...	...	...	...	...	...	...	...	...
B Gross fixed capital formation	16458	5627	...	10754	77	19699	6688	...	12988	23
2 Purchases of land, net	...	...	...	...	...	...	...	...	...	...
3 Purchases of intangible assets, net	...	...	...	...	...	...	...	...	...	...
4 Capital transfers	...	...	...	...	...	...	...	...	...	...
Net lending	28337	26484	...	-1475	3329	19330	21199	...	-5963	4094
Gross Accumulation [a]	44795	32111	...	9279	3406	39029	27887	...	7025	4117

a) Central government includes also sector for tax collection, i.e. values shown on accrued basis.

3.22 Corporate and Quasi-Corporate Enterprise Income and Outlay Account: Total and Sectors
Million Norwegian kroner

	\multicolumn{3}{c	}{1980}	\multicolumn{3}{c	}{1981}	\multicolumn{3}{c	}{1982}	\multicolumn{3}{c	}{1983}
	TOTAL	Non-Financial	Financial	TOTAL	Non-Financial	Financial	TOTAL	Non-Financial	Financial	TOTAL	Non-Financial	Financial

Receipts

1 Operating surplus	42423	46075	-3652	50576	55015	-4439	51361	57140	-5779	62069	68944	-6875
2 Property and entrepreneurial income	41855	7979	33876	53244	10058	43186	65299	12054	53245	74114	14053	60061
A Withdrawals from quasi-corporate enterprises	2194	2194	-	1910	1910	-	2301	2301	-	2211	2211	-
B Interest	37990	4295	33695	49225	6241	42984	61303	8316	52987	68784	9114	59670
C Dividends	1462	1281	181	1858	1656	202	1510	1252	258	2777	2386	391
D Net land rent and royalties	209	209	-	251	251	-	185	185	-	342	342	-

Norway

3.22 Corporate and Quasi-Corporate Enterprise Income and Outlay Account: Total and Sectors
(Continued)

Million Norwegian kroner

	1980 TOTAL	1980 Non-Financial	1980 Financial	1981 TOTAL	1981 Non-Financial	1981 Financial	1982 TOTAL	1982 Non-Financial	1982 Financial	1983 TOTAL	1983 Non-Financial	1983 Financial
3 Current transfers	11484	5842	5642	14408	7550	6858	16823	8372	8451	18968	9715	9253
A Casualty insurance claims	4040	4040	-	5014	5014	-	6076	6076	-	6412	6412	-
B Casualty insurance premiums, net, due to be received by insurance companies	5130	-	5130	6293	-	6293	7623	-	7623	7969	-	7969
C Current transfers from the rest of the world	...	...	...	...	...	...	...	...	...	...	...	...
D Other transfers except imputed	2314	1802	512	3101	2536	565	3124	2296	828	4587	3303	1284
E Imputed unfunded employee pension and welfare contributions	...	...	...	...	...	...	...	...	...	...	...	...
Total Current Receipts	95762	59896	35866	118228	72623	45605	133483	77566	55917	155151	92712	62439

Disbursements

	1980 TOTAL	1980 Non-Financial	1980 Financial	1981 TOTAL	1981 Non-Financial	1981 Financial	1982 TOTAL	1982 Non-Financial	1982 Financial	1983 TOTAL	1983 Non-Financial	1983 Financial
1 Property and entrepreneurial income	47237	23390	23847	60442	30305	30137	73947	37173	36774	83196	41451	41745
A Withdrawals from quasi-corporations	-22	-22	-	16	16	-	94	94	-	701	701	-
Public	-22	-22	-	16	16	-	94	94	-	701	701	-
Private	...	...	...	...	...	...	...	...	...	...	...	...
B Interest	42152	18720	23433	54228	24561	29667	65931	29686	36245	73269	32223	41046
C Dividends	4756	4342	414	5759	5289	470	7438	6909	529	8588	7889	699
D Net land rent and royalties	350	350	-	439	439	-	484	484	-	638	638	-
2 Direct taxes and other current transfers n.e.c. to general government	23531	23265	266	26004	25705	299	27965	27634	331	32642	32053	589
3 Other current transfers	12227	5340	6887	15150	7154	7996	17711	8010	9701	19944	9741	10203
A Casualty insurance premiums, net	4040	4040	-	5014	5014	-	6076	6076	-	6412	6412	-
B Casualty insurance claims liability of insurance companies	5130	-	5130	6293	-	6293	7623	-	7623	7969	-	7969
C Transfers to private non-profit institutions	...	...	...	...	...	...	...	...	...	...	...	...
D Unfunded employee pension and welfare benefits	...	...	...	...	...	...	...	...	...	...	...	...
E Social assistance grants	...	...	...	...	...	...	...	...	...	...	...	...
F Other transfers n.e.c.	3057	1300	1757	3843	2140	1703	4012	1934	2078	5563	3329	2234
G Transfers to the rest of the world	...	...	...	...	...	...	...	...	...	...	...	...
Net saving	12767	7901	4866	16632	9459	7173	13860	4749	9111	19369	9467	9902
Total Current Disbursements and Net Saving	95762	59896	35866	118228	72623	45605	133483	77566	55917	155151	92712	62439

	1984 TOTAL	1984 Non-Financial	1984 Financial	1985 TOTAL	1985 Non-Financial	1985 Financial	1986 TOTAL	1986 Non-Financial	1986 Financial	1987 TOTAL	1987 Non-Financial	1987 Financial

Receipts

	1984 TOTAL	1984 Non-Financial	1984 Financial	1985 TOTAL	1985 Non-Financial	1985 Financial	1986 TOTAL	1986 Non-Financial	1986 Financial	1987 TOTAL	1987 Non-Financial	1987 Financial
1 Operating surplus	80354	88191	-7836	88229	95707	-7478	54392	61234	-6842	46668	54880	-8212
2 Property and entrepreneurial income	84083	13962	70121	104138	20232	83906	141342	26518	114823	167345	30231	137114
A Withdrawals from quasi-corporate enterprises	2147	2147	-	2811	2811	-	4051	4051	-	7888	7888	-
B Interest	78695	9044	69651	98201	14746	83455	134906	20845	114061	155897	19561	136336
C Dividends	2982	2512	470	2839	2388	451	2036	1274	762	3065	2287	778
D Net land rent and royalties	259	259	-	287	287	-	348	348	-	495	495	-
3 Current transfers	20360	10415	9945	20381	10509	9872	19489	11797	7693	19449	10835	8614
A Casualty insurance claims	6986	6986	-	7331	7331	-	4631	4631	-	5145	5145	-
B Casualty insurance premiums, net, due to be received by insurance companies	8777	-	8777	9134	-	9134	6840	-	6840	7600	-	7600
C Current transfers from the rest of the world	...	...	...	...	...	...	...	...	...	...	...	...
D Other transfers except imputed	4597	3429	1168	3916	3178	738	8019	7166	853	6704	5690	1014
E Imputed unfunded employee pension and welfare contributions	...	...	...	...	...	...	...	...	...	...	...	...
Total Current Receipts	184797	112568	72230	212748	126448	86300	215223	99549	115674	233462	95946	137516

Norway

3.22 Corporate and Quasi-Corporate Enterprise Income and Outlay Account: Total and Sectors
(Continued)

Million Norwegian kroner

	1984 TOTAL	1984 Non-Financial	1984 Financial	1985 TOTAL	1985 Non-Financial	1985 Financial	1986 TOTAL	1986 Non-Financial	1986 Financial	1987 TOTAL	1987 Non-Financial	1987 Financial
Disbursements												
1 Property and entrepreneurial income	98276	46302	51974	113342	47692	65649	146191	55678	90511	169659	59255	110403
A Withdrawals from quasi-corporations	552	552	-	35	35	-	5	5	-	10	10	-
Public	552	552	-	35	35	-	5	5	-	10	10	-
Private	...	-	...	...	-	...	...	-	...	...	-	...
B Interest	87325	36118	51207	102402	37666	64736	136207	46514	89693	159832	50169	109663
C Dividends	9736	8969	767	10203	9290	913	9123	8305	818	8451	7711	740
D Net land rent and royalties	663	663	-	701	701	-	854	854	-	1365	1365	-
2 Direct taxes and other current transfers n.e.c. to general government	39025	38436	589	47862	47251	611	20290	19600	690	17920	17252	668
3 Other current transfers	24650	10368	14282	24429	9025	15404	24274	10107	14167	23076	10055	13021
A Casualty insurance premiums, net	6986	6986	-	7331	7331	-	4631	4631	-	5145	5145	-
B Casualty insurance claims liability of insurance companies	8777	-	8777	9135	-	9134	6840	-	6840	7600	-	7600
C Transfers to private non-profit institutions	...	...	...	...	...	...	...	...	...	...	...	...
D Unfunded employee pension and welfare benefits	...	...	...	...	...	...	...	...	...	...	...	...
E Social assistance grants	...	...	...	...	...	...	...	...	...	...	...	...
F Other transfers n.e.c.	8887	3382	5505	7964	1694	6270	12803	5476	7327	10331	4910	5421
G Transfers to the rest of the world	...	...	...	...	...	...	...	...	...	...	...	...
Net saving	22847	17461	5386	27115	22479	4636	24468	14163	10305	22807	9383	13424
Total Current Disbursements and Net Saving	184798	112567	72231	212748	126447	86300	215223	99548	115673	233462	95945	137516

3.32 Household and Private Unincorporated Enterprise Income and Outlay Account

Million Norwegian kroner

	1970	1975	1978	1979	1980	1981	1982	1983	1984	1985	1986	1987
Receipts												
1 Compensation of employees	...	86161	123960	129376	145397	164002	183182	198070	216178	239467	271438	304135
A Wages and salaries	...	73330	105921	110565	124106	139799	156163	169236	185034	205209	232447	259917
B Employers' contributions for social security	...	12831	18039	18811	21291	24203	27019	28834	31144	34258	38991	44218
C Employers' contributions for private pension & welfare plans	...	...	...	...	...	...	...	...	...	...	...	...
2 Operating surplus of private unincorporated enterprises	...	15399	24567	23381	26779	30977	34462	36985	40805	41691	45620	50567
3 Property and entrepreneurial income	...	3493	6180	7739	9612	11793	13711	16885	20392	23076	28630	36526
A Withdrawals from private quasi-corporations	...	...	...	...	...	...	...	...	...	...	...	...
B Interest	...	3132	5866	7143	8516	10376	12461	15296	18719	21381	27763	35026
C Dividends	...	361	314	596	1096	1417	1250	1589	1673	1695	867	1500
D Net land rent and royalties	...	...	...	...	...	...	...	...	...	...	...	...
3 Current transfers	...	21518	33979	39230	43575	50675	58014	65938	72096	77993	86718	97591
A Casualty insurance claims	...	467	911	987	1090	1279	1547	1558	1790	1803	2209	2455
B Social security benefits	...	20154	31916	37023	40975	47636	54516	62212	67916	73820	81525	91503
C Social assistance grants	...	...	...	...	...	...	...	...	...	...	...	...
D Unfunded employee pension and welfare benefits	...	...	...	...	...	...	...	...	...	...	...	...
E Transfers from general government	...	...	...	...	...	...	...	...	...	...	...	...
F Transfers from the rest of the world	...	529	553	594	756	1016	1061	1178	1291	1402	1268	1435
G Other transfers n.e.c.	...	368	599	626	754	744	890	990	1099	968	1716	2198
Total Current Receipts [a]	...	126571	188686	199726	225363	257447	289369	317878	349471	382227	432406	488819
Disbursements												
1 Final consumption expenditures	...	77615	110670	120104	135241	155205	175310	192980	210921	245439	278764	294796
2 Property income	...	4343	8199	9525	11231	14024	17572	21316	24080	28838	41289	52150

Norway

3.32 Household and Private Unincorporated Enterprise Income and Outlay Account
(Continued)

Million Norwegian kroner

	1970	1975	1978	1979	1980	1981	1982	1983	1984	1985	1986	1987
A Interest	...	4343	8199	9525	11231	14024	17572	21316	24080	28838	41289	52150
B Net land rent and royalties	...	...	...	...	...	...	...	...	...	...	...	...
3 Direct taxes and other current transfers n.e.c. to government	...	40245	58017	62419	71833	78255	86160	91280	99199	110104	126559	144372
A Social security contributions	...	19863	27757	29914	34224	38699	43495	47151	50512	57305	67442	78084
B Direct taxes	...	20382	30260	32505	37609	39556	42665	44129	48687	52799	59117	66287
Income taxes	...	...	...	...	...	...	...	...	...	...	...	...
Other	...	...	...	...	...	...	...	...	...	...	...	...
C Fees, fines and penalties	...	...	...	...	...	...	...	...	...	...	...	...
4 Other current transfers	...	985	1698	1946	2265	2656	3427	3594	3649	4067	4794	5679
A Net casualty insurance premiums	...	467	911	987	1090	1279	1547	1558	1790	1803	2209	2455
B Transfers to private non-profit institutions serving households	...	...	...	...	...	...	...	...	...	...	...	...
C Transfers to the rest of the world	...	474	720	862	1026	1179	1393	1520	1500	1917	2146	2728
D Other current transfers, except imputed	...	44	67	97	149	198	487	516	359	347	439	496
E Imputed employee pension and welfare contributions	...	...	...	...	...	...	...	...	...	...	...	...
Net saving	...	3384	10102	5732	4793	7307	6899	8709	11623	-6222	-19001	-8178
Total Current Disbursements and Net Saving [a]	...	126572	188686	199726	225363	257447	289368	317879	349472	382226	432405	488819

a) Column 'Farm' is included in column 'Non-farm entrepreneurial'.

3.51 External Transactions: Current Account: Detail

Million Norwegian kroner

	1970	1975	1978	1979	1980	1981	1982	1983	1984	1985	1986	1987
Payments to the Rest of the World												
1 Imports of goods and services	34431	72139	89119	99154	117371	130469	144543	152031	172852	194602	212469	211795
A Imports of merchandise c.i.f.	26651	54366	61979	70433	84543	90516	100458	102520	116541	133927	153072	151581
B Other	7780	17773	27140	28721	32828	39953	44085	49510	56311	60675	59397	60214
2 Factor income to the rest of the world	1676	3706	9635	12663	14841	19319	23431	23394	26651	27733	29438	29967
A Compensation of employees	77	66	64	84	90	248	270	261	280	320	320	320
B Property and entrepreneurial income	1599	3640	9571	12579	14751	19071	23161	23133	26371	27413	29118	29647
3 Current transfers to the rest of the world	487	1356	2478	2799	3212	3796	4791	5522	5506	6189	7208	8039
A Indirect taxes by general government to supranational organizations	-	-	-	-	-	-	-	-	-	-	-	-
B Other current transfers	487	1356	2478	2799	3212	3796	4791	5522	5506	6189	7208	8039
By general government	299	882	1758	1938	2186	2617	3271	3850	3870	4210	4947	5222
By other resident sectors	188	474	720	861	1026	1179	1520	1672	1636	1979	2261	2817
4 Surplus of the nation on current transactions	-1728	-12692	-11005	-5278	5448	12460	4146	14645	23929	26682	-32913	-27579
Payments to the Rest of the World, and Surplus of the Nation on Current Transfers	34866	64509	90227	109338	140872	166044	176911	195592	228938	255206	216202	222222
Receipts From The Rest of the World												
1 Exports of goods and services	33403	62189	87221	105407	134795	156288	165022	183921	214078	235563	194630	199732
A Exports of merchandise f.o.b.	17715	38140	57863	70007	92863	106899	114798	133249	156822	173254	136003	144945

Norway

3.51 External Transactions: Current Account: Detail
(Continued)

Million Norwegian kroner

	1970	1975	1978	1979	1980	1981	1982	1983	1984	1985	1986	1987
B Other	15688	24049	29358	35400	41932	49390	50224	50672	57256	62309	58627	54787
2 Factor income from the rest of the world	1056	1791	2453	3337	5321	8740	10727	10392	13509	18227	20266	21007
A Compensation of employees	24	42	60	66	66	84	96	96	108	120	126	132
B Property and entrepreneurial income	1031	1749	2393	3271	5255	8656	10631	10296	13401	18107	20140	20875
3 Current transfers from the rest of the world	408	529	553	594	756	1016	1161	1278	1350	1415	1307	1483
A Subsidies to general government from supranational organizations	-	-	-	-	-	-	-	-	-	-	-	-
B Other current transfers	408	529	553	594	756	1016	1161	1278	1350	1415	1307	1483
To general government	-	-	-	-	-	-	-	-	-	-	-	-
To other resident sectors	408	529	553	594	756	1016	1161	1278	1350	1415	1307	1483
Receipts from the Rest of the World on Current Transfers	34867	64509	90227	109338	140872	166044	176910	195591	228937	255205	216203	222222

3.52 External Transactions: Capital Accumulation Account

Million Norwegian kroner

	1970	1975	1978	1979	1980	1981	1982	1983	1984	1985	1986	1987
Finance of Gross Accumulation												
1 Surplus of the nation on current transactions	-1728	-12692	-11005	-5278	5448	12460	4146	14645	23929	26682	-32913	-27579
2 Capital transfers from the rest of the world	...	...	...	...	...	...	...	...	...	...	...	...
Statistical discrepancy a	180	-	-	201	199	206	-	-	-	-	-	-
Total Finance of Gross Accumulation	-1548	-12692	-11005	-5077	5647	12666	4146	14645	23929	26682	-32913	-27579
Gross Accumulation												
1 Capital transfers to the rest of the world	...	...	...	...	...	...	...	...	...	...	...	...
2 Purchases of intangible assets, n.e.c., net, from the rest of the world	-	-	-	-	-	-	-	-	-	-	-	-
Net lending to the rest of the world	-1548	-12692	-11005	-5077	5647	12666	4146	14645	23929	26682	-32913	-27579
Total Gross Accumulation	-1548	-12692	-11005	-5077	5647	12666	4146	14645	23929	26682	-32913	-27579

a) Item 'Statistical discrepancy' refers to allocation of SDRs.

3.53 External Transactions: Capital Finance Account

Million Norwegian kroner

	1970	1975	1978	1979	1980	1981	1982	1983	1984	1985	1986	1987
Acquisitions of Foreign Financial Assets												
1 Gold and SDR's	180	5	33	298	115	356	995	1117	501	-224	752	28
2 Currency and transferable deposits	643	202	-181	-97	87	4	45	35	62	37	108	-4
3 Other deposits	-34	1446	3979	7597	14701	6798	2450	-4253	14851	-4119	-9557	4457
4 Bills and bonds, short term	5	-	18	152	512	741	4614	3197	12762	30072	-83	-2307
5 Bonds, long term	-	-	-	-	-	-	-	-	-	-	55	-2
6 Corporate equity securities	219	68	79	-41	178	890	538	1520	1330	3965	5281	3936
A Subsidiaries abroad	...	...	...	...	...	911	511	1187	1162	3790	3466	2537
B Other	...	...	...	...	...	-21	27	333	169	174	1815	1399
7 Short-term loans, n.e.c.	59	148	-97	-	-514	1328	4033	2351	3972	2031	1542	-6032
A Subsidiaries abroad	...	...	...	...	...	-	-	-	-	524	399	-2545
B Other	...	...	...	...	...	1328	4033	2351	3972	1507	1143	-3487
8 Long-term loans	881	893	926	653	2013	1591	3282	4431	4286	12662	9804	13150
A Subsidiaries abroad	...	...	...	...	...	134	1342	1379	3807	6229	7026	8062
B Other	...	...	...	...	...	1458	1941	3052	479	6434	2778	5088
9 Prproprietors' net additions to accumulation of quasi-corporate, non-resident enterprises	-	-	-	-	-	-	-	-	-	-	-	...
10 Trade credit and advances	391	826	2419	5448	781	1567	2394	2291	-841	516	-614	-2657
11 Other	-51	817	1413	1038	1941	484	941	1342	-1	1015	1561	1532
Total Acquisitions of Foreign Financial Assets	2293	4405	8589	15048	19814	13759	19292	12031	36922	45955	8849	12101
Incurrence of Foreign Liabilities												
1 Currency and transferable deposits	416	-76	-	-	-	-	-	-	-	-	-	-
2 Other deposits	-2	-160	-2213	2472	7293	4661	7287	2693	12175	12900	9154	25966
3 Bills and bonds, short term	-	-	-	-	-	-	-	-	-	1178	2476	650

Norway

3.53 External Transactions: Capital Finance Account
(Continued)

Million Norwegian kroner

		1970	1975	1978	1979	1980	1981	1982	1983	1984	1985	1986	1987
4	Bonds, long term	380	2815	12515	8926	-149	-4109	-4425	-7256	3442	12913	31105	20220
5	Corporate equity securities	274	655	486	251	687	235	1029	1585	3838	1284	4223	6231
	A Subsidiaries of non-resident incorporated units	...	...	...	...	...	148	650	484	1124	966	1767	4424
	B Other	...	...	...	...	...	87	379	1101	2714	317	2457	1808
6	Short-term loans, n.e.c.	-262	956	2204	343	1396	-254	-765	-3933	-1764	8970	4478	5613
	A Subsidiaries of non-residents	...	...	...	...	...	-	-	-	-	1856	485	283
	B Other	...	...	...	...	...	-254	-765	-3933	-1764	7115	3994	5330
7	Long-term loans	1333	11749	5826	3524	-1503	1993	10542	134	-2235	-10189	1106	-2309
	A Subsidiaries of non-residents	...	...	...	...	...	3783	2087	1972	-2966	-6796	5018	-3118
	B Other	...	...	...	...	...	-1790	8455	-1838	731	-3393	-3912	808
8	Non-resident proprietors' net additions to accumulation of resident quasi-corporate enterprises	-	-	-	-	-	-	-	-	-	-	-	
9	Trade credit and advances	639	372	825	1728	10	-880	1699	345	1620	1714	2449	-19
10	Other	585	-97	-2906	-163	1908	-561	521	999	-942	804	-1081	65
	Total Incurrence of Liabilities	3363	16214	16737	17081	9642	1084	15887	-5433	16135	29573	53911	56417
	Statistical discrepancy [a]	478	883	2857	3044	4525	10	-740	2819	-3141	-10300	-12150	-16737
	Net Lending	-1548	-12692	-11005	-5077	5647	12665	4146	14646	23929	26682	-32912	-27579
	Total Incurrence of Liabilities and Net Lending	2293	4405	8589	15048	19814	13759	19293	12032	36923	45955	8849	12101

a) Item 'Statistical discrepancy' refers to other short-term capital transactions and a statistical discrepancy.

4.1 Derivation of Value Added by Kind of Activity, in Current Prices

Million Norwegian kroner

		1980			1981			1982			1983		
		Gross Output	Intermediate Consumption	Value Added	Gross Output	Intermediate Consumption	Value Added	Gross Output	Intermediate Consumption	Value Added	Gross Output	Intermediate Consumption	Value Added

All Producers

1	Agriculture, hunting, forestry and fishing	22439	11469	10969	25510	12553	12957	27013	13576	13437	27599	14464	13135
	A Agriculture and hunting	16465	9496	6969	18186	10339	7847	19650	11054	8597	19638	11688	7950
	B Forestry and logging	2048	311	1737	2610	366	2244	2536	365	2171	2405	359	2046
	C Fishing	3926	1662	2264	4714	1848	2866	4827	2157	2670	5556	2417	3139
2	Mining and quarrying	45905	3827	42078	56253	5068	51185	65140	8627	56514	78160	9929	68231
	A Coal mining	111	79	32	186	125	61	186	130	55	191	108	84
	B Crude petroleum and natural gas production	43523	2532	40991	53544	3565	49979	62436	7090	55346	75137	8282	66855
	C Metal ore mining	1100	678	422	1258	767	492	1148	743	405	1263	792	470
	D Other mining	1171	538	633	1265	611	654	1370	664	707	1569	747	822
3	Manufacturing	159133	113498	45635	176296	127721	48575	184297	132914	51383	193424	136699	56724
	A Manufacture of food, beverages and tobacco	32824	27931	4894	38236	31800	6436	41740	34041	7699	44958	35924	9034
	B Textile, wearing apparel and leather industries	4872	3017	1856	4811	2954	1857	4594	2892	1702	4293	2684	1609
	C Manufacture of wood and wood products, including furniture	11812	7745	4067	12908	8716	4192	13367	9065	4303	13259	8964	4296
	D Manufacture of paper and paper products, printing and publishing	16899	11322	5577	19725	13258	6467	20197	13476	6722	21859	13951	7908
	E Manufacture of chemicals and chemical petroleum, coal, rubber and plastic products	26405	21031	5374	28746	24056	4689	29650	24520	5130	32801	27092	5709
	F Manufacture of non-metallic mineral products, except products of petroleum and coal	4685	2860	1824	5271	3253	2019	5576	3456	2120	5744	3432	2312
	G Basic metal industries	16273	10594	5679	15915	11430	4484	14792	10821	3971	18305	12137	6168
	H Manufacture of fabricated metal products, machinery and equipment	44565	28528	16037	49924	31807	18117	53568	34171	19397	51340	32043	19297
	I Other manufacturing industries	798	470	328	760	447	314	813	474	339	864	474	391
4	Electricity, gas and water	16401	8164	8237	19216	9058	10158	24062	12081	11981	28123	13811	14312
	A Electricity, gas and steam	15824	7907	7917	18682	8803	9878	23425	11782	11643	27380	13485	13895
	B Water works and supply	576	257	320	534	255	280	637	298	338	743	326	417

Norway

4.1 Derivation of Value Added by Kind of Activity, in Current Prices
(Continued)

Million Norwegian kroner

	1980 Gross Output	1980 Intermediate Consumption	1980 Value Added	1981 Gross Output	1981 Intermediate Consumption	1981 Value Added	1982 Gross Output	1982 Intermediate Consumption	1982 Value Added	1983 Gross Output	1983 Intermediate Consumption	1983 Value Added
5 Construction	47590	30638	16952	53953	34281	19673	59555	36844	22711	63157	39309	23848
6 Wholesale and retail trade, restaurants and hotels	51992	18729	33264	59825	21350	38475	67956	25191	42765	73974	28499	45475
A Wholesale and retail trade	45300	15185	30115	51975	17279	34697	58913	20541	38372	63530	23201	40328
B Restaurants and hotels	6692	3544	3149	7850	4071	3779	9043	4650	4393	10445	5298	5147
7 Transport, storage and communication	56952	30062	26890	65811	35057	30755	69031	37742	31289	72963	39110	33852
A Transport and storage	49903	27722	22181	57149	32594	24556	58088	34703	23385	60096	35637	24459
B Communication	7049	2340	4709	8662	2463	6199	10943	3039	7904	12867	3473	9394
8 Finance, insurance, real estate and business services	41507	13263	28244	49638	15483	34155	59462	18604	40859	67441	21807	45633
A Financial institutions	11206	3059	8147	14409	3482	10926	18136	4283	13853	20781	5220	15562
B Insurance	2183	1339	845	2047	1225	822	2053	1504	549	2339	1970	370
C Real estate and business services	28118	8865	19253	33182	10776	22406	39273	12816	26457	44320	14618	29702
Real estate, except dwellings	5071	2427	2644	6090	3030	3061	6761	3221	3539	7488	3492	3997
Dwellings	13389	3321	10067	15464	3855	11609	17784	4381	13402	20315	5314	15001
9 Community, social and personal services	16925	4447	12478	19048	5040	14009	21491	5770	15722	24232	6531	17701
A Sanitary and similar services	488	39	449	556	45	511	661	54	608	719	57	663
B Social and related community services	6924	2109	4815	7851	2455	5396	8987	2828	6159	10101	3238	6863
Educational services	1019	772	247	1109	947	162	1357	1159	198	1525	1345	180
Medical, dental, other health and veterinary services	4456	949	3508	5058	1064	3994	5818	1202	4616	6374	1318	5057
C Recreational and cultural services	2510	778	1732	2881	884	1997	3102	971	2131	3834	1210	2624
D Personal and household services	7003	1521	5482	7760	1656	6104	8741	1916	6824	9578	2027	7551
Total, Industries	458843	234096	224747	525550	265609	259941	578006	291347	286660	629072	310160	318912
Producers of Government Services	57363	18462	38901	67626	22464	45162	76579	25073	51505	85354	28512	56841
Other Producers	...	...	...	...	...	...	...	...	...	...	...	...
Total	516206	252558	263648	593176	288073	305103	654585	316420	338165	714425	338672	375753
Less: Imputed bank service charge	...	-8724	8724	...	-11349	11349	...	-14318	14318	...	-15960	15960
Import duties [a]	3692	...	3692	4248	...	4248	5203	...	5203	5764	...	5764
Value added tax [b]	24703	...	24703	28024	...	28024	31536	...	31536	34623	...	34623
Other adjustments [c]	1726	...	1726	1649	...	1649	1683	...	1683	2017	...	2017
Total	546327	261282	285045	627097	299422	327675	693007	330738	362269	756829	354632	402197
Memorandum Item: Mineral fuels and power	70899	21312	49587	84428	24651	59777	98395	31064	67331	116008	35166	80842

of which General Government:

	1980 Gross Output	1980 Intermediate Consumption	1980 Value Added	1981 Gross Output	1981 Intermediate Consumption	1981 Value Added	1982 Gross Output	1982 Intermediate Consumption	1982 Value Added	1983 Gross Output	1983 Intermediate Consumption	1983 Value Added
1 Agriculture, hunting, forestry and fishing	16	6	10	17	7	10	18	7	11	23	10	13
2 Mining and quarrying	...	...	...	...	...	...	...	...	...	...	...	...
3 Manufacturing	...	...	...	...	...	...	...	...	...	...	...	...
4 Electricity, gas and water	...	...	...	...	...	...	...	...	...	...	...	...
5 Construction	...	...	...	...	...	...	...	...	...	...	...	...
6 Wholesale and retail trade, restaurants and hotels	...	...	...	...	...	...	...	...	...	...	...	...
7 Transport and communication	3695	2890	805	4178	3243	935	4653	3587	1066	5052	3929	1123
8 Finance, insurance, real estate and business services	298	141	157	368	169	199	343	107	236	395	121	273
9 Community, social and personal services	53353	15425	37928	63063	19045	44018	71565	21373	50192	79884	24452	55432
Total, Industries of General Government	57363	18462	38901	67626	22464	45162	76579	25073	51505	85354	28512	56841
Producers of Government Services	...	...	...	...	...	...	...	...	...	...	...	...
Total, General Government	...	...	...	...	...	...	...	...	...	...	...	...

Norway

4.1 Derivation of Value Added by Kind of Activity, in Current Prices

Million Norwegian kroner

	1984 Gross Output	1984 Intermediate Consumption	1984 Value Added	1985 Gross Output	1985 Intermediate Consumption	1985 Value Added	1986 Gross Output	1986 Intermediate Consumption	1986 Value Added	1987 Gross Output	1987 Intermediate Consumption	1987 Value Added
						All Producers						
1 Agriculture, hunting, forestry and fishing	30397	15354	15042	32045	16895	15150	34950	18236	16714	39171	19824	19348
A Agriculture and hunting	21629	12249	9380	22364	13355	9009	24052	14516	9536	26220	15499	10721
B Forestry and logging	2880	420	2459	2880	437	2443	3217	453	2765	3673	525	3148
C Fishing	5888	2685	3203	6801	3103	3698	7682	3268	4414	9278	3799	5479
2 Mining and quarrying	96398	11621	84778	107612	16603	91009	72508	21077	51431	77154	25442	51712
A Coal mining	188	100	88	234	114	120	232	162	71	...	...	...
B Crude petroleum and natural gas production	93089	9702	83387	104071	14364	89706	69002	18981	50022	73641	23316	50325
C Metal ore mining	1390	941	449	1483	1173	309	1222	942	279	...	...	...
D Other mining	1732	878	854	1825	951	874	2052	992	1059	...	...	...
3 Manufacturing	217590	153066	64524	247337	177210	70127	258169	183095	75074	282805	199809	82994
A Manufacture of food, beverages and tobacco	48990	38744	10246	53129	41572	11556	58673	45742	12932	64029	48862	15166
B Textile, wearing apparel and leather industries	4643	2934	1709	5069	3215	1854	5313	3312	2001	5268	3254	2014
C Manufacture of wood and wood products, including furniture	13843	9431	4412	15240	10339	4901	17046	11572	5473	18265	12304	5961
D Manufacture of paper and paper products, printing and publishing	25266	15997	9269	28252	18094	10158	30982	19937	11046	34718	21828	12889
E Manufacture of chemicals and chemical petroleum, coal, rubber and plastic products	37358	30059	7299	39703	32120	7582	31941	24434	7507	...	...	...
F Manufacture of non-metallic mineral products, except products of petroleum and coal	5867	3594	2272	6742	4238	2505	8018	5043	2975	...	...	...
G Basic metal industries	23843	15471	8372	24576	17188	7388	23021	16248	6774	25049	17823	7226
H Manufacture of fabricated metal products, machinery and equipment	56826	36307	20519	73537	49808	23729	81952	56138	25814	...	...	...
I Other manufacturing industries	955	529	427	1089	636	454	1223	671	552	...	...	...
4 Electricity, gas and water	32772	16201	16571	38418	20141	18278	39363	19703	19660	45649	22934	22715
A Electricity, gas and steam	31953	15828	16124	37496	19699	17797	38356	19201	19155	44500	22362	22138
B Water works and supply	819	372	447	922	442	481	1007	502	505	1149	572	577
5 Construction	66660	42307	24353	73735	46665	27070	85771	54883	30888	96759	60759	36000
6 Wholesale and retail trade, restaurants and hotels	80850	31405	49445	89211	35315	53897	100765	38599	62166	109563	41167	68396
A Wholesale and retail trade	68973	25305	43668	75530	28232	47298	85497	30777	54720	91785	32169	59616
B Restaurants and hotels	11877	6100	5777	13681	7082	6599	15268	7821	7447	17778	8998	8780
7 Transport, storage and communication	82146	45069	37077	88693	50717	37976	93592	48622	44970	93639	47974	45664
A Transport and storage	67960	41146	26814	73433	45789	27645	75737	42889	32848	...	...	...
B Communication	14186	3923	10263	15260	4929	10332	17855	5733	12123	...	...	...
8 Finance, insurance, real estate and business services	75172	25853	49318	87361	30979	56383	103970	35388	68582	116399	41205	75195
A Financial institutions	21090	6076	15015	22931	7030	15901	30181	8663	21518	...	...	...
B Insurance	2750	2659	91	3948	3224	724	5008	2743	2266	...	...	...
C Real estate and business services	51332	17119	34213	60482	20725	39757	68780	23982	44798	78488	27855	50633
Real estate, except dwellings	8281	3978	4303	9516	4606	4910	10677	4812	5865	...	...	...
Dwellings	22569	5913	16656	24984	6879	18105	27777	8181	19596	31098	9499	21599
9 Community, social and personal services	25730	6980	18750	29253	7845	21408	33357	8834	24523	37531	9851	27681
A Sanitary and similar services	770	57	714	927	74	854	1158	85	1074	...	...	...
B Social and related community services	10697	3501	7197	11650	3786	7864	12877	4194	8682	...	...	...
Educational services	1672	1473	199	1891	1620	271	2178	1863	316	...	...	...
Medical, dental, other health and veterinary services	6668	1399	5269	7138	1462	5676	7745	1573	6173	8405	1757	6648
C Recreational and cultural services	4066	1283	2783	4618	1467	3151	5151	1612	3540	...	...	...
D Personal and household services	10197	2140	8057	12058	2519	9539	14171	2943	11228	...	...	...
Total, Industries	707714	347856	359858	793666	402369	391297	822443	428435	394008	898671	468964	429705
Producers of Government Services	92249	30441	61808	101919	33955	67965	112695	37349	75346	127990	42652	85337

Norway

4.1 Derivation of Value Added by Kind of Activity, in Current Prices
(Continued)

Million Norwegian kroner

	1984 Gross Output	1984 Intermediate Consumption	1984 Value Added	1985 Gross Output	1985 Intermediate Consumption	1985 Value Added	1986 Gross Output	1986 Intermediate Consumption	1986 Value Added	1987 Gross Output	1987 Intermediate Consumption	1987 Value Added
Other Producers	...	...	...	...	...	...	...	...	...	...	...	...
Total	799963	378296	421667	895585	436324	459261	935138	465785	469354	1026660	511616	515042
Less: Imputed bank service charge	...	-15443	15443	...	-15431	15431	...	-20630	20630	...	-21434	21434
Import duties [a]	6006	...	6006	9320	...	9320	11758	...	11758	9716	...	9716
Value added tax [b]	37794	...	37794	44150	...	44150	50527	...	50527	53219	...	53219
Other adjustments [c]	2489	...	2489	2900	...	2900	3569	...	3569	3746	3366	383
Total	846252	393739	452512	951955	451755	500201	1000990	486415	514578	1093340	536416	556926
Memorandum Item: Mineral fuels and power	140211	40535	99676	157571	49726	107846	115163	45790	69373	...	...	...

of which General Government:

	1984 GO	1984 IC	1984 VA	1985 GO	1985 IC	1985 VA	1986 GO	1986 IC	1986 VA	1987 GO	1987 IC	1987 VA
1 Agriculture, hunting, forestry and fishing	28	14	15	25	11	14	25	11	15	22	9	13
2 Mining and quarrying	...	...	...	...	...	...	...	...	...	...	...	...
3 Manufacturing	...	...	...	...	...	...	...	...	...	...	...	...
4 Electricity, gas and water	...	...	...	...	...	...	...	...	...	...	...	...
5 Construction	...	...	...	...	...	...	...	...	...	...	...	...
6 Wholesale and retail trade, restaurants and hotels	...	...	...	...	...	...	...	...	...	...	...	...
7 Transport and communication	5423	4248	1175	5797	4528	1270	6083	4683	1400	6723	5183	1539
8 Finance, insurance, real estate and business services	501	159	341	558	179	380	615	204	411	645	214	431
9 Community, social and personal services	86297	26020	60277	95539	29238	66301	105972	32452	73520	120600	37246	83354
Total, Industries of General Government	92249	30441	61808	101919	33955	67965	112695	37349	75346	127990	42652	85337
Producers of Government Services	...	...	...	...	...	...	...	...	...	...	...	...
Total, General Government	...	...	...	...	...	...	...	...	...	...	...	...

a) Item 'Import duties' includes collection of customs duties, value added tax on imports and special excises or taxes on imports.
b) Item 'Value added tax' excludes value added tax on imports which is included in item 'Import duties'.
c) Item 'Other adjustments' refers to collection of investment levy on fixed capital formation and subsidies on residential and social buildings and a statistical discrepancy.

4.2 Derivation of Value Added by Kind of Activity, in Constant Prices

Million Norwegian kroner

	1984 Gross Output	1984 Intermediate Consumption	1984 Value Added	1985 Gross Output	1985 Intermediate Consumption	1985 Value Added	1986 Gross Output	1986 Intermediate Consumption	1986 Value Added

At constant prices of: 1984
All Producers

	1984 GO	1984 IC	1984 VA	1985 GO	1985 IC	1985 VA	1986 GO	1986 IC	1986 VA
1 Agriculture, hunting, forestry and fishing	30397	15354	15042	29489	15806	13682	29607	16344	13264
A Agriculture and hunting	21629	12249	9380	20724	12477	8247	20288	12738	7550
B Forestry and logging	2880	420	2459	2675	412	2263	2773	427	2347
C Fishing	5888	2685	3203	6089	2917	3172	6546	3179	3366
2 Mining and quarrying	96398	11621	84778	103365	15550	87815	110382	18532	91850
A Coal mining	188	100	88	222	106	116	234	148	87
B Crude petroleum and natural gas production	93089	9702	83387	99968	13446	86522	107073	16626	90447
C Metal ore mining	1390	941	449	1405	1105	300	1205	845	360
D Other mining	1732	878	854	1770	893	877	1870	914	956

Norway

4.2 Derivation of Value Added by Kind of Activity, in Constant Prices
(Continued)

Million Norwegian kroner

At constant prices of: 1984

	1984 Gross Output	1984 Intermediate Consumption	1984 Value Added	1985 Gross Output	1985 Intermediate Consumption	1985 Value Added	1986 Gross Output	1986 Intermediate Consumption	1986 Value Added
3 Manufacturing	217590	153066	64524	234804	167911	66893	241241	174115	67126
A Manufacture of food, beverages and tobacco	48990	38744	10246	49719	39197	10522	51003	40442	10561
B Textile, wearing apparel and leather industries	4643	2934	1709	4853	3044	1809	4815	2984	1832
C Manufacture of wood and wood products, including furniture	13843	9431	4412	14460	9828	4632	15096	10271	4825
D Manufacture of paper and paper products, printing and publishing	25266	15997	9269	26480	16937	9543	27411	17889	9522
E Manufacture of chemicals and chemical petroleum, coal, rubber and plastic products	37358	30059	7299	38179	31229	6950	38180	31407	6773
F Manufacture of non-metallic mineral products, except products of petroleum and coal	5867	3594	2272	6337	4056	2280	6970	4565	2405
G Basic metal industries	23843	15471	8372	24707	16531	8176	24855	16620	8235
H Manufacture of fabricated metal products, machinery and equipment	56826	36307	20519	69034	46461	22573	71816	49313	22502
I Other manufacturing industries	955	529	427	1036	628	409	1096	624	472
4 Electricity, gas and water	32772	16201	16571	32116	16006	16109	30394	14667	15727
A Electricity, gas and steam	31953	15828	16124	31256	15596	15660	29537	14210	15326
B Water works and supply	819	372	447	860	411	449	857	457	401
5 Construction	66660	42307	24353	69535	44216	25319	75976	49496	26481
6 Wholesale and retail trade, restaurants and hotels	80850	31405	49445	86608	32945	53663	93081	34412	58669
A Wholesale and retail trade	68973	25305	43668	73709	26321	47388	79869	27584	52285
B Restaurants and hotels	11877	6100	5777	12899	6624	6275	13211	6828	6384
7 Transport, storage and communication	82146	45069	37077	85745	47371	38374	94169	51361	42808
A Transport and storage	67960	41146	26814	70174	42644	27530	76167	46003	30164
B Communication	14186	3923	10263	15572	4727	10844	18002	5358	12644
8 Finance, insurance, real estate and business services	75172	25853	49318	82882	29464	53417	89105	32272	56833
A Financial institutions	21090	6076	15015	22414	6896	15517	24372	8098	16274
B Insurance	2750	2659	91	3772	3129	643	3960	2564	1396
C Real estate and business services	51332	17119	34213	56697	19439	37257	60773	21610	39163
Real estate, except dwellings	8281	3978	4303	9017	4293	4724	9550	4685	4866
Dwellings	22569	5913	16656	23682	6501	17180	24846	7234	17612
9 Community, social and personal services	25730	6980	18750	27542	7450	20093	29124	7964	21160
A Sanitary and similar services	770	57	714	882	73	810	1011	91	919
B Social and related community services	10697	3501	7197	10922	3597	7325	11151	3754	7397
Educational services	1672	1473	199	1766	1538	228	1867	1626	241
Medical, dental, other health and veterinary services	6668	1399	5269	6654	1385	5269	6711	1437	5275
C Recreational and cultural services	4066	1283	2783	4444	1376	3068	4762	1483	3279
D Personal and household services	10197	2140	8057	11293	2403	8890	12201	2636	9565
Total, Industries	707714	347856	359858	752085	376719	375366	793079	399163	393916
Producers of Government Services	92249	30441	61808	95527	31759	63768	99865	34794	65071
Other Producers	...	...	...	...	...	...	...	...	...
Total	799963	378296	421667	847612	408478	439135	892944	433956	458987
Less: Imputed bank service charge	...	-15443	15443	...	-16393	16393	...	-17829	17829
Import duties [a]	6006	...	6006	9141	...	9141	9762	...	9762
Value added tax [b]	37794	...	37794	41820	...	41820	45238	...	45238
Other adjustments [c]	2489	...	2489	2680	...	2680	328	...	328
Total	846252	393739	452512	901253	424871	476382	948272	451785	496486
Memorandum Item: Mineral fuels and power	140211	40535	99676	146931	44474	102457	151926	45909	106017

Norway

4.2 Derivation of Value Added by Kind of Activity, in Constant Prices
(Continued)

Million Norwegian kroner

At constant prices of: 1984

of which General Government:

		1984			1985			1986	
	Gross Output	Intermediate Consumption	Value Added	Gross Output	Intermediate Consumption	Value Added	Gross Output	Intermediate Consumption	Value Added
1 Agriculture, hunting, forestry and fishing	28	14	15	23	10	13	19	9	11
2 Mining and quarrying	...	...	...	...	...	...	...	...	...
3 Manufacturing	...	...	...	...	...	...	...	...	...
4 Electricity, gas and water	...	...	...	...	...	...	...	...	...
5 Construction	...	...	...	...	...	...	...	...	...
6 Wholesale and retail trade, restaurants and hotels	...	...	...	...	...	...	...	...	...
7 Transport and communication	5423	4248	1175	5408	4222	1186	5420	4225	1195
8 Finance, insurance, real estate and business services	501	159	341	519	161	358	523	167	357
9 Community, social and personal services	86297	26020	60277	89578	27367	62212	93903	30394	63508
Total, Industries of General Government	92249	30441	61808	95527	31759	63768	99865	34794	65071
Producers of Government Services	...	...	...	...	...	...	...	...	...
Total, General Government	...	...	...	...	...	...	...	...	...

a) Item 'Import duties' includes collection of customs duties, value added tax on imports and special excises or taxes on imports.
b) Item 'Value added tax' excludes value added tax on imports which is included in item 'Import duties'.
c) Item 'Other adjustments' refers to collection of investment levy on fixed capital formation and subsidies on residential and social buildings and a statistical discrepancy.

4.3 Cost Components of Value Added

Million Norwegian kroner

All Producers

		1980						1981				
	Compensation of Employees	Capital Consumption	Net Operating Surplus	Indirect Taxes	Less: Subsidies Received	Value Added	Compensation of Employees	Capital Consumption	Net Operating Surplus	Indirect Taxes	Less: Subsidies Received	Value Added
1 Agriculture, hunting, forestry and fishing	1226	3564	9857	272	3950	10969	1401	3944	11748	409	4544	12957
A Agriculture and hunting	344	2358	7626	97	3457	6969	369	2628	8481	139	3771	7847
B Forestry and logging	634	202	1072	19	190	1737	736	223	1515	22	252	2244
C Fishing	248	1005	1159	156	303	2264	296	1093	1752	248	522	2866
2 Mining and quarrying	2225	5082	30619	4271	119	42078	2717	7490	35857	5494	372	51185
A Coal mining	80	20	27	1	95	32	104	22	57	1	123	61
B Crude petroleum and natural gas production	1413	4745	30594	4239	...	40991	1830	7120	35565	5464	...	49979
C Metal ore mining	421	176	-174	19	21	422	449	193	81	15	246	492
D Other mining	310	142	172	12	3	633	334	155	154	14	3	654
3 Manufacturing	34161	5552	8817	2671	5566	45635	37559	6068	7287	2991	5328	48575
A Manufacture of food, beverages and tobacco	4687	1010	1221	1883	3908	4894	5162	1097	1175	2181	3179	6436
B Textile, wearing apparel and leather industries	1489	184	274	22	113	1856	1485	196	284	21	128	1857
C Manufacture of wood and wood products, including furniture	2758	352	1007	59	109	4067	2990	390	921	64	173	4192
D Manufacture of paper and paper products, printing and publishing	4553	785	356	88	206	5577	4973	873	760	91	230	6467
E Manufacture of chemicals and chemical petroleum, coal, rubber and plastic products	3090	1038	1055	254	62	5374	3417	1107	-19	248	65	4689
F Manufacture of non-metallic mineral products, except products of petroleum and coal	1185	274	336	50	20	1824	1268	299	423	49	20	2019
G Basic metal industries	2975	741	2077	91	205	5679	3293	825	453	98	184	4484
H Manufacture of fabricated metal products, machinery and equipment	13151	1140	2443	222	920	16037	14699	1250	3255	237	1324	18117
I Other manufacturing industries	273	27	48	3	22	328	271	31	35	3	26	314
4 Electricity, gas and water	1943	2560	2239	1625	131	8237	2204	2842	3647	1644	180	10158
A Electricity, gas and steam	1840	2412	2149	1622	107	7917	2125	2675	3588	1641	151	9878
B Water works and supply	103	148	90	3	24	320	79	167	60	3	29	280

Norway

4.3 Cost Components of Value Added
(Continued)

Million Norwegian kroner

	1980						1981				
	Compensation of Employees	Capital Consumption	Net Operating Surplus	Indirect Taxes	Less: Subsidies Received	Value Added	Compensation of Employees	Capital Consumption	Net Operating Surplus	Indirect Taxes	Less: Subsidies Received	Value Added
5 Construction	13268	2085	1485	192	78	16952	13984	2259	3290	207	66	19673
6 Wholesale and retail trade, restaurants and hotels	21343	3481	4805	6878	3242	33264	23893	3635	7185	7828	4065	38475
A Wholesale and retail trade	18800	3353	4301	6854	3193	30115	20938	3505	6466	7802	4014	34697
B Restaurants and hotels	2543	127	504	24	50	3149	2955	130	719	26	52	3779
7 Transport, storage and communication	18120	11033	-1470	881	1674	26890	20591	12827	-2073	942	1533	30755
A Transport and storage	14133	10107	-1177	792	1674	22181	16115	11780	-2669	863	1533	24556
B Communication	3987	927	-293	89	...	4709	4476	1047	596	80	...	6199
8 Finance, insurance, real estate and business services	8472	4785	16092	723	1828	28244	10269	5411	19574	831	1931	34155
A Financial institutions	3499	227	5788	24	1391	8147	4211	277	7835	27	1423	10926
B Insurance	1370	117	-646	4	1	845	1518	142	-842	5	1	822
C Real estate and business services	3604	4441	10951	695	437	19253	4540	4992	12581	800	508	22406
Real estate, except dwellings	17	778	1782	146	79	2644	19	854	2078	170	61	3061
Dwellings	152	3635	6372	246	337	10067	179	4106	7433	297	406	11609
9 Community, social and personal services	8089	889	5482	556	2539	12478	9045	920	6388	610	2955	14009
A Sanitary and similar services	329	...	120	...	...	449	355	...	156	...	...	511
B Social and related community services	3534	580	2395	2	1696	4815	4021	597	2735	3	1960	5396
Educational services	745	70	654	2	1223	247	846	71	687	3	1444	162
Medical, dental, other health and veterinary services	1308	476	1741	...	18	3508	1472	492	2048	...	18	3994
C Recreational and cultural services	589	173	1284	529	843	1732	686	188	1536	582	994	1997
D Personal and household services	3637	136	1683	25	...	5482	3983	135	1962	26	1	6104
Total, Industries	108847	39031	77925	18069	19126	224747	121661	45395	92904	20955	20974	259941
Producers of Government Services	36574	2327	...	...	...	38901	42504	2658	...	...	...	45162
Other Producers	...	...	...	...	...	...	...	...	...	...	...	...
Total	145421	41358	77925	18069	19126	263648	164165	48053	92904	20955	20974	305103
Less: Imputed bank service charge [a]	...	...	8724	...	...	8724	...	...	11349	...	...	11349
Import duties [b]	...	...	...	3693	1	3692	...	...	...	4249	1	4248
Value added tax [c]	...	...	...	24703	...	24703	...	...	...	28024	...	28024
Other adjustments	...	...	...	2560	834	1726	...	...	...	2468	819	1649
Total	145421	41358	69201	49025	19961	285045	164165	48053	81555	55696	21794	327675

of which General Government:

1 Agriculture, hunting, forestry and fishing	10	...	...	...	...	10	10	...	...	...	...	10
2 Mining and quarrying	...	...	...	...	...	...	...	...	...	...	...	...
3 Manufacturing	...	...	...	...	...	...	...	...	...	...	...	...
4 Electricity, gas and water	...	...	...	...	...	...	...	...	...	...	...	...
5 Construction	...	...	...	...	...	...	...	...	...	...	...	...
6 Wholesale and retail trade, restaurants and hotels	...	...	...	...	...	...	...	...	...	...	...	...
7 Transport and communication	559	246	...	...	...	805	658	278	...	...	...	935
8 Finance, insurance, real estate & business services	153	5	...	...	...	157	194	5	...	...	...	199
9 Community, social and personal services	35852	2076	...	...	...	37928	41642	2375	...	...	...	44018
Total, Industries of General Government	36574	2327	...	...	...	38901	42504	2658	...	...	...	45162
Producers of Government Services	...	...	...	...	...	...	...	...	...	...	...	...
Total, General Government	...	...	...	...	...	...	...	...	...	...	...	...

Norway

4.3 Cost Components of Value Added

Million Norwegian kroner

		1982						1983				
	Compensation of Employees	Capital Consumption	Net Operating Surplus	Indirect Taxes	Less: Subsidies Received	Value Added	Compensation of Employees	Capital Consumption	Net Operating Surplus	Indirect Taxes	Less: Subsidies Received	Value Added

All Producers

	Comp. Emp. 82	Cap. Cons. 82	Net Op. Surp. 82	Ind. Tax 82	Subs. 82	VA 82	Comp. Emp. 83	Cap. Cons. 83	Net Op. Surp. 83	Ind. Tax 83	Subs. 83	VA 83
1 Agriculture, hunting, forestry and fishing	1413	4296	12484	368	5125	13437	1540	4511	12201	408	5526	13135
A Agriculture and hunting	394	2900	9694	127	4519	8597	427	3176	8936	147	4735	7950
B Forestry and logging	690	238	1465	27	250	2171	722	258	1322	33	288	2046
C Fishing	330	1157	1325	214	357	2670	391	1078	1944	229	502	3139
2 Mining and quarrying	3504	9690	37522	6199	402	56514	3946	10432	45392	8880	419	68231
A Coal mining	126	23	64	1	157	55	137	23	136	1	213	84
B Crude petroleum and natural gas production	2591	9295	37288	6172	...	55346	3007	10038	44961	8849	...	66855
C Metal ore mining	444	204	-16	15	241	405	419	198	38	18	203	470
D Other mining	344	169	186	12	4	707	384	173	257	12	4	822
3 Manufacturing	39868	6714	7001	3422	5623	51383	41462	6956	10286	3758	5738	56724
A Manufacture of food, beverages and tobacco	5632	1216	1400	2691	3239	7699	6051	1266	1920	2984	3187	9034
B Textile, wearing apparel and leather industries	1452	211	143	19	122	1702	1353	212	206	18	180	1609
C Manufacture of wood and wood products, including furniture	3129	431	868	59	185	4303	3176	448	899	65	292	4296
D Manufacture of paper and paper products, printing and publishing	5152	962	790	73	254	6722	5866	996	1218	77	248	7908
E Manufacture of chemicals and chemical petroleum, coal, rubber and plastic products	3639	1217	106	232	65	5130	3836	1254	446	240	66	5709
F Manufacture of non-metallic mineral products, except products of petroleum and coal	1365	330	404	41	20	2120	1392	338	563	45	24	2312
G Basic metal industries	3269	929	50	73	349	3971	3334	955	2373	72	566	6168
H Manufacture of fabricated metal products, machinery and equipment	15954	1385	3188	233	1363	19397	16169	1454	2568	256	1149	19297
I Other manufacturing industries	278	33	53	3	27	339	286	34	94	3	26	391
4 Electricity, gas and water	2479	3224	4686	1750	157	11981	2675	3511	6394	1888	156	14312
A Electricity, gas and steam	2390	3034	4608	1747	136	11643	2573	3310	6250	1885	123	13895
B Water works and supply	89	189	78	3	20	338	102	201	144	3	33	417
5 Construction	15675	2600	4274	207	45	22711	17069	2733	3942	237	133	23848
6 Wholesale and retail trade, restaurants and hotels	26834	3897	8516	7990	4472	42765	28678	3999	8764	8449	4414	45475
A Wholesale and retail trade	23419	3748	7654	7963	4413	38372	24924	3847	7489	8419	4350	40328
B Restaurants and hotels	3414	149	862	27	59	4393	3754	152	1275	30	64	5147
7 Transport, storage and communication	22632	14347	-5056	1038	1671	31289	23958	16332	-5810	1228	1856	33852
A Transport and storage	17381	13162	-6447	959	1671	23385	18363	15091	-8270	1130	1856	24459
B Communication	5251	1185	1391	79	...	7904	5596	1241	2460	98	...	9394
8 Finance, insurance, real estate and business services	12225	6242	23480	941	2030	40859	13978	6933	25773	1164	2214	45633
A Financial institutions	4898	335	10046	30	1457	13853	5644	386	11066	41	1576	15562
B Insurance	1779	175	-1409	5	1	549	1995	206	-1837	6	1	370
C Real estate and business services	5548	5732	14843	907	573	26457	6339	6341	16544	1117	638	29702
Real estate, except dwellings	22	973	2457	177	89	3539	33	1063	2799	197	95	3997
Dwellings	205	4724	8561	370	457	13402	218	5243	9593	446	499	15001
9 Community, social and personal services	10199	1019	7233	708	3438	15722	11275	1020	8073	846	3512	17701
A Sanitary and similar services	410	...	198	...	...	608	464	...	198	...	...	663
B Social and related community services	4603	661	3097	3	2205	6159	5139	662	3306	4	2248	6863
Educational services	945	79	691	3	1519	198	1054	79	617	4	1574	180
Medical, dental, other health and veterinary services	1673	544	2406	...	7	4616	1836	545	2689	...	13	5057
C Recreational and cultural services	739	210	1736	678	1232	2131	830	209	2038	811	1264	2624
D Personal and household services	4447	148	2203	27	1	6824	4842	149	2530	31	1	7551

Norway

4.3 Cost Components of Value Added
(Continued)

Million Norwegian kroner

	1982						1983					
	Compensation of Employees	Capital Consumption	Net Operating Surplus	Indirect Taxes	Less: Subsidies Received	Value Added	Compensation of Employees	Capital Consumption	Net Operating Surplus	Indirect Taxes	Less: Subsidies Received	Value Added
Total, Industries	134829	52028	100141	22624	22962	286660	144580	56428	115014	26857	23967	318912
Producers of Government Services	48526	2979	...	...	...	51505	53655	3186	...	...	...	56841
Other Producers	...	...	...	...	...	...	...	...	...	...	...	...
Total	183355	55007	100141	22624	22962	338165	198235	59614	115014	26857	23967	375753
Less: Imputed bank service charge [a]	...	...	14318	...	...	14318	...	...	15960	...	...	15960
Import duties [b]	...	...	...	5204	1	5203	...	...	...	5765	1	5764
Value added tax [c]	...	...	...	31536	...	31536	...	...	...	34623	...	34623
Other adjustments	...	...	...	2383	700	1683	...	...	...	2489	472	2017
Total	183355	55007	85823	61747	23663	362269	198235	59614	99054	69734	24440	402197

of which General Government:

1 Agriculture, hunting, forestry and fishing	11	...	...	...	...	11	13	...	...	...	...	13
2 Mining and quarrying	...	...	...	...	...	...	...	...	...	...	...	...
3 Manufacturing	...	...	...	...	...	...	...	...	...	...	...	...
4 Electricity, gas and water	...	...	...	...	...	...	...	...	...	...	...	...
5 Construction	...	...	...	...	...	...	...	...	...	...	...	...
6 Wholesale and retail trade, restaurants and hotels	...	...	...	...	...	...	...	...	...	...	...	...
7 Transport and communication	760	306	...	...	...	1066	811	311	...	...	...	1123
8 Finance, insurance, real estate & business services	231	6	...	...	...	236	268	6	...	...	...	273
9 Community, social and personal services	47524	2668	...	...	...	50192	52563	2869	...	...	...	55432
Total, Industries of General Government	48526	2979	...	...	...	51505	53655	3186	...	...	...	56841
Producers of Government Services	...	...	...	...	...	...	...	...	...	...	...	...
Total, General Government	...	...	...	...	...	...	...	...	...	...	...	...

	1984						1985					
	Compensation of Employees	Capital Consumption	Net Operating Surplus	Indirect Taxes	Less: Subsidies Received	Value Added	Compensation of Employees	Capital Consumption	Net Operating Surplus	Indirect Taxes	Less: Subsidies Received	Value Added

All Producers

1 Agriculture, hunting, forestry and fishing	1711	4591	13877	419	5556	15042	1938	4977	14007	118	5889	15150
A Agriculture and hunting	449	3325	10156	184	4735	9380	485	3620	9908	90	5093	9009
B Forestry and logging	825	271	1621	38	296	2459	880	293	1574	19	323	2443
C Fishing	437	995	2100	197	525	3203	573	1063	2526	9	472	3698
2 Mining and quarrying	5139	12935	56112	11137	544	84778	6206	14595	59480	11214	485	91009
A Coal mining	124	21	197	1	254	88	136	22	43	1	82	120
B Crude petroleum and natural gas production	4117	12573	55604	11094	...	83387	5124	14217	59181	11184	...	89706
C Metal ore mining	488	180	40	27	286	449	495	184	14	15	399	309
D Other mining	410	161	272	16	5	854	451	172	242	13	4	874

Norway

4.3 Cost Components of Value Added
(Continued)

Million Norwegian kroner

	1984						1985					
	Compensation of Employees	Capital Consumption	Net Operating Surplus	Indirect Taxes	Less: Subsidies Received	Value Added	Compensation of Employees	Capital Consumption	Net Operating Surplus	Indirect Taxes	Less: Subsidies Received	Value Added
3 Manufacturing	44940	6542	14581	4293	5832	64524	49454	7138	14985	4327	5777	70127
A Manufacture of food, beverages and tobacco	6488	1191	2370	3301	3104	10246	7011	1286	2925	3583	3249	11556
B Textile, wearing apparel and leather industries	1401	192	278	21	183	1709	1520	202	287	4	159	1854
C Manufacture of wood and wood products, including furniture	3316	423	866	72	265	4412	3622	461	1011	34	226	4901
D Manufacture of paper and paper products, printing and publishing	6450	935	2036	101	253	9269	7258	1016	1797	160	72	10158
E Manufacture of chemicals and chemical petroleum, coal, rubber and plastic products	4191	1165	1692	319	68	7299	4396	1263	1735	245	56	7582
F Manufacture of non-metallic mineral products, except products of petroleum and coal	1485	313	452	46	24	2272	1663	340	504	21	23	2505
G Basic metal industries	3761	908	4391	105	793	8372	3973	1012	2613	158	368	7388
H Manufacture of fabricated metal products, machinery and equipment	17543	1383	2379	325	1111	20519	19649	1524	4028	122	1594	23729
I Other manufacturing industries	306	30	118	3	30	427	363	35	86	1	31	454
4 Electricity, gas and water	2942	3804	7598	2387	159	16571	3307	4128	7739	3252	149	18278
A Electricity, gas and steam	2832	3584	7448	2383	121	16124	3185	3887	7620	3229	124	17797
B Water works and supply	111	220	150	4	38	447	122	241	120	23	25	481
5 Construction	18168	2695	3457	287	254	24353	19528	3306	3692	771	227	27070
6 Wholesale and retail trade, restaurants and hotels	31548	3800	9367	9473	4744	49445	35416	4290	8346	10817	4973	53897
A Wholesale and retail trade	27270	3660	7970	9435	4666	43668	30582	4133	6723	10756	4895	47298
B Restaurants and hotels	4278	140	1397	39	78	5777	4834	157	1623	62	78	6599
7 Transport, storage and communication	24968	16233	-3604	1434	1954	37077	26343	14745	-2810	1671	1973	37976
A Transport and storage	18990	14931	-6514	1312	1906	26814	19643	13233	-4786	1507	1953	27645
B Communication	5978	1303	2910	121	49	10263	6700	1512	1976	164	20	10332
8 Finance, insurance, real estate and business services	16380	7583	26630	1333	2607	49318	19820	8572	29825	1218	3052	56383
A Financial institutions	6301	449	10113	44	1892	15015	7321	580	10260	57	2317	15901
B Insurance	2223	238	-2377	7	1	91	2572	307	-2166	13	1	724
C Real estate and business services	7856	6895	18894	1282	714	34213	9927	7685	21731	1148	734	39757
Real estate, except dwellings	35	1171	2963	248	116	4303	38	1337	3409	230	104	4910
Dwellings	227	5689	10767	522	549	16656	246	6149	11872	417	578	18105
9 Community, social and personal services	12083	992	8584	991	3900	18750	13482	1019	10087	1185	4365	21408
A Sanitary and similar services	463	...	250	...	...	714	542	20	291	1	...	854
B Social and related community services	5551	643	3528	4	2529	7197	6121	637	4015	20	2929	7864
Educational services	1134	76	722	4	1737	199	1271	82	895	2	1978	271
Medical, dental, other health and veterinary services	1954	529	2807	...	21	5269	2048	511	3121	18	22	5676
C Recreational and cultural services	836	207	2165	945	1369	2783	1022	205	2225	1133	1434	3151
D Personal and household services	5232	142	2641	42	1	8057	5798	158	3556	30	2	9539
Total, Industries	157880	59174	136602	31753	25551	359858	175494	62770	145351	34572	26890	391297
Producers of Government Services	58470	3338	...	...	...	61808	64173	3742	...	49	...	67965
Other Producers	...	...	...	...	...	...	...	...	...	...	...	...
Total	216350	62513	136602	31753	25551	421667	239667	66512	145351	34621	26890	459261
Less: Imputed bank service charge [a]	...	...	15443	...	...	15443	...	...	15431	...	...	15431
Import duties [b]	...	...	...	6006	-	6006	...	...	...	9320	-	9320
Value added tax [c]	...	...	...	37794	...	37794	...	...	...	44150	...	44150
Other adjustments	...	...	...	2647	159	2489	...	...	...	2946	46	2900
Total	216350	62513	121159	78200	25710	452512	239667	66512	129920	91037	26936	500201

of which General Government:

1 Agriculture, hunting, forestry and fishing	15	...	...	...	...	15	14	...	...	...	...	14

Norway

4.3 Cost Components of Value Added
(Continued)

Million Norwegian kroner

		1984						1985				
		Compensation of Employees	Capital Consumption	Net Operating Surplus	Indirect Taxes	Less: Subsidies Received	Value Added	Compensation of Employees	Capital Consumption	Net Operating Surplus	Indirect Taxes	Less: Subsidies Received	Value Added
2	Mining and quarrying	...	...	...	...	...	...	...	...	...	...	...	...
3	Manufacturing	...	...	...	...	...	...	...	...	...	...	...	...
4	Electricity, gas and water	...	...	...	...	...	...	...	...	...	...	...	...
5	Construction	...	...	...	...	...	...	...	...	...	...	...	...
6	Wholesale and retail trade, restaurants and hotels	...	...	...	...	...	...	...	...	...	...	...	...
7	Transport and communication	860	316	...	...	...	1175	904	366	...	...	...	1270
8	Finance, insurance, real estate & business services	336	6	...	...	...	341	373	7	...	...	...	380
9	Community, social and personal services	57260	3017	...	...	...	60277	62883	3370	...	49	...	66301
	Total, Industries of General Government	58470	3338	...	...	...	61808	64173	3742	...	49	...	67965
	Producers of Government Services	...	...	...	...	...	...	...	...	...	...	...	...
	Total, General Government	...	...	...	...	...	...	...	...	...	...	...	...

		1986						1987				
		Compensation of Employees	Capital Consumption	Net Operating Surplus	Indirect Taxes	Less: Subsidies Received	Value Added	Compensation of Employees	Capital Consumption	Net Operating Surplus	Indirect Taxes	Less: Subsidies Received	Value Added

All Producers

1	Agriculture, hunting, forestry and fishing	2231	5495	15187	133	6331	16714	2421	6160	17484	...	...	19348
	A Agriculture and hunting	544	3939	10345	103	5394	9536	592	4379	11663	...	...	10721
	B Forestry and logging	992	314	1791	21	354	2765	1058	350	2115	...	...	3148
	C Fishing	696	1241	3051	9	584	4414	771	1431	3706	...	...	5479
2	Mining and quarrying	6921	17366	20750	6928	534	51431	7852	19823	17634	...	...	51712
	A Coal mining	154	26	24	1	133	71	...	...	...	...	...	...
	B Crude petroleum and natural gas production	5759	16957	20412	6894	...	50022	6665	19381	17435	...	...	50325
	C Metal ore mining	500	200	-44	18	394	279	...	...	...	...	...	...
	D Other mining	508	184	358	16	7	1059	...	...	...	...	...	...
3	Manufacturing	54856	8079	14035	5047	6943	75074	60779	9255	13770	...	...	82994
	A Manufacture of food, beverages and tobacco	7897	1435	2758	4154	3312	12932	9009	1630	3307	...	...	15166
	B Textile, wearing apparel and leather industries	1635	220	323	5	182	2001	1720	237	208	...	...	2014
	C Manufacture of wood and wood products, including furniture	3969	517	1252	42	306	5473	4414	590	1202	...	...	5961
	D Manufacture of paper and paper products, printing and publishing	8211	1155	1763	194	277	11046	9298	1356	2300	...	...	12889
	E Manufacture of chemicals and chemical petroleum, coal, rubber and plastic products	4880	1432	951	286	42	7507	...	...	...	...	...	...
	F Manufacture of non-metallic mineral products, except products of petroleum and coal	1924	379	666	27	20	2975	...	...	...	...	...	...
	G Basic metal industries	4339	1168	1805	187	726	6774	4602	1301	1222	...	...	7226
	H Manufacture of fabricated metal products, machinery and equipment	21595	1734	4372	151	2038	25814	...	...	...	...	...	...
	I Other manufacturing industries	406	39	146	1	40	552	...	...	...	...	...	...
4	Electricity, gas and water	3778	4567	7992	3498	175	19660	4221	5161	9708	...	...	22715
	A Electricity, gas and steam	3651	4300	7879	3474	149	19155	4091	4854	9535	...	...	22138
	B Water works and supply	127	267	113	24	27	505	130	307	173	...	...	577
5	Construction	22769	3743	3697	892	213	30888	26963	3927	4319	...	...	36000
6	Wholesale and retail trade, restaurants and hotels	41497	5061	7450	12411	4252	62166	46112	5796	5838	...	...	68396
	A Wholesale and retail trade	35668	4877	5999	12344	4166	54720	39459	5590	3908	...	...	59616
	B Restaurants and hotels	5830	184	1451	67	85	7447	6653	206	1930	...	...	8780
7	Transport, storage and communication	29284	12967	3027	1984	2293	44970	30772	13224	1835	...	...	45664
	A Transport and storage	21705	11217	419	1784	2278	32848	...	...	...	...	...	...
	B Communication	7579	1750	2608	201	15	12123	...	...	...	...	...	...
8	Finance, insurance, real estate and business services	23574	9977	37168	1528	3665	68582	27199	11836	38654	...	...	75195
	A Financial institutions	8719	744	14708	73	2725	21518	...	...	...	...	...	...

Norway

4.3 Cost Components of Value Added
(Continued)

Million Norwegian kroner

	1986						1987					
	Compensation of Employees	Capital Consumption	Net Operating Surplus	Indirect Taxes	Less: Subsidies Received	Value Added	Compensation of Employees	Capital Consumption	Net Operating Surplus	Indirect Taxes	Less: Subsidies Received	Value Added
B Insurance	2879	395	-1024	16	1	2266	...	...	...	...	...	...
C Real estate and business services	11976	8838	23484	1439	939	44798	14228	10376	25163	...	...	50633
Real estate, except dwellings	53	1624	4025	291	127	5865	...	...	...	...	...	...
Dwellings	284	6981	12584	499	751	19596	315	8112	13360	...	...	21599
9 Community, social and personal services	15669	1220	11337	1449	5151	24523	17533	1447	12893	...	...	27681
A Sanitary and similar services	632	23	418	2	...	1074	...	...	...	...	...	...
B Social and related community services	7060	764	4351	23	3515	8682	...	...	...	...	...	...
Educational services	1458	98	1130	2	2372	316	...	...	...	...	...	...
Medical, dental, other health and veterinary services	2347	613	3221	21	29	6173	2614	729	3323	...	...	6648
C Recreational and cultural services	1214	247	2323	1389	1634	3540	...	...	...	...	...	...
D Personal and household services	6764	186	4245	35	2	11228	...	...	...	...	...	...
Total, Industries	200578	68474	120642	33870	29556	394008	223852	76629	122135	...	...	429705
Producers of Government Services	71054	4234	...	58	...	75346	80470	4806	...	...	...	85337
Other Producers	...	...	...	...	...	...	...	...	...	...	...	...
Total	271632	72708	120642	33927	29556	469354	304322	81435	122135	...	...	515042
Less: Imputed bank service charge [a]	...	...	20630	...	...	20630	...	...	21434	...	...	21434
Import duties [b]	...	...	...	11758	-	11758	...	...	...	...	...	9716
Value added tax [c]	...	...	...	50527	...	50527	...	...	...	...	...	53219
Other adjustments	...	...	...	3582	13	3569	...	...	-3464	...	...	383
Total	271632	72708	100012	99794	29569	514578	304322	81435	97237	...	...	556926

of which General Government:

1 Agriculture, hunting, forestry and fishing	15	...	...	...	...	15	13	...	...	...	...	13
2 Mining and quarrying	...	...	...	...	...	...	...	...	...	...	...	...
3 Manufacturing	...	...	...	...	...	...	...	...	...	...	...	...
4 Electricity, gas and water	...	...	...	...	...	...	...	...	...	...	...	...
5 Construction	...	...	...	...	...	...	...	...	...	...	...	...
6 Wholesale and retail trade, restaurants and hotels	...	...	...	...	...	...	...	...	...	...	...	...
7 Transport and communication	973	427	...	...	...	1400	1055	485	...	...	...	1539
8 Finance, insurance, real estate & business services	404	8	...	...	...	411	422	9	...	...	...	431
9 Community, social and personal services	69663	3799	...	58	...	73520	78980	4312	...	...	...	83354
Total, Industries of General Government	71054	4234	...	58	...	75346	80470	4806	...	...	...	85337
Producers of Government Services	...	...	...	...	...	...	...	...	...	...	...	...
Total, General Government	...	...	...	...	...	...	...	...	...	...	...	...

a) Item 'Import duties' includes collection of customs duties, value added tax on imports and special excises or taxes on imports.
b) Item 'Value added tax' excludes value added tax on imports which is included in item 'Import duties'.
c) Item 'Other adjustments' refers to collection of investment levy on fixed capital formation and subsidies on residential and social buildings and a statistical discrepancy.

Oman

Source. Reply to the United Nations National Accounts Questionnaire from the Directorate General of National Statistics, Development Council, Technical Secretariat, Muscat. Official estimates are published in the 'Statistical Yearbook, Fourth Issue, 1397 A.H., 1977 A.D.'.

General note. The estimates shown in the following tables have been adjusted by the United Nations Statistical Office to conform to the United Nations System of National Accounts so far as the existing data would permit.

1.1 Expenditure on the Gross Domestic Product, in Current Prices

Million rials Omani	1970	1975	1978	1979	1980	1981	1982	1983	1984	1985	1986	1987
1 Government final consumption expenditure	13.7	...	272.3	354.7	499.2	656.4	715.2	779.8	808.0	938.1	929.0	913.7
2 Private final consumption expenditure [a]	20.7	...	310.3	337.4	576.8	590.6	794.7	802.2	938.5	1125.6	1020.0	936.4
3 Gross capital formation	14.7	...	273.5	335.4	465.7	583.5	706.7	736.9	913.2	953.1	898.4	564.3
A Increase in stocks [a]	...	...	...	...	...	...	...	...	...	...	...	...
B Gross fixed capital formation	14.7	...	273.5	335.4	465.7	583.5	706.7	736.9	913.2	953.1	898.4	564.3
4 Exports of goods and services	78.7	...	552.0	787.4	1294.0	1625.0	1532.0	1475.0	1532.0	1722.0	1098.0	1468.0
5 Less: Imports of goods and services	21.0	...	461.2	525.0	772.2	965.0	1135.0	1054.0	1145.0	1285.0	1145.0	873.0
Equals: Gross Domestic Product	106.8	724.2	946.9	1289.9	2063.5	2490.5	2613.6	2739.9	3046.7	3453.8	2800.4	3009.4

a) Item 'Increase in stocks' is included in item 'Private final consumption expenditure'.

1.3 Cost Components of the Gross Domestic Product

Million rials Omani	1970	1975	1978	1979	1980	1981	1982	1983	1984	1985	1986	1987
1 Indirect taxes, net	...	...	...	...	...	...	...	...	...	...	...	...
2 Consumption of fixed capital	...	...	...	...	...	...	...	...	...	...	...	...
3 Compensation of employees paid by resident producers to:	...	...	238.3	303.9	424.4	555.2	655.7	749.3	884.8	994.1	996.8	942.9
4 Operating surplus	...	...	...	...	...	...	...	...	...	...	...	...
Equals: Gross Domestic Product	...	...	946.9	1289.9	2063.5	2490.5	2613.6	2739.9	3046.7	3453.8	2800.4	3009.4

1.4 General Government Current Receipts and Disbursements

Million rials Omani	1970	1975	1978	1979	1980	1981	1982	1983	1984	1985	1986	1987
Receipts												
1 Operating surplus	...	...	...	...	...	...	...	...	...	...	...	...
2 Property and entrepreneurial income [a]	...	...	464.5	642.4	854.0	1165.1	1133.2	1198.9	1300.4	...	...	...
3 Taxes, fees and contributions [b]	...	...	19.8	24.6	28.4	39.6	43.9	63.2	82.3	...	...	...
4 Other current transfers [c]	...	...	15.2	21.0	27.4	39.4	39.5	51.7	78.6	...	...	...
Total Current Receipts of General Government	...	...	...	...	...	...	...	...	...	...	...	...
Disbursements												
1 Government final consumption expenditure	...	...	272.3	354.7	499.2	656.4	715.2	779.8	808.0	...	...	...
A Compensation of employees	...	...	109.2	137.9	194.6	260.5	305.0	360.0	423.9	...	...	...
B Consumption of fixed capital	...	...	...	...	...	...	...	...	...	...	...	...
C Purchases of goods and services, net	...	...	163.1	216.8	304.6	395.9	410.2	419.8	384.1	...	...	...
D Less: Own account fixed capital formation	...	...	...	...	...	...	...	...	...	...	...	...
E Indirect taxes paid, net	...	...	...	...	...	...	...	...	...	...	...	...
2 Property income	...	...	...	...	...	...	...	...	...	...	...	...
A Interest	...	...	16.2	19.7	21.1	15.5	17.5	19.2	39.2	...	...	...
B Net land rent and royalties	...	...	...	...	...	...	...	...	...	...	...	...
3 Subsidies	...	...	...	...	...	...	...	...	...	...	...	...
4 Other current transfers	...	...	...	...	...	...	...	...	...	...	...	...
5 Net saving	...	...	...	...	...	...	...	...	...	...	...	...
Total Current Disbursements and Net Saving of General Government	...	...	...	...	...	...	...	...	...	...	...	...

a) Item 'Property and entrepreneurial income' refers to oil and gas revenue and interest from investment and rent.
b) Item 'Taxes fees and contributions' includes indirect taxes and compulsory fees, fines and penalties only.
c) Item 'Other transfers' represents income accrued from sales and services.

Oman

1.7 External Transactions on Current Account, Summary

Million rials Omani

	1970	1975	1978	1979	1980	1981	1982	1983	1984	1985	1986	1987
Payments to the Rest of the World
1 Imports of goods and services	...	...	461.2	525.0	772.2	965.0	1135.0	1054.0	1145.0	1285.0	1145.0	873.0
A Imports of merchandise c.i.f.	...	...	438.3	493.2	661.2	833.0	991.0	906.0	1013.0	1162.0	980.0	756.0
B Other	...	...	22.9	31.8	111.0	132.0	144.0	148.0	132.0	123.0	165.0	117.0
2 Factor income to the rest of the world	...	...	123.0	148.6	257.0	310.0	363.0	418.0	484.0	539.0	579.0	483.0
A Compensation of employees	...	...	83.3	97.2	137.0	172.0	206.0	254.0	297.0	327.0	338.0	277.0
B Property and entrepreneurial income	...	...	39.7	51.4	120.0	138.0	157.0	164.0	187.0	212.0	241.0	206.0
3 Current transfers to the rest of the world	...	...	...	...	...	...	...	...	...	...	...	...
4 Surplus of the nation on current transactions	...	...	-20.6	125.1	309.8	425.0	159.0	124.0	37.0	38.0	-380.0	327.0
Payments to the Rest of the World and Surplus of the Nation on Current Transactions	...	...	563.6	798.7	1339.0	1700.0	1657.0	1596.0	1666.0	1862.0	1341.0	1683.0
Receipts From The Rest of the World
1 Exports of goods and services	...	...	552.0	787.4	1294.0	1625.0	1532.0	1475.0	1532.0	1722.0	1098.0	1468.0
2 Factor income from rest of the world	...	...	11.6	11.3	45.0	75.0	125.0	121.0	134.0	140.0	243.0	215.0
A Compensation of employees	...	...	10.0	11.3	12.0	14.0	15.0	15.0	15.0	15.0	15.0	15.0
B Property and entrepreneurial income	...	...	1.6	-	33.0	61.0	110.0	106.0	119.0	125.0	228.0	200.0
3 Current transfers from rest of the world	...	...	...	...	...	...	...	...	...	...	...	...
Receipts from the Rest of the World on Current Transactions	...	...	563.6	798.7	1339.0	1700.0	1657.0	1596.0	1666.0	1862.0	1341.0	1683.0

1.10 Gross Domestic Product by Kind of Activity, in Current Prices

Million rials Omani

	1970	1975	1978	1979	1980	1981	1982	1983	1984	1985	1986	1987
1 Agriculture, hunting, forestry and fishing	16.6	20.2	30.7	40.3	52.6	62.1	66.1	80.6	89.0	93.7	95.9	105.4
2 Mining and quarrying	71.6	486.8	493.8	719.7	1280.5	1476.4	1424.7	1402.0	1468.6	1683.9	1072.4	1413.0
3 Manufacturing	0.2	2.1	8.5	11.5	15.6	27.0	39.6	49.7	72.1	82.3	103.1	111.5
4 Electricity, gas and water	0.1	1.8	10.5	11.1	16.0	18.7	21.3	24.0	32.7	36.8	40.3	43.5
5 Construction	10.6	70.8	71.4	86.1	117.8	144.9	169.8	187.4	226.9	242.2	220.8	137.0
6 Wholesale and retail trade, restaurants and hotels	1.6	38.5	104.0	137.1	188.3	251.3	299.5	315.7	369.0	428.0	383.2	327.3
7 Transport, storage and communication	0.7	23.5	20.7	25.5	38.3	53.8	64.9	72.9	84.5	99.6	103.4	97.7
8 Finance, insurance, real estate and business services	2.1	19.1	100.1	123.1	162.8	206.6	231.2	250.1	275.9	295.9	281.2	267.1
9 Community, social and personal services	1.0	8.4	7.6	9.6	13.0	16.9	20.7	25.4	31.6	36.0	38.5	40.4
Total, Industries	104.5	671.2	847.3	1164.0	1884.9	2257.7	2337.8	2407.8	2650.3	2998.4	2338.8	2542.9
Producers of Government Services	2.3	53.0	109.2	137.9	194.6	260.5	305.0	360.0	423.9	477.9	495.8	509.9
Other Producers	...	...	...	...	...	...	...	...	...	...	...	...
Subtotal	106.8	724.2	956.5	1301.9	2079.5	2518.2	2642.8	2767.8	3074.2	3476.3	2834.6	3052.8
Less: Imputed bank service charge	...	...	14.2	19.0	24.6	39.0	43.9	49.6	59.2	63.6	71.2	70.3
Plus: Import duties	...	...	4.6	7.0	8.6	11.3	14.7	21.7	31.7	41.1	37.0	26.9
Plus: Value added tax	...	...	...	...	...	...	...	...	...	...	...	...
Equals: Gross Domestic Product	106.8	724.2	946.9	1289.9	2063.5	2490.5	2613.6	2739.9	3046.7	3453.8	2800.4	3009.4

Oman

1.11 Gross Domestic Product by Kind of Activity, in Constant Prices

Million rials Omani	1970	1975	1978	1979	1980	1981	1982	1983	1984	1985	1986	1987
			At constant prices of:1978									
1 Agriculture, hunting, forestry and fishing	...	...	30.7	40.7	49.0	49.7	54.1	64.2	70.4	81.7	81.1	83.8
2 Mining and quarrying	...	...	493.8	461.0	438.4	501.6	505.3	599.8	645.5	775.6	880.9	935.1
3 Manufacturing	...	...	8.5	10.5	12.5	20.6	30.2	37.8	55.9	67.3	81.0	84.3
4 Electricity, gas and water	...	...	10.5	14.0	16.7	18.4	26.3	29.9	44.8	47.5	78.0	95.4
5 Construction	...	...	71.4	74.6	91.4	107.1	142.3	174.7	221.3	239.3	235.4	144.5
6 Wholesale and retail trade, restaurants and hotels	...	...	104.0	117.5	139.0	180.4	224.6	238.6	286.9	316.6	250.4	191.8
7 Transport, storage and communication	...	...	20.7	23.9	33.2	43.2	51.3	59.0	73.4	86.5	84.5	80.3
8 Finance, insurance, real estate and business services	...	...	100.1	111.0	125.5	143.5	162.4	179.1	215.6	239.6	248.3	231.8
9 Community, social and personal services	...	...	7.6	9.4	12.1	15.1	18.3	22.8	29.5	34.0	34.8	36.1
Total, Industries	...	...	847.3	862.5	917.8	1079.6	1214.8	1405.9	1643.3	1888.1	1974.4	1883.1
Producers of Government Services			109.2	137.4	144.6	170.2	176.6	203.9	235.6	248.1	239.1	259.6
Other Producers	...	...	...	...	...	...	...	...	...	...	...	...
Subtotal			956.5	999.9	1062.4	1249.8	1391.4	1609.8	1878.9	2136.2	2213.5	2142.7
Less: Imputed bank service charge			14.2	18.4	21.5	32.2	35.3	40.7	52.8	58.1	60.1	57.8
Plus: Import duties			4.6	6.0	6.3	8.1	11.0	16.3	24.5	27.1	23.9	16.2
Plus: Value added tax	...	...	...	...	...	...	...	...	...	...	...	...
Equals: Gross Domestic Product			946.9	987.5	1047.2	1225.7	1367.1	1585.4	1850.6	2105.2	2177.3	2101.1

1.12 Relations Among National Accounting Aggregates

Million rials Omani	1970	1975	1978	1979	1980	1981	1982	1983	1984	1985	1986	1987
Gross Domestic Product	106.8	...	946.9	1289.9	2063.5	2490.5	2613.6	2739.9	3046.7	3453.8	2800.4	3009.4
Plus: Net factor income from the rest of the world	-25.0	...	-111.4	-137.3	-212.0	-235.0	-238.0	-297.0	-350.0	-399.0	-336.0	-268.0
Factor income from the rest of the world	...	...	11.6	11.3	45.0	75.0	125.0	121.0	134.0	140.0	243.0	215.0
Less: Factor income to the rest of the world	...	...	123.0	148.6	257.0	310.0	363.0	418.0	484.0	539.0	579.0	483.0
Equals: Gross National Product	81.8	...	835.5	1152.6	1851.5	2255.5	2375.6	2442.9	2696.7	3054.8	2464.4	2741.4
Less: Consumption of fixed capital	...	...	...	...	...	...	...	...	...	...	...	...
Equals: National Income	...	...	...	...	...	...	...	...	...	...	...	...
Plus: Net current transfers from the rest of the world	...	...	...	...	...	...	...	...	...	...	...	...
Equals: National Disposable Income	...	...	...	...	...	...	...	...	...	...	...	...
Less: Final consumption	...	...	...	...	...	...	...	...	...	...	...	...
Equals: Net Saving	...	...	...	...	...	...	...	...	...	...	...	...
Less: Surplus of the nation on current transactions	...	...	...	...	...	...	...	...	...	...	...	...
Equals: Net Capital Formation	...	...	...	...	...	...	...	...	...	...	...	...

2.1 Government Final Consumption Expenditure by Function, in Current Prices

Million rials Omani	1970	1975	1978	1979	1980	1981	1982	1983	1984	1985	1986	1987
1 General public services	...	...	...	...	...	...	...	...	...	...	...	...
2 Defence	...	...	223.1	305.1	428.5	563.4	603.5	652.8	664.6	774.5	752.4	734.4
3 Public order and safety	...	...										
4 Education	...	...	16.4	21.9	31.8	44.6	55.1	66.0	72.7	83.1	97.1	100.1
5 Health	...	...	11.9	13.5	19.1	25.4	30.6	33.6	40.5	47.3	48.6	53.4
6 Social security and welfare	...	...	...	...	...	...	...	...	...	...	...	...
7 Housing and community amenities	...	...	...	...	...	...	...	...	...	...	...	...
8 Recreational, cultural and religious affairs	...	...	...	...	...	...	...	...	...	...	...	...
9 Economic services	...	...	...	14.2	19.8	23.0	26.0	27.4	30.2	33.2	30.9	25.8

Oman

2.1 Government Final Consumption Expenditure by Function, in Current Prices
(Continued)

Million rials Omani

	1970	1975	1978	1979	1980	1981	1982	1983	1984	1985	1986	1987
A Fuel and energy	...	...	...	...	...	...	...	...	...	...	...	...
B Agriculture, forestry, fishing and hunting	...	...	...	4.8	7.6	9.0	9.9	10.1	11.2	11.6	11.1	9.7
C Mining, manufacturing and construction, except fuel and energy	...	...	...	...	...	...	...	...	...	...	...	...
D Transportation and communication	...	...	20.9	9.4	12.2	14.0	16.1	17.3	19.0	21.6	19.8	16.1
E Other economic affairs	...	...	...	...	...	...	...	...	...	...	...	...
10 Other functions	...	...	...	...	...	...	...	...	...	...	...	...
Total Government Final Consumption Expenditure	...	...	272.3	354.7	499.2	656.4	715.2	779.8	808.0	938.1	929.0	913.7

4.1 Derivation of Value Added by Kind of Activity, in Current Prices

Million rials Omani

	1980 Gross Output	1980 Intermediate Consumption	1980 Value Added	1981 Gross Output	1981 Intermediate Consumption	1981 Value Added	1982 Gross Output	1982 Intermediate Consumption	1982 Value Added	1983 Gross Output	1983 Intermediate Consumption	1983 Value Added
				All Producers								
1 Agriculture, hunting, forestry and fishing	73.0	20.3	52.6	86.7	24.6	62.1	91.8	25.7	66.1	112.4	31.8	80.6
A Agriculture and hunting	49.7	12.4	37.2	53.9	13.5	40.5	60.9	15.2	45.7	71.3	17.8	53.5
B Forestry and logging	...	...	...	...	...	...	...	...	...	...	...	...
C Fishing	23.3	7.9	15.4	32.8	11.2	21.7	30.9	10.5	20.4	41.1	14.0	27.1
2 Mining and quarrying	1329.1	48.7	1280.4	1544.3	67.9	1476.4	1506.1	81.4	1424.7	1483.9	81.9	1402.0
A Coal mining	...	...	...	...	...	...	...	...	...	...	...	...
B Crude petroleum and natural gas production	1327.1	47.7	1279.4	1539.1	65.3	1473.8	1498.6	77.7	1420.9	1471.3	74.8	1396.5
C Metal ore mining	...	...	...	...	...	...	...	...	...	...	...	...
D Other mining	2.0	1.0	1.0	5.2	2.6	2.6	7.5	3.7	3.8	12.6	7.1	5.5
3 Manufacturing	38.8	23.2	15.6	69.7	42.7	27.0	89.5	49.9	39.6	257.2	207.5	49.7
4 Electricity, gas and water	36.3	20.3	16.0	47.9	29.2	18.7	53.4	32.1	21.3	63.7	39.7	24.0
A Electricity, gas and steam	30.2	17.5	12.7	40.3	26.4	13.9	44.3	28.4	15.9	52.1	35.6	16.5
B Water works and supply	6.1	2.8	3.3	7.6	2.8	4.8	9.1	3.7	5.4	11.6	4.1	7.5
5 Construction	294.5	176.7	117.8	362.4	217.5	145.0	424.6	254.8	169.8	468.8	281.4	187.4
6 Wholesale and retail trade, restaurants and hotels	277.4	89.1	188.3	367.1	115.7	251.3	438.2	138.8	299.5	463.4	147.8	315.7
A Wholesale and retail trade	261.6	78.5	183.1	346.3	103.9	242.4	412.6	123.8	288.8	432.8	129.9	303.0
B Restaurants and hotels	15.8	10.6	5.2	20.7	11.8	8.9	25.7	15.0	10.7	30.6	17.9	12.7
7 Transport, storage and communication	70.9	32.6	38.3	91.2	37.4	53.8	108.5	43.6	64.9	121.1	48.2	72.9
A Transport and storage	57.0	24.9	32.1	74.3	32.3	42.0	87.6	38.0	49.6	94.4	41.1	53.3
B Communication	13.9	7.7	6.2	16.9	5.1	11.8	20.9	5.6	15.3	26.7	7.1	19.6
8 Finance, insurance, real estate and business services	187.4	24.5	162.9	234.4	27.8	206.6	261.7	30.5	231.2	285.3	35.2	250.1
A Financial institutions	39.3	8.2	31.1	53.7	9.0	44.7	62.2	10.4	51.8	69.3	12.9	56.4
B Insurance	5.4	2.1	3.3	5.7	1.3	4.4	11.3	1.3	10.0	8.8	1.6	7.2
C Real estate and business services	142.8	14.3	128.5	175.1	17.5	157.6	188.2	18.8	169.4	207.2	20.7	186.5
9 Community, social and personal services	17.4	4.3	13.0	22.4	5.5	16.8	27.5	6.8	20.7	33.7	8.3	25.4
A Sanitary and similar services	...	...	...	...	...	...	...	...	...	...	...	...
B Social and related community services	2.0	0.4	1.6	2.7	0.6	2.2	3.5	0.7	2.8	4.4	0.9	3.5
Educational services	1.5	0.3	1.2	1.9	0.4	1.5	2.4	0.5	1.9	3.0	0.6	2.4
Medical, dental, other health and veterinary services	0.5	0.1	0.4	0.8	0.2	0.7	1.1	0.2	0.9	1.4	0.3	1.1
C Recreational and cultural services	8.6	3.4	5.2	10.7	4.2	6.5	12.9	5.0	7.9	15.3	6.0	9.3
D Personal and household services	6.8	0.6	6.2	8.9	0.8	8.1	11.1	1.1	10.0	14.0	1.4	12.6
Total, Industries	2324.8	439.7	1884.9	2826.1	568.3	2257.7	3001.3	663.6	2337.8	3289.5	881.8	2407.8
Producers of Government Services	500.8	306.2	194.6	659.4	398.9	260.5	718.9	413.9	305.0	783.5	423.5	360.0
Other Producers	...	...	...	...	...	...	...	...	...	...	...	...
Total	2825.6	745.9	2079.5	3485.5	967.2	2518.2	3720.2	1077.5	2642.8	4073.0	1305.3	2767.8
Less: Imputed bank service charge	...	-24.6	24.6	...	-39.0	39.0	...	-43.9	43.9	...	-49.6	49.6
Import duties	8.6	...	8.6	11.3	...	11.3	14.7	...	14.7	21.7	...	21.7
Value added tax	...	...	...	...	...	...	...	...	...	...	...	...
Total	2834.2	770.5	2063.5	3496.8	1006.2	2490.5	3734.9	1121.4	2613.6	4094.7	1354.9	2739.9

Oman

4.1 Derivation of Value Added by Kind of Activity, in Current Prices

Million rials Omani

	1984 Gross Output	1984 Intermediate Consumption	1984 Value Added	1985 Gross Output	1985 Intermediate Consumption	1985 Value Added	1986 Gross Output	1986 Intermediate Consumption	1986 Value Added	1987 Gross Output	1987 Intermediate Consumption	1987 Value Added
All Producers												
1 Agriculture, hunting, forestry and fishing	124.5	35.5	89.0	129.7	36.0	93.7	132.9	37.0	95.9	147.9	42.5	105.4
A Agriculture and hunting	76.2	19.0	57.1	90.0	22.5	67.5	90.9	22.7	68.2	95.1	24.5	70.6
B Forestry and logging	...	...	...	...	...	...	...	...	...	...	...	...
C Fishing	48.3	16.4	31.9	39.7	13.5	26.2	42.0	14.3	27.7	52.8	18.0	34.8
2 Mining and quarrying	1561.5	92.9	1468.6	1791.2	107.3	1683.9	1191.5	119.1	1072.4	1509.3	96.3	1413.0
A Coal mining	...	...	...	...	...	...	...	...	...	...	...	...
B Crude petroleum and natural gas production	1544.1	83.1	1461.0	1770.7	95.6	1675.1	1172.8	109.7	1063.1	1492.3	87.6	1404.7
C Metal ore mining	...	...	...	...	...	...	...	...	...	...	...	...
D Other mining	17.1	9.8	7.2	20.5	11.7	8.8	18.7	9.4	9.3	17.0	8.7	8.3
3 Manufacturing	319.0	246.9	72.1	372.0	289.7	82.3	392.2	289.1	103.1	380.2	268.7	111.5
4 Electricity, gas and water	77.7	45.0	32.7	92.5	55.7	36.8	97.2	56.8	40.4	108.6	65.1	43.5
A Electricity, gas and steam	65.1	39.9	25.2	76.2	49.1	27.1	80.6	50.8	29.8	86.6	58.6	28.0
B Water works and supply	12.6	5.1	7.5	16.3	6.6	9.7	16.6	6.0	10.6	22.0	6.5	15.5
5 Construction	567.2	340.3	226.9	605.5	363.3	242.2	551.9	331.1	220.8	342.5	205.5	137.0
6 Wholesale and retail trade, restaurants and hotels	541.9	172.8	369.1	626.8	198.9	427.9	563.9	180.7	383.2	483.9	156.6	327.3
A Wholesale and retail trade	506.2	151.8	354.3	588.8	176.6	412.2	523.4	157.0	366.4	444.3	133.3	311.0
B Restaurants and hotels	35.7	21.0	14.7	38.0	22.3	15.7	40.5	23.7	16.8	39.6	23.3	16.3
7 Transport, storage and communication	139.1	54.6	84.5	163.9	64.3	99.6	169.9	66.7	103.4	162.8	65.1	97.7
A Transport and storage	106.4	46.2	60.2	120.7	52.5	68.2	122.0	53.3	68.7	115.0	50.9	64.1
B Communication	32.7	8.4	24.3	43.2	11.8	31.4	47.9	13.2	34.7	47.8	14.2	33.6
8 Finance, insurance, real estate and business services	315.4	39.5	275.9	333.0	37.1	295.9	321.6	40.4	281.2	304.1	37.0	267.1
A Financial institutions	80.5	14.2	66.3	84.9	11.1	73.8	96.0	17.5	78.5	89.6	15.3	74.3
B Insurance	15.6	3.4	12.2	20.2	3.2	17.0	17.0	2.0	15.0	19.2	2.2	17.0
C Real estate and business services	219.3	21.9	197.4	227.9	22.8	205.1	208.6	20.9	187.7	195.3	19.5	175.8
9 Community, social and personal services	41.9	10.3	31.6	47.9	11.9	36.0	51.3	12.9	38.4	53.8	13.4	40.4
A Sanitary and similar services	...	...	...	...	...	...	...	...	...	...	...	...
B Social and related community services	5.9	1.2	4.8	8.0	1.6	6.4	8.9	1.8	7.1	9.1	1.8	7.3
Educational services	4.1	0.8	3.3	5.8	1.1	4.7	6.5	1.3	5.2	6.6	1.3	5.3
Medical, dental, other health and veterinary services	1.8	0.4	1.5	2.2	0.4	1.8	2.4	0.5	1.9	2.5	0.5	2.0
C Recreational and cultural services	17.4	6.8	10.6	19.9	7.8	12.1	21.4	8.4	13.0	22.2	8.7	13.5
D Personal and household services	18.5	2.3	16.3	19.9	2.5	17.4	21.1	2.7	18.4	22.5	2.8	19.7
Total, Industries	3688.2	1037.8	2650.4	4162.6	1164.2	2998.4	3472.5	1133.7	2338.8	3493.0	950.0	2543.0
Producers of Government Services	810.9	387.0	423.9	897.7	419.8	477.9	853.4	357.6	495.8	916.6	406.7	509.9
Other Producers	...	...	...	...	...	...	...	...	...	...	...	...
Total	4499.1	1424.8	3074.3	5060.3	1584.0	3476.3	4325.9	1491.3	2834.6	4409.6	1356.7	3052.9
Less: Imputed bank service charge	...	-59.2	59.2	...	-63.6	63.6	...	-71.2	71.2	...	-70.3	70.3
Import duties	31.7	...	31.7	41.1	...	41.1	37.0	...	37.0	26.9	...	26.9
Value added tax	...	...	...	...	...	...	...	...	...	...	...	...
Total	4530.8	1484.0	3046.8	5101.4	1647.6	3453.8	4362.9	1562.5	2800.4	4436.4	1427.0	3009.4

Pakistan

General note. The preparation of national accounts statistics in Pakistan is undertaken by the Federal Bureau of Statistics, Statistics Division of the Ministry of Finance and Economic Affairs, Karachi. The official estimates and methodological notes on sources and methods are published in a series of reports entitled 'National Accounts'. The estimates are generally in accordance with the classifications and definitions recommended in the United Nations System of National Accounts (SNA). Input-output tables have been published in 'A Summary of Input-Output Studies of the Economy of Pakistan'. The following tables have been prepared from successive replies to the United Nations national accounts questionnaire. Estimates relate to fiscal year beginning 1 July. It should be noted that the estimates for 1960-1969, except Table 4, GDP by Kind of Economic Activity, include data for Bangladesh. When the scope and coverage of the estimates differ for conceptual or statistical reasons from the definitions and classifications recommended in SNA, a footnote is indicated to the relevant tables.

Sources and methods:

(a) Gross domestic product. Gross domestic product is estimated mainly through the production approach.

(b) Expenditure on the gross domestic product. The expenditure approach is used to estimate government final consumption expenditure and exports and imports of goods and services. This approach, in combination with the commodity-flow approach is used to estimate gross capital formation. Private final consumption expenditure is derived as a residual. Government consumption expenditure is estimated by analyzing the budgets of the government bodies with an element of estimation made for the local sector for which the budgets are difficult to obtain. The basic information used in estimating increase in stocks is received from the Planning Commission. The estimates of gross fixed capital formation are classified by economic sectors. For agriculture, investment in construction is based on the rural construction survey for the years 1959/60 to 1963/64, the estimates are projected by the straight-line method using the 1963/64 data as bench-marks. Non-monetized investment is estimated on the basis of special studies carried out by research workers using 1965/66 as bench-mark. Investment in the mining and quarrying sector is estimated on the basis of data obtained in 1969/70 through inquiries into establishments. For large-scale manufacturing, investment estimates are based on sample surveys while the Karachi small industries survey in 1966 projected on the basis of the population growth rate is used for the small-scale manufacturing. Investment in machinery and equipment of the agricultural and mining sectors is estimated by the commodity-flow method. For the service sector, estimates are prepared from trade and domestic production data, annual budgets and annual questionnaires. Estimates of private residential construction are based on the rural construction survey, census reports, population growth and number of persons per household. Capital expenditure for the government bodies are based on the classification of their budgets. The estimates of exports of goods and services are obtained from the Statistics Division and the balance-of-payments. For the constant price estimates, all items of GDP by expenditure type are deflated by appropriate price indexes except gross fixed capital formation which is extrapolated by quantity indicators. Private consumption expenditure is obtained as residual.

(c) Cost-structure of the gross domestic product. Domestic factor incomes consisting of compensation of employees and operating surplus, is obtained as a residual, i.e., after subtracting depreciation and net indirect taxes from GDP. For depreciation, a flat rate is applied for the different sectors, 5 per cent for agriculture, mining and quarrying, small-scale manufacturing, public administration and defence and other private services, 10 per cent for large-scale manufacturing and parts of road transport, 2.5 per cent for construction, 2 per cent for trade and 20 per cent for ownership of dwellings in the rural areas and 25 per cent in the urban areas. Data of indirect taxes and subsidies are derived from budgets of the government bodies.

(d) Gross domestic product by kind of economic activity. The table of GDP by kind of economic activity is prepared in factor values. The production approach is used to estimate value added in agriculture, mining and quarrying, manufacturing, construction and electricity. The income approach is used for most of the remaining sectors. Production data of major agricultural crops are obtained from the Ministry of Agriculture. Corresponding harvest prices are obtained from the Provincial Directorates of Land Records. For minor crops harvest prices are taken at 80 per cent of the wholesale prices. Data on livestock products and wholesale prices are obtained from the Department of Agricultural Marketing and Grading. The current price estimates are derived indirectly by applying the wholesale price index to the constant price estimates. Production and price data of forestry and fishing are obtained from the concerned departments. The Natural Resources Division and the Provincial Mineral Development Department provide production and price data for the mining sector. Gross output is obtained by multiplying the output of each mineral by pit-head or well-head prices in the bench-mark year while annual output and index of wholesale prices are used for the current estimates. Bench-mark estimates for large-scale manufacturing are mainly based on the 1959/60 census of manufacturing industries. Other years' estimates are obtained by applying the quantum index of manufacturing to the bench-mark value. For small-scale manufacturing, bench-mark 1959/60 was computed on the basis of the number of persons engaged and on imputed gross value added per person. For other years, a uniform growth rate of 3 per cent is used in combination with the wholesale price index for manufacturing. The estimates for electricity and gas are based on data furnished by concerned companies while the estimates of water are included in public administration and defence sector. For construction, assumptions are based on the availability of cement for local consumption and on data from household income and expenditures surveys. Value added at constant factor cost thus obtained are adjusted by wholesale price index for manufacturing to arrive at current estimates. The value added of the trade sector is measured by net trade margins earned by traders on various types of products entering into wholesale and retail trade. The trade margins are estimated through special studies undertaken for this purpose. For the transport sector, data on income and expenditure are supplied by the concerned enterprises. The income per person in each category of the transport sector is estimated on the basis of data obtained from the findings of the Minimum Wage Board in 1963 and the 1961 Manpower Survey, projected according to the rate of annual increases in wages of the workers employed. For the financial sector, value added is based on data provided by the State Bank of Pakistan and various financial institutions. Bench-mark data for occupied dwellings are obtained from the housing census in 1960. For other years, it is estimated by applying the geometric growth obtained during 1950-60. For government services, the budgets of all government bodies are used. For private services, the number of persons engaged in the different occupations is obtained from the 1961 population census and extrapolated by the intercensal growth rate in the working force of this sector. For the constant price estimates, double deflation is used for agriculture. Price deflation is used for forestry and fishing, electricity and gas, transport, financial and community services. For mining, the annual output of each mineral is multipled by the base year pit-head and well-head prices. Value added of the trade sector is obtained from the distribution of agricultural produce, manufactured and imported goods. Value added of manufacturing construction and ownership of dwellings is extrapolated by quantum indexes.

1.1 Expenditure on the Gross Domestic Product, in Current Prices

Million Pakistan rupees — Fiscal year beginning 1 July

	1970	1975	1978	1979	1980	1981	1982	1983	1984	1985	1986	1987
1 Government final consumption expenditure	5270	15165	20339	23535	28998	34337	42499	51549	58080	66770	78129	90759
2 Private final consumption expenditure	39030	101115	160700	192392	227345	265893	295565	343155	400471	430580	470304	534297
3 Gross capital formation	7892	24057	34876	43345	47473	57032	63443	70928	80397	89983	103362	112205
A Increase in stocks	847	-	1750	2000	4500	7858	6701	7489	8600	9000	9500	10400
B Gross fixed capital formation	7045	24057	33126	41345	42973	49174	56742	63439	71797	80983	93862	101805
Residential buildings	...	2658	3252	4052	4697	5710	7112	7673	8478	9132	10739	12059
Non-residential buildings	...	4749	5481	6822	8851	9702	10125	13529	14469	14328	18627	21082
Other construction and land improvement etc.	...	7967	8570	10665	11951	15857	16219	15308	18017	20418	23987	26380
Other	...	8683	15823	19806	17474	17905	23285	26929	30833	37015	40508	42283
4 Exports of goods and services	3922	13881	21529	29485	35707	33033	44395	47835	49889	63268	79044	87162
5 Less: Imports of goods and services	5323	23854	42529	54578	62129	68501	82018	92222	106729	103475	122694	138556
Equals: Gross Domestic Product	50791	130364	194915	234179	277394	321794	363884	421245	482108	547126	608145	685867

Pakistan

1.2 Expenditure on the Gross Domestic Product, in Constant Prices

Million Pakistan rupees — Fiscal year beginning 1 July

	1970	1975	1978	1979	1980	1981	1982	1983	1984	1985	1986	1987
					At constant prices of:1959							
1 Government final consumption expenditure	3838	5398	6134	6408	7182	7696	8472	9084	9469	10390	10899	11716
2 Private final consumption expenditure	27938	34694	43557	47157	48934	51028	53526	57182	62837	67544	71019	74856
3 Gross capital formation	5103	6512	7169	7335	7583	9087	9891	10341	11082	11708	13131	12952
A Increase in stocks	617	-	422	429	854	1389	1125	1142	1247	1248	1254	1265
B Gross fixed capital formation	4486	6512	6747	6906	6729	7698	8766	9199	9835	10460	11877	11687
4 Exports of goods and services	3697	3325	3351	4247	4858	4567	5689	5479	5460	5330	5986	5842
5 Less: Imports of goods and services	4356	5398	7890	8274	7745	7709	8565	9184	10004	9944	11388	10949
Equals: Gross Domestic Product	36220	44531	52321	56873	60812	64669	69013	72902	78844	85028	89647	94417

1.3 Cost Components of the Gross Domestic Product

Million Pakistan rupees — Fiscal year beginning 1 July

	1970	1975	1978	1979	1980	1981	1982	1983	1984	1985	1986	1987
1 Indirect taxes, net	4785	10628	17071	23926	30365	32006	35975	45453	47093	57750	62257	67831
A Indirect taxes	4978	13642	24058	30333	35562	37440	43487	53557	56396	67742	73494	80404
B Less: Subsidies	193	3014	6987	6407	5197	5434	7512	8104	9303	9992	11237	12573
2 Consumption of fixed capital	3208	7329	10851	13057	15217	17895	20655	24485	27992	31500	35163	40424
3 Compensation of employees paid by resident producers to:	42798	112407	166993	197196	231812	271893	307254	351307	407023	457876	510725	577612
4 Operating surplus												
Equals: Gross Domestic Product	50791	130364	194915	234179	277394	321794	363884	421245	482108	547126	608145	685867

1.10 Gross Domestic Product by Kind of Activity, in Current Prices

Million Pakistan rupees — Fiscal year beginning 1 July

	1970	1975	1978	1979	1980	1981	1982	1983	1984	1985	1986	1987
1 Agriculture, hunting, forestry and fishing	16236	38338	54147	62164	71699	83426	90715	92165	108873	120305	128159	143917
2 Mining and quarrying	243	968	1464	2239	3149	3578	4199	5086	7116	11029	12136	14767
3 Manufacturing	7723	17812	27344	33300	40561	47841	54403	66329	73572	81827	94066	108060
4 Electricity, gas and water	782	1713	3397	4789	5928	6436	7274	8610	8738	11136	12032	13974
5 Construction	1979	6739	9667	11906	11449	12247	14567	19325	26464	29135	34396	39242
6 Wholesale and retail trade, restaurants and hotels [a]	6954	18865	28327	33663	40433	49500	55349	61594	71883	80376	88468	98611
7 Transport, storage and communication	3017	8349	13181	15486	19370	22937	25704	30659	34793	39120	43674	48504
8 Finance, insurance, real estate and business services	2634	7377	11152	12493	13858	17384	21390	26909	30702	33932	37139	40473
9 Community, social and personal services [ab]	3475	10085	15306	17950	21325	24973	27841	31982	36160	40463	44800	51923
Total, Industries	43043	110246	163985	193990	227772	268322	301442	342659	398301	447323	494870	559471
Producers of Government Services	2963	9490	13859	16263	19257	21466	26467	33133	36714	42053	51018	58565
Other Producers [b]	...	...	...	...	...	...	...	...	...	...	...	...
Subtotal [c]	46006	119736	177844	210253	247029	289788	327909	375792	435015	489376	545888	618036
Less: Imputed bank service charge	...	...	...	...	...	...	...	...	...	...	...	...
Plus: Import duties	...	...	...	...	...	...	...	...	...	...	...	...
Plus: Value added tax	...	...	...	...	...	...	...	...	...	...	...	...
Plus: Other adjustments [d]	4785	10628	17071	23926	30365	32006	35975	45453	47093	57750	62257	67831
Equals: Gross Domestic Product	50791	130364	194915	234179	277394	321794	363884	421245	482108	547126	608145	685867

a) Restaurants and hotels are included in item 'Community, social and personal services'.
b) Item 'Other producers' is included in item 'Community, social and personal services'.
c) Gross domestic product in factor values.
d) Item 'Other adjustments' refers to indirect taxes net of subsidies.

1.11 Gross Domestic Product by Kind of Activity, in Constant Prices

Million Pakistan rupees — Fiscal year beginning 1 July

	1970	1975	1978	1979	1980	1981	1982	1983	1984	1985	1986	1987
					At constant prices of:1959							
1 Agriculture, hunting, forestry and fishing	12188	13659	14845	15826	16405	16992	17637	16571	18600	19788	20224	21124
2 Mining and quarrying	156	175	221	250	283	306	319	326	401	484	510	548
3 Manufacturing	5521	6588	7984	8803	9739	11079	11858	12792	13828	14872	15991	17201
4 Electricity, gas and water	741	985	1366	1531	1698	1777	1916	2249	2345	2709	2859	2927
5 Construction	1390	2094	2371	2644	2749	2836	3175	3727	3838	4086	4512	4820

Pakistan

1.11 Gross Domestic Product by Kind of Activity, in Constant Prices
(Continued)

Million Pakistan rupees — Fiscal year beginning 1 July

	1970	1975	1978	1979	1980	1981	1982	1983	1984	1985	1986	1987
					At constant prices of: 1959							
6 Wholesale and retail trade, restaurants and hotels [a]	4566	5894	6867	7378	7882	8723	9271	9611	10611	11373	12094	12836
7 Transport, storage and communication	1981	2608	3275	3495	3776	4042	4356	4821	5156	5546	5960	6322
8 Finance, insurance, real estate and business services	1784	2408	2859	2889	2831	3230	3815	4460	4791	5057	5334	5536
9 Community, social and personal services [ab]	2276	2964	3510	3711	3924	4183	4459	4753	5067	5401	5757	6137
Total, Industries	30603	37375	43298	46527	49287	53168	56806	59310	64637	69316	73241	77451
Producers of Government Services	2133	3854	4906	5209	5761	5844	6169	6658	7377	7707	8186	8715
Other Producers [b]	...	...	...	...	...	...	...	...	...	...	...	...
Subtotal [c]	32736	41229	48204	51736	55048	59012	62975	65968	72014	77023	81427	86166
Less: Imputed bank service charge	...	...	...	...	...	...	...	...	...	...	...	...
Plus: Import duties	...	...	...	...	...	...	...	...	...	...	...	...
Plus: Value added tax	...	...	...	...	...	...	...	...	...	...	...	...
Plus: Other adjustments [d]	3484	3302	4117	5137	5764	5657	6038	6934	6830	8005	8220	8251
Equals: Gross Domestic Product	36220	44531	52321	56873	60812	64669	69013	72902	78844	85028	89647	94417

a) Restaurants and hotels are included in item 'Community, social and personal services'.
b) Item 'Other producers' is included in item 'Community, social and personal services'.
c) Gross domestic product in factor values.
d) Item 'Other adjustments' refers to indirect taxes net of subsidies.

1.12 Relations Among National Accounting Aggregates

Million Pakistan rupees — Fiscal year beginning 1 July

	1970	1975	1978	1979	1980	1981	1982	1983	1984	1985	1986	1987
Gross Domestic Product	50791	130364	194915	234179	277394	321794	363884	421245	482108	547126	608145	685867
Plus: Net factor income from the rest of the world	-82	2992	14533	18284	22692	25349	39395	39595	38311	41359	36493	31096
Equals: Gross National Product	50709	133356	209448	252463	300086	347143	403279	460840	520419	588485	644638	716963
Less: Consumption of fixed capital	3208	7329	10851	13057	15217	17895	20655	24485	27992	31500	35163	40424
Equals: National Income	47501	126027	198597	239406	284869	329248	382624	436355	492427	556985	609475	676539
Plus: Net current transfers from the rest of the world	...	...	...	...	...	...	...	...	...	...	...	...
Equals: National Disposable Income	...	...	...	...	...	...	...	...	...	...	...	...
Less: Final consumption	...	...	...	...	...	...	...	...	...	...	...	...
Equals: Net Saving	...	...	...	...	...	...	...	...	...	...	...	...
Less: Surplus of the nation on current transactions	...	...	...	...	...	...	...	...	...	...	...	...
Equals: Net Capital Formation	...	...	...	...	...	...	...	...	...	...	...	...

2.1 Government Final Consumption Expenditure by Function, in Current Prices

Million Pakistan rupees — Fiscal year beginning 1 July

	1970	1975	1978	1979	1980	1981	1982	1983	1984	1985	1986	1987
1 General public services	3742	11202	14115	16776	17322	21132	25753	31259	34786	39460	46135	47699
2 Defence												
3 Public order and safety	...	...	...	...	2206	2279	2884	3826	4347	5017	5619	6387
4 Education	457	1567	2361	2812	3364	3830	4987	6275	5531	6563	7736	12696
5 Health	390	810	1420	1285	1087	1244	1619	2088	2560	2999	3419	4659
6 Social security and welfare	...	...	...	...	928	1204	1571	1670	1723	2021	2514	2867
7 Housing and community amenities	...	...	...	...	685	802	766	974	974	1147	1310	1431
8 Recreational, cultural and religious affairs	53	127	106	129	125	133	160	204	233	272	396	473
9 Economic services	458	1203	1885	1749	3180	3589	4197	4711	7365	8645	10361	13950
A Fuel and energy	...	...	...	...	127	146	162	205	235	276	312	406
B Agriculture, forestry, fishing and hunting	...	...	...	...	1799	2029	2796	3283	5727	6739	7875	9594
C Mining, manufacturing and construction, except fuel and energy	...	...	...	...	127	145	194	207	337	390	441	1421
D Transportation and communication	...	...	...	...	399	511	570	626	592	688	798	984
E Other economic affairs	...	...	...	...	728	758	475	390	474	552	935	1545
10 Other functions	170	256	452	784	101	124	562	542	561	646	639	597
Total Government Final Consumption Expenditure	5270	15165	20339	23535	28998	34337	42499	51549	58080	66770	78129	90759

Pakistan

2.3 Total Government Outlays by Function and Type

Million Pakistan rupees — Fiscal year beginning 1 July

		Final Consumption Expenditures		Subsidies	Other Current Transfers & Property Income	Total Current Disbursements	Gross Capital Formation	Other Capital Outlays	Total Outlays
		Total	Compensation of Employees	Other						

1980

		Total	Comp.	Other	Subs.	Other Curr.	Total Curr.	Gross Cap.	Other Cap.	Total
1	General public services	17322	9067	8255	23	468	17813	1824	5	19642
2	Defence									
3	Public order and safety	2206	1612	594	-	722	2928	154	-	3082
4	Education	3364	2755	609	-	90	3454	654	2	4110
5	Health	1087	535	552	10	47	1144	602	-	1746
6	Social security and welfare	928	811	117	-	487	1415	18	-	1433
7	Housing and community amenities	685	441	244	6	-	691	599	-	1290
8	Recreation, culture and religion	125	56	69	164	82	371	190	-	561
9	Economic services	3180	1361	1819	2901	5637	11718	4631	18024	34373
	A Fuel and energy	127	36	91	-	-	127	639	16	782
	B Agriculture, forestry, fishing and hunting	1799	740	1059	2844	2013	6656	1360	14026	22042
	C Mining (except fuels), manufacturing and construction	127	51	76	-	613	740	189	-	929
	D Transportation and communication	399	124	275	32	2893	3324	2376	2464	8164
	E Other economic affairs	728	410	318	25	118	871	67	1518	2456
10	Other functions	101	35	66	220	18923	19244	295	169366	188905
	Total	28998	16673	12325	3324	26456	58778	8967	187397	255142

1981

		Total	Comp.	Other	Subs.	Other Curr.	Total Curr.	Gross Cap.	Other Cap.	Total
1	General public services	21132	10257	10875	37	1294	22463	3613	28	26104
2	Defence									
3	Public order and safety	2279	1563	716	-	15	2294	172	-	2466
4	Education	3830	3188	642	-	852	4682	908	1	5591
5	Health	1244	605	639	16	56	1316	868	-	2184
6	Social security and welfare	1204	803	401	-	36	1240	28	-	1268
7	Housing and community amenities	802	502	300	10	958	1770	789	1	2560
8	Recreation, culture and religion	133	66	67	-	58	191	247	-	438
9	Economic services	3589	1562	2027	5011	3909	12509	5408	13615	31532
	A Fuel and energy	146	42	104	-	-	146	843	4	993
	B Agriculture, forestry, fishing and hunting	2029	857	1172	5009	1384	8422	1424	10595	20441
	C Mining (except fuels), manufacturing and construction	145	65	80	-	448	593	88	-	681
	D Transportation and communication	511	145	366	-	1993	2504	43	1608	4155
	E Other economic affairs	758	453	305	2	84	844	3010	1408	5262
10	Other functions	124	39	85	360	4693	5177	279	313559	319015
	Total	34337	18585	15752	5434	11871	51642	12312	327204	391158

1982

		Total	Comp.	Other	Subs.	Other Curr.	Total Curr.	Gross Cap.	Other Cap.	Total
1	General public services	25753	11919	13834	617	1751	28121	2372	44	30537
2	Defence									
3	Public order and safety	2884	2086	798	-	19	2903	260	2	3165
4	Education	4987	4023	964	-	1078	6065	844	-	6909
5	Health	1619	739	880	-	84	1703	672	29	2404
6	Social security and welfare	1571	1373	198	-	97	1668	21	-	1689
7	Housing and community amenities	766	456	310	10	566	1342	916	4	2262
8	Recreation, culture and religion	160	74	86	-	90	250	161	-	411
9	Economic services	4197	1893	2304	6635	2358	13190	6613	18054	37857
	A Fuel and energy	162	68	94	15	-	177	635	6	818
	B Agriculture, forestry, fishing and hunting	2796	1297	1499	3156	1111	7063	1818	15192	24073
	C Mining (except fuels), manufacturing and construction	194	99	95	1723	385	2302	46	162	2510
	D Transportation and communication	570	133	437	36	81	687	3969	156	4812
	E Other economic affairs	475	296	179	1705	781	2961	145	2538	5644
10	Other functions	562	353	209	250	9398	10210	866	208963	220039
	Total	42499	22916	19583	7512	15441	65452	12725	227096	305273

Pakistan

2.3 Total Government Outlays by Function and Type
(Continued)

Million Pakistan rupees — Fiscal year beginning 1 July

	Final Consumption Expenditures Total	Compensation of Employees	Other	Subsidies	Other Current Transfers & Property Income	Total Current Disbursements	Gross Capital Formation	Other Capital Outlays	Total Outlays
1983									
1 General public services	31259	15142	16117	1595	1670	34524	2908	34	37466
2 Defence									
3 Public order and safety	3826	2866	960	-	8	3834	365	-	4199
4 Education	6275	5025	1250	1	1080	7356	1257	-	8613
5 Health	2088	1020	1068	-	172	2260	1014	-	3274
6 Social security and welfare	1670	1483	187	-	30	1700	19	-	1719
7 Housing and community amenities	974	486	488	-	515	1489	1073	-	2562
8 Recreation, culture and religion	204	90	114	-	123	327	210	-	537
9 Economic services	4711	2249	2462	6508	12725	23944	6794	12285	43023
A Fuel and energy	205	89	116	15	1132	1352	710	30	2092
B Agriculture, forestry, fishing and hunting	3283	1613	1670	4546	1954	9783	2140	12052	23975
C Mining (except fuels), manufacturing and construction	207	85	122	-	1151	1358	66	157	1581
D Transportation and communication	626	187	439	297	7213	8136	3762	-	11898
E Other economic affairs	390	275	115	1650	1275	3315	116	46	3477
10 Other functions	542	325	217	-	10833	11375	542	287680	299597
Total	51549	28686	22863	8103	27156	86809	14182	299999	400990
1984									
1 General public services	34786	16328	18458	2258	1866	38910	3272	38	42220
2 Defence									
3 Public order and safety	4347	3163	1184	-	9	4356	464	-	4820
4 Education	5531	4279	1252	-	1207	6738	1547	-	8285
5 Health	2560	1347	1213	-	192	2752	1109	-	3861
6 Social security and welfare	1723	1509	214	-	34	1757	23	-	1780
7 Housing and community amenities	974	521	453	-	576	1550	1157	-	2707
8 Recreation, culture and religion	233	135	98	-	137	370	236	-	606
9 Economic services	7365	4204	3161	5848	14221	27434	7523	13788	48745
A Fuel and energy	235	76	159	89	1265	1589	651	34	2274
B Agriculture, forestry, fishing and hunting	5727	3520	2207	4354	2184	12265	2365	13526	28156
C Mining (except fuels), manufacturing and construction	337	132	205	-	1286	1623	96	176	1895
D Transportation and communication	592	184	408	268	8061	8921	4275	-	13196
E Other economic affairs	474	292	182	1137	1425	3036	136	52	3224
10 Other functions	561	301	260	1197	12106	13864	586	322874	337324
Total	58080	31787	26293	9303	30348	97731	15917	336700	450348
1985									
1 General public services	39460	18104	21356	2968	2275	44703	3659	43	48405
2 Defence									
3 Public order and safety	5017	3662	1355	-	10	5027	519	-	5546
4 Education	6563	5111	1452	-	1432	7995	1726	-	9721
5 Health	2999	1606	1393	-	225	3224	1235	-	4459
6 Social security and welfare	2021	1773	248	-	40	2061	26	-	2087
7 Housing and community amenities	1147	620	527	-	678	1825	1270	-	3095
8 Recreation, culture and religion	272	157	115	-	160	432	259	-	691
9 Economic services	8645	5028	3617	5446	16692	30783	8358	15318	54459
A Fuel and energy	276	91	185	-	1607	1883	717	37	2637
B Agriculture, forestry, fishing and hunting	6739	4219	2520	3594	2570	12903	2639	15028	30570
C Mining (except fuels), manufacturing and construction	390	156	234	-	1730	2120	108	198	2426
D Transportation and communication	688	221	467	353	9126	10167	4749	-	14916
E Other economic affairs	552	341	211	1499	1659	3710	145	55	3910
10 Other functions	646	348	298	1578	13940	16164	648	355933	372743
Total	66770	36409	30361	9992	35452	112214	17698	371294	501206

Pakistan

2.3 Total Government Outlays by Function and Type
(Continued)

Million Pakistan rupees — Fiscal year beginning 1 July

		Final Consumption Expenditures — Total	Compensation of Employees	Other	Subsidies	Other Current Transfers & Property Income	Total Current Disbursements	Gross Capital Formation	Other Capital Outlays	Total Outlays
	1986									
1	General public services	46135	22731	23404	343	2450	48928	4690	46	53664
2	Defence									
3	Public order and safety	5619	4086	1533	-	12	5631	554	-	6185
4	Education	7736	6108	1628	-	1566	9302	2009	-	11311
5	Health	3419	1887	1532	-	247	3666	1501	-	5167
6	Social security and welfare	2514	2225	289	-	45	2559	29	-	2588
7	Housing and community amenities	1310	727	583	-	742	2052	1648	-	3700
8	Recreation, culture and religion	396	185	211	-	176	572	318	-	890
9	Economic services	10361	5970	4391	8843	18078	37282	8806	18306	64394
	A Fuel and energy	312	108	204	-	1583	1895	724	45	2664
	B Agriculture, forestry, fishing and hunting	7875	4979	2896	5825	2806	16506	3027	17965	37498
	C Mining (except fuels), manufacturing and construction	441	217	224	48	1654	2143	88	229	2460
	D Transportation and communication	798	263	535	413	10210	11421	4807	-	16228
	E Other economic affairs	935	403	532	2557	1825	5317	160	67	5544
10	Other functions	639	253	386	2051	15375	18065	748	405597	424410
	Total	78129	44172	33957	11237	38691	128057	20303	423949	572309
	1987									
1	General public services	47699	23656	24043	5686	2747	56132	6003	594	62729
2	Defence									
3	Public order and safety	6387	4525	1862	-	15	6402	83	-	6485
4	Education	12696	10370	2326	-	1924	14620	2868	-	17488
5	Health	4659	2408	2251	-	286	4945	1580	-	6525
6	Social security and welfare	2867	2491	376	-	57	2924	37	-	2961
7	Housing and community amenities	1431	840	591	-	827	2258	2505	-	4763
8	Recreation, culture and religion	473	231	242	-	197	670	357	-	1027
9	Economic services	13950	5784	8166	5736	20918	40604	9457	21103	71164
	A Fuel and energy	406	151	255	-	1792	2198	1246	51	3495
	B Agriculture, forestry, fishing and hunting	9594	4357	5237	2646	3310	15550	3050	20716	39316
	C Mining (except fuels), manufacturing and construction	1421	293	1128	-	1884	3305	968	259	4532
	D Transportation and communication	984	327	657	418	11816	13218	3996	-	17214
	E Other economic affairs	1545	656	889	2672	2116	6333	197	77	6607
10	Other functions	597	399	198	1151	18676	20424	1002	483351	504777
	Total	90759	50704	40055	12573	45647	148979	23892	505048	677919

2.7 Gross Capital Formation by Type of Good and Owner, in Current Prices

Million Pakistan rupees — Fiscal year beginning 1 July

	1980 TOTAL	Total Private	Public Enterprises	General Government	1981 TOTAL	Total Private	Public Enterprises	General Government	1982 TOTAL	Total Private	Public Enterprises	General Government
Increase in stocks, total	4500	...	...	...	7858	...	...	...	6701	...	...	...
Gross Fixed Capital Formation, Total	42973	16874	17132	8967	49174	17916	18946	12312	56742	21738	22278	12725
1 Residential buildings	4697	3850	405	442	5710	4540	575	595	7112	5901	628	583
2 Non-residential buildings	8851	2993	2763	3095	9702	3264	2121	4317	10125	3632	2325	4168
3 Other construction	9646	93	5087	4466	13509	98	7053	6358	14033	199	6907	6927

Pakistan

2.7 Gross Capital Formation by Type of Good and Owner, in Current Prices
(Continued)

Million Pakistan rupees — Fiscal year beginning 1 July

	1980 TOTAL	1980 Total Private	1980 Public Enterprises	1980 General Government	1981 TOTAL	1981 Total Private	1981 Public Enterprises	1981 General Government	1982 TOTAL	1982 Total Private	1982 Public Enterprises	1982 General Government
4 Land improvement and plantation and orchard development	2305	1809	210	286	2348	1954	357	37	2186	1390	767	29
5 Producers' durable goods	17104	8008	8418	678	17542	7945	8592	1005	22823	10522	11283	1018
A Transport equipment	4230	2089	1996	145	4295	1890	2272	133	3851	2078	1544	229
Passenger cars	1544	813	659	72	1468	712	690	66	1354	826	411	117
Other	2686	1276	1337	73	2827	1178	1582	67	2497	1252	1133	112
B Machinery and equipment	12874	5919	6422	533	13247	6055	6320	872	18972	8444	9739	789
6 Breeding stock, dairy cattle, etc.	...	...	...	...	...	...	...	...	...	...	...	...
Statistical discrepancy [a]	370	121	249	-	363	115	248	-	462	94	368	-
Total Gross Capital Formation	47473	...	...	...	57032	...	...	...	63443	...	...	...

	1983 TOTAL	1983 Total Private	1983 Public Enterprises	1983 General Government	1984 TOTAL	1984 Total Private	1984 Public Enterprises	1984 General Government	1985 TOTAL	1985 Total Private	1985 Public Enterprises	1985 General Government
Increase in stocks, total	7489	...	...	...	8600	...	...	...	9000	...	...	...
Gross Fixed Capital Formation, Total	63439	25645	23612	14182	71797	29712	26168	15917	80893	33307	29888	17698
1 Residential buildings	7673	6445	460	768	8478	7011	534	933	9132	7645	445	1042
2 Non-residential buildings	13529	5282	2974	5273	14470	6083	2584	5803	14328	4901	2942	6485
3 Other construction	12527	93	5668	6766	14363	118	6707	7538	15469	173	6957	8339
4 Land improvement and plantation and orchard development	2783	1975	770	38	3652	1998	1628	26	4949	2430	2490	29
5 Producers' durable goods	26441	11724	13380	1337	30532	14351	14565	1616	36699	18082	16814	1803
A Transport equipment	5360	2621	2408	331	8032	3395	4292	345	8410	3966	4059	385
Passenger cars	2012	1241	576	195	2510	1867	436	207	3130	2340	560	230
Other	3348	1380	1832	136	5522	1528	3856	138	5280	1626	3499	155
B Machinery and equipment	21081	9103	10972	1006	22500	10956	10273	1271	28289	14116	12755	1418
6 Breeding stock, dairy cattle, etc.	...	...	...	...	...	...	...	...	...	...	...	...
Statistical discrepancy [a]	486	126	360	-	301	151	150	-	316	76	240	-
Total Gross Capital Formation	70928	...	...	...	80397	...	...	...	89893	...	...	...

	1986 TOTAL	1986 Total Private	1986 Public Enterprises	1986 General Government	1987 TOTAL	1987 Total Private	1987 Public Enterprises	1987 General Government
Increase in stocks, total	9500	...	...	...	10400	...	...	...
Gross Fixed Capital Formation, Total	93862	38171	35388	20303	101805	42825	35088	23892
1 Residential buildings	10739	9007	527	1205	12059	10105	539	1415
2 Non-residential buildings	18627	7815	3383	7429	21082	8767	3450	8865
3 Other construction	18339	152	8637	9550	20322	171	9026	11125
4 Land improvement and plantation and orchard development	5648	2567	3048	33	6058	2880	3140	38
5 Producers' durable goods	40029	18436	19508	2085	41862	20685	18729	2448
A Transport equipment	9212	4361	4406	445	9928	4893	4513	522
Passenger cars	3702	2681	763	258	3882	2801	782	299
Other	5510	1680	3643	187	6046	2092	3731	223
B Machinery and equipment	30817	14075	15102	1640	31934	15792	14216	1926
6 Breeding stock, dairy cattle, etc.	...	...	...	...	...	...	...	...
Statistical discrepancy [a]	479	194	285	-	421	217	204	-
Total Gross Capital Formation	103362	...	...	...	112205	...	...	...

a) Item 'Statistical discrepancy' refers to furniture and fixture.

2.11 Gross Fixed Capital Formation by Kind of Activity of Owner, ISIC Divisions, in Current Prices

Million Pakistan rupees — Fiscal year beginning 1 July

	1970	1975	1978	1979	1980	1981	1982	1983	1984	1985	1986	1987
All Producers
1 Agriculture, hunting, forestry and fishing [a]	1475	4772	4666	5924	6065	6301	7793	8636	8856	8792	9947	11112
2 Mining and quarrying	26	71	144	161	384	418	288	897	1032	2149	2874	2096
3 Manufacturing	1494	5000	9146	10104	9195	9157	10556	12828	12936	16253	16688	17827
A Manufacturing of food, beverages and tobacco	...	...	738	1147	563	856	983	1269	1772	1614	1657	1641

Pakistan

2.11 Gross Fixed Capital Formation by Kind of Activity of Owner, ISIC Divisions, in Current Prices
(Continued)

Million Pakistan rupees — Fiscal year beginning 1 July

	1970	1975	1978	1979	1980	1981	1982	1983	1984	1985	1986	1987
B Textile, wearing apparel and leather industries	...	...	1127	1495	1477	1151	1395	1488	1908	2826	2902	4623
C Manufacture of wood, and wood products, including furniture	...	...	98	158	153	180	152	95	132	180	185	183
D Manufacture of paper and paper products, printing and publishing	...	...	121	189	240	577	461	640	520	752	772	851
E Manufacture of chemicals and chemical petroleum, coal, rubber and plastic products	...	...	2227	1606	3307	1605	2513	3620	3446	3153	3237	3797
F Manufacture of non-metalic mineral products except products of petroleum and coal	...	...	738	1914	1047	1171	1243	1707	1646	1533	1574	1076
G Basic metal industries	...	...	3485	2995	1720	2633	2769	2382	1418	2937	3016	622
H Manufacture of fabricated metal products, machinery and equipment	...	...	394	436	562	646	758	-1272	1675	2620	2690	4171
I Other manufacturing industries	...	...	218	164	126	338	282	355	419	638	655	863
4 Electricity, gas and water [b]	683	3186	3028	2333	3382	3910	6195	6136	7949	8356	11687	13431
5 Construction	100	682	899	1229	1750	1916	3094	2445	3176	3588	4592	5766
6 Wholesale and retail trade, restaurants and hotels	...	...	...	...	...	...	...	...	...	...	...	...
7 Transport, storage and communication [c]	1269	2823	3910	8659	6338	7152	6412	7759	10719	11289	13903	11374
8 Finance, insurance, real estate and business services [d]	613	1459	2476	3281	4118	4925	6428	7048	7588	8450	8953	10366
9 Community, social and personal services [d]	443	1157	2277	2814	2774	3083	3250	3508	3624	4318	4915	5940
Total Industries [e]	6103	19151	26546	34506	34006	36862	44017	49257	55880	63195	73559	77912
Producers of Government Services	942	4907	6580	6840	8967	12312	12725	14182	15917	17698	20303	23892
Private Non-Profit Institutions Serving Households	...	...	...	...	...	...	...	...	...	...	...	...
Total	7045	24057	33126	41345	42973	49174	56742	63439	71797	80893	93862	101804

a) Item 'Agriculture, hunting, fishing and forestry' includes investment in Indus Basin Project made by WAPDA.
b) Item 'Electricity, gas and water' refers to electricity and gas only.
c) Item 'Transport, storage and communication' excludes storage.
d) Business services are included in item 'Community, social and personal services'.
e) The estimates of gross capital formation by kind of activity of owner refer to private and semi-public sector only.

Panama

General note. The preparation of national accounts statistics in Panama is undertaken by the Direccion de Estadistica y Censos Panama. Official estimates are published annually, from 1960 in 'Estadistica Panamena, Serie C, Ingreso Nacional' and from 1976 in the bulletin 'Situacion Economica'. The most detailed description of the sources and methods used for the national accounts estimation is found in 'Situacion Economica, Cuentas Nacionales: Anos 1973 a 1975', published in 1976. The estimates are generally in accordance with the classifications and definitions recommended in the United Nations System of National Accounts (SNA). The following tables have been prepared from successive replies to the United Nations national accounts questionnaire. When the scope and coverage of the estimates differ for conceptual or statistical reasons from the definitions and classifications recommended in SNA, a footnote is indicated to the relevant tables.

Sources and methods :

(a) Gross domestic product. Gross domestic product is estimated mainly through the income approach.

(b) Expenditure on the gross domestic product. The expenditure approach is used to estimate government final consumption expenditure as well as imports and exports of goods and services. The commodity-flow approach is used to estimate private final consumption expenditure and, to a large extent, gross capital formation. Data on government consumption expenditure are obtained from official documents and directly from the concerned agencies. Estimates of private consumption expenditure are based on data on locally produced and imported consumer goods. The gross value of construction is obtained by adding the cost of inputs of building materials to the estimated value added of the industry. Factor and non-factor services rendered by residents of Panama to the Former Canal Zone and to the Colon Free Zone are treated uniformly as non-factor services to the rest of the world. These services are, therefore, included in exports of goods and services. Constant prices are estimated by a combined use of extrapolation and price indexes. For government consumption expenditure, compensation of employees is extrapolated by the number of persons employed, whereas purchases of goods and services are deflated by a combination of price indexes. For private consumption expenditure, base-year estimates are extrapolated by means of indexes which refer to consumption at both current and constant prices. The final estimates are adjusted for the discrepancy between total demand and total supply. Current values of gross fixed capital formation are deflated by a price index for inputs in the case of buildings and other construction. The current value of transport equipment and machinery and equipment are extrapolated by a volume index obtained by deflating current values by an index based on the unit export value of machinery in supplier countries. Various price indexes are used for price deflation of exports and imports of goods and services.

(c) Cost-structure of the gross domestic product. Estimates of compensation of employees are based on data on average wages, and the percentage distribution of employees obtained from household surveys. To this informaton is added yearly estimates of salaries earned in the public and private sectors, employers' contribution to social security schemes and an estimate of the incomes of self-employed workers. Operating surplus is compiled from various items, such as property income, saving and direct taxes. The estimates on consumption of fixed capital, which exclude depreciation of government fixed capital, are based on accounting data of the private enterprises, obtained through direct surveys, and financial information of all autonomous and semi-autonomous entities included in the public sector. Estimates of indirect taxes are based on data from public finance, and on revenue figures from central government, municipalities and the Panamanian Institute of Tourism.

(d) Gross domestic product by kind of economic activity. The table of GDP by kind of economic activity is prepared in factor values. For the agriculture, forestry and fishing sector, value added is obtained by deducting inputs from gross value of production. Sources used to estimate agricultural production include the census of agriculture, agricultural surveys and, in the case of export products, external trade statistics. Price data are obtained from the current statistics on prices received by the agricultural producers. Value added in forestry is derived from a bench-mark estimate of sawn wood produced, the number of persons occupied and the ratio of output to employment, which is obtained from periodical industrial inquiries. In the case of fishing, estimates are based on fish landings in the Gulf of Panama, as published in 'Estadistica Panamena' and on the number of persons engaged in fishing, which is obtained from the latest population census. Value added of manufacturing is estimated by extrapolating the bench-mark estimate by an indicator based on the gross value of production by type of industrial activity. A similar approach is used for the electricity, gas and water sector, as well as the construction and the trade sectors. For the trade sector the indicator used is based on the current prices of products which are marketed through wholesale and retail trade. For transport, value added is estimated on the basis of the payments to factor of production. Value added for ownership of dwellings is obtained by aggregating estimates for different geographical areas of the country. For business services value added is estimated by utilizing an indicator of patent registrations in force for operating business at the end of each year. Financial reports relating to factor payments from central government, other government authorities and municipalities, form the data basis for estimates of public administration. A similar approach is applied for other public services, whereas for other private services value added is first estimated at constant prices and then inflated by price indices to arrive at value added at current prices. For the estimation of constant prices in the agricultural sector, the current quantities are valued at base-year prices. Base year estimates, for the manufacturing sector, are extrapolated by various indexes such as indexes of input quantities and quantum indexes of output. For construction, value added is extrapolated by a quantity index of inputs. For electricity, trade and transport value added is extrapolated by quantity indicators of output. For restaurants and hotels the indicators are based on tourist expenditure in Panama and on food and beverage quantities. For banks, value added is extrapolated using the balance of loans and deposits at the end of each year. For ownership of dwellings in urban areas, the construction of new dwellings is used as indicator, and for the rural areas the base-year estimate is extrapolated by an index of rural population growth. The value added of government services is extrapolated by an index of number of government employees. For other private services as well value added is extrapolated using various quantity indicators.

1.1 Expenditure on the Gross Domestic Product, in Current Prices

Million Panamanian balboas

	1970	1975	1978	1979	1980	1981	1982	1983	1984	1985	1986	1987
1 Government final consumption expenditure	152.3	353.3	482.9	567.2	680.5	812.9	962.6	941.5	1001.3	1043.6	1127.8	1231.2
2 Private final consumption expenditure	618.8	1054.1	1431.7	1693.8	2009.5	2107.4	2311.5	2480.0	2878.0	3080.2	2970.9	3053.2
3 Gross capital formation	284.3	567.4	651.7	785.7	986.9	1167.2	1184.6	934.1	761.0	753.0	859.2	939.8
A Increase in stocks	22.4	31.9	45.4	124.5	120.5	87.6	-0.8	16.3	-18.9	-20.1	-37.5	0.5
B Gross fixed capital formation	261.9	535.5	606.3	661.2	866.4	1079.6	1185.4	917.8	779.9	773.1	896.7	939.3
Residential buildings	54.4	69.7	86.2	96.4	93.3	117.4	121.7	119.7	128.9	182.3	207.0	215.4
Non-residential buildings	48.4	109.8	115.1	187.1	219.7	225.8	236.0	221.9	145.3	170.8	188.1	220.4
Other construction and land improvement etc.	45.6	148.8	176.2	136.1	251.4	339.0	493.6	272.4	225.7	125.2	147.7	106.9
Other	113.5	207.2	228.8	241.6	302.0	397.4	334.1	303.8	280.0	294.8	353.9	396.6
4 Exports of goods and services	388.2	865.4	986.4	1124.8	1567.1	1632.0	1689.6	1709.5	1622.1	1735.2	1786.5	1741.8
5 Less: Imports of goods and services	422.4	999.4	1100.2	1371.3	1685.2	1841.5	1869.4	1691.4	1696.9	1710.9	1599.3	1648.6
Equals: Gross Domestic Product	1021.2	1840.8	2452.5	2800.2	3558.8	3878.0	4278.9	4373.7	4565.5	4901.1	5145.1	5317.4

1.2 Expenditure on the Gross Domestic Product, in Constant Prices

Million Panamanian balboas

	1970	1975	1978	1979	1980	1981	1982	1983	1984	1985	1986	1987
					At constant prices of:1970							
1 Government final consumption expenditure	152.3	234.3	261.5	269.1	284.8	334.9	365.5	343.8	348.4	354.0	384.1	404.9
2 Private final consumption expenditure	618.8	733.0	877.0	931.6	952.4	945.7	997.6	1053.5	1176.0	1196.8	1157.3	1175.2
3 Gross capital formation	284.3	379.7	326.6	352.1	411.6	463.4	430.6	340.9	303.3	323.9	351.8	364.1
A Increase in stocks	22.4	18.7	23.4	52.2	46.3	37.3	0.5	7.9	-6.9	-7.5	-11.7	-0.9
B Gross fixed capital formation	261.9	361.0	303.2	299.9	365.3	426.1	430.1	333.0	310.2	331.4	363.5	365.0

Panama

1.2 Expenditure on the Gross Domestic Product, in Constant Prices
(Continued)

Million Panamanian balboas

	1970	1975	1978	1979	1980	1981	1982	1983	1984	1985	1986	1987
	\multicolumn{12}{c}{At constant prices of:1970}
Residential buildings	54.4	44.5	44.0	42.6	37.0	42.8	41.4	39.6	43.1	60.8	66.7	68.1
Non-residential buildings	48.4	70.0	58.7	82.7	87.2	82.3	80.2	73.4	48.6	57.0	60.6	69.7
Other construction and land improvement etc.	45.6	94.9	89.9	60.1	99.8	123.5	167.7	90.1	75.4	41.8	47.6	33.8
Other	113.5	151.6	110.6	114.5	141.3	177.5	140.8	129.9	143.1	171.8	188.6	193.4
4 Exports of goods and services	388.2	467.0	538.8	531.6	764.5	740.7	800.1	793.9	743.3	796.8	834.9	810.2
5 Less: Imports of goods and services	422.4	528.3	553.1	568.1	667.5	665.9	675.2	606.4	653.4	663.1	652.1	628.3
Equals: Gross Domestic Product	1021.2	1285.7	1450.8	1516.3	1745.8	1818.8	1918.6	1925.7	1917.6	2008.4	2076.0	2126.1

1.3 Cost Components of the Gross Domestic Product

Million Panamanian balboas

	1970	1975	1978	1979	1980	1981	1982	1983	1984	1985	1986	1987
1 Indirect taxes, net	78.8	139.6	216.0	251.7	268.2	281.6	307.9	331.4	353.7	384.7	427.9	444.6
A Indirect taxes	81.4	142.5	221.7	255.1	269.7	285.4	313.7	336.4	358.8	390.0	432.9	452.3
B Less: Subsidies	2.6	2.9	5.7	3.4	1.5	3.8	5.8	5.0	5.1	5.3	5.0	7.7
2 Consumption of fixed capital	53.0	91.8	134.9	157.3	252.1	279.7	320.9	335.5	374.6	398.8	424.4	438.6
3 Compensation of employees paid by resident producers to:	511.0	942.8	1218.7	1392.8	1624.6	1800.2	2049.5	2193.2	2301.1	2455.1	2582.1	2666.1
4 Operating surplus	378.4	666.6	882.9	998.4	1413.9	1516.5	1600.6	1513.6	1536.1	1662.5	1710.7	1768.1
Equals: Gross Domestic Product	1021.2	1840.8	2452.5	2800.2	3558.8	3878.0	4278.9	4373.7	4565.5	4901.1	5145.1	5317.4

1.4 General Government Current Receipts and Disbursements

Million Panamanian balboas

	1970	1975	1978	1979	1980	1981	1982	1983	1984	1985	1986	1987
	\multicolumn{12}{c}{Receipts}
1 Operating surplus	-0.5	-0.3	0.3	0.1	-0.7	-0.9	-1.5	0.2	-0.1	-0.2	-	0.7
2 Property and entrepreneurial income	27.0	57.2	59.3	63.4	89.2	97.7	107.1	133.6	141.0	188.1	167.9	165.2
3 Taxes, fees and contributions	193.4	380.0	548.0	671.7	833.2	951.4	1054.1	1159.5	1149.0	1250.7	1357.4	1423.1
A Indirect taxes	81.4	142.5	221.7	255.1	269.7	285.4	313.7	336.4	358.8	390.0	432.9	452.2
B Direct taxes	55.7	117.5	136.7	170.9	226.6	284.2	300.8	354.1	304.7	342.3	366.2	382.6
C Social security contributions	47.8	103.1	163.5	199.9	236.9	279.8	339.6	361.7	371.5	394.0	433.4	461.3
D Compulsory fees, fines and penalties	8.5	16.9	26.1	45.8	100.0	102.0	100.0	107.3	114.0	124.4	124.9	127.0
4 Other current transfers	42.6	61.2	78.0	100.8	137.0	173.2	173.9	194.0	219.4	222.9	254.9	243.0
Total Current Receipts of General Government	262.5	498.1	685.6	836.0	1058.7	1221.4	1333.6	1487.3	1509.3	1661.5	1780.2	1832.0
	\multicolumn{12}{c}{Disbursements}
1 Government final consumption expenditure	152.3	353.3	482.9	567.2	680.5	812.9	962.6	941.5	1001.3	1043.6	1127.8	1231.2
2 Property income	11.2	42.3	78.5	129.1	187.4	230.3	316.5	292.2	310.3	319.2	360.7	319.2
A Interest	11.2	42.3	78.5	129.1	187.4	230.3	316.5	292.2	310.3	319.2	360.7	319.2
B Net land rent and royalties	-	-	-	-	-	-	...	...	...	...	...	...
3 Subsidies	2.6	2.9	5.7	3.4	1.5	3.8	5.8	5.0	5.1	5.3	5.0	7.7
4 Other current transfers	39.5	83.7	118.0	155.9	197.8	239.9	281.4	306.7	327.7	362.8	381.6	399.8
A Social security benefits	18.2	45.9	74.8	87.2	99.1	121.7	134.6	156.4	174.4	198.6	212.4	230.0
B Social assistance grants	1.9	5.2	5.2	6.3	14.1	12.4	20.9	18.2	18.0	16.6	17.4	17.5
C Other	19.4	32.6	38.0	62.4	84.6	105.8	125.9	132.1	135.3	147.6	151.8	152.3
5 Net saving	56.9	15.9	0.5	-19.6	-8.5	-65.5	-232.7	-58.1	-135.1	-69.4	-94.9	-125.9
Total Current Disbursements and Net Saving of General Government	262.5	498.1	685.6	836.0	1058.7	1221.4	1333.6	1487.3	1509.3	1661.5	1780.2	1832.0

1.7 External Transactions on Current Account, Summary

Million Panamanian balboas

	1970	1975	1978	1979	1980	1981	1982	1983	1984	1985	1986	1987
	\multicolumn{12}{c}{Payments to the Rest of the World}
1 Imports of goods and services	422.4	999.4	1100.2	1371.3	1685.2	1841.5	1869.4	1691.4	1696.9	1710.9	1599.3	1648.6
A Imports of merchandise c.i.f.	363.5	906.1	966.4	1218.5	1483.9	1620.0	1636.9	1474.4	1468.3	1451.0	1323.7	1371.8
B Other	58.9	93.3	133.8	152.8	201.3	221.5	232.5	217.0	228.6	259.9	275.6	276.8
2 Factor income to the rest of the world	41.0	396.1	854.4	1552.6	2760.6	3510.5	3793.5	2827.8	2620.9	2134.0	1870.0	1509.6

Panama

1.7 External Transactions on Current Account, Summary
(Continued)

Million Panamanian balboas

		1970	1975	1978	1979	1980	1981	1982	1983	1984	1985	1986	1987
3	Current transfers to the rest of the world	19.1	39.5	54.7	61.4	58.1	54.8	63.9	70.4	61.3	39.0	33.2	40.3
4	Surplus of the nation on current transactions	-62.5	-169.3	-189.5	-353.7	-213.8	-256.9	-282.7	60.1	-108.8	86.6	239.2	99.9
	Payments to the Rest of the World and Surplus of the Nation on Current Transactions	420.0	1265.7	1819.8	2631.6	4290.1	5149.9	5444.1	4649.7	4270.3	3970.5	3741.7	3298.4

Receipts From The Rest of the World

		1970	1975	1978	1979	1980	1981	1982	1983	1984	1985	1986	1987
1	Exports of goods and services	388.2	865.4	986.4	1124.8	1567.1	1632.0	1689.6	1709.5	1622.1	1735.2	1786.5	1741.8
	A Exports of merchandise f.o.b.	158.3	466.0	387.4	451.8	525.5	495.0	488.8	426.5	368.2	393.4	400.4	417.7
	B Other	229.9	399.4	599.0	673.0	1041.6	1137.0	1200.8	1283.0	1253.9	1341.8	1386.1	1324.1
2	Factor income from rest of the world	14.5	376.6	797.0	1449.8	2650.6	3431.9	3654.6	2830.0	2497.3	2087.6	1826.3	1433.6
	A Compensation of employees	-	-	-	-	62.8	58.6	72.1	75.4	73.3	78.2	82.0	82.9
	B Property and entrepreneurial income	14.5	376.6	797.0	1449.8	2587.8	3373.3	3582.5	2754.6	2424.0	2009.4	1744.3	1350.7
3	Current transfers from rest of the world	17.3	23.7	36.4	57.0	72.4	86.0	99.9	110.2	150.9	147.7	128.9	123.0
	Receipts from the Rest of the World on Current Transactions	420.0	1265.7	1819.8	2631.6	4290.1	5149.9	5444.1	4649.7	4270.3	3970.5	3741.7	3298.4

1.10 Gross Domestic Product by Kind of Activity, in Current Prices

Million Panamanian balboas

		1970	1975	1978	1979	1980	1981	1982	1983	1984	1985	1986	1987
1	Agriculture, hunting, forestry and fishing	149.1	205.6	288.5	304.2	320.4	359.3	371.2	408.4	415.9	450.6	478.6	508.6
2	Mining and quarrying	1.9	3.2	4.1	4.4	6.8	8.7	9.3	7.9	6.0	5.7	6.0	7.3
3	Manufacturing	127.3	236.0	252.6	293.3	356.0	375.6	394.0	401.0	411.0	420.0	421.8	440.8
4	Electricity, gas and water	21.8	41.4	82.5	95.0	113.8	142.4	152.6	153.5	194.9	212.1	227.6	227.8
5	Construction	68.2	151.5	172.7	194.4	258.4	295.2	378.4	271.5	225.0	229.8	260.0	262.4
6	Wholesale and retail trade, restaurants and hotels	161.0	318.4	422.7	493.6	618.2	667.6	681.3	647.5	655.4	693.5	707.1	679.8
7	Transport, storage and communication	61.2	129.3	217.8	263.6	408.2	427.4	497.0	601.1	590.6	640.8	651.7	665.0
8	Finance, insurance, real estate and business services	122.1	242.7	346.5	430.1	503.2	587.4	663.7	725.0	791.3	886.7	957.2	1043.8
9	Community, social and personal services	68.2	141.0	181.2	206.5	246.9	273.1	344.0	358.5	379.5	397.1	420.7	436.3
	Statistical discrepancy [a,b]	75.0	104.7	140.7	158.9	312.4	330.5	353.3	321.1	337.7	342.6	360.5	360.4
	Total, Industries	855.8	1573.8	2109.3	2444.0	3144.3	3467.2	3844.8	3895.5	4007.3	4278.9	4491.2	4632.2
	Producers of Government Services	117.8	241.8	329.7	399.4	446.4	468.5	534.2	595.1	673.7	731.1	761.0	806.7
	Other Producers	21.3	23.4	26.9	30.3	37.2	42.4	46.2	50.7	56.3	57.6	59.7	61.4
	Subtotal	994.9	1839.0	2465.9	2873.7	3627.9	3978.1	4425.2	4541.3	4737.3	5067.6	5311.9	5500.3
	Less: Imputed bank service charge	10.6	42.4	70.4	141.6	147.5	183.7	237.4	263.9	280.6	285.1	309.4	318.3
	Plus: Import duties	36.9	44.2	57.0	68.1	78.4	83.6	91.1	96.3	108.8	118.6	142.6	135.4
	Plus: Value added tax	...	...	...	...	...	...	...	...	...	...	...	...
	Equals: Gross Domestic Product	1021.2	1840.8	2452.5	2800.2	3558.8	3878.0	4278.9	4373.7	4565.5	4901.1	5145.1	5317.4

a) For 1970-1979, item 'Statistical discrepancy' refers to the services rendered to the area of the Panama Canal. Beginning 1980, the Treaty Torrijos-Carter was inforced, therefore all the activities of the area of the Panama Canal have been incorporated to the corresponding type of economic activity.

b) Beginning 1980, item 'Statistical discrepancy' refers to transport services sold by a resident enterprise 'Commission del Canal de Panama'. Due to the special characteristics of this enterprise it has been separated from the rest to facilitate the analysis of the estimates.

1.11 Gross Domestic Product by Kind of Activity, in Constant Prices

Million Panamanian balboas

		1970	1975	1978	1979	1980	1981	1982	1983	1984	1985	1986	1987
						At constant prices of:1970							
1	Agriculture, hunting, forestry and fishing	149.1	158.6	189.1	181.0	173.7	188.1	185.2	191.0	194.2	203.9	199.4	214.9
2	Mining and quarrying	1.9	2.5	2.2	2.4	3.1	3.8	4.1	3.4	2.6	2.4	2.5	2.7
3	Manufacturing	127.3	147.0	154.9	172.0	182.1	176.1	179.9	176.7	175.8	179.3	183.3	189.5
4	Electricity, gas and water	21.8	38.3	46.7	52.4	53.5	56.2	59.2	64.9	64.2	69.2	73.3	78.3
5	Construction	68.2	96.9	102.5	102.4	124.3	128.3	154.7	106.4	87.9	87.9	94.5	92.3
6	Wholesale and retail trade, restaurants and hotels	161.0	191.0	219.6	240.9	256.4	252.9	251.0	239.4	240.4	251.4	255.4	243.1
7	Transport, storage and communication	61.2	116.0	145.1	155.4	207.6	216.5	251.1	321.1	305.1	335.5	338.8	354.6
8	Finance, insurance, real estate and business services	122.1	178.8	199.7	222.9	227.2	243.5	252.6	262.7	271.9	283.2	301.3	311.5
9	Community, social and personal services	68.2	102.0	118.3	127.8	142.6	150.1	163.3	168.8	176.2	182.4	195.7	200.5
	Statistical discrepancy [a,b]	75.0	74.7	74.3	76.4	175.5	188.4	204.7	175.0	174.6	177.0	186.0	187.7

Panama

1.11 Gross Domestic Product by Kind of Activity, in Constant Prices
(Continued)

Million Panamanian balboas

	1970	1975	1978	1979	1980	1981	1982	1983	1984	1985	1986	1987
					At constant prices of:1970							
Total, Industries	855.8	1105.8	1252.4	1333.6	1546.0	1603.9	1705.8	1709.4	1692.9	1772.2	1830.2	1875.1
Producers of Government Services	117.8	169.9	187.6	196.5	201.2	222.9	232.1	240.6	248.3	258.7	265.2	272.4
Other Producers	21.3	19.2	17.6	16.3	17.7	18.5	19.3	19.4	21.5	21.9	22.5	23.2
Subtotal	994.9	1294.9	1457.6	1546.4	1764.9	1845.3	1957.2	1969.4	1962.7	2052.8	2117.9	2170.7
Less: Imputed bank service charge	10.6	30.1	33.3	56.4	47.2	54.2	68.2	76.4	78.5	80.5	84.2	85.7
Plus: Import duties	36.9	20.9	26.5	26.3	28.1	27.7	29.6	32.7	33.4	36.1	42.3	41.1
Plus: Value added tax	...	...	...	...	...	...	...	...	...	...	...	...
Equals: Gross Domestic Product	1021.2	1285.7	1450.8	1516.3	1745.8	1818.8	1918.6	1925.7	1917.6	2008.4	2076.0	2126.1

a) For 1970-1979, item 'Statistical discrepancy' refers to the services rendered to the area of the Panama Canal. Beginning 1980, the Treaty Torrijos-Carter was inforced, therefore all the activities of the area of the Panama Canal have been incorporated to the corresponding type of economic activity.

b) Beginning 1980, item 'Statistical discrepancy' refers to transport services sold by a resident enterprise 'Commission del Canal de Panama'. Due to the special characteristics of this enterprise it has been separated from the rest to facilitate the analysis of the estimates.

1.12 Relations Among National Accounting Aggregates

Million Panamanian balboas

	1970	1975	1978	1979	1980	1981	1982	1983	1984	1985	1986	1987
Gross Domestic Product	1021.2	1840.8	2452.5	2800.2	3558.8	3878.0	4278.9	4373.7	4565.5	4901.1	5145.1	5317.4
Plus: Net factor income from the rest of the world	-26.5	-19.5	-57.4	-102.8	-110.0	-78.6	-138.9	2.2	-123.6	-46.4	-43.7	-76.0
Factor income from the rest of the world	14.5	376.6	797.0	1449.8	2650.6	3431.9	3654.6	2830.0	2497.3	2087.6	1826.3	1433.6
Less: Factor income to the rest of the world	41.0	396.1	854.4	1552.6	2760.6	3510.5	3793.5	2827.8	2620.9	2134.0	1870.0	1509.6
Equals: Gross National Product	994.7	1821.3	2395.1	2697.4	3448.8	3799.4	4140.0	4375.9	4441.9	4854.7	5101.4	5241.4
Less: Consumption of fixed capital	53.0	91.8	134.9	157.3	252.1	279.7	320.9	335.5	374.6	398.8	424.4	438.6
Equals: National Income	941.7	1729.5	2260.2	2540.1	3196.7	3519.7	3819.1	4040.4	4067.3	4455.9	4677.0	4802.8
Plus: Net current transfers from the rest of the world	-1.8	-15.8	-18.3	-4.4	14.3	31.2	36.0	39.8	89.6	108.7	95.7	82.7
Current transfers from the rest of the world	17.3	23.7	36.4	57.0	72.4	86.0	99.9	110.2	150.9	147.7	128.9	123.0
Less: Current transfers to the rest of the world	19.1	39.5	54.7	61.4	58.1	54.8	63.9	70.4	61.3	39.0	33.2	40.3
Equals: National Disposable Income	939.9	1713.7	2241.9	2535.7	3211.0	3550.9	3855.1	4080.2	4156.9	4564.6	4772.7	4885.5
Less: Final consumption	771.1	1407.4	1914.6	2261.0	2690.0	2920.3	3274.1	3421.5	3879.3	4123.8	4098.7	4284.4
Equals: Net Saving	168.8	306.3	327.3	274.7	521.0	630.6	581.0	658.7	277.6	440.8	674.0	601.1
Less: Surplus of the nation on current transactions	-62.5	-169.3	-189.5	-353.7	-213.8	-256.9	-282.7	60.1	-108.8	86.6	239.2	99.9
Equals: Net Capital Formation	231.3	475.6	516.8	628.4	734.8	887.5	863.7	598.6	386.4	354.2	434.8	501.2

2.1 Government Final Consumption Expenditure by Function, in Current Prices

Million Panamanian balboas

	1970	1975	1978	1979	1980	1981	1982	1983	1984	1985	1986	1987
1 General public services	45.2	122.6	184.3	217.2	275.3	372.8	445.7	348.0	351.5	323.5	402.5	480.9
2 Defence												
3 Public order and safety	...	...	...	...	...	...	...	...	...	...	...	...
4 Education	44.9	91.3	114.9	133.6	157.0	174.8	191.3	211.2	232.3	258.5	260.1	270.5
5 Health	16.7	27.1	40.0	49.6	54.9	57.5	74.0	72.9	77.6	78.8	94.8	101.3
6 Social security and welfare	21.1	52.3	78.4	81.6	101.8	116.2	133.9	173.6	211.3	217.0	222.6	226.8
7 Housing and community amenities	3.5	12.5	14.5	17.8	14.8	12.2	16.6	21.3	27.8	28.8	25.6	28.1
8 Recreational, cultural and religious affairs	5.0	6.2	6.3	7.7	13.2	19.1	25.4	22.4	25.9	22.9	25.8	38.7
9 Economic services	14.8	31.6	33.7	46.7	63.5	60.3	75.7	92.1	74.9	114.0	96.3	84.8
10 Other functions	1.1	9.7	10.8	13.0	-	-	-	-	-	0.1	0.1	0.1
Total Government Final Consumption Expenditure	152.3	353.3	482.9	567.2	680.5	812.9	962.6	941.5	1001.3	1043.6	1127.8	1231.2

Panama

2.2 Government Final Consumption Expenditure by Function, in Constant Prices

Million Panamanian balboas

	1970	1975	1978	1979	1980	1981	1982	1983	1984	1985	1986	1987
					At constant prices of:1970							
1 General public services	45.2	78.7	97.9	100.9	115.2	153.7	169.3	127.1	122.3	109.7	137.1	148.9
2 Defence												
3 Public order and safety	...	...	...	...	...	...	...	...	...	...	...	...
4 Education	44.9	63.1	64.4	65.1	65.7	72.0	72.6	77.1	80.8	87.7	88.6	107.6
5 Health	16.7	18.0	21.6	23.4	23.0	23.6	28.1	26.6	27.0	26.7	32.3	31.3
6 Social security and welfare	21.1	34.6	41.9	38.7	42.6	47.9	50.9	63.4	73.5	73.6	75.8	70.2
7 Housing and community amenities	3.5	8.5	7.9	8.6	6.2	5.0	6.3	7.8	9.7	9.8	8.7	8.7
8 Recreational, cultural and religious affairs	5.0	4.1	3.5	3.6	5.5	7.9	9.6	8.2	9.0	7.8	8.8	12.0
9 Economic services	14.8	20.6	18.2	22.4	26.6	24.8	28.7	33.6	26.1	38.7	32.8	26.2
10 Other functions	1.1	6.7	6.1	6.4	-	-	-	-	-	-	-	-
Total Government Final Consumption Expenditure	152.3	234.3	261.5	269.1	284.8	334.9	365.5	343.8	348.4	354.0	384.1	404.9

2.7 Gross Capital Formation by Type of Good and Owner, in Current Prices

Million Panamanian balboas

	1980				1981				1982			
	TOTAL	Total Private	Public Enterprises	General Government	TOTAL	Total Private	Public Enterprises	General Government	TOTAL	Total Private	Public Enterprises	General Government
Increase in stocks, total	120.5	93.3	27.2	...	87.6	84.0	3.6	...	-0.8	-14.5	13.7	...
1 Goods producing industries	64.1	...	...	...	84.0	...	...	...	7.3	...	...	...
2 Wholesale and retail trade	53.6	...	...	...	-0.2	...	...	...	-5.6	...	...	...
3 Other, except government stocks	...	...	...	...	...	...	...	...	...	...	...	...
4 Government stocks	2.8	...	...	...	3.8	...	...	...	-2.5	...	...	...
Gross Fixed Capital Formation, Total	866.4	513.8	352.6	...	1079.6	733.3	346.3	...	1185.4	712.5	472.9	...
1 Residential buildings	93.3	78.1	15.2	...	117.4	99.8	17.6	...	121.7	103.2	18.5	...
2 Non-residential buildings	219.7	199.2	20.5	...	225.8	204.8	21.0	...	236.0	187.5	48.5	...
3 Other construction	251.4	33.6	217.8	...	339.0	126.3	212.7	...	493.6	237.5	256.1	...
4 Land improvement and plantation and orchard development	...	...	...	...	...	...	...	...	...	...	...	...
5 Producers' durable goods	302.0	202.9	99.1	...	397.4	302.4	95.0	...	334.1	184.3	149.8	...
A Transport equipment	113.3	88.2	25.1	...	133.7	99.9	33.8	...	129.3	92.0	37.3	...
B Machinery and equipment	188.7	114.7	74.0	...	263.7	202.5	61.2	...	204.8	92.3	112.5	...
6 Breeding stock, dairy cattle, etc.	...	...	...	...	...	...	...	...	...	...	...	...
Total Gross Capital Formation	986.9	607.1	379.8	...	1167.2	817.3	349.9	...	1184.6	698.0	486.6	...

	1983				1984				1985			
	TOTAL	Total Private	Public Enterprises	General Government	TOTAL	Total Private	Public Enterprises	General Government	TOTAL	Total Private	Public Enterprises	General Government
Increase in stocks, total	16.3	-3.8	20.1	...	-18.9	0.7	-19.6	...	-20.1	-12.8	-7.3	...
1 Goods producing industries	-2.7	...	...	...	-24.7	...	...	...	-8.9	...	...	...
2 Wholesale and retail trade	0.5	...	...	...	0.4	...	...	...	-3.5	...	...	...
3 Other, except government stocks	...	...	...	...	...	...	...	...	...	...	...	...
4 Government stocks	18.5	...	...	...	5.4	...	...	...	-7.7	...	...	...
Gross Fixed Capital Formation, Total	917.8	604.8	313.0	...	779.9	497.5	282.4	...	773.1	586.1	187.0	...
1 Residential buildings	119.7	108.8	10.9	...	128.9	111.8	17.1	...	182.3	163.9	18.4	...
2 Non-residential buildings	221.9	202.3	19.6	...	145.3	118.8	26.5	...	170.8	146.8	24.0	...
3 Other construction	272.4	62.3	210.1	...	225.7	38.6	187.1	...	125.2	45.9	79.3	...
4 Land improvement and plantation and orchard development	...	...	...	...	...	...	...	...	...	...	...	...
5 Producers' durable goods	303.8	231.4	72.4	...	280.0	228.3	51.7	...	294.8	229.5	65.3	...
A Transport equipment	103.4	77.7	25.7	...	105.4	89.3	16.1	...	117.6	94.1	23.5	...
B Machinery and equipment	200.4	153.7	46.7	...	174.6	139.0	35.6	...	177.2	135.4	41.8	...
6 Breeding stock, dairy cattle, etc.	...	...	...	...	...	...	...	...	...	...	...	...
Total Gross Capital Formation	934.1	601.0	333.1	...	761.0	498.2	262.8	...	753.0	573.3	179.7	...

Panama

2.7 Gross Capital Formation by Type of Good and Owner, in Current Prices

Million Panamanian balboas

	1986 TOTAL	1986 Total Private	1986 Public Enterprises	1986 General Government	1987 TOTAL	1987 Total Private	1987 Public Enterprises	1987 General Government
Increase in stocks, total	-37.5	-28.9	-8.6	...	0.5	-6.3	6.8	...
1 Goods producing industries	-49.5	...	...	...	7.0	...	...	...
2 Wholesale and retail trade	19.6	...	...	...	-12.7	...	...	...
3 Other, except government stocks	...	...	...	...	...	...	...	...
4 Government stocks	-7.6	...	...	...	6.2	...	...	...
Gross Fixed Capital Formation, Total	896.7	715.4	181.3	...	939.3	797.3	142.0	...
1 Residential buildings	207.0	191.8	15.2	...	215.4	211.3	4.1	...
2 Non-residential buildings	188.1	169.5	18.6	...	220.4	204.5	15.9	...
3 Other construction	147.7	53.6	94.1	...	106.9	60.9	46.0	...
4 Land improvement and plantation and orchard development	...	...	...	...	...	...	...	...
5 Producers' durable goods	353.9	300.5	53.4	...	396.6	320.6	76.0	...
A Transport equipment	140.1	125.9	14.2	...	159.1	120.6	38.5	...
B Machinery and equipment	213.8	174.6	39.2	...	237.5	200.0	37.5	...
6 Breeding stock, dairy cattle, etc.	...	...	...	...	...	...	...	...
Total Gross Capital Formation	859.2	686.5	172.7	...	939.8	791.0	148.8	...

2.8 Gross Capital Formation by Type of Good and Owner, in Constant Prices

Million Panamanian balboas

At constant prices of: 1970

	1980 TOTAL	1980 Total Private	1980 Public Enterprises	1980 General Government	1981 TOTAL	1981 Total Private	1981 Public Enterprises	1981 General Government	1982 TOTAL	1982 Total Private	1982 Public Enterprises	1982 General Government
Increase in stocks, total	46.3	34.0	12.3	...	37.3	37.6	-0.3	...	0.5	-2.0	2.5	...
1 Goods producing industries	22.9	...	...	...	36.2	...	...	...	3.4	...	...	...
2 Wholesale and retail trade	21.5	...	...	...	-0.5	...	...	...	-1.0	...	...	...
3 Other, except government stocks	...	...	...	...	...	...	...	...	...	...	...	...
4 Government stocks	1.9	...	...	...	1.6	...	...	...	-1.9	...	...	...
Gross Fixed Capital Formation, Total	365.3	215.3	150.0	...	426.1	292.1	134.0	...	430.1	258.5	171.6	...
1 Residential buildings	37.0	30.9	6.1	...	42.8	36.4	6.4	...	41.4	35.1	6.3	...
2 Non-residential buildings	87.2	79.1	8.1	...	82.3	74.6	7.7	...	80.2	63.7	16.5	...
3 Other construction	99.8	13.4	86.4	...	123.5	46.0	77.5	...	167.7	80.7	87.0	...
4 Land improvement and plantation and orchard development	...	...	...	...	...	...	...	...	...	...	...	...
5 Producers' durable goods	141.3	91.9	49.4	...	177.5	135.1	42.4	...	140.8	79.0	61.8	...
A Transport equipment	35.3	27.5	7.8	...	60.7	45.4	15.3	...	54.4	39.8	14.6	...
B Machinery and equipment	106.0	64.4	41.6	...	116.8	89.7	27.1	...	86.4	39.2	47.2	...
6 Breeding stock, dairy cattle, etc.	...	...	...	...	...	...	...	...	...	...	...	...
Total Gross Capital Formation	411.6	249.3	162.3	...	463.4	329.7	133.7	...	430.6	256.5	174.1	...

At constant prices of: 1970

	1983 TOTAL	1983 Total Private	1983 Public Enterprises	1983 General Government	1984 TOTAL	1984 Total Private	1984 Public Enterprises	1984 General Government	1985 TOTAL	1985 Total Private	1985 Public Enterprises	1985 General Government
Increase in stocks, total	7.9	-2.9	10.8	...	-6.9	0.4	-7.3	...	-7.5	-1.9	-5.6	...
1 Goods producing industries	-0.4	...	...	...	-5.6	...	...	...	-2.5	...	...	...
2 Wholesale and retail trade	-1.7	...	...	...	1.5	...	...	...	-1.0	...	...	...
3 Other, except government stocks	...	...	...	...	...	...	...	...	...	...	...	...
4 Government stocks	10.0	...	...	...	-2.8	...	...	...	-4.0	...	...	...
Gross Fixed Capital Formation, Total	333.0	222.5	110.5	...	310.2	214.7	95.5	...	331.4	252.9	78.5	...
1 Residential buildings	39.6	36.0	3.6	...	43.1	37.4	5.7	...	60.8	54.7	6.1	...
2 Non-residential buildings	73.4	66.9	6.5	...	48.6	39.7	8.9	...	57.0	49.0	8.0	...

Panama

2.8 Gross Capital Formation by Type of Good and Owner, in Constant Prices
(Continued)

Million Panamanian balboas

	1983 TOTAL	1983 Total Private	1983 Public Enterprises	1983 General Government	1984 TOTAL	1984 Total Private	1984 Public Enterprises	1984 General Government	1985 TOTAL	1985 Total Private	1985 Public Enterprises	1985 General Government
					At constant prices of:1970							
3 Other construction	90.1	20.6	69.5	...	75.4	13.0	62.4	...	41.8	15.3	26.5	...
4 Land improvement and plantation and orchard development	...	...	...	...	...	...	...	...	...	...	...	...
5 Producers' durable goods	129.9	99.0	30.9	...	143.1	124.6	18.5	...	171.8	133.9	37.9	...
A Transport equipment	43.2	32.5	10.7	...	49.0	43.2	5.8	...	73.4	58.7	14.7	...
B Machinery and equipment	86.7	66.5	20.2	...	94.1	81.4	12.7	...	98.4	75.2	23.2	...
6 Breeding stock, dairy cattle, etc.	...	...	...	...	...	...	...	...	...	...	...	...
Total Gross Capital Formation	340.9	219.6	121.3	...	303.3	215.1	88.2	...	323.9	251.0	72.9	...

	1986 TOTAL	1986 Total Private	1986 Public Enterprises	1986 General Government	1987 TOTAL	1987 Total Private	1987 Public Enterprises	1987 General Government
				At constant prices of:1970				
Increase in stocks, total	-11.7	-7.7	-4.0	...	-0.9	-3.9	3.0	...
1 Goods producing industries	-14.6	...	...	...	1.1	...	...	...
2 Wholesale and retail trade	6.6	...	...	...	-4.8	...	...	...
3 Other, except government stocks	...	...	...	...	...	...	...	...
4 Government stocks	-3.7	...	...	...	2.8	...	...	...
Gross Fixed Capital Formation, Total	363.5	294.1	69.4	...	365.0	306.7	58.3	...
1 Residential buildings	66.7	61.8	4.9	...	68.1	66.8	1.3	...
2 Non-residential buildings	60.6	54.6	6.0	...	69.7	64.7	5.0	...
3 Other construction	47.6	17.3	30.3	...	33.8	19.2	14.6	...
4 Land improvement and plantation and orchard development	...	...	...	...	...	...	...	...
5 Producers' durable goods	188.6	160.4	28.2	...	193.4	156.0	37.4	...
A Transport equipment	77.6	69.7	7.9	...	82.3	62.4	19.9	...
B Machinery and equipment	111.0	90.7	20.3	...	111.1	93.6	17.5	...
6 Breeding stock, dairy cattle, etc.	...	...	...	...	...	...	...	...
Total Gross Capital Formation	351.8	286.4	65.4	...	364.1	302.8	61.3	...

2.17 Exports and Imports of Goods and Services, Detail

Million Panamanian balboas

	1970	1975	1978	1979	1980	1981	1982	1983	1984	1985	1986	1987
Exports of Goods and Services												
1 Exports of merchandise, f.o.b.	158.3	466.0	387.4	451.8	525.5	495.0	488.8	426.5	368.2	393.4	400.4	417.7
2 Transport and communication	3.0	15.9	20.6	26.5	408.0	440.3	532.9	640.8	602.0	645.6	622.8	609.6
3 Insurance service charges	0.3	0.6	1.7	2.1	2.1	2.3	2.1	1.4	1.6	2.7	1.5	2.3
4 Other commodities	59.2	125.7	217.4	246.6	366.6	413.9	380.1	351.4	341.9	343.8	418.6	369.8
5 Adjustments of merchandise exports to change-of-ownership basis	...	...	...	...	...	...	...	...	...	...	...	...
6 Direct purchases in the domestic market by non-residential households	84.0	142.4	209.1	222.7	219.8	232.8	235.8	240.8	249.6	284.2	283.6	265.9
7 Direct purchases in the domestic market by extraterritorial bodies [a]	8.3	9.9	8.7	15.6	45.1	47.7	49.9	48.6	58.8	65.5	59.6	76.5
Statistical discrepancy	75.1	104.9	141.5	159.5	-	-	-	-	-	-	...	...
Total Exports of Goods and Services	388.2	865.4	986.4	1124.8	1567.1	1632.0	1689.6	1709.5	1622.1	1735.2	1786.5	1741.8
Imports of Goods and Services												
1 Imports of merchandise, c.i.f.	363.5	906.1	966.4	1218.5	1483.9	1620.0	1636.9	1474.4	1468.3	1451.0	1323.7	1371.8

Panama

2.17 Exports and Imports of Goods and Services, Detail
(Continued)

Million Panamanian balboas

	1970	1975	1978	1979	1980	1981	1982	1983	1984	1985	1986	1987
A Imports of merchandise, f.o.b.	331.4	827.2	866.6	1095.2	1327.0	1453.0	1477.3	1329.5	1314.6	1301.5	1152.0	1220.9
B Transport of services on merchandise imports	30.4	75.7	92.4	114.1	149.3	161.2	154.4	139.7	147.5	146.7	168.0	146.6
C Insurance service charges on merchandise imports	1.7	3.2	7.4	9.2	7.6	5.8	5.2	5.2	6.2	2.8	3.7	4.3
2 Adjustments of merchandise imports to change-of-ownership basis	...	...	...	...	...	...	...	...	...	...	...	...
3 Other transport and communication	12.9	17.0	22.4	26.1	42.4	46.8	45.8	46.0	59.8	58.8	67.0	72.8
4 Other insurance service charges	5.4	7.9	11.4	12.5	13.0	17.1	20.8	19.7	19.4	30.3	31.9	36.4
5 Other commodities	8.5	25.1	33.9	40.9	66.7	64.0	48.1	38.1	41.8	56.1	50.2	31.8
6 Direct purchases abroad by government	5.9	7.3	15.4	12.1	15.3	16.4	20.9	23.4	20.9	24.9	27.3	19.9
7 Direct purchases abroad by resident households	26.2	36.0	50.7	61.2	63.9	77.2	96.9	89.8	86.7	89.8	99.2	115.9
Total Imports of Goods and Services	422.4	999.4	1100.2	1371.3	1685.2	1841.5	1869.4	1691.4	1696.9	1710.9	1599.3	1648.6
Balance of Goods and Services	-34.2	-134.0	-113.8	-246.5	-118.1	-209.5	-179.8	18.1	-74.8	24.3	187.2	93.2
Total Imports and Balance of Goods and Services	388.2	865.4	986.4	1124.8	1567.1	1632.0	1689.6	1709.5	1622.1	1735.2	1786.5	1741.8

a) Item 'Direct purchases in the domestic market by extra-territorial bodies' relates to compensation of employees and property and entrepreneurial income received by residents of Panama for services rendered in the Former Canal Zone and Colon Free Zone.

4.1 Derivation of Value Added by Kind of Activity, in Current Prices

Million Panamanian balboas

	1980 Gross Output	1980 Intermediate Consumption	1980 Value Added	1981 Gross Output	1981 Intermediate Consumption	1981 Value Added	1982 Gross Output	1982 Intermediate Consumption	1982 Value Added	1983 Gross Output	1983 Intermediate Consumption	1983 Value Added
All Producers												
1 Agriculture, hunting, forestry and fishing	...	...	320.4	...	...	359.3	...	...	371.2	...	...	408.4
A Agriculture and hunting	...	...	272.6	...	...	318.3	...	...	323.7	...	...	357.2
B Forestry and logging	...	...	8.7	...	...	8.9	...	...	9.9	...	...	11.8
C Fishing	...	...	39.1	...	...	32.1	...	...	37.6	...	...	39.4
2 Mining and quarrying	...	...	6.8	...	...	8.7	...	...	9.3	...	...	7.9
3 Manufacturing	...	...	356.0	...	...	375.6	...	...	394.0	...	...	401.0
A Manufacture of food, beverages and tobacco	...	...	143.2	...	...	155.6	...	...	160.3	...	...	169.0
B Textile, wearing apparel and leather industries	...	...	44.1	...	...	44.8	...	...	46.1	...	...	45.2
C Manufacture of wood and wood products, including furniture	...	...	14.8	...	...	16.2	...	...	17.8	...	...	18.2
D Manufacture of paper and paper products, printing and publishing	...	...	27.1	...	...	26.5	...	...	27.1	...	...	30.1
E Manufacture of chemicals and chemical petroleum, coal, rubber and plastic products	...	...	69.7	...	...	72.3	...	...	76.4	...	...	76.3
F Manufacture of non-metallic mineral products, except products of petroleum and coal	...	...	30.6	...	...	33.5	...	...	36.8	...	...	33.6
G Basic metal industries	...	...	6.1	...	...	6.3	...	...	6.0	...	...	4.1
H Manufacture of fabricated metal products, machinery and equipment	...	...	19.4	...	...	19.6	...	...	22.6	...	...	23.0
I Other manufacturing industries	...	...	1.0	...	...	0.8	...	...	0.9	...	...	1.5
4 Electricity, gas and water	...	...	113.8	...	...	142.4	...	...	152.6	...	...	153.5
A Electricity, gas and steam	...	...	101.6	...	...	131.0	...	...	134.1	...	...	133.8
B Water works and supply	...	...	12.2	...	...	11.4	...	...	18.5	...	...	19.7
5 Construction	...	...	258.4	...	...	295.2	...	...	378.4	...	...	271.5
6 Wholesale and retail trade, restaurants and hotels	...	...	618.2	...	...	667.6	...	...	681.3	...	...	647.5
A Wholesale and retail trade	...	...	544.4	...	...	592.1	...	...	602.2	...	...	574.3
B Restaurants and hotels	...	...	73.8	...	...	75.5	...	...	79.1	...	...	73.2
7 Transport, storage and communication	...	...	408.2	...	...	427.4	...	...	497.0	...	...	601.1
A Transport and storage	...	...	352.8	...	...	356.3	...	...	413.9	...	...	509.5

Panama

4.1 Derivation of Value Added by Kind of Activity, in Current Prices
(Continued)

Million Panamanian balboas

	1980 Gross Output	1980 Intermediate Consumption	1980 Value Added	1981 Gross Output	1981 Intermediate Consumption	1981 Value Added	1982 Gross Output	1982 Intermediate Consumption	1982 Value Added	1983 Gross Output	1983 Intermediate Consumption	1983 Value Added
B Communication	...	...	55.4	...	...	71.1	...	...	83.1	...	...	91.6
8 Finance, insurance, real estate and business services	...	...	503.2	...	...	587.4	...	...	663.7	...	...	725.0
A Financial institutions	...	...	166.3	...	...	203.5	...	...	226.8	...	...	242.3
B Insurance	...	...	24.5	...	...	30.1	...	...	34.5	...	...	37.5
C Real estate and business services	...	...	312.4	...	...	353.8	...	...	402.4	...	...	445.2
Real estate, except dwellings	...	...	13.3	...	...	16.3	...	...	18.0	...	...	20.1
Dwellings	...	...	247.9	...	...	278.4	...	...	319.1	...	...	359.1
9 Community, social and personal services	...	...	246.9	...	...	273.1	...	...	344.0	...	...	358.5
A Sanitary and similar services	...	...	17.5	...	...	16.5	...	...	20.8	...	...	20.5
B Social and related community services	...	...	64.6	...	...	74.5	...	...	94.9	...	...	101.9
Educational services	...	...	16.3	...	...	17.2	...	...	22.1	...	...	22.5
Medical, dental, other health and veterinary services	...	...	48.3	...	...	57.3	...	...	72.8	...	...	79.4
C Recreational and cultural services	...	...	102.7	...	...	111.0	...	...	133.7	...	...	135.5
D Personal and household services	...	...	62.1	...	...	71.1	...	...	94.6	...	...	100.6
Statistical discrepancy [ab]	...	...	312.4	...	...	330.5	...	...	353.3	...	...	321.1
Total, Industries	...	...	3144.3	...	...	3467.2	...	...	3844.8	...	...	3895.5
Producers of Government Services	...	...	446.4	...	...	468.5	...	...	534.2	...	...	595.1
Other Producers	...	...	37.2	...	...	42.4	...	...	46.2	...	...	50.7
Total	...	...	3627.9	...	...	3978.1	...	...	4425.2	...	...	4541.3
Less: Imputed bank service charge	...	...	147.5	...	...	183.7	...	...	237.4	...	...	263.9
Import duties	...	...	78.4	...	...	83.6	...	...	91.1	...	...	96.3
Value added tax	...	...	...	...	...	...	...	...	...	...	...	...
Total	...	...	3558.8	...	...	3878.0	...	...	4278.9	...	...	4373.7

	1984 Gross Output	1984 Intermediate Consumption	1984 Value Added	1985 Gross Output	1985 Intermediate Consumption	1985 Value Added	1986 Gross Output	1986 Intermediate Consumption	1986 Value Added	1987 Gross Output	1987 Intermediate Consumption	1987 Value Added
						All Producers						
1 Agriculture, hunting, forestry and fishing	...	...	415.9	...	...	450.6	...	...	478.6	...	...	508.6
A Agriculture and hunting	...	...	366.1	...	...	393.0	...	...	383.9	...	...	419.2
B Forestry and logging	...	...	12.2	...	...	12.3	...	...	12.3	...	...	12.7
C Fishing	...	...	37.6	...	...	45.3	...	...	82.4	...	...	76.7
2 Mining and quarrying	...	...	6.0	...	...	5.7	...	...	6.0	...	...	7.3
3 Manufacturing	...	...	411.0	...	...	420.0	...	...	421.8	...	...	440.8
A Manufacture of food, beverages and tobacco	...	...	175.5	...	...	188.6	...	...	197.8	...	...	202.0
B Textile, wearing apparel and leather industries	...	...	47.0	...	...	48.6	...	...	47.3	...	...	47.8
C Manufacture of wood and wood products, including furniture	...	...	21.4	...	...	21.7	...	...	21.2	...	...	19.9
D Manufacture of paper and paper products, printing and publishing	...	...	32.1	...	...	34.9	...	...	34.3	...	...	35.0
E Manufacture of chemicals and chemical petroleum, coal, rubber and plastic products	...	...	76.5	...	...	69.8	...	...	60.2	...	...	67.8
F Manufacture of non-metallic mineral products, except products of petroleum and coal	...	...	27.6	...	...	26.9	...	...	31.0	...	...	33.5
G Basic metal industries	...	...	3.9	...	...	4.3	...	...	4.7	...	...	6.1
H Manufacture of fabricated metal products, machinery and equipment	...	...	24.1	...	...	22.4	...	...	22.0	...	...	25.3
I Other manufacturing industries	...	...	2.9	...	...	2.8	...	...	3.3	...	...	3.4
4 Electricity, gas and water	...	...	194.9	...	...	212.1	...	...	227.6	...	...	227.8
A Electricity, gas and steam	...	...	176.0	...	...	194.5	...	...	206.6	...	...	208.6
B Water works and supply	...	...	18.9	...	...	17.6	...	...	21.0	...	...	19.2

Panama

4.1 Derivation of Value Added by Kind of Activity, in Current Prices
(Continued)

Million Panamanian balboas

	1984 Gross Output	1984 Intermediate Consumption	1984 Value Added	1985 Gross Output	1985 Intermediate Consumption	1985 Value Added	1986 Gross Output	1986 Intermediate Consumption	1986 Value Added	1987 Gross Output	1987 Intermediate Consumption	1987 Value Added
5 Construction	...	...	225.0	...	...	229.8	...	...	260.0	...	...	262.4
6 Wholesale and retail trade, restaurants and hotels	...	...	655.4	...	...	693.5	...	...	707.1	...	...	679.8
A Wholesale and retail trade	...	...	575.1	...	...	604.0	...	...	615.2	...	...	593.4
B Restaurants and hotels	...	...	80.3	...	...	89.5	...	...	91.9	...	...	86.4
7 Transport, storage and communication	...	...	590.6	...	...	640.8	...	...	651.7	...	...	665.0
A Transport and storage	...	...	489.9	...	...	533.7	...	...	529.5	...	...	524.1
B Communication	...	...	100.7	...	...	107.1	...	...	122.2	...	...	140.9
8 Finance, insurance, real estate and business services	...	...	791.3	...	...	886.7	...	...	957.2	...	...	1043.8
A Financial institutions	...	...	255.7	...	...	278.3	...	...	308.3	...	...	317.1
B Insurance	...	...	40.2	...	...	41.0	...	...	43.8	...	...	44.0
C Real estate and business services	...	...	495.4	...	...	567.4	...	...	605.1	...	...	682.7
Real estate, except dwellings	...	...	21.2	...	...	22.9	...	...	26.0	...	...	29.1
Dwellings	...	...	402.3	...	...	466.7	...	...	496.1	...	...	567.6
9 Community, social and personal services	...	...	379.5	...	...	397.1	...	...	420.7	...	...	436.3
A Sanitary and similar services	...	...	18.5	...	...	17.4	...	...	17.6	...	...	18.0
B Social and related community services	...	...	111.6	...	...	113.9	...	...	115.5	...	...	120.4
Educational services	...	...	20.7	...	...	21.3	...	...	21.9	...	...	22.1
Medical, dental, other health and veterinary services	...	...	90.9	...	...	92.6	...	...	93.6	...	...	98.3
C Recreational and cultural services	...	...	136.7	...	...	141.0	...	...	148.8	...	...	147.5
D Personal and household services	...	...	112.7	...	...	124.8	...	...	138.8	...	...	150.4
Statistical discrepancy [a,b]	...	...	337.7	...	...	342.6	...	...	360.5	...	...	360.4
Total, Industries	...	...	4007.3	...	...	4278.9	...	...	4491.2	...	...	4632.2
Producers of Government Services	...	...	673.7	...	...	731.1	...	...	761.0	...	...	806.7
Other Producers	...	...	56.3	...	...	57.6	...	...	59.7	...	...	61.4
Total	...	...	4737.3	...	...	5067.6	...	...	5311.9	...	...	5500.3
Less: Imputed bank service charge	...	...	280.6	...	...	285.1	...	...	309.4	...	...	318.3
Import duties	...	...	108.8	...	...	118.6	...	...	142.6	...	...	135.4
Value added tax	...	...	...	...	...	...	...	...	...	...	...	...
Total	...	...	4565.5	...	...	4901.1	...	...	5145.1	...	...	5317.4

a) For 1970-1979, item 'Statistical discrepancy' refers to the services rendered to the area of the Panama Canal. Beginning 1980, the Treaty Torrijos-Carter was inforced, therefore all the activities of the area of the Panama Canal have been incorporated to the corresponding type of economic activity.

b) Beginning 1980, item 'Statistical discrepancy' refers to transport services sold by a resident enterprise 'Commission del Canal de Panama'. Due to the special characteristics of this enterprise it has been separated from the rest to facilitate the analysis of the estimates.

4.2 Derivation of Value Added by Kind of Activity, in Constant Prices

Million Panamanian balboas

	1980 Gross Output	1980 Intermediate Consumption	1980 Value Added	1981 Gross Output	1981 Intermediate Consumption	1981 Value Added	1982 Gross Output	1982 Intermediate Consumption	1982 Value Added	1983 Gross Output	1983 Intermediate Consumption	1983 Value Added
					At constant prices of:1970							
					All Producers							
1 Agriculture, hunting, forestry and fishing	...	...	173.7	...	...	188.1	...	...	185.2	...	...	191.0
A Agriculture and hunting	...	...	161.4	...	...	176.4	...	...	173.3	...	...	178.6
B Forestry and logging	...	...	5.0	...	...	4.9	...	...	5.1	...	...	5.5
C Fishing	...	...	7.3	...	...	6.8	...	...	6.8	...	...	6.9
2 Mining and quarrying	...	...	3.1	...	...	3.8	...	...	4.1	...	...	3.4

Panama

4.2 Derivation of Value Added by Kind of Activity, in Constant Prices
(Continued)

Million Panamanian balboas

At constant prices of: 1970

	1980 Gross Output	1980 Intermediate Consumption	1980 Value Added	1981 Gross Output	1981 Intermediate Consumption	1981 Value Added	1982 Gross Output	1982 Intermediate Consumption	1982 Value Added	1983 Gross Output	1983 Intermediate Consumption	1983 Value Added
3 Manufacturing	...	...	182.1	...	...	176.1	...	...	179.9	...	...	176.7
A Manufacture of food, beverages and tobacco	...	...	91.1	...	...	88.9	...	...	91.2	...	...	91.1
B Textile, wearing apparel and leather industries	...	...	22.3	...	...	21.9	...	...	21.1	...	...	16.8
C Manufacture of wood and wood products, including furniture	...	...	6.3	...	...	6.0	...	...	6.0	...	...	5.6
D Manufacture of paper and paper products, printing and publishing	...	...	12.5	...	...	11.0	...	...	11.6	...	...	13.0
E Manufacture of chemicals and chemical petroleum, coal, rubber and plastic products	...	...	23.6	...	...	22.1	...	...	23.2	...	...	24.7
F Manufacture of non-metallic mineral products, except products of petroleum and coal	...	...	13.4	...	...	12.7	...	...	13.3	...	...	12.1
G Basic metal industries	...	...	1.3	...	...	1.2	...	...	1.2	...	...	1.0
H Manufacture of fabricated metal products, machinery and equipment	...	...	10.2	...	...	10.1	...	...	10.5	...	...	9.9
I Other manufacturing industries	...	...	1.4	...	...	2.2	...	...	1.8	...	...	2.5
4 Electricity, gas and water	...	...	53.5	...	...	56.2	...	...	59.2	...	...	64.9
A Electricity, gas and steam	...	...	45.0	...	...	47.5	...	...	50.1	...	...	56.0
B Water works and supply	...	...	8.5	...	...	8.7	...	...	9.1	...	...	8.9
5 Construction	...	...	124.3	...	...	128.3	...	...	154.7	...	...	106.4
6 Wholesale and retail trade, restaurants and hotels	...	...	256.4	...	...	252.9	...	...	251.0	...	...	239.4
A Wholesale and retail trade	...	...	218.9	...	...	217.4	...	...	218.0	...	...	207.6
B Restaurants and hotels	...	...	37.5	...	...	35.5	...	...	33.0	...	...	31.8
7 Transport, storage and communication	...	...	207.6	...	...	216.5	...	...	251.1	...	...	321.1
A Transport and storage	...	...	187.4	...	...	195.0	...	...	228.2	...	...	297.5
B Communication	...	...	20.2	...	...	21.5	...	...	22.9	...	...	23.6
8 Finance, insurance, real estate and business services	...	...	227.2	...	...	243.5	...	...	252.6	...	...	262.7
A Financial institutions	...	...	60.3	...	...	67.1	...	...	70.5	...	...	76.3
B Insurance	...	...	12.3	...	...	14.2	...	...	14.0	...	...	14.3
C Real estate and business services	...	...	154.6	...	...	162.2	...	...	168.1	...	...	172.1
Real estate, except dwellings	...	...	9.0	...	...	11.9	...	...	12.8	...	...	12.9
Dwellings	...	...	121.9	...	...	125.2	...	...	129.2	...	...	102.8
9 Community, social and personal services	...	...	142.6	...	...	150.1	...	...	163.3	...	...	168.8
A Sanitary and similar services	...	...	6.3	...	...	6.3	...	...	6.7	...	...	6.2
B Social and related community services	...	...	31.1	...	...	32.5	...	...	35.6	...	...	36.8
Educational services	...	...	8.3	...	...	7.9	...	...	8.7	...	...	8.6
Medical, dental, other health and veterinary services	...	...	22.8	...	...	24.6	...	...	26.9	...	...	28.2
C Recreational and cultural services	...	...	76.0	...	...	80.1	...	...	86.5	...	...	89.1
D Personal and household services	...	...	29.2	...	...	31.2	...	...	34.5	...	...	36.7
Statistical discrepancy [a,b]	...	...	175.5	...	...	188.4	...	...	204.7	...	...	175.0
Total, Industries	...	...	1546.0	...	...	1603.9	...	...	1705.8	...	...	1709.4
Producers of Government Services	...	...	201.2	...	...	222.9	...	...	232.1	...	...	240.6
Other Producers	...	...	17.7	...	...	18.5	...	...	19.3	...	...	19.4
Total	...	...	1764.9	...	...	1845.3	...	...	1957.2	...	...	1969.4
Less: Imputed bank service charge	...	...	47.2	...	...	54.2	...	...	68.2	...	...	76.4
Import duties	...	...	28.1	...	...	27.7	...	...	29.6	...	...	32.7
Value added tax	...	...	...	...	...	...	...	...	...	...	...	...
Total	...	...	1745.8	...	...	1818.8	...	...	1918.6	...	...	1925.7

Panama

4.2 Derivation of Value Added by Kind of Activity, in Constant Prices

Million Panamanian balboas

	1984 Gross Output	1984 Intermediate Consumption	1984 Value Added	1985 Gross Output	1985 Intermediate Consumption	1985 Value Added	1986 Gross Output	1986 Intermediate Consumption	1986 Value Added	1987 Gross Output	1987 Intermediate Consumption	1987 Value Added
						At constant prices of:1970						
						All Producers						
1 Agriculture, hunting, forestry and fishing	...	...	194.2	...	...	203.9	...	...	199.4	...	...	214.9
A Agriculture and hunting	...	...	182.0	...	...	188.9	...	...	180.7	...	...	197.4
B Forestry and logging	...	...	5.6	...	...	5.6	...	...	5.5	...	...	5.3
C Fishing	...	...	6.6	...	...	9.4	...	...	13.2	...	...	12.2
2 Mining and quarrying	...	...	2.6	...	...	2.4	...	...	2.5	...	...	2.7
3 Manufacturing	...	...	175.8	...	...	179.3	...	...	183.3	...	...	189.5
A Manufacture of food, beverages and tobacco	...	...	90.4	...	...	93.7	...	...	95.4	...	...	96.4
B Textile, wearing apparel and leather industries	...	...	18.2	...	...	18.6	...	...	18.8	...	...	18.8
C Manufacture of wood and wood products, including furniture	...	...	6.0	...	...	6.2	...	...	6.4	...	...	5.7
D Manufacture of paper and paper products, printing and publishing	...	...	13.1	...	...	14.0	...	...	13.3	...	...	13.9
E Manufacture of chemicals and chemical petroleum, coal, rubber and plastic products	...	...	24.6	...	...	24.2	...	...	24.5	...	...	27.5
F Manufacture of non-metallic mineral products, except products of petroleum and coal	...	...	10.5	...	...	10.1	...	...	11.7	...	...	12.6
G Basic metal industries	...	...	0.9	...	...	1.1	...	...	1.3	...	...	1.7
H Manufacture of fabricated metal products, machinery and equipment	...	...	9.6	...	...	8.9	...	...	9.0	...	...	10.2
I Other manufacturing industries	...	...	2.5	...	...	2.5	...	...	2.9	...	...	2.7
4 Electricity, gas and water	...	...	64.2	...	...	69.2	...	...	73.3	...	...	78.3
A Electricity, gas and steam	...	...	55.1	...	...	59.7	...	...	63.4	...	...	68.0
B Water works and supply	...	...	9.1	...	...	9.5	...	...	9.9	...	...	10.3
5 Construction	...	...	87.9	...	...	87.9	...	...	94.5	...	...	92.3
6 Wholesale and retail trade, restaurants and hotels	...	...	240.4	...	...	251.4	...	...	255.4	...	...	243.1
A Wholesale and retail trade	...	...	206.7	...	...	215.9	...	...	219.6	...	...	209.1
B Restaurants and hotels	...	...	33.7	...	...	35.5	...	...	35.8	...	...	34.0
7 Transport, storage and communication	...	...	305.1	...	...	335.5	...	...	338.8	...	...	354.6
A Transport and storage	...	...	280.3	...	...	309.5	...	...	311.8	...	...	326.7
B Communication	...	...	24.8	...	...	26.0	...	...	27.0	...	...	27.9
8 Finance, insurance, real estate and business services	...	...	271.9	...	...	283.2	...	...	301.3	...	...	311.5
A Financial institutions	...	...	79.7	...	...	83.6	...	...	91.4	...	...	93.7
B Insurance	...	...	14.3	...	...	15.0	...	...	17.1	...	...	16.5
C Real estate and business services	...	...	177.9	...	...	184.6	...	...	192.8	...	...	201.3
Real estate, except dwellings	...	...	12.9	...	...	13.2	...	...	14.8	...	...	16.1
Dwellings	...	...	136.4	...	...	140.3	...	...	145.7	...	...	151.8
9 Community, social and personal services	...	...	176.2	...	...	182.4	...	...	195.7	...	...	200.5
A Sanitary and similar services	...	...	5.4	...	...	4.9	...	...	4.9	...	...	5.0
B Social and related community services	...	...	40.4	...	...	41.5	...	...	43.9	...	...	45.1
Educational services	...	...	8.6	...	...	8.6	...	...	8.8	...	...	8.9
Medical, dental, other health and veterinary services	...	...	31.8	...	...	32.9	...	...	35.1	...	...	36.2
C Recreational and cultural services	...	...	89.5	...	...	91.3	...	...	97.1	...	...	96.2
D Personal and household services	...	...	40.9	...	...	44.7	...	...	49.8	...	...	54.2
Statistical discrepancy [a,b]	...	...	174.6	...	...	177.0	...	...	186.0	...	...	187.7

Panama

4.2 Derivation of Value Added by Kind of Activity, in Constant Prices
(Continued)

Million Panamanian balboas

	1984			1985			1986			1987		
	Gross Output	Intermediate Consumption	Value Added	Gross Output	Intermediate Consumption	Value Added	Gross Output	Intermediate Consumption	Value Added	Gross Output	Intermediate Consumption	Value Added
				At constant prices of:1970								
Total, Industries	...	...	1692.9	...	...	1772.2	...	...	1830.2	...	...	1875.1
Producers of Government Services	...	...	248.3	...	...	258.7	...	...	265.2	...	...	272.4
Other Producers	...	...	21.5	...	...	21.9	...	...	22.5	...	...	23.2
Total	...	...	1962.7	...	...	2052.8	...	...	2117.9	...	...	2170.7
Less: Imputed bank service charge	...	...	78.5	...	...	80.5	...	...	84.2	...	...	85.7
Import duties	...	...	33.4	...	...	36.1	...	...	42.3	...	...	41.1
Value added tax	...	...	...	...	...	...	...	...	...	...	...	...
Total	...	...	1917.6	...	...	2008.4	...	...	2076.0	...	...	2126.1

a) For 1970-1979, item 'Statistical discrepancy' refers to the services rendered to the area of the Panama Canal. Beginning 1980, the Treaty Torrijos-Carter was inforced, therefore all the activities of the area of the Panama Canal have been incorporated to the corresponding type of economic activity.

b) Beginning 1980, item 'Statistical discrepancy' refers to transport services sold by a resident enterprise 'Commission del Canal de Panama'. Due to the special characteristics of this enterprise it has been separated from the rest to facilitate the analysis of the estimates.

Papua New Guinea

General note. The preparation of national accounts statistics in Papua New Guinea is undertaken by the National Statistical Office (formerly Bureau of Statistics), Port Moresby. The official estimates are published in 'National Accounts Statistics'. A detailed description of the sources and methods used for the national accounts estimation is found in 'National Accounts Statistics 1960/61 - 1973/74', published in 1974. The estimates are generally in accordance with the classifications and definitions recommended in the United Nations System of National Accounts (SNA). Input-output tables for the years 1969/70, 1972/73 and 1976/77 were published in 1973, 1974 and 1982 respectively. The following tables have been prepared from successive replies to the United Nations national accounts questionnaire. When the scope and coverage of the estimates differ for conceptual or statistical reasons from the definitions and classfications recommended in SNA, a footnote is indicated to the relevant tables.

Sources and methods:

(a) Gross domestic product. Gross domestic product is estimated mainly through the income approach.

(b) Expenditure on the gross domestic product. All components of GDP by expenditure type are estimated through the expenditure approach. However, the commodity-flow approach is used for checking purposes in the case of a few items included under private consumption expenditure. The estimates of government consumption expenditure are based on Budget Papers, Annual Reports of the Commissioner for Local Government, Financial Statements of Provincial Government and Australian Budget Papers. The market component of household consumption expenditure is estimated mainly from the results of the retail sales and selected services survey. Estimates for items not covered by this survey are obtained from sources such as Budget Papers, the population census, various surveys of urban markets and village industry and taxation data. For some selected items, the estimates are checked and supplemented by data from international trade statistics using the commodity-flow approach. The non-market component of household consumption consists of food and firewood for own consumption and services of owner-occupied dwellings. Estimates of food produced for own consumption are calculated by using data from the Rural Industrial Bulletin and the estimated consumption per head of population. The annual quantity of firewood used per family is multiplied by average price and the number of families gathering firewood for own use. Construction and maintenance of housing is estimated by multiplying population data by the time spent and the minimum wage rate. Estimates of increase in stocks are based mainly on the Taxation Statistics Bulletin. For gross fixed capital formation by private industries, the principal source of information is the capital expenditure survey and for the public industries, the annual reports of the public enterprises. Exports and imports of goods and services are estimated mainly from the international trade statistics. For the constant price estimates of parts of government expenditure, private expenditure, gross fixed capital formation, increase in stocks and exports of merchandise, the current quantities are revalued at base-year prices. Regarding the market component of private consumption expenditure, building and construction, government expenditure on goods and services and imports of merchandise, the current values are deflated by appropriate price indexes.

(c) Cost-structure of the gross domestic product. Estimates of compensation of employees are based on taxation statistics, statistics of religious organizations and the Labour Information Bulletin. Adjustments are made for wages and salaries not covered by the above sources. Imputed wages referring to work provided to government and mission authorities are shown separately. Estimates of operating surplus for the market component are based mainly on taxation returns with some adjustments made to cover imputed bank service charge and to include producers not required to submit returns. For owner-occupied dwellings, operating surplus is calculated from information contained in the Building Statistics Bulletin. Consumption of fixed capital is estimated based on taxation data supplemented by annual reports for producers not covered. The Papua New Guinea Budget papers and the annual reports of the Commissioner for Local Government provide all the information needed to estimate indirect taxes and subsidies.

(d) Gross domestic product by kind of economic activity. The table of gross domestic product by kind of economic activity is prepared at market prices, i.e., producers' values. The income approach is used to estimate value added of most industries. Value added is defined as the sum of compensation of employees, operating surplus, consumption of fixed capital and net indirect taxes. The principal source is the income tax statistics, supplemented by annual reports of public and private enterprises. The reporting unit in these statistics is the enterprise (legal entity) rather than the establishment. For the major activities such as mining and quarrying, electricity, gas and water, and communication, in which cases almost the whole production is concentrated in a few enterprise units, the establishment type data are used. In cases where surveys data are used, adjustments and supplementary data are taken into account to cover activities not included. For the non-marketed production and contributions of free and partially-paid labour, estimates are available separately as sub-divisions of the relevant items as the amounts involved are quite substantial. As mentioned above, estimates of GDP by kind of economic activity are arrived at by subdividing the cost-structure components of total GDP into the various kinds of activity. Compensation of employees is classified in accordance with the industry information on individuals' tax returns. If an individual has more than one source of income, he is allocated to the industry category corresponding to his major source of income and all of his income is classed to that category. Data on operating surplus of private enterprises are classified on the basis of information given in the company tax statistics and in the statistics of individuals' income other than wages and salaries, while the industry categories of the operating surplus of public enterprises are determined by the nature of their productive activities. For industry allocation of consumption of fixed capital, the taxation data supplemented by other information in respect of producers not covered by the taxation statistics provide the basis. In the case of indirect taxes and subsidies, the industry allocation is made on the basis of the nature of indirect taxes and subsidies. GDP by kind of economic activity at constant prices is not estimated.

1.1 Expenditure on the Gross Domestic Product, in Current Prices

Million Papua New Guinea kina — Fiscal year beginning 1 July

	1970	1975	1978	1979	1980	1981	1982	1983	1984	1985	1986	1987
1 Government final consumption expenditure	183.1	367.2	353.3	371.4	411.2	454.4	468.1	471.3	505.1	537.3	551.8	598.8
2 Private final consumption expenditure	387.1	591.3	788.6	890.5	1051.3	1104.2	1117.9	1245.0	1343.6	1479.1	1576.1	1693.3
3 Gross capital formation	291.6	193.4	296.3	383.3	430.6	458.1	562.5	626.2	605.2	500.7	541.0	622.5
A Increase in stocks	15.5	29.9	27.8	57.1	36.4	7.4	-14.2	-6.2	71.5	33.8	-31.5	34.1
B Gross fixed capital formation	276.1	163.5	268.5	326.2	394.2	450.7	576.7	632.4	533.7	466.9	572.5	588.4
4 Exports of goods and services	113.6	400.4	579.1	742.5	737.6	642.9	644.3	766.1	893.2	1004.2	1098.8	1214.5
5 Less: Imports of goods and services	354.2	470.9	627.5	744.3	910.8	987.6	1058.2	1129.6	1207.6	1243.0	1287.0	1364.1
Statistical discrepancy	0.5	-13.0	23.4	-10.9	-11.8	9.2	14.5	-5.4	-5.2	0.9	-13.3	-1.3
Equals: Gross Domestic Product [a]	621.7	1068.5	1413.3	1632.5	1708.1	1681.2	1749.1	1973.7	2134.4	2279.2	2467.5	2763.8

a) Second series, estimates relate to calendar year.

Papua New Guinea

1.2 Expenditure on the Gross Domestic Product, in Constant Prices

Million Papua New Guinea kina — Fiscal year beginning 1 July

	1970	1975	1978	1979	1980	1981	1982	1983	1984	1985	1986	1987
	1968	**1972**				At constant prices of: **1977**						
1 Government final consumption expenditure	151.8	232.5	343.4	349.6	337.8	324.8 / 454.4	422.6	414.1	419.3	429.3	419.0	433.0
2 Private final consumption expenditure	356.6	445.9	728.6	764.5	794.1	768.8 / 1104.2	1075.3	1119.0	1144.2	1221.2	1240.8	1276.5
3 Gross capital formation	265.5	122.4	288.2	353.5	368.5	353.1 / 458.1	518.8	541.9	487.7	373.8	397.5	423.6
A Increase in stocks	14.6	20.3	27.8	52.6	29.2	5.3 / 7.4	-12.8	-5.3	54.4	20.7	-12.9	20.3
B Gross fixed capital formation	250.9	102.1	260.4	300.9	339.3	347.8 / 450.7	531.6	547.2	433.3	353.1	410.4	403.3
4 Exports of goods and services	110.7	330.6	639.1	637.4	635.3	669.6 / 642.9	640.5	653.1	683.4	756.1	815.8	848.1
5 Less: Imports of goods and services	328.0	311.7	613.3	660.6	723.5	724.7 / 987.6	976.0	969.7	956.2	924.9	910.7	934.3
Statistical discrepancy	0.5	-9.4	23.8	-9.1	-10.0	6.7 / 9.2	14.0	-4.8	-4.3	0.7	-10.4	-1.0
Equals: Gross Domestic Product	557.2	810.2	1409.7a	1435.2a	1402.3a	1398.3a / 1681.2a	1695.2a	1753.5a	1774.2a	1856.2a	1952.0a	2045.9a

a) The estimates with base year 1977 and 1981 relate to calendar year.

1.3 Cost Components of the Gross Domestic Product

Million Papua New Guinea kina — Fiscal year beginning 1 July

	1970	1975	1978	1979	1980	1981	1982	1983	1984	1985	1986	1987
1 Indirect taxes, net	30.2	57.9	82.9	98.3	110.0	114.6	134.4	151.9	179.2	189.7	212.0	240.9
A Indirect taxes	32.0	60.4	87.6	102.2	114.6	119.2	138.5	153.7	182.2	191.6	213.7	242.8
B Less: Subsidies	1.8	2.5	4.7	3.9	4.6	4.6	4.1	1.8	3.0	1.9	1.7	1.9
2 Consumption of fixed capital [a]	28.7	77.7	103.6	107.3	124.9	137.6	150.0	162.6	204.8	211.4	223.9	227.0
3 Compensation of employees paid by resident producers to:	296.9	505.8	552.0	594.7	676.2	747.7	763.4	792.9	872.3	871.5	939.0	1004.7
A Resident households	296.9	505.8	551.5	593.8	675.4	747.1	762.5	792.2	871.7	870.9	938.4	1004.0
B Rest of the world	-	-	0.5	0.9	0.7	0.6	0.8	0.8	0.6	0.6	0.6	0.7
4 Operating surplus	265.8	427.0	674.6	832.2	797.1	681.4	701.2	866.4	878.1	1006.6	1092.5	1291.2
Equals: Gross Domestic Product [b]	621.7	1068.5	1413.3	1632.5	1708.1	1681.2	1749.1	1973.7	2134.4	2279.2	2467.5	2763.8

a) Item 'Consumption of fixed capital' excludes consumption of fixed capital of producers of government-owned houses and hostels.
b) Second series, estimates relate to calendar year.

1.4 General Government Current Receipts and Disbursements

Million Papua New Guinea kina — Fiscal year beginning 1 July

	1970	1975	1978	1979	1980	1981	1982	1983	1984	1985	1986	1987
					Receipts							
1 Operating surplus	...	...	...	...	...	...	...	...	...	...	...	...
2 Property and entrepreneurial income	1.9	...	...	...	...	...	...	...	...	...	...	...
3 Taxes, fees and contributions	97.5	...	...	...	...	...	...	...	...	...	...	...
A Indirect taxes	32.0	60.4	87.6	102.2	114.6	119.2	138.5	153.7	182.2	191.6	213.7	242.8

Papua New Guinea

1.4 General Government Current Receipts and Disbursements
(Continued)

Million Papua New Guinea kina — Fiscal year beginning 1 July

	1970	1975	1978	1979	1980	1981	1982	1983	1984	1985	1986	1987
B Direct taxes	64.3	...	...									
C Social security contributions	-	...	...									
D Compulsory fees, fines and penalties	1.2	3.0	...									
4 Other current transfers	100.3	...	...									
Total Current Receipts of General Government [a]	199.8	...	...	...	...	...	...	...	...	1479.1	1554.2	...

Disbursements

	1970	1975	1978	1979	1980	1981	1982	1983	1984	1985	1986	1987
1 Government final consumption expenditure	183.1	367.2	353.3	371.4	411.2	454.4	468.1	471.3	505.1	537.3	551.8	598.8
A Compensation of employees	61.6	...	...									
B Consumption of fixed capital	2.4	...	...									
C Purchases of goods and services, net	...	...	...									
D Less: Own account fixed capital formation	...	...	...									
E Indirect taxes paid, net	...	...	...									
2 Property income	3.8	...	...									
3 Subsidies	1.8	2.5	4.7	3.9	4.6	4.6	4.1	1.8	3.0	1.9	1.7	1.5
4 Other current transfers	2.5	...	...									
5 Net saving	8.5	...	...									
Total Current Disbursements and Net Saving of General Government [a]	199.7	...	...	...	...	...	...	...	...	...	...	...

a) Second series, estimates relate to calendar year.

1.5 Current Income and Outlay of Corporate and Quasi-Corporate Enterprises, Summary

Million Papua New Guinea kina — Fiscal year beginning 1 July

	1970	1975	1978	1979	1980	1981	1982	1983	1984	1985	1986	1987

Receipts

	1970	1975	1978	1979	1980	1981	1982	1983	1984	1985	1986	1987
1 Operating surplus	57.5	...	...	...	...	...	...	...	...	...	...	...
2 Property and entrepreneurial income received	29.3	...	...	...	...	...	...	...	...	...	...	...
3 Current transfers	5.8	...	...	...	...	...	...	...	...	...	...	...
Total Current Receipts	92.6	...	...	...	...	...	...	...	...	...	...	...

Disbursements

	1970	1975	1978	1979	1980	1981	1982	1983	1984	1985	1986	1987
1 Property and entrepreneurial income	60.3	...	...	...	...	...	...	...	...	...	...	...
2 Direct taxes and other current payments to general government	11.0	...	...	...	...	...	...	...	...	...	...	...
3 Other current transfers	6.7	...	...	...	...	...	...	...	...	...	...	...
4 Net saving	14.6	...	...	...	...	...	...	...	...	...	...	...
Total Current Disbursements and Net Saving	92.6	...	...	...	...	...	...	...	...	...	...	...

1.6 Current Income and Outlay of Households and Non-Profit Institutions

Million Papua New Guinea kina — Fiscal year beginning 1 July

	1970	1975	1978	1979	1980	1981	1982	1983	1984	1985	1986	1987

Receipts

	1970	1975	1978	1979	1980	1981	1982	1983	1984	1985	1986	1987
1 Compensation of employees	296.9	507.1	552.7	595.4	677.2	753.1	768.8	798.8	878.4	878.1	945.9	1011.7
A From resident producers	296.9	505.8	551.5	593.8	675.4	747.1	762.5	792.2	871.5	870.9	938.4	1004.0
B From rest of the world	-	1.3	1.2	1.6	1.8	6.0	6.3	6.6	6.9	7.2	7.5	7.7
2 Operating surplus of private unincorporated enterprises	...	...	...									

Papua New Guinea

1.6 Current Income and Outlay of Households and Non-Profit Institutions
(Continued)

Million Papua New Guinea kina — Fiscal year beginning 1 July

	1970	1975	1978	1979	1980	1981	1982	1983	1984	1985	1986	1987
3 Property and entrepreneurial income	215.4	...	...	...	...	...	...	...	...	...	...	...
4 Current transfers	5.7	...	...	...	...	...	...	...	...	...	...	...
A Social security benefits	...	...	...	...	...	...	...	...	...	...	...	...
B Social assistance grants	...	...	...	...	...	...	...	...	...	...	...	...
C Other	3.2	...	...	...	...	...	...	...	...	...	...	...
Total Current Receipts [a]	518.0	...	...	...	...	...	...	...	...	...	...	...

Disbursements

	1970	1975	1978	1979	1980	1981	1982	1983	1984	1985	1986	1987
1 Private final consumption expenditure	387.1	591.3	788.6	890.5	1051.3	1104.2	1117.9	1245.0	1343.6	1479.1	1576.1	1693.3
2 Property income	0.7	...	...	...	...	...	...	...	...	...	...	...
3 Direct taxes and other current transfers n.e.c. to general government	54.5	...	...	...	...	...	...	...	...	...	...	...
A Social security contributions	...	...	...	...	...	...	...	...	...	...	...	...
B Direct taxes	53.3	...	...	...	...	...	...	...	...	...	...	...
C Fees, fines and penalties	1.2	...	...	...	...	...	...	...	...	...	...	...
4 Other current transfers	8.5	...	...	...	...	...	...	...	...	...	...	...
5 Net saving	76.9	...	...	...	...	...	...	...	...	...	...	...
Total Current Disbursements and Net Saving [a]	518.0	...	...	...	...	...	...	...	...	...	...	...

a) Second series, estimates relate to calendar year.

1.7 External Transactions on Current Account, Summary

Million Papua New Guinea kina — Fiscal year beginning 1 July

	1970	1975	1978	1979	1980	1981	1982	1983	1984	1985	1986	1987

Payments to the Rest of the World

	1970	1975	1978	1979	1980	1981	1982	1983	1984	1985	1986	1987
1 Imports of goods and services	354.2	470.9	627.5	744.3	910.8	987.6	1058.2	1129.6	1207.6	1243.0	1287.0	1364.1
A Imports of merchandise c.i.f.	311.5	400.1	551.4	665.3	808.7	872.3	897.5	961.2	1018.2	1058.3	1089.9	1162.9
B Other	42.7	70.8	76.1	79.0	102.1	115.3	160.7	168.4	189.4	184.7	197.1	201.2
2 Factor income to the rest of the world	36.4	55.6	49.9	76.8	100.4	98.2	122.5	174.8	124.1	151.4	170.2	138.8
A Compensation of employees	-	-	0.5	0.9	0.7	0.6	0.8	0.8	0.6	0.6	0.6	0.7
B Property and entrepreneurial income	36.4	55.6	49.4	75.9	99.7	97.6	121.7	174.0	123.5	150.8	169.6	138.1
3 Current transfers to the rest of the world	2.4	23.7	32.5	48.3	45.1	30.9	36.9	36.7	38.4	39.3	38.6	43.6
4 Surplus of the nation on current transactions	-163.7	54.5	69.6	82.8	-101.2	-242.8	-306.3	-277.8	-164.3	-114.3	-47.4	-29.6
Payments to the Rest of the World and Surplus of the Nation on Current Transactions [a]	229.4	604.8	779.6	952.2	955.1	873.9	911.4	1063.3	1205.8	1319.4	1448.4	1516.9

Receipts From The Rest of the World

	1970	1975	1978	1979	1980	1981	1982	1983	1984	1985	1986	1987
1 Exports of goods and services	113.6	400.4	579.1	742.5	737.6	642.9	644.3	766.1	893.2	1004.2	1098.8	1214.5

Papua New Guinea

1.7 External Transactions on Current Account, Summary
(Continued)

Million Papua New Guinea kina — Fiscal year beginning 1 July

	1970	1975	1978	1979	1980	1981	1982	1983	1984	1985	1986	1987
A Exports of merchandise f.o.b.	77.4	345.3	510.9	656.6	640.3	555.6	552.7	674.3	793.3	901.6	994.5	1105.2
B Other	36.2	55.1	68.2	85.9	97.3	87.4	91.6	91.8	99.9	102.6	104.3	109.3
2 Factor income from rest of the world	9.8	16.7	30.5	37.3	41.7	37.8	50.1	55.4	51.7	62.9	98.1	60.5
A Compensation of employees	-	1.3	1.2	1.6	1.8	6.0	6.3	6.6	6.9	7.2	7.5	7.7
B Property and entrepreneurial income	9.8	15.4	29.3	35.7	39.9	31.8	43.8	48.8	44.8	55.7	90.6	52.8
3 Current transfers from rest of the world	106.0	187.7	169.9	172.5	175.8	193.2	217.0	241.7	261.0	252.4	251.5	241.9
Receipts from the Rest of the World on Current Transactions [a]	229.3	604.8	779.6	952.2	955.0	873.9	911.4	1063.3	1205.8	1319.4	1448.4	1516.9

a) Second series, estimates relate to calendar year.

1.8 Capital Transactions of The Nation, Summary

Million Papua New Guinea kina — Fiscal year beginning 1 July

	1970	1975	1978	1979	1980	1981	1982	1983	1984	1985	1986	1987
Finance of Gross Capital Formation												
Gross saving	128.4	234.9	389.3	455.2	317.7	224.4	270.8	343.0	435.7	387.4	480.3	591.7
1 Consumption of fixed capital [a]	28.7	77.7	103.6	107.3	124.9	137.6	150.0	162.6	204.8	211.4	223.9	227.0
A General government	2.4	...	...	...	...	...	...	...	...	...	...	...
B Corporate and quasi-corporate enterprises	23.3	...	...	...	...	...	...	...	...	...	...	...
Public	2.3	...	...	...	...	...	...	...	...	...	...	...
Private	21.0	...	...	...	...	...	...	...	...	...	...	...
C Other	3.0	...	...	...	...	...	...	...	...	...	...	...
2 Net saving	99.7	157.2	285.7	347.9	192.8	86.8	120.8	180.5	230.9	176.0	256.4	364.7
A General government	8.5	...	...	...	...	...	...	...	...	...	...	...
B Corporate and quasi-corporate enterprises	14.7	...	...	...	...	...	...	...	...	...	...	...
Public	3.8	...	...	...	...	...	...	...	...	...	...	...
Private	10.8	...	...	...	...	...	...	...	...	...	...	...
C Other	76.5	...	...	...	...	...	...	...	...	...	...	...
Less: Surplus of the nation on current transactions	-163.7	54.5	69.6	82.8	-101.2	-242.8	-306.3	-277.8	-164.3	-114.3	-47.4	-29.6
Statistical discrepancy	-0.5	13.0	-23.4	10.9	11.8	-9.2	-14.5	5.4	5.2	-0.9	13.3	1.3
Finance of Gross Capital Formation [b]	291.6	193.4	296.3	383.3	430.7	458.0	562.6	626.2	605.2	500.7	541.0	622.6
Gross Capital Formation												
Increase in stocks	15.5	29.9	27.8	57.1	36.4	7.4	-14.2	-6.2	71.5	33.8	-31.5	34.1
Gross fixed capital formation	276.1	163.5	268.5	326.2	394.2	450.7	576.7	632.4	533.7	466.9	572.5	588.5
1 General government	43.1	51.6	66.5	90.0	123.1	107.3	84.5	89.0	100.6	106.1	119.3	119.2
2 Corporate and quasi-corporate enterprises	...	...	...	...	...	...	...	...	...	...	...	...
3 Other	...	...	...	...	...	...	...	...	...	...	...	...
Gross Capital Formation [b]	291.6	193.4	296.3	383.3	430.7	458.0	562.6	626.2	605.2	500.7	541.0	622.6

a) Item 'Consumption of fixed capital' excludes consumption of fixed capital of producers of government-owned houses and hostels.
b) Second series, estimates relate to calendar year.

Papua New Guinea

1.10 Gross Domestic Product by Kind of Activity, in Current Prices

Million Papua New Guinea kina — Fiscal year beginning 1 July

	1970	1975	1978	1979	1980	1981	1982	1983	1984	1985	1986	1987
1 Agriculture, hunting, forestry and fishing	215.5	316.2	497.5	552.8	565.7	561.4	567.2	647.8	...	...	...	...
2 Mining and quarrying	1.4	119.9	147.6	247.2	225.7	133.7	140.4	210.8	...	...	...	...
3 Manufacturing	34.7	92.1	134.0	152.2	162.3	166.6	164.6	178.8	...	...	...	...
4 Electricity, gas and water	6.9	10.0	17.0	20.8	6.3	19.9	19.4	28.8	...	...	...	...
5 Construction	109.7	68.9	52.4	54.6	64.2	70.5	82.0	84.7	...	...	...	...
6 Wholesale and retail trade, restaurants and hotels [a]	45.7	75.9	130.9	145.5	135.2	140.3	142.4	156.6	...	...	...	...
7 Transport, storage and communication	39.9	57.7	79.0	83.5	78.1	97.6	72.9	68.3	...	...	...	...
8 Finance, insurance, real estate and business services	24.8	62.4	65.8	80.9	139.4	126.1	172.3	187.4	...	...	...	...
9 Community, social and personal services [a]	60.8	244.9	160.2	166.5	182.8	199.8	212.7	225.8	...	...	...	...
Total, Industries	539.4	1048.0	1284.4	1504.0	1559.7	1515.9	1573.9	1789.0	...	...	...	...
Producers of Government Services	64.2	...	106.5	106.5	125.7	143.0	144.5	147.1	...	...	...	...
Other Producers	...	...	...	...	...	...	...	...	...	...	...	...
Subtotal	603.6	1048.0	1390.9	1610.5	1685.4	1658.9	1718.4	1936.1	...	...	...	...
Less: Imputed bank service charge	4.7	11.2	25.4	34.4	41.3	45.7	49.1	53.5	...	...	...	...
Plus: Import duties	22.7	31.7	47.8	56.4	64.1	68.1	79.7	91.1	...	...	...	...
Plus: Value added tax	...	...	...	...	...	...	...	...	...	...	...	...
Equals: Gross Domestic Product [b]	621.7	1068.5	1413.3	1632.5	1708.1	1681.2	1749.1	1973.7	...	...	...	...

a) Restaurants and hotels are included in item 'Community, social and personal services'.
b) Second series, estimates relate to calendar year.

1.12 Relations Among National Accounting Aggregates

Million Papua New Guinea kina — Fiscal year beginning 1 July

	1970	1975	1978	1979	1980	1981	1982	1983	1984	1985	1986	1987
Gross Domestic Product [a]	621.7	1068.5	1413.3	1632.5	1708.1	1681.2	1749.1	1973.7	2134.4	2279.2	2467.5	2763.8
Plus: Net factor income from the rest of the world	-26.6	-38.9	-19.4	-39.5	-58.7	-60.4	-72.4	-119.4	-72.4	-88.5	-72.1	-78.3
Factor income from the rest of the world	9.8	16.7	30.5	37.3	41.7	37.8	50.1	55.4	51.7	62.9	98.1	60.5
Less: Factor income to the rest of the world	36.4	55.6	49.9	76.8	100.4	98.2	122.5	174.8	124.1	151.4	170.2	138.8
Equals: Gross National Product [a]	595.1	1029.6	1393.9	1593.0	1649.4	1620.8	1676.7	1854.3	2062.0	2190.7	2395.4	2685.5
Less: Consumption of fixed capital [b]	28.7	77.7	103.6	107.3	124.9	137.6	150.0	162.6	204.8	211.4	223.9	227.0

Papua New Guinea

1.12 Relations Among National Accounting Aggregates
(Continued)

Million Papua New Guinea kina — Fiscal year beginning 1 July

	1970	1975	1978	1979	1980	1981	1982	1983	1984	1985	1986	1987
Equals: National Income [a]	566.4	951.8	1290.2	1485.6	1524.5	1483.2	1526.6	1691.7	1857.1	1979.3	2171.5	2458.5
Plus: Net current transfers from the rest of the world	103.5	164.0	137.4	124.2	130.7	162.3	180.1	205.1	222.6	213.1	212.9	198.3
Current transfers from the rest of the world	106.0	187.7	169.9	172.5	175.8	193.2	217.0	241.7	261.0	252.4	251.5	241.9
Less: Current transfers to the rest of the world	2.4	23.7	32.5	48.3	45.1	30.9	36.9	36.7	38.4	39.3	38.6	43.6
Equals: National Disposable Income [a]	669.9	1115.8	1427.6	1609.8	1655.2	1645.5	1706.7	1896.8	2079.7	2192.4	2384.3	2656.8
Less: Final consumption	570.2	958.5	1141.9	1261.9	1462.5	1558.6	1586.0	1716.3	1848.8	2016.4	2127.9	2292.1
Equals: Net Saving [a]	99.7	157.2	285.7	347.9	192.8	86.9	120.8	180.5	230.9	176.0	256.4	364.7
Less: Surplus of the nation on current transactions [a]	-163.7	54.5	69.6	82.8	-101.2	-242.8	-306.3	-277.8	-164.3	-114.3	-47.4	-29.6
Statistical discrepancy	-0.5	13.0	-23.4	10.9	11.8	-9.3	-14.5	5.4	5.2	-0.9	13.3	1.3
Equals: Net Capital Formation [a]	262.9	115.7	192.7	276.0	305.8	320.4	412.6	463.6	400.4	289.4	317.1	395.6

a) Second series, estimates relate to calendar year.
b) Item 'Consumption of fixed capital' excludes consumption of fixed capital of producers of government-owned houses and hostels.

2.1 Government Final Consumption Expenditure by Function, in Current Prices

Million Papua New Guinea kina — Fiscal year beginning 1 July

	1970	1975	1978	1979	1980	1981	1982	1983	1984	1985	1986	1987
1 General public services	46.7	...	...	...	...	...	...	...	...	...	...	...
2 Defence	16.0	...	...	...	...	...	...	...	...	...	...	...
3 Public order and safety		...	...	...	...	...	...	...	...	...	...	...
4 Education	27.7	...	...	...	...	...	...	...	...	...	...	...
5 Health	16.2	...	...	...	...	...	...	...	...	...	...	...
6 Social security and welfare	-	...	...	...	...	...	...	...	...	...	...	...
7 Housing and community amenities	2.7	...	...	...	...	...	...	...	...	...	...	...
8 Recreational, cultural and religious affairs	1.6	...	...	...	...	...	...	...	...	...	...	...
9 Economic services	72.2	...	...	...	...	...	...	...	...	...	...	...
10 Other functions	-	...	...	...	...	...	...	...	...	...	...	...
Total Government Final Consumption Expenditure	183.1	...	...	...	...	...	...	...	...	...	...	...

2.5 Private Final Consumption Expenditure by Type and Purpose, in Current Prices

Million Papua New Guinea kina — Fiscal year beginning 1 July

	1970	1975	1978	1979	1980	1981	1982	1983	1984	1985	1986	1987
Final Consumption Expenditure of Resident Households												
1 Food, beverages and tobacco [a]	236.2	...	...	...	...	...	...	...	...	...	...	...
A Food	201.8	...	...	...	...	...	...	...	...	...	...	...
B Non-alcoholic beverages	...	...	...	...	...	...	...	...	...	...	...	...
C Alcoholic beverages	...	...	...	...	...	...	...	...	...	...	...	...
D Tobacco	12.2	...	...	...	...	...	...	...	...	...	...	...
2 Clothing and footwear	11.5	...	...	...	...	...	...	...	...	...	...	...
3 Gross rent, fuel and power	36.5	...	...	...	...	...	...	...	...	...	...	...
4 Furniture, furnishings and household equipment and operation	25.5	...	...	...	...	...	...	...	...	...	...	...
5 Medical care and health expenses	3.4	...	...	...	...	...	...	...	...	...	...	...
6 Transport and communication	30.7	...	...	...	...	...	...	...	...	...	...	...
A Personal transport equipment	6.1	...	...	...	...	...	...	...	...	...	...	...

Papua New Guinea

2.5 Private Final Consumption Expenditure by Type and Purpose, in Current Prices
(Continued)

Million Papua New Guinea kina — Fiscal year beginning 1 July

	1970	1975	1978	1979	1980	1981	1982	1983	1984	1985	1986	1987
B Other	24.6	...	...	...	...	...	...	...	...	...	...	...
7 Recreational, entertainment, education and cultural services	16.5	...	...	...	...	...	...	...	...	...	...	...
A Education	0.5	...	...	...	...	...	...	...	...	...	...	...
B Other	16.0	...	...	...	...	...	...	...	...	...	...	...
8 Miscellaneous goods and services	6.6	...	...	...	...	...	...	...	...	...	...	...
A Personal care	4.5	...	...	...	...	...	...	...	...	...	...	...
B Expenditures in restaurants, cafes and hotels [a]	...	...	...	...	...	...	...	...	...	...	...	...
C Other	...	...	...	...	...	...	...	...	...	...	...	...
Total Final Consumption Expenditure in the Domestic Market by Households, of which	366.9	580.0	782.5	885.6	1044.6	1096.0	1110.8	1238.6	1337.2	1471.1	1569.3	1686.4
A Durable goods	50.9	...	...	...	...	...	...	...	...	...	...	...
B Semi-durable goods	...	...	...	...	...	...	...	...	...	...	...	...
C Non-durable goods	254.4	...	...	...	...	...	...	...	...	...	...	...
D Services	61.7	...	...	...	...	...	...	...	...	...	...	...
Plus: Direct purchases abroad by resident households	18.2	15.9	12.3	11.9	15.3	15.9	14.8	13.3	13.5	14.5	13.8	14.1
Less: Direct purchases in the domestic market by non-resident households	9.7	4.6	6.2	7.0	8.7	7.8	7.7	6.9	7.1	6.5	7.0	7.2
Equals: Final Consumption Expenditure of Resident Households [b]	375.4	591.3	788.6	890.5	1051.3	1104.2	1117.9	1245.0	1343.6	1479.1	1576.1	1693.3

Final Consumption Expenditure of Private Non-profit Institutions Serving Households

	1970	1975	1978	1979	1980	1981	1982	1983	1984	1985	1986	1987
1 Research and science	...	...	...	...	...	...	...	...	...	...	...	...
2 Education	1.2	...	...	...	...	...	...	...	...	...	...	...
3 Medical and other health services	0.7	...	...	...	...	...	...	...	...	...	...	...
4 Welfare services	...	...	...	...	...	...	...	...	...	...	...	...
5 Recreational and related cultural services	9.6	...	...	...	...	...	...	...	...	...	...	...
6 Religious organisations	...	...	...	...	...	...	...	...	...	...	...	...
7 Professional and labour organisations serving households	...	...	...	...	...	...	...	...	...	...	...	...
8 Miscellaneous	...	...	...	...	...	...	...	...	...	...	...	...
Equals: Final Consumption Expenditure of Private Non-profit Organisations Serving Households	11.6	...	...	...	...	...	...	...	...	...	...	...
Private Final Consumption Expenditure [b]	387.1	591.3	788.6	890.5	1051.3	1104.2	1117.9	1245.0	1343.6	1479.1	1576.1	1693.3

a) Item 'Food, beverages and tobacco' includes expenditure in restaurants, cafes and hotels.
b) Second series, estimates relate to calendar year.

2.11 Gross Fixed Capital Formation by Kind of Activity of Owner, ISIC Divisions, in Current Prices

Million Papua New Guinea kina — Fiscal year beginning 1 July

	1970	1975	1978	1979	1980	1981	1982	1983	1984	1985	1986	1987
					All Producers							
1 Agriculture, hunting, forestry and fishing	7.1	...	...	...	...	...	...	...	...	...	...	...
2 Mining and quarrying	152.2	...	...	...	...	...	...	...	...	...	...	...
3 Manufacturing	8.2	...	...	...	...	...	...	...	...	...	...	...
4 Electricity, gas and water [a]	5.8	...	...	...	...	...	...	...	...	...	...	...

Papua New Guinea

2.11 Gross Fixed Capital Formation by Kind of Activity of Owner, ISIC Divisions, in Current Prices
(Continued)

Million Papua New Guinea kina — Fiscal year beginning 1 July

	1970	1975	1978	1979	1980	1981	1982	1983	1984	1985	1986	1987
5 Construction	5.6	...	...	...	...	...	...	...	...	...	...	...
6 Wholesale and retail trade, restaurants and hotels	...	...	...	...	...	...	...	...	...	...	...	...
7 Transport, storage and communication	...	...	...	...	...	...	...	...	...	...	...	...
8 Finance, insurance, real estate and business services [b]	7.4	...	...	...	...	...	...	...	...	...	...	...
9 Community, social and personal services [b]	43.4	...	...	...	...	...	...	...	...	...	...	...
Total Industries	229.7	...	...	...	...	...	...	...	...	...	...	...
Producers of Government Services	43.1	...	...	...	...	...	...	...	...	...	...	...
Private Non-Profit Institutions Serving Households	3.4	...	...	...	...	...	...	...	...	...	...	...
Total	276.1	...	...	...	...	...	...	...	...	...	...	...

a) Item 'Electricity, gas and water' also includes sanitary and similar services.
b) Finance, insurance, real estate (except owner-occupied dwellings) and business services are included in item 'Community, social and personal services'.

2.17 Exports and Imports of Goods and Services, Detail

Million Papua New Guinea kina — Fiscal year beginning 1 July

	1970	1975	1978	1979	1980	1981	1982	1983	1984	1985	1986	1987
Exports of Goods and Services												
1 Exports of merchandise, f.o.b. [a]	77.4	345.3	510.9	656.6	640.3	555.6	552.7	674.3	793.3	901.6	994.5	1105.2
2 Transport and communication	17.1	24.7	34.0	37.5	46.1	51.2	54.4	58.0	64.7	66.7	68.3	70.0
A In respect of merchandise imports	5.1	15.1	18.4	20.2	22.3	22.5	24.1	25.5	28.2	28.8	29.3	30.0
B Other	12.1	9.7	15.6	17.3	23.8	28.7	30.3	32.5	36.5	37.9	39.0	40.0
3 Insurance service charges	...	0.7	1.0	1.3	1.5	1.1	1.3	0.4	1.4	2.1	1.9	1.7
A In respect of merchandise imports	...	0.5	0.9	1.3	1.4	1.0	1.2	0.3	1.2	1.8	1.7	1.5
B Other	...	0.2	0.1	0.1	0.1	0.1	0.1	0.1	0.2	0.3	0.2	0.2
4 Other commodities	9.4	25.1	27.0	40.1	41.1	27.3	28.3	26.5	26.7	27.3	27.1	30.4
5 Adjustments of merchandise exports to change-of-ownership basis	...	...	...	...	...	...	...	...	...	...	...	...
6 Direct purchases in the domestic market by non-residential households	9.7	4.6	6.2	7.0	8.7	7.8	7.7	6.9	7.1	6.5	7.0	7.2
7 Direct purchases in the domestic market by extraterritorial bodies	...	...	...	...	...	...	...	...	...	...	...	...
Total Exports of Goods and Services [b]	113.6	400.4	579.1	742.5	737.6	642.9	644.3	766.1	893.2	1004.2	1098.8	1214.5
Imports of Goods and Services												
1 Imports of merchandise, c.i.f. [a]	311.5	400.1	551.4	665.3	808.7	872.3	897.5	961.2	1018.2	1058.3	1089.9	1162.9
A Imports of merchandise, f.o.b.	277.6	341.2	470.3	560.7	687.3	751.5	760.0	817.3	856.7	876.1	903.4	963.1
B Transport of services on merchandise imports	33.9	58.2	78.9	101.4	117.8	117.0	133.6	139.6	157.0	177.5	181.7	194.7
By residents	5.1	15.1	18.4	20.2	22.3	22.5	24.1	26.5	28.2	28.8	29.3	37.9
By non-residents	28.8	43.1	60.5	81.2	95.5	94.5	109.5	113.1	128.7	148.7	152.4	156.8
C Insurance service charges on merchandise imports	...	0.8	2.2	3.3	3.6	3.9	4.0	4.3	4.5	4.6	4.8	5.1
By residents	...	0.5	0.9	1.3	1.4	1.0	1.2	0.3	1.2	1.8	1.7	1.2

Papua New Guinea

2.17 Exports and Imports of Goods and Services, Detail
(Continued)

Million Papua New Guinea kina — Fiscal year beginning 1 July

	1970	1975	1978	1979	1980	1981	1982	1983	1984	1985	1986	1987
By non-residents	...	0.3	1.3	2.0	2.2	2.9	2.8	4.0	3.4	2.8	3.1	3.9
2 Adjustments of merchandise imports to change-of-ownership basis	...	...	...	...	...	...	...	...	...	...	...	...
3 Other transport and communication	13.5	31.6	32.8	34.6	41.3	40.2	49.7	40.8	46.4	47.8	51.1	53.0
4 Other insurance service charges		4.3	8.0	7.7	9.5	9.9	10.4	9.6	9.8	10.2	10.6	10.8
5 Other commodities	11.7	18.1	21.7	23.8	34.0	46.7	83.8	100.5	116.1	109.6	118.2	120.1
6 Direct purchases abroad by government	...	...	1.3	1.1	1.9	2.4	2.1	4.2	3.7	2.7	3.4	3.2
7 Direct purchases abroad by resident households	17.5	16.8	12.3	11.9	15.4	16.1	14.8	13.3	13.5	14.5	13.8	14.1
Total Imports of Goods and Services [b]	354.2	470.9	627.5	744.3	910.8	987.6	1058.2	1129.6	1207.6	1243.0	1287.0	1364.1
Balance of Goods and Services	-240.6	-70.5	-48.4	-1.8	-173.2	-344.7	-413.9	-363.5	-314.4	-238.8	-188.2	-149.6
Total Imports and Balance of Goods and Services [b]	113.6	400.4	579.1	742.5	737.6	642.9	644.3	766.1	893.2	1004.2	1098.8	1214.5

a) Exports and imports of merchandise are recorded on the basis of the crossing of frontiers. No data are available on the basis of changes in the ownership of the goods.
b) Second series, estimates relate to calendar year.

Paraguay

General note. The preparation of national accounts statistics in Paraguay is undertaken by the Departamento de Estudios Economicos of the Banco Central del Paraguay, Asuncion. The official estimates are published by the Department in 'Cuentas Nacionales'. The following presentation is based mainly on a comprehensive description of sources and methods used in national accounting received from the Banco Central. The estimates are generally in accordance with the classifications and definitions recommended in the United Nations System of National Accounts (SNA). The following tables have been prepared from successive replies to the United Nations national accounts questionnaire. When the scope and coverage of the estimates differ for conceptual or statistical reasons from the definitions and classifications recommded in SNA, a footnote is indicated to the relevant tables.

Sources and methods:

(a) Gross domestic product. Gross domestic product is estimated mainly through the production approach.

(b) Expenditure on the gross domestic product. The expenditure approach is used to estimate government final consumption expenditure and exports and imports of goods and services. The commodity-flow approach is used for the estimation of gross fixed capital formation. Private final consumption expenditure is arrived at as a residual. The information needed to estimate government consumption expenditure is obtained from the Ministerio de Hacienda, which controls the budget of the public sector institutions. Increase in stock is estimated for livestock only. It is assumed to be the annual increase of the cattle production minus the number of cattle slaughtered. Gross fixed capital formation is estimated on the basis of import statistics for machinery, equipment, transport and communication. Estimates of the domestic production of these items as well as the gross value of production in the construction sector are also included. Exports and imports of goods and services are estimated on the basis of information furnished by the Division de Balanza de Pagos of the Banco Central. For the constant price estimates, the only information available is that the wholesale price index is used as a deflator.

(c) Cost-structure of the gross domestic product. Compensation of employees is estimated by combining the information on the number of persons employed, by economic sectors and the average wages paid in each productive sector. Depreciation is estimated on the basis of the average lifetime of each type of capital good established in the respective depreciation tables. Information on indirect taxes and subsidies are supplied by the Ministerio de Hacienda. Operating surplus is obtained as a residual.

(d) Gross domestic product by kind of economic activity. The table of GDP by kind of economic activity is prepared at market prices, i.e., producers' values. The production approach is used to estimate the value added of most industries. The income approach is used to estimate the value added of public administration and defence, part of transport and communication, and part of other private services. The gross output of the trade sector is based on the commodity-flow approach, applying a fixed percentage for value added. The value of agricultural production is obtained by multiplying quantities by prices. Information on prices and on most quantities are obtained from Ministerio de Agricultura y Ganaderia. Remaining quantities are estimated through the use of indirect indicators such as the rate of population growth. The value of livestock production is estimated by type of livestock. Slaughtering is estimated on the basis of information provided by the Direccion De Impuestos and the meat-processing industries while stocks of cattle are based on the 1956 agricultural census. Inputs for the agricultural section is assumed to be a certain percentage of the gross value of production. The production of mining and quarrying is estimated on the basis of the industrial production coefficients of lime and cement. Information on the manufacturing sector is obtained from the surveys of the Banco Central, and the 1955 and 1963 industrial censuses. The value added of each industrial group is determined on the basis of coefficients from the 1963 industrial census applied to the gross production values. The value added of electricity and water is mainly based on information from the concerned enterprises. For constuction, the source used is the production index for construction materials. This index is compared with permits granted by the municipalities expressed in quantitative measures, multiplied by the base-year value and inflated by the implicit price index of construction materials. Value added of the trade sector is assumed to be 30 percent of the values of locally manufactured goods, imported goods and agricultural products net of farm consumption. For motor transport, the number of vehicles by category is multiplied by the number of days worked and the gross income earned in the base year. The resulting amounts are then multiplied by value added coefficients for each category of vehicle. Non-mechanical transport is calculated on the basis of the index of agricultural production transported in rural areas by carts. For ownership of dwellings, the estimates are prepared on the basis of the number of dwellings by type of construction materials used. Value added is estimated by multiplying the paid and imputed rents by the number of dwellings. The value added of public administration and defence is estimated as the total compensation paid to government employees based on information furnished by the Presupuesto General de la Nacion. The value of public education is determined directly from the Presupuesto General de Gastos de la Nacion while that of private education is estimated at constant prices by multiplying the number of students enrolled by the annual education costs plus registration fees minus 20 percent for intermediate consumption. For health, information is obtained directly from the public health services and social security services and from the Ministerio de Salud Publica y Bienestar Social for the private sector. Estimates for domestic services are obtained by multiplying actual annual wages by employment figures which are assumed to increase at a rate of 3.3 percent in the urban area and 2.6 percent in the rural area. For other services, bench-mark estimates, based on the 1963 economic census, are projected by a specially constructed growth rate. For the constant price estimates, double deflation is used for the agricultural sector. The current quantities of mining and manufacturing are revalued at base-year prices. Value added of construction, transport and financial sectors is extrapolated by using quantity indicators. For electricity, gas and water, trade and services sectors, value added is deflated by using appropriate price indexes.

1.1 Expenditure on the Gross Domestic Product, in Current Prices

Million Paraguayan guaranies

	1970	1975	1978	1979	1980	1981	1982	1983	1984	1985	1986	1987
1 Government final consumption expenditure	6748	11972	21500	24710	34732	48625	52272	58024	69280	90214	121790	176600
2 Private final consumption expenditure	58042	142970	225241	306501	399296	504074	552019	642198	821968	1066915	1434840	1882612
3 Gross capital formation	11034	45893	87717	122972	161204	204283	188916	175229	245478	306451	458882	625815
A Increase in stocks [a]	151	6350	6461	6830	8550	10064	12045	10720	14300	18500	27072	34400
B Gross fixed capital formation	10883	39543	81256	116142	152654	194219	176871	164509	231178	287951	431810	591415
Residential buildings												
Non-residential buildings	5463	18850	40710	61066	90308	123000	115632	128351	133746	165776	220274	292084
Other construction and land improvement etc.												
Other [b]	5420	20693	40546	55076	62346	71219	61239	36158	97432	122175	211536	299331
4 Exports of goods and services	11176	25155	59413	69133	77599	79107	89461	70054	169991	355028	399014	704695
5 Less: Imports of goods and services	12078	35551	71329	92802	112372	127400	145628	127391	236273	424718	580726	896121
Equals: Gross Domestic Product	74921	190439	322542	430514	560459	708689	737040	818114	1070444	1393890	1833800	2493601

a) Item 'Increase in stocks' includes livestock only.
b) Item 'Other' of gross capital formation includes communications equipments.

1.2 Expenditure on the Gross Domestic Product, in Constant Prices

Million Paraguayan guaranies

	1970	1975	1978	1979	1980	1981	1982	1983	1984	1985	1986	1987
	\multicolumn{12}{c}{At constant prices of:1982}											
1 Government final consumption expenditure	25720	28956	40245	37494	42803	51126	52272	53919	50755	52800	53950	59350
2 Private final consumption expenditure	230899	317410	409266	403714	472573	524562	552019	543425	566155	576210	595573	603515
3 Gross capital formation	36546	78810	138528	161013	194465	227503	188916	154587	156940	158640	164500	175490
A Increase in stocks [a]	629	15338	12354	10179	10766	10741	12045	9404	10500	11700	13000	14500
B Gross fixed capital formation	35917	63472	126174	150834	183699	216762	176871	145183	146440	146940	151500	160990

Paraguay

1.2 Expenditure on the Gross Domestic Product, in Constant Prices
(Continued)

Million Paraguayan guaranies

	1970	1975	1978	1979	1980	1981	1982	1983	1984	1985	1986	1987
					At constant prices of:1982							
Residential buildings												
Non-residential buildings	18030	30257	63215	79307	108673	137277	115632	113185	91208	90296	91200	93024
Other construction and land improvement etc.												
Other b	17887	33215	62959	71527	75026	79485	61239	31998	55232	56644	60300	67966
4 Exports of goods and services	42015	52005	74452	132693	110070	83358	89461	75734	94749	109487	104963	143471
5 Less: Imports of goods and services	39861	60730	110759	120522	135225	142188	145628	112736	131693	130979	152763	182444
Equals: Gross Domestic Product	295319	416451	551732	614392	684686	744361	737040	714929	736906	766158	766223	799382

a) Item 'Increase in stocks' includes livestock only.
b) Item 'Other' of gross capital formation includes communications equipments.

1.3 Cost Components of the Gross Domestic Product

Million Paraguayan guaranies

	1970	1975	1978	1979	1980	1981	1982	1983	1984	1985	1986	1987
1 Indirect taxes, net	5486	7879	16212	27565	34536	41894	48210	45120	50726	66240	89455	150650
A Indirect taxes	5507	7940	16297	27586	34578	41946	48297	45166	50778	66350	89570	150830
B Less: Subsidies	21	61	85	21	42	52	87	46	52	110	115	180
2 Consumption of fixed capital	3962	9800	32253	49190	58630	77688	74285	72184	107900	145270	196530	289100
3 Compensation of employees paid by resident producers to:	25770	65260	106100	150900	195300	242850	245900	258243	342205	432120	561756	761440
4 Operating surplus	39704	107500	167977	202859	271993	346257	368645	442567	569613	750260	986059	1292411
Equals: Gross Domestic Product	74921	190439	322542	430514	560459	708689	737040	818114	1070444	1393890	1833800	2493601

1.4 General Government Current Receipts and Disbursements

Million Paraguayan guaranies

	1970	1975	1978	1979	1980	1981	1982	1983	1984	1985	1986	1987
					Receipts							
1 Operating surplus	...	...	...	...	...	...	...	...	...	...	...	...
2 Property and entrepreneurial income	956	1429	4909	10530	7609	8315	6561	7412	7800	9924	16396	21474
3 Taxes, fees and contributions	7586	12073	27718	42347	53255	66563	74383	75301	79755	105622	137416	211066
A Indirect taxes	5507	7940	16297	27586	34578	41946	48297	45166	50778	66350	89570	150830
B Direct taxes	857	1573	5062	6680	9097	11496	11528	12542	10001	15715	20298	35039
C Social security contributions	1222	2560	6359	8081	9580	13121	14558	17593	18976	23557	27548	25197
D Compulsory fees, fines and penalties	...	...	...	...	...	...	...	...	...	...	...	...
4 Other current transfers	744	1012	1024	1191	1452	1952	2591	3348	7660	8504	7500	7183
Total Current Receipts of General Government	9286	14513	33651	54068	62316	76830	83535	86061	95215	124050	161312	239723
					Disbursements							
1 Government final consumption expenditure	6748	11972	21500	24710	34732	48625	52272	58024	69280	90214	121790	176600
2 Property income a	102	115	53	75	126	107	87	91	988	1208	1600	1984
3 Subsidies	21	61	85	21	42	52	87	46	52	110	115	180
4 Other current transfers	1570	1966	3798	5043	7047	9955	18923	17593	23260	29100	36329	47774
A Social security benefits	...	...	...	...	...	...	...	...	...	...	...	...
B Social assistance grants	...	...	...	...	...	...	...	...	...	...	...	...
C Other	1570	1966	3798	5043	7047	9955	18923	17593	23260	29100	36329	47774
5 Net saving	844	399	8215	24219	20369	18091	12166	10307	1635	3418	1478	13185
Total Current Disbursements and Net Saving of General Government	9286	14513	33651	54068	62316	76830	83535	86061	95215	124050	161312	239723

a) Item 'Property income' relates to interest on public debt.

1.6 Current Income and Outlay of Households and Non-Profit Institutions

Million Paraguayan guaranies

	1970	1975	1978	1979	1980	1981	1982	1983	1984	1985	1986	1987
					Receipts							
1 Compensation of employees	25770	65260	106100	150900	195300	242850	245900	258243	342205	432120	561756	761440
2 Operating surplus of private unincorporated enterprises	...	...	...	...	...	...	...	...	...	...	...	...
3 Property and entrepreneurial income a	35982	100479	154727	179825	251674	323321	347430	414301	531465	685437	905160	1124751
4 Current transfers	1570	1966	3798	5043	7047	9955	18923	17593	23260	29100	36329	47774

Paraguay

1.6 Current Income and Outlay of Households and Non-Profit Institutions
(Continued)

Million Paraguayan guaranies

	1970	1975	1978	1979	1980	1981	1982	1983	1984	1985	1986	1987
A Social security benefits	...	...	...	...	...	...	...	...	...	...	...	...
B Social assistance grants	...	...	...	...	...	...	...	...	...	...	...	...
C Other	1570	1966	3798	5043	7047	9955	18923	17593	23260	29100	36329	47774
Total Current Receipts	63322	167706	264625	335768	454021	576126	612253	690137	896930	1146657	1503245	1933965

Disbursements

	1970	1975	1978	1979	1980	1981	1982	1983	1984	1985	1986	1987
1 Private final consumption expenditure	58042	142970	225241	306501	399296	504074	552019	642198	821968	1066915	1434840	1882612
2 Property income [a]	...	...	...	...	...	...	...	...	...	...	...	...
3 Direct taxes and other current transfers n.e.c. to general government	1278	2662	6484	8268	9840	13430	14982	17593	18976	23557	27548	25197
4 Other current transfers	744	1012	1024	1191	1452	1952	2591	3348	7660	8504	7500	7183
5 Net saving	3259	21062	31876	19808	43433	56670	42661	26998	48326	47681	33357	18973
Total Current Disbursements and Net Saving	63322	167706	264625	335768	454021	576126	612253	690137	896930	1146657	1503245	1933965

a) Item 'Property and entrepreneurial income' received is net of item 'Property income' paid.

1.8 Capital Transactions of The Nation, Summary

Million Paraguayan guaranies

	1970	1975	1978	1979	1980	1981	1982	1983	1984	1985	1986	1987

Finance of Gross Capital Formation

	1970	1975	1978	1979	1980	1981	1982	1983	1984	1985	1986	1987
Gross saving	8316	33961	77574	100597	131692	164749	141012	122882	176771	223815	267901	384328
1 Consumption of fixed capital	3962	9800	32253	49190	58630	77688	74285	72184	107900	145270	196530	289100
2 Net saving	4354	24161	45321	51407	73062	87061	66727	50698	68871	78545	71371	95228
A General government	844	399	8215	24219	20369	18091	12166	10307	1635	3418	1478	13185
B Corporate and quasi-corporate enterprises	251	2700	5230	7380	9260	12300	11900	13393	18910	27446	36536	63070
C Other	3259	21062	31876	19808	43433	56670	42661	26998	48326	47681	33357	18973
Less: Surplus of the nation on current transactions	-2718	-11932	-10143	-22375	-29512	-39534	-47904	-52347	-68707	-82636	-190981	-241487
Finance of Gross Capital Formation	11034	45893	87717	122972	161204	204283	188916	175229	245478	306451	458882	625815

Gross Capital Formation

	1970	1975	1978	1979	1980	1981	1982	1983	1984	1985	1986	1987
Increase in stocks	151	6350	6461	6830	8550	10064	12045	10720	14300	18500	27072	34400
Gross fixed capital formation	10883	39543	81256	116142	152654	194219	176871	164509	231178	287951	431810	591415
Gross Capital Formation	11034	45893	87717	122972	161204	204283	188916	175229	245478	306451	458882	625815

1.10 Gross Domestic Product by Kind of Activity, in Current Prices

Million Paraguayan guaranies

	1970	1975	1978	1979	1980	1981	1982	1983	1984	1985	1986	1987
1 Agriculture, hunting, forestry and fishing	24024	70284	103431	135162	165137	196784	190645	211615	307113	403261	498923	681934
2 Mining and quarrying	83	365	794	1446	2285	2933	3142	3487	4359	5672	8350	11507
3 Manufacturing	12498	29759	54419	69610	92338	118469	120966	134273	172003	226115	296008	404051
4 Electricity, gas and water	840	2739	5982	7889	12923	15271	18120	20638	26064	30896	44791	62609
5 Construction	2076	7163	15470	23205	34317	46740	49544	54994	66873	82888	110137	146042
6 Wholesale and retail trade, restaurants and hotels [a,b]	18291	43594	83986	112656	144870	188378	196158	217210	272599	360391	489776	662177
7 Transport, storage and communication	2950	7600	12994	17359	23784	29059	31107	34529	44059	57974	80083	109313
8 Finance, insurance, real estate and business services [b,c]	2281	5018	7493	11229	14993	20091	22500	24976	30971	39163	52553	70368
9 Community, social and personal services [a,c]	7936	17424	25263	37362	50697	64286	72000	79920	101178	129209	174917	240808
Total, industries	70978	183945	309832	415918	541344	682012	704183	781642	1025219	1335569	1755538	2388809
Producers of Government Services	3943	6494	12710	14595	19115	26678	32858	36472	45225	58321	78262	104792
Other Producers	...	...	...	...	...	...	...	...	...	...	...	...
Subtotal	74921	190439	322542	430513	560459	708689	737041	818114	1070444	1393890	1833800	2493601
Less: Imputed bank service charge	...	...	...	...	...	...	...	...	...	...	...	...
Plus: Import duties	...	...	...	...	...	...	...	...	...	...	...	...
Plus: Value added tax	...	...	...	...	...	...	...	...	...	...	...	...
Equals: Gross Domestic Product	74921	190439	322542	430513	560459	708689	737041	818114	1070444	1393890	1833800	2493601

a) Restaurants and hotels are included in item 'Community, social and personal services'.
b) Finance is included in item 'Wholesale and retail trade, restaurants and hotels'.
c) Business services are included in item 'Community, social and personal services'.

Paraguay

1.11 Gross Domestic Product by Kind of Activity, in Constant Prices

Million Paraguayan guaranies

	1970	1975	1978	1979	1980	1981	1982	1983	1984	1985	1986	1987
	\multicolumn{12}{c}{At constant prices of:1982}
1 Agriculture, hunting, forestry and fishing	89846	128157	149112	159001	172524	189876	190645	185991	196990	206042	193467	207021
2 Mining and quarrying	219	731	1487	2118	2669	3070	3142	2912	2942	3073	3440	3646
3 Manufacturing	54267	70036	96712	106289	120422	125613	120966	115861	121075	127129	125345	129732
4 Electricity, gas and water	2794	6135	9923	11797	14025	14746	18120	17779	18164	19248	21218	22821
5 Construction	7141	13491	27573	35845	45164	52707	49544	46720	45604	45148	45600	46512
6 Wholesale and retail trade, restaurants and hotels ab	78258	105602	148841	167446	185028	200570	196158	190171	193634	202759	209437	216767
7 Transport, storage and communication	11702	18699	23985	26743	29551	30497	31107	30742	31853	33468	35142	36899
8 Finance, insurance, real estate and business services bc	10699	13661	17833	19705	21479	22961	22500	21448	21448	21662	22096	22538
9 Community, social and personal services ac	23438	42011	54387	61403	68096	72727	72000	71133	72243	73688	75858	78134
Total, Industries	278364	398523	529853	590347	658958	712768	704182	682757	703953	732217	731603	764070
Producers of Government Services	16955	17928	21879	24045	25728	31594	32858	32172	32953	33941	34620	35312
Other Producers	...	...	...	...	...	...	...	...	...	...	...	...
Subtotal	295319	416451	551732	614392	684686	744361	737040	714929	736906	766158	766223	799382
Less: Imputed bank service charge	...	...	...	...	...	...	...	...	...	...	...	...
Plus: Import duties	...	...	...	...	...	...	...	...	...	...	...	...
Plus: Value added tax	...	...	...	...	...	...	...	...	...	...	...	...
Equals: Gross Domestic Product	295319	416451	551732	614392	684686	744361	737040	714929	736906	766158	766223	799382

a) Restaurants and hotels are included in item 'Community, social and personal services'.
b) Finance is included in item 'Wholesale and retail trade, restaurants and hotels'.
c) Business services are included in item 'Community, social and personal services'.

1.12 Relations Among National Accounting Aggregates

Million Paraguayan guaranies

	1970	1975	1978	1979	1980	1981	1982	1983	1984	1985	1986	1987
Gross Domestic Product	74921	190439	322542	430514	560459	708689	737040	818114	1070444	1393890	1833800	2493601
Plus: Net factor income from the rest of the world	-1816	-1536	1773	1294	5261	8759	8263	4990	-2425	-12946	-9269	-50061
Factor income from the rest of the world	...	...	7449	10893	17247	22282	22119	20860	22904	39147	45841	56819
Less: Factor income to the rest of the world	...	...	5676	9599	11986	13523	13856	15870	25329	52093	55110	106880
Equals: Gross National Product	73105	188903	324315	431808	565720	717448	745303	823104	1068019	1380944	1824531	2443540
Less: Consumption of fixed capital	3962	9800	32253	49190	58630	77688	74285	72184	107900	145270	196530	289100
Equals: National Income	69143	179103	292062	382618	507090	639760	671018	750920	960119	1235674	1628001	2154440
Plus: Net current transfers from the rest of the world	-	-	-	-	-	-	-	-	-	-	-	-
Equals: National Disposable Income	69143	179103	292062	382618	507090	639760	671018	750920	960119	1235674	1628001	2154440
Less: Final consumption	64790	154942	246741	331211	434028	552699	604291	700222	891248	1157129	1556630	2059212
Equals: Net Saving	4354	24161	45321	51407	73062	87061	66727	50698	68871	78545	71371	95228
Less: Surplus of the nation on current transactions	-2718	-11932	-10143	-22375	-29512	-39534	-47904	-52347	-68707	-82636	-190981	-241487
Equals: Net Capital Formation	7072	36093	55464	73782	102574	126595	114632	103045	137578	161181	262352	336715

4.1 Derivation of Value Added by Kind of Activity, in Current Prices

Million Paraguayan guaranies

	\multicolumn{3}{c}{1980}	\multicolumn{3}{c}{1981}	\multicolumn{3}{c}{1982}	\multicolumn{3}{c}{1983}
	Gross Output	Intermediate Consumption	Value Added	Gross Output	Intermediate Consumption	Value Added	Gross Output	Intermediate Consumption	Value Added	Gross Output	Intermediate Consumption	Value Added
	\multicolumn{12}{c}{All Producers}
1 Agriculture, hunting, forestry and fishing	...	...	165137	...	...	196784	...	...	190645	...	...	211615
A Agriculture and hunting	...	...	148397	...	...	176087	...	...	171838	...	...	190740
B Forestry and logging	...	...	16402	...	...	20300	...	...	18370	...	...	20390
C Fishing	...	...	338	...	...	397	...	...	437	...	...	485
2 Mining and quarrying	...	...	2285	...	...	2933	...	...	3142	...	...	3487

Paraguay

4.1 Derivation of Value Added by Kind of Activity, in Current Prices
(Continued)

Million Paraguayan guaranies

	1980 Gross Output	1980 Intermediate Consumption	1980 Value Added	1981 Gross Output	1981 Intermediate Consumption	1981 Value Added	1982 Gross Output	1982 Intermediate Consumption	1982 Value Added	1983 Gross Output	1983 Intermediate Consumption	1983 Value Added
3 Manufacturing	...	...	92338	...	...	118469	...	...	120966	...	...	134273
A Manufacture of food, beverages and tobacco	...	...	31780	...	...	40520	...	...	48023	...	...	56380
B Textile, wearing apparel and leather industries	...	...	10349	...	...	15194	...	...	12473	...	...	13036
C Manufacture of wood and wood products, including furniture	...	...	14832	...	...	16734	...	...	17678	...	...	19276
D Manufacture of paper and paper products, printing and publishing	...	...	3506	...	...	4515	...	...	6334	...	...	6409
E Manufacture of chemicals and chemical petroleum, coal, rubber and plastic products	...	...	16709	...	...	21433	...	...	13866	...	...	14242
F Manufacture of non-metallic mineral products, except products of petroleum and coal	...	...	3826	...	...	4956	...	...	4526	...	...	5774
G Basic metal industries	...	...	172	...	...	348	...	...	446	...	...	530
H Manufacture of fabricated metal products, machinery and equipment	...	...	2326	...	...	3326	...	...	3842	...	...	4122
I Other manufacturing industries	...	...	8838	...	...	11442	...	...	13778	...	...	14504
4 Electricity, gas and water	...	...	12923	...	...	15271	...	...	18120	...	...	20638
A Electricity, gas and steam	...	...	11238	...	...	13148	...	...	15778	...	...	17514
B Water works and supply	...	...	1685	...	...	2123	...	...	2342	...	...	3124
5 Construction	...	...	34317	...	...	46740	...	...	49544	...	...	54994
6 Wholesale and retail trade, restaurants and hotels [ab]	...	...	144870	...	...	188378	...	...	196158	...	...	217210
7 Transport, storage and communication	...	...	23784	...	...	29059	...	...	31107	...	...	34529
8 Finance, insurance, real estate and business services [bc]	...	...	14993	...	...	20091	...	...	22500	...	...	24976
9 Community, social and personal services [ac]	...	...	50697	...	...	64286	...	...	72000	...	...	79920
Total, Industries	...	...	541344	...	...	682012	...	...	704183	...	...	781643
Producers of Government Services	...	...	19115	...	...	26678	...	...	32858	...	...	36472
Other Producers	...	...	...	...	...	...	...	...	...	...	...	...
Total	...	...	560459	...	...	708689	...	...	737040	...	...	818114
Less: Imputed bank service charge	...	...	...	...	...	...	...	...	...	...	...	...
Import duties	...	...	...	...	...	...	...	...	...	...	...	...
Value added tax	...	...	...	...	...	...	...	...	...	...	...	...
Total	...	...	560459	...	...	708689	...	...	737040	...	...	818114

	1984 Gross Output	1984 Intermediate Consumption	1984 Value Added	1985 Gross Output	1985 Intermediate Consumption	1985 Value Added	1986 Gross Output	1986 Intermediate Consumption	1986 Value Added	1987 Gross Output	1987 Intermediate Consumption	1987 Value Added
All Producers												
1 Agriculture, hunting, forestry and fishing	...	...	307113	...	...	403261	...	...	498923	...	...	681934
A Agriculture and hunting	...	...	273860	...	...	359230	...	...	429977	...	...	586972
B Forestry and logging	...	...	32642	...	...	43243	...	...	67778	...	...	93398
C Fishing	...	...	611	...	...	788	...	...	1168	...	...	1564
2 Mining and quarrying	...	...	4359	...	...	5672	...	...	8350	...	...	11507

Paraguay

4.1 Derivation of Value Added by Kind of Activity, in Current Prices
(Continued)

Million Paraguayan guaranies

	1984 Gross Output	1984 Intermediate Consumption	1984 Value Added	1985 Gross Output	1985 Intermediate Consumption	1985 Value Added	1986 Gross Output	1986 Intermediate Consumption	1986 Value Added	1987 Gross Output	1987 Intermediate Consumption	1987 Value Added
3 Manufacturing	...	...	172003	...	...	226115	...	...	296008	...	...	404051
A Manufacture of food, beverages and tobacco	...	...	76307	...	...	106369	...	...	152186	...	...	206246
B Textile, wearing apparel and leather industries	...	...	22086	...	...	28903	...	...	32408	...	...	40245
C Manufacture of wood and wood products, including furniture	...	...	22948	...	...	25539	...	...	34641	...	...	42532
D Manufacture of paper and paper products, printing and publishing	...	...	6077	...	...	7215	...	...	10231	...	...	12267
E Manufacture of chemicals and chemical petroleum, coal, rubber and plastic products	...	...	16049	...	...	20917	...	...	23125	...	...	36531
F Manufacture of non-metallic mineral products, except products of petroleum and coal	...	...	5770	...	...	6425	...	...	12229	...	...	17650
G Basic metal industries	...	...	663	...	...	745	...	...	996	...	...	2095
H Manufacture of fabricated metal products, machinery and equipment	...	...	6559	...	...	7819	...	...	9887	...	...	12151
I Other manufacturing industries	...	...	15544	...	...	22183	...	...	20305	...	...	34334
4 Electricity, gas and water	...	...	26064	...	...	30896	...	...	44791	...	...	62609
A Electricity, gas and steam	...	...	22127	...	...	25780	...	...	37681	...	...	52904
B Water works and supply	...	...	3937	...	...	5116	...	...	7110	...	...	9705
5 Construction	...	...	66873	...	...	82888	...	...	110137	...	...	146042
6 Wholesale and retail trade, restaurants and hotels ab	...	...	272599	...	...	360391	...	...	489776	...	...	662177
7 Transport, storage and communication	...	...	44059	...	...	57974	...	...	80083	...	...	109313
8 Finance, insurance, real estate and business services bc	...	...	30971	...	...	39163	...	...	52553	...	...	70368
9 Community, social and personal services ac	...	...	101178	...	...	129209	...	...	174917	...	...	240808
Total, Industries	...	...	1025219	...	...	1335569	...	...	1755538	...	...	2388809
Producers of Government Services	...	...	45225	...	...	58321	...	...	78262	...	...	104792
Other Producers	...	...	...	...	...	...	...	...	...	...	...	...
Total	...	...	1070444	...	...	1393890	...	...	1833800	...	...	2493601
Less: Imputed bank service charge	...	...	...	...	...	...	...	...	...	...	...	...
Import duties	...	...	...	...	...	...	...	...	...	...	...	...
Value added tax	...	...	...	...	...	...	...	...	...	...	...	...
Total	...	...	1070444	...	...	1393890	...	...	1833800	...	...	2493601

a) Restaurants and hotels are included in item 'Community, social and personal services'.
b) Finance is included in item 'Wholesale and retail trade, restaurants and hotels'.
c) Business services are included in item 'Community, social and personal services'.

4.2 Derivation of Value Added by Kind of Activity, in Constant Prices

Million Paraguayan guaranies

	1980 Gross Output	1980 Intermediate Consumption	1980 Value Added	1981 Gross Output	1981 Intermediate Consumption	1981 Value Added	1982 Gross Output	1982 Intermediate Consumption	1982 Value Added	1983 Gross Output	1983 Intermediate Consumption	1983 Value Added

At constant prices of:1982

All Producers

	1980 GO	1980 IC	1980 VA	1981 GO	1981 IC	1981 VA	1982 GO	1982 IC	1982 VA	1983 GO	1983 IC	1983 VA
1 Agriculture, hunting, forestry and fishing	...	...	172524	...	...	189876	...	...	190645	...	...	185991
A Agriculture and hunting	...	...	153692	...	...	169981	...	...	171838	...	...	167534
B Forestry and logging	...	...	18424	...	...	19471	...	...	18370	...	...	18039
C Fishing	...	...	408	...	...	424	...	...	437	...	...	418
2 Mining and quarrying	...	...	2669	...	...	3070	...	...	3142	...	...	2912

Paraguay

4.2 Derivation of Value Added by Kind of Activity, in Constant Prices
(Continued)

Million Paraguayan guaranies

	1980 Gross Output	1980 Intermediate Consumption	1980 Value Added	1981 Gross Output	1981 Intermediate Consumption	1981 Value Added	1982 Gross Output	1982 Intermediate Consumption	1982 Value Added	1983 Gross Output	1983 Intermediate Consumption	1983 Value Added
					At constant prices of:1982							
3 Manufacturing	...	...	120422	...	...	125613	...	...	120966	...	...	115861
A Manufacture of food, beverages and tobacco	...	...	40025	...	...	45456	...	...	48023	...	...	49523
B Textile, wearing apparel and leather industries	...	...	11276	...	...	13540	...	...	12473	...	...	11624
C Manufacture of wood and wood products, including furniture	...	...	22979	...	...	17655	...	...	17678	...	...	16977
D Manufacture of paper and paper products, printing and publishing	...	...	5261	...	...	5885	...	...	6334	...	...	3873
E Manufacture of chemicals and chemical petroleum, coal, rubber and plastic products	...	...	20816	...	...	20606	...	...	13866	...	...	13541
F Manufacture of non-metallic mineral products, except products of petroleum and coal	...	...	4645	...	...	5040	...	...	4526	...	...	4874
G Basic metal industries	...	...	377	...	...	430	...	...	446	...	...	445
H Manufacture of fabricated metal products, machinery and equipment	...	...	3609	...	...	3863	...	...	3842	...	...	3780
I Other manufacturing industries	...	...	11434	...	...	13138	...	...	13778	...	...	11224
4 Electricity, gas and water	...	...	14025	...	...	14746	...	...	18120	...	...	17779
A Electricity, gas and steam	...	...	12137	...	...	12623	...	...	15778	...	...	15014
B Water works and supply	...	...	1888	...	...	2123	...	...	2342	...	...	2765
5 Construction	...	...	45164	...	...	52707	...	...	49544	...	...	46720
6 Wholesale and retail trade, restaurants and hotels ab	...	...	185028	...	...	200570	...	...	196158	...	...	190171
7 Transport, storage and communication	...	...	29551	...	...	30497	...	...	31107	...	...	30742
8 Finance, insurance, real estate and business services bc	...	...	21479	...	...	22961	...	...	22501	...	...	21448
9 Community, social and personal services ac	...	...	68096	...	...	72727	...	...	72000	...	...	71133
Total, Industries	...	...	658958	...	...	712767	...	...	704182	...	...	682757
Producers of Government Services	...	...	25728	...	...	31594	...	...	32858	...	...	32172
Other Producers	...	...	...	...	...	...	...	...	...	...	...	...
Total	...	...	684686	...	...	744361	...	...	737041	...	...	714929
Less: Imputed bank service charge	...	...	...	...	...	...	...	...	...	...	...	...
Import duties	...	...	...	...	...	...	...	...	...	...	...	...
Value added tax	...	...	...	...	...	...	...	...	...	...	...	...
Total	...	...	684686	...	...	744361	...	...	737041	...	...	714929

	1984 Gross Output	1984 Intermediate Consumption	1984 Value Added	1985 Gross Output	1985 Intermediate Consumption	1985 Value Added	1986 Gross Output	1986 Intermediate Consumption	1986 Value Added	1987 Gross Output	1987 Intermediate Consumption	1987 Value Added
					At constant prices of:1982							
					All Producers							
1 Agriculture, hunting, forestry and fishing	...	...	196990	...	...	206042	...	...	193467	...	...	207021
A Agriculture and hunting	...	...	178074	...	...	186954	...	...	172178	...	...	184468
B Forestry and logging	...	...	18490	...	...	18649	...	...	20837	...	...	22087
C Fishing	...	...	426	...	...	439	...	...	452	...	...	466
2 Mining and quarrying	...	...	2942	...	...	3073	...	...	3440	...	...	3646

Paraguay

4.2 Derivation of Value Added by Kind of Activity, in Constant Prices
(Continued)

Million Paraguayan guaranies

	1984 Gross Output	1984 Intermediate Consumption	1984 Value Added	1985 Gross Output	1985 Intermediate Consumption	1985 Value Added	1986 Gross Output	1986 Intermediate Consumption	1986 Value Added	1987 Gross Output	1987 Intermediate Consumption	1987 Value Added
						At constant prices of: 1982						
3 Manufacturing	...	...	121075	...	...	127129	...	...	125345	...	...	129732
A Manufacture of food, beverages and tobacco	...	...	52664	...	...	53588	...	...	57195	...	...	59359
B Textile, wearing apparel and leather industries	...	...	12523	...	...	15352	...	...	12783	...	...	10300
C Manufacture of wood and wood products, including furniture	...	...	16724	...	...	15302	...	...	15661	...	...	17404
D Manufacture of paper and paper products, printing and publishing	...	...	4407	...	...	4487	...	...	4136	...	...	4217
E Manufacture of chemicals and chemical petroleum, coal, rubber and plastic products	...	...	12470	...	...	14006	...	...	12838	...	...	15284
F Manufacture of non-metallic mineral products, except products of petroleum and coal	...	...	4555	...	...	4003	...	...	5261	...	...	6076
G Basic metal industries	...	...	519	...	...	550	...	...	553	...	...	826
H Manufacture of fabricated metal products, machinery and equipment	...	...	4794	...	...	6253	...	...	5406	...	...	5303
I Other manufacturing industries	...	...	12419	...	...	13588	...	...	11512	...	...	10963
4 Electricity, gas and water	...	...	18164	...	...	19248	...	...	21218	...	...	22821
A Electricity, gas and steam	...	...	15344	...	...	16255	...	...	18060	...	...	19505
B Water works and supply	...	...	2820	...	...	2993	...	...	3158	...	...	3316
5 Construction	...	...	45604	...	...	45148	...	...	45600	...	...	46512
6 Wholesale and retail trade, restaurants and hotels [ab]	...	...	193634	...	...	202759	...	...	209437	...	...	216767
7 Transport, storage and communication	...	...	31853	...	...	33468	...	...	35142	...	...	36899
8 Finance, insurance, real estate and business services [bc]	...	...	21448	...	...	21662	...	...	22096	...	...	22538
9 Community, social and personal services [ac]	...	...	72243	...	...	73688	...	...	75858	...	...	78134
Total, Industries	...	...	703953	...	...	732217	...	...	731603	...	...	764070
Producers of Government Services	...	...	32953	...	...	33941	...	...	34620	...	...	35312
Other Producers	...	...	...	...	...	...	...	...	...	...	...	...
Total	...	...	736906	...	...	766158	...	...	766223	...	...	799382
Less: Imputed bank service charge	...	...	...	...	...	...	...	...	...	...	...	...
Import duties	...	...	...	...	...	...	...	...	...	...	...	...
Value added tax	...	...	...	...	...	...	...	...	...	...	...	...
Total	...	...	736906	...	...	766158	...	...	766223	...	...	799382

a) Restaurants and hotels are included in item 'Community, social and personal services'.
b) Finance is included in item 'Wholesale and retail trade, restaurants and hotels'.
c) Business services are included in item 'Community, social and personal services'.

Peru

Source. Reply to the United Nations National Accounts Questionnaire from the Instituto Nacional de Estadistica, Lima. The official estimates are published in 'Cuentas Nacionales del Peru: Tablas Insumo Producto y Sectores Institucionales', Instituto Nacional de Estadistica del Peru, Lima

General note. The estimates shown in the following tables have been prepareb by the Instituto Nacional de Estadistica in accordance with the United Nations System of National Accounts so far as the existing data would permit.

1.1 Expenditure on the Gross Domestic Product, in Current Prices

Million Peruvian intis

	1970	1975	1978	1979	1980	1981	1982	1983	1984	1985	1986	1987
1 Government final consumption expenditure	231	575	1520	301	667	1215	2260	4077	8104	22457	42342	80145
2 Private final consumption expenditure				2131	3659	6738	11070	21099	45532	123412	254589	506009
3 Gross capital formation	43	164	368	757	1640	3347	5644	7733	16517	44668	92125	186824
A Increase in stocks	2	17	-9	33	239	575	664	172	-221	414	9480	32151
B Gross fixed capital formation	41	147	377	724	1402	2772	4981	7561	16738	44254	82645	154673
Residential buildings	19	40	132	247	469	982	1955	3161	7081	19124	34954	67749
Non-residential buildings												
Other construction and land improvement etc.	5	30	70	165	284	561	1055	1613	3611	9474	20249	38241
Other	17	76	174	311	649	1228	1970	2788	6046	15656	27442	48683
4 Exports of goods and services	50	72	394	968	1332	1735	2806	5880	13486	39611	43708	71886
5 Less: Imports of goods and services	45	146	381	666	1329	2378	3829	6224	10794	30304	51742	84697
Equals: Gross Domestic Product	280	665	1901	3490	5968	10658	17950	32565	72845	199845	381022	760166

1.2 Expenditure on the Gross Domestic Product, in Constant Prices

Million Peruvian intis

	1970	1975	1978	1979	1980	1981	1982	1983	1984	1985	1986	1987
				At constant prices of:1979								
1 Government final consumption expenditure	2008	2527	2414	301	368	362	410	374	357	370	385	392
2 Private final consumption expenditure				2131	2236	2356	2376	2167	2209	2256	2557	2721
3 Gross capital formation	441	922	643	757	1031	1242	1153	716	645	579	856	963
A Increase in stocks	5	6	-16	33	149	218	150	4	-23	-19	114	101
B Gross fixed capital formation	436	916	659	724	882	1024	1003	712	668	598	742	862
Residential buildings	186	250	247	247	272	300	311	251	249	225	263	307
Non-residential buildings												
Other construction and land improvement etc.	46	158	123	166	191	225	222	172	176	153	207	237
Other	205	508	290	311	419	499	470	289	244	220	272	317
4 Exports of goods and services	651	606	800	968	879	854	906	812	886	925	811	832
5 Less: Imports of goods and services	582	842	558	666	868	1006	1028	723	592	541	680	706
Equals: Gross Domestic Product	2519	3213	3299	3490	3647	3808	3817	3346	3506	3589	3929	4201

1.3 Cost Components of the Gross Domestic Product

Million Peruvian intis

	1970	1975	1978	1979	1980	1981	1982	1983	1984	1985	1986	1987
1 Indirect taxes, net	23	46	165	361	573	1025	1710	2747	6197	19838	28670	53096
A Indirect taxes	24	58	220	422	726	1195	1974	3152	6815	21608	31736	59512
B Less: Subsidies	1	12	55	61	153	170	264	405	618	1770	3066	6416
2 Consumption of fixed capital	17	41	144	196	321	553	945	1886	4253	11005	18834	36286
3 Compensation of employees paid by resident producers to:	100	248	610	981	1772	3286	5703	10700	21681	54100	115635	235509
A Resident households	100	248	608	977	1767	3275	5675	10631	21564	53849	115336	...
B Rest of the world	...	...	2	4	5	11	28	70	118	251	300	...
4 Operating surplus	141	331	982	1951	3303	5795	9592	17231	40714	114901	217882	435275
Equals: Gross Domestic Product	280	665	1901	3490	5968	10658	17950	32565	72845	199845	381022	760166

1.4 General Government Current Receipts and Disbursements

Million Peruvian intis

	1970	1975	1978	1979	1980	1981	1982	1983	1984	1985	1986	1987
					Receipts							
1 Operating surplus	...	...	...	4	5	8	20	37	147	582	951	...
2 Property and entrepreneurial income	...	...	...	34	213	399	571	939	1938	6780	6594	...
3 Taxes, fees and contributions	...	...	...	793	1333	2097	3338	5440	11528	32916	58285	...
A Indirect taxes	...	...	...	422	726	1195	1974	3152	6815	21608	31736	59512

Peru

1.4 General Government Current Receipts and Disbursements
(Continued)

Million Peruvian intis

	1970	1975	1978	1979	1980	1981	1982	1983	1984	1985	1986	1987
B Direct taxes	...	...	...	280	424	512	782	1060	2115	4514	12355	...
C Social security contributions	...	...	...	84	168	332	513	1033	2053	5581	12495	...
D Compulsory fees, fines and penalties	...	...	...	7	15	58	69	195	545	1213	1699	...
4 Other current transfers	...	...	...	45	136	207	82	373	707	1668	1016	...
Total Current Receipts of General Government	...	...	...	875	1687	2712	4011	6789	14321	41947	66845	...

Disbursements

	1970	1975	1978	1979	1980	1981	1982	1983	1984	1985	1986	1987
1 Government final consumption expenditure	...	...	...	301	667	1215	2260	4077	8104	22457	42342	80145
2 Property income	...	...	...	124	228	357	519	1411	1759	4934	8332	...
A Interest	...	...	...	124	228	357	519	1411	1759	4934	8332	...
B Net land rent and royalties	...	...	...	...	...	...	...	...	...	...	...	...
3 Subsidies	...	...	...	61	153	170	264	405	618	1770	3066	6416
4 Other current transfers	...	...	...	219	527	897	1098	2195	4342	11293	16634	...
A Social security benefits	...	...	...	79	150	281	481	918	1926	4462	10091	...
B Social assistance grants	...	...	...	...	...	...	...	...	...	...	...	...
C Other	...	...	...	140	377	616	617	1277	2416	6831	6543	...
5 Net saving a	...	...	...	170	111	73	-130	-1299	-502	1493	-3527	...
Total Current Disbursements and Net Saving of General Government	...	...	...	875	1687	2712	4011	6789	14321	41947	66845	...

a) Item 'Net saving' includes consumption of fixed capital.

1.5 Current Income and Outlay of Corporate and Quasi-Corporate Enterprises, Summary

Million Peruvian intis

	1970	1975	1978	1979	1980	1981	1982	1983	1984	1985	1986	1987

Receipts

	1970	1975	1978	1979	1980	1981	1982	1983	1984	1985	1986	1987
1 Operating surplus	...	...	...	605	914	1359	2114	4132	11593	32880	41245	...
2 Property and entrepreneurial income received	...	...	...	299	583	1357	2280	4623	10950	26582	33463	...
3 Current transfers	...	...	...	127	298	538	741	1355	2552	7402	7805	...
Total Current Receipts a	...	...	...	1033	1794	3253	5136	10109	25094	66865	82516	...

Disbursements

	1970	1975	1978	1979	1980	1981	1982	1983	1984	1985	1986	1987
1 Property and entrepreneurial income	...	...	...	456	914	2052	3368	6498	16356	41973	47584	...
2 Direct taxes and other current payments to general government	...	...	...	241	381	441	680	891	1830	3907	11386	...
3 Other current transfers	...	...	...	33	65	137	234	552	956	2228	3667	...
4 Net saving b	...	...	...	302	435	622	854	2166	5950	18755	19879	...
Total Current Disbursements and Net Saving a	...	...	...	1033	1794	3253	5137	10109	25094	66865	82516	...

a) Data for this table have not been revised, therefore, data for some years are not comparable with those of other tables.
b) Item 'Net saving' includes consumption of fixed capital.

1.6 Current Income and Outlay of Households and Non-Profit Institutions

Million Peruvian intis

	1970	1975	1978	1979	1980	1981	1982	1983	1984	1985	1986	1987

Receipts

	1970	1975	1978	1979	1980	1981	1982	1983	1984	1985	1986	1987
1 Compensation of employees	...	...	...	983	1776	3290	5706	10703	21729	54395	116039	...
A From resident producers	...	...	...	977	1767	3275	5675	10631	21564	53849	115336	...
B From rest of the world	...	...	...	6	9	15	31	72	165	546	703	...
2 Operating surplus of private unincorporated enterprises	...	...	...	1539	2704	4981	8402	14950	33227	92444	194522	...
3 Property and entrepreneurial income	...	...	...	103	191	493	864	1625	2858	7456	9505	...
4 Current transfers	...	...	...	148	308	551	900	1693	3011	6647	14821	...
A Social security benefits	...	...	...	85	162	307	526	1021	2112	4685	10504	...
B Social assistance grants	...	...	...	...	...	...	...	...	...	...	...	...
C Other	...	...	...	...	...	...	...	...	...	...	...	...
Total Current Receipts a	...	...	...	2773	4980	9314	15872	28972	60825	160943	334886	...

Disbursements

	1970	1975	1978	1979	1980	1981	1982	1983	1984	1985	1986	1987
1 Private final consumption expenditure	...	...	...	2131	3659	6738	11070	21099	45532	123412	254589	...

Peru

1.6 Current Income and Outlay of Households and Non-Profit Institutions
(Continued)

Million Peruvian intis

	1970	1975	1978	1979	1980	1981	1982	1983	1984	1985	1986	1987
2 Property income	...	...	...	69	126	258	507	1054	1658	4433	4672	...
3 Direct taxes and other current transfers n.e.c. to general government	...	...	...	136	236	486	728	1499	3069	7625	15575	...
A Social security contributions	...	...	...	90	179	358	557	1136	2240	5805	12908	...
B Direct taxes	...	...	...	41	48	108	134	231	540	1092	1393	...
C Fees, fines and penalties	...	...	...	5	9	20	37	132	289	728	1274	...
4 Other current transfers	...	...	...	5	20	24	60	122	247	979	1912	...
5 Net saving [b]	...	...	...	432	938	1807	3507	5197	10318	24493	58138	...
Total Current Disbursements and Net Saving [a]	...	...	...	2773	4980	9314	15872	28972	60825	160943	334886	...

a) Data for this table have not been revised, therefore, data for some years are not comparable with those of other tables.
b) Item 'Net saving' includes consumption of fixed capital.

1.7 External Transactions on Current Account, Summary

Million Peruvian intis

	1970	1975	1978	1979	1980	1981	1982	1983	1984	1985	1986	1987
Payments to the Rest of the World
1 Imports of goods and services	...	...	...	666	1329	2377	3829	6224	10794	30304	51742	...
2 Factor income to the rest of the world	...	...	...	232	354	516	795	2031	4687	12172	12565	...
A Compensation of employees	...	...	...	4	5	11	28	70	118	251	300	...
B Property and entrepreneurial income	...	...	...	228	349	505	767	1961	4569	11921	12265	...
3 Current transfers to the rest of the world	...	...	...	1	3	4	5	17	47	208	206	...
4 Surplus of the nation on current transactions	...	...	...	147	-155	-844	-1413	-1669	-751	74	-17636	...
Payments to the Rest of the World and Surplus of the Nation on Current Transactions	...	...	...	1046	1531	2053	3216	6602	14777	42757	46876	...
Receipts From The Rest of the World
1 Exports of goods and services	...	...	...	968	1332	1735	2806	5880	13486	39611	43708	...
2 Factor income from rest of the world	...	...	...	21	76	101	117	257	709	1945	1942	...
A Compensation of employees	...	...	...	6	9	15	31	72	165	546	703	...
B Property and entrepreneurial income	...	...	...	15	67	86	86	185	544	1399	1239	...
3 Current transfers from rest of the world	...	...	...	57	123	216	294	464	582	1202	1226	...
Receipts from the Rest of the World on Current Transactions	...	...	...	1046	1531	2053	3216	6602	14777	42757	46876	...

1.9 Gross Domestic Product by Institutional Sectors of Origin

Million Peruvian intis

	1970	1975	1978	1979	1980	1981	1982	1983	1984	1985	1986	1987
Domestic Factor Incomes Originating
1 General government	...	...	...	237	509	996	1715	3415	7350	18052	37847	...
2 Corporate and quasi-corporate enterprises	...	...	...	1056	1707	2844	4720	8925	21049	161954	314505	...
A Non-financial	...	...	...	1036	1678	2784	4602	8748	20421	161447	313833	...
Public	...	...	...	177	52	166	503	1140	2841	8218	11495	...
Private	...	...	...	859	1626	2618	4099	7608	17580	153229	302338	...
B Financial [a]	...	...	...	20	29	60	118	177	628	507	672	...
3 Households and private unincorporated enterprises [ba]	...	...	...	1836	3180	5793	9804	17477	38249	...	...	...
4 Non-profit institutions serving households [c]	...	...	...	...	...	...	...	...	...	...	...	...
Subtotal: Domestic Factor Incomes [d]	...	...	...	3129	5396	9633	16240	29817	66648	180007	352352	...
Indirect taxes, net [e]	...	...	...	361	573	1025	1710	2747	6197	19838	28670	...
A Indirect taxes	...	...	...	422	726	1195	1974	3152	6815	21608	31736	...
B Less: Subsidies	...	...	...	61	153	170	264	405	618	1770	3066	...
Consumption of fixed capital	...	...	...	...	...	...	...	...	...	...	...	...
Gross Domestic Product	...	...	...	3490	5968	10658	17950	32565	72845	199845	381022	...

a) For 1985 and 1986 households and private unincorporated enterprises and Non-profit institutions serving households are included in private non-financial enterprises.
b) Item 'Non-profit institutions serving households' is included in item 'Households and private unincorporated enterprises'.
c)
d) Item 'Domestic factor incomes' includes consumption of fixed capital.
e) Item 'Indirect taxes, net' includes import duties.

Peru

1.10 Gross Domestic Product by Kind of Activity, in Current Prices

Million Peruvian intis

	1970	1975	1978	1979	1980	1981	1982	1983	1984	1985	1986	1987
1 Agriculture, hunting, forestry and fishing	52	109	249	408	610	1098	1709	3426	7982	18634	45836	80360
2 Mining and quarrying	14	22	160	459	905	1257	1873	3589	7702	19513	11410	20540
3 Manufacturing	55	133	433	820	1206	1956	3317	6066	14859	50007	94098	171143
4 Electricity, gas and water	2	5	19	34	51	111	191	270	824	2344	3701	7432
5 Construction	17	51	116	181	342	737	1589	2172	4745	14087	28337	54439
6 Wholesale and retail trade, restaurants and hotels	37	114	327	623	1060	1932	3131	6145	13240	35564	73918	153525
7 Transport, storage and communication	15	45	129	224	396	712	1089	1817	4266	12183	23198	40412
8 Finance, insurance, real estate and business services	46	94	238	370	591	1238	2248	3836	8118	19454	39149	86279
9 Community, social and personal services	10	21	71	122	242	523	905	1750	3920	11019	25095	68063
Total, Industries	248	594	1742	3241	5403	9564	16052	29071	65656	182805	344742	682193
Producers of Government Services	24	57	135	215	461	917	1567	3020	6438	16103	33116	64268
Other Producers	3	6	19	32	62	150	316	536	975	2604	6973	19885
Subtotal	275	657	1896	3488	5926	10631	17935	32627	73069	201512	384831	766346
Less: Imputed bank service charge	4	12	41	76	118	284	404	767	1624	5716	11013	17571
Plus: Import duties	9	20	46	78	160	312	419	705	1400	4048	7204	11391
Plus: Value added tax	...	...	...	...	...	...	...	...	...	...	...	...
Equals: Gross Domestic Product	280	665	1901	3490	5968	10659	17950	32565	72845	199845	381022	760166

1.11 Gross Domestic Product by Kind of Activity, in Constant Prices

Million Peruvian intis

	1970	1975	1978	1979	1980	1981	1982	1983	1984	1985	1986	1987
	\multicolumn{12}{c}{At constant prices of: 1979}
1 Agriculture, hunting, forestry and fishing	405	387	391	408	382	416	428	382	427	443	467	488
2 Mining and quarrying	230	232	390	459	469	454	460	415	435	453	432	423
3 Manufacturing	627	805	787	820	866	873	864	718	757	795	921	1028
4 Electricity, gas and water	15	24	32	34	39	42	45	38	38	41	45	49
5 Construction	133	217	173	181	202	225	230	181	183	164	204	236
6 Wholesale and retail trade, restaurants and hotels	431	638	591	623	654	689	689	590	604	618	704	756
7 Transport, storage and communication	130	199	215	224	236	251	248	230	231	238	258	277
8 Finance, insurance, real estate and business services	257	333	358	370	386	411	410	391	392	424	446	478
9 Community, social and personal services	88	111	119	122	127	134	132	128	133	138	150	159
Total, Industries	2316	2946	3056	3241	3361	3495	3506	3073	3200	3314	3627	3894
Producers of Government Services	145	191	213	215	233	240	242	258	278	279	295	300
Other Producers	27	29	31	32	33	34	35	37	39	39	43	45
Subtotal	2488	3166	3300	3488	3627	3769	3783	3368	3517	3638	3965	4239
Less: Imputed bank service charge	52	67	73	76	82	89	90	98	88	111	117	122
Plus: Import duties	83	114	72	78	102	128	124	76	77	68	81	84
Plus: Value added tax	...	...	...	...	...	...	...	...	...	...	...	...
Equals: Gross Domestic Product	2519	3213	3299	3490	3647	3808	3817	3346	3506	3589	3929	4201

1.12 Relations Among National Accounting Aggregates

Million Peruvian intis

	1970	1975	1978	1979	1980	1981	1982	1983	1984	1985	1986	1987
Gross Domestic Product	280	665	1901	3490	5968	10658	17950	32565	72845	199845	381022	760166
Plus: Net factor income from the rest of the world	-5	-9	-88	-211	-278	-415	-678	-1773	-3977	-10227	-10622	-9621
Factor income from the rest of the world	1	2	4	21	76	101	117	257	709	1945	1942	...
Less: Factor income to the rest of the world	6	11	92	232	354	516	795	2031	4687	12171	12564	...
Equals: Gross National Product	275	657	1814	3279	5690	10244	17272	30792	68867	189618	370400	...
Less: Consumption of fixed capital	16	41	144	196	321	553	945	1886	4253	11005	18834	36286

Peru

1.12 Relations Among National Accounting Aggregates
(Continued)

Million Peruvian intis

	1970	1975	1978	1979	1980	1981	1982	1983	1984	1985	1986	1987
Equals: National Income	259	616	1670	3082	5369	9691	16327	28906	64614	178613	351566	...
Plus: Net current transfers from the rest of the world	3	2	8	56	120	213	289	448	535	994	1020	...
Current transfers from the rest of the world	3	2	8	57	122	216	292	465	582	1202	1226	...
Less: Current transfers to the rest of the world	-	-	-	1	2	4	3	17	47	208	206	...
Equals: National Disposable Income	262	618	1678	3138	5489	9904	16616	29354	65149	179607	352586	...
Less: Final consumption	231	575	1520	2432	4325	7954	13330	25176	53636	145870	296931	...
Equals: Net Saving	31	43	158	706	1164	1950	3286	4178	11513	33737	55655	...
Less: Surplus of the nation on current transactions	...	...	...	147	-155	-844	-1413	-1669	-751	74	-17636	...
Equals: Net Capital Formation	...	...	...	559	1318	2794	4700	5847	12265	33662	73291	...

2.1 Government Final Consumption Expenditure by Function, in Current Prices

Million Peruvian intis

	1970	1975	1978	1979	1980	1981	1982	1983	1984	1985	1986	1987
1 General public services	...	...	...	155	359	642	1347	2334	4388	12895	23826	45097
2 Defence	...	...	...									
3 Public order and safety	...	...	...	...	...	...	...	...	...	...	...	...
4 Education	...	...	...	81	167	325	530	1008	2206	5551	10818	20477
5 Health	...	...	...	27	52	101	152	346	685	1866	3565	6748
6 Social security and welfare	...	...	...	7	14	26	52	72	160	427	796	1507
7 Housing and community amenities	...	...	...	1	1	2	5	8	10	47	72	136
8 Recreational, cultural and religious affairs	...	...	...	5	24	23	42	76	58	319	567	1074
9 Economic services	...	...	...	25	50	96	133	233	596	1352	2697	5105
10 Other functions	...	...	...	...	...	...	...	...	...	...	...	...
Total Government Final Consumption Expenditure	...	...	...	301	667	1215	2260	4077	8104	22457	42342	80144

2.5 Private Final Consumption Expenditure by Type and Purpose, in Current Prices

Million Peruvian intis

	1970	1975	1978	1979	1980	1981	1982	1983	1984	1985	1986	1987
Final Consumption Expenditure of Resident Households												
1 Food, beverages and tobacco	...	...	...	852	1356	2502	4005	8646	18373	47126	97532	...
2 Clothing and footwear	...	...	...	263	501	830	1212	1565	3413	10403	23989	...
3 Gross rent, fuel and power	...	...	...	106	154	243	404	698	1232	2726	4264	...
4 Furniture, furnishings and household equipment and operation	...	...	...	270	484	866	1354	2230	4974	14614	28605	...
5 Medical care and health expenses	...	...	...	80	132	250	432	919	1844	4943	10496	...
6 Transport and communication	...	...	...	158	266	495	891	1693	3781	11497	19775	...
7 Recreational, entertainment, education and cultural services	...	...	...	55	91	168	307	569	1309	3894	7400	...
8 Miscellaneous goods and services	...	...	...	347	674	1384	2464	4779	10607	28210	62529	...
Total Final Consumption Expenditure in the Domestic Market by Households, of which	...	...	...	2131	3659	6738	11070	21099	45532	123412	254589	506009
Plus: Direct purchases abroad by resident households	...	...	...	...	...	...	...	...	...	...	...	...
Less: Direct purchases in the domestic market by non-resident households	...	...	...	...	...	...	...	...	...	...	...	...
Equals: Final Consumption Expenditure of Resident Households	...	...	...	2131	3659	6738	11070	21099	45532	123412	254589	506009
Final Consumption Expenditure of Private Non-profit Institutions Serving Households												
Equals: Final Consumption Expenditure of Private Non-profit Organisations Serving Households	...	...	...	...	...	...	...	...	...	...	...	...
Private Final Consumption Expenditure	...	...	...	2131	3659	6738	11070	21099	45532	123412	254589	506009

Peru

2.6 Private Final Consumption Expenditure by Type and Purpose, in Constant Prices

Million Peruvian intis

	1970	1975	1978	1979	1980	1981	1982	1983	1984	1985	1986	1987
				At constant prices of: 1979								
				Final Consumption Expenditure of Resident Households								
1 Food, beverages and tobacco	...	...	...	852	862	914	941	910	931	930	1062	...
2 Clothing and footwear	...	...	...	263	279	277	281	224	221	234	273	...
3 Gross rent, fuel and power	...	...	...	106	112	115	117	119	121	126	130	...
4 Furniture, furnishings and household equipment and operation	...	...	...	270	291	307	283	214	220	227	269	...
5 Medical care and health expenses	...	...	...	80	83	87	89	76	73	76	81	...
6 Transport and communication	...	...	...	158	174	185	188	163	166	164	179	...
7 Recreational, entertainment, education and cultural services	...	...	...	55	57	58	61	62	63	65	71	...
8 Miscellaneous goods and services	...	...	...	347	379	413	417	399	414	435	492	...
Total Final Consumption Expenditure in the Domestic Market by Households, of which	...	...	...	2131	2236	2356	2376	2167	2209	2256	2557	2721
Plus: Direct purchases abroad by resident households	...	...	...	...	...	...	...	...	...	...	...	...
Less: Direct purchases in the domestic market by non-resident households	...	...	...	...	...	...	...	...	...	...	...	...
Equals: Final Consumption Expenditure of Resident Households	...	...	...	2131	2236	2356	2376	2167	2209	2256	2557	2721
				Final Consumption Expenditure of Private Non-profit Institutions Serving Households								
Equals: Final Consumption Expenditure of Private Non-profit Organisations Serving Households	...	...	...	...	...	...	...	...	...	...	...	...
Private Final Consumption Expenditure	...	...	...	2131	2236	2356	2376	2167	2209	2256	2557	2721

2.7 Gross Capital Formation by Type of Good and Owner, in Current Prices

Million Peruvian intis

	1980 TOTAL	1980 Total Private	1980 Public Enterprises	1980 General Government	1981 TOTAL	1981 Total Private	1981 Public Enterprises	1981 General Government	1982 TOTAL	1982 Total Private	1982 Public Enterprises	1982 General Government
Increase in stocks, total	239	204	35	-	575	471	105	-	664	479	185	-
Gross Fixed Capital Formation, Total	1402	1059	164	179	2772	2133	291	348	4981	3627	739	615
1 Residential buildings	469	419	6	44	982	864	49	70	1955	1775	37	143
2 Non-residential buildings												
3 Other construction	239	60	124	55	470	240	85	145	907	198	472	237
4 Land improvement and plantation and orchard development	45	2	-	43	91	3	-	89	148	4	-	144
5 Producers' durable goods	649	578	33	36	1228	1027	156	45	1970	1650	230	90
A Transport equipment	173	159	2	12	417	388	18	11	671	622	24	25
B Machinery and equipment	476	419	31	25	811	639	138	33	1299	1028	206	62
6 Breeding stock, dairy cattle, etc.	...	...	...	...	...	...	...	...	...	...	...	...
Total Gross Capital Formation	1640	1263	199	179	3347	2604	396	348	5644	4106	924	615

	1983 TOTAL	1983 Total Private	1983 Public Enterprises	1983 General Government	1984 TOTAL	1984 Total Private	1984 Public Enterprises	1984 General Government	1985 TOTAL	1985 Total Private	1985 Public Enterprises	1985 General Government
Increase in stocks, total	172	123	48	-	-221	-1062	842	-	414	-2138	2552	-
Gross Fixed Capital Formation, Total	7561	5241	1375	945	16738	12203	2024	2510	44254	34057	5211	4987
1 Residential buildings	3161	2892	70	199	7081	6422	210	448	19124	17952	197	975
2 Non-residential buildings												
3 Other construction	1291	285	681	325	3000	250	1584	1166	8045	2255	3882	1908
4 Land improvement and plantation and orchard development	322	7	-	315	611	15	-	596	1429	47	-	1382
5 Producers' durable goods	2788	2058	624	106	6046	5516	230	300	15656	13802	1131	722
A Transport equipment	887	841	16	30	2077	1980	19	78	5660	5368	128	164
B Machinery and equipment	1902	1217	608	76	3969	3536	211	217	9996	8434	1003	554
6 Breeding stock, dairy cattle, etc.	...	...	...	...	...	...	...	...	...	...	...	...
Total Gross Capital Formation	7733	5364	1423	945	16517	11141	2866	2510	44668	31919	7763	4987

Peru

2.7 Gross Capital Formation by Type of Good and Owner, in Current Prices

Million Peruvian intis

	1986 TOTAL	Total Private	Public Enterprises	General Government	1987 TOTAL	Total Private	Public Enterprises	General Government
Increase in stocks, total	9480	8139	1340	-	32151	...	...	...
Gross Fixed Capital Formation, Total	82645	64189	6539	11917	154673	119974	...	...
1 Residential buildings	34954	32320	236	2398	67749	62118	380	5252
2 Non-residential buildings								
3 Other construction	16877	6873	5385	4619	31919	20438	1506	9975
4 Land improvement and plantation and orchard development	3372	117	-	3255	6323	198	-	6124
5 Producers' durable goods	27442	24879	919	1645	48683	37220	8623	2840
A Transport equipment	10160	9521	175	464	19236	18252	280	704
B Machinery and equipment	17282	15358	744	1181	29447	18968	8343	2136
6 Breeding stock, dairy cattle, etc.	...	...	...	...	...	...	...	...
Total Gross Capital Formation	92125	72328	7879	11917	186824	...	...	...

2.8 Gross Capital Formation by Type of Good and Owner, in Constant Prices

Million Peruvian intis

	1980 TOTAL	Total Private	Public Enterprises	General Government	1981 TOTAL	Total Private	Public Enterprises	General Government	1982 TOTAL	Total Private	Public Enterprises	General Government
				At constant prices of: 1979								
Increase in stocks, total	149	...	...	...	218	...	...	...	150	...	...	...
Gross Fixed Capital Formation, Total	882	658	110	114	1024	778	116	130	1003	716	165	122
1 Residential buildings	272	243	4	25	300	263	15	21	311	283	6	23
2 Non-residential buildings	...	...	...	...	...	...	...	...	...	...	...	...
3 Other construction	163	41	84	38	193	98	35	60	195	43	101	51
4 Land improvement and plantation and orchard development	28	1	-	27	32	1	-	31	27	1	-	26
5 Producers' durable goods	419	373	22	23	499	415	66	18	470	391	58	21
A Transport equipment	110	101	1	8	162	151	7	4	144	133	5	5
B Machinery and equipment	309	272	21	10	337	264	59	8	326	257	53	11
6 Breeding stock, dairy cattle, etc.	...	...	...	...	...	...	...	...	...	...	...	...
Total Gross Capital Formation	1031	...	...	...	1242	...	...	...	1153	...	...	...

	1983 TOTAL	Total Private	Public Enterprises	General Government	1984 TOTAL	Total Private	Public Enterprises	General Government	1985 TOTAL	Total Private	Public Enterprises	General Government
				At constant prices of: 1979								
Increase in stocks, total	4	...	...	...	-23	...	...	...	-19	...	...	...
Gross Fixed Capital Formation, Total	712	475	146	91	668	461	95	111	598	442	83	73
1 Residential buildings	252	230	6	16	249	226	7	16	225	211	2	11
2 Non-residential buildings	...	...	...	...	...	...	...	...	...	...	...	...
3 Other construction	143	32	75	36	149	12	78	58	132	37	64	31
4 Land improvement and plantation and orchard development	29	1	-	28	27	1	-	26	21	1	-	20
5 Producers' durable goods	289	213	65	11	244	222	9	12	220	193	16	10
A Transport equipment	91	86	1	3	80	76	1	3	74	70	1	2
B Machinery and equipment	198	126	64	5	164	146	9	5	145	123	15	6
6 Breeding stock, dairy cattle, etc.	...	...	...	...	...	...	...	...	...	...	...	...
Total Gross Capital Formation	712	...	...	...	645	...	...	...	579	...	...	...

Peru

2.8 Gross Capital Formation by Type of Good and Owner, in Constant Prices

Million Peruvian intis

	\multicolumn{4}{c	}{1986}	\multicolumn{4}{c	}{1987}
	TOTAL	Total Private	Public Enterprises	General Government	TOTAL	Total Private	Public Enterprises	General Government

At constant prices of: 1979

Increase in stocks, total	114	...	...	...	101	...	...	...
Gross Fixed Capital Formation, Total	742	563	67	112	862	650	72	140
1 Residential buildings	263	243	2	18	307	282	2	24
2 Non-residential buildings	...	...	...	...	...	...	...	...
3 Other construction	176	72	56	48	201	129	9	63
4 Land improvement and plantation and orchard development	30	1	-	29	36	1	-	35
5 Producers' durable goods	272	246	10	16	317	238	61	18
A Transport equipment	92	86	2	4	110	105	2	4
B Machinery and equipment	180	160	8	9	207	133	59	11
6 Breeding stock, dairy cattle, etc.	...	...	...	...	...	...	...	...
Total Gross Capital Formation	856	...	...	...	962	...	...	...

3.11 General Government Production Account: Total and Subsectors

Million Peruvian intis

	\multicolumn{5}{c	}{1980}	\multicolumn{5}{c	}{1981}
	Total General Government	Central Government	State or Provincial Government	Local Government	Social Security Funds	Total General Government	Central Government	State or Provincial Government	Local Government	Social Security Funds

Gross Output

1 Sales	5	4	...	2	...	11	7	...	4	...
2 Services produced for own use	667	517	...	139	11	1215	946	...	247	22
3 Own account fixed capital formation	137	55	...	29	53	263	116	...	46	101
Gross Output	809	575	...	170	64	1489	1069	...	297	124

Gross Input

Intermediate Consumption	288	234	...	30	23	452	362	...	47	43
Subtotal: Value Added	521	341	...	139	41	1037	707	...	250	80
1 Indirect taxes, net	12	8	...	3	1	41	32	...	7	2
A Indirect taxes	12	8	...	3	1	41	32	...	7	2
B Less: Subsidies	...	...	...	...	...	...	...	...	...	...
2 Consumption of fixed capital	...	...	...	...	...	...	...	...	...	...
3 Compensation of employees	504	330	...	134	39	988	670	...	239	78
4 Net Operating surplus	5	3	...	2	-	8	4	...	3	1
Gross Input	809	575	...	170	64	1489	1069	...	297	124

	\multicolumn{5}{c	}{1982}	\multicolumn{5}{c	}{1983}
	Total General Government	Central Government	State or Provincial Government	Local Government	Social Security Funds	Total General Government	Central Government	State or Provincial Government	Local Government	Social Security Funds

Gross Output

1 Sales	19	16	...	3	...	31	25	...	6	...
2 Services produced for own use	2260	2116	...	98	46	4077	3821	...	195	61
3 Own account fixed capital formation	445	201	...	90	154	944	416	...	265	264
Gross Output	2724	2333	...	191	200	5052	4262	...	465	325

Gross Input

Intermediate Consumption	956	820	...	67	69	1610	1317	...	191	102
Subtotal: Value Added	1769	1513	...	125	131	3442	2945	...	273	223
1 Indirect taxes, net	53	48	...	2	3	26	19	...	3	4
A Indirect taxes	53	48	...	2	3	26	19	...	3	4
B Less: Subsidies	...	...	...	...	...	...	...	...	...	...
2 Consumption of fixed capital	...	...	...	...	...	...	...	...	...	...
3 Compensation of employees	1696	1454	...	114	128	3379	2907	...	254	218
4 Net Operating surplus	20	10	...	9	1	37	19	...	16	1
Gross Input	2724	2333	...	191	200	5052	4262	...	465	325

Peru

3.11 General Government Production Account: Total and Subsectors

Million Peruvian intis

	1984					1985				
	Total General Government	Central Government	State or Provincial Government	Local Government	Social Security Funds	Total General Government	Central Government	State or Provincial Government	Local Government	Social Security Funds

Gross Output

1 Sales	65	53	...	11	...	165	131	...	33	-
2 Services produced for own use	8104	7543	...	437	124	22457	21062	...	1089	307
3 Own account fixed capital formation	2126	946	...	709	471	4858	2309	...	1399	1150
Gross Output	10294	8542	...	1157	595	27481	23502	...	2521	1457

Gross Input

Intermediate Consumption	2886	2222	...	498	166	9357	7815	...	1043	499
Subtotal: Value Added	7408	6320	...	659	429	18124	15687	...	1478	958
1 Indirect taxes, net	58	46	...	7	5	72	50	...	15	7
A Indirect taxes	58	46	...	7	5	72	50	...	15	7
B Less: Subsidies	...	...	...	...	...	...	...	...	...	...
2 Consumption of fixed capital	...	...	...	...	...	...	...	...	...	...
3 Compensation of employees	7203	6182	...	610	411	17470	15225	...	1332	912
4 Net Operating surplus	147	92	...	43	12	582	412	...	131	39
Gross Input	10294	8542	...	1157	595	27481	23502	...	2521	1457

	1986			
	Total General Government	Central Government	State or Provincial Government	Local Government	Social Security Funds

Gross Output

1 Sales	302	218	...	84	...
2 Services produced for own use	42342	39540	...	2083	718
3 Own account fixed capital formation	11319	4758	...	3148	3412
Gross Output	53962	44517	...	5315	4130

Gross Input

Intermediate Consumption	15888	12033	...	2324	1531
Subtotal: Value Added	38074	32484	...	2991	2599
1 Indirect taxes, net	226	147	...	27	52
A Indirect taxes	226	147	...	27	52
B Less: Subsidies	...	...	...	...	...
2 Consumption of fixed capital	...	...	...	...	...
3 Compensation of employees	36897	31708	...	2744	2445
4 Net Operating surplus	951	629	...	221	101
Gross Input	53962	44517	...	5315	4130

3.12 General Government Income and Outlay Account: Total and Subsectors

Million Peruvian intis

	1980					1981				
	Total General Government	Central Government	State or Provincial Government	Local Government	Social Security Funds	Total General Government	Central Government	State or Provincial Government	Local Government	Social Security Funds

Receipts

1 Operating surplus	5	2	...	2	-	8	4	...	3	1
2 Property and entrepreneurial income	213	202	...	1	11	399	368	...	3	28
A Withdrawals from public quasi-corporations	...	...	...	...	...	...	...	...	...	...
B Interest	14	3	...	1	11	39	8	...	3	28
C Dividends	19	19	...	-	-	5	5	...	-	-
D Net land rent and royalties	180	180	...	-	-	355	355	...	-	-
3 Taxes, fees and contributions	1333	1197	...	20	116	2097	1814	...	51	231
A Indirect taxes	726	721	...	5	...	1195	1181	...	14	...
B Direct taxes	424	421	...	4	-	512	501	...	10	-
C Social security contributions	168	46	...	6	116	332	90	...	12	230
D Fees, fines and penalties	15	9	...	5	-	58	42	...	15	1

Peru

3.12 General Government Income and Outlay Account: Total and Subsectors
(Continued)

Million Peruvian intis

	1980					1981				
	Total General Government	Central Government	State or Provincial Government	Local Government	Social Security Funds	Total General Government	Central Government	State or Provincial Government	Local Government	Social Security Funds
4 Other current transfers	136	15	...	120	-	207	20	...	188	-
A Casualty insurance claims	-	-	...	-	-	1	1	...	-	-
B Transfers from other government subsectors	...	...	...	...	...	...	...	...	...	...
C Transfers from the rest of the world	...	...	...	...	...	...	...	...	...	...
D Other transfers, except imputed	136	15	...	120	-	206	19	...	188	-
E Imputed unfunded employee pension and welfare contributions	...	...	...	...	...	...	...	...	...	...
Total Current Receipts	1687	1417	...	143	127	2712	2207	...	246	260

Disbursements

1 Government final consumption expenditure	667	517	...	139	11	1215	946	...	247	22
2 Property income	228	228	...	-	-	357	357	...	-	-
A Interest	228	228	...	-	-	357	357	...	-	-
B Net land rent and royalties	...	...	...	...	...	...	...	...	...	...
3 Subsidies	153	153	...	-	-	170	170	...	-	-
4 Other current transfers	527	423	...	6	98	897	697	...	17	183
A Casualty insurance premiums, net	3	3	...	-	-	5	5	...	-	-
B Transfers to other government subsectors	...	...	...	...	...	...	...	...	...	...
C Social security benefits	150	46	...	6	98	281	90	...	12	179
D Social assistance grants	...	...	...	...	...	...	...	...	...	...
E Unfunded employee pension and welfare benefits	...	...	...	...	...	...	...	...	...	...
F Transfers to private non-profit institutions serving households	...	...	...	...	...	...	...	...	...	...
G Other transfers n.e.c.	374	374	...	-	-	611	602	...	5	4
H Transfers to the rest of the world	...	...	...	...	...	...	...	...	...	...
Net saving [a]	111	96	...	-3	18	73	38	...	-19	54
Total Current Disbursements and Net Saving	1687	1417	...	143	127	2712	2207	...	246	260

	1982					1983				
	Total General Government	Central Government	State or Provincial Government	Local Government	Social Security Funds	Total General Government	Central Government	State or Provincial Government	Local Government	Social Security Funds

Receipts

1 Operating surplus	20	10	...	9	1	37	19	...	16	1
2 Property and entrepreneurial income	571	510	...	6	55	939	852	...	13	74
A Withdrawals from public quasi-corporations	...	...	...	...	...	...	...	...	...	...
B Interest	69	8	...	6	55	91	4	...	13	74
C Dividends	15	15	...	-	-	6	6	...	-	-
D Net land rent and royalties	488	488	...	-	-	842	842	...	-	-
3 Taxes, fees and contributions	3338	2942	...	54	343	5440	4517	...	211	712
A Indirect taxes	1974	1953	...	20	...	3152	2999	...	154	...
B Direct taxes	782	770	...	13	-	1060	1038	...	22	...
C Social security contributions	513	182	...	3	328	1033	387	...	8	638
D Fees, fines and penalties	69	37	...	18	15	195	93	...	27	74
4 Other current transfers	82	36	...	46	-	373	291	...	82	-
A Casualty insurance claims	1	1	...	-	-	7	7	...	-	-
B Transfers from other government subsectors	...	...	...	...	...	...	...	...	...	...
C Transfers from the rest of the world	...	...	...	...	...	...	...	...	...	...
D Other transfers, except imputed	81	35	...	46	-	366	284	...	82	-
E Imputed unfunded employee pension and welfare contributions	...	...	...	...	...	...	...	...	...	...
Total Current Receipts	4011	3498	...	115	398	6789	5680	...	322	787

Peru

3.12 General Government Income and Outlay Account: Total and Subsectors
(Continued)

Million Peruvian intis

1982 / 1983

	1982 Total General Government	1982 Central Government	1982 State or Provincial Government	1982 Local Government	1982 Social Security Funds	1983 Total General Government	1983 Central Government	1983 State or Provincial Government	1983 Local Government	1983 Social Security Funds
Disbursements										
1 Government final consumption expenditure	2260	2116	...	98	46	4077	3821	...	195	61
2 Property income	519	518	...	-	1	1411	1403	...	-	8
A Interest	519	518	...	-	1	1411	1403	...	-	8
B Net land rent and royalties	...	...	...	...	...	...	...	...	...	...
3 Subsidies	264	264	...	-	-	405	405	...	-	-
4 Other current transfers	1098	783	...	9	306	2195	1634	...	21	540
A Casualty insurance premiums, net	9	9	...	-	-	18	18	...	-	-
B Transfers to other government subsectors	...	...	...	...	...	...	...	...	...	...
C Social security benefits	481	182	...	3	296	918	387	...	8	523
D Social assistance grants	...	...	...	...	...	...	...	...	...	...
E Unfunded employee pension and welfare benefits	...	...	...	...	...	...	...	...	...	...
F Transfers to private non-profit institutions serving households	...	...	...	...	...	...	...	...	...	...
G Other transfers n.e.c.	609	592	...	6	10	1259	1229	...	13	17
H Transfers to the rest of the world	...	...	...	...	...	...	...	...	...	...
Net saving [a]	-130	-182	...	7	45	-1299	-1583	...	106	178
Total Current Disbursements and Net Saving	4011	3498	...	115	398	6789	5680	...	322	787

1984 / 1985

	1984 Total General Government	1984 Central Government	1984 State or Provincial Government	1984 Local Government	1984 Social Security Funds	1985 Total General Government	1985 Central Government	1985 State or Provincial Government	1985 Local Government	1985 Social Security Funds
Receipts										
1 Operating surplus	147	92	...	43	12	582	412	...	131	39
2 Property and entrepreneurial income	1938	1740	...	35	163	6780	6305	...	135	341
A Withdrawals from public quasi-corporations	...	...	...	...	...	...	...	...	...	...
B Interest	206	8	...	35	163	654	181	...	135	338
C Dividends	128	128	...	-	-	345	345	...	-	-
D Net land rent and royalties	1604	1604	...	-	-	5781	5778	...	-	3
3 Taxes, fees and contributions	11528	9752	...	459	1317	32916	27503	...	1590	3825
A Indirect taxes	6815	6516	...	299	...	21608	20484	...	1124	...
B Direct taxes	2115	2034	...	81	-	4514	4294	...	221	-
C Social security contributions	2053	881	...	19	1154	5581	2065	...	38	3479
D Fees, fines and penalties	545	321	...	60	163	1213	660	...	207	346
4 Other current transfers	707	560	...	147	1	1668	1512	...	155	-
A Casualty insurance claims	1	1	...	-	-	13	12	...	-	-
B Transfers from other government subsectors	...	...	...	...	...	...	...	...	...	...
C Transfers from the rest of the world	...	...	...	...	...	...	...	...	...	...
D Other transfers, except imputed	706	559	...	147	1	1655	1500	...	155	-
E Imputed unfunded employee pension and welfare contributions	...	...	...	...	...	...	...	...	...	...
Total Current Receipts	14321	12143	...	684	1493	41947	35732	...	2011	4204
Disbursements										
1 Government final consumption expenditure	8104	7543	...	437	124	22457	21062	...	1089	307
2 Property income	1759	1738	...	3	18	4934	4901	...	3	30
A Interest	1759	1738	...	3	18	4934	4901	...	3	30
B Net land rent and royalties	...	...	...	...	...	...	...	...	...	...
3 Subsidies	618	618	...	-	-	1770	1770	...	-	-

Peru

3.12 General Government Income and Outlay Account: Total and Subsectors
(Continued)

Million Peruvian intis

	1984					1985				
	Total General Government	Central Government	State or Provincial Government	Local Government	Social Security Funds	Total General Government	Central Government	State or Provincial Government	Local Government	Social Security Funds
4 Other current transfers	4342	3241	...	51	1050	11293	8808	...	85	2399
A Casualty insurance premiums, net	51	50	...	-	-	116	115	...	-	-
B Transfers to other government subsectors	...	...	...	...	...	...	...	...	...	...
C Social security benefits	1926	881	...	19	1027	4462	2065	...	38	2359
D Social assistance grants	...	...	...	...	...	...	...	...	...	...
E Unfunded employee pension and welfare benefits	...	...	...	...	...	...	...	...	...	...
F Transfers to private non-profit institutions serving households	...	...	...	...	...	...	...	...	...	...
G Other transfers n.e.c.	2365	2310	...	32	23	6715	6628	...	47	40
H Transfers to the rest of the world	...	...	...	...	...	...	...	...	...	...
Net saving [a]	-502	-997	...	193	303	1493	-809	...	833	1468
Total Current Disbursements and Net Saving	14321	12143	...	684	1493	41947	35732	...	2011	4204

	1986				
	Total General Government	Central Government	State or Provincial Government	Local Government	Social Security Funds

Receipts

1 Operating surplus	951	...	...	...	...
2 Property and entrepreneurial income	6594	...	...	...	...
A Withdrawals from public quasi-corporations	...	...	...	...	...
B Interest	521	...	...	...	...
C Dividends	247	...	...	...	...
D Net land rent and royalties	5826	...	...	...	...
3 Taxes, fees and contributions	58285	...	...	...	...
A Indirect taxes	31736	...	...	...	...
B Direct taxes	12355	...	...	...	...
C Social security contributions	12495	...	...	...	...
D Fees, fines and penalties	1699	...	...	...	...
4 Other current transfers	1016	...	...	...	...
A Casualty insurance claims	18	...	...	...	...
B Transfers from other government subsectors	...	...	...	...	...
C Transfers from the rest of the world	...	...	...	...	...
D Other transfers, except imputed	998	...	...	...	...
E Imputed unfunded employee pension and welfare contributions	...	...	...	...	...
Total Current Receipts	66845	...	...	...	...

Disbursements

1 Government final consumption expenditure	42342	...	...	...	...
2 Property income	8332	...	...	...	...
A Interest	8332	...	...	...	...
B Net land rent and royalties	...	...	...	...	...
3 Subsidies	3066	3066	...	...	...

Peru

3.12 General Government Income and Outlay Account: Total and Subsectors
(Continued)

Million Peruvian intis

	1986				
	Total General Government	Central Government	State or Provincial Government	Local Government	Social Security Funds
4 Other current transfers	16634	...	...	...	...
A Casualty insurance premiums, net	132	...	...	...	...
B Transfers to other government subsectors	...	...	...	...	...
C Social security benefits	10091	...	...	...	...
D Social assistance grants	...	...	...	...	...
E Unfunded employee pension and welfare benefits	...	...	...	...	...
F Transfers to private non-profit institutions serving households	...	...	...	...	...
G Other transfers n.e.c.	6411	...	...	...	...
H Transfers to the rest of the world	...	...	...	...	...
Net saving [a]	-3527	...	...	...	...
Total Current Disbursements and Net Saving	66845	...	...	...	...

a) Item 'Net saving' includes consumption of fixed capital.

3.13 General Government Capital Accumulation Account: Total and Subsectors

Million Peruvian intis

	1980					1981				
	Total General Government	Central Government	State or Provincial Government	Local Government	Social Security Funds	Total General Government	Central Government	State or Provincial Government	Local Government	Social Security Funds
	Finance of Gross Accumulation									
1 Gross saving	111	96	...	-3	18	73	38	...	-19	54
2 Capital transfers	61	6	...	55	-	102	13	...	88	-
Finance of Gross Accumulation	172	102	...	52	18	175	51	...	70	54
	Gross Accumulation									
1 Gross capital formation	179	101	...	67	12	348	213	...	110	25
A Increase in stocks	-	-	...	-	-	-	-	...	-	-
B Gross fixed capital formation	179	101	...	67	12	348	213	...	110	25
2 Purchases of land, net	6	7	...	-	-	-1	-	...	-1	-
3 Purchases of intangible assets, net	...	...	...	...	...	...	...	...	...	...
4 Capital transfers	89	89	...	-	-	164	162	...	2	-
Net lending	-103	-94	...	-15	6	-337	-325	...	-41	29
Gross Accumulation	172	102	...	52	18	175	51	...	70	54

	1982					1983				
	Total General Government	Central Government	State or Provincial Government	Local Government	Social Security Funds	Total General Government	Central Government	State or Provincial Government	Local Government	Social Security Funds
	Finance of Gross Accumulation									
1 Gross saving	-130	-182	...	7	45	-1299	-1583	...	106	178
2 Capital transfers	128	26	...	101	-	296	68	...	227	-
Finance of Gross Accumulation	-3	-156	...	108	45	-1003	-1515	...	334	178
	Gross Accumulation									
1 Gross capital formation	615	455	...	127	34	945	540	...	381	24
A Increase in stocks	-	-	...	-	-	-	-	...	-	-
B Gross fixed capital formation	615	455	...	127	34	945	540	...	381	24
2 Purchases of land, net	-	-1	...	-2	-	-1	1	...	-1	-
3 Purchases of intangible assets, net	...	...	...	...	...	...	...	...	...	...
4 Capital transfers	191	189	...	2	-	358	354	...	4	-
Net lending	-808	-800	...	-19	11	-2306	-2410	...	-50	154
Gross Accumulation	-3	-156	...	108	45	-1003	-1515	...	334	178

Peru

3.13 General Government Capital Accumulation Account: Total and Subsectors

Million Peruvian intis

	1984					1985				
	Total General Government	Central Government	State or Provincial Government	Local Government	Social Security Funds	Total General Government	Central Government	State or Provincial Government	Local Government	Social Security Funds

Finance of Gross Accumulation

1 Gross saving	-502	-997	...	193	303	1493	-809	...	833	1468
2 Capital transfers	697	206	...	491	-	1477	443	...	1033	-
Finance of Gross Accumulation	196	-791	...	684	303	2970	-365	...	1867	1468

Gross Accumulation

1 Gross capital formation	2510	1582	...	896	32	4987	3247	...	1691	49
A Increase in stocks	-	-	...	-	-	-	-	...	-	-
B Gross fixed capital formation	2510	1582	...	896	32	4987	3247	...	1691	49
2 Purchases of land, net	-4	6	...	-11	-	-19	-6	...	-13	-
3 Purchases of intangible assets, net	...	...	...	...	...	...	...	...	...	...
4 Capital transfers	713	710	...	3	-	1723	1668	...	55	-
Net lending	-3023	-3090	...	-204	270	-3721	-5274	...	134	1420
Gross Accumulation	196	-791	...	684	303	2970	-365	...	1867	1468

	1986				
	Total General Government	Central Government	State or Provincial Government	Local Government	Social Security Funds

Finance of Gross Accumulation

1 Gross saving	-3527	...	...	...	...
2 Capital transfers	2852	...	...	...	...
Finance of Gross Accumulation	-675	...	...	...	...

Gross Accumulation

1 Gross capital formation	11917	...	...	...	...
A Increase in stocks	-	...	...	...	...
B Gross fixed capital formation	11917	...	...	...	...
2 Purchases of land, net	-12	...	...	...	...
3 Purchases of intangible assets, net	...	...	...	...	...
4 Capital transfers	3071	...	...	...	...
Net lending	-15652	...	...	...	...
Gross Accumulation	-675	...	...	...	...

3.14 General Government Capital Finance Account, Total and Subsectors

Million Peruvian intis

	1980					1981				
	Total General Government	Central Government	State or Provincial Government	Local Government	Social Security Funds	Total General Government	Central Government	State or Provincial Government	Local Government	Social Security Funds

Acquisition of Financial Assets

1 Gold and SDRs	...	...	...	...	...	...	...	...	...	...
2 Currency and transferable deposits	-25	-33	...	-4	11	74	46	...	20	7
3 Other deposits	16	13	...	2	2	162	147	...	4	11
4 Bills and bonds, short term	-	-	...	-	-	2	-	...	1	1
5 Bonds, long term	1	-	...	-	1	7	-	...	-	7
6 Corporate equity securities	...	...	...	...	...	...	...	...	...	...
7 Short-term loans, n.e.c.	1	-	...	-	-	3	-	...	2	1
8 Long-term loans, n.e.c.	1	-	...	-	1	19	1	...	-	17
9 Other receivables	117	92	...	8	18	-83	-99	...	1	14
10 Other assets	223	222	...	1	-	187	186	...	1	-
Total Acquisition of Financial Assets	334	294	...	7	33	370	282	...	30	58

Incurrence of Liabilities

1 Currency and transferable deposits	...	...	...	...	...	...	...	...	...	...
2 Other deposits	2	-1	...	2	1	29	29	...	-	-
3 Bills and bonds, short term	-	-	...	-	-	1	1	...	-	-

Peru

3.14 General Government Capital Finance Account, Total and Subsectors
(Continued)

Million Peruvian intis

	1980					1981				
	Total General Government	Central Government	State or Provincial Government	Local Government	Social Security Funds	Total General Government	Central Government	State or Provincial Government	Local Government	Social Security Funds
4 Bonds, long term	67	67	...	-	-	120	120	...	-	-
5 Short-term loans, n.e.c.	-22	-23	...	1	-	208	198	...	9	1
6 Long-term loans, n.e.c.	335	335	...	-	-	170	159	...	10	-
7 Other payables	42	3	...	13	26	131	97	...	9	25
8 Other liabilities	15	9	...	5	1	36	27	...	7	2
Total Incurrence of Liabilities	439	390	...	22	27	695	631	...	37	27
Net Lending	-104	-96	...	-15	6	-325	-349	...	-6	30
Incurrence of Liabilities and Net Worth	334	294	...	7	33	370	282	...	30	58

	1982					1983				
	Total General Government	Central Government	State or Provincial Government	Local Government	Social Security Funds	Total General Government	Central Government	State or Provincial Government	Local Government	Social Security Funds

Acquisition of Financial Assets

1 Gold and SDRs	...	...	...	...	...	...	...	...	...	...
2 Currency and transferable deposits	-7	-7	...	9	-9	312	296	...	14	2
3 Other deposits	64	14	...	24	26	323	242	...	80	1
4 Bills and bonds, short term	2	1	...	1	1	68	2	...	2	64
5 Bonds, long term	-8	-	...	-	-8	98	-	...	1	97
6 Corporate equity securities	...	...	...	...	...	...	...	...	...	...
7 Short-term loans, n.e.c.	1	2	...	-	-1	3	-	...	4	-1
8 Long-term loans, n.e.c.	-9	-	...	2	-11	41	37	...	3	-
9 Other receivables	11	-201	...	26	186	-262	-564	...	-78	380
10 Other assets	310	309	...	1	-	860	851	...	9	-
Total Acquisition of Financial Assets	364	118	...	62	184	1444	864	...	35	544

Incurrence of Liabilities

1 Currency and transferable deposits	...	...	...	...	...	...	...	...	...	...
2 Other deposits	78	76	...	2	-	-56	-56	...	-	-
3 Bills and bonds, short term	1	1	...	-	-	-1	-1	...	-	-
4 Bonds, long term	59	59	...	-	-	100	100	...	-	-
5 Short-term loans, n.e.c.	-68	-79	...	-9	20	681	636	...	25	20
6 Long-term loans, n.e.c.	1058	1070	...	-11	-	2625	2637	...	-8	-4
7 Other payables	-20	-262	...	95	148	190	-226	...	52	365
8 Other liabilities	70	62	...	4	5	228	204	...	15	8
Total Incurrence of Liabilities	1180	926	...	81	173	3767	3294	...	84	389
Net Lending	-816	-808	...	-19	11	-2324	-2429	...	-49	155
Incurrence of Liabilities and Net Worth	364	118	...	62	184	1444	864	...	35	544

	1984					1985				
	Total General Government	Central Government	State or Provincial Government	Local Government	Social Security Funds	Total General Government	Central Government	State or Provincial Government	Local Government	Social Security Funds

Acquisition of Financial Assets

1 Gold and SDRs	...	...	...	...	...	...	...	...	...	...
2 Currency and transferable deposits	368	312	...	12	44	1802	1316	...	213	273
3 Other deposits	264	149	...	126	-11	649	264	...	283	102
4 Bills and bonds, short term	54	9	...	6	39	815	440	...	55	320
5 Bonds, long term	-11	1	...	1	-13	204	-2	...	5	202
6 Corporate equity securities	...	...	...	...	...	...	...	...	...	...
7 Short-term loans, n.e.c.	7	5	...	1	1	479	439	...	13	27
8 Long-term loans, n.e.c.	72	6	...	2	64	74	7	...	35	32
9 Other receivables	-3590	-4031	...	-278	718	-637	-2148	...	-403	1913
10 Other assets	1263	1245	...	19	-	850	778	...	72	-
Total Acquisition of Financial Assets	-1573	-2305	...	-111	842	4236	1094	...	273	2869

Incurrence of Liabilities

1 Currency and transferable deposits	...	...	...	...	...	...	...	...	...	...
2 Other deposits	5	5	...	1	-1	55	48	...	8	-
3 Bills and bonds, short term	-	-	...	-	-	...	...	...	...	...

Peru

3.14 General Government Capital Finance Account, Total and Subsectors
(Continued)

Million Peruvian intis

	1984					1985				
	Total General Government	Central Government	State or Provincial Government	Local Government	Social Security Funds	Total General Government	Central Government	State or Provincial Government	Local Government	Social Security Funds
4 Bonds, long term	320	320	...	-	-	1151	1152	...	-	-
5 Short-term loans, n.e.c.	490	469	...	4	17	631	589	...	24	18
6 Long-term loans, n.e.c.	5348	5286	...	6	56	16889	16875	...	6	9
7 Other payables	-5287	-5776	...	18	471	-11665	-13065	...	35	1365
8 Other liabilities	563	471	...	64	28	958	835	...	65	57
Total Incurrence of Liabilities	1438	774	...	93	572	8020	6432	...	138	1450
Net Lending	-3012	-3078	...	-204	270	-3784	-5339	...	135	1419
Incurrence of Liabilities and Net Worth	-1573	-2305	...	-111	842	4236	1094	...	273	2869

3.21 Corporate and Quasi-Corporate Enterprise Production Account: Total and Sectors

Million Peruvian intis

	1980				1981				1982			
	Corporate and Quasi-Corporate Enterprises			ADDENDUM: Total, including Unincorporated	Corporate and Quasi-Corporate Enterprises			ADDENDUM: Total, including Unincorporated	Corporate and Quasi-Corporate Enterprises			ADDENDUM: Total, including Unincorporated
	TOTAL	Non-Financial	Financial		TOTAL	Non-Financial	Financial		TOTAL	Non-Financial	Financial	
Gross Output												
1 Output for sale	...	...	...	...	...	...	...	...	...	...	...	...
2 Imputed bank service charge	...	...	...	...	...	...	...	...	...	...	...	...
3 Own-account fixed capital formation	...	...	...	...	...	...	...	...	...	...	...	...
Gross Output	5019	4802	217	...	8549	8075	474	...	14114	13347	767	...
Gross Input												
Intermediate consumption	2957	2777	180	...	5117	4724	393	...	8240	7628	612	...
1 Imputed banking service charge	119	...	119	...	284	...	284	...	404	...	404	...
2 Other intermediate consumption	61	...	61	...	109	...	109	...	208	...	208	...
Subtotal: Value Added	2063	2026	37	...	3431	3350	81	...	5874	5719	155	...
1 Indirect taxes, net	356	349	7	...	587	567	20	...	1152	1116	36	...
A Indirect taxes	503	492	11	...	749	726	23	...	1391	1354	37	...
B Less: Subsidies	147	143	4	...	162	159	3	...	239	238	1	...
2 Consumption of fixed capital	...	...	...	...	...	...	...	...	...	...	...	...
3 Compensation of employees	793	710	83	...	1486	1315	171	...	2606	2302	304	...
4 Net operating surplus	914	968	-54	...	1359	1469	-110	...	2114	2300	-186	...
Gross Input	5019	4802	217	...	8549	8075	474	...	14114	13347	767	...

	1983				1984			
	Corporate and Quasi-Corporate Enterprises			ADDENDUM: Total, including Unincorporated	Corporate and Quasi-Corporate Enterprises			ADDENDUM: Total, including Unincorporated
	TOTAL	Non-Financial	Financial		TOTAL	Non-Financial	Financial	
Gross Output								
1 Output for sale	...	...	...	...	...	...	...	...
2 Imputed bank service charge	...	...	...	...	...	...	...	...
3 Own-account fixed capital formation	...	...	...	...	...	...	...	...
Gross Output	26352	24911	1441	...	61379	58075	3304	...
Gross Input								
Intermediate consumption	15552	14350	1202	...	35879	33320	2559	...
1 Imputed banking service charge	767	...	767	...	1624	...	1624	...
2 Other intermediate consumption	435	...	435	...	935	...	935	...
Subtotal: Value Added	10800	10561	239	...	25500	24755	745	...
1 Indirect taxes, net	1875	1813	62	...	4450	4333	117	...
A Indirect taxes	2256	2194	62	...	4993	4876	117	...
B Less: Subsidies	381	381	-	...	543	543	-	...
2 Consumption of fixed capital	...	...	...	...	...	...	...	...
3 Compensation of employees	4795	4232	563	...	9456	8074	1382	...
4 Net operating surplus	4132	4517	-385	...	11593	12347	-754	...
Gross Input	26352	24911	1441	...	61379	58075	3304	...

Peru

3.22 Corporate and Quasi-Corporate Enterprise Income and Outlay Account: Total and Sectors

Million Peruvian intis

	1980 TOTAL	1980 Non-Financial	1980 Financial	1981 TOTAL	1981 Non-Financial	1981 Financial	1982 TOTAL	1982 Non-Financial	1982 Financial	1983 TOTAL	1983 Non-Financial	1983 Financial
Receipts												
1 Operating surplus	914	968	-54	1359	1469	-110	2114	2300	-186	4132	4517	-385
2 Property and entrepreneurial income	583	136	447	1357	219	1138	2280	413	1867	4623	1061	3562
A Withdrawals from quasi-corporate enterprises	...	...	...	...	...	...	...	...	...	...	...	...
B Interest	572	127	445	1335	203	1132	2237	383	1854	4517	967	3550
C Dividends	8	5	3	15	9	6	31	18	13	80	68	12
D Net land rent and royalties	4	4	-	6	6	-	12	12	-	26	26	-
3 Current transfers	298	271	27	538	481	57	741	642	99	1355	1116	239
A Casualty insurance claims	44	19	25	91	41	50	145	58	87	314	98	216
B Casualty insurance premiums, net, due to be received by insurance companies	...	...	...	...	...	...	...	...	...	...	...	...
C Current transfers from the rest of the world	...	...	...	...	...	...	...	...	...	...	...	...
D Other transfers except imputed	242	242	-	421	421	-	552	552	-	938	938	-
E Imputed unfunded employee pension and welfare contributions	12	10	2	26	19	7	44	32	12	103	80	23
Total Current Receipts [a]	1794	1374	420	3253	2169	1084	5136	3357	1779	10109	6693	3416
Disbursements												
1 Property and entrepreneurial income	914	570	344	2052	1198	854	3368	1900	1468	6498	3699	2799
A Withdrawals from quasi-corporations	...	...	...	...	...	...	...	...	...	...	...	...
B Interest	568	246	322	1483	643	840	2590	1150	1440	4721	1957	2764
C Dividends	156	133	23	195	181	14	256	227	29	863	828	35
D Net land rent and royalties	192	192	-	374	374	-	522	522	-	913	913	-
2 Direct taxes and other current transfers n.e.c. to general government	381	363	18	441	390	51	680	640	40	891	812	79
A Direct taxes	376	358	18	403	354	49	648	610	38	828	750	78
B Fines, fees, penalties and other current transfers n.e.c.	5	5	-	38	36	2	32	30	2	63	62	1
3 Other current transfers	65	36	29	137	78	59	234	127	107	552	293	259
A Casualty insurance premiums, net	43	17	26	88	38	50	139	56	83	298	110	188
B Casualty insurance claims liability of insurance companies	...	...	...	...	...	...	...	...	...	...	...	...
C Transfers to private non-profit institutions	...	...	...	...	...	...	...	...	...	...	...	...
D Unfunded employee pension and welfare benefits	12	10	2	26	19	7	44	32	12	103	80	23
E Social assistance grants	...	...	...	...	...	...	...	...	...	...	...	...
F Other transfers n.e.c.	10	9	1	23	21	2	51	39	12	151	103	48
G Transfers to the rest of the world	...	...	...	...	...	...	...	...	...	...	...	...
Net saving [b]	435	406	29	622	503	119	854	690	164	2166	1888	278
Total Current Disbursements and Net Saving [a]	1794	1374	420	3253	2169	1084	5137	3357	1780	10109	6693	3416

	1984 TOTAL	1984 Non-Financial	1984 Financial	1985 TOTAL	1985 Non-Financial	1985 Financial	1986 TOTAL	1986 Non-Financial	1986 Financial
Receipts									
1 Operating surplus	11593	12347	-754	125324	127887	-2563	235767	240953	-5186
2 Property and entrepreneurial income	10950	2798	8152	34038	13949	20089	42968	16197	26771
A Withdrawals from quasi-corporate enterprises	...	...	...	...	...	...	...	...	...
B Interest	10139	2043	8096	27360	7348	20012	35542	9073	26469
C Dividends	768	711	57	6263	6186	77	6668	6366	302
D Net land rent and royalties	45	45	-	415	415	-	758	758	-

Peru

3.22 Corporate and Quasi-Corporate Enterprise Income and Outlay Account: Total and Sectors
(Continued)

Million Peruvian intis

	1984 TOTAL	1984 Non-Financial	1984 Financial	1985 TOTAL	1985 Non-Financial	1985 Financial	1986 TOTAL	1986 Non-Financial	1986 Financial
3 Current transfers	2552	2092	460	9364	8231	1133	12122	10738	1384
A Casualty insurance claims	627	221	406	1871	772	1099	2334	982	1352
B Casualty insurance premiums, net, due to be received by insurance companies	...	...	...	...	...	...	...	...	...
C Current transfers from the rest of the world	...	...	...	...	...	...	...	...	...
D Other transfers except imputed	1737	1737	-	7269	7269	-	9375	9375	-
E Imputed unfunded employee pension and welfare contributions	188	134	54	224	190	34	413	381	32
Total Current Receipts a	25094	17236	7858	168726	150067	18659	290857	267888	22969

Disbursements

1 Property and entrepreneurial income	16356	9791	6565	46407	31872	14535	52256	36437	15819
A Withdrawals from quasi-corporations	...	...	...	...	...	...	...	...	...
B Interest	12673	6247	6426	33240	19093	14147	38492	23341	15151
C Dividends	1933	1795	138	6959	6571	388	7139	6470	669
D Net land rent and royalties	1748	1748	-	6208	6208	-	6627	6627	-
2 Direct taxes and other current transfers n.e.c. to general government	1830	1597	233	5727	4856	871	14053	13015	1038
A Direct taxes	1575	1343	232	4514	3647	867	12355	11322	1033
B Fines, fees, penalties and other current transfers n.e.c.	255	254	1	1213	1209	4	1698	1693	5
3 Other current transfers	956	466	490	3207	1977	1230	5579	4050	1529
A Casualty insurance premiums, net	588	202	386	1856	794	1062	2287	995	1292
B Casualty insurance claims liability of insurance companies	...	...	...	...	...	...	...	...	...
C Transfers to private non-profit institutions	...	...	...	...	...	...	...	...	...
D Unfunded employee pension and welfare benefits	184	130	54	224	190	34	413	381	32
E Social assistance grants	...	...	...	...	...	...	...	...	...
F Other transfers n.e.c.	184	134	50	1127	993	134	2879	2674	205
G Transfers to the rest of the world	...	...	...	...	...	...	...	...	...
Net saving b	5950	5380	570	113385	111362	2023	218972	214386	4586
Total Current Disbursements and Net Saving a	25094	17236	7858	168726	150067	18659	290860	267888	22972

a) For 1985 and 1986 households and private unincorporated enterprises and Non-profit institutions serving households are included in private non-financial enterprises.
b) Item 'Net saving' includes consumption of fixed capital.

3.23 Corporate and Quasi-Corporate Enterprise Capital Accumulation Account: Total and Sectors

Million Peruvian intis

	1980 TOTAL	1980 Non-Financial	1980 Financial	1981 TOTAL	1981 Non-Financial	1981 Financial	1982 TOTAL	1982 Non-Financial	1982 Financial	1983 TOTAL	1983 Non-Financial	1983 Financial

Finance of Gross Accumulation

1 Gross saving	435	406	29	622	503	119	855	690	165	2166	1888	278
2 Capital transfers	47	12	35	97	15	82	141	31	110	760	287	473
Finance of Gross Accumulation	483	418	65	720	518	202	996	721	275	2926	2175	751

Gross Accumulation

1 Gross capital formation	895	864	31	1752	1714	38	2962	2886	76	3806	3874	-68
A Increase in stocks	172	157	15	400	405	-5	491	480	11	59	239	-180
B Gross fixed capital formation	725	709	16	1352	1309	43	2473	2408	65	3745	3633	112
2 Purchases of land, net	1	-	1	7	1	6	4	-2	6	8	2	6
3 Purchases of intangible assets, net	...	...	...	...	...	...	...	...	...	...	...	...
4 Capital transfers	8	-	8	11	2	9	32	14	18	285	25	260
Net lending	-421	-446	25	-1050	-1198	148	-2002	-2177	175	-1174	-1725	551
Gross Accumulation	483	418	65	720	518	202	996	721	275	2926	2175	751

Peru

3.23 Corporate and Quasi-Corporate Enterprise Capital Accumulation Account: Total and Sectors

Million Peruvian intis

	1984 TOTAL	1984 Non-Financial	1984 Financial	1985 TOTAL	1985 Non-Financial	1985 Financial	1986 TOTAL	1986 Non-Financial	1986 Financial
Finance of Gross Accumulation									
1 Gross saving	5950	5380	570	43249	41225	2024	78017	73431	4586
2 Capital transfers	519	106	413	1565	721	844	1516	220	1296
Finance of Gross Accumulation	6468	5486	982	44814	41946	2868	79533	73651	5882
Gross Accumulation									
1 Gross capital formation	7998	7526	472	39682	38641	1041	80209	78500	1709
A Increase in stocks	206	108	98	414	253	161	9479	9317	162
B Gross fixed capital formation	7792	7418	374	39268	38388	880	70730	69183	1547
2 Purchases of land, net	16	-4	20	19	3	16	12	-12	24
3 Purchases of intangible assets, net	...	...	...	...	...	...	...	...	...
4 Capital transfers	122	122	-	195	107	88	696	509	187
Net lending	-1666	-2157	491	4918	3195	1723	-1384	-5346	3962
Gross Accumulation	6468	5486	982	44814	41946	2868	79533	73651	5882

3.24 Corporate and Quasi-Corporate Enterprise Capital Finance Account: Total and Sectors

Million Peruvian intis

	1980 TOTAL	1980 Non-Financial	1980 Financial	1981 TOTAL	1981 Non-Financial	1981 Financial	1982 TOTAL	1982 Non-Financial	1982 Financial	1983 TOTAL	1983 Non-Financial	1983 Financial
Acquisition of Financial Assets												
1 Gold and SDRs	-19	-	-19	119	-	119	7	-	7	4	8	-4
2 Currency and transferable deposits	100	-38	138	131	12	119	-14	15	-29	540	91	449
3 Other deposits	465	-1	466	-263	-30	-233	891	86	805	1975	118	1857
4 Bills and bonds, short term	8	3	5	5	8	-3	21	-4	25	60	44	16
A Corporate and quasi-corporate, resident	8	3	5	5	8	-3	...	...	...	...	...	...
B Government	...	...	...	...	...	...	...	...	...	...	...	...
C Rest of the world	...	...	...	...	...	...	...	...	...	...	...	...
5 Bonds, long term	-19	-4	-15	145	1	144	77	3	74	-16	5	-21
6 Corporate equity securities	...	...	...	...	...	...	...	...	...	...	...	...
7 Short term loans, n.e.c.	176	-	176	981	4	977	681	81	600	2169	17	2152
8 Long term loans, n.e.c.	352	-	352	671	-	671	823	-	823	3233	-	3233
9 Trade credits and advances	...	...	...	...	...	...	...	...	...	...	...	...
10 Other receivables	106	59	47	405	177	228	699	376	323	4099	837	3262
11 Other assets	65	23	42	9	70	-61	127	90	37	65	18	47
Total Acquisition of Financial Assets	1234	42	1192	2204	242	1962	3313	647	2666	12130	1137	10993
Incurrence of Liabilities												
1 Currency and transferable deposits	347	-	347	399	-	399	511	-	511	2514	-	2514
2 Other deposits	491	-	491	844	-9	853	1308	3	1305	4084	5	4079
3 Bills and bonds, short term	76	-	76	-83	-	-83	19	-	19	2	-	2
4 Bonds, long term	11	4	7	31	-2	33	43	3	40	39	3	36
5 Corporate equity securities	...	...	...	...	...	...	...	...	...	...	...	...
6 Short-term loans, n.e.c.	-75	-3	-72	211	57	154	406	295	111	1410	186	1224
7 Long-term loans, n.e.c.	77	29	48	317	110	207	425	214	211	1085	279	806
8 Net equity of households in life insurance and pension fund reserves	...	...	...	...	...	...	...	...	...	...	...	...
9 Proprietors' net additions to the accumulation of quasi-corporations	...	...	...	...	...	...	...	...	...	...	...	...
10 Trade credit and advances	...	...	...	...	...	...	...	...	...	...	...	...
11 Other accounts payable	157	-34	191	333	200	133	660	467	193	2131	587	1544
12 Other liabilities	252	169	83	284	160	124	463	361	102	1443	1215	228
Total Incurrence of Liabilities	1336	165	1171	2334	516	1818	3835	1343	2492	12708	2275	10433
Net Lending	-102	-123	21	-131	-274	143	-522	-696	174	-577	-1138	561
Incurrence of Liabilities and Net Lending	1234	42	1192	2204	242	1962	3313	647	2666	12130	1137	10993

Peru

3.24 Corporate and Quasi-Corporate Enterprise Capital Finance Account: Total and Sectors

Million Peruvian intis

	1984 TOTAL	1984 Non-Financial	1984 Financial	1985 TOTAL	1985 Non-Financial	1985 Financial
Acquisition of Financial Assets						
1 Gold and SDRs	...	23	...	...	-77	...
2 Currency and transferable deposits	...	221	...	...	1108	...
3 Other deposits	...	127	...	...	2239	...
4 Bills and bonds, short term	...	78	...	...	-15	...
A Corporate and quasi-corporate, resident	...	...	...	...	...	...
B Government	...	...	...	...	...	...
C Rest of the world	...	...	...	...	...	...
5 Bonds, long term	...	19	...	...	3	...
6 Corporate equity securities	...	...	...	...	...	...
7 Short term loans, n.e.c.	...	34	...	...	133	...
8 Long term loans, n.e.c.	...	-	...	...	-	...
9 Trade credits and advances	...	...	...	...	...	...
10 Other receivables	...	2117	...	...	6954	...
11 Other assets	...	1454	...	...	1395	...
Total Acquisition of Financial Assets	...	4074	...	...	11739	...
Incurrence of Liabilities						
1 Currency and transferable deposits	...	...	...	...	...	...
2 Other deposits	...	4	...	...	42	...
3 Bills and bonds, short term	...	-	...	...	-	...
4 Bonds, long term	...	6	...	...	48	...
5 Corporate equity securities	...	...	...	...	...	...
6 Short-term loans, n.e.c.	...	191	...	...	512	...
7 Long-term loans, n.e.c.	...	1563	...	...	4434	...
8 Net equity of households in life insurance and pension fund reserves	...	...	...	...	...	...
9 Proprietors' net additions to the accumulation of quasi-corporations	...	...	...	...	...	...
10 Trade credit and advances	...	...	...	...	...	...
11 Other accounts payable	...	2070	...	...	5495	...
12 Other liabilities	...	1828	...	...	4413	...
Total Incurrence of Liabilities	...	5663	...	...	14944	...
Net Lending	...	-1589	...	...	-3205	...
Incurrence of Liabilities and Net Lending	...	4074	...	...	11739	...

3.31 Household and Private Unincorporated Enterprise Production Account

Million Peruvian intis

	1970	1975	1978	1979	1980	1981	1982	1983	1984	1985	1986	1987
Gross Output												
1 Output for sale	...	...	...	3117	5348	9538	15869	29067	64964	...	...	...
2 Non-marketed output	...	...	...	35	76	158	332	575	1059	...	...	...
Gross Output	...	...	...	3152	5424	9696	16201	29641	66023	...	...	...
Gross Input												
Intermediate consumption	...	...	...	1293	2199	3819	6312	12023	27485	...	...	...
Subtotal: Value Added	...	...	...	1859	3225	5877	9890	17618	38538	...	...	...
1 Indirect taxes net liability of unincorporated enterprises	...	...	...	23	45	85	86	141	289	...	...	...
A Indirect taxes	...	...	...	30	51	94	111	166	364	...	...	...
B Less: Subsidies	...	...	...	7	6	9	25	25	75	...	...	...
2 Consumption of fixed capital	...	...	...	...	...	...	...	...	...	...	...	...
3 Compensation of employees	...	...	...	298	476	812	1401	2527	5022	...	...	...
4 Net operating surplus	...	...	...	1539	2704	4981	8402	14950	33227	...	...	...
Gross Input	...	...	...	3152	5424	9696	16201	29641	66023	...	...	...

Peru

3.32 Household and Private Unincorporated Enterprise Income and Outlay Account

Million Peruvian intis

	1970	1975	1978	1979	1980	1981	1982	1983	1984	1985	1986	1987
Receipts												
1 Compensation of employees	...	...	...	983	1776	3290	5706	10703	21729	...	...	...
A Wages and salaries	...	...	...	893	1597	2932	5149	9567	19489	...	...	...
B Employers' contributions for social security	...	...	...	58	116	230	328	638	1154	...	...	...
C Employers' contributions for private pension & welfare plans	...	...	...	32	64	128	229	498	1086	...	...	...
2 Operating surplus of private unincorporated enterprises	...	...	...	1539	2704	4981	8402	14950	33227	...	...	...
3 Property and entrepreneurial income	...	...	...	103	191	493	864	1625	2858	...	...	...
A Withdrawals from private quasi-corporations	...	...	...	...	...	...	...	...	...	...	...	...
B Interest	...	...	...	52	118	395	683	956	1818	...	...	...
C Dividends	...	...	...	45	63	81	153	612	920	...	...	...
D Net land rent and royalties	...	...	...	6	9	16	27	57	120	...	...	...
3 Current transfers	...	...	...	148	308	551	900	1693	3011	...	...	...
A Casualty insurance claims	...	...	...	2	4	5	11	32	79	...	...	...
B Social security benefits	...	...	...	85	162	307	526	1021	2112	...	...	...
C Social assistance grants												
D Unfunded employee pension and welfare benefits												
E Transfers from general government												
F Transfers from the rest of the world												
G Other transfers n.e.c.	...	...	...	61	142	239	363	640	820	...	...	...
Total Current Receipts a	...	...	...	2773	4980	9314	15872	28972	60825	...	...	...
Disbursements												
1 Final consumption expenditures	...	...	...	2131	3659	6738	11070	21099	45532	...	...	...
2 Property income	...	...	...	69	126	258	507	1054	1658	...	...	...
A Interest	...	...	...	68	123	252	498	1035	1620	...	...	...
B Net land rent and royalties	...	...	...	2	3	6	9	18	38	...	...	...
3 Direct taxes and other current transfers n.e.c. to government	...	...	...	136	236	486	728	1499	3069	...	...	...
A Social security contributions	...	...	...	90	179	358	557	1136	2240	...	...	...
B Direct taxes	...	...	...	41	48	108	134	231	540	...	...	...
Income taxes	...	...	...	...	...	...	...	...	...	...	...	...
Other	...	...	...	...	...	...	...	...	...	...	...	...
C Fees, fines and penalties	...	...	...	5	9	20	37	132	289	...	...	...
4 Other current transfers	...	...	...	5	20	24	60	122	247	...	...	...
A Net casualty insurance premiums	...	...	...	2	4	4	11	38	71	...	...	...
B Transfers to private non-profit institutions serving households	...	...	...	...	...	...	...	...	...	...	...	...
C Transfers to the rest of the world	...	...	...	...	...	...	...	...	...	...	...	...
D Other current transfers, except imputed	...	...	...	3	16	20	49	84	176	...	...	...
E Imputed employee pension and welfare contributions	...	...	...	...	...	...	...	...	...	...	...	...
Net saving b	...	...	...	432	938	1807	3507	5197	10318	...	...	...
Total Current Disbursements and Net Saving a	...	...	...	2773	4980	9314	15872	28972	60825	...	...	...

a) For 1985 and 1986 households and private unincorporated enterprises and Non-profit institutions serving households are included in private non-financial enterprises.
b) Item 'Net saving' includes consumption of fixed capital.

Peru

3.33 Household and Private Unincorporated Enterprise Capital Accumulation Account

Million Peruvian intis

	1970	1975	1978	1979	1980	1981	1982	1983	1984	1985	1986	1987
Finance of Gross Accumulation												
1 Gross saving	...	...	...	432	938	1807	3507	5197	10318	...	...	...
2 Capital transfers	...	...	...	9	8	11	16	78	89	...	...	...
Total Finance of Gross Accumulation	...	...	...	440	947	1819	3523	5276	10407	...	...	...
Gross Accumulation												
1 Gross Capital Formation	...	...	...	250	566	1246	2067	2982	6010	...	...	...
A Increase in stocks	...	...	...	-5	67	176	174	112	-426	...	...	...
B Gross fixed capital formation	...	...	...	255	499	1071	1893	2870	6436	...	...	...
2 Purchases of land, net	...	...	...	-1	-8	-6	-3	-7	-11	...	...	...
3 Purchases of intangibles, net	...	...	...	...	...	...	...	...	...	...	...	...
4 Capital transfers	...	...	...	1	3	3	-	-	-	...	...	...
Net lending	...	...	...	190	386	575	1460	2300	4408	...	...	...
Total Gross Accumulation	...	...	...	440	947	1819	3523	5276	10407	...	...	...

3.51 External Transactions: Current Account: Detail

Million Peruvian intis

	1970	1975	1978	1979	1980	1981	1982	1983	1984	1985	1986	1987
Payments to the Rest of the World												
1 Imports of goods and services	45	146	381	666	1329	2378	3829	6224	10794	30304	51742	84697
2 Factor income to the rest of the world	6	11	91	232	354	516	795	2031	4687	12172	12565	...
A Compensation of employees	...	1	2	4	5	11	28	69	118	251	300	...
B Property and entrepreneurial income	6	10	89	228	349	505	767	1961	4569	11921	12265	...
3 Current transfers to the rest of the world	-	-	1	1	3	4	5	16	47	207	205	...
4 Surplus of the nation on current transactions	...	...	...	147	-155	-844	-1413	-1669	-751	74	-17636	...
Payments to the Rest of the World, and Surplus of the Nation on Current Transfers	...	...	...	1046	1531	2053	3216	6602	14777	42757	46876	...
Receipts From The Rest of the World												
1 Exports of goods and services	50	72	394	968	1332	1735	2806	5880	13486	39611	43708	71886
2 Factor income from the rest of the world	1	2	3	21	76	101	117	257	709	1945	1942	...
A Compensation of employees	...	1	1	6	9	15	31	72	165	546	703	...
B Property and entrepreneurial income	1	1	2	15	67	86	86	185	544	1399	1239	...
3 Current transfers from the rest of the world	3	2	8	57	123	216	294	464	582	1202	1226	...
Receipts from the Rest of the World on Current Transfers	...	...	...	1046	1531	2053	3216	6602	14777	42757	46876	...

3.52 External Transactions: Capital Accumulation Account

Million Peruvian intis

	1970	1975	1978	1979	1980	1981	1982	1983	1984	1985	1986	1987
Finance of Gross Accumulation												
1 Surplus of the nation on current transactions	...	...	...	147	-155	-844	-1413	-1669	-751	74	-17636	...
2 Capital transfers from the rest of the world	...	...	...	13	17	32	63	490	470	1123	601	...
Total Finance of Gross Accumulation	...	...	...	160	-138	-812	-1350	-1179	-281	1197	-17035	...
Gross Accumulation												
1 Capital transfers to the rest of the world	...	...	...	...	...	...	...	...	...	...	...	...
2 Purchases of intangible assets, n.e.c., net, from the rest of the world	...	...	...	...	...	...	...	...	...	...	...	...
Net lending to the rest of the world	...	...	...	...	...	...	...	...	...	...	...	...
Total Gross Accumulation	...	...	...	160	-138	-812	-1350	-1179	-281	1197	-17035	...

Peru

3.53 External Transactions: Capital Finance Account

Million Peruvian intis

		1970	1975	1978	1979	1980	1981	1982	1983	1984	1985	1986	1987
	Acquisitions of Foreign Financial Assets												
1	Gold and SDR's	...	...	...				...	...	...	...	...	...
2	Currency and transferable deposits	...	...	...	81	62	-9	185	741	...	...	...	...
3	Other deposits	...	...	...	-44	-3	-2	-213	128	...	...	...	...
4	Bills and bonds, short term	...	...	...	-	-	11	-19	-	...	...	...	...
5	Bonds, long term	...	...	...	-	-	-	-	-	...	...	...	...
6	Corporate equity securities	...	...	...	72	68	123	88	174	...	...	...	...
7	Short-term loans, n.e.c.	...	...	...	-103	-31	-13	641	-541	...	...	...	...
8	Long-term loans	...	...	...	149	202	211	1243	1821	...	...	...	...
9	Prporietors' net additions to accumulation of quasi-corporate, non-resident enterprises	...	...	...	...	...	...	...	...	...	...	...	...
10	Trade credit and advances	...	...	...	...	...	...	...	...	...	...	...	...
11	Other	...	...	...	4	100	41	21	52	...	...	...	...
	Total Acquisitions of Foreign Financial Assets	...	...	...	160	397	362	1947	2374	...	...	...	...
	Incurrence of Foreign Liabilities												
1	Currency and transferable deposits	...	...	...	207	-19	119	7	3	...	...	...	...
2	Other deposits	...	...	...	111	339	-345	258	205	...	...	...	...
3	Bills and bonds, short term	...	...	...	-	-	-	-	-	...	...	...	...
4	Bonds, long term	...	...	...	1	1	-	-2	6	...	...	...	...
5	Corporate equity securities	...	...	...	8	7	5	31	72	...	...	...	...
6	Short-term loans, n.e.c.	...	...	...	-	-1	-1	-1	-10	...	...	...	...
7	Long-term loans	...	...	...	4	5	-13	13	-9	...	...	...	...
8	Non-resident proprietors' net additions to accumulation of resident quasi-corporate enterprises	...	...	...	...	...	...	...	...	...	...	...	...
9	Trade credit and advances	...	...	...	...	...	...	...	...	...	...	...	...
10	Other	...	...	...	35	42	46	118	552	...	...	...	...
	Total Incurrence of Liabilities	...	...	...	364	374	-188	425	820	...	...	...	...
	Net Lending	...	...	...	-204	23	550	1522	1554	...	...	...	...
	Total Incurrence of Liabilities and Net Lending	...	...	...	160	397	362	1947	2374	...	...	...	...

4.1 Derivation of Value Added by Kind of Activity, in Current Prices

Million Peruvian intis

		1980 Gross Output	1980 Intermediate Consumption	1980 Value Added	1981 Gross Output	1981 Intermediate Consumption	1981 Value Added	1982 Gross Output	1982 Intermediate Consumption	1982 Value Added	1983 Gross Output	1983 Intermediate Consumption	1983 Value Added
	All Producers												
1	Agriculture, hunting, forestry and fishing	817	207	610	1466	368	1098	2311	602	1709	4672	1246	3426
	A Agriculture and hunting	776	195	581	1388	346	1042	2178	556	1622	4448	1171	3277
	B Forestry and logging												
	C Fishing	41	12	29	78	22	56	133	46	87	224	75	149
2	Mining and quarrying	1096	191	905	1576	319	1257	2430	557	1873	4751	1162	3589
	A Coal mining [a]	...	...	...	...	...	...	...	...	...	...	...	...
	B Crude petroleum and natural gas production	660	54	606	1078	92	986	1694	156	1538	2876	318	2558
	C Metal ore mining [a]	436	137	299	498	227	271	736	401	335	1875	844	1031
	D Other mining												

Peru

4.1 Derivation of Value Added by Kind of Activity, in Current Prices
(Continued)

Million Peruvian intis

	1980 Gross Output	1980 Intermediate Consumption	1980 Value Added	1981 Gross Output	1981 Intermediate Consumption	1981 Value Added	1982 Gross Output	1982 Intermediate Consumption	1982 Value Added	1983 Gross Output	1983 Intermediate Consumption	1983 Value Added
3 Manufacturing	4162	2956	1206	6794	4838	1956	10756	7439	3317	19916	13850	6066
A Manufacture of food, beverages and tobacco	1113	797	316	2060	1453	607	3198	2212	986	6356	4507	1849
B Textile, wearing apparel and leather industries	730	448	282	1049	618	431	1468	899	569	2109	1392	717
C Manufacture of wood and wood products, including furniture	163	90	73	259	137	122	454	250	204	813	446	367
D Manufacture of paper and paper products, printing and publishing	215	129	86	361	214	147	497	278	219	850	528	322
E Manufacture of chemicals and chemical petroleum, coal, rubber and plastic products	747	776	-29	1286	1357	-71	2233	2159	74	4663	3962	701
F Manufacture of non-metallic mineral products, except products of petroleum and coal	129	66	63	254	121	133	438	208	230	916	405	511
G Basic metal industries	549	327	222	650	404	246	977	625	352	2200	1455	745
H Manufacture of fabricated metal products, machinery and equipment	425	267	158	722	455	267	1232	693	539	1596	973	623
I Other manufacturing industries	91	56	35	153	79	74	259	115	144	413	182	231
4 Electricity, gas and water	74	23	51	152	41	111	287	96	191	484	214	270
5 Construction	777	435	342	1590	853	737	3130	1541	1589	4941	2769	2172
6 Wholesale and retail trade, restaurants and hotels	1656	596	1060	3030	1098	1932	4981	1850	3131	9545	3400	6145
A Wholesale and retail trade	1234	415	819	2227	764	1463	3527	1301	2225	6538	2207	4331
B Restaurants and hotels	422	181	241	803	334	469	1454	549	906	3007	1193	1814
7 Transport, storage and communication	752	356	396	1375	663	712	2300	1211	1089	4323	2506	1817
8 Finance, insurance, real estate and business services	820	229	591	1649	411	1238	2973	725	2248	5279	1443	3836
A Financial institutions	175	39	136	402	72	330	655	143	512	1253	316	937
B Insurance	42	23	19	72	37	35	111	65	46	188	119	69
C Real estate and business services	603	167	436	1175	302	873	2207	517	1690	3838	1008	2830
Real estate, except dwellings	472	157	315	974	284	690	1875	481	1394	3283	930	2353
Dwellings	131	10	121	201	18	183	332	36	296	555	78	477
9 Community, social and personal services	321	79	242	671	148	523	1184	279	905	2286	536	1750
A Sanitary and similar services	...	...	...	...	...	...	...	...	...	...	...	...
B Social and related community services	109	30	79	215	52	163	396	91	305	837	182	655
Educational services	28	7	21	55	12	43	110	23	87	226	46	180
Medical, dental, other health and veterinary services	81	23	58	160	40	120	286	68	218	611	136	475
C Recreational and cultural services	212	49	163	456	96	360	788	188	600	1449	354	1095
D Personal and household services												
Total, Industries	10475	5072	5403	18303	8739	9564	30352	14300	16052	56197	27126	29071
Producers of Government Services	701	240	461	1273	356	917	2355	788	1567	4273	1253	3020
Other Producers	76	14	62	158	8	150	332	16	316	575	39	536
Total	11252	5326	5926	19734	9103	10631	33039	15104	17935	61045	28418	32627
Less: Imputed bank service charge	...	-118	118	...	-284	284	...	-404	404	...	-767	767
Import duties	160	...	160	312	...	312	419	...	419	705	...	705
Value added tax	...	...	...	...	...	...	...	...	...	...	...	...
Total b	11412	5444	5968	20046	9387	10659	33458	15508	17950	61750	29185	32565

	1984 Gross Output	1984 Intermediate Consumption	1984 Value Added	1985 Gross Output	1985 Intermediate Consumption	1985 Value Added	1986 Gross Output	1986 Intermediate Consumption	1986 Value Added	1987 Gross Output	1987 Intermediate Consumption	1987 Value Added
					All Producers							
1 Agriculture, hunting, forestry and fishing	10964	2982	7982	28029	9395	18634	61206	15370	45836	...	...	80359
A Agriculture and hunting	10344	2760	7584	25975	8541	17434	56479	13848	42631	...	...	75807
B Forestry and logging										...		
C Fishing	620	222	398	2054	854	1200	4727	1522	3205	...	...	4552

Peru

4.1 Derivation of Value Added by Kind of Activity, in Current Prices
(Continued)

Million Peruvian intis

	1984 Gross Output	1984 Intermediate Consumption	1984 Value Added	1985 Gross Output	1985 Intermediate Consumption	1985 Value Added	1986 Gross Output	1986 Intermediate Consumption	1986 Value Added	1987 Gross Output	1987 Intermediate Consumption	1987 Value Added
2 Mining and quarrying	10439	2737	7702	27770	8258	19513	23210	11801	11409	...	...	20540
A Coal mining [a]	...	...	...	...	...	...	...	...	...			...
B Crude petroleum and natural gas production	6808	775	6033	18015	2230	15784	11755	3473	8282	...	...	15478
C Metal ore mining [a]	3631	1962	1669	9755	6027	3728	11455	8328	3127	...	...	5062
D Other mining										...	...	
3 Manufacturing	47586	32727	14859	141303	91294	50008	241164	147066	94098	...	...	171143
A Manufacture of food, beverages and tobacco	15124	10655	4469	40654	27706	12949	73757	51435	22322	...	...	41704
B Textile, wearing apparel and leather industries	5341	3602	1739	17363	11093	6270	34322	19339	14983	...	...	30250
C Manufacture of wood and wood products, including furniture	1911	1032	879	5767	3085	2681	12681	6319	6362	...	...	13186
D Manufacture of paper and paper products, printing and publishing	2035	1197	838	5675	3300	2375	9581	5775	3806	...	...	7230
E Manufacture of chemicals and chemical petroleum, coal, rubber and plastic products	10538	9357	1181	33637	25112	8525	47199	28870	18329	...	...	27901
F Manufacture of non-metallic mineral products, except products of petroleum and coal	2008	862	1146	6243	2597	3646	11212	4819	6393	...	...	10396
G Basic metal industries	4814	3125	1689	13937	9328	4609	17355	12220	5135	...	...	7535
H Manufacture of fabricated metal products, machinery and equipment	4641	2466	2175	15143	7972	7170	29965	16233	13732	...	...	26515
I Other manufacturing industries	1174	431	743	2884	1101	1783	5092	2056	3036	...	...	6423
4 Electricity, gas and water	1198	374	824	3766	1421	2345	5885	2184	3701	...	...	7432
5 Construction	11117	6372	4745	29677	15590	14087	57621	29284	28337	...	...	54439
6 Wholesale and retail trade, restaurants and hotels	20605	7365	13240	55616	20053	35563	111612	37694	73918	...	...	153525
A Wholesale and retail trade	14245	4820	9425	38452	12592	25860	71940	23269	48671	...	...	97084
B Restaurants and hotels	6360	2545	3815	17164	7461	9703	39673	14425	25248	...	...	56441
7 Transport, storage and communication	9735	5469	4266	28838	16655	12183	50827	27628	23199	...	...	40412
8 Finance, insurance, real estate and business services	11416	3298	8118	29823	10369	19454	55715	16567	39148	...	...	86279
A Financial institutions	2911	685	2226	8236	2213	6023	14800	3737	11063	...	...	19510
B Insurance	393	250	143	1589	1087	502	3048	1842	1206	...	...	2059
C Real estate and business services	8112	2363	5749	19999	7069	12929	37867	10988	26879	...	...	64710
Real estate, except dwellings	7196	2235	4961	18173	6717	11456	35024	10382	24642	...	...	61172
Dwellings	916	128	788	1825	352	1473	2843	606	2237	...	...	3538
9 Community, social and personal services	5084	1164	3920	14368	3349	11019	31041	5946	25095	...	...	68063
A Sanitary and similar services	...	...	...	...	...	...	...	...	...			...
B Social and related community services	1861	368	1493	4999	1092	3906	11678	1801	9877	...	...	24778
Educational services	584	113	471	1666	323	1342	3684	565	3119	...	...	7969
Medical, dental, other health and veterinary services	1277	255	1022	3333	769	2564	7994	1236	6758	...	...	16809
C Recreational and cultural services	3223	796	2427	9369	2257	7113	19363	4145	15218	...	...	43285
D Personal and household services										...		
Total, Industries	128144	62488	65656	359190	176384	182806	638282	293540	344742	...	...	682193
Producers of Government Services	8493	2055	6438	23527	7424	16103	44394	11278	33116	...	...	64268
Other Producers	1059	84	975	3075	471	2604	7755	782	6973	...	...	19885
Total	137696	64627	73069	385792	184279	201513	690431	305600	384831	...	...	766346
Less: Imputed bank service charge	...	-1624	1624	...	-5716	5716	...	-11013	11013	...	...	17571
Import duties	1400	...	1400	4049	...	4049	7204	...	7204	...	...	11391
Value added tax	...	...	...	...	...	...	...	...	...	...	...	...
Total [b]	139096	66251	72845	389841	189995	199846	697635	316613	381022	...	...	760166

a) 'Coal mining' is included in 'Other mining'.
b) Data for this table have not been revised, therefore, data for some years are not comparable with those of other tables.

Peru

4.2 Derivation of Value Added by Kind of Activity, in Constant Prices

Million Peruvian intis

	1980 Gross Output	1980 Intermediate Consumption	1980 Value Added	1981 Gross Output	1981 Intermediate Consumption	1981 Value Added	1982 Gross Output	1982 Intermediate Consumption	1982 Value Added	1983 Gross Output	1983 Intermediate Consumption	1983 Value Added
\multicolumn{13}{c}{At constant prices of: 1979 — All Producers}
1 Agriculture, hunting, forestry and fishing	515	133	382	562	146	416	578	150	428	516	134	382
A Agriculture and hunting	488	125	363	532	137	395	544	140	404	492	127	365
B Forestry and logging												
C Fishing	27	8	19	30	9	21	34	10	24	24	7	17
2 Mining and quarrying	596	127	469	577	123	454	585	125	460	534	119	415
A Coal mining [a]	...	...	...	...	...	...	...	...	...	...	...	...
B Crude petroleum and natural gas production	327	35	292	317	34	283	319	34	285	270	29	241
C Metal ore mining [a]	269	92	177	260	89	171	266	91	175	264	90	174
D Other mining												
3 Manufacturing	2706	1840	866	2751	1878	873	2706	1842	864	2295	1577	718
A Manufacture of food, beverages and tobacco	778	551	227	813	581	232	823	586	237	758	549	209
B Textile, wearing apparel and leather industries	430	290	140	404	273	131	387	261	126	316	208	108
C Manufacture of wood and wood products, including furniture	100	60	40	101	61	40	107	65	42	88	53	35
D Manufacture of paper and paper products, printing and publishing	134	83	51	135	82	53	111	65	46	103	60	43
E Manufacture of chemicals and chemical petroleum, coal, rubber and plastic products	510	410	100	534	427	107	538	431	107	452	373	79
F Manufacture of non-metallic mineral products, except products of petroleum and coal	79	43	36	84	46	38	82	44	38	72	39	33
G Basic metal industries	358	196	162	337	184	153	343	184	159	303	162	141
H Manufacture of fabricated metal products, machinery and equipment	267	174	93	293	191	102	269	176	93	169	111	58
I Other manufacturing industries	50	33	17	50	33	17	46	30	16	34	22	12
4 Electricity, gas and water	54	15	39	58	16	42	62	17	45	52	14	38
5 Construction	478	276	202	542	317	225	556	326	230	440	259	181
6 Wholesale and retail trade, restaurants and hotels	1023	369	654	1102	413	689	1105	416	689	950	360	590
A Wholesale and retail trade	782	253	529	855	293	562	853	294	559	695	237	458
B Restaurants and hotels	241	116	125	247	120	127	252	122	130	255	123	132
7 Transport, storage and communication	467	231	236	496	245	251	493	245	248	457	227	230
8 Finance, insurance, real estate and business services	535	149	386	571	160	411	572	162	410	543	152	391
A Financial institutions	123	25	98	136	28	108	146	32	114	151	34	117
B Insurance	25	14	11	24	13	11	21	13	8	17	12	5
C Real estate and business services	387	110	277	411	119	292	405	117	288	375	106	269
Real estate, except dwellings	292	104	188	315	113	202	307	111	196	276	100	176
Dwellings	95	6	89	96	6	90	98	6	92	99	6	93
9 Community, social and personal services	176	49	127	186	52	134	185	53	132	176	48	128
A Sanitary and similar services	...	...	...	...	...	...	...	...	...	...	...	...
B Social and related community services	63	20	43	66	21	45	67	22	45	66	20	46
Educational services	17	4	13	17	4	13	17	4	13	18	5	13
Medical, dental, other health and veterinary services	46	16	30	49	17	32	50	18	32	48	15	33
C Recreational and cultural services	113	29	84	120	31	89	118	31	87	110	28	82
D Personal and household services												

Peru

4.2 Derivation of Value Added by Kind of Activity, in Constant Prices
(Continued)

Million Peruvian intis

	1980 Gross Output	1980 Intermediate Consumption	1980 Value Added	1981 Gross Output	1981 Intermediate Consumption	1981 Value Added	1982 Gross Output	1982 Intermediate Consumption	1982 Value Added	1983 Gross Output	1983 Intermediate Consumption	1983 Value Added
	At constant prices of:1979											
Total, Industries	6550	3189	3361	6845	3350	3495	6842	3336	3506	5963	2890	3073
Producers of Government Services	388	155	233	381	141	240	430	188	242	393	135	258
Other Producers	42	9	33	38	4	34	39	4	35	41	4	37
Total	6980	3353	3627	7264	3495	3769	7311	3528	3783	6397	3029	3368
Less: Imputed bank service charge	...	-82	82	...	-89	89	...	-90	90	...	-98	98
Import duties	102	...	102	128	...	128	124	...	124	76	...	76
Value added tax	...	...	...	...	...	...	...	...	...	...	...	...
Total [b]	7082	3435	3647	7392	3584	3808	7435	3618	3817	6473	3127	3346

	1984 Gross Output	1984 Intermediate Consumption	1984 Value Added	1985 Gross Output	1985 Intermediate Consumption	1985 Value Added	1986 Gross Output	1986 Intermediate Consumption	1986 Value Added	1987 Gross Output	1987 Intermediate Consumption	1987 Value Added
	At constant prices of:1979											
	All Producers											
1 Agriculture, hunting, forestry and fishing	577	150	427	599	156	443	632	165	467	...	...	488
A Agriculture and hunting	542	140	402	558	144	414	579	149	430	...	...	456
B Forestry and logging												
C Fishing	35	10	25	41	12	29	53	16	37	...	...	32
2 Mining and quarrying	559	124	435	586	133	453	560	128	432	...	...	423
A Coal mining [a]	...	...	...	...	...	...	...	...	...	...	...	...
B Crude petroleum and natural gas production	286	31	255	290	31	259	274	30	244	...	...	225
C Metal ore mining [a]	273	93	180	296	102	194	286	98	188	...	...	197
D Other mining												
3 Manufacturing	2419	1662	757	2518	1723	795	2885	1963	922	...	...	1028
A Manufacture of food, beverages and tobacco	781	565	216	788	565	223	921	647	274	...	...	300
B Textile, wearing apparel and leather industries	347	230	117	388	258	130	422	280	142	...	...	150
C Manufacture of wood and wood products, including furniture	91	55	36	95	58	37	113	68	45	...	...	44
D Manufacture of paper and paper products, printing and publishing	102	59	43	96	56	40	111	66	45	...	...	56
E Manufacture of chemicals and chemical petroleum, coal, rubber and plastic products	488	401	87	497	406	91	563	451	112	...	...	133
F Manufacture of non-metallic mineral products, except products of petroleum and coal	69	37	32	69	37	32	92	50	42	...	...	52
G Basic metal industries	331	177	154	353	190	163	341	189	152	...	...	154
H Manufacture of fabricated metal products, machinery and equipment	175	115	60	202	133	69	283	186	97	...	...	122
I Other manufacturing industries	35	23	12	30	20	10	39	26	13	...	...	18
4 Electricity, gas and water	52	14	38	56	15	41	62	16	46	...	...	49
5 Construction	443	260	183	398	234	164	495	292	203	...	...	236
6 Wholesale and retail trade, restaurants and hotels	955	351	604	973	355	618	1110	406	704	...	...	756
A Wholesale and retail trade	691	223	468	690	218	472	788	250	538	...	...	578
B Restaurants and hotels	264	128	136	283	137	146	322	156	166	...	...	178
7 Transport, storage and communication	459	228	231	474	236	238	510	252	258	...	...	277
8 Finance, insurance, real estate and business services	543	151	392	595	171	424	629	183	446	...	...	478
A Financial institutions	148	33	115	171	39	132	183	43	140	...	...	151
B Insurance	17	11	6	25	17	8	29	20	9	...	...	8
C Real estate and business services	378	107	271	399	115	284	417	120	297	...	...	319
Real estate, except dwellings	277	101	176	297	108	189	312	113	199	...	...	219
Dwellings	101	6	95	102	7	95	105	7	98	...	...	100
9 Community, social and personal services	180	47	133	188	50	138	204	55	149	...	...	159
A Sanitary and similar services	...	...	...	...	...	...	...	...	...	...	...	...
B Social and related community services	67	18	49	70	20	50	75	21	54	...	...	59

Peru

4.2 Derivation of Value Added by Kind of Activity, in Constant Prices
(Continued)

Million Peruvian intis

	1984 Gross Output	1984 Intermediate Consumption	1984 Value Added	1985 Gross Output	1985 Intermediate Consumption	1985 Value Added	1986 Gross Output	1986 Intermediate Consumption	1986 Value Added	1987 Gross Output	1987 Intermediate Consumption	1987 Value Added
				At constant prices of: 1979								
Educational services	19	5	14	21	6	15	23	6	17	...	...	18
Medical, dental, other health and veterinary services	48	13	35	49	14	35	52	15	37	...	...	41
C Recreational and cultural services	113	29	84	118	30	88	129	34	95	...	...	100
D Personal and household services												
Total, Industries	6187	2987	3200	6387	3073	3314	7087	3460	3627			3894
Producers of Government Services	375	97	278	389	110	279	406	111	295			300
Other Producers	43	4	39	47	8	39	51	8	43			45
Total	6605	3088	3517	6823	3191	3632	7544	3579	3965			4239
Less: Imputed bank service charge	...	-88	88	...	-111	111	...	-117	117			122
Import duties	77	...	77	68	...	68	81	...	81			84
Value added tax	...	...	...	...	...	...	...	...	...			...
Total [b]	6682	3176	3506	6891	3302	3589	7625	3696	3929			4201

a) 'Coal mining' is included in 'Other mining'.
b) Data for this table have not been revised, therefore, data for some years are not comparable with those of other tables.

4.3 Cost Components of Value Added

Million Peruvian intis

	1980 Compensation of Employees	1980 Capital Consumption	1980 Net Operating Surplus	1980 Indirect Taxes	1980 Less: Subsidies Received	1980 Value Added	1981 Compensation of Employees	1981 Capital Consumption	1981 Net Operating Surplus	1981 Indirect Taxes	1981 Less: Subsidies Received	1981 Value Added
				All Producers								
1 Agriculture, hunting, forestry and fishing	129	16	464	1	...	610	223	29	845	1	...	1098
A Agriculture and hunting	118	10	452	1		581	202	18	821	1		1042
B Forestry and logging												
C Fishing	11	6	12	...	...	29	21	11	24	...		56
2 Mining and quarrying	89	37	690	89	...	905	162	70	933	92	...	1257
A Coal mining [a]	...	...	...	...	...	...	...	...	...	...	...	...
B Crude petroleum and natural gas production	21	1	531	53	...	606	46	35	847	58	...	986
C Metal ore mining [a]	68	36	159	36		299	116	35	86	34		271
D Other mining												
3 Manufacturing	343	101	494	341	73	1206	553	148	794	507	46	1956
A Manufacture of food, beverages and tobacco	81	25	156	98	44	316	134	42	300	146	15	607
B Textile, wearing apparel and leather industries	53	18	189	37	15	282	79	22	300	46	16	431
C Manufacture of wood and wood products, including furniture	14	3	53	4	1	73	23	5	89	6	1	122
D Manufacture of paper and paper products, printing and publishing	22	5	55	4	-	86	36	11	92	8	...	147
E Manufacture of chemicals and chemical petroleum, coal, rubber and plastic products	56	15	-224	127	3	-29	92	21	-403	225	6	-71
F Manufacture of non-metallic mineral products, except products of petroleum and coal	16	5	37	8	3	63	25	7	93	10	2	133
G Basic metal industries	36	15	137	35	1	222	65	23	131	29	2	246
H Manufacture of fabricated metal products, machinery and equipment	59	14	62	26	3	158	90	15	133	33	4	267
I Other manufacturing industries	6	1	29	2	3	35	9	2	59	4	-	74
4 Electricity, gas and water	27	13	6	5	-	51	58	25	17	11		111

Peru

4.3 Cost Components of Value Added
(Continued)

Million Peruvian intis

		1980					1981					
		Compensation of Employees	Capital Consumption	Net Operating Surplus	Indirect Taxes	Less: Subsidies Received	Value Added	Compensation of Employees	Capital Consumption	Net Operating Surplus	Indirect Taxes	Less: Subsidies Received	Value Added
5	Construction	114	20	201	7	...	342	197	42	487	11	...	737
6	Wholesale and retail trade, restaurants and hotels	186	12	871	63	72	1060	348	23	1552	122	113	1932
	A Wholesale and retail trade	163	7	661	60	72	819	310	14	1134	118	113	1463
	B Restaurants and hotels	23	5	210	3	...	241	38	9	418	4	...	469
7	Transport, storage and communication	108	57	215	18	2	396	201	98	385	34	6	712
8	Finance, insurance, real estate and business services	144	46	382	23	4	591	284	84	828	45	3	1238
	A Financial institutions	77	6	51	5	3	136	160	8	153	11	2	330
	B Insurance	6	-	7	6	...	19	11	1	11	12	...	35
	C Real estate and business services	61	40	324	12	1	436	113	75	664	22	1	873
	Real estate, except dwellings	61	28	216	11	1	315	113	56	501	21	1	690
	Dwellings	...	12	108	1	...	121	...	19	163	1	-	183
9	Community, social and personal services	126	12	98	8	2	242	245	22	238	20	2	523
	A Sanitary and similar services	...	...	...	...	...	...	...	...	...	...	...	...
	B Social and related community services	55	4	20	2	2	79	110	5	46	4	2	163
	Educational services	21	1	...	1	2	21	42	1	1	1	2	43
	Medical, dental, other health and veterinary services	34	3	20	1	...	58	68	4	45	3	...	120
	C Recreational and cultural services	71	8	78	6	...	163	135	17	192	16	...	360
	D Personal and household services												
Total, Industries		1266	314	3421	555	153	5403	2271	541	6079	843	170	9564
Producers of Government Services		446	4	...	11	-	461	872	5	-	40	...	917
Other Producers		60	2	...	...	...	62	143	6	...	1	...	150
Total		1772	320	3421	566	153	5926	3286	552	6079	884	170	10631
Less: Imputed bank service charge		...	...	118	...	...	118	...	...	284	...	...	284
Import duties		...	...	...	160	...	160	...	...	...	312	...	312
Value added tax		...	...	...	...	...	...	...	...	...	...	...	...
Total		1772	320	3303	726	153	5968	3286	552	5795	1196	170	10659

		1982					1983					
		Compensation of Employees	Capital Consumption	Net Operating Surplus	Indirect Taxes	Less: Subsidies Received	Value Added	Compensation of Employees	Capital Consumption	Net Operating Surplus	Indirect Taxes	Less: Subsidies Received	Value Added
				All Producers										
1	Agriculture, hunting, forestry and fishing	348	46	1314	1	...	1709	724	84	2617	1	...	3426
	A Agriculture and hunting	310	28	1283	1	...	1622	665	55	2556	1	...	3277
	B Forestry and logging												
	C Fishing	38	18	31	...	...	87	59	29	61	...	...	149
2	Mining and quarrying	271	115	1365	122	...	1873	505	304	2588	192	...	3589
	A Coal mining [a]	...	...	...	...	...	...	...	...	...	...	...	...
	B Crude petroleum and natural gas production	81	63	1294	100	...	1538	194	173	2020	171	...	2558
	C Metal ore mining [a]	190	52	71	22	...	335	311	131	568	21	...	1031
	D Other mining												

Peru

4.3 Cost Components of Value Added
(Continued)

Million Peruvian intis

	1982						1983					
	Compensation of Employees	Capital Consumption	Net Operating Surplus	Indirect Taxes	Less: Subsidies Received	Value Added	Compensation of Employees	Capital Consumption	Net Operating Surplus	Indirect Taxes	Less: Subsidies Received	Value Added
3 Manufacturing	941	239	1281	926	70	3317	1678	507	2425	1576	120	6066
A Manufacture of food, beverages and tobacco	222	70	474	234	14	986	372	143	990	373	29	1849
B Textile, wearing apparel and leather industries	134	34	380	43	22	569	243	81	375	58	40	717
C Manufacture of wood and wood products, including furniture	40	9	150	7	2	204	72	17	272	9	3	367
D Manufacture of paper and paper products, printing and publishing	61	16	122	20	...	219	99	24	172	27	...	322
E Manufacture of chemicals and chemical petroleum, coal, rubber and plastic products	162	33	-518	412	15	74	328	66	-516	852	29	701
F Manufacture of non-metallic mineral products, except products of petroleum and coal	47	13	144	29	3	230	75	41	366	30	1	511
G Basic metal industries	98	37	181	40	4	352	160	89	461	40	5	745
H Manufacture of fabricated metal products, machinery and equipment	162	24	251	112	10	539	303	39	153	141	13	623
I Other manufacturing industries	15	3	97	29	...	144	26	7	152	46	-	231
4 Electricity, gas and water	142	45	-9	13	...	191	239	81	-68	20	2	270
5 Construction	359	82	1137	11	...	1589	530	130	1494	18	...	2172
6 Wholesale and retail trade, restaurants and hotels	580	39	2480	213	181	3131	1014	75	5039	267	250	6145
A Wholesale and retail trade	518	22	1659	207	181	2225	895	41	3387	258	250	4331
B Restaurants and hotels	62	17	821	6	-	906	119	34	1652	9	...	1814
7 Transport, storage and communication	337	164	540	57	9	1089	775	304	641	123	26	1817
8 Finance, insurance, real estate and business services	491	157	1482	119	1	2248	917	293	2455	171	...	3836
A Financial institutions	285	16	192	20	1	512	526	33	347	31	...	937
B Insurance	18	2	9	17	...	46	37	5	-4	31	...	69
C Real estate and business services	188	139	1281	82	...	1690	354	255	2112	109	...	2830
Real estate, except dwellings	188	108	1016	82	...	1394	354	203	1687	109	...	2353
Dwellings	...	31	265	...	...	296	...	52	425	...	...	477
9 Community, social and personal services	422	36	408	42	3	905	821	73	808	55	7	1750
A Sanitary and similar services	...	...	...	...	...	...	...	...	...	...	...	...
B Social and related community services	201	10	91	6	3	305	412	23	217	10	7	655
Educational services	85	2	2	1	3	87	173	7	4	3	7	180
Medical, dental, other health and veterinary services	116	8	89	5	-	218	239	16	213	7	...	475
C Recreational and cultural services	221	26	317	36	...	600	409	50	591	45	...	1095
D Personal and household services					...						...	
Total, Industries	3891	923	9998	1504	264	16052	7203	1851	17999	2423	405	29071
Producers of Government Services	1508	9	-	50	...	1567	2982	16	...	22	...	3020
Other Producers	303	12	...	1	...	316	516	19	...	1	...	536
Total	5702	944	9998	1555	264	17935	10701	1886	17999	2446	405	32627
Less: Imputed bank service charge	...	...	404	...		404	...	...	767	...		767
Import duties	...	...	...	419		419	...	...	...	705		705
Value added tax	...	...	...	...		...	...	...	...	...		...
Total	5702	944	9594	1974	264	17950	10701	1886	17232	3151	405	32565

	1984						1985					
	Compensation of Employees	Capital Consumption	Net Operating Surplus	Indirect Taxes	Less: Subsidies Received	Value Added	Compensation of Employees	Capital Consumption	Net Operating Surplus	Indirect Taxes	Less: Subsidies Received	Value Added
					All Producers							
1 Agriculture, hunting, forestry and fishing	1391	207	6380	4	...	7982	3272	490	14862	10	...	18634
A Agriculture and hunting	1276	127	6179	2	...	7584	2971	292	14166	5	...	17434
B Forestry and logging					...						...	
C Fishing	115	80	201	2	...	398	301	198	696	4	...	1200

Peru

4.3 Cost Components of Value Added
(Continued)

Million Peruvian intis

			1984						1985			
		Compensation of Employees	Capital Consumption	Net Operating Surplus	Indirect Taxes	Less: Subsidies Received	Value Added	Compensation of Employees	Capital Consumption	Net Operating Surplus	Indirect Taxes	Less: Subsidies Received	Value Added
2	Mining and quarrying	1087	476	5829	310	...	7702	2990	1032	14545	946	...	19512
	A Coal mining a	...	...	...	...	...	...	...	...	...	...	...	...
	B Crude petroleum and natural gas production	424	264	5083	262	...	6033	1222	374	13430	758	...	15784
	C Metal ore mining a	663	212	746	48	...	1669	1767	658	1115	188	...	3728
	D Other mining					...						...	
3	Manufacturing	3133	1293	7087	3704	358	14859	8312	3040	26261	13674	1280	50007
	A Manufacture of food, beverages and tobacco	646	374	2737	822	110	4469	1577	727	8424	2549	327	12950
	B Textile, wearing apparel and leather industries	451	176	1124	113	125	1739	1197	496	4800	239	462	6270
	C Manufacture of wood and wood products, including furniture	122	58	685	18	4	879	340	144	2177	37	16	2681
	D Manufacture of paper and paper products, printing and publishing	205	76	507	53	3	838	522	169	1584	110	12	2375
	E Manufacture of chemicals and chemical petroleum, coal, rubber and plastic products	725	172	-1710	2055	61	1181	2022	433	-2728	9006	209	8525
	F Manufacture of non-metallic mineral products, except products of petroleum and coal	126	114	850	62	6	1146	327	300	2906	133	21	3646
	G Basic metal industries	329	194	1122	55	11	1689	919	509	2989	300	109	4609
	H Manufacture of fabricated metal products, machinery and equipment	480	101	1259	372	37	2175	1260	227	4909	893	118	7170
	I Other manufacturing industries	49	28	513	154	1	743	147	35	1200	404	4	1783
4	Electricity, gas and water	443	220	114	47	...	824	1456	657	114	118	...	2344
5	Construction	1055	292	3358	40	...	4745	2541	430	11031	86	...	14087
6	Wholesale and retail trade, restaurants and hotels	1888	159	10893	513	213	13240	4327	428	30437	797	426	35563
	A Wholesale and retail trade	1668	87	7396	487	213	9425	3848	233	21473	732	426	25860
	B Restaurants and hotels	220	72	3497	26	...	3815	479	195	8964	65	...	9703
7	Transport, storage and communication	1562	685	1798	259	38	4266	4118	2444	4959	717	55	12183
8	Finance, insurance, real estate and business services	2117	624	5019	358	...	8118	4897	1450	12273	837	-	19457
	A Financial institutions	1308	88	775	55	...	2226	2872	215	2848	87	-	6023
	B Insurance	74	12	-4	61	...	143	198	25	66	213	...	502
	C Real estate and business services	735	524	4248	242	...	5749	1827	1210	9356	536	...	12932
	Real estate, except dwellings	735	438	3546	242	...	4961	1827	1049	8044	536	...	11456
	Dwellings	...	86	702	...	...	788	...	161	1312	...	...	1473
9	Community, social and personal services	1767	176	1860	126	9	3920	4302	503	5918	309	12	11020
	A Sanitary and similar services	...	...	...	...	...	...	...	...	...	...	...	...
	B Social and related community services	921	65	497	19	9	1493	2254	182	1443	40	12	3907
	Educational services	444	18	12	6	9	471	1186	52	104	13	12	1343
	Medical, dental, other health and veterinary services	477	47	485	13	...	1022	1068	130	1339	27	...	2564
	C Recreational and cultural services	846	111	1363	107	...	2427	2048	321	4475	269	...	7113
	D Personal and household services					...						...	
Total, Industries		14443	4132	42338	5361	618	65656	36213	10473	120400	17493	1770	182809
Producers of Government Services		6291	95	...	52	...	6438	15577	463	...	63	...	16103
Other Producers		947	26	...	2	...	975	2529	70	...	5	...	2604
Total		21681	4253	42338	5415	618	73069	54319	11006	120400	17561	1770	201516
Less: Imputed bank service charge		...	...	1624	...	...	1624	...	...	5716	...	...	5716
Import duties		...	...	...	1400	...	1400	...	...	...	4048	...	4048
Value added tax		...	...	...	...	...	...	...	...	...	...	...	...
Total		21681	4253	40714	6815	618	72845	54321	11005	114680	21608	1770	199845

Peru

4.3 Cost Components of Value Added

Million Peruvian intis

		1986						1987					
		Compensation of Employees	Capital Consumption	Net Operating Surplus	Indirect Taxes	Less: Subsidies Received	Value Added	Compensation of Employees	Capital Consumption	Net Operating Surplus	Indirect Taxes	Less: Subsidies Received	Value Added
		All Producers											
1	Agriculture, hunting, forestry and fishing	6075	1260	38490	11	...	45836	...	...	...	...	...	80359
	A Agriculture and hunting	5519	731	36376	5	...	42631	...	...	...	...	...	75807
	B Forestry and logging												
	C Fishing	556	529	2114	6	...	3205	...	...	...	...	...	4552
2	Mining and quarrying	5582	1291	3805	732	...	11410	...	...	...	...	...	20540
	A Coal mining a	...	...	...	...	...	...	...	...	...	...	...	...
	B Crude petroleum and natural gas production	1760	801	5116	605	...	8282	...	...	...	...	...	15478
	C Metal ore mining a	3822	490	-1311	127	...	3128	...	...	...	...	...	5062
	D Other mining												
3	Manufacturing	17801	4780	53139	19834	1455	94098	...	...	...	...	...	171143
	A Manufacture of food, beverages and tobacco	3306	1109	13557	4697	347	22322	...	...	...	...	...	41707
	B Textile, wearing apparel and leather industries	2652	972	11610	258	509	14983	...	...	...	...	...	30250
	C Manufacture of wood and wood products, including furniture	759	246	5323	40	6	6362	...	...	...	...	...	13186
	D Manufacture of paper and paper products, printing and publishing	1130	264	2299	121	8	3806	...	...	...	...	...	7230
	E Manufacture of chemicals and chemical petroleum, coal, rubber and plastic products	3977	657	2310	11729	344	18329	...	...	...	...	...	27901
	F Manufacture of non-metallic mineral products, except products of petroleum and coal	740	514	4998	163	22	6393	...	...	...	...	...	10396
	G Basic metal industries	1955	561	2314	416	111	5135	...	...	...	...	...	7535
	H Manufacture of fabricated metal products, machinery and equipment	2898	397	8964	1577	103	13733	...	...	...	...	...	26515
	I Other manufacturing industries	384	60	1764	833	5	3036	...	...	...	...	...	6423
4	Electricity, gas and water	2788	1043	-330	201	...	3701	...	...	...	...	...	7432
5	Construction	4836	861	22538	102	...	28337	...	...	...	...	...	54439
6	Wholesale and retail trade, restaurants and hotels	9701	918	63813	963	1476	73919	...	...	...	...	...	153525
	A Wholesale and retail trade	8604	438	40296	809	1476	48671	...	...	...	...	...	97084
	B Restaurants and hotels	1097	480	23517	154	...	25248	...	...	...	...	...	56441
7	Transport, storage and communication	8729	4091	9796	697	115	23198	...	...	...	...	...	40412
8	Finance, insurance, real estate and business services	9869	2757	25033	1489	...	39148	...	...	...	...	...	86279
	A Financial institutions	5490	457	4926	190	...	11063	...	...	...	...	...	19510
	B Insurance	368	85	359	394	...	1206	...	...	...	...	...	2059
	C Real estate and business services	4011	2215	19748	905	...	26879	...	...	...	...	...	64710
	Real estate, except dwellings	4012	1971	17755	905	...	24642	...	...	...	...	...	61172
	Dwellings	...	244	1993	...	...	2237	...	...	...	...	...	3538
9	Community, social and personal services	10139	961	13697	318	20	25095	...	...	...	...	...	68063
	A Sanitary and similar services	...	...	...	...	...	...	...	...	...	...	...	...
	B Social and related community services	5422	412	4017	46	20	9877	...	...	...	...	...	24778
	Educational services	2696	115	313	15	20	3119	...	...	...	...	...	7969
	Medical, dental, other health and veterinary services	2726	297	3704	30	...	6758	...	...	...	...	...	16809
	C Recreational and cultural services	4717	549	9680	272	...	15218	...	...	...	...	...	43285
	D Personal and household services												

Peru

4.3 Cost Components of Value Added
(Continued)

Million Peruvian intis

	\multicolumn{6}{c	}{1986}	\multicolumn{6}{c	}{1987}
	Compensation of Employees	Capital Consumption	Net Operating Surplus	Indirect Taxes	Less: Subsidies Received	Value Added	Compensation of Employees	Capital Consumption	Net Operating Surplus	Indirect Taxes	Less: Subsidies Received	Value Added
Total, Industries	75520	17962	229981	24347	3066	344742	...	...	...	...	...	682193
Producers of Government Services	32254	681	...	182	...	33117	...	...	...	...	...	64268
Other Producers	6775	192	...	6	...	6973	...	...	...	...	...	19885
Total	114551	18834	229981	24534	3066	384831	...	...	...	...	...	766346
Less: Imputed bank service charge	...	...	11013	...	...	11013	...	...	...	...	...	17571
Import duties	...	...	...	7204	...	7204	...	...	...	...	...	11391
Value added tax	...	...	...	...	...	...	...	...	...	...	...	...
Total	114551	18834	218967	31736	3066	381022	...	...	...	...	...	760166

a) 'Coal mining' is included in 'Other mining'.

Philippines

General note. The preparation of national accounts statistics in the Philippines is undertaken by the National Economic and Development Authority (NEDA), Manila. The official estimates with methodological notes are published in the annual NEDA National Income Series entitled 'The National Income Accounts'. An over-all revision was completed in 1976 and a detailed description of the framework, sources and methods used in national income estimation is found in 'Manual on the Philippine System of National Accounts: Framework, Sources and Methods' published in 1978 by NEDA. The estimates are generally in accordance with the classifications and definitions recommended in the United Nations System of National Accounts (SNA). In 1961, the first input-output study was published by the Office of Statistical Coordination and Standards. The following tables have been prepared from successive replies to the United Nations national accounts questionnaire. When the scope and coverage of the estimates differ for conceptual or statistical reasons from the definitions and classifications recommended in SNA, a footnote is indicated to the relevant tables.

Sources and methods:

(a) Gross domestic product. Gross domestic product is estimated mainly through the production approach.

(b) Expenditure on the gross domestic product. The expenditure approach is used to estimate all components of GDP by expenditure type except capital formation in machinery and equipment for which the commodity-flow approach is used. The commodity-flow approach and income-elasticity approach are also used for private consumption expenditure. Estimates of government consumption expenditure are taken from the Commission on Audit reports for national and local government and for the social security system from the Budget Commission and the two offices administering it. For personal consumption of goods, for which the statistics are available in quantity terms, the value of final consumption is obtained by multiplying consumption quantities by the appropriate retail prices. Consumption expenditure on each broad expenditure group is estimated by using the commodity-flow method. Since the required data lag by at least a year, preliminary estimates are computed by using the income-elasticity approach. Bench-mark information on the levels and patterns of household expenditure are available from the family income and expenditure surveys for 1961, 1965 and 1971. Current data on supply are derived from production figures available from various sources such as censuses, surveys and concerned companies. The sources of data for increase in stocks include the integrated agricultural surveys and establishment surveys and censuses. For gross fixed capital formation, the net supply of durable equipment for domestic use is divided between consumption and capital formation by means of allocation ratios for each type of equipment. The 1969 survey of importers of durable equipment provided bench-mark data on importer-dealer ratios as well as trade and transport mark-up ratios. The ratios are updated by using the results of the annual trade establishments surveys. The primary sources of data for exports and imports of goods and services are the foreign trade statistics and the balance of payments. For the constant price estimates, wages and salaries of the government sector are extrapolated by an index of employment of government services. All the other components of GDP by expenditure type are deflated by appropriate price indexes.

(c) Cost-structure of the gross domestic product. Estimates of compensation of employees, operating surplus and depreciation are available from the annual surveys of establishments and reports of financial institutions and public utilities for the non-agricultural sectors and from studies on production costs for the agricultural sector. For depreciation, a global estimate for all sectors is derived by estimating the cost of replacement of existing stock by the use of the perpetual inventory method. The global estimate is then allocated to each sector, using a sectoral structure based on the reported levels of depreciation. The estimates of indirect taxes and subsidies are made on the basis of reports of the Commission on Audit, the Bureau of Internal Revenue, the Bureau of Customs, the Central Bank and other government agencies.

(d) Gross domestic product by kind of economic activity. The table of GDP by kind of economic activity is prepared at market prices, i.e., producers' values. The production approach is used to estimate value added of most industries. The income approach is used for producers of government services and a large part of private services. The expenditure approach is also used for construction. The sources used for the estimation of the agricultural sector are the 1971 census of agriculture, the integrated agricultural surveys which are conducted five times a year, the family income and expenditure surveys and data collected through administrative agencies and producers' associations. The value of agricultural and livestock production is obtained by multiplying the volume of output by the average prices received by the farmers. The cost ratios are obtained from cost-of-production studies and from the 1969 input-output tables. For fishery, the sources are the monthly reports from the operators and sustenance estimates based on growth-rates in selected municipalities. Estimates for mining are based on the annual reports from the Bureau of Mines, the surveys of establishments, the 1972 economic census and the financial statements of mining firms. For the organized sector of manufacturing, the sources of data include the economic census and the survey of establishments. For 5 out of 20 major industry groups, the commodity-flow approach is used, taking the supply and disposition ratios from the 1969 input-output tables. Basic data for electricity, gas and water are collected from concerned companies, government agencies and the surveys of establishments. Gross output of private construction is estimated on the basis of building construction statistics and building permits issued. Data for public construction are obtained from the annual report of the Commission on Audit and from quarterly questionnaires. Bench-mark estimates for trade are taken from the 1972 economic census. These are extrapolated by using the results of the surveys of trade establishments. An undercoverage allowance is made for trade activities not covered using employment data from the labour force survey and an estimate of value added per worker. The main sources of data for the transport sector are the 1972 economic census, the surveys of establishments and the financial reports of the concerned companies. Data for the financial sector are derived from financial statements compiled by the Central Bank. Bench-mark estimates for the real estate sector are based on the results of the economic census and are extrapolated by the growth rates of real estate sales and mortgages. For the producers of government services, data are obtained from the annual report of the Commission on Audit. Bench-mark estimates for the private services are based on the economic census and are extrapolated by using appropriate price indexes for other years. For the domestic services, the value added is taken as the product of the number of persons employed and an estimate of value added per worker. For the constant price estimates, the value added of the agricultural and mining sectors are obtained by applying the base-year unit values to the volume of production. For the manufacturing, transport, financial and services sectors, value added is deflated by appropriate price indexes. Double deflation is used for electricity, gas and water, construction and trade.

1.1 Expenditure on the Gross Domestic Product, in Current Prices

Million Philippine pesos

		1970	1975	1978	1979	1980	1981	1982	1983	1984	1985	1986	1987
1	Government final consumption expenditure	3514	11115	16127	18259	21191	24792	29215	29481	35567	44044	48441	58472
2	Private final consumption expenditure	29552	76165	118846	146577	178119	206942	234486	268188	403431	469133	474991	526081
3	Gross capital formation	8303	33840	51348	67687	80883	93261	96521	102526	91951	85402	81106	110394
	A Increase in stocks	1288	6708	9043	11381	13160	13976	10495	7272	-8144	-4572	289	11806
	B Gross fixed capital formation	7015	27132	42305	56306	67723	79285	86026	95254	100095	89974	80817	98588
	Residential buildings												
	Non-residential buildings	2599	11714	22735	30571	37098	46007	51382	54361	63907	56228	46199	56930
	Other construction and land improvement etc.												
	Other	4416	15418	19570	25735	30625	33278	34644	40893	36188	33746	34618	41658
4	Exports of goods and services	8096	21272	32420	41460	53590	57806	56150	75267	117701	126571	155104	163472
5	Less: Imports of goods and services	8236	29057	41321	53558	68704	74359	79321	101138	118382	108506	116188	157397
	Statistical discrepancy a	289	1362	249	-2882	-429	-3184	3546	9772	10198	-3960	-16325	7346
	Equals: Gross Domestic Product	41518	114697	177669	217543	264650	305258	340597	384096	540466	612684	627129	708368

a) Item 'Statistical discrepancy' of increases in stocks, relates to the difference between the estimate of GDP through industrial origin approach and that of expenditure approach.

1.2 Expenditure on the Gross Domestic Product, in Constant Prices

Million Philippine pesos

		1970	1975	1978	1979	1980	1981	1982	1983	1984	1985	1986	1987
						At constant prices of:1972							
1	Government final consumption expenditure	4250	7263	7710	7995	8294	8598	9145	8788	8255	8221	8187	8774
2	Private final consumption expenditure	37468	46515	54098	56718	59270	61617	63535	65348	66032	65977	66597	70409
3	Gross capital formation	9929	18323	22928	25493	26609	27220	26267	24923	14215	11124	10111	13171
	A Increase in stocks	1638	3349	3893	4223	3872	3678	2580	1911	-1379	-702	54	1540
	B Gross fixed capital formation	8291	14974	19035	21270	22737	23542	23687	23012	15594	11826	10057	11631

Philippines

1.2 Expenditure on the Gross Domestic Product, in Constant Prices
(Continued)

Million Philippine pesos

	1970	1975	1978	1979	1980	1981	1982	1983	1984	1985	1986	1987
	\multicolumn{12}{c}{At constant prices of:1972}
Residential buildings												
Non-residential buildings	3089	6152	9435	10546	11123	12045	12521	11948	9446	7114	5505	6348
Other construction and land improvement etc.												
Other	5202	8822	9600	10724	11614	11497	11166	11064	6148	4712	4552	5283
4 Exports of goods and services	8510	10220	14657	15650	17741	17947	17486	19262	20846	19351	23560	23245
5 Less: Imports of goods and services	10033	13276	16116	18765	19377	18854	19510	21746	18175	13995	15802	19987
Statistical discrepancy [a]	630	-608	-493	871	30	-321	2076	3345	2754	-774	-1473	-149
Equals: Gross Domestic Product	50754	68437	82784	87962	92567	96207	98999	99920	93927	89904	91180	95463

a) Item 'Statistical discrepancy' of increases in stocks, relates to the difference between the estimate of GDP through industrial origin approach and that of expenditure approach.

1.3 Cost Components of the Gross Domestic Product

Million Philippine pesos

	1970	1975	1978	1979	1980	1981	1982	1983	1984	1985	1986	1987
1 Indirect taxes, net	3126	11161	16851	22379	25759	25928	28665	34689	43920	49346	52309	70231
A Indirect taxes	3292	11822	17424	22967	26519	26705	29512	35608	44697	50216	53955	71619
B Less: Subsidies	166	661	573	588	760	777	847	919	777	870	1646	1388
2 Consumption of fixed capital	3714	11304	16759	20538	24543	30658	34664	39180	53749	67222	71682	77615
3 Compensation of employees paid by resident producers to:	34678	92232	144059	174626	214348	248672	277268	310227	442797	496116	503138	560522
4 Operating surplus												
Equals: Gross Domestic Product	41518	114697	177669	217543	264650	305258	340597	384096	540466	612684	627129	708368

1.4 General Government Current Receipts and Disbursements

Million Philippine pesos

	1970	1975	1978	1979	1980	1981	1982	1983	1984	1985	1986	1987
	\multicolumn{12}{c}{Receipts}
1 Operating surplus	...	...	...	...	...	...	...	...	...	...	...	...
2 Property and entrepreneurial income	210	608	1528	1891	2525	3404	4737	5801	7033	9317	12820	...
3 Taxes, fees and contributions	5032	16319	25112	32125	37123	38255	41823	48499	62455	72091	78049	...
A Indirect taxes	3292	11822	17424	22967	26519	26705	29512	35608	44697	50216	53955	...
B Direct taxes	1309	3432	5712	6824	7912	8600	9061	9439	14281	18198	20187	...
C Social security contributions	431	1065	1976	2334	2692	2950	3250	3452	3477	3677	3907	...
D Compulsory fees, fines and penalties	...	...	...	...	...	...	...	...	...	...	...	...
4 Other current transfers	95	301	265	208	240	281	407	624	948	2025	1915	...
Total Current Receipts of General Government [a]	5337	17228	26905	34224	39888	41940	46967	54924	70436	83433	92784	...
	\multicolumn{12}{c}{Disbursements}
1 Government final consumption expenditure	3514	11115	16127	18259	21191	24792	29215	29481	35567	42469	48553	...
2 Property income	...	...	...	...	...	...	...	...	...	...	...	...
3 Subsidies	166	661	573	588	760	777	847	919	777	1267	1626	...
4 Other current transfers	698	1914	3254	4279	4758	4869	6171	7921	13603	19662	24057	...
A Social security benefits	156	416	994	1083	1173	1418	1697	1992	2295	2350	2770	...
B Social assistance grants	...	...	...	...	...	...	...	...	...	...	...	...
C Other	542	1498	2260	3196	3585	3451	4474	5930	11308	17312	21287	...
5 Net saving	959	3538	6951	11098	13179	11502	10734	16604	20489	20035	18548	...
Total Current Disbursements and Net Saving of General Government [a]	5337	17228	26905	34224	39888	41940	46967	54924	70436	83433	92784	...

a) Data for this table have not been revised, therefore, data for some years are not comparable with those of other tables.

1.6 Current Income and Outlay of Households and Non-Profit Institutions

Million Philippine pesos

	1970	1975	1978	1979	1980	1981	1982	1983	1984	1985	1986	1987
	\multicolumn{12}{c}{Receipts}
1 Compensation of employees [a]	31864	86122	134168	158292	193779	223531	247970	278068	416147	466644	460193	508300
A From resident producers	31726	85384	132035	154264	189058	217482	238595	265822	399752	447276	438936	483335
B From rest of the world	138	738	2133	4028	4721	6049	9375	12246	16395	19368	21257	24965
2 Operating surplus of private unincorporated enterprises	...	...	...	...	...	...	...	...	...	...	...	...

Philippines

1.6 Current Income and Outlay of Households and Non-Profit Institutions
(Continued)

Million Philippine pesos

	1970	1975	1978	1979	1980	1981	1982	1983	1984	1985	1986	1987
3 Property and entrepreneurial income [a]	...	...	...	...	...	...	...	...	...	...	...	...
4 Current transfers	1242	3605	4926	5952	6693	7473	8775	11547	11983	19244	29063	39352
A Social security benefits	156	416	994	1083	1173	1418	1697	1992	2295	2350	2659	3947
B Social assistance grants	527	1364	1843	2373	2486	2460	3244	3952	6710	11428	15099	25713
C Other	559	1825	2089	2496	3034	3595	3834	5603	2978	5466	11305	9692
Total Current Receipts	33106	89727	139094	164244	200472	231004	256745	289615	428130	485888	489256	547652

Disbursements

	1970	1975	1978	1979	1980	1981	1982	1983	1984	1985	1986	1987
1 Private final consumption expenditure	29552	76165	118846	146577	178119	206942	234486	268188	403431	469133	474991	526081
2 Property income	...	...	...	...	...	...	...	...	...	...	...	...
3 Direct taxes and other current transfers n.e.c. to general government	975	2494	5047	6285	7202	7446	7808	8094	9577	13525	15420	16849
A Social security contributions	431	1065	1976	2334	2692	2950	3250	3452	3477	3677	3908	6334
B Direct taxes	544	1429	3071	3951	4510	4496	4558	4642	6100	9848	11512	10515
C Fees, fines and penalties	...	...	...	...	...	...	...	...	...	...	...	...
4 Other current transfers	11	21	19	35	36	40	17	24	20	170	61	42
Statistical discrepancy	289	1362	249	-2882	-429	-3184	3546	9772	10198	-3960	-16325	7346
5 Net saving	2279	9685	14933	14229	15544	19760	10888	3538	4904	7020	15109	-2666
Total Current Disbursements and Net Saving	33106	89727	139094	164244	200472	231004	256745	289615	428130	485888	489256	547652

a) Item 'Property and entrepreneurial income' is included in item 'Compensation of employees'.

1.7 External Transactions on Current Account, Summary

Million Philippine pesos

	1970	1975	1978	1979	1980	1981	1982	1983	1984	1985	1986	1987

Payments to the Rest of the World

	1970	1975	1978	1979	1980	1981	1982	1983	1984	1985	1986	1987
1 Imports of goods and services	8236	29057	41321	53556	68704	74359	79321	101138	118382	108506	116188	157397
A Imports of merchandise c.i.f.	7371	26757	37042	48144	61081	65816	69697	87448	106134	98582	106662	142918
B Other	865	2300	4279	5412	7623	8543	9624	13690	12248	9924	9526	14479
2 Factor income to the rest of the world	896	2220	4108	5104	7178	11800	17672	20990	35045	40985	38464	37070
A Compensation of employees	18	56	32	44	65	71	69	74	20	19	122	62
B Property and entrepreneurial income	878	2164	4076	5060	7113	11729	17603	20916	35025	40966	38342	37008
3 Current transfers to the rest of the world	26	155	436	858	1135	1031	1247	2002	4618	4362	6291	12723
4 Surplus of the nation on current transactions	-209	-6073	-7630	-9763	-13093	-15338	-25339	-26996	-14484	6253	33419	-210
Payments to the Rest of the World and Surplus of the Nation on Current Transactions	8949	25359	38235	49757	63924	71852	72901	97134	143561	160106	194362	206980

Receipts From The Rest of the World

	1970	1975	1978	1979	1980	1981	1982	1983	1984	1985	1986	1987
1 Exports of goods and services	8096	21272	32420	41460	53590	57806	56150	75267	117701	126571	155104	163472
A Exports of merchandise f.o.b.	6608	16343	24954	33506	42709	44378	42136	54609	88818	84126	95391	113941
B Other	1488	4929	7466	7954	10881	13428	14014	20658	28883	42445	59713	49531
2 Factor income from rest of the world	199	1961	3461	5593	7060	10170	12510	15640	21934	26044	26038	32063
A Compensation of employees	138	738	2133	4028	4721	6049	9375	12246	16395	19368	21257	24965
B Property and entrepreneurial income	61	1223	1328	1565	2339	4121	3135	3394	5539	6676	4781	7098
3 Current transfers from rest of the world	654	2126	2354	2704	3274	3876	4241	6227	3926	7491	13220	11445
Receipts from the Rest of the World on Current Transactions	8949	25359	38235	49757	63924	71852	72901	97134	143561	160106	194362	206980

1.8 Capital Transactions of The Nation, Summary

Million Philippine pesos

	1970	1975	1978	1979	1980	1981	1982	1983	1984	1985	1986	1987

Finance of Gross Capital Formation

	1970	1975	1978	1979	1980	1981	1982	1983	1984	1985	1986	1987
Gross saving	8094	27767	43717	57924	67790	77923	71182	75530	77467	91655	114525	110184
1 Consumption of fixed capital	3714	11304	16759	20538	24543	30658	34664	39180	53749	67222	71682	77615
2 Net saving	4380	16463	26958	37386	43247	47265	36518	36350	23718	24433	42843	32569
A General government	959	3538	6951	11098	13179	11502	10734	16604	20489	20582	12311	12065

Philippines

1.8 Capital Transactions of The Nation, Summary
(Continued)

Million Philippine pesos

	1970	1975	1978	1979	1980	1981	1982	1983	1984	1985	1986	1987
B Corporate and quasi-corporate enterprises	1142	3240	5075	12059	14524	16003	14896	16209	-1675	-3169	15423	23170
C Other [a]	2279	9685	14932	14229	15544	19760	10888	3537	4904	7020	15109	-2666
Less: Surplus of the nation on current transactions	-209	-6073	-7630	-9763	-13093	-15338	-25339	-26996	-14484	6253	33419	-210
Finance of Gross Capital Formation	8303	33840	51348	67687	80883	93261	96521	102526	91951	85402	81106	110394
					Gross Capital Formation							
Increase in stocks	1288	6708	9043	11381	13160	13976	10495	7272	-8144	-4572	289	11806
Gross fixed capital formation	7015	27132	42305	56306	67723	79285	86026	95254	100095	89974	80817	98588
Gross Capital Formation	8303	33840	51348	67687	80883	93261	96521	102526	91951	85402	81106	110394

a) Item 'Other' of Net saving includes change in stocks which is mostly private.

1.10 Gross Domestic Product by Kind of Activity, in Current Prices

Million Philippine pesos

	1970	1975	1978	1979	1980	1981	1982	1983	1984	1985	1986	1987
1 Agriculture, hunting, forestry and fishing [a]	11863	33209	47360	55543	61761	69391	76721	84546	139505	162519	155989	170770
2 Mining and quarrying	1181	2000	3333	5810	8095	6849	6106	7021	9714	11529	12445	13600
3 Manufacturing	9780	28248	43688	52144	64555	75151	83133	95172	137251	150523	155172	173539
4 Electricity, gas and water	328	1057	1669	2125	2761	3329	4042	5256	7980	10986	14678	17333
5 Construction	1515	6813	12591	16855	21311	26268	29302	30730	31209	27506	22685	28113
6 Wholesale and retail trade, restaurants and hotels	6189	17171	28638	36164	45322	53650	60888	71085	106367	125869	129282	146435
7 Transport, storage and communication	1900	5834	9894	12377	16444	19618	21376	24378	33820	38263	39256	42027
8 Finance, insurance, real estate and business services	4182	10106	15018	18312	22670	25017	28792	33048	34912	37393	43608	54244
9 Community, social and personal services	1460	3428	5252	6317	7670	9023	10516	11642	14257	16751	18179	19527
Total, Industries	38398	107866	167443	205647	250589	288295	320876	362878	515015	581339	591294	665588
Producers of Government Services	2544	5573	8619	9795	11493	13930	16389	17539	21254	27033	31728	38610
Other Producers	576	1258	1607	2101	2568	3032	3332	3678	4197	4312	4107	4170
Subtotal	41518	114697	177669	217543	264650	305258	340597	384096	540466	612684	627129	708368
Less: Imputed bank service charge	...	...	...	...	...	...	...	...	...	...	...	...
Plus: Import duties	...	...	...	...	...	...	...	...	...	...	...	...
Plus: Value added tax	...	...	...	...	...	...	...	...	...	...	...	...
Equals: Gross Domestic Product	41518	114697	177669	217543	264650	305258	340597	384096	540466	612684	627129	708368

a) Item 'Agriculture, hunting, forestry and fishing' excludes hunting.

1.11 Gross Domestic Product by Kind of Activity, in Constant Prices

Million Philippine pesos

	1970	1975	1978	1979	1980	1981	1982	1983	1984	1985	1986	1987
					At constant prices of:1972							
1 Agriculture, hunting, forestry and fishing [a]	14821	18327	21631	22606	23662	24608	25378	24845	25409	26252	27110	26834
2 Mining and quarrying	1093	1445	1809	2134	2236	2175	2016	1966	1755	1768	1574	1547
3 Manufacturing	12367	17313	21108	22239	23175	23959	24535	25108	23319	21541	21717	23168
4 Electricity, gas and water	394	607	750	843	921	999	1084	1192	1342	1433	1723	1908
5 Construction	1738	3958	5944	6759	7139	7830	8079	7689	5866	4258	3382	3967
6 Wholesale and retail trade, restaurants and hotels	7795	9781	11987	12885	13664	14231	14672	15466	15540	15452	15728	16575
7 Transport, storage and communication	2360	3610	4501	4613	4827	5040	5165	5266	5032	4953	5105	5251
8 Finance, insurance, real estate and business services	4767	6106	7051	7506	8138	8032	8349	8698	6081	5251	5779	6781
9 Community, social and personal services	1655	2402	2732	2859	2991	3106	3209	3208	3018	2956	2970	3013
Total, Industries	46990	63549	77513	82444	86753	89980	92487	93438	87362	83864	85088	89044
Producers of Government Services	3051	3940	4251	4457	4700	5081	5339	5294	5585	5253	5362	5697
Other Producers	713	948	1020	1061	1114	1146	1173	1188	980	787	730	722
Subtotal	50754	68437	82784	87962	92567	96207	98999	99920	93927	89904	91180	95463
Less: Imputed bank service charge	...	...	...	...	...	...	...	...	...	...	...	...
Plus: Import duties	...	...	...	...	...	...	...	...	...	...	...	...
Plus: Value added tax	...	...	...	...	...	...	...	...	...	...	...	...
Equals: Gross Domestic Product	50754	68437	82784	87962	92567	96207	98999	99920	93927	89904	91180	95463

a) Item 'Agriculture, hunting, forestry and fishing' excludes hunting.

Philippines

1.12 Relations Among National Accounting Aggregates

Million Philippine pesos

	1970	1975	1978	1979	1980	1981	1982	1983	1984	1985	1986	1987
Gross Domestic Product	41518	114697	177669	217543	264650	305258	340597	384096	540466	612684	627129	708368
Plus: Net factor income from the rest of the world	-697	-259	-647	489	-118	-1630	-5162	-5350	-13111	-14941	-12426	-5007
Factor income from the rest of the world	199	1961	3461	5593	7060	10170	12510	15640	21934	26044	26038	32063
Less: Factor income to the rest of the world	896	2220	4108	5104	7178	11800	17672	20990	35045	40985	38464	37070
Equals: Gross National Product	40821	114438	177022	218032	264532	303628	335435	378746	527355	597743	614703	703361
Less: Consumption of fixed capital	3714	11304	16759	20538	24543	30658	34664	39180	53749	67222	71682	77615
Equals: National Income	37107	103134	160263	197494	239989	272970	300771	339566	473606	530521	543021	625746
Plus: Net current transfers from the rest of the world	628	1971	1918	1846	2139	2845	2994	4225	-692	3129	6929	-1278
Current transfers from the rest of the world	654	2126	2354	2704	3274	3876	4241	6227	3926	7491	13220	11445
Less: Current transfers to the rest of the world	26	155	436	858	1135	1031	1247	2002	4618	4362	6291	12723
Equals: National Disposable Income	37735	105105	162181	199340	242128	275815	303765	343791	472914	533650	549950	624468
Less: Final consumption	33066	87280	134973	164836	199310	231734	263701	297669	438998	513177	523432	584553
Statistical discrepancy	-289	-1362	-249	2882	429	3184	-3546	-9772	-10198	3960	16325	-7346
Equals: Net Saving	4380	16463	26958	37386	43247	47265	36518	36350	23718	24433	42843	32569
Less: Surplus of the nation on current transactions	-209	-6073	-7630	-9763	-13093	-15338	-25339	-26996	-14484	6253	33419	-210
Equals: Net Capital Formation	4589	22536	34589	47149	56340	62603	61857	63346	38202	18180	9424	32779

2.5 Private Final Consumption Expenditure by Type and Purpose, in Current Prices

Million Philippine pesos

	1970	1975	1978	1979	1980	1981	1982	1983	1984	1985	1986	1987
Final Consumption Expenditure of Resident Households												
1 Food, beverages and tobacco	17393	48735	67746	82152	98022	114456	128533	147578	226221	264620	266116	293412
A Food	15338	43327	62468	75421	89974	105013	117475	135166	207966	243717	244488	269950
B Non-alcoholic beverages	1149	3123	2749	3665	4466	5269	6035	6858	9801	11494	11962	13003
C Alcoholic beverages												
D Tobacco	906	2285	2529	3066	3582	4174	5023	5554	8454	9409	9666	10459
2 Clothing and footwear	1795	5407	7087	8745	11078	12895	14656	16491	25213	28348	29103	32545
3 Gross rent, fuel and power	3095	6713	12469	15717	19702	23682	10315	12209	17947	21461	20902	23627
A Fuel and power	3095	6713	12469	15717	19702	23682	10315	12209	17947	21461	20902	23627
B Other	...	...	...	...	...	...	...	...	...	...	...	...
4 Furniture, furnishings and household equipment and operation	1775	3656	8722	10756	13146	14841	33785	38191	56597	65514	67237	75505
A Household operation	712	1600	3067	3900	4774	5511	23647	26946	40580	46607	47881	53040
B Other	1063	2056	5655	6856	8372	9330	10138	11245	16017	18907	19356	22465
5 Medical care and health expenses	852	1828	3332	4105	5059	5812	...	...	...	...	...	...
6 Transport and communication	764	1676	3257	4415	5839	6790	7862	8835	13345	14866	14816	16686
7 Recreational, entertainment, education and cultural services	1412	3123	4813	6189	7663	8653	...	...	...	...	...	...
A Education	933	2057	2975	3827	4756	5441	...	...	...	...	...	...
B Other	479	1066	1838	2362	2907	3212	...	...	...	...	...	...
8 Miscellaneous goods and services	2466	5027	11420	14498	17610	19813	39335	44884	64108	74324	76817	84306
A Personal care	753	1523	2024	2535	3125	3579	...	...	...	...	...	...
B Expenditures in restaurants, cafes and hotels	...	...	...	...	...	...	...	...	...	...	...	...

Philippines

2.5 Private Final Consumption Expenditure by Type and Purpose, in Current Prices
(Continued)

Million Philippine pesos

	1970	1975	1978	1979	1980	1981	1982	1983	1984	1985	1986	1987
C Other	1713	3504	9396	11963	14485	16234	39335	44884	64108	74324	76817	84306
Total Final Consumption Expenditure in the Domestic Market by Households, of which	29552	76165	118846	146577	178119	206942	234486	268188	403431	469133	474991	526081
Plus: Direct purchases abroad by resident households	...	...	...	...	...	...	...	...	...	...	...	...
Less: Direct purchases in the domestic market by non-resident households	...	...	...	...	...	...	...	...	...	...	...	...
Equals: Final Consumption Expenditure of Resident Households [a]	29552	76165	118846	146577	178119	206942	234486	268188	403431	469133	474991	526081

Final Consumption Expenditure of Private Non-profit Institutions Serving Households

	1970	1975	1978	1979	1980	1981	1982	1983	1984	1985	1986	1987
Equals: Final Consumption Expenditure of Private Non-profit Organisations Serving Households	...	...	...	...	...	...	...	...	...	...	...	...
Private Final Consumption Expenditure	29552	76165	118846	146577	178119	206942	234486	268188	403431	469133	474991	526081

a) Item 'Final consumption expenditure of resident households' includes consumption expenditure of private non-profit institutions serving households.

2.6 Private Final Consumption Expenditure by Type and Purpose, in Constant Prices

Million Philippine pesos

	1970	1975	1978	1979	1980	1981	1982	1983	1984	1985	1986	1987
	At constant prices of: 1967						1972					

Final Consumption Expenditure of Resident Households

	1970	1975	1978	1979	1980	1981	1982	1983	1984	1985	1986	1987
1 Food, beverages and tobacco	143126	175200	...	...	35661	37138	38299	39416	40200	40299	40859	42932
A Food	126514	154480	...	...	32733	34061	35163	36221	36957	37061	37622	39646
B Non-alcoholic beverages	9218	11840	...	...	1399	1499	1518	1557	1590	1577	1586	1653
C Alcoholic beverages			...	...								
D Tobacco	7394	8880	...	...	1529	1578	1618	1638	1653	1661	1651	1633
2 Clothing and footwear	13846	17460	...	...	3295	3406	3493	3568	3599	3561	3545	3763
3 Gross rent, fuel and power	25129	31370	...	...	1748	1816	1940	2010	2030	2050	2079	2241
A Fuel and power	...	...	...	...	1748	1816	1940	2010	2030	2050	2079	2241
B Other	...	...	...	...	...	...	...	...	...	...	...	...
4 Furniture, furnishings and household equipment and operation	13403	17170	...	...	7991	8311	8452	8637	8660	8619	8647	9370
A Household operation	5783	7400	...	...	5579	5807	5910	6038	6057	6056	6082	6535
B Other	7620	9770	...	...	2412	2504	2542	2599	2603	2563	2565	2835
5 Medical care and health expenses	6787	8580	...	...	1689	1707	...	...	...	...	...	...
6 Transport and communication	6254	7990	...	...	1357	1411	1448	1469	1488	1491	1504	1637
7 Recreational, entertainment, education and cultural services	11023	14500	...	...	2578	2687	...	...	...	...	...	...
A Education	7194	9470	...	...	1719	1795	...	...	...	...	...	...
B Other	3829	5030	...	...	859	892	...	...	...	...	...	...
8 Miscellaneous goods and services	19152	23670	...	...	4951	5141	9903	10248	10055	9957	9963	10466
A Personal care	5605	7100	...	...	1085	1122	...	...	...	...	...	...
B Expenditures in restaurants, cafes and hotels	...	...	...	...	...	...	...	...	...	...	...	...

Philippines

2.6 Private Final Consumption Expenditure by Type and Purpose, in Constant Prices
(Continued)

Million Philippine pesos

	1970	1975	1978	1979	1980	1981	1982	1983	1984	1985	1986	1987
			1967		**At constant prices of:**				**1972**			
C Other	13547	16570	...	...	3866	4019	9903	10248	10055	9957	9963	10466
Total Final Consumption Expenditure in the Domestic Market by Households, of which	238720	295940	...	...	59270	61617	63535	65348	66032	65977	66597	70409
Plus: Direct purchases abroad by resident households	...	...	...	...	...	...	...	...	...	...	...	...
Less: Direct purchases in the domestic market by non-resident households	...	...	...	...	...	...	...	...	...	...	...	...
Equals: Final Consumption Expenditure of Resident Households [a]	238720	295940	...	...	59270	61617	63535	65348	66032	65977	66597	70409
Final Consumption Expenditure of Private Non-profit Institutions Serving Households												
Equals: Final Consumption Expenditure of Private Non-profit Organisations Serving Households	...	...	...	...	...	...	...	...	...	...	...	...
Private Final Consumption Expenditure	238720	295940	...	...	59270	61617	63535	65348	66032	65977	66597	70409

a) Item 'Final consumption expenditure of resident households' includes consumption expenditure of private non-profit institutions serving households.

2.17 Exports and Imports of Goods and Services, Detail

Million Philippine pesos

	1970	1975	1978	1979	1980	1981	1982	1983	1984	1985	1986	1987
					Exports of Goods and Services							
1 Exports of merchandise, f.o.b.	6608	16343	24954	33506	42709	44378	42136	54609	88818	84126	95391	113941
2 Transport and communication	273	975	1562	1791	2357	2813	2120	2376	3548	5152	4504	4715
A In respect of merchandise imports	52	324	552	614	831	878	1059	1078	1114	1300	1368	1235
B Other	221	651	1010	1177	1526	1935	1061	1298	2434	3852	3136	3480
3 Insurance service charges	28	103	41	110	91	36	39	186	99	74	203	224
A In respect of merchandise imports	23	44	25	21	8	13	21	10	-	-	-	-
B Other	5	59	16	89	83	23	18	176	99	74	203	224
4 Other commodities	233	1799	2842	2906	4308	5852	5724	9715	14830	21552	26870	25098
5 Adjustments of merchandise exports to change-of-ownership basis	...	...	...	...	...	...	...	...	...	...	...	...
6 Direct purchases in the domestic market by non-residential households	557	747	1523	1728	2380	2690	3792	5103	5847	9495	13197	9424
7 Direct purchases in the domestic market by extraterritorial bodies	396	1305	1498	1420	1745	2037	2339	3278	4559	6172	14939	10070
Total Exports of Goods and Services	8096	21272	32420	41461	53590	57806	56150	75267	117701	126571	155104	163472
					Imports of Goods and Services							
1 Imports of merchandise, c.i.f.	7371	26757	37042	48144	61081	65816	69697	87448	106134	98582	106662	142918
A Imports of merchandise, f.o.b.	6651	24592	34258	44892	57056	61911	64835	82234	100213	92659	98615	134183
B Transport of services on merchandise imports	685	2083	2715	3180	3944	3779	4628	5120	5795	5792	7947	8571
By residents	53	329	559	621	842	899	1093	1048	1149	1320	1243	1235
By non-residents	632	1754	2156	2559	3102	2880	3535	4072	4646	4472	6704	7336
C Insurance service charges on merchandise imports	35	82	69	74	82	125	234	94	126	132	100	164
By residents	23	44	25	21	8	16	23	10	5	-	-	-

Philippines

2.17 Exports and Imports of Goods and Services, Detail
(Continued)

Million Philippine pesos

	1970	1975	1978	1979	1980	1981	1982	1983	1984	1985	1986	1987
By non-residents	12	38	44	53	74	109	211	84	121	132	100	164
2 Adjustments of merchandise imports to change-of-ownership basis	...	...	...	...	...	...	...	...	...	...	...	...
3 Other transport and communication	108	222	678	1278	1452	1980	1188	2246	1711	715	1059	2264
4 Other insurance service charges	34	83	104	79	150	159	189	229	332	488	265	494
5 Other commodities	473	1342	2548	3130	4786	5063	6733	8482	8973	7611	6637	9276
6 Direct purchases abroad by government	92	553	770	691	918	870	920	1455	814	433	426	635
7 Direct purchases abroad by resident households	158	100	179	234	316	472	594	1278	418	677	1139	1810
Total Imports of Goods and Services	8236	29057	41321	53556	68704	74359	79321	101138	118382	108506	116188	157397
Balance of Goods and Services	-140	-7785	-8901	-12097	-15114	-16553	-23171	-25871	-681	18065	38916	6075
Total Imports and Balance of Goods and Services	8096	21272	32420	41461	53590	57806	56150	75267	117701	126571	155104	163472

4.1 Derivation of Value Added by Kind of Activity, in Current Prices

Million Philippine pesos

	1980 Gross Output	1980 Intermediate Consumption	1980 Value Added	1981 Gross Output	1981 Intermediate Consumption	1981 Value Added	1982 Gross Output	1982 Intermediate Consumption	1982 Value Added	1983 Gross Output	1983 Intermediate Consumption	1983 Value Added
						All Producers						
1 Agriculture, hunting, forestry and fishing	...	...	61761	...	...	69391	...	...	76721	...	...	84546
A Agriculture and hunting [a]	...	...	43820	...	...	49419	...	...	54593	...	...	60215
B Forestry and logging	...	...	6743	...	...	6151	...	...	7351	...	...	7541
C Fishing	...	...	11198	...	...	13821	...	...	14777	...	...	16790
2 Mining and quarrying	...	...	8095	...	...	6849	...	...	6106	...	...	7021
A Coal mining [b]	...	...	...	...	...	...	...	...	...	...	...	...
B Crude petroleum and natural gas production	...	...	...	...	...	...	...	...	...	...	...	...
C Metal ore mining	...	...	7075	...	...	5411	...	...	4431	...	...	5190
D Other mining [b]	...	...	1020	...	...	1438	...	...	1675	...	...	1831
3 Manufacturing	...	...	64555	...	...	75151	...	...	83133	...	...	95172
A Manufacture of food, beverages and tobacco	...	...	24204	...	...	29318	...	...	33245	...	...	38136
B Textile, wearing apparel and leather industries	...	...	8130	...	...	9919	...	...	10445	...	...	11854
C Manufacture of wood and wood products, including furniture	...	...	2679	...	...	3257	...	...	3446	...	...	3866
D Manufacture of paper and paper products, printing and publishing	...	...	1551	...	...	1714	...	...	1748	...	...	2051
E Manufacture of chemicals and chemical petroleum, coal, rubber and plastic products	...	...	16236	...	...	17534	...	...	18751	...	...	21352
F Manufacture of non-metallic mineral products, except products of petroleum and coal	...	...	1832	...	...	1978	...	...	2289	...	...	2506
G Basic metal industries	...	...	2237	...	...	2217	...	...	2614	...	...	3126
H Manufacture of fabricated metal products, machinery and equipment	...	...	6832	...	...	8156	...	...	9331	...	...	10820
I Other manufacturing industries	...	...	854	...	...	1058	...	...	1264	...	...	1461
4 Electricity, gas and water	...	...	2761	...	...	3329	...	...	4042	...	...	5256
A Electricity, gas and steam	...	...	2426	...	...	2868	...	...	3459	...	...	4561
B Water works and supply	...	...	335	...	...	461	...	...	583	...	...	695
5 Construction	...	...	21311	...	...	26268	...	...	29302	...	...	30730
6 Wholesale and retail trade, restaurants and hotels	...	...	45322	...	...	53650	...	...	60888	...	...	71085
A Wholesale and retail trade	...	...	42050	...	...	49765	...	...	56356	...	...	66094
B Restaurants and hotels	...	...	3272	...	...	3885	...	...	4532	...	...	4991
7 Transport, storage and communication	...	...	16444	...	...	19618	...	...	21376	...	...	24378
A Transport and storage	...	...	14528	...	...	17311	...	...	18735	...	...	20818
B Communication	...	...	1916	...	...	2307	...	...	2641	...	...	3560
8 Finance, insurance, real estate and business services	...	...	22670	...	...	25017	...	...	28792	...	...	33048
A Financial institutions	...	...	9585	...	...	9463	...	...	10599	...	...	12379

Philippines

4.1 Derivation of Value Added by Kind of Activity, in Current Prices
(Continued)

Million Philippine pesos

	1980 Gross Output	1980 Intermediate Consumption	1980 Value Added	1981 Gross Output	1981 Intermediate Consumption	1981 Value Added	1982 Gross Output	1982 Intermediate Consumption	1982 Value Added	1983 Gross Output	1983 Intermediate Consumption	1983 Value Added
B Insurance	...	...	2864	...	...	3396	...	...	3926	...	...	4141
C Real estate and business services	...	...	10221	...	...	12158	...	...	14267	...	...	16528
Real estate, except dwellings	...	...	4458	...	...	5361	...	...	6240	...	...	7277
Dwellings	...	...	5763	...	...	6797	...	...	8027	...	...	9251
9 Community, social and personal services	...	...	7670	...	...	9023	...	...	10516	...	...	11642
A Sanitary and similar services	...	...	...	...	...	...	...	...	...	...	...	...
B Social and related community services	...	...	4458	...	...	5254	...	...	6168	...	...	7075
Educational services	...	...	1574	...	...	1835	...	...	2199	...	...	2472
Medical, dental, other health and veterinary services	...	...	2884	...	...	3419	...	...	3969	...	...	4603
C Recreational and cultural services	...	...	1346	...	...	1568	...	...	1721	...	...	1802
D Personal and household services	...	...	1866	...	...	2201	...	...	2627	...	...	2765
Total, Industries	...	...	250589	...	...	288295	...	...	320876	...	...	362878
Producers of Government Services	...	...	11493	...	...	13930	...	...	16389	...	...	17539
Other Producers	...	...	2568	...	...	3032	...	...	3332	...	...	3678
Total	...	...	264650	...	...	305258	...	...	340597	...	...	384096
Less: Imputed bank service charge	...	...	...	...	...	...	...	...	...	...	...	...
Import duties	...	...	...	...	...	...	...	...	...	...	...	...
Value added tax	...	...	...	...	...	...	...	...	...	...	...	...
Total	...	...	...	...	...	...	...	...	...	...	...	...

	1984 Gross Output	1984 Intermediate Consumption	1984 Value Added	1985 Gross Output	1985 Intermediate Consumption	1985 Value Added	1986 Gross Output	1986 Intermediate Consumption	1986 Value Added	1987 Gross Output	1987 Intermediate Consumption	1987 Value Added
					All Producers							
1 Agriculture, hunting, forestry and fishing	...	...	139505	...	...	162519	...	...	155989	...	...	170770
A Agriculture and hunting [a]	...	...	104346	...	...	123670	...	...	113410	...	...	123544
B Forestry and logging	...	...	12043	...	...	10865	...	...	9874	...	...	10907
C Fishing	...	...	23116	...	...	27984	...	...	32705	...	...	36319
2 Mining and quarrying	...	...	9714	...	...	11529	...	...	12445	...	...	13600
A Coal mining [b]	...	...	...	...	...	...	...	...	...	...	...	...
B Crude petroleum and natural gas production	...	...	...	...	...	...	...	...	...	...	...	...
C Metal ore mining	...	...	7712	...	...	9314	...	...	10444	...	...	11449
D Other mining [b]	...	...	2002	...	...	2215	...	...	2001	...	...	2151
3 Manufacturing	...	...	137251	...	...	150523	...	...	155172	...	...	173539
A Manufacture of food, beverages and tobacco	...	...	58683	...	...	67206	...	...	67367	...	...	76368
B Textile, wearing apparel and leather industries	...	...	16594	...	...	18047	...	...	22482	...	...	25324
C Manufacture of wood and wood products, including furniture	...	...	4522	...	...	4682	...	...	3831	...	...	4370
D Manufacture of paper and paper products, printing and publishing	...	...	3370	...	...	3751	...	...	4341	...	...	4851
E Manufacture of chemicals and chemical petroleum, coal, rubber and plastic products	...	...	31284	...	...	30473	...	...	28583	...	...	30562
F Manufacture of non-metallic mineral products, except products of petroleum and coal	...	...	2956	...	...	2668	...	...	2805	...	...	3169
G Basic metal industries	...	...	5068	...	...	6459	...	...	6327	...	...	7608
H Manufacture of fabricated metal products, machinery and equipment	...	...	11551	...	...	12715	...	...	14439	...	...	16069
I Other manufacturing industries	...	...	3223	...	...	4522	...	...	4997	...	...	5218
4 Electricity, gas and water	...	...	7980	...	...	10986	...	...	14678	...	...	17333
A Electricity, gas and steam	...	...	7090	...	...	9799	...	...	13066	...	...	15552
B Water works and supply	...	...	890	...	...	1187	...	...	1612	...	...	1781

Philippines

4.1 Derivation of Value Added by Kind of Activity, in Current Prices
(Continued)

Million Philippine pesos

		1984 Gross Output	1984 Intermediate Consumption	1984 Value Added	1985 Gross Output	1985 Intermediate Consumption	1985 Value Added	1986 Gross Output	1986 Intermediate Consumption	1986 Value Added	1987 Gross Output	1987 Intermediate Consumption	1987 Value Added
5	Construction	...	...	31209	...	...	27506	...	...	22685	...	...	28113
6	Wholesale and retail trade, restaurants and hotels	...	...	106367	...	...	125869	...	...	129282	...	...	146435
	A Wholesale and retail trade	...	...	99711	...	...	118370	...	...	121243	...	...	137375
	B Restaurants and hotels	...	...	6656	...	...	7499	...	...	8039	...	...	9060
7	Transport, storage and communication	...	...	33820	...	...	38263	...	...	39256	...	...	42027
	A Transport and storage	...	...	28245	...	...	32204	...	...	32508	...	...	34658
	B Communication	...	...	5575	...	...	6059	...	...	6748	...	...	7369
8	Finance, insurance, real estate and business services	...	...	34912	...	...	37393	...	...	43608	...	...	54244
	A Financial institutions	...	...	8471	...	...	4451	...	...	8826	...	...	14923
	B Insurance	...	...	5369	...	...	6502	...	...	6783	...	...	7589
	C Real estate and business services	...	...	21072	...	...	26440	...	...	27999	...	...	31732
	Real estate, except dwellings	...	...	7482	...	...	8439	...	...	9337	...	...	10257
	Dwellings	...	...	13590	...	...	18003	...	...	18662	...	...	21475
9	Community, social and personal services	...	...	14257	...	...	16751	...	...	18179	...	...	19527
	A Sanitary and similar services	...	...	...	...	...	...	...	...	...	...	...	...
	B Social and related community services	...	...	8811	...	...	10941	...	...	11834	...	...	12854
	Educational services	...	...	3114	...	...	4021	...	...	4288	...	...	4684
	Medical, dental, other health and veterinary services	...	...	5698	...	...	6920	...	...	7546	...	...	8170
	C Recreational and cultural services	...	...	2200	...	...	2406	...	...	2663	...	...	2722
	D Personal and household services	...	...	3245	...	...	3404	...	...	3682	...	...	3951
	Total, Industries	...	...	515015	...	...	581339	...	...	591294	...	...	665588
	Producers of Government Services	...	...	21254	...	...	27033	...	...	31728	...	...	38610
	Other Producers	...	...	4197	...	...	4312	...	...	4107	...	...	4170
	Total	...	...	540466	...	...	612684	...	...	627129	...	...	708368
	Less: Imputed bank service charge	...	...	...	...	...	...	...	...	...	...	...	...
	Import duties	...	...	...	...	...	...	...	...	...	...	...	...
	Value added tax	...	...	...	...	...	...	...	...	...	...	...	...
	Total	...	...	...	...	...	...	...	...	...	...	...	...

a) Item 'Agriculture, hunting, forestry and fishing' excludes hunting.
b) 'Coal mining' is included in 'Other mining'.

4.2 Derivation of Value Added by Kind of Activity, in Constant Prices

Million Philippine pesos

At constant prices of: 1972

All Producers

		1980 Gross Output	1980 Intermediate Consumption	1980 Value Added	1981 Gross Output	1981 Intermediate Consumption	1981 Value Added	1982 Gross Output	1982 Intermediate Consumption	1982 Value Added	1983 Gross Output	1983 Intermediate Consumption	1983 Value Added
1	Agriculture, hunting, forestry and fishing	...	...	23662	...	...	24608	...	...	25378	...	...	24845
	A Agriculture and hunting [a]	...	...	18400	...	...	19301	...	...	20141	...	...	19619
	B Forestry and logging	...	...	1386	...	...	1175	...	...	983	...	...	819
	C Fishing	...	...	3876	...	...	4132	...	...	4254	...	...	4407
2	Mining and quarrying	...	...	2236	...	...	2175	...	...	2016	...	...	1966
	A Coal mining [b]	...	...	...	...	...	...	...	...	...	...	...	...
	B Crude petroleum and natural gas production	...	...	...	...	...	...	...	...	...	...	...	...
	C Metal ore mining	...	...	1946	...	...	1777	...	...	1574	...	...	1501
	D Other mining [b]	...	...	290	...	...	398	...	...	442	...	...	465

Philippines

4.2 Derivation of Value Added by Kind of Activity, in Constant Prices
(Continued)

Million Philippine pesos

	1980 Gross Output	1980 Intermediate Consumption	1980 Value Added	1981 Gross Output	1981 Intermediate Consumption	1981 Value Added	1982 Gross Output	1982 Intermediate Consumption	1982 Value Added	1983 Gross Output	1983 Intermediate Consumption	1983 Value Added
					At constant prices of: 1972							
3 Manufacturing	...	...	23175	...	...	23959	...	...	24535	...	...	25108
A Manufacture of food, beverages and tobacco	...	...	10190	...	...	10633	...	...	10960	...	...	11126
B Textile, wearing apparel and leather industries	...	...	2136	...	...	2354	...	...	2348	...	...	2363
C Manufacture of wood and wood products, including furniture	...	...	797	...	...	846	...	...	844	...	...	858
D Manufacture of paper and paper products, printing and publishing	...	...	515	...	...	532	...	...	531	...	...	564
E Manufacture of chemicals and chemical petroleum, coal, rubber and plastic products	...	...	4040	...	...	3915	...	...	3910	...	...	3982
F Manufacture of non-metallic mineral products, except products of petroleum and coal	...	...	574	...	...	540	...	...	569	...	...	587
G Basic metal industries	...	...	853	...	...	791	...	...	856	...	...	947
H Manufacture of fabricated metal products, machinery and equipment	...	...	3805	...	...	4052	...	...	4197	...	...	4347
I Other manufacturing industries	...	...	265	...	...	296	...	...	320	...	...	334
4 Electricity, gas and water	...	...	921	...	...	999	...	...	1084	...	...	1192
A Electricity, gas and steam	...	...	813	...	...	872	...	...	941	...	...	1029
B Water works and supply	...	...	108	...	...	127	...	...	143	...	...	163
5 Construction	...	...	7139	...	...	7830	...	...	8079	...	...	7689
6 Wholesale and retail trade, restaurants and hotels	...	...	13664	...	...	14231	...	...	14672	...	...	15466
A Wholesale and retail trade	...	...	12224	...	...	12731	...	...	13103	...	...	13930
B Restaurants and hotels	...	...	1440	...	...	1500	...	...	1569	...	...	1536
7 Transport, storage and communication	...	...	4827	...	...	5040	...	...	5165	...	...	5266
A Transport and storage	...	...	3937	...	...	4066	...	...	4123	...	...	4153
B Communication	...	...	890	...	...	974	...	...	1042	...	...	1113
8 Finance, insurance, real estate and business services	...	...	8138	...	...	8032	...	...	8349	...	...	8698
A Financial institutions	...	...	3323	...	...	2895	...	...	2905	...	...	3108
B Insurance	...	...	983	...	...	1024	...	...	1094	...	...	1058
C Real estate and business services	...	...	3832	...	...	4113	...	...	4350	...	...	4532
Real estate, except dwellings	...	...	1309	...	...	1948	...	...	2059	...	...	2155
Dwellings	...	...	2023	...	...	2165	...	...	2291	...	...	2377
9 Community, social and personal services	...	...	2991	...	...	3106	...	...	3209	...	...	3208
A Sanitary and similar services	...	...	...	...	...	...	...	...	...	...	...	...
B Social and related community services	...	...	1758	...	...	1833	...	...	1897	...	...	1941
Educational services	...	...	786	...	...	821	...	...	865	...	...	877
Medical, dental, other health and veterinary services	...	...	972	...	...	1012	...	...	1032	...	...	1064
C Recreational and cultural services	...	...	477	...	...	494	...	...	506	...	...	493
D Personal and household services	...	...	756	...	...	779	...	...	806	...	...	774
Total, Industries	...	...	86753	...	...	89980	...	...	92487	...	...	93438
Producers of Government Services	...	...	4700	...	...	5081	...	...	5339	...	...	5294
Other Producers	...	...	1114	...	...	1146	...	...	1173	...	...	1188
Total	...	...	92567	...	...	96207	...	...	98999	...	...	99920
Less: Imputed bank service charge	...	...	...	...	...	...	...	...	...	...	...	...
Import duties	...	...	...	...	...	...	...	...	...	...	...	...
Value added tax	...	...	...	...	...	...	...	...	...	...	...	...
Total	...	...	...	...	...	...	...	...	...	...	...	...

Philippines

4.2 Derivation of Value Added by Kind of Activity, in Constant Prices

Million Philippine pesos

	1984 Gross Output	1984 Intermediate Consumption	1984 Value Added	1985 Gross Output	1985 Intermediate Consumption	1985 Value Added	1986 Gross Output	1986 Intermediate Consumption	1986 Value Added	1987 Gross Output	1987 Intermediate Consumption	1987 Value Added
At constant prices of: 1972 — All Producers												
1 Agriculture, hunting, forestry and fishing	...	...	25409	...	...	26252	...	...	27110	...	...	26834
A Agriculture and hunting [a]	...	...	20315	...	...	21124	...	...	21905	...	...	21548
B Forestry and logging	...	...	765	...	...	706	...	...	654	...	...	648
C Fishing	...	...	4329	...	...	4422	...	...	4551	...	...	4638
2 Mining and quarrying	...	...	1755	...	...	1768	...	...	1574	...	...	1547
A Coal mining [b]	...	...	...	...	...	...	...	...	...	...	...	...
B Crude petroleum and natural gas production	...	...	...	...	...	...	...	...	...	...	...	...
C Metal ore mining	...	...	1349	...	...	1370	...	...	1236	...	...	1198
D Other mining [b]	...	...	406	...	...	398	...	...	338	...	...	349
3 Manufacturing	...	...	23319	...	...	21541	...	...	21717	...	...	23168
A Manufacture of food, beverages and tobacco	...	...	11039	...	...	10412	...	...	10184	...	...	10885
B Textile, wearing apparel and leather industries	...	...	2311	...	...	2016	...	...	2332	...	...	2474
C Manufacture of wood and wood products, including furniture	...	...	730	...	...	645	...	...	508	...	...	554
D Manufacture of paper and paper products, printing and publishing	...	...	552	...	...	547	...	...	602	...	...	647
E Manufacture of chemicals and chemical petroleum, coal, rubber and plastic products	...	...	3390	...	...	3138	...	...	3030	...	...	3163
F Manufacture of non-metallic mineral products, except products of petroleum and coal	...	...	481	...	...	375	...	...	377	...	...	399
G Basic metal industries	...	...	1121	...	...	1070	...	...	1018	...	...	1140
H Manufacture of fabricated metal products, machinery and equipment	...	...	3270	...	...	2891	...	...	3218	...	...	3445
I Other manufacturing industries	...	...	425	...	...	447	...	...	448	...	...	461
4 Electricity, gas and water	...	...	1342	...	...	1433	...	...	1723	...	...	1908
A Electricity, gas and steam	...	...	1159	...	...	1229	...	...	1501	...	...	1675
B Water works and supply	...	...	183	...	...	204	...	...	222	...	...	233
5 Construction	...	...	5866	...	...	4258	...	...	3382	...	...	3967
6 Wholesale and retail trade, restaurants and hotels	...	...	15540	...	...	15452	...	...	15728	...	...	16575
A Wholesale and retail trade	...	...	14073	...	...	14066	...	...	14337	...	...	15153
B Restaurants and hotels	...	...	1467	...	...	1386	...	...	1391	...	...	1422
7 Transport, storage and communication	...	...	5032	...	...	4953	...	...	5105	...	...	5251
A Transport and storage	...	...	3860	...	...	3813	...	...	3873	...	...	4073
B Communication	...	...	1172	...	...	1140	...	...	1232	...	...	1178
8 Finance, insurance, real estate and business services	...	...	6081	...	...	5251	...	...	5779	...	...	6781
A Financial institutions	...	...	1373	...	...	598	...	...	1154	...	...	1840
B Insurance	...	...	870	...	...	855	...	...	886	...	...	958
C Real estate and business services	...	...	3838	...	...	3798	...	...	3739	...	...	3983
Real estate, except dwellings	...	...	1575	...	...	1407	...	...	1430	...	...	1470
Dwellings	...	...	2263	...	...	2391	...	...	2309	...	...	2513
9 Community, social and personal services	...	...	3018	...	...	2956	...	...	2970	...	...	3013
A Sanitary and similar services	...	...	...	...	...	...	...	...	...	...	...	...
B Social and related community services	...	...	1871	...	...	1957	...	...	1951	...	...	2005
Educational services	...	...	855	...	...	890	...	...	866	...	...	897
Medical, dental, other health and veterinary services	...	...	1016	...	...	1067	...	...	1085	...	...	1108
C Recreational and cultural services	...	...	457	...	...	402	...	...	420	...	...	408
D Personal and household services	...	...	690	...	...	597	...	...	599	...	...	600

Philippines

4.2 Derivation of Value Added by Kind of Activity, in Constant Prices
(Continued)

Million Philippine pesos

	1984			1985			1986			1987		
	Gross Output	Intermediate Consumption	Value Added	Gross Output	Intermediate Consumption	Value Added	Gross Output	Intermediate Consumption	Value Added	Gross Output	Intermediate Consumption	Value Added
				At constant prices of:1972								
Total, Industries	...	...	87362	...	...	83864	...	...	85088	...	...	89044
Producers of Government Services	...	...	5585	...	...	5253	...	...	5362	...	...	5697
Other Producers	...	...	980	...	...	787	...	...	730	...	...	722
Total	...	...	93927	...	...	89904	...	...	91180	...	...	95463
Less: Imputed bank service charge	...	...	...	...	...	...	...	...	...	...	...	...
Import duties	...	...	...	...	...	...	...	...	...	...	...	...
Value added tax	...	...	...	...	...	...	...	...	...	...	...	...
Total	...	...	...	...	...	...	...	...	...	...	...	...

a) Item 'Agriculture, hunting, forestry and fishing' excludes hunting.
b) 'Coal mining' is included in 'Other mining'.

Poland

Source. Reply to the United Nations Material Balances Questionnaire from the Central Statistical Office of Poland, Warsaw. The official estimates are published annually in 'Rocznik Statystyczny' (Statistical Yearbook). Concepts, definitions and methods of estimation are described in the above Yearbook and also in 'Concise Statistical Yearbook of Poland' and in 'Rocznik Dochodu Narodowego, 1960-1965' (Yearbook of National Income, 1960-1965). The above publications are issued by the Central Statistical Office.

General note. The estimates shown in the following tables have been prepared in accordance with the System of Material Product Balances. Therefore, these estimates are not comparable in concept and coverage with those conforming to the United Nations System of National Accounts. In Poland, investments and general repairs in the socialized economy are financed from the state budget, credits granted by banks, depreciation funds, development fund of enterprises or enterprises, profit, receipts from the liquidation of fixed assets, various state and social funds designed as a whole or partially for investment, and from the so-called special funds construction activities of the housing and building associations are financed from their own funds (contributions of their members) and credits granted by banks. The estimates on national income for the years 1976-1980 were calculated according to the method of kind of activity. Beginning 1981, the method of enterprises has been adopted i.e., all activities of an enterprise are classified to one branch of activity only. Estimates using both methods are shown for the year 1980.

1a Net Material Product by Use at Current Market Prices

Thousand Million Polish zlotych

	1970	1975	1978	1979	1980	1981	1982	1983	1984	1985	1986	1987
1 Personal consumption	465.0	799.7 / 805.2	1130.7	1245.5	1404.0 / 1409.3	1721.2	2929.3	3749.6	4455.8	5189.9 / 5205.9	6403.2	8254.6
2 Material consumption in the units of the non-material sphere serving individuals [a]	...	...	...	...	...	...	...	...	...	623.4	792.8	1033.7
Consumption of the Population	465.0	799.7 / 805.2	1130.7	1245.5	1404.0 / 1409.3	1721.2	2929.3	3749.6	4455.8	5189.9 / 5829.3	7196.0	9288.3
3 Material consumption in the units of the non-material sphere serving the community as a whole [a]	83.0	146.6 / 152.3	228.7	247.4	264.5 / 255.1	276.4	525.7	687.9	885.1	1120.2 / 460.2	528.5	667.4
4 Net fixed capital formation	139.5	410.7 / 393.9	517.7	446.8	349.8 / 347.6	225.4	800.2	1053.6	1274.7	1539.7 / 1533.6	1950.0	2612.4
5 Increase in material circulating assets and in stocks	44.0	102.0 / 102.0	96.2	59.0	13.8 / 40.5	-5.8	433.2	339.4	476.1	677.5 / 677.5	904.6	1062.5
6 Losses [b]										59.1[c] / 17.9	-65.7	-24.5
7 Exports of goods and material services	17.7	-102.0 / -103.7	-70.7	-63.3	-95.9 / -60.8	-56.8	64.6	93.5	90.1	... / 1900.6	2357.5	3625.2
8 Less: Imports of goods and material services										... / 1761.2	2173.8	3218.1
Net Material Product [d]	749.2	1357.0 / 1349.7	1902.6	1935.4	1936.2 / 1991.7	2160.4	4753.0	5924.0	7181.8	8586.4 / 8657.9	10697.1	14013.2

a) Item 'Material consumption in units of the non-material sphere serving individuals' is included in item 'Material consumption in the units of the non-material sphere serving the community as a whole'.
b) Item 'Losses', includes also statistical discrepancy.
c) Including item 'Losses' through 'Less: Imports of goods and material services'.
d) Beginning 1975 the estimates of net material product shown in table 1a (Net Material Product by Use) differ from those shown in table 4 (Primary Income from Net Material Product). This is because net material product in table 1a is computed by means of the kind of activity method for which there was no possibility to single out elements of primary distribution while in table 4 there is primary distribution of net material product computed by means of the enterprise method.

Poland

1b Net Material Product by Use at Constant Market Prices

Thousand Million Polish zlotych

	1970	1975	1978	1979	1980	1981	1982	1983	1984	1985	1986	1987
		1971		**1977**	At constant prices of:			**1982**			**1984**	
1 Personal consumption	470.4	706.3 875.5	1023.7	1056.9	1081.1 3651.2	3502.3	2989.4	3176.0	3295.1	3367.6 4624.1	4855.2	5000.0
2 Material consumption in the units of the non-material sphere serving individuals	...	...	...	...	...					558.0	592.1	612.2
Consumption of the Population	470.4	706.3 875.5	1023.7	1056.9	1081.1 3651.2	3502.3	2989.4	3176.0	3295.1	3367.6 5182.1	5447.3	5612.2
3 Material consumption in the units of the non-material sphere serving the community as a whole	81.8[a]	130.4[a] 168.1[a]	209.8[a]	214.9[a]	217.4[a] 525.0[a]	482.5[a]	538.1[a]	554.8[a]	600.9[a]	640.4[a] 392.6	397.5	399.2
4 Net fixed capital formation	167.0	427.1 470.3	459.6	388.7	290.0 1326.1	1005.4	805.1	881.4	989.6	1037.7 838.3	888.0	932.7
5 Increase in material circulating assets and in stocks	46.8	82.6 109.1	84.1	50.9	19.7 108.2	33.0	165.0	136.0	102.3	132.6 468.8	489.8	412.1
6 Losses [b]										122.6[c] 68.1	87.1	88.0
7 Exports of goods and material services	25.3	-85.0 -116.3	-36.0	-10.0	-8.9 -102.0	-175.4	83.1	107.4	140.3	... 1520.3	1584.3	1663.4
8 Less: Imports of goods and material services										... 1440.6	1518.0	1587.9
Net Material Product	791.3	1261.4 1506.7[d]	1741.2[d]	1701.4[d]	1599.3[d] 5508.5	4847.8	4580.7	4855.6	5128.2	5300.9 7029.6	7376.0	7519.7

a) Item 'Material consumption in units of the non-material sphere serving individuals' is included in item 'Material consumption in the units of the non-material sphere serving the community as a whole'. b) Item 'Losses', includes also statistical discrepancy. c) Including item 'Losses' through 'Less: Imports of goods and material services'. d) The estimates are at constant prices as of January 1, 1977.

2a Net Material Product by Kind of Activity of the Material Sphere in Current Market Prices

Thousand Million Polish zlotych

	1970	1975	1978	1979	1980	1981	1982	1983	1984	1985	1986	1987
1 Agriculture and forestry	129.5	199.8 199.8	304.4	304.8	296.9 314.7	638.4	925.0	1088.5	1256.4	1398.7 1398.7	1650.2	1849.2
A Agriculture and livestock [a]	108.6	166.4 166.4	257.2	256.7	246.3 260.6	576.5	758.5	907.7	1049.9	1155.9 1155.9	1352.6	1453.6
B Forestry	10.6	15.1 15.1	15.7	14.5	15.1 24.2	24.9	73.3	85.9	93.6	115.8 115.8	139.7	188.9
C Other	10.3	18.3 18.3	31.5	33.6	35.5 29.9	37.0	93.2	94.9	112.9	127.0 127.0	157.9	206.7
2 Industrial activity [a]	408.7	803.3 803.3	993.8	1023.6	1062.8 1038.5	909.8	2387.6	2967.9	3561.8	4181.9 4117.1	5060.9	6804.0

Poland

2a Net Material Product by Kind of Activity of the Material Sphere in Current Market Prices
(Continued)

Thousand Million Polish zlotych

	1970	1975	1978	1979	1980	1981	1982	1983	1984	1985	1986	1987
3 Construction	73.7	151.3 151.3	233.0	215.0	178.2 201.8	158.3	510.0	644.3	832.9	1064.5 1063.7	1378.9	1801.0
4 Wholesale and retail trade and restaurants and other eating and drinking places	73.9	74.2 74.2	196.0	203.9	201.9 254.1	269.7	655.5	802.2	982.3	1207.2 1343.9	1708.3	2384.7
5 Transport and communication	50.5	92.1 92.1	131.0	134.7	143.4 143.2	141.3	206.5	318.3	420.3	579.0 563.1	667.0	851.2
A Transport	44.9	78.9 78.9	113.5	112.1	116.3 115.8	113.7	166.5	261.3	355.7	488.5 472.6	562.4	708.5
B Communication	5.6	13.2 13.2	17.5	22.6	27.1 27.4	27.6	40.0	57.0	64.6	90.5 90.5	104.6	142.7
6 Other activities of the material sphere	12.9	28.3 29.0	44.4	53.4	53.0 39.4	42.9	68.4	102.8	128.1	155.1 171.4	231.8	323.1
Net material product	749.2	1349.0 1349.7	1902.6	1935.4	1936.2 1991.7	2160.4	4753.0	5924.0	7181.8	8586.4 8657.9	10697.1	14013.2

a) Inland water fishing is included in item 'Agriculture and livestock'. Ocean and coastal fishing and factory-vessel fishing are included in item 'Industrial activity'.

2b Net Material Product by Kind of Activity of the Material Sphere in Constant Market Prices

Thousand Million Polish zlotych

	1970	1975	1978	1979	1980	1981	1982	1983	1984	1985	1986	1987
		1971	**1977**		**At constant prices of:** **1982**					**1984**		
1 Agriculture and forestry	149.6	154.6 246.3	267.6	248.3	213.1 773.9	787.4	829.4	877.3	926.3	928.3 1106.5	1176.0	1083.9
A Agriculture and livestock a	125.5	121.0 205.1	220.1	201.5	165.8 601.9	625.6	661.5	717.4	760.4	763.0 917.5	981.8	883.5
B Forestry	13.8	14.6 16.6	15.9	14.7	15.4 62.9	66.7	73.2	82.6	89.1	90.4 95.0	100.2	102.5
C Other	10.3	19.0 24.6	31.6	32.1	31.9 109.1	95.1	94.7	77.3	76.8	74.9 94.0	94.0	97.9
2 Industrial activity a	394.3	657.5 759.0	914.7	898.8	862.4 2763.3	2360.9	2253.8	2384.0	2511.5	2611.0 3418.9	3571.2	3689.7

Poland

2b Net Material Product by Kind of Activity of the Material Sphere in Constant Market Prices
(Continued)

Thousand Million Polish zlotych

	1970	1975	1978	1979	1980	1981	1982	1983	1984	1985	1986	1987
		1971		**1977**	At constant prices of:		**1982**			**1984**		
3 Construction	89.8	152.5	201.8	189.2	148.2	548.3	502.4	541.1	584.7	609.8	880.4	898.9
		195.4			731.8					844.2		
4 Wholesale and retail trade and restaurants and other eating and drinking places	93.5	159.8	180.3	185.5	185.7	827.9	720.1	750.8	777.4	810.3	1224.4	1294.2
		158.8			893.6					1162.9		
5 Transport and communication	51.3	91.0	135.8	130.8	140.5	238.5	206.6	227.3	248.9	259.2	381.6	405.0
		115.0			262.1					363.4		
A Transport	...	...	...	...	...	201.3	166.6	177.4	195.4	203.3	312.9	328.5
					224.5					299.5		
B Communication	...	...	...	...	...	37.2	40.0	49.9	53.5	55.9	68.7	76.5
					37.6					63.9		
6 Other activities of the material sphere	12.8	46.0	41.0	48.8	49.4	84.8	68.4	75.1	79.4	82.3	142.4	148.0
		32.2			83.8					133.7		
Net material product	791.3	1261.4	1741.2[b]	1701.4[b]	1599.3[b]	4847.8	4580.7	4855.6	5128.2	5300.9	7376.0	7519.7
		1506.7[b]			5508.5					7029.6		

a) Inland water fishing is included in item 'Agriculture and livestock'. Ocean and coastal fishing and factory-vessel fishing are included in item 'Industrial activity'.
b) The estimates are at constant prices as of January 1, 1977.

3 Primary Incomes by Kind of Activity of the Material Sphere in Current Market Prices

Thousand Million Polish zlotych

	1980		1981	
	Primary Income of the Population	Primary Income of Enterprises	Primary Income of the Population	Primary Income of Enterprises
1 Agriculture and forestry	292.5	22.2	602.4	36.0
A Agriculture and livestock [a]	255.9	4.7	553.2	23.3
B Forestry	10.4	13.8	14.3	10.6
C Other	26.2	3.7	34.9	2.1
2 Industrial activity [a]	409.1	629.4	515.1	394.7
3 Construction	134.3	61.6	163.0	-11.9
4 Wholesale and retail trade and restaurants and other eating and drinking places	89.9	165.0	131.3	139.9
5 Transport and communication	90.6	52.6	114.1	27.2
6 Other activities of the material sphere	38.4	1.0	45.9	-3.0
Total [b]	1054.8	931.8	1571.8	582.9

a) Inland water fishing is included in item 'Agriculture and livestock'. Ocean and coastal fishing and factory-vessel fishing are included in item 'Industrial activity'.
b) Column 'Primary income of the population', includes net income of the owner of private farms and other private enterprises (equivalent to unincorporated enterprises in SNA).

4 Primary Incomes From Net Material Product

Thousand Million Polish zlotych

	1970	1975	1978	1979	1980	1981	1982	1983	1984	1985	1986	1987
			a) Primary Incomes of the Population									
1 Socialist sector	262.6	455.3	622.2	679.9	759.0	971.5	...	...	...	...	...	...
		458.8			754.8							
A State sector	224.8	378.6	504.6	552.5	623.2	793.0	...	...	...	...	...	...
		382.1			618.5							
B Co-operative sector	36.3	75.3	115.8	124.7	132.3	175.2	...	...	...	...	...	...
		75.3			132.9							
C Personal plots of households	1.5	1.4	1.8	2.7	3.5	3.3	...	...	...	...	...	...
		1.4			3.4							
2 Private sector	124.7	186.5	287.8	301.2	298.1	600.3	...	...	...	...	...	...
		186.5			300.0							
Sub-total	387.3	641.8	910.0	981.1	1057.1	1571.8	...	...	...	...	...	...
		645.3			1054.8							

Poland

4 Primary Incomes From Net Material Product
(Continued)

Thousand Million Polish zlotych

	1970	1975	1978	1979	1980	1981	1982	1983	1984	1985	1986	1987
			b) Primary incomes of the enterprises									
1 Socialist sector	344.0	668.0 / 665.2	946.6	908.4	827.8 / 888.8	533.1	...	...	...	...	...	...
A State sector	311.5	629.2 / 626.3	884.1	835.3	769.1 / 823.9	528.3	...	...	...	...	...	...
B Co-operative sector	32.5	38.8 / 38.9	62.5	73.1	58.7 / 64.9	4.8	...	...	...	...	...	...
2 Private sector	17.9	26.1 / 26.1	39.0	40.2	42.8 / 43.0	49.8	...	...	...	...	...	...
Sub-total	361.9	694.1 / 691.3	985.6	948.6	870.6 / 931.8	582.9	...	...	...	...	...	...
Total net material product	749.2	1335.9 / 1336.6	1895.6	1929.7	1927.7 / 1986.6	2154.7	...	...	...	...	...	...

5a Supply and Disposition of Goods and Material Services in Current Market Prices

Thousand Million Polish zlotych

	Supply					Disposition				
	Gross Output at Producers Prices	Trade Margins and Transport Charges	Gross Output at Market Prices	Imports	Total Supply and Disposition	Intermediate Material Consumption including Depreciation	Final Consumption	Net Capital Formation	Losses	Exports
					1982					
1 Agriculture and forestry a	1965.0	85.0	2050.0	81.0	2131.0	1646.0	477.0	-15.0	-	23.0
2 Industrial activity a	7088.0	726.0	7814.0	824.0	8638.0	4453.0	2589.0	802.0	-65.0	859.0
3 Construction	1114.0	1.0	1115.0	2.0	1117.0	202.0	91.0	756.0	-	68.0
4 Transport and communication	664.0	-	664.0	53.0	717.0	455.0	130.0	1.0	5.0	126.0
5 Other activities of the material sphere	249.0	4.0	253.0	2.0	255.0	143.0	104.0	6.0	-	2.0
Total b	11080.0	816.0	11896.0	962.0	12858.0	6899.0	3391.0	1550.0	-60.0	1078.0
					1983					
1 Agriculture and forestry a	2232.0	105.0	2337.0	63.0	2400.0	1843.0	512.0	15.0	-	30.0
2 Industrial activity a	8656.0	975.0	9631.0	938.0	10569.0	5514.0	3407.0	728.0	-55.0	975.0
3 Construction	1415.0	2.0	1417.0	3.0	1420.0	268.0	113.0	985.0	-	54.0
4 Transport and communication	890.0	-	890.0	63.0	953.0	604.0	209.0	1.0	8.0	131.0
5 Other activities of the material sphere	317.0	5.0	322.0	3.0	325.0	186.0	133.0	4.0	-	2.0
Total b	13510.0	1087.0	14597.0	1070.0	15667.0	8415.0	4374.0	1733.0	-47.0	1192.0
					1984					
1 Agriculture and forestry a	2484.0	136.0	2620.0	75.0	2695.0	2016.0	572.0	61.0	-	46.0
2 Industrial activity a	10453.0	1110.0	11563.0	1173.0	12736.0	6621.0	4074.0	922.0	-91.0	1210.0
3 Construction	1789.0	9.0	1798.0	1.0	1799.0	332.0	132.0	1267.0	-	68.0
4 Transport and communication	1102.0	-	1102.0	92.0	1194.0	745.0	259.0	2.0	8.0	180.0
5 Other activities of the material sphere	401.0	8.0	409.0	5.0	414.0	223.0	174.0	5.0	-	12.0
Total b	16229.0	1263.0	17492.0	1346.0	18838.0	9937.0	5211.0	2257.0	-83.0	1516.0

a) Inland water fishing is included in item 'Agriculture and livestock'. Ocean and coastal fishing and factory-vessel fishing are included in item 'Industrial activity'.
b) Column 2 (Trade margins and transport charges) refers to trade margins only, column 6 (Intermediate consumption including depreciation) excludes depreciation and column 9 (Losses) includes scraps and statistical discrepancies.

Poland

6a Capital Formation by Kind of Activity of the Material and Non-Material Spheres in Current Market Prices

Thousand Million Polish zlotych

	1970	1975	1978	1979	1980	1981	1982	1983	1984	1985	1986	1987
Net Fixed Capital Formation												
1 Agriculture and forestry	22.6	54.6 / 54.6	88.8	85.7	54.4 / 51.0	49.2	134.6	187.1	202.3	195.2 / 195.2	218.8	289.3
2 Industrial activity	37.3	157.9 / 157.9	165.2	115.7	79.1 / 75.9	16.5	144.4	199.1	248.8	331.8 / 327.2	432.0	653.7
3 Construction	3.3	14.7 / 14.7	17.8	10.3	4.6 / 5.7	-6.3	-1.0	6.4	11.3	17.8 / 16.7	25.7	41.6
4 Wholesale and retail trade, restaurants and other eating and drinking places	3.2	7.4 / 7.4	7.0	5.3	4.0 / 4.9	3.8	17.2	25.4	30.1	34.4 / 33.8	59.7	83.3
5 Transport and communication	14.3	42.6 / 42.6	33.5	25.3	17.7 / 13.8	-6.2	12.5	21.4	43.3	67.7 / 73.0	93.1	83.7
6 Other activities of the material sphere	5.4	11.4 / 11.1	24.4	21.7	14.3 / 19.0	16.5	57.5	74.7	95.8	120.8 / 115.9	157.4	206.7
Total Material Sphere	86.1	288.6 / 288.3	336.7	264.0	174.1 / 170.3	73.5	365.2	514.1	631.6	767.7 / 761.8	986.7	1358.3
7 Housing except owner-occupied, communal and miscellaneous personal services	19.2	48.2 / 46.8	95.7	97.3	92.9 / 94.2	73.1	190.3	239.9	292.0	344.6 / 344.6	424.5	529.7
8 Education, culture and art	8.9	15.0 / 15.0	17.1	15.7	14.9 / 12.7	11.8	37.1	48.8	62.8	86.2 / 86.2	113.2	153.3
9 Health and social welfare services and sports	4.4	15.7 / 15.7	18.5	21.2	19.7 / 19.7	18.4	43.2	55.6	73.5	97.9 / 97.8	129.4	171.9
Total Non-Material Sphere Serving Individuals	32.5	78.9 / 77.5	131.3	134.2	127.5 / 126.6	103.3	270.6	344.3	428.3	528.7 / 528.6	667.1	854.9
10 Government	...	... / ...	...	...	... / ...	...	...	...	...	... / ...	...	...
11 Finance, credit and insurance	...	... / ...	...	...	... / ...	...	...	...	...	... / ...	...	...
12 Research, scientific and technological institutes	...	... / ...	...	...	... / ...	...	...	...	...	... / ...	...	...
13 Other activities of the non-material sphere	...	... / ...	...	...	... / ...	...	...	...	...	... / ...	...	...
Total Non-Material Sphere Serving the Community as a Whole	10.6	20.0 / 20.1	23.2	22.4	27.6 / 30.1	28.6	72.5	78.7	96.3	110.6 / 110.4	146.3	197.7
14 Owner-occupied dwellings	10.3	8.0 / 8.0	26.5	26.2	20.6 / 20.6	20.0	91.9	116.5	118.5	132.7 / 132.8	149.9	201.5
Total Net Fixed Capital Formation [a]	139.5	395.5 / 393.9	517.7	446.8	349.8 / 347.6	225.4	800.2	1053.6	1274.7	1539.7 / 1533.6	1950.0	2612.4
Gross Fixed Capital Formation												
1 Agriculture and forestry	36.8	78.3 / 78.3	119.8	120.7	93.7 / 93.2	94.3	192.3	251.1	301.0	331.8 / 331.8	397.0	529.5

Poland

6a Capital Formation by Kind of Activity of the Material and Non-Material Spheres in Current Market Prices
(Continued)

Thousand Million Polish zlotych

	1970	1975	1978	1979	1980	1981	1982	1983	1984	1985	1986	1987
2 Industrial activity	87.7	227.4 / 227.4	269.2	228.8	203.3 / 202.1	151.2	293.0	353.4	469.1	615.2 / 612.5	804.3	1133.0
3 Construction	10.0	27.9 / 27.9	36.6	31.0	26.7 / 26.6	15.2	18.2	24.6	36.3	47.1 / 47.1	63.2	89.4
4 Wholesale and retail trade and restaurants and other eating and drinking places	5.5	12.1 / 12.1	14.0	12.6	11.4 / 11.3	10.7	24.3	33.7	41.3	49.1 / 51.8	81.7	111.4
5 Transport and communcication	32.4	68.7 / 68.7	65.9	62.1	60.5 / 54.6	34.8	53.0	66.8	105.3	145.5 / 145.5	189.8	264.3
6 Other activities of the material sphere	7.2	15.3 / 15.3	30.2	28.9	21.5 / 27.0	25.3	68.9	88.5	116.8	149.3 / 149.3	199.0	259.2
Total Material Sphere	179.6	429.7 / 429.7	535.7	484.1	417.1 / 414.8	331.5	649.7	818.1	1069.8	1338.0 / 1338.0	1735.0	2386.8
7 Housing except owner-occupied, communal and miscellaneous personal services	25.0	54.1 / 54.1	105.3	107.5	104.0 / 102.6	82.0	200.0	250.6	312.4	375.8 / 375.8	467.7	586.4
8 Education, culture and art	9.2	17.1 / 17.1	20.0	18.7	17.9 / 17.8	17.1	42.6	54.0	69.6	94.3 / 94.3	122.9	165.8
9 Health and social welfare services and sports	4.9	16.1 / 16.1	19.4	22.1	20.7 / 20.6	19.3	44.0	56.9	75.6	100.6 / 100.7	132.8	177.0
Total Non-Material Sphere Serving Individuals	39.1	87.3 / 87.3	144.7	148.3	142.6 / 141.0	118.4	286.6	361.5	457.6	570.7 / 570.8	723.4	929.2
10 Government	...	...	...	...	...	...	...	...	...	...	...	...
11 Finance, credit and insurance	...	...	...	...	...	...	...	...	...	...	...	...
12 Research, scientific and technological institutes	...	...	...	...	...	...	...	...	...	...	...	...
13 Other activities of the non-material sphere	...	...	...	...	...	...	...	...	...	...	...	...
Total Non-Material Sphere Serving the Community as a Whole	12.9	20.3 / 20.3	23.6	22.8	28.2 / 30.6	29.2	73.2	79.7	97.1	111.8 / 111.8	148.0	199.9
14 Owner-occupied dwellings	12.3	19.3 / 19.3	39.4	39.8	34.8 / 34.8	34.8	107.9	135.2	156.4	190.2 / 190.2	229.1	305.1
Total Gross Fixed Capital Formation	243.9	556.6 / 556.6	743.4	695.0	622.7 / 621.2	513.9	1117.4	1394.5	1780.9	2210.7 / 2210.8	2835.5	3821.0

a) Computing of amortization according to spheres and divisions in 1972 and 1973 is not possible, therefore the sum of spheres is not equal to the total net investment outlays for fixed capital formation.

Poland

6b Capital Formation by Kind of Activity of the Material and Non-Material Spheres in Constant Market Prices

Thousand Million Polish zlotych

	1970	1975	1978	1979	1980	1981	1982	1983	1984	1985	1986	1987
		1971	1977		At constant prices of:		1982			1984		

Net Fixed Capital Formation

1 Agriculture and forestry	...	... 69.2	82.6	77.0	48.1 216.5	197.8	139.4	149.8	151.7	127.2 61.9	52.6	62.3
2 Industrial activity	...	... 188.7	146.1	97.4	56.7 338.8	203.6	144.5	160.0	198.8	229.3 84.0	104.1	119.1
3 Construction	...	... 18.3	15.2	7.7	1.7 40.3	13.6	-0.9	3.6	10.0	12.2 -7.5	-3.7	-3.3
4 Wholesale and retail trade, restaurants and other eating and drinking places	...	... 9.8	6.2	4.3	2.9 20.4	18.9	17.2	21.5	24.3	23.8 22.6	28.4	30.0
5 Transport and communication	...	... 39.1	27.0	20.4	18.8 84.5	38.5	12.5	15.6	39.9	52.6 11.8	17.4	21.7
6 Other activities of the material sphere	...	... 14.8	18.7	16.1	13.4 63.8	57.1	57.5	64.2	75.1	82.3 84.5	91.8	91.3
Total Material Sphere	...	... 339.9	295.8	222.9	141.6 764.3	529.5	370.2	414.7	499.8	527.4 257.3	290.6	321.1
7 Housing except owner-occupied, communal and miscellaneous personal services	...	... 57.9	78.9	81.4	75.5 289.4	229.0	190.3	209.9	221.6	226.4 270.7	269.6	264.1
8 Education, culture and art	...	... 17.2	15.8	14.7	13.8 41.9	39.7	37.1	42.4	47.5	55.4 69.4	73.7	78.3
9 Health and social welfare services and sports	...	... 18.0	17.1	19.5	18.3 52.4	46.4	43.2	48.6	55.4	62.5 81.5	88.2	91.5
Total Non-Material Sphere Serving Individuals	...	... 93.1	111.8	115.6	107.6 383.7	315.1	270.6	300.9	324.5	344.3 421.6	431.5	433.9
10 Government	...	... ...	...	...	... ...	...	...	...	...	... ...	...	...
11 Finance, credit and insurance	...	... ...	...	...	... ...	...	...	...	...	... ...	...	...
12 Research, scientific and technological institutes	...	... ...	...	...	... ...	...	...	...	...	... ...	...	...
13 Other activities of the non-material sphere	...	... ...	...	...	... ...	...	...	...	...	... ...	...	...
Total Non-Material Sphere Serving the Community as a Whole	...	... 23.2	29.7	28.8	26.4 83.5	78.4	72.4	69.1	72.6	95.0 93.4	100.9	106.0
14 Owner-occupied dwellings	...	... 14.1	22.3	21.4	14.4 94.6	82.4	91.9	96.7	92.7	71.0 66.0	65.0	71.7
Total Net Fixed Capital Formation	...	... 470.3	459.6	388.7	290.0 1326.1	1005.4	805.1	881.4	989.6	1037.7 838.3	888.0	932.7

Gross Fixed Capital Formation

1 Agriculture and forestry	40.0	77.0 92.9	113.6	111.9	87.5 263.5	247.3	197.1	213.7	218.2	195.8 283.7	281.9	298.7

Poland

6b Capital Formation by Kind of Activity of the Material and Non-Material Spheres in Constant Market Prices
(Continued)

Thousand Million Polish zlotych

	1970	1975	1978	1979	1980	1981	1982	1983	1984	1985	1986	1987
		1971	**1977**		**At constant prices of:**		**1982**			**1984**		
2 Industrial activity	97.1	246.3 258.2	250.0	210.6	180.8 465.0	338.3	293.1	314.2	357.4	393.0 507.1	541.1	570.9
3 Construction	10.6	30.8 31.5	34.0	28.4	23.8 61.2	35.1	18.2	21.8	28.5	31.1 39.5	43.8	45.9
4 Wholesale and retail trade and restaurants and other eating and drinking places	6.2	12.9 14.6	13.1	11.6	10.2 26.8	25.8	24.3	29.8	32.8	32.5 49.3	56.4	60.0
5 Transport and communciation	34.8	73.4 65.2	59.1	55.3	55.6 125.4	79.5	53.0	59.7	84.7	97.9 122.6	132.1	140.4
6 Other activities of the material sphere	8.3	19.9 18.9	24.7	23.3	20.8 73.3	67.6	68.9	78.1	90.0	98.0 127.5	136.9	138.0
Total Material Sphere	197.0	460.3 481.3	494.5	441.1	378.7 1015.2	793.6	654.6	717.3	811.6	848.3 1129.7	1192.2	1253.9
7 Housing except owner-occupied, communal and miscellaneous personal services	28.9	53.1 65.2	88.5	91.6	86.6 297.8	237.9	200.0	220.7	233.2	238.7 321.4	322.2	318.9
8 Education, culture and art	10.4	17.0 19.2	18.7	17.7	16.8 47.0	45.0	42.6	47.5	52.7	60.8 80.4	85.9	90.2
9 Health and social welfare services and sports	5.6	13.6 18.4	17.9	20.4	19.3 53.3	47.3	44.0	50.0	56.9	64.0 85.3	92.4	95.8
Total Non-Material Sphere Serving Individuals	44.9	83.7 102.8	125.1	129.7	122.7 398.1	330.2	286.6	318.2	342.8	363.5 487.1	500.5	504.9
10 Government	...	... ...	...	...	... ...	...	...	...	...	... ...	...	...
11 Finance, credit and insurance	...	... ...	...	...	... ...	...	...	...	...	... ...	...	...
12 Research, scientific and technological institutes	...	... ...	...	...	... ...	...	...	...	...	... ...	...	...
13 Other activities of the non-material sphere	...	... ...	...	...	... ...	...	...	...	...	... ...	...	...
Total Non-Material Sphere Serving the Community as a Whole	14.8	24.9 23.6	30.1	29.4	26.9 84.1	79.0	73.2	70.0	73.6	72.1 95.2	102.9	108.3
14 Owner-occupied dwellings	13.2	17.2 25.3	35.3	35.0	28.7 108.8	97.2	107.9	115.4	112.8	115.4 160.2	161.0	169.4
Total Gross Fixed Capital Formation	269.9	586.1 633.0	685.0	635.2	557.0 1606.2	1300.0	1122.3	1220.9	1340.8	1399.3 1872.2	1956.6	2036.5

Poland

7a Final Consumption at Current Market Prices

Thousand Million Polish zlotych

	1970	1975	1978	1979	1980	1981	1982	1983	1984	1985	1986	1987
1 Personal consumption	465.0	799.7 805.2	1130.7	1245.5	1404.0 1409.3	1721.2	2929.3	3749.6	4455.8	5189.9 5205.9	6403.2	8254.6

a) Material Consumption in the Units of the Non-Material Sphere Serving Individuals

	1970	1975	1978	1979	1980	1981	1982	1983	1984	1985	1986	1987
2 Total non-material sphere serving individuals	...	...	...	...	...	...	...	...	...	623.4	792.8	1033.7

b) Material Consumption in the Units of the Non-Material Sphere Serving the Community as a Whole

	1970	1975	1978	1979	1980	1981	1982	1983	1984	1985	1986	1987
3 Total non-material sphere serving the community as a whole	83.0	146.6 152.3	228.7	247.4	264.5 255.1	276.4	525.7	687.9	885.1	1120.2 460.2	528.5	667.4
Final consumption	548.0	946.3 957.5	1359.4	1492.9	1668.5 1664.4	1997.6	3455.0	4437.5	5340.9	6310.1 6289.5	7724.5	9955.7

7b Final Consumption at Constant Market Prices

Thousand Million Polish zlotych

	1970	1975	1978	1979	1980	1981	1982	1983	1984	1985	1986	1987
At constant prices of:		**1971**		**1977**			**1982**				**1984**	
1 Personal consumption	470.4	706.3 875.5	1023.7	1056.9	1081.1 3651.2	3502.3	2989.4	3176.0	3295.1	3367.6 4624.1	4855.2	5000.0

a) Material Consumption in the Units of the Non-Material Sphere Serving Individuals

	1970	1975	1978	1979	1980	1981	1982	1983	1984	1985	1986	1987
2 Total non-material sphere serving individuals	...	...	...	...	...	...	...	...	...	558.0	592.1	612.2

b) Material Consumption in the Units of the Non-Material Sphere Serving the Community as a Whole

	1970	1975	1978	1979	1980	1981	1982	1983	1984	1985	1986	1987
3 Total non-material sphere serving the community as a whole	81.8	130.4 168.1	209.8	214.9	217.4 525.0	482.5	538.1	554.8	600.9	640.4 392.6	397.5	399.2
Final consumption	552.2	836.7 1043.6	1233.5	1271.8	1298.5 4176.2	3984.8	3527.5	3730.8	3896.0	4008.0 5574.7	5844.8	6011.4

Poland

8 Personal Consumption According to Source of Supply of Goods and Material Services in Current Market Prices

Thousand Million Polish zlotych

	1970	1975	1978	1979	1980	1981	1982	1983	1984	1985	1986	1987
1 Purchases of goods in state and co-operative retail trade	342.2	640.7 / 643.6	896.3	992.6	1105.0 / 1101.4	1272.6	2215.6	2902.5	3441.3	4001.5 / 4008.6	4960.7	6423.3
2 Purchases of goods in the free market and from private retail trade	30.1	31.5 / 31.4	47.0	50.6	68.9 / 68.8	132.7	211.1	232.3	279.6	311.9 / 330.9	385.7	489.6
3 Goods produced on own account and received in kind	45.8	52.7 / 50.2	71.4	74.7	85.3 / 85.3	135.9	218.5	236.0	257.0	286.1 / 286.1	333.7	387.0
4 Payments for transport and communication services	16.8	29.5 / 31.6	41.9	46.1	52.6 / 54.9	63.2	83.0	138.9	167.1	208.7 / 208.7	255.6	346.4
5 Purchases of electricity, gas and water	8.0	12.7 / 9.1	11.4	12.6	13.8 / 13.8	15.2	30.8	33.4	38.8	46.1 / 46.1	58.2	78.1
6 Purchases directly from handicrafts, repair shops and the like	14.6	23.3 / 28.0	49.8	55.3	64.2 / 70.9	86.8	154.2	187.8	234.1	278.2 / 268.0	330.1	426.7
7 Consumption of fixed assets in respect of all dwellings	7.5	9.3 / 11.3	12.9	13.6	14.2 / 14.2	14.8	16.1	18.7	37.9	57.4 / 57.5	79.2	103.5
8 Other	...	... / ...	...	...	... / ...	...	...	...	...	... / ...	...	...
Personal consumption	465.0	799.7 / 805.2	1130.7	1245.5	1404.0 / 1409.3	1721.2	2929.3	3749.6	4455.8	5189.9 / 5205.9	6403.2	8254.6

9a Total Consumption of the Population in Current Market Prices

Thousand Million Polish zlotych

	1970	1975	1978	1979	1980	1981	1982	1983	1984	1985	1986	1987
					By Object							
1 Housing except owner-occupied, communal and miscellaneous personal services	6.9	8.2 / 12.6	16.5	18.0	19.5 / 20.1	21.8	30.4	38.5	57.0	76.8 / 76.8	101.7	131.4
2 Education, culture and art	7.6	11.0 / 9.7	13.3	14.3	15.2 / 14.5	15.9	23.3	30.5	37.3	44.1 / 44.2	57.7	73.4
3 Health and social welfare services and sport	7.3	10.3 / 10.2	15.3	16.6	18.0 / 20.0	21.3	30.8	47.9	66.1	84.0 / 84.0	99.7	133.2
Statistical discrepancy [a]	5.9	9.5 / 8.8	10.7	12.1	11.9 / 11.0	14.0	15.9	24.3	32.9	44.1 / 44.2	59.1	80.7
Total consumption of non-material services	27.7	39.0 / 41.3	55.8	61.0	64.6 / 65.6	73.0	100.4	141.2	193.3	249.0 / 249.2	318.2	418.7
4 Personal consumption of goods and material services excluding depreciation of dwellings	455.9	790.4 / 793.9	1117.8	1231.9	1389.8 / 1395.1	1706.4	2913.2	3730.9	4417.9	5132.5 / 5148.4	6324.0	8151.1
Statistical discrepancy [b]	67.7	116.9 / 115.5	166.4	188.1	211.3 / 207.7	250.2	452.8	612.2	786.9	972.6 / 972.6	1178.2	1496.4
Total consumption of the population	551.3	946.3 / 950.7	1340.0	1481.0	1665.7 / 1668.4	2029.6	3466.4	4484.3	5398.1	6354.1 / 6370.2	7820.4	10066.2

Poland

9a Total Consumption of the Population in Current Market Prices
(Continued)

Thousand Million Polish zlotych

	1970	1975	1978	1979	1980	1981	1982	1983	1984	1985	1986	1987
By Commodity and Service												
1 Food c	204.9	290.7 / 288.4	383.6	419.3	479.9 / 478.6	629.0	1274.1	1427.2	1651.7	1920.1 / 1928.4	2338.2	2846.0
2 Beverages, coffee and tea	55.5	121.4 / 121.3	188.9	213.5	233.6 / 233.4	235.1	462.5	644.5	777.0	882.9 / 883.4	1064.6	1369.9
3 Tobacco	13.2	21.6 / 21.6	34.2	38.6	41.4 / 41.3	60.9	77.2	98.4	107.2	113.7 / 113.7	148.4	186.4
4 Clothing and footwear	72.1	126.3 / 129.2	154.7	166.2	184.1 / 187.0	222.0	260.1	374.5	470.8	556.3 / 557.0	745.6	1021.3
5 Gross rent	12.9	15.6 / 20.5	38.7	43.0	45.3 / 44.1	49.1	99.2	126.1	164.7	204.3 / 204.3	260.2	346.0
6 Fuel, electricity, water and gas	13.9	19.1 / 14.7	15.6	17.2	19.2 / 22.2	21.8	76.9	74.4	79.2	88.0 / 88.0	123.2	181.5
7 Furniture and household equipment	37.6	91.1 / 93.7	141.5	145.3	158.7 / 160.0	190.0	285.0	398.4	517.4	629.1 / 633.0	757.3	927.8
8 Health	41.6	73.8 / 73.8	101.7	114.6	134.6 / 134.3	158.9	256.5	326.1	389.4	483.4 / 483.3	602.4	769.7
9 Transport and communication	27.8	61.2 / 62.9	106.0	120.6	139.7 / 139.7	175.7	252.9	387.4	429.3	486.1 / 487.4	629.1	823.5
10 Education, recreation, sport	63.5	112.3 / 111.3	151.2	172.7	194.0 / 196.0	229.5	369.7	541.3	709.0	867.6 / 868.9	1051.0	1398.6
11 Other	8.3	13.2 / 13.3	23.9	30.0	35.2 / 31.8	57.6	52.3	86.0	102.4	122.6 / 122.8	100.4	195.5
Total consumption of the population	551.3	946.3 / 950.7	1340.0	1481.0	1665.7 / 1668.4	2029.6	3466.4	4484.3	5398.1	6354.1 / 6370.2	7820.4	10066.2
By Mode of Acquisition												
1 Purchased	437.9	776.7 / 785.0	1102.2	1218.2	1369.1 / 1375.4	1643.4	2795.1	3636.1	4354.2	5095.4 / 5111.5	6308.5	8182.8
2 Free of charge	67.6	116.9 / 115.5	166.4	188.1	211.3 / 207.7	250.2	452.8	612.2	786.9	972.6 / 972.6	1178.2	1496.4
3 From own production	45.8	52.7 / 50.2	71.4	74.7	85.3 / 85.3	136.0	218.5	236.0	257.0	286.1 / 286.1	333.7	387.0
Total consumption of the population	551.3	946.3 / 950.7	1340.0	1481.0	1665.7 / 1668.4	2029.6	3466.4	4484.3	5398.1	6354.1 / 6370.2	7820.4	10066.2

a) Item 'Statistical discrepancy' refers to other non-material services.
b) Except for an amount of 8.1 for 1970 which refers to statistical discrepancy, item 'Statistical discrepancy' refers to consumption from social funds, (benefits in kind).
c) For series 1, including consumption of food in schools, health institutions, sports institutions etc.

Portugal

General note. The preparation of national accounts statistics in Portugal is undertaken by the Instituto Nacional de Estatistica, Lisbon. The official estimates are published annually in the 'Annuario Estatistico'. A detailed description of the sources and methods used for the national accounts estimation is found in 'As Contas Nacionais Portuguesas 1958-1971', published by the Institute in 1972. The estimates are generally in accordance with the classification and definitions recommended in the United Nations System of National Accounts (SNA). Input-output table for 1959 has been published in 'Algunas Aplicacoes de Analise Input-Output a Matriz Portuguesa de 1959'. The following tables have been prepared from successive replies to the United Nations national accounts questionnaire. When the scope and coverage of the estimates differ for conceptual or statistical reasons from the definitions and classifications recommended in SNA, a footnote is indicated to the relevant tables.

Sources and methods:

(a) Gross domestic product. Gross domestic product is estimated mainly through the production approach.

(b) Expenditure on the gross domestic product. All items of GDP by expenditure type are estimated through the expenditure approach. The commodity-flow approach is also used for part of private final consumption expenditure. The estimates of government consumption expenditure are obtained from the government accounts. For private consumption expenditure, only estimates for food, beverages, tobacco, gross rent, fuel and power are made. For other components an estimate is derived as a residual between GDP and other final uses. The estimates of food, beverages and tobacco are based on retail prices and quantities consumed. Quantities consumed of other consumer products are available either through direct information or from production and foreign trade statistics, taking into account changes in producers' and wholesalers' stocks. Expenditures on house rent are estimated on the basis of information published in Estatisticas das Contribucoes e Impostos, adding 12 per cent for repairs. The calculation of increase in stocks is based on information on stock values supplied by corporations. Fixed capital formation in the private sector is estimated on the basis of annual surveys of corporation, the results of which are used to calculate increasing coefficients to be applied to total fixed capital formation. The annual construction surveys are used for the estimations of expenditure on new dwellings. For the public sector, investment is estimated from the revenue and expenditure data of the central government and other state organizations. Data for estimating exports and imports of goods and services are obtained from the balance of payments. For the constant price estimates, current values of government consumption expenditure, gross capital formation and exports and imports of goods and services are deflated by appropriate price indexes. For private consumption expenditure, the current quantities of the items estimated are revalued at base-year prices.

(c) Cost-structure of the gross domestic product. Wages and salaries for private sector are calculated per capita and applied to the number of employees which are obtained from the employment surveys submitted by the enterprises. Remuneration data for the government sector are obtained from government accounts. The data on employers' contributions to social security schemes are taken from 'seguro social'. Mathematical formulae are used to calculate consumption of fixed capital. Indirect taxes and subsidies are obtained directly from the government accounts.

(d) Gross domestic product by kind of economic activity. The table of GDP by kind of economic activity is prepared in factor values. Since 1977, the Portuguese National Institute of Statistics has followed the European System of Integrated Economic Accounts (ESA) in the national accounts estimates. The data reported according to ISIC Major divisions have been approximated from the Portuguese Branch and Product Nomenclature. The production approach is used to estimate value added of goods-production sectors whereas the income approach is used for the service sectors. The principal sources used to estimate agricultural production are Estadisticas Agricolas and the monthly Estado das Culturas e Previsao das Colheitas which contain data on quantities and prices. Data on intermediate consumption are supplied by the entities that supply the products. For products of forestry and logging not covered by statistics on agriculture, estimates are based on per capita data on consumption. For fishery, quantity and price data are obtained from fishery statistics while intermediate consumtpion is calculated as a percentage of the gross value of production. For the industrial activity sectors estimates are obtained directly from Estatisticas Industriais and the Anuario Estatistico. Adjustments are made for activities in the manufacturing sector not covered in these two sources by using the industrial census of 1957. Value added of electricity, gas and water is obtained directly from annual surveys of corporations, non-corporations and local government services. The construction estimates are based on annual surveys of enterprises. For dwellings taxation statistics are used and the figures relating to floor area of new buildings are multiplied by the average cost of construction by region. For the trade sector, the annual surveys of corporations are used for the corporations while data on the economically active population and the value added per capita for the retail trade is used for the individual enterprises. Taxation statistics and information provided by corporation are used for restaurants and hotels. The value added of the transport sector is obtained from the concerned companies and from annual surveys. The estimates for the financial institutions are based on direct information whereas data published in 'Estatisticas das Contribucoes e Impostoa' are used for ownership of dwellings. For government services, value added is obtained through government accounts. For private services, estimates are obtained through the use of data from 'Estatisticas de Educacao' for education, inquiries held in various cities for domestic servants, number of tickets sold for recreational services and taxation statistics for other personal services. For the constant price estimates, double deflation is used for the agricultural sector. Value added for construction, trade, restaurants, services incidental to transport, financial institutions, and community services is deflated by appropriate price indexes. For industrial activity sectors, hotels, transport and ownership of dwellings, value added is extrapolated by quantity indexes.

1.1 Expenditure on the Gross Domestic Product, in Current Prices

Million Portuguese escudos

		1970	1975	1978	1979	1980	1981	1982	1983	1984	1985	1986	1987
1	Government final consumption expenditure	25245	57983	... 109670	137576	182608	225892	276165	348355	423078	546899	678841	...
2	Private final consumption expenditure a	122370	303768	... 535360	670255	845522	1045450	1287062	1596207	1990334	2393245	2865943	...
	A Households	...	...	533128	667269	840705	1040150	1280930	1587597	1980398	2381390	2851580	
	B Private non-profit institutions serving households	...	...	2232	2986	4817	5300	6132	8610	9936	11855	14363	
3	Gross capital formation	41806	61471	... 239997	293016	412011	518815	631152	650661	625971	727184	987556	...
	A Increase in stocks	10551	-12521	... 20223	29060	53164	55803	56383	-20845	-37723	-40775	10562	
	B Gross fixed capital formation	31255	73992	... 219774	263956	358847	463012	574769	671506	663694	767959	976994	
	Residential buildings	4441	14316	65227	68053	88914	95811	114597	131425	...	...	...	
	Non-residential buildings	11698	32642	17462	20000	35856	36871	...	...	...	...	...	
	Other construction and land improvement etc.	723	956	... 48958	63229	81092	112950	...	...	...	...	...	
	Other	14393	26078	... 88127	112674	152985	217380	268878	309019	282943	334256	435311	...
4	Exports of goods and services	41742	74067	... 158369	268723	343950	389515	488482	721243	1048633	1315210	1466570	...
5	Less: Imports of goods and services	53825	121050	... 256136	376265	528040	678536	832453	1014753	1272288	1458590	1578510	...
	Equals: Gross Domestic Product	177338	376239	... 787260	993305	1256051	1501136	1850408	2301713	2815728	3523948	4420400	...

a) Item 'Private final consumption expenditure' has been obtained as a residual.

Portugal

1.2 Expenditure on the Gross Domestic Product, in Constant Prices

Million Portuguese escudos

	1970	1975	1978	1979	1980	1981	1982	1983	1984	1985	1986	1987
		1963	\multicolumn{10}{c	}{At constant prices of: **1977**}	
1 Government final consumption expenditure	18003	28057	91710	97490	105190	108140	111170	114170	117020	119010	120200	...
2 Private final consumption expenditure	95288	136096	441370	440490	457670	466370	476160	471400	457260	461830	494160	...
3 Gross capital formation	33684	22615	189630	207100	231290	243080	251330	197570	160780	161640	185150	...
A Increase in stocks	8475	-5791	12000	33380	42630	44800	47300	8840	6020	11520	20770	
B Gross fixed capital formation	25209	28406	177630	173720	188660	198280	204030	188730	154760	150120	164380	
Residential buildings	3640	5103	...									
Non-residential buildings	9658	11634	...									
Other construction and land improvement etc.	421	407	...									
Other	11490	11262	...									
4 Exports of goods and services	33881	32715	130400	165740	173200	168000	178080	207820	237330	263440	281880	
5 Less: Imports of goods and services	43198	48909	206080	224010	247530	256690	270550	247010	240340	249710	292660	
Equals: Gross Domestic Product	137658	170574	647030	686810	719820	728900	746190	743950	732050	756210	788730	...

1.3 Cost Components of the Gross Domestic Product

Million Portuguese escudos

	1970	1975	1978	1979	1980	1981	1982	1983	1984	1985	1986	1987
1 Indirect taxes, net	18306	34101	60538	74745	111544	133645	195795	266711	316660	407032	628839	...
A Indirect taxes	21036	41741	96622	119679	176915	215073	275397	358507	436761	534160	778189	
B Less: Subsidies [a]	2730	7640	36084	44934	65371	81428	79602	91796	120101	127128	149350	
2 Consumption of fixed capital	9373	18022	35740	43270	53960	62040	79600	98500	121100	151500	190100	
3 Compensation of employees paid by resident producers to:	79313	224241	411200	503638	642966	788599	963576	1174170	1385850	1669810	2009240	
A Resident households	77821	221597	409547	501676	639987	786066	960176	1169100	1379620	1661690	1997950	
B Rest of the world	1492	2644	1653	1962	2979	2533	3400	5064	6237	8121	11284	
4 Operating surplus	70346	99875	279782	371652	447581	516847	611436	762335	992116	1295610	1592230	
Equals: Gross Domestic Product	177338	376239	787260	993305	1256051	1501136	1850408	2301713	2815728	3523948	4420400	...

a) The 1973, 1975 and 1976 estimates for item 'Subsidies' in table 1.3 differ from those of table 1.4. In the first case they are entered on an accrual payment basis, in the second case they are entered on a cash payment basis.

1.4 General Government Current Receipts and Disbursements

Million Portuguese escudos

	1970	1975	1978	1979	1980	1981	1982	1983	1984	1985	1986	1987
	\multicolumn{12}{c	}{**Receipts**}
1 Operating surplus	274	144	982	1219	1092	1710	1834	1707	4550	3021	6473	...
2 Property and entrepreneurial income	1710	1601	8101	16254	10173	14793	24915	45965	49684	43162	70405	...
3 Taxes, fees and contributions	40092	88888	214420	270025	368528	466207	604207	793128	961603	1178020	1509440	...
A Indirect taxes	21036	41741	96622	119679	176915	215073	275397	358507	436761	534160	767876	...
B Direct taxes	10819	20065	47993	65880	81993	113224	146937	206687	246744	313274	321972	...
C Social security contributions	8237	27082	69805	84466	109620	137910	181873	227934	278098	330582	419593	...
D Compulsory fees, fines and penalties	...	...	...							...	...	

Portugal

1.4 General Government Current Receipts and Disbursements
(Continued)

Million Portuguese escudos

	1970	1975	1978	1979	1980	1981	1982	1983	1984	1985	1986	1987
4 Other current transfers	1010	2533	8402	10230	14300	16494	23475	28420	35299	42488	73897	...
Total Current Receipts of General Government	43086	93166	231905	297728	394093	499204	654431	869220	1051140	1266690	1660220	...

Disbursements

	1970	1975	1978	1979	1980	1981	1982	1983	1984	1985	1986	1987
1 Government final consumption expenditure	25245	57983	109670	137576	182608	225892	276165	348355	423078	546899	678841	...
A Compensation of employees	...	...	87656	108472	144647	176711	...	...	...	...	...	...
B Consumption of fixed capital	...	55	...	...	...	...	...	...	...	...	...	...
C Purchases of goods and services, net	...	...	22010	29064	37925	49167	...	...	...	...	...	...
D Less: Own account fixed capital formation	...	...	...	...	...	...	...	...	...	...	...	...
E Indirect taxes paid, net	...	...	4	40	36	14	...	...	...	...	...	...
2 Property income	975	2753	21111	28557	38755	80122	97910	141365	231042	329014	428104	...
A Interest	...	...	21107	28532	38749	80115	97896	141348	231004	328966	428049	...
B Net land rent and royalties	...	...	4	25	6	7	14	17	38	48	55	...
3 Subsidies a	2730	7473	36084	44934	65371	81428	79602	91796	120101	127128	131058	...
4 Other current transfers	5666	34249	83112	98976	137435	177082	215614	253846	310729	386491	549431	...
A Social security benefits	4537	23285	58127	69813	100557	133493	168677	209590	255324	315451	402912	...
B Social assistance grants	971	8963	17754	20206	25072	32026	30511	25575	30531	42266	78815	...
C Other	158	2001	7231	8957	11806	11563	16426	18681	24874	28774	67704	...
5 Net saving b	8470	-9292	-18072	-12315	-30076	-65320	-14860	33858	-33814	-122845	-127218	...
Total Current Disbursements and Net Saving of General Government	43086	93166	231905	297728	394093	499204	654431	869220	1051140	1266690	1660220	...

a) The 1973, 1975 and 1976 estimates for item 'Subsidies' in table 1.3 differ from those of table 1.4. In the first case they are entered on an accrual payment basis, in the second case they are entered on a cash payment basis. b) Item 'Net saving' includes consumption of fixed capital.

1.5 Current Income and Outlay of Corporate and Quasi-Corporate Enterprises, Summary

Million Portuguese escudos

	1970	1975	1978	1979	1980	1981	1982	1983	1984	1985	1986	1987
					Receipts							
1 Operating surplus	...	...	84250	124250	151159	165501	172833	245115	358837	500760	619477	...
2 Property and entrepreneurial income received	...	...	136349	190970	242937	347826	477179	674833	960450	1273700	1267560	...
3 Current transfers	...	...	17324	26953	38057	44353	56017	66251	70933	89193	96448	...
Total Current Receipts	...	...	237923	342173	432153	557680	706029	986199	1390220	1863660	1983490	...
					Disbursements							
1 Property and entrepreneurial income	...	...	173566	270630	334635	487953	716150	1016980	1445370	1805970	1625130	...
2 Direct taxes and other current payments to general government	...	...	11220	15109	22670	30852	38050	45373	58124	68447	72945	...
3 Other current transfers	...	...	17598	28159	40386	47217	63047	76343	81523	89231	105698	...
Statistical discrepancy	...	...	897	1049	1492	1929	2956	3422	3451	-930	3234	...
4 Net saving a	...	...	34642	27226	32970	-10271	-114174	-155914	-198252	-99066	176483	...
Total Current Disbursements and Net Saving	...	...	237923	342173	432153	557680	706029	986199	1390220	1863660	1983490	...

a) Item 'Net saving' includes consumption of fixed capital.

Portugal

1.6 Current Income and Outlay of Households and Non-Profit Institutions

Million Portuguese escudos

	1970	1975	1978	1979	1980	1981	1982	1983	1984	1985	1986	1987
Receipts												
1 Compensation of employees	79313	224241	410589	503251	642028	788893	963012	1173330	1386840	1674000	2008900	...
A From resident producers	...	...	409547	501676	639987	786066	960176	1169100	1379620	1661690	1997950	...
B From rest of the world	...	...	1042	1575	2041	2827	2836	4225	7222	12317	10947	...
2 Operating surplus of private unincorporated enterprises	...	...	230290	289453	349290	411676	516369	613903	749829	943325	1156380	...
3 Property and entrepreneurial income	57249	106839	55166	112960	141575	205120	280824	397800	614069	777375	713436	...
4 Current transfers	21378	61192	166929	230547	304977	377589	460442	533192	688002	810361	1001630	...
A Social security benefits	4537	23285	78680	92958	132634	173239	214072	253486	308884	380072	481533	...
B Social assistance grants	...	...	...	...	...	...	...	...	...	...	...	...
C Other	16841	37907	88249	137589	172343	204350	246370	279706	379118	430289	520101	...
Statistical discrepancy	...	...	897	1049	1492	1929	2956	3422	3451	-930	3234	...
Total Current Receipts	157940	392272	863871	1137260	1439360	1785210	2223600	2721650	3442190	4204130	4883580	...
Disbursements												
1 Private final consumption expenditure	122370	303768	535360	670255	845522	1045450	1287060	1587600	1990330	2393240	2865940	...
2 Property income	...	...	20016	42946	52935	62148	74281	88149	126757	160037	155550	...
3 Direct taxes and other current transfers n.e.c. to general government	14303	41298	109628	138829	173932	226852	299859	400307	479451	585871	685749	...
A Social security contributions	8237	27082	72855	88058	114609	144480	190972	238995	290831	341044	436722	...
B Direct taxes	6066	14216	36773	50771	59323	82372	108887	161312	188620	244827	249027	...
C Fees, fines and penalties	...	...	...	...	...	...	...	...	...	...	...	...
4 Other current transfers	1309	2958	20491	24370	32553	38880	52846	66120	84283	103447	122526	...
5 Net saving	19958	44248	178376	260860	334420	411882	509556	579472	761363	961535	1053810	...
Total Current Disbursements and Net Saving	157940	392272	863871	1137260	1439360	1785210	2223600	2721650	3442190	4204130	4883580	...

1.7 External Transactions on Current Account, Summary

Million Portuguese escudos

	1970	1975	1978	1979	1980	1981	1982	1983	1984	1985	1986	1987
Payments to the Rest of the World												
1 Imports of goods and services	53825	121050	256136	376265	528040	678536	832453	1014750	1272290	1458590	1578510	...
A Imports of merchandise c.i.f.	42764	99598	236361	345510	488209	630478	772651	939000	1171140	1356380	1469790	...
B Other	11061	21452	19775	30755	39831	48058	59802	75753	101153	102209	108722	...
2 Factor income to the rest of the world	1492	2644	19786	29313	41736	74865	119064	143080	209709	244978	204414	...

Portugal

1.7 External Transactions on Current Account, Summary
(Continued)

Million Portuguese escudos

	1970	1975	1978	1979	1980	1981	1982	1983	1984	1985	1986	1987
A Compensation of employees	1492	2644	1653	1962	2979	2533	3400	5064	6237	8121	11284	...
B Property and entrepreneurial income	...	...	18133	27351	38757	72332	115664	138016	203472	236857	193130	...
3 Current transfers to the rest of the world	547	1550	7511	7517	6864	5650	9263	13116	17367	21313	65689	...
A Indirect taxes to supranational organizations	...	...	...	...	...	...	...	...	...	...	10313	...
B Other current transfers	547	1550	7511	7517	6864	5650	9263	13116	17367	21313	55376	...
4 Surplus of the nation on current transactions	3373	-20866	-45051	-17245	-74697	-182524	-250630	-190695	-96674	12440	115519	...
Payments to the Rest of the World and Surplus of the Nation on Current Transactions	59237	104378	238382	395850	501943	576527	710150	980254	1402690	1737320	1964140	...

Receipts From The Rest of the World

	1970	1975	1978	1979	1980	1981	1982	1983	1984	1985	1986	1987
1 Exports of goods and services	41742	74067	158369	268723	343950	389515	488482	721243	1048630	1315210	1466570	...
A Exports of merchandise f.o.b.	26596	49456	114514	193115	247564	275979	357465	536423	790234	1005290	1124170	...
B Other	15146	24611	43855	75608	96386	113536	131017	184820	258399	309924	342405	...
2 Factor income from rest of the world	2381	2275	4098	6977	9158	12675	13077	19638	31724	48389	46699	...
A Compensation of employees	2381	2275	1042	1575	2041	2827	2836	4225	7222	12317	10947	...
B Property and entrepreneurial income	...	...	3056	5402	7117	9848	10241	15413	24502	36072	35752	...
3 Current transfers from rest of the world	15114	28036	75915	120150	148835	174337	208591	239373	322333	373724	450863	...
A Subsidies from supranational organisations	...	...	554	664	563	1095	...	...	...	...	18292	...
B Other current transfers	15114	28036	75361	119486	148272	173242	208591	239373	322333	373724	432571	...
Receipts from the Rest of the World on Current Transactions	59237	104378	238382	395850	501943	576527	710150	980254	1402690	1737320	1964140	...

1.8 Capital Transactions of The Nation, Summary

Million Portuguese escudos

	1970	1975	1978	1979	1980	1981	1982	1983	1984	1985	1986	1987
			Finance of Gross Capital Formation									
Gross saving	45179	40605	194946	275771	337314	336291	380522	459966	529297	739624	1103080	...
1 Consumption of fixed capital	9373	18022	35740	43270	53960	62040	79600	98500	121100	151500	190100	...
A General government	...	55	...	...	...	...	...	...	...	...	...	...
B Corporate and quasi-corporate enterprises	9373	17967	...	...	...	...	...	...	...	...	...	...
Public	775	1340	...	...	...	...	...	...	...	...	...	...
Private	8598	16627	...	...	...	...	...	...	...	...	...	...
C Other	...	...	...	...	...	...	...	...	...	...	...	...
2 Net saving	35806	22583	159206	232501	283354	274251	300922	361466	408197	588124	912975	...
A General government [a]	8470	-9292	-18072	-12315	-30076	-65320	-14860	33858	-33814	-122845	-127218	...
B Corporate and quasi-corporate enterprises [a]	7378	-13156	34642	27226	32970	-10271	-114174	-155914	-198252	-99066	176483	...
Public	1336	5902	...	...	...	...	...	...	...	...	...	...
Private	6042	-19058	...	...	...	...	...	...	...	...	...	...

Portugal

1.8 Capital Transactions of The Nation, Summary
(Continued)

Million Portuguese escudos

	1970	1975	1978	1979	1980	1981	1982	1983	1984	1985	1986	1987
C Other	19958	45031	178376	260860	334420	411882	509556	582022	761363	961535	1053810	...
Less: Surplus of the nation on current transactions	3373	-20866	-45051	-17245	-74697	-182524	-250630	-190695	-96674	12440	115519	...
Finance of Gross Capital Formation	41806	61471	239997	293016	412011	518815	631152	650661	625971	727184	987556	...

Gross Capital Formation

	1970	1975	1978	1979	1980	1981	1982	1983	1984	1985	1986	1987
Increase in stocks	10551	-12521	20223	29060	53164	55803	56383	-20845	-37723	-40775	10562	...
Gross fixed capital formation	31255	73992	219774	263956	358847	463012	574769	671506	663694	767959	976994	...
1 General government	3865	9068	25822	37482	51605	74617	79923	88553	90656	108926	143957	...
2 Corporate and quasi-corporate enterprises	...	...	116563	143836	190220	239765	303083	370554	342234	379385	493435	...
3 Other	...	...	77389	82638	117022	148630	191763	212399	230804	279648	339602	...
Gross Capital Formation	41806	61471	239997	293016	412011	518815	631152	650661	625971	727184	987556	...

a) Gross savings.

1.10 Gross Domestic Product by Kind of Activity, in Current Prices

Million Portuguese escudos

	1970	1975	1978	1979	1980	1981	1982	1983	1984	1985	1986	1987
1 Agriculture, hunting, forestry and fishing	28180	53022	94000	115043	129899	134560	162895	183321	234448	281203	328722	...
2 Mining and quarrying	916	2010	224320	303730	388982	470161	545369	675744	862101	1070630	1290120	...
3 Manufacturing	53098	114817										...
4 Electricity, gas and water	4311	6976	16513	19954	26502	16097	33031	57330	91767	123049	136407	...
5 Construction	8104	22619	60719	65393	88852	113022	149451	175197	166841	200368	245720	...
6 Wholesale and retail trade, restaurants and hotels	22820	47526	168877	218701	272419	326190	416709	520187	615172	788545	948541	...
7 Transport, storage and communication	10474	23628	43534	54987	69341	93804	121685	166490	214185	272262	297134	...
8 Finance, insurance, real estate and business services [a]	10274	21747	95387	102692	131409	166562	211840	256567	290106	357453	427079	...
9 Community, social and personal services [ab]	4464	8853	18978	23619	30209	41011	52862	67106	85294	112966	139234	...
Total, Industries	142641	301198	722328	904119	1137610	1361410	1693840	2101940	2559910	3206470	3812960	...
Producers of Government Services	14674	38343	87660	108512	144683	176725	214658	269137	327324	410280	499131	...
Other Producers	1717	2597	8362	10090	13282	16379	19120	23451	28344	34316	38799	...
Subtotal [c]	159032	342138	818350	1022720	1295580	1554510	1927620	2394530	2915580	3651070	4350890	...
Less: Imputed bank service charge	...	...	44896	41902	55553	77588	107420	135775	139753	179388	222787	...
Plus: Import duties	4153	8340	13806	12486	16026	24208	30207	42958	39899	52265	54802	...
Plus: Value added tax	...	...	...	...	...	...	...	...	...	...	237497	...
Plus: Other adjustments [d]	14153	25761	...	...	...	...	...	...	...	...	...	...
Equals: Gross Domestic Product	177338	376239	787260	993305	1256050	1501130	1850410	2301710	2815730	3523950	4420400	...
Memorandum Item: Mineral fuels and power	...	...	18484	23919	29654	20823	...	...	...	...	...	...

a) Business services and real estate except dwellings are included in item 'Community, social and personal services'.
b) Repair services are included in item 'Community, social and personal services'.
c) For the first series, gross domestic product in factor values.
d) Item 'Other adjustments' refers to net indirect taxes other than import duties.

Portugal

1.11 Gross Domestic Product by Kind of Activity, in Constant Prices

Million Portuguese escudos

	1970	1975	1978	1979	1980	1981	1982	1983	1984	1985	1986	1987
		1963		At constant prices of:				1977				
1 Agriculture, hunting, forestry and fishing	19117	18093	79012	95280	97420	87140	...	...	...	...	...	...
2 Mining and quarrying	606	951	183986	196310	204120	209050	...	...	...	...	...	...
3 Manufacturing	46285	59534										
4 Electricity, gas and water	4023	5706	12250	13160	11000	8990	...	...	...	...	...	...
5 Construction	6607	8074	54032	53870	57670	60380	...	...	...	...	...	...
6 Wholesale and retail trade, restaurants and hotels	17069	19487	132918	136580	143260	145860	...	...	...	...	...	...
7 Transport, storage and communication	8455	11410	35264	37800	41820	42550	...	...	...	...	...	...
8 Finance, insurance, real estate and business services	7896	10275	79688	71250	75550	79170	...	...	...	...	...	...
9 Community, social and personal services	3066	3123	14780	14960	15640	16220	...	...	...	...	...	...
Statistical discrepancy	...	...	...	-	-	2020	...	...	...	...	...	...
Total, Industries	113124	136653	591930	619210	646480	651380	...	...	...	...	...	...
Producers of Government Services	10742	21411	73703	78800	86090	90530	...	...	...	...	...	...
Other Producers	1219	903	7203	7350	7350	7580	...	...	...	...	...	...
Subtotal	125085	158967	672836	705360	739920	749490	...	...	...	...	...	...
Less: Imputed bank service charge	...	...	37413	27010	28400	31510	...	...	...	...	...	...
Plus: Import duties	12573	11607	11610	8530	8560	11480	...	...	...	...	...	...
Plus: Value added tax	...	...	...	...	...	...	...	...	...	...	...	...
Plus: Other adjustments	...	...	...	-70	-260	-560	...	...	...	...	...	...
Equals: Gross Domestic Product	137658	170574	647033	686810	719820	728900	...	...	...	...	...	...

1.12 Relations Among National Accounting Aggregates

Million Portuguese escudos

	1970	1975	1978	1979	1980	1981	1982	1983	1984	1985	1986	1987
Gross Domestic Product	177338	376239	787260	993305	1256050	1501130	1850410	2301710	2815730	3523950	4420400	...
Plus: Net factor income from the rest of the world	889	-369	-15688	-22336	-32578	-62190	-105987	-123442	-177985	-196589	-149736	...
Factor income from the rest of the world	2381	2275	4098	6977	9158	12675	13077	19638	31724	48389	64991	...
Less: Factor income to the rest of the world	1492	2644	19786	29313	41736	74865	119064	143080	209709	244978	214727	...
Equals: Gross National Product	178227	375870	771572	970969	1223470	1438940	1744420	2178270	2637740	3327360	4270660	...
Less: Consumption of fixed capital	9373	18022	35740	43270	53960	62040	79600	98500	121100	151500	190100	...

Portugal

1.12 Relations Among National Accounting Aggregates
(Continued)

Million Portuguese escudos

	1970	1975	1978	1979	1980	1981	1982	1983	1984	1985	1986	1987
Equals: National Income	168854	357848	735832	927699	1169510	1376900	1664820	2079770	2516640	3175860	4080560	...
Plus: Net current transfers from the rest of the world	14567	26486	68404	112633	141971	168687	199328	226257	304966	352411	377195	...
Current transfers from the rest of the world	15114	28036	75915	120150	148835	174337	208591	239373	322333	373724	432571	...
Less: Current transfers to the rest of the world	547	1550	7511	7517	6864	5650	9263	13116	17367	21313	55376	...
Equals: National Disposable Income	183421	384334	804236	1040330	1311480	1545590	1864150	2306030	2821610	3528270	4457760	...
Less: Final consumption	147615	361751	645030	807831	1028130	1271340	1563230	1944560	2413410	2940140	3544780	...
Equals: Net Saving	35806	22583	159206	232501	283354	274251	300922	361466	408197	588124	912975	...
Less: Surplus of the nation on current transactions	3373	-20866	-45051	-17245	-74697	-182524	-250630	-190695	-96674	12440	115519	...
Equals: Net Capital Formation	32433	43449	204257	249746	358051	456775	551552	552161	504871	575684	797456	...

2.1 Government Final Consumption Expenditure by Function, in Current Prices

Million Portuguese escudos

	1970	1975	1978	1979	1980	1981	1982	1983	1984	1985	1986	1987
1 General public services	6306	14592	15425	20492	24705	29539	34189	39613	53601	67621	82572	...
2 Defence	12739	16741	21712	28047	36057	43001	51829	66871	74214	88786	116392	...
3 Public order and safety	...	...	9706	12005	15834	19232	24878	31167	40375	53116	65206	...
4 Education	2918	13288	24352	29567	42997	55279	67743	87331	105877	135196	171751	...
5 Health	2752	11181	19939	24131	32467	42661	53876	71944	84868	123044	147382	...
6 Social security and welfare	530	2181	6158	7977	11099	12748	17260	17626	20779	26037	32180	...
7 Housing and community amenities	...	...	1988	2510	3304	4230	4208	6304	7306	9846	10801	...
8 Recreational, cultural and religious affairs	...	...	1234	1251	1980	2507	2914	4119	5246	7253	9273	...
9 Economic services	...	...	9156	11536	14120	16693	19268	23305	30243	35764	43284	...
A Fuel and energy	...	...	34	25	11	15	8	17	8	467	288	...
B Agriculture, forestry, fishing and hunting	...	...	3188	4256	5374	6251	6904	2979	5028	3440	12579	...
C Mining, manufacturing and construction, except fuel and energy [a]	...	...	530	849	1046	1362	1566	1939	2687	3136	3544	...
D Transportation and communication	...	...	1864	2049	1698	2217	3204	2925	3185	4509	5697	...
E Other economic affairs	...	...	3540	4357	5991	6848	7586	15445	19335	24212	21176	...
10 Other functions	...	...	...	60	45	2	-	75	569	236	-	...
Total Government Final Consumption Expenditure	25245	57983	109670	137576	182608	225892	276165	348355	423078	546899	678841	...

a) Item 'Mining, manufacturing and construction, except fuel and energy' includes fuel.

Portugal

2.2 Government Final Consumption Expenditure by Function, in Constant Prices

Million Portuguese escudos

		1970	1975	1978	1979	1980	1981	1982	1983	1984	1985	1986	1987
						At constant prices of: 1963							
1	General public services	4676	7743	...	...	...	...	...	...	...	...	...	...
2	Defence	8965	8172	...	...	...	...	...	...	...	...	...	...
3	Public order and safety	...	...	...	...	...	...	...	...	...	...	...	...
4	Education	2096	6541	...	...	...	...	...	...	...	...	...	...
5	Health	1875	4566	...	...	...	...	...	...	...	...	...	...
6	Social security and welfare	391	1035	...	...	...	...	...	...	...	...	...	...
7	Housing and community amenities	...	...	...	...	...	...	...	...	...	...	...	...
8	Recreational, cultural and religious affairs	...	...	...	...	...	...	...	...	...	...	...	...
9	Economic services	...	...	...	...	...	...	...	...	...	...	...	...
10	Other functions	...	...	...	...	...	...	...	...	...	...	...	...
	Total Government Final Consumption Expenditure	18003	28057	...	...	...	...	...	...	...	...	...	...

2.3 Total Government Outlays by Function and Type

Million Portuguese escudos

		Final Consumption Expenditures Total	Compensation of Employees	Other	Subsidies	Other Current Transfers & Property Income	Total Current Disbursements	Gross Capital Formation	Other Capital Outlays	Total Outlays
						1980				
1	General public services	24705	21209	3496	-	999	25704	5394	115	31213
2	Defence	36057	23023	13034	-	156	36213	115	4	36332
3	Public order and safety	15834	14798	1036	-	301	16135	602	18	16755
4	Education	42997	40433	2564	2	3936	46935	8490	455	55880
5	Health	32467	22266	10201	2	16758	49227	4138	73	53438
6	Social security and welfare	11099	9300	1799	-	110986	122085	1316	1042	124443
7	Housing and community amenities	3304	2874	430	1687	10	5001	7892	5006	17899
8	Recreation, culture and religion	1980	1404	576	-	1359	3339	1039	221	4599
9	Economic services	14120	9313	4807	63680	2681	80481	22607	9650	112738
	A Fuel and energy	11	-	11	367	-	378	3259	503	4140
	B Agriculture, forestry, fishing and hunting	5374	4042	1332	1202	28	6604	3540	347	10491
	C Mining (except fuels), manufacturing and construction [a]	1046	710	336	15975	9	17030	169	3547	20746
	D Transportation and communication	1698	630	1068	8112	2491	12301	14351	3523	30175
	E Other economic affairs	5991	3931	2060	38024	153	44168	1288	1730	47186
10	Other functions	45	27	18	-	39004	39049	12	4100	43161
	Total	182608	144647	37961	65371	176190	424169	51605	20684	496458
						1981				
1	General public services	29539	25403	4136	-	2093	31632	5790	-1150	36272
2	Defence	43001	26662	16339	-	5544	48545	1372	14	49931
3	Public order and safety	19232	18208	1024	-	1731	20963	1559	135	22657
4	Education	55291	51050	4229	11	3124	58414	10461	394	69269
5	Health	42661	28925	13736	36	18435	61132	6851	163	68146
6	Social security and welfare	12748	10136	2612	-	136713	149461	1082	1459	152002
7	Housing and community amenities	4230	3494	736	2087	85	6402	9190	848	16440
8	Recreation, culture and religion	2507	1860	647	-	1997	4504	1588	246	6338
9	Economic services	16693	10973	5720	79294	6388	102375	36724	13658	152757
	A Fuel and energy	15	-	15	816	-	831	4989	1326	7146
	B Agriculture, forestry, fishing and hunting	6251	4685	1566	1465	243	7959	3192	408	11559
	C Mining (except fuels), manufacturing and construction [a]	1362	946	416	22940	110	24412	561	9261	34234
	D Transportation and communication	2217	760	1457	7567	5415	15199	26357	1672	43228
	E Other economic affairs	6848	4582	2266	46506	620	53974	1625	991	56590
10	Other functions	2	-	2	-	81094	81096	-	6458	87554
	Total	225892	176711	49181	81428	257204	564524	74617	22225	661366

Portugal

2.3 Total Government Outlays by Function and Type
(Continued)

Million Portuguese escudos

		Final Consumption Expenditures Total	Compensation of Employees	Other	Subsidies	Other Current Transfers & Property Income	Total Current Disbursements	Gross Capital Formation	Other Capital Outlays	Total Outlays
					1982					
1	General public services	34189	...	...	2	3941	38132	7587	128	45847
2	Defence	51829	...	...	-	6998	58827	535	32	59394
3	Public order and safety	24878	...	...	-	2102	26980	2377	573	29930
4	Education	67743	...	...	-	3039	70782	13123	474	84379
5	Health	53876	...	...	-	12746	66622	6278	51	72951
6	Social security and welfare	17260	...	...	1529	177308	196097	630	1749	198476
7	Housing and community amenities	4208	...	...	1760	103	6071	8593	9186	23850
8	Recreation, culture and religion	2914	...	...	814	2240	5968	2207	748	8923
9	Economic services	19268	...	...	75497	5786	100551	38593	30088	169232
	A Fuel and energy	8	...	...	886	5	899	6236	1370	8505
	B Agriculture, forestry, fishing and hunting	6904	...	...	2039	443	9386	3498	661	13545
	C Mining (except fuels), manufacturing and construction [a]	1566	...	...	29753	106	31425	771	23201	55397
	D Transportation and communication	3204	...	...	8747	4642	16593	27031	1786	45410
	E Other economic affairs	7586	...	...	34072	590	42248	1057	3070	46375
10	Other functions	-	...	...	-	99261	99261	-	32147	131408
	Total	276165	...	...	79602	313524	669291	79923	75176	824390
					1983					
1	General public services	39613	...	...	-	2919	42532	8632	179	51343
2	Defence	66871	...	...	-	9983	76854	687	-	77541
3	Public order and safety	31167	...	...	-	2959	34126	2059	620	36805
4	Education	87331	...	...	7	4809	92147	15127	278	107552
5	Health	71944	...	...	-	1379	73323	6476	17	79816
6	Social security and welfare	17626	...	...	-	224973	242599	1230	2110	245939
7	Housing and community amenities	6304	...	...	383	123	6810	6964	6616	20390
8	Recreation, culture and religion	4119	...	...	-	2741	6860	2385	751	9996
9	Economic services	23305	...	...	91406	1348	116059	44993	166048	327100
	A Fuel and energy	17	...	...	559	-	576	5473	884	6933
	B Agriculture, forestry, fishing and hunting	2979	...	...	2228	180	5387	5353	1213	11953
	C Mining (except fuels), manufacturing and construction [a]	1939	...	...	29363	81	31383	675	19864	51922
	D Transportation and communication	2925	...	...	9114	20	12059	30389	4337	46785
	E Other economic affairs	15445	...	...	50142	1067	66654	3103	139750	209507
10	Other functions	75	...	...	-	143977	144052	-	31711	175763
	Total	348355	...	...	91796	395211	835362	88553	208330	1132250
					1984					
1	General public services	53601	...	...	-	3647	57248	7586	-807	64027
2	Defence	74214	...	...	-	12583	86797	599	64	87460
3	Public order and safety	40375	...	...	-	4506	44881	2045	785	47711
4	Education	105877	...	...	1	5414	111292	15359	1674	128325
5	Health	84868	...	...	-	5423	90291	6437	100	96828
6	Social security and welfare	20779	...	...	3800	272106	296685	1883	1603	300171
7	Housing and community amenities	7306	...	...	406	139	7851	7184	6072	21107
8	Recreation, culture and religion	5246	...	...	1322	2951	9519	2879	1250	13648
9	Economic services	30243	...	...	111592	2172	144007	46684	152238	342929
	A Fuel and energy	8	...	...	407	-	415	4759	1301	6475
	B Agriculture, forestry, fishing and hunting	5028	...	...	3214	381	8623	9532	885	19040
	C Mining (except fuels), manufacturing and construction [a]	2687	...	...	84487	81	87255	1316	2964	91535
	D Transportation and communication	3185	...	...	8987	24	12196	26421	6861	45478
	E Other economic affairs	19335	...	...	14497	1686	35518	4656	140227	180401
10	Other functions	569	...	...	2980	232830	236379	-	31778	268157
	Total	423078	...	...	120101	541771	1084950	90656	194757	1370360

Portugal

2.3 Total Government Outlays by Function and Type
(Continued)

Million Portuguese escudos

		Final Consumption Expenditures			Subsidies	Other Current Transfers & Property Income	Total Current Disbursements	Gross Capital Formation	Other Capital Outlays	Total Outlays
		Total	Compensation of Employees	Other						

1985

1	General public services	67621	...	...	3	4707	72331	10500	-947	81884
2	Defence	88786	...	...	-	13309	102095	757	163	103015
3	Public order and safety	53116	...	...	-	5877	58993	2417	804	62214
4	Education	135196	...	...	2	6728	141926	16258	1287	159471
5	Health	123044	...	...	9	7901	130954	7298	132	138384
6	Social security and welfare	26037	...	...	2998	337351	366386	1980	2014	370380
7	Housing and community amenities	9846	...	...	470	184	10500	8325	45118	63943
8	Recreation, culture and religion	7253	...	...	1642	4215	13110	4672	1964	19746
9	Economic services	35764	...	...	119177	2307	157248	56719	241985	455952
	A Fuel and energy	467	...	...	207	41	715	4746	1372	6833
	B Agriculture, forestry, fishing and hunting	3440	...	...	12930	497	16867	11917	914	29698
	C Mining (except fuels), manufacturing and construction [a]	3136	...	...	67815	189	71140	1041	26939	99120
	D Transportation and communication	4509	...	...	18497	40	23046	32905	10723	66674
	E Other economic affairs	24212	...	...	19728	1540	45480	6110	202037	253627
10	Other functions	236	...	...	2827	332926	335989	-	37653	373642
	Total	546899	...	...	127128	715505	1389530	108926	330173	1828630

1986

1	General public services	82572	...	...	84	37939	120595	11729	-154	132170
2	Defence	116392	...	...	-	16402	132794	3147	328	136269
3	Public order and safety	65206	...	...	-	7431	72637	3769	1720	78126
4	Education	171751	...	...	-	8033	179784	25439	1361	206584
5	Health	147382	...	...	591	11455	159428	9001	194	168623
6	Social security and welfare	32180	...	...	4929	430048	467157	2772	2299	472228
7	Housing and community amenities	10801	...	...	984	25015	36800	9886	26468	73154
8	Recreation, culture and religion	9273	...	...	3113	6044	18430	5055	2762	26247
9	Economic services	43284	...	...	119174	2540	164998	73159	94859	333016
	A Fuel and energy	288	...	...	948	59	1295	5159	1679	8133
	B Agriculture, forestry, fishing and hunting	12579	...	...	12169	1090	25838	11347	4746	41931
	C Mining (except fuels), manufacturing and construction [a]	3544	...	...	52606	133	56283	1240	19893	77416
	D Transportation and communication	5697	...	...	31823	44	37564	46780	2695	87039
	E Other economic affairs	21176	...	...	21628	1214	44018	8633	65846	118497
10	Other functions	-	...	...	2183	432628	434811	-	53765	488576
	Total	678841	...	...	131058	977535	1787430	143957	183602	2114990

a) Item 'Mining, manufacturing and construction, except fuel and energy' includes fuel.

2.5 Private Final Consumption Expenditure by Type and Purpose, in Current Prices

Million Portuguese escudos

		1970	1975	1978	1979	1980	1981	1982	1983	1984	1985	1986	1987

Final Consumption Expenditure of Resident Households

		1970	1975	1978	1979	1980	1981	1982	1983	1984	1985	1986	1987
1	Food, beverages and tobacco	66312	154974	216167	271870	320460	392837	489425	618890	786763	946473	1111560	...
	A Food	50974	116640	187536	233396	278473	342130	426554	543204	691743	833653	977043	...
	B Non-alcoholic beverages	1933	4587	1368	1666	2073	3052	3187	3429	4545	5767	7252	...
	C Alcoholic beverages	11275	28821	17409	23568	22839	26700	31531	35928	42536	49439	57700	...
	D Tobacco	2130	4926	9854	13240	17075	20955	28153	36329	47939	57614	69567	...
2	Clothing and footwear	...	...	48980	66390	91220	108766	130169	149840	195013	235383	307081	...
3	Gross rent, fuel and power	7789	13664	39338	43794	51722	59424	68880	86193	104213	124234	148261	...
	A Fuel and power	...	...	12577	15470	20073	25607	32027	46182	61671	77262	88446	...

Portugal

2.5 Private Final Consumption Expenditure by Type and Purpose, in Current Prices
(Continued)

Million Portuguese escudos

	1970	1975	1978	1979	1980	1981	1982	1983	1984	1985	1986	1987
B Other	...	...	26761	28324	31649	33817	36853	40011	42542	46972	59815	...
4 Furniture, furnishings and household equipment and operation	...	...	50125	62150	87077	103457	121524	146122	183416	217791	257713	...
A Household operation	...	...	16079	20407	28214	34103	40350	50638	66911	82436	91425	...
B Other	...	...	34046	41743	58863	69354	81174	95484	116505	135355	166288	...
5 Medical care and health expenses	...	...	23547	29206	37141	45972	56870	72564	92141	115242	134585	...
6 Transport and communication	...	...	71339	92131	122577	164613	199456	253416	299433	371885	459673	...
A Personal transport equipment	...	...	46911	61546	82705	110566	134561	168832	185403	225789	293470	...
B Other	...	...	24428	30585	39872	54047	64895	84584	114030	146096	166203	...
7 Recreational, entertainment, education and cultural services	...	...	25858	32849	43384	57666	73400	92213	119253	145459	171628	...
A Education	...	...	5082	6379	7943	10788	14762	18939	25999	33331	40735	...
B Other	...	...	20776	26470	35441	46878	58638	73274	93254	112128	130893	...
8 Miscellaneous goods and services	...	...	67787	90731	114825	139498	173968	214174	275287	334932	401878	...
A Personal care	...	...	6033	7279	9780	12481	14882	17168	21881	28167	32229	...
B Expenditures in restaurants, cafes and hotels	...	...	49030	66189	82052	98089	122601	153370	195414	239122	289039	...
C Other	...	...	12724	17263	22993	28928	36485	43636	57992	67643	80610	...
Total Final Consumption Expenditure in the Domestic Market by Households, of which	...	...	543141	689121	868406	1072230	1313690	1633410	2055520	2491400	2992380	...
A Durable goods	...	...	38152	47858	68817	93413	...	...	...	...	...	...
B Semi-durable goods	...	...	94858	126640	169565	205546	...	...	...	...	...	...
C Non-durable goods	...	...	267057	336104	406152	496010	...	...	...	...	...	...
D Services	...	...	143074	178519	223872	277264	...	...	...	...	...	...
Plus: Direct purchases abroad by resident households	...	...	9524	14694	17785	18814	23993	30890	39652	46662	45889	...
Less: Direct purchases in the domestic market by non-resident households	...	...	19537	36546	45486	50902	56756	76705	114773	156672	186690	...
Equals: Final Consumption Expenditure of Resident Households	122370	303768	533128	667269	840705	1040150	1280930	1587600	1980400	2381390	2851580	...

Final Consumption Expenditure of Private Non-profit Institutions Serving Households

1 Research and science	...	...	-	-	-	-	...	...	...	...	...	...
2 Education	...	...	11	15	18	26	...	...	...	...	...	...
3 Medical and other health services	...	...	27	28	42	42	...	...	...	...	...	...

Portugal

2.5 Private Final Consumption Expenditure by Type and Purpose, in Current Prices
(Continued)

Million Portuguese escudos

		1970	1975	1978	1979	1980	1981	1982	1983	1984	1985	1986	1987
4	Welfare services	...	...					...	...	...	...	...	...
5	Recreational and related cultural services	...	...					...	...	...	...	...	...
6	Religious organisations	...	...	2194	2943	4757	5232	...	...	...	...	...	...
7	Professional and labour organisations serving households	...	...					...	...	...	...	...	...
8	Miscellaneous	...	...					...	...	...	...	...	...
	Equals: Final Consumption Expenditure of Private Non-profit Organisations Serving Households	...	...	2232	2986	4817	5300	6132	8610	9936	11855	14363	...
	Private Final Consumption Expenditure	122370	303768	535360	670255	845522	1045450	1287060	1596210	1990330	2393240	2865940	...

2.6 Private Final Consumption Expenditure by Type and Purpose, in Constant Prices

Million Portuguese escudos

		1970	1975	1978	1979	1980	1981	1982	1983	1984	1985	1986	1987

At constant prices of: 1963

Final Consumption Expenditure of Resident Households

		1970	1975	1978	1979	1980	1981	1982	1983	1984	1985	1986	1987
1	Food, beverages and tobacco	49433	62073	...	...	...	...	...	...	...	...	...	...
	A Food	38684	45527	...	...	...	...	...	...	...	...	...	...
	B Non-alcoholic beverages	1409	2828	...	...	...	...	...	...	...	...	...	...
	C Alcoholic beverages	7425	10983	...	...	...	...	...	...	...	...	...	...
	D Tobacco	1915	2735	...	...	...	...	...	...	...	...	...	...
2	Clothing and footwear	...	...	...	...	...	...	...	...	...	...	...	...
3	Gross rent, fuel and power	7163	9500	...	...	...	...	...	...	...	...	...	...
4	Furniture, furnishings and household equipment and operation	...	...	...	...	...	...	...	...	...	...	...	...
5	Medical care and health expenses	...	...	...	...	...	...	...	...	...	...	...	...
6	Transport and communication	...	...	...	...	...	...	...	...	...	...	...	...
7	Recreational, entertainment, education and cultural services	...	...	...	...	...	...	...	...	...	...	...	...
8	Miscellaneous goods and services	...	...	...	...	...	...	...	...	...	...	...	...
	Total Final Consumption Expenditure in the Domestic Market by Households, of which												
	Plus: Direct purchases abroad by resident households	...	...	...	...	...	...	...	...	...	...	...	...
	Less: Direct purchases in the domestic market by non-resident households	...	...	...	...	...	...	...	...	...	...	...	...
	Equals: Final Consumption Expenditure of Resident Households	95288	136096	...	...	...	...	...	...	...	...	...	...

Final Consumption Expenditure of Private Non-profit Institutions Serving Households

		1970	1975	1978	1979	1980	1981	1982	1983	1984	1985	1986	1987
	Equals: Final Consumption Expenditure of Private Non-profit Organisations Serving Households	...	...	...	...	...	...	...	...	...	...	...	...
	Private Final Consumption Expenditure	95288	136096	...	...	...	...	...	...	...	...	...	...

2.11 Gross Fixed Capital Formation by Kind of Activity of Owner, ISIC Divisions, in Current Prices

Million Portuguese escudos

		1970	1975	1978	1979	1980	1981	1982	1983	1984	1985	1986	1987

All Producers

		1970	1975	1978	1979	1980	1981	1982	1983	1984	1985	1986	1987
1	Agriculture, hunting, forestry and fishing	1614	3227	9186	12875	17049	19704	...	...	...	...	...	...
	A Agriculture and hunting	1258	2568	7386	9768	13847	16801	...	...	...	...	...	...
	B Forestry and logging	...	...	555	824	944	1184	...	...	...	...	...	...
	C Fishing	356	659	1245	2283	2258	1719	...	...	...	...	...	...

Portugal

2.11 Gross Fixed Capital Formation by Kind of Activity of Owner, ISIC Divisions, in Current Prices
(Continued)

Million Portuguese escudos

	1970	1975	1978	1979	1980	1981	1982	1983	1984	1985	1986	1987
2 Mining and quarrying	232	502	...	...	...	...	...	...	...	...	...	...
3 Manufacturing	9737	23162	47937	61187	82754	110069	...	...	...	...	...	...
A Manufacturing of food, beverages and tobacco	...	...	5639	6687	8729	12019	...	...	...	...	...	...
B Textile, wearing apparel and leather industries	...	...	6158	9884	13316	21565	...	...	...	...	...	...
C Manufacture of wood, and wood products, including furniture	...	...	1855	2604	3878	4690	...	...	...	...	...	...
D Manufacture of paper and paper products, printing and publishing	...	...	2766	4007	4550	9654	...	...	...	...	...	...
E Manufacture of chemicals and chemical petroleum, coal, rubber and plastic products	...	...	18100	19582	26003	23330	...	...	...	...	...	...
F Manufacture of non-metallic mineral products except products of petroleum and coal	...	...	4677	5708	7221	10199	...	...	...	...	...	...
G Basic metal industries	...	...	1674	1813	2956	2993	...	...	...	...	...	...
H Manufacture of fabricated metal products, machinery and equipment	...	...	6188	9849	14638	23735	...	...	...	...	...	...
I Other manufacturing industries	...	...	880	1053	1463	1884	...	...	...	...	...	...
4 Electricity, gas and water	2581	7097	17107	21487	26982	23729	...	...	...	...	...	...
5 Construction	679	1064	9788	14215	23421	23415	...	...	...	...	...	...
6 Wholesale and retail trade, restaurants and hotels	2856	4248	12913	16377	25918	31091	...	...	...	...	...	...
A Wholesale and retail trade	...	...	11745	14492	22903	27914	...	...	...	...	...	...
B Restaurants and hotels	...	...	1168	1885	3015	3177	...	...	...	...	...	...
7 Transport, storage and communication	4476	9736	28299	26712	31427	46939	...	...	...	...	...	...
A Transport and storage	...	...	22968	16895	23178	37512	...	...	...	...	...	...
B Communication	...	...	5331	9817	8249	9427	...	...	...	...	...	...
8 Finance, insurance, real estate and business services	4886	15210	70283	76692	109024	137752	...	...	...	...	...	...
A Financial institutions	...	...	1399	5137	7715	10003	...	...	...	...	...	...
B Insurance	...	...	726	1110	2042	2813	...	...	...	...	...	...
C Real estate and business services	...	...	68158	70445	99267	124936	...	...	...	...	...	...
Real estate except dwellings	...	...	5944	4450	10299	11949	...	...	...	...	...	...
Dwellings	...	...	62214	65995	88968	112987	...	...	...	...	...	...
9 Community, social and personal services	329	678	1648	3040	3508	4200	...	...	...	...	...	...
A Sanitary and similar services	...	...	...	...	...	...	...	...	...	...	...	...
B Social and related community services	...	...	357	1044	1091	1802	...	...	...	...	...	...

Portugal

2.11 Gross Fixed Capital Formation by Kind of Activity of Owner, ISIC Divisions, in Current Prices
(Continued)

Million Portuguese escudos

	1970	1975	1978	1979	1980	1981	1982	1983	1984	1985	1986	1987
Educational services	...	...	97	166	162	403	...	...	...	...	...	...
Medical, dental, other health and veterinary services	...	...	260	878	929	1399	...	...	...	...	...	...
C Recreational and cultural services	...	...	1291	1996	2417	2398	...	...	...	...	...	...
D Personal and household services	...	...	...	...	...	...	...	...	...	...	...	...
Total Industries	27390	64924	197161	232585	320083	396899	...	...	...	...	...	...
Producers of Government Services	3865	9068	22613	31371	38764	66113	...	...	...	...	...	...
Private Non-Profit Institutions Serving Households	...	...	...	...	...	...	...	...	...	...	...	...
Total	31255	73992	219774	263956	358847	463012	...	...	...	...	...	...

2.12 Gross Fixed Capital Formation by Kind of Activity of Owner, ISIC Divisions, in Constant Prices

Million Portuguese escudos

	1970	1975	1978	1979	1980	1981	1982	1983	1984	1985	1986	1987
	\multicolumn{12}{c}{At constant prices of:1963}											
	\multicolumn{12}{c}{All Producers}											
1 Agriculture, hunting, forestry and fishing	1196	1400	...	...	...	...	...	...	...	...	...	...
A Agriculture and hunting	910	1117	...	...	...	...	...	...	...	...	...	...
B Forestry and logging	...	...	...	...	...	...	...	...	...	...	...	...
C Fishing	286	283	...	...	...	...	...	...	...	...	...	...
2 Mining and quarrying	187	186	...	...	...	...	...	...	...	...	...	...
3 Manufacturing	7825	9318	...	...	...	...	...	...	...	...	...	...
4 Electricity, gas and water	2101	2593	...	...	...	...	...	...	...	...	...	...
5 Construction	544	448	...	...	...	...	...	...	...	...	...	...
6 Wholesale and retail trade, restaurants and hotels	2306	1678	...	...	...	...	...	...	...	...	...	...
7 Transport, storage and communication	3618	3771	...	...	...	...	...	...	...	...	...	...
8 Finance, insurance, real estate and business services	4011	5438	...	...	...	...	...	...	...	...	...	...
9 Community, social and personal services	263	269	...	...	...	...	...	...	...	...	...	...
Total Industries	22051	25102	...	...	...	...	...	...	...	...	...	...
Producers of Government Services	3158	3304	...	...	...	...	...	...	...	...	...	...
Private Non-Profit Institutions Serving Households	...	...	...	...	...	...	...	...	...	...	...	...
Total	25209	28406	...	...	...	...	...	...	...	...	...	...

2.17 Exports and Imports of Goods and Services, Detail

Million Portuguese escudos

	1970	1975	1978	1979	1980	1981	1982	1983	1984	1985	1986	1987
	\multicolumn{12}{c}{Exports of Goods and Services}											
1 Exports of merchandise, f.o.b.	26596	49456	114514	193115	247564	275979	357465	536423	790234	1005290	1124170	...
2 Transport and communication	1917	4208	17856	28934	38810	47617	...	...	...	...	...	...
A In respect of merchandise imports	...	...	...	9234	13262	...	...	...	...	...	...	...
B Other	...	...	...	19700	25548	...	...	...	...	...	...	...

Portugal

2.17 Exports and Imports of Goods and Services, Detail
(Continued)

Million Portuguese escudos

	1970	1975	1978	1979	1980	1981	1982	1983	1984	1985	1986	1987
3 Insurance service charges	13229	20403	520	938	999	874	...	...	...	...	...	...
4 Other commodities			5942	9190	11091	14143	...	...	...	...	...	...
5 Adjustments of merchandise exports to change-of-ownership basis	...	...	...	...	...	...	...	...	...	...	...	...
6 Direct purchases in the domestic market by non-residential households	...	...	19537	36546	45486	50902	...	...	...	...	...	...
7 Direct purchases in the domestic market by extraterritorial bodies	...	...	...				...	...	...	...	...	...
Total Exports of Goods and Services	41742	74067	158369	268723	343950	389515	488482	721243	1048630	1315210	1466570	...

Imports of Goods and Services

	1970	1975	1978	1979	1980	1981	1982	1983	1984	1985	1986	1987
1 Imports of merchandise, c.i.f.	42764	99598	236361	345510	488209	630478	772651	939000	1171140	1356380	1469790	...
A Imports of merchandise, f.o.b.	39568	92125	214799	314476	432343	573372	...	...	...	...	...	...
B Transport of services on merchandise imports	3196	7473	19442	27982	50721	51491	...	...	...	...	...	...
By residents	...	...	6416	9234	13262	16994	...	...	...	...	...	...
By non-residents	3196	7473	13026	18748	37459	34497	...	...	...	...	...	...
C Insurance service charges on merchandise imports	...	...	2120	3052	5145	5615	...	...	...	...	...	...
By residents	...	...	635	916	1316	1685	...	...	...	...	...	...
By non-residents	...	...	1485	2136	3829	3930	...	...	...	...	...	...
2 Adjustments of merchandise imports to change-of-ownership basis	...	...	...	...	...	...	...	...	...	...	...	...
3 Other transport and communication			6146	10533	14554	18832	...	...	...	...	...	...
4 Other insurance service charges	11061	21452	176	127	257	560	...	...	...	...	...	...
5 Other commodities			3929	5401	7235	9852	...	...	...	...	...	...
6 Direct purchases abroad by government	...	...	...				...	...	...	...	...	...
7 Direct purchases abroad by resident households	...	...	9524	14694	17785	18814	...	...	...	...	...	...
Total Imports of Goods and Services	53825	121050	256136	376265	528040	678536	832453	1014750	1272290	1458590	1578510	...
Balance of Goods and Services	-12083	-46983	-97767	-107542	-184090	-289021	-343971	-293510	-223655	-143382	-111940	...
Total Imports and Balance of Goods and Services	41742	74067	158369	268723	343950	389515	488482	721243	1048630	1315210	1466570	...

3.11 General Government Production Account: Total and Subsectors

Million Portuguese escudos

	1980					1981				
	Total General Government	Central Government	State or Provincial Government	Local Government	Social Security Funds	Total General Government	Central Government	State or Provincial Government	Local Government	Social Security Funds

Gross Output

1 Sales	15843	13258	...	2253	332	19280	15950	...	2894	436
2 Services produced for own use	183809	160323	...	14471	9015	227812	198709	...	18648	10455
3 Own account fixed capital formation	...	...		...	...	...	...		...	...
Gross Output	199652	173581	...	16724	9347	247092	214659	...	21542	10891

Gross Input

Intermediate Consumption	48752	42486	...	4771	1495	62164	54142	...	5946	2076
Subtotal: Value Added	150900	131095	...	11953	7852	184928	160517	...	15596	8815

Portugal

3.11 General Government Production Account: Total and Subsectors
(Continued)

Million Portuguese escudos

	1980					1981				
	Total General Government	Central Government	State or Provincial Government	Local Government	Social Security Funds	Total General Government	Central Government	State or Provincial Government	Local Government	Social Security Funds
1 Indirect taxes, net	4142	4135	-	5	2	5151	5166	-	-18	3
A Indirect taxes	4188	4142	...	44	2	5197	5174	...	20	3
B Less: Subsidies	46	7	...	39	-	46	8	...	38	-
2 Consumption of fixed capital	...	...	...	...	...	...	...	...	...	...
3 Compensation of employees	145666	126186	...	11859	7621	178067	154196	...	15308	8563
4 Net Operating surplus [a]	1092	774	...	89	229	1710	1155	...	306	249
Gross Input	199652	173581	...	16724	9347	247092	214659	...	21542	10891

	1982					1983				
	Total General Government	Central Government	State or Provincial Government	Local Government	Social Security Funds	Total General Government	Central Government	State or Provincial Government	Local Government	Social Security Funds

Gross Output

1 Sales	23971	19921	...	3645	405	30358	25917	...	4031	410
2 Services produced for own use	279412	244215	...	22849	12348	352219	309934	...	28557	13728
3 Own account fixed capital formation	...	...	...	...	...	...	...	...	...	...
Gross Output	303383	264136	...	26494	12753	382577	335851	...	32588	14138

Gross Input

Intermediate Consumption	78707	69424	...	6738	2545	101608	90588	...	7679	3341
Subtotal: Value Added	224676	194712	...	19756	10208	280969	245263	...	24909	10797
1 Indirect taxes, net	6485	6589	...	-107	3	8027	8111	...	-89	5
A Indirect taxes	6637	6604	...	30	3	8168	8136	...	27	5
B Less: Subsidies	152	15	...	137	-	141	25	...	116	-
2 Consumption of fixed capital	...	...	...	...	...	...	...	...	...	...
3 Compensation of employees	216357	186898	...	19457	10002	271235	235815	...	24789	10631
4 Net Operating surplus [a]	1834	1225	...	406	203	1707	1337	...	209	161
Gross Input	303383	264136	...	26494	12753	382577	335851	...	32588	14138

	1984					1985				
	Total General Government	Central Government	State or Provincial Government	Local Government	Social Security Funds	Total General Government	Central Government	State or Provincial Government	Local Government	Social Security Funds

Gross Output

1 Sales	39090	33687	...	4974	429	51077	43953	...	6587	537
2 Services produced for own use	427190	375197	...	36498	15495	552595	483590	...	48985	20020
3 Own account fixed capital formation	...	...	...	...	...	...	...	...	...	...
Gross Output	466280	408884	...	41472	15924	603672	527543	...	55572	20557

Gross Input

Intermediate Consumption	122893	107484	...	11039	4370	175351	152804	...	17147	5400
Subtotal: Value Added	343387	301400	...	30433	11554	428321	374739	...	38425	15157
1 Indirect taxes, net	8353	8577	...	-227	3	11236	11537	...	-304	3
A Indirect taxes	8626	8602	...	21	3	11565	11537	...	25	3
B Less: Subsidies	273	25	...	248	-	329	-	...	329	-
2 Consumption of fixed capital	...	...	...	...	...	...	...	...	...	...
3 Compensation of employees	330484	288763	...	30174	11547	414064	361090	...	37818	15156
4 Net Operating surplus [a]	4550	4060	...	486	4	3021	2112	...	911	-2
Gross Input	466280	408884	...	41472	15924	603672	527543	...	55572	20557

	1986			
	Total General Government	Central Government	State or Provincial Government	Local Government	Social Security Funds

Gross Output

1 Sales	63173	52733	...	9707	733
2 Services produced for own use	684742	600557	...	59832	24353
3 Own account fixed capital formation	...	...	...	...	...
Gross Output	747915	653290	...	69539	25086

Gross Input

Intermediate Consumption	224235	195739	...	21138	7358
Subtotal: Value Added	523680	457551	...	48401	17728

Portugal

3.11 General Government Production Account: Total and Subsectors
(Continued)

Million Portuguese escudos

		1986			
	Total General Government	Central Government	State or Provincial Government	Local Government	Social Security Funds
1 Indirect taxes, net	13432	13803	...	-372	1
A Indirect taxes	13840	13803	...	36	1
B Less: Subsidies	408	-	...	408	-
2 Consumption of fixed capital	...	...	...	...	...
3 Compensation of employees	503775	439602	...	46569	17604
4 Net Operating surplus a	6473	4146	...	2204	123
Gross Input	747915	653290	...	69539	25086

a) Item 'Operating surplus' includes consumption of fixed capital.

3.12 General Government Income and Outlay Account: Total and Subsectors

Million Portuguese escudos

	1980					1981				
	Total General Government	Central Government	State or Provincial Government	Local Government	Social Security Funds	Total General Government	Central Government	State or Provincial Government	Local Government	Social Security Funds
					Receipts					
1 Operating surplus ab	1092	774	...	89	229	1710	1155	...	306	249
2 Property and entrepreneurial income	10173	9384	...	462	385	14793	13863	...	774	771
A Withdrawals from public quasi-corporations b	-	-	...	-	-	...	...	...	...	...
B Interest	3110	2508	...	275	385	8560	7876	...	528	771
C Dividends	6843	6831	...	12	-	5930	5930	...	-	-
D Net land rent and royalties	220	45	...	175	-	303	57	...	246	-
3 Taxes, fees and contributions	368528	249896	...	8526	110115	466207	318134	...	9621	138475
A Indirect taxes	176915	175225	...	1195	495	215073	212992	...	1516	565
B Direct taxes	81993	74671	...	7331	-	113224	105142	...	8105	-
Income	79587	73121	...	6475	-	...	...	...	...	...
Other	2406	1550	...	856	-	...	...	...	...	...
C Social security contributions	109620	-	...	-	109620	137910	-	...	-	137910
D Fees, fines and penalties	...	...	...	...	...	...	...	...	...	...
4 Other current transfers	14300	15131	...	14181	8208	16494	16595	...	16817	7713
A Casualty insurance claims	37	-	...	8	29	46	-	...	18	28
B Transfers from other government subsectors	...	2291	...	12942	7987	...	1118	...	16160	7353
C Transfers from the rest of the world	857	841	...	-	16	1095	1077	...	-	18
D Other transfers, except imputed	6252	5628	...	563	61	6623	6406	...	67	150
E Imputed unfunded employee pension and welfare contributions	7154	6371	...	668	115	8730	7994	...	572	164
Total Current Receipts	394093	275185	...	23258	118937	499204	349747	...	27518	147208
					Disbursements					
1 Government final consumption expenditure	182608	159453	...	14285	8870	225892	197233	...	18361	10298
2 Property income	38755	38515	...	298	-	80122	79847	...	586	304
A Interest	38749	38511	...	296	-	80115	79843	...	583	304
B Net land rent and royalties	6	4	...	2	-	7	4	...	3	-
3 Subsidies	65371	65068	...	303	-	81428	80942	...	486	-
4 Other current transfers	137435	51145	...	3617	105902	177082	61372	...	2692	137672
A Casualty insurance premiums, net	70	20	...	44	6	82	24	...	53	5
B Transfers to other government subsectors	...	20915	...	1986	328	...	23397	...	761	496
C Social security benefits	100557	-	...	...	100557	133493	-	...	...	133493
D Social assistance grants c	25072	20837	...	918	3317	32026	27206	...	1306	3514
E Unfunded employee pension and welfare benefits	7154	6371	...	668	115	8730	7994	...	572	164
F Transfers to private non-profit institutions serving households	282	282	...	-	-	584	584	...	-	-
G Other transfers n.e.c.	...	...	...	...	...	...	...	...	...	...
H Transfers to the rest of the world	4300	2720	...	1	1579	2167	2167	...	-	-
Net saving d	-30076	-38996	...	4755	4165	-65320	-69647	...	5393	-1066
Total Current Disbursements and Net Saving	394093	275185	...	23258	118937	499204	349747	...	27518	147208

Portugal

3.12 General Government Income and Outlay Account: Total and Subsectors

Million Portuguese escudos

	1982					1983				
	Total General Government	Central Government	State or Provincial Government	Local Government	Social Security Funds	Total General Government	Central Government	State or Provincial Government	Local Government	Social Security Funds
Receipts										
1 Operating surplus [ab]	1834	1225	...	406	203	1707	1337	...	209	161
2 Property and entrepreneurial income	24915	23238	...	1190	487	45965	43718	...	1742	505
A Withdrawals from public quasi-corporations [b]	-	-	...	-	-	-	-	...	-	-
B Interest	9514	8205	...	822	487	10680	9161	...	1014	505
C Dividends	15047	15015	...	32	-	34638	34523	...	115	-
D Net land rent and royalties	354	18	...	336	-	647	34	...	613	-
3 Taxes, fees and contributions	604207	410151	...	11486	182574	793128	551041	...	13358	228731
A Indirect taxes	275397	272799	...	1897	701	358507	355283	...	2427	797
B Direct taxes	146937	137352	...	9589	-	206687	195758	...	10931	-
Income	...	...	...	...	...	...	...	...	...	...
Other	...	...	...	...	...	...	...	...	...	...
C Social security contributions	181873	-	...	-	181873	227934	-	...	-	227934
D Fees, fines and penalties	...	...	...	...	...	...	...	...	...	...
4 Other current transfers	23475	22757	...	24827	9761	28420	28541	...	30157	19062
A Casualty insurance claims	26	1	...	23	2	21	-	...	21	-
B Transfers from other government subsectors	...	1744	...	22865	9261	...	2602	...	28107	18631
C Transfers from the rest of the world	757	668	...	-	89	80	20	...	-	60
D Other transfers, except imputed	9672	8266	...	1225	181	11672	10276	...	1216	180
E Imputed unfunded employee pension and welfare contributions	13020	12078	...	714	228	16647	15643	...	813	191
Total Current Receipts	654431	457371	...	37909	193025	869220	624637	...	45466	248459
Disbursements										
1 Government final consumption expenditure	276165	241524	...	22501	12140	348355	306746	...	28201	13408
2 Property income	97910	95716	...	1674	520	141365	137728	...	2946	691
A Interest	97896	95702	...	1674	520	141348	137713	...	2944	691
B Net land rent and royalties	14	14	...	-	-	17	15	...	2	-
3 Subsidies	79602	78716	...	886	-	91796	91641	...	155	-
4 Other current transfers	215614	71673	...	2953	174862	253846	82436	...	3153	217599
A Casualty insurance premiums, net	123	33	...	83	7	118	30	...	84	4
B Transfers to other government subsectors	...	32023	...	442	1409	...	46654	...	381	2307
C Social security benefits	168677	-	...	-	168677	209590	-	...	-	209590
D Social assistance grants [c]	30511	24256	...	1714	4541	25575	18193	...	1875	5507
E Unfunded employee pension and welfare benefits	13020	12078	...	714	228	16647	15643	...	813	191
F Transfers to private non-profit institutions serving households	752	752	...	-	-	865	865	...	-	-
G Other transfers n.e.c.	-	-	...	...	...	-	-	...	...	...
H Transfers to the rest of the world	2531	2531	...	-	-	1051	1051	...	-	-
Net saving [d]	-14860	-30258	...	9895	5503	33858	6086	...	11011	16761
Total Current Disbursements and Net Saving	654431	457371	...	37909	193025	869220	624637	...	45466	248459

	1984					1985				
	Total General Government	Central Government	State or Provincial Government	Local Government	Social Security Funds	Total General Government	Central Government	State or Provincial Government	Local Government	Social Security Funds
Receipts										
1 Operating surplus [ab]	4550	4060	...	486	4	3021	2112	...	911	-2
2 Property and entrepreneurial income	49684	46771	...	2330	583	43162	38764	...	2484	1914
A Withdrawals from public quasi-corporations [b]	-	-	...	-	-	-	-	...	-	-
B Interest	34975	32728	...	1666	581	32631	28834	...	1883	1914

Portugal

3.12 General Government Income and Outlay Account: Total and Subsectors
(Continued)

Million Portuguese escudos

	1984					1985				
	Total General Government	Central Government	State or Provincial Government	Local Government	Social Security Funds	Total General Government	Central Government	State or Provincial Government	Local Government	Social Security Funds
C Dividends	14041	13910	...	129	2	9783	9765	...	18	-
D Net land rent and royalties	668	133	...	535	-	748	165	...	583	-
3 Taxes, fees and contributions	961603	665454	...	17123	279030	1178020	824704	...	20272	333049
A Indirect taxes	436761	432392	...	3437	932	534160	527276	...	4417	2467
B Direct taxes	246744	233062	...	13686	-	313274	297428	...	15855	-
Income	...	...	...	...	...	...	...	...	...	...
Other	...	...	...	...	...	...	...	...	...	...
C Social security contributions	278098	-	...	-	278098	330582	-	...	-	330582
D Fees, fines and penalties	...	...	...	...	...	...	...	...	...	...
4 Other current transfers	35299	34759	...	36185	43990	42488	40520	...	45993	48225
A Casualty insurance claims	12	-	...	12	-	25	-	...	25	-
B Transfers from other government subsectors	...	2884	...	33302	43449	...	3050	...	41972	47228
C Transfers from the rest of the world	250	200	...	-	50	65	12	...	-	53
D Other transfers, except imputed	14655	12619	...	1834	202	19002	15647	...	2854	501
E Imputed unfunded employee pension and welfare contributions	20382	19056	...	1037	289	23396	21811	...	1142	443
Total Current Receipts	1051140	751044	...	56124	323607	1266690	906100	...	69660	383186

Disbursements

1 Government final consumption expenditure	423078	372124	...	35884	15070	546899	479218	...	48143	19538
2 Property income	231042	225803	...	4653	586	329014	323027	...	5509	478
A Interest	231004	225775	...	4643	586	328966	322998	...	5490	478
B Net land rent and royalties	38	28	...	10	-	48	29	...	19	-
3 Subsidies	120101	119677	...	424	-	127128	126852	...	276	-
4 Other current transfers	310729	122017	...	3555	264796	386491	146607	...	4610	327533
A Casualty insurance premiums, net	69	39	...	26	4	65	40	...	22	3
B Transfers to other government subsectors	...	76750	...	485	2404	...	89122	...	648	2489
C Social security benefits	255324	-	...	-	255324	315451	-	...	-	315451
D Social assistance grants c	30531	21749	...	2007	6775	42266	30321	...	2798	9147
E Unfunded employee pension and welfare benefits	20382	19056	...	1037	289	23396	21811	...	1142	443
F Transfers to private non-profit institutions serving households	1056	1056	...	-	-	1964	1964	...	-	-
G Other transfers n.e.c.	-	-	...	...	...	-	-	...	...	...
H Transfers to the rest of the world	3367	3367	...	-	-	3349	3349	...	-	-
Net saving d	-33814	-88577	...	11608	43155	-122845	-169604	...	11122	35637
Total Current Disbursements and Net Saving	1051140	751044	...	56124	323607	1266690	906100	...	69660	383186

	1986			
	Total General Government	Central Government	State or Provincial Government	Local Government	Social Security Funds

Receipts

1 Operating surplus ab	6473	4146	...	2204	123
2 Property and entrepreneurial income	70405	62438	...	2483	5484
A Withdrawals from public quasi-corporations b	-	-	...	-	-
B Interest	39733	32743	...	1507	5483
C Dividends	29529	29510	...	18	1
D Net land rent and royalties	1143	185	...	958	-
3 Taxes, fees and contributions	1509440	1061600	...	24584	423273
A Indirect taxes	767876	759225	...	4971	3680
B Direct taxes	321972	302370	...	19613	-
Income	...	...	...	...	...

Portugal

3.12 General Government Income and Outlay Account: Total and Subsectors
(Continued)

Million Portuguese escudos

	1986				
	Total General Government	Central Government	State or Provincial Government	Local Government	Social Security Funds
Other	...	...	...	...	...
C Social security contributions	419593	-	...	-	419593
D Fees, fines and penalties	...	...	...	...	...
4 Other current transfers	73897	83600	...	54725	35101
A Casualty insurance claims	40	-	...	40	-
B Transfers from other government subsectors	...	13745	...	51750	34034
C Transfers from the rest of the world	26061	25735	...	-	326
D Other transfers, except imputed	18147	16572	...	1352	223
E Imputed unfunded employee pension and welfare contributions	29649	27548	...	1583	518
Total Current Receipts	1660220	1211780	...	83996	463981

Disbursements

1 Government final consumption expenditure	678841	596343	...	58678	23820
2 Property income	428104	421896	...	6207	1
A Interest	428049	421858	...	6190	1
B Net land rent and royalties	55	38	...	17	-
3 Subsidies	131058	121067	...	428	9563
4 Other current transfers	549431	213287	...	5392	430292
A Casualty insurance premiums, net	74	46	...	25	3
B Transfers to other government subsectors	...	85692	...	509	13339
C Social security benefits	402912	-	...	-	402912
D Social assistance grants c	78815	62020	...	3275	13520
E Unfunded employee pension and welfare benefits	29649	27548	...	1583	518
F Transfers to private non-profit institutions serving households	2248	2248	...	-	-
G Other transfers n.e.c.	-	-	...	...	...
H Transfers to the rest of the world	35733	35733	...	-	-
Net saving d	-127218	-140814	...	13291	305
Total Current Disbursements and Net Saving	1660220	1211780	...	83996	463981

a) Item 'Operating surplus' includes consumption of fixed capital.
b) Item 'Withdrawal from public quasi-corporate enterprises' is included in item 'Operating surplus'.
c) Item 'Social assistance grants' includes also transfers to households n.e.c.
d) Item 'Net saving' includes consumption of fixed capital.

3.13 General Government Capital Accumulation Account: Total and Subsectors

Million Portuguese escudos

	1980					1981				
	Total General Government	Central Government	State or Provincial Government	Local Government	Social Security Funds	Total General Government	Central Government	State or Provincial Government	Local Government	Social Security Funds

Finance of Gross Accumulation

1 Gross saving	-30076	-38996	...	4755	4165	-65320	-69647	...	5393	-1066
A Consumption of fixed capital	...	...	...	...	...	...	...	...	...	...
B Net saving a	-30076	-38996	...	4755	4165	-65320	-69647	...	5393	-1066
2 Capital transfers	171688	171265	...	21133	1666	2627	2202	...	25089	1694
A From other government subsectors	-	14	...	20696	1666	-	137	...	24527	1694
B From other resident sectors	171577	171232	...	345	-	2560	2057	...	503	-
C From rest of the world	111	19	...	92	-	67	8	...	59	-
Finance of Gross Accumulation b	141612	132269	...	25888	5831	-62693	-67445	...	30482	628

Gross Accumulation

1 Gross capital formation	51605	26442	...	24359	804	74617	40822	...	33170	625
A Increase in stocks	-	-	...	-	-	-	-	...	-	-
B Gross fixed capital formation	51605	26442	...	24359	804	74617	40822	...	33170	625

Portugal

3.13 General Government Capital Accumulation Account: Total and Subsectors
(Continued)

Million Portuguese escudos

	1980					1981				
	Total General Government	Central Government	State or Provincial Government	Local Government	Social Security Funds	Total General Government	Central Government	State or Provincial Government	Local Government	Social Security Funds
2 Purchases of land, net	1296	864	...	417	15	837	708	...	134	-5
3 Purchases of intangible assets, net	1	...	...	1	...	-	...	...	-	...
4 Capital transfers	19387	40210	...	568	985	21388	44658	...	1490	1598
A To other government subsectors	...	22354	...	11	11	...	26206	...	7	145
B To other resident sectors	14980	13450	...	556	974	15812	12876	...	1483	1453
C To rest of the world	4407	4406	...	1	-	5576	5576	...	-	-
Net lending	69323	64753	...	543	4027	-159535	-153633	...	-4312	-1590
Gross Accumulation [b]	141612	132269	...	25888	5831	-62693	-67445	...	30482	628

	1982					1983				
	Total General Government	Central Government	State or Provincial Government	Local Government	Social Security Funds	Total General Government	Central Government	State or Provincial Government	Local Government	Social Security Funds

Finance of Gross Accumulation

1 Gross saving	-14860	-30258	...	9895	5503	33858	6086	...	11011	16761
A Consumption of fixed capital	...	...	...	...	...	...	...	...	...	...
B Net saving [a]	-14860	-30258	...	9895	5503	33858	6086	...	11011	16761
2 Capital transfers	28904	4659	...	22340	1905	29886	6233	...	21852	1801
A From other government subsectors	...	...	...	...	...	...	...	...	...	...
B From other resident sectors	...	...	...	...	...	...	...	...	...	...
C From rest of the world	...	...	...	...	...	...	...	...	...	...
Finance of Gross Accumulation [b]	14044	-25599	...	32235	7408	63744	12319	...	32863	18562

Gross Accumulation

1 Gross capital formation	79923	41982	...	37834	107	88553	51123	...	36472	958
A Increase in stocks	-	-	...	-	-	-	-	...	-	-
B Gross fixed capital formation	79923	41982	...	37834	107	88553	51123	...	36472	958
2 Purchases of land, net	558	956	...	-398	-	324	1604	...	-1280	-
3 Purchases of intangible assets, net	-	-	...	-	-	-	-	...	-	-
4 Capital transfers	74618	71175	...	1663	1780	208006	204998	...	1177	1831
A To other government subsectors	...	...	...	...	...	...	...	...	...	...
B To other resident sectors	...	...	...	...	...	...	...	...	...	...
C To rest of the world	...	...	...	...	...	...	...	...	...	...
Net lending	-141055	-139712	...	-6864	5521	-233139	-245406	...	-3506	15773
Gross Accumulation [b]	14044	-25599	...	32235	7408	63744	12319	...	32863	18562

	1984					1985				
	Total General Government	Central Government	State or Provincial Government	Local Government	Social Security Funds	Total General Government	Central Government	State or Provincial Government	Local Government	Social Security Funds

Finance of Gross Accumulation

1 Gross saving	-33814	-88577	...	11608	43155	-122845	-169604	...	11122	35637
A Consumption of fixed capital	...	...	...	...	...	...	...	...	...	...
B Net saving [a]	-33814	-88577	...	11608	43155	-122845	-169604	...	11122	35637
2 Capital transfers	120810	94254	...	24785	1771	300615	270494	...	28091	2030
A From other government subsectors	...	...	...	...	...	...	...	...	...	...
B From other resident sectors	...	...	...	...	...	...	...	...	...	...
C From rest of the world	...	...	...	...	...	...	...	...	...	...
Finance of Gross Accumulation [b]	86996	5677	...	36393	44926	177770	100890	...	39213	37667

Gross Accumulation

1 Gross capital formation	90656	54542	...	34986	1128	108926	65551	...	42298	1077
A Increase in stocks	-	-	...	-	-	-	-	...	-	-
B Gross fixed capital formation	90656	54542	...	34986	1128	108926	65551	...	42298	1077

Portugal

3.13 General Government Capital Accumulation Account: Total and Subsectors
(Continued)

Million Portuguese escudos

	1984					1985				
	Total General Government	Central Government	State or Provincial Government	Local Government	Social Security Funds	Total General Government	Central Government	State or Provincial Government	Local Government	Social Security Funds
2 Purchases of land, net	1542	1825	...	-283	-	1236	2428	...	-1192	-
3 Purchases of intangible assets, net	-	-	...	-	-	-	-	...	-	-
4 Capital transfers	193215	189906	...	1910	1399	328937	325377	...	1947	1613
A To other government subsectors	...	...	...	...	...	...	...	...	...	...
B To other resident sectors	...	...	...	...	...	...	...	...	...	...
C To rest of the world	...	...	...	...	...	...	...	...	...	...
Net lending	-198417	-240596	...	-220	42399	-261329	-292466	...	-3840	34977
Gross Accumulation b	86996	5677	...	36393	44926	177770	100890	...	39213	37667

	1986				
	Total General Government	Central Government	State or Provincial Government	Local Government	Social Security Funds

Finance of Gross Accumulation

1 Gross saving	-127218	-140814	...	13291	305
A Consumption of fixed capital	...	...	...	...	...
B Net saving a	-127218	-140814	...	13291	305
2 Capital transfers	173266	131734	...	39171	2361
A From other government subsectors	...	...	...	...	...
B From other resident sectors	...	...	...	...	...
C From rest of the world	...	...	...	...	...
Finance of Gross Accumulation b	46048	-9080	...	52462	2666

Gross Accumulation

1 Gross capital formation	143957	94216	...	47717	2024
A Increase in stocks	-	-	...	-	-
B Gross fixed capital formation	143957	94216	...	47717	2024
2 Purchases of land, net	2380	3149	...	-769	-
3 Purchases of intangible assets, net	-	-	...	-	-
4 Capital transfers	181222	171550	...	2287	7385
A To other government subsectors	...	...	...	...	...
B To other resident sectors	...	...	...	...	...
C To rest of the world	...	...	...	...	...
Net lending	-281511	-277995	...	3227	-6743
Gross Accumulation b	46048	-9080	...	52462	2666

a) Item 'Net saving' includes consumption of fixed capital.
b) Data in this table have been revised, therefore they are not strictly comparable with the unrevised data in the other tables.

3.21 Corporate and Quasi-Corporate Enterprise Production Account: Total and Sectors

Million Portuguese escudos

	1980				1981				1982			
	Corporate and Quasi-Corporate Enterprises			ADDENDUM: Total, including Unincorporated	Corporate and Quasi-Corporate Enterprises			ADDENDUM: Total, including Unincorporated	Corporate and Quasi-Corporate Enterprises			ADDENDUM: Total, including Unincorporated
	TOTAL	Non-Financial	Financial		TOTAL	Non-Financial	Financial		TOTAL	Non-Financial	Financial	

Gross Output

1 Output for sale	1724830	1697560	27275	2405680	2144390	2109620	34773	2953240	2660770	2617210	43559	3653470
2 Imputed bank service charge	55553	-	55553	55553	77588	-	77588	77588	107420	-	107420	107420
3 Own-account fixed capital formation	-	-	-	-	-	-	-	-	-	-	-	-
Gross Output	1780390	1697560	82828	2461230	2221980	2109620	112361	3030830	2768190	2617210	150979	3760890

Gross Input

Intermediate consumption	1144780	1076800	67977	1375570	1456850	1362580	94264	1743180	1818930	1689940	128992	2170760
1 Imputed banking service charge	55553	-	55553	55553	77588	-	77588	77588	107420	-	107420	107420
2 Other intermediate consumption	1089230	1076800	12424	1320020	1379260	1362580	16676	1665590	1711510	1689940	21572	2063340
Subtotal: Value Added	635607	620756	14851	1085660	765131	747034	18097	1287650	949266	927279	21987	1590130

Portugal

3.21 Corporate and Quasi-Corporate Enterprise Production Account: Total and Sectors
(Continued)

Million Portuguese escudos

	1980				1981				1982			
	Corporate and Quasi-Corporate Enterprises			ADDENDUM: Total, including Unincorporated	Corporate and Quasi-Corporate Enterprises			ADDENDUM: Total, including Unincorporated	Corporate and Quasi-Corporate Enterprises			ADDENDUM: Total, including Unincorporated
	TOTAL	Non-Financial	Financial		TOTAL	Non-Financial	Financial		TOTAL	Non-Financial	Financial	
1 Indirect taxes, net	83274	73650	9624	91347	93740	81267	12473	104232	147803	127258	20545	159026
A Indirect taxes	147706	138042	9664	156672	174450	161977	12473	185614	225541	204996	20545	238476
B Less: Subsidies	64432	64392	40	65325	80710	80710	-	81382	77738	77738	-	79450
2 Consumption of fixed capital	...	...	...	...	...	...	...	...	...	...	...	...
3 Compensation of employees	401174	371952	29222	493858	505890	468975	36915	606214	628630	581133	47497	741880
4 Net operating surplus a	151159	175154	-23995	500458	165501	196792	-31291	577206	172833	218888	-46055	689224
Gross Input	1780390	1697560	82828	2461230	2221980	2109620	112361	3030830	2768190	2617210	150979	3760890

	1983				1984				1985			
	Corporate and Quasi-Corporate Enterprises			ADDENDUM: Total, including Unincorporated	Corporate and Quasi-Corporate Enterprises			ADDENDUM: Total, including Unincorporated	Corporate and Quasi-Corporate Enterprises			ADDENDUM: Total, including Unincorporated
	TOTAL	Non-Financial	Financial		TOTAL	Non-Financial	Financial		TOTAL	Non-Financial	Financial	

Gross Output

1 Output for sale	3439930	3386500	53427	4670440	4291400	4218570	72828	5791610	5223450	5134670	88778	7034770
2 Imputed bank service charge	135775	-	135775	135775	139753	-	139753	139753	179388	-	179388	179388
3 Own-account fixed capital formation	-	-	-	-	-	-	-	-	-	-	-	-
Gross Output	3575700	3386500	189202	4806220	4431150	4218570	212581	5931370	5402830	5134670	268166	7214160

Gross Input

Intermediate consumption	2376350	2210990	165356	2835900	2939990	2759430	180560	3507900	3521360	3290560	230805	4182130
1 Imputed banking service charge	135775	-	135775	135775	139753	-	139753	139753	179388	-	179388	179388
2 Other intermediate consumption	2240570	2210990	29581	2700120	2800230	2759430	40807	3368140	3341970	3290560	51417	4002750
Subtotal: Value Added	1199360	1175510	23846	1970320	1491170	1459150	32021	2423470	1881470	1844110	37361	3032030
1 Indirect taxes, net	201642	174295	27347	215635	247951	211772	36179	268210	325372	280553	44819	343506
A Indirect taxes	290828	263481	27347	307290	364852	325367	39485	388038	440976	396157	44819	470305
B Less: Subsidies	89186	89186	-	91655	116901	113595	3306	119828	115604	115604	-	126799
2 Consumption of fixed capital	...	...	...	...	...	...	...	...	...	...	...	...
3 Compensation of employees	752598	689250	63348	895664	884378	807005	77373	1046750	1055340	957869	97471	1244560
4 Net operating surplus a	245115	311964	-66849	859018	358837	440368	-81531	1108510	500760	605689	-104929	1443960
Gross Input	3575700	3386500	189202	4806220	4431150	4218570	212581	5931370	5402830	5134670	268166	7214160

	1986			
	Corporate and Quasi-Corporate Enterprises			ADDENDUM: Total, including Unincorporated
	TOTAL	Non-Financial	Financial	

Gross Output

1 Output for sale	5694650	5596560	98089	7790600
2 Imputed bank service charge	222787	-	222787	222787
3 Own-account fixed capital formation	-	-	-	-
Gross Output	5917440	5596560	320876	8013390

Gross Input

Intermediate consumption	3710140	3423680	286459	4422700
1 Imputed banking service charge	222787	-	222787	222787
2 Other intermediate consumption	3487350	3423680	63672	4199920
Subtotal: Value Added	2207300	2172890	34417	3590680
1 Indirect taxes, net	316480	261679	54801	323088
A Indirect taxes	454244	399434	54810	472030
B Less: Subsidies	137764	137755	9	148942
2 Consumption of fixed capital	...	...	...	...
3 Compensation of employees	1271350	1152380	118966	1492210
4 Net operating surplus a	619477	758827	-139350	1775390
Gross Input	5917440	5596560	320876	8013390

a) Item 'Operating surplus' includes consumption of fixed capital.

Portugal

3.22 Corporate and Quasi-Corporate Enterprise Income and Outlay Account: Total and Sectors

Million Portuguese escudos

	1980 TOTAL	1980 Non-Financial	1980 Financial	1981 TOTAL	1981 Non-Financial	1981 Financial	1982 TOTAL	1982 Non-Financial	1982 Financial	1983 TOTAL	1983 Non-Financial	1983 Financial
Receipts												
1 Operating surplus [a]	151159	175154	-23995	165501	196792	-31291	172833	218888	-46055	245115	311964	-66849
2 Property and entrepreneurial income	242937	22861	220076	347826	33485	314341	477179	38180	438999	674833	49278	625555
A Withdrawals from quasi-corporate enterprises	423	423	-	466	466	-	591	591	-	621	621	-
B Interest	240841	21192	219649	344936	31423	313513	473905	35501	438404	671245	46744	624501
C Dividends	1381	954	427	2053	1226	827	2238	1643	595	2634	1581	1053
D Net land rent and royalties	292	292	-	371	370	1	445	445	-	333	332	1
3 Current transfers	38057	17066	20991	44353	19427	24926	56017	23132	32885	66251	26266	39985
A Casualty insurance claims	5690	5641	49	6189	6133	56	7892	7822	70	9018	8920	98
B Casualty insurance premiums, net, due to be received by insurance companies	14286	-	14286	16019	-	16019	20704	-	20704	25025	-	25025
C Current transfers from the rest of the world	-	-	-	-	-	-	-	-	-	-	-	-
D Other transfers except imputed	11521	6279	5242	13995	6905	7090	17152	7376	9776	18571	6807	11764
E Imputed unfunded employee pension and welfare contributions	6560	5146	1414	8150	6389	1761	10269	7934	2335	13637	10539	3098
Total Current Receipts	432153	215081	217072	557680	249704	307976	706029	280200	425829	986199	387508	598691
Disbursements												
1 Property and entrepreneurial income	334635	166457	168178	487953	248762	239191	716150	372793	343357	1016980	496467	520508
A Withdrawals from quasi-corporations	...	...	...	...	...	...	...	...	...	...	...	...
B Interest	315164	152620	162544	468701	234365	234336	683175	354553	328622	964194	478367	485827
C Dividends	15771	10137	5634	14862	10074	4788	26677	11942	14735	45800	11121	34679
D Net land rent and royalties	3700	3700	-	4390	4323	67	6298	6298	-	6981	6979	2
2 Direct taxes and other current transfers n.e.c. to general government	22670	21278	1392	30852	28943	1909	38050	35705	2345	45373	42379	2994
A Direct taxes	22670	21278	1392	30852	28943	1909	38050	35705	2345	45373	42379	2994
B Fines, fees, penalties and other current transfers n.e.c.	...	...	...	...	...	...	...	...	...	...	...	...
3 Other current transfers	40386	12904	27482	47217	14040	33177	63047	21439	41608	76343	24684	51659
A Casualty insurance premiums, net	5904	5790	114	6175	6120	55	8712	8649	63	9058	8988	70
B Casualty insurance claims liability of insurance companies	14286	-	14286	16019	-	16019	20704	-	20704	25025	-	25025
C Transfers to private non-profit institutions	365	365	-	551	551	-	608	608	-	713	713	-
D Unfunded employee pension and welfare benefits	...	...	...	...	...	...	...	...	...	...	...	...
E Social assistance grants	10057	5146	4911	12791	6389	6402	16412	7934	8478	21276	10539	10737
F Other transfers n.e.c.	9774	1603	8171	11681	980	10701	16611	4248	12363	20271	4444	15827
G Transfers to the rest of the world	...	...	...	...	...	...	...	...	...	...	...	...
Statistical discrepancy [b]	1492	-	1492	1929	-	1929	2956	-	2956	3422	-	3422
Net saving [c]	32970	14442	18528	-10271	-42041	31770	-114174	-149737	35563	-155914	-176022	20108
Total Current Disbursements and Net Saving	432153	215081	217072	557680	249704	307976	706029	280200	425829	986199	387508	598691

	1984 TOTAL	1984 Non-Financial	1984 Financial	1985 TOTAL	1985 Non-Financial	1985 Financial	1986 TOTAL	1986 Non-Financial	1986 Financial
Receipts									
1 Operating surplus [a]	358837	440368	-81531	500760	605689	-104929	619477	758827	-139350
2 Property and entrepreneurial income	960450	67956	892494	1273700	92152	1181550	1267560	109148	1158410
A Withdrawals from quasi-corporate enterprises	1013	1013	-	1050	1050	-	1156	1156	-
B Interest	954489	63097	891392	1264450	84393	1180060	1259270	102223	1157050
C Dividends	4336	3235	1101	7471	5980	1491	6154	4790	1364
D Net land rent and royalties	612	611	1	729	729	-	979	979	-

Portugal

3.22 Corporate and Quasi-Corporate Enterprise Income and Outlay Account: Total and Sectors
(Continued)

Million Portuguese escudos

	1984 TOTAL	1984 Non-Financial	1984 Financial	1985 TOTAL	1985 Non-Financial	1985 Financial	1986 TOTAL	1986 Non-Financial	1986 Financial
3 Current transfers	70933	27488	43445	89193	41423	47770	96448	30603	65845
A Casualty insurance claims	9312	9261	51	7514	7450	64	6569	6489	80
B Casualty insurance premiums, net, due to be received by insurance companies	25863	-	25863	30760	-	30760	39989	-	39989
C Current transfers from the rest of the world	-	-	-	-	-	-	-	-	-
D Other transfers except imputed	18177	4710	13467	28146	16706	11440	22786	3758	19028
E Imputed unfunded employee pension and welfare contributions	17581	13517	4064	22773	17267	5506	27104	20356	6748
Total Current Receipts	1390220	535812	854408	1863660	739264	1124390	1983490	898578	1084910

Disbursements

	1984 TOTAL	1984 Non-Financial	1984 Financial	1985 TOTAL	1985 Non-Financial	1985 Financial	1986 TOTAL	1986 Non-Financial	1986 Financial
1 Property and entrepreneurial income	1445370	687589	757785	1805970	805518	1000460	1625130	674247	950879
A Withdrawals from quasi-corporations	...	...	...	...	...	...	...	...	...
B Interest	1412110	666752	745360	1770140	778568	991572	1568920	645435	923484
C Dividends	24646	12221	12425	25187	16304	8883	47294	19899	27395
D Net land rent and royalties	8616	8616	-	10646	10646	-	8913	8913	-
2 Direct taxes and other current transfers n.e.c. to general government	58124	49300	8824	68447	62147	6300	72945	67573	5372
A Direct taxes	58124	49300	8824	68447	62147	6300	72945	67573	5372
B Fines, fees, penalties and other current transfers n.e.c.	...	...	...	...	...	...	...	...	...
3 Other current transfers	81523	26866	54657	89231	28939	60292	105698	36092	69606
A Casualty insurance premiums, net	10457	10379	78	9121	8976	145	13591	13421	170
B Casualty insurance claims liability of insurance companies	25863	-	25863	30760	-	30760	39989	-	39989
C Transfers to private non-profit institutions	896	896	-	889	889	-	1080	1080	-
D Unfunded employee pension and welfare benefits	...	...	...	...	...	...	...	...	...
E Social assistance grants	26863	13517	13346	34165	17267	16898	40999	20356	20643
F Other transfers n.e.c.	17444	2074	15370	14296	1807	12489	10039	1235	8804
G Transfers to the rest of the world	...	...	...	...	...	...	...	...	...
Statistical discrepancy b	3451	-	3451	-930	-	-930	3234	-	3234
Net saving c	-198252	-227943	29691	-99066	-157340	58274	176483	120666	55817
Total Current Disbursements and Net Saving	1390220	535812	854408	1863660	739264	1124390	1983490	898578	1084910

a) Item 'Operating surplus' includes consumption of fixed capital.
b) Item 'Statistical discrepancy' refers to increase in technical reserves of pension funds.
c) Item 'Net saving' includes consumption of fixed capital.

3.23 Corporate and Quasi-Corporate Enterprise Capital Accumulation Account: Total and Sectors

Million Portuguese escudos

	1980 TOTAL	1980 Non-Financial	1980 Financial	1981 TOTAL	1981 Non-Financial	1981 Financial	1982 TOTAL	1982 Non-Financial	1982 Financial	1983 TOTAL	1983 Non-Financial	1983 Financial
Finance of Gross Accumulation											
1 Gross saving	32970	14442	18528	-10271	-42041	31770	-114174	-149737	35563	-155914	-176022	20108
A Consumption of fixed capital	...	...	...	...	...	...	...	...	...	...	...	...
B Net saving a	32970	14442	18528	-10271	-42041	31770	-114174	-149737	35563	-155914	-176022	20108
2 Capital transfers	16260	16168	92	17129	17102	27	45325	45149	176	177189	176905	284
Finance of Gross Accumulation	49230	30610	18620	6858	-24939	31797	-68849	-104588	35739	21275	883	20392
Gross Accumulation											
1 Gross capital formation	243698	233941	9757	292271	279455	12816	353909	338949	14960	358755	339252	19503

Portugal

3.23 Corporate and Quasi-Corporate Enterprise Capital Accumulation Account: Total and Sectors
(Continued)

Million Portuguese escudos

	1980 TOTAL	1980 Non-Financial	1980 Financial	1981 TOTAL	1981 Non-Financial	1981 Financial	1982 TOTAL	1982 Non-Financial	1982 Financial	1983 TOTAL	1983 Non-Financial	1983 Financial
A Increase in stocks	53478	53478	-	52506	52506	-	50826	50826	-	-11799	-11799	-
B Gross fixed capital formation	190220	180463	9757	239765	226949	12816	303083	288123	14960	370554	351051	19503
2 Purchases of land, net	6392	5320	1072	5952	4670	1282	9134	8116	1018	6529	5371	1158
3 Purchases of intangible assets, net												
4 Capital transfers	173936	2481	171455	6753	3174	3579	11417	6206	5211	9331	4392	4939
Net lending	-374796	-211132	-163664	-298118	-312238	14120	-443309	-457859	14550	-353340	-348132	-5208
Gross Accumulation	49230	30610	18620	6858	-24939	31797	-68849	-104588	35739	21275	883	20392

	1984 TOTAL	1984 Non-Financial	1984 Financial	1985 TOTAL	1985 Non-Financial	1985 Financial	1986 TOTAL	1986 Non-Financial	1986 Financial
				Finance of Gross Accumulation					
1 Gross saving	-198252	-227943	29691	-99066	-157340	58274	176483	120666	55817
A Consumption of fixed capital	...	...	...	...	...	...	...	...	...
B Net saving [a]	-198252	-227943	29691	-99066	-157340	58274	176483	120666	55817
2 Capital transfers	162721	162367	354	250027	247998	2029	141097	140874	223
Finance of Gross Accumulation	-35531	-65576	30045	150961	90658	60303	317580	261540	56040
				Gross Accumulation					
1 Gross capital formation	312798	290778	22020	347922	326830	21092	503381	469426	33955
A Increase in stocks	-29436	-29436	-	-31463	-31463	-	9946	9946	-
B Gross fixed capital formation	342234	320214	22020	379385	358293	21092	493435	459480	33955
2 Purchases of land, net	8623	7366	1257	6565	5261	1304	4863	1708	3155
3 Purchases of intangible assets, net									
4 Capital transfers	93310	88855	4455	272811	139696	133115	116356	101591	14765
Net lending	-450262	-452575	2313	-476337	-381129	-95208	-307020	-311185	4165
Gross Accumulation	-35531	-65576	30045	150961	90658	60303	317580	261540	56040

a) Item 'Net saving' includes consumption of fixed capital.

3.24 Corporate and Quasi-Corporate Enterprise Capital Finance Account: Total and Sectors

Million Portuguese escudos

	1980 TOTAL	1980 Non-Financial	1980 Financial	1981 TOTAL	1981 Non-Financial	1981 Financial
			Acquisition of Financial Assets			
1 Gold and SDRs	14438	-	14438	3036	-	3036
2 Currency and transferable deposits	36722	33125	3597	7265	5108	2157
3 Other deposits	1339	10326	-8987	-10242	14204	-24446
4 Bills and bonds, short term	4959	-	4959	15024	-	15024
5 Bonds, long term	-59896	499	-60395	156290	1274	155016
6 Corporate equity securities	-5020	-	-5020	-119	-	-119
7 Short term loans, n.e.c.	95944	7708	88236	139733	8	139725
8 Long term loans, n.e.c.	145948	716	145232	145360	-1750	147110
9 Trade credits and advances	15024	6768	8256	41142	20974	20168
10 Other receivables	-	-	-	-	-	-
11 Other assets [a]	2224	2205	19	1888	1874	14
Total Acquisition of Financial Assets	251682	61347	190335	499377	41692	457685
			Incurrence of Liabilities			
1 Currency and transferable deposits	62190	-	62190	43985	-	43985
2 Other deposits	273384	-	273384	369059	-	369059
3 Bills and bonds, short term	-809	-755	-54	11854	10909	945
4 Bonds, long term	...	...	...	...	...	...
5 Corporate equity securities	37337	36538	799	33289	32562	727
6 Short-term loans, n.e.c.	103416	134270	-30854	116886	120845	-3959

Portugal

3.24 Corporate and Quasi-Corporate Enterprise Capital Finance Account: Total and Sectors
(Continued)

Million Portuguese escudos

	1980 TOTAL	1980 Non-Financial	1980 Financial	1981 TOTAL	1981 Non-Financial	1981 Financial
7 Long-term loans, n.e.c.	130274	121809	8465	146466	124442	22024
8 Net equity of households in life insurance and pension fund reserves	8058	-	8058	8508	-	8508
9 Proprietors' net additions to the accumulation of quasi-corporations	...	...	...	...	...	...
10 Trade credit and advances	-11879	-21308	9429	91703	87431	4272
11 Other accounts payable	...	...	...	...	...	...
12 Other liabilities	-3930	...	-3930	-2126	...	-2126
Total Incurrence of Liabilities	598041	270554	327487	819624	376189	443435
Statistical discrepancy	28437	1925	26512	-22129	-22259	130
Net Lending	-374796	-211132	-163664	-298118	-312238	14120
Incurrence of Liabilities and Net Lending	251682	61347	190335	499377	41692	457685

a) Item 'Other assets' refers to insurance reserves.

3.31 Household and Private Unincorporated Enterprise Production Account

Million Portuguese escudos

	1970	1975	1978	1979	1980	1981	1982	1983	1984	1985	1986	1987
Gross Output
1 Output for sale	...	...	423389	551289	680844	808856	978783	1214150	1480340	1787650	2069660	...
2 Non-marketed output	...	...	5972	...	...	...	13915	16365	19872	23679	26286	...
Gross Output	...	...	429361	551289	680844	808856	992698	1230510	1500210	1811320	2095950	...
Gross Input
Intermediate consumption	...	...	134811	181851	230788	286335	351834	459552	567909	660771	712566	...
Subtotal: Value Added	...	...	294550	369438	450056	522521	640864	770962	932304	1150550	1383380	...
1 Indirect taxes net liability of unincorporated enterprises	...	...	3172	5891	8073	10492	11223	13993	20259	18134	6608	...
A Indirect taxes	...	...	4493	6405	8966	11164	12935	16462	23186	29329	17786	...
B Less: Subsidies	...	...	1321	514	893	672	1712	2469	2927	11195	11178	...
2 Consumption of fixed capital	...	...	...	...	...	...	...	...	...	...	...	...
3 Compensation of employees	...	...	61090	74094	92684	100324	113250	143066	162369	189218	220864	...
4 Net operating surplus a	...	...	230288	289453	349299	411705	516391	613903	749676	943201	1155910	...
Gross Input	...	...	429361	551289	680844	808856	992698	1230510	1500210	1811320	2095950	...

a) Item 'Operating surplus' includes consumption of fixed capital.

3.32 Household and Private Unincorporated Enterprise Income and Outlay Account

Million Portuguese escudos

	1970	1975	1978	1979	1980	1981	1982	1983	1984	1985	1986	1987
Receipts
1 Compensation of employees	79313	224241	410589	503251	642028	788893	963012	1173330	1386840	1674000	2008900	...
A Wages and salaries	73307	205207	...	...	...	...	...	...	...	...	...	...
B Employers' contributions for social security	6006	19034	...	...	...	...	...	...	...	...	...	...
C Employers' contributions for private pension & welfare plans	...	...	...	...	...	...	...	...	...	...	...	...
2 Operating surplus of private unincorporated enterprises	...	...	230288	289453	349299	411705	516391	613903	749676	943201	1155910	...
3 Property and entrepreneurial income	57249	106839	54064	111372	139532	202101	276806	397800	606619	768896	703750	...
A Withdrawals from private quasi-corporations	...	...	-	-	-	-	-	-	-	-	-	...
B Interest	...	...	48252	103129	128416	191779	262761	384963	592913	753140	686677	...
C Dividends	...	...	4169	6058	7312	6491	8965	7966	6187	7771	11060	...
D Net land rent and royalties	...	...	1643	2185	3804	3831	5080	4871	7519	7985	6013	...

Portugal

3.32 Household and Private Unincorporated Enterprise Income and Outlay Account
(Continued)

Million Portuguese escudos

	1970	1975	1978	1979	1980	1981	1982	1983	1984	1985	1986	1987
3 Current transfers	21378	61192	164493	227605	301347	371743	453445	533192	678171	799376	988256	...
A Casualty insurance claims	...	...	4440	6008	9217	10665	13493	17271	18445	25104	35502	...
B Social security benefits	4537	23285	78680	92958	132634	173239	214072	253486	308884	380072	481533	...
C Social assistance grants												...
D Unfunded employee pension and welfare benefits	...	...	148	174	180	175	177	163	170	210	232	
E Transfers from general government	...	...	...									
F Transfers from the rest of the world	15024	27962	...									
G Other transfers n.e.c.	1817	9945	81225	128465	159316	187664	225703	262272	350672	393990	470989	
Statistical discrepancy a	...	...	897	1049	1492	1929	2956	3422	3451	-930	3234	
Total Current Receipts	157940	392272	860331	1132730	1433700	1776370	2212610	2721650	3424750	4184550	4860050	...

Disbursements

	1970	1975	1978	1979	1980	1981	1982	1983	1984	1985	1986	1987
1 Final consumption expenditures	122370	303768	533128	667269	840705	1040150	1280930	1587600	1980400	2381390	2851580	
2 Property income	...	...	19939	42849	52933	62050	74132	88149	126439	159725	155180	
A Interest	...	...	18792	41611	50863	59942	71562	85319	122320	155567	148647	
B Net land rent and royalties	...	...	1147	1238	2070	2108	2570	2830	4119	4158	6533	
3 Direct taxes and other current transfers n.e.c. to government	14303	41298	109628	138829	173932	226846	299858	400307	479444	585865	685749	...
A Social security contributions	8237	27082	72855	88058	114609	144480	190972	238995	290831	341044	436722	
B Direct taxes	6066	14216	36773	50771	59323	82366	108886	161312	188613	244821	249027	
Income taxes	6066	14216	...	...	...	...	...	...	...	...	...	
Other	...	...	...	...	...	...	...	...	...	...	...	
C Fees, fines and penalties	...	...	...									
4 Other current transfers	1309	2958	20009	23375	31309	37565	50616	66120	81137	99441	118428	...
A Net casualty insurance premiums	...	...	3960	5704	7972	8849	11479	13908	11967	17748	23093	
B Transfers to private non-profit institutions serving households	...	...	2188	2496	2700	4317	5074	5880	7544	7650	9291	
C Transfers to the rest of the world	389	499	3511	2636	1792	1653	2634	7498	11044	12910	15920	
D Other current transfers, except imputed	920	2459	3923	4025	4933	5665	7909	8315	12380	14649	13006	
E Imputed employee pension and welfare contributions	...	...	6427	8514	13912	17081	23520	30519	38202	46484	57118	
Net saving b	19958	44248	177627	260408	334819	409765	507075	579472	757336	958126	1049110	...
Total Current Disbursements and Net Saving	157940	392272	860331	1132730	1433700	1776370	2212610	2721650	3424750	4184550	4860050	...

a) Item 'Statistical discrepancy' refers to increase in technical reserves of pension funds.
b) Item 'Net saving' includes consumption of fixed capital.

Portugal

3.33 Household and Private Unincorporated Enterprise Capital Accumulation Account

Million Portuguese escudos

	1970	1975	1978	1979	1980	1981	1982	1983	1984	1985	1986	1987
Finance of Gross Accumulation												
1 Gross saving	...	...	177627	260408	334819	409765	507075	579472	757336	958126	1049110	...
A Consumption of fixed capital	...	...	...	...	...	...	...	...	...	...	...	...
B Net saving [a]	...	...	177627	260408	334819	409765	507075	579472	757336	958126	1049110	...
2 Capital transfers	...	...	886	2686	2020	4623	6611	6929	7293	51686	14026	...
Total Finance of Gross Accumulation	...	...	178513	263094	336839	414388	513686	586401	764629	1009810	1063140	...
Gross Accumulation												
1 Gross Capital Formation	...	...	83188	93197	117427	150521	194845	200991	219947	266786	335456	...
A Increase in stocks	...	...	6218	10936	-314	3297	5557	-9046	-8287	-9312	616	...
B Gross fixed capital formation	...	...	76970	82261	117741	147224	189288	210037	228234	276098	334840	...
2 Purchases of land, net	...	...	-2418	-3652	-7786	-6952	-9771	-7103	-10473	-7968	-7743	...
3 Purchases of intangibles, net	...	...										...
4 Capital transfers	...	...	789	848	1045	1798	2010	5393	8035	9938	13979	...
Net lending	...	...	96954	172701	226153	269021	326602	387120	547120	741056	721443	...
Total Gross Accumulation	...	...	178513	263094	336839	414388	513686	586401	764629	1009810	1063140	...

a) Item 'Net saving' includes consumption of fixed capital.

3.34 Household and Private Unincorporated Enterprise Capital Finance Account

Million Portuguese escudos

	1970	1975	1978	1979	1980	1981	1982	1983	1984	1985	1986	1987
Acquisition of Financial Assets												
1 Gold	...	...	-	-	-801	-	...	...	...	...	...	...
2 Currency and transferable deposits	...	...	19876	43473	49428	34477	...	...	...	...	...	...
3 Other deposits	...	...	116048	156502	238169	326196	...	...	...	...	...	...
4 Bills and bonds, short term	...	...	-	-	3460	6519	...	...	...	...	...	...
5 Bonds, long term	...	...	-1372	-784	69928	12505	...	...	...	...	...	...
6 Corporate equity securities	...	...	-	-	-59163	-5996	...	...	...	...	...	...
7 Short term loans, n.e.c.	...	...	-	-	-	-	...	...	...	...	...	...
8 Long term loans, n.e.c.	...	...	31	-25	-	-	...	...	...	...	...	...
9 Trade credit and advances	...	...	711	-2160	5114	2960	...	...	...	...	...	...
10 Net equity of households in life insurance and pension fund reserves	...	...	3084	3737	5805	6603	...	...	...	...	...	...
11 Proprietors' net additions to the accumulation of quasi-corporations	...	...					...	...	...	...	...	...
12 Other	...	...	-	-	-	-	...	...	...	...	...	...
Total Acquisition of Financial Assets	...	...	138378	200743	311940	383264	...	...	...	...	...	...
Incurrence of Liabilities												
1 Short term loans, n.e.c.	...	...	15816	22100	21908	12587	...	...	...	...	...	...
2 Long term loans, n.e.c.	...	...	29053	38780	47017	56832	...	...	...	...	...	...
3 Trade credit and advances	...	...	3556	6063	8977	4092	...	...	...	...	...	...
4 Other accounts payable	...	...	-	-	-	-	...	...	...	...	...	...
5 Other liabilities	...	...	-	-	-	-	...	...	...	...	...	...
Total Incurrence of Liabilities	...	...	48425	66943	77902	73511	...	...	...	...	...	...
Statistical discrepancy	...	...	-7001	-38901	7885	40732	...	...	...	...	...	...
Net Lending	...	...	96954	172701	226153	269021	...	...	...	...	...	...
Incurrence of Liabilities and Net Lending	...	...	138378	200743	311940	383264	...	...	...	...	...	...

3.41 Private Non-Profit Institutions Serving Households: Production Account

Million Portuguese escudos

	1970	1975	1978	1979	1980	1981	1982	1983	1984	1985	1986	1987
Gross Output												
1 Sales	...	...	325	377	552	1060	1196	1866	2377	3699	4435	...
2 Non-marketed output	...	...	3580	4475	5961	6858	8309	11217	13385	15913	18740	...
A Services produced for own use	...	...	3580	4475	5961	6858	8309	11217	13385	15913	18740	...
B Own account fixed capital formation	...	...	...	...	...	...	...	...	...	...	...	...
Gross Output	...	...	3905	4852	6513	7918	9505	13083	15762	19612	23175	...

Portugal

3.41 Private Non-Profit Institutions Serving Households: Production Account
(Continued)

Million Portuguese escudos

	1970	1975	1978	1979	1980	1981	1982	1983	1984	1985	1986	1987
					Gross Input							
Intermediate consumption	...	...	1447	1858	3051	3575	4111	5614	6790	8278	9436	...
Subtotal: Value Added	...	...	2458	2994	3462	4343	5394	7469	8972	11334	13739	...
1 Indirect taxes, net	...	...	17	27	29	54	77	91	198	25	20	...
2 Consumption of fixed capital	...	...	...	...	...	...	...	...	...	...	...	...
3 Compensation of employees	...	...	2439	2967	3442	4318	5339	7268	8621	11185	13251	...
4 Net operating surplus [a]	...	...	2	-	-9	-29	-22	110	153	124	468	...
Gross Input	...	...	3905	4852	6513	7918	9505	13083	15762	19612	23175	...

a) Item 'Operating surplus' includes consumption of fixed capital.

3.42 Private Non-Profit Institutions Serving Households: Income and Outlay Account

Million Portuguese escudos

	1970	1975	1978	1979	1980	1981	1982	1983	1984	1985	1986	1987
					Receipts							
1 Operating surplus [a]	...	...	2	-	-9	-29	-22	110	153	124	468	...
2 Property and entrepreneurial income	...	...	1102	1588	2043	3019	4018	5574	7450	8479	9686	...
A Withdrawals from quasi-corporations	...	...	-	-	-	-	-	-	-	-	-	...
B Interest	...	...	427	600	960	1407	1609	1426	2075	2760	1828	...
C Dividends	...	...	675	988	1083	1611	2408	4147	5372	5719	7854	...
D Net land rent and royalties	...	...	-	-	-	1	1	1	3	-	4	...
3 Current transfers	...	...	2436	2942	3630	5846	6997	8064	9831	10985	13378	...
A Casualty insurance claims	...	...	-	-	-	-	-	-	-	-	-	...
B Current transfers from general government	...	...	2412	2911	3612	5815	6943	7992	9762	10880	13245	...
C Other transfers from resident sectors	...	...	...	...	...	...	...	...	...	...	...	...
D Current transfers received from the rest of the world	...	...	...	...	...	...	...	...	...	...	...	...
E Imputed unfunded employee pension and welfare contributions	...	...	24	31	18	26	54	72	69	105	133	...
Total Current Receipts	...	...	3540	4530	5664	8836	10993	13748	17434	19588	23532	...
					Disbursements							
1 Final consumption expenditures	...	...	2232	2986	4817	5300	6132	8610	9936	11855	14363	...
A Compensation of employees	...	...	2373	2896	3333	4145	...	...	...	...	...	...
B Consumption of fixed capital	...	...	...	...	...	...	...	...	...	...	...	...
C Purchases of goods and services, net	...	...	-141	90	1484	1155	...	...	...	...	...	...
Purchases	...	...	1421	1761	2932	3402	...	...	...	...	...	...
Less: Sales	...	...	1562	1671	1448	2247	...	...	...	...	...	...
2 Property income	...	...	77	97	2	98	149	286	318	312	370	...
A Interest	...	...	77	97	2	98	149	286	318	311	370	...
B Net land rent and royalties	...	...	-	-	-	-	-	-	-	1	-	...
3 Direct taxes and other transfers to general government	...	...	-	-	-	6	1	2	7	6	-	...
A Direct taxes	...	...	-	-	-	6	1	2	7	6	-	...
B Fees, fines and penalties	...	...	...	...	...	...	...	...	...	...	...	...
4 Other current transfers	...	...	482	995	1244	1315	2230	2300	3146	4006	4098	...
A Net casualty insurance premiums	...	...	5	6	18	8	10	11	13	31	28	...
B Social assistance grants	...	...	95	247	225	373	374	599	913	1162	1262	...
C Unfunded employee pension and welfare benefits	...	...	-	-	-	-	-	-	-	-	-	...
D Current transfers to the rest of the world	...	...	157	247	267	234	541	797	942	1016	920	...
E Other current transfers n.e.c.	...	...	225	495	734	700	1305	893	1278	1797	1888	...
Net saving [b]	...	...	749	452	-399	2117	2481	2550	4027	3409	4701	...
Total Current Disbursements	...	...	3540	4530	5664	8836	10993	13748	17434	19588	23532	...

a) Item 'Operating surplus' includes consumption of fixed capital.
b) Item 'Net saving' includes consumption of fixed capital.

Portugal

3.43 Private Non-Profit Institutions Serving Households: Capital Accumulation Account
Million Portuguese escudos

	1970	1975	1978	1979	1980	1981	1982	1983	1984	1985	1986	1987
Finance of Gross Accumulation											
1 Gross saving	...	...	749	452	-399	2117	2481	2550	4027	3409	4701	...
A Consumption of fixed capital	...	...	...	...	...	...	...	...	...	...	...	...
B Net saving a	...	...	749	452	-399	2117	2481	2550	4027	3409	4701	...
2 Capital transfers	...	...	61	-	104	103	396	486	497	695	743	...
Finance of Gross Accumulation	...	...	810	452	-295	2220	2877	3036	4524	4104	5444	...
Gross Accumulation											
1 Gross capital formation	...	...	419	377	-719	1406	2475	2362	2570	3550	4762	...
A Increase in stocks	...	...	-	-	-	-	-	-	-	-	-	...
B Gross fixed capital formation	...	...	419	377	-719	1406	2475	2362	2570	3550	4762	...
2 Purchases of land, net	...	...	...	...	...	...	...	...	...	...	...	...
3 Purchases of intangible assets, net	...	...	-1	2	-2	2	-84	26	48	-161	61	...
4 Capital transfers	...	...	10	-	-	52	62	77	-	-	-	...
Net lending	...	...	382	73	426	760	424	571	1906	715	621	...
Gross Accumulation	...	...	810	452	-295	2220	2877	3036	4524	4104	5444	...

a) Item 'Net saving' includes consumption of fixed capital.

3.44 Private Non-Profit Institutions Serving Households: Capital Finance Account
Million Portuguese escudos

	1970	1975	1978	1979	1980	1981	1982	1983	1984	1985	1986	1987
Acquisition of Financial Assets											
1 Gold	...	...	...	...	165	73	...	...	...	...	...	...
2 Currency and transferable deposits	...	...	477	-768	512	856	...	...	...	...	...	...
3 Other deposits	...	...	99	182	1013	678	...	...	...	...	...	...
4 Bills and bonds, short term	...	...	...	...	...	...	...	...	...	...	...	...
5 Bonds, long term	...	...	-90	-11	-130	698	...	...	...	...	...	...
6 Corporate equity securities	...	...	-20	87	231	-1139	...	...	...	...	...	...
7 Short-term loans, n.e.c.	...	...	31	291	266	68	...	...	...	...	...	...
8 Long-term loans, n.e.c.	...	...	-8	22	68	18	...	...	...	...	...	...
9 Other receivables	...	...	-	-	-	2	...	...	...	...	...	...
10 Proprietors' net additions to the accumulation of quasi-corporations	...	...					...	...	...	...	...	...
11 Other assets	...	...	-	1	1	1	...	...	...	...	...	...
Total Acquisition of Financial Assets	...	...	489	-196	2126	1255	...	...	...	...	...	...
Incurrence of Liabilities											
1 Short-term loans	...	...	14	97	1675	545	...	...	...	...	...	...
2 Long-term loans	...	...	54	-36	127	-95	...	...	...	...	...	...
3 Other liabilities	...	...	-	-	2	3	...	...	...	...	...	...
Total Incurrence of Liabilities	...	...	68	61	1804	453	...	...	...	...	...	...
Statistical discrepancy	...	...	39	-330	-104	42	...	...	...	...	...	...
Net Lending	...	...	382	73	426	760	...	...	...	...	...	...
Incurrence of Liabilities and Net Lending	...	...	489	-196	2126	1255	...	...	...	...	...	...

3.51 External Transactions: Current Account: Detail
Million Portuguese escudos

	1970	1975	1978	1979	1980	1981	1982	1983	1984	1985	1986	1987
Payments to the Rest of the World											
1 Imports of goods and services	53825	121050	256136	376265	528040	678536	832453	1014750	1272290	1458590	1578510	...
A Imports of merchandise c.i.f.	42764	99598	236361	345510	488209	630478	772651	939000	1171140	1356380	1469790	...
B Other	11061	21452	19775	30755	39831	48058	59802	75753	101153	102209	108722	...
2 Factor income to the rest of the world	1492	2644	19786	29313	41736	74865	119064	143080	209709	244978	204414	...

Portugal

3.51 External Transactions: Current Account: Detail
(Continued)

Million Portuguese escudos

	1970	1975	1978	1979	1980	1981	1982	1983	1984	1985	1986	1987
A Compensation of employees	1492	2644	1653	1962	2979	2533	3400	5064	6237	8121	11284	...
B Property and entrepreneurial income	...	...	18133	27351	38757	72332	115664	138016	203472	236857	193130	...
3 Current transfers to the rest of the world	547	1550	7511	7517	6864	5650	9263	13116	17367	21313	65689	...
A Indirect taxes by general government to supranational organizations			...	...	...	...	...	...	...	...	10313	...
B Other current transfers	547	1550	7511	7517	6864	5650	9263	13116	17367	21313	55376	...
By general government	158	1051	...	...	...	...	...	...	...	...	...	...
By other resident sectors	389	499	...	...	...	...	...	...	...	...	...	...
4 Surplus of the nation on current transactions	3373	-20866	-45051	-17245	-74697	-182524	-250630	-190695	-96674	12440	115519	...
Payments to the Rest of the World, and Surplus of the Nation on Current Transfers	59237	104378	238382	395850	501943	576527	710150	980254	1402690	1737320	1964140	...

Receipts From The Rest of the World

	1970	1975	1978	1979	1980	1981	1982	1983	1984	1985	1986	1987
1 Exports of goods and services	41742	74067	158369	268723	343950	389515	488482	721243	1048630	1315210	1466570	...
A Exports of merchandise f.o.b.	26596	49456	114514	193115	247564	275979	357465	536423	790234	1005290	1124170	...
B Other	15146	24611	43855	75608	96386	113536	131017	184820	258399	309924	342405	...
2 Factor income from the rest of the world	2381	2275	4098	6977	9158	12675	13077	19638	31724	48389	46699	...
A Compensation of employees	2381	2275	1042	1575	2041	2827	2836	4225	7222	12317	10947	...
B Property and entrepreneurial income	...	...	3056	5402	7117	9848	10241	15413	24502	36072	35752	...
3 Current transfers from the rest of the world	15114	28036	75915	120150	148835	174337	208591	239373	322333	373724	450863	...
A Subsidies to general government from supranational organizations	...	...	554	664	563	1095	...	...	...	...	18292	...
B Other current transfers	15114	28036	75361	119486	148272	173242	208591	239373	322333	373724	432571	...
To general government	90	74	...	...	...	...	...	...	...	...	...	...
To other resident sectors	15024	27962	...	...	...	...	...	...	...	...	...	...
Receipts from the Rest of the World on Current Transfers	59237	104378	238382	395850	501943	576527	710150	980254	1402690	1737320	1964140	...

Portugal

3.52 External Transactions: Capital Accumulation Account

Million Portuguese escudos

	1970	1975	1978	1979	1980	1981	1982	1983	1984	1985	1986	1987
Finance of Gross Accumulation												
1 Surplus of the nation on current transactions	3373	-20866	-45051	-17245	-74697	-182524	-250630	-190695	-96674	12440	115519	...
2 Capital transfers from the rest of the world	...	...	11	6	111	67	32	1191	3211	820	28732	...
Total Finance of Gross Accumulation	3373	-20866	-45040	-17239	-74586	-182457	-250598	-189504	-93463	13260	144251	...
Gross Accumulation												
1 Capital transfers to the rest of the world	...	...	528	1005	4407	5576	6903	9508	6450	9483	11157	...
2 Purchases of intangible assets, n.e.c., net, from the rest of the world a	...	...	-39	-62	-99	-161	-163	-224	-260	-328	-439	...
Net lending to the rest of the world	3373	-20866	-45529	-18182	-78894	-187872	-257338	-198788	-99653	4105	133533	...
Total Gross Accumulation	3373	-20866	-45040	-17239	-74586	-182457	-250598	-189504	-93463	13260	144251	...

a) Item 'Purchase of intangible assets, n.e.c. net, from the rest of the world' refers to sales of land.

3.53 External Transactions: Capital Finance Account

Million Portuguese escudos

	1970	1975	1978	1979	1980	1981	1982	1983	1984	1985	1986	1987
Acquisitions of Foreign Financial Assets												
1 Gold and SDR's a	...	...	-2401	-955	-3930	-2126	...	...	...	...	...	...
2 Currency and transferable deposits	...	...	477	-56	731	-54	...	...	...	...	...	...
3 Other deposits	...	...	3447	-1427	896	-409	...	...	...	...	...	...
4 Bills and bonds, short term	...	...	...	...	...	...	...	...	...	...	...	...
5 Bonds, long term	...	...	-556	-326	1480	326	...	...	...	...	...	...
6 Corporate equity securities	...	...	1977	2263	5010	7287	...	...	...	...	...	...
7 Short-term loans, n.e.c.	...	...	9972	-24889	38082	-3959	...	...	...	...	...	...
8 Long-term loans	...	...	32957	39884	52527	90219	...	...	...	...	...	...
9 Prprorietors' net additions to accumulation of quasi-corporate, non-resident enterprises	...	...	...	...	...	...	...	...	...	...	...	...
10 Trade credit and advances	...	...	...	...	...	...	...	...	...	...	...	...
11 Other	...	...	366	23799	-21717	72154	...	...	...	...	...	...
Total Acquisitions of Foreign Financial Assets	...	...	46239	38293	73079	163438	...	...	...	...	...	...
Incurrence of Foreign Liabilities												
1 Currency and transferable deposits	...	...	-4991	9003	8389	1010	...	...	...	...	...	...
2 Other deposits	...	...	20092	11742	-8791	-24015	...	...	...	...	...	...
3 Bills and bonds, short term	...	...	...	...	...	...	...	...	...	...	...	...
4 Bonds, long term	...	...	-68	-80	-27	1142	...	...	...	...	...	...
5 Corporate equity securities	...	...	236	-589	572	182	...	...	...	...	...	...
6 Short-term loans, n.e.c.	...	...	-875	-1607	7821	1801	...	...	...	...	...	...
7 Long-term loans	...	...	2571	2279	3327	1526	...	...	...	...	...	...
8 Non-resident proprietors' net additions to accumulation of resident quasi-corporate enterprises	...	...	...	...	...	...	...	...	...	...	...	...
9 Trade credit and advances	...	...	1273	11033	-2640	12884	...	...	...	...	...	...
10 Other	...	...	...	...	...	...	...	...	...	...	...	...
Total Incurrence of Liabilities	...	...	18238	31781	8651	-5470	...	...	...	...	...	...
Statistical discrepancy	...	...	-17528	-11670	-14466	-18964	...	...	...	...	...	...
Net Lending	...	...	45529	18182	78894	187872	...	...	...	...	...	...
Total Incurrence of Liabilities and Net Lending	...	...	46239	38293	73079	163438	...	...	...	...	...	...

a) Item 'Gold and SDRs' includes also foreign currency.

Portugal

4.1 Derivation of Value Added by Kind of Activity, in Current Prices

Million Portuguese escudos

	1980 Gross Output	1980 Intermediate Consumption	1980 Value Added	1981 Gross Output	1981 Intermediate Consumption	1981 Value Added	1982 Gross Output	1982 Intermediate Consumption	1982 Value Added	1983 Gross Output	1983 Intermediate Consumption	1983 Value Added
All Producers												
1 Agriculture, hunting, forestry and fishing	207060	77161	129899	231975	97415	134560	280383	117488	162895	339566	156245	183321
A Agriculture and hunting	159831	68681	91150	184398	88322	96076	230625	107887	122738	280378	143003	137375
B Forestry and logging	28168	1602	26566	25512	1493	24019	27512	1815	25697	31857	2468	29389
C Fishing	19061	6878	12183	22065	7600	14465	22246	7786	14460	27331	10774	16557
2 Mining and quarrying	1220980	831997	388982	1490830	1020670	470161	1820950	1275580	545369	2348610	1672870	675744
3 Manufacturing												
A Manufacture of food, beverages and tobacco	278005	206456	71549	342156	254654	87502	424373	317421	106952	560500	419087	141413
B Textile, wearing apparel and leather industries	238806	150905	87901	264679	164543	100136	310925	196090	114835	416902	266892	150010
C Manufacture of wood and wood products, including furniture	63260	38604	24656	66213	39730	26483	68751	41156	27595	83765	49476	34289
D Manufacture of paper and paper products, printing and publishing	55178	33780	21398	71701	43568	28133	83993	53164	30829	106952	69121	37831
E Manufacture of chemicals and chemical petroleum, coal, rubber and plastic products	223488	188349	35139	304681	261406	43275	408385	358595	49790	547016	482063	64953
F Manufacture of non-metallic mineral products, except products of petroleum and coal	62945	30448	32497	81362	40048	41314	98732	51103	47629	120487	63667	56820
G Basic metal industries	44549	33554	10995	46294	32838	13456	59194	40314	18880	73766	51682	22084
H Manufacture of fabricated metal products, machinery and equipment	195212	109728	85484	240359	135640	104719	281352	162004	119348	331039	197784	133255
I Other manufacturing industries	59536	40173	19363	73389	48246	25143	85243	55732	29511	108182	73093	35089
4 Electricity, gas and water	63786	37284	26502	89732	73635	16097	122612	89581	33031	186918	129588	57330
5 Construction	222967	134115	88852	287330	174308	113022	362236	212785	149451	438680	263483	175197
6 Wholesale and retail trade, restaurants and hotels	406779	134360	272419	491231	165041	326190	618855	202146	416709	771263	251076	520187
A Wholesale and retail trade	316344	81467	234877	382483	102327	280156	482964	125574	357390	600381	154560	445821
B Restaurants and hotels	90435	52893	37542	108748	62714	46034	135891	76572	59319	170882	96516	74366
7 Transport, storage and communication	133189	63848	69341	173399	79595	93804	217339	95654	121685	298564	132074	166490
A Transport and storage	109975	60666	49309	140876	75114	65762	178640	90096	88544	240514	124005	116509
B Communication	23214	3182	20032	32523	4481	28042	38699	5558	33141	58050	8069	49981
8 Finance, insurance, real estate and business services [a]	161666	30257	131409	207160	40598	166562	263906	52066	211840	328328	71761	256567
A Financial institutions	69580	7312	62268	96610	10334	86276	132724	13700	119024	166164	18104	148060
B Insurance	12784	5112	7672	15156	6342	8814	17435	7872	9563	22061	11477	10584
C Real estate and business services	79302	17833	61469	95394	23922	71472	113747	30494	83253	140103	42180	97923
Real estate, except dwellings	55119	12415	42704	70324	17051	53273	88076	21919	66157	113901	31255	82646
Dwellings	24183	5418	18765	25070	6871	18199	25671	8575	17096	26202	10925	15277
9 Community, social and personal services [ab]	42172	11963	30209	56231	15220	41011	71907	19045	52862	91539	24433	67106
A Sanitary and similar services	...	...	...	...	...	...	...	...	...	...	...	...
B Social and related community services	24591	5743	18848	33563	7326	26237	44625	9052	35573	59201	12239	46962
Educational services	7605	2135	5470	10570	2701	7869	14537	3165	11372	18701	3848	14853
Medical, dental, other health and veterinary services	16986	3608	13378	22993	4625	18368	30088	5887	24201	40500	8391	32109
C Recreational and cultural services	17581	6220	11361	22668	7894	14774	27282	9993	17289	32338	12194	20144
D Personal and household services	...	...	...	...	...	...	...	...	...	...	...	...
Total, Industries	2458600	1320990	1137610	3027890	1666490	1361410	3758190	2064340	1693840	4803470	2701530	2101940
Producers of Government Services	192613	47930	144683	238223	61498	176725	292617	77959	214658	369760	100623	269137
Other Producers	16185	2903	13282	19727	3348	16379	22976	3856	19120	28649	5198	23451
Total	2667400	1371820	1295580	3285840	1731330	1554510	4073780	2146160	1927620	5201880	2807350	2394530
Less: Imputed bank service charge	...	-55553	55553	...	-77588	77588	...	-107420	107420	...	-135775	135775
Import duties	16026	...	16026	24208	...	24208	30207	...	30207	42958	...	42958
Value added tax	...	...	...	...	...	...	...	...	...	...	...	...

Portugal

4.1 Derivation of Value Added by Kind of Activity, in Current Prices
(Continued)

Million Portuguese escudos

	1980			1981			1982			1983		
	Gross Output	Intermediate Consumption	Value Added	Gross Output	Intermediate Consumption	Value Added	Gross Output	Intermediate Consumption	Value Added	Gross Output	Intermediate Consumption	Value Added
Total	2683420	1427370	1256050	3310050	1808920	1501130	4103990	2253580	1850410	5244830	2943120	2301710
Memorandum Item: Mineral fuels and power	169728	140074	29654	250540	229717	20823	...	...	...	...	...	...

of which General Government:

	1980			1981			1982			1983		
1 Agriculture, hunting, forestry and fishing	...	...	...	...	...	...	...	...	...	...	...	...
2 Mining and quarrying	...	...	...	...	...	...	...	...	...	...	...	...
3 Manufacturing	...	...	...	...	...	...	...	...	...	...	...	...
4 Electricity, gas and water	1040	554	486	1291	373	918	...	...	...	...	...	...
5 Construction	46	28	18	190	44	146	...	...	...	...	...	...
6 Wholesale and retail trade, restaurants and hotels	67	4	63	52	5	47	...	...	...	...	...	...
7 Transport and communication	...	...	...	...	...	...	...	...	...	...	...	...
8 Finance, insurance, real estate and business services	5886	236	5650	7293	240	7053	...	...	...	...	...	...
9 Community, social and personal services	-	-	-	43	4	39	...	...	...	...	...	...
Total, Industries of General Government	7039	822	6217	8869	666	8203	...	...	...	...	...	...
Producers of Government Services	...	...	...	...	...	...	...	...	...	...	...	...
Total, General Government	...	...	...	...	...	...	...	...	...	...	...	...

	1984			1985			1986		
	Gross Output	Intermediate Consumption	Value Added	Gross Output	Intermediate Consumption	Value Added	Gross Output	Intermediate Consumption	Value Added

All Producers

	Gross Output 1984	Interm. Cons. 1984	Value Added 1984	Gross Output 1985	Interm. Cons. 1985	Value Added 1985	Gross Output 1986	Interm. Cons. 1986	Value Added 1986
1 Agriculture, hunting, forestry and fishing	441288	206840	234448	523700	242497	281203	605377	276655	328722
A Agriculture and hunting	365278	189120	176158	426931	219354	207577	489254	251511	237743
B Forestry and logging	41628	3490	38138	55426	4469	50957	63260	4760	58500
C Fishing	34382	14230	20152	41343	18674	22669	52863	20384	32479
2 Mining and quarrying	2967990	2105880	862101	3603010	2532390	1070630	3833800	2543670	1290120
3 Manufacturing									
A Manufacture of food, beverages and tobacco	685427	513014	172413	846959	633180	213779	946673	703641	243032
B Textile, wearing apparel and leather industries	588278	378452	209826	744412	468101	276311	857189	502718	354471
C Manufacture of wood and wood products, including furniture	101471	62207	39264	120963	76139	44824	143322	89134	54188
D Manufacture of paper and paper products, printing and publishing	153617	94164	59453	187849	120693	67156	215580	129347	86233
E Manufacture of chemicals and chemical petroleum, coal, rubber and plastic products	693952	602524	91428	813273	697977	115296	673606	531982	141624
F Manufacture of non-metallic mineral products, except products of petroleum and coal	138609	74436	64173	157225	82838	74387	178730	87903	90827
G Basic metal industries	89323	64400	24923	102524	72369	30155	104528	67286	37242
H Manufacture of fabricated metal products, machinery and equipment	389362	233986	155376	479365	280405	198960	527957	312036	215921
I Other manufacturing industries	127946	82701	45245	150442	100684	49758	186210	119627	66583
4 Electricity, gas and water	240068	148301	91767	288603	165554	123049	336227	199820	136407
5 Construction	461899	295058	166841	528516	328148	200368	605458	359738	245720
6 Wholesale and retail trade, restaurants and hotels	929656	314484	615172	1168390	379844	788545	1382040	433496	948541
A Wholesale and retail trade	712566	190215	522351	902426	231886	670540	1082010	264698	817310
B Restaurants and hotels	217090	124269	92821	265963	147958	118005	300029	168798	131231
7 Transport, storage and communication	386698	172513	214185	470434	198172	272262	503256	206122	297134
A Transport and storage	312898	160953	151945	372729	183607	189122	393123	190132	202991
B Communication	73800	11560	62240	97705	14565	83140	110133	15990	94143
8 Finance, insurance, real estate and business services [a]	385082	94976	290106	476473	119020	357453	566135	139056	427079
A Financial institutions	178728	24288	154440	224938	30050	194888	275461	40091	235370

Portugal

4.1 Derivation of Value Added by Kind of Activity, in Current Prices
(Continued)

Million Portuguese escudos

	1984 Gross Output	1984 Intermediate Consumption	1984 Value Added	1985 Gross Output	1985 Intermediate Consumption	1985 Value Added	1986 Gross Output	1986 Intermediate Consumption	1986 Value Added
B Insurance	32568	16519	16049	41659	21367	20292	43602	23581	20021
C Real estate and business services	173786	54169	119617	209876	67603	142273	247072	75384	171688
Real estate, except dwellings	146753	40486	106267	182491	51029	131462	212420	56041	156379
Dwellings	27033	13683	13350	27385	16574	10811	34652	19343	15309
9 Community, social and personal services ab	116992	31698	85294	151927	38961	112966	182890	43656	139234
A Sanitary and similar services	...	...	...	...	...	...	...	...	...
B Social and related community services	77211	16168	61043	100377	19457	80920	122202	20886	101316
Educational services	26123	5249	20874	33462	6058	27404	40952	6745	34207
Medical, dental, other health and veterinary services	51088	10919	40169	66915	13399	53516	81250	14141	67109
C Recreational and cultural services	39781	15530	24251	51550	19504	32046	60688	22770	37918
D Personal and household services	...	...	...	...	...	...	...	...	...
Total, Industries	5929670	3369750	2559910	7211050	4004580	3206470	8015180	4202220	3812960
Producers of Government Services	449032	121708	327324	584345	174065	410280	721591	222460	499131
Other Producers	34707	6363	28344	42043	7727	34316	47709	8910	38799
Total	6413410	3497830	2915580	7837440	4186370	3651070	8784480	4433590	4350890
Less: Imputed bank service charge	...	-139753	139753	...	-179388	179388	...	-222787	222787
Import duties	39899	...	39899	52265	...	52265	54802	...	54802
Value added tax	...	...	...	...	...	...	237497	...	237497
Total	6453310	3637580	2815730	7889710	4365760	3523950	9076770	4656370	4420400
Memorandum Item: Mineral fuels and power	...	...	...	...	...	...	...	...	...
of which General Government:									
1 Agriculture, hunting, forestry and fishing	...	...	...	...	...	...	...	...	...
2 Mining and quarrying	...	...	...	...	...	...	...	...	...
3 Manufacturing	...	...	...	...	...	...	...	...	...
4 Electricity, gas and water	...	...	...	...	...	...	...	...	...
5 Construction	...	...	...	...	...	...	...	...	...
6 Wholesale and retail trade, restaurants and hotels	...	...	...	...	...	...	...	...	...
7 Transport and communication	...	...	...	...	...	...	...	...	...
8 Finance, insurance, real estate and business services	...	...	...	...	...	...	...	...	...
9 Community, social and personal services	...	...	...	...	...	...	...	...	...
Total, Industries of General Government	...	...	...	...	...	...	...	...	...
Producers of Government Services	...	...	...	...	...	...	...	...	...
Total, General Government	...	...	...	...	...	...	...	...	...

a) Business services and real estate except dwellings are included in item 'Community, social and personal services'.
b) Repair services are included in item 'Community, social and personal services'.

4.2 Derivation of Value Added by Kind of Activity, in Constant Prices

Million Portuguese escudos

	1980 Gross Output	1980 Intermediate Consumption	1980 Value Added	1981 Gross Output	1981 Intermediate Consumption	1981 Value Added
	At constant prices of: 1977					
	All Producers					
1 Agriculture, hunting, forestry and fishing	...	...	97420	...	...	87140
A Agriculture and hunting	...	...	78240	...	...	71410
B Forestry and logging	...	...	12780	...	...	10180
C Fishing	...	...	6330	...	...	6150

Portugal

4.2 Derivation of Value Added by Kind of Activity, in Constant Prices
(Continued)

Million Portuguese escudos

	1980 Gross Output	1980 Intermediate Consumption	1980 Value Added	1981 Gross Output	1981 Intermediate Consumption	1981 Value Added
			At constant prices of: 1977			
2 Mining and quarrying	...	...	[204120	...	...	209050]
3 Manufacturing	...	...		...	...	
A Manufacture of food, beverages and tobacco	...	...	38030	...	...	39160
B Textile, wearing apparel and leather industries	...	...	43390	...	...	44510
C Manufacture of wood and wood products, including furniture	...	...	11700	...	...	10200
D Manufacture of paper and paper products, printing and publishing	...	...	11900	...	...	12080
E Manufacture of chemicals and chemical petroleum, coal, rubber and plastic products	...	...	19410	...	...	20960
F Manufacture of non-metallic mineral products, except products of petroleum and coal	...	...	18660	...	...	19960
G Basic metal industries	...	...	6300	...	...	6420
H Manufacture of fabricated metal products, machinery and equipment	...	...	43270	...	...	43980
I Other manufacturing industries	...	...	11240	...	...	11920
4 Electricity, gas and water	...	...	11000	...	...	8990
5 Construction	...	...	57670	...	...	60380
6 Wholesale and retail trade, restaurants and hotels	...	...	143260	...	...	145860
A Wholesale and retail trade	...	...	126030	...	...	128450
B Restaurants and hotels	...	...	17270	...	...	17460
7 Transport, storage and communication	...	...	41820	...	...	42550
A Transport and storage	...	...	30380	...	...	30500
B Communication	...	...	11520	...	...	12110
8 Finance, insurance, real estate and business services [a]	...	...	75550	...	...	79170
A Financial institutions	...	...	32250	...	...	35600
B Insurance	...	...	3480	...	...	3300
C Real estate and business services	...	...	39980	...	...	40130
Real estate, except dwellings	...	...	22780	...	...	22640
Dwellings	...	...	16930	...	...	17360
9 Community, social and personal services [ab]	...	...	15640	...	...	16220
A Sanitary and similar services	...	...	...	...	...	...
B Social and related community services	...	...	10380	...	...	10870
Educational services	...	...	3330	...	...	3450
Medical, dental, other health and veterinary services	...	...	7070	...	...	7440
C Recreational and cultural services	...	...	5320	...	...	5420
D Personal and household services	...	...	...	...	...	...
Statistical discrepancy	...	...	...	...	...	2020
Total, Industries	...	...	646480	...	...	651380
Producers of Government Services	...	...	86090	...	...	90530
Other Producers	...	...	7350	...	...	7580
Total	...	...	739920	...	...	749490
Less: Imputed bank service charge	...	...	28400	...	...	31510
Import duties	...	...	8560	...	...	11480
Value added tax	...	...	...	...	...	...
Other adjustments	...	...	-260	...	...	-560
Total	...	...	719820	...	...	728900

a) Business services and real estate except dwellings are included in item 'Community, social and personal services'.
b) Repair services are included in item 'Community, social and personal services'.

Portugal

4.3 Cost Components of Value Added

Million Portuguese escudos

		1980					1981				
	Compensation of Employees	Capital Consumption	Net Operating Surplus	Indirect Taxes	Less: Subsidies Received	Value Added	Compensation of Employees	Capital Consumption	Net Operating Surplus	Indirect Taxes	Less: Subsidies Received	Value Added

All Producers

	Comp. Emp. 1980	Cap. Cons. 1980	Net Op. Surp. 1980	Ind. Tax 1980	Subs. 1980	VA 1980	Comp. Emp. 1981	Cap. Cons. 1981	Net Op. Surp. 1981	Ind. Tax 1981	Subs. 1981	VA 1981
1 Agriculture, hunting, forestry and fishing		...						...				
A Agriculture and hunting		...						...				
B Forestry and logging	26602	...	102532	1967	1202	129899	28767	...	104991	2267	1465	134560
C Fishing		...						...				
2 Mining and quarrying		...						...				
3 Manufacturing	205666	...	147691	51761	16136	388982	249307	...	177908	62781	19835	470161
A Manufacture of food, beverages and tobacco	24094	...	33164	20154	5863	71549	29705	...	39003	25140	6346	87502
B Textile, wearing apparel and leather industries	59750	...	24787	3808	444	87901	69402	...	27194	4526	986	100136
C Manufacture of wood and wood products, including furniture	12560	...	10782	1392	78	24656	14379	...	10474	1734	104	26483
D Manufacture of paper and paper products, printing and publishing	10128	...	10280	1283	293	21398	12659	...	14180	1762	468	28133
E Manufacture of chemicals and chemical petroleum, coal, rubber and plastic products	18213	...	14578	9320	6972	35139	22814	...	18096	9850	7485	43275
F Manufacture of non-metallic mineral products, except products of petroleum and coal	16106	...	14745	1776	130	32497	19797	...	19479	2434	396	41314
G Basic metal industries	6938	...	3679	569	191	10995	8581	...	4465	688	278	13456
H Manufacture of fabricated metal products, machinery and equipment	48060	...	26767	12780	2123	85484	60245	...	32885	15292	3703	104719
I Other manufacturing industries	9817	...	8909	679	42	19363	11725	...	12132	1355	69	25143
4 Electricity, gas and water	10845	...	15283	741	367	26502	13668	...	2118	1127	816	16097
5 Construction	60010	...	26604	2716	478	88852	75583	...	37837	3242	3640	113022
6 Wholesale and retail trade, restaurants and hotels	78550	...	149210	81165	36506	272419	96742	...	181258	92700	44510	326190
A Wholesale and retail trade	67412	...	124177	79744	36456	234877	82656	...	150875	90861	44236	280156
B Restaurants and hotels	11138	...	25033	1421	50	37542	14086	...	30383	1839	274	46034
7 Transport, storage and communication	55680	...	17245	3914	7498	69341	70769	...	25935	4667	7567	93804
A Transport and storage	42264	...	11638	2802	7395	49309	53557	...	16751	2968	7514	65762
B Communication	13416	...	5607	1112	103	20032	17212	...	9184	1699	53	28042
8 Finance, insurance, real estate and business services [a]	37119	...	82083	14649	2442	131409	46973	...	103887	18525	2823	166562
A Financial institutions	22991	...	31955	7362	40	62268	29397	...	47504	9375	-	86276
B Insurance	6231	...	-861	2302	-	7672	7518	...	-1802	3098	-	8814
C Real estate and business services	7897	...	50989	4985	2402	61469	10058	...	58185	6052	2823	71472
Real estate, except dwellings	7816	...	30743	4839	694	42704	9971	...	38143	5895	736	53273
Dwellings	81	...	20246	146	1708	18765	87	...	20042	157	2087	18199
9 Community, social and personal services [ab]	10594	...	16446	3911	742	30209	13754	...	22541	5488	772	41011
A Sanitary and similar services	...	...	...	...	...	...	...	...	...	...	...	...
B Social and related community services	5479	...	13120	253	4	18848	7131	...	18782	371	47	26237
Educational services	2525	...	2853	94	2	5470	3206	...	4536	138	11	7869
Medical, dental, other health and veterinary services	2954	...	10267	159	2	13378	3925	...	14246	233	36	18368
C Recreational and cultural services	5115	...	3326	3658	738	11361	6623	...	3759	5117	725	14774
D Personal and household services	...	...	...	...	...	...	...	...	...	...	...	...
Total, Industries [c]	485066	...	557094	160824	65371	1137610	595563	...	656475	190797	81428	1361410
Producers of Government Services	144647	...	-	36	-	144683	176711	...	-	14	-	176725
Other Producers	13253	...	-	29	-	13282	16325	...	-	54	-	16379
Total [c]	642966	...	557094	160889	65371	1295580	788599	...	656475	190865	81428	1554510
Less: Imputed bank service charge	...	55553	...	...	...	55553	...	77588	...	...	...	77588
Import duties	...	...	...	16026	...	16026	...	...	...	24208	...	24208
Value added tax	...	...	...	...	...	...	...	...	...	...	...	...
Total	642966	...	501541	176915	65371	1256050	788599	...	578887	215073	81428	1501130

Portugal

4.3 Cost Components of Value Added
(Continued)

Million Portuguese escudos

1980 / 1981

of which General Government:

	Compensation of Employees	Capital Consumption	Net Operating Surplus	Indirect Taxes	Less: Subsidies Received	Value Added	Compensation of Employees	Capital Consumption	Net Operating Surplus	Indirect Taxes	Less: Subsidies Received	Value Added
1 Agriculture, hunting, forestry and fishing	...	...	...	...	...	...	...	...	...	...	...	...
2 Mining and quarrying	...	...	...	...	...	...	...	...	...	...	...	...
3 Manufacturing	...	...	...	...	...	...	...	...	...	...	...	...
4 Electricity, gas and water	417	...	78	8	17	486	616	...	337	6	30	918
5 Construction	17	...	1	-	-	18	-	...	-	-	-	146
6 Wholesale and retail trade, restaurants and hotels	21	...	42	-	-	63	21	...	26	-	-	47
7 Transport and communication	...	...	...	...	...	...	...	...	...	...	...	...
8 Finance, insurance, real estate & business services	564	...	971	4144	29	5650	699	...	1142	5177	16	7053
9 Community, social and personal services	-	...	-	-	-	-	20	...	205	-	-	39
Total, Industries of General Government	1019	...	1092	4152	46	6217	1356	...	1710	5183	46	8203
Producers of Government Services	...	...	...	...	...	...	...	...	...	...	...	...
Total, General Government	...	...	...	...	...	...	...	...	...	...	...	...

1982 / 1983

All Producers

	Compensation of Employees	Capital Consumption	Net Operating Surplus	Indirect Taxes	Less: Subsidies Received	Value Added	Compensation of Employees	Capital Consumption	Net Operating Surplus	Indirect Taxes	Less: Subsidies Received	Value Added
1 Agriculture, hunting, forestry and fishing		...						...				
A Agriculture and hunting		...						...				
B Forestry and logging	31619	...	130709	3139	2572	162895	36087	...	146201	3261	2228	183321
C Fishing		...						...				
2 Mining and quarrying		...						...				
3 Manufacturing	300070	...	198057	74814	27572	545369	356048	...	255406	93282	28992	675744
A Manufacture of food, beverages and tobacco	35527	...	46629	31116	6320	106952	42685	...	68301	38656	8229	141413
B Textile, wearing apparel and leather industries	81044	...	29115	5824	1148	114835	99129	...	44742	7211	1072	150010
C Manufacture of wood and wood products, including furniture	16387	...	10266	1076	134	27595	18835	...	13269	2323	138	34289
D Manufacture of paper and paper products, printing and publishing	15754	...	14286	1255	466	30829	19584	...	16112	2655	520	37831
E Manufacture of chemicals and chemical petroleum, coal, rubber and plastic products	28478	...	24236	12336	15260	49790	34501	...	27801	14417	11766	64953
F Manufacture of non-metallic mineral products, except products of petroleum and coal	24098	...	20948	2994	411	47629	28350	...	26147	3595	1272	56820
G Basic metal industries	10949	...	7241	904	214	18880	12182	...	9118	1000	216	22084
H Manufacture of fabricated metal products, machinery and equipment	73335	...	31827	17677	3491	119348	83196	...	34283	21437	5661	133255
I Other manufacturing industries	14498	...	13509	1632	128	29511	17586	...	15633	1988	118	35089
4 Electricity, gas and water	17616	...	14696	1830	1111	33031	22406	...	33433	2050	559	57330
5 Construction	98862	...	46926	4200	537	149451	122016	...	51078	5022	2919	175197
6 Wholesale and retail trade, restaurants and hotels	114654	...	213701	119906	31552	416709	137672	...	271379	156974	45838	520187
A Wholesale and retail trade	97405	...	173332	117646	30993	357390	116755	...	220542	153766	45242	445821
B Restaurants and hotels	17249	...	40369	2260	559	59319	20917	...	50837	3208	596	74366
7 Transport, storage and communication	89235	...	36463	5872	9885	121685	107223	...	57122	8779	6634	166490
A Transport and storage	67112	...	27052	4222	9842	88544	79770	...	36899	6473	6633	116509
B Communication	22123	...	9411	1650	43	33141	27453	...	20223	2306	1	49981
8 Finance, insurance, real estate and business services [a]	60271	...	128957	28149	5537	211840	78298	...	145292	36879	3902	256567
A Financial institutions	37908	...	64782	16334	-	119024	51391	...	74180	22489	-	148060
B Insurance	9589	...	-4237	4211	-	9563	11957	...	-6229	4858	2	10584
C Real estate and business services	12774	...	68412	7604	5537	83253	14950	...	77341	9532	3900	97923
Real estate, except dwellings	12679	...	49776	7449	3747	66157	14845	...	61912	9366	3477	82646

Portugal

4.3 Cost Components of Value Added
(Continued)

Million Portuguese escudos

	1982						1983					
	Compensation of Employees	Capital Consumption	Net Operating Surplus	Indirect Taxes	Less: Subsidies Received	Value Added	Compensation of Employees	Capital Consumption	Net Operating Surplus	Indirect Taxes	Less: Subsidies Received	Value Added
Dwellings	95	...	18636	155	1790	17096	105	...	15429	166	423	15277
9 Community, social and personal services [ab]	17570	...	28947	7181	836	52862	21943	...	36699	9188	724	67106
A Sanitary and similar services	...	...	...	...	...	...	...	...	...	...	...	...
B Social and related community services	9432	...	25673	489	21	35573	11988	...	34261	720	7	46962
Educational services	3945	...	7268	180	21	11372	4917	...	9700	243	7	14853
Medical, dental, other health and veterinary services	5487	...	18405	309	-	24201	7071	...	24561	477	-	32109
C Recreational and cultural services	8138	...	3274	6692	815	17289	9955	...	2438	8468	717	20144
D Personal and household services	...	...	...	...	...	...	...	...	...	...	...	...
Total, Industries [c]	729897	...	798456	245091	79602	1693840	881693	...	996610	315435	91796	2101940
Producers of Government Services	214636	...	-	22	-	214658	269114	...	-	23	-	269137
Other Producers	19043	...	-	77	-	19120	23360	...	-	91	-	23451
Total [c]	963576	...	798456	245190	79602	1927620	1174170	...	996610	315549	91796	2394530
Less: Imputed bank service charge	...	...	107420	...	...	107420	...	...	135775	...	...	135775
Import duties	...	...	...	30207	...	30207	...	...	...	42958	...	42958
Value added tax	...	...	...	...	...	...	...	...	...	...	...	...
Total	963576	...	691036	275397	79602	1850410	1174170	...	660835	358507	91796	2301710

of which General Government:

1 Agriculture, hunting, forestry and fishing	...	...	...	...	...	...	...	...	...	...	...	...
2 Mining and quarrying	...	...	...	...	...	...	...	...	...	...	...	...
3 Manufacturing	...	...	...	...	...	...	...	...	...	...	...	...
4 Electricity, gas and water	...	...	...	...	...	...	...	...	...	...	...	...
5 Construction	...	...	...	...	...	...	...	...	...	...	...	...
6 Wholesale and retail trade, restaurants and hotels	...	...	...	...	...	...	...	...	...	...	...	...
7 Transport and communication	...	...	...	...	...	...	...	...	...	...	...	...
8 Finance, insurance, real estate & business services	...	...	...	...	...	...	...	...	...	...	...	...
9 Community, social and personal services	...	...	...	...	...	...	...	...	...	...	...	...
Total, Industries of General Government	...	...	...	...	...	...	...	...	...	...	...	...
Producers of Government Services	...	...	...	...	...	...	...	...	...	...	...	...
Total, General Government	...	...	...	...	...	...	...	...	...	...	...	...

	1984						1985					
	Compensation of Employees	Capital Consumption	Net Operating Surplus	Indirect Taxes	Less: Subsidies Received	Value Added	Compensation of Employees	Capital Consumption	Net Operating Surplus	Indirect Taxes	Less: Subsidies Received	Value Added

All Producers

1 Agriculture, hunting, forestry and fishing		...						...				
A Agriculture and hunting	42110	...	189564	5584	2810	234448	49707	...	238113	6182	12799	281203
B Forestry and logging		...						...				
C Fishing		...						...				
2 Mining and quarrying												

Portugal

4.3 Cost Components of Value Added
(Continued)

Million Portuguese escudos

		1984					1985				
	Compensation of Employees	Capital Consumption	Net Operating Surplus	Indirect Taxes	Less: Subsidies Received	Value Added	Compensation of Employees	Capital Consumption	Net Operating Surplus	Indirect Taxes	Less: Subsidies Received	Value Added
3 Manufacturing	414094	...	372516	113292	37801	862101	496839	...	484858	137739	48810	1070630
A Manufacture of food, beverages and tobacco	49467	...	82959	46591	6604	172413	58216	...	105432	56445	6314	213779
B Textile, wearing apparel and leather industries	115905	...	86353	9097	1529	209826	142803	...	122650	12661	1803	276311
C Manufacture of wood and wood products, including furniture	21203	...	15516	2755	210	39264	25057	...	16450	3590	273	44824
D Manufacture of paper and paper products, printing and publishing	24323	...	32056	3881	807	59453	28069	...	35324	4631	868	67156
E Manufacture of chemicals and chemical petroleum, coal, rubber and plastic products	41016	...	47051	19604	16243	91428	49766	...	68072	22154	24696	115296
F Manufacture of non-metallic mineral products, except products of petroleum and coal	31877	...	29227	4040	971	64173	35953	...	35127	4756	1449	74387
G Basic metal industries	14045	...	9668	1460	250	24923	17564	...	11209	1863	481	30155
H Manufacture of fabricated metal products, machinery and equipment	95274	...	47968	23166	11032	155376	114073	...	69201	28394	12708	198960
I Other manufacturing industries	20984	...	21718	2698	155	45245	25338	...	21393	3245	218	49758
4 Electricity, gas and water	31353	...	58942	2788	1316	91767	37862	...	81900	4215	928	123049
5 Construction	124809	...	37889	5396	1253	166841	139494	...	54071	7833	1030	200368
6 Wholesale and retail trade, restaurants and hotels	168214	...	312312	195909	61263	615172	200467	...	398707	235116	45745	788545
A Wholesale and retail trade	143454	...	248348	191210	60661	522351	172057	...	314491	228962	44970	670540
B Restaurants and hotels	24760	...	63964	4699	602	92821	28410	...	84216	6154	775	118005
7 Transport, storage and communication	128669	...	83116	11989	9589	214185	152318	...	119110	14184	13350	272262
A Transport and storage	95140	...	57355	8976	9526	151945	111605	...	80981	9859	13323	189122
B Communication	33529	...	25761	3013	63	62240	40713	...	38129	4325	27	83140
8 Finance, insurance, real estate and business services [a]	95455	...	149930	49982	5261	290106	118384	...	183295	58765	2991	357453
A Financial institutions	63043	...	62031	32672	3306	154440	78974	...	79135	36779	-	194888
B Insurance	14379	...	-5143	6813	-	16049	18497	...	-6245	8040	-	20292
C Real estate and business services	18033	...	93042	10497	1955	119617	20913	...	110405	13946	2991	142273
Real estate, except dwellings	17909	...	79549	10290	1481	106267	20766	...	99635	13730	2669	131462
Dwellings	124	...	13493	207	474	13350	147	...	10770	216	322	10811
9 Community, social and personal services [ab]	25701	...	48700	11701	808	85294	30194	...	66440	17807	1475	112966
A Sanitary and similar services	...	...	...	...	...	...	...	...	...	...	...	...
B Social and related community services	14084	...	45946	1018	5	61043	15987	...	63680	1289	36	80920
Educational services	5657	...	14850	369	2	20874	5912	...	21054	468	30	27404
Medical, dental, other health and veterinary services	8427	...	31096	649	3	40169	10075	...	42626	821	6	53516
C Recreational and cultural services	11617	...	2754	10683	803	24251	14207	...	2760	16518	1439	32046
D Personal and household services	...	...	...	...	...	...	...	...	...	...	...	...
Total, Industries [c]	1030410	...	1252970	396641	120101	2559910	1225270	...	1626490	481841	127128	3206470
Producers of Government Services	327301	...	-	23	-	327324	410253	...	-	27	-	410280
Other Producers	28146	...	-	198	-	28344	34289	...	-	27	-	34316
Total [c]	1385850	...	1252970	396862	120101	2915580	1669810	...	1626490	481895	127128	3651070
Less: Imputed bank service charge	...	...	139753	...	...	139753	...	...	179388	...	...	179388
Import duties	...	...	...	39899	...	39899	...	...	...	52265	...	52265
Value added tax	...	...	...	...	...	...	...	...	...	...	...	...
Total	1385850	...	1113220	436761	120101	2815730	1669810	...	1447110	534160	127128	3523950

of which General Government:

1 Agriculture, hunting, forestry and fishing	...	...	...	...	...	...	...	...	...	...	...	...
2 Mining and quarrying	...	...	...	...	...	...	...	...	...	...	...	...
3 Manufacturing	...	...	...	...	...	...	...	...	...	...	...	...
4 Electricity, gas and water	...	...	...	...	...	...	...	...	...	...	...	...

Portugal

4.3 Cost Components of Value Added
(Continued)

Million Portuguese escudos

	1984						1985					
	Compensation of Employees	Capital Consumption	Net Operating Surplus	Indirect Taxes	Less: Subsidies Received	Value Added	Compensation of Employees	Capital Consumption	Net Operating Surplus	Indirect Taxes	Less: Subsidies Received	Value Added
5 Construction	...	...	...	...	...	...	...	...	...	...	...	...
6 Wholesale and retail trade, restaurants and hotels	...	...	...	...	...	...	...	...	...	...	...	...
7 Transport and communication	...	...	...	...	...	...	...	...	...	...	...	...
8 Finance, insurance, real estate & business services	...	...	...	...	...	...	...	...	...	...	...	...
9 Community, social and personal services	...	...	...	...	...	...	...	...	...	...	...	...
Total, Industries of General Government	...	...	...	...	...	...	...	...	...	...	...	...
Producers of Government Services	...	...	...	...	...	...	...	...	...	...	...	...
Total, General Government	...	...	...	...	...	...	...	...	...	...	...	...

	1986						
	Compensation of Employees	Capital Consumption	Net Operating Surplus	Indirect Taxes	Less: Subsidies Received	Value Added
			All Producers			
1 Agriculture, hunting, forestry and fishing		...				
A Agriculture and hunting		...				
B Forestry and logging	56061	...	283089	4341	14769	328722
C Fishing		...				
2 Mining and quarrying		...				
3 Manufacturing	598170	...	640727	111768	60544	1290120
A Manufacture of food, beverages and tobacco	69755	...	139563	50312	16598	243032
B Textile, wearing apparel and leather industries	180288	...	166261	9912	1990	354471
C Manufacture of wood and wood products, including furniture	30835	...	23153	1911	1711	54188
D Manufacture of paper and paper products, printing and publishing	34374	...	50632	2263	1036	86233
E Manufacture of chemicals and chemical petroleum, coal, rubber and plastic products	59676	...	81498	24279	23829	141624
F Manufacture of non-metallic mineral products, except products of petroleum and coal	43173	...	47912	2143	2401	90827
G Basic metal industries	20194	...	20113	1416	4481	37242
H Manufacture of fabricated metal products, machinery and equipment	128831	...	77664	17652	8226	215921
I Other manufacturing industries	31044	...	33931	1880	272	66583
4 Electricity, gas and water	42587	...	92208	3574	1962	136407
5 Construction	165377	...	77026	6064	2747	245720
6 Wholesale and retail trade, restaurants and hotels	244578	...	462776	262796	21609	948541
A Wholesale and retail trade	209291	...	369315	259651	20947	817310
B Restaurants and hotels	35287	...	93461	3145	662	131231
7 Transport, storage and communication	181785	...	143337	6794	34782	297134
A Transport and storage	130627	...	100645	6177	34458	202991
B Communication	51158	...	42692	617	324	94143
8 Finance, insurance, real estate and business services [a]	144786	...	218236	70332	6275	427079
A Financial institutions	96521	...	93848	45009	8	235370
B insurance	22445	...	-12224	9801	1	20021
C Real estate and business services	25820	...	136612	15522	6266	171688
Real estate, except dwellings	25640	...	121095	15370	5726	156379
Dwellings	180	...	15517	152	540	15309
9 Community, social and personal services [ab]	38179	...	87714	20003	6662	139234
A Sanitary and similar services	...	...	...	...	...	...
B Social and related community services	20029	...	82754	1139	2606	101316

Portugal

4.3 Cost Components of Value Added
(Continued)

Million Portuguese escudos

	1986					
	Compensation of Employees	Capital Consumption	Net Operating Surplus	Indirect Taxes	Less: Subsidies Received	Value Added
Educational services	7374	...	28419	398	1984	34207
Medical, dental, other health and veterinary services	12655	...	54335	741	622	67109
C Recreational and cultural services	18150	...	4960	18864	4056	37918
D Personal and household services	...	...	...	...	...	...
Total, Industries c	1471520	...	2005110	485672	149350	3812960
Producers of Government Services	499084	...	-	47	-	499131
Other Producers	38628	...	-	171	-	38799
Total c	2009240	...	2005110	485890	149350	4350890
Less: Imputed bank service charge	...	...	222787	...	...	222787
Import duties	...	...	...	54802	...	54802
Value added tax	...	...	...	237497	...	237497
Total	2009240	...	1782330	778189	149350	4420400
of which General Government:						
1 Agriculture, hunting, forestry and fishing	...	...	...	...	...	...
2 Mining and quarrying	...	...	...	...	...	...
3 Manufacturing	...	...	...	...	...	...
4 Electricity, gas and water	...	...	...	...	...	...
5 Construction	...	...	...	...	...	...
6 Wholesale and retail trade, restaurants and hotels	...	...	...	...	...	...
7 Transport and communication	...	...	...	...	...	...
8 Finance, insurance, real estate & business services	...	...	...	...	...	...
9 Community, social and personal services	...	...	...	...	...	...
Total, Industries of General Government	...	...	...	...	...	...
Producers of Government Services	...	...	...	...	...	...
Total, General Government	...	...	...	...	...	...

a) Business services and real estate except dwellings are included in item 'Community, social and personal services'.
b) Repair services are included in item 'Community, social and personal services'.
c) Column 'Consumption of fixed capital' is included in column 'Net operating surplus'.

Puerto Rico

General note. The preparation of national accounts statistics in Puerto Rico is undertaken by the Puerto Rico Planning Board, San Juan. The official estimates are published periodically in 'Ingreso y Producto-Puerto Rico Income and Product'. The following presentation of sources and methods is mainly based on information received from the Puerto Rico Planning Board. The estimates are generally in accordance with the classifications and definitions recommended in the United Nations System of National Accounts (SNA). The following tables have been prepared from successive replies to the United Nations national accounts questionnaire. When the scope and coverage of the estimates differ for conceptual or statistical reasons from the definitions and classifications recommended in SNA, a footnote is indicated to the relevant tables.

Sources and methods:

(a) Gross domestic product. Gross domestic product is estimated mainly through the expnditure approach.

(b) Expenditure on the gross domestic product. All components of GDP by expenditure type are estimated through the expenditure approach except private final consumption expenditure of goods and private investment in machinery and equipment which are estimated through the commodity-flow approach. Estimates of government consumption expenditure are based on special tabulations prepared by the Accounting Division of the Department of the Treasury. For personal consumption expenditure on goods, import data in f.o.b. values are obtained from the trade statistics whereas transport costs by commodity are computed by the Division of Economic Accounts. Estimates of locally produced goods are obtained by using the Puerto Rican censuses of manufactures as bench-marks and extrapolating these data for other years. Estimates of local sales of agricultural products are furnished by the Division of Agricultural Statistics. Adjustments for changes in trade inventories and mark-ups are made on the basis of data obtained from income tax returns and from the firms concerned. For some goods, the estimated quantity consumed is multiplied by the average price believed to have been paid by the consumer. Estimates of services are based on the gross receipts of the firms or organizations providing the services. Estimates of changes in stocks for the manufacturing sector are obtained through the use of census data which are extrapolated for the non-census years. For sugar and tobacco, quantity data from official sources are multiplied by the average export prices. For trade, inventories are calculated as percentages of sales from a sample of income tax returns. These percentages are then applied to the estimated total sales. Farm inventories of livestock are computed from data supplied by the Department of Agriculture. Estimates of gross fixed domestic investment in construction are obtained directly through surveys among the contractors. For those not covered by the surveys, data from building permits are used. Private investment in machinery and equipment is estimated on the basis of import statistics. For the government sector, capital expenditure estimates are based on direct surveys within the agencies and on special tabulations prepared by the Accounting Division of the Department of the Treasury. Sales to the rest of the world, i.e., to the federal government and other non-residents of Puerto Rico, include wages and salaries paid to federal employees and all purchases of goods and services by the federal government. These data are obtained from the records of the agencies themselves. Data on imports are obtained from the trade statistics issued by the United States Department of Commerce. For the constant price estimates, private final consumption expenditure is obtained by multiplying quantities by base-year prices where quantity data are available. Otherwise, the current estimates are deflated by appropriate price indexes. For all other components of GDP by expenditure type, price defaltion is used.

(c) Cost-structure of the gross domestic product. Basic data on wages and salaries are derived from records of the Bureau of Unemployment Insurance, from censuses of business and manufacturers and from income tax returns and other financial reports of private businesses and public corporations. The method used for estimating operating surplus in manufacturing, construction and some services consists in calculating, from a sample of income tax returns, ratios of profits and other property income to wages and salaries. These ratios are then applied to total wages and salaries. For some industries, the method is based on ratios of profits to gross receipts as reported on the income tax returns. Rental income of prsons is estimated by deducting from the total rent paid the rent received by businesses, government and the rest of the world. Depreciation is estimated by applying to the total wages and salaries the ratio of depreciation charges to wages and salaries or to gross receipts, in the case of trade, derived from income tax returns. Data on indirect taxes and subsidies are obtained in detail from government reports.

(d) Gross domestic product by kind of economic activity. The table of gross domestic product by kind of economic activity is prepared at market prices, i.e., producers' values. The income approach by distributive shares is used to estimate the value added of each industrial sector. The net income by distributive shares is available by industrial sector. Business transfer payments, depreciation and subsidies are distributed using direct information. Indirect business taxes are obtained from grovernment reports and are broken down by industrial sector, using economic indicators such as data on local production and imports. For the constant price estimates, price deflation is used for the different economic activities of GDP.

1.1 Expenditure on the Gross Domestic Product, in Current Prices

Million United States dollars — Fiscal year beginning 1 July

		1970	1975	1978	1979	1980	1981	1982	1983	1984	1985	1986	1987
1	Government final consumption expenditure	913.8	1612.9	2055.3	2280.8	2501.1	2418.3	2555.3	2886.2	3063.7	3214.0	3411.8	...
2	Private final consumption expenditure	4272.1	7485.7	9913.3	10976.0	12123.4	12414.0	12991.2	13833.8	14871.4	15600.7	16706.3	...
3	Gross capital formation	1707.5	1973.7	2063.8	2458.3	2264.8	1245.6	1429.0	2392.5	2296.1	2011.6	2776.2	...
	A Increase in stocks	113.8	137.9	176.1	406.6	125.5	-542.1	-229.7	416.7	37.5	-308.3	-103.1	...
	B Gross fixed capital formation	1593.7	1835.8	1887.7	2051.8	2139.3	1787.7	1658.7	1975.7	2258.7	2319.9	2879.4	...
	Residential buildings	408.7	424.2	443.9	435.5	417.4	387.1	359.5	330.8	373.7	360.9	458.6	...
	Non-residential buildings	121.0	185.4	135.4	140.7	191.6	193.0	171.8	259.7	277.4	285.4	416.6	...
	Other construction and land improvement etc.	612.8	685.7	621.0	726.9	767.5	656.4	502.1	637.2	664.5	567.0	760.8	...
	Other	451.2	540.5	687.4	748.7	762.8	551.2	625.2	748.0	943.1	1106.5	1243.4	...
4	Exports of goods and services	2333.5	4200.8	7230.7	8334.4	9565.5	10405.6	10193.4	10913.5	11568.1	12296.1	13623.9	...
5	Less: Imports of goods and services	3568.3	6276.8	8476.9	9569.4	10631.9	10069.0	10181.4	11403.9	12116.1	11852.3	12872.9	...
	Equals: Gross Domestic Product	5658.6	8996.4	12786.2	14480.0	15823.0	16414.5	16987.5	18622.0	19683.2	21270.1	23645.4	...

1.2 Expenditure on the Gross Domestic Product, in Constant Prices

Million United States dollars — Fiscal year beginning 1 July

At constant prices of:1954

		1970	1975	1978	1979	1980	1981	1982	1983	1984	1985	1986	1987
1	Government final consumption expenditure	548.1	690.3	813.5	860.8	902.4	863.4	896.7	965.9	1022.1	1066.7	1127.6	...
2	Private final consumption expenditure	2904.2	3473.7	4037.0	3962.3	3971.9	3848.8	3916.7	4123.1	4320.3	4474.0	4724.8	...
3	Gross capital formation	1012.9	776.7	659.3	727.7	633.6	297.0	371.2	577.5	556.2	504.9	658.0	...
	A Increase in stocks	72.2	53.8	41.8	113.5	65.6	-145.1	-35.9	107.9	14.9	-57.2	-11.7	...
	B Gross fixed capital formation	940.7	722.9	617.5	614.1	568.0	442.1	407.2	469.6	541.4	562.0	669.7	...
	Residential buildings	233.0	155.4	132.3	120.6	101.8	87.4	78.5	71.0	79.8	77.1	97.1	...
	Non-residential buildings	69.0	67.9	40.3	39.0	46.7	43.6	37.5	55.7	59.2	60.8	88.2	...
	Other construction and land improvement etc.	349.4	251.4	185.1	201.2	187.3	148.2	109.6	136.7	141.9	121.2	161.0	...
	Other	289.3	248.2	259.8	253.3	232.2	162.9	181.6	206.2	260.6	302.9	323.4	...
4	Exports of goods and services	1507.4	1560.9	2152.6	2101.0	2071.7	2112.0	2047.2	2167.6	2213.0	2408.6	2644.0	...
5	Less: Imports of goods and services	2704.2	2671.8	2985.3	2900.9	2800.3	2571.2	2605.2	2900.3	3071.3	3062.8	3375.8	...
	Equals: Gross Domestic Product	3268.3	3829.9	4677.2	4750.9	4779.4	4550.0	4626.6	4933.8	5040.4	5391.4	5778.6	...

Puerto Rico

1.3 Cost Components of the Gross Domestic Product

Million United States dollars — Fiscal year beginning 1 July

	1970	1975	1978	1979	1980	1981	1982	1983	1984	1985	1986	1987
1 Indirect taxes, net	440.8	788.2	867.8	901.3	1008.5	1030.9	1211.0	1338.7	1371.9	1288.4	1459.1	...
A Indirect taxes	500.0	980.9	1144.6	1184.5	1282.0	1333.7	1448.6	1672.8	1649.0	1567.1	1744.1	...
B Less: Subsidies	59.2	192.7	276.8	283.2	273.5	302.8	237.6	334.1	277.1	278.7	285.0	...
2 Consumption of fixed capital	406.3	622.8	799.3	861.2	932.8	1020.8	992.8	1131.3	1209.0	1281.2	1377.4	...
3 Compensation of employees paid by resident producers to:	2988.2	4819.3	6290.2	6982.1	7570.5	7676.9	7738.4	8510.6	8956.6	9509.0	10180.6	...
A Resident households	2986.2	4799.9	6262.2	6952.0	7538.1	7639.5	7703.5	8453.3	8887.4	9442.3	10117.6	...
B Rest of the world	2.0	19.4	28.0	30.1	32.4	37.4	34.9	57.3	69.0	66.7	63.0	...
4 Operating surplus	1589.4	3015.0	4784.9	5665.3	6039.0	6491.0	6988.8	7676.5	8113.3	8939.5	10401.8	...
Statistical discrepancy	233.9	-248.9	44.0	70.1	272.2	194.9	56.5	-35.1	32.6	252.0	226.5	...
Equals: Gross Domestic Product	5658.6	8996.4	12786.2	14480.0	15823.0	16414.5	16987.5	18622.0	19683.2	21270.1	23645.4	...

1.7 External Transactions on Current Account, Summary

Million United States dollars — Fiscal year beginning 1 July

	1970	1975	1978	1979	1980	1981	1982	1983	1984	1985	1986	1987
Payments to the Rest of the World												
1 Imports of goods and services	3568.3	6276.8	8476.9	9569.4	10631.9	10069.0	10181.4	11403.9	12116.1	11852.3	12872.9	...
A Imports of merchandise c.i.f.	3065.6	5502.8	7488.9	8531.5	9521.7	8895.8	8915.3	10015.0	10667.9	10396.0	11246.0	...
B Other	502.7	774.0	988.0	1037.9	1110.2	1173.2	1266.1	1388.9	1448.2	1456.3	1626.9	...
2 Factor income to the rest of the world	697.1	1975.4	3422.9	4285.9	4728.3	5092.4	5379.6	5904.1	6489.3	7042.8	8239.4	...
A Compensation of employees	2.0	19.4	28.0	30.1	32.4	37.4	34.9	57.3	69.0	66.7	63.0	...
B Property and entrepreneurial income	695.1	1956.0	3394.9	4255.8	4695.9	5055.0	5344.7	5846.8	6420.3	6976.1	8176.4	...
By general government	35.2	97.2	116.5	115.9	141.3	142.8	159.5	201.8	211.2	201.5	211.7	...
By corporate and quasi-corporate enterprises	...	...	...	...	...	...	...	...	...	...	...	...
By other	...	...	...	...	...	...	...	...	...	...	...	...
3 Current transfers to the rest of the world	297.9	749.2	857.9	898.3	958.5	1010.0	1061.1	1198.6	1274.6	1376.7	1452.3	...
4 Surplus of the nation on current transactions	-1192.5	-1754.5	-1580.7	-1811.2	-1787.0	-337.2	-783.8	-1991.0	-2263.7	-1573.1	-2355.9	...
Payments to the Rest of the World and Surplus of the Nation on Current Transactions	3370.8	7246.9	11177.0	12942.4	14531.7	15834.2	15838.3	16515.6	17616.3	18698.7	20208.7	...
Receipts From The Rest of the World												
1 Exports of goods and services	2333.5	4200.8	7230.7	8334.4	9565.5	10405.6	10193.4	10913.5	11568.1	12296.1	13623.9	...
A Exports of merchandise f.o.b.	1826.5	3413.1	6179.7	7139.7	8289.5	9052.7	8760.4	9408.8	9920.4	10610.5	11628.6	...
B Other	507.0	787.7	1051.0	1194.7	1276.0	1352.9	1433.0	1504.7	1647.7	1685.6	1995.3	...
2 Factor income from rest of the world	261.3	441.0	586.9	773.0	960.9	1172.5	1176.5	1104.7	1412.9	1411.8	1459.4	...
A Compensation of employees	200.9	231.3	266.6	265.7	317.5	332.9	356.9	386.1	416.1	428.7	447.4	...
B Property and entrepreneurial income	60.4	209.7	320.3	507.3	643.4	839.6	819.6	718.6	996.8	983.1	1012.0	...
By general government	6.5	3.3	5.7	9.2	7.3	10.8	11.1	14.5	12.6	11.1	8.8	...
By corporate and quasi-corporate enterprises	...	...	...	...	...	...	...	...	...	...	...	...
By other	...	...	...	...	...	...	...	...	...	...	...	...
3 Current transfers from rest of the world	776.0	2605.1	3359.4	3835.0	4005.3	4256.1	4468.3	4497.4	4635.3	4990.8	5125.4	...
Receipts from the Rest of the World on Current Transactions	3370.8	7246.9	11177.0	12942.4	14531.7	15834.2	15838.3	16515.6	17616.3	18698.7	20208.7	...

1.10 Gross Domestic Product by Kind of Activity, in Current Prices

Million United States dollars — Fiscal year beginning 1 July

	1970	1975	1978	1979	1980	1981	1982	1983	1984	1985	1986	1987
1 Agriculture, hunting, forestry and fishing	176.5	285.5	354.6	393.9	377.1	394.8	395.9	343.3	345.5	337.6	372.1	...
2 Mining and quarrying	10.4	9.3	9.1	11.2	11.0	10.8	11.0	9.7	10.8	10.8	13.4	...
3 Manufacturing	1333.8	2974.0	4470.5	5322.5	5786.1	6017.0	6482.5	7266.2	7757.9	8298.5	9388.5	...
4 Electricity, gas and water	183.5	331.3	391.3	447.8	453.9	641.4	602.4	590.9	577.3	641.8	696.9	...
5 Construction [a]	474.2	386.3	349.6	359.0	399.4	344.0	311.0	296.1	326.2	315.8	394.8	...

Puerto Rico

1.10 Gross Domestic Product by Kind of Activity, in Current Prices
(Continued)

Million United States dollars — Fiscal year beginning 1 July

	1970	1975	1978	1979	1980	1981	1982	1983	1984	1985	1986	1987
6 Wholesale and retail trade, restaurants and hotels	1062.3	1660.9	2252.7	2422.2	2621.2	2623.4	2566.5	2933.5	3089.5	3268.2	3685.7	...
7 Transport, storage and communication	298.2	495.4	707.1	787.0	849.3	899.9	865.0	1069.3	1017.5	1124.4	1175.5	...
8 Finance, insurance, real estate and business services	755.8	1089.2	1673.9	1858.9	1995.1	2261.2	2518.6	2720.2	2862.1	3131.0	3515.3	...
9 Community, social and personal services	349.4	547.2	727.2	799.7	883.4	944.1	1009.0	1104.4	1156.8	1269.8	1362.6	...
Total, Industries	4644.1	7779.1	10936.0	12402.2	13376.5	14136.6	14761.9	16333.6	17143.6	18397.9	20604.8	...
Producers of Government Services	736.1	1390.1	1707.7	1896.3	2051.0	1952.0	2028.9	2172.8	2344.9	2443.8	2629.4	...
Other Producers	44.4	76.0	98.6	111.5	123.4	130.8	140.3	150.8	162.0	176.4	184.8	...
Subtotal	5424.6	9245.2	12742.3	14410.0	15550.9	16219.4	16931.1	18657.2	19650.5	21018.1	23419.0	...
Less: Imputed bank service charge	...	...	...	...	...	...	...	...	...	...	...	...
Plus: Import duties	...	...	...	...	...	...	...	...	...	...	...	...
Plus: Value added tax	...	...	...	...	...	...	...	...	...	...	...	...
Plus: Other adjustments	233.9	-248.9	44.0	70.1	272.2	194.9	56.5	-35.1	32.6	252.0	226.5	...
Equals: Gross Domestic Product	5658.6	8996.4	12786.2	14480.0	15823.0	16414.5	16987.5	18622.0	19683.2	21270.1	23645.4	...

a) Item 'Construction' refers to contract construction only.

1.11 Gross Domestic Product by Kind of Activity, in Constant Prices

Million United States dollars — Fiscal year beginning 1 July

	1970	1975	1978	1979	1980	1981	1982	1983	1984	1985	1986	1987
					At constant prices of:1954							
1 Agriculture, hunting, forestry and fishing	141.8	154.9	176.6	172.5	169.9	174.8	169.5	146.8	150.0	152.2	166.7	...
2 Mining and quarrying	5.9	4.3	4.0	4.5	3.9	3.6	3.5	3.0	3.2	3.1	3.8	...
3 Manufacturing	1012.9	1485.7	1880.6	2016.4	2019.2	1978.8	2127.8	2330.4	2457.3	2672.8	2805.0	...
4 Electricity, gas and water	198.5	166.1	167.5	152.6	123.9	147.4	140.6	138.1	134.4	172.1	198.2	...
5 Construction a	270.4	141.6	104.2	99.4	97.4	77.7	67.9	63.5	69.6	67.4	83.8	...
6 Wholesale and retail trade, restaurants and hotels	685.1	753.3	853.2	816.4	795.9	762.8	733.6	817.2	852.4	897.3	980.0	...
7 Transport, storage and communication	188.7	208.1	288.6	294.0	289.6	302.1	249.9	330.7	327.4	354.1	370.3	...
8 Finance, insurance, real estate and business services	521.6	586.8	730.0	714.8	721.0	739.2	786.2	830.7	833.5	922.4	1069.1	...
9 Community, social and personal services	203.6	231.1	260.4	264.5	268.2	271.6	280.6	304.5	311.7	329.6	349.5	...
Total, Industries	3228.5	3731.9	4465.1	4535.1	4489.5	4458.0	4559.6	4964.9	5139.5	5571.0	6026.4	...
Producers of Government Services	428.2	587.5	672.9	722.9	756.0	719.5	738.9	755.2	815.1	848.0	909.2	...
Other Producers	24.4	26.2	29.7	30.3	31.0	31.4	32.9	34.9	37.2	40.4	43.4	...
Subtotal	3681.1	4345.6	5167.7	5288.3	5276.5	5208.9	5331.4	5755.0	5991.8	6459.4	6979.0	...
Less: Imputed bank service charge	...	...	...	...	...	...	...	...	...	...	...	...
Plus: Import duties	...	...	...	...	...	...	...	...	...	...	...	...
Plus: Value added tax	...	...	...	...	...	...	...	...	...	...	...	...
Plus: Other adjustments	-412.7	-515.8	-490.6	-537.4	-497.2	-658.6	-704.8	-821.3	-951.2	-1068.1	-1200.2	...
Equals: Gross Domestic Product	3268.3	3829.9	4677.2	4750.9	4779.4	4550.0	4626.6	4933.8	5040.4	5391.4	5778.6	...

a) Item 'Construction' refers to contract construction only.

1.12 Relations Among National Accounting Aggregates

Million United States dollars — Fiscal year beginning 1 July

	1970	1975	1978	1979	1980	1981	1982	1983	1984	1985	1986	1987
Gross Domestic Product	5658.6	8996.4	12786.2	14480.0	15823.0	16414.5	16987.5	18622.0	19683.2	21270.1	23645.4	...
Plus: Net factor income from the rest of the world	-435.8	-1534.4	-2836.0	-3512.9	-3767.4	-3919.9	-4203.1	-4799.4	-5076.4	-5631.0	-6780.0	...
Factor income from the rest of the world	261.3	441.0	586.9	773.0	960.9	1172.5	1176.5	1104.7	1412.9	1411.8	1459.4	...
Less: Factor income to the rest of the world	697.1	1975.4	3422.9	4285.9	4728.3	5092.4	5379.6	5904.1	6489.3	7042.8	8239.4	...
Equals: Gross National Product	5222.8	7462.0	9950.2	10967.1	12055.6	12494.6	12784.4	13822.6	14606.8	15639.1	16865.4	...
Less: Consumption of fixed capital	406.3	622.8	799.3	861.2	932.8	1020.8	992.8	1131.3	1209.0	1281.2	1377.4	...

Puerto Rico

1.12 Relations Among National Accounting Aggregates
(Continued)

Million United States dollars — Fiscal year beginning 1 July

	1970	1975	1978	1979	1980	1981	1982	1983	1984	1985	1986	1987
Equals: National Income	4816.5	6839.2	9150.9	10105.9	11122.8	11473.8	11791.6	12691.3	13397.8	14357.9	15488.0	...
Plus: Net current transfers from the rest of the world	478.1	1855.9	2501.5	2936.7	3046.8	3246.1	3407.2	3298.8	3360.7	3614.1	3673.1	...
Current transfers from the rest of the world	776.0	2605.1	3359.4	3835.0	4005.3	4256.1	4468.3	4497.4	4635.3	4990.8	5125.4	...
Less: Current transfers to the rest of the world	297.9	749.2	857.9	898.3	958.5	1010.0	1061.1	1198.6	1274.6	1376.7	1452.3	...
Equals: National Disposable Income	5294.6	8695.1	11652.4	13042.6	14169.6	14719.9	15198.8	15990.1	16758.5	17972.0	19161.1	...
Less: Final consumption	5185.9	9098.6	11968.6	13256.8	14624.5	14832.3	15546.4	16719.9	17935.1	18814.7	20118.2	...
Equals: Net Saving	108.7	-403.6	-316.2	-214.1	-455.0	-112.4	-347.6	-729.8	-1176.6	-842.7	-957.1	...
Less: Surplus of the nation on current transactions	-1192.5	-1754.5	-1580.7	-1811.2	-1787.0	-337.2	-783.8	-1991.0	-2263.7	-1573.1	-2355.9	...
Equals: Net Capital Formation	1301.2	1350.9	1264.5	1597.1	1332.0	224.8	436.2	1261.2	1087.1	730.4	1398.8	...

2.5 Private Final Consumption Expenditure by Type and Purpose, in Current Prices

Million United States dollars — Fiscal year beginning 1 July

	1970	1975	1978	1979	1980	1981	1982	1983	1984	1985	1986	1987
Final Consumption Expenditure of Resident Households												
1 Food, beverages and tobacco	1323.2	2577.4	2999.2	3428.9	3699.8	3663.9	3822.2	3887.3	4198.9	4375.2	4733.6	...
A Food	996.8	2106.0	2420.2	2779.5	2980.7	2936.0	3026.4	3087.3	3364.0	3492.4	3806.8	...
B Non-alcoholic beverages	...	...	...	...	...	...	...	...	...	...	...	...
C Alcoholic beverages	236.8	347.0	402.5	453.5	507.5	492.0	545.8	560.0	557.2	598.3	625.3	...
D Tobacco	89.5	124.4	176.5	195.9	211.6	235.9	250.0	240.0	277.7	284.6	301.5	...
2 Clothing and footwear	470.6	698.5	990.4	1016.1	1102.4	1119.3	1163.7	1313.8	1295.2	1325.8	1391.3	...
3 Gross rent, fuel and power	532.7	958.5	1318.4	1511.9	1801.9	1961.4	2075.0	2188.4	2321.6	2431.0	2551.2	...
4 Furniture, furnishings and household equipment and operation	401.2	669.8	730.9	817.7	855.4	819.9	824.1	850.9	909.2	977.0	1103.9	...
A Household operation	100.0	170.4	204.8	231.3	243.3	246.6	256.0	236.0	269.7	278.9	289.9	...
B Other	301.2	499.4	526.1	586.4	612.1	573.3	568.1	614.9	639.5	698.1	814.0	...
5 Medical care and health expenses	184.5	289.6	479.3	486.0	534.7	586.9	631.4	698.0	844.3	912.2	1064.7	...
6 Transport and communication	569.3	1006.6	1559.3	1780.5	2073.2	2005.4	2014.1	2268.4	2428.6	2579.4	2647.3	...
A Personal transport equipment	221.5	296.4	540.6	447.7	520.1	397.1	491.5	748.3	871.2	959.5	1034.5	...
B Other	347.8	710.2	1018.7	1332.8	1553.1	1608.3	1522.6	1520.1	1557.4	1619.9	1612.8	...
7 Recreational, entertainment, education and cultural services	248.5	513.4	751.2	735.7	814.8	868.1	906.9	936.3	1014.0	1019.0	1069.2	...
A Education	19.9	113.8	183.3	205.9	229.5	260.3	281.6	303.5	325.6	354.4	379.6	...
B Other	228.6	399.6	567.9	529.8	585.3	607.8	625.3	632.8	688.4	664.6	689.6	...
8 Miscellaneous goods and services	463.2	719.6	1012.0	1139.2	1199.3	1308.8	1411.9	1476.5	1616.9	1710.8	1876.9	...
A Personal care	111.5	180.5	239.4	291.3	328.2	375.6	403.3	426.8	440.2	437.7	456.7	...
B Expenditures in restaurants, cafes and hotels	141.0	222.2	341.7	378.2	412.5	417.2	396.2	415.1	453.2	497.5	549.4	...
C Other	210.7	316.9	430.9	469.7	458.6	516.0	612.4	634.6	723.5	775.6	870.8	...
Total Final Consumption Expenditure in the Domestic Market by Households, of which	4193.2	7433.4	9840.7	10916.0	12081.5	12333.7	12849.3	13619.6	14628.7	15330.4	16438.1	...
Plus: Direct purchases abroad by resident households	250.3	327.2	460.5	471.7	467.3	524.9	542.3	579.0	615.2	628.3	761.9	...
Less: Direct purchases in the domestic market by non-resident households	239.3	398.6	573.9	628.0	665.1	715.3	707.3	698.9	738.8	762.8	918.5	...
Equals: Final Consumption Expenditure of Resident Households	4204.2	7362.0	9727.3	10759.7	11883.7	12143.3	12684.3	13499.7	14505.1	15195.9	16281.5	...
Final Consumption Expenditure of Private Non-profit Institutions Serving Households												
1 Research and science	...	...	...	...	...	...	...	...	...	...	...	...
2 Education	20.6	...	...	...	...	...	...	...	...	...	...	...
3 Medical and other health services	45.2	114.6	171.8	200.0	219.9	248.1	281.3	307.2	338.1	373.6	391.8	...

Puerto Rico

2.5 Private Final Consumption Expenditure by Type and Purpose, in Current Prices
(Continued)

Million United States dollars — Fiscal year beginning 1 July

		1970	1975	1978	1979	1980	1981	1982	1983	1984	1985	1986	1987
4	Welfare services	...	...	...	...	...	...	...	...	...	...	...	...
5	Recreational and related cultural services	...	...	...	...	...	...	...	...	...	...	...	...
6	Religious organisations	2.1	9.1	14.2	16.3	19.7	22.6	25.6	26.9	28.1	31.3	32.9	...
7	Professional and labour organisations serving households	...	...	...	...	...	...	...	...	...	...	...	...
8	Miscellaneous	...	...	...	...	...	...	...	...	...	...	...	...
	Equals: Final Consumption Expenditure of Private Non-profit Organisations Serving Households	67.9	123.7	186.0	216.3	239.6	270.7	306.9	334.1	366.2	404.9	424.7	...
	Private Final Consumption Expenditure	4272.1	7485.7	9913.3	10976.0	12123.4	12414.0	12991.2	13833.8	14871.4	15600.7	16706.3	...

2.6 Private Final Consumption Expenditure by Type and Purpose, in Constant Prices

Million United States dollars — Fiscal year beginning 1 July

		1970	1975	1978	1979	1980	1981	1982	1983	1984	1985	1986	1987
	At constant prices of: 1954												
	Final Consumption Expenditure of Resident Households												
1	Food, beverages and tobacco	816.4	927.6	953.2	992.8	963.3	906.2	924.3	919.9	973.8	1012.5	1067.1	...
	A Food	616.6	751.9	768.0	792.8	756.5	723.1	730.7	727.2	775.6	806.5	855.1	...
	B Non-alcoholic beverages	...	...	...	...	...	...	...	...	...	...	...	...
	C Alcoholic beverages	143.2	125.4	130.9	141.5	148.8	126.9	136.7	139.0	137.7	145.8	149.6	...
	D Tobacco	56.6	50.3	54.3	58.5	58.0	56.2	56.9	53.7	60.5	60.3	62.3	...
2	Clothing and footwear	333.8	397.4	495.2	469.3	476.9	472.3	479.3	546.2	529.3	538.4	571.8	...
3	Gross rent, fuel and power	432.4	541.9	631.6	647.4	683.4	685.1	690.7	700.0	712.8	728.2	741.6	...
4	Furniture, furnishings and household equipment and operation	309.6	378.3	360.0	371.4	367.1	333.4	328.8	332.9	350.0	370.9	421.5	...
	A Household operation	69.2	81.3	78.7	77.7	75.1	70.3	70.1	67.9	70.4	52.0	53.9	...
	B Other	240.4	297.0	281.3	293.7	292.0	263.1	258.7	265.0	279.6	318.9	367.6	...
5	Medical care and health expenses	99.5	114.8	156.4	143.3	145.0	148.0	149.7	159.6	185.8	190.8	212.2	...
6	Transport and communication	385.7	457.2	610.0	573.3	588.7	536.9	548.6	634.2	680.7	721.2	729.9	...
	A Personal transport equipment	132.7	133.0	204.6	155.0	160.6	114.7	141.5	210.3	238.2	253.0	244.7	...
	B Other	253.0	324.2	405.4	418.3	428.1	422.2	407.1	423.9	442.5	468.2	485.2	...
7	Recreational, entertainment, education and cultural services	178.7	288.8	384.7	344.3	367.3	380.1	384.4	389.7	417.3	410.4	427.6	...
	A Education	12.7	47.7	68.1	70.0	72.6	78.7	81.3	84.0	85.8	90.2	91.7	...
	B Other	166.0	241.1	316.6	274.3	294.7	301.4	303.1	305.7	331.5	320.2	335.9	...
8	Miscellaneous goods and services	260.7	292.2	352.0	356.9	350.9	350.0	366.4	379.2	406.4	438.3	494.7	...
	A Personal care	132.7	83.8	101.6	116.1	125.5	132.4	137.5	144.0	145.9	142.5	146.3	...
	B Expenditures in restaurants, cafes and hotels	66.1	71.1	92.6	95.4	90.2	80.6	71.6	73.3	78.1	85.6	93.2	...
	C Other	61.9	137.3	157.8	145.4	135.2	137.0	157.3	161.9	182.4	210.2	255.2	...
	Total Final Consumption Expenditure in the Domestic Market by Households, of which	2816.8	3398.2	3943.1	3898.7	3942.6	3812.0	3872.2	4061.7	4256.1	4410.7	4666.4	...
	Plus: Direct purchases abroad by resident households	181.5	174.2	225.2	191.8	149.3	151.9	153.0	162.2	167.0	168.9	201.7	...
	Less: Direct purchases in the domestic market by non-resident households	131.1	142.9	183.1	183.1	177.1	176.7	172.9	168.3	175.4	181.7	216.9	...
	Equals: Final Consumption Expenditure of Resident Households	2867.2	3429.5	3985.2	3907.4	3914.8	3787.2	3852.3	4055.6	4247.7	4397.9	4651.2	...
	Final Consumption Expenditure of Private Non-profit Institutions Serving Households												
1	Research and science	...	...	...	...	...	...	...	...	...	...	...	...
2	Education	13.1	...	...	...	...	...	...	...	...	...	...	...
3	Medical and other health services	22.6	40.3	46.6	49.4	50.9	55.1	57.3	59.8	64.4	67.3	64.7	...

Puerto Rico

2.6 Private Final Consumption Expenditure by Type and Purpose, in Constant Prices
(Continued)

Million United States dollars — Fiscal year beginning 1 July

		1970	1975	1978	1979	1980	1981	1982	1983	1984	1985	1986	1987
						At constant prices of:1954							
4	Welfare services	...	...	...	...	...	...	...	...	...	...	...	...
5	Recreational and related cultural services	...	...	...	...	...	...	...	...	...	...	...	...
6	Religious organisations	1.3	3.8	5.3	5.5	6.1	6.5	7.3	7.5	8.1	8.7	9.0	...
7	Professional and labour organisations serving households												...
8	Miscellaneous	...	...	...	...	...	...	...	...	...	...	...	...
	Equals: Final Consumption Expenditure of Private Non-profit Organisations Serving Households	37.0	44.1	51.9	54.9	57.0	61.5	64.6	67.3	72.5	76.0	73.7	
	Private Final Consumption Expenditure	2904.2	3473.7	4037.0	3962.3	3971.9	3848.8	3916.9	4123.1	4320.3	4474.0	4724.8	...

2.17 Exports and Imports of Goods and Services, Detail

Million United States dollars — Fiscal year beginning 1 July

		1970	1975	1978	1979	1980	1981	1982	1983	1984	1985	1986	1987
						Exports of Goods and Services							
1	Exports of merchandise, f.o.b.	1826.5	3413.1	6179.7	7139.7	8289.5	9052.7	8760.4	9408.8	9920.4	10610.5	11628.6	...
2	Transport and communication	103.4	205.2	277.4	330.2	333.2	358.0	388.5	409.0	390.9	392.5	407.7	...
	A In respect of merchandise imports	0.3	34.9	39.2	43.4	59.3	66.3	72.6	83.4	76.0	87.5	91.0	...
	B Other	103.1	170.3	238.2	286.8	273.9	291.7	315.9	325.6	314.9	305.0	316.7	...
3	Insurance service charges	1.9	2.4	3.2	3.4	2.5	3.0	5.0	4.9	4.5	5.3	5.8	...
	A In respect of merchandise imports	1.9	2.4	3.2	3.4	2.5	3.0	5.0	4.9	4.5	5.3	5.8	...
	B Other	-	-	-	-	-	-	-	-	-	-	-	...
4	Other commodities	162.4	181.4	196.6	233.0	275.1	276.6	332.3	392.1	513.5	524.9	663.4	...
5	Adjustments of merchandise exports to change-of-ownership basis	...	...	...	...	...	...	...	...	...	...	...	...
6	Direct purchases in the domestic market by non-residential households	239.3	398.7	574.0	628.0	665.1	715.3	707.3	698.9	738.8	762.8	918.5	...
7	Direct purchases in the domestic market by extraterritorial bodies	...	...	...	...	...	...	...	...	...	...	...	...
	Total Exports of Goods and Services	2333.5	4200.8	7230.7	8334.4	9565.5	10405.6	10193.4	10913.5	11568.1	12296.1	13623.9	...
						Imports of Goods and Services							
1	Imports of merchandise, c.i.f.	3065.6	5502.8	7488.9	8531.5	9521.7	8895.8	8915.3	10015.0	10667.9	10396.0	11246.0	...
	A Imports of merchandise, f.o.b.	2832.8	5222.9	7172.5	8189.3	9123.8	8523.8	8526.6	9519.9	10108.1	9830.0	10616.3	...
	B Transport of services on merchandise imports	223.1	261.5	291.4	313.0	366.2	343.4	359.9	462.7	525.5	531.8	593.7	...
	By residents	...	...	...	...	...	...	...	...	...	...	...	...
	By non-residents	223.1	261.5	291.4	313.0	366.2	343.4	359.9	462.7	525.5	531.8	593.7	...
	C Insurance service charges on merchandise imports	9.7	18.4	25.0	29.2	31.7	28.6	28.8	32.3	34.3	34.2	35.9	...
	By residents	...	...	...	...	...	...	...	...	...	...	...	...
	By non-residents	9.7	18.4	25.0	29.2	31.7	28.6	28.8	32.3	34.3	34.2	35.9	...
2	Adjustments of merchandise imports to change-of-ownership basis	...	...	...	...	...	...	...	...	...	...	...	...
3	Other transport and communication	106.8	266.2	290.6	288.9	342.3	323.5	376.7	413.5	411.5	396.7	430.2	...
4	Other insurance service charges	...	...	...	...	...	...	...	...	...	...	...	...
5	Other commodities	130.4	156.1	252.4	271.9	279.5	279.3	302.3	362.3	390.1	396.9	420.7	...
6	Direct purchases abroad by government	7.4	26.9	18.7	27.1	25.6	29.6	22.1	32.9	38.9	36.3	40.3	...
7	Direct purchases abroad by resident households	258.1	324.9	426.3	450.2	462.8	540.8	564.9	580.2	607.8	626.3	735.7	...
	Total Imports of Goods and Services	3568.3	6276.8	8476.9	9569.4	10631.9	10069.0	10181.4	11403.9	12116.1	11852.3	12872.9	...
	Balance of Goods and Services	-1234.8	-2076.0	-1246.2	-1235.0	-1066.4	336.6	12.0	-490.4	-548.0	443.8	751.0	...
	Total Imports and Balance of Goods and Services	2333.5	4200.8	7230.7	8334.4	9565.5	10405.6	10193.4	10913.5	11568.1	12296.1	13623.9	...

Qatar

Source. Reply to the United Nations National Accounts Questionnaire from the Central Statistical Organization, Doha.

General note. The estimates shown in the following tables have been prepared in accordance with the United Nations System of National Accounts so far as the existing data would permit.

1.1 Expenditure on the Gross Domestic Product, in Current Prices

Million Qatari riyals

	1970	1975	1978	1979	1980	1981	1982	1983	1984	1985	1986	1987
1 Government final consumption expenditure	...	...	6075	7955	5622	8143	7236	8203	9021	7882	8384	...
2 Private final consumption expenditure	...	...			4509	5424	5921	5769	5927	5626	5307	...
3 Gross capital formation	...	...	4975	4551	4883	5596	7606	5176	4147	3998	3409	...
A Increase in stocks	...	...	...	...	117	284	215	-544	-155	30	7	...
B Gross fixed capital formation	...	...	...	...	4766	5312	7391	5720	4302	3968	3402	...
4 Exports of goods and services	...	...	9249	14655	21127	21468	16753	12753	13450	11502	7330	...
5 Less: Imports of goods and services	...	...	4590	5378	7478	9063	9811	8296	7537	6610	6167	...
Equals: Gross Domestic Product	...	...	15709	21783	28663	31568	27705	23605	25008	22398	18263	...

1.10 Gross Domestic Product by Kind of Activity, in Current Prices

Million Qatari riyals

	1970	1975	1978	1979	1980	1981	1982	1983	1984	1985	1986	1987
1 Agriculture, hunting, forestry and fishing	...	71	111	122	150	172	190	195	206	213	237	241
2 Mining and quarrying	...	6734	8660	13664	19245	20175	15001	10790	11330	9595	5395	5630
3 Manufacturing	...	255	597	856	943	1491	1391	1464	1829	1770	1777	1847
4 Electricity, gas and water	...	19	62	85	64	83	89	133	165	191	363	359
5 Construction	...	766	1340	1357	1556	1632	1829	1395	1411	1313	1054	1086
6 Wholesale and retail trade, restaurants and hotels	...	372	1485	1660	1293	1858	1775	1587	1506	1186	1149	1172
7 Transport, storage and communication	...	156	370	415	399	409	458	450	480	450	410	412
8 Finance, insurance, real estate and business services	...	743	1290	1523	1705	2022	2308	2030	1919	1899	1842	1958
9 Community, social and personal services	...	58	105	126	128	176	242	227	222	201	214	216
Total, Industries	...	9174	14020	19808	25483	28018	23283	18272	19068	16818	12441	12921
Producers of Government Services	...	622	1831	2143	3367	3865	4727	5553	6189	5748	6047	5848
Other Producers	...	44	71	83	132	143	157	168	176	187	198	213
Subtotal	...	9840	15922	22034	28982	32026	28167	23993	25433	22753	18686	18982
Less: Imputed bank service charge	...	153	313	321	406	561	569	492	543	484	553	533
Plus: Import duties	...	20	100	70	87	103	107	104	118	129	130	131
Plus: Value added tax	...	...	...	...	...	...	...	...	...	...	...	...
Equals: Gross Domestic Product	...	9707	15709	21783	28663	31568	27705	23605	25008	22398	18263	18580

1.11 Gross Domestic Product by Kind of Activity, in Constant Prices

Million Qatari riyals

	1970	1975	1978	1979	1980	1981	1982	1983	1984	1985	1986	1987
				At constant prices of:1981								
1 Agriculture, hunting, forestry and fishing	...	...	...	...	148	172	189	184	192	193	218	...
2 Mining and quarrying	...	...	...	...	23524	20175	16342	14647	16071	15252	16685	...
3 Manufacturing	...	...	...	...	1470	1491	1622	1792	2141	2219	2438	...
4 Electricity, gas and water	...	...	...	...	61	83	105	143	173	201	216	...
5 Construction	...	...	...	...	1600	1632	1795	1369	1481	1406	1128	...
6 Wholesale and retail trade, restaurants and hotels	...	...	...	...	1272	1858	1702	1428	1362	1017	1010	...
7 Transport, storage and communication	...	...	...	...	409	409	428	436	446	408	369	...
8 Finance, insurance, real estate and business services	...	...	...	...	1839	2022	2197	2052	2122	2108	2087	...
9 Community, social and personal services	...	...	...	...	139	176	228	209	202	180	189	...
Total, Industries	...	...	...	...	30462	28018	24608	22260	24190	22984	24340	...
Producers of Government Services	...	...	...	...	3436	3865	4089	4422	4434	4476	4480	...
Other Producers	...	...	...	...	143	143	148	155	160	167	174	...
Subtotal	...	...	...	...	34041	32026	28845	26837	28784	27627	28994	...
Less: Imputed bank service charge	...	...	...	...	441	561	537	453	495	432	486	...
Plus: Import duties	...	...	...	...	89	103	103	81	81	65	52	...
Plus: Value added tax	...	...	...	...	...	...	...	...	...	...	...	
Equals: Gross Domestic Product	...	...	...	...	33689	31568	28411	26465	28370	27260	28560	...

Reunion

Source. Reply to the United Nations National Accounts Questionnaire from the Institute national de la statistique et des etudes economiques (INSEE), Paris. Official estimates and descriptions are published by the same Institute in 'Comptes Economiques de la Reunion'.

General note. The estimates shown in the following tables have been adjusted by the INSEE to conform to the United Nations System of National Accounts so far as the existing data would permit.

1.1 Expenditure on the Gross Domestic Product, in Current Prices

Million French francs

	1970	1975	1978	1979	1980	1981	1982	1983	1984	1985	1986	1987
1 Government final consumption expenditure	657.7	1542.7	2194.8	2480.9	2868.0	3330.2	4058.4	4515.6	4864.5	5258.5	5806.0	6503.0
2 Private final consumption expenditure	1436.6	3399.8	5207.9	6168.9	7120.4	8291.2	10296.5	11769.7	12900.3	14205.8	15254.0	16811.0
A Households	...	3386.3	5173.1	6133.3	7079.7	8208.8	10152.9	11425.5	12737.3	...	...	...
B Private non-profit institutions serving households	...	13.5	34.8	35.6	40.7	82.4	143.6	344.2	163.0	...	...	...
3 Gross capital formation	539.4	1109.7	1363.9	1570.1	1875.4	2085.1	2570.7	3064.3	3117.8	3426.9	3925.0	4685.0
A Increase in stocks	-32.9	140.6	103.8	138.2	130.4	92.0	72.6	87.6	24.7	125.3	125.0	125.0
B Gross fixed capital formation	572.3	969.1	1260.1	1431.9	1744.9	1993.1	2498.1	2976.7	3093.1	3301.6	3800.0	4560.0
4 Exports of goods and services	282.1	268.5	521.0	594.9	556.0	763.2	787.4	881.5	855.5	1067.1	945.0	1115.0
5 Less: Imports of goods and services	902.8	1780.8	2690.2	3342.6	3971.2	4341.6	5426.9	6556.4	7046.6	7621.6	7861.0	8751.0
Equals: Gross Domestic Product	2013.4	4539.9	6597.4	7472.2	8448.6	10128.2	12286.2	13674.7	14691.6	16336.6	18069.0	20363.0

1.3 Cost Components of the Gross Domestic Product

Million French francs

	1970	1975	1978	1979	1980	1981	1982	1983	1984	1985	1986	1987
1 Indirect taxes, net	252.6	462.6	647.7	709.1	871.9	1022.0	1262.5	...	...	...	...	...
2 Consumption of fixed capital	...	...	...	...	...	...	...	...	...	...	...	...
3 Compensation of employees paid by resident producers to:	1429.5	2826.2	4202.5	4735.4	5481.0	6477.6	7682.5	8924.1	9500.0	10200.0	...	...
4 Operating surplus [a]	331.3	1251.1	1747.2	2027.7	2095.6	2628.6	3341.2	...	...	...	...	...
Equals: Gross Domestic Product	2013.4	4539.9	6597.4	7472.2	8448.6	10128.2	12286.2	13674.7	14691.6	16336.6	...	...

a) Item 'Operating surplus' includes consumption of fixed capital.

1.7 External Transactions on Current Account, Summary

Million French francs

	1970	1975	1978	1979	1980	1981	1982	1983	1984	1985	1986	1987
Payments to the Rest of the World
1 Imports of goods and services	902.8	1780.8	2690.2	3342.6	3971.2	4341.6	5380.3	...	...	...	...	...
2 Factor income to the rest of the world	43.9	87.6	198.8	239.4	278.8	315.4	400.5	...	...	...	...	...
A Compensation of employees	-	-	-	-	-	-	-	...	...	...	...	...
B Property and entrepreneurial income	43.9	87.6	198.8	239.4	278.8	315.4	400.5	...	...	...	...	...
3 Current transfers to the rest of the world	44.6	24.0	88.3	100.4	131.3	156.2	186.8	...	...	...	...	...
4 Surplus of the nation on current transactions	76.7	210.8	331.9	193.1	-73.4	442.1	-19.8	...	...	...	...	...
Payments to the Rest of the World and Surplus of the Nation on Current Transactions	1068.0	2103.2	3309.2	3875.5	4308.0	5255.3	5947.8	...	...	...	...	...
Receipts From The Rest of the World
1 Exports of goods and services	282.0	268.5	521.0	594.8	556.0	763.3	787.4	...	...	...	...	...
2 Factor income from rest of the world	6.9	19.4	104.4	138.8	197.8	274.9	416.4	...	...	...	...	...
A Compensation of employees	-	-	-	-	-	-	-	...	...	...	...	...
B Property and entrepreneurial income	6.9	19.4	104.4	138.8	197.8	274.9	416.4	...	...	...	...	...
3 Current transfers from rest of the world	779.1	1815.3	2683.8	3141.9	3554.2	4217.1	4744.0	...	...	...	...	...
Receipts from the Rest of the World on Current Transactions	1068.0	2103.2	3309.2	3875.5	4308.0	5255.3	5947.8	...	...	...	...	...

Reunion

1.10 Gross Domestic Product by Kind of Activity, in Current Prices

Million French francs

	1970	1975	1978	1979	1980	1981	1982	1983	1984	1985	1986	1987
1 Agriculture, hunting, forestry and fishing	...	283.3	477.3	519.3	498.5	646.2	828.2	...	...	...	...	...
2 Mining and quarrying	...	360.0	592.4	718.2	802.0	984.7	1125.8	...	...	...	...	...
3 Manufacturing	...							...	...	...	...	...
4 Electricity, gas and water	...	59.0	46.9	43.7	130.0	184.6	225.1	...	...	...	...	...
5 Construction	...	277.4	306.8	373.7	401.0	486.7	638.5	...	...	...	...	...
6 Wholesale and retail trade, restaurants and hotels	...	870.6	1244.4	1324.9	1360.1	1525.0	1751.2	...	...	...	...	...
7 Transport, storage and communication	...	147.6	281.3	330.0	346.8	460.3	561.0	...	...	...	...	...
8 Finance, insurance, real estate and business services	...	357.2	600.8	737.7	883.2	1321.0	1340.7	...	...	...	...	...
9 Community, social and personal services	...	596.2	711.7	805.6	997.1	1095.9	1558.6	...	...	...	...	...
Total, Industries	1311.9	2951.3	4261.6	4853.1	5418.7	6704.4	8029.1	...	...	...	...	...
Producers of Government Services	579.5	1342.8	1989.1	2205.5	2569.1	2943.4	3495.7	...	...	...	...	...
Other Producers	31.5	71.8	108.7	118.4	166.4	217.8	301.5	...	...	...	...	...
Subtotal	1922.9	4365.9	6359.4	7177.0	8154.2	9865.6	11826.3	...	...	...	...	...
Less: Imputed bank service charge	73.8	113.5	234.0	270.9	383.1	520.0	538.7	...	...	...	...	...
Plus: Import duties	82.7	120.1	223.7	266.5	334.7	379.5	488.1	...	...	...	...	...
Plus: Value added tax	81.6	167.4	248.3	299.6	338.8	403.0	510.6	...	...	...	...	...
Equals: Gross Domestic Product	2013.4	4539.9	6597.4	7472.2	8448.6	10128.2	12286.2	...	...	...	...	...

1.12 Relations Among National Accounting Aggregates

Million French francs

	1970	1975	1978	1979	1980	1981	1982	1983	1984	1985	1986	1987
Gross Domestic Product	2013.4	4539.9	6597.4	7472.2	8448.6	10128.2	12286.2	...	...	...	...	...
Plus: Net factor income from the rest of the world	-37.0	-68.2	-94.4	-100.6	-81.0	-40.6	15.9	...	...	...	...	...
Factor income from the rest of the world	6.9	19.4	104.4	138.8	197.8	274.9	416.4	...	...	...	...	...
Less: Factor income to the rest of the world	43.9	87.6	198.8	239.4	278.8	315.5	400.5	...	...	...	...	...
Equals: Gross National Product	1976.4	4471.7	6503.0	7371.6	8367.6	10087.4	12301.9	...	...	...	...	...
Less: Consumption of fixed capital	...	...	...	...	...	...	...	...	...	...	...	...
Equals: National Income	...	...	...	...	...	...	...	...	...	...	...	...
Plus: Net current transfers from the rest of the world	734.5	1791.3	2595.6	3041.5	3422.9	4060.9	4557.2	...	...	...	...	...
Current transfers from the rest of the world	779.1	1815.3	2683.8	3141.9	3554.2	4217.1	4744.0	...	...	...	...	...
Less: Current transfers to the rest of the world	44.6	24.0	88.2	100.4	131.3	156.2	186.8	...	...	...	...	...
Equals: National Disposable Income	...	...	...	...	...	...	...	...	...	...	...	...
Less: Final consumption	2094.3	4942.5	7402.7	8649.8	9988.4	11621.5	14360.9	...	...	...	...	...
Equals: Net Saving	...	...	...	...	...	...	...	...	...	...	...	...
Less: Surplus of the nation on current transactions	76.7	210.8	331.8	193.1	-73.4	442.1	-19.8	...	...	...	...	...
Equals: Net Capital Formation	...	...	...	...	...	...	...	...	...	...	...	...

Romania

Source. Communication from the Central Statistical Board of Romania, Bucharest. Official estimates and descriptions are published annually in 'Anuarul Statistics' (Statistical Yearbook).

General note. The estimates shown in the following tables have been prepared in accordance with the System of Material Product Balances. Therefore, these estimates are not comparable in concept and coverage with those conforming to the United Nations System of National Accounts.

2a Net Material Product by Kind of Activity of the Material Sphere in Current Market Prices

Percentages

		1970	1975	1978	1979	1980	1981	1982	1983	1984	1985	1986	1987
1	Agriculture and forestry [a]	19.5 / 18.5	16.0 / 16.2	15.3	14.8	14.1	15.8	19.7	15.5	15.3	15.0	15.9	15.9
2	Industrial activity	60.3 / 58.0	56.2 / 59.8	57.9	58.5	58.6	57.2	55.7	60.2	61.0	62.7	62.5	62.5
3	Construction	9.8 / 10.4	7.6 / 7.6	10.2	9.6	8.8	8.5	7.4	7.8	7.7	7.8	7.6	7.4
4	Wholesale and retail trade and restaurants and other eating and drinking places	3.6 / ...	...	...	...	...	...	...	...	...	...	...	...
5	Transport and communication	4.0 / 6.0	5.8 / 5.8	5.9	5.8	7.0	6.9	6.4	6.2	6.0	6.0	6.2	6.0
6	Other activities of the material sphere	2.8 / ...	...	...	...	...	...	...	...	...	...	...	...
	Net material product	100.0 / 100.0	100.0 / 100.0	100.0	100.0	100.0	100.0	100.0	100.0	100.0	100.0	100.0	100.0

a) Item 'Agriculture and forestry' refers to agriculture and livestock only.

2b Net Material Product by Kind of Activity of the Material Sphere in Constant Market Prices

Index numbers 1970=100

		1970	1975	1978	1979	1980	1981	1982	1983	1984	1985	1986	1987
					At constant prices of:1985								
1	Agriculture and forestry [a]	100	130	166	169	144	141	152	146	164	166	188	192
2	Industrial activity	100	186	244	263	279	290	295	313	336	362	389	416
3	Construction	100	144	192	195	195	189	191	208	221	231	239	241
4	Wholesale and retail trade and restaurants and other eating and drinking places	...	...	...	...	...	...	...	...	...	...	...	...
5	Transport and communication	100	169	197	205	221	229	234	230	238	241	259	264
6	Other activities of the material sphere	...	...	...	...	...	...	...	...	...	...	...	...
	Net material product [b]	100	171	222	235	242	247	254	263	284	300	322	338

a) Item 'Agriculture and forestry' refers to agriculture and livestock only.
b) For the period 1970-1975, base year in prices 1963, for the period 1975-1980, base year in prices 1977, for the period 1980-1983, base year in prices 1981, for period 1983-1984, base year in prices 1983, for the period 1984-1985, base year in prices 1984, and for the period 1986-1987, base year in prices 1985. A link was made between these periods on the basis of relations between indices.

6a Capital Formation by Kind of Activity of the Material and Non-Material Spheres in Current Market Prices

Million Romanian lei

		1970	1975	1978	1979	1980	1981	1982	1983	1984	1985	1986	1987
					Gross Fixed Capital Formation								
1	Agriculture and forestry	...	...	...	...	...	32821	33687	37481	40963	44686	43271	42245
2	Industrial activity	...	...	...	...	...	105490	101545	111684	124094	119121	124668	116047
3	Construction	...	...	...	...	...	7218	8312	8142	9542	11347	11304	11623
4	Wholesale and retail trade and restaurants and other eating and drinking places	...	...	...	...	...	4866	5701	5237	5059	5233	5648	5686
5	Transport and communciation	...	...	...	...	...	20631	26983	29183	26321	26369	22600	24087
6	Other activities of the material sphere	...	...	...	...	...	...	...	...	...	...	...	...
	Total Material Sphere	...	...	...	...	...	...	...	...	...	...	...	...
7	Housing except owner-occupied, communal and miscellaneous personal services [a]	...	...	...	...	...	30822	33405	34311	33638	32083	33883	39389
8	Education, culture and art	...	...	...	...	...	1977	2048	1082	771	917	...	...
9	Health and social welfare services and sports	...	...	...	...	...	1091	1286	1099	1052	1109	...	...
	Total Non-Material Sphere Serving Individuals	...	...	...	...	...	...	...	...	...	...	...	...

Romania

6a Capital Formation by Kind of Activity of the Material and Non-Material Spheres in Current Market Prices
(Continued)

Million Romanian lei

	1970	1975	1978	1979	1980	1981	1982	1983	1984	1985	1986	1987
10 Government	...	...	...	...	...	1117	1440	900	1110	1475	...	...
11 Finance, credit and insurance	...	...	...	...	...						...	...
12 Research, scientific and technological institutes	...	...	...	...	...	1239	1135	1064	1380	1416	...	...
13 Other activities of the non-material sphere	...	...	...	...	...	...	...	...	...	...	...	...
Total Non-Material Sphere Serving the Community as a Whole	...	...	...	...	...	...	...	...	...	...	...	...
14 Owner-occupied dwellings	...	...	...	...	...	...	...	...	...	...	...	...
Total Gross Fixed Capital Formation	...	...	...	...	...	207954	216354	230743	244714	246365	249347	...

a) Item 'Owner-occupied dwellings' is included in item 'Housing except owner-occupied, communal, and miscellaneous personal services'.

6b Capital Formation by Kind of Activity of the Material and Non-Material Spheres in Constant Market Prices

Million Romanian lei

	1970	1975	1978	1979	1980	1981	1982	1983	1984	1985	1986	1987
	1963	1977				1981						

At constant prices of:

Gross Fixed Capital Formation

	1970	1975	1978	1979	1980	1981	1982	1983	1984	1985	1986	1987
1 Agriculture and forestry	13102	18540 / 19498	27302	26833	28008 / 29848	32821	...	...	...	...	...	...
2 Industrial activity	37961	67829 / 66125	97164	104321	107058 / 111948	105490	...	...	...	...	...	...
3 Construction	3595	7317 / 6343	12738	12745	9652 / 9910	7218	...	...	...	...	...	...
4 Wholesale and retail trade and restaurants and other eating and drinking places	2828	4849 / 5233	5421	4591	4567 / 4926	4866	...	...	...	...	...	...
5 Transport and communciation	8469	14726 / 14766	19908	20377	25286 / 26472	20631	...	...	...	...	...	...
6 Other activities of the material sphere	...	...	...	...	...	...	...	...	...	...	...	...
Total Material Sphere	...	...	...	...	...	...	...	...	...	...	...	...
7 Housing except owner-occupied, communal and miscellaneous personal services a	10181	17642 / 20419	26462	28470	28391 / 33025	30822	...	...	...	...	...	...
8 Education, culture and art	1591	2673 / 2963	2881	2524	2761 / 2972	1977	...	...	...	...	...	...
9 Health and social welfare services and sports	1143	1373 / 1523	1251	962	1050 / 1150	1091	...	...	...	...	...	...
Total Non-Material Sphere Serving Individuals	...	...	...	...	...	...	...	...	...	...	...	...

Romania

6b Capital Formation by Kind of Activity of the Material and Non-Material Spheres in Constant Market Prices
(Continued)

Million Romanian lei

	1970	1975	1978	1979	1980	1981	1982	1983	1984	1985	1986	1987
		1963		1977	At constant prices of:				1981			
10 Government	500	886	1449	1403	1218		...	...	...	...	...	...
		971			1347	1117						
11 Finance, credit and insurance							...	...	...	...	...	...
12 Research, scientific and technological institutes	438	903	1200	1122	1349		...	...	...	...	...	...
		869			1401	1239						
13 Other activities of the non-material sphere	...	...	...	...	...	...	...	...	...	...	...	...
		...			...							
Total Non-Material Sphere Serving the Community as a Whole	...	...	...	...	...	...	...	...	...	...	...	...
		...			...							
14 Owner-occupied dwellings	...	...	...	...	...	...	...	...	...	...	...	...
		...			...							
Total Gross Fixed Capital Formation	79990	137731	196294	204368	210451		...	...	...	...	...	...
		139674			223877	207954						

a) Item 'Owner-occupied dwellings' is included in item 'Housing except owner-occupied, communal, and miscellaneous personal services'.

Rwanda

Source. Reply to the United Nations National Accounts Questionnaire from the Ministry of Planning, Kigali. Some official estimates together with information on concepts, definitions and methods of estimation are published in 'Comptes Economiques du Rwanda, 1969 et 1970'.

General note. The estimates shown in the following tables have been prepared in accordance with the United Nations System of National Accounts so far as the existing data would permit.

1.1 Expenditure on the Gross Domestic Product, in Current Prices

Thousand Million Rwanda francs

	1970	1975	1978	1979	1980	1981	1982	1983	1984	1985	1986	1987
1 Government final consumption expenditure	2.97	8.78	12.80	12.62	13.49	22.96	16.91	16.71	16.25	19.58	20.13	19.80
2 Private final consumption expenditure	17.60	41.24	62.10	73.62	89.97	98.00	107.27	119.29	128.91	139.87	134.72	135.48
3 Gross capital formation	1.62	7.25	13.46	11.57	17.43	16.31	23.28	19.24	25.15	30.07	27.04	27.73
A Increase in stocks	-0.03	0.29	2.14	-2.70	4.24	0.33	4.50	-1.50	0.49	3.02	0.24	0.38
B Gross fixed capital formation	1.65	6.96	11.32	14.27	13.19	15.98	18.78	20.74	24.66	27.05	26.80	27.35
4 Exports of goods and services	2.67	4.84	11.98	20.24	15.59	12.05	15.13	16.47	20.10	18.73	21.44	16.12
5 Less: Imports of goods and services	3.29	9.34	19.29	21.88	28.49	26.68	31.63	29.52	31.29	34.54	34.33	32.62
Equals: Gross Domestic Product [a]	21.56	52.77	81.05	96.17	107.99	122.64	130.96	142.19	159.11	173.70	168.99	166.51

a) Data in this table have been revised, therefore they are not strictly comparable with the unrevised data in the other tables.

1.2 Expenditure on the Gross Domestic Product, in Constant Prices

Thousand Million Rwanda francs

	1970	1975	1978	1979	1980	1981	1982	1983	1984	1985	1986	1987
		1972			At constant prices of: 1976					1985		
1 Government final consumption expenditure	...	...	...	...	...	...	19.32	17.93	16.53	19.58	20.35	19.23
2 Private final consumption expenditure	...	...	...	...	...	...	132.75	144.97	135.78	139.87	147.63	143.03
3 Gross capital formation	...	...	...	...	...	...	24.38	20.53	27.51	30.07	28.44	29.64
A Increase in stocks	...	...	...	...	...	...	5.00	-1.60	0.42	3.02	0.25	0.59
B Gross fixed capital formation	...	...	...	...	...	...	19.38	22.13	27.09	27.05	28.19	29.05
4 Exports of goods and services	...	...	...	...	...	...	17.13	18.25	18.10	18.73	21.48	21.41
5 Less: Imports of goods and services	...	...	...	...	...	...	29.65	27.95	31.55	34.54	36.38	35.63
Equals: Gross Domestic Product	22.37	...	71.46	78.16	...	...	163.94	173.74	166.37	173.70	181.53	177.68

1.3 Cost Components of the Gross Domestic Product

Thousand Million Rwanda francs

	1970	1975	1978	1979	1980	1981	1982	1983	1984	1985	1986	1987
1 Indirect taxes, net	...	3.25	5.95	8.24	8.26	7.81	9.22	9.46	11.67	13.88	17.21	...
A Indirect taxes	...	3.35	6.80	9.61	...	9.40	9.63	10.20	12.05	13.88	17.21	...
B Less: Subsidies	...	0.10	0.85	1.37	...	1.59	0.39	0.74	0.38	-	-	...
2 Consumption of fixed capital	...	1.49	2.58	3.06	6.06	3.74	4.80	6.45	6.81	9.39	10.53	...
3 Compensation of employees paid by resident producers to:	...	9.02	12.55	14.46	17.82	26.86	28.25	30.42	30.59	41.35	41.91	...
4 Operating surplus	...	39.01	59.97	70.41	75.85	84.23	90.16	97.39	109.86	109.08	99.33	...
Equals: Gross Domestic Product	21.56	52.77	81.05	96.17	107.99	122.64	132.43	142.55	158.93	173.70	168.99	...

1.7 External Transactions on Current Account, Summary

Thousand Million Rwanda francs

	1970	1975	1978	1979	1980	1981	1982	1983	1984	1985	1986	1987
					Payments to the Rest of the World							
1 Imports of goods and services	...	9.34	19.29	21.88	28.49	26.68	31.63	29.52	31.29	34.54	34.33	32.62
2 Factor income to the rest of the world	...	0.05	0.89	0.94	1.45	1.30	1.78	1.59	1.48	2.75	4.19	...
A Compensation of employees	...	...	...	...	...	...	...	...	...	1.52	1.68	...
B Property and entrepreneurial income	...	...	...	...	...	...	...	...	...	1.23	2.52	...

Rwanda

1.7 External Transactions on Current Account, Summary
(Continued)

Thousand Million Rwanda francs

	1970	1975	1978	1979	1980	1981	1982	1983	1984	1985	1986	1987
3 Current transfers to the rest of the world	...	1.60	1.82	8.02	5.59	6.09	6.20	5.95	6.20	1.85	2.18	...
4 Surplus of the nation on current transactions	...	0.14	0.95	6.13	-9.49	-11.31	-13.66	-10.02	-9.11	-10.91	-9.98	...
Payments to the Rest of the World and Surplus of the Nation on Current Transactions	...	11.13	22.95	36.97	26.04	22.76	25.95	27.04	29.86	28.23	30.72	...

Receipts From The Rest of the World

	1970	1975	1978	1979	1980	1981	1982	1983	1984	1985	1986	1987
1 Exports of goods and services	...	4.84	11.98	20.24	15.59	12.05	15.13	16.47	20.10	18.73	21.44	16.12
2 Factor income from rest of the world	...	0.04	0.41	0.97	1.59	2.21	1.50	0.82	0.82	0.97	0.85	...
A Compensation of employees	...	...	...	...	...	...	0.02	0.02	0.02	0.06	0.06	...
B Property and entrepreneurial income	...	...	...	...	...	...	1.48	0.80	0.80	0.91	0.80	...
3 Current transfers from rest of the world	...	6.25	10.56	15.76	8.84	8.50	9.32	9.75	8.94	8.53	8.43	...
Receipts from the Rest of the World on Current Transactions	...	11.13	22.95	36.97	26.04	22.76	25.95	27.04	29.86	28.23	30.72	...

1.10 Gross Domestic Product by Kind of Activity, in Current Prices

Thousand Million Rwanda francs

	1970	1975	1978	1979	1980	1981	1982	1983	1984	1985	1986	1987
1 Agriculture, hunting, forestry and fishing	11.22	25.97	34.38	47.16	49.51	49.96	51.49	53.60	64.41	72.67	62.58	...
2 Mining and quarrying	0.47	1.05	1.84	1.84	1.84	0.81	0.62	0.72	0.57	0.46	0.33	...
3 Manufacturing	2.71	6.48	12.64	12.30	16.48	19.30	18.27	22.55	22.78	23.83	27.13	...
4 Electricity, gas and water	0.06	0.16	0.18	0.17	0.13	0.08	0.45	0.77	0.91	0.91	1.10	...
5 Construction	0.58	2.32	3.27	3.71	4.82	5.39	10.19	11.69	14.20	15.11	11.86	...
6 Wholesale and retail trade, restaurants and hotels	2.23	7.48	14.18	15.44	15.88	19.65	19.19	18.26	19.56	21.24	23.61	...
7 Transport, storage and communication	0.23	0.55	1.04	1.66	2.30	3.24	7.42	8.67	8.19	8.47	10.17	...
8 Finance, insurance, real estate and business services [a]	0.08	2.30	4.59	3.71	4.11	5.34	8.00	10.04	11.82	13.25	12.52	...
9 Community, social and personal services	2.48	4.85	6.11	7.21	9.17	15.39	11.46	12.20	12.04	12.28	13.96	...
Total, Industries	20.06	51.16	78.23	93.20	104.24	119.16	127.09	138.51	154.47	168.23	163.26	...
Producers of Government Services	...	...	...	...	...	...	...	...	...	...	...	...
Other Producers	...	...	...	...	...	...	...	...	...	...	...	...
Subtotal	20.06	51.16	78.23	93.20	104.24	119.16	127.09	138.51	154.47	168.23	163.26	...
Less: Imputed bank service charge [a]	...	...	...	...	...	...	...	...	...	...	...	...
Plus: Import duties	1.51	1.61	2.82	2.97	3.75	3.48	3.87	3.68	4.64	5.47	5.73	...
Plus: Value added tax	...	...	...	...	...	...	...	...	...	...	...	...
Equals: Gross Domestic Product [b]	21.57	52.77	81.05	96.17	107.99	122.64	130.94	142.19	159.11	173.70	168.99	...

a) Item 'Less: Imputed bank service charge' is netted out of item 'Finance, insurance, real estate and business services'. b) Data in this table have been revised, therefore they are not strictly comparable with the unrevised data in the other tables.

1.11 Gross Domestic Product by Kind of Activity, in Constant Prices

Thousand Million Rwanda francs

	1970	1975	1978	1979	1980	1981	1982	1983	1984	1985	1986	1987
			At constant prices of: 1976						1985			
1 Agriculture, hunting, forestry and fishing	...	...	31.52	38.31	...	...	74.65	77.91	71.04	72.67	73.11	...
2 Mining and quarrying	...	...	1.29	1.20	...	...	0.34	0.69	0.54	0.46	0.34	...
3 Manufacturing	...	...	8.94	8.86	...	...	22.77	26.26	22.28	23.83	28.29	...
4 Electricity, gas and water	...	...	0.18	0.17	...	...	0.49	0.87	1.04	0.91	1.04	...
5 Construction	...	...	3.13	3.55	...	...	10.20	11.99	14.62	15.11	12.45	...

Rwanda

1.11 Gross Domestic Product by Kind of Activity, in Constant Prices
(Continued)

Thousand Million Rwanda francs

	1970	1975	1978	1979	1980	1981	1982	1983	1984	1985	1986	1987
					At constant prices of: 1976					1985		
6 Wholesale and retail trade, restaurants and hotels	...	...	12.99	12.75	...	...	21.94	19.59	19.90	21.24	23.87	...
7 Transport, storage and communication	...	...	0.95	0.89	...	...	7.94	9.09	8.30	8.47	10.04	...
8 Finance, insurance, real estate and business services [a]	...	...	4.31	3.81	...	...	8.64	10.58	11.77	13.25	12.55	...
9 Community, social and personal services	...	...	5.61	6.27	...	...	13.10	13.09	12.24	12.28	14.11	...
Total, Industries	...	...	68.92	75.81	...	...	160.06	170.06	161.73	168.23	175.80	...
Producers of Government Services	...	...	...	...	...	...	...	...	...	...	...	...
Other Producers	...	...	...	...	...	...	...	...	...	...	...	...
Subtotal	...	...	68.92	75.81	...	...	160.06	170.06	161.73	168.23	175.80	...
Less: Imputed bank service charge [a]	...	...	...	...	...	...	...	...	...	...	...	...
Plus: Import duties	...	...	2.54	2.35	...	...	3.87	3.68	4.64	5.47	5.73	...
Plus: Value added tax	...	...	...	...	...	...	...	...	...	...	...	...
Equals: Gross Domestic Product	...	...	71.46	78.16	...	...	163.94	173.74	166.37	173.70	181.53	...

a) Item 'Less: Imputed bank service charge' is netted out of item 'Finance, insurance, real estate and business services'.

1.12 Relations Among National Accounting Aggregates

Thousand Million Rwanda francs

	1970	1975	1978	1979	1980	1981	1982	1983	1984	1985	1986	1987
Gross Domestic Product [a]	...	52.77	81.05	96.17	107.99	122.64	130.96	142.19	159.11	173.70	168.99	...
Plus: Net factor income from the rest of the world	...	-0.01	-0.48	0.03	0.14	0.91	-0.28	-0.77	-0.66	-1.78	-3.34	...
Factor income from the rest of the world	...	0.04	0.41	0.97	1.59	2.21	1.50	0.82	0.82	0.97	0.85	...
Less: Factor income to the rest of the world	...	0.05	0.89	0.94	1.45	1.30	1.78	1.59	1.48	2.75	4.19	...
Equals: Gross National Product	...	52.76	80.57	96.20	108.13	123.55	130.68	141.42	158.45	171.92	165.65	...
Less: Consumption of fixed capital	...	1.49	2.58	3.06	3.55	3.74	4.79	5.28	6.81	9.39	10.53	...
Equals: National Income	...	51.27	77.99	93.14	104.58	119.81	125.89	136.14	151.64	162.53	155.12	...
Plus: Net current transfers from the rest of the world	...	4.65	8.74	7.74	3.26	2.40	3.12	3.80	2.74	6.68	6.25	...
Current transfers from the rest of the world	...	6.25	10.56	15.76	8.84	8.50	9.32	9.75	8.94	8.53	8.43	...
Less: Current transfers to the rest of the world	...	1.60	1.82	8.02	5.59	6.10	6.20	5.95	6.20	1.85	2.18	...
Equals: National Disposable Income	...	55.92	86.73	100.88	107.84	122.21	129.01	139.94	154.38	169.21	161.37	...
Less: Final consumption	...	50.02	74.90	86.24	103.46	120.96	124.17	136.00	145.14	159.45	154.85	...
Equals: Net Saving	...	5.90	11.83	14.64	4.38	1.25	4.84	3.94	9.24	9.76	6.52	...
Less: Surplus of the nation on current transactions	...	0.14	0.95	6.13	-9.49	-11.31	-13.66	-10.02	-9.11	-10.91	-9.98	...
Equals: Net Capital Formation [a]	...	5.76	10.88	8.51	13.87	12.56	18.50	13.96	18.35	20.67	16.50	...

a) Data in this table have been revised, therefore they are not strictly comparable with the unrevised data in the other tables.

4.1 Derivation of Value Added by Kind of Activity, in Current Prices

Thousand Million Rwanda francs

	1980			1981			1982			1983		
	Gross Output	Intermediate Consumption	Value Added	Gross Output	Intermediate Consumption	Value Added	Gross Output	Intermediate Consumption	Value Added	Gross Output	Intermediate Consumption	Value Added
						All Producers						
1 Agriculture, hunting, forestry and fishing	51.33	1.82	49.51	51.32	1.36	49.96	55.66	1.38	54.28	58.19	1.62	56.57
A Agriculture and hunting	...	...	...	...	...	...	54.66	1.38	53.28	57.14	1.62	55.52
B Forestry and logging	...	...	...	...	...	...	0.75	-	0.75	0.78	-	0.78
C Fishing	...	...	...	...	...	...	0.25	-	0.25	0.28	-	0.28
2 Mining and quarrying	2.98	1.14	1.84	2.08	1.27	0.81	1.59	0.97	0.62	1.80	1.08	0.72

Rwanda

4.1 Derivation of Value Added by Kind of Activity, in Current Prices
(Continued)

Thousand Million Rwanda francs

	1980 Gross Output	1980 Intermediate Consumption	1980 Value Added	1981 Gross Output	1981 Intermediate Consumption	1981 Value Added	1982 Gross Output	1982 Intermediate Consumption	1982 Value Added	1983 Gross Output	1983 Intermediate Consumption	1983 Value Added
A Coal mining	...	...	...	...	...	...	...	...	...	...	...	...
B Crude petroleum and natural gas production	...	...	...	...	...	...	-	0.05	-0.05	0.02	0.04	-0.02
C Metal ore mining	...	...	...	...	...	...	1.41	0.92	0.49	1.60	1.04	0.56
D Other mining	...	...	...	...	...	...	0.17	-	0.17	0.18	-	0.18
3 Manufacturing	46.86	30.38	16.48	53.96	34.66	19.30	55.02	34.21	20.81	60.59	34.60	25.99
A Manufacture of food, beverages and tobacco	...	...	...	...	...	...	44.69	28.89	15.80	49.54	28.74	20.80
B Textile, wearing apparel and leather industries	...	...	...	...	...	...	3.04	1.51	1.53	3.55	2.02	1.53
C Manufacture of wood and wood products, including furniture	...	...	...	...	...	...	0.87	0.24	0.63	0.89	0.22	0.67
D Manufacture of paper and paper products, printing and publishing	...	...	...	...	...	...	0.31	0.19	0.12	0.39	0.18	0.21
E Manufacture of chemicals and chemical petroleum, coal, rubber and plastic products	...	...	...	...	...	...	2.06	1.43	0.63	1.99	1.48	0.51
F Manufacture of non-metallic mineral products, except products of petroleum and coal	...	...	...	...	...	...	1.18	0.15	1.03	1.25	0.15	1.10
G Basic metal industries	...	...	...	...	...	...	-	-	-	-	-	-
H Manufacture of fabricated metal products, machinery and equipment	...	...	...	...	...	...	2.86	1.81	1.05	2.98	1.81	1.17
I Other manufacturing industries	...	...	...	...	...	...	...	...	...	...	...	...
4 Electricity, gas and water	0.50	0.37	0.13	0.51	0.44	0.08	1.24	0.79	0.45	1.28	0.51	0.77
A Electricity, gas and steam	...	...	...	...	...	...	0.97	0.40	0.57	0.98	0.29	0.69
B Water works and supply	...	...	...	...	...	...	0.26	0.39	-0.13	0.30	0.22	0.09
5 Construction	9.39	4.57	4.82	9.48	4.09	5.39	8.93	3.27	5.66	10.47	3.98	6.49
6 Wholesale and retail trade, restaurants and hotels	17.57	1.69	15.88	21.56	1.91	19.65	23.40	2.09	21.31	22.32	2.04	20.28
A Wholesale and retail trade	...	...	...	...	...	...	22.76	1.82	20.94	21.59	1.74	19.85
B Restaurants and hotels	...	...	...	...	...	...	0.65	0.27	0.38	0.73	0.30	0.43
7 Transport, storage and communication	7.37	5.07	2.30	5.53	2.28	3.25	6.95	2.94	4.01	7.64	2.95	4.69
A Transport and storage	...	...	...	...	...	...	6.43	2.88	3.55	7.13	2.62	4.51
B Communication	...	...	...	...	...	...	0.51	0.06	0.45	0.51	0.33	0.18
8 Finance, insurance, real estate and business services [a]	7.90	3.79	4.11	9.40	4.06	5.34	8.45	3.71	4.74	9.11	3.68	5.43
A Financial institutions	...	...	...	...	...	...	3.69	2.78	0.91	2.91	2.48	0.43
B Insurance	...	...	...	...	...	...	-	-0.08	0.08	0.31	0.08	0.23
C Real estate and business services	...	...	...	...	...	...	5.36	1.02	4.34	5.88	1.12	4.76
9 Community, social and personal services	15.68	6.51	9.17	24.57	9.18	15.39	26.32	9.63	16.69	26.22	8.29	17.93
A Sanitary and similar services	...	...	...	...	...	...	...	...	...	...	...	...
B Social and related community services	...	...	...	...	...	...	...	...	...	...	...	...
Educational services	...	...	...	...	...	...	...	...	...	5.68	1.28	4.40
Medical, dental, other health and veterinary services	...	...	...	...	...	...	...	...	...	...	...	...
C Recreational and cultural services	...	...	...	...	...	...	...	...	...	0.40	0.29	0.11
D Personal and household services	...	...	...	...	...	...	...	...	...	...	...	...
Total, Industries	159.58	55.34	104.24	178.41	59.25	119.16	187.54	59.00	128.55	197.62	58.75	138.87
Producers of Government Services	...	...	...	...	...	...	...	...	...	...	...	...
Other Producers	...	...	...	...	...	...	...	...	...	...	...	...
Total	159.58	55.34	104.24	178.41	59.25	119.16	187.54	59.00	128.55	197.62	58.75	138.87
Less: Imputed bank service charge [a]	...	...	...	...	...	...	...	...	...	...	...	...
Import duties	3.75	-	3.75	3.48	-	3.48	3.87	-	3.87	3.68	-	3.68
Value added tax	...	...	...	...	...	...	...	...	...	...	...	...
Total	163.33	55.34	107.99	181.89	59.25	122.64	191.41	59.00	132.42	201.30	58.75	142.55

Rwanda

4.1 Derivation of Value Added by Kind of Activity, in Current Prices

Thousand Million Rwanda francs

		1984			1985			1986		
		Gross Output	Intermediate Consumption	Value Added	Gross Output	Intermediate Consumption	Value Added	Gross Output	Intermediate Consumption	Value Added

All Producers

1	Agriculture, hunting, forestry and fishing	70.75	2.06	68.69	76.71	4.04	72.67	66.23	3.65	62.58
	A Agriculture and hunting	69.66	2.06	67.60	...	...	...	...	...	...
	B Forestry and logging	0.81	-	0.81	...	...	...	...	...	...
	C Fishing	0.28	-	0.28	...	...	...	...	...	...
2	Mining and quarrying	0.88	0.31	0.57	0.68	0.22	0.46	0.36	0.03	0.33
	A Coal mining	...	...	...	...	...	...	...	...	...
	B Crude petroleum and natural gas production	0.03	0.01	0.02	...	...	...	...	...	...
	C Metal ore mining	0.66	0.30	0.36	...	...	...	...	...	...
	D Other mining	0.19	-	0.19	...	...	...	...	...	...
3	Manufacturing	62.64	36.59	26.05	65.79	41.95	23.83	65.21	38.08	27.13
	A Manufacture of food, beverages and tobacco	49.45	30.11	19.34	...	...	...	49.96	...	...
	B Textile, wearing apparel and leather industries	3.54	1.86	1.68	...	...	...	4.09	...	...
	C Manufacture of wood and wood products, including furniture	1.08	0.37	0.71	...	...	...	1.30	...	...
	D Manufacture of paper and paper products, printing and publishing	0.35	0.19	0.16	...	...	...	0.52	...	...
	E Manufacture of chemicals and chemical petroleum, coal, rubber and plastic products	2.50	1.60	0.90	...	...	...	2.72	...	...
	F Manufacture of non-metallic mineral products, except products of petroleum and coal	1.49	0.24	1.25	...	...	...	[3.62]	...	...
	G Basic metal industries	1.12	0.36	0.76	...	...	...		...	...
	H Manufacture of fabricated metal products, machinery and equipment	3.11	1.86	1.25	...	...	...	3.00	...	...
	I Other manufacturing industries	...	...	...	...	...	...	...	...	...
4	Electricity, gas and water	1.49	0.58	0.91	1.80	0.89	0.91	1.56	0.46	1.10
	A Electricity, gas and steam	1.10	0.44	0.66	...	...	...	...	...	...
	B Water works and supply	0.38	0.13	0.25	...	...	...	...	...	...
5	Construction	12.84	4.95	7.89	24.33	9.21	15.11	23.74	11.88	11.86
6	Wholesale and retail trade, restaurants and hotels	24.19	2.46	21.73	46.57	25.32	21.24	44.15	20.54	23.61
	A Wholesale and retail trade	23.12	1.90	21.22	...	...	...	20.58	...	...
	B Restaurants and hotels	1.07	0.57	0.50	...	...	...	23.57	...	...
7	Transport, storage and communication	9.92	5.50	4.42	16.53	8.06	8.47	19.14	8.97	10.17
	A Transport and storage	9.33	5.34	3.99	...	...	...	18.31	...	...
	B Communication	0.59	0.16	0.43	...	...	...	0.84	...	...
8	Finance, insurance, real estate and business services [a]	10.36	4.13	6.23	15.76	2.52	13.25	17.39	4.87	12.52
	A Financial institutions	3.52	2.80	0.72	...	...	...	...	...	...
	B Insurance	0.30	0.09	0.21	...	...	...	...	...	...
	C Real estate and business services	6.54	1.24	5.30	...	...	...	...	...	...
9	Community, social and personal services	26.63	8.83	17.80	20.49	8.20	12.28	22.55	8.59	13.96
	A Sanitary and similar services	...	...	...	...	...	...	...	...	...
	B Social and related community services	...	...	...	...	...	...	...	...	...
	Educational services	6.22	1.23	4.99	...	...	...	...	...	...
	Medical, dental, other health and veterinary services	...	...	...	...	...	...	...	...	...
	C Recreational and cultural services	0.30	0.15	0.15	...	...	...	...	...	...
	D Personal and household services	...	...	...	...	...	...	...	...	...

Rwanda

4.1 Derivation of Value Added by Kind of Activity, in Current Prices
(Continued)

Thousand Million Rwanda francs

	1984 Gross Output	1984 Intermediate Consumption	1984 Value Added	1985 Gross Output	1985 Intermediate Consumption	1985 Value Added	1986 Gross Output	1986 Intermediate Consumption	1986 Value Added
Total, Industries	219.70	65.41	154.29	268.66	100.44	168.23	260.34	97.08	163.26
Producers of Government Services	...	...	...	...	...	...	...	...	...
Other Producers	...	...	...	...	...	...	...	...	...
Total	219.70	65.41	154.29	268.66	100.44	168.23	260.34	97.08	163.26
Less: Imputed bank service charge [a]	...	...	...	...	...	...	...	...	...
Import duties	4.64	-	4.64	5.47	-	5.47	5.73	-	5.73
Value added tax	...	...	...	...	...	...	...	...	...
Total	224.34	65.41	158.93	274.13	100.44	173.70	266.07	97.08	168.99

a) Item 'Less: Imputed bank service charge' is netted out of item 'Finance, insurance, real estate and business services'.

4.3 Cost Components of Value Added

Thousand Million Rwanda francs

	1980 Compensation of Employees	1980 Capital Consumption	1980 Net Operating Surplus	1980 Indirect Taxes	1980 Less: Subsidies Received	1980 Value Added	1981 Compensation of Employees	1981 Capital Consumption	1981 Net Operating Surplus	1981 Indirect Taxes	1981 Less: Subsidies Received	1981 Value Added
All Producers												
1 Agriculture, hunting, forestry and fishing	0.50	0.03	47.62	1.36	...	49.51	0.26	0.07	49.41	1.38	1.16	49.96
A Agriculture and hunting	...	...	...	...	...	...	...	...	...	...	...	...
B Forestry and logging	...	...	...	...	...	...	...	...	...	...	...	...
C Fishing	...	...	...	...	...	...	...	...	...	...	...	...
2 Mining and quarrying	0.95	0.33	0.47	0.09	-	1.84	1.07	0.30	-0.70	0.14	-	0.81
A Coal mining	...	...	...	...	...	...	...	...	...	...	...	...
B Crude petroleum and natural gas production												
C Metal ore mining	...	...	...	...	...	...	...	...	...	...	...	...
D Other mining	...	...	...	...	...	...	...	...	...	...	...	...
3 Manufacturing	1.88	0.64	11.17	2.79	...	16.48	2.24	0.71	13.33	3.30	0.28	19.30
A Manufacture of food, beverages and tobacco	...	...	...	...	...	...	...	...	...	...	...	...
B Textile, wearing apparel and leather industries												
C Manufacture of wood and wood products, including furniture												
D Manufacture of paper and paper products, printing and publishing												
E Manufacture of chemicals and chemical petroleum, coal, rubber and plastic products												
F Manufacture of non-metallic mineral products, except products of petroleum and coal												
G Basic metal industries	...	...	...	...	...	...	...	...	...	...	...	...
H Manufacture of fabricated metal products, machinery and equipment												
I Other manufacturing industries												
4 Electricity, gas and water	0.06	0.26	-0.19	-	-	0.13	0.21	0.15	-0.28	-	-	0.08
A Electricity, gas and steam												
B Water works and supply	...	...	...	...	...	...	...	...	...	...	...	...
5 Construction	3.85	0.97	-	-	...	4.82	4.71	0.23	0.44	0.01	-	5.39
6 Wholesale and retail trade, restaurants and hotels	1.27	0.67	13.88	0.06	...	15.88	1.71	0.39	16.82	0.73	-	19.65
A Wholesale and retail trade	...	...	...	...	...	...	...	...	...	...	...	...
B Restaurants and hotels	...	...	...	...	...	...	...	...	...	...	...	...
7 Transport, storage and communication	0.62	0.56	1.03	0.09	-	2.30	0.69	0.15	2.45	0.09	0.13	3.25
A Transport and storage	...	...	...	...	...	...	...	...	...	...	...	...
B Communication	...	...	...	...	...	...	...	...	...	...	...	...
8 Finance, insurance, real estate and business services	0.43	1.71	1.87	0.10	-	4.11	0.61	1.72	2.76	0.26	0.01	5.34
A Financial institutions	...	...	...	...	...	...	...	...	...	...	...	...

Rwanda

4.3 Cost Components of Value Added
(Continued)

Thousand Million Rwanda francs

	1980						1981					
	Compensation of Employees	Capital Consumption	Net Operating Surplus	Indirect Taxes	Less: Subsidies Received	Value Added	Compensation of Employees	Capital Consumption	Net Operating Surplus	Indirect Taxes	Less: Subsidies Received	Value Added
B Insurance	...	...	...	...	...	...	...	...	...	...	...	...
C Real estate and business services	...	...	...	...	...	...	...	...	...	...	...	...
9 Community, social and personal services	8.26	0.91	-	-	-	9.17	15.37	0.02	-	-	-	15.39
A Sanitary and similar services	...	...	...	...	...	...	...	...	...	...	...	...
B Social and related community services	...	...	...	...	...	...	...	...	...	...	...	...
Educational services	...	...	...	...	...	...	...	...	...	...	...	...
Medical, dental, other health and veterinary services	...	...	...	...	...	...	...	...	...	...	...	...
C Recreational and cultural services	...	...	...	...	...	...	...	...	...	...	...	...
D Personal and household services	...	...	...	...	...	...	...	...	...	...	...	...
Total, Industries	17.82	6.08	75.85	4.49	...	104.24	26.86	3.74	84.23	5.91	1.58	119.16
Producers of Government Services	...	...	...	...	...	...	...	...	...	...	...	...
Other Producers	...	...	...	...	...	...	...	...	...	...	...	...
Total	17.82	6.08	75.85	4.49	...	104.24	26.86	3.74	84.23	5.91	1.58	119.16
Less: Imputed bank service charge	...	...	...	...	...	...	...	...	...	...	...	...
Import duties	...	...	...	3.75	...	3.75	...	...	...	3.48	...	3.48
Value added tax	...	...	...	...	...	...	...	...	...	...	...	...
Total	17.82	6.08	75.85	8.24	...	107.99	26.86	3.74	84.23	9.40	1.58	122.64

	1982						1983					
	Compensation of Employees	Capital Consumption	Net Operating Surplus	Indirect Taxes	Less: Subsidies Received	Value Added	Compensation of Employees	Capital Consumption	Net Operating Surplus	Indirect Taxes	Less: Subsidies Received	Value Added

All Producers

1 Agriculture, hunting, forestry and fishing	0.23	0.07	52.81	1.41	0.24	54.28	0.30	0.06	55.57	1.11	0.47	56.57
A Agriculture and hunting	...	...	...	...	...	...	0.30	0.06	54.51	1.11	0.47	55.51
B Forestry and logging	...	...	...	...	...	...	-	-	0.78	-	-	0.78
C Fishing	...	...	...	...	...	...	-	-	0.28	-	-	0.28
2 Mining and quarrying	1.09	0.29	-0.84	0.08	-	0.62	1.15	0.33	-0.85	0.09	-	0.72
A Coal mining	...	...	...	...	...	...	...	...	...	...	...	...
B Crude petroleum and natural gas production	...	...	...	...	...	...	0.01	0.01	-0.04	-	-	-0.02
C Metal ore mining	...	...	...	...	...	...	1.07	0.32	-0.92	0.09	-	0.56
D Other mining	...	...	...	...	...	...	0.07	-	0.11	-	-	0.18
3 Manufacturing	2.65	0.72	14.16	3.38	0.10	20.81	2.81	0.91	18.38	4.04	0.14	25.99
A Manufacture of food, beverages and tobacco	...	...	...	...	...	...	0.94	0.56	15.40	4.00	0.10	20.80
B Textile, wearing apparel and leather industries	...	...	...	...	...	...	0.37	0.03	1.12	0.01	-	1.53
C Manufacture of wood and wood products, including furniture	...	...	...	...	...	...	0.31	0.02	0.34	-	-	0.67
D Manufacture of paper and paper products, printing and publishing	...	...	...	...	...	...	0.09	0.03	0.09	-	-	0.21
E Manufacture of chemicals and chemical petroleum, coal, rubber and plastic products	...	...	...	...	...	...	0.27	0.15	0.08	-	-	0.51
F Manufacture of non-metallic mineral products, except products of petroleum and coal	...	...	...	...	...	...	0.33	-	0.77	-	-	1.10
G Basic metal industries	...	...	...	...	...	...	...	...	...	...	...	...
H Manufacture of fabricated metal products, machinery and equipment	...	...	...	...	...	...	0.50	0.11	0.57	0.02	0.04	1.17
I Other manufacturing industries	...	...	...	...	...	...	...	...	...	...	...	...
4 Electricity, gas and water	0.11	0.35	-0.01	-	-	0.45	0.21	0.35	0.21	-	-	0.77
A Electricity, gas and steam	...	...	...	...	...	...	0.10	0.28	0.30	-	-	0.68
B Water works and supply	...	...	...	...	...	...	0.11	0.07	-0.09	-	-	0.09

Rwanda

4.3 Cost Components of Value Added
(Continued)

Thousand Million Rwanda francs

	1982						1983					
	Compensation of Employees	Capital Consumption	Net Operating Surplus	Indirect Taxes	Less: Subsidies Received	Value Added	Compensation of Employees	Capital Consumption	Net Operating Surplus	Indirect Taxes	Less: Subsidies Received	Value Added
5 Construction	4.92	0.26	0.47	0.01	-	5.66	5.55	0.30	0.63	0.01	-	6.49
6 Wholesale and retail trade, restaurants and hotels	1.82	0.94	17.77	0.78	-	21.31	1.92	0.90	16.62	0.84	-	20.28
A Wholesale and retail trade	...	...	...	...	...	...	1.67	0.81	16.53	0.84	-	19.85
B Restaurants and hotels	...	...	...	...	...	...	0.24	0.09	0.09	-	-	0.43
7 Transport, storage and communication	0.65	0.17	3.10	0.09	-	4.01	0.60	0.21	3.52	0.43	0.07	4.69
A Transport and storage	...	...	...	...	...	...	0.36	0.21	3.52	0.43	0.01	4.51
B Communication	...	...	...	...	...	...	0.23	-	-	-	0.06	0.18
8 Finance, insurance, real estate and business services	0.10	1.99	2.69	0.01	0.05	4.74	0.80	2.17	2.52	-	0.06	5.43
A Financial institutions	...	...	...	...	...	...	0.71	0.30	-0.52	-	0.06	0.44
B Insurance	...	...	...	...	...	...	0.08	0.01	0.14	-	-	0.23
C Real estate and business services	...	...	...	...	...	...	-	1.87	2.90	-	-	4.77
9 Community, social and personal services	16.67	0.02	-	-	-	16.69	17.08	0.06	0.79	-	-	17.93
A Sanitary and similar services	...	...	...	...	...	...	...	...	...	...	...	...
B Social and related community services	...	...	...	...	...	...						
Educational services	...	...	...	...	...	...	4.40	...	...	...	...	4.40
Medical, dental, other health and veterinary services	...	...	...	...	...	...	...	...	...	...	...	...
C Recreational and cultural services	...	...	...	...	...	...	0.11	...	...	...	...	0.11
D Personal and household services	...	...	...	...	...	...	...	...	0.79	...	...	0.79
Total, Industries	28.24	4.81	90.15	5.76	0.39	128.57	30.42	5.29	97.39	6.52	0.74	138.87
Producers of Government Services	...	...	...	...	...	...	...	...	...	...	...	...
Other Producers	...	...	...	...	...	...	...	...	...	...	...	...
Total	28.24	4.81	90.15	5.76	0.39	128.57	30.42	5.29	97.39	6.52	0.74	138.87
Less: Imputed bank service charge	...	...	...	...	...	...	...	...	...	...	...	...
Import duties	...	...	...	3.87	...	3.87	...	...	...	3.68	...	3.68
Value added tax	...	...	...	...	...	...	...	...	...	...	...	...
Total	28.24	4.81	90.15	9.63	0.39	132.44	30.42	5.29	97.39	10.20	0.74	142.55

	1984						1985					
	Compensation of Employees	Capital Consumption	Net Operating Surplus	Indirect Taxes	Less: Subsidies Received	Value Added	Compensation of Employees	Capital Consumption	Net Operating Surplus	Indirect Taxes	Less: Subsidies Received	Value Added

All Producers

1 Agriculture, hunting, forestry and fishing	0.31	0.06	66.75	1.75	0.17	68.69	4.59	0.77	67.08	0.23	-	72.67
A Agriculture and hunting	0.31	0.06	65.66	1.75	0.17	67.61	...	...	...	...	...	...
B Forestry and logging	-	-	0.81	-	-	0.81	...	...	...	...	...	...
C Fishing	-	-	0.28	-	-	0.28	...	...	...	...	...	...
2 Mining and quarrying	1.01	0.31	-0.89	0.14	-	0.57	0.32	0.08	-0.02	0.08	-	0.46
A Coal mining	...	...	...	...	...	...	...	...	...	...	...	...
B Crude petroleum and natural gas production	0.01	-	0.01	-	-	0.02	...	...	...	...	...	...
C Metal ore mining	0.92	0.31	-1.02	0.14	-	0.36	...	...	...	...	...	...
D Other mining	0.08	-	0.12	-	-	0.20	...	...	...	...	...	...

Rwanda

4.3 Cost Components of Value Added
(Continued)

Thousand Million Rwanda francs

		1984						1985				
		Compensation of Employees	Capital Consumption	Net Operating Surplus	Indirect Taxes	Less: Subsidies Received	Value Added	Compensation of Employees	Capital Consumption	Net Operating Surplus	Indirect Taxes	Less: Subsidies Received	Value Added
3	Manufacturing	2.92	1.09	17.75	4.43	0.14	26.05	3.46	1.22	12.15	7.00	-	23.83
	A Manufacture of food, beverages and tobacco	0.94	0.69	13.52	4.28	0.09	19.34	...	...	...	...	...	...
	B Textile, wearing apparel and leather industries	0.36	0.02	1.29	0.01	-	1.68	...	...	...	...	...	...
	C Manufacture of wood and wood products, including furniture	0.33	0.02	0.36	-	-	0.71	...	...	...	...	...	...
	D Manufacture of paper and paper products, printing and publishing	0.09	0.04	0.02	0.02	-	0.16	...	...	...	...	...	...
	E Manufacture of chemicals and chemical petroleum, coal, rubber and plastic products	0.32	0.15	0.46	0.02	0.04	0.91	...	...	...	...	...	...
	F Manufacture of non-metallic mineral products, except products of petroleum and coal	0.34	-	0.92	-	-	1.25	...	...	...	...	...	...
	G Basic metal industries	-	0.04	0.72	-	-	0.76	...	...	...	...	...	...
	H Manufacture of fabricated metal products, machinery and equipment	0.55	0.14	0.46	0.10	0.01	1.25	...	...	...	...	...	...
	I Other manufacturing industries	...	...	...	...	...	...	...	...	...	...	...	...
4	Electricity, gas and water	0.24	0.53	0.15	-	-	0.91	0.34	0.55	0.02	-	-	0.91
	A Electricity, gas and steam	0.16	0.46	0.04	-	-	0.66	...	...	...	...	...	...
	B Water works and supply	0.08	0.07	0.11	-	-	0.25	...	...	...	...	...	...
5	Construction	5.97	0.99	0.86	0.06	-	7.89	8.78	0.31	5.98	0.05	-	15.11
6	Wholesale and retail trade, restaurants and hotels	2.07	0.96	17.79	0.90	-	21.72	5.16	0.48	15.23	0.36	-	21.24
	A Wholesale and retail trade	1.73	0.87	17.73	0.89	-	21.22	...	...	...	...	...	...
	B Restaurants and hotels	0.34	0.09	0.06	0.01	-	0.50	...	...	...	...	...	...
7	Transport, storage and communication	0.83	0.50	2.97	0.12	-	4.43	2.24	3.05	2.63	0.55	-	8.47
	A Transport and storage	0.59	0.50	2.78	0.12	-	3.99	...	...	...	...	...	...
	B Communication	0.24	-	0.19	-	-	0.43	...	...	...	...	...	...
8	Finance, insurance, real estate and business services	0.72	2.30	3.27	-	0.07	6.23	4.25	2.87	6.01	0.12	-	13.25
	A Financial institutions	0.63	0.22	-0.07	-	0.07	0.72	...	...	...	...	...	...
	B Insurance	0.10	0.01	0.10	-	-	0.21	...	...	...	...	...	...
	C Real estate and business services	-	2.07	3.23	-	-	5.30	...	...	...	...	...	...
9	Community, social and personal services	16.51	0.07	1.21	-	-	17.80	12.22	0.07	-	-	-	12.28
	A Sanitary and similar services	...	...	...	...	...	...	...	...	...	...	...	...
	B Social and related community services	...	...	...	...	...	...	...	...	...	...	...	...
	Educational services	4.99	...	...	...	...	4.99	...	...	...	...	...	...
	Medical, dental, other health and veterinary services	...	...	...	...	...	...	...	...	...	...	...	...
	C Recreational and cultural services	0.15	...	...	...	...	0.15	...	...	...	...	...	...
	D Personal and household services	...	...	0.89	...	...	0.89	...	...	...	...	...	...
Total, industries		30.58	6.81	109.85	7.40	0.38	154.29	41.35	9.39	109.08	8.41	-	168.23
Producers of Government Services		...	...	...	...	...	...	...	...	...	...	...	...
Other Producers		...	...	...	...	...	...	...	...	...	...	...	...
Total		30.58	6.81	109.85	7.40	0.38	154.29	41.35	9.39	109.08	8.41	-	168.23
Less: Imputed bank service charge		...	...	...	...	...	...	...	...	...	...	...	...
Import duties		...	...	...	4.64	...	4.64	...	...	...	5.47	...	5.47
Value added tax		...	...	...	...	...	...	...	...	...	...	...	...
Total		30.58	6.81	109.85	12.04	0.38	158.93	41.35	9.39	109.08	13.88	-	173.70

Rwanda

4.3 Cost Components of Value Added

Thousand Million Rwanda francs

		1986					
		Compensation of Employees	Capital Consumption	Net Operating Surplus	Indirect Taxes	Less: Subsidies Received	Value Added
				All Producers			
1	Agriculture, hunting, forestry and fishing	4.01	0.70	57.41	0.45	-	62.58
	A Agriculture and hunting	...	...	...	...	...	...
	B Forestry and logging	...	...	...	...	...	...
	C Fishing	...	...	...	...	...	...
2	Mining and quarrying	0.16	-	0.12	0.04	-	0.33
	A Coal mining	...	...	...	...	...	...
	B Crude petroleum and natural gas production	...	...	...	...	...	...
	C Metal ore mining	...	...	...	...	...	...
	D Other mining	...	...	...	...	...	...
3	Manufacturing	4.07	1.30	11.90	9.87	-	27.13
	A Manufacture of food, beverages and tobacco	...	...	...	...	...	...
	B Textile, wearing apparel and leather industries	...	...	...	...	...	...
	C Manufacture of wood and wood products, including furniture	...	...	...	...	...	...
	D Manufacture of paper and paper products, printing and publishing	...	...	...	...	...	...
	E Manufacture of chemicals and chemical petroleum, coal, rubber and plastic products	...	...	...	...	...	...
	F Manufacture of non-metallic mineral products, except products of petroleum and coal	...	...	...	...	...	...
	G Basic metal industries	...	...	...	...	...	...
	H Manufacture of fabricated metal products, machinery and equipment	...	...	...	...	...	...
	I Other manufacturing industries	...	...	...	...	...	...
4	Electricity, gas and water	0.55	0.61	-0.06	-	-	1.10
	A Electricity, gas and steam	...	...	...	...	...	...
	B Water works and supply	...	...	...	...	...	...
5	Construction	6.65	0.74	4.37	0.11	-	11.86
6	Wholesale and retail trade, restaurants and hotels	5.10	0.50	17.67	0.33	-	23.61
	A Wholesale and retail trade	...	...	...	...	...	...
	B Restaurants and hotels	...	...	...	...	...	...
7	Transport, storage and communication	2.55	3.14	3.84	0.64	-	10.17
	A Transport and storage	...	...	...	...	...	...
	B Communication	...	...	...	...	...	...
8	Finance, insurance, real estate and business services	4.71	3.45	4.35	-	-	12.52
	A Financial institutions	...	...	...	...	...	...
	B Insurance	...	...	...	...	...	...
	C Real estate and business services	...	...	...	...	...	...
9	Community, social and personal services	14.11	0.09	-0.28	0.04	-	13.96
	A Sanitary and similar services	...	...	...	...	...	...
	B Social and related community services	...	...	...	...	...	...
	Educational services	...	...	...	...	...	...
	Medical, dental, other health and veterinary services	...	...	...	...	...	...
	C Recreational and cultural services	...	...	...	...	...	...
	D Personal and household services	...	...	...	...	...	...

Rwanda

4.3 Cost Components of Value Added
(Continued)

Thousand Million Rwanda francs

	\multicolumn{6}{c	}{1986}
	Compensation of Employees	Capital Consumption	Net Operating Surplus	Indirect Taxes	Less: Subsidies Received	Value Added
Total, Industries	41.91	10.53	99.33	11.48	-	163.26
Producers of Government Services	...	...	...	...	...	...
Other Producers	...	...	...	...	...	...
Total	41.91	10.53	99.33	11.48	-	163.26
Less: Imputed bank service charge	...	...	...	...	...	...
Import duties	...	...	...	5.73	...	5.73
Value added tax	...	...	...	...	...	...
Total	41.91	10.53	99.33	17.21	-	168.99

Saint Kitts and Nevis

Source. Reply to the United Nations National Accounts Questionnaire from the Ministry of Finance, St. Kitts-Nevis.
General note. The estimates shown in the following tables have been prepared in accordance with the United Nations System of National Accounts so far as the existing data would permit.

1.1 Expenditure on the Gross Domestic Product, in Current Prices

Thousand E.C. dollars

	1970	1975	1978	1979	1980	1981	1982	1983	1984	1985	1986	1987
1 Government final consumption expenditure	...	12140	20130	22170	26310	38780	35520	35520	37520	...	...	...
2 Private final consumption expenditure	...	57085	57550	73870	92690	108950	117200	140150	129560	...	...	...
3 Gross capital formation	...	9441	25140	37250	49440	46060	55120	49910	53270	...	...	...
A Increase in stocks	...	1714	-	-	-	-	-	-	-	...	...	...
B Gross fixed capital formation	...	7727	25140	37250	49440	46060	55120	49910	53270	...	...	...
Residential buildings	...	930	...	...	...	...	...	...	...	...	...	...
Non-residential buildings	...	1009	...	...	...	...	...	...	...	...	...	...
Other construction and land improvement etc.	...	439	...	...	...	...	...	...	...	...	...	...
Other	...	5346	...	...	...	...	...	...	...	...	...	...
4 Exports of goods and services	...	46841	58600	64300	86730	92240	80630	78840	92820	...	...	...
5 Less: Imports of goods and services	...	51361	69100	90200	125930	136610	130370	150390	145980	...	...	...
Equals: Gross Domestic Product	...	74146	92320	107390	129240	149420	158100	154030	167190	...	...	...

1.3 Cost Components of the Gross Domestic Product

Thousand E.C. dollars

	1970	1975	1978	1979	1980	1981	1982	1983	1984	1985	1986	1987
1 Indirect taxes, net	...	12403	16030	19860	26130	28880	20340	21940	...	...	...	...
A Indirect taxes	...	12403	17820	22840	32220	35020	27270	25220	26700	...	...	...
B Less: Subsidies	...	-	1790	2980	6090	6140	6930	3280	...	...	...	...
2 Consumption of fixed capital	...	2646	...	...	...	...	...	...	...	...	...	...
3 Compensation of employees paid by resident producers to:	...	49331	...	...	...	...	...	...	...	...	...	...
4 Operating surplus	...	9766	...	...	...	...	...	...	...	...	...	...
Equals: Gross Domestic Product	...	74146	92320	107390	129240	149420	158100	154030	167190	...	...	...

1.10 Gross Domestic Product by Kind of Activity, in Current Prices

Thousand E.C. dollars

	1970	1975	1978	1979	1980	1981	1982	1983	1984	1985	1986	1987
1 Agriculture, hunting, forestry and fishing	8700	7832	12180	13640	16510	13830	20310	16190	19720	16980	17410	...
2 Mining and quarrying	800	-	160	240	320	330	410	450	380	450	500	...
3 Manufacturing		27503	13240	12790	15740	17880	18660	17550	22620	21940	23660	...
4 Electricity, gas and water	400	10	710	810	880	1110	1430	1360	1440	1530	1630	...
5 Construction	4000	3274	5490	8120	10580	10850	13600	14960	12820	14860	16670	...

Saint Kitts and Nevis

1.10 Gross Domestic Product by Kind of Activity, in Current Prices
(Continued)

Thousand E.C. dollars

	1970	1975	1978	1979	1980	1981	1982	1983	1984	1985	1986	1987
6 Wholesale and retail trade, restaurants and hotels	4500	11226	11530	14590	17480	19480	20830	22620	25890	30020	34710	...
7 Transport, storage and communication	1100	3343	7320	7840	10000	15420	17450	16420	19540	21140	23900	...
8 Finance, insurance, real estate and business services	2600	7316	9320	11090	11920	13320	16380	16310	19540	20870	22370	...
9 Community, social and personal services	1500	4035	3530	3970	5200	6570	7300	7830	8400	9010	9650	...
Total, Industries	23600	64539	63480	73090	88630	98790	116370	113690	130350	136800	150500	
Producers of Government Services	5800	9606	15970	18250	19200	26640	28550	29930	36080	37330	41540	...
Other Producers	...	...	...	...	...	...	...	...	...	...	...	...
Subtotal a	29400	74145	79450	91340	107830	125430	144920	143620	166430	174130	192040	...
Less: Imputed bank service charge	...	...	2930	3480	4360	3990	6180	7130	8920	8020	8620	...
Plus: Import duties	...	...	...	...	...	...	...	...	...	...	...	...
Plus: Value added tax	...	...	...	...	...	...	...	...	...	...	...	...
Equals: Gross Domestic Product a	...	74146	76520	87860	103460	121440	138740	136490	157510	166110	183420	...

a) Gross domestic product in factor values.

1.11 Gross Domestic Product by Kind of Activity, in Constant Prices

Thousand E.C. dollars

	1970	1975	1978	1979	1980	1981	1982	1983	1984	1985	1986	1987
			\multicolumn{10}{c}{At constant prices of:1977}	
1 Agriculture, hunting, forestry and fishing	...	...	13700	14860	13440	14090	14090	11500	11990	11720	11530	...
2 Mining and quarrying	...	...	150	180	230	240	280	310	260	290	320	...
3 Manufacturing	...	...	13150	13310	13530	12150	13170	11720	13150	12440	13050	...
4 Electricity, gas and water	...	...	710	740	880	940	1000	1010	1070	1160	1270	...
5 Construction	...	...	4940	6090	7720	7990	9490	10440	8720	9810	10300	...
6 Wholesale and retail trade, restaurants and hotels	...	...	9960	11100	11970	12110	12680	13430	15170	17100	18840	...
7 Transport, storage and communication	...	...	6180	6290	6880	9290	9410	9640	10480	11030	11850	...
8 Finance, insurance, real estate and business services	...	...	8940	9460	9780	9760	10580	10750	11360	11870	12400	...
9 Community, social and personal services	...	...	3310	3370	3750	4290	4500	4720	4950	5200	5460	...
Total, Industries	...	...	61040	65400	68180	70860	75200	73520	77150	80620	85020	...
Producers of Government Services	...	...	13070	14950	15690	16580	17750	18500	22400	23520	23910	...
Other Producers	...	...	...	...	...	...	...	...	...	...	...	...
Subtotal a	...	...	74110	80350	83870	87440	92950	92020	99550	104140	108930	...
Less: Imputed bank service charge	...	...	2640	3100	3590	3060	3250	3300	3630	3810	4040	...
Plus: Import duties	...	...	...	...	...	...	...	...	...	...	...	...
Plus: Value added tax	...	...	...	...	...	...	...	...	...	...	...	...
Equals: Gross Domestic Product a	...	...	71470	77250	80280	84380	89700	88720	95920	100330	104890	...

a) Gross domestic product in factor values.

Saint Kitts and Nevis

1.12 Relations Among National Accounting Aggregates

Thousand E.C. dollars

	1970	1975	1978	1979	1980	1981	1982	1983	1984	1985	1986	1987
Gross Domestic Product	...	...	...	...	...	...	158100	154030	167190	...	...	...
Plus: Net factor income from the rest of the world	...	...	...	...	...	...	-9100	-2200	-800	-2200	...	...
Equals: Gross National Product	...	...	...	...	...	...	149000	151830	166390	...	...	...
Less: Consumption of fixed capital	...	...	...	...	...	...	...	...	...	...	...	...
Equals: National Income	...	...	...	...	...	...	...	...	...	...	...	...
Plus: Net current transfers from the rest of the world	...	...	...	...	...	...	35100	30500	31600	...	...	...
Equals: National Disposable Income	...	...	...	...	...	...	...	...	...	...	...	...
Less: Final consumption	...	...	...	...	...	...	...	...	...	...	...	...
Equals: Net Saving	...	...	...	...	...	...	...	...	...	...	...	...
Less: Surplus of the nation on current transactions	...	...	...	...	...	...	...	...	...	...	...	...
Equals: Net Capital Formation	...	...	...	...	...	...	...	...	...	...	...	...

Saint Lucia

Source. 'Economic Survey and Projections', British Development Division in the Caribbean.
General note. The estimates shown in the following tables have been prepared in accordance with the United Nations System of National Accounts so far as the existing data would permit.

1.1 Expenditure on the Gross Domestic Product, in Current Prices

Million E.C. dollars

	1970	1975	1978	1979	1980	1981	1982	1983	1984	1985	1986	1987
1 Government final consumption expenditure	...	23.2	35.8	46.3	59.4	73.4	87.9	97.5	102.7	...	...	...
2 Private final consumption expenditure	...	96.5	175.3	205.5	225.3	280.1	274.6	243.7	266.7	...	...	...
3 Gross capital formation	...	56.8	101.2	128.6	159.1	164.8	145.3	113.8	126.0	...	...	...
A Increase in stocks	...	6.7	16.9	21.4	26.2	27.5	24.2	19.0	21.0	...	...	...
B Gross fixed capital formation	...	50.1	84.3	107.2	132.9	137.3	121.1	94.8	105.0	...	...	...
4 Exports of goods and services	...	51.5	147.2	176.3	213.0	191.7	200.1	241.4	261.4	...	...	...
5 Less: Imports of goods and services	...	104.8	237.9	284.6	351.5	369.1	344.3	316.4	348.6	...	...	...
Equals: Gross Domestic Product	...	123.2	221.6	272.1	305.3	340.9	363.6	380.0	408.2	...	...	...

1.10 Gross Domestic Product by Kind of Activity, in Current Prices

Million E.C. dollars

	1970	1975	1978	1979	1980	1981	1982	1983	1984	1985	1986	1987
1 Agriculture, hunting, forestry and fishing	...	16.1	33.2	34.8	31.0	28.9	36.1	42.3	46.2	58.3	70.7	...
2 Mining and quarrying	...	1.5	1.3	3.1	3.9	4.1	3.2	2.2	2.3	2.3	2.5	...
3 Manufacturing	...	7.4	15.2	18.9	24.7	25.3	26.8	30.2	31.1	33.0	34.0	...
4 Electricity, gas and water	...	2.8	4.7	5.0	5.5	7.3	8.6	11.2	13.6	15.0	16.5	...
5 Construction	...	11.2	17.2	25.2	31.5	37.9	33.1	19.6	23.2	27.0	31.9	...
6 Wholesale and retail trade, restaurants and hotels	...	18.3	48.6	58.3	67.2	72.9	72.8	75.8	83.0	88.4	94.1	...
7 Transport, storage and communication	...	8.5	21.6	25.9	30.9	34.5	35.3	37.6	38.7	40.4	42.2	...
8 Finance, insurance, real estate and business services	...	16.3	20.6	25.0	28.9	36.8	40.0	41.5	42.5	43.8	45.2	...
9 Community, social and personal services	...	7.0	8.0	9.2	11.4	13.5	14.9	16.2	17.9	19.0	20.5	...
Total, Industries	...	89.1	170.4	205.4	235.0	261.2	270.8	276.6	298.5	327.2	357.6	...
Producers of Government Services	...	19.0	29.7	34.5	41.2	56.1	62.3	67.8	76.3	84.0	92.0	...
Other Producers	...	...	...	...	...	...	...	...	...	...	...	...
Subtotal [a]	...	108.1	200.1	239.9	276.2	317.3	333.1	344.4	374.8	411.2	449.6	...
Less: Imputed bank service charge	...	...	9.1	10.8	12.0	17.9	20.6	21.0	21.8	22.4	23.0	...
Plus: Import duties	...	...	...	...	...	...	...	...	...	...	...	...
Plus: Value added tax	...	...	...	...	...	...	...	...	...	...	...	...
Equals: Gross Domestic Product [a]	...	108.1	191.0	229.1	264.2	299.4	312.5	323.4	353.0	388.8	426.6	...

a) Gross domestic product in factor values.

1.11 Gross Domestic Product by Kind of Activity, in Constant Prices

Million E.C. dollars

	1970	1975	1978	1979	1980	1981	1982	1983	1984	1985	1986	1987
			At constant prices of:1977									
1 Agriculture, hunting, forestry and fishing	...	...	29.3	27.9	22.1	18.8	25.0	28.7	31.0	34.8	39.1	...
2 Mining and quarrying	...	...	1.2	2.8	3.0	2.8	1.5	0.9	0.9	0.9	1.0	...
3 Manufacturing	...	...	16.0	13.4	15.5	15.8	17.0	18.8	18.8	19.3	19.6	...
4 Electricity, gas and water	...	...	5.1	5.9	5.7	5.8	6.0	6.6	7.1	7.6	8.0	...
5 Construction	...	...	15.3	18.2	18.7	19.8	17.2	9.7	10.9	12.5	14.5	...

Saint Lucia

1.11 Gross Domestic Product by Kind of Activity, in Constant Prices
(Continued)

Million E.C. dollars

	1970	1975	1978	1979	1980	1981	1982	1983	1984	1985	1986	1987
			\multicolumn{10}{c}{At constant prices of:1977}	
6 Wholesale and retail trade, restaurants and hotels	...	...	44.2	46.2	46.0	44.3	43.5	45.3	48.0	49.6	51.9	...
7 Transport, storage and communication	...	...	19.7	20.3	19.0	18.7	19.1	22.0	23.0	24.9	27.0	...
8 Finance, insurance, real estate and business services	...	...	18.5	19.6	20.0	20.9	21.6	22.8	23.1	24.0	24.7	...
9 Community, social and personal services	...	...	7.2	7.6	7.9	8.2	8.6	9.3	10.0	10.4	10.6	...
Total, Industries	...	...	156.5	161.9	157.9	155.1	159.5	164.1	172.8	184.0	196.4	...
Producers of Government Services	...	...	28.2	30.2	32.8	38.7	39.9	43.4	44.8	46.4	47.1	...
Other Producers	...	...	...	...	...	...	...	...	...	...	...	...
Subtotal [a]	...	...	184.7	192.1	190.7	193.8	199.4	207.5	217.6	230.4	243.5	...
Less: Imputed bank service charge	...	...	7.7	8.6	8.6	9.2	9.5	9.9	10.1	10.5	10.8	...
Plus: Import duties	...	...	...	...	...	...	...	...	...	...	...	...
Plus: Value added tax	...	...	...	...	...	...	...	...	...	...	...	...
Equals: Gross Domestic Product [a]	...	...	177.0	183.5	182.1	184.3	189.9	197.6	207.5	219.9	232.7	...

a) Gross domestic product in factor values.

Saint Vincent and the Grenadines

Source. 'The preparation of national accounts statistics in St. Vincent and the Grenadines is undertaken by the Statistical Office, Ministry of Finance, Planning and Development, Kingstown. The official estimates together with a description of the sources and methods used for the national accounts estimation are published in 'National Accounts of St. Vincent and the Grenadines'.

General note. The estimates shown in the following tables have been prepared in accordance with the United Nations System of National Accounts so far as the existing data would permit.

1.1 Expenditure on the Gross Domestic Product, in Current Prices

Million E.C. dollars

	1970	1975	1978	1979	1980	1981	1982	1983	1984	1985	1986	1987
1 Government final consumption expenditure	...	...	27.6	34.0	37.4	46.8	54.0	58.3	62.9	60.2	67.8	...
2 Private final consumption expenditure	...	...	90.1	123.3	140.2	147.1	176.4	194.0	174.0	173.6	208.7	...
3 Gross capital formation	...	...	34.4	48.6	62.8	64.1	64.7	62.9	76.8	86.1	102.0	...
A Increase in stocks	...	...	-	-	-	-	-	-	6.3	10.0	1.2	...
B Gross fixed capital formation	...	...	34.4	48.6	62.8	64.1	64.7	62.9	70.5	76.1	100.8	...
Residential buildings	...	...										...
Non-residential buildings	...	...	24.2	32.1	41.1	47.2	46.1	42.1	38.1	44.7	67.1	
Other construction and land improvement etc.	...	...										...
Other	...	...	10.2	16.5	21.7	16.9	18.6	20.8	32.4	31.4	33.7	
4 Exports of goods and services	...	...	74.0	76.3	89.5	116.0	135.9	155.7	192.9	222.5	225.2	...
5 Less: Imports of goods and services	...	...	103.9	140.2	170.9	178.8	204.7	217.5	231.6	239.9	263.0	...
Equals: Gross Domestic Product	...	...	122.2	142.0	159.0	195.2	226.3	253.4	275.0	302.5	340.7	...

1.10 Gross Domestic Product by Kind of Activity, in Current Prices

Million E.C. dollars

	1970	1975	1978	1979	1980	1981	1982	1983	1984	1985	1986	1987
1 Agriculture, hunting, forestry and fishing	...	...	20.7	19.8	19.8	27.5	31.9	36.6	43.2	49.5	54.8	...
2 Mining and quarrying	...	...	0.3	0.4	0.5	0.6	0.6	0.6	0.5	0.5	0.8	...
3 Manufacturing	...	...	10.3	13.1	14.2	18.4	20.7	21.3	28.9	28.7	26.8	...
4 Electricity, gas and water	...	...	2.6	3.0	3.3	4.4	5.2	6.8	7.1	9.5	10.6	...
5 Construction	...	...	10.8	14.4	18.4	20.6	21.8	23.2	16.6	19.4	28.9	...
6 Wholesale and retail trade, restaurants and hotels	...	...	14.8	16.1	20.3	22.1	26.7	28.9	30.7	33.7	37.2	...
7 Transport, storage and communication	...	...	17.3	21.6	23.5	28.9	34.2	37.2	40.3	45.4	52.6	...
8 Finance, insurance, real estate and business services	...	...	9.9	12.4	15.1	18.3	20.5	22.8	27.1	25.9	29.3	...
9 Community, social and personal services	...	...	3.1	3.3	4.6	5.3	5.7	6.1	6.4	6.5	6.9	...
Total, Industries	...	...	89.8	104.1	119.7	146.1	167.3	183.5	200.8	219.1	247.9	...
Producers of Government Services	...	...	19.0	21.6	22.6	29.4	32.9	39.5	41.5	42.9	46.5	...
Other Producers	...	...	...	...	...	...	...	...	...	...	...	...
Subtotal [a]	...	...	108.8	125.7	142.3	175.5	200.2	223.0	242.3	262.0	294.4	...
Less: Imputed bank service charge	...	...	4.5	5.5	7.4	8.5	10.8	11.7	11.9	12.0	12.8	...
Plus: Import duties	...	...	...	...	...	...	...	...	...	...	...	...
Plus: Value added tax	...	...	...	...	...	...	...	...	...	...	...	...
Plus: Other adjustments [b]	...	...	18.0	21.9	24.2	28.2	36.8	42.2	44.7	52.3	59.1	...
Equals: Gross Domestic Product	...	...	122.3	142.1	159.1	195.2	226.3	253.5	275.1	302.3	340.7	...

a) Gross domestic product in factor values.
b) Item 'Other adjustments' refers to indirect taxes net of subsidies.

1.11 Gross Domestic Product by Kind of Activity, in Constant Prices

Million E.C. dollars

	1970	1975	1978	1979	1980	1981	1982	1983	1984	1985	1986	1987
			At constant prices of:1977									
1 Agriculture, hunting, forestry and fishing	...	...	17.2	14.6	12.5	17.7	18.7	20.2	21.5	23.3	24.2	...
2 Mining and quarrying	...	...	0.2	0.3	0.3	0.3	0.3	0.3	0.3	0.4	0.4	...
3 Manufacturing	...	...	8.9	10.6	11.1	11.3	12.0	12.3	13.3	13.5	13.4	...
4 Electricity, gas and water	...	...	2.8	3.0	3.2	3.3	3.6	3.7	3.8	4.1	4.5	...
5 Construction	...	...	8.8	10.6	11.2	11.4	11.5	12.2	12.1	12.4	14.3	...
6 Wholesale and retail trade, restaurants and hotels	...	...	14.3	14.0	15.7	14.3	16.1	16.6	17.2	18.5	20.3	...
7 Transport, storage and communication	...	...	15.5	16.7	19.0	21.5	23.6	26.4	28.8	32.0	34.4	...
8 Finance, insurance, real estate and business services	...	...	7.7	8.1	9.2	9.7	9.6	9.9	10.7	10.0	10.5	...
9 Community, social and personal services	...	...	2.9	2.9	3.1	3.2	3.4	3.4	3.5	3.5	3.6	...

Saint Vincent and the Grenadines

1.11 Gross Domestic Product by Kind of Activity, in Constant Prices
(Continued)

Million E.C. dollars

	1970	1975	1978	1979	1980	1981	1982	1983	1984	1985	1986	1987
				At constant prices of:1977								
Total, Industries	...	...	78.3	80.8	85.3	92.7	98.8	105.0	111.2	117.7	125.6	...
Producers of Government Services	...	...	15.6	16.5	17.1	17.5	17.5	17.8	18.4	18.9	19.5	...
Other Producers	...	...	...	...	...	...	...	...	...	...	...	...
Subtotal [a]	...	...	93.9	97.3	102.4	110.2	116.3	122.8	129.6	136.6	145.1	...
Less: Imputed bank service charge	...	...	3.2	3.5	4.3	4.2	4.4	4.3	3.9	3.5	3.7	...
Plus: Import duties	...	...	...	...	...	...	...	...	...	...	...	...
Plus: Value added tax	...	...	...	...	...	...	...	...	...	...	...	...
Plus: Other adjustments	...	...	15.6	17.1	17.6	17.9	21.8	23.8	24.4	27.8	29.6	...
Equals: Gross Domestic Product [a]	...	...	106.3	110.9	115.7	123.9	133.7	142.3	150.1	160.9	171.0	...

a) Gross domestic product in factor values.

1.12 Relations Among National Accounting Aggregates

Million E.C. dollars

	1970	1975	1978	1979	1980	1981	1982	1983	1984	1985	1986	1987
Gross Domestic Product	...	...	122.3	142.1	159.1	195.2	226.3	253.5	275.1	302.3	340.7	...
Plus: Net factor income from the rest of the world	...	...	-	-1.6	-2.4	-4.6	-7.3	-6.2	-8.1	-7.8	-9.5	...
Equals: Gross National Product	...	...	122.3	140.5	156.7	190.6	219.0	247.3	267.0	294.5	331.2	...
Less: Consumption of fixed capital	...	...	...	...	...	...	...	...	...	...	...	...
Equals: National Income	...	...	...	...	...	...	...	...	...	...	...	...
Plus: Net current transfers from the rest of the world	...	...	...	...	...	...	...	...	...	...	...	...
Equals: National Disposable Income	...	...	...	...	...	...	...	...	...	...	...	...
Less: Final consumption	...	...	...	...	...	...	...	...	...	...	...	...
Equals: Net Saving	...	...	...	...	...	...	...	...	...	...	...	...
Less: Surplus of the nation on current transactions	...	...	...	...	...	...	...	...	...	...	...	...
Equals: Net Capital Formation	...	...	...	...	...	...	...	...	...	...	...	...

2.1 Government Final Consumption Expenditure by Function, in Current Prices

Million E.C. dollars

Fiscal year beginning 1 July

		1970	1975	1978	1979	1980	1981	1982	1983	1984	1985	1986	1987
1	General public services	...	...	4.7	5.6	4.5	7.1	...	...	...	...	...	...
2	Defence	...	...	-	-	-	-	...	...	...	...	...	...
3	Public order and safety	...	...	3.1	3.4	3.5	6.0	...	...	...	...	...	...
4	Education	...	...	9.4	8.8	9.3	15.7	...	...	...	...	...	...
5	Health	...	...	5.6	5.4	6.0	9.8	...	...	...	...	...	...
6	Social security and welfare	...	...	2.2	2.0	2.2	2.7	...	...	...	...	...	...
7	Housing and community amenities	...	...	0.7	1.4	1.4	2.7	...	...	...	...	...	...
8	Recreational, cultural and religious affairs	...	...	-	-	-	-	...	...	...	...	...	...
9	Economic services	...	...	6.5	7.6	11.4	5.2	...	...	...	...	...	...
	A Fuel and energy	...	...	...	...	...	...	...	...	...	...	...	...
	B Agriculture, forestry, fishing and hunting	...	...	1.6	1.6	1.9	3.7	...	...	...	...	...	...
	C Mining, manufacturing and construction, except fuel and energy	...	...	4.8	5.9	9.5	1.3	...	...	...	...	...	...
	D Transportation and communication	...	...	-	-	-	-	...	...	...	...	...	...
	E Other economic affairs	...	...	0.1	0.1	0.1	0.2	...	...	...	...	...	...
10	Other functions	...	...	...	...	...	...	...	...	...	...	...	...
	Total Government Final Consumption Expenditure	...	...	32.2	34.1	38.3	49.5	...	...	...	...	...	...

Samoa

Source. Reply to the United Nations National Accounts Questionnaire from the Department of Statistics, Apia.

General note. The estimates shown in the following tables have been prepared in accordance with the United Nations System of National Accounts so far as the existing data would permit.

1.1 Expenditure on the Gross Domestic Product, in Current Prices

Thousand Samoan tala

		1970	1975	1978	1979	1980	1981	1982	1983	1984	1985	1986	1987
1	Government final consumption expenditure	...	...	...	...	...	...	...	...	...	...	...	...
2	Private final consumption expenditure	...	...	...	...	...	...	...	...	...	...	...	...
3	Gross capital formation	...	...	...	...	...	...	...	...	...	...	...	...
4	Exports of goods and services	5204.6	9600.0	...	...	...	...	...	...	...	...	...	...
5	Less: Imports of goods and services	10847.2	25168.0	...	...	...	...	...	...	...	...	...	...
	Equals: Gross Domestic Product	...	...	...	...	...	...	...	...	...	...	...	...

Saudi Arabia

General note. The preparation of national accounts statistics in Saudi Arabia is undertaken by the Central Department of Statistics, Ministry of Finance and National Economy, Riyadh. The official estimates are published in the National Income Series entitled 'National Accounts of Saudi Arabia'. The most detailed description of the sources and methods used for the national accounts estimation is found in 'National Accounts of Saudi Arabia 1386-87 through 1391-92, A.H.' published in 1973. The estimates are generally in accordance with the classifications and definitions recommended in the United Nations System of National Accounts (SNA). The following tables have been prepared from successive replies to the United Nations national accounts questionnaire. The national accounts estimates shown relate to Hejra fiscal years. A Hejra fiscal year covers the period from the beginning of the seventh month of one Hejra calendar year through the end of the sixth month of the following year. When the scope and coverage of the estimates differ for conceptual or statistical reasons from the definitions and classifications recommended in SNA, a footnote is indicated to the relevant tables.

Sources and methods:

(a) Gross domestic product. Gross domestic product is estimated mainly through the production approach.

(b) Expenditure on the gross domestic product. All components of GDP by expenditure type are estimated through the expenditure approach except private final consumption expenditure and gross fixed capital formation of private transport establishments which are estimated by using the commodity-flow approach. Government consumption expenditure is calculated as the sum of compensation of employees and net current purchases of goods and services. Data are obtained from the appropriations in the government budget rather than from actual expenditure data. The estimates are, however, adjusted for under-spending. Estimates of private consumption expenditure are based on imports in c.i.f. values and gross output of domestically produced goods and services. Import duties are based on the customs tariffs whereas transport and distribution margins are based on assumed margin rates. In order to estimate the gross fixed capital formation of transport establishments, a detailed classification of import statistics is used to estimate the capital formation in transport equipment. For general government, public enterprises and private industries the estimates are based on surveys of industrial production, which include information on fixed assets. Gross capital formation of the oil sector is based on data provided by the oil companies through their annual returns. Exports of crude petroleum and petroleum products constitute over 99 per cent of total exports of merchandise. The data are obtained from annual returns of the oil companies. Non-petroleum exports and imports of merchandise are obtained from foreign trade statistics and balance of payment estimates. GDP by expenditure type at constant prices is not estimated.

(c) Cost-structure of the gross domestic product. Compensation of employees for the crude petroleum and petroleum refining industries is obtained from the annual returns provided by the oil companies. For most of the other industries, the estimates are determined on the basis of an estimated ratio of wages to gross output. Estimates of indirect taxes are made from revenue figures of the central and local governments while subsidies are calculated from information supplied by the Ministry of Finance. Gross operating surplus, including depreciation, is estimated as a residual.

(d) Gross domestic product by kind of economic activity. The table of GDP by kind of economic activity is prepared at market prices, i.e. producers' values. The production approach is used to estimate value added of the majority of industries. The income approach is used for mining other than extraction of crude petroleum and natural gas, mechanized road transport, ownership of dwellings, domestic services and producers of government services. For the agricultural sector, bench-mark estimates for 1967-68 on gross output and intermediate consumption were prepared based on the results of agricultural surveys conducted in the period 1960-1965. Other years' estimates are calculated by multiplying the 1967-68 figures by index numbers of physical output and producers' prices. The extraction of crude petroleum and natural gas are undertaken by Aramco, Getty, and Arabian Oil Company. The annual returns from these companies and from the Saudi Arabian Oil refineries provide details on sales, costs and capital expenditures which enable the calculation of gross output, intermediate consumption and compensation of employees for mining, manufacturing of petroleum products and construction. Internal prices of the oil companies are used for the calculation of sales figures and not the 'posted' prices which are used for calculating the payment of income tax. For other manufacturing, electricity, non-residential building construction, trade, water transport, financial services other than commercial banks, real estate, business services and private services, the estimates on gross output, intermediate consumption and compensation of employees for 1970 are available from the sample survey of establishments in 1971. Other years' estimates are calculated by multiplying the bench-mark year figures by quantity indexes, price indexes or assumed growth rates. Estimates on construction for the government sector are based on details of government appropriations. For the private sector, the value of construction of dwellings is derived by multiplying the estimated number of dwellings constructed by the estimated cost of construction per dwelling. For mechanized road transport, the estimated number of vehicles is multiplied by an estimated value added per vehicle while for the airlines, railways and the Tapline annual returns from the companies concerned provide data on gross output, intermediate consumption and compensation of employees. Commercial banks' figures for 1970 are obtained from a survey of the operations of commercial banks. An estimated index of growth of banking services is applied for other years. Estimates of government services are derived from a classification of government appropriations shown in the budget volumes. For the constant price estimates, the value added of the agricultural sector, manufacturing, electricity, trade, transport and other services is extrapolated by quantity indexes. Value added of crude petroleum and petroleum refining is extrapolated by quantity indexes compiled from figures on barrels produced. Different kinds of price indexes such as index of wage rates and cost of living index are used to deflate the value added of construction and the financial sectors.

1.1 Expenditure on the Gross Domestic Product, in Current Prices

Million Saudi Arabia riyals

Fiscal year beginning 1 July

	1970	1975	1978	1979	1980	1981	1982	1983	1984	1985	1986	1987
1 Government final consumption expenditure	3798	28883	71904	77563	81915	128526	126900	121800	115600	113500	...	...
2 Private final consumption expenditure	6412	23903	68608	102385	114905	126514	137300	143500	146000	122100	...	...
3 Gross capital formation	2727	34320	69270	79722	112803	102513	112900	113400	94000	77200	...	...
A Increase in stocks [a]	-205	780	-7384	-17346	6427	-19802	-2600	3300	2800	2300	...	...
B Gross fixed capital formation [b]	2932	33540	76654	97068	106376	122315	115500	110100	91200	74900	...	...
Residential buildings	697	4912	...	...	...	...	...	...	...	...	...	...
Non-residential buildings	192	8539	...	...	...	...	...	...	...	...	...	...
Other construction and land improvement etc.	1307	13439	...	...	...	...	...	...	...	...	...	...
Other	736	6337	12682	17596	...	...	...	...	...	...	...	...
4 Exports of goods and services	15189	120284	147236	258488	368425	354919	219400	168400	134700	102600	...	...
5 Less: Imports of goods and services	5205	42863	107479	132351	157459	187754	181300	175900	159400	128700	...	...
Equals: Gross Domestic Product	22921	164526	249539	385807	520589	524718	415200	371200	330900	286700	...	...

a) Item 'Increase in stocks' includes a statistical discrepancy.
b) Beginning 1974, item 'gross capital formation' includes other not classified capital goods.

1.3 Cost Components of the Gross Domestic Product

Million Saudi Arabia riyals

Fiscal year beginning 1 July

	1970	1975	1978	1979	1980	1981	1982	1983	1984	1985	1986	1987
1 Indirect taxes, net	350	-900	-455	-1390	-981	-900	-700	-800	-500	-500	...	...
A Indirect taxes	430	665	...	...	...	...	...	...	...	...	...	...
B Less: Subsidies	80	1565	...	...	...	...	...	...	...	...	...	...
2 Consumption of fixed capital [a]	...	...	...	...	...	...	...	...	...	...	...	...
3 Compensation of employees paid by resident producers to:	4833	25007	61140	75299	90177	525600	415900	372000	331400	287200	...	...
A Resident households	4305	23690	...	...	...						...	...
B Rest of the world	528	1316	...	...	...						...	...
4 Operating surplus [a]	17739	140419	188854	311898	431393						...	...
Equals: Gross Domestic Product	22921	164526	249539	385807	520589	524700	415200	371200	330900	286700	...	...

a) Item 'Operating surplus' includes consumption of fixed capital.

Saudi Arabia

1.7 External Transactions on Current Account, Summary

Million Saudi Arabia riyals — Fiscal year beginning 1 July

	1970	1975	1978	1979	1980	1981	1982	1983	1984	1985	1986	1987
Payments to the Rest of the World												
1 Imports of goods and services	5205	42863	107479	132351	157500	187700	181300	175900	159400	...	...	...
A Imports of merchandise c.i.f.	4160	29652	...	...	...	...	...	...	...	...	...	...
B Other	1045	13211	...	...	...	...	...	...	...	...	...	...
2 Factor income to the rest of the world	6028	7670	18200	36500	46400	39600	32900	31300	30300	...	...	...
A Compensation of employees	528	1316	11300	13500	13900	18300	18100	18600	18400	...	...	...
B Property and entrepreneurial income	5500	6354	6900	23000	32500	21300	14800	12700	11900	...	...	...
3 Current transfers to the rest of the world	1531	10389	11800	18300	19300	...	...	...	...	...	...	...
4 Surplus of the nation on current transactions	2790	66912	22800	90300	182300	175800	60000	8300	-10300	...	...	...
Payments to the Rest of the World and Surplus of the Nation on Current Transactions	15553	127834	160300	277500	405500	403100	274200	215500	179400	...	...	...
Receipts From The Rest of the World												
1 Exports of goods and services	15189	120284	147236	258488	368400	354900	219400	168400	134700	...	...	...
A Exports of merchandise f.o.b.	14319	116597	...	...	...	...	...	...	...	...	...	...
B Other	870	3687	...	...	...	...	...	...	...	...	...	...
2 Factor income from rest of the world	348	7537	13100	19000	37100	48200	54800	47100	44700	...	...	...
A Compensation of employees	-	-	-	-	-	-	-	-	-	...	...	...
B Property and entrepreneurial income	348	7537	13100	19000	37100	48200	54800	47100	44700	...	...	...
3 Current transfers from rest of the world	16	13	...	...	...	...	...	...	...	...	...	...
Receipts from the Rest of the World on Current Transactions	15553	127834	160300	277500	405500	403100	274200	215500	179400	...	...	...

1.10 Gross Domestic Product by Kind of Activity, in Current Prices

Million Saudi Arabia riyals — Fiscal year beginning 1 July

	1970	1975	1978	1979	1980	1981	1982	1983	1984	1985	1986	1987
1 Agriculture, hunting, forestry and fishing	1016	1586	4196	4648	5572	6740	8725	9400	11100	12600	...	...
2 Mining and quarrying	12632	110095	132218	238579	342693	325297	194659	144900	112700	82800	...	...
3 Manufacturing	1958	8173	12615	19295	25748	22384	23972	26700	27100	26200	...	...
4 Electricity, gas and water	298	151	248	271	399	-429	-850	-1000	-700	-800	...	...
5 Construction	1007	15854	34764	43108	50348	58181	54903	50200	41600	34600	...	...
6 Wholesale and retail trade, restaurants and hotels	1068	6180	13912	17760	21984	25064	28088	28400	27500	24200	...	...
7 Transport, storage and communication	1479	4077	12764	15749	17123	19871	21489	24200	23500	20500	...	...
8 Finance, insurance, real estate and business services	1104	8444	16180	18815	22325	25862	30183	31200	28400	23300	...	...
9 Community, social and personal services	265	1989	4155	5261	5504	6813	8408	8400	9000	8600	...	...
Total, Industries	20826	156549	231052	363486	491696	489783	369577	324400	280200	232000	...	...
Producers of Government Services	1805	7890	18912	23384	29905	36361	46585	47600	51400	55200	...	...
Other Producers	...	...	...	...	...	...	...	...	...	...	...	...
Subtotal	22631	164439	249964	386870	521601	526144	416162	372000	331600	287200	...	...
Less: Imputed bank service charge	50	547	2342	3279	3607	3968	4364	4400	4600	4300	...	...
Plus: Import duties	340	634	1917	2217	2595	2542	3400	3600	3900	3800	...	...
Plus: Value added tax	...	...	...	...	...	...	...	...	...	...	...	...
Equals: Gross Domestic Product	22921	164526	249539	385807	520589	524718	415200	371200	330900	286700	...	...

Saudi Arabia

1.11 Gross Domestic Product by Kind of Activity, in Constant Prices

Million Saudi Arabia riyals — Fiscal year beginning 1 July

	1970	1975	1978	1979	1980	1981	1982	1983	1984	1985	1986	1987
		1969	At constant prices of:				1979					
1 Agriculture, hunting, forestry and fishing	1018	1221	4400	4700	4900	5200	5700	6200	6300	...	...	...
2 Mining and quarrying	9971	17622	221700	238600	248000	223900	134000	116700	96700	...	...	...
3 Manufacturing	1839	2187	17700	19300	20700	22100	24200	27400	27000	...	...	...
4 Electricity, gas and water	298	345	200	300	300	-400	-500	600	600	...	...	...
5 Construction	957	3309	39500	43100	47500	52300	49100	45300	41200	...	...	...
6 Wholesale and retail trade, restaurants and hotels	1051	2331	14200	17800	21000	24200	27300	27800	27600	...	...	...
7 Transport, storage and communication	1468	1580	13800	15700	17100	18500	20100	22400	22200	...	...	...
8 Finance, insurance, real estate and business services	1053	2608	16900	18800	20500	22200	23700	24100	23300	...	...	...
9 Community, social and personal services	253	363	5100	5300	5700	6300	6700	6700	6500	...	...	...
Total, Industries	17908	31565	333500	363500	385800	374300	290300	277200	251300			
Producers of Government Services	1722	2755	22000	23400	25800	27600	29600	30400	32000			
Other Producers	...	...										
Subtotal	19630	34320	355500	387000	411500	401900	319900	307600	283400			
Less: Imputed bank service charge	48	70	2600	3300	4100	4300	4500	4500	4600			
Plus: Import duties	325	211	2200	2200	2200	1900	2200	2100	1900			
Plus: Value added tax	...	...										
Equals: Gross Domestic Product	19907	34461	355100	385800	409700	399500	317600	305100	280600	...	...	...

1.12 Relations Among National Accounting Aggregates

Million Saudi Arabia riyals — Fiscal year beginning 1 July

	1970	1975	1978	1979	1980	1981	1982	1983	1984	1985	1986	1987
Gross Domestic Product	22921	164526	249539	385807	520500	524700	415200	371200	330900	...	...	...
Plus: Net factor income from the rest of the world	-5680	-133	-5100	-17500	-9300	8600	21900	15800	14400	...	...	...
Factor income from the rest of the world	348	7537	13100	19000	37100	48200	54800	47100	44700	...	...	...
Less: Factor income to the rest of the world	6028	7670	18200	36500	46400	39600	32900	31300	30300	...	...	...
Equals: Gross National Product	17241	164393	244439	368307	511200	533300	437100	387000	345300	...	...	...
Less: Consumption of fixed capital	...	...	...	...	...	...	...	...	...			
Equals: National Income [a]	17242	164393	244439	368307	511200	533300	437100	387000	345300	...	...	...
Plus: Net current transfers from the rest of the world	-1515	-10376	-11800	-18300	-19300	...	...	...	...			
Current transfers from the rest of the world	16	13	...	...	...	...	...	...	...			
Less: Current transfers to the rest of the world	1531	10389	11800	18300	19300	...	...	...	...			
Equals: National Disposable Income [b]	15727	154017	232639	350007	491900	533300	437100	387000	345300	...	...	...
Less: Final consumption	10210	52785	140512	179948	196800	255000	264200	265300	261600	...	...	...
Equals: Net Saving [c]	5517	101232	92100	170100	295100	278300	172900	121700	83700	...	...	...
Less: Surplus of the nation on current transactions	2790	66912	22800	90300	182300	175800	60000	8300	-10300	...	...	...
Equals: Net Capital Formation [d]	2727	34320	69300	79800	112800	102500	112900	113400	94000	...	...	...

a) Item 'National income' includes consumption of fixed capital.
b) Item 'National disposable income' includes consumption of fixed capital.
c) Item 'Net saving' includes consumption of fixed capital.
d) Item 'Net capital formation' includes consumption of fixed capital.

Saudi Arabia

2.1 Government Final Consumption Expenditure by Function, in Current Prices

Million Saudi Arabia riyals — Fiscal year beginning 1 July

	1970	1975	1978	1979	1980	1981	1982	1983	1984	1985	1986	1987
1 General public services	646	2991	...	...	...	...	...	...	...	...	...	...
2 Defence	1804	17473	...	...	...	...	...	...	...	...	...	...
3 Public order and safety	...	...	...	...	...	...	...	...	...	...	...	...
4 Education	469	3074	...	...	...	...	...	...	...	...	...	...
5 Health	153	826	...	...	...	...	...	...	...	...	...	...
6 Social security and welfare	24	81	...	...	...	...	...	...	...	...	...	...
7 Housing and community amenities	57	-	...	...	...	...	...	...	...	...	...	...
8 Recreational, cultural and religious affairs	146	339	...	...	...	...	...	...	...	...	...	...
9 Economic services	332	2484	...	...	...	...	...	...	...	...	...	...
10 Other functions	166	1614	...	...	...	...	...	...	...	...	...	...
Total Government Final Consumption Expenditure	3798	28883	...	...	...	...	...	...	...	...	...	...

2.17 Exports and Imports of Goods and Services, Detail

Million Saudi Arabia riyals — Fiscal year beginning 1 July

	1970	1975	1978	1979	1980	1981	1982	1983	1984	1985	1986	1987
Exports of Goods and Services												
1 Exports of merchandise, f.o.b.	14319	116597	...	...	...	...	...	...	...	...	...	...
2 Transport and communication	122	1070	...	...	...	...	...	...	...	...	...	...
3 Insurance service charges	...	...	...	...	...	...	...	...	...	...	...	...
4 Other commodities	32	78	...	...	...	...	...	...	...	...	...	...
5 Adjustments of merchandise exports to change-of-ownership basis	...	...	...	...	...	...	...	...	...	...	...	...
6 Direct purchases in the domestic market by non-residential households	717	2539	...	...	...	...	...	...	...	...	...	...
7 Direct purchases in the domestic market by extraterritorial bodies	...	...	...	...	...	...	...	...	...	...	...	...
Total Exports of Goods and Services [a]	15189	120284	...	...	...	...	...	...	...	...	...	...
Imports of Goods and Services												
1 Imports of merchandise, c.i.f.	4160	29652	...	...	...	...	...	...	...	...	...	...
2 Adjustments of merchandise imports to change-of-ownership basis	...	...	...	...	...	...	...	...	...	...	...	...
3 Other transport and communication	...	...	...	...	...	...	...	...	...	...	...	...
4 Other insurance service charges	...	...	...	...	...	...	...	...	...	...	...	...
5 Other commodities	94	856	...	...	...	...	...	...	...	...	...	...
6 Direct purchases abroad by government	951	12355	...	...	...	...	...	...	...	...	...	...
7 Direct purchases abroad by resident households			...	...	...	...	...	...	...	...	...	...
Total Imports of Goods and Services [a]	5205	42863	...	...	...	...	...	...	...	...	...	...
Balance of Goods and Services	9984	77421	...	...	...	...	...	...	...	...	...	...
Total Imports and Balance of Goods and Services [a]	15189	120284	...	...	...	...	...	...	...	...	...	...

a) Data for this table have not been revised, therefore, data for some years are not comparable with those of other tables.

Senegal

Source. Reply to the United Nations National Accounts Questionnaire from the Direction de la Statistique, Dakar.
General note. The estimates shown in the following tables have been adjusted by the United Nations Statistical Office to conform to the United Nations System of National Accounts so far as the existing data would permit.

1.1 Expenditure on the Gross Domestic Product, in Current Prices

Thousand Million CFA francs

	1970	1975	1978	1979	1980	1981	1982	1983	1984	1985	1986	1987
1 Government final consumption expenditure	35.7	61.8	91.1	111.0	140.3	150.7	169.1	177.8	206.8	213.0	224.7	...
2 Private final consumption expenditure	177.3	294.5	385.1	446.7	504.0	551.9	635.5	672.8	758.1	925.5	986.1	...
3 Gross capital formation	37.7	72.3	86.2	108.4	97.3	110.1	132.9	188.9	160.7	157.8	179.4	...
A Increase in stocks	7.7	15.7	19.0	25.8	-2.9	7.7	8.4	55.8	8.9	-3.5	-3.6	...
B Gross fixed capital formation	30.0	56.6	67.2	82.6	100.2	102.4	124.5	133.1	151.8	161.3	183.0	...
4 Exports of goods and services	65.3	147.9	149.9	200.7	164.3	178.3	319.5	334.7	396.4	351.8	349.3	...
5 Less: Imports of goods and services	75.9	170.1	217.6	284.9	278.4	321.2	412.9	449.3	506.5	496.1	432.5	...
Equals: Gross Domestic Product	240.1	406.4	494.7	581.9	627.5	669.8	844.3	924.9	1015.5	1152.0	1307.0	...

1.2 Expenditure on the Gross Domestic Product, in Constant Prices

Thousand Million CFA francs

	1970	1975	1978	1979	1980	1981	1982	1983	1984	1985	1986	1987
					At constant prices of: 1977							
1 Government final consumption expenditure	59.6	66.9	84.8	90.9	92.8	94.9	99.0	102.3	104.1	106.8	110.0	...
2 Private final consumption expenditure	293.5	328.0	365.0	388.4	395.3	397.1	398.5	417.1	400.8	442.2	442.2	...
3 Gross capital formation	72.7	88.2	80.4	90.9	70.0	70.9	75.9	79.5	77.3	70.9	75.8	...
A Increase in stocks	17.9	17.7	17.9	22.1	-2.2	5.3	5.1	2.2	4.7	-1.7	-1.6	...
B Gross fixed capital formation	54.8	70.5	62.5	68.8	72.2	65.6	70.8	77.3	72.6	72.6	77.4	...
4 Exports of goods and services	158.6	168.5	140.1	182.0	129.7	142.4	202.1	188.3	197.6	166.3	185.9	...
5 Less: Imports of goods and services	178.3	195.3	216.9	255.1	207.1	228.3	226.0	223.6	242.2	228.3	230.3	...
Equals: Gross Domestic Product	405.9	456.3	453.4	497.1	480.7	477.0	549.5	563.6	537.5	557.9	583.6	...

1.3 Cost Components of the Gross Domestic Product

Thousand Million CFA francs

	1970	1975	1978	1979	1980	1981	1982	1983	1984	1985	1986	1987
1 Indirect taxes, net	...	41.8	75.4	89.9	95.2	113.7	...	...	...	...	...	...
A Indirect taxes	...	53.7	91.2	101.6	...	...	...	...	...	...	...	...
B Less: Subsidies	...	11.9	15.8	11.7	...	...	...	...	...	...	...	...
2 Consumption of fixed capital	...	22.0	34.2	39.9	41.9	46.8	...	...	...	...	...	...
3 Compensation of employees paid by resident producers to:	...	117.2	172.5	193.4	...	...	...	...	...	...	...	...
4 Operating surplus	...	225.4	212.6	258.7	...	...	...	...	...	...	...	...
Equals: Gross Domestic Product	240.1	406.4	494.7	581.9	627.5	669.8	...	...	...	...	...	...

1.7 External Transactions on Current Account, Summary

Thousand Million CFA francs

	1970	1975	1978	1979	1980	1981	1982	1983	1984	1985	1986	1987
			Payments to the Rest of the World									
1 Imports of goods and services	...	170.1	217.6	284.9	278.4	...	...	...	...	...	...	...
A Imports of merchandise c.i.f.	...	145.6	...	...	...	...	...	...	...	...	...	...
B Other	...	24.5	...	...	...	...	...	...	...	...	...	...
2 Factor income to the rest of the world	...	20.9	23.6	22.1	22.6	...	...	...	...	...	...	...
A Compensation of employees	...	6.8	9.6	6.1	7.4	...	...	...	...	...	...	...
B Property and entrepreneurial income	...	14.1	14.0	16.0	15.2	...	...	...	...	...	...	...
3 Current transfers to the rest of the world	...	4.0	10.3	7.8	11.9	...	...	...	...	...	...	...
4 Surplus of the nation on current transactions	...	-18.2	-54.5	-59.3	-66.0	...	...	...	...	...	...	...
Payments to the Rest of the World and Surplus of the Nation on Current Transactions	...	176.8	197.0	255.5	246.9	...	...	...	...	...	...	...
			Receipts From The Rest of the World									
1 Exports of goods and services	...	147.9	149.9	200.7	164.3	...	...	...	...	...	...	...

Senegal

1.7 External Transactions on Current Account, Summary
(Continued)

Thousand Million CFA francs

	1970	1975	1978	1979	1980	1981	1982	1983	1984	1985	1986	1987
A Exports of merchandise f.o.b.	...	107.8	90.5	133.4	103.8	...	...	...	...	...	...	...
B Other	...	40.1	59.4	67.3	60.5	...	...	...	...	...	...	...
2 Factor income from rest of the world	...	9.2	17.5	15.9	23.9	...	...	...	...	...	...	...
A Compensation of employees	...	7.7	15.3	14.1	21.3	...	...	...	...	...	...	...
B Property and entrepreneurial income	...	1.5	2.2	1.8	2.6	...	...	...	...	...	...	...
3 Current transfers from rest of the world	...	19.7	29.6	38.9	58.7	...	...	...	...	...	...	...
Receipts from the Rest of the World on Current Transactions	...	176.8	197.0	255.5	246.9	...	...	...	...	...	...	...

1.10 Gross Domestic Product by Kind of Activity, in Current Prices

Thousand Million CFA francs

	1970	1975	1978	1979	1980	1981	1982	1983	1984	1985	1986	1987
1 Agriculture, hunting, forestry and fishing	57.8	122.8	104.6	139.6	120.0	121.1	211.4	212.8	174.1	218.8	292.8	...
2 Mining and quarrying												...
3 Manufacturing	42.3	79.5	92.9	109.0	118.5	128.8	113.9	141.4	208.1	252.0	262.5	
4 Electricity, gas and water												...
5 Construction	9.4	18.0	27.5	32.1	37.7	42.8	36.9	44.2	72.3	78.1	85.1	...
6 Wholesale and retail trade, restaurants and hotels	65.4	84.7	128.6	135.2								...
7 Transport, storage and communication	17.4	28.6	30.8	36.6	236.5	254.6	346.5	392.6	396.2	434.2	488.3	
8 Finance, insurance, real estate and business services	19.0	25.8	40.6	45.7								...
9 Community, social and personal services												...
Total, Industries	211.3	359.2	425.0	498.2	512.7	547.3	708.7	791.0	850.7	983.1	1128.7	...
Producers of Government Services	26.6	43.9	63.9	77.7	106.1	113.0	124.4	122.5	153.5	155.0	163.5	...
Other Producers	2.2	3.3	5.8	6.0	8.7	9.5	11.2	11.4	11.4	13.9	14.8	...
Subtotal	240.1	406.4	494.7	581.9	627.5	669.8	844.1	924.9	1015.5	1152.0	1307.0	...
Less: Imputed bank service charge	...	...	...	...	...	...	...	...	...	...	...	...
Plus: Import duties	...	...	...	...	...	...	...	...	...	...	...	...
Plus: Value added tax	...	...	...	...	...	...	...	...	...	...	...	...
Equals: Gross Domestic Product	240.1	406.4	494.7	581.9	627.5	669.8	844.1	924.9	1015.5	1152.0	1307.0	...

1.11 Gross Domestic Product by Kind of Activity, in Constant Prices

Thousand Million CFA francs

	1970	1975	1978	1979	1980	1981	1982	1983	1984	1985	1986	1987
				At constant prices of:1977								
1 Agriculture, hunting, forestry and fishing	111.6	124.2	101.2	128.7	105.2	99.3	123.9	129.9	107.1	115.6	131.3	...
2 Mining and quarrying												...
3 Manufacturing	82.8	97.1	102.9	114.3	110.9	117.2	134.7	137.8	135.3	138.0	141.9	...
4 Electricity, gas and water												...
5 Construction												
6 Wholesale and retail trade, restaurants and hotels												...
7 Transport, storage and communication	163.7	184.9	185.3	187.3	192.9	184.8	211.1	212.7	207.4	211.5	213.6	
8 Finance, insurance, real estate and business services												...
9 Community, social and personal services												...
Total, Industries	358.1	406.2	389.4	430.3	409.0	401.3	469.7	480.4	449.8	465.1	486.8	...
Producers of Government Services	44.0	47.1	58.4	61.5	65.7	69.2	73.3	76.7	81.2	84.0	87.8	...
Other Producers	3.8	3.0	5.6	5.3	6.0	6.5	6.5	6.5	6.5	8.8	8.9	...
Subtotal	405.9	456.3	453.4	497.1	480.7	477.0	549.5	563.6	537.5	557.9	583.5	...
Less: Imputed bank service charge	...	...	...	...	...	...	...	...	...	...	...	...
Plus: Import duties	...	...	...	...	...	...	...	...	...	...	...	...
Plus: Value added tax	...	...	...	...	...	...	...	...	...	...	...	...
Equals: Gross Domestic Product	405.9	456.3	453.4	497.1	480.7	477.0	549.5	563.6	537.5	557.9	583.5	...

Senegal

1.12 Relations Among National Accounting Aggregates

Thousand Million CFA francs

	1970	1975	1978	1979	1980	1981	1982	1983	1984	1985	1986	1987
Gross Domestic Product	240.1	406.4	494.7	581.9	627.5	669.8	844.3	924.9	1015.5	1152.0	1307.0	...
Plus: Net factor income from the rest of the world	5.1	4.0	13.2	24.9	24.3	23.4	-11.4	-10.1	-24.6	-36.8	-55.3	...
Equals: Gross National Product	245.2	410.4	507.9	606.8	651.8	693.2	832.9	914.8	990.9	1115.2	1251.7	...
Less: Consumption of fixed capital	...	22.0	34.2	39.9	41.9	46.8	87.1	107.7	110.7	157.8	179.4	...
Equals: National Income	...	388.4	473.7	566.9	609.9	646.4	745.8	807.1	880.2	957.4	1072.3	...
Plus: Net current transfers from the rest of the world	...	...	...	...	...	...	...	...	...	...	...	...
Equals: National Disposable Income	...	...	...	...	...	...	...	...	...	...	...	...
Less: Final consumption	...	...	...	...	...	...	...	...	...	...	...	...
Equals: Net Saving	...	...	...	...	...	...	...	...	...	...	...	...
Less: Surplus of the nation on current transactions	...	...	...	...	...	...	...	...	...	...	...	...
Equals: Net Capital Formation	...	...	...	...	...	...	...	...	...	...	...	...

Seychelles

Source. Reply to the United Nations National Accounts Questionnaire from the Department of Economic Development Planning and Housing, Unity House.
General note. The estimates shown in the following tables have been prepared in accordance with the United Nations System of National Accounts so far as the existing data would permit.

1.1 Expenditure on the Gross Domestic Product, in Current Prices

Million Seychelles rupees

	1970	1975	1978	1979	1980	1981	1982	1983	1984	1985	1986	1987
1 Government final consumption expenditure	...	...	149.5	211.4	270.0	308.5	338.0	325.9	327.7	417.4	497.6	...
2 Private final consumption expenditure	...	...	195.3	377.6	416.3	497.7	598.6	673.3	653.0	700.7	740.2	...
3 Gross capital formation	...	...	257.5	265.5	360.9	317.1	313.2	210.4	231.5	273.5	298.5	...
A Increase in stocks	...	...	4.1	8.9	16.7	-12.5	10.3	-9.5	4.6	-	5.8	...
B Gross fixed capital formation	...	...	253.4	256.6	344.2	329.6	302.9	219.9	226.9	273.5	292.7	...
Residential buildings	...	...	147.4	149.9	196.3	205.4	160.0	97.0	135.7	149.3	54.0	...
Non-residential buildings	...	...										...
Other construction and land improvement etc.	...	...	0.1	0.2	1.0	3.9	4.8	4.7	5.4	4.5	4.5	...
Other	...	...	87.9	106.5	146.9	120.3	138.0	118.3	85.7	119.7	234.2	...
4 Exports of goods and services	...	...	488.4	582.5	640.1	554.1	404.4	415.0	524.9	581.1	498.7	...
5 Less: Imports of goods and services	...	...	495.8	630.8	745.4	705.6	686.0	635.3	669.2	767.8	723.6	...
Equals: Gross Domestic Product	...	292.0	594.9	806.2	941.9	971.8	968.2	989.3	1067.9	1204.9	1311.4	...

1.2 Expenditure on the Gross Domestic Product, in Constant Prices

Million Seychelles rupees

	1970	1975	1978	1979	1980	1981	1982	1983	1984	1985	1986	1987
					At constant prices of:1976							
1 Government final consumption expenditure	...	...	120.4	140.7	142.0	145.8 / 145.8	153.3	139.8	134.5	167.9	179.9	...
2 Private final consumption expenditure	...	...	257.7	291.2	277.2	267.8 / 267.8	327.4	347.0	323.4	344.2	362.5	...
3 Gross capital formation	...	...	192.1	184.3	202.7	182.1 / 182.1	216.5	128.4	141.1	163.8	168.1	...
A Increase in stocks	...	...	3.7	5.2	9.3	5.2 / 5.2	6.7	2.9	-3.8	-	3.3	...
B Gross fixed capital formation	...	...	188.4	179.1	193.4	176.9 / 176.9	209.8	125.5	144.9	163.8	164.8	...
4 Exports of goods and services	...	...	310.3	351.7	317.8	270.1 / -160.5[a]	-277.0	-208.9	-153.0	-187.4	-211.7	...
5 Less: Imports of goods and services	...	...	459.5	477.5	461.8	420.3 / ...						...
Equals: Gross Domestic Product [b]	...	...	421.0	490.4	477.9	445.6 / 435.2	420.2	406.3	446.1	488.5	498.8	...

a) Including item 'Less: Imports of goods and services'.
b) Beginning 1981, gross national product rather than gross domestic product.

1.3 Cost Components of the Gross Domestic Product

Million Seychelles rupees

	1970	1975	1978	1979	1980	1981	1982	1983	1984	1985	1986	1987
1 Indirect taxes, net	...	...	79.0	115.5	152.9	167.5	183.1	186.4	190.6	204.6	213.2	...
A Indirect taxes	...	...	79.0	115.5	152.9	167.5	183.1	186.4	...	...	...	...
B Less: Subsidies	...	...	-	-	-	-	-	-	...	...	...	...
2 Consumption of fixed capital	...	...	36.5	35.3	45.0	54.2	57.6	59.3	64.3	75.2	83.4	...
3 Compensation of employees paid by resident producers to:	...	...	212.9	289.8	356.9	410.5	402.8	401.8	419.5	447.4	452.7	...
4 Operating surplus	...	...	266.6	365.7	387.1	339.6	324.6	341.9	393.7	477.7	562.2	...
Equals: Gross Domestic Product	...	...	595.0	806.3	941.9	971.8	968.2	989.4	1068.1	1204.9	1311.4	...

Seychelles

1.7 External Transactions on Current Account, Summary
Million Seychelles rupees

	1970	1975	1978	1979	1980	1981	1982	1983	1984	1985	1986	1987
Payments to the Rest of the World
1 Imports of goods and services	...	...	495.8	630.8	745.4	705.6	686.0	635.3	669.2	767.8	723.6	...
A Imports of merchandise c.i.f.	...	...	427.3	534.8	631.4	589.0	639.3	592.1	616.7	702.7	653.6	...
B Other	...	...	68.5	96.0	114.0	116.6	46.7	43.2	52.5	65.1	70.0	...
2 Factor income to the rest of the world	...	...	47.3	72.2	56.3	34.2	44.5	48.6	56.0	57.6	65.1	...
A Compensation of employees	...	...	...	...	...	...	...	...	...	...	...	...
B Property and entrepreneurial income	...	...	47.3	72.2	56.3	34.2	44.5	48.6	56.0	57.6	65.1	...
3 Current transfers to the rest of the world	...	...	16.2	20.1	20.9	31.5	21.0	18.8	16.6	5.7	31.3	...
4 Surplus of the nation on current transactions	...	...	18.1	-60.7	-58.0	-113.6	-264.8	-175.1	-95.4	-132.5	-207.0	...
Payments to the Rest of the World and Surplus of the Nation on Current Transactions	...	...	577.4	662.4	764.6	657.7	486.7	527.6	646.4	698.6	613.0	...
Receipts From The Rest of the World
1 Exports of goods and services	...	...	488.4	582.5	640.1	554.1	404.4	415.0	524.9	581.1	498.7	...
A Exports of merchandise f.o.b.	...	...	49.1	43.6	38.3	30.9	25.3	33.9	35.3	33.1	31.4	...
B Other	...	...	439.3	538.9	601.8	523.2	379.1	381.1	489.6	548.0	467.3	...
2 Factor income from rest of the world	...	...	9.0	15.9	22.2	19.6	18.3	16.0	14.8	15.4	12.7	...
A Compensation of employees	...	...	...	...	...	...	...	...	...	...	...	...
B Property and entrepreneurial income	...	...	9.0	15.9	22.2	19.6	18.3	16.0	14.8	15.4	12.7	...
3 Current transfers from rest of the world	...	...	80.0	64.0	102.3	84.0	64.0	96.6	106.7	102.1	101.6	...
Receipts from the Rest of the World on Current Transactions	...	...	577.4	662.4	764.6	657.7	486.7	527.6	646.4	698.6	613.0	...

1.10 Gross Domestic Product by Kind of Activity, in Current Prices
Million Seychelles rupees

	1970	1975	1978	1979	1980	1981	1982	1983	1984	1985	1986	1987
1 Agriculture, hunting, forestry and fishing	...	...	50.0	58.8	64.4	76.5	62.0	76.9	69.0	69.3	77.3	...
2 Mining and quarrying	...	...	1.1	1.2	0.7	0.2	-	-	-	-	-	...
3 Manufacturing	...	...	36.4	48.6	69.5	83.2	82.6	95.6	100.3	116.4	116.3	...
4 Electricity, gas and water	...	...	4.9	4.0	2.1	11.3	12.6	14.9	23.4	31.7	34.7	...
5 Construction	...	...	39.7	67.9	75.0	71.8	55.0	42.8	52.8	73.1	76.1	...
6 Wholesale and retail trade, restaurants and hotels	...	...	155.0	218.4	239.1	230.4	221.9	225.6	257.5	298.1	325.1	...
7 Transport, storage and communication	...	...	88.8	104.4	131.5	109.8	108.5	120.3	154.5	169.5	160.7	...
8 Finance, insurance, real estate and business services	...	...	72.7	99.4	117.6	115.9	120.4	111.2	106.3	119.2	131.7	...
9 Community, social and personal services [a]	...	...	15.5	22.2	24.4	22.2	23.2	28.6	28.0	33.3	33.8	...
Total, Industries	...	...	464.1	624.9	724.3	721.3	686.2	715.9	791.9	910.6	955.7	...
Producers of Government Services	...	...	82.7	114.6	142.3	171.0	183.4	170.7	173.6	191.8	184.0	...
Other Producers [a]	...	...	...	...	...	...	...	...	...	...	...	...
Subtotal	...	...	546.8	739.5	866.6	892.3	869.6	886.6	965.5	1102.4	1139.7	...
Less: Imputed bank service charge	...	...	11.6	20.0	29.8	34.1	29.6	25.8	26.0	31.9	25.9	...
Plus: Import duties	...	...	59.8	86.8	105.1	113.7	128.2	128.6	128.6	134.5	197.6	...
Plus: Value added tax	...	...	...	...	...	...	...	...	...	...	...	...
Equals: Gross Domestic Product	...	...	595.0	806.3	941.9	971.9	968.2	989.4	1068.1	1205.0	1311.4	...

a) Item 'Other producers' is included in item 'Community, social and personal services'.

1.11 Gross Domestic Product by Kind of Activity, in Constant Prices
Million Seychelles rupees

	1970	1975	1978	1979	1980	1981	1982	1983	1984	1985	1986	1987
At constant prices of: 1976
1 Agriculture, hunting, forestry and fishing	...	...	30.2	35.1	35.1	44.9	35.0	37.9	32.4	32.3	33.6	...
2 Mining and quarrying	...	...	0.8	0.9	0.5	0.2	-	-	-	-	-	...
3 Manufacturing	...	...	28.3	31.1	39.6	30.9	32.0	36.5	36.9	39.0	40.0	...
4 Electricity, gas and water	...	...	0.6	1.6	-4.0	-5.9	-6.2	-9.5	9.0	12.3	11.6	...
5 Construction	...	...	32.9	48.7	40.7	38.4	27.4	21.3	25.8	31.7	33.5	...

Seychelles

1.11 Gross Domestic Product by Kind of Activity, in Constant Prices
(Continued)

Million Seychelles rupees

	1970	1975	1978	1979	1980	1981	1982	1983	1984	1985	1986	1987
					At constant prices of: 1976							
6 Wholesale and retail trade, restaurants and hotels	...	...	109.2	126.8	124.1	112.0	108.5	113.0	119.6	131.1	136.1	...
7 Transport, storage and communication	...	...	53.8	58.1	58.6	49.2	49.0	54.7	64.4	63.0	60.5	...
8 Finance, insurance, real estate and business services	...	...	56.1	68.6	72.1	64.3	68.3	60.9	54.4	64.5	72.9	...
9 Community, social and personal services [a]	...	...	12.0	14.4	12.2	10.2	12.1	10.3	9.1	10.5	10.3	...
Total, Industries	...	...	323.9	385.3	378.9	344.2	326.1	325.1	351.6	384.4	398.5	...
Producers of Government Services	...	...	67.2	76.6	74.9	82.3	84.1	76.0	75.8	79.2	75.6	...
Other Producers [a]	...	...	...	...	...	...	...	...	...	...	...	...
Subtotal	...	...	391.1	461.9	453.8	426.5	410.2	401.1	427.4	463.6	474.1	...
Less: Imputed bank service charge	...	...	10.2	15.0	18.0	18.6	16.3	13.4	13.6	14.0	15.6	...
Plus: Import duties	...	...	40.1	43.5	42.1	37.7	43.1	41.8	46.4	56.0	59.0	...
Plus: Value added tax	...	...	...	...	...	...	...	...	...	...	...	...
Equals: Gross Domestic Product	...	...	421.0	490.4	477.9	445.6	437.0	429.5	460.3	505.6	517.5	...

a) Item 'Other producers' is included in item 'Community, social and personal services'.

1.12 Relations Among National Accounting Aggregates

Million Seychelles rupees

	1970	1975	1978	1979	1980	1981	1982	1983	1984	1985	1986	1987
Gross Domestic Product	...	...	595.0	806.3	941.9	971.8	968.2	989.4	1068.0	1204.9	1311.4	...
Plus: Net factor income from the rest of the world	...	...	-38.3	-56.3	-34.1	-14.6	-26.2	-32.6	-41.2	-42.2	-52.4	...
Factor income from the rest of the world	...	...	9.0	15.9	22.2	19.6	18.3	16.0	14.8	15.4	12.7	...
Less: Factor income to the rest of the world	...	...	47.3	72.2	56.3	34.2	44.5	48.6	56.0	57.6	65.1	...
Equals: Gross National Product	...	...	556.7	750.0	907.8	957.2	942.0	956.8	1026.8	1162.7	1259.0	...
Less: Consumption of fixed capital	...	...	36.5	35.3	45.0	54.2	57.6	59.3	64.3	75.2	83.4	...
Equals: National Income	...	...	520.2	714.7	862.8	903.0	884.4	897.5	962.5	1087.5	1175.6	...
Plus: Net current transfers from the rest of the world	...	...	63.8	43.9	81.4	52.5	43.0	77.8	90.1	96.4	70.3	...
Current transfers from the rest of the world	...	...	80.0	64.0	102.3	84.0	64.0	96.6	106.7	102.1	101.6	...
Less: Current transfers to the rest of the world	...	...	16.2	20.1	20.9	31.5	21.0	18.8	16.6	5.7	31.3	...
Equals: National Disposable Income	...	...	584.0	758.6	944.2	955.5	927.4	975.3	1052.6	1183.9	1245.9	...
Less: Final consumption	...	...	344.8	589.0	686.3	806.2	936.6	999.2	980.7	1118.1	1237.8	...
Equals: Net Saving	...	...	239.2	169.6	257.9	149.3	-9.2	-23.9	71.9	65.8	8.1	...
Less: Surplus of the nation on current transactions	...	...	18.1	-60.7	-58.0	-113.6	-264.8	-175.1	-95.4	-132.5	-207.0	...
Equals: Net Capital Formation	...	...	221.1	230.3	315.9	262.9	255.6	151.2	167.3	198.3	215.1	...

4.1 Derivation of Value Added by Kind of Activity, in Current Prices

Million Seychelles rupees

	1981			1982			1983			1984		
	Gross Output	Intermediate Consumption	Value Added	Gross Output	Intermediate Consumption	Value Added	Gross Output	Intermediate Consumption	Value Added	Gross Output	Intermediate Consumption	Value Added
						All Producers						
1 Agriculture, hunting, forestry and fishing	107.9	31.5	76.5	96.2	34.2	62.0	114.6	37.7	76.9	105.7	36.7	69.0
A Agriculture and hunting	62.6	18.0	44.6	57.0	22.0	35.0	70.3	24.5	45.8	68.9	25.8	43.1
B Forestry and logging	1.7	0.5	1.3	1.2	0.3	1.0	2.1	0.6	1.5	2.0	0.6	1.4
C Fishing	43.6	13.0	30.6	38.0	11.9	26.1	42.3	12.7	29.6	34.8	10.4	24.4
2 Mining and quarrying	...	...	...	...	...	...	...	...	...	...	...	...
3 Manufacturing	160.3	76.8	83.5	158.9	76.3	82.6	171.6	76.0	95.6	177.2	76.9	100.3
4 Electricity, gas and water	67.7	56.5	11.3	68.1	55.4	12.6	74.2	59.3	14.9	80.0	56.5	23.4
A Electricity, gas and steam	58.3	50.6	7.7	58.7	49.4	9.3	60.9	49.6	11.3	62.9	46.2	16.7
B Water works and supply	9.4	5.9	3.6	9.4	6.0	3.3	13.3	9.7	3.5	17.1	10.3	6.7

Seychelles

4.1 Derivation of Value Added by Kind of Activity, in Current Prices
(Continued)

Million Seychelles rupees

	1981 Gross Output	1981 Intermediate Consumption	1981 Value Added	1982 Gross Output	1982 Intermediate Consumption	1982 Value Added	1983 Gross Output	1983 Intermediate Consumption	1983 Value Added	1984 Gross Output	1984 Intermediate Consumption	1984 Value Added
5 Construction	209.3	137.5	71.8	160.0	104.9	55.0	98.0	55.2	42.8	103.5	50.7	52.8
6 Wholesale and retail trade, restaurants and hotels	386.6	156.2	230.4	339.5	117.5	221.9	373.2	147.6	225.6	411.6	154.1	257.5
A Wholesale and retail trade	207.5	47.6	159.9	207.3	44.6	162.7	211.1	46.5	164.6	216.3	46.5	169.8
B Restaurants and hotels	179.2	108.6	70.5	128.5	71.5	57.0	162.1	101.1	61.0	195.4	107.6	87.7
7 Transport, storage and communication	218.1	108.2	109.9	209.5	101.1	108.4	304.0	183.7	120.3	346.6	192.1	154.5
8 Finance, insurance, real estate and business services	144.4	28.7	115.7	147.7	27.3	120.4	135.7	24.5	111.2	130.2	24.0	106.3
A Financial institutions	44.9	17.1	27.9	49.5	15.7	33.8	44.6	16.4	28.2	46.7	15.2	31.4
B Insurance	8.8	3.7	5.1	12.0	4.2	7.8	5.7	1.1	4.6	3.2	1.3	1.9
C Real estate and business services	90.7	7.9	82.7	86.2	7.5	78.8	85.4	7.0	78.4	80.3	7.5	73.0
Real estate, except dwellings	16.3	1.6	14.7	12.2	4.1	8.1	15.8	1.6	14.3	14.0	1.4	12.6
Dwellings	61.1	1.9	59.2	58.5	1.8	56.7	58.7	1.7	57.1	55.5	1.7	53.8
9 Community, social and personal services	37.0	14.8	22.2	41.0	17.8	23.2	41.5	12.9	28.6	40.5	12.5	28.0
Total, Industries	1331.5	610.3	721.2	1220.8	534.6	686.2	1312.8	596.9	715.9	1395.3	603.5	791.9
Producers of Government Services	322.8	151.8	171.0	356.0	172.6	183.4	341.9	171.2	170.7	345.2	171.6	173.6
Other Producers	...	...	...	...	...	...	...	...	...	...	...	...
Total	1654.2	762.0	892.2	1576.8	707.2	869.6	1654.7	768.1	886.6	1740.5	775.1	965.5
Less: Imputed bank service charge	...	-34.1	34.1	...	-29.6	29.6	...	-25.8	25.8	...	-26.0	26.0
Import duties	113.7	...	113.7	128.2	...	128.2	128.6	...	128.6	128.6	...	128.6
Value added tax	...	...	...	...	...	...	...	...	...	...	...	...
Total	1768.0	796.1	971.8	1705.0	736.8	968.2	1783.3	793.9	989.4	1869.1	801.1	1068.1

	1985 Gross Output	1985 Intermediate Consumption	1985 Value Added	1986 Gross Output	1986 Intermediate Consumption	1986 Value Added
All Producers						
1 Agriculture, hunting, forestry and fishing	103.1	33.8	69.3	112.6	35.3	77.3
A Agriculture and hunting	71.3	27.0	44.3	75.0	28.3	46.7
B Forestry and logging	2.1	0.6	1.5	2.2	0.6	1.6
C Fishing	29.7	6.2	23.5	35.4	6.4	29.0
2 Mining and quarrying	...	...	...	...	...	...
3 Manufacturing	203.8	87.4	116.4	203.7	87.3	116.3
4 Electricity, gas and water	89.7	58.0	31.7	97.2	62.5	34.7
A Electricity, gas and steam	73.3	49.5	23.9	81.0	53.6	27.3
B Water works and supply	16.3	8.5	7.8	16.2	8.9	7.4
5 Construction	137.8	64.7	73.1	146.9	70.8	76.1
6 Wholesale and retail trade, restaurants and hotels	505.1	207.0	298.1	534.5	209.4	325.1
A Wholesale and retail trade	246.6	51.3	195.4	267.0	52.9	214.1
B Restaurants and hotels	258.5	155.7	102.7	267.5	156.5	111.0
7 Transport, storage and communication	382.2	212.7	169.5	369.8	209.1	160.7
8 Finance, insurance, real estate and business services	148.8	29.6	119.2	166.2	34.4	131.7
A Financial institutions	59.8	16.2	43.6	66.0	18.2	47.8
B Insurance	7.4	2.3	5.1	16.3	4.6	11.7
C Real estate and business services	81.6	11.1	70.5	83.9	11.7	72.2
Real estate, except dwellings	5.8	4.0	1.8	5.7	4.0	1.7
Dwellings	65.2	1.9	63.3	66.6	2.0	64.6
9 Community, social and personal services	46.4	13.1	33.3	47.1	13.3	33.8

Seychelles

4.1 Derivation of Value Added by Kind of Activity, in Current Prices
(Continued)

Million Seychelles rupees

	1985			1986		
	Gross Output	Intermediate Consumption	Value Added	Gross Output	Intermediate Consumption	Value Added
Total, Industries	1616.9	706.3	910.6	1677.9	722.1	955.7
Producers of Government Services	417.4	225.6	191.8	497.6	313.6	184.0
Other Producers	...	...	...	...	...	...
Total	2034.3	931.9	1102.4	2175.5	1035.7	1139.7
Less: Imputed bank service charge	...	-31.9	31.9	...	-26.0	26.0
Import duties	134.5	...	134.5	197.6	...	197.6
Value added tax	...	...	...	...	...	...
Total	2168.8	963.8	1205.0	2373.1	1061.7	1311.4

4.2 Derivation of Value Added by Kind of Activity, in Constant Prices

Million Seychelles rupees

	1981			1982			1983			1984		
	Gross Output	Intermediate Consumption	Value Added	Gross Output	Intermediate Consumption	Value Added	Gross Output	Intermediate Consumption	Value Added	Gross Output	Intermediate Consumption	Value Added

At constant prices of: 1976

All Producers

1 Agriculture, hunting, forestry and fishing	62.3	17.0	44.9	56.0	20.9	35.1	59.3	21.4	37.9	54.0	21.6	32.4
A Agriculture and hunting	43.4	13.5	29.9	41.2	16.8	24.4	45.4	17.3	28.1	42.1	18.2	23.9
B Forestry and logging	1.9	0.5	1.4	1.3	0.2	1.1	1.0	0.3	0.7	1.3	0.3	1.0
C Fishing	16.7	3.0	13.7	13.4	3.9	9.5	12.9	3.8	9.1	10.6	3.1	7.5
2 Mining and quarrying	0.3	0.1	0.2	-	-	-	-	-	-	-	-	-
3 Manufacturing	68.9	38.0	30.9	71.5	39.6	31.9	75.7	39.2	36.5	76.0	39.2	36.9
4 Electricity, gas and water	23.6	29.4	-6.0	23.5	29.7	-6.2	26.7	36.2	-9.5	31.4	22.4	9.0
A Electricity, gas and steam	17.8	25.8	-8.1	18.7	26.6	-7.9	18.7	30.3	-11.6	21.2	16.2	5.0
B Water works and supply	5.8	3.6	2.1	4.8	3.1	1.7	8.0	5.9	2.1	10.2	6.2	4.0
5 Construction	111.9	73.5	38.4	79.6	52.2	27.4	48.7	27.4	21.3	50.7	24.8	25.8
6 Wholesale and retail trade, restaurants and hotels	193.0	81.0	112.0	179.1	70.5	108.6	196.0	82.9	113.1	211.3	91.6	119.6
A Wholesale and retail trade	106.3	25.7	80.5	109.5	25.1	84.5	106.6	26.3	80.3	108.9	26.8	82.1
B Restaurants and hotels	86.7	55.3	31.4	68.5	43.4	25.1	89.4	56.6	32.8	102.4	64.9	37.5
7 Transport, storage and communication	137.3	88.2	49.2	130.8	81.8	49.0	160.8	106.2	54.6	175.4	110.9	64.4
8 Finance, insurance, real estate and business services	80.1	15.7	64.4	83.9	15.6	68.3	73.2	12.4	60.8	67.3	12.8	54.4
A Financial institutions	22.9	9.3	13.6	25.1	8.6	16.5	21.7	8.1	13.6	21.9	8.1	13.8
B Insurance	4.5	2.0	2.5	6.1	2.3	3.8	2.5	0.6	1.9	1.5	0.7	0.8
C Real estate and business services	52.7	4.4	48.3	52.7	4.7	48.0	49.0	3.7	45.3	43.9	4.0	39.8
Real estate, except dwellings	8.4	0.9	7.6	7.6	0.8	6.8	8.2	0.8	7.4	7.1	0.7	6.4
Dwellings	33.6	1.0	32.6	32.5	1.0	31.5	32.6	1.0	31.6	28.9	0.9	28.0
9 Community, social and personal services	8.2	4.5	3.7	6.3	2.0	4.3	7.5	4.1	3.4	16.9	7.8	9.1
Total, Industries	685.3	347.3	338.0	630.7	312.3	318.4	647.9	329.8	318.1	683.0	331.1	351.6
Producers of Government Services	152.0	69.7	82.3	155.5	71.4	84.1	146.8	70.8	76.0	146.3	70.6	75.8
Other Producers	10.0	3.7	6.3	10.7	3.0	7.7	10.8	3.8	7.0	...	...	...
Total	847.3	420.7	426.6	796.9	386.7	410.2	805.5	404.4	401.1	829.3	401.7	427.4
Less: Imputed bank service charge	...	-18.6	18.6	...	-16.3	16.3	...	-13.4	13.4	...	-13.6	13.6
Import duties	37.7	...	37.7	43.1	...	43.1	41.8	...	41.8	46.4	...	46.4
Value added tax	...	...	...	...	...	...	...	...	...	...	...	...
Total	885.0	439.3	445.7	840.0	403.0	437.0	847.3	417.8	429.5	875.7	415.3	460.2

	1985			1986		
	Gross Output	Intermediate Consumption	Value Added	Gross Output	Intermediate Consumption	Value Added

At constant prices of: 1976

All Producers

1 Agriculture, hunting, forestry and fishing	53.7	21.4	32.3	58.0	24.4	33.6
A Agriculture and hunting	42.3	18.7	23.6	44.5	20.8	23.7
B Forestry and logging	1.2	0.3	0.9	1.2	0.3	0.9
C Fishing	10.2	2.4	7.9	12.3	3.3	9.0
2 Mining and quarrying	-	-	-	-	-	-

1303

Seychelles

4.2 Derivation of Value Added by Kind of Activity, in Constant Prices
(Continued)

Million Seychelles rupees

	1985 Gross Output	1985 Intermediate Consumption	1985 Value Added	1986 Gross Output	1986 Intermediate Consumption	1986 Value Added
			At constant prices of: 1976			
3 Manufacturing	85.6	46.6	39.0	89.6	49.6	40.0
4 Electricity, gas and water	35.0	22.7	12.3	36.9	25.3	11.6
A Electricity, gas and steam	26.3	18.0	8.3	26.8	20.0	6.8
B Water works and supply	8.7	4.7	4.0	10.1	5.3	4.8
5 Construction	65.8	34.1	31.7	71.6	38.1	33.5
6 Wholesale and retail trade, restaurants and hotels	246.7	115.6	131.1	256.9	120.8	136.1
A Wholesale and retail trade	122.8	31.8	91.0	132.6	36.8	95.8
B Restaurants and hotels	123.9	83.8	40.1	124.3	84.0	40.3
7 Transport, storage and communication	177.3	114.3	63.0	170.1	109.6	60.5
8 Finance, insurance, real estate and business services	80.4	15.9	64.5	93.4	20.5	72.9
A Financial institutions	26.2	7.3	18.8	31.0	10.0	21.0
B Insurance	3.2	1.0	2.2	7.6	2.5	5.1
C Real estate and business services	51.0	7.6	43.5	54.8	8.0	46.8
Real estate, except dwellings	2.5	1.8	0.7	2.5	1.9	0.7
Dwellings	33.5	1.1	32.4	36.2	1.2	35.0
9 Community, social and personal services	15.4	4.9	10.5	15.4	5.1	10.3
Total, Industries	759.9	375.5	384.4	791.9	393.4	398.5
Producers of Government Services	175.6	96.6	79.0	218.1	142.5	75.6
Other Producers	...	...	...	...	...	...
Total	935.5	472.1	463.4	1010.0	535.9	474.1
Less: Imputed bank service charge	...	-14.0	14.0	...	-15.6	15.6
Import duties	56.0	...	56.0	59.0	...	59.0
Value added tax	...	...	...	...	...	...
Total	991.5	486.1	505.4	1069.0	551.5	517.5

4.3 Cost Components of Value Added

Million Seychelles rupees

	1981 Compensation of Employees	1981 Capital Consumption	1981 Net Operating Surplus	1981 Indirect Taxes	1981 Less: Subsidies Received	1981 Value Added	1982 Compensation of Employees	1982 Capital Consumption	1982 Net Operating Surplus	1982 Indirect Taxes	1982 Less: Subsidies Received	1982 Value Added
					All Producers							
1 Agriculture, hunting, forestry and fishing	-	-	74.9	1.5	...	76.5	-	-	60.8	1.2	...	62.0
A Agriculture and hunting	-	-	43.4	1.2	...	44.6	-	-	34.4	0.6	...	35.0
B Forestry and logging	-	-	1.3	-	...	1.3	-	-	1.0	-	...	1.0
C Fishing	-	-	30.3	0.4	...	30.6	-	-	25.4	0.6	...	26.1
2 Mining and quarrying	...	...	...	...	...	...	...	...	...	...	...	...
3 Manufacturing	22.4	8.1	21.1	31.8	...	83.5	24.5	8.5	15.1	34.5	...	82.6
4 Electricity, gas and water	12.9	3.9	-5.5	-	...	11.3	12.2	6.5	-6.2	-	...	12.6
A Electricity, gas and steam	8.5	3.5	-4.3	-	...	7.7	7.1	5.8	-3.6	-	...	9.3
B Water works and supply	4.4	0.3	-1.2	-	...	3.6	5.1	0.8	-2.6	-	...	3.3
5 Construction	46.1	3.0	22.7	-	...	71.8	36.1	3.3	15.6	-	...	55.0
6 Wholesale and retail trade, restaurants and hotels	53.7	6.4	151.6	18.6	...	230.4	41.8	7.0	159.3	13.8	...	221.9
A Wholesale and retail trade	...	...	...	...	...	...	...	...	...	...	...	...
B Restaurants and hotels	...	...	...	...	...	...	...	...	...	...	...	...
7 Transport, storage and communication	74.3	15.8	17.4	2.4	...	109.9	67.4	14.7	22.6	3.7	...	108.4
A Transport and storage	57.1	9.3	16.3	2.4	...	85.2	49.2	9.2	12.0	3.7	...	74.2
B Communication	17.1	6.5	1.1	-	...	24.7	18.1	5.5	10.7	-	...	34.3
8 Finance, insurance, real estate and business services	19.2	16.9	79.0	0.6	...	115.7	20.6	17.4	80.9	1.4	...	120.4
A Financial institutions	11.0	1.1	15.7	-	...	27.9	13.4	1.9	18.3	0.2	...	33.8
B Insurance	3.4	0.3	1.4	-	...	5.1	3.5	0.3	4.0	-	...	7.8
C Real estate and business services	4.9	15.5	61.8	0.5	...	82.7	3.7	15.2	58.6	1.2	...	78.8
Real estate, except dwellings	-	-	14.7	-	...	14.7	3.7	0.6	2.6	1.2	...	8.1

Seychelles

4.3 Cost Components of Value Added
(Continued)

Million Seychelles rupees

	1981						1982					
	Compensation of Employees	Capital Consumption	Net Operating Surplus	Indirect Taxes	Less: Subsidies Received	Value Added	Compensation of Employees	Capital Consumption	Net Operating Surplus	Indirect Taxes	Less: Subsidies Received	Value Added
Dwellings	-	15.3	43.9	-	...	59.2	-	14.6	42.1	-	...	56.7
9 Community, social and personal services	10.9	-	11.0	0.2	...	22.2	16.9	-	6.1	0.2	...	23.2
Total, Industries	239.6	54.1	372.2	55.3	...	721.2	219.6	57.5	354.2	54.9	...	686.2
Producers of Government Services	170.9	0.1	...	...	...	171.0	183.3	0.1	...	...	...	183.4
Other Producers	...	...	...	...	...	...	...	...	...	...	...	...
Total	410.5	54.0	372.2	55.2	...	892.2	402.9	57.6	354.3	54.8	...	869.6
Less: Imputed bank service charge	...	...	34.1	...	...	34.1	...	...	29.6	...	...	29.6
Import duties	...	...	...	113.7	...	113.7	...	...	...	128.2	...	128.2
Value added tax	...	...	...	...	...	...	...	...	...	...	...	...
Total	410.5	54.2	338.1	168.9	...	971.8	402.9	57.6	324.7	183.1	...	968.2

	1983						1984					
	Compensation of Employees	Capital Consumption	Net Operating Surplus	Indirect Taxes	Less: Subsidies Received	Value Added	Compensation of Employees	Capital Consumption	Net Operating Surplus	Indirect Taxes	Less: Subsidies Received	Value Added
					All Producers							
1 Agriculture, hunting, forestry and fishing	-	-	76.9	0.1	...	76.9	-	-	69.0	-	...	69.0
A Agriculture and hunting	-	-	45.8	-	...	45.8	-	-	43.1	-	...	43.1
B Forestry and logging	-	-	1.5	-	...	1.5	-	-	1.4	-	...	1.4
C Fishing	-	-	29.6	-	...	29.6	-	-	24.4	-	...	24.4
2 Mining and quarrying	...	...	...	...	...	...	...	...	...	...	...	...
3 Manufacturing	27.3	9.6	21.0	37.7	...	95.6	27.2	9.8	21.5	41.8	...	100.3
4 Electricity, gas and water	18.1	6.4	-10.5	1.0	...	14.9	18.4	6.0	-3.5	2.6	...	23.4
A Electricity, gas and steam	9.4	5.9	-4.7	0.7	...	11.3	9.6	5.7	-0.9	2.3	...	16.7
B Water works and supply	8.7	0.4	-5.8	0.3	...	3.5	8.8	0.3	-2.6	0.3	...	6.7
5 Construction	27.1	2.2	13.5	-	...	42.8	30.9	4.7	17.1	-	...	52.8
6 Wholesale and retail trade, restaurants and hotels	50.3	7.4	154.5	13.4	...	225.6	53.1	6.2	186.4	11.8	...	257.5
A Wholesale and retail trade	-	7.4	154.4	2.6	...	164.4	-	6.2	160.8	2.7	...	169.7
B Restaurants and hotels	50.3	-	-0.1	10.8	...	61.0	53.1	-	25.5	9.1	...	87.7
7 Transport, storage and communication	65.8	14.5	36.8	3.3	...	120.3	69.9	17.8	63.0	3.8	...	154.5
A Transport and storage	44.7	8.2	26.9	0.9	...	80.8	52.1	8.1	45.7	1.8	...	107.7
B Communication	21.1	6.2	9.8	2.4	...	39.6	17.8	9.8	17.2	2.0	...	46.8
8 Finance, insurance, real estate and business services	21.3	18.2	69.8	1.9	...	111.2	23.4	18.1	63.1	1.8	...	106.3
A Financial institutions	15.2	1.6	11.4	-	...	28.2	16.7	2.0	12.7	-	...	31.4
B Insurance	1.4	0.1	1.2	1.8	...	4.6	1.9	0.2	-1.9	1.8	...	1.9
C Real estate and business services	4.7	16.4	57.2	0.1	...	78.4	4.7	15.9	52.3	0.1	...	73.0
Real estate, except dwellings	-	-	14.3	-	...	14.3	-	-	12.6	-	...	12.6
Dwellings	-	15.5	41.5	-	...	57.1	-	15.0	38.8	-	...	53.9
9 Community, social and personal services	21.5	0.8	5.8	0.5	...	28.6	23.1	1.5	3.1	0.3	...	28.0
Total, Industries	231.2	59.2	367.7	57.8	...	715.9	246.0	64.2	419.7	62.0	...	791.9
Producers of Government Services	170.6	0.1	...	...	...	170.7	173.5	0.1	...	...	...	173.6
Other Producers	...	...	...	...	...	...	...	...	...	...	...	...
Total	401.9	59.1	367.7	57.9	...	886.5	419.5	64.3	419.7	62.0	...	965.5
Less: Imputed bank service charge	...	...	25.8	...	...	25.8	...	...	26.0	...	...	26.0
Import duties	...	...	...	128.6	...	128.6	...	...	...	128.6	...	128.6
Value added tax	...	...	...	...	...	...	...	...	...	...	...	...
Total	401.8	59.3	341.9	186.4	...	989.4	419.5	64.3	393.7	190.6	...	1068.1

	1985					
	Compensation of Employees	Capital Consumption	Net Operating Surplus	Indirect Taxes	Less: Subsidies Received	Value Added
			All Producers			
1 Agriculture, hunting, forestry and fishing	0.8	-	68.5	-	...	69.3
A Agriculture and hunting	-	-	44.3	-	...	44.3
B Forestry and logging	-	-	1.5	-	...	1.5
C Fishing	0.8	-	22.6	-	...	23.5

Seychelles

4.3 Cost Components of Value Added
(Continued)

Million Seychelles rupees

	1985 Compensation of Employees	Capital Consumption	Net Operating Surplus	Indirect Taxes	Less: Subsidies Received	Value Added
2 Mining and quarrying	...	...	...	...	...	...
3 Manufacturing	29.4	9.8	28.3	48.9	...	116.4
4 Electricity, gas and water	16.4	6.4	6.3	2.6	...	31.7
A Electricity, gas and steam	9.8	6.3	5.2	2.6	...	23.9
B Water works and supply	6.6	0.1	1.2	-	...	7.8
5 Construction	26.5	10.2	36.4	-	...	73.1
6 Wholesale and retail trade, restaurants and hotels	66.3	6.5	212.7	12.6	-	298.1
A Wholesale and retail trade	...	...	...	...	...	...
B Restaurants and hotels	...	...	...	...	...	...
7 Transport, storage and communication	70.3	21.2	74.8	3.3	-	169.5
A Transport and storage	...	...	...	...	...	...
B Communication	...	...	...	...	...	...
8 Finance, insurance, real estate and business services	23.2	19.7	74.4	2.0	...	119.2
A Financial institutions	16.1	2.2	25.3	-	...	43.6
B Insurance	1.9	0.1	1.1	1.9	...	5.1
C Real estate and business services	5.2	17.3	48.0	0.1	...	70.5
Real estate, except dwellings	0.8	0.7	0.1	-	...	1.8
Dwellings	-	16.3	47.0	-	...	63.3
9 Community, social and personal services	22.8	1.3	8.3	0.8	...	33.3
Total, Industries	255.7	75.1	509.6	70.2	...	910.6
Producers of Government Services	191.7	0.1	-	-	...	191.8
Other Producers	...	...	...	...	...	...
Total	447.4	75.2	509.6	70.2	...	1102.4
Less: Imputed bank service charge	...	...	31.9	...	...	31.9
Import duties	...	...	...	134.5	...	134.5
Value added tax	...	...	...	...	...	...
Total	447.4	75.2	477.7	204.6	...	1204.9

Sierra Leone

General note. The preparation of national accounts statistics in Sierra Leone is undertaken by the Central Statistics Office, Freetown. Official estimates together with methodological notes are published in a series of reports entitled 'National Accounts of Sierra Leone'. The most detailed description of the sources and methods used for the national accounts estimation is found in the sixteenth edition of this report published in December 1987. The estimates are generally in accordance with the classifications and definitions recommended in the United Nations System of National Accounts (SNA). New and revised estimates for the years 1970/71 to 1975/76 were published in 1977, incorporating results of the 1974 population census and the Njala University survey on small-scale manufacturing in 1974. The following tables have been prepared from successive replies to the United Nations national accounts questionnaire. Estimates prior to 1967 relate to fiscal year beginning 1 April while estimates from 1966 relate to fiscal year beginning 1 July. When the scope and coverage of the estimates differ for conceptual or statistical reasons from the definitions and classifications recommended in SNA, a footnote is indicated to the relevant tables.

Sources and methods:

(a) Gross domestic product. Gross domestic product is estimated mainly through the income approach.

(b) Expenditure on the gross domestic product. The expenditure approach is used for the estimation of government final consumption expenditure and exports and imports of goods and services. A combination of the commodity-flow method and the expenditure approach is used to estimate private final consumption expenditure. The commodity-flow method is used to obtain estimates of gross capital formation. The actual expenditures incurred by the government are obtained from the government budget documents. The expenditure is classified by purpose, distinguishing between military and civilian purposes. Private final consumption expenditure estimates are compiled mainly by tracing the consumption goods through the distributive system to the ultimate consumer. Estimates for a few items of food and services are, however, prepared from data collected through the household expenditure survey and the report of the survey of business and industry. The figures on changes in stocks relate principally to diamonds, iron ore, bauxite, rice, export crops, stocks of all public companies, and all major manufacturing and trading establishments for which the completed questionnaires are received by the Central Statistics Office. The estimates of gross fixed capital formation are obtained through an analysis of production and imports of all capital goods classified by type and then marked up for distributive costs. Exports and imports of goods and services are estimated mainly from external trade statistics. GDP by expenditure type at constant prices is not estimated.

(c) Cost-structure of the gross domestic product. Estimates of domestic factor income are compiled from returns directly obtained from the companies concerned and then marked up for non-responding establishments. Analysis of indirect taxes and subsidies by industry was undertaken for the first time in 1976 to arrive at GDP by economic activity in producers' values. Information on depreciation is available only for some larger establishments.

(d) Gross domestic product by kind of economic activity. The table of gross domestic product by kind of economic activity is prepared at market prices, i.e. producers' values. Value added of the majority of industries is estimated through the income approach. The production approach is used to estimate the agricultural and mining sectors. Fairly reliable information on production of major agricultural crops is available only for 1970-71 and 1984-85 based on objective samples surveys. For other years the Ministry of Agriculture and Natural Resources estimate the production of these crops on the basis of reports received from their regional office. For other crops the main source is the Production Yearbook of the Food and Agriculture Organisation. The data required to estimate the value added of mining are obtained from the companies concerned while the value of diamonds smuggled out of the country is based on informal discussions with knowledgeable persons in the industry. The estimates of total income, wages and salaries, operating profits, etc. of a large sample of manufacturing establishments employing six or more persons are compiled from returns directly obtained from them, and then marked up for non-responding establishments using employment data as mark-up factors. The census of manufacturing establishments 1986-87 provided valuable data to strengthen the estimates for 1984 and 1985. The Njala University survey in 1974/75 was used to confirm estimates made for small-scale manufacturing which are based on employment projections and statistics of earnings. The commodity-flow method is used to estimate gross output and intermediate consumption of construction. Data from the government public works department and a number of private contractors are used for analysis of total construction expenditure. The commodity-flow method is also used for the trade sector, preparing aggregate trade margin estimates of all commodities marketed. Receipts and expenditure data are collected directly for national accounting purposes from a sample of trading establishments. For smaller trade establishments, estimates are obtained as a product of the number of persons engaged which is based on the 1974 census, and average earnings per person obtained from a bench-mark year and adjusted yearly. Transportation surveys and other data sources are used for bench-mark estimates in the transport sector. For the services sector, the imputed banking service charge is treated as a negative operating surplus of a nominal finance industry and deducted as a lump sum separately. The number of persons engaged in domestic services, obtained from the 1974 population census has been assumed to continue to grow at the average rate as indicated by the two censuses in 1963 and 1974. Government budgetary documents and unpublished records are used to obtain estimates for central government and local authorities. For the constant price estimates, double deflation is used for the agricultural components with current quantities valued at base-year prices of 1963/64 and 1972/73. Index of building costs is used for price deflation in the construction sector. For other industries, value added is extrapolated by quantity indexes of output obtained by price deflation or employment data. No single typical approach is used for mining and quarrying.

1.1 Expenditure on the Gross Domestic Product, in Current Prices

Million Sierra Leone leones — Fiscal year beginning 1 July

		1970	1975	1978	1979	1980	1981	1982	1983	1984	1985	1986	1987
1	Government final consumption expenditure	31.5	59.0	95.5	97.3	90.1	137.6	166.6	189.2	345.4	497.6	1209.8	...
2	Private final consumption expenditure	267.8	528.9	879.8	1048.3	1171.5	1415.5	1647.3	2242.1	3969.5	6198.7	15971.6	...
3	Gross capital formation	53.3	74.5	138.1	187.3	246.7	214.7	267.9	346.8	476.8	839.0	2058.4	...
	A Increase in stocks	5.9	-2.3	10.1	15.7	10.5	9.6	32.6	15.0	52.6	109.3	204.5	...
	B Gross fixed capital formation	47.4	76.8	128.0	171.6	236.2	205.1	235.3	331.8	424.2	729.7	1853.9	...
	Residential buildings	...	...	...	...	...	...	...	...	...	...	...	...
	Non-residential buildings	24.8	47.5	62.8	109.2	131.3	128.2	124.9	188.1	253.1	425.8	987.5	
	Other construction and land improvement etc.												...
	Other	22.6	29.3	65.2	62.4	104.9	76.9	110.4	143.7	171.1	303.9	866.4	
4	Exports of goods and services [a]	109.0	142.6	233.4	264.2	297.4	252.8	207.7	290.0	463.2	855.0	2515.6	...
5	Less: Imports of goods and services	113.0	191.5	317.6	441.6	513.5	416.1	413.4	338.6	502.5	948.5	2350.4	...
	Equals: Gross Domestic Product	348.6	613.5	1029.2	1155.5	1292.2	1604.5	1876.1	2729.5	4752.4	7441.8	19405.0	...

a) The estimates of exports of goods and services shown in table 1.1 differ from those shown in the other tables. These estimates include an upward adjustments for the estimated value of diamond smuggled out of the country.

1.3 Cost Components of the Gross Domestic Product

Million Sierra Leone leones — Fiscal year beginning 1 July

		1970	1975	1978	1979	1980	1981	1982	1983	1984	1985	1986	1987
1	Indirect taxes, net	32.0	54.9	96.7	92.6	118.6	100.5	76.9	104.8	132.0	212.7	911.2	...
	A Indirect taxes	33.8	56.0	97.1	92.7	119.2	100.7	77.3	105.6	139.4	223.4	912.1	...
	B Less: Subsidies	1.8	1.1	0.4	0.1	0.6	0.2	0.4	0.8	7.4	10.7	0.9	...
2	Consumption of fixed capital	30.9	49.3	81.2	102.9	124.0	152.5	182.6	280.1	360.0	507.0	1385.0	...
3	Compensation of employees paid by resident producers to:	89.2	156.8	253.5	294.9	345.4	409.5	489.0	710.5	836.0	1300.0	3080.0	...
4	Operating surplus	196.4	352.5	597.7	665.1	704.2	942.0	1127.6	1634.1	3424.4	5422.1	14028.2	...
	Equals: Gross Domestic Product	348.6	613.5	1029.2	1155.5	1292.2	1604.5	1876.1	2729.5	4752.4	7441.8	19405.0	...

Sierra Leone

1.7 External Transactions on Current Account, Summary

Million Sierra Leone leones — Fiscal year beginning 1 July

	1970	1975	1978	1979	1980	1981	1982	1983	1984	1985	1986	1987
Payments to the Rest of the World												
1 Imports of goods and services	113.0	191.5	317.6	441.6	513.5	416.1	413.4	338.6	502.5	948.5	2350.4	...
A Imports of merchandise c.i.f.	96.9	167.6	290.8	388.6	405.1	360.4	368.5	286.9	375.8	719.5	1793.0	
B Other	16.1	23.9	26.8	53.0	108.4	55.7	44.9	51.7	126.7	229.0	557.4	
2 Factor income to the rest of the world	9.2	13.8	41.2	44.9	23.7	43.4	43.6	40.0	81.8	-59.2	-1859.9	
A Compensation of employees	...	...	...	...	...	...	...	...	...	...	...	
B Property and entrepreneurial income	9.2	13.8	41.2	44.9	23.7	43.4	43.6	40.0	81.8	-59.2	-1859.9	
3 Current transfers to the rest of the world	1.5	2.0	2.5	2.9	4.3	1.2	4.9	4.7	3.8	7.2	5.2	
4 Surplus of the nation on current transactions	-14.9	-57.3	-112.2	-195.5	-191.5	-165.3	-198.7	-33.1	-57.1	38.1	2076.3	
Payments to the Rest of the World and Surplus of the Nation on Current Transactions	108.8	150.0	249.1	293.9	350.0	295.4	263.2	350.2	531.0	934.6	2572.0	
Receipts From The Rest of the World												
1 Exports of goods and services	100.4	134.6	225.4	256.2	289.4	242.8	195.7	276.0	443.2	825.0	2465.6	...
A Exports of merchandise f.o.b.	84.3	116.6	193.8	208.4	224.1	176.9	136.6	201.8	333.0	671.7	2027.4	
B Other	16.1	18.0	31.6	47.8	65.2	65.9	59.1	74.2	110.2	153.3	438.2	
2 Factor income from rest of the world	2.6	4.0	0.5	0.4	0.8	0.7	0.2	0.5	0.6	1.3	2.4	
A Compensation of employees	...	...	...	...	...	...	...	...	...	...	...	
B Property and entrepreneurial income	2.6	4.0	0.5	0.4	0.8	0.7	0.2	0.5	0.6	1.3	2.4	
3 Current transfers from rest of the world	5.8	11.4	23.2	37.3	59.9	51.9	67.3	73.7	87.2	108.3	104.0	
Receipts from the Rest of the World on Current Transactions	108.8	150.0	249.1	293.9	350.0	295.4	263.2	350.2	531.0	934.6	2572.0	

1.10 Gross Domestic Product by Kind of Activity, in Current Prices

Million Sierra Leone leones — Fiscal year beginning 1 July

	1970	1975	1978	1979	1980	1981	1982	1983	1984	1985	1986	1987
1 Agriculture, hunting, forestry and fishing	96.5	220.0	342.4	369.0	399.4	552.3	690.7	1062.1	2075.5	2926.5	7655.9	...
2 Mining and quarrying	57.5	63.4	119.3	128.1	121.8	95.2	101.4	140.5	297.9	1313.3	2159.9	
3 Manufacturing	29.8	46.3	80.7	83.8	93.7	142.7	144.8	181.9	232.6	334.5	976.6	
4 Electricity, gas and water	2.4	4.6	4.7	4.2	7.3	8.0	10.9	14.4	5.5	12.8	109.2	
5 Construction	13.2	17.5	28.6	46.4	56.0	54.8	47.5	71.0	127.9	173.5	418.8	
6 Wholesale and retail trade, restaurants and hotels	43.1	69.4	145.3	153.3	162.7	173.0	233.0	295.0	758.8	1046.1	3246.1	
7 Transport, storage and communication	33.9	65.0	107.9	160.0	197.3	286.9	324.0	468.9	547.3	602.8	1871.1	
8 Finance, insurance, real estate and business services	26.4	47.3	67.5	80.2	96.7	126.0	146.9	269.7	434.4	663.0	1751.2	
9 Community, social and personal services [a]	8.7	17.3	24.8	25.2	52.0	64.0	73.9	98.1	102.7	128.5	291.0	
Total, Industries	311.5	550.8	921.2	1050.2	1186.9	1502.9	1773.1	2601.9	4582.6	7201.0	18479.8	
Producers of Government Services	19.8	39.8	62.2	67.0	62.9	90.8	102.9	121.9	143.0	197.3	416.1	
Other Producers [a]	1.4	2.0	2.5	2.5	...	...	...	...	...	...	...	
Subtotal	332.7	592.6	985.9	1119.7	1249.8	1593.7	1876.0	2723.5	4725.6	7398.3	18895.9	
Less: Imputed bank service charge	3.3	8.3	6.7	6.9	6.4	29.5	31.9	39.0	35.0	58.0	140.0	
Plus: Import duties	19.2	29.2	50.0	42.7	48.8	40.3	32.0	45.0	61.8	101.5	649.1	
Plus: Value added tax	...	...	...	...	...	...	...	...	...	...	...	
Equals: Gross Domestic Product	348.6	613.5	1029.2	1155.5	1292.2	1604.5	1876.1	2729.5	4752.4	7441.8	19405.0	...

a) Beginning 1980, item 'Other producers' is included in item 'Community, social and personal services'.

Sierra Leone

1.11 Gross Domestic Product by Kind of Activity, in Constant Prices

Million Sierra Leone leones — Fiscal year beginning 1 July

	1970	1975	1978	1979	1980	1981	1982	1983	1984	1985	1986	1987
					At constant prices of: 1972				1984			
1 Agriculture, hunting, forestry and fishing	109.7	120.9	141.8	137.6	138.7	146.0	140.0	142.9	174.3 / 2075.5	1974.4	2125.5	...
2 Mining and quarrying	70.0	51.7	29.1	33.2	26.2	22.3	19.9	22.6	20.6 / 297.9	329.9	346.1	...
3 Manufacturing	28.5	39.2	41.3	39.0	41.9	50.4	41.5	44.5	38.3 / 232.6	216.2	191.0	...
4 Electricity, gas and water	1.3	1.6	1.8	1.8	1.9	2.5	2.5	2.5	0.2 / 5.5	2.1	7.6	...
5 Construction	13.3	12.6	14.5	18.4	21.9	17.3	13.4	16.1	18.5 / 127.9	131.8	136.5	...
6 Wholesale and retail trade, restaurants and hotels	47.3	45.7	52.1	53.0	64.7	65.2	74.4	61.5	80.7 / 758.8	763.1	760.0	...
7 Transport, storage and communication	34.8	40.5	47.2	51.5	50.3	59.5	58.8	60.4	52.6 / 547.3	443.0	401.7	...
8 Finance, insurance, real estate and business services	27.1	33.2	35.6	39.4	41.2	46.0	47.1	49.0	45.8 / 434.4	437.2	457.5	...
9 Community, social and personal services [a]	8.8	13.0	12.8	13.4	22.8	24.2	26.1	29.6	22.3 / 102.7	109.5	116.4	...
Total, Industries	340.8	358.4	376.2	387.3	409.6	433.4	423.7	429.1	453.3 / 4582.6	4407.2	4542.3	...
Producers of Government Services	20.8	33.1	47.1	48.6	46.0	57.5	65.1	63.2	71.7 / 143.0	154.4	177.2	...
Other Producers [a]	1.4	1.7	1.8	1.8	...	...	...	...	...	...	...	...
Subtotal	363.0	393.2	425.1	437.7	455.6	490.9	488.8	492.3	525.0 / 4725.6	4561.6	4719.5	...
Less: Imputed bank service charge	3.5	5.4	3.1	2.7	2.2	14.0	15.0	18.0	9.9 / 35.0	36.9	38.3	...
Plus: Import duties	26.2	20.8	24.7	25.1	20.0	20.0	16.0	22.0	18.0 / 61.8	57.8	143.1	...
Plus: Value added tax	...	...	...	...	...	...	...	...	...	...	...	...
Equals: Gross Domestic Product	385.7	408.6	446.7	460.1	473.4	496.9	489.8	496.3	533.1 / 4752.4	4582.5	4824.3	...

a) Beginning 1980, item 'Other producers' is included in item 'Community, social and personal services'.

1.12 Relations Among National Accounting Aggregates

Million Sierra Leone leones — Fiscal year beginning 1 July

	1970	1975	1978	1979	1980	1981	1982	1983	1984	1985	1986	1987
Gross Domestic Product	348.6	613.5	1029.2	1155.5	1292.2	1604.5	1876.1	2729.5	4752.4	7441.8	19405.0	...
Plus: Net factor income from the rest of the world	-6.6	-9.8	-40.7	-44.5	-22.9	-42.7	-43.4	-39.5	-81.2	60.5	1862.3	...
Factor income from the rest of the world	2.6	4.0	0.5	0.4	0.8	0.7	0.2	0.5	0.6	1.3	2.4	...
Less: Factor income to the rest of the world	9.2	13.8	41.2	44.9	23.7	43.4	43.6	40.0	81.8	-59.2	-1859.9	...
Equals: Gross National Product	342.0	603.7	988.5	1111.0	1269.3	1561.8	1832.7	2690.0	4671.2	7502.3	21267.3	...
Less: Consumption of fixed capital	30.9	49.3	81.2	102.9	124.0	152.5	182.6	280.1	360.0	507.0	1385.0	...
Equals: National Income	311.1	554.4	907.3	1008.1	1145.3	1409.3	1650.1	2409.9	4311.2	6995.3	19882.3	...
Plus: Net current transfers from the rest of the world	4.3	9.4	20.7	34.4	55.6	50.7	62.4	69.0	83.4	101.1	98.8	...
Current transfers from the rest of the world	5.8	11.4	23.2	37.3	59.9	51.9	67.3	73.7	87.2	108.3	104.0	...
Less: Current transfers to the rest of the world	1.5	2.0	2.5	2.9	4.3	1.2	4.9	4.7	3.8	7.2	5.2	...
Equals: National Disposable Income	318.5	563.8	928.0	1042.5	1200.9	1460.0	1712.5	2478.9	4394.6	7096.4	19981.1	...
Less: Final consumption	299.2	587.9	975.4	1145.6	1261.6	1553.1	1813.9	2431.3	4314.9	6696.3	17181.4	...
Equals: Net Saving	19.3	-24.1	-47.4	-103.1	-60.7	-93.1	-101.4	47.6	79.7	400.1	2799.7	...
Less: Surplus of the nation on current transactions	-14.9	-57.3	-112.2	-195.5	-191.4	-165.3	-198.7	-33.1	-57.1	38.1	2076.3	...
Statistical discrepancy	-11.8	-8.0	-7.9	-8.0	-8.0	-10.0	-12.0	-14.0	-20.0	-30.0	-50.0	...
Equals: Net Capital Formation	22.4	25.2	56.9	84.4	122.7	62.2	85.3	66.7	116.8	332.0	673.4	...

Sierra Leone

2.1 Government Final Consumption Expenditure by Function, in Current Prices

Million Sierra Leone leones — Fiscal year beginning 1 July

	1970	1975	1978	1979	1980	1981	1982	1983	1984	1985	1986	1987
1 General public services	9.85	22.98	44.31	102.41	43.40	49.07	43.38	55.13	56.34	136.33	503.31	...
2 Defence	3.41	9.00	16.55	11.73	13.88	18.32	18.02	19.72	21.60	35.16	109.91	...
3 Public order and safety	...	...	...	...	...	...	...	...	...	...	...	...
4 Education	10.23	23.84	32.61	38.10	47.22	72.28	58.49	73.69	74.68	90.91	260.88	...
5 Health	4.07	8.49	15.99	18.51	26.38	27.72	22.08	33.78	28.43	38.72	146.73	...
6 Social security and welfare	0.15	3.10	2.89	2.15	1.98	2.26	2.00	4.57	2.61	3.34	14.64	...
7 Housing and community amenities	1.19	4.99	6.56	6.26	4.37	7.43	3.92	4.87	3.30	7.05	43.57	...
8 Recreational, cultural and religious affairs	-	-	-	-	-	-	-	-	4.27	5.00	36.56	...
9 Economic services	17.89	49.57	67.30	97.47	123.02	110.50	138.51	120.51	146.74	348.00	815.63	...
A Fuel and energy	...	...	...	...	14.72	...	...	...	20.06	37.74	43.65	...
B Agriculture, forestry, fishing and hunting	...	...	...	...	40.25	...	...	...	49.85	76.21	186.88	...
C Mining, manufacturing and construction, except fuel and energy	...	...	...	...	4.90	...	...	...	1.46	8.71	4.63	...
D Transportation and communication	...	...	...	...	33.42	...	...	...	53.10	202.12	555.89	...
E Other economic affairs	...	...	...	...	29.73	...	...	...	22.24	23.22	24.58	...
10 Other functions	7.47	24.72	55.53	68.40	144.53	94.56	57.29	58.12	150.36	235.05	288.00	...
Total Government Final Consumption Expenditure [a,b]	54.26	146.69	241.74	345.03	404.78	382.14	343.69	370.39	491.33	899.56	2219.23	...

a) Item 'Total government final consumption expenditure' includes development expenditure.
b) Only central government data are included in the general government estimates.

2.5 Private Final Consumption Expenditure by Type and Purpose, in Current Prices

Million Sierra Leone leones — Fiscal year beginning 1 July

	1970	1975	1978	1979	1980	1981	1982	1983	1984	1985	1986	1987
Final Consumption Expenditure of Resident Households												
1 Food, beverages and tobacco	143.5	301.1	...	...	...	695.8	912.3	1242.2	2549.6	4023.6	10847.5	...
2 Clothing and footwear	37.7	66.5	...	...	...	126.9	121.2	144.6	158.0	189.6	445.6	...
3 Gross rent, fuel and power	27.3	47.2	...	...	...	143.5	177.8	298.9	597.6	932.1	2254.8	...
4 Furniture, furnishings and household equipment and operation	23.0	36.8	...	...	...	90.4	106.0	107.2	130.9	170.4	353.2	...
5 Medical care and health expenses	3.5	5.7	...	...	...	15.6	20.6	35.2	37.5	56.9	173.0	...
6 Transport and communication	21.1	49.9	...	...	...	208.5	236.5	340.0	322.3	429.2	1321.8	...
7 Recreational, entertainment, education and cultural services	10.1	23.4	...	...	...	49.7	52.5	71.6	87.6	110.1	222.7	...
8 Miscellaneous goods and services	5.4	8.1	...	...	...	24.6	23.6	27.0	30.0	51.0	150.0	...
Statistical discrepancy	-3.4	-11.2	...	...	...	...	...	...	59.0	246.1	264.2	...
Total Final Consumption Expenditure in the Domestic Market by Households, of which	268.2	527.5	...	...	...	1355.0	1650.5	2266.7	3972.5	6209.0	16032.8	...
Plus: Direct purchases abroad by resident households	2.8	4.8	...	...	...	4.0	6.2	6.8	8.1	10.8	80.7	...
Less: Direct purchases in the domestic market by non-resident households	3.3	3.4	...	...	...	6.0	6.5	9.9	11.1	21.1	141.9	...
Equals: Final Consumption Expenditure of Resident Households [a]	267.7	528.9	...	...	...	1353.0	1650.2	2263.6	3969.5	6198.7	15971.6	...
Final Consumption Expenditure of Private Non-profit Institutions Serving Households												
Equals: Final Consumption Expenditure of Private Non-profit Organisations Serving Households	...	...	...	...	...	...	...	...	...	...	...	...
Statistical discrepancy	...	...	...	...	...	62.5	-2.9	-21.5	...	...	...	...
Private Final Consumption Expenditure	267.7	528.9	...	...	...	1415.5	1647.3	2242.1	3969.5	6198.7	15971.6	...

a) Item 'Final consumption expenditure of resident households' includes consumption expenditure of private non-profit institutions serving households.

Sierra Leone

2.6 Private Final Consumption Expenditure by Type and Purpose, in Constant Prices

Million Sierra Leone leones
Fiscal year beginning 1 July

	1970	1975	1978	1979	1980	1981	1982	1983	1984	1985	1986	1987
	At constant prices of:											
			1963				1972			1984		

Final Consumption Expenditure of Resident Households

	1970	1975	1978	1979	1980	1981	1982	1983	1984	1985	1986	1987
1 Food, beverages and tobacco	107.6	...	...	...	...	214.3	213.4	203.6	200.4 / 2549.6	2693.8	2907.7	...
A Food	98.3	...	...	...	...	...	...	...	...	...	...	...
B Non-alcoholic beverages	5.0	...	...	...	...	...	...	...	...	...	...	...
C Alcoholic beverages		...	...	...	...	...	...	...	...	...	...	...
D Tobacco	4.3	...	...	...	...	...	...	...	...	...	...	...
2 Clothing and footwear	35.3	...	...	...	...	43.6	40.8	40.2	37.9 / 158.0	161.6	168.4	...
3 Gross rent, fuel and power	23.1	...	...	...	...	53.5	55.7	54.8	57.2 / 597.6	607.8	603.4	...
4 Furniture, furnishings and household equipment and operation	23.8	...	...	...	...	29.6	30.4	29.2	18.6 / 130.9	112.9	124.4	...
A Household operation	8.1	...	...	...	...	...	...	...	...	...	...	...
B Other	15.7	...	...	...	...	...	...	...	...	...	...	...
5 Medical care and health expenses	2.9	...	...	...	...	4.8	4.5	4.4	5.3 / 37.5	39.1	39.1	...
6 Transport and communication	25.8	...	...	...	...	29.9	27.5	27.7	25.7 / 322.3	269.5	255.6	...
A Personal transport equipment	3.4	...	...	...	...	...	...	...	...	...	...	...
B Other	22.4	...	...	...	...	...	...	...	...	...	...	...
7 Recreational, entertainment, education and cultural services	11.3	...	...	...	...	19.2	18.2	23.1	26.3 / 87.6	87.3	93.9	...
A Education	7.2	...	...	...	...	...	...	...	...	...	...	...
B Other	4.1	...	...	...	...	...	...	...	...	...	...	...
8 Miscellaneous goods and services	5.4	...	...	...	...	6.8	6.5	6.6	4.3 / 30.0	31.0	32.0	...
A Personal care	2.0	...	...	...	...	...	...	...	...	...	...	...
B Expenditures in restaurants, cafes and hotels	...	...	...	...	...	...	...	...	...	...	...	...
C Other	3.4	...	...	...	...	...	...	...	...	...	...	...

Sierra Leone

2.6 Private Final Consumption Expenditure by Type and Purpose, in Constant Prices
(Continued)

Million Sierra Leone leones — Fiscal year beginning 1 July

	1970	1975	1978	1979	1980	1981	1982	1983	1984	1985	1986	1987
	At constant prices of: 1963						1972		1984			
Statistical discrepancy	...	...	...	...	...	18.5	-0.8	-3.8	-3.5 / 59.0	165.0	70.0	...
Total Final Consumption Expenditure in the Domestic Market by Households, of which	235.2					419.2	396.2	385.8	372.2 / 3972.5	4168.0	4294.5	...
Plus: Direct purchases abroad by resident households	2.2					0.9	1.4	1.1	1.4 / 8.1	6.2	17.8	...
Less: Direct purchases in the domestic market by non-resident households	3.7					1.4	1.5	1.6	2.0 / 11.1	12.0	31.3	...
Equals: Final Consumption Expenditure of Resident Households a	233.7					418.7	396.1	385.3	371.6 / 3969.5	4162.2	4281.0	...

Final Consumption Expenditure of Private Non-profit Institutions Serving Households

Equals: Final Consumption Expenditure of Private Non-profit Organisations Serving Households	...					...			...	...	...	...
Private Final Consumption Expenditure	233.7					418.7	396.1	385.3	371.6 / 3969.5	4162.2	4281.0	...

a) Item 'Final consumption expenditure of resident households' includes consumption expenditure of private non-profit institutions serving households.

2.7 Gross Capital Formation by Type of Good and Owner, in Current Prices

Million Sierra Leone leones — Fiscal year beginning 1 July

	1980 TOTAL	Total Private	Public Enterprises	General Government	1981 TOTAL	Total Private	Public Enterprises	General Government	1982 TOTAL	Total Private	Public Enterprises	General Government
Increase in stocks, total	10.5	2.5	8.0	...	9.6	19.6	-10.0	...	32.6	23.2	9.4	...
Gross Fixed Capital Formation, Total	236.2	147.2	35.2	53.8	205.1	124.4	20.2	60.5	235.3	164.9	12.6	57.8
1 Residential buildings												
2 Non-residential buildings	120.5	75.8	10.0	34.7	114.1	61.5	13.4	39.2	110.0	67.7	4.8	37.5
3 Other construction												
4 Land improvement and plantation and orchard development	10.8	-	-	10.8	14.1	-	-	14.1	14.9	-	-	14.9
5 Producers' durable goods	104.9	71.4	25.2	8.3	76.9	62.9	6.8	7.2	110.4	97.2	7.8	5.4
A Transport equipment	48.7	39.9	1.8	7.0	41.6	33.7	2.7	5.2	48.1	40.3	3.9	3.9
Passenger cars	23.0	...	...	...	19.4	...	...	...	18.7	...	...	...
Other	25.7	...	...	...	22.2	...	...	...	29.4	...	...	...
B Machinery and equipment	56.2	31.5	23.4	1.3	35.3	29.2	4.1	2.0	62.3	56.9	3.9	1.5
6 Breeding stock, dairy cattle, etc.	...	...	...	...	...	...	...	...	...	...	...	...
Total Gross Capital Formation	246.7	149.7	43.2	53.8	214.7	144.0	10.2	60.5	267.9	188.1	22.0	57.8

	1983 TOTAL	Total Private	Public Enterprises	General Government	1984 TOTAL	Total Private	Public Enterprises	General Government	1985 TOTAL	Total Private	Public Enterprises	General Government
Increase in stocks, total	15.0	18.0	-3.0	...	52.6	15.6	37.0	...	109.3	72.3	37.0	...
Gross Fixed Capital Formation, Total	331.8	295.9	13.9	22.0	424.2	...	...	...	729.7	...	...	...
1 Residential buildings												
2 Non-residential buildings	183.9	165.4	3.3	15.2	237.7	...	...	...	401.7	...	...	...
3 Other construction												

Sierra Leone

2.7 Gross Capital Formation by Type of Good and Owner, in Current Prices
(Continued)

Million Sierra Leone leones — Fiscal year beginning 1 July

	1983 TOTAL	Total Private	Public Enterprises	General Government	1984 TOTAL	Total Private	Public Enterprises	General Government	1985 TOTAL	Total Private	Public Enterprises	General Government
4 Land improvement and plantation and orchard development	4.2	-	-	4.2	15.4	-	-	15.4	24.1	-	0.1	24.0
5 Producers' durable goods	143.7	130.5	10.6	2.6	171.1	...	...	...	303.9	...	...	...
A Transport equipment	54.0	46.9	5.1	2.0	61.8	...	...	...	153.0	...	...	...
Passenger cars	24.2	...	...	...	25.8	...	...	...	49.2	...	...	...
Other	29.8	...	...	...	36.0	...	...	...	103.8	...	...	...
B Machinery and equipment	89.7	83.6	5.5	0.6	109.3	...	...	...	150.9	...	...	...
6 Breeding stock, dairy cattle, etc.	...	...	...	...	...	...	...	...	...	...	...	...
Total Gross Capital Formation	346.8	313.9	10.9	22.0	476.8	...	...	...	839.0	...	...	...

	1986 TOTAL	Total Private	Public Enterprises	General Government
Increase in stocks, total	204.5	...	...	...
Gross Fixed Capital Formation, Total	1853.9	...	...	...
1 Residential buildings		...	...	...
2 Non-residential buildings	965.3	...	...	...
3 Other construction		...	...	...
4 Land improvement and plantation and orchard development	22.2	...	...	...
5 Producers' durable goods	866.4	...	...	...
A Transport equipment	348.9	...	...	...
Passenger cars	141.7	...	...	...
Other	207.2	...	...	...
B Machinery and equipment	517.5	...	...	...
6 Breeding stock, dairy cattle, etc.	...	...	...	...
Total Gross Capital Formation	2058.4	...	...	...

2.17 Exports and Imports of Goods and Services, Detail

Million Sierra Leone leones — Fiscal year beginning 1 July

	1970	1975	1978	1979	1980	1981	1982	1983	1984	1985	1986	1987
Exports of Goods and Services												
1 Exports of merchandise, f.o.b.	84.3	116.6	193.8	208.4	224.1	176.9	136.6	201.8	333.0	671.7	...	...
2 Transport and communication	...	...	...	...	...	...	...	...	...	...	...	...
3 Insurance service charges	...	...	...	...	...	...	...	...	...	...	...	...
4 Other commodities	16.1	18.0	31.6	47.8	65.3	65.9	59.1	74.2	110.2	153.3	...	...
5 Adjustments of merchandise exports to change-of-ownership basis												
6 Direct purchases in the domestic market by non-resident households	...	...	...	...	...	...	...	...	...	...	...	...
7 Direct purchases in the domestic market by extraterritorial bodies	...	...	...	...	...	...	...	...	...	...	...	...
Total Exports of Goods and Services	100.4	134.6	225.4	256.2	289.4	242.8	195.7	276.0	443.2	825.0	...	...
Imports of Goods and Services												
1 Imports of merchandise, c.i.f.	96.9	167.6	290.8	388.6	447.5	360.4	368.5	286.9	418.3	781.6	...	...

Sierra Leone

2.17 Exports and Imports of Goods and Services, Detail
(Continued)

Million Sierra Leone leones — Fiscal year beginning 1 July

	1970	1975	1978	1979	1980	1981	1982	1983	1984	1985	1986	1987
A Imports of merchandise, f.o.b.	85.8	148.1	259.1	355.5	405.1	326.9	322.4	250.7	375.8	719.5	...	...
B Transport of services on merchandise imports	...	...	...	...	...	...	...	...	...	...	...	...
C Insurance service charges on merchandise imports	...	...	...	...	...	...	...	...	...	...	...	...
2 Adjustments of merchandise imports to change-of-ownership basis	...	...	...	...	...	...	...	...	...	...	...	...
3 Other transport and communication	...	...	...	...	...	...	...	...	...	...	...	...
4 Other insurance service charges	...	...	...	...	...	...	...	...	...	...	...	...
5 Other commodities	16.1	23.9	26.8	53.0	66.0	55.7	44.9	51.7	84.2	166.9	...	...
6 Direct purchases abroad by government	...	...	...	...	...	...	...	...	...	...	...	...
7 Direct purchases abroad by resident households	...	...	...	...	...	...	...	...	...	...	...	...
Total Imports of Goods and Services	113.0	191.5	317.6	441.6	513.5	416.1	413.4	338.6	502.5	948.5	...	...
Balance of Goods and Services	-12.5	-56.9	-92.2	-185.4	-224.1	-173.3	-217.7	-62.6	-59.3	-123.5	...	...
Total Imports and Balance of Goods and Services [a]	100.4	134.6	225.4	256.2	289.4	242.8	195.7	276.0	443.2	825.0	...	...

a) Data for this table have not been revised, therefore, data for some years are not comparable with those of other tables.

4.1 Derivation of Value Added by Kind of Activity, in Current Prices

Million Sierra Leone leones — Fiscal year beginning 1 July

	1984 Gross Output	1984 Intermediate Consumption	1984 Value Added	1985 Gross Output	1985 Intermediate Consumption	1985 Value Added	1986 Gross Output	1986 Intermediate Consumption	1986 Value Added
				All Producers					
1 Agriculture, hunting, forestry and fishing	2434.9	364.7	2070.2	3420.3	531.0	2889.3	9031.9	1390.8	7641.1
A Agriculture and hunting	1562.6	225.4	1337.3	2069.6	298.3	1771.3	6191.1	907.8	5283.3
B Forestry and logging	258.2	25.8	232.4	317.0	31.7	285.3	623.6	62.4	561.2
C Fishing	614.0	113.5	500.5	1033.6	201.0	832.7	2217.2	420.7	1796.5
2 Mining and quarrying	421.6	129.5	292.1	1754.4	446.9	1307.5	2865.8	725.1	2140.7
3 Manufacturing	642.8	472.9	169.9	794.3	528.1	266.2	2789.0	2023.8	765.2
4 Electricity, gas and water	38.9	26.7	12.2	47.7	26.4	21.3	160.0	50.8	109.2
A Electricity, gas and steam	30.0	22.3	7.7	37.2	23.3	13.9	117.8	35.3	82.5
B Water works and supply	8.9	4.4	4.5	10.5	3.1	7.4	42.3	15.5	26.7
5 Construction	237.8	109.9	127.9	401.7	228.3	173.5	965.3	547.0	418.4
6 Wholesale and retail trade, restaurants and hotels	976.9	218.6	758.3	1344.3	301.9	1042.4	4088.1	846.5	3241.6
7 Transport, storage and communication	892.1	346.2	545.9	1040.7	440.7	600.0	5073.3	3211.7	1861.6
A Transport and storage	876.0	337.1	538.9	1012.0	427.0	585.0	4995.0	3178.6	1816.4
B Communication	16.1	9.1	7.0	28.7	13.7	15.0	78.3	33.1	45.2
8 Finance, insurance, real estate and business services	457.8	23.9	433.9	746.1	84.1	662.0	1828.5	78.5	1750.0
A Financial institutions	128.6	23.9	104.7	211.6	84.1	127.5	545.9	78.5	467.4
B Insurance									
C Real estate and business services	329.2	-	329.2	534.5	-	534.5	1282.6	-	1282.6
9 Community, social and personal services [a]	102.1	-	102.1	127.6	-	127.6	289.5	-	289.5
A Sanitary and similar services	...	...	...	...	...	...	...	...	...
B Social and related community services	81.8	-	81.8	97.5	-	97.5	215.6	-	215.6
Educational services	51.9	-	51.9	59.8	-	59.8	127.6	-	127.6
Medical, dental, other health and veterinary services	29.9	-	29.9	37.7	-	37.7	88.0	-	88.0
C Recreational and cultural services	...	...	...	...	...	...	...	...	...
D Personal and household services	...	...	...	...	...	...	...	...	...
Total, Industries	6204.8	1692.3	4512.4	9677.0	2587.3	7089.8	27091.2	8874.2	18217.1
Producers of Government Services	143.0	...	143.0	197.3	...	197.3	416.1	...	416.1

Sierra Leone

4.1 Derivation of Value Added by Kind of Activity, in Current Prices
(Continued)

Million Sierra Leone leones — Fiscal year beginning 1 July

	1984 Gross Output	1984 Intermediate Consumption	1984 Value Added	1985 Gross Output	1985 Intermediate Consumption	1985 Value Added	1986 Gross Output	1986 Intermediate Consumption	1986 Value Added
Other Producers a	...	...	...	...	...	...	...	...	...
Total b	6347.7	1692.3	4655.4	9874.3	2587.3	7287.1	27507.3	8874.2	18633.2
Less: Imputed bank service charge	...	-35.0	35.0	...	-58.0	58.0	...	-140.0	140.0
Import duties	...	...	...	...	...	...	...	...	...
Value added tax	...	...	...	...	...	...	...	...	...
Other adjustments c	132.0	...	132.0	212.7	...	212.7	911.2	...	911.2
Total	6479.8	1727.3	4752.4	10087.2	2645.3	7441.8	28418.5	9014.2	19404.4

a) Beginning 1980, item 'Other producers' is included in item 'Community, social and personal services'.
b) Gross domestic product in factor values.
c) Item 'Other adjustments' refers to indirect taxes net of subsidies.

4.3 Cost Components of Value Added

Million Sierra Leone leones — Fiscal year beginning 1 July

	1984 Compensation of Employees	1984 Capital Consumption	1984 Net Operating Surplus	1984 Indirect Taxes	1984 Less: Subsidies Received	1984 Value Added	1985 Compensation of Employees	1985 Capital Consumption	1985 Net Operating Surplus	1985 Indirect Taxes	1985 Less: Subsidies Received	1985 Value Added
All Producers												
1 Agriculture, hunting, forestry and fishing	263.7	...	1806.5	...	...	2070.2	380.0	...	2509.4	...	...	2889.3
A Agriculture and hunting	78.1	...	1259.2	...	...	1337.3	103.5	...	1667.9	...	...	1771.3
B Forestry and logging	12.9	...	219.5	...	...	232.4	15.9	...	269.5	...	...	285.3
C Fishing	172.6	...	327.9	...	...	500.5	260.6	...	572.0	...	...	832.7
2 Mining and quarrying	47.4	...	244.7	...	...	292.1	121.9	...	1185.6	...	...	1307.5
3 Manufacturing	44.2	...	125.7	...	...	169.9	64.6	...	201.7	...	...	266.2
4 Electricity, gas and water	8.0	...	4.2	...	...	12.2	9.0	...	12.3	...	...	21.3
A Electricity, gas and steam	7.0	...	0.7	...	...	7.7	7.8	...	6.1	...	...	13.9
B Water works and supply	1.0	...	3.5	...	...	4.5	1.3	...	6.2	...	...	7.4
5 Construction	54.8	...	73.1	...	...	127.9	142.3	...	31.2	...	...	173.5
6 Wholesale and retail trade, restaurants and hotels	64.1	...	694.2	...	...	758.3	100.5	...	941.9	...	...	1042.4
7 Transport, storage and communication	85.7	...	460.2	...	...	545.9	104.2	...	495.8	...	...	600.0
A Transport and storage	80.8	...	458.1	...	...	538.9	97.8	...	487.2	...	...	585.0
B Communication	4.9	...	2.1	...	...	7.0	6.4	...	8.6	...	...	15.0
8 Finance, insurance, real estate and business services	35.4	...	398.5	...	...	433.9	52.8	...	609.3	...	...	662.0
A Financial institutions	35.0	...	69.7	...	...	104.7	52.2	...	75.3	...	...	127.5
B Insurance	...	...	...	...	...	...	...	...	...	...	...	...
C Real estate and business services	0.4	...	328.8	...	...	329.2	0.6	...	533.9	...	...	534.5
9 Community, social and personal services a	89.8	...	12.3	...	...	102.1	127.6	...	-	...	...	127.6
A Sanitary and similar services	...	...	...	...	...	...	...	...	...	...	...	...
B Social and related community services	81.8	...	-	...	...	81.8	97.5	...	-	...	...	97.5
Educational services	51.9	...	-	...	...	51.9	59.8	...	-	...	...	59.8
Medical, dental, other health and veterinary services	29.9	...	-	...	...	29.9	37.7	...	-	...	...	37.7
C Recreational and cultural services	...	...	...	...	...	...	...	...	...	...	...	...
D Personal and household services	...	...	...	...	...	...	...	...	...	...	...	...
Total, Industries	693.0	...	3819.4	...	...	4512.4	1102.7	...	5987.1	...	...	7089.8
Producers of Government Services	143.0	...	-	...	...	143.0	197.3	...	-	...	...	197.3
Other Producers a	...	...	...	...	...	...	...	...	...	...	...	...
Total b	836.0	...	3819.4	...	...	4655.4	1300.0	...	5987.1	...	...	7287.1
Less: Imputed bank service charge	-	...	35.0	...	...	35.0	-	...	58.0	...	...	58.0
Import duties	...	...	...	...	...	...	...	...	...	...	...	...
Value added tax	...	...	...	...	...	...	...	...	...	...	...	...
Other adjustments c	...	...	...	139.4	7.4	132.0	...	...	...	223.4	10.7	212.7
Total	836.0	...	3784.4	139.4	7.4	4752.4	1300.0	...	5929.1	223.4	10.7	7441.8

Sierra Leone

4.3 Cost Components of Value Added

Million Sierra Leone leones — Fiscal year beginning 1 July

	Compensation of Employees	Capital Consumption	Net Operating Surplus	Indirect Taxes	Less: Subsidies Received	Value Added
			1986			
			All Producers			
1 Agriculture, hunting, forestry and fishing	906.0	...	6733.1	...	...	7641.1
A Agriculture and hunting	309.6	...	4973.8	...	...	5283.3
B Forestry and logging	31.2	...	530.0	...	...	561.2
C Fishing	567.3	...	1229.2	...	...	1796.5
2 Mining and quarrying	329.4	...	1811.3	...	...	2140.7
3 Manufacturing	147.1	...	618.1	...	...	765.2
4 Electricity, gas and water	11.0	...	98.2	...	...	109.2
A Electricity, gas and steam	8.5	...	74.0	...	...	82.5
B Water works and supply	2.5	...	24.2	...	...	26.7
5 Construction	332.5	...	85.8	...	...	418.4
6 Wholesale and retail trade, restaurants and hotels	293.7	...	2947.9	...	...	3241.6
7 Transport, storage and communication	286.1	...	1575.5	...	...	1861.6
A Transport and storage	272.5	...	1543.9	...	...	1816.4
B Communication	13.6	...	31.6	...	...	45.2
8 Finance, insurance, real estate and business services	111.0	...	1638.9	...	...	1750.0
A Financial institutions	[110.0	...	[357.4	...	...	[467.4
B Insurance	]	...	]	...	...	]
C Real estate and business services	1.0	...	1281.6	...	...	1282.6
9 Community, social and personal services [a]	245.2	...	44.3	...	...	289.5
A Sanitary and similar services	...	...	...	...	...	...
B Social and related community services	215.6	...	-	...	...	215.6
Educational services	127.6	...	-	...	...	127.6
Medical, dental, other health and veterinary services	88.0	...	-	...	...	88.0
C Recreational and cultural services	...	...	...	...	...	...
D Personal and household services	...	...	...	...	...	...
Total, Industries	2663.9	...	15553.2	...	...	18217.1
Producers of Government Services	416.1	...	-	...	...	416.1
Other Producers [a]	...	...	...	...	...	...
Total [b]	3080.0	...	15553.2	...	...	18633.2
Less: Imputed bank service charge	-	...	140.0	...	...	140.0
Import duties	...	...	...	...	...	...
Value added tax	...	...	...	...	...	...
Other adjustments [c]	...	...	...	912.1	0.9	911.2
Total	3080.0	...	15413.2	912.1	0.9	19404.4

a) Beginning 1980, item 'Other producers' is included in item 'Community, social and personal services'.
b) Gross domestic product in factor values.
c) Item 'Other adjustments' refers to indirect taxes net of subsidies.

Singapore

General note. The preparation of national accounts statistics in Singapore is undertaken by the Department of Statistics, Singapore. The official estimates together with a comprehensive description of the sources and methods used for the national accounts estimation is found in 'Singapore National Accounts, 1987' published by the Department of Statistics in March 1988. The estimates are generally in accordance with the classifications and definitions recommended in the United Nations System of National Accounts (SNA). The following tables have been prepared from successive replies to the United Nations national accounts questionnaire. When the scope and coverage of the estimates differ for conceptual or statistical reasons from the definitions and classifications recommended in SNA, a footnote is indicated to the relevant tables.

Sources and methods:

(a) Gross domestic product. Gross domestic product is estimated mainly through the production approach.

(b) Expenditure on the gross domestic product. The expenditure approach is used to estimate all components of GDP by expenditure type except private final expenditure on goods and capital expenditure on plant, machinery and equipment, for which the commodity-flow approach is used. The basic sources for estimating government final consumption expenditure are the annual financial statements of the Accountant-General, detailed income and expenditure statements of statutory boards and data collected from educational institutions. The estimates of private expenditure on goods are based on external trade statistics, data from the annual census of industrial production and on agricultural prduction data supplied by the Primary Production Department. Transport cost and distributor's margin are added to imports and local production values to arrive at market values of the commodities. Adjustments are made for stocks changes and for commodities with mulitple uses. Private expenditure on services are derived mainly from the results of surveys which are used as bench-mark estimates. Data used for the estimates of increase in stocks are derived from the annual censuses of industrial production and annual surveys of stocks conducted by the Department of Statistics. Capital formation in construction is estimated from the survey of capital expenditure on buildings, other construction and w orks. The estimates for capital formation of transport equipment are based on trade and prduction data as well as registration figures. The estimates of exports and imports of goods and services are based on balance-of-payments statistics. For the constant price estimates, all components of GDP by expenditure type are deflated by appropriate price indexes.

(c) Cost-structure of the gross domestic product. Estimates of the cost-structure of GDP are not made.

(d) Gross domestic product by kind of economic activity. The table of gross domestic product by kind of economic activity is prepared at market prices, i.e. producers' values. The production approach is used to estimate the value added of most industries. The income approach is used in the case of community, social and personal services and the transport sectors. Production data for the agricultural activities are estimated by the Primary Production Department based on two surveys conducted annually - the sample survey on pigs and poultry and the sample survey on vegetables. Fish production is based on fish caught and landed by locally registered fishing vessels while the estimates of output of live plants, flowers and aquarium fish are based on external trade statistics. Value added is calculated separately for each component as a fixed percentage of the value of production derived from the information available from the Department of Primary Production. Value added of the mining sector is derived from the annual census of industrial production with adjustments made to conform to the national income concept. For manufacturing, basic data for establishments employing 10 or more workers are obtained from the annual census of industrial production. For smaller establishments, estimates are based on the censuses of industrial production for establishments with five to nine workers supplemented by estimates made from employment data and per capita value added referring to establishments engaging less than five workers. The data used for the estimates of electricity, gas and water are taken from detailed accounts provided by the Public Utilities Board. Since April 1986, the Ministry of National Development has taken over the inquiries to collect expenditure data on new construction and major extensions and alteration works. Value added is estimated as a fixed ratio of the total cost of work done, the ratio calculated from detailed cost estimates of Housing and Development Board Construction and the margin earned by the contractors. The wholesale and retail trades are divided into entrepot trade and domestic trade activities. Value added of the entrepot trade is taken as the gross margin on re-export, which is the difference between re-exports in f.o.b. values and the corresponding imports in c.i.f. values, less an allowance for transport and other costs. The data are extracted from the external trade statistics. For the domestic trade activities, estimates for retained imports are compiled from the external trade statistics while estimates for local production are based on agricultural output and the sales of the manufacturing sector to wholesalers and retailers. Value added is taken as the gross mark-up margin on the value of retained imports or local production less the costs of transport and other intermediate expenses. Data gathered in the surveys of wholesale and retail trade, restaurants and hotels were also used. Bench-mark value added of the transport and communications sector is derived from the surveys of services and detailed accounts from airlines, Port of Singapore Authority, telecoms etc. Value added of banks is equal to the sum of actual and imputed bank charges minus purchases of goods and services for intermediate consumption. The data are based on detailed accounts submitted by the respective banks. Value added of finance companies is equal to the net interest income received less intermediate inputs. Other financial institutions are estimated on the basis of bench-mark value added data computed from the survey of services, employment data and other appropriate indicators. Value added estimates of insurance are based on income and expenditure data contained in the annual report of the Insurance Commissioner. For real estate and business services, the estimates for the private establishments are based on the surveys of services. The estimates of owner-occupied dwellings are based on the annual value of properties as assessed for property tax. Government output is valued at the cost of producing its services and value added is analysed from government financial statements, income and expenditure accounts of statutory boards and data provided by educational institutions and the Ministry of Education. The value added of domestic services consists of wages only and is estimated on the basis of the numbers employed and average earnings. For the constant price estimates, price deflation is used for agriculture, mining and quarrying, construction, trade, communication and services sectors. For manufacturing, electricity, gas and water and private services, value added is extrapolated by various output indicators. For transport, value added is either extrapolated by various indicators or deflated by price indexes.

1.1 Expenditure on the Gross Domestic Product, in Current Prices

Million Singapore dollars

	1970	1975	1978	1979	1980	1981	1982	1983	1984	1985	1986	1987
1 Government final consumption expenditure	692.5	1423.0	1964.7	2033.6	2447.4	2788.6	3570.4	3995.3	4333.0	5548.5	5198.1	5181.3
2 Private final consumption expenditure	3919.6	8120.7	10149.1	11245.2	12911.3	14329.3	15282.5	16202.1	17569.5	17552.9	18096.1	19785.6
3 Gross capital formation	2244.5	5370.4	6957.4	8899.9	11627.6	13587.0	15658.8	17595.8	19417.3	16551.2	14566.3	16522.6
A Increase in stocks	356.0	537.7	592.3	1380.3	1424.5	802.3	153.1	131.6	295.1	126.4	187.3	1340.1
B Gross fixed capital formation	1888.5	4832.7	6365.1	7519.6	10203.1	12784.7	15505.7	17464.2	19122.2	16424.8	14379.0	15182.5
Residential buildings	363.6	1051.4	1045.2	1017.3	1438.4	2060.7	3395.5	5516.8	6591.2	5265.4	3567.8	3051.2
Non-residential buildings	244.1	648.7	963.4	1405.3	2069.7	3149.4	3912.4	4336.7	4200.5	3284.8	2133.7	1738.5
Other construction and land improvement etc.	170.2	420.5	487.3	520.6	801.4	897.0	972.2	1023.1	1162.9	1457.2	2171.8	2155.0
Other	1110.6	2712.1	3869.2	4576.4	5893.6	6677.6	7225.6	6587.6	7167.6	6417.4	6505.7	8237.8
4 Exports of goods and services	-1179.1	-1416.4	-897.6	-1445.1	-2215.8	-1633.5	-1440.6	-663.8	-1113.0	-945.7	200.1	182.0
5 Less: Imports of goods and services												
Statistical discrepancy	127.4	-54.7	-343.2	-210.6	320.2	268.0	-401.2	-396.6	-158.9	216.6	94.5	227.4
Equals: Gross Domestic Product	5804.9	13443.0	17830.4	20523.0	25090.7	29339.4	32669.9	36732.8	40047.9	38923.5	38155.1	41898.9

1.2 Expenditure on the Gross Domestic Product, in Constant Prices

Million Singapore dollars

	1970	1975	1978	1979	1980	1981	1982	1983	1984	1985	1986	1987
					At constant prices of:1985							
1 Government final consumption expenditure	1617.1	2327.4	2976.3	2961.9	3241.5	3411.6	3863.8	4235.9	4457.2	5548.5	5541.6	5516.8
2 Private final consumption expenditure	7482.1	11109.0	13168.1	13971.4	14809.7	15491.3	16086.4	16852.1	17711.6	17552.9	18360.3	19889.3
3 Gross capital formation	5043.3	7679.2	9130.9	10854.4	12642.7	13541.0	15549.7	17309.9	18950.4	16551.2	14995.3	16578.8
A Increase in stocks	1010.7	949.3	931.0	1596.7	1516.1	730.7	144.0	242.2	273.0	126.4	380.8	1430.5
B Gross fixed capital formation	4032.6	6729.9	8199.9	9257.7	11126.6	12810.3	15405.7	17067.7	18677.4	16424.8	14614.5	15148.3

1317

Singapore

1.2 Expenditure on the Gross Domestic Product, in Constant Prices
(Continued)

Million Singapore dollars

	1970	1975	1978	1979	1980	1981	1982	1983	1984	1985	1986	1987
					At constant prices of:1985							
Residential buildings	1026.0	1583.9	1530.7	1416.6	1573.1	1960.8	3403.2	5551.4	6549.5	5265.4	3720.6	3175.8
Non-residential buildings	651.3	923.6	1306.0	1785.9	2188.8	3000.8	3788.2	4123.8	4098.5	3284.8	2219.1	1805.3
Other construction and land improvement etc.	444.8	587.5	617.9	625.3	839.2	853.7	915.0	972.2	1132.7	1457.2	2255.7	2254.1
Other	2012.1	3681.7	4745.3	5429.9	6525.5	6995.0	7299.3	6420.3	6896.7	6417.4	6419.1	7913.1
4 Exports of goods and services	-2316.9	-1975.0	-1119.3	-1318.5	-1495.2	-1088.6	-2044.9	-1669.6	-1431.4	-945.7	359.9	885.8
5 Less: Imports of goods and services												
Statistical discrepancy	346.8	30.8	-110.0	-184.5	-366.2	247.8	317.3	-191.1	-115.3	216.6	348.0	224.6
Equals: Gross Domestic Product	12172.4	19171.4	24046.0	26284.7	28832.5	31603.1	33772.3	36537.2	39572.5	38923.5	39605.1	43095.3

1.10 Gross Domestic Product by Kind of Activity, in Current Prices

Million Singapore dollars

	1970	1975	1978	1979	1980	1981	1982	1983	1984	1985	1986	1987
1 Agriculture, hunting, forestry and fishing	132.0	249.7	269.1	287.3	310.8	342.8	332.6	312.7	320.0	272.7	226.5	204.3
2 Mining and quarrying	19.2	45.9	37.5	42.1	82.2	104.7	128.1	140.6	132.2	111.3	75.6	68.8
3 Manufacturing	1152.5	3207.6	4574.4	5700.9	7310.8	8359.4	8151.0	8905.1	9860.1	9180.7	10182.2	11968.9
4 Electricity, gas and water	148.8	249.9	351.1	422.1	555.0	477.5	600.9	702.7	773.0	796.0	1074.6	944.5
5 Construction	385.2	1060.1	1094.2	1209.3	1583.2	2129.8	3102.7	4154.8	4892.4	4117.3	3098.5	2775.8
6 Wholesale and retail trade, restaurants and hotels	1516.2	3337.1	4283.3	4844.8	5435.1	5840.0	6387.5	6667.4	6885.5	6636.3	6518.9	7391.8
7 Transport, storage and communication	610.4	1478.2	2550.6	2847.6	3517.3	4057.2	4429.0	4885.3	5213.6	5223.7	5287.5	5761.5
8 Finance, insurance, real estate and business services	1004.2	2549.6	3147.5	3686.4	4880.0	6586.6	7673.1	8777.5	9851.7	10523.0	10600.3	12015.6
9 Community, social and personal services	319.7	614.6	735.8	813.2	852.1	1016.7	1209.3	1406.5	1531.6	1571.7	1698.6	1812.1
Total, Industries	5288.2	12792.7	17043.5	19853.7	24526.5	28914.7	32014.2	35952.6	39460.1	38432.7	38762.7	42943.3
Producers of Government Services	451.5	964.4	1184.3	1338.8	1548.3	1775.4	2284.1	2576.0	2901.1	3219.2	3023.9	3014.9
Other Producers	...	...	...	...	...	...	...	...	...	...	...	...
Subtotal	5739.7	13757.1	18227.8	21192.5	26074.8	30690.1	34298.3	38528.6	42361.2	41651.9	41786.6	45958.2
Less: Imputed bank service charge	110.2	542.2	737.6	1039.2	1410.9	1778.6	2109.9	2306.8	2827.4	3196.5	4025.1	4507.4
Plus: Import duties	175.4	228.1	340.2	369.7	426.8	427.9	481.5	511.0	514.1	468.1	393.6	448.1
Plus: Value added tax	...	...	...	...	...	...	...	...	...	...	...	...
Equals: Gross Domestic Product	5804.9	13443.0	17830.4	20523.0	25090.7	29339.4	32669.9	36732.8	40047.9	38923.5	38155.1	41898.9

1.11 Gross Domestic Product by Kind of Activity, in Constant Prices

Million Singapore dollars

	1970	1975	1978	1979	1980	1981	1982	1983	1984	1985	1986	1987
					At constant prices of:1985							
1 Agriculture, hunting, forestry and fishing	256.1	275.2	306.7	308.1	308.1	300.9	284.3	290.7	306.0	272.7	240.8	214.8
2 Mining and quarrying	28.1	56.6	52.5	60.0	65.0	83.5	104.0	122.0	120.2	111.3	94.3	93.4
3 Manufacturing	3088.3	5088.1	6787.6	7724.7	8497.3	9287.7	8962.5	9213.2	9904.2	9180.7	9952.1	11647.0
4 Electricity, gas and water	219.9	336.5	491.4	536.5	578.0	620.4	650.2	707.8	762.1	796.0	839.9	926.6
5 Construction	1112.5	1685.5	1686.8	1807.7	2010.5	2371.7	3248.8	4213.5	4873.6	4117.3	3177.9	2798.7
6 Wholesale and retail trade, restaurants and hotels	2645.3	4000.5	4767.6	5095.6	5452.8	5755.0	6091.9	6374.2	6738.9	6636.3	6604.2	7336.7
7 Transport, storage and communication	879.2	1732.9	2655.7	3038.5	3441.2	3888.7	4343.7	4670.7	5122.2	5223.7	5669.0	6164.0
8 Finance, insurance, real estate and business services	1949.7	3742.5	4433.0	4936.3	5823.2	6781.5	7466.9	8294.5	9325.1	10523.0	11143.9	12272.7
9 Community, social and personal services	637.8	913.0	1091.3	1136.4	1172.1	1239.6	1358.0	1453.8	1523.6	1571.7	1602.1	1701.3
Total, Industries	10678.1	17597.5	22272.6	24643.8	27348.2	30329.0	32510.3	35340.4	38675.9	38432.7	39324.2	43155.2
Producers of Government Services	1193.0	1781.9	2060.2	2185.6	2329.1	2444.8	2658.9	2878.5	3051.7	3219.2	3351.4	3404.7
Other Producers	...	...	...	...	...	...	...	...	...	...	...	...
Subtotal	11834.7	19352.0	24332.8	26829.4	29677.3	32773.8	35169.2	38218.9	41727.6	41651.9	42675.6	46559.9
Less: Imputed bank service charge	160.2	581.2	707.1	991.6	1340.8	1653.8	1925.4	2191.7	2666.6	3196.5	3464.1	3863.6
Plus: Import duties	356.1	324.9	420.3	446.9	496.0	483.1	528.5	510.0	511.5	468.1	393.6	399.0
Plus: Value added tax	...	...	...	...	...	...	...	...	...	...	...	...
Equals: Gross Domestic Product	12172.4	19171.4	24046.0	26284.7	28832.5	31603.1	33772.3	36537.2	39572.5	38923.5	39605.1	43095.3

Singapore

1.12 Relations Among National Accounting Aggregates

Million Singapore dollars

	1970	1975	1978	1979	1980	1981	1982	1983	1984	1985	1986	1987
Gross Domestic Product	5804.9	13443.0	17830.4	20523.0	25090.7	29339.4	32669.9	36732.8	40047.9	38923.5	38155.1	41898.9
Plus: Net factor income from the rest of the world	56.2	123.5	-43.0	-78.9	-902.2	-1148.2	-894.2	-171.7	767.2	1406.9	1395.8	1373.3
Equals: Gross National Product	5861.1	13566.5	17787.4	20444.1	24188.5	28191.2	31775.7	36561.1	40815.1	40330.4	39550.9	43272.2
Less: Consumption of fixed capital	318.8	1265.9	2083.4	2510.7	3026.4	3551.8	4148.6	4900.4	5482.4	5789.5	6225.1	6701.3
Equals: National Income	5542.3	12300.6	15704.0	17933.4	21162.1	24639.4	27627.1	31660.7	35332.7	34540.9	33325.8	36570.9
Plus: Net current transfers from the rest of the world	...	...	...	...	...	...	...	...	...	...	...	...
Equals: National Disposable Income	...	...	...	...	...	...	...	...	...	...	...	...
Less: Final consumption	...	...	...	...	...	...	...	...	...	...	...	...
Equals: Net Saving	...	...	...	...	...	...	...	...	...	...	...	...
Less: Surplus of the nation on current transactions	...	...	...	...	...	...	...	...	...	...	...	...
Equals: Net Capital Formation	...	...	...	...	...	...	...	...	...	...	...	...

2.5 Private Final Consumption Expenditure by Type and Purpose, in Current Prices

Million Singapore dollars

	1970	1975	1978	1979	1980	1981	1982	1983	1984	1985	1986	1987
Final Consumption Expenditure of Resident Households												
1 Food, beverages and tobacco	1399.3	2648.8	3163.4	3476.6	3997.5	4561.8	4800.1	4932.0	5185.9	5121.5	5101.3	5348.8
A Food	1085.0	2103.0	2480.4	2741.5	3107.7	3583.6	3736.6	3723.7	3894.8	3818.3	3811.4	4021.4
B Non-alcoholic beverages	57.3	107.3	137.3	155.8	197.2	219.5	218.6	269.2	259.6	290.7	301.6	327.1
C Alcoholic beverages	116.2	198.5	252.4	281.3	343.5	364.9	417.4	453.4	498.6	465.2	442.3	496.3
D Tobacco	140.8	240.0	293.3	298.0	349.1	393.8	427.5	485.7	532.9	547.3	546.0	504.0
2 Clothing and footwear	431.0	748.2	979.9	1117.0	1240.7	1408.4	1555.2	1681.8	1665.1	1569.4	1758.3	2035.2
3 Gross rent, fuel and power	445.8	920.5	1129.9	1219.7	1390.4	1493.1	1623.4	1745.3	1976.6	2184.9	2263.6	2385.3
4 Furniture, furnishings and household equipment and operation	355.8	813.8	1006.6	1114.5	1322.9	1525.8	1602.1	1719.3	1943.2	2015.3	2051.6	2156.2
A Household operation	100.7	201.4	208.2	231.2	251.7	297.3	336.3	418.0	458.9	489.1	542.6	601.1
B Other	255.1	612.4	798.4	883.3	1071.2	1228.5	1265.8	1301.3	1484.3	1526.2	1509.0	1555.1
5 Medical care and health expenses	121.2	249.1	326.4	350.9	411.7	445.3	502.8	567.4	643.1	702.2	806.7	865.4
6 Transport and communication	543.3	1005.9	1526.0	1820.4	2198.3	2345.5	2560.2	2743.1	2816.7	2678.7	2569.6	2845.0
A Personal transport equipment	100.9	61.7	281.4	363.5	487.4	424.1	500.4	521.6	395.8	235.3	208.0	357.8
B Other	442.4	944.2	1244.6	1456.9	1710.9	1921.4	2059.8	2221.5	2420.9	2443.4	2361.6	2487.2
7 Recreational, entertainment, education and cultural services	441.1	1013.7	1379.4	1647.7	1802.7	2153.8	2229.1	2421.0	2543.0	2453.5	2741.4	3199.4
A Education	44.6	65.5	83.0	86.1	95.1	102.3	147.3	167.5	183.5	192.5	202.6	223.7
B Other	396.5	948.2	1296.4	1561.6	1707.6	2051.5	2081.8	2253.5	2359.5	2261.0	2538.8	2975.7
8 Miscellaneous goods and services	736.9	1693.7	2205.5	2565.0	3133.1	3638.4	3684.4	3829.6	3910.1	3562.4	3685.7	4440.2
A Personal care	77.6	157.4	237.0	264.5	288.7	330.4	408.4	432.5	474.3	456.1	457.4	499.4
B Expenditures in restaurants, cafes and hotels	274.7	672.9	939.5	1092.8	1276.6	1449.9	1406.6	1432.6	1479.4	1423.3	1400.1	1511.1
C Other	384.6	863.4	1029.0	1207.7	1567.8	1858.1	1869.4	1964.5	1956.4	1683.0	1828.2	2429.7
Total Final Consumption Expenditure in the Domestic Market by Households, of which	4474.4	9093.7	11717.1	13311.8	15497.3	17572.1	18557.3	19639.5	20683.7	20287.9	20978.2	23275.5
Plus: Direct purchases abroad by resident households	54.7	332.4	440.1	475.2	585.7	651.2	843.3	973.4	1049.5	1103.5	1145.7	1355.6
Less: Direct purchases in the domestic market by non-resident households	609.5	1305.4	2008.1	2541.8	3171.7	3894.0	4118.1	4410.8	4163.7	3838.5	4027.8	4845.5
Equals: Final Consumption Expenditure of Resident Households [a]	3919.6	8120.7	10149.1	11245.2	12911.3	14329.3	15282.5	16202.1	17569.5	17552.9	18096.1	19785.6
Final Consumption Expenditure of Private Non-profit Institutions Serving Households												
Equals: Final Consumption Expenditure of Private Non-profit Organisations Serving Households	...	...	...	...	...	...	...	...	...	...	...	...
Private Final Consumption Expenditure	3919.6	8120.7	10149.1	11245.2	12911.3	14329.3	15282.5	16202.1	17569.5	17552.9	18096.1	19785.6

a) Item 'Final consumption expenditure of resident households' includes consumption expenditure of private non-profit institutions serving households.

Singapore

2.6 Private Final Consumption Expenditure by Type and Purpose, in Constant Prices

Million Singapore dollars

	1970	1975	1978	1979	1980	1981	1982	1983	1984	1985	1986	1987
	\multicolumn{12}{c}{At constant prices of:1985}

Final Consumption Expenditure of Resident Households

	1970	1975	1978	1979	1980	1981	1982	1983	1984	1985	1986	1987
1 Food, beverages and tobacco	2985.4	3545.8	4111.7	4363.8	4638.0	4810.1	4876.0	4962.4	5111.3	5121.5	5228.0	5458.1
A Food	2287.6	2696.0	3118.6	3325.6	3487.5	3643.3	3679.0	3663.2	3830.0	3818.3	3932.4	4184.1
B Non-alcoholic beverages	119.5	147.8	188.6	193.2	234.3	229.1	210.8	261.1	255.9	290.7	302.7	332.4
C Alcoholic beverages	234.1	282.9	344.7	378.0	428.1	428.5	475.7	501.8	495.1	465.2	446.9	474.6
D Tobacco	347.9	421.4	459.8	467.0	488.1	509.2	510.5	536.3	530.3	547.3	946.0	467.0
2 Clothing and footwear	686.2	851.3	1068.3	1171.2	1281.2	1457.0	1580.0	1642.4	1647.3	1569.4	1812.9	2073.7
3 Gross rent, fuel and power	870.4	1273.4	1476.9	1528.3	1576.4	1630.9	1694.2	1794.9	1984.8	2184.9	2325.9	2507.1
4 Furniture, furnishings and household equipment and operation	685.3	1096.6	1211.1	1291.6	1451.9	1609.4	1641.4	1747.1	1953.3	2015.3	2011.9	2090.4
A Household operation	223.5	286.9	301.4	324.7	329.8	369.6	385.4	435.9	459.9	489.1	513.4	566.7
B Other	471.9	811.8	909.7	966.9	1122.1	1239.8	1256.0	1311.2	1493.4	1526.2	1498.5	1523.7
5 Medical care and health expenses	268.1	412.3	506.2	524.6	550.9	570.0	620.1	633.1	654.6	702.2	781.7	838.2
6 Transport and communication	1111.3	1524.4	2139.6	2404.4	2618.4	2752.8	2861.2	2995.0	2967.3	2678.7	2648.5	2821.1
A Personal transport equipment	164.8	77.2	280.1	348.3	460.8	394.8	471.7	499.5	386.8	235.3	168.2	255.4
B Other	942.4	1475.7	1859.5	2056.1	2157.6	2358.0	2389.5	2495.5	2580.5	2443.4	2480.3	2565.7
7 Recreational, entertainment, education and cultural services	623.2	1132.5	1424.8	1612.7	1735.3	2047.0	2168.9	2480.4	2534.9	2453.5	2736.5	3144.5
A Education	72.0	105.8	125.8	125.1	124.6	127.9	177.8	180.2	192.6	192.5	198.7	211.7
B Other	553.0	1026.4	1299.0	1487.6	1610.7	1919.1	1991.1	2300.2	2342.3	2261.0	2537.8	2932.8
8 Miscellaneous goods and services	1378.3	2241.6	2787.2	3089.3	3378.1	3523.8	3633.1	3779.3	3884.1	3562.4	3739.1	4464.4
A Personal care	149.0	213.2	309.0	332.6	351.5	364.2	407.9	445.0	484.0	456.1	452.3	487.4
B Expenditures in restaurants, cafes and hotels	562.9	980.4	1281.5	1401.6	1372.3	1390.9	1356.2	1386.5	1428.5	1423.3	1469.0	1627.4
C Other	655.6	1035.7	1196.7	1355.1	1654.3	1768.7	1869.0	1947.8	1971.6	1683.0	1817.8	2349.6
Total Final Consumption Expenditure in the Domestic Market by Households, of which	8506.3	12051.8	14725.8	15985.9	17230.2	18401.0	19074.9	20034.6	20737.6	20287.9	21284.5	23397.5
Plus: Direct purchases abroad by resident households	106.5	487.6	612.4	638.6	699.0	729.6	896.0	992.2	1049.7	1103.5	1162.4	1362.7
Less: Direct purchases in the domestic market by non-resident households	996.4	1487.4	2170.1	2653.1	3119.5	3639.3	3884.5	4174.7	4075.7	3838.5	4086.6	4870.9
Equals: Final Consumption Expenditure of Resident Households	7482.1	11109.0	13168.1	13971.4	14809.7	15491.3	16086.4	16852.1	17711.6	17552.9	18360.3	19889.3

Final Consumption Expenditure of Private Non-profit Institutions Serving Households

	1970	1975	1978	1979	1980	1981	1982	1983	1984	1985	1986	1987
Equals: Final Consumption Expenditure of Private Non-profit Organisations Serving Households	...	...	...	...	...	...	...	...	...	...	...	...
Private Final Consumption Expenditure	7482.1	11109.0	13168.1	13971.4	14809.7	15491.3	16086.4	16852.1	17711.6	17552.9	18360.3	19889.3

Solomon Islands

Source. Reply to the United Nations National Accounts Questionnaire from the Statistics Division, Ministry of Finance, Honiara.
General note. The estimates have been adjusted by the United Nations Statistical Office to conform to the United Nations System of National Accounts so far as the existing data would permit.

1.1 Expenditure on the Gross Domestic Product, in Current Prices

Million Solomon Islands dollars

	1970	1975	1978	1979	1980	1981	1982	1983	1984	1985	1986	1987
1 Government final consumption expenditure	...	...	...	...	...	...	...	...	51.7	66.1	83.6	97.0
2 Private final consumption expenditure	...	...	...	...	...	...	...	...	121.6	150.9	155.8	191.8
A Households	...	...	...	...	...	...	...	...	118.2	146.9	151.4	186.8
B Private non-profit institutions serving households	...	...	...	...	...	...	...	...	3.4	4.0	4.4	5.0
3 Gross capital formation	...	...	...	...	...	...	...	...	50.9	62.1	68.0	75.0
A Increase in stocks	...	...	...	...	...	...	...	...	7.9	12.2	2.5	10.0
B Gross fixed capital formation	...	...	...	...	...	...	...	...	43.0	49.9	65.5	65.0
Residential buildings	...	...	...	...	...	...	...	...	14.1	11.0	15.1	...
Non-residential buildings	...	...	...	...	...	...	...	...				...
Other construction and land improvement etc.	...	...	...	...	...	...	...	...	8.8	13.9	19.6	...
Other	...	...	...	...	...	...	...	...	20.1	25.0	30.7	...
4 Exports of goods and services	7.1	11.8	30.6	60.2	60.8	...	...	...	135.2	121.1	132.9	150.1
5 Less: Imports of goods and services [a]	10.0	21.8	30.9	50.5	61.5	...	...	...	138.5	164.9	189.8	219.9
Equals: Gross Domestic Product	28.6	51.2	85.8	112.7	119.4	140.6	158.5	175.0	220.8	235.3	250.4	294.0

a) Imports of merchandise, f.o.b. rather than c.i.f.

1.2 Expenditure on the Gross Domestic Product, in Constant Prices

Million Solomon Islands dollars

	1970	1975	1978	1979	1980	1981	1982	1983	1984	1985	1986	1987
			1977		At constant prices of:				1984			
1 Government final consumption expenditure	...	...	...	...	...	...	...	...	...	...	...	...
2 Private final consumption expenditure	...	...	...	...	...	...	...	...	...	...	...	...
3 Gross capital formation	...	...	...	...	...	...	...	...	...	...	...	...
4 Exports of goods and services	...	...	...	...	...	...	...	...	...	...	...	...
5 Less: Imports of goods and services	...	...	...	...	...	...	...	...	...	...	...	...
Equals: Gross Domestic Product	...	57.9	80.6	98.1	91.9 / 186.8	199.3	197.1	204.8	220.5	227.4	222.4	211.0

1.3 Cost Components of the Gross Domestic Product

Million Solomon Islands dollars

	1970	1975	1978	1979	1980	1981	1982	1983	1984	1985	1986	1987
1 Indirect taxes, net	2.2	3.4	6.2	10.5	10.8	14.5	18.0	18.0	25.8	26.9	31.4	40.0
A Indirect taxes	...	...	...	...	...	...	...	...	29.2	30.7	35.5	45.0
B Less: Subsidies	...	...	...	...	...	...	...	...	3.4	3.8	4.1	5.0
2 Consumption of fixed capital	2.8	4.7	7.5	10.9	14.2	18.1	22.0	24.0	13.1	15.8	19.1	21.0
3 Compensation of employees paid by resident producers to:	7.9	14.6	25.2	27.1	31.3	39.2	45.2	50.0	85.1	104.6	125.1	140.0
4 Operating surplus	15.7	28.5	46.9	64.2	63.0	68.9	73.3	83.0	96.8	88.1	74.7	93.0
Equals: Gross Domestic Product	28.6	51.2	85.8	112.7	119.4	140.6	158.5	175.0	220.8	235.3	250.4	294.0

1.4 General Government Current Receipts and Disbursements

Million Solomon Islands dollars

	1970	1975	1978	1979	1980	1981	1982	1983	1984	1985	1986	1987
					Receipts							
1 Operating surplus	...	...	...	...	...	...	...	...	1.2	1.5	1.1	...
2 Property and entrepreneurial income	...	...	...	...	...	...	...	...	2.4	3.2	4.2	...
3 Taxes, fees and contributions	...	...	...	...	...	...	...	...	44.6	49.0	56.1	...
A Indirect taxes	...	...	...	...	...	...	...	...	29.3	30.6	35.5	...

Solomon Islands

1.4 General Government Current Receipts and Disbursements
(Continued)

Million Solomon Islands dollars

	1970	1975	1978	1979	1980	1981	1982	1983	1984	1985	1986	1987
B Direct taxes	...	...	...	...	...	...	...	...	14.7	17.6	19.6	...
C Social security contributions									...	...	...	...
D Compulsory fees, fines and penalties									0.6	0.8	1.0	...
4 Other current transfers	...	...	...	...	...	...	...	...	23.4	22.8	62.2	...
Total Current Receipts of General Government	...	...	...	...	...	...	...	...	71.6	76.5	123.6	...

Disbursements

	1970	1975	1978	1979	1980	1981	1982	1983	1984	1985	1986	1987
1 Government final consumption expenditure	...	...	...	...	...	...	...	...	51.7	66.1	83.6	...
2 Property income	...	...	...	...	...	...	...	...	1.8	3.4	4.8	...
A Interest	...	...	...	...	...	...	...	...	1.8	3.4	4.8	...
B Net land rent and royalties									...	...	...	...
3 Subsidies	...	...	...	...	...	...	...	...	3.4	3.8	4.1	...
4 Other current transfers	...	...	...	...	...	...	...	...	4.0	5.0	7.3	...
5 Net saving	...	...	...	...	...	...	...	...	10.7	-1.8	23.8	...
Total Current Disbursements and Net Saving of General Government	...	...	...	...	...	...	...	...	71.6	76.5	123.6	...

1.7 External Transactions on Current Account, Summary

Million Solomon Islands dollars

	1970	1975	1978	1979	1980	1981	1982	1983	1984	1985	1986	1987

Payments to the Rest of the World

	1970	1975	1978	1979	1980	1981	1982	1983	1984	1985	1986	1987
1 Imports of goods and services	...	...	...	...	...	...	...	...	138.5	164.9	189.8	...
2 Factor income to the rest of the world	...	...	...	...	...	...	...	...	17.9	16.8	22.4	...
A Compensation of employees	...	...	...	...	...	...	...	...	4.9	4.8	11.6	...
B Property and entrepreneurial income	...	...	...	...	...	...	...	...	13.0	12.0	10.8	...
3 Current transfers to the rest of the world	...	...	...	...	...	...	...	...	12.5	13.8	16.0	...
4 Surplus of the nation on current transactions	...	...	...	...	...	...	...	...	-0.7	-40.0	-15.2	...
Payments to the Rest of the World and Surplus of the Nation on Current Transactions	...	...	...	...	...	...	...	...	168.2	155.5	212.8	...

Receipts From The Rest of the World

	1970	1975	1978	1979	1980	1981	1982	1983	1984	1985	1986	1987
1 Exports of goods and services	...	...	...	...	...	...	...	...	135.2	121.1	132.8	...
2 Factor income from rest of the world	...	...	...	...	...	...	...	...	5.9	6.6	5.7	...
A Compensation of employees									...	...	...	...
B Property and entrepreneurial income	...	...	...	...	...	...	...	...	5.9	6.6	5.7	...
3 Current transfers from rest of the world	...	...	...	...	...	...	...	...	27.1	27.8	74.3	...
Receipts from the Rest of the World on Current Transactions	...	...	...	...	...	...	...	...	168.2	155.5	212.8	...

1.8 Capital Transactions of The Nation, Summary

Million Solomon Islands dollars

	1970	1975	1978	1979	1980	1981	1982	1983	1984	1985	1986	1987

Finance of Gross Capital Formation

	1970	1975	1978	1979	1980	1981	1982	1983	1984	1985	1986	1987
Gross saving	...	...	...	...	...	...	...	...	50.2	22.2	52.7	...
1 Consumption of fixed capital	...	...	...	...	...	...	...	...	13.1	15.8	19.1	...
A General government	...	...	...	...	...	...	...	...	0.2	0.3	0.5	...
B Corporate and quasi-corporate enterprises									...	...	...	...
Public	...	...	...	...	...	...	...	...	4.0	5.7	6.6	...
Private	...	...	...	...	...	...	...	...	...	...	...	...
C Other	...	...	...	...	...	...	...	...	...	...	...	...
2 Net saving	...	...	...	...	...	...	...	...	37.1	6.4	33.6	...
A General government	...	...	...	...	...	...	...	...	10.7	-1.8	23.8	...
B Corporate and quasi-corporate enterprises	...	...	...	...	...	...	...	...	...	...	...	...

Solomon Islands

1.8 Capital Transactions of The Nation, Summary
(Continued)

Million Solomon Islands dollars	1970	1975	1978	1979	1980	1981	1982	1983	1984	1985	1986	1987
Public	...	...	...	...	...	...	...	...	8.6	-2.5	-5.1	...
Private	...	...	...	...	...	...	...	...	...	...	...	...
C Other	...	...	...	...	...	...	...	...	...	...	...	...
Less: Surplus of the nation on current transactions	...	...	...	...	...	...	...	...	-0.7	-40.0	-15.2	...
Finance of Gross Capital Formation	...	...	...	...	...	...	...	...	50.9	62.2	67.9	...

Gross Capital Formation

	1970	1975	1978	1979	1980	1981	1982	1983	1984	1985	1986	1987
Increase in stocks	...	...	...	...	...	...	...	...	7.9	12.2	2.5	...
Gross fixed capital formation	...	...	...	...	...	...	...	...	43.0	50.0	65.4	...
1 General government	...	...	...	...	...	...	...	...	12.2	14.3	29.6	...
2 Corporate and quasi-corporate enterprises	...	...	...	...	...	...	...	...	30.8	35.7	35.8	...
A Public	...	...	...	...	...	...	...	...	11.0	13.1	12.0	...
B Private	...	...	...	...	...	...	...	...	19.8	22.6	23.8	...
3 Other	...	...	...	...	...	...	...	...	...	...	...	...
Gross Capital Formation	...	...	...	...	...	...	...	...	50.9	62.2	67.9	...

1.9 Gross Domestic Product by Institutional Sectors of Origin

Million Solomon Islands dollars	1970	1975	1978	1979	1980	1981	1982	1983	1984	1985	1986	1987

Domestic Factor Incomes Originating

	1970	1975	1978	1979	1980	1981	1982	1983	1984	1985	1986	1987
1 General government	...	...	...	...	...	...	...	...	35.7	45.1	51.1	...
2 Corporate and quasi-corporate enterprises	...	...	...	...	...	...	...	...	84.1	78.9	79.4	...
3 Households and private unincorporated enterprises	...	...	...	...	...	...	...	...	60.4	66.5	67.0	...
4 Non-profit institutions serving households	...	...	...	...	...	...	...	...	1.7	2.1	2.3	...
Subtotal: Domestic Factor Incomes	...	...	...	...	...	...	...	...	181.9	192.6	199.9	...
Indirect taxes, net	...	...	...	...	...	...	...	...	25.8	26.9	31.4	...
A Indirect taxes	...	...	...	...	...	...	...	...	29.2	30.7	35.5	...
B Less: Subsidies	...	...	...	...	...	...	...	...	3.4	3.8	4.1	...
Consumption of fixed capital	...	...	...	...	...	...	...	...	13.1	15.8	19.1	...
Gross Domestic Product	...	...	...	...	...	...	...	...	220.8	235.3	250.4	...

1.10 Gross Domestic Product by Kind of Activity, in Current Prices

Million Solomon Islands dollars	1970	1975	1978	1979	1980	1981	1982	1983	1984	1985	1986	1987
1 Agriculture, hunting, forestry and fishing	...	...	...	...	...	...	...	...	106.3	107.4	108.3	...
2 Mining and quarrying	...	...	...	...	...	...	...	...	-0.4	-1.5	-2.6	...
3 Manufacturing	...	...	...	...	...	...	...	...	7.2	8.0	10.1	...
4 Electricity, gas and water	...	...	...	...	...	...	...	...	1.7	2.2	2.6	...
5 Construction	...	...	...	...	...	...	...	...	7.6	9.0	11.4	...
6 Wholesale and retail trade, restaurants and hotels	...	...	...	...	...	...	...	...	21.1	22.1	18.9	...
7 Transport, storage and communication	...	...	...	...	...	...	...	...	10.4	10.8	13.0	...
8 Finance, insurance, real estate and business services	...	...	...	...	...	...	...	...	11.3	13.0	14.6	...
9 Community, social and personal services	...	...	...	...	...	...	...	...	33.6	42.0	48.0	...
Total, Industries	...	...	...	...	...	...	...	...	198.8	213.0	224.3	...
Producers of Government Services	...	...	...	...	...	...	...	...	...	...	...	...
Other Producers	...	...	...	...	...	...	...	...	...	...	...	...
Subtotal [a]	...	...	...	...	...	...	...	...	198.8	213.0	224.3	...
Less: Imputed bank service charge	...	...	...	...	...	...	...	...	3.6	4.4	5.3	...
Plus: Import duties	...	...	...	...	...	...	...	...	...	...	...	...
Plus: Value added tax	...	...	...	...	...	...	...	...	...	...	...	...
Plus: Other adjustments [b]	...	...	...	...	...	...	...	...	25.8	26.9	31.4	...
Equals: Gross Domestic Product	...	...	...	...	...	...	...	...	221.0	235.5	250.4	...

a) Gross domestic product in factor values.
b) Item 'Other adjustments' refers to indirect taxes net of subsidies.

Solomon Islands

1.12 Relations Among National Accounting Aggregates

Million Solomon Islands dollars

	1970	1975	1978	1979	1980	1981	1982	1983	1984	1985	1986	1987
Gross Domestic Product	...	...	...	...	...	...	...	...	220.8	235.3	250.4	...
Plus: Net factor income from the rest of the world	...	...	...	...	...	...	...	...	-11.9	-10.2	-16.7	...
Equals: Gross National Product	...	...	...	...	...	...	...	...	208.9	225.1	233.7	...
Less: Consumption of fixed capital	...	...	...	...	...	...	...	...	13.1	15.8	19.1	...
Equals: National Income	...	...	...	...	...	...	...	...	195.8	209.3	214.6	...
Plus: Net current transfers from the rest of the world	...	...	...	...	...	...	...	...	14.6	14.0	58.4	...
Equals: National Disposable Income	...	...	...	...	...	...	...	...	210.4	223.4	273.0	...
Less: Final consumption	...	...	...	...	...	...	...	...	173.3	217.0	239.4	...
Equals: Net Saving	...	...	...	...	...	...	...	...	37.1	6.4	33.6	...
Less: Surplus of the nation on current transactions	...	...	...	...	...	...	...	...	-0.7	-40.0	-15.2	...
Equals: Net Capital Formation	...	...	...	...	...	...	...	...	37.8	46.4	48.8	...

2.7 Gross Capital Formation by Type of Good and Owner, in Current Prices

Million Solomon Islands dollars

	1984 TOTAL	1984 Total Private	1984 Public Enterprises	1984 General Government	1985 TOTAL	1985 Total Private	1985 Public Enterprises	1985 General Government	1986 TOTAL	1986 Total Private	1986 Public Enterprises	1986 General Government
Increase in stocks, total	7.9	...	...	...	12.2	...	...	...	2.5	...	...	...
Gross Fixed Capital Formation, Total	43.0	19.8	10.9	12.3	49.9	22.6	13.0	14.3	65.3	23.7	12.0	29.6
1 Residential buildings	14.1	4.0	4.0	6.1	11.0	4.1	2.9	4.0	15.1	7.9	3.6	3.6
2 Non-residential buildings												
3 Other construction	2.4	-	0.9	1.5	5.6	-	0.4	5.2	11.0	-	0.7	10.3
4 Land improvement and plantation and orchard development	6.4	4.6	-	1.8	8.3	6.2	-	2.1	8.5	4.7	1.9	1.9
5 Producers' durable goods	20.1	11.2	6.0	2.9	25.0	12.3	9.7	3.0	30.7	11.1	5.8	13.8
A Transport equipment	7.0	2.6	3.4	1.0	11.6	5.0	7.2	-0.6	7.6	3.1	1.9	2.6
B Machinery and equipment	13.1	8.6	2.6	1.9	13.4	7.3	2.5	3.6	23.1	8.0	3.9	11.2
6 Breeding stock, dairy cattle, etc.	...	...	...	...	...	...	...	...	...	...	...	...
Total Gross Capital Formation	50.9	...	...	...	62.1	...	...	...	68.0	...	...	...

4.3 Cost Components of Value Added

Million Solomon Islands dollars

	1984 Compensation of Employees	1984 Capital Consumption	1984 Net Operating Surplus	1984 Indirect Taxes	1984 Less: Subsidies Received	1984 Value Added	1985 Compensation of Employees	1985 Capital Consumption	1985 Net Operating Surplus	1985 Indirect Taxes	1985 Less: Subsidies Received	1985 Value Added
All Producers												
1 Agriculture, hunting, forestry and fishing	22.1	7.2	76.9	...	...	106.2	27.1	8.6	71.7	...	...	107.4
2 Mining and quarrying	0.4	-	-0.8	...	...	-0.4	0.5	-	-2.1	...	...	-1.6
3 Manufacturing	4.5	0.9	1.8	...	...	7.2	5.4	1.0	1.6	...	...	8.0
4 Electricity, gas and water	1.2	0.4	0.1	...	...	1.7	1.2	0.5	0.5	...	...	2.2
5 Construction	4.0	0.2	3.4	...	...	7.6	5.8	0.3	2.9	...	...	9.0
6 Wholesale and retail trade, restaurants and hotels	7.7	1.5	11.9	...	...	21.1	9.2	1.9	11.0	...	...	22.1
7 Transport, storage and communication	6.0	1.6	2.8	...	...	10.4	7.3	1.7	1.7	...	...	10.7
A Transport and storage	4.6	1.3	2.1	...	...	8.0	5.4	1.4	1.1	...	...	7.9
B Communication	1.4	0.3	0.7	...	...	2.4	1.9	0.3	0.6	...	...	2.8
8 Finance, insurance, real estate and business services	6.0	0.9	4.3	...	...	11.2	6.7	1.3	5.1	...	...	13.1
9 Community, social and personal services	33.1	0.4	-	...	...	33.5	41.5	0.6	-	...	...	42.1
Total, Industries	85.0	13.1	100.4	...	...	198.5	104.7	15.9	92.4	...	...	213.0
Producers of Government Services	...	...	...	...	...	...	...	...	...	...	...	...
Other Producers	...	...	...	...	...	...	...	...	...	...	...	...
Total [a]	85.0	13.1	100.4	...	...	198.5	104.7	15.9	92.4	...	...	213.0
Less: Imputed bank service charge	...	...	3.6	...	...	3.6	...	...	4.4	...	...	4.4
Import duties	...	...	...	...	...	...	...	...	...	...	...	...
Value added tax	...	...	...	...	...	...	...	...	...	...	...	...
Other adjustments	...	...	...	29.2	3.4	25.8	...	...	...	30.7	3.8	26.9
Total	85.0	13.1	96.8	29.2	3.4	220.7	104.7	15.9	88.0	30.7	3.8	235.5

Solomon Islands

4.3 Cost Components of Value Added

Million Solomon Islands dollars

	\multicolumn{6}{c	}{1986}
	Compensation of Employees	Capital Consumption	Net Operating Surplus	Indirect Taxes	Less: Subsidies Received	Value Added
	\multicolumn{6}{c	}{**All Producers**}
1 Agriculture, hunting, forestry and fishing	35.5	9.8	62.9	...	...	108.2
2 Mining and quarrying	0.6	0.4	-3.6	...	...	-2.6
3 Manufacturing	6.5	1.2	2.4	...	...	10.1
4 Electricity, gas and water	1.7	0.5	0.3	...	...	2.5
5 Construction	5.8	0.3	5.4	...	...	11.5
6 Wholesale and retail trade, restaurants and hotels	10.7	2.4	5.8	...	...	18.9
7 Transport, storage and communication	8.2	2.0	2.8	...	...	13.0
A Transport and storage	5.8	1.6	2.2	...	...	9.6
B Communication	2.4	0.4	0.6	...	...	3.4
8 Finance, insurance, real estate and business services	8.9	1.6	4.1	...	...	14.6
9 Community, social and personal services	47.2	0.8	-	...	...	48.0
Total, Industries	125.1	19.0	80.1	...	...	224.2
Producers of Government Services	...	...	...	...	...	...
Other Producers	...	...	...	...	...	...
Total [a]	125.1	19.0	80.1	...	...	224.2
Less: Imputed bank service charge	...	...	5.3	...	...	5.3
Import duties	...	...	...	...	...	...
Value added tax	...	...	...	...	...	...
Other adjustments	...	...	...	35.5	4.1	31.4
Total	125.1	19.0	74.8	35.5	4.1	250.3

a) Gross domestic product in factor values.

Somalia

Source. National Accounts estimates are published in 'National Accounts Aggregates of Somali Democratic Republic' by the Ministero Della Pianificazione Nazionale, Mogadishu.

General note. The estimates shown in the following tables have been prepared in accordance with the United Nations System of National Accounts so far as the existing data would permit.

1.1 Expenditure on the Gross Domestic Product, in Current Prices

Million Somali shillings

	1970	1975	1978	1979	1980	1981	1982	1983	1984	1985	1986	1987
1 Government final consumption expenditure [a]	233	909	1540	1996	2394	2570	3435	4722	5092	9222	11520	18810
2 Private final consumption expenditure [b]	1811	3120	6007	7478	15469	19974	27202	31764	57619	78986	105809	150551
3 Gross capital formation	318	1008	1704	1415	1579	1428	1977	4032	6460	10299	21143	36524
A Increase in stocks [c]	113	324	502	-115	-119	978	1224	-1376	897	2498	1203	8085
B Gross fixed capital formation [a]	205	684	1202	1530	1698	450	753	5408	5563	7801	19940	28439
4 Exports of goods and services [d]	260	702	689	666	845	718	1472	1578	1236	3647	6866	9925
5 Less: Imports of goods and services [e]	378	1349	1765	2570	2946	2634	4975	6967	8154	14864	26557	46202
Equals: Gross Domestic Product	2244	4390	8175	8985	17341	22056	29111	35129	62253	87290	118781	169608

a) The value of Technical Assistance from abroad is included in 'Gross fixed capital formation' rather than 'Government final consumption expenditure'.
b) Item 'Private final consumption expenditure' has been obtained as a residual.
c) Item 'Increase in stocks' includes livestock only.
d) Item 'Exports of goods and services' includes exports of goods only.
e) Item 'Imports of goods and services' refers to imports of goods and non-factor services.

1.2 Expenditure on the Gross Domestic Product, in Constant Prices

Million Somali shillings

	1970	1975	1978	1979	1980	1981	1982	1983	1984	1985	1986	1987
					At constant prices of:1977							
1 Government final consumption expenditure	426	1146	1516	1422	1388	1046	...	...	...	...	...	...
2 Private final consumption expenditure	3669	4710	4848	4402	4365	4633	...	...	...	...	...	...
3 Gross capital formation	849	1145	1748	664	527	1662	...	...	...	...	...	...
A Increase in stocks	333	466	766	-300	-315	846	...	...	...	...	...	...
B Gross fixed capital formation	516	679	982	964	842	816	...	...	...	...	...	...
4 Exports of goods and services	765	789	673	637	754	686	...	...	...	...	...	...
5 Less: Imports of goods and services	912	2108	1985	1168	1206	1035	...	...	...	...	...	...
Equals: Gross Domestic Product	4797	5682	6800	5957	5823	6992	...	...	...	...	...	...

1.7 External Transactions on Current Account, Summary

Million Somali shillings

	1970	1975	1978	1979	1980	1981	1982	1983	1984	1985	1986	1987
				Payments to the Rest of the World								
1 Imports of goods and services	...	1349	2012	2808	3256	3080	...	...	...	...	...	...
A Imports of merchandise c.i.f.	...	1021	1732	2481	2905	2681	...	...	...	...	...	...
B Other	...	328	280	327	351	399	...	...	...	...	...	...
2 Factor income to the rest of the world	...	20	16	46	41	104	...	...	...	...	...	...
A Compensation of employees	...	1	1	2	4	17	...	...	...	...	...	...
B Property and entrepreneurial income	...	19	15	44	37	88	...	...	...	...	...	...
3 Current transfers to the rest of the world	...	12	2	6	-	-	...	...	...	...	...	...
4 Surplus of the nation on current transactions	...	-1	-406	-1296	-1128	-634	...	...	...	...	...	...
Payments to the Rest of the World and Surplus of the Nation on Current Transactions [a]	...	1380	1624	1564	2169	2550	...	...	...	...	...	...
				Receipts From The Rest of the World								
1 Exports of goods and services	...	702	916	905	1221	1668	...	...	...	...	...	...

Somalia

1.7 External Transactions on Current Account, Summary
(Continued)

Million Somali shillings

	1970	1975	1978	1979	1980	1981	1982	1983	1984	1985	1986	1987
A Exports of merchandise f.o.b.	...	558	689	667	839	1103	...	...	...	...	...	...
B Other	...	144	227	238	382	565	...	...	...	...	...	...
2 Factor income from rest of the world	...	23	40	62	51	82	...	...	...	...	...	...
A Compensation of employees	...	2	3	2	19	45	...	...	...	...	...	...
B Property and entrepreneurial income	...	21	37	60	31	37	...	...	...	...	...	...
3 Current transfers from rest of the world	...	655	668	597	897	800	...	...	...	...	...	...
Receipts from the Rest of the World on Current Transactions [a]	...	1380	1624	1564	2169	2550	...	...	...	...	...	...

a) Data for this table have not been revised, therefore, data for some years are not comparable with those of other tables.

1.10 Gross Domestic Product by Kind of Activity, in Current Prices

Million Somali shillings

	1970	1975	1978	1979	1980	1981	1982	1983	1984	1985	1986	1987
1 Agriculture, hunting, forestry and fishing	1066	2095	4496	4588	11162	13855	18346	21407	40561	55542	70413	105979
2 Mining and quarrying	23	35	28	37	43	69	77	110	212	291	396	507
3 Manufacturing	186	226	301	446	773	932	1423	1572	2805	4145	6240	8303
4 Electricity, gas and water	15	38	29	34	27	40	59	65	96	71	262	-891
5 Construction	105	204	208	277	461	514	633	642	1235	1889	3000	4800
6 Wholesale and retail trade, restaurants and hotels	172	407	622	855	1569	1768	2522	3171	6097	8452	11598	17418
7 Transport, storage and communication	133	323	374	404	717	958	1277	1807	3369	5667	8174	11109
8 Finance, insurance, real estate and business services	91	228	371	447	635	820	1312	1625	2125	3747	6608	8791
9 Community, social and personal services	52	108	169	215	353	526	664	932	1846	2620	3664	4833
Total, Industries	1842	3664	6598	7303	15740	19482	26312	31331	58346	82425	110354	160848
Producers of Government Services	148	280	694	720	810	1032	1090	1433	1807	1625	2230	2327
Other Producers	...	...	...	...	...	...	...	...	...	...	...	...
Subtotal [a]	1990	3944	7292	8023	16550	20514	27402	32764	60153	84050	112584	163175
Less: Imputed bank service charge	...	...	151	202	239	238	339	584	440	859	1000	1300
Plus: Import duties	...	...	...	...	...	...	...	...	...	...	...	...
Plus: Value added tax	...	...	...	...	...	...	...	...	...	...	...	...
Plus: Other adjustments [b]	254	448	1034	1164	1030	1780	2048	2949	2540	4099	7197	7733
Equals: Gross Domestic Product	2244	4390	8175	8985	17341	22056	29111	35129	62253	87290	118781	169608

a) Gross domestic product in factor values.
b) Item 'Other adjustments' refers to indirect taxes net of subsidies.

1.11 Gross Domestic Product by Kind of Activity, in Constant Prices

Million Somali shillings

	1970	1975	1978	1979	1980	1981	1982	1983	1984	1985	1986	1987
			At constant prices of:1977									
1 Agriculture, hunting, forestry and fishing	2640	2747	4046	3594	3844	4418	4495	3699	4220	4753	4426	5106
2 Mining and quarrying	15	38	25	27	20	22	20	21	21	21	21	21
3 Manufacturing	340	285	273	327	357	297	370	300	278	299	331	344
4 Electricity, gas and water	42	44	29	43	43	43	40	40	46	47	55	44
5 Construction	192	257	204	242	286	294	262	238	276	300	318	337

Somalia

1.11 Gross Domestic Product by Kind of Activity, in Constant Prices
(Continued)

Million Somali shillings

	1970	1975	1978	1979	1980	1981	1982	1983	1984	1985	1986	1987
			At constant prices of: 1977									
6 Wholesale and retail trade, restaurants and hotels	314	513	565	628	724	564	656	605	605	609	615	722
7 Transport, storage and communication	233	401	339	296	331	306	332	345	334	408	434	460
8 Finance, insurance, real estate and business services	165	344	358	375	367	332	349	370	327	337	340	351
9 Community, social and personal services	94	136	153	158	163	168	173	178	183	189	194	200
Total, Industries	4036	4765	5993	5690	6135	6444	6696	5796	6290	6963	6735	7585
Producers of Government Services	270	353	485	520	539	545	547	550	522	493	461	432
Other Producers	...	...	...	...	...	...	...	...	...	...	...	...
Subtotal [a]	4306	5118	6477	6210	6674	6989	7243	6346	6812	7456	7196	8017
Less: Imputed bank service charge	...	...	137	148	110	76	88	111	44	62	53	54
Plus: Import duties	...	...	...	...	...	...	...	...	...	...	...	...
Plus: Value added tax	...	...	...	...	...	...	...	...	...	...	...	...
Plus: Other adjustments [b]	464	565	938	854	475	568	533	563	252	295	382	320
Equals: Gross Domestic Product	4770	5682	7279	6916	7040	7481	7688	6798	7020	7689	7524	8283

a) Gross domestic product in factor values.
b) Item 'Other adjustments' refers to indirect taxes net of subsidies.

1.12 Relations Among National Accounting Aggregates

Million Somali shillings

	1970	1975	1978	1979	1980	1981	1982	1983	1984	1985	1986	1987
Gross Domestic Product	...	...	8175	8985	17341	22056	29111	35129	62253	87290	118781	169608
Plus: Net factor income from the rest of the world	...	...	-6	13	-6	-28	-131	-71	-875	-1922	-4372	-5490
Equals: Gross National Product	...	...	8169	8998	17335	22028	28980	35058	61378	85368	114409	164118
Less: Consumption of fixed capital	...	...	...	...	...	...	...	...	...	...	...	...
Equals: National Income	...	...	8169	8998	17335	22028	28980	35058	61378	85368	114409	164118
Plus: Net current transfers from the rest of the world	...	...	667	592	1259	1347	2225	3140	4903	8785	16871	36066
Equals: National Disposable Income	...	...	8836	9590	18594	23374	31205	38198	66281	94154	131280	200184
Less: Final consumption	...	...	7547	9474	17863	22544	30637	36486	62711	88208	117329	169361
Equals: Net Saving	...	...	1289	116	731	830	568	1712	3570	5946	13951	30823
Less: Surplus of the nation on current transactions	...	...	-415	-1299	-848	-598	-1409	-2320	-2890	-4353	-7192	-5701
Equals: Net Capital Formation	...	...	1704	1415	1579	1428	1977	4032	6460	10299	21143	36524

2.17 Exports and Imports of Goods and Services, Detail

Million Somali shillings

	1970	1975	1978	1979	1980	1981	1982	1983	1984	1985	1986	1987
			Exports of Goods and Services									
1 Exports of merchandise, f.o.b.	...	558	689	667	839	1103	...	...	...	...	...	...
2 Transport and communication	...	21	18	34	73	198	...	...	...	...	...	...
A In respect of merchandise imports	...	2	12	18	49	154	...	...	...	...	...	...
B Other	...	19	6	16	29	44	...	...	...	...	...	...
3 Insurance service charges	...	-	-	-	-	-	...	...	...	...	...	...
4 Other commodities	...	34	39	56	...	...	...	...	...	...	...	...
5 Adjustments of merchandise exports to change-of-ownership basis	...	-	-	-	-	-	...	...	...	...	...	...
6 Direct purchases in the domestic market by non-residential households	...	8	78	25	154	168	...	...	...	...	...	...
7 Direct purchases in the domestic market by extraterritorial bodies	...	82	92	122	145	198	...	...	...	...	...	...
Total Exports of Goods and Services [a]	...	702	916	905	1221	1668	...	...	...	...	...	...

Somalia

2.17 Exports and Imports of Goods and Services, Detail
(Continued)

Million Somali shillings

	1970	1975	1978	1979	1980	1981	1982	1983	1984	1985	1986	1987
					Imports of Goods and Services							
1 Imports of merchandise, c.i.f.	...	1021	1732	2481	2905	2681	...	...	...	...	...	...
By residents	...	...	...	...	1221	1668	...	...	...	...	...	...
By non-residents	...	...	...	...	...	...	...	...	...	...	...	...
2 Adjustments of merchandise imports to change-of-ownership basis	...	-	-	-	-	-	...	...	...	...	...	...
3 Other transport and communication	...	39	23	23	80	37	...	...	...	...	...	...
4 Other insurance service charges	...	-	-	-	-	-	...	...	...	...	...	...
5 Other commodities	...	155	111	100	...	...	...	...	...	...	...	...
6 Direct purchases abroad by government	...	94	88	93	170	175	...	...	...	...	...	...
7 Direct purchases abroad by resident households	...	40	58	111	101	187	...	...	...	...	...	...
Total Imports of Goods and Services	...	1349	2012	2808	3256	3080	...	...	...	...	...	...
Balance of Goods and Services	...	-647	-1096	-1903	-2035	-1412	...	...	...	...	...	...
Total Imports and Balance of Goods and Services [a]	...	702	916	905	1221	1668	...	...	...	...	...	...

a) Data for this table have not been revised, therefore, data for some years are not comparable with those of other tables.

South Africa

General note. The preparation of national accounts statistics in South Africa is undertaken by the South African Reserve Bank, Pretoria. The official estimates are published in the Bank's Quarterly Bulletin. A detailed description of the sources and methods used for the national accounts estimation is contained in a suplement to the Bulletin published in September 1981 entitled 'A Statistical Presentaton of South Africa's Quarterly National Accounts for the period 1946 to 1980'. The estimates are generally in accordance with the classifications and definitions recommended in the United Nations System of National Accounts (SNA). Input-output tables have been published in 'The South African Journal of Economics'. The following tables have been prepared from successive replies to the United Nations national accounts questionnaire. When the scope and coverage of the estimates differ for conceptual or statistical reasons from the definitions and classifications recommended in SNA, a footnote is indicated to the relevant tables.

Sources and methods:

(a) **Gross domestic product.** Gross domestic product is estimated mainly through the income approach.

(b) **Expenditure on the gross domestic product.** All items of GDP by expenditure type are estimated through the expenditure approach. Government expenditure is estimated through the use of published annual accounts and monthly issues from the Exchequer Account for the central authorities quarterly returns submitted directly to the Reserve Bank for the provincial authorities, and annual and quarterly data collected by the Department of Statistics for the local authorities. Estimates of private consumption expenditure are based on a variety of sources such as quarterly data on the agricultural products marketed for food, monthly excise figures for beverages and tobacco, monthly retail sales data for clothing, medicine, entertainment, etc., number of motor vehicles and cycles sold for transport equipment, number of dwelling units and average rent and income of concerned enterprises. The estimates of increase in stocks are based on census results and quarterly surveys. Information on investment in the public sector is obtained from published accounts updated by quarterly returns submitted to the Reserve Bank by concerned authorities. For the private sector, data on investment by the different sectors are obtained from various sources -- censuses and quarterly surveys for agriculture, manufacturing and mining, the value of buildings completed in urban areas for the sectors of commerce, private transport, financial institutions, etc. All relevant information for exports and imports of goods and services is based on balance-of-payments data. Official statistics and sample surveys of financial and non-financial companies are also used for exports and imports of services. For the constant price estimates, price deflation is used for government expenditure on goods and services, increase in stocks except agricultural stocks, gross fixed capital formation and exports and imports of goods and services. The net value of gold exports at constant prices is obtained by extrapolating the value of the base year on the basis of the number of kilograms of fine gold produced. The base-year values of government wages, salaries and allowances and private consumption expenditure are extrapolated by appropriate volume indexes. For agricultural stocks, values at constant prices are obtained by multiplying the change in the number of livestock by the average flock value.

(c) **Cost-structure of the gross domestic product.** Estimates of compensation of employees of all sectors of the economy are based on census results and monthly and quarterly data of wages, salaries and benefits paid to employees. Operating surplus is obtanied from different sources for the different sectors of the economy-- data obtained from the Department of Agricultural Economics and Marketing for the agricultural sector, census results and quarterly surveys of financial statistics for mining, manufactUring, construction and trade, information from concerned enterprises for electricity, gas and water, financial data for the financial institutions, annual and monthly statistics for trade and communication and data on the number of residential units and indexes of house and flat rents for real estate. The straight-line method based on the original cost of the original assets is used for estimating consumption of fixed capital. Depreciation is based on replacement cost. Indirect taxes and subsidies are estimated on the basis of an analysis of government accounts by the Reserve Bank.

(d) **Gross domestic product by kind of economic activity.** The table of GDP by kind of economic activity is prepared in factor values. The income approach is used to estimate the value added of all industries except agriculture for which the production approach is used. The estimates of agricultural production are obtained by valuing physical output at net producers' prices. Data pertaining to agricultural and livestock production are obtained from the censuses of agriculture and forestry and the Agricultural Control Boards. For forestry and fishing, estimates are obtained from the Department of Forestry and from the censuses of Fisheries, respectively. Estimates of income originating from gold, coal, diamond and other mines are obtained from triennial censuses. For non-census years, estimates are based on various sources such as reports of the Government Mining Engineer and quarterly sample surveys of financial statistics of mining. Estimates of manufacturing are based on biennial censuses covering establishments employing three or more full-time workers or using power equipment. For other years, estimates are based on quarterly sample surveys supplemented by financial reports for public corporations and Auditor-General's reports and anual surveys of local authorities for government enterprises. Intermediate consumption is estimated in census years only. For electricity, gas and water, estimates are based on annual financial statements for corporations and on results of annual censuses for local authorities and private enterprises. The estimates of construction are based on biennial censuses of construction. For non-census years, sample surveys of wages and salaries and analysis of financial statements of important companies are used. The basic information for trade is obtained from the five-yearly censuses of distribution. For other years, estimates are based on sample surveys of trading establishments. Estimates for the transport sector are obtained from published data of concerned establishments, annual surveys and for the private sector, on the results of the five-yearly censuses. For communication, estimates are obtained from the reports of the Auditor-General. Estimates for banking, insurance and real estate are based on quarterly data collected from the financial institutions. Estimates for ownership of dwellings are based on the results of inquiries into housing and rent as part of the decennial population censuses which are updated by monthly data. Data from the annual rent surveys and monthly data of dwellings completed are used for estimating owner-occupied dwelling rents. For government services, information is obtained from government accounts. For private services, estimates are based on annual surveys, inquiry conducted concurrently with the population censuses and on workmen's compensation statistics. Estimates of the contribution to the GDP at constant prices by each major industry division are made on a quarterly basis. The value added of most industries is extrapolated by quantity indicators. Double deflation is used for agriculture and forestry. For financial institutions, business services and part of private service, value added is deflated by appropriate indexes.

1.1 Expenditure on the Gross Domestic Product, in Current Prices

Million South African rand

	1970	1975	1978	1979	1980	1981	1982	1983	1984	1985	1986	1987
1 Government final consumption expenditure	1564	3782	5673	6543	8449	10378	12990	14809	18787	21695	26008	31613
2 Private final consumption expenditure	7760	15478	21510	24917	30922	37799	44134	50703	58517	65454	77093	92033
A Households	7656	15214	21143	24491	30405	37180	43347	49756	57436	64224	75748	90466
B Private non-profit institutions serving households	104	264	367	426	517	619	787	947	1081	1230	1345	1567
3 Gross capital formation	3684	8893	9939	12574	18840	24033	20746	23206	26188	24657	27650	32124
A Increase in stocks	490	783	-403	323	2462	3901	-1946	-1303	57	-3962	-1348	56
B Gross fixed capital formation	3194	8110	10342	12251	16378	20132	22692	24509	26131	28619	28998	32068
Residential buildings	487	982	1036	1280	1796	2311	2766	3366	3887	3568	3560	3995
Non-residential buildings	530	1132	1400	1608	1957	2606	3212	3506	4074	4419	4569	5184
Other construction and land improvement etc. [a]	810	2292	2860	3510	4683	5008	4812	5304	5468	5734	6039	6651
Other	1367	3704	5046	5853	7942	10207	11902	12333	12702	14898	14830	16238
4 Exports of goods and services	2757	7388	12959	16724	22219	20584	21833	23163	28261	40395	46499	48026
5 Less: Imports of goods and services	3165	8119	9867	11878	16959	21627	21813	19440	25931	28299	31866	34817
Statistical discrepancy	308	32	-917	-2182	-1464	-84	1786	-2566	-8	-3761	-5689	-4524
Equals: Gross Domestic Product [b]	12908	27454	39297	46698	62007	71083	79676	89875	105814	120141	139695	164455

a) Land development includes transfer costs.
b) Estimates are prepared by the South African Reserve Bank. These estimates include the Republic of South Africa and Namibia.

South Africa

1.2 Expenditure on the Gross Domestic Product, in Constant Prices

Million South African rand

	1970	1975	1978	1979	1980	1981	1982	1983	1984	1985	1986	1987
	At constant prices of:1985											
1 Government final consumption expenditure	10275	14192	15649	16138	17995	18610	19639	19961	21505	21695	22072	23338
2 Private final consumption expenditure	40847	52327	53490	54717	59587	63486	64824	66018	68311	65454	65507	67905
3 Gross capital formation	25115	31359	23560	27250	35922	39484	29707	29840	30512	24657	22248	23432
A Increase in stocks	5173	2560	-1991	739	4787	5727	-3064	-1370	-68	-3962	-1383	129
B Gross fixed capital formation	19942	28799	25551	26511	31135	33757	32771	31210	30580	28619	23631	23303
Residential buildings	3183	3588	2661	2863	3448	3848	3926	4137	4361	3568	3036	3041
Non-residential buildings	3404	4090	3569	3588	3761	4330	4545	4321	4567	4419	3944	3935
Other construction and land improvement etc. [a]	5546	8770	7490	7873	8996	8343	6861	6588	6199	5732	5217	5092
Other	7911	12479	11905	12234	14955	17255	17419	16164	15453	14900	11434	11235
4 Exports of goods and services	30628	31878	37907	38215	37926	35722	35756	33805	36676	40395	39835	38801
5 Less: Imports of goods and services	30065	38065	29561	29161	34878	39462	33295	27604	33198	28299	27554	28638
Statistical discrepancy	...	...	...	...	-3955	476	1106	-6310	-2145	-3761	-772	-368
Equals: Gross Domestic Product [bc]	81694	99827	104236	107621	113689	119114	118210	115710	121661	120141	121336	124470

a) Land development includes transfer costs.
b) Estimates are prepared by the South African Reserve Bank. These estimates include the Republic of South Africa and Namibia.
c) For the years prior to 1983, existing series expressed in 1980 prices have been linked to the new 1985 base year without re-weighting. As a result, for the periods before 1983, the converted sub-totals and totals are not equal to the sum of their components.

1.3 Cost Components of the Gross Domestic Product

Million South African rand

	1970	1975	1978	1979	1980	1981	1982	1983	1984	1985	1986	1987
1 Indirect taxes, net	885	1608	2779	3477	4044	5081	6683	6606	8386	9987	11793	13371
A Indirect taxes	1032	1896	3361	4058	4839	5974	7833	8480	10574	12594	14951	17002
B Less: Subsidies	147	288	582	581	795	893	1150	1874	2188	2607	3158	3631
2 Consumption of fixed capital	1359	3372	5801	6886	8194	9860	12218	14453	16344	19722	24864	27851
3 Compensation of employees paid by resident producers to:	7033	14822	20653	23822	29358	36480	43387	48638	57262	63401	72663	85924
A Resident households	6870	14348	20077	23175	28607	35608	42401	47487	55969	61898	70897	83896
B Rest of the world	163	474	576	647	751	872	986	1151	1293	1503	1766	2028
4 Operating surplus	3631	7652	10064	12513	20411	19662	17388	20178	23822	27031	30375	37309
Equals: Gross Domestic Product [a]	12908	27454	39297	46698	62007	71083	79676	89875	105814	120141	139695	164455

a) Estimates are prepared by the South African Reserve Bank. These estimates include the Republic of South Africa and Namibia.

1.4 General Government Current Receipts and Disbursements

Million South African rand

	1970	1975	1978	1979	1980	1981	1982	1983	1984	1985	1986	1987
	Receipts											
1 Operating surplus	...	...	...	...	...	...	...	...	...	...	...	...
2 Property and entrepreneurial income	164	455	654	656	1304	1056	573	772	1190	1468	1968	2720
3 Taxes, fees and contributions	2418	5417	8119	9689	12528	14514	17652	20363	24056	29636	34588	38648
A Indirect taxes	1032	1896	3361	4058	4839	5974	7833	8480	10574	12594	14951	17002
B Direct taxes	1313	3350	4531	5372	7369	8181	9386	11395	12912	16397	18925	20858
C Social security contributions	36	71	109	129	169	184	228	263	296	333	372	402
D Compulsory fees, fines and penalties	37	100	118	130	151	175	205	225	274	312	340	386
4 Other current transfers	39	99	117	160	279	345	276	277	269	373	426	431
Total Current Receipts of General Government [a]	2621	5971	8890	10505	14111	15915	18501	21412	25515	31477	36982	41799
	Disbursements											
1 Government final consumption expenditure	1564	3782	5673	6543	8449	10378	12990	14809	18787	21695	26008	31613
2 Property income	177	395	786	1424	1492	1708	2328	3290	4132	5201	5554	6038
A Interest	177	395	786	1424	1492	1708	2328	3290	4132	5201	5554	6038
B Net land rent and royalties	...	...	...	...	...	...	...	...	...	...	...	...

South Africa

1.4 General Government Current Receipts and Disbursements
(Continued)

Million South African rand

	1970	1975	1978	1979	1980	1981	1982	1983	1984	1985	1986	1987
3 Subsidies	147	288	582	581	795	893	1150	1874	2188	2607	3158	3631
4 Other current transfers	294	692	1033	1234	1349	1532	2073	2475	2939	3662	4098	4097
A Social security benefits	42	73	138	143	176	164	200	264	352	471	588	678
B Social assistance grants	251	614	889	1084	1166	1360	1862	2198	2571	3172	3490	3396
C Other	1	5	6	7	7	8	11	13	16	19	20	23
5 Net saving	439	814	816	723	2026	1404	-40	-1036	-2531	-1688	-1836	-3580
Total Current Disbursements and Net Saving of General Government [a]	2621	5971	8890	10505	14111	15915	18501	21412	25515	31477	36982	41799

a) Estimates are prepared by the South African Reserve Bank. These estimates include the Republic of South Africa and Namibia.

1.6 Current Income and Outlay of Households and Non-Profit Institutions

Million South African rand

	1970	1975	1978	1979	1980	1981	1982	1983	1984	1985	1986	1987
Receipts												
1 Compensation of employees	6872	14352	20085	23185	28619	35623	42419	47508	55990	61921	70923	83924
A From resident producers	6870	14348	20077	23175	28607	35608	42401	47488	55969	61898	70897	83896
B From rest of the world	2	4	8	10	12	15	18	20	21	23	26	28
2 Operating surplus of private unincorporated enterprises	...	...	...	...	...	...	...	...	...	...	...	...
3 Property and entrepreneurial income	1936	3825	4974	6502	7738	6161	5390	8514	9860	13133	14907	19015
4 Current transfers	367	840	1181	1414	1554	1768	2360	2791	3293	4050	4503	4507
Total Current Receipts [a]	9175	19017	26240	31101	37911	43552	50169	58813	69143	79104	90333	107446
Disbursements												
1 Private final consumption expenditure	7760	15478	21510	24917	30922	37799	44134	50703	58517	65454	77093	92033
2 Property income	...	...	...	...	...	...	...	...	...	...	...	...
3 Direct taxes and other current transfers n.e.c. to general government	586	1555	2410	2437	2579	3358	4582	5689	8002	9492	10803	12558
A Social security contributions	...	...	...	...	...	...	...	...	...	...	...	...
B Direct taxes	586	1555	2410	2437	2579	3358	4582	5689	8002	9492	10803	12558
C Fees, fines and penalties	...	...	...	...	...	...	...	...	...	...	...	...
4 Other current transfers	47	76	120	106	104	120	121	129	139	165	184	163
5 Net saving	782	1908	2200	3641	4306	2275	1332	2292	2485	3993	2253	2692
Total Current Disbursements and Net Saving [a]	9175	19017	26240	31101	37911	43552	50169	58813	69143	79104	90333	107446

a) Estimates are prepared by the South African Reserve Bank. These estimates include the Republic of South Africa and Namibia.

1.7 External Transactions on Current Account, Summary

Million South African rand

	1970	1975	1978	1979	1980	1981	1982	1983	1984	1985	1986	1987
Payments to the Rest of the World												
1 Imports of goods and services	3165	8119	9867	11878	16959	21627	21813	19440	25931	28299	31866	34817
A Imports of merchandise c.i.f.	2861	7382	8751	10667	15518	19997	19956	17462	23667	25907	28713	31250
B Other	304	737	1116	1211	1441	1630	1858	1978	2264	2392	3153	3567
2 Factor income to the rest of the world	623	1425	2162	2555	3184	3835	4146	4702	5659	7855	9312	8853
A Compensation of employees	163	474	577	647	751	872	986	1150	1293	1503	1766	2028
B Property and entrepreneurial income	460	951	1585	1908	2433	2963	3160	3552	4366	6352	7546	6825
3 Current transfers to the rest of the world [a]	61	103	158	159	164	177	191	198	251	364	397	358
4 Surplus of the nation on current transactions	-868	-1813	1330	2880	2818	-4089	-3345	-78	-2220	5925	7196	6152
Payments to the Rest of the World and Surplus of the Nation on Current Transactions [b]	2981	7834	13517	17472	23125	21550	22805	24262	29621	42443	48771	50180
Receipts From The Rest of the World												
1 Exports of goods and services	2757	7388	12959	16724	22219	20584	21833	23163	28261	40395	46499	48026

South Africa

1.7 External Transactions on Current Account, Summary
(Continued)

Million South African rand	1970	1975	1978	1979	1980	1981	1982	1983	1984	1985	1986	1987
A Exports of merchandise f.o.b.	2290	6193	11313	14816	19907	17919	18767	20136	24591	35925	41767	42938
B Other	467	1195	1646	1908	2312	2665	3066	3027	3670	4470	4732	5088
2 Factor income from rest of the world	114	205	303	426	449	419	442	538	771	1326	1490	1365
A Compensation of employees	2	4	8	10	12	15	18	20	21	23	26	28
B Property and entrepreneurial income	112	201	295	416	437	404	424	518	750	1303	1464	1337
3 Current transfers from rest of the world	110	241	255	322	457	547	530	561	589	722	782	789
Receipts from the Rest of the World on Current Transactions [b]	2981	7834	13517	17472	23125	21550	22805	24262	29621	42443	48771	50180

a) Item 'Current transfers to/from the rest of the world' includes also capital transfers.
b) Estimates are prepared by the South African Reserve Bank. These estimates include the Republic of South Africa and Namibia.

1.8 Capital Transactions of The Nation, Summary

Million South African rand	1970	1975	1978	1979	1980	1981	1982	1983	1984	1985	1986	1987
Finance of Gross Capital Formation												
Gross saving	2816	7080	11269	15454	21658	19944	17401	23128	23968	30582	34846	38276
1 Consumption of fixed capital	1359	3372	5801	6886	8194	9860	12218	14453	16344	19722	24864	27851
A General government	52	132	212	253	309	372	455	543	616	711	854	994
B Corporate and quasi-corporate enterprises	1307	3240	5589	6633	7885	9488	11763	13910	15728	19011	24010	26857
Public	334	865	1516	1823	2431	2981	3667	4348	4941	5896	7394	8149
Private	973	2375	4073	4810	5454	6507	8096	9562	10787	13115	16616	18708
C Other	-	-	-	-	-	-	-	-	-	-	-	...
2 Net saving	1457	3708	5468	8568	13464	10084	5183	8675	7624	10860	9982	10425
A General government	439	814	816	723	2026	1404	-40	-1036	-2531	-1688	-1836	-3580
B Corporate and quasi-corporate enterprises	236	986	2452	4204	7132	6405	3891	7419	7670	8555	9565	11313
C Other	782	1908	2200	3641	4306	2275	1332	2292	2485	3993	2253	2692
Less: Surplus of the nation on current transactions	-868	-1813	1330	2880	2818	-4089	-3345	-78	-2220	5925	7196	6152
Finance of Gross Capital Formation [a]	3684	8893	9939	12574	18840	24033	20746	23206	26188	24657	27650	32124
Gross Capital Formation												
Increase in stocks	490	783	-403	323	2462	3901	-1946	-1303	57	-3962	-1348	56
Gross fixed capital formation	3193	8110	10342	12251	16378	20132	22692	24509	26131	28619	28998	32068
1 General government	563	1296	1411	1671	1909	2253	2353	2590	2832	3168	3729	4658
2 Corporate and quasi-corporate enterprises	2631	6814	8931	10580	14469	17879	20339	21919	23299	25451	25269	27410
A Public	816	2748	3876	4706	6160	6698	7519	7827	8003	9685	8903	8351
B Private	1815	4066	5055	5874	8309	11181	12820	14092	15296	15766	16366	19059
3 Other	...	...	...	...	...	...	...	...	...	...	...	...
Gross Capital Formation [a]	3684	8893	9939	12574	18840	24033	20746	23206	26188	24657	27650	32124

a) Estimates are prepared by the South African Reserve Bank. These estimates include the Republic of South Africa and Namibia.

1.10 Gross Domestic Product by Kind of Activity, in Current Prices

Million South African rand	1970	1975	1978	1979	1980	1981	1982	1983	1984	1985	1986	1987
1 Agriculture, hunting, forestry and fishing	973	2129	2722	2885	4035	4787	4581	4096	5265	5907	7277	8533
2 Mining and quarrying	1207	3182	5497	7756	12729	10447	10409	12194	13210	17760	20953	20453
3 Manufacturing	2796	5991	7886	9579	12606	15646	16939	19456	22704	24311	27840	35103
4 Electricity, gas and water	307	610	1570	1777	1924	2164	2594	3181	3781	4480	5427	6695
5 Construction	507	1362	1472	1586	2080	2533	2898	3334	3674	3917	4215	4645
6 Wholesale and retail trade, restaurants and hotels	1819	3667	4595	4922	6806	8645	9376	10869	11486	12477	14242	17837
7 Transport, storage and communication	1154	2395	3670	4093	5045	5972	6623	7439	9336	9405	11335	12822
8 Finance, insurance, real estate and business services	1733	3268	4570	5386	6352	7664	9385	11459	13677	16470	18786	22952
9 Community, social and personal services	228	389	609	678	820	945	1147	1466	1708	1920	2202	2665
Total, Industries	10724	22993	32591	38662	52397	58803	63952	73494	84841	96647	112277	131705
Producers of Government Services	1132	2497	3723	4342	5384	6837	8292	9604	12311	13906	16821	20573

South Africa

1.10 Gross Domestic Product by Kind of Activity, in Current Prices
(Continued)

Million South African rand

	1970	1975	1978	1979	1980	1981	1982	1983	1984	1985	1986	1987
Other Producers	375	742	970	1070	1244	1459	1763	2005	2296	2603	2936	3359
Subtotal [a]	12231	26232	37284	44074	59025	67099	74007	85103	99448	113156	132034	155637
Less: Imputed bank service charge	208	386	766	853	1062	1097	1014	1834	2020	3002	4132	4553
Plus: Import duties	...	...	...	...	...	...	...	...	...	...	...	...
Plus: Value added tax	...	...	...	...	...	...	...	...	...	...	...	...
Plus: Other adjustments [b]	885	1608	2779	3477	4044	5081	6683	6606	8386	9987	11793	13371
Equals: Gross Domestic Product [c]	12908	27454	39297	46698	62007	71083	79676	89875	105814	120141	139695	164455

a) Gross domestic product in factor values.
b) Item 'Other adjustments' refers to indirect taxes net of subsidies.
c) Estimates of GDP by economic activity are prepared by the Central Statistical Services. These estimates include the Republic of South Africa and Namibia.

1.11 Gross Domestic Product by Kind of Activity, in Constant Prices

Million South African rand

	1970	1975	1978	1979	1980	1981	1982	1983	1984	1985	1986	1987
					At constant prices of:1985							
1 Agriculture, hunting, forestry and fishing	4487	5448	6103	5957	6584	6957	6350	4920	5438	5907	6858	7036
2 Mining and quarrying	20107	16435	17416	17791	17362	17139	17055	17089	17695	17760	17237	16658
3 Manufacturing	14940	19932	21179	22928	25111	26810	26000	24272	25238	24311	24621	25587
4 Electricity, gas and water	1714	2496	2886	3087	3355	3741	3959	3955	4200	4480	4603	4801
5 Construction	3373	4738	3956	4009	4347	4588	4408	4168	4218	3917	3774	3893
6 Wholesale and retail trade, restaurants and hotels	7474	10595	9875	9519	10624	11623	11642	12050	13168	12477	12073	12561
7 Transport, storage and communication	5199	7122	7770	8455	9051	9625	9325	8779	9468	9405	9295	9295
8 Finance, insurance, real estate and business services	9828	11958	12577	13222	14038	14772	15134	15637	16259	16470	16883	17562
9 Community, social and personal services	1015	1211	1354	1417	1469	1580	1678	1793	1915	1920	1930	1946
Total, Industries	68137	79935	83116	86385	91941	96835	95551	92663	97599	96647	97274	99339
Producers of Government Services	8080	9965	11205	11510	11899	12182	12663	13300	13818	13906	14305	14843
Other Producers	1704	2088	2194	2231	2284	2339	2411	2494	2592	2603	2620	2663
Subtotal [a]	77921	91988	96515	100126	106124	111356	110625	108457	114009	113156	114199	116845
Less: Imputed bank service charge	1632	2100	2106	2166	2352	2660	2722	2782	2980	3002	2847	2805
Plus: Import duties	...	...	...	...	...	...	...	...	...	...	...	...
Plus: Value added tax	...	...	...	...	...	...	...	...	...	...	...	...
Plus: Other adjustments [b]	6690	8690	8658	8717	9341	10139	10181	10035	10632	9987	9984	10430
Equals: Gross Domestic Product [cd]	81694	99827	104236	107621	113689	119114	118210	115710	121661	120141	121336	124470

a) Gross domestic product in factor values.
b) Item 'Other adjustments' refers to indirect taxes net of subsidies.
c) Estimates of GDP by economic activity are prepared by the Central Statistical Services. These estimates include the Republic of South Africa and Namibia.
d) For the years prior to 1983, existing series expressed in 1980 prices have been linked to the new 1985 base year without re-weighting. As a result, for the periods before 1983, the converted sub-totals and totals are not equal to the sum of their components.

1.12 Relations Among National Accounting Aggregates

Million South African rand

	1970	1975	1978	1979	1980	1981	1982	1983	1984	1985	1986	1987
Gross Domestic Product [a]	12908	27454	39297	46698	62007	71083	79676	89875	105814	120141	139695	164455
Plus: Net factor income from the rest of the world	-509	-1220	-1859	-2129	-2735	-3416	-3704	-4164	-4888	-6529	-7822	-7488
Factor income from the rest of the world	114	205	303	426	449	419	442	538	771	1326	1490	1365
Less: Factor income to the rest of the world	623	1425	2162	2555	3184	3835	4146	4702	5659	7855	9312	8853
Equals: Gross National Product	12399	26234	37438	44569	59272	67667	75972	85711	100926	113612	131873	156967
Less: Consumption of fixed capital	1359	3372	5801	6886	8194	9860	12218	14453	16344	19722	24864	27851
Equals: National Income	11040	22862	31637	37683	51078	57807	63754	71258	84582	93890	107009	129116
Plus: Net current transfers from the rest of the world	49	138	97	163	293	370	339	363	338	358	385	431
Current transfers from the rest of the world	110	241	255	322	457	547	530	561	589	722	782	789
Less: Current transfers to the rest of the world [b]	61	103	158	159	164	177	191	198	251	364	397	358
Equals: National Disposable Income [a]	11089	23000	31734	37846	51371	58177	64093	71621	84920	94248	107394	129547
Less: Final consumption	9324	19260	27183	31460	39371	48177	57124	65512	77304	87149	103101	123646
Statistical discrepancy	-308	-32	917	2182	1464	84	-1786	2566	8	3761	5689	4524
Equals: Net Saving	1457	3708	5468	8568	13464	10084	5183	8675	7624	10860	9982	10425
Less: Surplus of the nation on current transactions	-868	-1813	1330	2880	2818	-4089	-3345	-78	-2220	5925	7196	6152
Equals: Net Capital Formation [a]	2325	5521	4138	5688	10646	14173	8528	8753	9844	4935	2786	4273

a) Estimates are prepared by the South African Reserve Bank. These estimates include the Republic of South Africa and Namibia.
b) Item 'Current transfers to/from the rest of the world' includes also capital transfers.

South Africa

2.5 Private Final Consumption Expenditure by Type and Purpose, in Current Prices

Million South African rand

	1970	1975	1978	1979	1980	1981	1982	1983	1984	1985	1986	1987
Final Consumption Expenditure of Resident Households												
1 Food, beverages and tobacco	2500	5009	7383	8685	10377	12791	14955	16917	19872	22253	27252	32995
A Food	1797	3613	5303	6283	7742	9766	11170	12832	14910	16956	20897	25811
B Non-alcoholic beverages	90	200	263	332	408	427	515	588	782	880	1157	1259
C Alcoholic beverages	394	807	1264	1455	1462	1732	2253	2425	2821	2878	3447	3825
D Tobacco	219	389	553	615	765	866	1017	1072	1359	1539	1751	2100
2 Clothing and footwear	780	1587	2030	2219	2746	3361	3792	4099	4518	4734	5599	6853
3 Gross rent, fuel and power	961	1582	2302	2575	3004	3640	4282	5250	6549	8128	9625	10930
4 Furniture, furnishings and household equipment and operation	1084	2093	2577	2954	3728	4504	5176	5842	6363	6697	7825	9378
A Household operation	208	392	596	712	890	1108	1314	1577	1862	1893	2235	2448
B Other	876	1701	1981	2242	2838	3396	3862	4265	4501	4804	5590	6930
5 Medical care and health expenses	252	537	828	913	1124	1324	1691	1984	2342	2674	3142	3571
6 Transport and communication [a]	1101	2388	3474	4210	5615	6831	7744	8683	9778	10999	12108	14814
A Personal transport equipment	410	750	958	1150	1732	2213	2326	2673	2942	2480	2698	4238
B Other	691	1638	2516	3060	3883	4618	5418	6010	6836	8519	9410	10576
7 Recreational, entertainment, education and cultural services	371	913	1230	1372	1760	2153	2585	3100	3577	4062	4668	5497
A Education	8	15	20	23	26	31	40	45	84	152	247	394
B Other	363	898	1210	1349	1734	2122	2545	3055	3493	3910	4421	5103
8 Miscellaneous goods and services	690	1402	1769	2068	2571	3176	3781	4616	5339	5921	6531	7767
A Personal care	159	277	366	417	495	612	739	883	1020	1157	1334	1550
B Expenditures in restaurants, cafes and hotels	241	461	531	624	793	959	1082	1351	1563	1618	1705	2078
C Other [a]	290	664	872	1027	1283	1605	1960	2382	2756	3146	3492	4139
Total Final Consumption Expenditure in the Domestic Market by Households, of which	7739	15511	21593	24996	30925	37780	44006	50491	58338	65468	76750	91805
A Durable goods	934	1911	2273	2672	3765	4757	5297	6085	6597	6120	6854	9347
B Semi-durable goods	1475	3002	3885	4282	5359	6586	7490	8493	9573	10571	12342	14871
C Non-durable goods	3195	6572	9862	11719	14166	17415	20350	23099	26998	30792	36920	43674
D Services	2134	4026	5573	6323	7635	9022	10869	12814	15170	17985	20634	23913
Plus: Direct purchases abroad by resident households	161	353	363	446	570	674	785	872	971	902	1327	1544
Less: Direct purchases in the domestic market by non-resident households [b]	244	650	813	951	1090	1274	1444	1607	1873	2146	2329	2883
Equals: Final Consumption Expenditure of Resident Households	7656	15214	21143	24491	30405	37180	43347	49756	57436	64224	75748	90466
Final Consumption Expenditure of Private Non-profit Institutions Serving Households												
1 Research and science	...	...	...	...	...	...	...	...	...	...	...	...
2 Education	76	189	246	288	356	438	546	671	764	854	945	1046
3 Medical and other health services	17	52	83	92	108	118	168	195	225	272	282	387
4 Welfare services	...	...	...	...	...	...	...	...	...	...	...	...
5 Recreational and related cultural services	8	15	27	34	40	49	58	65	75	86	99	114
6 Religious organisations	...	...	...	...	...	...	...	...	...	...	...	...
7 Professional and labour organisations serving households	...	...	...	...	...	...	...	...	...	...	...	...
8 Miscellaneous	3	8	11	12	13	14	15	16	17	18	19	20
Equals: Final Consumption Expenditure of Private Non-profit Organisations Serving Households	104	264	367	426	517	619	787	947	1081	1230	1345	1567
Private Final Consumption Expenditure [c]	7760	15478	21510	24917	30922	37799	44134	50703	58517	65454	77093	92033

a) Packaged tours is included in item 'Transport and communication'.
b) Item 'Direct purchases in the domestic market by non-resident households' includes a statistical discrepancy.
c) Estimates are prepared by the South African Reserve Bank. These estimates include the Republic of South Africa and Namibia.

South Africa

2.6 Private Final Consumption Expenditure by Type and Purpose, in Constant Prices

Million South African rand

	1970	1975	1978	1979	1980	1981	1982	1983	1984	1985	1986	1987
					At constant prices of: 1985							
					Final Consumption Expenditure of Resident Households							
1 Food, beverages and tobacco	13665	16534	18234	18868	19501	20134	20838	21178	22363	22253	22830	22934
A Food	10524	12337	13708	14002	14551	15032	15459	15891	16640	16913	17317	17465
B Non-alcoholic beverages	421	676	593	686	767	701	724	724	810	786	869	883
C Alcoholic beverages	1538	2386	2771	2962	2747	2911	3176	3135	3309	2987	3077	2959
D Tobacco	914	1114	1159	1218	1436	1490	1479	1428	1604	1567	1567	1627
2 Clothing and footwear	3180	4341	4218	4265	4869	5291	5202	5133	5066	4734	4784	4909
3 Gross rent, fuel and power	5345	6259	6814	6922	7124	7450	7592	7577	7888	8128	8249	8501
4 Furniture, furnishings and household equipment and operation	4257	6020	5596	5843	6632	7113	7150	7262	7242	6697	6477	6686
A Household operation	1154	1508	1716	1713	1819	2047	2076	2152	2289	1893	1660	1560
B Other	3103	4512	3880	4130	4813	5066	5074	5110	4953	4804	4817	5126
5 Medical care and health expenses	1705	2670	2759	2770	2415	2554	2742	2702	2972	2946	2879	3002
6 Transport and communication [a]	7487	9457	9349	9287	10920	12076	11918	11994	12353	10999	10761	12106
A Personal transport equipment	2257	2560	2232	2453	3368	3723	3366	3152	2906	1920	1523	2796
B Other	5121	6828	7116	6833	7396	8353	8252	8842	9447	9079	9238	9310
7 Recreational, entertainment, education and cultural services	2587	3785	3850	3869	4281	4632	4878	5240	5392	5002	4703	4785
A Education	528	684	696	702	946	965	987	1031	1066	1026	956	996
B Other	2057	3100	3155	3167	3335	3667	3891	4209	4326	3976	3747	3789
8 Miscellaneous goods and services	3742	4850	4487	4666	5160	5547	5678	6010	6158	5939	5545	5733
A Personal care	650	952	899	922	1005	1116	1147	1170	1185	1157	1093	1098
B Expenditures in restaurants, cafes and hotels	1500	1654	1400	1444	1574	1581	1555	1713	1758	1618	1451	1499
C Other [a]	1592	2244	2188	2300	2581	2850	2976	3127	3215	3164	3001	3136
Total Final Consumption Expenditure in the Domestic Market by Households, of which [b]	41460	53589	54800	56025	60815	64695	65950	67096	69434	66698	66228	68656
A Durable goods	4105	5933	5265	5689	7282	7928	7695	7691	7302	5703	5015	6151
B Semi-durable goods	7036	9554	9095	9126	10365	11307	11232	11527	11636	11129	11009	10720
C Non-durable goods	19243	23953	25955	26359	27399	28880	29871	30671	32684	31938	32345	31614
D Services	11076	14149	14485	14851	15769	16580	17153	17207	17811	17928	17860	20171
Plus: Direct purchases abroad by resident households	672	907	703	775	873	922	976	1008	1051	902	1241	1337
Less: Direct purchases in the domestic market by non-resident households [c]	1285	2169	2013	2083	2101	2131	2102	2086	2174	2146	1962	2088
Equals: Final Consumption Expenditure of Resident Households [d,b]	40847	52327	53490	54717	59587	63486	64824	66018	68311	65454	65507	67905
					Final Consumption Expenditure of Private Non-profit Institutions Serving Households							
Equals: Final Consumption Expenditure of Private Non-profit Organisations Serving Households	...	...	...	...	...	...	...	...	...	...	...	...
Private Final Consumption Expenditure [e,b]	40847	52327	53490	54717	59587	63486	64824	66018	68311	65454	65507	67905

a) Packaged tours is included in item 'Transport and communication'.
b) For the years prior to 1983, existing series expressed in 1980 prices have been linked to the new 1985 base year without re-weighting. As a result, for the periods before 1983, the converted sub-totals and totals are not equal to the sum of their components.
c) Item 'Direct purchases in the domestic market by non-resident households' includes a statistical discrepancy.
d) Item 'Final consumption expenditure of resident households' includes consumption expenditure of private non-profit institutions serving households.
e) Estimates are prepared by the South African Reserve Bank. These estimates include the Republic of South Africa and Namibia.

2.7 Gross Capital Formation by Type of Good and Owner, in Current Prices

Million South African rand

	1980				1981				1982			
	TOTAL	Total Private	Public Enterprises	General Government	TOTAL	Total Private	Public Enterprises	General Government	TOTAL	Total Private	Public Enterprises	General Government
Increase in stocks, total [a,b,c]	2462	2026	436	-	3901	3034	867	-	-1946	-1927	-19	-
1 Goods producing industries	239	...	...	...	985	...	...	...	-1314	...	...	...
2 Wholesale and retail trade [c]	1351	...	...	...	1913	...	...	...	-778	...	...	...
3 Other, except government stocks [c]	852	...	...	...	929	...	...	...	93	...	...	...
4 Government stocks [c]	20	...	...	...	74	...	...	...	53	...	...	...
Gross Fixed Capital Formation, Total	16378	8309	6160	1909	20132	11181	6698	2253	22692	12820	7519	2353
1 Residential buildings	1796	1179	...	...	2311	1609	...	...	2766	2065	...	...
2 Non-residential buildings	1957	892	...	...	2606	1369	...	...	3212	1911	...	...

1336

South Africa

2.7 Gross Capital Formation by Type of Good and Owner, in Current Prices
(Continued)

Million South African rand

	1980 TOTAL	1980 Total Private	1980 Public Enterprises	1980 General Government	1981 TOTAL	1981 Total Private	1981 Public Enterprises	1981 General Government	1982 TOTAL	1982 Total Private	1982 Public Enterprises	1982 General Government
3 Other construction	4330	671	...	...	4625	810	...	...	4379	823	...	...
4 Land improvement and plantation and orchard development [d]	353	353	...	...	383	383	...	...	433	433	...	...
5 Producers' durable goods	7942	5214	...	...	10207	7010	...	...	11902	7588	...	...
A Transport equipment	1893	1430	...	...	2569	1889	...	...	2915	1967	...	...
B Machinery and equipment	6049	3784	...	...	7637	5121	...	...	8986	5621	...	...
6 Breeding stock, dairy cattle, etc. [a]	...	...	...	...	...	...	...	...	...	...	...	...
Total Gross Capital Formation [e]	18840	10335	6596	1909	24033	14215	7563	2253	20746	10893	7500	2353

	1983 TOTAL	1983 Total Private	1983 Public Enterprises	1983 General Government	1984 TOTAL	1984 Total Private	1984 Public Enterprises	1984 General Government	1985 TOTAL	1985 Total Private	1985 Public Enterprises	1985 General Government
Increase in stocks, total [abc]	-1303	-1309	6	-	57	190	-133	...	-3962	-3393	-569	...
1 Goods producing industries	-861	...	...	...	-124	...	...	...	-1991	...	...	...
2 Wholesale and retail trade [c]	-464	...	...	...	433	...	...	...	-1483	...	...	...
3 Other, except government stocks [c]	109	...	...	...	-242	...	...	...	-461	...	...	...
4 Government stocks [c]	-87	...	...	...	-10	...	...	...	-27	...	...	...
Gross Fixed Capital Formation, Total	24509	14092	7827	2590	26131	15296	8003	2832	28619	15766	9685	3168
1 Residential buildings	3366	2511	...	...	3887	2977	...	...	3568	2708	...	...
2 Non-residential buildings	3506	2117	...	...	4074	2403	...	...	4419	2435	...	...
3 Other construction	4624	1012	...	...	4743	1191	...	...	5098	1510	...	...
4 Land improvement and plantation and orchard development [d]	678	678	...	...	725	725	...	...	634	634	...	...
5 Producers' durable goods	12335	7774	...	...	12702	8000	...	...	14900	8479	...	...
A Transport equipment	3172	2135	...	...	2868	2282	...	...	2904	2246	...	...
B Machinery and equipment	9163	5639	...	...	9834	5718	...	...	11996	6233	...	...
6 Breeding stock, dairy cattle, etc. [a]	...	...	...	...	...	...	...	...	...	...	...	...
Total Gross Capital Formation [e]	23206	12783	7833	2590	26188	15486	7870	2832	24657	12373	9116	3168

	1986 TOTAL	1986 Total Private	1986 Public Enterprises	1986 General Government	1987 TOTAL	1987 Total Private	1987 Public Enterprises	1987 General Government
Increase in stocks, total [abc]	-1348	-1343	-5	...	56	791	-735	...
1 Goods producing industries	-132	...	...	...	313	...	...	...
2 Wholesale and retail trade [c]	-905	...	...	...	156	...	...	...
3 Other, except government stocks [c]	-128	...	...	...	-301	...	...	...
4 Government stocks [c]	-183	...	...	...	-112	...	...	...
Gross Fixed Capital Formation, Total	28998	16366	8903	3729	32068	19059	8351	4658
1 Residential buildings	3560	2795	...	...	3995	3198	...	...
2 Non-residential buildings	4569	2420	...	...	5184	2648	...	...
3 Other construction	5375	1678	...	...	5723	1968	...	...
4 Land improvement and plantation and orchard development [d]	664	664	...	...	928	...	...	...
5 Producers' durable goods	14830	8809	...	...	16238	...	...	...
A Transport equipment	2839	2383	...	...	...	...	...	...
B Machinery and equipment	11991	6426	...	...	...	...	...	...
6 Breeding stock, dairy cattle, etc. [a]	...	...	...	...	...	...	...	...
Total Gross Capital Formation [e]	27650	15023	8898	3729	32124	19850	7616	4658

a) Item 'Breeding stocks, dairy cattle, etc.' is included in item 'Increase in stocks'.
b) Item 'Increase in stocks' excludes enterprises of commercial farms in business services, education, health and large unincorporated units of government enterprises.
c) The estimates of 'Increase in stocks' and their components are after inventory valuation adjustment.
d) Land development includes transfer costs.
e) Estimates are prepared by the South African Reserve Bank. These estimates include the Republic of South Africa and Namibia.

South Africa

2.8 Gross Capital Formation by Type of Good and Owner, in Constant Prices

Million South African rand

	1980				1981				1982			
	TOTAL	Total Private	Public Enterprises	General Government	TOTAL	Total Private	Public Enterprises	General Government	TOTAL	Total Private	Public Enterprises	General Government
At constant prices of:1985												
Increase in stocks, total [abc]	4787	4118	...	...	5727	4573	...	...	-3064	-2755	...	...
1 Goods producing industries	508	...	...	...	1608	...	...	...	-1821	...	...	...
2 Wholesale and retail trade [c]	2117	...	...	...	1365	...	...	...	-1084	...	...	...
3 Other, except government stocks [c]	2152	...	...	...	2672	...	...	...	-205	...	...	...
4 Government stocks [c]	10	...	...	...	82	...	...	...	46	...	...	...
Gross Fixed Capital Formation, Total [d]	31135	15834	...	...	33757	18849	...	...	32771	18597	...	...
1 Residential buildings	3448	2263	...	...	3848	2680	...	...	3926	2937	...	...
2 Non-residential buildings	3761	1715	...	...	4330	2271	...	...	4545	2702	...	...
3 Other construction	8318	1288	...	...	7703	1345	...	...	6245	1183	...	...
4 Land improvement and plantation and orchard development [e]	678	678	...	...	640	640	...	...	616	616	...	...
5 Producers' durable goods	14955	9896	...	...	17255	11909	...	...	17419	11145	...	...
A Transport equipment	3837	2897	...	...	4567	3357	...	...	4376	2948	...	...
B Machinery and equipment	11118	6999	...	...	12688	8552	...	...	13043	8197	...	...
6 Breeding stock, dairy cattle, etc. [a]	...	...	...	...	...	...	...	...	...	...	...	...
Total Gross Capital Formation [f]	35922	19952	...	...	39484	23422	...	...	29707	15842	...	...

	1983				1984				1985			
	TOTAL	Total Private	Public Enterprises	General Government	TOTAL	Total Private	Public Enterprises	General Government	TOTAL	Total Private	Public Enterprises	General Government
At constant prices of:1985												
Increase in stocks, total [abc]	-1370	-1378	...	...	-68	82	...	...	-3962	-3393	...	...
1 Goods producing industries	-1107	...	...	...	-152	...	...	...	-2057	...	...	...
2 Wholesale and retail trade [c]	11	...	...	...	154	...	...	...	-1507	...	...	...
3 Other, except government stocks [c]	-161	...	...	...	-61	...	...	...	-371	...	...	...
4 Government stocks [c]	-113	...	...	...	-9	...	...	...	-27	...	...	...
Gross Fixed Capital Formation, Total [d]	31210	17988	...	...	30580	17921	...	...	28619	15766	...	...
1 Residential buildings	4137	3088	...	...	4361	3340	...	...	3568	2708	...	...
2 Non-residential buildings	4321	2611	...	...	4567	2695	...	...	4419	2435	...	...
3 Other construction	5748	1259	...	...	5375	1347	...	...	5098	1510	...	...
4 Land improvement and plantation and orchard development [e]	840	840	...	...	824	824	...	...	634	634	...	...
5 Producers' durable goods	16164	10190	...	...	15453	9715	...	...	14900	8479	...	...
A Transport equipment	4119	2761	...	...	3414	2716	...	...	2904	2246	...	...
B Machinery and equipment	12045	7429	...	...	12039	6999	...	...	11996	6233	...	...
6 Breeding stock, dairy cattle, etc. [a]	...	...	...	...	...	...	...	...	...	...	...	...
Total Gross Capital Formation [f]	29840	16610	...	...	30512	18003	...	...	24657	12373	...	...

	1986				1987			
	TOTAL	Total Private	Public Enterprises	General Government	TOTAL	Total Private	Public Enterprises	General Government
At constant prices of:1985								
Increase in stocks, total [abc]	-1383	-1436	...	...	129	695	...	...
1 Goods producing industries	-128	...	...	...	-368	...	...	...
2 Wholesale and retail trade [c]	-812	...	...	...	-92	...	...	...
3 Other, except government stocks [c]	-251	...	...	...	673	...	...	...
4 Government stocks [c]	-192	...	...	...	-84	...	...	...
Gross Fixed Capital Formation, Total [d]	23631	13254	...	...	23303	13668	...	...
1 Residential buildings	3036	2376	...	...	3041	2435	...	...
2 Non-residential buildings	3944	2094	...	...	3935	2003	...	...

South Africa

2.8 Gross Capital Formation by Type of Good and Owner, in Constant Prices
(Continued)

Million South African rand

	1986 TOTAL	1986 Total Private	1986 Public Enterprises	1986 General Government	1987 TOTAL	1987 Total Private	1987 Public Enterprises	1987 General Government
				At constant prices of:1985				
3 Other construction	4643	1443	...	...	4384	1503	...	...
4 Land improvement and plantation and orchard development e	574	574	...	...	708	708	...	...
5 Producers' durable goods	11434	6767	...	...	11235	7019	...	...
A Transport equipment	2148	1801	...	...	2212	1988	...	...
B Machinery and equipment	9286	4966	...	...	9023	5031	...	...
6 Breeding stock, dairy cattle, etc. a	...	...	...	...	...	...	...	...
Total Gross Capital Formation f	22248	11818	...	...	23432	14363	...	...

a) Item 'Breeding stocks, dairy cattle, etc.' is included in item 'Increase in stocks'.
b) Item 'Increase in stocks' excludes enterprises of commercial farms in business services, education, health and large unincorporated units of government enterprises.
c) The estimates of 'Increase in stocks' and their components are after inventory valuation adjustment.
d) For the years prior to 1983, existing series expressed in 1980 prices have been linked to the new 1985 base year without re-weighting. As a result, for the periods before 1983, the converted sub-totals and totals are not equal to the sum of their components.
e) Land development includes transfer costs.
f) Estimates are prepared by the South African Reserve Bank. These estimates include the Republic of South Africa and Namibia.

2.11 Gross Fixed Capital Formation by Kind of Activity of Owner, ISIC Divisions, in Current Prices

Million South African rand

	1970	1975	1978	1979	1980	1981	1982	1983	1984	1985	1986	1987
					All Producers							
1 Agriculture, hunting, forestry and fishing	218	527	583	628	897	1250	1085	1006	870	945	933	982
2 Mining and quarrying	196	746	924	1305	1962	2290	2271	2173	2560	3182	4434	4870
3 Manufacturing	594	1471	2192	2821	4334	4750	4951	5300	4940	4524	4268	4754
4 Electricity, gas and water	256	619	1490	1739	1973	2309	3037	3629	4348	4877	4122	3972
5 Construction	41	160	187	214	264	338	357	397	438	446	436	480
6 Wholesale and retail trade, restaurants and hotels	241	503	563	609	715	993	1325	1383	1655	2165	1706	1981
7 Transport, storage and communication	351	1332	1313	1430	1670	2326	3152	2952	2674	3266	3042	2975
8 Finance, insurance, real estate and business services	684	1310	1576	1733	2533	3434	3956	4849	5542	5685	5895	7034
9 Community, social and personal services a	50	146	103	101	121	189	205	230	272	361	433	362
Total Industries bc	2631	6814	8931	10580	14469	17879	20339	21919	23299	25451	25269	27410
Producers of Government Services	563	1296	1411	1671	1909	2253	2353	2590	2832	3168	3729	4658
Private Non-Profit Institutions Serving Households a	...	...	...	...	...	...	...	...	...	...	...	...
Total b	3194	8110	10342	12251	16378	20132	22692	24509	26131	28619	28998	32068

a) Item 'Private non-profit institutions serving households' is included in item 'Community, social and personal services'.
b) Estimates are prepared by the South African Reserve Bank. These estimates include the Republic of South Africa and Namibia.
c) For the years prior to 1983, existing series expressed in 1980 prices have been linked to the new 1985 base year without re-weighting. As a result, for the periods before 1983, the converted sub-totals and totals are not equal to the sum of their components.

2.12 Gross Fixed Capital Formation by Kind of Activity of Owner, ISIC Divisions, in Constant Prices

Million South African rand

	1970	1975	1978	1979	1980	1981	1982	1983	1984	1985	1986	1987
					At constant prices of:1985							
					All Producers							
1 Agriculture, hunting, forestry and fishing	1511	2105	1532	1432	1851	2301	1672	1341	1045	945	766	686
2 Mining and quarrying	1356	2919	2245	2767	3682	3790	3255	2754	2980	3182	3612	3605
3 Manufacturing	3593	5056	5321	5989	8083	7865	7139	6822	5881	4524	3406	3430
4 Electricity, gas and water	1521	2069	3496	3597	3653	3830	4376	4652	5183	4877	3246	2873

South Africa

2.12 Gross Fixed Capital Formation by Kind of Activity of Owner, ISIC Divisions, in Constant Prices
(Continued)

Million South African rand

	1970	1975	1978	1979	1980	1981	1982	1983	1984	1985	1986	1987
					At constant prices of:1985							
5 Construction	238	535	447	451	498	571	525	516	530	446	336	334
6 Wholesale and retail trade, restaurants and hotels	1438	1723	1377	1308	1353	1660	1907	1763	1937	2165	1400	1428
7 Transport, storage and communication	2100	4690	3258	3155	3232	3949	4590	3802	3151	3266	2437	2076
8 Finance, insurance, real estate and business services	4319	4679	3989	3839	4892	5799	5696	6071	6366	5685	4834	5049
9 Community, social and personal services [a,b]	4019	5300	3922	3977	3894	4053	3632	3489	3507	3529	3594	3822
Total Industries [c,d]	16229	24020	21882	22759	27470	30017	29428	31210	30580	28619	23631	23303
Producers of Government Services [a]	...	...	...	...	...	...	...	...	...	...	...	...
Private Non-Profit Institutions Serving Households [b]	...	...	...	...	...	...	...	...	...	...	...	...
Total [c,d]	19942	28799	25551	26511	31135	33757	32771	31210	30580	28619	23631	23303

a) Item 'Producers of government services' is included in item 'Community, social and personal services'.
b) Item 'Private non-profit institutions serving households' is included in item 'Community, social and personal services'.
c) Estimates are prepared by the South African Reserve Bank. These estimates include the Republic of South Africa and Namibia.
d) For the years prior to 1983, existing series expressed in 1980 prices have been linked to the new 1985 base year without re-weighting. As a result, for the periods before 1983, the converted sub-totals and totals are not equal to the sum of their components.

2.17 Exports and Imports of Goods and Services, Detail

Million South African rand

	1970	1975	1978	1979	1980	1981	1982	1983	1984	1985	1986	1987
					Exports of Goods and Services							
1 Exports of merchandise, f.o.b.	2290	6193	11313	14816	19907	17919	18768	20136	24591	35925	41767	42938
2 Transport and communication	134	340	512	611	826	863	1028	835	980	1351	1772	1671
3 Insurance service charges												
4 Other commodities	89	205	323	347	396	527	593	585	817	973	631	534
5 Adjustments of merchandise exports to change-of-ownership basis	-	-	-	-	-	-	-	-	-	-	-	...
6 Direct purchases in the domestic market by non-residential households	244	650	811	950	1090	1275	1444	1607	1873	2146	2329	2883
7 Direct purchases in the domestic market by extraterritorial bodies	...	...	...	...	...	...	...	...	...	...	...	...
Total Exports of Goods and Services [a]	2757	7388	12959	16724	22219	20584	21833	23163	28261	40395	46499	48026
					Imports of Goods and Services							
1 Imports of merchandise, c.i.f.	2861	7382	8751	10667	15518	19997	19956	17462	23667	25907	28713	31250
A Imports of merchandise, f.o.b.	2582	6742	8019	9739	14159	18109	18005	15863	21471	23045	25514	28320
B Transport of services on merchandise imports	279	640	733	928	1359	1888	1951	1599	2196	2862	3199	2930
C Insurance service charges on merchandise imports												
2 Adjustments of merchandise imports to change-of-ownership basis	...	...	...	...	...	...	...	...	...	...	...	...
3 Other transport and communication	142	383	753	765	871	955	1073	1106	1293	1490	1826	2023
4 Other insurance service charges	...	...	...	...	...	...	...	...	...	...	...	...
5 Other commodities	...	...	...	...	...	...	...	...	...	...	...	...
6 Direct purchases abroad by government	...	...	...	...	...	...	...	...	...	...	...	...
7 Direct purchases abroad by resident households	162	354	362	446	570	674	785	872	971	902	1327	1544
Total Imports of Goods and Services [a]	3165	8119	9867	11878	16959	21626	21814	19440	25931	28299	31866	34817
Balance of Goods and Services	-408	-731	3092	4846	5260	-1042	19	3723	2330	12096	14633	13209
Total Imports and Balance of Goods and Services [a]	2757	7388	12959	16724	22219	20584	21833	23163	28261	40395	46499	48026

a) Estimates are prepared by the South African Reserve Bank. These estimates include the Republic of South Africa and Namibia.

Spain

General note. The preparation of national accounts statistics in Spain is undertaken by the Instituto Nacional de Estadistica, Madrid. The official estimates are published by the Instituto in 'La Contabilidad Nacional de Espana'. A detailed description of the sources and methods used for the national accounts estimation is found in 'La Contabilidad Nacional de Espana, Base, 1970' published in 1977. In this publication, the Instituto introduced a new system of national accounts, the ESA system, which corresponds closely to the present United Nations System of National Accounts (SNA). Input output tables have been published by the organizacion Sindical Espanola in 'Tabla Input-output de la Economia Espanola'. The following tables have been prepared from successive replies to the United Nations national accounts questionnaire. When the scope and coverage of the estimates differ for conceptual or statistical reasons from the definitions and classifications recommended in SNA, a footnotes is indicated to the relevant tables.

Sources and methods:

(a) Gross domestic product. Gross domestic product is estimated mainly through the production approach.

(b) Expenditure on the gross domestic product. The expenditure approach is used to estimate government final consumption expenditure, increase in stocks and exports and imports of goods and services. This approach, in combination with the commodity-flow approach is used to estimate private consumption expenditure and gross fixed capital formation. Estimates of government expenditure are derived from the government accounts and for the social security funds, from basic accounting documents. Data obtained from the family budget expenditure surveys are used together with the commodity-flow method to arrive at the final estimates of private expenditure. For the estimation of changes in stocks, information is available from the Comisaria de Abastecimiento y Transportes and the Servicio Nacional de Cereales for the agricultural sector and from stock surveys for the industrial sectors. The basic data used for the estimation of gross fixed capital formation are obtained from various concerned agencies such as Ministerio de Agricultura for agricultural investments, Servicio Sindical de Estadistica for investments in the industrial sector, Comisaria del Plan de Desarrollo for public investments, reports from other enterprises, etc. The source of information for the estimation of exports and imports of goods and services is the balance of payments which is based on custom's statistics and information on external monetary flows. Supplementary information is obtained from the accounts of insurance companies and government accounts. For the constant prices estimates, all items of GDP by expenditure type are deflated by appropriate price indexes.

(c) Cost-structure of the gross domestic product. Wage statistics and social security data provided by the Instituto and the Ministerio de Sanidad u Seguridad Social are used to estimate compensation of employees. Operating surplus is obtained as a residual except interests of financial sector, rents of ownership of dwellings and imputed rents of public buildings for which separate estimates are made. The rate of consumption of fixed capital is based on average life of the existing stocks. Estimates of indirect taxes and subsidies are derived from the information used to compile the government accounts.

(d) Gross domestic product by kind of economic activity. The table of GDP by kind of economic activity is prepared in factor values. The production approach is used to estimate the value added of most industries. The income approach is used for government services and some service industries. Both production and income approaches are used for the trade sector, restaurants and hotels. The estimates of the agricultural sector are prepared by the Ministerio de Agricultura. Separate information on the volume and value of production of each subsector is available while intermediate consumption is estimated on a comprehensive basis. Value added of the fishing sector is estimated by using a fixed percentage between costs and value added based on data provided by the Sindicato Nacional de la Pescas. Annual mining statistics are obtained from the Direccion General de Minas y Combustibles supplemented by information obtained from the Ministerio de Industria. The estimates for manufacturing are based on industrial statistics compiled by the Ministerio de Industria, Ministerio de Agricultura and Servicio Sindical de Estadistica. The data used for estimating electricity, gas, and water are provided by the Ministerio de Industria, Servicio Sindical de Estadistica and Sindicato Nacional de Agua, Gas y Electricidad, respectively. The estimates of construction are based mainly on sample surveys supplemented by information on employment and material consumption obtained from the Ministerio de Obras Publicas and the Ministerio de Vivienda. For the trade sector, only scattered information is available on employment, wages and salaries, external trade and gross margins. However, a survey of domestic trade conducted for 1964 provided a detailed knowledge of the structure of this sector. For restaurants and hotels, estimates are based on information obtained from concerned agencies. The estimates for the transport sector are based on data supplied by the RENFE (a national enterprise) and other public and private companies for railways, data from the national airlines for air transport, passenger transport surveys and national surveys of goods transported for road transport and data from concerned maritime companies for water transport. The value added of communication is estimated directly on the basis of data provided by the State monopolies. For the financial and insurance sectors, the data are provided by the concerned institutions. For ownership of dwellings, the estimates are based on the resultes of family budget expenditure surveys. The rents are imputed by ascertaining the total dwelling costs, from which the net rent is derived as income on the capital. Estimates for producers of government services are based on data obtained from the Ministerio de Hacienda. The information for health and sanitary services in the private and public sectors is obtained from government accounts supplemented by the family budget expenditure surveys and censuses of health establishments. For other services, estimates are based on the number of persons employed, derived from the population censuses and checked against the data of input-output tables. The value added of domestic services and business services is obtained from sample surveys of family budget and accounting documents, respectively. For the constant price estimates, current estimates of most industries are deflated by appropriate price indexes. For agriculture and construction, double deflation is used.

1.1 Expenditure on the Gross Domestic Product, in Current Prices

Thousand Million Spanish pesetas

		1970	1975	1978	1979	1980	1981	1982	1983	1984	1985	1986	1987
1	Government final consumption expenditure	239.1	606.5	1292.2	1574.7	1929.3	2242.2	2619.5	3090.9	3448.3	3906.6	4470.0	5141.7
2	Private final consumption expenditure	1705.0	3929.7	7290.7	8602.8	10080.4	11457.9	13143.3	14808.1	16370.0	18137.7	20435.7	22713.6
3	Gross capital formation	705.1	1717.6	2578.0	2940.9	3548.1	3638.2	4156.6	4470.2	4712.8	5240.7	6332.0	7792.1
	A Increase in stocks	21.1	126.3	27.7	98.7	179.9	-58.7	-14.4	-104.4	4.2	-34.9	208.0	406.0
	B Gross fixed capital formation	684.0	1591.3	2550.3	2842.2	3368.2	3696.9	4171.0	4574.6	4708.6	5275.6	6124.0	7386.1
	Residential buildings	...	...	...	...	934.9	1029.3	1126.1	1136.0	1144.3	1183.5	1267.5	1475.1
	Non-residential buildings	...	...	...	...	1355.5	1479.8	1665.6	1925.5	2028.8	2309.8	2683.9	3124.6
	Other construction and land improvement etc.	...	...	...	...								
	Other	...	...	...	...	1077.8	1187.8	1379.4	1513.1	1535.5	1782.3	2172.6	2786.3
4	Exports of goods and services	348.4	816.0	1710.8	1975.2	2409.8	3079.1	3672.2	4725.6	5943.5	6518.7	6475.9	7023.9
5	Less: Imports of goods and services	373.3	1046.7	1621.2	1935.9	2758.5	3428.3	4024.3	4860.1	5363.3	5914.8	5766.1	6956.7
	Statistical discrepancy	-0.1	-	-	-	-	-0.1	-	-	-	-0.1	-	-0.1
	Equals: Gross Domestic Product	2624.2	6023.1	11250.5	13157.7	15209.1	16989.0	19567.3	22234.7	25111.3	27888.8	31947.5	35714.5

1.2 Expenditure on the Gross Domestic Product, in Constant Prices

Thousand Million Spanish pesetas

		1970	1975	1978	1979	1980	1981	1982	1983	1984	1985	1986	1987
		At constant prices of:1980											
1	Government final consumption expenditure	1129.8	1517.1	1777.7	1851.9	1929.3	1965.5	2061.0	2141.7	2203.3	2305.5	2437.5	2649.3
2	Private final consumption expenditure	6980.6	9152.3	9898.5	10023.1	10080.4	10020.1	10038.5	10072.8	10034.1	10273.3	10644.1	11224.5
3	Gross capital formation	2986.2	3895.2	3535.0	3461.7	3548.1	3215.5	3265.1	3132.6	3009.6	3112.0	3570.7	4187.2
	A Increase in stocks	104.5	234.5	35.9	115.8	179.9	-43.1	-9.9	-59.1	2.8	-19.4	126.5	239.6
	B Gross fixed capital formation	2881.7	3660.7	3499.1	3345.9	3368.2	3258.6	3275.0	3191.7	3006.8	3131.4	3444.2	3947.6

Spain

1.2 Expenditure on the Gross Domestic Product, in Constant Prices
(Continued)

Thousand Million Spanish pesetas

	1970	1975	1978	1979	1980	1981	1982	1983	1984	1985	1986	1987
					At constant prices of:1980							
Residential buildings	...	...	...	...	934.9	919.0	892.4	835.3	782.6	770.9	786.3	831.9
Non-residential buildings	...	...	...	...	1355.5	1295.7	1314.1	1335.7	1280.8	1333.8	1469.7	1642.9
Other construction and land improvement etc.	...	...	...	...								
Other	...	...	...	...	1077.8	1043.9	1068.6	1020.8	943.4	1026.7	1188.2	1472.8
4 Exports of goods and services	1219.8	1712.3	2230.3	2356.2	2409.8	2612.0	2736.7	3014.4	3367.9	3460.4	3505.0	3710.7
5 Less: Imports of goods and services	1494.0	2336.0	2397.4	2669.8	2758.5	2641.7	2745.4	2728.5	2700.5	2868.4	3341.0	4023.0
Statistical discrepancy	-0.1	-	-0.1	-	-	-0.1	-	0.2	0.1	-	0.1	-
Equals: Gross Domestic Product	10822.3	13940.9	15044.0	15023.1	15209.1	15171.3	15355.9	15633.2	15914.5	16282.8	16816.4	17748.7

1.3 Cost Components of the Gross Domestic Product

Thousand Million Spanish pesetas

	1970	1975	1978	1979	1980	1981	1982	1983	1984	1985	1986	1987
1 Indirect taxes, net	181.6	320.9	479.8	601.5	694.4	908.6	1033.3	1324.3	1567.8	1948.2	2806.4	3080.7
A Indirect taxes	204.6	389.5	693.4	824.0	1009.5	1243.0	1522.3	1900.1	2271.4	2686.9	3508.1	3816.9
B Less: Subsidies	23.0	68.6	213.6	222.5	315.1	334.4	489.0	575.8	703.6	738.7	701.7	736.2
2 Consumption of fixed capital	265.8	599.2	1105.7	1351.0	1615.4	1930.6	2253.7	2637.9	3029.6	3349.2	3626.5	3943.3
3 Compensation of employees paid by resident producers to:	1186.0	3077.0	5892.0	6870.0	7784.0	8714.9	9853.2	11132.4	11876.2	12891.0	14600.4	16354.4
A Resident households	1186.0	3076.9	5891.9	6869.8	7783.3	8714.6	9852.8	11132.0	11875.6	12890.1	14598.9	16352.9
B Rest of the world	-	0.1	0.1	0.2	0.6	0.3	0.4	0.4	0.5	0.9	1.4	1.5
4 Operating surplus	990.8	2026.0	3773.0	4335.1	5115.4	5434.9	6427.1	7140.0	8637.7	9700.4	10914.3	12336.1
Statistical discrepancy	-	-	-	0.1	-0.1	-	-	0.1	-	-	-0.1	-
Equals: Gross Domestic Product	2624.2	6023.1	11250.5	13157.7	15209.1	16989.0	19567.3	22234.7	25111.3	27888.8	31947.5	35714.5

1.4 General Government Current Receipts and Disbursements

Thousand Million Spanish pesetas

	1970	1975	1978	1979	1980	1981	1982	1983	1984	1985	1986	1987
					Receipts							
1 Operating surplus	...	...	...	...	...	...	...	...	...	...	...	...
2 Property and entrepreneurial income	...	...	...	...	152.4	222.5	288.9	307.1	251.7	324.7	332.4	...
3 Taxes, fees and contributions	...	...	...	...	3879.6	4535.4	5236.3	6435.5	7368.0	8405.9	9844.0	...
A Indirect taxes	...	...	...	...	1009.5	1243.0	1522.3	1900.1	2271.4	2686.9	3411.6	...
B Direct taxes [a]	...	...	...	...	1059.0	1221.1	1332.6	1748.1	2085.6	2378.4	2638.0	...
C Social security contributions	...	...	...	...	1811.1	2071.3	2381.4	2787.3	3011.0	3340.6	3794.4	...
D Compulsory fees, fines and penalties [a]	...	...	...	...	...	...	...	...	...	...	...	...
4 Other current transfers	...	...	...	...	489.1	536.3	611.8	696.0	729.7	884.0	1013.0	...
Total Current Receipts of General Government	...	...	...	...	4521.1	5294.2	6137.0	7438.6	8349.4	9614.6	11189.4	...
					Disbursements							
1 Government final consumption expenditure	...	...	...	...	1929.3	2242.2	2619.5	3090.9	3448.3	3906.6	4470.0	...
A Compensation of employees	...	...	...	...	1488.2	1747.2	2000.1	2364.9	2634.4	2975.1	3339.0	...
B Consumption of fixed capital	...	...	...	...	77.1	89.7	105.6	126.6	148.1	168.8	194.5	...
C Purchases of goods and services, net	...	...	...	...	364.0	405.3	513.8	599.5	665.8	762.6	936.6	...
D Less: Own account fixed capital formation	...	...	...	...	...	...	...	...	...	...	...	...
E Indirect taxes paid, net	...	...	...	...	...	...	...	...	...	...	...	...
2 Property income	...	...	...	...	110.9	135.6	190.5	290.4	509.3	900.0	1201.9	...
3 Subsidies	...	...	...	...	315.1	334.4	489.0	575.8	703.6	738.7	663.8	...
4 Other current transfers	...	...	...	...	2156.3	2661.2	3045.6	3596.9	4015.9	4627.0	5202.2	...
A Social security benefits	...	...	...	...	1926.3	2401.6	2747.5	3232.1	3642.9	4151.0	4655.4	...
B Social assistance grants	...	...	...	...	...	...	...	...	...	...	...	...
C Other	...	...	...	...	230.0	259.6	298.2	364.8	372.9	476.0	546.8	...
5 Net saving	...	...	...	...	9.6	-79.1	-207.5	-115.4	-327.7	-557.7	-348.6	...
Total Current Disbursements and Net Saving of General Government	...	...	...	...	4521.2	5294.3	6137.1	7438.6	8349.4	9614.6	11189.3	...

a) Item 'Fees, fines and penalties' is included in item 'Direct taxes'.

Spain

1.5 Current Income and Outlay of Corporate and Quasi-Corporate Enterprises, Summary

Thousand Million Spanish pesetas

	1970	1975	1978	1979	1980	1981	1982	1983	1984	1985	1986	1987
Receipts												
1 Operating surplus	...	...	...	...	1558.4	1484.4	1755.9	1812.2	2383.0	2695.5	3167.4	...
2 Property and entrepreneurial income received	...	...	...	...	1925.2	2656.8	3485.9	3992.8	4939.9	5200.8	5597.0	...
3 Current transfers	...	...	...	...	376.9	443.9	520.7	634.4	659.1	754.1	1012.0	...
Total Current Receipts	...	...	...	...	3860.5	4585.1	5762.5	6439.4	7982.0	8650.4	9776.4	...
Disbursements												
1 Property and entrepreneurial income	...	...	...	...	2485.7	3465.5	4393.8	4923.5	5710.0	5866.4	6067.5	...
2 Direct taxes and other current payments to general government	...	...	...	...	259.4	295.2	351.1	434.1	481.5	556.0	685.9	...
3 Other current transfers	...	...	...	...	449.9	539.3	675.1	800.6	814.6	937.3	1174.8	...
Statistical discrepancy	...	...	...	...	10.4	2.2	1.5	-	25.3	47.0	132.0	...
4 Net saving	...	...	...	...	655.1	282.9	341.0	281.2	950.5	1243.7	1716.2	...
Total Current Disbursements and Net Saving	...	...	...	...	3860.5	4585.1	5762.5	6439.4	7981.9	8650.4	9776.4	...

1.6 Current Income and Outlay of Households and Non-Profit Institutions

Thousand Million Spanish pesetas

	1970	1975	1978	1979	1980	1981	1982	1983	1984	1985	1986	1987
Receipts												
1 Compensation of employees	...	...	...	...	7797.5	8734.4	9877.4	11162.3	11907.5	12922.5	14637.2	...
A From resident producers	...	...	...	...	7783.3	8714.6	9852.8	11132.0	11875.6	12890.1	14598.9	...
B From rest of the world	...	...	...	...	14.2	19.8	24.6	30.3	31.8	32.4	38.3	...
2 Operating surplus of private unincorporated enterprises	...	...	...	...	3557.0	3950.5	4671.3	5327.8	6254.8	7004.9	7746.9	...
3 Property and entrepreneurial income	...	...	...	...	782.4	1077.1	1192.9	1324.0	1614.8	1922.8	2081.9	...
4 Current transfers	...	...	...	...	2592.5	3181.3	3667.6	4279.5	4726.9	5405.8	6123.9	...
A Social security benefits	...	...	...	...	2126.0	2639.2	3012.2	3509.2	3937.0	4480.1	5026.6	...
B Social assistance grants	...	...	...	...	...	...	...	...	...	...	...	...
C Other	...	...	...	...	466.5	542.1	655.4	770.3	790.0	925.7	1097.3	...
Statistical discrepancy	...	...	...	...	10.4	2.2	1.5	-	25.3	47.0	132.0	...
Total Current Receipts	...	...	...	...	14739.8	16945.5	19410.7	22093.6	24529.3	27303.0	30721.9	...
Disbursements												
1 Private final consumption expenditure	...	...	...	...	10080.4	11457.9	13143.3	14808.1	16370.0	18137.7	20435.7	...
2 Property income	...	...	...	...	406.9	612.9	692.4	798.2	1015.2	1044.0	1076.9	...
3 Direct taxes and other current transfers n.e.c. to general government	...	...	...	...	2683.3	3070.3	3439.1	4152.6	4661.5	5207.2	5807.1	...
A Social security contributions	...	...	...	...	1883.7	2144.4	2457.6	2838.7	3057.4	3384.8	3855.0	...
B Direct taxes	...	...	...	...	799.6	925.9	981.5	1313.9	1604.0	1822.4	1952.1	...
C Fees, fines and penalties	...	...	...	...	...	...	...	...	...	...	...	...
4 Other current transfers	...	...	...	...	665.3	758.5	853.6	1006.3	1067.4	1248.9	1534.1	...
5 Net saving	...	...	...	...	903.7	1045.9	1282.4	1328.5	1415.1	1665.3	1868.1	...
Total Current Disbursements and Net Saving	...	...	...	...	14739.6	16945.5	19410.8	22093.7	24529.2	27303.1	30721.9	...

1.7 External Transactions on Current Account, Summary

Thousand Million Spanish pesetas

	1970	1975	1978	1979	1980	1981	1982	1983	1984	1985	1986	1987
Payments to the Rest of the World												
1 Imports of goods and services	...	...	...	...	2758.5	3428.3	4024.3	4860.1	5363.3	5914.8	5766.1	6956.7
A Imports of merchandise c.i.f.	...	...	...	...	2480.7	3045.6	3561.1	4300.4	4753.3	5205.2	5035.2	6127.5
B Other	...	...	...	...	277.8	382.7	463.3	559.6	610.0	709.6	731.0	829.2
2 Factor income to the rest of the world	...	...	...	...	256.9	429.3	496.3	552.4	641.5	645.2	543.1	544.6

Spain

1.7 External Transactions on Current Account, Summary
(Continued)

Thousand Million Spanish pesetas

	1970	1975	1978	1979	1980	1981	1982	1983	1984	1985	1986	1987
A Compensation of employees	...	...	...	...	0.6	0.3	0.4	0.4	0.5	0.9	1.4	1.5
B Property and entrepreneurial income	...	...	...	...	256.3	428.9	495.9	552.1	641.0	644.3	541.6	543.1
3 Current transfers to the rest of the world	...	...	...	...	34.9	44.9	51.1	71.0	69.3	113.5	232.0	273.5
A Indirect taxes to supranational organizations	...	...	...	...	...	...	...	...	...	...	96.5	134.9
B Other current transfers	...	...	...	...	34.9	44.9	51.1	71.0	69.3	113.5	135.5	138.6
4 Surplus of the nation on current transactions	...	...	...	...	-364.3	-458.0	-487.1	-338.0	354.8	459.9	530.3	40.2
Payments to the Rest of the World and Surplus of the Nation on Current Transactions	...	...	...	...	2686.0	3444.5	4084.6	5145.5	6428.9	7133.4	7071.5	7815.0

Receipts From The Rest of the World

	1970	1975	1978	1979	1980	1981	1982	1983	1984	1985	1986	1987
1 Exports of goods and services	...	...	...	...	2409.8	3079.1	3672.2	4725.6	5943.5	6518.7	6475.9	7023.9
A Exports of merchandise f.o.b.	...	...	...	...	1531.6	1976.2	2372.2	3066.8	3936.1	4296.2	3957.9	4305.9
B Other	...	...	...	...	878.2	1102.8	1300.0	1658.7	2007.4	2222.5	2518.0	2718.0
2 Factor income from rest of the world	...	...	...	...	127.0	191.1	211.6	194.3	244.7	314.7	244.9	237.2
A Compensation of employees	...	...	...	...	14.2	19.8	24.6	30.3	31.8	32.4	38.3	42.0
B Property and entrepreneurial income	...	...	...	...	112.8	171.3	187.0	163.9	212.9	282.3	206.6	195.2
3 Current transfers from rest of the world	...	...	...	...	149.3	174.2	200.6	225.7	240.7	300.0	350.6	554.0
A Subsidies from supranational organisations	...	...	...	...	...	...	...	...	...	...	37.9	123.5
B Other current transfers	...	...	...	...	149.3	174.2	200.6	225.7	240.7	300.0	312.7	430.5
Receipts from the Rest of the World on Current Transactions	...	...	...	...	2686.1	3444.4	4084.4	5145.6	6428.9	7133.4	7071.4	7815.1

1.8 Capital Transactions of The Nation, Summary

Thousand Million Spanish pesetas

	1970	1975	1978	1979	1980	1981	1982	1983	1984	1985	1986	1987

Finance of Gross Capital Formation

	1970	1975	1978	1979	1980	1981	1982	1983	1984	1985	1986	1987
Gross saving	710.1	1540.4	2692.8	3002.9	3183.8	3180.2	3669.5	4132.2	5067.6	5700.5	6862.3	7832.2
1 Consumption of fixed capital	265.8	599.2	1105.7	1351.0	1615.4	1930.6	2253.7	2637.9	3029.6	3349.2	3626.5	3943.3
A General government	...	...	...	...	77.1	89.7	105.6	126.6	148.1	168.8	194.5	...
B Corporate and quasi-corporate enterprises	...	...	...	...	1188.0	1415.4	1642.5	1932.4	2231.3	2489.0	2697.6	...
C Other	...	...	...	...	350.2	425.5	505.6	578.9	650.3	691.4	734.3	...
2 Net saving	444.3	941.2	1587.1	1651.9	1568.4	1249.6	1415.8	1494.3	2038.0	2351.3	3235.8	3888.9
A General government	...	...	...	...	9.6	-79.1	-207.5	-115.4	-327.7	-557.7	-348.6	...
B Corporate and quasi-corporate enterprises	...	...	...	...	655.1	282.9	341.0	281.2	950.5	1243.7	1716.2	...
C Other	...	...	...	...	903.7	1045.9	1282.4	1328.5	1415.1	1665.3	1868.1	...
Less: Surplus of the nation on current transactions	5.0	-177.2	114.8	62.0	-364.3	-458.0	-487.1	-338.0	354.8	459.9	530.3	40.2
Statistical discrepancy	-	-	-	-	-	-	-	-	-	0.1	-	-
Finance of Gross Capital Formation	705.1	1717.6	2578.0	2940.9	3548.1	3638.2	4156.6	4470.2	4712.8	5240.7	6332.0	7792.0

Gross Capital Formation

	1970	1975	1978	1979	1980	1981	1982	1983	1984	1985	1986	1987
Increase in stocks	21.1	126.3	27.7	98.7	179.9	-58.7	-14.4	-104.4	4.2	-34.9	208.0	406.0
Gross fixed capital formation	684.0	1591.3	2550.3	2842.2	3368.2	3696.9	4171.0	4574.6	4708.6	5275.6	6124.0	7386.1
Gross Capital Formation	705.1	1717.6	2578.0	2940.9	3548.1	3638.2	4156.6	4470.2	4712.8	5240.7	6332.0	7792.1

1.9 Gross Domestic Product by Institutional Sectors of Origin

Thousand Million Spanish pesetas

	1970	1975	1978	1979	1980	1981	1982	1983	1984	1985	1986	1987

Domestic Factor Incomes Originating

	1970	1975	1978	1979	1980	1981	1982	1983	1984	1985	1986	1987
1 General government	...	...	...	...	1488.2	1747.2	2000.1	2364.9	2634.4	2975.1	3339.0	...
2 Corporate and quasi-corporate enterprises	...	...	...	...	11411.1	12402.7	14280.2	15907.5	17879.5	19616.3	22175.7	...
A Non-financial	...	...	...	...	11116.6	12204.5	14160.4	15935.4	17838.0	19590.7	22190.2	...
B Financial	...	...	...	...	294.6	198.1	119.8	-27.9	41.5	25.6	-14.5	...

Spain

1.9 Gross Domestic Product by Institutional Sectors of Origin
(Continued)

Thousand Million Spanish pesetas

	1970	1975	1978	1979	1980	1981	1982	1983	1984	1985	1986	1987
3 Households and private unincorporated enterprises	...	...	...	...	...	...	...	...	...	...	...	...
4 Non-profit institutions serving households	...	...	...	...	...	...	...	...	...	...	...	...
Subtotal: Domestic Factor Incomes	2176.8	5103.0	9665.0	11205.1	12899.4	14149.8	16280.3	18272.4	20513.9	22591.4	25514.7	28690.5
Indirect taxes, net	181.6	320.9	479.8	601.5	694.4	908.6	1033.3	1324.3	1567.8	1948.2	2806.4	3080.7
A Indirect taxes	204.6	389.5	693.4	824.0	1009.5	1243.0	1522.3	1900.1	2271.4	2686.9	3508.1	3816.9
B Less: Subsidies	23.0	68.6	213.6	222.5	315.1	334.4	489.0	575.8	703.6	738.7	701.7	736.2
Consumption of fixed capital	265.8	599.2	1105.7	1351.0	1615.4	1930.6	2253.7	2637.9	3029.6	3349.2	3626.5	3943.3
Statistical discrepancy	-	-	-	0.1	-0.1	-	-	0.1	-	-	-0.1	-
Gross Domestic Product	2624.2	6023.1	11250.5	13157.7	15209.1	16989.0	19567.3	22234.7	25111.3	27888.8	31947.5	35714.5

1.10 Gross Domestic Product by Kind of Activity, in Current Prices

Thousand Million Spanish pesetas

	1970	1975	1978	1979	1980	1981	1982	1983	1984	1985	1986	1987
1 Agriculture, hunting, forestry and fishing	...	...	...	...	1073.4	1038.0	1225.9	1370.2	1642.7	1744.4	1814.5	1941.5
2 Mining and quarrying	...	...	...	...	4284.3	4762.1	5326.2	6149.5	6903.6	7631.9	9301.6	...
3 Manufacturing	...	...	...	...								...
4 Electricity, gas and water	...	...	...	...	309.0	426.7	562.2	591.7	765.8	860.9	1020.1	...
5 Construction	...	...	...	...	1283.7	1328.6	1527.9	1631.7	1635.6	1806.1	2226.6	2860.0
6 Wholesale and retail trade, restaurants and hotels	...	...	...	...	2772.8	3192.0	3717.6	4329.8	5019.7	5665.1	6600.1	...
7 Transport, storage and communication	...	...	...	...	876.7	1036.2	1167.6	1362.3	1528.8	1661.9	1781.6	...
8 Finance, insurance, real estate and business services [a]	...	...	...	...	2010.6	2298.5	2547.8	2724.6	3376.5	3664.2	3997.5	...
9 Community, social and personal services [ab]	...	...	...	...	1297.5	1528.1	1895.7	2173.9	2460.6	2714.3	3054.7	...
Total, Industries	...	...	...	...	13908.0	15610.3	17970.8	20333.7	23333.3	25748.9	29796.6	33349.0
Producers of Government Services	...	...	...	...	1565.3	1836.8	2105.6	2491.5	2782.5	3144.0	3533.5	3932.1
Other Producers [b]	...	...	...	...	...	...	...	...	...	...	...	...
Subtotal	...	...	...	...	15473.4	17447.1	20076.4	22825.2	26115.8	28892.8	33330.0	37281.1
Less: Imputed bank service charge	...	...	...	...	535.8	756.3	889.1	1043.0	1478.0	1560.4	1832.7	2129.0
Plus: Import duties	...	...	...	...	271.5	298.2	379.9	452.5	473.5	556.4	450.1	562.4
Plus: Value added tax	...	...	...	...	...	...	...	...	...	...	...	...
Plus: Other adjustments	...	...	...	...	0.1	-	0.1	-	-	-0.1	-	-
Equals: Gross Domestic Product	...	...	...	...	15209.1	16989.0	19567.3	22234.7	25111.3	27888.8	31947.5	35714.5

a) Business services and real estate except dwellings are included in item 'Community, social and personal services'.
b) Item 'Other producers' is included in item 'Community, social and personal services'.

1.11 Gross Domestic Product by Kind of Activity, in Constant Prices

Thousand Million Spanish pesetas

	1970	1975	1978	1979	1980	1981	1982	1983	1984	1985	1986	1987
					At constant prices of:1980							
1 Agriculture, hunting, forestry and fishing	...	...	...	...	1073.4	971.7	956.9	1016.6	1104.1	1138.4	1034.9	1134.2
2 Mining and quarrying	...	...	...	...	4284.3	4278.8	4214.2	4287.3	4303.9	4384.1	4617.5	...
3 Manufacturing	...	...	...	...								...
4 Electricity, gas and water	...	...	...	...	309.0	303.6	312.2	312.5	345.8	362.9	396.0	...
5 Construction	...	...	...	...	1283.7	1281.1	1315.3	1316.6	1235.5	1263.2	1338.1	1477.5
6 Wholesale and retail trade, restaurants and hotels	...	...	...	...	2772.8	2766.5	2804.8	2854.1	2928.4	2985.5	3114.9	...
7 Transport, storage and communication	...	...	...	...	876.7	900.3	906.5	930.1	956.0	991.5	1008.8	...
8 Finance, insurance, real estate and business services [a]	...	...	...	...	2010.6	2034.8	2065.9	2077.6	2142.5	2186.6	2214.7	...
9 Community, social and personal services [ab]	...	...	...	...	1297.5	1309.8	1378.8	1394.4	1413.7	1415.2	1485.0	...
Total, Industries	...	...	...	...	13908.0	13846.7	13954.7	14189.3	14429.9	14727.5	15209.8	16071.5
Producers of Government Services	...	...	...	...	1565.3	1615.5	1683.0	1744.4	1798.5	1874.0	1950.6	2047.3

Spain

1.11 Gross Domestic Product by Kind of Activity, in Constant Prices
(Continued)

Thousand Million Spanish pesetas

	1970	1975	1978	1979	1980	1981	1982	1983	1984	1985	1986	1987
					At constant prices of:1980							
Other Producers [b]	...	...	...	...	...	...	...	...	...	...	...	...
Subtotal	...	...	...	...	15473.4	15462.1	15637.7	15933.7	16228.3	16601.5	17160.5	18118.8
Less: Imputed bank service charge	...	...	...	...	535.8	540.6	553.1	564.1	574.8	587.5	639.7	691.6
Plus: Import duties	...	...	...	...	271.5	249.8	271.3	263.6	261.0	268.8	295.7	321.4
Plus: Value added tax	...	...	...	...	...	...	...	...	...	...	...	...
Plus: Other adjustments	...	...	...	...	0.1	-0.1	-	-	-0.1	-	-	0.1
Equals: Gross Domestic Product	...	...	...	...	15209.1	15171.3	15355.9	15633.2	15914.5	16282.8	16816.4	17748.7

a) Business services and real estate except dwellings are included in item 'Community, social and personal services'.
b) Item 'Other producers' is included in item 'Community, social and personal services'.

1.12 Relations Among National Accounting Aggregates

Thousand Million Spanish pesetas

	1970	1975	1978	1979	1980	1981	1982	1983	1984	1985	1986	1987
Gross Domestic Product	2624.2	6023.1	11250.5	13157.7	15209.1	16989.0	19567.3	22234.7	25111.3	27888.8	31947.5	35714.5
Plus: Net factor income from the rest of the world	-17.1	-18.5	-87.4	-78.2	-130.0	-238.1	-284.7	-358.2	-396.9	-330.5	-298.1	-307.4
Factor income from the rest of the world	4.6	35.5	55.3	91.1	127.0	191.1	211.6	194.3	244.7	314.7	244.9	237.2
Less: Factor income to the rest of the world	21.7	54.0	142.7	169.3	256.9	429.3	496.3	552.4	641.5	645.2	543.1	544.6
Equals: Gross National Product	2607.1	6004.6	11163.2	13079.5	15079.1	16750.9	19282.7	21876.5	24714.5	27558.3	31649.4	35407.1
Less: Consumption of fixed capital	265.8	599.2	1105.7	1351.0	1615.4	1930.6	2253.7	2637.9	3029.6	3349.2	3626.5	3943.3
Equals: National Income	2341.3	5405.4	10057.5	11728.5	13463.8	14820.3	17029.0	19238.6	21684.9	24209.1	28022.9	31463.8
Plus: Net current transfers from the rest of the world	47.1	72.1	112.6	100.9	114.4	129.4	149.6	154.7	171.4	186.5	118.7	280.4
Current transfers from the rest of the world	50.5	90.0	156.8	159.0	149.3	174.2	200.6	225.7	240.7	300.0	350.6	553.9
Less: Current transfers to the rest of the world	3.5	18.1	44.3	58.0	34.9	44.9	51.1	71.0	69.3	113.5	231.9	273.5
Equals: National Disposable Income	2388.4	5477.5	10170.1	11829.4	13578.2	14949.7	17178.6	19393.3	21856.3	24395.6	28141.6	31744.2
Less: Final consumption	1944.1	4536.2	8582.9	10177.5	12009.8	13700.0	15762.7	17899.0	19818.3	22044.3	24905.7	27855.3
Equals: Net Saving	444.3	941.2	1587.1	1651.9	1568.4	1249.6	1415.8	1494.3	2038.0	2351.3	3235.8	3888.9
Less: Surplus of the nation on current transactions	5.0	-177.2	114.8	62.0	-364.3	-458.0	-487.1	-338.0	354.8	459.9	530.3	40.2
Equals: Net Capital Formation	439.3	1118.4	1472.3	1589.9	1932.7	1707.6	1903.0	1832.2	1683.2	1891.4	2705.5	3848.7

2.5 Private Final Consumption Expenditure by Type and Purpose, in Current Prices

Thousand Million Spanish pesetas

	1970	1975	1978	1979	1980	1981	1982	1983	1984	1985	1986	1987
				Final Consumption Expenditure of Resident Households								
1 Food, beverages and tobacco	...	...	...	...	2918.7	3296.4	3804.2	4231.9	4795.1	5308.9	5951.3	6332.2
A Food	...	...	...	...	2620.6	2936.8	3404.9	3788.1	4299.9	4788.8	...	...
B Non-alcoholic beverages	...	...	...	...	44.6	50.1	56.2	62.8	64.8	74.8	...	...
C Alcoholic beverages	...	...	...	...	131.2	144.0	159.4	174.0	198.8	209.1	...	...
D Tobacco	...	...	...	...	122.3	165.6	183.6	206.9	231.6	236.2	...	...
2 Clothing and footwear	...	...	...	...	839.8	943.6	1040.7	1154.0	1239.0	1417.9	1607.9	1800.8
3 Gross rent, fuel and power	...	...	...	...	1716.5	1993.2	2290.1	2553.8	2833.1	3044.1	3281.5	3465.3
A Fuel and power	...	...	...	...	246.6	344.0	400.1	459.7	552.5	622.2	...	...
B Other	...	...	...	...	1469.9	1649.2	1890.0	2094.1	2280.5	2421.9	...	...
4 Furniture, furnishings and household equipment and operation	...	...	...	...	810.5	888.2	989.5	1123.8	1228.1	1349.1	1548.7	1723.4
5 Medical care and health expenses	...	...	...	...	394.4	447.7	528.9	591.5	627.5	697.2	773.1	864.4
6 Transport and communication	...	...	...	...	1409.0	1611.7	1824.7	2158.2	2395.7	2635.1	3006.7	3599.0
A Personal transport equipment	...	...	...	...	326.9	309.9	371.8	430.6	449.1	547.5	...	...
B Other	...	...	...	...	1082.1	1301.9	1452.9	1727.6	1946.6	2087.7	...	...
7 Recreational, entertainment, education and cultural services	...	...	...	...	708.4	813.6	943.8	1076.1	1141.7	1275.3	1476.7	1600.8
A Education	...	...	...	...	199.4	222.5	255.0	289.2	321.6	352.1	...	...
B Other	...	...	...	...	509.0	591.1	688.8	786.9	820.2	923.1	...	...
8 Miscellaneous goods and services	...	...	...	...	1697.0	1996.8	2395.5	2778.7	3220.0	3605.0	4239.7	4912.9
A Personal care	...	...	...	...	140.6	158.6	179.7	206.1	229.0	267.4	...	...
B Expenditures in restaurants, cafes and hotels	...	...	...	...	1178.8	1422.9	1755.8	2052.5	2409.7	2703.7	...	...

Spain

2.5 Private Final Consumption Expenditure by Type and Purpose, in Current Prices
(Continued)

Thousand Million Spanish pesetas

	1970	1975	1978	1979	1980	1981	1982	1983	1984	1985	1986	1987
C Other	...	...	...	...	377.6	415.4	460.0	520.1	581.3	633.9	204.5	224.0
Total Final Consumption Expenditure in the Domestic Market by Households, of which	...	...	...	...	10494.3	11991.3	13817.4	15668.1	17480.1	19332.5	21885.7	24298.7
Plus: Direct purchases abroad by resident households	...	...	...	...	94.7	103.6	123.4	142.8	153.6	193.5	235.8	271.7
Less: Direct purchases in the domestic market by non-resident households	...	...	...	...	508.5	637.0	797.6	1002.8	1263.7	1388.3	1685.8	1856.9
Equals: Final Consumption Expenditure of Resident Households [a]	...	...	...	...	10080.4	11457.9	13143.3	14808.1	16370.0	18137.7	20435.7	22713.6

Final Consumption Expenditure of Private Non-profit Institutions Serving Households

| Equals: Final Consumption Expenditure of Private Non-profit Organisations Serving Households | ... | ... | ... | ... | ... | ... | ... | ... | ... | ... | ... | ... |
| Private Final Consumption Expenditure | ... | ... | ... | ... | 10080.4 | 11457.9 | 13143.3 | 14808.1 | 16370.0 | 18137.7 | 20435.7 | 22713.6 |

a) Item 'Final consumption expenditure of resident households' includes consumption expenditure of private non-profit institutions serving households.

2.6 Private Final Consumption Expenditure by Type and Purpose, in Constant Prices

Thousand Million Spanish pesetas

	1970	1975	1978	1979	1980	1981	1982	1983	1984	1985	1986	1987

At constant prices of: 1980

Final Consumption Expenditure of Resident Households

	1970	1975	1978	1979	1980	1981	1982	1983	1984	1985	1986	1987
1 Food, beverages and tobacco	...	...	...	...	2918.7	2901.3	2900.3	2915.7	2927.3	2960.9	2999.9	3038.2
A Food	...	...	...	...	2620.6	2601.7	2599.8	2617.8	2619.9	2663.6	...	...
B Non-alcoholic beverages	...	...	...	...	44.6	42.8	42.0	41.5	39.5	41.4	...	...
C Alcoholic beverages	...	...	...	...	131.2	136.9	136.9	134.2	139.5	133.9	...	...
D Tobacco	...	...	...	...	122.3	119.8	121.6	122.2	128.4	121.9	...	...
2 Clothing and footwear	...	...	...	...	839.8	834.6	815.9	808.2	780.1	803.8	826.1	847.5
3 Gross rent, fuel and power	...	...	...	...	1716.5	1732.6	1752.7	1786.2	1825.9	1858.5	1893.6	1934.4
A Fuel and power	...	...	...	...	246.6	243.6	241.4	246.3	259.8	267.3	...	...
B Other	...	...	...	...	1469.9	1489.0	1511.2	1539.9	1566.1	1591.2	...	...
4 Furniture, furnishings and household equipment and operation	...	...	...	...	810.5	793.6	776.6	782.6	777.1	784.9	819.8	873.0
5 Medical care and health expenses	...	...	...	...	394.4	388.3	389.5	381.7	359.6	366.3	377.6	398.1
6 Transport and communication	...	...	...	...	1409.0	1374.1	1398.8	1424.2	1438.8	1500.2	1633.0	1856.5
A Personal transport equipment	...	...	...	...	326.9	287.6	304.9	314.0	296.8	326.8	...	...
B Other	...	...	...	...	1082.1	1086.4	1093.9	1110.2	1142.0	1173.4	...	...
7 Recreational, entertainment, education and cultural services	...	...	...	...	708.4	718.1	732.1	748.2	724.5	740.1	791.5	820.3
A Education	...	...	...	...	199.4	198.2	199.0	198.2	198.2	196.8	...	...
B Other	...	...	...	...	509.0	520.0	533.1	550.0	526.3	543.3	...	...
8 Miscellaneous goods and services	...	...	...	...	1697.0	1742.8	1768.7	1779.9	1832.3	1878.8	1970.7	2142.7
A Personal care	...	...	...	...	140.6	139.2	140.6	136.4	137.7	146.0	...	...
B Expenditures in restaurants, cafes and hotels	...	...	...	...	1178.8	1237.8	1277.2	1296.4	1348.3	1376.6	...	...
C Other	...	...	...	...	377.6	365.9	350.9	347.1	346.3	356.2	106.0	110.2
Total Final Consumption Expenditure in the Domestic Market by Households, of which	...	...	...	...	10494.3	10485.6	10534.5	10626.7	10665.5	10893.4	11312.2	11910.7
Plus: Direct purchases abroad by resident households	...	...	...	...	94.7	85.6	90.0	83.6	84.2	97.4	113.0	126.5
Less: Direct purchases in the domestic market by non-resident households	...	...	...	...	508.5	551.0	586.0	637.5	715.6	717.5	781.2	812.7
Equals: Final Consumption Expenditure of Resident Households [a]	...	...	...	...	10080.4	10020.1	10038.5	10072.8	10034.1	10273.3	10644.1	11224.5

Final Consumption Expenditure of Private Non-profit Institutions Serving Households

| Equals: Final Consumption Expenditure of Private Non-profit Organisations Serving Households | ... | ... | ... | ... | ... | ... | ... | ... | ... | ... | ... | ... |
| Private Final Consumption Expenditure | ... | ... | ... | ... | 10080.4 | 10020.1 | 10038.5 | 10072.8 | 10034.1 | 10273.3 | 10644.1 | 11224.5 |

a) Item 'Final consumption expenditure of resident households' includes consumption expenditure of private non-profit institutions serving households.

Spain

2.17 Exports and Imports of Goods and Services, Detail

Thousand Million Spanish pesetas

	1970	1975	1978	1979	1980	1981	1982	1983	1984	1985	1986	1987
Exports of Goods and Services												
1 Exports of merchandise, f.o.b.	...	...	...	...	1531.6	1976.2	2372.2	3066.8	3936.1	4296.2	3957.9	4305.9
2 Transport and communication [a]	...	...	...	...	254.3	309.1	335.9	434.4	483.8	543.1	500.2	538.4
3 Insurance service charges	...	...	...	...	26.1	30.2	31.3	33.7	44.8	47.0	43.1	62.0
4 Other commodities [a]	...	...	...	...	89.2	126.5	135.3	187.9	215.2	244.1	289.0	260.8
5 Adjustments of merchandise exports to change-of-ownership basis	...	...	...	...	...	...	...	...	...	...	...	...
6 Direct purchases in the domestic market by non-residential households	...	...	...	...	508.5	637.0	797.6	1002.8	1263.7	1388.3	1685.8	1856.9
7 Direct purchases in the domestic market by extraterritorial bodies	...	...	...	...	...	...	...	...	...	...	...	...
Total Exports of Goods and Services	...	...	...	...	2409.8	3079.1	3672.2	4725.6	5943.5	6518.7	6475.9	7023.9
Imports of Goods and Services												
1 Imports of merchandise, c.i.f.	...	...	...	...	2480.7	3045.6	3561.1	4300.4	4753.3	5205.2	5035.2	6127.5
2 Adjustments of merchandise imports to change-of-ownership basis	...	...	...	...	...	...	...	...	...	...	...	...
3 Other transport and communication	...	...	...	...	55.9	93.4	108.2	142.4	164.9	155.3	151.0	184.5
4 Other insurance service charges	...	...	...	...	9.3	19.8	3.1	1.0	27.4	33.1	36.8	51.4
5 Other commodities	...	...	...	...	117.8	165.9	228.5	273.4	264.1	327.7	307.4	321.6
6 Direct purchases abroad by government	...	...	...	...	...	...	...	...	...	...	...	...
7 Direct purchases abroad by resident households	...	...	...	...	94.7	103.6	123.4	142.8	153.6	193.5	235.8	271.7
Total Imports of Goods and Services	...	...	...	...	2758.5	3428.3	4024.3	4860.1	5363.3	5914.8	5766.1	6956.7
Balance of Goods and Services	...	...	...	...	-348.7	-349.2	-352.1	-134.5	580.2	603.9	709.8	67.2
Total Imports and Balance of Goods and Services	...	...	...	...	2409.8	3079.1	3672.2	4725.6	5943.5	6518.7	6475.9	7023.9

a) The estimates refer to transport only. Communication is included in item 'Other Commodities'.

3.11 General Government Production Account: Total and Subsectors

Thousand Million Spanish pesetas

	1980 Total General Government	1980 Central Government	1980 State or Provincial Government	1980 Local Government	1980 Social Security Funds	1981 Total General Government	1981 Central Government	1981 State or Provincial Government	1981 Local Government	1981 Social Security Funds
Gross Output										
1 Sales	116.7	25.0	...	81.7	10.0	152.9	29.1	...	102.4	21.4
2 Services produced for own use	1939.0	1216.8	...	327.6	394.6	2254.5	1348.3	...	444.1	462.1
3 Own account fixed capital formation	...	...	...	...	...	...	...	...	...	...
Gross Output [a]	2055.7	1241.8	...	409.3	404.6	2407.4	1377.4	...	546.5	483.5
Gross Input										
Intermediate Consumption	490.3	262.9	...	153.1	74.4	570.6	272.7	...	206.5	91.3
Subtotal: Value Added	1565.3	979.0	...	256.2	330.1	1836.8	1104.6	...	340.1	392.1
1 Indirect taxes, net	...	...	...	...	...	...	...	...	...	...
2 Consumption of fixed capital	77.1	50.9	...	18.4	7.8	89.7	60.2	...	21.5	8.0
3 Compensation of employees	1488.2	928.2	...	237.7	322.3	1747.2	1044.4	...	318.6	384.2
4 Net Operating surplus	...	...	...	...	...	...	...	...	...	...
Gross Input [a]	2055.6	1242.0	...	409.2	404.5	2407.5	1377.3	...	546.6	483.5

	1982 Total General Government	1982 Central Government	1982 State or Provincial Government	1982 Local Government	1982 Social Security Funds	1983 Total General Government	1983 Central Government	1983 State or Provincial Government	1983 Local Government	1983 Social Security Funds
Gross Output										
1 Sales	178.3	29.1	...	119.8	29.5	212.7	31.5	...	134.6	46.7
2 Services produced for own use	2634.5	1527.5	...	585.1	521.9	3110.6	1723.4	...	803.4	583.9
3 Own account fixed capital formation	...	...	...	...	...	...	...	...	...	...
Gross Output [a]	2812.8	1556.6	...	704.9	551.4	3323.3	1754.9	...	938.0	630.6

1348

Spain

3.11 General Government Production Account: Total and Subsectors
(Continued)

Thousand Million Spanish pesetas

	\multicolumn{4}{c	}{1982}	\multicolumn{4}{c}{1983}
	Total General Government	Central Government	State or Provincial Government	Local Government	Social Security Funds	Total General Government	Central Government	State or Provincial Government	Local Government	Social Security Funds

Gross Input

	1982 Total	Central	State/Prov	Local	SSF	1983 Total	Central	State/Prov	Local	SSF
Intermediate Consumption	707.2	343.0	...	250.5	113.7	831.9	411.5	...	296.9	123.5
Subtotal: Value Added	2105.6	1213.6	...	454.3	437.7	2491.5	1343.3	...	641.1	507.0
1 Indirect taxes, net	...	...	...	...	...	...	...	...	...	...
2 Consumption of fixed capital	105.6	71.1	...	26.6	7.9	126.6	82.1	...	35.7	8.8
3 Compensation of employees	2000.1	1142.5	...	427.8	429.8	2364.9	1261.2	...	605.4	498.2
4 Net Operating surplus	...	...	...	...	...	...	...	...	...	...
Gross Input [a]	2812.9	1556.6	...	704.9	551.4	3323.4	1754.8	...	938.0	630.5

	\multicolumn{4}{c	}{1984}	\multicolumn{4}{c}{1985}

Gross Output

	1984 Total	Central	State/Prov	Local	SSF	1985 Total	Central	State/Prov	Local	SSF
1 Sales	267.0	44.9	...	169.1	53.0	301.4	37.1	...	190.2	74.1
2 Services produced for own use	3475.2	1767.7	...	1059.6	647.9	3940.1	1897.1	...	1319.4	723.6
3 Own account fixed capital formation	...	...	...	...	...	...	...	...	...	...
Gross Output [a]	3742.2	1812.6	...	1228.7	700.9	4241.5	1934.2	...	1509.6	797.7

Gross Input

	1984 Total	Central	State/Prov	Local	SSF	1985 Total	Central	State/Prov	Local	SSF
Intermediate Consumption	959.7	470.4	...	355.8	133.4	1097.5	478.4	...	456.8	162.3
Subtotal: Value Added	2782.5	1342.1	...	872.9	567.5	3144.0	1455.8	...	1052.8	635.4
1 Indirect taxes, net	...	...	...	...	...	...	...	...	...	...
2 Consumption of fixed capital	148.1	94.6	...	43.3	10.2	168.8	102.8	...	54.3	11.7
3 Compensation of employees	2634.4	1247.5	...	829.6	557.3	2975.1	1353.0	...	998.4	623.7
4 Net Operating surplus	...	...	...	...	...	...	...	...	...	...
Gross Input [a]	3742.2	1812.5	...	1228.7	700.9	4241.4	1934.2	...	1509.5	797.7

	\multicolumn{4}{c}{1986}

Gross Output

	Total General Government	Central Government	State or Provincial Government	Local Government	Social Security Funds
1 Sales	331.8	48.8	...	205.2	77.7
2 Services produced for own use	4505.4	2121.6	...	1545.1	838.6
3 Own account fixed capital formation	...	...	...	...	...
Gross Output [a]	4837.2	2170.4	...	1750.3	916.3

Gross Input

	Total	Central	State/Prov	Local	SSF
Intermediate Consumption	1303.7	590.7	...	512.0	201.0
Subtotal: Value Added	3533.5	1579.8	...	1238.3	715.3
1 Indirect taxes, net	...	...	...	...	...
2 Consumption of fixed capital	194.5	109.6	...	73.0	11.9
3 Compensation of employees	3339.0	1470.2	...	1165.4	703.4
4 Net Operating surplus	...	...	...	...	...
Gross Input [a]	4837.2	2170.5	...	1750.4	916.3

a) Local Government includes provincial government and other regional government entities.

3.12 General Government Income and Outlay Account: Total and Subsectors

Thousand Million Spanish pesetas

	\multicolumn{4}{c	}{1980}	\multicolumn{4}{c}{1981}

Receipts

	1980 Total	Central	State/Prov	Local	SSF	1981 Total	Central	State/Prov	Local	SSF
1 Operating surplus	...	...	...	...	...	...	...	...	...	...
2 Property and entrepreneurial income	152.4	138.3	...	9.0	5.2	222.5	201.5	...	14.0	7.0
A Withdrawals from public quasi-corporations	...	...	...	...	...	...	...	...	...	...
B Interest	71.0	61.3	...	6.7	3.0	87.3	73.3	...	10.2	3.8
C Dividends	81.4	77.0	...	2.2	2.2	135.2	128.2	...	3.8	3.2
D Net land rent and royalties	...	...	...	...	...	...	...	...	...	...
3 Taxes, fees and contributions	3879.6	1715.2	...	358.3	1806.1	4535.4	1943.8	...	526.9	2064.7
A Indirect taxes	1009.5	762.4	...	239.0	8.1	1243.0	918.3	...	316.4	8.3

Spain

3.12 General Government Income and Outlay Account: Total and Subsectors
(Continued)

Thousand Million Spanish pesetas

	1980					1981				
	Total General Government	Central Government	State or Provincial Government	Local Government	Social Security Funds	Total General Government	Central Government	State or Provincial Government	Local Government	Social Security Funds
B Direct taxes [a]	1059.0	939.7	...	119.3	-	1221.1	1010.6	...	210.5	-
C Social security contributions	1811.1	13.1	...	-	1798.0	2071.3	14.9	...	-	2056.4
D Fees, fines and penalties [a]	...	...	...	...	...	...	...	...	...	...
4 Other current transfers	489.1	474.4	...	83.4	299.0	536.3	547.3	...	103.4	423.8
A Casualty insurance claims	-	-	...	-	-	-	-	...	-	-
B Transfers from other government subsectors	...	28.7	...	41.4	297.7	...	63.8	...	55.9	418.4
C Transfers from the rest of the world	-	-	...	-	-	0.1	0.1	...	-	-
D Other transfers, except imputed	308.3	283.7	...	24.4	0.1	334.3	309.1	...	25.2	0.1
E Imputed unfunded employee pension and welfare contributions	180.8	162.0	...	17.5	1.2	201.9	174.3	...	22.4	5.2
Total Current Receipts [b]	4521.1	2327.9	...	450.7	2110.3	5294.2	2692.6	...	644.3	2495.5

Disbursements

	Total General Government	Central Government	State or Provincial Government	Local Government	Social Security Funds	Total General Government	Central Government	State or Provincial Government	Local Government	Social Security Funds
1 Government final consumption expenditure	1929.3	1207.2	...	327.6	394.6	2242.2	1336.0	...	444.1	462.1
2 Property income	110.9	81.2	...	29.5	0.2	135.6	103.7	...	31.8	0.1
3 Subsidies	315.1	288.4	...	26.7	...	334.4	306.9	...	27.5	...
4 Other current transfers	2156.3	767.4	...	36.9	1719.8	2661.2	929.6	...	95.5	2174.2
A Casualty insurance premiums, net	-	-	...	-	-	-	-	...	-	-
B Transfers to other government subsectors	...	308.0	...	5.9	53.9	...	445.1	...	40.9	52.2
C Social security benefits	1926.3	241.8	...	19.6	1664.8	2401.6	258.4	...	22.4	2120.8
D Social assistance grants	...	...	...	...	...	...	...	...	...	...
E Unfunded employee pension and welfare benefits	226.6	214.2	...	11.4	1.1	255.9	222.5	...	32.2	1.2
F Transfers to private non-profit institutions serving households	...	...	...	...	...	...	...	...	...	...
G Other transfers n.e.c.	...	...	...	...	...	...	...	...	...	...
H Transfers to the rest of the world	3.4	3.4	...	-	-	3.7	3.7	...	-	-
Net saving	9.6	-16.3	...	30.0	-4.1	-79.1	16.4	...	45.4	-140.9
Total Current Disbursements and Net Saving [b]	4521.2	2327.9	...	450.7	2110.5	5294.3	2692.6	...	644.3	2495.5

	1982					1983				
	Total General Government	Central Government	State or Provincial Government	Local Government	Social Security Funds	Total General Government	Central Government	State or Provincial Government	Local Government	Social Security Funds

Receipts

1 Operating surplus	...	...	...	...	...	...	...	...	...	...
2 Property and entrepreneurial income	288.9	252.7	...	26.9	9.3	307.1	265.2	...	29.0	12.9
A Withdrawals from public quasi-corporations	...	...	...	...	...	...	...	...	...	...
B Interest	126.9	100.8	...	20.3	5.8	149.4	115.6	...	25.1	8.6
C Dividends	162.0	151.9	...	6.5	3.6	157.7	149.6	...	3.9	4.2
D Net land rent and royalties	...	...	...	...	...	...	...	...	...	...
3 Taxes, fees and contributions	5236.3	2144.7	...	717.5	2374.2	6435.5	2736.3	...	918.4	2780.9
A Indirect taxes	1522.3	1116.0	...	396.9	9.4	1900.1	1394.1	...	493.1	13.0
B Direct taxes [a]	1332.6	1012.0	...	320.6	-	1748.1	1322.7	...	425.3	-
C Social security contributions	2381.4	16.6	...	-	2364.8	2787.3	19.4	...	-	2767.9
D Fees, fines and penalties [a]	...	...	...	...	...	...	...	...	...	...
4 Other current transfers	611.8	632.8	...	157.0	828.1	696.0	684.4	...	315.6	770.0
A Casualty insurance claims	-	-	...	-	-	-	-	...	-	-
B Transfers from other government subsectors	...	85.3	...	98.6	822.2	...	71.5	...	241.4	761.1
C Transfers from the rest of the world	0.2	0.2	...	-	-	0.4	0.4	...	-	-
D Other transfers, except imputed	381.9	350.2	...	31.6	0.1	428.3	381.1	...	44.3	2.9
E Imputed unfunded employee pension and welfare contributions	229.7	197.1	...	26.8	5.8	267.2	231.3	...	29.9	6.0
Total Current Receipts [b]	6137.0	3030.2	...	901.4	3211.6	7438.6	3685.9	...	1263.0	3563.8

Spain

3.12 General Government Income and Outlay Account: Total and Subsectors
(Continued)

Thousand Million Spanish pesetas

	1982					1983				
	Total General Government	Central Government	State or Provincial Government	Local Government	Social Security Funds	Total General Government	Central Government	State or Provincial Government	Local Government	Social Security Funds

Disbursements

1 Government final consumption expenditure	2619.5	1512.5	...	585.1	521.9	3090.9	1703.7	...	803.4	583.9
2 Property income	190.5	141.0	...	49.3	0.1	290.4	203.2	...	85.5	1.7
3 Subsidies	489.0	421.5	...	67.5	...	575.8	484.8	...	91.0	...
4 Other current transfers	3045.6	1422.6	...	123.9	2505.3	3596.9	1582.8	...	158.7	2929.4
A Casualty insurance premiums, net	-	-	...	-	-	-	-	...	-	-
B Transfers to other government subsectors	...	887.5	...	56.3	62.2	...	963.3	...	46.2	64.5
C Social security benefits	2747.5	279.7	...	26.8	2441.0	3232.1	339.1	...	29.9	2863.1
D Social assistance grants	...	...	...	...	...	...	...	...	...	...
E Unfunded employee pension and welfare benefits	291.3	248.5	...	40.7	2.0	355.2	270.7	...	82.7	1.8
F Transfers to private non-profit institutions serving households	...	...	...	...	...	...	...	...	...	...
G Other transfers n.e.c.	...	...	...	...	...	...	...	...	...	...
H Transfers to the rest of the world	6.9	6.9	...	-	-	9.6	9.6	...	-	-
Net saving	-207.5	-467.3	...	75.5	184.3	-115.4	-288.6	...	124.5	48.7
Total Current Disbursements and Net Saving [b]	6137.1	3030.3	...	901.3	3211.6	7438.6	3685.9	...	1263.1	3563.7

	1984					1985				
	Total General Government	Central Government	State or Provincial Government	Local Government	Social Security Funds	Total General Government	Central Government	State or Provincial Government	Local Government	Social Security Funds

Receipts

1 Operating surplus	...	...	...	...	...	...	...	...	...	...
2 Property and entrepreneurial income	251.7	200.4	...	36.4	14.9	324.7	266.0	...	45.4	13.2
A Withdrawals from public quasi-corporations	...	...	...	...	...	...	...	...	...	...
B Interest	171.8	131.6	...	30.2	10.0	201.7	153.8	...	38.4	9.5
C Dividends	79.9	68.7	...	6.2	5.0	123.0	112.2	...	7.0	3.7
D Net land rent and royalties	...	...	...	...	...	...	...	...	...	...
3 Taxes, fees and contributions	7368.0	3118.8	...	1241.9	3007.3	8405.9	3386.6	...	1688.6	3330.7
A Indirect taxes	2271.4	1535.6	...	716.5	19.3	2686.9	1706.8	...	959.4	20.7
B Direct taxes [a]	2085.6	1560.2	...	525.4	-	2378.4	1649.2	...	729.2	-
C Social security contributions	3011.0	23.0	...	-	2988.0	3340.6	30.5	...	-	3310.0
D Fees, fines and penalties [a]	...	...	...	...	...	...	...	...	...	...
4 Other current transfers	729.7	756.7	...	397.2	957.9	884.0	855.6	...	357.5	1118.4
A Casualty insurance claims	-	-	...	-	-	-	-	...	-	-
B Transfers from other government subsectors	...	125.4	...	306.4	950.2	...	108.7	...	228.4	1110.3
C Transfers from the rest of the world	0.1	0.1	...	-	-	0.1	0.1	...	-	-
D Other transfers, except imputed	458.4	400.4	...	57.6	0.4	564.0	477.9	...	86.1	-
E Imputed unfunded employee pension and welfare contributions	271.2	230.7	...	33.2	7.3	319.9	268.9	...	42.9	8.1
Total Current Receipts [b]	8349.4	4075.9	...	1675.5	3980.1	9614.6	4508.2	...	2091.5	4462.3

Disbursements

1 Government final consumption expenditure	3448.3	1740.8	...	1059.6	647.9	3906.6	1872.4	...	1310.6	723.6
2 Property income	509.3	410.4	...	98.9	0.1	900.0	776.1	...	123.4	0.4
3 Subsidies	703.6	586.2	...	117.4	...	738.7	561.2	...	166.9	10.7

Spain

3.12 General Government Income and Outlay Account: Total and Subsectors
(Continued)

Thousand Million Spanish pesetas

	1984					1985				
	Total General Government	Central Government	State or Provincial Government	Local Government	Social Security Funds	Total General Government	Central Government	State or Provincial Government	Local Government	Social Security Funds
4 Other current transfers	4015.9	1837.3	...	251.9	3308.7	4627.0	2044.8	...	260.1	3769.5
A Casualty insurance premiums, net	-	-	...	-	-	...	...	...	-	-
B Transfers to other government subsectors	...	1221.6	...	102.6	57.9	...	1289.9	...	84.1	73.5
C Social security benefits	3642.9	324.4	...	69.9	3248.6	4151.0	370.3	...	88.0	3692.8
D Social assistance grants	...	...	...	...	...	...	...	...	...	...
E Unfunded employee pension and welfare benefits	364.1	282.4	...	79.4	2.3	461.9	370.6	...	88.1	3.2
F Transfers to private non-profit institutions serving households	...	...	...	...	...	...	...	...	...	...
G Other transfers n.e.c.	...	...	...	...	...	...	...	...	...	...
H Transfers to the rest of the world	8.8	8.8	...	-	-	14.1	14.1	...	-	-
Net saving	-327.7	-498.8	...	147.7	23.4	-557.7	-746.4	...	230.4	-41.8
Total Current Disbursements and Net Saving [b]	8349.4	4075.9	...	1675.5	3980.1	9614.6	4508.1	...	2091.4	4462.4

	1986				
	Total General Government	Central Government	State or Provincial Government	Local Government	Social Security Funds

Receipts

1 Operating surplus	...	...	...	...	...
2 Property and entrepreneurial income	332.4	275.1	...	45.1	12.2
A Withdrawals from public quasi-corporations	...	...	...	...	...
B Interest	215.8	167.4	...	39.5	8.9
C Dividends	116.6	107.7	...	5.7	3.3
D Net land rent and royalties	...	...	...	...	...
3 Taxes, fees and contributions	9844.0	4328.3	...	1760.3	3755.4
A Indirect taxes	3411.6	2410.8	...	1000.8	-
B Direct taxes [a]	2638.0	1878.5	...	759.5	-
C Social security contributions	3794.4	39.0	...	-	3755.4
D Fees, fines and penalties [a]	...	...	...	...	...
4 Other current transfers	1013.0	936.5	...	511.7	1386.2
A Casualty insurance claims	-	-	...	-	-
B Transfers from other government subsectors	...	62.8	...	390.4	1368.3
C Transfers from the rest of the world	24.2	24.2	...	-	-
D Other transfers, except imputed	641.0	553.0	...	77.5	10.5
E Imputed unfunded employee pension and welfare contributions	347.8	296.5	...	43.8	7.5
Total Current Receipts [b]	11189.4	5539.9	...	2317.1	5153.8

Disbursements

1 Government final consumption expenditure	4470.0	2096.9	...	1534.5	838.6
2 Property income	1201.9	1059.7	...	141.5	0.7
3 Subsidies	663.8	506.8	...	144.1	12.9

Spain

3.12 General Government Income and Outlay Account: Total and Subsectors
(Continued)

Thousand Million Spanish pesetas

	\multicolumn{5}{c}{1986}
	Total General Government	Central Government	State or Provincial Government	Local Government	Social Security Funds
4 Other current transfers	5202.2	2532.6	...	259.5	4231.5
A Casualty insurance premiums, net	-	-	...	-	-
B Transfers to other government subsectors	...	1695.5	...	53.3	72.6
C Social security benefits	4655.4	401.0	...	106.7	4147.6
D Social assistance grants	...	...	...	...	...
E Unfunded employee pension and welfare benefits	525.2	414.4	...	99.5	11.3
F Transfers to private non-profit institutions serving households	...	...	...	...	...
G Other transfers n.e.c.	...	...	...	...	...
H Transfers to the rest of the world	21.6	21.6	...	-	-
Net saving	-348.6	-656.1	...	237.4	70.1
Total Current Disbursements and Net Saving [b]	11189.3	5539.9	...	2317.0	5153.8

a) Item 'Fees, fines and penalties' is included in item 'Direct taxes'.
b) Local Government includes provincial government and other regional government entities.

3.13 General Government Capital Accumulation Account: Total and Subsectors

Thousand Million Spanish pesetas

	\multicolumn{5}{c}{1980}	\multicolumn{5}{c}{1981}
	Total General Government	Central Government	State or Provincial Government	Local Government	Social Security Funds	Total General Government	Central Government	State or Provincial Government	Local Government	Social Security Funds
	\multicolumn{10}{c}{**Finance of Gross Accumulation**}
1 Gross saving	86.7	34.6	...	48.4	3.7	10.6	76.6	...	66.9	-132.9
A Consumption of fixed capital	77.1	50.9	...	18.4	7.8	89.7	60.2	...	21.5	8.0
B Net saving	9.6	-16.3	...	30.0	-4.1	-79.1	16.4	...	45.4	-140.9
2 Capital transfers	32.6	20.0	...	44.4	0.6	81.5	24.5	...	53.0	3.9
Finance of Gross Accumulation [a]	119.3	54.6	...	92.8	4.3	92.1	101.1	...	119.9	-129.0
	\multicolumn{10}{c}{**Gross Accumulation**}
1 Gross capital formation	276.0	170.6	...	84.0	21.3	365.2	231.6	...	106.7	26.9
A Increase in stocks	...	...	...	...	...	...	...	...	...	...
B Gross fixed capital formation	276.0	170.6	...	84.0	21.3	365.2	231.6	...	106.7	26.9
2 Purchases of land, net	8.0	4.6	...	3.4	-	24.8	6.5	...	18.2	0.1
3 Purchases of intangible assets, net	...	...	...	...	...	...	...	...	...	...
4 Capital transfers	234.1	259.6	...	6.8	0.1	366.6	352.8	...	13.3	0.5
Net lending	-398.7	-380.2	...	-1.3	-17.1	-664.6	-489.8	...	-18.3	-156.6
Gross Accumulation [a]	119.4	54.6	...	92.9	4.3	92.0	101.1	...	119.9	-129.1

	\multicolumn{5}{c}{1982}	\multicolumn{5}{c}{1983}
	Total General Government	Central Government	State or Provincial Government	Local Government	Social Security Funds	Total General Government	Central Government	State or Provincial Government	Local Government	Social Security Funds
	\multicolumn{10}{c}{**Finance of Gross Accumulation**}
1 Gross saving	-101.9	-396.2	...	102.1	192.2	11.2	-206.5	...	160.2	57.5
A Consumption of fixed capital	105.6	71.1	...	26.6	7.9	126.6	82.1	...	35.7	8.8
B Net saving	-207.5	-467.3	...	75.5	184.3	-115.4	-288.6	...	124.5	48.7
2 Capital transfers	91.9	23.0	...	68.0	0.9	139.5	26.2	...	108.9	4.4
Finance of Gross Accumulation [a]	-10.0	-373.2	...	170.1	193.1	150.7	-180.3	...	269.1	61.9
	\multicolumn{10}{c}{**Gross Accumulation**}
1 Gross capital formation	574.5	298.9	...	236.7	38.9	607.7	346.7	...	226.2	34.8
A Increase in stocks	...	...	...	...	...	...	...	...	...	...
B Gross fixed capital formation	574.5	298.9	...	236.7	38.9	607.7	346.7	...	226.2	34.8
2 Purchases of land, net	27.2	3.7	...	23.5	0.1	24.3	10.6	...	13.6	0.1
3 Purchases of intangible assets, net	...	...	...	...	...	...	...	...	...	...
4 Capital transfers	488.2	451.5	...	36.4	0.3	585.7	512.3	...	73.0	0.5
Net lending	-1099.9	-1127.3	...	-126.5	153.8	-1067.1	-1050.0	...	-43.7	26.6
Gross Accumulation [a]	-10.0	-373.2	...	170.1	193.1	150.6	-180.4	...	269.1	62.0

Spain

3.13 General Government Capital Accumulation Account: Total and Subsectors

Thousand Million Spanish pesetas

	1984					1985				
	Total General Government	Central Government	State or Provincial Government	Local Government	Social Security Funds	Total General Government	Central Government	State or Provincial Government	Local Government	Social Security Funds
Finance of Gross Accumulation											
1 Gross saving	-179.6	-404.2	...	191.0	33.6	-388.9	-643.6	...	284.7	-30.1
A Consumption of fixed capital	148.1	94.6	...	43.3	10.2	168.8	102.8	...	54.3	11.7
B Net saving	-327.7	-498.8	...	147.7	23.4	-557.7	-746.4	...	230.4	-41.8
2 Capital transfers	300.8	18.3	...	277.7	4.9	337.3	31.0	...	300.3	6.0
Finance of Gross Accumulation [a]	121.2	-385.9	...	468.7	38.5	-51.6	-612.6	...	585.0	-24.1
Gross Accumulation											
1 Gross capital formation	722.0	310.8	...	371.8	39.5	994.6	325.2	...	619.8	49.5
A Increase in stocks	...	...	...	...	...	...	...	...	...	...
B Gross fixed capital formation	722.0	310.8	...	371.8	39.5	994.6	325.2	...	619.8	49.5
2 Purchases of land, net	37.9	10.3	...	27.9	-0.2	50.4	17.0	...	33.4	-
3 Purchases of intangible assets, net	...	...	...	...	...	...	...	...	...	...
4 Capital transfers	739.4	655.0	...	84.0	0.4	860.0	745.9	...	113.3	0.8
Net lending	-1378.1	-1362.0	...	-14.9	-1.2	-1956.0	-1700.6	...	-181.4	-74.5
Gross Accumulation [a]	121.2	-385.9	...	468.8	38.5	-51.6	-612.5	...	585.1	-24.2

	1986				
	Total General Government	Central Government	State or Provincial Government	Local Government	Social Security Funds
Finance of Gross Accumulation					
1 Gross saving	-154.1	-546.5	...	310.4	82.0
A Consumption of fixed capital	194.5	109.6	...	73.0	11.9
B Net saving	-348.6	-656.1	...	237.4	70.1
2 Capital transfers	476.9	115.1	...	352.4	9.4
Finance of Gross Accumulation [a]	322.8	-431.4	...	662.8	91.4
Gross Accumulation					
1 Gross capital formation	1135.3	336.0	...	740.7	58.7
A Increase in stocks	...	...	...	...	...
B Gross fixed capital formation	1135.3	336.0	...	740.7	58.7
2 Purchases of land, net	43.9	3.1	...	40.8	-
3 Purchases of intangible assets, net	...	...	...	...	...
4 Capital transfers	1083.1	904.0	...	123.8	55.4
Net lending	-1939.5	-1674.4	...	-242.4	-22.7
Gross Accumulation [a]	322.8	-431.3	...	662.9	91.4

a) Local Government includes provincial government and other regional government entities.

3.21 Corporate and Quasi-Corporate Enterprise Production Account: Total and Sectors

Thousand Million Spanish pesetas

	1980				1981				1982			
	Corporate and Quasi-Corporate Enterprises			ADDENDUM: Total, including Unincorporated	Corporate and Quasi-Corporate Enterprises			ADDENDUM: Total, including Unincorporated	Corporate and Quasi-Corporate Enterprises			ADDENDUM: Total, including Unincorporated
	TOTAL	Non-Financial	Financial		TOTAL	Non-Financial	Financial		TOTAL	Non-Financial	Financial	
Gross Output												
1 Output for sale	26417.0	25800.9	616.1	...	30020.1	29425.2	594.9	...	34280.6	33730.4	550.2	...
2 Imputed bank service charge	535.8	...	535.8	...	756.3	...	756.3	...	889.1	...	889.1	...
3 Own-account fixed capital formation	...	...	...	...	...	...	...	...	...	...	...	...
Gross Output	26952.8	25800.9	1151.9	...	30776.4	29425.2	1351.2	...	35169.7	33730.4	1439.3	...
Gross Input												
Intermediate consumption	13580.5	12791.4	789.1	...	15922.4	14856.8	1065.6	...	18087.9	16864.8	1223.1	...
1 Imputed banking service charge	535.8	...	535.8	...	756.3	...	756.3	...	889.1	...	889.1	...
2 Other intermediate consumption	13044.7	12791.4	253.3	...	15166.1	14856.8	309.4	...	17198.9	16864.8	334.1	...
Subtotal: Value Added	13372.3	13009.5	362.8	...	14854.0	14568.4	285.6	...	17081.7	16865.6	216.2	...

Spain

3.21 Corporate and Quasi-Corporate Enterprise Production Account: Total and Sectors
(Continued)

Thousand Million Spanish pesetas

	1980 TOTAL	1980 Non-Financial	1980 Financial	ADDENDUM: Total, including Unincorporated	1981 TOTAL	1981 Non-Financial	1981 Financial	ADDENDUM: Total, including Unincorporated	1982 TOTAL	1982 Non-Financial	1982 Financial	ADDENDUM: Total, including Unincorporated
1 Indirect taxes, net	422.9	394.9	28.1	...	610.4	574.7	35.7	...	653.4	611.5	41.9	...
A Indirect taxes	738.0	709.1	28.9	...	944.8	907.8	37.0	...	1142.4	1094.7	47.7	...
B Less: Subsidies	315.1	314.2	0.8	...	334.4	333.1	1.3	...	489.0	483.2	5.8	...
2 Consumption of fixed capital	1538.2	1498.1	40.2	...	1840.9	1789.2	51.7	...	2148.1	2093.7	54.4	...
3 Compensation of employees	6295.8	5849.7	446.0	...	6967.7	6443.2	524.5	...	7853.1	7232.0	621.2	...
4 Net operating surplus	5115.4	5266.8	-151.5	...	5434.9	5761.3	-326.4	...	6427.1	6928.4	-501.3	...
Gross Input	26952.8	25800.9	1151.9	...	30776.3	29425.2	1351.1	...	35169.6	33730.4	1439.3	...

	1983 TOTAL	1983 Non-Financial	1983 Financial	ADDENDUM: Total, including Unincorporated	1984 TOTAL	1984 Non-Financial	1984 Financial	ADDENDUM: Total, including Unincorporated	1985 TOTAL	1985 Non-Financial	1985 Financial	ADDENDUM: Total, including Unincorporated
Gross Output												
1 Output for sale	39053.6	38575.9	477.8	...	44076.0	43448.9	627.2	...	48498.1	47777.7	720.4	...
2 Imputed bank service charge	1043.0	...	1043.0	...	1478.0	...	1478.0	...	1560.4	...	1560.4	...
3 Own-account fixed capital formation	...	...	...	...	...	...	...	...	...	...	...	...
Gross Output	40096.6	38575.9	1520.8	...	45554.0	43448.9	2105.2	...	50058.5	47777.7	2280.8	...
Gross Input												
Intermediate consumption	20805.9	19374.0	1431.9	...	23698.6	21770.2	1928.4	...	25870.0	23806.3	2063.6	...
1 Imputed banking service charge	1043.0	...	1043.0	...	1478.0	...	1478.0	...	1560.4	...	1560.4	...
2 Other intermediate consumption	19762.9	19374.0	388.9	...	22220.7	21770.2	450.5	...	24309.6	23806.3	503.3	...
Subtotal: Value Added	19290.7	19201.9	88.8	...	21855.4	21678.7	176.7	...	24188.5	23971.4	217.1	...
1 Indirect taxes, net	871.9	815.8	56.1	...	1094.2	1033.5	60.6	...	1391.8	1287.0	104.8	...
A Indirect taxes	1447.7	1386.1	61.6	...	1797.8	1719.7	78.0	...	2130.5	2013.9	116.6	...
B Less: Subsidies	575.8	570.3	5.5	...	703.6	686.2	17.4	...	738.7	726.9	11.8	...
2 Consumption of fixed capital	2511.3	2450.7	60.7	...	2881.5	2807.0	74.5	...	3180.4	3093.7	86.7	...
3 Compensation of employees	8767.5	8066.8	700.7	...	9241.8	8461.6	780.2	...	9915.9	9046.9	869.1	...
4 Net operating surplus	7140.0	7868.6	-728.6	...	8637.9	9376.6	-738.7	...	9700.4	10543.8	-843.4	...
Gross Input	40096.6	38575.9	1520.8	...	45554.0	43448.9	2105.0	...	50058.5	47777.7	2280.8	...

	1986 TOTAL	1986 Non-Financial	1986 Financial	ADDENDUM: Total, including Unincorporated
Gross Output				
1 Output for sale	53498.5	52817.5	681.0	...
2 Imputed bank service charge	1832.7	...	1832.7	...
3 Own-account fixed capital formation	...	...	...	...
Gross Output	55331.2	52817.5	2513.7	...
Gross Input				
Intermediate consumption	27367.2	24965.9	2401.3	...
1 Imputed banking service charge	1832.7	...	1832.7	...
2 Other intermediate consumption	25534.6	24965.9	568.7	...
Subtotal: Value Added	27963.9	27851.7	112.3	...
1 Indirect taxes, net	2356.2	2319.4	36.8	...
A Indirect taxes	3057.9	3012.6	45.3	...
B Less: Subsidies	701.7	693.2	8.5	...
2 Consumption of fixed capital	3432.0	3342.0	90.0	...
3 Compensation of employees	11261.4	10169.4	1092.0	...
4 Net operating surplus	10914.3	12020.9	-1106.5	...
Gross Input	55331.1	52817.6	2513.6	...

Spain

3.22 Corporate and Quasi-Corporate Enterprise Income and Outlay Account: Total and Sectors

Thousand Million Spanish pesetas

	1980 TOTAL	1980 Non-Financial	1980 Financial	1981 TOTAL	1981 Non-Financial	1981 Financial	1982 TOTAL	1982 Non-Financial	1982 Financial	1983 TOTAL	1983 Non-Financial	1983 Financial
Receipts												
1 Operating surplus	1558.4	1709.9	-151.5	1484.4	1810.8	-326.4	1755.9	2257.2	-501.3	1812.2	2540.7	-728.6
2 Property and entrepreneurial income	1925.2	178.6	1746.6	2656.8	174.6	2482.2	3485.9	284.7	3201.2	3992.8	335.1	3657.7
A Withdrawals from quasi-corporate enterprises	0.4	0.4	...	0.7	0.7	...	2.0	2.0	...	5.7	5.7	...
B Interest	1876.9	161.3	1715.6	2595.5	151.0	2444.4	3412.3	255.8	3156.5	3903.9	298.5	3605.4
C Dividends	45.9	14.9	31.0	58.5	20.8	37.8	68.3	23.5	44.8	79.7	27.3	52.3
D Net land rent and royalties	1.9	1.9	...	2.1	2.1	...	3.3	3.3	...	3.6	3.6	...
3 Current transfers	376.9	145.3	231.6	443.9	180.1	263.8	520.7	204.7	316.0	634.4	241.5	392.9
A Casualty insurance claims	32.6	32.6	...	37.2	37.2	...	45.0	45.0	...	61.4	61.4	...
B Casualty insurance premiums, net, due to be received by insurance companies	123.8	...	123.8	142.6	...	142.6	172.9	...	172.9	234.1	...	234.1
C Current transfers from the rest of the world	...	...	...	...	...	...	...	...	...	...	...	...
D Other transfers except imputed	84.9	4.2	80.6	90.9	1.7	89.2	101.0	2.3	98.8	105.7	0.4	105.3
E Imputed unfunded employee pension and welfare contributions	135.6	108.5	27.1	173.2	141.2	32.0	201.8	157.5	44.3	233.1	179.7	53.5
Total Current Receipts	3860.5	2033.8	1826.7	4585.1	2165.5	2419.6	5762.5	2746.6	3015.9	6439.4	3117.3	3322.0
Disbursements												
1 Property and entrepreneurial income	2485.7	1194.2	1291.6	3465.5	1621.7	1843.8	4393.8	1924.4	2469.3	4923.5	2167.3	2756.2
A Withdrawals from quasi-corporations	5.7	5.7	...	7.0	7.0	...	6.8	6.8	...	29.0	29.0	...
B Interest	2208.8	1019.5	1189.4	3083.7	1406.5	1677.3	3912.8	1655.5	2257.3	4394.0	1846.2	2547.8
C Dividends	255.2	153.0	102.2	358.3	191.7	166.6	453.4	241.4	212.0	471.3	262.9	208.4
D Net land rent and royalties	16.0	16.0	...	16.5	16.5	...	20.8	20.8	...	29.2	29.2	...
2 Direct taxes and other current transfers n.e.c. to general government	259.4	233.3	26.1	295.2	254.7	40.5	351.1	303.7	47.4	434.1	381.7	52.5
A Direct taxes	259.4	233.3	26.1	295.2	254.7	40.5	351.1	303.7	47.4	434.1	381.7	52.5
B Fines, fees, penalties and other current transfers n.e.c.	...	...	...	...	...	...	...	...	...	...	...	...
3 Other current transfers	449.9	210.8	239.0	539.3	269.5	269.9	675.1	322.2	353.0	800.6	414.2	386.5
A Casualty insurance premiums, net	45.2	38.1	7.1	51.7	48.4	3.3	62.0	55.5	6.5	85.2	81.3	3.9
B Casualty insurance claims liability of insurance companies	123.8	...	123.8	142.6	...	142.6	172.9	...	172.9	234.1	...	234.1
C Transfers to private non-profit institutions	...	...	...	...	...	...	...	...	...	...	...	...
D Unfunded employee pension and welfare benefits	200.1	108.5	91.7	239.7	141.2	98.5	271.4	157.5	113.9	279.7	179.7	100.0
E Social assistance grants	...	...	...	...	...	...	...	...	...	...	...	...
F Other transfers n.e.c.	80.7	64.3	16.4	105.3	79.9	25.4	168.9	109.2	59.7	201.6	153.2	48.4
G Transfers to the rest of the world	...	...	...	...	...	...	...	...	...	...	...	...
Statistical discrepancy	10.4	...	10.4	2.2	...	2.2	1.5	...	1.5	-	...	-
Net saving	655.1	395.5	259.6	282.9	19.7	263.2	341.0	196.3	144.7	281.2	154.3	126.9
Total Current Disbursements and Net Saving	3860.5	2033.8	1826.7	4585.1	2165.6	2419.6	5762.5	2746.6	3015.9	6439.4	3117.5	3322.1

	1984 TOTAL	1984 Non-Financial	1984 Financial	1985 TOTAL	1985 Non-Financial	1985 Financial	1986 TOTAL	1986 Non-Financial	1986 Financial
Receipts									
1 Operating surplus	2383.0	3121.6	-738.7	2695.5	3538.9	-843.4	3167.4	4274.0	-1106.5
2 Property and entrepreneurial income	4939.9	455.6	4484.3	5200.8	454.7	4746.1	5597.0	625.0	4972.0
A Withdrawals from quasi-corporate enterprises	2.6	2.6	...	-	-	...	-	-	...
B Interest	4847.6	423.3	4424.3	5100.5	421.9	4678.6	5453.3	581.1	4872.2
C Dividends	85.6	25.6	60.0	99.2	31.7	67.5	142.5	42.8	99.7
D Net land rent and royalties	4.1	4.1	...	1.1	1.1	...	1.2	1.2	...

Spain

3.22 Corporate and Quasi-Corporate Enterprise Income and Outlay Account: Total and Sectors
(Continued)

Thousand Million Spanish pesetas

	1984 TOTAL	1984 Non-Financial	1984 Financial	1985 TOTAL	1985 Non-Financial	1985 Financial	1986 TOTAL	1986 Non-Financial	1986 Financial
3 Current transfers	659.1	266.1	393.0	754.1	301.8	452.3	1012.0	345.9	666.0
A Casualty insurance claims	61.9	61.9	...	68.2	68.2	...	85.6	85.6	...
B Casualty insurance premiums, net, due to be received by insurance companies	238.7	...	238.7	272.6	...	272.6	342.7	...	342.7
C Current transfers from the rest of the world	...	...	...	...	...	...	...	...	...
D Other transfers except imputed	83.6	1.2	82.4	83.0	3.7	79.3	131.8	2.8	129.1
E Imputed unfunded employee pension and welfare contributions	275.0	203.0	72.0	330.4	229.9	100.4	451.8	257.5	194.3
Total Current Receipts	7982.0	3843.3	4138.6	8650.4	4295.4	4355.0	9776.4	5244.9	4531.5

Disbursements

	1984 TOTAL	1984 Non-Financial	1984 Financial	1985 TOTAL	1985 Non-Financial	1985 Financial	1986 TOTAL	1986 Non-Financial	1986 Financial
1 Property and entrepreneurial income	5710.0	2631.6	3078.4	5866.4	2588.5	3277.8	6067.5	2875.6	3191.9
A Withdrawals from quasi-corporations	26.4	26.4	...	-	-	...	-	-	...
B Interest	5255.5	2299.6	2955.9	5288.8	2184.6	3104.2	5341.9	2312.1	3029.8
C Dividends	391.9	269.4	122.5	528.3	354.6	173.7	671.2	509.1	162.0
D Net land rent and royalties	36.1	36.1	...	49.3	49.3	...	54.5	54.5	...
2 Direct taxes and other current transfers n.e.c. to general government	481.5	416.0	65.6	556.0	474.7	81.3	685.9	554.9	131.0
A Direct taxes	481.5	416.0	65.6	556.0	474.7	81.3	685.9	554.9	131.0
B Fines, fees, penalties and other current transfers n.e.c.	...	...	...	...	...	...	...	...	...
3 Other current transfers	814.6	431.5	383.2	937.3	505.9	431.4	1174.8	583.8	590.9
A Casualty insurance premiums, net	85.8	81.4	4.4	96.7	92.1	4.6	123.7	119.1	4.6
B Casualty insurance claims liability of insurance companies	238.7	...	238.7	272.6	...	272.6	342.7	...	342.7
C Transfers to private non-profit institutions	...	...	...	...	...	...	...	...	...
D Unfunded employee pension and welfare benefits	295.7	203.0	92.7	328.6	229.9	98.6	369.4	257.5	111.9
E Social assistance grants	...	...	...	...	...	...	...	...	...
F Other transfers n.e.c.	194.4	147.1	47.4	239.5	183.9	55.6	339.0	207.2	131.8
G Transfers to the rest of the world	...	...	...	...	...	...	...	...	...
Statistical discrepancy	25.3	...	25.3	47.0	...	47.0	132.0	...	132.0
Net saving	950.5	364.3	586.2	1243.7	726.3	517.4	1716.2	1230.6	485.6
Total Current Disbursements and Net Saving	7981.9	3843.4	4138.7	8650.4	4295.4	4354.9	9776.4	5244.9	4531.4

3.23 Corporate and Quasi-Corporate Enterprise Capital Accumulation Account: Total and Sectors

Thousand Million Spanish pesetas

	1980 TOTAL	1980 Non-Financial	1980 Financial	1981 TOTAL	1981 Non-Financial	1981 Financial	1982 TOTAL	1982 Non-Financial	1982 Financial	1983 TOTAL	1983 Non-Financial	1983 Financial

Finance of Gross Accumulation

	1980 TOTAL	1980 Non-Financial	1980 Financial	1981 TOTAL	1981 Non-Financial	1981 Financial	1982 TOTAL	1982 Non-Financial	1982 Financial	1983 TOTAL	1983 Non-Financial	1983 Financial
1 Gross saving	1843.1	1543.3	299.8	1698.3	1383.3	314.9	1983.5	1784.4	199.1	2213.6	2026.0	187.6
A Consumption of fixed capital	1188.0	1147.8	40.2	1415.4	1363.6	51.7	1642.5	1588.1	54.4	1932.4	1871.7	60.7
B Net saving	655.1	395.5	259.6	282.9	19.7	263.2	341.0	196.3	144.7	281.2	154.3	126.9
2 Capital transfers	224.5	224.5	-	311.9	311.9	-	403.8	403.8	-	450.4	450.4	-
Finance of Gross Accumulation	2067.6	1767.8	299.8	2010.2	1695.2	314.9	2387.3	2188.2	199.1	2664.0	2476.4	187.6

Gross Accumulation

	1980 TOTAL	1980 Non-Financial	1980 Financial	1981 TOTAL	1981 Non-Financial	1981 Financial	1982 TOTAL	1982 Non-Financial	1982 Financial	1983 TOTAL	1983 Non-Financial	1983 Financial
1 Gross capital formation	2369.4	2221.5	147.9	2278.2	2152.7	125.5	2460.0	2327.9	132.1	2713.4	2585.8	127.6
A Increase in stocks	...	...	...	...	...	...	...	...	...	...	...	...
B Gross fixed capital formation	2369.4	2221.5	147.9	2278.2	2152.7	125.5	2460.0	2327.9	132.1	2713.4	2585.8	127.6
2 Purchases of land, net	...	...	...	...	...	...	...	...	...	...	...	...
3 Purchases of intangible assets, net	...	...	...	...	...	...	...	...	...	...	...	...
4 Capital transfers	7.9	3.9	4.1	11.0	3.6	7.5	5.1	3.4	1.7	5.1	2.8	2.3
Net lending	-309.8	-457.5	147.8	-279.1	-461.0	181.9	-77.8	-143.1	65.3	-54.5	-112.2	57.8
Gross Accumulation	2067.5	1767.9	299.8	2010.1	1695.3	314.9	2387.3	2188.2	199.1	2664.0	2476.4	187.7

Spain

3.23 Corporate and Quasi-Corporate Enterprise Capital Accumulation Account: Total and Sectors
Thousand Million Spanish pesetas

	1984 TOTAL	1984 Non-Financial	1984 Financial	1985 TOTAL	1985 Non-Financial	1985 Financial	1986 TOTAL	1986 Non-Financial	1986 Financial
Finance of Gross Accumulation									
1 Gross saving	3181.8	2521.1	660.7	3732.7	3128.6	604.1	4413.8	3838.3	575.6
A Consumption of fixed capital	2231.3	2156.8	74.5	2489.0	2402.3	86.7	2697.6	2607.7	90.0
B Net saving	950.5	364.3	586.2	1243.7	726.3	517.4	1716.2	1230.6	485.6
2 Capital transfers	451.5	451.5	-	591.0	591.0	-	695.8	695.8	-
Finance of Gross Accumulation	3633.3	2972.6	660.7	4323.7	3719.6	604.1	5109.6	4534.1	575.6
Gross Accumulation									
1 Gross capital formation	2738.1	2610.9	127.2	2924.1	2786.3	137.8	3808.9	3707.3	101.5
A Increase in stocks	...	...	...	...	...	...	...	...	...
B Gross fixed capital formation	2738.1	2610.9	127.2	2924.1	2786.3	137.8	3808.9	3707.3	101.5
2 Purchases of land, net	...	...	...	...	...	...	...	...	...
3 Purchases of intangible assets, net	...	...	...	...	...	...	...	...	...
4 Capital transfers	13.1	9.8	3.3	59.0	52.8	6.2	41.4	37.9	3.4
Net lending	882.1	351.9	530.2	1340.6	880.5	460.1	1259.5	788.9	470.6
Gross Accumulation	3633.3	2972.6	660.7	4323.7	3719.6	604.1	5109.8	4534.1	575.5

3.32 Household and Private Unincorporated Enterprise Income and Outlay Account
Thousand Million Spanish pesetas

	1970	1975	1978	1979	1980	1981	1982	1983	1984	1985	1986	1987
Receipts												
1 Compensation of employees	...	...	...	...	7797.5	8734.4	9877.4	11162.3	11907.5	12922.5	14637.2	...
A Wages and salaries	...	...	...	...	6029.0	6698.7	7554.1	8494.5	9102.2	9757.5	10998.8	...
B Employers' contributions for social security	...	...	...	...	1768.5	2035.7	2323.4	2667.8	2805.3	3165.0	3638.4	...
C Employers' contributions for private pension & welfare plans	...	...	...	...								...
2 Operating surplus of private unincorporated enterprises	...	...	...	...	3557.0	3950.5	4671.3	5327.8	6254.8	7004.9	7746.9	...
3 Property and entrepreneurial income	...	...	...	...	782.4	1077.1	1192.9	1324.0	1614.8	1922.8	2081.9	...
A Withdrawals from private quasi-corporations	...	...	...	...	...	...	...	...	...	...	...	...
B Interest	...	...	...	...	679.1	946.4	1030.4	1132.3	1434.1	1699.5	1781.5	...
C Dividends	...	...	...	...	102.3	129.5	161.2	190.1	179.1	217.8	294.7	...
D Net land rent and royalties	...	...	...	...	0.9	1.2	1.3	1.5	1.7	5.6	5.7	...
3 Current transfers	...	...	...	...	2592.5	3181.3	3667.6	4279.5	4726.9	5405.8	6123.9	...
A Casualty insurance claims	...	...	...	...	91.7	105.3	128.3	174.0	176.7	205.6	258.9	...
B Social security benefits	...	...	...	...	2126.0	2639.2	3012.2	3509.2	3937.0	4480.1	5026.6	...
C Social assistance grants	...	...	...	...	...	...	...	...	...	...	...	...
D Unfunded employee pension and welfare benefits	...	...	...	...	...	...	...	...	...	...	...	...
E Transfers from general government	...	...	...	...	...	...	...	...	...	...	...	...
F Transfers from the rest of the world	...	...	...	...	116.7	133.4	143.9	156.2	157.0	168.5	154.0	...
G Other transfers n.e.c.	...	...	...	...	258.1	303.4	383.2	440.1	456.3	551.6	684.4	...
Statistical discrepancy	...	...	...	...	10.4	2.2	1.5	-	25.3	47.0	132.0	...
Total Current Receipts [a]	...	...	...	...	14739.8	16945.5	19410.7	22093.6	24529.3	27303.0	30721.9	...
Disbursements												
1 Final consumption expenditures	...	...	...	...	10080.4	11457.9	13143.3	14808.1	16370.0	18137.7	20435.7	...
2 Property income	...	...	...	...	406.9	612.9	692.4	798.2	1015.2	1044.0	1076.9	...
A Interest	...	...	...	...	406.9	612.9	692.4	798.2	1015.2	1044.0	1076.9	...
B Net land rent and royalties	...	...	...	...	...	...	...	...	...	...	...	...
3 Direct taxes and other current transfers n.e.c. to government	...	...	...	...	2683.3	3070.3	3439.1	4152.6	4661.5	5207.2	5807.1	...
A Social security contributions	...	...	...	...	1883.7	2144.4	2457.6	2838.7	3057.4	3384.8	3855.0	...
B Direct taxes	...	...	...	...	799.6	925.9	981.5	1313.9	1604.0	1822.4	1952.1	...
Income taxes	...	...	...	...	...	...	...	...	...	...	...	...
Other	...	...	...	...	...	...	...	...	...	...	...	...
C Fees, fines and penalties	...	...	...	...	...	...	...	...	...	...	...	...

Spain

3.32 Household and Private Unincorporated Enterprise Income and Outlay Account
(Continued)

Thousand Million Spanish pesetas

	1970	1975	1978	1979	1980	1981	1982	1983	1984	1985	1986	1987
4 Other current transfers	...	...	...	...	665.3	758.5	853.6	1006.3	1067.4	1248.9	1534.1	...
A Net casualty insurance premiums	...	...	...	...	75.5	86.6	104.5	141.5	143.9	165.1	212.2	...
B Transfers to private non-profit institutions serving households	...	...	...	...	1.3	3.3	3.6	3.0	4.4	3.7	3.3	...
C Transfers to the rest of the world	...	...	...	...	0.5	0.9	1.5	2.1	3.2	21.5	17.2	...
D Other current transfers, except imputed	...	...	...	...	271.6	292.6	312.6	359.4	369.9	408.4	501.8	...
E Imputed employee pension and welfare contributions	...	...	...	...	316.4	375.1	431.5	500.4	546.1	650.3	799.6	...
Net saving	...	...	...	...	903.7	1045.9	1282.4	1328.5	1415.1	1665.3	1868.1	...
Total Current Disbursements and Net Saving [a]	...	...	...	...	14739.6	16945.5	19410.8	22093.7	24529.2	27303.1	30721.9	...

a) Private non-profit institutions serving households is included in household and private unincorporated enterprise.

3.33 Household and Private Unincorporated Enterprise Capital Accumulation Account

Thousand Million Spanish pesetas

	1970	1975	1978	1979	1980	1981	1982	1983	1984	1985	1986	1987
Finance of Gross Accumulation												
1 Gross saving	...	...	...	...	1253.9	1471.4	1788.0	1907.4	2065.4	2356.7	2602.4	...
A Consumption of fixed capital	...	...	...	...	350.2	425.5	505.6	578.9	650.3	691.4	734.3	...
B Net saving	...	...	...	...	903.7	1045.9	1282.4	1328.5	1415.1	1665.3	1868.1	...
2 Capital transfers	...	...	...	...	12.1	18.3	28.4	40.8	48.3	50.6	56.9	...
Total Finance of Gross Accumulation [a]	...	...	...	...	1266.0	1489.7	1816.4	1948.2	2113.7	2407.3	2659.3	...
Gross Accumulation												
1 Gross Capital Formation	...	...	...	...	902.7	994.8	1122.2	1149.1	1252.8	1321.9	1387.8	...
A Increase in stocks	...	...	...	...	...	...	...	...	...	...	...	...
B Gross fixed capital formation	...	...	...	...	902.7	994.8	1122.2	1149.1	1252.8	1321.9	1387.8	...
2 Purchases of land, net	...	...	...	...	-8.0	-24.8	-27.2	-24.3	-37.9	-50.4	-43.9	...
3 Purchases of intangibles, net	...	...	...	...	...	...	...	...	...	...	...	...
4 Capital transfers	...	...	...	...	28.3	35.6	33.5	42.2	53.4	65.2	69.6	...
Net lending	...	...	...	...	343.0	484.1	688.0	781.4	845.5	1070.6	1245.9	...
Total Gross Accumulation [a]	...	...	...	...	1266.0	1489.7	1816.5	1948.4	2113.8	2407.3	2659.4	...

a) Private non-profit institutions serving households is included in household and private unincorporated enterprise.

3.51 External Transactions: Current Account: Detail

Thousand Million Spanish pesetas

	1970	1975	1978	1979	1980	1981	1982	1983	1984	1985	1986	1987
Payments to the Rest of the World												
1 Imports of goods and services	...	...	...	...	2758.5	3428.3	4024.3	4860.1	5363.3	5914.8	5766.1	6956.7
A Imports of merchandise c.i.f.	...	...	...	...	2480.7	3045.6	3561.1	4300.4	4753.3	5205.2	5035.2	6127.5
B Other	...	...	...	...	277.8	382.7	463.3	559.6	610.0	709.6	731.0	829.2
2 Factor income to the rest of the world	...	...	...	...	256.9	429.3	496.3	552.4	641.5	645.2	543.1	544.6
A Compensation of employees	...	...	...	...	0.6	0.3	0.4	0.4	0.5	0.9	1.4	1.5
B Property and entrepreneurial income	...	...	...	...	256.3	428.9	495.9	552.1	641.0	644.3	541.6	543.1
3 Current transfers to the rest of the world	...	...	...	...	34.9	44.9	51.1	71.0	69.3	113.5	232.0	273.5
A Indirect taxes by general government to supranational organizations	...	...	...	...	...	...	...	...	...	...	96.5	134.9
B Other current transfers	...	...	...	...	34.9	44.9	51.1	71.0	69.3	113.5	135.5	138.6
By general government	...	...	...	...	3.4	3.7	6.9	9.6	8.8	14.1	21.6	23.2
By other resident sectors	...	...	...	...	31.5	41.2	44.2	61.4	60.4	99.4	113.9	115.5
4 Surplus of the nation on current transactions	...	...	...	...	-364.3	-458.0	-487.1	-338.0	354.8	459.9	530.3	40.2
Payments to the Rest of the World, and Surplus of the Nation on Current Transfers	...	...	...	...	2686.0	3444.5	4084.6	5145.5	6428.9	7133.4	7071.5	7815.0
Receipts From The Rest of the World												
1 Exports of goods and services	...	...	...	...	2409.8	3079.1	3672.2	4725.6	5943.5	6518.7	6475.9	7023.9

Spain

3.51 External Transactions: Current Account: Detail
(Continued)

Thousand Million Spanish pesetas

	1970	1975	1978	1979	1980	1981	1982	1983	1984	1985	1986	1987
A Exports of merchandise f.o.b.	...	...	...	...	1531.6	1976.2	2372.2	3066.8	3936.1	4296.2	3957.9	4305.9
B Other	...	...	...	...	878.2	1102.8	1300.0	1658.7	2007.4	2222.5	2518.0	2718.0
2 Factor income from the rest of the world	...	...	...	...	127.0	191.1	211.6	194.3	244.7	314.7	244.9	237.2
A Compensation of employees	...	...	...	...	14.2	19.8	24.6	30.3	31.8	32.4	38.3	42.0
B Property and entrepreneurial income	...	...	...	...	112.8	171.3	187.0	163.9	212.9	282.3	206.6	195.2
3 Current transfers from the rest of the world	...	...	...	...	149.3	174.2	200.6	225.7	240.7	300.0	350.6	554.0
A Subsidies to general government from supranational organizations	...	...	...	...	...	...	...	...	...	...	37.9	123.5
B Other current transfers	...	...	...	...	149.3	174.2	200.6	225.7	240.7	300.0	312.7	430.5
To general government	...	...	...	...	-	0.1	0.2	0.4	0.1	0.1	24.2	38.0
To other resident sectors	...	...	...	...	149.3	174.1	200.4	225.3	240.6	299.9	288.5	392.5
Receipts from the Rest of the World on Current Transfers	...	...	...	...	2686.1	3444.4	4084.4	5145.6	6428.9	7133.4	7071.4	7815.1

3.52 External Transactions: Capital Accumulation Account

Thousand Million Spanish pesetas

	1970	1975	1978	1979	1980	1981	1982	1983	1984	1985	1986	1987
Finance of Gross Accumulation												
1 Surplus of the nation on current transactions	...	...	...	...	-364.3	-458.0	-487.1	-338.0	354.8	459.9	530.3	40.2
2 Capital transfers from the rest of the world	...	...	...	...	0.4	0.6	0.2	0.4	-	0.1	40.7	50.6
Total Finance of Gross Accumulation	...	...	...	...	-363.9	-457.4	-486.9	-337.6	354.8	460.0	571.0	90.8
Gross Accumulation												
1 Capital transfers to the rest of the world	...	...	...	...	1.6	2.2	2.9	2.6	5.3	5.4	5.1	-
2 Purchases of intangible assets, n.e.c., net, from the rest of the world	...	...	...	...	...	...	...	...	...	...	...	...
Net lending to the rest of the world	...	...	...	...	-365.5	-459.7	-489.8	-340.2	349.5	454.6	565.9	90.8
Total Gross Accumulation	...	...	...	...	-363.9	-457.5	-486.9	-337.6	354.8	460.0	571.0	90.8

4.1 Derivation of Value Added by Kind of Activity, in Current Prices

Thousand Million Spanish pesetas

	1980 Gross Output	1980 Intermediate Consumption	1980 Value Added	1981 Gross Output	1981 Intermediate Consumption	1981 Value Added	1982 Gross Output	1982 Intermediate Consumption	1982 Value Added	1983 Gross Output	1983 Intermediate Consumption	1983 Value Added
All Producers												
1 Agriculture, hunting, forestry and fishing	2045.1	971.6	1073.4	2175.7	1137.7	1038.0	2544.7	1318.8	1225.9	2872.5	1502.3	1370.2
2 Mining and quarrying	...	...	...	...	...	...	...	...	...	...	...	...
3 Manufacturing	11872.2	7588.0	4284.3	13310.6	8548.5	4762.1	14941.4	9615.2	5326.2	17287.6	11138.1	6149.5
A Manufacture of food, beverages and tobacco	2471.5	1770.3	701.2	2826.9	2014.0	812.9	3240.9	2302.3	938.6	3743.3	2659.2	1084.1
B Textile, wearing apparel and leather industries	1013.4	571.0	442.4	1028.0	574.0	454.0	1151.9	648.2	503.7	1296.0	738.4	557.6
C Manufacture of wood and wood products, including furniture	410.5	226.1	184.4	413.2	222.1	191.1	445.4	241.2	204.2	484.2	263.2	221.1
D Manufacture of paper and paper products, printing and publishing	503.1	309.8	193.3	577.1	354.8	222.2	655.2	402.2	253.0	735.0	445.4	289.6
E Manufacture of chemicals and chemical petroleum, coal, rubber and plastic products	...	...	...	...	...	...	...	...	...	...	...	...
F Manufacture of non-metallic mineral products, except products of petroleum and coal	...	...	...	...	...	...	...	...	...	...	...	...
G Basic metal industries	...	...	...	...	...	...	...	...	...	...	...	...
H Manufacture of fabricated metal products, machinery and equipment	...	...	...	...	...	...	...	...	...	...	...	...
I Other manufacturing industries	7473.7	4710.8	2763.0	8465.5	5383.5	3081.9	9448.0	6021.2	3426.7	11029.1	7031.9	3997.2
4 Electricity, gas and water	669.2	360.2	309.0	968.4	541.7	426.7	1181.9	619.7	562.2	1305.4	713.6	591.7

Spain

4.1 Derivation of Value Added by Kind of Activity, in Current Prices
(Continued)

Thousand Million Spanish pesetas

	1980 Gross Output	1980 Intermediate Consumption	1980 Value Added	1981 Gross Output	1981 Intermediate Consumption	1981 Value Added	1982 Gross Output	1982 Intermediate Consumption	1982 Value Added	1983 Gross Output	1983 Intermediate Consumption	1983 Value Added
5 Construction	2443.4	1159.7	1283.7	2724.4	1395.7	1328.6	3070.3	1542.4	1527.9	3346.7	1715.0	1631.7
6 Wholesale and retail trade, restaurants and hotels	4234.1	1461.3	2772.8	4914.8	1722.8	3192.0	5731.0	2013.4	3717.6	6605.2	2275.4	4329.8
A Wholesale and retail trade	2839.9	685.6	2154.3	3209.1	774.8	2434.3	3642.4	879.4	2763.0	4163.6	1005.2	3158.4
B Restaurants and hotels	1394.2	775.7	618.5	1705.7	948.0	757.6	2088.7	1134.0	954.6	2441.6	1270.2	1171.5
7 Transport, storage and communication	1469.5	592.7	876.7	1794.2	758.1	1036.2	2031.5	864.0	1167.6	2381.9	1019.6	1362.3
A Transport and storage	1217.2	568.5	648.7	1488.5	728.9	759.6	1678.5	826.8	851.8	1960.1	975.4	984.8
B Communication	252.2	24.2	228.0	305.7	29.2	276.6	353.0	37.2	315.8	421.8	44.2	377.5
8 Finance, insurance, real estate and business services [a]	2634.6	624.0	2010.6	3022.2	723.8	2298.5	3354.3	806.4	2547.8	3642.6	918.0	2724.6
A Financial institutions	...	...	...	...	...	...	...	...	...	...	...	...
B Insurance	...	...	...	...	...	...	...	...	...	...	...	...
C Real estate and business services	1482.7	370.7	1112.1	1671.0	414.4	1256.6	1915.0	472.4	1442.6	2121.8	529.1	1592.7
9 Community, social and personal services [ab]	1584.7	287.2	1297.5	1866.0	337.9	1528.1	2314.5	418.9	1895.7	2654.7	480.8	2173.9
Total, Industries	26952.8	13044.7	13908.0	30776.4	15166.1	15610.3	35169.7	17198.9	17970.8	40096.6	19762.9	20333.7
Producers of Government Services	2055.7	490.3	1565.3	2407.4	570.6	1836.8	2812.9	707.2	2105.6	3323.4	831.9	2491.5
Other Producers [b]	...	...	...	...	...	...	...	...	...	...	...	...
Total	29008.4	13535.1	15473.4	33183.8	15736.7	17447.1	37982.5	17906.1	20076.4	43420.0	20594.8	22825.2
Less: Imputed bank service charge	...	-535.8	535.8	...	-756.3	756.3	...	-889.1	889.1	...	-1043.0	1043.0
Import duties	271.5	...	271.5	298.2	...	298.2	379.9	...	379.9	452.5	...	452.5
Value added tax	...	...	...	...	...	...	...	...	...	...	...	...
Other adjustments	...	...	0.1	...	...	...	...	...	0.1	...	...	...
Total	29279.9	14070.9	15209.1	33482.0	16493.0	16989.0	38362.4	18795.2	19567.3	43872.5	21637.8	22234.7

	1984 Gross Output	1984 Intermediate Consumption	1984 Value Added	1985 Gross Output	1985 Intermediate Consumption	1985 Value Added	1986 Gross Output	1986 Intermediate Consumption	1986 Value Added	1987 Gross Output	1987 Intermediate Consumption	1987 Value Added
					All Producers							
1 Agriculture, hunting, forestry and fishing	3363.6	1720.9	1642.7	3575.7	1831.3	1744.4	...	...	1814.5	...	...	1941.5
2 Mining and quarrying	...	...	...	...	...	...	...	...	...	...	...	...
3 Manufacturing	19568.9	12665.3	6903.6	21451.6	13819.7	7631.9	...	...	9301.6	...	...	...
A Manufacture of food, beverages and tobacco	4307.0	3053.7	1253.3	4731.3	3339.1	1392.1	...	...	1525.0	...	...	...
B Textile, wearing apparel and leather industries	1449.3	832.7	616.6	1552.0	876.1	675.9	...	...	791.9	...	...	...
C Manufacture of wood and wood products, including furniture	508.4	278.2	230.2	539.9	294.6	245.3	...	...	312.3	...	...	...
D Manufacture of paper and paper products, printing and publishing	858.3	512.5	345.8	951.0	571.4	379.5	...	...	429.9	...	...	...
E Manufacture of chemicals and chemical petroleum, coal, rubber and plastic products	...	...	...	...	...	...	...	...	...	...	...	...
F Manufacture of non-metallic mineral products, except products of petroleum and coal	...	...	...	...	...	...	...	...	...	...	...	...
G Basic metal industries	...	...	...	...	...	...	...	...	...	...	...	...
H Manufacture of fabricated metal products, machinery and equipment	...	...	...	...	...	...	...	...	...	...	...	...
I Other manufacturing industries	12446.0	7988.2	4457.8	13677.5	8738.4	4939.1	...	...	6242.4	...	...	...
4 Electricity, gas and water	1435.2	669.4	765.8	1593.6	732.8	860.9	...	...	1020.1	...	...	...
5 Construction	3458.2	1822.6	1635.6	3844.8	2038.7	1806.1	...	...	2226.6	...	...	2860.0
6 Wholesale and retail trade, restaurants and hotels	7648.0	2628.4	5019.7	8566.0	2900.9	5665.1	...	...	6600.1	...	...	...
A Wholesale and retail trade	4769.3	1151.5	3617.8	5298.7	1279.3	4019.4	...	...	4500.1	...	...	...
B Restaurants and hotels	2878.7	1476.9	1401.8	3267.3	1621.6	1645.7	...	...	2100.0	...	...	...
7 Transport, storage and communication	2662.3	1133.5	1528.8	2899.7	1237.8	1661.9	...	...	1781.6	...	...	...
A Transport and storage	2173.6	1082.2	1091.5	2355.4	1178.6	1176.7	...	...	1262.4	...	...	...
B Communication	488.6	51.3	437.3	544.4	59.2	485.2	...	...	519.2	...	...	...
8 Finance, insurance, real estate and business services [a]	4413.4	1036.8	3376.5	4812.4	1148.2	3664.2	...	...	3997.5	...	...	...
A Financial institutions	...	...	...	...	...	...	...	...	...	...	...	...

Spain

4.1 Derivation of Value Added by Kind of Activity, in Current Prices
(Continued)

Thousand Million Spanish pesetas

	1984 Gross Output	1984 Intermediate Consumption	1984 Value Added	1985 Gross Output	1985 Intermediate Consumption	1985 Value Added	1986 Gross Output	1986 Intermediate Consumption	1986 Value Added	1987 Gross Output	1987 Intermediate Consumption	1987 Value Added
B Insurance	...	...	...	...	...	...	...	...	...	...	...	...
C Real estate and business services	2308.3	586.4	1721.9	2531.6	644.9	1886.7	...	...	2052.5	...	...	...
9 Community, social and personal services [a,b]	3004.4	543.9	2460.6	3314.7	600.3	2714.3	...	...	3054.7	...	...	...
Total, Industries	45554.0	22220.7	23333.3	50058.5	24309.6	25748.9	...	...	29796.6	...	...	33349.0
Producers of Government Services	3742.1	959.7	2782.5	4241.5	1097.5	3144.0	...	...	3533.5	...	...	3932.1
Other Producers [b]	...	...	...	...	...	...	...	...	...	...	...	...
Total	49296.1	23180.3	26115.8	54300.0	25407.1	28892.8	...	...	33330.0	...	...	37281.1
Less: Imputed bank service charge	...	-1478.0	1478.0	...	-1560.4	1560.4	...	...	1832.7	...	...	2129.0
Import duties	473.5	...	473.5	556.4	...	556.4	...	...	450.1	...	...	562.4
Value added tax	...	...	...	...	...	...	...	...	...	...	...	...
Other adjustments	...	...	...	...	...	-0.1	...	...	...	...	...	...
Total	49769.6	24658.3	25111.3	54856.4	26967.5	27888.8	...	...	31947.5	...	...	35714.5

a) Business services and real estate except dwellings are included in item 'Community, social and personal services'.
b) Item 'Other producers' is included in item 'Community, social and personal services'.

4.2 Derivation of Value Added by Kind of Activity, in Constant Prices

Thousand Million Spanish pesetas

	1980 Gross Output	1980 Intermediate Consumption	1980 Value Added	1981 Gross Output	1981 Intermediate Consumption	1981 Value Added	1982 Gross Output	1982 Intermediate Consumption	1982 Value Added	1983 Gross Output	1983 Intermediate Consumption	1983 Value Added
At constant prices of: 1980												
All Producers												
1 Agriculture, hunting, forestry and fishing	...	...	1073.4	...	...	971.7	...	...	956.9	...	...	1016.6
2 Mining and quarrying	...	...	...	...	...	...	...	...	...	...	...	...
3 Manufacturing	...	...	4284.3	...	...	4278.8	...	...	4214.2	...	...	4287.3
A Manufacture of food, beverages and tobacco	...	...	701.2	...	...	711.3	...	...	718.6	...	...	743.8
B Textile, wearing apparel and leather industries	...	...	442.4	...	...	413.1	...	...	413.0	...	...	417.3
C Manufacture of wood and wood products, including furniture	...	...	184.4	...	...	173.4	...	...	174.8	...	...	172.1
D Manufacture of paper and paper products, printing and publishing	...	...	193.3	...	...	193.3	...	...	189.4	...	...	199.4
E Manufacture of chemicals and chemical petroleum, coal, rubber and plastic products	...	...	...	...	...	...	...	...	...	...	...	...
F Manufacture of non-metallic mineral products, except products of petroleum and coal	...	...	...	...	...	...	...	...	...	...	...	...
G Basic metal industries	...	...	...	...	...	...	...	...	...	...	...	...
H Manufacture of fabricated metal products, machinery and equipment	...	...	...	...	...	...	...	...	...	...	...	...
I Other manufacturing industries	...	...	2763.0	...	...	2787.8	...	...	2718.5	...	...	2754.7
4 Electricity, gas and water	...	...	309.0	...	...	303.6	...	...	312.2	...	...	312.5
5 Construction	...	...	1283.7	...	...	1281.1	...	...	1315.3	...	...	1316.6
6 Wholesale and retail trade, restaurants and hotels	...	...	2772.8	...	...	2766.5	...	...	2804.8	...	...	2854.1
A Wholesale and retail trade	...	...	2154.3	...	...	2111.2	...	...	2123.9	...	...	2166.3
B Restaurants and hotels	...	...	618.5	...	...	655.3	...	...	680.9	...	...	687.7
7 Transport, storage and communication	...	...	876.7	...	...	900.3	...	...	906.5	...	...	930.1
A Transport and storage	...	...	648.7	...	...	666.0	...	...	667.0	...	...	671.2
B Communication	...	...	228.0	...	...	234.2	...	...	239.5	...	...	259.0
8 Finance, insurance, real estate and business services [a]	...	...	2010.6	...	...	2034.8	...	...	2065.9	...	...	2077.6
A Financial institutions	...	...	...	...	...	...	...	...	...	...	...	...
B Insurance	...	...	...	...	...	...	...	...	...	...	...	...
C Real estate and business services	...	...	1112.1	...	...	1121.0	...	...	1141.1	...	...	1162.8
9 Community, social and personal services [a,b]	...	...	1297.5	...	...	1309.8	...	...	1378.8	...	...	1394.4
Total, Industries	...	...	13908.0	...	...	13846.7	...	...	13954.7	...	...	14189.3
Producers of Government Services	...	...	1565.3	...	...	1615.5	...	...	1683.0	...	...	1744.4

Spain

4.2 Derivation of Value Added by Kind of Activity, in Constant Prices
(Continued)

Thousand Million Spanish pesetas

	1980 Gross Output	1980 Intermediate Consumption	1980 Value Added	1981 Gross Output	1981 Intermediate Consumption	1981 Value Added	1982 Gross Output	1982 Intermediate Consumption	1982 Value Added	1983 Gross Output	1983 Intermediate Consumption	1983 Value Added
					At constant prices of:1980							
Other Producers [b]	...	...	...	...	...	...	...	...	...	...	...	...
Total	...	...	15473.4	...	...	15462.1	...	...	15637.7	...	...	15933.7
Less: Imputed bank service charge	...	...	535.8	...	...	540.6	...	...	553.1	...	...	564.1
Import duties	...	...	271.5	...	...	249.8	...	...	271.3	...	...	263.6
Value added tax	...	...	...	...	...	...	...	...	...	...	...	...
Other adjustments	...	...	0.1	...	...	-0.1	...	...	...	...	...	...
Total	...	...	15209.1	...	...	15171.3	...	...	15355.9	...	...	15633.2

	1984 Gross Output	1984 Intermediate Consumption	1984 Value Added	1985 Gross Output	1985 Intermediate Consumption	1985 Value Added	1986 Gross Output	1986 Intermediate Consumption	1986 Value Added	1987 Gross Output	1987 Intermediate Consumption	1987 Value Added
					At constant prices of:1980							
					All Producers							
1 Agriculture, hunting, forestry and fishing	...	...	1104.1	...	...	1138.4	...	...	1034.9	...	...	1134.2
2 Mining and quarrying	...	...	...	...	...	...	...	...	...	...	...	...
3 Manufacturing	...	...	4303.9	...	...	4384.1	...	...	4617.5	...	...	...
A Manufacture of food, beverages and tobacco	...	...	759.4	...	...	779.8	...	...	784.8	...	...	...
B Textile, wearing apparel and leather industries	...	...	404.2	...	...	407.9	...	...	420.5	...	...	...
C Manufacture of wood and wood products, including furniture	...	...	162.2	...	...	157.5	...	...	184.9	...	...	...
D Manufacture of paper and paper products, printing and publishing	...	...	204.4	...	...	206.5	...	...	219.9	...	...	...
E Manufacture of chemicals and chemical petroleum, coal, rubber and plastic products	...	...	...	...	...	...	...	...	...	...	...	...
F Manufacture of non-metallic mineral products, except products of petroleum and coal	...	...	...	...	...	...	...	...	...	...	...	...
G Basic metal industries	...	...	...	...	...	...	...	...	...	...	...	...
H Manufacture of fabricated metal products, machinery and equipment	...	...	...	...	...	...	...	...	...	...	...	...
I Other manufacturing industries	...	...	2773.7	...	...	2832.4	...	...	3007.3	...	...	...
4 Electricity, gas and water	...	...	345.8	...	...	362.9	...	...	396.0	...	...	...
5 Construction	...	...	1235.5	...	...	1263.2	...	...	1338.1	...	...	1477.5
6 Wholesale and retail trade, restaurants and hotels	...	...	2928.4	...	...	2985.5	...	...	3114.9	...	...	...
A Wholesale and retail trade	...	...	2211.8	...	...	2253.9	...	...	2332.7	...	...	...
B Restaurants and hotels	...	...	716.6	...	...	731.6	...	...	782.1	...	...	...
7 Transport, storage and communication	...	...	956.0	...	...	991.5	...	...	1008.8	...	...	...
A Transport and storage	...	...	687.7	...	...	706.3	...	...	713.1	...	...	...
B Communication	...	...	268.3	...	...	285.2	...	...	295.7	...	...	...
8 Finance, insurance, real estate and business services [a]	...	...	2142.5	...	...	2186.6	...	...	2214.7	...	...	...
A Financial institutions	...	...	...	...	...	...	...	...	...	...	...	...
B Insurance	...	...	...	...	...	...	...	...	...	...	...	...
C Real estate and business services	...	...	1182.2	...	...	1200.6	...	...	1215.0	...	...	...
9 Community, social and personal services [ab]	...	...	1413.7	...	...	1415.2	...	...	1485.0	...	...	...
Total, Industries	...	...	14429.9	...	...	14727.5	...	...	15209.8	...	...	16071.5
Producers of Government Services	...	...	1798.5	...	...	1874.0	...	...	1950.6	...	...	2047.3
Other Producers [b]	...	...	...	...	...	...	...	...	...	...	...	...
Total	...	...	16228.3	...	...	16601.5	...	...	17160.5	...	...	18118.8
Less: Imputed bank service charge	...	...	574.8	...	...	587.5	...	...	639.7	...	...	691.6
Import duties	...	...	261.0	...	...	268.8	...	...	295.7	...	...	321.4
Value added tax	...	...	...	...	...	...	...	...	...	...	...	...
Other adjustments	...	...	-0.1	...	...	0.1	...	...	0.1	...	...	0.1
Total	...	...	15914.5	...	...	16282.8	...	...	16816.4	...	...	17748.7

a) Business services and real estate except dwellings are included in item 'Community, social and personal services'.
b) Item 'Other producers' is included in item 'Community, social and personal services'.

Spain

4.3 Cost Components of Value Added

Thousand Million Spanish pesetas

	1980						1981					
	Compensation of Employees	Capital Consumption	Net Operating Surplus	Indirect Taxes	Less: Subsidies Received	Value Added	Compensation of Employees	Capital Consumption	Net Operating Surplus	Indirect Taxes	Less: Subsidies Received	Value Added
	All Producers											
1 Agriculture, hunting, forestry and fishing	302.7	...	799.1	-28.3	...	1073.4	315.3	...	757.8	-35.1	...	1038.0
2 Mining and quarrying	...	...	...	...	...	...	...	...	...	...	...	...
3 Manufacturing	2404.6	...	1594.3	285.3	...	4284.3	2627.8	...	1734.0	400.3	...	4762.1
A Manufacture of food, beverages and tobacco	301.7	...	313.5	85.9	...	701.2	337.8	...	359.4	115.7	...	812.9
B Textile, wearing apparel and leather industries	277.7	...	166.5	3.2	...	442.4	279.7	...	170.4	3.9	...	454.0
C Manufacture of wood and wood products, including furniture	121.5	...	57.8	5.1	...	184.4	120.2	...	63.6	7.2	...	191.1
D Manufacture of paper and paper products, printing and publishing	119.2	...	78.9	-4.9	...	193.3	129.9	...	94.5	-2.2	...	222.2
E Manufacture of chemicals and chemical petroleum, coal, rubber and plastic products	...	...	...	...	...	...	...	...	...	...	...	...
F Manufacture of non-metallic mineral products, except products of petroleum and coal	...	...	...	...	...	...	...	...	...	...	...	...
G Basic metal industries	...	...	...	...	...	...	...	...	...	...	...	...
H Manufacture of fabricated metal products, machinery and equipment	...	...	...	...	...	...	...	...	...	...	...	...
I Other manufacturing industries	1584.4	...	977.5	201.0	...	2763.0	1760.2	...	1046.1	275.7	...	3081.9
4 Electricity, gas and water	116.4	...	170.0	22.6	...	309.0	144.1	...	241.8	40.8	...	426.7
5 Construction	889.2	...	351.6	42.9	...	1283.7	921.2	...	359.6	47.9	...	1328.6
6 Wholesale and retail trade, restaurants and hotels	1008.8	...	1729.4	34.7	...	2772.8	1106.9	...	2034.5	50.6	...	3192.0
A Wholesale and retail trade	803.9	...	1332.0	18.4	...	2154.3	857.2	...	1546.5	30.7	...	2434.3
B Restaurants and hotels	204.8	...	397.4	16.3	...	618.5	249.7	...	488.0	19.9	...	757.6
7 Transport, storage and communication	501.6	...	473.8	-98.6	...	876.7	586.8	...	541.3	-91.9	...	1036.2
A Transport and storage	380.9	...	383.5	-115.7	...	648.7	446.6	...	431.5	-118.6	...	759.6
B Communication	120.7	...	90.3	17.1	...	228.0	140.1	...	109.8	26.6	...	276.6
8 Finance, insurance, real estate and business services [a]	458.0	...	1509.8	42.9	...	2010.6	538.5	...	1709.1	50.9	...	2298.5
A Financial institutions	406.3	...	...	...	...	...	477.8	...	...	...	...	...
B Insurance	39.7	...	...	...	...	...	46.8	...	...	...	...	...
C Real estate and business services	12.0	...	1085.3	14.9	...	1112.1	14.0	...	1227.5	15.2	...	1256.6
9 Community, social and personal services [ab]	614.5	...	561.5	121.4	...	1297.5	727.1	...	654.0	147.0	...	1528.1
Total, Industries [cd]	6295.8	...	7189.4	422.9	...	13908.0	6967.7	...	8032.1	610.4	...	15610.3
Producers of Government Services	1488.2	...	77.1	...	...	1565.3	1747.2	...	89.7	...	...	1836.8
Other Producers [b]	...	...	...	...	...	...	...	...	...	...	...	...
Total [cd]	7784.0	...	7266.5	422.9	...	15473.4	8714.9	...	8121.8	610.4	...	17447.1
Less: Imputed bank service charge	...	...	535.8	...	...	535.8	...	...	756.3	...	...	756.3
Import duties	...	...	...	271.5	...	271.5	...	...	...	298.2	...	298.2
Value added tax	...	...	...	...	...	...	...	...	...	...	...	...
Other adjustments	...	...	...	...	...	0.1	...	...	...	...	...	...
Total [cd]	7784.0	...	6730.7	694.4	...	15209.1	8714.9	...	7365.5	908.6	...	16989.0

	1982						1983					
	Compensation of Employees	Capital Consumption	Net Operating Surplus	Indirect Taxes	Less: Subsidies Received	Value Added	Compensation of Employees	Capital Consumption	Net Operating Surplus	Indirect Taxes	Less: Subsidies Received	Value Added
	All Producers											
1 Agriculture, hunting, forestry and fishing	345.4	...	914.9	-34.5	...	1225.9	393.9	...	1021.8	-45.5	...	1370.2
2 Mining and quarrying	...	...	...	...	...	...	...	...	...	...	...	...
3 Manufacturing	2875.5	...	1975.3	475.4	...	5326.2	3156.3	...	2376.9	616.3	...	6149.5
A Manufacture of food, beverages and tobacco	381.0	...	407.0	150.5	...	938.6	430.7	...	461.3	192.1	...	1084.1

Spain

4.3 Cost Components of Value Added
(Continued)

Thousand Million Spanish pesetas

	1982						1983					
	Compensation of Employees	Capital Consumption	Net Operating Surplus	Indirect Taxes	Less: Subsidies Received	Value Added	Compensation of Employees	Capital Consumption	Net Operating Surplus	Indirect Taxes	Less: Subsidies Received	Value Added
B Textile, wearing apparel and leather industries	300.5	...	196.9	6.3	...	503.7	328.9	...	225.5	3.3	...	557.6
C Manufacture of wood and wood products, including furniture	127.0	...	68.0	9.2	...	204.2	136.5	...	73.9	10.6	...	221.1
D Manufacture of paper and paper products, printing and publishing	147.8	...	104.6	0.6	...	253.0	161.2	...	126.4	2.0	...	289.6
E Manufacture of chemicals and chemical petroleum, coal, rubber and plastic products	...	...	...	...	...	...	...	...	...	...	...	...
F Manufacture of non-metallic mineral products, except products of petroleum and coal	...	...	...	...	...	...	...	...	...	...	...	...
G Basic metal industries	...	...	...	...	...	...	...	...	...	...	...	...
H Manufacture of fabricated metal products, machinery and equipment	...	...	...	...	...	...	...	...	...	...	...	...
I Other manufacturing industries	1919.2	...	1198.8	308.7	...	3426.7	2099.1	...	1489.7	408.4	...	3997.2
4 Electricity, gas and water	173.3	...	350.4	38.5	...	562.2	200.2	...	334.7	56.9	...	591.7
5 Construction	1028.9	...	431.8	67.2	...	1527.9	1091.7	...	455.0	84.9	...	1631.7
6 Wholesale and retail trade, restaurants and hotels	1230.7	...	2418.8	68.1	...	3717.6	1418.4	...	2819.6	91.8	...	4329.8
A Wholesale and retail trade	934.3	...	1786.4	42.3	...	2763.0	1093.3	...	2006.4	58.6	...	3158.4
B Restaurants and hotels	296.3	...	632.4	25.9	...	954.6	325.1	...	813.1	33.2	...	1171.5
7 Transport, storage and communication	673.6	...	647.4	-153.5	...	1167.6	766.0	...	791.5	-195.2	...	1362.3
A Transport and storage	511.1	...	536.7	-196.0	...	851.8	583.3	...	640.0	-238.5	...	984.8
B Communication	162.5	...	110.7	42.6	...	315.8	182.7	...	151.5	43.2	...	377.5
8 Finance, insurance, real estate and business services [a]	637.7	...	1849.3	60.9	...	2547.8	719.4	...	1926.8	78.4	...	2724.6
A Financial institutions	567.6	...	...	...	...	...	637.7	...	...	...	...	...
B Insurance	53.6	...	...	...	...	...	62.9	...	...	...	...	...
C Real estate and business services	16.5	...	1407.1	18.9	...	1442.6	18.7	...	1551.6	22.4	...	1592.7
9 Community, social and personal services [ab]	888.0	...	876.4	131.3	...	1895.7	1021.5	...	968.2	184.2	...	2173.9
Total, Industries [cd]	7853.1	...	9464.3	653.4	...	17970.8	8767.5	...	10694.4	871.9	...	20333.7
Producers of Government Services	2000.1	...	105.6	...	...	2105.6	2364.9	...	126.6	...	...	2491.5
Other Producers [b]	...	...	...	...	...	...	...	...	...	...	...	...
Total [cd]	9853.2	...	9569.8	653.4	...	20076.4	11132.4	...	10820.9	871.9	...	22825.2
Less: Imputed bank service charge	...	...	889.1	...	...	889.1	...	...	1043.0	...	...	1043.0
Import duties	...	...	...	379.9	...	379.9	...	...	...	452.5	...	452.5
Value added tax	...	...	...	...	...	...	...	...	...	...	...	...
Other adjustments	...	...	...	...	...	0.1	...	...	...	...	...	-
Total [cd]	9853.2	...	8680.7	1033.3	...	19567.3	11132.4	...	9777.9	1324.4	...	22234.7

	1984						1985					
	Compensation of Employees	Capital Consumption	Net Operating Surplus	Indirect Taxes	Less: Subsidies Received	Value Added	Compensation of Employees	Capital Consumption	Net Operating Surplus	Indirect Taxes	Less: Subsidies Received	Value Added
					All Producers							
1 Agriculture, hunting, forestry and fishing	424.7	...	1254.4	-36.4	...	1642.7	470.9	...	1323.7	-50.2	...	1744.4
2 Mining and quarrying	...	...	...	...	...	...	...	...	...	...	...	...
3 Manufacturing	3348.8	...	2815.6	739.2	...	6903.6	3590.4	...	3115.9	925.6	...	7631.9
A Manufacture of food, beverages and tobacco	475.3	...	550.5	227.5	...	1253.3	521.0	...	584.8	286.4	...	1392.1

Spain

4.3 Cost Components of Value Added
(Continued)

Thousand Million Spanish pesetas

	1984						1985					
	Compensation of Employees	Capital Consumption	Net Operating Surplus	Indirect Taxes	Less: Subsidies Received	Value Added	Compensation of Employees	Capital Consumption	Net Operating Surplus	Indirect Taxes	Less: Subsidies Received	Value Added
B Textile, wearing apparel and leather industries	347.3	...	264.5	4.8	...	616.6	370.1	...	284.1	21.7	...	675.9
C Manufacture of wood and wood products, including furniture	137.7	...	79.4	13.1	...	230.2	143.5	...	88.8	13.0	...	245.3
D Manufacture of paper and paper products, printing and publishing	172.7	...	164.4	8.6	...	345.8	170.8	...	197.3	11.4	...	379.5
E Manufacture of chemicals and chemical petroleum, coal, rubber and plastic products	...	...	...	...	...	...	...	...	...	...	...	...
F Manufacture of non-metallic mineral products, except products of petroleum and coal	...	...	...	...	...	...	...	...	...	...	...	...
G Basic metal industries	...	...	...	...	...	...	...	...	...	...	...	...
H Manufacture of fabricated metal products, machinery and equipment	...	...	...	...	...	...	...	...	...	...	...	...
I Other manufacturing industries	2215.7	...	1756.8	485.2	...	4457.8	2384.9	...	1960.9	593.2	...	4939.1
4 Electricity, gas and water	209.1	...	470.2	86.6	...	765.8	229.5	...	543.1	88.3	...	860.9
5 Construction	997.6	...	518.8	119.2	...	1635.6	984.7	...	693.0	128.5	...	1806.1
6 Wholesale and retail trade, restaurants and hotels	1491.6	...	3406.9	121.2	...	5019.7	1607.2	...	3870.9	187.0	...	5665.1
A Wholesale and retail trade	1119.0	...	2425.7	73.1	...	3617.8	1204.1	...	2691.8	123.6	...	4019.4
B Restaurants and hotels	372.6	...	981.2	48.0	...	1401.8	403.1	...	1179.2	63.4	...	1645.7
7 Transport, storage and communication	820.6	...	936.3	-228.1	...	1528.8	889.6	...	995.6	-223.3	...	1661.9
A Transport and storage	620.3	...	753.2	-282.0	...	1091.5	666.7	...	789.3	-279.2	...	1176.7
B Communication	200.3	...	183.2	53.9	...	437.3	222.9	...	206.3	55.9	...	485.2
8 Finance, insurance, real estate and business services [a]	800.9	...	2482.8	92.9	...	3376.5	892.0	...	2631.3	140.9	...	3664.2
A Financial institutions	713.1	...	...	...	...	...	...	...	...	...	...	...
B Insurance	70.1	...	...	...	...	...	...	...	...	...	...	...
C Real estate and business services	20.7	...	1669.0	32.2	...	1721.9	23.0	...	1827.6	36.1	...	1886.7
9 Community, social and personal services [ab]	1148.5	...	1112.2	199.8	...	2460.6	1251.6	...	1267.7	195.0	...	2714.3
Total, Industries [cd]	9241.8	...	12997.2	1094.4	...	23333.3	9915.9	...	14441.1	1391.8	...	25748.9
Producers of Government Services	2634.4	...	148.1	...	...	2782.5	2975.1	...	168.8	...	...	3144.0
Other Producers [b]	...	...	...	...	...	...	...	...	...	...	...	...
Total [cd]	11876.2	...	13145.3	1094.4	...	26115.8	12891.0	...	14610.0	1391.8	...	28892.8
Less: Imputed bank service charge	...	...	1478.0	...	...	1478.0	...	...	1560.4	...	...	1560.4
Import duties	...	...	...	473.5	...	473.5	...	...	...	556.4	...	556.4
Value added tax	...	...	...	...	...	...	...	...	...	...	...	...
Other adjustments	...	...	...	...	...	-	...	...	...	...	...	-0.1
Total [cd]	11876.2	...	11667.3	1567.9	...	25111.3	12891.0	...	13049.6	1948.2	...	27888.8

	1986						1987					
	Compensation of Employees	Capital Consumption	Net Operating Surplus	Indirect Taxes	Less: Subsidies Received	Value Added	Compensation of Employees	Capital Consumption	Net Operating Surplus	Indirect Taxes	Less: Subsidies Received	Value Added
					All Producers							
1 Agriculture, hunting, forestry and fishing	488.3	...	...	...	...	1814.5	543.1	...	...	...	...	1941.5
2 Mining and quarrying	...	...	...	...	...	...	...	...	...	...	...	...
3 Manufacturing	3994.5	...	...	...	...	9301.6	...	...	...	...	...	...
A Manufacture of food, beverages and tobacco	580.6	...	...	...	...	1525.0	...	...	...	...	...	...

Spain

4.3 Cost Components of Value Added
(Continued)

Thousand Million Spanish pesetas

	1986						1987					
	Compensation of Employees	Capital Consumption	Net Operating Surplus	Indirect Taxes	Less: Subsidies Received	Value Added	Compensation of Employees	Capital Consumption	Net Operating Surplus	Indirect Taxes	Less: Subsidies Received	Value Added
B Textile, wearing apparel and leather industries	402.9	...	...	...	...	791.9	...	...	...	...	...	...
C Manufacture of wood and wood products, including furniture	157.5	...	...	...	...	312.3	...	...	...	...	...	...
D Manufacture of paper and paper products, printing and publishing	210.7	...	...	...	...	429.9	...	...	...	...	...	...
E Manufacture of chemicals and chemical petroleum, coal, rubber and plastic products	...	...	...	...	...	...	...	...	...	...	...	...
F Manufacture of non-metallic mineral products, except products of petroleum and coal	...	...	...	...	...	...	...	...	...	...	...	...
G Basic metal industries	...	...	...	...	...	...	...	...	...	...	...	...
H Manufacture of fabricated metal products, machinery and equipment	...	...	...	...	...	...	...	...	...	...	...	...
I Other manufacturing industries	2642.8	...	...	...	...	6242.4	...	...	...	...	...	...
4 Electricity, gas and water	249.8	...	...	...	...	1020.1	...	...	...	...	...	...
5 Construction	1190.3	...	...	...	...	2226.6	1452.2	...	...	...	...	2860.0
6 Wholesale and retail trade, restaurants and hotels	1881.2	...	...	...	...	6600.1	...	...	...	...	...	...
A Wholesale and retail trade	1411.2	...	...	...	...	4500.1	...	...	...	...	...	...
B Restaurants and hotels	470.0	...	...	...	...	2100.0	...	...	...	...	...	...
7 Transport, storage and communication	935.0	...	...	...	...	1781.6	...	...	...	...	...	...
A Transport and storage	692.5	...	...	...	...	1262.4	...	...	...	...	...	...
B Communication	242.5	...	...	...	...	519.2	...	...	...	...	...	...
8 Finance, insurance, real estate and business services [a]	1117.7	...	...	...	...	3997.5	...	...	...	...	...	...
A Financial institutions	...	...	...	...	...	...	...	...	...	...	...	...
B Insurance	...	...	...	...	...	...	...	...	...	...	...	...
C Real estate and business services	25.7	...	...	...	...	2052.5	...	...	...	...	...	...
9 Community, social and personal services [a,b]	1404.5	...	...	...	...	3054.7	...	...	...	...	...	...
Total, Industries [c,d]	11261.4	...	...	...	...	29796.6	12634.9	...	...	...	...	33349.0
Producers of Government Services	3339.0	...	...	...	...	3533.5	3719.5	...	...	...	...	3932.1
Other Producers [b]	...	...	...	...	...	...	...	...	...	...	...	...
Total [c,d]	14600.4	...	...	...	...	33330.0	16354.4	...	...	...	...	37281.1
Less: Imputed bank service charge	...	...	...	...	...	1832.7	...	...	...	...	...	2129.0
Import duties	...	...	...	...	...	450.1	...	...	...	...	...	562.4
Value added tax	...	...	...	...	...	-	...	...	...	...	...	-
Other adjustments	...	...	...	...	...	...	...	...	...	...	...	...
Total [c,d]	14600.4	...	...	...	...	31947.5	16354.4	...	...	...	...	35714.5

a) Business services and real estate except dwellings are included in item 'Community, social and personal services'.
b) Item 'Other producers' is included in item 'Community, social and personal services'.
c) Column 4 refers to indirect taxes less subsidies received.
d) Column 'Operating surplus' includes capital consumption and net indirect taxes'.

Sri Lanka

General note. The preparation of national accounts statistics in Sri Lanka is undertaken by the Department of Census and Statistics, Colombo. The official estimates are published by the Department in 'National Accounts in Sri Lanka'. The following presentation on sources and methods is based mainly on a report by the U.N. Regional Adviser of National Accounts entitled 'Assessment of sources, methods and reliability of estimates of gross domestic product by kind of economic activity in Sri Lanka (1975)' and on a detailed and comprehensive information received from the Department of Census and Statistics in 1978. The estimates are generally in accordance with the classifications and definitions recommended in the United Nations System of National Accounts (SNA). The following tables have been prepared from successve replies to the United Nations national accounts questionnaire. When the scope and coverage of the estimates differ for conceptual or statistical reasons from the definitions and classifications recommended in SNA, a footnote is indicated to the relevant tables.

Sources and methods :

(a) Gross domestic product. Gross domestic product is estimated mainly through the production approach.

(b) Expenditure on the gross domestic product. The expenditure approach is used to estimate government final consumption expenditure, gross fixed capital formation in the public sector and exports and imports of goods and services. This approach, in combination with the commodity-flow approach is used to estimate private final consumption expenditure. The commodity-flow approach is used for gross fixed capital formation in the private sector. Changes in stocks are estimated as a residual. General government expenditure consists of actual expenditure made by central government and current expenditure by the local government on goods and services which are obtained from the Treasury Votes Ledgers and the Ministry of Local Government, respectively. Private consumption expenditure is estimated by using the commodity-flow method on the basis of imports as well as domestic goods available for consumption. Bench-mark estimates for selected consumer items are avilable in value terms through the use of household survey data. These estimates are extrapolated by using the increase in population and price levels. For gross fixed capital formation in the public sector, direct estimates are prepared on the basis of information available in the budegetary accounts. For building and other construction, the supply of locally produced building materials are first compiled, adding 45 per cent to the production values for trade and transport margins while data on imported materials are obtained from customs returns adding import duties and 45 per cent for trade and transport margins. It has been found that building materials constitute 45 per cent of the construction cost with wages and profits at 55 per cent. For machinery and equipment, import statistics are analyzed in detail. Estimates for exports and imports of goods and services are based on foreign trade statistics and balance of payments data. For the constant price estimates, all items of GDP by expenditure type are deflated by appropriate price indices or extrapolated by using quantum indices.

(c) Cost-structure of the gross domestic product. Data on wages and salaries in the government sector are obtained from Treasury records. In order to estimate compensation of employees in the private sector, the percentages of wage component for the key sectors, obtained from the socio-economic survey data for 1980/1981, are applied to the respective activity. Based on special inquiries made, depreciation is assumed to be 33.3 per cent of the value of fixed assets up to 1978 and 20 per cent for the years 1979, 1980 and 1981. Indirect taxes are obtained from government revenue records and subsidies from treasury records.

(d) Gross domestic product by kind of economic activity. The table of GDP by kind of economic activity is prepared in producers values. The production approach is used to estimate value added of most industries. For livestock and forestry, the expenditure approach is used and for some of the service sectors like banking and transport, the income approach is used. Estimates of value added for tea and rubber have been revised by using the production approach. The estimation of coconut production is based on domestic and industrial consumption and exports. The annual cost-of-production returns are used for estimating inputs. The volume of paddy prodcution is estimated on the basis of acreage statistics obtained from a multistage sample survey of crop-cutting. Own-account consumption is estimated as 10 per cent of production. Bench-mark estimates for fruits and vegetables are based on the 1973 consumer finance survey. These are extrapolated for current years by increase in population and price levels. For livestock products, the per capita consumption obtained from the 1973 consumer finance survey is multiplied by each year's mid-year population. Production data for the mining and quarrying sector are obtained from the Department of Geological Survey. The value of input is assumed to be 15 per cent of the value of gross putput. For large-scale manufacturing, quantities and values of gross output and values of inputs are submitted in annual returns furnished by the registered industrial establishments. Bench-mark estimates for small-scale industries are obtained from the 1971 survey on the unorganized sector conducted by the Industrial Development Board. Extrapolation is done by using the growth in the labour force and the wage index. Data on electricity, gas and water are obtained from the Ceylon Electricity Board and the Ministry of Industries. The value added of construction activity in the private sector is based on locally produced and imported building materials obtained from the annual returns of manufacturing establishments and the customs returns, respectively. For the government sector, value of materials used in building and other construction accounts for 45 per cent of the gross value. This estimate is deducted from the value of the total supply of materials to obtain the value of material used in the private sector. Value added for the distributive trade is measured by net trade margins earned by traders on various types of products. Gross trade margin estimates are made seperately for exports, local market production, government and private imports, etc. From these estimates 15 per cent is deducted for input. Bench-mark estimates for hotels and restaurants have been obtained from the 1969/70 socio-economic survey. These estimates are extrapolated by population growth and a specially constructed index for meals consumed outside homes. For trnasport in the government sector, the expenditure on personal employment is taken as value added. The gross value of goods, transport and trade is obtained by applying specified distribution margins to the c.i.f. value in the case of imports and to the producer value in the case of locally produced goods. Wherever retail and producer prices are available the difference between them is taken as the distribution margin. For the financial sector, value added is based on data obtained from the Central Bank and concerned institutions. Bench-mark data for gross rental values have been obtained from the 1980/81 socio-economic survey. These estimates are applied to the housing stock, with an allowance made for rental increases. The value added of government services is obtained from the Treasury Accounts. For the private sector, value added is based on expenditure data obtained from the 1980/81 consumer finance survey, extrapolated by the growth in the labour force adjusted for changes in wages. For the constant price estimates, price deflation is used for most of the industries. For some agricultural products, electricity, gas and water, transport and government services, value added is extrapolated by a quantity index.

1.1 Expenditure on the Gross Domestic Product, in Current Prices

Million Sri Lanka rupees

	1970	1975	1978	1979	1980	1981	1982	1983	1984	1985	1986	1987
1 Government final consumption expenditure	1680	2697	4851	5447	6667	7456	10407	12727	15442	19170	22990	26204
2 Private final consumption expenditure	10165	21679	31891	40052	53457	64581	77310	93075	108312	118101	130728	138754
3 Gross capital formation	2746	3981	9515	14339	22410	24286	28174	31374	34412	37876	38631	44096
A Increase in stocks [a]	363	441	33	281	167	331	248	-210	150	225	137	148
B Gross fixed capital formation	2383	3540	9482	14058	22243	23955	27926	31584	34262	37651	38494	43948
Residential buildings	424	579	1234	2151	3808	5048	6138	6950	7238	9525	10694	10492
Non-residential buildings	514	690	969	1479	2839	2350	2356	2858	2399	3039	4167	4931
Other construction and land improvement etc.	673	968	1900	2102	5113	7211	7472	7836	11075	9294	8966	10846
Other	772	1302	5378	8326	10483	9348	11960	13939	13550	15793	14667	17679
4 Exports of goods and services	3478	7306	14835	17660	21434	25892	27148	32016	44285	42394	42602	50763
5 Less: Imports of goods and services	3908	9291	16872	23969	36456	39558	45905	50381	54469	62396	63737	70694
Statistical discrepancy	-	670	342	1391	825	1869	394	391	-639	2619	1228	-301
Equals: Gross Domestic Product	14161	27041	44562	54920	68338	84527	97528	119202	147344	157763	172440	188822

a) The estimates of 'Increase in stocks' for the years prior to 1975 include a statistical discrepancy.

1.2 Expenditure on the Gross Domestic Product, in Constant Prices

Million Sri Lanka rupees

	1970	1975	1978	1979	1980	1981	1982	1983	1984	1985	1986	1987
					At constant prices of:1975							
1 Government final consumption expenditure	2747	2697	3654	3688	3626	3593	4208	3919	3953	4876	5714	5846
2 Private final consumption expenditure	18338	21679	25960	28569	31610	35390	37720	39188	39598	41986	44192	44428
3 Gross capital formation	3866	3981	5259	5891	6986	7434	7516	7262	6722	6696	6501	6973
A Increase in stocks	771	441	22	169	75	127	91	-61	42	61	39	42
B Gross fixed capital formation	3095	3540	5237	5722	6911	7306	7425	7324	6680	6635	6462	6931

Sri Lanka

1.2 Expenditure on the Gross Domestic Product, in Constant Prices
(Continued)

Million Sri Lanka rupees

	1970	1975	1978	1979	1980	1981	1982	1983	1984	1985	1986	1987
	\multicolumn{12}{c}{At constant prices of:1975}
Residential buildings	611	579	784	989	1178	1312	1527	1593	1505	1839	2050	1991
Non-residential buildings	730	690	691	834	1108	774	726	813	613	742	1017	1059
Other construction and land improvement etc.	925	968	1450	1430	1808	2523	2516	2236	2686	2081	1987	2311
Other	829	1302	2312	2469	2817	2698	2656	2682	1876	1973	1408	1570
4 Exports of goods and services	7326	7306	7091	7746	8131	8375	9213	8936	10312	10828	11550	11735
5 Less: Imports of goods and services	11842	9291	13629	12743	13573	14061	15509	15420	15559	15062	16839	17243
Statistical discrepancy	2709	670	3156	254	-1473	-3464	-3949	-2824	-1891	-4024	-3882	-3737
Equals: Gross Domestic Product [a]	23143	27041	31492	33406	35308	37266	39199	41062	43136	45300	47236	48002

a) The estimates before 1975 for this table have been calculated on the basis of 1963 prices and linked to the estimates for the years beginning 1975.

1.3 Cost Components of the Gross Domestic Product

Million Sri Lanka rupees

	1970	1975	1978	1979	1980	1981	1982	1983	1984	1985	1986	1987
1 Indirect taxes, net	664	749	2116	3185	9174	10688	11163	15210	23102	22481	24318	27223
A Indirect taxes	...	...	...	...	10163	11884	12176	16937	25245	24402	26437	29274
B Less: Subsidies	...	...	...	...	988	1197	1013	1727	2143	1921	2119	2051
2 Consumption of fixed capital	794	1180	3161	2812	4449	4791	5585	6317	6852	7530	7699	8790
3 Compensation of employees paid by resident producers to:	5103	12143	19000	23945	31031	37636	44561	53729	64265	70748	78741	86388
4 Operating surplus [a]	7237	12527	19910	23307	22692	29211	35577	43765	53614	54160	60317	66574
Statistical discrepancy [b]	363	441	375	1672	992	2200	642	181	-489	2844	1365	-153
Equals: Gross Domestic Product	14161	27041	44562	54920	68338	84527	97528	119202	147344	157763	172440	188822

a) Item 'Operating surplus' has been obtained as a residual.
b) Item 'Statistical discrepancy' includes 'Increase in stocks'.

1.4 General Government Current Receipts and Disbursements

Million Sri Lanka rupees

	1970	1975	1978	1979	1980	1981	1982	1983	1984	1985	1986	1987
	\multicolumn{12}{c}{Receipts}
1 Operating surplus	...	...	...	...	...	...	...	...	...	...	...	...
2 Property and entrepreneurial income	10	25	30	30	1073	1360	1578	2149	3545	5168	5071	5523
3 Taxes, fees and contributions	2509	4240	10410	11225	12775	14267	15476	20765	31296	31095	32004	35968
A Indirect taxes	2042	3423	9217	9745	10163	11884	12176	16937	25245	24402	26437	29274
B Direct taxes	425	770	1103	1357	2515	2250	3180	3703	5887	6232	5292	6377
C Social security contributions	18	24	50	52	51	60	71	71	84	89	106	127
D Compulsory fees, fines and penalties	24	23	41	71	47	72	49	55	79	372	169	190
4 Other current transfers	449	706	1034	1220	286	357	573	2077	2270	2368	2796	2835
Total Current Receipts of General Government [a]	2968	4971	11474	12475	14134	15984	17627	24991	37110	38631	39871	44326
	\multicolumn{12}{c}{Disbursements}
1 Government final consumption expenditure	1680	2697	4851	5447	6667	7456	10407	12727	15442	19170	22990	26204
A Compensation of employees	924	1788	2466	2883	3573	4162	5379	7260	8237	9244	11124	12708
B Consumption of fixed capital	...	...	...	...	...	...	...	...	...	...	...	...
C Purchases of goods and services, net	756	909	2385	2564	3094	3294	5029	5467	7205	9926	11866	13495
D Less: Own account fixed capital formation	...	...	...	...	...	...	...	...	...	...	...	...
E Indirect taxes paid, net	...	...	...	...	...	...	...	...	...	...	...	...
2 Property income	...	...	...	...	2213	3738	5104	7369	7446	8488	9448	10671
A Interest	...	...	...	...	2213	3738	5104	7369	7446	8488	9448	10671
B Net land rent and royalties	...	...	...	...	...	...	...	...	...	...	...	...

Sri Lanka

1.4 General Government Current Receipts and Disbursements
(Continued)

Million Sri Lanka rupees

	1970	1975	1978	1979	1980	1981	1982	1983	1984	1985	1986	1987
3 Subsidies	...	...	...	...	988	1197	1013	1867	1463	1646	1548	1830
4 Other current transfers	1330	2569	5671	6141	4042	3638	3632	1731	3175	6378	2775	111
A Social security benefits	...	...	...	...	...	...	...	...	...	...	...	...
B Social assistance grants	...	...	...	...	...	...	...	...	...	...	...	...
C Other	1084	2125	4557	4931	...	...	...	...	...	...	...	...
5 Net saving	-41	-294	952	887	223	-45	-2530	1297	9584	2949	3110	5510
Total Current Disbursements and Net Saving of General Government [a]	2968	4971	11474	12475	14134	15984	17627	24991	37110	38631	39871	44326

a) Prior to 1980, estimates are based on data extracted from Central Bank of Ceylon and from the Department of Census and Statistics (DC & S). Beginning 1980, the estimates are prepared by DC & S and are therefore, not comparable with the data prior to 1980.

1.6 Current Income and Outlay of Households and Non-Profit Institutions

Million Sri Lanka rupees

	1970	1975	1978	1979	1980	1981	1982	1983	1984	1985	1986	1987
Receipts												
1 Compensation of employees	...	...	...	...	31031	37636	44561	53729	64265	70748	78741	86388
2 Operating surplus of private unincorporated enterprises	...	...	...	...	...	...	...	...	...	...	...	...
3 Property and entrepreneurial income	...	...	...	...	21817	26033	30647	37935	41640	44772	51281	56292
4 Current transfers	...	...	...	...	6100	8985	11055	12232	13982	15177	16049	17262
Total Current Receipts	...	...	...	...	58948	72654	86263	103896	119887	130697	146071	159942
Disbursements												
1 Private final consumption expenditure	...	...	...	...	53457	64581	77310	93075	108312	118101	130728	138754
2 Property income	...	...	...	...	136	165	204	253	412	409	479	478
3 Direct taxes and other current transfers n.e.c. to general government	...	...	...	...	1671	2080	2636	2884	3860	4837	5637	6109
A Social security contributions	...	...	...	...	498	601	722	795	1057	1264	1281	1450
B Direct taxes	...	...	...	...	1173	1479	1914	2089	2803	3573	4356	4659
C Fees, fines and penalties	...	...	...	...	...	...	...	...	...	...	...	...
4 Other current transfers	...	...	...	...	530	830	866	894	1140	1329	1566	1869
Statistical discrepancy	...	...	...	...	-602	-1273	-1205	-941	-4959	-7529	-7411	-6973
5 Net saving [a]	...	...	...	...	3756	6271	6452	7731	11122	13550	15072	19705
Total Current Disbursements and Net Saving [a]	...	...	...	...	58948	72654	86263	103896	119887	130697	146071	159942

a) Item 'Net saving' includes consumption of fixed capital.

1.7 External Transactions on Current Account, Summary

Million Sri Lanka rupees

	1970	1975	1978	1979	1980	1981	1982	1983	1984	1985	1986	1987
Payments to the Rest of the World												
1 Imports of goods and services [a]	3908	9291	16872	23969	36456	39558	45905	50381	54469	62396	63737	70694
A Imports of merchandise c.i.f.	3615	8801	15600	22570	33915	36121	41420	45201	49046	55528	55284	61102
B Other	293	490	1272	1399	2541	3438	4486	5180	5423	6868	8454	9592
2 Factor income to the rest of the world	235	295	551	854	1206	2502	2871	4270	4881	5706	5764	6755
A Compensation of employees	...	...	...	...	...	...	...	...	...	...	...	...
B Property and entrepreneurial income	235	295	551	854	1206	2502	2871	4270	4881	5706	5764	6755
3 Current transfers to the rest of the world	36	67	268	182	258	512	530	475	622	708	890	1098
4 Surplus of the nation on current transactions	-543	-2166	-1932	-5795	-13193	-11616	-15223	-15138	-6554	-16235	-17024	-15404
Payments to the Rest of the World and Surplus of the Nation on Current Transactions	3636	7487	15759	19210	24726	30956	34084	39987	53418	52575	53367	63142
Receipts From The Rest of the World												
1 Exports of goods and services [a]	3478	7306	14835	17660	21434	25892	27148	32016	44285	42394	42602	50763

Sri Lanka

1.7 External Transactions on Current Account, Summary
(Continued)

Million Sri Lanka rupees

	1970	1975	1978	1979	1980	1981	1982	1983	1984	1985	1986	1987
A Exports of merchandise f.o.b.	3103	6436	13207	15282	17603	20507	21098	25038	37198	35729	33893	41091
B Other	375	870	1629	2378	3831	5385	6050	6978	7088	6665	8708	9672
2 Factor income from rest of the world	15	82	314	615	774	634	912	1056	1480	2261	1893	2056
A Compensation of employees	...	...	...	...	...	...	...	...	...	...	...	...
B Property and entrepreneurial income	15	82	314	615	774	634	912	1056	1480	2261	1893	2056
3 Current transfers from rest of the world	143	99	610	935	2518	4430	6024	6916	7653	7920	8873	10324
Receipts from the Rest of the World on Current Transactions	3636	7487	15759	19210	24726	30956	34084	39987	53418	52575	53367	63142

a) Prior to 1978, estimates of imports and exports of goods and services are valued at the Foreign Exchange Entitlement Certificate Rate (FEECR) which is a proxy to the unitary rate.

1.8 Capital Transactions of The Nation, Summary

Million Sri Lanka rupees

	1970	1975	1978	1979	1980	1981	1982	1983	1984	1985	1986	1987
Finance of Gross Capital Formation												
Gross saving	2203	1815	7583	8544	9216	12670	12951	16236	27858	21641	21607	28692
1 Consumption of fixed capital [a]	794	1180	3161	2812	4449	4791	5585	6317	6852	7530	7699	8790
2 Net saving	1409	635	4422	5733	4768	7879	7366	9919	21006	14111	13908	19902
Less: Surplus of the nation on current transactions	-543	-2166	-1932	-5795	-13193	-11616	-15223	-15138	-6554	-16235	-17024	-15404
Statistical discrepancy	-	-	-	-	-	-	-	-	-	-	-	-
Finance of Gross Capital Formation	2746	3981	9515	14339	22410	24286	28174	31374	34412	37876	38631	44096
Gross Capital Formation												
Increase in stocks	363	441	33	281	167	331	248	-210	150	225	137	148
Gross fixed capital formation	2383	3540	9482	14058	22243	23955	27926	31584	34262	37651	38494	43948
1 General government [b]	572	1043	2567	3773	5177	4242	4246	5428	6142	7758	8937	11328
2 Corporate and quasi-corporate enterprises	1811	2496	6915	10284	17066	19713	23680	26156	28121	29893	29557	32620
A Public	...	...	...	...	...	...	...	...	...	...	...	...
B Private	1811	2496	6915	10284	17066	19713	23680	26156	28121	29893	29557	32620
3 Other	...	...	...	...	...	...	...	...	...	...	...	...
Gross Capital Formation	2746	3981	9515	14339	22410	24286	28174	31374	34412	37876	38631	44096

a) Item 'Consumption of fixed capital' includes depreciation of all private corporations as well as depreciation of fixed assets in other private unincorporated units.
b) Public enterprises is included in general government.

1.10 Gross Domestic Product by Kind of Activity, in Current Prices

Million Sri Lanka rupees

	1970	1975	1978	1979	1980	1981	1982	1983	1984	1985	1986	1987
1 Agriculture, hunting, forestry and fishing [a]	5080	7581	12098	15199	17900	22787	25258	30468	37293	38506	39529	43174
2 Mining and quarrying	90	323	587	646	910	1078	1159	1420	1209	1227	1670	2194
3 Manufacturing [a]	2046	6652	10071	10890	12422	14028	14644	17933	24301	26180	26914	29701
4 Electricity, gas and water	73	117	169	352	547	1003	1543	1611	2507	2999	3062	3457
5 Construction	848	1262	2476	3702	6503	8037	8651	9902	11306	11939	13197	14207
6 Wholesale and retail trade, restaurants and hotels	2357	4883	8949	9896	11331	16168	19732	23901	26951	29061	32716	35373
7 Transport, storage and communication	1307	2362	3371	4848	6962	7383	9748	11635	15621	17429	19661	20236
8 Finance, insurance, real estate and business services	699	1003	1644	2852	3620	4624	5884	7226	8623	9235	10628	11363
9 Community, social and personal services	327	621	991	1200	1513	1873	2093	2762	3057	3246	3594	4362
Total, Industries	12827	24804	40354	49584	61708	76981	88711	106857	130868	139822	150971	164067
Producers of Government Services	1192	1825	2660	2969	3573	4162	5379	7260	8237	9244	11124	12708
Other Producers	143	77	93	105	133	158	215	249	294	300	331	364
Subtotal	14161	26706	43108	52658	65414	81302	94305	114366	139399	149366	162426	177139
Less: Imputed bank service charge	...	...	...	...	...	...	...	...	...	...	...	...
Plus: Import duties	...	334	1454	2262	2924	3225	3222	4836	7945	8397	10014	11683
Plus: Value added tax	...	...	...	...	...	...	...	...	...	...	...	...
Equals: Gross Domestic Product	14161	27041	44562	54920	68338	84527	97528	119202	147344	157763	172440	188822

a) The estimates on processing of tea and rubber are included in the agricultural sector prior to 1975. From 1975 onward, they are included in the manufacturing sector.

Sri Lanka

1.11 Gross Domestic Product by Kind of Activity, in Constant Prices

Million Sri Lanka rupees

	1970	1975	1978	1979	1980	1981	1982	1983	1984	1985	1986	1987
	\multicolumn{12}{c}{At constant prices of: 1975}
1 Agriculture, hunting, forestry and fishing [a]	7191	7581	8812	9209	9357	10058	10372	10994	10200	11146	11224	10562
2 Mining and quarrying	149	323	436	411	475	500	479	575	693	673	918	1133
3 Manufacturing [a]	4556	6652	6866	7043	7071	7327	7281	7064	8300	8812	9345	9670
4 Electricity, gas and water	97	117	132	166	181	203	222	226	253	274	294	304
5 Construction	1295	1262	1505	1650	1947	2208	2157	2172	2200	2248	2419	2556
6 Wholesale and retail trade, restaurants and hotels	4080	4883	5925	6795	7564	8059	9408	10162	10907	11422	11983	12422
7 Transport, storage and communication	2007	2362	2782	3000	3460	3564	3658	4043	4531	4607	4718	4803
8 Finance, insurance, real estate and business services	855	1003	1092	1199	1269	1357	1512	1566	1649	1719	1772	1834
9 Community, social and personal services	651	621	934	926	980	1076	1117	1196	1296	1299	1338	1377
Statistical discrepancy	657	...	...	...	...	...	...	...	...	...	...	...
Total, Industries	21538	24804	28484	30398	32305	34352	36206	37997	40029	42200	44011	44661
Producers of Government Services	1529	1825	2208	2195	2206	2236	2256	2272	2298	2334	2380	2475
Other Producers	77	77	88	83	83	84	102	104	105	106	108	111
Subtotal [b]	23143	26706	30780	32676	34594	36672	38564	40373	42432	44640	46499	47247
Less: Imputed bank service charge	...	...	...	...	...	...	...	...	...	...	...	...
Plus: Import duties	...	334	712	729	714	595	635	689	704	660	737	755
Plus: Value added tax	...	...	...	...	...	...	...	...	...	...	...	...
Equals: Gross Domestic Product [b]	23143	27041	31492	33406	35308	37266	39199	41062	43136	45300	47236	48002

a) The estimates on processing of tea and rubber are included in the agricultural sector prior to 1975. From 1975 onward, they are included in the manufacturing sector.
b) The estimates before 1975 for this table have been calculated on the basis of 1963 prices and linked to the estimates for the years beginning 1975.

1.12 Relations Among National Accounting Aggregates

Million Sri Lanka rupees

	1970	1975	1978	1979	1980	1981	1982	1983	1984	1985	1986	1987
Gross Domestic Product	14161	27041	44562	54920	68338	84527	97528	119202	147344	157763	172440	188822
Plus: Net factor income from the rest of the world	-220	-213	-237	-240	-432	-1868	-1959	-3214	-3401	-3445	-3871	-4699
Factor income from the rest of the world	15	82	314	615	774	634	912	1056	1480	2261	1893	2056
Less: Factor income to the rest of the world	235	295	551	854	1206	2502	2871	4270	4881	5706	5764	6755
Equals: Gross National Product	13941	26828	44325	54681	67906	82659	95568	115988	143943	154318	168569	184123
Less: Consumption of fixed capital	794	1180	3161	2812	4449	4791	5585	6317	6852	7530	7699	8790
Equals: National Income	13147	25648	41164	51869	63457	77868	89983	109671	137091	146788	160870	175333
Plus: Net current transfers from the rest of the world	107	32	342	754	2260	3918	5494	6441	7031	7212	7983	9226
Current transfers from the rest of the world	143	99	610	935	2518	4430	6024	6916	7653	7920	8873	10324
Less: Current transfers to the rest of the world	36	67	268	182	258	512	530	475	622	708	890	1098
Equals: National Disposable Income	13254	25680	41506	52623	65717	81786	95477	116112	144122	154000	168853	184559
Less: Final consumption	11845	24375	36742	45499	60124	72038	87717	105802	123755	137271	153718	164958
Statistical discrepancy	...	-670	-342	-1391	-825	-1869	-394	-391	639	-2619	-1228	301
Equals: Net Saving	1409	635	4422	5733	4768	7879	7366	9919	21006	14111	13908	19902
Less: Surplus of the nation on current transactions	-543	-2166	-1932	-5795	-13193	-11616	-15223	-15138	-6554	-16235	-17024	-15404
Equals: Net Capital Formation [a]	1952	2801	6354	11527	17961	19495	22589	25057	27560	30346	30932	35306

a) Item 'Net capital formation' includes a statistical discrepancy.

Sri Lanka

2.1 Government Final Consumption Expenditure by Function, in Current Prices

Million Sri Lanka rupees

	1970	1975	1978	1979	1980	1981	1982	1983	1984	1985	1986	1987
1 General public services	318	666	1497	1748	1860	2644	4346	4701	5816	6126	5281	5711
2 Defence	92	193	283	485	585	625	687	1229	1748	4654	7877	9110
3 Public order and safety	...	...	...	...	...	...	...	...	...	...	...	...
4 Education	472	681	1008	1167	1171	1508	1872	2380	2662	3154	3457	3691
5 Health	236	332	522	626	738	823	954	1259	1521	1660	1733	2258
6 Social security and welfare	183	336	640	596	756	930	1203	1681	1950	2228	3053	3514
7 Housing and community amenities	2	25	37	52	61	67	87	133	130	83	73	74
8 Recreational, cultural and religious affairs	23	13	25	36	39	37	48	64	74	82	93	104
9 Economic services	354	451	839	738	1457	824	1211	1279	1541	1183	1423	1742
10 Other functions	...	...	...	...	...	...	...	...	...	...	...	...
Total Government Final Consumption Expenditure	1680	2697	4851	5447	6667	7456	10407	12727	15442	19170	22990	26204

2.2 Government Final Consumption Expenditure by Function, in Constant Prices

Million Sri Lanka rupees

	1970	1975	1978	1979	1980	1981	1982	1983	1984	1985	1986	1987
					At constant prices of:1975							
1 General public services	522	666	1128	1183	1012	1276	1757	1448	1490	1555	1314	1275
2 Defence	151	193	213	328	319	302	278	379	447	1185	1960	2035
3 Public order and safety	...	...	...	...	...	...	...	...	...	...	...	...
4 Education	772	681	759	790	638	726	757	733	680	804	857	824
5 Health	385	332	393	424	403	395	386	388	391	424	429	503
6 Social security and welfare	299	336	482	403	410	449	486	518	498	566	760	783
7 Housing and community amenities	3	25	28	35	33	32	35	41	32	20	17	17
8 Recreational, cultural and religious affairs	39	13	19	24	22	18	19	20	20	20	23	23
9 Economic services	577	451	632	500	791	395	490	394	395	302	354	386
10 Other functions	...	...	...	...	...	...	...	...	...	...	...	...
Total Government Final Consumption Expenditure [a]	2747	2697	3654	3688	3626	3593	4208	3919	3953	4876	5714	5846

a) The estimates before 1975 for this table have been calculated on the basis of 1963 prices and linked to the estimates for the years beginning 1975.

2.5 Private Final Consumption Expenditure by Type and Purpose, in Current Prices

Million Sri Lanka rupees

	1970	1975	1978	1979	1980	1981	1982	1983	1984	1985	1986	1987
				Final Consumption Expenditure of Resident Households								
1 Food, beverages and tobacco	6539	15476	22041	26957	33101	37270	44674	55616	62411	64194	69240	75284
A Food	5506	13724	19411	23111	27298	30626	36974	47137	51684	52457	57307	65470
B Non-alcoholic beverages	43	60	66	76	88	77	52	233	659	292	626	595
C Alcoholic beverages	344	594	978	1525	1884	1847	2809	2993	3111	3832	3474	3679
D Tobacco	647	1099	1587	2245	3831	4720	4839	5253	6957	7613	7833	5540
2 Clothing and footwear	618	1615	1974	2532	3208	3923	4558	5794	6548	8044	9172	10999
3 Gross rent, fuel and power	727	1047	1362	2448	3112	3635	4704	5177	6174	6710	7033	7307
A Fuel and power	237	347	520	802	1050	1215	2171	2611	3334	3517	3729	3905
B Other	490	700	842	1646	2062	2419	2534	2566	2840	3193	3304	3402
4 Furniture, furnishings and household equipment and operation	461	692	1203	1828	2606	3281	3428	3492	3759	5312	5711	5975
A Household operation	258	326	555	851	805	1265	1472	1474	1452	1853	2000	1873
B Other	203	366	648	977	1801	2016	1956	2018	2307	3459	3711	4102
5 Medical care and health expenses	291	310	523	644	896	1088	1236	1224	1508	1829	2597	2544
6 Transport and communication	643	1229	2711	3450	6467	9253	10696	12684	17678	18715	19959	21008
A Personal transport equipment	3	5	294	454	988	1199	1093	1466	1546	1630	1459	1624
B Other	640	1224	2418	2996	5478	8055	9603	11217	16132	17085	18500	19384
7 Recreational, entertainment, education and cultural services	687	689	1245	1342	2064	2201	3393	3642	4189	5494	5411	6187
A Education	227	213	351	373	385	219	587	689	677	1387	1120	1371
B Other	460	477	894	969	1680	1982	2806	2953	3512	4107	4291	4816
8 Miscellaneous goods and services	261	812	1123	1371	2235	2259	2467	2455	2942	3476	5497	5099
A Personal care	81	263	462	536	1202	887	952	1173	1367	2212	3537	2770
B Expenditures in restaurants, cafes and hotels	120	366	532	725	724	967	1308	991	1422	1106	1731	2087

Sri Lanka

2.5 Private Final Consumption Expenditure by Type and Purpose, in Current Prices
(Continued)

Million Sri Lanka rupees

	1970	1975	1978	1979	1980	1981	1982	1983	1984	1985	1986	1987
C Other	60	183	129	110	309	405	208	291	153	158	228	242
Total Final Consumption Expenditure in the Domestic Market by Households, of which	10226	21869	32182	40572	53689	62910	75156	90083	105208	113774	124620	134404
Plus: Direct purchases abroad by resident households a b	221	60	597	684	1656	4300	5201	5945	6839	7468	9316	8128
Less: Direct purchases in the domestic market by non-resident households c	282	250	888	1204	1888	2629	3048	2952	3734	3141	3208	3778
Equals: Final Consumption Expenditure of Resident Households d	10165	21679	31891	40052	53457	64581	77310	93075	108312	118101	130728	138754

Final Consumption Expenditure of Private Non-profit Institutions Serving Households

	1970	1975	1978	1979	1980	1981	1982	1983	1984	1985	1986	1987
Equals: Final Consumption Expenditure of Private Non-profit Organisations Serving Households	...	...	...	...	...	...	...	...	...	...	...	...
Private Final Consumption Expenditure	10165	21679	31891	40052	53457	64581	77310	93075	108312	118101	130728	138754

a) Estimates up to 1972 for 'Direct purchases abroad by resident households' have been obtained from the Central Bank. For 1973 and 1974, no estimates have been made. From 1975 onward, figures have been estimated independently by the Department of Census and Statistics.
b) For 1981 and 1982, transfers made by residents abroad are not included in item 'Direct Purchases Abroad by Resident Households' shown in table 2.17 but are included in the estimates shown in table 2.5.
c) Estimates up to 1974 for 'Direct purchases in the domestic market by non-resident households' have been obtained from the Central Bank. From 1975 onward, figures have been estimated independently by the Department of Census and Statistics.
d) Item 'Final consumption expenditure of resident households' includes consumption expenditure of private non-profit institutions serving households.

2.6 Private Final Consumption Expenditure by Type and Purpose, in Constant Prices

Million Sri Lanka rupees

At constant prices of: 1975

Final Consumption Expenditure of Resident Households

	1970	1975	1978	1979	1980	1981	1982	1983	1984	1985	1986	1987
1 Food, beverages and tobacco	13725	15476	16878	18604	18799	19201	19303	19851	18306	18718	18612	19689
A Food	12509	13724	15188	16530	16055	16534	16609	17025	15134	16001	16138	17639
B Non-alcoholic beverages	47	60	40	40	44	31	20	37	284	119	120	179
C Alcoholic beverages	537	594	591	807	946	741	1089	1141	967	1115	859	821
D Tobacco	631	1099	1061	1228	1755	1896	1585	1648	1921	1483	1495	1050
2 Clothing and footwear	1039	1615	1734	2146	2691	3169	3426	4144	4433	4628	4692	4878
3 Gross rent, fuel and power	839	1047	1144	1189	1197	1217	1419	1473	1455	1525	1582	1589
A Fuel and power	347	347	418	447	441	452	644	690	710	772	814	840
B Other	492	700	726	742	755	765	775	783	745	753	768	749
4 Furniture, furnishings and household equipment and operation	756	692	1008	1338	1648	1912	1675	1527	1481	1878	1863	1882
A Household operation	311	326	465	627	526	694	748	652	560	678	640	552
B Other	445	366	544	710	1122	1218	927	876	921	1200	1223	1330
5 Medical care and health expenses	507	310	439	475	585	602	628	541	582	669	830	750
6 Transport and communication	969	1229	2730	2990	3404	3982	4596	4182	4950	5223	5255	5531
A Personal transport equipment	4	5	296	394	520	516	470	479	430	454	384	426
B Other	965	1224	2435	2596	2883	3466	4127	3703	4520	4769	4871	5105
7 Recreational, entertainment, education and cultural services	1014	689	1233	1112	1347	1207	1335	1315	1264	1545	1312	1495
A Education	311	213	348	309	251	120	231	172	231	507	354	404
B Other	703	477	885	803	1096	1087	1104	1142	1033	1038	958	1091
8 Miscellaneous goods and services	284	812	941	1010	1459	1103	1253	1086	1135	1271	1758	1503
A Personal care	92	263	387	395	785	433	483	432	528	591	1132	816
B Expenditures in restaurants, cafes and hotels	128	366	446	534	473	472	664	555	548	614	554	615
C Other	64	183	108	81	202	198	106	100	59	66	72	72

Sri Lanka

2.6 Private Final Consumption Expenditure by Type and Purpose, in Constant Prices
(Continued)

Million Sri Lanka rupees

	1970	1975	1978	1979	1980	1981	1982	1983	1984	1985	1986	1987
					At constant prices of:1975							
Statistical discrepancy	-632	-	...	...	...	...	...	...	...	...	...	...
Total Final Consumption Expenditure in the Domestic Market by Households, of which	18502	21869	26108	28863	31130	32393	33635	34119	33609	35457	35903	37316
Plus: Direct purchases abroad by resident households [a,b]	238	60	597	684	1656	4011	5201	5945	6839	7468	9316	8128
Less: Direct purchases in the domestic market by non-resident households [c]	402	250	745	978	1177	1014	1116	876	850	939	1026	1016
Equals: Final Consumption Expenditure of Resident Households [d,e]	18338	21679	25960	28569	31610	35390	37720	39188	39598	41986	44192	44428
			Final Consumption Expenditure of Private Non-profit Institutions Serving Households									
Equals: Final Consumption Expenditure of Private Non-profit Organisations Serving Households	...	...	...	...	...	...	...	...	...	...	...	...
Private Final Consumption Expenditure [e]	18338	21679	25960	28569	31610	35390	37720	39188	39598	41986	44192	44428

a) Estimates up to 1972 for 'Direct purchases abroad by resident households' have been obtained from the Central Bank. For 1973 and 1974, no estimates have been made. From 1975 onward, figures have been estimated independently by the Department of Census and Statistics.
b) For 1981 and 1982, transfers made by residents abroad are not included in item 'Direct Purchases Abroad by Resident Households' shown in table 2.17 but are included in the estimates shown in table 2.5.
c) Estimates up to 1974 for 'Direct purchases in the domestic market by non-resident households' have been obtained from the Central Bank. From 1975 onward, figures have been estimated independently by the Department of Census and Statistics.
d) Item 'Final consumption expenditure of resident households' includes consumption expenditure of private non-profit institutions serving households.
e) The estimates before 1975 for this table have been calculated on the basis of 1963 prices and linked to the estimates for the years beginning 1975.

2.7 Gross Capital Formation by Type of Good and Owner, in Current Prices

Million Sri Lanka rupees

	1980				1981				1982			
	TOTAL	Total Private	Public Enterprises	General Government	TOTAL	Total Private	Public Enterprises	General Government	TOTAL	Total Private	Public Enterprises	General Government
Increase in stocks, total [a]	167	128	...	39	331	272	...	59	248	210	...	38
Gross Fixed Capital Formation, Total	22243	17066	...	5177	23955	19713	...	4242	27926	23680	...	4246
1 Residential buildings	3808	3645	...	162	5048	4996	...	51	6138	5981	...	157
2 Non-residential buildings	2839	1388	...	1451	2350	1199	...	1151	2356	1359	...	997
3 Other construction	1661	520	...	1141	3147	2125	...	1022	3074	1722	...	1353
4 Land improvement and plantation and orchard development	3453	2755	...	698	4063	3156	...	908	4398	3315	...	1083
5 Producers' durable goods	10483	8759	...	1725	9348	8236	...	1111	11960	11303	...	657
A Transport equipment	3653	3158	...	495	2850	2430	...	420	6627	6257	...	369
B Machinery and equipment	6831	5600	...	1230	6497	5806	...	691	5333	5046	...	287
6 Breeding stock, dairy cattle, etc.	...	...	...	...	...	...	...	...	...	...	...	...
Total Gross Capital Formation [b]	22410	17194	...	5216	24286	19985	...	4301	28174	23890	...	4284

	1983				1984				1985			
	TOTAL	Total Private	Public Enterprises	General Government	TOTAL	Total Private	Public Enterprises	General Government	TOTAL	Total Private	Public Enterprises	General Government
Increase in stocks, total [a]	-210	-174	...	-36	150	123	...	27	225	178	...	47
Gross Fixed Capital Formation, Total	31584	26156	...	5428	34262	28121	...	6142	37651	29893	...	7758
1 Residential buildings	6950	6883	...	67	7238	7186	...	53	9525	9477	...	48
2 Non-residential buildings	2858	1564	...	1294	2399	1633	...	766	3039	2154	...	885
3 Other construction	3848	1981	...	1867	4633	2069	...	2565	6490	2728	...	3762
4 Land improvement and plantation and orchard development	3988	2798	...	1191	6442	4784	...	1658	2804	1096	...	1708
5 Producers' durable goods	13939	12930	...	1009	13550	12449	...	1101	15793	14437	...	1355
A Transport equipment	5753	5414	...	339	5621	5184	...	437	5328	4506	...	822
B Machinery and equipment	8186	7516	...	671	7929	7266	...	664	10465	9931	...	533
6 Breeding stock, dairy cattle, etc.	...	...	...	...	...	...	...	...	...	...	...	...
Total Gross Capital Formation [b]	31374	25982	...	5392	34412	28244	...	6168	37876	30071	...	7805

Sri Lanka

2.7 Gross Capital Formation by Type of Good and Owner, in Current Prices

Million Sri Lanka rupees

	1986 TOTAL	Total Private	Public Enterprises	General Government	1987 TOTAL	Total Private	Public Enterprises	General Government
Increase in stocks, total [a]	137	105	...	32	148	110	...	38
Gross Fixed Capital Formation, Total	38494	29557	...	8937	43948	32620	...	11328
1 Residential buildings	10694	10495	...	199	10492	10286	...	206
2 Non-residential buildings	4167	2385	...	1782	4931	2961	...	1970
3 Other construction	6197	3021	...	3176	6217	2338	...	3879
4 Land improvement and plantation and orchard development	2769	1008	...	1761	4629	1960	...	2669
5 Producers' durable goods	14667	12648	...	2019	17679	15075	...	2604
A Transport equipment	4883	3682	...	1201	6049	4639	...	1410
B Machinery and equipment	9784	8966	...	818	11630	10436	...	1194
6 Breeding stock, dairy cattle, etc.	...	...	...	...	...	...	...	...
Total Gross Capital Formation [b]	38631	29662	...	8969	44096	32730	...	11366

a) The estimates of 'Increase in stocks' for the years prior to 1975 include a statistical discrepancy.
b) Column 'Public Enterprises' is included in column 'General Government'.

2.8 Gross Capital Formation by Type of Good and Owner, in Constant Prices

Million Sri Lanka rupees

	1980 TOTAL	Total Private	Public Enterprises	General Government	1981 TOTAL	Total Private	Public Enterprises	General Government	1982 TOTAL	Total Private	Public Enterprises	General Government
At constant prices of: 1975												
Increase in stocks, total	75	58	...	18	127	105	...	23	91	77	...	14
Gross Fixed Capital Formation, Total	6911	5103	...	1809	7306	5922	...	1384	7425	6169	...	1257
1 Residential buildings	1178	1128	...	50	1312	1299	...	13	1527	1488	...	39
2 Non-residential buildings	1108	542	...	566	774	395	...	379	726	419	...	307
3 Other construction	690	216	...	474	1161	784	...	377	1053	590	...	463
4 Land improvement and plantation and orchard development	1118	864	...	255	1361	1067	...	294	1463	1139	...	325
5 Producers' durable goods	2817	2354	...	464	2698	2377	...	321	2656	2533	...	123
A Transport equipment	982	849	...	133	823	701	...	121	1250	1182	...	68
B Machinery and equipment	1836	1505	...	331	1875	1676	...	199	1406	1352	...	54
6 Breeding stock, dairy cattle, etc.	...	...	...	...	...	...	...	...	...	...	...	...
Total Gross Capital Formation [a]	6986	5160	...	1826	7434	6027	...	1407	7516	6245	...	1270

	1983 TOTAL	Total Private	Public Enterprises	General Government	1984 TOTAL	Total Private	Public Enterprises	General Government	1985 TOTAL	Total Private	Public Enterprises	General Government
At constant prices of: 1975												
Increase in stocks, total	-61	-51	...	-11	42	35	...	8	61	48	...	13
Gross Fixed Capital Formation, Total	7324	5852	...	1472	6680	5248	...	1432	6635	5016	...	1619
1 Residential buildings	1593	1577	...	15	1505	1494	...	11	1839	1830	...	9
2 Non-residential buildings	813	445	...	368	613	418	...	196	742	526	...	216
3 Other construction	1214	625	...	589	1288	575	...	713	1464	616	...	848
4 Land improvement and plantation and orchard development	1022	717	...	305	1398	1038	...	360	617	241	...	376
5 Producers' durable goods	2682	2488	...	194	1876	1723	...	152	1973	1804	...	169
A Transport equipment	1107	1042	...	65	778	718	...	61	666	563	...	103
B Machinery and equipment	1575	1446	...	129	1098	1006	...	92	1307	1241	...	66
6 Breeding stock, dairy cattle, etc.	...	...	...	...	...	...	...	...	...	...	...	...
Total Gross Capital Formation [a]	7262	5801	...	1461	6722	5282	...	1440	6696	5064	...	1632

Sri Lanka

2.8 Gross Capital Formation by Type of Good and Owner, in Constant Prices

Million Sri Lanka rupees

	1986 TOTAL	1986 Total Private	1986 Public Enterprises	1986 General Government	1987 TOTAL	1987 Total Private	1987 Public Enterprises	1987 General Government
At constant prices of: 1975								
Increase in stocks, total	39	30	...	9	42	31	...	11
Gross Fixed Capital Formation, Total	6462	4704	...	1758	6931	4840	...	2091
1 Residential buildings	2050	2012	...	38	1991	1952	...	39
2 Non-residential buildings	1017	582	...	435	1059	636	...	423
3 Other construction	1393	679	...	714	1388	522	...	866
4 Land improvement and plantation and orchard development	594	216	...	378	923	391	...	532
5 Producers' durable goods	1408	1215	...	193	1570	1339	...	231
A Transport equipment	469	354	...	115	537	412	...	125
B Machinery and equipment	939	861	...	78	1033	927	...	106
6 Breeding stock, dairy cattle, etc.	...	...	...	...	...	...	...	...
Total Gross Capital Formation [a]	6501	4734	...	1767	6973	4871	...	2102

a) Column 'Public Enterprises' is included in column 'General Government'.

2.17 Exports and Imports of Goods and Services, Detail

Million Sri Lanka rupees

	1970	1975	1978	1979	1980	1981	1982	1983	1984	1985	1986	1987
Exports of Goods and Services												
1 Exports of merchandise, f.o.b. [a,b]	3103	6436	13207	15282	17603	20507	21098	25038	37198	35729	33893	41091
2 Transport and communication	...	...	...	...	...	...	...	...	...	...	...	...
3 Insurance service charges	...	...	...	...	...	...	...	...	...	...	...	...
4 Other commodities [c]	93	620	741	1175	1943	2756	3003	4026	3353	3524	5501	5894
5 Adjustments of merchandise exports to change-of-ownership basis	...	...	...	...	...	...	...	...	...	...	...	...
6 Direct purchases in the domestic market by non-residential households [d]	282	250	888	1204	1888	2629	3048	2952	3734	3141	3208	3778
7 Direct purchases in the domestic market by extraterritorial bodies	...	...	...	...	...	...	...	...	...	...	...	...
Total Exports of Goods and Services	3478	7306	14835	17660	21434	25892	27148	32016	44285	42394	42602	50763
Imports of Goods and Services												
1 Imports of merchandise, c.i.f. [b]	3615	8801	15600	22570	33915	36121	41420	45201	49046	55528	55284	61102
2 Adjustments of merchandise imports to change-of-ownership basis	...	...	...	...	...	...	...	...	...	...	...	...
3 Other transport and communication	22	61	268	348	483	659	884	1256	1409	2077	2724	3176
4 Other insurance service charges	8	11	33	26	41	55	114	185	261	278	867	526
5 Other commodities	42	358	375	342	361	189	217	-	-	-	-	-
6 Direct purchases abroad by government	...	...	...	...	...	...	...	...	...	...	...	...
7 Direct purchases abroad by resident households [e,f]	221	60	597	684	1656	4300	5202	5945	6839	7468	9316	8128
Statistical discrepancy	...	...	...	...	...	-1766	-1930	-2206	-3086	-2955	-4454	-2238
Total Imports of Goods and Services	3908	9291	16872	23969	36456	39558	45905	50381	54469	62396	63737	70694
Balance of Goods and Services	-430	-1985	-2037	-6309	-15022	-13667	-18758	-18365	-10184	-20002	-21135	-19931
Total Imports and Balance of Goods and Services	3478	7306	14835	17660	21434	25892	27148	32016	44285	42394	42602	50763

a) Item 'Exports of merchandise, f.o.b.' excludes merchandise purchases in the domestic market by non-resident households.
b) Prior to 1978, estimates of imports and exports of goods and services are valued at the Foreign Exchange Entitlement Certificate Rate (FEECR) which is a proxy to the unitary rate.
c) Item 'Other commodities' has been obtained as a residual.
d) Estimates up to 1974 for 'Direct purchases in the domestic market by non-resident households' have been obtained from the Central Bank. From 1975 onward, figures have been estimated independently by the Department of Census and Statistics.
e) Estimates up to 1972 for 'Direct purchases abroad by resident households' have been obtained from the Central Bank. For 1973 and 1974, no estimates have been made. From 1975 onward, figures have been estimated independently by the Department of Census and Statistics.
f) For 1981 and 1982, transfers made by residents abroad are not included in item 'Direct Purchases Abroad by Resident Households' shown in table 2.17 but are included in the estimates shown in table 2.5.

Sri Lanka

4.1 Derivation of Value Added by Kind of Activity, in Current Prices

Million Sri Lanka rupees

	1980 Gross Output	1980 Intermediate Consumption	1980 Value Added	1981 Gross Output	1981 Intermediate Consumption	1981 Value Added	1982 Gross Output	1982 Intermediate Consumption	1982 Value Added	1983 Gross Output	1983 Intermediate Consumption	1983 Value Added
					All Producers							
1 Agriculture, hunting, forestry and fishing [a]	...	...	17900	27496	4709	22787	31091	5834	25258	38474	8006	30468
A Agriculture and hunting	...	...	15824	24476	3944	20532	27574	4978	22596	34177	6676	27501
B Forestry and logging	...	...	946	944	-	944	1091	14	1077	1254	20	1234
C Fishing	...	...	1130	2076	765	1311	2427	841	1586	3043	1311	1733
2 Mining and quarrying	...	...	910	1268	190	1078	1364	205	1159	1566	146	1420
A Coal mining	...	...	...	...	...	...	...	...	...	...	...	...
B Crude petroleum and natural gas production	...	...	...	...	...	...	...	...	...	...	...	...
C Metal ore mining	...	...	...	...	...	...	...	...	...	...	...	...
D Other mining	...	...	910	1268	190	1078	1364	205	1159	1566	146	1420
3 Manufacturing [a]	...	...	12422	24837	10810	14028	35915	21271	14644	40913	22980	17933
A Manufacture of food, beverages and tobacco	...	...	6065	12956	6206	6750	14945	7421	7524	19718	10268	9451
B Textile, wearing apparel and leather industries	...	...	1550	2473	830	1643	2960	972	1988	2784	924	1860
C Manufacture of wood and wood products, including furniture	...	...	154	267	90	177	456	143	313	544	168	376
D Manufacture of paper and paper products, printing and publishing	...	...	255	448	156	292	414	144	270	426	148	278
E Manufacture of chemicals and chemical petroleum, coal, rubber and plastic products	...	...	1950	3577	1278	2299	13310	10633	2676	11332	8132	3200
F Manufacture of non-metallic mineral products, except products of petroleum and coal	...	...	925	1631	528	1103	1486	504	982	1534	518	1016
G Basic metal industries	...	...	108	192	67	125	119	42	77	243	85	158
H Manufacture of fabricated metal products, machinery and equipment	...	...	793	1278	447	831	331	116	215	612	214	398
I Other manufacturing industries	...	...	622	2015	1208	807	1895	1297	598	3721	2524	1197
4 Electricity, gas and water	...	...	547	1579	576	1003	2621	1078	1543	4145	2534	1611
A Electricity, gas and steam	...	...	547	1579	576	1003	2621	1078	1543	4145	2534	1611
B Water works and supply	...	...	...	...	...	...	...	...	...	...	...	...
5 Construction	...	...	6503	14536	6499	8037	15696	7045	8651	17686	7784	9902
6 Wholesale and retail trade, restaurants and hotels	...	...	11331	19725	3557	16168	23384	3653	19732	28408	4508	23901
A Wholesale and retail trade	...	...	10895	19753	3168	15585	22058	3139	18919	27398	4110	23288
B Restaurants and hotels	...	...	436	972	389	583	1326	513	812	1010	398	612
Restaurants	...	...	...	...	...	...	527	207	321	568	224	344
Hotels and other lodging places	...	...	...	...	...	...	799	307	492	442	174	268
7 Transport, storage and communication	...	...	6962	15592	8209	7383	20240	10492	9748	23711	12075	11635
A Transport and storage	...	...	...	15362	8209	7153	19814	10492	9322	22803	12075	10727
B Communication	...	...	...	230	-	230	426	-	426	908	-	908
8 Finance, insurance, real estate and business services	...	...	3620	5246	623	4624	6509	625	5884	7925	699	7226
A Financial institutions	...	...	1877	2689	113	2576	3848	115	3732	5149	117	5032
B Insurance	...	...										
C Real estate and business services	...	...	1743	2557	510	2047	2662	510	2152	2776	582	2194
Real estate, except dwellings	...	...	84	100	-	100	114	-	114	131	-	131
Dwellings	...	...	1659	2457	510	1947	2548	510	2039	2645	582	2063
9 Community, social and personal services	...	...	1513	2524	651	1873	2731	638	2093	3477	715	2762
A Sanitary and similar services	...	...	...	...	...	...	...	...	...	...	...	...
B Social and related community services	...	...	217	312	73	239	742	222	519	1003	267	736
C Recreational and cultural services	...	...	800	1302	461	840	1143	325	818	1323	336	987
D Personal and household services	...	...	496	911	117	794	847	91	756	1151	111	1039

Sri Lanka

4.1 Derivation of Value Added by Kind of Activity, in Current Prices
(Continued)

Million Sri Lanka rupees

	1980 Gross Output	1980 Intermediate Consumption	1980 Value Added	1981 Gross Output	1981 Intermediate Consumption	1981 Value Added	1982 Gross Output	1982 Intermediate Consumption	1982 Value Added	1983 Gross Output	1983 Intermediate Consumption	1983 Value Added
Total, Industries	...	...	61708	112805	35824	76981	139551	50840	88711	166304	59447	106857
Producers of Government Services	...	...	3573	7456	3294	4162	10407	5029	5379	12733	5473	7260
Other Producers	...	...	133	158	-	158	215	-	215	249	-	249
Total	...	...	65414	120419	39118	81302	150174	55869	94305	179286	64920	114366
Less: Imputed bank service charge	...	...	...	...	...	...	...	...	...	...	...	...
Import duties	...	...	2924	3225	-	3225	3222	-	3222	4836	-	4836
Value added tax	...	...	...	...	...	...	...	...	...	...	...	...
Total	...	...	68338	123644	39118	84527	153396	55869	97528	184121	64920	119202

	1984 Gross Output	1984 Intermediate Consumption	1984 Value Added	1985 Gross Output	1985 Intermediate Consumption	1985 Value Added	1986 Gross Output	1986 Intermediate Consumption	1986 Value Added	1987 Gross Output	1987 Intermediate Consumption	1987 Value Added
					All Producers							
1 Agriculture, hunting, forestry and fishing [a]	45132	7839	37293	47008	8502	38506	48918	9389	39529	53460	10286	43174
A Agriculture and hunting	40222	6950	33272	41663	7457	34206	42773	8112	34661	46393	8764	37629
B Forestry and logging	1444	13	1431	1652	15	1637	1723	13	1710	1797	18	1779
C Fishing	3466	876	2590	3693	1030	2663	4422	1264	3158	5270	1504	3766
2 Mining and quarrying	1344	135	1209	1372	145	1227	1869	199	1670	2412	218	2194
A Coal mining	...	...	...	...	...	...	...	...	...	...	...	...
B Crude petroleum and natural gas production												
C Metal ore mining	...	...	...	...	...	...	...	...	...	...	...	...
D Other mining	1344	135	1209	1372	145	1227	1869	199	1670	2412	218	2194
3 Manufacturing [a]	57899	33598	24301	58938	32758	26180	59866	32952	26914	69165	39464	29701
A Manufacture of food, beverages and tobacco	29679	14423	15256	25868	11841	14027	28762	13905	14857	33481	17037	16444
B Textile, wearing apparel and leather industries	8416	5323	3093	9731	5634	4097	10527	6217	4310	13912	8233	5679
C Manufacture of wood and wood products, including furniture	655	207	448	980	317	663	913	292	621	945	301	644
D Manufacture of paper and paper products, printing and publishing	34	11	23	680	236	444	354	122	232	504	175	329
E Manufacture of chemicals and chemical petroleum, coal, rubber and plastic products	13834	11184	2650	12625	10345	2280	10596	8495	2101	13571	10536	3035
F Manufacture of non-metallic mineral products, except products of petroleum and coal	964	313	651	1865	627	1238	1748	587	1161	903	291	612
G Basic metal industries	84	30	54	147	51	96	180	63	117	115	40	75
H Manufacture of fabricated metal products, machinery and equipment	1335	467	868	2894	1013	1881	3108	1087	2021	1989	696	1293
I Other manufacturing industries	2898	1640	1258	4148	2694	1454	3678	2184	1494	3745	2155	1590
4 Electricity, gas and water	3304	797	2507	3369	370	2999	3520	458	3062	4435	978	3457
A Electricity, gas and steam	3304	797	2507	3369	370	2999	3520	458	3062	4435	978	3457
B Water works and supply	...	...	...	...	...	...	...	...	...	...	...	...
5 Construction	20411	9105	11306	21550	9611	11939	23667	10470	13197	25547	11340	14207
6 Wholesale and retail trade, restaurants and hotels	32114	5163	26951	36616	7555	29061	41323	8607	32716	44739	9366	35373
A Wholesale and retail trade	30683	4602	26081	35410	7082	28328	39565	7913	31652	42650	8530	34120
B Restaurants and hotels	1431	561	870	1206	473	733	1758	694	1064	2089	836	1253
Restaurants	1012	397	615	804	315	489	1288	508	780	1539	616	923
Hotels and other lodging places	419	164	255	402	158	244	470	186	284	550	220	330
7 Transport, storage and communication	31730	16109	15621	34413	16984	17429	36972	17311	19661	38481	18245	20236
A Transport and storage	30772	16109	14663	33365	16984	16381	35827	17311	18516	37248	18245	19003
B Communication	958	-	958	1048	-	1048	1145	-	1145	1233	-	1233
8 Finance, insurance, real estate and business services	9370	747	8623	10059	824	9235	11499	871	10628	12237	874	11363
A Financial institutions	6357	118	6239	6693	118	6575	8006	141	7865	8639	124	8515
B Insurance												
C Real estate and business services	3013	629	2384	3366	706	2660	3493	730	2763	3597	749	2848
Real estate, except dwellings	155	-	155	158	-	158	175	-	175	192	-	192

# Sri Lanka

4.1 Derivation of Value Added by Kind of Activity, in Current Prices
(Continued)

Million Sri Lanka rupees

	1984 Gross Output	1984 Intermediate Consumption	1984 Value Added	1985 Gross Output	1985 Intermediate Consumption	1985 Value Added	1986 Gross Output	1986 Intermediate Consumption	1986 Value Added	1987 Gross Output	1987 Intermediate Consumption	1987 Value Added
Dwellings	2858	629	2229	3208	706	2502	3318	730	2588	3405	749	2656
9 Community, social and personal services	3840	783	3057	4055	809	3246	4507	913	3594	5370	1008	4362
A Sanitary and similar services	...	...	...	...	...	...	...	...	...	...	...	...
B Social and related community services	1053	290	763	1127	303	824	1237	329	908	1413	351	1062
C Recreational and cultural services	1469	364	1105	1456	374	1082	1576	388	1188	1852	425	1427
D Personal and household services	1318	129	1189	1472	132	1340	1694	196	1498	2105	232	1873
Total, Industries	205144	74276	130868	217380	77558	139822	232141	81170	150971	255846	91779	164067
Producers of Government Services	15442	7205	8237	19170	9926	9244	22990	11866	11124	26204	13496	12708
Other Producers	294	-	294	300	-	300	331	-	331	364	-	364
Total	220880	81481	139399	236850	87484	149366	255462	93036	162426	282414	105275	177139
Less: Imputed bank service charge	...	...	...	...	...	...	...	...	...	...	...	...
Import duties	7945	-	7945	8397	-	8397	10014	-	10014	11683	-	11683
Value added tax	...	...	...	...	...	...	...	...	...	...	...	...
Total	228825	81481	147344	245247	87484	157763	265476	93036	172440	294097	105275	188822

a) The estimates on processing of tea and rubber are included in the agricultural sector prior to 1975. From 1975 onward, they are included in the manufacturing sector.

4.2 Derivation of Value Added by Kind of Activity, in Constant Prices

Million Sri Lanka rupees

	1980 Gross Output	1980 Intermediate Consumption	1980 Value Added	1981 Gross Output	1981 Intermediate Consumption	1981 Value Added	1982 Gross Output	1982 Intermediate Consumption	1982 Value Added	1983 Gross Output	1983 Intermediate Consumption	1983 Value Added

At constant prices of: 1975

All Producers

	GO	IC	VA	GO	IC	VA	GO	IC	VA	GO	IC	VA
1 Agriculture, hunting, forestry and fishing a	...	...	9357	...	...	10058	...	...	10372	...	...	10994
A Agriculture and hunting	...	...	8542	...	...	9177	...	...	9411	...	...	9962
B Forestry and logging	...	...	287	...	...	279	...	...	317	...	...	373
C Fishing	...	...	528	...	...	602	...	...	644	...	...	660
2 Mining and quarrying	...	...	475	...	...	500	...	...	479	...	...	575
A Coal mining	...	...	...	...	...	...	...	...	...	...	...	...
B Crude petroleum and natural gas production	...	...	...	...	...	...	...	...	...	...	...	...
C Metal ore mining	...	...	...	...	...	...	...	...	...	...	...	...
D Other mining	...	...	475	...	...	500	...	...	479	...	...	575
3 Manufacturing a	...	...	7071	...	...	7327	...	...	7281	...	...	7064
A Manufacture of food, beverages and tobacco	...	...	3452	...	...	3526	...	...	3741	...	...	3973
B Textile, wearing apparel and leather industries	...	...	882	...	...	858	...	...	989	...	...	651
C Manufacture of wood and wood products, including furniture	...	...	88	...	...	92	...	...	156	...	...	151
D Manufacture of paper and paper products, printing and publishing	...	...	145	...	...	153	...	...	134	...	...	94
E Manufacture of chemicals and chemical petroleum, coal, rubber and plastic products	...	...	1110	...	...	1201	...	...	1331	...	...	1148
F Manufacture of non-metallic mineral products, except products of petroleum and coal	...	...	527	...	...	576	...	...	488	...	...	285
G Basic metal industries	...	...	62	...	...	65	...	...	38	...	...	61
H Manufacture of fabricated metal products, machinery and equipment	...	...	451	...	...	434	...	...	107	...	...	236
I Other manufacturing industries	...	...	354	...	...	421	...	...	297	...	...	465
4 Electricity, gas and water	...	...	181	...	...	203	...	...	222	...	...	226
A Electricity, gas and steam	...	...	181	...	...	203	...	...	...	...	...	...
B Water works and supply	...	...	...	...	...	...	...	...	...	...	...	...

Sri Lanka

4.2 Derivation of Value Added by Kind of Activity, in Constant Prices
(Continued)

Million Sri Lanka rupees

	1980 Gross Output	1980 Intermediate Consumption	1980 Value Added	1981 Gross Output	1981 Intermediate Consumption	1981 Value Added	1982 Gross Output	1982 Intermediate Consumption	1982 Value Added	1983 Gross Output	1983 Intermediate Consumption	1983 Value Added
				At constant prices of:1975								
5 Construction	...	...	1947	...	...	2208	...	...	2157	...	...	2172
6 Wholesale and retail trade, restaurants and hotels	...	...	7564	...	...	8059	...	...	9408	...	...	10162
A Wholesale and retail trade	...	...	7267	...	...	7719	...	...	8999	...	...	9731
B Restaurants and hotels	...	...	297	...	...	340	...	...	409	...	...	430
7 Transport, storage and communication	...	...	3460	...	...	3564	...	...	3658	...	...	4043
8 Finance, insurance, real estate and business services	...	...	1269	...	...	1357	...	...	1512	...	...	1566
A Financial institutions	...	...	541	...	...	622	...	...	762	...	...	805
B Insurance	...	...		...	...		...	...		...	...	
C Real estate and business services	...	...	728	...	...	735	...	...	750	...	...	761
Real estate, except dwellings	...	...	52	...	...	53	...	...	54	...	...	55
Dwellings	...	...	675	...	...	682	...	...	696	...	...	706
9 Community, social and personal services	...	...	980	...	...	1076	...	...	1117	...	...	1196
A Sanitary and similar services	...	...	...	...	...	...	...	...	...	...	...	...
B Social and related community services	...	...	138	...	...	133	...	...	309	...	...	367
C Recreational and cultural services	...	...	530	...	...	504	...	...	461	...	...	488
D Personal and household services	...	...	312	...	...	439	...	...	347	...	...	340
Total, Industries [b]	...	...	32305	...	...	34352	...	...	36206	...	...	37997
Producers of Government Services	...	...	2206	...	...	2236	...	...	2256	...	...	2272
Other Producers	...	...	83	...	...	84	...	...	102	...	...	104
Total [b]	...	...	34594	...	...	36672	...	...	38564	...	...	40373
Less: Imputed bank service charge	...	...	...	...	...	...	...	...	...	...	...	...
Import duties	...	...	714	...	...	595	...	...	635	...	...	689
Value added tax	...	...	...	...	...	...	...	...	...	...	...	...
Total [b]	...	...	35308	...	...	37266	...	...	39199	...	...	41062

	1984 Gross Output	1984 Intermediate Consumption	1984 Value Added	1985 Gross Output	1985 Intermediate Consumption	1985 Value Added	1986 Gross Output	1986 Intermediate Consumption	1986 Value Added	1987 Gross Output	1987 Intermediate Consumption	1987 Value Added
				At constant prices of:1975								
				All Producers								
1 Agriculture, hunting, forestry and fishing [a]	...	...	10200	...	...	11146	...	...	11224	...	...	10562
A Agriculture and hunting	...	...	9359	...	...	10249	...	...	10276	...	...	9589
B Forestry and logging	...	...	351	...	...	399	...	...	415	...	...	419
C Fishing	...	...	490	...	...	498	...	...	533	...	...	554
2 Mining and quarrying	...	...	693	...	...	673	...	...	918	...	...	1133
A Coal mining	...	...	...	...	...	...	...	...	...	...	...	...
B Crude petroleum and natural gas production	...	...	...	...	...	...	...	...	...	...	...	...
C Metal ore mining	...	...	...	...	...	...	...	...	...	...	...	...
D Other mining	...	...	693	...	...	673	...	...	918	...	...	1133

Sri Lanka

4.2 Derivation of Value Added by Kind of Activity, in Constant Prices
(Continued)

Million Sri Lanka rupees

	1984 Gross Output	1984 Intermediate Consumption	1984 Value Added	1985 Gross Output	1985 Intermediate Consumption	1985 Value Added	1986 Gross Output	1986 Intermediate Consumption	1986 Value Added	1987 Gross Output	1987 Intermediate Consumption	1987 Value Added
					At constant prices of:1975							
3 Manufacturing [a]	...	...	8300	...	...	8812	...	...	9345	...	...	9670
A Manufacture of food, beverages and tobacco	...	...	4737	...	...	4435	...	...	5248	...	...	5721
B Textile, wearing apparel and leather industries	...	...	1381	...	...	1497	...	...	1303	...	...	1586
C Manufacture of wood and wood products, including furniture	...	...	126	...	...	175	...	...	168	...	...	169
D Manufacture of paper and paper products, printing and publishing	...	...	7	...	...	117	...	...	63	...	...	87
E Manufacture of chemicals and chemical petroleum, coal, rubber and plastic products	...	...	1298	...	...	1216	...	...	1185	...	...	1186
F Manufacture of non-metallic mineral products, except products of petroleum and coal	...	...	125	...	...	231	...	...	226	...	...	125
G Basic metal industries	...	...	17	...	...	29	...	...	36	...	...	22
H Manufacture of fabricated metal products, machinery and equipment	...	...	272	...	...	563	...	...	617	...	...	390
I Other manufacturing industries	...	...	337	...	...	549	...	...	499	...	...	384
4 Electricity, gas and water	...	...	253	...	...	274	...	...	294	...	...	304
A Electricity, gas and steam	...	...	...	...	...	...	...	...	...	...	...	...
B Water works and supply	...	...	...	...	...	...	...	...	...	...	...	...
5 Construction	...	...	2200	...	...	2248	...	...	2419	...	...	2556
6 Wholesale and retail trade, restaurants and hotels	...	...	10907	...	...	11422	...	...	11983	...	...	12422
A Wholesale and retail trade	...	...	10291	...	...	10926	...	...	11421	...	...	11876
B Restaurants and hotels	...	...	616	...	...	496	...	...	562	...	...	546
7 Transport, storage and communication	...	...	4531	...	...	4607	...	...	4718	...	...	4803
8 Finance, insurance, real estate and business services	...	...	1649	...	...	1719	...	...	1772	...	...	1834
A Financial institutions	...	...	879	...	...	938	...	...	976	...	...	1026
B Insurance	...	...		...	...		...	...		...	...	
C Real estate and business services	...	...	770	...	...	781	...	...	795	...	...	808
Real estate, except dwellings	...	...	55	...	...	56	...	...	57	...	...	58
Dwellings	...	...	715	...	...	726	...	...	738	...	...	750
9 Community, social and personal services	...	...	1296	...	...	1299	...	...	1338	...	...	1377
A Sanitary and similar services	...	...	...	...	...	...	...	...	...	...	...	...
B Social and related community services	...	...	372	...	...	393	...	...	413	...	...	438
C Recreational and cultural services	...	...	532	...	...	488	...	...	517	...	...	543
D Personal and household services	...	...	392	...	...	418	...	...	408	...	...	396
Total, Industries [b]	...	...	40029	...	...	42200	...	...	44011	...	...	44661
Producers of Government Services	...	...	2298	...	...	2334	...	...	2380	...	...	2475
Other Producers	...	...	105	...	...	106	...	...	108	...	...	111
Total [b]	...	...	42432	...	...	44640	...	...	46499	...	...	47247
Less: Imputed bank service charge	...	...	...	...	...	...	...	...	...	...	...	...
Import duties	...	...	704	...	...	660	...	...	737	...	...	755
Value added tax	...	...	...	...	...	...	...	...	...	...	...	...
Total [b]	...	...	43136	...	...	45300	...	...	47236	...	...	48002

a) The estimates on processing of tea and rubber are included in the agricultural sector prior to 1975. From 1975 onward, they are included in the manufacturing sector.

b) The estimates before 1975 for this table have been calculated on the basis of 1963 prices and linked to the estimates for the years beginning 1975.

Sri Lanka

4.3 Cost Components of Value Added

Million Sri Lanka rupees

1983 / 1984

	Compensation of Employees	Capital Consumption	Net Operating Surplus	Indirect Taxes	Less: Subsidies Received	Value Added	Compensation of Employees	Capital Consumption	Net Operating Surplus	Indirect Taxes	Less: Subsidies Received	Value Added
	All Producers											
1 Agriculture, hunting, forestry and fishing [a]	11898	...	17263	1461	154	30468	15269	...	22156	65	197	37293
2 Mining and quarrying	451	...	954	16	-	1420	381	...	806	22	-	1209
3 Manufacturing [a]	8509	...	3276	6930	782	17933	11417	...	4396	9368	880	24301
4 Electricity, gas and water	329	...	1178	104	-	1611	541	...	1942	24	-	2507
5 Construction	6809	...	2918	189	14	9902	7835	...	3358	116	3	11306
6 Wholesale and retail trade, restaurants and hotels [b]	8334	...	13590	6812	-	28736	8057	...	13145	13694	-	34896
7 Transport, storage and communication	4409	...	7851	152	776	11635	5956	...	10588	140	1063	15621
8 Finance, insurance, real estate and business services [c]	3790	...	2923	246	-	6960	4617	...	3277	456	-	8350
9 Community, social and personal services [dc]	1941	...	308	1029	-	3277	1955	...	310	1359	-	3624
Total, Industries [e]	46469	...	50262	16937	1727	111942	56028	...	59978	25244	2143	139107
Producers of Government Services	7260	...	...	...	...	7260	8237	...	...	...	...	8237
Other Producers [d]	...	...	...	...	...	...	...	...	...	...	...	...
Total [e]	53729	...	50262	16937	1727	119202	64265	...	59978	25244	2143	147344
Less: Imputed bank service charge	...	...	...	...	...	...	...	...	...	...	...	...
Import duties [b]	...	...	...	...	...	...	...	...	...	...	...	...
Value added tax	...	...	...	...	...	...	...	...	...	...	...	...
Total [e]	53729	...	50262	16937	1727	119202	64265	...	59977	25245	2143	147344

1985 / 1986

	Compensation of Employees	Capital Consumption	Net Operating Surplus	Indirect Taxes	Less: Subsidies Received	Value Added	Compensation of Employees	Capital Consumption	Net Operating Surplus	Indirect Taxes	Less: Subsidies Received	Value Added
	All Producers											
1 Agriculture, hunting, forestry and fishing [a]	15805	...	22932	54	285	38506	16245	...	23571	57	344	39529
2 Mining and quarrying	386	...	816	24	-	1227	530	...	1121	19	-	1670
3 Manufacturing [a]	14841	...	5715	6446	822	26180	16556	...	6375	4830	847	26914
4 Electricity, gas and water	645	...	2313	41	-	2999	656	...	2354	52	-	3062
5 Construction	8273	...	3545	124	3	11939	9031	...	3870	299	3	13197
6 Wholesale and retail trade, restaurants and hotels [b]	8448	...	13783	15227	-	37458	9060	...	14781	18889	-	42730
7 Transport, storage and communication	6506	...	11565	149	791	17429	7322	...	13016	231	908	19661
8 Finance, insurance, real estate and business services [c]	4653	...	3558	747	-	8957	5893	...	3927	512	-	10332
9 Community, social and personal services [dc]	1929	...	307	1588	-	3824	2307	...	366	1548	-	4221
Total, Industries [e]	61486	...	64534	24402	1901	148519	67600	...	69381	26437	2102	161316
Producers of Government Services	9264	...	...	...	20	9244	11141	...	...	...	17	11124
Other Producers [d]	...	...	...	...	...	...	...	...	...	...	...	...
Total [e]	70750	...	64534	24402	1921	157763	78741	...	69381	26437	2119	172440
Less: Imputed bank service charge	...	...	...	...	...	...	...	...	...	...	...	...
Import duties [b]	...	...	...	...	...	...	...	...	...	...	...	...
Value added tax	...	...	...	...	...	...	...	...	...	...	...	...
Total [e]	70748	...	64534	24402	1921	157763	78741	...	69381	26437	2119	172440

1987

	Compensation of Employees	Capital Consumption	Net Operating Surplus	Indirect Taxes	Less: Subsidies Received	Value Added
	All Producers					
1 Agriculture, hunting, forestry and fishing [a]	17741	...	25742	51	360	43174
2 Mining and quarrying	699	...	1479	16	-	2194
3 Manufacturing [a]	17879	...	6884	5532	594	29701
4 Electricity, gas and water	726	...	2605	126	-	3457

Sri Lanka

4.3 Cost Components of Value Added
(Continued)

Million Sri Lanka rupees

	\multicolumn{6}{c}{1987}
	Compensation of Employees	Capital Consumption	Net Operating Surplus	Indirect Taxes	Less: Subsidies Received	Value Added
5 Construction	9760	...	4183	269	5	14207
6 Wholesale and retail trade, restaurants and hotels [b]	9987	...	16294	20775	-	47056
7 Transport, storage and communication	7570	...	13457	279	1071	20235
8 Finance, insurance, real estate and business services [c]	6368	...	4102	556	-	11026
9 Community, social and personal services [dc]	2929	...	465	1670	-	5064
Total, Industries [e]	73659	...	75211	29274	2030	176114
Producers of Government Services	12729	...	...	...	21	12708
Other Producers [d]	...	...	...	...	...	...
Total [e]	86388	...	75211	29274	2051	188822
Less: Imputed bank service charge	...	...	...	...	...	...
Import duties [b]	...	...	...	...	...	...
Value added tax	...	...	...	...	...	...
Total [e]	86388	...	75211	29274	2051	188822

a) The estimates on processing of tea and rubber are included in the agricultural sector prior to 1975. From 1975 onward, they are included in the manufacturing sector.
b) Item 'Import duties' is included in item 'Wholesale and retail trade'.
c) Finance is included in item 'Community, social and personal services'.
d) Item 'Other producers' is included in item 'Community, social and personal services'.
e) Column 'Consumption of fixed capital' is included in column 'Net operating surplus'.

Sudan

General note. The preparation of national accounts statistics in Sudan is undertaken by the Department of Statistics, Khartoum. The official estimates together with the sources and methods used for the national accounts estimates are published in a series of publications entitled 'National Accounts and Supporting Tables'. The estimates are generally in accordance with the classifications and definitions recommended in the United Nations System of National Accounts (SNA). Input-output tables were published in 1964 in 'National Income of Sudan in 1961/62 (with preliminary estimates for 1962/63)'. The following tables have been prepared from successive replies to the United Nations national accounts questionnaire. From 1969 estimates relate to fiscal year beginning 1 July. When the scope and coverage of the estimates differ for conceptual or statistical reasons from the definitions and classifications recommended in SNA, a footnote is indicated to the relevant tables.

Sources and methods:

(a) Gross domestic product. Gross domestic product is estimated mainly through the production approach.

(b) Expenditure on the gross domestic product. All components of GDP by expenditure type are estimated through the expenditure approach except the estimates of gross fixed capital formation which are based partly on the commodity-flow method and partly on the expenditure approach. The sources of data for government final consumption expenditure are the actual figures available at Ministry of Treasury, Ministry of Local Government, different government units and public entities. For the central government, current and capital expenditure budgets are available, while for the local government figures on receipts and expenditures are available only for the six northern provinces, for the three southern provinces, budget figures have to be used. The estimates of private fixed consumption expenditure are based on the Household Budget Sample Survey 1967/68 which provided for the six northern provinces, data on average income and expenditure of households in the urban, semi-urban and rural areas. The number of households in these areas is based on the result of the 1973 Population Census. For the three southern provinces, which were not included in the Household Budget Sample Survey 1967/68, certain assumptions have been made to estimate their average expenditure per household. The expenditure by object per household has been calculated for 1967/68 to 1970/71 by multiplying an estimated rate of consumption increase by the number of urban, semi-urban and rural households in the North and the South. Increase in stocks is estimated partly on the basis of replies to questionnaires sent to public enterprises, producing industries and wholesale and retail trade companies. Capital formation estimates for central government and public entities are extracted from government capital expenditure accounts and for local government from the accounts of local councils. Total private expenditure on construction is obtained as a residual after deducting public expenditure on construction from total output of the construction sector. The expenditure on machinery and equipment is obtained from the statistics of imports classified by end-use. The data on external transactions are provided by the Bank of Sudan. The estimates of direct purchases by non-residents are based on a survey of the non-residents in Sudan. GDP by expenditure type at constant prices is not estimated.

(c) Cost-structure of the gross domestic product. In estimating the cost-structure components of GDP, compensation of employees is taken as the wage bill reported by manufacturing establishments and companies in the various economic activities. For the agriculture and primary sectors, compensation of employees is imputed from the employment side. Operating surplus is in most cases taken as the residual of gross output over total costs. Depreciation estimates of public corporations and private manufacturing enterprises are based on actual information available. Indirect taxes consist mainly of import and excise duties and are obtained from government budgets and accounts.

(d) Gross domestic product by kind of economic activity. The table of GDP by kind of economic activity is prepared at market prices, i.e. producers' values. Value added of most industries is estimated through the production approach. The income approach is used for government services and for electricity, gas and water. The commodity-flow method is used for the construction and trade sectors, while the expenditure approach is used for private services. For the agricultural sector, information on crop production is based on rough estimates furnished by the Ministry of Agriculture. To obtain the value of most crops, production figures are multiplied by auction or wholesale prices reduced by 10 per cent for transport and distribution margins. The estimates of value added of cotton, wheat, durra and ground-nuts are based on the records of Sudan Gezira Board which provides data on production, value and cost of production. The value of animal production is obtained through multiplying the assumed production per species by average producer price per head, supplied by the Department of Animal Resources. In the calculation of input and value added of livestock, dairy and poultry products, certain percentages have been adopted. There is a considerable difficulty in estimating the non-marketed production and own consumption in agriculture, as such information is only available from supply and disposition surveys which unfortunately have not been recently conducted. For forestry, hunting and fishing, data are supplied by the respective departments. The intermediate consumption of hunting and fishing is assumed to be a certain percentage of gross output. The gross output and value added of manufacturing are based on the Industrial Survey 1970/71 and on computed indexes of the value of production. The value added of industrial corporations are obtained from the balance sheets and profit and loss accounts of the corporations. Gross output of construction is estimated indirectly by calculating the total supplies of cement and the imported building materials. Intermediate consumption constitute 60 per cent of gross output. The market value of imported building materials is calculated by adding estimated margins to the c.i.f. value. For the domestic production of cement, an assumed average price per ton is applied. The construction of traditional buildings is estimated based on the 1973 Population Census and certain assumptions. For the trade sector, the trade margin of imported goods is calculated on the basis of c.i.f. value plus 5 per cent covering assumed duties and transport margin. For local production, it is assumed that 20 per cent of agricultural production represents own consumption. For the remaining marketable agricultural and industrial production, the trade margin is assumed to be 21.2 per cent. A rough estimate of the intermediate consumption is obtained by applying certain percentages and ratios. For transport, detailed data on receipts and expenditure are obtained from the accounts of the large public enterprises and by means of questionnaires and special surveys for other enterprises. Information on banks and insurance companies are obtained from the enterprises concerned. Gross output of banks is equated to the sum of actual service charges received plus imputed service charges. Data on intermediate consumption and factor income of banks and insurance companies are obtained from their balance sheet and profit and loss statements. The estimates of producers of government services are obtained from the Ordinary Budget or the extra-budgetary funds. For health services, entertainment and personal care, information is obtained from the institutions concerned and from the Household Sample Survey 1967/68 and the Population Census 1973. GDP by kind of economic activity at constant prices is not estimated.

1.1 Expenditure on the Gross Domestic Product, in Current Prices

Million Sudanese pounds — Fiscal year beginning 1 July

	1970	1975	1978	1979	1980	1981	1982	1983	1984	1985	1986	1987
1 Government final consumption expenditure	159.0	236.0	407.0	500.9	648.2	719.9	853.5	1112.5	...	...	...	...
2 Private final consumption expenditure	528.1	1371.1	2605.7	2978.7	4211.5	5431.0	7956.8	9464.7	...	...	...	...
A Households	...	...	...	2950.2	4176.5	5386.3	7897.2	9385.0	...	...	...	...
B Private non-profit institutions serving households	...	...	...	28.5	35.0	44.7	59.6	79.7	...	...	...	...
3 Gross capital formation	89.6	427.5	431.4	998.1	1078.2	1648.1	1627.3	1630.9	...	...	...	...
A Increase in stocks	16.4	65.5	92.0	228.9	80.4	372.7	32.9	-234.4	...	...	...	...
B Gross fixed capital formation	73.2	362.0	339.4	769.2	997.8	1275.4	1594.4	1865.3	...	...	...	...
Residential buildings	16.3	28.9	44.9	101.4	156.0	198.7	387.3	396.2	...	...	...	...
Non-residential buildings	2.4	17.2	63.9	58.4	85.3	123.3	179.0	192.6	...	...	...	...
Other construction and land improvement etc.	9.9	66.3	31.4	200.1	276.1	336.5	481.0	545.1	...	...	...	...
Other	44.6	249.6	199.2	409.3	480.4	616.9	547.1	731.4	...	...	...	...
4 Exports of goods and services	123.2	206.6	256.9	382.9	504.9	630.9	1095.8	1306.7	...	...	...	...
5 Less: Imports of goods and services	138.8	393.2	447.2	957.3	1356.9	1709.4	2347.6	2185.4	...	...	...	...
Equals: Gross Domestic Product	761.1	1848.0	3253.8	3903.3	5085.9	6720.5	9185.8	11329.4	...	...	...	...

Sudan

1.2 Expenditure on the Gross Domestic Product, in Constant Prices

Million Sudanese pounds — Fiscal year beginning 1 July

	1970	1975	1978	1979	1980	1981	1982	1983	1984	1985	1986	1987
					At constant prices of: 1981							
1 Government final consumption expenditure	...	...	...	...	...	719.9	617.3	626.8	...	...	...	...
2 Private final consumption expenditure	...	...	...	...	...	5431.0	5869.1	5352.7	...	...	...	...
A Households	...	...	...	...	...	5386.3	5822.3	5303.8	...	...	...	...
B Private non-profit institutions serving households	...	...	...	...	...	44.7	46.8	48.9	...	...	...	...
3 Gross capital formation	...	...	...	...	...	1648.1	1109.4	872.6	...	...	...	...
A Increase in stocks	...	...	...	...	...	372.7	47.5	-116.0	...	...	...	...
B Gross fixed capital formation	...	...	...	...	...	1275.4	1061.9	988.6	...	...	...	...
4 Exports of goods and services	...	...	...	...	...	630.9	822.2	807.1	...	...	...	...
5 Less: Imports of goods and services	...	...	...	...	...	1709.4	1656.7	1153.8	...	...	...	...
Statistical discrepancy	...	...	...	...	...	-	4.1	-27.7	...	...	...	...
Equals: Gross Domestic Product	...	...	...	...	...	6720.5	6765.4	6477.7	...	...	...	...

1.3 Cost Components of the Gross Domestic Product

Million Sudanese pounds — Fiscal year beginning 1 July

	1970	1975	1978	1979	1980	1981	1982	1983	1984	1985	1986	1987
1 Indirect taxes, net	110.1	225.7	357.6	349.1	427.8	483.8	847.2	895.9	...	...	...	...
A Indirect taxes	...	...	...	356.1	437.0	500.9	852.4	895.9	...	...	...	...
B Less: Subsidies	...	...	...	7.0	9.2	17.1	5.2	-	...	...	...	...
2 Consumption of fixed capital	53.2	166.1	222.5	359.9	458.0	640.9	1012.3	1245.0	...	...	...	...
3 Compensation of employees paid by resident producers to:	334.1	832.4	1276.5	1371.2	1757.1	2347.8	3084.0	3895.1	...	...	...	...
A Resident households	333.0	831.4	...	1371.2	1757.1	2347.8	3084.0	3895.1	...	...	...	...
B Rest of the world	1.1	1.0	...	-	-	-	-	-	...	...	...	...
4 Operating surplus	263.7	623.8	1397.2	1823.1	2443.0	3248.0	4242.3	5293.4	...	...	...	...
Equals: Gross Domestic Product	761.1	1848.0	3253.8	3903.3	5085.9	6720.5	9185.8	11329.4	...	...	...	...

1.4 General Government Current Receipts and Disbursements

Million Sudanese pounds — Fiscal year beginning 1 July

	1970	1975	1978	1979	1980	1981	1982	1983	1984	1985	1986	1987
					Receipts							
1 Operating surplus	...	...	...	...	...	...	...	...	...	...	...	...
2 Property and entrepreneurial income	43.2	...	...	37.8	55.6	9.7	61.5	33.9	...	...	...	...
3 Taxes, fees and contributions	143.3	319.3	468.2	510.4	704.1	795.3	1243.7	1337.6	...	...	...	...
A Indirect taxes	110.1	227.7	357.6	329.7	460.2	503.0	833.8	869.3	...	...	...	...
B Direct taxes	22.2	43.3	69.4	93.5	134.8	160.1	198.9	229.9	...	...	...	...
C Social security contributions	0.8	2.6	9.2	13.9	21.0	24.4	31.0	34.7	...	...	...	...
D Compulsory fees, fines and penalties	10.2	45.7	32.0	73.3	88.1	107.8	180.0	203.7	...	...	...	...
4 Other current transfers	19.2	...	...	-	-	-	-	-	...	...	...	...
Total Current Receipts of General Government	205.7	...	...	548.2	759.7	805.0	1305.2	1371.5	...	...	...	...
					Disbursements							
1 Government final consumption expenditure	159.0	...	...	500.9	648.2	719.9	853.5	1112.5	...	...	...	...
A Compensation of employees	78.1	157.8	246.9	317.7	417.0	464.7	593.9	767.8	...	...	...	...
B Consumption of fixed capital	46.9	15.7	35.6	74.0	77.0	80.3	155.7	214.7	...	...	...	...
C Purchases of goods and services, net	...	...	...	109.2	154.2	174.9	103.9	130.0	...	...	...	...
D Less: Own account fixed capital formation	...	...	...	...	...	...	...	...	...	...	...	...
E Indirect taxes paid, net	-	2.0	-	...	...	...	...	...	...	...	...	...
2 Property income	-	...	...	123.3	153.5	179.3	256.6	321.5	...	...	...	...
A Interest	...	...	...	123.3	153.5	179.3	256.6	321.5	...	...	...	...
B Net land rent and royalties	...	...	...	...	...	...	...	...	...	...	...	...

Sudan

1.4 General Government Current Receipts and Disbursements
(Continued)

Million Sudanese pounds — Fiscal year beginning 1 July

	1970	1975	1978	1979	1980	1981	1982	1983	1984	1985	1986	1987
3 Subsidies	4.2	...	...	7.0	9.2	17.1	5.2	-	...	...	...	...
4 Other current transfers	46.2	...	...	26.8	26.4	35.2	53.6	73.5	...	...	...	...
A Social security benefits	2.7	...	...	...	...	...	...	...	...	...	...	...
B Social assistance grants	32.1	...	...	...	...	...	...	...	...	...	...	...
C Other	11.4	...	...	...	...	...	...	...	...	...	...	...
5 Net saving	-3.8	...	...	-109.8	-77.6	-146.5	136.3	-136.0	...	...	...	...
Total Current Disbursements and Net Saving of General Government	205.6	...	...	548.2	759.7	805.0	1305.2	1371.5	...	...	...	...

1.7 External Transactions on Current Account, Summary

Million Sudanese pounds — Fiscal year beginning 1 July

	1970	1975	1978	1979	1980	1981	1982	1983	1984	1985	1986	1987
Payments to the Rest of the World												
1 Imports of goods and services	138.8	393.2	447.2	957.3	1356.9	1709.4	2347.6	2185.4	...	...	...	...
A Imports of merchandise c.i.f.	119.1	362.8	382.0	867.9	1235.1	1514.4	2118.2	1900.6	...	...	...	...
B Other	19.7	30.4	65.2	89.4	121.8	195.0	229.4	284.8	...	...	...	...
2 Factor income to the rest of the world	6.1	27.5	32.7	33.8	52.6	147.2	187.4	316.8	...	...	...	...
A Compensation of employees	1.1	1.0	1.6	-	-	-	-	-	...	...	...	...
B Property and entrepreneurial income	5.0	26.5	31.1	33.8	52.6	147.2	187.4	316.8	...	...	...	...
3 Current transfers to the rest of the world	9.8	5.3	16.5	14.8	33.4	34.0	40.0	51.6	...	...	...	...
4 Surplus of the nation on current transactions	-22.5	-196.4	-137.8	-212.8	-518.0	-795.3	-1100.1	-675.0	...	...	...	...
Payments to the Rest of the World and Surplus of the Nation on Current Transactions	132.2	229.6	358.6	793.1	924.9	1095.3	1474.9	1878.8	...	...	...	...
Receipts From The Rest of the World												
1 Exports of goods and services	123.2	206.6	256.9	382.9	504.9	630.9	1095.8	1306.7	...	...	...	...
A Exports of merchandise f.o.b.	106.6	188.3	214.6	281.3	326.5	340.8	589.4	873.3	...	...	...	...
B Other	16.6	18.3	42.3	101.6	178.4	290.1	506.4	433.4	...	...	...	...
2 Factor income from rest of the world	2.9	7.4	8.9	10.4	16.6	36.1	48.1	12.4	...	...	...	...
A Compensation of employees	2.3	2.6	5.4	-	-	-	-	-	...	...	...	...
B Property and entrepreneurial income	0.6	4.8	3.5	10.4	16.6	36.1	48.1	12.4	...	...	...	...
3 Current transfers from rest of the world	6.1	15.6	92.8	399.8	403.4	428.3	331.0	559.7	...	...	...	...
Receipts from the Rest of the World on Current Transactions	132.2	229.6	358.6	793.1	924.9	1095.3	1474.9	1878.8	...	...	...	...

1.8 Capital Transactions of The Nation, Summary

Million Sudanese pounds — Fiscal year beginning 1 July

	1970	1975	1978	1979	1980	1981	1982	1983	1984	1985	1986	1987
Finance of Gross Capital Formation												
Gross saving	...	...	...	785.3	560.2	852.8	527.2	955.9	...	...	...	...
1 Consumption of fixed capital	...	...	...	359.9	458.0	640.9	1012.3	1245.0	...	...	...	...
A General government	...	...	...	74.0	77.0	80.3	155.7	214.7	...	...	...	...
B Corporate and quasi-corporate enterprises	...	...	...	...	...	...	...	...	...	...	...	...
C Other	...	...	...	...	...	...	...	...	...	...	...	...
2 Net saving	...	...	...	425.4	102.2	211.9	-485.1	-289.1	...	...	...	...
A General government	...	...	...	-109.8	-77.6	-146.5	136.3	-136.0	...	...	...	...
B Corporate and quasi-corporate enterprises	...	...	...	...	...	...	...	...	...	...	...	...
C Other	...	...	...	...	...	...	...	...	...	...	...	...
Less: Surplus of the nation on current transactions	...	...	...	-212.8	-518.0	-795.3	-1100.1	-675.0	...	...	...	...
Finance of Gross Capital Formation	...	...	...	998.1	1078.2	1648.1	1627.3	1630.9	...	...	...	...

Sudan

1.8 Capital Transactions of The Nation, Summary
(Continued)

Million Sudanese pounds

Fiscal year beginning 1 July

	1970	1975	1978	1979	1980	1981	1982	1983	1984	1985	1986	1987
Gross Capital Formation												
Increase in stocks	...	...	...	228.9	80.4	372.7	32.9	-234.4	...	...	...	...
Gross fixed capital formation	...	...	...	769.2	997.8	1275.4	1594.4	1865.3	...	...	...	...
1 General government	...	...	...	96.9	86.0	118.3	77.6	101.5	...	...	...	...
2 Corporate and quasi-corporate enterprises	...	...	...	...	...	...	...	...	...	...	...	...
3 Other	...	...	...	...	...	...	...	...	...	...	...	...
Gross Capital Formation	...	...	...	998.1	1078.2	1648.1	1627.3	1630.9	...	...	...	...

1.10 Gross Domestic Product by Kind of Activity, in Current Prices

Million Sudanese pounds

Fiscal year beginning 1 July

	1970	1975	1978	1979	1980	1981	1982	1983	1984	1985	1986	1987
1 Agriculture, hunting, forestry and fishing	294.4	628.2	1111.0	1298.4	1665.3	2401.9	2788.2	3339.4	...	...	...	...
2 Mining and quarrying	1.8	5.5	3.6	3.8	4.1	3.7	5.1	5.5	...	...	...	...
3 Manufacturing	67.4	155.6	282.5	336.5	394.6	466.1	670.1	869.7	...	...	...	...
4 Electricity, gas and water	16.6	28.6	45.0	65.5	69.4	76.4	93.6	175.3	...	...	...	...
5 Construction	23.3	88.8	124.0	204.6	296.0	381.9	604.9	666.7	...	...	...	...
6 Wholesale and retail trade, restaurants and hotels	113.6	315.3	641.3	574.3	791.5	949.3	1418.4	1978.6	...	...	...	...
7 Transport, storage and communication	50.7	192.4	363.7	416.1	488.1	691.4	927.1	1071.9	...	...	...	...
8 Finance, insurance, real estate and business services	41.8	138.8	219.0	368.2	551.8	795.0	1159.3	1383.0	...	...	...	...
9 Community, social and personal services	23.1	33.7	72.8	58.0	72.0	101.5	140.0	180.0	...	...	...	...
Total, Industries	632.7	1586.9	2862.9	3325.4	4332.8	5867.2	7806.7	9670.1	...	...	...	...
Producers of Government Services	87.4	171.4	282.4	391.7	494.0	545.0	749.6	982.5	...	...	...	...
Other Producers	...	...	...	44.7	58.7	79.2	108.7	150.8	...	...	...	...
Subtotal	720.1	1758.3	3145.3	3761.8	4885.5	6491.4	8665.0	10803.4	...	...	...	...
Less: Imputed bank service charge	10.3	20.3	41.6	51.9	79.6	107.8	132.9	142.4	...	...	...	...
Plus: Import duties	51.3	110.0	150.1	193.4	280.0	336.9	653.7	668.4	...	...	...	...
Plus: Value added tax	...	...	...	...	...	...	...	...	...	...	...	...
Equals: Gross Domestic Product	761.1	1848.0	3253.8	3903.3	5085.9	6720.5	9185.8	11329.4	...	...	...	...

1.11 Gross Domestic Product by Kind of Activity, in Constant Prices

Million Sudanese pounds

Fiscal year beginning 1 July

	1970	1975	1978	1979	1980	1981	1982	1983	1984	1985	1986	1987
At constant prices of: 1981												
1 Agriculture, hunting, forestry and fishing	...	...	...	...	...	2401.9	2220.1	2164.3	...	...	...	...
2 Mining and quarrying	...	...	...	...	...	3.7	5.0	5.0	...	...	...	...
3 Manufacturing	...	...	...	...	...	466.1	511.5	503.6	...	...	...	...
4 Electricity, gas and water	...	...	...	...	...	76.4	94.5	102.2	...	...	...	...
5 Construction	...	...	...	...	...	381.9	460.7	399.4	...	...	...	...
6 Wholesale and retail trade, restaurants and hotels	...	...	...	...	...	949.3	979.5	905.5	...	...	...	...
7 Transport, storage and communication	...	...	...	...	...	691.4	706.9	672.3	...	...	...	...
8 Finance, insurance, real estate and business services	...	...	...	...	...	795.0	800.8	837.9	...	...	...	...
9 Community, social and personal services	...	...	...	...	...	101.5	110.0	110.3	...	...	...	...
Total, Industries	...	...	...	...	...	5867.2	5889.0	5700.5	...	...	...	...
Producers of Government Services	...	...	...	...	...	545.0	546.2	558.3	...	...	...	...
Other Producers	...	...	...	...	...	79.2	82.9	86.6	...	...	...	...
Subtotal	...	...	...	...	...	6491.4	6518.1	6345.4	...	...	...	...
Less: Imputed bank service charge	...	...	...	...	...	107.8	93.3	101.8	...	...	...	...
Plus: Import duties	...	...	...	...	...	336.9	340.6	234.1	...	...	...	...
Plus: Value added tax	...	...	...	...	...	...	...	...	...	...	...	...
Equals: Gross Domestic Product	...	...	...	...	...	6720.5	6765.4	6477.7	...	...	...	...

Sudan

1.12 Relations Among National Accounting Aggregates

Million Sudanese pounds — Fiscal year beginning 1 July

	1970	1975	1978	1979	1980	1981	1982	1983	1984	1985	1986	1987
Gross Domestic Product	761.1	1848.0	3253.8	3903.3	5085.9	6720.5	9185.8	11329.4	...	...	...	...
Plus: Net factor income from the rest of the world	-3.2	-20.1	-23.8	-23.4	-36.0	-111.1	-139.3	-304.4	...	...	...	...
Factor income from the rest of the world	2.9	7.4	8.9	10.4	16.6	36.1	48.1	12.4	...	...	...	...
Less: Factor income to the rest of the world	6.1	27.5	32.7	33.8	52.6	147.2	187.4	316.8	...	...	...	...
Equals: Gross National Product	757.9	1827.9	3230.0	3879.9	5049.9	6609.4	9046.5	11025.0	...	...	...	...
Less: Consumption of fixed capital	53.2	166.1	222.5	359.9	458.0	640.9	1012.3	1245.0	...	...	...	...
Equals: National Income	704.7	1661.8	3007.5	3520.0	4591.9	5968.5	8034.2	9780.0	...	...	...	...
Plus: Net current transfers from the rest of the world	-3.7	10.3	76.3	385.0	370.0	394.3	291.0	508.1	...	...	...	...
Current transfers from the rest of the world	6.1	15.6	92.8	399.8	403.4	428.3	331.0	559.7	...	...	...	...
Less: Current transfers to the rest of the world	9.8	5.3	16.5	14.8	33.4	34.0	40.0	51.6	...	...	...	...
Equals: National Disposable Income	701.0	1672.1	3083.8	3905.0	4961.9	6362.8	8325.2	10288.1	...	...	...	...
Less: Final consumption	687.1	1607.1	3012.7	3479.6	4859.7	6150.9	8810.3	10577.2	...	...	...	...
Equals: Net Saving	13.9	65.0	71.1	425.4	102.2	211.9	-485.1	-289.1	...	...	...	...
Less: Surplus of the nation on current transactions	-22.5	-196.4	-137.8	-212.8	-518.0	-795.3	-1100.1	-675.0	...	...	...	...
Equals: Net Capital Formation	36.4	261.4	208.9	638.2	620.2	1007.2	615.0	385.9	...	...	...	...

2.1 Government Final Consumption Expenditure by Function, in Current Prices

Million Sudanese pounds — Fiscal year beginning 1 July

	1970	1975	1978	1979	1980	1981	1982	1983	1984	1985	1986	1987
1 General public services [a]	69.8	109.4	185.4	134.6	193.9	181.2	236.1	360.4	...	...	...	...
2 Defence	28.0			101.1	124.3	133.6	161.8	250.4	...	...	...	...
3 Public order and safety [a]	...	...	...	...	...	...	...	...	...	...	...	...
4 Education	26.2	56.5	112.1	142.4	178.9	222.4	236.8	263.8	...	...	...	...
5 Health	14.2	22.3	31.1	35.8	38.6	70.1	73.1	56.2	...	...	...	...
6 Social security and welfare	...	...	...	...	...	...	...	...	...	...	...	...
7 Housing and community amenities	0.1	2.9	0.7	0.3	0.6	0.7	0.4	-2.0	...	...	...	...
8 Recreational, cultural and religious affairs	1.7	4.5	12.0	11.3	16.4	22.7	22.3	24.0	...	...	...	...
9 Economic services [b]	19.0	40.3	65.7	75.4	95.5	89.2	123.0	159.7	...	...	...	...
10 Other functions [b]	...	...	...	...	...	...	...	...	...	...	...	...
Total Government Final Consumption Expenditure	159.0	235.9	407.0	500.9	648.2	719.9	853.5	1112.5	...	...	...	...

a) Item 'Public order and safety' is included in item 'General public services'.
b) Item 'Other functions' is included in item 'Economic services'.

2.2 Government Final Consumption Expenditure by Function, in Constant Prices

Million Sudanese pounds — Fiscal year beginning 1 July

	1970	1975	1978	1979	1980	1981	1982	1983	1984	1985	1986	1987
				At constant prices of:1981								
1 General public services	...	...	...	...	...	181.2	170.2	204.3	...	...	...	...
2 Defence	...	...	...	...	...	133.6	122.0	143.5	...	...	...	...
3 Public order and safety	...	...	...	...	...	...	...	...	...	...	...	...
4 Education	...	...	...	...	...	222.4	178.5	151.7	...	...	...	...
5 Health	...	...	...	...	...	70.1	53.9	31.0	...	...	...	...
6 Social security and welfare	...	...	...	...	...	...	...	...	...	...	...	...
7 Housing and community amenities	...	...	...	...	...	0.7	0.4	-1.0	...	...	...	...
8 Recreational, cultural and religious affairs	...	...	...	...	...	22.7	15.6	13.2	...	...	...	...
9 Economic services	...	...	...	...	...	89.2	76.7	84.1	...	...	...	...
10 Other functions	...	...	...	...	...	...	...	...	...	...	...	...
Total Government Final Consumption Expenditure	...	...	...	...	...	719.9	617.3	626.8	...	...	...	...

Sudan

2.3 Total Government Outlays by Function and Type

Million Sudanese pounds
Fiscal year beginning 1 July

	Final Consumption Expenditures Total	Compensation of Employees	Other	Subsidies	Other Current Transfers & Property Income	Total Current Disbursements	Gross Capital Formation	Other Capital Outlays	Total Outlays
1980									
1 General public services [a]	193.9	129.5	64.4	...	11.7	...	73.1	...	...
2 Defence	124.3	92.6	31.7	...	...	...	-	...	...
3 Public order and safety [a]	...	...	...	...	...	...	...	...	...
4 Education	178.8	116.5	62.3	...	5.0	...	5.0	...	...
5 Health	38.6	20.3	18.3	...	0.3	...	4.4	...	...
6 Social security and welfare	...	...	...	...	...	...	...	...	...
7 Housing and community amenities	0.6	0.5	0.1	...	...	...	0.4	...	...
8 Recreation, culture and religion	16.4	3.7	12.7	...	1.8	...	0.3	...	...
9 Economic services [b]	95.5	53.9	41.6	9.2	0.2	...	29.0	...	...
A Fuel and energy	...	...	...	...	...	...	...	...	...
B Agriculture, forestry, fishing and hunting	18.8	16.5	2.3	...	...	...	15.8	...	...
C Mining (except fuels), manufacturing and construction	29.5	8.1	21.4	...	...	...	0.9	...	...
D Transportation and communication	-7.8	4.6	-12.4	...	...	...	4.4	...	...
E Other economic affairs	55.0	24.7	30.3	...	...	...	7.9	...	...
10 Other functions [b]	...	...	...	...	7.4	...	...	...	...
Total	648.1	417.0	231.1	9.2	26.4	...	112.2	...	...
1981									
1 General public services [a]	181.2	120.0	61.2	...	13.5	...	110.0	...	...
2 Defence	133.6	100.9	32.7	...	...	...	-	...	...
3 Public order and safety [a]	...	...	...	...	...	...	...	...	...
4 Education	222.4	141.8	80.6	...	12.5	...	5.8	...	...
5 Health	70.1	41.1	29.0	...	0.3	...	5.1	...	...
6 Social security and welfare	...	...	...	...	...	...	...	...	...
7 Housing and community amenities	0.7	0.5	0.2	...	...	...	0.4	...	...
8 Recreation, culture and religion	22.7	6.8	15.9	...	0.2	...	1.4	...	...
9 Economic services [b]	89.2	53.6	35.6	17.1	-	...	33.3	...	...
A Fuel and energy	...	...	...	...	...	...	...	...	...
B Agriculture, forestry, fishing and hunting	20.1	18.2	1.9	...	...	...	18.3	...	...
C Mining (except fuels), manufacturing and construction	28.1	8.9	19.2	...	...	...	1.3	...	...
D Transportation and communication	-8.6	0.3	-8.9	...	...	...	5.6	...	...
E Other economic affairs	49.6	26.2	23.4	...	...	...	8.1	...	...
10 Other functions [b]	...	...	...	...	8.7	...	...	...	...
Total	719.7	464.7	255.2	17.1	35.2	...	156.0	...	...
1982									
1 General public services [a]	236.1	157.0	79.1	...	34.2	...	57.7	...	...
2 Defence	161.8	122.6	39.2	...	...	...	-	...	...
3 Public order and safety [a]	...	...	...	...	...	...	...	...	...
4 Education	236.8	188.4	48.4	...	2.9	...	13.6	...	...
5 Health	73.1	50.4	22.7	...	-	...	10.9	...	...
6 Social security and welfare	...	...	...	...	...	...	...	...	...
7 Housing and community amenities	0.4	0.9	-0.5	...	...	...	0.4	...	...
8 Recreation, culture and religion	22.3	10.9	11.4	...	1.1	...	1.4	...	...
9 Economic services [b]	123.0	63.7	59.3	5.2	0.7	...	48.3	...	...
A Fuel and energy	...	...	...	...	...	...	...	...	...
B Agriculture, forestry, fishing and hunting	18.1	23.5	-5.4	...	...	...	24.1	...	...
C Mining (except fuels), manufacturing and construction	40.7	10.3	30.4	...	...	...	2.7	...	...
D Transportation and communication	-9.0	3.4	-12.4	...	...	...	9.9	...	...
E Other economic affairs	73.2	26.5	46.7	...	...	...	11.6	...	...
10 Other functions [b]	...	...	...	...	14.7	...	...	...	...
Total	853.5	593.9	259.6	5.2	53.6	...	132.3	...	...

Sudan

2.3 Total Government Outlays by Function and Type
(Continued)

Million Sudanese pounds — Fiscal year beginning 1 July

	Final Consumption Expenditures Total	Compensation of Employees	Other	Subsidies	Other Current Transfers & Property Income	Total Current Disbursements	Gross Capital Formation	Other Capital Outlays	Total Outlays
				1983					
1 General public services [a]	360.4	262.8	97.6	...	51.4	...	75.6	...	...
2 Defence	250.4	188.5	61.9	...	...	...	-	...	...
3 Public order and safety [a]	...	...	...	...	...	...	...	...	...
4 Education	263.8	211.0	52.8	...	0.3	...	15.7	...	...
5 Health	56.2	26.6	29.6	...	0.4	...	9.6	...	...
6 Social security and welfare	...	...	...	...	...	...	...	...	...
7 Housing and community amenities	-1.0	1.0	-3.0	...	...	...	0.3	...	...
8 Recreation, culture and religion	24.0	12.2	11.8	...	1.3	...	0.9	...	...
9 Economic services [b]	159.7	65.7	94.0	...	0.4	...	59.4	...	...
A Fuel and energy	...	...	...	...	...	...	...	...	...
B Agriculture, forestry, fishing and hunting	22.3	24.5	-2.2	...	...	...	26.9	...	...
C Mining (except fuels), manufacturing and construction	49.0	10.2	38.8	...	...	...	3.3	...	...
D Transportation and communication	-11.1	3.7	-14.8	...	...	...	14.6	...	...
E Other economic affairs	99.5	27.3	72.2	...	...	...	14.6	...	...
10 Other functions [b]	...	...	...	...	19.7	...	...	...	...
Total	1112.5	767.8	344.7	-	73.5	...	161.5	...	...

a) Item 'Public order and safety' is included in item 'General public services'.
b) Item 'Other functions' is included in item 'Economic services'.

2.5 Private Final Consumption Expenditure by Type and Purpose, in Current Prices

Million Sudanese pounds — Fiscal year beginning 1 July

	1970	1975	1978	1979	1980	1981	1982	1983	1984	1985	1986	1987
			Final Consumption Expenditure of Resident Households									
1 Food, beverages and tobacco	...	...	...	1862.7	2670.5	3384.8	4767.8	6073.4	...	...	...	...
A Food	...	...	...	1796.2	2575.8	3251.1	4600.7	5905.8	...	...	...	...
B Non-alcoholic beverages	...	...	...	14.7	16.5	22.0	32.9	52.8	...	...	...	...
C Alcoholic beverages	...	...	...	19.9	26.3	34.4	27.4	2.4	...	...	...	...
D Tobacco	...	...	...	31.9	51.9	77.3	106.8	112.4	...	...	...	...
2 Clothing and footwear	...	...	...	162.5	229.0	300.7	595.8	500.4	...	...	...	...
3 Gross rent, fuel and power	...	...	...	451.4	650.8	850.0	1209.6	1429.2	...	...	...	...
A Fuel and power	...	...	...	151.2	212.1	250.1	315.6	352.7	...	...	...	...
B Other	...	...	...	300.2	438.7	599.9	894.0	1076.5	...	...	...	...
4 Furniture, furnishings and household equipment and operation	...	...	...	134.9	179.5	250.0	444.0	513.0	...	...	...	...
A Household operation	...	...	...	99.6	130.3	198.8	351.4	437.8	...	...	...	...
B Other	...	...	...	35.3	49.2	51.2	92.6	75.2	...	...	...	...
5 Medical care and health expenses	...	...	...	131.9	185.3	282.4	420.5	385.8	...	...	...	...
6 Transport and communication	...	...	...	74.9	91.2	127.6	199.7	143.4	...	...	...	...
7 Recreational, entertainment, education and cultural services	...	...	...	38.7	54.3	58.6	91.0	69.4	...	...	...	...
8 Miscellaneous goods and services	...	...	...	86.8	111.3	142.5	191.2	259.7	...	...	...	...
Total Final Consumption Expenditure in the Domestic Market by Households, of which	...	...	...	2943.8	4171.9	5396.6	7919.6	9374.3	...	...	...	...
Plus: Direct purchases abroad by resident households	...	...	...	17.0	29.8	22.1	24.8	58.3	...	...	...	...
Less: Direct purchases in the domestic market by non-resident households	...	...	...	10.6	25.2	32.4	47.2	47.6	...	...	...	...
Equals: Final Consumption Expenditure of Resident Households	...	...	...	2950.2	4176.5	5386.3	7897.2	9385.0	...	...	...	...
			Final Consumption Expenditure of Private Non-profit Institutions Serving Households									
Equals: Final Consumption Expenditure of Private Non-profit Organisations Serving Households	...	...	...	28.5	35.0	44.7	59.6	79.7	...	...	...	...
Private Final Consumption Expenditure	...	...	...	2978.7	4211.5	5431.0	7956.8	9464.7	...	...	...	...

Sudan

2.6 Private Final Consumption Expenditure by Type and Purpose, in Constant Prices

Million Sudanese pounds — Fiscal year beginning 1 July

At constant prices of: 1981

Final Consumption Expenditure of Resident Households

	1970	1975	1978	1979	1980	1981	1982	1983	1984	1985	1986	1987
1 Food, beverages and tobacco	...	...	...	...	...	3384.8	3595.3	3486.2	...	...	...	...
A Food	...	...	...	...	...	3251.1	3473.8	3392.9	...	...	...	...
B Non-alcoholic beverages	...	...	...	...	...	22.0	23.0	22.9	...	...	...	...
C Alcoholic beverages	...	...	...	...	...	34.4	20.0	1.5	...	...	...	...
D Tobacco	...	...	...	...	...	77.3	78.5	68.9	...	...	...	...
2 Clothing and footwear	...	...	...	...	...	300.7	355.5	226.5	...	...	...	...
3 Gross rent, fuel and power	...	...	...	...	...	850.0	898.1	898.9	...	...	...	...
A Fuel and power	...	...	...	...	...	250.1	269.8	247.2	...	...	...	...
B Other	...	...	...	...	...	599.9	628.3	651.7	...	...	...	...
4 Furniture, furnishings and household equipment and operation	...	...	...	...	...	250.0	305.0	181.8	...	...	...	...
A Household operation	...	...	...	...	...	30.1	31.5	32.9	...	...	...	...
B Other	...	...	...	...	...	219.9	273.5	148.9	...	...	...	...
5 Medical care and health expenses	...	...	...	...	...	282.4	329.6	235.9	...	...	...	...
6 Transport and communication	...	...	...	...	...	127.6	137.9	77.0	...	...	...	...
7 Recreational, entertainment, education and cultural services	...	...	...	...	...	58.6	71.6	42.6	...	...	...	...
8 Miscellaneous goods and services	...	...	...	...	...	142.5	147.9	152.6	...	...	...	...
Total Final Consumption Expenditure in the Domestic Market by Households, of which	...	...	...	...	...	5396.6	5840.9	5301.5	...	...	...	...
Plus: Direct purchases abroad by resident households	...	...	...	...	...	22.1	16.2	29.2	...	...	...	...
Less: Direct purchases in the domestic market by non-resident households	...	...	...	...	...	32.4	34.8	26.9	...	...	...	...
Equals: Final Consumption Expenditure of Resident Households	...	...	...	...	...	5386.3	5822.3	5303.8	...	...	...	...

Final Consumption Expenditure of Private Non-profit Institutions Serving Households

	1970	1975	1978	1979	1980	1981	1982	1983	1984	1985	1986	1987
Equals: Final Consumption Expenditure of Private Non-profit Organisations Serving Households	...	...	...	...	...	...	...	...	...	...	...	...
Private Final Consumption Expenditure	...	...	...	...	...	...	...	...	...	...	...	...

2.7 Gross Capital Formation by Type of Good and Owner, in Current Prices

Million Sudanese pounds — Fiscal year beginning 1 July

	1980 TOTAL	1980 Total Private	1980 Public Enterprises	1980 General Government	1981 TOTAL	1981 Total Private	1981 Public Enterprises	1981 General Government	1982 TOTAL	1982 Total Private	1982 Public Enterprises	1982 General Government
Increase in stocks, total	80.4	...	...	...	372.7	...	...	...	32.9	...	...	...
1 Goods producing industries	105.2	...	...	...	506.0	...	...	...	222.0	...	...	...
A Materials and supplies	...	...	...	...	...	...	...	...	...	...	...	...
B Work in progress	35.9	...	...	...	416.9	...	...	...	129.4	...	...	...
C Livestock, except breeding stocks, dairy cattle, etc.	69.3	...	...	...	89.1	...	...	...	92.6	...	...	...
D Finished goods	...	...	...	...	...	...	...	...	...	...	...	...
2 Wholesale and retail trade	19.4	...	...	...	-122.3	...	...	...	-93.0	...	...	...
3 Other, except government stocks	-44.2	...	...	...	-11.0	...	...	...	-96.1	...	...	...
4 Government stocks	...	...	...	...	...	...	...	...	...	...	...	...
Gross Fixed Capital Formation, Total	997.8	754.2	131.4	112.2	1275.4	908.5	211.1	155.8	1594.4	1144.3	317.9	132.2
1 Residential buildings	156.0	149.5	3.2	3.3	198.7	188.3	2.5	7.9	387.3	374.1	9.2	4.0
2 Non-residential buildings	85.3	21.6	22.5	41.2	123.3	28.4	43.7	51.2	179.0	68.9	57.8	52.3

Sudan

2.7 Gross Capital Formation by Type of Good and Owner, in Current Prices
(Continued)

Million Sudanese pounds — Fiscal year beginning 1 July

	1980 TOTAL	Total Private	Public Enterprises	General Government	1981 TOTAL	Total Private	Public Enterprises	General Government	1982 TOTAL	Total Private	Public Enterprises	General Government
3 Other construction	251.4	149.8	58.5	43.1	316.7	204.3	47.5	64.9	428.8	313.4	88.4	27.0
4 Land improvement and plantation and orchard development	24.7	-	20.3	4.4	19.8	-	16.3	3.5	52.2	-	30.0	22.2
5 Producers' durable goods	480.4	433.3	26.9	20.2	616.9	487.5	101.1	28.3	547.1	387.9	132.5	26.7
A Transport equipment	188.0	181.2	4.6	2.2	333.2	279.4	51.5	2.3	124.4	78.7	40.8	4.9
B Machinery and equipment	292.4	252.1	22.3	18.0	283.7	208.1	49.6	26.0	422.7	309.2	91.7	21.8
6 Breeding stock, dairy cattle, etc.	-	-	-	...	-	-	-	...	-	-	-	...
Total Gross Capital Formation	1078.2	...	...	112.2	1648.1	...	...	155.8	1627.3	...	...	132.2

	1983 TOTAL	Total Private	Public Enterprises	General Government
Increase in stocks, total	-234.4	...	...	...
1 Goods producing industries	-71.1	...	...	...
A Materials and supplies	...	...	...	...
B Work in progress	-86.7	...	...	...
C Livestock, except breeding stocks, dairy cattle, etc.	15.6	...	...	...
D Finished goods	...	...	...	...
2 Wholesale and retail trade	-157.6	...	...	...
3 Other, except government stocks	-5.7	...	...	...
4 Government stocks	...	...	...	...
Gross Fixed Capital Formation, Total	1865.3	1390.7	312.8	161.8
1 Residential buildings	396.2	388.7	3.2	4.3
2 Non-residential buildings	192.6	60.0	55.9	76.7
3 Other construction	484.9	369.6	82.0	33.3
4 Land improvement and plantation and orchard development	60.2	-	51.9	8.3
5 Producers' durable goods	731.4	572.4	119.8	39.2
A Transport equipment	237.0	196.3	28.8	11.9
B Machinery and equipment	494.4	376.1	91.0	27.3
6 Breeding stock, dairy cattle, etc.	-	-	-	...
Total Gross Capital Formation	1630.9	...	...	161.8

2.11 Gross Fixed Capital Formation by Kind of Activity of Owner, ISIC Divisions, in Current Prices

Million Sudanese pounds — Fiscal year beginning 1 July

	1970	1975	1978	1979	1980	1981	1982	1983	1984	1985	1986	1987
All Producers												
1 Agriculture, hunting, forestry and fishing	...	...	...	...	...	...	154.4	130.4	...	...	...	...
2 Mining and quarrying	...	...	...	...	...	...	0.5	0.6	...	...	...	...
3 Manufacturing	...	...	...	...	...	...	227.1	280.3	...	...	...	...
4 Electricity, gas and water	...	...	...	...	...	...	77.6	77.9	...	...	...	...
A Electricity, gas and steam	...	...	...	...	...	...	66.4	65.5	...	...	...	...
B Water works and supply	...	...	...	...	...	...	11.2	12.4	...	...	...	...
5 Construction	...	...	...	...	...	...	98.6	35.5	...	...	...	...
6 Wholesale and retail trade, restaurants and hotels	...	...	...	...	...	...	106.6	120.7	...	...	...	...
7 Transport, storage and communication	...	...	...	...	...	...	34.6	38.3	...	...	...	...
A Transport and storage	...	...	...	...	...	...	31.1	34.5	...	...	...	...
B Communication	...	...	...	...	...	...	3.5	3.8	...	...	...	...
8 Finance, insurance, real estate and business services	...	...	...	...	...	...	756.4	818.3	...	...	...	...
A Financial institutions	...	...	...	...	...	...	...	...	...	...	...	...

Sudan

2.11 Gross Fixed Capital Formation by Kind of Activity of Owner, ISIC Divisions, in Current Prices
(Continued)

Million Sudanese pounds — Fiscal year beginning 1 July

	1970	1975	1978	1979	1980	1981	1982	1983	1984	1985	1986	1987
B Insurance	...	...	...	...	...	...	...	...	...	...	...	...
C Real estate and business services	...	...	...	...	...	...	756.4	818.3	...	...	...	...
9 Community, social and personal services	...	...	...	...	...	...	...	...	...	...	...	...
Total Industries	...	...	...	...	...	...	1455.8	1502.0	...	...	...	...
Producers of Government Services	...	...	...	...	...	...	132.2	161.8	...	...	...	...
Private Non-Profit Institutions Serving Households	...	...	...	...	...	...	6.4	201.5	...	...	...	...
Total	...	...	...	...	...	...	1594.4	1865.3	...	...	...	...

2.17 Exports and Imports of Goods and Services, Detail

Million Sudanese pounds — Fiscal year beginning 1 July

	1970	1975	1978	1979	1980	1981	1982	1983	1984	1985	1986	1987
Exports of Goods and Services												
1 Exports of merchandise, f.o.b.	106.6	188.3	214.6	281.3	326.5	340.8	589.4	873.3	...	...	...	...
2 Transport and communication	1.2	4.1	5.3	8.7	13.1	14.8	31.6	8.8	...	...	...	...
3 Insurance service charges	0.8	0.3	0.9	0.2	0.3	0.5	0.6	0.2	...	...	...	...
4 Other commodities	1.7	2.0	3.9	82.1	139.8	242.4	427.0	376.8	...	...	...	...
5 Adjustments of merchandise exports to change-of-ownership basis	...	...	...	...	...	...	...	...	...	...	...	...
6 Direct purchases in the domestic market by non-residential households	12.9	11.9	32.2	10.6	25.2	32.4	47.2	47.6	...	...	...	...
7 Direct purchases in the domestic market by extraterritorial bodies	...	...	...	...	...	...	...	...	...	...	...	...
Total Exports of Goods and Services	123.2	206.6	256.9	382.9	504.9	630.9	1095.8	1306.7	...	...	...	...
Imports of Goods and Services												
1 Imports of merchandise, c.i.f.	119.1	362.8	382.0	867.9	1235.1	1514.4	2118.2	1900.6	...	...	...	...
A Imports of merchandise, f.o.b.	...	...	...	855.5	1218.7	1488.3	2093.5	1880.7	...	...	...	...
B Transport of services on merchandise imports	...	...	...	12.1	16.1	25.5	23.7	19.1	...	...	...	...
C Insurance service charges on merchandise imports	...	...	...	0.3	0.3	0.6	1.0	0.8	...	...	...	...
2 Adjustments of merchandise imports to change-of-ownership basis	...	...	...	...	...	...	...	...	...	...	...	...
3 Other transport and communication	4.2	3.1	10.0	12.1	16.1	25.5	23.7	19.1	...	...	...	...
4 Other insurance service charges	0.9	1.2	2.2	0.3	0.3	0.6	1.0	0.8	...	...	...	...
5 Other commodities	3.7	11.0	21.9	60.0	75.6	146.8	179.9	206.6	...	...	...	...
6 Direct purchases abroad by government	...	...	...	...	...	...	...	...	...	...	...	...
7 Direct purchases abroad by resident households	10.9	15.1	31.1	17.0	29.8	22.1	24.8	58.3	...	...	...	...
Total Imports of Goods and Services	138.8	393.2	447.2	957.3	1356.9	1709.4	2347.6	2185.4	...	...	...	...
Balance of Goods and Services	-15.6	-186.6	-190.3	-574.4	-852.0	-1078.5	-1251.8	-878.7	...	...	...	...
Total Imports and Balance of Goods and Services	123.2	206.6	256.9	382.9	504.9	630.9	1095.8	1306.7	...	...	...	...

4.1 Derivation of Value Added by Kind of Activity, in Current Prices

Million Sudanese pounds — Fiscal year beginning 1 July

	1980 Gross Output	1980 Intermediate Consumption	1980 Value Added	1981 Gross Output	1981 Intermediate Consumption	1981 Value Added	1982 Gross Output	1982 Intermediate Consumption	1982 Value Added	1983 Gross Output	1983 Intermediate Consumption	1983 Value Added
All Producers												
1 Agriculture, hunting, forestry and fishing	2070.7	405.4	1665.3	2955.1	553.2	2401.9	3610.3	822.1	2788.2	4499.6	1160.2	3339.4
A Agriculture and hunting	1953.8	395.4	1558.4	2804.4	540.0	2264.4	3431.1	806.8	2624.3	4276.2	1140.1	3136.1
B Forestry and logging	88.7	5.8	82.9	110.6	7.2	103.4	135.5	8.8	126.7	156.2	10.1	146.1
C Fishing	28.2	4.2	24.0	40.1	6.0	34.1	43.7	6.5	37.2	67.2	10.0	57.2
2 Mining and quarrying	5.8	1.7	4.1	5.3	1.6	3.7	7.2	2.1	5.1	7.7	2.2	5.5
A Coal mining	...	...	...	...	...	...	...	...	...	...	...	...
B Crude petroleum and natural gas production	...	...	...	...	...	...	...	...	...	...	...	...
C Metal ore mining	...	...	...	...	...	...	...	...	...	...	...	...

Sudan

4.1 Derivation of Value Added by Kind of Activity, in Current Prices
(Continued)

Million Sudanese pounds — Fiscal year beginning 1 July

	1980 Gross Output	1980 Intermediate Consumption	1980 Value Added	1981 Gross Output	1981 Intermediate Consumption	1981 Value Added	1982 Gross Output	1982 Intermediate Consumption	1982 Value Added	1983 Gross Output	1983 Intermediate Consumption	1983 Value Added
D Other mining	5.8	1.7	4.1	5.3	1.6	3.7	7.2	2.1	5.1	7.7	2.2	5.5
3 Manufacturing	1001.7	607.1	394.6	1523.7	1057.6	466.1	2266.1	1595.9	670.2	2891.7	2022.0	869.7
A Manufacture of food, beverages and tobacco	423.8	246.1	177.7	581.1	342.2	238.9	815.8	485.1	330.7	1174.6	706.3	468.3
B Textile, wearing apparel and leather industries	127.4	80.3	47.1	373.4	319.8	53.6	594.9	507.6	87.3	735.4	633.7	101.7
C Manufacture of wood and wood products, including furniture	29.4	11.5	17.9	17.3	6.8	10.5	22.3	8.9	13.4	28.5	10.4	18.1
D Manufacture of paper and paper products, printing and publishing	34.4	17.6	16.8	34.8	23.1	11.7	57.8	40.6	17.2	62.3	43.5	18.8
E Manufacture of chemicals and chemical petroleum, coal, rubber and plastic products	269.2	183.1	86.1	343.3	270.8	72.5	519.5	408.8	110.7	572.4	447.8	124.6
F Manufacture of non-metallic mineral products, except products of petroleum and coal	37.3	19.6	17.7	45.3	23.1	22.2	85.7	45.4	40.3	124.8	66.9	57.9
G Basic metal industries	17.8	12.4	5.4	19.4	13.2	6.2	34.0	23.6	10.4	49.0	33.1	15.9
H Manufacture of fabricated metal products, machinery and equipment	57.5	34.5	23.0	102.6	53.4	49.2	127.1	68.7	58.4	132.7	70.7	62.0
I Other manufacturing industries	4.9	2.0	2.9	6.5	5.2	1.3	9.0	7.2	1.8	12.0	9.6	2.4
4 Electricity, gas and water	96.6	27.2	69.4	116.4	40.0	76.4	146.7	53.1	93.6	248.4	73.1	175.3
A Electricity, gas and steam	38.7	17.6	21.1	44.6	30.8	13.8	53.3	41.1	12.2	118.7	59.2	59.5
B Water works and supply	57.9	9.6	48.3	71.8	9.2	62.6	93.4	12.0	81.4	129.7	13.9	115.8
5 Construction	587.6	291.6	296.0	753.3	371.4	381.9	1193.8	588.9	604.9	1306.3	639.6	666.7
6 Wholesale and retail trade, restaurants and hotels	1150.4	358.9	791.5	1421.9	472.6	949.3	2100.9	682.5	1418.4	2717.8	739.2	1978.6
A Wholesale and retail trade	1064.1	310.4	753.7	1325.0	418.1	906.9	1982.2	618.9	1363.3	2569.6	660.1	1909.5
B Restaurants and hotels	86.3	48.5	37.8	96.9	54.5	42.4	118.7	63.6	55.1	148.2	79.1	69.1
Restaurants	49.1	30.4	18.7	54.9	34.0	20.9	74.6	46.2	28.4	99.4	61.6	37.8
Hotels and other lodging places	37.2	18.1	19.1	42.0	20.5	21.5	44.1	17.4	26.7	48.8	17.5	31.3
7 Transport, storage and communication	761.5	273.4	488.1	1089.2	397.8	691.4	1536.6	609.5	927.1	1880.3	808.4	1071.9
A Transport and storage	740.9	268.6	472.3	1065.0	392.6	672.4	1511.5	604.3	907.2	1847.8	799.1	1048.7
B Communication	20.6	4.8	15.8	24.2	5.2	19.0	25.1	5.2	19.9	32.5	9.3	23.2
8 Finance, insurance, real estate and business services	719.4	167.6	551.8	1076.7	281.7	795.0	1609.1	449.8	1159.3	1869.2	486.2	1383.0
A Financial institutions	139.3	17.3	122.0	193.3	21.2	172.1	253.0	31.6	221.4	306.4	46.7	259.7
B Insurance	11.6	0.7	10.9	13.2	0.8	12.4	16.5	1.3	15.2	23.5	1.9	21.6
C Real estate and business services	568.5	149.6	418.9	870.2	259.7	610.5	1339.6	416.9	922.7	1539.3	437.6	1101.7
9 Community, social and personal services	107.3	35.3	72.0	154.6	53.1	101.5	208.1	68.1	140.0	269.2	89.2	180.0
Total, Industries	6501.0	2168.2	4332.8	9096.2	3229.0	5867.2	12678.8	4872.0	7806.8	15690.2	6020.1	9670.1
Producers of Government Services	727.2	233.2	494.0	819.9	274.9	545.0	1011.4	261.8	749.6	1294.0	311.5	982.5
Other Producers	88.6	29.9	58.7	117.0	37.8	79.2	156.5	47.8	108.7	211.3	60.5	150.8
Total	7316.8	2431.3	4885.5	10033.1	3541.7	6491.4	13846.7	5181.6	8665.1	17195.5	6392.1	10803.4
Less: Imputed bank service charge	...	−79.6	79.6	...	−107.8	107.8	...	−132.9	132.9	...	−142.4	142.4
Import duties	280.0	−	280.0	336.9	−	336.9	653.7	−	653.7	668.4	−	668.4
Value added tax	...	...	...	...	...	...	...	...	...	...	...	...
Total	7596.8	2510.9	5085.9	10370.0	3649.5	6720.5	14500.4	5314.5	9185.9	17863.9	6534.5	11329.4

4.2 Derivation of Value Added by Kind of Activity, in Constant Prices

Million Sudanese pounds — Fiscal year beginning 1 July

At constant prices of: 1981

All Producers

	1981 Gross Output	1981 Intermediate Consumption	1981 Value Added	1982 Gross Output	1982 Intermediate Consumption	1982 Value Added	1983 Gross Output	1983 Intermediate Consumption	1983 Value Added
1 Agriculture, hunting, forestry and fishing	...	...	2401.9	...	...	2220.1	...	...	2164.3
A Agriculture and hunting	...	...	2264.4	...	...	2088.5	...	...	2021.3
B Forestry and logging	...	...	103.4	...	...	98.9	...	...	108.8
C Fishing	...	...	34.1	...	...	32.7	...	...	34.2
2 Mining and quarrying	...	...	3.7	...	...	5.0	...	...	5.0

Sudan

4.2 Derivation of Value Added by Kind of Activity, in Constant Prices
(Continued)

Million Sudanese pounds — Fiscal year beginning 1 July

	1981 Gross Output	1981 Intermediate Consumption	1981 Value Added	1982 Gross Output	1982 Intermediate Consumption	1982 Value Added	1983 Gross Output	1983 Intermediate Consumption	1983 Value Added
			At constant prices of: 1981						
A Coal mining	...	...	...	...	...	...	...	...	...
B Crude petroleum and natural gas production	...	...	...	...	...	...	...	...	...
C Metal ore mining	...	...	...	...	...	...	...	...	...
D Other mining	...	...	3.7	...	...	5.0	...	...	5.0
3 Manufacturing	...	...	466.1	...	...	511.5	...	...	503.6
A Manufacture of food, beverages and tobacco	...	...	238.9	...	...	266.5	...	...	280.9
B Textile, wearing apparel and leather industries	...	...	53.6	...	...	59.2	...	...	53.9
C Manufacture of wood and wood products, including furniture	...	...	10.5	...	...	10.8	...	...	10.8
D Manufacture of paper and paper products, printing and publishing	...	...	11.7	...	...	12.2	...	...	12.8
E Manufacture of chemicals and chemical petroleum, coal, rubber and plastic products	...	...	72.5	...	...	78.4	...	...	75.9
F Manufacture of non-metallic mineral products, except products of petroleum and coal	...	...	22.2	...	...	29.5	...	...	31.1
G Basic metal industries	...	...	6.2	...	...	4.6	...	...	5.3
H Manufacture of fabricated metal products, machinery and equipment	...	...	49.2	...	...	48.9	...	...	31.5
I Other manufacturing industries	...	...	1.3	...	...	1.4	...	...	1.4
4 Electricity, gas and water	...	...	76.4	...	...	94.5	...	...	102.2
A Electricity, gas and steam	...	...	13.8	...	...	25.9	...	...	29.2
B Water works and supply	...	...	62.6	...	...	68.6	...	...	73.0
5 Construction	...	...	381.9	...	...	460.7	...	...	399.4
6 Wholesale and retail trade, restaurants and hotels	...	...	949.3	...	...	979.5	...	...	905.5
A Wholesale and retail trade	...	...	906.9	...	...	940.9	...	...	868.3
B Restaurants and hotels	...	...	42.4	...	...	38.6	...	...	37.2
7 Transport, storage and communication	...	...	691.4	...	...	706.9	...	...	672.3
A Transport and storage	...	...	672.4	...	...	691.5	...	...	658.7
B Communication	...	...	19.0	...	...	15.4	...	...	13.6
8 Finance, insurance, real estate and business services	...	...	795.0	...	...	800.3	...	...	837.9
A Financial institutions	...	...	172.1	...	...	148.4	...	...	162.6
B Insurance	...	...	12.4	...	...	17.6	...	...	17.6
C Real estate and business services	...	...	610.5	...	...	634.3	...	...	657.7
9 Community, social and personal services	...	...	101.5	...	...	110.0	...	...	110.3
Total, Industries	...	...	5867.2	...	...	5889.0	...	...	5700.5
Producers of Government Services	...	...	545.0	...	...	546.2	...	...	558.3
Other Producers	...	...	79.2	...	...	82.9	...	...	86.6
Total	...	...	6491.4	...	...	6518.1	...	...	6345.4
Less: Imputed bank service charge	...	...	107.8	...	...	93.3	...	...	101.8
Import duties	...	...	336.9	...	...	340.6	...	...	234.1
Value added tax	...	...	...	...	...	...	...	...	...
Total	...	...	6720.5	...	...	6765.4	...	...	6477.7

4.3 Cost Components of Value Added

Million Sudanese pounds — Fiscal year beginning 1 July

	1980 Compensation of Employees	1980 Capital Consumption	1980 Net Operating Surplus	1980 Indirect Taxes	1980 Less: Subsidies Received	1980 Value Added	1981 Compensation of Employees	1981 Capital Consumption	1981 Net Operating Surplus	1981 Indirect Taxes	1981 Less: Subsidies Received	1981 Value Added
					All Producers							
1 Agriculture, hunting, forestry and fishing	434.3	52.0	1169.5	9.5	...	1665.3	669.5	69.9	1656.2	6.3	...	2401.9
A Agriculture and hunting	382.2	48.1	1119.3	8.8	...	1558.4	601.6	64.6	1592.7	5.5	...	2264.4
B Forestry and logging	35.4	2.2	44.8	0.5	...	82.9	44.2	2.8	55.8	0.6	...	103.4
C Fishing	16.7	1.7	5.4	0.2	...	24.0	23.7	2.5	7.7	0.2	...	34.1

Sudan

4.3 Cost Components of Value Added
(Continued)

Million Sudanese pounds — Fiscal year beginning 1 July

	1980 Compensation of Employees	1980 Capital Consumption	1980 Net Operating Surplus	1980 Indirect Taxes	1980 Less: Subsidies Received	1980 Value Added	1981 Compensation of Employees	1981 Capital Consumption	1981 Net Operating Surplus	1981 Indirect Taxes	1981 Less: Subsidies Received	1981 Value Added
2 Mining and quarrying	2.7	0.4	0.9	0.1	...	4.1	2.4	0.4	0.8	0.1	...	3.7
A Coal mining	...	...	...	...	...	...	...	...	...	...	...	...
B Crude petroleum and natural gas production	...	...	...	...	...	...	...	...	...	...	...	...
C Metal ore mining	...	...	...	...	...	...	...	...	...	...	...	...
D Other mining	2.7	0.4	0.9	0.1	...	4.1	2.4	0.4	0.8	0.1	...	3.7
3 Manufacturing	108.8	35.1	156.1	94.6	...	394.6	133.0	75.6	156.2	101.3	...	466.1
A Manufacture of food, beverages and tobacco	33.3	14.0	96.2	34.2	...	177.7	42.7	32.7	128.2	35.3	...	238.9
B Textile, wearing apparel and leather industries	22.3	6.8	10.5	7.5	...	47.1	43.4	25.1	-22.2	7.3	...	53.6
C Manufacture of wood and wood products, including furniture	6.1	0.9	10.3	0.6	...	17.9	4.1	0.8	5.0	0.6	...	10.5
D Manufacture of paper and paper products, printing and publishing	6.5	2.0	6.0	2.3	...	16.8	6.4	1.5	1.1	2.7	...	11.7
E Manufacture of chemicals and chemical petroleum, coal, rubber and plastic products	22.1	6.7	21.7	35.6	...	86.1	11.8	10.3	12.7	37.7	...	72.5
F Manufacture of non-metallic mineral products, except products of petroleum and coal	8.5	1.5	4.9	2.8	...	17.7	5.8	1.7	11.3	3.4	...	22.2
G Basic metal industries	1.4	0.6	1.1	2.3	...	5.4	1.9	0.3	2.0	2.0	...	6.2
H Manufacture of fabricated metal products, machinery and equipment	8.1	2.3	3.5	9.1	...	23.0	16.3	3.1	17.8	12.0	...	49.2
I Other manufacturing industries	0.5	0.3	1.9	0.2	...	2.9	0.6	0.1	0.3	0.3	...	1.3
4 Electricity, gas and water	51.9	5.1	12.4	-	...	69.4	66.7	7.0	2.7	-	...	76.4
A Electricity, gas and steam	8.5	3.7	8.9	-	...	21.1	12.4	4.4	-3.0	-	...	13.8
B Water works and supply	43.4	1.4	3.5	-	...	48.3	54.3	2.6	5.7	-	...	62.6
5 Construction	143.9	16.1	133.0	3.0	...	296.0	184.3	20.4	173.5	3.7	...	381.9
6 Wholesale and retail trade, restaurants and hotels	252.5	20.5	487.1	31.4	...	791.5	339.2	27.8	560.4	21.9	...	949.3
A Wholesale and retail trade	242.9	16.4	466.7	27.7	...	753.7	327.7	23.2	538.3	17.7	...	906.9
B Restaurants and hotels	9.6	4.1	20.4	3.7	...	37.8	11.5	4.6	22.1	4.2	...	42.4
Restaurants	4.1	-	14.6	-	...	18.7	4.6	-	16.3	-	...	20.9
Hotels and other lodging places	5.5	4.1	5.8	3.7	...	19.1	6.9	4.6	5.8	4.2	...	21.5
7 Transport, storage and communication	202.5	66.7	213.3	5.6	...	488.1	277.3	89.9	316.2	8.0	...	691.4
A Transport and storage	188.0	66.6	212.2	5.5	...	472.3	259.6	89.8	315.0	8.0	...	672.4
B Communication	14.5	0.1	1.1	0.1	...	15.8	17.7	0.1	1.2	-	...	19.0
8 Finance, insurance, real estate and business services	57.9	182.8	308.5	2.6	...	551.8	84.8	263.0	443.0	4.2	...	795.0
A Financial institutions	33.2	2.5	86.3	-	...	122.0	39.9	4.1	128.1	-	...	172.1
B Insurance	0.9	-	10.0	-	...	10.9	1.2	0.1	11.1	-	...	12.4
C Real estate and business services	23.8	180.3	212.2	2.6	...	418.9	43.7	258.8	303.8	4.2	...	610.5
9 Community, social and personal services	27.6	1.6	41.8	1.0	...	72.0	47.6	5.7	46.8	1.4	...	101.5
Total, Industries [a]	1282.1	380.3	2522.6	147.8	...	4332.8	1804.8	559.7	3355.8	146.9	...	5867.2
Producers of Government Services	417.0	77.0	-	-	...	494.0	464.7	80.3	-	-	...	545.0
Other Producers	58.0	0.7	-	-	...	58.7	78.3	0.9	-	-	...	79.2
Total [a]	1757.1	458.0	2522.6	147.8	...	4885.5	2347.8	640.9	3355.8	146.9	...	6491.4
Less: Imputed bank service charge	...	...	79.6	...	...	79.6	...	...	107.8	...	...	107.8
Import duties	...	...	...	280.0	...	280.0	...	...	...	336.9	...	336.9
Value added tax	...	...	...	...	...	...	...	...	...	...	...	...
Total [a]	1757.1	458.0	2443.0	427.8	...	5085.9	2347.8	640.9	3248.0	483.8	...	6720.5

Sudan

4.3 Cost Components of Value Added

Million Sudanese pounds — Fiscal year beginning 1 July

		1982					1983					
		Compensation of Employees	Capital Consumption	Net Operating Surplus	Indirect Taxes	Less: Subsidies Received	Value Added	Compensation of Employees	Capital Consumption	Net Operating Surplus	Indirect Taxes	Less: Subsidies Received	Value Added

All Producers

1 Agriculture, hunting, forestry and fishing	788.2	110.8	1880.5	8.7	...	2788.2	1062.6	135.0	2130.5	11.3	...	3339.4
A Agriculture and hunting	708.2	104.7	1803.7	7.7	...	2624.3	960.4	126.9	2038.7	10.1	...	3136.1
B Forestry and logging	54.2	3.4	68.4	0.7	...	126.7	62.5	3.9	78.9	0.8	...	146.1
C Fishing	25.8	2.7	8.4	0.3	...	37.2	39.7	4.2	12.9	0.4	...	57.2
2 Mining and quarrying	3.3	0.5	1.2	0.1	...	5.1	3.6	0.5	1.3	0.1	...	5.5
A Coal mining	...	...	...	...	...	...	...	...	...	...	...	...
B Crude petroleum and natural gas production	...	...	...	...	...	...	...	...	...	...	...	...
C Metal ore mining	...	...	...	...	...	...	...	...	...	...	...	...
D Other mining	3.3	0.5	1.2	0.1	...	5.1	3.6	0.5	1.3	0.1	...	5.5
3 Manufacturing	199.6	114.2	232.2	124.2	...	670.2	261.4	157.9	310.1	140.3	...	869.7
A Manufacture of food, beverages and tobacco	60.4	46.3	181.3	42.7	...	330.7	87.8	67.6	262.6	50.3	...	468.3
B Textile, wearing apparel and leather industries	68.0	40.5	-24.2	3.0	...	87.3	82.4	56.3	-40.4	3.4	...	101.7
C Manufacture of wood and wood products, including furniture	5.4	0.8	6.8	0.4	...	13.4	6.7	1.2	8.9	1.3	...	18.1
D Manufacture of paper and paper products, printing and publishing	11.3	2.6	1.9	1.4	...	17.2	12.1	2.8	2.0	1.9	...	18.8
E Manufacture of chemicals and chemical petroleum, coal, rubber and plastic products	17.9	15.6	19.2	58.0	...	110.7	21.9	19.1	23.4	60.2	...	124.6
F Manufacture of non-metallic mineral products, except products of petroleum and coal	11.4	3.4	20.9	4.6	...	40.3	22.9	5.3	25.3	4.4	...	57.9
G Basic metal industries	3.4	0.6	3.5	2.9	...	10.4	4.8	0.9	4.8	5.4	...	15.9
H Manufacture of fabricated metal products, machinery and equipment	20.9	4.0	22.8	10.7	...	58.4	21.6	4.1	23.5	12.8	...	62.0
I Other manufacturing industries	0.9	0.4	-	0.5	...	1.8	1.2	0.6	-	0.6	...	2.4
4 Electricity, gas and water	86.1	18.5	-11.0	-	...	93.6	118.3	21.5	35.5	-	...	175.3
A Electricity, gas and steam	15.2	13.3	-16.3	-	...	12.2	20.0	15.0	24.5	-	...	59.5
B Water works and supply	70.9	5.2	5.3	-	...	81.4	98.3	6.5	11.0	-	...	115.8
5 Construction	287.7	33.2	278.0	6.0	...	604.9	325.9	31.7	303.2	5.9	...	666.7
6 Wholesale and retail trade, restaurants and hotels	489.5	33.7	856.2	39.0	...	1418.4	573.1	36.2	1317.1	51.2	...	1978.6
A Wholesale and retail trade	469.6	29.9	829.6	34.2	...	1363.3	547.5	31.9	1283.2	45.9	...	1909.5
B Restaurants and hotels	19.9	3.8	26.6	4.8	...	55.1	25.6	4.3	33.9	5.3	...	69.1
Restaurants	13.0	1.1	14.0	0.3	...	28.4	17.3	1.5	18.6	0.4	...	37.8
Hotels and other lodging places	6.9	2.7	12.6	4.5	...	26.7	8.3	2.8	15.3	4.9	...	31.3
7 Transport, storage and communication	351.1	129.0	439.4	7.6	...	927.1	405.4	153.6	505.5	7.4	...	1071.9
A Transport and storage	339.1	128.5	432.0	7.6	...	907.2	391.5	152.1	497.7	7.4	...	1048.7
B Communication	12.0	0.5	7.4	-	...	19.9	13.9	1.5	7.8	-	...	23.2
8 Finance, insurance, real estate and business services	120.3	408.4	624.6	6.0	...	1159.3	155.6	481.8	736.6	9.0	...	1383.0
A Financial institutions	44.6	5.9	170.8	0.1	...	221.4	64.0	9.0	186.2	0.5	...	259.7
B Insurance	2.2	0.2	12.8	-	...	15.2	2.9	0.3	18.4	-	...	21.6
C Real estate and business services	73.5	402.3	441.0	5.9	...	922.7	88.7	472.5	532.0	8.5	...	1101.7
9 Community, social and personal services	56.8	7.1	74.2	1.9	...	140.0	72.0	10.7	95.0	2.3	...	180.0
Total, Industries [a]	2382.6	855.4	4375.3	193.5	...	7806.8	2977.9	1028.9	5435.8	227.5	...	9670.1
Producers of Government Services	593.9	155.7	-	-	...	749.6	767.8	214.7	-	-	...	982.5
Other Producers	107.5	1.2	-	-	...	108.7	149.4	1.4	-	-	...	150.8
Total [a]	3084.0	1012.3	4375.3	193.5	...	8665.1	3895.1	1245.0	5435.8	227.5	...	10803.4
Less: Imputed bank service charge	...	...	132.9	...	...	132.9	...	...	142.4	...	...	142.4
Import duties	...	...	...	653.7	...	653.7	...	...	...	668.4	...	668.4
Value added tax	...	...	...	...	...	...	...	...	...	...	...	...
Total [a]	3084.0	1012.3	4242.4	847.2	...	9185.9	3895.1	1245.0	5293.4	895.9	...	11329.4

a) Column 4 refers to indirect taxes less subsidies received.

Suriname

Source. Reply to the United Nations National Accounts Questionnaire from the Algemeen Bureau Voor de Statistiek, Parmaribo. The official estimates based on the present SNA are published by the Bureau in 'Nationale Rekeningen van Suriname'.

General note. The estimates shown in the following table have been prepared in accordance with the United Nations System of National Accounts so far as the existing data would permit.

1.1 Expenditure on the Gross Domestic Product, in Current Prices

Million Suriname guilders	1970	1975	1978	1979	1980	1981	1982	1983	1984	1985	1986	1987
1 Government final consumption expenditure	...	194.9	335.1	342.7	338.5	430.7	520.1	437.2	498.8	588.5	688.1	749.6
2 Private final consumption expenditure	...	491.6	692.5	870.3	928.3	1060.9	1102.3	1331.2	1111.8	1050.3	797.4	794.2
3 Gross capital formation	...	300.9	477.3	357.3	420.6	555.0	507.3	275.6	203.9	137.0	302.8	277.9
A Increase in stocks	...	49.0	87.2	16.2	78.3	73.6	-8.8	-81.9	-110.1	-157.8	-0.9	-
B Gross fixed capital formation	...	252.0	390.1	341.1	342.2	481.4	516.1	357.6	314.0	294.7	303.5	277.9
Residential buildings	...											
Non-residential buildings	...	111.5	192.6	175.4	211.7	229.2	254.0	187.4	181.2	182.0	198.0	207.9
Other construction and land improvement etc.	...											
Other	...	140.4	197.5	165.7	130.5	252.2	262.2	170.1	132.8	112.7	105.5	70.0
4 Exports of goods and services	...	578.0	814.0	917.0	1094.2	1009.8	909.5	775.5	749.4	639.8	570.8	599.1
5 Less: Imports of goods and services	...	634.0	848.0	922.0	1179.2	1258.1	1190.8	1032.8	819.1	674.3	568.6	498.2
Equals: Gross Domestic Product	...	930.8	1471.0	1565.3	1602.3	1798.3	1848.8	1786.8	1744.8	1741.3	1790.5	1922.6

1.3 Cost Components of the Gross Domestic Product

Million Suriname guilders	1970	1975	1978	1979	1980	1981	1982	1983	1984	1985	1986	1987
1 Indirect taxes, net	...	195.8	234.9	226.3	247.7	269.6	245.1	226.4	214.1	183.0	146.5	138.8
A Indirect taxes	...	224.0	264.9	251.2	273.8	298.7	277.9	259.2	245.2	204.0	178.0	164.1
B Less: Subsidies	...	28.2	30.0	24.9	26.1	29.1	32.8	32.8	31.1	21.0	31.5	25.3
2 Consumption of fixed capital	...	91.0	145.6	168.4	171.6	186.4	182.3	182.5	173.0	174.6	197.2	235.0
3 Compensation of employees paid by resident producers to:	...	400.9	673.5	718.8	796.6	900.6	1076.2	1119.3	1160.5	1199.3	1215.9	1228.1
4 Operating surplus	...	243.1	416.9	451.9	386.6	441.7	345.2	258.6	197.2	184.4	230.9	320.7
Equals: Gross Domestic Product	...	930.8	1471.0	1565.3	1602.3	1798.3	1848.8	1786.8	1744.8	1741.3	1790.5	1922.6

1.7 External Transactions on Current Account, Summary

Million Suriname guilders	1970	1975	1978	1979	1980	1981	1982	1983	1984	1985	1986	1987
Payments to the Rest of the World												
1 Imports of goods and services	...	634.4	847.5	921.6	1179.2	1258.1	1190.8	1032.8	819.1	674.3	568.6	498.2
A Imports of merchandise c.i.f.	...	471.6	681.3	733.5	900.3	1013.7	921.2	803.7	617.3	532.9	431.2	376.9
B Other	...	162.8	166.2	188.1	278.9	244.4	269.6	229.1	201.8	141.4	137.4	121.3
2 Factor income to the rest of the world	...	46.1	70.1	98.9	76.4	41.7	51.6	49.6	6.4	5.8	8.3	10.4
A Compensation of employees	...	7.0	6.7	8.2	7.5	6.6	5.4	2.8	2.2	1.7	1.6	1.9
B Property and entrepreneurial income	...	39.1	63.4	90.7	68.9	35.1	46.2	46.8	4.2	4.1	6.7	8.5
3 Current transfers to the rest of the world	...	14.8	15.9	15.8	22.6	20.2	25.3	31.8	24.8	15.7	12.6	10.4
4 Surplus of the nation on current transactions	...	-85.2	-82.1	-66.1	-104.6	-218.7	-273.7	-291.7	-80.4	-44.5	-12.0	86.0
Payments to the Rest of the World and Surplus of the Nation on Current Transactions	...	610.1	851.4	970.2	1174.2	1101.3	994.0	822.5	769.9	651.3	577.5	605.0
Receipts From The Rest of the World												
1 Exports of goods and services	...	577.7	813.6	916.7	1094.2	1009.8	909.5	775.5	749.4	639.8	570.8	599.1
A Exports of merchandise f.o.b.	...	495.3	702.4	792.7	918.2	845.7	765.1	654.7	650.8	560.8	525.0	454.7
B Other	...	82.4	112.0	124.0	176.0	164.1	144.4	120.8	98.6	79.0	45.8	144.4
2 Factor income from rest of the world	...	20.8	14.9	25.2	45.7	64.7	63.9	29.5	8.9	4.9	2.9	2.2
A Compensation of employees	...	2.7	1.3	1.3	1.2	1.9	0.7	1.4	1.2	1.0	0.1	0.1
B Property and entrepreneurial income	...	18.1	13.6	23.9	44.5	62.8	63.2	28.1	7.7	3.9	2.8	2.1
3 Current transfers from rest of the world	...	11.6	22.9	28.3	34.3	26.8	20.6	17.5	11.6	6.6	3.8	3.7
Receipts from the Rest of the World on Current Transactions	...	610.1	851.4	970.2	1174.2	1101.3	994.0	822.5	769.9	651.3	577.5	605.0

Suriname

1.10 Gross Domestic Product by Kind of Activity, in Current Prices

Million Suriname guilders

	1970	1975	1978	1979	1980	1981	1982	1983	1984	1985	1986	1987
1 Agriculture, hunting, forestry and fishing	...	58.5	91.7	116.0	122.7	140.1	144.3	126.9	134.5	142.7	164.2	206.1
2 Mining and quarrying	...	90.6	113.3	125.0	96.8	123.6	132.0	95.7	92.7	94.6	79.0	58.7
3 Manufacturing	...	152.3	225.3	239.6	249.1	271.2	225.8	195.3	197.4	206.6	226.6	210.6
4 Electricity, gas and water	...	22.5	46.7	62.1	87.1	73.4	69.7	92.9	88.0	66.4	50.4	65.8
5 Construction	...	33.9	104.2	102.6	88.6	106.8	110.2	99.7	106.5	97.2	104.9	115.6
6 Wholesale and retail trade, restaurants and hotels	...	142.4	246.8	270.9	273.3	286.7	314.5	310.6	271.2	267.8	278.0	267.1
7 Transport, storage and communication	...	48.3	82.5	77.8	84.1	98.6	100.2	106.2	111.4	127.7	138.9	153.7
8 Finance, insurance, real estate and business services	...	82.0	138.5	160.4	176.5	219.7	222.9	202.5	204.4	239.7	273.1	337.5
9 Community, social and personal services [a]	...	13.1	17.4	19.1	21.9	26.4	29.5	32.1	25.2	21.0	32.7	33.8
Total, Industries	...	643.6	1066.4	1173.5	1200.1	1346.4	1349.9	1261.8	1231.3	1263.7	1347.0	1448.9
Producers of Government Services	...	118.4	210.9	221.6	225.9	276.1	346.3	373.9	374.1	383.8	408.7	463.8
Other Producers [a]	...	...	...	...	...	...	...	...	...	...	...	...
Subtotal [b]	...	761.9	1277.3	1395.0	1425.9	1622.5	1696.2	1635.7	1605.4	1647.5	1756.5	1912.7
Less: Imputed bank service charge	...	27.0	41.2	56.0	71.3	93.9	92.5	75.3	74.7	89.3	112.5	128.9
Plus: Import duties	...	...	...	...	...	...	...	...	...	...	...	...
Plus: Value added tax	...	...	...	...	...	...	...	...	...	...	...	...
Plus: Other adjustments [c]	...	195.8	234.9	226.3	247.7	269.6	245.1	226.4	214.1	183.4	146.5	138.8
Equals: Gross Domestic Product	...	930.8	1471.0	1565.3	1602.3	1798.3	1848.8	1786.8	1744.8	1741.6	1790.5	1922.6

a) Item 'Other producers' is included in item 'Community, social and personal services'.
b) Gross domestic product in factor values.
c) Item 'Other adjustments' refers to indirect taxes net of subsidies.

1.11 Gross Domestic Product by Kind of Activity, in Constant Prices

Million Suriname guilders

	1970	1975	1978	1979	1980	1981	1982	1983	1984	1985	1986	1987
					At constant prices of: 1980							
1 Agriculture, hunting, forestry and fishing	...	96.9	110.2	121.8	122.7	138.9	134.7	122.9	127.6	129.4	127.4	133.4
2 Mining and quarrying	...	161.7	151.1	134.4	96.8	102.6	80.6	60.4	77.3	87.3	104.0	85.6
3 Manufacturing	...	262.1	295.0	278.4	249.1	256.1	214.0	193.6	187.5	199.6	206.9	168.3
4 Electricity, gas and water	...	50.8	77.3	86.0	87.1	78.0	63.3	64.0	63.9	59.0	53.7	46.5
5 Construction	...	56.5	116.3	105.0	88.6	106.3	104.5	94.4	98.1	87.0	91.7	76.7
6 Wholesale and retail trade, restaurants and hotels	...	236.1	318.5	306.8	273.3	263.8	269.7	255.2	214.9	191.3	166.1	104.3
7 Transport, storage and communication	...	77.3	95.6	83.6	84.1	82.4	84.1	90.6	93.0	105.0	105.4	99.0
8 Finance, insurance, real estate and business services	...	138.6	166.5	168.2	176.5	216.2	197.2	175.1	170.2	194.5	201.9	223.2
9 Community, social and personal services [a]	...	21.9	22.3	21.7	21.9	24.3	25.4	26.3	20.0	15.0	19.7	18.9
Total, Industries	...	1101.9	1352.7	1306.0	1200.1	1268.6	1173.5	1082.5	1052.5	1068.1	1076.8	955.9
Producers of Government Services	...	173.3	259.5	221.6	225.9	276.1	298.5	322.3	322.5	330.9	351.7	371.8
Other Producers [a]	...	...	...	...	...	...	...	...	...	...	...	...
Subtotal	...	1275.2	1612.2	1527.5	1425.9	1544.7	1472.0	1404.8	1375.0	1399.0	1428.5	1327.7
Less: Imputed bank service charge	...	45.6	52.5	59.7	71.3	90.1	75.6	56.2	52.6	62.4	75.8	85.1
Plus: Import duties	...	...	...	...	...	...	...	...	...	...	...	...
Plus: Value added tax	...	...	...	...	...	...	...	...	...	...	...	...
Equals: Gross Domestic Product [b]	...	1229.6	1559.7	1467.9	1354.6	1454.6	1396.4	1348.6	1322.4	1336.6	1352.7	1242.6

a) Item 'Other producers' is included in item 'Community, social and personal services'.
b) Gross domestic product in factor values.

1.12 Relations Among National Accounting Aggregates

Million Suriname guilders

	1970	1975	1978	1979	1980	1981	1982	1983	1984	1985	1986	1987
Gross Domestic Product	...	930.8	1471.0	1565.3	1602.3	1798.3	1848.8	1786.8	1744.8	1741.3	1790.5	1922.6
Plus: Net factor income from the rest of the world	...	-25.3	-55.2	-73.7	-30.7	23.0	12.3	-20.1	2.5	-0.9	-5.4	-8.2
Factor income from the rest of the world	...	20.8	14.9	25.2	45.7	64.7	63.9	29.5	8.9	4.9	2.9	2.2
Less: Factor income to the rest of the world	...	46.1	70.1	98.9	76.4	41.7	51.6	49.6	6.4	5.8	8.3	10.4
Equals: Gross National Product	...	905.5	1415.8	1491.6	1571.6	1821.3	1861.1	1766.7	1747.3	1740.4	1785.1	1914.4
Less: Consumption of fixed capital	...	91.0	145.6	168.4	171.6	186.4	182.3	182.5	173.0	174.6	197.2	235.0

Suriname

1.12 Relations Among National Accounting Aggregates
(Continued)

Million Suriname guilders

	1970	1975	1978	1979	1980	1981	1982	1983	1984	1985	1986	1987
Equals: National Income	...	814.5	1270.2	1323.3	1400.1	1634.9	1678.8	1584.2	1574.3	1565.8	1587.9	1679.4
Plus: Net current transfers from the rest of the world	...	-3.2	7.0	12.5	11.7	6.6	-4.7	-14.3	-13.2	-9.1	-8.8	-6.7
Current transfers from the rest of the world	...	11.6	22.9	28.3	34.3	26.8	20.6	17.5	11.6	6.6	3.8	3.7
Less: Current transfers to the rest of the world	...	14.8	15.9	15.8	22.6	20.2	25.3	31.8	24.8	15.7	12.6	10.4
Equals: National Disposable Income	...	811.3	1277.2	1335.8	1411.8	1641.5	1674.1	1569.9	1561.1	1556.7	1579.1	1672.7
Less: Final consumption	...	686.5	1027.6	1213.0	1266.8	1491.6	1622.8	1768.4	1610.6	1638.8	1485.6	1543.8
Equals: Net Saving	...	124.8	249.6	122.8	145.0	149.9	51.3	-198.5	-49.5	-82.1	93.5	128.9
Less: Surplus of the nation on current transactions	...	-85.2	-82.1	-66.1	-104.0	-218.7	-273.7	-291.7	-80.4	-44.5	-12.0	86.0
Equals: Net Capital Formation	...	210.0	331.7	188.9	249.0	368.6	325.0	93.2	30.9	-37.6	105.5	42.9

Swaziland

Source. Reply to the United Nations National Accounts Questionnaire from the Central Statistical Office, Mbabane. Official estimates are published annually in 'National Accounts Report', issued by the same Office.

General note. The official estimates of Swaziland have been prepared by the Statistical Office to conform to the United Nations System of National Accounts so far as the existing data would permit.

1.1 Expenditure on the Gross Domestic Product, in Current Prices

Million Swaziland emalangeni — Fiscal year ending 30 June

	1970	1975	1978	1979	1980	1981	1982	1983	1984	1985	1986	1987
1 Government final consumption expenditure	10.8	36.8	70.2	74.9	103.9	133.8	141.0	135.8	182.0	177.6	240.7	...
2 Private final consumption expenditure [a]	38.9	102.8	153.3	249.2	286.9	360.2	394.9	450.4	510.8	591.5	595.2	...
3 Gross capital formation	19.5	39.6	141.9	148.1	171.6	155.5	176.2	202.8	209.4	237.6	233.9	...
A Increase in stocks	2.4	-2.0	-3.0	6.0	23.8	15.3	23.4	-5.7	1.0	12.2	5.0	...
B Gross fixed capital formation	17.1	41.6	144.9	142.1	147.8	140.2	152.8	208.5	208.5	225.4	228.9	...
4 Exports of goods and services [b]	56.0	155.4	186.4	218.2	325.7	388.0	416.8	400.6	432.8	474.6	710.7	...
5 Less: Imports of goods and services [b]	48.4	121.3	256.7	344.2	465.9	536.6	582.2	610.0	672.8	738.0	824.5	...
Equals: Gross Domestic Product	76.8	213.3	295.2	346.2	422.1	500.9	546.7	579.6	662.3	743.3	956.0	...

a) Item 'Private final consumption expenditure' shows significant increases from 1975 due to the sharp increases in salary. Estimates also include errors and omissions. b) The estimates for imports and exports of goods and services and for the External Transaction Account are on calendar year basis.

1.2 Expenditure on the Gross Domestic Product, in Constant Prices

Million Swaziland emalangeni — Fiscal year ending 30 June

	1970	1975	1978	1979	1980	1981	1982	1983	1984	1985	1986	1987
					At constant prices of: 1970							
1 Government final consumption expenditure	10.8	19.6	...	...	...	...	...	...	...	...	...	...
2 Private final consumption expenditure	38.9	73.6	...	...	...	...	...	...	...	...	...	...
3 Gross capital formation	19.5	44.4	...	...	...	...	...	...	...	...	...	...
A Increase in stocks	2.4	3.9	...	...	...	...	...	...	...	...	...	...
B Gross fixed capital formation	17.1	40.5	...	...	...	...	...	...	...	...	...	...
4 Exports of goods and services	56.0	90.2	...	...	...	...	...	...	...	...	...	...
5 Less: Imports of goods and services	48.4	69.5	...	...	...	...	...	...	...	...	...	...
Equals: Gross Domestic Product	76.8	158.4	...	...	...	...	...	...	...	...	...	...

1.3 Cost Components of the Gross Domestic Product

Million Swaziland emalangeni — Fiscal year ending 30 June

	1970	1975	1978	1979	1980	1981	1982	1983	1984	1985	1986	1987
1 Indirect taxes, net	7.3	...	...	...	59.6	63.1	61.9	62.9	74.5	91.8	...	...
2 Consumption of fixed capital	7.7	...	...	...	24.6	30.1	37.3	46.6	47.1	55.1	...	...
3 Compensation of employees paid by resident producers to:	33.0	...	...	...	187.3	237.4	271.8	291.2	315.8	342.5	...	...
4 Operating surplus	28.8	...	...	...	150.7	170.4	175.7	178.9	224.8	254.0	...	...
Equals: Gross Domestic Product	76.8	...	...	...	422.1	500.9	546.7	579.6	662.3	743.3	...	...

1.4 General Government Current Receipts and Disbursements

Million Swaziland emalangeni — Fiscal year ending 30 June

	1970	1975	1978	1979	1980	1981	1982	1983	1984	1985	1986	1987
					Receipts							
1 Operating surplus	...	...	...	...	...	...	...	...	...	...	...	...
2 Property and entrepreneurial income	1.0	...	...	...	4.4	6.3	9.2	8.0	14.0	11.6	...	...
3 Taxes, fees and contributions	13.1	...	...	...	143.7	124.2	173.2	170.5	195.6	224.1	...	...
A Indirect taxes	7.3	...	...	...	103.4	78.4	122.2	123.2	137.6	152.8	...	...
B Direct taxes	5.3	...	...	...	37.4	43.8	48.7	45.1	54.4	62.3	...	...
C Social security contributions	-	...	...	...	-	-	-	-	-	-	...	...
D Compulsory fees, fines and penalties	0.5	...	...	...	2.9	2.0	2.3	2.2	3.6	9.0	...	...
4 Other current transfers	0.6	...	...	...	20.2	13.6	23.5	23.0	31.0	28.2	...	...
Total Current Receipts of General Government	14.8	...	...	...	168.3	144.1	196.7	193.5	226.6	252.3	...	...
					Disbursements							
1 Government final consumption expenditure	10.9	...	...	...	103.9	133.8	141.0	136.8	182.1	177.6	...	...

Swaziland

1.4 General Government Current Receipts and Disbursements
(Continued)

Million Swaziland emalangeni — Fiscal year ending 30 June

	1970	1975	1978	1979	1980	1981	1982	1983	1984	1985	1986	1987
A Compensation of employees	7.4	...	...	...	65.1	80.9	92.1	95.9	111.6	114.7	...	...
B Consumption of fixed capital	...	...	...	...	-	-	-	-	-	-	...	...
C Purchases of goods and services, net	...	...	...	...	38.8	52.9	48.8	40.9	70.5	63.0	...	...
D Less: Own account fixed capital formation	...	...	...	...	...	...	...	...	...	...	...	...
E Indirect taxes paid, net	...	...	...	...	...	...	...	...	...	...	...	...
2 Property income	1.9	...	...	...	0.4	9.4	1.2	6.8	9.7	17.9	...	...
3 Subsidies	-	...	...	...	...	...	...	...	...	...	...	...
4 Other current transfers	1.8	...	...	...	6.9	6.2	21.2	14.3	15.0	14.8	...	...
A Social security benefits	...	...	...	...	...	...	...	...	...	...	...	...
B Social assistance grants	0.7	...	...	...	...	...	...	...	...	...	...	...
C Other	1.1	...	...	...	...	...	...	...	...	...	...	...
5 Net saving	0.1	...	...	...	57.1	-5.3	33.3	35.6	19.8	42.0	...	...
Total Current Disbursements and Net Saving of General Government	14.8	...	...	...	168.3	144.1	196.7	193.5	226.6	252.3	...	...

1.7 External Transactions on Current Account, Summary

Million Swaziland emalangeni — Fiscal year ending 30 June

	1970	1975	1978	1979	1980	1981	1982	1983	1984	1985	1986	1987
Payments to the Rest of the World												
1 Imports of goods and services	48.4	121.3	256.7	344.6	465.9	536.6	582.2	610.0	672.8	738.0	824.6	...
A Imports of merchandise c.i.f.	...	94.4	205.3	276.3	405.5	442.7	469.0	516.3	547.6	616.6	689.4	...
B Other	...	26.9	51.5	68.4	60.4	93.9	113.2	93.7	125.2	121.5	135.2	...
2 Factor income to the rest of the world	10.7	17.1	56.0	31.1	27.9	38.0	27.4	38.8	51.2	73.2	124.8	...
A Compensation of employees	0.8	...	-	0.2	0.6	1.5	1.5	2.1	13.5	19.6	23.6	...
B Property and entrepreneurial income	9.9	17.1	56.0	30.9	27.3	36.5	25.9	36.7	37.7	53.6	101.2	...
3 Current transfers to the rest of the world	0.4	0.6	4.3	4.6	5.2	5.4	7.2	7.9	8.0	8.1	11.5	...
4 Surplus of the nation on current transactions	6.2	42.3	-84.7	-114.8	-95.7	-100.8	-82.9	-113.7	-99.6	-102.7	15.0	...
Payments to the Rest of the World and Surplus of the Nation on Current Transactions [a]	65.7	181.3	232.3	265.5	403.3	479.2	533.9	543.0	632.4	716.6	975.9	...
Receipts From The Rest of the World												
1 Exports of goods and services	56.0	155.4	186.4	218.2	325.7	388.0	416.8	400.6	432.8	474.6	710.7	...
A Exports of merchandise f.o.b.	...	145.7	170.0	201.9	286.8	340.3	368.5	338.9	340.5	385.2	606.6	...
B Other	...	9.7	16.4	16.3	38.9	47.7	48.3	61.7	92.3	89.4	104.1	...
2 Factor income from rest of the world	1.3	12.4	9.8	8.9	22.1	43.8	42.9	69.4	104.4	149.7	161.7	...
A Compensation of employees	0.1	...	-	-	13.5	18.8	24.0	54.3	77.7	105.7	125.7	...
B Property and entrepreneurial income	1.2	12.4	9.8	8.9	8.6	25.0	18.9	15.1	26.7	44.1	35.9	...
3 Current transfers from rest of the world	8.4	13.5	36.0	38.4	55.5	47.4	74.3	72.9	95.3	92.3	103.5	...
Receipts from the Rest of the World on Current Transactions [a]	65.7	181.3	232.3	265.5	403.3	479.2	533.9	543.0	632.4	716.6	975.9	...

a) The estimates for imports and exports of goods and services and for the External Transaction Account are on calendar year basis.

1.10 Gross Domestic Product by Kind of Activity, in Current Prices

Million Swaziland emalangeni — Fiscal year ending 30 June

	1970	1975	1978	1979	1980	1981	1982	1983	1984	1985	1986	1987
1 Agriculture, hunting, forestry and fishing	18.1	...	...	...	90.2	104.7	102.1	111.2	127.0	160.3	201.7	...
2 Mining and quarrying	8.3	...	...	...	14.1	15.1	14.4	15.7	12.4	18.0	21.5	...
3 Manufacturing	9.1	...	...	...	79.6	89.1	100.8	89.7	111.3	106.5	166.3	...
4 Electricity, gas and water	1.6	...	...	...	4.4	7.2	8.7	9.3	15.9	22.0	26.8	...
5 Construction	1.8	...	...	...	16.2	21.4	24.8	25.3	24.6	24.8	33.0	...

Swaziland

1.10 Gross Domestic Product by Kind of Activity, in Current Prices
(Continued)

Million Swaziland emalangeni — Fiscal year ending 30 June

	1970	1975	1978	1979	1980	1981	1982	1983	1984	1985	1986	1987
6 Wholesale and retail trade, restaurants and hotels	10.5	...	...	...	35.6	42.3	54.8	63.8	73.7	83.1	99.6	...
7 Transport, storage and communication	5.6	...	...	...	20.5	24.8	32.0	36.8	41.4	43.6	54.9	...
8 Finance, insurance, real estate and business services	5.5	...	...	...	39.2	57.1	66.8	80.1	93.3	110.3	127.6	...
9 Community, social and personal services	1.9	...	...	...	5.7	7.4	9.4	10.8	9.2	9.8	11.1	...
Total, Industries	62.3	...	...	...	305.5	369.1	413.8	442.7	508.8	578.4	742.5	...
Producers of Government Services	7.4	...	...	...	61.1	76.0	85.4	89.1	103.5	106.6	130.2	...
Other Producers	...	...	...	...	6.7	9.3	9.1	10.5	11.3	11.6	13.2	...
Subtotal [a]	69.7	...	...	...	373.3	454.4	508.3	542.3	623.6	696.6	885.9	...
Less: Imputed bank service charge	0.8	...	...	...	10.9	16.5	23.6	25.5	35.6	45.1	49.6	...
Plus: Import duties	...	...	...	...	...	...	...	...	...	...	...	...
Plus: Value added tax	...	...	...	...	...	...	...	...	...	...	...	...
Plus: Other adjustments [b]	8.1	...	...	...	59.6	63.1	61.9	62.9	74.5	91.8	119.5	...
Equals: Gross Domestic Product	76.8	...	...	...	422.1	500.9	546.7	579.7	662.3	743.3	956.0	...

a) Gross domestic product in factor values.
b) Item 'Other adjustments' refers to indirect taxes net of subsidies.

1.11 Gross Domestic Product by Kind of Activity, in Constant Prices

Million Swaziland emalangeni — Fiscal year ending 30 June

At constant prices of: 1980

	1970	1975	1978	1979	1980	1981	1982	1983	1984	1985	1986	1987
1 Agriculture, hunting, forestry and fishing	...	...	86.9	83.4	90.2	101.6	96.5	95.2	100.2	108.6	120.9	...
2 Mining and quarrying	...	...	15.4	14.5	14.1	14.6	12.8	10.7	11.2	11.7	11.2	...
3 Manufacturing	...	...	69.8	71.6	79.6	88.4	93.0	94.0	93.5	92.3	109.1	...
4 Electricity, gas and water	...	...	3.3	3.6	4.4	4.9	4.2	3.8	5.1	5.5	5.5	...
5 Construction	...	...	27.9	25.1	16.2	18.7	18.9	16.9	15.0	13.4	15.0	...
6 Wholesale and retail trade, restaurants and hotels	...	...	32.8	34.4	35.6	35.4	41.9	45.5	46.4	44.6	46.2	...
7 Transport, storage and communication	...	...	24.4	24.8	20.5	21.4	21.4	22.2	23.2	25.0	27.8	...
8 Finance, insurance, real estate and business services	...	...	35.7	37.6	39.2	41.9	42.4	43.0	43.7	42.2	43.4	...
9 Community, social and personal services	...	...	5.2	5.5	5.7	6.2	6.6	6.9	6.7	7.3	7.5	...
Total, Industries	...	...	301.4	300.5	305.5	333.1	337.7	338.2	345.0	350.6	386.6	...
Producers of Government Services	...	...	56.2	57.9	61.1	66.1	71.5	69.8	75.8	78.9	79.8	...
Other Producers	...	...	6.4	6.6	6.7	6.9	7.2	7.4	7.7	7.9	8.2	...
Subtotal [a]	...	...	364.1	365.0	373.3	406.1	416.4	415.4	428.5	437.4	474.6	...
Less: Imputed bank service charge	...	...	10.6	10.6	10.9	12.4	12.1	12.4	12.5	11.7	11.3	...
Plus: Import duties	...	...	...	...	...	...	...	...	...	...	...	...
Plus: Value added tax	...	...	...	...	...	...	...	...	...	...	...	...
Plus: Other adjustments [b]	...	...	49.5	56.0	59.6	57.5	48.8	44.8	45.7	45.3	50.4	...
Equals: Gross Domestic Product	...	...	403.0	410.2	422.1	451.1	453.0	447.8	461.6	471.0	513.7	...

a) Gross domestic product in factor values.
b) Item 'Other adjustments' refers to indirect taxes net of subsidies.

1.12 Relations Among National Accounting Aggregates

Million Swaziland emalangeni — Fiscal year ending 30 June

	1970	1975	1978	1979	1980	1981	1982	1983	1984	1985	1986	1987
Gross Domestic Product	76.8	213.4	295.2	346.2	422.1	500.9	546.7	579.6	662.3	743.3	956.0	...
Plus: Net factor income from the rest of the world	-9.4	-4.8	-46.2	-22.2	-5.7	5.7	15.5	30.6	53.1	76.5	36.9	...
Factor income from the rest of the world	1.3	12.4	9.8	8.9	22.1	43.8	42.9	69.4	104.4	149.7	161.7	...
Less: Factor income to the rest of the world	10.7	17.2	56.0	31.1	27.9	38.0	27.4	38.8	51.3	73.2	124.8	...
Equals: Gross National Product	67.4	208.6	249.0	324.0	416.4	506.7	562.2	610.2	715.4	819.9	992.8	...
Less: Consumption of fixed capital	...	...	...	...	...	...	...	...	...	...	...	...

Swaziland

1.12 Relations Among National Accounting Aggregates
(Continued)

Million Swaziland emalangeni — Fiscal year ending 30 June

	1970	1975	1978	1979	1980	1981	1982	1983	1984	1985	1986	1987
Equals: National Income	...	...	...	...	...	...	...	...	...	...	...	...
Plus: Net current transfers from the rest of the world	8.0	12.9	31.7	33.8	50.3	42.0	67.1	65.0	87.3	84.2	92.0	...
Current transfers from the rest of the world	8.4	13.5	36.0	38.4	55.5	47.4	74.3	72.9	95.3	92.3	103.5	...
Less: Current transfers to the rest of the world	0.4	0.6	4.3	4.6	5.2	5.4	7.2	7.9	8.0	8.1	11.5	...
Equals: National Disposable Income [a]	75.4	221.5	280.7	357.8	466.7	548.7	629.2	675.3	802.8	904.1	1084.8	...
Less: Final consumption	49.7	139.6	223.5	324.1	390.8	494.0	535.9	586.2	692.9	769.2	835.9	...
Equals: Net Saving [b]	25.7	81.9	57.2	33.7	75.9	54.7	93.3	89.0	109.8	134.9	248.9	...
Less: Surplus of the nation on current transactions	6.2	42.3	-84.7	-114.8	-95.7	-100.8	-82.9	-113.7	-99.6	-102.7	15.0	...
Equals: Net Capital Formation [c]	19.5	39.6	141.9	148.5	171.6	155.5	176.2	202.8	209.4	237.6	233.9	...

a) Item 'National disposable income' includes consumption of fixed capital.
b) Item 'Net saving' includes consumption of fixed capital.
c) Item 'Net capital formation' includes consumption of fixed capital.

2.9 Gross Capital Formation by Kind of Activity of Owner, ISIC Major Divisions, in Current Prices

Million Swaziland emalangeni — Fiscal year ending 30 June

	1980 Total Gross Capital Formation	1980 Increase in Stocks	1980 Gross Fixed Capital Formation	1981 Total Gross Capital Formation	1981 Increase in Stocks	1981 Gross Fixed Capital Formation	1983 Total Gross Capital Formation	1983 Increase in Stocks	1983 Gross Fixed Capital Formation
				All Producers					
1 Agriculture, hunting, fishing and forestry	10.7	0.3	10.4	15.5	1.3	14.2	10.0	0.6	9.4
2 Mining and quarrying	2.6	1.5	1.1	2.3	1.2	1.1	-2.2	-2.5	0.3
3 Manufacturing	99.3	18.6	80.7	36.1	8.7	27.4	4.8	-6.3	11.1
4 Electricity, gas and water	1.8	-0.1	1.9	11.5	0.1	11.4	36.0	-	36.0
5 Construction	1.7	-0.4	2.1	5.9	0.3	5.6	0.6	-0.6	0.6
6 Wholesale and retail trade, restaurants and hotels	6.7	4.3	2.4	6.1	3.4	2.7	5.2	2.3	3.0
7 Transport, storage and communication	5.2	-0.5	5.7	10.6	-0.6	11.2	7.0	-0.1	7.1
8 Finance, insurance, real estate and business services	12.9	-	12.9	24.3	-	24.3	10.0	-	10.0
9 Community, social and personal services	0.7	0.1	0.6	1.4	0.8	0.6	1.0	0.4	0.6
Total Industries	141.6	23.8	117.8	113.7	15.2	98.5	72.4	-5.7	78.1
Producers of Government Services	30.1	-	30.1	39.7	-	39.7	33.7	-	33.7
Private Non-Profit Institutions Serving Households	-0.1	-	-0.1	2.1	-	2.1	1.3	-	1.3
Total	171.6	23.8	147.8	155.5	15.2	140.2	107.3	-5.7	113.1

4.1 Derivation of Value Added by Kind of Activity, in Current Prices

Million Swaziland emalangeni — Fiscal year ending 30 June

	1980 Gross Output	1980 Intermediate Consumption	1980 Value Added	1981 Gross Output	1981 Intermediate Consumption	1981 Value Added	1982 Gross Output	1982 Intermediate Consumption	1982 Value Added	1983 Gross Output	1983 Intermediate Consumption	1983 Value Added
					All Producers							
1 Agriculture, hunting, forestry and fishing	140.2	50.1	90.2	163.0	58.3	104.7	168.5	66.4	102.1	183.5	72.3	111.2
A Agriculture and hunting	125.4	40.6	84.9	145.2	47.6	98.3	150.1	54.6	95.5	166.7	61.5	105.2
B Forestry and logging	14.8	9.5	5.3	17.8	10.7	6.4	18.4	11.8	6.6	16.8	10.8	6.1
C Fishing	...	...	...	...	...	...	...	...	...	...	...	...
2 Mining and quarrying	23.9	9.8	14.1	25.8	10.7	15.1	25.0	10.6	14.4	26.7	11.0	15.7

Swaziland

4.1 Derivation of Value Added by Kind of Activity, in Current Prices
(Continued)

Million Swaziland emalangeni — Fiscal year ending 30 June

	1980 Gross Output	1980 Intermediate Consumption	1980 Value Added	1981 Gross Output	1981 Intermediate Consumption	1981 Value Added	1982 Gross Output	1982 Intermediate Consumption	1982 Value Added	1983 Gross Output	1983 Intermediate Consumption	1983 Value Added
3 Manufacturing	296.2	216.5	79.6	373.0	284.0	89.1	404.5	303.6	100.8	403.2	313.5	89.7
A Manufacture of food, beverages and tobacco	148.4	115.1	33.3	174.1	131.5	42.6	182.5	137.9	44.6	208.9	159.5	49.4
B Textile, wearing apparel and leather industries	12.5	10.3	2.2	21.7	19.3	2.4	19.0	16.7	2.3	17.6	16.0	1.6
C Manufacture of wood and wood products, including furniture	16.0	9.9	6.1	20.0	13.9	6.1	22.2	14.1	8.1	20.7	15.2	5.5
D Manufacture of paper and paper products, printing and publishing	60.8	36.4	24.4	63.7	45.7	18.0	67.6	49.3	18.3	68.2	54.4	13.8
E Manufacture of chemicals and chemical petroleum, coal, rubber and plastic products	35.5	26.9	8.5	55.6	43.7	11.9	67.4	48.9	18.5	52.3	42.1	10.2
F Manufacture of non-metallic mineral products, except products of petroleum and coal	3.1	2.2	0.9	6.7	5.4	1.3	9.8	8.3	1.5	7.9	5.5	2.4
G Basic metal industries	...	...	...	...	...	...	...	...	...	...	...	...
H Manufacture of fabricated metal products, machinery and equipment	19.2	15.2	4.0	30.8	24.2	6.6	35.5	28.0	7.5	26.9	20.4	6.5
I Other manufacturing industries	0.7	0.5	0.2	0.5	0.3	0.2	0.5	0.4	0.1	0.6	0.3	0.3
4 Electricity, gas and water	11.3	6.9	4.4	14.9	7.7	7.2	20.5	11.8	8.7	22.9	13.6	9.3
5 Construction	54.8	38.6	16.2	75.0	53.7	21.4	98.6	73.7	24.9	71.9	46.6	25.3
6 Wholesale and retail trade, restaurants and hotels	84.0	48.3	35.6	115.4	73.2	42.3	118.6	63.7	54.7	121.0	57.2	63.8
A Wholesale and retail trade	65.6	38.6	27.1	90.4	58.8	31.6	90.4	48.1	42.2	96.7	45.7	51.0
B Restaurants and hotels	18.4	9.8	8.6	25.1	14.4	10.7	28.2	15.6	12.5	24.3	11.5	12.8
7 Transport, storage and communication	45.8	25.3	20.5	64.5	39.7	24.8	78.9	46.9	32.0	83.2	46.5	36.8
A Transport and storage	39.7	22.4	17.3	53.5	34.3	19.2	67.9	41.4	26.5	69.4	41.1	28.3
B Communication	6.1	2.9	3.2	10.9	5.4	5.6	11.0	5.5	5.5	13.8	5.4	8.5
8 Finance, insurance, real estate and business services	61.8	22.6	39.2	83.1	26.0	57.1	114.2	47.5	66.9	107.3	27.2	80.1
A Financial institutions	28.6	16.4	12.3	37.9	15.7	22.2	58.2	34.5	23.8	36.9	10.9	26.0
B Insurance	3.1	1.8	1.4	4.3	2.4	1.9	6.3	3.9	2.5	8.7	2.8	6.0
C Real estate and business services	30.0	4.5	25.6	40.9	7.9	33.0	49.7	9.1	40.6	61.7	13.5	48.2
Real estate, except dwellings	5.4	1.2	4.3	10.0	2.0	8.0	13.4	2.5	10.9	20.7	5.8	14.8
Dwellings [a]	16.4	0.8	15.6	18.5	0.9	17.6	22.2	1.1	21.1	25.3	1.3	24.0
9 Community, social and personal services	11.8	6.0	5.7	15.3	7.9	7.4	21.7	12.3	9.4	24.2	13.4	10.8
A Sanitary and similar services	...	...	...	...	...	...	...	...	...	...	...	...
B Social and related community services	1.3	0.6	0.8	3.2	1.7	1.5	...	...	...	...	...	...
C Recreational and cultural services	2.7	1.3	1.4	3.3	1.6	1.7	...	...	...	...	...	...
D Personal and household services	7.7	4.2	3.5	8.9	4.6	4.2	...	...	...	...	...	...
Total, Industries	729.8	424.2	305.5	930.2	561.2	369.1	1050.1	636.4	413.7	1043.9	601.3	442.7
Producers of Government Services	97.6	36.4	61.1	126.4	50.4	76.0	134.8	49.4	85.4	136.1	47.0	89.1
Other Producers	9.9	3.2	6.7	13.9	4.6	9.3	14.6	5.5	9.1	18.0	7.6	10.5
Total [b]	837.3	463.8	373.3	1070.5	616.2	454.4	1199.5	691.3	508.2	1198.0	655.9	542.3
Less: Imputed bank service charge	...	-10.9	10.9	...	-16.5	16.5	...	-23.6	23.6	...	-25.5	25.5
Import duties	...	...	...	...	...	...	...	...	...	...	...	...
Value added tax	...	...	...	...	...	...	...	...	...	...	...	...
Other adjustments [c]	59.6	...	59.6	63.1	...	63.1	61.9	...	61.9	62.9	...	62.9
Total	896.9	474.8	422.1	1133.6	632.7	500.9	1261.5	714.8	546.7	1261.0	681.4	579.6

of which General Government:

	1980 GO	1980 IC	1980 VA	1981 GO	1981 IC	1981 VA	1982 GO	1982 IC	1982 VA	1983 GO	1983 IC	1983 VA
1 Agriculture, hunting, forestry and fishing	...	...	...	...	...	...	...	...	...	...	...	...
2 Mining and quarrying	...	...	...	...	...	...	...	...	...	...	...	...
3 Manufacturing	...	...	...	...	...	...	...	...	...	...	...	...
4 Electricity, gas and water	...	...	...	...	...	...	...	...	...	...	...	...

Swaziland

4.1 Derivation of Value Added by Kind of Activity, in Current Prices
(Continued)

Million Swaziland emalangeni
Fiscal year ending 30 June

	1980 Gross Output	1980 Intermediate Consumption	1980 Value Added	1981 Gross Output	1981 Intermediate Consumption	1981 Value Added	1982 Gross Output	1982 Intermediate Consumption	1982 Value Added	1983 Gross Output	1983 Intermediate Consumption	1983 Value Added
5 Construction	5.5	2.9	2.7	5.9	2.6	3.3	8.0	3.1	4.9	8.9	3.9	5.0
6 Wholesale and retail trade, restaurants and hotels	...	...	...	...	...	...	...	...	...	...	...	...
7 Transport and communication	7.1	5.9	1.2	8.6	7.1	1.5	11.7	9.9	1.8	10.4	8.6	1.8
8 Finance, insurance, real estate and business services	...	...	...	...	...	...	...	...	...	...	...	...
9 Community, social and personal services	...	...	...	...	...	...	...	...	...	...	...	...
Total, Industries of General Government	12.6	8.8	3.9	14.5	9.7	4.8	...	...	...	...	...	...
Producers of Government Services	97.6	36.4	61.1	126.5	50.4	76.1	164.8	49.4	85.4	136.1	47.0	89.1
Total, General Government	110.3	45.2	65.1	141.0	60.1	80.9	...	...	...	...	...	...

	1984 Gross Output	1984 Intermediate Consumption	1984 Value Added	1985 Gross Output	1985 Intermediate Consumption	1985 Value Added
All Producers						
1 Agriculture, hunting, forestry and fishing	213.8	86.9	127.0	259.7	99.4	160.3
A Agriculture and hunting	195.6	75.2	120.4	233.1	82.4	150.7
B Forestry and logging	18.3	11.7	6.6	26.6	17.0	9.6
C Fishing	...	...	...	...	...	...
2 Mining and quarrying	27.8	15.3	12.4	41.9	23.8	18.0
3 Manufacturing	405.0	293.8	111.3	427.3	320.8	106.5
A Manufacture of food, beverages and tobacco	235.6	172.8	62.7	249.0	185.4	63.5
B Textile, wearing apparel and leather industries	21.8	17.9	3.9	22.1	18.8	3.4
C Manufacture of wood and wood products, including furniture	19.4	13.7	5.7	21.3	15.9	5.4
D Manufacture of paper and paper products, printing and publishing	88.3	58.8	29.5	101.3	76.9	24.4
E Manufacture of chemicals and chemical petroleum, coal, rubber and plastic products	7.4	6.4	1.1	5.7	4.3	1.4
F Manufacture of non-metallic mineral products, except products of petroleum and coal	6.9	5.1	1.8	6.0	4.9	1.2
G Basic metal industries	...	...	...	...	...	...
H Manufacture of fabricated metal products, machinery and equipment	24.9	18.6	6.3	21.2	14.3	6.9
I Other manufacturing industries	0.7	0.4	0.3	0.6	0.3	0.3
4 Electricity, gas and water	19.5	3.6	15.9	26.6	4.6	22.0
5 Construction	78.1	53.5	24.6	85.3	60.5	24.8
6 Wholesale and retail trade, restaurants and hotels	170.2	96.5	73.7	179.8	96.7	83.1
A Wholesale and retail trade	116.0	60.3	55.7	129.7	66.7	63.0
B Restaurants and hotels	54.2	36.2	18.0	50.1	30.0	20.1
7 Transport, storage and communication	101.7	60.4	41.3	114.3	70.8	43.6
A Transport and storage	85.2	53.6	31.6	94.0	62.9	31.2
B Communication	16.5	6.8	9.7	20.3	7.9	12.4
8 Finance, insurance, real estate and business services	124.4	31.1	93.3	154.9	44.6	110.1
A Financial institutions	51.2	13.8	37.4	66.0	23.5	42.4
B Insurance	4.4	3.9	0.5	9.7	5.0	4.7
C Real estate and business services	68.8	13.4	55.4	79.2	16.1	63.0
Real estate, except dwellings	26.9	6.6	20.3	30.3	7.3	22.9

Swaziland

4.1 Derivation of Value Added by Kind of Activity, in Current Prices
(Continued)

Million Swaziland emalangeni — Fiscal year ending 30 June

	1984 Gross Output	1984 Intermediate Consumption	1984 Value Added	1985 Gross Output	1985 Intermediate Consumption	1985 Value Added
Dwellings [a]	27.9	1.4	26.5	32.1	1.6	30.5
9 Community, social and personal services	26.0	16.9	9.2	27.8	18.0	9.8
A Sanitary and similar services	...	...	...	...	...	...
B Social and related community services	...	...	...	...	...	...
C Recreational and cultural services	...	...	...	...	...	...
D Personal and household services	...	...	...	...	...	...
Total, Industries	1166.4	657.7	508.6	1317.6	739.3	578.4
Producers of Government Services	172.7	69.2	103.5	165.6	59.0	106.6
Other Producers	19.5	8.2	11.3	20.0	8.4	11.6
Total [b]	1358.6	735.1	623.4	1503.2	806.7	696.6
Less: Imputed bank service charge	...	-35.6	35.6	...	-45.1	45.1
Import duties	...	...	...	...	...	...
Value added tax	...	...	...	...	...	...
Other adjustments [c]	74.5	...	74.5	91.8	...	91.8
Total	1433.0	770.7	662.3	1595.0	851.7	743.3

of which General Government:

	1984 Gross Output	1984 Intermediate Consumption	1984 Value Added	1985 Gross Output	1985 Intermediate Consumption	1985 Value Added
1 Agriculture, hunting, forestry and fishing	...	...	...	...	...	...
2 Mining and quarrying	...	...	...	...	...	...
3 Manufacturing	...	...	...	...	...	...
4 Electricity, gas and water	...	...	...	...	...	...
5 Construction	7.5	4.0	3.5	7.1	4.0	3.1
6 Wholesale and retail trade, restaurants and hotels	...	...	...	...	...	...
7 Transport and communication	14.1	12.2	1.9	17.8	15.9	2.0
8 Finance, insurance, real estate and business services	...	...	...	...	...	...
9 Community, social and personal services	...	...	...	...	...	...
Total, Industries of General Government	...	...	...	...	...	...
Producers of Government Services	172.7	69.2	103.5	165.6	59.0	106.6
Total, General Government	...	...	...	...	...	...

a) Rented and owner-occupied dwellings are included in the category 'Dwelling' of item 'Finance, insurance, real estate and business services'. b) Gross domestic product in factor values. c) Item 'Other adjustments' refers to indirect taxes net of subsidies.

4.3 Cost Components of Value Added

Million Swaziland emalangeni — Fiscal year ending 30 June

	1980 Compensation of Employees	1980 Capital Consumption	1980 Net Operating Surplus	1980 Indirect Taxes	1980 Less: Subsidies Received	1980 Value Added	1981 Compensation of Employees	1981 Capital Consumption	1981 Net Operating Surplus	1981 Indirect Taxes	1981 Less: Subsidies Received	1981 Value Added
				All Producers								
1 Agriculture, hunting, forestry and fishing	22.2	5.8	62.2	...	...	90.2	23.6	6.0	75.1	...	...	104.7
A Agriculture and hunting	16.3	4.6	64.0	...	...	84.9	18.2	5.1	75.0	...	...	98.3
B Forestry and logging	5.9	1.2	-1.8	...	...	5.3	5.4	0.9	0.1	...	...	6.4
C Fishing	...	...	...	...	...	...	...	...	...	...	...	...
2 Mining and quarrying	7.9	0.6	5.6	...	...	14.1	10.0	0.4	4.8	...	...	15.1

Swaziland

4.3 Cost Components of Value Added
(Continued)

Million Swaziland emalangeni — Fiscal year ending 30 June

	1980						1981					
	Compensation of Employees	Capital Consumption	Net Operating Surplus	Indirect Taxes	Less: Subsidies Received	Value Added	Compensation of Employees	Capital Consumption	Net Operating Surplus	Indirect Taxes	Less: Subsidies Received	Value Added
3 Manufacturing	30.3	9.2	40.1	...	...	79.6	38.9	10.8	39.4	...	...	89.1
A Manufacture of food, beverages and tobacco	13.0	5.0	15.3	...	...	33.3	16.2	5.1	21.3	...	...	42.6
B Textile, wearing apparel and leather industries	1.1	0.1	1.0	...	...	2.2	2.0	0.3	0.1	...	...	2.4
C Manufacture of wood and wood products, including furniture	2.6	0.4	3.1	...	...	6.1	4.0	0.3	1.8	...	...	6.1
D Manufacture of paper and paper products, printing and publishing	8.2	1.7	14.5	...	...	24.4	8.8	2.2	6.9	...	...	18.0
E Manufacture of chemicals and chemical petroleum, coal, rubber and plastic products	1.5	1.0	6.0	...	...	8.5	3.3	1.2	7.3	...	...	11.9
F Manufacture of non-metallic mineral products, except products of petroleum and coal	0.4	0.1	0.4	...	...	0.9	0.8	0.2	0.3	...	...	1.3
G Basic metal industries	...	...	...	...	...	...	...	...	...	...	...	...
H Manufacture of fabricated metal products, machinery and equipment	3.1	0.9	-	...	...	4.0	3.5	1.3	1.7	...	...	6.6
I Other manufacturing industries	0.3	-	-0.1	...	...	0.2	0.2	-	-	...	...	0.2
4 Electricity, gas and water	1.3	1.8	1.3	...	...	4.4	3.6	1.7	1.9	...	...	7.2
5 Construction	14.4	0.3	1.5	...	...	16.2	20.0	0.4	0.9	...	...	21.4
6 Wholesale and retail trade, restaurants and hotels	18.4	1.4	15.9	...	...	35.6	22.9	2.4	17.0	...	...	42.3
A Wholesale and retail trade	12.9	0.8	13.3	...	...	27.0	15.8	1.7	14.1	...	...	31.6
B Restaurants and hotels	5.5	0.6	2.6	...	...	8.6	7.1	0.6	2.9	...	...	10.7
7 Transport, storage and communication	10.0	3.3	7.1	...	...	20.5	12.4	4.7	7.8	...	...	24.8
A Transport and storage	8.2	2.7	6.4	...	...	17.3	10.2	3.5	5.5	...	...	19.2
B Communication	1.8	0.6	0.7	...	...	3.2	2.2	1.2	2.2	...	...	5.6
8 Finance, insurance, real estate and business services	10.8	1.4	27.1	...	...	39.2	15.7	3.0	38.5	...	...	57.1
A Financial institutions	6.9	0.9	4.5	...	...	12.3	9.5	1.9	10.8	...	...	22.2
B Insurance	0.6	-	0.8	...	...	1.4	0.8	-	1.1	...	...	1.9
C Real estate and business services	3.3	0.5	21.8	...	...	25.6	5.5	1.0	26.6	...	...	33.0
Real estate, except dwellings	...	...	...	...	...	...	0.4	0.7	6.8	...	...	7.9
Dwellings [a]	...	...	15.6	...	...	15.6	-	-	17.6	...	...	17.6
9 Community, social and personal services	4.2	0.5	1.0	...	...	5.7	5.1	0.7	1.6	...	...	7.4
A Sanitary and similar services	...	...	...	...	...	...	...	...	...	...	...	...
B Social and related community services	0.6	...	0.2	...	...	0.8	...	...	...	...	...	...
C Recreational and cultural services	0.9	0.5	-	...	...	1.5	...	...	...	...	...	...
D Personal and household services	2.7	...	0.8	...	...	3.5	...	...	...	...	...	...
Total, Industries	119.5	24.5	161.6	...	...	305.5	152.2	29.9	186.9	...	...	369.1
Producers of Government Services	61.1	-	-	...	...	61.1	76.0	-	-	...	...	76.0
Other Producers	6.7	0.1	-	...	...	6.7	9.2	0.1	-	...	...	9.3
Total [b]	187.3	24.6	161.6	...	...	373.7	237.4	30.0	186.9	...	...	454.4
Less: Imputed bank service charge	...	...	10.9	...	...	10.9	-	-	16.5	...	...	16.5
Import duties	...	...	...	...	...	...	...	...	...	...	...	...
Value added tax	...	...	...	...	...	...	...	...	...	...	...	...
Other adjustments [c]	...	...	...	...	...	59.6	...	...	...	...	...	63.1
Total	187.3	24.6	150.7	59.6	...	422.1	237.4	30.0	170.5	63.1	...	500.9

of which General Government:

1 Agriculture, hunting, forestry and fishing	...	...	...	...	...	...	...	...	...	...	...	...
2 Mining and quarrying	...	...	...	...	...	...	...	...	...	...	...	...
3 Manufacturing	...	...	...	...	...	...	...	...	...	...	...	...
4 Electricity, gas and water	...	...	...	...	...	...	...	...	...	...	...	...

Swaziland

4.3 Cost Components of Value Added
(Continued)

Million Swaziland emalangeni — Fiscal year ending 30 June

	1980						1981					
	Compensation of Employees	Capital Consumption	Net Operating Surplus	Indirect Taxes	Less: Subsidies Received	Value Added	Compensation of Employees	Capital Consumption	Net Operating Surplus	Indirect Taxes	Less: Subsidies Received	Value Added
5 Construction	2.7	...	...	...	...	2.7	3.4	...	...	...	...	3.4
6 Wholesale and retail trade, restaurants and hotels	...	...	...	...	...	...	...	...	...	...	...	...
7 Transport and communication	1.2	...	...	...	...	1.2	1.5	...	...	...	...	1.5
8 Finance, insurance, real estate & business services	...	...	...	...	...	...	...	...	...	...	...	...
9 Community, social and personal services	...	...	...	...	...	...	...	...	...	...	...	...
Total, Industries of General Government	3.9	...	...	...	...	3.9	4.9	...	...	...	...	4.9
Producers of Government Services	61.1	...	...	...	...	61.1	76.0	...	...	...	...	76.0
Total, General Government	65.0	...	...	...	...	65.0	80.9	...	...	...	...	80.9

	1982						1983					
	Compensation of Employees	Capital Consumption	Net Operating Surplus	Indirect Taxes	Less: Subsidies Received	Value Added	Compensation of Employees	Capital Consumption	Net Operating Surplus	Indirect Taxes	Less: Subsidies Received	Value Added

All Producers

1 Agriculture, hunting, forestry and fishing	24.1	6.1	71.9	...	...	102.1	30.1	9.9	71.2	...	...	111.2
A Agriculture and hunting	18.5	5.2	71.8	...	...	95.5	25.0	9.1	71.1	...	...	105.2
B Forestry and logging	5.6	0.9	0.1	...	...	6.6	5.1	0.8	0.1	...	...	6.1
C Fishing	...	...	...	...	...	...	...	...	...	...	...	...
2 Mining and quarrying	10.0	0.2	4.2	...	...	14.4	9.8	0.2	5.8	...	...	15.7
3 Manufacturing	47.4	12.1	41.3	...	...	100.8	48.3	13.0	28.4	...	...	89.7
A Manufacture of food, beverages and tobacco	21.0	6.1	17.6	...	...	44.7	19.8	6.4	23.2	...	...	49.4
B Textile, wearing apparel and leather industries	1.6	0.3	0.4	...	...	2.3	1.6	0.3	-0.3	...	...	1.6
C Manufacture of wood and wood products, including furniture	5.1	0.5	2.6	...	...	8.2	5.2	0.9	-0.5	...	...	5.5
D Manufacture of paper and paper products, printing and publishing	10.3	2.5	5.6	...	...	18.4	11.1	2.4	0.3	...	...	13.8
E Manufacture of chemicals and chemical petroleum, coal, rubber and plastic products	4.1	1.2	13.2	...	...	18.5	5.5	1.3	3.4	...	...	10.2
F Manufacture of non-metallic mineral products, except products of petroleum and coal	0.9	0.8	-0.2	...	...	1.5	0.7	0.6	1.2	...	...	2.4
G Basic metal industries	...	...	...	...	...	...	...	...	...	...	...	...
H Manufacture of fabricated metal products, machinery and equipment	4.2	0.9	2.4	...	...	7.5	4.1	1.1	1.3	...	...	6.5
I Other manufacturing industries	0.3	-	-0.2	...	...	0.1	0.3	-	-0.1	...	...	0.2
4 Electricity, gas and water	4.2	1.9	2.5	...	...	8.7	4.3	2.1	2.9	...	...	9.3
5 Construction	24.2	0.6	0.1	...	...	24.8	21.6	2.0	1.7	...	...	25.3
6 Wholesale and retail trade, restaurants and hotels	28.1	2.5	24.1	...	...	54.8	32.1	2.8	28.9	...	...	63.8
A Wholesale and retail trade	19.3	1.8	21.1	...	...	42.2	22.4	2.0	26.7	...	...	51.0
B Restaurants and hotels	8.8	0.7	3.0	...	...	12.5	9.8	0.8	2.2	...	...	12.8
7 Transport, storage and communication	15.6	7.7	8.7	...	...	32.0	17.3	9.2	10.2	...	...	36.8
A Transport and storage	13.1	6.2	7.1	...	...	26.5	14.5	7.2	6.6	...	...	28.3
B Communication	2.5	1.5	1.5	...	...	5.5	2.8	2.1	3.6	...	...	8.5
8 Finance, insurance, real estate and business services	17.8	5.2	43.8	...	...	66.8	21.4	6.4	52.3	...	...	80.1
A Financial institutions	10.9	4.3	8.6	...	...	23.8	13.1	4.1	8.8	...	...	26.0
B Insurance	1.0	0.1	1.4	...	...	2.5	1.1	0.1	4.8	...	...	6.0
C Real estate and business services	5.9	0.9	33.7	...	...	40.6	7.2	2.2	38.7	...	...	48.2
Real estate, except dwellings	0.5	0.5	9.9	...	...	10.9	0.9	1.8	12.2	...	...	14.8

Swaziland

4.3 Cost Components of Value Added
(Continued)

Million Swaziland emalangeni — Fiscal year ending 30 June

	1982 Compensation of Employees	Capital Consumption	Net Operating Surplus	Indirect Taxes	Less: Subsidies Received	Value Added	1983 Compensation of Employees	Capital Consumption	Net Operating Surplus	Indirect Taxes	Less: Subsidies Received	Value Added
Dwellings [a]	-	-	21.1	...	...	21.1	-	-	24.0	...	...	24.0
9 Community, social and personal services	5.9	0.7	2.7	...	...	9.4	6.8	0.7	3.2	...	...	10.8
A Sanitary and similar services	...	...	...	...	...	...	...	...	...	...	...	...
B Social and related community services	...	...	...	...	...	...	...	...	...	...	...	...
C Recreational and cultural services	...	...	...	...	...	...	...	...	...	...	...	...
D Personal and household services	...	...	...	...	...	...	...	...	...	...	...	...
Total, Industries	177.3	37.1	199.3	...	...	413.7	191.7	46.3	204.6	...	...	442.7
Producers of Government Services	85.4	-	-	...	...	85.4	89.1	-	-	...	...	89.1
Other Producers	9.0	0.1	-	...	...	9.1	10.2	0.2	-	...	...	10.5
Total [b]	271.8	37.3	199.3	...	...	508.4	291.2	46.6	204.6	...	...	542.3
Less: Imputed bank service charge	-	-	23.6	...	...	23.6	-	-	25.5	...	...	25.5
Import duties	...	...	...	...	...	...	...	...	...	...	...	...
Value added tax	...	...	...	...	...	...	...	...	...	...	...	...
Other adjustments [c]	...	...	...	...	...	61.9	...	...	...	...	...	62.9
Total	271.8	37.3	175.7	61.9	...	546.7	291.2	46.6	178.9	62.9	...	579.6

of which General Government:

	Comp. Emp. 1982	CC	NOS	IT	Subs	VA	Comp. Emp. 1983	CC	NOS	IT	Subs	VA
1 Agriculture, hunting, forestry and fishing	...	...	...	...	...	...	...	...	...	...	...	...
2 Mining and quarrying	...	...	...	...	...	...	...	...	...	...	...	...
3 Manufacturing	...	...	...	...	...	...	...	...	...	...	...	...
4 Electricity, gas and water	...	...	...	...	...	...	...	...	...	...	...	...
5 Construction	4.9	...	...	...	...	4.9	5.0	...	...	...	...	5.0
6 Wholesale and retail trade, restaurants and hotels	...	...	...	...	...	...	...	...	...	...	...	...
7 Transport and communication	1.8	...	...	...	...	1.8	1.8	...	...	...	...	1.8
8 Finance, insurance, real estate & business services	...	...	...	...	...	...	...	...	...	...	...	...
9 Community, social and personal services	...	...	...	...	...	...	...	...	...	...	...	...
Total, Industries of General Government	6.7	...	...	...	...	6.7	6.8	...	...	...	...	6.8
Producers of Government Services	85.4	...	...	...	...	85.4	89.1	...	...	...	...	89.1
Total, General Government	92.1	...	...	...	...	92.1	95.9	...	...	...	...	95.9

	1984 Compensation of Employees	Capital Consumption	Net Operating Surplus	Indirect Taxes	Less: Subsidies Received	Value Added	1985 Compensation of Employees	Capital Consumption	Net Operating Surplus	Indirect Taxes	Less: Subsidies Received	Value Added

All Producers

	1984 CoE	CC	NOS	IT	Subs	VA	1985 CoE	CC	NOS	IT	Subs	VA
1 Agriculture, hunting, forestry and fishing	28.9	6.9	91.2	...	...	127.0	34.8	7.8	117.8	...	...	160.3
A Agriculture and hunting	23.3	6.0	91.1	...	...	120.4	26.6	6.4	117.7	...	...	150.7
B Forestry and logging	5.6	0.9	0.1	...	...	6.6	8.1	1.3	0.1	...	...	9.6
C Fishing	...	...	...	...	...	...	...	...	...	...	...	...
2 Mining and quarrying	9.1	0.1	3.2	...	...	12.4	11.4	0.8	5.8	...	...	18.0

Swaziland

4.3 Cost Components of Value Added
(Continued)

Million Swaziland emalangeni
Fiscal year ending 30 June

	1984						1985					
	Compensation of Employees	Capital Consumption	Net Operating Surplus	Indirect Taxes	Less: Subsidies Received	Value Added	Compensation of Employees	Capital Consumption	Net Operating Surplus	Indirect Taxes	Less: Subsidies Received	Value Added
3 Manufacturing	44.9	11.9	54.5	...	...	111.3	51.2	12.7	42.7	...	...	106.5
A Manufacture of food, beverages and tobacco	22.6	6.7	33.4	...	...	62.7	26.0	6.9	30.5	...	...	63.5
B Textile, wearing apparel and leather industries	1.1	0.1	2.6	...	...	3.9	1.5	0.3	1.6	...	...	3.4
C Manufacture of wood and wood products, including furniture	3.4	0.9	1.4	...	...	5.7	5.2	0.8	-0.6	...	...	5.4
D Manufacture of paper and paper products, printing and publishing	11.7	2.5	15.4	...	...	29.5	13.2	3.1	8.1	...	...	24.4
E Manufacture of chemicals and chemical petroleum, coal, rubber and plastic products	0.6	0.1	0.4	...	...	1.1	0.8	0.2	0.5	...	...	1.5
F Manufacture of non-metallic mineral products, except products of petroleum and coal	1.8	0.5	-0.4	...	...	1.8	1.0	0.2	-	...	...	1.2
G Basic metal industries	...	...	...	...	...	...	...	...	...	...	...	...
H Manufacture of fabricated metal products, machinery and equipment	3.5	1.1	1.6	...	...	6.3	3.3	1.2	2.4	...	...	6.9
I Other manufacturing industries	0.3	-	-	...	...	0.3	0.2	-	-	...	...	0.3
4 Electricity, gas and water	5.5	2.9	7.5	...	...	15.9	5.8	4.2	12.0	...	...	22.0
5 Construction	20.3	1.3	3.0	...	...	24.6	20.9	1.2	2.7	...	...	24.8
6 Wholesale and retail trade, restaurants and hotels	39.5	3.8	30.4	...	...	73.7	41.6	3.9	37.6	...	...	83.1
A Wholesale and retail trade	26.2	2.7	26.9	...	...	55.7	30.2	2.8	29.9	...	...	63.0
B Restaurants and hotels	13.3	1.1	3.5	...	...	18.0	11.5	1.0	7.6	...	...	20.1
7 Transport, storage and communication	19.7	10.8	10.8	...	...	41.4	21.3	13.2	9.1	...	...	43.6
A Transport and storage	16.8	8.4	6.4	...	...	31.6	18.0	10.5	2.6	...	...	31.2
B Communication	2.9	2.4	4.4	...	...	9.7	3.3	2.7	6.5	...	...	12.4
8 Finance, insurance, real estate and business services	25.0	8.6	59.6	...	...	93.3	29.4	10.5	70.4	...	...	110.3
A Financial institutions	15.3	4.9	17.3	...	...	37.4	18.0	6.6	17.9	...	...	42.4
B Insurance	1.4	0.1	-1.0	...	...	0.5	1.8	0.1	2.8	...	...	4.7
C Real estate and business services	8.4	3.7	43.4	...	...	55.4	9.6	3.8	49.7	...	...	63.1
Real estate, except dwellings	2.1	3.2	15.0	...	...	20.3	2.3	3.2	17.4	...	...	22.9
Dwellings [a]	-	-	26.5	...	...	26.5	-	-	30.5	...	...	30.5
9 Community, social and personal services	8.1	0.7	0.3	...	...	9.2	8.2	0.6	1.0	...	...	9.8
A Sanitary and similar services	...	...	...	...	...	...	...	...	...	...	...	...
B Social and related community services	...	...	...	...	...	...	...	...	...	...	...	...
C Recreational and cultural services	...	...	...	...	...	...	...	...	...	...	...	...
D Personal and household services	...	...	...	...	...	...	...	...	...	...	...	...
Total, Industries	201.3	46.9	260.5	...	...	508.6	224.6	54.8	299.1	...	...	578.4
Producers of Government Services	103.5	-	-	...	...	103.5	106.6	-	-	...	...	106.6
Other Producers	11.1	0.2	-	...	...	11.3	11.3	0.3	-	...	...	11.6
Total [b]	315.8	47.1	260.4	...	...	623.4	342.5	55.1	299.1	...	...	696.6
Less: Imputed bank service charge	-	-	35.6	...	...	35.6	-	-	45.1	...	...	45.1
Import duties	...	...	...	...	...	...	...	...	...	...	...	...
Value added tax	...	...	...	...	...	...	...	...	...	...	...	...
Other adjustments [c]	...	...	...	...	...	74.5	...	...	...	...	...	91.8
Total	315.8	47.1	224.8	74.5	...	662.3	342.5	55.1	254.0	91.8	...	743.3

of which General Government:

1 Agriculture, hunting, forestry and fishing	...	...	...	...	...	...	...	...	...	...	...	...
2 Mining and quarrying	...	...	...	...	...	...	...	...	...	...	...	...
3 Manufacturing	...	...	...	...	...	...	...	...	...	...	...	...
4 Electricity, gas and water	...	...	...	...	...	...	...	...	...	...	...	...

Swaziland

4.3 Cost Components of Value Added
(Continued)

Million Swaziland emalangeni

Fiscal year ending 30 June

	1984						1985					
	Compensation of Employees	Capital Consumption	Net Operating Surplus	Indirect Taxes	Less: Subsidies Received	Value Added	Compensation of Employees	Capital Consumption	Net Operating Surplus	Indirect Taxes	Less: Subsidies Received	Value Added
5 Construction	3.5	...	...	...	...	3.5	3.1	...	...	...	...	3.1
6 Wholesale and retail trade, restaurants and hotels	...	...	...	...	...	...	...	...	...	...	...	...
7 Transport and communication	1.9	...	...	...	...	1.9	2.0	...	...	...	...	2.0
8 Finance, insurance, real estate & business services	...	...	...	...	...	...	...	...	...	...	...	...
9 Community, social and personal services	...	...	...	...	...	...	...	...	...	...	...	...
Total, Industries of General Government	4.4	...	...	...	...	4.4	5.1	...	...	...	...	5.1
Producers of Government Services	103.5	...	...	...	...	103.5	106.6	...	...	...	...	106.6
Total, General Government	107.9	...	...	...	...	107.9	111.7	...	...	...	...	111.7

a) Rented and owner-occupied dwellings are included in the category 'Dwelling' of item 'Finance, insurance, real estate and business services'.
b) Gross domestic product in factor values.
c) Item 'Other adjustments' refers to indirect taxes net of subsidies.

Sweden

General note. The preparation of national accounts statistics in Sweden is undertaken by Statistics, Sweden. The annual estimates of certain standard tables are published in a series of Statistical Reports entitled 'Nationalrakenskaper - National Accounts'. Supplementary and supporting tables are published separately in a set of five appendixes. Each series of the Statistical Reports contains some methodological notes. However, the most detailed description of the sources and methods used for the national accounts estimation at current and constant prices is found in 'Reports on Statistical Coordination 1979:11. Swedish National Accounts System. Sources and Methods'. The Swedish National Accounts System corresponds closely to the United Nations System of National Accounts. Separate input-output tables have been published for the years 1964, 1968, 1969, 1975 and 1980 in 'Input-Output tabeller for Sverige'. The following tables have been prepared from successive replies to the United Nations national accounts questionnaire. When the scope and coverage of the estimates differ for conceptual or statistical reasons from the definitions and classifications recommended in SNA, a footnote is indicated to the relevant tables.

Sources and methods:

(a) Gross domestic product. Gross domestic product is estimated mainly through the expenditure approach.

(b) Expenditure on the gross domestic product. All components of GDP by expenditure type are estimated through the expenditure approach. Government final consumption expenditure is calculated from the cost side. The calculations for the central government are based on the semi-annual groupings made by the National Accounting and Audit Bureau and on reports of the central government revenue. For local government the calculations are based on finance statistics compiled by Statistics Sweden. Private consumption expenditure consists of approximately 130 items, for which a number of estimation methods are used. The Swedish National Agriculture Marketing Board is the source for the estimate of food consumption, and for most of the remaining goods, the estimates are based on a combination of the Family Expenditure Survey and turnover statistics of retail trade. Gross capital formation estimates are derived from investment inquiries from the different sectors of economic activity and from government accounts data. Exports and imports of goods and services are mainly estimated from foreign trade statistics, and balance of payment statistics of the Swedish Central Bank. For the constant price estimates, price deflation is used for most of the expenditure items, the current values being deflated by various price indexes such as weighted consumer price indexes, adjusted export and import price indexes, price indexes for different capital goods, etc. Components of government consumption expenditure are deflated by relevant price indexes, except wages and salaries which are extrapolated by employment indexes.

(c) Cost-structure of the gross domestic product. In estimating the cost-structure components of GDP, compensation of employees is based on adjusted tax assessments and income statistics, adding employers' contributions to insurance and pensions from compilations in the insurance sector. Consumption of fixed capital is calculated from capital stock values obtained by the perpetual inventory method. Data on indirect taxes and subsidies are based on local government finance statistics and information from the National Accounting and Audit Bureau. Operating surplus, however, is arrived at as a residual.

(d) Gross domestic product by kind of economic activity. The table of gross domestic product by kind of economic activity is calculated in basic values. The production approach is used to estimate value added of the majority of industries. The income approach is applied to most government services as well as to the trade sector, construction and other private services. Statistics of the Agricultural Marketing Board is the main source of information for the estimation of agricultural production. Estimates of output and intermediate consumption of mining and manufacturing and electricity, gas and water are based on annual censuses. Special calculations are made to include establishments not included in the census. The annual statistics of financial accounting of enterprises as well as employment data obtained from the census of population are used for the trade sector. For the transport sector, the estimates are mainly based on official statistics and on financial accounting statistics. The output value of letting of dwellings and use of owner-occupied dwellings correspond to the item housing in private consumption. Input estimates are based on cost data from surveys of real estate costs. The financial statistics of enterprises are the main source for compiling estimates of the business services sector. Input is estimated on the basis of a fixed input-output relationship at constant prices. For government services the source is the National Accounting and Audit Bureau's statistics of government income and expenditure. For the constant price estimates, the general approach for all industries is double deflation. For the mining and manufacturing sectors deflation has been used at the level of establishment with previous year as base-year. For agriculture, forestry and fishing, current output quantities are revalued at base-year prices, while base-year values are extrapolated by employment figures for financing, insurance and producers of government services. For other industries different kinds of price indexes have been used, such as wholesale indexes, implicit price indexes, consumer price indexes, etc.

1.1 Expenditure on the Gross Domestic Product, in Current Prices

Million Swedish kronor

	1970	1975	1978	1979	1980	1981	1982	1983	1984	1985	1986	1987
1 Government final consumption expenditure	36916	71530	115068	130657	151374	167414	182711	200560	218041	235879	253701	268487
2 Private final consumption expenditure	92237	156908	220480	243755	271831	301024	336650	365820	401987	442427	484794	531009
A Households	91176	154811	216379	239430	266953	295825	330696	359334	394984	435006	476605	521993
B Private non-profit institutions serving households	1061	2097	4101	4325	4878	5199	5954	6486	7003	7421	8189	9016
3 Gross capital formation	44036	72931	72676	92523	111891	104303	112143	122578	139158	162921	161150	184736
A Increase in stocks	5269	10013	-7423	962	5905	-5587	-6093	-9591	-7426	-1354	-9620	-6139
B Gross fixed capital formation	38767	62918	80099	91561	105986	109890	118236	132169	146584	164275	170770	190875
Residential buildings	9602	12055	19212	22418	24490	25776	26947	28856	33070	35211	35693	43090
Non-residential buildings	16558	24239	30086	33181	38362	39563	41606	45288	48289	50739	54903	58199
Other construction and land improvement etc.												
Other [a]	12607	26624	30801	35962	43134	44551	49683	58025	65225	78325	80174	89586
4 Exports of goods and services	41515	84679	116399	140568	156523	172527	201331	249528	284664	303509	309193	326119
5 Less: Imports of goods and services	42478	85263	112173	145196	166520	172228	205157	233121	254267	283852	277054	305125
Equals: Gross Domestic Product	172226	300785	412450	462307	525099	573040	627678	705365	789583	860884	931784	1005230

a) Item 'Other' of gross capital formation includes a statistical discrepancy.

1.2 Expenditure on the Gross Domestic Product, in Constant Prices

Million Swedish kronor

	1970	1975	1978	1979	1980	1981	1982	1983	1984	1985	1986	1987
	At constant prices of:1980											
1 Government final consumption expenditure	110825	128384	141387	148084	151374	154439	155641	156882	160511	163923	165811	167848
2 Private final consumption expenditure	231661	261433	267564	274028	271831	270432	274144	269269	273207	281267	294672	305969
A Households	227617	256842	263008	269338	266953	265522	268914	263889	267742	275828	289043	300155
B Private non-profit institutions serving households	4044	4591	4556	4690	4878	4910	5230	5380	5465	5439	5629	5814
3 Gross capital formation	113590	121556	88700	102804	111891	95012	94045	93417	102237	112162	106596	114378

Sweden

1.2 Expenditure on the Gross Domestic Product, in Constant Prices
(Continued)

Million Swedish kronor

	1970	1975	1978	1979	1980	1981	1982	1983	1984	1985	1986	1987
					At constant prices of:1980							
A Increase in stocks	13405	15073	-9365	360	5905	-5312	-5181	-7369	-3684	-138	-5073	-4219
B Gross fixed capital formation	100185	106483	98065	102444	105986	100324	99226	100786	105921	112300	111669	118597
Residential buildings	28476	25138	25593	26051	24490	23340	22942	22657	24333	24485	23624	26679
Non-residential buildings	40713	40300	37027	37214	38362	35934	35248	35320	35361	35142	36682	36760
Other construction and land improvement etc.												
Other [a]	30996	41045	35445	39179	43134	41050	41036	42809	46227	52673	51363	55158
4 Exports of goods and services	107872	129951	148266	157364	156523	158281	165260	182904	195230	199456	206058	211257
5 Less: Imports of goods and services	131301	149778	148537	165801	166520	154651	161357	161940	169302	182910	192988	205232
Equals: Gross Domestic Product	432647	491546	497380	516479	525099	523513	527733	540532	561883	573898	580149	594220

a) Item 'Other' of gross capital formation includes a statistical discrepancy.

1.3 Cost Components of the Gross Domestic Product

Million Swedish kronor

	1970	1975	1978	1979	1980	1981	1982	1983	1984	1985	1986	1987
1 Indirect taxes, net	18907	32412	40311	42282	48694	57100	60719	70794	87104	99138	118382	128782
A Indirect taxes	21754	41622	57622	62001	71337	83784	91795	107644	126261	141245	163395	175240
B Less: Subsidies	2847	9210	17311	19719	22643	26684	31076	36850	39157	42107	45013	46458
2 Consumption of fixed capital	16351	30538	45963	51723	59421	66479	74675	84339	91752	99464	107186	116476
3 Compensation of employees paid by resident producers to:	103018	183743	272908	299946	337085	368363	389526	421599	461433	502379	549412	595664
A Resident households	103012	183734	272886	299918	337055	368293	389363	421219	461076	501964	548498	594664
B Rest of the world	6	9	22	28	30	70	163	380	357	415	914	1000
4 Operating surplus	33950	54092	53268	68356	79899	81098	102758	128633	149294	159903	156804	164304
A Corporate and quasi-corporate enterprises	8639	18876	1956	16488	21313	19061	28818	46806	59090	63881	58394	54989
B Private unincorporated enterprises	23920	33052	49197	50273	56586	59727	71198	77420	85861	91411	93304	103950
C General government	1391	2164	2115	1595	2000	2310	2742	4407	4343	4611	5106	5365
Equals: Gross Domestic Product	172226	300785	412450	462307	525099	573040	627678	705365	789583	860884	931784	1005230

1.4 General Government Current Receipts and Disbursements

Million Swedish kronor

	1970	1975	1978	1979	1980	1981	1982	1983	1984	1985	1986	1987
					Receipts							
1 Operating surplus	1391	2164	2115	1595	2000	2310	2742	4407	4343	4611	5106	5365
2 Property and entrepreneurial income	5153	12030	19208	22210	27121	32782	38910	45650	50891	57194	61799	59552
3 Taxes, fees and contributions	69963	131725	208869	229445	260498	292155	315679	358999	400969	433991	495893	558093
A Indirect taxes	21754	41622	57622	62001	71337	83784	91795	107644	126261	141245	163395	175240
B Direct taxes	35010	63995	94322	104369	113925	121835	136230	154440	169294	182952	206136	243782
C Social security contributions	13059	25761	56439	62525	74643	85833	86630	95653	103781	108206	124456	137282
D Compulsory fees, fines and penalties	140	347	486	550	593	703	1024	1262	1633	1588	1906	1789
4 Other current transfers	3833	6033	6950	7689	7628	6913	12200	13251	14335	16837	11447	7543
Total Current Receipts of General Government	80340	151952	237142	260939	297247	334160	369531	422307	470538	512633	574245	630553
					Disbursements							
1 Government final consumption expenditure	36916	71530	115068	130657	151374	167414	182711	200560	218041	235879	253701	268487
A Compensation of employees	25027	49476	82887	93883	108627	118747	129076	139801	151694	161691	174978	183010
B Consumption of fixed capital	1463	2768	4142	4678	5367	6118	6915	7797	8509	9189	9735	10427
C Purchases of goods and services, net	10200	17757	26217	30503	35338	40025	43998	47306	52254	58870	61985	67235
D Less: Own account fixed capital formation	...	...	...	...	...	...	...	...	...	...	...	...
E Indirect taxes paid, net	226	1529	1822	1593	2042	2524	2722	5656	5584	6129	7003	7815
2 Property income	3305	6666	11230	14323	21887	31144	43953	51457	60991	73318	71109	67299
A Interest	3225	6507	11013	14170	21591	30771	43496	51063	60464	72738	70205	66629
B Net land rent and royalties	80	159	217	153	296	373	457	394	527	580	904	670

Sweden

1.4 General Government Current Receipts and Disbursements
(Continued)

Million Swedish kronor

		1970	1975	1978	1979	1980	1981	1982	1983	1984	1985	1986	1987
3	Subsidies	2847	9210	17311	19719	22643	26684	31076	36850	39157	42107	45013	46458
4	Other current transfers	20451	47143	79280	89642	102495	116209	127516	143225	152914	172339	189396	207882
	A Social security benefits	12718	31634	55733	63011	73396	84729	92730	104640	112335	125016	139567	153639
	B Social assistance grants	4837	8768	13501	15218	16457	17188	19782	21711	22315	27356	27763	30518
	C Other	2896	6741	10046	11413	12642	14292	15004	16874	18264	19967	22066	23725
5	Net saving	16821	17403	14253	6598	-1152	-7291	-15725	-9785	-565	-11010	15026	40427
	Total Current Disbursements and Net Saving of General Government	80340	151952	237142	260939	297247	334160	369531	422307	470538	512633	574245	630553

1.5 Current Income and Outlay of Corporate and Quasi-Corporate Enterprises, Summary

Million Swedish kronor

		1970	1975	1978	1979	1980	1981	1982	1983	1984	1985	1986	1987
	Receipts												
1	Operating surplus	8639	18876	1956	16488	21313	19061	28818	46806	59090	63881	58394	54989
2	Property and entrepreneurial income received	16665	32197	52319	63032	86631	111850	129435	141035	164058	192668	205017	225788
3	Current transfers	7217	13975	23967	24052	26181	33029	39754	41153	46413	56176	64279	68417
	Total Current Receipts	32521	65048	78242	103572	134125	163940	198007	228994	269561	312725	327690	349194
	Disbursements												
1	Property and entrepreneurial income	18705	37150	58151	67105	90562	115864	131212	147445	169616	194505	207822	224421
2	Direct taxes and other current payments to general government	2667	3397	4519	5167	6552	6334	8744	13012	14626	14536	17091	27763
3	Other current transfers	5685	9232	14388	15203	17026	23330	30234	32895	38908	46005	53551	56364
4	Net saving	5464	15269	1184	16097	19985	18412	27817	35642	46411	57679	49226	40646
	Total Current Disbursements and Net Saving	32521	65048	78242	103572	134125	163940	198007	228994	269561	312725	327690	349194

1.6 Current Income and Outlay of Households and Non-Profit Institutions

Million Swedish kronor

		1970	1975	1978	1979	1980	1981	1982	1983	1984	1985	1986	1987
	Receipts												
1	Compensation of employees	103026	183786	273100	300130	337338	368631	389646	421456	461259	502173	548623	594950
	A From resident producers	103012	183734	272886	299918	337055	368293	389363	421219	461076	501964	548498	594664
	B From rest of the world	14	52	214	212	283	338	283	237	183	209	125	286
2	Operating surplus of private unincorporated enterprises	23920	33052	49197	50273	56586	59727	71198	77420	85861	91411	93304	103950
3	Property and entrepreneurial income	7235	11471	16235	18422	27267	34145	35833	38490	44130	52810	56772	57973
4	Current transfers	22119	49409	82342	92826	105996	120721	132961	149337	160190	179818	198658	218183
	A Social security benefits	12718	31634	55733	63011	73396	84729	92730	104640	112335	125016	139567	153639
	B Social assistance grants	4899	10159	15580	17496	19369	21148	23296	25737	26663	31932	32938	36308
	C Other	4502	7616	11029	12319	13231	14844	16935	18960	21192	22870	26153	28236
	Total Current Receipts	156300	277718	420874	461651	527187	583224	629638	686703	751440	826212	897357	975056
	Disbursements												
1	Private final consumption expenditure	92237	156908	220480	243755	271831	301024	336650	365820	401987	442427	484794	531009
2	Property income	7107	11118	19949	23686	32846	41477	43002	43292	48573	57159	61160	67116
3	Direct taxes and other current transfers n.e.c. to general government	46388	87566	147391	163166	183729	203509	217329	240110	261798	279994	316348	357114
	A Social security contributions	13059	25761	56439	62525	74643	85833	86630	95653	103781	108206	124456	137282
	B Direct taxes	32398	60680	89975	99353	107614	115701	127773	141798	155060	168591	189211	216073
	C Fees, fines and penalties	931	1125	977	1288	1472	1975	2926	2659	2957	3197	2681	3759
4	Other current transfers	6535	13874	21945	23076	23967	24689	30042	32268	34440	40927	39051	36038
5	Net saving	4033	8252	11109	7968	14814	12525	2615	5213	4642	5705	-3996	-16221
	Total Current Disbursements and Net Saving	156300	277718	420874	461651	527187	583224	629638	686703	751440	826212	897357	975056

Sweden

1.7 External Transactions on Current Account, Summary

Million Swedish kronor

	1970	1975	1978	1979	1980	1981	1982	1983	1984	1985	1986	1987
Payments to the Rest of the World												
1 Imports of goods and services	42478	85263	112173	145196	166520	172228	205157	233121	254267	283852	277054	305125
A Imports of merchandise c.i.f.	36730	73519	93883	124661	143839	148735	177208	202038	221134	246761	233640	258008
B Other	5748	11744	18290	20535	22681	23493	27949	31083	33133	37091	43414	47117
2 Factor income to the rest of the world	912	2084	7344	7986	11947	21523	27599	31593	36530	42195	36821	37834
A Compensation of employees	6	9	22	28	30	70	163	380	357	415	914	1000
B Property and entrepreneurial income	906	2075	7322	7958	11917	21453	27436	31213	36173	41780	35907	36834
By general government [a]	10	2	977	1165	2981	6526	8664	11125	13295	14832	11983	12283
By corporate and quasi-corporate enterprises	...	...	...	...	...	...	...	...	...	...	...	...
By other	...	...	...	...	...	...	...	...	...	...	...	...
3 Current transfers to the rest of the world	1235	3383	5470	6267	6903	11378	14179	15641	16412	19530	20947	21131
A Indirect taxes to supranational organizations	...	...	...	...	...	...	...	...	...	...	...	...
B Other current transfers	1235	3383	5470	6267	6903	11378	14179	15641	16412	19530	20947	21131
4 Surplus of the nation on current transactions	-1367	-1469	-167	-10137	-18823	-14178	-22761	-7169	3082	-11083	6292	-3408
Payments to the Rest of the World and Surplus of the Nation on Current Transactions	43258	89261	124820	149312	166547	190951	224174	273186	310291	334494	341114	360682
Receipts From The Rest of the World												
1 Exports of goods and services	41515	84679	116399	140568	156523	172527	201331	249528	284664	303509	309193	326119
A Exports of merchandise f.o.b.	35045	71727	97703	117509	130246	143909	167088	209168	241362	258681	262529	278841
B Other	6470	12952	18696	23059	26277	28618	34243	40360	43302	44828	46664	47278
2 Factor income from rest of the world	856	2891	5968	6720	7924	12083	13730	14431	16255	19679	19529	21597
A Compensation of employees	14	52	214	212	283	338	283	237	183	209	125	286
B Property and entrepreneurial income	842	2839	5754	6508	7641	11745	13447	14194	16072	19470	19404	21311
By general government [a]	149	395	1209	1341	1626	2415	2717	2712	2999	3572	4387	4767
By corporate and quasi-corporate enterprises	...	...	...	...	...	...	...	...	...	...	...	...
By other	...	...	...	...	...	...	...	...	...	...	...	...
3 Current transfers from rest of the world	887	1691	2453	2024	2100	6341	9113	9227	9372	11306	12392	12966
A Subsidies from supranational organisations	...	...	...	...	...	...	...	...	...	...	...	...
B Other current transfers	887	1691	2453	2024	2100	6341	9113	9227	9372	11306	12392	12966
Receipts from the Rest of the World on Current Transactions	43258	89261	124820	149312	166547	190951	224174	273186	310291	334494	341114	360682

a) Only central government data are included in the general government estimates.

1.8 Capital Transactions of The Nation, Summary

Million Swedish kronor

	1970	1975	1978	1979	1980	1981	1982	1983	1984	1985	1986	1987
Finance of Gross Capital Formation												
Gross saving	42669	71462	72509	82386	93068	90125	89382	115409	142240	151838	167442	181328
1 Consumption of fixed capital	16351	30538	45963	51723	59421	66479	74675	84339	91752	99464	107186	116476
A General government	1885	3508	5196	5863	6733	7654	8657	9747	10637	11410	12261	13081
B Corporate and quasi-corporate enterprises	10203	19835	29626	33326	37890	42178	47778	54433	58826	64484	70013	77554
C Other	4263	7195	11141	12534	14798	16647	18240	20159	22289	23570	24912	25841
2 Net saving	26318	40924	26546	30663	33647	23646	14707	31070	50488	52374	60256	64852
A General government	16821	17403	14253	6598	-1152	-7291	-15725	-9785	-565	-11010	15026	40427
B Corporate and quasi-corporate enterprises	5464	15269	1184	16097	19985	18412	27817	35642	46411	57679	49226	40646
C Other	4033	8252	11109	7968	14814	12525	2615	5213	4642	5705	-3996	-16221
Less: Surplus of the nation on current transactions	-1367	-1469	-167	-10137	-18823	-14178	-22761	-7169	3082	-11083	6292	-3408
Finance of Gross Capital Formation	44036	72931	72676	92523	111891	104303	112143	122578	139158	162921	161150	184736

Sweden

1.8 Capital Transactions of The Nation, Summary
(Continued)

Million Swedish kronor

	1970	1975	1978	1979	1980	1981	1982	1983	1984	1985	1986	1987
Gross Capital Formation												
Increase in stocks	5269	10013	-7423	962	5905	-5587	-6093	-9591	-7426	-1354	-9620	-6139
Gross fixed capital formation	38767	62918	80099	91561	105986	109890	118236	132169	146584	164275	170770	190875
1 General government	10753	12808	17834	19139	21836	23251	23809	25888	26903	27411	27599	27689
2 Corporate and quasi-corporate enterprises	21289	36417	42643	50278	61977	66577	75301	86646	98771	117635	124780	143111
3 Other	6725	13693	19622	22144	22173	20062	19126	19635	20910	19229	18391	20075
Gross Capital Formation	44036	72931	72676	92523	111891	104303	112143	122578	139158	162921	161150	184736

1.9 Gross Domestic Product by Institutional Sectors of Origin

Million Swedish kronor

	1970	1975	1978	1979	1980	1981	1982	1983	1984	1985	1986	1987
Domestic Factor Incomes Originating												
1 General government	27384	53120	87577	99489	115232	126097	137237	150122	162576	...	...	...
2 Corporate and quasi-corporate enterprises	77847	142658	178565	208539	235006	253132	...	...	...	...	...	...
A Non-financial	77334	141422	176379	205616	231731	249635	...	...	...	...	...	...
B Financial	513	1236	2186	2923	3275	3497	...	...	...	...	...	...
3 Households and private unincorporated enterprises	30433	39988	56671	56789	62958	66216	76061	...	...	...	...	...
4 Non-profit institutions serving households	1304	2069	3363	3485	3788	4016	...	...	...	...	...	...
Subtotal: Domestic Factor Incomes	136968	237835	326176	368302	416984	449461	492284	550232	610727	662282	706216	759968
Indirect taxes, net	18907	32412	40311	42282	48694	57100	60719	70794	87104	99138	118382	128782
A Indirect taxes	21754	41622	57622	62001	71337	83784	91795	107644	126261	141245	163395	175240
B Less: Subsidies	2847	9210	17311	19719	22643	26684	31076	36850	39157	42107	45013	46458
Consumption of fixed capital	16351	30538	45963	51723	59421	66479	74675	84339	91752	99464	107186	116476
Gross Domestic Product	172226	300785	412450	462307	525099	573040	627678	705365	789583	860884	931784	1005230

1.10 Gross Domestic Product by Kind of Activity, in Current Prices

Million Swedish kronor

	1970	1975	1978	1979	1980	1981	1982	1983	1984	1985	1986	1987
1 Agriculture, hunting, forestry and fishing	7088	13021	14709	14703	16829	18625	20550	22486	25561	25887	27434	28726
2 Mining and quarrying	1592	2384	1262	1987	2449	2235	2484	3214	3833	4414	3606	3467
3 Manufacturing	43110	79242	88044	100924	111018	115712	125671	147050	168050	183325	193524	208634
4 Electricity, gas and water	3129	6088	10293	11520	13093	15148	15950	18797	21789	25240	26850	28739
5 Construction	14268	22831	31525	34707	38675	42844	44731	47311	50823	53708	56270	62335
6 Wholesale and retail trade, restaurants and hotels	18761	34994	45560	52085	58297	60413	65176	74330	86088	95965	105792	114746
7 Transport, storage and communication	10737	18085	24244	27268	31727	34638	37379	40662	44278	48521	54598	60435
8 Finance, insurance, real estate and business services [a]	18889	31945	46732	52209	58920	65122	74543	83284	91729	98598	110597	123802
9 Community, social and personal services	5823	9478	14184	15701	17230	18181	19934	22197	23716	27143	30119	33169
Total, Industries	123397	218068	276553	311104	348238	372918	406418	459331	515867	562801	608790	664053
Producers of Government Services	26716	53773	88851	100154	116036	127389	138713	153254	165787	177009	191716	201252
Other Producers	1315	2136	3437	3546	3860	4101	4571	4934	5246	5534	6060	6607
Subtotal [b]	151428	273977	368841	414804	468134	504408	549702	617519	686900	745344	806566	871912
Less: Imputed bank service charge [a]	...	...	...	...	...	...	...	...	...	...	...	...
Plus: Import duties	1517	1424	1311	1562	1760	1927	2160	2192	2520	2736	3044	3544
Plus: Value added tax [c]	16677	28266	42421	47110	54019	64447	71563	78599	89138	101729	108962	119968
Plus: Other adjustments	2604	-2882	-123	-1169	1186	2258	4253	7055	11025	11075	13212	9802
Equals: Gross Domestic Product	172226	300785	412450	462307	525099	573040	627678	705365	789583	860884	931784	1005230
Memorandum Item: Mineral fuels and power [d]	3259	5982	10302	11225	12740	14303	15264	18616	22194	25458	26745	28736

a) Item 'Less: Imputed bank service charge' is netted out of item 'Finance, insurance, real estate and business services'.
b) Gross domestic product in basic values.
c) Item 'Value added tax' relates to value added tax and other taxes and subsidies on sales and production of commodities.
d) Item 'Mineral fuels and power' refers to ISIC categories 353 (Petroleum refineries), 354 (Manufacture of miscellaneous products of petroleum and coal) and 41 (Electricity, gas and steam).

Sweden

1.11 Gross Domestic Product by Kind of Activity, in Constant Prices

Million Swedish kronor

	1970	1975	1978	1979	1980	1981	1982	1983	1984	1985	1986	1987
					At constant prices of:1980							
1 Agriculture, hunting, forestry and fishing	17449	17181	16327	16257	16829	17067	18165	18993	19707	18914	18936	18271
2 Mining and quarrying	2752	2707	1858	2416	2449	2142	1793	1832	2073	2180	2129	2170
3 Manufacturing	98776	113255	103902	110588	111018	107398	106852	112342	119121	123075	122445	127290
4 Electricity, gas and water	7249	10592	12496	12929	13093	14098	13582	14335	16393	19224	19070	19918
5 Construction	35638	36332	37651	38393	38675	37896	38578	38778	39770	39590	40653	41821
6 Wholesale and retail trade, restaurants and hotels	48382	56061	55290	57979	58297	57279	57474	58447	59476	60862	62491	65034
7 Transport, storage and communication	20204	26347	28180	29654	31727	31027	31149	31028	33026	33887	35447	37565
8 Finance, insurance, real estate and business services [a]	46086	53812	56697	57522	58920	59689	60650	62717	64757	65956	66591	68884
9 Community, social and personal services	13021	16141	16860	17125	17230	16960	17255	17554	17443	18151	18430	19259
Total, Industries	289557	332428	329261	342863	348238	343556	345498	356026	371766	381839	386192	400212
Producers of Government Services	81535	98090	108629	113213	116036	118849	120301	122611	125214	126373	127886	128464
Other Producers	4299	4080	3861	3831	3860	3823	4042	4157	4198	4165	4282	4415
Subtotal [b]	375391	434598	441751	459907	468134	466228	469841	482794	501178	512377	518360	533091
Less: Imputed bank service charge [a]	...	...	...	...	...	...	...	...	...	...	...	...
Plus: Import duties	1283	1399	1436	1762	1760	1645	1654	1695	1882	2060	2020	2484
Plus: Value added tax [c]	48679	52719	54374	55801	54019	52579	53506	53140	53584	56330	58129	60628
Plus: Other adjustments	7294	2830	-181	-991	1186	3061	2732	2903	5239	3131	1640	-1983
Equals: Gross Domestic Product	432647	491546	497380	516479	525099	523513	527733	540532	561883	573898	580149	594220
Memorandum Item: Mineral fuels and power [d]	6787	10146	12227	12510	12740	13713	13252	14167	16285	18874	18856	19779

a) Item 'Less: Imputed bank service charge' is netted out of item 'Finance, insurance, real estate and business services'.
b) Gross domestic product in basic values.
c) Item 'Value added tax' relates to value added tax and other taxes and subsidies on sales and production of commodities.
d) Item 'Mineral fuels and power' refers to ISIC categories 353 (Petroleum refineries), 354 (Manufacture of miscellaneous products of petroleum and coal) and 41 (Electricity, gas and steam).

1.12 Relations Among National Accounting Aggregates

Million Swedish kronor

	1970	1975	1978	1979	1980	1981	1982	1983	1984	1985	1986	1987
Gross Domestic Product	172226	300785	412450	462307	525099	573040	627678	705365	789583	860884	931784	1005230
Plus: Net factor income from the rest of the world	-56	807	-1376	-1266	-4023	-9440	-13869	-17162	-20275	-22516	-17292	-16237
Factor income from the rest of the world	856	2891	5968	6720	7924	12083	13730	14431	16255	19679	19529	21597
Less: Factor income to the rest of the world	912	2084	7344	7986	11947	21523	27599	31593	36530	42195	36821	37834
Equals: Gross National Product	172170	301592	411074	461041	521076	563600	613809	688203	769308	838368	914492	988989
Less: Consumption of fixed capital	16351	30538	45963	51723	59421	66479	74675	84339	91752	99464	107186	116476
Equals: National Income	155819	271054	365111	409318	461655	497121	539134	603864	677556	738904	807306	872513
Plus: Net current transfers from the rest of the world	-348	-1692	-3017	-4243	-4803	-5037	-5066	-6414	-7040	-8224	-8555	-8165
Current transfers from the rest of the world	887	1691	2453	2024	2100	6341	9113	9227	9372	11306	12392	12966
Less: Current transfers to the rest of the world	1235	3383	5470	6267	6903	11378	14179	15641	16412	19530	20947	21131
Equals: National Disposable Income	155471	269362	362094	405075	456852	492084	534068	597450	670516	730680	798751	864348
Less: Final consumption	129153	228438	335548	374412	423205	468438	519361	566380	620028	678306	738495	799496
Equals: Net Saving	26318	40924	26546	30663	33647	23646	14707	31070	50488	52374	60256	64852
Less: Surplus of the nation on current transactions	-1367	-1469	-167	-10137	-18823	-14178	-22761	-7169	3082	-11083	6292	-3408
Equals: Net Capital Formation	27685	42393	26713	40800	52470	37824	37468	38239	47406	63457	53964	68260

Sweden

2.1 Government Final Consumption Expenditure by Function, in Current Prices
Million Swedish kronor

	1970	1975	1978	1979	1980	1981	1982	1983	1984	1985	1986	1987
1 General public services [a]	4998	10023	14768	17410	20256	22716	23727	26807	29284	31475	...	...
2 Defence	5712	9729	12514	13814	16031	17901	19089	19446	20738	22460	...	...
3 Public order and safety											...	...
4 Education [a]	9093	15478	23755	27337	31179	34183	37718	40885	43252	46451	...	...
5 Health	8256	17572	29028	32200	38541	42603	46811	51776	56885	61997	...	...
6 Social security and welfare	3966	9035	19258	22136	25410	27707	31396	35885	39539	43054	...	...
7 Housing and community amenities	847	1460	2468	2411	2988	3231	3109	3188	3371	3589	...	...
8 Recreational, cultural and religious affairs	1762	4015	6189	7073	8159	9085	10017	10867	11917	13020	...	...
9 Economic services	1949	3674	5810	6728	7470	8382	9309	10202	11287	11836	...	...
10 Other functions	333	544	1278	1548	1340	1606	1535	1504	1768	1997	...	...
Total Government Final Consumption Expenditure	36916	71530	115068	130657	151374	167414	182711	200560	218041	235879	253701	268487

a) For 1982, general central government research is excluded from general administration and is included in item 'Education'.

2.2 Government Final Consumption Expenditure by Function, in Constant Prices
Million Swedish kronor

	1970	1975	1978	1979	1980	1981	1982	1983	1984	1985	1986	1987
	\multicolumn{12}{c}{At constant prices of:1980}											
1 General public services [a]	14535	17828	18265	19824	20256	20974	20709	21371	21488	21810	...	...
2 Defence	15878	16226	15336	15520	16031	15959	15469	14586	14664	14994	...	...
3 Public order and safety											...	...
4 Education [a]	25138	27564	28980	30222	31179	31815	32489	32604	33058	32827	...	...
5 Health	27171	31211	36252	37319	38541	39822	40332	41085	42399	43983	...	...
6 Social security and welfare	13506	18412	23593	25028	25410	25779	26917	27924	28580	29847	...	...
7 Housing and community amenities	2513	2485	3011	2791	2988	2922	2551	2366	2353	2298	...	...
8 Recreational, cultural and religious affairs	4887	6862	7427	7955	8159	8305	8331	8258	8585	8846	...	...
9 Economic services	6063	6706	6992	7676	7470	7480	7579	7534	7821	7705	...	...
10 Other functions	1134	1090	1531	1749	1340	1383	1264	1154	1563	1613	...	...
Total Government Final Consumption Expenditure	110825	128384	141387	148084	151374	154439	155641	156882	160511	163923	165811	167848

a) For 1982, general central government research is excluded from general administration and is included in item 'Education'.

2.3 Total Government Outlays by Function and Type
Million Swedish kronor

	Final Consumption Expenditures Total	Compensation of Employees	Other	Subsidies	Other Current Transfers & Property Income	Total Current Disbursements	Gross Capital Formation	Other Capital Outlays	Total Outlays
					1980				
1 General public services [a]	20256	15035	5221	...	...	...	2832	...	...
2 Defence	16031	5522	10509	...	...	...	1910	...	...
3 Public order and safety				...	...	...		...	...
4 Education [a]	31179	23724	7455	...	...	...	3112	...	...
5 Health	38541	30669	7872	...	...	...	3357	...	...
6 Social security and welfare	25410	21811	3599	...	...	...	1519	...	...
7 Housing and community amenities	2988	1579	1409	...	...	...	3179	...	...
8 Recreation, culture and religion	8159	5173	2986	...	...	...	1224	...	...
9 Economic services	7470	4382	3088	...	...	...	5718	...	...
10 Other functions	1340	732	608	...	...	...		...	...
Total	151374	108627	42747	22643	124382	298399	22851	4010	325260
					1981				
1 General public services [a]	22716	16290	6426	...	...	...	2897	...	...
2 Defence	17901	6178	11723	...	...	...	1576	...	...
3 Public order and safety				...	...	...		...	...
4 Education [a]	34183	25840	8343	...	...	...	3522	...	...
5 Health	42603	33400	9203	...	...	...	3862	...	...
6 Social security and welfare	27707	24053	3654	...	...	...	1425	...	...
7 Housing and community amenities	3231	1672	1559	...	...	...	3245	...	...
8 Recreation, culture and religion	9085	5701	3384	...	...	...	1443	...	...
9 Economic services	8382	4759	3623	...	...	...	5817	...	...
10 Other functions	1606	854	752	...	...	...		...	...
Total	167414	118747	48667	26684	147353	341451	23787	6404	371642

Sweden

2.3 Total Government Outlays by Function and Type
(Continued)

Million Swedish kronor

		Final Consumption Expenditures Total	Compensation of Employees	Other	Subsidies	Other Current Transfers & Property Income	Total Current Disbursements	Gross Capital Formation	Other Capital Outlays	Total Outlays
	1982									
1	General public services a	23727	16864	6863	...	...	...	3045	...	...
2	Defence	19089	6695	12394	...	...	...	1527	...	...
3	Public order and safety				...	...	...		...	...
4	Education a	37718	27918	9800	...	...	...	3487	...	...
5	Health	46811	36682	10129	...	...	...	4374	...	...
6	Social security and welfare	31396	27014	4382	...	...	...	1209	...	...
7	Housing and community amenities	3109	1732	1377	...	...	...	3108	...	...
8	Recreation, culture and religion	10017	6125	3892	...	...	...	1475	...	...
9	Economic services	9309	5167	4142	...	...	...	6138	...	...
10	Other functions	1535	879	656	...	...	...	...	...	...
	Total	182711	129076	53635	31076	171469	385256	24363	10236	419855
	1983									
1	General public services a	26807	18338	8469	...	...	...	3325	...	...
2	Defence	19446	6617	12829	...	...	...	872	...	...
3	Public order and safety				...	...	...		...	...
4	Education a	40885	29781	11104	...	...	...	3405	...	...
5	Health	51776	39884	11892	...	...	...	4901	...	...
6	Social security and welfare	35885	30415	5470	...	...	...	1146	...	...
7	Housing and community amenities	3188	1819	1369	...	...	...	3093	...	...
8	Recreation, culture and religion	10867	6548	4319	...	...	...	1732	...	...
9	Economic services	10202	5519	4683	...	...	...	7453	...	...
10	Other functions	1504	880	624	...	...	...	...	...	...
	Total	200560	139801	60759	36850	194682	432092	25927	11110	469129
	1984									
1	General public services a	29284	19858	9426	...	...	...	3675	...	...
2	Defence	20738	6826	13912	...	...	...	-20	...	...
3	Public order and safety				...	...	...		...	...
4	Education a	43252	31682	11570	...	...	...	3427	...	...
5	Health	56885	43913	12972	...	...	...	5435	...	...
6	Social security and welfare	39539	33439	6100	...	...	...	1064	...	...
7	Housing and community amenities	3371	1922	1449	...	...	...	2882	...	...
8	Recreation, culture and religion	11917	7214	4703	...	...	...	1773	...	...
9	Economic services	11287	5838	5449	...	...	...	7832	...	...
10	Other functions	1768	1002	766	...	...	...	...	...	...
	Total	218041	151694	66347	39157	213905	471101	26068	6627	503798
	1985									
1	General public services a	31475	20911	10564	...	...	...	3679	...	...
2	Defence	22460	7218	15242	...	...	...	205	...	...
3	Public order and safety				...	...	...		...	...
4	Education a	46451	33634	12817	...	...	...	3538	...	...
5	Health	61997	47405	14592	...	...	...	5318	...	...
6	Social security and welfare	43054	35643	7411	...	...	...	1328	...	...
7	Housing and community amenities	3589	2033	1556	...	...	...	3073	...	...
8	Recreation, culture and religion	13020	7667	5353	...	...	...	1962	...	...
9	Economic services	11836	6092	5744	...	...	...	7633	...	...
10	Other functions	1997	1088	909	...	...	...	...	...	...
	Total	235879	161691	74188	42107	245657	523643	26736	8271	558650

Sweden

2.3 Total Government Outlays by Function and Type
(Continued)

Million Swedish kronor

	Final Consumption Expenditures Total	Compensation of Employees	Other	Subsidies	Other Current Transfers & Property Income	Total Current Disbursements	Gross Capital Formation	Other Capital Outlays	Total Outlays
				1986					
1 General public services [a]	...	...	...	...	...	...	...	...	...
2 Defence	...	...	...	...	...	...	...	...	...
3 Public order and safety	...	...	...	...	...	...	...	...	...
4 Education [a]	...	...	...	...	...	...	...	...	...
5 Health	...	...	...	...	...	...	...	...	...
6 Social security and welfare	...	...	...	...	...	...	...	...	...
7 Housing and community amenities	...	...	...	...	...	...	...	...	...
8 Recreation, culture and religion	...	...	...	...	...	...	...	...	...
9 Economic services	...	...	...	...	...	...	...	...	...
10 Other functions	...	...	...	...	...	...	...	...	...
Total	253701	174978	78723	45013	260505	559219	27469	7987	594675
				1987					
1 General public services [a]	...	...	...	...	...	...	...	...	...
2 Defence	...	...	...	...	...	...	...	...	...
3 Public order and safety	...	...	...	...	...	...	...	...	...
4 Education [a]	...	...	...	...	...	...	...	...	...
5 Health	...	...	...	...	...	...	...	...	...
6 Social security and welfare	...	...	...	...	...	...	...	...	...
7 Housing and community amenities	...	...	...	...	...	...	...	...	...
8 Recreation, culture and religion	...	...	...	...	...	...	...	...	...
9 Economic services	...	...	...	...	...	...	...	...	...
10 Other functions	...	...	...	...	...	...	...	...	...
Total	268487	183010	85477	46458	275181	590126	29059	1866	621051

a) For 1982, general central government research is excluded from general administration and is included in item 'Education'.

2.5 Private Final Consumption Expenditure by Type and Purpose, in Current Prices

Million Swedish kronor

	1970	1975	1978	1979	1980	1981	1982	1983	1984	1985	1986	1987
Final Consumption Expenditure of Resident Households												
1 Food, beverages and tobacco	26584	41131	55603	59897	66438	72743	81169	88878	98182	105164	112452	117521
A Food	18989	28836	40160	43848	48752	54058	60719	66643	74112	79506	85329	88573
B Non-alcoholic beverages	650	1048	1254	1169	1283	1384	1530	1633	1752	2009	2189	2596
C Alcoholic beverages	4282	7407	9300	9717	10582	11161	12189	13182	14068	14982	16074	16966
D Tobacco	2663	3840	4889	5163	5821	6140	6731	7420	8250	8667	8860	9386
2 Clothing and footwear	7259	12252	16626	18264	20159	21760	23510	25681	28449	32107	35935	39053
3 Gross rent, fuel and power	19498	33622	51083	58004	66756	75569	86579	94661	103256	114791	122095	131720
A Fuel and power	2740	5706	9648	11833	15131	17228	19450	20147	21970	26309	25536	26587
B Other	16758	27916	41435	46171	51625	58341	67129	74514	81286	88482	96559	105133
4 Furniture, furnishings and household equipment and operation	6739	12484	16212	17488	19051	19857	21779	23521	26027	27761	31040	34664
A Household operation	1543	2251	2970	3023	3193	3435	3761	4143	4451	4794	4273	5569
B Other	5196	10233	13242	14465	15858	16422	18018	19378	21576	22967	26767	29095
5 Medical care and health expenses	1980	3185	4444	4935	5729	6741	7748	8861	10029	10870	11951	13125
6 Transport and communication	12706	22530	32181	35907	39325	44413	51616	55792	61039	68835	77379	90534
A Personal transport equipment	3436	6822	8161	9128	8423	9083	11616	11783	12827	14273	19758	27751
B Other	9270	15708	24020	26779	30902	35330	40000	44009	48212	54562	57621	62783
7 Recreational, entertainment, education and cultural services	7796	16097	21537	23958	26495	29660	32240	34919	38479	41758	47197	51862
A Education	180	291	363	406	464	489	504	564	636	672	682	719
B Other	7616	15806	21174	23552	26031	29171	31736	34355	37843	41086	46515	51143
8 Miscellaneous goods and services	6611	10551	14249	15786	17228	18351	20095	22258	24575	27543	29846	32413
A Personal care	2397	3841	5169	5643	6195	6796	7492	8220	8894	9757	10614	11440
B Expenditures in restaurants, cafes and hotels	3328	5337	6830	7387	8074	8402	9341	10489	11915	13600	14665	16004

Sweden

2.5 Private Final Consumption Expenditure by Type and Purpose, in Current Prices
(Continued)

Million Swedish kronor

	1970	1975	1978	1979	1980	1981	1982	1983	1984	1985	1986	1987
C Other	886	1373	2250	2756	2959	3153	3262	3549	3766	4186	4567	4969
Total Final Consumption Expenditure in the Domestic Market by Households, of which	89173	151852	211935	234239	261181	289094	324736	354571	390036	428829	467895	510892
A Durable goods	9175	18091	22274	24681	25389	26771	31068	32320	35551	38548	47423	59214
B Semi-durable goods	14021	25591	35789	39408	43476	47353	51720	56558	62750	69296	76923	84683
C Non-durable goods	37803	61198	85052	93613	106951	118522	132354	143676	157310	173076	180943	189444
D Services	28174	46972	68820	76537	85365	96448	109594	122017	134425	147909	162606	177551
Plus: Direct purchases abroad by resident households	2816	5242	8174	9339	10191	11980	12766	13601	14872	17435	20839	24615
Less: Direct purchases in the domestic market by non-resident households	813	2283	3730	4148	4419	5249	6806	8838	9924	11258	12129	13514
Equals: Final Consumption Expenditure of Resident Households	91176	154811	216379	239430	266953	295825	330696	359334	394984	435006	476605	521993

Final Consumption Expenditure of Private Non-profit Institutions Serving Households

	1970	1975	1978	1979	1980	1981	1982	1983	1984	1985	1986	1987
Equals: Final Consumption Expenditure of Private Non-profit Organisations Serving Households	1061	2097	4101	4325	4878	5199	5954	6486	7003	7421	8189	9016
Private Final Consumption Expenditure	92237	156908	220480	243755	271831	301024	336650	365820	401987	442427	484794	531009

2.6 Private Final Consumption Expenditure by Type and Purpose, in Constant Prices

Million Swedish kronor

At constant prices of: 1980

Final Consumption Expenditure of Resident Households

	1970	1975	1978	1979	1980	1981	1982	1983	1984	1985	1986	1987
1 Food, beverages and tobacco	60732	64477	64609	67166	66438	64706	65078	63667	63359	63325	64659	65070
A Food	43366	45218	46527	48740	48752	48042	47825	47085	46924	46889	47711	48236
B Non-alcoholic beverages	1368	1287	1234	1249	1283	1237	1284	1295	1310	1469	1593	1748
C Alcoholic beverages	10530	12162	11103	11310	10582	9823	10047	9575	9397	9347	9733	9554
D Tobacco	5468	5810	5745	5867	5821	5604	5922	5712	5728	5620	5622	5532
2 Clothing and footwear	16238	19812	20478	20489	20159	20522	20973	20673	21244	22485	23848	24260
3 Gross rent, fuel and power	53406	59390	64730	66265	66756	67016	67468	67684	68615	70993	71814	72672
A Fuel and power	13572	13478	15234	15651	15131	14528	14289	13997	14290	16046	16229	16485
B Other	39834	45912	49496	50614	51625	52488	53179	53687	54325	54947	55585	56187
4 Furniture, furnishings and household equipment and operation	17481	19561	19099	19260	19051	18205	18715	18416	18946	19054	20254	21618
A Household operation	4240	3643	3571	3366	3193	3176	3348	3421	3407	3412	3548	3590
B Other	13241	15918	15528	15894	15858	15029	15367	14995	15539	15642	16706	18028
5 Medical care and health expenses	3725	5187	5360	5563	5729	6026	6410	6528	6808	6894	7271	7670
6 Transport and communication	31899	37825	39957	40741	39325	39287	41764	40945	42042	44219	48180	53113
A Personal transport equipment	8029	10435	9218	9716	8423	8582	10182	9060	9059	9449	11840	15059
B Other	23870	27390	30739	31025	30902	30705	31582	31885	32983	34770	36340	38054
7 Recreational, entertainment, education and cultural services	17748	25551	25316	26231	26495	27006	27490	26989	27585	28401	30897	33137
A Education	326	402	433	440	464	462	451	437	442	445	429	431
B Other	17422	25149	24883	25791	26031	26544	27039	26552	27143	27956	30468	32706
8 Miscellaneous goods and services	20466	19595	17940	17941	17228	16907	17337	17388	17545	18323	18604	18973
A Personal care	7399	6620	6692	6662	6195	6454	6779	6644	6500	6759	7077	7318
B Expenditures in restaurants, cafes and hotels	10300	10183	8315	8261	8074	7451	7410	7407	7458	7662	7524	7637
C Other	2767	2792	2933	3018	2959	3002	3148	3337	3587	3902	4003	4018
Total Final Consumption Expenditure in the Domestic Market by Households, of which	221695	251398	257489	263656	261181	259675	265235	262290	266144	273694	285527	296513
A Durable goods	21534	26983	25749	26872	25389	25436	27946	26025	26806	27818	32539	37985
B Semi-durable goods	33088	41525	43128	43690	43476	43459	44231	43339	44492	46402	48748	50777
C Non-durable goods	98761	104039	106071	108932	106951	103989	104663	103212	103590	105548	108193	109727

Sweden

2.6 Private Final Consumption Expenditure by Type and Purpose, in Constant Prices
(Continued)

Million Swedish kronor

	1970	1975	1978	1979	1980	1981	1982	1983	1984	1985	1986	1987
				At constant prices of:1980								
D Services	68312	78851	82541	84162	85365	86791	88395	89714	91256	93926	96047	98024
Plus: Direct purchases abroad by resident households	7884	9202	10063	10398	10191	10529	9256	8251	8518	9448	11083	11724
Less: Direct purchases in the domestic market by non-resident households	1962	3758	4544	4716	4419	4682	5577	6652	6920	7314	7567	8082
Equals: Final Consumption Expenditure of Resident Households	227617	256842	263008	269338	266953	265522	268914	263889	267742	275828	289043	300155

Final Consumption Expenditure of Private Non-profit Institutions Serving Households

	1970	1975	1978	1979	1980	1981	1982	1983	1984	1985	1986	1987
Equals: Final Consumption Expenditure of Private Non-profit Organisations Serving Households	4044	4591	4556	4690	4878	4910	5230	5380	5465	5439	5629	5814
Private Final Consumption Expenditure	231661	261433	267564	274028	271831	270432	274144	269269	273207	281267	294672	305969

2.7 Gross Capital Formation by Type of Good and Owner, in Current Prices

Million Swedish kronor

	1980				1981				1982			
	TOTAL	Total Private	Public Enterprises	General Government	TOTAL	Total Private	Public Enterprises	General Government	TOTAL	Total Private	Public Enterprises	General Government
Increase in stocks, total	5905	...	...	1015	-5587	...	...	536	-6093	...	...	554
1 Goods producing industries	3467	...	...	...	-2449	...	...	...	-6093	...	...	...
A Materials and supplies	915	...	...	...	-1052	...	...	...	-173	...	...	...
B Work in progress	-226	...	...	...	-3189	...	...	...	-3560	...	...	...
C Livestock, except breeding stocks, dairy cattle, etc.	10	...	...	...	-2	...	...	...	-51	...	...	...
D Finished goods	2768	...	...	...	1794	...	...	...	-2309	...	...	...
2 Wholesale and retail trade	1423	...	...	...	-3674	...	...	...	-554	...	...	...
3 Other, except government stocks	...	...	...	...	...	...	...	...	...	...	...	...
4 Government stocks	1015	...	...	1015	536	...	...	536	554	...	...	554
Gross Fixed Capital Formation, Total	105986	62992	25356	17638	109890	64456	26795	18639	118236	68487	30688	19061
1 Residential buildings	24490	18971	5519	-	25776	19189	6587	-	26947	19478	7469	-
2 Non-residential buildings	37109	11662	11657	13790	38262	11581	11860	14821	40188	11452	13755	14981
3 Other construction												
4 Land improvement and plantation and orchard development	1253	511	112	630	1301	538	126	637	1418	667	168	583
5 Producers' durable goods	38045	26759	8068	3218	38660	27257	8222	3181	43494	30701	9296	3497
A Transport equipment	7063	...	...	...	6204	...	...	...	7270	...	...	...
Passenger cars	1558	...	...	...	1450	...	...	...	1696	...	...	...
Other	5505	...	...	...	4754	...	...	...	5574	...	...	...
B Machinery and equipment	30982	...	...	...	32456	...	...	...	36224	...	...	...
6 Breeding stock, dairy cattle, etc.	378	378	...	...	393	393	...	...	390	390	...	...
Statistical discrepancy	4711	4711	...	...	5498	5498	...	...	5799	5799	...	...
Total Gross Capital Formation	111891	...	...	18653	104303	...	...	19175	112143	...	...	19615

	1983				1984				1985			
	TOTAL	Total Private	Public Enterprises	General Government	TOTAL	Total Private	Public Enterprises	General Government	TOTAL	Total Private	Public Enterprises	General Government
Increase in stocks, total	-9591	...	...	39	-7426	...	...	-835	-1354	...	...	-675
1 Goods producing industries	-7082	...	...	...	-4767	...	...	...	332	...	...	...
A Materials and supplies	-927	...	...	...	-3363	...	...	...	-1072	...	...	...
B Work in progress	-2616	...	...	...	1362	...	...	...	566	...	...	...
C Livestock, except breeding stocks, dairy cattle, etc.	-61	...	...	...	-1	...	...	...	-57	...	...	...
D Finished goods	-3478	...	...	...	-2765	...	...	...	895	...	...	...
2 Wholesale and retail trade	-2548	...	...	...	-1824	...	...	...	-1011	...	...	...
3 Other, except government stocks	...	...	...	...	...	...	...	...	...	...	...	...
4 Government stocks	39	...	...	39	-835	...	...	-835	-675	...	...	-675
Gross Fixed Capital Formation, Total	132169	78636	32932	20601	146584	91294	33793	21497	164275	103404	39009	21862

Sweden

2.7 Gross Capital Formation by Type of Good and Owner, in Current Prices
(Continued)

Million Swedish kronor

	1983 TOTAL	1983 Total Private	1983 Public Enterprises	1983 General Government	1984 TOTAL	1984 Total Private	1984 Public Enterprises	1984 General Government	1985 TOTAL	1985 Total Private	1985 Public Enterprises	1985 General Government
1 Residential buildings	28856	21410	7446	-	33070	25208	7862	-	35211	25818	9393	-
2 Non-residential buildings	43763	12534	15155	16074	46695	14867	15331	16497	49010	16719	16110	16181
3 Other construction												
4 Land improvement and plantation and orchard development	1525	787	198	540	1594	915	214	465	1729	1009	232	488
5 Producers' durable goods	51097	36977	10133	3987	57605	42684	10386	4535	69830	51363	13274	5193
A Transport equipment	8119	...	...	...	11101	...	...	...	12904	...	...	...
Passenger cars	3068	...	...	...	3967	...	...	...	5748	...	...	...
Other	5051	...	...	...	7134	...	...	...	7156	...	...	...
B Machinery and equipment	42978	...	...	...	46504	...	...	...	56926	...	...	...
6 Breeding stock, dairy cattle, etc.	462	462	...	...	440	440	...	...	452	452	...	...
Statistical discrepancy	6466	6466	...	...	7180	7180	...	...	8043	8043	...	...
Total Gross Capital Formation	122578	...	...	20640	139158	...	...	20662	162921	...	...	21187

	1986 TOTAL	1986 Total Private	1986 Public Enterprises	1986 General Government	1987 TOTAL	1987 Total Private	1987 Public Enterprises	1987 General Government
Increase in stocks, total	-9620	...	...	-130	-6139	...	...	1370
1 Goods producing industries	-6274	...	...	...	-5575	...	...	...
A Materials and supplies	-375	...	...	...	-1993	...	...	...
B Work in progress	-3113	...	...	...	-1990	...	...	...
C Livestock, except breeding stocks, dairy cattle, etc.	-150	...	...	...	-79	...	...	...
D Finished goods	-2636	...	...	...	-1513	...	...	...
2 Wholesale and retail trade	-3216	...	...	...	-1934	...	...	...
3 Other, except government stocks	...	...	...	...	...	...	...	...
4 Government stocks	-130	...	...	-130	1370	...	...	1370
Gross Fixed Capital Formation, Total	170770	108219	40050	22501	190875	125681	41951	23243
1 Residential buildings	35693	26142	9551	-	43090	32376	10714	-
2 Non-residential buildings	53044	20210	16701	16133	56101	23332	16876	15893
3 Other construction								
4 Land improvement and plantation and orchard development	1859	1091	253	515	2098	1216	260	622
5 Producers' durable goods	71300	51902	13545	5853	79404	58575	14101	6728
A Transport equipment	14131	...	...	...	15010	...	...	...
Passenger cars	4529	...	...	...	4453	...	...	...
Other	9602	...	...	...	10557	...	...	...
B Machinery and equipment	57169	...	...	...	64394	...	...	...
6 Breeding stock, dairy cattle, etc.	443	443	...	...	605	605	...	...
Statistical discrepancy	8431	8431	...	...	9577	9577	...	...
Total Gross Capital Formation	161150	...	...	22371	184736	...	...	24613

2.8 Gross Capital Formation by Type of Good and Owner, in Constant Prices

Million Swedish kronor

	1980 TOTAL	1980 Total Private	1980 Public Enterprises	1980 General Government	1981 TOTAL	1981 Total Private	1981 Public Enterprises	1981 General Government	1982 TOTAL	1982 Total Private	1982 Public Enterprises	1982 General Government
				At constant prices of: 1980								
Increase in stocks, total	5905	...	...	1015	-5312	...	...	450	-5181	...	...	391
1 Goods producing industries	3467	...	...	...	-2335	...	...	...	-5043	...	...	...
A Materials and supplies	915	...	...	...	-1090	...	...	...	-67	...	...	...
B Work in progress	-226	...	...	...	-2912	...	...	...	-2929	...	...	...
C Livestock, except breeding stocks, dairy cattle, etc.	10	...	...	...	-2	...	...	...	-47	...	...	...
D Finished goods	2768	...	...	...	1669	...	...	...	-2000	...	...	...
2 Wholesale and retail trade	1423	...	...	...	-3427	...	...	...	-529	...	...	...
3 Other, except government stocks	...	...	...	...	...	...	...	...	...	...	...	...

Sweden

2.8 Gross Capital Formation by Type of Good and Owner, in Constant Prices
(Continued)

Million Swedish kronor

	1980 TOTAL	Total Private	Public Enterprises	General Government	1981 TOTAL	Total Private	Public Enterprises	General Government	1982 TOTAL	Total Private	Public Enterprises	General Government
				At constant prices of:1980								
4 Government stocks	1015	...	...	1015	450	...	...	450	391	...	...	391
Gross Fixed Capital Formation, Total	105986	62992	25356	17638	100324	59140	24243	16941	99226	57549	25514	16163
1 Residential buildings	24490	18971	5519	-	23340	17537	5803	-	22942	16717	6225	
2 Non-residential buildings	37109	11662	11657	13790	34723	10505	10759	13459	34009	9651	11592	12766
3 Other construction												
4 Land improvement and plantation and orchard development	1253	511	112	630	1211	505	118	588	1239	582	148	509
5 Producers' durable goods	38045	26759	8068	3218	35722	25265	7563	2894	35802	25365	7549	2888
A Transport equipment	7063	...	...	...	6004	...	...	...	6520	...	...	...
Passenger cars	1558	...	...	...	1376	...	...	...	1489	...	...	...
Other	5505	...	...	...	4628	...	...	...	5031	...	...	...
B Machinery and equipment	30982	...	...	...	29718	...	...	...	29282	...	...	...
6 Breeding stock, dairy cattle, etc.	378	378	...	...	351	351	...	...	322	322	...	...
Statistical discrepancy	4711	4711	...	...	4977	4977	...	...	4912	4912	...	...
Total Gross Capital Formation	111891	...	...	18653	95012	...	...	17391	94045	...	...	16554

	1983 TOTAL	Total Private	Public Enterprises	General Government	1984 TOTAL	Total Private	Public Enterprises	General Government	1985 TOTAL	Total Private	Public Enterprises	General Government
				At constant prices of:1980								
Increase in stocks, total	-7369	...	...	60	-3684	...	...	-454	-138	...	...	-416
1 Goods producing industries	-5683	...	...	...	-2345	...	...	...	776	...	...	...
A Materials and supplies	-1033	...	...	...	-1443	...	...	...	-191	...	...	...
B Work in progress	-2017	...	...	...	1011	...	...	...	434	...	...	...
C Livestock, except breeding stocks, dairy cattle, etc.	-55	...	...	...	-1	...	...	...	-42	...	...	...
D Finished goods	-2578	...	...	...	-1912	...	...	...	575	...	...	...
2 Wholesale and retail trade	-1746	...	...	...	-885	...	...	...	-498	...	...	...
3 Other, except government stocks	...	...	...	...	...	...	...	...	...	...	...	...
4 Government stocks	60	...	...	60	-454	...	...	-454	-416	...	...	-416
Gross Fixed Capital Formation, Total	100786	59948	24363	16475	105921	66050	24119	15752	112300	70835	26305	15160
1 Residential buildings	22657	16924	5733	-	24333	18595	5738	-	24485	18060	6425	-
2 Non-residential buildings	34120	9762	11277	13081	34205	10882	11108	12215	34001	11661	10987	11353
3 Other construction												
4 Land improvement and plantation and orchard development	1200	607	153	440	1156	648	151	357	1141	647	148	346
5 Producers' durable goods	37343	27189	7200	2954	40535	30233	7122	3180	46672	34466	8745	3461
A Transport equipment	6399	...	...	...	8454	...	...	...	8916	...	...	...
Passenger cars	2356	...	...	...	2805	...	...	...	3814	...	...	...
Other	4043	...	...	...	5649	...	...	...	5102	...	...	...
B Machinery and equipment	30944	...	...	...	32081	...	...	...	37756	...	...	...
6 Breeding stock, dairy cattle, etc.	353	353	...	...	318	318	...	...	305	305	...	...
Statistical discrepancy	5113	5113	...	...	5374	5374	...	...	5696	5696	...	...
Total Gross Capital Formation	93417	...	...	16535	102237	...	...	15298	112162	...	...	14744

	1986 TOTAL	Total Private	Public Enterprises	General Government	1987 TOTAL	Total Private	Public Enterprises	General Government
				At constant prices of:1980				
Increase in stocks, total	-5073	...	...	-310	-4219	...	...	1086
1 Goods producing industries	-3619	...	...	...	-3387	...	...	...
A Materials and supplies	130	...	...	...	-1218	...	...	...
B Work in progress	-1998	...	...	...	-1152	...	...	...
C Livestock, except breeding stocks, dairy cattle, etc.	-115	...	...	...	-56	...	...	...

Sweden

2.8 Gross Capital Formation by Type of Good and Owner, in Constant Prices
(Continued)

Million Swedish kronor

	1986 TOTAL	1986 Total Private	1986 Public Enterprises	1986 General Government	1987 TOTAL	1987 Total Private	1987 Public Enterprises	1987 General Government
				At constant prices of: 1980				
D Finished goods	-1636	...	...	...	-961	...	...	...
2 Wholesale and retail trade	-1144	...	...	...	-1918	...	...	...
3 Other, except government stocks	...	...	...	...	...	...	...	...
4 Government stocks	-310	...	...	-310	1086	...	...	1086
Gross Fixed Capital Formation, Total	111669	70688	25939	15042	118597	77835	25812	14950
1 Residential buildings	23624	17472	6152	-	26679	20285	6394	-
2 Non-residential buildings	35522	13524	11118	10880	35510	14654	10749	10107
3 Other construction								
4 Land improvement and plantation and orchard development	1160	659	152	349	1250	692	147	411
5 Producers' durable goods	45407	33077	8517	3813	48759	35805	8522	4432
A Transport equipment	8918	...	...	...	8831	...	...	...
Passenger cars	2712	...	...	...	2406	...	...	...
Other	6206	...	...	...	6425	...	...	...
B Machinery and equipment	36489	...	...	...	39928	...	...	...
6 Breeding stock, dairy cattle, etc.	297	297	...	...	379	379	...	...
Statistical discrepancy	5659	5659	...	...	6020	6020	...	...
Total Gross Capital Formation	106596	...	...	14732	114378	...	...	16036

2.9 Gross Capital Formation by Kind of Activity of Owner, ISIC Major Divisions, in Current Prices

Million Swedish kronor

	1980 Total Gross Capital Formation	1980 Increase in Stocks	1980 Gross Fixed Capital Formation	1981 Total Gross Capital Formation	1981 Increase in Stocks	1981 Gross Fixed Capital Formation	1982 Total Gross Capital Formation	1982 Increase in Stocks	1982 Gross Fixed Capital Formation	1983 Total Gross Capital Formation	1983 Increase in Stocks	1983 Gross Fixed Capital Formation
						All Producers						
1 Agriculture, hunting, fishing and forestry	4218	-156	4374	4642	116	4526	5651	364	5287	6036	66	5970
2 Mining and quarrying	1055	169	886	1000	304	696	675	8	667	55	-418	473
3 Manufacturing	20685	3407	17278	14618	-2793	17411	10258	-5976	16234	12676	-6112	18788
4 Electricity, gas and water	8447	47	8400	9936	-76	10012	11643	-489	12132	13257	-618	13875
5 Construction	1820	...	1820	1891	...	1891	1883	...	1883	2063	...	2063
6 Wholesale and retail trade, restaurants and hotels	6479	1423	5056	1427	-3674	5101	5215	-554	5769	4152	-2548	6700
7 Transport, storage and communication	9917	...	9917	9751	...	9751	11892	...	11892	12142	...	12142
8 Finance, insurance, real estate and business services	34860	...	34860	35229	...	35229	38282	...	38282	43729	...	43729
9 Community, social and personal services	1046	...	1046	1136	...	1136	1230	...	1230	1361	...	1361
Statistical discrepancy	4711	...	4711	5498	...	5498	5799	...	5799	6466	...	6466
Total Industries	93238	4890	88348	85128	-6123	91251	92528	-6647	99175	101938	-9630	111568
Producers of Government Services	18653	1015	17638	19175	536	18639	19615	554	19061	20640	39	20601
Private Non-Profit Institutions Serving Households	...	...	...	...	...	...	...	...	...	...	...	...
Total	111891	5905	105986	104303	-5587	109890	112143	-6093	118236	122578	-9591	132169
Memorandum Item: Mineral Fuels and Power [a]	...	...	6617	...	...	8354	...	...	10897	...	...	12885

	1984 Total Gross Capital Formation	1984 Increase in Stocks	1984 Gross Fixed Capital Formation	1985 Total Gross Capital Formation	1985 Increase in Stocks	1985 Gross Fixed Capital Formation	1986 Total Gross Capital Formation	1986 Increase in Stocks	1986 Gross Fixed Capital Formation	1987 Total Gross Capital Formation	1987 Increase in Stocks	1987 Gross Fixed Capital Formation
						All Producers						
1 Agriculture, hunting, fishing and forestry	6146	-314	6460	5678	-467	6145	5166	-202	5368	5651	-75	5726
2 Mining and quarrying	281	-249	530	456	-105	561	508	-87	595	409	-274	683
3 Manufacturing	19780	-2923	22703	30676	2331	28345	22474	-6711	29185	29785	-4674	34459
4 Electricity, gas and water	12142	-1281	13423	12333	-1427	13760	12461	726	11735	9866	-552	10418

Sweden

2.9 Gross Capital Formation by Kind of Activity of Owner, ISIC Major Divisions, in Current Prices
(Continued)

Million Swedish kronor

	1984 Total Gross Capital Formation	1984 Increase in Stocks	1984 Gross Fixed Capital Formation	1985 Total Gross Capital Formation	1985 Increase in Stocks	1985 Gross Fixed Capital Formation	1986 Total Gross Capital Formation	1986 Increase in Stocks	1986 Gross Fixed Capital Formation	1987 Total Gross Capital Formation	1987 Increase in Stocks	1987 Gross Fixed Capital Formation
5 Construction	2310	...	2310	2389	...	2389	2338	...	2338	2520	...	2520
6 Wholesale and retail trade, restaurants and hotels	6293	-1824	8117	9022	-1011	10033	7737	-3216	10953	10756	-1934	12690
7 Transport, storage and communication	14778	...	14778	15535	...	15535	18224	...	18224	19191	...	19191
8 Finance, insurance, real estate and business services	48300	...	48300	56047	...	56047	59746	...	59746	70495	...	70495
9 Community, social and personal services	1286	...	1286	1555	...	1555	1694	...	1694	1873	...	1873
Statistical discrepancy	7180	...	7180	8043	...	8043	8431	...	8431	9577	...	9577
Total Industries	118496	-6591	125087	141734	-679	142413	138779	-9490	148269	160123	-7509	167632
Producers of Government Services	20662	-835	21497	21187	-675	21862	22371	-130	22501	24613	1370	23243
Private Non-Profit Institutions Serving Households	...	...	...	...	...	...	...	...	...	...	...	...
Total	139158	-7426	146584	162921	-1354	164275	161150	-9620	170770	184736	-6139	190875
Memorandum Item: Mineral Fuels and Power [a]	...	...	11919	...	...	12267	...	...	10156	...	...	9181

a) Item 'Mineral fuels and power' refers to ISIC categories 353 (Petroleum refineries), 354 (Manufacture of miscellaneous products of petroleum and coal) and 41 (Electricity, gas and steam).

2.10 Gross Capital Formation by Kind of Activity of Owner, ISIC Major Divisions, in Constant Prices

Million Swedish kronor

	1980 Total Gross Capital Formation	1980 Increase in Stocks	1980 Gross Fixed Capital Formation	1981 Total Gross Capital Formation	1981 Increase in Stocks	1981 Gross Fixed Capital Formation	1982 Total Gross Capital Formation	1982 Increase in Stocks	1982 Gross Fixed Capital Formation	1983 Total Gross Capital Formation	1983 Increase in Stocks	1983 Gross Fixed Capital Formation

At constant prices of: 1980

All Producers

1 Agriculture, hunting, fishing and forestry	4218	-156	4374	4258	92	4166	4698	284	4414	4463	34	4429
2 Mining and quarrying	1055	169	886	950	308	642	568	18	550	60	-288	348
3 Manufacturing	20685	3407	17278	13376	-2593	15969	8152	-5041	13193	8542	-5100	13642
4 Electricity, gas and water	8447	47	8400	8992	-142	9134	9735	-304	10039	10036	-329	10365
5 Construction	1820	...	1820	1729	...	1729	1589	...	1589	1591	...	1591
6 Wholesale and retail trade, restaurants and hotels	6479	1423	5056	1291	-3427	4718	4311	-529	4840	3357	-1746	5103
7 Transport, storage and communication	9917	...	9917	9087	...	9087	10162	...	10162	9289	...	9289
8 Finance, insurance, real estate and business services	34860	...	34860	31922	...	31922	32329	...	32329	33831	...	33831
9 Community, social and personal services	1046	...	1046	1039	...	1039	1035	...	1035	1040	...	1040
Statistical discrepancy	4711	...	4711	4977	...	4977	4912	...	4912	5113	...	5113
Total Industries	93238	4890	88348	77621	-5762	83383	77491	-5572	83063	77322	-7429	84751
Producers of Government Services	18653	1015	17638	17391	450	16941	16554	391	16163	16095	60	16035
Private Non-Profit Institutions Serving Households	...	...	...	...	...	...	...	...	...	...	...	...
Total	111891	5905	105986	95012	-5312	100324	94045	-5181	99226	93417	-7369	100786
Memorandum Item: Mineral Fuels and Power [a]	...	...	6617	...	...	7634	...	...	8987	...	...	9563

	1984 Total Gross Capital Formation	1984 Increase in Stocks	1984 Gross Fixed Capital Formation	1985 Total Gross Capital Formation	1985 Increase in Stocks	1985 Gross Fixed Capital Formation	1986 Total Gross Capital Formation	1986 Increase in Stocks	1986 Gross Fixed Capital Formation	1987 Total Gross Capital Formation	1987 Increase in Stocks	1987 Gross Fixed Capital Formation

At constant prices of: 1980

All Producers

1 Agriculture, hunting, fishing and forestry	4229	-218	4447	3721	-292	4013	3153	-162	3315	3273	-73	3346
2 Mining and quarrying	214	-156	370	312	-65	377	332	-52	384	191	-230	421
3 Manufacturing	14513	-1435	15948	20732	1651	19081	14608	-4046	18654	18249	-2760	21009
4 Electricity, gas and water	8924	-536	9460	8647	-518	9165	8312	641	7671	6233	-324	6557

Sweden

2.10 Gross Capital Formation by Kind of Activity of Owner, ISIC Major Divisions, in Constant Prices
(Continued)

Million Swedish kronor

	1984 Total Gross Capital Formation	1984 Increase in Stocks	1984 Gross Fixed Capital Formation	1985 Total Gross Capital Formation	1985 Increase in Stocks	1985 Gross Fixed Capital Formation	1986 Total Gross Capital Formation	1986 Increase in Stocks	1986 Gross Fixed Capital Formation	1987 Total Gross Capital Formation	1987 Increase in Stocks	1987 Gross Fixed Capital Formation
					At constant prices of: 1980							
5 Construction	1679	...	1679	1660	...	1660	1523	...	1523	1541	...	1541
6 Wholesale and retail trade, restaurants and hotels	4925	-885	5810	6285	-498	6783	6013	-1144	7157	5924	-1918	7842
7 Transport, storage and communication	10997	...	10997	10662	...	10662	11755	...	11755	11763	...	11763
8 Finance, insurance, real estate and business services	35167	...	35167	38666	...	38665	39436	...	39436	44006	...	44006
9 Community, social and personal services	917	...	917	1038	...	1038	1073	...	1073	1142	...	1142
Statistical discrepancy	5374	...	5374	5696	...	5696	5659	...	5659	6020	...	6020
Total Industries	86939	-3230	90169	97418	278	97140	91864	-4763	96627	98342	-5305	103647
Producers of Government Services	15298	-454	15752	14744	-416	15160	14732	-310	15042	16036	1086	14950
Private Non-Profit Institutions Serving Households	...	...	...	...	...	...	...	...	...	...	...	...
Total	102237	-3684	105921	112162	-138	112300	106596	-5073	111669	114378	-4219	118597
Memorandum Item: Mineral Fuels and Power [a]	...	...	8386	...	...	8164	...	...	6620	...	...	5746

a) Item 'Mineral fuels and power' refers to ISIC categories 353 (Petroleum refineries), 354 (Manufacture of miscellaneous products of petroleum and coal) and 41 (Electricity, gas and steam).

2.11 Gross Fixed Capital Formation by Kind of Activity of Owner, ISIC Divisions, in Current Prices

Million Swedish kronor

	1970	1975	1978	1979	1980	1981	1982	1983	1984	1985	1986	1987
					All Producers							
1 Agriculture, hunting, forestry and fishing	1201	3298	4083	4372	4374	4526	5287	5970	6460	6145	5368	5726
A Agriculture and hunting	748	2361	3034	3194	3156	3182	3736	4224	4504	3997	3166	3247
B Forestry and logging	425	903	953	1119	1163	1298	1490	1680	1850	2018	2111	2364
C Fishing	28	34	96	59	55	46	61	66	106	130	91	115
2 Mining and quarrying	265	566	474	518	886	696	667	473	530	561	595	683
A Coal mining	...	...	...	...	...	...	...	...	...	...	...	...
B Crude petroleum and natural gas production	...	...	...	...	...	...	...	...	...	...	...	...
C Metal ore mining	220	474	380	404	742	628	565	332	353	356	354	304
D Other mining	45	92	94	114	144	68	102	141	177	205	241	379
3 Manufacturing	6556	13476	11911	13296	17278	17411	16234	18788	22703	28345	29185	34459
A Manufacturing of food, beverages and tobacco	727	963	1446	1645	1933	1753	1589	1939	2053	2453	2466	2954
B Textile, wearing apparel and leather industries	196	344	277	354	444	382	343	307	378	377	473	605
C Manufacture of wood, and wood products, including furniture	385	1171	861	940	1387	1137	978	1337	1699	1518	1633	1770
D Manufacture of paper and paper products, printing and publishing	1411	2637	2538	2513	3261	4096	3783	4054	4859	7070	6025	7659
E Manufacture of chemicals and chemical petroleum, coal, rubber and plastic products	742	1306	1492	1924	2034	1852	2339	3278	2957	3768	3810	4486
F Manufacture of non-metalic mineral products except products of petroleum and coal	269	585	854	672	609	502	430	410	484	596	750	787
G Basic metal industries	835	1592	752	1057	2017	1671	1019	927	1336	1642	1520	1657
H Manufacture of fabricated metal products, machinery and equipment	1964	4831	3644	4150	5548	5976	5709	6476	8861	10728	12402	14456
I Other manufacturing industries	27	47	47	41	45	42	44	60	76	193	106	85
4 Electricity, gas and water	3361	5654	7025	6430	8400	10012	12132	13875	13423	13760	11735	10418
A Electricity, gas and steam	2000	4096	5151	4675	6463	8083	10322	11921	11699	12003	9906	8604
B Water works and supply	1361	1558	1874	1755	1937	1929	1810	1954	1724	1757	1829	1814
5 Construction	672	1093	1147	1417	1820	1891	1883	2063	2310	2389	2338	2520
6 Wholesale and retail trade, restaurants and hotels	1949	3537	4100	4687	5056	5101	5769	6700	8117	10033	10953	12690
A Wholesale and retail trade	1775	3286	3777	4327	4553	4686	5136	5822	7158	8854	9716	11177
B Restaurants and hotels	174	251	323	360	503	415	633	878	959	1179	1237	1513
7 Transport, storage and communication	3160	5828	6749	8680	9917	9751	11892	12142	14778	15535	18224	19191
A Transport and storage	1926	4262	4368	5967	6392	5646	6871	7017	9488	8970	11062	11485

Sweden

2.11 Gross Fixed Capital Formation by Kind of Activity of Owner, ISIC Divisions, in Current Prices
(Continued)

Million Swedish kronor

	1970	1975	1978	1979	1980	1981	1982	1983	1984	1985	1986	1987
B Communication	1234	1566	2381	2713	3525	4105	5021	5125	5290	6565	7162	7706
8 Finance, insurance, real estate and business services	12361	17055	26177	31764	34860	35229	38282	43729	48300	56047	59746	70495
A Financial institutions	257	522	524	686	680	603	592	555	1016	1219	1997	1662
B Insurance	63	148	125	235	144	181	199	181	252	585	432	388
C Real estate and business services	12041	16385	25528	30843	34036	34445	37491	42993	47032	54243	57317	68445
Real estate except dwellings	1173	1617	1995	2888	3020	2671	3247	3925	4270	5123	6409	8109
Dwellings [a]	10488	13802	21424	25099	26903	27787	28757	30488	34705	37012	37679	45741
9 Community, social and personal services	413	535	756	907	1046	1136	1230	1361	1286	1555	1694	1873
A Sanitary and similar services	99	97	153	173	215	219	210	192	233	186	296	329
B Social and related community services	12	29	12	21	22	19	17	24	34	72	46	56
Educational services [b]	12	29	12	21	22	19	17	24	34	72	46	56
Medical, dental, other health and veterinary services	...	...	...	...	...	...	...	...	...	...	...	...
C Recreational and cultural services	144	186	324	409	458	518	573	650	668	786	843	901
D Personal and household services	158	223	267	304	351	380	430	495	351	511	509	587
Statistical discrepancy	530	1977	3434	3947	4711	5498	5799	6466	7180	8043	8431	9577
Total Industries	30468	53019	65856	76018	88348	91251	99175	111568	125087	142413	148269	167632
Producers of Government Services	8299	9899	14243	15543	17638	18639	19061	20601	21497	21862	22501	23243
Private Non-Profit Institutions Serving Households	...	...	...	...	...	...	...	...	...	...	...	...
Total	38767	62918	80099	91561	105986	109890	118236	132169	146584	164275	170770	190875

a) Dwellings includes country lodges.
b) Item 'Educational services' includes research and scientific institutes (ISIC category 932).

2.12 Gross Fixed Capital Formation by Kind of Activity of Owner, ISIC Divisions, in Constant Prices

Million Swedish kronor

	1970	1975	1978	1979	1980	1981	1982	1983	1984	1985	1986	1987

At constant prices of:1980

All Producers

	1970	1975	1978	1979	1980	1981	1982	1983	1984	1985	1986	1987
1 Agriculture, hunting, forestry and fishing	2877	5212	4894	4883	4374	4166	4414	4429	4447	4013	3315	3346
A Agriculture and hunting	1798	3714	3643	3560	3156	2930	3107	3117	3086	2621	1964	1896
B Forestry and logging	1035	1452	1141	1259	1163	1195	1258	1264	1293	1310	1294	1380
C Fishing	44	46	110	64	55	41	49	48	68	82	57	70
2 Mining and quarrying	686	914	562	570	886	642	550	348	370	377	384	421
A Coal mining	...	...	...	...	...	...	...	...	...	...	...	...
B Crude petroleum and natural gas production	...	...	...	...	...	...	...	...	...	...	...	...
C Metal ore mining	570	769	452	445	742	578	466	244	247	240	230	188
D Other mining	116	145	110	125	144	64	84	104	123	137	154	233

Sweden

2.12 Gross Fixed Capital Formation by Kind of Activity of Owner, ISIC Divisions, in Constant Prices
(Continued)

Million Swedish kronor

	1970	1975	1978	1979	1980	1981	1982	1983	1984	1985	1986	1987
					At constant prices of:1980							
3 Manufacturing	16832	21643	14107	14581	17278	15969	13193	13642	15948	19081	18654	21009
A Manufacturing of food, beverages and tobacco	1862	1541	1715	1799	1933	1608	1297	1419	1455	1660	1573	1805
B Textile, wearing apparel and leather industries	502	553	329	389	444	350	278	223	265	254	303	369
C Manufacture of wood, and wood products, including furniture	991	1887	1022	1032	1387	1043	799	981	1197	1026	1050	1081
D Manufacture of paper and paper products, printing and publishing	3622	4207	2999	2757	3261	3755	3064	2919	3395	4734	3837	4651
E Manufacture of chemicals and chemical petroleum, coal, rubber and plastic products	1906	2091	1770	2113	2034	1701	1886	2364	2070	2532	2432	2734
F Manufacture of non-metalic mineral products except products of petroleum and coal	690	934	1006	737	609	461	350	299	338	399	477	478
G Basic metal industries	2142	2556	888	1159	2017	1532	824	665	931	1096	961	1000
H Manufacture of fabricated metal products, machinery and equipment	5048	7797	4322	4550	5548	5480	4660	4728	6243	7248	7953	8839
I Other manufacturing industries	69	77	56	45	45	39	35	44	54	132	68	52
4 Electricity, gas and water	7981	8922	8421	7184	8400	9134	10039	10365	9460	9165	7671	6557
A Electricity, gas and steam	4785	6456	6145	5208	6463	7385	8526	8876	8233	7989	6462	5398
B Water works and supply	3196	2466	2276	1976	1937	1749	1513	1489	1227	1176	1209	1159
5 Construction	1654	1752	1373	1561	1820	1729	1589	1591	1679	1660	1523	1541
6 Wholesale and retail trade, restaurants and hotels	4638	5490	4919	5196	5056	4718	4840	5103	5810	6783	7157	7842
A Wholesale and retail trade	4308	5139	4556	4809	4553	4336	4310	4432	5109	5957	6295	6806
B Restaurants and hotels	330	351	363	387	503	382	530	671	701	826	862	1036
7 Transport, storage and communication	8245	8572	7063	9163	9917	9087	10162	9289	10997	10662	11755	11763
A Transport and storage	5096	6140	4252	6195	6392	5330	5957	5424	7176	6166	7080	6956
B Communication	3149	2432	2811	2968	3525	3757	4205	3865	3821	4496	4675	4807
8 Finance, insurance, real estate and business services	34911	33391	34073	36450	34860	31922	32329	33831	35167	38665	39436	44006
A Financial institutions	518	756	608	741	680	546	490	419	725	843	1379	1149
B Insurance	141	225	146	251	144	165	165	138	181	403	296	257
C Real estate and business services	34252	32410	33319	35458	34036	31211	31674	33274	34261	37419	37761	42600
Real estate except dwellings	2785	2743	2462	3225	3020	2426	2690	2984	3059	3514	4215	5054
Dwellings [a]	30779	28346	28475	29174	26903	25102	24461	23935	25495	25692	24898	28248
9 Community, social and personal services	1012	839	900	1004	1046	1039	1035	1040	917	1038	1073	1142
A Sanitary and similar services	257	151	182	189	215	204	184	152	168	128	191	203
B Social and related community services	29	45	12	21	22	19	16	19	26	50	29	32
Educational services [b]	29	45	12	21	22	19	16	19	26	50	29	32
Medical, dental, other health and veterinary services	...	...	...	...	...	...	...	...	...	...	...	...
C Recreational and cultural services	341	286	389	463	458	464	472	491	470	514	532	554
D Personal and household services	385	357	317	331	351	352	363	378	253	346	321	353
Statistical discrepancy	1391	3569	4386	4475	4711	4977	4912	5113	5374	5696	5659	6020
Total Industries	80227	90304	80698	85067	88348	83383	83063	84751	90169	97140	96627	103647
Producers of Government Services	19958	16179	17367	17377	17638	16941	16163	16035	15752	15160	15042	14950
Private Non-Profit Institutions Serving Households	...	...	...	...	...	...	...	...	...	...	...	...
Total	100185	106483	98065	102444	105986	100324	99226	100786	105921	112300	111669	118597

a) Dwellings includes country lodges.
b) Item 'Educational services' includes research and scientific institutes (ISIC category 932).

Sweden

2.14 Stocks of Reproducible Fixed Assets, by Type of Good and Owner, in Constant Prices

Million Swedish kronor

	TOTAL Gross	TOTAL Net	Total Private Gross	Total Private Net	Public Enterprises Gross	Public Enterprises Net	General Government Gross	General Government Net
	At constant prices of: 1980							
	1980							
1 Residential buildings	991025	...	...	...	991025	...	...	...
2 Non-residential buildings	1039360	...	...	...	709610	...	329753	...
3 Other construction		...	...	...		...		...
4 Land improvement and plantation and orchard development	...	...	...	...	...	...	...	...
5 Producers' durable goods	526203	...	...	...	491602	...	34601	...
A Transport equipment	56529	...	...	...	55136	...	1393	...
Passenger cars	27891	...	...	...	27455	...	436	...
Other	28638	...	...	...	27681	...	957	...
B Machinery and equipment	469674	...	...	...	436466	...	33208	...
6 Breeding stock, dairy cattle, etc.	...	...	...	...	...	...	...	...
Total [a,b]	2556590	...	...	...	2192240	...	364354	...
	1981							
1 Residential buildings	1007600	...	...	...	1007600	...	...	...
2 Non-residential buildings	1070100	...	...	...	728838	...	341259	...
3 Other construction		...	...	...		...		...
4 Land improvement and plantation and orchard development	...	...	...	...	...	...	...	...
5 Producers' durable goods	543193	...	...	...	506638	...	36555	...
A Transport equipment	56661	...	...	...	55186	...	1475	...
Passenger cars	27880	...	...	...	27432	...	448	...
Other	28781	...	...	...	27754	...	1027	...
B Machinery and equipment	486532	...	...	...	451452	...	35080	...
6 Breeding stock, dairy cattle, etc.	...	...	...	...	...	...	...	...
Total [a,b]	2620890	...	...	...	2243080	...	377814	...
	1982							
1 Residential buildings	1023760	...	...	...	1023760	...	...	...
2 Non-residential buildings	1098570	...	...	...	746233	...	352337	...
3 Other construction		...	...	...		...		...
4 Land improvement and plantation and orchard development	...	...	...	...	...	...	...	...
5 Producers' durable goods	558335	...	...	...	520198	...	38137	...
A Transport equipment	57822	...	...	...	56243	...	1579	...
Passenger cars	28391	...	...	...	27940	...	451	...
Other	29431	...	...	...	28303	...	1128	...
B Machinery and equipment	500513	...	...	...	463955	...	36558	...
6 Breeding stock, dairy cattle, etc.	...	...	...	...	...	...	...	...
Total [a,b]	2680660	...	...	...	2290190	...	390474	...
	1983							
1 Residential buildings	1037050	...	...	...	1037050	...	...	...
2 Non-residential buildings	1126600	...	...	...	764133	...	362468	...
3 Other construction		...	...	...		...		...
4 Land improvement and plantation and orchard development	...	...	...	...	...	...	...	...
5 Producers' durable goods	572724	...	...	...	533069	...	39655	...
A Transport equipment	59160	...	...	...	57518	...	1642	...
Passenger cars	28448	...	...	...	28021	...	427	...
Other	30712	...	...	...	29497	...	1215	...
B Machinery and equipment	513564	...	...	...	475551	...	38013	...
6 Breeding stock, dairy cattle, etc.	...	...	...	...	...	...	...	...
Total [a,b]	2736380	...	...	...	2334250	...	402123	...

a) Column 'Total Private' is included in column 'Public Enterprise'.
b) Estimates of this table (Stocks of reproducible fixed assets) are stocks at January 1st each year.

Sweden

2.16 Stocks of Reproducible Fixed Assets by Kind of Activity, in Constant Prices

Million Swedish kronor

	1980 Gross	1980 Net	1981 Gross	1981 Net	1982 Gross	1982 Net	1983 Gross	1983 Net
At constant prices of: 1980								
1 Residential buildings	991025	...	1007600	...	1023760	...	1037050	...
2 Non-residential buildings a	1039360	...	1070100	...	1098570	...	1126600	...
A Industries	1700640	...	1736440	...	1769990	...	1801180	...
1 Agriculture	68264	...	69075	...	69790	...	70631	...
2 Mining and quarrying	9475	...	9807	...	10035	...	10257	...
3 Manufacturing	165176	...	168274	...	170497	...	172477	...
4 Electricity, gas and water	146015	...	151716	...	157719	...	164160	...
5 Construction	8748	...	9184	...	9559	...	10010	...
6 Wholesale and retail trade	51471	...	53222	...	54852	...	56508	...
7 Transport and communication	104920	...	106974	...	109037	...	111397	...
8 Finance, etc.	1130160	...	1151510	...	1171550	...	1188540	...
9 Community, social and personal services	16403	...	16675	...	16949	...	17200	...
B Producers of government services	329753	...	341259	...	352337	...	362468	...
C Other producers	...	...	...	...	...	...	...	...
3 Other construction a								
4 Land improvement and development and plantation and orchard development	...	...	...	...	...	...	...	...
5 Producers' durable goods	526203	...	543193	...	558335	...	572724	...
A Industries	491602	...	506638	...	520198	...	533069	...
1 Agriculture	39766	...	40400	...	41057	...	41606	...
2 Mining and quarrying	10066	...	10437	...	10658	...	10779	...
3 Manufacturing	229882	...	236483	...	242487	...	246381	...
4 Electricity, gas and water	45492	...	47020	...	48912	...	51193	...
5 Construction	17306	...	17212	...	17347	...	16956	...
6 Wholesale and retail trade	40019	...	40736	...	41291	...	41616	...
7 Transport and communication	82432	...	83735	...	84522	...	86327	...
8 Finance, etc.	20931	...	25123	...	28567	...	32931	...
9 Community, social and personal services	5708	...	5492	...	5357	...	5280	...
B Producers of government services	34601	...	36555	...	38137	...	39655	...
C Other producers	...	...	...	...	...	...	...	...
6 Breeding stock, dairy cattle, etc.	...	...	...	...	...	...	...	...
Total	2556590	...	2620890	...	2680660	...	2736380	...

a) Item 'Other construction' is included in item 'Non-residential buildings'.

2.17 Exports and Imports of Goods and Services, Detail

Million Swedish kronor

	1970	1975	1978	1979	1980	1981	1982	1983	1984	1985	1986	1987
Exports of Goods and Services												
1 Exports of merchandise, f.o.b.	35045	71727	97703	117509	130246	143909	167088	209168	241362	258681	262529	278841
2 Transport and communication	4492	6888	8696	10107	11386	15758	16541	18823	19400	20904	20953	20031
A In respect of merchandise imports a	2984	3648	5022	6139	6826	8357	8926	9554	9875	10586	9374	8820
B Other	1508	3240	3674	3968	4560	7401	7615	9269	9525	10318	11579	11211
3 Insurance service charges b	...	...	...	...	...	...	...	...	...	...	...	...
4 Other commodities	1165	3781	6270	8804	10472	7611	10896	12699	13978	12666	13582	13733
5 Adjustments of merchandise exports to change-of-ownership basis	...	...	...	...	...	...	...	...	...	...	...	...
6 Direct purchases in the domestic market by non-residential households c	813	2283	3730	4148	4419	5249	6806	8838	9924	11258	12129	13514
7 Direct purchases in the domestic market by extraterritorial bodies	...	...	...	...	...	...	...	...	...	...	...	...
Total Exports of Goods and Services	41515	84679	116399	140568	156523	172527	201331	249528	284664	303509	309193	326119
Imports of Goods and Services												
1 Imports of merchandise, c.i.f.	36730	73519	93883	124661	143839	148735	177208	202038	221134	246761	233640	258008

Sweden

2.17 Exports and Imports of Goods and Services, Detail
(Continued)

Million Swedish kronor

	1970	1975	1978	1979	1980	1981	1982	1983	1984	1985	1986	1987
A Imports of merchandise, f.o.b.	35070	71165	90743	120709	140033	144791	172518	197313	216180	241980	227707	252104
B Transport of services on merchandise imports	1533	2101	2815	3521	3310	3433	4081	4023	4189	3900	5096	4977
By residents	411	611	773	950	968	1097	1262	1183	1282	1631	1664	1415
By non-residents	1122	1490	2042	2571	2342	2336	2819	2840	2907	2269	3432	3562
C Insurance service charges on merchandise imports	127	253	325	431	496	511	609	702	765	881	837	927
By residents	34	74	89	116	145	164	189	206	234	368	274	188
By non-residents	93	179	236	315	351	347	420	496	531	513	563	739
2 Adjustments of merchandise imports to change-of-ownership basis	...	...	...	...	...	...	...	...	...	...	...	...
3 Other transport and communication	1440	2767	4303	4873	5696	6002	7495	7653	8556	8740	9477	10642
4 Other insurance service charges b	...	...	...	...	...	...	...	...	...	...	...	...
5 Other commodities	1492	3735	5813	6323	6794	5511	7688	9829	9705	10916	13098	11860
6 Direct purchases abroad by government	...	...	...	...	...	...	...	...	...	...	...	...
7 Direct purchases abroad by resident households c	2816	5242	8174	9339	10191	11980	12766	13601	14872	17435	20839	24615
Total Imports of Goods and Services	42478	85263	112173	145196	166520	172228	205157	233121	254267	283852	277054	305125
Balance of Goods and Services	-963	-584	4226	-4628	-9997	299	-3826	16407	30397	19657	32139	20994
Total Imports and Balance of Goods and Services	41515	84679	116399	140568	156523	172527	201331	249528	284664	303509	309193	326119

a) Transport and communication in respect of merchandise imports includes all freight services provided by Swedish transporters abroad.
b) Insurance service charges paid and received are calculated net.
c) Beginning 1975, items 'Direct purchases in the domestic market by non-residential households' and 'Direct purchase abroad by resident households' include gross amounts of Swedish bank-notes used for direct purchases abroad by residents and direct purchases in the domestic market.

3.11 General Government Production Account: Total and Subsectors

Million Swedish kronor

	1980					1981				
	Total General Government	Central Government	State or Provincial Government	Local Government	Social Security Funds	Total General Government	Central Government	State or Provincial Government	Local Government	Social Security Funds
Gross Output										
1 Sales	...	...	...	...	...	...	...	...	...	...
2 Services produced for own use	...	...	...	...	...	...	...	...	...	...
3 Own account fixed capital formation	...	...	...	...	...	...	...	...	...	...
Gross Output	...	...	...	...	...	...	...	...	...	...
Gross Input										
Intermediate Consumption	...	...	...	...	...	...	...	...	...	...
Subtotal: Value Added	...	...	...	...	...	...	...	...	...	...
1 Indirect taxes, net	...	...	...	...	...	...	...	...	...	...
2 Consumption of fixed capital	6733	1460	...	5255	18	7654	1643	...	5990	21
3 Compensation of employees	113232	...	...	...	...	123787	...	...	...	...
4 Net Operating surplus	2000	141	...	1859	...	2310	135	...	2175	...
Gross Input	...	...	...	...	...	...	...	...	...	...

	1982					1983				
	Total General Government	Central Government	State or Provincial Government	Local Government	Social Security Funds	Total General Government	Central Government	State or Provincial Government	Local Government	Social Security Funds
Gross Output										
1 Sales	...	...	...	...	...	...	...	...	...	...
2 Services produced for own use	...	...	...	...	...	...	...	...	...	...
3 Own account fixed capital formation	...	...	...	...	...	...	...	...	...	...
Gross Output	...	...	...	...	...	...	...	...	...	...
Gross Input										
Intermediate Consumption	...	...	...	...	...	...	...	...	...	...
Subtotal: Value Added	...	...	...	...	...	...	...	...	...	...
1 Indirect taxes, net	...	...	...	...	...	...	...	...	...	...
2 Consumption of fixed capital	8657	1860	...	6773	24	9747	2066	...	7651	30
3 Compensation of employees	134495	...	...	...	...	145715	...	...	...	...
4 Net Operating surplus	2742	145	...	2597	...	4407	145	...	4262	...
Gross Input	...	...	...	...	...	...	...	...	...	...

Sweden

3.11 General Government Production Account: Total and Subsectors
Million Swedish kronor

	1984 Total General Government	1984 Central Government	1984 State or Provincial Government	1984 Local Government	1984 Social Security Funds	1985 Total General Government	1985 Central Government	1985 State or Provincial Government	1985 Local Government	1985 Social Security Funds
Gross Output										
1 Sales	...	...	...	...	...	...	...	...	...	...
2 Services produced for own use	...	...	...	...	...	...	...	...	...	...
3 Own account fixed capital formation	...	...	...	...	...	...	...	...	...	...
Gross Output	...	...	...	...	...	...	...	...	...	...
Gross Input										
Intermediate Consumption	...	...	...	...	...	...	...	...	...	...
Subtotal: Value Added	...	...	...	...	...	...	...	...	...	...
1 Indirect taxes, net	...	...	...	...	...	...	...	...	...	...
2 Consumption of fixed capital	10637	2251	...	8358	28	11410	2339	...	9040	31
3 Compensation of employees	158233	...	...	...	...	...	...	...	...	...
4 Net Operating surplus	4343	208	...	4135	...	4611	160	...	4451	...
Gross Input	...	...	...	...	...	...	...	...	...	...

	1986 Total General Government	1986 Central Government	1986 State or Provincial Government	1986 Local Government	1986 Social Security Funds	1987 Total General Government	1987 Central Government	1987 State or Provincial Government	1987 Local Government	1987 Social Security Funds
Gross Output										
1 Sales	...	...	...	...	...	...	...	...	...	...
2 Services produced for own use	...	...	...	...	...	...	...	...	...	...
3 Own account fixed capital formation	...	...	...	...	...	...	...	...	...	...
Gross Output	...	...	...	...	...	...	...	...	...	...
Gross Input										
Intermediate Consumption	...	...	...	...	...	...	...	...	...	...
Subtotal: Value Added	...	...	...	...	...	...	...	...	...	...
1 Indirect taxes, net	...	...	...	...	...	...	...	...	...	...
2 Consumption of fixed capital	12261	2621	...	9610	30	13081	2715	...	10336	30
3 Compensation of employees	...	...	...	...	...	...	...	...	...	...
4 Net Operating surplus	5106	205	...	4901	...	5365	222	...	5143	...
Gross Input	...	...	...	...	...	...	...	...	...	...

3.12 General Government Income and Outlay Account: Total and Subsectors
Million Swedish kronor

	1980 Total General Government	1980 Central Government	1980 State or Provincial Government	1980 Local Government	1980 Social Security Funds	1981 Total General Government	1981 Central Government	1981 State or Provincial Government	1981 Local Government	1981 Social Security Funds
Receipts										
1 Operating surplus	2000	141	...	1859	...	2310	135	...	2175	...
2 Property and entrepreneurial income	27121	8288	...	4815	14018	32782	10473	...	5504	16805
A Withdrawals from public quasi-corporations	2246	2246	...	...	...	2736	2736	...	...	...
B Interest	23860	5927	...	3972	13961	28924	7621	...	4564	16739
C Dividends	196	92	...	47	57	197	95	...	36	66
D Net land rent and royalties	819	23	...	796	...	925	21	...	904	...
3 Taxes, fees and contributions	260498	133390	...	77668	49440	292155	148615	...	86946	56594
A Indirect taxes	71337	69587	...	1750	-	83784	81521	...	2263	-
B Direct taxes	113925	38007	...	75918	-	121835	37152	...	84683	-
C Social security contributions	74643	25203	...	...	49440	85833	29239	...	...	56594
D Fees, fines and penalties	593	593	...	...	...	703	703	...	...	...
4 Other current transfers	7628	3700	...	51574	2944	6913	2530	...	56694	1655
A Casualty insurance claims	...	...	...	...	...	...	...	...	...	...
B Transfers from other government subsectors	...	3620	...	44026	2944	...	3451	...	48860	1655
C Transfers from the rest of the world	...	...	...	...	...	...	...	...	...	...
D Other transfers, except imputed	1479	289	...	1190	...	1672	243	...	1429	...
E Imputed unfunded employee pension and welfare contributions	6149	-209	...	6358	...	5241	-1164	...	6405	...

Sweden

3.12 General Government Income and Outlay Account: Total and Subsectors
(Continued)

Million Swedish kronor

	1980					1981				
	Total General Government	Central Government	State or Provincial Government	Local Government	Social Security Funds	Total General Government	Central Government	State or Provincial Government	Local Government	Social Security Funds
Total Current Receipts	297247	145519	...	135916	66402	334160	161753	...	151319	75054

Disbursements

	Total General Government	Central Government	State or Provincial Government	Local Government	Social Security Funds	Total General Government	Central Government	State or Provincial Government	Local Government	Social Security Funds
1 Government final consumption expenditure	151374	45269	...	103748	2357	167414	48972	...	115918	2524
2 Property income	21887	17057	...	4814	16	31144	25512	...	5604	28
A Interest	21591	17057	...	4518	16	30771	25512	...	5231	28
B Net land rent and royalties	296	...	...	296	...	373	...	...	373	...
3 Subsidies	22643	14588	...	3885	4170	26684	17617	...	4770	4297
4 Other current transfers	102495	95142	...	14982	42961	116209	104813	...	15747	49615
A Casualty insurance premiums, net	199	199	...	...	...	422	422	...	...	...
B Transfers to other government subsectors	...	39682	...	5386	5522	...	42381	...	5548	6037
C Social security benefits	73396	36238	...	...	37158	84729	41470	...	...	43259
D Social assistance grants	16457	11054	...	5122	281	17188	11716	...	5153	319
E Unfunded employee pension and welfare benefits	3440	1650	...	1790	...	3580	1691	...	1889	...
F Transfers to private non-profit institutions serving households	4882	2198	...	2684	...	6068	2911	...	3157	...
G Other transfers n.e.c.	...	...	...	...	...	...	...	...	...	...
H Transfers to the rest of the world	4121	4121	...	...	...	4222	4222	...	...	...
Net saving	-1152	-26537	...	8487	16898	-7291	-35161	...	9280	18590
Total Current Disbursements and Net Saving	297247	145519	...	135916	66402	334160	161753	...	151319	75054

	1982					1983				
	Total General Government	Central Government	State or Provincial Government	Local Government	Social Security Funds	Total General Government	Central Government	State or Provincial Government	Local Government	Social Security Funds

Receipts

	Total General Government	Central Government	State or Provincial Government	Local Government	Social Security Funds	Total General Government	Central Government	State or Provincial Government	Local Government	Social Security Funds
1 Operating surplus	2742	145	...	2597	...	4407	145	...	4262	...
2 Property and entrepreneurial income	38910	13778	...	5717	19415	45650	17698	...	5784	22168
A Withdrawals from public quasi-corporations	4146	4146	...	...	...	6631	6631	...	...	...
B Interest	33504	9489	...	4683	19332	37702	10935	...	4693	22074
C Dividends	246	121	...	42	83	254	123	...	37	94
D Net land rent and royalties	1014	22	...	992	...	1063	9	...	1054	...
3 Taxes, fees and contributions	315679	160802	...	97393	57484	358999	191154	...	107363	60482
A Indirect taxes	91795	89416	...	2379	-	107644	105183	...	2461	-
B Direct taxes	136230	41216	...	95014	-	154440	49140	...	104902	398
C Social security contributions	86630	29146	...	...	57484	95653	35569	...	...	60084
D Fees, fines and penalties	1024	1024	...	...	...	1262	1262	...	...	...
4 Other current transfers	12200	4870	...	61210	5494	13251	4640	...	67456	8936
A Casualty insurance claims	...	...	...	...	...	...	...	...	...	...
B Transfers from other government subsectors	...	3150	...	50730	5494	...	3239	...	55606	8936
C Transfers from the rest of the world	...	...	...	...	...	...	...	...	...	...
D Other transfers, except imputed	2699	341	...	2358	...	3437	460	...	2977	...
E Imputed unfunded employee pension and welfare contributions	9501	1379	...	8122	...	9814	941	...	8873	...
Total Current Receipts	369531	179595	...	166917	82393	422307	213637	...	184865	91586

Disbursements

	Total General Government	Central Government	State or Provincial Government	Local Government	Social Security Funds	Total General Government	Central Government	State or Provincial Government	Local Government	Social Security Funds
1 Government final consumption expenditure	182711	52153	...	127872	2686	200560	54554	...	143183	2823
2 Property income	43953	37653	...	6256	44	51457	44997	...	6424	36
A Interest	43496	37653	...	5799	44	51063	44997	...	6030	36
B Net land rent and royalties	457	...	...	457	...	394	...	...	394	...
3 Subsidies	31076	20841	...	5326	4909	36850	26023	...	5368	5459

Sweden

3.12 General Government Income and Outlay Account: Total and Subsectors
(Continued)

Million Swedish kronor

	1982					1983				
	Total General Government	Central Government	State or Provincial Government	Local Government	Social Security Funds	Total General Government	Central Government	State or Provincial Government	Local Government	Social Security Funds
4 Other current transfers	127516	113182	...	17626	56082	143225	126940	...	19858	64208
A Casualty insurance premiums, net	338	338	...	...	...	450	450	...	...	...
B Transfers to other government subsectors	...	47393	...	5155	6826	...	54831	...	5647	7303
C Social security benefits	92730	43834	...	...	48896	104640	48148	...	...	56492
D Social assistance grants	19782	12610	...	6812	360	21711	13486	...	7812	413
E Unfunded employee pension and welfare benefits	3944	1899	...	2045	...	4362	2090	...	2272	...
F Transfers to private non-profit institutions serving households	6343	2729	...	3614	...	7196	3069	...	4127	...
G Other transfers n.e.c.	...	...	...	...	...	...	...	...	...	...
H Transfers to the rest of the world	4379	4379	...	...	...	4866	4866	...	...	...
Net saving	-15725	-44234	...	9837	18672	-9785	-38877	...	10032	19060
Total Current Disbursements and Net Saving	369531	179595	...	166917	82393	422307	213637	...	184865	91586

	1984					1985				
	Total General Government	Central Government	State or Provincial Government	Local Government	Social Security Funds	Total General Government	Central Government	State or Provincial Government	Local Government	Social Security Funds

Receipts

1 Operating surplus	4343	208	...	4135	...	4611	160	...	4451	...
2 Property and entrepreneurial income	50891	19242	...	6409	25240	57194	22033	...	6761	28400
A Withdrawals from public quasi-corporations	7921	7921	...	...	...	9743	9743	...	...	...
B Interest	41377	11079	...	5179	25119	45522	11898	...	5377	28247
C Dividends	382	217	...	44	121	571	361	...	57	153
D Net land rent and royalties	1211	25	...	1186	...	1358	31	...	1327	...
3 Taxes, fees and contributions	400969	218867	...	115534	66568	433991	241611	...	123084	69296
A Indirect taxes	126261	123076	...	2564	621	141245	138788	...	1780	677
B Direct taxes	169294	55699	...	112970	625	182952	61111	...	121304	537
C Social security contributions	103781	38459	...	...	65322	108206	40124	...	...	68082
D Fees, fines and penalties	1633	1633	...	...	...	1588	1588	...	...	...
4 Other current transfers	14335	4364	...	74119	10449	16837	6336	...	80046	19740
A Casualty insurance claims	...	...	...	...	...	...	...	...	...	...
B Transfers from other government subsectors	...	3470	...	60678	10449	...	3606	...	65939	19740
C Transfers from the rest of the world	...	...	...	...	...	...	...	...	...	...
D Other transfers, except imputed	4131	496	...	3635	...	4299	314	...	3985	...
E Imputed unfunded employee pension and welfare contributions	10204	398	...	9806	...	12538	2416	...	10122	...
Total Current Receipts	470538	242681	...	200197	102257	512633	270140	...	214342	117436

Disbursements

1 Government final consumption expenditure	218041	58199	...	156936	2906	235879	61710	...	170996	3173
2 Property income	60991	54034	...	6849	108	73318	65815	...	7326	177
A Interest	60464	54034	...	6322	108	72738	65815	...	6746	177
B Net land rent and royalties	527	...	...	527	...	580	...	...	580	...
3 Subsidies	39157	27794	...	5543	5820	42107	29508	...	6307	6292

Sweden

3.12 General Government Income and Outlay Account: Total and Subsectors
(Continued)

Million Swedish kronor

	1984					1985				
	Total General Government	Central Government	State or Provincial Government	Local Government	Social Security Funds	Total General Government	Central Government	State or Provincial Government	Local Government	Social Security Funds
4 Other current transfers	152914	134871	...	21746	70894	172339	151151	...	24306	86167
A Casualty insurance premiums, net	718	718	...	...	...	401	401	...	...	...
B Transfers to other government subsectors	...	60688	...	6230	7679	...	69725	...	6498	13062
C Social security benefits	112335	49579	...	...	62756	125016	52481	...	...	72535
D Social assistance grants	22315	13309	...	8547	459	27356	16322	...	10464	570
E Unfunded employee pension and welfare benefits	4706	2265	...	2441	...	4939	2263	...	2676	...
F Transfers to private non-profit institutions serving households	7773	3245	...	4528	...	8804	4136	...	4668	...
G Other transfers n.e.c.	...	...	...	...	...	...	...	...	...	...
H Transfers to the rest of the world	5067	5067	...	...	...	5823	5823	...	...	...
Net saving	-565	-32217	...	9123	22529	-11010	-38044	...	5407	21627
Total Current Disbursements and Net Saving	470538	242681	...	200197	102257	512633	270140	...	214342	117436

	1986					1987				
	Total General Government	Central Government	State or Provincial Government	Local Government	Social Security Funds	Total General Government	Central Government	State or Provincial Government	Local Government	Social Security Funds

Receipts

1 Operating surplus	5106	205	...	4901	...	5365	222	...	5143	...
2 Property and entrepreneurial income	61799	25055	...	6072	30672	59552	21474	...	5912	32166
A Withdrawals from public quasi-corporations	11050	11050	...	...	...	9437	9437	...	...	...
B Interest	48495	13574	...	4528	30393	47392	11481	...	4131	31780
C Dividends	759	396	...	84	279	1023	532	...	105	386
D Net land rent and royalties	1495	35	...	1460	...	1700	24	...	1676	...
3 Taxes, fees and contributions	495893	277375	...	138063	80455	558093	314615	...	153360	90118
A Indirect taxes	163395	160756	...	1832	807	175240	173910	...	429	901
B Direct taxes	206136	68002	...	136231	1903	243782	87394	...	152931	3457
C Social security contributions	124456	46711	...	...	77745	137282	51522	...	...	85760
D Fees, fines and penalties	1906	1906	...	...	...	1789	1789	...	...	...
4 Other current transfers	11447	4688	...	77674	18343	7543	7137	...	76990	21419
A Casualty insurance claims	...	...	...	...	...	...	...	...	...	...
B Transfers from other government subsectors	...	3829	...	67086	18343	...	6155	...	70429	21419
C Transfers from the rest of the world	...	...	...	...	...	...	...	...	...	...
D Other transfers, except imputed	2399	370	...	2029	...	4595	299	...	4296	...
E Imputed unfunded employee pension and welfare contributions	9048	489	...	8559	...	2948	683	...	2265	...
Total Current Receipts	574245	307323	...	226710	129470	630553	343448	...	241405	143703

Disbursements

1 Government final consumption expenditure	253701	67022	...	183309	3370	268487	70613	...	194137	3737
2 Property income	71109	63054	...	7960	95	67299	58936	...	8311	52
A Interest	70205	63054	...	7056	95	66629	58936	...	7641	52
B Net land rent and royalties	904	...	...	904	...	670	...	...	670	...
3 Subsidies	45013	31405	...	6629	6979	46458	31398	...	7103	7957

Sweden

3.12 General Government Income and Outlay Account: Total and Subsectors
(Continued)

Million Swedish kronor

	1986 Total General Government	1986 Central Government	1986 State or Provincial Government	1986 Local Government	1986 Social Security Funds	1987 Total General Government	1987 Central Government	1987 State or Provincial Government	1987 Local Government	1987 Social Security Funds
4 Other current transfers	189396	157586	...	25789	95279	207882	171533	...	28704	105648
A Casualty insurance premiums, net	541	541	...	...	...	1059	1059	...	...	...
B Transfers to other government subsectors	...	70267	...	6808	12183	...	76129	...	9444	12430
C Social security benefits	139567	56637	...	...	82930	153639	60540	...	...	93099
D Social assistance grants	27763	16814	...	10783	166	30518	19785	...	10614	119
E Unfunded employee pension and welfare benefits	5599	2469	...	3130	...	5917	2524	...	3393	...
F Transfers to private non-profit institutions serving households	9837	4769	...	5068	...	10361	5108	...	5253	...
G Other transfers n.e.c.	...	...	...	...	...	...	...	...	...	...
H Transfers to the rest of the world	6089	6089	...	...	...	6388	6388	...	...	...
Net saving	15026	-11744	...	3023	23747	40427	10968	...	3150	26309
Total Current Disbursements and Net Saving	574245	307323	...	226710	129470	630553	343448	...	241405	143703

3.13 General Government Capital Accumulation Account: Total and Subsectors

Million Swedish kronor

	1980 Total General Government	1980 Central Government	1980 State or Provincial Government	1980 Local Government	1980 Social Security Funds	1981 Total General Government	1981 Central Government	1981 State or Provincial Government	1981 Local Government	1981 Social Security Funds
			Finance of Gross Accumulation							
1 Gross saving	5581	-25077	...	13742	16916	363	-33518	...	15270	18611
A Consumption of fixed capital	6733	1460	...	5255	18	7654	1643	...	5990	21
B Net saving	-1152	-26537	...	8487	16898	-7291	-35161	...	9280	18590
2 Capital transfers	1617	580	...	2893	...	1696	631	...	3323	...
A From other government subsectors	...	...	...	1856	...	...	...	...	2258	...
B From other resident sectors	1617	580	...	1037	...	1696	631	...	1065	...
C From rest of the world	...	...	...	...	...	...	...	...	...	...
Finance of Gross Accumulation	7198	-24497	...	16635	16916	2059	-32887	...	18593	18611
			Gross Accumulation							
1 Gross capital formation	22851	5815	...	16996	40	23787	5077	...	18656	54
A Increase in stocks	1015	1015	...	...	...	536	536	...	...	...
B Gross fixed capital formation	21836	4800	...	16996	40	23251	4541	...	18656	54
2 Purchases of land, net	-526	151	...	-677	...	-78	118	...	-196	...
3 Purchases of intangible assets, net	...	...	...	...	...	...	...	...	...	...
4 Capital transfers	4536	6286	...	106	...	6482	8579	...	161	...
A To other government subsectors	...	1822	...	34	...	...	2177	...	81	...
B To other resident sectors	4536	4464	...	72	...	6482	6402	...	80	...
C To rest of the world	...	...	...	...	...	...	...	...	...	...
Net lending [a]	-19663	-36749	...	210	16876	-28132	-46661	...	-28	18557
Gross Accumulation	7198	-24497	...	16635	16916	2059	-32887	...	18593	18611

	1982 Total General Government	1982 Central Government	1982 State or Provincial Government	1982 Local Government	1982 Social Security Funds	1983 Total General Government	1983 Central Government	1983 State or Provincial Government	1983 Local Government	1983 Social Security Funds
			Finance of Gross Accumulation							
1 Gross saving	-7068	-42374	...	16610	18696	-38	-36811	...	17683	19090
A Consumption of fixed capital	8657	1860	...	6773	24	9747	2066	...	7651	30
B Net saving	-15725	-44234	...	9837	18672	-9785	-38877	...	10032	19060
2 Capital transfers	1823	710	...	3244	...	1951	835	...	3319	...
A From other government subsectors	...	...	...	2131	...	...	...	...	2203	...
B From other resident sectors	1823	710	...	1113	...	1951	835	...	1116	...
C From rest of the world	...	...	...	...	...	...	...	...	...	...
Finance of Gross Accumulation	-5245	-41664	...	19854	18696	1913	-35976	...	21002	19090
			Gross Accumulation							
1 Gross capital formation	24363	5451	...	18832	80	25927	5684	...	20198	45

Sweden

3.13 General Government Capital Accumulation Account: Total and Subsectors
(Continued)

Million Swedish kronor

	1982					1983				
	Total General Government	Central Government	State or Provincial Government	Local Government	Social Security Funds	Total General Government	Central Government	State or Provincial Government	Local Government	Social Security Funds
A Increase in stocks	554	554	...	...	...	39	39	...	...	...
B Gross fixed capital formation	23809	4897	...	18832	80	25888	5645	...	20198	45
2 Purchases of land, net	-6	116	...	-122	...	81	115	...	-34	...
3 Purchases of intangible assets, net	...	...	...	...	...	...	...	...	...	...
4 Capital transfers	10242	12189	...	184	...	11029	13030	...	202	...
A To other government subsectors	...	2027	...	104	...	...	2090	...	113	...
B To other resident sectors	10242	10162	...	80	...	11029	10940	...	89	...
C To rest of the world	...	...	...	...	...	...	...	...	...	...
Net lending [a]	-39844	-59420	...	960	18616	-35124	-54805	...	636	19045
Gross Accumulation	-5245	-41664	...	19854	18696	1913	-35976	...	21002	19090

	1984					1985				
	Total General Government	Central Government	State or Provincial Government	Local Government	Social Security Funds	Total General Government	Central Government	State or Provincial Government	Local Government	Social Security Funds

Finance of Gross Accumulation

1 Gross saving	10072	-29966	...	17481	22557	400	-35705	...	14447	21658
A Consumption of fixed capital	10637	2251	...	8358	28	11410	2339	...	9040	31
B Net saving	-565	-32217	...	9123	22529	-11010	-38044	...	5407	21627
2 Capital transfers	2108	1059	...	3688	...	2279	1193	...	2959	...
A From other government subsectors	...	...	...	2639	...	...	...	...	1873	...
B From other resident sectors	2108	1059	...	1049	...	2279	1193	...	1086	...
C From rest of the world	...	...	...	...	...	...	...	...	...	...
Finance of Gross Accumulation	12180	-28907	...	21169	22557	2679	-34512	...	17406	21658

Gross Accumulation

1 Gross capital formation	26068	5370	...	20652	46	26736	5292	...	21392	52
A Increase in stocks	-835	-835	...	...	...	-675	-675	...	...	...
B Gross fixed capital formation	26903	6205	...	20652	46	27411	5967	...	21392	52
2 Purchases of land, net	238	109	...	129	...	43	121	...	-78	...
3 Purchases of intangible assets, net	...	...	...	...	...	...	...	...	...	...
4 Capital transfers	6389	8867	...	161	...	8228	10003	...	98	...
A To other government subsectors	...	2574	...	65	...	...	1873	...	-	...
B To other resident sectors	6389	6293	...	96	...	8228	8130	...	98	...
C To rest of the world	...	...	...	...	...	...	...	...	...	...
Net lending [a]	-20515	-43253	...	227	22511	-32328	-49928	...	-4006	21606
Gross Accumulation	12180	-28907	...	21169	22557	2679	-34512	...	17406	21658

	1986					1987				
	Total General Government	Central Government	State or Provincial Government	Local Government	Social Security Funds	Total General Government	Central Government	State or Provincial Government	Local Government	Social Security Funds

Finance of Gross Accumulation

1 Gross saving	27287	-9123	...	12633	23777	53508	13683	...	13486	26339
A Consumption of fixed capital	12261	2621	...	9610	30	13081	2715	...	10336	30
B Net saving	15026	-11744	...	3023	23747	40427	10968	...	3150	26309
2 Capital transfers	2139	1252	...	2757	...	18473	17485	...	2751	...
A From other government subsectors	...	...	...	1870	...	...	...	...	1763	...
B From other resident sectors	2139	1252	...	887	...	18473	17485	...	988	...
C From rest of the world	...	...	...	...	...	...	...	...	...	...
Finance of Gross Accumulation	29426	-7871	...	15390	23777	71981	31168	...	16237	26339

Gross Accumulation

1 Gross capital formation	27469	5596	...	21820	53	29059	7790	...	21208	61
A Increase in stocks	-130	-130	...	...	...	1370	1370	...	...	...
B Gross fixed capital formation	27599	5726	...	21820	53	27689	6420	...	21208	61

Sweden

3.13 General Government Capital Accumulation Account: Total and Subsectors
(Continued)

Million Swedish kronor

		1986					1987				
		Total General Government	Central Government	State or Provincial Government	Local Government	Social Security Funds	Total General Government	Central Government	State or Provincial Government	Local Government	Social Security Funds
2	Purchases of land, net	-1150	127	...	-1277	...	-1627	152	...	-1779	...
3	Purchases of intangible assets, net	...	...	...	...	...	...	...	...	...	...
4	Capital transfers	9137	10820	...	187	...	3493	5089	...	167	...
	A To other government subsectors	...	1783	...	87	...	...	1697	...	66	...
	B To other resident sectors	9137	9037	...	100	...	3493	3392	...	101	...
	C To rest of the world	...	...	...	...	...	...	...	...	...	...
Net lending [a]		-6030	-24414	...	-5340	23724	41056	18137	...	-3359	26278
Gross Accumulation		29426	-7871	...	15390	23777	71981	31168	...	16237	26339

a) Net lending of the capital accumulation account and the capital finance account have not been reconciled and are different due to different statistical sources.

3.14 General Government Capital Finance Account, Total and Subsectors

Million Swedish kronor

		1980					1981				
		Total General Government	Central Government	State or Provincial Government	Local Government	Social Security Funds	Total General Government	Central Government	State or Provincial Government	Local Government	Social Security Funds

Acquisition of Financial Assets

1	Gold and SDRs	...	...	...	...	...	...	...	...	...	...
2	Currency and transferable deposits	1933	812	...	1003	118	2841	551	...	2382	-92
3	Other deposits [a]	868	-	...	868	-	86	-	...	86	-
4	Bills and bonds, short term [b]	100	-	...	100	-	-100	-	...	-100	-
5	Bonds, long term [c]	11200	-39	...	52	11187	14263	-12	...	228	14047
6	Corporate equity securities	1564	1238	...	232	94	2375	2054	...	167	154
7	Short-term loans, n.e.c.	14656	11622	...	1746	1288	13516	10365	...	2094	1057
8	Long-term loans, n.e.c.	...	...	...	...	...	...	...	...	...	...
9	Other receivables	...	...	...	...	...	...	...	...	...	...
10	Other assets	9917	4091	...	1643	4183	2051	-1019	...	-275	3345
Total Acquisition of Financial Assets		40238	17724	...	5644	16870	35032	11939	...	4582	18511

Incurrence of Liabilities

1	Currency and transferable deposits	...	...	...	...	...	...	...	...	...	...
2	Other deposits [a]	-	-	...	-	...	-	-	...	-	...
3	Bills and bonds, short term [b]	7444	7444	...	...	...	-743	-743	...	...	...
4	Bonds, long term [c]	35805	35821	...	-16	...	59731	58734	...	997	...
5	Short-term loans, n.e.c.	14766	12110	...	2656	-	7419	3437	...	3973	9
6	Long-term loans, n.e.c.	...	...	...	...	...	...	...	...	...	...
7	Other payables	...	...	...	...	...	...	...	...	...	...
8	Other liabilities	1337	-200	...	1538	-1	-979	15	...	-1053	59
Total Incurrence of Liabilities		59352	55175	...	4178	-1	65428	61443	...	3917	68
Net Lending [d]		-19114	-37451	...	1466	16871	-30396	-49504	...	665	18443
Incurrence of Liabilities and Net Worth		40238	17724	...	5644	16870	35032	11939	...	4582	18511

		1982					1983				
		Total General Government	Central Government	State or Provincial Government	Local Government	Social Security Funds	Total General Government	Central Government	State or Provincial Government	Local Government	Social Security Funds

Acquisition of Financial Assets

1	Gold and SDRs	...	...	...	...	...	...	...	...	...	...
2	Currency and transferable deposits	617	1310	...	-487	-206	-1493	-79	...	-1055	-359
3	Other deposits [a]	562	-	...	562	...	389	2	...	387	...
4	Bills and bonds, short term [b]	2159	-	...	2012	147	1291	164	...	774	353
5	Bonds, long term [c]	15285	58	...	-161	15388	17952	-281	...	1333	16900
6	Corporate equity securities	2037	1582	...	333	122	5473	5360	...	250	-137
7	Short-term loans, n.e.c.	12740	10185	...	914	1641	11239	9700	...	1077	462
8	Long-term loans, n.e.c.	...	...	...	...	...	...	...	...	...	...
9	Other receivables	...	...	...	...	...	...	...	...	...	...
10	Other assets	8699	3810	...	2768	2121	6948	3849	...	1631	1468
Total Acquisition of Financial Assets		42099	16945	...	5941	19213	41799	18715	...	4397	18687

Incurrence of Liabilities

| 1 | Currency and transferable deposits | ... | ... | ... | ... | ... | ... | ... | ... | ... | ... |

Sweden

3.14 General Government Capital Finance Account, Total and Subsectors
(Continued)

Million Swedish kronor

	1982					1983				
	Total General Government	Central Government	State or Provincial Government	Local Government	Social Security Funds	Total General Government	Central Government	State or Provincial Government	Local Government	Social Security Funds
2 Other deposits [a]	-	-	...	-	...	205	-	...	205	...
3 Bills and bonds, short term [b]	33741	33741	...	...	...	-5784	-5784	...	...	...
4 Bonds, long term [c]	26996	27105	...	-109	...	81395	81033	...	362	...
5 Short-term loans, n.e.c.	13932	11440	...	2489	3	4626	4031	...	591	4
6 Long-term loans, n.e.c.	...	...	...	...	...	...	...	...	...	...
7 Other payables	...	...	...	...	...	...	...	...	...	...
8 Other liabilities	5526	3165	...	2048	313	-911	-3180	...	2224	45
Total Incurrence of Liabilities	80195	75451	...	4428	316	79531	76100	...	3382	49
Net Lending [d]	-38096	-58506	...	1513	18897	-37732	-57385	...	1015	18638
Incurrence of Liabilities and Net Worth	42099	16945	...	5941	19213	41799	18715	...	4397	18687

	1984					1985				
	Total General Government	Central Government	State or Provincial Government	Local Government	Social Security Funds	Total General Government	Central Government	State or Provincial Government	Local Government	Social Security Funds

Acquisition of Financial Assets

1 Gold and SDRs	...	...	...	...	...	...	...	...	...	...
2 Currency and transferable deposits	1184	1781	...	-840	243	-1927	2364	...	-4482	191
3 Other deposits [a]	63	-2	...	-192	257	1627	779	...	440	408
4 Bills and bonds, short term [b]	768	264	...	-1042	1546	123	-148	...	643	-372
5 Bonds, long term [c]	16218	166	...	150	15902	14264	556	...	-311	14019
6 Corporate equity securities	2750	440	...	770	1540	2955	1258	...	543	1154
7 Short-term loans, n.e.c.	11838	9470	...	2357	11	7767	8529	...	-635	-127
8 Long-term loans, n.e.c.	...	...	...	...	...	...	...	...	...	...
9 Other receivables	...	...	...	...	...	...	...	...	...	...
10 Other assets	11947	8155	...	1455	2337	-801	-10961	...	4271	5889
Total Acquisition of Financial Assets	44768	20274	...	2658	21836	24008	2377	...	469	21162

Incurrence of Liabilities

1 Currency and transferable deposits	...	...	...	...	...	...	...	...	...	...
2 Other deposits [a]	6556	6517	...	39	...	11008	10678	...	330	...
3 Bills and bonds, short term [b]	38900	38900	...	...	...	21625	21625	...	...	...
4 Bonds, long term [c]	49724	49544	...	180	...	27092	26909	...	183	...
5 Short-term loans, n.e.c.	-31177	-32962	...	1782	3	1943	-3371	...	5312	2
6 Long-term loans, n.e.c.	...	...	...	...	...	...	...	...	...	...
7 Other payables	...	...	...	...	...	...	...	...	...	...
8 Other liabilities	-2	-	...	-17	15	-1256	-	...	-870	-386
Total Incurrence of Liabilities	64001	61999	...	1984	18	60412	55841	...	4955	-384
Net Lending [d]	-19233	-41725	...	674	21818	-36404	-53464	...	-4486	21546
Incurrence of Liabilities and Net Worth	44768	20274	...	2658	21836	24008	2377	...	469	21162

	1986					1987				
	Total General Government	Central Government	State or Provincial Government	Local Government	Social Security Funds	Total General Government	Central Government	State or Provincial Government	Local Government	Social Security Funds

Acquisition of Financial Assets

1 Gold and SDRs	...	...	...	...	...	...	...	...	...	...
2 Currency and transferable deposits	541	1961	...	-1615	195	-6572	-4756	...	-1847	31
3 Other deposits [a]	957	-499	...	-845	2301	2338	-123	...	803	1658
4 Bills and bonds, short term [b]	-2422	-50	...	-1764	-608	584	191	...	453	-60
5 Bonds, long term [c]	18542	1422	...	521	16599	23253	1591	...	465	21197
6 Corporate equity securities	4733	1833	...	401	2499	6724	2860	...	466	3398
7 Short-term loans, n.e.c.	-3654	-3775	...	-1560	1681	9603	11196	...	368	-1961
8 Long-term loans, n.e.c.	...	...	...	...	...	...	...	...	...	...
9 Other receivables	...	...	...	...	...	...	...	...	...	...
10 Other assets	15921	7727	...	5837	2357	1859	1755	...	-1116	1220
Total Acquisition of Financial Assets	34618	8619	...	975	25024	37789	12714	...	-408	25483

Incurrence of Liabilities

1 Currency and transferable deposits	...	...	...	...	...	...	...	...	...	...
2 Other deposits [a]	17639	15813	...	1826	...	11632	9679	...	1953	...
3 Bills and bonds, short term [b]	-6625	-6625	...	...	...	-21225	-21225	...	...	...

Sweden

3.14 General Government Capital Finance Account, Total and Subsectors
(Continued)

Million Swedish kronor

	1986 Total General Government	1986 Central Government	1986 State or Provincial Government	1986 Local Government	1986 Social Security Funds	1987 Total General Government	1987 Central Government	1987 State or Provincial Government	1987 Local Government	1987 Social Security Funds
4 Bonds, long term c	22297	20960	...	1337	...	-1242	-672	...	-570	...
5 Short-term loans, n.e.c.	4383	2570	...	1814	-1	-287	1065	...	-1346	-6
6 Long-term loans, n.e.c.	...	...	...	...	...	...	...	...	...	...
7 Other payables	...	...	...	...	...	...	...	...	...	...
8 Other liabilities	2458	-	...	873	1585	1355	-	...	2540	-1185
Total Incurrence of Liabilities	40152	32718	...	5850	1584	-9767	-11153	...	2577	-1191
Net Lending d	-5534	-24099	...	-4875	23440	47556	23867	...	-2985	26674
Incurrence of Liabilities and Net Worth	34618	8619	...	975	25024	37789	12714	...	-408	25483

a) Item 'Other deposits' refers to certificate of deposit.
b) 'Bills and bonds' refer to Swedish treasury bills and special treasury bills.
c) Item 'Bonds, long-term' includes both short-term and long-term bonds.
d) Net lending of the capital accumulation account and the capital finance account have not been reconciled and are different due to different statistical sources.

3.21 Corporate and Quasi-Corporate Enterprise Production Account: Total and Sectors

Million Swedish kronor

	1980 TOTAL	1980 Non-Financial	1980 Financial	1980 ADDENDUM: Total, including Unincorporated	1981 TOTAL	1981 Non-Financial	1981 Financial	1981 ADDENDUM: Total, including Unincorporated	1982 TOTAL	1982 Non-Financial	1982 Financial	1982 ADDENDUM: Total, including Unincorporated
Gross Output												
1 Output for sale	...	...	...	...	...	...	...	...	...	...	...	...
2 Imputed bank service charge	...	...	...	...	...	...	...	...	...	...	...	...
3 Own-account fixed capital formation	...	...	...	...	...	...	...	...	...	...	...	...
Gross Output	...	...	...	...	...	...	...	...	...	...	...	...
Gross Input												
Intermediate consumption	...	...	...	...	...	...	...	...	...	...	...	...
Subtotal: Value Added	...	...	...	...	...	...	...	...	...	...	...	...
1 Indirect taxes, net	...	...	...	...	...	...	...	...	...	...	...	...
2 Consumption of fixed capital	37890	37358	532	52688	42178	41574	604	58825	47778	47093	685	66018
3 Compensation of employees	213693	206230	7463	220065	234071	225880	8191	240560	...	...	...	...
4 Net operating surplus	21313	25501	-4188	77899	19061	23755	-4694	78788	28818	33945	-5127	100016
Gross Input	...	...	...	...	...	...	...	...	...	...	...	...

	1983 TOTAL	1983 Non-Financial	1983 Financial	1983 ADDENDUM: Total, including Unincorporated	1984 TOTAL	1984 Non-Financial	1984 Financial	1984 ADDENDUM: Total, including Unincorporated	1985 TOTAL	1985 Non-Financial	1985 Financial	1985 ADDENDUM: Total, including Unincorporated
Gross Output												
1 Output for sale	...	...	...	...	...	...	...	...	...	...	...	...
2 Imputed bank service charge	...	...	...	...	...	...	...	...	...	...	...	...
3 Own-account fixed capital formation	...	...	...	...	...	...	...	...	...	...	...	...
Gross Output	...	...	...	...	...	...	...	...	...	...	...	...
Gross Input												
Intermediate consumption	...	...	...	...	...	...	...	...	...	...	...	...
Subtotal: Value Added	...	...	...	...	...	...	...	...	...	...	...	...
1 Indirect taxes, net	...	...	...	...	...	...	...	...	...	...	...	...
2 Consumption of fixed capital	54433	53662	771	74592	58826	57975	851	81115	64484	63538	946	88054
3 Compensation of employees	...	...	...	...	...	...	...	...	...	...	...	...
4 Net operating surplus	46806	53145	-6339	124226	59090	68228	-9138	144951	63881	74921	-11040	155292
Gross Input	...	...	...	...	...	...	...	...	...	...	...	...

	1986 TOTAL	1986 Non-Financial	1986 Financial	1986 ADDENDUM: Total, including Unincorporated	1987 TOTAL	1987 Non-Financial	1987 Financial	1987 ADDENDUM: Total, including Unincorporated
Gross Output								
1 Output for sale	...	...	...	...	...	...	...	...
2 Imputed bank service charge	...	...	...	...	...	...	...	...
3 Own-account fixed capital formation	...	...	...	...	...	...	...	...
Gross Output	...	...	...	...	...	...	...	...

Sweden

3.21 Corporate and Quasi-Corporate Enterprise Production Account: Total and Sectors
(Continued)

Million Swedish kronor

	1986			ADDENDUM: Total, including Unincorporated	1987			ADDENDUM: Total, including Unincorporated
	\multicolumn{3}{c	}{Corporate and Quasi-Corporate Enterprises}		\multicolumn{3}{c	}{Corporate and Quasi-Corporate Enterprises}	
	TOTAL	Non-Financial	Financial		TOTAL	Non-Financial	Financial	
\multicolumn{9}{c}{**Gross Input**}							
Intermediate consumption	...	...	...	...	...	...	...	...
Subtotal: Value Added	...	...	...	...	...	...	...	...
1 Indirect taxes, net	...	...	...	...	...	...	...	...
2 Consumption of fixed capital	70013	68994	1019	94925	77554	76448	1106	103395
3 Compensation of employees	...	...	...	...	...	...	...	...
4 Net operating surplus	58394	72072	-13678	151698	54989	72907	-17918	158939
Gross Input	...	...	...	...	...	...	...	...

3.22 Corporate and Quasi-Corporate Enterprise Income and Outlay Account: Total and Sectors

Million Swedish kronor

	1980			1981			1982			1983		
	TOTAL	Non-Financial	Financial	TOTAL	Non-Financial	Financial	TOTAL	Non-Financial	Financial	TOTAL	Non-Financial	Financial
\multicolumn{13}{c}{**Receipts**}											
1 Operating surplus	21313	25501	-4188	19061	23755	-4694	28818	33945	-5127	46806	53145	-6339
2 Property and entrepreneurial income	86631	3911	82720	111850	4385	107465	129435	6240	123195	141035	6299	134736
A Withdrawals from quasi-corporate enterprises	...	...	...	...	...	...	...	...	...	...	...	...
B Interest	81630	...	81630	106227	...	106227	121406	...	121406	132848	...	132848
C Dividends	4813	3723	1090	4804	3566	1238	7117	5328	1789	7111	5223	1888
D Net land rent and royalties	188	188	...	819	819	...	912	912	...	1076	1076	...
3 Current transfers	26181	12459	13722	33029	12823	20206	39754	15394	24360	41153	15777	25376
A Casualty insurance claims	4077	4077	...	4517	4517	...	5177	5177	...	5584	5584	...
B Casualty insurance premiums, net, due to be received by insurance companies	5807	...	5807	11475	...	11475	15052	...	15052	15444	...	15444
C Current transfers from the rest of the world	884	884	...	73	73	...	...	...	...	...	...	...
D Other transfers except imputed	1750	1401	349	1887	1676	211	3942	3597	345	3742	3315	427
E Imputed unfunded employee pension and welfare contributions	13663	6097	7566	15077	6557	8520	15583	6620	8963	16383	6878	9505
Total Current Receipts	134125	41871	92254	163940	40963	122977	198007	55579	142428	228994	75221	153773
\multicolumn{13}{c}{**Disbursements**}											
1 Property and entrepreneurial income	90562	30268	60294	115864	37601	78263	131212	41371	89841	147445	48905	98540
A Withdrawals from quasi-corporations	3683	2933	750	4251	3401	850	6089	4089	2000	9499	5499	4000
Public	2246	1496	750	2736	1886	850	4146	2146	2000	6631	2631	4000
Private	1437	1437	...	1515	1515	...	1943	1943	...	2868	2868	...
B Interest	79070	20519	58551	104019	27728	76291	115337	28891	86446	125539	32773	92766
C Dividends	6733	5740	993	6331	5209	1122	8412	7017	1395	10296	8522	1774
D Net land rent and royalties	1076	1076	...	1263	1263	...	1374	1374	...	2111	2111	...
2 Direct taxes and other current transfers n.e.c. to general government	6552	5376	1176	6334	4748	1586	8744	6922	1822	13012	10099	2913
A Direct taxes	6263	5248	1015	6091	4585	1506	8403	6727	1676	12552	9863	2689
B Fines, fees, penalties and other current transfers n.e.c.	289	128	161	243	163	80	341	195	146	460	236	224

Sweden

3.22 Corporate and Quasi-Corporate Enterprise Income and Outlay Account: Total and Sectors
(Continued)

Million Swedish kronor

	1980 TOTAL	1980 Non-Financial	1980 Financial	1981 TOTAL	1981 Non-Financial	1981 Financial	1982 TOTAL	1982 Non-Financial	1982 Financial	1983 TOTAL	1983 Non-Financial	1983 Financial
3 Other current transfers	17026	7340	9686	23330	6956	16374	30234	8099	22135	32895	10457	22438
A Casualty insurance premiums, net	4073	4073	...	3662	3662	...	4042	4042	...	4882	4882	...
B Casualty insurance claims liability of insurance companies	5896	...	5896	11768	...	11768	15408	...	15408	15677	...	15677
C Transfers to private non-profit institutions	...	...	...	...	...	...	...	...	...	...	...	...
D Unfunded employee pension and welfare benefits	5937	2607	3330	6803	2916	3887	7902	3256	4646	8779	3568	5211
E Social assistance grants	...	...	...	...	...	...	...	...	...	...	...	...
F Other transfers n.e.c.	1120	660	460	1097	378	719	2882	801	2081	3557	2007	1550
G Transfers to the rest of the world	...	...	...	...	...	...	...	...	...	...	...	...
Net saving	19985	-1113	21098	18412	-8342	26754	27817	-813	28630	35642	5760	29882
Total Current Disbursements and Net Saving	134125	41871	92254	163940	40963	122977	198007	55579	142428	228994	75221	153773

	1984 TOTAL	1984 Non-Financial	1984 Financial	1985 TOTAL	1985 Non-Financial	1985 Financial	1986 TOTAL	1986 Non-Financial	1986 Financial	1987 TOTAL	1987 Non-Financial	1987 Financial
Receipts												
1 Operating surplus	59090	68228	-9138	63881	74921	-11040	58394	72072	-13678	54989	72907	-17918
2 Property and entrepreneurial income	164058	8126	155932	192668	11027	181641	205017	15379	189638	225788	15403	210385
A Withdrawals from quasi-corporate enterprises	...	...	...	...	...	...	...	...	...	...	...	...
B Interest	153150	...	153150	178968	...	178968	186346	...	186346	205569	...	205569
C Dividends	9436	6654	2782	11247	8574	2673	16865	13573	3292	18416	13600	4816
D Net land rent and royalties	1472	1472	...	2453	2453	...	1806	1806	...	1803	1803	...
3 Current transfers	46413	18138	28275	56176	20946	35230	64279	23655	40624	68417	25003	43414
A Casualty insurance claims	7061	7061	...	7341	7341	...	8026	8026	...	9951	9951	...
B Casualty insurance premiums, net, due to be received by insurance companies	17037	...	17037	20600	...	20600	23731	...	23731	23306	...	23306
C Current transfers from the rest of the world	-	-	...	-	-	...	-	-	...	-	-	...
D Other transfers except imputed	4820	4230	590	7709	5933	1776	11513	7897	3616	11318	7276	4042
E Imputed unfunded employee pension and welfare contributions	17495	6847	10648	20526	7672	12854	21009	7732	13277	23842	7776	16066
Total Current Receipts	269561	94492	175069	312725	106894	205831	327690	111106	216584	349194	113313	235881
Disbursements												
1 Property and entrepreneurial income	169616	56453	113163	194505	60281	134224	207822	73685	134137	224421	78266	146155
A Withdrawals from quasi-corporations	12550	8550	4000	14643	7982	6661	16631	9008	7623	15798	9957	5841
Public	7921	3921	4000	9743	3082	6661	11050	3427	7623	9437	3596	5841
Private	4629	4629	...	4900	4900	...	5581	5581	...	6361	6361	...
B Interest	143031	36433	106598	162362	38461	123901	168356	47435	120921	183613	48110	135503
C Dividends	11990	9425	2565	15009	11347	3662	20624	15031	5593	22849	18038	4811
D Net land rent and royalties	2045	2045	...	2491	2491	...	2211	2211	...	2161	2161	...
2 Direct taxes and other current transfers n.e.c. to general government	14626	12336	2290	14536	12687	1849	17091	11333	5758	27763	24286	3477
A Direct taxes	14130	11999	2131	14222	12381	1841	16721	10972	5749	27464	23987	3477
B Fines, fees, penalties and other current transfers n.e.c.	496	337	159	314	306	8	370	361	9	299	299	-

Sweden

3.22 Corporate and Quasi-Corporate Enterprise Income and Outlay Account: Total and Sectors
(Continued)

Million Swedish kronor

	1984 TOTAL	1984 Non-Financial	1984 Financial	1985 TOTAL	1985 Non-Financial	1985 Financial	1986 TOTAL	1986 Non-Financial	1986 Financial	1987 TOTAL	1987 Non-Financial	1987 Financial
3 Other current transfers	38908	12463	26445	46005	14773	31232	53551	16645	36906	56364	17549	38815
A Casualty insurance premiums, net	5812	5812	...	6749	6749	...	7693	7693	...	7118	7118	...
B Casualty insurance claims liability of insurance companies	18017	...	18017	21341	...	21341	24249	...	24249	25752	...	25752
C Transfers to private non-profit institutions	...	...	...	...	...	...	...	...	...	...	...	...
D Unfunded employee pension and welfare benefits	9796	3750	6046	10568	3872	6696	11496	4082	7414	12179	4163	8016
E Social assistance grants	...	...	...	...	...	...	...	...	...	...	...	...
F Other transfers n.e.c.	5283	2901	2382	7347	4152	3195	10113	4870	5243	11315	6268	5047
G Transfers to the rest of the world	...	...	...	...	...	...	...	...	...	...	...	...
Net saving	46411	13240	33171	57679	19153	38526	49226	9443	39783	40646	-6788	47434
Total Current Disbursements and Net Saving	269561	94492	175069	312725	106894	205831	327690	111106	216584	349194	113313	235881

3.23 Corporate and Quasi-Corporate Enterprise Capital Accumulation Account: Total and Sectors

Million Swedish kronor

	1980 TOTAL	1980 Non-Financial	1980 Financial	1981 TOTAL	1981 Non-Financial	1981 Financial	1982 TOTAL	1982 Non-Financial	1982 Financial	1983 TOTAL	1983 Non-Financial	1983 Financial
Finance of Gross Accumulation												
1 Gross saving	57875	36245	21630	60590	33232	27358	75595	46280	29315	90075	59422	30653
A Consumption of fixed capital	37890	37358	532	42178	41574	604	47778	47093	685	54433	53662	771
B Net saving	19985	-1113	21098	18412	-8342	26754	27817	-813	28630	35642	5760	29882
2 Capital transfers	3869	3869	...	5889	5889	...	9599	9599	...	10193	10193	...
A From resident sectors	3869	3869	...	5889	5889	...	9599	9599	...	10193	10193	...
B From the rest of the world	...	...	...	...	...	...	...	...	...	...	...	...
Finance of Gross Accumulation	61744	40114	21630	66479	39121	27358	85194	55879	29315	100268	69615	30653
Gross Accumulation												
1 Gross capital formation	66811	65775	1036	60566	59510	1056	68564	67472	1092	77016	75989	1027
A Increase in stocks	4834	4834	...	-6011	-6011	...	-6737	-6737	...	-9630	-9630	...
B Gross fixed capital formation	61977	60941	1036	66577	65521	1056	75301	74209	1092	86646	85619	1027
2 Purchases of land, net	-2352	-2451	99	-2560	-2739	179	-2051	-4002	1951	-1971	-4003	2032
3 Purchases of intangible assets, net	...	...	...	...	...	...	...	...	...	...	...	...
4 Capital transfers	259	259	-	266	266	-	278	278	-	279	279	-
A To resident sectors	259	259	...	266	266	...	278	278	...	279	279	...
B To the rest of the world	...	...	...	...	...	...	...	...	...	...	...	...
Net lending [ab]	-2974	-23469	20495	8207	-17916	26123	18403	-7869	26272	24944	-2650	27594
Gross Accumulation	61744	40114	21630	66479	39121	27358	85194	55879	29315	100268	69615	30653

	1984 TOTAL	1984 Non-Financial	1984 Financial	1985 TOTAL	1985 Non-Financial	1985 Financial	1986 TOTAL	1986 Non-Financial	1986 Financial	1987 TOTAL	1987 Non-Financial	1987 Financial
Finance of Gross Accumulation												
1 Gross saving	105237	71215	34022	122163	82691	39472	119239	78437	40802	118200	69660	48540
A Consumption of fixed capital	58826	57975	851	64484	63538	946	70013	68994	1019	77554	76448	1106
B Net saving	46411	13240	33171	57679	19153	38526	49226	9443	39783	40646	-6788	47434
2 Capital transfers	5503	5503	...	7189	7189	...	8011	8011	...	2325	2325	...
A From resident sectors	5503	5503	...	7189	7189	...	8011	8011	...	2325	2325	...
B From the rest of the world	...	...	...	...	...	...	...	...	...	...	...	...
Finance of Gross Accumulation	110740	76718	34022	129352	89880	39472	127250	86448	40802	120525	71985	48540
Gross Accumulation												
1 Gross capital formation	92180	90473	1707	116956	114662	2294	115290	112251	3039	135602	132824	2778
A Increase in stocks	-6591	-6591	...	-679	-679	...	-9490	-9490	...	-7509	-7509	...
B Gross fixed capital formation	98771	97064	1707	117635	115341	2294	124780	121741	3039	143111	140333	2778

Sweden

3.23 Corporate and Quasi-Corporate Enterprise Capital Accumulation Account: Total and Sectors
(Continued)

Million Swedish kronor

	1984 TOTAL	1984 Non-Financial	1984 Financial	1985 TOTAL	1985 Non-Financial	1985 Financial	1986 TOTAL	1986 Non-Financial	1986 Financial	1987 TOTAL	1987 Non-Financial	1987 Financial
2 Purchases of land, net	-1932	-3988	2056	-1631	-3428	1797	-353	-892	539	-223	-490	267
3 Purchases of intangible assets, net	...	...	...	...	...	...	...	...	...	...	...	...
4 Capital transfers	262	262	-	272	272	-	222	222	-	10275	248	10027
A To resident sectors	262	262	...	272	272	...	222	222	...	10275	248	10027
B To the rest of the world	...	...	...	...	...	...	...	...	...	...	...	...
Net lending ab	20230	-10029	30259	13755	-21626	35381	12091	-25133	37224	-25129	-60597	35468
Gross Accumulation	110740	76718	34022	129352	89880	39472	127250	86448	40802	120525	71985	48540

a) Net lending of the capital accumulation account and the capital finance account have not been reconciled and are different due to different statistical sources.
b) Net lending excludes net acquisition of SDR.

3.24 Corporate and Quasi-Corporate Enterprise Capital Finance Account: Total and Sectors

Million Swedish kronor

	1980 TOTAL	1980 Non-Financial	1980 Financial	1981 TOTAL	1981 Non-Financial	1981 Financial	1982 TOTAL	1982 Non-Financial	1982 Financial	1983 TOTAL	1983 Non-Financial	1983 Financial
Acquisition of Financial Assets												
1 Gold and SDRs	-253	...	-253	8	...	8	53	...	53	-920	...	-920
2 Currency and transferable deposits	10918	145	10773	20985	14121	6864	13031	5258	7773	12162	7612	4550
3 Other deposits [a]	12903	5413	7490	156	306	-150	23893	19093	4800	4840	7189	-2349
4 Bills and bonds, short term [b]	6312	-	6312	-3057	-	-3057	10252	-	10252	-2733	1484	-4217
5 Bonds, long term [c]	23805	32	23773	61620	3066	58554	20937	1005	19932	64502	14944	49558
6 Corporate equity securities	7017	5467	1550	13687	11430	2257	13327	9075	4252	14410	9605	4805
7 Short term loans, n.e.c.	66108	10615	55493	66889	9052	57837	87955	20483	67472	110744	36455	74289
8 Long term loans, n.e.c.	...	...	...	...	...	...	...	...	...	...	...	...
9 Trade credits and advances	9444	9444	...	9842	9842	...	12328	12328	...	18041	18041	...
10 Other receivables	...	...	...	...	...	...	...	...	...	...	...	...
11 Other assets	7634	7291	343	28230	1468	26762	19973	872	19101	25991	383	25608
Total Acquisition of Financial Assets [d]	143888	38407	105481	198360	49285	149075	201749	68114	133635	247037	95713	151324
Incurrence of Liabilities												
1 Currency and transferable deposits	27432	...	27432	43415	...	43415	27729	...	27729	26418	...	26418
2 Other deposits [a]	14661	-	14661	298	-	298	4281	-	4281	4948	378	4570
3 Bills and bonds, short term	...	...	...	...	...	...	...	...	...	...	...	...
4 Bonds, long term [c]	15378	-481	15859	24372	957	23415	26941	2863	24078	31901	3501	28400
5 Corporate equity securities	4120	3826	294	9194	7285	1909	11465	7211	4254	18296	11632	6664
6 Short-term loans, n.e.c.	64585	43027	21558	60458	35989	24469	65892	37615	28277	77306	54953	22353
7 Long-term loans, n.e.c.	...	...	...	...	...	...	...	...	...	...	...	...
8 Net equity of households in life insurance and pension fund reserves	3182	...	3182	4140	...	4140	4914	...	4914	9071	...	9071
9 Proprietors' net additions to the accumulation of quasi-corporations	1208	1208	...	1308	1308	...	1525	1525	...	1910	1910	...
10 Trade credit and advances [e]	7274	7274	...	8170	8170	...	10079	10079	...	13994	13994	...
11 Other accounts payable	...	...	...	...	...	...	...	...	...	...	...	...
12 Other liabilities	10048	7296	2752	35843	11299	24544	29276	14167	15109	39995	15213	24782
Total Incurrence of Liabilities	147888	62150	85738	187198	65008	122190	182102	73460	108642	223839	101581	122258
Net Lending [f]	-4000	-23743	19743	11162	-15723	26885	19647	-5346	24993	23198	-5868	29066
Incurrence of Liabilities and Net Lending	143888	38407	105481	198360	49285	149075	201749	68114	133635	247037	95713	151324

	1984 TOTAL	1984 Non-Financial	1984 Financial	1985 TOTAL	1985 Non-Financial	1985 Financial	1986 TOTAL	1986 Non-Financial	1986 Financial	1987 TOTAL	1987 Non-Financial	1987 Financial
Acquisition of Financial Assets												
1 Gold and SDRs	486	...	486	313	...	313	330	...	330	-434	...	-434
2 Currency and transferable deposits	17995	16401	1594	163	-7785	7948	24828	14566	10262	15926	-8863	24789
3 Other deposits [a]	-2376	-7666	5290	-3815	-315	-3500	8916	-677	9593	21835	19347	2488
4 Bills and bonds, short term [b]	33576	-2912	36488	31100	17923	13177	-2460	-29986	27526	-15597	4239	-19836
5 Bonds, long term [c]	25920	1649	24271	37380	2729	34651	88617	62194	26423	30992	12137	18855
6 Corporate equity securities	25162	20094	5068	27791	23174	4617	34418	24273	10145	24872	11150	13722
7 Short term loans, n.e.c.	121168	41003	80165	116996	38610	78386	238243	53488	184755	202206	42638	159568
8 Long term loans, n.e.c.	...	...	...	...	...	...	...	...	...	...	...	...
9 Trade credits and advances	17225	17225	...	10554	10554	...	7788	7788	...	12224	12224	...

Sweden

3.24 Corporate and Quasi-Corporate Enterprise Capital Finance Account: Total and Sectors
(Continued)

Million Swedish kronor

	1984 TOTAL	1984 Non-Financial	1984 Financial	1985 TOTAL	1985 Non-Financial	1985 Financial	1986 TOTAL	1986 Non-Financial	1986 Financial	1987 TOTAL	1987 Non-Financial	1987 Financial
10 Other receivables	...	...	...	...	...	...	...	...	...	...	...	...
11 Other assets	44953	15514	29439	46397	13986	32411	73134	16598	56536	51568	-3230	54798
Total Acquisition of Financial Assets [d]	284109	101308	182801	266879	98876	168003	473814	148244	325570	343592	89642	253950

Incurrence of Liabilities

	1984 TOTAL	1984 Non-Financial	1984 Financial	1985 TOTAL	1985 Non-Financial	1985 Financial	1986 TOTAL	1986 Non-Financial	1986 Financial	1987 TOTAL	1987 Non-Financial	1987 Financial
1 Currency and transferable deposits	38119	...	38119	11748	...	11748	60457	...	60457	11626	...	11626
2 Other deposits [a]	-1793	4464	-6257	-1968	4218	-6186	7681	3432	4249	25835	-2120	27955
3 Bills and bonds, short term	...	...	...	...	...	...	...	...	...	...	...	...
4 Bonds, long term [c]	36590	4287	32303	52322	5481	46841	98621	14128	84493	65299	5095	60204
5 Corporate equity securities	23837	16025	7812	20703	13228	7475	33851	13216	20635	14037	17748	-3711
6 Short-term loans, n.e.c.	99072	63325	35747	89537	73955	15582	162570	118116	44454	173645	114548	59097
7 Long-term loans, n.e.c.	...	...	...	...	...	...	...	...	...	...	...	...
8 Net equity of households in life insurance and pension fund reserves	9433	...	9433	10741	...	10741	13312	...	13312	9442	...	9442
9 Proprietors' net additions to the accumulation of quasi-corporations	332	332	...	1948	1948	...	2454	2454	...	2729	2729	...
10 Trade credit and advances [e]	16609	16609	...	13725	13725	...	9473	9473	...	12233	12233	...
11 Other accounts payable	...	...	...	...	...	...	...	...	...	...	...	...
12 Other liabilities	52507	16089	36418	51459	5272	46187	87414	25727	61687	70322	12157	58165
Total Incurrence of Liabilities	274706	121131	153575	250215	117827	132388	475833	186546	289287	385168	162390	222778
Net Lending [f]	9403	-19823	29226	16664	-18951	35615	-2019	-38302	36283	-41576	-72748	31172
Incurrence of Liabilities and Net Lending	284109	101308	182801	266879	98876	168003	473814	148244	325570	343592	89642	253950

a) Item 'Other deposits' refers to certificate of deposit.
b) 'Bills and bonds' refer to Swedish treasury bills and special treasury bills.
c) Item 'Bonds, long-term' includes both short-term and long-term bonds.
d) Item 'Total acquisition of financial assets' excludes net acquisition of SDRS except for 1982.
e) Item 'Trade credit advances' includes trade bills.
f) Net lending of the capital accumulation account and the capital finance account have not been reconciled and are different due to different statistical sources.

3.31 Household and Private Unincorporated Enterprise Production Account

Million Swedish kronor

	1970	1975	1978	1979	1980	1981	1982	1983	1984	1985	1986	1987

Gross Output

	1970	1975	1978	1979	1980	1981	1982	1983	1984	1985	1986	1987
1 Output for sale	...	...	...	...	...	...	...	...	...	...	...	...
2 Non-marketed output	...	...	...	...	...	...	...	...	...	...	...	...
Gross Output	...	...	...	...	...	...	...	...	...	...	...	...

Gross Input

	1970	1975	1978	1979	1980	1981	1982	1983	1984	1985	1986	1987
Intermediate consumption	...	...	...	...	...	...	...	...	...	...	...	...
Subtotal: Value Added	...	...	...	...	...	...	...	...	...	...	...	...
1 Indirect taxes net liability of unincorporated enterprises	...	...	...	...	...	...	...	...	...	...	...	...
2 Consumption of fixed capital	4263	7195	11141	12534	14798	16647	18240	20159	22289	23570	24912	25841
3 Compensation of employees	6513	6936	7474	6516	6372	6489	4863	...	...	...	...	...
4 Net operating surplus	23920	33052	49197	50273	56586	59727	71198	77420	85861	91411	93304	103950
Gross Input	...	...	...	...	...	...	...	...	...	...	...	...

3.32 Household and Private Unincorporated Enterprise Income and Outlay Account

Million Swedish kronor

	1970	1975	1978	1979	1980	1981	1982	1983	1984	1985	1986	1987

Receipts

	1970	1975	1978	1979	1980	1981	1982	1983	1984	1985	1986	1987
1 Compensation of employees	103026	183786	273100	300130	337338	368631	389646	421456	461259	502173	548623	594950
A Wages and salaries	89529	147597	201024	221110	245924	265729	281388	303641	334296	365807	399312	436404
B Employers' contributions for social security	8133	24189	53924	59713	71602	82584	83174	91618	99264	103302	119254	131756
C Employers' contributions for private pension & welfare plans	5364	12000	18152	19307	19812	20318	25084	26197	27699	33064	30057	26790
2 Operating surplus of private unincorporated enterprises	23920	33052	49197	50273	56586	59727	71198	77420	85861	91411	93304	103950
3 Property and entrepreneurial income	7235	11471	16235	18422	27267	34145	35833	38490	44130	52810	56772	57973
A Withdrawals from private quasi-corporations	517	827	1139	1287	1437	1515	1943	2868	4629	4900	5581	6361
B Interest	5714	8911	13079	14966	22723	29604	30129	30441	35375	42478	44963	44473
C Dividends	885	1488	1642	1833	2623	2398	3072	4238	3568	4833	5235	6380
D Net land rent and royalties	119	245	375	336	484	628	689	943	558	599	993	759

Sweden

3.32 Household and Private Unincorporated Enterprise Income and Outlay Account
(Continued)

Million Swedish kronor

	1970	1975	1978	1979	1980	1981	1982	1983	1984	1985	1986	1987
3 Current transfers	22119	49409	82342	92826	105996	120721	132961	149337	160190	179818	198658	218183
A Casualty insurance claims	1046	1353	2140	2231	2469	2818	3241	3517	4319	5241	6440	6416
B Social security benefits	12718	31634	55733	63011	73396	84729	92730	104640	112335	125016	139567	153639
C Social assistance grants	4899	10159	15580	17496	19369	21148	23296	25737	26663	31932	32938	36308
D Unfunded employee pension and welfare benefits	3139	5666	7886	8610	9377	10383	11846	13141	14502	15507	17095	18096
E Transfers from general government	234	489	783	880	1029	1161	1313	1405	1577	1490	2008	2242
F Transfers from the rest of the world	83	108	220	598	356	482	535	897	794	632	610	1482
G Other transfers n.e.c.	...	...	...	...	...	...	...	...	...	...	...	...
Total Current Receipts [a]	156300	277718	420874	461651	527187	583224	629638	686703	751440	826212	897357	975056

Disbursements

	1970	1975	1978	1979	1980	1981	1982	1983	1984	1985	1986	1987
1 Final consumption expenditures	92237	156908	220480	243755	271831	301024	336650	365820	401987	442427	484794	531009
A Market purchases	81704	139119	193461	213410	237649	262412	291994	315994	347631	383384	420577	461360
B Gross rents of owner-occupied housing	10399	17580	26716	30020	33871	38612	44656	49826	54356	59043	64217	69649
C Consumption from own-account production	134	209	303	325	311	...	...	...	...	...	...	...
2 Property income	7107	11118	19949	23686	32846	41477	43002	43292	48573	57159	61160	67116
A Interest	6909	10787	19493	23200	32230	40777	42234	42476	47655	56132	60030	65819
Consumer debt	...	...	...	...	...	...	...	...	...	...	...	...
Mortgage	3540	6917	11900	13105	17516	23269	25107	...	...	...	...	...
Other	...	...	...	...	...	...	...	...	...	...	...	...
B Net land rent and royalties	198	331	456	486	616	700	768	816	918	1027	1130	1297
3 Direct taxes and other current transfers n.e.c. to government	46388	87566	147391	163166	183729	203509	217329	240110	261798	279994	316348	357114
A Social security contributions	13059	25761	56439	62525	74643	85833	86630	95653	103781	108206	124456	137282
B Direct taxes	32398	60680	89975	99353	107614	115701	127773	141798	155060	168591	189211	216073
Income taxes	...	...	...	...	...	...	...	...	...	...	...	...
Other	...	...	...	...	...	...	...	...	...	...	...	...
C Fees, fines and penalties	931	1125	977	1288	1472	1975	2926	2659	2957	3197	2681	3759
4 Other current transfers	6535	13874	21945	23076	23967	24689	30042	32268	34440	40927	39051	36038
A Net casualty insurance premiums	921	1157	2638	2517	2527	2803	2992	3259	3861	4626	5784	6196
B Transfers to private non-profit institutions serving households	...	...	...	...	...	...	...	...	...	...	...	...
C Transfers to the rest of the world	250	717	1155	1252	1628	1568	1966	2812	2880	3237	3210	3052
D Other current transfers, except imputed	...	...	...	...	...	...	...	...	...	...	...	...
E Imputed employee pension and welfare contributions	5364	12000	18152	19307	19812	20318	25084	26197	27699	33064	30057	26790
Net saving	4033	8252	11109	7968	14814	12525	2615	5213	4642	5705	-3996	-16221
Total Current Disbursements and Net Saving [a]	156300	277718	420874	461651	527187	583224	629638	686703	751440	826212	897357	975056

a) Private non-profit institutions serving households is included in household and private unincorporated enterprise.

3.33 Household and Private Unincorporated Enterprise Capital Accumulation Account

Million Swedish kronor

	1970	1975	1978	1979	1980	1981	1982	1983	1984	1985	1986	1987

Finance of Gross Accumulation

	1970	1975	1978	1979	1980	1981	1982	1983	1984	1985	1986	1987
1 Gross saving	8296	15447	22250	20502	29612	29172	20855	25372	26931	29275	20916	9620
A Consumption of fixed capital	4263	7195	11141	12534	14798	16647	18240	20159	22289	23570	24912	25841
Owner-occupied housing	2312	3812	6325	7494	9075	10169	11156	12147	13519	14553	15192	16341
Other unincorporated enterprises	1951	3383	4816	5040	5723	6478	7084	8012	8770	9017	9720	9500
B Net saving	4033	8252	11109	7968	14814	12525	2615	5213	4642	5705	-3996	-16221
2 Capital transfers	213	364	445	585	667	593	643	836	886	1039	1126	1168
A From resident sectors	213	364	445	585	667	593	643	836	886	1039	1126	1168
B From the rest of the world	...	...	...	...	...	...	...	...	...	...	...	...
Total Finance of Gross Accumulation [a]	8509	15811	22695	21087	30279	29765	21498	26208	27817	30314	22042	10788

Gross Accumulation

	1970	1975	1978	1979	1980	1981	1982	1983	1984	1985	1986	1987
1 Gross Capital Formation	6670	13614	19497	22312	22229	19950	19216	19635	20910	19229	18391	20075

Sweden

3.33 Household and Private Unincorporated Enterprise Capital Accumulation Account
(Continued)

Million Swedish kronor

	1970	1975	1978	1979	1980	1981	1982	1983	1984	1985	1986	1987
A Increase in stocks	-55	-79	-125	168	56	-112	90	...	...	...	...	...
B Gross fixed capital formation	6725	13693	19622	22144	22173	20062	19126	19635	20910	19229	18391	20075
Owner-occupied housing [bc]	5106	9884	14748	16590	16545	14371	12404	11278	12437	10720	10598	11586
Other gross fixed capital formation	1619	3809	4874	5554	5628	5691	6722	8357	8473	8509	7793	8489
2 Purchases of land, net [d]	943	1897	2556	2888	2878	2638	2057	1890	1694	1588	1503	1850
3 Purchases of intangibles, net	...	...	...	...	...	...	...	...	...	...	...	...
4 Capital transfers	557	852	1173	1222	1358	1430	1545	1672	1846	2007	1917	8198
A To resident sectors	557	852	1173	1222	1358	1430	1545	1672	1846	2007	1917	8198
B To the rest of the world	...	...	...	...	...	...	...	...	...	...	...	...
Net lending [e]	339	-552	-531	-5335	3814	5747	-1320	3011	3367	7490	231	-19335
Total Gross Accumulation [a]	8509	15811	22695	21087	30279	29765	21498	26208	27817	30314	22042	10788

a) Private non-profit institutions serving households is included in household and private unincorporated enterprise.
b) Dwellings includes country lodges.
c) Item 'Owner occupied housing' excludes estate agents' commission.
d) Item 'Purchases of land, rent' includes estate agents' commission.
e) Net lending of the capital accumulation account and the capital finance account have not been reconciled and are different due to different statistical sources.

3.34 Household and Private Unincorporated Enterprise Capital Finance Account

Million Swedish kronor

	1970	1975	1978	1979	1980	1981	1982	1983	1984	1985	1986	1987
Acquisition of Financial Assets												
1 Gold	...	...	...	...	...	...	...	...	...	...	...	...
2 Currency and transferable deposits	5093	14778	16998	19190	22848	25530	19383	16029	16837	14059	31996	14755
3 Other deposits [a]	...	...	...	...	...	...	...	...	6517	10678	15813	9679
4 Bills and bonds, short term	-	-	-3	-	38	-9	-14	-17	4500	2100	-600	-1200
A Corporate and quasi-corporate	...	...	...	...	...	...	...	...	...	...	...	...
B Government	-	-	-3	-	38	-9	-14	-17	4500	2100	-600	-1200
C Rest of the world	...	...	...	...	...	...	...	...	...	...	...	...
5 Bonds, long term [b]	576	3479	4842	5368	9512	2272	4620	8406	8334	9645	16076	9530
6 Corporate equity securities	-831	-1032	-1015	-2040	-1708	-2494	-267	-128	-730	-8448	6467	-7001
7 Short term loans, n.e.c.	536	959	430	750	3389	1758	3874	412	4078	64	5276	1299
8 Long term loans, n.e.c.	...	...	...	...	...	...	...	...	...	...	...	...
9 Trade credit and advances [c]	493	-1119	24	50	52	101	107	114	121	129	166	-
10 Net equity of households in life insurance and pension fund reserves	1116	2269	2275	2644	3182	4140	4914	9071	9433	10741	13312	9442
11 Proprietors' net additions to the accumulation of quasi-corporations	...	...	...	...	...	...	...	...	...	...	...	...
12 Other [c]	2	-404	3357	849	-2966	4583	6130	6145	-4395	4607	817	18250
Total Acquisition of Financial Assets	6985	18930	26908	26811	34347	35881	38747	40032	44695	43575	89323	54754
Incurrence of Liabilities												
1 Short term loans, n.e.c.	6678	18926	27414	32023	31252	30096	39861	36781	40955	35801	88816	74254
2 Long term loans, n.e.c.	...	...	...	...	...	...	...	...	...	...	...	...
3 Trade credit and advances	-	-	20	88	90	219	232	245	259	274	289	-
4 Other accounts payable	...	...	...	...	...	...	...	...	...	...	...	...
5 Other liabilities	...	...	...	...	...	...	...	...	...	...	...	...
Total Incurrence of Liabilities	6678	18926	27434	32111	31342	30315	40093	37026	41214	36075	89105	74254
Net Lending [d]	307	4	-526	-5300	3005	5566	-1346	3006	3481	7500	218	-19500
Incurrence of Liabilities and Net Lending	6985	18930	26908	26811	34347	35881	38747	40032	44695	43575	89323	54754

a) Item 'Other deposits' refers to certificate of deposit.
b) Item 'Bonds, long-term' includes both short-term and long-term bonds.
c) Acquisition are reported net of incurrence of liabilities.
d) Net lending of the capital accumulation account and the capital finance account have not been reconciled and are different due to different statistical sources.

Sweden

3.41 Private Non-Profit Institutions Serving Households: Production Account

Million Swedish kronor

	1970	1975	1978	1979	1980	1981	1982	1983	1984	1985	1986	1987
Gross Output												
1 Sales	...	...	...	...	...	...	...	...	...	...	...	...
2 Non-marketed output	...	...	...	...	...	...	...	...	...	...	...	...
Gross Output	1061	2097	4101	4325	4878	5199	5954	6486	7003	7421	8189	...
Gross Input												
Intermediate consumption	211	409	1175	1221	1419	1486	1788	1996	2217	2370	2601	2904
Subtotal: Value Added	850	1688	2926	3104	3459	3713	4166	4490	4786	5051	5588	6112
1 Indirect taxes, net	7	52	62	53	64	77	87	176	171	186	214	243
2 Consumption of fixed capital	...	...	...	...	...	...	...	...	...	...	...	...
3 Compensation of employees	843	1636	2864	3051	3395	3636	4079	4314	4615	4865	5374	5869
4 Net operating surplus	...	...	...	...	...	...	...	...	...	...	...	...
Gross Input	1061	2097	4101	4325	4878	5199	5954	6486	7003	7421	8189	9016

3.44 Private Non-Profit Institutions Serving Households: Capital Finance Account

Million Swedish kronor

	1970	1975	1978	1979	1980	1981	1982	1983	1984	1985	1986	1987
Acquisition of Financial Assets												
1 Gold	...	...	...	...	...	...	...	...	...	...	...	...
2 Currency and transferable deposits	...	...	296	...	...	...	...	...	...	...	...	...
3 Other deposits	...	...	...	...	...	...	...	...	...	...	...	...
4 Bills and bonds, short term	...	...	...	...	...	...	...	...	...	...	...	...
5 Bonds, long term	...	...	236	...	...	...	...	...	...	...	...	...
6 Corporate equity securities	...	...	93	...	...	...	...	...	...	...	...	...
7 Short-term loans, n.e.c.	...	...	...	...	...	...	...	...	...	...	...	...
8 Long-term loans, n.e.c.	...	...	...	...	...	...	...	...	...	...	...	...
9 Other receivables	...	...	...	...	...	...	...	...	...	...	...	...
10 Proprietors' net additions to the accumulation of quasi-corporations	...	...	...	...	...	...	...	...	...	...	...	...
11 Other assets	...	...	530	...	...	...	...	...	...	...	...	...
Total Acquisition of Financial Assets	...	...	1155	...	...	...	...	...	...	...	...	...
Incurrence of Liabilities												
1 Short-term loans	...	...	...	...	...	...	...	...	...	...	...	...
2 Long-term loans	...	...	...	...	...	...	...	...	...	...	...	...
3 Other liabilities	...	...	131	...	...	...	...	...	...	...	...	...
Total Incurrence of Liabilities	...	...	131	...	...	...	...	...	...	...	...	...
Net Lending	...	...	1024	...	...	...	...	...	...	...	...	...
Incurrence of Liabilities and Net Lending	...	...	1155	...	...	...	...	...	...	...	...	...

3.51 External Transactions: Current Account: Detail

Million Swedish kronor

	1970	1975	1978	1979	1980	1981	1982	1983	1984	1985	1986	1987
Payments to the Rest of the World												
1 Imports of goods and services	42478	85263	112173	145196	166520	172228	205157	233121	254267	283852	277054	305125
A Imports of merchandise c.i.f.	36730	73519	93883	124661	143839	148735	177208	202038	221134	246761	233640	258008
B Other	5748	11744	18290	20535	22681	23493	27949	31083	33133	37091	43414	47117
2 Factor income to the rest of the world	912	2084	7344	7986	11947	21523	27599	31593	36530	42195	36821	37834
A Compensation of employees	6	9	22	28	30	70	163	380	357	415	914	1000
B Property and entrepreneurial income	906	2075	7322	7958	11917	21453	27436	31213	36173	41780	35907	36834
By general government [a]	10	2	977	1165	2981	6526	8664	11125	13295	14832	11983	12283
By corporate and quasi-cororate enterprises	...	...	...	...	...	...	...	...	...	...	...	...

Sweden

3.51 External Transactions: Current Account: Detail
(Continued)

Million Swedish kronor

	1970	1975	1978	1979	1980	1981	1982	1983	1984	1985	1986	1987
By other	...	...	...	...	...	...	...	...	...	...	...	...
3 Current transfers to the rest of the world	1235	3383	5470	6267	6903	11378	14179	15641	16412	19530	20947	21131
A Indirect taxes by general government to supranational organizations	...	...	...	...	...	...	...	...	...	...	...	...
B Other current transfers	1235	3383	5470	6267	6903	11378	14179	15641	16412	19530	20947	21131
By general government	597	2067	3388	4052	4121	4222	4379	4866	5067	5857	6112	6435
By other resident sectors	638	1316	2082	2215	2782	7156	9800	10775	11345	13673	14835	14696
4 Surplus of the nation on current transactions	-1367	-1469	-167	-10137	-18823	-14178	-22761	-7169	3082	-11083	6292	-3408
Payments to the Rest of the World, and Surplus of the Nation on Current Transfers	43258	89261	124820	149312	166547	190951	224174	273186	310291	334494	341114	360682

Receipts From The Rest of the World

	1970	1975	1978	1979	1980	1981	1982	1983	1984	1985	1986	1987
1 Exports of goods and services	41515	84679	116399	140568	156523	172527	201331	249528	284664	303509	309193	326119
A Exports of merchandise f.o.b.	35045	71727	97703	117509	130246	143909	167088	209168	241362	258681	262529	278841
B Other	6470	12952	18696	23059	26277	28618	34243	40360	43302	44828	46664	47278
2 Factor income from the rest of the world	856	2891	5968	6720	7924	12083	13730	14431	16255	19679	19529	21597
A Compensation of employees	14	52	214	212	283	338	283	237	183	209	125	286
B Property and entrepreneurial income	842	2839	5754	6508	7641	11745	13447	14194	16072	19470	19404	21311
By general government [a]	149	395	1209	1341	1626	2415	2717	2712	2999	3572	4387	4767
By corporate and quasi-corporate enterprises	...	...	...	...	...	...	...	...	...	...	...	...
By other	...	...	...	...	...	...	...	...	...	...	...	...
3 Current transfers from the rest of the world	887	1691	2453	2024	2100	6341	9113	9227	9372	11306	12392	12966
A Subsidies to general government from supranational organizations	...	...	...	...	...	...	...	...	...	...	...	...
B Other current transfers	887	1691	2453	2024	2100	6341	9113	9227	9372	11306	12392	12966
To general government	16	31	35	39	48	43	54	90	104	139	204	214
To other resident sectors	871	1660	2418	1985	2052	6298	9059	9137	9268	11167	12188	12752
Receipts from the Rest of the World on Current Transfers	43258	89261	124820	149312	166547	190951	224174	273186	310291	334494	341114	360682

a) Only central government data are included in the general government estimates.

3.52 External Transactions: Capital Accumulation Account

Million Swedish kronor

	1970	1975	1978	1979	1980	1981	1982	1983	1984	1985	1986	1987

Finance of Gross Accumulation

	1970	1975	1978	1979	1980	1981	1982	1983	1984	1985	1986	1987
1 Surplus of the nation on current transactions	-1367	-1469	-167	-10137	-18823	-14178	-22761	-7169	3082	-11083	6292	-3408
2 Capital transfers from the rest of the world	...	...	...	...	...	...	...	...	...	...	...	...
Total Finance of Gross Accumulation	-1367	-1469	-167	-10137	-18823	-14178	-22761	-7169	3082	-11083	6292	-3408

Gross Accumulation

	1970	1975	1978	1979	1980	1981	1982	1983	1984	1985	1986	1987
1 Capital transfers to the rest of the world	...	...	...	...	...	...	...	...	...	...	...	...
2 Purchases of intangible assets, n.e.c., net, from the rest of the world	...	...	...	...	...	...	...	...	...	...	...	...
Net lending to the rest of the world	-1367	-1469	-167	-10137	-18823	-14178	-22761	-7169	3082	-11083	6292	-3408
Total Gross Accumulation	-1367	-1469	-167	-10137	-18823	-14178	-22761	-7169	3082	-11083	6292	-3408

3.53 External Transactions: Capital Finance Account

Million Swedish kronor

	1970	1975	1978	1979	1980	1981	1982	1983	1984	1985	1986	1987

Acquisitions of Foreign Financial Assets

	1970	1975	1978	1979	1980	1981	1982	1983	1984	1985	1986	1987
1 Gold and SDR's	-134	-	41	89	-253	8	53	-920	486	313	330	-434
2 Currency and transferable deposits	478	3230	108	4185	9252	8289	5363	5056	-56	6023	4036	21888
3 Other deposits [a]	...	...	...	...	...	...	...	...	...	...	...	...
4 Bills and bonds, short term [b]	208	5710	2559	-3038	-992	-2410	-1060	4325	-56	11698	1143	5012

Sweden

3.53 External Transactions: Capital Finance Account
(Continued)

Million Swedish kronor

		1970	1975	1978	1979	1980	1981	1982	1983	1984	1985	1986	1987
5	Bonds, long term [c]	21	83	-110	131	378	457	679	1069	531	671	3305	2031
6	Corporate equity securities	657	1051	808	1215	1836	3467	3455	5470	5201	4880	11661	4558
7	Short-term loans, n.e.c.	1034	2170	2445	3766	3024	5813	12004	12222	7162	3169	8263	16099
8	Long-term loans	...	...	...	...	...	...	...	...	...	...	...	...
9	Proprietors' net additions to accumulation of quasi-corporate, non-resident enterprises	...	...	...	...	...	...	...	...	...	...	...	...
10	Trade credit and advances	1411	1135	1911	1373	373	3513	2474	3129	1607	401	-100	2529
11	Other	...	...	...	...	...	...	...	...	...	...	...	...
	Total Acquisitions of Foreign Financial Assets [d]	3675	13379	7762	7721	13618	19137	22968	30351	14875	27155	28638	51683

Incurrence of Foreign Liabilities

		1970	1975	1978	1979	1980	1981	1982	1983	1984	1985	1986	1987
1	Currency and transferable deposits	21	24	150	335	985	2348	61	4776	2047	5476	7128	9405
2	Other deposits [a]	-	-	-	-	892	69	110	-76	559	550	-366	3615
3	Bills and bonds, short term [b]	-34	-	-	-	-	-	-	-	-	-	-	-
4	Bonds, long term [c]	342	3126	2922	4650	7044	6405	13774	23505	36373	18796	988	2313
5	Corporate equity securities	75	140	116	26	291	401	1348	5921	2188	5233	2348	-3271
6	Short-term loans, n.e.c.	1954	11246	1621	13736	29474	21623	27120	8540	-21072	5623	24167	50603
7	Long-term loans	...	...	...	...	...	...	...	...	...	...	...	...
8	Non-resident proprietors' net additions to accumulation of resident quasi-corporate enterprises	...	...	...	...	...	...	...	...	...	...	...	...
9	Trade credit and advances	1072	1818	759	1019	-1759	1959	350	-787	1129	3717	1708	2538
10	Other	...	...	...	...	...	...	...	...	...	...	...	...
	Total Incurrence of Liabilities [d]	3430	16354	5568	19766	36927	32805	42763	41879	21224	39395	35973	65203
	Statistical discrepancy	1612	-1506	2361	-1908	-4486	510	2966	-4359	-9431	-1157	-13627	-10112
	Net Lending [d]	-1367	-1469	-167	-10137	-18823	-14178	-22761	-7169	3082	-11083	6292	-3408
	Total Incurrence of Liabilities and Net Lending [d]	3675	13379	7762	7721	13618	19137	22968	30351	14875	27155	28638	51683

a) Item 'Other deposits' refers to certificate of deposit.
b) 'Bills and bonds' refer to Swedish treasury bills and special treasury bills.
c) Item 'Bonds, long-term' includes both short-term and long-term bonds.
d) Beginning 1970 estimates of acquisition and incurrence of foreign liabilities are reported according to the financial accounts calculated by the Central Bureau of Statistics. Prior to 1970 estimates are based on the capital accounts of the balance of payment calculated by the Central Bank.

4.1 Derivation of Value Added by Kind of Activity, in Current Prices

Million Swedish kronor

		1980			1981			1982			1983		
		Gross Output	Intermediate Consumption	Value Added	Gross Output	Intermediate Consumption	Value Added	Gross Output	Intermediate Consumption	Value Added	Gross Output	Intermediate Consumption	Value Added

All Producers

		1980 GO	1980 IC	1980 VA	1981 GO	1981 IC	1981 VA	1982 GO	1982 IC	1982 VA	1983 GO	1983 IC	1983 VA
1	Agriculture, hunting, forestry and fishing	28583	11754	16829	31878	13253	18625	35739	15189	20550	39059	16573	22486
	A Agriculture and hunting	19345	9932	9413	21689	11225	10464	24909	12705	12204	26304	13938	12366
	B Forestry and logging	8659	1613	7046	9580	1769	7811	10145	2187	7958	11933	2304	9629
	C Fishing	579	209	370	609	259	350	685	297	388	822	331	491
2	Mining and quarrying	4597	2148	2449	4296	2061	2235	4530	2046	2484	5430	2216	3214
	A Coal mining	...	...	...	...	...	...	...	...	...	...	...	...
	B Crude petroleum and natural gas production	...	...	...	...	...	...	...	...	...	...	...	...
	C Metal ore mining	3324	1614	1710	2997	1567	1430	3246	1540	1706	4112	1694	2418
	D Other mining	1273	534	739	1299	494	805	1284	506	778	1318	522	796

Sweden

4.1 Derivation of Value Added by Kind of Activity, in Current Prices
(Continued)

Million Swedish kronor

	1980 Gross Output	1980 Intermediate Consumption	1980 Value Added	1981 Gross Output	1981 Intermediate Consumption	1981 Value Added	1982 Gross Output	1982 Intermediate Consumption	1982 Value Added	1983 Gross Output	1983 Intermediate Consumption	1983 Value Added
3 Manufacturing	327225	216207	111018	345893	230181	115712	382540	256869	125671	445495	298445	147050
A Manufacture of food, beverages and tobacco	43290	31640	11650	48017	35512	12505	55293	41749	13544	60345	44977	15368
B Textile, wearing apparel and leather industries	9311	5496	3815	9070	5351	3719	9299	5643	3656	10244	6163	4081
C Manufacture of wood and wood products, including furniture	26692	16846	9846	25258	16094	9164	26786	17579	9207	31499	20566	10933
D Manufacture of paper and paper products, printing and publishing	48078	32667	15411	52084	35745	16339	55684	36956	18728	66123	43972	22151
E Manufacture of chemicals and chemical petroleum, coal, rubber and plastic products	47184	36131	11053	50168	39775	10393	56210	43745	12465	67476	52522	14954
F Manufacture of non-metallic mineral products, except products of petroleum and coal	8521	4646	3875	8620	4730	3890	9578	5166	4412	10358	5609	4749
G Basic metal industries	26437	19975	6462	25374	19012	6362	28786	21195	7591	33850	25286	8564
H Manufacture of fabricated metal products, machinery and equipment	115145	66992	48153	124640	72119	52521	137956	82785	55171	162441	96992	65449
I Other manufacturing industries	2567	1814	753	2662	1843	819	2948	2051	897	3159	2358	801
4 Electricity, gas and water	20428	7335	13093	23763	8615	15148	26380	10430	15950	29395	10598	18797
A Electricity, gas and steam	18999	6829	12170	22094	8065	14029	24481	9799	14682	27426	9932	17494
B Water works and supply	1429	506	923	1669	550	1119	1899	631	1268	1969	666	1303
5 Construction	77215	38540	38675	83174	40330	42844	88992	44261	44731	95212	47901	47311
6 Wholesale and retail trade, restaurants and hotels	89617	31320	58297	95135	34722	60413	104837	39661	65176	118072	43742	74330
A Wholesale and retail trade	80548	26320	54228	85043	29116	55927	93433	33256	60177	105225	36672	68553
B Restaurants and hotels	9069	5000	4069	10092	5606	4486	11404	6405	4999	12847	7070	5777
7 Transport, storage and communication	60231	28504	31727	67709	33071	34638	75125	37746	37379	82868	42206	40662
A Transport and storage	46015	24071	21944	51542	28121	23421	56922	31458	25464	62297	34622	27675
B Communication	14216	4433	9783	16167	4950	11217	18203	6288	11915	20571	7584	12987
8 Finance, insurance, real estate and business services [a]	107811	48891	58920	124292	59170	65122	141598	67055	74543	160754	77470	83284
A Financial institutions	17511	18715	-1204	22537	23486	-949	25368	26553	-1185	30634	32457	-1823
B Insurance	5696	1350	4346	5918	1631	4287	5681	1863	3818	5717	2017	3700
C Real estate and business services	84604	28826	55778	95837	34053	61784	110549	38639	71910	124403	42996	81407
Real estate, except dwellings	6086	3257	2829	7578	3984	3594	9319	4731	4588	10663	5130	5533
Dwellings	55298	16319	38979	62743	19135	43608	72311	21819	50492	80600	24165	56435
9 Community, social and personal services	31218	13988	17230	34294	16113	18181	38309	18375	19934	41774	19577	22197
A Sanitary and similar services	6002	2075	3927	6323	2223	4100	7236	2516	4720	8043	2821	5222
B Social and related community services	5797	1721	4076	5920	1856	4064	6763	2092	4671	7565	2263	5302
Educational services	...	...	...	...	...	...	...	...	...	...	...	...
Medical, dental, other health and veterinary services	2102	838	1264	2191	965	1226	2693	1105	1588	3033	1169	1864
C Recreational and cultural services	7432	3805	3627	8772	4854	3918	9500	5643	3857	10450	5894	4556
D Personal and household services	11987	6387	5600	13279	7180	6099	14810	8124	6686	15716	8599	7117
Total, Industries	746925	398687	348238	810434	437516	372918	898050	491632	406418	1018060	558728	459331
Producers of Government Services	159207	43171	116036	176038	48649	127389	192891	54178	138713	211907	58653	153254
Other Producers	5279	1419	3860	5587	1486	4101	6359	1788	4571	6930	1996	4934
Total [b]	911411	443277	468134	992059	487651	504408	1097300	547598	549702	1236900	619377	617519
Less: Imputed bank service charge [a]	...	...	...	...	...	...	...	...	...	...	...	...
Import duties	1760	...	1760	1927	...	1927	2160	...	2160	2192	...	2192
Value added tax [c]	54019	...	54019	64447	...	64447	71563	...	71563	78599	...	78599
Other adjustments	1186	...	1186	2258	...	2258	4253	...	4253	7055	...	7055
Total	968376	443277	525099	1060690	487651	573040	1175280	547598	627678	1324740	619377	705365
Memorandum Item: Mineral fuels and power [d]	39259	26519	12740	43943	29640	14303	48935	33671	15264	56513	37897	18616

# Sweden

4.1 Derivation of Value Added by Kind of Activity, in Current Prices

Million Swedish kronor

	1984 Gross Output	1984 Intermediate Consumption	1984 Value Added	1985 Gross Output	1985 Intermediate Consumption	1985 Value Added	1986 Gross Output	1986 Intermediate Consumption	1986 Value Added	1987 Gross Output	1987 Intermediate Consumption	1987 Value Added
All Producers												
1 Agriculture, hunting, forestry and fishing	43778	18217	25561	44843	18956	25887	46334	18900	27434	47596	18870	28726
A Agriculture and hunting	28864	15397	13467	28866	15973	12893	29597	16018	13579	29677	15833	13844
B Forestry and logging	14031	2460	11571	15070	2593	12477	15824	2551	13273	16951	2697	14254
C Fishing	883	360	523	907	390	517	913	331	582	968	340	628
2 Mining and quarrying	6418	2585	3833	7125	2711	4414	6467	2861	3606	6233	2766	3467
A Coal mining	...	...	...	...	...	...	...	...	...	...	...	...
B Crude petroleum and natural gas production	...	...	...	...	...	...	...	...	...	...	...	...
C Metal ore mining	4967	1980	2987	5695	2162	3533	5068	2309	2759	4859	2207	2652
D Other mining	1451	605	846	1430	549	881	1399	552	847	1374	559	815
3 Manufacturing	508380	340330	168050	547128	363803	183325	559873	366349	193524	593156	384522	208634
A Manufacture of food, beverages and tobacco	67880	51659	16221	72812	54486	18326	76343	56295	20048	78310	58266	20044
B Textile, wearing apparel and leather industries	11445	6988	4457	12291	7314	4977	12848	7429	5419	13261	7803	5458
C Manufacture of wood and wood products, including furniture	35756	23483	12273	35590	24198	11392	37834	25919	11915	41056	27820	13236
D Manufacture of paper and paper products, printing and publishing	78048	51302	26746	83792	56154	27638	90184	61872	28312	100584	66739	33845
E Manufacture of chemicals and chemical petroleum, coal, rubber and plastic products	74747	56450	18297	77889	57740	20149	65507	43444	22063	71270	46513	24757
F Manufacture of non-metallic mineral products, except products of petroleum and coal	11119	6133	4986	11832	6510	5322	12536	6736	5800	14048	7496	6552
G Basic metal industries	38509	29113	9396	40420	30296	10124	39208	29247	9961	40162	29498	10664
H Manufacture of fabricated metal products, machinery and equipment	187365	112506	74859	208606	124312	84294	221260	132464	88796	230097	137313	92784
I Other manufacturing industries	3511	2696	815	3896	2793	1103	4153	2943	1210	4368	3074	1294
4 Electricity, gas and water	32936	11147	21789	38245	13005	25240	39048	12198	26850	41226	12487	28739
A Electricity, gas and steam	30871	10410	20461	36030	12129	23901	36756	11333	25423	38800	11542	27258
B Water works and supply	2065	737	1328	2215	876	1339	2292	865	1427	2426	945	1481
5 Construction	105008	54185	50823	109913	56205	53708	116034	59764	56270	127018	64683	62335
6 Wholesale and retail trade, restaurants and hotels	133902	47814	86088	149453	53488	95965	163489	57697	105792	177238	62492	114746
A Wholesale and retail trade	119152	39859	79293	132556	44509	88047	145110	48496	96614	157053	52657	104396
B Restaurants and hotels	14750	7955	6795	16897	8979	7918	18379	9201	9178	20185	9835	10350
7 Transport, storage and communication	91319	47041	44278	100542	52021	48521	107980	53382	54598	116419	55984	60435
A Transport and storage	67804	37352	30452	74076	40523	33553	78657	41082	37575	83322	42657	40665
B Communication	23515	9689	13826	26466	11498	14968	29323	12300	17023	33097	13327	19770
8 Finance, insurance, real estate and business services [a]	180960	89231	91729	199019	100421	98598	229823	119226	110597	257850	134048	123802
A Financial institutions	36465	38040	-1575	40169	42263	-2094	52906	54664	-1758	60207	62696	-2489
B Insurance	5371	2258	3113	5617	2524	3093	5739	2905	2834	6412	3066	3346
C Real estate and business services	139124	48933	90191	153233	55634	97599	171178	61657	109521	191231	68286	122945
Real estate, except dwellings	12393	6130	6263	13834	7783	6051	15962	7499	8463	18750	8485	10265
Dwellings	87688	26680	61008	95671	29707	65964	104347	32413	71934	113675	34216	79459
9 Community, social and personal services	45414	21698	23716	50388	23245	27143	54745	24626	30119	60297	27128	33169
A Sanitary and similar services	8273	3089	5184	9341	3394	5947	10819	3542	7277	12247	3882	8365
B Social and related community services	8263	2452	5811	9007	2685	6322	9411	2844	6567	10317	3267	7050
Educational services	...	...	...	...	...	...	...	...	...	...	...	...
Medical, dental, other health and veterinary services	3175	1233	1942	3587	1374	2213	3827	1481	2346	3990	1695	2295
C Recreational and cultural services	11558	6681	4877	12982	6865	6117	14144	7360	6784	15474	8070	7404
D Personal and household services	17320	9476	7844	19058	10301	8757	20371	10880	9491	22259	11909	10350
Total, Industries	1148120	632248	515867	1246660	683855	562801	1323790	715003	608790	1427030	762980	664053
Producers of Government Services	230810	65023	165787	249309	72300	177009	269013	77297	191716	285189	83937	201252

Sweden

4.1 Derivation of Value Added by Kind of Activity, in Current Prices
(Continued)

Million Swedish kronor

	1984 Gross Output	1984 Intermediate Consumption	1984 Value Added	1985 Gross Output	1985 Intermediate Consumption	1985 Value Added	1986 Gross Output	1986 Intermediate Consumption	1986 Value Added	1987 Gross Output	1987 Intermediate Consumption	1987 Value Added
Other Producers	7463	2217	5246	7904	2370	5534	8661	2601	6060	9511	2904	6607
Total [b]	1386390	699488	686900	1503870	758525	745344	1601470	794901	806566	1721730	849821	871912
Less: Imputed bank service charge [a]	...	...	...	...	...	...	...	...	...	...	...	...
Import duties	2520	...	2520	2736	...	2736	3044	...	3044	3544	...	3544
Value added tax [c]	89138	...	89138	101729	...	101729	108962	...	108962	119968	...	119968
Other adjustments	11025	...	11025	11075	...	11075	13212	...	13212	9802	...	9802
Total	1489070	699488	789583	1619410	758525	860884	1726690	794901	931784	1855050	849821	1005230
Memorandum Item: Mineral fuels and power [d]	62095	39901	22194	67297	41839	25458	54778	28033	26745	57437	28701	28736

a) Item 'Less: Imputed bank service charge' is netted out of item 'Finance, insurance, real estate and business services'.
b) Gross domestic product in basic values.
c) Item 'Value added tax' relates to value added tax and other taxes and subsidies on sales and production of commodities.
d) Item 'Mineral fuels and power' refers to ISIC categories 353 (Petroleum refineries), 354 (Manufacture of miscellaneous products of petroleum and coal) and 41 (Electricity, gas and steam).

4.2 Derivation of Value Added by Kind of Activity, in Constant Prices

Million Swedish kronor

At constant prices of: 1980

All Producers

	1980 Gross Output	1980 Intermediate Consumption	1980 Value Added	1981 Gross Output	1981 Intermediate Consumption	1981 Value Added	1982 Gross Output	1982 Intermediate Consumption	1982 Value Added	1983 Gross Output	1983 Intermediate Consumption	1983 Value Added
1 Agriculture, hunting, forestry and fishing	28583	11754	16829	28776	11709	17067	29970	11805	18165	30705	11712	18993
A Agriculture and hunting	19345	9932	9413	19442	9929	9513	20265	9894	10371	20128	9785	10343
B Forestry and logging	8659	1613	7046	8704	1549	7155	9079	1678	7401	9928	1687	8241
C Fishing	579	209	370	630	231	399	626	233	393	649	240	409
2 Mining and quarrying	4597	2148	2449	3929	1787	2142	3478	1685	1793	3481	1649	1832
A Coal mining	...	...	...	...	...	...	...	...	...	...	...	...
B Crude petroleum and natural gas production	...	...	...	...	...	...	...	...	...	...	...	...
C Metal ore mining	3324	1614	1710	2739	1340	1399	2385	1254	1131	2456	1241	1215
D Other mining	1273	534	739	1190	447	743	1093	431	662	1025	408	617
3 Manufacturing	327225	216207	111018	315712	208314	107398	315477	208625	106852	332940	220598	112342
A Manufacture of food, beverages and tobacco	43290	31640	11650	43031	31437	11594	43635	31879	11756	43262	31599	11663
B Textile, wearing apparel and leather industries	9311	5496	3815	8395	4943	3452	7809	4638	3171	7647	4545	3102
C Manufacture of wood and wood products, including furniture	26692	16846	9846	23793	15032	8761	24390	15516	8874	25720	16419	9301
D Manufacture of paper and paper products, printing and publishing	48078	32667	15411	46667	31802	14865	44742	30159	14583	48655	32948	15707
E Manufacture of chemicals and chemical petroleum, coal, rubber and plastic products	47184	36131	11053	43461	32712	10749	43391	32409	10982	48360	36538	11822
F Manufacture of non-metallic mineral products, except products of petroleum and coal	8521	4646	3875	7565	4166	3399	7682	4236	3446	7737	4243	3494
G Basic metal industries	26437	19975	6462	24930	18999	5931	25542	19242	6300	26690	20112	6578
H Manufacture of fabricated metal products, machinery and equipment	115145	66992	48153	115324	67417	47907	115615	68659	46956	122307	72258	50049
I Other manufacturing industries	2567	1814	753	2546	1806	740	2671	1887	784	2562	1936	626
4 Electricity, gas and water	20428	7335	13093	21597	7499	14098	21846	8264	13582	23103	8768	14335
A Electricity, gas and steam	18999	6829	12170	20176	7000	13176	20419	7735	12684	21721	8258	13463
B Water works and supply	1429	506	923	1421	499	922	1427	529	898	1382	510	872
5 Construction	77215	38540	38675	75009	37113	37896	75394	36816	38578	74677	35899	38778
6 Wholesale and retail trade, restaurants and hotels	89617	31320	58297	88173	30894	57279	88853	31379	57474	90230	31783	58447
A Wholesale and retail trade	80548	26320	54228	79170	25925	53245	79812	26390	53422	81094	26746	54348
B Restaurants and hotels	9069	5000	4069	9003	4969	4034	9041	4989	4052	9136	5037	4099
7 Transport, storage and communication	60231	28504	31727	60766	29739	31027	61463	30314	31149	61564	30536	31028
A Transport and storage	46015	24071	21944	46766	25308	21458	45918	25078	20840	44879	24705	20174
B Communication	14216	4433	9783	14000	4431	9569	15545	5236	10309	16685	5831	10854
8 Finance, insurance, real estate and business services [a]	107811	48891	58920	110661	50972	59689	114495	53845	60650	119178	56461	62717
A Financial institutions	17511	18715	-1204	18311	19584	-1273	19264	20480	-1216	21172	22317	-1145

Sweden

4.2 Derivation of Value Added by Kind of Activity, in Constant Prices
(Continued)

Million Swedish kronor

	1980 Gross Output	1980 Intermediate Consumption	1980 Value Added	1981 Gross Output	1981 Intermediate Consumption	1981 Value Added	1982 Gross Output	1982 Intermediate Consumption	1982 Value Added	1983 Gross Output	1983 Intermediate Consumption	1983 Value Added
				At constant prices of: 1980								
B Insurance	5696	1350	4346	5776	1299	4477	6108	1552	4556	6350	1517	4833
C Real estate and business services	84604	28826	55778	86574	30089	56485	89123	31813	57310	91656	32627	59029
Real estate, except dwellings	6086	3257	2829	6368	3414	2954	6792	3646	3146	6969	3733	3236
Dwellings	55298	16319	38979	56247	17132	39115	57009	18072	38937	57744	18445	39299
9 Community, social and personal services	31218	13988	17230	31474	14514	16960	31796	14541	17255	31772	14218	17554
A Sanitary and similar services	6002	2075	3927	5955	2014	3941	6089	2025	4064	6284	2122	4162
B Social and related community services	5797	1721	4076	5617	1692	3925	5541	1680	3861	5589	1687	3902
Educational services	...	...	...	...	...	...	...	...	...	...	...	...
Medical, dental, other health and veterinary services	2102	838	1264	2108	853	1255	2120	859	1261	2100	850	1250
C Recreational and cultural services	7432	3805	3627	7781	4271	3510	7897	4308	3589	7913	4146	3767
D Personal and household services	11987	6387	5600	12121	6537	5584	12269	6528	5741	11986	6263	5723
Total, Industries	746925	398687	348238	736097	392541	343556	742772	397274	345498	767650	411624	356026
Producers of Government Services	159207	43171	116036	162214	43365	118849	164074	43773	120301	165511	42900	122611
Other Producers	5279	1419	3860	5261	1438	3823	5573	1531	4042	5729	1572	4157
Total [b]	911411	443277	468134	903572	437344	466228	912419	442578	469841	938890	456096	482794
Less: Imputed bank service charge [a]	...	...	...	...	...	...	...	...	...	...	...	...
Import duties	1760	...	1760	1645	...	1645	1654	...	1654	1695	...	1695
Value added tax [c]	54019	...	54019	52579	...	52579	53506	...	53506	53140	...	53140
Other adjustments	1186	...	1186	3061	...	3061	2732	...	2732	2903	...	2903
Total	968376	443277	525099	960857	437344	523513	970311	442578	527733	996628	456096	540532
Memorandum Item: Mineral fuels and power [d]	39259	26519	12740	37392	23679	13713	36957	23705	13252	40644	26477	14167

	1984 Gross Output	1984 Intermediate Consumption	1984 Value Added	1985 Gross Output	1985 Intermediate Consumption	1985 Value Added	1986 Gross Output	1986 Intermediate Consumption	1986 Value Added	1987 Gross Output	1987 Intermediate Consumption	1987 Value Added
				At constant prices of: 1980								
				All Producers								
1 Agriculture, hunting, forestry and fishing	31598	11891	19707	30657	11743	18914	30513	11577	18936	29566	11295	18271
A Agriculture and hunting	20853	9896	10957	20194	9716	10478	19994	9677	10317	18904	9392	9512
B Forestry and logging	10068	1743	8325	9824	1778	8046	9936	1667	8269	10108	1670	8438
C Fishing	677	252	425	639	249	390	583	233	350	554	233	321
2 Mining and quarrying	3890	1817	2073	4032	1852	2180	3984	1855	2129	3889	1719	2170
A Coal mining	...	...	...	...	...	...	...	...	...	...	...	...
B Crude petroleum and natural gas production	...	...	...	...	...	...	...	...	...	...	...	...
C Metal ore mining	2843	1391	1452	3080	1463	1617	3098	1488	1610	3031	1361	1670
D Other mining	1047	426	621	952	389	563	886	367	519	858	358	500

Sweden

4.2 Derivation of Value Added by Kind of Activity, in Constant Prices
(Continued)

Million Swedish kronor

	1984			1985			1986			1987		
	Gross Output	Intermediate Consumption	Value Added	Gross Output	Intermediate Consumption	Value Added	Gross Output	Intermediate Consumption	Value Added	Gross Output	Intermediate Consumption	Value Added
	At constant prices of: 1980											
3 Manufacturing	351796	232675	119121	359185	236110	123075	357644	235199	122445	371652	244362	127290
A Manufacture of food, beverages and tobacco	44083	32254	11829	44215	32335	11880	43661	31870	11791	44973	32824	12149
B Textile, wearing apparel and leather industries	7889	4664	3225	7861	4668	3193	7758	4602	3156	7915	4693	3222
C Manufacture of wood and wood products, including furniture	26693	17117	9576	25526	16482	9044	26067	16900	9167	27458	17708	9750
D Manufacture of paper and paper products, printing and publishing	51645	35102	16543	53175	36038	17137	54641	37082	17559	56559	38372	18187
E Manufacture of chemicals and chemical petroleum, coal, rubber and plastic products	49877	37719	12158	49976	37604	12372	44275	32095	12180	47634	34585	13049
F Manufacture of non-metallic mineral products, except products of petroleum and coal	7852	4368	3484	7843	4359	3484	7851	4382	3469	8447	4711	3736
G Basic metal industries	28040	20932	7108	28125	20924	7201	27745	20927	6818	27709	20871	6838
H Manufacture of fabricated metal products, machinery and equipment	133069	78500	54569	139672	81685	57987	142783	85285	57498	148184	88582	59602
I Other manufacturing industries	2648	2019	629	2792	2015	777	2863	2056	807	2773	2016	757
4 Electricity, gas and water	24722	8329	16393	28277	9053	19224	28347	9277	19070	29243	9325	19918
A Electricity, gas and steam	23358	7793	15565	26856	8452	18404	26934	8681	18253	27820	8698	19122
B Water works and supply	1364	536	828	1421	601	820	1413	596	817	1423	627	796
5 Construction	77093	37323	39770	75754	36164	39590	77519	36866	40653	79849	38028	41821
6 Wholesale and retail trade, restaurants and hotels	91536	32060	59476	94190	33328	60862	97086	34595	62491	100959	35925	65034
A Wholesale and retail trade	82231	26928	55303	84605	28040	56565	87589	29357	58232	91268	30583	60685
B Restaurants and hotels	9305	5132	4173	9585	5288	4297	9497	5238	4259	9691	5342	4349
7 Transport, storage and communication	64687	31661	33026	66985	33098	33887	70507	35060	35447	72083	34518	37565
A Transport and storage	46412	24800	21612	46864	25447	21417	49645	27303	22342	49686	26418	23268
B Communication	18275	6861	11414	20121	7651	12470	20862	7757	13105	22397	8100	14297
8 Finance, insurance, real estate and business services [a]	124628	59871	64757	127711	61755	65956	134555	67964	66591	140453	71569	68884
A Financial institutions	22816	23910	-1094	23490	24656	-1166	26254	28439	-2185	27553	30762	-3209
B Insurance	6566	1698	4868	6803	1650	5153	7245	1787	5458	7440	1750	5690
C Real estate and business services	95246	34263	60983	97418	35449	61969	101056	37738	63318	105460	39057	66403
Real estate, except dwellings	7426	3978	3448	7738	4147	3591	8115	4350	3765	8788	4718	4070
Dwellings	58237	18826	39411	59062	19320	39742	59628	20122	39506	60282	19852	40430
9 Community, social and personal services	32149	14706	17443	32813	14662	18151	33237	14807	18430	34570	15311	19259
A Sanitary and similar services	6451	2241	4210	6581	2285	4296	6793	2347	4446	7296	2478	4818
B Social and related community services	5616	1690	3926	5727	1735	3992	5707	1745	3962	5902	1787	4115
Educational services	...	...	...	...	...	...	...	...	...	...	...	...
Medical, dental, other health and veterinary services	2076	841	1235	2185	885	1300	2277	922	1355	2247	910	1337
C Recreational and cultural services	7891	4306	3585	8137	4081	4056	8306	4116	4190	8509	4225	4284
D Personal and household services	12191	6469	5722	12368	6561	5807	12431	6599	5832	12863	6821	6042
Total, Industries	802099	430333	371766	819604	437765	381839	833392	447200	386192	862264	462052	400212
Producers of Government Services	169469	44255	125214	172684	46311	126373	175400	47514	127886	177843	49379	128464
Other Producers	5794	1596	4198	5754	1589	4165	5925	1643	4282	6110	1695	4415

Sweden

4.2 Derivation of Value Added by Kind of Activity, in Constant Prices
(Continued)

Million Swedish kronor

	1984 Gross Output	1984 Intermediate Consumption	1984 Value Added	1985 Gross Output	1985 Intermediate Consumption	1985 Value Added	1986 Gross Output	1986 Intermediate Consumption	1986 Value Added	1987 Gross Output	1987 Intermediate Consumption	1987 Value Added
				At constant prices of:1980								
Total [b]	977362	476184	501178	998042	485665	512377	1014720	496357	518360	1046220	513126	533091
Less: Imputed bank service charge [a]	...	...	...	...	...	...	...	...	...	...	...	...
Import duties	1882	...	1882	2060	...	2060	2020	...	2020	2484	...	2484
Value added tax [c]	53584	...	53584	56330	...	56330	58129	...	58129	60628	...	60628
Other adjustments	5239	...	5239	3131	...	3131	1640	...	1640	-1983	...	-1983
Total	1038070	476184	561883	1059560	485665	573898	1076510	496357	580149	1107350	513126	594220
Memorandum Item: Mineral fuels and power [d]	42442	26157	16285	46002	27128	18874	40812	21956	18856	43002	23223	19779

a) Item 'Less: Imputed bank service charge' is netted out of item 'Finance, insurance, real estate and business services'.
b) Gross domestic product in basic values.
c) Item 'Value added tax' relates to value added tax and other taxes and subsidies on sales and production of commodities.
d) Item 'Mineral fuels and power' refers to ISIC categories 353 (Petroleum refineries), 354 (Manufacture of miscellaneous products of petroleum and coal) and 41 (Electricity, gas and steam).

4.3 Cost Components of Value Added

Million Swedish kronor

	1980 Compensation of Employees	1980 Capital Consumption	1980 Net Operating Surplus	1980 Indirect Taxes	1980 Less: Subsidies Received	1980 Value Added	1981 Compensation of Employees	1981 Capital Consumption	1981 Net Operating Surplus	1981 Indirect Taxes	1981 Less: Subsidies Received	1981 Value Added
				All Producers								
1 Agriculture, hunting, forestry and fishing	4767	3498	8434	379	249	16829	5173	3851	9502	450	351	18625
A Agriculture and hunting	1904	2734	4768	256	249	9413	2117	3010	5396	292	351	10464
B Forestry and logging	2835	679	3413	119	-	7046	3030	748	3879	154	-	7811
C Fishing	28	85	253	4	-	370	26	93	227	4	-	350
2 Mining and quarrying	1593	522	297	37	-	2449	1628	576	-11	42	-	2235
A Coal mining	...	...	...	...	...	...	...	...	...	...	...	...
B Crude petroleum and natural gas production	...	...	...	...	...	...	...	...	...	...	...	...
C Metal ore mining	1232	404	50	24	...	1710	1267	454	-319	28	-	1430
D Other mining	361	118	247	13	...	739	361	122	308	14	...	805
3 Manufacturing	86936	13230	11854	1983	2985	111018	92634	14599	9494	2265	3280	115712
A Manufacture of food, beverages and tobacco	6805	1340	3313	192	...	11650	7312	1472	3496	225	...	12505
B Textile, wearing apparel and leather industries	3264	476	22	79	26	3815	3323	506	-185	88	13	3719
C Manufacture of wood and wood products, including furniture	6504	1035	2148	159	-	9846	6549	1127	1310	178	-	9164
D Manufacture of paper and paper products, printing and publishing	12352	2770	404	266	381	15411	12847	3090	451	300	349	16339
E Manufacture of chemicals and chemical petroleum, coal, rubber and plastic products	7207	1606	2047	193	-	11053	7785	1769	655	184	-	10393
F Manufacture of non-metallic mineral products, except products of petroleum and coal	2733	563	512	67	...	3875	2778	612	426	74	...	3890
G Basic metal industries	6357	1414	-1435	126	...	6462	6765	1561	-2114	150	...	6362
H Manufacture of fabricated metal products, machinery and equipment	39553	3966	4127	854	347	48153	43078	4398	4613	1014	582	52521
I Other manufacturing industries	2161	60	716	47	2231	753	2197	64	842	52	2336	819
4 Electricity, gas and water	2958	4297	5920	115	197	13093	3301	4830	7151	138	272	15148
A Electricity, gas and steam	2787	3423	5972	112	124	12170	3126	3897	7055	134	183	14029
B Water works and supply	171	874	-52	3	73	923	175	933	96	4	89	1119
5 Construction	26277	1694	9895	809	...	38675	28392	1929	11593	930	...	42844
6 Wholesale and retail trade, restaurants and hotels	40911	3637	12522	1227	...	58297	44545	3951	10519	1398	...	60413
A Wholesale and retail trade	37850	3392	11832	1154	...	54228	41134	3677	9808	1308	...	55927
B Restaurants and hotels	3061	245	690	73	...	4069	3411	274	711	90	...	4486
7 Transport, storage and communication	22049	7647	4057	1346	3372	31727	23922	8358	4965	1516	4123	34638
A Transport and storage	16402	4974	2738	1202	3372	21944	17673	5393	3083	1365	4093	23421
B Communication	5647	2673	1319	144	-	9783	6249	2965	1882	151	30	11217
8 Finance, insurance, real estate and business services [ab]	20517	18898	22428	1732	4655	58920	22442	21604	25319	2317	6560	65122
A Financial institutions	4910	352	-6577	111	...	-1204	5422	402	-6907	137	3	-949

Sweden

4.3 Cost Components of Value Added
(Continued)

Million Swedish kronor

	1980						1981					
	Compensation of Employees	Capital Consumption	Net Operating Surplus	Indirect Taxes	Less: Subsidies Received	Value Added	Compensation of Employees	Capital Consumption	Net Operating Surplus	Indirect Taxes	Less: Subsidies Received	Value Added
B Insurance	2553	180	1558	55	...	4346	2769	202	1249	67	...	4287
C Real estate and business services	13054	18366	27447	1566	4655	55778	14251	21000	30977	2113	6557	61784
Real estate, except dwellings	...	521	2210	120	22	2829	...	596	2893	132	27	3594
Dwellings	2360	16114	23699	1230	4424	38979	2566	18256	27369	1717	6300	43608
9 Community, social and personal services	14661	631	3975	354	2391	17230	15670	663	3995	409	2556	18181
A Sanitary and similar services	2205	44	1707	50	79	3927	2501	49	1587	61	98	4100
B Social and related community services	5185	26	703	111	1949	4076	5374	23	565	127	2025	4064
Educational services	...	...	...	...	...	...	...	...	...	...	...	...
Medical, dental, other health and veterinary services	2541	...	516	51	1844	1264	2644	...	417	59	1894	1226
C Recreational and cultural services [c]	3020	...	898	72	363	3627	3306	...	961	84	433	3918
D Personal and household services	4251	48	1180	121	...	5600	4489	50	1423	137	...	6099
Total, Industries	220669	54054	79382	7982	13849	348238	237707	60361	82527	9465	17142	372918
Producers of Government Services	108627	5367	...	2042	...	116036	118747	6118	...	2524	...	127389
Other Producers	3788	...	...	72	-	3860	4016	...	...	85	-	4101
Total [d]	333084	59421	79382	10096	13849	468134	360470	66479	82527	12074	17142	504408
Less: Imputed bank service charge [a]	...	...	...	...	...	...	...	...	...	...	...	...
Import duties	...	...	...	1760	...	1760	...	...	...	1927	...	1927
Value added tax [e]	...	...	...	61372	7353	54019	...	...	...	72279	7832	64447
Other adjustments	4001	...	517	-1891	1441	1186	7893	...	...	-1429	-2496	1710	2258
Total	337085	59421	79899	71337	22643	525099	368363	66479	81098	83784	26684	573040

	1982						1983					
	Compensation of Employees	Capital Consumption	Net Operating Surplus	Indirect Taxes	Less: Subsidies Received	Value Added	Compensation of Employees	Capital Consumption	Net Operating Surplus	Indirect Taxes	Less: Subsidies Received	Value Added

All Producers

1 Agriculture, hunting, forestry and fishing	5330	4313	10757	502	352	20550	5712	4909	11241	984	360	22486
A Agriculture and hunting	2167	3371	6717	301	352	12204	2272	3836	6110	508	360	12366
B Forestry and logging	3132	834	3795	197	-	7958	3407	946	4809	467	-	9629
C Fishing	31	108	245	4	-	388	33	127	322	9	-	491
2 Mining and quarrying	1634	658	500	42	350	2484	1691	740	1097	76	390	3214
A Coal mining	...	...	...	...	...	...	...	...	...	...	...	...
B Crude petroleum and natural gas production	...	...	...	...	...	...	...	...	...	...	...	...
C Metal ore mining	1258	518	252	28	350	1706	1278	581	896	53	390	2418
D Other mining	376	140	248	14	...	778	413	159	201	23	...	796
3 Manufacturing	96003	16588	13391	2411	2722	125671	100329	18837	26351	4448	2915	147050
A Manufacture of food, beverages and tobacco	7700	1662	3949	233	...	13544	8071	1886	4998	413	...	15368
B Textile, wearing apparel and leather industries	3238	551	-201	85	17	3656	3278	598	74	156	25	4081
C Manufacture of wood and wood products, including furniture	6549	1257	1225	176	-	9207	6884	1433	2292	324	-	10933
D Manufacture of paper and paper products, printing and publishing	13249	3545	2001	307	374	18728	14176	4025	3800	612	462	22151
E Manufacture of chemicals and chemical petroleum, coal, rubber and plastic products	8105	2037	2050	273	-	12465	8658	2345	3576	375	-	14954
F Manufacture of non-metallic mineral products, except products of petroleum and coal	2787	683	868	74	...	4412	2736	759	1127	127	...	4749
G Basic metal industries	6789	1763	-1111	150	...	7591	6767	1971	-461	287	...	8564
H Manufacture of fabricated metal products, machinery and equipment	45173	5019	4150	1056	227	55171	47018	5742	10699	2035	45	65449
I Other manufacturing industries	2413	71	460	57	2104	897	2741	78	246	119	2383	801
4 Electricity, gas and water	3592	5585	6909	157	293	15950	3964	6461	8528	250	406	18797
A Electricity, gas and steam	3415	4547	6737	153	170	14682	3777	5299	8433	242	257	17494
B Water works and supply	177	1038	172	4	123	1268	187	1162	95	8	149	1303

Sweden

4.3 Cost Components of Value Added
(Continued)

Million Swedish kronor

		1982						1983					
		Compensation of Employees	Capital Consumption	Net Operating Surplus	Indirect Taxes	Less: Subsidies Received	Value Added	Compensation of Employees	Capital Consumption	Net Operating Surplus	Indirect Taxes	Less: Subsidies Received	Value Added
5	Construction	29357	2090	12449	835	...	44731	29952	2254	13611	1494	...	47311
6	Wholesale and retail trade, restaurants and hotels	46719	4452	12529	1476	...	65176	50359	5092	16194	2685	...	74330
	A Wholesale and retail trade	42989	4129	11681	1378	...	60177	46236	4720	15110	2487	...	68553
	B Restaurants and hotels	3730	323	848	98	...	4999	4123	372	1084	198	...	5777
7	Transport, storage and communication	26024	9350	5496	1600	5091	37379	27938	10629	5830	2286	6021	40662
	A Transport and storage	18973	5979	4109	1437	5034	25464	20439	6837	4408	1961	5970	27675
	B Communication	7051	3371	1387	163	57	11915	7499	3792	1422	325	51	12987
8	Finance, insurance, real estate and business services [a,b]	24551	23986	33293	2435	9722	74543	27936	26802	37006	3117	11577	83284
	A Financial institutions	5955	460	-6663	150	1087	-1185	6559	521	-7459	285	1729	-1823
	B Insurance	3040	225	480	73	...	3818	3458	250	-156	148	...	3700
	C Real estate and business services	15556	23301	39476	2212	8635	71910	17919	26031	44621	2684	9848	81407
	Real estate, except dwellings	...	677	3798	144	31	4588	...	771	4652	147	37	5533
	Dwellings	2817	19825	34438	1781	8369	50492	3299	21499	39295	1912	9570	56435
9	Community, social and personal services	16410	738	4978	432	2624	19934	17418	818	5932	835	2806	22197
	A Sanitary and similar services	2638	55	2071	65	109	4720	2781	61	2386	125	131	5222
	B Social and related community services	5616	22	951	133	2051	4671	6060	23	1100	264	2145	5302
	Educational services	...	...	...	...	...	...	...	...	...	...	...	...
	Medical, dental, other health and veterinary services	2795	...	720	63	1990	1588	3018	...	813	130	2097	1864
	C Recreational and cultural services [c]	3516	...	714	91	464	3857	3726	...	1186	174	530	4556
	D Personal and household services	4640	56	1847	143	...	6686	4851	69	1925	272	...	7117
Total, Industries		249620	67760	100302	9890	21154	406418	265299	76542	125790	16175	24475	459331
Producers of Government Services		129076	6915	...	2722	...	138713	139801	7797	...	5656	...	153254
Other Producers		4475	...	...	96	-	4571	4740	...	...	194	-	4934
Total [d]		383171	74675	100302	12708	21154	549702	409840	84339	125790	22025	24475	617519
Less: Imputed bank service charge [a]		...	...	...	...	...	...	...	...	...	...	...	...
Import duties		...	...	...	2160	...	2160	...	...	...	2192	...	2192
Value added tax [e]		...	...	...	79394	7831	71563	...	...	...	88155	9556	78599
Other adjustments		6355	...	2456	-2467	2091	4253	11759	...	2843	-4728	2819	7055
Total		389526	74675	102758	91795	31076	627678	421599	84339	128633	107644	36850	705365

		1984						1985					
		Compensation of Employees	Capital Consumption	Net Operating Surplus	Indirect Taxes	Less: Subsidies Received	Value Added	Compensation of Employees	Capital Consumption	Net Operating Surplus	Indirect Taxes	Less: Subsidies Received	Value Added

All Producers

1	Agriculture, hunting, forestry and fishing	6220	5210	13657	1044	570	25561	6332	5502	13605	996	548	25887
	A Agriculture and hunting	2550	4193	6807	487	570	13467	2566	4454	5927	494	548	12893
	B Forestry and logging	3625	877	6521	548	-	11571	3706	909	7370	492	-	12477
	C Fishing	45	140	329	9	-	523	60	139	308	10	-	517
2	Mining and quarrying	1814	779	1164	76	-	3833	1976	818	1534	86	-	4414
	A Coal mining	...	...	...	...	...	...	...	...	...	...	...	...
	B Crude petroleum and natural gas production	...	...	...	...	...	...	...	...	...	...	...	...
	C Metal ore mining	1343	611	982	51	-	2987	1429	643	1405	56	-	3533
	D Other mining	471	168	182	25	...	846	547	175	129	30	...	881

Sweden

4.3 Cost Components of Value Added
(Continued)

Million Swedish kronor

	1984 Compensation of Employees	1984 Capital Consumption	1984 Net Operating Surplus	1984 Indirect Taxes	1984 Less: Subsidies Received	1984 Value Added	1985 Compensation of Employees	1985 Capital Consumption	1985 Net Operating Surplus	1985 Indirect Taxes	1985 Less: Subsidies Received	1985 Value Added
3 Manufacturing	111910	19981	34797	4512	3150	168050	124544	21313	35572	5219	3323	183325
A Manufacture of food, beverages and tobacco	8946	1983	4888	404	...	16221	9790	2102	5960	474	...	18326
B Textile, wearing apparel and leather industries	3604	611	127	158	43	4457	3889	625	344	175	56	4977
C Manufacture of wood and wood products, including furniture	7533	1510	2906	324	-	12273	8007	1571	1459	355	-	11392
D Manufacture of paper and paper products, printing and publishing	15990	4254	6341	628	467	26746	17617	4550	5223	712	464	27638
E Manufacture of chemicals and chemical petroleum, coal, rubber and plastic products	9885	2504	5518	390	-	18297	11097	2691	5864	497	-	20149
F Manufacture of non-metallic mineral products, except products of petroleum and coal	2974	789	1098	125	...	4986	3315	826	1037	144	...	5322
G Basic metal industries	6858	2057	216	265	...	9396	7609	2152	61	302	...	10124
H Manufacture of fabricated metal products, machinery and equipment	53178	6192	13393	2101	5	74859	59935	6709	15251	2426	27	84294
I Other manufacturing industries	2942	81	310	117	2635	815	3285	87	373	134	2776	1103
4 Electricity, gas and water	4245	7090	10635	248	429	21789	4557	7723	13246	268	554	25240
A Electricity, gas and steam	4080	5822	10585	242	268	20461	4383	6351	13269	261	363	23901
B Water works and supply	165	1268	50	6	161	1328	174	1372	-23	7	191	1339
5 Construction	32686	2374	14266	1497	...	50823	35519	2474	14039	1676	...	53708
6 Wholesale and retail trade, restaurants and hotels	56768	5558	20954	2808	...	86088	62735	6144	23859	3227	...	95965
A Wholesale and retail trade	51931	5139	19626	2597	...	79293	57153	5676	22236	2982	...	88047
B Restaurants and hotels	4837	419	1328	211	...	6795	5582	468	1623	245	...	7918
7 Transport, storage and communication	30807	11538	6393	2240	6700	44278	34232	12560	5852	2514	6637	48521
A Transport and storage	22724	7503	4965	1915	6655	30452	25089	8199	4734	2129	6598	33553
B Communication	8083	4035	1428	325	45	13826	9143	4361	1118	385	39	14968
8 Finance, insurance, real estate and business services [a,b]	32066	29839	37913	4068	12157	91729	34927	32793	37583	7418	14123	98598
A Financial institutions	7578	578	-9506	1132	1357	-1575	8314	641	-11370	1514	1193	-2094
B Insurance	3851	273	-1163	152	...	3113	4218	305	-1599	169	...	3093
C Real estate and business services	20637	28988	48582	2784	10800	90191	22395	31847	50552	5735	12930	97599
Real estate, except dwellings	...	862	5283	157	39	6263	...	968	5101	26	44	6051
Dwellings	3468	23601	42506	1965	10532	61008	3721	25303	44609	4964	12633	65964
9 Community, social and personal services	18807	874	6210	848	3023	23716	20597	948	7808	945	3155	27143
A Sanitary and similar services	3123	68	2003	128	138	5184	3427	75	2458	145	158	5947
B Social and related community services	6451	26	1407	257	2330	5811	6948	35	1529	282	2472	6322
Educational services	...	...	...	...	...	...	...	...	...	...	...	...
Medical, dental, other health and veterinary services	3144	...	1004	124	2330	1942	3416	...	1122	137	2462	2213
C Recreational and cultural services [c]	4060	...	1180	192	555	4877	4452	...	1977	213	525	6117
D Personal and household services	5173	81	2319	271	...	7844	5770	97	2585	305	...	8757
Total, Industries	295323	83243	145989	17341	26029	515867	325419	90275	153098	22349	28340	562801
Producers of Government Services	151694	8509	...	5584	...	165787	161691	9189	...	6129	...	177009
Other Producers	5058	...	...	188	-	5246	5330	...	...	204	-	5534
Total [d]	452075	91752	145989	23113	26029	686900	492440	99464	153098	28682	28340	745344
Less: Imputed bank service charge [a]	.	...	...	...	...	...	...	...	...	...	...	...
Import duties	...	...	...	2520	...	2520	...	...	...	2736	...	2736
Value added tax [e]	...	...	...	98680	9542	89138	...	...	...	112446	10717	101729
Other adjustments	9358	...	3305	1948	3586	11025	9939	...	6805	-2619	3050	11075
Total	461433	91752	149294	126261	39157	789583	502379	99464	159903	141245	42107	860884

Sweden

4.3 Cost Components of Value Added

Million Swedish kronor

		1986						1987				
	Compensation of Employees	Capital Consumption	Net Operating Surplus	Indirect Taxes	Less: Subsidies Received	Value Added	Compensation of Employees	Capital Consumption	Net Operating Surplus	Indirect Taxes	Less: Subsidies Received	Value Added

All Producers

1 Agriculture, hunting, forestry and fishing	6848	...	...	1178	961	27434	7414	...	...	1219	807	28726
A Agriculture and hunting	2776	...	...	539	951	13579	2974	...	...	514	807	13844
B Forestry and logging	3989	...	...	627	10	13273	4337	...	...	691	-	14254
C Fishing	83	...	...	12	-	582	103	...	...	14	-	628
2 Mining and quarrying	2001	...	...	91	-	3606	1965	...	...	92	-	3467
A Coal mining	...					*	...					...
B Crude petroleum and natural gas production				...						...		...
C Metal ore mining	1439	...	...	58	-	2759	1369	...	...	58	-	2652
D Other mining	562	...	...	33		847	596	...	...	34		815
3 Manufacturing	133255	...	...	5857	3603	193524	141993	...	...	6395	3782	208634
A Manufacture of food, beverages and tobacco	10441	...	...	537	...	20048	11366	...	...	590	...	20044
B Textile, wearing apparel and leather industries	3949	...	...	189	75	5419	4084	...	...	200	186	5458
C Manufacture of wood and wood products, including furniture	8385	...	...	395	-	11915	9078	...	...	432	-	13236
D Manufacture of paper and paper products, printing and publishing	19096	...	...	806	585	28312	20297	...	...	883	478	33845
E Manufacture of chemicals and chemical petroleum, coal, rubber and plastic products	12166	...	...	563	-	22063	12992	...	...	616	-	24757
F Manufacture of non-metallic mineral products, except products of petroleum and coal	3509	...	...	161	...	5800	3791	...	...	177	...	6552
G Basic metal industries	7674	...	...	318	...	9961	8045	...	...	345	...	10664
H Manufacture of fabricated metal products, machinery and equipment	64527	...	...	2739	-	88796	68620	...	...	2989	15	92784
I Other manufacturing industries	3508	...	...	149	2943	1210	3720	...	...	163	3103	1294
4 Electricity, gas and water	4996	...	...	329	609	26850	5336	...	...	361	607	28739
A Electricity, gas and steam	4822	...	...	322	393	25423	5148	...	...	353	393	27258
B Water works and supply	174	...	...	7	216	1427	188	...	...	8	214	1481
5 Construction	39342	...	...	1945	...	56270	43755	...	...	2172	...	62335
6 Wholesale and retail trade, restaurants and hotels	68495	...	...	3499	...	105792	75710	...	...	3775	...	114746
A Wholesale and retail trade	62527	...	...	3225	...	96614	68778	...	...	3451	...	104396
B Restaurants and hotels	5968	...	...	274	...	9178	6932	...	...	324	...	10350
7 Transport, storage and communication	38139	...	...	2949	6866	54598	41862	...	...	3055	7302	60435
A Transport and storage	27709	...	...	2502	6833	37575	30820	...	...	2568	7272	40665
B Communication	10430	...	...	447	33	17023	11042	...	...	487	30	19770
8 Finance, insurance, real estate and business services [ab]	39347	...	...	10381	14505	110597	45535	...	...	10159	14734	123802
A Financial institutions	9163	...	...	3057	866	-1758	11032	...	...	4221	455	-2489
B Insurance	4624	...	...	195	...	2834	5130	...	...	223	...	3346
C Real estate and business services	25560	...	...	7129	13639	109521	29373	...	...	5715	14279	122945
Real estate, except dwellings	...	...	...	26	43	8463	...	...	...	-	45	10265
Dwellings	4447	...	...	6227	13345	71934	4662	...	...	4659	13943	79459
9 Community, social and personal services	22032	...	...	1067	3424	30119	25157	...	...	1228	3880	33169
A Sanitary and similar services	3834	...	...	169	154	7277	4440	...	...	199	162	8365
B Social and related community services	7236	...	...	313	2780	6567	8404	...	...	372	3194	7050
Educational services	...	...	...	...	...	...	...	...	...	...	...	...
Medical, dental, other health and veterinary services	3742	...	...	158	2780	2346	4476	...	...	195	3194	2295
C Recreational and cultural services [c]	4776	...	...	243	490	6784	5326	...	...	275	524	7404
D Personal and household services	6186	...	...	342	...	9491	6987	...	...	382	...	10350

Sweden

4.3 Cost Components of Value Added
(Continued)

Million Swedish kronor

	1986						1987					
	Compensation of Employees	Capital Consumption	Net Operating Surplus	Indirect Taxes	Less: Subsidies Received	Value Added	Compensation of Employees	Capital Consumption	Net Operating Surplus	Indirect Taxes	Less: Subsidies Received	Value Added
Total, Industries	354455	97451	159556	27296	29968	608790	388727	106049	171933	28456	31112	664053
Producers of Government Services	174978	9735	...	7003	...	191716	183010	10427	...	7815	...	201252
Other Producers	5826	...	...	234	-	6060	6343	...	...	264	-	6607
Total [d]	535259	107186	159556	34533	29968	806566	578080	116476	171933	36535	31112	871912
Less: Imputed bank service charge [a]	...	...	...	...	...	...	...	...	...	...	...	...
Import duties	...	...	...	3044	...	3044	...	...	...	3544	...	3544
Value added tax [e]	...	...	...	120373	11411	108962	...	...	...	132014	12046	119968
Other adjustments	14153	...	-2752	5445	3634	13212	17584	...	-7629	3147	3300	9802
Total	549412	107186	156804	163395	45013	931784	595664	116476	164304	175240	46458	1005230

a) Item 'Less: Imputed bank service charge' is netted out of item 'Finance, insurance, real estate and business services'.
b) Column 'Operating Surplus' is reduced for imputed bank service charges.
c) Column 'Consumption of fixed capital' is included in column 'Net operating surplus'.
d) Gross domestic product in basic values.
e) Item 'Value added tax' relates to value added tax and other taxes and subsidies on sales and production of commodities.

Switzerland

Source. Reply to the United Nations National Accounts Questionnaire from the Federal Bureau of Statistics, Bern. The official estimates are published annually by the Bureau in the September issue of 'La Vie Economique', and in 'Series revisees de la compatabilite nationale suisse, 1948-1976'.

General note. The estimates shown in the following tables have been adjusted to conform to the United Nations System of National Accounts so far as the existing data would permit.

1.1 Expenditure on the Gross Domestic Product, in Current Prices

Million Swiss francs

		1970	1975	1978	1979	1980	1981	1982	1983	1984	1985	1986	1987
1	Government final consumption expenditure	9505	17685	19510	20520	21685	23545	25555	27355	28500	30420	31845	32650
2	Private final consumption expenditure	53455	86270	95540	101000	108335	116020	122440	127755	134035	141015	145405	150560
3	Gross capital formation	29245	32200	32925	37840	46320	47010	47095	48845	51300	55565	63365	70020
	A Increase in stocks	4290	-1455	435	3255	5820	2450	1795	1345	1500	1365	4370	5650
	B Gross fixed capital formation	24955	33655	32490	34585	40500	44560	45300	47500	49800	54200	58995	64370
	Residential buildings												
	Non-residential buildings	15455	22445	21380	23410	27500	30800	31800	32750	34200	35900	38590	41870
	Other construction and land improvement etc.												
	Other	9500	11210	11110	11175	13000	13760	13500	14750	15600	18300	20405	22500
4	Exports of goods and services	29710	44030	53225	56015	62580	69100	69550	71760	80550	89015	89115	90245
5	Less: Imports of goods and services	31250	40030	49525	56830	68590	70920	68660	71850	81155	88065	86380	88345
	Equals: Gross Domestic Product	90665	140155	151675	158545	170330	184755	195980	203865	213230	227950	243350	255130

1.2 Expenditure on the Gross Domestic Product, in Constant Prices

Million Swiss francs

		1970	1975	1978	1979	1980	1981	1982	1983	1984	1985	1986	1987
						At constant prices of:1970							
1	Government final consumption expenditure	9505	10850	11420	11540	11650	11935	12040	12495	12645	13060	13570	13880
2	Private final consumption expenditure	53455	58615	62390	63185	64845	65140	65140	66180	67195	68180	70080	71455
3	Gross capital formation	29245	23295	23895	27325	31260	29460	28285	29175	30445	32025	36490	39795
	A Increase in stocks	4290	-1210	250	2475	3945	1490	1060	790	875	780	2580	3300
	B Gross fixed capital formation	24955	24505	23645	24850	27315	27970	27225	28385	29570	31245	33910	36495
	Residential buildings												
	Non-residential buildings	15455	15905	14910	15650	17070	17770	17490	18015	18750	19300	20120	21150
	Other construction and land improvement etc.												
	Other	9500	8600	8735	9200	10245	10200	9735	10370	10820	11945	13790	15345
4	Exports of goods and services	29710	33425	41575	42600	44760	46840	45445	45880	48805	52875	53085	53965
5	Less: Imports of goods and services	31250	31790	43555	46540	49890	49260	47970	50095	53640	56375	60370	63645
	Equals: Gross Domestic Product	90665	94395	95725	98110	102625	104115	102940	103635	105450	109765	112855	115450

1.3 Cost Components of the Gross Domestic Product

Million Swiss francs

		1970	1975	1978	1979	1980	1981	1982	1983	1984	1985	1986	1987
1	Indirect taxes, net	5615	7435	8590	8890	9660	10510	10720	11320	11850	12630	14060	14780
	A Indirect taxes	6375	9115	10775	11105	11910	12670	13315	14145	14895	15875	17375	18310
	B Less: Subsidies	760	1680	2185	2215	2250	2160	2595	2825	3045	3245	3315	3530
2	Consumption of fixed capital	10770	15245	16430	16700	17960	19550	20400	20900	21700	23400	24395	25640
3	Compensation of employees paid by resident producers to:	49605	85150	92185	97095	104650	114120	122700	128155	133425	141525	150455	158140
	A Resident households	48535	82545	89775	94500	101740	110670	118910	124330	129490	137300	145765	152910
	B Rest of the world	1070	2605	2410	2595	2910	3450	3790	3825	3935	4225	4690	5230
4	Operating surplus	24675	32325	34470	35860	38060	40575	42160	43490	46255	50395	54440	56570
	Equals: Gross Domestic Product	90665	140155	151675	158545	170330	184755	195980	203865	213230	227950	243350	255130

1.4 General Government Current Receipts and Disbursements

Million Swiss francs

		1970	1975	1978	1979	1980	1981	1982	1983	1984	1985	1986	1987
						Receipts							
1	Operating surplus	...	...	...	...	...	...	...	...	...	...	...	...
2	Property and entrepreneurial income	1420	2235	2245	2145	2505	2940	3020	2975	2995	3210	3490	3635
3	Taxes, fees and contributions	22035	41780	47745	48980	51925	56070	60330	63995	68640	72520	78700	81345
	A Indirect taxes	6375	9115	10775	11105	11910	12670	13315	14145	14895	15875	17375	18310

Switzerland

1.4 General Government Current Receipts and Disbursements
(Continued)

Million Swiss francs

	1970	1975	1978	1979	1980	1981	1982	1983	1984	1985	1986	1987
B Direct taxes	10130	20215	21865	21965	23340	25480	27720	29085	31070	32500	35650	36010
C Social security contributions	5065	11655	14125	14845	15550	16710	18035	19390	21165	22495	23900	25155
D Compulsory fees, fines and penalties	465	795	980	1065	1125	1210	1260	1375	1510	1650	1775	1870
4 Other current transfers	565	960	1285	1345	1480	1655	1905	2155	2430	2765	3075	3140
Total Current Receipts of General Government	24020	44975	51275	52470	55910	60665	65255	69125	74065	78495	85265	88120

Disbursements

	1970	1975	1978	1979	1980	1981	1982	1983	1984	1985	1986	1987
1 Government final consumption expenditure	9505	17685	19510	20520	21685	23545	25555	27355	28500	30420	31845	32650
2 Property income	1330	2735	3120	3025	3130	3375	3535	3630	3590	3695	3750	3710
3 Subsidies	760	1680	2185	2215	2250	2160	2595	2825	3045	3245	3315	3530
4 Other current transfers	7700	18190	21035	21655	22795	24245	27365	29085	31790	33320	35350	36920
A Social security benefits	5670	14205	16350	16840	17575	18600	21050	22425	24595	25555	27140	28120
B Social assistance grants	1755	3295	3685	3725	4000	4355	4835	5050	5395	5780	6070	6455
C Other	275	690	1000	1090	1220	1290	1480	1610	1800	1985	2140	2345
5 Net saving	4725	4685	5425	5055	6050	7340	6205	6230	7140	7815	11005	11310
Total Current Disbursements and Net Saving of General Government	24020	44975	51275	52470	55910	60665	65255	69125	74065	78495	85265	88120

1.6 Current Income and Outlay of Households and Non-Profit Institutions

Million Swiss francs

	1970	1975	1978	1979	1980	1981	1982	1983	1984	1985	1986	1987

Receipts

	1970	1975	1978	1979	1980	1981	1982	1983	1984	1985	1986	1987
1 Compensation of employees	48965	83370	90735	95485	102760	111540	119810	125310	130490	138335	146745	153880
A From resident producers	48535	82545	89775	94500	101740	110670	118910	124330	129490	137300	145765	152910
B From rest of the world	430	825	960	985	1020	870	900	980	1000	1035	980	970
2 Operating surplus of private unincorporated enterprises [a]	...	...	...	...	...	...	...	...	...	...	...	...
3 Property and entrepreneurial income [b]	20640	29715	31055	32200	34115	37785	39395	40685	43750	45500	46650	47980
4 Current transfers	7665	17775	20310	20840	21915	23295	26225	27830	30345	31710	33595	34960
A Social security benefits	5670	14205	16350	16840	17575	18600	21050	22425	24595	25555	27140	28120
B Social assistance grants	...	...	...	...	...	...	4835	5050	5395	5780	6070	6455
C Other	1995	3570	3960	4000	4340	4695	340	355	355	375	385	385
Total Current Receipts	77270	130860	142100	148525	158790	172620	185430	193825	204585	215545	226990	236820

Disbursements

	1970	1975	1978	1979	1980	1981	1982	1983	1984	1985	1986	1987
1 Private final consumption expenditure	53455	86270	95540	101000	108335	116020	122440	127755	134035	141015	145405	150560
2 Property income [b]	...	...	...	...	...	...	...	...	...	...	...	...
3 Direct taxes and other current transfers n.e.c. to general government	13855	29000	33605	34790	36710	39730	42940	45475	49220	51755	55615	57145
A Social security contributions	5065	11655	14125	14845	15550	16710	18035	19390	21165	22495	23900	25155
B Direct taxes	8790	17345	19480	19945	21160	23020	24905	26085	28055	29260	31715	31990
C Fees, fines and penalties	...	...	...	...	...	...	...	...	...	...	...	...
4 Other current transfers	1555	1810	1420	1470	1835	2120	2260	2295	2345	2490	2605	2740
5 Net saving	8405	13780	11535	11265	11910	14750	17790	18300	18985	20285	23365	26375
Total Current Disbursements and Net Saving	77270	130860	142100	148525	158790	172620	185430	193825	204585	215545	226990	236820

a) Item 'Operating surplus of private unincorporated enterprises' is included in item 'Property and entrepreneurial income'.
b) Item 'Property and entrepreneurial income' received is net of item 'Property income' paid.

1.7 External Transactions on Current Account, Summary

Million Swiss francs

	1970	1975	1978	1979	1980	1981	1982	1983	1984	1985	1986	1987

Payments to the Rest of the World

	1970	1975	1978	1979	1980	1981	1982	1983	1984	1985	1986	1987
1 Imports of goods and services	31250	40030	49525	56830	68590	70920	68660	71850	81155	88065	86380	88345
2 Factor income to the rest of the world	1610	3590	3755	3835	4235	5290	5950	6650	6965	7845	9020	9485
A Compensation of employees	1070	2605	2410	2595	2910	3450	3790	3825	3935	4225	4690	5230
B Property and entrepreneurial income	540	985	1345	1240	1325	1840	2160	2825	3030	3620	4330	4255

Switzerland

1.7 External Transactions on Current Account, Summary
(Continued)

Million Swiss francs

	1970	1975	1978	1979	1980	1981	1982	1983	1984	1985	1986	1987
3 Current transfers to the rest of the world	1830	2500	2420	2560	3055	3410	3740	3905	4145	4475	4745	5085
A Indirect taxes to supranational organizations	...	...	...	...	...	...	...	...	...	...	...	...
B Other current transfers	1830	2500	2420	2560	3055	3410	3740	3905	4145	4475	4745	5085
4 Surplus of the nation on current transactions	330	6820	8040	4285	-795	5430	8010	8075	10260	12375	12350	10805
Payments to the Rest of the World and Surplus of the Nation on Current Transactions	35020	52940	63740	67510	75085	85050	86360	90480	102525	112760	112495	113720

Receipts From The Rest of the World

	1970	1975	1978	1979	1980	1981	1982	1983	1984	1985	1986	1987
1 Exports of goods and services	29710	44030	53225	56015	62580	69100	69550	71760	80550	89015	89115	90245
2 Factor income from rest of the world	4875	8060	9575	10480	11250	14510	15140	16735	19795	21250	20595	20625
A Compensation of employees	430	825	960	985	1020	870	900	980	1000	1035	980	970
B Property and entrepreneurial income	4445	7235	8615	9495	10230	13640	14240	15755	18795	20215	19615	19655
3 Current transfers from rest of the world	435	850	940	1015	1255	1440	1670	1985	2180	2495	2785	2850
A Subsidies from supranational organisations	...	...	...	...	...	...	...	...	...	...	...	...
B Other current transfers	435	850	940	1015	1255	1440	1670	1985	2180	2495	2785	2850
Receipts from the Rest of the World on Current Transactions	35020	52940	63740	67510	75085	85050	86360	90480	102525	112760	112495	113720

1.8 Capital Transactions of The Nation, Summary

Million Swiss francs

	1970	1975	1978	1979	1980	1981	1982	1983	1984	1985	1986	1987

Finance of Gross Capital Formation

	1970	1975	1978	1979	1980	1981	1982	1983	1984	1985	1986	1987
Gross saving	29575	39020	40965	42125	45525	52440	55105	56920	61560	67940	75715	80825
1 Consumption of fixed capital	10770	15245	16430	16700	17960	19550	20400	20900	21700	23400	24395	25640
2 Net saving	18805	23775	24535	25425	27565	32890	34705	36020	39860	44540	51320	55185
A General government	4725	4685	5425	5055	6050	7340	6205	6230	7140	7815	11005	11310
B Corporate and quasi-corporate enterprises	5675	5310	7575	9105	9605	10800	10710	11490	13735	16440	16950	17500
C Other	8405	13780	11535	11265	11910	14750	17790	18300	18985	20285	23365	26375
Less: Surplus of the nation on current transactions	330	6820	8040	4285	-795	5430	8010	8075	10260	12375	12350	10805
Finance of Gross Capital Formation	29245	32200	32925	37840	46320	47010	47095	48845	51300	55565	63365	70020

Gross Capital Formation

	1970	1975	1978	1979	1980	1981	1982	1983	1984	1985	1986	1987
Increase in stocks	4290	-1455	435	3255	5820	2450	1795	1345	1500	1365	4370	5650
Gross fixed capital formation	24955	33655	32490	34585	40500	44560	45300	47500	49800	54200	58995	64370
Gross Capital Formation	29245	32200	32925	37840	46320	47010	47095	48845	51300	55565	63365	70020

1.10 Gross Domestic Product by Kind of Activity, in Current Prices

Million Swiss francs

	1970	1975	1978	1979	1980	1981	1982	1983	1984	1985	1986	1987
1 Agriculture, hunting, forestry and fishing	...	...	...	...	...	...	...	...	...	8180	...	...
2 Mining and quarrying	...	...	...	...	...	...	...	...	...	-	...	...
3 Manufacturing	...	...	...	...	...	...	...	...	...	58625	...	...
4 Electricity, gas and water	...	...	...	...	...	...	...	...	...	5023	...	...
5 Construction	...	...	...	...	...	...	...	...	...	17325	...	...
6 Wholesale and retail trade, restaurants and hotels	...	...	...	...	...	...	...	...	...	44077	...	...
7 Transport, storage and communication	...	...	...	...	...	...	...	...	...	14763	...	...
8 Finance, insurance, real estate and business services	...	...	...	...	...	...	...	...	...	36994	...	...
9 Community, social and personal services	...	...	...	...	...	...	...	...	...	18943	...	...

Switzerland

1.10 Gross Domestic Product by Kind of Activity, in Current Prices
(Continued)

Million Swiss francs

	1970	1975	1978	1979	1980	1981	1982	1983	1984	1985	1986	1987
Total, Industries	...	...	...	...	...	...	...	...	...	203930	...	...
Producers of Government Services	...	...	...	...	...	...	...	...	...	26065	...	...
Other Producers	...	...	...	...	...	...	...	...	...	4655	...	...
Subtotal	...	...	...	...	...	...	...	...	...	234650	...	...
Less: Imputed bank service charge	...	...	...	...	...	...	...	...	...	10400	...	...
Plus: Import duties	...	...	...	...	...	...	...	...	...	3700	...	...
Plus: Value added tax	...	...	...	...	...	...	...	...	...	...	...	...
Equals: Gross Domestic Product	...	...	...	...	...	...	...	...	...	227950	...	...

1.12 Relations Among National Accounting Aggregates

Million Swiss francs

	1970	1975	1978	1979	1980	1981	1982	1983	1984	1985	1986	1987
Gross Domestic Product	90665	140155	151675	158545	170330	184755	195980	203865	213230	227950	243350	255130
Plus: Net factor income from the rest of the world	3265	4470	5820	6645	7015	9220	9190	10085	12830	13405	11575	11140
Factor income from the rest of the world	4875	8060	9575	10480	11250	14510	15140	16735	19795	21250	20595	20625
Less: Factor income to the rest of the world	1610	3590	3755	3835	4235	5290	5950	6650	6965	7845	9020	9485
Equals: Gross National Product	93930	144625	157495	165190	177345	193975	205170	213950	226060	241355	254925	266270
Less: Consumption of fixed capital	10770	15245	16430	16700	17960	19550	20400	20900	21700	23400	24395	25640
Equals: National Income	83160	129380	141065	148490	159385	174425	184770	193050	204360	217955	230530	240630
Plus: Net current transfers from the rest of the world	-1395	-1650	-1480	-1545	-1800	-1970	-2070	-1920	-1965	-1980	-1960	-2235
Current transfers from the rest of the world	435	850	940	1015	1255	1440	1670	1985	2180	2495	2785	2850
Less: Current transfers to the rest of the world	1830	2500	2420	2560	3055	3410	3740	3905	4145	4475	4745	5085
Equals: National Disposable Income	81765	127730	139585	146945	157585	172455	182700	191130	202395	215975	228570	238395
Less: Final consumption	62960	103955	115050	121520	130020	139565	147995	155110	162535	171435	177250	183210
Equals: Net Saving	18805	23775	24535	25425	27565	32890	34705	36020	39860	44540	51320	55185
Less: Surplus of the nation on current transactions	330	6820	8040	4285	-795	5430	8010	8075	10260	12375	12350	10805
Equals: Net Capital Formation	18475	16955	16495	21140	28360	27460	26695	27945	29600	32165	38970	44380

2.5 Private Final Consumption Expenditure by Type and Purpose, in Current Prices

Million Swiss francs

	1970	1975	1978	1979	1980	1981	1982	1983	1984	1985	1986	1987
Final Consumption Expenditure of Resident Households												
1 Food, beverages and tobacco	16805	25515	26985	27955	29900	32085	33940	35330	36960	38655	40135	41005
A Food	11665	18070	19445	20140	21750	23290	24470	25530	26985	28250	29360	29945
B Non-alcoholic beverages	5140	7445	7540	7815	8150	8795	9470	9800	9975	10405	10775	11060
C Alcoholic beverages	...	...	...	...	...	...	...	...	...	...	...	...
D Tobacco	...	...	...	...	...	...	...	...	...	...	...	...
2 Clothing and footwear	3550	4670	4795	4855	5220	5555	5640	5855	6045	6340	6735	6880
3 Gross rent, fuel and power	9185	16220	18265	20060	20990	22270	23855	25120	26470	27805	27065	27580
A Fuel and power	2515	4840	5510	7090	7630	8095	8105	8235	8890	9380	7625	7225
B Other	6670	11380	12755	12970	13360	14175	15750	16885	17580	18425	19440	20355
4 Furniture, furnishings and household equipment and operation	4115	5580	5730	5910	6315	6550	6625	6735	6925	7125	7435	7605
A Household operation	1125	1695	1740	1715	1790	1845	1905	1960	2005	2050	2095	2130
B Other	2990	3885	3990	4195	4525	4705	4720	4775	4920	5075	5340	5475
5 Medical care and health expenses	3320	6520	7595	8030	8585	9280	10070	10815	11400	12130	12965	13810
6 Transport and communication	5850	9125	11120	11835	12775	13925	14240	14400	14770	15310	15800	16320
A Personal transport equipment	1870	2390	3715	3700	3825	4135	4215	4090	4100	4195	4880	5065
B Other	3980	6735	7405	8135	8950	9790	10025	10310	10670	11115	10920	11255
7 Recreational, entertainment, education and cultural services [a]	4795	7840	8575	9075	9925	10700	11315	11870	12620	13325	14020	14640
8 Miscellaneous goods and services	4095	8010	8850	9235	9820	10530	11230	11850	12435	13240	14165	15105
A Personal care	1140	1810	1900	1960	2075	2195	2340	2440	2560	2710	2845	2960
B Expenditures in restaurants, cafes and hotels [a]	...	...	...	...	...	...	...	...	...	...	...	...

Switzerland

2.5 Private Final Consumption Expenditure by Type and Purpose, in Current Prices
(Continued)

Million Swiss francs

	1970	1975	1978	1979	1980	1981	1982	1983	1984	1985	1986	1987
C Other	2955	6200	6950	7275	7745	8335	8890	9410	9875	10530	11320	12145
Total Final Consumption Expenditure in the Domestic Market by Households, of which	51715	83480	91915	96955	103530	110895	116915	121975	127625	133930	138320	142945
Plus: Direct purchases abroad by resident households	1740	2790	3625	4045	4805	5125	5525	5780	6410	7085	7085	7615
Less: Direct purchases in the domestic market by non-resident households [b]	...	...	...	...	...	...	...	...	...	...	...	...
Equals: Final Consumption Expenditure of Resident Households [c]	53455	86270	95540	101000	108335	116020	122440	127755	134035	141015	145405	150560

Final Consumption Expenditure of Private Non-profit Institutions Serving Households

	1970	1975	1978	1979	1980	1981	1982	1983	1984	1985	1986	1987
Equals: Final Consumption Expenditure of Private Non-profit Organisations Serving Households	...	...	...	...	...	...	...	...	...	...	...	...
Private Final Consumption Expenditure	53455	86270	95540	101000	108335	116020	122440	127755	134035	141015	145405	150560

a) Item 'Expenditure in restaurants, cafes and hotels' is included in item 'Recreational, entertainment, education and cultural services'.
b) Item 'Direct purchases in the domestic market by non-resident households' is netted out from the appropriate items above.
c) Item 'Final consumption expenditure of resident households' includes consumption expenditure of private non-profit institutions serving households.

2.6 Private Final Consumption Expenditure by Type and Purpose, in Constant Prices

Million Swiss francs

	1970	1975	1978	1979	1980	1981	1982	1983	1984	1985	1986	1987

At constant prices of: 1970

Final Consumption Expenditure of Resident Households

	1970	1975	1978	1979	1980	1981	1982	1983	1984	1985	1986	1987
1 Food, beverages and tobacco	16805	17715	18125	18140	18340	18080	17980	18255	18530	18775	19180	19390
A Food	11665	12785	13240	13235	13360	13065	12920	13200	13445	13670	14020	14145
B Non-alcoholic beverages	5140	4930	4885	4905	4980	5015	5060	5055	5085	5105	5160	5245
C Alcoholic beverages	...	...	...	...	...	...	...	...	...	...	...	...
D Tobacco	...	...	...	...	...	...	...	...	...	...	...	...
2 Clothing and footwear	3550	3180	3165	3180	3300	3365	3285	3300	3310	3340	3425	3430
3 Gross rent, fuel and power	9185	10755	11655	11650	11910	12020	12080	12415	12700	12880	13135	13390
A Fuel and power	2515	3070	3610	3455	3560	3530	3455	3650	3795	3835	3945	4045
B Other	6670	7685	8045	8195	8350	8490	8625	8765	8905	9045	9190	9345
4 Furniture, furnishings and household equipment and operation	4115	4050	4010	4115	4255	4230	4090	4055	4110	4135	4230	4265
A Household operation	1125	1195	1145	1110	1120	1115	1095	1095	1095	1090	1090	1090
B Other	2990	2855	2865	3005	3135	3115	2995	2960	3015	3045	3140	3175
5 Medical care and health expenses	3320	3740	3885	3965	4105	4190	4230	4330	4395	4485	4600	4705
6 Transport and communication	5850	6230	7225	7330	7535	7755	7765	7750	7740	7715	8160	8425
A Personal transport equipment	1870	1630	2415	2295	2255	2300	2300	2200	2150	2115	2535	2645
B Other	3980	4600	4810	5035	5280	5455	5465	5550	5590	5600	5625	5780
7 Recreational, entertainment, education and cultural services [a]	4795	5610	5815	6100	6395	6555	6600	6740	6865	7030	7190	7270
8 Miscellaneous goods and services	4095	5025	5250	5345	5480	5545	5585	5705	5815	5960	6185	6415
A Personal care	1140	1240	1240	1285	1330	1355	1385	1400	1445	1495	1540	1575
B Expenditures in restaurants, cafes and hotels [a]	...	...	...	...	...	...	...	...	...	...	...	...
C Other	2955	3785	4010	4060	4150	4190	4200	4305	4370	4465	4645	4840
Total Final Consumption Expenditure in the Domestic Market by Households, of which	51715	56305	59130	59825	61320	61740	61615	62550	63465	64320	66105	67290
Plus: Direct purchases abroad by resident households	1740	2310	3260	3360	3525	3400	3525	3630	3730	3860	3975	4165
Less: Direct purchases in the domestic market by non-resident households [b]	...	...	...	...	...	...	...	...	...	...	...	...
Equals: Final Consumption Expenditure of Resident Households [c]	53455	58615	62390	63185	64845	65140	65140	66180	67195	68180	70080	71455

Final Consumption Expenditure of Private Non-profit Institutions Serving Households

	1970	1975	1978	1979	1980	1981	1982	1983	1984	1985	1986	1987
Equals: Final Consumption Expenditure of Private Non-profit Organisations Serving Households	...	...	...	...	...	...	...	...	...	...	...	...
Private Final Consumption Expenditure	53455	58615	62390	63185	64845	65140	65140	66180	67195	68180	70080	71455

a) Item 'Expenditure in restaurants, cafes and hotels' is included in item 'Recreational, entertainment, education and cultural services'.
b) Item 'Direct purchases in the domestic market by non-resident households' is netted out from the appropriate items above.
c) Item 'Final consumption expenditure of resident households' includes consumption expenditure of private non-profit institutions serving households.

Syrian Arab Republic

General note. The preparation of national accounts statistics in Syrian Arab Republic is undertaken by the Directorate of National Accounts, Central Bureau of Statistics, Damascus. The official estimates are published annually in the 'Statistical Abstract', issued by the Central Bureau of Statistics. The following presentation of sources and methods is based on a report entitled: 'National Accounts of the Syrian Arab Republic and Syria's First Effort at Implementing Stages of the New United Nations System of National Accounts (SNA)'. The estimates are generally in accordance with the classifications and definitions recommended in the United Nations System of National Accounts. The following tables have been prepared from successive replies to the United Nations national accounts questionnaire. When the scope and coverage of the estimates differ for conceptual or statisitcal reasons from the definitions and classifications recommended in SNA, a footnote is indicated to the relevant tables.

Sources and methods:

(a) Gross domestic product. Gross domestic product is estimated mainly through the production approach.

(b) Expenditure on the gross domestic product. The expenditure approach is used to estimate government final consumption expenditure, exports and imports of goods and services, and part of changes in stocks. This approach, in combination with the commodity-flow approach, is used to estimate gross fixed capital formation. Private final consumption expenditure is obtained as a residual. The basic data for government final consumption expenditure estimates are available from the budgets of the State, the municipalities and religious endowment administrations. Stock fluctuations are not estimated. For gross fixed capital formation, detailed classification of import statistics are utilized for machinery and equipment. Added to the c.i.f. values are import duties, other indirect taxes and estimated trade margins. For construction in the private sector, estimates are obtained by multiplying the area of floor space indicated in the annual census by the average price per square metre and by adding thereto the value of repairs carried out. The estimates of exports and imports of goods and services are based on foreign trade statistics and balance-of-payments data. For the constant price estimates, price deflation is used for government final consumption expenditure and gross fixed capital formation. Price deflation and extrapolation by volume index are used for exports and imports of merchandise. Private consumption expenditure is obtained as a residual and no estimates for increase in stocks are made.

(c) Cost-structure of the gross domestic product. The cost-structure table of the GDP is not being estimated.

(d) Gross domestic product by kind of economic activity. The table of gross domestic product by kind of economic activity is prepared at market prices, i.e., producers' values. The production approach is used to estimate the value added of most industries. The income approach is used for some private services and for producers of government services. The commodity-flow approach is used to estimate the gross output of the trade sector. The data on field and animal agricultural production are collected by the Ministry of Agriculture. Gross output and intermediate input are compiled per individual commodity group, estimated from figures gathered separately on quantities and prices. The agricultural prices were obtained through a census for the year 1971. For other years, only wholesale prices are known while producers' prices are derived on the basis of varying assumptions. Own-account consumption of agricultural production is mainly based on the sample survey conducted in 1970 and the 1968 family budget survey. Data for extractive industries, such as crude oil and phosphates, owned by the State are obtained from reports that include the size and value of production and intermediate consumption. Extractive industries in the private sector are based on industrial surveys. Data concerning industrial public enterprises are available from the Union of Industries. For the private sector, the Central Bureau of Statistics has undertaken a general economic survey for 1971, which covers all establishments employing more than nine persons and includes a sample of the smaller establishments. The frame for the survey was based on the 1970 population census. Other data sources has been used to cover establishments created after 1970. In the manufacture of food, the value of flour is multiplied by the ratio between the value of bread and the value of flour derived from the economic survey. Similar ratios between gross output and intermediate consumption and compensation of employees are used for the estimation of intermediate consumption and compensation of employees. The sources of data on the electricity and water industries are the accounts of the concerned enterprises. For construction, estimates of production values and intermediate consumption in the private sector are made by determining the value of construction projects completed during the year and adding to it the value of the completed portions of unfinished buildings and construction projects. The progress reports issued by the State Planning Commission are the prime source of data for construction in the public sector. For trade, gross margins are estimated as percentage mark-ups on commodity-flow values. The value of intermediate consumption is estimated as 8 percent of the production value. Information on railway and air transport and communication activities is supplied entirely by public enterprises. Gross output of road transport are based on the registration of licenses issued, and on gross revenue and cost data by type of unit, based on ad hoc transport sample surveys. Estimates of pipeline and sea transport are obtained from concerned enterprises. For banks, the production value is calculated by adding to actual expenditure imputed service charges. Estimates of insurance and real estate activities are derived from the concerned companies. The production value of the housing sector is estimated as rents paid to others for house leases plus the estimated rental value of owner-occupied houses. For community services, the basic data are available from the accounting records of public enterprises and the budgets of public authorities. The results of the 1971 general economic survey are used for some private services while proxy output indicators derived from the results of the 1970 population census and administrative records are used for other services. For the constant price estimates, double deflation is used for agriculture. Value added of all other economic activity sectors of GDP, except trade, is extrapolated by a quantity index. To obtain wholesale and retail trade margin at constant prices, the same percentages as those used for current prices are applied to the production values of the agricultural, mining and quarrying and manufacturing sectors.

1.1 Expenditure on the Gross Domestic Product, in Current Prices

Million Syrian pounds

	1970	1975	1978	1979	1980	1981	1982	1983	1984	1985	1986	1987
1 Government final consumption expenditure	1187	4338	6499	8487	11870	13656	15103	16154	17079	19785	21440	22945
2 Private final consumption expenditure	4966	13044	21627	27399	34107	48256	44992	49686	49121	54155	65553	90818
3 Gross capital formation	937	5916	9876	10113	14116	15262	16270	17286	17865	19784	23331	23473
A Increase in stocks	40	760	989	-81	...	...	...	...	...	...	...	...
B Gross fixed capital formation	897	5156	8887	10194	14116	15262	16270	17286	17865	19784	23331	23473
Residential buildings	215	849	1627	1538	4036	4685	4650	3859	4471	5126	8748	9256
Non-residential buildings	59	337	642	968	1163	1047	1668	1825	2259	2335	2584	2160
Other construction and land improvement etc.	259	1329	2462	3947	4269	4456	5580	6317	6705	7503	7653	7021
Other	364	2641	4156	3741	4648	5074	4372	5285	4430	4820	4346	5036
4 Exports of goods and services	1190	4409	4808	7253	9345	10290	9572	9714	9360	10245	10134	18691
5 Less: Imports of goods and services	1432	6996	10114	13950	18168	21687	17149	19549	18083	20744	20158	29602
Equals: Gross Domestic Product	6848	20711	32696	39302	51270	65777	68788	73291	75342	83225	100300	126325

1.2 Expenditure on the Gross Domestic Product, in Constant Prices

Million Syrian pounds

	1970	1975	1978	1979	1980	1981	1982	1983	1984	1985	1986	1987
					At constant prices of:1980							
1 Government final consumption expenditure	3701	8332	9377	11862	11870	12445	13154	13855	15035	13913	12509	10582
2 Private final consumption expenditure	8581	26036	30177	31410	34107	42838	39227	40871	36883	41158	37247	34844
3 Gross capital formation	3192	8636	11567	11740	14116	14421	14896	15457	15742	16769	15851	11917
A Increase in stocks	...	...	...	...	...	...	...	...	...	...	...	...
B Gross fixed capital formation	3192	8636	11567	11740	14116	14421	14896	15457	15742	16769	15851	11917

Syrian Arab Republic

1.2 Expenditure on the Gross Domestic Product, in Constant Prices
(Continued)

Million Syrian pounds

	1970	1975	1978	1979	1980	1981	1982	1983	1984	1985	1986	1987
	At constant prices of:1980											
Residential buildings	886	1422	2625	2240	4036	4156	4266	3415	3888	4381	4552	4142
Non-residential buildings	194	565	827	1410	1163	930	1530	1615	1964	1996	2118	1370
Other construction and land improvement etc.	848	2226	2772	3459	4269	3934	5215	5692	5934	6525	6431	4347
Other	1264	4423	5343	4631	4648	5401	3885	4735	3956	3867	2750	2058
4 Exports of goods and services	10042	10991	10671	10219	9345	9758	10231	10636	10080	11578	10092	10330
5 Less: Imports of goods and services	4938	13992	15560	17438	18168	23319	19711	21965	21027	24993	17982	15299
Equals: Gross Domestic Product	20578	40003	46232	47793	51270	56143	57797	58855	56713	58425	57717	52374

1.3 Cost Components of the Gross Domestic Product

Million Syrian pounds

	1970	1975	1978	1979	1980	1981	1982	1983	1984	1985	1986	1987
1 Indirect taxes, net	434	501	1848	428	1308	1316	2567	2504	2898	2798	3689	3757
A Indirect taxes	540	1557	2284	2543	3218	3326	3932	3924	3943	4198	5089	4957
B Less: Subsidies	106	1056	436	2115	1910	2010	1365	1420	1045	1400	1400	1200
2 Consumption of fixed capital	305	582	1030	1149	1443	1967	2115	2243	2334	2731	3065	4218
3 Compensation of employees paid by resident producers to:	...	...	...	...	...	...	...	...	...	...	...	...
4 Operating surplus	...	...	...	...	...	...	...	...	...	...	...	...
Equals: Gross Domestic Product	6848	20711	32696	39302	51270	65777	68788	73291	75342	83225	100300	126325

1.10 Gross Domestic Product by Kind of Activity, in Current Prices

Million Syrian pounds

	1970	1975	1978	1979	1980	1981	1982	1983	1984	1985	1986	1987
1 Agriculture, hunting, forestry and fishing	1382	3705	6851	6857	10369	12759	13854	15627	14805	17463	23816	34369
2 Mining and quarrying	157	2416	2815	4524	6154	7004	6480	6024	6043	5948	3050	8524
3 Manufacturing	1312	1535	3585	3327	1825	5500	5176	5788	6047	6382	12298	8454
4 Electricity, gas and water	91	222	338	395	394	526	-47	201	-55	191	206	121
5 Construction	201	960	1781	2715	3574	3759	4327	4460	5006	5692	7059	6772
6 Wholesale and retail trade, restaurants and hotels	1395	4603	7893	9476	12693	16274	16846	17813	17701	18509	20045	29719
7 Transport, storage and communication	733	2407	1932	2786	3555	4810	5513	5968	6254	8196	9883	11793
8 Finance, insurance, real estate and business services	731	1481	2205	2591	3266	4113	4328	4202	4402	4181	4883	5545
9 Community, social and personal services	116	281	710	810	926	1154	1407	1468	1818	2195	2734	3147
Total, Industries	6118	17610	28111	33481	42756	55899	57884	61551	62022	68757	83974	108444
Producers of Government Services	712	3082	4557	5790	8480	9840	10861	11693	13268	14408	16260	17808
Other Producers	18	19	27	31	34	38	43	47	52	60	66	73
Subtotal	6848	20711	32696	39302	51270	65777	68788	73291	75342	83225	100300	126325
Less: Imputed bank service charge	...	...	...	...	...	...	...	...	...	...	...	...
Plus: Import duties	...	...	...	...	...	...	...	...	...	...	...	...
Plus: Value added tax	...	...	...	...	...	...	...	...	...	...	...	...
Equals: Gross Domestic Product	6848	20711	32696	39302	51270	65777	68788	73291	75342	83225	100300	126325

1.11 Gross Domestic Product by Kind of Activity, in Constant Prices

Million Syrian pounds

	1970	1975	1978	1979	1980	1981	1982	1983	1984	1985	1986	1987
	At constant prices of:1980											
1 Agriculture, hunting, forestry and fishing	3842	6778	8698	7423	10369	10765	10513	10458	9563	10169	10762	9365
2 Mining and quarrying	2978	6955	6489	6433	6154	7056	6937	7222	7287	7157	8160	8878
3 Manufacturing	2037	3083	2946	1959	1825	602	1025	1367	-327	211	1053	-1145
4 Electricity, gas and water	112	277	395	453	394	457	476	608	662	746	547	662
5 Construction	910	1749	2894	3796	3574	3743	4140	4068	4528	5061	5013	3665
6 Wholesale and retail trade, restaurants and hotels	4796	9197	11134	11617	12693	15445	15512	15205	14259	14874	12298	12622
7 Transport, storage and communication	1742	2934	3056	3379	3555	4202	4225	4468	4698	5009	5044	4841
8 Finance, insurance, real estate and business services	1435	2276	2792	3142	3266	3574	3652	3370	3029	2897	3182	3316
9 Community, social and personal services	344	463	906	987	926	986	1188	1238	1160	1199	1089	797

Syrian Arab Republic

1.11 Gross Domestic Product by Kind of Activity, in Constant Prices
(Continued)

Million Syrian pounds

	1970	1975	1978	1979	1980	1981	1982	1983	1984	1985	1986	1987
					At constant prices of:1980							
Total, Industries	18196	33712	39310	39189	42756	46830	47668	48004	44859	47323	47148	43001
Producers of Government Services	2350	6269	6894	8574	8480	9276	10089	10807	11806	11050	10514	9313
Other Producers	32	22	28	30	34	37	40	44	48	52	55	60
Subtotal	20578	40003	46232	47793	51270	56143	57797	58855	56713	58425	57717	52374
Less: Imputed bank service charge	...	...	...	...	...	...	...	...	...	...	...	...
Plus: Import duties	...	...	...	...	...	...	...	...	...	...	...	...
Plus: Value added tax	...	...	...	...	...	...	...	...	...	...	...	...
Equals: Gross Domestic Product	20578	40003	46232	47793	51270	56143	57797	58855	56713	58425	57717	52374

2.11 Gross Fixed Capital Formation by Kind of Activity of Owner, ISIC Divisions, in Current Prices

Million Syrian pounds

	1970	1975	1978	1979	1980	1981	1982	1983	1984	1985	1986	1987
					All Producers							
1 Agriculture, hunting, forestry and fishing	141	353	585	808	525	959	940	1471	2064	2606	2878	2469
2 Mining and quarrying												
3 Manufacturing	230	2349	3950	4391	4048	5117	5306	5033	4306	4328	4308	5182
4 Electricity, gas and water												
5 Construction	...	...	...	...	...	...	...	...	...	...	...	...
6 Wholesale and retail trade, restaurants and hotels	...	...	...	...	...	...	...	...	...	...	...	...
7 Transport, storage and communication	187	960	1213	1335	1629	2080	2395	2785	2212	2311	1853	2110
8 Finance, insurance, real estate and business services	339	1494	3139	3660	7914	7106	7629	7997	9283	10539	14292	13712
9 Community, social and personal services												
Total Industries	897	5156	8887	10194	14116	15262	16270	17286	17865	19784	23331	23473
Producers of Government Services	...	...	...	...	...	...	...	...	...	...	...	...
Private Non-Profit Institutions Serving Households	...	...	...	...	...	...	...	...	...	...	...	...
Total	897	5156	8887	10194	14116	15262	16270	17286	17865	19784	23331	23473

2.12 Gross Fixed Capital Formation by Kind of Activity of Owner, ISIC Divisions, in Constant Prices

Million Syrian pounds

	1970	1975	1978	1979	1980	1981	1982	1983	1984	1985	1986	1987
					At constant prices of:1980							
					All Producers							
1 Agriculture, hunting, forestry and fishing	479	591	699	800	525	924	868	1328	1831	2261	2333	1453
2 Mining and quarrying												
3 Manufacturing	847	3936	4969	5169	4048	4866	4776	4575	3790	3712	3238	2775
4 Electricity, gas and water												
5 Construction	...	...	...	...	...	...	...	...	...	...	...	...
6 Wholesale and retail trade, restaurants and hotels	...	...	...	...	...	...	...	...	...	...	...	...
7 Transport, storage and communication	556	1608	1472	1350	1629	1940	2243	2457	1941	1836	1320	1019
8 Finance, insurance, real estate and business services	1310	2501	4427	4421	7914	6691	7009	7097	8180	8960	8960	6670
9 Community, social and personal services												
Total Industries	3192	8636	11567	11740	14116	14421	14896	15457	15742	16769	15851	11917
Producers of Government Services	...	...	...	...	...	...	...	...	...	...	...	...
Private Non-Profit Institutions Serving Households	...	...	...	...	...	...	...	...	...	...	...	...
Total	3192	8636	11567	11740	14116	14421	14896	15457	15742	16769	15851	11917

Syrian Arab Republic

4.1 Derivation of Value Added by Kind of Activity, in Current Prices

Million Syrian pounds

	1980 Gross Output	1980 Intermediate Consumption	1980 Value Added	1981 Gross Output	1981 Intermediate Consumption	1981 Value Added	1982 Gross Output	1982 Intermediate Consumption	1982 Value Added	1983 Gross Output	1983 Intermediate Consumption	1983 Value Added
						All Producers						
1 Agriculture, hunting, forestry and fishing	12804	2435	10369	16270	3511	12759	17870	4016	13854	19492	3866	15626
2 Mining and quarrying	...	...	6154	...	...	7004	...	...	6480	...	...	6023
3 Manufacturing	...	...	1825	...	...	5500	...	...	5176	...	...	5788
A Manufacture of food, beverages and tobacco	...	...	716	...	...	382	...	...	-443	...	...	-275
B Textile, wearing apparel and leather industries	...	...	1837	...	...	1997	...	...	1225	...	...	1249
C Manufacture of wood and wood products, including furniture	...	...	530	...	...	452	...	...	421	...	...	453
D Manufacture of paper and paper products, printing and publishing	...	...	43	...	...	54	...	...	125	...	...	90
E Manufacture of chemicals and chemical petroleum, coal, rubber and plastic products	...	...	-2098	...	...	1626	...	...	1462	...	...	1181
F Manufacture of non-metallic mineral products, except products of petroleum and coal	...	...	213	...	...	289	...	...	707	...	...	965
G Basic metal industries	...	...	69	...	...	141	...	...	46	...	...	66
H Manufacture of fabricated metal products, machinery and equipment	...	...	474	...	...	516	...	...	1476	...	...	1670
I Other manufacturing industries	...	...	41	...	...	43	...	...	157	...	...	389
4 Electricity, gas and water	...	...	394	...	...	526	...	...	-47	...	...	201
5 Construction	9717	6143	3574	10413	6654	3759	12141	7814	4327	12223	7763	4460
6 Wholesale and retail trade, restaurants and hotels	14340	1647	12693	18341	2067	16274	18992	2146	16846	20094	2281	17813
7 Transport, storage and communication	5642	2087	3555	7718	2908	4810	8733	3220	5513	9538	3570	5968
8 Finance, insurance, real estate and business services	3478	212	3266	4368	255	4113	4558	230	4328	4506	304	4202
9 Community, social and personal services	1219	293	926	1584	430	1154	1890	483	1407	2019	551	1468
Total, Industries	70912	28156	42756	92401	36502	55899	100400	42516	57884	106514	44963	61551
Producers of Government Services	11989	3509	8480	13803	3963	9840	15214	4353	10861	16269	4576	11693
Other Producers	46	12	34	51	13	38	57	14	43	63	16	47
Total	82947	31677	51270	106255	40478	65777	115671	46883	68788	122846	49555	73291
Less: Imputed bank service charge	...	...	...	...	...	...	...	...	...	...	...	...
Import duties	...	...	...	...	...	...	...	...	...	...	...	...
Value added tax	...	...	...	...	...	...	...	...	...	...	...	...
Total	...	...	...	...	...	...	...	...	...	...	...	...

	1984 Gross Output	1984 Intermediate Consumption	1984 Value Added	1985 Gross Output	1985 Intermediate Consumption	1985 Value Added	1986 Gross Output	1986 Intermediate Consumption	1986 Value Added	1987 Gross Output	1987 Intermediate Consumption	1987 Value Added
						All Producers						
1 Agriculture, hunting, forestry and fishing	19338	4533	14805	22517	5054	17463	30883	7067	23816	44302	9933	34369
2 Mining and quarrying	...	...	6043	6593	645	5948	4092	1042	3050	10926	2402	8524
3 Manufacturing	...	...	6047	...	...	6382	...	...	12298	...	...	8454
A Manufacture of food, beverages and tobacco	...	...	517	...	...	215	...	...	730	...	...	1432

Syrian Arab Republic

4.1 Derivation of Value Added by Kind of Activity, in Current Prices
(Continued)

Million Syrian pounds

	1984 Gross Output	1984 Intermediate Consumption	1984 Value Added	1985 Gross Output	1985 Intermediate Consumption	1985 Value Added	1986 Gross Output	1986 Intermediate Consumption	1986 Value Added	1987 Gross Output	1987 Intermediate Consumption	1987 Value Added
B Textile, wearing apparel and leather industries	...	...	976	...	...	1249	...	...	1634	...	...	2200
C Manufacture of wood and wood products, including furniture	...	...	595	...	...	540	...	...	806	...	...	970
D Manufacture of paper and paper products, printing and publishing	...	...	84	...	...	138	...	...	183	...	...	239
E Manufacture of chemicals and chemical petroleum, coal, rubber and plastic products	...	...	1836	...	...	1690	...	...	6475	...	...	958
F Manufacture of non-metallic mineral products, except products of petroleum and coal	...	...	1129	...	...	1066	...	...	1492	...	...	1400
G Basic metal industries	...	...	81	...	...	157	...	...	120	...	...	94
H Manufacture of fabricated metal products, machinery and equipment	...	...	723	...	...	1198	...	...	729	...	...	980
I Other manufacturing industries	...	...	106	...	...	129	...	...	129	...	...	181
4 Electricity, gas and water	...	...	-55	1977	1786	191	2213	2007	206	...	...	121
5 Construction	13653	8647	5006	15195	9503	5692	19220	12161	7059	18584	11812	6772
6 Wholesale and retail trade, restaurants and hotels	19751	2049	17702	20604	2095	18509	22334	2289	20045	33046	3327	29719
7 Transport, storage and communication	10095	3841	6254	12612	4416	8196	15166	5283	9883	18198	6405	11793
8 Finance, insurance, real estate and business services	4708	306	4402	4508	327	4181	5252	369	4883	5953	408	5545
9 Community, social and personal services	2604	786	1818	3301	1106	2195	4397	1663	2734	5070	1923	3147
Total, Industries	109953	47931	62022	118530	49773	68757	139469	55495	83974	181147	72703	108444
Producers of Government Services	18569	5301	13268	19915	5507	14408	21698	5438	16260	23089	5281	17808
Other Producers	70	18	52	80	20	60	88	22	66	97	24	73
Total	128592	53250	75342	138525	55300	83225	161255	60955	100300	204333	78008	126325
Less: Imputed bank service charge	...	...	...	...	...	...	...	...	...	...	...	...
Import duties	...	...	...	...	...	...	...	...	...	...	...	...
Value added tax	...	...	...	...	...	...	...	...	...	...	...	...
Total	...	...	...	...	...	...	...	...	...	...	...	...

4.2 Derivation of Value Added by Kind of Activity, in Constant Prices

Million Syrian pounds

	1980 Gross Output	1980 Intermediate Consumption	1980 Value Added	1981 Gross Output	1981 Intermediate Consumption	1981 Value Added	1982 Gross Output	1982 Intermediate Consumption	1982 Value Added	1983 Gross Output	1983 Intermediate Consumption	1983 Value Added
				At constant prices of:1980								
				All Producers								
1 Agriculture, hunting, forestry and fishing	12804	2435	10369	13731	2911	10765	13433	2920	10513	13437	2979	10458
2 Mining and quarrying	...	...	6154	...	...	7056	7374	437	6937	7725	503	7222
3 Manufacturing	...	...	1825	...	...	602	20160	19135	1025	21957	20590	1367
A Manufacture of food, beverages and tobacco	...	...	716	...	...	437	4010	3961	49	4488	4177	311
B Textile, wearing apparel and leather industries	...	...	1837	...	...	1863	3299	1927	1372	3998	2627	1371
C Manufacture of wood and wood products, including furniture	...	...	530	...	...	448	859	469	390	878	499	379
D Manufacture of paper and paper products, printing and publishing	...	...	43	...	...	44	205	109	96	278	180	98
E Manufacture of chemicals and chemical petroleum, coal, rubber and plastic products	...	...	-2098	...	...	-3138	6780	9689	-2909	6829	10101	-3272
F Manufacture of non-metallic mineral products, except products of petroleum and coal	...	...	213	...	...	244	1226	830	396	1419	869	550
G Basic metal industries	...	...	69	...	...	104	284	216	68	335	256	79
H Manufacture of fabricated metal products, machinery and equipment	...	...	474	...	...	559	2794	1371	1423	3015	1472	1543
I Other manufacturing industries	...	...	41	...	...	41	703	563	140	717	409	308
4 Electricity, gas and water	...	...	394	...	...	457	770	294	476	987	379	608

Syrian Arab Republic

4.2 Derivation of Value Added by Kind of Activity, in Constant Prices
(Continued)

Million Syrian pounds

	1980 Gross Output	1980 Intermediate Consumption	1980 Value Added	1981 Gross Output	1981 Intermediate Consumption	1981 Value Added	1982 Gross Output	1982 Intermediate Consumption	1982 Value Added	1983 Gross Output	1983 Intermediate Consumption	1983 Value Added
				At constant prices of:1980								
5 Construction	9717	6143	3574	10111	6368	3743	11327	7187	4140	11005	6937	4068
6 Wholesale and retail trade, restaurants and hotels	14340	1647	12693	17317	1872	15445	17298	1786	15512	17077	1872	15205
7 Transport, storage and communication	5642	2087	3555	6688	2486	4202	6704	2479	4225	7049	2581	4468
8 Finance, insurance, real estate and business services	3478	212	3266	3793	219	3574	3892	240	3652	3615	245	3370
9 Community, social and personal services	1219	293	926	1325	339	986	1588	400	1188	1694	456	1238
Total, Industries	70912	28156	42756	79947	33117	46830	82546	34878	47668	84546	36542	48004
Producers of Government Services	11989	3509	8480	12579	3303	9276	13251	3162	10089	13955	3148	10807
Other Producers	46	12	34	49	12	37	54	14	40	60	16	44
Total	82947	31677	51270	92575	36432	56143	95851	38054	57797	98561	39706	58855
Less: Imputed bank service charge	...	...	...	...	...	...	...	...	...	...	...	...
Import duties	...	...	...	...	...	...	...	...	...	...	...	...
Value added tax	...	...	...	...	...	...	...	...	...	...	...	...
Total	...	...	...	...	...	...	...	...	...	...	...	...

	1984 Gross Output	1984 Intermediate Consumption	1984 Value Added	1985 Gross Output	1985 Intermediate Consumption	1985 Value Added	1986 Gross Output	1986 Intermediate Consumption	1986 Value Added	1987 Gross Output	1987 Intermediate Consumption	1987 Value Added
				At constant prices of:1980								
				All Producers								
1 Agriculture, hunting, forestry and fishing	12385	2822	9563	12986	2817	10169	13836	3074	10762	12265	2900	9365
2 Mining and quarrying	7828	541	7287	7697	540	7157	9364	1204	8160	10748	1870	8878
3 Manufacturing	21529	21856	-327	21106	20895	211	21495	20442	1053	20959	22104	-1145
A Manufacture of food, beverages and tobacco	4399	4346	53	3622	3836	-214	3900	4118	-218	4043	5169	-1126
B Textile, wearing apparel and leather industries	4185	3008	1177	4120	2593	1527	4423	2910	1513	4057	2702	1355
C Manufacture of wood and wood products, including furniture	1056	509	547	1164	816	348	1029	478	551	982	463	519
D Manufacture of paper and paper products, printing and publishing	277	201	76	399	349	50	394	285	109	212	150	62
E Manufacture of chemicals and chemical petroleum, coal, rubber and plastic products	7344	11043	-3699	7848	10940	-3092	8088	10320	-2232	7755	11085	-3330
F Manufacture of non-metallic mineral products, except products of petroleum and coal	1621	911	710	1433	780	653	1447	808	639	1561	874	687
G Basic metal industries	327	269	58	465	301	164	357	234	123	128	85	43
H Manufacture of fabricated metal products, machinery and equipment	2031	1360	671	1746	1068	678	1535	1060	475	1901	1347	554
I Other manufacturing industries	289	209	80	309	212	97	322	229	93	320	229	91
4 Electricity, gas and water	1209	547	662	1339	593	746	1115	568	547	1374	712	662
5 Construction	12082	7554	4528	13239	8178	5061	13338	8325	5013	9950	6285	3665
6 Wholesale and retail trade, restaurants and hotels	15861	1602	14259	16513	1639	14874	13625	1327	12298	13942	1320	12622
7 Transport, storage and communication	7503	2805	4698	7683	2674	5009	7739	2695	5044	7428	2587	4841
8 Finance, insurance, real estate and business services	3234	205	3029	3109	212	2897	3394	212	3182	3519	203	3316
9 Community, social and personal services	1653	493	1160	1792	593	1199	1742	653	1089	1283	486	797
Total, Industries	83284	38425	44859	85464	38141	47323	85648	38500	47148	81468	38467	43001
Producers of Government Services	15136	3330	11806	14004	2954	11050	12659	2145	10514	10648	1335	9313
Other Producers	66	18	48	69	17	52	73	18	55	80	20	60
Total	98486	41773	56713	99537	41112	58425	98380	40663	57717	92196	39822	52374
Less: Imputed bank service charge	...	...	...	...	...	...	...	...	...	...	...	...
Import duties	...	...	...	...	...	...	...	...	...	...	...	...
Value added tax	...	...	...	...	...	...	...	...	...	...	...	...
Total	...	...	...	...	...	...	...	...	...	...	...	...

Thailand

General note. The preparation of national accounts statistics in Thailand is undertaken by the Office of the National Economic Development Board, Bangkok. The official estimates together with methodological notes are published annually by the same office in 'National Income of Thailand'. The estimates are generally in accordance with the classifications and definitions recommended in the United Nations System of National Accounts (SNA). The following tables have been prepared from successive replies to the United Nations national accounts questionnaire. When the scope and coverage of the estimates differ from conceptual of statistical reasons from the definitions and classifications recommended in SNA, a footnote is indicated to the relevant tables.

Sources and methods :

(a) Gross domestic product. Gross domestic product is estimated mainly through the production approach.

(b) Expenditure on the gross domestic product. The expenditure approach is used to estimate government final consumption expenditure, increase in stocks and exports and imports of goods and services. The commodity-flow approach, supplemented by the expenditure approach, is used for the estimation of private final consumption expenditure and gross fixed capital formation. Estimates of government consumption expenditure are compiled from government accounts. Expenditure financed by foreign aids is added. For the main items of private consumption expenditure, the commodity-flow method is used. The per capita consumption of other items such as flour and chicken is based on family expenditure inquiries extrapolated by population and price changes. Stock changes in the private sector are estimated on the basis of commodity balance accounts. The estimate of private building activity is based on building permits issued for the urban areas and on municipal building construction costs. Additions are made for the imput profit of builders based on sample surveys, for permanent fixtures and fittings and for construction for own use. For the public sector questionnaires are sent to various government departments and enterprises. Estimates of other capital formation are based on foreign trade statistics. To the import values are added import duties, mark-ups and installation costs. Exports and imports of goods and services are derived directly from the balance-of-payments. For the constant prices estimates, current values of most of the expenditure items are deflated by appropriate price indexes. For private consumption expenditure, direct revaluation at base-year prices is used when information is available on quantities of commodities consumed.

(c) Cost-structure of the gross domestic product. Estimates of compensation of employees are derived from the cost of production estimated through surveys for the agricultural sector, from data on the average wage per worker multiplied by the construction sector, and for the public and financial sectors, the estimates are obtained from their records. Depreciation is estimated as 6.67 per cent and 10 per cent of GDP for building construction and equipment, respectively. Indirect taxes net of subsidies are estimated by the Comptroller-General's Department. Operating surplus is obtained as a residual.

(d) Gross domestic product by kind of economic activity. The table of GDP by kind of economic activity is prepared at market prices, i.e., producers' values. The production approach is used to estimate value added of most industries. However, the expenditure approach is used to estimate part of the agricultural sector, the income approach for public administration and defence and part of the private services and the commodity-flow approach for gross output of the trade sector. For the agricultural sector, annual production figures of paddy and 19 other principal crops are reported by the Department of Agriculture while vegetables and fruit production is based on consumption estimates. The production figure of each crop is multiplied by the average ex-farm prices. Annual livestock production estimates are based on inventory changes and the number of animals that are exported or slaughtered while cost estimates are based on information from the Department of Livestock Development. Own-account consumption of rice and fish, vegetables and fruits is based on the quantity consumed multiplied by local prices and on the 1962 household expenditure survey, respectively. The value of forestry production is estimated by multiplying the average price per unit by the total quantity produced. For mining and quarrying, the total production quantity of each mineral is multiplied by its average price to obtain the production value. Data on the gross value of production, intermediate consumption and value added in manufacturing by both private and public enterprises and registered partnership are obtained from reports submitted to the Comptroller-General's Department, the Ministry of Industry, the Department of Revenue and the Budget Bureau. For other manufacturing, value added is estimated by applying approximate value-added ratios to the gross value of production derived from financial statements and tax returns. The estimates of electricity, gas and water are computed directly from the financial statements of the various agencies. Construction expenditure in the public sector is reported directly to the National Statistical Office. Adjustments are made for non-reported construction. For the private sector, it is based on reported data such as building permits of municipalities or on average price of new houses. Intermediate cost for each type of construction is derived from questionnaires sent to contractors and information received from architects and engineers. The income originating in the trade sector is estimated by the commodity-flow method which traces the flows of consumer and producer goods of both domestic and foreign origin through the distribution channel. Gross margins are derived from the differences between retail prices and producers' prices. For the public transport and communications sectors, information is obtained directly from the financial statements of the agencies concerned. In the private sector, information is obtained from various sources such as the operating accounts of enterprises, registration and licence data and information on the earnings of companies that supply data. Value added of travel agencies is calculated from a tourist expenditure survey. For the financial sector, estimates are based on profit and loss statements for banking and insurance and on income tax returns for real-estate brokers and warehouse operators. Value added of ownership of dwelling represents the estimated rental value after expenses. Net rent is estimated by multiplying the estimated average net rent per dwelling by the estimated number of dwellings. For business services, value added of legal services for the base year is estimated from the number of lawyers practicing while average income is based on the labour survey and extrapolated by the growth rate of total criminal and civil cases. Other services such as auditing and engineering are estimated from auditing fees paid and the value of dwellings construction in the municipal area, respectively. Value added of public administration and defence are supplied by the Comptroller-General's Department. For other private services, including restaurants and hotels, data from the Department of Revenue licensing statistics and other data collected by the National Statistical Office are used. Both public and private education estimates are based on wages and salaries data of teachers. For the constant price estimates, price deflation is used to estimate the value added for most industries. For agriculture, when quantity figures of agricultural products are available, the base-year of mining and quarrying are extrapolated by quantity indicators. For public administration and defence, the number of employees by civil classification is used as an indicator of value added in real terms.

1.1 Expenditure on the Gross Domestic Product, in Current Prices

Million Thai baht

	1970	1975	1978	1979	1980	1981	1982	1983	1984	1985	1986	1987
1 Government final consumption expenditure	16578	31290	54583	66798	81431	96981	110162	118572	130095	142917	144528	154109
2 Private final consumption expenditure	103190	211292	314983	364028	438624	499619	540678	598603	635939	662665	704384	767162
3 Gross capital formation	37731	81134	137496	152050	174045	199723	189577	236090	242506	243949	246516	291673
A Increase in stocks	2736	11754	14247	9191	8330	11677	-2618	17636	3884	3666	11138	16134
B Gross fixed capital formation	34995	69380	123249	142859	165715	188046	192195	218454	238622	240283	235378	275539
Residential buildings	4094	7800	16050	17589	20687	27242	29946	35752	40443	40004	45885	53790
Non-residential buildings	6296	12965	27941	32048	38931	37994	30094	28535	31676	32267	26765	32196
Other construction and land improvement etc.	6500	7739	14291	18169	24700	28718	39492	45982	53610	56652	53841	53206
Other	18105	40876	64967	75053	81397	94092	92663	108185	112893	111360	108887	136347
4 Exports of goods and services	22140	55695	97082	126150	159736	181325	192870	185222	216411	245251	290169	355118
5 Less: Imports of goods and services	28569	69683	117721	163740	201180	229029	207282	251184	258557	274073	267148	354020
Statistical discrepancy	-3685	-6409	1803	13575	5853	11576	-6003	22751	7018	-6310	-18908	9176
Equals: Gross Domestic Product	147385	303319	488226	558861	658509	760195	820002	910054	973412	1014399	1099541	1223218

1.2 Expenditure on the Gross Domestic Product, in Constant Prices

Million Thai baht

	1970	1975	1978	1979	1980	1981	1982	1983	1984	1985	1986	1987
	At constant prices of:1972											
1 Government final consumption expenditure	17234	22695	33823	39066	40171	45636	47206	50781	54446	58191	58277	61289
2 Private final consumption expenditure	108619	141245	174705	187526	197744	201696	206984	221450	237229	241983	251643	267645
3 Gross capital formation	40782	49668	73674	70293	71398	78612	70096	85905	91806	87711	83219	91180
A Increase in stocks	2677	7608	8150	2186	825	4801	-2262	4246	1214	1936	2121	2505
B Gross fixed capital formation	38105	42060	65524	68107	70573	73811	72358	81659	90592	85775	81098	88675

Thailand

1.2 Expenditure on the Gross Domestic Product, in Constant Prices
(Continued)

Million Thai baht

	1970	1975	1978	1979	1980	1981	1982	1983	1984	1985	1986	1987
					At constant prices of:1972							
Residential buildings	4370	4570	7634	6892	7240	9102	9516	11255	12569	11767	13382	15004
Non-residential buildings	6658	7620	14150	14156	15030	13580	10096	9415	10212	10016	8204	9505
Other construction and land improvement etc.	6807	4738	7264	7921	8596	9368	12484	14573	16626	16816	15678	15090
Other	20270	25132	36476	39138	39707	41761	40262	46416	51185	47176	43834	49076
4 Exports of goods and services	22449	30300	46963	51859	55900	60643	67563	63876	75201	83066	95315	110774
5 Less: Imports of goods and services	30306	37789	54832	69158	75680	72909	69453	90205	94177	86278	100607	125356
Statistical discrepancy	-3084	-1691	-2955	6211	9939	4761	8984	23595	16233	9440	24764	36361
Equals: Gross Domestic Product	155694	204428	271378	285797	299472	318439	331380	355408	380738	394113	412609	441893

1.3 Cost Components of the Gross Domestic Product

Million Thai baht

	1970	1975	1978	1979	1980	1981	1982	1983	1984	1985	1986	1987
1 Indirect taxes, net	16097	31842	52957	64496	76223	84771	87374	104506	115708	113917	128388	150707
A Indirect taxes	16097	32657	54296	66052	81662	88768	93465	114162	119089	120701	133035	159717
B Less: Subsidies	..	815	1339	1556	5439	3997	6091	9656	3381	6784	4647	9010
2 Consumption of fixed capital	10174	20253	31647	37203	43358	50001	57020	64696	72976	81436	89531	98190
3 Compensation of employees paid by resident producers to:	27661	62666	107657	131877	171495	198599	233256	268096	286813	304227	321396	354181
4 Operating surplus	93453	188558	295966	325285	367433	426824	442352	472756	497915	514819	560226	620140
Equals: Gross Domestic Product	147385	303319	488226	558861	658509	760195	820002	910054	973412	1014399	1099541	1223218

1.4 General Government Current Receipts and Disbursements

Million Thai baht

	1970	1975	1978	1979	1980	1981	1982	1983	1984	1985	1986	1987
					Receipts							
1 Operating surplus	...	...	...	...	...	...	...	...	...	...	...	...
2 Property and entrepreneurial income	1091	2743	3310	3565	5315	8075	7884	13224	8491	13273	15787	17172
3 Taxes, fees and contributions	18416	39272	66478	80645	99118	111882	119167	143108	152010	157114	169084	198250
A Indirect taxes [a]	16097	32657	54296	66052	81662	88768	93465	114162	119089	120701	133035	159717
B Direct taxes	2319	6615	12182	14593	17456	23114	25702	28964	32921	36413	36049	38533
C Social security contributions	...	...	...	...	...	...	...	...	...	...	...	...
D Compulsory fees, fines and penalties	...	...	...	...	...	...	...	...	...	...	...	...
4 Other current transfers	1250	1809	2473	3167	4869	5817	5689	5153	6532	7732	7696	8393
Total Current Receipts of General Government	20757	43824	72261	87377	109302	125774	132740	161485	167033	178119	192567	223815
					Disbursements							
1 Government final consumption expenditure	16578	31290	54583	66798	81431	96981	110162	118572	130095	142917	144528	154109
2 Property income	1442	3455	6011	7793	10929	14690	18641	21519	26303	30291	36034	37411
A Interest	1442	3455	6011	7793	10929	14690	18641	21519	26303	30291	36034	37411
B Net land rent and royalties	...	...	...	...	...	...	...	...	...	...	...	...
3 Subsidies [a]	...	815	1339	1556	5439	3997	6091	9656	3381	6784	4647	9010
4 Other current transfers	189	307	760	893	1000	941	1034	904	1089	1217	1257	1042
A Social security benefits	...	...	...	...	...	...	...	...	...	...	...	...
B Social assistance grants	...	...	...	...	...	...	...	...	...	...	...	...
C Other	189	307	760	893	1000	941	1034	904	1089	1217	1257	1042
5 Net saving	2548	7957	9568	10337	10503	9165	-3188	10834	6165	-3090	6101	22243
Total Current Disbursements and Net Saving of General Government	20757	43824	72261	87377	109302	125774	132740	161485	167033	178119	192567	223815

a) For years before 1974, item 'Subsidies' is netted out of item 'Indirect taxes'.

1.6 Current Income and Outlay of Households and Non-Profit Institutions

Million Thai baht

	1970	1975	1978	1979	1980	1981	1982	1983	1984	1985	1986	1987
					Receipts							
1 Compensation of employees	27661	62666	107657	131877	171495	198599	233256	268096	286813	304227	321396	354181
A From resident producers	27754	62542	105878	128441	164528	189038	220202	249713	267103	282440	302317	334175
B From rest of the world	-93	124	1779	3436	6967	9561	13054	18383	19710	21787	19079	20006
2 Operating surplus of private unincorporated enterprises	76321	151944	238705	257058	288300	323014	330870	346508	358347	355122	396235	449327

Thailand

1.6 Current Income and Outlay of Households and Non-Profit Institutions
(Continued)

Million Thai baht

	1970	1975	1978	1979	1980	1981	1982	1983	1984	1985	1986	1987
3 Property and entrepreneurial income	13837	26248	38264	44726	58443	72093	84493	96313	110450	122484	122331	116494
4 Current transfers	371	1597	1130	1604	2919	2340	3078	4858	2934	3148	3571	2813
Total Current Receipts	118190	242455	385756	435265	521157	596046	651697	715775	758544	784981	843533	922815

Disbursements

	1970	1975	1978	1979	1980	1981	1982	1983	1984	1985	1986	1987
1 Private final consumption expenditure	103190	211292	314983	364028	438624	499619	540678	598603	635939	662665	704384	767162
2 Property income	364	1046	2697	3207	3775	4534	5135	6062	8210	9194	8362	9626
3 Direct taxes and other current transfers n.e.c. to general government	1416	2986	5723	6736	7831	9647	12821	15621	18168	20887	20344	20671
A Social security contributions	...	...	...	...	...	...	...	...	...	...	...	...
B Direct taxes	1416	2986	5723	6736	7831	9647	12821	15621	18168	20887	20344	20671
C Fees, fines and penalties	...	...	...	...	...	...	...	...	...	...	...	...
4 Other current transfers	273	1037	874	1041	1171	1347	1204	1363	2021	2339	2392	2630
5 Net saving	12947	26094	61479	60253	69756	80899	91859	94126	94206	89896	108051	122726
Total Current Disbursements and Net Saving	118190	242455	385756	435265	521157	596046	651697	715775	758544	784981	843533	922815

1.7 External Transactions on Current Account, Summary

Million Thai baht

	1970	1975	1978	1979	1980	1981	1982	1983	1984	1985	1986	1987

Payments to the Rest of the World

	1970	1975	1978	1979	1980	1981	1982	1983	1984	1985	1986	1987
1 Imports of goods and services	28569	69683	117721	163740	201180	229029	207282	251184	258557	274073	267148	354020
2 Factor income to the rest of the world	1452	4301	9102	14278	18438	28290	32843	31541	38139	48175	50126	51673
3 Current transfers to the rest of the world	169	223	245	254	395	316	359	444	461	693	680	796
4 Surplus of the nation on current transactions	-5206	-12316	-22970	-41745	-42102	-54906	-21997	-66014	-48647	-40514	6867	-16499
Payments to the Rest of the World and Surplus of the Nation on Current Transactions	24984	61891	104098	136527	177911	202729	218487	217155	248510	282427	324821	389990

Receipts From The Rest of the World

	1970	1975	1978	1979	1980	1981	1982	1983	1984	1985	1986	1987
1 Exports of goods and services	22140	55695	97082	126150	159736	181325	192870	185222	216411	245251	290169	355118
2 Factor income from rest of the world	1673	4288	5480	8053	13044	16255	19913	24840	26688	30578	27689	27675
3 Current transfers from rest of the world	1171	1908	1536	2324	5131	5149	5704	7093	5411	6598	6963	7197
Receipts from the Rest of the World on Current Transactions	24984	61891	104098	136527	177911	202729	218487	217155	248510	282427	324821	389990

1.8 Capital Transactions of The Nation, Summary

Million Thai baht

	1970	1975	1978	1979	1980	1981	1982	1983	1984	1985	1986	1987

Finance of Gross Capital Formation

	1970	1975	1978	1979	1980	1981	1982	1983	1984	1985	1986	1987
Gross saving	28840	62409	116329	123880	137796	156393	161577	192827	200877	197125	234475	284350
1 Consumption of fixed capital	10174	20253	31647	37203	43358	50001	57020	64696	72976	81436	89531	98190
2 Net saving	18666	42156	84682	86677	94438	106392	104557	128131	127901	115689	144944	186160
A General government	2548	7957	9568	10337	10503	9165	-3188	10834	6165	-3090	6101	22243
B Corporate and quasi-corporate enterprises	3171	8105	13635	16087	14179	16328	15886	23171	27530	28883	30792	41191
C Other	12947	26094	61479	60253	69756	80899	91859	94126	94206	89896	108051	122726
Less: Surplus of the nation on current transactions	-5206	-12316	-22970	-41745	-42102	-54906	-21997	-66014	-48647	-40514	6867	-16499
Statistical discrepancy	3685	6409	-1803	-13575	-5853	-11576	6003	-22751	-7018	-6310	18908	-9176
Finance of Gross Capital Formation	37731	81134	137496	152050	174045	199723	189577	236090	242506	243949	246516	291673

Gross Capital Formation

	1970	1975	1978	1979	1980	1981	1982	1983	1984	1985	1986	1987
Increase in stocks	2736	11754	14247	9191	8330	11677	-2618	17636	3884	3666	11138	16134

Thailand

1.8 Capital Transactions of The Nation, Summary
(Continued)

Million Thai baht

	1970	1975	1978	1979	1980	1981	1982	1983	1984	1985	1986	1987
Gross fixed capital formation	34995	69380	123249	142859	165715	188046	192195	218454	238622	240283	235378	275539
1 General government	10429	15704	37358	42425	58611	67987	66402	73646	82076	91920	83578	82780
2 Corporate and quasi-corporate enterprises	24566	53676	85891	100434	107104	120059	125793	144808	156546	148363	151800	192759
A Public	...	...	...	...	...	...	...	...	...	...	...	...
B Private	24566	53676	85891	100434	107104	120059	125793	144808	156546	148363	151800	192759
3 Other	...	...	...	...	...	...	...	...	...	...	...	...
Gross Capital Formation	37731	81134	137496	152050	174045	199723	189577	236090	242506	243949	246516	291673

1.10 Gross Domestic Product by Kind of Activity, in Current Prices

Million Thai baht

	1970	1975	1978	1979	1980	1981	1982	1983	1984	1985	1986	1987
1 Agriculture, hunting, forestry and fishing	38163	81521	119638	134148	152852	162987	156839	185628	175190	169895	184770	195059
2 Mining and quarrying	4382	6582	16608	18498	22147	21556	25110	26403	32954	40167	33239	37606
3 Manufacturing	23503	56636	97658	117611	139936	169461	176360	194344	218050	224456	253593	294496
4 Electricity, gas and water	1624	3417	5667	6499	6289	10901	15672	17067	18618	23590	28689	31497
5 Construction	7818	11594	24393	27004	34764	38135	41500	47985	56092	56824	56564	62087
6 Wholesale and retail trade, restaurants and hotels	34406	72105	115138	126595	144594	176778	189665	196695	208629	211899	235426	267096
7 Transport, storage and communication	9161	16790	27462	32179	37863	45850	55639	60809	69530	78076	86763	96523
8 Finance, insurance, real estate and business services	12607	22480	33135	38086	45019	51252	58774	68368	75696	81310	86387	95960
9 Community, social and personal services	9000	18826	28698	34757	44334	49994	60746	68173	73634	79637	83571	89767
Total, Industries	140664	289951	468397	535377	627798	726914	780305	865472	928393	965854	1049002	1170091
Producers of Government Services	6721	13368	19829	23484	30711	33281	39697	44582	45019	48545	50539	53127
Other Producers	...	...	...	...	...	...	...	...	...	...	...	...
Subtotal	147385	303319	488226	558861	658509	760195	820002	910054	973412	1014399	1099541	1223218
Less: Imputed bank service charge	...	...	...	...	...	...	...	...	...	...	...	...
Plus: Import duties	...	...	...	...	...	...	...	...	...	...	...	...
Plus: Value added tax	...	...	...	...	...	...	...	...	...	...	...	...
Equals: Gross Domestic Product	147385	303319	488226	558861	658509	760195	820002	910054	973412	1014399	1099541	1223218

1.11 Gross Domestic Product by Kind of Activity, in Constant Prices

Million Thai baht

At constant prices of: 1972

	1970	1975	1978	1979	1980	1981	1982	1983	1984	1985	1986	1987
1 Agriculture, hunting, forestry and fishing	42064	50700	61856	60726	61770	65093	67082	70061	73977	78539	79633	77635
2 Mining and quarrying	4452	4264	7435	7691	7917	7638	8077	7988	9535	9901	9431	10270
3 Manufacturing	24893	40708	58337	63163	64984	69069	70823	76773	81962	81463	88884	97974
4 Electricity, gas and water	1623	3263	4874	5376	5908	6591	7548	8253	9023	9934	11162	12529
5 Construction	8233	7625	13037	12855	13478	14298	14202	15787	17547	16635	16157	17342
6 Wholesale and retail trade, restaurants and hotels	35087	44440	58238	60231	63717	68889	69593	73434	79196	82527	87325	97998
7 Transport, storage and communication	10052	12445	15717	17932	20045	20641	22711	24536	27074	28171	30115	32703
8 Finance, insurance, real estate and business services	13006	17125	21248	22716	23540	24228	25642	27712	29512	30492	31323	33582
9 Community, social and personal services	9389	14164	18364	20982	22676	25170	27882	30761	32954	35093	36584	38974
Total, Industries	148799	194734	259106	271672	284035	301617	313560	335305	360780	372755	390614	419007
Producers of Government Services	6895	9694	12272	14125	15437	16822	17820	20103	19958	21358	21995	22886
Other Producers	...	...	...	...	...	...	...	...	...	...	...	...
Subtotal	155694	204428	271378	285797	299472	318439	331380	355408	380738	394113	412609	441893
Less: Imputed bank service charge	...	...	...	...	...	...	...	...	...	...	...	...
Plus: Import duties	...	...	...	...	...	...	...	...	...	...	...	...
Plus: Value added tax	...	...	...	...	...	...	...	...	...	...	...	...
Equals: Gross Domestic Product	155694	204428	271378	285797	299472	318439	331380	355408	380738	394113	412609	441893

Thailand

1.12 Relations Among National Accounting Aggregates

Million Thai baht

	1970	1975	1978	1979	1980	1981	1982	1983	1984	1985	1986	1987
Gross Domestic Product	147385	303319	488226	558861	658509	760195	820002	910054	973412	1014399	1099541	1223218
Plus: Net factor income from the rest of the world	221	-13	-3622	-6225	-5394	-12035	-12930	-6701	-11451	-17597	-22437	-23998
Factor income from the rest of the world	1673	4288	5480	8053	13044	16255	19913	24840	26688	30578	27689	27675
Less: Factor income to the rest of the world	1452	4301	9102	14278	18438	28290	32843	31541	38139	48175	50126	51673
Equals: Gross National Product	147606	303306	484604	552636	653115	748160	807072	903353	961961	996802	1077104	1199220
Less: Consumption of fixed capital	10174	20253	31647	37203	43358	50001	57020	64696	72976	81436	89531	98190
Equals: National Income	137432	283053	452957	515433	609757	698159	750052	838657	888985	915366	987573	1101030
Plus: Net current transfers from the rest of the world	1002	1685	1291	2070	4736	4833	5345	6649	4950	5905	6283	6401
Current transfers from the rest of the world	1171	1908	1536	2324	5131	5149	5704	7093	5411	6598	6963	7197
Less: Current transfers to the rest of the world	169	223	245	254	395	316	359	444	461	693	680	796
Equals: National Disposable Income	138434	284738	454248	517503	614493	702992	755397	845306	893935	921271	993856	1107431
Less: Final consumption	119768	242582	369566	430826	520055	596600	650840	717175	766034	805582	848912	921271
Equals: Net Saving	18666	42156	84682	86677	94438	106392	104557	128131	127901	115689	144944	186160
Less: Surplus of the nation on current transactions	-5206	-12316	-22970	-41745	-42102	-54906	-21997	-66014	-48647	-40514	6867	-16499
Statistical discrepancy	3685	6409	-1803	-13575	-5853	-11576	6003	-22751	-7018	6310	18908	-9176
Equals: Net Capital Formation	27557	60881	105849	114847	130687	149722	132557	171394	169530	162513	156985	193483

2.1 Government Final Consumption Expenditure by Function, in Current Prices

Million Thai baht

	1970	1975	1978	1979	1980	1981	1982	1983	1984	1985	1986	1987
1 General public services [a]	4952	7577	11632	14270	19305	23582	24230	25464	26818	28280	28651	30011
2 Defence [a]	6404	11096	23415	29411	32564	40443	43865	47372	52557	60385	57125	60258
3 Public order and safety												
4 Education	3122	7964	13326	15823	20740	22651	29539	32270	36136	38756	41890	45085
5 Health	638	1566	3160	3890	4551	5467	6877	8164	8880	10118	10206	11210
6 Social security and welfare	125	169	293	318	419	466	607	610	704	727	860	887
7 Housing and community amenities	...	...	...	...	...	...	...	...	...	...	...	...
8 Recreational, cultural and religious affairs	...	...	...	...	...	...	...	...	...	...	...	...
9 Economic services	1193	2505	2102	2300	2739	3202	3485	3290	3192	3025	3332	3453
A Fuel and energy	...	...	...	...	...	...	...	...	...	...	...	...
B Agriculture, forestry, fishing and hunting	...	...	...	...	...	...	...	...	...	...	...	...
C Mining, manufacturing and construction, except fuel and energy	...	...	...	...	...	...	...	...	...	...	...	...
D Transportation and communication	1193	2505	2102	2300	2739	3202	3485	3290	3192	3025	3332	3453
E Other economic affairs	...	...	...	...	...	...	...	...	...	...	...	...
10 Other functions [b]	144	413	655	786	1113	1170	1559	1402	1808	1626	2464	3205
Total Government Final Consumption Expenditure	16578	31290	54583	66798	81431	96981	110162	118572	130095	142917	144528	154109

a) Justice and police are included in item 'Defence'.
b) Item 'Other functions' includes items 'Housing and community amenities' and 'Recreational, cultural and religious affairs'.

2.2 Government Final Consumption Expenditure by Function, in Constant Prices

Million Thai baht

	1970	1975	1978	1979	1980	1981	1982	1983	1984	1985	1986	1987
					At constant prices of:1972							
1 General public services [a]	5140	5533	7263	8488	9584	11129	10413	10919	11183	11464	11474	11910
2 Defence [a]	6696	7974	14415	16793	15877	18385	18354	19669	21420	23618	22106	22881
3 Public order and safety												
4 Education	3209	5809	8303	9540	10429	11355	13170	14462	15815	16828	17943	19136
5 Health	663	1144	1976	2291	2247	2585	2942	3492	3692	4099	4114	4442
6 Social security and welfare	130	123	183	188	206	220	258	264	290	294	344	354
7 Housing and community amenities	...	...	...	...	...	...	...	...	...	...	...	...
8 Recreational, cultural and religious affairs	...	...	...	...	...	...	...	...	...	...	...	...
9 Economic services	1247	1810	1274	1300	1281	1422	1417	1385	1312	1243	1326	1358

Thailand

2.2 Government Final Consumption Expenditure by Function, in Constant Prices
(Continued)

Million Thai baht

	1970	1975	1978	1979	1980	1981	1982	1983	1984	1985	1986	1987
					At constant prices of:1972							
A Fuel and energy	...	...	...	...	...	...	...	...	...	...	...	...
B Agriculture, forestry, fishing and hunting	...	...	...	...	...	...	...	...	...	...	...	...
C Mining, manufacturing and construction, except fuel and energy	...	...	...	...	...	...	...	...	...	...	...	...
D Transportation and communication	1247	1810	1274	1300	1281	1422	1417	1385	1312	1243	1326	1358
E Other economic affairs	...	...	...	...	...	...	...	...	...	...	...	...
10 Other functions [b]	149	302	409	466	547	540	652	590	734	645	970	1208
Total Government Final Consumption Expenditure	17234	22695	33823	39066	40171	45636	47206	50781	54446	58191	58277	61289

a) Justice and police are included in item 'Defence'.
b) Item 'Other functions' includes items 'Housing and community amenities' and 'Recreational, cultural and religious affairs'.

2.5 Private Final Consumption Expenditure by Type and Purpose, in Current Prices

Million Thai baht

	1970	1975	1978	1979	1980	1981	1982	1983	1984	1985	1986	1987
					Final Consumption Expenditure of Resident Households							
1 Food, beverages and tobacco	52305	109567	158366	176323	208836	231761	244474	264682	267074	264010	277436	291838
A Food	42943	92264	130878	140239	165925	185213	193247	206946	204018	202705	210743	219462
B Non-alcoholic beverages	3072	5578	7687	9963	12431	13366	15025	17554	19253	20791	23379	25973
C Alcoholic beverages	2747	5206	11000	15828	18368	19256	21437	23582	26403	23042	25221	27357
D Tobacco	3543	6519	8801	10293	12112	1392	14765	16600	17400	17472	18093	19046
2 Clothing and footwear	9462	22172	32318	39445	50930	59588	64894	73185	80909	89663	99204	111609
3 Gross rent, fuel and power	11928	20273	28687	32787	39102	45803	51377	58010	63592	70094	75654	82602
A Fuel and power	2578	4731	7780	9382	11814	14061	14616	15855	16559	16880	17225	18086
B Other	9350	15542	20907	23405	27288	31742	36761	42155	47033	53214	58429	64516
4 Furniture, furnishings and household equipment and operation	5518	10774	19128	23485	28098	31436	33584	39654	43764	47007	49517	58041
A Household operation	1859	3634	5164	6383	7814	8945	9829	10878	12042	13736	14857	16234
B Other	3659	7140	13964	17102	20284	22491	23755	28776	31722	33271	34660	41807
5 Medical care and health expenses	4533	7538	12007	14260	18740	22355	23699	27810	37125	42508	46837	53714
6 Transport and communication	7740	15844	24963	30465	40457	51146	57967	62861	65558	68192	70977	77469
A Personal transport equipment	1764	3610	5870	6943	9476	10950	11840	14031	13288	10539	11405	14860
B Other	5976	12234	19093	23522	30981	40196	46127	48830	52270	57653	59572	62609
7 Recreational, entertainment, education and cultural services	4251	8251	12543	14953	18775	21557	24179	26014	27643	28588	32266	34599
A Education	782	1247	1949	2513	2834	3460	3735	4225	4257	4339	4187	3538
B Other	3469	7004	10594	12440	15941	18097	20444	21789	23386	24249	28079	31061
8 Miscellaneous goods and services	8356	18620	32286	38894	46462	51402	58232	63541	70301	76749	82016	94252
A Personal care	1903	3701	5337	6382	8008	8183	8878	9547	11103	12095	12233	12858
B Expenditures in restaurants, cafes and hotels	5874	13686	24592	29618	34729	39138	44380	47897	52927	57952	62658	72832
C Other	579	1233	2357	2894	3725	4081	4974	6097	6271	6702	7125	8562
Total Final Consumption Expenditure in the Domestic Market by Households, of which	104093	213039	320298	370612	451400	515048	558406	615757	655966	686811	733907	804124
A Durable goods	5897	11993	22005	25748	31303	36488	37808	45466	48386	46072	48056	59101
B Semi-durable goods	72163	151443	225172	258654	318992	361341	386348	421564	444628	463534	496159	540678
C Non-durable goods												

Thailand

2.5 Private Final Consumption Expenditure by Type and Purpose, in Current Prices
(Continued)

Million Thai baht

	1970	1975	1978	1979	1980	1981	1982	1983	1984	1985	1986	1987
D Services	26033	49603	73121	86210	101105	117219	134250	148727	162952	177205	189692	204345
Plus: Direct purchases abroad by resident households	1267	2735	3579	4648	4989	6027	6151	7896	7290	7622	7798	9038
Less: Direct purchases in the domestic market by non-resident households	2170	4482	8894	11232	17765	21456	23879	25050	27317	31768	37321	46000
Equals: Final Consumption Expenditure of Resident Households [a]	103190	211292	314983	364028	438624	499619	540678	598603	635939	662665	704384	767162

Final Consumption Expenditure of Private Non-profit Institutions Serving Households

	1970	1975	1978	1979	1980	1981	1982	1983	1984	1985	1986	1987
Equals: Final Consumption Expenditure of Private Non-profit Organisations Serving Households	...	...	...	...	...	...	...	...	...	...	...	...
Private Final Consumption Expenditure	103190	211292	314983	364028	438624	499619	540678	598603	635939	662665	704384	767162

a) Item 'Final consumption expenditure of resident households' includes consumption expenditure of private non-profit institutions serving households.

2.6 Private Final Consumption Expenditure by Type and Purpose, in Constant Prices

Million Thai baht

At constant prices of: 1972

Final Consumption Expenditure of Resident Households

	1970	1975	1978	1979	1980	1981	1982	1983	1984	1985	1986	1987
1 Food, beverages and tobacco	54893	67980	82463	87261	90433	91756	92690	97948	103891	104405	107773	110550
A Food	45242	54350	63588	64439	67021	68258	69661	71191	74610	77562	79334	80247
B Non-alcoholic beverages	3264	4537	5735	6854	6746	6658	6725	7652	8482	9123	10751	11873
C Alcoholic beverages	2841	3707	6743	8499	8396	8349	9038	10883	12147	9480	9345	9673
D Tobacco	3546	5386	6397	7469	8270	8491	7266	8222	8652	8240	8384	8757
2 Clothing and footwear	10095	16034	19307	20537	22251	23763	24928	26160	27320	28619	30574	33306
3 Gross rent, fuel and power	12573	16025	19099	20288	21414	22535	23708	25206	26619	27971	29355	31341
A Fuel and power	2962	3654	4582	4973	5221	5432	5746	6189	6615	6881	7239	7922
B Other	9611	12371	14517	15315	16193	17103	17962	19017	20004	21090	22176	23419
4 Furniture, furnishings and household equipment and operation	5573	7381	10603	12028	13429	12611	12420	13882	15642	16215	17195	20136
A Household operation	1920	2564	3106	3497	3759	3737	3801	4136	4456	4843	5039	5391
B Other	3653	4817	7497	8531	9670	8874	8619	9746	11186	11372	12156	14745
5 Medical care and health expenses	4529	6012	8605	10040	10906	12028	11929	13378	17653	19500	20348	22728
6 Transport and communication	8392	10194	12230	13330	15517	15065	15988	17588	17419	16683	17075	18525
A Personal transport equipment	2028	2454	2971	3378	4434	4639	4894	5521	4919	3811	3818	4396
B Other	6364	7740	9259	9952	11083	10426	11094	12067	12500	12872	13257	14129
7 Recreational, entertainment, education and cultural services	4403	6397	8455	9066	10307	10901	11445	11795	12595	12546	13263	14062
A Education	783	931	1089	1198	1295	1590	1631	1756	1715	1683	1584	1279
B Other	3620	5466	7366	7868	9012	9311	9814	10039	10880	10861	11679	12783
8 Miscellaneous goods and services	9107	12630	17088	18444	18972	19098	20461	21795	23618	25121	26343	29817
A Personal care	2055	2510	3244	3673	4178	3986	4122	4377	4811	5036	5058	5276
B Expenditures in restaurants, cafes and hotels	6441	9281	12505	13289	13152	13542	14513	15262	16667	17832	18939	21717
C Other	611	839	1339	1482	1642	1570	1826	2156	2140	2253	2346	2824
Total Final Consumption Expenditure in the Domestic Market by Households, of which	109565	142653	177850	190994	203229	207759	213569	227752	244798	251058	261926	280465
A Durable goods	6254	8040	11562	12688	15043	14637	14279	16337	16934	16008	16435	19445
B Semi-durable goods	75890	98345	122649	131924	140560	144752	147730	156373	169258	175022	182931	194953
C Non-durable goods												

Thailand

2.6 Private Final Consumption Expenditure by Type and Purpose, in Constant Prices
(Continued)

Million Thai baht

	1970	1975	1978	1979	1980	1981	1982	1983	1984	1985	1986	1987
				At constant prices of:1972								
D Services	27421	36268	43639	46382	47626	48370	51560	55042	58606	60028	62560	66067
Plus: Direct purchases abroad by resident households	1337	1809	1958	2314	2074	2224	2157	2668	2442	2493	2505	2587
Less: Direct purchases in the domestic market by non-resident households	2283	3217	5103	5782	7559	8287	8742	8970	10011	11568	12788	15407
Equals: Final Consumption Expenditure of Resident Households [a]	108619	141245	174705	187526	197744	201696	206984	221450	237229	241983	251643	267645

Final Consumption Expenditure of Private Non-profit Institutions Serving Households

	1970	1975	1978	1979	1980	1981	1982	1983	1984	1985	1986	1987
Equals: Final Consumption Expenditure of Private Non-profit Organisations Serving Households	...	...	...	...	...	...	...	...	...	...	...	...
Private Final Consumption Expenditure	108619	141245	174705	187526	197744	201696	206984	221450	237229	241983	251643	267645

a) Item 'Final consumption expenditure of resident households' includes consumption expenditure of private non-profit institutions serving households.

2.11 Gross Fixed Capital Formation by Kind of Activity of Owner, ISIC Divisions, in Current Prices

Million Thai baht

	1970	1975	1978	1979	1980	1981	1982	1983	1984	1985	1986	1987
					All Producers							
1 Agriculture, hunting, forestry and fishing	3495	6571	12030	...	...	...	...	...	...	...	...	...
2 Mining and quarrying	724	1515	2490	...	...	...	...	...	...	...	...	...
3 Manufacturing	5463	12913	21093	...	...	...	...	...	...	...	...	...
4 Electricity, gas and water	1446	2758	8546	...	...	...	...	...	...	...	...	...
5 Construction	1699	2911	4772	...	...	...	...	...	...	...	...	...
6 Wholesale and retail trade, restaurants and hotels	3871	7182	11547	...	...	...	...	...	...	...	...	...
7 Transport, storage and communication	5979	12134	21716	...	...	...	...	...	...	...	...	...
8 Finance, insurance, real estate and business services	5704	11228	21478	...	...	...	...	...	...	...	...	...
9 Community, social and personal services	3315	7218	11293	...	...	...	...	...	...	...	...	...
Total Industries	31696	64430	114965	...	...	...	...	...	...	...	...	...
Producers of Government Services	8226	12129	25846	...	...	...	...	...	...	...	...	...
Private Non-Profit Institutions Serving Households	...	...	...	...	...	...	...	...	...	...	...	...
Statistical discrepancy	-7196	-10431	-24161	...	...	...	...	...	...	...	...	...
Total [a]	32726	66128	116650	144356	177099	189067	179898	205992	228799	232079	...	...

a) Data for this table have not been revised, therefore, data for some years are not comparable with those of other tables.

4.1 Derivation of Value Added by Kind of Activity, in Current Prices

Million Thai baht

	1980			1981			1982			1983		
	Gross Output	Intermediate Consumption	Value Added	Gross Output	Intermediate Consumption	Value Added	Gross Output	Intermediate Consumption	Value Added	Gross Output	Intermediate Consumption	Value Added
					All Producers							
1 Agriculture, hunting, forestry and fishing	...	...	152852	...	...	162987	...	...	156839	...	...	185628
A Agriculture and hunting	...	...	136124	...	...	142810	...	...	137201	...	...	164217
B Forestry and logging	...	...	8613	...	...	9560	...	...	8654	...	...	9046
C Fishing	...	...	8115	...	...	10617	...	...	10984	...	...	12365
2 Mining and quarrying	...	...	22147	...	...	21556	...	...	25110	...	...	26403
A Coal mining	...	...	68	...	...	138	...	...	155	...	...	240
B Crude petroleum and natural gas production	...	...	-	...	...	811	...	...	3545	...	...	5181
C Metal ore mining	...	...	8686	...	...	6446	...	...	5249	...	...	3880
D Other mining	...	...	13393	...	...	14161	...	...	16161	...	...	17102

Thailand

4.1 Derivation of Value Added by Kind of Activity, in Current Prices
(Continued)

Million Thai baht

	1980 Gross Output	1980 Intermediate Consumption	1980 Value Added	1981 Gross Output	1981 Intermediate Consumption	1981 Value Added	1982 Gross Output	1982 Intermediate Consumption	1982 Value Added	1983 Gross Output	1983 Intermediate Consumption	1983 Value Added
3 Manufacturing	...	...	139936	...	...	169461	...	...	176360	...	...	194344
A Manufacture of food, beverages and tobacco	...	...	35630	...	...	51128	...	...	53274	...	...	53345
B Textile, wearing apparel and leather industries	...	...	33955	...	...	39849	...	...	42515	...	...	46821
C Manufacture of wood and wood products, including furniture	...	...	8696	...	...	7862	...	...	7603	...	...	8057
D Manufacture of paper and paper products, printing and publishing	...	...	4332	...	...	5051	...	...	5556	...	...	6025
E Manufacture of chemicals and chemical petroleum, coal, rubber and plastic products	...	...	20481	...	...	21529	...	...	20897	...	...	24535
F Manufacture of non-metallic mineral products, except products of petroleum and coal	...	...	5209	...	...	6938	...	...	7835	...	...	8789
G Basic metal industries	...	...	3655	...	...	3332	...	...	3004	...	...	2862
H Manufacture of fabricated metal products, machinery and equipment	...	...	22399	...	...	26320	...	...	27105	...	...	33149
I Other manufacturing industries	...	...	5579	...	...	7452	...	...	8571	...	...	10761
4 Electricity, gas and water	...	...	6289	...	...	10901	...	...	15672	...	...	17067
A Electricity, gas and steam	...	...	4998	...	...	9274	...	...	13063	...	...	14376
B Water works and supply	...	...	1291	...	...	1627	...	...	2609	...	...	2691
5 Construction	...	...	34764	...	...	38135	...	...	41500	...	...	47985
6 Wholesale and retail trade, restaurants and hotels	...	...	144594	...	...	176778	...	...	189665	...	...	196695
A Wholesale and retail trade	...	...	110176	...	...	137491	...	...	143902	...	...	147443
B Restaurants and hotels	...	...	34418	...	...	39287	...	...	45763	...	...	49252
Restaurants	...	...	29399	...	...	34321	...	...	39498	...	...	42670
Hotels and other lodging places	...	...	5019	...	...	4966	...	...	6265	...	...	6582
7 Transport, storage and communication	...	...	37863	...	...	45850	...	...	55639	...	...	60809
A Transport and storage	...	...	34251	...	...	41235	...	...	49832	...	...	54836
B Communication	...	...	3612	...	...	4615	...	...	5807	...	...	5973
8 Finance, insurance, real estate and business services	...	...	45019	...	...	51252	...	...	58774	...	...	68368
A Financial institutions	...	...	15759	...	...	17969	...	...	20719	...	...	24504
B Insurance	...	...	2860	...	...	3513	...	...	4058	...	...	4873
C Real estate and business services	...	...	26400	...	...	29770	...	...	33997	...	...	38991
Real estate, except dwellings	...	...	1307	...	...	1157	...	...	1343	...	...	1768
Dwellings	...	...	22798	...	...	26025	...	...	29774	...	...	33851
9 Community, social and personal services	...	...	44334	...	...	49994	...	...	60746	...	...	68173
A Sanitary and similar services	...	...	...	...	...	...	...	...	...	...	...	...
B Social and related community services	...	...	29322	...	...	32764	...	...	41017	...	...	45964
Educational services	...	...	21956	...	...	24115	...	...	30520	...	...	34028
Medical, dental, other health and veterinary services	...	...	7169	...	...	8430	...	...	10233	...	...	11639
C Recreational and cultural services	...	...	4123	...	...	4511	...	...	4646	...	...	4926
D Personal and household services	...	...	10889	...	...	12719	...	...	15083	...	...	17283
Total, Industries	...	...	627798	...	...	726914	...	...	780305	...	...	865472
Producers of Government Services	...	...	30711	...	...	33281	...	...	39697	...	...	44582
Other Producers	...	...	...	...	...	...	...	...	...	...	...	...
Total	...	...	658509	...	...	760195	...	...	820002	...	...	910054
Less: Imputed bank service charge	...	...	...	...	...	...	...	...	...	...	...	...
Import duties	...	...	...	...	...	...	...	...	...	...	...	...
Value added tax	...	...	...	...	...	...	...	...	...	...	...	...
Total	...	...	658509	...	...	760195	...	...	820002	...	...	910054

Thailand

4.1 Derivation of Value Added by Kind of Activity, in Current Prices

Million Thai baht

		1984			1985			1986			1987	
	Gross Output	Intermediate Consumption	Value Added	Gross Output	Intermediate Consumption	Value Added	Gross Output	Intermediate Consumption	Value Added	Gross Output	Intermediate Consumption	Value Added

All Producers

1	Agriculture, hunting, forestry and fishing	...	...	175190	...	...	169895	...	...	184770	...	...	195059
	A Agriculture and hunting	...	...	154639	...	...	148170	...	...	159880	...	...	171220
	B Forestry and logging	...	...	9212	...	...	8962	...	...	9067	...	...	9301
	C Fishing	...	...	11339	...	...	12763	...	...	15823	...	...	14538
2	Mining and quarrying	...	...	32954	...	...	40167	...	...	33239	...	...	37606
	A Coal mining	...	...	472	...	...	2106	...	...	2185	...	...	2912
	B Crude petroleum and natural gas production	...	...	8332	...	...	14329	...	...	10598	...	...	12213
	C Metal ore mining	...	...	4282	...	...	3635	...	...	1134	...	...	1282
	D Other mining	...	...	19868	...	...	20097	...	...	19322	...	...	21199
3	Manufacturing	...	...	218050	...	...	224456	...	...	253593	...	...	294496
	A Manufacture of food, beverages and tobacco	...	...	64625	...	...	67214	...	...	65995	...	...	67589
	B Textile, wearing apparel and leather industries	...	...	53111	...	...	58343	...	...	70117	...	...	90413
	C Manufacture of wood and wood products, including furniture	...	...	8672	...	...	8738	...	...	9175	...	...	12104
	D Manufacture of paper and paper products, printing and publishing	...	...	6321	...	...	6634	...	...	7418	...	...	8713
	E Manufacture of chemicals and chemical petroleum, coal, rubber and plastic products	...	...	26285	...	...	28802	...	...	40473	...	...	42406
	F Manufacture of non-metallic mineral products, except products of petroleum and coal	...	...	10498	...	...	10502	...	...	10287	...	...	11578
	G Basic metal industries	...	...	2640	...	...	3709	...	...	3201	...	...	3312
	H Manufacture of fabricated metal products, machinery and equipment	...	...	34683	...	...	28751	...	...	32068	...	...	38165
	I Other manufacturing industries	...	...	11015	...	...	11763	...	...	14859	...	...	20216
4	Electricity, gas and water	...	...	18618	...	...	23590	...	...	28689	...	...	31497
	A Electricity, gas and steam	...	...	15891	...	...	19504	...	...	24134	...	...	25971
	B Water works and supply	...	...	2727	...	...	4086	...	...	4555	...	...	5526
5	Construction	...	...	56092	...	...	56824	...	...	56564	...	...	62087
6	Wholesale and retail trade, restaurants and hotels	...	...	208629	...	...	211899	...	...	235426	...	...	267096
	A Wholesale and retail trade	...	...	154891	...	...	153130	...	...	171917	...	...	193116
	B Restaurants and hotels	...	...	53738	...	...	58769	...	...	63509	...	...	73980
	Restaurants	...	...	46773	...	...	51607	...	...	55248	...	...	63359
	Hotels and other lodging places	...	...	6965	...	...	7162	...	...	8261	...	...	10621
7	Transport, storage and communication	...	...	69530	...	...	78076	...	...	86763	...	...	96523
	A Transport and storage	...	...	62088	...	...	68769	...	...	73799	...	...	82493
	B Communication	...	...	7442	...	...	9307	...	...	12964	...	...	14030
8	Finance, insurance, real estate and business services	...	...	75696	...	...	81310	...	...	86387	...	...	95960
	A Financial institutions	...	...	27161	...	...	27994	...	...	28570	...	...	32690
	B Insurance	...	...	5524	...	...	6211	...	...	6750	...	...	7064
	C Real estate and business services	...	...	43011	...	...	47105	...	...	51067	...	...	56206
	Real estate, except dwellings	...	...	1741	...	...	1783	...	...	1900	...	...	2488
	Dwellings	...	...	37253	...	...	41091	...	...	44837	...	...	48846
9	Community, social and personal services	...	...	73634	...	...	79637	...	...	83571	...	...	89767
	A Sanitary and similar services	...	...	...	...	...	...	...	...	...	...	...	...
	B Social and related community services	...	...	49350	...	...	53718	...	...	56857	...	...	61010
	Educational services	...	...	36599	...	...	39523	...	...	41843	...	...	44964
	Medical, dental, other health and veterinary services	...	...	12421	...	...	13837	...	...	14630	...	...	15618
	C Recreational and cultural services	...	...	5747	...	...	5978	...	...	6213	...	...	6832
	D Personal and household services	...	...	18537	...	...	19941	...	...	20501	...	...	21925

Thailand

4.1 Derivation of Value Added by Kind of Activity, in Current Prices
(Continued)

Million Thai baht

	1984 Gross Output	1984 Intermediate Consumption	1984 Value Added	1985 Gross Output	1985 Intermediate Consumption	1985 Value Added	1986 Gross Output	1986 Intermediate Consumption	1986 Value Added	1987 Gross Output	1987 Intermediate Consumption	1987 Value Added
Total, Industries	...	...	928393	...	...	965854	...	...	1049002	...	...	1170091
Producers of Government Services	...	...	45019	...	...	48545	...	...	50539	...	...	53127
Other Producers	...	...	...	...	...	...	...	...	...	...	...	...
Total	...	...	973412	...	...	1014399	...	...	1099541	...	...	1223218
Less: Imputed bank service charge	...	...	...	...	...	...	...	...	...	...	...	...
Import duties	...	...	...	...	...	...	...	...	...	...	...	...
Value added tax	...	...	...	...	...	...	...	...	...	...	...	...
Total	...	...	973412	...	...	1014399	...	...	1099541	...	...	1223218

4.2 Derivation of Value Added by Kind of Activity, in Constant Prices

Million Thai baht

	1980 Gross Output	1980 Intermediate Consumption	1980 Value Added	1981 Gross Output	1981 Intermediate Consumption	1981 Value Added	1982 Gross Output	1982 Intermediate Consumption	1982 Value Added	1983 Gross Output	1983 Intermediate Consumption	1983 Value Added
At constant prices of: 1972 — All Producers												
1 Agriculture, hunting, forestry and fishing	...	...	61770	...	...	65093	...	...	67082	...	...	70061
A Agriculture and hunting	...	...	56017	...	...	58791	...	...	61128	...	...	63865
B Forestry and logging	...	...	2610	...	...	2325	...	...	2209	...	...	2188
C Fishing	...	...	3143	...	...	3977	...	...	3745	...	...	4008
2 Mining and quarrying	...	...	7917	...	...	7638	...	...	8077	...	...	7988
A Coal mining	...	...	87	...	...	103	...	...	120	...	...	115
B Crude petroleum and natural gas production	...	...	-	...	...	91	...	...	416	...	...	557
C Metal ore mining	...	...	1965	...	...	1852	...	...	1564	...	...	1238
D Other mining	...	...	5865	...	...	5592	...	...	5977	...	...	6078
3 Manufacturing	...	...	64984	...	...	69069	...	...	70823	...	...	76773
A Manufacture of food, beverages and tobacco	...	...	19786	...	...	21525	...	...	22635	...	...	23627
B Textile, wearing apparel and leather industries	...	...	16470	...	...	17669	...	...	18354	...	...	19608
C Manufacture of wood and wood products, including furniture	...	...	2207	...	...	1992	...	...	1884	...	...	2040
D Manufacture of paper and paper products, printing and publishing	...	...	2223	...	...	2296	...	...	2406	...	...	2660
E Manufacture of chemicals and chemical petroleum, coal, rubber and plastic products	...	...	7900	...	...	8181	...	...	8259	...	...	9101
F Manufacture of non-metallic mineral products, except products of petroleum and coal	...	...	2357	...	...	2558	...	...	2558	...	...	2833
G Basic metal industries	...	...	1180	...	...	1040	...	...	945	...	...	898
H Manufacture of fabricated metal products, machinery and equipment	...	...	10331	...	...	10801	...	...	10534	...	...	12119
I Other manufacturing industries	...	...	2530	...	...	3007	...	...	3248	...	...	3887
4 Electricity, gas and water	...	...	5908	...	...	6591	...	...	7548	...	...	8253
A Electricity, gas and steam	...	...	4948	...	...	5528	...	...	6325	...	...	7001
B Water works and supply	...	...	960	...	...	1063	...	...	1223	...	...	1252
5 Construction	...	...	13478	...	...	14298	...	...	14202	...	...	15787
6 Wholesale and retail trade, restaurants and hotels	...	...	63717	...	...	68889	...	...	69593	...	...	73434
A Wholesale and retail trade	...	...	50677	...	...	55096	...	...	54508	...	...	57617
B Restaurants and hotels	...	...	13040	...	...	13793	...	...	15085	...	...	15817
Restaurants	...	...	11064	...	...	11776	...	...	12633	...	...	13288
Hotels and other lodging places	...	...	1976	...	...	2017	...	...	2452	...	...	2529
7 Transport, storage and communication	...	...	20045	...	...	20641	...	...	22711	...	...	24536
A Transport and storage	...	...	17253	...	...	17754	...	...	19165	...	...	20787
B Communication	...	...	2792	...	...	2887	...	...	3546	...	...	3749
8 Finance, insurance, real estate and business services	...	...	23540	...	...	24228	...	...	25642	...	...	27712
A Financial institutions	...	...	6553	...	...	6630	...	...	7264	...	...	8280

Thailand

4.2 Derivation of Value Added by Kind of Activity, in Constant Prices
(Continued)

Million Thai baht

	1980 Gross Output	1980 Intermediate Consumption	1980 Value Added	1981 Gross Output	1981 Intermediate Consumption	1981 Value Added	1982 Gross Output	1982 Intermediate Consumption	1982 Value Added	1983 Gross Output	1983 Intermediate Consumption	1983 Value Added
				At constant prices of:1972								
B Insurance	...	...	1190	...	...	1296	...	...	1423	...	...	1647
C Real estate and business services	...	...	15797	...	...	16302	...	...	16955	...	...	17785
Real estate, except dwellings	...	...	543	...	...	427	...	...	471	...	...	597
Dwellings	...	...	14289	...	...	14929	...	...	15490	...	...	16059
9 Community, social and personal services	...	...	22676	...	...	25170	...	...	27882	...	...	30761
A Sanitary and similar services	...	...	...	...	...	...	...	...	...	...	...	...
B Social and related community services	...	...	14924	...	...	16916	...	...	18977	...	...	21044
Educational services	...	...	10902	...	...	11977	...	...	13544	...	...	15014
Medical, dental, other health and veterinary services	...	...	3953	...	...	4866	...	...	5357	...	...	5949
C Recreational and cultural services	...	...	2933	...	...	3147	...	...	3162	...	...	3306
D Personal and household services	...	...	4819	...	...	5107	...	...	5743	...	...	6411
Total, Industries	...	...	284035	...	...	301617	...	...	313560	...	...	335305
Producers of Government Services	...	...	15437	...	...	16822	...	...	17820	...	...	20103
Other Producers	...	...	...	...	...	...	...	...	...	...	...	...
Total	...	...	299472	...	...	318439	...	...	331380	...	...	355408
Less: Imputed bank service charge	...	...	...	...	...	...	...	...	...	...	...	...
Import duties	...	...	...	...	...	...	...	...	...	...	...	...
Value added tax	...	...	...	...	...	...	...	...	...	...	...	...
Total	...	...	299472	...	...	318439	...	...	331380	...	...	355408

	1984 Gross Output	1984 Intermediate Consumption	1984 Value Added	1985 Gross Output	1985 Intermediate Consumption	1985 Value Added	1986 Gross Output	1986 Intermediate Consumption	1986 Value Added	1987 Gross Output	1987 Intermediate Consumption	1987 Value Added
				At constant prices of:1972								
				All Producers								
1 Agriculture, hunting, forestry and fishing	...	...	73977	...	...	78539	...	...	79633	...	...	77635
A Agriculture and hunting	...	...	67818	...	...	72317	...	...	72751	...	...	71108
B Forestry and logging	...	...	2185	...	...	2117	...	...	2304	...	...	2214
C Fishing	...	...	3974	...	...	4105	...	...	4578	...	...	4313
2 Mining and quarrying	...	...	9535	...	...	9901	...	...	9431	...	...	10270
A Coal mining	...	...	144	...	...	317	...	...	337	...	...	421
B Crude petroleum and natural gas production	...	...	836	...	...	1342	...	...	1279	...	...	1524
C Metal ore mining	...	...	1376	...	...	1052	...	...	1047	...	...	889
D Other mining	...	...	7179	...	...	7190	...	...	6768	...	...	7436
3 Manufacturing	...	...	81962	...	...	81463	...	...	88884	...	...	97974
A Manufacture of food, beverages and tobacco	...	...	26121	...	...	26023	...	...	27307	...	...	27755
B Textile, wearing apparel and leather industries	...	...	20767	...	...	21637	...	...	24700	...	...	28633
C Manufacture of wood and wood products, including furniture	...	...	2269	...	...	2209	...	...	2373	...	...	2690
D Manufacture of paper and paper products, printing and publishing	...	...	2785	...	...	2847	...	...	2913	...	...	3222
E Manufacture of chemicals and chemical petroleum, coal, rubber and plastic products	...	...	9260	...	...	9737	...	...	10718	...	...	11530
F Manufacture of non-metallic mineral products, except products of petroleum and coal	...	...	3354	...	...	3315	...	...	3288	...	...	3757
G Basic metal industries	...	...	972	...	...	1427	...	...	1457	...	...	1487
H Manufacture of fabricated metal products, machinery and equipment	...	...	12486	...	...	10072	...	...	10957	...	...	12062
I Other manufacturing industries	...	...	3948	...	...	4196	...	...	5171	...	...	6838
4 Electricity, gas and water	...	...	9023	...	...	9934	...	...	11162	...	...	12529
A Electricity, gas and steam	...	...	7743	...	...	8666	...	...	9865	...	...	11194
B Water works and supply	...	...	1280	...	...	1268	...	...	1297	...	...	1335

Thailand

4.2 Derivation of Value Added by Kind of Activity, in Constant Prices
(Continued)

Million Thai baht

	1984 Gross Output	1984 Intermediate Consumption	1984 Value Added	1985 Gross Output	1985 Intermediate Consumption	1985 Value Added	1986 Gross Output	1986 Intermediate Consumption	1986 Value Added	1987 Gross Output	1987 Intermediate Consumption	1987 Value Added
					At constant prices of:1972							
5 Construction	...	...	17547	...	...	16635	...	...	16157	...	...	17342
6 Wholesale and retail trade, restaurants and hotels	...	...	79196	...	...	82527	...	...	87325	...	...	97998
A Wholesale and retail trade	...	...	62074	...	...	64162	...	...	67827	...	...	75594
B Restaurants and hotels	...	...	17122	...	...	18365	...	...	19498	...	...	22404
Restaurants	...	...	14306	...	...	15425	...	...	16250	...	...	18471
Hotels and other lodging places	...	...	2816	...	...	2940	...	...	3248	...	...	3933
7 Transport, storage and communication	...	...	27074	...	...	28171	...	...	30115	...	...	32703
A Transport and storage	...	...	22599	...	...	22964	...	...	24061	...	...	26104
B Communication	...	...	4475	...	...	5207	...	...	6054	...	...	6599
8 Finance, insurance, real estate and business services	...	...	29512	...	...	30492	...	...	31323	...	...	33582
A Financial institutions	...	...	9100	...	...	9157	...	...	9178	...	...	10254
B Insurance	...	...	1851	...	...	2032	...	...	2168	...	...	2215
C Real estate and business services	...	...	18561	...	...	19303	...	...	19977	...	...	21113
Real estate, except dwellings	...	...	583	...	...	583	...	...	610	...	...	781
Dwellings	...	...	16649	...	...	17357	...	...	17995	...	...	18833
9 Community, social and personal services	...	...	32954	...	...	35093	...	...	36584	...	...	38974
A Sanitary and similar services	...	...	...	...	...	...	...	...	...	...	...	...
B Social and related community services	...	...	22222	...	...	23926	...	...	25064	...	...	26605
Educational services	...	...	15873	...	...	17006	...	...	17833	...	...	18974
Medical, dental, other health and veterinary services	...	...	6262	...	...	6829	...	...	7137	...	...	7532
C Recreational and cultural services	...	...	3858	...	...	3942	...	...	4213	...	...	4766
D Personal and household services	...	...	6874	...	...	7225	...	...	7307	...	...	7603
Total, Industries	...	...	360780	...	...	372755	...	...	390614	...	...	419007
Producers of Government Services	...	...	19958	...	...	21358	...	...	21995	...	...	22886
Other Producers	...	...	...	...	...	...	...	...	...	...	...	...
Total	...	...	380738	...	...	394113	...	...	412609	...	...	441893
Less: Imputed bank service charge	...	...	...	...	...	...	...	...	...	...	...	...
Import duties	...	...	...	...	...	...	...	...	...	...	...	...
Value added tax	...	...	...	...	...	...	...	...	...	...	...	...
Total	...	...	380738	...	...	394113	...	...	412609	...	...	441893

4.3 Cost Components of Value Added

Million Thai baht

	1980 Compensation of Employees	1980 Capital Consumption	1980 Net Operating Surplus	1980 Indirect Taxes	1980 Less: Subsidies Received	1980 Value Added	1981 Compensation of Employees	1981 Capital Consumption	1981 Net Operating Surplus	1981 Indirect Taxes	1981 Less: Subsidies Received	1981 Value Added
					All Producers							
1 Agriculture, hunting, forestry and fishing	18426	...	134426	...	...	152852	19167	...	143820	...	...	162987
A Agriculture and hunting	16671	...	119453	...	...	136124	17049	...	125761	...	...	142810
B Forestry and logging	436	...	8177	...	...	8613	361	...	9199	...	...	9560
C Fishing	1319	...	6796	...	...	8115	1757	...	8860	...	...	10617
2 Mining and quarrying	3030	...	19117	...	...	22147	3515	...	18041	...	...	21556
A Coal mining	...	...	...	...	...	68	...	...	...	...	...	138
B Crude petroleum and natural gas production	...	...	...	...	...	-	...	...	...	...	...	811
C Metal ore mining	...	...	...	...	...	8686	...	...	...	...	...	6446
D Other mining	...	...	...	...	...	13393	...	...	...	...	...	14161

Thailand

4.3 Cost Components of Value Added
(Continued)

Million Thai baht

		1980					1981				
		Compensation of Employees	Capital Consumption	Net Operating Surplus	Indirect Taxes	Less: Subsidies Received	Value Added	Compensation of Employees	Capital Consumption	Net Operating Surplus	Indirect Taxes	Less: Subsidies Received	Value Added
3	Manufacturing	35407	...	104529	...	...	139936	43047	...	126414	...	...	169461
	A Manufacture of food, beverages and tobacco	...	...	...	...	...	35630						51128
	B Textile, wearing apparel and leather industries						33955						39849
	C Manufacture of wood and wood products, including furniture	...	...	...	...	...	8696						7862
	D Manufacture of paper and paper products, printing and publishing					...	4332					...	5051
	E Manufacture of chemicals and chemical petroleum, coal, rubber and plastic products						20481						21529
	F Manufacture of non-metallic mineral products, except products of petroleum and coal						5209						6938
	G Basic metal industries						3655						3332
	H Manufacture of fabricated metal products, machinery and equipment						22399						26320
	I Other manufacturing industries	...	...	...	...	...	5579	...	...	...	...	...	7452
4	Electricity, gas and water	2938	...	3351	...	...	6289	3754	...	7147	...	...	10901
	A Electricity, gas and steam						4998						9274
	B Water works and supply	...	...	...	...	...	1291	...	...	...	...	...	1627
5	Construction	12154	...	22610	...	...	34764	13928	...	24207	...	...	38135
6	Wholesale and retail trade, restaurants and hotels	12422	...	132172	...	...	144594	16695	...	160083	...	...	176778
	A Wholesale and retail trade	10432	...	99744	...	...	110176	13758	...	123733	...	...	137491
	B Restaurants and hotels	1990	...	32428	...	...	34418	2937	...	36350	...	...	39287
	Restaurants	762	...	28637	...	...	29399	1250	...	33071	...	...	34321
	Hotels and other lodging places	1228	...	3791	...	...	5019	1687	...	3279	...	...	4966
7	Transport, storage and communication	12076	...	25787	...	...	37863	13617	...	32233	...	...	45850
	A Transport and storage	...	...	...	...	...	34251	...	...	...	...	...	41235
	B Communication	...	...	...	...	...	3612	...	...	...	...	...	4615
8	Finance, insurance, real estate and business services	8176	...	36843	...	...	45019	9592	...	41660	...	...	51252
	A Financial institutions	...	...	...	...	...	15759					...	17969
	B Insurance	...	...	...	...	...	2860					...	3513
	C Real estate and business services	...	...	...	...	...	26400					...	29770
	Real estate, except dwellings					...	1307					...	1157
	Dwellings	...	...	...	...	...	22798	...	...	...	...	...	26025
9	Community, social and personal services	30332	...	14002	...	...	44334	33936	...	16058	...	...	49994
	A Sanitary and similar services												
	B Social and related community services						29322						32764
	Educational services						21956						24115
	Medical, dental, other health and veterinary services						7169						8430
	C Recreational and cultural services						4123						4511
	D Personal and household services	...	...	...	...	...	10889	...	...	...	...	...	12719
Total, Industries [a]		134961	...	492837	...	...	627798	157251	...	569663	...	...	726914
Producers of Government Services		29567	...	1144	...	...	30711	31787	...	1494	...	...	33281
Other Producers		...	...	...	...	...	...	...	...	...	...	...	...
Total [a]		164528	...	493981	...	...	658509	189038	...	571157	...	...	760195
Less: Imputed bank service charge		...	...	...	...	...	...	...	...	...	...	...	...
Import duties		...	...	...	...	...	...	...	...	...	...	...	...
Value added tax		...	...	...	...	...	...	...	...	...	...	...	...
Total [a]		164528	...	493981	...	...	658509	189038	...	571157	...	...	760195

Thailand

4.3 Cost Components of Value Added

Million Thai baht

	1982						1983					
	Compensation of Employees	Capital Consumption	Net Operating Surplus	Indirect Taxes	Less: Subsidies Received	Value Added	Compensation of Employees	Capital Consumption	Net Operating Surplus	Indirect Taxes	Less: Subsidies Received	Value Added
All Producers												
1 Agriculture, hunting, forestry and fishing	19318	...	137521	...	...	156839	22830	...	162798	...	...	185628
A Agriculture and hunting	17041	...	120160	...	...	137201	20299	...	143918	...	...	164217
B Forestry and logging	311	...	8343	...	...	8654	312	...	8734	...	...	9046
C Fishing	1966	...	9018	...	...	10984	2219	...	10146	...	...	12365
2 Mining and quarrying	3881	...	21229	...	...	25110	4036	...	22367	...	...	26403
A Coal mining	...	...	...	...	...	155	...	...	...	...	...	240
B Crude petroleum and natural gas production	...	...	...	...	...	3545	...	...	...	...	...	5181
C Metal ore mining	...	...	...	...	...	5249	...	...	...	...	...	3880
D Other mining	...	...	...	...	...	16161	...	...	...	...	...	17102
3 Manufacturing	49220	...	127140	...	...	176360	55418	...	138926	...	...	194344
A Manufacture of food, beverages and tobacco	...	...	...	...	...	53274	...	...	...	...	...	53345
B Textile, wearing apparel and leather industries	...	...	...	...	...	42515	...	...	...	...	...	46821
C Manufacture of wood and wood products, including furniture	...	...	...	...	...	7603	...	...	...	...	...	8057
D Manufacture of paper and paper products, printing and publishing	...	...	...	...	...	5556	...	...	...	...	...	6025
E Manufacture of chemicals and chemical petroleum, coal, rubber and plastic products	...	...	...	...	...	20897	...	...	...	...	...	24535
F Manufacture of non-metallic mineral products, except products of petroleum and coal	...	...	...	...	...	7835	...	...	...	...	...	8789
G Basic metal industries	...	...	...	...	...	3004	...	...	...	...	...	2862
H Manufacture of fabricated metal products, machinery and equipment	...	...	...	...	...	27105	...	...	...	...	...	33149
I Other manufacturing industries	...	...	...	...	...	8571	...	...	...	...	...	10761
4 Electricity, gas and water	4613	...	11059	...	...	15672	5209	...	11858	...	...	17067
A Electricity, gas and steam	...	...	...	...	...	13063	...	...	...	...	...	14376
B Water works and supply	...	...	...	...	...	2609	...	...	...	...	...	2691
5 Construction	16510	...	24990	...	...	41500	20361	...	27624	...	...	47985
6 Wholesale and retail trade, restaurants and hotels	18871	...	170794	...	...	189665	20994	...	175701	...	...	196695
A Wholesale and retail trade	15130	...	128772	...	...	143902	17247	...	130196	...	...	147443
B Restaurants and hotels	3741	...	42022	...	...	45763	3747	...	45505	...	...	49252
Restaurants	1465	...	38033	...	...	39498	1586	...	41084	...	...	42670
Hotels and other lodging places	2276	...	3989	...	...	6265	2161	...	4421	...	...	6582
7 Transport, storage and communication	15866	...	39773	...	...	55639	17934	...	42875	...	...	60809
A Transport and storage	...	...	...	...	...	49832	...	...	...	...	...	54836
B Communication	...	...	...	...	...	5807	...	...	...	...	...	5973
8 Finance, insurance, real estate and business services	11316	...	47458	...	...	58774	12712	...	55656	...	...	68368
A Financial institutions	...	...	...	...	...	20719	...	...	...	...	...	24504
B Insurance	...	...	...	...	...	4058	...	...	...	...	...	4873
C Real estate and business services	...	...	...	...	...	33997	...	...	...	...	...	38991
Real estate, except dwellings	...	...	...	...	...	1343	...	...	...	...	...	1768
Dwellings	...	...	...	...	...	29774	...	...	...	...	...	33851
9 Community, social and personal services	42728	...	18018	...	...	60746	47666	...	20507	...	...	68173
A Sanitary and similar services	...	...	...	...	...	...	...	...	...	...	...	...
B Social and related community services	...	...	...	...	...	41017	...	...	...	...	...	45964

Thailand

4.3 Cost Components of Value Added
(Continued)

Million Thai baht

	1982						1983					
	Compensation of Employees	Capital Consumption	Net Operating Surplus	Indirect Taxes	Less: Subsidies Received	Value Added	Compensation of Employees	Capital Consumption	Net Operating Surplus	Indirect Taxes	Less: Subsidies Received	Value Added
Educational services	...	...	...	...	...	30520	...	...	...	...	...	34028
Medical, dental, other health and veterinary services	...	...	...	...	...	10233	...	...	...	...	...	11639
C Recreational and cultural services	...	...	...	...	...	4646	...	...	...	...	...	4926
D Personal and household services	...	...	...	...	...	15083	...	...	...	...	...	17283
Total, Industries a	182323	...	597982	...	...	780305	207160	...	658312	...	...	865472
Producers of Government Services	37879	...	1818	...	...	39697	42553	...	2029	...	...	44582
Other Producers	...	...	...	...	...	...	...	...	...	...	...	...
Total a	220202	...	599800	...	...	820002	249713	...	660341	...	...	910054
Less: Imputed bank service charge	...	...	...	...	...	...	...	...	...	...	...	...
Import duties	...	...	...	...	...	...	...	...	...	...	...	...
Value added tax	...	...	...	...	...	...	...	...	...	...	...	...
Total a	220202	...	599800	...	...	820002	249713	...	660341	...	...	910054

	1984						1985					
	Compensation of Employees	Capital Consumption	Net Operating Surplus	Indirect Taxes	Less: Subsidies Received	Value Added	Compensation of Employees	Capital Consumption	Net Operating Surplus	Indirect Taxes	Less: Subsidies Received	Value Added

All Producers

1 Agriculture, hunting, forestry and fishing	21583	...	153607	...	...	175190	20757	...	149138	...	...	169895
A Agriculture and hunting	18972	...	135667	...	...	154639	17814	...	130356	...	...	148170
B Forestry and logging	316	...	8896	...	...	9212	331	...	8631	...	...	8962
C Fishing	2295	...	9044	...	...	11339	2612	...	10151	...	...	12763
2 Mining and quarrying	4359	...	28595	...	...	32954	4029	...	36138	...	...	40167
A Coal mining	...	...	...	...	...	472	...	...	...	...	...	2106
B Crude petroleum and natural gas production	...	...	...	...	...	8332	...	...	...	...	...	14329
C Metal ore mining	...	...	...	...	...	4282	...	...	...	...	...	3635
D Other mining	...	...	...	...	...	19868	...	...	...	...	...	20097
3 Manufacturing	61115	...	156935	...	...	218050	62712	...	161744	...	...	224456
A Manufacture of food, beverages and tobacco	...	...	...	...	...	64625	...	...	...	...	...	67214
B Textile, wearing apparel and leather industries	...	...	...	...	...	53111	...	...	...	...	...	58343
C Manufacture of wood and wood products, including furniture	...	...	...	...	...	8672	...	...	...	...	...	8738
D Manufacture of paper and paper products, printing and publishing	...	...	...	...	...	6321	...	...	...	...	...	6634
E Manufacture of chemicals and chemical petroleum, coal, rubber and plastic products	...	...	...	...	...	26285	...	...	...	...	...	28802
F Manufacture of non-metallic mineral products, except products of petroleum and coal	...	...	...	...	...	10498	...	...	...	...	...	10502
G Basic metal industries	...	...	...	...	...	2840	...	...	...	...	...	3709
H Manufacture of fabricated metal products, machinery and equipment	...	...	...	...	...	34683	...	...	...	...	...	28751
I Other manufacturing industries	...	...	...	...	...	11015	...	...	...	...	...	11763
4 Electricity, gas and water	5756	...	12862	...	...	18618	6444	...	17146	...	...	23590
A Electricity, gas and steam	...	...	...	...	...	15891	...	...	...	...	...	19504
B Water works and supply	...	...	...	...	...	2727	...	...	...	...	...	4086
5 Construction	24676	...	31416	...	...	56092	26157	...	30667	...	...	56824
6 Wholesale and retail trade, restaurants and hotels	22249	...	186380	...	...	208629	23881	...	188018	...	...	211899
A Wholesale and retail trade	18484	...	136407	...	...	154891	19766	...	133364	...	...	153130
B Restaurants and hotels	3765	...	49973	...	...	53738	4115	...	54654	...	...	58769
Restaurants	1733	...	45040	...	...	46773	1911	...	49696	...	...	51607
Hotels and other lodging places	2032	...	4933	...	...	6965	2204	...	4958	...	...	7162
7 Transport, storage and communication	19231	...	50299	...	...	69530	21225	...	56851	...	...	78076
A Transport and storage	...	...	...	...	...	62088	...	...	...	...	...	68769

Thailand

4.3 Cost Components of Value Added
(Continued)

Million Thai baht

	1984						1985					
	Compensation of Employees	Capital Consumption	Net Operating Surplus	Indirect Taxes	Less: Subsidies Received	Value Added	Compensation of Employees	Capital Consumption	Net Operating Surplus	Indirect Taxes	Less: Subsidies Received	Value Added
B Communication	...	...	...	...	...	7442	...	...	...	...	...	9307
8 Finance, insurance, real estate and business services	14133	...	61563	...	...	75696	15862	...	65448	...	...	81310
A Financial institutions	...	...	...	...	...	27161	...	...	...	...	...	27994
B Insurance	...	...	...	...	...	5524	...	...	...	...	...	6211
C Real estate and business services	...	...	...	...	...	43011	...	...	...	...	...	47105
Real estate, except dwellings	...	...	...	...	...	1741	...	...	...	...	...	1783
Dwellings	...	...	...	...	...	37253	...	...	...	...	...	41091
9 Community, social and personal services	51242	...	22392	...	...	73634	55421	...	24216	...	...	79637
A Sanitary and similar services	...	...	...	...	...	...	...	...	...	...	...	...
B Social and related community services	...	...	...	...	...	49350	...	...	...	...	...	53718
Educational services	...	...	...	...	...	36599	...	...	...	...	...	39523
Medical, dental, other health and veterinary services	...	...	...	...	...	12421	...	...	...	...	...	13837
C Recreational and cultural services	...	...	...	...	...	5747	...	...	...	...	...	5978
D Personal and household services	...	...	...	...	...	18537	...	...	...	...	...	19941
Total, Industries [a]	224344	...	704049	...	...	928393	236488	...	729366	...	...	965854
Producers of Government Services	42759	...	2260	...	...	45019	45952	...	2593	...	...	48545
Other Producers	...	...	...	...	...	...	...	...	...	...	...	...
Total [a]	267103	...	706309	...	...	973412	282440	...	731959	...	...	1014399
Less: Imputed bank service charge	...	...	...	...	...	...	...	...	...	...	...	...
Import duties	...	...	...	...	...	...	...	...	...	...	...	...
Value added tax	...	...	...	...	...	...	...	...	...	...	...	...
Total [a]	267103	...	706309	...	...	973412	282440	...	731959	...	...	1014399

	1986						1987					
	Compensation of Employees	Capital Consumption	Net Operating Surplus	Indirect Taxes	Less: Subsidies Received	Value Added	Compensation of Employees	Capital Consumption	Net Operating Surplus	Indirect Taxes	Less: Subsidies Received	Value Added
All Producers												
1 Agriculture, hunting, forestry and fishing	22470	...	162300	...	...	184770	24139	...	170920	...	...	195059
A Agriculture and hunting	19209	...	140671	...	...	159880	20512	...	150708	...	...	171220
B Forestry and logging	337	...	8730	...	...	9067	331	...	8970	...	...	9301
C Fishing	2924	...	12899	...	...	15823	3296	...	11242	...	...	14538
2 Mining and quarrying	3403	...	29836	...	...	33239	3199	...	34407	...	...	37606
A Coal mining	...	...	...	...	...	2185	...	...	...	...	...	2912
B Crude petroleum and natural gas production	...	...	...	...	...	10598	...	...	...	...	...	12213
C Metal ore mining	...	...	...	...	...	1134	...	...	...	...	...	1282
D Other mining	...	...	...	...	...	19322	...	...	...	...	...	21199

Thailand

4.3 Cost Components of Value Added
(Continued)

Million Thai baht

	1986						1987					
	Compensation of Employees	Capital Consumption	Net Operating Surplus	Indirect Taxes	Less: Subsidies Received	Value Added	Compensation of Employees	Capital Consumption	Net Operating Surplus	Indirect Taxes	Less: Subsidies Received	Value Added
3 Manufacturing	71487	...	182106	...	...	253593	82952	...	211544	...	...	294496
A Manufacture of food, beverages and tobacco	...	...	...	...	...	65995	...	...	...	...	...	67589
B Textile, wearing apparel and leather industries	...	...	...	...	...	70117	...	...	...	...	...	90413
C Manufacture of wood and wood products, including furniture	...	...	...	...	...	9175	...	...	...	...	...	12104
D Manufacture of paper and paper products, printing and publishing	...	...	...	...	...	7418	...	...	...	...	...	8713
E Manufacture of chemicals and chemical petroleum, coal, rubber and plastic products	...	...	...	...	...	40473	...	...	...	...	...	42406
F Manufacture of non-metallic mineral products, except products of petroleum and coal	...	...	...	...	...	10287	...	...	...	...	...	11578
G Basic metal industries	...	...	...	...	...	3201	...	...	...	...	...	3312
H Manufacture of fabricated metal products, machinery and equipment	...	...	...	...	...	32068	...	...	...	...	...	38165
I Other manufacturing industries	...	...	...	...	...	14859	...	...	...	...	...	20216
4 Electricity, gas and water	7209	...	21480	...	...	28689	7684	...	23813	...	...	31497
A Electricity, gas and steam	...	...	...	...	...	24134	...	...	...	...	...	25971
B Water works and supply	...	...	...	...	...	4555	...	...	...	...	...	5526
5 Construction	26691	...	29873	...	...	56564	29527	...	32560	...	...	62087
6 Wholesale and retail trade, restaurants and hotels	25074	...	210352	...	...	235426	29277	...	237819	...	...	267096
A Wholesale and retail trade	20566	...	151351	...	...	171917	23839	...	169277	...	...	193116
B Restaurants and hotels	4508	...	59001	...	...	63509	5438	...	68542	...	...	73980
Restaurants	2042	...	53206	...	...	55248	2387	...	60972	...	...	63359
Hotels and other lodging places	2466	...	5795	...	...	8261	3051	...	7570	...	...	10621
7 Transport, storage and communication	21909	...	64854	...	...	86763	23883	...	72640	...	...	96523
A Transport and storage	...	...	...	...	...	73799	...	...	...	...	...	82493
B Communication	...	...	...	...	...	12964	...	...	...	...	...	14030
8 Finance, insurance, real estate and business services	17763	...	68624	...	...	86387	20312	...	75648	...	...	95960
A Financial institutions	...	...	...	...	...	28570	...	...	...	...	...	32690
B Insurance	...	...	...	...	...	6750	...	...	...	...	...	7064
C Real estate and business services	...	...	...	...	...	51067	...	...	...	...	...	56206
Real estate, except dwellings	...	...	...	...	...	1900	...	...	...	...	...	2488
Dwellings	...	...	...	...	...	44837	...	...	...	...	...	48846
9 Community, social and personal services	58603	...	24968	...	...	83571	63094	...	26673	...	...	89767
A Sanitary and similar services	...	...	...	...	...	...	...	...	...	...	...	...
B Social and related community services	...	...	...	...	...	56857	...	...	...	...	...	61010
Educational services	...	...	...	...	...	41843	...	...	...	...	...	44964
Medical, dental, other health and veterinary services	...	...	...	...	...	14630	...	...	...	...	...	15618
C Recreational and cultural services	...	...	...	...	...	6213	...	...	...	...	...	6832
D Personal and household services	...	...	...	...	...	20501	...	...	...	...	...	21925
Total, Industries [a]	254609	...	794393	...	...	1049002	284067	...	886024	...	...	1170091
Producers of Government Services	47708	...	2831	...	...	50539	50108	...	3019	...	...	53127
Other Producers	...	...	...	...	...	...	...	...	...	...	...	...
Total [a]	302317	...	797224	...	...	1099541	334175	...	889043	...	...	1223218
Less: Imputed bank service charge	...	...	...	...	...	...	...	...	...	...	...	...
Import duties	...	...	...	...	...	...	...	...	...	...	...	...
Value added tax	...	...	...	...	...	...	...	...	...	...	...	...
Total [a]	302317	...	797224	...	...	1099541	334175	...	889043	...	...	1223218

a) Column 'Operating surplus' includes capital consumption and net indirect taxes'.

Togo

Source. Reply to the United Nations National Accounts Questionnaire from the Haut Commissariat du Plan, Lome. The official estimates and descriptions are published by the Commissariat in 'Comptes Nationaux'.

General note. The estimates shown in the following tables have been prepared in accordance with the United Nations System of National Accounts so far as the existing data would permit.

1.1 Expenditure on the Gross Domestic Product, in Current Prices

Million CFA francs

	1970	1975	1978	1979	1980	1981	1982	1983	1984	1985	1986	1987
1 Government final consumption expenditure	7371	19210	29254	32323	34655	38700	41800	40600	42600	47200	52500	...
2 Private final consumption expenditure	56038	95638	117239	134645	157193	180600	194900	201500	201200	219500	250900	...
3 Gross capital formation	10604	36586	93037	109406	86729	79100	70900	63300	60000	93700	105900	...
A Increase in stocks	1366	7359	4567	8000	16600	11400	7300	7000	-4600	17400	19200	...
B Gross fixed capital formation	9237	29227	88470	101406	70129	67700	63600	56300	64600	76300	86700	...
Residential buildings	2676	...	...	...	...	...	...	...	...	...	...	...
Non-residential buildings		...	...	...	...	...	...	...	...	...	...	...
Other construction and land improvement etc.	1928	...	...	...	...	...	...	...	...	...	...	...
Other	4633	...	...	...	...	...	...	...	...	...	...	...
4 Exports of goods and services	21642	35602	60578	69959	90562	103400	110700	104600	158200	160500	129500	...
5 Less: Imports of goods and services	22483	58734	108024	130102	130267	143800	148600	128700	157200	188400	175200	...
Equals: Gross Domestic Product [a]	73171	128302	192084	216231	238872	258000	269700	281300	304800	332500	363600	...

a) Data in this table have been revised, therefore they are not strictly comparable with the unrevised data in the other tables.

1.2 Expenditure on the Gross Domestic Product, in Constant Prices

Million CFA francs

	1970	1975	1978	1979	1980	1981	1982	1983	1984	1985	1986	1987
				At constant prices of: 1970								
1 Government final consumption expenditure	7371	13170	16890	18220	18211	18152	...	...	...	...	...	...
2 Private final consumption expenditure	56038	56159	64276	62626	60297	60772	...	...	...	...	...	...
3 Gross capital formation	10603	23279	39035	42685	34627	24263	...	...	...	...	...	...
A Increase in stocks	1366	4390	1978	3135	6217	5372	...	...	...	...	...	...
B Gross fixed capital formation	9237	18889	37057	39550	28410	18891	...	...	...	...	...	...
4 Exports of goods and services	21642	14061	20417	27984	33541	35847	...	...	...	...	...	...
5 Less: Imports of goods and services	22483	26100	47441	52750	52394	50589	...	...	...	...	...	...
Equals: Gross Domestic Product [a]	73171	80569	93177	98757	94282	88445	...	...	...	...	...	...

a) Data in this table have been revised, therefore they are not strictly comparable with the unrevised data in the other tables.

1.3 Cost Components of the Gross Domestic Product

Million CFA francs

	1970	1975	1978	1979	1980	1981	1982	1983	1984	1985	1986	1987
1 Indirect taxes, net	6757	18142	25206	26528	33065	35325	...	...	...	...	...	...
2 Consumption of fixed capital	4183	6188	11463	14814	17900	19124	...	...	...	...	...	...
3 Compensation of employees paid by resident producers to:	23025	39509	59417	64668	67112	71699	...	...	...	...	...	...
4 Operating surplus	39206	64463	95998	110221	120795	129052	...	...	...	...	...	...
Equals: Gross Domestic Product [a]	73171	128302	192084	216231	238872	255200	...	...	...	...	...	...

a) Data in this table have been revised, therefore they are not strictly comparable with the unrevised data in the other tables.

1.4 General Government Current Receipts and Disbursements

Million CFA francs

	1970	1975	1978	1979	1980	1981	1982	1983	1984	1985	1986	1987
					Receipts							
1 Operating surplus	...	...	...	...	...	...	...	...	...	...	...	...
2 Property and entrepreneurial income	358.8	...	...	...	...	...	...	...	...	...	...	...
3 Taxes, fees and contributions	9413.9	...	...	...	...	...	...	...	...	...	...	...
A Indirect taxes	7979.2	...	...	...	...	...	...	...	...	...	...	...
B Direct taxes	1414.0	...	...	...	...	...	...	...	...	...	...	...
C Social security contributions	-	...	...	...	...	...	...	...	...	...	...	...
D Compulsory fees, fines and penalties	20.7	...	...	...	...	...	...	...	...	...	...	...
4 Other current transfers	2472.6	...	...	...	...	...	...	...	...	...	...	...
Total Current Receipts of General Government	12245.3	...	...	...	...	...	...	...	...	...	...	...

Togo

1.4 General Government Current Receipts and Disbursements
(Continued)

Million CFA francs

	1970	1975	1978	1979	1980	1981	1982	1983	1984	1985	1986	1987
Disbursements												
1 Government final consumption expenditure	5241.2	...	...	...	...	...	...	...	...	...	...	...
A Compensation of employees	4365.3	...	...	...	...	...	...	...	...	...	...	...
B Consumption of fixed capital	...	...	...	...	...	...	...	...	...	...	...	...
C Purchases of goods and services, net	1299.9	...	...	...	...	...	...	...	...	...	...	...
D Less: Own account fixed capital formation												
E Indirect taxes paid, net	...	...	...	...	...	...	...	...	...	...	...	...
2 Property income	688.5	...	...	...	...	...	...	...	...	...	...	...
3 Subsidies	341.5	...	...	...	...	...	...	...	...	...	...	...
4 Other current transfers	4392.1	...	...	...	...	...	...	...	...	...	...	...
A Social security benefits	3575.2	...	...	...	...	...	...	...	...	...	...	...
B Social assistance grants		...	...	...	...	...	...	...	...	...	...	...
C Other	816.9	...	...	...	...	...	...	...	...	...	...	...
5 Net saving	1582.0	...	...	...	...	...	...	...	...	...	...	...
Total Current Disbursements and Net Saving of General Government	12245.3	...	...	...	...	...	...	...	...	...	...	...

1.6 Current Income and Outlay of Households and Non-Profit Institutions

Million CFA francs

	1970	1975	1978	1979	1980	1981	1982	1983	1984	1985	1986	1987
Receipts												
1 Compensation of employees	36417	...	...	...	...	...	...	...	...	...	...	...
A From resident producers	36090	...	...	...	...	...	...	...	...	...	...	...
B From rest of the world	327	...	...	...	...	...	...	...	...	...	...	...
2 Operating surplus of private unincorporated enterprises	...	...	...	...	...	...	...	...	...	...	...	...
3 Property and entrepreneurial income	...	...	...	...	...	...	...	...	...	...	...	...
4 Current transfers	...	...	...	...	...	...	...	...	...	...	...	...
Total Current Receipts	...	...	...	...	...	...	...	...	...	...	...	...
Disbursements												
1 Private final consumption expenditure	59601	...	...	...	...	...	...	...	...	...	...	...
2 Property income	...	...	...	...	...	...	...	...	...	...	...	...
3 Direct taxes and other current transfers n.e.c. to general government	308	...	...	...	...	...	...	...	...	...	...	...
A Social security contributions	174	...	...	...	...	...	...	...	...	...	...	...
B Direct taxes	...	...	...	...	...	...	...	...	...	...	...	...
C Fees, fines and penalties	...	...	...	...	...	...	...	...	...	...	...	...
4 Other current transfers	...	...	...	...	...	...	...	...	...	...	...	...
5 Net saving	-364	...	...	...	...	...	...	...	...	...	...	...
Total Current Disbursements and Net Saving	...	...	...	...	...	...	...	...	...	...	...	...

1.7 External Transactions on Current Account, Summary

Million CFA francs

	1970	1975	1978	1979	1980	1981	1982	1983	1984	1985	1986	1987
Payments to the Rest of the World												
1 Imports of goods and services	23508	58734	122489	128759	138862	...	...	...	...	...	...	...
A Imports of merchandise c.i.f.	19551	...	...	...	...	...	...	...	...	...	...	...
B Other	3958	...	...	...	...	...	...	...	...	...	...	...
2 Factor income to the rest of the world	2114	2447	6974	6485	6600	...	...	...	...	...	...	...

Togo

1.7 External Transactions on Current Account, Summary
(Continued)

Million CFA francs

	1970	1975	1978	1979	1980	1981	1982	1983	1984	1985	1986	1987
A Compensation of employees	340	55	98	95	100	...	...	...	...	...	...	...
B Property and entrepreneurial income	1775	2392	6876	6390	6500	...	...	...	...	...	...	...
3 Current transfers to the rest of the world	609	3407	3263	1200	3500	...	...	...	...	...	...	...
4 Surplus of the nation on current transactions	-1235	-16290	-49200	-45800	-37700	...	...	...	...	...	...	...
Payments to the Rest of the World and Surplus of the Nation on Current Transactions	24996	48298	83526	90644	111262	...	...	...	...	...	...	...

Receipts From The Rest of the World

	1970	1975	1978	1979	1980	1981	1982	1983	1984	1985	1986	1987
1 Exports of goods and services	21498	35602	66916	69959	90562	...	...	...	...	...	...	...
A Exports of merchandise f.o.b.	15910	...	...	...	...	...	...	...	...	...	...	...
B Other	5588	...	...	...	...	...	...	...	...	...	...	...
2 Factor income from rest of the world	848	2000	1660	2185	2200	...	...	...	...	...	...	...
A Compensation of employees	327	615	460	495	500	...	...	...	...	...	...	...
B Property and entrepreneurial income	520	1385	1200	1690	1700	...	...	...	...	...	...	...
3 Current transfers from rest of the world	2650	10696	14950	18500	18500	...	...	...	...	...	...	...
Receipts from the Rest of the World on Current Transactions	24996	48298	83526	90644	111262	...	...	...	...	...	...	...

1.10 Gross Domestic Product by Kind of Activity, in Current Prices

Million CFA francs

	1970	1975	1978	1979	1980	1981	1982	1983	1984	1985	1986	1987
1 Agriculture, hunting, forestry and fishing	27111	31646	46889	58880	63640	69300	...	...	...	...	...	...
2 Mining and quarrying	3685	14924	18932	17741	21876	22600	...	...	...	...	...	...
3 Manufacturing	6697	9004	12307	11312	16633	16300	...	...	...	...	...	...
4 Electricity, gas and water	2001	3040	3159	3482	4057	4100	...	...	...	...	...	...
5 Construction	2048	7083	17539	16796	13948	11000	...	...	...	...	...	...
6 Wholesale and retail trade, restaurants and hotels	17716	21973	30855	42215	45977	52900	...	...	...	...	...	...
7 Transport, storage and communication	5351	9268	14234	13109	15331	17200	...	...	...	...	...	...
8 Finance, insurance, real estate and business services	2608	6720	11443	12027	12656	15111	...	...	...	...	...	...
9 Community, social and personal services	2387	3785	3981	4168	...	...	...	...	...	...	...	...
Total, Industries	69604	107443	159339	179730	...	...	...	...	...	...	...	...
Producers of Government Services	5889	13112	20812	22974	...	...	...	...	...	...	...	...
Other Producers	...	...	...	...	...	...	...	...	...	...	...	...
Subtotal	75493	120555	180151	202704	223479	242311	...	...	...	...	...	...
Less: Imputed bank service charge	657	1747	1900	2386	1756	1711	...	...	...	...	...	...
Plus: Import duties	...	8034	13833	15913	17149	17400	...	...	...	...	...	...
Plus: Value added tax	...	...	...	...	...	...	...	...	...	...	...	...
Plus: Other adjustments	-1665	1460	...	...	...	...	...	...	...	...	...	...
Equals: Gross Domestic Product [a]	73171	128302	192084	216231	238872	258000	269700	281300	304800	332500	363600	...

a) Data in this table have been revised, therefore they are not strictly comparable with the unrevised data in the other tables.

1.12 Relations Among National Accounting Aggregates

Million CFA francs

	1970	1975	1978	1979	1980	1981	1982	1983	1984	1985	1986	1987
Gross Domestic Product [a]	73171	128302	192084	216231	238872	258000	269700	281300	304800	332500	363600	...
Plus: Net factor income from the rest of the world	-1100	-447	-4259	-4300	-4400	...	...	...	...	...	...	...
Factor income from the rest of the world	...	2000	...	...	2200	...	...	...	...	...	...	...
Less: Factor income to the rest of the world	...	2447	...	...	6600	...	...	...	...	...	...	...
Equals: Gross National Product	72071	127855	187825	211931	234472	...	...	...	...	...	...	...
Less: Consumption of fixed capital	4183	6188	11463	14814	17900	...	...	...	...	...	...	...

Togo

1.12 Relations Among National Accounting Aggregates
(Continued)

Million CFA francs

	1970	1975	1978	1979	1980	1981	1982	1983	1984	1985	1986	1987
Equals: National Income [a]	67888	121667	176362	197117	216572	224300	230000	234500	256400	281800	311700	...
Plus: Net current transfers from the rest of the world	2928	7289	11687	17300	15000	...	...	...	...	...	...	...
Current transfers from the rest of the world	...	10696	14950	18500	18500	...	...	...	...	...	...	...
Less: Current transfers to the rest of the world	...	3407	3263	1200	3500	...	...	...	...	...	...	...
Equals: National Disposable Income [a]	70816	128956	188049	214417	231572	...	...	...	...	...	...	...
Less: Final consumption	63409	114848	146493	166968	191848	...	...	...	...	...	...	...
Equals: Net Saving	7407	14108	41556	47449	39724	...	...	...	...	...	...	...
Less: Surplus of the nation on current transactions	986	-16290	-40018	-47143	-29105	...	...	...	...	...	...	...
Equals: Net Capital Formation	6421	30398	81574	94592	68829	...	...	...	...	...	...	...

a) Data in this table have been revised, therefore they are not strictly comparable with the unrevised data in the other tables.

2.1 Government Final Consumption Expenditure by Function, in Current Prices

Million CFA francs

		1970	1975	1978	1979	1980	1981	1982	1983	1984	1985	1986	1987
1	General public services	1689.0	...	...	...	...	...	...	...	...	...	...	...
2	Defence	797.3	...	...	...	...	...	...	...	...	...	...	...
3	Public order and safety		...	...	...	...	...	...	...	...	...	...	...
4	Education	1039.6	...	...	...	...	...	...	...	...	...	...	...
5	Health	641.8	...	...	...	...	...	...	...	...	...	...	...
6	Social security and welfare	53.8	...	...	...	...	...	...	...	...	...	...	...
7	Housing and community amenities	44.3	...	...	...	...	...	...	...	...	...	...	...
8	Recreational, cultural and religious affairs	42.6	...	...	...	...	...	...	...	...	...	...	...
9	Economic services	932.8	...	...	...	...	...	...	...	...	...	...	...
10	Other functions	-	...	...	...	...	...	...	...	...	...	...	...
	Total Government Final Consumption Expenditure	5241.2	...	...	...	...	...	...	...	...	...	...	...

2.5 Private Final Consumption Expenditure by Type and Purpose, in Current Prices

Million CFA francs

		1970	1975	1978	1979	1980	1981	1982	1983	1984	1985	1986	1987
	Final Consumption Expenditure of Resident Households												
1	Food, beverages and tobacco	38451.2	...	...	...	...	...	...	...	...	...	...	...
	A Food	35064.6	...	...	...	...	...	...	...	...	...	...	...
	B Non-alcoholic beverages	1787.7	...	...	...	...	...	...	...	...	...	...	...
	C Alcoholic beverages	...	...	...	...	...	...	...	...	...	...	...	...
	D Tobacco	1598.9	...	...	...	...	...	...	...	...	...	...	...
2	Clothing and footwear	5213.7	...	...	...	...	...	...	...	...	...	...	...
3	Gross rent, fuel and power	5974.7	...	...	...	...	...	...	...	...	...	...	...
4	Furniture, furnishings and household equipment and operation	2337.5	...	...	...	...	...	...	...	...	...	...	...
	A Household operation	736.3	...	...	...	...	...	...	...	...	...	...	...
	B Other	1601.2	...	...	...	...	...	...	...	...	...	...	...
5	Medical care and health expenses	952.0	...	...	...	...	...	...	...	...	...	...	...
6	Transport and communication	4964.7	...	...	...	...	...	...	...	...	...	...	...
	A Personal transport equipment	1236.6	...	...	...	...	...	...	...	...	...	...	...
	B Other	3728.1	...	...	...	...	...	...	...	...	...	...	...
7	Recreational, entertainment, education and cultural services	573.8	...	...	...	...	...	...	...	...	...	...	...
	A Education	334.4	...	...	...	...	...	...	...	...	...	...	...
	B Other	239.4	...	...	...	...	...	...	...	...	...	...	...
8	Miscellaneous goods and services	2057.4	...	...	...	...	...	...	...	...	...	...	...
	A Personal care	956.1	...	...	...	...	...	...	...	...	...	...	...
	B Expenditures in restaurants, cafes and hotels	324.8	...	...	...	...	...	...	...	...	...	...	...

Togo

2.5 Private Final Consumption Expenditure by Type and Purpose, in Current Prices
(Continued)

Million CFA francs

	1970	1975	1978	1979	1980	1981	1982	1983	1984	1985	1986	1987
C Other	776.5	...	...	...	...	...	...	...	...	...	...	...
Total Final Consumption Expenditure in the Domestic Market by Households, of which	60525.0	...	...	...	...	...	...	...	...	...	...	...
Plus: Direct purchases abroad by resident households	433.7	...	...	...	...	...	...	...	...	...	...	...
Less: Direct purchases in the domestic market by non-resident households	1213.4	...	...	...	...	...	...	...	...	...	...	...
Equals: Final Consumption Expenditure of Resident Households	59745.3	...	...	...	...	...	...	...	...	...	...	...

Final Consumption Expenditure of Private Non-profit Institutions Serving Households

	1970	1975	1978	1979	1980	1981	1982	1983	1984	1985	1986	1987
Equals: Final Consumption Expenditure of Private Non-profit Organisations Serving Households	...	...	...	...	...	...	...	...	...	...	...	...
Private Final Consumption Expenditure	59745.3	...	...	...	...	...	...	...	...	...	...	...

2.17 Exports and Imports of Goods and Services, Detail

Million CFA francs

	1970	1975	1978	1979	1980	1981	1982	1983	1984	1985	1986	1987
Exports of Goods and Services												
1 Exports of merchandise, f.o.b.	15910.2	...	...	...	...	...	...	...	...	...	...	...
2 Transport and communication	478.1	...	...	...	...	...	...	...	...	...	...	...
3 Insurance service charges	142.2	...	...	...	...	...	...	...	...	...	...	...
4 Other commodities	611.8	...	...	...	...	...	...	...	...	...	...	...
5 Adjustments of merchandise exports to change-of-ownership basis	3142.6	...	...	...	...	...	...	...	...	...	...	...
6 Direct purchases in the domestic market by non-residential households	1213.4	...	...	...	...	...	...	...	...	...	...	...
7 Direct purchases in the domestic market by extraterritorial bodies	...	...	...	...	...	...	...	...	...	...	...	...
Total Exports of Goods and Services	21498.3	...	...	...	...	...	...	...	...	...	...	...
Imports of Goods and Services												
1 Imports of merchandise, c.i.f.	19550.8	...	...	...	...	...	...	...	...	...	...	...
2 Adjustments of merchandise imports to change-of-ownership basis	1125.6	...	...	...	...	...	...	...	...	...	...	...
3 Other transport and communication	342.6	...	...	...	...	...	...	...	...	...	...	...
4 Other insurance service charges	296.3	...	...	...	...	...	...	...	...	...	...	...
5 Other commodities	433.7	...	...	...	...	...	...	...	...	...	...	...
6 Direct purchases abroad by government	1759.4	...	...	...	...	...	...	...	...	...	...	...
7 Direct purchases abroad by resident households		...	...	...	...	...	...	...	...	...	...	...
Total Imports of Goods and Services	23508.4	...	...	...	...	...	...	...	...	...	...	...
Balance of Goods and Services	-2010.1	...	...	...	...	...	...	...	...	...	...	...
Total Imports and Balance of Goods and Services	21498.3	...	...	...	...	...	...	...	...	...	...	...

Tonga

Source. Reply to the United Nations National Accounts Questionnaire from the Statistics Department, Nuku'alofa.
General note. The estimates shown in the following tables have been prepared in accordance with the United Nations System of National Accounts so far as the existing data would permit.

1.1 Expenditure on the Gross Domestic Product, in Current Prices

Million Tongan pa'anga — Fiscal year ending 30 June

	1970	1975	1978	1979	1980	1981	1982	1983	1984	1985	1986	1987
1 Government final consumption expenditure	2.3	... 3.2	5.8	6.0	6.9	7.7	10.8	10.3	...	...	...	...
2 Private final consumption expenditure	10.4	... 22.1	34.0	39.0	49.8	66.8	77.7	91.5	...	...	...	...
3 Gross capital formation	2.8	... 6.8	10.8	12.4	13.8	14.2	15.7	21.1	...	...	...	...
A Increase in stocks	-0.2	... 1.2	1.8	1.2	1.2	1.2	0.9	0.7	...	...	...	...
B Gross fixed capital formation	3.0	... 5.7	9.0	11.2	12.6	13.0	14.8	20.4	...	...	...	...
Residential buildings	...	...	...	...	3.9	2.1	3.2	6.6	...	...	...	...
Non-residential buildings	...	...	...	...	5.3	6.5	6.4	9.0	...	...	...	...
Other construction and land improvement etc.	...	...	...	...	0.1	0.1	0.1	0.2	...	...	...	...
Other	...	...	...	...	...	...	...	...	...	...	...	...
4 Exports of goods and services	3.3	... 10.3	10.5	10.4	14.1	14.3	16.5	14.3	...	...	...	...
5 Less: Imports of goods and services	5.4	... 17.6	24.6	27.9	31.7	36.6	41.0	50.9	...	...	...	...
Equals: Gross Domestic Product	13.3	28.3 / 24.8	36.3	39.9	52.9	54.4	64.2	72.7	...	...	...	...

1.3 Cost Components of the Gross Domestic Product

Million Tongan pa'anga — Fiscal year ending 30 June

	1970	1975	1978	1979	1980	1981	1982	1983	1984	1985	1986	1987
1 Indirect taxes, net	1.2	... 3.8	5.3	5.2	6.1	7.1	8.4	9.3	...	...	...	...
A Indirect taxes	...	...	...	...	...	7.3	8.7	9.7	...	...	...	...
B Less: Subsidies	...	...	...	...	...	0.2	0.3	0.4	...	...	...	...
2 Consumption of fixed capital	0.5	... 1.0	1.5	1.8	2.2	2.5	2.9	2.9	...	...	...	...
3 Compensation of employees paid by resident producers to:	6.5	... 9.5	12.8	17.2	18.6	24.1	28.5	32.2	...	...	...	...
A Resident households	6.5	...	...	...	...	...	...	...	...	...	...	...
B Rest of the world	-	...	...	...	...	...	...	...	...	...	...	...
4 Operating surplus	5.2	... 10.5	16.7	27.3	25.9	32.5	39.5	41.5	...	...	...	...
Equals: Gross Domestic Product	13.3	28.3 / 24.8	36.3	39.9	52.8	54.4	64.2	72.7	...	...	...	...

1.4 General Government Current Receipts and Disbursements

Million Tongan pa'anga — Fiscal year ending 30 June

	1970	1975	1978	1979	1980	1981	1982	1983	1984	1985	1986	1987
Receipts												
1 Operating surplus	...	0.1	0.2	0.2	0.2	0.4	0.9	...	...	...	...	...
2 Property and entrepreneurial income	...	0.2	-	-	0.3	0.7	0.6	...	...	...	...	...
3 Taxes, fees and contributions	...	4.3	6.5	6.5	7.8	9.1	10.7	...	...	...	...	...
A Indirect taxes	...	3.8	5.3	5.2	6.2	7.3	8.7	...	...	...	...	...
B Direct taxes	...	0.4	1.1	1.2	1.5	1.7	1.9	...	...	...	...	...
C Social security contributions	...	-	-	-	-	-	-	...	...	...	...	...
D Compulsory fees, fines and penalties	...	0.1	0.1	0.1	0.1	0.1	0.1	...	...	...	...	...
4 Other current transfers	...	-	0.1	0.1	0.2	0.2	0.3	...	...	...	...	...
Total Current Receipts of General Government [a]	...	4.6	6.8	6.8	8.5	10.4	12.5	...	...	...	...	...
Disbursements												
1 Government final consumption expenditure	...	3.3	5.4	5.9	6.3	6.9	9.2	...	...	...	...	...

Tonga

1.4 General Government Current Receipts and Disbursements
(Continued)

Million Tongan pa'anga — Fiscal year ending 30 June

	1970	1975	1978	1979	1980	1981	1982	1983	1984	1985	1986	1987
A Compensation of employees	...	2.2	3.7	3.9	4.3	4.3	5.8	...	...	...	...	...
B Consumption of fixed capital	...	...	...	...	...	...	...	...	...	...	...	...
C Purchases of goods and services, net	...	1.1	1.7	2.0	2.0	2.6	3.4	...	...	...	...	...
D Less: Own account fixed capital formation	...	...	...	...	...	...	...	...	...	...	...	...
E Indirect taxes paid, net	...	...	...	...	...	...	...	...	...	...	...	...
2 Property income	...	-	0.1	0.1	0.2	0.2	0.4	...	...	...	...	...
3 Subsidies	...	0.1	0.1	0.2	0.2	0.2	0.3	...	...	...	...	...
4 Other current transfers	...	0.2	0.4	0.5	0.5	0.6	0.6	...	...	...	...	...
5 Net saving [b]	...	1.0	0.8	0.1	1.3	2.5	2.0	...	...	...	...	...
Total Current Disbursements and Net Saving of General Government [a]	...	4.6	6.8	6.8	8.5	10.4	12.5	...	...	...	...	...

a) Data for this table have not been revised, therefore, data for some years are not comparable with those of other tables.
b) Item 'Net saving' includes consumption of fixed capital.

1.7 External Transactions on Current Account, Summary

Million Tongan pa'anga — Fiscal year ending 30 June

	1970	1975	1978	1979	1980	1981	1982	1983	1984	1985	1986	1987
Payments to the Rest of the World												
1 Imports of goods and services	5.4	17.6	24.6	27.9	31.7	36.7	41.0	50.9	...	...	...	...
A Imports of merchandise c.i.f.	...	14.8	20.3	24.5	27.2	32.2	36.2	43.8	...	...	...	...
B Other	...	2.8	4.3	3.4	4.5	4.5	4.8	7.1	...	...	...	...
2 Factor income to the rest of the world	-	0.1	0.2	0.3	0.4	0.5	0.9	0.1	...	...	...	...
A Compensation of employees	-	...	-	0.3	0.3	0.5	0.8	0.1	...	...	...	...
B Property and entrepreneurial income	-	...	0.2	0.1	0.2	-	0.1	-	...	...	...	...
3 Current transfers to the rest of the world	0.3	0.5	0.8	0.8	1.0	2.0	2.9	6.2	...	...	...	...
4 Surplus of the nation on current transactions	-0.5	-0.6	-6.0	-6.8	-4.7	-6.1	2.9	-13.7	...	...	...	...
Payments to the Rest of the World and Surplus of the Nation on Current Transactions	5.2	17.6	19.6	22.2	28.5	33.0	47.7	43.6	...	...	...	...
Receipts From The Rest of the World												
1 Exports of goods and services	3.3	10.3	10.5	10.4	14.1	14.3	16.4	14.3	...	...	...	...
A Exports of merchandise f.o.b.	...	5.6	5.3	5.0	7.7	7.1	6.7	3.8	...	...	...	...
B Other	...	4.7	5.2	5.5	6.4	7.2	9.7	10.6	...	...	...	...
2 Factor income from rest of the world	0.2	0.6	0.9	1.7	2.7	3.9	5.3	3.3	...	...	...	...
A Compensation of employees	-	...	0.1	0.3	0.8	2.7	2.8	3.3	...	...	...	...
B Property and entrepreneurial income	0.2	...	0.8	1.4	1.9	1.2	2.5	-	...	...	...	...
3 Current transfers from rest of the world	1.7	6.7	8.3	10.1	11.7	14.9	25.9	25.9	...	...	...	...
Receipts from the Rest of the World on Current Transactions	5.2	17.6	19.6	22.2	28.5	33.0	47.7	43.6	...	...	...	...

Tonga

1.8 Capital Transactions of The Nation, Summary

Million Tongan pa'anga — Fiscal year ending 30 June

	1970	1975	1978	1979	1980	1981	1982	1983	1984	1985	1986	1987
Finance of Gross Capital Formation												
Gross saving	2.2	6.2	4.7	5.7	10.9	10.2	18.9	...	...	...	...	...
1 Consumption of fixed capital	0.5	1.0	1.5	1.8	2.2	2.5	2.8	...	...	...	...	...
2 Net saving	1.7	5.2	3.2	3.9	8.7	7.8	16.1	...	...	...	...	...
Less: Surplus of the nation on current transactions	-0.5	-0.6	-6.0	-6.8	-4.6	-6.6	2.5	...	...	...	...	...
Finance of Gross Capital Formation [a]	2.8	6.9	10.7	12.5	15.5	16.8	16.3	...	...	...	...	...
Gross Capital Formation												
Increase in stocks	-0.2	1.2	1.8	1.2	2.0	2.0	1.3	...	...	...	...	...
Gross fixed capital formation	3.0	5.7	9.0	11.2	13.6	14.8	15.0	...	...	...	...	...
1 General government	...	1.0	3.5	5.1	6.0	4.2	6.4	...	...	...	...	...
2 Corporate and quasi-corporate enterprises	...	4.7	5.5	6.1	7.5	10.6	8.6	...	...	...	...	...
A Public	...	0.4	0.7	0.8	1.3	2.1	0.9	...	...	...	...	...
B Private	...	4.3	4.8	5.3	6.2	8.5	7.7	...	...	...	...	...
3 Other	...	...	...	...	...	...	...	...	...	...	...	...
Gross Capital Formation [a]	2.8	6.9	10.7	12.5	15.5	16.8	16.3	...	...	...	...	...

a) Data for this table have not been revised, therefore, data for some years are not comparable with those of other tables.

1.9 Gross Domestic Product by Institutional Sectors of Origin

Million Tongan pa'anga — Fiscal year ending 30 June

	1970	1975	1978	1979	1980	1981	1982	1983	1984	1985	1986	1987
Domestic Factor Incomes Originating												
1 General government	...	...	...	3.8	4.5	4.5	6.2	...	...	...	...	...
2 Corporate and quasi-corporate enterprises	...	...	...	9.1	11.3	13.1	14.7	...	...	...	...	...
A Non-financial [a]	...	...	...	9.1	11.3	13.1	14.7	...	...	...	...	...
Public	...	...	...	4.5	5.4	5.5	6.1	...	...	...	...	...
Private	...	...	...	4.6	5.9	7.6	8.6	...	...	...	...	...
B Financial [a]	...	...	...	...	...	...	...	...	...	...	...	...
3 Households and private unincorporated enterprises	...	...	...	19.9	22.7	26.4	27.9	...	...	...	...	...
4 Non-profit institutions serving households	...	...	...	1.9	2.1	2.3	2.5	...	...	...	...	...
Subtotal: Domestic Factor Incomes [b]	...	...	...	34.7	40.6	46.3	51.2	...	...	...	...	...
Indirect taxes, net	...	...	...	5.2	6.1	7.3	8.7	...	...	...	...	...
Consumption of fixed capital	...	...	...	...	...	...	...	...	...	...	...	...
Gross Domestic Product [b]	...	...	...	40.0	46.8	53.5	59.9	...	...	...	...	...

a) Item 'Non-financial' includes also financial corporate and quasi-corporate enterprises.
b) Data for this table have not been revised, therefore, data for some years are not comparable with those of other tables.

1.10 Gross Domestic Product by Kind of Activity, in Current Prices

Million Tongan pa'anga — Fiscal year ending 30 June

	1970	1975	1978	1979	1980	1981	1982	1983	1984	1985	1986	1987
1 Agriculture, hunting, forestry and fishing	6.3	10.5	13.0	14.5	21.3	17.8	21.1	24.3	...	...	...	...
2 Mining and quarrying	0.1	0.1	0.2	0.2	0.3	0.4	0.4	0.4	...	...	...	...
3 Manufacturing	0.3	1.1	2.3	2.7	2.8	4.5	5.2	5.0	...	...	...	...
4 Electricity, gas and water	0.1	0.2	0.3	0.4	0.3	0.3	8.4	0.4	...	...	...	...
5 Construction	0.6	0.8	1.5	2.0	1.8	2.0	1.9	2.5	...	...	...	...

Tonga

1.10 Gross Domestic Product by Kind of Activity, in Current Prices
(Continued)

Million Tongan pa'anga — Fiscal year ending 30 June

	1970	1975	1978	1979	1980	1981	1982	1983	1984	1985	1986	1987
6 Wholesale and retail trade, restaurants and hotels	1.2	... 2.8	4.4	4.8	6.8	7.4	10.6	12.4	...	...	...	...
7 Transport, storage and communication	0.7	... 0.8	1.8	2.0	3.1	4.5	4.7	4.9	...	...	...	...
8 Finance, insurance, real estate and business services	0.7	... 1.5	2.3	2.5	3.8	2.9	3.2	4.0	...	...	...	...
9 Community, social and personal services [a]	0.9	... 3.2	5.2	5.7	6.5	7.5	8.3	9.5	...	...	...	...
Statistical discrepancy	...	...	...	...	...	-6.3	0.2	-9.1	...	...	...	...
Total, Industries	11.0	...	...	...	...	...	...	...	...	...	...	...
Producers of Government Services [a]	1.2	...	...	...	...	-0.2	-2.7	4.6	...	...	...	...
Other Producers [a]	...	...	...	...	...	...	...	...	...	...	...	...
Subtotal [b]	12.1	... 21.0	31.0	34.7	46.7	47.3	55.8	63.4	...	...	...	...
Less: Imputed bank service charge	...	...	...	0.2	0.3	0.4	0.5	0.7	...	...	...	...
Plus: Import duties	...	...	...	...	...	...	...	...	...	...	...	...
Plus: Value added tax	...	...	...	...	...	...	...	...	...	...	...	...
Plus: Other adjustments [c]	1.2	3.8	5.3	5.2	6.1	7.1	8.4	9.3	...	...	...	...
Equals: Gross Domestic Product	13.3	28.3 24.8	36.3	40.0	52.9	64.4	64.2	72.7	...	...	...	...

a) Items 'Other producers' and 'Producers of government services' are included in item 'Community, social and personal services'.
b) Gross domestic product in factor values.
c) Item 'Other adjustments' refers to indirect taxes net of subsidies.

1.11 Gross Domestic Product by Kind of Activity, in Constant Prices

Million Tongan pa'anga — Fiscal year ending 30 June

	1970	1975	1978	1979	1980	1981	1982	1983	1984	1985	1986	1987
				At constant prices of:1975								
1 Agriculture, hunting, forestry and fishing	...	10.5	10.4	10.4	13.5	17.2	18.6	20.2	...	...	...	...
2 Mining and quarrying	...	0.1	0.2	0.2	0.2	0.3	0.2	0.3	...	...	...	...
3 Manufacturing	...	1.1	1.4	1.4	1.7	2.1	2.2	1.5	...	...	...	...
4 Electricity, gas and water	...	0.2	0.3	0.3	0.3	0.3	0.4	0.4	...	...	...	...
5 Construction	...	0.8	1.1	1.3	0.9	0.8	0.8	0.8	...	...	...	...
6 Wholesale and retail trade, restaurants and hotels	...	2.8	3.0	3.1	3.3	3.3	4.3	4.6	...	...	...	...
7 Transport, storage and communication	...	0.8	1.5	1.5	2.0	2.1	2.5	2.8	...	...	...	...
8 Finance, insurance, real estate and business services	...	1.5	1.8	2.2	2.5	2.5	3.3	3.6	...	...	...	...
9 Community, social and personal services [a]	...	3.2	3.6	3.7	3.9	3.8	5.0	5.3	...	...	...	...
Total, Industries	...	...	...	...	...	...	...	...	...	...	...	...
Producers of Government Services [a]	...	...	...	...	...	...	...	...	...	...	...	...
Other Producers [a]	...	...	...	...	...	...	...	...	...	...	...	...
Subtotal [b]	...	21.0	23.2	24.2	28.3	32.5	37.3	39.5	...	...	...	...
Less: Imputed bank service charge	...	...	...	...	...	...	...	...	...	...	...	...
Plus: Import duties	...	...	...	...	...	...	...	...	...	...	...	...
Plus: Value added tax	...	...	...	...	...	...	...	...	...	...	...	...
Plus: Other adjustments [c]	...	3.8	3.5	3.0	3.2	3.4	3.9	4.2	...	...	...	...
Equals: Gross Domestic Product	...	24.8	26.7	27.2	31.5	35.9	41.2	43.6	...	...	...	...

a) Items 'Other producers' and 'Producers of government services' are included in item 'Community, social and personal services'.
b) Gross domestic product in factor values.
c) Item 'Other adjustments' refers to indirect taxes net of subsidies.

Tonga

1.12 Relations Among National Accounting Aggregates

Million Tongan pa'anga — Fiscal year ending 30 June

	1970	1975	1978	1979	1980	1981	1982	1983	1984	1985	1986	1987
Gross Domestic Product	13.3	28.3 / 24.8	36.3	40.0	52.9	54.4	64.2	72.7	...	...	...	...
Plus: Net factor income from the rest of the world	0.2	... / 0.5	0.7	1.3	2.3	3.4	4.4	3.2	...	...	...	...
Factor income from the rest of the world	0.2	... / 0.6	0.9	1.7	2.7	3.9	5.3	3.3	...	...	...	...
Less: Factor income to the rest of the world	-	... / 0.1	0.2	0.3	0.4	0.5	0.9	0.1	...	...	...	...
Equals: Gross National Product	13.5	... / 25.3	37.0	41.2	55.2	57.8	68.6	75.9	...	...	...	...
Less: Consumption of fixed capital	0.5	... / 1.0	1.5	1.8	2.2	2.5	2.9	2.9	...	...	...	...
Equals: National Income	13.0	27.7 / 24.4	35.5	39.5	53.0	55.3	65.7	73.0	...	...	...	...
Plus: Net current transfers from the rest of the world	1.4	... / 6.1	7.5	9.3	10.7	12.9	23.0	19.7	...	...	...	...
Current transfers from the rest of the world	1.7	... / 6.7	8.3	10.1	11.7	14.9	25.9	25.9	...	...	...	...
Less: Current transfers to the rest of the world	0.3	... / 0.5	0.8	0.8	1.0	2.0	2.9	6.2	...	...	...	...
Equals: National Disposable Income	14.5	... / 30.5	43.0	48.8	63.7	68.2	88.7	92.0	...	...	...	...
Less: Final consumption	12.7	... / 25.3	39.8	45.0	56.7	74.5	88.5	101.8	...	...	...	...
Equals: Net Saving	1.7	... / 5.2	3.2	3.9	7.0	5.7	15.7	4.5	...	...	...	...
Less: Surplus of the nation on current transactions	-0.5	... / -0.6	-6.0	-6.8	-4.7	-6.1	2.9	-13.7	...	...	...	...
Equals: Net Capital Formation	2.3	... / 5.9	9.2	10.7	11.7	11.8	12.8	18.2	...	...	...	...

2.1 Government Final Consumption Expenditure by Function, in Current Prices

Million Tongan pa'anga — Fiscal year ending 30 June

	1970	1975	1978	1979	1980	1981	1982	1983	1984	1985	1986	1987
1 General public services	...	...	⎡				⎤	...	...	...	...	...
2 Defence	...	...	1.9	2.1	2.8	3.2	4.3	...	...	...	...	...
3 Public order and safety	...	...	⎣				⎦	...	...	...	...	...
4 Education	...	0.5	1.0	1.1	1.2	1.2	1.6	...	...	...	...	...
5 Health	...	0.6	1.0	1.1	1.4	1.6	2.1	...	...	...	...	...
6 Social security and welfare	...	...	...	...	...	...	...	...	...	...	...	...
7 Housing and community amenities	...	0.1	0.2	0.3	0.3	0.3	0.2	...	...	...	...	...
8 Recreational, cultural and religious affairs	...	...	...	...	...	...	...	...	...	...	...	...
9 Economic services	...	0.6	1.3	1.4	1.3	1.3	2.9	...	...	...	...	...
A Fuel and energy	...	...	...	...	...	...	...	...	...	...	...	...
B Agriculture, forestry, fishing and hunting	...	0.2	0.4	0.5	0.5	0.5	0.7	...	...	...	...	...
C Mining, manufacturing and construction, except fuel and energy	...	0.3	0.7	0.7	0.7	0.7	1.8	...	...	...	...	...
D Transportation and communication	...	...	...	...	...	...	...	...	...	...	...	...
E Other economic affairs	...	0.1	0.2	0.2	0.2	0.2	0.4	...	...	...	...	...
10 Other functions	...	...	...	...	...	...	...	...	...	...	...	...
Total Government Final Consumption Expenditure	...	3.2	5.3	6.0	6.9	7.8	11.0	...	...	...	...	...

2.11 Gross Fixed Capital Formation by Kind of Activity of Owner, ISIC Divisions, in Current Prices

Million Tongan pa'anga — Fiscal year ending 30 June

All Producers

	1970	1975	1978	1979	1980	1981	1982	1983	1984	1985	1986	1987
1 Agriculture, hunting, forestry and fishing	0.2	... / 0.5	1.7	2.3	1.4	1.6	4.0	...	...	...	...	...
A Agriculture and hunting	...	0.5	1.7	...	1.4	1.6	4.0	...	...	...	...	...
B Forestry and logging	...	...	...	...	...	...	...	...	...	...	...	...
C Fishing	...	...	...	...	...	...	...	...	...	...	...	...

Tonga

2.11 Gross Fixed Capital Formation by Kind of Activity of Owner, ISIC Divisions, in Current Prices
(Continued)

Million Tongan pa'anga — Fiscal year ending 30 June

	1970	1975	1978	1979	1980	1981	1982	1983	1984	1985	1986	1987
2 Mining and quarrying	0.1	...	-	0.1	0.1	-	-	...	...	...	...	...
A Coal mining	...	...	...	...	...	...	...	...	...	...	...	...
B Crude petroleum and natural gas production	...	...	...	...	...	...	...	...	...	...	...	...
C Metal ore mining	...	...	...	...	...	...	...	...	...	...	...	...
D Other mining	0.1	...	-	0.1	0.1	-	-	...	...	...	...	...
3 Manufacturing	0.1	0.2	0.4	0.7	1.1	0.9	1.5	...	...	...	...	...
4 Electricity, gas and water	-	0.2	0.5	0.6	0.8	2.1	0.6	...	...	...	...	...
5 Construction	0.5	0.3	0.4	0.9	1.5	1.2	0.5	...	...	...	...	...
6 Wholesale and retail trade, restaurants and hotels	0.1	0.3	0.6	1.1	0.9	1.1	1.0	...	...	...	...	...
7 Transport, storage and communication	0.5	0.9	1.5	1.4	2.5	4.0	3.1	...	...	...	...	...
8 Finance, insurance, real estate and business services	-	2.6	2.4	2.6	2.3	2.8	3.1	...	...	...	...	...
9 Community, social and personal services	1.1	0.7	1.4	2.3	2.9	1.1	1.3	...	...	...	...	...
Total Industries	2.7	5.7	8.9	11.2	13.6	14.8	15.0	...	...	...	...	...
Producers of Government Services	0.3	...										
Private Non-Profit Institutions Serving Households	...	...										
Total	3.0	5.7	8.9	11.2	13.6	14.8	15.0	...	...	...	...	...

Trinidad and Tobago

Source. Reply to the United Nations National Accounts Questionnaire from the Central Statistical Office, Port-of-Spain. The official estimates are published by the Office in the 'National Income of Trinidad and Tobago' and in the 'Annual Statistical Digest'.

General note. The official estimates of Trinidad and Tobago have been adjusted by the Central Statistical Office to conform to the United Nations System of National Accounts so far as the existing data would permit. It should be noted that interest on the public debt is treated as a factor payment and is therefore included in National Income.

1.1 Expenditure on the Gross Domestic Product, in Current Prices

Million Trinidad and Tobago dollars

		1970	1975	1978	1979	1980	1981	1982	1983	1984	1985	1986	1987
1	Government final consumption expenditure	215	652	1148	1536	1805	2110	4032	3907	4187	4113	4193	3811
2	Private final consumption expenditure	986	2257	4443	5663	6865	8197	11103	11594	10576	10076	10297	9425
3	Gross capital formation	425	1449	2584	3213	4580	4541	5417	5069	4367	3142	3982	3125
	A Increase in stocks	81	364	261	261	376	199	228	30	70	44	56	44
	B Gross fixed capital formation	344	1085	2323	2952	4204	4342	5189	5038	4297	3098	3927	3081
	Residential buildings	91	250	565	1051	1257	1415	1725	2149	2004	1289	1192	1128
	Non-residential buildings												
	Other construction and land improvement etc.	38	70	360	534	735	917	1360	952	505	240	222	210
	Other	217	766	1398	1367	2212	2011	2105	1937	1788	1569	2513	1743
4	Exports of goods and services	703	2808	3766	4979	7550	7542	6694	5756	5981	5883	5740	5867
5	Less: Imports of goods and services	685	1866	3391	4345	5834	5952	8070	7606	6283	5136	6970	5657
	Equals: Gross Domestic Product	1644	5300	8550	11046	14966	16438	19176	18719	18829	18077	17242	16572

1.2 Expenditure on the Gross Domestic Product, in Constant Prices

Million Trinidad and Tobago dollars

		1970	1975	1978	1979	1980	1981	1982	1983	1984	1985	1986	1987
		\multicolumn{7}{c}{At constant prices of: 1970}		1985			
1	Government final consumption expenditure	215	347	398	499	529	607	737	568 / 4032	4235	4113	4152	4277
2	Private final consumption expenditure	986	1217	1762	1958	2021	2110	2565	2426 / 14156	11384	10076	9561	7901
3	Gross capital formation	425	927	1402	1447	1774	1479	1558	1389 / 5084	4191	3142	3113	2418
4	Exports of goods and services	703	689	723	777	839	826	749	744 / 5333	5932	5883	5769	5667
5	Less: Imports of goods and services	685	1168	1665	2221	2380	2175	2815	2694 / 6146	5404	5136	5570	4157
	Statistical discrepancy	-	-130	-218	29	-33	28	197	283 / -2356	-1423	-	463	81
	Equals: Gross Domestic Product	1644	1881	2403	2490	2748	2874	2990	2715 / 20104	18915	18077	17487	16186

1.3 Cost Components of the Gross Domestic Product

Million Trinidad and Tobago dollars

		1970	1975	1978	1979	1980	1981	1982	1983	1984	1985	1986	1987
1	Indirect taxes, net	94	90	49	-231	-588	-537	-856	-665	-33	78	175	382
	A Indirect taxes	109	212	418	492	637	681	819	968	1041	1168	1087	1021
	B Less: Subsidies	16	122	370	723	1225	1218	1675	1633	1075	1090	913	639
2	Consumption of fixed capital	147	324	624	698	848	930	1142	1458	1563	1748	1777	1877
3	Compensation of employees paid by resident producers to:	846	1962	3866	4951	6110	7652	10612	11235	11366	10847	10816	10226
4	Operating surplus	558	2924	4012	5627	8597	8394	8278	6691	5934	5404	4474	4086
	Equals: Gross Domestic Product	1644	5300	8550	11046	14966	16438	19176	18719	18829	18077	17242	16572

1.4 General Government Current Receipts and Disbursements

Million Trinidad and Tobago dollars

		1970	1975	1978	1979	1980	1981	1982	1983	1984	1985	1986	1987
		\multicolumn{12}{c}{Receipts}												
1	Operating surplus	...	...	...	...	...	...	...	...	...	...	...	...
2	Property and entrepreneurial income	42	266	438	576	781	908	851	897	854	913	939	855
3	Taxes, fees and contributions	248	1444	2394	3206	5258	6037	6132	5526	5552	5397	4086	4164
	A Indirect taxes	109	212	418	492	637	681	819	968	1041	1168	1087	1021

Trinidad and Tobago

1.4 General Government Current Receipts and Disbursements
(Continued)

Million Trinidad and Tobago dollars

	1970	1975	1978	1979	1980	1981	1982	1983	1984	1985	1986	1987
B Direct taxes	127	1205	1934	2673	4537	5225	5183	4395	4308	3915	2762	2907
C Social security contributions	...	...	...	...	...	...	...	...	...	...	...	...
D Compulsory fees, fines and penalties	12	27	42	41	84	131	131	163	202	315	237	236
4 Other current transfers	-	11	19	23	37	39	49	50	80	104	80	75
Statistical discrepancy	3	4	7	6	5	4	8	46	30	41	43	34
Total Current Receipts of General Government	293	1725	2859	3811	6082	6989	7039	6519	6516	6455	5148	5128

Disbursements

	1970	1975	1978	1979	1980	1981	1982	1983	1984	1985	1986	1987
1 Government final consumption expenditure	215	652	1148	1536	1805	2110	4032	3907	4187	4113	4193	3811
A Compensation of employees	178	561	992	1325	1522	1807	3577	3339	3558	3519	3617	3213
B Consumption of fixed capital	-	-	1	1	1	2	2	2	2	2	2	2
C Purchases of goods and services, net	37	91	156	210	282	302	452	566	628	592	575	597
D Less: Own account fixed capital formation	...	...	...	...	...	...	...	...	...	...	...	...
E Indirect taxes paid, net	...	...	...	...	...	...	...	...	...	...	...	...
2 Property income	22	47	80	126	125	179	161	197	266	282	529	666
A Interest												
B Net land rent and royalties	...	...	...	...	...	...	...	...	...	...	...	...
3 Subsidies	16	122	370	723	1225	1218	1675	1633	1075	1090	913	639
4 Other current transfers	22	94	154	263	294	346	456	708	690	639	714	805
A Social security benefits	7	25	66	85	93	101	139	221	222	210	248	265
B Social assistance grants												
C Other	16	69	87	178	201	245	317	487	468	428	466	540
5 Net saving	19	811	1107	1164	2633	3135	716	73	299	332	-1201	-793
Total Current Disbursements and Net Saving of General Government	293	1725	2858	3811	6082	6989	7039	6519	6516	6455	5148	5128

1.7 External Transactions on Current Account, Summary

Million Trinidad and Tobago dollars

	1970	1975	1978	1979	1980	1981	1982	1983	1984	1985	1986	1987

Payments to the Rest of the World

	1970	1975	1978	1979	1980	1981	1982	1983	1984	1985	1986	1987
1 Imports of goods and services	685	1866	3391	4345	5834	5952	8070	7606	6283	5136	6970	5657
2 Factor income to the rest of the world	141	275	487	995	1314	1309	1011	891	1105	1338	1263	1089
3 Current transfers to the rest of the world	10	52	95	114	162	222	340	290	302	177	144	162
4 Surplus of the nation on current transactions	-116	716	97	-87	803	891	-1865	-2464	-1337	-263	-2278	-970
Payments to the Rest of the World and Surplus of the Nation on Current Transactions	720	2908	4070	5367	8112	8374	7556	6324	6352	6388	6099	5938

Receipts From The Rest of the World

	1970	1975	1978	1979	1980	1981	1982	1983	1984	1985	1986	1987
1 Exports of goods and services	703	2808	3766	4979	7550	7542	6694	5756	5981	5883	5740	5867
2 Factor income from rest of the world	11	94	300	384	558	827	857	553	340	480	352	51
3 Current transfers from rest of the world	6	6	4	4	4	5	5	15	32	25	7	20
Receipts from the Rest of the World on Current Transactions	720	2908	4070	5367	8112	8374	7556	6324	6352	6388	6099	5938

1.10 Gross Domestic Product by Kind of Activity, in Current Prices

Million Trinidad and Tobago dollars

	1970	1975	1978	1979	1980	1981	1982	1983	1984	1985	1986	1987
1 Agriculture, hunting, forestry and fishing	80	174	302	322	337	386	433	615	596	697	686	728
2 Mining and quarrying	133	1865	2349	3245	5928	5801	4760	3946	4047	3990	3046	2926
3 Manufacturing	397	792	1074	1567	1338	1118	1349	1541	1748	1571	1707	1900
4 Electricity, gas and water	33	36	50	51	26	31	-4	-5	177	181	198	236
5 Construction	112	438	1224	1449	1885	2639	3152	2817	2527	2171	2012	1867

Trinidad and Tobago

1.10 Gross Domestic Product by Kind of Activity, in Current Prices
(Continued)

Million Trinidad and Tobago dollars

	1970	1975	1978	1979	1980	1981	1982	1983	1984	1985	1986	1987
6 Wholesale and retail trade, restaurants and hotels	313	718	1166	1294	1431	1793	2313	2470	2416	2266	2295	2028
7 Transport, storage and communication	236	367	756	960	1444	1624	2005	1845	1725	1684	1712	1604
8 Finance, insurance, real estate and business services	122	364	774	1076	1434	1841	2167	2296	2179	2131	2028	1896
9 Community, social and personal services	111	257	465	593	728	809	1301	1325	1418	1431	1472	1351
Total, Industries	1537	5011	8161	10557	14551	16042	17476	16849	16831	16121	15155	14536
Producers of Government Services	139	453	763	1064	1174	1475	2868	2617	2776	2741	2810	2653
Other Producers	...	...	...	...	...	...	...	...	...	...	...	...
Subtotal	1676	5464	8924	11621	15725	17517	20344	19466	19606	18862	17965	17189
Less: Imputed bank service charge	32	164	375	577	758	1079	1168	747	778	785	723	617
Plus: Import duties	...	...	...	...	...	...	...	...	...	...	...	...
Plus: Value added tax	...	...	...	...	...	...	...	...	...	...	...	...
Equals: Gross Domestic Product	1644	5300	8550	11046	14966	16438	19176	18719	18829	18077	17242	16572

1.11 Gross Domestic Product by Kind of Activity, in Constant Prices

Million Trinidad and Tobago dollars

	1970	1975	1978	1979	1980	1981	1982	1983	1984	1985	1986	1987
	At constant prices of: 1970								1985			
1 Agriculture, hunting, forestry and fishing	80	80	75	72	67	66	68	66 / 521	522	561	580	600
2 Mining and quarrying	133	202	217	207	207	185	174	157 / 3698	3857	3990	3820	3501
3 Manufacturing	397	369	448	460	471	440	450	445 / 1955	1927	1708	1843	1763
4 Electricity, gas and water	33	40	53	59	66	75	89	96 / 174	180	181	198	209
5 Construction	112	201	350	374	410	474	486	399 / 3238	2634	2171	1908	1706
6 Wholesale and retail trade, restaurants and hotels	313	381	458	428	489	533	560	483 / 3121	2457	2265	2004	1597
7 Transport, storage and communication	236	201	293	326	440	468	515	438 / 1502	1619	1684	1685	1636
8 Finance, insurance, real estate and business services	122	197	312	378	429	481	508	449 / 2761	2346	2131	1882	1593
9 Community, social and personal services	111	135	152	177	176	184	175	179 / 1416	1435	1431	1429	1447
Total, Industries	1537	1806	2358	2481	2755	2906	3025	2712 / 18385	16977	16121	15348	14052
Producers of Government Services	139	165	198	213	223	249	238	238 / 2617	2776	2741	2810	2653
Other Producers	...	...	...	...	...	...	...	...	...	...	...	...
Subtotal	1676	1971	2556	2694	2978	3155	3263	2950 / 21002	19752	18862	18158	16704
Less: Imputed bank service charge	32	88	151	203	227	282	274	234 / 898	837	785	671	519
Plus: Import duties	...	...	...	...	...	...	...	...	...	...	...	...
Plus: Value added tax	...	...	...	...	...	...	...	...	...	...	...	...
Equals: Gross Domestic Product	1644	1881	2403	2490	2748	2874	2990	2715 / 20104	18915	18077	17487	16186

1.12 Relations Among National Accounting Aggregates

Million Trinidad and Tobago dollars

	1970	1975	1978	1979	1980	1981	1982	1983	1984	1985	1986	1987
Gross Domestic Product	1644	5300	8550	11046	14966	16438	19176	18719	18829	18077	17242	16572
Plus: Net factor income from the rest of the world	-130	-181	-187	-611	-756	-481	-154	-339	-765	-859	-911	-1038
Factor income from the rest of the world	11	94	300	384	558	827	857	553	340	480	352	51
Less: Factor income to the rest of the world	141	275	487	995	1314	1309	1011	891	1105	1338	1263	1089
Equals: Gross National Product	1514	5119	8363	10435	14210	15957	19022	18381	18064	17218	16331	15533
Less: Consumption of fixed capital	147	324	624	698	848	930	1142	1458	1563	1748	1777	1877

Trinidad and Tobago

1.12 Relations Among National Accounting Aggregates
(Continued)

Million Trinidad and Tobago dollars

	1970	1975	1978	1979	1980	1981	1982	1983	1984	1985	1986	1987
Equals: National Income	1367	4795	7739	9737	13362	15027	17880	16923	16501	15470	14554	13656
Plus: Net current transfers from the rest of the world	-4	-46	-91	-110	-157	-218	-335	-275	-270	-151	-137	-142
Current transfers from the rest of the world	6	6	4	4	4	5	5	15	32	25	7	20
Less: Current transfers to the rest of the world	10	52	95	114	162	222	340	290	302	177	144	162
Equals: National Disposable Income	1362	4749	7648	9627	13205	14809	17544	16648	16231	15318	14417	13514
Less: Final consumption	1201	2908	5591	7199	8670	10307	15134	15501	14763	14188	14490	13236
Equals: Net Saving	162	1841	2057	2428	4536	4502	2410	1146	1467	1130	-73	278
Less: Surplus of the nation on current transactions	-116	716	97	-87	803	891	-1865	-2464	-1337	-263	-2278	-970
Equals: Net Capital Formation	278	1125	1960	2515	3733	3610	4275	3610	2804	1394	2205	1247

2.1 Government Final Consumption Expenditure by Function, in Current Prices

Million Trinidad and Tobago dollars

	1970	1975	1978	1979	1980	1981	1982	1983	1984	1985	1986	1987
1 General public services	...	...	...	...	...	306	787	519	579	596	625	611
2 Defence	...	...	...	...	...	...	...	...	...	...	...	...
3 Public order and safety	...	...	...	...	...	284	562	543	582	565	578	544
4 Education	...	...	...	...	...	374	792	751	794	802	834	667
5 Health	...	...	...	...	...	354	620	658	701	698	727	654
6 Social security and welfare	...	...	...	...	...	12	17	17	17	19	19	17
7 Housing and community amenities	...	...	...	...	...	139	218	236	260	263	262	245
8 Recreational, cultural and religious affairs	...	...	...	...	...	...	...	...	...	...	...	...
9 Economic services	...	...	...	...	...	628	1032	1184	1254	1169	1147	1072
A Fuel and energy [a]	...	...	...	...	...	149	248	214	224	212	227	199
B Agriculture, forestry, fishing and hunting	...	...	...	...	...	101	162	200	170	180	144	133
C Mining, manufacturing and construction, except fuel and energy	...	...	...	...	...	40	52	71	71	73	75	80
D Transportation and communication	...	...	...	...	...	277	460	569	495	425	419	382
E Other economic affairs	...	...	...	...	...	61	110	129	294	279	282	279
10 Other functions	...	...	...	...	...	15	5	...	...	...	...	...
Total Government Final Consumption Expenditure	...	...	...	...	...	2110	4032	3907	4187	4113	4193	3811

a) Item 'Fuel and energy' includes general administration of economic services.

2.7 Gross Capital Formation by Type of Good and Owner, in Current Prices

Million Trinidad and Tobago dollars

	1980				1981				1982			
	TOTAL	Total Private	Public Enterprises	General Government	TOTAL	Total Private	Public Enterprises	General Government	TOTAL	Total Private	Public Enterprises	General Government
Increase in stocks, total	376	...	...	...	199	...	...	...	228	...	...	...
1 Goods producing industries	376	...	...	...	199	...	...	...	228	...	...	...
A Materials and supplies	122	...	...	...	160	...	...	...	114	...	...	...
B Work in progress	...	...	...	...	...	...	...	...	...	...	...	...
C Livestock, except breeding stocks, dairy cattle, etc.	...	...	...	...	...	...	...	...	...	...	...	...
D Finished goods	254	...	...	...	39	...	...	...	114	...	...	...
2 Wholesale and retail trade	...	...	...	...	...	...	...	...	...	...	...	...
3 Other, except government stocks	...	...	...	...	...	...	...	...	...	...	...	...
4 Government stocks	...	...	...	...	...	...	...	...	...	...	...	...
Gross Fixed Capital Formation, Total	4204	...	...	...	4342	...	...	...	5189	...	...	...
1 Residential buildings	1257	...	...	...	1415	...	...	...	1725	...	...	...
2 Non-residential buildings	...	...	...	...	...	...	...	...	...	...	...	...

Trinidad and Tobago

2.7 Gross Capital Formation by Type of Good and Owner, in Current Prices
(Continued)

Million Trinidad and Tobago dollars

	1980 TOTAL	Total Private	Public Enterprises	General Government	1981 TOTAL	Total Private	Public Enterprises	General Government	1982 TOTAL	Total Private	Public Enterprises	General Government
3 Other construction	735	...	...	...	917	...	...	...	1360	...	...	...
4 Land improvement and plantation and orchard development	...	...	...	...	...	...	...	...	...	...	...	...
5 Producers' durable goods	1859	...	...	...	1646	...	...	...	1678	...	...	...
A Transport equipment	293	...	...	...	361	...	...	...	319	...	...	...
B Machinery and equipment	1567	...	...	...	1285	...	...	...	1359	...	...	...
6 Breeding stock, dairy cattle, etc.	...	...	...	...	...	...	...	...	...	...	...	...
Statistical discrepancy	353	...	...	...	365	...	...	...	427	...	...	...
Total Gross Capital Formation	4580	...	...	...	4541	...	...	...	5417	...	...	...

	1983 TOTAL	Total Private	Public Enterprises	General Government	1984 TOTAL	Total Private	Public Enterprises	General Government	1985 TOTAL	Total Private	Public Enterprises	General Government
Increase in stocks, total	30	...	...	...	70	...	...	...	44	...	...	...
1 Goods producing industries	30	...	...	...	70	...	...	...	44	...	...	...
A Materials and supplies	-22	...	...	...	98	...	...	...	51	...	...	...
B Work in progress	...	...	...	...	...	...	...	...	...	...	...	...
C Livestock, except breeding stocks, dairy cattle, etc.	...	...	...	...	...	...	...	...	...	...	...	...
D Finished goods	52	...	...	...	-28	...	...	...	-7	...	...	...
2 Wholesale and retail trade	...	...	...	...	...	...	...	...	...	...	...	...
3 Other, except government stocks	...	...	...	...	...	...	...	...	...	...	...	...
4 Government stocks	...	...	...	...	...	...	...	...	...	...	...	...
Gross Fixed Capital Formation, Total	5038	...	...	...	4297	...	...	...	3098	...	...	...
1 Residential buildings	2149	...	...	...	2004	...	...	...	1289	...	...	...
2 Non-residential buildings		...	...	...		...	...	...		...	...	...
3 Other construction	952	...	...	...	505	...	...	...	240	...	...	...
4 Land improvement and plantation and orchard development	...	...	...	...	...	...	...	...	...	...	...	...
5 Producers' durable goods	1568	...	...	...	1463	...	...	...	1163	...	...	...
A Transport equipment	466	...	...	...	391	...	...	...	341	...	...	...
B Machinery and equipment	1102	...	...	...	1071	...	...	...	823	...	...	...
6 Breeding stock, dairy cattle, etc.	...	...	...	...	...	...	...	...	...	...	...	...
Statistical discrepancy	370	...	...	...	325	...	...	...	406	...	...	...
Total Gross Capital Formation	5069	...	...	...	4367	...	...	...	3142	...	...	...

	1986 TOTAL	Total Private	Public Enterprises	General Government	1987 TOTAL	Total Private	Public Enterprises	General Government
Increase in stocks, total	56	...	...	...	44	...	...	...
1 Goods producing industries	56	...	...	...	44	...	...	...
A Materials and supplies	65	...	...	...	51	...	...	...
B Work in progress	...	...	...	...	...	...	...	...
C Livestock, except breeding stocks, dairy cattle, etc.	...	...	...	...	...	...	...	...
D Finished goods	-9	...	...	...	-7	...	...	...
2 Wholesale and retail trade	...	...	...	...	...	...	...	...
3 Other, except government stocks	...	...	...	...	...	...	...	...
4 Government stocks	...	...	...	...	...	...	...	...
Gross Fixed Capital Formation, Total	3927	...	...	...	3081	...	...	...
1 Residential buildings	1192	...	...	...	1128	...	...	...
2 Non-residential buildings		...	...	...		...	...	...

Trinidad and Tobago

2.7 Gross Capital Formation by Type of Good and Owner, in Current Prices
(Continued)

Million Trinidad and Tobago dollars

	1986 TOTAL	1986 Total Private	1986 Public Enterprises	1986 General Government	1987 TOTAL	1987 Total Private	1987 Public Enterprises	1987 General Government
3 Other construction	222	...	...	...	210	...	...	...
4 Land improvement and plantation and orchard development	...	...	...	...	...	...	...	...
5 Producers' durable goods	1829	...	...	...	1297	...	...	...
A Transport equipment	535	...	...	...	380	...	...	...
B Machinery and equipment	1294	...	...	...	917	...	...	...
6 Breeding stock, dairy cattle, etc.	...	...	...	...	...	...	...	...
Statistical discrepancy	684	...	...	...	446	...	...	...
Total Gross Capital Formation	3982	...	...	...	3125	...	...	...

2.11 Gross Fixed Capital Formation by Kind of Activity of Owner, ISIC Divisions, in Current Prices

Million Trinidad and Tobago dollars

	1970	1975	1978	1979	1980	1981	1982	1983	1984	1985	1986	1987
					All Producers							
1 Agriculture, hunting, forestry and fishing	7	39	46	56	68	62	60	50	51	32	...	...
2 Mining and quarrying	85	413	376	386	513	544	816	417	432	560	...	...
3 Manufacturing	122	327	736	433	1012	740	625	344	600	343	...	...
A Manufacturing of food, beverages and tobacco	22	71	161	202	122	120	143	102	140	130	...	...
B Textile, wearing apparel and leather industries	8	13	18	16	24	11	3	16	18	8	...	...
C Manufacture of wood, and wood products, including furniture	1	11	41	20	21	9	16	15	11	5	...	...
D Manufacture of paper and paper products, printing and publishing	3	15	24	28	41	20	38	26	23	25	...	...
E Manufacture of chemicals and chemical petroleum, coal, rubber and plastic products	73	175	423	95	709	483	265	106	241	153	...	...
F Manufacture of non-metalic mineral products except products of petroleum and coal											...	...
G Basic metal industries	14	37	63	63	81	83	145	65	152	13	...	...
H Manufacture of fabricated metal products, machinery and equipment											...	...
I Other manufacturing industries	1	5	7	8	15	15	16	14	15	9	...	...
4 Electricity, gas and water	11	40	226	308	225	220	241	347	192	127	...	...
5 Construction	18	57	111	87	132	98	58	118	44	60	...	...
6 Wholesale and retail trade, restaurants and hotels	34	156	165	392	378	286	812	669	244	9	...	...
A Wholesale and retail trade	23	146	157	370	355	268	792	635	224	6	...	...
B Restaurants and hotels	11	11	8	21	23	18	20	34	20	3	...	...
7 Transport, storage and communication	35	124	201	198	530	504	392	583	691	496	...	...
8 Finance, insurance, real estate and business services	57	185	347	810	850	840	902	1133	1169	790	...	...
9 Community, social and personal services	11	34	128	132	152	181	195	242	134	232	...	...
Total Industries [a]	380	1375	2336	2800	3858	3474	4101	3903	3555	2649	...	...
Producers of Government Services	45	74	248	413	722	1067	1316	1166	812	493	...	...
Private Non-Profit Institutions Serving Households	...	...	...	...	...	...	...	...	...	...	...	...
Total [a]	425	1449	2584	3213	4580	4541	5417	5069	4367	3142	...	...

a) The estimates of this table (Gross Fixed Capital Formation by kind of activity of owner) include increase in stocks.

Trinidad and Tobago

4.3 Cost Components of Value Added

Million Trinidad and Tobago dollars

1980 / 1981

		Compensation of Employees	Capital Consumption	Net Operating Surplus	Indirect Taxes	Less: Subsidies Received	Value Added	Compensation of Employees	Capital Consumption	Net Operating Surplus	Indirect Taxes	Less: Subsidies Received	Value Added
						All Producers							
1	Agriculture, hunting, forestry and fishing	181	10	165	...	18	337	210	11	188	...	23	386
2	Mining and quarrying	213	245	5460	10	...	5928	260	249	5284	8	...	5801
3	Manufacturing	779	130	634	63	268	1338	950	156	256	69	312	1118
	A Manufacture of food, beverages and tobacco	217	36	204	50	210	296	258	50	192	49	258	291
	B Textile, wearing apparel and leather industries	56	3	11	3	...	73	71	4	18	-	...	93
	C Manufacture of wood and wood products, including furniture	37	9	15	...	...	61	42	8	-	...	...	49
	D Manufacture of paper and paper products, printing and publishing	46	4	-4	...	...	46	61	6	8	...	...	75
	E Manufacture of chemicals and chemical petroleum, coal, rubber and plastic products	293	64	310	7	59	614	336	68	-49	7	53	309
	F Manufacture of non-metallic mineral products, except products of petroleum and coal												
	G Basic metal industries	119	11	89	3	...	222	166	18	72	11	...	267
	H Manufacture of fabricated metal products, machinery and equipment					...						...	
	I Other manufacturing industries	12	3	10	1	...	25	15	4	15	1	...	35
4	Electricity, gas and water	175	21	11	1	183	26	210	17	13	1	209	31
5	Construction	1115	68	680	22	...	1885	1479	62	1065	33	...	2639
6	Wholesale and retail trade, restaurants and hotels	660	71	510	497	306	1431	768	83	765	522	345	1793
	A Wholesale and retail trade	583	60	461	495	306	1293	679	69	706	520	345	1628
	B Restaurants and hotels	77	11	49	2	...	138	90	13	59	3	...	164
7	Transport, storage and communication	978	204	685	27	450	1444	1329	231	363	30	329	1624
8	Finance, insurance, real estate and business services	319	97	1016	2	...	1434	412	117	1309	3	...	1841
9	Community, social and personal services	518	2	194	14	...	728	560	4	230	15	...	809
	Total, Industries	4938	848	9355	636	1225	14551	6178	930	9473	681	1218	16042
	Producers of Government Services	1172	1	...	...	...	1174	1474	2	...	...	...	1475
	Other Producers	...	...	...	...	...	...	...	...	...	...	...	...
	Total	6110	849	9355	636	1225	15725	7652	932	9473	681	1218	17517
	Less: Imputed bank service charge	...	...	758	...	...	758	...	...	1079	...	...	1079
	Import duties	...	...	...	...	...	...	...	...	...	...	...	...
	Value added tax	...	...	...	...	...	...	...	...	...	...	...	...
	Total	6110	848	8597	637	1225	14966	7652	930	8394	681	1218	16438

1982 / 1983

		Compensation of Employees	Capital Consumption	Net Operating Surplus	Indirect Taxes	Less: Subsidies Received	Value Added	Compensation of Employees	Capital Consumption	Net Operating Surplus	Indirect Taxes	Less: Subsidies Received	Value Added
						All Producers							
1	Agriculture, hunting, forestry and fishing	241	13	207	...	28	433	299	9	352	...	45	615
2	Mining and quarrying	338	327	4084	11	...	4760	374	327	3226	20	...	3946
3	Manufacturing	1097	201	352	79	379	1349	1297	268	287	116	426	1541
	A Manufacture of food, beverages and tobacco	298	56	261	56	290	381	341	68	224	61	422	272

Trinidad and Tobago

4.3 Cost Components of Value Added
(Continued)

Million Trinidad and Tobago dollars

	\multicolumn{6}{c	}{1982}	\multicolumn{6}{c	}{1983}
	Compensation of Employees	Capital Consumption	Net Operating Surplus	Indirect Taxes	Less: Subsidies Received	Value Added	Compensation of Employees	Capital Consumption	Net Operating Surplus	Indirect Taxes	Less: Subsidies Received	Value Added
B Textile, wearing apparel and leather industries	72	4	7	1	...	83	73	4	20	1	...	98
C Manufacture of wood and wood products, including furniture	47	9	3	...	...	59	49	14	8	1	...	72
D Manufacture of paper and paper products, printing and publishing	69	7	14	...	...	90	70	7	31	...	...	109
E Manufacture of chemicals and chemical petroleum, coal, rubber and plastic products	403	101	-26	6	90	394	442	113	69	17	4	636
F Manufacture of non-metallic mineral products, except products of petroleum and coal												
G Basic metal industries	194	21	82	15	...	311	300	60	-76	34	...	318
H Manufacture of fabricated metal products, machinery and equipment					...						...	
I Other manufacturing industries	15	3	13	1	...	32	22	2	11	2	...	36
4 Electricity, gas and water	305	23	52	1	384	-4	356	25	-4	2	384	-5
5 Construction	1745	50	1318	39	...	3152	1695	54	1032	36	...	2817
6 Wholesale and retail trade, restaurants and hotels	1001	110	947	622	367	2313	1061	111	738	721	160	2470
A Wholesale and retail trade	899	94	881	618	367	2125	925	89	704	719	160	2277
B Restaurants and hotels	103	16	66	4	...	188	136	22	34	2	...	193
7 Transport, storage and communication	1524	287	666	45	516	2005	1728	481	215	38	618	1845
8 Finance, insurance, real estate and business services	524	127	1513	4	...	2167	807	152	1326	11	...	2296
9 Community, social and personal services	972	3	307	19	...	1301	1004	30	266	25	...	1325
Total, Industries	7747	1141	9446	820	1674	17476	8620	1456	7438	968	1633	16849
Producers of Government Services	2866	2	...	...	...	2868	2615	2	...	...	...	2617
Other Producers	...	...	...	...	...	...	...	...	...	...	...	...
Total	10612	1143	9446	820	1674	20344	11235	1458	7438	968	1633	19466
Less: Imputed bank service charge	...	...	1168	...	...	1168	...	...	747	...	...	747
Import duties	...	...	...	...	...	...	...	...	...	...	...	...
Value added tax	...	...	...	...	...	...	...	...	...	...	...	...
Total	10612	1142	8278	819	1675	19176	11235	1458	6691	968	1633	18719

	\multicolumn{6}{c	}{1984}	\multicolumn{6}{c	}{1985}
	Compensation of Employees	Capital Consumption	Net Operating Surplus	Indirect Taxes	Less: Subsidies Received	Value Added	Compensation of Employees	Capital Consumption	Net Operating Surplus	Indirect Taxes	Less: Subsidies Received	Value Added
	\multicolumn{12}{c	}{All Producers}
1 Agriculture, hunting, forestry and fishing	328	11	289	...	33	596	342	11	363	...	19	697
2 Mining and quarrying	366	330	3329	21	...	4047	392	350	3229	19	...	3990
3 Manufacturing	1297	323	361	140	374	1748	1253	373	150	166	370	1571
A Manufacture of food, beverages and tobacco	351	69	153	78	374	277	362	71	197	90	273	446

Trinidad and Tobago

4.3 Cost Components of Value Added
(Continued)

Million Trinidad and Tobago dollars

	1984						1985					
	Compensation of Employees	Capital Consumption	Net Operating Surplus	Indirect Taxes	Less: Subsidies Received	Value Added	Compensation of Employees	Capital Consumption	Net Operating Surplus	Indirect Taxes	Less: Subsidies Received	Value Added
B Textile, wearing apparel and leather industries	71	4	13	2	...	91	57	5	5	2	...	69
C Manufacture of wood and wood products, including furniture	49	11	18	2	...	80	35	7	8	1	...	50
D Manufacture of paper and paper products, printing and publishing	75	8	32	1	...	116	78	12	21	2	...	112
E Manufacture of chemicals and chemical petroleum, coal, rubber and plastic products	447	166	152	22	-	787	445	204	-1	25	97	575
F Manufacture of non-metallic mineral products, except products of petroleum and coal												
G Basic metal industries	278	62	-10	35	...	364	252	71	-86	45	...	283
H Manufacture of fabricated metal products, machinery and equipment					...						...	
I Other manufacturing industries	26	3	3	2	...	34	24	4	7	1	...	36
4 Electricity, gas and water	387	29	7	2	248	177	359	35	64	2	278	181
5 Construction	1644	52	818	12	...	2527	1391	43	728	9	...	2171
6 Wholesale and retail trade, restaurants and hotels	959	100	581	793	17	2416	801	182	392	910	21	2266
A Wholesale and retail trade	834	82	561	791	17	2251	687	160	377	909	21	2113
B Restaurants and hotels	125	19	20	1	...	164	114	22	16	1	...	153
7 Transport, storage and communication	1678	500	-91	41	403	1725	1646	508	-106	40	403	1684
8 Finance, insurance, real estate and business services	847	174	1154	4	...	2179	814	195	1121	1	...	2131
9 Community, social and personal services	1065	41	263	29	...	1418	1111	50	248	22	...	1431
Total, Industries	8592	1560	6711	1041	1075	16831	8108	1747	6189	1168	1090	16121
Producers of Government Services	2773	3	...	...	...	2776	2740	2	...	...	...	2741
Other Producers	...	...	...	...	...	...	...	...	...	...	...	...
Total	11366	1563	6711	1041	1075	19606	10847	1748	6189	1168	1090	18862
Less: Imputed bank service charge	...	...	778	...	...	778	...	...	785	...	...	785
Import duties	...	...	...	...	...	...	...	...	...	...	...	...
Value added tax	...	...	...	...	...	...	...	...	...	...	...	...
Total	11366	1563	5934	1041	1075	18829	10847	1748	5404	1168	1090	18077

	1986						1987					
	Compensation of Employees	Capital Consumption	Net Operating Surplus	Indirect Taxes	Less: Subsidies Received	Value Added	Compensation of Employees	Capital Consumption	Net Operating Surplus	Indirect Taxes	Less: Subsidies Received	Value Added
	All Producers											
1 Agriculture, hunting, forestry and fishing	351	10	341	...	17	686	363	11	375	...	21	728
2 Mining and quarrying	387	332	2310	18	...	3046	356	400	2029	142	...	2926
3 Manufacturing	1290	379	179	166	308	1707	1300	387	192	157	136	1900
A Manufacture of food, beverages and tobacco	383	79	343	101	308	598	419	87	190	111	136	671

Trinidad and Tobago

4.3 Cost Components of Value Added
(Continued)

Million Trinidad and Tobago dollars

		1986						1987				
		Compensation of Employees	Capital Consumption	Net Operating Surplus	Indirect Taxes	Less: Subsidies Received	Value Added	Compensation of Employees	Capital Consumption	Net Operating Surplus	Indirect Taxes	Less: Subsidies Received	Value Added
	B Textile, wearing apparel and leather industries	62	6	20	2	...	90	58	6	26	2	...	92
	C Manufacture of wood and wood products, including furniture	32	7	7	1	...	46	25	5	6	1	...	37
	D Manufacture of paper and paper products, printing and publishing	75	14	77	2	...	167	71	14	80	2	...	167
	E Manufacture of chemicals and chemical petroleum, coal, rubber and plastic products	462	192	-224	21	...	450	472	186	-18	22	...	662
	F Manufacture of non-metallic mineral products, except products of petroleum and coal					...						...	
	G Basic metal industries	248	77	-52	39	...	313	225	84	-101	19	...	226
	H Manufacture of fabricated metal products, machinery and equipment					...						...	
	I Other manufacturing industries	29	4	8	2	...	43	31	5	9	2	...	46
4	Electricity, gas and water	365	46	8	3	223	198	363	81	-37	3	173	236
5	Construction	1231	40	737	4	...	2012	1109	33	722	3	...	1867
6	Wholesale and retail trade, restaurants and hotels	809	186	471	838	9	2295	795	186	399	655	7	2028
	A Wholesale and retail trade	694	164	455	837	9	2140	663	162	388	653	7	1859
	B Restaurants and hotels	115	22	16	1	...	155	132	25	11	2	...	170
7	Transport, storage and communication	1621	511	-103	39	356	1712	1541	491	-168	41	301	1604
8	Finance, insurance, real estate and business services	810	220	997	1	...	2028	776	230	889	1	...	1896
9	Community, social and personal services	1145	51	258	18	...	1472	972	57	302	19	...	1351
	Total, Industries	8009	1775	5198	1089	913	15155	7575	1876	4703	1021	639	14536
	Producers of Government Services	2808	2	...	...	...	2810	2651	2	...	...	...	2653
	Other Producers	...	...	...	...	...	...	...	...	...	...	...	...
	Total	10817	1777	5198	1089	913	17965	10226	1877	4703	1021	639	17189
	Less: Imputed bank service charge	...	...	723	...	...	723	...	...	617	...	...	617
	Import duties	...	...	...	...	...	...	...	...	...	...	...	...
	Value added tax	...	...	...	...	...	...	...	...	...	...	...	...
	Total	10817	1777	4475	1087	913	17242	10226	1877	4086	1021	639	16572

Tunisia

Source. Reply to the United Nations National Accounts Questionnaire from the Direction de la Planification, Ministere du Plan, Tunis. The official estimates are published annually by the same Office in 'l'Economie de la Tunisie en Chiffres'.

General note. The estimates shown in the following tables have been prepared in accordance with the United Nations System of National Accounts so far as the existing data would permit.

1.1 Expenditure on the Gross Domestic Product, in Current Prices

Million Tunisian dinars

	1970	1975	1978	1979	1980	1981	1982	1983	1984	1985	1986	1987
1 Government final consumption expenditure	127.4	254.5	406.1	444.4	512.2	615.7	793.8	926.8	1030.0	1142.0	1216.0	1315.0
2 Private final consumption expenditure	502.4	1082.6	1553.2	1763.8	2178.7	2553.7	2997.2	3434.2	3944.0	4356.0	4670.0	5110.0
3 Gross capital formation	159.8	487.9	764.0	859.6	1039.5	1345.5	1519.3	1610.0	1995.0	1835.0	1649.0	1750.0
A Increase in stocks	4.8	39.9	-7.0	-32.4	37.5	55.5	-115.7	-140.0	75.0	-15.0	-26.0	80.0
B Gross fixed capital formation	155.0	448.0	771.0	892.0	1002.0	1290.0	1635.0	1750.0	1920.0	1850.0	1675.0	1670.0
Residential buildings	22.3	75.0	122.0	143.0	188.0	198.0	266.0	327.0	365.0	378.0	391.0	410.0
Non-residential buildings	...	...	...	...	...	...	...	...	...	...	...	...
Other construction and land improvement etc.	...	...	...	...	...	...	...	...	...	...	...	...
Other	...	...	...	...	...	...	...	...	...	...	...	...
4 Exports of goods and services	166.2	545.6	769.0	1139.0	1424.6	1721.9	1773.3	1947.8	2114.0	2253.0	2161.0	2725.0
5 Less: Imports of goods and services	200.2	624.2	1008.4	1285.1	1614.5	2074.3	2279.2	2421.4	2843.0	2676.0	2671.0	2965.0
Equals: Gross Domestic Product	755.6	1741.4	2483.9	2922.0	3540.5	4162.0	4804.4	5497.4	6240.0	6910.0	7025.0	7935.0

1.2 Expenditure on the Gross Domestic Product, in Constant Prices

Million Tunisian dinars

	1970	1975	1978	1979	1980	1981	1982	1983	1984	1985	1986	1987
		At constant prices of: 1972					1980					
1 Government final consumption expenditure	140.9	205.0	460.6	465.9	512.2	554.8	596.0	631.0	668.0	695.0	690.0	705.0
2 Private final consumption expenditure	555.1	860.0	1833.8	1921.4	2178.7	2336.0	2403.0	2514.0	2664.0	2733.0	2750.0	2789.0
3 Gross capital formation	163.7	245.8	969.5	1030.1	1039.1	1196.1	1188.0	1162.0	1263.0	1104.0	902.0	870.0
A Increase in stocks	2.4	-67.0	69.5	66.0	37.1	51.7	-50.0	-18.0	27.0	-30.0	-24.0	40.0
B Gross fixed capital formation	161.3	312.8	900.0	964.1	1002.0	1144.4	1238.0	1180.0	1236.0	1134.0	926.0	830.0
4 Exports of goods and services	185.3	275.5	1172.1	1423.9	1424.6	1473.7	1372.0	1385.0	1422.0	1469.0	1545.0	1735.0
5 Less: Imports of goods and services	220.7	285.4	1342.7	1545.0	1614.5	1824.6	1841.0	1800.0	1902.0	1654.0	1620.0	1587.0
Equals: Gross Domestic Product	824.3	1227.9	3093.3	3296.3	3540.5	3736.0	3718.0	3892.0	4115.0	4347.0	4278.0	4512.0

1.3 Cost Components of the Gross Domestic Product

Million Tunisian dinars

	1970	1975	1978	1979	1980	1981	1982	1983	1984	1985	1986	1987
1 Indirect taxes, net	102.4	205.4	357.9	415.0	476.4	521.3	573.0	738.0	821.0	865.8	921.0	990.0
A Indirect taxes	106.3	240.0	413.0	483.9	553.6	651.0	...	...	...	...	...	...
B Less: Subsidies	3.9	34.6	55.1	68.9	77.2	129.7	...	...	...	...	...	...
2 Consumption of fixed capital	48.0	98.3	215.0	260.0	325.0	380.0	464.0	563.0	672.0	784.0	855.0	925.0
3 Compensation of employees paid by resident producers to:	605.2	1437.7	1911.0	2247.0	2739.1	3260.7	3767.4	4196.4	4747.0	5260.2	5249.0	6020.0
4 Operating surplus												
Equals: Gross Domestic Product	755.6	1741.4	2483.9	2922.0	3540.5	4162.0	4804.4	5497.4	6240.0	6910.0	7025.0	7935.0

1.4 General Government Current Receipts and Disbursements

Million Tunisian dinars

	1970	1975	1978	1979	1980	1981	1982	1983	1984	1985	1986	1987
					Receipts							
1 Operating surplus	...	...	...	...	...	...	...	...	...	...	...	...
2 Property and entrepreneurial income	10.7	20.1	56.5	80.3	80.8 / 75.5	76.3	90.8	134.8	158.1	164.4	190.7	202.9
3 Taxes, fees and contributions	183.5	471.4	742.7	895.6	1109.8 / 1062.7	1321.4	1628.0	1825.5	2105.3	2270.9	2345.5	2381.0
A Indirect taxes	106.4	231.6	425.6	477.3	567.4 / 553.6	651.0	798.6	983.2	1126.8	1214.6	1222.6	1282.6

Tunisia

1.4 General Government Current Receipts and Disbursements
(Continued)

Million Tunisian dinars

	1970	1975	1978	1979	1980	1981	1982	1983	1984	1985	1986	1987
B Direct taxes	55.1	185.7	229.4	294.4	401.9 / 386.5	503.1	645.6	615.1	742.3	808.6	809.6	825.7
C Social security contributions	22.0	54.1	87.7	123.9	140.5 / 122.6	167.3	183.8	227.2	236.2	247.7	313.3	272.7
D Compulsory fees, fines and penalties	...	...	...	...	...	...	...	...	...	...	...	...
4 Other current transfers	1.8	6.9	21.1	38.6	56.9 / 44.8	28.2	21.8	28.7	28.9	14.2	18.1	24.7
Total Current Receipts of General Government [a]	196.0	498.4	820.3	1014.5	1247.5 / 1183.0	1425.9	1740.6	1989.0	2292.3	2449.5	2554.3	2608.6

Disbursements

	1970	1975	1978	1979	1980	1981	1982	1983	1984	1985	1986	1987
1 Government final consumption expenditure	130.8	250.2	405.0	448.0	510.0 / 533.9	634.7	815.1	950.9	1067.7	1140.9	1237.4	1349.4
2 Property income	9.9	17.2	30.3	44.9	57.4 / 57.6	63.3	87.9	105.8	130.9	145.8	179.2	222.8
A Interest	...	...	...	...	57.6	63.3	87.9	105.8	130.9	145.8	179.2	222.8
B Net land rent and royalties	...	...	...	...	...	...	...	...	...	...	...	...
3 Subsidies	4.7	16.9	56.7	71.1	85.6 / 77.2	129.7	190.8	183.2	280.6	273.7	279.9	263.7
4 Other current transfers	24.1	89.6	105.6	127.6	277.4 / 119.3	200.5	196.1	220.6	267.8	326.9	372.6	369.7
A Social security benefits	13.7	29.2	54.0	63.2	75.7 / 78.7	108.5	128.0	155.7	187.4	187.1	230.6	273.4
B Social assistance grants	7.8	58.3	37.6	40.8	47.1 / 29.8	77.7	59.0	58.2	73.1	78.8	87.4	84.2
C Other	2.6	2.1	14.0	23.6	154.6 / 10.8	14.3	9.1	6.7	7.3	61.0	54.6	12.1
5 Net saving	26.5	124.5	222.7	322.9	317.1 / 395.0	397.7	450.7	528.5	545.3	562.2	485.2	403.0
Total Current Disbursements and Net Saving of General Government [a]	196.0	498.4	820.3	1014.5	1247.5 / 1183.0	1425.9	1740.6	1989.0	2292.3	2449.5	2554.3	2608.6

a) Data for this table have not been revised, therefore, data for some years are not comparable with those of other tables.

1.7 External Transactions on Current Account, Summary

Million Tunisian dinars

	1970	1975	1978	1979	1980	1981	1982	1983	1984	1985	1986	1987

Payments to the Rest of the World

	1970	1975	1978	1979	1980	1981	1982	1983	1984	1985	1986	1987
1 Imports of goods and services	200.2	624.2	1008.4	1285.1	1614.5	2074.3	2279.2	2421.4	2842.5	2676.3	2671.0	2965.0
A Imports of merchandise c.i.f.	167.7	572.8	899.7	1156.8	1467.1	1866.0	2002.0	2106.4	2511.0	2287.0	2303.7	2538.0
B Other	32.5	51.4	101.5	128.3	147.4	208.3	277.2	315.0	331.5	389.3	367.3	427.0
2 Factor income to the rest of the world	39.4	75.0	104.8	135.0	166.2	213.0	250.6	259.8	291.2	351.0	371.6	420.0
A Compensation of employees	14.9	11.3	8.8	8.1	8.1	5.7	6.9	6.3	5.0	...	...	...
B Property and entrepreneurial income	24.5	68.9	96.0	126.9	158.1	207.3	243.7	253.5	286.2	...	...	...
3 Current transfers to the rest of the world	2.2	5.7	8.6	5.8	...	...	...	...	...	...	...	...
4 Surplus of the nation on current transactions	-49.2	-85.1	-242.6	-140.5	-167.7	-320.5	-453.3	-409.5	-680.0	-491.2	-559.7	-300.0
Payments to the Rest of the World and Surplus of the Nation on Current Transactions	192.7	619.8	878.9	1285.4	1613.0	1966.8	2076.5	2271.7	2453.7	2536.1	2482.9	3085.0

Receipts From The Rest of the World

	1970	1975	1978	1979	1980	1981	1982	1983	1984	1985	1986	1987
1 Exports of goods and services	166.2	545.6	769.0	1139.0	1424.6	1721.9	1773.3	1947.8	2114.0	2253.0	2161.2	2725.0

Tunisia

1.7 External Transactions on Current Account, Summary
(Continued)

Million Tunisian dinars

	1970	1975	1978	1979	1980	1981	1982	1983	1984	1985	1986	1987
A Exports of merchandise f.o.b.	98.8	345.6	468.4	726.7	970.0	1212.4	1169.4	1262.6	1399.1	1443.0	1403.8	1750.0
B Other	67.4	200.0	300.6	412.3	454.6	509.5	603.9	685.2	714.6	810.1	757.4	975.0
2 Factor income from rest of the world	19.0	74.6	100.9	136.4	188.4	244.9	303.2	323.9	340.0	283.0	321.7	360.0
A Compensation of employees	15.2	58.7	91.8	115.5	122.8	178.3	219.6	243.8	245.9	225.8	287.1	320.0
B Property and entrepreneurial income	3.8	16.8	9.1	20.9	65.6	66.6	83.6	80.1	94.1	57.2	34.6	40.0
3 Current transfers from rest of the world	7.4	4.7	9.0	10.0	...	...	...	...	...	...	...	...
Receipts from the Rest of the World on Current Transactions	192.7	619.8	878.9	1285.4	1613.0	1966.8	2076.5	2271.7	2453.7	2536.1	2482.9	3085.0

1.10 Gross Domestic Product by Kind of Activity, in Current Prices

Million Tunisian dinars

	1970	1975	1978	1979	1980	1981	1982	1983	1984	1985	1986	1987
1 Agriculture, hunting, forestry and fishing	128.7	321.8	374.8	395.7	500.3	568.8	632.0	673.0	863.0	1048.0	933.0	1264.0
2 Mining and quarrying	40.7	166.9	169.8	267.2	422.9	514.2	560.7	609.5	668.7	701.1	592.7	660.7
3 Manufacturing	63.5	158.1	274.8	338.1	417.3	493.9	534.1	615.6	733.7	818.0	922.0	1034.2
4 Electricity, gas and water [a]	13.1	25.9	38.7	47.7	53.5	62.4	66.0	81.3	95.4	116.1	127.5	153.5
5 Construction	38.2	100.6	171.7	190.6	207.8	262.0	331.0	370.0	406.0	423.0	385.0	384.0
6 Wholesale and retail trade, restaurants and hotels [b]	148.1	355.7	449.8	517.3	621.7	745.4	905.9	1010.4	1147.2	1280.2	1364.5	1452.7
7 Transport, storage and communication	46.4	82.6	147.1	163.8	170.2	191.3	220.0	273.1	327.5	361.0	388.2	455.1
8 Finance, insurance, real estate and business services [cd]	53.8	75.0	118.6	139.0	163.0	194.3	221.1	239.9	249.4	265.8	302.4	330.4
9 Community, social and personal services [d]	17.0	61.7	89.9	118.3	138.9	160.6	184.6	212.8	196.8	225.5	210.0	270.0
Total, Industries	549.5	1348.3	1835.2	2177.7	2695.6	3192.9	3655.4	4085.6	4687.4	5238.7	5225.3	6004.6
Producers of Government Services	103.7	187.7	290.8	328.6	368.5	447.8	571.3	674.4	731.6	805.5	878.7	940.2
Other Producers	...	...	...	...	...	...	...	...	...	...	...	...
Subtotal [e]	653.2	1536.0	2126.0	2506.3	3064.1	3640.7	4226.7	4760.0	5419.0	6044.2	6104.0	6944.8
Less: Imputed bank service charge	...	...	...	...	...	...	...	...	...	...	...	...
Plus: Import duties	...	...	...	...	...	...	...	...	...	...	...	...
Plus: Value added tax	...	...	...	...	...	...	...	...	...	...	...	...
Plus: Other adjustments [f]	102.4	205.4	357.9	415.0	476.4	521.3	577.7	737.4	821.0	865.8	921.0	990.0
Equals: Gross Domestic Product	755.6	1741.4	2483.9	2922.0	3540.5	4162.0	4804.4	5497.4	6240.0	6910.0	7025.0	7934.8

a) Item 'Electricity, gas and water' excludes gas.
b) Restaurants and hotels are included in item 'Community, social and personal services'.
c) Real estate refers to owner-occupied dwellings and rent only.
d) Finance, insurance and business services are included in item 'Community, social and personal services'.
e) Gross domestic product in factor values.
f) Item 'Other adjustments' refers to indirect taxes net of subsidies.

1.11 Gross Domestic Product by Kind of Activity, in Constant Prices

Million Tunisian dinars

	1970	1975	1978	1979	1980	1981	1982	1983	1984	1985	1986	1987
		At constant prices of:										
		1972			1980							
1 Agriculture, hunting, forestry and fishing	146.0	245.8	478.2	455.4	500.3	533.0	478.0	490.0	553.0	649.0	570.0	670.0
2 Mining and quarrying	51.1	62.9	367.8	403.8	422.9	412.8	393.0	428.1	421.7	408.6	410.0	397.4
3 Manufacturing	63.4	114.9	326.6	362.4	417.3	458.9	482.0	521.8	556.0	584.6	612.6	636.8
4 Electricity, gas and water [a]	13.1	19.9	42.5	48.8	53.5	58.5	61.7	67.3	72.0	76.9	80.4	84.5
5 Construction	50.6	63.4	174.6	195.6	207.8	236.7	241.7	240.2	254.9	257.9	219.0	208.0
6 Wholesale and retail trade, restaurants and hotels [b]	109.7	254.6	534.6	573.2	621.7	665.8	688.9	720.6	763.8	786.7	805.1	825.6
7 Transport, storage and communication	50.0	66.1	146.0	162.8	170.2	173.5	174.2	180.9	198.3	207.1	200.3	214.1
8 Finance, insurance, real estate and business services [cd]	53.8	69.8	145.4	153.9	163.0	170.0	176.3	183.3	190.5	197.2	206.0	217.1
9 Community, social and personal services [d]	66.2	45.9	102.1	129.6	138.9	143.8	130.1	121.2	121.0	148.0	147.0	194.0

Tunisia

1.11 Gross Domestic Product by Kind of Activity, in Constant Prices
(Continued)

Million Tunisian dinars

	1970	1975	1978	1979	1980	1981	1982	1983	1984	1985	1986	1987
		1972	At constant prices of:					1980				
Total, Industries	603.9	943.3	2317.8	2485.2	2695.6	2863.0	2825.9	2953.4	3131.2	3316.0	3250.4	3447.5
Producers of Government Services	112.0	141.1	323.5	337.7	368.5	405.6	426.7	451.4	468.6	487.3	492.2	500.0
Other Producers	...	...	...	...	...	...	...	...	...	...	...	...
Subtotal e	715.9	1084.4	2641.3	2822.9	3064.1	3268.6	3252.6	3404.8	3599.8	3803.3	3742.6	3947.5
Less: Imputed bank service charge	...	...	...	...	...	...	...	...	...	...	...	...
Plus: Import duties	...	...	...	...	...	...	...	...	...	...	...	...
Plus: Value added tax	...	...	...	...	...	...	...	...	...	...	...	...
Plus: Other adjustments f	108.4	143.5	452.0	473.4	476.4	467.4	465.1	486.9	514.9	544.2	535.4	564.5
Equals: Gross Domestic Product	824.3	1227.9	3093.3	3296.3	3540.5	3736.0	3717.7	3891.7	4114.7	4347.5	4278.0	4512.0

a) Item 'Electricity, gas and water' excludes gas.
b) Restaurants and hotels are included in item 'Community, social and personal services'.
c) Real estate refers to owner-occupied dwellings and rent only.
d) Finance, insurance and business services are included in item 'Community, social and personal services'.
e) Gross domestic product in factor values.
f) Item 'Other adjustments' refers to indirect taxes net of subsidies.

1.12 Relations Among National Accounting Aggregates

Million Tunisian dinars

	1970	1975	1978	1979	1980	1981	1982	1983	1984	1985	1986	1987
Gross Domestic Product	755.6	1741.4	2483.9	2922.0	3540.5	4162.0	4804.4	5497.4	6240.0	6910.0	7025.0	7934.8
Plus: Net factor income from the rest of the world	-20.4	-0.4	-3.9	1.4	22.2	31.9	52.6	64.1	48.8	-68.0	-50.0	-60.0
Factor income from the rest of the world	19.0	74.6	100.9	136.4	188.4	244.9	303.2	323.9	340.0	283.0	321.7	360.0
Less: Factor income to the rest of the world	39.4	75.0	104.8	135.0	166.2	213.0	250.6	259.8	291.2	351.0	371.6	420.0
Equals: Gross National Product	735.2	1741.0	2480.0	2923.4	3562.7	4193.9	4857.0	5561.4	6288.8	6842.0	6975.0	7875.8
Less: Consumption of fixed capital	48.0	98.3	215.0	260.0	325.0	380.0	464.0	563.0	672.0	784.0	855.0	925.0
Equals: National Income	687.2	1642.7	2265.0	2663.4	3237.7	3813.9	4393.0	4998.4	5616.8	6058.0	6120.0	6949.8
Plus: Net current transfers from the rest of the world	5.3	-1.0	0.4	4.2	...	...	...	...	...	...	...	...
Current transfers from the rest of the world	7.4	4.7	9.0	10.0	...	...	...	...	...	...	...	...
Less: Current transfers to the rest of the world	2.2	5.7	8.6	5.8	...	...	...	...	...	...	...	...
Equals: National Disposable Income	692.5	1641.7	2265.4	2667.6	3237.7	3813.9	4393.0	4998.4	5616.8	6058.0	6120.0	6949.8
Less: Final consumption	629.8	1337.1	1959.3	2208.2	2690.9	3168.9	3791.0	4361.0	4974.0	5498.0	5886.0	6425.0
Equals: Net Saving	62.7	304.6	306.1	459.4	546.8	645.0	602.0	637.4	642.8	560.0	234.0	525.0
Less: Surplus of the nation on current transactions	-49.2	-85.1	-242.9	-140.5	-167.7	-320.5	-453.3	-409.5	-680.0	-491.0	-560.0	-300.0
Equals: Net Capital Formation	111.9	389.7	549.0	599.9	714.5	965.5	1055.3	1046.9	1322.8	1051.0	794.0	825.0

2.11 Gross Fixed Capital Formation by Kind of Activity of Owner, ISIC Divisions, in Current Prices

Million Tunisian dinars

	1970	1975	1978	1979	1980	1981	1982	1983	1984	1985	1986	1987
				All Producers								
1 Agriculture, hunting, forestry and fishing	13.8	40.7	59.6	108.5 / 110.5	149.5	178.1	204.7	261.7	265.5	303.0	285.0	273.0
2 Mining and quarrying	14.3	75.5	112.9	123.9 / 123.9	120.1	226.6	300.0	197.8	191.4	224.4	186.0	147.0
3 Manufacturing	17.8	83.3	166.5	162.1 / 165.8	133.9	216.0	289.5	362.4	364.3	274.1	266.0	247.0
4 Electricity, gas and water	10.0	35.0	48.8	104.4 / 104.4	71.9	89.4	113.1	150.7	206.7	152.7	111.0	98.0

Tunisia

2.11 Gross Fixed Capital Formation by Kind of Activity of Owner, ISIC Divisions, in Current Prices
(Continued)

Million Tunisian dinars

	1970	1975	1978	1979	1980	1981	1982	1983	1984	1985	1986	1987
5 Construction	...	6.0	2.0	1.0 / 9.8	10.2	12.0	13.0	15.0	20.0	5.0	5.0	10.0
6 Wholesale and retail trade, restaurants and hotels [a]	13.6	10.6	16.8	16.3 / 5.4	6.5	36.5	55.0	82.8	114.6	118.1	98.0	94.0
7 Transport, storage and communication	12.8	51.2	71.9	138.0 / 125.5	211.0	235.4	288.7	219.8	230.7	231.7	185.0	228.0
8 Finance, insurance, real estate and business services	26.5	82.5	101.0	... / 143.0	188.0	198.0	266.0	327.0	365.0	378.0	391.0	410.0
9 Community, social and personal services [a]	-	4.5	20.0	3.4 / 16.3	25.5	...	...	...	...	...	...	...
Total Industries	108.8	389.3	599.5	657.7 / 804.6	916.6	1192.0	1530.0	1617.2	1758.2	1687.0	1527.0	1507.0
Producers of Government Services	...	...	...	... / ...	...	...	...	...	...	...	...	...
Private Non-Profit Institutions Serving Households	42.7	77.7	125.5	236.3 / 87.4	85.4	98.0	105.0	132.8	161.8	163.0	148.0	163.0
Total	151.5	461.0	764.0	894.0 / 892.0	1002.0	1290.0	1635.0	1750.0	1920.0	1850.0	1675.0	1670.0

a) Beginning 1981, item 'Community, social and personal services' is included in item 'Wholesale and retail trade, restaurants and hotels'.

2.17 Exports and Imports of Goods and Services, Detail

Million Tunisian dinars

	1970	1975	1978	1979	1980	1981	1982	1983	1984	1985	1986	1987
Exports of Goods and Services												
1 Exports of merchandise, f.o.b.	98.8	345.6	468.4	726.7	970.0 / 970.0	1212.4	1169.4	1262.6	1399.1	1443.0	1403.8	1750.0
2 Transport and communication	13.6	44.2	62.6	...	... / 104.0	122.3	150.1	153.1	157.6	155.3	150.9	218.2
3 Insurance service charges				...								
4 Other commodities	31.6	119.0	166.7	...	... / 276.5	312.3	367.2	416.0	389.4	466.4	437.0	629.1
5 Adjustments of merchandise exports to change-of-ownership basis	...	...	...	...	...	...	...	...	...	...	...	...
6 Direct purchases in the domestic market by non-residential households [a]	22.0	36.8	71.3	...	... / 29.5	44.2	46.5	62.5	102.9	120.9	101.4	61.1
7 Direct purchases in the domestic market by extraterritorial bodies					... / 44.6	30.7	40.1	53.6	64.7	67.5	68.1	66.6
Total Exports of Goods and Services	166.2	545.6	769.0	1139.0	1424.6 / 1424.6	1721.9	1773.3	1947.8	2114.0	2253.1	2161.2	2725.0
Imports of Goods and Services												
1 Imports of merchandise, c.i.f.	167.7	572.8	906.9	1156.8	1467.1 / 1467.1	1866.0	2002.0	2106.4	2511.0	2287.0	2303.7	2538.0

Tunisia

2.17 Exports and Imports of Goods and Services, Detail
(Continued)

Million Tunisian dinars

	1970	1975	1978	1979	1980	1981	1982	1983	1984	1985	1986	1987
A Imports of merchandise, f.o.b.	154.5	521.8	860.0	1098.0	1398.6 1398.6	1771.2	1900.8	1986.6	2353.9	2166.0	2183.9	2406.2
B Transport of services on merchandise imports	13.2	51.0	46.9	58.8	63.1 68.5[b]	94.8	101.2	119.8	128.0	121.0	119.8	131.8
C Insurance service charges on merchandise imports					... ...							
2 Adjustments of merchandise imports to change-of-ownership basis	...	...	...	...	... ...	...	...	...	...	...	...	...
3 Other transport and communication	12.3	9.5	40.2	...	... 132.8	78.3	99.5	98.1	102.1	109.4	92.1	103.2
4 Other insurance service charges	...	...	...	...	... ...	...	...	...	...	...	...	...
5 Other commodities [c]	12.1	22.8	36.3	37.4	43.2 43.2	54.0	87.2	92.0	109.9	105.3	84.9	90.0
6 Direct purchases abroad by government	8.1	24.6	25.0	...	... ...	49.0	62.6	90.1	98.6	136.8	131.6	170.0
7 Direct purchases abroad by resident households				...	... ...	27.0	27.9	34.8	50.0	37.8	58.7	63.8
Total Imports of Goods and Services	200.2	629.7	1008.4	1285.0	1614.5 1614.5	2074.3	2279.2	2421.4	2842.5	2676.3	2671.0	2965.0
Balance of Goods and Services	-34.0	-84.1	-239.4	-146.0	-189.9 -189.9	-352.4	-505.9	-473.6	-728.8	-423.2	-509.8	-240.0
Total Imports and Balance of Goods and Services [d]	166.2	545.6	769.0	1139.0	1424.6 1424.6	1721.9	1773.3	1947.8	2113.7	2253.1	2161.2	2725.0

a) Item 'Direct purchases in the domestic market by non-residential households' refers to governmental and other services.
b) Including item 'Transport of services on merchandise imports' through 'Insurance service charges on merchandise imports'.
c) Item 'Other commodities' refers to tourism and travel.
d) Data for this table have not been revised, therefore, data for some years are not comparable with those of other tables.

Turkey

Source. Reply to the United Nations National Accounts Questionnaire from the State Institute of Statistics, Ankara. Methods of estimation, explanatory notes and primary sources are described annually in 'National Income of Turkey'.

General note. The official estimates have been prepared by the Institute to conform to the United Nations System of National Accounts so far as the existing data would permit.

1.1 Expenditure on the Gross Domestic Product, in Current Prices

Thousand Million Turkish liras

		1970	1975	1978	1979	1980	1981	1982	1983	1984	1985	1986	1987
1	Government final consumption expenditure	19	77	199	328	440	861	994	1454	1964	3139	...	...
2	Private final consumption expenditure	102	364	915	1565	3476	4465	6201	8449	14369	19095	...	...
3	Gross capital formation	29	120	211	352	751	1416	1680	2092	3290	5960	...	...
	A Increase in stocks [a]	2	18	-24	-63	61	198	47	-56	-87	136	...	...
	B Gross fixed capital formation [a]	27	102	236	415	690	1218	1636	2148	3377	5824	...	...
	Residential buildings	5	12	56	85	174	236	221	319	500	919	...	...
	Non-residential buildings	6	25	52	83	119	243	403	346	580	928	...	...
	Other construction and land improvement etc.	7	19	52	66	171	252	229	542	725	1415	...	...
	Other	9	46	76	181	226	487	784	942	1572	2562	...	...
4	Exports of goods and services	9	34	72	108	298	714	1262	1748	2784	5590	...	...
5	Less: Imports of goods and services	12	76	122	197	638	1042	1519	2212	4195	6233	...	...
	Equals: Gross Domestic Product	145	519	1275	2156	4328	6414	8620	11532	18212	27552	39288	58299

a) Item 'Breeding stocks, dairy cattle, etc.' is included in item 'Increase in stocks'.

1.2 Expenditure on the Gross Domestic Product, in Constant Prices

Million Turkish liras

		1970	1975	1978	1979	1980	1981	1982	1983	1984	1985	1986	1987
		\multicolumn{12}{c}{At constant prices of:1968}
1	Government final consumption expenditure	15541	25434	29747	29029	23661	35215	31478	36696	37386	42666	...	...
2	Private final consumption expenditure	86238	121900	150066	147704	147635	128021	142846	149942	167850	158512	...	...
3	Gross capital formation	25045	38118	42845	44140	33931	44239	40125	36914	36935	44404	...	...
	A Increase in stocks	1562	7153	-5323	-5833	2654	5856	1968	-1537	-875	1947	...	...
	B Gross fixed capital formation	23483	34000	35515	37027	31277	39083	38157	38451	37810	42457	...	...
	Residential buildings	4723	...	8886	8546	8916	9219	6921	7115	7570	9494	...	...
	Non-residential buildings	5020	...	8378	8048	5866	9507	12511	7935	8652	8228	...	...
	Other construction and land improvement etc.	5939	...	8124	6467	8682	10084	7187	12313	10815	13925	...	...
	Other	7801	...	10128	13930	7813	10273	11538	11088	10772	10810	...	...
4	Exports of goods and services	7298	10957	11741	10945	10981	18332	22678	24971	25310	30910	...	...
5	Less: Imports of goods and services	10174	18648	14933	13385	12252	13667	13659	16781	22442	18945	...	...
	Equals: Gross Domestic Product	123943	177761	207314	205487	203956	212841	223468	231742	245038	257546	278955	299582

1.3 Cost Components of the Gross Domestic Product

Thousand Million Turkish liras

		1970	1975	1978	1979	1980	1981	1982	1983	1984	1985	1986	1987
1	Indirect taxes, net [a]	14	51	85	141	230	390	540	714	863	2026	3660	5371
	A Indirect taxes [a]	16	53	102	165	306	498	648	911	1206	2479	4003	5856
	B Less: Subsidies [a]	2	3	18	25	76	108	108	197	343	453	343	485
2	Consumption of fixed capital	9	30	71	121	242	358	477	630	1001	1515	2142	3177
3	Compensation of employees paid by resident producers to:	42	141	349									
	A Resident households	42	140	347	1895	3856	5666	7604	10188	16348	24012	33486	49751
	B Rest of the world	-	1	2									
4	Operating surplus	80	297	770									
	Equals: Gross Domestic Product	145	519	1275	2156	4328	6414	8620	11532	18212	27552	39288	58299

a) The estimates of indirect taxes and subsidies are entered on accrual payment basis.

1.4 General Government Current Receipts and Disbursements

Thousand Million Turkish liras

		1970	1975	1978	1979	1980	1981	1982	1983	1984	1985	1986	1987
		\multicolumn{12}{c}{Receipts}
1	Operating surplus	-	...	...	...	...	...	...	...	...	...	...	...
2	Property and entrepreneurial income	2	...	...	...	...	...	...	...	...	...	...	...
3	Taxes, fees and contributions	30	...	...	...	...	...	...	...	...	...	...	...
	A Indirect taxes [a]	16	...	...	...	...	...	...	...	...	...	...	...

Turkey

1.4 General Government Current Receipts and Disbursements
(Continued)

Thousand Million Turkish liras

	1970	1975	1978	1979	1980	1981	1982	1983	1984	1985	1986	1987
B Direct taxes	9	...	...	...	...	...	...	...	...	...	...	...
C Social security contributions	5	...	...	...	...	...	...	...	...	...	...	...
D Compulsory fees, fines and penalties	-	...	...	...	...	...	...	...	...	...	...	...
4 Other current transfers	3	...	...	...	...	...	...	...	...	...	...	...
Total Current Receipts of General Government	34	...	...	...	...	...	...	...	...	...	...	...

Disbursements

	1970	1975	1978	1979	1980	1981	1982	1983	1984	1985	1986	1987
1 Government final consumption expenditure	19	...	...	...	...	...	...	...	...	...	...	...
A Compensation of employees	14	...	...	...	...	...	...	...	...	...	...	...
B Consumption of fixed capital	-	...	...	...	...	...	...	...	...	...	...	...
C Purchases of goods and services, net	5	...	...	...	...	...	...	...	...	...	...	...
D Less: Own account fixed capital formation	...	...	...	...	...	...	...	...	...	...	...	...
E Indirect taxes paid, net	-	...	...	...	...	...	...	...	...	...	...	...
2 Property income	1	...	...	...	...	...	...	...	...	...	...	...
3 Subsidies a	2	...	...	...	...	...	...	...	...	...	...	...
4 Other current transfers	3	...	...	...	...	...	...	...	...	...	...	...
A Social security benefits	2	...	...	...	...	...	...	...	...	...	...	...
B Social assistance grants	...	...	...	...	...	...	...	...	...	...	...	...
C Other	1	...	...	...	...	...	...	...	...	...	...	...
5 Net saving	11	...	...	...	...	...	...	...	...	...	...	...
Total Current Disbursements and Net Saving of General Government	34	...	...	...	...	...	...	...	...	...	...	...

a) The estimates of indirect taxes and subsidies are entered on cash payment basis.

1.7 External Transactions on Current Account, Summary

Thousand Million Turkish liras

	1970	1975	1978	1979	1980	1981	1982	1983	1984	1985	1986	1987

Payments to the Rest of the World

	1970	1975	1978	1979	1980	1981	1982	1983	1984	1985	1986	1987
1 Imports of goods and services	12	76	122	197	...	...	...	...	...	...	...	...
A Imports of merchandise c.i.f.	11	69	113	179	...	...	...	...	...	...	...	...
B Other	2	7	8	19	...	...	...	...	...	...	...	...
2 Factor income to the rest of the world	1	3	13	21	...	...	...	...	...	...	...	...
A Compensation of employees	-	1	2	-	...	...	...	...	...	...	...	...
B Property and entrepreneurial income	1	2	11	21	...	...	...	...	...	...	...	...
3 Current transfers to the rest of the world	-	-	-	-	...	...	...	...	...	...	...	...
A Indirect taxes to supranational organizations	-	-	-	-	...	...	...	...	...	...	...	...
B Other current transfers	...	...	...	...	...	...	...	...	...	...	...	...
4 Surplus of the nation on current transactions	-1	-27	-34	-45	...	...	...	...	...	...	...	...
Payments to the Rest of the World and Surplus of the Nation on Current Transactions	13	51	101	173	...	...	...	...	...	...	...	...

Receipts From The Rest of the World

	1970	1975	1978	1979	1980	1981	1982	1983	1984	1985	1986	1987
1 Exports of goods and services	9	34	72	108	...	...	...	...	...	...	...	...
A Exports of merchandise f.o.b.	7	20	55	76	...	...	...	...	...	...	...	...
B Other	2	13	16	32	...	...	...	...	...	...	...	...
2 Factor income from rest of the world	4	16	26	60	...	...	...	...	...	...	...	...
A Compensation of employees	4	16	25	59	...	...	...	...	...	...	...	...
B Property and entrepreneurial income	-	-	2	1	...	...	...	...	...	...	...	...
3 Current transfers from rest of the world	1	2	4	5	...	...	...	...	...	...	...	...
A Subsidies from supranational organisations	...	...	...	...	...	...	...	...	...	...	...	...
B Other current transfers	1	2	4	5	...	...	...	...	...	...	...	...
Receipts from the Rest of the World on Current Transactions	13	51	101	173	...	...	...	...	...	...	...	...

Turkey

1.10 Gross Domestic Product by Kind of Activity, in Current Prices

Thousand Million Turkish liras

	1970	1975	1978	1979	1980	1981	1982	1983	1984	1985	1986	1987
1 Agriculture, hunting, forestry and fishing	39	139	306	473	940	1351	1710	2162	3466	4891	6733	9745
2 Mining and quarrying	2	6	13	23	65	128	168	242	371	646	792	1105
3 Manufacturing	27	98	264	470	971	1510	2080	2911	4642	6953	10236	15172
4 Electricity, gas and water	2	8	22	33	86	131	211	265	520	1155	1761	2477
5 Construction	10	25	66	106	218	293	366	459	717	1045	1573	2374
6 Wholesale and retail trade, restaurants and hotels [a]	17	70	173	311	667	1029	1403	1933	3177	4763	6716	10086
7 Transport, storage and communication	11	44	112	205	419	640	859	1155	1797	2741	3827	5581
8 Finance, insurance, real estate and business services [b]	12	39	97	150	324	484	624	826	1344	1985	2832	4142
9 Community, social and personal services [ab]	8	27	67	112	233	351	469	629	1012	1526	2176	3199
Total, Industries	128	457	1121	1883	3924	5917	7889	10583	17044	25704	36646	53880
Producers of Government Services	14	51	133	235	378	481	687	861	1057	1441	2073	3219
Other Producers	...	...	...	...	...	...	...	...	...	...	...	...
Subtotal	142	507	1254	2119	4301	6398	8576	11444	18101	27145	38719	57100
Less: Imputed bank service charge	2	9	19	28	59	98	121	160	275	416	589	856
Plus: Import duties	6	21	40	66	86	113	166	248	387	823	1158	2056
Plus: Value added tax	...	...	...	...	...	...	...	...	...	...	...	...
Equals: Gross Domestic Product	145	519	1275	2156	4328	6414	8620	11532	18212	27552	39288	58296

a) Restaurants and hotels are included in item 'Community, social and personal services'.
b) Business services are included in item 'Community, social and personal services'.

1.11 Gross Domestic Product by Kind of Activity, in Constant Prices

Million Turkish liras

	1970	1975	1978	1979	1980	1981	1982	1983	1984	1985	1986	1987
					At constant prices of:1968							
1 Agriculture, hunting, forestry and fishing	32870	40889	44745	45989	46766	46829	49722	49690	51426	52841	56865	58057
2 Mining and quarrying	2165	2979	3553	3713	3782	4067	4081	3995	4137	4618	5283	5414
3 Manufacturing	24252	38478	46131	43317	41619	45549	48473	52089	56908	60151	66467	73157
4 Electricity, gas and water	1615	2811	3862	4020	4148	4428	4918	5044	5447	6078	6984	7791
5 Construction	8304	10532	12545	13069	13173	13232	13298	13378	13645	14041	15187	16201
6 Wholesale and retail trade, restaurants and hotels [a]	14270	24313	28694	27909	27100	28942	30389	32274	34759	37018	40657	44499
7 Transport, storage and communication	10095	16557	19820	19239	18450	19122	19485	20030	21378	22512	24043	25651
8 Finance, insurance, real estate and business services [b]	10066	13838	17052	17652	18218	18648	19074	19442	20116	20707	21440	22247
9 Community, social and personal services [ab]	6403	9202	10596	10501	10396	10853	11377	11774	12491	13105	14258	15235
Total, Industries	110040	159599	186998	185409	183652	191670	200817	207716	220307	231071	251184	268247
Producers of Government Services	11518	15471	18629	19415	20546	21367	22521	23467	24070	24864	25774	26998
Other Producers	...	...	...	...	...	...	...	...	...	...	...	...
Subtotal	121558	175070	205627	204824	204198	213037	223338	231183	244378	255935	276959	295250
Less: Imputed bank service charge	1964	2960	3677	3787	3855	3928	3991	4011	4192	4338	4498	4660
Plus: Import duties	4355	5651	5364	4450	3613	3732	4121	4570	4853	5949	6495	8997
Plus: Value added tax	...	...	...	...	...	...	...	...	...	...	...	...
Equals: Gross Domestic Product	123949	177761	207314	205487	203956	212841	223468	231742	245039	257546	278956	299582

a) Restaurants and hotels are included in item 'Community, social and personal services'.
b) Business services are included in item 'Community, social and personal services'.

1.12 Relations Among National Accounting Aggregates

Thousand Million Turkish liras

	1970	1975	1978	1979	1980	1981	1982	1983	1984	1985	1986	1987
Gross Domestic Product	145	519	1275	2156	4328	6414	8620	11532	18212	27552	39288	58299
Plus: Net factor income from the rest of the world	2	13	13	39	107	140	115	20	163	238	22	91
Factor income from the rest of the world	4	16	26	60	...	...	...	...	...	...	...	...
Less: Factor income to the rest of the world	1	3	13	21	...	...	...	...	...	...	...	...
Equals: Gross National Product	148	532	1288	2195	4435	6554	8735	11552	18375	27789	39310	58387
Less: Consumption of fixed capital	9	30	71	121	242	358	477	630	1001	1515	2142	3177

Turkey

1.12 Relations Among National Accounting Aggregates
(Continued)

Thousand Million Turkish liras

	1970	1975	1978	1979	1980	1981	1982	1983	1984	1985	1986	1987
Equals: National Income	139	502	1217	2075	4193	6196	8258	10922	17373	26275	37167	55211
Plus: Net current transfers from the rest of the world	1	2	3	4	-	-	-	-	-	-	-	-
Current transfers from the rest of the world	1	2	4	5	...	...	...	...	...	...	...	...
Less: Current transfers to the rest of the world	...	...	...	...	...	...	...	...	...	...	...	...
Equals: National Disposable Income	139	504	1220	2079	4193	6196	8258	10922	17373	26275	37167	55211
Less: Final consumption	121	441	1114	1893	...	...	...	...	...	...	...	...
Equals: Net Saving	19	62	106	186	...	...	...	...	...	...	...	...
Less: Surplus of the nation on current transactions	-1	-27	-34	-45	...	...	...	...	...	...	...	...
Equals: Net Capital Formation	20	90	140	231	...	...	...	...	...	...	...	...

2.1 Government Final Consumption Expenditure by Function, in Current Prices

Thousand Million Turkish liras

	1970	1975	1978	1979	1980	1981	1982	1983	1984	1985	1986	1987
1 General public services [a]	5	...	...	...	...	...	...	...	...	...	...	...
2 Defence	5	...	...	...	...	...	...	...	...	...	...	...
3 Public order and safety [a]	...	...	...	...	...	...	...	...	...	...	...	...
4 Education	3	...	...	...	...	...	...	...	...	...	...	...
5 Health	2	...	...	...	...	...	...	...	...	...	...	...
6 Social security and welfare	-	...	...	...	...	...	...	...	...	...	...	...
7 Housing and community amenities	...	...	...	...	...	...	...	...	...	...	...	...
8 Recreational, cultural and religious affairs [b]	2	...	...	...	...	...	...	...	...	...	...	...
9 Economic services	2	...	...	...	...	...	...	...	...	...	...	...
10 Other functions	-	...	...	...	...	...	...	...	...	...	...	...
Total Government Final Consumption Expenditure	19	...	...	...	...	...	...	...	...	...	...	...

a) Item 'Public order and safety' is included in item 'General public services'.
b) Item 'Recreational, cultural and religious affairs' refers to Social and other community services.

2.7 Gross Capital Formation by Type of Good and Owner, in Current Prices

Thousand Million Turkish liras

	\multicolumn{4}{c}{1980}	\multicolumn{4}{c}{1981}	\multicolumn{4}{c}{1982}
	TOTAL	Total Private	Public Enterprises	General Government	TOTAL	Total Private	Public Enterprises	General Government	TOTAL	Total Private	Public Enterprises	General Government
Increase in stocks, total	61	16	...	45	198	66	...	131	45	-7	...	51
1 Goods producing industries [ab]	43	16	...	27	167	66	...	101	3	-7	...	10
A Materials and supplies	15	-3	...	18	68	23	...	45	36	12	...	24
B Work in progress	3	6	...	-3	-8	-12	...	4	53	56	...	-3
C Livestock, except breeding stocks, dairy cattle, etc. [b]	-	-	...	-	-	-	...	-	-	-	...	-
D Finished goods	25	12	...	12	108	56	...	52	-86	-75	...	-11
2 Wholesale and retail trade [c]	18	-	...	18	24	-	...	24	32	-	...	32
3 Other, except government stocks	-	-	...	-	7	-	...	7	9	-	...	9
4 Government stocks	...	...	...	...	...	...	...	...	...	...	...	...
Gross Fixed Capital Formation, Total	690	211	...	479	1218	474	...	744	1636	659	...	977
1 Residential buildings	174	169	...	5	236	221	...	14	221	194	...	27
2 Non-residential buildings	119	27	...	92	243	35	...	208	403	42	...	360
3 Other construction	171	1	...	170	252	1	...	251	229	4	...	225
4 Land improvement and plantation and orchard development	...	...	...	...	...	...	...	...	...	...	...	...
5 Producers' durable goods	226	15	...	211	487	217	...	270	784	419	...	365
6 Breeding stock, dairy cattle, etc. [b]	...	...	...	...	...	...	...	...	...	...	...	...
Total Gross Capital Formation	751	227	...	524	1416	541	...	875	1680	652	...	1028

Turkey

2.7 Gross Capital Formation by Type of Good and Owner, in Current Prices

Thousand Million Turkish liras

	1983 TOTAL	1983 Total Private	1983 Public Enterprises	1983 General Government	1984 TOTAL	1984 Total Private	1984 Public Enterprises	1984 General Government	1985 TOTAL	1985 Total Private	1985 Public Enterprises	1985 General Government
Increase in stocks, total	-56	...	...	...	-87	...	...	...	136	...	...	...
1 Goods producing industries [a,b]	25	...	...	...	-147	...	...	...	162	...	...	...
A Materials and supplies	38	...	...	...	-75	...	...	...	55	...	...	...
B Work in progress	15	...	...	...	-48	...	...	...	46	...	...	...
C Livestock, except breeding stocks, dairy cattle, etc. [b]	-	...	...	...	-	...	...	...	-	...	...	...
D Finished goods	-27	...	...	...	-23	...	...	...	62	...	...	...
2 Wholesale and retail trade [c]	-60	...	...	...	56	...	...	...	-28	...	...	...
3 Other, except government stocks	-21	...	...	...	4	...	...	...	1	...	...	...
4 Government stocks	...	...	...	...	...	...	...	...	...	...	...	...
Gross Fixed Capital Formation, Total	2148	726	...	1422	3377	1488	...	1889	5824	...	...	...
1 Residential buildings	319	298	...	20	500	472	...	28	919	...	...	...
2 Non-residential buildings	346	76	...	270	580	91	...	489	928	...	...	...
3 Other construction	542	4	...	537	725	3	...	721	1415	...	...	...
4 Land improvement and plantation and orchard development	...	...	...	...	...	...	...	...	...	...	...	...
5 Producers' durable goods	942	348	...	594	1572	922	...	650	2562	...	...	...
6 Breeding stock, dairy cattle, etc. [b]	...	...	...	...	...	...	...	...	...	...	...	...
Total Gross Capital Formation	2092	...	...	...	3290	...	...	...	5960	...	...	...

a) Item 'Goods producing industries' excludes the stock changes of private agriculture.
b) Item 'Breeding stocks, dairy cattle, etc.' is included in item 'Increase in stocks'.
c) Item 'Wholesale and retail trade' excludes changes in stocks of private trade.

2.8 Gross Capital Formation by Type of Good and Owner, in Constant Prices

Million Turkish liras

	1983 TOTAL	1983 Total Private	1983 Public Enterprises	1983 General Government	1984 TOTAL	1984 Total Private	1984 Public Enterprises	1984 General Government	1985 TOTAL	1985 Total Private	1985 Public Enterprises	1985 General Government
					At constant prices of: 1968							
Increase in stocks, total	-1537	...	...	...	-875	...	...	...	1947	...	...	...
1 Goods producing industries [a,b]	391	...	...	...	-1693	...	...	...	2337	...	...	...
A Materials and supplies	663	...	...	...	-834	...	...	...	956	...	...	...
B Work in progress	287	...	...	...	-611	...	...	...	486	...	...	...
C Livestock, except breeding stocks, dairy cattle, etc. [b]	-1	...	...	...	...	...	...	...	2	...	...	...
D Finished goods	-558	...	...	...	-248	...	...	...	893	...	...	...
2 Wholesale and retail trade [c]	-1549	...	...	...	765	...	...	...	-421	...	...	...
3 Other, except government stocks	-379	...	...	...	53	...	...	...	31	...	...	...
4 Government stocks	...	...	...	...	...	...	...	...	...	...	...	...
Gross Fixed Capital Formation, Total	38451	...	...	...	37810	...	...	...	42457	...	...	...
1 Residential buildings	7115	...	...	...	7571	...	...	...	9494	...	...	...
2 Non-residential buildings	7935	...	...	...	8652	...	...	...	8228	...	...	...
3 Other construction	12313	...	...	...	10815	...	...	...	13925	...	...	...
4 Land improvement and plantation and orchard development	...	...	...	...	...	...	...	...	...	...	...	...
5 Producers' durable goods	11088	...	...	...	10772	...	...	...	10810	...	...	...
6 Breeding stock, dairy cattle, etc. [b]	...	...	...	...	...	...	...	...	...	...	...	...
Total Gross Capital Formation	36914	...	...	...	36935	...	...	...	44404	...	...	...

a) Item 'Goods producing industries' excludes the stock changes of private agriculture.
b) Item 'Breeding stocks, dairy cattle, etc.' is included in item 'Increase in stocks'.
c) Item 'Wholesale and retail trade' excludes changes in stocks of private trade.

Turkey

2.17 Exports and Imports of Goods and Services, Detail

Thousand Million Turkish liras

	1970	1975	1978	1979	1980	1981	1982	1983	1984	1985	1986	1987
Exports of Goods and Services												
1 Exports of merchandise, f.o.b.	7	20	55	76	...	...	...	...	...	...	...	...
2 Transport and communication	-	5	4	8	...	...	...	...	...	...	...	...
A In respect of merchandise imports	-	2	1	1	...	...	...	...	...	...	...	...
B Other	-	2	4	7	...	...	...	...	...	...	...	...
3 Insurance service charges	-	1	-	-	...	...	...	...	...	...	...	...
A In respect of merchandise imports	-	1	-	-	...	...	...	...	...	...	...	...
B Other	-	-	-	-	...	...	...	...	...	...	...	...
4 Other commodities	1	5	6	15	...	...	...	...	...	...	...	...
5 Adjustments of merchandise exports to change-of-ownership basis	-	-	-	-	...	...	...	...	...	...	...	...
6 Direct purchases in the domestic market by non-residential households	1	3	6	10	...	...	...	...	...	...	...	...
7 Direct purchases in the domestic market by extraterritorial bodies	...	...	...	...	...	...	...	...	...	...	...	...
Total Exports of Goods and Services	9	34	72	108	...	...	...	...	...	...	...	...
Imports of Goods and Services												
1 Imports of merchandise, c.i.f.	11	69	113	179	...	...	...	...	...	...	...	...
A Imports of merchandise, f.o.b.	10	63	101	159	...	...	...	...	...	...	...	...
B Transport of services on merchandise imports	1	5	11	17	...	...	...	...	...	...	...	...
By residents	...	...	...	...	...	...	...	...	...	...	...	...
By non-residents	1	5	11	17	...	...	...	...	...	...	...	...
C Insurance service charges on merchandise imports	-	1	2	2	...	...	...	...	...	...	...	...
By residents	...	...	...	...	...	...	...	...	...	...	...	...
By non-residents	-	1	2	2	...	...	...	...	...	...	...	...
2 Adjustments of merchandise imports to change-of-ownership basis	1	2	2	4	...	...	...	...	...	...	...	...
3 Other transport and communication	-	1	1	2	...	...	...	...	...	...	...	...
4 Other insurance service charges	-	-	-	-	...	...	...	...	...	...	...	...
5 Other commodities	1	3	5	13	...	...	...	...	...	...	...	...
6 Direct purchases abroad by government	...	...	...	...	...	...	...	...	...	...	...	...
7 Direct purchases abroad by resident households	...	...	...	...	...	...	...	...	...	...	...	...
Total Imports of Goods and Services	12	76	122	197	...	...	...	...	...	...	...	...
Balance of Goods and Services	-4	-42	-50	-89	...	...	...	...	...	...	...	...
Total Imports and Balance of Goods and Services	9	34	72	108	...	...	...	...	...	...	...	...

Uganda

General note. The preparation of national accounts statistics in Uganda is undertaken by the Statistics Division, Ministry of Planning and Economic Development, Entebbe. The official estimates are published in the 'Statistical Abstract'. The following presentation of sources and methods is mainly based on information received by the United Nations from the Statistical Division of Uganda. The estimates are generally in accordance with the classifications and definitions recommended in the United Nations System of National Accounts (SNA). The following tables have been prepared from successive replies to the United Nations national accounts questionnaire. When the scope and coverage of the estimates differ for conceptual or statistical reasons from the definitions and classifications recommended in SNA, a footnote is indicated to the relevant tables.

Sources and methods:

(a) Gross domestic product. Gross domestic product is estimated mainly through the production approach.

(b) Expenditure on the gross domestic product. The expenditure approach is used to estimate government final consumption expenditure and exports and imports of goods and services. The commodity-flow approach is used to estimate gross capital formation. Private final consumption expenditure is obtained as a residual. Government final consumption expenditure is obtained from accounts of the government bodies. The estimates are recorded on a cash basis and are classified by purpose. Estimates of changes in stocks are prepared for coffee and livestock only, for which average prices are used. The value of capital expenditure on plant, machinery and transport equipment is estimated on the basis of import values, adding import duties, mark-ups for trade, transport and other miscellaneous charges. The estimates of construction are prepared on the basis of the estimated value of building materials as well as on wages and salaries paid. Own-account rural residential construction is estimated on the assumption that it keeps pace with the population growth. Estimates of government gross fixed capital formation are derived from the government fiscal and operating accounts. For exports and imports of goods and services, the Annual Trade Reports issued by the East African Customs Department and the balance-of-payments statistics are used. GDP by expenditure type at constant prices is not estimated.

(c) Cost-structure of the gross domestic product. For the government sector, wages and salaries are derived from the government accounts, for large-scale manufacturing they are obtained from the surveys of industrial production, for trade they are based on the 1966 census of distribution, with a constant ratio to total value added for other years and for services, they are taken from accounts of the services establishments or from the enumeration of employees. The estimates of consumption of fixed capital are built up by branch from various sources such as the annual surveys of industrial production and the accounts of enterprises in mining, electricity and water supply. Estimates of indirect taxes and subsidies are obtained from government accounts. Operating surplus is in most cases derived as a residual.

(d) Gross domestic product by kind of economic activity. The table of GDP by kind of economic activity is prepared in factor values. The production approach is used to estimate the value added of the goods-commodity-producing sectors. The income approach is used for the service-producing sectors except the trade sector, for which the commodity-flow approach is used. For the five major commercial agricultural crops: coffee, cotton, tea, tobacco and sugar cane, statistics of production and value are available annually from sources such as the Coffee Marketing Board, the annual surveys of industrial production and the Produce Marketing Board. For other crops, bench-mark estimates are based on the results of the census of agriculture in 1964/65. Production figures for other years are obtained by using population growth as an indicator. Estimates of subsistence production are based on ad hoc statistical inquiries conducted during the 1960s. Crop prices are collected monthly by the Ministry of Agriculture from selected markets. For intermediate consumption, input ratios are used. Livestock slaughtered for own consumption is evaluated at annual average auction prices while the marketed meat is evaluated at annual average retail prices adjusted for trade and transport margins. For forestry, the gross value of output of the public forests is taken to be equal to the gross revenue earned by the government from this activity. The main sources for estimating the mining industry are the annual surveys of industrial production. For manufacturing, the Statistics Division conducts annual surveys of industrial production covering all establishments employing 10 or more workers. The 1965 survey also covered small establishments employing 5 to 9 workers. The price data applicable for the large-scale sector are also used for the small-scale sector. The input ratios are mainly based on the 1965 survey results and assumed to remain constant. Estimates of electricity and water are obtained from the annual reports and accounts of the agencies involved. For construction, a bench-mark survey of building and construction activities was carried out in 1964 covering both small and large construction units and own-account construction in the organized sector. For trade, annual gross sales are determined by applying mark-ups based on the 1966 census of distribution and assuming stocks to remain constant. The value of gross sales is then related to inputs, wages and operating surplus on the basis of global norms derived from the 1966 census results. These norms are assumed to remain constant over the years. For restaurants and hotels, bench-mark information has been collected for 1967 from the profit and loss accounts of 50 hotels and resturants. The information collected are projected by means of either sales-tax data or data on wages and salaries. The estimates of railways, air transport and communications are obtained from the relevant corporations which are managed by the East African Community. For financial institutions, bench-mark information in terms of profit and loss accounts and balance-sheets of individual banks and other financial institutions has been analysed and estimates have been complied for 1969. For other years, these relationships have been applied to the number of employees in these institutions. Bench-mark information on insurance companies is available for 1967 and extrapolated by using management expenses. For real estate and ownership of dwellings, the estimates of rental values in urban areas are based on the records of the Land and Survey Department and the annual reports of the town councils. Bench-mark estimates for business services were collected in 1967 and are projected using as indicator the number of persons engaged in these services. For producers of government services, sources of data are the annual reports of government agencies and accounts of non-profit institutions. For other services, 1967 bench-mark estimates are extrapolated by the results of the annual enumeration of employees. For the constant price estimates, double deflation is used for agriculture, mining and quarrying, electricity, gas and water and trade sectors. For manufacturing and transport, value added is extrapolated by a quantity index for output. Price deflation is used for construction, restaurants and hotels and for financial and services sectors.

1.1 Expenditure on the Gross Domestic Product, in Current Prices

Million Uganda shillings

		1970	1975	1978	1979	1980	1981	1982	1983	1984	1985	1986	1987
1	Government final consumption expenditure	7897	21271	62797	...	...	146188	301131	435250	580423	...	...	...
2	Private final consumption expenditure				...	...					...	...	...
3	Gross capital formation	1261	1712	2481	...	...	4793	18313	41050	84101	...	...	...
	A Increase in stocks	100	171	600	...	...	2758	11256	31884	65322	...	...	...
	B Gross fixed capital formation	1161	1541	1881	...	...	2035	7057	9166	18779	...	...	...
	Residential buildings	660	883	...	...	...	...	...	...	...	...	...	...
	Non-residential buildings	...	...	...	...	...	...	...	...	...	...	...	...
	Other construction and land improvement etc.	...	...	...	...	...	...	...	...	...	...	...	...
	Other	501	658	...	...	...	...	...	...	...	...	...	...
4	Exports of goods and services	2101	1837	2550	...	...	6250	21853	48782	110400	...	...	...
5	Less: Imports of goods and services	1810	2318	3524	...	...	16619	41356	49897	126734	...	...	...
	Equals: Gross Domestic Product	9449	22502	64304	...	...	140612	299941	475185	648190	...	...	...

1.3 Cost Components of the Gross Domestic Product

Million Uganda shillings

		1970	1975	1978	1979	1980	1981	1982	1983	1984	1985	1986	1987
1	Indirect taxes, net	921	...	...	...	...	...	...	...	...	...	...	...
	A Indirect taxes	937	...	...	...	...	...	...	...	...	...	...	...
	B Less: Subsidies	16	...	...	...	...	...	...	...	...	...	...	...
2	Consumption of fixed capital [a]	...	...	...	...	...	...	...	...	...	...	...	...
3	Compensation of employees paid by resident producers to:	2136	...	...	...	...	...	...	...	...	...	...	...
4	Operating surplus [a]	6392	...	...	...	...	...	...	...	...	...	...	...
	Equals: Gross Domestic Product	9449	...	...	...	...	...	...	...	...	...	...	...

a) Item 'Operating surplus' includes consumption of fixed capital.

Uganda

1.10 Gross Domestic Product by Kind of Activity, in Current Prices

Million Uganda shillings

	1970	1975	1978	1979	1980	1981	1982	1983	1984	1985	1986	1987
1 Agriculture, hunting, forestry and fishing	4591	14996	...	...	...	...	...	...	...	...	...	...
2 Mining and quarrying	144	59	...	...	...	...	...	...	...	...	...	...
3 Manufacturing	782	1317	...	...	...	...	...	...	...	...	...	...
4 Electricity, gas and water	105	103	...	...	...	...	...	...	...	...	...	...
5 Construction	154	230	...	...	...	...	...	...	...	...	...	...
6 Wholesale and retail trade, restaurants and hotels	961	1342	...	...	...	...	...	...	...	...	...	...
7 Transport, storage and communication	263	430	...	...	...	...	...	...	...	...	...	...
8 Finance, insurance, real estate and business services [a]	633	1199	...	...	...	...	...	...	...	...	...	...
9 Community, social and personal services	66	42	...	...	...	...	...	...	...	...	...	...
Total, Industries	7699	19718	...	...	...	...	...	...	...	...	...	...
Producers of Government Services	731	1010	...	...	...	...	...	...	...	...	...	...
Other Producers	107	48	...	...	...	...	...	...	...	...	...	...
Subtotal [b]	8537	20776	...	...	...	...	...	...	...	...	...	...
Less: Imputed bank service charge [a]	...	...	...	...	...	...	...	...	...	...	...	...
Plus: Import duties	264	...	...	...	...	...	...	...	...	...	...	...
Plus: Value added tax	...	...	...	...	...	...	...	...	...	...	...	...
Plus: Other adjustments [c]	648	...	...	...	...	...	...	...	...	...	...	...
Equals: Gross Domestic Product	9449	...	...	...	...	...	...	...	...	...	...	...

a) Item 'Less: Imputed bank service charge' is netted out of item 'Finance, insurance, real estate and business services'.
b) Gross domestic product in factor values.
c) Item 'Other adjustments' refers to indirect taxes net of subsidies and a statistical discrepancy.

1.11 Gross Domestic Product by Kind of Activity, in Constant Prices

Million Uganda shillings

	1970	1975	1978	1979	1980	1981	1982	1983	1984	1985	1986	1987
	\multicolumn{12}{c}{At constant prices of:1966}
1 Agriculture, hunting, forestry and fishing	3774	3965	4067	3497	3277	3500	3854	4239	...	...	...	...
2 Mining and quarrying	119	59	15	8	6	6	7	7	...	...	...	...
3 Manufacturing	631	504	372	246	261	247	282	290	...	...	...	...
4 Electricity, gas and water	109	104	103	77	91	109	105	97	...	...	...	...
5 Construction	122	92	79	72	37	38	43	47	...	...	...	...
6 Wholesale and retail trade, restaurants and hotels	825	592	587	537	465	448	498	541	...	...	...	...
7 Transport, storage and communication	276	322	167	134	168	182	200	208	...	...	...	...
8 Finance, insurance, real estate and business services [a]	542	602	720	661	663	664	680	704	...	...	...	...
9 Community, social and personal services	56	60	46	36	39	30	37	38	...	...	...	...
Total, Industries	6455	6301	6156	5268	5007	5224	5706	6171	...	...	...	...
Producers of Government Services	731	1012	997	1032	1078	1094	1130	1163	...	...	...	...
Other Producers	96	44	28	30	30	33	37	41	...	...	...	...
Subtotal [b]	7281	7356	7181	6330	6115	6351	6873	7375	...	...	...	...
Less: Imputed bank service charge [a]	...	...	...	...	...	...	...	...	...	...	...	...
Plus: Import duties	...	...	...	...	...	...	...	...	...	...	...	...
Plus: Value added tax	...	...	...	...	...	...	...	...	...	...	...	...
Equals: Gross Domestic Product [b]	7282	7357	7181	6330	6115	6351	6873	7375	...	...	...	...

a) Item 'Less: Imputed bank service charge' is netted out of item 'Finance, insurance, real estate and business services'.
b) Gross domestic product in factor values.

1.12 Relations Among National Accounting Aggregates

Million Uganda shillings

	1970	1975	1978	1979	1980	1981	1982	1983	1984	1985	1986	1987
Gross Domestic Product	9449	...	...	...	...	...	...	...	...	...	...	...
Plus: Net factor income from the rest of the world	-107	...	...	...	...	...	...	...	...	...	...	...
Equals: Gross National Product	9342	...	...	...	...	...	...	...	...	...	...	...
Less: Consumption of fixed capital	...	...	...	...	...	...	...	...	...	...	...	...
Equals: National Income [a]	9342	...	...	...	...	...	...	...	...	...	...	...

Uganda

1.12 Relations Among National Accounting Aggregates
(Continued)

Million Uganda shillings

	1970	1975	1978	1979	1980	1981	1982	1983	1984	1985	1986	1987
Plus: Net current transfers from the rest of the world	-39	...	...	...	...	...	...	...	...	...	...	...
Equals: National Disposable Income [b]	9303	...	...	...	...	...	...	...	...	...	...	...
Less: Final consumption	...	...	...	...	...	...	...	...	...	...	...	...
Equals: Net Saving	...	...	...	...	...	...	...	...	...	...	...	...
Less: Surplus of the nation on current transactions	...	...	...	...	...	...	...	...	...	...	...	...
Equals: Net Capital Formation	...	...	...	...	...	...	...	...	...	...	...	...

a) Item 'National income' includes consumption of fixed capital.
b) Item 'National disposable income' includes consumption of fixed capital.

Ukrainian SSR

Source. Communication from the Central Statistical Board of the Council of Ministers of the Ukrainian SSR, Kiev. The official estimates are published annually in 'Narodue Gospodarstvo Ukrainskoi SSR' (National Economy of the Ukrainian SSR).

General note. The estimates shown in the following tables have been prepared in accordance with the System of Material Product Balances. Therefore, these estimates are not comparable in concept and coverage with those conforming to the United Nations System of National Accounts.

2a Net Material Product by Kind of Activity of the Material Sphere in Current Market Prices

Thousand Million USSR Roubles

	1970	1975	1978	1979	1980	1981	1982	1983	1984	1985	1986	1987
1 Agriculture and forestry	13.9	14.3	17.3	...	...	...	...	...	...	...	...	...
2 Industrial activity	27.4	33.1	36.6	...	...	...	...	...	...	...	...	...
3 Construction	5.0	6.5	7.1	...	...	...	...	...	...	...	...	...
4 Wholesale and retail trade and restaurants and other eating and drinking places [a]	5.9	8.2	10.6	...	...	...	...	...	...	...	...	...
5 Transport and communication [b]	2.6	3.7	4.1	...	...	...	...	...	...	...	...	...
6 Other activities of the material sphere [a]	...	...	...	...	...	...	...	...	...	...	...	...
Net material product	54.8	65.8	75.9	76.4	77.5	82.6	87.5	92.3	96.2	96.6	97.4	99.5

a) Item 'Other activities of the material sphere' is included in item 'Wholesale and retail trade and restaurants and other eating and drinking places'.
b) Only goods transport and communication serving branches of material production are included in item 'Transport and Communication'.

2a Net Material Product by Kind of Activity of the Material Sphere in Current Market Prices

Percentages

	1970	1975	1978	1979	1980	1981	1982	1983	1984	1985	1986	1987
1 Agriculture and forestry	25.3	21.7	22.8	...	...	...	...	...	...	...	...	...
2 Industrial activity	50.0	50.3	48.2	...	...	...	...	...	...	...	...	...
3 Construction	9.2	9.9	9.4	...	...	...	...	...	...	...	...	...
4 Wholesale and retail trade and restaurants and other eating and drinking places [a]	10.7	12.5	14.0	...	...	...	...	...	...	...	...	...
5 Transport and communication [b]	4.8	5.6	5.4	...	...	...	...	...	...	...	...	...
6 Other activities of the material sphere [a]	...	...	...	...	...	...	...	...	...	...	...	...
Net material product	100.0	100.0	100.0	...	...	...	...	...	...	...	...	...

a) Item 'Other activities of the material sphere' is included in item 'Wholesale and retail trade and restaurants and other eating and drinking places'.
b) Only goods transport and communication serving branches of material production are included in item 'Transport and Communication'.

2b Net Material Product by Kind of Activity of the Material Sphere in Constant Market Prices

Index numbers 1960=100

	1970	1975	1978	1979	1980	1981	1982	1983	1984	1985	1986	1987
				At constant prices of:1975								
1 Agriculture and forestry	116	...	...	...	...	...	...	...	...	...	...	...
2 Industrial activity	258	356	419	433	444	452	461	...	...	...	...	...
3 Construction	151	186	197	193	193	196	200	...	...	...	...	...
4 Wholesale and retail trade and restaurants and other eating and drinking places	197	258	284	291	410	444	475	...	...	...	...	...
5 Transport and communication	199	282	322	325	324	336	340	...	...	...	...	...
6 Other activities of the material sphere	...	...	...	...	...	...	...	...	...	...	...	...
Net material product	195	244	282	283	287	295	311	327	338	344	353	363

6b Capital Formation by Kind of Activity of the Material and Non-Material Spheres in Constant Market Prices

Million USSR Roubles

	1970	1975	1978	1979	1980	1981	1982	1983	1984	1985	1986	1987
				At constant prices of:1984								
			Gross Fixed Capital Formation by Socio-economic Sector and Industrial Use									
1 State and co-operative (excluding collective farms)	14781	19848	22023	21482	21325	21335	21966	24110	24438	25114	27620	28590
A Industry	5462	7335	8229	8012	8285	8301	8658	9190	9492	9660	10522	10901
B Construction	438	535	574	636	643	601	602	572	554	622	674	817
C Agriculture and forestry [a]	2840	4340	4632	4511	4489	4438	4539	4722	4648	4686	5116	4929
D Transport and communication	1544	2090	2881	2540	2201	2056	2121	3036	2705	2693	2834	3073
E Residential building	2167	2746	2881	2893	2823	2985	3092	3383	3670	3883	4478	4577
F Trade and other	2330	2802	2826	2890	2884	2954	2954	3207	3369	3570	3996	4293
2 Collective farms	...	...	...	...	...	...	...	...	...	...	...	...
3 Other	...	...	...	...	...	...	...	...	...	...	...	...
Gross Fixed Capital Formation [b]	14781	19848	22023	21482	21325	21335	21966	24110	24438	25114	27620	28590

a) Item 'Agriculture and forestry' excludes forestry and procurement.
b) The estimates for this table are at constant prices of 1 January 1984.

United Arab Emirates

Source. Reply to the United Nations National Accounts Questionnaire from the Ministry of Foreign Affairs, Abu Dhabi.
General note. The estimates shown in the following tables have been prepared in accordance with the United Nations System of National Accounts so far as the existing data would permit.

1.1 Expenditure on the Gross Domestic Product, in Current Prices

Million U.A.E Dirhams	1970	1975	1978	1979	1980	1981	1982	1983	1984	1985	1986	1987
1 Government final consumption expenditure	...	3261	8163	9600	11992	21475	22000	19030	17696	19484	18314	19200
2 Private final consumption expenditure	...	6215	12501	15245	18968	24946	26846	27467	26744	27173	29877	31000
3 Gross capital formation	...	12059	23679	27643	31155	31801	32163	32203	29496	24933	22607	23000
A Increase in stocks	...	-	-2100	-799	1000	1158	480	535	380	475	510	...
B Gross fixed capital formation	...	12059	25779	28442	30155	30643	31683	31668	29116	24458	22097	23000
4 Exports of goods and services	...	29522	40200	57201	85592	83662	71576	60874	60008	58266	39396	46800
5 Less: Imports of goods and services	...	11597	23874	29717	37874	40784	40152	36665	32101	30440	31850	35000
Equals: Gross Domestic Product	...	39460	60669	79972	109833	121100	112433	102909	101843	99416	78344	85000

1.2 Expenditure on the Gross Domestic Product, in Constant Prices

Million U.A.E Dirhams	1970	1975	1978	1979	1980	1981	1982	1983	1984	1985	1986	1987
					At constant prices of:1980							
1 Government final consumption expenditure	...	4667	8570	10204	11992	20300	20042	18020	18381	19700	18402	...
2 Private final consumption expenditure	...	9344	16785	17550	18968	23262	25669	26066	27364	28334	30038	...
3 Gross capital formation	...	16029	27779	30009	31155	30114	29615	30527	30123	25596	21952	...
A Increase in stocks	...	-	-3000	-1000	1000	1064	455	515	395	490	505	...
B Gross fixed capital formation	...	16029	30779	31009	30155	29050	29160	30012	29728	25106	21447	...
4 Exports of goods and services	...	42145	49544	66670	85592	77835	66714	58377	60583	58907	39855	...
5 Less: Imports of goods and services	...	19458	33112	37554	37874	38557	38405	34565	33775	32314	32147	...
Equals: Gross Domestic Product	...	52727	69566	86879	109833	112954	103635	98425	102676	100223	78100	...

1.3 Cost Components of the Gross Domestic Product

Million U.A.E Dirhams	1970	1975	1978	1979	1980	1981	1982	1983	1984	1985	1986	1987
1 Indirect taxes, net	...	-175	-601	-825	-1637	-2954	-3221	-2595	-2661	-2538	-2318	...
2 Consumption of fixed capital	...	2729	5840	7129	9035	10384	13622	16582	17649	17027	15152	...
3 Compensation of employees paid by resident producers to:	...	5633	12617	14166	16011	21123	23300	24297	24573	24997	24637	...
A Resident households	...	3923	8952	10124	11639	14673	16300	16997	17761	18097	17487	...
B Rest of the world	...	1710	3665	4042	4372	6450	7000	7300	6812	6900	7150	...
4 Operating surplus	...	31273	42813	59502	86424	92547	78732	64625	62282	59930	40873	...
Equals: Gross Domestic Product	...	39460	60669	79972	109833	121100	112433	102909	101843	99416	78344	...

1.7 External Transactions on Current Account, Summary

Million U.A.E Dirhams	1970	1975	1978	1979	1980	1981	1982	1983	1984	1985	1986	1987
					Payments to the Rest of the World							
1 Imports of goods and services	...	11597	23874	29717	37874	40784	40152	36665	32101	30440	31850	...
A Imports of merchandise c.i.f.	...	10912	21473	26642	34116	35594	34795	30970	25530	24140	25100	...
B Other	...	685	2401	3075	3758	5190	5357	5695	6571	6300	6750	...
2 Factor income to the rest of the world	...	4234	7671	9496	10306	12770	12076	11600	10157	9800	8900	...
A Compensation of employees	...	1710	3665	4042	4372	6450	7000	7300	6812	6900	7150	...
B Property and entrepreneurial income	...	2524	4006	5454	5934	6320	5076	4300	3345	2900	1750	...
3 Current transfers to the rest of the world	...	2421	3248	4774	6757	4016	2510	800	1064	1013	887	...
4 Surplus of the nation on current transactions	...	12697	8989	18589	38909	34842	26138	21709	27286	27213	7159	...
Payments to the Rest of the World and Surplus of the Nation on Current Transactions	...	30949	43782	62576	93846	92412	80876	70774	70608	68466	48796	...
					Receipts From The Rest of the World							
1 Exports of goods and services	...	29522	40200	57201	85592	83662	71576	60874	60008	58266	39396	...

United Arab Emirates

1.7 External Transactions on Current Account, Summary
(Continued)

Million U.A.E Dirhams

	1970	1975	1978	1979	1980	1981	1982	1983	1984	1985	1986	1987
A Exports of merchandise f.o.b.	...	29112	39444	56250	84512	82142	69980	59254	58440	56766	37776	...
B Other	...	410	756	951	1080	1520	1596	1620	1568	1500	1620	...
2 Factor income from rest of the world	...	1427	3582	5375	8254	8750	9300	9900	10600	10200	9400	...
A Compensation of employees	...	...	...	...	...	...	...	...	...	...	...	...
B Property and entrepreneurial income	...	1427	3582	5375	8254	8750	9300	9900	10600	10200	9400	...
3 Current transfers from rest of the world	...	...	...	...	...	...	...	...	...	...	...	...
Receipts from the Rest of the World on Current Transactions	...	30949	43782	62576	93846	92412	80876	70774	70608	68466	48796	...

1.10 Gross Domestic Product by Kind of Activity, in Current Prices

Million U.A.E Dirhams

	1970	1975	1978	1979	1980	1981	1982	1983	1984	1985	1986	1987
1 Agriculture, hunting, forestry and fishing	...	329	604	680	827	1036	1144	1198	1349	1440	1540	...
2 Mining and quarrying	...	26462	32825	48104	70767	70071	56280	46454	46942	45016	26453	...
3 Manufacturing	...	369	2197	2534	4191	8077	9436	9584	9761	9255	8405	...
4 Electricity, gas and water	...	209	689	985	1297	1547	1851	1746	2076	2143	2308	...
5 Construction	...	4308	8271	9338	9834	10475	10168	10520	9860	8882	8500	...
6 Wholesale and retail trade, restaurants and hotels	...	3248	5589	6850	9094	10849	10913	9701	9154	8715	8820	...
7 Transport, storage and communication	...	1255	2866	3420	3731	4950	5465	4780	4420	4188	4138	...
8 Finance, insurance, real estate and business services [a]	...	2219	4429	4422	6129	9132	11375	12107	10617	10330	8707	...
9 Community, social and personal services [b]	...	382	675	740	814	1174	1380	1556	1602	1645	1758	...
Total, Industries	...	38781	58145	77073	106684	117311	108012	97646	95781	91614	70629	...
Producers of Government Services	...	1364	3981	4700	5989	8910	9632	9847	10356	11001	10957	...
Other Producers [b]	...	40	114	148	200	234	253	298	335	364	368	...
Subtotal [c]	...	40185	62240	81921	112873	126455	117897	107791	106472	102979	81954	...
Less: Imputed bank service charge [a]	...	550	970	1124	1403	2401	2243	2287	1968	1025	1292	...
Plus: Import duties	...	...	...	...	...	...	...	...	...	...	...	...
Plus: Value added tax	...	...	...	...	...	...	...	...	...	...	...	...
Plus: Other adjustments [d]	...	-175	-601	-825	-1637	-2954	-3221	-2595	-2661	-2538	-2318	...
Equals: Gross Domestic Product	...	39460	60669	79972	109833	121100	112433	102909	101843	99416	78344	...

a) For 1972-1974, imputed bank service charges are netted out of item 'Finance, insurance, real estate and business services.'
b) For 1972-1974, item 'Other producers' is included in item 'Community, social and personal services'.
c) Gross domestic product in factor values.
d) Item 'Other adjustments' refers to indirect taxes net of subsidies.

1.11 Gross Domestic Product by Kind of Activity, in Constant Prices

Million U.A.E Dirhams

	1970	1975	1978	1979	1980	1981	1982	1983	1984	1985	1986	1987
				At constant prices of:1980								
1 Agriculture, hunting, forestry and fishing	...	367	649	732	827	1020	1079	1236	1400	1525	1617	...
2 Mining and quarrying	...	35938	37824	52724	70767	65504	53487	45255	47327	45606	25621	...
3 Manufacturing	...	472	2274	2542	4191	7990	9251	9116	9655	9443	8695	...
4 Electricity, gas and water	...	287	792	1122	1297	1509	1710	1742	2025	2225	2270	...
5 Construction	...	4770	9749	9753	9834	9615	9692	10250	11650	9022	8652	...
6 Wholesale and retail trade, restaurants and hotels	...	4940	8046	8316	9094	10384	10295	9574	9251	9025	9084	...
7 Transport, storage and communication	...	1608	3188	3552	3731	3909	3880	3647	3890	3950	4075	...
8 Finance, insurance, real estate and business services [a]	...	2151	4073	4824	6129	8484	8966	10907	10505	10290	8733	...
9 Community, social and personal services [b]	...	516	703	736	814	1126	1234	1472	1475	1580	1715	...
Total, Industries	...	51049	67298	84301	106684	109541	99594	93199	97178	92666	70462	...
Producers of Government Services	...	2551	4496	5125	5989	8104	8830	9491	9865	10792	10837	...

United Arab Emirates

1.11 Gross Domestic Product by Kind of Activity, in Constant Prices
(Continued)

Million U.A.E Dirhams

	1970	1975	1978	1979	1980	1981	1982	1983	1984	1985	1986	1987
					At constant prices of:1980							
Other Producers [b]	...	54	119	147	200	223	233	307	359	410	408	...
Subtotal [c]	...	53654	71913	89573	112873	117868	108657	102997	107402	103868	81707	...
Less: Imputed bank service charge [a]	...	600	1407	1514	1403	2180	2050	2130	1996	1064	1312	...
Plus: Import duties	...	...	...	...	...	...	...	...	...	...	...	...
Plus: Value added tax	...	...	...	...	...	...	...	...	...	...	...	...
Plus: Other adjustments [d]	...	-327	-940	-1180	-1637	-2734	-2972	-2442	-2730	-2581	-2295	...
Equals: Gross Domestic Product	...	52727	69566	86879	109833	112954	103635	98425	102676	100223	78100	...

a) For 1972-1974, imputed bank service charges are netted out of item 'Finance, insurance, real estate and business services.'
b) For 1972-1974, item 'Other producers' is included in item 'Community, social and personal services'.
c) Gross domestic product in factor values.
d) Item 'Other adjustments' refers to indirect taxes net of subsidies.

1.12 Relations Among National Accounting Aggregates

Million U.A.E Dirhams

	1970	1975	1978	1979	1980	1981	1982	1983	1984	1985	1986	1987
Gross Domestic Product	...	39460	60669	79972	109833	121100	112433	102909	101843	99416	78344	...
Plus: Net factor income from the rest of the world	...	-2807	-4089	-4121	-2052	-4020	-2776	-1700	443	400	500	...
Factor income from the rest of the world	...	1427	3582	5375	8254	8750	9300	9900	10600	10200	9400	...
Less: Factor income to the rest of the world	...	4234	7671	9496	10306	12770	12076	11600	10157	9800	8900	...
Equals: Gross National Product	...	36653	56580	75851	107781	117080	109657	101209	102286	99816	78844	...
Less: Consumption of fixed capital	...	2729	5840	7129	9035	10384	13622	16582	17649	17027	15152	...
Equals: National Income	...	33924	50740	68722	98746	106696	96035	84627	84637	82789	63692	...
Plus: Net current transfers from the rest of the world	...	-2421	-3248	-4774	-6757	-4016	-2510	-800	-1064	-1013	-887	...
Current transfers from the rest of the world	...	-	-	-	-	-	-	-	-	-	-	...
Less: Current transfers to the rest of the world	...	2421	3248	4774	6757	4016	2510	800	1064	1013	887	...
Equals: National Disposable Income	...	31503	47492	63948	91989	102680	93525	83827	83573	81776	62805	...
Less: Final consumption	...	9476	20664	24845	30960	46421	48846	46497	44440	46657	48191	...
Equals: Net Saving	...	22027	26828	39103	61029	56259	44679	37330	39133	35119	14614	...
Less: Surplus of the nation on current transactions	...	12697	8989	18590	38909	34842	26138	21709	27286	27213	7159	...
Equals: Net Capital Formation	...	9330	17839	20513	22120	21417	18541	15621	11847	7906	7455	...

2.11 Gross Fixed Capital Formation by Kind of Activity of Owner, ISIC Divisions, in Current Prices

Million U.A.E Dirhams

	1970	1975	1978	1979	1980	1981	1982	1983	1984	1985	1986	1987
					All Producers							
1 Agriculture, hunting, forestry and fishing	...	161	297	269	560	472	482	430	392	319	200	...
2 Mining and quarrying	...	2211	3593	4334	5463	3949	3839	7724	8201	6955	6420	...
3 Manufacturing	...	2356	5809	10712	9983	11855	12800	7633	6970	5700	4785	...
4 Electricity, gas and water	...	779	3058	2193	2663	1900	2033	3565	3253	2599	2416	...
5 Construction	...	407	698	582	715	1016	1006	1080	736	592	600	...
6 Wholesale and retail trade, restaurants and hotels	...	311	1476	1006	749	611	733	685	732	480	702	...
7 Transport, storage and communication	...	2111	5467	4624	4139	4779	4612	4928	4547	3948	4000	...
8 Finance, insurance, real estate and business services	...	2638	2902	1951	2483	2101	2070	2239	1328	1061	781	...
9 Community, social and personal services	...	7	10	12	15	30	40	45	41	80	100	...
Total Industries	...	10981	23310	25683	26770	26713	27615	28329	26200	21734	20004	...
Producers of Government Services	...	1078	2469	2759	3385	3930	4068	3339	2916	2724	2093	...
Private Non-Profit Institutions Serving Households	...	...	...	...	...	...	...	...	...	...	...	...
Total	...	12059	25779	28442	30155	30643	31683	31668	29116	24458	22097	...

United Arab Emirates

2.12 Gross Fixed Capital Formation by Kind of Activity of Owner, ISIC Divisions, in Constant Prices

Million U.A.E Dirhams

	1970	1975	1978	1979	1980	1981	1982	1983	1984	1985	1986	1987
					At constant prices of:1980							
					All Producers							
1 Agriculture, hunting, forestry and fishing		244	368	301	560	313	...	...	...	...	...	...
2 Mining and quarrying	...	2521	4010	4525	5463						...	
3 Manufacturing		3348	7105	11864	9983						...	
4 Electricity, gas and water		1159	3785	2458	2663							
5 Construction		660	896	666	715							
6 Wholesale and retail trade, restaurants and hotels		410	1700	1063	749							
7 Transport, storage and communication		3491	6884	5173	4139							
8 Finance, insurance, real estate and business services		2934	3217	2032	2483							
9 Community, social and personal services	...	11	13	14	15							
Total Industries	...	14778	27978	28096	26770							
Producers of Government Services	...	1251	2800	2908	3385							
Private Non-Profit Institutions Serving Households	...	...	...	...	...	...	...	...	...	...	...	...
Total	...	16029	30779	31004	30155	29050	29160	30012	29728	25106	21447	...

2.17 Exports and Imports of Goods and Services, Detail

Million U.A.E Dirhams

	1970	1975	1978	1979	1980	1981	1982	1983	1984	1985	1986	1987
					Exports of Goods and Services							
1 Exports of merchandise, f.o.b.	...	29112	39444	56250	84512	82142	69980	59254	58440	56766	37776	...
2 Transport and communication	...	301	482	601	659	900	950	850	900	800	850	...
3 Insurance service charges		...	...	...	...	...	...	...	...	...	...	...
4 Other commodities a	...	46	136	177	219	320	331	390	318	350	370	...
5 Adjustments of merchandise exports to change-of-ownership basis	...	...	...	...	...	...	...	...	...	...	...	...
6 Direct purchases in the domestic market by non-residential households	...	63	138	173	202	300	315	380	350	350	400	...
7 Direct purchases in the domestic market by extraterritorial bodies	...	...	...	...	...	...	...	...	...	...	...	...
Total Exports of Goods and Services	...	29522	40200	57201	85592	83662	71576	60874	60008	58266	39396	...
					Imports of Goods and Services							
1 Imports of merchandise, c.i.f.	...	10912	21473	26642	34116	35594	34795	30970	25530	24140	25100	...
2 Adjustments of merchandise imports to change-of-ownership basis	...	...	...	...	...	...	...	...	...	...	...	...
3 Other transport and communication	...	191	654	849	976	1250	1438	1015	1463	1400	1500	...
4 Other insurance service charges	...	...	...	...	...	...	...	...	...	...	...	...
5 Other commodities a	...	436	1517	2002	2507	3570	3519	4280	4708	4500	4800	...
6 Direct purchases abroad by government	...	58	230	224	275	370	400	400	400	400	450	...
7 Direct purchases abroad by resident households	...	...	...	...	...	...	...	...	...	...	...	...
Total Imports of Goods and Services	...	11597	23874	29717	37874	40784	40152	36665	32101	30440	31850	...
Balance of Goods and Services	...	17925	16326	27485	47718	42878	31424	24209	27907	27826	7546	...
Total Imports and Balance of Goods and Services	...	29522	40200	57201	85592	83662	71576	60874	60008	58266	39396	...

a) Item 'Other commodities' refers to tourism and travel.

United Kingdom

General note. The preparation of national accounts statistics in United Kingdom is undertaken by the Central Statistical Office, London. Official estimates are published annually in 'National Income and Expenditure'. A comprehensive descripton of the sources and methods used in the preparation of the estimates is given in 'National Accounts Statistics, Sources and Methods', H.M.S.O., London, 1968. A new source of reference is 'The National Accounts - A Short Guide', H.M.S.O. London, 1981. Input-output tables for selected years are produced and published by the Central Statistical Office. The following tables have been prepared from successive replies to the United Nations national accounts questionnaire. When the scope and coverage of the estimates differ for conceptual or statistical reasons from the definitions and classifications recommended in SNA, a footnote is indicated to the relevant tables.

Sources and methods:

(a) Gross domestic product. GDP is calculated as average estimate of the three component measures of income, expenditure and output.

(b) Expenditure on the gross domestic product. The expenditure approach is used to estimate all types of expenditure. Government final consumption expenditure is based on accounting data and departmental returns. Estimates for the central government are derived from the various exchequer and departmental accounts. Both the central government and the local government data are extensively rearranged to fit the concepts used in the national accounts. The estimates of private final consumption expenditure are built up commodity by commodity from a variety of independent sources. The sources available are statistics of supplies, sample surveys of consumers' expenditure, and statistics of sales by retail shops and other outlets. The major sources for estimating gross fixed capital formation in private industries are the annual censuses of production and annual inquiries into the distributive and service trades. Base-year estimates of dwellings are, however, based on the number of houses under construction and average prices. Changes are estimated from building output data obtained from contractors. The estimates of capital formation for the public sector are based on accounts. The statistics of exports and imports of goods and services are taken from the balance of payments accounts. Government final consumption expenditures referring to wages and salaries are estimated at constant prices partly by deflating by indexes of changes in rates of pay, but mostly by the use of volume indicators based on numbers employed. Goods and services are mainly deflated by composite base-weighted price indexes. No single-approach is used for all components of private final consumption expenditure. Most food, beverages and tobacco are revalued item by item at average base-year prices. Deflators constructed from components of the General Index of Retail Prices are used for other items. Price deflation is used for gross fixed capital formation. For buildings and other construction out-turn price indexes of successful tenders are used. For exports and imports of goods and services base-year figures on a balance of payments basis are extrapolated by means of volume changes for many goods. For other goods and services, however, mainly price deflation is used.

(c) Cost-structure of the gross domestic product. Information about wages and salaries paid in cash is obtained from the PAYE (Pay-As-You-Earn) system. The estimates of employers' contributions to national insurance and health are taken from the central government accounts. Estimates of operating surplus are provided through tax assessment data for profit incomes. Since they, however, are not available for the latest periods, the quarterly sample inquiry on company trading profits undertaken by the Inland Revenue is also used. Statistics of the trading surplus of public corporations, central government and local authority trading enterprises are taken from their accounts. The method used for estimating capital consumption is mainly the perpetual inventory method. Estimates of total taxes on expenditure and subsidies are available from government accounts.

(d) Gross domestic product by kind of economic activity. The income approach is used to estimate value added of most of the various economic activities. The production approach is applied in connexion with the estimates of agricultural income. The production figures of agriculture are based on estimates prepared by the departments concerned. Agricultural earnings, including payments in kind, are estimated by these departments from regular sample surveys. The estimate of income from farming is built up from very detailed estimates of output and expenditure. Information about crop areas and livestock numbers is collected from farmers by means of questionnaires, and estimates on the quantity harvested are based on the production acreage and the yield per acre. The estimates of mining and quarrying, manufacturing, electricity, gas and water and construction are built up from tax assessment data and production censuses. The censuses of production which are conducted annually, provide information on sales, employment, wages and salaries, purchases, expenditure, etc. For electricity, gas and water annual accounts data are also used, while for construction government accounts are among the sources. The estimates for the distributive trade are calculated from tax assessment data, number in employment and changes in average earnings. In the transport, storage and communication group, income data for the nationalized industries and public corporations are obtained from their annual reports, whereas for the remainder tax assessment data, annual censuses of employment and earnings inquiries are used. Tax assessment data and PAYE (Pay-As-You-Earn) statistics are mainly used as sources for financial institutions. Rents are based on the estimated rent income from various groups of property. Business services are mainly estimated from Inland Revenue data. The figures of central government wages and salaries are obtained from departments, while for local authorities they are derived from official publications. Tax assessment data are utilized to estimate the wage and salary bill for most services. Estimates at constant prices for the agricultural sector are obtained through double deflation. Output is valued at base-year prices, while input is valued at pre-subsidy base-year prices. Value added of all other sectors is obtained through extrapolation by indexes of production, volume or output.

1.1 Expenditure on the Gross Domestic Product, in Current Prices

Million Pounds Sterling

	1970	1975	1978	1979	1980	1981	1982	1983	1984	1985	1986	1987
1 Government final consumption expenditure	9042	23124	33420	38903	49041	55478	60470	65900	69912	74024	79717	85804
2 Private final consumption expenditure	31793	65077	99615	118035	137151	152705	167499	183408	196177	213756	235158	256759
3 Gross capital formation	10118	19681	32864	39087	38989	38536	43636	50080	56586	60852	64369	71394
A Increase in stocks a	382	-1354	1804	2162	-2572	-2768	-1188	1465	1561	569	572	627
B Gross fixed capital formation a	9736	21035	31060	36925	41561	41304	44824	48615	55025	60283	63797	70767
Residential buildings	1870	4682	6325	7649	8674	8138	8920	10447	11733	11928	13556	15197
Non-residential buildings	2946	7020	8182	9637	11802	12471	13386	13306	14637	15206	15967	17342
Other construction and land improvement etc.	274	625	1103	1416	1561	1782	1937	2397	2673	2972	3466	4021
Other	4646	8708	15450	18223	19524	18913	20581	22465	25982	30177	30808	34207
4 Exports of goods and services	11912	27431	48033	55560	63595	68328	73600	81000	92942	103323	99018	108108
5 Less: Imports of goods and services	11440	29199	45858	54828	58078	60849	68376	78086	93279	99377	101739	112211
Statistical discrepancy	167	-860	-624	280	-538	-927	346	-270	775	527	1103	3382
Equals: Gross Domestic Product	51592	105254	167450	197037	230160	253271	277175	302032	323113	353105	377626	413236

a) Beginning 1973, 'Gross fixed capital formation' excludes the value of completed but unsold dwellings which is included in 'Increase in stocks'.

1.2 Expenditure on the Gross Domestic Product, in Constant Prices

Million Pounds Sterling

	1970	1975	1978	1979	1980	1981	1982	1983	1984	1985	1986	1987
	At constant prices of:1980											
1 Government final consumption expenditure	38538	46398	47259	48278	49041	49193	49577	50581	51059	51074	52031	52489
2 Private final consumption expenditure	110685	124771	131617	137185	137151	137189	138371	144547	147087	152263	160473	168705
3 Gross capital formation	41532	38935	44931	46464	38994	35139	38629	42607	46006	47339	47770	50375
A Increase in stocks a	1412	-2600	2204	2542	-2567	-2440	-986	999	820	435	437	426
B Gross fixed capital formation ab	40120	41535	42727	43922	41561	37579	39615	41608	45186	46904	47333	49949

United Kingdom

1.2 Expenditure on the Gross Domestic Product, in Constant Prices
(Continued)

Million Pounds Sterling

	1970	1975	1978	1979	1980	1981	1982	1983	1984	1985	1986	1987
	\multicolumn{12}{c}{At constant prices of:1980}
Residential buildings	8613	9139	9048	9363	8674	7180	7637	8582	8809	8358	8989	9394
Non-residential buildings	14417	14134	12759	12437	11802	11298	12459	12516	13672	13714	13798	14256
Other construction and land improvement etc.	1403	1552	1802	1657	1561	1651	1814	1995	2140	2138	2206	2363
Other	15803	16756	19118	20465	19524	17450	17705	18515	20618	22733	22340	23936
4 Exports of goods and services	41301	51640	61304	63602	63595	62953	63614	65102	69430	73428	76199	80464
5 Less: Imports of goods and services	41125	49659	54958	60231	58078	56373	59282	63038	69226	70959	75579	81177
Statistical discrepancy c	-318	-1896	-840	327	-543	-846	290	-223	358	106	565	1931
Equals: Gross Domestic Product	190613	210189	229313	235625	230160	227255	231199	239576	244714	253251	261459	272787

a) Beginning 1973, 'Gross fixed capital formation' excludes the value of completed but unsold dwellings which is included in 'Increase in stocks'.
b) For years prior to 1983, components do not add up to total due to the method used to rebase to 1985 prices.
c) Price indexes based on 1963 were used to deflate the period 1960-1962, indexes based on 1970 were used to deflate the period 1963-1972, and indexes based on 1975 were used for the period 1973-1977. For subsequent years, price indices based on 1980 have been used for deflation purposes. The series were then linked at the component and total levels producing a residual difference shown as a statistical discrepancy.

1.3 Cost Components of the Gross Domestic Product

Million Pounds Sterling

	1970	1975	1978	1979	1980	1981	1982	1983	1984	1985	1986	1987
1 Indirect taxes, net	7231	9875	18389	24426	30030	35256	39634	42007	43758	48040	55028	60578
A Indirect taxes	8115	13660	22289	29146	35803	41809	45637	48411	51437	55340	61289	66677
B Less: Subsidies	884	3785	3900	4720	5773	6553	6003	6404	7679	7300	6261	6099
2 Consumption of fixed capital	4618	11621	19378	22827	27952	31641	33653	36150	38686	41899	45165	48238
3 Compensation of employees paid by resident producers to:	30623	68646	99069	116089	137854	149790	158865	169848	180398	194903	209919	226764
A Resident households	30544	68460	98783	115802	137570	149512	158545	169507	180025	194492	209462	226253
B Rest of the world	79	186	286	287	284	278	320	341	373	411	457	511
4 Operating surplus	9287	14253	29695	33002	33786	36491	45751	55197	59960	68789	69122	79938
A Corporate and quasi-corporate enterprises	3830	2870	12238	13108	11424	11252	16926	24159	26269	33279	31089	40059
B Private unincorporated enterprises	4826	10375	15919	18156	20446	23209	26899	29623	32541	33839	36569	38779
C General government	630	1008	1538	1738	1916	2030	1926	1415	1150	1671	1464	1100
Statistical discrepancy	-167	860	919	692	538	93	-728	-1168	311	-527	-1608	-2282
Equals: Gross Domestic Product	51592	105255	167450	197036	230160	253271	277175	302034	323113	353104	377626	413236

1.4 General Government Current Receipts and Disbursements

Million Pounds Sterling

	1970	1975	1978	1979	1980	1981	1982	1983	1984	1985	1986	1987
	\multicolumn{12}{c}{Receipts}
1 Operating surplus	605	1008	1538	1738	1916	2030	1926	1415	1150	1671	1464	1100
2 Property and entrepreneurial income	903	2118	3156	3898	5122	5833	6884	6969	7588	8658	6852	7029
3 Taxes, fees and contributions	18757	38226	56209	67226	82346	95698	106238	115080	123092	134247	143267	155034
A Indirect taxes	8140	13660	22289	29146	35803	41809	45637	48411	51437	55340	61289	66677
B Direct taxes	7915	17638	23648	26399	32411	37768	42286	45627	49083	54442	55636	59544
C Social security contributions	2655	6848	10107	11531	13944	15923	18104	20793	22327	24207	26048	28464
D Compulsory fees, fines and penalties	38	80	165	150	188	198	211	249	245	258	294	349
4 Other current transfers	488	1397	2282	2587	3214	3879	4301	4698	5101	5401	5869	6265
Total Current Receipts of General Government	20753	42749	63186	75449	92598	107440	119349	128162	136931	149977	157452	169428
	\multicolumn{12}{c}{Disbursements}
1 Government final consumption expenditure	9015	23124	33420	38903	49041	55478	60470	65900	69912	74024	79717	85804
A Compensation of employees	5555	15188	20878	23800	30092	34276	36530	39839	42056	44615	47632	52436
B Consumption of fixed capital	301	777	1182	1403	1739	1935	1999	2056	2162	2350	2584	2732
C Purchases of goods and services, net	2598	6544	10177	12049	15199	16733	19119	21698	23468	24881	27116	28112
D Less: Own account fixed capital formation	150	189	303	311	452	430	493	562	562	568	687	829
E Indirect taxes paid, net	711	804	1486	1962	2463	2964	3315	2869	2788	2746	3074	3353
2 Property income	2025	4127	7093	8671	10873	12702	13973	14189	15756	17474	17191	17667
A Interest	2025	4127	7093	8671	10873	12702	13973	14189	15756	17474	17191	17667
B Net land rent and royalties	...	...	...	...	...	...	...	...	...	...	...	...
3 Subsidies	884	3785	3900	4720	5773	6553	6003	6404	7679	7300	6261	6099

United Kingdom

1.4 General Government Current Receipts and Disbursements
(Continued)

Million Pounds Sterling

	1970	1975	1978	1979	1980	1981	1982	1983	1984	1985	1986	1987
4 Other current transfers	4911	11534	21326	24926	29727	35994	41964	45730	49402	54698	57906	60937
A Social security benefits	2731	6519	10738	12171	14804	17859	19348	20820	21944	23401	25724	26215
B Social assistance grants	1289	3030	6209	7685	9313	11847	15494	16981	18900	20968	22312	23285
C Other	891	1985	4379	5070	5610	6288	7122	7929	8558	10329	9870	11437
Statistical discrepancy	84	479	498	601	795	740	720	755	842	808	940	1108
5 Net saving	3834	-311	-3071	-2385	-3623	-4043	-3771	-4801	-6661	-4343	-4582	-2206
Total Current Disbursements and Net Saving of General Government	20753	42749	63186	75449	92598	107440	119349	128162	136931	149977	157452	169428

1.5 Current Income and Outlay of Corporate and Quasi-Corporate Enterprises, Summary

Million Pounds Sterling

	1970	1975	1978	1979	1980	1981	1982	1983	1984	1985	1986	1987
Receipts												
1 Operating surplus	3830	2870	12238	13108	11424	11252	16926	24159	26269	33279	31089	40059
2 Property and entrepreneurial income received	5719	15036	21613	33538	43623	48480	54807	55088	63474	76350	78097	83595
3 Current transfers	...	...	...	...	...	...	...	...	...	...	...	...
Total Current Receipts	9549	17906	33851	46646	55047	59732	71733	79247	89743	109629	109186	123654
Disbursements												
1 Property and entrepreneurial income	7133	16238	21831	33776	45669	48927	56077	56270	63933	77114	77212	83912
2 Direct taxes and other current payments to general government	1736	2487	4191	5194	6838	8835	10826	12413	14468	16987	15086	16238
3 Other current transfers	36	42	45	51	52	62	69	86	105	119	151	185
4 Net saving	644	-861	7784	7625	2488	1908	4761	10478	11237	15409	16737	23319
Total Current Disbursements and Net Saving	9549	17906	33851	46646	55047	59732	71733	79247	89743	109629	109186	123654

1.6 Current Income and Outlay of Households and Non-Profit Institutions

Million Pounds Sterling

	1970	1975	1978	1979	1980	1981	1982	1983	1984	1985	1986	1987
Receipts												
1 Compensation of employees	30553	68494	98843	115866	137639	149584	158621	169580	180096	194573	209542	226343
A From resident producers	30544	68460	98783	115802	137570	149512	158545	169507	180025	194492	209462	226253
B From rest of the world	9	34	60	64	69	72	76	73	71	81	80	90
2 Operating surplus of private unincorporated enterprises	4826	10375	15919	18157	20446	23209	26899	29623	32542	33839	36569	38779
3 Property and entrepreneurial income	4028	6602	9348	13706	18007	19685	22599	23571	26952	32761	34373	37592
4 Current transfers	4596	10713	18690	21818	26511	32421	37901	41377	44722	48565	52548	54229
A Social security benefits	2751	6469	10641	12072	14689	17674	19151	20569	21639	23050	25345	25808
B Social assistance grants	1243	3020	6184	7658	9271	11887	15507	17059	18848	20939	22077	22961
C Other	602	1224	1865	2088	2551	2860	3243	3749	4235	4576	5126	5460
Total Current Receipts	44003	96184	142800	169547	202603	224899	246020	264151	284312	309738	333032	356943
Disbursements												
1 Private final consumption expenditure	31793	65078	99616	118036	137151	152705	167499	183408	196177	213756	235158	256759
2 Property income	1061	3100	4597	6721	9798	11591	13364	13349	16431	21340	22858	25328
3 Direct taxes and other current transfers n.e.c. to general government	8897	22079	29723	32881	39700	45047	49766	54243	57172	61904	66879	72104
A Social security contributions	2655	6848	10101	11526	13939	15916	18095	20780	22312	24191	26033	28449
B Direct taxes	6201	15151	19457	21205	25573	28933	31460	33214	34615	37455	40552	43306
C Fees, fines and penalties	41	80	165	150	188	198	211	249	245	258	294	349
4 Other current transfers	243	531	901	1044	1139	1057	1200	1179	1261	1436	1615	1782
5 Net saving	2009	5396	7963	10865	14815	14499	14191	11972	13271	11302	6522	970
Total Current Disbursements and Net Saving	44003	96184	142800	169547	202603	224899	246020	264151	284312	309738	333032	356943

United Kingdom

1.7 External Transactions on Current Account, Summary

Million Pounds Sterling

	1970	1975	1978	1979	1980	1981	1982	1983	1984	1985	1986	1987
Payments to the Rest of the World												
1 Imports of goods and services	11440	29199	45858	54828	58078	60849	68376	78086	93279	99377	101739	112211
A Imports of merchandise c.i.f.	8962	23927	38569	46298	48320	49983	55975	64784	78283	83982	84860	93152
B Other	2478	5272	7289	8530	9758	10866	12401	13302	14996	15395	16879	19059
2 Factor income to the rest of the world	821	5592	9631	14210	21940	35014	42133	38751	45294	46197	41645	40205
A Compensation of employees	79	186	286	287	284	278	320	341	373	411	457	511
B Property and entrepreneurial income	742	5406	9345	13923	21656	34736	41813	38410	44921	45786	41188	39694
By general government	319	491	650	681	895	940	1092	1189	1327	1478	1669	1977
By corporate and quasi-corporate enterprises	423	4915	8695	13242	20761	33796	40721	37221	43594	44308	39519	37717
By other	...	...	...	...	...	...	...	...	...	...	...	...
3 Current transfers to the rest of the world	412	1234	3025	3624	3905	4405	5216	5433	5856	6735	6086	7494
A Indirect taxes to supranational organizations	-	349	986	1987	1897	2241	2936	3063	3296	3894	2890	4194
B Other current transfers	412	885	2039	1637	2008	2164	2280	2370	2560	2841	3196	3300
4 Surplus of the nation on current transactions	650	-2116	735	259	3718	6488	4123	2820	-518	2362	-3238	-6737
Payments to the Rest of the World and Surplus of the Nation on Current Transactions	13323	33909	59249	72921	87641	106756	119848	125090	143911	154671	146232	153173
Receipts From The Rest of the World												
1 Exports of goods and services	11912	27431	48033	55560	63595	68328	73600	81000	92942	103323	99018	108108
A Exports of merchandise f.o.b.	8128	19183	34981	40470	47147	50668	55330	60698	70263	77988	72678	79422
B Other	3784	8248	13052	15090	16448	17660	18270	20302	22679	25335	26340	28686
2 Factor income from rest of the world	1181	5719	9982	15947	22125	35570	42773	40318	46885	47692	43308	41074
A Compensation of employees	9	34	60	64	69	72	76	73	71	81	80	90
B Property and entrepreneurial income	1172	5685	9922	15883	22056	35498	42697	40245	46814	47611	43228	40984
By general government	54	266	692	816	946	971	979	764	817	735	764	932
By corporate and quasi-corporate enterprises	1118	5419	9230	15067	21110	34527	41718	39481	45997	46876	42464	40052
By other												
3 Current transfers from rest of the world	230	759	1234	1414	1921	2858	3475	3772	4084	3656	3906	3991
A Subsidies from supranational organisations	-	342	344	380	573	742	855	1158	1442	1284	1470	1483
B Other current transfers	230	417	890	1034	1348	2116	2620	2614	2642	2372	2436	2508
Receipts from the Rest of the World on Current Transactions	13323	33909	59249	72921	87641	106756	119848	125090	143911	154671	146232	153173

1.8 Capital Transactions of The Nation, Summary

Million Pounds Sterling

	1970	1975	1978	1979	1980	1981	1982	1983	1984	1985	1986	1987
Finance of Gross Capital Formation												
Gross saving	11101	15845	32054	38932	41632	44005	48834	53799	56533	64267	63842	70321
1 Consumption of fixed capital	4618	11621	19378	22827	27952	31641	33653	36150	38686	41899	45165	48238
A General government	559	1416	2091	2487	3098	3494	3546	3642	3835	4079	4360	4617
B Corporate and quasi-corporate enterprises	3084	7671	13135	15342	18785	21257	22739	24358	25866	27944	29871	31428
Public	1129	2752	4327	4974	5998	6672	6940	7210	7391	6171	6337	5511
Private	1955	4919	8808	10368	12787	14585	15799	17148	18475	21773	23534	25917
C Other	975	2534	4152	4998	6069	6890	7368	8150	8985	9876	10934	12193
2 Net saving	6483	4224	12676	16105	13680	12364	15181	17649	17847	22368	18677	22083
A General government	3830	-311	-3071	-2385	-3623	-4043	-3771	-4801	-6661	-4343	-4582	-2206
B Corporate and quasi-corporate enterprises	644	-861	7784	7625	2488	1908	4761	10478	11237	15409	16737	23319
Public	-413	-1511	-939	-1938	-2154	-1524	-803	207	-1409	-1044	-453	-630
Private	1057	650	8723	9563	4642	3432	5564	10271	12646	16453	17190	23949
C Other	2009	5396	7963	10865	14815	14499	14191	11972	13271	11302	6522	970
Less: Surplus of the nation on current transactions	650	-2116	735	259	3718	6488	4123	2820	-518	2362	-3238	-6737

United Kingdom

1.8 Capital Transactions of The Nation, Summary
(Continued)

Million Pounds Sterling

	1970	1975	1978	1979	1980	1981	1982	1983	1984	1985	1986	1987
Statistical discrepancy	-334	1720	1543	412	1076	1020	-1074	-898	-464	-1054	-2711	-5664
Finance of Gross Capital Formation	10118	19681	32864	39087	38989	38536	43636	50080	56586	60852	64369	71394
Gross Capital Formation												
Increase in stocks	382	-1354	1804	2162	-2572	-2768	-1188	1465	1561	569	572	627
Gross fixed capital formation	9736	21035	31060	36925	41561	41304	44824	48615	55025	60283	63797	70767
1 General government	2443	4995	4653	5145	5499	4578	4315	5707	6493	6584	7007	6911
2 Corporate and quasi-corporate enterprises	5690	12224	20198	23622	26778	27010	28612	29112	33894	38247	38900	43383
A Public	1676	3920	4944	5641	6653	6780	7114	7884	7305	5656	5545	4605
B Private	4014	8304	15254	17981	20125	20230	21498	21228	26589	32591	33355	38778
3 Other	1603	3816	6209	8158	9284	9716	11897	13796	14638	15452	17890	20473
Gross Capital Formation	10118	19681	32864	39087	38989	38536	43636	50080	56586	60852	64369	71394

1.9 Gross Domestic Product by Institutional Sectors of Origin

Million Pounds Sterling

	1970	1975	1978	1979	1980	1981	1982	1983	1984	1985	1986	1987
Domestic Factor Incomes Originating												
1 General government	6555	16827	23196	26539	33102	37550	39920	42868	45021	48174	51117	55497
2 Corporate and quasi-corporate enterprises	25750	50422	81748	95161	107172	113408	124620	138271	146892	164160	172047	191024
A Non-financial	25168	49364	80196	92871	105106	112663	123584	134838	144330	159597	165830	182076
Public	3360	7790	12134	13092	15598	17684	19870	20863	18460	16819	18852	15660
Private	21808	41574	68062	79779	89508	94979	103714	113975	125870	142778	146978	166416
B Financial	582	1058	1552	2290	2066	745	1036	3433	2562	4563	6217	8948
Public	-4	19	13	-3	-22	8	1	-4	12	3	8	-12
Private	586	1039	1539	2293	2088	737	1035	3437	2550	4560	6209	8960
3 Households and private unincorporated enterprises	7604	15650	23820	27391	31366	35323	40076	43906	48445	51358	55877	60181
A Owner-occupied housing	1296	3456	5403	6522	7830	9114	10160	11181	11917	12783	13810	14632
B Subsistence production	...	...	...	...	...	...	...	...	...	...	...	...
C Other	6308	12194	18417	20869	23536	26209	29916	32725	36528	38575	42067	45549
4 Non-profit institutions serving households	...	...	...	...	...	...	...	...	...	...	...	...
Subtotal: Domestic Factor Incomes	39909	82899	128764	149091	171640	186281	204616	225045	240358	263692	279041	306702
Indirect taxes, net	7231	9875	18389	24426	30030	35256	39634	42007	43758	48040	55028	60578
A Indirect taxes	8115	13660	22289	29146	35803	41809	45637	48411	51437	55340	61289	66677
B Less: Subsidies	884	3785	3900	4720	5773	6553	6003	6404	7679	7300	6261	6099
Consumption of fixed capital	4618	11621	19378	22827	27952	31641	33653	36150	38686	41899	45165	48238
Statistical discrepancy	-167	860	919	692	538	93	-728	-1168	311	-527	-1608	-2282
Gross Domestic Product	51591	105255	167450	197036	230160	253271	277175	302034	323113	353104	377626	413236

1.10 Gross Domestic Product by Kind of Activity, in Current Prices

Million Pounds Sterling

	1970	1975	1978	1979	1980	1981	1982	1983	1984	1985	1986	1987
1 Agriculture, hunting, forestry and fishing	1242	2466	3555	3867	4246	4775	5412	5274	6229	5565	5947	5901
2 Mining and quarrying	616	1861	5291	8510	12463	16037	18335	20756	22250	22886	12807	13447
3 Manufacturing [a]	14832	27435	43920	49435	53483	54764	59094	62149	66670	73685	79398	86225
4 Electricity, gas and water [b]	1359	2764	4500	4742	6376	7216	7785	8932	7595	8553	9592	10064
5 Construction	2897	6260	9136	10563	12053	12837	14116	15643	16896	18101	19380	21524
6 Wholesale and retail trade, restaurants and hotels [a]	6003	12270	19993	22841	25654	27247	30223	33174	36300	40907	45673	48963
7 Transport, storage and communication	3683	7761	11760	13199	14316	15892	17254	18283	19803	21375	23369	25915
8 Finance, insurance, real estate and business services	6636	15592	25659	31326	36923	41857	47112	52000	56922	65438	74760	84083
9 Community, social and personal services [a]	2207	4403	7084	8120	9271	10347	11011	12378	13614	14961	17215	18515
Total, Industries	39475	80812	130898	152603	174785	190972	210342	228589	246279	271471	288141	314637
Producers of Government Services	5647	15640	21416	24444	31144	35262	37420	40911	43218	45727	49477	54244
Other Producers	709	1469	2080	2446	2961	3420	3827	4174	4629	5216	5834	6604

United Kingdom

1.10 Gross Domestic Product by Kind of Activity, in Current Prices
(Continued)

Million Pounds Sterling

	1970	1975	1978	1979	1980	1981	1982	1983	1984	1985	1986	1987
Subtotal c	45831	97921	154394	179493	208890	229654	251589	273674	294126	322414	343452	375485
Less: Imputed bank service charge	1299	3402	6252	7574	9298	11732	13320	12481	15082	16822	19246	20545
Plus: Import duties d	7231	6360	13150	15631	18133	22200	25326	25831	25485	27316	32032	35386
Plus: Value added tax	-	3515	5239	8795	11897	13056	14308	16176	18273	20724	22996	25192
Plus: Other adjustments e	-167	860	919	692	538	93	-728	-1168	311	-527	-1608	-2282
Equals: Gross Domestic Product	51592	105254	167450	197037	230160	253271	277175	302032	323113	353105	377626	413236
Memorandum Item: Mineral fuels and power f	1987	4649	10091	13855	19368	23519	26049	30112	30091	32436	23575	24184

a) Repairs to consumer durables other than clothing are included in item 'Wholesale and retail trade, restaurants and hotels'.
b) Item 'Electricity, gas and water' includes nuclear fuel production.
c) Gross domestic product in factor values.
d) Item 'Import duties' refers to indirect taxes net of subsidies less value added tax.
e) Item 'Other adjustments' refers to statistical discrepancy.
f) Item 'Mineral fuels and Power' includes water supply.

1.12 Relations Among National Accounting Aggregates

Million Pounds Sterling

	1970	1975	1978	1979	1980	1981	1982	1983	1984	1985	1986	1987
Gross Domestic Product	51592	105254	167450	197037	230160	253271	277175	302032	323113	353105	377626	413236
Plus: Net factor income from the rest of the world	360	127	351	1737	185	556	640	1567	1591	1495	1663	869
Factor income from the rest of the world	1181	5719	9982	15947	22125	35570	42773	40318	46885	47692	43308	41074
Less: Factor income to the rest of the world	821	5592	9631	14210	21940	35014	42133	38751	45294	46197	41645	40205
Equals: Gross National Product	51952	105381	167801	198774	230345	253827	277815	303599	324704	354600	379289	414105
Less: Consumption of fixed capital	4618	11621	19378	22827	27952	31641	33653	36150	38686	41899	45165	48238
Equals: National Income	47334	93760	148423	175947	202393	222186	244162	267449	286018	312701	334124	365867
Plus: Net current transfers from the rest of the world	-182	-475	-1791	-2210	-1984	-1547	-1741	-1661	-1772	-3079	-2180	-3504
Current transfers from the rest of the world	230	773	1344	1482	1952	2981	3601	3827	4134	3673	3976	4189
Less: Current transfers to the rest of the world	412	1248	3135	3692	3936	4528	5342	5488	5906	6752	6156	7693
Equals: National Disposable Income	47152	93285	146632	173737	200409	220639	242421	265788	284246	309622	331944	362364
Less: Final consumption	41002	87341	132411	157218	185654	207256	228315	249038	266864	288307	315978	345945
Statistical discrepancy	334	-1720	-1543	-412	-1076	-1020	1074	898	464	1054	2711	5664
Equals: Net Saving	6484	4224	12678	16107	13679	12363	15180	17648	17846	22369	18677	22082
Less: Surplus of the nation on current transactions	650	-2116	735	259	3718	6488	4123	2820	-518	2362	-3238	-6737
Statistical discrepancy	-334	1720	1543	412	1076	1020	-1074	-898	-464	-1054	-2711	-5664
Equals: Net Capital Formation	5500	8060	13486	16260	11037	6895	9983	13930	17900	18953	19204	23156

2.1 Government Final Consumption Expenditure by Function, in Current Prices

Million Pounds Sterling

		1970	1975	1978	1979	1980	1981	1982	1983	1984	1985	1986	1987
1	General public services	...	...	1949	2337	2840	3055	3338	3455	3490	3640	4185	4448
2	Defence	...	...	7507	8892	11370	12532	14283	15596	16882	17916	18655	18671
3	Public order and safety	...	...	2217	2680	3408	4050	4517	4957	5513	5766	6301	7147
4	Education	...	...	7057	8011	9852	11120	12025	12817	13418	13692	15410	16911
5	Health	...	...	7343	8488	10967	12631	13198	14994	15741	16763	18240	20113
6	Social security and welfare	...	...	2107	2482	3142	3658	4115	4436	4717	5364	5181	5906
7	Housing and community amenities	...	...	1057	1274	1589	1734	1923	2113	2215	2463	2801	3089
8	Recreational, cultural and religious affairs	...	...	710	849	1058	1159	1265	1449	1512	1519	1653	1899
9	Economic services	...	...	2292	2487	3074	3604	3807	4027	4262	4551	4709	4888
	A Fuel and energy	...	...	99	110	163	163	153	206	243	265	303	281
	B Agriculture, forestry, fishing and hunting	...	...	306	327	430	456	479	495	442	434	468	520
	C Mining, manufacturing and construction, except fuel and energy	...	...	224	188	193	374	385	365	405	463	427	448
	D Transportation and communication	...	...	938	1094	1335	1500	1684	1742	1734	1851	1901	2137
	E Other economic affairs	...	...	725	768	953	1111	1106	1219	1438	1538	1610	1502
10	Other functions	...	...	1184	1408	1746	1935	1999	2056	2162	2350	2582	2732
	Total Government Final Consumption Expenditure	...	...	33423	38908	49046	55478	60470	65900	69912	74024	79717	85804

United Kingdom

2.3 Total Government Outlays by Function and Type

Million Pounds Sterling

		Final Consumption Expenditures Total	Compensation of Employees	Other	Subsidies	Other Current Transfers & Property Income	Total Current Disbursements	Gross Capital Formation	Other Capital Outlays	Total Outlays
					1981					
1	General public services	3055	...	...	-	1141	4196	346	33	4575
2	Defence	12532	...	...	-	59	12591	46	10	12647
3	Public order and safety	4050	...	...	-	1351	5401	195	-	5596
4	Education	11120	...	...	-	3026	14146	558	201	14905
5	Health	12631	...	...	-	43	12674	700	-	13374
6	Social security and welfare	3658	...	...	-	33769	37427	96	1	37524
7	Housing and community amenities	1734	...	...	2163	1107	5004	952	759	6715
8	Recreation, culture and religion	1159	...	...	-	212	1371	241	13	1625
9	Economic services	3604	...	...	4390	3751	11745	1383	4864	17992
	A Fuel and energy	163	...	...	550	38	751	-5	10	756
	B Agriculture, forestry, fishing and hunting	456	...	...	1020	44	1520	134	218	1872
	C Mining (except fuels), manufacturing and construction	374	...	...	268	117	759	52	4406	5217
	D Transportation and communication	1500	...	...	1348	454	3302	1071	162	4535
	E Other economic affairs	1111	...	...	1204	3098	5413	131	68	5612
10	Other functions	1935	...	...	-	24814	26749	-32	-	26717
	Total	55478	...	...	6553	69273	131304	4485	5881	141670
					1982					
1	General public services	3338	...	...	-	1105	4443	503	37	4983
2	Defence	14283	...	...	-	67	14350	72	35	14457
3	Public order and safety	4517	...	...	-	1552	6069	245	-	6314
4	Education	12025	...	...	-	3196	15221	505	187	15913
5	Health	13198	...	...	-	61	13259	817	4	14080
6	Social security and welfare	4115	...	...	-	38444	42559	102	-	42661
7	Housing and community amenities	1923	...	...	1553	1408	4884	-24	1140	6000
8	Recreation, culture and religion	1265	...	...	-	230	1495	265	4	1764
9	Economic services	3807	...	...	4450	3986	12243	1935	2475	16653
	A Fuel and energy	153	...	...	566	72	791	-33	11	769
	B Agriculture, forestry, fishing and hunting	479	...	...	1038	50	1567	370	245	2182
	C Mining (except fuels), manufacturing and construction	385	...	...	313	147	845	32	1792	2669
	D Transportation and communication	1684	...	...	1590	551	3825	1371	352	5548
	E Other economic affairs	1106	...	...	943	3166	5215	195	75	5485
10	Other functions	1999	...	...	-	26587	28586	50	-	28636
	Total	60470	...	...	6003	76636	143109	4470	3882	151461
					1983					
1	General public services	3455	...	...	-	1221	4676	422	43	5141
2	Defence	15596	...	...	-	56	15652	171	23	15846
3	Public order and safety	4957	...	...	-	1610	6567	256	-	6823
4	Education	12817	...	...	-	3435	16252	555	179	16986
5	Health	14994	...	...	-	76	15070	854	4	15928
6	Social security and welfare	4436	...	...	-	44099	48535	100	-	48635
7	Housing and community amenities	2113	...	...	1393	1411	4917	1128	1933	7978
8	Recreation, culture and religion	1449	...	...	-	281	1730	323	3	2056
9	Economic services	4027	...	...	5011	3759	12797	2252	1405	16454
	A Fuel and energy	206	...	...	945	152	1303	38	-	1341
	B Agriculture, forestry, fishing and hunting	495	...	...	1318	54	1867	447	270	2584
	C Mining (except fuels), manufacturing and construction	365	...	...	313	101	779	81	787	1647
	D Transportation and communication	1742	...	...	1614	567	3923	1483	304	5710
	E Other economic affairs	1219	...	...	821	2885	4925	203	44	5172
10	Other functions	2056	...	...	-	27910	29966	-108	-	29858
	Total	65900	...	...	6404	83858	156162	5953	3590	165705

United Kingdom

2.3 Total Government Outlays by Function and Type
(Continued)

Million Pounds Sterling

		Final Consumption Expenditures Total	Compensation of Employees	Other	Subsidies	Other Current Transfers & Property Income	Total Current Disbursements	Gross Capital Formation	Other Capital Outlays	Total Outlays
					1984					
1	General public services	3490	...	...	-	1334	4824	497	49	5370
2	Defence	16882	...	...	-	72	16954	203	17	17174
3	Public order and safety	5513	...	...	-	1862	7375	292	-	7667
4	Education	13418	...	...	-	3600	17018	606	187	17811
5	Health	15741	...	...	-	91	15832	945	4	16781
6	Social security and welfare	4717	...	...	-	47649	52366	123	1	52490
7	Housing and community amenities	2215	...	...	1402	1649	5266	1516	2271	9053
8	Recreation, culture and religion	1512	...	...	-	294	1806	400	1	2207
9	Economic services	4262	...	...	6277	3811	14350	1819	1308	17477
	A Fuel and energy	243	...	...	1971	206	2420	34	5	2459
	B Agriculture, forestry, fishing and hunting	442	...	...	1543	49	2034	-3	277	2308
	C Mining (except fuels), manufacturing and construction	405	...	...	292	101	798	50	670	1518
	D Transportation and communication	1734	...	...	1569	541	3844	1570	299	5713
	E Other economic affairs	1438	...	...	902	2914	5254	168	57	5479
10	Other functions	2162	...	...	-	30585	32747	372	-	33119
	Total	69912	...	...	7679	90947	168538	6773	3838	179149
					1985					
1	General public services	3640	...	...	-	1329	4969	602	54	5625
2	Defence	17916	...	...	-	61	17977	268	21	18266
3	Public order and safety	5766	...	...	-	1995	7761	327	-	8088
4	Education	13692	...	...	-	3678	17370	599	208	18177
5	Health	16763	...	...	-	117	16880	1005	4	17889
6	Social security and welfare	5364	...	...	-	51645	57009	152	-	57161
7	Housing and community amenities	2463	...	...	1456	1796	5715	1272	1683	8670
8	Recreation, culture and religion	1519	...	...	-	368	1887	383	3	2273
9	Economic services	4551	...	...	5844	3673	14068	2600	1346	18014
	A Fuel and energy	265	...	...	1540	421	2226	49	-	2275
	B Agriculture, forestry, fishing and hunting	434	...	...	1409	49	1892	693	220	2805
	C Mining (except fuels), manufacturing and construction	463	...	...	249	86	798	77	797	1672
	D Transportation and communication	1851	...	...	1520	209	3580	1678	285	5543
	E Other economic affairs	1538	...	...	1126	2908	5572	103	44	5719
10	Other functions	2350	...	...	-	33672	36022	-174	-	35848
	Total	74024	...	...	7300	98334	179658	7034	3319	190011
					1986					
1	General public services	4185	...	...	-	1443	5628	481	67	6176
2	Defence	18655	...	...	-	95	18750	359	12	19121
3	Public order and safety	6301	...	...	-	2293	8594	304	-	8898
4	Education	15410	...	...	-	3748	19158	661	235	20054
5	Health	18240	...	...	-	125	18365	1078	5	19448
6	Social security and welfare	5181	...	...	-	55435	60616	179	-	60795
7	Housing and community amenities	2801	...	...	1415	2066	6282	1569	3070	10921
8	Recreation, culture and religion	1653	...	...	-	319	1972	360	1	2333
9	Economic services	4709	...	...	4846	3223	12778	2120	1353	16251
	A Fuel and energy	303	...	...	713	593	1609	4	-	1613
	B Agriculture, forestry, fishing and hunting	468	...	...	1678	21	2167	155	170	2492
	C Mining (except fuels), manufacturing and construction	427	...	...	231	94	752	50	845	1647
	D Transportation and communication	1901	...	...	1338	85	3324	1801	303	5428
	E Other economic affairs	1610	...	...	886	2430	4926	110	35	5071
10	Other functions	2582	...	...	-	34091	36673	-341	-	36332
	Total	79717	...	...	6261	102838	188816	6770	4743	200329

United Kingdom

2.3 Total Government Outlays by Function and Type
(Continued)

Million Pounds Sterling

		Final Consumption Expenditures Total	Compensation of Employees	Other	Subsidies	Other Current Transfers & Property Income	Total Current Disbursements	Gross Capital Formation	Other Capital Outlays	Total Outlays
						1987				
1	General public services	4448	...	...	-	1380	5828	495	70	6393
2	Defence	18671	...	...	-	96	18767	352	-	19119
3	Public order and safety	7147	...	...	-	2390	9537	391	-	9928
4	Education	16911	...	...	-	4105	21016	731	245	21992
5	Health	20113	...	...	-	150	20263	998	4	21265
6	Social security and welfare	5906	...	...	-	57343	63249	208	-1	63456
7	Housing and community amenities	3089	...	...	1419	2449	6957	1354	1436	9747
8	Recreation, culture and religion	1899	...	...	-	389	2288	340	22	2650
9	Economic services	4888	...	...	4680	2470	12038	1742	1328	15114
	A Fuel and energy	281	...	...	660	519	1460	-	-	1460
	B Agriculture, forestry, fishing and hunting	520	...	...	2101	14	2635	-248	169	2556
	C Mining (except fuels), manufacturing and construction	448	...	...	298	35	781	30	689	1500
	D Transportation and communication	2137	...	...	995	92	3224	1871	379	5480
	E Other economic affairs	1502	...	...	626	1810	3938	89	91	4118
10	Other functions	2732	...	...	-	37597	40329	-312	-	40011
	Total	85804	...	...	6099	108369	200272	6299	3104	209675

2.5 Private Final Consumption Expenditure by Type and Purpose, in Current Prices

Million Pounds Sterling

	1970	1975	1978	1979	1980	1981	1982	1983	1984	1985	1986	1987
Final Consumption Expenditure of Resident Households												
1 Food, beverages and tobacco	8236	15430	23142	26227	29455	31683	33666	36094	38006	40136	42979	44719
A Food	6194	11531	17324	19606	22020	23364	24793	26379	27591	28871	30960	32082
B Non-alcoholic beverages	155	430	603	758	856	843	856	1006	1051	1193	1379	1561
C Alcoholic beverages	425	1144	1913	2264	2481	2788	3018	3435	3733	4117	4290	4571
D Tobacco	1462	2325	3302	3599	4098	4688	4999	5278	5629	5955	6350	6505
2 Clothing and footwear	2753	5206	7830	9170	9875	10157	10925	12108	13252	14812	16337	17788
3 Gross rent, fuel and power	5368	11622	17772	20866	25180	30307	34619	37149	39157	42794	46750	49944
A Fuel and power	1480	2887	4613	5292	6355	7727	8696	9399	9575	10657	11148	11082
B Other	3888	8735	13159	15574	18825	22580	25922	27550	29372	32129	34951	38862
4 Furniture, furnishings and household equipment and operation	2450	5006	7533	8971	9883	10522	11104	12153	12991	14247	15550	16763
A Household operation [a]	635	1150	1547	1773	2171	2436	2608	2834	3105	3485	3700	3882
B Other	1815	3856	5986	7198	7712	8086	8496	9319	9886	10762	11850	12881
5 Medical care and health expenses	290	547	845	1025	1305	1562	1861	2165	2399	2681	2910	3278
6 Transport and communication	3961	9006	14826	18747	21954	24413	26745	30198	31355	34179	36852	41705
A Personal transport equipment	1081	2326	4811	6493	6510	6557	7407	9113	9011	9992	11664	14303
B Other	2880	6680	10015	12254	15444	17856	19338	21085	22344	24187	25188	27402
7 Recreational, entertainment, education and cultural services	2706	5987	9394	11028	12885	14197	15563	16721	18059	19834	21819	23682
A Education	171	374	783	883	1135	1337	1442	1432	1506	1626	1782	1962
B Other	2535	5613	8611	10145	11750	12860	14121	15289	16553	18208	20037	21720
8 Miscellaneous goods and services	5530	11383	17617	20905	24626	26996	29641	33465	37342	41530	46702	52445
A Personal care	564	1067	1563	1877	2180	2427	2713	3003	3383	3936	4399	4841
B Expenditures in restaurants, cafes and hotels	3833	7714	11793	13910	16485	18011	19328	21706	24075	26446	29110	31952
C Other	1133	2602	4261	5118	5961	6558	7600	8756	9884	11148	13193	15652
Total Final Consumption Expenditure in the Domestic Market by Households, of which [b]	31294	64187	98959	116939	135163	149837	164124	180053	192561	210213	229899	250324
A Durable goods	2607	5872	10168	13087	13495	13942	15439	18248	18779	20370	22871	26000
B Semi-durable goods	5338	10733	16883	19875	22132	23021	24743	27127	29490	32909	36547	40318
C Non-durable goods	11448	22292	32813	37873	43870	49146	53199	57236	60296	64554	67574	70057

United Kingdom

2.5 Private Final Consumption Expenditure by Type and Purpose, in Current Prices
(Continued)

Million Pounds Sterling

	1970	1975	1978	1979	1980	1981	1982	1983	1984	1985	1986	1987
D Services	11901	25289	39093	46103	55666	63728	70742	77443	83995	92381	102906	113949
Plus: Direct purchases abroad by resident households	420	1009	1592	2079	2648	3131	3483	3855	4275	4540	5651	6668
Less: Direct purchases in the domestic market by non-resident households	518	1442	2891	3207	3436	3513	3792	4661	5344	6282	6460	7194
Equals: Final Consumption Expenditure of Resident Households	31196	63754	97660	115811	134375	149455	163815	179247	191492	208471	229090	249798

Final Consumption Expenditure of Private Non-profit Institutions Serving Households

	1970	1975	1978	1979	1980	1981	1982	1983	1984	1985	1986	1987
Equals: Final Consumption Expenditure of Private Non-profit Organisations Serving Households	597	1324	1956	2225	2776	3250	3685	4161	4685	5285	6068	6961
Private Final Consumption Expenditure [bc]	31793	65078	99616	118036	137151	152705	167500	183408	196177	213756	235158	256759

a) Item 'Household operation' includes repairs to clothing and footwear, household equipment and miscellaneous goods, n.e.c.
b) The estimates of this table (Private final consumption expenditure by type and purpose) exclude the products of private gardens.
c) For years prior to 1983, components do not add up to total due to the method used to rebase to 1985 prices.

2.6 Private Final Consumption Expenditure by Type and Purpose, in Constant Prices

Million Pounds Sterling

	1970	1975	1978	1979	1980	1981	1982	1983	1984	1985	1986	1987

At constant prices of: 1985
Final Consumption Expenditure of Resident Households

	1970	1975	1978	1979	1980	1981	1982	1983	1984	1985	1986	1987
1 Food, beverages and tobacco [a]	37444	38787	40178	40894	40541	39837	39326	40177	39689	40136	41037	41301
A Food	28542	27974	28526	28912	28915	28752	28624	29065	28554	28871	29673	29621
B Non-alcoholic beverages	513	776	860	968	948	903	934	1079	1108	1193	1374	1524
C Alcoholic beverages	1570	2781	3474	3684	3509	3440	3425	3695	3906	4117	4199	4407
D Tobacco	7661	7755	7736	7700	7485	6941	6410	6338	6121	5955	5791	5749
2 Clothing and footwear	8964	10067	11238	12038	11901	11794	12226	13057	13854	14812	15899	17026
3 Gross rent, fuel and power [a]	33811	36508	38070	39300	39464	39790	40072	40821	41359	42794	44183	45468
A Fuel and power	9427	9879	10214	10717	10281	10246	10046	10059	9958	10657	10933	10921
B Other	24439	26671	27890	28625	29206	29562	30033	30762	31401	32137	33250	34547
4 Furniture, furnishings and household equipment and operation [a]	10403	11929	12248	12887	12395	12391	12528	13209	13579	14247	15075	15817
A Household operation [b]	3810	3392	2985	2974	3106	3163	3134	3189	3304	3485	3550	3566
B Other	6998	8655	9269	9892	9305	9255	9411	10020	10275	10762	11525	12251
5 Medical care and health expenses	1493	1623	1729	1818	1937	2039	2210	2387	2512	2681	2786	2993
6 Transport and communication [a]	20765	24540	27246	29093	29034	29420	29804	32758	32812	34179	36387	39119
A Personal transport equipment	5082	6224	7113	8054	7623	7754	8005	10097	9506	9992	10774	11880
B Other	16029	18553	20388	21220	21674	21927	22033	22661	23306	24187	25613	27239
7 Recreational, entertainment, education and cultural services [a]	10688	14323	15986	16729	17141	17248	17564	18260	18951	19834	21102	22304
A Education	1161	1153	1680	1682	1778	1883	1740	1602	1587	1626	1664	1710
B Other	9609	13117	14353	15082	15406	15423	15854	16658	17364	18208	19438	20594
8 Miscellaneous goods and services [a]	30821	36963	37958	38702	37658	36740	36858	38628	40173	41530	44028	47012
A Personal care	2794	3182	3109	3230	3150	3218	3296	3444	3660	3936	4174	4414
B Expenditures in restaurants, cafes and hotels	22722	25705	26029	26566	26130	24925	24215	25205	25836	26446	27411	28554
C Other	5583	8203	8940	9032	8527	8689	9363	9978	10676	11148	12443	14044
Total Final Consumption Expenditure in the Domestic Market by Households, of which [ac]	153397	173806	184151	191141	189745	188966	190365	199297	202928	210213	220497	231039
A Durable goods	9479	12833	14338	16171	15417	15707	16504	19579	19442	20370	22016	23521
B Semi-durable goods	20730	24907	27536	28572	27785	27585	28466	29690	30990	32909	35265	38104
C Non-durable goods	57713	60327	62451	63841	63365	62815	62291	63316	63177	64554	66256	66869

United Kingdom

2.6 Private Final Consumption Expenditure by Type and Purpose, in Constant Prices
(Continued)

Million Pounds Sterling

	1970	1975	1978	1979	1980	1981	1982	1983	1984	1985	1986	1987
					At constant prices of:1985							
D Services	67730	76912	80838	83237	84178	83768	83711	86713	89319	92381	96959	102546
Plus: Direct purchases abroad by resident households	2052	2384	2562	3225	4038	4277	4267	4344	4354	4540	5064	5808
Less: Direct purchases in the domestic market by non-resident households	3030	4473	5866	5664	5134	4646	4602	5323	5730	6282	6059	6361
Equals: Final Consumption Expenditure of Resident Households [a]	152322	171735	181020	188810	188661	188560	189992	198318	201552	208471	219502	230486

Final Consumption Expenditure of Private Non-profit Institutions Serving Households

	1970	1975	1978	1979	1980	1981	1982	1983	1984	1985	1986	1987
Equals: Final Consumption Expenditure of Private Non-profit Organisations Serving Households	3126	3481	3740	3776	3881	4034	4273	4605	4938	5285	5780	6353
Private Final Consumption Expenditure [ac]	155422	175213	184758	192584	192540	192593	194264	202923	206490	213756	225282	236839

a) For years prior to 1983, components do not add up to total due to the method used to rebase to 1985 prices.
b) Item 'Household operation' includes repairs to clothing and footwear, household equipment and miscellaneous goods, n.e.c.
c) The estimates of this table (Private final consumption expenditure by type and purpose) exclude the products of private gardens.

2.7 Gross Capital Formation by Type of Good and Owner, in Current Prices

Million Pounds Sterling

	1980 TOTAL	1980 Total Private	1980 Public Enterprises	1980 General Government	1981 TOTAL	1981 Total Private	1981 Public Enterprises	1981 General Government	1982 TOTAL	1982 Total Private	1982 Public Enterprises	1982 General Government
Increase in stocks, total [a]	-2586	-2856	219	51	-2735	-2734	60	-61	-1244	-1610	261	105
1 Goods producing industries	-2358	-2577	219	-	-2154	-2249	95	-	-1165	-1468	303	-
A Materials and supplies	-1292	-1394	102	-	-1307	-1386	79	-	-360	-743	383	-
B Work in progress	-1031	-964	-67	-	-124	-159	35	-	-526	-495	-31	-
C Livestock, except breeding stocks, dairy cattle, etc.	-42	-42	-	-	-15	-15	-	-	46	46	-	-
D Finished goods	7	-177	184	-	-708	-689	-19	-	-325	-276	-49	-
2 Wholesale and retail trade	-883	-885	2	-	-643	-651	8	-	10	7	3	-
3 Other, except government stocks	604	606	-2	-	123	166	-43	-	-194	-149	-45	-
4 Government stocks	51	-	-	51	-61	-	-	-61	105	-	-	105
Gross Fixed Capital Formation, Total [a]	41561	29409	6653	5499	41304	29946	6780	4578	44824	33395	7114	4315
1 Residential buildings	8674	6115	335	2224	8138	6174	309	1655	8920	6850	301	1769
2 Non-residential buildings	11802	6020	2637	3145	12471	6460	2700	3311	13386	6415	3034	3937
3 Other construction	...	...	...	...	...	...	...	...	...	...	...	...
4 Land improvement and plantation and orchard development	1561	2418	-173	-684	1782	2982	-42	-1158	1937	4254	-91	-2226
5 Producers' durable goods	19559	14891	3854	814	18910	14327	3813	770	20553	15848	3870	835
A Transport equipment	4566	3713	681	172	3846	3302	392	152	4285	3823	300	162
B Machinery and equipment	14993	11178	3173	642	15064	11025	3421	618	16268	12025	3570	673
6 Breeding stock, dairy cattle, etc.	-35	-35	-	-	3	3	-	-	28	28	-	-
Total Gross Capital Formation	38975	26553	6872	5550	38569	27212	6840	4517	43580	31785	7375	4420

	1983 TOTAL	1983 Total Private	1983 Public Enterprises	1983 General Government	1984 TOTAL	1984 Total Private	1984 Public Enterprises	1984 General Government	1985 TOTAL	1985 Total Private	1985 Public Enterprises	1985 General Government
Increase in stocks, total [a]	1418	836	336	246	1208	1380	-452	280	505	78	-23	450
1 Goods producing industries	574	262	312	-	430	959	-529	-	-267	-281	14	-
A Materials and supplies	28	-340	368	-	-370	179	-549	-	479	178	301	-
B Work in progress	623	663	-40	-	334	298	36	-	-344	-403	59	-
C Livestock, except breeding stocks, dairy cattle, etc.	-6	-6	-	-	-17	-17	-	-	-76	-76	-	-
D Finished goods	-71	-55	-16	-	483	499	-16	-	-326	20	-346	-
2 Wholesale and retail trade	402	400	2	-	515	515	-	-	282	282	-	-
3 Other, except government stocks	196	174	22	-	-17	-94	77	-	40	77	-37	-
4 Government stocks	246	-	-	246	280	-	-	280	450	-	-	450
Gross Fixed Capital Formation, Total [a]	48615	35024	7884	5707	55025	41227	7305	6493	60283	48043	5656	6584
1 Residential buildings	10447	7757	326	2364	11733	8987	318	2428	11928	9392	280	2256
2 Non-residential buildings	13306	6269	3082	3955	14637	7234	2863	4540	15206	7786	2699	4721

United Kingdom

2.7 Gross Capital Formation by Type of Good and Owner, in Current Prices
(Continued)

Million Pounds Sterling

	1983 TOTAL	1983 Total Private	1983 Public Enterprises	1983 General Government	1984 TOTAL	1984 Total Private	1984 Public Enterprises	1984 General Government	1985 TOTAL	1985 Total Private	1985 Public Enterprises	1985 General Government
3 Other construction	...	...	...	...	...	...	...	...	...	...	...	...
4 Land improvement and plantation and orchard development	2397	4292	-156	-1739	2673	4637	-315	-1649	2972	5149	-380	-1797
5 Producers' durable goods	22472	16713	4632	1127	26010	20397	4439	1174	30165	25704	3057	1404
A Transport equipment	4530	3863	456	211	5662	4895	573	194	6433	5656	588	189
B Machinery and equipment	17942	12850	4176	916	20348	15502	3866	980	23732	20048	2469	1215
6 Breeding stock, dairy cattle, etc.	-7	-7	-	-	-28	-28	-	-	12	12	-	-
Total Gross Capital Formation	50033	35860	8220	5953	56233	42607	6853	6773	60788	48121	5633	7034

	1986 TOTAL	1986 Total Private	1986 Public Enterprises	1986 General Government	1987 TOTAL	1987 Total Private	1987 Public Enterprises	1987 General Government
Increase in stocks, total a	515	999	-247	-237	551	1385	-222	-612
1 Goods producing industries	-473	-211	-262	-	132	262	-130	...
A Materials and supplies	-60	8	-68	-	-96	15	-111	...
B Work in progress	-12	132	-144	-	-21	-84	63	...
C Livestock, except breeding stocks, dairy cattle, etc.	-33	-33	-	-	-38	-38	...	...
D Finished goods	-368	-318	-50	-	287	369	-82	...
2 Wholesale and retail trade	1326	1326	-	-	1225	1225	...	...
3 Other, except government stocks	-101	-116	15	-	-194	-102	-92	...
4 Government stocks	-237	-	-	-237	-612	...	...	-612
Gross Fixed Capital Formation, Total a	63797	51245	5545	7007	70767	59251	4605	6911
1 Residential buildings	13556	10852	242	2462	15197	12363	234	2600
2 Non-residential buildings	15967	8266	2763	4938	17342	10116	2275	4951
3 Other construction	...	...	...	...	...	...	...	...
4 Land improvement and plantation and orchard development	3466	5865	-391	-2008	4021	6973	-654	-2298
5 Producers' durable goods	30803	26257	2931	1615	34262	29854	2750	1658
A Transport equipment	6128	5490	449	189	7229	6624	415	190
B Machinery and equipment	24675	20767	2482	1426	27033	23230	2335	1468
6 Breeding stock, dairy cattle, etc.	5	5	-	-	-55	-55	...	...
Total Gross Capital Formation	64312	52244	5298	6770	71318	60636	4383	6299

a) Beginning 1973, 'Gross fixed capital formation' excludes the value of completed but unsold dwellings which is included in 'Increase in stocks'.

2.8 Gross Capital Formation by Type of Good and Owner, in Constant Prices

Million Pounds Sterling

	1980 TOTAL	1980 Total Private	1980 Public Enterprises	1980 General Government	1981 TOTAL	1981 Total Private	1981 Public Enterprises	1981 General Government	1982 TOTAL	1982 Total Private	1982 Public Enterprises	1982 General Government
					At constant prices of:1985							
Increase in stocks, total ab	-3357	-3800	290	56	-3191	-3244	48	-62	-1289	-1729	257	151
1 Goods producing industries b	-3046	-3188	289	...	-2724	-2859	92	...	-1207	-1690	306	...
A Materials and supplies	-1717	-1871	134	...	-1652	-1785	73	...	-326	-892	418	...
B Work in progress	-1341	-1277	-89	...	-174	-197	36	...	-579	-550	-34	...
C Livestock, except breeding stocks, dairy cattle, etc.	-53	-53	...	...	-19	-19	...	...	51	51	...	...
D Finished goods	65	13	244	...	-879	-858	-25	...	-353	-299	-78	...
2 Wholesale and retail trade	-1172	-1175	2	...	-755	765	8	...	105	103	2	...
3 Other, except government stocks	722	687	-4	...	255	289	-55	...	-303	-243	-50	...
4 Government stocks	56	...	...	56	-62	...	...	-62	151	...	...	151
Gross Fixed Capital Formation, Total ab	53416	38577	8491	6290	48298	35990	7775	4632	50915	38892	7906	4313
1 Residential buildings	12379	9134	419	2778	10247	8149	339	1817	10899	8680	333	1949
2 Non-residential buildings	13086	6486	3013	3570	12527	6418	2729	3352	13815	6616	3128	4066

United Kingdom

2.8 Gross Capital Formation by Type of Good and Owner, in Constant Prices
(Continued)

Million Pounds Sterling

	1980 TOTAL	1980 Total Private	1980 Public Enterprises	1980 General Government	1981 TOTAL	1981 Total Private	1981 Public Enterprises	1981 General Government	1982 TOTAL	1982 Total Private	1982 Public Enterprises	1982 General Government
At constant prices of: 1985												
3 Other construction	...	...	...	...	...	...	...	...	...	...	...	...
4 Land improvement and plantation and orchard development	2170	3359	-240	-950	2295	3838	-53	-1491	2521	5544	-118	-2905
5 Producers' durable goods b	25963	19547	5329	1080	23160	17405	4800	952	23470	17962	4531	957
A Transport equipment	6296	5119	937	240	4895	4209	488	198	5028	4479	355	194
B Machinery and equipment	19706	14452	4390	842	18265	13195	4311	755	18447	13490	4177	764
6 Breeding stock, dairy cattle, etc.	-47	-47	...	...	4	4	...	...	32	32	...	...
Total Gross Capital Formation	50059	29659	8710	6346	45107	28993	7811	4528	49626	34989	8100	4464

	1983 TOTAL	1983 Total Private	1983 Public Enterprises	1983 General Government	1984 TOTAL	1984 Total Private	1984 Public Enterprises	1984 General Government	1985 TOTAL	1985 Total Private	1985 Public Enterprises	1985 General Government
At constant prices of: 1985												
Increase in stocks, total ab	1306	833	237	236	1072	1547	-746	271	569	-264	383	450
1 Goods producing industries b	453	244	209	...	182	962	-780	...	-267	-681	414	...
A Materials and supplies	-149	-384	235	...	-700	133	-833	...	456	40	416	...
B Work in progress	702	739	-37	...	376	337	39	...	-334	-392	58	...
C Livestock, except breeding stocks, dairy cattle, etc.	-16	-16	...	...	-17	-17	...	...	-76	-76	...	...
D Finished goods	-84	-95	11	...	523	509	14	...	-313	-253	-60	...
2 Wholesale and retail trade	411	409	2	...	567	567	...	...	283	283	...	...
3 Other, except government stocks	206	180	26	...	52	18	34	...	103	134	-31	...
4 Government stocks	236	...	...	236	271	...	...	271	450	...	...	450
Gross Fixed Capital Formation, Total ab	53476	39085	8490	5901	58075	43845	7625	6605	60283	48043	5656	6584
1 Residential buildings	12247	9323	354	2570	12571	9746	327	2498	11928	9392	280	2256
2 Non-residential buildings	13878	6560	3197	4121	15160	7499	2947	4714	15206	7786	2699	4721
3 Other construction	...	...	...	...	...	...	...	...	...	...	...	...
4 Land improvement and plantation and orchard development	2773	4972	-176	-2023	2975	5163	-350	-1838	2972	5149	-380	-1797
5 Producers' durable goods b	24586	18238	5115	1233	27401	21469	4701	1231	30165	25704	3057	1404
A Transport equipment	5177	4434	502	241	6107	5295	604	208	6433	5656	588	189
B Machinery and equipment	19409	13804	4613	992	21294	16174	4097	1023	23732	20048	2469	1215
6 Breeding stock, dairy cattle, etc.	-8	-8	...	...	-32	-32	...	...	12	12	...	...
Total Gross Capital Formation	54782	40056	8690	6139	59147	45214	6834	6893	60852	48148	5633	7042

	1986 TOTAL	1986 Total Private	1986 Public Enterprises	1986 General Government	1987 TOTAL	1987 Total Private	1987 Public Enterprises	1987 General Government
At constant prices of: 1985								
Increase in stocks, total ab	572	833	-26	-235	557	1347	-200	-590
1 Goods producing industries b	-400	-387	-13	...	135	297	-162	...
A Materials and supplies	76	-46	122	...	-178	7	-185	...
B Work in progress	-22	99	-121	...	51	13	38	...
C Livestock, except breeding stocks, dairy cattle, etc.	-33	-33	...	...	-38	-38	...	...
D Finished goods	-421	-407	-14	...	300	315	-15	...
2 Wholesale and retail trade	1320	1320	...	...	1170	1170	...	...
3 Other, except government stocks	-113	-100	-13	...	-158	-120	-38	...
4 Government stocks	-235	...	...	-235	-590	...	...	-590
Gross Fixed Capital Formation, Total ab	60834	48473	5399	6962	64196	52969	4431	6796
1 Residential buildings	12829	10198	235	2396	13406	10737	220	2449
2 Non-residential buildings	15299	7816	2698	4785	15807	8925	2198	4684

United Kingdom

2.8 Gross Capital Formation by Type of Good and Owner, in Constant Prices
(Continued)

Million Pounds Sterling

	1986				1987			
	TOTAL	Total Private	Public Enterprises	General Government	TOTAL	Total Private	Public Enterprises	General Government
	At constant prices of: 1985							
3 Other construction	...	...	...	...	...	...	...	...
4 Land improvement and plantation and orchard development	3066	5194	-346	-1782	3285	5725	-538	-1902
5 Producers' durable goods b	29635	25260	2812	1563	31755	27639	2551	1565
A Transport equipment	5627	5027	423	177	6099	5544	378	177
B Machinery and equipment	24008	20233	2389	1386	25656	22095	2173	1388
6 Breeding stock, dairy cattle, etc.	5	5	...	...	-57	-57	...	...
Total Gross Capital Formation	61406	49195	5307	6714	64753	54253	4093	6526

a) Beginning 1973, 'Gross fixed capital formation' excludes the value of completed but unsold dwellings which is included in 'Increase in stocks'.   b) For years prior to 1983, components do not add up to total due to the method used to rebase to 1985 prices.

2.9 Gross Capital Formation by Kind of Activity of Owner, ISIC Major Divisions, in Current Prices

Million Pounds Sterling

	1980			1981			1982			1983		
	Total Gross Capital Formation	Increase in Stocks	Gross Fixed Capital Formation	Total Gross Capital Formation	Increase in Stocks	Gross Fixed Capital Formation	Total Gross Capital Formation	Increase in Stocks	Gross Fixed Capital Formation	Total Gross Capital Formation	Increase in Stocks	Gross Fixed Capital Formation
	All Producers											
1 Agriculture, hunting, fishing and forestry	972	-51	1023	907	-33	940	1168	39	1129	1287	28	1259
2 Mining and quarrying	3647	84	3563	3556	-522	4078	3672	-439	4111	3658	-274	3932
3 Manufacturing	4157	-2321	6478	3758	-1565	5323	4195	-1291	5486	5988	129	5859
4 Electricity, gas and water	2254	128	2126	2569	76	2493	3124	424	2700	3569	473	3096
5 Construction	270	-198	468	330	-110	440	645	102	543	815	218	597
6 Wholesale and retail trade, restaurants and hotels	2356	-883	3239	2580	-643	3223	3589	10	3579	4178	402	3776
7 Transport, storage and communication	3879	-3	3882	3318	-43	3361	3168	-44	3212	3805	20	3785
8 Finance, insurance, real estate and business services	14821	607	14214	14640	166	14474	15921	-150	16071	17767	176	17591
9 Community, social and personal services	3229	49	3180	3195	-101	3296	3553	37	3516	4013	238	3775
Statistical discrepancy a	1620	-	1620	1909	-	1909	2091	-	2091	2492	-	2492
Total Industries	37205	-2588	39793	36762	-2775	39537	41126	-1312	42438	47572	1410	46162
Producers of Government Services	1770	2	1768	1807	40	1767	2454	68	2386	2461	8	2453
Private Non-Profit Institutions Serving Households b	...	...	...	...	...	...	...	...	...	...	...	...
Total c	38975	-2586	41561	38569	-2735	41304	43580	-1244	44824	50033	1418	48615
Memorandum Item: Mineral Fuels and Power	5587	212	5375	5799	-448	6247	6443	-15	6458	6833	199	6634

	1984			1985			1986			1987		
	Total Gross Capital Formation	Increase in Stocks	Gross Fixed Capital Formation	Total Gross Capital Formation	Increase in Stocks	Gross Fixed Capital Formation	Total Gross Capital Formation	Increase in Stocks	Gross Fixed Capital Formation	Total Gross Capital Formation	Increase in Stocks	Gross Fixed Capital Formation
	All Producers											
1 Agriculture, hunting, fishing and forestry	1292	89	1203	753	-228	981	930	22	908	670	-40	710
2 Mining and quarrying	3535	-200	3735	3192	-414	3606	3270	-258	3528	3004	58	2946
3 Manufacturing	8392	1010	7382	8269	-466	8735	8410	-419	8829	9466	-414	9880
4 Electricity, gas and water	2608	-461	3069	3431	400	3031	3279	-21	3300	3197	-172	3369

United Kingdom

2.9 Gross Capital Formation by Kind of Activity of Owner, ISIC Major Divisions, in Current Prices
(Continued)

Million Pounds Sterling

	1984 Total Gross Capital Formation	1984 Increase in Stocks	1984 Gross Fixed Capital Formation	1985 Total Gross Capital Formation	1985 Increase in Stocks	1985 Gross Fixed Capital Formation	1986 Total Gross Capital Formation	1986 Increase in Stocks	1986 Gross Fixed Capital Formation	1987 Total Gross Capital Formation	1987 Increase in Stocks	1987 Gross Fixed Capital Formation
5 Construction	512	-8	520	972	441	531	750	203	547	1269	700	569
6 Wholesale and retail trade, restaurants and hotels	5029	515	4514	5463	282	5181	7081	1326	5755	8333	1225	7108
7 Transport, storage and communication	4651	39	4612	5062	-22	5084	5143	27	5116	5602	-67	5669
8 Finance, insurance, real estate and business services	20261	-56	20317	22605	62	22543	24031	-128	24159	27731	-127	27858
9 Community, social and personal services	4408	277	4131	4839	443	4396	4387	-237	4624	4495	-612	5107
Statistical discrepancy a	2955	-	2955	3391	-	3391	4067	-	4067	4572	-	4572
Total Industries	53643	1205	52438	57977	498	57479	61348	515	60833	68339	551	67788
Producers of Government Services	2590	3	2587	2811	7	2804	2964	-	2964	2979	-	2979
Private Non-Profit Institutions Serving Households b	...	...	...	...	...	...	...	...	...	...	...	...
Total c	56233	1208	55025	60788	505	60283	64312	515	63797	71318	551	70767
Memorandum Item: Mineral Fuels and Power	5725	-661	6386	6252	7	6245	6087	-286	6373	5688	-112	5800

a) Column 'Gross fixed capital formation' is purchases less sales of land and existing buildings (excluding general government non-trading land) and column 'Increase in stocks' is an adjustment to reflect the deficiency on both coverage and quality of recorded data.
b) Item 'Private non-profit institutions serving households' is included with various industries above.
c) Beginning 1973, 'Gross fixed capital formation' excludes the value of completed but unsold dwellings which is included in 'Increase in stocks'.

2.10 Gross Capital Formation by Kind of Activity of Owner, ISIC Major Divisions, in Constant Prices

Million Pounds Sterling

	1980 Total Gross Capital Formation	1980 Increase in Stocks	1980 Gross Fixed Capital Formation	1981 Total Gross Capital Formation	1981 Increase in Stocks	1981 Gross Fixed Capital Formation	1982 Total Gross Capital Formation	1982 Increase in Stocks	1982 Gross Fixed Capital Formation	1983 Total Gross Capital Formation	1983 Increase in Stocks	1983 Gross Fixed Capital Formation
						At constant prices of: 1985 All Producers						
1 Agriculture, hunting, fishing and forestry	1148	-65	1213	1009	-34	1043	1270	41	1229	1372	34	1338
2 Mining and quarrying	4473	121	4352	3967	-607	4574	4074	-442	4516	3896	-295	4191
3 Manufacturing	5738	-3023	8761	4604	-1975	6579	4912	-1448	6360	6556	134	6422
4 Electricity, gas and water	2906	174	2732	2964	91	2873	3478	476	3002	3657	336	3321
5 Construction	358	-249	607	406	-131	537	728	121	607	903	244	659
6 Wholesale and retail trade, restaurants and hotels	2924	-1169	4093	3063	-697	3760	4117	98	4019	4564	411	4153
7 Transport, storage and communication	5066	-4	5070	3929	-55	3984	3593	-50	3643	4212	26	4186
8 Finance, insurance, real estate and business services	18900	304	18596	17280	158	17122	18476	-56	18532	19917	180	19737
9 Community, social and personal services	3854	54	3800	3486	-102	3588	3858	86	3772	4262	227	4035
Statistical discrepancy a	2250	...	2250	2456	...	2456	2723	...	2723	2878	...	2878
Total Industries b	48033	-3359	51392	43294	-3231	46525	47068	-1354	48422	52217	1297	50920
Producers of Government Services	2075	2	2073	1863	40	1823	2553	65	2488	2565	9	2556
Private Non-Profit Institutions Serving Households c	...	...	...	...	...	...	...	...	...	...	...	...
Total db	50059	-3357	53416	45107	-3191	48298	49626	-1289	50915	54782	1306	53476
Memorandum Item: Mineral Fuels and Power	7029	296	6733	6643	-495	7138	7234	64	7170	7144	40	7104

	1984 Total Gross Capital Formation	1984 Increase in Stocks	1984 Gross Fixed Capital Formation	1985 Total Gross Capital Formation	1985 Increase in Stocks	1985 Gross Fixed Capital Formation	1986 Total Gross Capital Formation	1986 Increase in Stocks	1986 Gross Fixed Capital Formation	1987 Total Gross Capital Formation	1987 Increase in Stocks	1987 Gross Fixed Capital Formation
						At constant prices of: 1985 All Producers						
1 Agriculture, hunting, fishing and forestry	1352	110	1242	753	-228	981	885	20	865	614	-36	650
2 Mining and quarrying	3685	-185	3870	3192	-414	3606	3053	-347	3400	2903	127	2776
3 Manufacturing	8868	1058	7810	8269	-466	8735	8074	-403	8477	8745	-345	9090
4 Electricity, gas and water	2402	-800	3202	3431	400	3031	3319	134	3185	2964	-248	3212

United Kingdom

2.10 Gross Capital Formation by Kind of Activity of Owner, ISIC Major Divisions, in Constant Prices
(Continued)

Million Pounds Sterling

	1984			1985			1986			1987		
	Total Gross Capital Formation	Increase in Stocks	Gross Fixed Capital Formation	Total Gross Capital Formation	Increase in Stocks	Gross Fixed Capital Formation	Total Gross Capital Formation	Increase in Stocks	Gross Fixed Capital Formation	Total Gross Capital Formation	Increase in Stocks	Gross Fixed Capital Formation
	At constant prices of:1985											
5 Construction	552	-1	553	972	441	531	717	196	521	1146	637	509
6 Wholesale and retail trade, restaurants and hotels	5369	567	4802	5464	283	5181	6750	1320	5430	7502	1170	6332
7 Transport, storage and communication	4899	40	4859	5062	-22	5084	4877	26	4851	5073	-64	5137
8 Finance, insurance, real estate and business services	21475	12	21463	22668	125	22543	22978	-139	23117	24999	-94	25093
9 Community, social and personal services	4594	268	4326	4839	443	4396	4177	-235	4412	4101	-590	4691
Statistical discrepancy [a]	3288	...	3288	3392	...	3392	3600	...	3600	3753	...	3753
Total Industries [b]	56484	1069	55415	58042	562	57480	58430	572	57858	61800	557	61243
Producers of Government Services	2663	3	2660	2810	7	2803	2976	-	2976	2953	-	2953
Private Non-Profit Institutions Serving Households [c]	...	...	...	...	...	...	...	...	...	...	...	...
Total [db]	59147	1072	58075	60852	569	60283	61406	572	60834	64753	557	64196
Memorandum Item: Mineral Fuels and Power	5658	-985	6643	6252	7	6245	5934	-220	6154	5370	-119	5489

a) Column 'Gross fixed capital formation' is purchases less sales of land and existing buildings (excluding general government non-trading land) and column 'Increase in stocks' is an adjustment to reflect the deficiency on both coverage and quality of recorded data.
b) For years prior to 1983, components do not add up to total due to the method used to rebase to 1985 prices.
c) Item 'Private non-profit institutions serving households' is included with various industries above.
d) Beginning 1973, 'Gross fixed capital formation' excludes the value of completed but unsold dwellings which is included in 'Increase in stocks'.

2.11 Gross Fixed Capital Formation by Kind of Activity of Owner, ISIC Divisions, in Current Prices

Million Pounds Sterling

	1970	1975	1978	1979	1980	1981	1982	1983	1984	1985	1986	1987
	All Producers											
1 Agriculture, hunting, forestry and fishing	288	586	953	959	1023	940	1129	1259	1203	981	908	710
A Agriculture and hunting	258	518	873	887	949	862	1052	1171	1092	841	769	566
B Forestry and logging	23	38	48	51	66	77	74	84	102	127	134	135
C Fishing	7	30	32	21	8	1	3	4	9	13	5	9
2 Mining and quarrying	193	1642	2781	2906	3563	4078	4111	3932	3735	3606	3528	2946
A Coal mining	65	166	452	553	784	766	820	783	393	522	653	631
B Crude petroleum and natural gas production	128	1476	2329	2353	2779	3312	3291	3149	3342	3084	2875	2315
C Metal ore mining	...	...	...	...	...	...	...	...	...	...	...	...
D Other mining	...	...	...	...	...	...	...	...	...	...	...	...
3 Manufacturing	2089	3458	5624	6515	6478	5323	5486	5859	7382	8735	8829	9880
A Manufacturing of food, beverages and tobacco	252	479	821	903	961	900	1002	996	1235	1395	1297	1447
B Textile, wearing apparel and leather industries	124	182	266	299	235	181	238	249	336	384	449	568
C Manufacture of wood, and wood products, including furniture	33	74	126	169	171	105	113	136	157	192	190	255
D Manufacture of paper and paper products, printing and publishing	134	211	366	504	542	446	432	497	694	828	954	1292
E Manufacture of chemicals and chemical petroleum, coal, rubber and plastic products	81	104	214	248	256	196	205	233	360	391	406	535
F Manufacture of non-metallic mineral products except products of petroleum and coal	128	204	353	417	443	333	361	373	507	542	462	639
G Basic metal industries	214	549	506	438	389	297	263	251	239	360	418	535
H Manufacture of fabricated metal products, machinery and equipment	1106	1611	2913	3471	3414	2813	2799	3062	3799	4590	4596	4545
I Other manufacturing industries	17	44	59	66	67	52	73	62	55	53	57	64
4 Electricity, gas and water	782	1288	1489	1696	2126	2493	2700	3096	3069	3031	3300	3369
A Electricity, gas and steam	679	1140	1232	1409	1812	2169	2347	2702	2651	2639	2845	2854
B Water works and supply	103	148	257	287	314	324	353	394	418	392	455	515

United Kingdom

2.11 Gross Fixed Capital Formation by Kind of Activity of Owner, ISIC Divisions, in Current Prices
(Continued)

Million Pounds Sterling

	1970	1975	1978	1979	1980	1981	1982	1983	1984	1985	1986	1987
5 Construction	159	349	484	586	468	440	543	597	520	531	547	569
6 Wholesale and retail trade, restaurants and hotels	640	1244	2329	3040	3239	3223	3579	3776	4514	5181	5755	7108
A Wholesale and retail trade	496	1030	1910	2442	2573	2559	2886	3051	3743	4236	4543	5426
B Restaurants and hotels	144	214	419	598	666	664	693	725	771	945	1212	1682
7 Transport, storage and communication	1179	2179	3153	3525	3882	3361	3212	3785	4612	5084	5116	5669
A Transport and storage	745	1405	2188	2383	2426	1896	1721	2100	2755	2784	2544	2833
B Communication	434	774	965	1142	1456	1465	1491	1685	1857	2300	2572	2836
8 Finance, insurance, real estate and business services	2533	6410	9647	12131	14214	14474	16071	17591	20317	22543	24159	27858
A Financial institutions	344	691	1693	2387	2977	3161	3778	3655	4978	6386	5915	7278
B Insurance	79	289	306	425	604	660	695	794	711	706	811	967
C Real estate and business services	2110	5430	7648	9319	10633	10653	11598	13142	14628	15451	17433	19613
Real estate except dwellings	240	748	1323	1670	1959	2515	2678	2695	2895	3523	3877	4416
Dwellings	1870	4682	6325	7649	8674	8138	8920	10447	11733	11928	13556	15197
9 Community, social and personal services	907	1811	2229	2607	3180	3296	3516	3775	4131	4396	4624	5107
A Sanitary and similar services	148	388	439	475	605	553	610	633	660	636	737	853
B Social and related community services	582	1096	1174	1295	1556	1695	1812	1924	2126	2304	2490	2608
Educational services	421	703	656	712	845	874	839	894	975	1050	1151	1251
Medical, dental, other health and veterinary services	161	393	518	583	711	821	973	1030	1151	1254	1339	1357
C Recreational and cultural services	177	327	616	837	1019	1048	1094	1218	1345	1456	1397	1646
D Personal and household services												
Statistical discrepancy	144	413	1082	1406	1620	1909	2091	2492	2955	3391	4067	4572
Total Industries	8914	19380	29771	35371	39793	39537	42438	46162	52438	57479	60833	67788
Producers of Government Services	822	1655	1289	1554	1768	1767	2386	2453	2587	2804	2964	2979
Private Non-Profit Institutions Serving Households [a]	...	...	...	...	...	...	...	...	...	...	...	...
Total	9736	21035	31060	36925	41561	41304	44824	48615	55025	60283	63797	70767

a) Item 'Private non-profit institutions serving households' is included with various industries above.

2.12 Gross Fixed Capital Formation by Kind of Activity of Owner, ISIC Divisions, in Constant Prices

Million Pounds Sterling

	1970	1975	1978	1979	1980	1981	1982	1983	1984	1985	1986	1987
	\multicolumn{12}{c}{At constant prices of:1985}
	\multicolumn{12}{c}{All Producers}
1 Agriculture, hunting, forestry and fishing	1553	1479	1548	1358	1213	1043	1229	1338	1242	981	865	650
A Agriculture and hunting	1414	1306	1425	1263	1122	953	1143	1245	1128	841	733	519
B Forestry and logging	121	95	82	70	82	88	82	89	105	127	127	123
C Fishing	32	89	45	27	11	3	4	4	9	13	5	8
2 Mining and quarrying	1024	3896	4794	4306	4352	4574	4516	4191	3870	3606	3400	2776
A Coal mining	312	428	796	851	1025	889	923	836	411	522	633	601
B Crude petroleum and natural gas production	697	3439	3985	3454	3340	3683	3594	3355	3459	3084	2767	2175
C Metal ore mining	...	...	...	...	...	...	...	...	...	...	...	...
D Other mining	...	...	...	...	...	...	...	...	...	...	...	...

United Kingdom

2.12 Gross Fixed Capital Formation by Kind of Activity of Owner, ISIC Divisions, in Constant Prices
(Continued)

Million Pounds Sterling

	1970	1975	1978	1979	1980	1981	1982	1983	1984	1985	1986	1987
				At constant prices of:1985								
3 Manufacturing	10666	9181	9763	10136	8761	6579	6360	6422	7810	8735	8477	9090
A Manufacturing of food, beverages and tobacco	1326	1257	1442	1407	1304	1118	1157	1102	1310	1395	1242	1329
B Textile, wearing apparel and leather industries	634	509	449	450	308	217	269	276	355	384	428	515
C Manufacture of wood, and wood products, including furniture	-	-	224	265	233	129	133	152	167	192	181	230
D Manufacture of paper and paper products, printing and publishing	677	557	635	785	751	569	518	563	739	828	911	1170
E Manufacture of chemicals and chemical petroleum, coal, rubber and plastic products	-	-	359	372	341	240	237	256	379	391	440	491
F Manufacture of non-metallic mineral products except products of petroleum and coal	630	526	599	633	588	404	414	407	533	542	442	587
G Basic metal industries	1133	1427	857	667	516	363	304	275	251	360	402	495
H Manufacture of fabricated metal products, machinery and equipment	5598	4312	5102	5460	4631	3474	3246	3322	4019	4590	4376	4214
I Other manufacturing industries	-	-	96	97	89	65	82	69	57	53	55	59
4 Electricity, gas and water	4065	3229	2652	2639	2732	2873	3002	3321	3202	3031	3185	3212
A Electricity, gas and steam	3448	2879	2178	2198	2356	2540	2636	2913	2773	2639	2754	2713
B Water works and supply	583	349	461	431	372	335	366	408	429	392	431	499
5 Construction	838	932	803	875	607	537	607	659	553	531	521	509
6 Wholesale and retail trade, restaurants and hotels	3148	3170	3993	4547	4093	3760	4019	4153	4802	5181	5430	6332
A Wholesale and retail trade	2408	2642	3272	3666	3275	3006	3244	3364	3985	4236	4287	4847
B Restaurants and hotels	736	530	722	886	817	753	775	789	817	945	1143	1485
7 Transport, storage and communication	5838	5683	5450	5376	5070	3984	3643	4186	4859	5084	4851	5137
A Transport and storage	3610	3633	3747	3618	3149	2234	1973	2309	2884	2784	2379	2516
B Communication	2224	2046	1693	1749	1916	1749	1670	1877	1975	2300	2472	2621
8 Finance, insurance, real estate and business services	14213	16071	17520	19010	18596	17122	18532	19737	21463	22543	23117	25093
A Financial institutions	1299	1565	2610	3279	3587	3533	4064	3856	5163	6386	5759	6776
B Insurance	419	629	497	574	654	665	718	825	744	706	768	840
C Real estate and business services	12893	14111	14571	15265	14391	12913	13709	15056	15556	15451	16590	17477
Real estate except dwellings	1077	1462	1898	2117	2164	2608	2753	2809	2985	3523	3761	4071
Dwellings	12292	13042	12913	13363	12379	10247	10899	12247	12571	11928	12829	13406
9 Community, social and personal services	4709	4220	3820	3808	3800	3588	3772	4035	4326	4396	4412	4691
A Sanitary and similar services	861	930	800	725	725	583	641	663	682	636	720	822
B Social and related community services	2948	2476	1972	1864	1832	1825	1935	2059	2230	2304	2360	2382
Educational services	2098	1577	1094	1006	994	941	898	953	1018	1050	1094	1153
Medical, dental, other health and veterinary services	839	895	877	857	837	883	1038	1106	1212	1254	1266	1229
C Recreational and cultural services	851	789	1044	1220	1245	1181	1195	1313	1414	1456	1332	1487
D Personal and household services												
Statistical discrepancy	682	1152	2450	2272	2250	2456	2723	2878	3288	3392	3600	3753
Total Industries	47097	49259	52715	54194	51392	46525	48422	50920	55415	57480	57858	61243
Producers of Government Services	4234	3941	2239	2298	2073	1823	2488	2556	2660	2803	2976	2953
Private Non-Profit Institutions Serving Households [a]	...	...	...	...	...	...	...	...	...	...	...	...
Total	51564	53383	54914	56450	53416	48298	50915	53476	58075	60283	60834	64196

a) Item 'Private non-profit institutions serving households' is included with various industries above.

United Kingdom

2.13 Stocks of Reproducible Fixed Assets, by Type of Good and Owner, in Current Prices

Thousand Million Pounds Sterling

	TOTAL Gross	TOTAL Net	Total Private Gross	Total Private Net	Public Enterprises Gross	Public Enterprises Net	General Government Gross	General Government Net
1980								
1 Residential buildings	359.8	248.6	242.2	157.6	10.1	8.7	107.6	82.3
2 Non-residential buildings								
3 Other construction	449.2	306.2	198.4	131.8	107.8	63.4	142.2	111.0
4 Land improvement and plantation and orchard development								
5 Producers' durable goods	348.6	197.4	224.0	130.2	112.1	59.7	12.4	7.5
A Transport equipment	56.1	29.5	41.0	23.3	13.4	5.4	1.7	0.8
B Machinery and equipment	292.5	167.9	183.0	106.9	98.7	54.3	10.7	6.7
6 Breeding stock, dairy cattle, etc.	...	...	...	...	...	...	...	...
Total a	1157.6	752.2	664.6	419.6	230.0	131.7	262.1	200.9
1981								
1 Residential buildings	389.6	268.1	264.8	172.6	11.0	9.4	113.8	86.1
2 Non-residential buildings								
3 Other construction	474.4	322.5	208.1	137.2	114.1	67.1	151.3	118.1
4 Land improvement and plantation and orchard development								
5 Producers' durable goods	383.2	214.1	249.1	142.9	120.4	63.1	13.6	8.1
A Transport equipment	58.3	30.1	43.2	24.1	13.4	5.2	1.8	0.8
B Machinery and equipment	324.8	184.0	205.9	118.8	107.1	57.9	11.8	7.3
6 Breeding stock, dairy cattle, etc.	...	...	...	...	...	...	...	...
Total a	1247.2	804.7	722.1	452.6	245.5	139.7	278.7	212.3
1982								
1 Residential buildings	406.9	278.7	283.4	185.0	11.4	9.7	112.2	84.0
2 Non-residential buildings								
3 Other construction	475.0	322.2	208.6	136.9	113.6	66.8	152.0	118.5
4 Land improvement and plantation and orchard development								
5 Producers' durable goods	414.9	228.7	272.3	154.3	127.8	65.7	14.7	8.8
A Transport equipment	60.1	30.4	44.9	24.5	13.4	5.0	1.8	0.9
B Machinery and equipment	354.8	198.3	227.4	129.8	114.4	60.7	12.9	7.9
6 Breeding stock, dairy cattle, etc.	...	...	...	...	...	...	...	...
Total a	1296.8	829.6	764.4	476.2	252.7	142.1	278.8	211.2
1983								
1 Residential buildings	440.5	300.5	312.9	204.5	12.1	10.2	115.5	85.7
2 Non-residential buildings								
3 Other construction	483.2	327.1	213.6	139.3	113.9	67.2	154.8	120.7
4 Land improvement and plantation and orchard development								
5 Producers' durable goods	442.9	241.3	292.1	163.4	135.0	68.5	15.8	9.4
A Transport equipment	62.1	30.8	46.5	24.8	13.7	5.1	1.8	0.9
B Machinery and equipment	380.9	210.5	245.6	138.6	121.3	63.4	14.0	8.5
6 Breeding stock, dairy cattle, etc.	...	...	...	...	...	...	...	...
Total a	1366.6	868.9	818.6	507.1	261.0	146.0	286.1	215.9
1984								
1 Residential buildings	479.1	325.8	346.1	226.6	12.9	10.8	120.1	88.3
2 Non-residential buildings								
3 Other construction	504.1	341.0	228.2	148.6	112.8	66.1	162.2	126.3
4 Land improvement and plantation and orchard development								
5 Producers' durable goods	474.6	256.4	347.7	191.3	109.9	55.0	17.0	10.1
A Transport equipment	65.9	32.2	50.4	26.2	13.5	5.0	1.9	1.0
B Machinery and equipment	408.7	224.2	297.3	165.1	96.3	50.0	15.1	9.1
6 Breeding stock, dairy cattle, etc.	...	...	...	...	...	...	...	...
Total a	1457.8	923.1	922.0	566.4	235.6	132.0	299.3	224.7

United Kingdom

2.13 Stocks of Reproducible Fixed Assets, by Type of Good and Owner, in Current Prices
(Continued)

Thousand Million Pounds Sterling

		TOTAL Gross	TOTAL Net	Total Private Gross	Total Private Net	Public Enterprises Gross	Public Enterprises Net	General Government Gross	General Government Net
					1985				
1	Residential buildings	516.8	349.5	379.9	248.4	13.6	11.3	123.3	89.8
2	Non-residential buildings								
3	Other construction	534.3	360.8	244.6	159.0	116.5	68.2	172.2	133.5
4	Land improvement and plantation and orchard development								
5	Producers' durable goods	510.1	274.6	377.0	206.9	114.5	56.6	18.6	11.0
	A Transport equipment	71.1	34.4	55.3	28.2	13.7	5.1	2.1	1.0
	B Machinery and equipment	439.0	240.2	321.7	178.7	100.8	51.5	16.5	10.0
6	Breeding stock, dairy cattle, etc.	...	...	...	...	...	...	...	...
	Total [a]	1561.1	984.9	1001.4	614.4	244.6	136.1	314.2	234.4
					1986				
1	Residential buildings	564.2	379.3	422.9	276.0	14.2	11.8	127.0	91.5
2	Non-residential buildings								
3	Other construction	563.6	379.9	276.5	178.9	104.8	61.2	181.3	139.8
4	Land improvement and plantation and orchard development								
5	Producers' durable goods	540.6	290.2	407.6	223.5	113.0	54.8	19.9	11.9
	A Transport equipment	74.3	35.9	58.6	29.8	13.7	5.0	2.0	1.0
	B Machinery and equipment	466.3	254.3	349.0	193.7	99.4	49.7	17.9	10.9
6	Breeding stock, dairy cattle, etc.	...	...	...	...	...	...	...	...
	Total [a]	1668.3	1049.4	1107.0	678.4	232.1	127.7	328.3	243.3
					1987				
1	Residential buildings	631.5	422.0	483.0	314.4	15.2	12.4	133.3	95.1
2	Non-residential buildings								
3	Other construction	595.4	401.1	296.3	191.3	106.3	62.2	191.8	147.5
4	Land improvement and plantation and orchard development								
5	Producers' durable goods	573.1	307.9	438.3	240.6	113.3	54.4	21.5	12.9
	A Transport equipment	79.0	38.2	65.5	33.2	11.2	4.0	2.2	1.1
	B Machinery and equipment	494.1	269.6	372.8	207.4	102.0	50.4	19.3	11.8
6	Breeding stock, dairy cattle, etc.	...	...	...	...	...	...	...	...
	Total [a]	1800.0	1130.9	1217.7	746.3	234.8	129.1	346.6	255.5

a) This table (Stocks of reproducible fixed assets) excludes breeding and producers livestock.

2.14 Stocks of Reproducible Fixed Assets, by Type of Good and Owner, in Constant Prices

Thousand Million Pounds Sterling

		TOTAL Gross	TOTAL Net	Total Private Gross	Total Private Net	Public Enterprises Gross	Public Enterprises Net	General Government Gross	General Government Net
				At constant prices of: 1985					
					1980				
1	Residential buildings	450.5	311.4	313.2	205.2	11.7	10.1	125.6	96.1
2	Non-residential buildings								
3	Other construction	473.5	322.8	204.9	136.1	116.2	68.2	151.5	118.5
4	Land improvement and plantation and orchard development								
5	Producers' durable goods	453.6	256.5	291.4	168.8	146.4	78.1	15.8	9.6
	A Transport equipment	73.4	38.8	54.4	30.9	16.8	6.8	2.2	1.1
	B Machinery and equipment	380.2	217.7	237.0	137.9	129.6	71.2	13.6	8.5
6	Breeding stock, dairy cattle, etc.	...	...	...	...	...	...	...	...
	Total [a]	1377.6	890.7	809.5	510.1	274.3	156.5	292.9	224.1

United Kingdom

2.14 Stocks of Reproducible Fixed Assets, by Type of Good and Owner, in Constant Prices
(Continued)

Thousand Million Pounds Sterling

		TOTAL Gross	TOTAL Net	Total Private Gross	Total Private Net	Public Enterprises Gross	Public Enterprises Net	General Government Gross	General Government Net
		At constant prices of:1985							
		1981							
1	Residential buildings	459.7	316.3	322.6	211.2	12.1	10.4	125.0	94.7
2	Non-residential buildings								
3	Other construction	482.3	327.8	210.7	138.9	116.5	68.6	154.2	120.3
4	Land improvement and plantation and orchard development								
5	Producers' durable goods	461.6	257.5	299.8	171.4	145.7	76.4	16.1	9.6
	A Transport equipment	71.7	37.1	53.4	29.7	16.2	6.4	2.1	1.0
	B Machinery and equipment	389.9	220.4	246.4	141.7	129.5	70.1	14.0	8.6
6	Breeding stock, dairy cattle, etc.	...	...	...	...	...	...	...	...
	Total [a]	1403.6	901.6	833.0	521.6	274.3	155.4	295.4	224.6
		1982							
1	Residential buildings	469.4	321.5	334.3	219.0	12.4	10.6	122.7	91.9
2	Non-residential buildings								
3	Other construction	492.2	333.9	216.4	142.0	117.2	69.0	157.7	122.9
4	Land improvement and plantation and orchard development								
5	Producers' durable goods	469.3	258.3	307.6	173.8	145.3	74.7	16.4	9.7
	A Transport equipment	70.0	35.5	52.6	28.7	15.4	5.8	2.1	1.0
	B Machinery and equipment	399.3	222.8	255.0	145.1	130.0	68.9	14.3	8.7
6	Breeding stock, dairy cattle, etc.	...	...	...	...	...	...	...	...
	Total [a]	1430.8	913.6	858.2	534.9	274.9	154.2	296.8	224.5
		1983							
1	Residential buildings	480.2	327.7	345.6	226.4	12.8	10.8	121.9	90.5
2	Non-residential buildings								
3	Other construction	502.0	339.9	222.4	145.1	117.5	69.4	161.2	125.4
4	Land improvement and plantation and orchard development								
5	Producers' durable goods	477.2	259.6	314.4	175.5	145.9	74.1	17.0	10.0
	A Transport equipment	68.5	34.0	51.7	27.5	14.7	5.5	2.1	1.0
	B Machinery and equipment	408.7	225.6	262.7	148.0	131.2	68.6	14.9	9.0
6	Breeding stock, dairy cattle, etc.	...	...	...	...	...	...	...	...
	Total [a]	1459.4	927.2	882.4	547.1	276.1	154.2	300.0	226.0
		1984							
1	Residential buildings	491.3	334.1	356.6	233.6	13.1	11.0	121.7	89.5
2	Non-residential buildings								
3	Other construction	513.0	347.0	232.5	151.5	114.3	67.0	165.3	128.6
4	Land improvement and plantation and orchard development								
5	Producers' durable goods	487.5	263.2	357.2	196.4	112.8	56.5	17.5	10.4
	A Transport equipment	68.3	33.4	52.4	27.2	13.9	5.2	2.0	1.0
	B Machinery and equipment	419.2	229.9	304.8	169.2	98.9	51.3	15.5	9.4
6	Breeding stock, dairy cattle, etc.	...	...	...	...	...	...	...	...
	Total [a]	1491.8	944.4	946.3	581.5	240.2	134.5	304.4	228.4
		1985							
1	Residential buildings	501.7	339.7	366.9	240.1	13.4	11.1	121.5	88.5
2	Non-residential buildings								
3	Other construction	524.0	354.1	238.5	154.9	115.2	67.5	169.4	131.7
4	Land improvement and plantation and orchard development								
5	Producers' durable goods	499.4	269.0	369.2	202.8	112.1	55.4	18.2	10.8
	A Transport equipment	68.2	33.0	53.0	27.0	13.3	4.9	2.0	1.0
	B Machinery and equipment	431.2	236.1	316.2	175.8	98.8	50.5	16.2	9.8
6	Breeding stock, dairy cattle, etc.	...	...	...	...	...	...	...	...
	Total [a]	1525.2	962.8	974.5	597.9	240.7	134.0	309.1	231.0

United Kingdom

2.14 Stocks of Reproducible Fixed Assets, by Type of Good and Owner, in Constant Prices
(Continued)

Thousand Million Pounds Sterling

	TOTAL Gross	TOTAL Net	Total Private Gross	Total Private Net	Public Enterprises Gross	Public Enterprises Net	General Government Gross	General Government Net
	\multicolumn{8}{c}{At constant prices of: 1985}							
	\multicolumn{8}{c}{1986}							
1 Residential buildings	513.0	346.0	378.0	247.3	13.6	11.2	121.3	87.5
2 Non-residential buildings								
3 Other construction	535.0	361.1	259.4	167.4	101.8	59.3	173.0	134.4
4 Land improvement and plantation and orchard development								
5 Producers' durable goods	508.7	273.8	383.5	211.0	106.3	51.5	18.9	11.3
A Transport equipment	65.8	31.8	51.6	26.3	12.5	4.6	1.8	0.9
B Machinery and equipment	442.9	242.1	331.9	184.7	93.8	47.0	17.1	10.4
6 Breeding stock, dairy cattle, etc.	...	...	...	...	...	...	...	...
Total a	1556.7	980.9	1020.9	625.7	221.7	122.1	313.2	233.1
	\multicolumn{8}{c}{1987}							
1 Residential buildings	524.7	352.6	389.7	254.8	13.8	11.3	121.1	86.4
2 Non-residential buildings								
3 Other construction	546.8	368.7	268.3	172.6	100.5	58.7	177.0	137.4
4 Land improvement and plantation and orchard development								
5 Producers' durable goods	519.9	280.5	397.7	219.4	102.5	49.3	19.7	11.9
A Transport equipment	64.8	31.3	53.4	27.1	9.6	3.4	1.7	0.9
B Machinery and equipment	455.1	249.1	344.3	192.3	92.8	45.9	18.0	11.0
6 Breeding stock, dairy cattle, etc.	...	...	...	...	...	...	...	...
Total a	1591.3	1001.7	1055.8	646.8	216.8	119.3	317.9	235.6

a) This table (Stocks of reproducible fixed assets) excludes breeding and producers livestock.

2.15 Stocks of Reproducible Fixed Assets by Kind of Activity, in Current Prices

Thousand Million Pounds Sterling

	1980 Gross	1980 Net	1981 Gross	1981 Net	1982 Gross	1982 Net	1983 Gross	1983 Net	1984 Gross	1984 Net	1985 Gross	1985 Net
1 Residential buildings	359.8	248.6	389.6	268.1	406.9	278.7	440.7	300.5	479.1	325.8	516.8	349.5
2 Non-residential buildings a	...	...	...	...	...	...	...	...	...	...	...	...
3 Other construction ba	449.2	306.2	474.4	322.5	475.0	322.2	483.2	327.1	504.1	341.0	534.3	360.8
A Industries	385.4	246.2	405.7	258.0	405.2	256.9	411.3	260.0	428.6	270.6	454.7	286.9
1 Agriculture	13.6	8.1	14.2	8.3	14.3	8.3	14.6	8.5	15.6	8.9	16.4	9.2
2 Mining and quarrying c	21.3	13.5	23.6	14.8	24.6	15.3	25.9	16.0	27.7	17.0	29.6	17.9
3 Manufacturing d	75.2	43.0	76.7	43.4	74.9	41.9	75.1	41.4	77.0	42.0	79.7	43.1
4 Electricity, gas and water e	43.6	26.4	46.8	28.1	47.0	28.1	47.8	28.5	49.1	29.1	50.8	30.0
5 Construction	3.2	2.3	3.3	2.3	3.3	2.3	3.3	2.3	3.4	2.3	3.6	2.4
6 Wholesale and retail trade f	34.7	25.8	36.4	27.0	36.6	27.1	37.3	27.6	39.5	29.2	43.4	32.0
7 Transport and communication	45.1	23.2	47.5	24.5	46.8	24.2	46.8	24.4	47.9	25.1	49.4	26.1
8 Finance, etc. g	48.3	36.5	51.2	38.7	52.1	39.4	53.7	40.6	57.0	43.1	62.8	47.4
9 Community, social and personal services	100.4	68.2	106.0	71.7	105.7	71.3	106.7	71.8	111.4	74.8	119.1	79.6
B Producers of government services h	63.8	60.0	68.7	64.5	69.8	65.3	71.9	67.2	75.5	70.4	79.5	73.9
C Other producers	...	...	...	...	...	...	...	...	...	...	...	...
4 Land improvement and development and plantation and orchard development b	...	...	...	...	...	...	...	...	...	...	...	...
5 Producers' durable goods	348.6	197.4	383.2	214.1	414.9	228.7	442.9	241.3	474.6	256.4	510.1	274.6
A Industries	344.4	195.0	378.6	211.5	409.8	225.9	437.5	238.2	468.7	253.0	503.4	270.7
1 Agriculture	11.6	7.0	12.1	7.2	12.8	7.6	13.3	8.0	13.3	7.8	13.5	8.0
2 Mining and quarrying c	12.0	7.5	14.2	8.7	16.5	9.9	18.5	10.8	19.8	11.1	21.0	11.4
3 Manufacturing d	136.6	73.7	149.3	78.9	160.8	83.2	170.1	86.4	180.1	90.4	190.9	95.2
4 Electricity, gas and water e	54.2	30.2	59.3	32.7	63.9	34.8	67.9	36.7	71.9	38.5	75.8	40.1

United Kingdom

2.15 Stocks of Reproducible Fixed Assets by Kind of Activity, in Current Prices
(Continued)

Thousand Million Pounds Sterling

	1980 Gross	1980 Net	1981 Gross	1981 Net	1982 Gross	1982 Net	1983 Gross	1983 Net	1984 Gross	1984 Net	1985 Gross	1985 Net
5 Construction	9.7	5.3	10.5	5.6	11.2	5.8	11.5	5.9	11.9	6.0	12.3	6.1
6 Wholesale and retail trade [f]	28.0	17.0	31.4	18.9	34.6	20.7	37.7	22.3	41.3	24.6	45.8	27.4
7 Transport and communication	55.4	29.2	58.0	30.1	59.3	30.1	61.1	30.5	64.3	31.5	67.5	32.6
8 Finance, etc. [g]	23.0	16.7	28.2	20.2	33.5	23.7	38.7	26.9	45.5	31.2	54.1	37.0
9 Community, social and personal services	13.9	8.3	15.5	9.2	17.3	10.0	18.8	10.9	20.6	11.8	22.5	12.9
B Producers of government services [h]	4.1	2.4	4.5	2.6	5.0	2.8	5.4	3.1	6.0	3.4	6.7	3.9
C Other producers	...	...	...	...	...	...	...	...	...	...	...	...
6 Breeding stock, dairy cattle, etc.	...	...	...	...	...	...	...	...	...	...	...	...
Total	1157.6	752.2	1247.2	804.7	1296.8	829.6	1366.6	868.9	1457.8	923.1	1561.1	984.9

	1986 Gross	1986 Net	1987 Gross	1987 Net
1 Residential buildings	564.2	379.3	631.5	422.0
2 Non-residential buildings [a]	...	...	...	...
3 Other construction [b]	563.6	379.9	595.4	401.1
A Industries	480.4	303.0	507.3	319.9
1 Agriculture	17.0	9.4	17.6	9.5
2 Mining and quarrying [c]	31.1	18.4	32.6	18.8
3 Manufacturing [d]	82.0	44.0	84.7	45.1
4 Electricity, gas and water [e]	52.2	30.7	54.1	31.7
5 Construction	3.7	2.5	3.9	2.6
6 Wholesale and retail trade [f]	47.8	35.3	52.6	39.1
7 Transport and communication	50.6	27.0	52.2	28.0
8 Finance, etc. [g]	69.1	52.1	75.2	56.7
9 Community, social and personal services	126.9	84.6	134.5	89.4
B Producers of government services [h]	83.2	76.9	88.1	81.1
C Other producers	...	...	...	...
4 Land improvement and development and plantation and orchard development [b]	...	...	...	...
5 Producers' durable goods	540.6	290.2	573.1	307.9
A Industries	533.0	285.7	564.7	302.8
1 Agriculture	13.9	8.1	14.0	8.2
2 Mining and quarrying [c]	22.1	11.7	22.5	11.4
3 Manufacturing [d]	200.4	99.4	210.3	104.1
4 Electricity, gas and water [e]	78.8	41.3	82.1	42.7
5 Construction	12.7	6.2	13.0	6.2
6 Wholesale and retail trade [f]	49.9	29.9	54.0	32.5
7 Transport and communication	68.6	33.4	70.7	34.5
8 Finance, etc. [g]	62.2	42.0	72.0	48.4
9 Community, social and personal services	24.4	13.8	26.2	14.8
B Producers of government services [h]	7.5	4.5	8.4	5.0
C Other producers	...	...	...	...
6 Breeding stock, dairy cattle, etc.	...	...	...	...
Total	1668.3	1049.4	1800.0	1130.9

a) Item 'Non-residential buildings' is included in item 'Other construction'.
b) Item 'Land improvement and plantation and orchard development' is included in item 'Other construction'.
c) Item 'Mining and quarrying' refers to coal extraction and manufacture of solid fuels, coke ovens, extraction of mineral oil and natural gas. It excludes mineral mining.
d) Item 'Manufacturing' includes mineral mining, but excludes manufacture of solid fuels and coke ovens.
e) Item 'Electricity, gas and water' includes nuclear fuel production.
f) Item 'Wholesale and retail trade' includes hotels, catering and repairs.
g) Item 'Finance etc.' includes banking, finance, insurance, business services and leasing.
h) Item 'Producers of government services' includes public administration, national defence and compulsory social security. It also includes expenditure on roads.

United Kingdom

2.16 Stocks of Reproducible Fixed Assets by Kind of Activity, in Constant Prices

Thousand Million Pounds Sterling

	1980 Gross	1980 Net	1981 Gross	1981 Net	1982 Gross	1982 Net	1983 Gross	1983 Net	1984 Gross	1984 Net	1985 Gross	1985 Net
	At constant prices of: 1985											
1 Residential buildings	450.5	311.4	459.7	316.3	469.4	321.5	480.2	327.7	491.3	334.1	501.7	339.7
2 Non-residential buildings [a]	...	...	...	...	...	...	...	...	...	...	...	...
3 Other construction [ba]	473.5	322.8	482.3	327.8	492.2	333.9	502.0	339.9	513.0	347.0	524.0	354.1
A Industries	405.1	258.5	412.4	262.2	420.1	266.3	427.7	270.5	436.3	275.6	444.8	280.4
1 Agriculture	14.1	8.4	14.4	8.4	14.8	8.6	15.3	8.8	15.8	9.0	16.1	9.0
2 Mining and quarrying [c]	22.4	14.2	24.1	15.1	25.6	15.9	26.7	16.5	28.1	17.2	29.2	17.7
3 Manufacturing [d]	77.9	44.5	78.0	44.1	78.0	43.6	77.9	42.9	78.0	42.6	78.3	42.4
4 Electricity, gas and water [e]	47.3	28.6	47.8	28.7	48.4	29.0	49.1	29.3	49.7	29.5	50.3	29.7
5 Construction	3.3	2.3	3.4	2.3	3.4	2.3	3.4	2.4	3.5	2.4	3.5	2.4
6 Wholesale and retail trade [f]	35.7	26.6	36.7	27.3	37.8	28.0	39.0	28.8	40.4	29.8	42.0	31.0
7 Transport and communication	48.6	25.0	48.5	25.0	48.4	25.1	48.4	25.2	48.6	25.5	48.7	25.7
8 Finance, etc. [g]	49.7	37.5	51.6	39.0	53.9	40.7	56.2	42.4	58.5	44.2	60.7	45.8
9 Community, social and personal services	106.2	72.2	107.9	73.1	109.7	74.0	111.6	75.0	113.8	76.3	115.9	77.6
B Producers of government services [h]	68.4	64.3	69.9	65.6	72.2	67.5	74.3	69.4	76.7	71.5	79.2	73.7
C Other producers	...	...	...	...	...	...	...	...	...	...	...	...
4 Land improvement and development and plantation and orchard development [b]	...	...	...	...	...	...	...	...	...	...	...	...
5 Producers' durable goods	453.6	256.5	461.6	257.5	469.2	258.2	477.2	259.6	487.5	263.3	499.5	269.0
A Industries	448.4	253.5	456.2	254.5	463.7	255.2	471.4	256.3	481.4	259.7	492.9	265.2
1 Agriculture	14.9	9.1	14.6	8.7	14.2	8.5	13.9	8.3	13.5	8.0	13.0	7.7
2 Mining and quarrying [c]	16.0	10.0	17.3	10.6	18.6	11.1	19.7	11.5	20.3	11.3	20.6	11.1
3 Manufacturing [d]	180.8	97.6	182.2	96.3	183.2	94.8	183.9	93.4	185.2	92.9	186.9	93.3
4 Electricity, gas and water [e]	71.8	40.0	72.2	39.8	72.6	39.6	73.3	39.6	73.8	39.5	74.2	39.3
5 Construction	12.2	6.6	12.2	6.5	12.2	6.3	12.3	6.3	12.2	6.1	12.1	6.0
6 Wholesale and retail trade [f]	36.5	22.2	37.9	22.8	39.4	23.6	40.9	24.3	42.7	25.4	44.6	26.7
7 Transport and communication	71.3	37.8	69.8	36.4	68.0	34.6	66.6	33.3	66.3	32.5	65.9	31.9
8 Finance, etc. [g]	27.2	19.6	31.6	22.6	36.2	25.5	40.6	28.1	46.3	31.7	53.5	36.7
9 Community, social and personal services	17.6	10.5	18.3	10.8	19.2	11.2	20.2	11.7	21.2	12.2	22.1	12.6
B Producers of government services [h]	5.2	3.0	5.4	3.1	5.6	3.1	5.8	3.3	6.1	3.5	6.5	3.8
C Other producers	...	...	...	...	...	...	...	...	...	...	...	...
6 Breeding stock, dairy cattle, etc.	...	...	...	...	...	...	...	...	...	...	...	...
Total	1377.6	890.7	1403.6	901.6	1430.8	913.6	1459.4	927.2	1491.8	944.4	1525.2	962.8

	1986 Gross	1986 Net	1987 Gross	1987 Net
	At constant prices of: 1985			
1 Residential buildings	513.0	346.0	524.7	352.6
2 Non-residential buildings [a]	...	...	...	...
3 Other construction [ba]	535.0	361.1	546.8	368.7
A Industries	453.2	285.1	462.4	290.5
1 Agriculture	16.3	9.0	16.4	8.8
2 Mining and quarrying [c]	30.0	17.7	30.6	17.7
3 Manufacturing [d]	78.5	42.1	78.9	42.0
4 Electricity, gas and water [e]	51.0	30.0	51.6	30.2
5 Construction	3.6	2.4	3.6	2.4
6 Wholesale and retail trade [f]	43.9	32.4	46.3	34.5
7 Transport and communication	48.8	25.9	48.8	26.1
8 Finance, etc. [g]	63.1	47.5	65.7	49.5
9 Community, social and personal services	118.1	78.8	120.4	80.2
B Producers of government services [h]	81.8	76.0	84.4	78.2

United Kingdom

2.16 Stocks of Reproducible Fixed Assets by Kind of Activity, in Constant Prices
(Continued)

Thousand Million Pounds Sterling

	1986 Gross	1986 Net	1987 Gross	1987 Net
			At constant prices of:1985	
C Other producers	...	...	...	...
4 Land improvement and development and plantation and orchard development [b]	...	...	...	...
5 Producers' durable goods	508.7	273.8	519.8	280.5
A Industries	501.6	269.6	512.2	275.8
1 Agriculture	12.5	7.4	11.8	7.0
2 Mining and quarrying [c]	20.9	11.0	20.5	10.4
3 Manufacturing [d]	188.4	93.4	189.7	93.9
4 Electricity, gas and water [e]	74.5	39.1	75.0	39.0
5 Construction	11.9	5.8	11.8	5.7
6 Wholesale and retail trade [f]	46.5	27.9	48.7	29.5
7 Transport and communication	64.0	31.1	63.4	31.0
8 Finance, etc. [g]	59.9	40.8	67.3	45.7
9 Community, social and personal services	23.0	13.0	23.9	13.6
B Producers of government services [h]	7.1	4.3	7.7	4.7
C Other producers	...	...	...	...
6 Breeding stock, dairy cattle, etc.	...	...	...	...
Total	1556.7	980.9	1591.3	1001.7

a) Item 'Non-residential buildings' is included in item 'Other construction'.
b) Item 'Land improvement and plantation and orchard development' is included in item 'Other construction'.
c) Item 'Mining and quarrying' refers to coal extraction and manufacture of solid fuels, coke ovens, extraction of mineral oil and natural gas. It excludes mineral mining.
d) Item 'Manufacturing' includes mineral mining, but excludes manufacture of solid fuels and coke ovens.
e) Item 'Electricity, gas and water' includes nuclear fuel production.
f) Item 'Wholesale and retail trade' includes hotels, catering and repairs.
g) Item 'Finance etc.' includes banking, finance, insurance, business services and leasing.
h) Item 'Producers of government services' includes public administration, national defence and compulsory social security. It also includes expenditure on roads.

2.17 Exports and Imports of Goods and Services, Detail

Million Pounds Sterling

	1970	1975	1978	1979	1980	1981	1982	1983	1984	1985	1986	1987
	\multicolumn{12}{c}{**Exports of Goods and Services**}
1 Exports of merchandise, f.o.b.	8128	19183	34981	40470	47147	50668	55330	60698	70263	77988	72678	79422
2 Transport and communication	2132	4140	5474	6504	7158	7207	6828	6763	7573	7703	7407	8214
A In respect of merchandise imports	415	594	597	707	726	688	643	527	653	581	582	662
B Other [a]	1717	3546	4877	5797	6432	6519	6185	6236	6920	7122	6825	7552
3 Insurance service charges	209	321	704	715	662	919	1020	1199	1372	2239	3200	3246
A In respect of merchandise imports	...	9	14	13	12	18	18	5	11	41	32	30
B Other	...	312	690	702	650	901	1002	1194	1361	2198	3168	3216
4 Other commodities	925	2345	3983	4664	5192	6021	6630	7679	8390	9111	9273	10032
5 Adjustments of merchandise exports to change-of-ownership basis	...	...	...	...	...	...	...	...	...	...	...	...
6 Direct purchases in the domestic market by non-residential households	518	1442	2891	3207	3436	3513	3792	4661	5344	6282	6460	7194
7 Direct purchases in the domestic market by extraterritorial bodies	...	...	...	...	...	...	...	...	...	...	...	...
Total Exports of Goods and Services	11912	27431	48033	55560	63595	68328	73600	81000	92942	103323	99018	108108
	\multicolumn{12}{c}{**Imports of Goods and Services**}
1 Imports of merchandise, c.i.f.	8962	23927	38569	46298	48320	49983	55975	64784	78283	83982	84860	93152
A Imports of merchandise, f.o.b.	8142	22440	36574	43868	45794	47318	53112	61773	74843	80334	81394	89584
B Transport of services on merchandise imports	795	1426	1883	2295	2385	2526	2681	2801	3189	3380	3178	3267
By residents	415	594	597	707	726	688	643	527	653	581	582	662
By non-residents	380	832	1286	1588	1659	1838	2038	2274	2536	2799	2596	2605
C Insurance service charges on merchandise imports	25	61	112	135	141	139	182	210	251	268	288	301
By residents	...	9	14	13	12	18	18	5	11	41	32	30

United Kingdom

2.17 Exports and Imports of Goods and Services, Detail
(Continued)

Million Pounds Sterling

	1970	1975	1978	1979	1980	1981	1982	1983	1984	1985	1986	1987
By non-residents [b]	...	52	98	122	129	121	164	205	240	227	256	271
2 Adjustments of merchandise imports to change-of-ownership basis	...	...	...	...	...	...	...	...	...	...	...	...
3 Other transport and communication [a]	1371	2536	3319	3854	4188	4443	4648	5042	5502	5627	5981	6737
4 Other insurance service charges	...	...	...	...	...	...	...	...	...	...	...	...
5 Other commodities	687	1727	2378	2597	2922	3292	4270	4405	5219	5228	5247	5654
6 Direct purchases abroad by government	...	...	...	...	...	...	...	...	...	...	...	...
7 Direct purchases abroad by resident households	420	1009	1592	2079	2648	3131	3483	3855	4275	4540	5651	6668
Total Imports of Goods and Services	11440	29199	45858	54828	58078	60849	68376	78086	93279	99377	101739	112211
Balance of Goods and Services	472	-1768	2175	732	5517	7479	5224	2914	-337	3946	-2721	-4103
Total Imports and Balance of Goods and Services	11912	27431	48033	55560	63595	68328	73600	81000	92942	103323	99018	108108

a) Other transport and communication includes telecommunications and postal services.
b) Insurance service charges on merchandise imports by non-residents comprises both claims and insurance service charges on imports paid to overseas residents.

3.11 General Government Production Account: Total and Subsectors

Million Pounds Sterling

	1980					1981				
	Total General Government	Central Government	State or Provincial Government	Local Government	Social Security Funds	Total General Government	Central Government	State or Provincial Government	Local Government	Social Security Funds

Gross Output

1 Sales	...	...		...	...	...	...		...	...
2 Services produced for own use	56018	31453	...	23956	609	63706	35745	...	27227	734
3 Own account fixed capital formation	452	145	...	307	...	430	163	...	267	...
Gross Output	56470	31598	...	24263	609	64136	35908	...	27494	734

Gross Input

Intermediate Consumption	20684	15080	...	5290	314	22648	17224	...	5046	378
Subtotal: Value Added	35786	16518	...	18973	295	41488	18684	...	22448	356
1 Indirect taxes, net	-388	513	...	-907	6	464	614	...	-158	8
A Indirect taxes	2469	556	...	1907	6	2972	666	...	2298	8
B Less: Subsidies	2857	43	...	2814	...	2508	52	...	2456	...
2 Consumption of fixed capital	3098	713	...	2385	...	3494	805	...	2689	...
3 Compensation of employees	31160	15322	...	15549	289	35500	17245	...	17907	348
A To residents	30902	15064	...	15549	289	35242	16987	...	17907	348
B To the rest of the world	258	258	...	...	...	258	258	...	...	...
4 Net Operating surplus	1916	-30	...	1946	...	2030	20	...	2010	...
Gross Input	56470	31598	...	24263	609	64136	35908	...	27494	734

	1982					1983				
	Total General Government	Central Government	State or Provincial Government	Local Government	Social Security Funds	Total General Government	Central Government	State or Provincial Government	Local Government	Social Security Funds

Gross Output

1 Sales	...	...		...	...	...	...		...	...
2 Services produced for own use	70079	39278	...	30037	764	75978	43133	...	32083	762
3 Own account fixed capital formation	493	199	...	294	...	562	218	...	344	...
Gross Output	70572	39477	...	30331	764	76540	43351	...	32427	762

Gross Input

Intermediate Consumption	25929	19729	...	5810	390	29191	22090	...	6720	381
Subtotal: Value Added	44643	19748	...	24521	374	47349	21261	...	25707	381
1 Indirect taxes, net	1199	605	...	587	7	860	467	...	388	5
A Indirect taxes	3322	659	...	2656	7	2874	522	...	2347	5
B Less: Subsidies	2123	54	...	2069	...	2014	55	...	1959	...
2 Consumption of fixed capital	3546	847	...	2699	...	3640	887	...	2753	...
3 Compensation of employees	37972	18381	...	19224	367	41434	20155	...	20903	376
A To residents	37674	18083	...	19224	367	41112	19833	...	20903	376
B To the rest of the world	298	298	...	...	...	322	322	...	...	...
4 Net Operating surplus	1926	-85	...	2011	...	1415	-248	...	1663	...
Gross Input	70572	39477	...	30331	764	76540	43351	...	32427	762

United Kingdom

3.11 General Government Production Account: Total and Subsectors

Million Pounds Sterling

	1984 Total General Government	Central Government	State or Provincial Government	Local Government	Social Security Funds	1985 Total General Government	Central Government	State or Provincial Government	Local Government	Social Security Funds
Gross Output										
1 Sales	...	...	...	...	...	...	...	...	...	...
2 Services produced for own use	80208	45458	...	33999	751	84434	47653	...	35851	930
3 Own account fixed capital formation	562	194	...	368	...	568	208	...	360	...
Gross Output	80770	45652	...	34367	751	85002	47861	...	36211	930
Gross Input										
Intermediate Consumption	31162	23827	...	6962	373	31898	24292	...	7125	481
Subtotal: Value Added	49608	21825	...	27405	378	53104	23569	...	29086	449
1 Indirect taxes, net	796	361	...	432	3	880	311	...	569	-
A Indirect taxes	2791	427	...	2361	3	2746	376	...	2370	-
B Less: Subsidies	1995	66	...	1929	...	1866	65	...	1801	...
2 Consumption of fixed capital	3834	935	...	2899	...	4078	1022	...	3057	...
3 Compensation of employees	43828	20971	...	22482	375	46474	22330	...	23695	449
A To residents	43478	20621	...	22482	375	46089	21945	...	23695	449
B To the rest of the world	350	350	...	...	...	385	385	...	...	...
4 Net Operating surplus	1150	-442	...	1592	...	1671	-94	...	1765	...
Gross Input	80770	45652	...	34367	751	85002	47861	...	36211	930

	1986 Total General Government	Central Government	State or Provincial Government	Local Government	Social Security Funds	1987 Total General Government	Central Government	State or Provincial Government	Local Government	Social Security Funds
Gross Output										
1 Sales	...	...	...	...	...	...	...	...	...	...
2 Services produced for own use	89866	50625	...	38466	775	96638	53702	...	42106	830
3 Own account fixed capital formation	687	302	...	385	...	829	420	...	409	...
Gross Output	90553	50927	...	38851	775	97467	54122	...	42515	830
Gross Input										
Intermediate Consumption	33697	25808	...	7492	397	37426	28764	...	8248	414
Subtotal: Value Added	56857	25119	...	31359	378	60041	25358	...	34267	416
1 Indirect taxes, net	1404	342	...	1062	-	1922	351	...	1571	-
A Indirect taxes	3074	410	...	2664	-	3353	421	...	2932	-
B Less: Subsidies	1670	68	...	1602	...	1432	70	...	1361	...
2 Consumption of fixed capital	4360	1124	...	3236	...	4617	1221	...	3396	...
3 Compensation of employees	49626	23842	...	25406	378	52402	24188	...	27798	416
A To residents	49196	23412	...	25406	378	51917	23703	...	27798	416
B To the rest of the world	430	430	...	...	...	485	485	...	...	...
4 Net Operating surplus	1464	-189	...	1653	...	1100	-402	...	1502	...
Gross Input	90553	50927	...	38851	775	97467	54122	...	42515	830

3.12 General Government Income and Outlay Account: Total and Subsectors

Million Pounds Sterling

	1980 Total General Government	Central Government	State or Provincial Government	Local Government	Social Security Funds	1981 Total General Government	Central Government	State or Provincial Government	Local Government	Social Security Funds
Receipts										
1 Operating surplus	1916	-30	...	1946	...	2030	21	...	2010	...
2 Property and entrepreneurial income	5122	6027	...	707	626	5833	6896	...	738	617
A Withdrawals from public quasi-corporations	...	...	...	...	...	...	...	...	...	...
B Interest [a]	3800	4705	...	707	626	4294	5357	...	738	617
C Dividends	166	166	...	...	...	177	177	...	...	...
D Net land rent and royalties	1156	1156	...	...	...	1362	1362	...	...	...
3 Taxes, fees and contributions	82346	60141	...	8261	13944	95698	69581	...	10194	15923
A Indirect taxes	35803	27542	...	8261	...	41809	31615	...	10194	...
B Direct taxes	32411	32411	...	...	...	37768	37768	...	...	...
Income	31685	31685	...	...	...	36928	36928	...	...	...
Other	726	726	...	...	...	840	840	...	...	...
C Social security contributions	13944	...	...	...	13944	15923	...	...	...	15923
D Fees, fines and penalties	188	188	...	...	...	198	198	...	...	...

United Kingdom

3.12 General Government Income and Outlay Account: Total and Subsectors
(Continued)

Million Pounds Sterling

	1980					1981				
	Total General Government	Central Government	State or Provincial Government	Local Government	Social Security Funds	Total General Government	Central Government	State or Provincial Government	Local Government	Social Security Funds
4 Other current transfers	3214	3055	...	14391	2803	3879	3793	...	16574	2989
A Casualty insurance claims	...	...	...	...	...	...	...	...	...	...
B Transfers from other government subsectors	...	1034	...	13233	2768	...	1333	...	15201	2943
C Transfers from the rest of the world	...	...	...	...	...	...	...	...	...	...
D Other transfers, except imputed	...	...	...	...	...	...	...	...	...	...
E Imputed unfunded employee pension and welfare contributions	3214	2021	...	1158	35	3879	2460	...	1373	46
Total Current Receipts [a]	92598	69193	...	25305	17373	107440	80290	...	29516	19529

Disbursements

1 Government final consumption expenditure	49041	29403	...	19029	609	55478	33171	...	21573	734
2 Property income	10873	8890	...	4233	-	12702	10738	...	4397	1
A interest	10873	8890	...	4233	...	12702	10738	...	4397	...
B Net land rent and royalties	...	...	...	...	...	...	...	...	...	...
3 Subsidies	5773	4674	...	1099	...	6553	5355	...	1198	...
4 Other current transfers	29727	28999	...	1890	15873	35994	34013	...	2220	19238
A Casualty insurance premiums, net	...	...	...	...	...	...	...	...	...	...
B Transfers to other government subsectors	...	16001	...	...	1034	...	18144	...	...	1333
C Social security benefits	14804	...	...	...	14804	17859	...	...	...	17859
D Social assistance grants	9313	8213	...	1100	...	11847	10716	...	1131	...
E Unfunded employee pension and welfare benefits	2419	1599	...	785	35	3139	2015	...	1078	46
F Transfers to private non-profit institutions serving households	1545	1540	...	5	...	1751	1740	...	11	...
G Other transfers n.e.c.	...	...	...	...	...	...	...	...	...	...
H Transfers to the rest of the world	1646	1646	...	...	...	1398	1398	...	...	...
Statistical discrepancy	795	422	...	373	...	740	445	...	295	...
Net saving	-3623	-3195	...	-1319	891	-4043	-3432	...	-167	-444
Total Current Disbursements and Net Saving	92598	69193	...	25305	17373	107440	80290	...	29516	19529

	1982					1983				
	Total General Government	Central Government	State or Provincial Government	Local Government	Social Security Funds	Total General Government	Central Government	State or Provincial Government	Local Government	Social Security Funds

Receipts

1 Operating surplus	1926	-85	...	2011	...	1415	-248	...	1663	...
2 Property and entrepreneurial income	6884	7840	...	818	511	6969	8253	...	745	462
A Withdrawals from public quasi-corporations	...	...	...	...	...	...	...	...	...	...
B Interest [a]	5026	5982	...	818	511	4777	6061	...	745	462
C Dividends	258	258	...	...	...	305	305	...	...	...
D Net land rent and royalties	1600	1600	...	...	...	1887	1887	...	...	...
3 Taxes, fees and contributions	106238	76402	...	11732	18104	115080	82068	...	12219	20793
A Indirect taxes	45637	33905	...	11732	...	48411	36192	...	12219	...
B Direct taxes	42286	42286	...	...	...	45627	45627	...	...	...
Income	41264	41264	...	...	...	44444	44443	...	...	...
Other	1022	1022	...	...	...	1184	1184	...	...	...
C Social security contributions	18104	...	...	...	18104	20793	...	...	...	20793
D Fees, fines and penalties	211	211	...	...	...	249	249	...	...	...

United Kingdom

3.12 General Government Income and Outlay Account: Total and Subsectors
(Continued)

Million Pounds Sterling

	1982					1983				
	Total General Government	Central Government	State or Provincial Government	Local Government	Social Security Funds	Total General Government	Central Government	State or Provincial Government	Local Government	Social Security Funds
4 Other current transfers	4301	4303	...	17720	2309	4698	4735	...	20355	2840
A Casualty insurance claims	...	...	...	...	...	...	...	...	...	...
B Transfers from other government subsectors	...	1582	...	16190	2259	...	1741	...	18702	2789
C Transfers from the rest of the world	...	...	...	...	...	...	...	...	...	...
D Other transfers, except imputed	...	...	...	...	...	...	...	...	...	...
E Imputed unfunded employee pension and welfare contributions	4301	2721	...	1530	50	4698	2994	...	1653	51
Total Current Receipts [a]	119349	88460	...	32281	20924	128162	94808	...	34982	24095

Disbursements

	Total General Government	Central Government	State or Provincial Government	Local Government	Social Security Funds	Total General Government	Central Government	State or Provincial Government	Local Government	Social Security Funds
1 Government final consumption expenditure	60470	36266	...	23440	764	65900	39926	...	25212	762
2 Property income	13973	11902	...	4321	27	14189	12698	...	3939	28
A Interest	13973	11902	...	4321	...	14189	12698	...	3939	...
B Net land rent and royalties	...	...	...	...	...	...	...	...	...	...
3 Subsidies	6003	4578	...	1425	...	6404	4879	...	1525	...
4 Other current transfers	41964	38504	...	2511	20980	45730	41850	...	4500	22612
A Casualty insurance premiums, net	...	...	...	...	...	...	...	...	...	...
B Transfers to other government subsectors	...	18449	...	...	1582	...	21491	...	...	1741
C Social security benefits	19348	...	...	...	19348	20820	...	...	...	20820
D Social assistance grants	15494	14208	...	1286	...	16981	13810	...	3171	...
E Unfunded employee pension and welfare benefits	3583	2318	...	1215	50	3943	2573	...	1319	51
F Transfers to private non-profit institutions serving households	1974	1964	...	10	...	2322	2312	...	10	...
G Other transfers n.e.c.	...	...	...	...	...	...	...	...	...	...
H Transfers to the rest of the world	1565	1565	...	...	...	1664	1664	...	...	...
Statistical discrepancy	720	403	...	315	...	755	421	...	334	...
Net saving	-3771	-3193	...	269	-847	-4801	-4966	...	-528	693
Total Current Disbursements and Net Saving	119349	88460	...	32281	20924	128162	94808	...	34982	24095

	1984					1985				
	Total General Government	Central Government	State or Provincial Government	Local Government	Social Security Funds	Total General Government	Central Government	State or Provincial Government	Local Government	Social Security Funds

Receipts

1 Operating surplus	1150	-442	...	1592	...	1671	-94	...	1765	...
2 Property and entrepreneurial income	7588	9267	...	694	482	8658	10575	...	765	538
A Withdrawals from public quasi-corporations	...	...	...	...	...	...	...	...	...	...
B Interest [a]	4812	6491	...	694	482	5680	7597	...	765	538
C Dividends	317	317	...	...	...	612	612	...	...	...
D Net land rent and royalties	2459	2459	...	...	...	2366	2366	...	...	...
3 Taxes, fees and contributions	123092	87989	...	12776	22327	134247	96391	...	13649	24207
A Indirect taxes	51437	38661	...	12776	...	55340	41691	...	13649	...
B Direct taxes	49083	49083	...	...	...	54442	54442	...	...	...
Income	47794	47794	...	...	...	52960	52960	...	...	...
Other	1289	1289	...	...	...	1482	1482	...	...	...
C Social security contributions	22327	...	...	...	22327	24207	...	...	...	24207
D Fees, fines and penalties	245	245	...	...	...	258	258	...	...	...

United Kingdom

3.12 General Government Income and Outlay Account: Total and Subsectors
(Continued)

Million Pounds Sterling

	1984					1985				
	Total General Government	Central Government	State or Provincial Government	Local Government	Social Security Funds	Total General Government	Central Government	State or Provincial Government	Local Government	Social Security Funds
4 Other current transfers	5101	5042	...	22081	2773	5401	5417	...	22422	2507
A Casualty insurance claims	...	...	...	...	...	...	...	...	...	...
B Transfers from other government subsectors	...	1844	...	20231	2720	...	2015	...	20486	2444
C Transfers from the rest of the world	...	...	...	...	...	...	...	...	...	...
D Other transfers, except imputed	...	...	...	...	...	...	...	...	...	...
E Imputed unfunded employee pension and welfare contributions	5101	3198	...	1850	53	5401	3402	...	1936	63
Total Current Receipts [a]	136931	101856	...	37143	25582	149977	112289	...	38601	27252

Disbursements

1 Government final consumption expenditure	69912	42442	...	26719	751	74024	45075	...	28019	930
2 Property income	15756	14585	...	4009	18	17474	16286	...	4420	4
A Interest	15756	14585	...	4009	...	17474	16286	...	4420	...
B Net land rent and royalties	...	...	...	...	...	...	...	...	...	...
3 Subsidies	7679	6182	...	1497	...	7300	6036	...	1264	...
4 Other current transfers	49402	45011	...	5345	23841	54698	48432	...	5732	25479
A Casualty insurance premiums, net	...	...	...	...	...	...	...	...	...	...
B Transfers to other government subsectors	...	22951	...	...	1844	...	22930	...	...	2015
C Social security benefits	21944	...	...	...	21944	23401	...	...	...	23401
D Social assistance grants	18900	15174	...	3726	...	20968	16918	...	4050	...
E Unfunded employee pension and welfare benefits	4259	2597	...	1609	53	4593	2858	...	1672	63
F Transfers to private non-profit institutions serving households	2511	2501	...	10	...	2753	2743	...	10	...
G Other transfers n.e.c.	...	...	...	...	...	...	...	...	...	...
H Transfers to the rest of the world	1788	1788	...	...	...	2983	2983	...	...	...
Statistical discrepancy	842	601	...	241	...	808	544	...	264	...
Net saving	-6661	-6965	...	-668	972	-4343	-4084	...	-1098	839
Total Current Disbursements and Net Saving	136931	101856	...	37143	25582	149977	112289	...	38601	27252

	1986					1987				
	Total General Government	Central Government	State or Provincial Government	Local Government	Social Security Funds	Total General Government	Central Government	State or Provincial Government	Local Government	Social Security Funds

Receipts

1 Operating surplus	1464	-189	...	1653	...	1100	-402	...	1502	...
2 Property and entrepreneurial income	6852	9192	...	852	577	7029	9666	...	1046	555
A Withdrawals from public quasi-corporations	...	...	...	...	...	...	...	...	...	...
B Interest [a]	5178	7518	...	852	577	5144	7781	...	1046	555
C Dividends	733	733	...	...	...	734	734	...	...	...
D Net land rent and royalties	941	941	...	...	...	1151	1151	...	...	...
3 Taxes, fees and contributions	143267	101975	...	15244	26048	155034	109922	...	16648	28464
A Indirect taxes	61289	46045	...	15244	...	66677	50029	...	16648	...
B Direct taxes	55636	55636	...	...	...	59544	59544	...	...	...
Income	54072	54072	...	...	...	57904	57904	...	...	...
Other	1564	1564	...	...	...	1640	1640	...	...	...
C Social security contributions	26048	...	...	...	26048	28464	...	...	...	28464
D Fees, fines and penalties	294	294	...	...	...	349	349	...	...	...

United Kingdom

3.12 General Government Income and Outlay Account: Total and Subsectors
(Continued)

Million Pounds Sterling

	1986					1987				
	Total General Government	Central Government	State or Provincial Government	Local Government	Social Security Funds	Total General Government	Central Government	State or Provincial Government	Local Government	Social Security Funds
4 Other current transfers	5869	5877	...	23822	2342	6265	6636	...	25577	2273
A Casualty insurance claims	...	...	...	...	...	...	...	...	...	...
B Transfers from other government subsectors	...	2221	...	21663	2288	...	2713	...	23297	2211
C Transfers from the rest of the world	...	...	...	...	...	...	...	...	...	...
D Other transfers, except imputed	...	...	...	...	...	...	...	...	...	...
E Imputed unfunded employee pension and welfare contributions	5869	3656	...	2159	54	6265	3923	...	2280	62
Total Current Receipts [a]	157452	116857	...	41571	28967	169428	125822	...	44773	31292
Disbursements											
1 Government final consumption expenditure	79717	48346	...	30598	775	85804	50891	...	34083	830
2 Property income	17191	16587	...	4394	-	17667	17546	...	4378	-
A Interest	17191	16587	...	4394	...	17667	17546	...	4378	...
B Net land rent and royalties	...	...	...	...	...	...	...	...	...	...
3 Subsidies	6261	5182	...	1079	...	6099	5281	...	818	...
4 Other current transfers	57906	49944	...	6135	27999	60937	53630	...	6538	28990
A Casualty insurance premiums, net	...	...	...	...	...	...	...	...	...	...
B Transfers to other government subsectors	...	23951	...	...	2221	...	25508	...	...	2713
C Social security benefits	25724	...	...	...	25724	26215	...	...	...	26215
D Social assistance grants	22312	18093	...	4219	...	23285	18676	...	4609	...
E Unfunded employee pension and welfare benefits	4929	2969	...	1906	54	5157	3176	...	1919	62
F Transfers to private non-profit institutions serving households	3098	3086	...	10	...	3417	3407	...	10	...
G Other transfers n.e.c.	...	...	...	...	...	...	...	...	...	...
H Transfers to the rest of the world	1843	1843	...	...	...	2863	2863	...	...	...
Statistical discrepancy	940	687	...	253	...	1108	747	...	361	...
Net saving	-4582	-3889	...	-886	193	-2206	-2273	...	-1405	1472
Total Current Disbursements and Net Saving	157452	116857	...	41571	28967	169428	125822	...	44773	31292

a) Part of the receipts/payments of interests refers to receipts from/payments to subsectors of government. These are not included in the total for general government.

3.13 General Government Capital Accumulation Account: Total and Subsectors

Million Pounds Sterling

	1980					1981				
	Total General Government	Central Government	State or Provincial Government	Local Government	Social Security Funds	Total General Government	Central Government	State or Provincial Government	Local Government	Social Security Funds
Finance of Gross Accumulation											
1 Gross saving	-525	-2482	...	1066	891	-549	-2627	...	2522	-444
A Consumption of fixed capital	3098	713	...	2385	-	3494	805	...	2689	-
B Net saving	-3623	-3195	...	-1319	891	-4043	-3432	...	-167	-444
2 Capital transfers	494	451	...	338	...	780	745	...	352	...
A From other government subsectors	...	...	...	295	...	...	...	...	317	...
B From other resident sectors [a]	494	451	...	43	...	780	745	...	35	...
C From rest of the world	...	...	...	...	...	...	...	...	...	...
Finance of Gross Accumulation	-31	-2031	...	1404	891	231	-1882	...	2874	-444
Gross Accumulation											
1 Gross capital formation	5542	1800	...	3742	...	4485	1770	...	2715	...
A Increase in stocks	43	43	...	...	...	-93	-93	...	...	...
B Gross fixed capital formation	5499	1757	...	3742	...	4578	1863	...	2715	...

United Kingdom

3.13 General Government Capital Accumulation Account: Total and Subsectors
(Continued)

Million Pounds Sterling

	1980					1981				
	Total General Government	Central Government	State or Provincial Government	Local Government	Social Security Funds	Total General Government	Central Government	State or Provincial Government	Local Government	Social Security Funds
2 Purchases of land, net	...	...	...	...	...	...	...	...	...	...
3 Purchases of intangible assets, net	...	...	...	...	...	...	...	...	...	...
4 Capital transfers	2453	2490	...	258	...	5881	5888	...	310	...
A To other government subsectors	...	295	...	...	...	...	317	...	...	...
B To other resident sectors	2453	2195	...	258	...	5881	5571	...	310	...
C To rest of the world	...	-	...	...	...	...	-	...	...	...
Net lending	-8026	-6321	...	-2596	891	-10135	-9540	...	-151	-444
Gross Accumulation	-31	-2031	...	1404	891	231	-1882	...	2874	-444

	1982					1983				
	Total General Government	Central Government	State or Provincial Government	Local Government	Social Security Funds	Total General Government	Central Government	State or Provincial Government	Local Government	Social Security Funds

Finance of Gross Accumulation

1 Gross saving	-225	-2346	...	2968	-847	-1161	-4079	...	2225	693
A Consumption of fixed capital	3546	847	...	2699	-	3642	887	...	2753	-
B Net saving	-3771	-3193	...	269	-847	-4801	-4966	...	-528	693
2 Capital transfers	664	623	...	369	...	616	573	...	358	...
A From other government subsectors	...	...	...	328	...	...	...	...	316	...
B From other resident sectors [a]	664	623	...	41	...	616	573	...	42	...
C From rest of the world	...	...	...	...	...	...	...	...	...	...
Finance of Gross Accumulation	440	-1723	...	3338	-847	-546	-3506	...	2583	693

Gross Accumulation

1 Gross capital formation	4420	2329	...	2091	...	5953	2736	...	3217	...
A Increase in stocks	105	105	...	...	...	246	246	...	...	...
B Gross fixed capital formation	4315	2224	...	2091	...	5707	2490	...	3217	...
2 Purchases of land, net	...	...	...	...	...	...	...	...	...	...
3 Purchases of intangible assets, net	...	...	...	...	...	...	...	...	...	...
4 Capital transfers	3882	3666	...	544	...	3590	2773	...	1133	...
A To other government subsectors	...	328	...	...	...	...	316	...	...	...
B To other resident sectors	3882	3338	...	544	...	3590	2457	...	1133	...
C To rest of the world	...	-	...	...	...	...	-	...	...	...
Net lending	-7912	-7768	...	703	-847	-10089	-9015	...	-1767	693
Gross Accumulation	440	-1723	...	3338	-847	-546	-3506	...	2583	693

	1984					1985				
	Total General Government	Central Government	State or Provincial Government	Local Government	Social Security Funds	Total General Government	Central Government	State or Provincial Government	Local Government	Social Security Funds

Finance of Gross Accumulation

1 Gross saving	-2827	-6030	...	2231	972	-264	-3062	...	1959	839
A Consumption of fixed capital	3835	935	...	2899	-	4079	1022	...	3057	-
B Net saving	-6661	-6965	...	-668	972	-4343	-4084	...	-1098	839
2 Capital transfers	709	664	...	385	...	929	877	...	688	...
A From other government subsectors	...	...	...	340	...	...	...	...	637	...
B From other resident sectors [a]	709	664	...	45	...	929	877	...	51	...
C From rest of the world	...	...	...	...	...	...	...	...	...	...
Finance of Gross Accumulation	-2118	-5366	...	2616	972	664	-2185	...	2647	839

Gross Accumulation

1 Gross capital formation	6773	2998	...	3775	...	7034	3565	...	3469	...
A Increase in stocks	280	280	...	...	...	450	450	...	...	...
B Gross fixed capital formation	6493	2718	...	3775	...	6584	3115	...	3469	...

United Kingdom

3.13 General Government Capital Accumulation Account: Total and Subsectors
(Continued)

Million Pounds Sterling

	1984					1985				
	Total General Government	Central Government	State or Provincial Government	Local Government	Social Security Funds	Total General Government	Central Government	State or Provincial Government	Local Government	Social Security Funds
2 Purchases of land, net	...	...	...	...	...	...	...	...	...	...
3 Purchases of intangible assets, net	...	...	...	...	...	...	...	...	...	...
4 Capital transfers	3838	2842	...	1336	...	3319	3185	...	771	...
A To other government subsectors	...	340	...	...	...	...	637	...	...	...
B To other resident sectors	3838	2502	...	1336	...	3319	2548	...	771	...
C To rest of the world	...	-	...	...	...	...	-	...	...	...
Net lending	-12729	-11206	...	-2495	972	-9689	-8935	...	-1593	839
Gross Accumulation	-2118	-5366	...	2616	972	664	-2185	...	2647	839

	1986					1987				
	Total General Government	Central Government	State or Provincial Government	Local Government	Social Security Funds	Total General Government	Central Government	State or Provincial Government	Local Government	Social Security Funds

Finance of Gross Accumulation

1 Gross saving	-222	-2765	...	2350	193	2411	-1052	...	1991	1472
A Consumption of fixed capital	4360	1124	...	3236	-	4617	1221	...	3396	-
B Net saving	-4582	-3889	...	-886	193	-2206	-2273	...	-1405	1472
2 Capital transfers	1029	976	...	871	...	1112	1058	...	958	...
A From other government subsectors	...	...	...	818	...	...	...	...	904	...
B From other resident sectors a	1029	976	...	53	...	1112	1058	...	54	...
C From rest of the world	...	...	...	...	...	...	...	...	...	...
Finance of Gross Accumulation	807	-1789	...	3221	193	3523	6	...	2949	1472

Gross Accumulation

1 Gross capital formation	6770	3080	...	3690	...	6299	2702	...	3597	...
A Increase in stocks	-237	-237	...	...	...	-612	-612	...	...	...
B Gross fixed capital formation	7007	3317	...	3690	...	6911	3314	...	3597	...
2 Purchases of land, net	...	...	...	...	...	...	...	...	...	...
3 Purchases of intangible assets, net	...	...	...	...	...	...	...	...	...	...
4 Capital transfers	4743	4964	...	597	...	3104	3434	...	574	...
A To other government subsectors	...	818	...	...	...	...	904	...	...	...
B To other resident sectors	4743	4146	...	597	...	3104	2530	...	574	...
C To rest of the world	...	-	...	...	...	...	-	...	...	...
Net lending	-10706	-9833	...	-1066	193	-5880	-6130	...	-1222	1472
Gross Accumulation	807	-1789	...	3221	193	3523	6	...	2949	1472

a) Capital transfers from other resident sectors includes capital taxes and other capital receipts.

3.14 General Government Capital Finance Account, Total and Subsectors

Million Pounds Sterling

	1980					1981				
	Total General Government	Central Government	State or Provincial Government	Local Government	Social Security Funds	Total General Government	Central Government	State or Provincial Government	Local Government	Social Security Funds

Acquisition of Financial Assets

1 Gold and SDRs	...	...	...	...	...	...	...	...	...	...
2 Currency and transferable deposits	489	474	...	15	...	-2500	-2550	...	50	...
3 Other deposits	-110	-142	...	32	...	-124	-189	...	65	...
4 Bills and bonds, short term	403	403	...	-	...	2559	2559	...	-	...
A Corporate and quasi-corporate enterprises, resident	403	403	...	-	...	2559	2559	...	-	...
B Other government subsectors	...	...	...	...	...	...	...	...	...	...
C Rest of the world	...	...	...	...	...	...	...	...	...	...
5 Bonds, long term	12	8	...	4	...	8	-6	...	14	...
A Corporations	...	...	...	...	...	...	...	...	...	...
B Other government subsectors	12	8	...	4	...	8	-6	...	14	...
C Rest of the world	...	...	...	...	...	...	...	...	...	...
6 Corporate equity securities	152	148	...	4	...	1664	1649	...	15	...
7 Short-term loans, n.e.c.	-147	-562	...	33	382	-2006	-482	...	9	-1533
8 Long-term loans, n.e.c.	4835	4430	...	405	...	-2569	-2787	...	218	...
A Mortgages	456	...	...	456	...	271	...	...	271	...

United Kingdom

3.14 General Government Capital Finance Account, Total and Subsectors
(Continued)

Million Pounds Sterling

	1980					1981				
	Total General Government	Central Government	State or Provincial Government	Local Government	Social Security Funds	Total General Government	Central Government	State or Provincial Government	Local Government	Social Security Funds
B Other	4379	4430	...	-51	...	-2840	-2787	...	-53	...
9 Other receivables	1328	1098	...	-279	509	3471	2708	...	-326	1089
10 Other assets	9	9	...	...	...	-7	-7	...	...	...
Total Acquisition of Financial Assets	6971	5866	...	214	891	496	895	...	45	-444

Incurrence of Liabilities

1 Currency and transferable deposits	266	266	...	...	...	527	527	...	...	...
2 Other deposits	1635	1738	...	-103	...	4138	4375	...	-237	...
3 Bills and bonds, short term	546	276	...	270	...	-986	-1160	...	174	...
4 Bonds, long term	10541	10678	...	-137	...	7958	8135	...	-177	...
5 Short-term loans, n.e.c.	285	-441	...	726	...	-202	-1787	...	1584	...
6 Long-term loans, n.e.c.	1268	-991	...	2259	...	-2179	-1229	...	-950	...
7 Other payables	-17	-154	...	137	...	359	132	...	227	...
8 Other liabilities	667	667	...	...	...	1405	1405	...	...	...
Total Incurrence of Liabilities	15191	12039	...	3152	...	11020	10399	...	621	...
Statistical discrepancy [a]	-194	148	...	-342	...	-389	36	...	-425	...
Net Lending	-8026	-6321	...	-2596	891	-10135	-9540	...	-151	-444
Incurrence of Liabilities and Net Worth	6971	5866	...	214	891	496	895	...	45	-444

	1982					1983				
	Total General Government	Central Government	State or Provincial Government	Local Government	Social Security Funds	Total General Government	Central Government	State or Provincial Government	Local Government	Social Security Funds

Acquisition of Financial Assets

1 Gold and SDRs	...	...	...	...	...	...	...	...	...	...
2 Currency and transferable deposits	-1416	-1497	...	81	...	-533	-577	...	44	...
3 Other deposits	714	300	...	414	...	-45	-52	...	7	...
4 Bills and bonds, short term	4714	4714	...	-	...	-725	-725	...	-	...
A Corporate and quasi-corporate enterprises, resident	4714	4714	...	-	...	-725	-725	...	-	...
B Other government subsectors	...	...	...	...	...	...	...	...	...	...
C Rest of the world	...	...	...	...	...	...	...	...	...	...
5 Bonds, long term	-240	-242	...	2	...	134	116	...	18	...
A Corporations	...	...	...	...	...	...	...	...	...	...
B Other government subsectors	-240	-242	...	2	...	134	116	...	18	...
C Rest of the world	...	...	...	...	...	...	...	...	...	...
6 Corporate equity securities	-11	-60	...	49	...	-490	-505	...	15	...
7 Short-term loans, n.e.c.	-62	-484	...	-13	435	-350	-250	...	-1	-99
8 Long-term loans, n.e.c.	3387	2996	...	391	...	5135	5507	...	-372	...
A Mortgages	555	...	...	555	...	-306	...	...	-306	...
B Other	2832	2996	...	-164	...	5441	5507	...	-66	...
9 Other receivables	-1725	135	...	-578	-1282	1899	976	...	131	792
10 Other assets	-10	-10	...	...	...	-8	-8	...	...	...
Total Acquisition of Financial Assets	5351	5852	...	346	-847	5017	4482	...	-158	693

Incurrence of Liabilities

1 Currency and transferable deposits	300	300	...	...	...	787	786	...	...	...
2 Other deposits	3993	4995	...	-1002	...	3251	3262	...	-11	...
3 Bills and bonds, short term	-758	-323	...	-435	...	241	142	...	99	...
4 Bonds, long term	6290	6457	...	-167	...	9254	9490	...	-236	...
5 Short-term loans, n.e.c.	1015	521	...	494	...	-1109	-189	...	-920	...
6 Long-term loans, n.e.c.	822	29	...	793	...	1520	-844	...	2364	...
7 Other payables	6	151	...	-145	...	690	515	...	175	...
8 Other liabilities	1148	1148	...	...	...	585	585	...	...	...
Total Incurrence of Liabilities	12816	13278	...	-462	...	15219	13748	...	1471	...
Statistical discrepancy [a]	447	342	...	105	...	-113	-251	...	138	...
Net Lending	-7912	-7768	...	703	-847	-10089	-9015	...	-1767	693
Incurrence of Liabilities and Net Worth	5351	5852	...	346	-847	5017	4482	...	-158	693

United Kingdom

3.14 General Government Capital Finance Account, Total and Subsectors

Million Pounds Sterling

	1984					1985				
	Total General Government	Central Government	State or Provincial Government	Local Government	Social Security Funds	Total General Government	Central Government	State or Provincial Government	Local Government	Social Security Funds

Acquisition of Financial Assets

1 Gold and SDRs	...	...	...	...	...	...	...	...	...	...
2 Currency and transferable deposits	-823	-757	...	-66	...	1743	1592	...	151	...
3 Other deposits	32	-92	...	124	...	368	-155	...	523	...
4 Bills and bonds, short term	3062	3062	...	-	...	1143	1129	...	14	...
A Corporate and quasi-corporate enterprises, resident	3062	3062	...	-	...	1143	1129	...	14	...
B Other government subsectors	...	...	...	...	...	...	...	...	...	...
C Rest of the world	...	...	...	...	...	...	...	...	...	...
5 Bonds, long term	-9	-22	...	13	...	-25	-28	...	3	...
A Corporations	...	...	...	...	...	...	...	...	...	...
B Other government subsectors	-9	-22	...	13	...	-25	-28	...	3	...
C Rest of the world	...	...	...	...	...	...	...	...	...	...
6 Corporate equity securities	-2427	-2431	...	4	...	-2334	-2344	...	10	...
7 Short-term loans, n.e.c.	849	-3	...	148	704	692	62	...	121	509
8 Long-term loans, n.e.c.	3475	3691	...	-216	...	5336	5971	...	-635	...
A Mortgages	-195	...	...	-195	...	-502	...	...	-502	...
B Other	3670	3691	...	-21	...	5838	5971	...	-133	...
9 Other receivables	1472	1206	...	-2	268	1295	757	...	208	330
10 Other assets	-9	-9	...	...	...	1	1	...	...	...
Total Acquisition of Financial Assets	5622	4645	...	5	972	8219	6985	...	395	839

Incurrence of Liabilities

1 Currency and transferable deposits	617	617	...	...	...	429	429	...	...	...
2 Other deposits	4386	3723	...	663	...	2803	3173	...	-368	...
3 Bills and bonds, short term	94	-12	...	106	...	231	100	...	131	...
4 Bonds, long term	8220	8558	...	-338	...	8926	9555	...	-629	...
5 Short-term loans, n.e.c.	332	545	...	-213	...	-765	615	...	-1380	...
6 Long-term loans, n.e.c.	1902	-399	...	2301	...	5659	1034	...	4625	...
7 Other payables	1684	1591	...	98	...	502	434	...	69	...
8 Other liabilities	759	759	...	...	...	712	712	...	...	...
Total Incurrence of Liabilities	17994	15382	...	2612	...	18497	16050	...	2447	...
Statistical discrepancy [a]	357	469	...	-112	...	-589	-130	...	-459	...
Net Lending	-12729	-11206	...	-2495	972	-9689	-8935	...	-1593	839
Incurrence of Liabilities and Net Worth	5622	4645	...	5	972	8219	6985	...	395	839

	1986					1987				
	Total General Government	Central Government	State or Provincial Government	Local Government	Social Security Funds	Total General Government	Central Government	State or Provincial Government	Local Government	Social Security Funds

Acquisition of Financial Assets

1 Gold and SDRs	...	...	...	...	...	...	...	...	...	...
2 Currency and transferable deposits	3335	3184	...	151	...	12448	11903	...	545	...
3 Other deposits	881	-149	...	1030	...	1162	-111	...	1273	...
4 Bills and bonds, short term	509	523	...	-14	...	-5735	-5735	...	-	...
A Corporate and quasi-corporate enterprises, resident	509	523	...	-14	...	-5735	-5735	...	-	...
B Other government subsectors	...	...	...	...	...	...	...	...	...	...
C Rest of the world	...	...	...	...	...	...	...	...	...	...
5 Bonds, long term	82	75	...	7	...	-183	-187	...	4	...
A Corporations	...	...	...	...	...	...	...	...	...	...
B Other government subsectors	82	75	...	7	...	-183	-187	...	4	...
C Rest of the world	...	...	...	...	...	...	...	...	...	...
6 Corporate equity securities	-3761	-3810	...	49	...	-5678	-5929	...	251	...
7 Short-term loans, n.e.c.	875	-75	...	619	331	1824	39	...	604	1181
8 Long-term loans, n.e.c.	3882	4670	...	-788	...	4738	5316	...	-578	...
A Mortgages	-506	...	...	-506	...	-445	...	...	-445	...
B Other	4388	4670	...	-282	...	5183	5316	...	-133	...
9 Other receivables	-1600	-1270	...	-192	-138	862	686	...	-115	291

United Kingdom

3.14 General Government Capital Finance Account, Total and Subsectors
(Continued)

Million Pounds Sterling

	1986 Total General Government	1986 Central Government	1986 State or Provincial Government	1986 Local Government	1986 Social Security Funds	1987 Total General Government	1987 Central Government	1987 State or Provincial Government	1987 Local Government	1987 Social Security Funds
10 Other assets	-9	-9	...	...	...	-3	-3	...	...	...
Total Acquisition of Financial Assets	4194	3139	...	862	193	9435	5979	...	1984	1472

Incurrence of Liabilities

1 Currency and transferable deposits	674	674	...	...	...	1089	1089	...	...	...
2 Other deposits	1175	2190	...	-1015	...	1153	2093	...	-940	...
3 Bills and bonds, short term	-128	1	...	-129	...	2551	2460	...	91	...
4 Bonds, long term	6640	6870	...	-230	...	4509	4648	...	-139	...
5 Short-term loans, n.e.c.	-880	256	...	-1136	...	655	1428	...	-778	...
6 Long-term loans, n.e.c.	7385	2418	...	4969	...	4952	-240	...	5192	...
7 Other payables	-175	-156	...	-19	...	512	469	...	49	...
8 Other liabilities	870	870	...	...	...	903	903	...	...	...
Total Incurrence of Liabilities	15561	13121	...	2440	...	16324	12850	...	3474	...
Statistical discrepancy [a]	-661	-149	...	-512	...	-1009	-741	...	-268	...
Net Lending	-10706	-9833	...	-1066	193	-5880	-6130	...	-1222	1472
Incurrence of Liabilities and Net Worth	4194	3139	...	862	193	9435	5979	...	1984	1472

a) Statistical discrepancy refers to adjustment made in order to reconcile the net lending of the Capital Accumulation Account and the Capital Finance Account.

3.22 Corporate and Quasi-Corporate Enterprise Income and Outlay Account: Total and Sectors

Million Pounds Sterling

	1980 TOTAL	1980 Non-Financial	1980 Financial	1981 TOTAL	1981 Non-Financial	1981 Financial	1982 TOTAL	1982 Non-Financial	1982 Financial	1983 TOTAL	1983 Non-Financial	1983 Financial
Receipts												
1 Operating surplus	11424	15598	-4174	11252	17698	-6446	16926	24145	-7219	24159	30188	-6029
2 Property and entrepreneurial income	43623	6779	36844	48480	7551	40929	54807	7883	46924	55088	9022	46066
A Withdrawals from quasi-corporate enterprises	43623	6779	36844	48480	7551	40929	54807	7883	46924	55088	9022	46066
B Interest	...	...	...	...	...	...	...	...	...	...	...	...
C Dividends	...	...	...	...	...	...	...	...	...	...	...	...
D Net land rent and royalties	...	...	...	...	...	...	...	...	...	...	...	...
3 Current transfers	...	...	...	...	...	...	...	...	...	...	...	...
Total Current Receipts	55047	22377	32670	59732	25249	34483	71733	32028	39705	79247	39210	40037
Disbursements												
1 Property and entrepreneurial income	45669	17294	28375	48927	18790	30137	56077	21140	34937	56270	21538	34732
2 Direct taxes and other current transfers n.e.c. to general government	6838	5861	977	8835	8209	626	10826	9895	931	12413	11385	1028
3 Other current transfers	52	43	9	62	51	11	69	57	12	86	71	15
A Casualty insurance premiums, net	...	...	...	...	...	...	...	...	...	...	...	...
B Casualty insurance claims liability of insurance companies	...	...	...	...	...	...	...	...	...	...	...	...
C Transfers to private non-profit institutions	52	43	9	62	51	11	69	57	12	86	71	15
D Unfunded employee pension and welfare benefits	...	...	...	...	...	...	...	...	...	...	...	...
E Social assistance grants	...	...	...	...	...	...	...	...	...	...	...	...
F Other transfers n.e.c.	...	...	...	...	...	...	...	...	...	...	...	...
G Transfers to the rest of the world	...	...	...	...	...	...	...	...	...	...	...	...
Net saving	2488	-821	3309	1908	-1801	3709	4761	936	3825	10478	6216	4262
Total Current Disbursements and Net Saving	55047	22377	32670	59732	25249	34483	71733	32028	39705	79247	39210	40037

United Kingdom

3.22 Corporate and Quasi-Corporate Enterprise Income and Outlay Account: Total and Sectors

Million Pounds Sterling

	1984 TOTAL	1984 Non-Financial	1984 Financial	1985 TOTAL	1985 Non-Financial	1985 Financial	1986 TOTAL	1986 Non-Financial	1986 Financial	1987 TOTAL	1987 Non-Financial	1987 Financial
Receipts												
1 Operating surplus	26269	34417	-8148	33279	40873	-7594	31089	38711	-7622	40059	46913	-6854
2 Property and entrepreneurial income	63474	8752	54722	76350	10410	65940	78097	10452	67645	83595	11374	72221
A Withdrawals from quasi-corporate enterprises	63474	8752	54722	76350	10410	65940	78097	10452	67645	83595	11374	72221
B Interest	...	...	...	...	...	...	...	...	...	...	...	...
C Dividends	...	...	...	...	...	...	...	...	...	...	...	...
D Net land rent and royalties	...	...	...	...	...	...	...	...	...	...	...	...
3 Current transfers	...	...	...	...	...	...	...	...	...	...	...	...
Total Current Receipts	89743	43169	46574	109629	51283	58346	109186	49163	60023	123654	58287	65367
Disbursements												
1 Property and entrepreneurial income	63933	22537	41396	77114	26329	50785	77212	26785	50427	83912	29848	54064
2 Direct taxes and other current transfers n.e.c. to general government	14468	13208	1260	16987	15745	1242	15086	13821	1265	16238	14283	1955
3 Other current transfers	105	86	19	119	98	21	151	124	27	185	152	33
A Casualty insurance premiums, net	...	...	...	...	...	...	...	...	...	...	...	...
B Casualty insurance claims liability of insurance companies	...	...	...	...	...	...	...	...	...	...	...	...
C Transfers to private non-profit institutions	105	86	19	119	98	21	151	124	27	185	152	33
D Unfunded employee pension and welfare benefits	...	...	...	...	...	...	...	...	...	...	...	...
E Social assistance grants	...	...	...	...	...	...	...	...	...	...	...	...
F Other transfers n.e.c.	...	...	...	...	...	...	...	...	...	...	...	...
G Transfers to the rest of the world	...	...	...	...	...	...	...	...	...	...	...	...
Net saving	11237	7338	3899	15409	9111	6298	16737	8433	8304	23319	14004	9315
Total Current Disbursements and Net Saving	89743	43169	46574	109629	51283	58346	109186	49163	60023	123654	58287	65367

3.23 Corporate and Quasi-Corporate Enterprise Capital Accumulation Account: Total and Sectors

Million Pounds Sterling

	1980 TOTAL	1980 Non-Financial	1980 Financial	1981 TOTAL	1981 Non-Financial	1981 Financial	1982 TOTAL	1982 Non-Financial	1982 Financial	1983 TOTAL	1983 Non-Financial	1983 Financial
Finance of Gross Accumulation												
1 Gross saving	21273	16825	4448	23165	18036	5129	27500	22008	5492	34836	28619	6217
A Consumption of fixed capital	18785	17646	1139	21257	19837	1420	22739	21072	1667	24358	22403	1955
B Net saving	2488	-821	3309	1908	-1801	3709	4761	936	3825	10478	6216	4262
2 Capital transfers	1340	1340	-	4872	4872	-	2338	2338	-	1419	1419	-
Finance of Gross Accumulation	22613	18165	4448	28037	22908	5129	29838	24346	5492	36255	30038	6217
Gross Accumulation												
1 Gross capital formation	24403	19157	5246	24546	19014	5532	27211	20987	6224	30183	24794	5389
A Increase in stocks	-2375	-2381	6	-2464	-2473	9	-1401	-1405	4	1071	1033	38
B Gross fixed capital formation	26778	21538	5240	27010	21487	5523	28612	22392	6220	29112	23761	5351
2 Purchases of land, net	...	...	...	...	...	...	...	...	...	...	...	...
3 Purchases of intangible assets, net	...	...	...	...	...	...	...	...	...	...	...	...
4 Capital transfers	150	150	-	411	144	267	185	97	88	222	222	-
A To resident sectors	150	150	-	411	144	267	184	96	88	222	222	-
B To the rest of the world	...	...	...	...	...	...	...	...	...	...	...	...
Net lending	-1940	-1142	-798	3080	3750	-670	2442	3262	-820	5850	5022	828
Gross Accumulation	22613	18165	4448	28037	22908	5129	29838	24346	5492	36255	30038	6217

United Kingdom

3.23 Corporate and Quasi-Corporate Enterprise Capital Accumulation Account: Total and Sectors
Million Pounds Sterling

	1984 TOTAL	1984 Non-Financial	1984 Financial	1985 TOTAL	1985 Non-Financial	1985 Financial	1986 TOTAL	1986 Non-Financial	1986 Financial	1987 TOTAL	1987 Non-Financial	1987 Financial
Finance of Gross Accumulation											
1 Gross saving	37103	30955	6148	43354	34350	9004	46608	35138	11470	54747	41787	12960
A Consumption of fixed capital	25866	23617	2249	27944	25239	2706	29871	26705	3166	31428	27783	3645
B Net saving	11237	7338	3899	15409	9111	6298	16737	8433	8304	23319	14004	9315
2 Capital transfers	1279	1279	-	1343	1343	-	2986	2986	-	1299	1299	...
Finance of Gross Accumulation	38382	32234	6148	44697	35693	9004	49594	38124	11470	56046	43086	12960
Gross Accumulation											
1 Gross capital formation	34992	27917	7075	38409	30555	7854	39383	32065	7318	44348	36287	8061
A Increase in stocks	1098	1074	24	162	162	-	483	483	-	965	965	-
B Gross fixed capital formation	33894	26843	7051	38247	30393	7854	38900	31582	7318	43383	35322	8061
2 Purchases of land, net	...	...	...	...	...	...	...	...	...	...	...	...
3 Purchases of intangible assets, net	...	...	...	...	...	...	...	...	...	...	...	...
4 Capital transfers	245	245	-	258	258	-	244	244	-	217	217	-
A To resident sectors	245	245	-	258	258	-	244	244	-	217	217	-
B To the rest of the world	...	...	...	...	...	...	...	...	...	...	...	...
Net lending	3145	4072	-927	6030	4880	1150	9967	5815	4152	11481	6582	4899
Gross Accumulation	38382	32234	6148	44697	35693	9004	49594	38124	11470	56046	43086	12960

3.24 Corporate and Quasi-Corporate Enterprise Capital Finance Account: Total and Sectors
Million Pounds Sterling

	1980 TOTAL	1980 Non-Financial	1980 Financial	1981 TOTAL	1981 Non-Financial	1981 Financial	1982 TOTAL	1982 Non-Financial	1982 Financial	1983 TOTAL	1983 Non-Financial	1983 Financial
Acquisition of Financial Assets											
1 Gold and SDRs	...	...	...	...	...	...	...	...	...	...	...	...
2 Currency and transferable deposits	-442	-224	-218	2573	1629	944	1224	368	856	2594	2066	528
3 Other deposits	26842	3298	23544	29418	3972	25446	12818	2506	10312	20035	3477	16558
4 Bills and bonds, short term	2131	388	1743	-113	69	-182	-1869	46	-1915	2127	325	1802
A Corporate and quasi-corporate, resident	1411	383	1028	845	80	765	-943	-24	-919	1904	227	1677
B Government	720	5	715	-958	-11	-947	-926	70	-996	223	98	125
C Rest of the world	...	...	...	...	...	...	...	...	...	...	...	...
5 Bonds, long term	8903	412	8491	7871	-54	7925	8661	546	8115	12205	406	11799
A Corporate, resident	...	...	...	...	...	...	...	...	...	...	...	...
B Government	214	214	...	-339	-339	...	403	403	...	377	377	...
C Rest of the world	...	...	...	...	...	...	...	...	...	...	...	...
6 Corporate equity securities	7669	2225	5444	7649	1382	6267	9472	1920	7552	9277	1794	7483
7 Short term loans, n.e.c.	19635	68	19567	24198	98	24100	21334	-3	21337	9305	44	9261
8 Long term loans, n.e.c.	10397	2004	8393	13938	3549	10389	17180	2523	14657	20183	3803	16380
A Mortgages	6615	37	6578	8896	29	8867	13201	-30	13231	14753	-57	14810
B Other	3782	1967	1815	5042	3520	1522	3979	2553	1426	5430	3860	1570
9 Trade credits and advances	746	746	...	3698	3698	...	556	556	...	1508	1508	...
A Consumer credit	-126	-126	...	378	378	...	32	32	...	109	109	...
B Other	872	872	...	3320	3320	...	524	524	...	1399	1399	...
10 Other receivables	...	...	...	...	...	...	...	...	...	...	...	...
11 Other assets	-71	-124	53	81	34	47	357	169	188	728	515	213
Total Acquisition of Financial Assets	75810	8793	67017	89313	14377	74936	69733	8631	61102	77962	13938	64024
Incurrence of Liabilities											
1 Currency and transferable deposits	2737	...	2737	6961	...	6961	6599	...	6599	7441	...	7441
2 Other deposits	47970	-145	48115	37364	-31	37395	29747	-3	29750	31972	18	31954
3 Bills and bonds, short term	2788	500	2288	15347	428	14919	8949	412	8537	4389	-595	4984
4 Bonds, long term	267	56	211	298	87	211	420	-75	495	1055	405	650
5 Corporate equity securities	1808	1329	479	3520	2282	1238	2465	1328	1137	4000	2014	1986
6 Short-term loans, n.e.c.	7349	5843	1506	7312	5931	1381	8261	6330	1931	4862	2058	2804

United Kingdom

3.24 Corporate and Quasi-Corporate Enterprise Capital Finance Account: Total and Sectors
(Continued)

Million Pounds Sterling

	1980 TOTAL	1980 Non-Financial	1980 Financial	1981 TOTAL	1981 Non-Financial	1981 Financial	1982 TOTAL	1982 Non-Financial	1982 Financial	1983 TOTAL	1983 Non-Financial	1983 Financial
7 Long-term loans, n.e.c.	3715	3631	84	-2020	-2082	62	2767	2219	548	4432	3224	1208
8 Net equity of households in life insurance and pension fund reserves	12147	...	12147	14217	...	14217	14935	...	14935	15931	...	15931
9 Proprietors' net additions to the accumulation of quasi-corporations	...	...	...	...	...	...	...	...	...	...	...	...
10 Trade credit and advances	569	521	48	2258	2310	-52	170	142	28	1497	1477	20
11 Other accounts payable	...	...	...	...	...	...	...	...	...	...	...	...
12 Other liabilities	1617	679	938	3274	2744	530	-484	-1412	928	2474	1550	924
Total Incurrence of Liabilities	80967	12414	68553	88531	11669	76862	73829	8941	64888	78053	10151	67902
Statistical discrepancy [a]	-3218	-2479	-739	-2299	-1042	-1257	-6538	-3572	-2966	-5941	-1235	-4706
Net Lending	-1939	-1142	-797	3081	3750	-669	2442	3262	-820	5850	5022	828
Incurrence of Liabilities and Net Lending	75810	8793	67017	89313	14377	74936	69733	8631	61102	77962	13938	64024

	1984 TOTAL	1984 Non-Financial	1984 Financial	1985 TOTAL	1985 Non-Financial	1985 Financial	1986 TOTAL	1986 Non-Financial	1986 Financial	1987 TOTAL	1987 Non-Financial	1987 Financial
Acquisition of Financial Assets												
1 Gold and SDRs	...	...	...	...	...	...	...	...	...	...	...	...
2 Currency and transferable deposits	4659	1832	2827	3599	1778	1821	6347	3557	2790	11284	5384	5900
3 Other deposits	18878	866	18012	33297	3735	29562	68046	7378	60668	65291	1726	63565
4 Bills and bonds, short term	197	-281	478	1376	173	1203	3970	471	3499	11301	3380	7921
A Corporate and quasi-corporate, resident	227	-154	381	1178	205	973	4039	425	3614	10132	2834	7298
B Government	-30	-127	97	198	-32	230	-69	46	-115	1169	546	623
C Rest of the world	...	...	...	...	...	...	...	...	...	...	...	...
5 Bonds, long term	17568	333	17235	21249	-292	21541	23318	341	22977	-5999	128	-6127
A Corporate, resident	...	...	...	...	...	...	...	...	...	...	...	...
B Government	-143	-143	...	-409	-409	...	-78	-78	...	-351	-351	...
C Rest of the world	...	...	...	...	...	...	...	...	...	...	...	...
6 Corporate equity securities	11991	4566	7425	19077	5898	13179	26917	5995	20922	22455	7353	15102
7 Short term loans, n.e.c.	16460	65	16395	12562	22	12540	27196	274	26922	41129	-23	41152
8 Long term loans, n.e.c.	20849	2023	18826	23858	993	22865	26082	-1705	27787	38311	6126	32185
A Mortgages	17248	-62	17310	19466	-93	19559	26906	-120	27026	29887	-265	30152
B Other	3601	2085	1516	4392	1086	3306	-824	-1585	761	8424	6391	2033
9 Trade credits and advances	459	459	...	612	612	...	617	617	...	739	739	...
A Consumer credit	200	200	...	118	118	...	-103	-103	...	49	49	...
B Other	259	259	...	494	494	...	720	720	...	690	690	...
10 Other receivables	...	...	...	...	...	...	...	...	...	...	...	...
11 Other assets	2051	1669	382	922	342	580	1229	500	729	1447	751	696
Total Acquisition of Financial Assets	93112	11532	81580	116552	13261	103291	183722	17428	166294	185958	25564	160394
Incurrence of Liabilities												
1 Currency and transferable deposits	11362	...	11362	19238	...	19238	4226	...	4226	24482	...	24482
2 Other deposits	40170	-	40170	48891	-	48891	90918	18	90900	66549	432	66117
3 Bills and bonds, short term	830	-191	1021	-4890	26	-4916	16815	991	15824	20675	1590	19085
4 Bonds, long term	1362	230	1132	8154	797	7357	6322	698	5624	4173	645	3528
5 Corporate equity securities	3462	1457	2005	6966	4239	2727	14886	7105	7781	25845	17495	8350
6 Short-term loans, n.e.c.	14594	8204	6390	11129	6739	4390	24518	8373	16145	30033	12131	17902
7 Long-term loans, n.e.c.	-2835	-2328	-507	2404	-31	2435	-986	-639	-347	1276	-42	1318
8 Net equity of households in life insurance and pension fund reserves	17755	...	17755	18420	...	18420	18756	...	18756	19669	...	19669
9 Proprietors' net additions to the accumulation of quasi-corporations	...	...	...	...	...	...	...	...	...	...	...	...
10 Trade credit and advances	259	239	20	496	476	20	725	705	20	689	669	20
11 Other accounts payable	...	...	...	...	...	...	...	...	...	...	...	...
12 Other liabilities	3019	852	2167	3522	229	3293	1639	275	1364	3857	785	3072
Total Incurrence of Liabilities	89978	8463	81515	114330	12475	101855	177819	17526	160293	197248	33705	163543
Statistical discrepancy [a]	-11	-1003	992	-3808	-4094	286	-4064	-5913	1849	-22771	-14723	-8048
Net Lending	3145	4072	-927	6030	4880	1150	9967	5815	4152	11481	6582	4899
Incurrence of Liabilities and Net Lending	93112	11532	81580	116552	13261	103291	183722	17428	166294	185958	25564	160394

a) Statistical discrepancy refers to adjustment made in order to reconcile the net lending of the Capital Accumulation Account and the Capital Finance Account.

United Kingdom

3.32 Household and Private Unincorporated Enterprise Income and Outlay Account

Million Pounds Sterling

	1970	1975	1978	1979	1980	1981	1982	1983	1984	1985	1986	1987
Receipts												
1 Compensation of employees	30553	68494	98843	115866	137639	149584	158621	169580	180096	194573	209542	226343
A Wages and salaries	27760	60333	85646	100444	119005	127884	136245	145469	155117	168568	182614	198191
B Employers' contributions for social security	1354	4068	6069	6889	8210	8814	9344	10536	11263	12208	13362	14657
C Employers' contributions for private pension & welfare plans	1439	4093	7128	8533	10424	12886	13032	13575	13711	13761	13566	13495
2 Operating surplus of private unincorporated enterprises	4826	10375	15919	18157	20446	23209	26899	29623	32542	33839	36569	38779
3 Property and entrepreneurial income	4028	6602	9348	13706	18007	19685	22599	23571	26952	32761	34373	37592
A Withdrawals from private quasi-corporations	...	...	...	...	...	...	...	...	...	...	...	...
B Interest	4028	6602	9348	13706	18007	19685	22599	23571	26952	32761	34373	37592
C Dividends	...	...	...	...	...	...	...	...	...	...	...	...
D Net land rent and royalties	...	...	...	...	...	...	...	...	...	...	...	...
3 Current transfers	4596	10713	18690	21818	26511	32421	37901	41377	44722	48565	52548	54229
A Casualty insurance claims	...	...	...	...	...	...	...	...	...	...	...	...
B Social security benefits	2751	6469	10641	12072	14689	17675	19151	20569	21639	23050	25345	25808
C Social assistance grants	1243	3020	6184	7658	9271	11887	15507	17059	18848	20939	22077	22961
D Unfunded employee pension and welfare benefits	...	...	...	...	...	...	...	...	...	...	...	...
E Transfers from general government	336	789	1046	1187	1564	1681	1926	2215	2542	2768	3307	3709
F Transfers from the rest of the world	230	393	774	850	935	1117	1248	1448	1588	1689	1668	1566
G Other transfers n.e.c.	36	42	45	51	52	62	69	86	105	119	151	185
Total Current Receipts	44003	96184	142800	169547	202603	224899	246020	264151	284312	309738	333032	356943
Disbursements												
1 Final consumption expenditures	31793	65078	99616	118036	137151	152705	167499	183408	196177	213756	235158	256759
2 Property income	1061	3100	4597	6721	9798	11591	13364	13349	16431	21340	22858	25328
Consumer debt	...	...	...	...	...	...	...	...	...	...	...	...
Mortgage	754	2115	3007	4256	6153	6822	7581	7524	9384	12729	13622	...
Other	...	...	...	...	...	...	...	...	...	...	...	...
3 Direct taxes and other current transfers n.e.c. to government	8897	22079	29723	32883	39700	45047	49766	54243	57172	61904	66879	72104
A Social security contributions	2655	6848	10101	11526	13939	15916	18095	20780	22312	24191	26033	28449
B Direct taxes	6201	15151	19457	21205	25573	28933	31460	33214	34615	37455	40552	43306
Income taxes	5964	14761	18867	20604	24847	28093	30438	32032	33326	35973	38977	41666
Other	237	390	590	601	726	840	1022	1184	1289	1482	1566	1640
C Fees, fines and penalties	41	80	165	150	188	198	211	249	245	258	294	349
4 Other current transfers	243	531	901	1044	1139	1057	1200	1179	1261	1436	1615	1782
A Net casualty insurance premiums	...	...	...	...	...	...	...	...	...	...	...	...
B Transfers to private non-profit institutions serving households	...	...	...	...	...	...	...	...	...	...	...	...
C Transfers to the rest of the world	243	531	901	1044	1139	1057	1200	1179	1261	1436	1615	1782
D Other current transfers, except imputed	...	...	...	...	...	...	...	...	...	...	...	...
E Imputed employee pension and welfare contributions	...	...	...	...	...	...	...	...	...	...	...	...
Net saving	2009	5396	7963	10865	14815	14499	14191	11972	13271	11302	6522	970
Total Current Disbursements and Net Saving	44003	96184	142800	169547	202603	224899	246020	264151	284312	309738	333032	356943

3.33 Household and Private Unincorporated Enterprise Capital Accumulation Account

Million Pounds Sterling

	1970	1975	1978	1979	1980	1981	1982	1983	1984	1985	1986	1987
Finance of Gross Accumulation												
1 Gross saving	2984	7930	12115	15863	20884	21389	21559	20122	22256	21178	17456	13163
A Consumption of fixed capital	975	2534	4152	4998	6069	6890	7368	8150	8985	9876	10934	12193
B Net saving	2009	5396	7963	10865	14815	14499	14191	11972	13271	11302	6522	970
2 Capital transfers	207	426	1054	1095	1281	1179	1646	2419	2843	2238	2010	2033

United Kingdom

3.33 Household and Private Unincorporated Enterprise Capital Accumulation Account
(Continued)

Million Pounds Sterling

	1970	1975	1978	1979	1980	1981	1982	1983	1984	1985	1986	1987
A From resident sectors	207	426	1054	1095	1281	1179	1646	2419	2843	2238	2010	2033
B From the rest of the world	...	...	...	...	...	...	...	...	...	...	...	...
Total Finance of Gross Accumulation	3191	8357	13170	16959	22165	22568	23205	22541	25099	23416	19465	15196
Gross Accumulation												
1 Gross Capital Formation	1623	3571	6522	8546	9044	9505	12055	13944	14831	15409	18216	20747
A Increase in stocks	20	-245	313	388	-240	-211	58	148	193	-43	326	274
B Gross fixed capital formation [a]	1603	3816	6209	8158	9284	9716	11997	13796	14638	15452	17890	20473
2 Purchases of land, net	...	...	...	...	...	...	...	...	...	...	...	...
3 Purchases of intangibles, net	...	...	...	...	...	...	...	...	...	...	...	...
4 Capital transfers	385	326	410	468	512	539	582	641	738	932	1037	1123
A To resident sectors	385	326	410	468	512	539	582	641	738	932	1037	1123
B To the rest of the world	...	...	...	...	...	...	...	...	...	...	...	...
Net lending	1183	4460	6238	7945	12609	12524	10668	7956	9530	7075	212	-6674
Total Gross Accumulation	3191	8357	13170	16959	22165	22568	23205	22541	25099	23416	19465	15196

a) Item 'Gross fixed capital formation' of household and private unincorporated enterprises includes net transactions in land and existing buildings.

3.34 Household and Private Unincorporated Enterprise Capital Finance Account

Million Pounds Sterling

	1970	1975	1978	1979	1980	1981	1982	1983	1984	1985	1986	1987
Acquisition of Financial Assets												
1 Gold	...	...	...	...	...	...	...	...	...	...	...	...
2 Currency and transferable deposits	966	1704	2536	1731	1345	1538	2977	2546	3476	6986	7566	7716
3 Other deposits	1508	4487	8535	13358	15285	14315	14940	14413	16716	14514	15970	16624
4 Bills and bonds, short term	...	...	...	...	...	...	...	...	...	...	...	...
5 Bonds, long term	-426	880	172	1550	1419	1381	1762	1401	1178	4766	3320	3754
A Corporate	-7	80	75	21	92	-220	-193	289	-77	1233	173	56
B Government	-264	946	6	1539	1412	1969	1981	820	1113	1381	2061	2821
C Rest of the world	-155	-146	91	-10	-85	-368	-26	292	142	2152	1086	877
6 Corporate equity securities	-607	-1219	-2388	-3202	-3012	-1492	-2717	-1497	-4976	-3672	1189	4510
7 Short term loans, n.e.c.	2	38	38	69	99	126	75	292	380	333	267	660
8 Long term loans, n.e.c.	70	-145	-14	-16	149	176	-622	-389	-180	-496	-676	-737
A Mortgages	...	...	...	...	...	...	...	...	...	...	...	...
B Other	70	-145	-14	-16	149	176	-622	-389	-180	-496	-676	-737
9 Trade credit and advances	...	...	...	...	...	...	...	...	...	...	...	...
10 Net equity of households in life insurance and pension fund reserves	1727	4475	8283	10769	12846	14863	15556	16622	18523	19133	19640	20574
11 Proprietors' net additions to the accumulation of quasi-corporations	...	...	...	...	...	...	...	...	...	...	...	...
12 Other	7	33	104	233	347	263	636	699	1187	1824	1826	2079
Total Acquisition of Financial Assets	3247	10253	17266	24492	28478	31170	32607	34087	36304	43388	49102	55180
Incurrence of Liabilities												
1 Short term loans, n.e.c.	59	-493	1509	2706	2966	3975	5015	4892	4075	6528	5059	8216
2 Long term loans, n.e.c.	1331	3613	6232	7512	7970	10088	14516	15335	17661	20566	27455	31887
A Mortgages	1249	3613	5441	6517	7368	9483	14127	14501	17030	19032	26468	29504
B Other	82	-	791	997	602	605	389	834	631	1534	987	2383
3 Trade credit and advances	29	140	214	674	-126	378	32	109	200	118	-103	49
A Consumer credit	29	140	214	674	-126	378	32	109	200	118	-103	49
B Other	...	...	...	...	...	...	...	...	...	...	...	...
4 Other accounts payable	-5	-40	30	187	4	182	-254	162	7	17	-9	19
5 Other liabilities	...	-8	-6	6	-1	16	-29	-2	-1	4	75	24
Total Incurrence of Liabilities	1414	3212	7979	11086	10813	14639	19280	20496	21942	27233	32477	40195
Statistical discrepancy [a]	650	2581	3049	5461	5056	4007	2659	5635	4832	9080	16413	21659
Net Lending	1183	4460	6238	7945	12609	12524	10668	7956	9530	7075	212	-6674
Incurrence of Liabilities and Net Lending	3247	10253	17266	24492	28478	31170	32607	34087	36304	43388	49102	55180

a) Statistical discrepancy refers to adjustment made in order to reconcile the net lending of the Capital Accumulation Account and the Capital Finance Account.

United Kingdom

3.51 External Transactions: Current Account: Detail

Million Pounds Sterling

	1970	1975	1978	1979	1980	1981	1982	1983	1984	1985	1986	1987
Payments to the Rest of the World
1 Imports of goods and services	11440	29199	45858	54828	58078	60849	68376	78086	93279	99377	101739	112211
A Imports of merchandise c.i.f.	8962	23927	38569	46298	48320	49983	55975	64784	78283	83982	84860	93152
B Other	2478	5272	7289	8530	9758	10866	12401	13302	14996	15395	16879	19059
2 Factor income to the rest of the world	821	5592	9631	14210	21940	35014	42133	38751	45294	46197	41645	40205
A Compensation of employees	79	186	286	287	284	278	320	341	373	411	457	511
B Property and entrepreneurial income	742	5406	9345	13923	21656	34736	41813	38410	44921	45786	41188	39694
By general government	319	491	650	681	895	940	1092	1189	1327	1478	1669	1977
By corporate and quasi-cororate enterprises	423	4915	8695	13242	20761	33796	40721	37221	43594	44308	39519	37717
By other												
3 Current transfers to the rest of the world	412	1234	3025	3624	3905	4405	5216	5433	5856	6735	6086	7494
A Indirect taxes by general government to supranational organizations	-	349	986	1987	1897	2241	2936	3063	3296	3894	2890	4194
B Other current transfers	412	885	2039	1637	2008	2164	2280	2370	2560	2841	3196	3300
By general government	169	354	1138	593	869	1107	1080	1191	1299	1405	1581	1518
By other resident sectors	243	531	901	1044	1139	1057	1200	1179	1261	1436	1615	1782
4 Surplus of the nation on current transactions	650	-2116	735	259	3718	6488	4123	2820	-518	2362	-3238	-6737
Payments to the Rest of the World, and Surplus of the Nation on Current Transfers	13323	33909	59249	72921	87641	106756	119848	125090	143911	154671	146232	153173
Receipts From The Rest of the World
1 Exports of goods and services	11912	27431	48033	55560	63595	68328	73600	81000	92942	103323	99018	108108
A Exports of merchandise f.o.b.	8128	19183	34981	40470	47147	50668	55330	60698	70263	77988	72678	79422
B Other	3784	8248	13052	15090	16448	17660	18270	20302	22679	25335	26340	28686
2 Factor income from the rest of the world	1181	5719	9982	15947	22125	35570	42773	40318	46885	47692	43308	41074
A Compensation of employees	9	34	60	64	69	72	76	73	71	81	80	90
B Property and entrepreneurial income	1172	5685	9922	15883	22056	35498	42697	40245	46814	47611	43228	40984
By general government	54	266	692	816	946	971	979	764	817	735	764	932
By corporate and quasi-corporate enterprises	1118	5419	9230	15067	21110	34527	41718	39481	45997	46876	42464	40052
By other												
3 Current transfers from the rest of the world	230	759	1234	1414	1921	2858	3475	3772	4084	3656	3906	3991
A Subsidies to general government from supranational organizations	-	342	344	380	573	742	855	1158	1442	1284	1470	1483
B Other current transfers	230	417	890	1034	1348	2116	2620	2614	2642	2372	2436	2508
To general government	-	24	116	184	413	999	1372	1166	1054	683	768	942
To other resident sectors	230	393	774	850	935	1117	1248	1448	1588	1689	1668	1566
Receipts from the Rest of the World on Current Transfers	13323	33909	59249	72921	87641	106756	119848	125090	143911	154671	146232	153173

United Kingdom

3.52 External Transactions: Capital Accumulation Account

Million Pounds Sterling

	1970	1975	1978	1979	1980	1981	1982	1983	1984	1985	1986	1987
Finance of Gross Accumulation													
1 Surplus of the nation on current transactions	650	-2116	735	259	3718	6488	4123	2820	-518	2362	-3238	-6737
2 Capital transfers from the rest of the world	...	...	...	...	...	...	...	...	...	...	...	...
Total Finance of Gross Accumulation	650	-2116	735	259	3718	6488	4123	2820	-518	2362	-3238	-6737
Gross Accumulation													
1 Capital transfers to the rest of the world	-	-	-	-	-	-	-	-	-	-	-	-
A By general government	-	-	-	-	-	-	-	-	-	-	-	-
B By other resident sectors	...	...	...	...	...	...	...	...	...	...	...	...
2 Purchases of intangible assets, n.e.c., net, from the rest of the world	...	...	...	...	...	...	...	...	...	...	...	...
Net lending to the rest of the world	650	-2116	735	259	3718	6488	4123	2820	-518	2362	-3238	-6737
Total Gross Accumulation	650	-2116	735	259	3718	6488	4123	2820	-518	2362	-3238	-6737

3.53 External Transactions: Capital Finance Account

Million Pounds Sterling

	1970	1975	1978	1979	1980	1981	1982	1983	1984	1985	1986	1987
Acquisitions of Foreign Financial Assets													
1 Gold and SDR's	...	...	...	...	...	...	...	...	...	...	...	...
2 Currency and transferable deposits	...	-655	-2329	1059	291	-2419	-1421	-607	-908	1758	2891	12012
3 Other deposits	...	-	14638	23872	22435	24805	9125	13642	13433	24478	53212	49338
4 Bills and bonds, short term	...	-272	87	-226	312	1746	2029	579	1213	-460	983	-2644
5 Bonds, long term	...	103	634	377	1038	1459	3903	4305	10086	14406	18179	-5574
6 Corporate equity securities	...	257	1432	1872	4044	5412	4575	4769	2466	8120	13734	3632
7 Short-term loans, n.e.c.	...	7343	5171	5642	8985	11232	6941	599	-1655	-3305	-358	4698
8 Long-term loans	...	562	1749	3995	3468	5681	3421	6061	3543	1690	-2667	5173
9 Prporietors' net additions to accumulation of quasi-corporate, non-resident enterprises	...	...	...	...	...	...	...	...	...	...	...	...
10 Trade credit and advances	...	99	337	903	313	530	-290	-	-	-	-	...
11 Other	...	...	...	...	...	...	...	...	...	...	...	...
Total Acquisitions of Foreign Financial Assets	...	7437	21719	37494	40886	48446	28283	29348	28178	46687	85974	66635
Incurrence of Foreign Liabilities													
1 Currency and transferable deposits	...	18	-1136	3468	1902	3458	2693	3014	3759	9097	-9457	6135
2 Other deposits	...	7375	16478	23029	30023	22698	14393	14462	22363	27993	60408	33963
3 Bills and bonds, short term	...	117	2476	6718	1111	13677	7346	3805	-1123	-7634	13266	15040
4 Bonds, long term	...	54	5	1211	1512	455	430	874	931	5496	4421	5536
5 Corporate equity securities	...	195	150	446	1043	1111	296	1479	1340	2015	4275	8190
6 Short-term loans, n.e.c.	...	1	14	-13	-2	-1	-115	-3	-343	-	1	-11
7 Long-term loans	...	1749	927	773	1040	25	1581	2419	-3873	1621	1899	976
8 Non-resident proprietors' net additions to accumulation of resident quasi-corporate enterprises	...	...	...	...	...	...	...	...	...	...	...	...
9 Trade credit and advances	...	65	163	364	-211	76	-107	-	-	-	-	-
10 Other	...	-	-	195	180	158	-	-	-	-	-	-
Total Incurrence of Liabilities	...	9574	19077	36191	36598	41657	26517	26050	23054	38588	74813	69829
Statistical discrepancy [a]	...	1699	3451	1457	1644	1319	-3432	-419	5178	4683	11688	-2121
Net Lending	...	-3836	-809	-154	2644	5470	5198	3717	-54	3416	-527	-1073
Total Incurrence of Liabilities and Net Lending	...	7437	21719	37494	40886	48446	28283	29348	28178	46687	85974	66635

a) Statistical discrepancy refers to adjustment made in order to reconcile the net lending of the Capital Accumulation Account and the Capital Finance Account.

United Kingdom

4.3 Cost Components of Value Added

Million Pounds Sterling

1980 / 1981

	Compensation of Employees	Capital Consumption	Net Operating Surplus	Indirect Taxes	Less: Subsidies Received	Value Added	Compensation of Employees	Capital Consumption	Net Operating Surplus	Indirect Taxes	Less: Subsidies Received	Value Added
					All Producers							
1 Agriculture, hunting, forestry and fishing	1302	1109	1835	...	...	4246	1387	1183	2205	...	...	4775
2 Mining and quarrying	3246	1984	7233	...	...	12463	3526	2349	10162	...	...	16037
3 Manufacturing [a]	43380	6497	3606	...	...	53483	44741	7146	2877	...	...	54764
4 Electricity, gas and water	3147	2253	976	...	...	6376	3590	2517	1109	...	...	7216
5 Construction	7639	549	3865	...	...	12053	7836	590	4411	...	...	12837
6 Wholesale and retail trade, restaurants and hotels [a]	18223	1831	5600	...	...	25654	20173	2041	5033	...	...	27247
7 Transport, storage and communication	10631	3910	-225	...	...	14316	11483	4408	1	...	...	15892
8 Finance, insurance, real estate and business services	12632	5824	18467	...	...	36923	14484	6886	20487	...	...	41857
9 Community, social and personal services [a]	5656	389	3226	...	...	9271	6226	468	3653	...	...	10347
Total, Industries	105856	25845	43084	...	...	174785	113446	29303	48223	...	...	190972
Producers of Government Services	29405	1739		...	...	31144	33327	1935		...	...	35262
Other Producers	2593	368		...	...	2961	3017	403		...	...	3420
Total [b]	137854	27952	43084	...	...	208890	149790	31641	48223	...	...	229654
Less: Imputed bank service charge			9298			9298			11732			11732
Import duties [c]						18133						22200
Value added tax				11897		11897				13056		13056
Other adjustments [d]						538						93
Total	137854	27952	33786	35803	5773	230160	149790	31641	36491	41809	6553	253271

1982 / 1983

	Compensation of Employees	Capital Consumption	Net Operating Surplus	Indirect Taxes	Less: Subsidies Received	Value Added	Compensation of Employees	Capital Consumption	Net Operating Surplus	Indirect Taxes	Less: Subsidies Received	Value Added
					All Producers							
1 Agriculture, hunting, forestry and fishing	1488	1209	2715	...	...	5412	1602	1245	2427	...	...	5274
2 Mining and quarrying	3771	2566	11998	...	...	18335	3666	2783	14307	...	...	20756
3 Manufacturing [a]	46267	7618	5209	...	...	59094	47333	7999	6817	...	...	62149
4 Electricity, gas and water	3768	2655	1362	...	...	7785	3805	2784	2343	...	...	8932
5 Construction	8107	633	5376	...	...	14116	8672	645	6326	...	...	15643
6 Wholesale and retail trade, restaurants and hotels [a]	21458	2212	6553	...	...	30223	23099	2327	7748	...	...	33174
7 Transport, storage and communication	11953	4522	779	...	...	17254	12735	4838	710	...	...	18283
8 Finance, insurance, real estate and business services	16642	7446	23024	...	...	47112	19093	8182	24725	...	...	52000
9 Community, social and personal services [a]	6572	529	3910	...	...	11011	7231	578	4569	...	...	12378
Total, Industries	120026	31245	59071	...	...	210342	127236	33677	67676	...	...	228589
Producers of Government Services	35421	1999		...	...	37420	38855	2056		...	...	40911
Other Producers	3418	409		...	...	3827	3757	417		...	...	4174
Total [b]	158865	33653	59071	...	...	251589	169848	36150	67676	...	...	273674
Less: Imputed bank service charge			13320			13320			12481			12481
Import duties [c]						25326						25831
Value added tax				14308		14308				16176		16176
Other adjustments [d]						-728						-1168
Total	158865	33653	45751	45637	6003	277175	169848	36150	55195	48411	6404	302032

1984 / 1985

	Compensation of Employees	Capital Consumption	Net Operating Surplus	Indirect Taxes	Less: Subsidies Received	Value Added	Compensation of Employees	Capital Consumption	Net Operating Surplus	Indirect Taxes	Less: Subsidies Received	Value Added
					All Producers							
1 Agriculture, hunting, forestry and fishing	1655	1264	3310	...	...	6229	1776	1270	2519	...	...	5565
2 Mining and quarrying	1911	2950	17389	...	...	22250	3341	3133	16412	...	...	22886
3 Manufacturing [a]	50164	8368	8138	...	...	66670	53385	8975	11325	...	...	73685
4 Electricity, gas and water	3954	2903	738	...	...	7595	4097	3066	1390	...	...	8553

United Kingdom

4.3 Cost Components of Value Added
(Continued)

Million Pounds Sterling

1984 / 1985

	Compensation of Employees	Capital Consumption	Net Operating Surplus	Indirect Taxes	Less: Subsidies Received	Value Added	Compensation of Employees	Capital Consumption	Net Operating Surplus	Indirect Taxes	Less: Subsidies Received	Value Added
5 Construction	9121	660	7115	...	...	16896	9380	687	8034	...	...	18101
6 Wholesale and retail trade, restaurants and hotels [a]	24925	2478	8897	...	...	36300	26818	2728	11361	...	...	40907
7 Transport, storage and communication	13671	5106	1026	...	...	19803	14406	5435	1534	...	...	21375
8 Finance, insurance, real estate and business services	21620	9204	26098	...	...	56922	24569	10393	30476	...	...	65438
9 Community, social and personal services [a]	8124	621	4869	...	...	13614	8996	684	5281	...	...	14961
Total, Industries	135145	36092	75042	...	...	246279	146768	39091	85612	...	...	271471
Producers of Government Services	41056	2162		...	...	43218	43377	2350		...	...	45727
Other Producers	4197	432	...	...	...	4629	4758	458	...	...	...	5216
Total [b]	180398	38686	75042	...	...	294126	194903	41899	85612	...	...	322414
Less: Imputed bank service charge	...	...	15082	...	...	15082	...	...	16822	...	...	16822
Import duties [c]	...	...	...	...	...	25485	...	...	...	...	...	27316
Value added tax	...	...	...	18273	...	18273	...	...	...	20724	...	20724
Other adjustments [d]	...	...	...	...	...	311	...	...	...	...	...	-527
Total	180398	38686	59960	51437	7679	323113	194903	41899	68790	55340	7300	353105

1986 / 1987

	Compensation of Employees	Capital Consumption	Net Operating Surplus	Indirect Taxes	Less: Subsidies Received	Value Added	Compensation of Employees	Capital Consumption	Net Operating Surplus	Indirect Taxes	Less: Subsidies Received	Value Added
					All Producers							
1 Agriculture, hunting, forestry and fishing	1775	1300	2872	...	...	5947	1800	1317	2784	...	...	5901
2 Mining and quarrying	3324	3293	6190	...	...	12807	3016	3357	7074	...	...	13447
3 Manufacturing [a]	55910	9506	13982	...	...	79398	59035	9660	17530	...	...	86225
4 Electricity, gas and water	4230	3201	2161	...	...	9592	4339	3297	2428	...	...	10064
5 Construction	9828	708	8844	...	...	19380	10701	731	10092	...	...	21524
6 Wholesale and retail trade, restaurants and hotels [a]	28964	2978	13731	...	...	45673	31147	3219	14597	...	...	48963
7 Transport, storage and communication	15205	5666	2498	...	...	23369	16291	5610	4014	...	...	25915
8 Finance, insurance, real estate and business services	27975	11615	35170	...	...	74760	31958	13043	39082	...	...	84083
9 Community, social and personal services [a]	10464	736	6015	...	...	17215	10864	872	6779	...	...	18515
Total, Industries	157675	42098	88368	...	...	288141	169151	45003	100483	...	...	314637
Producers of Government Services	46895	2582		...	...	49477	51512	2732		...	...	54244
Other Producers	5349	485	...	...	...	5834	6101	503	...	...	...	6604
Total [b]	209919	45165	88368	...	...	343452	226764	48238	100483	...	...	375485
Less: Imputed bank service charge	...	...	19246	...	...	19246	...	...	20545	...	...	20545
Import duties [c]	...	...	...	...	...	32032	...	...	...	...	...	35386
Value added tax	...	...	...	22996	...	22996	...	...	...	25192	...	25192
Other adjustments [d]	...	...	...	...	...	-1608	...	...	...	...	...	-2282
Total	209919	45165	69122	61289	6261	377626	226764	48238	79938	66677	6099	413236

a) Repairs to consumer durables other than clothing are included in item 'Wholesale and retail trade, restaurants and hotels'.
b) Gross domestic product in factor values.
c) Item 'Import duties' refers to indirect taxes net of subsidies.
d) Item 'Other adjustments' refers to statistical discrepancy.

United Rep. of Tanzania

General note. The preparation of national accounts statistics in the United Republic of Tanzania is undertaken by the Bureau of Statistics, Ministry of Finance, Economic Affairs and Planning, Dar es Salaam. Official estimates are published in the annual reports entitled 'Economic Surveys'. Detailed description of the sources and methods used for the national accounts estimation is found in the report 'National Accounts of Tanzania, 1976 to 1984: Sources and Methods' published in 1985. The estimates follow closely the classifications and definitions recommended in the United Nations System of National Accounts (SNA). Input-output tables have been compiled for 1969, 1970 and 1976. The following tables have been prepared from successive replies to the United Nations national accounts questionnaire. The estimates presented relate to Tanzania (mainland) only, i.e., the former territory of Tanganyika and excluding Zanzibar. When the scope and coverage of the estimates differ for conceptual or statistical reasons from the definitions and classifications recommended in SNA, a footnote is indicated to the relevant tables.

Sources and methods:

(a) Gross domestic product. Gross domestic product is estimated mainly through the income approach.

(b) Expenditure on the gross domestic product. Government final consumption expenditure and exports and imports of goods and services are estimated through the expenditure approach, while private final consumption expenditure and gross capital formation are compiled by using a combination of the commodity-flow and expenditure approaches. For government expenditure, actual central government revenue and expenditure, classified by purpose, are available from government documents. Revenue and expenditure details of local authorities are obtained from the Prime Minister's Office and from the local authorities themselves. For private consumption expenditure, estimates of domestic production of all commodities are compiled and allowances made for various intermediate uses and government and business purposes. The estimates are then marked up for distribution costs and adjusted for imports and exports. Data from the 1976/77 Household Budget Survey are used with regard to most expenditures on services. The estimate of change in stocks only covers the parastatal enterprises, export crops, livestock and those factories which were included in the survey of manufacturing industries. Estimates of gross fixed capital formation for the public sector are derived from detailed analysis of the accounts of the agencies concerned and from detailed statistics on imports of capital equipment. Own account rural residential construction has been estimated on the basis of building costs data, rental values and data on population growth. Exports and imports of goods and services are obtained from the balance of payment statements of the Bank of Tanzania. GDP by expenditure at constant prices is not estimated.

(c) Cost-structure of the gross domestic product. In estimating the cost structure components of GDP, estimates of compensation of employees are obtained from each industry group separately. In addition, information obtained from Employment and Earnings survey is used for the non-primary and mining industries groups. For agriculture, animal husbandry, forestry and fishing, the wage component of value added is fixed at 4.3 per cent of its value added based on the results of various farm surveys. Operating surplus estimates for each industrial sector is obtained from the companies concerned. Estimates of depreciation for fixed assets of the parastatal enterprises are provided by the establishments themselves and for other sectors, estimates are based on percentages obtained from previous surveys. Data on indirect taxes and subsidies are obtained by analyzing government recurrent revenue and expenditure.

(d) Gross domestic product by kind of economic activity. The table of gross domestic product by kind of economic activity is prepared at factor costs. The value added of agriculture, mining and manufacturing is estimated through the production approach while for the remaining industries, the income approach is used. For agriculture, the data on production, prices and cost of production of each export crop, available with the respective commodity boards, are utilized to derive estimates of their value added. For the non-export crops, similar data available from the Ministry of Agriculture and Livestock Development, Marketing Development Bureau, Bureau of Statistics and data collected through Economic and Household Budget Surveys and the 1976 Input-Output Table have been used. The 1969 and 1976-77 Household Budget Surveys provided information on the quantities of crops harvested and the value and quantity of crops sold for a number of food crops. Based on some assumptions regarding conversion factors for differing physical units and the adjustment from retail to producer prices, approximate values of the crop harvested at producers' prices have been worked out in a number of cases. For livestock, forestry and fishing, data are obtained from the concerned departments or sections of the Ministry of Agriculture and from the household budget surveys. The production costs incurred by producers of livestocks are based on scattered data available, from farm studies and informal discussions. For some minor crops and by-products, a very rough mark-up is established to cover their production. Data on mining are available in the annual Economic Surveys, obtained directly from Mines Division, Dodoma. The data obtained from Employment and Earnings Survey, census reports and monthly surveys are utilized for manufacturing. Bench-mark estimates of value added of manufacturing establishments were obtained from the Census of Industrial Production 1978 while current estimates are prepared mainly on the basis of annual surveys of manufacturing industries. The Annual Accounts and Supporting Schedules of Tanzania's electric company gives full details of its activities. Total volume of construction activity is estimated from a variety of sources and the estimates of factor incomes are specially collected from a large sample of contractors and building firms. Data collected through the 1969 and 1976/77 Household Budget Survey were used to re-examine estimates made for rural own account construction. For trade, transport and service industries, the data provided by the Employment and Earnings Surveys and the data on income and expenditure, specially collected from a large sample of such enterprises, together with the estimated gross trade margins, number of trade licenses, vehicle licenses, etc. provide the basis for estimation. Rental value of houses in the urban and rural areas are compiled on the basis of information on rented houses collected through the 1967 Population Census and the 1969 Household Budget Survey. For government services, data are collected from the agencies concerned and detailed analysis of their revenue and expenditure are undertaken. Information on the activities of East African Community are obtained from the East African Statistical Department. For the constant price estimates, double deflation is used for the agricultural, mining and quarrying, and construction sectors with current year quantities revalued at base-year prices. For the manufacturing, electricity, trade and transport sectors, value added is extrapolated by various quantity indicators and indexes. For the financial and service sectors, value added is deflated by different indexes such as employment index.

1.1 Expenditure on the Gross Domestic Product, in Current Prices

Million Tanzanian shillings

	1970	1975	1978	1979	1980	1981	1982	1983	1984	1985	1986	1987
1 Government final consumption expenditure	1208	3259	5585	5956	5494	6105	8046	9443	13844	18555	23621	28109
2 Private final consumption expenditure	6396	14171	23363	25497	32486	37035	42261	55128	68652	93130	128894	199004
3 Gross capital formation	2067	4004	8094	9458	9685	10130	12235	9588	13618	18963	31820	50645
A Increase in stocks	189	464	764	866	1055	1498	1410	1836	1645	2091	2487	3685
B Gross fixed capital formation	1878	3540	7330	8592	8630	8632	10825	7752	11973	16872	29333	46960
Residential buildings	253	408	546	622	709	1001	1043	949	1291	1708	1837	2085
Non-residential buildings	229	359	749	943	1126	1446	1373	898	1219	1388	2595	4338
Other construction and land improvement etc.	528	926	1755	2001	2524	2230	2985	1687	2203	2762	4952	4094
Other	868	1847	4280	5026	4271	3955	5424	4218	7260	11014	19949	36443
4 Exports of goods and services	2200	3462	4692	5131	5540	5994	4546	5111	6321	7453	14580	29640
5 Less: Imports of goods and services	2607	5885	9565	9759	11087	10162	8862	8761	13543	17480	37026	79519
Statistical discrepancy	-91	-	...	...	...	...	...	...	...	...	...	...
Equals: Gross Domestic Product	9173	19011	32169	36283	42118	49102	58226	70509	88892	120621	161889	227879

United Rep. of Tanzania

1.2 Expenditure on the Gross Domestic Product, in Constant Prices

Million Tanzanian shillings

	1970	1975	1978	1979	1980	1981	1982	1983	1984	1985	1986	1987
		1966	At constant prices of:					1976				
1 Government final consumption expenditure	...	...	...	...	...	...	...	...	...	...	...	...
2 Private final consumption expenditure	...	...	...	...	...	...	...	...	...	...	...	...
3 Gross capital formation	1821	1894	6223	6825	6103	6368	6563	4632	6333	7635	7586	7168
A Increase in stocks	165	256	513	425	488	562	511	590	442	414	390	423
B Gross fixed capital formation	1656	1638	5710	6400	5615	5806	6052	4042	5891	7221	7196	6745
Residential buildings	218	232	425	443	439	551	516	412	478	519	466	467
Non-residential buildings	183	188	550	675	700	799	683	394	467	397	560	837
Other construction and land improvement etc.	421	485	1289	1431	1569	1232	1485	740	844	789	1069	791
Other	834	733	3446	3851	2907	3224	3369	2496	4102	5517	5101	4650
4 Exports of goods and services	...	...	...	...	...	...	...	...	...	...	...	...
5 Less: Imports of goods and services	...	...	...	...	...	...	...	...	...	...	...	...
Equals: Gross Domestic Product [a]	7680	9553	22202	22849	23419	23301	23439	22882	23656	24278	25158	26142

a) Gross domestic product in factor values.

1.3 Cost Components of the Gross Domestic Product

Million Tanzanian shillings

	1970	1975	1978	1979	1980	1981	1982	1983	1984	1985	1986	1987
1 Indirect taxes, net	958	2023	3587	3966	4664	5196	5680	7901	10749	12538	18855	29778
A Indirect taxes	994	2447	3915	4222	4963	5730	6594	8391	11016	12855	19018	30183
B Less: Subsidies	36	424	328	256	299	534	914	490	267	317	163	405
2 Consumption of fixed capital	512	907	1139	1270	1540	1542	1568	1619	1879	2482	3761	3899
3 Compensation of employees paid by resident producers to:	2852	6082	6110	6858	7940	9047	10168	12906	14713	17816	20185	22442
4 Operating surplus	4851	9999	21333	24192	27974	33317	40810	48083	61551	87785	119088	171760
Equals: Gross Domestic Product	9173	19011	32169	36283	42118	49102	58226	70509	88892	120621	161889	227879

1.7 External Transactions on Current Account, Summary

Million Tanzanian shillings

	1970	1975	1978	1979	1980	1981	1982	1983	1984	1985	1986	1987
			Payments to the Rest of the World									
1 Imports of goods and services	2607	5885	9565	9759	11087	10162	8862	8761	13543	17480	37026	79519
A Imports of merchandise c.i.f.	...	...	8798	8986	10003	9120	8392	8192	12960	16470	34329	74967
B Other	...	...	767	773	1084	1042	470	569	583	1010	2697	4552
2 Factor income to the rest of the world	101	90	192	166	226	266	257	232	190	734	3697	10826
3 Current transfers to the rest of the world	184	359	239	210	209	192	168	270	303	286	917	1853
4 Surplus of the nation on current transactions	-340	-1787	-3645	-3252	-4604	-2456	-3440	-2715	-5968	-7660	-10225	-19634
Payments to the Rest of the World and Surplus of the Nation on Current Transactions	2552	4547	6351	6883	6918	8164	5847	6548	8068	10840	31415	72564

United Rep. of Tanzania

1.7 External Transactions on Current Account, Summary
(Continued)

Million Tanzanian shillings

	1970	1975	1978	1979	1980	1981	1982	1983	1984	1985	1986	1987
Receipts From The Rest of the World												
1 Exports of goods and services	2200	3462	4692	5131	5540	5994	4546	5111	6321	7453	14580	29640
A Exports of merchandise f.o.b.	...	...	3671	3980	4187	4373	3484	4001	5125	5718	11391	23822
B Other	...	...	1021	1151	1353	1621	1062	1110	1196	1735	3189	5818
2 Factor income from rest of the world	77	37	147	95	114	90	26	21	17	30	416	1047
3 Current transfers from rest of the world	275	1048	1512	1657	1264	2080	1275	1416	1730	3357	16419	41877
Receipts from the Rest of the World on Current Transactions	2552	4547	6351	6883	6918	8164	5847	6548	8068	10840	31415	72564

1.10 Gross Domestic Product by Kind of Activity, in Current Prices

Million Tanzanian shillings

	1970	1975	1978	1979	1980	1981	1982	1983	1984	1985	1986	1987
1 Agriculture, hunting, forestry and fishing	3381	7007	12506	14728	16636	20338	26449	32737	41295	61231	84153	120941
2 Mining and quarrying	105	101	228	284	329	299	266	249	337	251	474	563
3 Manufacturing [a]	828	1774	3859	3868	4097	4501	4361	4869	5932	6665	7417	9044
4 Electricity, gas and water	84	146	261	275	424	423	421	514	551	1071	2096	2259
5 Construction	404	735	1052	1229	1498	1614	1863	1252	1661	2061	3257	3658
6 Wholesale and retail trade, restaurants and hotels	1046	2172	3889	4344	4713	5479	6814	8148	10447	14195	18851	27453
7 Transport, storage and communication	713	1453	1917	2113	3019	3133	3395	3507	4789	7021	9863	16794
8 Finance, insurance, real estate and business services	844	1650	2686	2978	3744	4507	4891	5252	6028	6659	8127	11062
9 Community, social and personal services [b]	920	2204	2873	3342	3959	4732	5446	7372	8614	10735	11340	12771
Total, Industries	8325	17242	29271	33161	38419	45026	53906	63900	79654	109889	145578	204545
Producers of Government Services [b]	...	...	...	...	...	...	...	...	...	...	...	...
Other Producers [b]	...	...	...	...	...	...	...	...	...	...	...	...
Subtotal [c]	8325	17242	29271	33161	38419	45026	53906	63900	79654	109889	145578	204545
Less: Imputed bank service charge	110	254	689	844	965	1120	1360	1292	1511	1806	2544	6444
Plus: Import duties	...	...	...	...	...	...	...	...	...	...	...	...
Plus: Value added tax	...	...	...	...	...	...	...	...	...	...	...	...
Plus: Other adjustments [d]	958	2023	3587	3966	4664	5196	5680	7901	10749	12538	18855	29778
Equals: Gross Domestic Product	9173	19011	32169	36285	42118	49102	58226	70509	88892	120621	161889	227879

a) Item 'Manufacturing' includes handicrafts.
b) Items 'Other producers' and 'Producers of government services' are included in item 'Community, social and personal services'.
c) Gross domestic product in factor values.
d) Item 'Other adjustments' refers to indirect taxes net of subsidies.

United Rep. of Tanzania

1.11 Gross Domestic Product by Kind of Activity, in Constant Prices

Million Tanzanian shillings

	1970	1975	1978	1979	1980	1981	1982	1983	1984	1985	1986	1987
		1966	**At constant prices of:**				**1976**					
1 Agriculture, hunting, forestry and fishing	3205	3596	8998	9066	9418	9511	9639	9914	10312	10931	11557	12066
2 Mining and quarrying	97	73	189	200	189	193	193	174	186	174	167	165
3 Manufacturing [a]	716	903	2730	2821	2683	2382	2304	2103	2159	2075	1991	2075
4 Electricity, gas and water	92	139	286	318	400	417	420	413	439	461	544	585
5 Construction	327	392	783	879	932	890	930	549	660	601	752	774
6 Wholesale and retail trade, restaurants and hotels	984	1074	2797	2839	2839	2725	2668	2612	2640	2662	2953	3086
7 Transport, storage and communication	729	997	1699	1634	1818	1652	1694	1473	1482	1509	1514	1582
8 Finance, insurance, real estate and business services	763	941	2208	2338	2483	2529	2702	2817	2984	3046	3283	3362
9 Community, social and personal services [b]	866	1581	2997	3255	3188	3551	3556	3543	3549	3616	3283	3309
Total, Industries	7779	9696	22687	23350	23950	23850	24106	23598	24411	25075	26044	27004
Producers of Government Services [b]	...	...	...	...	...	...	...	...	...	...	...	...
Other Producers [b]	...	...	...	...	...	...	...	...	...	...	...	...
Subtotal [c]	7779	9696	22687	23350	23950	23850	24106	23598	24411	25075	26044	27004
Less: Imputed bank service charge	99	143	485	501	531	549	667	716	755	797	886	862
Plus: Import duties	...	...	...	...	...	...	...	...	...	...	...	...
Plus: Value added tax	...	...	...	...	...	...	...	...	...	...	...	...
Equals: Gross Domestic Product [c]	7680	9553	22202	22849	23419	23301	23439	22882	23656	24278	25158	26142

a) Item 'Manufacturing' includes handicrafts.
b) Items 'Other producers' and 'Producers of government services' are included in item 'Community, social and personal services'.
c) Gross domestic product in factor values.

1.12 Relations Among National Accounting Aggregates

Million Tanzanian shillings

	1970	1975	1978	1979	1980	1981	1982	1983	1984	1985	1986	1987
Gross Domestic Product	9173	19011	32169	36285	42118	49102	58226	70509	88892	120621	161889	227879
Plus: Net factor income from the rest of the world	-24	-53	-45	-71	-112	-176	-231	-211	-173	-704	-3281	-9779
Factor income from the rest of the world	77	37	147	95	114	90	26	21	17	30	416	1047
Less: Factor income to the rest of the world	101	90	192	166	226	266	257	232	190	734	3697	10826
Equals: Gross National Product	9149	18958	32124	36214	42006	48926	57995	70298	88719	119917	158608	218100
Less: Consumption of fixed capital	512	907	1139	1270	1540	1542	1568	1619	1879	2482	3761	3899

United Rep. of Tanzania

1.12 Relations Among National Accounting Aggregates
(Continued)

Million Tanzanian shillings

	1970	1975	1978	1979	1980	1981	1982	1983	1984	1985	1986	1987
Equals: National Income	8637	18051	30985	34944	40466	47384	56427	68679	86840	117435	154847	214201
Plus: Net current transfers from the rest of the world	91	689	1273	1447	1055	1888	1107	1146	1427	3071	15502	40024
Current transfers from the rest of the world	275	1048	1512	1657	1264	2080	1275	1416	1730	3357	16419	41877
Less: Current transfers to the rest of the world	184	359	239	210	209	192	168	270	303	286	917	1854
Equals: National Disposable Income	8728	18740	32258	36391	41521	49272	57534	69825	88267	120506	170349	254225
Less: Final consumption	7604	17430	28948	31453	37980	43140	50307	64571	82496	111685	152515	227113
Statistical discrepancy	91	-	...		...		...		...		...	
Equals: Net Saving	1215	1310	3310	4936	3541	6132	7227	5254	5771	8821	17834	27112
Less: Surplus of the nation on current transactions	-340	-1787	-3645	-3252	-4604	-2456	-3440	-2715	-5968	-7660	-10225	-19634
Equals: Net Capital Formation	1555	3097	6955	8188	8145	8588	10667	7969	11739	16481	28059	46746

2.1 Government Final Consumption Expenditure by Function, in Current Prices

Million Tanzanian shillings — Fiscal year beginning 1 July

	1970	1975	1978	1979	1980	1981	1982	1983	1984	1985	1986	1987
1 General public services	296	648	1176	1592	1584	1712	2380	2257	3463	5873	10436	9903
2 Defence	127	729	1349	3194	1110	1862	2308	2557	2744	3659	4949	6661
3 Public order and safety	151	345	420	488	558	719	927	1040	1265	2130	4277	2880
4 Education	289	757	1324	1472	1653	1782	2298	2543	2503	1795	2321	4227
5 Health	118	426	669	688	739	813	992	983	1171	1329	2446	2213
6 Social security and welfare	9	21	24	37	52	44	51	61	62	125	123	150
7 Housing and community amenities	44	101	89	108	147	187	189	209	212	258	334	453
8 Recreational, cultural and religious affairs	56	130	174	240	277	322	381	385	440	589	771	950
9 Economic services	742	2630	3404	4566	5222	5354	5495	5213	5563	6463	6904	12406
A Fuel and energy [a]	102	603	460	773	647	545	677	647	712	680	880	1459
B Agriculture, forestry, fishing and hunting	218	945	882	934	1328	1272	1282	1233	1580	1654	1992	4350
C Mining, manufacturing and construction, except fuel and energy	43	253	827	871	1406	1340	1555	1399	1492	1674	1172	2597
D Transportation and communication	379	294	705	984	1109	1379	1482	1439	1295	1678	1966	3051
E Other economic affairs		535	530	1004	732	819	500	494	484	769	888	960
10 Other functions	305	399	810	1378	1195	1802	3406	4042	4029	5219	7203	13458
Total Government Final Consumption Expenditure [b]	2137	6186	9439	13763	12537	14597	18427	19289	21451	27440	39764	53301

a) Item 'Fuel and energy' includes water supply.
b) Only central government data are included in the general government estimates.

2.5 Private Final Consumption Expenditure by Type and Purpose, in Current Prices

Million Tanzanian shillings

	1970	1975	1978	1979	1980	1981	1982	1983	1984	1985	1986	1987

Final Consumption Expenditure of Resident Households

	1970	1975	1978	1979	1980	1981	1982	1983	1984	1985	1986	1987
1 Food, beverages and tobacco	3575	9237	...	...	...	...	...	...	...	...	...	...
A Food	3266	8201	...	...	...	...	...	...	...	...	...	...
B Non-alcoholic beverages	24	43	...	...	...	...	...	...	...	...	...	...
C Alcoholic beverages	224	628	...	...	...	...	...	...	...	...	...	...
D Tobacco	61	365	...	...	...	...	...	...	...	...	...	...

United Rep. of Tanzania

2.5 Private Final Consumption Expenditure by Type and Purpose, in Current Prices
(Continued)

Million Tanzanian shillings

	1970	1975	1978	1979	1980	1981	1982	1983	1984	1985	1986	1987
2 Clothing and footwear	442	805	...	...	...	...	...	...	...	...	...	...
3 Gross rent, fuel and power	1019	1746	...	...	...	...	...	...	...	...	...	...
4 Furniture, furnishings and household equipment and operation	449	874	...	...	...	...	...	...	...	...	...	...
5 Medical care and health expenses	133	321	...	...	...	...	...	...	...	...	...	...
6 Transport and communication	392	577	...	...	...	...	...	...	...	...	...	...
7 Recreational, entertainment, education and cultural services	130	231	...	...	...	...	...	...	...	...	...	...
8 Miscellaneous goods and services	233	313	...	...	...	...	...	...	...	...	...	...
Total Final Consumption Expenditure in the Domestic Market by Households, of which	6373	14104	...	...	...	...	...	...	...	...	...	...
Plus: Direct purchases abroad by resident households	120	...	...	...	...	...	...	...	...	...	...	...
Less: Direct purchases in the domestic market by non-resident households	97	...	...	...	...	...	...	...	...	...	...	...
Equals: Final Consumption Expenditure of Resident Households [a]	6396	14171	...	...	...	...	...	...	...	...	...	...

Final Consumption Expenditure of Private Non-profit Institutions Serving Households

	1970	1975	1978	1979	1980	1981	1982	1983	1984	1985	1986	1987
Equals: Final Consumption Expenditure of Private Non-profit Organisations Serving Households	...	...	...	...	...	...	...	...	...	...	...	...
Private Final Consumption Expenditure	6396	14171	...	...	...	...	...	...	...	...	...	...

a) Item 'Final consumption expenditure of resident households' includes consumption expenditure of private non-profit institutions serving households.

2.11 Gross Fixed Capital Formation by Kind of Activity of Owner, ISIC Divisions, in Current Prices

Million Tanzanian shillings

	1970	1975	1978	1979	1980	1981	1982	1983	1984	1985	1986	1987
			All Producers									
1 Agriculture, hunting, forestry and fishing	117	234	676	686	698	677	846	972	1490	2197	1907	1471
2 Mining and quarrying	31	48	16	8	46	41	41	104	134	109	154	218
3 Manufacturing	319	636	1672	1865	1955	1961	3022	1724	2584	4289	5095	14115
4 Electricity, gas and water	119	498	493	534	779	652	403	776	1430	1680	8707	3055
A Electricity, gas and steam	..	...	318	334	508	410	209	511	1163	1473	8268	2117
B Water works and supply	...	...	175	200	271	242	194	265	267	207	439	938
5 Construction	77	82	326	420	500	680	1051	645	1319	1589	2358	5922
6 Wholesale and retail trade, restaurants and hotels	54	72	410	200	151	105	504	131	340	396	324	678
7 Transport, storage and communication	756	1184	2258	2524	1913	1927	2162	1887	2854	4176	8371	15861
8 Finance, insurance, real estate and business services	322	642	485	562	687	771	884	305	374	436	749	331
9 Community, social and personal services [a,b]	83	144	994	1793	1901	1818	1912	1208	1448	2000	1668	5309
Total Industries	1878	3540	7330	8592	8630	8632	10825	7752	11973	16872	29333	46960
Producers of Government Services [a]	...	...	...	...	...	...	...	...	...	...	...	...
Private Non-Profit Institutions Serving Households [b]	...	...	...	...	...	...	...	...	...	...	...	...
Total	1878	3540	7330	8592	8630	8632	10825	7752	11973	16872	29333	46960

a) Item 'Producers of government services' is included in item 'Community, social and personal services'.
b) Item 'Private non-profit institutions serving households' is included in item 'Community, social and personal services'.

United States

General note. The Bureau of Economic Analysis, is responsible for the preparation of national income accounts statistics in the United States. The official estimates are published in the 'Survey of Current Business, (Survey)'. A selected set of tables appears monthly and the full set appears in the July issue. The capital finance accounts and balance sheets are published by the Board of Governors of the Federal Reserve System. The official estimates are not totally consistent with the classifications and definitions used in the United Nations System of National Accounts (SNA). A summary explanation of the accounting framework appears in 'Introduction to National Economic Accounting' in the March 1985 'Survey'. Information on the sources and methods used to estimate the national accounts appears in 'GNP: An Overview of Source Data and Estimating Methods,' in the July 1987 'Survey'. Information on U.S. capital finance accounts and balance sheets is found in 'Introduction to the Flow of Funds', 1980, a publication of the Federal Reserve System. The most recent benchmark input-output accounts were published in 1984 in 'The Detailed Input-Output Structure of the U.S. Economy, 1977, Volumes 1 and 2'. Annual update tables also are prepared; see the january 1987 'Survey' for the 1981 accounts. The following tables have been prepared from successive national accounts questionnaires provided to the United Nations. The United States converts its official estimates as closely as possible to SNA definitions. When differences in scope and coverage from the SNA recommendations remain, footnotes are attached to the appropriate tables.

Sources and methods:

(a) Gross domestic product. Both the expenditure and income approach are used.

(b) Expenditure on the gross domestic product. The estimates of central government final consumption expenditures are based largely on budget statistics. The State and local government estimates are based largely on Census Bureau annual surveys of these governments. For private final consumption expenditures, benchmark estimates are taken from the detailed input-output tables, prepared every 5 years to coincide with comprehensive economic censuses. In addition major statistical sources include the Census Bureau merchandise trade series and the Decennial Census of Housing. Estimates for nonbenchmark years are extrapolations and interpolations of the benchmark data using Census Bureau surveys of retail store sales, service receipts, rental payments, and other public and private data sources. Annual estimates of gross fixed capital formation are largely based on surveys conducted by the Census Bureau and other government agencies, and private data for oil well drilling. Reports of government agencies are used for construction by the Federal government, federally-aided projects and public utility construction. Benchmark estimates of producers' durable equipment are largely based on Census of Manufactures shipments and merchandise trade using the commodity-flow method. Estimates for nonbenchmark years are extrapolations and interpolations of the benchmark data using Census Bureau annual and monthly survey data, merchandise trade statistics and an abbreviated commodity-flow method. Estimates of exports and imports of merchandise are based on customs documents tabulated by the Census Bureau. Service transactions are taken from the U.S. balance of payments accounts based on Bureau of Economic Analysis surveys and other government sources. Constant-dollar government final consumption expenditures are calculated in two parts. Employee compensation is obtained by extrapolating base-year figures with full-time equivalent employment measures, with detail by level of pay or experience. Purchases from business are obtained by deflation. The price indexes used are BEA indexes for national defense purchases, CPI, PPI, indexes of prices paid by farmers and a variety of others. Deflation is used for gross fixed capital formation, exports and imports of goods and services, and private final consumption expenditures, primarily using CPI and PPI, and other indexes.

(c) Cost-structure of the gross domestic product. The annual estimates of wages and salaries are taken mainly from administrative records of government agencies. The operating surplus is estimated in four separate parts: income of unincorporated enterprises, rental income of person, corporate profits, and net interest. Tabulations of tax returns are the primary source for nonfarm income, proprietors' income, corporate profits and net interest. Farm income is based on data compiled by the Department of Agriculture. Rental income of persons is based primarily on the decennial Census and a biennial survey of housing. Imputed rental receipts of owner-occupants of nonfarm dwellings are estimated using the rental-equivalency method. Rental receipts for both tenant-occupied and owner-occupied housing are adjusted to exclude expenses. Capital consumption allowances consist of depreciation, primarily based on tabulations of tax returns, and accidental damage to fixed capital, estimated by BEA. The estimates of depreciation that are based on capital consumption allowances with capital consumption adjustment are derived from perpetual inventory calculations from BEA's capital stock estimates. Indirect taxes include for the Federal government excise taxes and customs duties and for State and local government sales taxes and property taxes. Subsidies paid by the Federal government include payments to farmers and housing subsidies. Both components are estimated using the same sources as used for government final consumption.

(d) Gross domestic product by kind of economic activity. The table of GDP by kind of economic activity is prepared at market prices. The income approach is used to estimate value added of the various kinds of economic activities. The source data for the income components are described in (c) above. In many cases, the distribution by economic activity is provided by these source data. For six income components, it is based on the economic activity of the company. For corporate profits and corporate capital consumption allowances the distributions are converted by BEA to an establishment basis using Census Bureau and Department of Energy data. For nonfarm proprietors' income, noncorporate net interest, and noncorporate capital consumption allowances, they are assumed to be equivalent to an establishment distribution. For the other component, corporate net interest, no data are available for conversion to an establishment basis and the company basis is used. For income components where the source data provide no economic activity distributions, BEA estimates establishment distributions using various data and estimating methods. In the preparation of constant-dollar estimates, double deflation is used for farms; construction; manufacturing (except petroleum and coal products); railroad transportation; and electric, gas and sanitary services. Extrapolation of base year product by an indicator series is used for agricultural services, forestry, and fisheries; mining; manufacturing of petroleum and coal products; local and interurban transit; water and air transportation; pipelines (except natural gas); retail trade; finance, insurance and real estate; hotels and lodging places; private households; government and the following service sectors: transportation, business, personal, repairs, health, legal and education. Direct deflation is used for trucking and warehousing; communication; auto repair, services, and garages; motion pictures; amusement and recreation services; social services and membership organizations; and miscellaneous professional services. Data sources for double deflation includes Census Bureau shipments and cost of materials data; Department of Agriculture receipts, expenses, and prices; BEA input-output composition of intermediate consumption and Bureau of Labor Statistics price data. Data sources for extrapolation include Federal Reserve Board Index of Industrial Production; BEA estimates of persons engaged in production and hours worked; Department of Energy production; and BEA constant-dollar consumption measures. Bureau of Labor Statistics prices and average earnings are used for direct deflation.

1.1 Expenditure on the Gross Domestic Product, in Current Prices

Million United States dollars

	1970	1975	1978	1979	1980	1981	1982	1983	1984	1985	1986	1987
1 Government final consumption expenditure	189586	294219	377292	418924	473722	525613	574090	617003	670110	727926	780403	831989
2 Private final consumption expenditure	635842	1005820	1392720	1554720	1721220	1909680	2046300	2223660	2422200	2615800	2788200	2983670
3 Gross capital formation	179863	268163	475075	515731	508253	591713	525237	568601	736220	742394	762045	809707
A Increase in stocks	1369	-4181	30042	13102	-6014	32390	-12341	-9007	66204	24275	20760	37072
B Gross fixed capital formation	178494	272344	445033	502629	514267	559323	537578	577608	670016	718119	741285	772635
Residential buildings	40488	61229	127988	137567	121618	121311	104030	150990	179228	186542	214337	224015
Non-residential buildings	33794	45534	56768	69566	77645	85326	88152	84531	99652	115525	115399	118584
Other construction and land improvement etc.	31514	50245	69164	78657	91005	105826	104800	88919	94332	99999	89258	91480
Other	72698	115336	191113	216839	223999	246860	240596	253168	296804	316053	322291	338556
4 Exports of goods and services	59104	136346	182013	223575	273347	292988	270904	264005	283250	281300	291042	332034
5 Less: Imports of goods and services	55177	120625	208188	248147	288074	310521	295137	319797	389441	399952	430223	484494
Equals: Gross Domestic Product	1009220	1583920	2218910	2464810	2688470	3009470	3121400	3353470	3722340	3967470	4191470	4472910

1.2 Expenditure on the Gross Domestic Product, in Constant Prices

Million United States dollars

	1970	1975	1978	1979	1980	1981	1982	1983	1984	1985	1986	1987
					At constant prices of:1980							
1 Government final consumption expenditure	432237	436443	459057	467765	473722	478863	490247	507583	530591	558495	585249	602051
2 Private final consumption expenditure	1271920	1472470	1688980	1725730	1721220	1747910	1766650	1855740	1945400	2036820	2124400	2180920
3 Gross capital formation	404932	405478	573053	563914	508252	545308	460586	500322	645655	651601	656760	684199
A Increase in stocks	1268	-8263	33840	11831	-6014	31744	-8271	-9716	54611	19799	19005	26986
B Gross fixed capital formation	403664	413741	539213	552083	514266	513564	468857	510038	591044	631802	637755	657213

United States

1.2 Expenditure on the Gross Domestic Product, in Constant Prices
(Continued)

Million United States dollars

	1970	1975	1978	1979	1980	1981	1982	1983	1984	1985	1986	1987
					At constant prices of: 1980							
Residential buildings	99206	101769	158494	151611	121618	112286	93118	132604	151490	154038	172459	171982
Non-residential buildings	78414	68464	69875	76827	77645	78120	76460	70649	79608	89186	86649	85542
Other construction and land improvement etc.	84083	79615	88269	88102	91005	95610	89709	81954	88247	89456	78748	79556
Other	141961	163893	222575	235544	223998	227548	209569	224831	271699	299122	299899	320133
4 Exports of goods and services	134298	196195	226912	246688	273347	272298	249641	243619	259544	266601	281679	325290
5 Less: Imports of goods and services	191577	218856	309750	313686	288074	295044	288541	323621	398202	417965	460122	491187
Equals: Gross Domestic Product	2051810	2291730	2638250	2690410	2688470	2749340	2678580	2783640	2982980	3095560	3187970	3301270

1.3 Cost Components of the Gross Domestic Product

Million United States dollars

	1970	1975	1978	1979	1980	1981	1982	1983	1984	1985	1986	1987
1 Indirect taxes, net	89075	134910	168539	179810	202558	239294	243352	260385	291184	310774	321155	334540
A Indirect taxes	94026	139996	178066	189352	213281	251476	258835	282560	313914	333637	348446	366323
B Less: Subsidies	4951	5086	9527	9542	10723	12182	15483	22175	22730	22863	27291	31783
2 Consumption of fixed capital	105843	192851	269346	311362	355816	403461	440644	455627	476888	503300	524716	551464
3 Compensation of employees paid by resident producers to:	619072	952085	1334580	1497630	1646340	1817190	1918000	2032310	2224420	2379650	2519560	2697060
A Resident households	618875	951714	1334100	1497160	1645810	1816640	1917380	2031690	2223840	2379040	2518970	2696440
B Rest of the world	197	371	478	473	536	544	618	614	580	608	591	614
4 Operating surplus	196361	301570	448356	476964	478832	545407	519455	599985	724487	778499	839679	897961
A Corporate and quasi-corporate enterprises	87469	141733	232504	246621	243149	273785	242589	301886	360190	371717	384348	401389
B Private unincorporated enterprises	108892	159837	215852	230343	235683	271622	276866	298099	364297	406782	455331	496572
C General government	...	...	...	...	...	...	...	...	...	...	...	...
Statistical discrepancy	-1133	2502	-1908	-965	4920	4124	-56	5170	5359	-4750	-13647	-8114
Equals: Gross Domestic Product	1009220	1583920	2218910	2464810	2688470	3009470	3121400	3353470	3722340	3967470	4191470	4472910

1.4 General Government Current Receipts and Disbursements

Million United States dollars

	1970	1975	1978	1979	1980	1981	1982	1983	1984	1985	1986	1987
					Receipts							
1 Operating surplus	...	...	...	...	...	...	...	...	...	...	...	...
2 Property and entrepreneurial income	5368	10900	16705	23806	30344	38231	43721	46553	53180	58114	62500	62273
3 Taxes, fees and contributions	279717	430963	627297	704537	769959	881303	893825	948250	1054460	1143390	1210030	1327930
A Indirect taxes	94026	139996	178066	189352	213281	251476	258835	282560	313914	333637	348446	366323
B Direct taxes	137414	198624	313446	357266	384793	427409	418758	431457	473774	517104	546653	627154
C Social security contributions	46745	89637	131716	153311	166617	196129	209139	226259	257654	282182	303234	321255
D Compulsory fees, fines and penalties	1532	2706	4069	4608	5268	6289	7093	7974	9120	10462	11692	13199
4 Other current transfers	6658	14216	19952	22446	26422	30134	32947	34863	34698	37746	38694	40257
Total Current Receipts of General Government	291743	456079	663954	750789	826725	949668	970493	1029670	1142340	1239250	1311220	1430460
					Disbursements							
1 Government final consumption expenditure	189586	294219	377292	418924	473722	525613	574090	617003	670111	727926	780403	831989
A Compensation of employees	120050	190050	244345	264870	294059	323789	351777	374733	397767	427587	452308	482382
B Consumption of fixed capital	13611	24335	30439	35102	39919	42470	43597	44589	46215	50072	52081	54060
C Purchases of goods and services, net	56797	80908	103612	120187	141140	160653	179925	198893	227436	251779	277665	297253
D Less: Own account fixed capital formation	872	1074	1104	1235	1396	1299	1209	1212	1307	1512	1651	1706
E Indirect taxes paid, net	...	...	...	...	...	...	...	...	...	...	...	...
2 Property income	22686	38345	57526	69522	84750	110997	130684	147964	176821	198193	210441	220808
A Interest	22686	38345	57526	69522	84750	110997	130684	147964	176821	198193	210441	220808
B Net land rent and royalties	...	...	...	...	...	...	...	...	...	...	...	...

United States

1.4 General Government Current Receipts and Disbursements
(Continued)

Million United States dollars

	1970	1975	1978	1979	1980	1981	1982	1983	1984	1985	1986	1987
3 Subsidies	4951	5086	9527	9542	10723	12182	15483	22175	22730	22863	27291	31783
4 Other current transfers	81943	181330	224397	251702	300631	340667	379862	408663	418561	449043	474812	494175
A Social security benefits	46470	105876	133784	150502	180285	208948	242014	261039	265268	283539	300639	313389
B Social assistance grants	25098	57060	68353	75403	89310	97367	99653	106850	111299	117523	124809	131524
C Other	10375	18394	22260	25797	31036	34352	38195	40774	41994	47981	49364	49262
5 Net saving	-7423	-62901	-4788	1099	-43101	-39791	-129626	-166139	-145883	-158780	-181728	-148294
Total Current Disbursements and Net Saving of General Government	291743	456079	663954	750789	826725	949668	970493	1029670	1142340	1239250	1311220	1430460

1.5 Current Income and Outlay of Corporate and Quasi-Corporate Enterprises, Summary

Million United States dollars

	1970	1975	1978	1979	1980	1981	1982	1983	1984	1985	1986	1987
Receipts
1 Operating surplus	87469	141733	232504	246621	243149	273785	242589	301886	360190	371717	384348	401389
2 Property and entrepreneurial income received	104532	206133	309784	401589	501347	650062	715410	706394	798799	870892	898529	952115
3 Current transfers	1416	2995	4022	4671	5340	6117	6690	7118	7425	8194	8429	9309
Total Current Receipts	193417	350861	546310	652881	749836	929964	964689	1015400	1166410	1250800	1291310	1362810
Disbursements
1 Property and entrepreneurial income	137841	258601	386380	495238	620425	798236	871305	860024	958749	1026810	1054530	1120780
2 Direct taxes and other current payments to general government	34356	50906	83506	87996	84785	81143	63081	77241	93899	96422	106574	133759
3 Other current transfers	3957	7757	10313	11628	13649	14678	16765	18616	20776	23383	25829	28864
4 Net saving	17263	33597	66111	58019	30977	35907	13538	59517	92990	104190	104375	79411
Total Current Disbursements and Net Saving	193417	350861	546310	652881	749836	929964	964689	1015400	1166410	1250800	1291310	1362810

1.6 Current Income and Outlay of Households and Non-Profit Institutions

Million United States dollars

	1970	1975	1978	1979	1980	1981	1982	1983	1984	1985	1986	1987
Receipts
1 Compensation of employees	619097	952048	1334490	1497580	1646250	1817140	1917900	2032250	2224440	2379670	2519640	2697180
A From resident producers	618875	951714	1334100	1497160	1645810	1816640	1917380	2031690	2223840	2379040	2518970	2696440
B From rest of the world	222	334	388	419	449	497	520	560	600	627	672	743
2 Operating surplus of private unincorporated enterprises	80171	125373	176206	191871	180673	186772	175535	190882	234502	255860	286732	312944
3 Property and entrepreneurial income	102238	151840	215709	254103	310957	393037	432713	456218	513523	548917	573803	608231
4 Current transfers	81220	183643	230966	259007	308513	349572	389561	420011	429716	460410	488307	512796
A Social security benefits	46470	105876	133784	150502	180285	208948	242014	261039	265268	283539	300639	313389
B Social assistance grants	25098	57060	68353	75403	89310	97367	99653	106850	111299	117523	124809	131524
C Other	9652	20707	28829	33102	38918	43257	47894	52122	53149	59348	62859	67883
Total Current Receipts	882726	1412900	1957370	2202560	2446400	2746520	2915710	3099360	3402180	3644860	3868490	4131160
Disbursements
1 Private final consumption expenditure	635842	1005820	1392720	1554720	1721220	1909680	2046300	2223660	2422200	2615800	2788200	2983670
2 Property income	16686	24428	36687	43533	47376	51970	55548	61858	72508	82598	89062	92103
3 Direct taxes and other current transfers n.e.c. to general government	151335	240061	365725	427189	471893	548684	571909	588449	646649	713326	755005	827849
A Social security contributions	46745	89637	131716	153311	166617	196129	209139	226259	257654	282182	303234	321255
B Direct taxes	103058	147718	229940	269270	300008	346266	355677	354216	379875	420682	440079	493395
C Fees, fines and penalties	1532	2706	4069	4608	5268	6289	7093	7974	9120	10462	11692	13199
4 Other current transfers	9611	18890	26062	29454	34439	38698	42169	44445	44907	49052	50271	52899
5 Net saving	69252	123710	136176	147663	171470	197489	199784	180950	215917	184075	185949	174634
Total Current Disbursements and Net Saving	882726	1412900	1957370	2202560	2446400	2746520	2915710	3099360	3402180	3644860	3868490	4131160

United States

1.7 External Transactions on Current Account, Summary

Million United States dollars

	1970	1975	1978	1979	1980	1981	1982	1983	1984	1985	1986	1987
Payments to the Rest of the World												
1 Imports of goods and services	55177	120625	208188	248147	288074	310521	295137	319797	389441	399952	430223	484494
A Imports of merchandise c.i.f. [a]	40855	99000	176477	211930	247460	266462	249474	271341	334250	340877	367725	412997
B Other	14322	21625	31711	36217	40614	44059	45663	48456	55191	59075	62498	71497
2 Factor income to the rest of the world	6316	14204	23871	35425	43368	55259	58748	56682	72772	70230	75220	90637
A Compensation of employees	197	371	478	473	536	544	618	614	580	608	591	614
B Property and entrepreneurial income	6119	13833	23393	34952	42832	54715	58130	56068	72192	69622	74629	90023
By general government	1024	4542	8674	11122	12592	16878	18285	17825	19769	21306	22607	24052
By corporate and quasi-corporate enterprises	5095	9291	14719	23830	30240	37837	39845	38243	52423	48316	52022	65971
By other	...	...	...	...	...	...	...	...	...	...	...	...
3 Current transfers to the rest of the world	6599	7858	7044	8050	10023	9701	11103	11221	13747	16689	17446	15744
A Indirect taxes to supranational organizations	...	...	...	...	...	...	...	...	...	...	...	...
B Other current transfers	6599	7858	7044	8050	10023	9701	11103	11221	13747	16689	17446	15744
4 Surplus of the nation on current transactions	3939	21596	-10138	1448	11830	9478	-953	-33485	-90948	-114359	-142380	-160606
Payments to the Rest of the World and Surplus of the Nation on Current Transactions	72031	164283	228965	293070	353295	384959	364035	354215	385012	372512	380509	430269
Receipts From The Rest of the World												
1 Exports of goods and services	59104	136346	182013	223575	273347	292988	270904	264005	283250	281300	291042	332034
A Exports of merchandise f.o.b. [a]	44280	109359	144454	182986	224672	237894	213572	205637	223699	220280	224599	254322
B Other	14824	26987	37559	40589	48675	55094	57332	58368	59551	61020	66443	77712
2 Factor income from rest of the world	12545	27202	45740	68104	78368	90489	91626	88721	100420	89651	87503	96067
A Compensation of employees	222	334	388	419	449	497	520	560	600	627	672	743
B Property and entrepreneurial income	12323	26868	45352	67685	77919	89992	91106	88161	99820	89024	86831	95324
By general government	907	1112	1843	2295	2562	3680	4118	4832	5229	5504	6420	5332
By corporate and quasi-corporate enterprises	11416	25756	43509	65390	75357	86312	86988	83329	94591	83520	80411	89992
By other	...	...	...	...	...	...	...	...	...	...	...	...
3 Current transfers from rest of the world	382	735	1212	1391	1580	1482	1505	1489	1342	1561	1964	2168
A Subsidies from supranational organisations	...	...	...	...	...	...	...	...	...	...	...	...
B Other current transfers	382	735	1212	1391	1580	1482	1505	1489	1342	1561	1964	2168
Receipts from the Rest of the World on Current Transactions	72031	164283	228965	293070	353295	384959	364035	354215	385012	372512	380509	430269

a) Valuation basis is essentially Free Along Side (F.A.S.).

1.8 Capital Transactions of The Nation, Summary

Million United States dollars

	1970	1975	1978	1979	1980	1981	1982	1983	1984	1985	1986	1987
Finance of Gross Capital Formation												
Gross saving	184935	287257	466845	518143	515162	597066	524340	529955	639913	632785	633312	657215
1 Consumption of fixed capital	105843	192851	269346	311362	355816	403461	440644	455627	476888	503300	524716	551464
A General government	13611	24335	30439	35102	39919	42470	43597	44589	46215	50072	52081	54060
B Corporate and quasi-corporate enterprises	55361	103091	146174	168827	193465	223865	248861	257154	269726	284567	299183	314930
Public	3411	6711	9007	10510	12049	13150	13884	14436	15212	16002	16735	17445
Private	51950	96380	137167	158317	181416	210715	234977	242718	254514	268565	282448	297485
C Other	36871	65425	92733	107433	122432	137126	148186	153884	160947	168661	173452	182474
2 Net saving	79092	94406	197499	206781	159346	193605	83696	74328	163025	129485	108596	105751
A General government	-7423	-62901	-4788	1099	-43101	-39791	-129626	-166139	-145882	-158780	-181728	-148294
B Corporate and quasi-corporate enterprises	17263	33597	66111	58019	30977	35907	13538	59517	92990	104190	104375	79411
Public	-444	-2803	-1320	-2640	-5256	-5377	-4243	-3415	1282	1541	-530	-2397
Private	17707	36400	67431	60659	36233	41284	17781	62932	91708	102649	104905	81808

United States

1.8 Capital Transactions of The Nation, Summary
(Continued)

Million United States dollars

	1970	1975	1978	1979	1980	1981	1982	1983	1984	1985	1986	1987
C Other	69252	123710	136176	147663	171470	197489	199784	180950	215917	184075	185949	174634
Less: Surplus of the nation on current transactions	3939	21596	-10138	1447	11829	9477	-953	-33485	-90948	-114359	-142380	-160606
Statistical discrepancy	-1133	2502	-1908	-965	4920	4124	-56	5161	5359	-4750	-13647	-8114
Finance of Gross Capital Formation	179863	268163	475075	515731	508253	591713	525237	568601	736220	742394	762045	809707
Gross Capital Formation												
Increase in stocks	1369	-4181	30042	13102	-6014	32390	-12341	-9007	66204	24275	20760	37072
Gross fixed capital formation	178494	272344	445033	502629	514267	559323	537578	577608	670016	718119	741285	772635
1 General government	25077	33500	37398	41087	47261	45749	46935	49367	51240	62471	64103	70669
2 Corporate and quasi-corporate enterprises	88304	142896	226503	256999	274429	310358	303373	305946	360465	389462	386152	396741
A Public	7740	13661	19431	19668	21708	22071	18830	18874	21633	23876	26777	28268
B Private	80564	129235	207072	237331	252721	288287	284543	287072	338832	365586	359375	368473
3 Other	65113	95948	181132	204543	192577	203216	187270	222295	258311	266186	291030	305225
Gross Capital Formation	179863	268163	475075	515731	508253	591713	525237	568601	736220	742394	762045	809707

1.9 Gross Domestic Product by Institutional Sectors of Origin

Million United States dollars

	1970	1975	1978	1979	1980	1981	1982	1983	1984	1985	1986	1987
Domestic Factor Incomes Originating												
1 General government	120050	190050	244345	264870	294059	323789	351777	374733	397767	427587	452308	482382
2 Corporate and quasi-corporate enterprises	662975	1011580	1468360	1631100	1741830	1937830	1972940	2134690	2418410	2588230	2753820	2943690
3 Households and private unincorporated enterprises	4501	4634	6247	6462	6586	7043	7596	8160	8928	9033	9079	9196
A Owner-occupied housing	...	...	...	...	...	...	...	...	...	...	...	...
B Subsistence production	...	...	...	...	...	...	...	...	...	...	...	...
C Other	4501	4634	6247	6462	6586	7043	7596	8160	8928	9033	9079	9196
4 Non-profit institutions serving households	27907	47393	63981	72167	82700	93930	105147	114710	123804	133294	144037	159751
Subtotal: Domestic Factor Incomes	815433	1253660	1782930	1974600	2125170	2362600	2437460	2632290	2948910	3158150	3359240	3595020
Indirect taxes, net	89075	134910	168539	179810	202558	239294	243352	260385	291184	310774	321155	334540
A Indirect taxes	94026	139996	178066	189352	213281	251476	258835	282560	313914	333637	348446	366323
B Less: Subsidies	4951	5086	9527	9542	10723	12182	15483	22175	22730	22863	27291	31783
Consumption of fixed capital	105843	192851	269346	311362	355816	403461	440644	455627	476888	503300	524716	551464
Statistical discrepancy	-1133	2502	-1908	-965	4920	4124	-56	5170	5359	-4750	-13647	-8114
Gross Domestic Product	1009220	1583920	2218910	2464810	2688470	3009470	3121400	3353470	3722340	3967470	4191470	4472910

1.10 Gross Domestic Product by Kind of Activity, in Current Prices

Million United States dollars

	1970	1975	1978	1979	1980	1981	1982	1983	1984	1985	1986	1987
1 Agriculture, hunting, forestry and fishing	27856	53037	65114	77193	70320	83722	81370	66394	85305	85222	86481	89201
2 Mining and quarrying	18791	41524	56816	73139	107854	144398	132893	119060	120347	115158	83072	86434
3 Manufacturing	254115	360183	522763	566612	586438	649631	641021	689493	778413	797379	828377	862331
4 Electricity, gas and water [a]	24055	42718	58131	58663	68682	80847	92490	104001	119496	127796	134167	137292
5 Construction	51853	77338	116586	132712	139366	140321	142956	151321	173526	188603	206164	220746
6 Wholesale and retail trade, restaurants and hotels	174064	280491	384900	429917	455226	500354	525500	563712	635022	682807	724092	767723
7 Transport, storage and communication	64905	99740	143749	158544	173314	190158	197763	217833	237226	249174	262378	274194
8 Finance, insurance, real estate and business services	186844	291899	432204	490311	548516	622462	663127	746450	817524	915395	1022510	1123880
9 Community, social and personal services	78633	128259	180214	199065	224472	250312	276551	302886	331136	363927	392052	431784
Statistical discrepancy [b]	14497	22471	29734	32001	33840	37976	40023	44085	51940	57723	60017	62629
Total, Industries	895613	1397660	1990210	2218160	2408030	2700180	2793690	3005240	3349940	3583180	3799310	4056210
Producers of Government Services	133661	214385	274784	299972	333978	366259	395374	419322	443982	477659	504389	536442
Other Producers	...	...	...	...	...	...	...	...	...	...	...	...
Subtotal	1029270	1612050	2265000	2518130	2742010	3066440	3189070	3424560	3793920	4060840	4303700	4592650
Less: Imputed bank service charge	21407	36492	51280	59814	65620	69681	76225	85345	88844	100779	112282	127079
Plus: Import duties	2484	5864	7100	7454	7160	8589	8609	9091	11904	12158	13697	15445
Plus: Value added tax	...	...	...	...	...	...	...	...	...	...	...	...
Plus: Other adjustments [c]	-1133	2502	-1908	-965	4920	4124	-56	5170	5359	-4750	-13647	-8114
Equals: Gross Domestic Product	1009220	1583920	2218910	2464800	2688470	3009470	3121400	3353470	3722340	3967470	4191470	4472910

a) Item 'Electricity, gas and water' also includes sanitary and similar services.
b) Item 'Statistical discrepancy' refers to government enterprises.
c) Item 'Other adjustments' refers to statistical discrepancy.

United States

1.11 Gross Domestic Product by Kind of Activity, in Constant Prices

Million United States dollars

		1970	1975	1978	1979	1980	1981	1982	1983	1984	1985	1986	1987
						At constant prices of:1980							
1	Agriculture, hunting, forestry and fishing	65236	69958	67729	71843	70320	81329	82539	67065	76496	87857	91615	91122
2	Mining and quarrying	106499	99637	102272	103566	107854	111078	104573	99450	105884	103740	92982	94538
3	Manufacturing	444747	480455	599805	613150	586438	597779	560720	594971	667550	694514	710835	742670
4	Electricity, gas and water [a]	48473	64847	66058	66947	68682	73749	73992	76401	83563	84773	83268	85274
5	Construction	144375	128696	151883	149366	139366	127320	121798	127020	137274	142455	148984	151308
6	Wholesale and retail trade, restaurants and hotels	334209	391048	454099	464232	455226	460673	459839	479268	521574	549829	577190	591994
7	Transport, storage and communication	119441	137954	168446	174879	173314	170659	164326	172136	181135	184895	191246	204230
8	Finance, insurance, real estate and business services	366964	442017	510680	536556	548516	565760	565002	584203	611029	637676	665554	695380
9	Community, social and personal services	158717	188510	215066	219657	224472	233150	237537	245786	256926	270793	280958	294903
	Statistical discrepancy [b]	26093	28879	31572	32344	33840	33721	32658	33587	34497	35478	36374	37358
	Total, Industries	1814750	2032000	2367610	2432540	2408030	2455220	2402980	2479890	2675930	2792010	2879010	2988780
	Producers of Government Services	294298	310846	324443	328513	333978	337400	338089	340550	342795	350545	356356	362904
	Other Producers	...	...	...	...	...	...	...	...	...	...	...	...
	Subtotal	2109050	2342850	2692050	2761050	2742010	2792620	2741070	2820440	3018720	3142560	3235360	3351680
	Less: Imputed bank service charge	45559	55508	62355	64032	65620	64762	67357	71386	72023	74278	76662	77424
	Plus: Import duties	5023	8412	8747	8194	7160	7958	7817	8093	10294	10554	11924	13070
	Plus: Value added tax	...	...	...	...	...	...	...	...	...	...	...	...
	Plus: Other adjustments [c]	-16703	-4026	-191	-14799	4920	13525	-2951	26499	25991	16725	17344	13944
	Equals: Gross Domestic Product	2051810	2291730	2638250	2690420	2688470	2749340	2678580	2783640	2982980	3095560	3187970	3301270

a) Item 'Electricity, gas and water' also includes sanitary and similar services.
b) Item 'Statistical discrepancy' refers to government enterprises.
c) Item 'Other adjustments' refers to statistical discrepancy.

1.12 Relations Among National Accounting Aggregates

Million United States dollars

	1970	1975	1978	1979	1980	1981	1982	1983	1984	1985	1986	1987
Gross Domestic Product	1009220	1583920	2218910	2464810	2688470	3009470	3121400	3353470	3722340	3967470	4191470	4472910
Plus: Net factor income from the rest of the world	7253	17540	30543	43801	47592	52108	51163	49864	47417	40727	34890	29482
Factor income from the rest of the world	12545	27202	45740	68104	78368	90489	91626	88721	100420	89651	87503	96067
Less: Factor income to the rest of the world [a]	5292	9662	15197	24303	30776	38381	40463	38857	53003	48924	52613	66585
Equals: Gross National Product	1016470	1601460	2249450	2508610	2736060	3061580	3172560	3403340	3769750	4008200	4226360	4502390
Less: Consumption of fixed capital	105843	192851	269346	311362	355816	403461	440644	455627	476888	503300	524716	551464
Equals: National Income	910628	1408610	1980110	2197240	2380240	2658120	2731920	2947710	3292870	3504900	3701640	3950920
Plus: Net current transfers from the rest of the world	-6217	-7123	-5832	-6659	-8443	-8219	-9598	-9732	-12405	-15128	-15482	-13576
Current transfers from the rest of the world	382	735	1212	1391	1580	1482	1505	1489	1342	1561	1964	2168
Less: Current transfers to the rest of the world	6599	7858	7044	8050	10023	9701	11103	11221	13747	16689	17446	15744
Equals: National Disposable Income	904411	1401480	1974270	2190590	2371800	2649900	2722320	2937980	3280460	3489770	3686160	3937350
Less: Final consumption	825428	1300030	1770010	1973650	2194940	2435290	2620390	2840660	3092310	3343730	3568600	3815660
Statistical discrepancy [b]	1133	-2502	1908	965	-4920	-4124	56	-5161	-5359	4750	13647	8114
Equals: Net Saving [c]	79092	94406	197499	206782	159347	193606	83696	74328	163025	129485	108596	105751
Less: Surplus of the nation on current transactions	3939	21596	-10138	1448	11830	9478	-953	-33485	-90948	-114359	-142380	-160606
Statistical discrepancy [b]	-1133	2502	-1908	-965	4920	4124	-56	5161	5359	-4750	-13647	-8114
Equals: Net Capital Formation	74020	75312	205729	204369	152437	188252	84593	112974	259332	239094	237329	258243

a) Item 'Factor income to the rest of the world' excludes factor income paid to the rest of the world by General Government.
b) Statistical Discrepancy is defined as the difference between GNP less charges against GNP other than Statistical Discrepancy. It arises because GNP and charges against GNP are independently derived by different methodologies. This Statistical Discrepancy after item 'Final consumption' is treated as a negative item and after item 'Surplus of the nations on current transactions', it is treated as a positive item.
c) Factor income paid to the rest of the world by general government is deducted from item 'Net saving'.

2.1 Government Final Consumption Expenditure by Function, in Current Prices

Million United States dollars

		1970	1975	1978	1979	1980	1981	1982	1983	1984	1985	1986	1987
1	General public services	10623	16798	22994	26664	30441	33271	36951	39389	42996	45820	48897	53189
2	Defence	74119	87738	108743	121491	142013	166814	193341	213984	232750	259094	277403	295250
3	Public order and safety	8421	16564	22138	24427	26918	30365	34445	37763	41212	45637	51075	55096
4	Education	44702	79445	100361	111393	122828	133962	144928	153555	164744	175491	188604	201063
5	Health	8651	16727	21379	22583	25897	28358	29359	30839	33391	34265	37454	41012

United States

2.1 Government Final Consumption Expenditure by Function, in Current Prices
(Continued)

Million United States dollars

	1970	1975	1978	1979	1980	1981	1982	1983	1984	1985	1986	1987
6 Social security and welfare	4326	9824	14069	15495	17282	18799	19969	21021	23170	24207	25420	27297
7 Housing and community amenities	4744	8847	12527	13370	14528	13698	13527	13222	14834	15896	18105	19123
8 Recreational, cultural and religious affairs	1864	3805	5000	5390	5991	6226	6395	6462	6783	7460	8433	9465
9 Economic services	27651	43194	54592	61463	68661	73557	74492	78985	85800	94626	97773	101120
A Fuel and energy	2137	5240	8861	9042	8862	9993	8433	7499	8224	10946	9609	9531
B Agriculture, forestry, fishing and hunting	2266	2863	3510	3949	4474	4896	5570	6724	7781	7864	7739	6896
C Mining, manufacturing and construction, except fuel and energy	2360	4106	5189	6360	7124	8250	8264	8843	8554	9378	9428	10316
D Transportation and communication	17788	25882	30180	34523	39027	40800	42809	45874	50501	54884	58661	61428
E Other economic affairs	3100	5103	6852	7589	9174	9618	9416	10045	10740	11554	12336	12949
10 Other functions	4485	11277	15485	16648	19163	20563	20683	21783	24429	25430	27239	29374
Total Government Final Consumption Expenditure	189586	294219	377288	418924	473722	525613	574090	617003	670109	727926	780403	831989

2.3 Total Government Outlays by Function and Type

Million United States dollars

	Final Consumption Expenditures Total	Compensation of Employees	Other	Subsidies	Other Current Transfers & Property Income	Total Current Disbursements	Gross Capital Formation	Other Capital Outlays	Total Outlays
1980									
1 General public services	30441	...	...	...	...	...	...	...	...
2 Defence	142013	...	...	...	...	...	...	...	...
3 Public order and safety	26918	...	...	...	...	...	...	...	...
4 Education	122828	...	...	...	...	...	...	...	...
5 Health	25897	...	...	...	...	...	...	...	...
6 Social security and welfare	17282	...	...	...	...	...	...	...	...
7 Housing and community amenities	14528	...	...	...	...	...	...	...	...
8 Recreation, culture and religion	5991	...	...	...	...	...	...	...	...
9 Economic services	68661	...	...	...	...	...	...	...	...
A Fuel and energy	8862	...	...	...	...	...	...	...	...
B Agriculture, forestry, fishing and hunting	4474	...	...	...	...	...	...	...	...
C Mining (except fuels), manufacturing and construction	7124	...	...	...	...	...	...	...	...
D Transportation and communication	39027	...	...	...	...	...	...	...	...
E Other economic affairs	9174	...	...	...	...	...	...	...	...
10 Other functions	19163	...	...	...	...	...	...	...	...
Total	473722	294059	179663	10723	385381	869826	48551	-2422	915955
1981									
1 General public services	33271	...	...	...	...	...	...	...	...
2 Defence	166814	...	...	...	...	...	...	...	...
3 Public order and safety	30365	...	...	...	...	...	...	...	...
4 Education	133962	...	...	...	...	...	...	...	...
5 Health	28358	...	...	...	...	...	...	...	...
6 Social security and welfare	18799	...	...	...	...	...	...	...	...
7 Housing and community amenities	13698	...	...	...	...	...	...	...	...
8 Recreation, culture and religion	6226	...	...	...	...	...	...	...	...
9 Economic services	73557	...	...	...	...	...	...	...	...
A Fuel and energy	9993	...	...	...	...	...	...	...	...
B Agriculture, forestry, fishing and hunting	4896	...	...	...	...	...	...	...	...
C Mining (except fuels), manufacturing and construction	8250	...	...	...	...	...	...	...	...
D Transportation and communication	40800	...	...	...	...	...	...	...	...
E Other economic affairs	9618	...	...	...	...	...	...	...	...
10 Other functions	20563	...	...	...	...	...	...	...	...
Total	525613	323789	201824	12182	451664	989459	50890	-3643	1036710

United States

2.3 Total Government Outlays by Function and Type
(Continued)

Million United States dollars

		Final Consumption Expenditures Total	Compensation of Employees	Other	Subsidies	Other Current Transfers & Property Income	Total Current Disbursements	Gross Capital Formation	Other Capital Outlays	Total Outlays
					1982					
1	General public services	36951	...	...	...	...	...	...	...	...
2	Defence	193341	...	...	...	...	...	...	...	...
3	Public order and safety	34445	...	...	...	...	...	...	...	...
4	Education	144928	...	...	...	...	...	...	...	...
5	Health	29359	...	...	...	...	...	...	...	...
6	Social security and welfare	19969	...	...	...	...	...	...	...	...
7	Housing and community amenities	13527	...	...	...	...	...	...	...	...
8	Recreation, culture and religion	6395	...	...	...	...	...	...	...	...
9	Economic services	74492	...	...	...	...	...	...	...	...
	A Fuel and energy	8433	...	...	...	...	...	...	...	...
	B Agriculture, forestry, fishing and hunting	5570	...	...	...	...	...	...	...	...
	C Mining (except fuels), manufacturing and construction	8264	...	...	...	...	...	...	...	...
	D Transportation and communication	42809	...	...	...	...	...	...	...	...
	E Other economic affairs	9416	...	...	...	...	...	...	...	...
10	Other functions	20683	...	...	...	...	...	...	...	...
	Total	574090	351777	222313	15483	510546	1100120	49711	-1636	1148190
					1983					
1	General public services	39389	...	...	...	...	...	...	...	...
2	Defence	213984	...	...	...	...	...	...	...	...
3	Public order and safety	37763	...	...	...	...	...	...	...	...
4	Education	153555	...	...	...	...	...	...	...	...
5	Health	30839	...	...	...	...	...	...	...	...
6	Social security and welfare	21021	...	...	...	...	...	...	...	...
7	Housing and community amenities	13222	...	...	...	...	...	...	...	...
8	Recreation, culture and religion	6462	...	...	...	...	...	...	...	...
9	Economic services	78985	...	...	...	...	...	...	...	...
	A Fuel and energy	7499	...	...	...	...	...	...	...	...
	B Agriculture, forestry, fishing and hunting	6724	...	...	...	...	...	...	...	...
	C Mining (except fuels), manufacturing and construction	8843	...	...	...	...	...	...	...	...
	D Transportation and communication	45874	...	...	...	...	...	...	...	...
	E Other economic affairs	10045	...	...	...	...	...	...	...	...
10	Other functions	21783	...	...	...	...	...	...	...	...
	Total	617003	374733	242270	22175	556627	1195810	52835	-2854	1245790
					1984					
1	General public services	42996	...	...	...	...	...	...	...	...
2	Defence	232750	...	...	...	...	...	...	...	...
3	Public order and safety	41212	...	...	...	...	...	...	...	...
4	Education	164744	...	...	...	...	...	...	...	...
5	Health	33391	...	...	...	...	...	...	...	...
6	Social security and welfare	23170	...	...	...	...	...	...	...	...
7	Housing and community amenities	14834	...	...	...	...	...	...	...	...
8	Recreation, culture and religion	6783	...	...	...	...	...	...	...	...
9	Economic services	85800	...	...	...	...	...	...	...	...
	A Fuel and energy	8224	...	...	...	...	...	...	...	...
	B Agriculture, forestry, fishing and hunting	7781	...	...	...	...	...	...	...	...
	C Mining (except fuels), manufacturing and construction	8554	...	...	...	...	...	...	...	...
	D Transportation and communication	50501	...	...	...	...	...	...	...	...
	E Other economic affairs	10740	...	...	...	...	...	...	...	...
10	Other functions	24429	...	...	...	...	...	...	...	...
	Total	670109	397767	272344	22730	595382	1288220	53383	-1515	1340090

United States

2.3 Total Government Outlays by Function and Type
(Continued)

Million United States dollars

		Final Consumption Expenditures Total	Compensation of Employees	Other	Subsidies	Other Current Transfers & Property Income	Total Current Disbursements	Gross Capital Formation	Other Capital Outlays	Total Outlays
	1985									
1	General public services	45820	...	...	...	...	...	...	...	...
2	Defence	259094	...	...	...	...	...	...	...	...
3	Public order and safety	45637	...	...	...	...	...	...	...	...
4	Education	175491	...	...	...	...	...	...	...	...
5	Health	34265	...	...	...	...	...	...	...	...
6	Social security and welfare	24207	...	...	...	...	...	...	...	...
7	Housing and community amenities	15896	...	...	...	...	...	...	...	...
8	Recreation, culture and religion	7460	...	...	...	...	...	...	...	...
9	Economic services	94626	...	...	...	...	...	...	...	...
	A Fuel and energy	10946	...	...	...	...	...	...	...	...
	B Agriculture, forestry, fishing and hunting	7864	...	...	...	...	...	...	...	...
	C Mining (except fuels), manufacturing and construction	9378	...	...	...	...	...	...	...	...
	D Transportation and communication	54884	...	...	...	...	...	...	...	...
	E Other economic affairs	11554	...	...	...	...	...	...	...	...
10	Other functions	25430	...	...	...	...	...	...	...	...
	Total	727926	427587	300339	22863	647236	1398030	64188	1772	1463990
	1986									
1	General public services	48897	...	...	...	...	...	...	...	...
2	Defence	277403	...	...	...	...	...	...	...	...
3	Public order and safety	51075	...	...	...	...	...	...	...	...
4	Education	188604	...	...	...	...	...	...	...	...
5	Health	37454	...	...	...	...	...	...	...	...
6	Social security and welfare	25420	...	...	...	...	...	...	...	...
7	Housing and community amenities	18105	...	...	...	...	...	...	...	...
8	Recreation, culture and religion	8433	...	...	...	...	...	...	...	...
9	Economic services	97773	...	...	...	...	...	...	...	...
	A Fuel and energy	9609	...	...	...	...	...	...	...	...
	B Agriculture, forestry, fishing and hunting	7739	...	...	...	...	...	...	...	...
	C Mining (except fuels), manufacturing and construction	9428	...	...	...	...	...	...	...	...
	D Transportation and communication	58661	...	...	...	...	...	...	...	...
	E Other economic affairs	12336	...	...	...	...	...	...	...	...
10	Other functions	27239	...	...	...	...	...	...	...	...
	Total	780403	452308	328095	27291	685253	1492950	64193	393	1557530
	1987									
1	General public services	53189	...	...	...	...	...	...	...	...
2	Defence	295250	...	...	...	...	...	...	...	...
3	Public order and safety	55096	...	...	...	...	...	...	...	...
4	Education	201063	...	...	...	...	...	...	...	...
5	Health	41012	...	...	...	...	...	...	...	...
6	Social security and welfare	27297	...	...	...	...	...	...	...	...
7	Housing and community amenities	19123	...	...	...	...	...	...	...	...
8	Recreation, culture and religion	9465	...	...	...	...	...	...	...	...
9	Economic services	101120	...	...	...	...	...	...	...	...
	A Fuel and energy	9531	...	...	...	...	...	...	...	...
	B Agriculture, forestry, fishing and hunting	6896	...	...	...	...	...	...	...	...
	C Mining (except fuels), manufacturing and construction	10316	...	...	...	...	...	...	...	...
	D Transportation and communication	61428	...	...	...	...	...	...	...	...
	E Other economic affairs	12949	...	...	...	...	...	...	...	...
10	Other functions	29374	...	...	...	...	...	...	...	...
	Total	831989	482382	349607	31783	714983	1578760	71700	3193	1653650

United States

2.4 Composition of General Government Social Security Benefits and Social Assistance Grants to Households
Million United States dollars

		1980 SSB	1980 SAG	1981 SSB	1981 SAG	1982 SSB	1982 SAG	1983 SSB	1983 SAG	1984 SSB	1984 SAG	1985 SSB	1985 SAG
1	Education benefits	...	9318	...	10332	...	9716	...	10489	...	10489	...	10941
2	Health benefits	...	26671	...	31041	...	33982	...	37264	...	40553	...	44228
3	Social security and welfare benefits	180285	50279	208948	53343	242014	53744	261039	56806	265268	58140	283539	60170
4	Housing and community amenities	...	167	...	163	...	96	...	16	...	16	...	83
5	Recreation and cultural benefits	...	312	...	408	...	264	...	425	...	520	...	326
6	Other	...	2563	...	2080	...	1851	...	1832	...	1581	...	1775
	Total	180285	89310	208948	97367	242014	99653	261039	106832	265268	111299	283539	117523

		1986 SSB	1986 SAG	1987 SSB	1987 SAG
1	Education benefits	...	11007	...	11396
2	Health benefits	...	48528	...	53524
3	Social security and welfare benefits	300639	62477	313389	63949
4	Housing and community amenities	...	319	...	328
5	Recreation and cultural benefits	...	472	...	387
6	Other	...	2006	...	1940
	Total	300639	124809	313389	131524

2.5 Private Final Consumption Expenditure by Type and Purpose, in Current Prices
Million United States dollars

		1970	1975	1978	1979	1980	1981	1982	1983	1984	1985	1986	1987
	Final Consumption Expenditure of Resident Households												
1	Food, beverages and tobacco	118018	177961	221360	246179	269655	292539	310611	326598	344907	363872	382787	397596
	A Food	89915	135675	170384	189675	207663	225806	240171	250415	265885	280224	295233	306670
	B Non-alcoholic beverages	5054	8099	9955	11076	12130	13188	14036	14630	15526	16367	17247	17901
	C Alcoholic beverages	12257	19119	23359	26134	29112	30809	31749	33306	32950	35099	36667	37365
	D Tobacco	10792	15068	17662	19294	20750	22736	24655	28247	30546	32182	33640	35660
2	Clothing and footwear	52283	75766	101293	109315	116945	128589	133619	146029	158508	169250	180989	193098
3	Gross rent, fuel and power	114628	187514	261375	295465	338021	381325	416048	445858	479053	516764	546266	581250
	A Fuel and power	19584	36984	54119	62586	74345	82919	91391	97473	102595	107386	104085	104916
	B Other	95044	150530	207256	232879	263676	298406	324657	348385	376458	409378	442181	476334
4	Furniture, furnishings and household equipment and operation	46397	67259	92517	102263	108191	115915	118458	129008	141128	149613	161771	170856
	A Household operation	13589	18630	25365	27726	29864	32283	34022	35805	38191	39978	42665	44954
	B Other	32808	48629	67152	74537	78327	83632	84436	93203	102937	109635	119106	125902
5	Medical care and health expenses	59930	107576	157137	178170	205113	240347	270020	295381	326602	358074	391898	438138
6	Transport and communication	95099	155230	232532	257831	277136	304717	315806	346689	384489	416301	425788	441772
	A Personal transport equipment	30826	47851	84341	84916	77104	85258	92611	112666	138992	159138	175489	173832
	B Other	64273	107379	148191	172915	200032	219459	223195	234023	245497	257163	250299	267940
7	Recreational, entertainment, education and cultural services	54550	89143	120774	134446	147175	165244	178166	196146	216359	238571	259580	285770
	A Education	12530	20580	26970	30273	34314	38861	41939	46184	50465	55663	60619	65465
	B Other	42020	68563	93804	104173	112861	126383	136227	149962	165894	182908	198961	220305
8	Miscellaneous goods and services	90423	140921	201246	226479	254850	277992	298450	329472	359885	390248	427133	461558
	A Personal care	20280	30579	42908	46606	51321	55417	56897	62596	67849	71605	77007	82446
	B Expenditures in restaurants, cafes and hotels	37340	59778	84953	98252	108806	116017	122758	134418	145934	152813	165104	178913
	C Other	32803	50564	73385	81621	94723	106558	118795	132458	146102	165830	185022	200199
	Total Final Consumption Expenditure in the Domestic Market by Households, of which	631328	1001370	1388230	1550150	1717090	1906670	2041180	2215180	2410930	2602690	2776210	2970040
	A Durable goods	67119	106331	165466	174880	171918	187634	197917	228590	269708	302931	331489	341705
	B Semi-durable goods	93060	138574	185819	202304	216974	237810	247421	269778	293002	312082	335078	359170
	C Non-durable goods	185929	294526	379495	433467	492329	538543	566020	595236	624902	655107	660093	687917

United States

2.5 Private Final Consumption Expenditure by Type and Purpose, in Current Prices
(Continued)

Million United States dollars

	1970	1975	1978	1979	1980	1981	1982	1983	1984	1985	1986	1987
D Services	285220	461939	657454	739497	835865	942681	1029820	1121580	1223320	1332570	1449550	1581250
Plus: Direct purchases abroad by resident households [a]	7177	9817	12577	13976	15691	17026	18777	21308	24640	26456	26837	31086
Less: Direct purchases in the domestic market by non-resident households	2663	5372	8095	9402	11558	14013	13651	12828	13373	13345	14851	17454
Equals: Final Consumption Expenditure of Resident Households [b]	635842	1005820	1392720	1554720	1721220	1909680	2046300	2223660	2422200	2615800	2788200	2983670

Final Consumption Expenditure of Private Non-profit Institutions Serving Households

	1970	1975	1978	1979	1980	1981	1982	1983	1984	1985	1986	1987
Equals: Final Consumption Expenditure of Private Non-profit Organisations Serving Households	...	...	...	...	...	...	...	...	...	...	...	...
Private Final Consumption Expenditure	635842	1005820	1392720	1554720	1721220	1909680	2046300	2223660	2422200	2615800	2788200	2983670

a) Item 'Direct purchases abroad by resident households' includes direct purchases abroad by resident households less value of gifts in kind, sent abroad, net.
b) Item 'Final consumption expenditure of resident households' includes consumption expenditure of private non-profit institutions serving households.

2.6 Private Final Consumption Expenditure by Type and Purpose, in Constant Prices

Million United States dollars

	1970	1975	1978	1979	1980	1981	1982	1983	1984	1985	1986	1987

At constant prices of: 1980

Final Consumption Expenditure of Resident Households

	1970	1975	1978	1979	1980	1981	1982	1983	1984	1985	1986	1987
1 Food, beverages and tobacco	241780	244225	261233	264428	269655	270472	275644	283556	287571	298842	305175	302497
A Food	198817	188207	202052	203464	207663	208411	214126	222062	226386	236157	242399	240115
B Non-alcoholic beverages	4834	11159	11768	11880	12130	12149	12469	12939	13185	13756	14119	13962
C Alcoholic beverages	20290	25021	27230	28275	29112	28859	28534	28864	28019	29056	29220	29192
D Tobacco	17839	19838	20183	20808	20750	21053	20515	19691	19980	19874	19437	19228
2 Clothing and footwear	77756	91406	109815	114326	116945	123833	125705	134408	143649	148642	158954	161881
3 Gross rent, fuel and power	246265	293232	322866	332350	338021	340915	343258	348144	355868	366431	373973	383844
A Fuel and power	63864	68729	76811	76667	74345	71504	71655	72796	73684	76188	77614	78790
B Other	182400	224504	246055	255683	263676	269411	271603	275348	282184	290242	296359	305054
4 Furniture, furnishings and household equipment and operation	87295	92790	107359	110980	108191	107386	103795	109757	118080	123016	130511	134582
A Household operation	31943	28523	30016	30380	29864	29420	29353	30065	31498	31920	32793	33190
B Other	55352	64267	77342	80600	78327	77967	74442	79692	86581	91096	97719	101392
5 Medical care and health expenses	121869	164446	189058	197584	205113	216332	222380	227284	234112	242081	251590	266370
6 Transport and communication	210224	250468	307066	302162	277136	276684	278164	300284	323631	342376	359234	360010
A Personal transport equipment	55104	67296	97157	91007	77104	78237	80154	94636	111207	123791	133426	127446
B Other	155120	183171	209909	211154	200032	198447	198010	205648	212424	218584	225808	232564
7 Recreational, entertainment, education and cultural services	86116	119529	139636	145614	147176	154303	159095	170954	185585	202639	218843	235823
A Education	28603	31428	33351	33884	34314	35211	35889	37890	39567	42188	44514	46392
B Other	57513	88102	106285	111730	112862	119093	123206	133065	146018	160451	174329	189431
8 Miscellaneous goods and services	188524	210845	246372	253204	254850	254762	251673	270550	282581	295359	311549	320607
A Personal care	39681	44821	52741	53108	51321	51636	50965	53920	57043	58958	62165	63656
B Expenditures in restaurants, cafes and hotels	78559	89398	103405	107801	108806	106398	106386	111445	115674	116020	120237	125217
C Other	70285	76626	90226	92295	94723	96727	94323	105185	109864	120381	129147	131734
Total Final Consumption Expenditure in the Domestic Market by Households, of which	1259830	1466940	1683400	1720650	1717090	1744690	1759720	1844940	1931080	2019390	2109830	2165620
A Durable goods	101396	142285	191037	189209	171919	175701	177998	201354	231920	258571	281724	284382
B Semi-durable goods	148430	176677	208919	216212	216974	225281	226108	241275	259015	269362	287546	297612
C Non-durable goods	435662	457273	495868	497544	492329	488799	493695	507434	515494	529556	541695	543501

United States

2.6 Private Final Consumption Expenditure by Type and Purpose, in Constant Prices
(Continued)

Million United States dollars

	1970	1975	1978	1979	1980	1981	1982	1983	1984	1985	1986	1987
					At constant prices of:1980							
D Services	574340	690706	787581	817682	835865	854906	861914	894875	924646	961897	998864	1040120
Plus: Direct purchases abroad by resident households [a]	17521	13777	15531	15641	15691	15904	18403	21123	24552	27201	25068	27089
Less: Direct purchases in the domestic market by non-resident households	5426	8254	9954	10556	11558	12676	11469	10322	10231	9763	10495	11786
Equals: Final Consumption Expenditure of Resident Households [b]	1271920	1472470	1688980	1725730	1721220	1747910	1766650	1855740	1945400	2036820	2124400	2180920

Final Consumption Expenditure of Private Non-profit Institutions Serving Households

	1970	1975	1978	1979	1980	1981	1982	1983	1984	1985	1986	1987
Equals: Final Consumption Expenditure of Private Non-profit Organisations Serving Households	...	...	...	...	...	...	...	...	...	...	...	...
Private Final Consumption Expenditure	1271920	1472470	1688980	1725730	1721220	1747910	1766650	1855740	1945400	2036820	2124400	2180920

a) Item 'Direct purchases abroad by resident households' includes direct purchases abroad by resident households less value of gifts in kind, sent abroad, net.   b) Item 'Final consumption expenditure of resident households' includes consumption expenditure of private non-profit institutions serving households.

2.7 Gross Capital Formation by Type of Good and Owner, in Current Prices

Million United States dollars

	1980				1981				1982			
	TOTAL	Total Private	Public Enterprises	General Government	TOTAL	Total Private	Public Enterprises	General Government	TOTAL	Total Private	Public Enterprises	General Government
Increase in stocks, total	-6014	-8329	1025	1290	32390	24007	3242	5141	-12341	-24532	9415	2776
1 Goods producing industries [a]	-4524	-4524	...	...	9034	9034	...	...	-16528	-16528	...	...
A Materials and supplies	-709	-709	...	...	-4701	-4701	...	...	-6997	-6997	...	...
B Work in progress	1917	1917	...	...	-35	-35	...	...	-5188	-5188	...	...
C Livestock, except breeding stocks, dairy cattle, etc. [b]	1339	1339	...	...	286	286	...	...	-690	-690	...	...
D Finished goods	-7071	-7071	...	...	13484	13484	...	...	-3653	-3653	...	...
2 Wholesale and retail trade	-682	-682	...	...	8383	8383	...	...	-6082	-6082	...	...
3 Other, except government stocks	-2098	-3123	1025	...	9832	6590	3242	...	7493	-1922	9415	...
4 Government stocks	1290	...	...	1290	5141	...	...	5141	2776	...	...	2776
Gross Fixed Capital Formation, Total	514267	445298	21708	47261	559323	491503	22071	45749	537578	471813	18830	46935
1 Residential buildings [c]	121618	119453	1321	844	121311	118999	1400	912	104030	101847	1151	1032
2 Non-residential buildings	77645	61016	336	16293	85326	69505	463	15358	88152	73095	386	14671
3 Other construction	91005	52887	18156	19962	105826	68993	17603	19230	104800	70200	14589	20011
4 Land improvement and plantation and orchard development	...	...	...	...	...	...	...	...	...	...	...	...
5 Producers' durable goods	223999	211942	1895	10162	246860	234006	2605	10249	240596	226671	2704	11221
A Transport equipment	49336	44917	...	4419	51292	46248	...	5044	47377	42516	...	4861
Passenger cars	12522	11359	...	1163	14337	13129	...	1208	13543	12347	...	1196
Other	36814	33558	...	3256	36955	33119	...	3836	33834	30169	...	3665
B Machinery and equipment [d]	174663	167025	1895	5743	195568	187758	2605	5205	193219	184155	2704	6360
6 Breeding stock, dairy cattle, etc. [b]	...	...	...	...	...	...	...	...	...	...	...	...
Total Gross Capital Formation	508253	436969	22733	48551	591713	515510	25313	50890	525237	447281	28245	49711

	1983				1984				1985			
	TOTAL	Total Private	Public Enterprises	General Government	TOTAL	Total Private	Public Enterprises	General Government	TOTAL	Total Private	Public Enterprises	General Government
Increase in stocks, total	-9007	-7081	-5394	3468	66204	67688	-3627	2143	24275	11317	11241	1717
1 Goods producing industries [a]	-13265	-13265	...	...	28751	28751	...	...	-12653	-12653	...	...
A Materials and supplies	-508	-508	...	...	5232	5232	...	...	-4079	-4079	...	...
B Work in progress	-601	-601	...	...	9994	9994	...	...	-2226	-2226	...	...
C Livestock, except breeding stocks, dairy cattle, etc. [b]	-467	-467	...	...	-1697	-1697	...	...	-1915	-1915	...	...
D Finished goods	-11689	-11689	...	...	15222	15222	...	...	-4433	-4433	...	...
2 Wholesale and retail trade	6319	6319	...	...	30057	30057	...	...	15673	15673	...	...
3 Other, except government stocks	-5529	-135	-5394	...	5253	8880	-3627	...	19538	8297	11241	...
4 Government stocks	3468	...	...	3468	2143	...	...	2143	1717	...	...	1717
Gross Fixed Capital Formation, Total	577608	509367	18874	49367	670016	597143	21633	51240	718119	631772	23876	62471
1 Residential buildings [c]	150990	148375	1271	1344	179228	176485	1465	1278	186542	183756	1178	1608
2 Non-residential buildings	84531	68970	478	15083	99652	84265	417	14970	115525	96929	598	17998

United States

2.7 Gross Capital Formation by Type of Good and Owner, in Current Prices
(Continued)

Million United States dollars

	1983				1984				1985			
	TOTAL	Total Private	Public Enterprises	General Government	TOTAL	Total Private	Public Enterprises	General Government	TOTAL	Total Private	Public Enterprises	General Government
3 Other construction	88919	55079	13907	19933	94332	56850	15994	21488	99999	56274	17531	26194
4 Land improvement and plantation and orchard development	...	...	...	...	...	...	...	...	...	...	...	...
5 Producers' durable goods	253168	236943	3218	13007	296804	279543	3757	13504	316053	294813	4569	16671
A Transport equipment	54427	49456	...	4971	65875	59781	...	6094	71043	63777	...	7266
Passenger cars	18639	17347	...	1292	19629	18276	...	1353	19286	17900	...	1386
Other	35788	32109	...	3679	46246	41505	...	4741	51757	45877	...	5880
B Machinery and equipment [d]	198741	187487	3218	8036	230929	219762	3757	7410	245010	231036	4569	9405
6 Breeding stock, dairy cattle, etc. [b]	...	...	...	...	...	...	...	...	...	...	...	...
Total Gross Capital Formation	568601	502286	13480	52835	736220	664831	18006	53383	742394	643089	35117	64188

	1986				1987			
	TOTAL	Total Private	Public Enterprises	General Government	TOTAL	Total Private	Public Enterprises	General Government
Increase in stocks, total	20760	15544	5126	90	37072	39219	-3178	1031
1 Goods producing industries [a]	-5175	-5175	...	...	4595	4595	...	...
A Materials and supplies	-1241	-1241	...	...	636	636	...	...
B Work in progress	-1939	-1939	...	...	3905	3905	...	...
C Livestock, except breeding stocks, dairy cattle, etc. [b]	-1562	-1562	...	...	-1132	-1132	...	...
D Finished goods	-433	-433	...	...	1186	1186	...	...
2 Wholesale and retail trade	10278	10278	...	...	28702	28702	...	...
3 Other, except government stocks	15567	10441	5126	...	2744	5922	-3178	...
4 Government stocks	90	...	...	90	1031	...	...	1031
Gross Fixed Capital Formation, Total	741285	650405	26777	64103	772635	673698	28268	70669
1 Residential buildings [c]	214337	211062	1641	1634	224015	221071	1076	1868
2 Non-residential buildings	115399	93973	380	21046	118584	94553	865	23166
3 Other construction	89258	44503	19349	25406	91480	44899	20256	26325
4 Land improvement and plantation and orchard development	...	...	...	...	...	...	...	...
5 Producers' durable goods	322291	300867	5407	16017	338556	313175	6071	19310
A Transport equipment	73983	66908	...	7075	74111	67822	...	6289
Passenger cars	21755	20349	...	1406	20698	19187	...	1511
Other	52228	46559	...	5669	53413	48635	...	4778
B Machinery and equipment [d]	248308	233959	5407	8942	264445	245353	6071	13021
6 Breeding stock, dairy cattle, etc. [b]	...	...	...	...	...	...	...	...
Total Gross Capital Formation	762045	665949	31903	64193	809707	712917	25090	71700

a) Item 'Goods producing industries' includes only manufacturing and farming.
b) Item 'Breeding stocks, dairy cattle, etc.' is included in item 'Increase in stocks'.
c) The estimates of residential buildings of government enterprises and general government are included in the respective columns of item 'Residential buildings' in tables 2.7 and 2.8. These estimates are included in item 'Real estate' in tables 2.9-2.12 and are therefore excluded from the estimates of government enterprises and general government of these tables. This latter classification is followed in tables 2.13-2.16.
d) Item 'Machinery and equipment' includes all producers durable goods of public enterprises.

2.8 Gross Capital Formation by Type of Good and Owner, in Constant Prices

Million United States dollars

	1980				1981				1982			
	TOTAL	Total Private	Public Enterprises	General Government	TOTAL	Total Private	Public Enterprises	General Government	TOTAL	Total Private	Public Enterprises	General Government
	At constant prices of: 1980											
Increase in stocks, total	-6014	-8329	1025	1290	31744	21702	3884	6158	-8271	-22971	11353	3347
1 Goods producing industries [a]	-4524	-4524	...	...	8020	8020	...	...	-15837	-15837	...	...
A Materials and supplies	-709	-709	...	...	17942	17942	...	...	-7471	-7471	...	...
B Work in progress	1917	1917	...	...	-861	-861	...	...	-5384	-5384	...	...
C Livestock, except breeding stocks, dairy cattle, etc. [b]	1339	1339	...	...	278	278	...	...	-723	-723	...	...
D Finished goods	-7071	-7071	...	...	-9339	-9339	...	...	-2259	-2259	...	...
2 Wholesale and retail trade	-682	-682	...	...	7867	7867	...	...	-5573	-5573	...	...
3 Other, except government stocks	-2098	-3123	1025	...	9699	5815	3884	...	9792	-1561	11353	...
4 Government stocks	1290	...	...	1290	6158	...	...	6158	3347	...	...	3347
Gross Fixed Capital Formation, Total	514266	445297	21708	47261	513564	449065	21295	43204	468857	407356	18147	43353

1598

United States

2.8 Gross Capital Formation by Type of Good and Owner, in Constant Prices
(Continued)

Million United States dollars

	1980 TOTAL	1980 Total Private	1980 Public Enterprises	1980 General Government	1981 TOTAL	1981 Total Private	1981 Public Enterprises	1981 General Government	1982 TOTAL	1982 Total Private	1982 Public Enterprises	1982 General Government
					At constant prices of:1980							
1 Residential buildings c	121618	119453	1321	844	112286	110124	1309	853	93118	91114	1057	947
2 Non-residential buildings	77645	61016	336	16293	78120	63582	425	14113	76460	63379	335	12746
3 Other construction	91005	52887	18156	19962	95610	59723	17151	18736	89709	55644	14364	19701
4 Land improvement and plantation and orchard development	...	...	...	...	...	...	...	...	...	...	...	...
5 Producers' durable goods	223998	211941	1895	10162	227548	215636	2410	9502	209569	197219	2391	9959
A Transport equipment	49336	44917	...	4419	48153	43582	...	4571	43264	39071	...	4193
Passenger cars	12522	11359	...	1163	15007	13841	...	1166	14907	13777	...	1130
Other	36814	33558	...	3256	33146	29741	...	3405	28356	25293	...	3063
B Machinery and equipment d	174662	167024	1895	5743	179395	172054	2410	4931	166306	158148	2391	5766
6 Breeding stock, dairy cattle, etc. b	...	...	...	...	...	...	...	...	...	...	...	...
Total Gross Capital Formation	508252	436968	22733	48551	545308	470767	25179	49362	460586	384385	29500	46700

	1983 TOTAL	1983 Total Private	1983 Public Enterprises	1983 General Government	1984 TOTAL	1984 Total Private	1984 Public Enterprises	1984 General Government	1985 TOTAL	1985 Total Private	1985 Public Enterprises	1985 General Government
					At constant prices of:1980							
Increase in stocks, total	-9716	-7617	-5876	3777	54611	50258	-4026	2379	19799	7239	10896	1664
1 Goods producing industries a	-12381	-12381	...	...	23051	23051	...	...	-13101	-13101	...	...
A Materials and supplies	-828	-828	...	...	5717	5717	...	...	-4732	-4732	...	...
B Work in progress	-1399	-1399	...	...	9434	9434	...	...	-2279	-2279	...	...
C Livestock, except breeding stocks, dairy cattle, etc. b	-823	-823	...	...	-2664	-2664	...	...	-2862	-2862	...	...
D Finished goods	-9331	-9331	...	...	10564	10564	...	...	-3228	-3229	...	...
2 Wholesale and retail trade	4729	4729	...	...	25826	25826	...	...	13263	13263	...	...
3 Other, except government stocks	-5841	35	-5876	...	3355	7381	-4026	...	17973	7077	10896	...
4 Government stocks	3777	...	...	3777	2379	...	...	2379	1664	...	...	1664
Gross Fixed Capital Formation, Total	510038	446623	18218	45197	591044	525111	20298	45635	631802	557472	21070	53260
1 Residential buildings c	132604	130240	1149	1215	151490	149100	1277	1113	154038	151679	997	1362
2 Non-residential buildings	70649	57617	400	12632	79608	67288	334	11986	89186	74838	461	13887
3 Other construction	81954	48259	13847	19848	88247	52149	15403	20695	89456	50337	15684	23435
4 Land improvement and plantation and orchard development	...	...	...	...	...	...	...	...	...	...	...	...
5 Producers' durable goods	224831	210507	2822	11502	271699	256574	3284	11841	299122	280618	3928	14576
A Transport equipment	48983	44810	...	4173	59762	54778	...	4984	62762	57028	...	5734
Passenger cars	19950	18749	...	1201	23588	22288	...	1300	23130	21840	...	1290
Other	29033	26061	...	2972	36173	32490	...	3683	39632	35188	...	4444
B Machinery and equipment d	175848	165697	2822	7329	211938	201796	3284	6857	236360	223590	3928	8842
6 Breeding stock, dairy cattle, etc. b	...	...	...	...	...	...	...	...	...	...	...	...
Total Gross Capital Formation	500322	439006	12342	48974	645655	581369	16272	48014	651601	564711	31966	54924

	1986 TOTAL	1986 Total Private	1986 Public Enterprises	1986 General Government	1987 TOTAL	1987 Total Private	1987 Public Enterprises	1987 General Government
				At constant prices of:1980				
Increase in stocks, total	19005	12766	6132	107	26986	29259	-3364	1091
1 Goods producing industries a	-5847	-5847	...	...	2030	2030	...	...
A Materials and supplies	-1348	-1348	...	...	547	547	...	...
B Work in progress	-1837	-1837	...	...	3392	3392	...	...
C Livestock, except breeding stocks, dairy cattle, etc. b	-2293	-2293	...	...	-1589	-1589	...	...
D Finished goods	-369	-369	...	...	-320	-320	...	...
2 Wholesale and retail trade	9139	9139	...	...	21840	21840	...	...
3 Other, except government stocks	15606	9474	6132	...	2025	5389	-3364	...
4 Government stocks	107	...	...	107	1091	...	...	1091
Gross Fixed Capital Formation, Total	637755	561316	23310	53129	657213	574829	24403	57981

United States

2.8 Gross Capital Formation by Type of Good and Owner, in Constant Prices
(Continued)

Million United States dollars

	1986				1987			
	TOTAL	Total Private	Public Enterprises	General Government	TOTAL	Total Private	Public Enterprises	General Government
	At constant prices of: 1980							
1 Residential buildings [c]	172459	169763	1351	1345	171982	169660	849	1473
2 Non-residential buildings	86649	70592	285	15772	85542	68233	623	16686
3 Other construction	78748	39244	17079	22425	79556	38631	17796	23129
4 Land improvement and plantation and orchard development	...	...	...	...	...	...	...	...
5 Producers' durable goods	299899	281717	4595	13587	320133	298305	5135	16693
A Transport equipment	60949	55605	...	5344	59599	54908	...	4691
Passenger cars	22191	20941	...	1250	20495	19196	...	1299
Other	38758	34664	...	4094	39104	35712	...	3392
B Machinery and equipment [d]	238950	226113	4595	8243	260534	243397	5135	12002
6 Breeding stock, dairy cattle, etc. [b]								
Total Gross Capital Formation	656760	574082	29442	53236	684199	604088	21039	59072

a) Item 'Goods producing industries' includes only manufacturing and farming.
b) Item 'Breeding stocks, dairy cattle, etc.' is included in item 'Increase in stocks'.
c) The estimates of residential buildings of government enterprises and general government are included in the respective columns of item 'Residential buildings' in tables 2.7 and 2.8. These estimates are included in item 'Real estate' in tables 2.9-2.12 and are therefore excluded from the estimates of government enterprises and general government of these tables. This latter classification is followed in tables 2.13-2.16.
d) Item 'Machinery and equipment' includes all producers durable goods of public enterprises.

2.9 Gross Capital Formation by Kind of Activity of Owner, ISIC Major Divisions, in Current Prices
Million United States dollars

	1980			1981			1982			1983		
	Total Gross Capital Formation	Increase in Stocks	Gross Fixed Capital Formation	Total Gross Capital Formation	Increase in Stocks	Gross Fixed Capital Formation	Total Gross Capital Formation	Increase in Stocks	Gross Fixed Capital Formation	Total Gross Capital Formation	Increase in Stocks	Gross Fixed Capital Formation
	All Producers											
1 Agriculture, hunting, fishing and forestry	14075	-5928	20003	24715	5751	18964	13865	-1429	15294	7416	-7482	14898
2 Mining and quarrying	34830	-154	34984	53707	2197	51510	53150	600	52550	33447	-1860	35307
3 Manufacturing	76745	1404	75341	85204	3283	81921	63224	-15099	78323	58642	-5783	64425
4 Electricity, gas and water	24634	-723	25357	28027	773	27254	25478	-1908	27386	24687	-1365	26052
5 Construction	6449	-1984	8433	10347	627	9720	4035	-82	4117	5234	954	4280
6 Wholesale and retail trade, restaurants and hotels	33496	-682	34178	50244	8383	41861	38252	-6082	44334	61269	6319	54950
7 Transport, storage and communication	51646	266	51380	54468	-156	54624	51454	-503	51957	55239	180	55059
8 Finance, insurance, real estate and business services [a]	169547	-395	169942	175406	809	174597	164090	-62	164152	207515	238	207277
9 Community, social and personal services	14995	-133	15128	20278	2340	17938	18987	33	18954	23888	1718	22170
Statistical discrepancy [ba]	21412	1025	20387	23913	3242	20671	27094	9415	17679	12209	-5394	17603
Total Industries	447829	-7304	455133	526309	27249	499060	459629	-15117	474746	489546	-12475	502021
Producers of Government Services [a]	47707	1290	46417	49978	5141	44837	48679	2776	45903	51491	3468	48023
Private Non-Profit Institutions Serving Households	12718	-	12718	15426	-	15426	16928	-	16928	27564	-	27564
Statistical discrepancy	-1	-	-1	-	-	-	1	-	1	-	-	-
Total	508253	-6014	514267	591713	32390	559323	525237	-12341	537578	568601	-9007	577608

	1984			1985			1986			1987		
	Total Gross Capital Formation	Increase in Stocks	Gross Fixed Capital Formation	Total Gross Capital Formation	Increase in Stocks	Gross Fixed Capital Formation	Total Gross Capital Formation	Increase in Stocks	Gross Fixed Capital Formation	Total Gross Capital Formation	Increase in Stocks	Gross Fixed Capital Formation
	All Producers											
1 Agriculture, hunting, fishing and forestry	21905	7146	14759	8782	-3326	12108	9141	-1886	11027	11029	-1493	12522
2 Mining and quarrying	36507	-28	36535	35031	2134	32897	21355	2147	19208	18905	865	18040
3 Manufacturing	97955	21605	76350	74327	-9327	83654	73619	-3289	76908	85045	6088	78957
4 Electricity, gas and water	32752	2345	30407	44143	2198	41945	46753	3440	43313	45978	3483	42495

United States

2.9 Gross Capital Formation by Kind of Activity of Owner, ISIC Major Divisions, in Current Prices
(Continued)

Million United States dollars

	1984 Total Gross Capital Formation	1984 Increase in Stocks	1984 Gross Fixed Capital Formation	1985 Total Gross Capital Formation	1985 Increase in Stocks	1985 Gross Fixed Capital Formation	1986 Total Gross Capital Formation	1986 Increase in Stocks	1986 Gross Fixed Capital Formation	1987 Total Gross Capital Formation	1987 Increase in Stocks	1987 Gross Fixed Capital Formation
5 Construction	8864	3538	5326	10265	3661	6604	10021	2696	7325	9136	2019	7117
6 Wholesale and retail trade, restaurants and hotels	97795	30057	67738	90426	15673	74753	85068	10278	74790	108193	28702	79491
7 Transport, storage and communication	58508	1449	57059	58517	65	58452	62637	166	62471	58997	-1740	60737
8 Finance, insurance, real estate and business services [a]	267436	846	266590	283387	176	283211	314674	132	314542	328699	-266	328965
9 Community, social and personal services	28746	730	28016	27390	63	27327	31360	1860	29500	33354	1561	31793
Statistical discrepancy [ba]	16541	-3627	20168	33939	11241	22698	30262	5126	25136	24014	-3178	27192
Total Industries	667009	64061	602948	666207	22558	643649	684890	20670	664220	723350	36041	687309
Producers of Government Services [a]	52105	2143	49962	62580	1717	60863	62559	90	62469	69832	1031	68801
Private Non-Profit Institutions Serving Households	17106	-	17106	13606	-	13606	14596	-	14596	16524	-	16524
Statistical discrepancy	-	-	-	-	-	-	-	-	-	-	-	-
Total	736220	66204	670016	742393	24275	718118	762045	20760	741285	809706	37072	772634

a) The estimates of residential buildings of government enterprises and general government are included in the respective columns of item 'Residential buildings' in tables 2.7 and 2.8. These estimates are included in item 'Real estate' in tables 2.9-2.12 and are therefore excluded from the estimates of government enterprises and general government of these tables. This latter classification is followed in tables 2.13-2.16. b) Item 'Statistical discrepancy' refers to government enterprises.

2.10 Gross Capital Formation by Kind of Activity of Owner, ISIC Major Divisions, in Constant Prices

Million United States dollars

	1980 Total Gross Capital Formation	1980 Increase in Stocks	1980 Gross Fixed Capital Formation	1981 Total Gross Capital Formation	1981 Increase in Stocks	1981 Gross Fixed Capital Formation	1982 Total Gross Capital Formation	1982 Increase in Stocks	1982 Gross Fixed Capital Formation	1983 Total Gross Capital Formation	1983 Increase in Stocks	1983 Gross Fixed Capital Formation
	At constant prices of:1980											
	All Producers											
1 Agriculture, hunting, fishing and forestry	14075	-5928	20003	22108	5008	17100	11378	-1481	12859	5462	-6502	11964
2 Mining and quarrying	34830	-154	34984	44773	1874	42899	39434	498	38936	29387	-1580	30967
3 Manufacturing	76745	1404	75341	77797	3012	74785	53158	-14356	67514	49507	-5878	55385
4 Electricity, gas and water	24634	-723	25357	25205	533	24672	21312	-1558	22870	20102	-1086	21188
5 Construction	6449	-1984	8433	9496	682	8814	3416	-12	3428	4415	922	3493
6 Wholesale and retail trade, restaurants and hotels	33496	-682	34178	46340	7867	38473	33275	-5573	38848	52936	4729	48207
7 Transport, storage and communication	51645	265	51380	48949	-142	49091	42825	-462	43287	44313	181	44132
8 Finance, insurance, real estate and business services [a]	169547	-395	169942	161879	839	161040	145447	-32	145479	182463	266	182197
9 Community, social and personal services	14995	-133	15128	18364	2028	16336	16293	2	16291	20356	1331	19025
Statistical discrepancy [ba]	21412	1025	20387	23302	3884	19418	27491	11353	16138	9909	-5876	15785
Total Industries	447827	-7305	455132	478213	25585	452628	394029	-11621	405650	418849	-13493	432342
Producers of Government Services [a]	47707	1290	46417	48679	6158	42521	46107	3347	42760	48084	3777	44307
Private Non-Profit Institutions Serving Households	12718	...	12718	18415	...	18415	20447	...	20447	33389	...	33389
Statistical discrepancy [c]	-	1	-1	1	1	-	3	3	-	-	-	-
Total	508252	-6014	514266	545308	31744	513564	460586	-8271	468857	500322	-9716	510038

	1984 Total Gross Capital Formation	1984 Increase in Stocks	1984 Gross Fixed Capital Formation	1985 Total Gross Capital Formation	1985 Increase in Stocks	1985 Gross Fixed Capital Formation	1986 Total Gross Capital Formation	1986 Increase in Stocks	1986 Gross Fixed Capital Formation	1987 Total Gross Capital Formation	1987 Increase in Stocks	1987 Gross Fixed Capital Formation
	At constant prices of:1980											
	All Producers											
1 Agriculture, hunting, fishing and forestry	16081	4615	11466	4827	-4437	9264	5729	-2626	8355	6848	-2562	9410
2 Mining and quarrying	34485	-21	34506	32988	1871	31117	21430	2178	19252	19315	861	18454
3 Manufacturing	83621	18436	65185	64815	-8664	73479	62879	-3220	66099	71194	4592	66602
4 Electricity, gas and water	25895	1758	24137	34483	1754	32729	36331	3117	33214	35595	3373	32222

United States

2.10 Gross Capital Formation by Kind of Activity of Owner, ISIC Major Divisions, in Constant Prices
(Continued)

Million United States dollars

	1984			1985			1986			1987		
	Total Gross Capital Formation	Increase in Stocks	Gross Fixed Capital Formation	Total Gross Capital Formation	Increase in Stocks	Gross Fixed Capital Formation	Total Gross Capital Formation	Increase in Stocks	Gross Fixed Capital Formation	Total Gross Capital Formation	Increase in Stocks	Gross Fixed Capital Formation
	At constant prices of: 1980											
5 Construction	7343	3092	4251	8379	3147	5232	8049	2318	5731	7145	1712	5433
6 Wholesale and retail trade, restaurants and hotels	84687	25826	58861	78381	13263	65118	75017	9139	65878	91209	21840	69369
7 Transport, storage and communication	45551	1233	44318	44839	97	44742	47095	360	46735	42956	-1453	44409
8 Finance, insurance, real estate and business services [a]	230691	753	229938	248633	159	248474	275022	120	274902	281537	-233	281770
9 Community, social and personal services	24063	568	23495	22979	49	22930	25821	1381	24440	27056	1129	25927
Statistical discrepancy [b]	13645	-4026	17671	29968	10896	19072	27086	6132	20954	18978	-3364	22342
Total Industries	566062	52234	513828	570293	18135	552158	584458	18899	565559	601834	25895	575939
Producers of Government Services [a]	47441	2379	45062	53126	1664	51462	52022	107	51915	57534	1091	56443
Private Non-Profit Institutions Serving Households	32154	...	32154	28182	...	28182	20281	...	20281	24831	...	24831
Statistical discrepancy [c]	-2	-2	-	-	-	-	-1	-1	-	-	-	-
Total	645655	54611	591044	651601	19799	631802	656760	19005	637755	684199	26986	657213

a) The estimates of residential buildings of government enterprises and general government are included in the respective columns of item 'Residential buildings' in tables 2.7 and 2.8. These estimates are included in item 'Real estate' in tables 2.9-2.12 and are therefore excluded from the estimates of government enterprises and general government of these tables. This latter classification is followed in tables 2.13-2.16.
b) Item 'Statistical discrepancy' refers to government enterprises.
c) Item 'Statistical discrepancy' refers to residual (deflation) error to adjust total Gross Fixed Capital Formation by Kind of Activity of Owner (Table 2.12) to Gross Fixed Capital Formation by Type of Good and Owner (Table 2.8).

2.11 Gross Fixed Capital Formation by Kind of Activity of Owner, ISIC Divisions, in Current Prices

Million United States dollars

	1970	1975	1978	1979	1980	1981	1982	1983	1984	1985	1986	1987
	All Producers											
1 Agriculture, hunting, forestry and fishing	7258	12860	18432	21773	20003	18964	15294	14898	14759	12108	11027	12522
2 Mining and quarrying	5093	12234	22995	28367	34984	51510	52550	35307	36535	32897	19208	18040
A Coal mining	476	1385	3074	3410	3615	4744	3871	2729	2526	2522	2183	2187
B Crude petroleum and natural gas production	3868	9023	17434	21860	28341	43506	45151	30027	31113	27749	15109	13844
C Metal ore mining	431	1071	1477	1780	1685	1663	1790	1654	1933	1718	1317	1433
D Other mining	318	756	1009	1317	1342	1597	1737	897	963	908	598	576
3 Manufacturing	23812	38487	58172	67280	75341	81921	78323	64425	76350	83654	76908	78957
A Manufacturing of food, beverages and tobacco	2211	3645	5209	5644	6454	6918	7610	6554	7105	7694	7560	7845
B Textile, wearing apparel and leather industries	1195	1458	2150	2224	2509	2500	2203	2241	2790	2509	2188	2589
C Manufacture of wood, and wood products, including furniture	815	1501	2422	2697	2637	2298	1895	1779	2465	2444	2451	2993
D Manufacture of paper and paper products, printing and publishing	2248	3782	5899	7048	7982	7488	8247	7849	8790	10447	9901	10791
E Manufacture of chemicals and chemical petroleum, coal, rubber and plastic products	5478	10306	12883	14649	15332	17643	19373	14346	14598	15424	13763	13011
F Manufacture of non-metallic mineral products except products of petroleum and coal	948	1629	2679	2803	3259	2650	2297	1697	2240	2202	2173	2316
G Basic metal industries	2670	4328	5089	5745	6082	6844	5320	4304	4118	4523	2962	3637
H Manufacture of fabricated metal products, machinery and equipment	7992	11518	21256	25790	30304	34934	30766	25130	33613	37797	35312	35187
I Other manufacturing industries	255	320	587	680	782	647	612	524	630	613	599	588
4 Electricity, gas and water	10424	15206	19999	20754	25357	27254	27386	26052	30407	41945	43313	42495
5 Construction	3176	5154	8805	9257	8433	9720	4117	4280	5326	6604	7325	7117
6 Wholesale and retail trade, restaurants and hotels	11510	18190	29847	35206	34178	41861	44334	54950	67738	74753	74790	79491
A Wholesale and retail trade	10187	16881	27848	32374	30875	37751	39781	49044	59752	66111	65968	70465
B Restaurants and hotels	1323	1310	1998	2832	3303	4109	4553	5906	7986	8642	8821	9026
Restaurants	...	...	...	...	...	...	...	...	...	...	...	...
Hotels and other lodging places	1323	1310	1998	2832	3303	4109	4553	5906	7986	8642	8821	9026
7 Transport, storage and communication	16591	25636	43895	51611	51380	54624	51957	55059	57059	58452	62471	60737
A Transport and storage	7329	12301	20946	23578	23990	23844	20183	21367	21006	19715	20422	19659

United States

2.11 Gross Fixed Capital Formation by Kind of Activity of Owner, ISIC Divisions, in Current Prices
(Continued)

Million United States dollars

	1970	1975	1978	1979	1980	1981	1982	1983	1984	1985	1986	1987
B Communication	9262	13335	22949	28032	27390	30780	31774	33693	36053	38737	42049	41078
8 Finance, insurance, real estate and business services	53500	74677	151961	182747	169942	174597	164152	207277	266590	283211	314542	328965
A Financial institutions	2998	6533	10400	12273	13312	15203	16518	18561	27329	31064	34119	36187
B Insurance	644	920	1313	1488	1799	1881	1862	2048	5331	8296	10033	11566
C Real estate and business services	49858	67224	140248	168986	154830	157513	145771	186668	233930	243851	270390	281212
Real estate except dwellings	9038	8713	19893	28109	29512	34227	37519	42337	48531	51404	50020	50345
Dwellings	40820	58511	120355	140877	125318	123286	108252	144331	185399	192447	220370	230867
9 Community, social and personal services	5554	8559	13110	14448	15128	17938	18954	22170	28016	27327	29500	31793
A Sanitary and similar services	...	...	...	...	...	...	...	...	...	...	...	...
B Social and related community services	2055	3112	4092	4287	5106	6390	7263	8321	9038	9420	10182	11334
Educational services	94	118	132	142	198	187	231	244	245	290	312	340
Medical, dental, other health and veterinary services	1283	1847	2431	2901	3814	5414	6354	7133	7781	7963	8561	9647
C Recreational and cultural services	1078	1654	2264	2865	2879	2988	2931	3031	4081	4593	4397	4563
D Personal and household services	2421	3794	6753	7297	7143	8560	8759	10818	14897	13314	14921	15897
Statistical discrepancy [a]	6811	13530	18580	18783	20387	20671	17679	17603	20168	22698	25136	27192
Total Industries	143729	224534	385795	450226	455133	499060	474746	502021	602948	643649	664220	687309
Producers of Government Services	24847	32816	36798	40494	46417	44837	45903	48023	49962	60863	62469	68801
Private Non-Profit Institutions Serving Households	9918	14994	22440	11909	12718	15426	16928	27564	17106	13606	14596	16524
Statistical discrepancy	1	-	-	-	-1	-	1	-	-	-	-	-
Total	178495	272344	445033	502629	514267	559323	537578	577608	670016	718118	741285	772634

a) Item 'Statistical discrepancy' refers to government enterprises.

2.12 Gross Fixed Capital Formation by Kind of Activity of Owner, ISIC Divisions, in Constant Prices

Million United States dollars

	1970	1975	1978	1979	1980	1981	1982	1983	1984	1985	1986	1987
	\multicolumn{12}{c}{At constant prices of:1980}
	\multicolumn{12}{c}{All Producers}
1 Agriculture, hunting, forestry and fishing	16717	19826	22659	24407	20003	17100	12859	11964	11466	9264	8355	9410
2 Mining and quarrying	15265	21944	29250	31526	34984	42899	38936	30967	34506	31117	19252	18454
A Coal mining	1187	2244	3799	3784	3615	4182	3133	2168	1969	1918	1663	1650
B Crude petroleum and natural gas production	12276	16761	22380	24309	28341	35819	32904	26750	30269	27203	16140	15305
C Metal ore mining	1025	1713	1836	1979	1685	1481	1476	1334	1525	1315	1006	1079
D Other mining	776	1226	1235	1454	1342	1416	1423	715	744	681	443	419
3 Manufacturing	51886	56405	69528	73843	75341	74785	67514	55385	65185	73479	66099	66602
A Manufacturing of food, beverages and tobacco	4831	5363	6297	6224	6454	6292	6555	5565	5893	6383	6089	6166
B Textile, wearing apparel and leather industries	2664	2184	2630	2451	2509	2256	1868	1874	2265	2021	1704	1976
C Manufacture of wood, and wood products, including furniture	1835	2299	2962	2989	2637	2070	1610	1494	2006	1988	1931	2319
D Manufacture of paper and paper products, printing and publishing	5017	5577	7073	7732	7982	6780	7029	6656	7347	8913	8165	8696
E Manufacture of chemicals and chemical petroleum, coal, rubber and plastic products	12105	14889	15332	16129	15332	16114	16679	12175	12174	12890	11286	10433
F Manufacture of non-metalic mineral products except products of petroleum and coal	2182	2451	3172	3053	3259	2433	2014	1521	2031	2109	2120	2246
G Basic metal industries	5798	6383	6082	6322	6082	6202	4496	3597	3382	3719	2365	2855
H Manufacture of fabricated metal products, machinery and equipment	16913	16782	25270	28191	30304	32050	26738	22056	29556	34938	31942	31436
I Other manufacturing industries	541	476	711	751	782	588	525	446	531	519	497	477
4 Electricity, gas and water	24349	23571	23582	22908	25357	24672	22870	21188	24137	32729	33214	32222

United States

2.12 Gross Fixed Capital Formation by Kind of Activity of Owner, ISIC Divisions, in Constant Prices
(Continued)

Million United States dollars

	1970	1975	1978	1979	1980	1981	1982	1983	1984	1985	1986	1987
					At constant prices of:1980							
5 Construction	7476	8001	10830	10310	8433	8814	3428	3493	4251	5232	5731	5433
6 Wholesale and retail trade, restaurants and hotels	24328	26458	35555	38548	34178	38473	38848	48207	58861	65118	65878	69369
A Wholesale and retail trade	21394	24526	33145	35435	30875	34720	34902	43217	52354	58182	58921	62446
B Restaurants and hotels	2934	1932	2411	3113	3303	3753	3945	4990	6507	6936	6957	6924
Restaurants	...	...	...	...	...	...	...	...	...	...	...	...
Hotels and other lodging places	2934	1932	2411	3113	3303	3753	3945	4990	6507	6936	6957	6924
7 Transport, storage and communication	32338	34583	49547	54757	51380	49091	43287	44132	44318	44742	46735	44409
A Transport and storage	16077	17913	24448	25483	23990	20997	16753	17435	16614	15365	15585	14736
B Communication	16262	16670	25099	29274	27390	28094	26534	26696	27704	29376	31149	29673
8 Finance, insurance, real estate and business services	123216	118661	184527	199450	169942	161040	145479	182197	229938	248474	274902	281770
A Financial institutions	5862	9113	11655	12852	13312	14049	14722	17709	27031	34899	40530	44504
B Insurance	1125	1081	1363	1478	1799	1854	1824	2237	6628	11833	15880	18722
C Real estate and business services	116229	108467	171509	185119	154830	145137	128933	162251	196280	201743	218491	218544
Real estate except dwellings	17536	12253	23212	30298	29512	31034	32156	36008	40431	42738	41231	40788
Dwellings	98693	96214	148297	154821	125318	114103	96777	126244	155849	159005	177260	177756
9 Community, social and personal services	11286	12420	15707	15852	15128	16336	16291	19025	23495	22930	24440	25927
A Sanitary and similar services	...	...	...	...	...	...	...	...	...	...	...	...
B Social and related community services	4290	4512	4881	4638	5106	5844	6268	7241	7694	8149	8792	9627
Educational services	137	129	134	138	198	183	224	267	290	420	500	573
Medical, dental, other health and veterinary services	2655	2641	2863	3137	3814	4955	5465	6105	6467	6553	6946	7667
C Recreational and cultural services	2018	2326	2645	3107	2879	2738	2536	2591	3445	3924	3730	3786
D Personal and household services	4978	5582	8181	8106	7143	7754	7488	9193	12355	10856	11918	12514
Statistical discrepancy [a]	17131	20396	23044	20700	20387	19418	16138	15785	17671	19072	20954	22342
Total Industries	323993	342265	464229	492300	455132	452628	405650	432342	513828	552158	565559	575939
Producers of Government Services	60577	50688	47101	45452	46417	42521	42760	44307	45062	51462	51915	56443
Private Non-Profit Institutions Serving Households	19093	20789	27883	14331	12718	18415	20447	33389	32154	28182	20281	24831
Statistical discrepancy	-	-1	-	-	-1	-	-	-	-	-	-	-
Total	403663	413741	539213	552083	514266	513564	468857	510038	591044	631802	637755	657213

a) Item 'Statistical discrepancy' refers to government enterprises.

2.13 Stocks of Reproducible Fixed Assets, by Type of Good and Owner, in Current Prices

Thousand Million United States dollars

	TOTAL		Total Private		Public Enterprises		General Government	
	Gross	Net	Gross	Net	Gross	Net	Gross	Net
					1980			
1 Residential buildings [a]	4155	2718	4070	2661	54	38	31	20
2 Non-residential buildings	2111	1296	1455	886	41	28	614	382
3 Other construction	2578	1564	1036	585	511	333	1032	646
4 Land improvement and plantation and orchard development	...	...	...	...	...	...	...	...
5 Producers' durable goods	2562	1445	2382	1353	24	14	157	79
A Transport equipment	...	...	549	312	...	...	...	...
Passenger cars	...	...	92	63	...	...	...	...
Other	...	...	458	249	...	...	...	...
B Machinery and equipment	...	...	1832	1041	...	...	...	...
6 Breeding stock, dairy cattle, etc.	...	...	...	...	...	...	...	...
Total	11407	7023	8943	5484	630	413	1834	1127

United States

2.13 Stocks of Reproducible Fixed Assets, by Type of Good and Owner, in Current Prices
(Continued)

Thousand Million United States dollars

	TOTAL Gross	TOTAL Net	Total Private Gross	Total Private Net	Public Enterprises Gross	Public Enterprises Net	General Government Gross	General Government Net
1981								
1 Residential buildings [a]	4565	2974	4471	2911	60	41	34	21
2 Non-residential buildings	2361	1438	1638	991	45	30	678	417
3 Other construction	2746	1656	1186	672	548	356	1012	628
4 Land improvement and plantation and orchard development	...	...	...	...	...	...	...	...
5 Producers' durable goods	2911	1631	2712	1530	28	16	171	85
A Transport equipment	...	...	605	338	...	...	...	...
Passenger cars	...	...	100	68	...	...	...	...
Other	...	...	505	270	...	...	...	...
B Machinery and equipment	...	...	2107	1192	...	...	...	...
6 Breeding stock, dairy cattle, etc.	...	...	...	...	...	...	...	...
Total	12583	7700	10007	6104	680	444	1895	1152
1982								
1 Residential buildings [a]	4543	2937	4450	2876	59	40	34	21
2 Non-residential buildings	2450	1480	1709	1027	47	31	694	422
3 Other construction	2811	1685	1256	710	563	364	992	611
4 Land improvement and plantation and orchard development	...	...	...	...	...	...	...	...
5 Producers' durable goods	3138	1736	2928	1629	31	18	179	89
A Transport equipment	...	...	627	344	...	...	...	...
Passenger cars	...	...	105	70	...	...	...	...
Other	...	...	523	274	...	...	...	...
B Machinery and equipment	...	...	2301	1285	...	...	...	...
6 Breeding stock, dairy cattle, etc.	...	...	...	...	...	...	...	...
Total	12941	7838	10343	6242	699	453	1899	1143
1983								
1 Residential buildings [a]	4899	3160	4798	3094	64	43	37	23
2 Non-residential buildings	2651	1585	1862	1109	48	32	740	444
3 Other construction	2822	1682	1225	689	583	373	1015	620
4 Land improvement and plantation and orchard development	...	...	...	...	...	...	...	...
5 Producers' durable goods	3261	1783	3044	1671	34	20	183	92
A Transport equipment	...	...	650	354	...	...	...	...
Passenger cars	...	...	117	79	...	...	...	...
Other	...	...	532	274	...	...	...	...
B Machinery and equipment	...	...	2394	1317	...	...	...	...
6 Breeding stock, dairy cattle, etc.	...	...	...	...	...	...	...	...
Total	13632	8209	10929	6563	729	467	1975	1179
1984								
1 Residential buildings [a]	5203	3358	5096	3289	67	45	39	25
2 Non-residential buildings	2812	1668	2008	1189	51	34	753	445
3 Other construction	2989	1772	1272	713	615	391	1102	669
4 Land improvement and plantation and orchard development	...	...	...	...	...	...	...	...
5 Producers' durable goods	3415	1866	3190	1748	37	22	188	96
A Transport equipment	...	...	678	372	...	...	...	...
Passenger cars	...	...	127	88	...	...	...	...
Other	...	...	550	284	...	...	...	...
B Machinery and equipment	...	...	2512	1376	...	...	...	...
6 Breeding stock, dairy cattle, etc.	...	...	...	...	...	...	...	...
Total	14419	8663	11566	6939	770	490	2083	1234

United States

2.13 Stocks of Reproducible Fixed Assets, by Type of Good and Owner, in Current Prices
(Continued)

Thousand Million United States dollars

		TOTAL Gross	TOTAL Net	Total Private Gross	Total Private Net	Public Enterprises Gross	Public Enterprises Net	General Government Gross	General Government Net
					1985				
1	Residential buildings [a]	5471	3534	5360	3462	70	46	42	26
2	Non-residential buildings	2995	1768	2125	1256	54	35	816	477
3	Other construction	3141	1851	1294	719	650	409	1197	722
4	Land improvement and plantation and orchard development	...	...	...	...	...	...	...	...
5	Producers' durable goods	3562	1945	3325	1818	36	22	200	106
	A Transport equipment	...	...	709	393	...	...	...	...
	Passenger cars	...	...	139	98	...	...	...	...
	Other	...	...	571	295	...	...	...	...
	B Machinery and equipment	...	...	2616	1425	...	...	...	...
6	Breeding stock, dairy cattle, etc.	...	...	...	...	...	...	...	...
	Total	15169	9097	12105	7255	810	512	2254	1331
					1986				
1	Residential buildings [a]	5777	3739	5659	3664	73	48	44	28
2	Non-residential buildings	3154	1852	2247	1321	55	36	852	495
3	Other construction	3167	1853	1300	716	669	419	1198	718
4	Land improvement and plantation and orchard development	...	...	...	...	...	...	...	...
5	Producers' durable goods	3737	2040	3487	1902	39	24	211	114
	A Transport equipment	...	...	741	413	...	...	...	...
	Passenger cars	...	...	154	108	...	...	...	...
	Other	...	...	587	305	...	...	...	...
	B Machinery and equipment	...	...	2746	1489	...	...	...	...
6	Breeding stock, dairy cattle, etc.	...	...	...	...	...	...	...	...
	Total	15835	9484	12693	7603	837	526	2305	1355
					1987				
1	Residential buildings [a]	6239	4046	6113	3966	78	50	48	30
2	Non-residential buildings	3373	1969	2406	1406	58	37	909	525
3	Other construction	3273	1901	1341	731	697	435	1235	736
4	Land improvement and plantation and orchard development	...	...	...	...	...	...	...	...
5	Producers' durable goods	3916	2137	3651	1988	43	26	222	123
	A Transport equipment	...	...	768	429	...	...	...	...
	Passenger cars	...	...	165	116	...	...	...	...
	Other	...	...	603	314	...	...	...	...
	B Machinery and equipment	...	...	2883	1559	...	...	...	...
6	Breeding stock, dairy cattle, etc.	...	...	...	...	...	...	...	...
	Total	16801	10053	13512	8091	876	548	2414	1414

a) The estimates of residential buildings of government enterprises and general government are included in the respective columns of item 'Residential buildings' in tables 2.7 and 2.8. These estimates are included in item 'Real estate' in tables 2.9-2.12 and are therefore excluded from the estimates of government enterprises and general government of these tables. This latter classification is followed in tables 2.13-2.16.

United States

2.14 Stocks of Reproducible Fixed Assets, by Type of Good and Owner, in Constant Prices

Thousand Million United States dollars

		TOTAL Gross	TOTAL Net	Total Private Gross	Total Private Net	Public Enterprises Gross	Public Enterprises Net	General Government Gross	General Government Net
		\multicolumn{8}{c}{At constant prices of:1980}								

1980

		Gross	Net	Gross	Net	Gross	Net	Gross	Net
1	Residential buildings [a]	3982	2603	3900	2548	52	36	30	19
2	Non-residential buildings	2018	1239	1391	847	40	27	586	365
3	Other construction	2382	1446	900	504	496	324	986	618
4	Land improvement and plantation and orchard development	...	...	...	...	...	...	...	...
5	Producers' durable goods	2474	1396	2302	1307	23	13	149	75
	A Transport equipment	...	...	512	291	...	...	...	...
	Passenger cars	...	...	89	61	...	...	...	...
	Other	...	...	422	229	...	...	...	...
	B Machinery and equipment	...	...	1791	1016	...	...	...	...
6	Breeding stock, dairy cattle, etc.	...	...	...	...	...	...	...	...
	Total	10856	6684	8494	5206	611	401	1751	1077

1981

1	Residential buildings [a]	4061	2644	3977	2588	53	37	30	19
2	Non-residential buildings	2072	1262	1437	869	41	28	593	365
3	Other construction	2441	1478	934	526	508	330	999	621
4	Land improvement and plantation and orchard development	...	...	...	...	...	...	...	...
5	Producers' durable goods	2572	1441	2396	1352	25	14	151	75
	A Transport equipment	...	...	518	290	...	...	...	...
	Passenger cars	...	...	92	62	...	...	...	...
	Other	...	...	426	228	...	...	...	...
	B Machinery and equipment	...	...	1879	1062	...	...	...	...
6	Breeding stock, dairy cattle, etc.	...	...	...	...	...	...	...	...
	Total	11145	6825	8745	5336	628	409	1773	1080

1982

1	Residential buildings [a]	4122	2666	4037	2610	54	37	31	19
2	Non-residential buildings	2122	1282	1480	890	42	28	599	364
3	Other construction	2491	1499	962	541	517	334	1012	625
4	Land improvement and plantation and orchard development	...	...	...	...	...	...	...	...
5	Producers' durable goods	2639	1460	2462	1369	26	15	151	76
	A Transport equipment	...	...	518	285	...	...	...	...
	Passenger cars	...	...	94	63	...	...	...	...
	Other	...	...	424	222	...	...	...	...
	B Machinery and equipment	...	...	1944	1085	...	...	...	...
6	Breeding stock, dairy cattle, etc.	...	...	...	...	...	...	...	...
	Total	11374	6907	8940	5410	640	414	1794	1084

1983

1	Residential buildings [a]	4210	2716	4123	2659	55	37	32	20
2	Non-residential buildings	2166	1295	1517	904	43	28	605	363
3	Other construction	2533	1511	981	547	526	336	1026	628
4	Land improvement and plantation and orchard development	...	...	...	...	...	...	...	...
5	Producers' durable goods	2711	1485	2530	1392	28	16	153	77
	A Transport equipment	...	...	524	286	...	...	...	...
	Passenger cars	...	...	102	69	...	...	...	...
	Other	...	...	422	218	...	...	...	...
	B Machinery and equipment	...	...	2006	1105	...	...	...	...
6	Breeding stock, dairy cattle, etc.	...	...	...	...	...	...	...	...
	Total	11620	7007	9151	5501	652	417	1817	1088

United States

2.14 Stocks of Reproducible Fixed Assets, by Type of Good and Owner, in Constant Prices
(Continued)

Thousand Million United States dollars

		TOTAL Gross	TOTAL Net	Total Private Gross	Total Private Net	Public Enterprises Gross	Public Enterprises Net	General Government Gross	General Government Net
		\multicolumn{8}{c}{At constant prices of:1980}								
		\multicolumn{8}{c}{1984}								
1	Residential buildings [a]	4327	2793	4238	2735	56	37	33	21
2	Non-residential buildings	2218	1315	1563	925	44	29	611	361
3	Other construction	2580	1529	1004	557	535	340	1040	632
4	Land improvement and plantation and orchard development	...	...	...	...	...	...	...	...
5	Producers' durable goods	2812	1541	2627	1444	30	17	155	79
	A Transport equipment	...	...	534	294	...	...	...	...
	Passenger cars	...	...	107	74	...	...	...	...
	Other	...	...	426	220	...	...	...	...
	B Machinery and equipment	...	...	2093	1150	...	...	...	...
6	Breeding stock, dairy cattle, etc.	...	...	...	...	...	...	...	...
	Total	11936	7177	9432	5662	665	423	1839	1093
		\multicolumn{8}{c}{1985}								
1	Residential buildings [a]	4443	2869	4352	2810	57	37	34	21
2	Non-residential buildings	2279	1345	1616	955	45	29	618	361
3	Other construction	2627	1546	1025	565	546	344	1056	638
4	Land improvement and plantation and orchard development	...	...	...	...	...	...	...	...
5	Producers' durable goods	2931	1612	2741	1510	32	19	158	83
	A Transport equipment	...	...	546	304	...	...	...	...
	Passenger cars	...	...	114	80	...	...	...	...
	Other	...	...	432	224	...	...	...	...
	B Machinery and equipment	...	...	2194	1206	...	...	...	...
6	Breeding stock, dairy cattle, etc.	...	...	...	...	...	...	...	...
	Total	12280	7373	9734	5840	680	430	1866	1103
		\multicolumn{8}{c}{1986}								
1	Residential buildings [a]	4578	2962	4484	2903	58	38	35	22
2	Non-residential buildings	2333	1370	1663	978	46	30	624	363
3	Other construction	2664	1554	1034	562	558	349	1072	643
4	Land improvement and plantation and orchard development	...	...	...	...	...	...	...	...
5	Producers' durable goods	3049	1678	2853	1571	35	21	161	86
	A Transport equipment	...	...	557	310	...	...	...	...
	Passenger cars	...	...	120	84	...	...	...	...
	Other	...	...	437	226	...	...	...	...
	B Machinery and equipment	...	...	2296	1260	...	...	...	...
6	Breeding stock, dairy cattle, etc.	...	...	...	...	...	...	...	...
	Total	12624	7564	10035	6013	697	438	1892	1114
		\multicolumn{8}{c}{1987}								
1	Residential buildings [a]	4711	3053	4616	2993	59	38	36	23
2	Non-residential buildings	2386	1393	1707	997	47	30	632	365
3	Other construction	2697	1559	1040	556	569	355	1088	648
4	Land improvement and plantation and orchard development	...	...	...	...	...	...	...	...
5	Producers' durable goods	3176	1750	2970	1634	39	24	167	92
	A Transport equipment	...	...	567	317	...	...	...	...
	Passenger cars	...	...	125	88	...	...	...	...
	Other	...	...	442	229	...	...	...	...
	B Machinery and equipment	...	...	2403	1318	...	...	...	...
6	Breeding stock, dairy cattle, etc.	...	...	...	...	...	...	...	...
	Total	12970	7755	10333	6181	714	446	1923	1128

a) The estimates of residential buildings of government enterprises and general government are included in the respective columns of item 'Residential buildings' in tables 2.7 and 2.8. These estimates are included in item 'Real estate' in tables 2.9-2.12 and are therefore excluded from the estimates of government enterprises and general government of these tables. This latter classification is followed in tables 2.13-2.16.

United States

2.15 Stocks of Reproducible Fixed Assets by Kind of Activity, in Current Prices

Thousand Million United States dollars

	1980 Gross	1980 Net	1981 Gross	1981 Net	1982 Gross	1982 Net	1983 Gross	1983 Net	1984 Gross	1984 Net	1985 Gross	1985 Net
1 Residential buildings [a]	4155	2718	4565	2974	4543	2937	4899	3160	5203	3358	5471	3534
2 Non-residential buildings [b]	2111	1296	2361	1438	2450	1480	2651	1585	2812	1668	2995	1768
3 Other construction [b]	2578	1564	2746	1656	2811	1685	2822	1682	2989	1772	3141	1851
A Industries	2757	1653	3100	1854	3249	1935	3365	1991	3571	2103	3734	2190
1 Agriculture	136	83	151	91	155	92	166	97	174	100	179	101
2 Mining and quarrying	272	146	360	199	397	221	331	183	339	186	344	186
3 Manufacturing	367	209	409	232	423	238	454	251	482	263	499	270
4 Electricity, gas and water	436	262	477	285	498	295	519	304	538	312	556	320
5 Construction	23	17	25	18	26	19	29	20	31	21	32	21
6 Wholesale and retail trade	217	142	248	162	262	170	289	186	317	203	346	223
7 Transport and communication	376	199	405	216	420	223	438	234	462	248	461	245
8 Finance, etc.	237	148	272	171	292	184	327	205	364	231	404	259
9 Community, social and personal services	142	85	159	95	166	98	182	107	197	115	209	121
Statistical discrepancy [ca]	552	361	593	386	610	395	631	405	666	424	703	444
B Producers of government services [a]	1646	1028	1691	1046	1686	1032	1755	1063	1855	1114	2013	1200
C Other producers [d]	286	178	316	195	326	198	353	212	375	223	390	229
4 Land improvement and development and plantation and orchard development	...	...	...	...	...	...	...	...	...	...	...	...
5 Producers' durable goods	2562	1445	2911	1631	3138	1736	3261	1783	3415	1866	3562	1945
A Industries	2376	1351	2706	1528	2923	1627	3038	1669	3185	1747	3317	1814
1 Agriculture	183	98	202	106	211	106	215	104	212	100	205	93
2 Mining and quarrying	86	50	103	59	112	61	109	56	106	52	104	49
3 Manufacturing	742	425	844	482	910	513	929	513	962	526	998	542
4 Electricity, gas and water	181	103	206	115	221	122	227	123	235	128	253	141
5 Construction	78	41	87	46	87	43	83	39	79	36	77	35
6 Wholesale and retail trade	194	107	218	120	235	129	255	143	281	162	303	176
7 Transport and communication	472	269	540	307	588	331	621	346	652	360	678	369
8 Finance, etc.	281	169	325	193	361	211	386	225	423	249	449	265
9 Community, social and personal services	137	76	155	86	168	92	180	100	197	112	213	123
Statistical discrepancy [c]	24	14	28	16	31	18	34	20	37	22	36	22
B Producers of government services	157	79	171	85	179	89	183	92	188	96	200	106
C Other producers [d]	29	15	33	18	37	20	39	21	42	23	45	25
6 Breeding stock, dairy cattle, etc.	...	...	...	...	...	...	...	...	...	...	...	...
Total	11407	7023	12583	7700	12941	7838	13632	8209	14419	8663	15169	9097

	1986 Gross	1986 Net	1987 Gross	1987 Net
1 Residential buildings [a]	5777	3739	6239	4046
2 Non-residential buildings [b]	3154	1852	3373	1969
3 Other construction [b]	3167	1853	3273	1901
A Industries	3865	2256	4071	2361
1 Agriculture	183	101	190	102
2 Mining and quarrying	322	168	326	163
3 Manufacturing	517	276	543	285
4 Electricity, gas and water	575	329	597	340
5 Construction	34	22	36	23
6 Wholesale and retail trade	373	240	406	259
7 Transport and communication	471	251	489	260
8 Finance, etc.	444	287	491	319
9 Community, social and personal services	222	128	238	137
Statistical discrepancy [ca]	724	455	755	472
B Producers of government services [a]	2050	1214	2143	1261

United States

2.15 Stocks of Reproducible Fixed Assets by Kind of Activity, in Current Prices
(Continued)

Thousand Million United States dollars

		1986 Gross	1986 Net	1987 Gross	1987 Net
	C Other producers [d]	406	236	431	248
4	Land improvement and development and plantation and orchard development	...	...	...	...
5	Producers' durable goods	3737	2040	3916	2137
	A Industries	3478	1898	3641	1984
	1 Agriculture	196	86	188	81
	2 Mining and quarrying	98	43	94	39
	3 Manufacturing	1032	555	1066	568
	4 Electricity, gas and water	270	152	288	163
	5 Construction	76	35	75	35
	6 Wholesale and retail trade	333	195	364	215
	7 Transport and communication	707	382	733	391
	8 Finance, etc.	493	292	539	319
	9 Community, social and personal services	232	135	251	147
	Statistical discrepancy [c]	39	24	43	26
	B Producers of government services	211	114	222	123
	C Other producers [d]	49	28	53	30
6	Breeding stock, dairy cattle, etc.	...	...	...	...
Total		15835	9484	16801	10053

a) The estimates of residential buildings of government enterprises and general government are included in the respective columns of item 'Residential buildings' in tables 2.7 and 2.8. These estimates are included in item 'Real estate' in tables 2.9-2.12 and are therefore excluded from the estimates of government enterprises and general government of these tables. This latter classification is followed in tables 2.13-2.16.
b) The sub-items of 'Non-residential buildings' are included in the sub-items of 'Other construction'.
c) Item 'Statistical discrepancy' refers to government enterprises.
d) Item 'Other producers' consists of non-profit institutions serving individuals.

2.16 Stocks of Reproducible Fixed Assets by Kind of Activity, in Constant Prices

Thousand Million United States dollars

		1980 Gross	1980 Net	1981 Gross	1981 Net	1982 Gross	1982 Net	1983 Gross	1983 Net	1984 Gross	1984 Net	1985 Gross	1985 Net
		\multicolumn{12}{c}{At constant prices of: 1980}
1	Residential buildings [a]	3982	2603	4061	2644	4122	2666	4210	2716	4327	2793	4443	2869
2	Non-residential buildings [b]	2018	1239	2072	1262	2122	1282	2166	1295	2218	1315	2279	1345
3	Other construction [b]	2382	1446	2441	1478	2491	1499	2533	1511	2580	1529	2627	1546
	A Industries	2603	1562	2691	1613	2767	1651	2829	1673	2904	1708	2987	1751
	1 Agriculture	130	80	133	80	134	80	136	79	136	78	136	77
	2 Mining and quarrying	248	133	269	149	288	160	301	165	316	173	327	176
	3 Manufacturing	350	200	359	203	367	206	370	205	375	204	380	205
	4 Electricity, gas and water	385	232	395	236	403	239	409	239	416	241	424	244
	5 Construction	22	16	22	16	23	16	24	16	24	16	25	16
	6 Wholesale and retail trade	207	136	218	142	227	147	235	152	247	158	263	169
	7 Transport and communication	362	192	365	194	367	195	368	196	370	197	373	199
	8 Finance, etc.	227	142	240	151	255	160	268	169	286	182	309	199
	9 Community, social and personal services	136	82	140	83	144	85	148	87	154	89	159	92
	Statistical discrepancy [ca]	536	351	550	358	559	362	569	365	579	369	591	373
	B Producers of government services [a]	1572	983	1592	986	1612	988	1632	991	1651	993	1674	999
	C Other producers [d]	273	171	278	171	282	172	287	173	292	174	296	174
4	Land improvement and development and plantation and orchard development	...	...	...	...	...	...	...	...	...	...	...	...
5	Producers' durable goods	2474	1396	2572	1441	2639	1460	2711	1485	2812	1541	2931	1612
	A Industries	2291	1303	2386	1348	2452	1366	2523	1390	2623	1444	2739	1512
	1 Agriculture	174	93	175	91	172	86	168	81	163	77	156	71
	2 Mining and quarrying	81	47	85	48	87	48	85	44	83	41	80	37
	3 Manufacturing	722	414	753	430	775	437	786	435	805	441	829	452
	4 Electricity, gas and water	172	98	175	98	178	98	181	98	185	100	196	109

United States

2.16 Stocks of Reproducible Fixed Assets by Kind of Activity, in Constant Prices
(Continued)

Thousand Million United States dollars

	1980 Gross	1980 Net	1981 Gross	1981 Net	1982 Gross	1982 Net	1983 Gross	1983 Net	1984 Gross	1984 Net	1985 Gross	1985 Net
					At constant prices of:1980							
5 Construction	74	39	76	40	71	35	67	31	63	29	61	28
6 Wholesale and retail trade	194	107	202	111	210	116	227	128	250	145	272	160
7 Transport and communication	441	251	460	262	473	266	487	271	499	275	510	278
8 Finance, etc.	276	165	296	176	315	184	340	199	378	224	424	255
9 Community, social and personal services	135	75	140	78	146	80	154	85	167	95	178	103
Statistical discrepancy [c]	23	13	25	14	26	15	28	16	30	17	32	19
B Producers of government services	149	75	151	75	151	76	153	77	155	79	158	83
C Other producers [d]	28	15	29	15	30	16	32	17	34	19	36	20
6 Breeding stock, dairy cattle, etc.	...	...	...	...	...	...	...	...	...	...	...	...
Total	10856	6684	11145	6825	11374	6907	11620	7007	11936	7177	12280	7373

	1986 Gross	1986 Net	1987 Gross	1987 Net
	At constant prices of:1980			
1 Residential buildings [a]	4578	2962	4711	3053
2 Non-residential buildings [b]	2333	1370	2386	1393
3 Other construction [b]	2664	1554	2697	1559
A Industries	3054	1779	3114	1800
1 Agriculture	136	75	136	73
2 Mining and quarrying	325	168	321	160
3 Manufacturing	383	204	385	202
4 Electricity, gas and water	435	249	444	253
5 Construction	25	16	26	16
6 Wholesale and retail trade	276	177	288	183
7 Transport and communication	375	200	377	200
8 Finance, etc.	332	215	352	229
9 Community, social and personal services	164	95	169	97
Statistical discrepancy [ca]	603	379	616	385
B Producers of government services [a]	1696	1005	1720	1013
C Other producers [d]	301	175	306	176
4 Land improvement and development and plantation and orchard development	...	...	...	...
5 Producers' durable goods	3049	1678	3176	1750
A Industries	2856	1576	2978	1644
1 Agriculture	148	65	141	61
2 Mining and quarrying	76	33	71	30
3 Manufacturing	845	456	860	460
4 Electricity, gas and water	205	115	214	121
5 Construction	59	27	57	27
6 Wholesale and retail trade	298	177	327	195
7 Transport and communication	523	282	532	283
8 Finance, etc.	476	289	533	324
9 Community, social and personal services	191	111	205	120
Statistical discrepancy [c]	35	21	39	24
B Producers of government services	161	86	167	92
C Other producers [d]	39	22	42	24
6 Breeding stock, dairy cattle, etc.	...	...	...	...
Total	12624	7564	12970	7755

a) The estimates of residential buildings of government enterprises and general government are included in the respective columns of item 'Residential buildings' in tables 2.7 and 2.8. These estimates are included in item 'Real estate' in tables 2.9-2.12 and are therefore excluded from the estimates of government enterprises and general government of these tables. This latter classification is followed in tables 2.13-2.16.
b) The sub-items of 'Non-residential buildings' are included in the sub-items of 'Other construction'.
c) Item 'Statistical discrepancy' refers to government enterprises.
d) Item 'Other producers' consists of non-profit institutions serving individuals.

United States

2.17 Exports and Imports of Goods and Services, Detail

Million United States dollars

		1970	1975	1978	1979	1980	1981	1982	1983	1984	1985	1986	1987
	Exports of Goods and Services												
1	Exports of merchandise, f.o.b. [a]	44280	109359	144454	182986	224672	237894	213572	205637	223699	220280	224599	254322
2	Transport and communication	3669	6879	9739	12127	14209	15671	15491	15627	16837	18322	19633	22383
3	Insurance service charges	...	...	...	...	...	...	...	...	...	...	...	...
4	Other commodities	8492	14736	19725	19060	22908	25410	28190	29913	29341	29353	31959	37875
5	Adjustments of merchandise exports to change-of-ownership basis	...	...	...	...	...	...	...	...	...	...	...	...
6	Direct purchases in the domestic market by non-residential households	2663	5372	8095	9402	11558	14013	13651	12828	13373	13345	14851	17454
7	Direct purchases in the domestic market by extraterritorial bodies	...	...	...	...	...	...	...	...	...	...	...	...
	Total Exports of Goods and Services	59104	136346	182013	223575	273347	292988	270904	264005	283250	281300	291042	332034
	Imports of Goods and Services												
1	Imports of merchandise, c.i.f. [a]	40855	99000	176477	211930	247460	266462	249474	271341	334250	340877	367725	412997
	A Imports of merchandise, f.o.b. [a]	40855	99000	176477	211930	247460	266462	249474	271341	334250	340877	367725	412997
	B Transport of services on merchandise imports	...	...	...	...	...	...	...	...	...	...	...	...
	C Insurance service charges on merchandise imports	...	...	...	...	...	...	...	...	...	...	...	...
2	Adjustments of merchandise imports to change-of-ownership basis	...	...	...	...	...	...	...	...	...	...	...	...
3	Other transport and communication	2843	5708	9124	10906	11790	12474	11710	12222	14843	15643	16715	18161
4	Other insurance service charges	...	...	...	...	...	...	...	...	...	...	...	...
5	Other commodities	4036	5830	9784	11035	12755	14139	14766	14479	15309	16468	18496	21800
6	Direct purchases abroad by government	...	...	...	...	...	...	...	...	...	...	...	...
7	Direct purchases abroad by resident households	7443	10087	12803	14276	16069	17446	19187	21755	25039	26964	27287	31536
	Total Imports of Goods and Services	55177	120625	208188	248147	288074	310521	295137	319797	389441	399952	430223	484494
	Balance of Goods and Services	3927	15721	-26175	-24572	-14727	-17533	-24233	-55792	-106191	-118652	-139181	-152460
	Total Imports and Balance of Goods and Services	59104	136346	182013	223575	273347	292988	270904	264005	283250	281300	291042	332034

a) Valuation basis is essentially Free Along Side (F.A.S.).

3.12 General Government Income and Outlay Account: Total and Subsectors

Million United States dollars

		1980					1981				
		Total General Government	Central Government	State or Provincial Government	Local Government	Social Security Funds	Total General Government	Central Government	State or Provincial Government	Local Government	Social Security Funds
	Receipts										
1	Operating surplus	...	...	...	...	...	...	...	...	...	...
2	Property and entrepreneurial income	30344	10188	...	19307	849	38231	13466	...	23777	988
	A Withdrawals from public quasi-corporations	...	...	...	...	...	...	...	...	...	...
	B Interest	30247	10188	...	19210	849	38105	13466	...	23651	988
	C Dividends	97	...	...	97	...	126	...	...	126	...
	D Net land rent and royalties	...	...	...	...	...	...	...	...	...	...
3	Taxes, fees and contributions	769959	360490	...	242852	166617	881303	413794	...	271380	196129
	A Indirect taxes	213281	38822	...	174459	...	251476	56183	...	195293	...
	B Direct taxes	384793	321436	...	63357	...	427409	357352	...	70057	...
	Income	378496	321436	...	57060	...	420706	357352	...	63354	...
	Other	6297	...	...	6297	...	6703	...	...	6703	...
	C Social security contributions	166617	...	...	...	166617	196129	...	...	...	196129
	D Fees, fines and penalties	5268	232	...	5036	...	6289	259	...	6030	...

United States

3.12 General Government Income and Outlay Account: Total and Subsectors
(Continued)

Million United States dollars

	1980					1981				
	Total General Government	Central Government	State or Provincial Government	Local Government	Social Security Funds	Total General Government	Central Government	State or Provincial Government	Local Government	Social Security Funds
4 Other current transfers	26422	31690	...	88990	5626	30134	35875	...	88257	6408
A Casualty insurance claims	...	...	...	...	...	...	...	...	...	...
B Transfers from other government subsectors	...	5268	...	88990	5626	...	5741	...	88257	6408
C Transfers from the rest of the world	21	21	...	-	...	34	34	...	-	...
D Other transfers, except imputed	2731	2731	...	...	...	2910	2910	...	...	...
E Imputed unfunded employee pension and welfare contributions	23670	23670	...	...	...	27190	27190	...	...	...
Total Current Receipts [a][b]	826725	402368	...	351149	173092	949668	463135	...	383414	203525

Disbursements

1 Government final consumption expenditure	473722	207081	...	266641	5580	525613	236000	...	289613	6106
2 Property income	84750	65392	...	19358	...	110997	88153	...	22844	...
A Interest	84750	65392	...	19358	...	110997	88153	...	22844	...
B Net land rent and royalties	...	...	...	...	...	...	...	...	...	...
3 Subsidies	10723	10369	...	354	...	12182	11780	...	402	...
4 Other current transfers	300631	166801	...	47849	180285	340667	172771	...	53248	208948
A Casualty insurance premiums, net	...	...	...	...	...	...	...	...	...	...
B Transfers to other government subsectors	...	94304	...	...	...	...	94300	...	...	...
C Social security benefits	180285	...	...	...	180285	208948	...	...	...	208948
D Social assistance grants	89310	41501	...	47809	...	97367	44119	...	53248	...
E Unfunded employee pension and welfare benefits [c]	23710	23670	...	40	...	27131	27131	...	-	...
F Transfers to private non-profit institutions serving households	...	...	...	...	...	...	...	...	...	...
G Other transfers n.e.c.	...	...	...	...	...	...	...	...	...	...
H Transfers to the rest of the world	7326	7326	...	...	...	7221	7221	...	...	...
Net saving	-43101	-47275	...	16947	-12773	-39791	-45569	...	17307	-11529
Total Current Disbursements and Net Saving [a][b]	826725	402368	...	351149	173092	949668	463135	...	383414	203525

	1982					1983				
	Total General Government	Central Government	State or Provincial Government	Local Government	Social Security Funds	Total General Government	Central Government	State or Provincial Government	Local Government	Social Security Funds

Receipts

1 Operating surplus	...	...	...	...	...	...	...	...	...	...
2 Property and entrepreneurial income	43721	16157	...	26309	1255	46553	18079	...	26976	1498
A Withdrawals from public quasi-corporations	...	...	...	...	...	...	...	...	...	...
B Interest	43567	16157	...	26155	1255	46377	18079	...	26800	1498
C Dividends	154	...	...	154	...	176	...	...	176	...
D Net land rent and royalties	...	...	...	...	...	...	...	...	...	...
3 Taxes, fees and contributions	893825	393973	...	290713	209139	948250	401515	...	320476	226259
A Indirect taxes	258835	48085	...	210750	...	282560	51599	...	230961	...
B Direct taxes	418758	345577	...	73181	...	431457	349435	...	82022	...
Income	411498	345577	...	65921	...	423616	349435	...	74181	...
Other	7260	...	...	7260	...	7841	...	...	7841	...
C Social security contributions	209139	...	...	...	209139	226259	...	...	...	226259
D Fees, fines and penalties	7093	311	...	6782	...	7974	481	...	7493	...
4 Other current transfers	32947	38917	...	84271	6322	34863	41370	...	86683	5963
A Casualty insurance claims	...	...	...	...	...	...	...	...	...	...
B Transfers from other government subsectors	...	5970	...	84271	6322	...	6507	...	86683	5963
C Transfers from the rest of the world	117	117	...	-	...	35	35	...	-	...
D Other transfers, except imputed	3093	3093	...	...	...	3221	3221	...	...	...
E Imputed unfunded employee pension and welfare contributions	29737	29737	...	...	...	31607	31607	...	...	...

United States

3.12 General Government Income and Outlay Account: Total and Subsectors
(Continued)

Million United States dollars

	1982					1983				
	Total General Government	Central Government	State or Provincial Government	Local Government	Social Security Funds	Total General Government	Central Government	State or Provincial Government	Local Government	Social Security Funds
Total Current Receipts [ab]	970493	449047	...	401293	216716	1029670	460964	...	434135	233720
Disbursements											
1 Government final consumption expenditure	574090	264347	...	309743	6385	617003	289218	...	327785	6971
2 Property income	130684	103559	...	27125	...	147964	115617	...	32347	...
A Interest	130684	103559	...	27125	...	147964	115617	...	32347	...
B Net land rent and royalties	...	...	...	...	...	...	...	...	...	...
3 Subsidies	15483	15029	...	454	...	22175	21666	...	509	...
4 Other current transfers	379862	171115	...	56911	242014	408663	178524	...	61282	261039
A Casualty insurance premiums, net	...	...	...	...	...	...	...	...	...	...
B Transfers to other government subsectors	...	90178	...	...	...	...	92182	...	...	...
C Social security benefits	242014	...	...	...	242014	261039	...	...	...	261039
D Social assistance grants	99653	42742	...	56911	...	106850	45568	...	61282	...
E Unfunded employee pension and welfare benefits [c]	29741	29741	...	-	...	32052	32052	...	-	...
F Transfers to private non-profit institutions serving households	...	...	...	...	...	...	...	...	...	...
G Other transfers n.e.c.	...	...	...	...	...	...	...	...	...	...
H Transfers to the rest of the world	8454	8454	...	...	...	8722	8722	...	...	...
Net saving	-129626	-105003	...	7060	-31683	-166139	-144061	...	12212	-34290
Total Current Disbursements and Net Saving [ab]	970493	449047	...	401293	216716	1029670	460964	...	434135	233720

	1984					1985				
	Total General Government	Central Government	State or Provincial Government	Local Government	Social Security Funds	Total General Government	Central Government	State or Provincial Government	Local Government	Social Security Funds
Receipts											
1 Operating surplus	...	...	...	...	...	...	...	...	...	...
2 Property and entrepreneurial income	53180	20274	...	31088	1818	58114	21308	...	34982	1824
A Withdrawals from public quasi-corporations	...	...	...	...	...	...	...	...	...	...
B Interest	53016	20274	...	30924	1818	57958	21308	...	34826	1824
C Dividends	164	...	...	164	...	156	...	...	156	...
D Net land rent and royalties	...	...	...	...	...	...	...	...	...	...
3 Taxes, fees and contributions	1054460	435170	...	361638	257654	1143390	471298	...	389905	282182
A Indirect taxes	313914	55718	...	258196	...	333637	55093	...	278544	...
B Direct taxes	473774	378962	...	94812	...	517104	415543	...	101561	...
Income	465222	378962	...	86260	...	507923	415543	...	92380	...
Other	8552	...	...	8552	...	9181	...	...	9181	...
C Social security contributions	257654	...	...	...	257654	282182	...	...	...	282182
D Fees, fines and penalties	9120	490	...	8630	...	10462	662	...	9800	...
4 Other current transfers	34698	41373	...	94028	9550	37746	44910	...	100185	13431
A Casualty insurance claims	...	...	...	...	...	...	...	...	...	...
B Transfers from other government subsectors	...	6675	...	94028	9550	...	7164	...	100185	13431
C Transfers from the rest of the world	38	38	...	-	...	85	85	...	-	...
D Other transfers, except imputed	3371	3371	...	...	...	3402	3402	...	...	...
E Imputed unfunded employee pension and welfare contributions	31289	31289	...	...	...	34259	34259	...	...	...
Total Current Receipts [ab]	1142340	496817	...	486754	269022	1239250	537516	...	525072	297437
Disbursements											
1 Government final consumption expenditure	670111	315613	...	354498	7148	727926	342964	...	384962	7671
2 Property income	176821	139775	...	37046	...	198193	156005	...	42188	...
A Interest	176821	139775	...	37046	...	198193	156005	...	42188	...
B Net land rent and royalties	...	...	...	...	...	...	...	...	...	...
3 Subsidies	22730	22120	...	610	...	22863	22173	...	690	...

United States

3.12 General Government Income and Outlay Account: Total and Subsectors
(Continued)

Million United States dollars

	1984					1985				
	Total General Government	Central Government	State or Provincial Government	Local Government	Social Security Funds	Total General Government	Central Government	State or Provincial Government	Local Government	Social Security Funds
4 Other current transfers	418561	191046	...	65352	265268	449043	207810	...	70803	283539
A Casualty insurance premiums, net	...	...	...	...	...	...	...	...	...	...
B Transfers to other government subsectors	...	103105	...	...	...	...	113109	...	...	...
C Social security benefits	265268	...	...	...	265268	283539	...	...	...	283539
D Social assistance grants	111299	45947	...	65352	...	117523	46720	...	70803	...
E Unfunded employee pension and welfare benefits c	31069	31069	...	-	...	34489	34489	...	-	...
F Transfers to private non-profit institutions serving households	...	...	...	...	...	...	...	...	...	...
G Other transfers n.e.c.	...	...	...	...	...	...	...	...	...	...
H Transfers to the rest of the world	10925	10925	...	...	...	13492	13492	...	...	...
Net saving	-145883	-171737	...	29248	-3394	-158780	-191436	...	26429	6227
Total Current Disbursements and Net Saving ab	1142340	496817	...	486754	269022	1239250	537516	...	525072	297437

	1986					1987				
	Total General Government	Central Government	State or Provincial Government	Local Government	Social Security Funds	Total General Government	Central Government	State or Provincial Government	Local Government	Social Security Funds

Receipts

1 Operating surplus	...	...	...	...	...	...	...	...	...	...
2 Property and entrepreneurial income	62500	22262	...	38250	1988	62273	18831	...	41250	2192
A Withdrawals from public quasi-corporations	...	...	...	...	...	...	...	...	...	...
B Interest	62350	22262	...	38100	1988	62123	18831	...	41100	2192
C Dividends	150	...	...	150	...	150	...	...	150	...
D Net land rent and royalties	...	...	...	...	...	...	...	...	...	...
3 Taxes, fees and contributions	1210030	489059	...	417732	303234	1327930	558104	...	448572	321255
A Indirect taxes	'9446	50806	...	297640	...	366323	54029	...	312294	...
B Direct taxes	546653	437461	...	109192	...	627154	502665	...	124489	...
Income	536959	437461	...	99498	...	616652	502665	...	113987	...
Other	9694	...	...	9694	...	10502	...	...	10502	...
C Social security contributions	303234	...	...	...	303234	321255	...	...	...	321255
D Fees, fines and penalties	11692	792	...	10900	...	13199	1410	...	11789	...
4 Other current transfers	38694	45965	...	107356	14629	40257	47489	...	103283	19996
A Casualty insurance claims	...	...	...	...	...	...	...	...	...	...
B Transfers from other government subsectors	...	7271	...	107356	14629	...	7232	...	103283	19996
C Transfers from the rest of the world	131	131	...	-	...	65	65	...	-	...
D Other transfers, except imputed	3366	3366	...	...	...	3276	3276	...	...	...
E Imputed unfunded employee pension and welfare contributions	35197	35197	...	...	...	36916	36916	...	...	...
Total Current Receipts ab	1311220	557286	...	563338	319851	1430460	624424	...	593105	343443

Disbursements

1 Government final consumption expenditure	780403	365038	...	415365	7829	831989	385888	...	446101	7832
2 Property income	210441	162867	...	47574	...	220808	167508	...	53300	...
A Interest	210441	162867	...	47574	...	220808	167508	...	53300	...
B Net land rent and royalties	...	...	...	...	...	...	...	...	...	...
3 Subsidies	27291	26484	...	807	...	31783	30823	...	960	...

United States

3.12 General Government Income and Outlay Account: Total and Subsectors
(Continued)

Million United States dollars

	1986 Total General Government	1986 Central Government	1986 State or Provincial Government	1986 Local Government	1986 Social Security Funds	1987 Total General Government	1987 Central Government	1987 State or Provincial Government	1987 Local Government	1987 Social Security Funds
4 Other current transfers	474812	218701	...	76899	300639	494175	220889	...	82576	313389
A Casualty insurance premiums, net	...	...	...	...	...	...	...	...	...	...
B Transfers to other government subsectors	...	121427	...	...	...	...	122679	...	...	...
C Social security benefits	300639	...	...	...	300639	313389	...	...	...	313389
D Social assistance grants	124809	47910	...	76899	...	131524	48948	...	82576	...
E Unfunded employee pension and welfare benefits [c]	35197	35197	...	...	...	36916	36916	...	-	...
F Transfers to private non-profit institutions serving households	...	...	...	...	...	...	...	...	...	...
G Other transfers n.e.c.	...	...	...	...	...	...	...	...	...	...
H Transfers to the rest of the world	14167	14167	...	...	...	12346	12346	...	...	...
Net saving	-181728	-215804	...	22693	11383	-148294	-180684	...	10168	22222
Total Current Disbursements and Net Saving [a,b]	1311220	557286	...	563338	319851	1430460	624424	...	593105	343443

a) State or provincial government is included in local government.
b) Intergovernmental transfers (not shown separately) are included in column 1. Therefore, column 1 is not equal to the sum of columns 2, 3, 4 and 5.
c) Item 'Unfunded employee pension and welfare benefits' also includes wage accruals less disbursements.

3.13 General Government Capital Accumulation Account: Total and Subsectors

Million United States dollars

	1980 Total General Government	1980 Central Government	1980 State or Provincial Government	1980 Local Government	1980 Social Security Funds	1981 Total General Government	1981 Central Government	1981 State or Provincial Government	1981 Local Government	1981 Social Security Funds
Finance of Gross Accumulation										
1 Gross saving	-3182	-39291	...	48882	-12773	2679	-36833	...	51041	-11529
A Consumption of fixed capital	39919	7984	...	31935	...	42470	8736	...	33734	...
B Net saving	-43101	-47275	...	16947	-12773	-39791	-45569	...	17307	-11529
2 Capital transfers	9988	7724	...	2264	...	10446	8075	...	2371	...
A From other government subsectors	...	...	...	...	...	...	...	...	...	...
B From other resident sectors	8836	6572	...	2264	...	9353	6982	...	2371	...
C From rest of the world	1152	1152	...	...	...	1093	1093	...	...	...
Finance of Gross Accumulation [a]	6806	-31567	...	51146	-12773	13125	-28758	...	53412	-11529
Gross Accumulation										
1 Gross capital formation	48551	10195	...	38356	...	50890	14269	...	36621	...
A Increase in stocks	1290	1059	...	231	...	5141	4993	...	148	...
B Gross fixed capital formation	47261	9136	...	38125	...	45749	9276	...	36473	...
Own account	1396	107	...	1289	...	1299	98	...	1201	...
Other	45865	9029	...	36836	...	44450	9178	...	35272	...
2 Purchases of land, net	2377	342	...	2035	...	2384	165	...	2219	...
3 Purchases of intangible assets, net	-4799	-4376	...	-423	...	-6027	-5706	...	-321	...
4 Capital transfers	-	-	...	...	...	-	-	...	...	...
A To other government subsectors	...	...	...	...	...	...	...	...	...	...
B To other resident sectors	...	...	...	...	...	...	...	...	...	...
C To rest of the world	-	-	...	...	...	-	-	...	...	...
Net lending [b]	-39323	-37728	...	11178	-12773	-34122	-37486	...	14893	-11529
Gross Accumulation [a]	6806	-31567	...	51146	-12773	13125	-28758	...	53412	-11529

	1982 Total General Government	1982 Central Government	1982 State or Provincial Government	1982 Local Government	1982 Social Security Funds	1983 Total General Government	1983 Central Government	1983 State or Provincial Government	1983 Local Government	1983 Social Security Funds
Finance of Gross Accumulation										
1 Gross saving	-86029	-95783	...	41437	-31683	-121550	-134659	...	47399	-34290
A Consumption of fixed capital	43597	9220	...	34377	...	44589	9402	...	35187	...
B Net saving	-129626	-105003	...	7060	-31683	-166139	-144061	...	12212	-34290
2 Capital transfers	10207	7619	...	2588	...	8455	5889	...	2566	...

United States

3.13 General Government Capital Accumulation Account: Total and Subsectors
(Continued)

Million United States dollars

	\multicolumn{5}{c	}{1982}	\multicolumn{5}{c	}{1983}
	Total General Government	Central Government	State or Provincial Government	Local Government	Social Security Funds	Total General Government	Central Government	State or Provincial Government	Local Government	Social Security Funds
A From other government subsectors	...	...	...	...	...	...	...	...	...	...
B From other resident sectors	10207	7619	...	2588	...	8455	5889	...	2566	...
C From rest of the world	-	-	...	-	...	-	-	...	-	...
Finance of Gross Accumulation a	-75822	-88164	...	44025	-31683	-113095	-128770	...	49965	-34290
\multicolumn{11}{c}{**Gross Accumulation**}
1 Gross capital formation	49711	13629	...	36082	...	52835	14654	...	38181	...
A Increase in stocks	2776	2739	...	37	...	3468	3099	...	369	...
B Gross fixed capital formation	46935	10890	...	36045	...	49367	11555	...	37812	...
Own account	1209	90	...	1119	...	1212	89	...	1123	...
Other	45726	10800	...	34926	...	48155	11466	...	36689	...
2 Purchases of land, net	2354	146	...	2208	...	2327	68	...	2259	...
3 Purchases of intangible assets, net	-3990	-3813	...	-177	...	-5181	-5051	...	-130	...
4 Capital transfers	-	-	...	...	...	-	-	...	...	...
A To other government subsectors	...	...	...	...	...	...	...	...	...	...
B To other resident sectors	...	...	...	...	...	...	...	...	...	...
C To rest of the world	-	-	...	...	...	-	-	...	...	...
Net lending b	-123897	-98126	...	5912	-31683	-163076	-138441	...	9655	-34290
Gross Accumulation a	-75822	-88164	...	44025	-31683	-113095	-128770	...	49965	-34290

	\multicolumn{5}{c	}{1984}	\multicolumn{5}{c	}{1985}
	Total General Government	Central Government	State or Provincial Government	Local Government	Social Security Funds	Total General Government	Central Government	State or Provincial Government	Local Government	Social Security Funds
\multicolumn{11}{c}{**Finance of Gross Accumulation**}
1 Gross saving	-99668	-162135	...	65861	-3394	-108708	-181540	...	66605	6227
A Consumption of fixed capital	46215	9602	...	36613	...	50072	9896	...	40176	...
B Net saving	-145883	-171737	...	29248	-3394	-158780	-191436	...	26429	6227
2 Capital transfers	8487	6096	...	2391	...	9102	6491	...	2611	...
A From other government subsectors	...	...	...	...	...	...	...	...	...	...
B From other resident sectors	8487	6096	...	2391	...	9102	6491	...	2611	...
C From rest of the world	-	-	...	...	...	-	-	...	...	...
Finance of Gross Accumulation a	-91181	-156039	...	68252	-3394	-99606	-175049	...	69216	6227
\multicolumn{11}{c}{**Gross Accumulation**}
1 Gross capital formation	53383	12275	...	41108	...	64188	16532	...	47656	...
A Increase in stocks	2143	2011	...	132	...	1717	1499	...	218	...
B Gross fixed capital formation	51240	10264	...	40976	...	62471	15033	...	47438	...
Own account	1307	84	...	1223	...	1512	85	...	1427	...
Other	49933	10180	...	39753	...	60959	14948	...	46011	...
2 Purchases of land, net	2744	150	...	2594	...	3282	215	...	3067	...
3 Purchases of intangible assets, net	-4259	-4083	...	-176	...	-1510	-1370	...	-140	...
4 Capital transfers	-	-	...	...	...	-	-	...	...	...
A To other government subsectors	...	...	...	...	...	...	...	...	...	...
B To other resident sectors	...	...	...	...	...	...	...	...	...	...
C To rest of the world	-	-	...	...	...	-	-	...	...	...
Net lending b	-143049	-164381	...	24726	-3394	-165566	-190426	...	18633	6227
Gross Accumulation a	-91181	-156039	...	68252	-3394	-99606	-175049	...	69216	6227

	\multicolumn{5}{c	}{1986}	\multicolumn{5}{c	}{1987}
	Total General Government	Central Government	State or Provincial Government	Local Government	Social Security Funds	Total General Government	Central Government	State or Provincial Government	Local Government	Social Security Funds
\multicolumn{11}{c}{**Finance of Gross Accumulation**}
1 Gross saving	-129647	-205649	...	64619	11383	-94234	-170256	...	53800	22222
A Consumption of fixed capital	52081	10155	...	41926	...	54060	10428	...	43632	...
B Net saving	-181728	-215804	...	22693	11383	-148294	-180684	...	10168	22222
2 Capital transfers	10136	7089	...	3047	...	10689	7385	...	3304	...

United States

3.13 General Government Capital Accumulation Account: Total and Subsectors
(Continued)

Million United States dollars

	1986					1987				
	Total General Government	Central Government	State or Provincial Government	Local Government	Social Security Funds	Total General Government	Central Government	State or Provincial Government	Local Government	Social Security Funds
A From other government subsectors	...	...	...	...	...	...	...	...	...	...
B From other resident sectors	10136	7089	...	3047	...	10689	7385	...	3304	...
C From rest of the world	-	-	...	...	...	-	-	...	...	...
Finance of Gross Accumulation a	-119511	-198560	...	67666	11383	-83545	-162871	...	57104	22222
Gross Accumulation											
1 Gross capital formation	64193	11227	...	52966	...	71700	14967	...	56733	...
A Increase in stocks	90	553	...	-463	...	1031	673	...	358	...
B Gross fixed capital formation	64103	10674	...	53429	...	70669	14294	...	56375	...
Own account	1651	80	...	1571	...	1706	86	...	1620	...
Other	62452	10594	...	51858	...	68963	14208	...	54755	...
2 Purchases of land, net	3665	189	...	3476	...	3912	205	...	3707	...
3 Purchases of intangible assets, net	-3272	-3173	...	-99	...	-719	-600	...	-119	...
4 Capital transfers	-	-	...	...	...	-	-	...	...	...
A To other government subsectors	...	...	...	...	...	...	...	...	...	...
B To other resident sectors	...	...	...	...	...	...	...	...	...	...
C To rest of the world	-	-	...	...	...	-	-	...	...	...
Net lending b	-184097	-206803	...	11323	11383	-158438	-177443	...	-3217	22222
Gross Accumulation a	-119511	-198560	...	67666	11383	-83545	-162871	...	57104	22222

a) State or provincial government is included in local government.
b) Net lending of the capital accumulation account and the capital finance account have not been reconciled and are different due to different statistical sources.

3.14 General Government Capital Finance Account, Total and Subsectors

Million United States dollars

	1980					1981				
	Total General Government	Central Government	State or Provincial Government	Local Government	Social Security Funds	Total General Government	Central Government	State or Provincial Government	Local Government	Social Security Funds
Acquisition of Financial Assets											
1 Gold and SDRs	4961	4961	...	...	...	4733	4733	...	...	...
2 Currency and transferable deposits	-3143	-2536	...	-607	...	-1099	375	...	-1474	...
3 Other deposits	-1926	-210	...	-1716	...	7307	-142	...	7449	...
4 Bills and bonds, short term	2132	-	...	2132	...	-6984	-	...	-6984	...
5 Bonds, long term	...	...	...	...	...	...	...	...	...	...
6 Corporate equity securities	...	...	...	...	...	...	...	...	...	...
7 Short-term loans, n.e.c.	16180	16180	...	...	...	19107	19107	...	...	...
8 Long-term loans, n.e.c.	17288	7506	...	9782	...	12621	4939	...	7682	...
9 Other receivables	3778	3778	...	...	...	2542	2542	...	...	...
10 Other assets	-753	-4340	...	3587	...	-9738	-9130	...	-608	...
Total Acquisition of Financial Assets a	38517	25339	...	13178	...	28489	22424	...	6065	...
Incurrence of Liabilities											
1 Currency and transferable deposits	...	...	...	...	...	...	...	...	...	...
2 Other deposits	...	...	...	...	...	...	...	...	...	...
3 Bills and bonds, short term	38397	36660	...	1737	...	24208	23070	...	1138	...
4 Bonds, long term	57202	42640	...	14562	...	68821	64412	...	4409	...
5 Short-term loans, n.e.c.	924	-	...	924	...	1238	-	...	1238	...
6 Long-term loans, n.e.c.	-104	-104	...	...	...	-109	-109	...	...	...
7 Other payables	3277	1296	...	1981	...	1598	491	...	1107	...
8 Other liabilities	8187	8187	...	...	...	12334	12334	...	...	...
Total Incurrence of Liabilities	107883	88679	...	19204	...	108090	100198	...	7892	...
Net Lending b	-69366	-63340	...	-6026	...	-79601	-77774	...	-1827	...
Incurrence of Liabilities and Net Worth a	38517	25339	...	13178	...	28489	22424	...	6065	...

United States

3.14 General Government Capital Finance Account, Total and Subsectors

Million United States dollars

		1982					1983				
		Total General Government	Central Government	State or Provincial Government	Local Government	Social Security Funds	Total General Government	Central Government	State or Provincial Government	Local Government	Social Security Funds
	Acquisition of Financial Assets										
1	Gold and SDRs	4438	4438	...	...	...	2892	2892	...	...	...
2	Currency and transferable deposits	4874	6429	...	-1555	...	-8943	-8263	...	-680	...
3	Other deposits	11644	472	...	11172	...	531	-451	...	982	...
4	Bills and bonds, short term	6755	-	...	6755	...	27488	-	...	27488	...
5	Bonds, long term	...	...	...	...	...	...	...	...	...	...
6	Corporate equity securities	...	...	...	...	...	...	...	...	...	...
7	Short-term loans, n.e.c.	13572	13572	...	...	...	8435	8435	...	...	...
8	Long-term loans, n.e.c.	7603	2364	...	5239	...	9106	1220	...	7886	...
9	Other receivables	4792	4792	...	...	...	3766	3766	...	...	...
10	Other assets	-8473	-8556	...	83	...	9775	6003	...	3772	...
	Total Acquisition of Financial Assets [a]	45205	23511	...	21694	...	53050	13602	...	39448	...
	Incurrence of Liabilities										
1	Currency and transferable deposits	...	...	...	...	...	...	...	...	...	...
2	Other deposits	...	...	...	...	...	...	...	...	...	...
3	Bills and bonds, short term	71679	64948	...	6731	...	43539	45020	...	-1481	...
4	Bonds, long term	110284	96434	...	13850	...	176012	141618	...	34394	...
5	Short-term loans, n.e.c.	967	-	...	967	...	1109	-	...	1109	...
6	Long-term loans, n.e.c.	-119	-119	...	...	...	-81	-81	...	...	...
7	Other payables	2850	1912	...	938	...	3744	2952	...	792	...
8	Other liabilities	13734	13734	...	...	...	16720	16720	...	...	...
	Total Incurrence of Liabilities	199395	176909	...	22486	...	241043	206229	...	34814	...
	Net Lending [b]	-154190	-153398	...	-792	...	-187993	-192627	...	4634	...
	Incurrence of Liabilities and Net Worth [a]	45205	23511	...	21694	...	53050	13602	...	39448	...

		1984					1985				
		Total General Government	Central Government	State or Provincial Government	Local Government	Social Security Funds	Total General Government	Central Government	State or Provincial Government	Local Government	Social Security Funds
	Acquisition of Financial Assets										
1	Gold and SDRs	2596	2596	...	...	...	1907	1907	...	...	...
2	Currency and transferable deposits	10294	5263	...	5031	...	14062	12991	...	1071	...
3	Other deposits	10270	532	...	9738	...	12193	40	...	12153	...
4	Bills and bonds, short term	17633	-	...	17633	...	87985	-	...	87985	...
5	Bonds, long term	...	...	...	...	...	...	...	...	...	...
6	Corporate equity securities	...	...	...	...	...	...	...	...	...	...
7	Short-term loans, n.e.c.	16612	16612	...	...	...	14932	14932	...	...	...
8	Long-term loans, n.e.c.	10704	469	...	10235	...	11649	1841	...	9808	...
9	Other receivables	5082	5082	...	...	...	3679	3679	...	...	...
10	Other assets	6967	2044	...	4923	...	2085	-2615	...	4700	...
	Total Acquisition of Financial Assets [a]	80158	32598	...	47560	...	148492	32775	...	115717	...
	Incurrence of Liabilities										
1	Currency and transferable deposits	...	...	...	...	...	...	...	...	...	...
2	Other deposits	...	...	...	...	...	...	...	...	...	...
3	Bills and bonds, short term	26412	30068	...	-3656	...	69014	67712	...	1302	...
4	Bonds, long term	192176	168834	...	23342	...	238283	155978	...	82305	...
5	Short-term loans, n.e.c.	7741	-	...	7741	...	8179	-	...	8179	...
6	Long-term loans, n.e.c.	-100	-100	...	...	...	-69	-69	...	...	...
7	Other payables	4253	3271	...	982	...	5637	4554	...	1083	...
8	Other liabilities	23615	23615	...	...	...	19174	19174	...	...	...
	Total Incurrence of Liabilities	254097	225688	...	28409	...	340218	247349	...	92869	...
	Net Lending [b]	-173939	-193090	...	19151	...	-191726	-214574	...	22848	...
	Incurrence of Liabilities and Net Worth [a]	80158	32598	...	47560	...	148492	32775	...	115717	...

United States

3.14 General Government Capital Finance Account, Total and Subsectors
Million United States dollars

		1986				1987				
		Total General Government	Central Government	State or Provincial Government	Local Government	Social Security Funds	Total General Government	Central Government	State or Provincial Government	Local Government	Social Security Funds

Acquisition of Financial Assets

		Total General Government	Central Government	State or Provincial Government	Local Government	Social Security Funds	Total General Government	Central Government	State or Provincial Government	Local Government	Social Security Funds
1	Gold and SDRs	-741	-741	...	...	...	-5363	-5363	...	...	...
2	Currency and transferable deposits	3915	408	...	3507	...	-7305	-8074	...	769	...
3	Other deposits	4197	185	...	4012	...	12030	218	...	11812	...
4	Bills and bonds, short term	36574	-	...	36574	...	11686	-	...	11686	...
5	Bonds, long term	...	...	...	...	...	...	...	...	...	...
6	Corporate equity securities	...	...	...	...	...	...	...	...	...	...
7	Short-term loans, n.e.c.	9139	9139	...	...	...	-6178	-6178	...	...	...
8	Long-term loans, n.e.c.	12315	517	...	11798	...	3404	-5288	...	8692	...
9	Other receivables	121	121	...	...	...	-1049	-1049	...	...	...
10	Other assets	4405	185	...	4220	...	3823	2365	...	1458	...
	Total Acquisition of Financial Assets [a]	69925	9814	...	60111	...	11048	-23369	...	34417	...

Incurrence of Liabilities

1	Currency and transferable deposits	...	...	...	...	...	...	...	...	...	...
2	Other deposits	...	...	...	...	...	...	...	...	...	...
3	Bills and bonds, short term	50659	46509	...	4150	...	-2516	-8759	...	6243	...
4	Bonds, long term	207278	168543	...	38735	...	182749	152616	...	30133	...
5	Short-term loans, n.e.c.	1437	-	...	1437	...	-1934	-	...	-1934	...
6	Long-term loans, n.e.c.	-36	-36	...	...	...	-15	-15	...	...	...
7	Other payables	2672	1046	...	1626	...	7013	5098	...	1915	...
8	Other liabilities	27025	27025	...	...	...	11360	11360	...	...	...
	Total Incurrence of Liabilities	289035	243087	...	45948	...	196657	160300	...	36357	...
	Net Lending [b]	-219110	-233273	...	14163	...	-185609	-183669	...	-1940	...
	Incurrence of Liabilities and Net Worth [a]	69925	9814	...	60111	...	11048	-23369	...	34417	...

a) State or provincial government is included in local government.
b) Net lending of the capital accumulation account and the capital finance account have not been reconciled and are different due to different statistical sources.

3.22 Corporate and Quasi-Corporate Enterprise Income and Outlay Account: Total and Sectors
Million United States dollars

		1980			1981			1982			1983		
		TOTAL	Non-Financial	Financial	TOTAL	Non-Financial	Financial	TOTAL	Non-Financial	Financial	TOTAL	Non-Financial	Financial

Receipts

		TOTAL	Non-Financial	Financial	TOTAL	Non-Financial	Financial	TOTAL	Non-Financial	Financial	TOTAL	Non-Financial	Financial
1	Operating surplus	243149	224025	19124	273785	260962	12823	242589	237847	4742	301886	284910	16976
2	Property and entrepreneurial income	501347	113475	387872	650062	140242	509820	715410	147570	567840	706394	145838	560556
	A Withdrawals from quasi-corporate enterprises	...	...	...	...	...	...	...	...	...	...	...	...
	B Interest	448345	80331	368014	597094	108047	489047	660144	114039	546105	647973	111886	536087
	C Dividends	53002	33144	19858	52968	32195	20773	55266	33531	21735	58421	33952	24469
	D Net land rent and royalties	...	...	...	...	...	...	...	...	...	...	...	...
3	Current transfers	5340	5340	...	6117	6117	...	6690	6690	...	7118	7118	...
	A Casualty insurance claims	...	...	...	...	...	...	...	...	...	...	...	...
	B Casualty insurance premiums, net, due to be received by insurance companies	...	...	...	...	...	...	...	...	...	...	...	...
	C Current transfers from the rest of the world	...	...	...	...	...	...	...	...	...	...	...	...
	D Other transfers except imputed	1048	1048	...	1107	1107	...	1185	1185	...	1238	1238	...
	E Imputed unfunded employee pension and welfare contributions	4292	4292	...	5010	5010	...	5505	5505	...	5880	5880	...
	Total Current Receipts	749836	342840	406996	929964	407321	522643	964689	392107	572582	1015400	437866	577532

Disbursements

		TOTAL	Non-Financial	Financial	TOTAL	Non-Financial	Financial	TOTAL	Non-Financial	Financial	TOTAL	Non-Financial	Financial
1	Property and entrepreneurial income	620425	241968	378457	798236	297435	500801	871305	317229	554076	860024	310788	549236
	A Withdrawals from quasi-corporations	...	...	...	...	...	...	...	...	...	...	...	...
	B Interest	514555	147654	366901	683980	197300	486680	752109	211455	540654	732872	198583	534289

United States

3.22 Corporate and Quasi-Corporate Enterprise Income and Outlay Account: Total and Sectors
(Continued)

Million United States dollars

	1980 TOTAL	1980 Non-Financial	1980 Financial	1981 TOTAL	1981 Non-Financial	1981 Financial	1982 TOTAL	1982 Non-Financial	1982 Financial	1983 TOTAL	1983 Non-Financial	1983 Financial
C Dividends	105870	94314	11556	114256	100135	14121	119196	105774	13422	127152	112205	14947
D Net land rent and royalties	...	...	...	...	...	...	...	...	...	...	...	...
2 Direct taxes and other current transfers n.e.c. to general government	84785	67006	17779	81143	63887	17256	63081	46258	16823	77241	59437	17804
A Direct taxes	84785	67006	17779	81143	63887	17256	63081	46258	16823	77241	59437	17804
On income	84785	67006	17779	81143	63887	17256	63081	46258	16823	77241	59437	17804
Other	...	...	...	...	...	...	...	...	...	...	...	...
B Fines, fees, penalties and other current transfers n.e.c.	...	...	...	...	...	...	...	...	...	...	...	...
3 Other current transfers	13649	12165	1484	14678	13287	1391	16765	14890	1875	18616	16544	2072
A Casualty insurance premiums, net	...	...	...	...	...	...	...	...	...	...	...	...
B Casualty insurance claims liability of insurance companies	-	...	-	-	...	-	-	...	-	-	...	-
C Transfers to private non-profit institutions	2359	2109	250	2514	2298	216	2906	2688	218	3627	3321	306
D Unfunded employee pension and welfare benefits	4292	4292	...	5010	5010	...	5505	5505	...	5880	5880	...
E Social assistance grants	2847	1674	1173	2438	1332	1106	3247	1665	1582	3545	1860	1685
F Other transfers n.e.c.	4151	4090	61	4716	4647	69	5107	5032	75	5564	5483	81
G Transfers to the rest of the world	...	...	...	...	...	...	...	...	...	...	...	...
Net saving	30977	21701	9276	35907	32712	3195	13538	13730	-192	59517	51097	8420
Total Current Disbursements and Net Saving	749836	342840	406996	929964	407321	522643	964689	392107	572582	1015400	437866	577532

	1984 TOTAL	1984 Non-Financial	1984 Financial	1985 TOTAL	1985 Non-Financial	1985 Financial	1986 TOTAL	1986 Non-Financial	1986 Financial	1987 TOTAL	1987 Non-Financial	1987 Financial
Receipts												
1 Operating surplus	360190	354359	5831	371717	353671	18046	384348	356226	28122	401389	370939	30450
2 Property and entrepreneurial income	798799	166506	632293	870892	189244	681648	898529	194667	703862	952115	205244	746871
A Withdrawals from quasi-corporate enterprises	...	...	...	...	...	...	...	...	...	...	...	...
B Interest	738684	130572	608112	805264	150502	654762	829364	154110	675254	885356	168255	717101
C Dividends	60115	35934	24181	65628	38742	26886	69165	40557	28608	66759	36989	29770
D Net land rent and royalties	...	...	...	...	...	...	...	...	...	...	...	...
3 Current transfers	7425	7425	...	8194	8194	...	8429	8429	...	9309	9309	...
A Casualty insurance claims	...	...	...	...	...	...	...	...	...	...	...	...
B Casualty insurance premiums, net, due to be received by insurance companies	...	...	...	...	...	...	...	...	...	...	...	...
C Current transfers from the rest of the world	...	...	...	...	...	...	...	...	...	...	...	...
D Other transfers except imputed	1294	1294	...	1386	1386	...	1372	1372	...	1400	1400	...
E Imputed unfunded employee pension and welfare contributions	6131	6131	...	6808	6808	...	7057	7057	...	7909	7909	...
Total Current Receipts	1166410	528290	638124	1250800	551109	699694	1291310	559322	731984	1362810	585492	777321
Disbursements												
1 Property and entrepreneurial income	958749	341162	617587	1026810	360221	666587	1054530	367455	687073	1120780	387636	733143
A Withdrawals from quasi-corporations	...	...	...	...	...	...	...	...	...	...	...	...
B Interest	823103	223980	599123	882442	237116	645326	902606	236665	665941	965441	254735	710706
C Dividends	135646	117182	18464	144366	123105	21261	151922	130790	21132	155338	132901	22437
D Net land rent and royalties	...	...	...	...	...	...	...	...	...	...	...	...
2 Direct taxes and other current transfers n.e.c. to general government	93899	73523	20376	96422	69853	26569	106574	76760	29814	133759	98950	34809
A Direct taxes	93899	73523	20376	96422	69853	26569	106574	76760	29814	133759	98950	34809
On income	93899	73523	20376	96422	69853	26569	106574	76760	29814	133759	98950	34809
Other	...	...	...	...	...	...	...	...	...	...	...	...
B Fines, fees, penalties and other current transfers n.e.c.	...	...	...	...	...	...	...	...	...	...	...	...

United States

3.22 Corporate and Quasi-Corporate Enterprise Income and Outlay Account: Total and Sectors
(Continued)

Million United States dollars

		1984			1985			1986			1987		
		TOTAL	Non-Financial	Financial	TOTAL	Non-Financial	Financial	TOTAL	Non-Financial	Financial	TOTAL	Non-Financial	Financial
3	Other current transfers	20776	18300	2476	23383	20982	2401	25829	23036	2793	28864	25679	3185
A	Casualty insurance premiums, net	...	...	...	...	...	...	...	...	...	...	...	...
B	Casualty insurance claims liability of insurance companies	80	...	80	105	...	105	161	...	161	167	...	167
C	Transfers to private non-profit institutions	4059	3717	342	4472	4091	381	4600	4208	392	4800	4390	410
D	Unfunded employee pension and welfare benefits	6131	6131	...	6808	6808	...	7057	7057	...	7909	7909	...
E	Social assistance grants	3735	1780	1955	4543	2737	1806	5178	3066	2112	6095	3630	2465
F	Other transfers n.e.c.	6771	6672	99	7455	7346	109	8833	8705	128	9893	9750	143
G	Transfers to the rest of the world	...	...	...	...	...	...	...	...	...	...	...	...
	Net saving	92990	95305	-2315	104190	100053	4137	104375	92071	12304	79411	73227	6184
	Total Current Disbursements and Net Saving	1166410	528290	638124	1250800	551109	699694	1291310	559322	731984	1362810	585492	777321

3.23 Corporate and Quasi-Corporate Enterprise Capital Accumulation Account: Total and Sectors

Million United States dollars

		1980			1981			1982			1983		
		TOTAL	Non-Financial	Financial	TOTAL	Non-Financial	Financial	TOTAL	Non-Financial	Financial	TOTAL	Non-Financial	Financial

Finance of Gross Accumulation

1	Gross saving	224442	206295	18147	259772	246092	13680	262399	250573	11826	316671	295319	21352
A	Consumption of fixed capital	193465	184594	8871	223865	213380	10485	248861	236843	12018	257154	244222	12932
B	Net saving	30977	21701	9276	35907	32712	3195	13538	13730	-192	59517	51097	8420
2	Capital transfers	...	...	...	...	...	...	...	...	...	...	...	...
	Finance of Gross Accumulation	224442	206295	18147	259772	246092	13680	262399	250573	11826	316671	295319	21352

Gross Accumulation

1	Gross capital formation	274147	259048	15099	329967	310436	19531	290296	263787	26509	299498	285221	14277
A	Increase in stocks	-282	-1131	849	19609	16202	3407	-13077	-22249	9172	-6448	-788	-5660
B	Gross fixed capital formation	274429	260179	14250	310358	294234	16124	303373	286036	17337	305946	286009	19937
2	Purchases of land, net	-2377	-2377	...	-2384	-2384	...	-2354	-2354	...	-2327	-2327	...
3	Purchases of intangible assets, net	4799	4799	...	6027	6027	...	3990	3990	...	5181	5181	...
4	Capital transfers	...	...	...	...	...	...	...	...	...	...	...	...
	Net lending [a]	-52127	-55175	3048	-73838	-67987	-5851	-29533	-14850	-14683	14319	7244	7075
	Gross Accumulation	224442	206295	18147	259772	246092	13680	262399	250573	11826	316671	295319	21352

		1984			1985			1986			1987		
		TOTAL	Non-Financial	Financial	TOTAL	Non-Financial	Financial	TOTAL	Non-Financial	Financial	TOTAL	Non-Financial	Financial

Finance of Gross Accumulation

1	Gross saving	362716	350572	12144	388757	368609	20148	403558	372925	30633	394341	366886	27455
A	Consumption of fixed capital	269726	255267	14459	284567	268556	16011	299183	280854	18329	314930	293659	21271
B	Net saving	92990	95305	-2315	104190	100053	4137	104375	92071	12304	79411	73227	6184
2	Capital transfers	...	...	...	...	...	...	...	...	...	...	...	...
	Finance of Gross Accumulation	362716	350572	12144	388757	368609	20148	403558	372925	30633	394341	366886	27455

Gross Accumulation

1	Gross capital formation	414426	388413	26013	412626	365027	47599	407195	361045	46150	430323	389276	41047
A	Increase in stocks	53961	57550	-3589	23164	11935	11229	21043	15694	5349	33582	36929	-3347
B	Gross fixed capital formation	360465	330863	29602	389462	353092	36370	386152	345351	40801	396741	352347	44394
2	Purchases of land, net	-2744	-2744	...	-3282	-3282	...	-3665	-3665	...	-3912	-3912	...
3	Purchases of intangible assets, net	4259	4259	...	1510	1510	...	3272	3272	...	719	719	...
4	Capital transfers	...	...	...	...	...	...	...	...	...	...	...	...
	Net lending [a]	-53225	-39356	-13869	-22097	5354	-27451	-3244	12273	-15517	-32789	-19197	-13592
	Gross Accumulation	362716	350572	12144	388757	368609	20148	403558	372925	30633	394341	366886	27455

a) Net lending of the capital accumulation account and the capital finance account have not been reconciled and are different due to different statistical sources.

United States

3.24 Corporate and Quasi-Corporate Enterprise Capital Finance Account: Total and Sectors

Million United States dollars

		1980			1981			1982			1983	
		TOTAL	Non-Financial	Financial	TOTAL	Non-Financial	Financial	TOTAL	Non-Financial	Financial	TOTAL	Non-Financial	Financial

Acquisition of Financial Assets

		TOTAL	Non-Financial	Financial	TOTAL	Non-Financial	Financial	TOTAL	Non-Financial	Financial	TOTAL	Non-Financial	Financial
1	Gold and SDRs	-12	...	-12	-9	...	-9	-3	...	-3	-27	...	-27
2	Currency and transferable deposits	13244	6762	6482	-5804	-9698	3894	12645	5879	6766	7392	6691	701
3	Other deposits	25492	7295	18197	47350	8247	39103	45368	10859	34509	22009	17743	4266
4	Bills and bonds, short term	166212	-1940	168152	209600	8962	200638	248108	20264	227844	240769	17333	223436
5	Bonds, long term	...	...	...	...	...	...	...	...	...	...	...	...
6	Corporate equity securities	43725	19222	24503	35377	9624	25753	25738	-2370	28108	50730	373	50357
7	Short term loans, n.e.c.	72215	268	71947	107576	284	107292	69225	-26	69251	85433	3335	82098
8	Long term loans, n.e.c.	96296	...	96296	77450	...	77450	66229	...	66229	173626	...	173626
9	Trade credits and advances	48187	48187	...	24763	24763	...	-15082	-15082	...	37232	37232	...
10	Other receivables	...	...	...	...	...	...	...	...	...	...	...	...
11	Other assets	64941	18618	46323	103232	54840	48392	122712	27471	95241	76858	32372	44486
	Total Acquisition of Financial Assets	530300	98412	431888	599535	97022	502513	574940	46995	527945	694022	115079	578943

Incurrence of Liabilities

1	Currency and transferable deposits	17058	...	17058	27904	...	27904	37659	...	37659	40379	...	40379
2	Other deposits	166854	...	166854	139030	...	139030	195184	...	195184	215395	...	215395
3	Bills and bonds, short term	11997	7202	4795	40015	19068	20947	-8038	-6907	-1131	22159	6136	16023
4	Bonds, long term	83721	38519	45202	86132	36192	49940	111427	33809	77618	110543	25457	85086
5	Corporate equity securities	33212	28190	5022	20252	13846	6406	33653	20210	13443	65892	35019	30873
6	Short-term loans, n.e.c.	36363	29040	7323	61476	42173	19303	49514	46439	3075	11992	19156	-7164
7	Long-term loans, n.e.c.	-16964	-16924	-40	4698	4678	20	-29840	-29953	113	3639	3614	25
8	Net equity of households in life insurance and pension fund reserves	109710	...	109710	107871	...	107871	136120	...	136120	144934	...	144934
9	Proprietors' net additions to the accumulation of quasi-corporations	...	...	...	...	...	...	...	...	...	...	...	...
10	Trade credit and advances	37966	37966	...	28627	28627	...	5357	5357	...	37265	37265	...
11	Other accounts payable	...	...	...	...	...	...	...	...	...	...	...	...
12	Other liabilities	63961	733	63228	135024	-8232	143256	63036	-12740	75776	67021	7970	59051
	Total Incurrence of Liabilities	543878	124726	419152	651029	136352	514677	594072	56215	537857	719219	134617	584602
	Net Lending [a]	-13578	-26314	12736	-51494	-39330	-12164	-19132	-9220	-9912	-25197	-19538	-5659
	Incurrence of Liabilities and Net Lending	530300	98412	431888	599535	97022	502513	574940	46995	527945	694022	115079	578943

		1984			1985			1986			1987		
		TOTAL	Non-Financial	Financial	TOTAL	Non-Financial	Financial	TOTAL	Non-Financial	Financial	TOTAL	Non-Financial	Financial

Acquisition of Financial Assets

1	Gold and SDRs	-25	...	-25	-6	...	-6	-26	...	-26	14	...	14
2	Currency and transferable deposits	10348	6682	3666	30035	13754	16281	36270	18962	17308	-8037	-1014	-7023
3	Other deposits	28605	8140	20465	33954	11335	22619	47073	18165	28908	28737	1244	27493
4	Bills and bonds, short term	294452	21450	273002	318912	13698	305214	518738	31109	487629	362778	7859	354919
5	Bonds, long term	...	...	...	...	...	...	...	...	...	...	...	...
6	Corporate equity securities	18616	2821	15795	63636	18068	45568	76315	27811	48504	67078	44456	22622
7	Short term loans, n.e.c.	191842	2042	189800	157480	1670	155810	167747	95	167652	102288	2593	99695
8	Long term loans, n.e.c.	200874	...	200874	222761	...	222761	287950	...	287950	315547	...	315547
9	Trade credits and advances	48069	48069	...	26726	26726	...	3232	3232	...	49242	49242	...
10	Other receivables	...	...	...	...	...	...	...	...	...	...	...	...
11	Other assets	144792	42884	101908	136096	7706	128390	148916	23453	125463	-19818	-28746	8928
	Total Acquisition of Financial Assets	937573	132088	805485	989594	92957	896637	1286220	122827	1163390	897829	75634	822195

Incurrence of Liabilities

1	Currency and transferable deposits	47358	...	47358	83494	...	83494	126993	...	126993	3906	...	3906
2	Other deposits	276072	...	276072	188746	...	188746	181288	...	181288	126263	...	126263
3	Bills and bonds, short term	44872	24506	20366	53838	12489	41349	20557	-9536	30093	29736	7374	22362
4	Bonds, long term	174576	66671	107905	244716	96353	148363	360801	111375	249426	352660	99026	253634
5	Corporate equity securities	-11371	-48907	37536	36889	-61009	97898	127986	-45355	173341	57819	-34342	92161
6	Short-term loans, n.e.c.	92762	76430	16332	51362	33504	17858	90622	67165	23457	43327	22975	20352

United States

3.24 Corporate and Quasi-Corporate Enterprise Capital Finance Account: Total and Sectors
(Continued)

Million United States dollars

	1984 TOTAL	1984 Non-Financial	1984 Financial	1985 TOTAL	1985 Non-Financial	1985 Financial	1986 TOTAL	1986 Non-Financial	1986 Financial	1987 TOTAL	1987 Non-Financial	1987 Financial
7 Long-term loans, n.e.c.	3094	2683	411	-9846	-9901	55	4900	4821	79	7176	6894	282
8 Net equity of households in life insurance and pension fund reserves	139471	...	139471	166462	...	166462	171582	...	171582	176136	...	176136
9 Proprietors' net additions to the accumulation of quasi-corporations	...	...	...	...	...	...	...	...	...	...	...	...
10 Trade credit and advances	33027	33027	...	34039	34039	...	3089	3089	...	18021	18021	...
11 Other accounts payable	...	...	...	...	...	...	...	...	...	...	...	...
12 Other liabilities	182080	1903	180177	171940	1394	170546	216242	3195	213047	148683	1352	147331
Total Incurrence of Liabilities	981941	156313	825628	1021640	106869	914771	1304060	134754	1169310	963727	121300	842427
Net Lending [a]	-44368	-24225	-20143	-32046	-13912	-18134	-17845	-11927	-5918	-65898	-45666	-20232
Incurrence of Liabilities and Net Lending	937573	132088	805485	989594	92957	896637	1286220	122827	1163390	897829	75634	822195

[a] Net lending of the capital accumulation account and the capital finance account have not been reconciled and are different due to different statistical sources.

3.32 Household and Private Unincorporated Enterprise Income and Outlay Account

Million United States dollars

	1970	1975	1978	1979	1980	1981	1982	1983	1984	1985	1986	1987
Receipts												
1 Compensation of employees	619097	952048	1334490	1497580	1646250	1817140	1917900	2032250	2224440	2379670	2519640	2697180
A Wages and salaries	552044	815624	1120980	1253590	1373840	1512350	1588340	1678840	1841730	1978460	2097610	2252400
B Employers' contributions for social security	23839	46691	71466	82513	88861	103522	109676	119773	138976	147797	157302	164913
C Employers' contributions for private pension & welfare plans	43214	89733	142042	161474	183553	201266	219888	233641	243733	253407	264736	279867
2 Operating surplus of private unincorporated enterprises	80171	125373	176206	191871	180673	186772	175535	190882	234502	255860	286732	312944
3 Property and entrepreneurial income	102238	151840	215709	254103	310957	393037	432713	456218	513523	548917	573803	608231
A Withdrawals from private quasi-corporations	...	...	...	...	...	...	...	...	...	...	...	...
B Interest	61840	109586	163407	200362	251489	318489	355166	374304	429458	460934	478624	501215
C Dividends	22215	28720	43007	48103	52868	61288	63930	68731	75531	78738	82757	88579
D Net land rent and royalties	18183	13534	9295	5638	6600	13260	13617	13183	8534	9245	12422	18437
3 Current transfers	81220	183643	230966	259007	308513	349572	389561	420011	429716	460410	488307	512796
A Casualty insurance claims	...	...	...	...	...	...	...	...	...	...	...	...
B Social security benefits	46470	105876	133784	150502	180285	208948	242014	261039	265268	283539	300639	313389
C Social assistance grants	25098	57060	68353	75403	89310	97367	99653	106850	111299	117523	124809	131524
D Unfunded employee pension and welfare benefits [a]	6186	14448	20428	23781	28002	32141	35246	37932	37200	41297	42254	44825
E Transfers from general government	...	...	...	...	...	...	...	...	...	...	...	...
F Transfers from the rest of the world	381	730	1206	1371	1559	1448	1388	1454	1304	1476	1833	2103
G Other transfers n.e.c.	3085	5529	7195	7950	9357	9668	11260	12736	14645	16575	18772	20955
Total Current Receipts	882726	1412900	1957370	2202560	2446400	2746520	2915710	3099360	3402180	3644860	3868490	4131160
Disbursements												
1 Final consumption expenditures	635842	1005820	1392720	1554720	1721220	1909680	2046300	2223660	2422200	2615800	2788200	2983670
A Market purchases	570853	901084	1246210	1388270	1531800	1696430	1815340	1977610	2157660	2332210	2484580	2657280
B Gross rents of owner-occupied housing	64213	103602	145383	165208	188283	212130	229913	244974	263477	282672	302727	325540
C Consumption from own-account production	776	1129	1120	1244	1134	1124	1048	1073	1063	927	888	854
2 Property income	16686	24428	36687	43533	47376	51970	55548	61858	72508	82598	89062	92103
A Interest	16686	24428	36687	43533	47376	51970	55548	61858	72508	82598	89062	92103
Consumer debt	16686	24428	36687	43533	47376	51970	55548	61858	72508	82598	89062	92103
Mortgage	...	...	...	...	...	...	...	...	...	...	...	...
Other	...	...	...	...	...	...	...	...	...	...	...	...
B Net land rent and royalties	...	...	...	...	...	...	...	...	...	...	...	...
3 Direct taxes and other current transfers n.e.c. to government	151335	240061	365725	427189	471893	548684	571909	588449	646649	713326	755005	827849
A Social security contributions	46745	89637	131716	153311	166617	196129	209139	226259	257654	282182	303234	321255
B Direct taxes	103058	147718	229940	269270	300008	346266	355677	354216	379875	420682	440079	493395
Income taxes	99744	143294	224471	263452	293711	339563	348417	346375	371323	411501	430385	482893

United States

3.32 Household and Private Unincorporated Enterprise Income and Outlay Account
(Continued)

Million United States dollars

	1970	1975	1978	1979	1980	1981	1982	1983	1984	1985	1986	1987
Other	3314	4424	5469	5818	6297	6703	7260	7841	8552	9181	9694	10502
C Fees, fines and penalties	1532	2706	4069	4608	5268	6289	7093	7974	9120	10462	11692	13199
4 Other current transfers	9611	18890	26062	29454	34439	38698	42169	44445	44907	49052	50271	52899
A Net casualty insurance premiums	...	...	...	...	...	...	...	...	...	...	...	...
B Transfers to private non-profit institutions serving households	...	...	...	...	...	...	...	...	...	...	...	...
C Transfers to the rest of the world	1538	1684	2094	2357	2698	2481	2649	2499	2822	3197	3279	3398
D Other current transfers, except imputed	1887	2658	3269	3497	3779	4017	4278	4459	4665	4788	4738	4676
E Imputed employee pension and welfare contributions	6186	14548	20699	23600	27962	32200	35242	37487	37420	41067	42254	44825
Net saving	69252	123710	136176	147663	171470	197489	199784	180950	215917	184075	185949	174634
Total Current Disbursements and Net Saving	882726	1412900	1957370	2202560	2446400	2746520	2915710	3099360	3402180	3644860	3868490	4131160

a) Item 'Unfunded employee pension and welfare benefits' also includes wage accruals less disbursements.

3.33 Household and Private Unincorporated Enterprise Capital Accumulation Account

Million United States dollars

	1970	1975	1978	1979	1980	1981	1982	1983	1984	1985	1986	1987
Finance of Gross Accumulation												
1 Gross saving	106123	189135	228909	255096	293902	334615	347970	334834	376864	352736	359401	357108
A Consumption of fixed capital	36871	65425	92733	107433	122432	137126	148186	153884	160947	168661	173452	182474
Owner-occupied housing	14329	25718	37897	43917	49164	53844	56770	59585	62612	67008	69350	74625
Other unincorporated enterprises	22542	39707	54836	63516	73268	83282	91416	94299	98335	101653	104102	107849
B Net saving	69252	123710	136176	147663	171470	197489	199784	180950	215917	184075	185949	174634
2 Capital transfers	...	...	...	...	...	...	...	...	...	...	...	...
Total Finance of Gross Accumulation	106123	189135	228909	255096	293902	334615	347970	334834	376864	352736	359401	357108
Gross Accumulation												
1 Gross Capital Formation	65539	98072	185238	208520	185555	210856	185230	216268	268411	265580	290657	307684
A Increase in stocks	426	2124	4106	3977	-7022	7640	-2040	-6027	10100	-606	-373	2459
B Gross fixed capital formation	65113	95948	181132	204543	192577	203216	187270	222295	258311	266186	291030	305225
Owner-occupied housing	27123	48815	101600	92670	79471	82081	70941	124164	132615	141169	170494	177867
Other gross fixed capital formation	37990	47133	79532	111873	113106	121135	116329	98131	125696	125017	120536	127358
2 Purchases of land, net	...	...	...	...	...	...	...	...	...	...	...	...
3 Purchases of intangibles, net	...	...	...	...	...	...	...	...	...	...	...	...
4 Capital transfers	4764	6448	7242	7593	8836	9353	10207	8455	8487	9102	10136	10689
A To resident sectors	4764	6448	7242	7593	8836	9353	10207	8455	8487	9102	10136	10689
B To the rest of the world	...	...	...	...	...	...	...	...	...	...	...	...
Net lending [a]	35820	84615	36429	38983	99511	114406	152533	110111	99966	78054	58608	38735
Total Gross Accumulation	106123	189135	228909	255096	293902	334615	347970	334834	376864	352736	359401	357108

a) Net lending of the capital accumulation account and the capital finance account have not been reconciled and are different due to different statistical sources.

3.34 Household and Private Unincorporated Enterprise Capital Finance Account

Million United States dollars

	1970	1975	1978	1979	1980	1981	1982	1983	1984	1985	1986	1987
Acquisition of Financial Assets												
1 Gold	...	...	...	...	...	...	...	...	...	...	...	...
2 Currency and transferable deposits	8932	6103	22384	35654	8940	35188	25808	34448	26723	35686	94100	16443
3 Other deposits	43226	78901	106125	109127	155687	181888	150967	158308	275684	135957	149844	122633
4 Bills and bonds, short term	659	14434	38213	70226	25268	36678	45713	85990	102931	156350	-15204	134889
5 Bonds, long term	...	...	...	...	...	...	...	...	...	...	...	...
6 Corporate equity securities	-729	-6190	-12524	-25473	-9870	-36601	-11912	1093	-51656	-34971	26129	-19819
7 Short term loans, n.e.c.	122	42	181	145	-62	18	52	667	396	318	410	385
8 Long term loans, n.e.c.	2384	3289	12598	16531	19158	19032	14324	5062	11524	7766	8368	-7059
9 Trade credit and advances	-1487	803	5322	3416	1618	4376	7581	6795	6489	4105	3200	3200
10 Net equity of households in life insurance and pension fund reserves	24189	71921	95022	101834	118503	117911	148047	159173	157657	185566	192653	196398
11 Proprietors' net additions to the accumulation of quasi-corporations	...	...	...	...	...	...	...	...	...	...	...	...

United States

3.34 Household and Private Unincorporated Enterprise Capital Finance Account
(Continued)

Million United States dollars

	1970	1975	1978	1979	1980	1981	1982	1983	1984	1985	1986	1987
12 Other	3209	10010	19814	14124	1078	-37985	-330	28822	11090	53030	54690	33544
Total Acquisition of Financial Assets	80505	179313	287135	325584	320320	320505	380250	480358	540838	543807	514190	480614

Incurrence of Liabilities

	1970	1975	1978	1979	1980	1981	1982	1983	1984	1985	1986	1987
1 Short term loans, n.e.c.	10291	18229	84234	82339	35894	65643	35896	76220	123997	116173	95834	62309
2 Long term loans, n.e.c.	29940	55693	142889	175318	149810	104514	118115	184236	220108	252091	303769	304731
3 Trade credit and advances	-171	1971	4865	9019	8018	8644	6515	1501	6339	7328	7197	7051
4 Other accounts payable	...	...	...	...	...	...	...	...	...	...	...	...
5 Other liabilities	-1350	4812	10468	9075	15568	12305	23899	35931	27035	60617	15084	-5458
Total Incurrence of Liabilities	38710	80705	242456	275751	209290	191106	184425	297888	377479	436209	421884	368633
Net Lending a	41795	98608	44679	49833	111030	129399	195825	182470	163359	107598	92306	111981
Incurrence of Liabilities and Net Lending	80505	179313	287135	325584	320320	320505	380250	480358	540838	543807	514190	480614

a) Net lending of the capital accumulation account and the capital finance account have not been reconciled and are different due to different statistical sources.

3.51 External Transactions: Current Account: Detail

Million United States dollars

	1970	1975	1978	1979	1980	1981	1982	1983	1984	1985	1986	1987
Payments to the Rest of the World												
1 Imports of goods and services	55177	120625	208188	248147	288074	310521	295137	319797	389441	399952	430223	484494
A Imports of merchandise c.i.f. a	40855	99000	176477	211930	247460	266462	249474	271341	334250	340877	367725	412997
B Other	14322	21625	31711	36217	40614	44059	45663	48456	55191	59075	62498	71497
2 Factor income to the rest of the world	6316	14204	23871	35425	43368	55259	58748	56682	72772	70230	75220	90637
A Compensation of employees	197	371	478	473	536	544	618	614	580	608	591	614
B Property and entrepreneurial income	6119	13833	23393	34952	42832	54715	58130	56068	72192	69622	74629	90023
By general government	1024	4542	8674	11122	12592	16878	18285	17825	19769	21306	22607	24052
By corporate and quasi-cororate enterprises	5095	9291	14719	23830	30240	37837	39845	38243	52423	48316	52022	65971
By other	...	...	...	...	...	...	...	...	...	...	...	...
3 Current transfers to the rest of the world	6599	7858	7044	8050	10023	9701	11103	11221	13747	16689	17446	15744
A Indirect taxes by general government to supranational organizations	...	...	...	...	...	...	...	...	...	...	...	...
B Other current transfers	6599	7858	7044	8050	10023	9701	11103	11221	13747	16689	17446	15744
By general government	5061	6174	4950	5693	7325	7220	8454	8722	10925	13492	14167	12346
By other resident sectors	1538	1684	2094	2357	2698	2481	2649	2499	2822	3197	3279	3398
4 Surplus of the nation on current transactions	3939	21596	-10138	1448	11830	9478	-953	-33485	-90948	-114359	-142380	-160606
Payments to the Rest of the World, and Surplus of the Nation on Current Transfers	72031	164283	228965	293070	353295	384959	364035	354215	385012	372512	380509	430269
Receipts From The Rest of the World												
1 Exports of goods and services	59104	136346	182013	223575	273347	292988	270904	264005	283250	281300	291042	332034
A Exports of merchandise f.o.b. a	44280	109359	144454	182986	224672	237894	213572	205637	223699	220280	224599	254322
B Other	14824	26987	37559	40589	48675	55094	57332	58368	59551	61020	66443	77712
2 Factor income from the rest of the world	12545	27202	45740	68104	78368	90489	91626	88721	100420	89651	87503	96067
A Compensation of employees	222	334	388	419	449	497	520	560	600	627	672	743
B Property and entrepreneurial income	12323	26868	45352	67685	77919	89992	91106	88161	99820	89024	86831	95324
By general government	907	1112	1843	2295	2562	3680	4118	4832	5229	5504	6420	5332
By corporate and quasi-corporate enterprises	11416	25756	43509	65390	75357	86312	86988	83329	94591	83520	80411	89992

United States

3.51 External Transactions: Current Account: Detail
(Continued)

Million United States dollars

	1970	1975	1978	1979	1980	1981	1982	1983	1984	1985	1986	1987
By other	...	...	...	...	...	...	...	...	...	...	...	...
3 Current transfers from the rest of the world	382	735	1212	1391	1580	1482	1505	1489	1342	1561	1964	2168
A Subsidies to general government from supranational organizations	...	...	...	...	...	...	...	...	...	...	...	...
B Other current transfers	382	735	1212	1391	1580	1482	1505	1489	1342	1561	1964	2168
To general government	1	5	6	20	21	34	117	35	38	85	131	65
To other resident sectors	381	730	1206	1371	1559	1448	1388	1454	1304	1476	1833	2103
Receipts from the Rest of the World on Current Transfers	72031	164283	228965	293070	353295	384959	364035	354215	385012	372512	380509	430269

a) Valuation basis is essentially Free Along Side (F.A.S.).

3.52 External Transactions: Capital Accumulation Account

Million United States dollars

	1970	1975	1978	1979	1980	1981	1982	1983	1984	1985	1986	1987
Finance of Gross Accumulation													
1 Surplus of the nation on current transactions	3939	21596	-10138	1448	11830	9478	-953	-33485	-90948	-114359	-142380	-160606
2 Capital transfers from the rest of the world	867	-	-	1139	1152	1093	-	-	-	-	-	-
A By general government	867	-	-	1139	1152	1093	-	-	-	-	-	-
B By other resident sectors	...	...	...	...	...	...	...	...	...	...	...	...
Total Finance of Gross Accumulation	4806	21596	-10138	2587	12982	10571	-953	-33485	-90948	-114359	-142380	-160606
Gross Accumulation													
1 Capital transfers to the rest of the world	-	-	-	-	-	-	-	-	-	-	-	-
A By general government	-	-	-	-	-	-	-	-	-	-	-	-
B By other resident sectors	...	...	...	...	...	...	...	...	...	...	...	...
2 Purchases of intangible assets, n.e.c., net, from the rest of the world	...	...	...	...	...	...	...	...	...	...	...	...
Net lending to the rest of the world a	4806	21596	-10138	2587	12982	10571	-953	-33485	-90948	-114359	-142380	-160606
Total Gross Accumulation	4806	21596	-10138	2587	12982	10571	-953	-33485	-90948	-114359	-142380	-160606

a) Net lending of the capital accumulation account and the capital finance account have not been reconciled and are different due to different statistical sources.

3.53 External Transactions: Capital Finance Account

Million United States dollars

	1970	1975	1978	1979	1980	1981	1982	1983	1984	1985	1986	1987
Acquisitions of Foreign Financial Assets													
1 Gold and SDR's	64	66	-1184	1201	16	1820	1372	65	979	897	246	510
2 Currency and transferable deposits	-2545	783	452	-68	8138	3353	3592	1130	2151	2960	-559	-9659
3 Other deposits	-375	826	2449	9782	4479	10419	4501	1279	-5785	-4271	9089	-3394
4 Bills and bonds, short term	799	-90	-3170	3593	4091	6922	8517	-122	969	-7351	-5376	1375
5 Bonds, long term	874	7168	3977	3701	1202	5487	6614	3080	3812	3793	3017	6814
6 Corporate equity securities	8666	13323	15706	26248	21588	9837	-1000	4056	3765	21757	29091	42098
A Subsidiaries abroad	7590	14244	16057	25223	19222	9624	-2370	373	2821	18068	27811	44456
B Other	1076	-921	-351	1025	2366	213	1370	3683	944	3689	1280	-2358
7 Short-term loans, n.e.c.	1133	6650	22171	5996	16463	7240	-1011	7892	-2601	-1442	470	-5984
8 Long-term loans	...	...	...	...	...	...	...	...	...	...	...	...
9 Prproprietors' net additions to accumulation of quasi-corporate, non-resident enterprises	...	...	...	...	...	...	...	...	...	...	...	...
10 Trade credit and advances	963	665	-274	1512	1745	203	-2726	242	-494	-615	-423	962
11 Other	-1685	-504	16686	5671	-2387	-16107	5696	12315	10244	-6632	8079	3116
Total Acquisitions of Foreign Financial Assets	7894	28887	56813	57636	55335	29174	25555	29937	13040	9096	43634	35838
Incurrence of Foreign Liabilities													
1 Currency and transferable deposits	521	-316	-248	4244	17	-3785	-3660	1605	1940	1565	2679	-1403
2 Other deposits	-1664	1456	1145	1173	1214	2270	6813	514	4560	3708	-2659	925
3 Bills and bonds, short term	10257	5651	21165	-21521	9755	-4490	-4365	12719	18567	-6960	20857	14174
4 Bonds, long term	717	2587	8244	9168	14223	21126	25539	8257	26253	67749	65851	47115
5 Corporate equity securities	2161	7270	10274	13472	20672	31057	17714	16929	22587	25460	53152	57673
A Subsidiaries of non-resident incorporated units	1464	2603	7852	11813	15315	25296	13810	11519	25568	20491	35395	42158

United States

3.53 External Transactions: Capital Finance Account
(Continued)

Million United States dollars

	1970	1975	1978	1979	1980	1981	1982	1983	1984	1985	1986	1987
B Other	697	4667	2422	1659	5357	5761	3904	5410	-2981	4969	17757	15515
6 Short-term loans, n.e.c.	...	...	...	...	...	...	...	...	...	...	...	...
7 Long-term loans	...	...	...	...	...	...	...	...	...	...	...	...
8 Non-resident proprietors' net additions to accumulation of resident quasi-corporate enterprises	...	...	...	...	...	...	...	...	...	...	...	...
9 Trade credit and advances	1558	1837	4116	214	3494	-207	27	-1340	1506	401	693	85
10 Other	-8634	-13629	14587	24990	-25272	-44189	-47347	19603	9471	21337	36458	68596
Total Incurrence of Liabilities	4916	4856	59283	31740	24103	1782	-5279	58287	84884	113260	177031	187165
Net Lending [a]	2978	24031	-2470	25896	31232	27392	30834	-28350	-71844	-104164	-133397	-151327
Total Incurrence of Liabilities and Net Lending	7894	28887	56813	57636	55335	29174	25555	29937	13040	9096	43634	35838

a) Net lending of the capital accumulation account and the capital finance account have not been reconciled and are different due to different statistical sources.

4.1 Derivation of Value Added by Kind of Activity, in Current Prices

Million United States dollars

	1980 Gross Output	1980 Intermediate Consumption	1980 Value Added	1981 Gross Output	1981 Intermediate Consumption	1981 Value Added	1982 Gross Output	1982 Intermediate Consumption	1982 Value Added	1983 Gross Output	1983 Intermediate Consumption	1983 Value Added
						All Producers						
1 Agriculture, hunting, forestry and fishing [a]	...	...	70320	...	...	83722	...	...	81370	...	...	66394
2 Mining and quarrying	...	...	107854	...	...	144398	...	...	132893	...	...	119060
A Coal mining	...	...	12994	...	...	13900	...	...	15222	...	...	14405
B Crude petroleum and natural gas production	...	...	85345	...	...	121341	...	...	110794	...	...	96928
C Metal ore mining	...	...	3876	...	...	3893	...	...	2344	...	...	2554
D Other mining	...	...	5639	...	...	5264	...	...	4533	...	...	5173
3 Manufacturing	...	...	586438	...	...	649631	...	...	641021	...	...	689493
A Manufacture of food, beverages and tobacco	...	...	60009	...	...	66791	...	...	70960	...	...	77143
B Textile, wearing apparel and leather industries	...	...	36269	...	...	39133	...	...	38212	...	...	41406
C Manufacture of wood and wood products, including furniture	...	...	27505	...	...	26572	...	...	25832	...	...	31406
D Manufacture of paper and paper products, printing and publishing	...	...	55098	...	...	60724	...	...	65616	...	...	70636
E Manufacture of chemicals and chemical petroleum, coal, rubber and plastic products	...	...	80446	...	...	93591	...	...	99882	...	...	110809
F Manufacture of non-metallic mineral products, except products of petroleum and coal	...	...	19155	...	...	19181	...	...	18320	...	...	20336
G Basic metal industries	...	...	44527	...	...	50183	...	...	35606	...	...	30618
H Manufacture of fabricated metal products, machinery and equipment	...	...	253728	...	...	281546	...	...	275320	...	...	296680
I Other manufacturing industries	...	...	9701	...	...	11910	...	...	11273	...	...	10459
4 Electricity, gas and water [b]	...	...	68682	...	...	80847	...	...	92490	...	...	104001
5 Construction	...	...	139366	...	...	140321	...	...	142956	...	...	151321
6 Wholesale and retail trade, restaurants and hotels	...	...	455226	...	...	500354	...	...	525500	...	...	563712
A Wholesale and retail trade [c]	...	...	436120	...	...	479816	...	...	503628	...	...	539199
B Restaurants and hotels [c]	...	...	19106	...	...	20538	...	...	21872	...	...	24513
Restaurants	...	...	...	...	...	...	...	...	...	...	...	...
Hotels and other lodging places	...	...	19106	...	...	20538	...	...	21872	...	...	24513
7 Transport, storage and communication	...	...	173314	...	...	190158	...	...	197763	...	...	217833
A Transport and storage	...	...	106575	...	...	113560	...	...	111878	...	...	121532
B Communication	...	...	66739	...	...	76598	...	...	85885	...	...	96301
8 Finance, insurance, real estate and business services	...	...	548516	...	...	622462	...	...	663127	...	...	746450
A Financial institutions	...	...	71758	...	...	85350	...	...	91003	...	...	113134
B Insurance	...	...	52441	...	...	51522	...	...	48423	...	...	55857
C Real estate and business services	...	...	424317	...	...	485590	...	...	523701	...	...	577459
Real estate, except dwellings	...	...	220307	...	...	252338	...	...	269660	...	...	303845

United States

4.1 Derivation of Value Added by Kind of Activity, in Current Prices
(Continued)

Million United States dollars

	1980 Gross Output	1980 Intermediate Consumption	1980 Value Added	1981 Gross Output	1981 Intermediate Consumption	1981 Value Added	1982 Gross Output	1982 Intermediate Consumption	1982 Value Added	1983 Gross Output	1983 Intermediate Consumption	1983 Value Added
Dwellings	...	...	204010	...	...	233252	...	...	254041	...	...	273614
9 Community, social and personal services	...	...	224472	...	...	250312	...	...	276551	...	...	302886
A Sanitary and similar services [b]												
B Social and related community services	...	...	150851	...	...	171208	...	...	192446	...	...	210699
Educational services	...	...	16020	...	...	17560	...	...	19162	...	...	21026
Medical, dental, other health and veterinary services	...	...	108533	...	...	125242	...	...	142712	...	...	156831
C Recreational and cultural services	...	...	17631	...	...	19803	...	...	21653	...	...	23605
D Personal and household services	...	...	55990	...	...	59301	...	...	62452	...	...	68582
Statistical discrepancy [d]	...	...	33840	...	...	37976	...	...	40023	...	...	44085
Total, Industries	...	...	2408030	...	...	2700180	...	...	2793690	...	...	3005240
Producers of Government Services	...	...	333978	...	...	366259	...	...	395374	...	...	419322
Other Producers	...	...	...	...	...	...	...	...	...	...	...	...
Total	...	...	2742010	...	...	3066440	...	...	3189070	...	...	3424560
Less: Imputed bank service charge	...	...	65620	...	...	69681	...	...	76225	...	...	85345
Import duties	...	...	7160	...	...	8589	...	...	8609	...	...	9091
Value added tax	...	...	...	...	...	...	...	...	...	...	...	...
Other adjustments [e]	...	...	4920	...	...	4124	...	...	-56	...	...	5170
Total	...	...	2688470	...	...	3009470	...	...	3121400	...	...	3353470

	1984 Gross Output	1984 Intermediate Consumption	1984 Value Added	1985 Gross Output	1985 Intermediate Consumption	1985 Value Added	1986 Gross Output	1986 Intermediate Consumption	1986 Value Added	1987 Gross Output	1987 Intermediate Consumption	1987 Value Added
All Producers												
1 Agriculture, hunting, forestry and fishing [a]	...	...	85305	...	...	85222	...	...	86481	...	...	89201
2 Mining and quarrying	...	...	120347	...	...	115158	...	...	83072	...	...	86434
A Coal mining	...	...	14680	...	...	13983	...	...	13304	...	...	12794
B Crude petroleum and natural gas production	...	...	97175	...	...	93188	...	...	61093	...	...	65788
C Metal ore mining	...	...	2255	...	...	1816	...	...	2140	...	...	2239
D Other mining	...	...	6237	...	...	6171	...	...	6535	...	...	5613
3 Manufacturing	...	...	778413	...	...	797379	...	...	828377	...	...	862331
A Manufacture of food, beverages and tobacco	...	...	79953	...	...	82706	...	...	86202	...	...	90312
B Textile, wearing apparel and leather industries	...	...	42072	...	...	41532	...	...	43576	...	...	46124
C Manufacture of wood and wood products, including furniture	...	...	35475	...	...	36167	...	...	39004	...	...	43006
D Manufacture of paper and paper products, printing and publishing	...	...	80031	...	...	86276	...	...	90953	...	...	98357
E Manufacture of chemicals and chemical petroleum, coal, rubber and plastic products	...	...	121300	...	...	123472	...	...	136721	...	...	142412
F Manufacture of non-metallic mineral products, except products of petroleum and coal	...	...	23114	...	...	24939	...	...	26066	...	...	27681
G Basic metal industries	...	...	36545	...	...	35071	...	...	33990	...	...	36730
H Manufacture of fabricated metal products, machinery and equipment	...	...	345955	...	...	353910	...	...	358353	...	...	363509
I Other manufacturing industries	...	...	13968	...	...	13306	...	...	13512	...	...	14200
4 Electricity, gas and water [b]	...	...	119496	...	...	127796	...	...	134167	...	...	137292
5 Construction	...	...	173526	...	...	188603	...	...	206164	...	...	220746
6 Wholesale and retail trade, restaurants and hotels	...	...	635022	...	...	682807	...	...	724092	...	...	767723
A Wholesale and retail trade [c]	...	...	607693	...	...	652157	...	...	691099	...	...	731663
B Restaurants and hotels [c]	...	...	27329	...	...	30650	...	...	32993	...	...	36060
Restaurants	...	...	...	...	...	...	...	...	...	...	...	...
Hotels and other lodging places	...	...	27329	...	...	30650	...	...	32993	...	...	36060
7 Transport, storage and communication	...	...	237226	...	...	249174	...	...	262378	...	...	274194

United States

4.1 Derivation of Value Added by Kind of Activity, in Current Prices
(Continued)

Million United States dollars

	1984 Gross Output	1984 Intermediate Consumption	1984 Value Added	1985 Gross Output	1985 Intermediate Consumption	1985 Value Added	1986 Gross Output	1986 Intermediate Consumption	1986 Value Added	1987 Gross Output	1987 Intermediate Consumption	1987 Value Added
A Transport and storage	...	...	134622	...	...	138745	...	...	145836	...	...	152218
B Communication	...	...	102604	...	...	110429	...	...	116542	...	...	121976
8 Finance, insurance, real estate and business services	...	...	817524	...	...	915395	...	...	1022510	...	...	1123880
A Financial institutions	...	...	114306	...	...	131707	...	...	148805	...	...	161161
B Insurance	...	...	56347	...	...	68057	...	...	88124	...	...	102978
C Real estate and business services	...	...	646871	...	...	715631	...	...	785579	...	...	859739
Real estate, except dwellings	...	...	351277	...	...	391709	...	...	434437	...	...	480896
Dwellings	...	...	295594	...	...	323922	...	...	351142	...	...	378843
9 Community, social and personal services	...	...	331136	...	...	363927	...	...	392052	...	...	431784
A Sanitary and similar services [b]	...	...	...	...	...	...	...	...	...	...	...	...
B Social and related community services	...	...	229156	...	...	249717	...	...	269050	...	...	299785
Educational services	...	...	23557	...	...	25815	...	...	27268	...	...	29701
Medical, dental, other health and veterinary services	...	...	169823	...	...	185498	...	...	200026	...	...	224763
C Recreational and cultural services	...	...	25486	...	...	29296	...	...	31706	...	...	35086
D Personal and household services	...	...	76494	...	...	84914	...	...	91296	...	...	96913
Statistical discrepancy [d]	...	...	51940	...	...	57723	...	...	60017	...	...	62629
Total, Industries	...	...	3349940	...	...	3583180	...	...	3799310	...	...	4056210
Producers of Government Services	...	...	443982	...	...	477659	...	...	504389	...	...	536442
Other Producers	...	...	...	...	...	...	...	...	...	...	...	...
Total	...	...	3793920	...	...	4060840	...	...	4303700	...	...	4592650
Less: Imputed bank service charge	...	...	88844	...	...	100779	...	...	112282	...	...	127079
Import duties	...	...	11904	...	...	12158	...	...	13697	...	...	15445
Value added tax	...	...	...	...	...	...	...	...	...	...	...	...
Other adjustments [e]	...	...	5359	...	...	-4750	...	...	-13647	...	...	-8114
Total	...	...	3722340	...	...	3967470	...	...	4191470	...	...	4472910

a) Item 'Agriculture, hunting, forestry and fishing' excludes hunting.
b) Item 'Electricity, gas and water' also includes sanitary and similar services.
c) Restaurants is included in Retail Trade.
d) Item 'Statistical discrepancy' refers to government enterprises.
e) Item 'Other adjustments' refers to statistical discrepancy.

4.2 Derivation of Value Added by Kind of Activity, in Constant Prices

Million United States dollars

	1980 Gross Output	1980 Intermediate Consumption	1980 Value Added	1981 Gross Output	1981 Intermediate Consumption	1981 Value Added	1982 Gross Output	1982 Intermediate Consumption	1982 Value Added	1983 Gross Output	1983 Intermediate Consumption	1983 Value Added
					At constant prices of:1980							
					All Producers							
1 Agriculture, hunting, forestry and fishing [a]	...	...	70320	...	...	81329	...	...	82539	...	...	67065
2 Mining and quarrying	...	...	107854	...	...	111078	...	...	104573	...	...	99450
A Coal mining	...	...	12994	...	...	12931	...	...	13151	...	...	12437
B Crude petroleum and natural gas production	...	...	85345	...	...	88250	...	...	84287	...	...	79584
C Metal ore mining	...	...	3876	...	...	4138	...	...	2537	...	...	2368
D Other mining	...	...	5639	...	...	5760	...	...	4597	...	...	5060

United States

4.2 Derivation of Value Added by Kind of Activity, in Constant Prices
(Continued)

Million United States dollars

	1980 Gross Output	1980 Intermediate Consumption	1980 Value Added	1981 Gross Output	1981 Intermediate Consumption	1981 Value Added	1982 Gross Output	1982 Intermediate Consumption	1982 Value Added	1983 Gross Output	1983 Intermediate Consumption	1983 Value Added
					At constant prices of:1980							
3 Manufacturing	...	...	586438	...	...	597779	...	...	560720	...	...	594971
A Manufacture of food, beverages and tobacco	...	...	60009	...	...	62039	...	...	63962	...	...	64405
B Textile, wearing apparel and leather industries	...	...	36269	...	...	36239	...	...	33981	...	...	36118
C Manufacture of wood and wood products, including furniture	...	...	27505	...	...	25947	...	...	22911	...	...	25472
D Manufacture of paper and paper products, printing and publishing	...	...	55098	...	...	56250	...	...	58358	...	...	61495
E Manufacture of chemicals and chemical petroleum, coal, rubber and plastic products	...	...	80446	...	...	84170	...	...	83404	...	...	89292
F Manufacture of non-metallic mineral products, except products of petroleum and coal	...	...	19155	...	...	17966	...	...	16524	...	...	17896
G Basic metal industries	...	...	44527	...	...	46348	...	...	34004	...	...	28922
H Manufacture of fabricated metal products, machinery and equipment	...	...	253728	...	...	257144	...	...	236867	...	...	261764
I Other manufacturing industries	...	...	9701	...	...	11676	...	...	10709	...	...	9609
4 Electricity, gas and water [b]	...	...	68682	...	...	73749	...	...	73992	...	...	76401
5 Construction	...	...	139366	...	...	127320	...	...	121798	...	...	127020
6 Wholesale and retail trade, restaurants and hotels	...	...	455226	...	...	460673	...	...	459839	...	...	479268
A Wholesale and retail trade [c]	...	...	436120	...	...	441889	...	...	441545	...	...	460272
B Restaurants and hotels [c]	...	...	19106	...	...	18784	...	...	18293	...	...	18996
Restaurants	...	...	...	...	...	...	...	...	...	...	...	...
Hotels and other lodging places	...	...	19106	...	...	18784	...	...	18293	...	...	18996
7 Transport, storage and communication	...	...	173314	...	...	170659	...	...	164326	...	...	172136
A Transport and storage	...	...	106575	...	...	100185	...	...	91443	...	...	93799
B Communication	...	...	66739	...	...	70474	...	...	72882	...	...	78338
8 Finance, insurance, real estate and business services	...	...	548516	...	...	565760	...	...	565002	...	...	584203
A Financial institutions	...	...	71758	...	...	74073	...	...	77364	...	...	78569
B Insurance	...	...	52441	...	...	52950	...	...	54553	...	...	55246
C Real estate and business services	...	...	424317	...	...	438738	...	...	433084	...	...	450389
Real estate, except dwellings	...	...	220307	...	...	228085	...	...	220246	...	...	233666
Dwellings	...	...	204010	...	...	210653	...	...	212838	...	...	216724
9 Community, social and personal services	...	...	224472	...	...	233150	...	...	237537	...	...	245786
A Sanitary and similar services [b]	...	...	...	...	...	...	...	...	...	...	...	...
B Social and related community services	...	...	150851	...	...	158599	...	...	162728	...	...	167719
Educational services	...	...	16020	...	...	16478	...	...	16916	...	...	17547
Medical, dental, other health and veterinary services	...	...	108533	...	...	115634	...	...	119245	...	...	123120
C Recreational and cultural services	...	...	17631	...	...	18605	...	...	19360	...	...	20198
D Personal and household services	...	...	55990	...	...	55947	...	...	55449	...	...	57869
Statistical discrepancy [d]	...	...	33840	...	...	33721	...	...	32658	...	...	33587
Total, Industries	...	...	2408030	...	...	2455220	...	...	2402980	...	...	2479890
Producers of Government Services	...	...	333978	...	...	337400	...	...	338089	...	...	340550
Other Producers	...	...	...	...	...	...	...	...	...	...	...	...
Total	...	...	2742010	...	...	2792620	...	...	2741070	...	...	2820440
Less: Imputed bank service charge	...	...	65620	...	...	64762	...	...	67357	...	...	71386
Import duties	...	...	7160	...	...	7958	...	...	7817	...	...	8093
Value added tax	...	...	...	...	...	...	...	...	...	...	...	...
Other adjustments [e]	...	...	4920	...	...	13525	...	...	-2951	...	...	26499
Total	...	...	2688470	...	...	2749340	...	...	2678580	...	...	2783640

United States

4.2 Derivation of Value Added by Kind of Activity, in Constant Prices

Million United States dollars

At constant prices of: 1980

All Producers

		1984 Gross Output	1984 Intermediate Consumption	1984 Value Added	1985 Gross Output	1985 Intermediate Consumption	1985 Value Added	1986 Gross Output	1986 Intermediate Consumption	1986 Value Added	1987 Gross Output	1987 Intermediate Consumption	1987 Value Added
1	Agriculture, hunting, forestry and fishing [a]	...	...	76496	...	...	87857	...	...	91615	...	...	91122
2	Mining and quarrying	...	...	105884	...	...	103740	...	...	92982	...	...	94538
	A Coal mining	...	...	13980	...	...	13885	...	...	13974	...	...	14431
	B Crude petroleum and natural gas production	...	...	83529	...	...	81404	...	...	70827	...	...	71391
	C Metal ore mining	...	...	2784	...	...	2706	...	...	2720	...	...	3016
	D Other mining	...	...	5590	...	...	5746	...	...	5460	...	...	5700
3	Manufacturing	...	...	667550	...	...	694514	...	...	710835	...	...	742670
	A Manufacture of food, beverages and tobacco	...	...	63091	...	...	63970	...	...	62628	...	...	64804
	B Textile, wearing apparel and leather industries	...	...	36647	...	...	35523	...	...	36206	...	...	38097
	C Manufacture of wood and wood products, including furniture	...	...	28756	...	...	28857	...	...	29905	...	...	32275
	D Manufacture of paper and paper products, printing and publishing	...	...	64081	...	...	65617	...	...	66045	...	...	67955
	E Manufacture of chemicals and chemical petroleum, coal, rubber and plastic products	...	...	92579	...	...	93702	...	...	99677	...	...	106903
	F Manufacture of non-metallic mineral products, except products of petroleum and coal	...	...	19631	...	...	20524	...	...	20112	...	...	21017
	G Basic metal industries	...	...	33365	...	...	32868	...	...	32988	...	...	33060
	H Manufacture of fabricated metal products, machinery and equipment	...	...	315372	...	...	339654	...	...	350083	...	...	364934
	I Other manufacturing industries	...	...	14026	...	...	13799	...	...	13192	...	...	13626
4	Electricity, gas and water [b]	...	...	83563	...	...	84773	...	...	83268	...	...	85274
5	Construction	...	...	137274	...	...	142455	...	...	148984	...	...	151308
6	Wholesale and retail trade, restaurants and hotels	...	...	521574	...	...	549829	...	...	577190	...	...	591994
	A Wholesale and retail trade [c]	...	...	502218	...	...	530028	...	...	557453	...	...	571498
	B Restaurants and hotels [c]	...	...	19355	...	...	19801	...	...	19737	...	...	20496
	Restaurants	...	...	...	...	...	...	...	...	...	...	...	...
	Hotels and other lodging places	...	...	19355	...	...	19801	...	...	19737	...	...	20496
7	Transport, storage and communication	...	...	181135	...	...	184895	...	...	191246	...	...	204230
	A Transport and storage	...	...	101965	...	...	103447	...	...	106384	...	...	112152
	B Communication	...	...	79171	...	...	81448	...	...	84862	...	...	92078
8	Finance, insurance, real estate and business services	...	...	611029	...	...	637676	...	...	665554	...	...	695380
	A Financial institutions	...	...	81730	...	...	83470	...	...	86673	...	...	90279
	B Insurance	...	...	56884	...	...	61205	...	...	65724	...	...	68886
	C Real estate and business services	...	...	472414	...	...	493001	...	...	513157	...	...	536215
	Real estate, except dwellings	...	...	250241	...	...	262706	...	...	277198	...	...	292878
	Dwellings	...	...	222174	...	...	230295	...	...	235959	...	...	243337
9	Community, social and personal services	...	...	256926	...	...	270793	...	...	280958	...	...	294903
	A Sanitary and similar services [b]	...	...	...	...	...	...	...	...	...	...	...	...
	B Social and related community services	...	...	174852	...	...	181412	...	...	188470	...	...	199585
	Educational services	...	...	18261	...	...	19018	...	...	19136	...	...	19811
	Medical, dental, other health and veterinary services	...	...	128531	...	...	133448	...	...	139147	...	...	148517
	C Recreational and cultural services	...	...	20644	...	...	22914	...	...	24094	...	...	25230
	D Personal and household services	...	...	61431	...	...	66468	...	...	68394	...	...	70088
	Statistical discrepancy [d]	...	...	34497	...	...	35478	...	...	36374	...	...	37358
	Total, Industries	...	...	2675930	...	...	2792010	...	...	2879010	...	...	2988780
	Producers of Government Services	...	...	342795	...	...	350545	...	...	356356	...	...	362904

United States

4.2 Derivation of Value Added by Kind of Activity, in Constant Prices
(Continued)

Million United States dollars

	1984			1985			1986			1987		
	Gross Output	Intermediate Consumption	Value Added	Gross Output	Intermediate Consumption	Value Added	Gross Output	Intermediate Consumption	Value Added	Gross Output	Intermediate Consumption	Value Added
	At constant prices of: 1980											
Other Producers	...	...	...	...	...	...	...	...	...	...	...	...
Total	...	...	3018720	...	...	3142560	...	...	3235360	...	...	3351680
Less: Imputed bank service charge	...	...	72023	...	...	74278	...	...	76662	...	...	77424
Import duties	...	...	10294	...	...	10554	...	...	11924	...	...	13070
Value added tax	...	...	...	...	...	...	...	...	...	...	...	...
Other adjustments e	...	...	25991	...	...	16725	...	...	17344	...	...	13944
Total	...	...	2982980	...	...	3095560	...	...	3187970	...	...	3301270

a) Item 'Agriculture, hunting, forestry and fishing' excludes hunting.
b) Item 'Electricity, gas and water' also includes sanitary and similar services.
c) Restaurants is included in Retail Trade.
d) Item 'Statistical discrepancy' refers to government enterprises.
e) Item 'Other adjustments' refers to statistical discrepancy and residual.

4.3 Cost Components of Value Added

Million United States dollars

	1980						1981					
	Compensation of Employees	Capital Consumption	Net Operating Surplus	Indirect Taxes	Less: Subsidies Received	Value Added	Compensation of Employees	Capital Consumption	Net Operating Surplus	Indirect Taxes	Less: Subsidies Received	Value Added
	All Producers											
1 Agriculture, hunting, forestry and fishing a	15049	12275	40874	3195	1073	70320	15507	13168	53111	3488	1552	83722
2 Mining and quarrying	28773	17917	44225	16939	-	107854	35830	23333	50499	34739	3	144398
A Coal mining	7785	1842	2018	1349	-	12994	8183	1953	2333	1434	3	13900
B Crude petroleum and natural gas production	15290	14598	40525	14932	...	85345	21322	20154	47254	32611	...	121341
C Metal ore mining	2948	368	167	393	...	3876	3450	229	-188	402	...	3893
D Other mining	2750	1109	1515	265	...	5639	2875	997	1100	292	...	5264
3 Manufacturing	436141	56943	67817	25813	276	586438	475363	68461	78730	27279	202	649631
A Manufacture of food, beverages and tobacco	34917	5649	10639	8804	...	60009	37661	6615	13420	9095	...	66791
B Textile, wearing apparel and leather industries	29185	1768	4900	416	...	36269	31231	1961	5487	454	...	39133
C Manufacture of wood and wood products, including furniture	18901	3228	4874	502	...	27505	19850	3348	2919	455	...	26572
D Manufacture of paper and paper products, printing and publishing	39381	4896	9650	1171	...	55098	43223	5978	10201	1322	...	60724
E Manufacture of chemicals and chemical petroleum, coal, rubber and plastic products	51255	11157	10173	7861	...	80446	56838	13391	15135	8227	...	93591
F Manufacture of non-metallic mineral products, except products of petroleum and coal	14333	2319	2001	502	...	19155	15118	2484	1037	542	...	19181
G Basic metal industries	33139	6199	4061	1128	...	44527	36019	7238	5682	1244	...	50183
H Manufacture of fabricated metal products, machinery and equipment	208249	20821	19742	5192	276	253728	228187	26232	21676	5653	202	281546
I Other manufacturing industries	6781	906	1777	237	...	9701	7236	1214	3173	287	...	11910
4 Electricity, gas and water b	21996	14014	21797	10875	-	68682	24912	15801	27623	12511	-	80847
5 Construction	92672	7460	36646	2588	-	139366	97859	8107	31637	2718	-	140321
6 Wholesale and retail trade, restaurants and hotels	276074	27828	86374	64950	-	455226	301568	33023	95546	70217	-	500354
A Wholesale and retail trade c	264708	25521	82279	63612	-	436120	288538	30004	92560	68714	-	479816
B Restaurants and hotels	11366	2307	4095	1338	...	19106	13030	3019	2986	1503	...	20538
Restaurants c	...	...	...	...	...	...	...	...	...	...	...	...
Hotels and other lodging places	11366	2307	4095	1338	...	19106	13030	3019	2986	1503	...	20538
7 Transport, storage and communication	106133	28165	29796	10887	1667	173314	115924	33661	30998	11288	1713	190158
A Transport and storage	70933	14610	17913	4786	1667	106575	75731	17623	17372	4547	1713	113560
B Communication	35200	13555	11883	6101	...	66739	40193	16038	13626	6741	...	76598
8 Finance, insurance, real estate and business services	174411	63305	247940	65851	2991	548516	199053	74941	276850	75199	3581	622462
A Financial institutions	47105	6738	14728	3187	...	71758	53744	9110	18826	3670	...	85350
B Insurance	33154	2084	11938	5377	112	52441	36492	2522	6840	5668	-	51522
C Real estate and business services	94152	54483	221274	57287	2879	424317	108817	63309	251184	65861	3581	485590
Real estate, except dwellings	92000	24768	88201	16299	961	220307	106459	31106	95924	20003	1154	252338

1633

United States

4.3 Cost Components of Value Added
(Continued)

Million United States dollars

1980

	Compensation of Employees	Capital Consumption	Net Operating Surplus	Indirect Taxes	Less: Subsidies Received	Value Added
Dwellings	2152	29715	133073	40988	1918	204010
9 Community, social and personal services	165270	10875	43304	5023	-	224472
A Sanitary and similar services [b]	...	...	...	...	...	...
B Social and related community services	123875	2795	23201	980	...	150851
Educational services	14815	178	924	103	...	16020
Medical, dental, other health and veterinary services	83299	2264	22231	739	...	108533
C Recreational and cultural services	11982	2203	1703	1743	...	17631
D Personal and household services	29413	5877	18400	2300	...	55990
Statistical discrepancy [d]	35763	5023	-2230	...	4716	33840
Total, Industries	1352280	243805	616543	206121	10723	2408030
Producers of Government Services	294059	39919	...	...	...	333978
Other Producers	...	...	...	...	...	...
Total	1646340	283724	616543	206121	10723	2742010
Less: Imputed bank service charge	...	...	65620	...	...	65620
Import duties	...	...	...	7160	...	7160
Value added tax	...	...	...	...	...	...
Other adjustments [e]	...	...	...	4920	...	4920
Total [f]	1646340	283724	550923	218201	10723	2688470

1981

	Compensation of Employees	Capital Consumption	Net Operating Surplus	Indirect Taxes	Less: Subsidies Received	Value Added
Dwellings	2358	32203	155260	45858	2427	233252
9 Community, social and personal services	187077	12208	45579	5448	...	250312
A Sanitary and similar services	...	...	...	...	...	...
B Social and related community services	141761	3595	24799	1053	...	171208
Educational services	16529	220	722	89	...	17560
Medical, dental, other health and veterinary services	97442	2930	24056	814	...	125242
C Recreational and cultural services	13286	2769	1915	1833	...	19803
D Personal and household services	32030	5844	18865	2562	...	59301
Statistical discrepancy	40306	5507	-2706	...	5131	37976
Total, Industries	1493400	288210	687867	242887	12182	2700180
Producers of Government Services	323789	42470	...	...	...	366259
Other Producers	...	...	...	...	...	...
Total	1817190	330680	687867	242887	12182	3066440
Less: Imputed bank service charge	...	...	69681	...	...	69681
Import duties	...	...	...	8589	...	8589
Value added tax	...	...	...	...	...	...
Other adjustments	...	...	...	4124	...	4124
Total	1817190	330680	618186	255600	12182	3009470

1982

	Compensation of Employees	Capital Consumption	Net Operating Surplus	Indirect Taxes	Less: Subsidies Received	Value Added

All Producers

	Comp.	Cap. Cons.	Net Op. Surp.	Ind. Taxes	Less: Subs. Rec.	Value Added
1 Agriculture, hunting, forestry and fishing [a]	16993	14338	48854	3575	2390	81370
2 Mining and quarrying	37454	29627	38334	27485	7	132893
A Coal mining	8883	2169	2055	2122	7	15222
B Crude petroleum and natural gas production	23123	26489	36522	24660	...	110794
C Metal ore mining	2628	199	-893	410	...	2344
D Other mining	2820	770	650	293	...	4533
3 Manufacturing	473056	78761	61154	28249	199	641021
A Manufacture of food, beverages and tobacco	39582	8504	13918	8956	...	70960
B Textile, wearing apparel and leather industries	30105	2143	5476	488	...	38212
C Manufacture of wood and wood products, including furniture	18977	3399	2911	545	...	25832
D Manufacture of paper and paper products, printing and publishing	45862	7174	11123	1457	...	65616
E Manufacture of chemicals and chemical petroleum, coal, rubber and plastic products	59725	16059	15575	8523	...	99882
F Manufacture of non-metallic mineral products, except products of petroleum and coal	14458	2704	584	574	...	18320
G Basic metal industries	30198	7115	-3078	1371	...	35606
H Manufacture of fabricated metal products, machinery and equipment	226706	30317	12450	6046	199	275320
I Other manufacturing industries	7443	1346	2195	289	...	11273
4 Electricity, gas and water [b]	28368	18373	31606	14143	-	92490
5 Construction	97703	9004	33498	2751	-	142956
6 Wholesale and retail trade, restaurants and hotels	318080	38210	95727	73483	-	525500
A Wholesale and retail trade [c]	303953	34714	93154	71807	-	503628
B Restaurants and hotels	14127	3496	2573	1676	...	21872

1983

	Comp.	Cap. Cons.	Net Op. Surp.	Ind. Taxes	Less: Subs. Rec.	Value Added
1 Agriculture, hunting, forestry and fishing	17183	14877	38703	3550	7919	66394
2 Mining and quarrying	33107	36728	28034	21193	2	119060
A Coal mining	7473	2623	2321	1990	2	14405
B Crude petroleum and natural gas production	20618	32578	25202	18530	...	96928
C Metal ore mining	2140	329	-304	389	...	2554
D Other mining	2876	1198	815	284	...	5173
3 Manufacturing	490606	88306	74630	35989	38	689493
A Manufacture of food, beverages and tobacco	40706	9917	14422	12098	...	77143
B Textile, wearing apparel and leather industries	32152	2200	6541	513	...	41406
C Manufacture of wood and wood products, including furniture	21709	3836	5309	552	...	31406
D Manufacture of paper and paper products, printing and publishing	49255	7890	11893	1598	...	70636
E Manufacture of chemicals and chemical petroleum, coal, rubber and plastic products	62470	17881	17835	12623	...	110809
F Manufacture of non-metallic mineral products	15162	2742	1822	610	...	20336
G Basic metal industries	28173	6217	-5201	1429	...	30618
H Manufacture of fabricated metal products, machinery and equipment	233324	35928	21210	6256	38	296680
I Other manufacturing industries	7655	1695	799	310	...	10459
4 Electricity, gas and water	30589	21487	36362	15563	-	104001
5 Construction	100485	9622	38073	3141	-	151321
6 Wholesale and retail trade, restaurants and hotels	338495	40921	102397	81899	-	563712
A Wholesale and retail trade	322933	36908	99385	79973	-	539199
B Restaurants and hotels	15562	4013	3012	1926	...	24513

1634

United States

4.3 Cost Components of Value Added
(Continued)

Million United States dollars

	\multicolumn{6}{c}{1982}	\multicolumn{6}{c}{1983}
	Compensation of Employees	Capital Consumption	Net Operating Surplus	Indirect Taxes	Less: Subsidies Received	Value Added	Compensation of Employees	Capital Consumption	Net Operating Surplus	Indirect Taxes	Less: Subsidies Received	Value Added
Restaurants c	...	...	...	...	...	...	...	...	...	...	...	...
Hotels and other lodging places	14127	3496	2573	1676	...	21872	15562	4013	3012	1926	...	24513
7 Transport, storage and communication	121324	35621	30519	11929	1630	197763	124765	43160	36631	15250	1973	217833
A Transport and storage	76055	16865	15783	4805	1630	111878	78203	19096	20153	6053	1973	121532
B Communication	45269	18756	14736	7124	...	85885	46562	24064	16478	9197	...	96301
8 Finance, insurance, real estate and business services	222278	82246	280720	82723	4840	663127	249470	96061	316187	90381	5649	746450
A Financial institutions	61477	10988	14754	3784	...	91003	70865	12802	25352	4115	...	113134
B Insurance	39848	2888	-361	6048	-	48423	42838	4150	2048	6821	-	55857
C Real estate and business services	120953	68370	266327	72891	4840	523701	135767	79109	288787	79445	5649	577459
Real estate, except dwellings	118368	33713	97469	22209	2099	269660	133121	41897	106370	24991	2534	303845
Dwellings	2585	34657	168858	50682	2741	254041	2646	37212	182417	54454	3115	273614
9 Community, social and personal services	208325	14670	47668	5888	-	276551	227095	17239	52049	6503	-	302886
A Sanitary and similar services b	...	...	...	...	...	...	...	...	...	...	...	...
B Social and related community services	159811	4495	26957	1183	...	192446	174728	5544	29080	1347	...	210699
Educational services	18005	267	791	99	...	19162	19825	337	763	101	...	21026
Medical, dental, other health and veterinary services	111951	3760	26081	920	...	142712	122838	4759	28150	1084	...	156831
C Recreational and cultural services	14401	3438	1900	1914	...	21653	15732	4060	1771	2042	...	23605
D Personal and household services	34113	6737	18811	2791	...	62452	36635	7635	21198	3114	...	68582
Statistical discrepancy d	42644	5979	-2183	...	6417	40023	45778	6438	-1537	...	6594	44085
Total, Industries	1566230	326829	665897	250226	15483	2793690	1657570	374839	721529	273469	22175	3005240
Producers of Government Services	351777	43597	...	...	...	395374	374733	44589	...	...	...	419322
Other Producers	...	...	...	...	...	...	...	...	...	...	...	...
Total	1918000	370426	665897	250226	15483	3189070	2032310	419428	721529	273469	22175	3424560
Less: Imputed bank service charge	...	...	76225	...	...	76225	...	...	85345	...	...	85345
Import duties	...	...	...	8609	...	8609	...	...	...	9091	...	9091
Value added tax	...	...	...	...	...	...	...	...	...	...	...	...
Other adjustments e	...	...	...	-56	...	-56	...	...	...	5170	...	5170
Total f	1918000	370426	589672	258779	15483	3121400	2032310	419428	636184	287730	22175	3353470

	\multicolumn{6}{c}{1984}	\multicolumn{6}{c}{1985}
	Compensation of Employees	Capital Consumption	Net Operating Surplus	Indirect Taxes	Less: Subsidies Received	Value Added	Compensation of Employees	Capital Consumption	Net Operating Surplus	Indirect Taxes	Less: Subsidies Received	Value Added
	\multicolumn{12}{c}{All Producers}
1 Agriculture, hunting, forestry and fishing a	17840	15422	55729	3357	7043	85305	18710	16015	53313	3480	6296	85222
2 Mining and quarrying	35251	40589	24359	20149	1	120347	34722	42719	20445	17274	2	115158
A Coal mining	8219	2613	1745	2104	1	14680	7960	2441	1377	2207	2	13983
B Crude petroleum and natural gas production	21768	36148	21978	17281	...	97175	21629	38282	19021	14256	...	93188
C Metal ore mining	2115	286	-570	424	...	2255	1832	544	-1010	450	...	1816
D Other mining	3149	1542	1206	340	...	6237	3301	1452	1057	361	...	6171

United States

4.3 Cost Components of Value Added
(Continued)

Million United States dollars

	1984							1985					
	Compensation of Employees	Capital Consumption	Net Operating Surplus	Indirect Taxes	Less: Subsidies Received	Value Added	Compensation of Employees	Capital Consumption	Net Operating Surplus	Indirect Taxes	Less: Subsidies Received	Value Added
3 Manufacturing	540658	96170	102160	39433	8	778413	563178	108157	86065	39983	4	797379
A Manufacture of food, beverages and tobacco	42027	10997	14948	11981	...	79953	43331	11903	15970	11502	...	82706
B Textile, wearing apparel and leather industries	33758	2738	5006	570	...	42072	32690	2736	5480	626	...	41532
C Manufacture of wood and wood products, including furniture	24362	3703	6520	890	...	35475	25145	4315	6034	673	...	36167
D Manufacture of paper and paper products, printing and publishing	54359	9707	14165	1800	...	80031	57893	11447	14975	1961	...	86276
E Manufacture of chemicals and chemical petroleum, coal, rubber and plastic products	66468	19417	21355	14060	...	121300	68778	20383	20209	14102	...	123472
F Manufacture of non-metallic mineral products, except products of petroleum and coal	16616	3039	2777	682	...	23114	16975	3470	3747	747	...	24939
G Basic metal industries	30358	3642	960	1585	...	36545	29155	5019	-804	1701	...	35071
H Manufacture of fabricated metal products, machinery and equipment	264525	40454	33472	7512	8	345955	280994	46306	18350	8264	4	353910
I Other manufacturing industries	8185	2473	2957	353	...	13968	8217	2578	2104	407	...	13306
4 Electricity, gas and water [b]	32776	25335	44453	16932	-	119496	35052	29532	43666	19546	-	127796
5 Construction	113890	10826	45245	3565	-	173526	124640	11821	48247	3895	-	188603
6 Wholesale and retail trade, restaurants and hotels	376248	46184	119019	93571	-	635022	403559	54448	122374	102426	-	682807
A Wholesale and retail trade [c]	358578	41440	116274	91401	-	607693	384266	48585	119291	100015	-	652157
B Restaurants and hotels	17670	4744	2745	2170	...	27329	19293	5863	3083	2411	...	30650
Restaurants [c]	...	...	...	...	...	...	...	...	...	...	...	...
Hotels and other lodging places	17670	4744	2745	2170	...	27329	19293	5863	3083	2411	...	30650
7 Transport, storage and communication	132382	46170	43685	16858	1869	237226	137695	53471	41603	18181	1776	249174
A Transport and storage	85159	20345	24112	6875	1869	134622	89039	23623	20455	7404	1776	138745
B Communication	47223	25825	19573	9983	...	102604	48656	29848	21148	10777	...	110429
8 Finance, insurance, real estate and business services	282348	110656	330298	100969	6747	817524	317110	128336	367884	108920	6855	915395
A Financial institutions	77490	14563	17436	4817	...	114306	86383	18770	21167	5387	...	131707
B Insurance	46240	4800	-1940	7247	-	56347	50884	5405	3386	8382	-	68057
C Real estate and business services	158618	91293	314802	88905	6747	646871	179843	104161	343331	95151	6855	715631
Real estate, except dwellings	155711	50978	118156	29840	3408	351277	176634	59681	126760	31401	2767	391709
Dwellings	2907	40315	196646	59065	3339	295594	3209	44480	216571	63750	4088	323922
9 Community, social and personal services	245895	20023	58042	7176	-	331136	263994	23723	68436	7774	-	363927
A Sanitary and similar services [b]	...	...	...	...	...	...	...	...	...	...	...	...
B Social and related community services	187711	6967	32975	1503	...	229156	201774	8159	38103	1681	...	249717
Educational services	21930	402	1075	150	...	23557	23964	512	1166	173	...	25815
Medical, dental, other health and veterinary services	131282	5726	31654	1161	...	169823	140725	6899	36592	1282	...	185498
C Recreational and cultural services	17001	4691	1612	2182	...	25486	18115	5424	3482	2275	...	29296
D Personal and household services	41183	8365	23455	3491	...	76494	44105	10140	26851	3818	...	84914
Statistical discrepancy [d]	49363	6942	2697	...	7062	51940	53402	7523	4728	...	7930	57723
Total, Industries	1826650	418317	825687	302010	22730	3349940	1952060	475745	856761	321479	22863	3583180
Producers of Government Services	397767	46215	...	...	...	443982	427587	50072	...	...	...	477659
Other Producers	...	...	...	...	...	...	...	...	...	...	...	...
Total	2224420	464532	825687	302010	22730	3793920	2379650	525817	856761	321479	22863	4060840
Less: Imputed bank service charge	...	...	88844	...	...	88844	...	...	100779	...	...	100779
Import duties	...	...	...	11904	...	11904	...	...	...	12158	...	12158
Value added tax	...	...	...	...	...	...	...	...	...	...	...	...
Other adjustments [e]	...	...	...	5359	...	5359	...	...	...	-4750	...	-4750
Total [f]	2224420	464532	736843	319273	22730	3722340	2379650	525817	755982	328887	22863	3967470

United States

4.3 Cost Components of Value Added

Million United States dollars

		1986					1987				
	Compensation of Employees	Capital Consumption	Net Operating Surplus	Indirect Taxes	Less: Subsidies Received	Value Added	Compensation of Employees	Capital Consumption	Net Operating Surplus	Indirect Taxes	Less: Subsidies Received	Value Added

All Producers

	Compensation of Employees	Capital Consumption	Net Operating Surplus	Indirect Taxes	Less: Subsidies Received	Value Added	Compensation of Employees	Capital Consumption	Net Operating Surplus	Indirect Taxes	Less: Subsidies Received	Value Added
1 Agriculture, hunting, forestry and fishing [a]	19596	15460	57518	3457	9550	86481	21329	15081	62996	3649	13854	89201
2 Mining and quarrying	30207	42627	-1101	11341	2	83072	28294	39472	8078	10592	2	86434
A Coal mining	7620	2063	1505	2118	2	13304	7207	1760	1689	2140	2	12794
B Crude petroleum and natural gas production	17512	38773	-3669	8477	...	61093	15670	36198	6276	7644	...	65788
C Metal ore mining	1676	459	-390	395	...	2140	1833	335	-350	421	...	2239
D Other mining	3399	1332	1453	351	...	6535	3584	1179	463	387	...	5613
3 Manufacturing	577733	104709	102285	43650	-	828377	596542	104503	117737	43549	-	862331
A Manufacture of food, beverages and tobacco	45102	12031	17348	11721	...	86202	46970	11983	19406	11953	...	90312
B Textile, wearing apparel and leather industries	33799	2655	6445	677	...	43576	35507	2630	7262	725	...	46124
C Manufacture of wood and wood products, including furniture	26614	3983	7677	730	...	39004	28768	4157	9306	775	...	43006
D Manufacture of paper and paper products, printing and publishing	61296	11955	15585	2117	...	90953	65166	12429	18510	2252	...	98357
E Manufacture of chemicals and chemical petroleum, coal, rubber and plastic products	70416	19430	30259	16616	...	136721	73672	17442	36014	15284	...	142412
F Manufacture of non-metallic mineral products, except products of petroleum and coal	17595	3236	4429	806	...	26066	18151	3129	5546	855	...	27681
G Basic metal industries	28004	3794	360	1832	...	33990	28075	3233	3463	1959	...	36730
H Manufacture of fabricated metal products, machinery and equipment	286388	45303	17954	8708	-	358353	291199	47163	15881	9266	-	363509
I Other manufacturing industries	8519	2322	2228	443	...	13512	9034	2337	2349	480	...	14200
4 Electricity, gas and water [b]	36956	33291	45132	18788	-	134167	38736	35681	43201	19674	-	137292
5 Construction	133780	12596	55601	4187	-	206164	142167	14960	59168	4451	-	220746
6 Wholesale and retail trade, restaurants and hotels	429630	58761	126123	109578	-	724092	459336	62339	129184	116864	-	767723
A Wholesale and retail trade [c]	408696	52250	123202	106951	-	691099	436347	55271	126015	114030	-	731663
B Restaurants and hotels	20934	6511	2921	2627	...	32993	22989	7068	3169	2834	...	36060
Restaurants [c]	...	...	...	...	...	...	...	...	...	...	...	...
Hotels and other lodging places	20934	6511	2921	2627	...	32993	22989	7068	3169	2834	...	36060
7 Transport, storage and communication	141872	52616	50721	18991	1822	262378	149449	53109	53141	20291	1796	274194
A Transport and storage	92318	21876	25606	7858	1822	145836	97877	20175	27390	8572	1796	152218
B Communication	49554	30740	25115	11133	...	116542	51572	32934	25751	11719	...	121976
8 Finance, insurance, real estate and business services	357155	143122	414554	116431	8754	1022510	401536	155957	452171	122868	8654	1123880
A Financial institutions	99824	21680	21435	5866	...	148805	111612	25474	17787	6288	...	161161
B Insurance	56801	7141	14090	10092	-	88124	62593	9345	19741	11299	-	102978
C Real estate and business services	200530	114301	379029	100473	8754	785579	227331	121138	414643	105281	8654	859739
Real estate, except dwellings	197059	66166	143573	32246	4607	434437	223689	68659	159791	32726	3969	480896
Dwellings	3471	48135	235456	68227	4147	351142	3642	52479	254852	72555	4685	378843
9 Community, social and personal services	284366	25184	74176	8326	-	392052	316658	26499	79687	8940	-	431784
A Sanitary and similar services [b]	...	...	...	...	...	...	...	...	...	...	...	...
B Social and related community services	218465	8378	40349	1858	...	269050	245522	9013	43234	2016	...	299785
Educational services	25506	446	1119	197	...	27268	27765	494	1229	213	...	29701
Medical, dental, other health and veterinary services	152774	7162	38670	1420	...	200026	174170	7678	41372	1543	...	224763
C Recreational and cultural services	19419	5756	4201	2330	...	31706	21644	6109	4827	2506	...	35086
D Personal and household services	46482	11050	29626	4138	...	91296	49492	11377	31626	4418	...	96913
Statistical discrepancy [d]	55959	8187	3034	...	7163	60017	60626	8918	562	...	7477	62629
Total, Industries	2067250	496553	928043	334749	27291	3799310	2214670	516519	1005930	350878	31783	4056210
Producers of Government Services	452308	52081	...	...	...	504389	482382	54060	...	...	...	536442

United States

4.3 Cost Components of Value Added
(Continued)

Million United States dollars

	\multicolumn{6}{c	}{1986}	\multicolumn{6}{c	}{1987}
	Compensation of Employees	Capital Consumption	Net Operating Surplus	Indirect Taxes	Less: Subsidies Received	Value Added	Compensation of Employees	Capital Consumption	Net Operating Surplus	Indirect Taxes	Less: Subsidies Received	Value Added
Other Producers	...	...	...	...	...	...	...	...	...	...	...	...
Total	2519560	548634	928043	334749	27291	4303700	2697060	570579	1005930	350878	31783	4592650
Less: Imputed bank service charge	...	...	112282	...	...	112282	...	...	127079	...	...	127079
Import duties	...	...	...	13697	...	13697	...	...	...	15445	...	15445
Value added tax	...	...	...	...	...	...	...	...	...	...	...	...
Other adjustments [e]	...	...	...	-13647	...	-13647	...	...	...	-8114	...	-8114
Total [f]	2519560	548634	815761	334799	27291	4191470	2697060	570579	878846	358209	31783	4472910

a) Item 'Agriculture, hunting, forestry and fishing' excludes hunting.
b) Item 'Electricity, gas and water' also includes sanitary and similar services.
c) Restaurants is included in Retail Trade.
d) Item 'Statistical discrepancy' refers to government enterprises.
e) Item 'Other adjustments' refers to statistical discrepancy.
f) Totals shown in columns 2 and 3, capital consumption and net operating surplus, differ from the estimates shown in table 1.3 by the amount of total capital consumption adjustment (including that of government enterprises) which is included in table 1.3 and not in this table. Industry detail in this table is not available for capital consumption adjustment.

Uruguay

General note. The preparation of national accounts statistics in Uruguay is undertaken by the Banco Central del Uruguay, Montevideo. The official estimates together with some methological notes are published annually by the Banco Central in 'Producto e Ingreso Nacionales'. The following presentation of sources and methods is mainly based on a report entitled 'Metodologia del Calculo de las cuentas de actividades, a precios corrientes'. The estimates are generally in accordance with the classifications and definitions recommended in the United Nations System of National Accounts (SNA). The following tables have been prepared from successive replies to the United Nations national accounts questionnaire. When the scope and coverage of the estimates differ for conceptual or statistical reasons from the definitions and classifications recommended in SNA, a footnote is indicated to the relevant tables.

Sources and methods:

(a) Gross domestic product. Gross domestic product is estimated mainly through the production approach.

(b) Expenditure on the gross domestic product. All components of GDP by expenditure type are estimated through the expenditure approach except private final consumption expenditure and gross investment in machinery and equipments which are estimated by the commodity-flow approach. The estimates of government final consumption expenditure are based on the budgetary programmes of the different institutional subsectors. The items are analyzed in accordance with the government disbursements which are classified into ten different items. The commodity-flow approach is used to estimate private final consumption expenditure by separating the current products according to their origin and source. These estimates are periodically checked by surveys of homes and of family budgets. The estimates of increase in stocks refer to stock variations for meat and wool only. The estimates of imported machinery and equipment are based on c.i.f. import values classified by industry of origin, principal groups of goods and sectors of destination. Customs duties, indirect taxes, trade margins, etc. are then added. Domestically produced capital goods are estimated in the same manner. The estimates of exports and imports of goods and services are based on the foreign trade statistics which are adjusted for unregistered transactions. The balance-of-payments data are also used. For the constant price estimates, price deflation is used for government purchases of goods and services, public construction and exports and imports of services. For government compensation of employees, increase in stocks, private construction, investment in machinery and equipment and exports and imports of goods, the base-year estimates are extrapolated by quantity index. Private consumption expenditure is obtained as a residual.

(c) Cost-structure of the gross domestic product. The estimates of wages and salaries in the agricultural sector are estimated by using employment data and average wages obtained from censuses and extrapolated and interpolated by using indices of physical volumes. For private construction, the ratio of wages and salaries to the value of building is determined for the different types of construction work. For the trade sector, wages and salaries are measured from employment data obtained from the 1963 population census and extrapolated by volume index of commercialized merchandise. For the public sectors, compensation of employees is obtained directly from the government enterprises. In general, consumption of fixed capital is valued at original cost. Information of indirect taxes and subsidies is available directly for registered tax classifications by economic branch. Profits of government monopoly enterprises are treated as indirect taxes while deficits are treated as subsidies. Operating surplus is obtained as a residual.

(d) Gross domestic product by kind of economic activity. The table of GDP by kind of economic activity is prepared in factor values. The production approach is used to estimate the value added of most industries. However, the income approach is used for producers of government services, part of the construction sector and part of the services sector. The Ministerio de Ganaderia y Agricultura conducts censuses and surveys every four years, covering agricultural establishments of over one hectare. The censuses include various type of information such as ownership, locations, land tenure conditions, production, stocks, etc. The Ministerio also conducts annual sample surveys on principal crops, wool production, etc. The gross value of livestock production is based on the number of livestock, adjusted for imports and exports and changes in stocks. Data on mining production and prices are provided by the Instituto Geologico del Uruguay and the Camara de la Construccion, respectively. The estimates of intermediate consumption are based on the 1968 national economic census. For manufacturing, quarterly and annual surveys are conducted. They provide data on labour force, salaries and wages, raw materials, manufactured products, costs, etc. The value of electricity and water production is obtained directly from the concerned enterprises which are government monopolies. The data of gas production are furnished by the concerned companies. Basic information used to estimate the gross vaue of production in the building sector is obtained from the administrative records of the public sector. For private building, the municipal records provide data on approved licences, quantity, size and type of construction. This information is adjusted on the basis of surveys on time extension of buildings and areas. The accounting records of the central government and public enterprises supply the information used to estimate the gross production value of public buildings. The estimates of the trade sector are based on the gross value of commercialized production while intermediate consumption is obtained from an analysis of the accounts of certain enterprises. The Banco Central del Uruguay conducts surveys of trade channels and trade margins. For restaurants and hotels, the estimates are based on studies carried out in 1962 extrapolated by price and volume indexes. The production values of railways, air transport and ports are estimated from the data supplied by the respective government enterprises. For other transport, data are obtained directly from concerned enterprises and from licence permits issued. Bench-mark estimates of cargo transport were prepared for 1961. These estimates are projected by the use of an index of receipts. Information on water transport, storage and communication is obtained directly from a special maritime commission, from the Mercado de Frutos, and from the accounts of government enterprises, respectively. The estimates of banking services are obtained from administrative records. For real estate, the value of production is determined as the amount of gross rents paid or imputed for housing services. Owner-occupied dwellings are imputed in accordance with the average rents for rented houses. The estimates of business services are based on the number of persons employed and average wages. For producers of government services, the estimates are based on budgetary programmes of the institutional subsectors. For domestic service, data from the 1963 population census are extrapolated on the basis of information from employment agencies. For other private services, bench-mark studies referring to 1961 are extrapolated by the most suitable indicators. For the constant price estimates, value added of most industries is extrapolated by a quantity index. Double deflation is used for all components of the agricultural sector and price deflation is used for public construction.

1.1 Expenditure on the Gross Domestic Product, in Current Prices

Million Uruguayan pesos

	1970	1975	1978	1979	1980	1981	1982	1983	1984	1985	1986	1987
1 Government final consumption expenditure	92	1116	3821	6789	11482	17336	20100	25653	36851	69154	127842	216929
2 Private final consumption expenditure	448	6244	22919	43441	69890	91147	94076	137826	216282	394839	720319	1290795
3 Gross capital formation	69	1102	4951	9975	15994	18802	18555	18427	29115	43071	72049	158233
A Increase in stocks [a]	-	12	8	663	572	-403	-827	-1902	1784	3863	1027	13674
B Gross fixed capital formation	69	1090	4943	9312	15422	19205	19382	20329	27331	39208	71022	144559
Residential buildings	37	734	3122	5935	10324	13880	14931	14568	20663	26582	43976	84888
Non-residential buildings												
Other construction and land improvement etc.	4	36	93	208	227	157	178	289	455	601	1521	3295
Other	28	320	1728	3169	4871	5168	4273	5472	6213	12025	25525	56376
4 Exports of goods and services	73	1317	5530	9400	13861	17987	18072	44700	72065	126745	227097	350449
5 Less: Imports of goods and services	81	1613	6291	11980	19023	22819	22107	41600	59954	105657	175573	315847
Equals: Gross Domestic Product	601	8166	30930	57625	92204	122453	128696	185006	294359	528152	971734	1700559

a) Item 'Increase in stocks' refers to increase in stocks of wool and livestock in the private sector, and to stocks held by the public sector.

1.2 Expenditure on the Gross Domestic Product, in Constant Prices

Million Uruguayan pesos

	1970	1975	1978	1979	1980	1981	1982	1983	1984	1985	1986	1987
	\multicolumn{12}{c}{At constant prices of:1978}												
1 Government final consumption expenditure	3047	3334	3821	4302	4244	4562	4452	4322	4347	4484	4644	4782
2 Private final consumption expenditure	21972	22758	22919	24163	26232	26854	24257	21926	20497	20764	22711	24903
3 Gross capital formation	2740	3057	4951	6132	6461	5888	4815	3052	3111	2524	2510	3144
A Increase in stocks [a]	-111	-84	8	250	206	-179	-350	-419	102	214	11	168
B Gross fixed capital formation	2851	3141	4943	5882	6255	6067	5165	3471	3009	2310	2499	2976

Uruguay

1.2 Expenditure on the Gross Domestic Product, in Constant Prices
(Continued)

Million Uruguayan pesos

	1970	1975	1978	1979	1980	1981	1982	1983	1984	1985	1986	1987
At constant prices of: 1978												
Residential buildings	1619	2049	3122	3537	3757	3840	3638	2412	2239	1537	1483	1610
Non-residential buildings												
Other construction and land improvement etc.	64	56	93	122	91	54	54	46	41	37	51	67
Other	1168	1036	1728	2223	2407	2173	1473	1013	729	736	965	1299
4 Exports of goods and services	3053	4086	5530	5893	6106	6483	5801	6697	6744	7102	8146	7375
5 Less: Imports of goods and services	4955	5305	6291	7652	8235	8318	7187	5740	4883	4969	6132	6750
Equals: Gross Domestic Product	25857	27930	30930	32838	34808	35469	32138	30257	29816	29905	31879	33454

a) Item 'Increase in stocks' refers to increase in stocks of wool and livestock in the private sector, and to stocks held by the public sector.

1.3 Cost Components of the Gross Domestic Product

Million Uruguayan pesos

	1970	1975	1978	1979	1980	1981	1982	1983	1984	1985	1986	1987
1 Indirect taxes, net	81	1058	4638	7867	12665	16550	16735	22874	38224	70497	135820	246214
A Indirect taxes	92	1224	5357	8864	14552	19239	20181	27787	44405	79387	152947	...
B Less: Subsidies	11	166	719	996	1887	2689	3446	4913	6181	8890	17127	...
2 Consumption of fixed capital	22	343	1557	2933	4858	6050	6105	6404	8609	12351	22372	45536
3 Compensation of employees paid by resident producers to:	269	3206	10255	17030	28367	39890	45956	55671	81446	166141	321820	1408809
4 Operating surplus	229	3559	14480	29795	46314	59963	59900	100057	166080	279163	491722	
Equals: Gross Domestic Product	601	8166	30930	57625	92204	122453	128696	185006	294359	528152	971734	1700559

1.4 General Government Current Receipts and Disbursements

Million Uruguayan pesos

	1970	1975	1978	1979	1980	1981	1982	1983	1984	1985	1986	1987
Receipts												
1 Operating surplus	...	...	...	...	...	...	...	...	...	...	...	...
2 Property and entrepreneurial income	2	5	54	203	185	169	447	193	294	379	647	...
3 Taxes, fees and contributions	167	2063	8778	14380	24119	30563	33390	46553	69942	130576	257916	...
A Indirect taxes	92	1224	5357	8864	14552	19239	20181	27787	44405	79387	152947	...
B Direct taxes	16	221	956	1528	3680	3885	4320	6980	9210	18573	36325	...
C Social security contributions	59	618	2465	3988	5887	7439	8889	11786	16327	32616	68644	...
D Compulsory fees, fines and penalties	...	...	...	...	...	...	...	...	...	...	...	...
4 Other current transfers	...	...	...	...	...	...	...	...	...	...	...	...
Total Current Receipts of General Government	169	2068	8832	14583	24304	30732	33837	46746	70236	130955	258563	...
Disbursements												
1 Government final consumption expenditure	92	1116	3821	6789	11482	17336	20100	25653	36851	69154	127842	...
2 Property income a	2	28	86	97	290	412	1769	3556	4823	6080	17790	...
3 Subsidies	11	166	719	996	1887	2689	3446	4913	6181	8890	17127	...
4 Other current transfers	57	670	2447	3790	6722	12419	15662	18637	25053	42951	83491	...
A Social security benefits	60	692	2482	3834	6783	12501	15776	18935	25612	44044	87323	...
B Social assistance grants	...	...	...	...	...	...	...	...	...	...	...	...
C Other	-3	-22	-35	-44	-61	-82	-114	-298	-559	-1093	-3832	...
5 Net saving	7	88	1759	2911	3923	-2124	-7140	-6013	-2672	3880	12313	...
Total Current Disbursements and Net Saving of General Government	169	2068	8832	14583	24304	30732	33837	46746	70236	130955	258563	...

a) Item 'Property income' relates to interest on public debt.

1.10 Gross Domestic Product by Kind of Activity, in Current Prices

Million Uruguayan pesos

	1970	1975	1978	1979	1980	1981	1982	1983	1984	1985	1986	1987
1 Agriculture, hunting, forestry and fishing	67	851	2946	6020	8860	9987	9942	16686	30415	55724	109796	191929
2 Mining and quarrying	6	43	255	565	1191	1613	1465	2425	3080	4985	9461	18891
3 Manufacturing	114	1756	6363	13603	20603	24152	21724	38336	67279	118098	217842	388345
4 Electricity, gas and water a	8	145	366	562	1185	1774	2587	4209	6589	13228	24277	42568
5 Construction	20	336	1326	2544	4182	5965	6494	5621	6989	9456	16900	34751

Uruguay

1.10 Gross Domestic Product by Kind of Activity, in Current Prices
(Continued)

Million Uruguayan pesos

	1970	1975	1978	1979	1980	1981	1982	1983	1984	1985	1986	1987
6 Wholesale and retail trade, restaurants and hotels [b]	86	1349	5248	10063	14910	19150	16401	24839	41746	78500	101157	173642
7 Transport, storage and communication	45	542	1709	2993	5083	6982	7898	11617	17304	29891	56349	92133
8 Finance, insurance, real estate and business services	50	698	3350	5709	10241	16315	21480	28585	41887	73216	...	...
9 Community, social and personal services	24	279	1079	1844	3053	4493	5430	7269	9996	16475	...	...
Total, Industries	420	5999	22643	43903	69308	90431	93421	139587	225285	399573	...	...
Producers of Government Services	77	881	2914	4856	8490	12958	15406	18956	25765	48147	91487	152326
Other Producers	23	228	735	999	1741	2514	3134	3589	5085	9935	...	...
Subtotal [c]	520	7108	26292	49758	79539	105903	111961	162132	256135	457655	835914	1454345
Less: Imputed bank service charge	...	...	...	...	...	...	...	...	...	...	...	...
Plus: Import duties	...	...	...	...	...	...	...	...	...	...	...	...
Plus: Value added tax	...	...	...	...	...	...	...	...	...	...	...	...
Plus: Other adjustments [d]	81	1058	4638	7867	12665	16550	16735	22874	38224	70497	135820	246214
Equals: Gross Domestic Product	601	8166	30930	57625	92204	122453	128696	185006	294359	528152	...	...

a) Item 'Electricity, gas and water' includes sewage services.
b) For the years 1986 and 1987, the estimates refer to wholesale and retail trade only.
c) Gross domestic product in factor values.
d) Item 'Other adjustments' refers to indirect taxes net of subsidies.

1.11 Gross Domestic Product by Kind of Activity, in Constant Prices

Million Uruguayan pesos

	1970	1975	1978	1979	1980	1981	1982	1983	1984	1985	1986	1987
					At constant prices of: 1978							
1 Agriculture, hunting, forestry and fishing	3197	3001	2946	2933	3408	3596	3332	3402	3171	3315	3538	3565
2 Mining and quarrying	151	207	255	317	374	367	290	248	205	187	191	292
3 Manufacturing	5058	5565	6364	6818	6980	6662	5536	5148	5292	5207	5837	6481
4 Electricity, gas and water [a]	281	314	366	379	408	430	435	444	441	456	474	513
5 Construction	686	876	1326	1490	1546	1593	1545	1026	913	638	627	692
6 Wholesale and retail trade, restaurants and hotels [b]	4451	4602	5248	5726	6214	6341	5063	4591	4518	4485	3997	4281
7 Transport, storage and communication	1485	1563	1709	1885	2041	2025	1802	1717	1711	1740	1910	1996
8 Finance, insurance, real estate and business services	2607	3269	3350	3461	3645	3909	4070	4047	...	...	...	...
9 Community, social and personal services	1122	1066	1079	1103	1104	1139	1118	1039	...	...	...	...
Total, Industries	19038	20463	22643	24112	25720	26062	23191	21662	...	...	...	...
Producers of Government Services	2333	2524	2914	3143	3147	3365	3373	3427	...	...	...	...
Other Producers	597	759	735	659	733	746	755	631	...	...	...	...
Subtotal [c]	21968	23746	26292	27914	29600	30173	27319	25720	...	...	...	...
Less: Imputed bank service charge	...	...	...	...	...	...	...	...	...	...	...	...
Plus: Import duties	...	...	...	...	...	...	...	...	...	...	...	...
Plus: Value added tax	...	...	...	...	...	...	...	...	...	...	...	...
Plus: Other adjustments [d]	3889	4184	4638	4924	5208	5296	4819	4537	4471	4477	4761	5005
Equals: Gross Domestic Product	25857	27930	30930	32838	34808	35469	32138	30257	29816	29905	31879	33454

a) Item 'Electricity, gas and water' includes sewage services.
b) For the years 1986 and 1987, the estimates refer to wholesale and retail trade only.
c) Gross domestic product in factor values.
d) Item 'Other adjustments' refers to indirect taxes net of subsidies.

1.12 Relations Among National Accounting Aggregates

Million Uruguayan pesos

	1970	1975	1978	1979	1980	1981	1982	1983	1984	1985	1986	1987
Gross Domestic Product	601	8166	30930	57625	92204	122453	128696	185006	294359	528152	971734	1700559
Plus: Net factor income from the rest of the world	-6	-168	-465	-454	-912	-797	-2729	-9895	-20210	-35501	-42100	-63399
Equals: Gross National Product	595	7998	30465	57171	91292	121656	125967	175111	274149	492651	929634	1637160
Less: Consumption of fixed capital	22	343	1557	2933	4858	6050	6105	6404	8609	12351	22372	45536
Equals: National Income	573	7655	28908	54238	86434	115606	119862	168707	265540	480300	907262	1591624
Plus: Net current transfers from the rest of the world	3	35	44	56	79	105	145	380	559	1093	3832	1805
Equals: National Disposable Income	576	7690	28952	54294	86513	115711	120007	169087	266099	481393	911094	1593429
Less: Final consumption	540	7360	26740	50230	81372	108483	114176	163479	253133	463993	848161	1507724
Equals: Net Saving	36	330	2212	4064	5141	7228	5831	5608	12966	17400	62933	85705
Less: Surplus of the nation on current transactions	-11	-429	-1182	-2978	-5995	-5524	-6619	-6415	-7540	-13320	13256	-26992
Equals: Net Capital Formation	47	759	3394	7042	11136	12752	12450	12023	20506	30720	49677	112697

Uruguay

2.7 Gross Capital Formation by Type of Good and Owner, in Current Prices

Million Uruguayan pesos

	1980 TOTAL	1980 Total Private	1980 Public Enterprises	1980 General Government	1981 TOTAL	1981 Total Private	1981 Public Enterprises	1981 General Government	1982 TOTAL	1982 Total Private	1982 Public Enterprises	1982 General Government
Increase in stocks, total [a]	572	572	-	...	-403	-403	-	...	-827	-827	-	...
Gross Fixed Capital Formation, Total	15422	10520	4902	...	19205	13046	6159	...	19382	10147	9235	...
1 Residential buildings	10324	6557	3767	...	13880	8365	5515	...	14931	7942	6989	...
2 Non-residential buildings	...	...	...	...	...	...	...	...	...	...	...	...
3 Other construction	...	...	...	...	...	...	...	...	...	...	...	...
4 Land improvement and plantation and orchard development	227	227	-	...	157	157	-	...	178	178	-	...
5 Producers' durable goods	4871	3736	1135	...	5168	4524	644	...	4273	2027	2246	...
6 Breeding stock, dairy cattle, etc.	...	...	...	...	...	...	...	...	...	...	...	...
Total Gross Capital Formation	15994	11092	4902	...	18802	12643	6159	...	18555	9320	9235	...

	1983 TOTAL	1983 Total Private	1983 Public Enterprises	1983 General Government	1984 TOTAL	1984 Total Private	1984 Public Enterprises	1984 General Government	1985 TOTAL	1985 Total Private	1985 Public Enterprises	1985 General Government
Increase in stocks, total [a]	-1902	-1902	-	...	1784	1784	-	-	3863	3863	-	...
Gross Fixed Capital Formation, Total	20329	12808	7521	...	27331	15345	11986	-	39208	23576	15632	...
1 Residential buildings	14568	8776	5792	...	20663	9401	11262	-	26582	13018	13564	...
2 Non-residential buildings	...	...	...	...	...	...	...	...	...	...	...	...
3 Other construction	...	...	...	...	...	...	...	...	...	...	...	...
4 Land improvement and plantation and orchard development	289	289	-	...	455	455	-	-	601	601	-	...
5 Producers' durable goods	5472	3743	1729	...	6213	5489	724	-	12025	9957	2068	...
6 Breeding stock, dairy cattle, etc.	...	...	...	...	...	...	...	...	...	...	...	...
Total Gross Capital Formation	18427	10906	7521	...	29115	17129	11986	...	43071	27439	15632	...

	1986 TOTAL	1986 Total Private	1986 Public Enterprises	1986 General Government	1987 TOTAL	1987 Total Private	1987 Public Enterprises	1987 General Government
Increase in stocks, total [a]	1027	1027	-	...	13674	13674	-	...
Gross Fixed Capital Formation, Total	71022	43072	27950	...	144559	91967	52592	...
1 Residential buildings	43976	20249	23727	...	84888	38272	46616	...
2 Non-residential buildings	...	...	...	...	...	...	...	...
3 Other construction	...	...	...	...	...	...	...	...
4 Land improvement and plantation and orchard development	1521	1521	-	...	3295	3295	-	...
5 Producers' durable goods	25525	21302	4233	...	56376	50400	5976	...
6 Breeding stock, dairy cattle, etc.	...	...	...	...	...	...	...	...
Total Gross Capital Formation	72049	44099	27950	...	158233	105641	52592	...

a) Item 'Increase in stocks' refers to increase in stocks of wool and livestock in the private sector, and to stocks held by the public sector.

2.8 Gross Capital Formation by Type of Good and Owner, in Constant Prices

Million Uruguayan pesos

	1980 TOTAL	1980 Total Private	1980 Public Enterprises	1980 General Government	1981 TOTAL	1981 Total Private	1981 Public Enterprises	1981 General Government	1982 TOTAL	1982 Total Private	1982 Public Enterprises	1982 General Government
At constant prices of: 1978												
Increase in stocks, total [a]	206	206	-	...	-179	-179	-	...	-350	-350	-	...
Gross Fixed Capital Formation, Total	6255	4312	1943	...	6067	4287	1780	...	5165	2680	2485	...
1 Residential buildings	3757	2396	1361	...	3840	2326	1514	...	3638	1945	1693	...
2 Non-residential buildings	...	...	...	...	...	...	...	...	...	...	...	...
3 Other construction	...	...	...	...	...	...	...	...	...	...	...	...
4 Land improvement and plantation and orchard development	91	91	-	...	54	54	-	...	54	54	-	...
5 Producers' durable goods	2407	1825	582	...	2173	1907	266	...	1473	681	792	...
6 Breeding stock, dairy cattle, etc.	...	...	...	...	...	...	...	...	...	...	...	...
Total Gross Capital Formation	6461	4518	1943	...	5888	4108	1780	...	4815	2330	2485	...

Uruguay

2.8 Gross Capital Formation by Type of Good and Owner, in Constant Prices

Million Uruguayan pesos

	1983 TOTAL	1983 Total Private	1983 Public Enterprises	1983 General Government	1984 TOTAL	1984 Total Private	1984 Public Enterprises	1984 General Government	1985 TOTAL	1985 Total Private	1985 Public Enterprises	1985 General Government
	\multicolumn{12}{c}{At constant prices of:1978}
Increase in stocks, total [a]	-419	-419	-	...	102	102	-	...	214	214	-	...
Gross Fixed Capital Formation, Total	3471	2205	1266	...	3009	1699	1310	...	2310	1416	894	...
1 Residential buildings	2412	1453	959	...	2239	1013	1226	...	1537	754	783	...
2 Non-residential buildings	...	...	...	...	...	...	...	...	...	...	...	...
3 Other construction	...	...	...	...	...	...	...	...	...	...	...	...
4 Land improvement and plantation and orchard development	46	46	-	...	41	41	-	...	37	37	-	...
5 Producers' durable goods	1013	706	307	...	729	645	84	...	736	625	111	...
6 Breeding stock, dairy cattle, etc.	...	...	...	...	...	...	...	...	...	...	...	...
Total Gross Capital Formation	3052	1786	1266	...	3111	1801	1310	...	2524	1630	894	...

	1986 TOTAL	1986 Total Private	1986 Public Enterprises	1986 General Government	1987 TOTAL	1987 Total Private	1987 Public Enterprises	1987 General Government
	\multicolumn{8}{c}{At constant prices of:1978}
Increase in stocks, total [a]	11	11	-	...	168	168	-	...
Gross Fixed Capital Formation, Total	2499	1534	965	...	2976	1951	1025	...
1 Residential buildings	1483	684	799	...	1610	728	882	...
2 Non-residential buildings	...	...	...	...	...	...	...	...
3 Other construction	...	...	...	...	...	...	...	...
4 Land improvement and plantation and orchard development	51	51	-	...	67	67	-	...
5 Producers' durable goods	965	799	166	...	1299	1156	143	...
6 Breeding stock, dairy cattle, etc.	...	...	...	...	...	...	...	...
Total Gross Capital Formation	2510	1545	965	...	3144	2119	1025	...

a) Item 'Increase in stocks' refers to increase in stocks of wool and livestock in the private sector, and to stocks held by the public sector.

USSR

Source. Communication from the Central Statistical Office of the USSR, Moscow. The official estimates and descriptions are published annually in 'Narodnoe Khozyaistvo SSSR' (National Economy of the USSR).

General note. The estimates shown in the following tables have been prepared in accordance with the System of Material Product Balances. Therefore, these estimates are not comparable in concept and coverage with those conforming to the United Nations System of National Accounts. It should be noted that the estimates for the USSR include those for the Byelorussian SSR and the Ukrainian SSR. Separate country chapters for those two Republics of the USSR are shown in this Yearbook.

1a Net Material Product by Use at Current Market Prices

Thousand Million USSR roubles

	1970	1975	1978	1979	1980	1981	1982	1983	1984	1985	1986	1987
1 Personal consumption	...	...	...	...	...	...	...	...	...	...	...	...
2 Material consumption in the units of the non-material sphere serving individuals	...	...	...	...	...	...	...	...	...	...	...	...
Consumption of the Population	201.3	266.4	307.9	323.6	345.5	364.9	378.5	393.0	407.2	418.4	427.6	441.9
3 Material consumption in the units of the non-material sphere serving the community as a whole												
4 Net fixed capital formation [ab]	84.2	96.6	112.7	109.3	108.6	113.0	134.4	143.4	151.8	150.3	148.4	143.9
5 Increase in material circulating assets and in stocks [abc]												
6 Losses	...	...	...	...	...	...	...	...	...	...	...	...
7 Exports of goods and material services	...	...	...	...	...	...	...	...	...	...	...	...
8 Less: Imports of goods and material services	...	...	...	...	...	...	...	...	...	...	...	...
Net Material Product	285.5	363.0	420.6	432.9	454.1	477.9	512.9	536.4	559.0	568.7	576.0	585.8

a) Changes in work-in-progress on construction are included in item 'Increase in material circulating assets and in stocks'.
b) Increase in productive livestock and draught animals is included in item 'Net fixed capital formation'.
c) Item 'Increase in material circulating assets and in stocks' includes increase in value of young animals.

2a Net Material Product by Kind of Activity of the Material Sphere in Current Market Prices

Thousand Million USSR roubles

	1970	1975	1978	1979	1980	1981	1982	1983	1984	1985	1986	1987
1 Agriculture and forestry [a]	63.1	61.5	74.4	73.2	68.9	73.1	80.9	111.1	115.7	112.8	121.2	122.6
2 Industrial activity [b]	148.3	191.2	220.4	226.5	238.1	248.0	266.6	253.8	262.1	263.1	258.0	268.6
3 Construction	30.0	41.3	46.2	46.7	47.6	49.0	51.9	53.2	59.4	62.3	70.3	74.7
4 Wholesale and retail trade and restaurants and other eating and drinking places [c]	32.2	46.3	60.1	68.6	80.6	88.5	92.9	97.0	99.6	105.3	101.4	97.1
5 Transport and communication	16.3	23.0	25.2	25.6	27.0	28.1	31.6	33.2	33.7	35.0	36.5	36.6
6 Other activities of the material sphere	...	...	...	...	...	...	...	...	...	...	...	...
Net material product	289.9	363.3	426.3	440.6	462.2	486.7	523.9	548.3	570.5	578.5	587.4	599.6

a) Item 'Agriculture and forestry' refers to agriculture only.
b) Item 'Industrial activity' includes turnover taxes realized in prices on industrial goods.
c) Item 'Wholesale and retail trade, restaurants and other eating and drinking places', refers to trade, procurement and other activities.

2b Net Material Product by Kind of Activity of the Material Sphere in Constant Market Prices

Index numbers

	1970	1975	1978	1979	1980	1981	1982	1983	1984	1985	1986	1987
				At constant prices of:1983								
1 Agriculture and forestry [a]	...	...	...	...	...	98	104	111	107	105	113	111
2 Industrial activity	246	365	118	123	128	132 / 104	107	111	115	120	125	131
3 Construction	176	235	112	113	117	120 / 103	105	110	113	117	131	138
4 Wholesale and retail trade and restaurants and other eating and drinking places [b]	189	256	114	117	121	125 / 104	104	107	111	114	117	117
5 Transport and communication	216	306	114	115	120	125 / 104	107	112	113	116	120	121
6 Other activities of the material sphere	...	...	...	...	...	...	...	...	...	...	...	...
Net material product	199	262	116	119	124	128 / 103	107	112	115	119	124	127

a) Item 'Agriculture and forestry' refers to agriculture only.
b) Item 'Wholesale and retail trade, restaurants and other eating and drinking places', refers to trade, procurement and other activities.

USSR

6b Capital Formation by Kind of Activity of the Material and Non-Material Spheres in Constant Market Prices

Thousand Million USSR roubles

	1970	1975	1978	1979	1980	1981	1982	1983	1984	1985	1986	1987
	\multicolumn{12}{c}{At constant prices of: 1980}
	\multicolumn{12}{c}{Gross Fixed Capital Formation}
1 Agriculture and forestry	16.0	26.1	29.0	29.5	29.8	30.6	31.0	32.0	31.1	31.5	33.5	...
2 Industrial activity	32.5	44.9	51.1	51.2	53.3	55.3	56.8	60.4	62.7	65.5	71.0	...
3 Construction	3.3	4.8	5.7	5.8	6.0	5.9	6.4	6.2	5.8	6.1	6.8	...
4 Wholesale and retail trade and restaurants and other eating and drinking places [a]	...	...	...	...	...	...	...	...	...	...	...	...
5 Transport and communcication	9.0	14.4	18.2	18.1	18.1	18.8	19.8	21.5	22.3	21.9	22.8	...
6 Other activities of the material sphere	...	...	...	...	...	...	...	...	...	...	...	...
Total Material Sphere	...	...	...	...	...	...	...	...	...	...	...	...
7 Housing except owner-occupied, communal and miscellaneous personal services	15.8	19.2	20.7	20.5	21.1	22.5	24.0	25.8	27.3	28.1	30.9	...
8 Education, culture and art [a]	15.6	19.1	21.9	22.5	22.6	23.4	23.9	25.1	25.1	26.4	29.4	...
9 Health and social welfare services and sports [a]												...
Total Non-Material Sphere Serving Individuals	...	...	...	...	...	...	...	...	...	...	...	...
10 Government	...	...	...	...	...	...	...	...	...	...	...	...
11 Finance, credit and insurance	...	...	...	...	...	...	...	...	...	...	...	...
12 Research, scientific and technological institutes	...	...	...	...	...	...	...	...	...	...	...	...
13 Other activities of the non-material sphere	...	...	...	...	...	...	...	...	...	...	...	...
Total Non-Material Sphere Serving the Community as a Whole	...	...	...	...	...	...	...	...	...	...	...	...
14 Owner-occupied dwellings	...	...	...	...	...	...	...	...	...	...	...	...
Total Gross Fixed Capital Formation	92.2	128.5	146.6	147.6	150.9	156.5	161.9	171.0	174.3	179.5	194.4	...

a) Item 'Wholesale and retail trade, restaurants etc.' is included in item 'Education, culture, and art' through 'Health and social welfare services and sports'.

Venezuela

General note. The preparation of national accounts statistics in Venezuela is undertaken by the Banco Central de Venezuela. The official estimates are published annually by the Banco in 'Memorias o Informes Economicas'. A detailed description of the sources and methods used for the national accounts estimation is found in 'Metodologia de las Cuentas Nationales de Venezuela' and in 'Practicas en materia de cuentas' published by the Banco. The estimates are generally in accordance with the classifications and defininitions recommended in the United Nations System of National Accounts (SNA). The following tables have been prepared from successive replies to the United Nations national accounts questionnaire. When the scope and coverage of the estimates differ for conceptual or statistical reasons from the definitions and classifications recommended in SNA, a footnote is indicated to the relevant tables.

Sources and methods:

(a) Gross domestic product. Gross domestic product is estimated mainly through the production approach.

(b) Expenditure on the gross domestic product. The expenditure approach is used to estimate government final consumption expenditure and exports and imports of goods and services. The commodity-flow approach is used for private consumption expenditure and gross fixed capital formation. Increase in stocks is obtained as a residual. The estimates of government final consumption expenditures are based on information obtained from government budgets and financial statements of the government entities. For private consumption expenditure on imported goods, estimates are based on the value of imports f.o.b. Values of locally produced goods are based on the production account of agriculture, manufacturing and the services. Trade margins based on surveys are used to estimate purchasers' values. The information used to estimate gross fixed capital formation include data on construction, manufacturing production, sales of vechiles and livestock and imported capital goods. The data on petroleum and iron-ore exports are obtained from the Ministerio de Energia y Minas while exports of other merchandise are obtained from the Oficina Central de Estadisticas e Informatica. The Corporacion de turismo, the embassies as well as companies engaged in transports, communication and insurance also provide export data. Import data are mainly provided by the Oficina Central de Estadisticas e Informatica. For the constant price estimates, only information for gross fixed capital formation is available. The item is deflated by price indexes constructed separately for construction, machinery and equipment and transport equipment. For other aggregates of this item, the estimates are obtained directly at constant prices.

(c) Cost-structure of the gross domestic product. In estimating the cost structure components of GDP, estimates of compensation of employees, operating surplus and depreciation are obtained for each industry group separately. For agriculture, forestry and fishing, they are estimated as a percentage of the gross value of production based on factore and coefficients from a 1968 study. For the mining sector, information from the Ministerio de Energia e Minas are used for petroleum activity and iron-ore mining. For manufacturing, estimates are based on cost structure data by the Ministerio de Hacienda supplemented by information from public enterprises and petroleum refineries. A survey conducted by the Banco in 1968-70 provides coefficients for the trade sector. Financial statements are used for public enterprises railway transport, communication, financial institutions and insurance. Input coefficients obtained from surveys are used for road transport and private services. Data on indirect taxes and subsidies are obtained from government sources.

(d) Gross domestic product by kind of economic activity. The table of GDP by kind of economic activity at market prices, i.e., producers' values. The production approach is used to estimate the value added of most industries. The income approach is used to estimate producers of government services. domestic services and part of other private services. The information on gross output in the agricultural sector is furnished annually by the Ministerio de Agricultura y Cria on the basis of field survey conducted during the summer (January-April) and the winter(May-December). These surveys give information on cultivated areas and physical production of the principal crops. The value of production is first calculated in constant prices by multiplying the physical production of each item by the respective producers' prices in 1968 and then converting it to current values by using the producers' price index estimated by the Banco. Value added is obtained by applying the cost structure estimated for 1968. For crude petroleum and refinery products, a production account covering all enterprises in the petroleum sector is constructed on the basis of information provided by the Ministerio de Energia y Minas. Crude petroleum is separated from refinery production on the basis of annual survey data. During the period 1968-1975, exports were calculated at official fiscal prices for export as declared by foreign concessionaires while from 1976 onwards, the prices reported by the nationalized enterprises have been used. Value added for the manufacturing industries is estimated by applying to the gross value of production by kind of economic activity the cost structure information on companies. Bench-mark estimates on gross value of manufacturing production have been prepared based on the third industrial survey conducted in 1971. These estimates are extrapolated by the annual changes in the index of industrial production through annual surveys. The Instituto Nacional de Obras Sanitarias provides information on production and cost structure of water supply. For public construction, information is obtained from censuses conducted by the Banco. For private construction requiring permits, estimates are based on construction coefficients per capita which are available for 14 urben centres through a Survey. The estimates for the federal district are calculated independently through a survey and through using information on construction permits. Non-permit construction estimates are agriculture. Bench-mark estimates for each of the activities in the trade sector have been prepared for 1968-1970 by using the results of a national survey conducted by the Banco. Since 1970, over-all estimates are made by extrapolating the total value of production by an index of market sales. Adjustments are made to account for the public enterprises by using their respective financial statements. Value added in the private transport sector is estimated by applying the sample coefficient, obtained through surveys, to the receipts for each type of services. For the public sector, information is obtained directly from concerned enterprises. The value added of the financial institutions is obtained as the difference between the value of production and intermediate consumption. For ownership of dwellings, the value of production is estimated from the total number of occupied dwellings and the annual average rent, adjusted by the rent item in the cost-of-living index. For real estate and business services, the production value is estimated by projecting the annual changes of incomes obtained from surveys. The value added of government services constitutes the renumeration of employees of the various government agencies and the consumption of fixed capital of the administrative organizations. For private services, coefficients of value added obtained from surveys are used. For the constant price estimates, value added of agriculture and mining is extrapolated by quantum indexes. For other industries, current values are deflated by various price indexes.

1.1 Expenditure on the Gross Domestic Product, in Current Prices

Million Venezuelan bolivares

		1970	1975	1978	1979	1980	1981	1982	1983	1984	1985	1986	1987
1	Government final consumption expenditure	6635	15943	24056	27758	35123	42643	42594	41339	43565 43588	48638	54791	72346
2	Private final consumption expenditure	27267	56286	94762	110329	135375	160533	182239	183435	209834 255349	291717	338853	466817
	A Households	...	...	...	...	...	...	...	...	250659	287345	333615	460624
	B Private non-profit institutions serving households	...	...	...	...	...	...	...	...	4690	4372	5238	6193
3	Gross capital formation	15743	36444	72413	65651	62791	65409	75330	34149	51345 64230	79857	99755	174593
	A Increase in stocks	4206	5846	576	98	-1354	-4374	5167	-21197	1751 6855	9371	6021	39027
	B Gross fixed capital formation	11537	30598	71837	65553	64145	69783	70163	55346	49594 57375	70486	93734	135566
	Residential buildings	2503	7045	14406	16238	17228	16272	12354	10209	8095 8700	8975	10538	13975
	Non-residential buildings	3820	8959	23423	22763	20548	23452	27412	24319	18227 20998	23583	29424	41497
	Other construction and land improvement etc.	355	586	710	400	451	707	748	786	437 974	1259	2009	2762
	Other	4859	14008	33298	26152	25918	29352	29649	20032	22835 26703	36669	51763	77332
4	Exports of goods and services	12226	39278	41957	64024	85463	89614	75197	74067	105159 116074	118734	102222	160198
5	Less: Imports of goods and services	9846	29853	64128	60025	64551	72991	84092	42498	62373 69754	74326	101856	154531
	Equals: Gross Domestic Product	52025	118098	169060	207737	254201	285208	291268	290492	347530 409487	464620	493765	719423

Venezuela

1.2 Expenditure on the Gross Domestic Product, in Constant Prices

Million Venezuelan bolivares

	1970	1975	1978	1979	1980	1981	1982	1983	1984	1985	1986	1987
					At constant prices of: 1968				1984			
1 Government final consumption expenditure	...	...	...	...	...	...	...	...	...	...	...	...
2 Private final consumption expenditure	...	...	...	...	...	...	...	...	...	...	...	...
3 Gross capital formation	...	...	...	...	...	...	...	...	...	...	...	...
A Increase in stocks	...	...	...	...	...	...	...	...	...	...	...	...
B Gross fixed capital formation	10949	18929	32610	26074	22290	22959	22102	16280	13209 / 57375	60425	69713	69218
Residential buildings	2450	4127	6053	5980	5403	4669	3290	2552	1830 / 8700	8162	8803	9036
Non-residential buildings	3682	5305	10063	8566	6583	6814	7228	6075	4149 / 20998	21082	24155	25091
Other construction and land improvement etc.	344	346	304	150	143	205	198	197	100 / 974	1132	1647	1688
Other	4473	9151	16190	11378	10161	11271	11386	7456	7130 / 26703	30049	35108	33403
4 Exports of goods and services	...	...	...	...	...	...	...	...	...	...	...	...
5 Less: Imports of goods and services	...	...	...	...	...	...	...	...	...	...	...	...
Equals: Gross Domestic Product	50634	64417	76376	77396	75857	75628	76144	71867	70894 / 409487	414750	443093	456544

1.3 Cost Components of the Gross Domestic Product

Million Venezuelan bolivares

	1970	1975	1978	1979	1980	1981	1982	1983	1984	1985	1986	1987
1 Indirect taxes, net	2836	4572	4544	6649	7996	8416	9776	20387	20395 / 23913	32064	17911	47253
A Indirect taxes	2947	5599	6648	8997	11378	12013	12910	22693	22568 / 44894	51567	57823	65054
B Less: Subsidies	111	1027	2104	2348	3382	3597	3134	2306	2173 / 20981	19503	39912	17801
2 Consumption of fixed capital	4824	7523	12485	14912	17104	19869	21666	24031	26628 / 33643	37220	44664	60192
3 Compensation of employees paid by resident producers to:	21098	45807	75831	86602	105143	119642	124529	123625	128398 / 151020	168801	193580	260752
A Resident households	21001	45731	75831	86602	105143	119642	124529	123578	128334 / 151020	168741	193451	260752
B Rest of the world	97	76	-	-	-	-	-	47	64 / -	60	129	-
4 Operating surplus	23267	60196	76200	99574	123958	137281	135297	122449	172109 / 200911	226535	237610	351226
Equals: Gross Domestic Product	52025	118098	169060	207737	254201	285208	291268	290492	347530 / 409487	464620	493765	719423

1.4 General Government Current Receipts and Disbursements

Million Venezuelan bolivares

	1970	1975	1978	1979	1980	1981	1982	1983	1984	1985	1986	1987
					Receipts							
1 Operating surplus	-63	-143	46	94	88	91	106	94	112	109	...	...
2 Property and entrepreneurial income	3019	9573	12382	11941	14342	18290	21482	26983	29871	28491	...	...
3 Taxes, fees and contributions	9036	36512	33661	51120	72296	80393	68287	66978	110993	98104	...	...
A Indirect taxes	2948	5599	6648	8997	11378	12013	12910	20863	19588	28721	...	...
B Direct taxes	5121	28972	23440	37378	54910	61996	48491	41014	84667	62594	...	...
C Social security contributions	845	1694	2718	3062	4258	4397	4734	4735	4879	5314	...	...
D Compulsory fees, fines and penalties	122	247	855	1683	1750	1987	2152	366	1859	1475	...	...
4 Other current transfers	243	365	11691	14039	13758	17804	17785	16569	18003	22073	...	...
Total Current Receipts of General Government	12235	46307	57780	77194	100484	116578	107660	110624	158979	148777	...	...
					Disbursements							
1 Government final consumption expenditure	6635	15943	24056	27758	35123	42643	42594	41339	43565	48737	...	...

Venezuela

1.4 General Government Current Receipts and Disbursements
(Continued)

Million Venezuelan bolivares

	1970	1975	1978	1979	1980	1981	1982	1983	1984	1985	1986	1987
A Compensation of employees	5745	12894	20054	23579	30030	34851	35171	34421	35788	40083	...	...
B Consumption of fixed capital	26	20	43	42	48	52	51	82	97	132	...	...
C Purchases of goods and services, net	1263	3086	4023	4137	5045	7740	7372	6836	7680	8522	...	...
D Less: Own account fixed capital formation	399	57	64	...	...	...	...	...	...	...	...	...
E Indirect taxes paid, net	...	...	...	...	...	...	...	...	...	...	...	...
2 Property income	205	323	2515	2915	5585	5992	6399	7231	11619	12814	...	...
A Interest	...	...	2515	2915	5585	5992	6399	7231	11619	12814	...	...
B Net land rent and royalties	...	...	...	...	...	...	...	...	...	...	...	...
3 Subsidies	111	1027	2104	2348	3382	3597	3134	2306	2173	1706	...	...
4 Other current transfers	510	1678	12019	13999	17046	20720	23760	27446	37232	43773	...	...
A Social security benefits	158	516	780	905	1298	1584	1783	1759	1864	2055	...	...
B Social assistance grants	184	734	870	710	1081	955	906	2805	3261	3945	...	...
C Other	168	428	10369	12384	14667	18181	21071	22882	32107	37773	...	...
5 Net saving	4774	27336	17086	30174	39348	43626	31773	32302	64390	41747	...	...
Total Current Disbursements and Net Saving of General Government	12235	46307	57780	77194	100484	116578	107660	110624	158979	148777	...	...

1.7 External Transactions on Current Account, Summary

Million Venezuelan bolivares

	1970	1975	1978	1979	1980	1981	1982	1983	1984	1985	1986	1987
Payments to the Rest of the World												
1 Imports of goods and services	9846	29853	64128	60025	64551	72991	84092	42498	62373 / 69754	74326	101856	154531
A Imports of merchandise c.i.f.	8363	25860	53574	47661	50783	56218	62977	33082	49365 / 55332	62896	87487	137459
B Other	1483	3993	10554	12364	13768	16773	21115	9416	13008 / 14422	11430	14369	17072
2 Factor income to the rest of the world	2768	2764	5136	6519	8487	13080	17539	16957	22279 / 28726	30374	32202	39556
A Compensation of employees	97	76	-	-	-	-	-	47	64 / 68	-	-	-
B Property and entrepreneurial income	2671	2688	5136	6519	8487	13080	17539	16910	22215 / 28658	30374	32202	39556
3 Current transfers to the rest of the world	317	659	1746	1746	1879	1750	2738	988	863 / 1284	958	921	2131
A Indirect taxes to supranational organizations	...	...	...	...	...	...	...	...	...	...	...	...
B Other current transfers	317	659	1746	1746	1879	1750	2738	988	863 / 1284	958	921	2131
4 Surplus of the nation on current transactions	-458	9118	-24546	1498	20236	17120	-18186	20720	33389 / 31363	27455	-14566	-15979
Payments to the Rest of the World and Surplus of the Nation on Current Transactions	12473	42394	46464	69788	95153	104941	86183	81163	118904 / 131127	133113	120413	180239
Receipts From The Rest of the World												
1 Exports of goods and services	12226	39278	41957	64024	85463	89614	75197	74067	105159 / 116074	118734	102222	160198

Venezuela

1.7 External Transactions on Current Account, Summary
(Continued)

Million Venezuelan bolivares

	1970	1975	1978	1979	1980	1981	1982	1983	1984	1985	1986	1987
A Exports of merchandise f.o.b.	11616	37724	39265	61461	82497	86374	70738	69078	99871 / 109780	110792	90894	150086
B Other	610	1554	2692	2563	2966	3240	4459	4989	5288 / 6294	7942	11328	10112
2 Factor income from rest of the world	238	3108	4503	5760	9690	15327	10986	7096	13745 / 14785	14379	17646	20041
A Compensation of employees	-	-	-	-	-	-	-	75	50 / -	60	129	-
B Property and entrepreneurial income	238	3108	4503	5760	9690	15327	10986	7021	13695 / 14785	14319	17517	20041
3 Current transfers from rest of the world	9	8	4	4	-	-	-	-	- / 268	-	545	-
Receipts from the Rest of the World on Current Transactions	12473	42394	46464	69788	95153	104941	86183	81163	118904 / 131127	133113	120413	180239

1.10 Gross Domestic Product by Kind of Activity, in Current Prices

Million Venezuelan bolivares

	1970	1975	1978	1979	1980	1981	1982	1983	1984	1985	1986	1987
1 Agriculture, hunting, forestry and fishing	3714	6974	10137	11940	14436	16413	17676	19536	23886 / 21507	26933	32474	42616
2 Mining and quarrying	9293	30486	30430	45507	62188	66944	54389	46922	69662 / 68345	59170	37719	68583
3 Manufacturing	8319	18851	26544	34743	41197	43089	46784	49293	67675 / 78365	96326	113706	158859
4 Electricity, gas and water [a]	845	1407	2124	2499	2579	3977	4900	5398	5773 / 6248	7196	7427	11035
5 Construction	2084	6201	14316	14753	14479	15683	15657	14317	10335 / 18232	20664	24724	34624
6 Wholesale and retail trade, restaurants and hotels	5625	11205	17461	19192	20834	23245	25704	33339	38292 / 57692	73914	91075	131542
7 Transport, storage and communication	5458	11063	21923	23452	25184	30769	35631	33266	37725 / 24142	29169	36232	49132
8 Finance, insurance, real estate and business services	7536	15014	23331	27386	37883	46277	49953	51820	57999 / 59154	62338	69985	88083
9 Community, social and personal services	2209	4781	7480	8160	9579	10981	11166	11421	13197 / 28123	31769	37693	50153
Total, Industries	45083	105982	153746	187632	228359	257378	261860	265312	324544 / 361808	407479	451035	634627
Producers of Government Services	5771	12914	20097	23621	30078	34903	35222	34503	35885 / 35482	39868	44054	55858
Other Producers	645	1238	1725	2108	2499	2966	3187	3777	3994 / 4868	5354	6263	7446
Subtotal	51499	120134	175568	213361	260936	295247	300269	303592	364423 / 402158	452701	501352	697931
Less: Imputed bank service charge	1065	5098	9857	10693	13104	16378	15879	16101	19916 / 11384	11821	14066	17836
Plus: Import duties	1591	3062	3349	5069	6369	6339	6878	3001	3023 / 4465	6292	8837	15720
Plus: Value added tax	...	...	...	...	...	...	...	...	... / ...	...	...	...
Plus: Other adjustments	...	...	...	...	...	...	...	...	... / 14248	17448	-2358	23608
Equals: Gross Domestic Product	52025	118098	169060	207737	254201	285208	291268	290492	347530 / 409487	464620	493765	719423

a) Item 'Electricity, gas and water' excludes gas.

Venezuela

1.11 Gross Domestic Product by Kind of Activity, in Constant Prices

Million Venezuelan bolivares

	1970	1975	1978	1979	1980	1981	1982	1983	1984	1985	1986	1987
	\multicolumn{8}{c}{At constant prices of: 1968}	\multicolumn{4}{c}{1984}
1 Agriculture, hunting, forestry and fishing	3544	4236	4545	4677	4765	4676	4843	4863	4901 / 21507	23299	25224	26259
2 Mining and quarrying	9780	6594	6004	6526	6103	5948	5340	5002	5098 / 68345	64649	69595	71246
3 Manufacturing	8264	10634	12899	13324	13660	13322	13863	13626	14247 / 78365	82219	87969	90207
4 Electricity, gas and water [a]	859	1483	1674	1933	1950	2256	2533	2635	2634 / 6248	6596	6860	6746
5 Construction	2015	3661	6115	5519	4609	4511	4131	3583	2350 / 18232	18532	20346	21228
6 Wholesale and retail trade, restaurants and hotels	5416	7364	8655	8211	6907	6724	6897	7012	6643 / 57692	58771	64051	65875
7 Transport, storage and communication	5223	7664	10368	9851	9805	10155	10508	9080	8806 / 24142	26558	29046	31659
8 Finance, insurance, real estate and business services	7226[b]	11739[b]	14245[b]	14504[b]	14023[b]	15133[b]	14645[b]	14600[b]	15660[b] / 59154	58101	61229	67790
9 Community, social and personal services	2134	3756	4778	4757	4872	4848	4492	4226	4330 / 28123	30247	33302	34445
Total, Industries	44461	57131	69283	69302	66694	67573	67252	64627	64669 / 361808	368972	397622	415455
Producers of Government Services	5082	7850	9431	10073	10498	10586	10593	10399	10357 / 35482	35450	35301	35726
Other Producers	619	822	806	826	835	847	863	861	843 / 4868	4891	5071	5256
Subtotal	50162	65803	79520	80201	78027	79006	78708	75887	75869 / 402158	409313	437994	456437
Less: Imputed bank service charge	1040	3287	4848	5203	4777	5697	4910	4904	5637 / 11384	10785	12478	16116
Plus: Import duties	1512	1901	1704	2398	2607	2319	2346	884	662 / 4465	4418	4428	4578
Plus: Value added tax	...	...	...	...	...	...	...	...	...	...	...	...
Plus: Other adjustments	...	...	...	...	...	...	...	...	... / 14248	11804	13149	11645
Equals: Gross Domestic Product	50634	64417	76376	77396	75857	75628	76144	71867	70894 / 409487	414750	443093	456544

a) Item 'Electricity, gas and water' excludes gas.
b) Item 'Finance, insurance, real estate and business services' includes the imputation applied to the financial intermediaries.

1.12 Relations Among National Accounting Aggregates

Million Venezuelan bolivares

	1970	1975	1978	1979	1980	1981	1982	1983	1984	1985	1986	1987
Gross Domestic Product	52025	118098	169060	207737	254201	285208	291268	290492	347530 / 409487	464620	493765	719423
Plus: Net factor income from the rest of the world	-2530	344	-633	-759	1203	2247	-6553	-9861	-8534 / -13941	-15995	-14556	-19515
Factor income from the rest of the world	238	3108	4503	5760	9690	15327	10986	7096	13745 / 14785	14379	17646	20041
Less: Factor income to the rest of the world	2768	2764	5136	6519	8487	13080	17539	16957	22279 / 28726	30374	32202	39556
Equals: Gross National Product	49495	118442	168427	206978	255404	287455	284715	280631	338996 / 395546	448625	479209	699908
Less: Consumption of fixed capital	4824	7523	12485	14912	17104	19869	21666	24031	26628 / 33643	37220	44664	60192

Venezuela

1.12 Relations Among National Accounting Aggregates
(Continued)

Million Venezuelan bolivares

	1970	1975	1978	1979	1980	1981	1982	1983	1984	1985	1986	1987
Equals: National Income	44671	110919	155942	192066	238300	267586	263049	256600	312368 361903	411405	434545	639716
Plus: Net current transfers from the rest of the world	-308	-651	-1742	-1742	-1879	-1750	-2738	-988	-863 -1016	-958	-376	-2131
Current transfers from the rest of the world	9	8	4	4	-	-	-	-	- 268	-	545	-
Less: Current transfers to the rest of the world	317	659	1746	1746	1879	1750	2738	988	863 1284	958	921	2131
Equals: National Disposable Income	44363	110268	154200	190324	236421	265836	260311	255612	311505 360887	410447	434169	637585
Less: Final consumption	33902	72229	118818	138087	170498	203176	224833	224774	253399 298937	340355	393644	539163
Equals: Net Saving	10461	38039	35382	52237	65923	62660	35478	30838	58106 61950	70092	40525	98422
Less: Surplus of the nation on current transactions	-458	9118	-24546	1498	20236	17120	-18186	20720	33389 31363	27455	-14566	-15979
Equals: Net Capital Formation	10919	28921	59928	50739	45687	45540	53664	10118	24717 30587	42637	55091	114401

2.1 Government Final Consumption Expenditure by Function, in Current Prices

Million Venezuelan bolivares

		1970	1975	1978	1979	1980	1981	1982	1983	1984	1985	1986	1987
1	General public services	1271	3312	5971	6871	9469	9524	8316	8373	7277 3510	4047	4424	...
2	Defence	938	2259	2583	3023	3240	3905	4903	4220	6033 5200	5227	5287	...
3	Public order and safety	...	...	...	...	...	...	...	...	... 4101	4795	5343	...
4	Education	1879	4777	7494	8563	11449	13239	14068	13482	15381 15575	16773	18603	...
5	Health	1300	2154	3306	3370	3925	5397	5484	7244	7416 7403	8832	10717	...
6	Social security and welfare	426	1215	1772	2029	2605	4371	4322	2466	3190 2997	3791	4122	...
7	Housing and community amenities	195	372	320	399	737	1078	1162	1116	1267 1491	1643	1807	...
8	Recreational, cultural and religious affairs	62	189	386	343	662	791	988	964	705 782	883	1034	...
9	Economic services	564	1665	2224	3160	3036	4163	3351	3474	2296 2484	2612	3404	...
	A Fuel and energy	...	...	...	...	...	...	...	...	... 53	68	72	...
	B Agriculture, forestry, fishing and hunting	...	...	...	...	...	...	...	...	... 862	940	1032	...
	C Mining, manufacturing and construction, except fuel and energy	...	...	...	...	...	...	...	...	... 140	141	164	...
	D Transportation and communication	...	...	...	...	...	...	...	...	... 804	758	1210	...
	E Other economic affairs	...	...	...	...	...	...	...	...	... 625	705	926	...
10	Other functions	...	...	...	...	...	175	-	-	- 45	35	50	...
	Total Government Final Consumption Expenditure	6635	15943	24056	27758	35123	42643	42594	41339	43565 43588	48638	54791	...

2.5 Private Final Consumption Expenditure by Type and Purpose, in Current Prices

Million Venezuelan bolivares

		1970	1975	1978	1979	1980	1981	1982	1983	1984	1985	1986	1987
	Final Consumption Expenditure of Resident Households												
1	Food, beverages and tobacco	10744	22713	37281	45983	59004	74727	85767	97157	111230 79080	94600	109684	153353
	A Food	...	...	...	...	...	...	60004	69953	82572 60678	72090	83166	117978
	B Non-alcoholic beverages	...	...	...	...	...	...	5342	3533	4036 14604a	17005	20882	29050
	C Alcoholic beverages	...	...	...	...	...	...	17777	20660	21999 ...			
	D Tobacco	...	...	...	...	...	...	2644	3011	2623 3798	5505	5636	6325

1651

Venezuela

2.5 Private Final Consumption Expenditure by Type and Purpose, in Current Prices
(Continued)

Million Venezuelan bolivares

	1970	1975	1978	1979	1980	1981	1982	1983	1984	1985	1986	1987
2 Clothing and footwear	1898	4444	6301	7198	7467	7758	8379	7596	8275 / 20457	22223	25971	34380
3 Gross rent, fuel and power	2985	4690	5894	7194	11178	14107	15996	17665	18569 / 31000	32694	34844	40358
4 Furniture, furnishings and household equipment and operation	2173	5252	7877	8729	9660	9318	10090	8302	10293 / 24860	30618	35346	55241
5 Medical care and health expenses	1260	2377	3447	3861	4917	5326	5864	7595	8880 / 14827	17332	21150	26980
6 Transport and communication	3863	7206	12403	13804	14413	17197	21255	20138	21595 / 27982	35136	43774	68294
7 Recreational, entertainment, education and cultural services	2315	4994	9057	9724	12763	12955	13170	10246	11908 / 18456	22263	25064	30296
8 Miscellaneous goods and services	1456	3366	6176	6811	8072	9138	9661	7949	9403 / 25693	30573	36394	50338
Total Final Consumption Expenditure in the Domestic Market by Households, of which	26694	55042	88436	103304	127474	150526	170182	176648	200153 / 242355	285439	332227	459240
A Durable goods	2152	4938	9572	9911	10970	11122	11322	6437	6831 / 12933	17528	21907	34310
B Semi-durable goods	3073	7077	11816	13172	14948	15738	17288	15055	17284 / 40672	46706	55402	80439
C Non-durable goods	13144	27723	43317	52954	67990	84226	97951	109663	126327 / 99966	118736	137219	196632
D Services	8325	15304	23731	27267	33566	39440	43621	45493	49711 / 88784	102469	117699	147859
Plus: Direct purchases abroad by resident households	616	1609	6613	7092	8046	9651	12052	8592	13001 / 13001	7651	10099	10108
Less: Direct purchases in the domestic market by non-resident households	246	819	963	873	1168	920	1482	3302	4697 / 4697	5745	8711	8724
Equals: Final Consumption Expenditure of Resident Households	27064	55832	94086	109523	134352	159257	180752	181938	208457 / 250659	287345	333615	460624

Final Consumption Expenditure of Private Non-profit Institutions Serving Households

	1970	1975	1978	1979	1980	1981	1982	1983	1984	1985	1986	1987
Equals: Final Consumption Expenditure of Private Non-profit Organisations Serving Households	203	454	676	806	1023	1276	1487	1497	1377 / 4690	4372	5238	6193
Private Final Consumption Expenditure	27267	56286	94762	110329	135375	160533	182239	183435	209834 / 255349	291717	338853	466817

a) Including item 'Alcoholic beverages'.

2.11 Gross Fixed Capital Formation by Kind of Activity of Owner, ISIC Divisions, in Current Prices

Million Venezuelan bolivares

	1970	1975	1978	1979	1980	1981	1982	1983	1984	1985	1986	1987
					All Producers							
1 Agriculture, hunting, forestry and fishing	767	1862	1958	1863	2091	2651	2131	1270	1794	3357	...	...
2 Mining and quarrying	1478	1296	4099	6194	9116	12338	15645	12344	9589	10044	...	...
3 Manufacturing a	1588	4052	5624	3148	4262	2843	2642	903	913	1869	...	...
4 Electricity, gas and water	387	2196	7575	7789	6301	10495	14355	12434	7876	8764	...	...
5 Construction b	...	...	...	...	...	...	...	...	...	...	...	...
6 Wholesale and retail trade, restaurants and hotels a	628	1311	125	65	120	65	14	30	56	-14	...	...
7 Transport, storage and communication	447	1523	4690	6897	5455	5747	6352	6124	4450	6606		
8 Finance, insurance, real estate and business services c	323	726	2285	2889	2633	4023	4410	4242	3413	4865		
9 Community, social and personal services bc	4292	12666	36706	30692	26616	20874	14609	5970	14754	12417	...	...
Total Industries	9910	25632	63062	59537	56594	59036	60158	43317	42845	47908	...	...
Producers of Government Services	1448	4618	8263	5434	6806	9816	8911	10935	5562	8237		
Private Non-Profit Institutions Serving Households	179	348	512	582	745	931	1094	1094	1187	1325		
Total	11537	30598	71837	65553	64145	69783	70163	55346	49594	57470		

a) Beginning 1977, items 'Manufacturing', 'Wholesale and retail trade', 'Restaurant and hotels', refer only to gross fixed public investment.
b) Item 'Construction' is included in item 'Community, social and personal services'.
c) Business services and real estate except dwellings are included in item 'Community, social and personal services'.

Venezuela

2.12 Gross Fixed Capital Formation by Kind of Activity of Owner, ISIC Divisions, in Constant Prices

Million Venezuelan bolivares

	1970	1975	1978	1979	1980	1981	1982	1983	1984	1985	1986	1987
\multicolumn{13}{c}{At constant prices of: 1968}
\multicolumn{13}{c}{All Producers}
1 Agriculture, hunting, forestry and fishing	728	1152	889	741	727	872	671	365	478	827	...	...
2 Mining and quarrying	1402	802	1860	2464	3168	4059	4928	3542	2553	2475	...	...
3 Manufacturing a	1507	2507	2553	1252	1481	935	832	259	243	461	...	...
4 Electricity, gas and water	368	1359	3439	3099	2189	3453	4522	3569	2098	2160	...	...
5 Construction b	...	...	...	...	...	...	...	...	...	...	...	...
6 Wholesale and retail trade, restaurants and hotels a	596	811	57	26	42	21	4	9	15	-3	...	...
7 Transport, storage and communication	424	942	2129	2743	1895	1891	2001	1757	1185	1628	...	...
8 Finance, insurance, real estate and business services c	307	449	1038	1148	915	1324	1389	1217	909	1199	...	...
9 Community, social and personal services bc	4073	7835	16662	12208	9249	6868	4602	2110	3931	3062	...	...
Total Industries	9405	15857	28627	23681	19666	19423	18949	12828	11412	11809	...	...
Producers of Government Services	1374	2857	3751	2161	2365	3230	2808	3138	1481	2030	...	...
Private Non-Profit Institutions Serving Households	170	215	232	232	259	306	345	314	316	327	...	...
Total	10949	18929	32610	26074	22290	22959	22102	16280	13209	14166	...	...

a) Beginning 1977, items 'Manufacturing', 'Wholesale and retail trade', 'Restaurant and hotels', refer only to gross fixed public investment.
b) Item 'Construction' is included in item 'Community, social and personal services'.
c) Business services and real estate except dwellings are included in item 'Community, social and personal services'.

2.17 Exports and Imports of Goods and Services, Detail

Million Venezuelan bolivares

	1970	1975	1978	1979	1980	1981	1982	1983	1984	1985	1986	1987
\multicolumn{13}{c}{Exports of Goods and Services}
1 Exports of merchandise, f.o.b.	11616	37724	39265	61461	82497	86374	70738	69078	99871 / 109780	110792	90894	150086
2 Transport and communication	251	528	1232	1140	1181	1571	1885	2246	2748 / 3240	4169	5912	5170
A In respect of merchandise imports	97	301	295	271	137	180	364	439	914 / 1572	1879	2228	-
B Other	154	227	937	869	1044	1391	1521	1807	1834 / 1668	2290	3684	5170
3 Insurance service charges	88	90	206	332	463	364	869	280	57 / 384	127	356	199
A In respect of merchandise imports	9	27	26	24	56	43	167	23	13 / 7	-	-	-
B Other	79	63	180	308	407	321	702	257	44 / 377	127	356	199
4 Other commodities	25	117	291	218	154	385	223	1012	227 / 7	255	327	-
5 Adjustments of merchandise exports to change-of-ownership basis	-	-	-	-	-	-	-	-	- / -	-	-	-
6 Direct purchases in the domestic market by non-residential households	246	819	963	873	1040	800	1323	1451	2256 / 2663	3391	4733	4743
7 Direct purchases in the domestic market by extraterritorial bodies	-	-	-	-	128	120	159	-	-	-	-	-
Total Exports of Goods and Services	12226	39278	41957	64024	85463	89614	75197	74067	105159 / 116074	118734	102222	160198
\multicolumn{13}{c}{Imports of Goods and Services}
1 Imports of merchandise, c.i.f.	8363	25860	53574	47661	50783	56218	62977	33082	49365 / 55332	62896	87487	137459
A Imports of merchandise, f.o.b.	7537	22941	48082	42817	46554	51887	58180	29997	45767 / 49834	56422	77971	125443
B Transport of services on merchandise imports	761	2682	5046	4452	4163	4295	4664	3047	3573 / 5464	6444	9496	12016
By residents	...	...	...	...	...	...	...	...	... / 1572	1879	2228	-
By non-residents	761	2682	5046	4452	4163	4295	4664	3047	3573 / 3892	4565	7268	12016
C Insurance service charges on merchandise imports	65	237	446	392	66	36	133	38	25 / 34	30	20	-

Venezuela

2.17 Exports and Imports of Goods and Services, Detail
(Continued)

Million Venezuelan bolivares

	1970	1975	1978	1979	1980	1981	1982	1983	1984	1985	1986	1987
By residents	...	...	...	...	...	...	...	...	7	-	-	-
By non-residents	65	237	446	392	66	36	133	38	25 / 27	30	20	-
2 Adjustments of merchandise imports to change-of-ownership basis									-			
3 Other transport and communication	220	340	1164	1378	1968	2375	1730	1268	3674 / 4441	3451	3763	4346
4 Other insurance service charges	119	92	217	325	449	501	1041	191	164 / 453	180	347	397
5 Other commodities	436	1704	1948	2927	2582	3570	5247	2724	2275 / 2018	2874	4367	5966
6 Direct purchases abroad by government	92	248	612	642	723	676	1045	805	624 / 680	793	812	1108
7 Direct purchases abroad by resident households	616	1609	6613	7092	8046	9651	12052	4428	6271 / 6830	4132	5080	5255
Total Imports of Goods and Services	9846	29853	64128	60025	64551	72991	84092	42498	62373 / 69754	74326	101856	154531
Balance of Goods and Services	2380	9425	-22171	3999	20912	16623	-8895	31569	42786 / 46320	44408	366	5667
Total Imports and Balance of Goods and Services	12226	39278	41957	64024	85463	89614	75197	74067	105159 / 116074	118734	102222	160198

4.1 Derivation of Value Added by Kind of Activity, in Current Prices

Million Venezuelan bolivares

	1984 Gross Output	1984 Intermediate Consumption	1984 Value Added	1985 Gross Output	1985 Intermediate Consumption	1985 Value Added	1986 Gross Output	1986 Intermediate Consumption	1986 Value Added	1987 Gross Output	1987 Intermediate Consumption	1987 Value Added
All Producers												
1 Agriculture, hunting, forestry and fishing	31101	9594	21507	38706	11773	26933	46966	14492	32474	60896	18280	42616
A Agriculture and hunting [a]	29263	9395	19868	36101	11476	24625	43263	14074	29189	55226	17665	37561
B Forestry and logging	231	34	197	282	45	237	420	60	360	726	94	632
C Fishing	1607	165	1442	2323	252	2071	3283	358	2925	4944	521	4423
2 Mining and quarrying	76000	7655	68345	65926	6756	59170	49650	11931	37719	88013	19430	68583
A Coal mining	4	1	3	4	1	3	7	1	6	6	1	5
B Crude petroleum and natural gas production	73429	7003	66426	62970	5902	57068	45215	10713	34502	80029	17025	63004
C Metal ore mining	1396	378	1018	1880	574	1306	3075	880	2195	6383	1931	4452
D Other mining	1171	273	898	1072	279	793	1353	337	1016	1595	473	1122
3 Manufacturing	223312	144947	78365	268391	172065	96326	320045	206339	113706	460451	301592	158859
A Manufacture of food, beverages and tobacco	59035	43311	15724	70047	49215	20832	83495	58858	24637	108351	76678	31673
B Textile, wearing apparel and leather industries	20207	14371	5836	24284	16626	7658	28855	19725	9130	41455	28298	13157
C Manufacture of wood and wood products, including furniture	4745	3223	1522	5301	3477	1824	6670	4347	2323	9188	6013	3175
D Manufacture of paper and paper products, printing and publishing	11193	7539	3654	12657	8121	4536	14798	9455	5343	22356	14273	8083
E Manufacture of chemicals and chemical petroleum, coal, rubber and plastic products	70800	39182	31618	88878	48327	40551	97196	54846	42350	150978	87904	63074
F Manufacture of non-metallic mineral products, except products of petroleum and coal	7273	4153	3120	7984	4903	3081	10677	6522	4155	14641	8932	5709
G Basic metal industries	18769	10365	8404	22302	14921	7381	30138	18054	12084	40864	27510	13354
H Manufacture of fabricated metal products, machinery and equipment	29945	21816	8129	35458	25478	9980	46413	33325	13088	69815	49971	19844
I Other manufacturing industries	1345	987	358	1480	997	483	1803	1207	596	2803	2013	790
4 Electricity, gas and water	8904	2656	6248	10537	3341	7196	11191	3764	7427	15681	4646	11035
A Electricity, gas and steam [b]	7714	2433	5281	9396	2983	6413	9906	3296	6610	14223	4115	10108
B Water works and supply	1190	223	967	1141	358	783	1285	468	817	1458	531	927

Venezuela

4.1 Derivation of Value Added by Kind of Activity, in Current Prices
(Continued)

Million Venezuelan bolivares

		1984			1985			1986			1987		
		Gross Output	Intermediate Consumption	Value Added	Gross Output	Intermediate Consumption	Value Added	Gross Output	Intermediate Consumption	Value Added	Gross Output	Intermediate Consumption	Value Added
5	Construction	29002	10770	18232	32774	12110	20664	40042	15318	24724	55411	20787	34624
6	Wholesale and retail trade, restaurants and hotels	91945	34253	57692	111749	37835	73914	138265	47190	91075	197436	65894	131542
	A Wholesale and retail trade	75820	24429	51391	91600	25606	65994	113105	32045	81060	165837	47006	118831
	B Restaurants and hotels	16125	9824	6301	20149	12229	7920	25160	15145	10015	31599	18888	12711
	Restaurants	12044	7618	4426	15017	9491	5526	17711	11211	6500	20460	12989	7471
	Hotels and other lodging places	4081	2206	1875	5132	2738	2394	7449	3934	3515	11139	5899	5240
7	Transport, storage and communication	40475	16333	24142	50443	21274	29169	62987	26755	36232	86439	37307	49132
	A Transport and storage	35502	15875	19627	44391	20560	23831	55335	25766	29569	77058	35551	41507
	B Communication	4973	458	4515	6052	714	5338	7652	989	6663	9381	1756	7625
8	Finance, insurance, real estate and business services	73617	14463	59154	79352	17014	62338	90384	20399	69985	115034	26951	88083
	A Financial institutions	16018	3872	12146	17101	4608	12493	19855	5551	14304	28002	7823	20179
	B Insurance	3898	2250	1648	4846	2863	1983	5105	3193	1912	7074	4659	2415
	C Real estate and business services	53701	8341	45360	57405	9543	47862	65424	11655	53769	79958	14469	65489
9	Community, social and personal services	42066	13943	28123	48297	16528	31769	56727	19034	37693	76344	26191	50153
	A Sanitary and similar services	1514	664	850	1842	939	903	1769	1060	709	2189	1238	951
	B Social and related community services c	20364	4710	15654	23041	5190	17851	27700	6687	21013	34535	8278	26257
	Educational services	7806	1749	6057	8982	2430	6552	10197	3216	6981	12614	3979	8635
	Medical, dental, other health and veterinary services	12293	2842	9451	13798	2643	11155	17166	3345	13821	21503	4142	17361
	C Recreational and cultural services	5021	1620	3401	5943	1803	4140	6680	1930	4750	8640	2425	6215
	D Personal and household services	15167	6949	8218	17471	8596	8875	20578	9357	11221	30980	14250	16730
Total, Industries		616422	254614	361808	706175	298696	407479	816257	365222	451035	1155705	521078	634627
Producers of Government Services		44371	8889	35482	49566	9698	39868	55716	11662	44054	73377	17519	55858
Other Producers		7186	2318	4868	7727	2373	5354	8956	2693	6263	10626	3180	7446
Total		667979	265821	402158	763468	310767	452701	880929	379577	501352	1239708	541777	697931
Less: Imputed bank service charge		...	-11384	11384	...	-11821	11821	...	-14066	14066	...	-17836	17836
Import duties		4465	...	4465	6292	...	6292	8837	...	8837	15720	...	15720
Value added tax		...	...	...	...	...	...	...	...	...	...	...	...
Other adjustments		14248	...	14248	17448	...	17448	-2358	...	-2358	23608	...	23608
Total		686692	277205	409487	787208	322588	464620	887408	393643	493765	1279036	559613	719423

a) Item 'Agriculture and hunting' includes agricultural products and improvements and other non-agricultural products.
b) Item 'Electricity, gas and water' excludes gas.
c) Social and related community services includes in addition to Educational and health services (item 33 and 34) also the services of commercial and professional associations.

4.2 Derivation of Value Added by Kind of Activity, in Constant Prices

Million Venezuelan bolivares

		1984			1985			1986			1987		
		Gross Output	Intermediate Consumption	Value Added	Gross Output	Intermediate Consumption	Value Added	Gross Output	Intermediate Consumption	Value Added	Gross Output	Intermediate Consumption	Value Added

At constant prices of: 1984

All Producers

1	Agriculture, hunting, forestry and fishing	...	...	21507	...	...	23299	...	...	25224	...	...	26259
	A Agriculture and hunting a	...	...	19868	...	...	21349	...	...	22926	...	...	23641
	B Forestry and logging	...	...	197	...	...	273	...	...	370	...	...	484
	C Fishing	...	...	1442	...	...	1677	...	...	1928	...	...	2134
2	Mining and quarrying	...	...	68345	...	...	64649	...	...	69595	...	...	71246
	A Coal mining	...	...	3	...	...	2	...	...	3	...	...	3
	B Crude petroleum and natural gas production	...	...	66426	...	...	62553	...	...	67110	...	...	68558
	C Metal ore mining	...	...	1018	...	...	1209	...	...	1404	...	...	1709
	D Other mining	...	...	898	...	...	885	...	...	1078	...	...	976

Venezuela

4.2 Derivation of Value Added by Kind of Activity, in Constant Prices
(Continued)

Million Venezuelan bolivares

	1984 Gross Output	1984 Intermediate Consumption	1984 Value Added	1985 Gross Output	1985 Intermediate Consumption	1985 Value Added	1986 Gross Output	1986 Intermediate Consumption	1986 Value Added	1987 Gross Output	1987 Intermediate Consumption	1987 Value Added
			At constant prices of:1984									
3 Manufacturing	...	...	78365	...	...	82219	...	...	87969	...	...	90207
A Manufacture of food, beverages and tobacco	...	...	15724	...	...	15074	...	...	15684	...	...	16264
B Textile, wearing apparel and leather industries	...	...	5836	...	...	6334	...	...	6925	...	...	6952
C Manufacture of wood and wood products, including furniture	...	...	1522	...	...	1527	...	...	1765	...	...	1687
D Manufacture of paper and paper products, printing and publishing	...	...	3654	...	...	3475	...	...	3808	...	...	4141
E Manufacture of chemicals and chemical petroleum, coal, rubber and plastic products	...	...	31618	...	...	34208	...	...	35652	...	...	36745
F Manufacture of non-metallic mineral products, except products of petroleum and coal	...	...	3120	...	...	3212	...	...	3883	...	...	3754
G Basic metal industries	...	...	8404	...	...	9138	...	...	9914	...	...	10926
H Manufacture of fabricated metal products, machinery and equipment	...	...	8129	...	...	8873	...	...	9935	...	...	9386
I Other manufacturing industries	...	...	358	...	...	378	...	...	403	...	...	352
4 Electricity, gas and water	...	...	6248	...	...	6596	...	...	6860	...	...	6746
A Electricity, gas and steam [b]	...	...	5281	...	...	5652	...	...	5843	...	...	5664
B Water works and supply	...	...	967	...	...	944	...	...	1017	...	...	1082
5 Construction	...	...	18232	...	...	18532	...	...	20346	...	...	21228
6 Wholesale and retail trade, restaurants and hotels	...	...	57692	...	...	58771	...	...	64051	...	...	65875
A Wholesale and retail trade	...	...	51391	...	...	51620	...	...	55877	...	...	57194
B Restaurants and hotels	...	...	6301	...	...	7151	...	...	8174	...	...	8681
Restaurants	...	...	4426	...	...	4921	...	...	5237	...	...	5121
Hotels and other lodging places	...	...	1875	...	...	2230	...	...	2937	...	...	3560
7 Transport, storage and communication	...	...	24142	...	...	26558	...	...	29046	...	...	31659
A Transport and storage	...	...	19627	...	...	21749	...	...	23890	...	...	25957
B Communication	...	...	4515	...	...	4809	...	...	5156	...	...	5702
8 Finance, insurance, real estate and business services	...	...	59154	...	...	58101	...	...	61229	...	...	67790
A Financial institutions	...	...	12146	...	...	11420	...	...	12672	...	...	17333
B Insurance	...	...	1648	...	...	1790	...	...	1657	...	...	1667
C Real estate and business services	...	...	45360	...	...	44891	...	...	46900	...	...	48790
9 Community, social and personal services	...	...	28123	...	...	30247	...	...	33302	...	...	34445
A Sanitary and similar services	...	...	850	...	...	830	...	...	603	...	...	691
B Social and related community services [c]	...	...	15654	...	...	17219	...	...	19122	...	...	19379
Educational services	...	...	6057	...	...	6884	...	...	7579	...	...	7655
Medical, dental, other health and veterinary services	...	...	9451	...	...	10198	...	...	11374	...	...	11534
C Recreational and cultural services	...	...	3401	...	...	3840	...	...	3881	...	...	3974
D Personal and household services	...	...	8218	...	...	8358	...	...	9696	...	...	10401
Total, Industries	...	...	361808	...	...	368972	...	...	397622	...	...	415455
Producers of Government Services	...	...	35482	...	...	35450	...	...	35301	...	...	35726
Other Producers	...	...	4868	...	...	4891	...	...	5071	...	...	5256
Total	...	...	402158	...	...	409313	...	...	437994	...	...	456437
Less: Imputed bank service charge	...	...	11384	...	...	10785	...	...	12478	...	...	16116
Import duties	...	...	4465	...	...	4418	...	...	4428	...	...	4578
Value added tax	...	...	...	...	...	...	...	...	...	...	...	...
Other adjustments	...	...	14248	...	...	11804	...	...	13149	...	...	11645
Total	...	...	409487	...	...	414750	...	...	443093	...	...	456544

a) Item 'Agriculture and hunting' includes agricultural products and improvements and other non-agricultural products.
b) Item 'Electricity, gas and water' excludes gas.
c) Social and related community services includes in addition to Educational and health services (item 33 and 34) also the services of commercial and professional associations.

Venezuela

4.3 Cost Components of Value Added

Million Venezuelan bolivares

		1984					1985				
	Compensation of Employees	Capital Consumption	Net Operating Surplus	Indirect Taxes	Less: Subsidies Received	Value Added	Compensation of Employees	Capital Consumption	Net Operating Surplus	Indirect Taxes	Less: Subsidies Received	Value Added

All Producers

	Comp.	Cap. Cons.	Net Op. Surp.	Ind. Tax	Subsidies	VA	Comp.	Cap. Cons.	Net Op. Surp.	Ind. Tax	Subsidies	VA
1 Agriculture, hunting, forestry and fishing	5166	1893	14977	...	529	21507	6458	2411	18223	...	159	26933
A Agriculture and hunting [a]	4640	1822	13935	...	529	19868	5716	2306	16762	...	159	24625
B Forestry and logging	31	9	157	...	...	197	39	11	187	...	...	237
C Fishing	495	62	885	...	...	1442	703	94	1274	...	...	2071
2 Mining and quarrying	5356	3280	59553	156	...	68345	7066	3522	48304	278	...	59170
A Coal mining	3	...	...	...	...	3	3	...	...	...	...	3
B Crude petroleum and natural gas production	4747	3072	58456	151	...	66426	6444	3309	47046	269	...	57068
C Metal ore mining	401	98	516	3	...	1018	432	106	762	6	...	1306
D Other mining	205	110	581	2	...	898	187	107	496	3	...	793
3 Manufacturing	28403	7304	39316	5256	1914	78365	32552	7723	50610	7571	2130	96326
A Manufacture of food, beverages and tobacco	6231	1407	5614	3361	889	15724	6987	1516	7482	5292	445	20832
B Textile, wearing apparel and leather industries	3646	356	1790	44	...	5836	4353	471	2765	80	11	7658
C Manufacture of wood and wood products, including furniture	854	120	534	14	...	1522	962	128	713	21	...	1824
D Manufacture of paper and paper products, printing and publishing	2063	312	1253	34	8	3654	2264	336	1889	59	12	4536
E Manufacture of chemicals and chemical petroleum, coal, rubber and plastic products	6365	2052	22101	1650	550	31618	7627	2170	29326	1892	464	40551
F Manufacture of non-metallic mineral products, except products of petroleum and coal	1652	550	897	30	9	3120	1766	513	813	39	50	3081
G Basic metal industries	2737	1625	4439	16	413	8404	3263	1514	3711	24	1131	7381
H Manufacture of fabricated metal products, machinery and equipment	4628	856	2589	101	45	8129	5072	1040	3730	155	17	9980
I Other manufacturing industries	227	26	99	6	...	358	258	35	181	9	...	483
4 Electricity, gas and water	2521	1179	2277	271	...	6248	2602	1407	2848	339	...	7196
A Electricity, gas and steam [b]	1747	1155	2108	271	...	5281	1818	1362	2894	339	...	6413
B Water works and supply	774	24	169	...	...	967	784	45	-46	...	...	783
5 Construction	6961	3319	7787	165	...	18232	7911	3887	8748	118	...	20664
6 Wholesale and retail trade, restaurants and hotels	29134	3547	23985	1329	303	57692	30500	4567	37320	1529	2	73914
A Wholesale and retail trade	26025	2818	21668	1183	303	51391	26916	3613	34126	1341	2	65994
B Restaurants and hotels	3109	729	2317	146	...	6301	3584	954	3194	188	...	7920
Restaurants	1991	417	1903	115	...	4426	2307	553	2538	128	...	5526
Hotels and other lodging places	1118	312	414	31	...	1875	1277	401	656	60	...	2394
7 Transport, storage and communication	8131	3178	13367	141	675	24142	8585	3573	17431	169	589	29169
A Transport and storage	6099	2652	11096	139	359	19627	6718	3028	14173	169	257	23831
B Communication	2032	526	2271	2	316	4515	1867	545	3258	...	332	5338
8 Finance, insurance, real estate and business services	11598	7707	38345	1504	...	59154	12158	8329	40312	1539	...	62338
A Financial institutions	5653	669	5456	368	...	12146	6107	723	5255	408	...	12493
B Insurance	997	106	495	50	...	1648	1185	128	605	65	...	1983
C Real estate and business services	4948	6932	32394	1086	...	45360	4866	7478	34452	1066	...	47862
9 Community, social and personal services	13666	1974	12688	366	571	28123	16094	1459	14560	371	715	31769
A Sanitary and similar services	1027	33	32	8	250	850	1029	32	36	6	200	903
B Social and related community services [c]	7421	838	7608	108	321	15654	8861	725	8748	32	515	17851
Educational services	4863	253	1257	5	321	6057	6101	414	545	7	515	6552
Medical, dental, other health and veterinary services	2448	575	6399	29	...	9451	2652	301	8178	24	...	11155
C Recreational and cultural services	1516	473	1222	190	...	3401	1647	132	2158	203	...	4140
D Personal and household services	3702	630	3826	60	...	8218	4557	570	3618	130	...	8875

Venezuela

4.3 Cost Components of Value Added
(Continued)

Million Venezuelan bolivares

	1984						1985					
	Compensation of Employees	Capital Consumption	Net Operating Surplus	Indirect Taxes	Less: Subsidies Received	Value Added	Compensation of Employees	Capital Consumption	Net Operating Surplus	Indirect Taxes	Less: Subsidies Received	Value Added
Total, Industries	110936	33381	212295	9188	3992	361808	123926	36878	238356	11914	3595	407479
Producers of Government Services	35322	160	...	...	...	35482	39682	186	...	...	...	39868
Other Producers	4762	102	...	4	...	4868	5193	156	...	5	...	5354
Total	151020	33643	212295	9192	3992	402158	168801	37220	238356	11919	3595	452701
Less: Imputed bank service charge	...	...	11384	...	...	11384	...	...	11821	...	...	11821
Import duties	...	...	...	4465	...	4465	...	...	...	6292	...	6292
Value added tax	...	...	...	...	...	...	...	...	...	...	...	...
Other adjustments	...	...	...	31237	16989	14248	...	...	...	33356	15908	17448
Total	151020	33643	200911	44894	20981	409487	168801	37220	226535	51567	19503	464620

	1986						1987					
	Compensation of Employees	Capital Consumption	Net Operating Surplus	Indirect Taxes	Less: Subsidies Received	Value Added	Compensation of Employees	Capital Consumption	Net Operating Surplus	Indirect Taxes	Less: Subsidies Received	Value Added

All Producers

1 Agriculture, hunting, forestry and fishing	7856	2849	21962	...	193	32474	10301	3677	28967	...	329	42616
A Agriculture and hunting a	6807	2703	19872	...	193	29189	8636	3465	25789	...	329	37561
B Forestry and logging	53	14	293	...	...	360	91	25	516	...	...	632
C Fishing	996	132	1797	...	...	2925	1574	187	2662	...	...	4423
2 Mining and quarrying	6464	3986	27125	144	...	37719	8021	4595	55661	316	10	68583
A Coal mining	7	1	-2	...	...	6	2	1	2	...	...	5
B Crude petroleum and natural gas production	5654	3709	25001	138	...	34502	6815	4156	51741	292	...	63004
C Metal ore mining	587	150	1452	6	...	2195	964	291	3185	22	10	4452
D Other mining	216	126	674	-	...	1016	240	147	733	2	...	1122
3 Manufacturing	39062	9367	57467	10963	3153	113706	55894	13467	85545	14015	10062	158859
A Manufacture of food, beverages and tobacco	8224	1770	10007	5946	1310	24637	10730	2304	16328	7374	5063	31673
B Textile, wearing apparel and leather industries	5017	558	3440	118	3	9130	7217	817	4989	139	5	13157
C Manufacture of wood and wood products, including furniture	1199	157	936	31	...	2323	1670	221	1247	37	...	3175
D Manufacture of paper and paper products, printing and publishing	2644	386	2282	71	40	5343	4012	585	3470	84	68	8083
E Manufacture of chemicals and chemical petroleum, coal, rubber and plastic products	8757	2599	27143	4526	675	42350	13101	3561	43729	5792	3109	63074
F Manufacture of non-metallic mineral products, except products of petroleum and coal	2360	692	1160	42	99	4155	3241	938	1645	54	169	5709
G Basic metal industries	3979	1815	7256	26	992	12084	5513	2944	6183	305	1591	13354
H Manufacture of fabricated metal products, machinery and equipment	6568	1349	5013	189	31	13088	9993	2042	7646	215	52	19844
I Other manufacturing industries	314	41	230	14	3	596	417	55	308	15	5	790
4 Electricity, gas and water	2362	1688	2979	398	...	7427	2973	2549	5034	479	...	11035
A Electricity, gas and steam b	1796	1662	2754	398	...	6610	2331	2519	4779	479	...	10108
B Water works and supply	566	26	225	...	...	817	642	30	255	...	...	927
5 Construction	9193	5121	10270	140	...	24724	12902	7343	14275	104	...	34624
6 Wholesale and retail trade, restaurants and hotels	38446	5214	45768	1648	1	91075	55609	7298	66710	2051	126	131542
A Wholesale and retail trade	33870	3578	42118	1495	1	81060	49702	5285	62066	1904	126	118831
B Restaurants and hotels	4576	1636	3650	153	...	10015	5907	2013	4644	147	...	12711
Restaurants	2765	1214	2444	77	...	6500	3194	1402	2814	61	...	7471
Hotels and other lodging places	1811	422	1206	76	...	3515	2713	611	1830	86	...	5240
7 Transport, storage and communication	9681	4563	21943	319	274	36232	12215	6687	30249	414	433	49132
A Transport and storage	7833	4103	17481	319	167	29569	10277	5927	25185	414	296	41507
B Communication	1848	460	4462	...	107	6663	1938	760	5064	...	137	7625
8 Finance, insurance, real estate and business services	13342	9391	45489	1763	...	69985	17269	11320	57394	2100	...	88083
A Financial institutions	6425	947	6463	469	...	14304	8582	1182	9892	523	...	20179

Venezuela

4.3 Cost Components of Value Added
(Continued)

Million Venezuelan bolivares

	1986						1987					
	Compensation of Employees	Capital Consumption	Net Operating Surplus	Indirect Taxes	Less: Subsidies Received	Value Added	Compensation of Employees	Capital Consumption	Net Operating Surplus	Indirect Taxes	Less: Subsidies Received	Value Added
B Insurance	1265	167	440	40	...	1912	1429	234	689	63	...	2415
C Real estate and business services	5652	8277	38586	1254	...	53769	7258	9904	46813	1514	...	65489
9 Community, social and personal services	17240	2110	18673	425	755	37693	22680	2849	25227	531	1134	50153
A Sanitary and similar services	1362	14	-465	6	208	709	1730	17	-205	6	597	951
B Social and related community services c	9629	1092	10783	56	547	21013	11918	1350	13454	72	537	26257
Educational services	6335	535	655	3	547	6981	7836	662	669	5	537	8635
Medical, dental, other health and veterinary services	3201	528	10061	31	...	13821	3967	652	12709	33	...	17361
C Recreational and cultural services	1813	206	2484	247	...	4750	2224	264	3406	321	...	6215
D Personal and household services	4436	798	5871	116	...	11221	6808	1218	8572	132	...	16730
Total, Industries	143646	44289	251676	15800	4376	451035	197864	59785	369062	20010	12094	634627
Producers of Government Services	43831	223	...	...	...	44054	55639	219	...	...	...	55858
Other Producers	6103	152	...	8	...	6263	7249	188	...	9	...	7446
Total	193580	44664	251676	15808	4376	501352	260752	60192	369062	20019	12094	697931
Less: Imputed bank service charge	...	...	14066	...	...	14066	...	...	17836	...	...	17836
Import duties	...	...	...	8837	...	8837	...	...	...	15720	...	15720
Value added tax	...	...	...	...	...	...	...	...	...	...	...	...
Other adjustments	...	...	...	33178	35536	-2358	...	...	...	29315	5707	23608
Total	193580	44664	237610	57823	39912	493765	260752	60192	351226	65054	17801	719423

a) Item 'Agriculture and hunting' includes agricultural products and improvements and other non-agricultural products.
b) Item 'Electricity, gas and water' excludes gas.
c) Social and related community services includes in addition to Educational and health services (item 33 and 34) also the services of commercial and professional associations.

Viet Nam

Source. 'Statistical Data of the Socialist Republic of Viet Nam, 1978' published by the General Statistical Office, Hanoi.

General note. The estimates shown in the following tables have been prepared in accordance with the United Nations System of National Accounts so far as the existing data would permit.

1.1 Expenditure on the Gross Domestic Product, in Current Prices

Million Dongs

	1970	1975	1978	1979	1980	1981	1982	1983	1984	1985	1986	1987
1 Government final consumption expenditure	...	...	...	...	...	...	...	...	...	...	...	...
2 Private final consumption expenditure	...	...	...	...	...	...	...	...	...	...	...	...
3 Gross capital formation	...	...	...	...	...	...	...	...	...	...	...	...
4 Exports of goods and services	...	...	...	...	...	...	...	...	...	...	...	...
5 Less: Imports of goods and services	...	...	...	...	...	...	...	...	...	...	...	...
Equals: Gross Domestic Product	...	18258	20742	...	...	...	...	...	...	...	...	...

Yemen

Source. Reply to the United Nations National Accounts Questionnaire from the Central Planning Organization, Sanaa. The official estimates and descriptions are published in the 'National Accounts of Yemen Arab Republic', issued by the same Organization.

General note. The official estimates of Yemen have been prepared in accordance with the United Nations System of National Accounts so far as the existing data would permit.

1.1 Expenditure on the Gross Domestic Product, in Current Prices

Million Yemeni rials — Fiscal year beginning 1 July

	1970	1975	1978	1979	1980	1981	1982	1983	1984	1985	1986	1987
1 Government final consumption expenditure	161	701	1839	2255	3007	3891	6416	7449	7135	5543	6898	...
2 Private final consumption expenditure	1477	4939	10648	12342	12910	12467	13530	14189	14837	29404	33999	...
3 Gross capital formation	251	900	3994	4761	5005	5530	5362	3981	3755	4472	4988	...
A Increase in stocks	31	155	30	355	107	219	240	-148	-90	-75	50	...
B Gross fixed capital formation	220	745	3964	4406	4898	5311	5122	4129	3845	4547	4938	...
4 Exports of goods and services	29	214	474	803	805	1130	958	1126	1178	1164	1155	...
5 Less: Imports of goods and services	391	1866	6774	8465	9046	9636	10397	9575	8955	9644	9568	...
Equals: Gross Domestic Product [a]	1527	4888	10181	11696	12681	13382	15869	17170	17950	30939	37472	...

a) Beginning 1981, estimates relate to calendar year.

1.2 Expenditure on the Gross Domestic Product, in Constant Prices

Million Yemeni rials — Fiscal year beginning 1 July

At constant prices of: 1975 (1970); 1981 (1978 onward)

	1970	1975	1978	1979	1980	1981	1982	1983	1984	1985	1986	1987
1 Government final consumption expenditure	435	1516	2221	2463	3103	3891	5263	5762	5493	3791	4290	...
2 Private final consumption expenditure	2739	10288	12249	12238	12120	12467	13308	13541	13696	17206	16984	...
3 Gross capital formation	542	2163	5978	6425	6433	5530	5155	3673	3370	3344	3108	...
A Increase in stocks	73	301	35	377	110	219	235	-140	-81	-42	23	...
B Gross fixed capital formation	469	1862	5943	6048	6323	5311	4920	3813	3451	3386	3085	...
4 Exports of goods and services	50	417	548	847	824	1130	939	1023	1038	711	560	...
5 Less: Imports of goods and services	674	5261	9374	9760	9529	9636	9949	8769	8001	5913	4688	...
Equals: Gross Domestic Product [a]	3092	9123	11622	12213	12951	13382	14716	15230	15596	19139	20254	...

a) Beginning 1981, estimates relate to calendar year.

1.3 Cost Components of the Gross Domestic Product

Million Yemeni rials — Fiscal year beginning 1 July

	1970	1975	1978	1979	1980	1981	1982	1983	1984	1985	1986	1987
1 Indirect taxes, net	70	431	1453	1811	1868	1792	1943	2327	2397	2974	2863	...
2 Consumption of fixed capital	33	98	235	279	309	313	360	393	421	839	1038	...
3 Compensation of employees paid by resident producers to:	294	4359	8493	9606	10504	11277	13566	14450	15132	27126	33571	...
4 Operating surplus	1130	...	...	...	...	...	...	...	...	...	...	...
Equals: Gross Domestic Product [a]	1527	4888	10181	11696	12681	13382	15869	17170	17950	30939	37472	...

a) Beginning 1981, estimates relate to calendar year.

Yemen

1.7 External Transactions on Current Account, Summary

Million Yemeni rials | Fiscal year beginning 1 July

	1970	1975	1978	1979	1980	1981	1982	1983	1984	1985	1986	1987
Payments to the Rest of the World											
1 Imports of goods and services	391	1866	6774	8465	9046	9636	10397	9575	8955	9644	9568	...
2 Factor income to the rest of the world	...	...	...	...	...	...	...	...	...	...	...	...
3 Current transfers to the rest of the world	...	...	...	...	...	...	...	...	...	...	...	...
4 Surplus of the nation on current transactions	-82	1100	-621	-1480	-2980	-2990	-2665	-2451	-1663	-2210	-1158	...
Payments to the Rest of the World and Surplus of the Nation on Current Transactions [a]	309	2966	6153	6985	6066	6646	7732	7124	7292	7434	8410	...
Receipts From The Rest of the World											
1 Exports of goods and services	29	214	474	803	805	1130	958	1126	1178	1164	1155	...
2 Factor income from rest of the world [b]	129	763	1743	2160	1899	1938	6774	5998	6114	6270	7255	...
A Compensation of employees	119	581	1217	1423	1356	1484	...	...	...	...	...	...
B Property and entrepreneurial income	10	182	526	737	543	454	...	...	...	...	...	...
3 Current transfers from rest of the world [b]	151	1989	3936	4022	3362	3579	...	...	...	...	...	...
Receipts from the Rest of the World on Current Transactions [a]	309	2966	6153	6985	6066	6646	7732	7124	7292	7434	8410	...

a) Beginning 1981, estimates relate to calendar year.
b) Net factor income and net current transfers are shown in items 2 and 3, respectively, of the receipt from the rest of the world.

1.10 Gross Domestic Product by Kind of Activity, in Current Prices

Million Yemeni rials | Fiscal year beginning 1 July

	1970	1975	1978	1979	1980	1981	1982	1983	1984	1985	1986	1987
1 Agriculture, hunting, forestry and fishing	785	2011	3049	3458	3579	3685	3799	3596	3712	8033	10680	...
2 Mining and quarrying [a]	15	32	133	149	149	156	168	190	210	241	506	...
3 Manufacturing	67	257	504	655	730	820	1043	1254	1453	3365	4620	...
4 Electricity, gas and water	4	17	38	66	80	117	138	173	226	257	320	...
5 Construction	79	236	1060	1033	1110	1098	1215	1255	1365	1541	1285	...
6 Wholesale and retail trade, restaurants and hotels	251	1012	1790	1935	2131	2185	2369	2476	2614	4169	4896	...
7 Transport, storage and communication	47	150	370	431	461	497	610	665	710	3489	4106	...
8 Finance, insurance, real estate and business services	100	258	635	788	946	1117	1274	1503	1635	3598	4166	...
9 Community, social and personal services	12	42	101	121	130	131	155	162	182	242	286	...
Total, Industries	1360	4015	7630	8636	9316	9806	10771	11274	12107	24935	30865	...
Producers of Government Services	127	509	1202	1505	1906	2129	3477	3912	3857	3643	4410	...
Other Producers	7	14	21	23	24	24	27	31	34	38	50	...
Subtotal	1494	4538	8903	10164	11246	11959	14275	15217	15998	28616	35325	...
Less: Imputed bank service charge	20	44	108	138	274	211	246	260	288	651	716	...
Plus: Import duties	53	394	1386	1670	1709	1634	1840	2213	2240	2974	2863	...
Plus: Value added tax	...	...	...	...	...	...	...	...	...	...	...	...
Equals: Gross Domestic Product [b]	1527	4888	10181	11696	12681	13382	15869	17170	17950	30939	37472	...

a) For 1986, item 'Mining and Quarrying' includes crude petroleum production.
b) Beginning 1981, estimates relate to calendar year.

Yemen

1.11 Gross Domestic Product by Kind of Activity, in Constant Prices

Million Yemeni rials — Fiscal year beginning 1 July

	1970	1975	1978	1979	1980	1981	1982	1983	1984	1985	1986	1987
		1975			At constant prices of:	1981						
1 Agriculture, hunting, forestry and fishing	1547	3409	3265	3404	3578	3685	3854	3418	3414	3704	4126	...
2 Mining and quarrying	27	67[a]	154[a]	163[a]	154[a]	156[a]	163[a]	178[a]	187[a]	172[a]	397[a]	...
3 Manufacturing	142	425	597	688	741	820	987	1216	1345	2404	2662	...
4 Electricity, gas and water	8	35	59	78	91	117	138	173	216	239	286	...
5 Construction	151	591	1473	1238	1196	1098	1167	1159	1225	1101	857	...
6 Wholesale and retail trade, restaurants and hotels	465	1764	1812	1996	2131	2185	2303	2259	2317	2553	2728	...
7 Transport, storage and communication	92	323	446	452	465	497	596	593	620	2406	2549	...
8 Finance, insurance, real estate and business services	197	556	685	738	969	1117	1274	1477	1556	2436	2597	...
9 Community, social and personal services	27	85	117	123	127	131	154	154	160	138	159	...
Total, Industries	2656	7255	8608	8880	9452	9806	10636	10627	11040	15153	16361	...
Producers of Government Services	314	1100	1453	1643	1963	2129	2472	2763	2724	2291	2314	...
Other Producers	9	14	21	23	24	24	27	31	32	36	40	...
Subtotal	2979	8369	10082	10546	11439	11959	13135	13421	13796	17480	18715	...
Less: Imputed bank service charge	51	98	133	155	295	211	251	248	260	465	482	...
Plus: Import duties	164	852	1673	1822	1807	1634	1832	2057	2060	2124	2021	...
Plus: Value added tax	...	...	...	...	...	...	...	...	...	...	...	...
Equals: Gross Domestic Product	3092[b]	9123[a]	11622[a]	12213[a]	12951[a]	13382[a]	14716[a]	15230[a]	15596[a]	19139[a]	20254[a]	...

a) For 1986, item 'Mining and Quarrying' includes crude petroleum production.
b) Beginning 1981, estimates relate to calendar year.

1.12 Relations Among National Accounting Aggregates

Million Yemeni rials — Fiscal year beginning 1 July

	1970	1975	1978	1979	1980	1981	1982	1983	1984	1985	1986	1987
Gross Domestic Product	1527	4888	10181	11696	12681	13382	15869	17170	17950	30939	37472	...
Plus: Net factor income from the rest of the world [a]	129	763	1743	2160	1899	1938	6774	5998	6114	6270	7255	...
Equals: Gross National Product	1656	5651	11924	13856	14580	15320	...	...	...	...	...	...
Less: Consumption of fixed capital	33	98	235	279	309	313	360	393	421	839	1038	...
Equals: National Income	1623	5553	11689	13577	14271	15007	...	...	...	...	...	...

Yemen

1.12 Relations Among National Accounting Aggregates
(Continued)

Million Yemeni rials

	1970	1975	1978	1979	1980	1981	1982	1983	1984	1985	1986	1987
Plus: Net current transfers from the rest of the world [a]	151	1989	3936	4022	3362	3579	...	...	...	...	...	...
Equals: National Disposable Income	1774	7542	15625	17599	17633	18586	22283	22775	23643	36370	43689	...
Less: Final consumption	1638	5640	12487	14597	15917	16358	19946	21638	21972	34947	40897	...
Equals: Net Saving	136	1902	3138	3002	1716	2227	2337	1137	1671	1423	2792	...
Less: Surplus of the nation on current transactions	-82	1100	-621	-1480	-2980	-2990	-2665	-2451	-1663	-2210	-1158	...
Equals: Net Capital Formation [b]	218	802	3759	4482	4696	5217	5002	3588	3334	3633	3950	...

a) Beginning 1982, item 'Net factor income from abroad' includes item 'Net current transfers from the rest of the world'.
b) Beginning 1981, estimates relate to calendar year.

2.11 Gross Fixed Capital Formation by Kind of Activity of Owner, ISIC Divisions, in Current Prices

Million Yemeni rials

	1970	1975	1978	1979	1980	1981	1982	1983	1984	1985	1986	1987
					All Producers							
1 Agriculture, hunting, forestry and fishing	...	57	317	311	383	269	341	402	416	619	526	...
2 Mining and quarrying	...	...	29	30	44	60	66	67	70	35	52	...
3 Manufacturing	...	52	418	355	372	364	237	187	168	578	451	...
4 Electricity, gas and water	...	...	192	324	609	768	661	552	505	839	801	...
5 Construction	...	10	210	270	303	80	52	54	56	104	116	...
6 Wholesale and retail trade, restaurants and hotels	...	...	...	...	...	430	229	227	219	269	257	...
7 Transport, storage and communication	...	220	1016	1504	1506	941	1053	531	445	322	571	...
8 Finance, insurance, real estate and business services	...	311	841	909	965	817	700	840	792	864	1001	...
A Financial institutions	...	...	...	...	...	27	22	68	59	44	78	...
B Insurance	...	...	...	...	...	...	...	...	...	...	...	...
C Real estate and business services	...	311	841	909	965	790	678	772	733	820	923	...
9 Community, social and personal services	...	95	941	703	716	1583	1783	1271	1174	917	1163	...
Total Industries [a]	...	745	3964	4406	4898	5311	5122	4129	3845	4547	4938	...
Producers of Government Services	...	...	...	...	...	...	...	...	...	...	...	...
Private Non-Profit Institutions Serving Households	...	...	...	...	...	...	...	...	...	...	...	...
Total	...	...	...	...	...	...	...	...	...	...	...	...

a) Beginning 1981, estimates relate to calendar year.

2.12 Gross Fixed Capital Formation by Kind of Activity of Owner, ISIC Divisions, in Constant Prices

Million Yemeni rials

	1970	1975	1978	1979	1980	1981	1982	1983	1984	1985	1986	1987
				At constant prices of:1981								
					All Producers							
1 Agriculture, hunting, forestry and fishing	...	141	561	449	526	269	328	373	371	461	329	...
2 Mining and quarrying	...	...	46	46	66	59	64	60	65	26	32	...
3 Manufacturing	...	129	705	563	573	364	227	172	147	430	282	...
4 Electricity, gas and water	...	...	320	494	897	768	635	509	464	625	500	...

Yemen

2.12 Gross Fixed Capital Formation by Kind of Activity of Owner, ISIC Divisions, in Constant Prices
(Continued)

Million Yemeni rials — Fiscal year beginning 1 July

	1970	1975	1978	1979	1980	1981	1982	1983	1984	1985	1986	1987
					At constant prices of:1981							
5 Construction	...	25	355	441	476	80	50	50	49	... / 77	72	...
6 Wholesale and retail trade, restaurants and hotels	...	...	...	...	...	430	220	209	191	... / 200	161	...
7 Transport, storage and communication	...	550	1788	2055	1905	941	1012	490	394	... / 240	357	...
8 Finance, insurance, real estate and business services	...	778	1110	1005	930	817	672	775	690	... / 644	626	...
A Financial institutions	...	...	...	...	...	27	21	62	54	... / 32	49	...
B Insurance	...	...	...	...	...	...	...	...	...	...	...	...
C Real estate and business services	...	778	1110	1005	930	790	651	713	636	... / 612	577	...
9 Community, social and personal services	...	239	1058	995	950	1583	1712	1175	1080	... / 683	726	...
Total Industries [a]	...	1862	5943	6048	6323	5311	4920	3813	3451	... / 3386	3085	...
Producers of Government Services	...	...	...	...	...	...	...	...	...	...	...	...
Private Non-Profit Institutions Serving Households	...	...	...	...	...	...	...	...	...	...	...	...
Total	...	...	...	...	...	...	...	...	...	...	...	...

a) Beginning 1981, estimates relate to calendar year.

4.1 Derivation of Value Added by Kind of Activity, in Current Prices

Million Yemeni rials — Fiscal year beginning 1 July

	1985 Gross Output	1985 Intermediate Consumption	1985 Value Added	1986 Gross Output	1986 Intermediate Consumption	1986 Value Added
			All Producers			
1 Agriculture, hunting, forestry and fishing	11476	3443	8033	16430	5750	10680
2 Mining and quarrying	330	89	241	662	156	506
A Coal mining	...	...	...	...	...	...
B Crude petroleum and natural gas production	...	...	...	325	65	260
C Metal ore mining	...	...	...	...	...	...
D Other mining	...	...	...	337	91	246
3 Manufacturing	7692	4327	3365	10675	6055	4620
4 Electricity, gas and water	492	235	257	685	365	320
5 Construction	3436	1895	1541	3022	1737	1285
6 Wholesale and retail trade, restaurants and hotels	5072	903	4169	5968	1072	4896
7 Transport, storage and communication	4743	1254	3489	5583	1477	4106
8 Finance, insurance, real estate and business services	3957	359	3598	4570	404	4166
9 Community, social and personal services	303	61	242	359	73	286
Total, Industries [a]	37501	12566	24935	47954	17089	30865
Producers of Government Services	5609	1966	3643	7010	2600	4410
Other Producers	45	7	38	65	15	50
Total	43155	14539	28616	55029	19704	35325
Less: Imputed bank service charge	...	-651	651	...	-716	716
Import duties	2974	...	2974	2863	...	2863
Value added tax	...	...	...	...	...	...
Total [a]	46129	15190	30939	57892	20420	37472

a) Beginning 1981, estimates relate to calendar year.

Yemen

4.2 Derivation of Value Added by Kind of Activity, in Constant Prices

Million Yemeni rials — Fiscal year beginning 1 July

At constant prices of: 1981

All Producers

	1985 Gross Output	1985 Intermediate Consumption	1985 Value Added	1986 Gross Output	1986 Intermediate Consumption	1986 Value Added
1 Agriculture, hunting, forestry and fishing	5292	1588	3704	6347	2221	4126
2 Mining and quarrying	235	63	172	512	115	397
A Coal mining	...	...	...	...	...	...
B Crude petroleum and natural gas production	...	...	...	325	65	260
C Metal ore mining	...	...	...	...	...	...
D Other mining	...	...	...	187	50	137
3 Manufacturing	5495	3091	2404	6201	3539	2662
4 Electricity, gas and water	457	218	239	612	326	286
5 Construction	2455	1354	1101	2015	1158	857
6 Wholesale and retail trade, restaurants and hotels	3115	562	2553	3326	598	2728
7 Transport, storage and communication	3271	865	2406	3466	917	2549
8 Finance, insurance, real estate and business services	2686	250	2436	2858	261	2597
9 Community, social and personal services	173	35	138	200	41	159
Total, Industries [a]	23179	8026	15153	25537	9176	16361
Producers of Government Services	3837	1546	2291	4359	2045	2314
Other Producers	43	7	36	52	12	40
Total	27059	9579	17480	29948	11233	18715
Less: Imputed bank service charge	...	-465	465	...	-482	482
Import duties	2124	...	2124	2021	...	2021
Value added tax	...	...	...	...	...	...
Total [a]	29183	10044	19139	31969	11715	20254

a) Beginning 1981, estimates relate to calendar year.

4.3 Cost Components of Value Added

Million Yemeni rials — Fiscal year beginning 1 July

All Producers

	1980 Compensation of Employees	1980 Capital Consumption	1980 Net Operating Surplus	1980 Indirect Taxes	1980 Less: Subsidies Received	1980 Value Added	1981 Compensation of Employees	1981 Capital Consumption	1981 Net Operating Surplus	1981 Indirect Taxes	1981 Less: Subsidies Received	1981 Value Added
1 Agriculture, hunting, forestry and fishing	421	...	3016	...	...	3579	428	...	3069	...	...	3648
2 Mining and quarrying	36	...	106	...	...	149	38	...	112	...	...	156
3 Manufacturing	133	...	398	...	...	730	275	...	411	...	...	854
4 Electricity, gas and water	19	...	58	...	...	80	26	...	81	...	...	111
5 Construction	617	...	420	...	...	1088	603	...	410	...	...	1080
6 Wholesale and retail trade, restaurants and hotels	224	...	1930	...	...	2260	231	...	1878	...	...	2188
7 Transport, storage and communication	78	...	234	...	...	461	84	...	229	...	...	470
8 Finance, insurance, real estate and business services	133	...	1346	...	...	1536	134	...	1370	...	...	1565
9 Community, social and personal services	8	...	111	...	...	130	9	...	103	...	...	131
Total, Industries [ab]	1670	...	7619	...	...	10013	1828	...	7662	...	...	10203
Producers of Government Services	1741	...	...	...	...	1748	1958	...	...	...	...	1965
Other Producers	24	...	...	...	...	24	24	...	...	...	...	24
Total	3435	...	7619	...	...	11785	3810	...	7662	...	...	12192
Less: Imputed bank service charge	...	...	864	...	...	864	...	...	705	...	...	705
Import duties	...	...	...	...	...	1709	...	...	...	...	...	1633
Value added tax	...	...	...	...	...	...	...	...	...	...	...	...
Total [ab]	3435	...	6755	...	...	12630	3810	...	6957	...	...	13120

Yemen

4.3 Cost Components of Value Added

Million Yemeni rials
Fiscal year beginning 1 July

	Compensation of Employees	Capital Consumption	Net Operating Surplus	Indirect Taxes	Less: Subsidies Received	Value Added
	\multicolumn{6}{c}{1982}					

All Producers

	Compensation of Employees	Capital Consumption	Net Operating Surplus	Indirect Taxes	Less: Subsidies Received	Value Added
1 Agriculture, hunting, forestry and fishing	447	...	3209	...	...	3813
2 Mining and quarrying	41	...	120	...	...	167
3 Manufacturing	320	...	478	...	...	991
4 Electricity, gas and water	36	...	114	...	...	155
5 Construction	649	...	441	...	...	1161
6 Wholesale and retail trade, restaurants and hotels	258	...	2094	...	...	2445
7 Transport, storage and communication	96	...	261	...	...	525
8 Finance, insurance, real estate and business services	128	...	1379	...	...	1569
9 Community, social and personal services	10	...	116	...	...	146
Total, Industries [a,b]	1985	...	8212	...	...	10972
Producers of Government Services	2454	...	...	...	...	2463
Other Producers	26	...	...	...	...	26
Total	4465	...	8212	...	...	13461
Less: Imputed bank service charge	...	...	670	...	...	670
Import duties	...	...	...	...	...	1846
Value added tax	...	...	...	...	...	...
Total [a,b]	4465	...	7542	...	...	14637

a) Beginning 1981, estimates relate to calendar year.
b) Data for this table have not been revised, therefore, data for some years are not comparable with those of other tables.

Yugoslavia

Source. Reply to the United Nations National Accounts Questionnaire from the Federal Institute for Statistics, Belgrade. The official estimates and descriptions are published annually in 'Statisticki Godisnjak' (Statistical Yearbook), issued by the same Office.

General note. The estimates shown in the following tables have been prepared in accordance with the United Nations System of National Accounts so far as the existing data would permit.

1.1 Expenditure on the Gross Domestic Product, in Current Prices

Thousand Million Yugoslav dinars

	1970	1975	1978	1979	1980	1981	1982	1983	1984	1985	1986	1987
1 Government final consumption expenditure	30	98	177	228	291	381	500	643	932	1666	3348	7318
2 Private final consumption expenditure	96	295	528	672	881	1226	1624	2243	3389	5951	11782	26141
3 Gross capital formation	65	218	411	539	731	983	1227	1660	2691	4702	8996	19551
A Increase in stocks	14	54	54	91	186	298	373	631	1233	2093	3949	9636
B Gross fixed capital formation	52	163	357	448	546	685	855	1030	1458	2609	5047	9915
4 Exports of goods and services	32	102	147	201	322	446	600	851	1704	2638	3763	12349
5 Less: Imports of goods and services	40	149	223	329	476	570	744	950	1864	2774	3930	13037
Statistical discrepancy	-1	13	-28	-16	-26	-56	-48	-165	-199	-232	-559	18
Equals: Gross Domestic Product	182	577	1013	1294	1724	2410	3159	4283	6653	11951	23400	52340

1.2 Expenditure on the Gross Domestic Product, in Constant Prices

Thousand Million Yugoslav dinars

	1970	1975	1978	1979	1980	1981	1982	1983	1984	1985	1986	1987
				At constant prices of:1980								
1 Government final consumption expenditure	187	229	265	278	281	268	268	263	265	269	281	...
2 Private final consumption expenditure	538	718	979	879	878	799	790	726	655	658	686	...
3 Gross capital formation	362	493	521	738	718	793	782	824	903	897	731	...
A Increase in stocks	48	76	-24	158	172	301	317	404	523	533	431	...
B Gross fixed capital formation	314	417	545	580	546	492	465	420	380	364	300	...
4 Exports of goods and services	213	270	306	314	336	321	302	284	304	319	310	...
5 Less: Imports of goods and services	282	372	404	453	413	358	309	283	280	279	296	...
Equals: Gross Domestic Product	1015	1337	1665	1746	1781	1791	1790	1765	1791	1809	1884	...

1.3 Cost Components of the Gross Domestic Product

Thousand Million Yugoslav dinars

	1970	1975	1978	1979	1980	1981	1982	1983	1984	1985	1986	1987
1 Indirect taxes, net	15	47	97	129	152	218	261	399	599	876	1747	3624
A Indirect taxes	16	62	123	163	195	269	340	508	771	1193	2364	5148
B Less: Subsidies	1	15	26	34	43	51	79	109	172	317	617	1524
2 Consumption of fixed capital	17	61	103	129	175	236	375	529	779	1325	2492	6561
3 Compensation of employees paid by resident producers to:	...	...	...	...	...	...	...	...	...	...	...	...
4 Operating surplus	...	...	...	...	...	...	...	...	...	...	...	...
Statistical discrepancy	151	469	813	1037	1397	1956	2524	3354	5275	9749	19161	42155
Equals: Gross Domestic Product	182	577	1013	1294	1724	2410	3159	4283	6653	11950	23400	52340

1.10 Gross Domestic Product by Kind of Activity, in Current Prices

Thousand Million Yugoslav dinars

	1970	1975	1978	1979	1980	1981	1982	1983	1984	1985	1986	1987
1 Agriculture, hunting, forestry and fishing	30	84	113	147	201	304	435	620	896	1376	2899	5679
2 Mining and quarrying	4	13	20	24	39	57	77	104	200	336	514	1364
3 Manufacturing	49	160	272	344	481	699	918	1264	2065	4125	7621	18195
4 Electricity, gas and water	4	14	25	32	45	60	79	91	145	264	565	1239
5 Construction	19	54	100	128	168	226	272	322	447	820	1589	3467
6 Wholesale and retail trade, restaurants and hotels	17	63	111	145	195	264	359	503	774	1305	2610	5510
7 Transport, storage and communication	12	44	74	97	127	177	228	310	469	890	1735	3746
8 Finance, insurance, real estate and business services	4	17	37	44	60	80	108	134	220	420	890	2427
9 Community, social and personal services	19	81	166	204	255	324	423	534	838	1539	3230	7089
Statistical discrepancy	-	1	-	-	-	-	-	-	-	-	-	-

Yugoslavia

1.10 Gross Domestic Product by Kind of Activity, in Current Prices
(Continued)

Thousand Million Yugoslav dinars

	1970	1975	1978	1979	1980	1981	1982	1983	1984	1985	1986	1987
Total, Industries	159	530	916	1165	1571	2192	2898	3884	6054	11075	21653	48716
Producers of Government Services	8	...	...	...	...	...	...	...	...	...	...	...
Other Producers	...	...	...	...	...	...	...	...	...	...	...	...
Subtotal	167	530	916	1165	1571	2192	2898	3884	6054	11075	21653	48716
Less: Imputed bank service charge	...	...	...	...	...	...	...	...	...	...	...	...
Plus: Import duties [a]	15	47	97	129	152	218	261	399	599	877	1747	3624
Plus: Value added tax	...	...	...	...	...	...	...	...	...	...	...	...
Equals: Gross Domestic Product	182	577	1013	1294	1724	2410	3159	4283	6653	11952	23400	52340

a) Item 'Import duties' refers to indirect taxes net of subsidies.

1.11 Gross Domestic Product by Kind of Activity, in Constant Prices

Million Yugoslav dinars

	1970	1975	1978	1979	1980	1981	1982	1983	1984	1985	1986	1987
	\multicolumn{12}{c}{At constant prices of:1972}
1 Agriculture, hunting, forestry and fishing	41900	48800	51200	54000	55200	56600	60700	60300	61415	57510	61415	...
2 Mining and quarrying	...	...	...	...	...	...	...	...	...	...	...	...
3 Manufacturing	73242	107154	132101	142900	148820	155270	155084	157335	165365	169830	176453	...
4 Electricity, gas and water	4782	6907	8983	9549	10425	10506	10669	11300	10545	10870	11215	...
5 Construction	24800	30000	38200	41800	42000	40000	37000	32200	30836	30325	29905	...
6 Wholesale and retail trade, restaurants and hotels	47600	63000	72500	76800	77600	76500	76900	75700	73835	73490	75336	...
7 Transport, storage and communication	17600	24000	29700	30900	32100	32500	31600	32000	33294	34426	36007	...
8 Finance, insurance, real estate and business services	3804	9504	14047	13921	14611	14015	14178	12690	12810	13715	13960	...
9 Community, social and personal services	...	...	...	...	...	...	...	...	...	...	...	...
Total, Industries	...	...	...	...	...	...	...	...	...	...	...	...
Producers of Government Services	...	...	...	...	...	...	...	...	...	...	...	...
Other Producers	...	...	...	...	...	...	...	...	...	...	...	...
Subtotal	...	...	...	...	...	...	...	...	...	...	...	...
Less: Imputed bank service charge	...	...	...	...	...	...	...	...	...	...	...	...
Plus: Import duties	...	...	...	...	...	...	...	...	...	...	...	...
Plus: Value added tax	...	...	...	...	...	...	...	...	...	...	...	...
Equals: Gross Domestic Product	...	...	...	...	...	...	...	...	...	...	...	...

1.12 Relations Among National Accounting Aggregates

Thousand Million Yugoslav dinars

	1970	1975	1978	1979	1980	1981	1982	1983	1984	1985	1986	1987
Gross Domestic Product	182	577	1013	1294	1724	2410	3159	4283	6653	11951	23400	52340
Plus: Net factor income from the rest of the world	4	29	53	59	91	103	124	116	223	291	420	1963
Factor income from the rest of the world	...	35	62	75	127	162	212	229	462	654	918	3438
Less: Factor income to the rest of the world	...	6	9	16	36	59	88	112	239	363	498	1475
Equals: Gross National Product	186	606	1066	1353	1814	2513	3283	4399	6876	12242	23820	54303
Less: Consumption of fixed capital	17	61	103	129	175	236	375	529	779	1325	2492	6561
Equals: National Income	169	545	963	1224	1640	2277	2908	3870	6097	10917	21328	47742
Plus: Net current transfers from the rest of the world	...	...	...	...	...	...	...	...	...	...	...	...
Equals: National Disposable Income	...	...	...	...	...	...	...	...	...	...	...	...
Less: Final consumption	...	...	...	...	...	...	...	...	...	...	...	...
Equals: Net Saving	...	...	...	...	...	...	...	...	...	...	...	...
Less: Surplus of the nation on current transactions	...	...	...	...	...	...	...	...	...	...	...	...
Equals: Net Capital Formation	...	...	...	...	...	...	...	...	...	...	...	...

Zaire

General note. The preparation of national accounts statistics in Zaire is undertaken by Institut de Recherche Scientifique, Kinshasa. Official estimates are published by the Banque du Zaire in 'Rapport Annuel'. The estimates are generally in accordance with the classifications and definitions recommended in the United Nations System of National Accounts (SNA). The following tables have been prepared from succesive replies to the United Nations national accounts questionnaire. When the scope and coverage of the estimates differ from conceptual or statistical reasons from the definitions and classifications recommend in SNA, a footnote is indicated to the relevant tables.

Sources and methods:

(a) Gross domestic product. Gross domestic product is estimated mainly through the production approach.

(b) Expenditure on the gross domestic product. The expenditure approach is used to estimate government final consumption expenditure and exports and imports of goods and services. This approach, together with the commodity flow approach, is used to estimate private final consumption expenditure and gross capital formation. The estimates of government consumption expenditure are derived from the government accounts. Information on private consumption expenditure is obtained from household sample surveys on expenditure conducted by the Institut National de la Statistique in the principal urban centres. The results of these surveys are extrapolated to cover the whole country. Some items are calculated as residuals by using the commodity-flow approach. For increase in stocks, information on the value of stocks at the beginning and end of the accounting year are obtained from the annual surveys of enterprises. For gross fixed capital formation, the estimates, using the commodity-flow approach, are based on information on acquisition of capital goods obtained from the surveys of enterprises. The estimates of capital formation by the general government, public enterprises and public corporations are derived from accounts while information from external trade statistics is used for machinery and equipment. The estimates of exports and imports of goods and services are derived from the balance of payments. The estimates of GDP by expenditure type at constant prices are obtained by applying to the value added at current prices the corresponding implicit price indexes.

(c) Cost-structure of the gross domestic product. The total of wages and salaries is estimated by extrapolating the bench-mark average wages and salaries from a special inquiry by indexes of yearly changes and multiplying the result by the number of employees. The estimates are adjusted to include the value of free lodging. Salaries paid by the government are obtained from budgetary accounts while those paid by enterprises are based on the annual reports of the Caisse des pensions. Estimates of income for unincorporated enterprises are derived from the estimates made of gross product from the production side. Estimates for the foreign population are based on the number of persons engaged in the various professions and their estimated average income. Income from property relates only to net rents and distributed profits received by the foreign population. The accounts of large enterprises are analysed to derive dividends and novelties received as well as direct taxes on corporations and corporate saving. General government income from property and entrepreneurship is derived from the budgets and accounts. The estimates of consumption of fixed capital are based on the results of the annual surveys of enterprises. Small enterprises are not included in the estimates. The annual surveys of enterprises also provide data on indirect taxes and subsidies.

(d) Gross domestic product by kind of economic activity. The table of GDP by kind of economic activity is prepared at market prices, i.e., producers' values. The production approach by commodity-flows is used to estimate the value of most industries. The income approach is used to estimate the value of public administration, defence and some private services. The Department de l'agriculture publishes annual statistical reports on agricultural production, livestock, forestry and fishing. Bench-mark estimates on gross output and value added have been prepared for 1970 based on a census of agriculture and livestock in the modern sector. In addition to this, the annual surveys of enterprises provide the values and the costs of production for the agricultural enterprises. For the modern agricultural sector, total production is valued on the basis of farm-gate prices while for the traditional sector, prices paid at the first sales point are used. The gross value of production in the mining and quarrying sector is estimated on the basis of data supplied by the Mining Service or is obtained from the annual surveys of enterprises. For large industrial enterprises, the annual surveys of industrial enterprises provide estimates of production and value added. For medium-sized and small enterprises, 1973 bench-mark data are obtained from a survey conducted at Kinshasa. These estimates are extrapolated for the country as a whole with a 90 per cent weighting for the city of Kinshasa. The data on electricity, gas and water are obtained from the public enterprises by means of a questionnaire. The estimates of construction in the private sector are based on the surveys of enterprises while the government budget and accounts are used for the public sector. Information on building permits issued in urban areas is used adjusted by means of average cost data per square meter of construction to give an estimate of construction for the whole country. For small construction, the 1973 data obtained from the survey conducted at Kinshasa are extrapolated by assuming that Kinshasa represent 77 per cent of the whole country. The annual surveys of enterprises which furnish information on purchases, services and value added are used to estimate the gross output in large organized trade enterprises. The gross output of the transportation sector is assumed to be equivalent to the gross receipts of transport enterprises. For the financial institutions, data are obtained from the surveys of enterprises as well as from the concerned enterprises directly. The estimates of services such as education, medical services, recreation, etc. are derived from profit-and-loss accounts, budgets of agencies and other offical statitics. For other services, the annual surveys of enterprises and household surveys of domestic servants provide the necessary data. The estimates of government services are derived from government accounts. The estimates of GDP by kind of economic activity at constant prices are obtained by applying to the value at current prices the corresponding implicit price indexes.

1.1 Expenditure on the Gross Domestic Product, in Current Prices

Million Zaires

		1970	1975	1978	1979	1980	1981	1982	1983	1984	1985	1986	1987
1	Government final consumption expenditure	266	452	893	1857	2756	4190	5948	8676	14999	17134	...	...
2	Private final consumption expenditure	413	1220	3812	6686	10426	15275	17094	36794	34363	70360	...	...
3	Gross capital formation	245	613	1007	2179	4277	5967	7493	11492	29322	43364	...	...
	A Increase in stocks	42	65	57	653	842	1292	1225	2010	8523	11378	...	...
	B Gross fixed capital formation	203	548	950	1526	3435	4675	6268	9482	20799	31986	...	...
4	Exports of goods and services	415	520	1216	2742	6102	8349	10013	23387	76783	106269	...	...
5	Less: Imports of goods and services	401	885	1448	2359	6379	10001	9437	21214	55883	89911	...	...
	Equals: Gross Domestic Product a	938	1919	5481	11105	17183	23781	31110	59134	99723	147263	203416	326946

a) Data in this table have been revised, therefore they are not strictly comparable with the unrevised data in the other tables.

1.2 Expenditure on the Gross Domestic Product, in Constant Prices

Million Zaires

		1970	1975	1978	1979	1980	1981	1982	1983	1984	1985	1986	1987
		At constant prices of:1970											
1	Government final consumption expenditure	260.9	224.4	...	...	...	...	...	...	...	...	...	...
2	Private final consumption expenditure	432.7	464.5	...	...	...	...	...	...	...	...	...	...
3	Gross capital formation	244.1	349.2	...	...	...	...	...	...	...	...	...	...
	A Increase in stocks	42.0	28.3	...	...	...	...	...	...	...	...	...	...
	B Gross fixed capital formation	202.1	320.9	...	...	...	...	...	...	...	...	...	...
4	Exports of goods and services	415.0	554.0	...	...	...	...	...	...	...	...	...	...
5	Less: Imports of goods and services	400.6	526.6	...	...	...	...	...	...	...	...	...	...
	Equals: Gross Domestic Product	952.1	1065.5	...	...	...	...	...	...	...	...	...	...

Zaire

1.3 Cost Components of the Gross Domestic Product

Million Zaires

	1970	1975	1978	1979	1980	1981	1982	1983	1984	1985	1986	1987
1 Indirect taxes, net	217.1	250.4	...	...	...	...	...	...	...	...	...	...
A Indirect taxes	217.4	262.4	...	...	...	...	...	...	...	...	...	...
B Less: Subsidies	0.3	12.0	...	...	...	...	...	...	...	...	...	...
2 Consumption of fixed capital	69.2	193.8	...	...	...	...	...	...	...	...	...	...
3 Compensation of employees paid by resident producers to:	665.8	1448.2	...	...	...	...	...	...	...	...	...	...
4 Operating surplus			...	...	...	...	...	...	...	...	...	...
Equals: Gross Domestic Product	952.1	1892.4										

1.10 Gross Domestic Product by Kind of Activity, in Current Prices

Million Zaires

	1970	1975	1978	1979	1980	1981	1982	1983	1984	1985	1986	1987
1 Agriculture, hunting, forestry and fishing	158.8	373.6	...	...	...	...	...	...	...	...	...	...
2 Mining and quarrying	211.2	200.2	...	...	...	...	...	...	...	...	...	...
3 Manufacturing	77.5	191.6	...	...	...	...	...	...	...	...	...	...
4 Electricity, gas and water	8.7	10.2	...	...	...	...	...	...	...	...	...	...
5 Construction	45.0	111.7	...	...	...	...	...	...	...	...	...	...
6 Wholesale and retail trade, restaurants and hotels [a]	106.4	326.5	...	...	...	...	...	...	...	...	...	...
7 Transport, storage and communication	75.9	82.3	...	...	...	...	...	...	...	...	...	...
8 Finance, insurance, real estate and business services [b]	19.4	44.3	...	...	...	...	...	...	...	...	...	...
9 Community, social and personal services [ab]	84.0	236.1	...	...	...	...	...	...	...	...	...	...
Total, Industries	786.9	1576.5	...	...	...	...	...	...	...	...	...	...
Producers of Government Services	119.3	248.8	...	...	...	...	...	...	...	...	...	...
Other Producers	...	...										
Subtotal	906.2	1825.3	...	...	...	...	...	...	...	...	...	...
Less: Imputed bank service charge	4.8	18.4	...	...	...	...	...	...	...	...	...	...
Plus: Import duties	50.7	85.5	...	...	...	...	...	...	...	...	...	...
Plus: Value added tax	...	...	...	...	...	...	...	...	...	...	...	...
Equals: Gross Domestic Product	952.1	1892.4	...	...	...	...	...	...	...	...	...	...

a) Restaurants and hotels are included in item 'Community, social and personal services'.
b) Insurance, real estate and business services are included in item 'Community, social and personal services'.

1.11 Gross Domestic Product by Kind of Activity, in Constant Prices

Million Zaires

	1970	1975	1978	1979	1980	1981	1982	1983	1984	1985	1986	1987
	\multicolumn{12}{c}{At constant prices of: 1970}											
1 Agriculture, hunting, forestry and fishing	158.8	172.6	...	...	...	...	...	...	...	...	...	...
2 Mining and quarrying	211.2	242.1	...	...	...	...	...	...	...	...	...	...
3 Manufacturing	77.5	92.1	...	...	...	...	...	...	...	...	...	...
4 Electricity, gas and water	8.7	10.2	...	...	...	...	...	...	...	...	...	...
5 Construction	45.0	58.1	...	...	...	...	...	...	...	...	...	...
6 Wholesale and retail trade, restaurants and hotels [a]	106.4	131.1	...	...	...	...	...	...	...	...	...	...
7 Transport, storage and communication	75.9	82.3	...	...	...	...	...	...	...	...	...	...
8 Finance, insurance, real estate and business services [b]	19.4	17.8	...	...	...	...	...	...	...	...	...	...
9 Community, social and personal services [ab]	84.0	94.8	...	...	...	...	...	...	...	...	...	...
Total, Industries	786.9	901.1	...	...	...	...	...	...	...	...	...	...
Producers of Government Services	119.3	135.2	...	...	...	...	...	...	...	...	...	...
Other Producers	...	...										
Subtotal	906.2	1036.3	...	...	...	...	...	...	...	...	...	...
Less: Imputed bank service charge	4.8	18.4	...	...	...	...	...	...	...	...	...	...
Plus: Import duties	50.7	47.6	...	...	...	...	...	...	...	...	...	...
Plus: Value added tax	...	...	...	...	...	...	...	...	...	...	...	...
Equals: Gross Domestic Product	952.1	1065.5	...	...	...	...	...	...	...	...	...	...

a) Restaurants and hotels are included in item 'Community, social and personal services'.
b) Insurance, real estate and business services are included in item 'Community, social and personal services'.

Zaire

1.12 Relations Among National Accounting Aggregates

Million Zaires

	1970	1975	1978	1979	1980	1981	1982	1983	1984	1985	1986	1987
Gross Domestic Product [a]	938.0	1919.0	5481.0	11105.0	17183.0	23781.0	31110.0	59134.0	99723.0	47263.0	...	...
Plus: Net factor income from the rest of the world	-55.9	-94.0	-180.0	-384.0	-742.0	-935.0	-1647.0	-2562.0	11452.0	-4084.0	...	...
Equals: Gross National Product	882.1	1825.0	5301.0	10721.0	16441.0	22846.0	29463.0	56572.0	88271.0	43179.0	...	...
Less: Consumption of fixed capital	69.2	195.0	382.0	439.0	548.0	837.0	1220.0	1725.0	2501.0	4331.0	...	...
Equals: National Income	813.0	1630.0	4919.0	10282.0	15893.0	22009.0	28243.0	54847.0	85770.0	38848.0	...	...
Plus: Net current transfers from the rest of the world	28.4	57.3	...	...	...	...	...	...	...	...	...	...
Equals: National Disposable Income	841.3	1687.3	...	...	...	...	...	...	...	...	...	...
Less: Final consumption	...	...	...	...	...	...	...	...	...	...	...	...
Equals: Net Saving	...	...	...	...	...	...	...	...	...	...	...	...
Less: Surplus of the nation on current transactions	...	...	...	...	...	...	...	...	...	...	...	...
Equals: Net Capital Formation	...	...	...	...	...	...	...	...	...	...	...	...

a) Data in this table have been revised, therefore they are not strictly comparable with the unrevised data in the other tables.

Zambia

General note. The preparation of national accounts statistics in Zambia is undertaken by the Central Statistical Office (CSO), Lusaka. The official estimates are published in November-December issue of the Monthly Digest of Statistics. A description of the sources and methods used for the National Accounts estimation is found in 'National Accounts and Input-Output Tables, 1971' and 'National Accounts, 1972' published in August 1975 and June 1978, respectively. The estimates are generally in accordance with the classifications and definitions recommended in the United Nations System of National Accounts (SNA). The following tables have been prepared from successive replies to the United Nations national accounts questionnaire. When the scope and coverage of the estimates differ for conceptual or statistical reasons from the definitions and classifications recommended in SNA, a footnote is indicated to the relevant tables.

Sources and methods:

(a) Gross domestic product. Gross domestic product is estimated mainly through the production approach.

(b) Expenditure on the gross domestic product. All components of GDP by expenditure type are estimated through the expenditure approach except for the total estimate of private consumption expenditure which is obtained as a residual. However, a detailed breakdown is obtained through the use of the expenditure approach. Data used to estimate government expenditure are contained in 'Financial Statistics of the Government Sector' supplemented by detailed tabulations prepared by the CSO. The 'Urban Household Budget Survey in Low-cost Housing Areas, 1966-1968' and the household budget surveys 1974/75 for the urban and rural areas provide a detailed breakdown for the private consumption expenditure. Data on changes in stocks are collected through the annual national income inquiries and the balance sheets supplied by the enterprises. These two sources as well as government accounts are also used to estimate gross fixed capital formation. For transport equipment and machinery, furniture etc., the estimates are based closely on end-use groupings of imports and domestic products. Transactions with the rest of the world are estimated from the balance of payments statistics. Data on exports and imports are obtained from the annual statements of external trade prepared by the CSO. The CSO also undertakes a special inquiry on international transactions of all major private and public sector enterprises. For the constant price estimates, the current values of the expenditure items are deflated by various price indexes such as weighted index of wages and prices, consumer price index, implicit price index, etc.

(c) Cost-structure of the gross domestic product. The estimates of compensation of employees are based on information obtained through the annual income inquiries, the annual censuses of production and construction and other sources. Grossing-up factors to account for non-responding units are worked out on the basis of employment data collected through the quarterly employment surveys. Compensation of employees includes an estimated figure for domestic servant based on the 1969 population census data projected by an assumed 5 per cent annual growth rate. Consumption of fixed capital figures are obtained from the balance sheets of enterprises. Depreciation is imputed for some government enterprises and government administration and for owner-occupied buildings in urban and rural areas. Indirect taxes estimates are derived from the annual national income inquiries, the annual censuses of industrial production and construction data. Operating surplus is obtained as a residual.

(d) Gross domestic product by kind of economic activity. The table of GDP by kind of economic activity is prepared at market prices, i.e., producers' values. The production approach is used to estimate the value added of nearly all industries. The income approach is used for the value added of producers of government services. The accounts of the agricultural sector have been divided into a commercial sector and a subsistence sector. The commercial sector includes all surplus production of the rural areas, the output of agricultural extension services, own-account capital formation and retentions by commercial farmers. The estimates for the subsistence sector are restricted to own consumption by traditional producers. The Quarterly Agricultural Statistical Bulletin gives information on intakes of agricultural products, official producer prices and input prices. Intake data are used for estimating surplus productions of commercial and non-commercial farmers. The output of agricultural extension services relates to tenant schemes of the Tobacco Board of Zambia and the extension services of the government. The estimates of own-account capital formation of livestocks are based on the annual surveys of agricultural and pastoral production and on annual censuses of livestock. The estimates of retentions by commercial farmers are also based on the annual surveys of agricultural and pastoral production. The 1971/72 survey included, for the first time, information on intermediate inputs of commercial farmers. This information is used for non-commercial farmers as well. The average input-output ratio for 1972 has been applied to agricultural output for earlier years. For later years, a constant real input-output ratio is assumed. Estimates of the subsistence sector's own-consumed production are derived from total production estimates by subtracting surplus production, covered by the commercial sector estimates. This is done for crops on the basis of the first sample census of non-commercial farms held during the crop year 1970/71. The annual censuses of industrial production provide the data for the estimates of mining and quarrying, manufacturing and electricity and water. For mining, the financial statements of the mining companies are also used. For manufacturing, extensive data on output and input of goods and services are available from the censuses. Provisions for non-responding establishments are made on the basis of employment data. The annual censuses of construction by contractors provide data for the construction sector. For own-account construction by households, the Ministry of Local Government and Housing provides information on the number, type and cost of houses. The principal source for the services sectors-trade, transport, communication, financial and community services - is the annual national income inquiry. Questionnaires are sent out annually to all large and medium-sized establishments and on a sample basis for small establishments using a short form. Information by kind of economic activity, is requested on employment, earnings, operating and non-operating incomes and expenditure, appropriation of surplus, capital investment and input and output of materials. For owner-occupied dwellings, rents are estimated on the basis of cost of houses and their life and on data from the household budget surveys. For producers of government services, estimates are based on financial statistics of the government sector. For constant price estimates, double deflation is used for the agricultural and mining sectors. For the remaining sectors, the current values are deflated by various price indexes.

1.1 Expenditure on the Gross Domestic Product, in Current Prices

Million Zambian kwacha

	1970	1975	1978	1979	1980	1981	1982	1983	1984	1985	1986	1987
1 Government final consumption expenditure	206.0	435.7	537.8	633.0	781.6	986.0	995.9	1008.8	1240.1	1686.7	3002.3	...
2 Private final consumption expenditure [a]	490.0	814.5	1251.5	1412.6	1691.9	2262.2	2312.1	2645.5	2848.5	4146.8	7496.6	...
3 Gross capital formation	367.0	642.0	537.0	376.0	713.3	673.3	602.9	575.0	724.0	1053.0	1791.0	...
A Increase in stocks	-12.0	40.0	100.0	-74.0	155.0	63.3	-15.1	-40.0	101.4	328.5	730.3	...
B Gross fixed capital formation	379.0	602.0	437.0	450.0	558.3	610.0	618.0	615.0	622.6	724.5	1060.7	...
Residential buildings	47.0	...	...	...	...	...	...	...	...	...	...	...
Non-residential buildings	43.0	...	...	...	...	...	...	...	...	...	...	...
Other construction and land improvement etc.	137.0	...	...	...	...	...	...	...	...	...	...	...
Other	151.0	...	...	...	...	...	...	...	...	...	...	...
4 Exports of goods and services	685.0	575.0	755.3	1208.3	1268.0	998.0	993.1	1280.7	1755.1	2627.8	5602.4	...
5 Less: Imports of goods and services	471.0	883.8	830.9	969.5	1391.2	1434.1	1311.5	1328.8	1636.7	2465.7	5794.4	...
Equals: Gross Domestic Product	1278.0	1583.4	2250.7	2660.4	3063.6	3485.4	3595.3	4181.2	4931.0	7048.6	12097.9	...

a) Item 'Private final consumption expenditure' has been obtained as a residual.

1.2 Expenditure on the Gross Domestic Product, in Constant Prices

Million Zambian kwacha

	1970	1975	1978	1979	1980	1981	1982	1983	1984	1985	1986	1987
			At constant prices of:									
		1970					1977					
1 Government final consumption expenditure	206.0	287.2	473.0	473.4	531.3	611.3	541.5	454.6	483.8	460.1	488.9	...
2 Private final consumption expenditure	490.0	565.2	1034.5	1143.6	1104.0	1176.4	1089.0	1102.1	1113.5	1281.9	1080.7	
3 Gross capital formation	367.0	427.3	474.8	266.7	439.1	390.5	298.9	226.5	242.0	261.2	308.5	
A Increase in stocks	-12.0	33.8	90.3	-45.0	94.0	38.1	-10.6	-21.1	30.1	62.4	127.2	
B Gross fixed capital formation	379.0	393.5	384.5	311.7	345.1	352.4	309.5	247.6	211.9	198.8	181.3	

Zambia

1.2 Expenditure on the Gross Domestic Product, in Constant Prices
(Continued)

Million Zambian kwacha

	1970	1975	1978	1979	1980	1981	1982	1983	1984	1985	1986	1987
					At constant prices of:							
		1970					1977					
Residential buildings	47.0	...	...	...	...	...	...	...	...	...	...	...
Non-residential buildings	43.0	...	...	...	...	...	...	...	...	...	...	...
Other construction and land improvement etc.	137.0	...	...	...	...	...	...	...	...	...	...	...
Other	151.0	...	...	...	...	...	...	...	...	...	...	...
4 Exports of goods and services	685.0	683.2	731.2	652.8	632.7	552.0	640.4	567.3	536.9	506.1	545.8	...
5 Less: Imports of goods and services	471.0	454.9	689.6	629.5	710.4	596.4	465.4	392.7	383.0	424.4	465.4	...
Statistical discrepancy	-	-69.9	-26.1	30.0	-0.9	-14.9	-45.1	61.0	18.3	-47.8	93.7	...
Equals: Gross Domestic Product	1278.0	1438.1	1997.8	1937.0	1995.8	2118.9	2059.3	2018.8	2011.5	2041.4	2052.2	...

1.3 Cost Components of the Gross Domestic Product

Million Zambian kwacha

	1970	1975	1978	1979	1980	1981	1982	1983	1984	1985	1986	1987
1 Indirect taxes, net [a]	68.0	117.7	246.4	237.0	221.0	357.3	345.2	632.1	666.9	740.2	2031.5	...
A Indirect taxes [a]	87.0	207.7	288.5	342.3	417.8	467.5	502.1	714.3	758.5	928.6	2365.3	...
B Less: Subsidies [a]	19.0	90.0	42.1	105.3	196.8	110.2	156.9	82.2	91.6	188.4	333.8	...
2 Consumption of fixed capital	136.0	243.0	299.6	307.5	339.1	383.4	405.8	426.4	630.3	948.5	1711.6	...
3 Compensation of employees paid by resident producers to:	481.0	802.0	1110.4	1234.1	1436.8	1722.7	1920.1	1974.2	2162.9	2859.3	4278.9	...
A Resident households	481.0	802.0	1110.4	1234.1	1436.8	1722.7	1920.1	1974.2	2162.9	2859.3	4278.9	...
B Rest of the world	-	-	-	-	-	-	-	-	-	-	-	...
4 Operating surplus	592.0	420.7	594.3	881.8	1066.7	1022.0	924.2	1148.5	1470.9	2500.6	4075.9	...
Equals: Gross Domestic Product	1278.0	1583.4	2250.9	2660.4	3063.6	3485.4	3595.3	4181.2	4931.0	7048.6	12097.9	...

a) The estimates of indirect taxes and subsidies are entered on accrual payment basis.

1.7 External Transactions on Current Account, Summary

Million Zambian kwacha

	1970	1975	1978	1979	1980	1981	1982	1983	1984	1985	1986	1987
					Payments to the Rest of the World							
1 Imports of goods and services	470.5	883.8	830.9	969.5	1391.2	1434.1	1311.5	1328.8	1636.7	2465.7	5794.4	...
A Imports of merchandise c.i.f.	408.0	760.9	648.4	745.2	1085.8	1097.3	1083.9	1067.2	1345.1	2103.6	5224.6	...
B Other	62.5	122.9	182.5	224.3	305.4	336.8	227.6	261.6	291.6	362.1	569.8	...
2 Factor income to the rest of the world	62.2	82.5	112.9	128.4	233.8	115.3	230.9	250.0	380.0	599.5	1249.9	...
A Compensation of employees	-	-	-	-	-	-	-	-	-	-	...	...
B Property and entrepreneurial income	62.2	82.5	112.9	128.4	233.8	115.3	230.9	250.0	380.0	599.5	1249.9	...
3 Current transfers to the rest of the world	110.5	87.2	70.6	113.2	166.1	140.4	67.1	59.5	89.5	109.8	318.5	...
4 Surplus of the nation on current transactions	77.0	-465.2	-230.9	35.8	-490.3	-648.5	-570.9	-298.5	-317.0	-429.2	-1670.2	...
Payments to the Rest of the World and Surplus of the Nation on Current Transactions	720.1	588.3	783.6	1246.9	1300.8	1041.3	1038.6	1340.0	1789.2	2745.8	5692.6	...
					Receipts From The Rest of the World							
1 Exports of goods and services	685.4	575.0	755.3	1208.3	1268.0	998.0	993.1	1280.7	1755.1	2627.8	5602.4	...
A Exports of merchandise f.o.b.	727.2	530.9	707.9	1107.6	1149.2	866.3	877.6	1150.4	1618.4	2447.5	5247.0	...

Zambia

1.7 External Transactions on Current Account, Summary
(Continued)

Million Zambian kwacha

	1970	1975	1978	1979	1980	1981	1982	1983	1984	1985	1986	1987
B Other	-41.8	44.1	47.4	100.7	118.8	131.7	115.5	130.1	136.7	180.3	355.4	...
2 Factor income from rest of the world	28.8	7.9	6.8	8.8	5.2	17.4	11.7	3.6	8.6	5.0	10.0	...
A Compensation of employees	-	-	-	-	-	-	-	-	-	-	-	...
B Property and entrepreneurial income	28.8	7.9	6.8	8.8	5.2	17.4	11.7	3.6	8.6	5.0	10.0	...
By general government	...	...	...	...	0.5	0.2	0.9	0.9	1.3	1.0	...	...
By corporate and quasi-corporate enterprises	...	...	...	...	-	0.2	-	-	-	-	...	...
By other	...	...	...	...	4.7	17.0	10.8	3.0	7.3	4.0	...	...
3 Current transfers from rest of the world	5.9	5.4	21.5	29.8	27.6	25.9	31.0	55.7	25.5	113.0	80.2	...
Receipts from the Rest of the World on Current Transactions	720.1	588.3	783.6	1246.9	1300.8	1041.3	1038.6	1340.0	1789.2	2745.8	5692.6	...

1.10 Gross Domestic Product by Kind of Activity, in Current Prices

Million Zambian kwacha

	1970	1975	1978	1979	1980	1981	1982	1983	1984	1985	1986	1987
1 Agriculture, hunting, forestry and fishing	126.3	206.4	363.0	397.2	435.3	553.8	492.2	593.7	717.2	925.2	1304.6	...
2 Mining and quarrying	458.0	215.2	286.8	469.3	501.7	488.4	396.6	641.6	673.8	1101.9	2978.6	...
3 Manufacturing	129.1	250.3	430.1	486.7	566.1	684.1	740.4	829.8	1010.6	1610.0	2431.5	...
4 Electricity, gas and water	17.7	43.0	57.7	59.9	61.0	66.3	72.2	70.4	69.7	71.1	72.3	...
5 Construction	90.3	151.2	111.5	101.2	136.5	111.7	127.0	133.1	153.3	182.9	304.0	...
6 Wholesale and retail trade, restaurants and hotels	133.6	157.5	260.0	287.9	361.2	410.9	452.9	524.9	646.8	944.1	1293.0	...
7 Transport, storage and communication	45.6	88.5	125.5	148.6	161.5	171.1	193.2	227.4	251.3	325.5	598.3	...
8 Finance, insurance, real estate and business services	87.6	159.8	222.3	258.4	290.9	325.0	363.3	403.6	517.2	683.7	1027.7	...
9 Community, social and personal services	11.3	10.9	18.1	20.1	23.4	29.3	33.3	35.4	40.1	46.8	58.1	...
Total, Industries	1099.5	1282.8	1875.0	2229.3	2537.6	2840.6	2871.1	3459.9	4080.0	5891.2	10068.1	...
Producers of Government Services	134.7	217.4	344.1	381.8	444.6	557.5	631.9	673.5	760.2	887.5	1101.6	...
Other Producers	21.4	40.2	...	...	...	...	...	...	...	...	...	...
Subtotal	1255.6	1540.4	2219.1	2611.1	2982.2	3398.1	3503.0	4133.4	4840.2	6778.7	11169.7	...
Less: Imputed bank service charge	9.7	19.0	23.5	29.0	31.1	33.7	38.8	44.9	49.6	64.2	111.1	...
Plus: Import duties	32.1	62.0	55.1	78.3	112.5	121.0	131.1	92.7	140.4	334.1	1039.5	...
Plus: Value added tax	...	...	...	...	...	...	...	...	...	...	...	...
Equals: Gross Domestic Product	1278.0	1583.4	2250.7	2660.4	3063.6	3485.4	3595.3	4181.2	4931.0	7048.6	12097.9	...

1.11 Gross Domestic Product by Kind of Activity, in Constant Prices

Million Zambian kwacha

	1970	1975	1978	1979	1980	1981	1982	1983	1984	1985	1986	1987
	At constant prices of:											
	1970						1977					
1 Agriculture, hunting, forestry and fishing	126.3	157.0	327.5	309.7	303.9	328.7	290.3	314.6	332.2	343.8	363.8	...
2 Mining and quarrying	458.0	427.9	245.2	195.1	205.2	214.8	215.2	221.7	200.0	185.4	173.9	...
3 Manufacturing	129.1	157.6	370.5	392.9	383.5	430.2	415.1	384.5	389.3	419.5	421.2	...
4 Electricity, gas and water	17.7	48.9	60.6	63.4	65.8	71.0	75.8	72.2	70.9	72.7	74.1	...
5 Construction	90.3	138.5	104.1	89.0	102.8	78.9	84.0	88.6	88.6	77.1	81.1	...
6 Wholesale and retail trade, restaurants and hotels	133.6	123.8	224.7	210.9	236.3	248.6	231.8	227.6	216.9	226.0	218.2	...
7 Transport, storage and communication	45.6	57.6	119.4	123.9	117.5	118.3	118.8	119.4	116.2	108.7	107.1	...
8 Finance, insurance, real estate and business services	87.6	132.9	194.5	207.0	211.3	218.3	226.5	234.5	242.0	239.6	246.1	...
9 Community, social and personal services	11.3	7.0	16.6	16.4	17.3	19.6	19.7	17.8	17.8	18.3	18.1	...

Zambia

1.11 Gross Domestic Product by Kind of Activity, in Constant Prices
(Continued)

Million Zambian kwacha

	1970	1975	1978	1979	1980	1981	1982	1983	1984	1985	1986	1987
					At constant prices of:							
		1970					1977					
Total, Industries	1099.5	1251.2	1663.1	1608.3	1643.6	1728.4	1677.2	1680.9	1673.9	1691.1	1703.6	...
Producers of Government Services	134.7	140.9	312.9	312.2	328.7	372.3	374.2	337.9	337.1	347.3	343.4	...
Other Producers	21.4	32.7	...	...	...	...	...	...	...	...	...	...
Subtotal	1255.6	1424.8	1976.0	1920.5	1972.3	2100.7	2051.4	2018.8	2011.0	2038.4	2047.0	
Less: Imputed bank service charge	9.7	13.6	18.8	20.6	18.8	18.2	19.8	18.5	17.5	16.9	16.8	
Plus: Import duties	32.1	26.9	40.6	37.1	42.3	36.4	27.7	18.5	18.0	19.9	22.0	...
Plus: Value added tax	...	...	...									...
Equals: Gross Domestic Product	1278.0	1438.1	1997.8	1937.0	1995.8	2118.9	2059.3	2018.8	2011.5	2041.4	2052.2	...

1.12 Relations Among National Accounting Aggregates

Million Zambian kwacha

	1970	1975	1978	1979	1980	1981	1982	1983	1984	1985	1986	1987
Gross Domestic Product	1278.0	1583.4	2250.7	2660.4	3063.6	3485.4	3595.3	4181.2	4931.0	7048.6	12097.9	...
Plus: Net factor income from the rest of the world	-33.4	-74.6	-106.1	-119.6	-228.6	-97.9	-219.2	-246.1	-371.4	-594.5	-1239.9	
Factor income from the rest of the world	28.8	7.9	6.8	8.8	5.2	17.4	11.7	3.6	8.6	5.0	10.0	
Less: Factor income to the rest of the world	62.2	82.5	112.9	128.4	233.8	115.3	230.9	250.0	380.0	599.5	1249.9	
Equals: Gross National Product	1244.6	1508.8	2144.6	2540.8	2835.0	3387.5	3376.1	3934.8	4559.6	6454.1	10858.0	
Less: Consumption of fixed capital	136.0	243.0	299.6	307.5	339.1	383.4	405.8	426.4	630.3	948.5	1711.6	
Equals: National Income	1108.0	1265.8	1845.0	2233.3	2495.9	3004.1	2970.3	3508.4	3929.3	5505.6	9146.4	
Plus: Net current transfers from the rest of the world	-105.0	-81.8	-49.1	-83.4	-138.5	-114.5	-36.1	-3.8	-64.0	3.2	-238.3	
Current transfers from the rest of the world	5.9	5.4	21.5	29.8	27.6	25.9	31.0	55.7	25.5	113.0	80.2	
Less: Current transfers to the rest of the world	110.5	87.2	70.6	113.2	166.1	140.4	67.1	59.5	89.5	109.8	318.5	
Equals: National Disposable Income	1003.0	1184.0	1795.9	2149.9	2357.4	2889.6	2934.2	3504.6	3865.3	5508.8	8908.1	
Less: Final consumption	696.0	1250.2	1789.3	2045.6	2473.3	3248.2	3308.0	3654.3	4088.6	5833.5	10498.9	
Equals: Net Saving	307.9	-66.2	6.6	104.3	-115.9	-358.6	-373.8	-149.7	-223.3	-324.7	-1590.8	
Less: Surplus of the nation on current transactions	77.0	-465.2	-230.8	35.8	-490.3	-648.5	-570.9	-298.7	-317.0	-429.2	-1670.2	
Equals: Net Capital Formation	231.0	399.0	237.4	68.5	374.2	289.9	197.1	148.8	93.7	104.5	79.4	

2.17 Exports and Imports of Goods and Services, Detail

Million Zambian kwacha

	1970	1975	1978	1979	1980	1981	1982	1983	1984	1985	1986	1987
					Exports of Goods and Services							
1 Exports of merchandise, f.o.b.	727.2	530.9	707.9	1107.6	1038.5	950.9	969.7	1061.8	1192.0	1494.7	5247.0	...
2 Transport and communication	-	44.8	66.5	66.8	72.7	69.4	64.9	80.0	87.6	118.3	234.4	...
A In respect of merchandise imports	-	35.8	49.3	37.9	48.5	35.8	27.3	37.0	41.1	52.3	157.4	...
B Other	-	9.0	17.2	28.9	24.2	33.6	37.6	43.0	46.5	66.0	77.0	...
3 Insurance service charges	2.4	-	-	-	...	...	...	...	...	...	...	...
A In respect of merchandise imports	-	-	-	-	...	...	...	...	...	...	...	...
B Other	2.4	-	-	-	...	...	...	...	...	...	...	...
4 Other commodities	4.8	8.0	13.7	12.9	9.5	14.1	2.0	2.0	2.5	4.0	5.0	...
5 Adjustments of merchandise exports to change-of-ownership basis	-54.0	-14.7	-42.8	9.0	110.7	-84.6	-89.5	100.4	426.4	952.8	-	
6 Direct purchases in the domestic market by non-residential households	5.0	6.0	10.0	12.0	16.6	27.0	23.0	23.3	23.0	24.0	48.0	
7 Direct purchases in the domestic market by extraterritorial bodies	...	...	...	...	20.0	21.2	23.0	25.0	23.6	34.0	68.0	
Total Exports of Goods and Services	685.4	575.0	755.3	1208.3	1268.0	998.0	993.1	1292.5	1755.1	2627.8	5602.4	...
					Imports of Goods and Services							
1 Imports of merchandise, c.i.f.	408.0	760.9	648.4	745.2	1085.8	1097.3	1083.9	1067.2	1345.1	2103.6	5224.6	

Zambia

2.17 Exports and Imports of Goods and Services, Detail
(Continued)

Million Zambian kwacha

	1970	1975	1978	1979	1980	1981	1982	1983	1984	1985	1986	1987
A Imports of merchandise, f.o.b.	347.7	609.6	494.8	599.8	878.7	926.4	932.0	895.2	1109.9	1790.0	4294.1	...
B Transport of services on merchandise imports	54.5	139.0	...	...	207.1	170.9	151.9	172.0	235.2	313.6	930.5	...
By residents	-	35.8	48.0	41.1	...	...	...	...	...	...	...	...
By non-residents	54.5	103.2	...	...	207.1	170.9	151.9	172.0	235.2	313.6	930.5	...
C Insurance service charges on merchandise imports	5.8	12.3	...	...	...	...	...	...	...	...	...	...
By residents	-	-	...	...	...	...	...	...	...	...	...	...
By non-residents	5.8	12.3	...	...	...	...	...	...	...	...	...	...
2 Adjustments of merchandise imports to change-of-ownership basis	...	...	...	...	...	...	...	...	...	...	...	...
3 Other transport and communication	14.0	32.0	53.0	89.2	88.4	77.6	79.4	100.0	110.3	157.0	183.3	...
4 Other insurance service charges	1.4	-	-	-	...	...	...	...	...	...	...	...
5 Other commodities	27.2	61.6	80.5	88.2	164.5	180.0	50.6	118.7	120.0	126.4	109.0	...
6 Direct purchases abroad by government	1.5	5.7	17.7	21.1	10.0	19.3	17.8	16.6	17.6	27.0	130.0	...
7 Direct purchases abroad by resident households	18.4	23.6	31.3	25.8	42.5	59.9	79.7	26.3	43.5	51.7	146.6	...
Total Imports of Goods and Services	470.5	883.8	830.9	969.5	1391.2	1434.1	1311.4	1328.4	1636.5	2465.7	5793.5	...
Balance of Goods and Services	214.9	-308.8	-75.6	238.8	-123.2	-436.1	-318.3	-36.3	118.6	162.1	-191.1	...
Total Imports and Balance of Goods and Services	685.4	575.0	755.3	1208.3	1268.0	998.0	993.1	1292.1	1755.1	2627.8	5602.4	...

4.1 Derivation of Value Added by Kind of Activity, in Current Prices

Million Zambian kwacha

	1980 Gross Output	1980 Intermediate Consumption	1980 Value Added	1981 Gross Output	1981 Intermediate Consumption	1981 Value Added	1982 Gross Output	1982 Intermediate Consumption	1982 Value Added	1983 Gross Output	1983 Intermediate Consumption	1983 Value Added
						All Producers						
1 Agriculture, hunting, forestry and fishing	...	...	435.3	...	...	553.8	...	...	492.2	...	...	593.7
A Agriculture and hunting	...	...	386.8	...	...	504.2	...	...	426.5	...	...	521.5
B Forestry and logging	...	...	27.8	...	...	29.4	...	...	32.4	...	...	34.2
C Fishing	...	...	20.7	...	...	20.2	...	...	33.3	...	...	38.0
2 Mining and quarrying	...	...	501.7	...	...	488.4	...	...	396.6	...	...	641.6
A Coal mining	...	...	...	...	...	...	...	...	...	...	...	...
B Crude petroleum and natural gas production	...	...	...	...	...	...	...	...	...	...	...	...
C Metal ore mining	...	...	490.1	...	...	472.7	...	...	381.6	...	...	619.1
D Other mining	...	...	11.6	...	...	15.7	...	...	15.0	...	...	22.5
3 Manufacturing	...	...	566.1	...	...	684.1	...	...	740.4	...	...	829.8
A Manufacture of food, beverages and tobacco	...	...	266.0	...	...	317.5	...	...	351.3	...	...	393.9
B Textile, wearing apparel and leather industries	...	...	72.1	...	...	89.3	...	...	100.3	...	...	104.0
C Manufacture of wood and wood products, including furniture	...	...	19.1	...	...	33.3	...	...	32.3	...	...	16.2
D Manufacture of paper and paper products, printing and publishing	...	...	20.4	...	...	20.6	...	...	19.6	...	...	23.2
E Manufacture of chemicals and chemical petroleum, coal, rubber and plastic products	...	...	69.5	...	...	87.1	...	...	74.9	...	...	83.4
F Manufacture of non-metallic mineral products, except products of petroleum and coal	...	...	27.0	...	...	48.5	...	...	58.9	...	...	81.2
G Basic metal industries	...	...	8.1	...	...	8.2	...	...	6.0	...	...	11.8
H Manufacture of fabricated metal products, machinery and equipment	...	...	78.3	...	...	73.0	...	...	89.6	...	...	107.5
I Other manufacturing industries	...	...	5.6	...	...	6.6	...	...	7.5	...	...	8.6
4 Electricity, gas and water	...	...	61.0	...	...	66.3	...	...	72.2	...	...	70.4

Zambia

4.1 Derivation of Value Added by Kind of Activity, in Current Prices
(Continued)

Million Zambian kwacha

	1980 Gross Output	1980 Intermediate Consumption	1980 Value Added	1981 Gross Output	1981 Intermediate Consumption	1981 Value Added	1982 Gross Output	1982 Intermediate Consumption	1982 Value Added	1983 Gross Output	1983 Intermediate Consumption	1983 Value Added
5 Construction	...	...	136.5	...	...	111.7	...	...	127.0	...	...	133.1
6 Wholesale and retail trade, restaurants and hotels	...	...	361.2	...	...	410.9	...	...	452.9	...	...	524.9
A Wholesale and retail trade	...	...	301.5	...	...	328.0	...	...	355.5	...	...	401.6
B Restaurants and hotels	...	...	59.7	...	...	82.9	...	...	97.4	...	...	123.3
7 Transport, storage and communication	...	...	161.5	...	...	171.1	...	...	193.2	...	...	227.4
A Transport and storage	...	...	135.1	...	...	142.8	...	...	161.1	...	...	189.2
B Communication	...	...	26.4	...	...	28.3	...	...	32.1	...	...	38.2
8 Finance, insurance, real estate and business services	...	...	290.9	...	...	325.0	...	...	363.3	...	...	403.6
A Financial institutions	...	...	110.0	...	...	119.2	...	...	137.3	...	...	156.6
B Insurance												
C Real estate and business services	...	...	180.9	...	...	205.8	...	...	226.0	...	...	247.0
9 Community, social and personal services [a]	...	...	468.0	...	...	586.8	...	...	665.2	...	...	708.9
A Sanitary and similar services	...	...	202.8	...	...	262.0	...	...	290.0	...	...	281.0
B Social and related community services	...	...	196.4	...	...	244.4	...	...	287.7	...	...	324.7
Educational services	...	...	148.2	...	...	180.2	...	...	211.2	...	...	237.0
Medical, dental, other health and veterinary services	...	...	48.2	...	...	64.2	...	...	76.5	...	...	87.7
C Recreational and cultural services	...	...	18.8	...	...	24.9	...	...	25.6	...	...	30.0
D Personal and household services	...	...	50.0	...	...	55.5	...	...	61.9	...	...	73.0
Total, Industries	...	...	...	...	...	...	...	...	...	...	...	...
Producers of Government Services [a]	...	...	...	...	...	...	...	...	...	...	...	...
Other Producers [a]	...	...	...	...	...	...	...	...	...	...	...	...
Total	...	...	2982.2	...	...	3398.1	...	...	3503.0	...	...	4133.4
Less: Imputed bank service charge	...	...	31.1	...	...	33.7	...	...	38.8	...	...	44.9
Import duties	...	...	112.5	...	...	121.0	...	...	131.1	...	...	92.7
Value added tax	...	...	...	...	...	...	...	...	...	...	...	...
Total	...	...	3063.6	...	...	3485.4	...	...	3595.3	...	...	4181.2

	1984 Gross Output	1984 Intermediate Consumption	1984 Value Added	1985 Gross Output	1985 Intermediate Consumption	1985 Value Added	1986 Gross Output	1986 Intermediate Consumption	1986 Value Added
				All Producers					
1 Agriculture, hunting, forestry and fishing	...	...	717.2	...	...	925.2	...	...	1304.6
A Agriculture and hunting	...	...	624.1	...	...	775.3	...	...	1049.6
B Forestry and logging	...	...	44.5	...	...	72.2	...	...	162.8
C Fishing	...	...	48.6	...	...	77.7	...	...	92.2
2 Mining and quarrying	...	...	673.8	...	...	1101.9	...	...	2978.1
A Coal mining	...	...	...	...	...	...	...	...	...
B Crude petroleum and natural gas production	...	...	...	...	...	...	...	...	...
C Metal ore mining	...	...	644.8	...	...	1056.8	...	...	2886.2
D Other mining	...	...	29.0	...	...	45.1	...	...	91.9

Zambia

4.1 Derivation of Value Added by Kind of Activity, in Current Prices
(Continued)

Million Zambian kwacha

	1984 Gross Output	1984 Intermediate Consumption	1984 Value Added	1985 Gross Output	1985 Intermediate Consumption	1985 Value Added	1986 Gross Output	1986 Intermediate Consumption	1986 Value Added
3 Manufacturing	...	...	1010.6	...	...	1610.0	...	...	2431.5
A Manufacture of food, beverages and tobacco	...	...	442.2	...	...	593.1	...	...	803.2
B Textile, wearing apparel and leather industries	...	...	130.5	...	...	212.6	...	...	274.9
C Manufacture of wood and wood products, including furniture	...	...	22.8	...	...	43.8	...	...	99.6
D Manufacture of paper and paper products, printing and publishing	...	...	34.9	...	...	95.4	...	...	156.7
E Manufacture of chemicals and chemical petroleum, coal, rubber and plastic products	...	...	108.6	...	...	194.8	...	...	339.0
F Manufacture of non-metallic mineral products, except products of petroleum and coal	...	...	69.8	...	...	129.7	...	...	113.5
G Basic metal industries	...	...	13.0	...	...	13.2	...	...	17.5
H Manufacture of fabricated metal products, machinery and equipment	...	...	177.6	...	...	309.6	...	...	599.5
I Other manufacturing industries	...	...	11.2	...	...	17.8	...	...	27.6
4 Electricity, gas and water	...	...	69.7	...	...	71.1	...	...	72.3
5 Construction	...	...	153.3	...	...	183.2	...	...	304.0
6 Wholesale and retail trade, restaurants and hotels	...	...	646.8	...	...	944.1	...	...	1293.3
A Wholesale and retail trade	...	...	520.8	...	...	763.0	...	...	1049.4
B Restaurants and hotels	...	...	126.0	...	...	181.1	...	...	243.9
7 Transport, storage and communication	...	...	251.3	...	...	325.5	...	...	598.3
A Transport and storage	...	...	205.5	...	...	260.0	...	...	477.8
B Communication	...	...	45.8	...	...	65.5	...	...	120.5
8 Finance, insurance, real estate and business services	...	...	517.2	...	...	683.7	...	...	1027.7
A Financial institutions	...	...	[172.9]	...	...	69.0	...	...	97.6
B Insurance	...	...		...	...	159.9	...	...	298.7
C Real estate and business services	...	...	344.3	...	...	454.8	...	...	631.4
9 Community, social and personal services [a]	...	...	800.3	...	...	934.3	...	...	1159.7
A Sanitary and similar services	...	...	318.5	...	...	391.7	...	...	480.2
B Social and related community services	...	...	360.2	...	...	404.7	...	...	507.5
Educational services	...	...	259.0	...	...	292.1	...	...	384.1
Medical, dental, other health and veterinary services	...	...	101.2	...	...	112.6	...	...	123.4
C Recreational and cultural services	...	...	34.0	...	...	41.8	...	...	51.2
D Personal and household services	...	...	87.6	...	...	96.1	...	...	120.8
Total, Industries	...	...	...	...	...	...	...	...	...
Producers of Government Services [a]	...	...	...	...	...	...	...	...	...
Other Producers [a]	...	...	...	...	...	...	...	...	...
Total	...	...	4840.2	...	...	6779.0	...	...	11169.5
Less: Imputed bank service charge	...	...	49.6	...	...	64.2	...	...	111.1
Import duties	...	...	140.4	...	...	334.1	...	...	1039.5
Value added tax	...	...	...	...	...	...	...	...	...
Total	...	...	4931.0	...	...	7048.9	...	...	12097.9

a) Items 'Other producers' and 'Producers of government services' are included in item 'Community, social and personal services'.

Zambia

4.2 Derivation of Value Added by Kind of Activity, in Constant Prices

Million Zambian kwacha

	1980 Gross Output	1980 Intermediate Consumption	1980 Value Added	1981 Gross Output	1981 Intermediate Consumption	1981 Value Added	1982 Gross Output	1982 Intermediate Consumption	1982 Value Added	1983 Gross Output	1983 Intermediate Consumption	1983 Value Added
					At constant prices of: 1977							
					All Producers							
1 Agriculture, hunting, forestry and fishing	...	...	303.9	...	...	328.7	...	...	290.3	...	...	314.6
A Agriculture and hunting	...	...	273.8	...	...	299.3	...	...	257.7	...	...	279.8
B Forestry and logging	...	...	14.5	...	...	14.9	...	...	15.3	...	...	15.8
C Fishing	...	...	15.6	...	...	14.5	...	...	17.3	...	...	19.0
2 Mining and quarrying	...	...	205.2	...	...	214.8	...	...	215.2	...	...	221.7
A Coal mining	...	...		...	...		...	...		...	...	
B Crude petroleum and natural gas production	...	...	...	...	...		...	...		...	...	
C Metal ore mining	...	...	198.2	...	...	206.3	...	...	206.1	...	...	215.0
D Other mining	...	...	7.0	...	...	8.5	...	...	9.1	...	...	6.7
3 Manufacturing	...	...	383.5	...	...	430.2	...	...	415.1	...	...	384.5
A Manufacture of food, beverages and tobacco	...	...	180.7	...	...	203.4	...	...	196.0	...	...	182.8
B Textile, wearing apparel and leather industries	...	...	62.2	...	...	69.4	...	...	73.3	...	...	63.1
C Manufacture of wood and wood products, including furniture	...	...	11.8	...	...	16.0	...	...	13.8	...	...	6.7
D Manufacture of paper and paper products, printing and publishing	...	...	11.7	...	...	11.1	...	...	12.0	...	...	11.3
E Manufacture of chemicals and chemical petroleum, coal, rubber and plastic products	...	...	45.7	...	...	58.8	...	...	47.5	...	...	44.5
F Manufacture of non-metallic mineral products, except products of petroleum and coal	...	...	14.9	...	...	17.6	...	...	16.5	...	...	19.6
G Basic metal industries	...	...	4.5	...	...	3.9	...	...	3.3	...	...	3.6
H Manufacture of fabricated metal products, machinery and equipment	...	...	48.4	...	...	45.8	...	...	48.7	...	...	49.3
I Other manufacturing industries	...	...	3.6	...	...	4.2	...	...	4.0	...	...	3.8
4 Electricity, gas and water	...	...	65.8	...	...	71.0	...	...	75.8	...	...	72.2
5 Construction	...	...	102.8	...	...	78.9	...	...	84.0	...	...	88.6
6 Wholesale and retail trade, restaurants and hotels	...	...	236.3	...	...	248.6	...	...	231.8	...	...	227.6
A Wholesale and retail trade	...	...	196.2	...	...	195.2	...	...	178.5	...	...	171.8
B Restaurants and hotels	...	...	40.1	...	...	53.4	...	...	53.3	...	...	55.8
7 Transport, storage and communication	...	...	117.5	...	...	118.3	...	...	118.8	...	...	119.4
A Transport and storage	...	...	96.1	...	...	97.3	...	...	97.1	...	...	95.6
B Communication	...	...	21.4	...	...	21.0	...	...	21.7	...	...	23.8
8 Finance, insurance, real estate and business services	...	...	211.3	...	...	218.3	...	...	226.5	...	...	234.5
A Financial institutions	...	...	66.8]	...	...	65.0]	...	...	70.8]	...	...	66.2]
B Insurance	...	...		...	...		...	...		...	...	
C Real estate and business services	...	...	144.5	...	...	153.3	...	...	155.7	...	...	168.3
9 Community, social and personal services [a]	...	...	346.0	...	...	391.9	...	...	393.9	...	...	355.7
A Sanitary and similar services	...	...	147.8	...	...	172.2	...	...	168.6	...	...	138.5
B Social and related community services	...	...	143.1	...	...	160.7	...	...	167.3	...	...	159.9
Educational services	...	...	108.0	...	...	118.5	...	...	122.8	...	...	116.7
Medical, dental, other health and veterinary services	...	...	35.1	...	...	42.2	...	...	44.5	...	...	43.2
C Recreational and cultural services	...	...	13.7	...	...	16.4	...	...	14.9	...	...	14.8
D Personal and household services	...	...	41.4	...	...	42.6	...	...	43.1	...	...	42.5

Zambia

4.2 Derivation of Value Added by Kind of Activity, in Constant Prices
(Continued)

Million Zambian kwacha

	1980			1981			1982			1983		
	Gross Output	Intermediate Consumption	Value Added	Gross Output	Intermediate Consumption	Value Added	Gross Output	Intermediate Consumption	Value Added	Gross Output	Intermediate Consumption	Value Added
	At constant prices of: 1977											
Total, Industries	...	...	...	...	...	...	...	...	...	...	...	...
Producers of Government Services [a]	...	...	...	...	...	...	...	...	...	...	...	...
Other Producers [a]	...	...	...	...	...	...	...	...	...	...	...	...
Total	...	...	1972.3	...	...	2100.7	...	...	2051.4	...	...	2018.8
Less: Imputed bank service charge	...	...	18.8	...	...	18.2	...	...	19.8	...	...	18.5
Import duties	...	...	42.3	...	...	36.4	...	...	27.1	...	...	18.5
Value added tax	...	...	...	...	...	...	...	...	...	...	...	...
Total	...	...	1995.8	...	...	2118.9	...	...	2059.3	...	...	2018.8

	1984			1985			1986		
	Gross Output	Intermediate Consumption	Value Added	Gross Output	Intermediate Consumption	Value Added	Gross Output	Intermediate Consumption	Value Added
	At constant prices of: 1977								
	All Producers								
1 Agriculture, hunting, forestry and fishing	...	...	332.2	...	...	343.8	...	...	363.8
A Agriculture and hunting	...	...	294.2	...	...	300.0	...	...	316.1
B Forestry and logging	...	...	15.3	...	...	19.3	...	...	23.2
C Fishing	...	...	22.7	...	...	24.5	...	...	24.5
2 Mining and quarrying	...	...	200.0	...	...	185.4	...	...	173.9
A Coal mining	...	...	...	...	...	...	...	...	...
B Crude petroleum and natural gas production	...	...	...	...	...	...	...	...	...
C Metal ore mining	...	...	193.5	...	...	179.0	...	...	167.6
D Other mining	...	...	6.5	...	...	6.4	...	...	6.3
3 Manufacturing	...	...	389.3	...	...	419.5	...	...	421.2
A Manufacture of food, beverages and tobacco	...	...	180.2	...	...	174.8	...	...	184.9
B Textile, wearing apparel and leather industries	...	...	60.5	...	...	74.3	...	...	64.3
C Manufacture of wood and wood products, including furniture	...	...	8.0	...	...	9.3	...	...	10.3
D Manufacture of paper and paper products, printing and publishing	...	...	11.5	...	...	15.3	...	...	18.9
E Manufacture of chemicals and chemical petroleum, coal, rubber and plastic products	...	...	46.1	...	...	42.9	...	...	43.0
F Manufacture of non-metallic mineral products, except products of petroleum and coal	...	...	15.1	...	...	26.1	...	...	15.5
G Basic metal industries	...	...	3.8	...	...	3.6	...	...	3.4
H Manufacture of fabricated metal products, machinery and equipment	...	...	60.2	...	...	68.9	...	...	76.7
I Other manufacturing industries	...	...	3.9	...	...	4.3	...	...	4.2
4 Electricity, gas and water	...	...	70.9	...	...	72.7	...	...	74.1
5 Construction	...	...	88.6	...	...	77.1	...	...	81.1
6 Wholesale and retail trade, restaurants and hotels	...	...	216.9	...	...	226.0	...	...	218.2
A Wholesale and retail trade	...	...	167.9	...	...	174.7	...	...	169.0
B Restaurants and hotels	...	...	49.0	...	...	51.3	...	...	49.2
7 Transport, storage and communication	...	...	116.2	...	...	108.7	...	...	107.1
A Transport and storage	...	...	91.2	...	...	82.9	...	...	81.7
B Communication	...	...	25.0	...	...	25.8	...	...	25.4
8 Finance, insurance, real estate and business services	...	...	242.0	...	...	239.6	...	...	246.1
A Financial institutions	...	...	62.5	...	...	22.4	...	...	20.1
B Insurance	...	...		...	...	38.2	...	...	40.1
C Real estate and business services	...	...	179.5	...	...	179.0	...	...	185.9
9 Community, social and personal services [a]	...	...	354.9	...	...	365.6	...	...	361.5
A Sanitary and similar services	...	...	137.4	...	...	141.3	...	...	137.3
B Social and related community services	...	...	158.7	...	...	163.1	...	...	158.5

Zambia

4.2 Derivation of Value Added by Kind of Activity, in Constant Prices
(Continued)

Million Zambian kwacha

	1984			1985			1986		
	Gross Output	Intermediate Consumption	Value Added	Gross Output	Intermediate Consumption	Value Added	Gross Output	Intermediate Consumption	Value Added
	At constant prices of:1977								
Educational services	...	...	115.8	...	...	119.0	...	...	115.7
Medical, dental, other health and veterinary services	...	...	42.9	...	...	44.1	...	...	42.8
C Recreational and cultural services	...	...	14.7	...	...	15.1	...	...	14.7
D Personal and household services	...	...	44.1	...	...	46.1	...	...	50.8
Total, Industries	...	...	...	...	...	...	...	...	...
Producers of Government Services [a]	...	...	...	...	...	...	...	...	...
Other Producers [a]	...	...	...	...	...	...	...	...	...
Total	...	...	2011.0	...	...	2038.4	...	...	2047.0
Less: Imputed bank service charge	...	...	17.5	...	...	16.9	...	...	16.8
Import duties	...	...	18.0	...	...	19.9	...	...	22.0
Value added tax	...	...	...	...	...	...	...	...	...
Total	...	...	2011.5	...	...	2041.4	...	...	2052.2

a) Items 'Other producers' and 'Producers of government services' are included in item 'Community, social and personal services'.

Zimbabwe

General note. The prepration of national accounts statistics in Zimbabwe is undertaken by the Central Statistical Office, Hararel. The official estimates together with methodological notes are published annually in 'National Accounts of Zimbabwe Rhodesia'. The estimates are generally in accordance with the classifications and definitions recommended in the United Nations System of National AccoUnts (SNA). The following tables have been prepared from successive replies to the United Nations national accounts questionnaire. When the scope and coverage of the estimates differ for conceptual or statistical reasons from the definitions and classifications recommended in SNA, a footnote is indicated to the relevant tables.

Sources and methods:

(a) Gross domestic product. Gross domestic product is estimated mainly through the production approach.

(b) Expenditure on the gross domestic product. All items of GDP by expenditure type are estimated through the use of the expenditure approach combined with the commodity-flow approach except private consumption expenditure which is derived as a residual. In general, the commodity-flow approach determines to which consuming sector or group the commodities would be allocated. For government expenditure, detailed accounts are available from each department of the central government while the local authorities and certain controlled organizations and funds provide copies of their annual financial statement. Total private consumption expenditure is to a large extent derived as a residual. However, supplementary information is obtained from returns of major suppliers of consumer products and from family budget surveys. The estimates are checked by turnover statistics of retailers. Data on changes in stocks are available from the annual censuses of production, agriculture and livestock and from the 1975 census of road transport and for the trade sector, from turnover indexes. Expenditure on capital goods are available in the anual censuses of agriculture and production, the annual analysis of public sector accounts and the annual surveys of financial institutions. The data from these sources are classified by industry, sector and type of asset. The value of new buildings construction is estimated from monthly surveys of private contractors and public sector producers. The estimates include own-account construction of dwellings and service charges of capital nature. Tabulations of exports and imports classified by industry of origin and commodity are used to determine the proportion of each group's output sold abroad and the value of imports at the border. Valuation adjustments are made to bring all trade to a uniform f.o.b. or free-on-rail valuation at the border of the exporting country. For the constant price estimates of all expenditure items deflation is done with the use of appropriate price indexes.

(c) Cost-structure of the gross domestic product. Wages and salaries paid in the industrial activity sectors are obtained from the annual censuses of industrial production. The estimates are adjusted from fiscal to calendar year and projected using ratios derived from the quarterly employment inquiries. This latter soUrce also provides wage data for the financial, trade and service sectors. Wages and salaries paid in the agricultural sector are taken from the results of qUarterly censuses of farmers. Estimates of indirect taxes and subsidies are obtained from government accounts. Gross operating surplus, including depreciation, is estimated as a residual.

(d) Gross domestic product by kind of economic activity. The table of GDP by kind of economic activity is prepared in factor values. The production approach is used to estimate value added of most industries. For the service sector, the income approach is used while for the trade sector, the estimates are made by projecting the results of the latest census of distribution. Information on the gross output of agriculture is available either from regular annual censuses or from records of sales to official marketing authorities. ValUe of own-accout consumption for some items is estimated on the basis of forecasts of total production less recorded sales and for other items, on the basis of assumed average consumption rates. The gross output of forestry and logging is estimated to include the cost of plantation development, sales and increase in stocks of cut timber, etc. For agricultural services, estimates are based on a survey held in 1974 of the main estalishments. For the industrial activity sector and construction, complete output and input accounts are available from the annual censuses of production. The results are converted from fiscal to calendary-year basis and extrapolated by indcators such as turnover, mineral output, construction work done and prices. The gross output of establishments classified to manufacturing which also engage in distribution activity includes the sales margin only on goods purchased for resale without further processing. Estimates of output and input of the trade sector are made by extrapolating the results of the 1969 census of distribution, using turnover indicators. For transport, the production account is based on the results of the 1975 census of road transport supplemented by the accounts of concerned companies. Estimates of financial institutions are based on the results of annual surveys taken together with statutory statistical returns rendered by registered institutions. The 1969 census of population provided information on the number of dwellings by type of dwelling, as well as the average gross rents paid for rented dwellings and these are updated using the consumer price rent index. The ratio between rented and owner-occupied dwellings is assumed to have remained constant since 1969. Cost of inputs into dwellings are estimated on a unit basis from annual surveys. Value added of private domestic services is estimated as wages in cash and in kind paid. Value added of education, health and other services are based on income tax statistics and wage data collected through the quarterly employment inquiries. GDP by kind of economic activity is estimated at constant prices mainly by the use of volume indices at commodity group levels for goods producing industries, trade (volume of goods handled), transport (volume of traffic by types) and services like education (combined index of students and teachers). In the case of the rest of the services, the total employment in each year is used as the indicator for constant price estimates.

1.1 Expenditure on the Gross Domestic Product, in Current Prices

Million Zimbabwean dollars

		1970	1975	1978	1979	1980	1981	1982	1983	1984	1985	1986	1987
1	Government final consumption expenditure	126	256	451	537	677	763	973	1145	1341	1511	1717	...
2	Private final consumption expenditure	740	1225	1546	1933	2219	2969	3406	4274	3931	4362	4811	...
	A Households	717	1196	1512	1899	2184	2934	3369	4235	3885	4310	4752	...
	B Private non-profit institutions serving households	23	29	34	34	35	35	37	39	46	52	59	...
3	Gross capital formation	202	540	281	358	648	1026	1102	1002	1116	1650	1994	...
	A Increase in stocks	27	72	-60	-37	120	196	63	-236	-69	338	414	...
	B Gross fixed capital formation	175	468	341	395	528	830	1039	1238	1185	1312	1580	...
	Residential buildings	29	57	36	30	34	53	57	59	58	53	56	...
	Non-residential buildings	18	91	56	73	107	183	203	239	241	221	235	...
	Other construction and land improvement etc.	59	142	67	108	109	193	398	396	98	77	77	...
	Other	69	178	182	184	278	401	381	544	788	961	1212	...
4	Exports of goods and services	11	590	675	798	1043	1117	1141	1345	1708	2101	2559	...
5	Less: Imports of goods and services		613	593	803	1146	1442	1450	1542	1673	2015	2202	...
	Equals: Gross Domestic Product a	1079	1998	2359	2822	3441	4433	5172	6224	6423	7609	8880	...

a) Data in this table have been revised, therefore they are not strictly comparable with the unrevised data in the other tables.

1.2 Expenditure on the Gross Domestic Product, in Constant Prices

Million Zimbabwean dollars

		1970	1975	1978	1979	1980	1981	1982	1983	1984	1985	1986	1987
						At constant prices of:1980							
1	Government final consumption expenditure	226	348	599	615	677	791	845	931	1020	1058	1088	...
2	Private final consumption expenditure	1646	2069	1990	2238	2219	2600	2627	2951	2336	2002	1936	...
	A Households	1601	2032	1947	2203	2184	2569	2600	2923	2307	1973	1906	...
	B Private non-profit institutions serving households	45	37	43	35	35	31	27	28	29	29	30	...
3	Gross capital formation	563	986	358	393	646	950	815	599	599	754	806	...

Zimbabwe

1.2 Expenditure on the Gross Domestic Product, in Constant Prices
(Continued)

Million Zimbabwean dollars

	1970	1975	1978	1979	1980	1981	1982	1983	1984	1985	1986	1987
					At constant prices of:1980							
A Increase in stocks	55	87	-84	-52	118	228	28	-166	-19	185	203	...
B Gross fixed capital formation	508	899	442	443	528	722	788	765	618	569	603	...
Residential buildings	93	109	50	36	34	43	40	35	30	25	23	...
Non-residential buildings	64	174	78	87	107	147	141	143	128	103	96	...
Other construction and land improvement etc.	164	252	91	124	109	160	279	235	52	37	33	...
Other	189	364	223	196	278	372	328	352	408	404	451	...
4 Exports of goods and services	30	1229	1027	855	1042	1123	1151	1155	1078	1138	1602	...
5 Less: Imports of goods and services		1277	902	860	1146	1450	1463	1325	1056	1146	1379	...
Statistical discrepancy [a]	195	-25	-68	-150	2	-141	29	-254	11	370	233	...
Equals: Gross Domestic Product [b]	2620	3294	3004	3089	3441	3873	4005	4057	3988	4176	4286	...

a) Item 'Statistical discrepancy' refers to the difference between gross domestic product obtained by the product approach and that obtained by the expenditure approach.
b) Data in this table have been revised, therefore they are not strictly comparable with the unrevised data in the other tables.

1.3 Cost Components of the Gross Domestic Product

Million Zimbabwean dollars

	1970	1975	1978	1979	1980	1981	1982	1983	1984	1985	1986	1987
1 Indirect taxes, net	68	96	104	172	217	384	540	874	755	803	...	...
A Indirect taxes	87	137	238	262	317	504	709	956	1051	1162	...	...
B Less: Subsidies	19	41	134	90	100	120	169	82	296	359	...	...
2 Consumption of fixed capital [a]	...	...	...	...	...	...	...	...	...	...	...	...
3 Compensation of employees paid by resident producers to:	559	1049	1380	1556	1902	2325	2797	3136	3454	3979	...	...
4 Operating surplus [a]	452	852	875	1097	1322	1727	1833	2216	2214	2828	...	...
Equals: Gross Domestic Product [b]	1079	1998	2359	2822	3441	4433	5172	6224	6423	7609	...	...

a) Item 'Operating surplus' includes consumption of fixed capital.
b) Data in this table have been revised, therefore they are not strictly comparable with the unrevised data in the other tables.

1.4 General Government Current Receipts and Disbursements

Million Zimbabwean dollars

	1970	1975	1978	1979	1980	1981	1982	1983	1984	1985	1986	1987
					Receipts							
1 Operating surplus	...	...	...	...	...	...	...	...	...	...	...	...
2 Property and entrepreneurial income [a]	50	43	52	57	56	56	79	107	124	142	...	...
3 Taxes, fees and contributions	172	393	509	548	705	1052	1424	1753	1913	2110	...	...
A Indirect taxes	87	137	238	262	316	507	709	956	1051	1148	...	...
B Direct taxes	82	250	265	281	383	539	707	783	856	955	...	...
C Social security contributions	1	4	5	5	5	5	7	13	6	7	...	...
D Compulsory fees, fines and penalties	2	2	1	1	1	1	1	1	-	-	...	...
4 Other current transfers	11	22	31	32	54	72	62	68	93	103	...	...
Total Current Receipts of General Government [b]	233	458	593	637	815	1180	1565	1928	2130	2355	...	...
					Disbursements							
1 Government final consumption expenditure	126	237	439	516	663	750	1007	1138	1334	1526	...	...
2 Property income	23	34	55	72	93	125	193	242	310	380	...	...
3 Subsidies	20	35	134	90	100	120	169	82	296	281	...	...
4 Other current transfers	40	57	94	113	158	184	269	370	364	454	...	...
A Social security benefits	1	2	3	3	3	4	4	6	5	6	...	...
B Social assistance grants [c]	18	20	48	60	74	71	77	75	79	85	...	...
C Other	20	36	43	49	81	109	188	289	280	363	...	...
Statistical discrepancy [d]	...	...	...	...	33	46	46	18	28	40	...	...
5 Net saving [e]	24	94	-129	-154	-232	-45	-119	78	-202	-326	...	...
Total Current Disbursements and Net Saving of General Government [b]	233	458	593	637	815	1180	1565	1928	2130	2355	...	...

a) Item 'Property and entrepreneurial income' includes consumption of fixed capital.
b) Estimates of general government cover central & local government.
c) Item 'Social assistance grants' refers to pensions.
d) Item 'Statistical discrepancy' represents unclassified estimates.
e) Item 'Net saving' includes consumption of fixed capital.

Zimbabwe

1.5 Current Income and Outlay of Corporate and Quasi-Corporate Enterprises, Summary

Million Zimbabwean dollars

	1970	1975	1978	1979	1980	1981	1982	1983	1984	1985	1986	1987
Receipts												
1 Operating surplus [a]	269	584	617	791	993	...	...	...	...	...	...	...
2 Property and entrepreneurial income received	81	162	210	241	292	...	...	...	...	...	...	...
3 Current transfers	34	72	117	120	150	...	...	...	...	...	...	...
Total Current Receipts	384	818	944	1152	1436	...	...	...	...	...	...	...
Disbursements												
1 Property and entrepreneurial income	145	286	351	419	496	...	...	...	...	...	...	...
2 Direct taxes and other current payments to general government	46	148	133	131	177	...	...	...	...	...	...	...
3 Other current transfers	59	129	194	199	250	...	...	...	...	...	...	...
4 Net saving [b]	134	256	266	403	513	...	...	...	...	...	...	...
Total Current Disbursements and Net Saving [c]	384	818	944	1152	1436	...	...	...	...	...	...	...

a) Item 'Operating surplus' includes consumption of fixed capital.
b) Item 'Net saving' includes consumption of fixed capital.
c) Corporate and quasi-corporate enterprises includes companies, financial institutions & public corporations.

1.7 External Transactions on Current Account, Summary

Million Zimbabwean dollars

	1970	1975	1978	1979	1980	1981	1982	1983	1984	1985	1986	1987
Payments to the Rest of the World												
1 Imports of goods and services	...	613	593	803	1146	1442	1450	1542	1673	2015	2202	...
A Imports of merchandise c.i.f.	275	494	443	595	861	1059	1114	1087	1237	1486	1686	...
B Other	...	119	150	208	285	383	336	455	436	530	515	...
2 Factor income to the rest of the world	...	67	67	97	115	187	272	339	287	365	480	...
A Compensation of employees	...	11	13	23	23	31	36	44	51	58	71	...
B Property and entrepreneurial income	...	56	54	73	92	156	236	295	236	307	410	...
By general government	...	1	1	3	5	20	63	94	128	147	154	...
By corporate and quasi-corporate enterprises	...	43	34	47	57	98	125	150	74	112	196	...
By other	...	12	19	23	31	38	48	52	34	48	59	...
3 Current transfers to the rest of the world	...	30	33	40	71	86	97	116	127	136	137	...
4 Surplus of the nation on current transactions	-13	-88	25	-74	-157	-439	-533	-454	-102	-159	15	...
Payments to the Rest of the World and Surplus of the Nation on Current Transactions	...	622	718	866	1175	1276	1286	1543	1984	2358	2834	...
Receipts From The Rest of the World												
1 Exports of goods and services	...	590	675	798	1043	1118	1141	1345	1708	2101	2559	...
A Exports of merchandise f.o.b.	265	542	625	734	929	1001	998	1174	1484	1811	2206	...
B Other	...	48	50	64	114	117	143	164	226	290	353	...
2 Factor income from rest of the world	...	21	26	43	68	72	78	91	92	81	96	...
A Compensation of employees	...	1	1	1	2	4	14	16	19	15	27	...
B Property and entrepreneurial income	...	20	25	43	66	68	64	75	73	67	69	...
By general government	...	-	-	-	-	8	14	12	12	12	13	...
By corporate and quasi-corporate enterprises	...	16	18	34	50	44	37	43	42	43	43	...
By other	...	4	7	8	15	17	13	20	19	12	13	...
3 Current transfers from rest of the world	...	11	18	25	64	86	67	107	184	175	179	...
Receipts from the Rest of the World on Current Transactions	...	622	718	866	1175	1276	1286	1543	1984	2358	2834	...

Zimbabwe

1.9 Gross Domestic Product by Institutional Sectors of Origin

Million Zimbabwean dollars

	1970	1975	1978	1979	1980	1981	1982	1983	1984	1985	1986	1987
Domestic Factor Incomes Originating											
1 General government	138	261	418	479	563	698	869	1130	1282	...	...	...
2 Corporate and quasi-corporate enterprises	617	1226	1432	1699	2020	2551	2966	3314	3343	...	...	...
A Non-financial	602	1191	1396	1658	1969	2487	2884	3211	3228	...	...	...
Public	90	155	200	212	198	234	261	343	524	...	...	...
Private	512	1036	1196	1446	1771	2253	2623	2868	2704	...	...	...
B Financial	15	35	36	41	51	64	82	103	115	...	...	...
Public	-1	14	21	30	45	41	41	53	37	...	...	...
Private	16	21	15	11	6	23	41	50	78	...	...	...
3 Households and private unincorporated enterprises	232	386	365	428	551	743	699	697	1226	...	...	...
A Owner-occupied housing	15	21	22	20	18	24	25	26	25	...	...	...
B Subsistence production	...	...	...	...	...	...	...	...	...	...	...	...
C Other	217	365	343	408	533	719	674	671	1200	...	...	...
4 Non-profit institutions serving households	24	31	43	47	88	63	85	97	101	...	...	...
Subtotal: Domestic Factor Incomes [a]	1011	1902	2259	2654	3224	4055	4620	5236	5952	...	...	...
Indirect taxes, net	68	96	104	172	217	384	540	896	744	...	...	...
A Indirect taxes	87	137	238	262	317	504	709	956	1040	...	...	...
B Less: Subsidies	19	41	134	90	100	120	169	60	296	...	...	...
Consumption of fixed capital	...	...	...	...	...	...	...	...	...	...	...	...
Gross Domestic Product	1079	1998	2363	2826	3441	4439	5160	6132	6696	...	...	...

a) Item 'Domestic factor incomes' includes consumption of fixed capital.

1.10 Gross Domestic Product by Kind of Activity, in Current Prices

Million Zimbabwean dollars

	1970	1975	1978	1979	1980	1981	1982	1983	1984	1985	1986	1987
1 Agriculture, hunting, forestry and fishing	153	323	289	321	451	640	669	544	748	1039	1080	947
2 Mining and quarrying	71	131	156	226	285	252	217	393	320	368	409	476
3 Manufacturing	209	447	515	625	802	1016	1121	1441	1475	2043	2405	2720
4 Electricity, gas and water [a]	32	50	62	71	70	78	73	195	142	164	277	364
5 Construction	55	94	67	92	91	138	190	258	205	188	206	213
6 Wholesale and retail trade, restaurants and hotels	152	258	356	425	451	603	719	740	759	799	1007	1118
7 Transport, storage and communication	88	145	178	188	211	306	362	364	436	377	431	416
8 Finance, insurance, real estate and business services [b]	69	130	150	167	202	240	283	334	342	359	405	475
9 Community, social and personal services [b]	140	246	312	347	478	588	777	857	964	1195	1399	1615
Total, Industries	969	1824	2086	2462	3041	3861	4410	5126	5391	6532	7619	8344
Producers of Government Services	63	130	239	270	291	309	367	398	444	479	512	590
Other Producers	...	...	...	...	...	...	...	...	...	...	...	...
Subtotal [c]	1032	1954	2325	2732	3332	4170	4778	5523	5836	7011	8131	8934
Less: Imputed bank service charge	21	52	69	82	108	121	146	173	168	205	222	233
Plus: Import duties	...	...	...	...	...	...	...	...	...	...	...	...
Plus: Value added tax	...	...	...	...	...	...	...	...	...	...	...	...
Plus: Other adjustments [d]	68	96	104	172	217	384	540	874	755	803	971	1024
Equals: Gross Domestic Product [e]	1079	1998	2359	2822	3441	4433	5172	6224	6423	7609	8880	9725

a) Item 'Electricity, gas and water' excludes gas.
b) Business services are included in item 'Community, social and personal services'.
c) Gross domestic product in factor values.
d) Item 'Other adjustments' refers to indirect taxes net of subsidies.
e) Data in this table have been revised, therefore they are not strictly comparable with the unrevised data in the other tables.

1.11 Gross Domestic Product by Kind of Activity, in Constant Prices

Million Zimbabwean dollars

	1970	1975	1978	1979	1980	1981	1982	1983	1984	1985	1986	1987
At constant prices of: 1980											
1 Agriculture, hunting, forestry and fishing	357	460	444	444	451	515	478	403	496	614	583	474
2 Mining and quarrying	251	299	292	292	285	278	284	280	291	288	293	300
3 Manufacturing	513	729	629	697	802	881	877	852	809	902	929	949
4 Electricity, gas and water [a]	97	94	70	64	70	70	63	68	70	79	94	123
5 Construction	113	156	91	89	91	105	101	93	86	64	66	62

Zimbabwe

1.11 Gross Domestic Product by Kind of Activity, in Constant Prices
(Continued)

Million Zimbabwean dollars

	1970	1975	1978	1979	1980	1981	1982	1983	1984	1985	1986	1987
					At constant prices of:1980							
6 Wholesale and retail trade, restaurants and hotels	287	378	329	339	451	456	451	392	366	386	406	412
7 Transport, storage and communication	193	196	167	173	211	221	226	224	226	237	239	217
8 Finance, insurance, real estate and business services [b]	160	271	225	203	202	217	251	247	233	231	233	240
9 Community, social and personal services [b]	363	439	427	425	478	561	637	674	703	750	791	841
Total, Industries	2334	3022	2674	2726	3041	3304	3368	3233	3280	3551	3634	3618
Producers of Government Services	158	198	277	277	291	339	333	338	364	372	372	395
Other Producers	...	...	...	...	...	...	...	...	...	...	...	...
Subtotal [c]	2492	3220	2951	3003	3332	3643	3701	3571	3644	3923	4002	4013
Less: Imputed bank service charge	54	86	88	90	108	106	113	112	105	115	109	105
Plus: Import duties	...	...	...	...	...	...	...	...	...	...	...	...
Plus: Value added tax	...	...	...	...	...	...	...	...	...	...	...	...
Plus: Other adjustments [d]	182	160	141	176	217	336	417	598	448	368	389	...
Equals: Gross Domestic Product [e]	2620	3294	3004	3089	3441	3873	4005	4057	3988	4176	4286	...

a) Item 'Electricity, gas and water' excludes gas.
b) Business services are included in item 'Community, social and personal services'.
c) Gross domestic product in factor values.
d) Item 'Other adjustments' refers to indirect taxes net of subsidies.
e) Data in this table have been revised, therefore they are not strictly comparable with the unrevised data in the other tables.

1.12 Relations Among National Accounting Aggregates

Million Zimbabwean dollars

	1970	1975	1978	1979	1980	1981	1982	1983	1984	1985	1986	1987
Gross Domestic Product	1079	1998	2359	2822	3441	4433	5172	6224	6423	7609	8880	...
Plus: Net factor income from the rest of the world	-21	-46	-42	-53	-47	-115	-194	-248	-195	-284	-384	...
Factor income from the rest of the world	...	21	26	43	68	72	78	91	92	81	96	...
Less: Factor income to the rest of the world	...	67	67	97	115	187	272	339	287	365	480	...
Equals: Gross National Product	1059	1952	2317	2769	3394	4318	4978	5976	6228	7325	8496	...
Less: Consumption of fixed capital	...	...	...	...	...	...	...	...	...	...	...	...
Equals: National Income [a]	1059	1952	2317	2769	3394	4318	4978	5976	6228	7325	8496	...
Plus: Net current transfers from the rest of the world	-3	-19	-15	-15	-6	1	-30	-9	57	39	42	...
Current transfers from the rest of the world	...	11	18	25	64	87	67	107	184	175	179	...
Less: Current transfers to the rest of the world	...	30	33	40	70	86	97	116	127	136	137	...
Equals: National Disposable Income [b]	1055	1933	2302	2753	3388	4319	4948	5967	6285	7364	8538	...
Less: Final consumption	866	1481	1997	2470	2896	3732	4379	5419	5272	5873	6528	...
Equals: Net Saving [c]	189	452	305	284	492	587	569	548	1013	1491	2010	...
Less: Surplus of the nation on current transactions	-13	-88	25	-74	-157	-439	-533	-454	-102	-159	15	...
Equals: Net Capital Formation [de]	202	540	281	358	648	1026	1102	1002	1116	1650	1994	...

a) Item 'National income' includes consumption of fixed capital.
b) Item 'National disposable income' includes consumption of fixed capital.
c) Item 'Net saving' includes consumption of fixed capital.
d) Item 'Net capital formation' includes consumption of fixed capital.
e) Data in this table have been revised, therefore they are not strictly comparable with the unrevised data in the other tables.

2.1 Government Final Consumption Expenditure by Function, in Current Prices

Million Zimbabwean dollars

	1970	1975	1978	1979	1980	1981	1982	1983	1984	1985	1986	1987
1 General public services											...	...
2 Defence	60	135	314	375	487	439	510	541	653	747	...	...
3 Public order and safety											...	...
4 Education	17	44	61	66	99	144	260	300	363	415	...	...
5 Health	13	24	37	40	54	70	95	106	128	146	...	...
6 Social security and welfare	...	...	...	...	...	...	...	...	...	...	...	...
7 Housing and community amenities	10	18	18	21	26	35	34	53	46	53	...	...
8 Recreational, cultural and religious affairs	3	8	10	10	13	18	32	38	37	43	...	...
9 Economic services	6	28	31	26	53	75	101	93	92	105	...	...
10 Other functions	-3	-20	-32	-22	-69	-31	-25	7	15	17	...	...
Total Government Final Consumption Expenditure [a]	106	237	439	516	663	750	1007	1138	1334	1526	...	...

a) Estimates of general government cover central & local government.

Zimbabwe

2.3 Total Government Outlays by Function and Type

Million Zimbabwean dollars

	Final Consumption Expenditures - Total	Compensation of Employees	Other	Subsidies	Other Current Transfers & Property Income	Total Current Disbursements	Gross Capital Formation	Other Capital Outlays	Total Outlays
1980									
1 General public services		...	...						
2 Defence	487	...	...	...	7	494	24	2	520
3 Public order and safety		...	...						
4 Education	99	...	...	...	103	202	6	...	208
5 Health	54	...	...	...	9	63	7	...	70
6 Social security and welfare	...	...	...	...	...	...	...	...	...
7 Housing and community amenities	26	...	...	...	-	26	35	...	61
8 Recreation, culture and religion	13	...	...	...	89	102	1	-	103
9 Economic services	53	...	...	100	13	166	37	...	203
10 Other functions	-69	...	...	...	7	-62	10	2	-50
Total ab	663	518	145	100	284	1047	120	4	1171
1981									
1 General public services		...	...						
2 Defence	439	...	...	...	4	443	30	5	478
3 Public order and safety		...	...						
4 Education	144	...	...	...	156	300	10	...	310
5 Health	70	...	...	...	23	93	7	...	100
6 Social security and welfare	...	...	...	...	...	...	...	...	...
7 Housing and community amenities	35	...	...	...	-	35	39	...	74
8 Recreation, culture and religion	18	...	...	...	92	110	1	-	111
9 Economic services	75	...	...	120	17	212	56	...	268
10 Other functions	-31	...	...	...	5	-26	12	2	-12
Total ab	750	626	124	120	355	1225	155	7	1387
1982									
1 General public services		...	...						
2 Defence	510	...	...	...	2	512	37	14	563
3 Public order and safety		...	...						
4 Education	260	...	...	...	263	523	22	-	545
5 Health	95	...	...	...	32	127	6	1	134
6 Social security and welfare	...	...	...	...	...	...	...	...	...
7 Housing and community amenities	34	...	...	...	-	34	45	-	79
8 Recreation, culture and religion	32	...	...	...	136	168	10	-	178
9 Economic services	101	...	...	169	26	296	140	...	436
10 Other functions	-25	...	...	...	10	-15	10	5	-
Total ab	1007	829	178	169	508	1684	270	20	1974
1983									
1 General public services		...	...						
2 Defence	541	...	...	...	3	544	51	5	600
3 Public order and safety		...	...						
4 Education	300	...	...	...	279	579	33	-	612
5 Health	106	...	...	...	29	135	8	5	148
6 Social security and welfare	...	...	...	...	...	...	...	...	...
7 Housing and community amenities	53	...	...	...	2	55	42	-	97
8 Recreation, culture and religion	38	...	...	...	216	253	7	-	261
9 Economic services	93	...	...	82	40	215	153	...	369
10 Other functions	7	...	...	...	9	16	7	6	29
Total ab	1138	925	213	82	630	1850	301	17	2168

Zimbabwe

2.3 Total Government Outlays by Function and Type
(Continued)

Million Zimbabwean dollars

	Final Consumption Expenditures Total	Compensation of Employees	Other	Subsidies	Other Current Transfers & Property Income	Total Current Disbursements	Gross Capital Formation	Other Capital Outlays	Total Outlays
1984									
1 General public services		...	...	...					
2 Defence	653	...	...	...	12	665	61	12	738
3 Public order and safety		...	...	...					
4 Education	363	...	...	...	324	687	33	...	720
5 Health	128	...	...	...	39	167	12	3	182
6 Social security and welfare	...	...	...	...	...	...	...	...	...
7 Housing and community amenities	46	...	...	...	-	46	43	...	89
8 Recreation, culture and religion	37	...	...	...	166	203	8	-	211
9 Economic services	92	...	...	296	51	439	168	...	607
10 Other functions	15	...	...	...	8	23	2	4	29
Total ab	1334	1064	270	296	702	2332	327	19	2678
1985									
1 General public services		...	...	...					
2 Defence	747	...	...	...	20	767	67	13	847
3 Public order and safety		...	...	...					
4 Education	415	...	...	...	405	820	37	-	857
5 Health	146	...	...	...	62	208	13	3	224
6 Social security and welfare	...	...	...	...	...	...	...	...	...
7 Housing and community amenities	53	...	...	...	-	53	47	-	100
8 Recreation, culture and religion	43	...	...	...	100	143	9	-	152
9 Economic services	105	...	...	281	145	531	185	-	716
10 Other functions	17	...	...	...	9	26	2	5	33
Total ab	1526	1217	309	281	874	2681	360	21	3062

a) Estimates of general government cover central & local government.
b) Property income and net of inter-governmental transfers in column 5 are included in the total and not in the breakdowns. Also included in the same total are some unclassified estimates.

2.5 Private Final Consumption Expenditure by Type and Purpose, in Current Prices

Million Zimbabwean dollars

	1970	1975	1978	1979	1980	1981	1982	1983	1984	1985	1986	1987
Final Consumption Expenditure of Resident Households												
1 Food, beverages and tobacco	266	436	575	748	800	954	1096	1175	1220	1661	...	...
A Food	185	304	377	489	461	509	532	477	512	735	...	...
B Non-alcoholic beverages	10	24	34	44	106	133	207	300	303	449	...	...
C Alcoholic beverages	71	108	164	215	233	312	357	398	405	477	...	...
D Tobacco											...	...
2 Clothing and footwear	96	151	204	268	290	415	475	444	462	573	...	...
3 Gross rent, fuel and power	99	175	223	277	308	423	488	651	866	847	...	...
A Fuel and power	30	65	92	113	127	190	255	400	532	503	...	...
B Other	69	110	131	164	181	233	233	251	334	344	...	...
4 Furniture, furnishings and household equipment and operation	77	123	139	152	275	376	364	360	427	346	...	...
A Household operation	47	79	86	101	215	299	284	272	340	258	...	...
B Other	30	44	53	51	60	77	80	88	87	88	...	...
5 Medical care and health expenses	30	57	95	111	94	119	133	153	156	167	...	...
6 Transport and communication a	20	32	28	38	55	96	115	114	87	97	...	...
7 Recreational, entertainment, education and cultural services	35	51	59	68	92	127	156	218	229	216	...	...
A Education	17	21	27	29	53	79	104	157	159	150	...	...
B Other	18	30	32	39	39	48	52	61	70	66	...	...
8 Miscellaneous goods and services a	120	191	237	303	331	508	563	624	749	799	...	...
A Personal care	...	...	...	...	...	...	...	...	...	...	...	...
B Expenditures in restaurants, cafes and hotels	48	76	115	143	149	263	302	342	415	444	...	...
C Other	72	115	122	160	182	245	261	282	334	355	...	...

Zimbabwe

2.5 Private Final Consumption Expenditure by Type and Purpose, in Current Prices
(Continued)

Million Zimbabwean dollars

	1970	1975	1978	1979	1980	1981	1982	1983	1984	1985	1986	1987
Statistical discrepancy	-1	...	...	...	...	...	...	...	...	...	...	...
Total Final Consumption Expenditure in the Domestic Market by Households, of which	740	1215	1560	1964	2242	3015	3388	3738	4196	4707	...	...
A Durable goods	66	111	114	139	271	394	400	386	426	355	...	...
B Semi-durable goods	...	...	...	...	...	...	...	...	...	...	...	...
C Non-durable goods	462	764	1012	1302	1367	1740	2026	2226	2450	3012	...	...
D Services	212	340	434	523	605	881	963	1126	1320	1340	...	...
Plus: Direct purchases abroad by resident households	...	...	...	...	...	...	...	...	...	...	...	...
Less: Direct purchases in the domestic market by non-resident households	23	19	44	61	58	75	31	12	-3	25	...	...
Equals: Final Consumption Expenditure of Resident Households	717	1196	1516	1903	2184	2940	3357	3726	4199	4682	...	...

Final Consumption Expenditure of Private Non-profit Institutions Serving Households

	1970	1975	1978	1979	1980	1981	1982	1983	1984	1985	1986	1987
1 Research and science	...	...	...	...	...	...	...	...	...	...	...	...
2 Education	13	16	19	18	17	17	17	16	...	...	...	...
3 Medical and other health services	3	4	5	5	6	6	3	3	...	...	...	...
4 Welfare services	...	...	...	...	...	...	...	...	...	...	...	...
5 Recreational and related cultural services	...	...	...	...	...	...	...	...	...	...	...	...
6 Religious organisations	...	...	...	...	...	...	...	...	...	...	...	...
7 Professional and labour organisations serving households	...	...	...	...	...	...	...	...	...	...	...	...
8 Miscellaneous	7	9	10	11	12	12	17	20	...	...	...	...
Equals: Final Consumption Expenditure of Private Non-profit Organisations Serving Households	23	29	34	34	35	35	37	39	46	52	...	...
Private Final Consumption Expenditure	740	1225	1550	1937	2219	2975	3394	3768	4245	4737	...	...

a) Item 'Transport and communication' includes personal transport equipment only. Communication is included in item 'Miscellaneous good and services'.

2.6 Private Final Consumption Expenditure by Type and Purpose, in Constant Prices

Million Zimbabwean dollars

At constant prices of: 1980

Final Consumption Expenditure of Resident Households

	1970	1975	1978	1979	1980	1981	1982	1983	1984	1985	1986	1987
1 Food, beverages and tobacco	625	829	774	915	800	817	838	757	686	605	...	...
A Food	406	515	457	545	461	432	406	298	282	272	...	...
B Non-alcoholic beverages	22	40	42	45	106	105	143	174	149	149	...	...
C Alcoholic beverages	197	274	275	325	233	280	289	285	255	184	...	...
D Tobacco											...	...
2 Clothing and footwear	193	227	242	293	290	363	369	306	278	231	...	...
3 Gross rent, fuel and power	187	249	281	293	308	367	365	467	452	379	...	...
A Fuel and power	86	122	144	125	127	155	197	254	263	183	...	...
B Other	101	127	137	168	181	212	168	213	189	196	...	...
4 Furniture, furnishings and household equipment and operation	163	204	169	172	275	326	275	244	264	188	...	...
A Household operation	89	119	97	108	215	267	235	206	228	164	...	...
B Other	74	85	72	64	60	59	40	38	36	24	...	...
5 Medical care and health expenses	72	98	121	125	94	109	105	113	106	99	...	...
6 Transport and communication a	43	60	33	41	55	93	107	78	47	44	...	...
7 Recreational, entertainment, education and cultural services	110	101	82	82	92	133	141	187	175	155	...	...
A Education	63	48	45	40	53	87	96	143	129	117	...	...
B Other	47	53	37	42	39	46	45	44	46	38	...	...
8 Miscellaneous goods and services a	264	303	311	356	331	430	417	433	484	454	...	...
A Personal care	...	...	...	...	...	...	...	...	...	...	...	...
B Expenditures in restaurants, cafes and hotels	117	126	154	169	149	215	214	220	250	233	...	...
C Other	147	177	157	187	182	215	203	213	234	221	...	...
Total Final Consumption Expenditure in the Domestic Market by Households, of which	1657	2068	2012	2275	2242	2638	2615	2585	2490	2157	...	...

Zimbabwe

2.6 Private Final Consumption Expenditure by Type and Purpose, in Constant Prices
(Continued)

Million Zimbabwean dollars

	1970	1975	1978	1979	1980	1981	1982	1983	1984	1985	1986	1987
					At constant prices of:1980							
A Durable goods	132	179	130	150	271	360	341	284	276	207	...	...
B Semi-durable goods	...	...	...	...	...	...	...	...	...	...	...	...
C Non-durable goods	1051	1354	1331	1520	1367	1502	1566	1475	1394	1185	...	...
D Services	474	535	551	605	605	776	708	826	820	765	...	...
Plus: Direct purchases abroad by resident households	...	...	...	...	...	...	...	...	...	...		
Less: Direct purchases in the domestic market by non-resident households	56	72	60	67	58	63	22	7	-1	12		
Equals: Final Consumption Expenditure of Resident Households	1601	1996	1952	2207	2184	2574	2593	2578	2491	2145		

Final Consumption Expenditure of Private Non-profit Institutions Serving Households

	1970	1975	1978	1979	1980	1981	1982	1983	1984	1985	1986	1987
Equals: Final Consumption Expenditure of Private Non-profit Organisations Serving Households	45	37	43	35	35	31	27	28	29	31		
Private Final Consumption Expenditure	1646	2033	1995	2242	2219	2605	2620	2606	2520	2176		

a) Item 'Transport and communication' includes personal transport equipment only. Communication is included in item 'Miscellaneous good and services'.

2.7 Gross Capital Formation by Type of Good and Owner, in Current Prices

Million Zimbabwean dollars

	1980				1981				1982			
	TOTAL	Total Private	Public Enterprises	General Government	TOTAL	Total Private	Public Enterprises	General Government	TOTAL	Total Private	Public Enterprises	General Government
Increase in stocks, total	120	...	...	...	196	...	...	...	63	...	...	...
1 Goods producing industries	164	...	...	...	377	...	...	...	378	...	...	...
A Materials and supplies	63	...	...	...	96	...	...	...	48	...	...	...
B Work in progress	...	...	...	...	...	...	...	...	...	...	...	...
C Livestock, except breeding stocks, dairy cattle, etc.	67	...	...	...	199	...	...	...	256	...	...	...
D Finished goods	34	...	...	...	82	...	...	...	74	...	...	...
2 Wholesale and retail trade	104	...	...	...	262	...	...	...	69	...	...	...
3 Other, except government stocks	9	...	...	...	15	...	...	...	43	...	...	...
4 Government stocks		...	...	...		...	...	...		...	...	...
Statistical discrepancy a	-157	...	...	...	-458	...	...	...	-427	...	...	...
Gross Fixed Capital Formation, Total	528	366	45	117	830	593	82	155	1039	523	277	239
1 Residential buildings	34	6	2	26	53	17	2	34	57	11	-	46
2 Non-residential buildings	107	90	1	16	183	158	2	23	203	139	14	50
3 Other construction	109	37	19	53	193	92	38	63	398	59	244	96
4 Land improvement and plantation and orchard development	...	...	...	...	...	...	...	...	...	...	...	...
5 Producers' durable goods	278	233	23	22	401	326	40	35	381	314	19	47
A Transport equipment	84	75	2	7	106	90	4	12	136	113	6	17
B Machinery and equipment	194	158	21	15	295	236	36	23	245	201	13	30
6 Breeding stock, dairy cattle, etc.	...	...	...	...	...	...	...	...	...	...	...	...
Total Gross Capital Formation	648	...	...	...	1026	...	...	...	1102	...	...	...

	1983				1984				1985			
	TOTAL	Total Private	Public Enterprises	General Government	TOTAL	Total Private	Public Enterprises	General Government	TOTAL	Total Private	Public Enterprises	General Government
Increase in stocks, total	195	...	...	...	-36	...	...	...	522	...	...	...
1 Goods producing industries	1119	...	...	...	-77	...	...	...	442	...	...	...
A Materials and supplies	76	...	...	...	21	...	...	...	45	...	...	...
B Work in progress	...	...	...	...	...	...	...	...	...	...	...	...
C Livestock, except breeding stocks, dairy cattle, etc.	455	...	...	...	-123	...	...	...	145	...	...	...
D Finished goods	588	...	...	...	25	...	...	...	252	...	...	...
2 Wholesale and retail trade	-84	...	...	...	222	...	...	...	311	...	...	...
3 Other, except government stocks	33	...	...	...	47	...	...	...	33	...	...	...
4 Government stocks		...	...	...		...	...	...		...	...	...

Zimbabwe

2.7 Gross Capital Formation by Type of Good and Owner, in Current Prices
(Continued)

Million Zimbabwean dollars

	1983 TOTAL	1983 Total Private	1983 Public Enterprises	1983 General Government	1984 TOTAL	1984 Total Private	1984 Public Enterprises	1984 General Government	1985 TOTAL	1985 Total Private	1985 Public Enterprises	1985 General Government
Statistical discrepancy a	-873	...	...	...	-228	...	...	...	-264	...	...	...
Gross Fixed Capital Formation, Total	1223	506	413	305	1110	608	221	281	1347	...	...	...
1 Residential buildings	52	9	3	40	47	8	3	35	43	...	...	...
2 Non-residential buildings	247	130	36	80	243	161	36	46	223	...	...	...
3 Other construction	381	49	207	126	63	56	-147	155	49	...	...	...
4 Land improvement and plantation and orchard development	...	...	...	...	...	...	...	...	...	...	...	...
5 Producers' durable goods	545	318	167	58	757	383	329	45	1032	...	...	...
A Transport equipment	132	102	13	17	158	141	10	7	175	...	...	...
B Machinery and equipment	411	216	154	41	599	242	319	38	857	...	...	...
6 Breeding stock, dairy cattle, etc.	...	...	...	...	...	...	...	...	...	...	...	...
Total Gross Capital Formation	1418	...	...	...	1074	...	...	...	1869	...	...	...

a) Item 'Statistical discrepancy' refers to revaluation adjustment.

2.8 Gross Capital Formation by Type of Good and Owner, in Constant Prices

Million Zimbabwean dollars

	1980 TOTAL	1980 Total Private	1980 Public Enterprises	1980 General Government	1981 TOTAL	1981 Total Private	1981 Public Enterprises	1981 General Government	1982 TOTAL	1982 Total Private	1982 Public Enterprises	1982 General Government
At constant prices of:1980											
Increase in stocks, total	118	...	...	...	228	...	...	...	27	...	...	...
1 Goods producing industries	45	...	...	...	76	...	...	...	34	...	...	...
A Materials and supplies	40	...	...	...	38	...	...	...	-3	...	...	...
B Work in progress	...	...	...	...	...	...	...	...	...	...	...	...
C Livestock, except breeding stocks, dairy cattle, etc.	-7	...	...	...	8	...	...	...	16	...	...	...
D Finished goods	11	...	...	...	30	...	...	...	21	...	...	...
2 Wholesale and retail trade	72	...	...	...	149	...	...	...	-32	...	...	...
3 Other, except government stocks	3	...	...	...	3	...	...	...	25	...	...	...
4 Government stocks		...	...	...		...	...	...		...	...	...
Gross Fixed Capital Formation, Total	528	...	...	...	722	...	...	...	788	...	...	...
1 Residential buildings	34	...	...	...	43	...	...	...	40	...	...	...
2 Non-residential buildings	107	...	...	...	147	...	...	...	141	...	...	...
3 Other construction	109	...	...	...	160	...	...	...	279	...	...	...
4 Land improvement and plantation and orchard development	...	...	...	...	...	...	...	...	...	...	...	...
5 Producers' durable goods	278	...	...	...	372	...	...	...	328	...	...	...
A Transport equipment	84	...	...	...	105	...	...	...	126	...	...	...
B Machinery and equipment	194	...	...	...	267	...	...	...	202	...	...	...
6 Breeding stock, dairy cattle, etc.	...	...	...	...	...	...	...	...	...	...	...	...
Total Gross Capital Formation	646	...	...	...	950	...	...	...	815	...	...	...

	1983 TOTAL	1983 Total Private	1983 Public Enterprises	1983 General Government	1984 TOTAL	1984 Total Private	1984 Public Enterprises	1984 General Government	1985 TOTAL	1985 Total Private	1985 Public Enterprises	1985 General Government
At constant prices of:1980											
Increase in stocks, total	120	...	...	...	-14	...	...	...	312	...	...	...
1 Goods producing industries	313	...	...	...	-103	...	...	...	149	...	...	...
A Materials and supplies	-5	...	...	...	-28	...	...	...	13	...	...	...
B Work in progress	...	...	...	...	...	...	...	...	...	...	...	...
C Livestock, except breeding stocks, dairy cattle, etc.	-19	...	...	...	-15	...	...	...	15	...	...	...
D Finished goods	337	...	...	...	-60	...	...	...	121	...	...	...
2 Wholesale and retail trade	-201	...	...	...	73	...	...	...	149	...	...	...
3 Other, except government stocks	8	...	...	...	16	...	...	...	14	...	...	...
4 Government stocks		...	...	...		...	...	...		...	...	...
Gross Fixed Capital Formation, Total	740	...	...	...	576	...	...	...	502	...	...	...

Zimbabwe

2.8 Gross Capital Formation by Type of Good and Owner, in Constant Prices
(Continued)

Million Zimbabwean dollars

	1983 TOTAL	Total Private	Public Enterprises	General Government	1984 TOTAL	Total Private	Public Enterprises	General Government	1985 TOTAL	Total Private	Public Enterprises	General Government
				At constant prices of:1980								
1 Residential buildings	31	...	...	...	24	...	...	...	20	...	...	...
2 Non-residential buildings	145	...	...	...	127	...	...	...	104	...	...	...
3 Other construction	227	...	...	...	33	...	...	...	24	...	...	...
4 Land improvement and plantation and orchard development	...	...	...	...	...	...	...	...	...	...	...	...
5 Producers' durable goods	337	...	...	...	392	...	...	...	354	...	...	...
A Transport equipment	90	...	...	...	93	...	...	...	80	...	...	...
B Machinery and equipment	247	...	...	...	299	...	...	...	274	...	...	...
6 Breeding stock, dairy cattle, etc.	...	...	...	...	...	...	...	...	...	...	...	...
Total Gross Capital Formation	860	...	...	...	562	...	...	...	814	...	...	...

2.11 Gross Fixed Capital Formation by Kind of Activity of Owner, ISIC Divisions, in Current Prices

Million Zimbabwean dollars

	1970	1975	1978	1979	1980	1981	1982	1983	1984	1985	1986	1987
					All Producers							
1 Agriculture, hunting, forestry and fishing	23	38	42	44	53	91	116	81	92	...	...	...
2 Mining and quarrying	25	40	59	83	83	133	94	89	89	...	...	...
3 Manufacturing	31	115	44	50	123	201	168	196	234	...	...	...
4 Electricity, gas and water [a]	9	36	18	14	26	47	133	288	171	...	...	...
5 Construction	3	9	3	6	12	26	35	33	17	...	...	...
6 Wholesale and retail trade, restaurants and hotels	10	17	19	24	43	50	47	28	100	...	...	...
7 Transport, storage and communication	15	60	33	37	48	60	160	137	83	...	...	...
8 Finance, insurance, real estate and business services [b]	31	62	45	62	49	87	95	106	106	...	...	...
9 Community, social and personal services [b]	10	26	26	25	29	62	78	84	87	...	...	...
A Sanitary and similar services	...	...	...	...	...	...	...	...	...	...	...	...
B Social and related community services	...	18	19	18	15	25	38	42	37	...	...	...
Educational services	...	12	11	10	8	18	30	31	24	...	...	...
Medical, dental, other health and veterinary services	...	6	8	8	7	7	8	11	13	...	...	...
C Recreational and cultural services	...	8	7	7	14	37	40	42	50	...	...	...
D Personal and household services	...	...	...	...	...	...	...	...	...	...	...	...
Total Industries	157	403	289	345	466	757	926	1042	979	...	...	...
Producers of Government Services	18	65	52	50	62	73	113	181	131	...	...	...
Private Non-Profit Institutions Serving Households	...	...	...	...	...	...	...	...	...	...	...	...
Total	175	468	341	395	528	830	1039	1223	1110	...	...	...

a) Item 'Electricity, gas and water' excludes gas.
b) Business services are included in item 'Community, social and personal services'.

2.12 Gross Fixed Capital Formation by Kind of Activity of Owner, ISIC Divisions, in Constant Prices

Million Zimbabwean dollars

	1970	1975	1978	1979	1980	1981	1982	1983	1984	1985	1986	1987
					At constant prices of:1980							
					All Producers							
1 Agriculture, hunting, forestry and fishing	64	73	55	49	53	83	93	51	50	...	...	...
2 Mining and quarrying	67	77	76	92	83	114	72	54	46	...	...	...
3 Manufacturing	85	226	56	54	123	179	135	121	121	...	...	...
4 Electricity, gas and water [a]	25	69	22	15	26	41	94	174	83	...	...	...

Zimbabwe

2.12 Gross Fixed Capital Formation by Kind of Activity of Owner, ISIC Divisions, in Constant Prices
(Continued)

Million Zimbabwean dollars

	1970	1975	1978	1979	1980	1981	1982	1983	1984	1985	1986	1987
					At constant prices of:1980							
5 Construction	7	19	3	6	12	24	29	21	9	...	...	...
6 Wholesale and retail trade, restaurants and hotels	31	35	24	28	44	45	37	18	53	...	...	...
7 Transport, storage and communication	45	114	40	40	48	54	122	86	45	...	...	...
8 Finance, insurance, real estate and business services [b]	100	118	62	74	49	71	67	63	55	...	...	...
9 Community, social and personal services [b]	32	51	35	28	29	52	57	50	45	...	...	...
A Sanitary and similar services	...	...	...	...	...	...	...	...	...	...	...	...
B Social and related community services	19	35	22	17	16	31	28	25	19	...	...	...
Educational services	11	23	11	8	8	15	22	19	12	...	...	...
Medical, dental, other health and veterinary services	8	12	11	9	8	6	6	6	7	...	...	...
C Recreational and cultural services	13	16	9	8	14	31	29	25	26	...	...	...
D Personal and household services	...	...	...	...	...	...	...	...	...	...	...	...
Total Industries	456	782	373	386	466	661	707	638	508	...	...	...
Producers of Government Services	54	117	69	57	62	61	81	102	68	...	...	...
Private Non-Profit Institutions Serving Households	...	...	...	...	...	...	...	...	...	...	...	...
Total	510	899	442	443	528	722	788	740	576	...	...	...

a) Item 'Electricity, gas and water' excludes gas.
b) Business services are included in item 'Community, social and personal services'.

4.1 Derivation of Value Added by Kind of Activity, in Current Prices

Million Zimbabwean dollars

	1980			1981			1982			1983		
	Gross Output	Intermediate Consumption	Value Added	Gross Output	Intermediate Consumption	Value Added	Gross Output	Intermediate Consumption	Value Added	Gross Output	Intermediate Consumption	Value Added
						All Producers						
1 Agriculture, hunting, forestry and fishing	778	327	451	1120	474	646	1194	537	658	1099	593	506
2 Mining and quarrying	468	183	285	485	233	252	440	223	217	629	235	393
3 Manufacturing	2204	1402	802	2837	1821	1016	3219	2098	1121	3349	1989	1360
A Manufacture of food, beverages and tobacco	638	461	177	785	573	211	1053	778	275	1149	758	391
B Textile, wearing apparel and leather industries	400	262	138	546	350	197	550	355	195	511	306	205
C Manufacture of wood and wood products, including furniture	74	42	32	111	63	48	110	64	46	98	51	47
D Manufacture of paper and paper products, printing and publishing	115	67	48	157	88	68	179	101	78	207	100	106
E Manufacture of chemicals and chemical petroleum, coal, rubber and plastic products	284	181	103	380	236	144	412	265	147	499	317	182
F Manufacture of non-metallic mineral products, except products of petroleum and coal	63	30	33	88	55	33	118	55	63	114	49	66
G Basic metal industries	289	169	120	263	168	95	230	155	75	289	182	107
H Manufacture of fabricated metal products, machinery and equipment	311	173	138	465	262	202	522	299	223	453	212	241
I Other manufacturing industries	30	18	13	42	25	17	45	26	19	30	14	16
4 Electricity, gas and water [a]	163	93	70	186	108	78	181	108	73	331	136	195
A Electricity, gas and steam	146	87	59	169	101	68	156	98	58	319	126	193
B Water works and supply	17	6	10	17	7	10	25	10	15	12	10	2

Zimbabwe

4.1 Derivation of Value Added by Kind of Activity, in Current Prices
(Continued)

Million Zimbabwean dollars

	1980 Gross Output	1980 Intermediate Consumption	1980 Value Added	1981 Gross Output	1981 Intermediate Consumption	1981 Value Added	1982 Gross Output	1982 Intermediate Consumption	1982 Value Added	1983 Gross Output	1983 Intermediate Consumption	1983 Value Added
5 Construction	255	168	91	341	203	138	463	273	190	536	278	258
6 Wholesale and retail trade, restaurants and hotels	893	438	451	1176	573	603	1231	512	718	1208	464	744
A Wholesale and retail trade	837	404	433	1112	537	575	1155	475	680	1110	412	697
B Restaurants and hotels	52	34	18	64	36	28	75	37	38	98	51	46
7 Transport, storage and communication	410	199	211	548	243	306	656	294	362	740	376	364
8 Finance, insurance, real estate and business services [b]	269	67	202	311	71	240	382	99	283	439	104	334
A Financial institutions	184	25	159	211	26	185	267	39	228	315	39	276
B Insurance												
C Real estate and business services	85	42	43	100	45	55	115	60	55	124	65	59
9 Community, social and personal services [b]	619	141	478	756	166	588	996	219	777	1146	289	857
A Sanitary and similar services	...	...	...	...	...	...	...	...	...	...	...	...
B Social and related community services	309	69	240	366	68	297	502	87	415	583	131	452
Educational services	213	44	169	249	33	215	351	42	309	417	74	343
Medical, dental, other health and veterinary services	96	25	71	117	35	82	151	45	106	166	57	109
C Recreational and cultural services	245	72	173	318	98	219	409	132	277	475	158	317
D Personal and household services	65	-	65	72	-	72	85	-	85	88	-	88
Total, Industries	6059	3018	3041	7760	3892	3867	8762	4363	4399	9477	4464	5011
Producers of Government Services	586	295	291	603	294	309	730	363	367	820	422	398
Other Producers	...	...	...	...	...	...	...	...	...	...	...	...
Total [c]	6645	3313	3332	8363	4186	4176	9492	4726	4766	10297	4886	5409
Less: Imputed bank service charge	...	-108	108	...	-121	121	...	-146	146	...	-173	173
Import duties	...	...	...	...	...	...	...	...	...	...	...	...
Value added tax	...	...	...	...	...	...	...	...	...	...	...	...
Other adjustments [d]	217	...	217	384	...	384	540	...	540	900	...	900
Total	6862	3420	3443	8747	4308	4439	10032	4872	5160	11197	5059	6132

	1984 Gross Output	1984 Intermediate Consumption	1984 Value Added
All Producers			
1 Agriculture, hunting, forestry and fishing	1317	644	673
2 Mining and quarrying	729	272	457
3 Manufacturing	3405	1872	1533
A Manufacture of food, beverages and tobacco	...	...	...
B Textile, wearing apparel and leather industries	...	...	...
C Manufacture of wood and wood products, including furniture	...	...	...
D Manufacture of paper and paper products, printing and publishing	...	...	...
E Manufacture of chemicals and chemical petroleum, coal, rubber and plastic products	...	...	...
F Manufacture of non-metallic mineral products, except products of petroleum and coal	...	...	...
G Basic metal industries	...	...	...
H Manufacture of fabricated metal products, machinery and equipment	...	...	...
I Other manufacturing industries	...	...	...
4 Electricity, gas and water [a]	405	166	239
A Electricity, gas and steam	...	...	...
B Water works and supply	...	...	...

Zimbabwe

4.1 Derivation of Value Added by Kind of Activity, in Current Prices
(Continued)

Million Zimbabwean dollars

		1984 Gross Output	1984 Intermediate Consumption	1984 Value Added
5	Construction	555	285	270
6	Wholesale and retail trade, restaurants and hotels	1452	684	768
	A Wholesale and retail trade	1331	616	715
	B Restaurants and hotels	121	69	52
7	Transport, storage and communication	857	422	436
8	Finance, insurance, real estate and business services [b]	483	141	342
	A Financial institutions	341	59	282
	B Insurance			
	C Real estate and business services	142	82	60
9	Community, social and personal services [b]	1296	332	964
	A Sanitary and similar services	...	...	...
	B Social and related community services	665	134	531
	Educational services	508	93	415
	Medical, dental, other health and veterinary services	157	41	116
	C Recreational and cultural services	544	198	346
	D Personal and household services	87	-	87
Total, Industries		10499	4818	5682
Producers of Government Services		816	377	438
Other Producers		...	...	...
Total [c]		11315	5195	6120
Less: Imputed bank service charge		...	-168	168
Import duties		...	...	...
Value added tax		...	...	...
Other adjustments [d]		744	...	744
Total		12059	5363	6696

a) Item 'Electricity, gas and water' excludes gas.
b) Business services are included in item 'Community, social and personal services'.
c) Gross domestic product in factor values.
d) Item 'Other adjustments' refers to indirect taxes net of subsidies.

4.3 Cost Components of Value Added

Million Zimbabwean dollars

		1980 Compensation of Employees	1980 Capital Consumption	1980 Net Operating Surplus	1980 Indirect Taxes	1980 Less: Subsidies Received	1980 Value Added	1981 Compensation of Employees	1981 Capital Consumption	1981 Net Operating Surplus	1981 Indirect Taxes	1981 Less: Subsidies Received	1981 Value Added
				All Producers									
1	Agriculture, hunting, forestry and fishing	146	...	305	...	...	451	215	...	430	...	...	646
2	Mining and quarrying	116	...	169	...	...	285	158	...	94	...	...	252
3	Manufacturing	402	...	400	...	...	802	541	...	475	...	...	1016
	A Manufacture of food, beverages and tobacco	90	...	86	...	...	176	115	...	96	...	...	211

Zimbabwe

4.3 Cost Components of Value Added
(Continued)

Million Zimbabwean dollars

	1980 Compensation of Employees	1980 Capital Consumption	1980 Net Operating Surplus	1980 Indirect Taxes	1980 Less: Subsidies Received	1980 Value Added	1981 Compensation of Employees	1981 Capital Consumption	1981 Net Operating Surplus	1981 Indirect Taxes	1981 Less: Subsidies Received	1981 Value Added
B Textile, wearing apparel and leather industries	62	...	76	...	...	138	89	...	108	...	...	197
C Manufacture of wood and wood products, including furniture	18	...	14	...	...	32	26	...	22	...	...	48
D Manufacture of paper and paper products, printing and publishing	31	...	16	...	...	47	41	...	27	...	...	68
E Manufacture of chemicals and chemical petroleum, coal, rubber and plastic products	45	...	59	...	...	104	59	...	85	...	...	144
F Manufacture of non-metallic mineral products, except products of petroleum and coal	15	...	18	...	...	33	22	...	11	...	...	33
G Basic metal industries	51	...	69	...	...	120	69	...	26	...	...	95
H Manufacture of fabricated metal products, machinery and equipment	83	...	56	...	...	139	113	...	89	...	...	202
I Other manufacturing industries	7	...	6	...	...	13	7	...	10	...	...	17
4 Electricity, gas and water [a]	27	...	43	...	...	70	30	...	48	...	...	78
A Electricity, gas and steam	25	...	34	...	...	59	28	...	40	...	...	68
B Water works and supply	2	...	9	...	...	11	2	...	8	...	...	10
5 Construction	81	...	9	...	...	91	110	...	28	...	...	138
6 Wholesale and retail trade, restaurants and hotels	203	...	248	...	...	451	197	...	406	...	...	603
A Wholesale and retail trade	185	...	249	...	...	434	176	...	399	...	...	575
B Restaurants and hotels	19	...	-1	...	...	18	21	...	7	...	...	28
7 Transport, storage and communication	194	...	17	...	...	211	218	...	88	...	...	306
8 Finance, insurance, real estate and business services [b]	78	...	124	...	...	202	100	...	140	...	...	240
A Financial institutions	74	...	85	...	...	159	95	...	90	...	...	185
B Insurance		...		...	...			...		...	...	
C Real estate and business services	4	...	39	...	...	43	5	...	50	...	...	55
9 Community, social and personal services [b]	392	...	86	...	...	478	479	...	109	...	...	586
A Sanitary and similar services	...	...	...	...	...	...	...	...	...	...	...	...
B Social and related community services	218	...	22	...	...	240	272	...	29	...	...	301
Educational services	169	...	-	...	...	169	216	...	1	...	...	215
Medical, dental, other health and veterinary services	49	...	22	...	...	71	56	...	26	...	...	82
C Recreational and cultural services	110	...	63	...	...	173	135	...	84	...	...	219
D Personal and household services	65	...	-	...	...	65	72	...	-	...	...	72
Total, Industries	1639	...	1405	...	...	3041	2048	...	1817	...	...	3867
Producers of Government Services	263	...	27	...	...	291	281	...	28	...	...	309
Other Producers	...	...	...	...	...	...	...	...	...	...	...	...
Total [c]	1902	...	1432	...	...	3332	2329	...	1843	...	...	4176
Less: Imputed bank service charge	...	...	108	...	...	108	...	...	121	...	...	121
Import duties	...	...	...	...	...	...	...	...	...	...	...	...
Value added tax	...	...	...	...	...	...	...	...	...	...	...	...
Other adjustments [d]	...	...	...	217	...	217	...	...	...	384	...	384
Total [c]	1900	...	1322	217	...	3441	2329	...	1727	384	...	4439

of which General Government:

1 Agriculture, hunting, forestry and fishing	5	...	-1	...	...	4	10	...	...	...	...	10
2 Mining and quarrying	...	...	...	...	...	...	...	...	...	...	...	...
3 Manufacturing	4	...	5	...	...	9	5	...	4	...	...	9
4 Electricity, gas and water	17	...	28	...	...	45	19	...	34	...	...	53

Zimbabwe

4.3 Cost Components of Value Added
(Continued)

Million Zimbabwean dollars

	1980						1981					
	Compensation of Employees	Capital Consumption	Net Operating Surplus	Indirect Taxes	Less: Subsidies Received	Value Added	Compensation of Employees	Capital Consumption	Net Operating Surplus	Indirect Taxes	Less: Subsidies Received	Value Added
5 Construction	35	...	-2	...	...	33	40	...	3	...	...	43
6 Wholesale and retail trade, restaurants and hotels	3	...	4	...	...	7	4	...	4	...	...	8
7 Transport and communication	8	...	...	...	...	8	8	...	...	...	...	8
8 Finance, insurance, real estate & business services	...	...	28	...	...	28	...	...	28	...	...	28
9 Community, social and personal services	170	...	...	...	...	170	258	...	...	...	...	258
Total, Industries of General Government	242	...	62	...	...	304	344	...	73	...	...	417
Producers of Government Services	263	...	...	...	...	263	281	...	...	...	...	281
Total, General Government	505	...	62	...	...	567	625	...	73	...	...	698

	1982						1983					
	Compensation of Employees	Capital Consumption	Net Operating Surplus	Indirect Taxes	Less: Subsidies Received	Value Added	Compensation of Employees	Capital Consumption	Net Operating Surplus	Indirect Taxes	Less: Subsidies Received	Value Added

All Producers

1 Agriculture, hunting, forestry and fishing	248	...	410	...	...	658	275	...	231	...	...	506
2 Mining and quarrying	179	...	38	...	...	217	161	...	232	...	...	393
3 Manufacturing	649	...	472	...	...	1121	702	...	659	...	...	1360
A Manufacture of food, beverages and tobacco	...	...	...	...	...	275	160	...	230	...	...	390
B Textile, wearing apparel and leather industries	...	...	...	...	...	195	128	...	77	...	...	205
C Manufacture of wood and wood products, including furniture	...	...	...	...	...	46	33	...	15	...	...	48
D Manufacture of paper and paper products, printing and publishing	50	...	28	...	...	78	53	...	53	...	...	106
E Manufacture of chemicals and chemical petroleum, coal, rubber and plastic products	71	...	77	...	...	148	84	...	97	...	...	181
F Manufacture of non-metallic mineral products, except products of petroleum and coal	27	...	36	...	...	63	27	...	38	...	...	65
G Basic metal industries	67	...	7	...	...	74	79	...	27	...	...	107
H Manufacture of fabricated metal products, machinery and equipment	134	...	89	...	...	223	129	...	113	...	...	242
I Other manufacturing industries	11	...	8	...	...	19	9	...	7	...	...	14
4 Electricity, gas and water [a]	34	...	39	...	...	73	35	...	160	...	...	195
A Electricity, gas and steam	32	...	26	...	...	58	34	...	159	...	...	193
B Water works and supply	2	...	13	...	...	15	2	...	1	...	...	3
5 Construction	142	...	48	...	...	190	134	...	125	...	...	258
6 Wholesale and retail trade, restaurants and hotels	189	...	529	...	...	718	336	...	407	...	...	744
A Wholesale and retail trade	168	...	512	...	...	680	308	...	390	...	...	698
B Restaurants and hotels	22	...	17	...	...	39	29	...	18	...	...	47
7 Transport, storage and communication	263	...	99	...	...	362	295	...	69	...	...	364
8 Finance, insurance, real estate and business services [b]	122	...	161	...	...	283	144	...	190	...	...	334
A Financial institutions	117	...	111	...	...	228	138	...	136	...	...	276
B Insurance		...		...	...			...		...	...	
C Real estate and business services	5	...	50	...	...	55	6	...	53	...	...	59
9 Community, social and personal services [b]	642	...	136	...	...	778	700	...	157	...	...	857
A Sanitary and similar services	...	...	...	...	...	...	...	...	...	...	...	...
B Social and related community services	386	...	30	...	...	416	420	...	32	...	...	452

Zimbabwe

4.3 Cost Components of Value Added
(Continued)

Million Zimbabwean dollars

	1982						1983					
	Compensation of Employees	Capital Consumption	Net Operating Surplus	Indirect Taxes	Less: Subsidies Received	Value Added	Compensation of Employees	Capital Consumption	Net Operating Surplus	Indirect Taxes	Less: Subsidies Received	Value Added
Educational services	310	...	-1	...	...	309	344	...	-1	...	...	343
Medical, dental, other health and veterinary services	76	...	30	...	...	106	76	...	32	...	...	109
C Recreational and cultural services	171	...	106	...	...	277	192	...	125	...	...	317
D Personal and household services	85	...	-	...	...	85	88	...	-	...	...	88
Total, Industries	2468	...	1931	...	...	4399	2782	...	2230	...	...	5011
Producers of Government Services	330	...	37	...	...	367	348	...	50	...	...	398
Other Producers	...	...	...	...	...	...	...	...	...	...	...	...
Total c	2798	...	1968	...	...	4766	3130	...	2280	...	...	5409
Less: Imputed bank service charge	...	...	146	...	...	146	...	...	173	...	...	173
Import duties	...	...	...	...	...	...	...	...	...	...	...	...
Value added tax	...	...	...	...	...	...	...	...	...	...	...	...
Other adjustments d	...	...	...	540	...	540	...	...	...	896	...	896
Total c	2797	...	1822	540	...	5160	3130	...	2107	896	...	6132

of which General Government:

1 Agriculture, hunting, forestry and fishing	20	...	-2	...	...	18	13	...	1	...	...	14
2 Mining and quarrying	...	...	...	...	...	...	...	...	...	...	...	...
3 Manufacturing	7	...	5	...	...	12	44	...	8	...	...	52
4 Electricity, gas and water	22	...	19	...	...	41	26	...	141	...	...	167
5 Construction	52	...	-4	...	...	48	44	...	36	...	...	80
6 Wholesale and retail trade, restaurants and hotels	5	...	5	...	...	10	5	...	12	...	...	17
7 Transport and communication	9	...	...	...	...	9	10	...	...	...	...	10
8 Finance, insurance, real estate & business services	...	...	37	...	...	37	...	...	50	...	...	50
9 Community, social and personal services	363	...	...	...	...	363	390	...	...	...	...	390
Total, Industries of General Government	478	...	60	...	...	538	531	...	248	...	...	779
Producers of Government Services	330	...	...	...	...	330	348	...	...	...	...	348
Total, General Government	808	...	60	...	...	868	879	...	248	...	...	1127

	1984					
	Compensation of Employees	Capital Consumption	Net Operating Surplus	Indirect Taxes	Less: Subsidies Received	Value Added

All Producers

1 Agriculture, hunting, forestry and fishing	313	...	360	...	...	673
2 Mining and quarrying	193	...	264	...	...	457
3 Manufacturing	763	...	770	...	...	1533
A Manufacture of food, beverages and tobacco	...	...	...	...	...	...
B Textile, wearing apparel and leather industries	...	...	...	...	...	...
C Manufacture of wood and wood products, including furniture	...	...	...	...	...	...
D Manufacture of paper and paper products, printing and publishing	...	...	...	...	...	...
E Manufacture of chemicals and chemical petroleum, coal, rubber and plastic products	...	...	...	...	...	...
F Manufacture of non-metallic mineral products, except products of petroleum and coal	...	...	...	...	...	...
G Basic metal industries	...	...	...	...	...	...
H Manufacture of fabricated metal products, machinery and equipment	...	...	...	...	...	...
I Other manufacturing industries	...	...	...	...	...	...
4 Electricity, gas and water a	46	...	193	...	...	239
A Electricity, gas and steam	...	...	...	...	...	...
B Water works and supply	...	...	...	...	...	...

Zimbabwe

4.3 Cost Components of Value Added
(Continued)

Million Zimbabwean dollars

	1984 Compensation of Employees	Capital Consumption	Net Operating Surplus	Indirect Taxes	Less: Subsidies Received	Value Added
5 Construction	167	...	103	...	...	270
6 Wholesale and retail trade, restaurants and hotels	356	...	411	...	...	768
A Wholesale and retail trade	327	...	390	...	...	715
B Restaurants and hotels	29	...	23	...	...	52
7 Transport, storage and communication	332	...	104	...	...	436
8 Finance, insurance, real estate and business services [b]	158	...	184	...	...	342
A Financial institutions	151	...	131	...	...	282
B Insurance						
C Real estate and business services	7	...	53	...	...	60
9 Community, social and personal services [b]	805	...	158	...	...	964
A Sanitary and similar services	...	...	...	...	...	...
B Social and related community services	507	...	23	...	...	531
Educational services	416	...	-1	...	...	415
Medical, dental, other health and veterinary services	91	...	24	...	...	116
C Recreational and cultural services	211	...	135	...	...	346
D Personal and household services	87	...	-	...	...	87
Total, Industries	3134	...	2547	...	...	5682
Producers of Government Services	391	...	47	...	...	438
Other Producers	...	...	...	...	...	...
Total [c]	3525	...	2594	...	...	6120
Less: Imputed bank service charge	...	...	168	...	...	168
Import duties	...	...	...	...	...	...
Value added tax	...	...	...	...	...	...
Other adjustments [d]	...	...	...	744	...	744
Total [c]	3525	...	2426	744	...	6696

of which General Government:

1 Agriculture, hunting, forestry and fishing	11	...	3	...	...	14
2 Mining and quarrying	...	...	...	...	...	...
3 Manufacturing	8	...	9	...	...	17
4 Electricity, gas and water	14	...	170	...	...	184
5 Construction	82	...	30	...	...	112
6 Wholesale and retail trade, restaurants and hotels	6	...	15	...	...	21
7 Transport and communication	12	...	...	...	...	12
8 Finance, insurance, real estate & business services	...	...	47	...	...	47
9 Community, social and personal services	484	...	...	...	...	484
Total, Industries of General Government	617	...	274	...	...	891
Producers of Government Services	391	...	...	...	...	391
Total, General Government	1008	...	274	...	...	1282

a) Item 'Electricity, gas and water' excludes gas.
b) Business services are included in item 'Community, social and personal services'.
c) Column 'Consumption of fixed capital' is included in column 'Net operating surplus'.
d) Item 'Other adjustments' refers to indirect taxes net of subsidies.

كيفية الحصول على منشورات الأمم المتحدة

يمكن الحصول على منشورات الأمم المتحدة من المكتبات ودور التوزيع في جميع أنحاء العالم . استعلم عنها من المكتبة التي تتعامل معها أو اكتب إل : الأمم المتحدة ، قسم البيع في نيويورك أو في جنيف .

如何购取联合国出版物

联合国出版物在全世界各地的书店和经售处均有发售。请向书店询问或写信到纽约或日内瓦的联合国销售组。

HOW TO OBTAIN UNITED NATIONS PUBLICATIONS

United Nations publications may be obtained from bookstores and distributors throughout the world. Consult your bookstore or write to: United Nations, Sales Section, New York or Geneva.

COMMENT SE PROCURER LES PUBLICATIONS DES NATIONS UNIES

Les publications des Nations Unies sont en vente dans les librairies et les agences dépositaires du monde entier. Informez-vous auprès de votre libraire ou adressez-vous à : Nations Unies, Section des ventes, New York ou Genève.

КАК ПОЛУЧИТЬ ИЗДАНИЯ ОРГАНИЗАЦИИ ОБЪЕДИНЕННЫХ НАЦИЙ

Издания Организации Объединенных Наций можно купить в книжных магазинах и агентствах во всех районах мира. Наводите справки об изданиях в вашем книжном магазине или пишите по адресу: Организация Объединенных Наций, Секция по продаже изданий, Нью-Йорк или Женева.

COMO CONSEGUIR PUBLICACIONES DE LAS NACIONES UNIDAS

Las publicaciones de las Naciones Unidas están en venta en librerías y casas distribuidoras en todas partes del mundo. Consulte a su librero o diríjase a: Naciones Unidas, Sección de Ventas, Nueva York o Ginebra.

Litho in United Nations, New York
89-41236—March 1990—3,800
ISBN 92-1-161312-4

10000
(not to be sold separately)

United Nations publication
Sales No. E.90.XVII.2, Part II
ST/ESA/STAT/SER.X/13

WITHDRAWN

WILLIAM F. MAAG LIBRARY
YOUNGSTOWN STATE UNIVERSITY